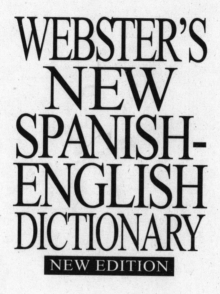

WEBSTER'S NEW SPANISH-ENGLISH DICTIONARY

NEW EDITION

WEBSTER'S NEW SPANISH-ENGLISH DICTIONARY

NEW EDITION

Created in Cooperation with the Editors of
MERRIAM-WEBSTER

THE
POPULAR
GROUP

This edition published by arrangement with Federal Street Press,
a Division of Merriam-Webster, Incorporated

The Popular Group LLC
1700 Broadway
New York, NY 10019

ISBN 13   978-1-59027-083-7

ISBN 10   1-59027-083-5

Printed in the United States of America

08 09 10 11 12   10 9 8 7

Contents

Preface

The volume you are holding is a new edition of a dictionary designed to meet the needs of English and Spanish speakers in a time of ever-expanding communication among the countries of the Western Hemisphere. It is intended for language learners, teachers, office workers, tourists, business travelers—anyone who needs to communicate effectively in the Spanish and English languages as they are spoken and written in the Americas. This new dictionary provides accurate and up-to-date coverage of current vocabulary in both languages, as well as abundant examples of words used in context to illustrate idiomatic usage. The selection of Spanish words and idioms was based on evidence drawn from a wide variety of modern Latin-American sources and interpreted by trained Merriam-Webster bilingual lexicographers. The English entries were chosen by Merriam-Webster editors from the most recent Merriam-Webster dictionaries, and they represent the current basic vocabulary of American English.

All of this material is presented in a format which is based firmly upon and, in many important ways, is similar to the traditional styling found in the Merriam-Webster monolingual dictionaries. The reader who is familiar with Merriam-Webster dictionaries will immediately recognize this style, with its emphasis on convenience and ease of use, clarity and conciseness of the information presented, precise discrimination of senses, and frequent inclusion of example phrases showing words in actual use. Other features include pronunciations (in the International Phonetic Alphabet) for all English words, full coverage of irregular verbs in both languages, a section on basic Spanish grammar, tables of the most common Spanish and English abbreviations, and a detailed Explanatory Notes section which answers any questions the reader might have concerning the use of this book.

This dictionary represents the combined efforts of many members of the Merriam-Webster Editorial Department, along with advice and assistance from consultants outside the company. The primary defining work was done by Charlene M. Chateauneuf, Seán O'Mannion-Espejo, James L. Rader, Donna L. Rickerby, Adrienne M. Scholz, Amy West, Karen L. Wilkinson, and Linda Picard Wood. Brian M. Sietsema, Ph.D., provided the pronunciations. Cross-reference services were provided by Donna L. Rickerby. Karen L. Levister assisted in inputting revisions. Carol Fugiel contributed many hours of clerical assistance and other valuable support. The editorial work relating to typesetting and production was begun by

Jennifer S. Goss and continued by Susan L. Brady, who also offered helpful suggestions regarding format. Madeline L. Novak provided guidance on typographic matters. John M. Morse was responsible for the conception of this book as well as for numerous ideas and continued support along the way.

Eileen M. Haraty
Editor

Explanatory Notes

Entries

1. Main Entries

A boldface letter, word, or phrase appearing flush with the left-hand margin of each column of type is a main entry or entry word. The main entry may consist of letters set solid, of letters joined by a hyphen, or of letters separated by a space:

> **cafetalero**[1], **-ra** *adj* . . .
>
> **eye–opener** . . . *n* . . .
>
> **walk out** *vi* . . .

The main entry, together with the material that follows it on the same line and succeeding indented lines, constitutes a dictionary entry.

2. Order of Main Entries

Alphabetical order throughout the book follows the order of the English alphabet, with one exception: words beginning with the Spanish letter *ñ* follow all entries for the letter *n*. The main entries follow one another alphabetically letter by letter without regard to intervening spaces or hyphens; for example, *shake-up* follows *shaker*.

Homographs (words with the same spelling) having different parts of speech are usually given separate dictionary entries. These entries are distinguished by superscript numerals following the entry word:

> **hail**[1] . . . *vt* . . .
>
> **hail**[2] *n* . . .
>
> **hail**[3] *interj* . . .
>
> **madrileño**[1], **-ña** *adj* . . .
>
> **madrileño**[2], **-ña** *n* . . .

Numbered homograph entries are listed in the following order: verb, adverb, adjective, noun, conjunction, preposition, pronoun, interjection, article.

Homographs having the same part of speech are normally included at the same dictionary entry, without regard to their different semantic origins. On the English-to-Spanish side, however, separate entries are made if the homographs have distinct inflected forms or if they have distinct pronunciations.

3. Guide Words

A pair of guide words is printed at the top of each page, indicating the first and last main entries that appear on that page:

factura · faringe

4. Variants

When a main entry is followed by the word *or* and another spelling, the two spellings are variants. Both are standard, and either one may be used according to personal inclination:

jailer *or* **jailor** . . . *n* . . .

quizá *or* **quizás** *adv* . . .

Occasionally, a variant spelling is used only for a particular sense of a word. In these cases, the variant spelling is listed after the sense number of the sense to which it pertains:

electric . . . *adj* **1** *or* **electrical** . . .

Sometimes the entry word is used interchangeably with a longer phrase containing the entry word. For the purposes of this dictionary, such phrases are considered variants of the headword:

bunk² *n* **1** *or* **bunk bed** . . .

angina *nf* **1** *or* **angina de pecho** : angina . . .

Variant wordings of boldface phrases may also be shown:

> **madera** *nf*. . . **3 madera dura** *or* **madera noble** . . .
>
> **atención**[1] *nf* . . . **2 poner atención** *or* **prestar atención** . . .

5. Run-On Entries

A main entry may be followed by one or more derivatives or by a homograph with a different functional label. These are run-on entries. Each is introduced by a boldface dash and each has a functional label. They are not defined, however, since their equivalents can be readily derived by adding the corresponding foreign-language suffix to the terms used to define the entry word or, in the case of homographs, simply substituting the appropriate part of speech:

> **illegal** . . . *adj* : ilegal — **illegally** *adv* (the Spanish adverb is *ilegalmente*)
>
> **transferir** . . . *vt* trasladar : to transfer — **transferible** *adj* (the English adjective is **transferable**)
>
> **Bosnian** *n* : bosnio *m*, -nia *f* — **Bosnian** *adj* (the Spanish adjective is *bosnio, -nia*)

On the Spanish side of the book, reflexive verbs are sometimes run on undefined:

> **enrollar** *vt* : to roll up, to coil — **enrollarse** *vr*

The absence of a definition means that *enrollarse* has the simple reflexive meaning "to become rolled up or coiled," "to roll itself up."

6. Bold Notes

A main entry may be followed by one or more phrases containing the entry word or an inflected form of the entry word. These are bold notes. Each bold note is defined at its own numbered sense:

álamo *nm* **1** : poplar **2 álamo temblón**
: aspen

hold[1] . . . *vi* . . . **4 to hold to :** . . . **5 to
hold with :** . . .

If the bold note consists only of the entry word and a single preposition, the entry word is represented by a boldface swung dash ~.

pegar . . . *vi* . . . **3 ~ con :** to match, to
go with . . .

The same bold note phrase may appear at two or more senses if it has more than one distinct meaning:

wear[1] . . . *vt* . . . **3 to wear out :** gastar
⟨he wore out his shoes . . . ⟩ **4 to wear
out** EXHAUST : agotar, fatigar ⟨to wear
oneself out . . . ⟩ . . .

estar . . . *vi* . . . **15 ~ por :** to be in favor
of **16 ~ por :** to be about to ⟨está por
cerrar . . . ⟩ . . .

If the use of the entry word is commonly restricted to one particular phrase, then a bold note may be given as the entry word's only sense:

ward[1] . . . *vt* **to ward off :** . . .

Pronunciation

1. Pronunciation of English Entry Words

The matter between a pair of brackets [ ] following the entry word of an English-to-Spanish entry indicates the pronunciation. The symbols used are explained in the International Phonetic Alphabet chart on page 58a.

The presence of variant pronunciations indicates that not all educated speakers pronounce words the same way. A second-place variant is not to be regarded as less acceptable than the pronunciation that is given first. It may, in fact, be used by as many

educated speakers as the first variant, but the requirements of
the printed page are such that one must precede the other:

> **tomato** [tə'meɪt̮o, -'mɑ-] . . .

When a compound word has less than a full pronunciation, the
missing part is to be supplied from the pronunciation at the entry
for the unpronounced element of the compound:

> **gamma ray** ['gæmə] . . .
>
> **ray** ['reɪ] . . .
>
> **smoke**[1] ['smoːk] . . .
>
> **smoke detector** [dɪ'tɛktər] . . .

In general, no pronunciation is given for open compounds consisting of two or more English words that are main entries at their
own alphabetical place:

> **water lily** *n* : nenúfar *m*

Only the first entry in a series of numbered homographs is giv-
en a pronunciation if their pronunciations are the same:

> **dab**[1] ['dæb] *vt* . . .
>
> **dab**[2] *n* . . .

No pronunciation is shown for principal parts of verbs that are
formed by regular suffixation, nor for other derivative words
formed by common suffixes.

2. Pronunciation of Spanish Entry Words

Spanish pronunciation is highly regular, so no pronunciations
are given for most Spanish-to-English entries. Exceptions have
been made for certain words (such as foreign borrowings) whose
Spanish pronunciations are not evident from their spellings:

> **pizza** ['pitsa, 'pisa] . . .
>
> **footing** ['fu,tɪŋ] . . .

Functional Labels

An italic label indicating a part of speech or some other functional classification follows the pronunciation or, if no pronunciation is given, the main entry. The eight traditional parts of speech, adjective, adverb, conjunction, interjection, noun, preposition, pronoun, and verb, are indicated as follows:

daily² *adj* . . .

vagamente *adv* . . .

and . . . *conj* . . .

huy *interj* . . .

jackal . . . *n* . . .

para *prep* . . .

neither³ *pron* . . .

leer . . . *v* . . .

Verbs that are intransitive are labeled *vi*, and verbs that are transitive are labeled *vt*. Entries for verbs that are both transitive and intransitive are labeled *v;* if such an entry includes irregular verb inflections, it is labeled *v* immediately after the main entry, with the labels *vi* and *vt* serving to introduce transitive and intransitive subdivisions when both are present:

deliberar *vi* : to deliberate

necessitate . . . *vt* -tated; -tating : necesitar, requerir

satisfy . . . *v* -fied; -fying *vt* . . . — *vi* . . .

Two other labels are used to indicate functional classifications of verbs: *v aux* (auxiliary verb) and *v impers* (impersonal verb).

may . . . *v aux, past* might . . .

haber¹ . . . *v aux* **1** : have . . . — *v impers* **1 hay** : there is, there are . . .

Gender Labels

In Spanish-to-English noun entries, the gender of the entry word is indicated by an italic *m* (masculine), *f* (feminine), or *mf* (masculine or feminine), immediately following the functional label:

> **magnesio** *nm* . . .
>
> **galaxia** *nf* . . .
>
> **turista** *nmf* . . .

If both the masculine and feminine forms are shown for a noun referring to a person, the label is simply *n:*

> **director, -tora** *n* . . .

Spanish noun equivalents of English entry words are also labeled for gender:

> **amnesia** . . . *n* : amnesia *f*
>
> **earache** . . . *n* : dolor *m* de oído
>
> **gamekeeper** . . . *n* : guardabosque *mf*

Inflected Forms

1. Nouns

The plurals of nouns are shown in this dictionary when they are irregular, when plural suffixation brings about a change in accentuation or in the spelling of the root word, when an English noun ends in a consonant plus *-o* or in *-ey,* when an English noun ends in *-oo,* when an English noun is a compound that pluralizes any element but the last, when a noun has variant plurals, or whenever the dictionary user might have reasonable doubts regarding the spelling of a plural:

> **tooth** . . . *n, pl* **teeth** . . .
>
> **garrafón** *nm, pl* **-fones** . . .
>
> **potato** . . . *n, pl* **-toes** . . .

abbey . . . *n, pl* **-beys** . . .

cuckoo[2] *n, pl* **-oos** . . .

brother–in–law . . . *n, pl*
  brothers–in–law . . .

quail[2] *n, pl* **quail** *or* **quails** . . .

hábitat *nm, pl* **-tats** . . .

tahúr *nm, pl* **tahúres** . . .

Cutback inflected forms are used for most nouns on the English-to-Spanish side, regardless of the number of syllables. On the Spanish-to-English side, cutback inflections are given for nouns that have three or more syllables; plurals for shorter words are written out in full:

shampoo[2] *n, pl* **-poos** . . .

calamity . . . *n, pl* **-ties** . . .

mouse . . . *n, pl* **mice** . . .

sartén *nmf, pl* **sartenes** . . .

hámster *nm, pl* **hámsters** . . .

federación *nf, pl* **-ciones** . . .

If only one gender form has a plural which is irregular, that plural form will be given with the appropriate label:

campeón, -ona *n, mpl* **-ones** : champion

The plurals of nouns are usually not shown when the base word is unchanged by the addition of the regular plural suffix or when the noun is unlikely to occur in the plural:

apple . . . *n* : manzana *f*

inglés[3] *nm* : English (language)

Nouns that are plural in form and that regularly occur in plural constructions are labeled as *npl* (for English nouns), *nmpl* (for Spanish masculine nouns), or *nfpl* (for Spanish feminine nouns):

knickers . . . *npl* . . .

enseres *nmpl* . . .

mancuernas *nfpl* . . .

Entry words that are unchanged in the plural are labeled *ns & pl* (for English nouns), *nms & pl* (for Spanish masculine nouns), *nfs & pl* (for Spanish feminine nouns), and *nmfs & pl* (for Spanish gender-variable nouns):

> **deer** . . . *ns & pl* . . .
>
> **lavaplatos** *nms & pl* . . .
>
> **tesis** *nfs & pl* . . .
>
> **rompehuelgas** *nmfs & pl* . . .

2. Verbs

ENGLISH VERBS

The principal parts of verbs are shown in English-to-Spanish entries when they are irregular, when suffixation brings about a change in spelling of the root word, when the verb ends in *-ey*, when there are variant inflected forms, or whenever it is believed that the dictionary user might have reasonable doubts about the spelling of an inflected form:

> **break¹** . . . *v* **broke** . . . ; **broken** . . . ; **breaking** . . .
>
> **drag¹** . . . *v* **dragged; dragging** . . .
>
> **monkey¹** . . . *vi* **-keyed; -keying** . . .
>
> **label¹** . . . *vt* **-beled** *or* **-belled; -beling** *or* **-belling** . . .
>
> **imagine** . . . *vt* **-ined; -ining** . . .

Cutback inflected forms are usually used when the verb has two or more syllables:

> **multiply** . . . *v* **-plied; -plying** . . .
>
> **bevel¹** . . . *v* **-eled** *or* **-elled; -eling** *or* **-elling** . . .
>
> **forgo** *or* **forego** . . . *vt* **-went; -gone; -going** . . .
>
> **commit** . . . *vt* **-mitted; -mitting** . . .

The principal parts of an English verb are not shown when the base word is unchanged by suffixation:

> **delay**[1] . . . *vt*
>
> **pitch**[1] . . . *vt*

SPANISH VERBS

Entries for irregular Spanish verbs are cross-referenced by number to the model conjugations appearing in the Conjugation of Spanish Verbs section:

> **abnegarse** {49} *vr* . . .
>
> **volver** {89} *vi* . . .

Entries for Spanish verbs with regular conjugations are not cross-referenced; however, model conjugations for regular Spanish verbs are included in the Conjugation of Spanish Verbs section beginning on page 38a.

Adverbs and Adjectives

The comparative and superlative forms of English adjective and adverb main entries are shown when suffixation brings about a change in spelling of the root word, when the inflection is irregular, and when there are variant inflected forms:

> **wet**[2] *adj* **wetter; wettest** . . .
>
> **good**[2] *adj* **better** . . . ; **best** . . .
>
> **evil**[1] . . . *adj* **eviler** *or* **eviller; evilest** *or* **evillest** . . .

The superlative forms of adjectives and adverbs of two or more syllables are usually cut back; the superlative is shown in full, however, when it is desirable to indicate the pronunciation of the inflected form:

> **early**[1] . . . *adv* **earlier; -est** . . .
>
> **gaudy** . . . *adj* **gaudier; -est** . . .
>
> **secure**[2] *adj* **-curer; -est** . . .
>
> *but*
>
> **young**[1] . . . *adj* **younger** [ˈjʌŋgər]; **youngest** [-gəst] . . .

At a few entries only the superlative form is shown:

mere *adj, superlative* **merest** . . .

The absence of the comparative form indicates that there is no evidence of its use.

The comparative and superlative forms of adjectives and adverbs are usually not shown when the base word is unchanged by suffixation:

quiet³ *adj* **1** . . .

Usage

1. Usage Labels

Two types of usage labels are used in this dictionary—regional and stylistic. Spanish words that are limited in use to a specific area or areas of Latin America, or to Spain, are given labels indicating the countries in which they are most commonly used:

guarachear *vi Cuba, PRi fam* . . .

bucket . . . *n* : . . . cubeta *f Mex*

The following regional labels are used in this book: *Arg* (Argentina), *Bol* (Bolivia), *CA* (Central America), *Car* (Caribbean), *Chile* (Chile), *Col* (Colombia), *CoRi* (Costa Rica), *Cuba* (Cuba), *DomRep* (Dominican Republic), *Ecua* (Ecuador), *Sal* (El Salvador), *Guat* (Guatemala), *Hond* (Honduras), *Mex* (Mexico), *Nic* (Nicaragua), *Pan* (Panama), *Par* (Paraguay), *Peru* (Peru), *PRi* (Puerto Rico), *Spain* (Spain), *Uru* (Uruguay), *Ven* (Venezuela).

Since this book focuses on the Spanish spoken in Latin America, only the most common regionalisms from Spain have been included in order to allow for more thorough coverage of Latin-American forms.

A number of Spanish words are given a *fam* (familiar) label as well, indicating that these words are suitable for informal contexts but would not normally be used in formal writing or speaking. The stylistic label *usu considered vulgar* is added for a word which is usually considered vulgar or offensive but whose widespread use justifies its inclusion in this book. The label is intended to warn the reader that the word in question may be inappropriate in polite conversation.

2. Usage Notes

Definitions are sometimes preceded by parenthetical usage notes that give supplementary semantic information:

> **not** . . . *adv* **1** (*used to form a negative*)
> : no . . .
>
> **within²** *prep* . . . **2** (*in expressions of distance*) : . . . **3** (*in expressions of time*)
> : . . .
>
> **e²** *conj* (*used instead of* **y** *before words beginning with i or hi*) : . . .
>
> **poder¹** . . . *v aux* . . . **2** (*expressing possibility*) : . . . **3** (*expressing permission*)
> : . . .

Additional semantic orientation is also sometimes given in the form of parenthetical notes appearing within the definition:

> **calibrate** . . . *vt* . . . : calibrar (armas), graduar (termómetros)
>
> **palco** *nm* : box (in a theater or stadium)

Occasionally a usage note is used in place of a definition. This is usually done when the entry word has no single foreign-language equivalent. This type of usage note will be accompanied by examples of common use:

> **shall** . . . *v aux* . . . **1** (*used to express a command*) ⟨you shall do as I say : harás lo que te digo⟩ . . .

3. Illustrations of Usage

Definitions are sometimes followed by verbal illustrations that show a typical use of the word in context or a common idiomatic usage. These verbal illustrations include a translation and are enclosed in angle brackets:

> **lejos** *adv* **1** : far away, distant ⟨a lo lejos
> : in the distance, far off⟩ . . .

> **make**[1] . . . **9** . . . : ganar ⟨to make a liv-
> ing : ganarse la vida⟩ . . .

Sense Division

A boldface colon is used to introduce a definition:

> **fable** . . . *n* : fábula *f*

Boldface Arabic numerals separate the senses of a word that has more than one sense:

> **laguna** *nf* **1** : lagoon **2** : lacuna, gap

Whenever some information (such as a synonym, a boldface word or phrase, a usage note, a cross-reference, or a label) follows a sense number, it applies only to that specific numbered sense and not to any other boldface numbered senses:

> **abanico** *nm* . . . **2** GAMA : . . .
>
> **tonic**[2] *n* . . . **2** *or* **tonic water** : . . .
>
> **grillo** *nm* . . . **2 grillos** *nmpl* : . . .
>
> **fairy** . . . *n, pl* **fairies** . . . **2 fairy tale** : . . .
>
> **myself** . . . *pron* **1** *(used reflexively)* : . . .
>
> **pike** . . . *n* . . . **3** → **turnpike**
>
> **atado**[2] *nm* . . . **2** *Arg* : . . .

Cross-References

Three different kinds of cross-references are used in this dictionary: synonymous, cognate, and inflectional. In each instance the cross-reference is readily recognized by the boldface arrow following the entry word.

Synonymous and cognate cross-references indicate that a definition at the entry cross-referred to can be substituted for the entry word:

> scapula . . . → shoulder blade
>
> amuck . . . → amok

An inflectional cross-reference is used to identify the entry word as an inflected form of another word (as a noun or verb):

> fue, etc. → ir, ser
>
> mice → mouse

Synonyms

At many entries or senses in this book, a synonym in small capital letters is provided before the boldface colon and the following defining text. These synonyms are all main entries or bold notes elsewhere in the book. They serve as a helpful guide to the meaning of the entry or sense and also give the reader an additional term that might be substituted in a similar context. On the English-to-Spanish side synonyms are particularly abundant, since special care has been taken to guide the English speaker—by means of synonyms, verbal illustrations, or usage notes—to the meaning of the Spanish terms at each sense of a multisense entry.

Spanish Grammar

Accentuation

Spanish word stress is generally determined according to the following rules:

- Words ending in a vowel, or in -*n* or -*s*, are stressed on the penultimate syllable (*za**pa**to*, *lla**man***).
- Words ending in a consonant other than -*n* or -*s* are stressed on the last syllable (*per**diz**, *curiosi**dad***).

Exceptions to these rules have a written accent mark over the stressed vowel (***fá**cil*, *habla**rá***, ***úl**timo*). There are also a few words which take accent marks in order to distinguish them from homonyms (*si*, *sí*; *que*, *qué*; *el*, *él*; etc.).

Adverbs ending in -*mente* have two stressed syllables since they retain both the stress of the root word and of the -*mente* suffix (***len**ta**men**te*, *di**fí**cil**men**te*). Many compounds also have two stressed syllables (*lim**pia**para**bri**sas*).

Punctuation and Capitalization

Questions and exclamations in Spanish are preceded by an inverted question mark ¿ and an inverted exclamation mark ¡, respectively:

¿Cuándo llamó Ana?
Y tú, ¿qué piensas?

¡No hagas eso!
Pero, ¡qué lástima!

In Spanish, unlike English, the following words are not capitalized:

- Names of days, months, and languages (*jueves*, *octubre*, *español*).

- Spanish adjectives or nouns derived from proper nouns (*los nicaragüenses, una teoría marxista*).

Articles

1. Definite Article

Spanish has five forms of the definite article: *el* (masculine singular), *la* (feminine singular), *los* (masculine plural), *las* (feminine plural), and *lo* (neuter). The first four agree in gender and number with the nouns they limit (*el carro*, the car; *las tijeras*, the scissors), although the form *el* is used with feminine singular nouns beginning with a stressed *a-* or *ha-* (*el águila, el hambre*).

The neuter article *lo* is used with the masculine singular form of an adjective to express an abstract concept (*lo mejor de este método*, the best thing about this method; *lo meticuloso de su trabajo*, the meticulousness of her work; *lo mismo para mí*, the same for me).

Whenever the masculine article *el* immediately follows the words *de* or *a*, it combines with them to form the contractions *del* and *al*, respectively (*viene del campo*, vi *al* hermano de Roberto).

The use of *el, la, los,* and *las* in Spanish corresponds largely to the use of *the* in English; some exceptions are noted below.

The definite article is used:

- When referring to something as a class (*los gatos son ágiles*, cats are agile; *me gusta el café*, I like coffee).

- In references to meals and in most expressions of time (*¿comiste el almuerzo?*, did you eat lunch?; *vino el año pasado*, he came last year; *son las dos*, it's two o'clock; *prefiero el verano*, I prefer summer; *la reunión es el lunes*, the meeting is on Monday; but: *hoy es lunes*, today is Monday).

- Before titles (except *don, doña, san, santo, santa, fray*, and *sor*) in third-person references to people (*la señora Rivera llamó*, Mrs. Rivera called; but: *hola, señora Rivera*, hello, Mrs. Rivera).

- In references to body parts and personal possessions (*me duele la cabeza,* my head hurts; *dejó el sombrero,* he left his hat).

- To mean "the one" or "the ones" when the subject is already understood (*la de madera,* the wooden one; *los que vi ayer,* the ones I saw yesterday).

The definite article is omitted:

- Before a noun in apposition, if the noun is not modified (*Caracas, capital de Venezuela;* but: *Pico Bolívar, la montaña más alta de Venezuela*).

- Before a number in a royal title (*Carlos Quinto,* Charles the Fifth).

2. Indefinite Article

The forms of the indefinite article in Spanish are *un* (masculine singular), *una* (feminine singular), *unos* (masculine plural), and *unas* (feminine plural). They agree in number and gender with the nouns they limit (*una mesa,* a table; *unos platos,* some plates), although the form *un* is used with feminine singular nouns beginning with a stressed *a-* or *ha-* (*un ala, un hacha*).

The use of *un, una, unos,* and *unas* in Spanish corresponds largely to the use of *a, an,* and *some* in English, with some exceptions:

- Indefinite articles are generally omitted before nouns identifying someone or something as a member of a class or category (*Paco es profesor/católico,* Paco is a professor/Catholic; *se llama páncreas,* it's called a pancreas).

- They are also often omitted in instances where quantity is understood from context (*vine sin chaqueta,* I came without a jacket; *no tengo carro,* I don't have a car).

Nouns

1. Gender

Nouns in Spanish are either masculine or feminine. A noun's gender can often be determined according to the following guidelines:

- Nouns ending in *-aje*, *-o*, or *-or* are usually masculine (*el traje, el libro, el sabor*), with some exceptions (*la mano, la foto, la labor*, etc.).

- Nouns ending in *-a*, *-dad*, *-ión*, *-tud*, or *-umbre* are usually feminine (*la alfombra, la capacidad, la excepción, la juventud, la certidumbre*). Exceptions include: *el día, el mapa*, and many learned borrowings ending in *-ma* (*el idioma, el tema*).

Most nouns referring to people or animals agree in gender with the subject (*el hombre, la mujer; el hermano, la hermana; el perro, la perra*). However, some nouns referring to people, including those ending in *-ista*, use the same form for both sexes (*el artista, la artista; el modelo, la modelo;* etc.).

A few names of animals exist in only one gender form (*la jirafa, el sapo*, etc.). In these instances, the adjectives *macho* and *hembra* are sometimes used to distinguish males and females (*una jirafa macho*, a male giraffe).

2. Pluralization

Plurals of Spanish nouns are formed as follows:

- Nouns ending in an unstressed vowel or an accented *-é* are pluralized by adding *-s* (*la vaca, las vacas; el café, los cafés*).

- Nouns ending in a consonant other than *-s,* or in a stressed vowel other than *-é,* are generally pluralized by adding *-es* (*el papel, los papeles; el rubí, los rubíes*). Exceptions include *papá* (*papás*) and *mamá* (*mamás*).

- Nouns with an unstressed final syllable ending in *-s* usually have a zero plural (*la crisis, las crisis; el jueves, los jueves*). Other nouns ending in *-s* add *-es* to form the plural (*el mes, los meses; el país, los países*).

- Nouns ending in *-z* are pluralized by changing the *-z* to *-c* and adding *-es* (*el lápiz, los lápices; la vez, las veces*).

- Many compound nouns have a zero plural (*el paraguas, los paraguas; el aguafiestas, los aguafiestas*).

- The plurals of *cualquiera* and *quienquiera* are *cualesquiera* and *quienesquiera,* respectively.

Adjectives

1. Gender and Number

Most adjectives agree in gender and number with the nouns they modify (un chico *alto*, una chica *alta*, unos chicos *altos*, unas chicas *altas*). Some adjectives, including those ending in -*e* and -*ista* (*fuerte*, *altruista*) and comparative adjectives ending in -*or* (*mayor*, *mejor*), vary only for number.

Adjectives whose masculine singular forms end in -*o* generally change the -*o* to -*a* to form the feminine (*pequeño* → *pequeña*). Masculine adjectives ending in -*án*, -*ón*, or -*dor*, and masculine adjectives of nationality which end in a consonant, usually add -*a* to form the feminine (*holgazán* → *holgazana*; *llorón* → *llorona*; *trabajador* → *trabajadora*; *irlandés* → *irlandesa*).

Adjectives are pluralized in much the same manner as nouns:

- The plurals of adjectives ending in an unstressed vowel or an accented -*é* are formed by adding an -*s* (un postre *rico*, unos postres *ricos;* una camisa *café*, unas camisas *cafés*).

- Adjectives ending in a consonant, or in a stressed vowel other than -*é*, are generally pluralized by adding -*es* (un niño *cortés*, unos niños *corteses;* una persona *iraní*, unas personas *iraníes*).

- Adjectives ending in -*z* are pluralized by changing the -*z* to -*c* and adding -*es* (una respuesta *sagaz*, unas respuestas *sagaces*).

2. Shortening

- The following masculine singular adjectives drop their final -*o* when they occur before a masculine singular noun: *bueno* (*buen*), *malo* (*mal*), *uno* (*un*), *alguno* (*algún*), *ninguno* (*ningún*), *primero* (*primer*), *tercero* (*tercer*).

- *Grande* shortens to *gran* before any singular noun.

- *Ciento* shortens to *cien* before any noun.

- The title *Santo* shortens to *San* before all masculine names except those beginning with *To-* or *Do-* (*San Juan*, *Santo Tomás*).

3. Position

Descriptive adjectives generally follow the nouns they modify (*una cosa útil, un actor famoso*). However, adjectives that express an inherent quality often precede the noun (*la blanca nieve*).

Some adjectives change meaning depending on whether they occur before or after the noun: *un pobre niño,* a poor (pitiable) child; *un niño pobre,* a poor (not rich) child; *un gran hombre,* a great man; *un hombre grande,* a big man; *el único libro,* the only book; *el libro único,* the unique book, etc.

4. Comparative and Superlative Forms

The comparative of Spanish adjectives is generally rendered as *más . . . que* (more . . . than) or *menos . . . que* (less . . . than): *soy más alta que él,* I'm taller than he; *son menos inteligentes que tú,* they're less intelligent than you.

The superlative of Spanish adjectives usually follows the formula *definite article + (noun +) más/menos + adjective: ella es la estudiante más trabajadora,* she is the hardest-working student; *él es el menos conocido,* he's the least known.

A few Spanish adjectives have irregular comparative and superlative forms:

Adjective	Comparative/Superlative
bueno (good)	**mejor** (better, best)
malo (bad)	**peor** (worse, worst)
grande[1] (big, great), **viejo** (old)	**mayor** (greater, older; greatest, oldest)
pequeño[1] (little), **joven** (young)	**menor** (lesser, younger; least, youngest)
mucho (much), **muchos** (many)	**más** (more, most)
poco (little), **pocos** (few)	**menos** (less, least)

[1] These words have regular comparative and superlative forms when used in reference to physical size: *él es más grande que yo; nuestra casa es la más pequeña.*

ABSOLUTE SUPERLATIVE

The absolute superlative is formed by placing *muy* before the adjective, or by adding the suffix *-ísimo* (*ella es muy simpática* or *ella es simpatiquísima,* she is very nice). The absolute superlative using *-ísimo* is formed according to the following rules:

- Adjectives ending in a consonant other than *-z* simply add the *-ísimo* ending (*fácil* → *facilísimo*).

- Adjectives ending in *-z* change this consonant to *-c* and add *-ísimo* (*feliz* → *felicísimo*).

- Adjectives ending in a vowel or diphthong drop the vowel or diphthong and add *-ísimo* (*claro* → *clarísimo; amplio* → *amplísimo*).

- Adjectives ending in *-co* or *-go* change these endings to *qu* and *gu*, respectively, and add *-ísimo* (*rico* → *riquísimo; largo* → *larguísimo*).

- Adjectives ending in *-ble* change this ending to *-bil* and add *-ísimo* (*notable* → *notabilísimo*).

- Adjectives containing the stressed diphthong *ie* or *ue* will sometimes change these to *e* and *o*, respectively (*ferviente* → *fervientísimo* or *ferventísimo; bueno* → *buenísimo* or *bonísimo*).

Adverbs

Adverbs can be formed by adding the adverbial suffix *-mente* to virtually any adjective (*fácil* → *fácilmente*). If the adjective varies for gender, the feminine form is used as the basis for forming the adverb (*rápido* → *rápidamente*).

Pronouns

1. Personal Pronouns

The personal pronouns in Spanish are:

Person	Singular		Plural	
FIRST	**yo**	I	**nosotros, nosotras**	we
SECOND	**tú**	you (familiar)	**vosotros[2], vosotras[2]**	you, all of you
	vos[1]	you		
	usted	you (formal)	**ustedes[3]**	you, all of you
THIRD	**él**	he	**ellos, ellas**	they
	ella	she		
	ello	it (neuter)		

[1] Familiar form used in addition to *tú* in South and Central America.

[2] Familiar form used in Spain.

[3] Formal form used in Spain; familiar and formal form used in Latin America.

FAMILIAR VS. FORMAL

The second person personal pronouns exist in both familiar and formal forms. The familiar forms are generally used when addressing relatives, friends, and children, although usage varies considerably from region to region; the formal forms are used in other contexts to show courtesy, respect, or emotional distance.

In Spain and in the Caribbean, *tú* is used exclusively as the familiar singular "you." In South and Central America, however, *vos* either competes with *tú* to varying degrees or replaces it entirely. (For a more detailed explanation of *vos* and its corresponding verb forms, refer to the Conjugation of Spanish Verbs section.)

The plural familiar form *vosotros, -as* is used only in Spain, where *ustedes* is reserved for formal contexts. In Latin America, *vosotros, -as* is not used, and *ustedes* serves as the all-purpose plural "you."

It should be noted that while *usted* and *ustedes* are regarded as second person pronouns, they take the third person form of the verb.

USAGE

In Spanish, personal pronouns are generally omitted (*voy al cine*, I'm going to the movies; *¿llamaron?*, did they call?), although they are sometimes used for purposes of emphasis or clarity (*se* *lo diré yo*, I will tell them; *vino ella, pero él se quedó*, she came, but he stayed behind). The forms *usted* and *ustedes* are usually included out of courtesy (*¿cómo está usted?*, how are you?).

Personal pronouns are not generally used in reference to inanimate objects or living creatures other than humans; in these instances, the pronoun is most often omitted (*¿es nuevo? no, es viejo*, is it new? no, it's old).

The neuter third person pronoun *ello* is reserved for indefinite subjects (as abstract concepts): *todo ello implica* . . . , all of this implies . . . ; *por si ello fuera poco* . . . , as if that weren't enough . . . . It most commonly appears in formal writing and speech. In less formal contexts, *ello* is often either omitted or replaced with *esto, eso,* or *aquello*.

2. Prepositional Pronouns

Prepositional pronouns are used as the objects of prepositions (*¿es para mí?*, is it for me?; *se lo dio a ellos*, he gave it to them).

The prepositional pronouns in Spanish are:

Singular		Plural	
mí	me	**nosotros, nosotras**	us
ti	you	**vosotros[1], vosotras[1]**	you
usted	you (formal)	**ustedes**	you
él	him	**ellos, ellas**	them
ella	her		
ello	it (neuter)		
sí	yourself, himself, herself, itself, oneself	**sí**	yourselves, themselves

[1] Used primarily in Spain.

When the preposition *con* is followed by *mí, ti,* or *sí,* both words are replaced by *conmigo, contigo,* and *consigo,* respectively (*¿vienes conmigo?*, are you coming with me?; *habló contigo*, he spoke with you; *no lo trajo consigo*, she didn't bring it with her).

3. Object Pronouns

DIRECT OBJECT PRONOUNS

Direct object pronouns represent the primary goal or result of the action of a verb. The direct object pronouns in Spanish are:

Singular		Plural	
me	me	nos	us
te	you	os[1]	you
le[2]	you, him	les[2]	you, them
lo	you, him, it	los	you, them
la	you, her, it	las	you, them

[1] Used only in Spain.
[2] Used mainly in Spain.

Agreement

The third person forms agree in both gender and number with the nouns they replace or the people they refer to (*pintó las paredes,* she painted the walls → *las pintó,* she painted them; *visitaron al señor Juárez*, they visited Mr. Juárez → *lo visitaron*, they visited him). The remaining forms vary only for number.

Position

Direct object pronouns are normally affixed to the end of an affirmative command, a simple infinitive, or a present participle (*¡hazlo!*, do it!; *es difícil hacerlo,* it's difficult to do it; *haciéndolo, aprenderás,* you'll learn by doing it). With constructions involving an auxiliary verb and an infinitive or present participle, the pronoun may occur either immediately before the construction or suffixed to it (*lo voy a hacer* or *voy a hacerlo,* I'm going to do it; *estoy haciéndolo* or *lo estoy haciendo,* I'm doing it). In all other cases, the pronoun immediately precedes the conjugated verb (*no lo haré,* I won't do it).

Regional Variation

In Spain and in a few areas of Latin America, *le* and *les* are used in place of *lo* and *los* when referring to or addressing people (*le vieron,* they saw him; *les vistió,* she dressed them). In most parts of Latin America, however, *los* and *las* are used for the second person plural in both formal and familiar contexts.

The second person plural familiar form *os* is restricted to Spain.

INDIRECT OBJECT PRONOUNS

Indirect object pronouns represent the secondary goal of the action of a verb (*me dio el regalo,* he gave me the gift; *les dije que no,* I told them no). The indirect object pronouns in Spanish are:

Singular		Plural	
me	(to, for, from) me	nos	(to, for, from) us
te	(to, for, from) you	os[1]	(to, for, from) you
le	(to, for, from) you, him, her, it	les	(to, for, from) you, them
se[2]		se[2]	

[1]Used only in Spain.
[2]See explanation below.

Position

Indirect object pronouns follow the same rules as direct object pronouns with regard to their position in relation to verbs. When they occur with direct object pronouns, the indirect object pronoun always precedes (*nos lo dio,* she gave it to us; *estoy trayéndotela,* I'm bringing it to you).

Use of *Se*

When the indirect object pronouns *le* or *les* occur before any direct object pronoun beginning with an *l-*, the indirect object pronouns *le* and *les* convert to *se* (*les mandé la carta,* I sent them the letter → *se la mandé,* I sent it to them; *vamos a comprarle los aretes,* let's buy her the earrings → *vamos a comprárselos,* let's buy them for her).

4. Reflexive Pronouns

Reflexive pronouns are used to refer back to the subject of the verb (*me hice daño,* I hurt myself; *se vistieron,* they got dressed, they dressed themselves; *nos lo compramos,* we bought it for ourselves).

The reflexive pronouns in Spanish are:

	Singular		Plural
me	myself	**nos**	ourselves
te	yourself	**os**[1]	yourselves
se	yourself, himself, herself, itself	**se**	yourselves, themselves

[1]Used only in Spain.

Reflexive pronouns are also used:

- When the verb describes an action performed to one's own body, clothing, etc. (*me quité los zapatos,* I took off my shoes; *se arregló el pelo,* he fixed his hair).

- In the plural, to indicate reciprocal action (*se hablan con frecuencia,* they speak with each other frequently).

- In the third person singular and plural, as an indefinite subject reference (*se dice que es verdad,* they say it's true; *nunca se sabe,* one never knows; *se escribieron miles de páginas,* thousands of pages were written).

It should be noted that many verbs which take reflexive pronouns in Spanish have intransitive equivalents in English (*ducharse,* to shower; *quejarse,* to complain; etc.).

5. Relative Pronouns

Relative pronouns introduce subordinate clauses acting as nouns or modifiers (*el libro que escribió* . . . , the book that he wrote . . . ; *las chicas a quienes conociste* . . . , the girls whom you met . . .). In Spanish, the relative pronouns are:

que (that, which, who, whom)

quien, quienes (who, whom, that, whoever, whomever)

el cual, la cual, los cuales, las cuales (which, who)

el que, la que, los que, las que (which, who, whoever)

lo cual (which)

lo que (what, which, whatever)

cuanto, cuanta, cuantos, cuantas (all those that, all that, whatever, whoever, as much as, as many as)

Relative pronouns are not omitted in Spanish as they often are in English: *el carro que vi ayer,* the car (that) I saw yesterday. When relative pronouns are used with prepositions, the preposition precedes the clause (*la película sobre la cual le hablé,* the film I spoke to you about).

The relative pronoun *que* can be used in reference to both people and things. Unlike other relative pronouns, *que* does not take the personal *a* when used as a direct object referring to a person (*el hombre que llamé,* the man that I called; but: *el hombre a quien llamé,* the man whom I called).

Quien is used only in reference to people. It varies in number with the explicit or implied antecedent (*las mujeres con quienes charlamos . . . ,* the women we chatted with; *quien lo hizo pagará,* whoever did it will pay).

El cual and *el que* vary for both number and gender, and are therefore often used in situations where *que* or *quien(es)* might create ambiguity: *nos contó algunas cosas sobre los libros, las cuales eran interesantes,* he told us some things about the books which (the things) were interesting.

Lo cual and *lo que* are used to refer back to a whole clause, or to something indefinite (*dijo que iría, lo cual me alegró,* he said he would go, which made me happy; *pide lo que quieras,* ask for whatever you want).

Cuanto varies for both number and gender with the implied antecedent: *conté a cuantas (personas) pude,* I counted as many (people) as I could. If an indefinite mass quantity is referred to, the masculine singular form is used (*anoté cuanto decía,* I jotted down whatever he said).

Possessives

1. Possessive Adjectives

UNSTRESSED FORMS

Singular		Plural	
mi(s)	my	**nuestro(s), nuestra(s)**	our
tu(s)	your	**vuestro(s)[1], vuestra(s)[1]**	your
su(s)	your, his, her, its	**su(s)**	your, their

[1] Used only in Spain.

STRESSED FORMS

Singular		Plural	
mío(s), mía(s)	my, mine, of mine	nuestro(s), nuestra(s)	our, ours, of ours
tuyo(s), tuya(s)	your, yours, of yours	vuestro(s)[1], vuestra(s)[1]	your, yours, of yours
suyo(s), suya(s)	your, yours, of yours; his, of his; her, hers, of hers; its, of its	suyo(s), suya(s)	your, yours, of yours; their, theirs, of theirs

[1]Used only in Spain.

The unstressed forms of possessive adjectives precede the nouns they modify (*mis zapatos,* my shoes; *nuestra escuela,* our school).

The stressed forms occur after the noun and are often used for purposes of emphasis (*el carro tuyo,* your car; *la pluma es mía,* the pen is mine; *unos amigos nuestros,* some friends of ours).

All possessive adjectives agree with the noun in number. The stressed forms, as well as the unstressed forms *nuestro* and *vuestro,* also vary for gender.

2. Possessive Pronouns

The possessive pronouns have the same forms as the stressed possessive adjectives (see table above). They are always preceded by the definite article, and they agree in number and gender with the nouns they replace (*las llaves mías,* my keys → *las mías,* mine; *los guantes nuestros,* our gloves → *los nuestros,* ours).

Demonstratives

1. Demonstrative Adjectives

The demonstrative adjectives in Spanish are:

Singular		Plural	
este, esta	this	estos, estas	these
ese, esa	that	esos, esas	those
aquel, aquella	that	aquellos, aquellas	those

Demonstrative adjectives agree with the nouns they modify in gender and number (*esta chica, aquellos árboles*). They normally precede the noun, but may occasionally occur after for purposes of emphasis or to express contempt: *en la época aquella de cambio*, in that era of change; *el perro ese ha ladrado toda la noche*, that (awful, annoying, etc.) dog barked all night long.

The forms *aquel, aquella, aquellos*, and *aquellas* are generally used in reference to people and things that are relatively distant from the speaker in space or time: *ese libro*, that book (a few feet away); *aquel libro*, that book (way over there).

2. Demonstrative Pronouns

The demonstrative pronouns in Spanish are orthographically identical to the demonstrative adjectives except that they take an accent mark over the stressed vowel (*éste, ése, aquél*, etc.). In addition, there are three neuter forms—*esto, eso*, and *aquello*—which are used when referring to abstract ideas or unidentified things (*¿te dijo eso?*, he said that to you?; *¿qué es esto?*, what is this?; *tráeme todo aquello*, bring me all that stuff).

Except for the neuter forms, demonstrative pronouns agree in gender and number with the nouns they replace (*esta silla*, this chair → *ésta*, this one; *aquellos vasos*, those glasses → *aquéllos*, those ones).

Abbreviations in This Work

adj	adjective	*nm*	masculine noun
adv	adverb	*nmf*	masculine or feminine noun
Arg	Argentina		
Bol	Bolivia	*nmfpl*	plural noun invariable for gender
Brit	British		
CA	Central America		
Car	Caribbean region	*nmfs & pl*	noun invariable for both gender and number
Col	Colombia		
conj	conjunction	*nmpl*	masculine plural noun
CoRi	Costa Rica		
DomRep	Dominican Republic	*nms & pl*	invariable singular or plural masculine noun
Ecua	Ecuador		
esp	especially	*npl*	plural noun
f	feminine	*ns & pl*	noun invariable for plural
fam	familiar or colloquial		
		Pan	Panama
fpl	feminine plural	*Par*	Paraguay
Guat	Guatemala	*pl*	plural
Hond	Honduras	*pp*	past participle
interj	interjection	*prep*	preposition
m	masculine	*PRi*	Puerto Rico
Mex	Mexico	*pron*	pronoun
mf	masculine or feminine	*s*	singular
		Sal	El Salvador
mfpl	masculine or feminine plural	*Uru*	Uruguay
		usu	usually
mpl	masculine plural	*v*	verb (transitive and intransitive)
n	noun		
nf	feminine noun	*v aux*	auxiliary verb
nfpl	feminine plural noun	*Ven*	Venezuela
		vi	intransitive verb
nfs & pl	invariable singular or plural feminine noun	*v impers*	impersonal verb
		vr	reflexive verb
Nic	Nicaragua	*vt*	transitive verb

Conjugation of Spanish Verbs

Simple Tenses

Tense	Regular Verbs Ending in -AR hablar	
PRESENT INDICATIVE	hablo	hablamos
	hablas	habláis
	habla	hablan
PRESENT SUBJUNCTIVE	hable	hablemos
	hables	habléis
	hable	hablen
PRETERIT INDICATIVE	hablé	hablamos
	hablaste	hablasteis
	habló	hablaron
IMPERFECT INDICATIVE	hablaba	hablábamos
	hablabas	hablabais
	hablaba	hablaban
IMPERFECT SUBJUNCTIVE	hablara	habláramos
	hablaras	hablarais
	hablara	hablaran
	or	
	hablase	hablásemos
	hablases	hablaseis
	hablase	hablasen
FUTURE INDICATIVE	hablaré	hablaremos
	hablarás	hablaréis
	hablará	hablarán
FUTURE SUBJUNCTIVE	hablare	habláremos
	hablares	hablareis
	hablare	hablaren
CONDITIONAL	hablaría	hablaríamos
	hablarías	hablaríais
	hablaría	hablarían
IMPERATIVE		hablemos
	habla	hablad
	hable	hablen
PRESENT PARTICIPLE (GERUND)	hablando	
PAST PARTICIPLE	hablado	

Regular Verbs Ending in -ER		Regular Verbs Ending in -IR	
comer		vivir	
como	comemos	vivo	vivimos
comes	coméis	vives	vivís
come	comen	vive	viven
coma	comamos	viva	vivamos
comas	comáis	vivas	viváis
coma	coman	viva	vivan
comí	comimos	viví	vivimos
comiste	comisteis	viviste	vivisteis
comió	comieron	vivió	vivieron
comía	comíamos	vivía	vivíamos
comías	comíais	vivías	vivíais
comía	comían	vivía	vivían
comiera	comiéramos	viviera	viviéramos
comieras	comierais	vivieras	vivierais
comiera	comieran	viviera	vivieran
or		*or*	
comiese	comiésemos	viviese	viviésemos
comieses	comieseis	vivieses	vivieseis
comiese	comiesen	viviese	viviesen
comeré	comeremos	viviré	viviremos
comerás	comeréis	vivirás	viviréis
comerá	comerán	vivirá	vivirán
comiere	comiéremos	viviere	viviéremos
comieres	comiereis	vivieres	viviereis
comiere	comieren	viviere	vivieren
comería	comeríamos	viviría	viviríamos
comerías	comeríais	vivirías	viviríais
comería	comerían	viviría	vivirían
	comamos		vivamos
come	comed	vive	vivid
coma	coman	viva	vivan
comiendo		viviendo	
comido		vivido	

Compound Tenses

1. Perfect Tenses

The perfect tenses are formed with *haber* and the past participle:

PRESENT PERFECT
> he hablado, etc. (*indicative*);
> haya hablado, etc. (*subjunctive*)

PAST PERFECT
> había hablado, etc. (*indicative*);
> hubiera hablado, etc. (*subjunctive*)
> *or*
> hubiese hablado, etc. (*subjunctive*)

PRETERIT PERFECT
> hube hablado, etc. (*indicative*)

FUTURE PERFECT
> habré hablado, etc. (*indicative*)

CONDITIONAL PERFECT
> habría hablado, etc. (*indicative*)

2. Progressive Tenses

The progressive tenses are formed with *estar* and the present participle:

PRESENT PROGRESSIVE
> estoy llamando, etc. (*indicative*);
> esté llamando, etc. (*subjunctive*)

IMPERFECT PROGRESSIVE
> estaba llamando, etc. (*indicative*);
> estuviera llamando, etc. (*subjunctive*)
> *or*
> estuviese llamando, etc. (*subjunctive*)

PRETERIT PROGRESSIVE

    estuve llamando, etc. (*indicative*)

FUTURE PROGRESSIVE

    estaré llamando, etc. (*indicative*)

CONDITIONAL PROGRESSIVE

    estaría llamando, etc. (*indicative*)

PRESENT PERFECT PROGRESSIVE

    he estado llamando, etc. (*indicative*);
    haya estado llamando, etc. (*subjunctive*)

PAST PERFECT PROGRESSIVE

    había estado llamando, etc. (*indicative*);
    hubiera estado llamando, etc. (*subjunctive*)
or
    hubiese estado llamando, etc. (*subjunctive*)

Use of *Vos*

In parts of South and Central America, *vos* often replaces or competes with *tú* as the second person familiar personal pronoun. It is particularly well established in the Río de la Plata region and much of Central America.

The pronoun *vos* often takes a distinct set of verb forms, usually in the present tense and the imperative. These vary widely from region to region; examples of the most common forms are shown below.

INFINITIVE FORM	hablar	comer	vivir
PRESENT INDICATIVE	vos hablás	vos comés	vos vivís
PRESENT SUBJUNCTIVE	vos hablés	vos comás	vos vivás
IMPERATIVE	hablá	comé	viví

In some areas, *vos* may take the *tú* or *vosotros* forms of the verb, while in others (as Uruguay), *tú* is combined with the *vos* verb forms.

Irregular Verbs

The *imperfect subjunctive,* the *future subjunctive,* the *conditional*, and most forms of the *imperative* are not included in the model conjugations list, but can be derived as follows:

The *imperfect subjunctive* and the *future subjunctive* are formed from the third person plural form of the preterit tense by removing the last syllable (*-ron*) and adding the appropriate suffix:

PRETERIT INDICATIVE, THIRD PERSON PLURAL (querer)	quisieron
IMPERFECT SUBJUNCTIVE (querer)	quisiera, quisieras, etc. *or* quisiese, quisieses, etc.
FUTURE SUBJUNCTIVE (querer)	quisiere, quisieres, etc.

The conditional uses the same stem as the future indicative:

FUTURE INDICATIVE (poner)	pondré, pondrás, etc.
CONDITIONAL (poner)	pondría, pondrías, etc.

The third person singular, first person plural, and third person plural forms of the *imperative* are the same as the corresponding forms of the present subjunctive.

The second person plural *(vosotros)* form of the *imperative* is formed by removing the final *-r* of the infinitive form and adding a *-d* (ex.: *oír → oíd*).

Model Conjugations of Irregular Verbs

The model conjugations below include the following simple tenses: the *present indicative* (IND), the *present subjunctive* (SUBJ), the *preterit indicative* (PRET), the *imperfect indicative* (IMPF), the *future indicative* (FUT), the second person singular form of the *imperative* (IMPER), the *present participle* or *gerund* (PRP), and the *past participle* (PP). Each set of conjugations is preceded by the corresponding infinitive form of the verb, shown in bold type. Only tenses containing irregularities are listed, and the irregular verb forms within each tense are displayed in bold type.

Each irregular verb entry in the Spanish-English section of this dictionary is cross-referred by number to one of the following model conjugations. These cross-reference numbers are shown in curly braces { } immediately following the entry's functional label.

1 **abolir** *(defective verb)* : IND abolimos, abolís *(other forms not used)*; SUBJ *(not used)*; IMPER *(only second person plural is used)*

2 **abrir** : PP abierto

3 **actuar** : IND **actúo, actúas, actúa**, actuamos, actuáis, **actúan**; SUBJ **actúe, actúes, actúe**, actuemos, actuéis, **actúen**; IMPER **actúa**

4 **adquirir** : IND **adquiero, adquieres, adquiere**, adquirimos, adquirís, **adquieren**; SUBJ **adquiera, adquieras, adquiera**, adquiramos, adquiráis, **adquieran**; IMPER **adquiere**

5 **airar** : IND **aíro, aíras, aíra**, airamos, airáis, **aíran**; SUBJ **aíre, aíres, aíre**, airemos, airéis, **aíren**; IMPER **aíra**

6 **andar** : PRET **anduve, anduviste, anduvo, anduvimos, anduvisteis, anduvieron**

7 **asir** : IND **asgo**, ases, ase, asimos, asís, asen; SUBJ **asga, asgas, asga, asgamos, asgáis, asgan**

8 **aunar** : IND **aúno, aúnas, aúna**, aunamos, aunáis, **aúnan**; SUBJ **aúne, aúnes, aúne**, aunemos, aunéis, **aúnen**; IMPER **aúna**

9 **avergonzar** : IND **avergüenzo, avergüenzas, avergüenza**, avergonzamos, avergonzáis, **avergüenzan**; SUBJ **avergüence, avergüences, avergüence**, avergoncemos, avergoncéis, **avergüencen**; PRET **avergoncé**; IMPER **avergüenza**

10 **averiguar** : SUBJ **averigüe, averigües, averigüe, averigüemos, averigüéis, averigüen**; PRET **averigüé**, averiguaste, averiguó, averiguamos, averiguasteis, averiguaron

11 **bendecir** : *IND* **bendigo, bendices, bendice,** bendecimos, ben-
decís, **bendicen;** *SUBJ* **bendiga, bendigas, bendiga, bendig-
amos, bendigáis, bendigan;** *PRET* **bendije, bendijiste,
bendijo, bendijimos, bendijisteis, bendijeron;** *IMPER* **bendice**

12 **caber** : *IND* **quepo,** cabes, cabe, cabemos, cabéis, caben; *SUBJ*
quepa, quepas, quepa, quepamos, quepáis, quepan; *PRET*
cupe, cupiste, cupo, cupimos, cupisteis, cupieron; *FUT* **cabré,
cabrás, cabrá, cabremos, cabréis, cabrán**

13 **caer** : *IND* **caigo,** caes, cae, caemos, caéis, caen; *SUBJ* **caiga,
caigas, caiga, caigamos, caigáis, caigan;** *PRET* caí, **caíste,
cayó, caímos, caísteis, cayeron;** *PRP* **cayendo;** *PP* **caído**

14 **cocer** : *IND* **cuezo, cueces, cuece,** cocemos, cocéis, **cuecen;**
SUBJ **cueza, cuezas, cueza,** cozamos, cozáis, **cuezan;** *IMPER*
cuece

15 **coger** : *IND* **cojo,** coges, coge, cogemos, cogéis, cogen; *SUBJ*
coja, cojas, coja, cojamos, cojáis, cojan

16 **colgar** : *IND* **cuelgo, cuelgas, cuelga,** colgamos, colgáis, **cuel-
gan;** *SUBJ* **cuelgue, cuelgues, cuelgue, colguemos, colguéis,
cuelguen;** *PRET* **colgué,** colgaste, colgó, colgamos, colgasteis,
colgaron; *IMPER* **cuelga**

17 **concernir** *(defective verb; used only in the third person singular
and plural of the present indicative, present subjunctive, and
imperfect subjunctive)* see 25 **discernir**

18 **conocer** : *IND* **conozco,** conoces, conoce, conocemos, cono-
céis, conocen; *SUBJ* **conozca, conozcas, conozca, conoz-
camos, conozcáis, conozcan**

19 **contar** : *IND* **cuento, cuentas, cuenta,** contamos, contáis, **cuen-
tan;** *SUBJ* **cuente, cuentes, cuente,** contemos, contéis,
cuenten; *IMPER* **cuenta**

20 **creer** : *PRET* creí, **creíste, creyó, creímos, creísteis, creyeron;**
PRP **creyendo;** *PP* **creído**

21 **cruzar** : *SUBJ* **cruce, cruces, cruce, crucemos, crucéis, crucen;**
PRET **crucé,** cruzaste, cruzó, cruzamos, cruzasteis, cruzaron

22 **dar** : *IND* **doy,** das, da, damos, **dais,** dan; *SUBJ* **dé,** des, **dé,**
demos, **deis,** den; *PRET* **di, diste, dio, dimos, disteis, dieron**

23 **decir** : *IND* **digo, dices, dice,** decimos, decís, **dicen;** *SUBJ* **diga, digas, diga, digamos, digáis, digan;** *PRET* **dije, dijiste, dijo, dijimos, dijisteis, dijeron;** *FUT* **diré, dirás, dirá, diremos, diréis, dirán;** *IMPER* **di;** *PRP* **diciendo;** *PP* **dicho**

24 **delinquir** : *IND* **delinco,** delinques, delinque, delinquimos, delinquís, delinquen; *SUBJ* **delinca, delincas, delinca, delincamos, delincáis, delincan**

25 **discernir** : *IND* **discierno, disciernes, discierne,** discernimos, discernís, **disciernen;** *SUBJ* **discierna, disciernas, discierna,** discernamos, discernáis, **disciernan;** *IMPER* **discierne**

26 **distinguir** : *IND* **distingo,** distingues, distingue, distinguimos, distinguís, distinguen; *SUBJ* **distinga, distingas, distinga, distingamos, distingáis, distingan**

27 **dormir** : *IND* **duermo, duermes, duerme,** dormimos, dormís, **duermen;** *SUBJ* **duerma, duermas, duerma, durmamos, durmáis, duerman;** *PRET* **dormí,** dormiste, **durmió,** dormimos, dormisteis, **durmieron;** *IMPER* **duerme;** *PRP* **durmiendo**

28 **elegir** : *IND* **elijo, eliges, elige,** elegimos, elegís, **eligen;** *SUBJ* **elija, elijas, elija, elijamos, elijáis, elijan;** *PRET* elegí, elegiste, **eligió,** elegimos, elegisteis, **eligieron;** *IMPER* **elige;** *PRP* **eligiendo**

29 **empezar** : *IND* **empiezo, empiezas, empieza,** empezamos, empezáis, **empiezan;** *SUBJ* **empiece, empieces, empiece, empecemos, empecéis, empiecen;** *PRET* **empecé,** empezaste, empezó, empezamos, empezasteis, empezaron; *IMPER* **empieza**

30 **enraizar** : *IND* **enraízo, enraízas, enraíza,** enraizamos, enraizáis, **enraízan;** *SUBJ* **enraíce, enraíces, enraíce, enraicemos, enraicéis, enraícen;** *PRET* **enraicé,** enraizaste, enraizó, enraizamos, enraizasteis, enraizaron; *IMPER* **enraíza**

31 **erguir** : *IND* **irgo** *or* **yergo, irgues** *or* **yergues, irgue** *or* **yergue,** erguimos, erguís, **irguen** *or* **yerguen;** *SUBJ* **irga** *or* **yerga, irgas** *or* **yergas, irga** *or* **yerga, irgamos, irgáis, irgan** *or* **yergan;** *PRET* erguí, erguiste, **irguió,** erguimos, erguisteis, **irguieron;** *IMPER* **irgue** *or* **yergue;** *PRP* **irguiendo**

32 **errar** : *IND* **yerro, yerras, yerra,** erramos, erráis, **yerran;** *SUBJ*
yerre, yerres, yerre, erremos, erréis, **yerren;** *IMPER* **yerra**

33 **escribir** : *PP* **escrito**

34 **estar** : *IND* **estoy, estás, está,** estamos, estáis, **están;** *SUBJ* **esté,**
estés, esté, estemos, estéis, **estén;** *PRET* **estuve, estuviste,**
estuvo, estuvimos, estuvisteis, estuvieron; *IMPER* **está**

35 **exigir** : *IND* **exijo,** exiges, exige, exigimos, exigís, exigen; *SUBJ*
exija, exijas, exija, exijamos, exijáis, exijan

36 **forzar** : *IND* **fuerzo, fuerzas, fuerza,** forzamos, forzáis,
fuerzan; *SUBJ* **fuerce, fuerces, fuerce, forcemos, forcéis,**
fuercen; *PRET* **forcé,** forzaste, forzó, forzamos, forzasteis,
forzaron; *IMPER* **fuerza**

37 **freír** : *IND* **frío, fríes, fríe, freímos,** freís, **fríen;** *SUBJ* **fría, frías,**
fría, friamos, friáis, frían; *PRET* freí, **freíste, frió, freímos,**
freísteis, frieron; *IMPER* **fríe;** *PRP* **friendo;** *PP* **frito**

38 **gruñir** : *PRET* gruñí, gruñiste, **gruñó,** gruñimos, gruñisteis,
gruñeron; *PRP* **gruñendo**

39 **haber** : *IND* **he, has, ha, hemos,** habéis, **han;** *SUBJ* **haya, hayas,**
haya, hayamos, hayáis, hayan; *PRET* **hube, hubiste, hubo,**
hubimos, hubisteis, hubieron; *FUT* **habré, habrás, habrá,**
habremos, habréis, habrán; *IMPER* **he**

40 **hacer** : *IND* **hago,** haces, hace, hacemos, hacéis, hacen; *SUBJ*
haga, hagas, haga, hagamos, hagáis, hagan; *PRET* **hice,**
hiciste, hizo, hicimos, hicisteis, hicieron; *FUT* **haré, harás,**
hará, haremos, haréis, harán; *IMPER* **haz;** *PP* **hecho**

41 **huir** : *IND* **huyo, huyes, huye,** huimos, huís, **huyen;** *SUBJ* **huya,**
huyas, huya, huyamos, huyáis, huyan; *PRET* huí, huiste,
huyó, huimos, huisteis, **huyeron;** *IMPER* **huye;** *PRP* **huyendo**

42 **imprimir** : *PP* **impreso**

43 **ir** : *IND* **voy, vas, va, vamos, vais, van;** *SUBJ* **vaya, vayas, vaya,**
vayamos, vayáis, vayan; *PRET* **fui, fuiste, fue, fuimos, fuis-**
teis, fueron; *IMPF* **iba, ibas, iba, íbamos, ibais, iban;** *IMPER*
ve; *PRP* **yendo;** *PP* **ido**

44 **jugar** : *IND* **juego, juegas, juega,** jugamos, jugáis, **juegan;** *SUBJ*
juegue, juegues, juegue, juguemos, juguéis, jueguen; *PRET*

jugué, jugaste, jugó, jugamos, jugasteis, jugaron; *IMPER* **juega**

45 **lucir** : *IND* **luzco**, luces, luce, lucimos, lucís, lucen; *SUBJ* **luzca, luzcas, luzca, luzcamos, luzcáis, luzcan**

46 **morir** : *IND* **muero, mueres, muere**, morimos, morís, **mueren**; *SUBJ* **muera, mueras, muera**, muramos, muráis, **mueran**; *PRET* morí, moriste, **murió**, morimos, moristeis, **murieron**; *IMPER* **muere**; *PRP* **muriendo**; *PP* **muerto**

47 **mover** : *IND* **muevo, mueves, mueve**, movemos, movéis, **mueven**; *SUBJ* **mueva, muevas, mueva**, movamos, mováis, **muevan**; *IMPER* **mueve**

48 **nacer** : *IND* **nazco**, naces, nace, nacemos, nacéis, nacen; *SUBJ* **nazca, nazcas, nazca, nazcamos, nazcáis, nazcan**

49 **negar** : *IND* **niego, niegas, niega**, negamos, negáis, **niegan**; *SUBJ* **niegue, niegues, niegue**, neguemos, neguéis, **nieguen**; *PRET* **negué**, negaste, negó, negamos, negasteis, negaron; *IMPER* **niega**

50 **oír** : *IND* **oigo, oyes, oye, oímos**, oís, **oyen**; *SUBJ* **oiga, oigas, oiga, oigamos, oigáis, oigan**; *PRET* oí, **oíste, oyó, oímos, oísteis, oyeron**; *IMPER* **oye**; *PRP* **oyendo**; *PP* **oído**

51 **oler** : *IND* **huelo, hueles, huele**, olemos, oléis, **huelen**; *SUBJ* **huela, huelas, huela**, olamos, oláis, **huelan**; *IMPER* **huele**

52 **pagar** : *SUBJ* **pague, pagues, pague, paguemos, paguéis, paguen**; *PRET* **pagué**, pagaste, pagó, pagamos, pagasteis, pagaron

53 **parecer** : *IND* **parezco**, pareces, parece, parecemos, parecéis, parecen; *SUBJ* **parezca, parezcas, parezca, parezcamos, parezcáis, parezcan**

54 **pedir** : *IND* **pido, pides, pide**, pedimos, pedís, **piden**; *SUBJ* **pida, pidas, pida, pidamos, pidáis, pidan**; *PRET* pedí, pediste, **pidió**, pedimos, pedisteis, **pidieron**; *IMPER* **pide**; *PRP* **pidiendo**

55 **pensar** : *IND* **pienso, piensas, piensa**, pensamos, pensáis, **piensan**; *SUBJ* **piense, pienses, piense**, pensemos, penséis, **piensen**; *IMPER* **piensa**

56 **perder** : *IND* **pierdo, pierdes, pierde**, perdemos, perdéis, **pier-**
den; *SUBJ* **pierda, pierdas, pierda**, perdamos, perdáis, **pier-**
dan; *IMPER* **pierde**

57 **placer** : *IND* **plazco**, places, place, placemos, placéis, placen;
SUBJ **plazca, plazcas, plazca, plazcamos, plazcáis, plazcan;**
PRET plací, placiste, plació *or* **plugo**, placimos, placisteis,
placieron *or* **pluguieron**

58 **poder** : *IND* **puedo, puedes, puede**, podemos, podéis, **pueden;**
SUBJ **pueda, puedas, pueda**, podamos, podáis, **puedan;** *PRET*
pude, pudiste, pudo, pudimos, pudisteis, pudieron; *FUT*
podré, podrás, podrá, podremos, podréis, podrán; *IMPER*
puede; *PRP* **pudiendo**

59 **podrir** *or* **pudrir** : *PP* **podrido** *(all other forms based on* pudrir*)*

60 **poner** : *IND* **pongo**, pones, pone, ponemos, ponéis, ponen; *SUBJ*
ponga, pongas, ponga, pongamos, pongáis, pongan; *PRET*
puse, pusiste, puso, pusimos, pusisteis, pusieron; *FUT* **pon-**
dré, pondrás, pondrá, pondremos, pondréis, pondrán;
IMPER **pon;** *PP* **puesto**

61 **producir** : *IND* **produzco**, produces, produce, producimos,
producís, producen; *SUBJ* **produzca, produzcas, produzca,**
produzcamos, produzcáis, produzcan; *PRET* **produje, pro-**
dujiste, produjo, produjimos, produjisteis, produjeron

62 **prohibir** : *IND* **prohíbo, prohíbes, prohíbe**, prohibimos, pro-
hibís, **prohíben;** *SUBJ* **prohíba, prohíbas, prohíba**, pro-
hibamos, prohibáis, **prohíban;** *IMPER* **prohíbe**

63 **proveer** : *PRET* **proveí, proveíste, proveyó, proveímos,**
proveísteis, proveyeron; *PRP* **proveyendo;** *PP* **provisto**

64 **querer** : *IND* **quiero, quieres, quiere**, queremos, queréis,
quieren; *SUBJ* **quiera, quieras, quiera**, queramos, queráis,
quieran; *PRET* **quise, quisiste, quiso, quisimos, quisisteis,**
quisieron; *FUT* **querré, querrás, querrá, querremos, quer-**
réis, querrán; *IMPER* **quiere**

65 **raer** : *IND* rao *or* **raigo** *or* **rayo**, raes, rae, raemos, raéis, raen;
SUBJ **raiga** *or* **raya, raigas** *or* **rayas, raiga** *or* **raya, raigamos**
or **rayamos, raigáis** *or* **rayáis, raigan** *or* **rayan;** *PRET* **raí,**
raíste, rayó, raímos, raísteis, rayeron; *PRP* **rayendo;** *PP* **raí-**
do

66 **reír** : *IND* **río, ríes, ríe, reímos,** reís, **ríen;** *SUBJ* **ría, rías, ría, riamos, riáis, rían;** *PRET* reí, **reíste, rió, reímos, reísteis, rieron;** *IMPER* **ríe;** *PRP* **riendo;** *PP* **reído**

67 **reñir** : *IND* **riño, riñes, riñe,** reñimos, reñís, **riñen;** *SUBJ* **riña, riñas, riña, riñamos, riñáis, riñan;** *PRET* reñí, reñiste, **riñó,** reñimos, reñisteis, **riñeron;** *IMPER* riñe; *PRP* riñendo

68 **reunir** : *IND* **reúno, reúnes, reúne,** reunimos, reunís, **reúnen;** *SUBJ* **reúna, reúnas, reúna,** reunamos, reunáis, **reúnan;** *IMPER* **reúne**

69 **roer** : *IND* **roo** *or* **roigo** *or* **royo,** roes, roe, roemos, roéis, roen; *SUBJ* **roa** *or* **roiga** *or* **roya,** roas *or* **roigas** *or* **royas,** roa *or* **roiga** *or* **roya,** roamos *or* **roigamos** *or* **royamos,** roáis *or* **roigáis** *or* **royáis,** roan *or* **roigan** *or* **royan;** *PRET* roí, **roíste, royó, roímos, roísteis, royeron;** *PRP* **royendo;** *PP* **roído**

70 **romper** : *PP* **roto**

71 **saber** : *IND* **sé,** sabes, sabe, sabemos, sabéis, saben; *SUBJ* **sepa, sepas, sepa, sepamos, sepáis, sepan;** *PRET* **supe, supiste, supo, supimos, supisteis, supieron;** *FUT* **sabré, sabrás, sabrá, sabremos, sabréis, sabrán**

72 **sacar** : *SUBJ* **saque, saques, saque, saquemos, saquéis, saquen;** *PRET* **saqué,** sacaste, sacó, sacamos, sacasteis, sacaron

73 **salir** : *IND* **salgo,** sales, sale, salimos, salís, salen; *SUBJ* **salga, salgas, salga, salgamos, salgáis, salgan;** *FUT* **saldré, saldrás, saldrá, saldremos, saldréis, saldrán;** *IMPER* **sal**

74 **satisfacer** : *IND* **satisfago,** satisfaces, satisface, satisfacemos, satisfacéis, satisfacen; *SUBJ* **satisfaga, satisfagas, satisfaga, satisfagamos, satisfagáis, satisfagan;** *PRET* **satisfice, satisficiste, satisfizo, satisficimos, satisficisteis, satisficieron;** *FUT* **satisfaré, satisfarás, satisfará, satisfaremos, satisfaréis, satisfarán;** *IMPER* **satisfaz** *or* satisface; *PP* **satisfecho**

75 **seguir** : *IND* **sigo, sigues, sigue,** seguimos, seguís, **siguen;** *SUBJ* **siga, sigas, siga, sigamos, sigáis, sigan;** *PRET* seguí, seguiste, **siguió,** seguimos, seguisteis, **siguieron;** *IMPER* **sigue;** *PRP* **siguiendo**

76 **sentir** : *IND* **siento, sientes, siente,** sentimos, sentís, **sienten;** *SUBJ* **sienta, sientas, sienta, sintamos, sintáis, sientan;** *PRET*

sentí, sentiste, **sintió,** sentimos, sentisteis, **sintieron;** *IMPER* **siente;** *PRP* **sintiendo**

77 **ser** : *IND* **soy, eres, es, somos, sois, son;** *SUBJ* **sea, seas, sea, seamos, seáis, sean;** *PRET* **fui, fuiste, fue, fuimos, fuisteis, fueron;** *IMPF* **era, eras, era, éramos, erais, eran;** *IMPER* **sé;** *PRP* **siendo;** *PP* **sido**

78 **soler** (*defective verb; used only in the present, preterit, and imperfect indicative, and the present and imperfect subjunctive*) *see* 47 **mover**

79 **tañer** : *PRET* **tañí,** tañiste, **tañó,** tañimos, tañisteis, **tañeron;** *PRP* **tañendo**

80 **tener** : *IND* **tengo, tienes, tiene,** tenemos, tenéis, **tienen;** *SUBJ* **tenga, tengas, tenga, tengamos, tengáis, tengan;** *PRET* **tuve, tuviste, tuvo, tuvimos, tuvisteis, tuvieron;** *FUT* **tendré, tendrás, tendrá, tendremos, tendréis, tendrán;** *IMPER* **ten**

81 **traer** : *IND* **traigo,** traes, trae, traemos, traéis, traen; *SUBJ* **traiga, traigas, traiga, traigamos, traigáis, traigan;** *PRET* **traje, trajiste, trajo, trajimos, trajisteis, trajeron;** *PRP* **trayendo;** *PP* **traído**

82 **trocar** : *IND* **trueco, truecas, trueca,** trocamos, trocáis, **truecan;** *SUBJ* **trueque, trueques, trueque, troquemos, troquéis, truequen;** *PRET* **troqué,** trocaste, trocó, trocamos, trocasteis, trocaron; *IMPER* **trueca**

83 **uncir** : *IND* **unzo,** unces, unce, uncimos, uncís, uncen; *SUBJ* **unza, unzas, unza, unzamos, unzáis, unzan**

84 **valer** : *IND* **valgo,** vales, vale, valemos, valéis, valen; *SUBJ* **valga, valgas, valga, valgamos, valgáis, valgan;** *FUT* **valdré, valdrás, valdrá, valdremos, valdréis, valdrán**

85 **variar** : *IND* **varío, varías, varía,** variamos, variáis, **varían;** *SUBJ* **varíe, varíes, varíe,** variemos, variéis, **varíen;** *IMPER* **varía**

86 **vencer** : *IND* **venzo,** vences, vence, vencemos, vencéis, vencen; *SUBJ* **venza, venzas, venza, venzamos, venzáis, venzan**

87 **venir** : *IND* **vengo, vienes, viene,** venimos, venís, **vienen;** *SUBJ* **venga, vengas, venga, vengamos, vengáis, vengan;** *PRET* **vine, viniste, vino, vinimos, vinisteis, vinieron;** *FUT* **vendré,**

vendrás, vendrá, vendremos, vendréis, vendrán; *IMPER* ven;
PRP viniendo

88 **ver** : *IND* veo, ves, ve, vemos, veis, ven; *PRET* vi, viste, vio,
vimos, visteis, vieron; *IMPER* ve; *PRP* viendo; *PP* visto

89 **volver** : *IND* vuelvo, vuelves, vuelve, volvemos, volvéis, vuel-
ven; *SUBJ* vuelva, vuelvas, vuelva, volvamos, volváis, vuel-
van; *IMPER* vuelve; *PP* vuelto

90 **yacer** : *IND* yazco *or* yazgo *or* yago, yaces, yace, yacemos,
yacéis, yacen; *SUBJ* yazca *or* yazga *or* yaga, yazcas *or* yaz-
gas *or* yagas, yazca *or* yazga *or* yaga, yazcamos *or* yazg-
amos *or* yagamos, yazcáis *or* yazgáis *or* yagáis, yazcan *or*
yazgan *or* yagan; *IMPER* yace *or* yaz

Irregular English Verbs

INFINITIVE	PAST	PAST PARTICIPLE
arise	arose	arisen
awake	awoke	awoken *or* awaked
be	was, were	been
bear	bore	borne
beat	beat	beaten *or* beat
become	became	become
befall	befell	befallen
begin	began	begun
behold	beheld	beheld
bend	bent	bent
beseech	beseeched *or* besought	beseeched *or* besought
beset	beset	beset
bet	bet	bet
bid	bade *or* bid	bidden *or* bid
bind	bound	bound
bite	bit	bitten
bleed	bled	bled
blow	blew	blown
break	broke	broken
breed	bred	bred
bring	brought	brought
build	built	built
burn	burned *or* burnt	burned *or* burnt
burst	burst	burst
buy	bought	bought
can	could	—
cast	cast	cast
catch	caught	caught
choose	chose	chosen
cling	clung	clung
come	came	come
cost	cost	cost
creep	crept	crept
cut	cut	cut
deal	dealt	dealt
dig	dug	dug
do	did	done
draw	drew	drawn
dream	dreamed *or* dreamt	dreamed *or* dreamt
drink	drank	drunk *or* drank
drive	drove	driven
dwell	dwelled *or* dwelt	dwelled *or* dwelt

INFINITIVE	PAST	PAST PARTICIPLE
eat	ate	eaten
fall	fell	fallen
feed	fed	fed
feel	felt	felt
fight	fought	fought
find	found	found
flee	fled	fled
fling	flung	flung
fly	flew	flown
forbid	forbade	forbidden
forecast	forecast	forecast
forego	forewent	foregone
foresee	foresaw	foreseen
foretell	foretold	foretold
forget	forgot	forgotten *or* forgot
forgive	forgave	forgiven
forsake	forsook	forsaken
freeze	froze	frozen
get	got	got *or* gotten
give	gave	given
go	went	gone
grind	ground	ground
grow	grew	grown
hang	hung	hung
have	had	had
hear	heard	heard
hide	hid	hidden *or* hid
hit	hit	hit
hold	held	held
hurt	hurt	hurt
keep	kept	kept
kneel	knelt *or* kneeled	knelt *or* kneeled
know	knew	known
lay	laid	laid
lead	led	led
lean	leaned	leaned
leap	leaped *or* leapt	leaped *or* leapt
learn	learned	learned
leave	left	left
lend	lent	lent
let	let	let
lie	lay	lain
light	lit *or* lighted	lit *or* lighted
lose	lost	lost
make	made	made
may	might	—

INFINITIVE	PAST	PAST PARTICIPLE
mean	meant	meant
meet	met	met
mow	mowed	mowed *or* mown
pay	paid	paid
put	put	put
quit	quit	quit
read	read	read
rend	rent	rent
rid	rid	rid
ride	rode	ridden
ring	rang	rung
rise	rose	risen
run	ran	run
saw	sawed	sawed *or* sawn
say	said	said
see	saw	seen
seek	sought	sought
sell	sold	sold
send	sent	sent
set	set	set
shake	shook	shaken
shall	should	—
shear	sheared	sheared *or* shorn
shed	shed	shed
shine	shone *or* shined	shone *or* shined
shoot	shot	shot
show	showed	shown *or* showed
shrink	shrank *or* shrunk	shrunk *or* shrunken
shut	shut	shut
sing	sang *or* sung	sung
sink	sank *or* sunk	sunk
sit	sat	sat
slay	slew	slain
sleep	slept	slept
slide	slid	slid
sling	slung	slung
smell	smelled *or* smelt	smelled *or* smelt
sow	sowed	sown *or* sowed
speak	spoke	spoken
speed	sped *or* speeded	sped *or* speeded
spell	spelled	spelled
spend	spent	spent
spill	spilled	spilled
spin	spun	spun
spit	spit *or* spat	spit *or* spat
split	split	split

INFINITIVE	PAST	PAST PARTICIPLE
spoil	spoiled	spoiled
spread	spread	spread
spring	sprang *or* sprung	sprung
stand	stood	stood
steal	stole	stolen
stick	stuck	stuck
sting	stung	stung
stink	stank *or* stunk	stunk
stride	strode	stridden
strike	struck	struck
swear	swore	sworn
sweep	swept	swept
swell	swelled	swelled *or* swollen
swim	swam	swum
swing	swung	swung
take	took	taken
teach	taught	taught
tear	tore	torn
tell	told	told
think	thought	thought
throw	threw	thrown
thrust	thrust	thrust
tread	trod	trodden *or* trod
wake	woke	woken *or* waked
waylay	waylaid	waylaid
wear	wore	worn
weave	wove *or* weaved	woven *or* weaved
wed	wedded	wedded
weep	wept	wept
will	would	—
win	won	won
wind	wound	wound
withdraw	withdrew	withdrawn
withhold	withheld	withheld
withstand	withstood	withstood
wring	wrung	wrung
write	wrote	written

Spelling-to-Sound Correspondences in Spanish

For example words for the phonetic symbols below, see
Pronunciation Symbols on page 58a.

VOWELS
a   [a]

e   [e] in open syllables
(syllables ending with
a vowel); [ɛ] in closed
syllables (syllables
ending with a conso-
nant)

i   [i]; before another vowel
in the same syllable
pronounced as [j] ([ʒ] or
[ʃ] in Argentina and
Uruguay; [ʤ] when at
the beginning of a word
in the Caribbean)

o   [o] in open syllables
(syllables ending with
a vowel); [ɔ] in closed
syllables (syllables
ending with a conso-
nant)

u   [u]; before another vowel
in the same syllable
pronounced as [w]

y   [i]; before another vowel
in the same syllable
pronounced as [j] ([ʒ] or
[ʃ] in Argentina and
Uruguay; [ʤ] when at
the beginning of a word
in the Caribbean)

CONSONANTS
b   [b] at the beginning of a
word or after *m* or *n*; [β]
elsewhere

c   [s] before *i* or *e* in Latin
America and parts of
southern Spain, [θ] in
northern Spain; [k]
elsewhere

ch   [ʧ]; frequently [ʃ] in Chile
and Panama; sometimes
[ts] in Chile

d   [d] at the beginning of a
word or after *n* or *l*; [ð]
elsewhere, frequently
silent between vowels

f   [f]; [Φ] in Honduras (no
English equivalent for
this sound; like [f] but
made with both lips)

g   [x] before *i* or *e* ([h] in the
Caribbean and Central
America); [g] at the
beginning of a word or
after *n* and not before *i*
or *e*; [ɣ] elsewhere,
frequently silent
between vowels

gu   [gw] at the beginning of a
word before *a, o;* [ɣw]
elsewhere before *a, o*;
frequently just [w]
between vowels; [g] at
the beginning of a word
before *i, e*; [ɣ] elsewhere
before *i, e*; frequently
silent between vowels

gü   [gw] at the beginning of a
word, [ɣw] elsewhere;
frequently just [w]
between vowels

h   silent

j   [x] ([h] in the Caribbean
and Central America)

k   [k]

l   [l]

ll   [j]; [ʒ] or [ʃ] in Argentina
and Uruguay; [ʤ] when
at the beginning of a
word in the Caribbean;

[lʲ] in Bolivia, Paraguay, Peru, and parts of northern Spain (no English equivalent; like "lli" in *million*)

m [m]

n [n]; frequently [ŋ] at the end of a word when next word begins with a vowel

ñ [ɲ]

p [p]

qu [k]

r [r] (no English equivalent; a trilled sound) at the beginning of words; [t̪]/[ɾ] elsewhere

rr [r] (no English equivalent; a trilled sound)

s [s]; frequently [z] before *b*, *d*, *g*, *m*, *n*, *l*, *r*; at the end of a word [h] or silent in many parts of Latin America and some parts of Spain

t [t]

v [b] at the beginning of a word or after *m* or *n*; [β] elsewhere

x [ks] or [gz] between vowels; [s] before consonants

z [s] in Latin America and parts of southern Spain, [θ] in northern Spain; at the end of a word [h] or silent in many parts of Latin America and some parts of Spain

Pronunciation Symbols

VOWELS

æ	ask, bat, glad
ɑ	cot, bomb
a	*New England* aunt, *British* ask, glass, *Spanish* casa
e	*Spanish* peso, jefe
ɛ	egg, bet, fed
ə	about, javelin, Alabama
ə	when italicized as in *ə*l, *ə*m, *ə*n, indicates a syllabic pronunciation of the consonant as in bottle, prism, button
i	very, any, thirty, *Spanish* piña
i:	eat, bead, bee
ɪ	id, bid, pit
o	Ohio, yellower, potato, *Spanish* óvalo
o:	oats, own, zone, blow
ɔ	awl, maul, caught, paw
ʊ	sure, should, could
u	*Spanish* uva, culpa
u:	boot, few, coo
ʌ	under, putt, bud
eɪ	eight, wade, bay
aɪ	ice, bite, tie
aʊ	out, gown, plow
ɔɪ	oyster, coil, boy
ər	further, stir
ɒ	*British* bond, god
:	indicates that the preceding vowel is long. Long vowels are almost always diphthongs in English, but not in Spanish.

CONSONANTS

b	baby, labor, cab
β	*Spanish* cabo, óvalo
d	day, ready, kid
ʤ	just, badger, fudge
ð	then, either, bathe
f	foe, tough, buff
g	go, bigger, bag
ɣ	*Spanish* tragar, daga
h	hot, aha
j	yes, vineyard
k	cat, keep, lacquer, flock
l	law, hollow, boil
m	mat, hemp, hammer, rim
n	new, tent, tenor, run
ŋ	rung, hang, swinger
ɲ	*Spanish* cabaña, piña
p	pay, lapse, top
r	rope, burn, tar
s	sad, mist, kiss
ʃ	shoe, mission, slush
t	toe, button, mat
ṭ	indicates that some speakers of English pronounce this as a voiced alveolar flap [ɾ], as in later, catty, battle
ʧ	choose, batch
θ	thin, ether, bath
v	vat, never, cave
w	wet, software
x	*German* Bach, *Scots* loch, *Spanish* gente, jefe
z	zoo, easy, buzz
ʒ	jaborandi, azure, beige
h, k, p, t	when italicized indicate sounds which are present in the pronunciation of some speakers of English but absent in that of others, so that *whence* ['hwɛnts] can be pronounced as ['wɛns], ['hwɛns], ['wɛnts], or ['hwɛnts]

STRESS MARKS

' high stress	**pen**manship
ˌ low stress	penman**ship**

Spanish–English
Dictionary

A

a[1] *nf* : first letter of the Spanish alphabet

a[2] *prep* **1** : to ⟨nos vamos a México : we're going to Mexico⟩ **2** (*used before direct or indirect objects referring to persons*) ⟨¿llamaste a tu papá? : did you call your dad?⟩ ⟨como a usted le guste : as you wish⟩ **3** : in the manner of ⟨papas a la francesa : french fries⟩ **4** : on, by means of ⟨a pie : on foot⟩ **5** : per, each ⟨tres pastillas al día : three pills per day⟩ **6** : at ⟨a las dos : at two o'clock⟩ ⟨al principio : at first⟩ **7** (*with infinitive*) ⟨enséñales a leer : teach them to read⟩ ⟨problemas a resolver : problems to be solved⟩

ábaco *nm* : abacus

abad *nm* : abbot

abadesa *nf* : abbess

abadía *nf* : abbey

abajo *adv* **1** : down ⟨póngalo más abajo : put it further down⟩ ⟨arriba y abajo : up and down⟩ **2** : downstairs **3** : under, beneath ⟨el abajo firmante : the undersigned⟩ **4** : down with ⟨¡abajo la inflación! : down with inflation!⟩ **5** ~ **de** : under, beneath **6 de** ~ : bottom ⟨el cajón de abajo : the bottom drawer⟩ **7 hacia** ~ *or* **para** ~ : downwards **8 cuesta abajo** : downhill **9 río abajo** : downstream

abalanzarse {21} *vr* : to hurl oneself, to rush

abanderado, -da *n* : standard-bearer

abandonado, -da *adj* **1** : abandoned, deserted **2** : neglected **3** : slovenly, unkempt

abandonar *vt* **1** DEJAR : to abandon, to leave **2** : to give up, to quit ⟨abandonaron la búsqueda : they gave up the search⟩ — **abandonarse** *vr* **1** : to neglect oneself **2** ~ **a** : to succumb to, to give oneself over to

abandono *nm* **1** : abandonment **2** : neglect **3** : withdrawal ⟨ganar por abandono : to win by default⟩

abanicar {72} *vt* : to fan — **abanicarse** *vr*

abanico *nm* **1** : fan **2** GAMA : range, gamut

abaratamiento *nm* : price reduction

abaratar *vt* : to lower the price of — **abaratarse** *vr* : to go down in price

abarcar {72} *vt* **1** : to cover, to include, to embrace **2** : to undertake **3** : to monopolize

abaritonado, -da *adj* : baritone

abarrotado, -da *adj* : packed, crammed

abarrotar *vt* : to fill up, to pack

abarrotería *nf CA, Mex* : grocery store

abarrotero, -ra *n Col, Mex* : grocer

abarrotes *nmpl* **1** : groceries, supplies **2 tienda de abarrotes** : general store, grocery store

abastecedor, -dora *n* : supplier

abastecer {53} *vt* : to supply, to stock — **abastecerse** *vr* : to stock up

abastecimiento → **abasto**

abasto *nm* : supply, supplying ⟨no da abasto : there isn't enough for all⟩

abatido, -da *adj* : dejected, depressed

abatimiento *nm* **1** : drop, reduction **2** : dejection, depression

abatir *vt* **1** DERRIBAR : to demolish, to knock down **2** : to shoot down **3** DEPRIMIR : to depress, to bring low — **abatirse** *vr* **1** DEPRIMIRSE : to get depressed **2** ~ **sobre** : to swoop down on

abdicación *nf, pl* **-ciones** : abdication

abdicar {72} *vt* : to relinquish, to abdicate

abdomen *nm, pl* **-dómenes** : abdomen

abdominal *adj* : abdominal

abecé *nm* : ABC's *pl*

abecedario *nm* ALFABETO : alphabet

abedul *nm* : birch (tree)

abeja *nf* : bee

abejorro *nm* : bumblebee

aberración *nf, pl* **-ciones** : aberration

aberrante *adj* : aberrant, perverse

abertura *nf* **1** : aperture, opening **2** AGUJERO : hole **3** : slit (in a skirt, etc.) **4** GRIETA : crack

abeto *nm* : fir (tree)

abierto[1] *pp* → **abrir**

abierto[2], **-ta** *adj* **1** : open **2** : candid, frank **3** : generous — **abiertamente** *adv*

abigarrado, -da *adj* : multicolored, variegated

abigeato *nm* : rustling (of livestock)

abismal *adj* : abysmal, vast

abismo *nm* : abyss, chasm ⟨al borde del abismo : on the brink of ruin⟩

abjurar *vi* ~ **de** : to abjure — **abjuración** *nf*

ablandamiento *nm* : softening, moderation

ablandar *vt* **1** SUAVIZAR : to soften **2** CALMAR : to soothe, to appease — *vi* : to moderate, to get milder — **ablandarse** *vr* **1** : to become soft, to soften **2** CEDER : to yield, to relent

ablución *nf, pl* **-ciones** : ablution

abnegación *nf, pl* **-ciones** : abnegation, self-denial

abnegado, -da *adj* : self-sacrificing, selfless

abnegarse {49} *vr* : to deny oneself

abobado, -da *adj* **1** : silly, stupid **2** : bewildered

abocarse {72} *vr* **1** DIRIGIRSE : to head, to direct oneself **2** DEDICARSE : to dedicate oneself

abochornar *vt* AVERGONZAR : to embarrass, to shame — **abochornarse** *vr*

abofetear *vt* : to slap

abogacía *nf* : law, legal profession

abogado, -da *n* : lawyer, attorney

abogar {52} *vi* ~ **por** : to plead for, to defend, to advocate

abolengo *nm* LINAJE : lineage, ancestry
abolición *nf, pl* **-ciones** : abolition
abolir {1} *vt* DEROGAR : to abolish, to repeal
abolladura *nf* : dent
abollar *vt* : to dent
abombar *vt* : to warp, to cause to bulge
— **abombarse** *vr* : to decompose, to go bad
abominable *adj* ABORRECIBLE : abominable
abominación *nf, pl* **-ciones** : abomination
abominar *vt* ABORRECER : to abominate, to abhor
abonado, -da *n* : subscriber
abonar *vt* **1** : to pay **2** FERTILIZAR : to fertilize — **abonarse** *vr* : to subscribe
abono *nm* **1** : payment, installment **2** FERTILIZANTE : fertilizer **3** : season ticket
abordaje *nm* : boarding
abordar *vt* **1** : to address, to broach **2** : to accost, to waylay **3** : to come on board
aborigen[1] *adj, pl* **-rígenes** : aboriginal, native
aborigen[2] *nmf, pl* **-rígenes** : aborigine, indigenous inhabitant
aborrecer {53} *vt* ABOMINAR, ODIAR : to abhor, to detest, to hate
aborrecible *adj* ABOMINABLE, ODIOSO : abominable, detestable
aborrecimiento *nm* : abhorrence, loathing
abortar *vi* : to have an abortion — *vt* **1** : to abort **2** : to quash, to suppress
abortista *nmf* : abortionist
abortivo, -va *adj* : abortive
aborto *nm* **1** : abortion **2** : miscarriage
abotonar *vt* : to button — **abotonarse** *vr* : to button up
abovedado, -da *adj* : vaulted
abrasador, -dora *adj* : burning, scorching
abrasar *vt* QUEMAR : to burn, to sear, to scorch
abrasivo[1], **-va** *adj* : abrasive
abrasivo[2] *nm* : abrasive
abrazadera *nf* : clamp, brace
abrazar {21} *vt* : to hug, to embrace — **abrazarse** *vr*
abrazo *nm* : hug, embrace
abrebotellas *nms & pl* : bottle opener
abrelatas *nms & pl* : can opener
abrevadero *nm* BEBEDERO : watering trough
abreviación *nf, pl* **-ciones** : abbreviation
abreviar *vt* **1** : to abbreviate **2** : to shorten, to cut short
abreviatura → **abreviación**
abridor *nm* : bottle opener, can opener
abrigadero *nm* : shelter, windbreak
abrigado, -da *adj* **1** : sheltered **2** : warm, wrapped up (with clothing)
abrigar {52} *vt* **1** : to shelter, to protect **2** : to keep warm, to dress warmly **3** : to cherish, to harbor ⟨abrigar esper-

anzas : to cherish hopes⟩ — **abrigarse** *vr* : to dress warmly
abrigo *nm* **1** : coat, overcoat **2** : shelter, refuge
abril *nm* : April
abrillantador *nm* : polish
abrillantar *vt* : to polish, to shine
abrir {2} *vt* **1** : to open **2** : to unlock, to undo **3** : to turn on (a tap or faucet) — *vi* : to open, to open up — **abrirse** *vr* **1** : to open up **2** : to clear (of the skies)
abrochar *vt* : to button, to fasten — **abrocharse** *vr* : to fasten, to hook up
abrogación *nf, pl* **-ciones** : abrogation, annulment, repeal
abrogar {52} *vt* : to abrogate, to annul, to repeal
abrojo *nm* : bur (of a plant)
abrumador, -dora *adj* : crushing, overwhelming
abrumar *vt* **1** AGOBIAR : to overwhelm **2** OPRIMIR : to oppress, to burden
abrupto, -ta *adj* **1** : abrupt **2** ESCARPADO : steep — **abruptamente** *adv*
absceso *nm* : abscess
absolución *nf, pl* **-ciones** **1** : absolution **2** : acquittal
absolutismo *nm* : absolutism
absoluto, -ta *adj* **1** : absolute, unconditional **2 en ~** : not at all ⟨no me gustó en absoluto : I did not like it at all⟩ — **absolutamente** *adv*
absolver {89} *vt* **1** : to absolve **2** : to acquit
absorbente *adj* **1** : absorbent **2** : absorbing, engrossing
absorber *vt* **1** : to absorb, to soak up **2** : to occupy, to take up, to engross
absorción *nf, pl* **-ciones** : absorption
absorto, -ta *adj* : absorbed, engrossed
abstemio[1], **-mia** *adj* : abstemious, teetotal
abstemio[2], **-mia** *n* : teetotaler
abstención *nf, pl* **-ciones** : abstention
abstenerse {80} *vr* : to abstain, to refrain
abstinencia *nf* : abstinence
abstracción *nf, pl* **-ciones** : abstraction
abstracto, -ta *adj* : abstract
abstraer {81} *vt* : to abstract — **abstraerse** *vr* : to lose oneself in thought
abstraído, -da *adj* : preoccupied, withdrawn
abstruso, -sa *adj* : abstruse
abstuvo, etc. → **abstenerse**
absuelto *pp* → **absolver**
absurdo[1], **-da** *adj* DISPARATADO, RIDÍCULO : absurd, ridiculous — **absurdamente** *adv*
absurdo[2] *nm* : absurdity
abuchear *vt* : to boo, to jeer
abucheo *nm* : booing, jeering
abuela *nf* **1** : grandmother **2** : old woman **3 ¡tu abuela!** *fam* : no way!, forget about it!
abuelo *nm* **1** : grandfather **2** : old man **3 abuelos** *nmpl* : grandparents, ancestors

abulia *nf* : apathy, lethargy

abúlico, -ca *adj* : lethargic, apathetic

abultado, -da *adj* : bulging, bulky

abultar *vi* : to bulge — *vt* : to enlarge, to expand

abundancia *nf* : abundance

abundante *adj* : abundant, plentiful — **abundantemente** *adv*

abundar *vi* 1 : to abound, to be plentiful 2 ~ **en** : to be in agreement with

aburrido, -da *adj* 1 : bored, tired, fed up 2 TEDIOSO : boring, tedious

aburrimiento *nm* : boredom, weariness

aburrir *vt* : to bore, to tire — **aburrirse** *vr* : to get bored

abusado, -da *adj Mex fam* : sharp, on the ball

abusador, -dora *n* : abuser

abusar *vi* 1 : to go too far, to do something to excess 2 ~ **de** : to abuse (as drugs) 3 ~ **de** : to take unfair advantage of

abusivo, -va *adj* 1 : abusive 2 : outrageous, excessive

abuso *nm* 1 : abuse 2 : injustice, outrage

abyecto, -ta *adj* : despicable, contemptible

acá *adv* AQUÍ : here, over here ⟨¡ven acá! : come here!⟩

acabado¹, -da *adj* 1 : finished, done, completed 2 : old, worn-out

acabado² *nm* : finish ⟨un acabado brillante : a glossy finish⟩

acabar *vi* 1 TERMINAR : to finish, to end 2 ~ **de** : to have just (done something) ⟨acabo de ver a tu hermano : I just saw your brother⟩ 3 ~ **con** : to put an end to, to stamp out — *vt* TERMINAR : to finish — **acabarse** *vr* TERMINARSE : to come to an end, to run out ⟨se me acabó el dinero : I ran out of money⟩

acacia *nf* : acacia

academia *nf* : academy

académico¹, -ca *adj* : academic, scholastic — **académicamente** *adv*

académico², -ca *n* : academic, academician

acaecer {53} *vt* (*3rd person only*) : to happen, to take place

acalambrarse *vr* : to cramp up, to get a cramp

acallar *vt* : to quiet, to silence

acalorado, -da *adj* : emotional, heated

acaloramiento *nm* 1 : heat 2 : ardor, passion

acalorar *vt* : to heat up, to inflame — **acalorarse** *vr* : to get upset, to get worked up

acampada *nf* : camp, camping ⟨ir de acampada : to go camping⟩

acampar *vi* : to camp

acanalar *vt* 1 : to groove, to furrow 2 : to corrugate

acantilado *nm* : cliff

acanto *nm* : acanthus

acantonar *vt* : to station, to quarter

acaparador, -dora *adj* : greedy, selfish

acaparar *vt* 1 : to stockpile, to hoard 2 : to monopolize

acápite *nm* : paragraph

acariciar *vt* 1 : to caress, to stroke, to pet

ácaro *nm* : mite

acarrear *vt* 1 : to haul, to carry 2 : to bring, to give rise to ⟨los problemas que acarrea : the problems that come along with it⟩

acarreo *nm* : transport, haulage

acartonarse *vr* 1 : to stiffen 2 : to become wizened

acaso *adv* 1 : perhaps, by any chance 2 **por si acaso** : just in case

acatamiento *nm* : compliance, observance

acatar *vt* : to comply with, to respect

acaudalado, -da *adj* RICO : wealthy, rich

acaudillar *vt* : to lead, to command

acceder *vi* ~ **a** 1 : to accede to, to agree to 2 : to assume (a position) 3 : to gain access to

accesar *vt* : to access (on a computer)

accesibilidad *nf* : accessibility

accesible *adj* ASEQUIBLE : accessible, attainable

acceso *nm* 1 : access 2 : admittance, entrance

accesorio¹, -ria *adj* 1 : accessory 2 : incidental

accesorio² *nm* 1 : accessory 2 : prop (in the theater)

accidentado¹, -da *adj* 1 : eventful, turbulent 2 : rough, uneven 3 : injured

accidentado², -da *n* : accident victim

accidental *adj* : accidental, unintentional — **accidentalmente** *adv*

accidentarse *vr* : to have an accident

accidente *nm* 1 : accident 2 : unevenness 3 **accidente geográfico** : geographical feature

acción *nf, pl* **acciones** 1 : action 2 ACTO : act, deed 3 : share, stock

accionamiento *nm* : activation

accionar *vt* : to put into motion, to activate — *vi* : to gesticulate

accionario, -ria *adj* : stock ⟨mercado accionario : stock market⟩

accionista *nmf* : stockholder, shareholder

acebo *nm* : holly

acechar *vt* 1 : to watch, to spy on 2 : to stalk, to lie in wait for

acecho *nm* **al acecho** : lying in wait

acedera *nf* : sorrel (herb)

acéfalo, -la *adj* : leaderless

aceitar *vt* : to oil

aceite *nm* 1 : oil 2 **aceite de ricino** : castor oil 3 **aceite de oliva** : olive oil

aceitera *nf* 1 : cruet (for oil) 2 : oilcan 3 *Mex* : oil refinery

aceitoso, -sa *adj* : oily

aceituna *nf* OLIVA : olive

aceituno *nm* OLIVO : olive tree

aceleración *nf, pl* **-ciones** : acceleration, speeding up

acelerado, -da *adj* : accelerated, speedy

acelerador *nm* : accelerator

aceleramiento *nm* → **aceleración**

acelerar *vt* **1** : to accelerate, to speed up **2** AGILIZAR : to expedite — *vi* : to accelerate (of an automobile) — **acelerarse** *vr* : to hasten, to hurry up

acelga *nf* : chard, Swiss chard

acendrado, -da *adj* : pure, unblemished

acendrar *vt* : to purify, to refine

acento *nm* **1** : accent **2** : stress, emphasis

acentuación *nf, pl* **-ciones** : accentuation

acentuado, -da *adj* : marked, pronounced

acentuar {3} *vt* **1** : to accent **2** : to emphasize, to stress — **acentuarse** *vr* : to become more pronounced

acepción *nf, pl* **-ciones** SIGNIFICADO : sense, meaning

aceptabilidad *nf* : acceptability

aceptable *adj* : acceptable

aceptación *nf, pl* **-ciones 1** : acceptance **2** APROBACIÓN : approval

aceptar *vt* **1** : to accept **2** : to approve

acequia *nf* **1** : irrigation ditch **2** *Mex* : sewer

acera *nf* : sidewalk

acerado, -da *adj* **1** : made of steel **2** : steely, tough

acerbo, -ba *adj* **1** : harsh, cutting ⟨comentarios acerbos : cutting remarks⟩ **2** : bitter — **acerbamente** *adv*

acerca *prep* ∼ **de** : about, concerning

acercamiento *nm* : rapprochement, reconciliation

acercar {72} *vt* APROXIMAR, ARRIMAR : to bring near, to bring closer — **acercarse** *vr* APROXIMARSE, ARRIMARSE : to approach, to draw near

acería *nf* : steel mill

acerico *nm* : pincushion

acero *nm* : steel ⟨acero inoxidable : stainless steel⟩

acérrimo, -ma *adj* **1** : staunch, steadfast **2** : bitter ⟨un acérrimo enemigo : a bitter enemy⟩

acertado, -da *adj* CORRECTO : accurate, correct, on target — **acertadamente** *adv*

acertante¹ *adj* : winning

acertante² *nmf* : winner

acertar {55} *vt* : to guess correctly — *vi* **1** ATINAR : to be correct, to be on target **2** ∼ **a** : to manage to

acertijo *nm* ADIVINANZA : riddle

acervo *nm* **1** : pile, heap **2** : wealth, heritage ⟨el acervo artístico del instituto : the artistic treasures of the institute⟩

acetato *nm* : acetate

acético, -ca *adj* : acetic ⟨ácido acético : acetic acid⟩

acetileno *nm* : acetylene

acetona *nf* **1** : acetone **2** : nail-polish remover

achacar {72} *vt* : to attribute, to impute ⟨te achaca todos sus problemas : he blames all his problems on you⟩

achacoso, -sa *adj* : frail, sickly

achaparrado, -da *adj* : stunted, scrubby ⟨árboles achaparrados : scrubby trees⟩

achaques *nmpl* : aches and pains

achatar *vt* : to flatten

achicar {72} *vt* **1** REDUCIR : to make smaller, to reduce **2** : to intimidate **3** : to bail out (water) — **achicarse** *vr* : to become intimidated

achicharrar *vt* : to scorch, to burn to a crisp

achicoria *nf* : chicory

achispado, -da *adj fam* : tipsy

achote *or* **achiote** *nm* : annatto seed

achuchón *nm, pl* **-chones 1** : push, shove **2** *fam* : squeeze, hug **3** *fam* : mild illness

aciago, -ga *adj* : fateful, unlucky

acicalar *vt* **1** PULIR : to polish **2** : to dress up, to adorn — **acicalarse** *vr* : to get dressed up

acicate *nm* **1** : spur **2** INCENTIVO : incentive, stimulus

acidez *nf, pl* **-deces 1** : acidity **2** : sourness **3 acidez estomacal** : heartburn

acidificar {72} *vt* : to acidify

ácido¹, -da *adj* AGRIO : acid, sour

ácido² *nm* : acid

acierto *nm* **1** : correct answer, right choice **2** : accuracy, skill, deftness

acimut *nm* : azimuth

acitronar *vt Mex* : to fry until crisp

aclamación *nf, pl* **-ciones** : acclaim, acclamation

aclamar *vt* : to acclaim, to cheer, to applaud

aclaración *nf, pl* **-ciones** CLARIFICACIÓN : clarification, explanation

aclarar *vt* **1** CLARIFICAR : to clarify, to explain, to resolve **2** : to lighten **3 aclarar la voz** : to clear one's throat — *vi* **1** : to get light, to dawn **2** : to clear up — **aclararse** *vr* : to become clear

aclaratorio, -ria *adj* : explanatory

aclimatar *vt* : to acclimatize — **aclimatarse** *vr* ∼ **a** : to get used to — **aclimatación** *nf*

acné *nm* : acne

acobardar *vt* INTIMIDAR : to frighten, to intimidate — **acobardarse** *vr* : to be frightened, to cower

acodarse *vr* ∼ **en** : to lean (one's elbows) on

acogedor, -dora *adj* : cozy, warm, friendly

acoger {15} *vt* **1** REFUGIAR : to take in, to shelter **2** : to receive, to welcome — **acogerse** *vr* **1** REFUGIARSE : to take refuge **2** ∼ **a** : to resort to, to avail oneself of

acogida *nf* **1** AMPARO, REFUGIO : refuge, protection **2** RECIBIMIENTO : reception, welcome

acolchar *vt* **1** : to pad (a wall, etc.) **2** : to quilt

acólito *nm* **1** MONAGUILLO : altar boy **2** : follower, helper, acolyte

acomedido, -da *adj* : helpful, obliging

acometer *vt* **1** ATACAR : to attack, to assail **2** EMPRENDER : to undertake, to begin — *vi* ~ **contra** : to rush against

acometida *nf* ATAQUE : attack, assault

acomodado, -da *adj* **1** : suitable, appropriate **2** : well-to-do, prosperous

acomodador, -dora *n* : usher, usherette *f*

acomodar *vt* **1** : to accommodate, to make room for **2** : to adjust, to adapt — **acomodarse** *vr* **1** : to settle in **2** ~ **a** : to adapt to

acomodaticio, -cia *adj* : accommodating, obliging

acomodo *nm* **1** : job, position **2** : arrangement, placement **3** : accommodation, lodging

acompañamiento *nm* : accompaniment

acompañante *nmf* **1** COMPAÑERO : companion **2** : accompanist

acompañar *vt* : to accompany, to go with

acompasado, -da *adj* : rhythmic, regular, measured

acomplejado, -da *adj* : full of complexes, neurotic

acondicionado, -da *adj* **1** : equipped, fitted-out **2 bien acondicionado** : in good shape, in a fit state

acondicionador *nm* **1** : conditioner **2 acondicionador de aire** : air conditioner

acondicionar *vt* **1** : to condition **2** : to fit out, to furnish

acongojado, -da *adj* : distressed, upset

acongojarse *vr* : to grieve, to become distressed

aconsejable *adj* : advisable

aconsejar *vt* : to advise, to counsel

acontecer {53} *vt* (*3rd person only*) : to occur, to happen

acontecimiento *nm* SUCESO : event

acopiar *vt* : to gather, to collect, to stockpile

acopio *nm* : collection, stock

acoplamiento *nm* : connection, coupling

acoplar *vt* : to couple, to connect — **acoplarse** *vr* : to fit together

acoquinar *vt* : to intimidate

acorazado¹, -da *adj* BLINDADO : armored

acorazado² *nm* : battleship

acordado, -da *adj* : agreed upon

acordar {19} *vt* **1** : to agree on **2** OTORGAR : to award, to bestow — **acordarse** *vr* RECORDAR : to remember, to recall

acorde¹ *adj* **1** : in agreement, in accordance **2** ~ **con** : in keeping with

acorde² *nm* : chord

acordeón *nm, pl* **-deones** : accordion — **acordeonista** *nmf*

acordonar *vt* **1** : to cordon off **2** : to lace up **3** : to mill (coins)

acorralar *vt* ARRINCONAR : to corner, to hem in, to corral

acortar *vt* : to shorten, to cut short — **acortarse** *vr* **1** : to become shorter **2** : to end early

acosar *vt* PERSEGUIR : to pursue, to hound, to harass

acoso *nm* ASEDIO : harassment ⟨acoso sexual : sexual harassment⟩

acostar {19} *vt* **1** : to lay (something) down **2** : to put to bed — **acostarse** *vr* **1** : to lie down **2** : to go to bed

acostumbrado, -da *adj* **1** HABITUADO : accustomed **2** HABITUAL : usual, customary

acostumbrar *vt* : to accustom — *vi* : to be accustomed, to be in the habit — **acostumbrarse** *vr*

acotación *nf, pl* **-ciones** **1** : marginal note **2** : stage direction

acotado, -da *adj* : enclosed

acotamiento *nm Mex* : shoulder (of a road)

acotar *vt* **1** ANOTAR : to note, to annotate **2** DELIMITAR : to mark off (land), to demarcate

acre¹ *adj* **1** : acrid, pungent **2** MORDAZ : caustic, biting

acre² *nm* : acre

acrecentamiento *nm* : growth, increase

acrecentar {55} *vt* AUMENTAR : to increase, to augment

acreditación *nf, pl* **-ciones** : accreditation

acreditado, -da *adj* **1** : accredited, authorized **2** : reputable

acreditar *vt* **1** : to accredit, to authorize **2** : to credit **3** : to prove, to verify — **acreditarse** *vr* : to gain a reputation

acreedor¹, -dora *adj* : deserving, worthy

acreedor², -dora *n* : creditor

acribillar *vt* **1** : to riddle, to pepper (with bullets, etc.) **2** : to hound, to harass

acrílico *nm* : acrylic

acrimonia *nf* **1** : pungency **2** : acrimony

acrimonioso, -sa *adj* : acrimonious

acriollarse *vr* : to adopt local customs, to go native

acritud *nf* **1** : pungency, bitterness **2** : intensity, sharpness **3** : harshness, asperity

acrobacia *nf* : acrobatics

acróbata *nmf* : acrobat

acrobático, -ca *adj* : acrobatic

acrónimo *nm* : acronym

acta *nf* **1** : document, certificate ⟨acta de nacimiento : birth certificate⟩ **2 actas** *nfpl* : minutes (of a meeting)

actitud *nf* **1** : attitude **2** : posture, position

activación *nf, pl* **-ciones** **1** : activation, stimulation **2** ACELERACIÓN : acceleration, speeding up

activar *vt* **1** : to activate **2** : to stimulate, to energize **3** : to speed up

actividad *nf* : activity

activista *nmf* : activist

activo¹, -va *adj* : active — **activamente** *adv*

activo² *nm* : assets *pl* ⟨activo y pasivo : assets and liabilities⟩

acto *nm* **1** ACCIÓN : act, deed **2** : act (in a play) **3 el acto sexual** : sexual intercourse **4 en el acto** : right away, on the spot **5 acto seguido** : immediately after
actor *nm* ARTISTA : actor
actriz *nf, pl* **actrices** ARTISTA : actress
actuación *nf, pl* **-ciones 1** : performance **2 actuaciones** *nfpl* DILIGENCIAS : proceedings
actual *adj* PRESENTE : present, current
actualidad *nf* **1** : present time ⟨en la actualidad : at present⟩ **2 actualidades** *nfpl* : current affairs
actualización *nf, pl* **-ciones** : updating, modernization
actualizar {21} *vt* : to modernize, to bring up to date
actualmente *adv* : at present, nowadays
actuar {3} *vi* : to act, to perform
actuarial *adj* : actuarial
actuario, -ria *n* : actuary
acuarela *nf* : watercolor
acuario *nm* : aquarium
Acuario *nmf* : Aquarius, Aquarian
acuartelar *vt* : to quarter (troops)
acuático, -ca *adj* : aquatic, water
acuchillar *vt* APUÑALAR : to knife, to stab
acuciante *adj* : pressing, urgent
acucioso, -sa → **acuciante**
acudir *vi* **1** : to go, to come (someplace for a specific purpose) ⟨acudió a la puerta : he went to the door⟩ ⟨acudimos en su ayuda : we came to her aid⟩ **2** : to be present, to show up ⟨acudí a la cita : I showed up for the appointment⟩ **3 ~ a** : to turn to, to have recourse to ⟨hay que acudir al médico : you must consult the doctor⟩
acueducto *nm* : aqueduct
acuerdo *nm* **1** : agreement **2 estar de acuerdo** : to agree **3 de acuerdo con** : in accordance with **4 de ~** : OK, all right
acuicultura *nf* : aquaculture
acullá *adv* : yonder, over there
acumulación *nf, pl* **-ciones** : accumulation
acumulador *nm* : storage battery
acumular *vt* : to accumulate, to amass — **acumularse** *vr* : to build up, to pile up
acumulativo, -va *adj* : cumulative — **acumulativamente** *adv*
acunar *vt* : to rock, to cradle
acuñar *vt* : to coin, to mint
acuoso, -sa *adj* : aqueous, watery
acupuntura *nf* : acupuncture
acurrucarse {72} *vr* : to cuddle, to nestle, to curl up
acusación *nf, pl* **-ciones 1** : accusation, charge **2 la acusación** : the prosecution
acusado¹, -da *adj* : prominent, marked
acusado², -da *n* : defendant
acusador, -dora *n* **1** : accuser **2** FISCAL : prosecutor

acusar *vt* **1** : to accuse, to charge **2** : to reveal, to betray ⟨sus ojos acusaban la desconfianza : his eyes revealed distrust⟩ — **acusarse** *vr* : to confess
acusativo *nm* : objective (in grammar)
acusatorio, -ria *adj* : accusatory
acuse *nm* **acuse de recibo** : acknowledgment of receipt
acústica *nf* : acoustics
acústico, -ca *adj* : acoustic
adagio *nm* **1** REFRÁN : adage, proverb **2** : adagio
adalid *nm* : leader, champion
adaptable *adj* : adaptable — **adaptabilidad** *nf*
adaptación *nf, pl* **-ciones** : adaptation, adjustment
adaptado, -da *adj* : suited, adapted
adaptador *nm* : adapter (in electricity)
adaptar *vt* **1** MODIFICAR : to adapt **2** : to adjust, to fit — **adaptarse** *vr* : to adapt oneself, to conform
adecentar *vt* : to tidy up
adecuación *nf, pl* **-ciones** ADAPTACIÓN : adaptation
adecuadamente *adv* : adequately
adecuado, -da *adj* **1** IDÓNEO : suitable, appropriate **2** : adequate
adecuar {8} *vt* : to adapt, to make suitable — **adecuarse** *vr* **~ a** : to be appropriate for, to fit in with
adefesio *nm* : eyesore, monstrosity
adelantado, -da *adj* **1** : advanced, ahead **2** : fast (of a clock or watch) **3 por ~** : in advance
adelantamiento *nm* **1** : advancement **2** : speeding up
adelantar *vt* **1** : to advance, to move forward **2** : to overtake, to pass **3** : to reveal (information) in advance **4** : to advance, to lend (money) — **adelantarse** *vr* **1** : to advance, to get in front **2 ~ a** : to forestall, to preempt
adelante *adv* **1** : ahead, in front, forward **2 más adelante** : further on, later on **3 ¡adelante!** : come in!
adelanto *nm* **1** : advance, progress **2** : advance payment **3** : earliness ⟨llevamos una hora de adelanto : we're running an hour ahead of time⟩
adelfa *nf* : oleander
adelgazar {21} *vt* : to thin, to reduce — *vi* : to lose weight
ademán *nm, pl* **-manes 1** GESTO : gesture **2 ademanes** *nmpl* : manners
además *adv* **1** : besides, furthermore **2 ~ de** : in addition to, as well as
adenoides *nfpl* : adenoids
adentrarse *vr* **~ en** : to go into, to penetrate
adentro *adv* : inside, within
adentros *nmpl* **decirse para sus adentros** : to say to oneself ⟨me dije para mis adentros que nunca regresaría : I told myself that I'd never go back⟩
adepto¹, -ta *adj* : supportive ⟨ser adepto a : to be a follower of⟩
adepto², -ta *n* PARTIDARIO : follower, supporter

aderezar {21} *vt* **1** SAZONAR : to season, to dress (salad) **2** : to embellish, to adorn

aderezo *nm* **1** : dressing, seasoning **2** : adornment, embellishment

adeudar *vt* **1** : to debit **2** DEBER : to owe

adeudo *nm* **1** DÉBITO : debit **2** *Mex* : debt, indebtedness

adherencia *nf* **1** : adherence, adhesiveness **2** : appendage, accretion

adherente *adj* : adhesive, sticky

adherirse {76} *vr* : to adhere, to stick

adhesión *nf*, *pl* -**siones 1** : adhesion **2** : attachment, commitment (to a cause, etc.)

adhesivo[1], -**va** *adj* : adhesive

adhesivo[2] *nm* : adhesive

adicción *nf*, *pl* -**ciones** : addiction

adición *nf*, *pl* -**ciones** : addition

adicional *adj* : additional — **adicionalmente** *adv*

adicionar *vt* : to add

adictivo, -**va** *adj* : addictive

adicto[1], -**ta** *adj* **1** : addicted **2** : devoted, dedicated

adicto[2], -**ta** *n* **1** : addict **2** PARTIDARIO : supporter, advocate

adiestrador, -**dora** *n* : trainer

adiestramiento *nm* : training

adiestrar *vt* : to train

adinerado, -**da** *adj* : moneyed, wealthy

adiós *nm*, *pl* **adioses 1** DESPEDIDA : farewell, good-bye **2** ¡adiós! : good-bye!

aditamento *nm* : attachment, accessory

aditivo *nm* : additive

adivinación *nf*, *pl* -**ciones 1** : guess **2** : divination, prediction

adivinanza *nf* ACERTIJO : riddle

adivinar *vt* **1** : to guess **2** : to foretell, to predict

adivino, -**na** *n* : fortune-teller

adjetivo[1], -**va** *adj* : adjectival

adjetivo[2] *nm* : adjective

adjudicación *nf*, *pl* -**ciones 1** : adjudication **2** : allocation, awarding, granting

adjudicar {72} *vt* **1** : to adjudge, to adjudicate **2** : to assign, to allocate ⟨adjudicar la culpa : to assign the blame⟩ **3** : to award, to grant

adjuntar *vt* : to enclose, to attach

adjunto[1], -**ta** *adj* : enclosed, attached

adjunto[2], -**ta** *n* : deputy, assistant

adjunto[3] *nm* : adjunct

administración *nf*, *pl* -**ciones 1** : administration, management **2 administración de empresas** : business administration

administrador, -**dora** *n* : administrator, manager

administrar *vt* : to administer, to manage, to run

administrativo, -**va** *adj* : administrative

admirable *adj* : admirable, impressive — **admirablemente** *adv*

admiración *nf*, *pl* -**ciones** : admiration

admirador, -**dora** *n* : admirer

admirar *vt* **1** : to admire **2** : to amaze, to astonish — **admirarse** *vr* : to be amazed

admirativo, -**va** *adj* : admiring

admisibilidad *nf* : admissibility

admisible *adj* : admissible, allowable

admisión *nf*, *pl* -**siones** : admission, admittance

admitir *vt* **1** : to admit, to let in **2** : to acknowledge, to concede **3** : to allow, to make room for ⟨la ley no admite cambios : the law doesn't allow for changes⟩

admonición *nf*, *pl* -**ciones** : admonition, warning

admonitorio, -**ria** *adj* : admonitory

ADN *nm* (ácido desoxirribonucleico) : DNA

adobar *vt* : to marinate

adobe *nm* : adobe

adobo *nm* **1** : marinade, seasoning **2** *Mex* : spicy marinade used for cooking pork

adoctrinamiento *nm* : indoctrination

adoctrinar *vt* : to indoctrinate

adolecer {53} *vi* PADECER : to suffer ⟨adolece de timidez : he suffers from shyness⟩

adolescencia *nf* : adolescence

adolescente[1] *adj* : adolescent, teenage

adolescente[2] *nmf* : adolescent, teenager

adonde *conj* : where ⟨el lugar adonde vamos es bello : the place where we're going is beautiful⟩

adónde *adv* : where ⟨¿adónde vamos? : where are we going?⟩

adondequiera *adv* : wherever, anywhere ⟨adondequiera que vayas : anywhere you go⟩

adopción *nf*, *pl* -**ciones** : adoption

adoptar *vt* **1** : to adopt (a measure), to take (a decision) **2** : to adopt (children)

adoptivo, -**va** *adj* **1** : adopted (children, country) **2** : adoptive (parents)

adoquín *nm*, *pl* -**quines** : paving stone, cobblestone

adorable *adj* : adorable, lovable

adoración *nf*, *pl* -**ciones** : adoration, worship

adorador[1], -**dora** *adj* : adoring, worshipping

adorador[2], -**dora** *n* : worshipper

adorar *vt* : to adore, to worship

adormecer {53} *vt* **1** : to make sleepy, to lull to sleep **2** : to numb — **adormecerse** *vr* **1** : to doze off **2** : to go numb

adormecimiento *nm* **1** SUEÑO : drowsiness, sleepiness **2** INSENSIBILIDAD : numbness

adormilarse *vr* : to doze, to drowse

adornar *vt* DECORAR : to decorate, to adorn

adorno *nm* : ornament, decoration

adquirido, -**da** *adj* **1** : acquired **2 mal adquirido** : ill-gotten

adquirir {4} *vt* **1** : to acquire, to gain **2** COMPRAR : to purchase

adquisición *nf, pl* **-ciones 1** : acquisition **2** COMPRA : purchase
adquisitivo, -va *adj* **poder adquisitivo** : purchasing power
adrede *adv* : intentionally, on purpose
adrenalina *nf* : adrenaline
adscribir {33} *vt* : to assign, to appoint
— **adscribirse** *vr* ~ **a** : to become a member of
adscripción *nf, pl* **-ciones** : assignment, appointment
adscrito *pp* → **adscribir**
aduana *nf* : customs, customs office
aduanero[1], **-ra** *adj* : customs
aduanero[2], **-ra** *n* : customs officer
aducir {61} *vt* : to adduce, to offer as proof
adueñarse *vr* ~ **de** : to take possession of, to take over
adulación *nf, pl* **-ciones** : adulation, flattery
adulador[1], **-dora** *adj* : flattering
adulador[2], **-dora** *n* : flatterer, toady
adular *vt* LISONJEAR : to flatter
adulteración *nf, pl* **-ciones** : adulteration
adulterar *vt* : to adulterate
adulterio *nm* : adultery
adúltero[1], **-ra** *adj* : adulterous
adúltero[2], **-ra** *n* : adulterer
adultez *nf* : adulthood
adulto, -ta *adj & n* : adult
adusto, -ta *adj* : harsh, severe
advenedizo, -za *n* **1** : upstart, parvenu **2** : newcomer
advenimiento *nm* : advent
adverbio *nm* : adverb — **adverbial** *adj*
adversario[1], **-ria** *adj* : opposing, contrary
adversario[2], **-ria** *n* OPOSITOR : adversary, opponent
adversidad *nf* : adversity
adverso, -sa *adj* DESFAVORABLE : adverse, unfavorable — **adversamente** *adv*
advertencia *nf* AVISO : warning
advertir {76} *vt* **1** AVISAR : to warn **2** : to notice, to tell ⟨no advertí que estuviera enojada : I couldn't tell she was angry⟩
Adviento *nm* : Advent
adyacente *adj* : adjacent
aéreo, -rea *adj* **1** : aerial, air **2 correo aéreo** : airmail
aeróbic *nm* : aerobics
aeróbico, -ca *adj* : aerobic
aerobio, -bia *adj* : aerobic
aerodinámica *nf* : aerodynamics
aerodinámico, -ca *adj* : aerodynamic, streamlined
aeródromo *nm* : airfield
aeroespacial *adj* : aerospace
aerolínea *nf* : airline
aeromozo, -za *n* : flight attendant, steward *m*, stewardess *f*
aeronáutica *nf* : aeronautics
aeronáutico, -ca *adj* : aeronautical
aeronave *nf* : aircraft

aeropostal *adj* : airmail
aeropuerto *nm* : airport
aerosol *nm* : aerosol, aerosol spray
aeróstata *nmf* : balloonist
aerotransportado, -da *adj* : airborne
aerotransportar *vt* : to airlift
afabilidad *nf* : affability
afable *adj* : affable — **afablemente** *adv*
afamado, -da *adj* : well-known, famous
afán *nm, pl* **afanes 1** ANHELO : eagerness, desire **2** EMPEÑO : effort, determination
afanador, -dora *n Mex* : cleaning person, cleaner
afanarse *vr* : to toil, to strive
afanosamente *adv* : zealously, industriously, busily
afanoso, -sa *adj* **1** : eager, industrious **2** : arduous, hard
afear *vt* : to make ugly, to disfigure
afección *nf, pl* **-ciones 1** : fondness, affection **2** : illness, complaint
afectación *nf, pl* **-ciones** : affectation
afectado, -da *adj* **1** : affected, mannered **2** : influenced **3** : afflicted **4** : feigned
afectar *vt* **1** : to affect **2** : to upset **3** : to feign, to pretend
afectísimo, -ma *adj* **suyo afectísimo** : yours truly
afectivo, -va *adj* : emotional
afecto[1], **-ta** *adj* **1** : affected, afflicted **2** : fond, affectionate
afecto[2] *nm* CARIÑO : affection
afectuoso, -sa *adj* CARIÑOSO : affectionate, caring
afeitadora *nf* : shaver, electric razor
afeitar *vt* RASURAR : to shave — **afeitarse** *vr*
afelpado, -da *adj* : plush
afeminado, -da *adj* : effeminate
aferrado, -da *adj* : obstinate, stubborn
aferrarse {55} *vr* : to cling, to hold on
affidávit *nm, pl* **-dávits** : affidavit
afgano, -na *adj & n* : Afghan
AFI *nm* (Alfabeto Fonético Internacional) : IPA
afianzar {21} *vt* **1** : to secure, to strengthen **2** : to guarantee, to vouch for — **afianzarse** *vr* ESTABLECERSE : to establish oneself
afiche *nm* : poster
afición *nf, pl* **-ciones 1** : enthusiasm, penchant, fondness ⟨afición al deporte : love of sports⟩ **2** PASATIEMPO : hobby
aficionado[1], **-da** *adj* ENTUSIASTA : enthusiastic, keen
aficionado[2], **-da** *n* **1** ENTUSIASTA : enthusiast, fan **2** : amateur
áfido *nm* : aphid
afiebrado, -da *adj* : feverish
afilado, -da *adj* **1** : sharp **2** : long, pointed ⟨una nariz afilada : a sharp nose⟩
afilador *nm* : sharpener
afilalápices *nms & pl* : pencil sharpener
afilar *vt* : to sharpen
afiliación *nf, pl* **-ciones** : affiliation

afiliado[1], **-da** *adj* : affiliated
afiliado[2], **-da** *n* : member
afiliarse *vr* : to become a member, to join, to affiliate
afín *adj, pl* **afines 1** PARECIDO : related, similar ⟨la biología y disciplinas afines : biology and related disciplines⟩ **2** PRÓXIMO : adjacent, nearby
afinación *nf, pl* **-ciones 1** : tune-up **2** : tuning (of an instrument)
afinador, -dora *n* : tuner (of musical instruments)
afinar *vt* **1** : to perfect, to refine **2** : to tune (an instrument) — *vi* : to sing or play in tune
afincarse {72} *vr* : to establish oneself, to settle in
afinidad *nf* : affinity, similarity
afirmación *nf, pl* **-ciones 1** : statement **2** : affirmation
afirmar *vt* **1** : to state, to affirm **2** REFORZAR : to make firm, to strengthen
afirmativo, -va *adj* : affirmative — **afirmativamente** *adj*
aflicción *nf, pl* **-ciones** DESCONSUELO, PESAR : grief, sorrow
afligido, -da *adj* : grief-stricken, sorrowful
afligir {35} *vt* **1** : to distress, to upset **2** : to afflict — **afligirse** *vr* : to grieve
aflojar *vt* **1** : to loosen, to slacken **2** *fam* : to pay up, to fork over — *vi* : to slacken, to ease up — **aflojarse** *vr* : to become loose, to slacken
afloramiento *nm* : outcropping, emergence
aflorar *vi* : to come to the surface, to emerge
afluencia *nf* **1** : flow, influx **2** : abundance, plenty
afluente *nm* : tributary
afluir {41} *vi* **1** : to flock ⟨la gente afluía a la frontera : people were flocking to the border⟩ **2** : to flow
aforismo *nm* : aphorism
aforo *nm* **1** : appraisal, assessment **2** : maximum capacity (of a theater, highway, etc.)
afortunado, -da *adj* : fortunate, lucky — **afortunadamente** *adv*
afrecho *nm* : bran, mash
afrenta *nf* : affront, insult
afrentar *vt* : to affront, to dishonor, to insult
africano, -na *adj & n* : African
afroamericano, -na *adj & n* : Afro-American
afrodisiaco *or* **afrodisíaco** *nm* : aphrodisiac
afrontamiento *nm* : confrontation
afrontar *vt* : to confront, to face up to
afrutado, -da *adj* : fruity
afuera *adv* **1** : out ⟨¡afuera! : get out!⟩ **2** : outside, outdoors
afueras *nfpl* ALEDAÑOS : outskirts
agachadiza *nf* : snipe (bird)
agachar *vt* : to lower (a part of the body) ⟨agachar la cabeza : to bow one's head⟩

— **agacharse** *vr* : to crouch, to stoop, to bend down
agalla *nf* **1** BRANQUIA : gill **2 tener agallas** *fam* : to have guts, to have courage
agarradera *nf* ASA, ASIDERO : handle, grip
agarrado, -da *adj fam* : cheap, stingy
agarrar *vt* **1** : to grab, to grasp **2** : to catch, to take — *vi* **agarrar y** *fam* : to do (something) abruptly ⟨el día siguiente agarró y se fue : the next day he up and left⟩ — **agarrarse** *vr* **1** : to hold on, to cling **2** *fam* : to get into a fight ⟨se agarraron a golpes : they came to blows⟩
agarre *nm* : grip, grasp
agarrotarse *vr* **1** : to stiffen up **2** : to seize up
agasajar *vt* : to fête, to wine and dine
agasajo *nm* : lavish attention
ágata *nf* : agate
agave *nm* : agave
agazaparse *vr* **1** AGACHARSE : to crouch **2** : to hide
agencia *nf* : agency, office
agenciar *vt* : to obtain, to procure — **agenciarse** *vr* : to manage, to get by
agenda *nf* **1** : agenda **2** : appointment book
agente *nmf* **1** : agent **2 agente de viajes** : travel agent **3 agente de bolsa** : stockbroker **4 agente de tráfico** : traffic officer
agigantado, -da *adj* GIGANTESCO : gigantic
agigantar *vt* **1** : to increase greatly, to enlarge **2** : to exaggerate
ágil *adj* **1** : agile, nimble **2** : sharp, lively (of a response, etc.) — **ágilmente** *adv*
agilidad *nf* : agility, nimbleness
agilizar {21} *vt* ACELERAR : to expedite, to speed up
agitación *nf, pl* **-ciones 1** : agitation **2** NERVIOSISMO : nervousness
agitado, -da *adj* **1** : agitated, excited **2** : choppy, rough, turbulent
agitador, -dora *n* PROVOCADOR : agitator
agitar *vt* **1** : to agitate, to shake **2** : to wave, to flap **3** : to stir up — **agitarse** *vr* **1** : to toss about, to flap around **2** : to get upset
aglomeración *nf, pl* **-ciones 1** : conglomeration, mass **2** GENTÍO : crowd
aglomerar *vt* **1** : to cluster, to amass — **aglomerarse** *vr* : to crowd together
aglutinar *vt* : to bring together, to bind
agnóstico, -ca *adj & n* : agnostic
agobiado, -da *adj* : weary, worn-out, weighted-down
agobiante *adj* **1** : exhausting, overwhelming **2** : stifling, oppressive
agobiar *vt* **1** OPRIMIR : to oppress, to burden **2** ABRUMAR : to overwhelm **3** : to wear out, to exhaust
agonía *nf* : agony, death throes
agonizante *adj* : dying

agonizar {21} *vi* **1** : to be dying **2** : to be in agony **3** : to dim, to fade

agorero, -ra *adj* : ominous

agostar *vt* **1** : to parch **2** : to wither — **agostarse** *vr*

agosto *nm* **1** : August **2 hacer uno su agosto** : to make a fortune, to make a killing

agotado, -da *adj* **1** : exhausted, used up **2** : sold out **3** FATIGADO : worn-out, tired

agotador, -dora *adj* : exhausting

agotamiento *nm* FATIGA : exhaustion

agotar *vt* **1** : to exhaust, to use up **2** : to weary, to wear out — **agotarse** *vr*

agraciado[1], **-da** *adj* **1** : attractive **2** : fortunate

agraciado[2], **-da** *n* : winner

agradable *adj* GRATO, PLACENTERO : pleasant, agreeable — **agradablemente** *adv*

agradar *vi* : to be pleasing ⟨nos agradó mucho el resultado : we were very pleased with the result⟩

agradecer {53} *vt* **1** : to be grateful for **2** : to thank

agradecido, -da *adj* : grateful, thankful

agradecimiento *nm* : gratitude, thankfulness

agrado *nm* **1** GUSTO : taste, liking ⟨no es de su agrado : it's not to his liking⟩ **2** : graciousness, agreeableness **3 con ~** : with pleasure, willingly ⟨lo haré con agrado : I will be happy to do it⟩

agrandar *vt* **1** : to exaggerate **2** : to enlarge — **agrandarse** *vr*

agrario, -ria *adj* : agrarian, agricultural

agravación *nf*, *pl* **-ciones** : aggravation, worsening

agravante *adj* : aggravating

agravar *vt* **1** : to increase (weight), to make heavier **2** EMPEORAR : to aggravate, to worsen — **agravarse** *vr*

agraviar *vt* INJURIAR, OFENDER : to offend, to insult

agravio *nm* INJURIA : affront, offense, insult

agredir {1} *vt* : to assail, to attack

agregado[1], **-da** *n* **1** : attaché **2** : assistant professor

agregado[2] *nm* **1** : aggregate **2** AÑADIDURA : addition, something added

agregar {52} *vt* **1** AÑADIR : to add, to attach **2** : to appoint — **agregarse** *vr* : to join

agresión *nf*, *pl* **-siones** **1** : aggression **2** ATAQUE : attack

agresividad *nf* : aggressiveness, aggression

agresivo, -va *adj* : aggressive — **agresivamente** *adv*

agresor[1], **-sora** *adj* : hostile, attacking

agresor[2], **-sora** *n* **1** : aggressor **2** : assailant, attacker

agreste *adj* **1** CAMPESTRE : rural **2** : wild, untamed

agriar *vt* **1** : to sour, to make sour **2** : to embitter — **agriarse** *vr* : to turn sour

agrícola *adj* : agricultural

agricultor, -tora *n* : farmer, grower

agricultura *nf* : agriculture, farming

agridulce *adj* **1** : bittersweet **2** : sweet-and-sour

agrietar *vt* : to crack — **agrietarse** *vr* **1** : to crack **2** : to chap

agrimensor, -sora *n* : surveyor

agrimensura *nf* : surveying

agrio, agria *adj* **1** ÁCIDO : sour **2** : caustic, acrimonious

agriparse *vr* : to catch the flu

agroindustria *nf* : agribusiness

agronomía *nf* : agronomy

agropecuario, -ria *adj* : pertaining to livestock and agriculture

agrupación *nf*, *pl* **-ciones** GRUPO : group, association

agrupamiento *nm* : grouping, concentration

agrupar *vt* : to group together

agua *nf* **1** : water **2 agua oxigenada** : hydrogen peroxide **3 aguas negras** *or* **aguas residuales** : sewage **4 como agua para chocolate** *Mex fam* : furious **5 echar aguas** *Mex fam* : to keep an eye out, to be on the lookout

aguacate *nm* : avocado

aguacero *nm* : shower, downpour

aguado, -da *adj* **1** DILUIDO : watered-down, diluted **2** *CA, Col, Mex fam* : soft, flabby **3** *Mex, Peru fam* : dull, boring

aguafiestas *nmfs & pl* : killjoy, stick-in-the-mud, spoilsport

aguafuerte *nm* : etching

aguamanil *nm* : ewer, pitcher

aguanieve *nf* : sleet ⟨caer aguanieve : to be sleeting⟩

aguantar *vt* **1** SOPORTAR : to bear, to tolerate, to withstand **2** : to hold **3 aguantar las ganas** : to resist an urge ⟨no pude aguantar las ganas de reír : I couldn't keep myself from laughing⟩ — *vi* : to hold out, to last — **aguantarse** *vr* **1** : to resign oneself **2** : to restrain oneself

aguante *nm* **1** TOLERANCIA : tolerance, patience **2** RESISTENCIA : endurance, strength

aguar {10} *vt* **1** : to water down, to dilute **2 aguar la fiesta** *fam* : to spoil the party

aguardar *vt* ESPERAR : to wait for, to await — *vi* : to be in store

aguardiente *nm* : clear brandy

aguarrás *nm* : turpentine

agudeza *nf* **1** : keenness, sharpness **2** : shrillness **3** : witticism

agudizar {21} *vt* : to intensify, to heighten

agudo, -da *adj* **1** : acute, sharp **2** : shrill, high-pitched **3** PERSPICAZ : clever, shrewd

agüero *nm* AUGURIO, PRESAGIO : augury, omen

aguijón *nm*, *pl* **-jones** **1** : stinger (of a bee, etc.) **2** : goad

aguijonear *vt* : to goad
águila *nf* **1** : eagle **2 águila o sol** *Mex* : heads or tails
aguileño, -ña *adj* : aquiline
aguilera *nf* : aerie, eagle's nest
aguilón *nm, pl* **-lones** : gable
aguinaldo *nm* **1** : Christmas bonus, year-end bonus **2** *PRi, Ven* : Christmas carol
agüitarse *vr Mex fam* : to have the blues, to feel discouraged
aguja *nf* **1** : needle **2** : steeple, spire
agujerear *vt* : to make a hole in, to pierce
agujero *nm* **1** : hole **2 agujero negro** : black hole (in astronomy)
agujeta *nf* **1** *Mex* : shoelace **2 agujetas** *nfpl* : muscular soreness or stiffness
agusanado, -da *adj* : worm-eaten
aguzar {21} *vt* **1** : to sharpen ⟨aguzar el ingenio : to sharpen one's wits⟩ **2 aguzar el oído** : to prick up one's ears
ah *interj* : oh!
ahí *adv* **1** : there ⟨ahí está : there it is⟩ **2 por** ~ : somewhere, thereabouts **3 de ahí que** : with the result that, so that ~ : for the time being
ahijado, -da *n* : godchild, godson *m*, goddaughter *f*
ahijar {5} *vt* : to adopt (a child)
ahínco *nm* : eagerness, zeal
ahogar {52} *vt* **1** : to drown **2** : to smother **3** : to choke back, to stifle — **ahogarse** *vr*
ahogo *nm* : breathlessness, suffocation
ahondar *vt* : to deepen — *vi* : to elaborate, to go into detail
ahora *adv* **1** : now **2 ahora mismo** : right now **3 hasta** ~ : so far **4 por** ~ : for the time being
ahorcar {72} *vt* : to hang, to kill by hanging — **ahorcarse** *vr*
ahorita *adv fam* : right now, right away
ahorquillado, -da *adj* : forked
ahorrador, -dora *adj* : thrifty
ahorrar *vt* **1** : to save (money) **2** : to spare, to conserve — *vi* : to save up — **ahorrarse** *vr* : to spare oneself
ahorrativo, -va *adj* : thrifty, frugal
ahorro *nm* : saving ⟨cuenta de ahorros : savings account⟩
ahuecar {72} *vt* **1** : to hollow out **2** : to cup (one's hands) **3** : to plump up, to fluff up
ahuizote *nm Mex fam* : annoying person, pain in the neck
ahumar {8} *vt* : to smoke, to cure
ahuyentar *vt* **1** : to scare away, to chase away **2** : to banish, to dispel ⟨ahuyentar las dudas : to dispel doubts⟩
airado, -da *adj FURIOSO* : angry, irate
airar {5} *vt* : to make angry, to anger
aire *nm* **1** : air **2 aire acondicionado** : air-conditioning **3 darse aires** : to give oneself airs
airear *vt* : to air, to air out — **airearse** *vr* : to get some fresh air
airoso, -sa *adj* **1** : elegant, graceful **2 salir airoso** : to come out winning
aislacionismo *nm* : isolationism

aislacionista *adj & nmf* : isolationist
aislado, -da *adj* : isolated, alone
aislador *nm* : insulator (part)
aislamiento *nm* **1** : isolation **2** : insulation
aislante *nm* : insulator, nonconductor
aislar {5} *vt* **1** : to isolate **2** : to insulate
ajado, -da *adj* **1** : worn, shabby **2** : wrinkled, crumpled
ajar *vt* : to wear out, to spoil
ajardinado, -da *adj* : landscaped
ajedrecista *nmf* : chess player
ajedrez *nm, pl* **-dreces 1** : chess **2** : chess set
ajeno, -na *adj* **1** : alien **2** : of another, of others ⟨propiedad ajena : somebody else's property⟩ **3** ~ **a** : foreign to **4** ~ **de** : devoid of, free from
ajetreado, -da *adj* : hectic, busy
ajetrearse *vr* : to bustle about, to rush around
ajetreo *nm* : hustle and bustle, fuss
ají *nm, pl* **ajíes** : chili pepper
ajo *nm* : garlic
ajonjolí *nm, pl* **-líes** : sesame
ajuar *nm* : trousseau
ajustable *adj* : adjustable
ajustado, -da *adj* **1** *CEÑIDO* : tight, tight-fitting **2** : close, tight ⟨una ajustada victoria : a close victory⟩
ajustar *vt* **1** : to adjust, to adapt **2** : to take in (clothing) **3** : to settle, to resolve — **ajustarse** *vr* : to fit, to conform
ajuste *nm* **1** : adjustment **2** : tightening
ajusticiar *vt EJECUTAR* : to execute, to put to death
al *prep* (contraction of a and el) → **a²**
ala *nf* **1** : wing **2** : brim (of a hat)
Alá *nm* : Allah
alabanza *nf ELOGIO* : praise
alabar *vt* : to praise — **alabarse** *vr* : to boast
alabastro *nm* : alabaster
alabear *vt* : to warp — **alabearse** *vr*
alabeo *nm* : warp, warping
alacena *nf* : cupboard, larder
alacrán *nm, pl* **-cranes** *ESCORPIÓN* : scorpion
alado, -da *adj* : winged
alambique *nm* : still (to distill alcohol)
alambre *nm* **1** : wire **2 alambre de púas** : barbed wire
alameda *nf* **1** : poplar grove **2** : tree-lined avenue
álamo *nm* **1** : poplar **2 álamo temblón** : aspen
alar *nm* : eaves *pl*
alarde *nm* **1** : show, display **2 hacer alarde de** : to make show of, to boast about
alardear *vi PRESUMIR* : to boast, to brag
alargado, -da *adj* : elongated, slender
alargamiento *nm* : lengthening, extension, elongation
alargar {52} *vt* **1** : to extend, to lengthen **2** *PROLONGAR* : to prolong — **alargarse** *vr*

alarido *nm* : howl, shriek
alarma *nf* : alarm
alarmante *adj* : alarming — **alarmante-mente** *adv*
alarmar *vt* : to alarm
alazán *nm, pl* **-zanes** : sorrel (color or animal)
alba *nf* AMANECER : dawn, daybreak
albacea *nmf* TESTAMENTARIO : executor, executrix *f*
albahaca *nf* : basil
albanés, -nesa *adj & n, mpl* **-neses** : Albanian
albañil *nmf* : bricklayer, mason
albañilería *nf* : bricklaying, masonry
albaricoque *nm* : apricot
albatros *nm* : albatross
albedrío *nm* : will ⟨libre albedrío : free will⟩
alberca *nf* **1** : reservoir, tank **2** *Mex* : swimming pool
albergar {52} *vt* ALOJAR : to house, to lodge, to shelter
albergue *nm* **1** : shelter, refuge **2** : hostel
albino, -na *adj & n* : albino — **albinismo** *nm*
albóndiga *nf* : meatball
albor *nm* **1** : dawning, beginning **2** BLANCURA : whiteness
alborada *nf* : dawn
alborear *v impers* : to dawn
alborotado, -da *adj* **1** : excited, agitated **2** : rowdy, unruly
alborotador¹, -dora *adj* **1** : noisy, boisterous **2** : rowdy, unruly
alborotador², -dora *n* : agitator, troublemaker, rioter
alborotar *vt* **1** : to excite, to agitate **2** : to incite, to stir up — **alborotarse** *vr* **1** : to get excited **2** : to riot
alboroto *nm* **1** : disturbance, ruckus **2** MOTÍN : riot
alborozado, -da *adj* : jubilant
alborozar {21} *vt* : to gladden, to cheer
alborozo *nm* : joy, elation
álbum *nm* : album ⟨álbum de recortes : scrapbook⟩
albúmina *nf* : albumin
albur *nm* **1** : chance, risk **2** *Mex* : pun
alca *nf* : auk
alcachofa *nf* : artichoke
alcahuete, -ta *n* CHISMOSO : gossip
alcaide *nm* : warden (in a prison)
alcalde, -desa *n* : mayor
alcaldía *nf* **1** : mayoralty **2** AYUNTAMIENTO : city hall
álcali *nm* : alkali
alcalino, -na *adj* : alkaline — **alcalinidad** *nf*
alcance *nm* **1** : reach **2** : range, scope
alcancía *nf* **1** : piggy bank, money box **2** : collection box (for alms, etc.)
alcanfor *nm* : camphor
alcantarilla *nf* CLOACA : sewer, drain
alcanzar {21} *vt* **1** : to reach **2** : to catch up with **3** LOGRAR : to achieve, to at-

tain — *vi* **1** DAR : to suffice, to be enough **2** ~ **a** : to manage to
alcaparra *nf* : caper
alcapurria *nf* PRi : stuffed fritter made with taro and green banana
alcaravea *nf* : caraway
alcatraz *nm, pl* **-traces** : gannet
alcázar *nm* : fortress, castle
alce¹, etc. → **alzar**
alce² *nm* : moose, European elk
alcoba *nf* : bedroom
alcohol *nm* : alcohol
alcohólico, -ca *adj & n* : alcoholic
alcoholismo *nm* : alcoholism
alcoholizarse {21} *vr* : to become an alcoholic
alcornoque *nm* **1** : cork oak **2** *fam* : idiot, fool
alcurnia *nf* : ancestry, lineage
aldaba *nf* : door knocker
aldea *nf* : village
aldeano¹, -na *adj* : village, rustic
aldeano², -na *n* : villager
aleación *nf, pl* **-ciones** : alloy
alear *vt* : to alloy
aleatorio, -ria *adj* : random, fortuitous — **aleatoriamente** *adv*
alebrestar *vt* : to excite, to make nervous — **alebrestarse** *vr*
aledaño, -ña *adj* : bordering, neighboring
aledaños *nmpl* AFUERAS : outskirts, surrounding area
alegar {52} *vt* : to assert, to allege — *vi* DISCUTIR : to argue
alegato *nm* **1** : allegation, claim **2** *Mex* : argument, summation (in law) **3** : argument, dispute
alegoría *nf* : allegory
alegórico, -ca *adj* : allegorical
alegrar *vt* : to make happy, to cheer up — **alegrarse** *vr* : to be glad, to rejoice
alegre *adj* **1** : glad, cheerful **2** : colorful, bright **3** *fam* : tipsy
alegremente *adv* : happily, cheerfully
alegría *nf* : joy, cheer, happiness
alejado, -da *adj* : remote
alejamiento *nm* **1** : removal, separation **2** : estrangement
alejar *vt* **1** : to remove, to move away **2** : to estrange, to alienate — **alejarse** *vr* **1** : to move away, to stray **2** : to drift apart
alelado, -da *adj* **1** : bewildered, stupefied **2** : foolish, stupid
aleluya *interj* : hallelujah!, alleluia!
alemán¹, -mana *adj & n, mpl* **-manes** : German
alemán² *nm* : German (language)
alentador, -dora *adj* : encouraging
alentar {55} *vt* : to encourage, to inspire — *vi* : to breathe
alerce *nm* : larch
alérgeno *nm* : allergen
alergia *nf* : allergy
alérgico, -ca *adj* : allergic
alero *nm* **1** : eaves *pl* **2** : forward (in basketball)

alerón *nm, pl* **-rones** : aileron
alerta[1] *adv* : on the alert
alerta[2] *adj & nf* : alert
alertar *vt* : to alert
aleta *nf* 1 : fin 2 : flipper 3 : small wing
aletargado, -da *adj* : lethargic, sluggish, torpid
aletargarse {52} *vr* : to feel drowsy, to become lethargic
aletear *vi* : to flutter, to flap one's wings
aleteo *nm* : flapping, flutter
alevín *nm, pl* **-vines** 1 : fry, young fish 2 PRINCIPIANTE : beginner
alevosía *nf* 1 : treachery 2 : premeditation
alevoso, -sa *adj* : treacherous
alfabético, -ca *adj* : alphabetical — **alfabéticamente** *adv*
alfabetismo *nm* : literacy
alfabetizado, -da *adj* : literate
alfabetizar {21} *vt* : to alphabetize
alfabeto *nm* : alphabet
alfalfa *nf* : alfalfa
alfanje *nm* : cutlass, scimitar
alfarería *nf* : pottery
alfarero, -ra *n* : potter
alféizar *nm* : sill, windowsill
alfeñique *nm fam* : wimp, weakling
alférez *nmf, pl* **-reces** 1 : second lieutenant 2 : ensign
alfil *nm* : bishop (in chess)
alfiler *nm* 1 : pin 2 BROCHE : brooch
alfiletero *nm* : pincushion
alfombra *nf* : carpet, rug
alfombrado *nm* : carpeting
alfombrar *vt* : to carpet
alfombrilla *nf* : small rug, mat
alforfón *nm, pl* **-fones** : buckwheat
alforja *nf* : saddlebag
alforza *nf* : pleat, tuck
alga *nf* 1 : aquatic plant, alga 2 : seaweed
algarabía *nf* 1 : gibberish, babble 2 : hubbub, uproar
álgebra *nf* : algebra
algebraico, -ca *adj* : algebraic
álgido, -da *adj* 1 : critical, decisive 2 : icy cold
algo[1] *adv* : somewhat, rather ⟨es simpático, pero algo tacaño : he's nice but rather stingy⟩
algo[2] *pron* 1 : something 2 ~ **de** : some, a little ⟨tengo algo de dinero : I've got some money⟩
algodón *nm, pl* **-dones** : cotton
algoritmo *nm* : algorithm
alguacil *nm* : constable
alguien *pron* : somebody, someone
alguno[1], **-na** *adj* (**algún** *before masculine singular nouns*) 1 : some, any ⟨algún día : someday, one day⟩ 2 (*in negative constructions*) : not any, not at all ⟨no tengo noticia alguna : I have no news at all⟩ 3 **algunas veces** : sometimes
alguno[2], **-na** *pron* 1 : one, someone, somebody ⟨alguno de ellos : one of them⟩ 2 **algunos, -nas** *pron pl* : some,

a few ⟨algunos quieren trabajar : some want to work⟩
alhaja *nf* : jewel, gem
alhajar *vt* : to adorn with jewels
alharaca *nf* : fuss
alhelí *nm* : wallflower
aliado[1], **-da** *adj* : allied
aliado[2], **-da** *n* : ally
alianza *nf* : alliance
aliarse {85} *vr* : to form an alliance, to ally oneself
alias *adv & nm* : alias
alicaído, -da *adj* : depressed, discouraged
alicates *nmpl* PINZAS : pliers
aliciente *nm* 1 INCENTIVO : incentive 2 ATRACCIÓN : attraction
alienación *nf, pl* **-ciones** : alienation, derangement
alienar *vt* ENAJENAR : to alienate
aliento *nm* 1 : breath 2 : courage, strength 3 **dar aliento a** : to encourage
aligerar *vt* 1 : to lighten 2 ACELERAR : to hasten, to quicken
alijo *nm* : cache, consignment (of contraband)
alimaña *nf* : pest, vermin
alimentación *nf, pl* **-ciones** NUTRICIÓN : nutrition, nourishment
alimentar *vt* 1 NUTRIR : to feed, to nourish 2 MANTENER : to support (a family) 3 FOMENTAR : to nurture, to foster — **alimentarse** *vr* ~ **con** : to live on
alimentario, -ria → **alimenticio**
alimenticio, -cia *adj* 1 : nutritional, food, dietary 2 : nutritious, nourishing
alimento *nm* : food, nourishment
aliñar *vt* 1 : to dress (salad) 2 CONDIMENTAR : to season
alineación *nf, pl* **-ciones** 1 : alignment 2 : lineup (in sports)
alineamiento *nm* : alignment
alinear *vt* 1 : to align 2 : to line up — **alinearse** *vr* 1 : to fall in, to line up 2 ~ **con** : to align oneself with
aliño *nm* : seasoning, dressing
alipús *nm, pl* **-puses** *Mex fam* : booze, drink
alisar *vt* : to smooth
aliso *nm* : alder
alistamiento *nm* : enlistment, recruitment
alistar *vt* 1 : to recruit 2 : to make ready — **alistarse** *vr* : to join up, to enlist
aliteración *nf, pl* **-ciones** : alliteration
aliviar *vt* MITIGAR : to relieve, to alleviate, to soothe — **aliviarse** *vr* : to recover, to get better
alivio *nm* : relief
aljaba *nf* : quiver (for arrows)
aljibe *nm* : cistern, well
allá *adv* 1 : there, over there 2 **más allá** : farther away. 3 **más allá de** : beyond 4 **allá tú** : that's up to you

allanamiento *nm* **1** : (police) raid **2 allanamiento de morada** : breaking and entering

allanar *vt* **1** : to raid, to search **2** : to solve, to solve **3** : to smooth, to level out

allegado[1], **-da** *adj* : close, intimate

allegado[2], **-da** *n* : close friend, relation ⟨parientes y allegados : friends and relations⟩

allegar {52} *vt* : to gather, to collect

allende[1] *adv* : beyond, on the other side

allende[2] *prep* : beyond ⟨allende las montañas : beyond the mountains⟩

allí *adv* : there, over there ⟨allí mismo : right there⟩ ⟨hasta allí : up to that point⟩

alma *nf* **1** : soul **2** : person, human being **3 no tener alma** : to be pitiless **4 tener el alma en un hilo** : to have one's heart in one's mouth

almacén *nm, pl* **-cenes 1** BODEGA : warehouse, storehouse **2** TIENDA : shop, store **3 gran almacén** *Spain* : department store

almacenaje → almacenamiento

almacenamiento *nm* : storage ⟨almacenamiento de datos : data storage⟩

almacenar *vt* : to store, to put in storage

almacenero, -ra *n* : shopkeeper

almacenista *nm* MAYORISTA : wholesaler

almádena *nf* : sledgehammer

almanaque *nm* : almanac

almeja *nf* : clam

almendra *nf* **1** : almond **2** : kernel

almendro *nm* : almond tree

almiar *nm* : haystack

almíbar *nm* : syrup

almidón *nm, pl* **-dones** : starch

almidonar *vt* : to starch

alminar *nm* MINARETE : minaret

almirante *nm* : admiral

almizcle *nm* : musk

almohada *nf* : pillow

almohadilla *nf* **1** : small pillow, cushion **2** : bag, base (in baseball)

almohadón *nm, pl* **-dones** : bolster, cushion

almohazar {21} *vt* : to curry (a horse)

almoneda *nf* SUBASTA : auction

almorranas *nfpl* HEMORROIDES : hemorrhoids, piles

almorzar {36} *vi* : to have lunch — *vt* : to have for lunch

almuerzo *nm* : lunch

alocado, -da *adj* **1** : crazy **2** : wild, reckless **3** : silly, scatterbrained

alocución *nf, pl* **-ciones** : speech, address

áloe *or* **aloe** *nm* : aloe

alojamiento *nm* : lodging, accommodations *pl*

alojar *vt* ALBERGAR : to house, to lodge — **alojarse** *vr* : to lodge, to room

alondra *nf* : lark, skylark

alpaca *nf* : alpaca

alpinismo *nm* : mountain climbing, mountaineering

alpinista *nmf* : mountain climber

alpino, -na *adj* : Alpine, alpine

alpiste *nm* : birdseed

alquilar *vt* ARRENDAR : to rent, to lease

alquiler *nm* ARRENDAMIENTO : rent, rental

alquimia *nf* : alchemy

alquimista *nmf* : alchemist

alquitrán *nm, pl* **-tranes** BREA : tar

alquitranar *vt* : to tar, to cover with tar

alrededor[1] *adv* **1** : around, about ⟨todo temblaba alrededor : all around things were shaking⟩ **2 ~ de** : around, approximately ⟨alrededor de quince personas : around fifteen people⟩

alrededor[2] *prep* **~ de** : around, about ⟨corrió alrededor de la casa : she ran around the house⟩ ⟨llegaré alrededor de diciembre : I will get there around December⟩

alrededores *nmpl* ALEDAÑOS : surroundings, outskirts

alta *nf* **1** : admission, entry, enrollment **2 dar de alta** : to release, to discharge (a patient)

altanería *nf* ALTIVEZ, ARROGANCIA : arrogance, haughtiness

altanero, -ra *adj* ALTIVO, ARROGANTE : arrogant, haughty — **altaneramente** *adv*

altar *nm* : altar

altavoz *nm, pl* **-voces** ALTOPARLANTE : loudspeaker

alteración *nf, pl* **-ciones 1** MODIFICACIÓN : alteration, modification **2** PERTURBACIÓN : disturbance, disruption

alterado, -da *adj* : upset

alterar *vt* **1** MODIFICAR : to alter, to modify **2** PERTURBAR : to disturb, to disrupt — **alterarse** *vr* : to get upset, to get worked up

altercado *nm* DISCUSIÓN, DISPUTA : altercation, argument, dispute

alternador *nm* : alternator

alternancia *nf* : alternation, rotation

alternar *vi* **1** : to alternate **2** : to mix, to socialize — *vt* : to alternate — **alternarse** *vr* : to take turns

alternativa *nf* OPCIÓN : alternative, option

alternativo, -va *adj* **1** : alternating **2** : alternative — **alternativamente** *adv*

alterno, -na *adj* : alternate ⟨corriente alterna : alternating current⟩

alteza *nf* **1** : loftiness, lofty height **2 Alteza** : Highness

altibajos *nmpl* **1** : unevenness (of terrain) **2** : ups and downs

altímetro *nm* : altimeter

altiplanicie *nf* → altiplano

altiplano *nm* : high plateau, upland

altisonante *adj* **1** : pompous, affected (of language) **2** *Mex* : rude, obscene (of language)

altitud *nf* : altitude

altivez *nf, pl* **-veces** ALTANERÍA, ARROGANCIA : arrogance, haughtiness
altivo, -va *adj* ALTANERO, ARROGANTE : arrogant, haughty
alto¹ *adv* **1** : high **2** : loud, loudly
alto², -ta *adj* **1** : tall, high **2** : loud ⟨en voz alta : aloud, out loud⟩
alto³ *nm* **1** ALTURA : height, elevation **2** : stop, halt **3 altos** *nmpl* : upper floors
alto⁴ *interj* : halt!, stop!
altoparlante *nm* ALTAVOZ : loudspeaker
altozano *nm* : hillock
altruismo *nm* : altruism
altruista¹ *adj* : altruistic
altruista² *nmf* : altruist
altura *nf* **1** : height **2** : altitude **3** : loftiness, nobleness **4 a la altura de** : near, up by ⟨en la avenida San Antonio a la altura de la Calle Tres : on San Antonio Avenue up near Third Street⟩ **5 a estas alturas** : at this point, at this stage of the game
alubia *nf* : kidney bean
alucinación *nf, pl* **-ciones** : hallucination
alucinante *adj* : hallucinatory
alucinar *vi* : to hallucinate
alucinógeno¹, -na *adj* : hallucinogenic
alucinógeno² *nm* : hallucinogen
alud *nm* AVALANCHA : avalanche, landslide
aludido, -da *n* **1** : person in question ⟨el aludido : the aforesaid⟩ **2 darse por aludido** : to take it personally
aludir *vi* : to allude, to refer
alumbrado *nm* ILUMINACIÓN : lighting
alumbramiento *nm* **1** : lighting **2** : childbirth
alumbrar *vt* **1** ILUMINAR : to light, to illuminate **2** : to give birth to
alumbre *nm* : alum
aluminio *nm* : aluminum
alumnado *nm* : student body
alumno, -na *n* **1** : pupil, student **2 ex–alumno, -na** : alumnus, alumna *f* **3 ex–alumnos, -nas** *npl* : alumni, alumnae *f*
alusión *nf, pl* **-siones** : allusion, reference
alusivo, -va *adj* **1** : allusive **2 ~ a** : in reference to, regarding
aluvión *nm, pl* **-viones** : flood, barrage
alza *nf* SUBIDA : rise ⟨precios en alza : rising prices⟩
alzamiento *nm* LEVANTAMIENTO : uprising, insurrection
alzar {21} *vt* **1** ELEVAR, LEVANTAR : to lift, to raise **2** : to erect — **alzarse** *vr* LEVANTARSE : to rise up
ama *nf* → **amo**
amabilidad *nf* : kindness
amable *adj* : kind, nice — **amablemente** *adv*
amado¹, -da *adj* : beloved, darling
amado², -da *n* : sweetheart, loved one
amaestrar *vt* : to train (animals)
amafiarse *vr Mex fam* : to conspire, to be in cahoots

amagar {52} *vt* **1** : to show signs of (an illness, etc.) **2** : to threaten — *vi* **1** : to be imminent, to threaten **2** : to feint, to dissemble
amago *nm* **1** AMENAZA : threat **2** : sign, hint
amainar *vi* : to abate, to ease up, to die down
amalgama *nf* : amalgam
amalgamar *vt* : to amalgamate, to unite
amamantar *v* : to breast-feed, to nurse, to suckle
amanecer¹ {53} *v impers* **1** : to dawn **2** : to begin to show, to appear **3** : to wake up (in the morning)
amanecer² *nm* ALBA : dawn, daybreak
amanerado, -da *adj* : affected, mannered
amansar *vt* **1** : to tame **2** : to soothe, to calm down — **amansarse** *vr*
amante¹ *adj* : loving, fond
amante² *nmf* : lover
amañar *vt* : to rig, to fix, to tamper with — **amañarse** *vr* **amañárselas** : to manage
amaño *nm* **1** : skill, dexterity **2** : trick, ruse
amapola *nf* : poppy
amar *vt* : to love — **amarse** *vr*
amargado, -da *adj* : embittered, bitter
amargar {52} *vt* : to make bitter, to embitter — *vi* : to taste bitter
amargo¹, -ga *adj* : bitter — **amargamente** *adv*
amargo² *nm* : bitterness, tartness
amargura *nf* **1** : bitterness **2** : grief, sorrow
amarilis *nf* : amaryllis
amarillear *vi* : to yellow, to turn yellow
amarillento, -ta *adj* : yellowish
amarillismo *nm* : yellow journalism, sensationalism
amarillo¹, -lla *adj* : yellow
amarillo² *nm* : yellow
amarra *nf* **1** : mooring, mooring line **2 soltar las amarras de** : to loosen one's grip on
amarrar *vt* **1** : to moor (a boat) **2** ATAR : to fasten, to tie up, to tie down
amartillar *vt* : to cock (a gun)
amasar *vt* **1** : to amass **2** : to knead **3** : to mix, to prepare
amasijo *nm* : jumble, hodgepodge
amasio, -sia *n* : lover, paramour
amateur *adj & nmf* : amateur — **amateurismo** *nm*
amatista *nf* : amethyst
amatorio, -ria *adj* : amatory, sexual ⟨poesía amatoria : love poems⟩
amazona *nf* **1** : Amazon (in mythology) **2** : horsewoman
amazónico, -ca *adj* : amazonian
ambages *nmpl* **sin ~** : without hesitation, straight to the point
ámbar *nm* **1** : amber **2 ámbar gris** : ambergris
ambición *nf, pl* **-ciones** : ambition
ambicionar *vt* : to aspire to, to seek

ambicioso, -sa *adj* : ambitious — **ambiciosamente** *adv*
ambidextro, -tra *adj* : ambidextrous
ambientación *nf, pl* **-ciones** : setting, atmosphere
ambiental *adj* : environmental — **ambientalmente** *adv*
ambientalista *nmf* : environmentalist
ambientar *vt* : to give atmosphere to, to set (in literature and drama) — **ambientarse** *vr* : to adjust, to get one's bearings
ambiente *nm* **1** : atmosphere **2** : environment **3** : surroundings *pl*
ambigüedad *nf* : ambiguity
ambiguo, -gua *adj* : ambiguous
ámbito *nm* : domain, field, area
ambivalencia *nf* : ambivalence
ambivalente *adj* : ambivalent
ambos, -bas *adj & pron* : both
ambulancia *nf* : ambulance
ambulante *adj* **1** : traveling, itinerant **2 vendedor ambulante** : street vendor
ameba *nf* : amoeba
amedrentar *vt* : to frighten, to intimidate — **amedrentarse** *vr*
amén *nm* **1** : amen **2 ~ de** : in addition to, besides **3 en un decir amén** : in an instant
amenaza *nf* : threat, menace
amenazador, -dora *adj* : threatening, menacing
amenazante → **amenazador**
amenazar {21} *v* : to threaten
amenguar {10} *vt* **1** : to diminish **2** : to belittle, to dishonor
amenidad *nf* : pleasantness, amenity
amenizar {21} *vt* **1** : to make pleasant **2** : to brighten up, to add life to
ameno, -na *adj* : agreeable, pleasant
americano, -na *adj & n* : American
amerindio, -dia *adj & n* : Amerindian
ameritar *vt* MERECER : to deserve
ametralladora *nf* : machine gun
amianto *nm* : asbestos
amiba → **ameba**
amigable *adj* : friendly, amicable — **amigablemente** *adv*
amígdala *nf* : tonsil
amigdalitis *nf* : tonsilitis
amigo[1], -ga *adj* : friendly, close
amigo[2], -ga *n* : friend
amigote *nm* : crony, pal
amilanar *vt* **1** : to frighten **2** : to daunt, to discourage — **amilanarse** *vr* : to lose heart
aminoácido *nm* : amino acid
aminorar *vt* : to reduce, to lessen — *vi* : to diminish
amistad *nf* : friendship
amistoso, -sa *adj* : friendly — **amistosamente** *adv*
amnesia *nf* : amnesia
amnésico, -ca *adj & n* : amnesiac, amnesic
amnistía *nf* : amnesty
amnistiar {85} *vt* : to grant amnesty to

amo, ama *n* **1** : master *m*, mistress *f* **2** : owner, keeper (of an animal) **3 ama de casa** : housewife **4 ama de llaves** : housekeeper
amodorrado, -da *adj* : drowsy
amolar {19} *vt* **1** : to grind, to sharpen **2** : to pester, to annoy
amoldable *adj* : adaptable
amoldar *vt* **1** : to mold **2** : to adapt, to adjust — **amoldarse** *vr*
amonestación *nf, pl* **-ciones 1** APERCIBIMIENTO : admonition, warning **2 amonestaciones** *nfpl* : banns
amonestar *vt* APERCIBIR : to admonish, to warn
amoníaco *or* **amoniaco** *nm* : ammonia
amontonamiento *nm* : accumulation, piling up
amontonar *vt* **1** APILAR : to pile up, to heap up **2** : to collect, to gather **3** : to hoard — **amontonarse** *vr*
amor *nm* **1** : love **2** : loved one, beloved **3 amor propio** : self-esteem **4 hacer el amor** : to make love
amoral *adj* : amoral
amoratado, -da *adj* : black-and-blue, bruised, livid
amordazar {21} *vt* **1** : to gag, to muzzle **2** : to silence
amorfo, -fa *adj* : shapeless, amorphous
amorío *nm* : love affair, fling
amoroso, -sa *adj* **1** : loving, affectionate **2** : amorous ⟨una mirada amorosa : an amorous glance⟩ **3** : charming, cute — **amorosamente** *adv*
amortiguación *nf* : cushioning, absorption
amortiguador *nm* : shock absorber
amortiguar {10} *vt* : to soften (an impact)
amortizar {21} *vt* : to amortize, to pay off — **amortización** *nf*
amotinado[1], -da *adj* : rebellious, insurgent, mutinous
amotinado[2], -da *n* : rebel, insurgent, mutineer
amotinamiento *nm* : uprising, rebellion
amotinar *vt* : to incite (to riot), to agitate — **amotinarse** *vr* **1** : to riot, to rebel **2** : to mutiny
amparar *vt* : to safeguard, to protect — **ampararse** *vr* **1 ~ de** : to take shelter from **2 ~ en** : to have recourse to
amparo *nm* ACOGIDA, REFUGIO : protection, refuge
amperímetro *nm* : ammeter
amperio *nm* : ampere
ampliable *adj* : expandable, enlargeable, extendible
ampliación *nf, pl* **-ciones** : expansion, extension
ampliar {85} *vt* **1** : to expand, to extend **2** : to widen **3** : to enlarge (photographs) **4** : to elaborate on, to develop (ideas)
amplificador *nm* : amplifier
amplificar {72} *vt* : to amplify — **amplificación** *nf*

amplio, -plia *adj* : broad, wide, ample —
ampliamente *adj*
amplitud *nf* **1** : breadth, extent **2** : spaciousness
ampolla *nf* **1** : blister **2** : vial, ampoule
ampollar *vt* : to blister — **ampollarse** *vr*
ampolleta *nf* **1** : small vial **2** : hourglass
3 *Chile* : light bulb
ampulosidad *nf* : pompousness, bombast
ampuloso, -sa *adj* GRANDILOCUENTE
: pompous, bombastic — **ampulosamente** *adv*
amputar *vt* : to amputate — **amputación** *nf*
amueblar *vt* : to furnish
amuleto *nm* TALISMÁN : amulet, charm
amurallar *vt* : to wall in, to fortify
anacardo *nm* : cashew nut
anaconda *nf* : anaconda
anacrónico, -ca *adj* : anachronistic
anacronismo *nm* : anachronism
ánade *nmf* **1** : duck **2 ánade real** : mallard
anagrama *nm* : anagram
anal *adj* : anal
anales *nmpl* : annals
analfabetismo *nm* : illiteracy
analfabeto, -ta *adj & n* : illiterate
analgésico[1], -ca *adj* : analgesic, painkilling
analgésico[2] *nm* : painkiller, analgesic
análisis *nm* : analysis
analista *nmf* **1** : analyst **2** : annalist
analítico, -ca *adj* : analytical, analytic
— **analíticamente** *adv*
analizar {21} *vt* : to analyze
analogía *nf* : analogy
analógico, -ca *adj* **1** : analogical **2** : analog ⟨computadora analógica : analog computer⟩
análogo, -ga *adj* : analogous, similar
ananá *or* **ananás** *nm, pl* **-nás** : pineapple
anaquel *nm* REPISA : shelf
anaranjado[1], -da *adj* NARANJA : orange-colored
anaranjado[2] *nm* NARANJA : orange (color)
anarquía *nf* : anarchy
anárquico, -ca *adj* : anarchic
anarquismo *nm* : anarchism
anarquista *adj & nmf* : anarchist
anatema *nm* : anathema
anatomía *nf* : anatomy — **anatomista** *nmf*
anatómico, -ca *adj* : anatomical — **anatómicamente** *adv*
anca *nf* **1** : haunch, hindquarter **2 ancas de rana** : frogs' legs
ancestral *adj* **1** : ancient, traditional **2** : ancestral
ancestro *nm* ASCENDIENTE : ancestor, forefather *m*
ancho[1], -cha *adj* **1** : wide, broad **2** : ample, loose-fitting
ancho[2] *nm* : width, breadth
anchoa *nf* : anchovy

anchura *nf* : width, breadth
ancianidad *nf* SENECTUD : old age
anciano[1], -na *adj* : aged, old, elderly
anciano[2], -na *n* : elderly person
ancla *nf* : anchor
ancladero → **anclaje**
anclaje *nm* : anchorage
anclar *v* FONDEAR : to anchor
andadas *nfpl* **1** : tracks **2 volver a las andadas** : to go back to one's old ways, to backslide
andador[1] *nm* **1** : walker, baby walker **2** *Mex* : walkway
andador[2], -dora *n* : walker, one who walks
andadura *nf* : course, journey ⟨su agotadora andadura al campeonato : his exhausting journey to the championship⟩
andaluz, -luza *adj & n, mpl* **-luces** : Andalusian
andamiaje *nm* **1** : scaffolding **2** ESTRUCTURA : structure, framework
andamio *nm* : scaffold
andanada *nf* **1** : volley, broadside **2 soltar una andanada a** : to reprimand
andanzas *nfpl* : adventures
andar[1] {6} *vi* **1** CAMINAR : to walk **2** IR
: to go, to travel **3** FUNCIONAR : to run, to function ⟨el auto anda bien : the car runs well⟩ **4** : to ride ⟨andar a caballo : to ride on horseback⟩ **5** : to be ⟨anda sin dinero : he's broke⟩ — *vt* : to walk, to travel
andar[2] *nm* : walk, gait
andas *nfpl* : stand (for a coffin), bier
andén *nm, pl* **andenes 1** : (train) platform **2** *CA, Col* : sidewalk
andino, -na *adj* : Andean
andorrano, -na *adj & n* : Andorran
andrajos *nmpl* : rags, tatters
andrajoso, -sa *adj* : ragged, tattered
andrógino, -na *adj* : androgynous
andurriales *nmpl* : remote place
anea *nf* : cattail
anduvo, etc. → **andar**
anécdota *nf* : anecdote
anecdótico, -ca *adj* : anecdotal
anegar {52} *vt* **1** INUNDAR : to flood **2** AHOGAR : to drown **3** : to overwhelm — **anegarse** *vr* : to be flooded
anejo *nm* → **anexo[2]**
anemia *nf* : anemia
anémico, -ca *adj* : anemic
anémona *nf* : anemone
anestesia *nf* : anesthesia
anestesiar *vt* : to anesthetize
anestésico[1], -ca *adj* : anesthetic
anestésico[2] *nm* : anesthetic
anestesista *nmf* : anesthetist
aneurisma *nmf* : aneurysm
anexar *vt* : to annex, to attach
anexión *nf, pl* **-xiones** : annexation
anexo[1], -xa *adj* : attached, joined, annexed
anexo[2] *nm* **1** : annex **2** : supplement (to a book), appendix
anfetamina *nf* : amphetamine

anfibio · ante

anfibio[1], -bia *adj* : amphibious
anfibio[2] *nm* : amphibian
anfiteatro *nm* **1** : amphitheater **2** : lecture hall
anfitrión, -triona *n, mpl* -triones : host, hostess *f*
ánfora *nf* **1** : amphora **2** *Mex, Peru* : ballot box
ángel *nm* : angel
angelical *adj* : angelic, angelical
angélico, -ca *adj* → angelical
angina *nf* **1** *or* angina de pecho : angina **2** *Mex* : tonsil
anglicano, -na *adj & n* : Anglican
angloparlante[1] *adj* : English-speaking
angloparlante[2] *nmf* : English speaker
anglosajón, -jona *adj & n, mpl* -jones : Anglo-Saxon
angoleño, -ña *adj & n* : Angolan
angora *nf* : angora
angostar *vt* : to narrow — angostarse *vr*
angosto, -ta *adj* : narrow
angostura *nf* : narrowness
anguila *nf* : eel
angular *adj* : angular — angularidad *nf*
ángulo *nm* **1** : angle **2** : corner **3** ángulo muerto : blind spot
anguloso, -sa *adj* : angular, sharp ⟨una cara angulosa : an angular face⟩ — angulosidad *nf*
angustia *nf* **1** CONGOJA : anguish, distress **2** : anxiety, worry
angustiar *vt* **1** : to anguish, to distress **2** : to worry — angustiarse *vr*
angustioso, -sa *adj* **1** : anguished, distressed **2** : distressing, worrisome
anhelante *adj* : yearning, longing
anhelar *vt* : to yearn for, to crave
anhelo *nm* : longing, yearning
anidar *vi* **1** : to nest **2** : to make one's home, to dwell — *vt* : to shelter
anillo *nm* SORTIJA : ring
ánima *n* ALMA : soul
animación *nf, pl* -ciones **1** : animation **2** VIVEZA : liveliness
animado, -da *adj* **1** : animated, lively **2** : cheerful — animadamente *adv*
animador, -dora *n* **1** : (television) host **2** : cheerleader
animadversión *nf, pl* -siones ANIMOSIDAD : animosity, antagonism
animal[1] *adj* **1** : animal **2** ESTÚPIDO : stupid, idiotic **3** : rough, brutish
animal[2] *nm* : animal
animal[3] *nmf* **1** IDIOTA : idiot, fool **2** : brute, beastly person
animar *vt* **1** ALENTAR : to encourage, to inspire **2** : to animate, to enliven **3** : to brighten up, to cheer up — animarse *vr*
anímico, -ca *adj* : mental ⟨estado anímico : state of mind⟩
ánimo *nm* **1** ALMA : spirit, soul **2** : mood, spirits *pl* **3** : encouragement **4** PROPÓSITO : intention, purpose ⟨sociedad sin ánimo de lucro : nonprofit organization⟩ **5** : energy, vitality

animosidad *nf* ANIMADVERSIÓN : animosity, ill will
animoso, -sa *adj* : brave, spirited
aniñado, -da *adj* : childlike
aniquilación *nf* → aniquilamiento
aniquilamiento *nm* : annihilation, extermination
aniquilar *vt* **1** : to annihilate, to wipe out **2** : to overwhelm, to bring to one's knees — aniquilarse *vr*
anís *nm* **1** : anise **2** semilla de anís : aniseed
aniversario *nm* : anniversary
ano *nm* : anus
anoche *adv* : last night
anochecer[1] {53} *v impers* : to get dark
anochecer[2] *nm* : dusk, nightfall
anodino, -na *adj* : insipid, dull
ánodo *nm* : anode
anomalía *nf* : anomaly
anómalo, -la *adj* : anomalous
anonadado, -da *adj* : dumbfounded, speechless
anonadar *vt* : to dumbfound, to stun
anonimato *nm* : anonymity
anónimo, -ma *adj* : anonymous — anónimamente *adv*
anorexia *nf* : anorexia
anoréxico, -ca *adj* : anorexic
anormal *adj* : abnormal — anormalmente *adv*
anormalidad *nf* : abnormality
anotación *nf, pl* -ciones **1** : annotation, note **2** : scoring (in sports) ⟨lograron una anotación : they managed to score a goal⟩
anotar *vt* **1** : to annotate **2** APUNTAR, ESCRIBIR : to write down, to jot down **3** : to score (in sports) — *vi* : to score
anquilosado, -da *adj* **1** : stiff-jointed **2** : stagnated, stale
anquilosamiento *nm* **1** : stiffness (of joints) **2** : stagnation, paralysis
anquilosarse *vr* **1** : to stagnate **2** : to become stiff or paralyzed
anquilostoma *nm* : hookworm
ánsar *nm* : goose
ansarino *nm* : gosling
ansia *nf* **1** INQUIETUD : apprehensiveness, uneasiness **2** ANGUSTIA : anguish, distress **3** ANHELO : longing, yearning
ansiar {85} *vt* : to long for, to yearn for
ansiedad *nf* : anxiety
ansioso, -sa *adj* **1** : anxious, worried **2** : eager — ansiosamente *adv*
antagónico, -ca *adj* : conflicting, opposing
antagonismo *nm* : antagonism
antagonista[1] *adj* : antagonistic
antagonista[2] *nmf* : antagonist, opponent
antagonizar {21} *vt* : to antagonize
antaño *adv* : yesteryear, long ago
antártico, -ca *adj* **1** : antarctic **2** círculo antártico : antarctic circle
ante[1] *nm* **1** : elk, moose **2** : suede
ante[2] *prep* **1** : before, in front of **2** : considering, in view of **3** ante todo : first and foremost, above all

anteanoche *adv* : the night before last
anteayer *adv* : the day before yesterday
antebrazo *nm* : forearm
antecedente[1] *adj* : previous, prior
antecedente[2] *nm* **1** : precedent **2 antecedentes** *nmpl* : record, background
anteceder *v* : to precede
antecesor, -sora *n* **1** ANTEPASADO : ancestor **2** PREDECESOR : predecessor
antedicho, -cha *adj* : aforesaid, above
antelación *nf, pl* **-ciones 1** : advance notice **2 con ~** : in advance, beforehand
antemano *adv* **de ~** : in advance ⟨se lo agradezco de antemano : I thank you in advance⟩
antena *nf* : antenna
antenoche → anteanoche
anteojera *nf* **1** : eyeglass case **2 anteojeras** *nfpl* : blinders
anteojos *nmpl* GAFAS : glasses, eyeglasses
antepasado[1], **-da** *adj* : before last ⟨el domingo antepasado : the Sunday before last⟩
antepasado[2], **-da** *n* ANTECESOR : ancestor
antepecho *nm* **1** : guardrail **2** : ledge, sill
antepenúltimo, -ma *adj* : third from last
anteponer {60} *vt* **1** : to place before ⟨anteponer al interés de la nación el interés de la comunidad : to place the interests of the community before national interest⟩ **2** : to prefer
anteproyecto *nm* **1** : draft, proposal **2 anteproyecto de ley** : bill
antera *nf* : anther
anterior *adj* **1** : previous **2** : earlier ⟨tiempos anteriores : earlier times⟩ **3** : anterior, forward, front
anterioridad *nf* **1** : priority **2 con ~** : beforehand, in advance
anteriormente *adv* : previously, beforehand
antes *adv* **1** : before, earlier **2** : formerly, previously **3** : rather, sooner ⟨antes prefiero morir : I'd rather die⟩ **4 ~ de** : before, previous to ⟨antes de hoy : before today⟩ **5 antes que** : before ⟨antes que llegue Luis : before Luis arrives⟩ **6 cuanto antes** : as soon as possible **7 antes bien** : on the contrary
antesala *nf* **1** : anteroom, waiting room, lobby **2** : prelude, prologue
antiaborto, -ta *adj* : antiabortion
antiácido *nm* : antacid
antiadherente *adj* : nonstick
antiaéreo, -rea *adj* : antiaircraft
antiamericano, -na *adj* : anti-American
antibalas *adj* : bulletproof
antibiótico[1], **-ca** *adj* : antibiotic
antibiótico[2] *nm* : antibiotic
antichoque *adj* : shockproof
anticipación *nf, pl* **-ciones 1** : expectation, anticipation **2 con ~** : in advance

anticipado, -da *adj* **1** : advance, early **2 por ~** : in advance
anticipar *vt* **1** : to anticipate, to forestall, to deal with in advance **2** : to pay in advance — **anticiparse** *vr* **1** : to be early **2** ADELANTARSE : to get ahead
anticipo *nm* **1** : advance (payment) **2** : foretaste, preview
anticlerical *adj* : anticlerical
anticlimático, -ca : anticlimactic
anticlímax *nm* : anticlimax
anticomunismo *nm* : anticommunism
anticomunista *adj & nmf* : anticommunist
anticoncepción *nf, pl* **-ciones** : birth control, contraception
anticonceptivo *nm* : contraceptive
anticongelante *nm* : antifreeze
anticuado, -da *adj* : antiquated, outdated
anticuario[1], **-ria** *adj* : antique, antiquarian
anticuario[2], **-ria** *n* : antiquarian, antiquary
anticuario[3] *nm* : antique shop
anticuerpo *nm* : antibody
antidemocrático, -ca *adj* : antidemocratic
antideportivo, -va *adj* : unsportsmanlike
antidepresivo *nm* : antidepressant
antídoto *nm* : antidote
antidrogas *adj* : antidrug
antier → anteayer
antiestético, -ca *adj* : unsightly, unattractive
antifascista *adj & nmf* : antifascist
antifaz *nm, pl* **-faces** : mask
antifeminista *adj & nmf* : antifeminist
antífona *nf* : anthem
antígeno *nm* : antigen
antigualla *nf* **1** : antique **2** : relic, old thing
antiguamente *adv* **1** : formerly, once **2** : long ago
antigüedad *nf* **1** : antiquity **2** : seniority **3** : age ⟨con siglos de antigüedad : centuries-old⟩ **4 antigüedades** *nfpl* : antiques
antiguo, -gua *adj* **1** : ancient, old **2** : former **3** : old-fashioned ⟨a la antigua : in the old-fashioned way⟩ **4 Antiguo Testamento** : Old Testament
antihigiénico, -ca *adj* INSALUBRE : unhygienic, unsanitary
antihistamínico *nm* : antihistamine
antiimperialismo *nm* : anti-imperialism
antiimperialista *adj & nmf* : anti-imperialist
antiinflacionario, -ria *adj* : anti-inflationary
antiinflamatorio, -ria *adj* : anti-inflammatory
antillano[1], **-na** *adj* CARIBEÑO : Caribbean, West Indian
antillano[2], **-na** *n* : West Indian
antílope *nm* : antelope
antimilitarismo *nm* : antimilitarism

antimilitarista *adj & nmf* : antimilitarist
antimonio *nm* : antimony
antimonopolista *adj* : antimonopoly, antitrust
antinatural *adj* : unnatural, perverse
antipatía *nf* : aversion, dislike
antipático, -ca *adj* : obnoxious, unpleasant
antipatriótico, -ca *adj* : unpatriotic
antirrábico, -ca *adj* : antirabies ⟨vacuna antirrábica : rabies vaccine⟩
antirreglamentario, -ria *adj* 1 : unlawful, illegal 2 : foul (in sports)
antirrevolucionario, -ria *adj & n* : antirevolutionary
antirrobo, -ba *adj* : antitheft
antisemita *adj* : anti-Semitic
antisemitismo *nm* : anti-Semitism
antiséptico[1], -ca *adj* : antiseptic
antiséptico[2] *nm* : antiseptic
antisocial *adj* : antisocial
antitabaco *adj* : antismoking
antiterrorista *adj* : antiterrorist
antítesis *nf* : antithesis
antitoxina *nf* : antitoxin
antitranspirante *nm* : antiperspirant
antojadizo, -za *adj* CAPRICHOSO : capricious
antojarse *vr* 1 APETECER : to be appealing, to be desirable ⟨se me antoja un helado : I feel like having ice cream⟩ 2 : to seem, to appear ⟨los árboles se antojaban fantasmas : the trees seemed like ghosts⟩
antojitos *nmpl Mex* : traditional Mexican snack foods
antojo *nm* 1 CAPRICHO : whim 2 : craving
antología *nf* 1 : anthology 2 de ~ *fam* : fantastic, incredible
antónimo *nm* : antonym
antonomasia *nf* por ~ : par excellence
antorcha *nf* : torch
antracita *nf* : anthracite
antro *nm* 1 : cave, den 2 : dive, seedy nightclub
antropofagia *nf* CANIBALISMO : cannibalism
antropófago[1], -ga *adj* : cannibalistic
antropófago[2], -ga *n* CANÍBAL : cannibal
antropoide *adj & nmf* : anthropoid
antropología *nf* : anthropology
antropológico, -ca *adj* : anthropological
antropólogo, -ga *n* : anthropologist
anual *adj* : annual, yearly — **anualmente** *adv*
anualidad *nf* : annuity
anuario *nm* : yearbook, annual
anudar *vt* : to knot, to tie in a knot — **anudarse** *vr*
anuencia *nf* : consent
anulación *nf, pl* -**ciones** : annulment, nullification
anular *vt* : to annul, to cancel
anunciador, -dora *n* → **anunciante**
anunciante *nmf* : advertiser
anunciar *vt* 1 : to announce 2 : to advertise

anuncio *nm* 1 : announcement 2 : advertisement, commercial
anzuelo *nm* 1 : fishhook 2 morder el anzuelo : to take the bait
añadido *nm* : addition
añadidura *nf* 1 : additive, addition 2 por ~ : in addition, furthermore
añadir *vt* 1 AGREGAR : to add 2 AUMENTAR : to increase
añejar *vt* : to age, to ripen
añejo, -ja *adj* 1 : aged, vintage 2 : age-old, musty, stale
añicos *nmpl* : smithereens, bits ⟨hacer(se) añicos : to shatter⟩
añil *nm* 1 : indigo 2 : bluing
año *nm* 1 : year ⟨en el año 1990 : in (the year) 1990⟩ ⟨tiene diez años : she is ten years old⟩ 2 : grade ⟨cuarto año : fourth grade⟩ 3 año bisiesto : leap year 4 año luz : light-year 5 Año Nuevo : New Year
añoranza *nf* : longing, yearning
añorar *vt* 1 DESEAR : to long for 2 : to grieve for, to miss — *vi* : to mourn, to grieve
añoso, -sa *adj* : aged, old
aorta *nf* : aorta
apabullante *adj* : overwhelming, crushing
apabullar *vt* : to overwhelm
apacentar {55} *vt* : to pasture, to put to pasture
apache *adj & nmf* : Apache
apachurrado, -da *adj fam* : depressed, down
apachurrar *vt* : to crush, to squash
apacible *adj* : gentle, mild, calm — **apaciblemente** *adv*
apaciguador, -dora *adj* : calming
apaciguamiento *nm* : appeasement
apaciguar {10} *vt* APLACAR : to appease, to pacify — **apaciguarse** *vr* : to calm down
apadrinar *vt* 1 : to be a godparent to 2 : to sponsor, to support
apagado, -da *adj* 1 : off, out ⟨la luz está apagada : the light is off⟩ 2 : dull, subdued
apagador *nm Mex* : switch
apagar {52} *vt* 1 : to turn off, to shut off 2 : to extinguish, to put out — **apagarse** *vr* 1 : to go out, to fade 2 : to wane, to die down
apagón *nm, pl* -**gones** : blackout (of power)
apalancamiento *nm* : leverage
apalancar {72} *vt* 1 : to jack up 2 : to pry open
apalear *vt* : to beat up, to thrash
apantallar *vt Mex* : to dazzle, to impress
apañar *vt* 1 : to seize, to grasp 2 : to repair, to mend — **apañarse** *vr* : to manage, to get along
apaño *nm fam* 1 : patch 2 HABILIDAD : skill, knack
apapachar *vt Mex fam* : to cuddle, to caress — **apapacharse** *vr*

aparador *nm* **1** : sideboard, cupboard **2** ESCAPARATE, VITRINA : shop window
aparato *nm* **1** : machine, appliance, apparatus ⟨aparato auditivo : hearing aid⟩ ⟨aparato de televisión : television set⟩ **2** : system ⟨aparato digestivo : digestive system⟩ **3** : display, ostentation ⟨sin aparato : without ceremony⟩ **4 aparatos** *nmpl* : braces (for the teeth)
aparatoso, -sa *adj* **1** : ostentatious **2** : spectacular
aparcamiento *nm Spain* **1** : parking **2** : parking lot
aparcar {72} *v Spain* : to park
aparcero, -ra *n* : sharecropper
aparear *vt* **1** : to mate (animals) **2** : to match up — **aparearse** *vr* : to mate
aparecer {53} *vi* **1** : to appear **2** PRESENTARSE : to show up **3** : to turn up, to be found — **aparecerse** *vr* : to appear
aparejado, -da *adj* **1 ir aparejado con** : to go hand in hand with **2 llevar aparejado** : to entail
aparejar *vt* **1** PREPARAR : to prepare, to make ready **2** : to harness (a horse) **3** : to fit out (a ship)
aparejo *nm* **1** : equipment, gear **2** : harness, saddle **3** : rig, rigging (of a ship)
aparentar *vt* **1** : to seem, to appear ⟨no aparentas tu edad : you don't look your age⟩ **2** FINGIR : to feign, to pretend
aparente *adj* **1** : apparent **2** : showy, striking — **aparentemente** *adv*
aparición *nf, pl* **-ciones 1** : appearance **2** PUBLICACIÓN : publication, release **3** FANTASMA : apparition, vision
apariencia *nf* **1** ASPECTO : appearance, look **2 en ~** : seemingly, apparently
apartado *nm* **1** : section, paragraph **2 apartado postal** : post office box
apartamento *nm* DEPARTAMENTO : apartment
apartar *vt* **1** ALEJAR : to move away, to put at a distance **2** : to put aside, to set aside, to separate — **apartarse** *vr* **1** : to step aside, to move away **2** DESVIARSE : to stray
aparte[1] *adv* **1** : apart, aside ⟨modestia aparte : if I say so myself⟩ **2** : separately **3 ~ de** : apart from, besides
aparte[2] *adj* : separate, special
aparte[3] *nm* : aside (in theater)
apartheid *nm* : apartheid
apasionado, -da *adj* : passionate, enthusiastic — **apasionadamente** *adv*
apasionante *adj* : fascinating, exciting
apasionar *vt* : to enthuse, to excite — **apasionarse** *vr*
apatía *nf* : apathy
apático, -ca *adj* : apathetic
apearse *vr* **1** DESMONTAR : to dismount **2** : to get out of or off (a vehicle)
apedrear *vt* : to stone, to throw stones at
apegado, -da *adj* : attached, close, devoted ⟨es muy apegado a su familia : he is very devoted to his family⟩

apegarse {52} *vr* **~ a** : to become attached to, to grow fond of
apego *nm* AFICIÓN : attachment, fondness, inclination
apelación *nf, pl* **-ciones** : appeal (in court)
apelar *vi* **1** : to appeal **2 ~ a** : to resort to
apelativo *nm* APELLIDO : last name, surname
apellidarse *vr* : to have for a last name ⟨¿cómo se apellida? : what is your last name?⟩
apellido *nm* : last name, surname
apelotonar *vt* : to roll into a ball, to bundle up
apenar *vt* : to aggrieve, to sadden — **apenarse** *vr* **1** : to be saddened **2** : to become embarrassed
apenas[1] *adv* : hardly, scarcely
apenas[2] *conj* : as soon as
apéndice *nm* **1** : appendix **2** : appendage
apendicectomía *nf* : appendectomy
apendicitis *nf* : appendicitis
apercibimiento *nm* **1** : preparation **2** AMONESTACIÓN : warning
apercibir *vt* **1** DISPONER : to prepare, to make ready **2** AMONESTAR : to warn **3** OBSERVAR : to observe, to perceive — **apercibirse** *vr* **1** : to get ready **2 ~ de** : to notice
aperitivo *nm* **1** : appetizer **2** : aperitif
apero *nm* : tool, implement
apertura *nf* **1** : opening, aperture **2** : commencement, beginning **3** : openness
apesadumbrar *vt* : to distress, to sadden — **apesadumbrarse** *vr* : to be weighed down
apestar *vt* **1** : to infect with the plague **2** : to corrupt — *vi* : to stink
apestoso, -sa *adj* : stinking, foul
apetecer {53} *vt* **1** : to crave, to long for ⟨apeteció la fama : he longed for fame⟩ **2** : to appeal to ⟨me apetece un bistec : I feel like having a steak⟩ ⟨¿cuándo te apetece ir? : when do you want to go?⟩ — *vi* : to be appealing
apetecible *adj* : appetizing, appealing
apetito *nm* : appetite
apetitoso, -sa *adj* : appetizing
apiario *nm* : apiary
ápice *nm* **1** : apex, summit **2** PIZCA : bit, smidgen
apicultor, -tora *n* : beekeeper
apicultura *nf* : beekeeping
apilar *vt* AMONTONAR : to heap up, to pile up — **apilarse** *vr*
apiñado, -da *adj* : jammed, crowded
apiñar *vt* : to pack, to cram — **apiñarse** *vr* : to crowd together, to huddle
apio *nm* : celery
apisonadora *nf* : steamroller
apisonar *vt* : to pack down, to tamp
aplacamiento *nm* : appeasement
aplacar {72} *vt* APACIGUAR : to appease, to placate — **aplacarse** *vr* : to calm down

aplanadora *nf* : steamroller
aplanar *vt* : to flatten, to level
aplastante *adj* : crushing, overwhelming
aplastar *vt* : to crush, to squash
aplaudir *v* : to applaud
aplauso *nm* 1 : applause, clapping 2 : praise, acclaim
aplazamiento *nm* : postponement
aplazar {21} *vt* : to postpone, to defer
aplicable *adj* : applicable — **aplicabilidad** *nf*
aplicación *nf, pl* -**ciones** 1 : application 2 : diligence, dedication
aplicado, -da *adj* : diligent, industrious
aplicador *nm* : applicator
aplicar {72} *vt* : to apply — **aplicarse** *vr* : to apply oneself
aplique *or* **apliqué** *nm* : appliqué
aplomar *vt* : to plumb, to make vertical
aplomo *nm* : aplomb, composure
apocado, -da *adj* : timid
apocalipsis *nms & pl* : apocalypse ⟨el Libro del Apocalipsis : the Book of Revelation⟩
apocalíptico, -ca *adj* : apocalyptic
apocamiento *nm* : timidity
apocarse {72} *vr* 1 : to shy away, to be intimidated 2 : to humble oneself, to sell oneself short
apócrifo, -fa *adj* : apocryphal
apodar *vt* : to nickname, to call — **apodarse** *vr*
apoderado, -da *n* : proxy, agent
apoderar *vt* : to authorize, to empower — **apoderarse** *vr* ~ **de** : to seize, to take over
apodo *nm* SOBRENOMBRE : nickname
apogeo *nm* : acme, peak, zenith
apología *nf* : defense, apology
apoplejía *nf* : apoplexy, stroke
apoplético, -ca *adj* : apoplectic
aporrear *vt* : to bang on, to beat, to bludgeon
aportación *nf, pl* -**ciones** : contribution
aportar *vt* CONTRIBUIR : to contribute, to provide
aporte *nm* → **aportación**
apostador, -dora *n* : bettor, better
apostar {19} *v* : to bet, to wager ⟨apuesto que no viene : I bet he's not coming⟩
apostasía *nf* : apostasy
apóstata *nmf* : apostate
apostilla *nf* : note
apostillar *vt* : to annotate
apóstol *nm* : apostle
apostólico, -ca *adj* : apostolic
apóstrofe *nmf* : apostrophe
apostura *nf* : elegance, gracefulness
apoyacabezas *nms & pl* : headrest
apoyapiés *nms & pl* : footrest
apoyar *vt* 1 : to support, to back 2 : to lean, to rest — **apoyarse** *vr* 1 ~ **en** : to lean on 2 ~ **en** : to be based on, to rest on
apoyo *nm* : support, backing
apreciable *adj* : appreciable, substantial, considerable

apreciación *nf, pl* -**ciones** 1 : appreciation 2 : appraisal, evaluation
apreciar *vt* 1 ESTIMAR : to appreciate, to value 2 EVALUAR : to appraise, to assess — **apreciarse** *vr* : to appreciate, to increase in value
aprecio *nm* 1 ESTIMO : esteem, appreciation 2 EVALUACIÓN : appraisal, assessment
aprehender *vt* 1 : to apprehend, to capture 2 : to conceive of, to grasp
aprehensión *nf, pl* -**siones** : apprehension, capture, arrest
apremiante *adj* : pressing, urgent
apremiar *vt* INSTAR : to pressure, to urge — *vi* URGIR : to be urgent ⟨el tiempo apremia : time is of the essence⟩
apremio *nm* : pressure, urgency
aprender *v* : to learn — **aprenderse** *vr*
aprendiz, -diza *n, mpl* -**dices** : apprentice, trainee
aprendizaje *nm* : apprenticeship
aprensión *nf, pl* -**siones** : apprehension, dread
aprensivo, -va *adj* : apprehensive, worried
apresamiento *nm* : seizure, capture
apresar *vt* : to capture, to seize
aprestar *vt* : to make ready, to prepare — **aprestarse** *vr* : to get ready
apresuradamente *adv* 1 : hurriedly 2 : hastily, too fast
apresurado, -da *adj* : hurried, in a rush
apresuramiento *nm* : hurry, haste
apresurar *vt* : to quicken, to speed up — **apresurarse** *vr* : to hurry up, to make haste
apretado, -da *adj* 1 : tight 2 *fam* : cheap, tightfisted — **apretadamente** *adv*
apretar {55} *vt* 1 : to press, to push (a button) 2 : to tighten 3 : to squeeze — *vi* 1 : to press, to push 2 : to fit tightly, to be too tight ⟨los zapatos me aprietan : my shoes are tight⟩
apretón *nm, pl* -**tones** 1 : squeeze 2 **apretón de manos** : handshake
apretujar *vt* : to squash, to squeeze — **apretujarse** *vr*
aprieto *nm* APURO : predicament, difficulty ⟨estar en un aprieto : to be in a fix⟩
aprisa *adv* : quickly, hurriedly
aprisionar *vt* 1 : to imprison 2 : to trap, to box in
aprobación *nf, pl* -**ciones** : approval, endorsement
aprobar {19} *vt* 1 : to approve of 2 : to pass (a law, an exam) — *vi* : to pass (in school)
aprobatorio, -ria *adj* : approving
apropiación *nf, pl* -**ciones** : appropriation
apropiado, -da *adj* : appropriate, proper, suitable — **apropiadamente** *adv*
apropiarse *vr* ~ **de** : to take possession of, to appropriate
aprovechable *adj* : usable

aprovechado[1], **-da** *adj* **1** : diligent, hardworking **2** : pushy, opportunistic

aprovechado[2], **-da** *n* : pushy person, opportunist

aprovechamiento *nm* : use, exploitation

aprovechar *vt* : to take advantage of, to make good use of — *vi* **1** : to be of use **2** : to progress, to improve — **aprovecharse** *vr* ~ **de** : to take advantage of, to exploit

aprovisionamiento *nm* : provisions *pl*, supplies *pl*

aprovisionar *vt* : to provide, to supply (with provisions)

aproximación *nf, pl* **-ciones 1** : approximation, estimate **2** : rapprochement

aproximado, -da *adj* : approximate, estimated — **aproximadamente** *adv*

aproximar *vt* ACERCAR, ARRIMAR : to approximate, to bring closer — **aproximarse** *vr* ACERCARSE, ARRIMARSE : to approach, to move closer

aptitud *nf* : aptitude, capability

apto, -ta *adj* **1** : suitable, suited, fit **2** HÁBIL : capable, competent

apuesta *nf* : bet, wager

apuesto, -ta *adj* : elegant, good-looking

apuntador, -dora *n* : prompter

apuntalar *vt* : to prop up, to shore up

apuntar *vt* **1** : to aim, to point **2** ANOTAR : to write down, to jot down **3** INDICAR, SEÑALAR : to point to, to point out **4** : to prompt (in the theater) — *vi* **1** : to take aim **2** : to become evident — **apuntarse** *vr* **1** : to sign up, to enroll **2** : to score

apunte *nm* : note

apuñalar *vt* : to stab

apuradamente *adv* **1** : with difficulty **2** : hurriedly, hastily

apurado, -da *adj* **1** APRESURADO : rushed, pressured **2** : poor, needy **3** : difficult, awkward **4** : embarrassed

apurar *vt* **1** APRESURAR : to hurry, to rush **2** : to use up, to exhaust **3** : to trouble — **apurarse** *vr* **1** APRESURARSE : to hurry up **2** PREOCUPARSE : to worry

apuro *nm* **1** APRIETO : predicament, jam **2** : rush, hurry **3** : embarrassment

aquejar *vt* : to afflict

aquel, aquella *adj, mpl* **aquellos** : that, those

aquél, aquélla *pron, mpl* **aquéllos 1** : that (one), those (ones) **2** : the former

aquello *pron* (*neuter*) : that, that matter, that business ⟨aquello fue algo serio : that was something serious⟩

aquí *adv* **1** : here **2** : now ⟨de aquí en adelante : from now on⟩ **3 por** ~ : around here, hereabouts

aquiescencia *nf* : acquiescence, approval

aquietar *vt* : to allay, to calm — **aquietarse** *vr* : to calm down

aquilatar *vt* **1** : to assay **2** : to assess, to size up

ara *nf* **1** : altar **2 en aras de** : in the interests of, for the sake of

árabe[1] *adj & nmf* : Arab, Arabian

árabe[2] *nm* : Arabic (language)

arabesco *nm* : arabesque — **arabesco, -ca** *adj*

arábigo, -ga *adj* **1** : Arabic, Arabian **2 número arábigo** : Arabic numeral

arable *adj* : arable

arado *nm* : plow

aragonés, -nesa *adj & n, mpl* **-neses** : Aragonese

arancel *nm* : tariff, duty

arándano *nm* : blueberry

arandela *nf* : washer (for a faucet, etc.)

araña *nf* **1** : spider **2** : chandelier

arañar *v* : to scratch, to claw

arañazo *nm* : scratch

arar *v* : to plow

arbitraje *nm* **1** : arbitration **2** : refereeing (in sports)

arbitrar *v* **1** : to arbitrate **2** : to referee, to umpire

arbitrariedad *nf* **1** : arbitrariness **2** INJUSTICIA : injustice, wrong

arbitrario, -ria *adj* **1** : arbitrary **2** : unfair, unjust — **arbitrariamente** *adv*

arbitrio *nm* **1** ALBEDRÍO : will **2** JUICIO : judgment

árbitro, -tra *n* **1** : arbitrator, arbiter **2** : referee, umpire

árbol *nm* **1** : tree **2 árbol genealógico** : family tree

arbolado[1], **-da** *adj* : wooded

arbolado[2] *nm* : woodland

arboleda *nf* : grove, wood

arbóreo, -rea *adj* : arboreal

arbusto *nm* : shrub, bush, hedge

arca *nf* **1** : ark **2** : coffer, chest

arcada *nf* **1** : arcade, series of arches **2 arcadas** *nfpl* : retching ⟨hacer arcadas : to retch⟩

arcaico, -ca *adj* : archaic

arcángel *nm* : archangel

arcano, -na *adj* : arcane

arce *nm* : maple tree

arcén *nm, pl* **arcenes** : hard shoulder, berm

archidiócesis *nfs & pl* : archdiocese

archipiélago *nm* : archipelago

archivador *nm* : filing cabinet

archivar *vt* **1** : to file **2** : to archive

archivero, -ra *n* : archivist

archivista *nmf* : archivist

archivo *nm* **1** : file **2** : archive, archives *pl*

arcilla *nf* : clay

arco *nm* **1** : arch, archway **2** : bow (in archery) **3** : arc **4** : wicket (in croquet) **5** PORTERÍA : goal, goalposts *pl* **6 arco iris** : rainbow

arder *vi* **1** : to burn ⟨el bosque está ardiendo : the forest is in flames⟩ ⟨arder de ira : to burn with anger, to be seething⟩ **2** : to smart, to sting, to burn ⟨le ardía el estómago : he had heartburn⟩

ardid *nm* : scheme, ruse

ardiente *adj* **1** : burning **2** : ardent, passionate — **ardientemente** *adv*
ardilla *nf* **1** : squirrel **2** *or* **ardilla listada** : chipmunk
ardor *nm* **1** : heat **2** : passion, ardor
ardoroso, -sa *adj* : heated, impassioned
arduo, -dua *adj* : arduous, grueling — **arduamente** *adv*
área *nf* : area
arena *nf* **1** : sand ⟨arena movediza : quicksand⟩ **2** : arena
arenga *nf* : harangue, lecture
arengar {52} *vt* : to harangue, to lecture
arenilla *nf* **1** : fine sand **2 arenillas** *nfpl* : kidney stones
arenisca *nf* : sandstone
arenoso, -sa *adj* : sandy, gritty
arenque *nm* : herring
arepa *nf* : cornmeal bread
arete *nm* : earring
argamasa *nf* : mortar (cement)
argelino, -na *adj & n* : Algerian
argentino, -na *adj & n* : Argentinian, Argentine
argolla *nf* : hoop, ring
argón *nm* : argon
argot *nm* : slang
argucia *nf* : sophistry, subtlety
argüir {41} *vi* : to argue — *vt* **1** ARGUMENTAR : to contend, to argue **2** INFERIR : to deduce **3** PROBAR : to prove
argumentación *nf, pl* **-ciones** : line of reasoning, argument
argumentar *vt* : to argue, to contend
argumento *nm* **1** : argument, reasoning **2** : plot, story line
aria *nf* : aria
aridez *nf, pl* **-deces** : aridity, dryness
árido, -da *adj* : arid, dry
Aries *nmf* : Aries
ariete *nm* : battering ram
arisco, -ca *adj* : surly, sullen, unsociable
arista *nf* **1** : ridge, edge **2** : beard (of a plant) **3 aristas** *nfpl* : rough edges, complications, problems
aristocracia *nf* : aristocracy
aristócrata *nmf* : aristocrat
aristocrático, -ca *adj* : aristocratic
aritmética *nf* : arithmetic
aritmético, -ca *adj* : arithmetic, arithmetical — **aritméticamente** *adv*
arlequín *nm, pl* **-quines** : harlequin
arma *nf* **1** : weapon **2 armas** *nfpl* : armed forces **3 arma de fuego** : firearm
armada *nf* : navy, fleet
armadillo *nm* : armadillo
armado, -da *adj* **1** : armed **2** : assembled, put together **3** *PRi* : obstinate, stubborn
armador, -dora *n* : shipowner
armadura *nf* **1** : armor **2** ARMAZÓN : skeleton, framework
armamento *nm* : armament, arms *pl*, weaponry
armar *vt* **1** : to assemble, to put together **2** : to create, to cause ⟨armar un es-

cándalo : to cause a scene⟩ **3** : to arm — **armarse** *vr* **armarse de valor** : to steel oneself
armario *nm* **1** CLÓSET, ROPERO : closet **2** ALACENA : cupboard
armatoste *nm fam* : monstrosity, contraption
armazón *nmf, pl* **-zones 1** ESQUELETO : framework, skeleton ⟨armazón de acero : steel framework⟩ **2** : frames *pl* (of eyeglasses)
armenio, -nia *adj & n* : Armenian
armería *nf* **1** : armory **2** : arms museum **3** : gunsmith's shop **4** : gunsmith's craft
armiño *nm* : ermine
armisticio *nm* : armistice
armonía *nf* : harmony
armónica *nf* : harmonica
armónico, -ca *adj* **1** : harmonic **2** : harmonious — **armónicamente** *adv*
armonioso, -sa *adj* : harmonious — **armoniosamente** *adv*
armonizar {21} *vt* **1** : to harmonize **2** : to reconcile — *vi* : to harmonize, to blend together
arnés *nm, pl* **arneses** : harness
aro *nm* **1** : hoop **2** : napkin ring **3** *Arg, Chile, Uru* : earring
aroma *nm* : aroma, scent
aromático, -ca *adj* : aromatic
arpa *nf* : harp
arpegio *nm* : arpeggio
arpía *nf* : shrew, harpy
arpillera *nf* : burlap
arpista *nmf* : harpist
arpón *nm, pl* **arpones** : harpoon — **arponear** *vt*
arquear *vt* : to arch, to bend — **arquearse** *vr* : to bend, to bow
arqueología *nf* : archaeology
arqueológico, -ca *adj* : archaeological
arqueólogo, -ga *n* : archaeologist
arquero, -ra *n* **1** : archer **2** PORTERO : goalkeeper, goalie
arquetípico, -ca *adj* : archetypal
arquetipo *nm* : archetype
arquitecto, -ta *n* : architect
arquitectónico, -ca *adj* : architectural — **aquitectónicamente** *adv*
arquitectura *nf* : architecture
arrabal *nm* **1** : slum **2 arrabales** *nmpl* : outskirts, outlying area
arracada *nf* : hoop earring
arracimarse *vr* : to cluster together
arraigado, -da *adj* : deep-seated, ingrained
arraigar {52} *vi* : to take root, to become established — **arraigarse** *vr*
arraigo *nm* : roots *pl* ⟨con mucho arraigo : deep-rooted⟩
arrancar {72} *vt* **1** : to pull out, to tear out **2** : to pick, to pluck (a flower) **3** : to start (an engine) **4** : to boot (a computer) — *vi* **1** : to start an engine **2** : to get going — **arrancarse** *vr* : to pull out, to pull off

arrancón *nm, pl* **-cones** *Mex* **1** : sudden loud start (of a car) **2 carrera de arrancones** : drag race

arranque *nm* **1** : starter (of a car) **2** ARREBATO : outburst, fit **3 punto de arranque** : beginning, starting point

arrasar *vt* **1** : to level, to smooth **2** : to devastate, to destroy **3** : to fill to the brim

arrastrar *vt* **1** : to drag, to tow **2** : to draw, to attract — *vi* : to hang down, to trail — **arrastrarse** *vr* **1** : to crawl **2** : to grovel

arrastre *nm* **1** : dragging **2** : pull, attraction **3 red de arrastre** : dragnet, trawling net

arrayán *nm, pl* **-yanes 1** MIRTO : myrtle **2 arrayán brabántico** : bayberry, wax myrtle

arrear *vt* : to urge on, to drive — *vi* : to hurry along

arrebatado, -da *adj* **1** PRECIPITADO : impetuous, hotheaded, rash **2** : flushed, blushing

arrebatar *vt* **1** : to snatch, to seize **2** CAUTIVAR : to captivate — **arrebatarse** *vr* : to get carried away (with anger, etc.)

arrebato *nm* ARRANQUE : fit, outburst

arreciar *vi* : to intensify, to worsen

arrecife *nm* : reef

arreglado, -da *adj* **1** : fixed, repaired **2** : settled, sorted out **3** : neat, tidy **4** : smart, dressed-up

arreglar *vt* **1** COMPONER : to repair, to fix **2** : to tidy up ⟨arregla tu cuarto : pick up your room⟩ **3** : to solve, to work out ⟨quiero arreglar este asunto : I want to settle this matter⟩ — **arreglarse** *vr* **1** : to get dressed (up) ⟨arreglarse el pelo : to get one's hair done⟩ **2 arreglárselas** *fam* : to get by, to manage

arreglo *nm* **1** : repair **2** : arrangement **3** : agreement, understanding

arrellanarse *vr* : to settle (in a chair)

arremangarse {52} *vr* : to roll up one's sleeves

arremeter *vi* EMBESTIR : to attack, to charge

arremetida *nf* EMBESTIDA : attack, onslaught

arremolinarse *vr* **1** : to crowd around, to mill about **2** : to swirl (about)

arrendador, -dora *n* **1** : landlord, landlady *f* **2** : tenant, lessee

arrendajo *nm* : jay

arrendamiento *nm* **1** ALQUILER : rental, leasing **2 contrato de arrendamiento** : lease

arrendar {55} *vt* ALQUILAR : to rent, to lease

arrendatario, -ria *n* : tenant, lessee, renter

arreos *nmpl* GUARNICIONES : tack, harness, trappings

arrepentido, -da *adj* : repentant, remorseful

arrepentimiento *nm* : regret, remorse, repentance

arrepentirse {76} *vr* **1** : to regret, to be sorry **2** : to repent

arrestar *vt* DETENER : to arrest, to detain

arresto *nm* **1** DETENCIÓN : arrest **2 arrestos** *nmpl* : boldness, daring

arriar {85} *vt* **1** : to lower (a flag, etc.) **2** : to slacken (a rope, etc.)

arriate *nm Mex, Spain* : bed (for plants), border

arriba *adv* **1** : up, upwards **2** : above, overhead **3** : upstairs **4** ~ **de** : more than **5 de arriba abajo** : from top to bottom, from head to foot

arribar *vi* **1** : to arrive **2** : to dock, to put into port

arribista *nmf* : parvenu, upstart

arribo *nm* : arrival

arriendo *nm* ARRENDAMIENTO : rent, rental

arriero, -ra *n* : mule driver, muleteer

arriesgado, -da *adj* **1** : risky **2** : bold, daring

arriesgar {52} *vt* : to risk, to venture — **arriesgarse** *vr* : to take a chance

arrimado, -da *n Mex fam* : sponger, freeloader

arrimar *vt* ACERCAR, APROXIMAR : to bring closer, to draw near — **arrimarse** *vr* ACERCARSE, APROXIMARSE : to approach, to get close

arrinconar *vt* **1** ACORRALAR : to corner, to box in **2** : to push aside, to abandon

arroba *nf* : arroba (Spanish unit of measurement)

arrobamiento *nm* : rapture, ecstasy

arrobar *vt* : to enrapture, to enchant — **arrobarse** *vr*

arrocero¹, -ra *adj* : rice

arrocero², -ra *n* : rice grower

arrodillarse *vr* : to kneel (down)

arrogancia *nf* ALTANERÍA, ALTIVEZ : arrogance, haughtiness

arrogante *adj* ALTANERO, ALTIVO : arrogant, haughty

arrogarse {52} *vr* : to usurp, to arrogate

arrojado, -da *adj* : daring, fearless

arrojar *vt* **1** : to hurl, to cast, to throw **2** : to give off, to spew out **3** : to yield, to produce **4** *fam* : to vomit — **arrojarse** *vr* PRECIPITARSE : to throw oneself, to leap

arrojo *nm* : boldness, fearlessness

arrollador, -dora *adj* : sweeping, overwhelming

arrollar *vt* **1** : to sweep away, to carry away **2** : to crush, to overwhelm **3** : to run over (with a vehicle)

arropar *vt* : to clothe, to cover (up) — **arroparse** *vr*

arrostrar *vt* : to confront, to face (up to)

arroyo *nm* **1** RIACHUELO : brook, creek, stream **2** : gutter

arroz *nm, pl* **arroces** : rice

arrozal *nm* : rice field, rice paddy

arruga *nf* : wrinkle, fold, crease

arrugado, -da *adj* : wrinkled, creased, lined

arrugar {52} *vt* : to wrinkle, to crease, to pucker — **arrugarse** *vr*

arruinar *vt* : to ruin, to wreck — **arruinarse** *vr* 1 : to be ruined 2 : to fall into ruin, to go bankrupt

arrullar *vt* : to lull to sleep — *vi* : to coo

arrullo *nm* 1 : lullaby 2 : coo (of a dove)

arrumaco *nm fam* : kissing, cuddling

arrumbar *vt* 1 : to lay aside, to put away 2 : to floor, to leave speechless

arsenal *nm* : arsenal

arsénico *nm* : arsenic

arte *nmf* (*usually m in singular, f in plural*) 1 : art ⟨artes y oficios : arts and crafts⟩ ⟨bellas artes : fine arts⟩ 2 HABILIDAD : skill 3 : cunning, cleverness

artefacto *nm* 1 : artifact 2 DISPOSITIVO : device

artemisa *nf* : sagebrush

arteria *nf* : artery — **arterial** *adj*

arteriosclerosis *nf* : arteriosclerosis, hardening of the arteries

artero, -ra *adj* : wily, crafty

artesanal *adj* : pertaining to crafts or craftsmanship, handmade

artesanía *nf* 1 : craftsmanship 2 : handicrafts *pl*

artesano, -na *n* : artisan, craftsman *m*, craftsperson

artesiano, -na *adj* : artesian ⟨pozo artesiano : artesian well⟩

ártico, -ca *adj* : arctic

articulación *nf, pl* **-ciones** 1 : articulation, pronunciation 2 COYUNTURA : joint

articular *vt* 1 : to articulate, to utter 2 : to connect with a joint 3 : to coordinate, to orchestrate

articulista *nmf* : columnist

artículo *nm* 1 : article, thing 2 : item, feature, report 3 **artículo de comercio** : commodity 4 **artículos de primera necesidad** : essentials 5 **artículos de tocador** : toiletries

artífice *nmf* 1 ARTESANO : artisan 2 : mastermind, architect

artificial *adj* 1 : artificial, man-made 2 : feigned, false — **artificialmente** *adv*

artificio *nm* 1 HABILIDAD : skill 2 APARATO : device, appliance 3 ARDID : artifice, ruse

artificioso, -sa *adj* 1 : skillful 2 : cunning, deceptive

artillería *nf* : artillery

artillero, -ra *n* : artilleryman *m*, gunner

artilugio *nm* : gadget, contraption

artimaña *nf* : ruse, trick

artista *nmf* 1 : artist 2 ACTOR, ACTRIZ : actor, actress *f*

artístico, -ca *adj* : artistic — **artísticamente** *adv*

artrítico, -ca *adj* : arthritic

artritis *nfs & pl* : arthritis

artrópodo *nm* : arthropod

arveja *nf* GUISANTE : pea

arzobispado *nm* : archbishopric

arzobispo *nm* : archbishop

as *nm* : ace

asa *nf* AGARRADERA, ASIDERO : handle, grip

asado¹, -da *adj* : roasted, grilled, broiled

**asado² *nm* 1 : roast 2 : barbecued meat 3 : barbecue, cookout

asador *nm* : spit, rotisserie

asaduras *nfpl* : entrails, offal

asalariado¹, -da *adj* : wage-earning, salaried

asalariado², -da *n* : wage earner

asaltante *nmf* 1 : mugger, robber 2 : assailant

asaltar *vt* 1 : to assault 2 : to mug, to rob 3 **asaltar al poder** : to seize power

asalto *nm* 1 : assault 2 : mugging, robbery 3 : round (in boxing) 4 **asalto al poder** : coup d'etat

asamblea *nf* : assembly, meeting

asambleísta *nmf* : assemblyman *m*, assemblywoman *f*

asar *vt* : to roast, to grill — **asarse** *vr fam* : to roast, to be dying from heat

asbesto *nm* : asbestos

ascendencia *nf* 1 : ancestry, descent 2 ~ **sobre** : influence over

ascendente *adj* : ascending, upward ⟨un curso ascendente : an upward trend⟩

ascender {56} *vt* 1 : to ascend, to rise up 2 : to be promoted ⟨ascendió a gerente : she was promoted to manager⟩ 3 ~ **a** : to amount to, to reach ⟨las deudas ascienden a 20 millones de pesos : the debt amounts to 20 million pesos⟩ — *vt* : to promote

ascendiente¹ *nmf* ANCESTRO : ancestor

**ascendiente² *nm* INFLUENCIA : influence, ascendancy

ascensión *nf, pl* **-siones** 1 : ascent, rise 2 **Fiesta de la Ascensión** : Ascension Day

ascenso *nm* 1 : ascent, rise 2 : promotion

ascensor *nm* ELEVADOR : elevator

asceta *nmf* : ascetic

ascético, -ca *adj* : ascetic

ascetismo *nm* : asceticism

asco *nm* 1 : disgust ⟨¡qué asco! : that's disgusting!, how revolting!⟩ 2 **darle asco (a alguien)** : to sicken, to revolt 3 **estar hecho un asco** : to be filthy 4 **hacerle ascos a** : to turn up one's nose at

ascua *nf* 1 BRASA : ember 2 **estar en ascuas** *fam* : to be on edge

asear *vt* 1 : to wash, to clean 2 : to tidy up — **asearse** *vr*

asechanza *nf* : snare, trap

asechar *vt* : to set a trap for

asediar *vt* 1 SITIAR : to besiege 2 ACOSAR : to harass

asedio *nm* 1 : siege 2 ACOSO : harassment

asegurador¹, -dora *adj* 1 : insuring, assuring 2 : pertaining to insurance

asegurador², **-dora** *n* : insurer, underwriter

aseguradora *nf* : insurance company

asegurar *vt* **1** : to assure **2** : to secure **3** : to insure — **asegurarse** *vr* **1** CERCIORARSE : to make sure **2** : to take out insurance, to insure oneself

asemejar *vt* **1** : to make similar ⟨ese bigote te asemeja a tu abuelo : that mustache makes you look like your grandfather⟩ **2** *Mex* : to be similar to, to resemble — **asemejarse** *vr* ~ **a** : to look like, to resemble

asentaderas *nfpl fam* : bottom, buttocks *pl*

asentado, **-da** *adj* : settled, established

asentamiento *nm* : settlement

asentar {55} *vt* **1** : to lay down, to set down, to place **2** : to settle, to establish **3** *Mex* : to state, to affirm — **asentarse** *vr* **1** : to settle **2** ESTABLECERSE : to settle down, to establish oneself

asentimiento *nm* : assent, consent

asentir {76} *vt* : to consent, to agree

aseo *nm* : cleanliness

aséptico, **-ca** *adj* : aseptic, germ-free

asequible *adj* ACCESIBLE : accessible, attainable

aserción *nf* → **aserto**

aserradero *nm* : sawmill

aserrar {55} *vt* : to saw

aserrín *nm, pl* **-rrines** : sawdust

aserto *nm* : assertion, affirmation

asesinar *vt* **1** : to murder **2** : to assassinate

asesinato *nm* **1** : murder **2** : assassination

asesino¹, **-na** *adj* : murderous, homicidal

asesino², **-na** *n* **1** : murderer, killer **2** : assassin

asesor, **-sora** *n* : advisor, consultant

asesoramiento *nm* : advice, counsel

asesorar *vt* : to advise, to counsel — **asesorarse** *vr* ~ **de** : to consult

asesoría *nf* **1** : consulting, advising **2** : consultant's office

asestar {55} *vt* **1** : to aim, to point (a weapon) **2** : to deliver, to deal (a blow)

aseveración *nf, pl* **-ciones** : assertion, statement

aseverar *vt* : to assert, to state

asexual *adj* : asexual — **asexualmente** *adv*

asfaltado¹, **-da** *adj* : asphalted, paved

asfaltado² *nm* PAVIMENTO : pavement, asphalt

asfaltar *vt* : to pave, to blacktop

asfalto *nm* : asphalt

asfixia *nf* : asphyxia, asphyxiation, suffocation

asfixiar *vt* : to asphyxiate, to suffocate, to smother — **asfixiarse** *vr*

asga, etc. → **asir**

así¹ *adv* **1** : like this, like that **2** : so, thus ⟨así sea : so be it⟩ **3** ~ **de** : so, about so ⟨una caja así de grande : a box about so big⟩ **4 así que** : so, therefore **5** ~ **como** : as well as **6 así así** : so-so, fair

así² *adj* : such, such a ⟨un talento así es inestimable : a talent like that is priceless⟩

así³ *conj* AUNQUE : even if, even though ⟨no irá, así le paguen : he won't go, even if they pay him⟩

asiático¹, **-ca** *adj* : Asian, Asiatic

asiático², **-ca** *n* : Asian

asidero *nm* **1** AGARRADERA, ASA : grip, handle **2** AGARRE : grip, hold

asiduamente *adv* : regularly, frequently

asiduidad *nf* **1** : assiduousness **2** : regularity, frequency

asiduo, **-dua** *adj* **1** : assiduous **2** : frequent, regular

asiento *nm* **1** : seat, chair ⟨asiento trasero : back seat⟩ **2** : location, site

asignación *nf, pl* **-ciones** **1** : allocation **2** : appointment, designation **3** : allowance, pay **4** *PRi* : homework, assignment

asignar *vt* **1** : to assign, to allocate **2** : to appoint

asignatura *nf* MATERIA : subject, course

asilado, **-da** *n* : exile, refugee

asilo *nm* : asylum, refuge, shelter

asimetría *nf* : asymmetry

asimétrico, **-ca** *adj* : asymmetrical, asymmetric

asimilación *nf, pl* **-ciones** : assimilation

asimilar *vt* : to assimilate — **asimilarse** *vr* ~ **a** : to be similar to, to resemble

asimismo *adv* **1** IGUALMENTE : similarly, likewise **2** TAMBIÉN : as well, also

asir {7} *vt* : to seize, to grasp — **asirse** *vr* ~ **a** : to cling to

asistencia *nf* **1** : attendance **2** : assistance **3** : assist (in sports)

asistente¹ *adj* : attending, in attendance

asistente² *nmf* **1** : assistant **2 los asistentes** : those present, those in attendance

asistir *vi* : to attend, to be present ⟨asistir a clase : to attend class⟩ — *vt* : to aid, to assist

asma *nf* : asthma

asmático, **-ca** *adj* : asthmatic

asno *nm* BURRO : ass, donkey

asociación *nf, pl* **-ciones** **1** : association, relationship **2** : society, group, association

asociado¹, **-da** *adj* : associate, associated

asociado², **-da** *n* : associate, partner

asociar *vt* **1** : to associate, to connect **2** : to pool (resources) **3** : to take into partnership — **asociarse** *vr* **1** : to become partners **2** ~ **a** : to join, to become a member of

asolar {19} *vt* : to devastate, to destroy

asoleado, **-da** *adj* : sunny

asolear *vt* : to put in the sun — **asolearse** *vr* : to sunbathe

asomar *vt* : to show, to stick out — *vi* : to appear, to become visible — **aso-**

marse *vr* **1** : to show, to appear **2** : to lean out, to look out ⟨se asomó por la ventana : he leaned out the window⟩

asombrar *vt* MARAVILLAR : to amaze, to astonish — **asombrarse** *vr* : to marvel, to be amazed

asombro *nm* : amazement, astonishment

asombroso, -sa *adj* : amazing, astonishing — **asombrosamente** *adv*

asomo *nm* **1** : hint, trace **2** ni por asomo : by no means

aspa *nf* : blade (of a fan or propeller)

aspaviento *nm* : exaggerated movement, fuss, flounce

aspecto *nm* **1** : aspect **2** APARIENCIA : appearance, look

aspereza *nf* RUDEZA : roughness, coarseness

áspero, -ra *adj* : rough, coarse, abrasive — **ásperamente** *adv*

aspersión *nf, pl* **-siones** : sprinkling

aspersor *nm* : sprinkler

aspiración *nf, pl* **-ciones** **1** : inhalation, breathing in **2** ANHELO : aspiration, desire

aspiradora *nf* : vacuum cleaner

aspirante *nmf* : applicant, candidate

aspirar *vi* ~ a : to aspire to — *vt* : to inhale, to breathe in

aspirina *nf* : aspirin

asquear *vt* : to sicken, to disgust

asquerosidad *nf* : filth, foulness

asqueroso, -sa *adj* : disgusting, sickening, repulsive — **asquerosamente** *adv*

asta *nf* **1** : flagpole ⟨a media asta : at half-mast⟩ **2** : horn, antler **3** : shaft (of a weapon)

ástaco *nm* : crayfish

astado, -da *adj* : horned

aster *nm* : aster

asterisco *nm* : asterisk

asteroide *nm* : asteroid

astigmatismo *nm* : astigmatism

astil *nm* : shaft (of an arrow or feather)

astilla *nf* **1** : splinter, chip **2** de tal palo, tal astilla : like father, like son

astillar *vt* : to splinter — **astillarse** *vr*

astillero *nm* : dry dock, shipyard

astral *adj* : astral

astringente *adj* & *nm* : astringent — **astringencia** *nf*

astro *nm* **1** : heavenly body **2** : star

astrología *nf* : astrology

astrológico, -ca *adj* : astrological

astrólogo, -ga *n* : astrologer

astronauta *nmf* : astronaut

astronáutica *nf* : astronautics

astronáutico, -ca *adj* : astronautic, astronautical

astronave *nf* : spaceship

astronomía *nf* : astronomy

astronómico, -ca *adj* : astronomical — **astronómicamente** *adv*

astrónomo, -ma *n* : astronomer

astroso, -sa *adj* DESALIÑADO : slovenly, untidy

astucia *nf* **1** : astuteness, shrewdness **2** : cunning, guile

astuto, -ta *adj* **1** : astute, shrewd **2** : crafty, tricky — **astutamente** *adv*

asueto *nm* : time off, break

asumir *vt* **1** : to assume, to take on ⟨asumir el cargo : to take office⟩ **2** SUPONER : to assume, to suppose

asunción *nf, pl* **-ciones** : assumption

asunto *nm* **1** CUESTIÓN, TEMA : affair, matter, subject **2** asuntos *nmpl* : affairs, business

asustadizo, -za *adj* : nervous, jumpy, skittish

asustado, -da *adj* : frightened, afraid

asustar *vt* ESPANTAR : to scare, to frighten — **asustarse** *vr*

atacante *nmf* : assailant, attacker

atacar {72} *v* : to attack

atado¹, -da *adj* : shy, inhibited

atado² *nm* **1** : bundle, bunch **2** *Arg* : pack (of cigarettes)

atadura *nf* LIGADURA : tie, bond

atajar *vt* **1** IMPEDIR : to block, to stop **2** INTERRUMPIR : to interrupt, to cut off **3** CONTENER : to hold back, to restrain — *vi* ~ por : to take a shortcut through

atajo *nm* : shortcut

atalaya *nf* **1** : watchtower **2** : vantage point

atañer {79} *vt* ~ a (*3rd person only*) : to concern, to have to do with ⟨eso no me atañe : that does not concern me⟩

ataque *nm* **1** : attack, assault **2** : fit ⟨ataque de risa : fit of laughter⟩ **3** ataque de nervios : nervous breakdown **4** ataque cardíaco *or* ataque al corazón : heart attack

atar *vt* AMARRAR : to tie, to tie up, to tie down — **atarse** *vr*

atarantado, -da *adj fam* **1** : restless **2** : dazed, stunned

atarantar *vt fam* : to daze, to stun

atarazana *nf* : shipyard

atardecer¹ {53} *v impers* : to get dark

atardecer² *nm* : late afternoon, dusk

atareado, -da *adj* : busy, overworked

atascar {72} *vt* **1** ATORAR : to block, to clog, to stop up **2** : to hinder — **atascarse** *vr* **1** : to become obstructed **2** : to get bogged down **3** PARARSE : to stall

atasco *nm* **1** : blockage **2** EMBOTELLAMIENTO : traffic jam

ataúd *nm* : coffin, casket

ataviar {85} *vt* : to dress, to clothe — **ataviarse** *vr* : to dress up

atavío *nm* ATUENDO : dress, attire

ateísmo *nm* : atheism

atemorizar {21} *vt* : to frighten, to intimidate — **atemorizarse** *vr*

atemperar — *vt* : to temper, to moderate

atención¹ *nf, pl* **-ciones** **1** : attention **2** poner atención *or* prestar atención : to pay attention **3** llamar la atención : to attract attention **4** en atención a : in view of

atención² *interj* **1** : attention! **2** : watch out!

atender {56} *vt* **1** : to help, to wait on **2** : to look after, to take care of **3** : to heed, to listen to — *vi* : to pay attention

atenerse {80} *vr* : to abide ⟨tendrás que atenerte a las reglas : you will have to abide by the rules⟩

atentado *nm* : attack, assault

atentamente *adv* **1** : attentively, carefully **2** (*used in correspondence*) : sincerely, sincerely yours

atentar {55} *vi* ~ **contra** : to make an attempt on, to threaten ⟨atentaron contra su vida : they made an attempt on his life⟩

atento, -ta *adj* **1** : attentive, mindful **2** CORTÉS : courteous

atenuación *nf, pl* **-ciones 1** : lessening **2** : understatement

atenuante[1] *adj* : extenuating, mitigating

atenuante[2] *nmf* : extenuating circumstance, excuse

atenuar {3} *vt* **1** MITIGAR : to extenuate, to mitigate **2** : to dim (light), to tone down (colors) **3** : to minimize, to lessen

ateo[1], **atea** *adj* : atheistic

ateo[2], **atea** *n* : atheist

aterciopelado, -da *adj* : velvety, downy

aterido, -da *adj* : freezing, frozen

aterrador, -dora *adj* : terrifying

aterrar {55} *vt* : to terrify, to frighten

aterrizaje *nm* : landing (of a plane)

aterrizar {21} *vt* : to land, to touch down

aterrorizar {21} *vt* **1** : to terrify **2** : to terrorize — **aterrorizarse** *vr* : to be terrified

atesorar *vt* : to hoard, to amass

atestado, -da *adj* : crowded, packed

atestar {55} *vt* **1** ATIBORRAR : to crowd, to pack **2** : to witness, to testify to — *vi* : to testify

atestiguar {10} *vt* : to testify to, to bear witness to — *vi* DECLARAR : to testify

atiborrar *vt* : to pack, to crowd — **atiborrarse** *vr* : to stuff oneself

ático *nm* **1** : penthouse **2** BUHARDILLA, DESVÁN : attic

atigrado, -da *adj* : tabby (of cats), striped (of fur)

atildado, -da *adj* : smart, neat, dapper

atildar *vt* **1** : to put a tilde over **2** : to clean up, to smarten up — **atildarse** *vr* : to get spruced up

atinar *vi* ACERTAR : to be accurate, to be on target

atingencia *nf* : bearing, relevance

atípico, -ca *adj* : atypical

atiplado, -da *adj* : shrill, high-pitched

atirantar *vt* : to make taut, to tighten

atisbar *vt* **1** : to spy on, to watch **2** : to catch a glimpse of, to make out

atisbo *nm* : glimpse, sign, hint

atizador *nm* : poker (for a fire)

atizar {21} *vt* **1** : to poke, to stir, to stoke (a fire) **2** : to stir up, to rouse **3** *fam* : to give, to land (a blow)

atlántico, -ca *adj* : Atlantic

atlas *nm* : atlas

atleta *nmf* : athlete

atlético, -ca *adj* : athletic

atletismo *nm* : athletics

atmósfera *nf* : atmosphere

atmosférico, -ca *adj* : atmospheric

atole *nm Mex* **1** : thick hot beverage prepared with corn flour **2 darle atole con el dedo (a alguien)** : to string (someone) along

atollarse *vr* : to get stuck, to get bogged down

atolón *nm, pl* **-lones** : atoll

atolondrado, -da *adj* **1** ATURDIDO : bewildered, dazed **2** DESPISTADO : scatterbrained, absentminded

atómico, -ca *adj* : atomic

atomizador *nm* : atomizer

atomizar {21} *vt* FRAGMENTAR : to fragment, to break into bits

átomo *nm* : atom

atónito, -ta *adj* : astonished, amazed

atontar *vt* **1** : to stupefy **2** : to bewilder, to confuse

atorar *vt* ATASCAR : to block, to clog — **atorarse** *vr* **1** ATASCARSE : to get stuck **2** ATRAGANTARSE : to choke

atormentador, -dora *n* : tormenter

atormentar *vt* : to torment, to torture — **atormentarse** *vr* : to torment oneself, to agonize

atornillar *vt* : to screw (in, on, down)

atorrante *nmf Arg* : bum, loafer

atosigar {52} *vt* : to harass, to annoy

atracadero *nm* : dock, pier

atracador, -dora *n* : robber, mugger

atracar {72} *vt* : to dock, to land — *vt* : to hold up, to rob, to mug — **atracarse** *vr fam* ~ **de** : to gorge oneself with

atracción *nf, pl* **-ciones** : attraction

atraco *nm* : holdup, robbery

atractivo[1], **-va** *adj* : attractive

atractivo[2] *nm* : attraction, appeal, charm

atraer {81} *vt* : to attract — **atraerse** *vr* **1** : to attract (each other) **2** GANARSE : to gain, to win

atragantarse *vr* : to choke (on food)

atrancar {72} *vt* : to block, to bar — **atrancarse** *vr*

atrapada *nf* : catch

atrapar *vt* : to trap, to capture

atrás *adv* **1** DETRÁS : back, behind ⟨se quedó atrás : he stayed behind⟩ **2** ANTES : ago ⟨mucho tiempo atrás : long ago⟩ **3 para** ~ *or* **hacia** ~ : backwards, toward the rear **4** ~ **de** : in back of, behind

atrasado, -da *adj* **1** : late, overdue **2** : backward **3** : old-fashioned **4** : slow (of a clock or watch)

atrasar *vt* : to delay, to put off — *vi* : to lose time — **atrasarse** *vr* : to fall behind

atraso *nm* **1** RETRASO : lateness, delay ⟨llegó con 20 minutos de atraso : he was 20 minutes late⟩ **2** : backwardness **3 atrasos** *nmpl* : arrears

atravesar {55} *vt* **1** CRUZAR : to cross, to go across **2** : to pierce **3** : to lay across **4** : to go through (a situation or crisis) — **atravesarse** *vr* **1** : to be in the way ⟨se me atravesó : it blocked my path⟩ **2** : to interfere, to meddle
atrayente *adj* : attractive
atreverse *vr* **1** : to dare **2** : to be insolent
atrevido, -da *adj* **1** : bold, daring **2** : insolent
atrevimiento *nm* **1** : daring, boldness **2** : insolence
atribución *nf, pl* **-ciones** : attribution
atribuible *adj* IMPUTABLE : attributable, ascribable
atribuir {41} *vt* **1** : to attribute, to ascribe **2** : to grant, to confer — **atribuirse** *vr* : to take credit for
atribular *vt* : to afflict, to trouble — **atribularse** *vr*
atributo *nm* : attribute
atril *nm* : lectern, stand
atrincherar *vt* : to entrench — **atrincherarse** *vr* **1** : to dig in, to entrench oneself **2** ~ **en** : to hide behind
atrio *nm* **1** : atrium **2** : portico
atrocidad *nf* : atrocity
atrofia *nf* : atrophy
atrofiar *v* : to atrophy
atronador, -dora *adj* : thunderous, deafening
atropellado, -da *adj* **1** : rash, hasty **2** : brusque, abrupt
atropellamiento → **atropello**
atropellar *vt* **1** : to knock down, to run over **2** : to violate, to abuse — **atropellarse** *vr* **1** : to rush through (a task), to trip over one's words
atropello *nm* : abuse, violation, outrage
atroz *adj, pl* **atroces** : atrocious, appalling — **atrozmente** *adv*
atuendo *nm* ATAVÍO : attire, costume
atufar *vt* : to vex, to irritate — **atufarse** *vr* **1** : to get angry **2** : to smell bad, to stink
atún *nm, pl* **atunes** : tuna fish, tuna
aturdimiento *nm* : bewilderment, confusion
aturdir *vt* **1** : to stun, to shock **2** : to bewilder, to confuse, to stupefy
atuvo, etc. → **atenerse**
audacia *nf* OSADÍA : boldness, audacity
audaz *adj, pl* **audaces** : bold, audacious, daring — **audazmente** *adv*
audible *adj* : audible
audición *nf, pl* **-ciones** **1** : hearing **2** : audition
audiencia *nf* : audience
audífono *nm* **1** : hearing aid **2** **audífonos** *nmpl* : headphones, earphones
audio *nm* : audio
audiovisual *adj* : audiovisual
auditar *vt* : to audit
auditivo, -va *adj* : auditory, hearing, aural ⟨aparato auditivo : hearing aid⟩
auditor, -tora *n* : auditor
auditoría *nf* : audit

auditorio *nm* **1** : auditorium **2** : audience
auge *nm* **1** : peak, height **2** : boom, upturn
augur *nm* : augur
augurar *vt* : to predict, to foretell
augurio *nm* AGÜERO, PRESAGIO : augury, omen
augusto, -ta *adj* : august
aula *nf* : classroom
aullar {8} *vt* : to howl, to wail
aullido *nm* : howl, wail
aumentar *vt* ACRECENTAR : to increase, to raise — *vi* : to rise, to increase, to grow
aumento *nm* INCREMENTO : increase, rise
aun *adv* **1** : even ⟨ni aun en coche llegaría a tiempo : I wouldn't arrive on time even if I drove⟩ **2** **aun así** : even so **3** **aun más** : even more
aún *adv* **1** TODAVÍA : still, yet ⟨¿aún no ha llegado el correo? : the mail still hasn't come?⟩ **2** **más aún** : furthermore
aunar {8} *vt* : to join, to combine — **aunarse** *vr* : to unite
aunque *conj* **1** : though, although, even if, even though **2** **aunque sea** : at least
aura *nf* **1** : aura **2** : turkey buzzard
áureo, -rea *adj* : golden
aureola *nf* **1** : halo **2** : aura (of power, fame, etc.)
aurícula *nf* : auricle
auricular *nm* : telephone receiver
aurora *nf* **1** : dawn **2** **aurora boreal** : aurora borealis
ausencia *nf* : absence
ausentarse *vr* **1** : to leave, to go away **2** ~ **de** : to stay away from
ausente[1] *adj* : absent, missing
ausente[2] *nmf* **1** : absentee **2** : missing person
auspiciar *vt* **1** PATROCINAR : to sponsor **2** FOMENTAR : to foster, to promote
auspicios *nmpl* : sponsorship, auspices
austeridad *nf* : austerity
austero, -ra *adj* : austere
austral[1] *adj* : southern
austral[2] *nm* : former monetary unit of Argentina
australiano, -na *adj & n* : Australian
austriaco *or* **austríaco, -ca** *adj & n* : Austrian
autenticar {72} *vt* : to authenticate — **autenticación** *nf*
autenticidad *nf* : authenticity
auténtico, -ca *adj* : authentic — **auténticamente** *adv*
autentificar {72} *vt* : to authenticate — **autentificación** *nf*
autismo *nm* : autism
autista *adj* : autistic
auto *nm* : auto, car
autoayuda *nf* : self-help
autobiografía *nf* : autobiography
autobiográfico, -ca *adj* : autobiographical
autobús *nm, pl* **-buses** : bus

autocompasión *nf* : self-pity
autocontrol *nm* : self-control
autocracia *nf* : autocracy
autócrata *nmf* : autocrat
autocrático, -ca *adj* : autocratic
autóctono, -na *adj* : indigenous, native ⟨arte autóctono : indigenous art⟩
autodefensa *nf* : self-defense
autodestrucción *nf* : self-destruction — **autodestructivo, -va** *adj*
autodeterminación *nf* : self-determination
autodidacta[1] *adj* : self-taught
autodidacta[2] *nmf* : self-taught person, autodidact
autodidacto[1]**, -ta** *adj* → **autodidacta**[1]
autodidacto[2]**, -ta** *n* → **autodidacta**[2]
autodisciplina *nf* : self-discipline
autoestima *nf* : self-esteem
autogobierno *nm* : self-government
autografiar *vt* : to autograph
autógrafo *nm* : autograph
autoinfligido, -da *adj* : self-inflicted
automación → **automatización**
autómata *nm* : automaton
automático, -ca *adj* : automatic — **automáticamente** *adv*
automatización *nf* : automation
automatizar {21} *vt* : to automate
automotor, -tora *adj* **1** : self-propelled **2** : automotive, car
automotriz[1] *adj, pl* **-trices** : automotive, car
automotriz[2] *nf, pl* **-trices** : automaker
automóvil *nm* : automobile
automovilista *nmf* : motorist
automovilístico, -ca *adj* : automobile, car ⟨accidente automovilístico : automobile accident⟩
autonombrado, -da *adj* : self-appointed
autonomía *nf* : autonomy
autónomo, -ma *adj* : autonomous — **autónomamente** *adv*
autopista *nf* : expressway, highway
autoproclamado, -da *adj* : self-proclaimed, self-appointed
autopropulsado, -da *adj* : self-propelled
autopsia *nf* : autopsy
autor, -tora *n* **1** : author **2** : perpetrator
autoría *nf* : authorship
autoridad *nf* : authority
autoritario, -ria *adj* : authoritarian
autorización *nf, pl* **-ciones** : authorization
autorizado, -da *adj* **1** : authorized **2** : authoritative
autorizar {21} *vt* : to authorize, to approve
autorretrato *nm* : self-portrait
autoservicio *nm* **1** : self-service restaurant **2** SUPERMERCADO : supermarket
autostop *nm* **1** : hitchhiking **2 hacer autostop** : to hitchhike
autostopista *nmf* : hitchhiker
autosuficiencia *nf* : self-sufficiency — **autosuficiente** *adj*
auxiliar[1] *vt* : to aid, to assist

auxiliar[2] *adj* : assistant, auxiliary
auxiliar[3] *nmf* **1** : assistant, helper **2 auxiliar de vuelo** : flight attendant
auxilio *nm* **1** : aid, assistance **2 primeros auxilios** : first aid
aval *nm* : guarantee, endorsement
avalancha *nf* ALUD : avalanche
avalar *vt* : to guarantee, to endorse
avaluar {3} *vt* : to evaluate, to appraise
avalúo *nm* : appraisal, evaluation
avance *nm* ADELANTO : advance
avanzado, -da *adj* **1** : advanced **2** : progressive
avanzar {21} *v* : to advance, to move forward
avaricia *nf* CODICIA : greed, avarice
avaricioso, -sa *adj* : avaricious, greedy
avaro[1]**, -ra** *adj* : miserly, greedy
avaro[2]**, -ra** *n* : miser
avasallador, -dora *adj* : overwhelming
avasallamiento *nm* : subjugation, domination
avasallar *vt* : to overpower, to subjugate
ave *nf* **1** : bird **2 aves de corral** : poultry **3 ave rapaz** *or* **ave de presa** : bird of prey
avecinarse *vr* : to approach, to come near
avecindarse *vr* : to settle, to take up residence
avellana *nf* : hazelnut, filbert
avellano *nm* : hazel
avena *nf* **1** : oat, oats *pl* **2** : oatmeal
avenencia *nf* : agreement, pact
avenida *nf* : avenue
avenir {87} *vt* : to reconcile, to harmonize — **avenirse** *vr* **1** : to agree, to come to terms **2** : to get along
aventajado, -da *adj* : outstanding
aventajar *vt* **1** : to be ahead of, to lead **2** : to surpass, to outdo
aventar {55} *vt* **1** : to fan **2** : to winnow **3** *Col, Mex* : to throw, to toss — **aventarse** *vr* **1** *Col, Mex* : to hurl oneself **2** *Mex fam* : to dare, to take a chance
aventón *nm, pl* **-tones** *Col, Mex fam* : ride, lift
aventura *nf* **1** : adventure **2** RIESGO : venture, risk **3** : love affair
aventurado, -da *adj* : hazardous, risky
aventurar *vt* : to venture, to risk — **aventurarse** *vr* : to take a risk
aventurero[1]**, -ra** *adj* : adventurous
aventurero[2]**, -ra** *n* : adventurer
avergonzado, -da *adj* **1** : ashamed **2** : embarrassed
avergonzar {9} *vt* APENAR : to shame, to embarrass — **avergonzarse** *vr* APENARSE : to be ashamed, to be embarrassed
avería *nf* **1** : damage **2** : breakdown, malfunction
averiado, -da *adj* **1** : damaged, faulty **2** : broken down
averiar {85} *vt* : to damage — **averiarse** *vr* : to break down
averiguación *nf, pl* **-ciones** : investigation, inquiry

averiguar {10} *vt* **1** : to find out, to ascertain **2** : to investigate

aversión *nf, pl* **-siones** : aversion, dislike

avestruz *nm, pl* **-truces** : ostrich

avezado, -da *adj* : seasoned, experienced

aviación *nf, pl* **-ciones** : aviation

aviador, -dora *n* : aviator, flyer

aviar {85} *vt* **1** : to prepare, to make ready **2** : to tidy up **3** : to equip, to supply

avicultor, -tora *n* : poultry farmer

avicultura *nf* : poultry farming

avidez *nf, pl* **-deces** : eagerness

ávido, -da *adj* : eager, avid — **ávidamente** *adv*

avieso, -sa *adj* **1** : twisted, distorted **2** : wicked, depraved

avinagrado, -da *adj* : vinegary, sour

avío *nm* **1** : preparation, provision **2** : loan (for agriculture or mining) **3** **avíos** *nmpl* : gear, equipment

avión *nm, pl* **aviones** : airplane

avioneta *nf* : light airplane

avisar *vt* **1** : to notify, to inform **2** : to advise, to warn

aviso *nm* **1** : notice **2** : advertisement, ad **3** ADVERTENCIA : warning **4 estar sobre aviso** : to be on the alert

avispa *nf* : wasp

avispado, -da *adj fam* : clever, sharp

avispero *nm* : wasps' nest

avispón *nm, pl* **-pones** : hornet

avistar *vt* : to sight, to catch sight of

avituallar *vt* : to suppy with food, to provision

avivar *vt* **1** : to enliven, to brighten **2** : to strengthen, to intensify

avizorar *vt* **1** ACECHAR : to spy on, to watch **2** : to observe, to perceive ⟨se avizoran dificultades : difficulties are expected⟩

axila *nf* : underarm, armpit

axioma *nm* : axiom

axiomático, -ca *adj* : axiomatic

ay *interj* **1** : oh! **2** : ouch!, ow!

ayer[1] *adv* : yesterday

ayer[2] *nm* ANTAÑO : yesteryear, days gone by

ayote *nm CA, Mex* : squash, pumpkin

ayuda *nf* **1** : help, assistance **2 ayuda de cámara** : valet

ayudante *nmf* : helper, assistant

ayudar *vt* : to help, to assist — **ayudarse** *vr* ~ **de** : to make use of

ayunar *vi* : to fast

ayunas *nfpl* **en** ~ : fasting ⟨este medicamento ha de tomarse en ayunas : this medication should be taken on an empty stomach⟩

ayuno *nm* : fast

ayuntamiento *nm* **1** : town hall, city hall **2** : town or city council

azabache *nm* : jet ⟨negro azabache : jet black⟩

azada *nf* : hoe

azafata *nf* **1** : stewardess *f* **2** : hostess *f* (on a TV show)

azafrán *nm, pl* **-franes** **1** : saffron **2** : crocus

azahar *nm* : orange blossom

azalea *nf* : azalea

azar *nm* **1** : chance ⟨juegos de azar : games of chance⟩ **2** : accident, misfortune **3 al azar** : at random, randomly

azaroso, -sa *adj* **1** : perilous, hazardous **2** : turbulent, eventful

azimut *nm* : azimuth

azogue *nm* : mercury, quicksilver

azorar *vt* **1** : to alarm, to startle **2** : to fluster, to embarrass — **azorarse** *vr* : to get embarrassed

azotar *vt* **1** : to whip, to flog **2** : to lash, to batter **3** : to devastate, to afflict

azote *nm* **1** LÁTIGO : whip, lash **2** *fam* : spanking, licking **3** : calamity, scourge

azotea *nf* : flat roof, terraced roof

azteca *adj & nmf* : Aztec

azúcar *nmf* : sugar — **azucarar** *vt*

azucarado, -da *adj* : sweetened, sugary

azucarera *nf* : sugar bowl

azucarero, -ra *adj* : sugar ⟨industria azucarera : sugar industry⟩

azucena *nf* : white lily

azuela *nf* : adze

azufre *nm* : sulphur — **azufroso, -sa** *adj*

azul *adj & nm* : blue

azulado, -da *adj* : bluish

azulejo *nm* : ceramic tile, floor tile

azuloso, -sa *adj* : bluish

azulete *nm* : bluing

azur[1] *adj* CELESTE : azure

azur[2] *n* CELESTE : azure, sky blue

azuzar {21} *vt* : to incite, to egg on

B

b *nf* : second letter of the Spanish alphabet

baba *nf* **1** : spittle, saliva **2** : dribble, drool (of a baby) **3** : slime, ooze

babear *vi* **1** : to drool, to slobber **2** : to ooze

babel *nmf* : babel, chaos, bedlam

babero *nm* : bib

babor *nm* : port, port side

babosa *nf* : slug (mollusk)

babosada *nf CA, Mex* : silly act or remark

baboso, -sa *adj* **1** : drooling, slobbering **2** : slimy **3** *CA, Mex fam* : silly, dumb

babucha *nf* : slipper

babuino *nm* : baboon

bacalao *nm* : cod (fish)

bache *nm* **1** : pothole **2** *PRi* : deep puddle **3** : bad period, rough time ⟨bache económico : economic slump⟩
bachiller *nmf* : high school graduate
bachillerato *nm* : high school diploma
bacilo *nm* : bacillus
bacon *nm Spain* : bacon
bacteria *nf* : bacterium
bacteriano, -na *adj* : bacterial
bacteriología *nf* : bacteriology
bacteriológico, -ca *adj* : bacteriologic, bacteriological
bacteriólogo, -ga *n* : bacteriologist
báculo *nm* **1** : staff, stick **2** : comfort, support
badajo *nm* : clapper (of a bell)
badén *nm, pl* **badenes** **1** : (paved) ford, channel **2** : dip, ditch (in a road) **3** : speed bump
bádminton *nm* : badminton
bafle *or* **baffle** *nm* **1** : baffle **2** : speaker, loudspeaker
bagaje *nm* **1** EQUIPAJE : baggage, luggage **2** : background ⟨bagaje cultural : cultural baggage⟩
bagatela *nf* : trifle, trinket
bagre *nm* : catfish
bahía *nf* : bay
bailar *vt* : to dance — *vi* **1** : to dance **2** : to spin **3** : to be loose, to be too big
bailarín¹, -rina *adj, mpl* **-rines** **1** : dancing **2** : fond of dancing
bailarín², -rina *n, mpl* **-rines** **1** : dancer **2** : ballet dancer, ballerina *f*
baile *nm* **1** : dance **2** : dance party, ball **3 llevarse al baile a** *Mex fam* : to take for a ride, to take advantage of
baja *nf* **1** DESCENSO : fall, drop **2** : slump, recession **3** : loss, casualty **4 dar de baja** : to discharge, to dismiss **5 darse de baja** : to withdraw, to drop out
bajada *nf* **1** : descent **2** : dip, slope **3** : decrease, drop
bajar *vt* **1** DESCENDER : to lower, to let down, to take down **2** REDUCIR : to reduce (prices) **3** INCLINAR : to lower, to bow (the head) **4** : to go down, to descend **5 bajar de categoría** : to downgrade — *vi* **1** : to drop, to fall **2** : to come down, to go down **3** : to ebb (of tides) — **bajarse** *vr* ~ **de** : to get off, to get out of (a vehicle)
bajeza *nf* **1** : low or despicable act **2** : baseness
bajío *nm* **1** : lowland **2** : shoal, sandbank, shallows
bajista *nmf* : bass player, bassist
bajo¹ *adv* **1** : down, low **2** : softly, quietly ⟨habla más bajo : speak more softly⟩
bajo², -ja *adj* **1** : low **2** : short (of stature) **3** : soft, faint, deep (of sounds) **4** : lower ⟨el bajo Amazonas : the lower Amazon⟩ **5** : lowered ⟨con la mirada baja : with lowered eyes⟩ **6** : base, vile **7 los bajos fondos** : the underworld

bajo³ *nm* **1** : bass (musical instrument) **2** : first floor, ground floor **3** : hemline
bajo⁴ *prep* : under, beneath, below
bajón *nm, pl* **bajones** : sharp drop, slump
bajorrelieve *nm* : bas-relief
bala *nf* **1** : bullet **2** : bale
balacera *nf* TIROTEO : shoot-out, gunfight
balada *nf* : ballad
balance *nm* **1** : balance **2** : balance sheet
balancear *vt* **1** : to balance **2** : to swing (one's arms, etc.) **3** : to rock (a boat) — **balancearse** *vr* **1** OSCILAR : to swing, to sway, to rock **2** VACILAR : to hesitate, to vacillate
balanceo *nm* **1** : swaying, rocking **2** : vacillation
balancín *nm, pl* **-cines** **1** : rocking chair **2** SUBIBAJA : seesaw
balandra *nf* : sloop
balanza *nf* BÁSCULA : scales *pl*, balance
balar *vi* : to bleat
balaustrada *nf* : balustrade
balaustre *nm* : baluster
balazo *nm* **1** TIRO : shot, gunshot **2** : bullet wound
balboa *nf* : balboa (monetary unit of Panama)
balbucear *vi* **1** : to mutter, to stammer **2** : to prattle, to babble ⟨los niños están balbuceando : the children are prattling away⟩
balbuceo *nm* : mumbling, stammering
balbucir → **balbucear**
balcánico, -ca *adj* : Balkan
balcón *nm, pl* **balcones** : balcony
balde *nm* **1** CUBO : bucket, pail **2 en** ~ : in vain, to no avail
baldío¹, -día *adj* **1** : fallow, uncultivated **2** : useless, vain
baldío² *nm* **1** : wasteland **2** *Mex* : vacant lot
baldosa *nf* LOSETA : floor tile
balear *vt* : to shoot, to shoot at
balero *nm* **1** *Mex* : ball bearing **2** *Mex, PRi* : cup-and-ball toy
balido *nm* : bleat
balín *nm, pl* **balines** : pellet
balística *nf* : ballistics
balístico, -ca *adj* : ballistic
baliza *nf* **1** : buoy **2** : beacon (for aircraft)
ballena *nf* : whale
ballenero¹, -ra *adj* : whaling
ballenero², -ra *n* : whaler
ballenero³ *nm* : whaleboat, whaler
ballesta *nf* **1** : crossbow **2** : spring (of an automobile)
ballet *nm* : ballet
balneario *nm* : spa, bathing resort
balompié *nm* FUTBOL : soccer
balón *nm, pl* **balones** : ball
baloncesto *nm* BASQUETBOL : basketball
balsa *nf* **1** : raft **2** : balsa **3** : pond, pool
balsámico, -ca *adj* : soothing

bálsamo *nm* : balsam, balm
báltico, -ca *adj* : Baltic
baluarte *nm* BASTIÓN : bulwark, bastion
bambolear *vi* 1 : to sway, to swing 2 : to wobble — **bambolearse** *vr*
bamboleo *nm* 1 : swaying, swinging 2 : wobbling
bambú *nm, pl* **bambúes** *or* **bambús** : bamboo
banal *adj* : banal, trivial
banalidad *nf* : banality
banana *nf* : banana
bananero[1], -ra *adj* : banana
bananero[2] *nm* : banana tree
banano *nm* 1 : banana tree 2 *CA, Col* : banana
banca *nf* 1 : banking 2 BANCO : bench
bancada *nf* 1 : group, faction 2 : workbench
bancal *nm* 1 : terrace (in agriculture) 2 : plot (of land)
bancario, -ria *adj* : bank, banking
bancarrota *nf* QUIEBRA : bankruptcy
banco *nm* 1 : bank ⟨banco central : central bank⟩ ⟨banco de datos : data bank⟩ ⟨banco de arena : sandbank⟩ ⟨banco de sangre : blood bank⟩ 2 BANCA : stool, bench 3 : pew 4 : school (of fish)
banda *nf* 1 : band, strip 2 *Mex* : belt ⟨banda transportadora : conveyor belt⟩ 3 : band (of musicians) 4 : gang (of persons), flock (of birds) 5 **banda de rodadura** : tread (of a tire, etc.) 6 **banda sonora** *or* **banda de sonido** : sound track
bandada *nf* : flock (of birds), school (of fish)
bandazo *nm* : swerving, lurch
bandearse *vr* : to look after oneself, to cope
bandeja *nf* : tray, platter
bandera *nf* : flag, banner
banderazo *nm* : starting signal (in sports)
banderilla *nf* : banderilla, dart (in bull-fighting)
banderín *nm, pl* **-rines** : pennant, small flag
bandidaje *nm* : banditry
bandido, -da *n* BANDOLERO : bandit, outlaw
bando *nm* 1 FACCIÓN : faction, side 2 EDICTO : proclamation
bandolerismo *nm* : banditry
bandolero, -ra *n* BANDIDO : bandit, outlaw
bangladesí *adj & nmf* : Bangladeshi
banjo *nm* : banjo
banquero, -ra *n* : banker
banqueta *nf* 1 : footstool, stool, bench 2 *Mex* : sidewalk
banquete *nm* : banquet
banquetear *v* : to feast
banquillo *nm* 1 : bench (in sports) 2 : dock, defendant's seat
bañadera *nf* → bañera

bañar *vt* 1 : to bathe, to wash 2 : to immerse, to dip 3 : to coat, to cover ⟨bañado en lágrimas : bathed in tears⟩ — **bañarse** *vr* 1 : to take a bath, to bathe 2 : to go for a swim
bañera *nf* TINA : bathtub
bañista *nmf* : bather
baño *nm* 1 : bath 2 : swim, dip 3 : bathroom 4 **baño María** : double boiler
baqueta *nf* 1 : ramrod 2 **baquetas** *nfpl* : drumsticks
bar *nm* : bar, tavern
baraja *nf* : deck of cards
barajar *vt* 1 : to shuffle (cards) 2 : to consider, to toy with
baranda *nf* : rail, railing
barandal *nm* 1 : rail, railing 2 : bannister, handrail
barandilla *nf Spain* : bannister, handrail, railing
barata *nf* 1 *Mex* : sale, bargain 2 *Chile* : cockroach
baratija *nf* : bauble, trinket
baratillo *nm* : rummage sale, flea market
barato[1] *adv* : cheap, cheaply ⟨te lo vendo barato : I'll sell it to you cheap⟩
barato[2], -ta *adj* : cheap, inexpensive
baratura *nf* 1 : cheapness 2 : cheap thing
barba *nf* 1 : beard, stubble 2 : chin
barbacoa *nf* : barbecue
bárbaramente *adv* : barbarously
barbaridad *nf* 1 : barbarity, atrocity 2 ¡qué barbaridad! : that's outrageous!
barbarie *nf* : barbarism, savagery
bárbaro[1] *adv fam* : wildly ⟨anoche lo pasamos bárbaro : we had a wild time last night⟩
bárbaro[2], -ra *adj* 1 : barbarous, wild, uncivilized 2 *fam* : great, fantastic
bárbaro[3], -ra *n* : barbarian
barbecho *nm* : fallow land ⟨dejar en barbecho : to leave fallow⟩
barbero, -ra *n* : barber
barbilla *nf* MENTÓN : chin
barbitúrico *nm* : barbiturate
barbudo[1], -da *adj* : bearded
barbudo[2] *nm* : bearded man
barca *nf* 1 : boat 2 **barca de pasaje** : ferryboat
barcaza *nf* : barge
barcia *nf* : chaff
barco *nm* 1 BARCA : boat 2 BUQUE, NAVE : ship
bardo *nm* : bard
bario *nm* : barium
barítono *nm* : baritone
barlovento *nm* : windward
barman *nm* : bartender
barniz *nm, pl* **barnices** 1 LACA : varnish, lacquer 2 : glaze (on ceramics, etc.)
barnizar {21} *vt* 1 : to varnish 2 : to glaze
barométrico, -ca *adj* : barometric
barómetro *nm* : barometer
barón *nm, pl* **barones** : baron

baronesa *nf* : baroness
baronet *nm* : baronet
barquero, -ra : boatman *m*, boatwoman *f*
barquillo *nm* : wafer, thin cookie or cracker
barra *nf* : bar
barraca *nf* **1** CABAÑA, CHOZA : hut, cabin **2** : booth, stall
barracuda *nf* : barracuda
barranca *nf* **1** : hillside, slope **2** → **barranco**
barranco *nm* : ravine, gorge
barredora *nf* : street sweeper (machine)
barrena *nf* **1** TALADRO : drill, auger, gimlet **2** : tailspin
barrenar *vt* **1** : to drill **2** : to undermine
barrendero, -ra *n* : sweeper, street cleaner
barrer *v* : to sweep — **barrerse** *vr* : to slide (in sports)
barrera *nf* OBSTÁCULO : barrier, obstacle ⟨barrera de sonido : sound barrier⟩
barreta *nf* : crowbar
barriada *nf* **1** : district, quarter **2** : slums *pl*
barrica *nf* BARRIL, TONEL : barrel, cask, keg
barricada *nf* : barricade
barrida *nf* **1** : sweep **2** : slide (in sports)
barrido *nm* : sweeping
barriga *nf* PANZA : belly, paunch
barrigón, -gona *adj, mpl* **-gones** *fam* : potbellied, paunchy
barril *nm* **1** BARRICA : barrel, keg **2 cerveza de barril** : draft beer
barrio *nm* **1** : neighborhood, district **2 barrios bajos** : slums *pl*
barro *nm* **1** LODO : mud **2** ARCILLA : clay **3** ESPINILLA, GRANO : pimple, blackhead
barroco, -ca *adj* : baroque
barroso, -sa *adj* ENLODADO : muddy
barrote *nm* : bar (on a window)
barrunto *nm* **1** SOSPECHA : suspicion **2** INDICIO : sign, indication, hint
bártulos *nmpl* : things, belongings ⟨liar los bártulos : to pack one's things⟩
barullo *nm* BULLA : racket, ruckus
basa *nf* : base, pedestal
basalto *nm* : basalt
basar *vt* FUNDAR : to base — **basarse** *vr* FUNDARSE ~ **en** : to be based on
báscula *nf* BALANZA : balance, scales *pl*
base *nf* **1** : base, bottom **2** : base (in baseball) **3** FUNDAMENTO · : basis, foundation **4 base de datos** : database **5 a base de** : based on, by means of **6 en base a** : based on, on the basis of
básico, -ca *adj* FUNDAMENTAL : basic — **básicamente** *adv*
basílica *nf* : basilica
basquetbol *or* **básquetbol** *nm* BALON-CESTO : basketball
basset *nm* : basset hound
bastante[1] *adv* **1** : enough, sufficiently ⟨he trabajado bastante : I have worked enough⟩ **2** : fairly, rather, quite ⟨lle-

garon bastante temprano : they arrived quite early⟩
bastante[2] *adj* : enough, sufficient
bastante[3] *pron* : enough ⟨hemos visto bastante : we have seen enough⟩
bastar *vi* : to be enough, to suffice
bastardilla *nf* CURSIVA : italic type, italics *pl*
bastardo, -da *adj & n* : bastard
bastidor *nm* **1** : framework, frame **2** : wing (in theater) ⟨entre bastidores : backstage, behind the scenes⟩
bastilla *nf* : hem
bastión *nf, pl* **bastiones** BALUARTE : bastion, bulwark
basto, -ta *adj* : coarse, rough
bastón *nm, pl* **bastones 1** : cane, walking stick **2** : baton **3 bastón de mando** : staff (of authority)
basura *nf* DESECHOS : garbage, waste, refuse
basurero[1], **-ra** *n* : garbage collector
basurero[2] *nm Mex* : garbage can
bata *nf* **1** : bathrobe, housecoat **2** : smock, coverall, lab coat
batalla *nf* **1** : battle **2** : fight, struggle **3 de ~** : ordinary, everyday ⟨mis zapatos de batalla : my everyday shoes⟩
batallar *vi* LIDIAR, LUCHAR : to battle, to fight
batallón *nm, pl* **-llones** : battalion
batata *nf* : yam, sweet potato
batazo *nm* HIT : hit (in baseball)
bate *nm* : baseball bat
batea *nf* **1** : tray, pan **2** : flat-bottomed boat, punt
bateador, -dora *n* : batter, hitter
batear *vi* : to bat — *vt* : to hit
bateo *nm* : batting (in baseball)
batería *nf* **1** PILA : battery **2** : drum kit, drums *pl* **3 batería de cocina** : kitchen utensils *pl*
baterista *nmf* : drummer
batido *nm* LICUADO : milk shake
batidor *nm* : eggbeater, whisk, mixer
batidora *nf* : (electric) mixer
batir *vt* **1** GOLPEAR : to beat, to hit **2** VENCER : to defeat **3** REVOLVER : to mix, to beat **4** : to break (a record) — **batirse** *vr* : to fight
batista *nf* : batiste, cambric
batuta *nf* **1** : baton **2 llevar la batuta** : to be the leader, to call the tune
baúl *nm* : trunk, chest
bautismal *adj* : baptismal
bautismo *nm* : baptism, christening
bautista *adj & nmf* : Baptist
bautizar {21} *vt* : to baptize, to christen
bautizo → **bautismo**
bávaro, -ra *adj & n* : Bavarian
baya *nf* **1** : berry **2 baya de saúco** : elderberry
bayeta *nf* : cleaning cloth
bayoneta *nf* : bayonet
baza *nf* **1** : trick (in card games) **2 meter baza en** : to butt in on
bazar *nm* : bazaar
bazo *nm* : spleen

bazofia *nf* **1** : table scraps *pl* **2** : slop, swill **3** : hogwash, rubbish
bazuca *nf* : bazooka
beagle *nm* : beagle
beatificar {72} *vt* : to beatify — **beatificación** *nf*
beatífico, -ca *adj* : beatific
beatitud *nf* : beatitude
beato, -ta *adj* **1** : blessed **2** : pious, devout **3** : sanctimonious, overly devout
bebé *nm* : baby
bebedero *nm* **1** ABREVADERO : watering trough **2** *Mex* : drinking fountain
bebedor, -dora *n* : drinker
beber *v* TOMAR : to drink
bebida *nf* : drink, beverage
beca *nf* : grant, scholarship
becado, -da *n* : scholar, scholarship holder
becerro, -rra *n* : calf
begonia *nf* : begonia
beige *adj & nm* : beige
beisbol *or* **béisbol** *nm* : baseball
beisbolista *nmf* : baseball player
beldad *nf* BELLEZA, HERMOSURA : beauty
belén *nf, pl* **belenes** NACIMIENTO : Nativity scene
belga *adj & nmf* : Belgian
beliceño, -ña *adj & n* : Belizean
belicista[1] *adj* : militaristic
belicista[2] *nmf* : warmonger
bélico, -ca *adj* GUERRERO : war, fighting ⟨esfuerzos bélicos : war efforts⟩
belicosidad *nf* : bellicosity
belicoso, -sa *adj* **1** : warlike, martial **2** : aggressive, belligerent
beligerancia *nf* : belligerence
beligerante *adj & nmf* : belligerent
bellaco[1], **-ca** *adj* : sly, cunning
bellaco[2], **-ca** *n* : rogue, scoundrel
belleza *nf* BELDAD, HERMOSURA : beauty
bello, -lla *adj* **1** HERMOSO : beautiful **2** **bellas artes** : fine arts
bellota *nf* : acorn
bemol *nm* : flat (in music) — **bemol** *adj*
benceno *nm* : benzene
bendecir {11} *vt* **1** CONSAGRAR : to bless, to consecrate **2** ALABAR : to praise, to extol **3 bendecir la mesa** : to say grace
bendición *nf, pl* **-ciones** : benediction, blessing
bendiga, bendijo etc. → **bendecir**
bendito, -ta *adj* **1** : blessed, holy **2** : fortunate **3** : silly, simple-minded
benedictino, -na *adj & n* : Benedictine
benefactor[1], **-tora** *adj* : beneficent
benefactor[2], **-tora** *n* : benefactor, benefactress *f*
beneficencia *nf* : beneficence, charity
beneficiar *vt* : to benefit, to be of assistance to — **beneficiarse** *vr* : to benefit, to profit
beneficiario, -ria *n* : beneficiary
beneficio *nm* **1** GANANCIA, PROVECHO : gain, profit **2** : benefit

beneficioso, -sa *adj* PROVECHOSO : beneficial
benéfico, -ca *adj* : charitable, beneficent
benemérito, -ta *adj* : meritorious, worthy
beneplácito *nm* : approval, consent
benevolencia *nf* BONDAD : benevolence, kindness
benévolo, -la *adj* BONDADOSO : benevolent, kind, good
bengala *nf* **luz de bengala 1** : flare (signal) **2** : sparkler
bengalí[1] *adj & nmf* : Bengali
bengalí[2] *nm* : Bengali (language)
benignidad *nf* : mildness, kindness
benigno, -na *adj* : benign, mild
beninés, -nesa *adj & n* : Beninese
benjamín, -mina *n, mpl* **-mines** : youngest child
beodo[1], **-da** *adj* : drunk, inebriated
beodo[2], **-da** *n* : drunkard
berberecho *nm* : cockle
berbiquí *nm* : brace (in carpentry)
berenjena *nf* : eggplant
bergantín *nm, pl* **-tines** : brig (ship)
berilo *nm* : beryl
bermudas *nfpl* : Bermuda shorts
berrear *vi* **1** : to bellow, to low **2** : to bawl, to howl
berrido *nm* **1** : bellowing **2** : howl, scream
berrinche *nm fam* : tantrum, conniption
berro *nm* : watercress
berza *nf* : cabbage
besar *vt* : to kiss
beso *nm* : kiss
bestia[1] *adj* **1** : ignorant, stupid **2** : boorish, rude
bestia[2] *nf* : beast, animal
bestia[3] *nmf* **1** IGNORANTE : ignoramus **2** : brute
bestial *adj* **1** : bestial, beastly **2** *fam* : huge, enormous ⟨hace un frío bestial : it's terribly cold⟩ **3** *fam* : great, fantastic
besuquear *vt fam* : to cover with kisses — **besuquearse** *vr fam* : to neck, to smooch
betabel *nm Mex* : beet
betún *nm, pl* **betunes 1** : shoe polish **2** *Mex* : icing
bianual *adj* : biannual
biatlón *nm, pl* **-lones** : biathlon
biberón *nm, pl* **-rones** : baby's bottle
biblia *nf* **1** : bible **2 la Biblia** : the Bible
bíblico, -ca *adj* : biblical
bibliografía *nf* : bibliography
bibliográfico, -ca *adj* : bibliographic, bibliographical
bibliógrafo, -fa *n* : bibliographer
biblioteca *nf* : library
bibliotecario, -ria *n* : librarian
bicameral *adj* : bicameral
bicarbonato *nm* **1** : bicarbonate **2 bicarbonato de soda** : sodium bicarbonate, baking soda
bicentenario *nm* : bicentennial

39 bíceps · bizarría

bíceps *nms & pl* : biceps
bicho *nm* : small animal, bug, insect
bici *nf fam* : bike
bicicleta *nf* : bicycle
bicolor *adj* : two-tone
bicúspide *adj* : bicuspid
bidón *nm, pl* **bidones** : large can, (oil) drum
bien[1] *adv* **1** : well ⟨¿dormiste bien? : did you sleep well?⟩ **2** CORRECTAMENTE : correctly, properly, right ⟨hay que hacerlo bien : it must be done correctly⟩ **3** : very, quite ⟨el libro era bien divertido : the book was very amusing⟩ **4** : easily ⟨bien puede acabarlo en un día : he can easily finish it in a day⟩ **5** : willingly, readily ⟨bien lo aceptaré : I'll gladly accept it⟩ **6 bien que** : although **7 más bien** : rather
bien[2] *adj* **1** : well, OK, all right ⟨¿te sientes bien? : are you feeling all right?⟩ **2** : pleasant, agreeable ⟨las flores huelen bien : the flowers smell very nice⟩ **3** : satisfactory **4** : correct, right
bien[3] *nm* **1** : good ⟨el bien y el mal : good and evil⟩ **2 bienes** *nmpl* : property, goods, possessions
bienal *adj & nf* : biennial — **bienalmente** *adv*
bienaventurado, -da *adj* **1** : blessed **2** : fortunate, happy
bienaventuranzas *nfpl* : Beatitudes
bienestar *nm* **1** : welfare, well-being **2** CONFORT : comfort
bienhechor[1], **-chora** *adj* : beneficent, benevolent
bienhechor[2], **-chora** *n* : benefactor, benefactress *f*
bienintencionado, -da *adj* : well-meaning
bienvenida *nf* **1** : welcome **2 dar la bienvenida a** : to welcome
bienvenido, -da *adj* : welcome
bies *nm* : bias (in sewing)
bife *nm Arg, Chile, Uru* : steak
bífido, -da *adj* : forked
bifocal *adj* : bifocal
bifocales *nmpl* : bifocals
bifurcación *nf, pl* **-ciones** : fork (in a river or road)
bifurcarse {72} *vr* : to fork
bigamia *nf* : bigamy
bígamo, -ma *n* : bigamist
bigote *nm* **1** : mustache **2** : whisker (of an animal)
bigotudo, -da *adj* : mustached, having a big mustache
bikini *nm* : bikini
bilateral *adj* : bilateral — **bilateralmente** *adv*
bilingüe *adj* : bilingual
bilioso, -sa *adj* **1** : bilious **2** : irritable
bilis *nf* : bile
billar *nm* : pool, billiards
billete *nm* **1** : bill ⟨un billete de cinco dólares : a five-dollar bill⟩ **2** BOLETO : ticket ⟨billete de ida y vuelta : round-trip ticket⟩

billetera *nf* : billfold, wallet
billón *nm, pl* **billones** **1** : billion (Great Britain) **2** : trillion (U.S.A.)
bimestral *adj* : bimonthly — **bimestralmente** *adv*
bimotor *adj* : twin-engined
binacional *adj* : binational
binario, -ria *adj* : binary
bingo *nm* : bingo
binocular *adj* : binocular
binoculares *nmpl* : binoculars
binomio *nm* **1** : binomial **2** PAREJA : pair, duo
biodegradable *adj* : biodegradable
biodegradarse *vr* : to biodegrade
biodiversidad *nf* : biodiversity
biofísica *nf* : biophysics
biofísico[1], **-ca** *adj* : biophysical
biofísico[2], **-ca** *n* : biophysicist
biografía *nf* : biography
biográfico, -ca *adj* : biographical
biógrafo, -fa *n* : biographer
biología *nf* : biology
biológico, -ca *adj* : biological, biologic — **biológicamente** *adv*
biólogo, -ga *n* : biologist
biombo *nm* MAMPARA : folding screen, room divider
biomecánica *nf* : biomechanics
biopsia *nf* : biopsy
bioquímica *nf* : biochemistry
bioquímico[1], **-ca** *adj* : biochemical
bioquímico[2], **-ca** *n* : biochemist
biosfera *or* **biósfera** *nf* : biosphere
biotecnología *nf* : biotechnology
biótico, -ca *adj* : biotic
bipartidismo *nm* : two-party system
bipartidista *adj* : bipartisan
bípedo *nm* : biped
birlar *vt fam* : to swipe, to pinch
birmano, -na *adj & n* : Burmese
bis[1] *adv* **1** : twice, again (in music) **2** : a, A ⟨artículo 47 bis : Article 47A⟩ ⟨calle Bolívar, número 70 bis : Bolívar Street, number 70A⟩
bis[2] *nm* : encore
bisabuelo, -la *n* : great-grandfather *m*, great-grandmother *f*, great-grandparent
bisagra *nf* : hinge
bisecar {72} *vt* : bisect — **bisección** *nf*
bisel *nm* : bevel
biselar *vt* : to bevel
bisexual *adj* : bisexual
bisiesto *adj* **año bisiesto** : leap year
bismuto *nm* : bismuth
bisnieto, -ta *n* : great-grandson *m*, great-granddaughter *f*, great-grandchild
bisonte *nm* : bison, buffalo
bisoñé *nm* : hairpiece, toupee
bisoño[1], **-ña** *adj* : inexperienced, green
bisoño[2], **-ña** *n* : rookie, greenhorn
bistec *nm* : steak, beefsteak
bisturí *nm* ESCALPELO : scalpel
bisutería *nf* : costume jewelry
bit *nm* : bit (unit of information)
bivalvo *nm* : bivalve
bizarría *nf* **1** : courage, gallantry **2** : generosity

bizarro, -rra *adj* **1** VALIENTE : courageous, valiant **2** GENEROSO : generous
bizco, -ca *adj* : cross-eyed
bizcocho *nm* **1** : sponge cake **2** : biscuit **3** *Mex* : breadstick
bizquera *nf* : crossed eyes, squint
blanco¹, -ca *adj* : white
blanco², -ca *n* : white person
blanco³ *nm* **1** : white **2** : target, bull's-eye ⟨dar en el blanco : to hit the target, to hit the nail on the head⟩ **3** : blank space, blank ⟨un cheque en blanco : a blank check⟩
blancura *nf* : whiteness
blancuzco, -ca *adj* **1** : whitish, off-white **2** PÁLIDO : pale
blandir {1} *vt* : to wave, to brandish
blando, -da *adj* **1** SUAVE : soft, tender **2** : weak (in character) **3** : lenient
blandura *nf* **1** : softness, tenderness **2** : leniency
blanqueador *nm* : bleach, whitener
blanquear *vt* **1** : to whiten, to bleach **2** : to shut out (in sports) **3** : to launder (money) — *vi* : to turn white
blanquillo *nm* *CA, Mex* : egg
blasfemar *vi* : to blaspheme
blasfemia *nf* : blasphemy
blasfemo, -ma *adj* : blasphemous
blazer *nm* : blazer
bledo *nm* **no me importa un bledo** *fam* : I couldn't care less, I don't give a damn
blindado, -da *adj* ACORAZADO : armored
blindaje *nm* **1** : armor, armor plating **2** : shield (for cables, machinery, etc.)
bloc *nm, pl* **blocs** : writing pad, pad of paper
blof *nm* *Col, Mex* : bluff
blofear *vi* *Col, Mex* : to bluff
blondo, -da *adj* : blond, flaxen
bloque *nm* **1** : block **2** GRUPO : bloc ⟨el bloque comunista : the Communist bloc⟩
bloquear *vt* **1** OBSTRUIR : to block, to obstruct **2** : to blockade
bloqueo *nm* **1** OBSTRUCCIÓN : blockage, obstruction **2** : blockade
blusa *nf* : blouse
blusón *nm, pl* **blusones** : loose shirt, smock
boa *nf* : boa
boato *nm* : ostentation, show
bobada *nf* **1** : stupid remark or action **2 decir bobadas** : to talk nonsense
bobalicón, -cona *adj, mpl* **-cones** *fam* : silly, stupid
bobina *nf* CARRETE : bobbin, reel
bobo¹, -ba *adj* : silly, stupid
bobo², -ba *n* : fool, simpleton
boca *nf* **1** : mouth **2 boca arriba** : face up, on one's back **3 boca abajo** : face down, prone **4 boca de riego** : hydrant **5 en boca de** : according to
bocacalle *nf* : entrance to a street ⟨gire a la última bocacalle : take the last turning⟩
bocadillo *nm* *Spain* : sandwich

bocado *nm* **1** : bite, mouthful **2** FRENO : bit (of a bridle)
bocajarro *nm* **a ~** : point-blank, directly
bocallave *nf* : keyhole
bocanada *nf* **1** : swig, swallow **2** : puff, mouthful (of smoke) **3** : gust (of air) **4** : stream (of people)
boceto *nm* : sketch, outline
bochinche *nm* *fam* : ruckus, uproar
bochorno *nm* **1** VERGÜENZA : embarrassment **2** : hot and humid weather **3** : hot flash
bochornoso, -sa *adj* **1** EMBARAZOSO : embarrassing **2** : hot and muggy
bocina *nf* **1** : horn, trumpet **2** : automobile horn **3** : mouthpiece (of a telephone) **4** *Mex* : loudspeaker
bocinazo *nm* : honk (of a horn)
bocio *nm* : goiter
bocón, -cona *n, mpl* **bocones** *fam* : blabbermouth, loudmouth
boda *nf* : wedding
bodega *nf* **1** : wine cellar **2** *Chile, Col, Mex* : storeroom, warehouse **3** (*in various countries*) : grocery store
bofetada *nf* CACHETADA : slap on the face
bofetear *vt* CACHETEAR : to slap
bofetón *nm* → **bofetada**
bofo, -fa *adj* : flabby
boga *nf* : fashion, vogue ⟨estar en boga : to be in style⟩
bogotano¹, -na *adj* : of or from Bogotá
bogotano², -na *n* : person from Bogotá
bohemio, -mia *adj & n* : bohemian, Bohemian
boicot *nm, pl* **boicots** : boycott
boicotear *vt* : to boycott
boina *nf* : beret
boiserie *nf* : wood paneling, wainscoting
boj *nm, pl* **bojes** : box (plant), boxwood
bola *nf* **1** : ball ⟨bola de nieve : snowball⟩ **2** *fam* : lie, fib **3** *Mex fam* : bunch, group ⟨una bola de rateros : a bunch of thieves⟩ **4** *Mex* : uproar, tumult
bolear *vt* *Mex* : to polish (shoes)
bolera *nf* : bowling alley
bolero *nm* : bolero
boleta *nf* **1** : ballot **2** : ticket **3** : receipt
boletería *nf* TAQUILLA : box office, ticket office
boletín *nm, pl* **-tines** **1** : bulletin **2** : journal, review **3 boletín de prensa** : press release
boleto *nm* BILLETE : ticket
boliche *nm* **1** BOLOS : bowling **2** *Arg* : bar, tavern
bólido *nm* **1** : race car **2** METEORO : meteor
bolígrafo *nm* : ballpoint pen
bolillo *nm* **1** : bobbin **2** *Mex* : roll, bun
bolívar *nm* : bolivar (monetary unit of Venezuela)
boliviano¹, -na *adj & n* : Bolivian
boliviano² *nm* : boliviano (monetary unit of Bolivia)

bollo *nm* : bun, sweet roll
bolo *nm* : bowling pin, tenpin
bolos *nmpl* BOLICHE : bowling
bolsa *nf* **1** : bag, sack **2** *Mex* : pocketbook, purse **3** *Mex* : pocket **4 la Bolsa** : the stock market, the stock exchange **5 bolsa de trabajo** : employment agency
bolsear *vi Mex* : to pick pockets
bolsillo *nm* **1** : pocket **2 dinero de bolsillo** : pocket change, loose change
bolso *nm* : pocketbook, handbag
bomba *nf* **1** : bomb **2** : pump **3** : pump ⟨bomba de gasolina : gas pump⟩
bombachos *nmpl* : baggy pants, bloomers
bombardear *vt* **1** : to bomb **2** : to bombard
bombardeo *nm* **1** : bombing, shelling **2** : bombardment
bombardero *nm* : bomber (airplane)
bombástico, -ca *adj* : bombastic
bombear *vt* : to pump
bombero, -ra *n* : firefighter, fireman *m*
bombilla *nf* : lightbulb
bombillo *nm* CA, Col, Ven : lightbulb
bombo *nm* **1** : bass drum **2** *fam* : exaggerated praise, hype ⟨con bombos y platillos : with great fanfare⟩
bombón *nm, pl* **bombones** **1** : bonbon, chocolate **2** *Mex* : marshmallow
bonachón[1], -chona *adj, mpl* **-chones** *fam* : good-natured, kindhearted
bonachón[2], -chona *n, mpl* **-chones** *fam* BUENAZO : kindhearted person
bonaerense[1] *adj* : of or from Buenos Aires
bonaerense[2] *nmf* : person from Buenos Aires
bonanza *nf* **1** PROSPERIDAD : prosperity ⟨bonanza económica : economic boom⟩ **2** : calm weather **3** : rich ore deposit, bonanza
bondad *nf* BENEVOLENCIA : goodness, kindness ⟨tener la bondad de hacer algo : to be kind enough to do something⟩
bondadoso, -sa *adj* BENÉVOLO : kind, kindly, good — **bondadosamente** *adv*
bonete *nm* : cap, mortarboard
boniato *nm* : sweet potato
bonificación *nf, pl* **-ciones** **1** : discount **2** : bonus, extra
bonito[1] *adv* : nicely, well ⟨¡qué bonito canta tu hermana! : your sister sings wonderfully!⟩
bonito[2], -ta *adj* LINDO : pretty, lovely ⟨tiene un apartamento bonito : she has a nice apartment⟩
bonito[3] *nm* : bonito (tuna)
bono *nm* **1** : bond ⟨bono bancario : bank bond⟩ **2** : voucher
boqueada *nf* : gasp ⟨dar la última boqueada : to give one's last gasp⟩
boquear *vi* **1** : to gasp **2** : to be dying
boquete *nm* : gap, opening, breach
boquiabierto, -ta *adj* : open-mouthed, speechless, agape

boquilla *nf* : mouthpiece (of a musical instrument)
borbollar *vi* : to bubble
borbotar *or* **borbotear** *vi* : to boil, to bubble, to gurgle
borboteo *nm* : bubbling, gurgling
borda *nf* : gunwale
bordado *nm* : embroidery, needlework
bordar *v* : to embroider
borde *nm* **1** : border, edge **2 al borde de** : on the verge of ⟨estoy al borde de la locura : I'm about to go crazy⟩
bordear *vt* **1** : to border, to skirt ⟨el Río Este bordea Manhattan : the East River borders Manhattan⟩ **2** : to border on ⟨bordea la irrealidad : it borders on unreality⟩ **3** : to line ⟨una calle bordeada de árboles : a street lined with trees⟩
bordillo *nm* : curb
bordo *nm* **a ∼** : aboard, on board
boreal *adj* : northern
borgoña *nf* : burgundy
bórico, -ca *adj* : boric ⟨ácido bórico : boric acid⟩
boricua *adj & nmf fam* : Puerto Rican
borinqueño, -ña → **boricua**
borla *nf* **1** : pom-pom, tassel **2** : powder puff
boro *nm* : boron
borrachera *nf* : drunkenness ⟨agarró una borrachera : he got drunk⟩
borrachín, -china *n, mpl* **-chines** *fam* : lush, drunk
borracho[1], -cha *adj* EBRIO : drunk, intoxicated
borracho[2], -cha *n* : drunk, drunkard
borrador *nm* **1** : rough copy, first draft ⟨en borrador : in the rough⟩ **2** : eraser
borrar *vt* : to erase, to blot out — **borrarse** *vr* **1** : to fade, to fade away **2** : to resign, to drop out **3** *Mex fam* : to split, to leave ⟨me borro : I'm out of here⟩
borrascoso, -sa *adj* : gusty, blustery
borrego, -ga *n* **1** : lamb, sheep **2** : simpleton, fool
borrico → **burro**
borrón *nm, pl* **borrones** : smudge, blot ⟨borrón y cuenta nueva : let's start on a clean slate, let's start over again⟩
borronear *vt* : to smudge, to blot
borroso, -sa *adj* **1** : blurry, smudgy **2** CONFUSO : unclear, confused
boscoso, -sa *adj* : wooded
bosnio, -nia *adj & n* : Bosnian
bosque *nm* : woods, forest
bosquecillo *nm* : grove, copse, thicket
bosquejar *vt* ESBOZAR : to outline, to sketch
bosquejo *nm* **1** TRAZADO : outline, sketch **2** : draft
bostezar {21} *vi* : to yawn
bostezo *nm* : yawn
bota *nf* **1** : boot **2** : wineskin
botana *nf Mex* : snack, appetizer
botanear *vi Mex* : to have a snack
botánica *nf* : botany

botánico[1], **-ca** *adj* : botanical
botánico[2], **-ca** *n* : botanist
botar *vt* **1** ARROJAR : to throw, to fling, to hurl **2** TIRAR : to throw out, to throw away **3** : to launch (a ship)
bote *nm* **1** : small boat ⟨bote de remos : rowboat⟩ **2** : can, jar **3** : jump, bounce **4** *Mex fam* : jail
botella *nf* : bottle
botica *nf* FARMACIA : drugstore, pharmacy
boticario, -ria *n* FARMACÉUTICO : pharmacist, druggist
botín *nm, pl* **botines** **1** : baby's bootee **2** : ankle boot **3** : booty, plunder
botiquín *nm, pl* **-quines** **1** : medicine cabinet **2** : first-aid kit
botón *nm, pl* **botones** **1** : button **2** : bud **3** INSIGNIA : badge
botones *nmfs & pl* : bellhop
botulismo *nm* : botulism
boulevard [‚bule'var] → **bulevar**
bouquet *nm* **1** : fragrance, bouquet (of wine) **2** RAMILLETE : bouquet (of flowers)
boutique *nf* : boutique
bóveda *nf* **1** : vault, dome **2** CRIPTA : crypt
bovino, -na *adj* : bovine
box *nm, pl* **boxes** **1** : pit (in auto racing) **2** *Mex* : boxing
boxeador, -dora *n* : boxer
boxear *vi* : to box
boxeo *nm* : boxing
boya *nf* : buoy
boyante *adj* **1** : buoyant **2** : prosperous, thriving
bozal *nm* **1** : muzzle **2** : halter (for a horse)
bracear *vi* **1** : to wave one's arms **2** : to make strokes (in swimming)
bracero, -ra *n* : migrant worker, day laborer
braguero *nm* : truss (in medicine)
bragueta *nf* : fly, pants zipper
braille *adj & nm* : braille
bramante *nm* : twine, string
bramar *vi* **1** RUGIR : to roar, to bellow **2** : to howl (of the wind)
bramido *nm* : bellowing, roar
brandy *nm* : brandy
branquia *nf* AGALLA : gill
brasa *nf* ASCUA : ember, live coal
brasero *nm* : brazier
brasier *nm Col, Mex* : brassiere, bra
brasileño, -ña *adj & n* : Brazilian
bravata *nf* **1** JACTANCIA : boast, bravado **2** AMENAZA : threat
bravo, -va *adj* **1** FEROZ : ferocious, fierce ⟨un perro bravo : a ferocious dog⟩ **2** EXCELENTE : excellent, great ⟨¡bravo! : bravo!, well done!⟩ **3** : rough, rugged, wild **4** : annoyed, angry
bravucón, -cona *n, mpl* **-cones** : bully
bravuconadas *nfpl* : bravado
bravura *nf* **1** FEROCIDAD : fierceness, ferocity **2** VALENTÍA : bravery

braza *nf* **1** : breaststroke **2** : fathom (unit of length)
brazada *nf* : stroke (in swimming)
brazalete *nm* PULSERA : bracelet, bangle
brazo *nm* **1** : arm **2 brazo derecho** : right-hand man **3 brazos** *nmpl* : hands, laborers
brea *nf* ALQUITRÁN : tar, pitch
brebaje *nm* : potion, brew
brecha *nf* **1** : gap, breach ⟨estar siempre en la brecha : to be always there when needed, to stay in the thick of things⟩ **2** : gash
brécol *nm* : broccoli
brega *nf* **1** LUCHA : struggle, fight **2** : hard work
bregar {52} *vi* **1** LUCHAR : to struggle **2** : to toil, to work hard **3** ~ **con** : to deal with
brete *nm* : jam, tight spot
breve *adj* **1** CORTO : brief, short **2 en** ~ : shortly, in short — **brevemente** *adv*
brevedad *nf* : brevity, shortness
breviario *nm* : breviary
brezal *nm* : heath, moor
brezo *nm* : heather
bribón, -bona *n, mpl* **bribones** : rascal, scamp
bricolaje *or* **bricolage** *nm* : do-it-yourself
brida *nf* : bridle
brigada *nf* **1** : brigade **2** : gang, team, squad
brigadier *nm* : brigadier
brillante[1] *adj* : brilliant, bright — **brillantemente** *adv*
brillante[2] *nm* DIAMANTE : diamond
brillantez *nf* : brilliance, brightness
brillar *vi* : to shine, to sparkle
brillo *nm* **1** LUSTRE : luster, shine **2** : brilliance
brilloso, -sa *adj* LUSTROSO : lustrous, shiny
brincar {72} *vi* **1** SALTAR : to jump around, to leap about **2** : to frolic, to gambol
brinco *nm* **1** SALTO : jump, leap, skip **2 pegar un brinco** : to give a start, to jump
brindar *vi* : to drink a toast ⟨brindó por los vencedores : he toasted the victors⟩ — *vt* OFRECER, PROPORCIONAR : to offer, to provide — **brindarse** *vr* : to offer one's assistance, to volunteer
brindis *nm* : toast, drink ⟨hacer un brindis : to drink a toast⟩
brinque, etc. → **brincar**
brío *nm* **1** : force, determination **2** : spirit, verve
brioso, -sa *adj* : spirited, lively
briqueta *nf* : briquette
brisa *nf* : breeze
británico[1], **-ca** *adj* : British
británico[2], **-ca** *n* **1** : British person **2 los británicos** : the British
brizna *nf* **1** : strand, thread **2** : blade (of grass)

broca *nf* : drill bit
brocado *nm* : brocade
brocha *nf* : paintbrush
broche *nm* **1** ALFILER : brooch **2** : fastener, clasp **3 broche de oro** : finishing touch
brocheta *nf* : skewer
brócoli *nm* : broccoli
broma *nf* **1** CHISTE : joke, prank **2** : fun, merriment **3 en ~** : in jest, jokingly
bromear *vi* : to joke, to fool around ⟨sólo estaba bromeando : I was only kidding⟩
bromista[1] *adj* : fun-loving, joking
bromista[2] *nmf* : joker, prankster
bromo *nm* : bromine
bronca *nf fam* : fight, quarrel, fuss
bronce *nm* : bronze
bronceado[1], **-da** *adj* **1** : tanned, suntanned **2** : bronze
bronceado[2] *nm* **1** : suntan, tan **2** : bronzing
broncearse *vr* : to get a suntan
bronco, -ca *adj* **1** : harsh, rough **2** : untamed, wild
bronquial *adj* : bronchial
bronquio *nm* : bronchial tube, bronchus
bronquitis *nf* : bronchitis
broqueta *nf* : skewer
brotar *vi* **1** : to bud, to sprout **2** : to spring up, to stream, to gush forth **3** : to break out, to appear
brote *nm* **1** : outbreak **2** : sprout, bud, shoot
broza *nf* **1** : brushwood **2** MALEZA : scrub, undergrowth
brujería *nf* HECHICERÍA : witchcraft, sorcery
brujo[1], **-ja** *adj* : bewitching
brujo[2], **-ja** *n* : warlock *m*, witch *f*, sorcerer
brújula *nf* : compass
bruma *nf* : haze, mist
brumoso, -sa *adj* : hazy, misty
bruñir {38} *vt* : to burnish, to polish (metals)
brusco, -ca *adj* **1** SÚBITO : sudden, abrupt **2** : curt, brusque — **bruscamente** *adv*
brusquedad *nf* **1** : abruptness, suddenness **2** : brusqueness
brutal *adj* **1** : brutal **2** *fam* : incredible, terrific — **brutalmente** *adv*
brutalidad *nf* CRUELDAD : brutality
brutalizar {21} *vt* : to brutalize, to maltreat
bruto[1], **-ta** *adj* **1** : gross ⟨peso bruto : gross weight⟩ ⟨ingresos brutos : gross income⟩ **2** : unrefined ⟨petróleo bruto : crude oil⟩ **3** : brutish, stupid
bruto[2], **-ta** *n* **1** : brute **2** : dunce, blockhead
bubónico, -ca *adj* : bubonic
bucal *adj* : oral
bucanero *nm* : buccaneer, pirate
buccino *nm* : whelk
buceador, -dora *n* : diver, scuba diver

bucear *vi* **1** : to dive, to swim underwater **2** : to explore, to delve
buceo *nm* **1** : diving, scuba diving **2** : exploration, searching
buche *nm* **1** : crop (of a bird) **2** *fam* : belly, gut **3** : mouthful ⟨hacer buches : to rinse one's mouth⟩
bucle *nm* **1** : curl, ringlet **2** : loop
bucólico, -ca *adj* : bucolic
budín *nm, pl* **budines** : pudding
budismo *nm* : Buddhism
budista *adj & nmf* : Buddhist
buen *adj* → **bueno**[1]
buenamente *adv* **1** : easily **2** : willingly
buenaventura *nf* **1** : good luck **2** : fortune, future ⟨le dijo la buenaventura : she told his fortune⟩
buenazo, -za *n fam* BONACHÓN : kindhearted person
bueno[1], **-na** *adj* (**buen** *before masculine singular nouns*) **1** : good ⟨una buena idea : a good idea⟩ **2** BONDADOSO : nice, kind **3** APROPIADO : proper, appropriate **4** SANO : well, healthy **5** : considerable, goodly ⟨una buena cantidad : a lot⟩ **6 buenos días** : hello, good day **7 buenas tardes** : good afternoon **8 buenas noches** : good evening, good night
bueno[2] *interj* **1** : OK!, all right! **2** *Mex* : hello! (on the telephone)
buey *nm* : ox, steer
búfalo *nm* **1** : buffalo **2 búfalo de agua** : water buffalo
bufanda *nf* : scarf, muffler
bufar *vi* : to snort
bufet *or* **bufé** *nm* : buffet-style meal
bufete *nm* **1** : law firm, law office **2** : writing desk
bufido *nm* : snort
bufo, -fa *adj* : comic
bufón, -fona *n, mpl* **bufones** : clown, buffoon, jester
bufonada *nf* **1** : jest, buffoonery **2** : sarcasm
buhardilla *nf* **1** ÁTICO, DESVÁN : attic **2** : dormer window
búho *nm* **1** : owl **2** *fam* : hermit, recluse
buhonero, -ra *n* MERCACHIFLE : peddler
buitre *nm* : vulture
bujía *nf* : spark plug
bula *nf* : papal bull
bulbo *nm* : bulb
bulboso, -sa *adj* : bulbous
bulevar *nm* : boulevard
búlgaro, -ra *adj & n* : Bulgarian
bulla *nf* BARULLO : racket, rowdiness
bullicio *nm* **1** : ruckus, uproar **2** : hustle and bustle
bullicioso, -sa *adj* : noisy, busy, turbulent
bullir {38} *vi* **1** HERVIR : to boil **2** MOVERSE : to stir, to bustle about
bulto *nm* **1** : package, bundle **2** : piece of luggage, bag **3** : size, bulk, volume **4** : form, shape **5** : lump (on the body), swelling, bulge

bumerán *nm, pl* **-ranes** : boomerang
búnker *nm, pl* **búnkers** : bunker
búnquer → **búnker**
buñuelo *nm* : fried pastry
buque *nm* BARCO : ship, vessel
burbuja *nf* : bubble, blister (on a surface)
burbujear *vi* 1 : to bubble 2 : to fizz
burbujeo *nm* : bubbling
burdel *nm* : brothel, whorehouse
burdo, -da *adj* 1 : coarse, rough 2 : crude, clumsy ⟨una burda mentira : a clumsy lie⟩ — **burdamente** *adj*
burgués, -guesa *adj & n, mpl* **burgueses** : bourgeois
burguesía *nf* : bourgeoisie, middle class
burla *nf* 1 : mockery, ridicule 2 : joke, trick 3 hacer **burla de** : to make fun of, to mock
burlar *vt* ENGAÑAR : to trick, to deceive — **burlarse** *vr* ~ **de** : to make fun of, to ridicule
burlesco, -ca *adj* : burlesque, comic
burlón[1], -lona *adj, mpl* **burlones** : joking, mocking
burlón[2], -lona *n, mpl* **burlones** : joker
burocracia *nf* : bureaucracy
burócrata *nmf* : bureaucrat
burocrático, -ca *adj* : bureaucratic
burrada *nf fam* : stupid act, nonsense
burrito *nm* : burrito
burro[1], -rra *adj fam* : dumb, stupid

burro[2], -rra *n* 1 ASNO : donkey, ass 2 *fam* : dunce, poor student
burro[3] *nm* 1 : sawhorse 2 *Mex* : ironing board 3 *Mex* : stepladder
bursátil *adj* : stock-market
bursitis *nf* : bursitis
burundés, -desa *adj & n* : Burundian
bus *nm* : bus
busca *nf* : search
buscador, -dora *n* : hunter (for treasure, etc.), prospector
buscapersonas *nms & pl* : beeper, pager
buscapleitos *nmfs & pl* : troublemaker
buscar {72} *vt* 1 : to look for, to seek 2 : to pick up, to collect 3 : to provoke — *vi* : to look, to search ⟨buscó en los bolsillos : he searched through his pockets⟩
buscavidas *nmf & pl* 1 : busybody 2 : go-getter
busque, etc. → **buscar**
búsqueda *nf* : search
busto *nm* : bust
butaca *nf* 1 SILLÓN : armchair 2 : seat (in a theatre) 3 *Mex* : pupil's desk
butano *nm* : butane
buzo[1], -za *adj Mex fam* : smart, astute ⟨¡ponte buzo! : get with it!, get on the ball!⟩
buzo[2] *nm* : diver, scuba diver
buzón *nm, pl* **buzones** : mailbox
byte *nm* : byte

C

c *nf* : third letter of the Spanish alphabet
cabal *adj* 1 : exact, correct 2 : complete 3 : upright, honest
cabales *nmpl* **no estar en sus cabales** : not to be in one's right mind
cabalgar {52} *vi* : to ride (on horseback)
cabalgata *nf* : cavalcade, procession
cabalidad *nf* a ~ : thoroughly, conscientiously
caballa *nf* : mackerel
caballada *nf* 1 : herd of horses 2 *fam* : nonsense, stupidity, outrageousness
caballar *adj* EQUINO : horse, equine
caballeresco, -ca *adj* : gallant, chivalrous
caballería *nf* 1 : cavalry 2 : horse, mount 3 : knighthood, chivalry
caballeriza *nf* : stable
caballero[1] → **caballeroso**
caballero[2] *nm* 1 : gentleman 2 : knight
caballerosidad *nf* : chivalry, gallantry
caballeroso, -sa *adj* : gentlemanly, chivalrous
caballete *nm* 1 : ridge 2 : easel 3 : trestle (for a table, etc.) 4 : bridge (of the nose) 5 : sawhorse
caballista *nmf* : horseman *m*, horsewoman *f*
caballito *nm* 1 : rocking horse 2 **caballito de mar** : seahorse 3 **caballitos** *nmpl* : merry-go-round

caballo *nm* 1 : horse 2 : knight (in chess) 3 **caballo de fuerza** *or* **caballo de vapor** : horsepower
cabalmente *adv* : fully, exactly
cabaña *nf* CHOZA : cabin, hut
cabaret *nm, pl* **-rets** : nightclub, cabaret
cabecear *vt* : to head (in soccer) — *vi* 1 : to nod one's head 2 : to lurch, to pitch
cabecera *nf* 1 : headboard 2 : head ⟨cabecera de la mesa : head of the table⟩ 3 : heading, headline 4 : headwaters *pl* 5 **médico de cabecera** : family doctor 6 **cabecera municipal** *CA, Mex* : downtown area
cabecilla *nmf* : ringleader, kingpin
cabellera *nf* : head of hair, mane
cabello *nm* : hair
cabelludo, -da *adj* 1 : hairy 2 **cuero cabelludo** : scalp
caber {12} *vi* 1 : to fit, to go ⟨no sé si cabremos todos en el coche : I don't know if we'll all fit in the car⟩ 2 : to be possible ⟨no cabe duda alguna : there's no doubt about it⟩ ⟨cabe que llegue mañana : he may come tomorrow⟩
cabestrillo *nm* : sling ⟨llevo el brazo en cabestrillo : my arm is in a sling⟩
cabestro *nm* : halter (for an animal)
cabeza *nf* 1 : head 2 **cabeza hueca** : scatterbrain 3 **de** ~ : head first 4 **dolor de cabeza** : headache

cabezada *nf* **1** : butt, blow with the head **2** : nod ⟨echar una cabezada : to take a nap, to doze off⟩
cabezal *nm* : bolster
cabezazo *nm* : butt, blow with the head
cabezón, -zona *adj, mpl* **-zones** *fam* **1** : having a big head **2** : pigheaded, stubborn
cabida *nf* **1** : room, space, capacity **2 dar cabida a** : to accommodate, to hold
cabildear *vi* : to lobby
cabildeo *nm* : lobbying
cabildero, -ra *n* : lobbyist
cabildo *nm* AYUNTAMIENTO **1** : town or city hall **2** : town or city council
cabina *nf* **1** : cabin **2** : booth **3** : cab (of a truck), cockpit (of an airplane)
cabizbajo, -ja *adj* : dejected, downcast
cable *nm* : cable
cableado *nm* : wiring
cabo *nm* **1** : end ⟨al cabo de dos semanas : at the end of two weeks⟩ **2** : stub, end piece **3** : corporal **4** : cape, headland ⟨el Cabo Cañaveral : Cape Canaveral⟩ **5 al fin y al cabo** : after all, in the end **6 llevar a cabo** : to carry out, to do
caboverdiano, -na *adj & n* : Cape Verdean
cabrá, etc. → **caber**
cabra *nf* : goat
cabrestante *nm* : windlass
cabrío, -ría *adj* : goat, caprine
cabriola *nf* **1** : skip, jump **2 hacer cabriolas** : to prance
cabriolar *vi* : to prance
cabrito *nm* : kid, baby goat
cabús *nm, pl* **cabuses** *Mex* : caboose
cacahuate *or* **cacahuete** *nm* : peanut
cacalote *nm Mex* : crow
cacao *nm* : cacao, cocoa bean
cacarear *vi* : to crow, to cackle, to cluck — *vt fam* : to boast about, to crow about ⟨cacarear un huevo : to brag about an accomplishment⟩
cacareo *nm* **1** : clucking (of a hen), crowing (of a rooster) **2** : boasting
cacatúa *nf* : cockatoo
cace, etc. → **cazar**
cacería *nf* **1** CAZA : hunt, hunting **2** : hunting party
cacerola *nf* : pan, saucepan
cacha *nf* : butt (of a gun)
cachar *vt fam* : to catch
cacharro *nm* **1** *fam* : thing, piece of junk **2** *fam* : jalopy **3 cacharros** *nmpl* : pots and pans
cache *nm* : cache, cache memory
caché *nm* : cachet
cachear *vt* : to search, to frisk
cachemir *nm* : cashmere
cachetada *nf* BOFETADA : slap on the face
cachete *nm* : cheek
cachetear *vt* BOFETEAR : to slap
cachiporra *nf* : bludgeon, club, blackjack
cachirul *nm Mex fam* : cheating ⟨hacer cachirul : to cheat⟩

cachivache *nm fam* : thing ⟨mete tus cachivaches en el maletero : put your stuff in the trunk⟩
cacho *nm fam* : piece, bit
cachorro, -rra *n* **1** : cub **2** PERRITO : puppy
cachucha *nf Mex* : cap, baseball cap
cacique *nm* **1** : chief (of a tribe) **2** : boss (in politics)
cacofonía *nf* : cacophony
cacofónico, -ca *adj* : cacophonous
cacto *nm* : cactus
cactus → **cacto**
cada *adj* **1** : each ⟨cuestan diez pesos cada una : they cost ten pesos each⟩ **2** : every ⟨cada vez : every time⟩ **3** : such, some ⟨sales con cada historia : you come up with such crazy stories⟩ **4 cada vez más** : more and more, increasingly **5 cada vez menos** : less and less
cadalso *nm* : scaffold, gallows
cadáver *nm* : corpse, cadaver
cadavérico, -ca *adj* **1** : cadaverous **2** PÁLIDO : deathly pale
caddie *or* **caddy** *nmf, pl* **caddies** : caddy
cadena *nf* **1** : chain **2** : network, channel **3 cadena de montaje** : assembly line **4 cadena perpetua** : life sentence
cadencia *nf* : cadence, rhythm
cadencioso, -sa *adj* : rhythmic, rhythmical
cadera *nf* : hip
cadete *nmf* : cadet
cadmio *nm* : cadmium
caducar {72} *vi* : to expire
caducidad *nf* : expiration
caduco, -ca *adj* **1** : outdated, obsolete **2** : deciduous
caer {13} *vi* **1** : to fall, to drop **2** : to collapse **3** : to hang (down) **4 caer bien** *fam* : to be pleasant, to be likeable ⟨me caes bien : I like you⟩ **5 caer mal** *or* **caer gordo** *fam* : to be unpleasant, to be unlikeable — **caerse** *vr* : to fall down
café[1] *adj* : brown ⟨ojos cafés : brown eyes⟩
café[2] *nm* **1** : coffee **2** : café
cafeína *nf* : caffeine
cafetal *nm* : coffee plantation
cafetalero[1], -ra *adj* : coffee ⟨cosecha cafetalera : coffee harvest⟩
cafetalero[2], -ra *n* : coffee grower
cafetera *nf* : coffeepot, coffeemaker
cafetería *nf* **1** : coffee shop, café **2** : lunchroom, cafeteria
cafetero[1], -ra *adj* : coffee-producing
cafetero[2], -ra *n* : coffee grower
cafeticultura *nf Mex* : coffee industry
caguama *nf* **1** : large Caribbean turtle **2** *Mex* : large bottle of beer
caída *nf* **1** BAJA, DESCENSO : fall, drop **2** : collapse, downfall
caiga, etc. → **caer**
caimán *nm, pl* **caimanes** : alligator, caiman

caimito *nm* : star apple
caja *nf* **1** : box, case **2** : cash register, checkout counter **3** : bed (of a truck) **4** *fam* : coffin **5 caja fuerte** *or* **caja de caudales** : safe **6 caja de seguridad** : safe-deposit box **7 caja torácica** : rib cage
cajero, -ra *n* **1** : cashier **2** : teller **3 cajero automático** : automated teller machine, ATM
cajeta *nf Mex* : a sweet caramel-flavored spread
cajetilla *nf* : pack (of cigarettes)
cajón *nm, pl* **cajones 1** : drawer, till **2** : crate, case **3 cajón de estacionamiento** *Mex* : parking space
cajuela *nf Mex* : trunk (of a car)
cal *nf* : lime, quicklime
cala *nf* : cove, inlet
calabacín *nm, pl* **-cines** : zucchini
calabacita *nf Mex* : zucchini
calabaza *nf* **1** : pumpkin, squash **2** : gourd **3 dar calabazas a** : to give the brush-off to, to jilt
calabozo *nm* **1** : prison **2** : jail cell
calado¹, -da *adj* **1** : drenched **2** : open-worked
calado² *nm* **1** : draft (of a ship) **2** : open-work
calafatear *vt* : to caulk
calamar *nm* **1** : squid **2 calamares** *nmpl* : calamari
calambre *nm* **1** ESPASMO : cramp **2** : electric shock, jolt
calamidad *nf* DESASTRE : calamity, disaster
calamina *nf* : calamine
calamitoso, -sa *adj* : calamitous, disastrous
calaña *nf* : ilk, kind, sort ⟨una persona de mala calaña : a bad sort⟩
calar *vt* **1** : to soak through **2** : to pierce, to penetrate — *vi* : to catch on — **calarse** *vr* : to get drenched
calavera¹ *nf* **1** : skull **2** *Mex* : taillight
calavera² *nm* : rake, rogue
calcar {72} *vt* **1** : to trace **2** : to copy, to imitate
calce, etc. → **calzar**
calceta *nf* : knee-high stocking
calcetería *nf* : hosiery
calcetín *nm, pl* **-tines** : sock
calcificar {72} *v* : to calcify — **calcificarse** *vr*
calcinar *vt* : to char, to burn
calcio *nm* : calcium
calco *nm* **1** : transfer, tracing **2** : copy, image
calcomanía *nf* : decal, transfer
calculador, -dora *adj* : calculating
calculadora *nf* : calculator
calcular *vt* **1** : to calculate, to estimate **2** : to plan, to scheme
cálculo *nm* **1** : calculation, estimation **2** : calculus **3** : plan, scheme **4 cálculo biliar** : gallstone **5 hoja de cálculo** : spreadsheet
caldas *nfpl* : hot springs

caldear *vt* : to heat, to warm — **caldearse** *vr* **1** : to heat up **2** : to become heated, to get tense
caldera *nf* **1** : cauldron **2** : boiler
caldo *nm* **1** CONSOMÉ : broth, stock **2** **caldo de cultivo** : culture medium, breeding ground
caldoso, -sa *adj* : watery
calefacción *nf, pl* **-ciones** : heating, heat
calefactor *nm* : heater
caleidoscopio → **calidoscopio**
calendario *nm* **1** : calendar **2** : timetable, schedule
caléndula *nf* : marigold
calentador *nm* : heater
calentamiento *nm* **1** : heating, warming **2** : warm-up (in sports)
calentar {55} *vt* **1** : to heat, to warm **2** *fam* : to annoy, to anger **3** *fam* : to excite, to turn on — **calentarse** *vr* **1** : to get warm, to heat up **2** : to warm up (in sports) **3** *fam* : to become sexually aroused **4** *fam* : to get mad
calentura *nf* **1** FIEBRE : temperature, fever **2** : cold sore
calibrador *nm* : gauge, calipers *pl*
calibrar *vt* : to calibrate — **calibración** *nf*
calibre *nm* **1** : caliber, gauge **2** : importance, excellence **3** : kind, sort ⟨un problema de grueso calibre : a serious problem⟩
calidad *nf* **1** : quality, grade **2** : position, status **3 en calidad de** : as, in the capacity of
cálido, -da *adj* **1** : hot ⟨un clima cálido : a hot climate⟩ **2** : warm ⟨una cálida bienvenida : a warm welcome⟩
calidoscopio *nm* : kaleidoscope
caliente *adj* **1** : hot, warm ⟨mantenerse caliente : to stay warm⟩ **2** : heated, fiery ⟨una disputa caliente : a heated argument⟩ **3** *fam* : sexually excited, horny
califa *nm* : caliph
calificación *nf, pl* **-ciones 1** NOTA : grade (for a course) **2** : rating, score **3** CLASIFICACIÓN : qualification, qualifying ⟨ronda de calificación : qualifying round⟩
calificar {72} *vt* **1** : to grade **2** : to describe, to rate ⟨la calificaron de buena alumna : they described her as a good student⟩ **3** : to qualify, to modify (in grammar)
calificativo¹, -va *adj* : qualifying
calificativo² *nm* : qualifier, epithet
caligrafía *nf* **1** ESCRITURA : handwriting **2** : calligraphy
calipso *nm* : calypso
calistenia *nf* : calisthenics
cáliz *nm, pl* **cálices 1** : chalice, goblet **2** : calyx
caliza *nf* : limestone
callado, -da *adj* : quiet, silent — **calladamente** *adv*
callar *vi* : to keep quiet, to be silent — *vt* **1** : to silence, to hush ⟨¡calla a los

niños! : keep the children quiet!⟩ **2** : to keep secret — **callarse** *vr* : to remain silent ⟨¡cállate! : be quiet!, shut up!⟩

calle *nf* : street, road

callejear *vi* : to wander about the streets, to hang out

callejero, -ra *adj* : street ⟨perro callejero : stray dog⟩

callejón *nm, pl* **-jones 1** : alley **2 callejón sin salida** : dead-end street

callo *nm* **1** : callus, corn **2 callos** *nmpl* : tripe

calloso, -sa *adj* : callous

calma *nf* : calm, quiet

calmante[1] *adj* : calming, soothing

calmante[2] *nm* : tranquilizer, sedative

calmar *vt* TRANQUILIZAR : to calm, to soothe — **calmarse** *vr* : to calm down

calmo, -ma *adj* TRANQUILO : calm, tranquil

calmoso, -sa *adj* **1** TRANQUILO : calm, quiet **2** LENTO : slow, sluggish

calor *nm* **1** : heat ⟨hace calor : it's hot outside⟩ ⟨tener calor : to feel hot⟩ **2** : warmth, affection **3** : ardor, passion

caloría *nf* : calorie

calórico, -ca *adj* : caloric

calorífico, -ca *adj* : caloric

calque, etc. → calcar

calumnia *nf* : slander, libel — **calumnioso, -sa** *adj*

calumniar *vt* : to slander, to libel

caluroso, -sa *adj* **1** : hot **2** : warm, enthusiastic

calva *nf* : bald spot, bald head

calvario *nm* **1** : Calvary **2** : Stations of the Cross *pl* **3 vivir un calvario** : to suffer great adversity

calvicie *nf* : baldness

calvo[1], **-va** *adj* : bald

calvo[2], **-va** *n* : bald person

calza *nf* : block, wedge

calzada *nf* : roadway, avenue

calzado *nm* : footwear

calzador *nm* : shoehorn

calzar {21} *vt* **1** : to wear (shoes) ⟨¿de cuál calza? : what is your shoe size?⟩ ⟨siempre calzaban tenis : they always wore sneakers⟩ **2** : to provide with shoes

calzo *nm* : chock, wedge

calzoncillos *nmpl* : underpants, briefs

calzones *nmpl* : underpants, panties

cama *nf* **1** : bed **2 cama elástica** : trampoline

camada *nf* : litter, brood

camafeo *nm* : cameo

camaleón *nm, pl* **-leones** : chameleon

cámara *nf* **1** : camera **2** : chamber, room **3** : house (in government) **4** : inner tube

camarada *nmf* **1** : comrade, companion **2** : colleague

camaradería *nf* : camaraderie

camarero, -ra *n* **1** MESERO : waiter, waitress *f* **2** : bellhop *m*, chambermaid *f* (in a hotel) **3** : steward *m*, stewardess *f* (on a ship, etc.)

camarilla *nf* : political clique

camarógrafo, -fa *n* : cameraman *m*, camerawoman *f*

camarón *nm, pl* **-rones 1** : shrimp **2** : prawn

camarote *nm* : cabin, stateroom

camastro *nm* : small hard bed, pallet

cambalache *nm fam* : swap

cambiante *adj* **1** : changing **2** VARIABLE : changeable, variable

cambiar *vt* **1** ALTERAR, MODIFICAR : to change **2** : to exchange, to trade — *vi* **1** : to change **2 cambiar de velocidad** : to shift gears — **cambiarse** *vr* **1** : to change (clothing) **2** MUDARSE : to move (to a new address)

cambio *nm* **1** : change, alteration **2** : exchange **3** : change (money) **4 en cambio** : instead **5 en cambio** : however, on the other hand

cambista *nmf* : exchange broker

camboyano, -na *adj & n* : Cambodian

cambur *nm Ven* : banana

camelia *nf* : camellia

camello *nm* : camel

camellón *nm, pl* **-llones** *Mex* : traffic island

camerino *nm* : dressing room

camerunés, -nesa *adj, mpl* **-neses** : Cameroonian

camilla *nf* : stretcher

camillero, -ra *n* : orderly (in a hospital)

caminante *nmf* : wayfarer, walker

caminar *vi* ANDAR : to walk, to move — *vt* : to walk, to cover (a distance)

caminata *nf* : hike, long walk

camino *nm* **1** : path, road **2** : journey ⟨ponerse en camino : to set off⟩ **3** : way ⟨a medio camino : halfway there⟩

camión *nm, pl* **camiones 1** : truck **2** *Mex* : bus

camionero, -ra *n* **1** : truck driver **2** *Mex* : bus driver

camioneta *nf* : light truck, van

camisa *nf* **1** : shirt **2 camisa de fuerza** : straitjacket

camiseta *nf* **1** : T-shirt **2** : undershirt

camisón *nm, pl* **-sones** : nightshirt, nightgown

camorra *nf fam* : fight, trouble ⟨buscar camorra : to pick a fight⟩

camote *nm* **1** : root vegetable similar to the sweet potato **2 hacerse camote** *Mex fam* : to get mixed up

campal *adj* : pitched, fierce ⟨batalla campal : pitched battle⟩

campamento *nm* : camp

campana *nf* : bell

campanada *nf* TAÑIDO : stroke (of a bell), peal

campanario *nm* : bell tower, belfry

campanilla *nf* **1** : small bell, handbell **2** : uvula

campante *adj* : nonchalant, smug ⟨seguir tan campante : to go on as if nothing had happened⟩

campaña *nf* 1 CAMPO : countryside, country 2 : campaign 3 **tienda de campaña** : tent
campañol *nm* : vole
campechana *nf Mex* : puff pastry
campechanía *nf* : geniality
campechano, -na *adj* : open, cordial, friendly
campeón, -peona *n, mpl* -peones : champion
campeonato *nm* : championship
cámper *nm* : camper (vehicle)
campero, -ra *adj* : country, rural
campesino, -na *n* : peasant, farm laborer
campestre *adj* : rural, rustic
camping *nm* 1 : camping 2 : campsite
campiña *nf* CAMPO : countryside, country
campista *nmf* : camper
campo *nm* 1 CAMPAÑA : countryside, country 2 : field ⟨campo de aviación : airfield⟩ ⟨su campo de responsabilidad : her field of responsibility⟩
camposanto *nm* : graveyard, cemetery
campus *nms & pl* : campus
camuflaje *nm* : camouflage
camuflajear *vt* : to camouflage
camuflar → **camuflajear**
can *nm* : hound, dog
cana *nf* 1 : gray hair 2 **salirle canas** : to go gray, to get gray hair 3 **echar una cana al aire** : to let one's hair down
canadiense *adj & nmf* : Canadian
canal[1] *nm* 1 : canal 2 : channel
canal[2] *nmf* : gutter, groove
canalé *nm* : rib, ribbing (in fabric)
canaleta *nf* : gutter
canalete *nm* : paddle
canalizar {21} *vt* : to channel
canalla[1] *adj fam* : low, rotten
canalla[2] *nmf fam* : bastard, swine
canapé *nm* 1 : hors d'oeuvre, canapé 2 SOFÁ : couch, sofa
canario[1], -ria *adj* : of or from the Canary Islands
canario[2], -ria *n* : Canarian, Canary Islander
canario[3] *nm* : canary
canasta *nf* 1 : basket 2 : canasta (card game)
cancel *nm* 1 : sliding door 2 : partition
cancelación *nf, pl* -ciones 1 : cancellation 2 : payment in full
cancelar *vt* 1 : to cancel 2 : to pay off, to settle
cáncer *nm* : cancer
Cáncer *nmf* : Cancer
cancerígeno[1], -na *adj* : carcinogenic
cancerígeno[2] *nm* : carcinogen
canceroso, -sa *adj* : cancerous
cancha *nf* : court, field (for sports)
canciller *nm* : chancellor
cancillería *nf* : chancellery, ministry
canción *nf, pl* canciones 1 : song 2 **canción de cuna** : lullaby
cancionero[1] *nm* : songbook
cancionero[2], -ra *n Mex* : songster, songstress *f*

candado *nm* : padlock
candela *nf* 1 : flame, fire 2 : candle
candelabro *nm* : candelabra
candelero *nm* 1 : candlestick 2 **estar en el candelero** : to be the center of attention
candente *adj* : red-hot
candidato, -ta *n* : candidate, applicant
candidatura *nf* : candidacy
candidez *nf* 1 : simplicity 2 INGENUIDAD : naïveté, ingenuousness
cándido, -da *adj* 1 : simple, unassuming 2 INGENUO : naive, ingenuous
candil *nm* : oil lamp
candilejas *nfpl* : footlights
candor *nm* : naïveté, innocence
candoroso, -sa *adj* : naive, innocent
canela *nf* : cinnamon
canesú *nm* : yoke (of clothing)
cangrejo *nm* JAIBA : crab
canguro *nm* 1 : kangaroo 2 **hacer de canguro** *Spain* : to baby-sit
caníbal[1] *adj* : cannibalistic
caníbal[2] *nmf* ANTROPÓFAGO : cannibal
canibalismo *nm* ANTROPOFAGIA : cannibalism
canibalizar {21} *vt* : to cannibalize
canica *nf* : marble ⟨jugar a las canicas : to play marbles⟩
caniche *nm* : poodle
canijo, -ja *adj* 1 *fam* : puny, weak 2 *Mex fam* : tough, hard ⟨un examen muy canijo : a very tough exam⟩
canilla *nf* 1 : shin, shinbone 2 *Arg, Uru* : faucet
canino[1], -na *adj* : canine
canino[2] *nm* 1 COLMILLO : canine (tooth) 2 : dog, canine
canje *nm* INTERCAMBIO : exchange, trade
canjear *vt* INTERCAMBIAR : to exchange, to trade
cannabis *nm* : cannabis
cano, -na *adj* : gray ⟨un hombre de pelo cano : a gray-haired man⟩
canoa *nf* : canoe
canon *nm, pl* cánones : canon
canónico, -ca *adj* : canonical 2 **derecho canónico** : canon law
canónigo *nm* : canon (of a church)
canonizar {21} *vt* : to canonize — **canonización** *nf*
canoso, -sa → **cano**
cansado, -da *adj* 1 : tired ⟨estar cansado : to be tired⟩ 2 : tiresome, wearying ⟨ser cansado : to be tiring⟩
cansancio *nm* FATIGA : fatigue, weariness
cansar *vt* FATIGAR : to wear out, to tire — *vi* : to be tiresome — **cansarse** *vr* 1 : to wear oneself out 2 : to get bored
cansino, -na *adj* : slow, weary, lethargic
cantaleta *nf fam* : nagging ⟨la misma cantaleta : the same old story⟩
cantalupo *nm* : cantaloupe
cantante *nmf* : singer
cantar[1] *v* : to sing

cantar² *nm* : song, ballad

cántaro *nm* **1** : pitcher, jug **2 llover a cántaros** *fam* : to rain cats and dogs

cantata *nf* : cantata

cantera *nf* : quarry ⟨cantera de piedra : stone quarry⟩

cántico *nm* : canticle, chant

cantidad¹ *adv fam* : really ⟨ese carro me costó cantidad : that car cost me plenty⟩

cantidad² *nf* **1** : quantity **2** : sum, amount (of money) **3** *fam* : a lot, a great many ⟨había cantidad de niños en el parque : there were tons of kids in the park⟩

cantimplora *nf* : canteen, water bottle

cantina *nf* **1** : tavern, bar **2** : canteen, mess, dining quarters *pl*

cantinero, -ra *n* : bartender

canto *nm* **1** : singing **2** : chant ⟨canto gregoriano : Gregorian chant⟩ **3** : song (of a bird) **4** : edge, end ⟨de canto : on end, sideways⟩ **5 canto rodado** : boulder

cantón *nm, pl* **cantones 1** : canton **2** *Mex fam* : place, home

cantonés¹, -nesa *adj & n, mpl* -neses : Cantonese

cantonés² *nm, pl* -neses : Cantonese (language)

cantor¹, -tora *adj* **1** : singing **2 pájaro cantor** : songbird

cantor², -tora *n* **1** : singer **2** : cantor

caña *nf* **1** : cane ⟨caña de azúcar : sugarcane⟩ **2** : reed **3 caña de pescar** : fishing rod **4 caña del timón** : tiller (of a boat)

cañada *nf* : ravine, gully

cáñamo *nm* : hemp

cañaveral *nm* : sugarcane field

cañería *nf* TUBERÍA : pipes *pl*, piping

caño *nm* **1** : pipe **2** : spout **3** : channel (for navigation)

cañón *nm, pl* **cañones 1** : cannon **2** : barrel (of a gun) **3** : canyon

cañonear *vt* : to shell, to bombard

cañoneo *nm* : shelling, bombardment

cañonero *nm* : gunboat

caoba *nf* : mahogany

caolín *nm* : kaolin

caos *nm* : chaos

caótico, -ca *adj* : chaotic

capa *nf* **1** : cape, cloak **2** : coating **3** : layer, stratum **4** : (social) class, stratum

capacidad *nf* **1** : capacity **2** : capability, ability

capacitación *nf, pl* -ciones : training

capacitar *vt* : to train, to qualify

caparazón *nm, pl* -zones : shell, carapace

capataz *nmf, pl* -taces : foreman *m*, forewoman *f*

capaz *adj, pl* **capaces 1** APTO : capable, able **2** COMPETENTE : competent **3** : spacious ⟨capaz para : with room for⟩

capcioso, -sa *adj* : cunning, deceptive ⟨pregunta capciosa : trick question⟩

capea *nf* : amateur bullfight

capear *vt* **1** : to make a pass with the cape (in bullfighting) **2** : to dodge, to weather ⟨capear el temporal : to ride out the storm⟩

capellán *nm, pl* -llanes : chaplain

capilar *nm* : capillary — **capilar** *adj*

capilla *nf* : chapel

capirotada *nf Mex* : traditional bread pudding

capirotazo *nm* : flip, flick

capital¹ *adj* **1** : capital **2** : chief, principal

capital² *nm* : capital ⟨capital de riesgo : venture capital⟩

capital³ *nf* : capital, capital city

capitalino¹, -na *adj* : of or from a capital city

capitalino², -na *n* : inhabitant of a capital city

capitalismo *nm* : capitalism

capitalista *adj & nmf* : capitalist

capitalizar {21} *vt* : to capitalize — **capitalización** *nf*

capitán, -tana *n, mpl* -tanes : captain

capitanear *vt* : to captain, to command

capitanía *nf* : captaincy

capitel *nm* : capital (of a column)

capitolio *nm* : capitol

capitulación *nf, pl* -ciones : capitulation

capitular *vi* : to capitulate, to surrender

capítulo *nm* **1** : chapter, section **2** : matter, subject

capó *nm* : hood (of a car)

capón *nm, pl* **capones** : capon

caporal *nm* **1** : chief, leader **2** : foreman (on a ranch)

capota *nf* : top (of a convertible)

capote *nm* **1** : cloak, overcoat **2** : bullfighter's cape **3** *Mex* COFRE : hood (of a car)

capricho *nm* ANTOJO : whim, caprice

caprichoso, -sa *adj* ANTOJADIZO : capricious, fickle

Capricornio *nmf* : Capricorn

cápsula *nf* : capsule

captar *vt* **1** : to catch, to grasp **2** : to gain, to attract **3** : to harness, to collect (waters)

captor, -tora *n* : captor

captura *nf* : capture, seizure

capturar *vt* : to capture, to seize

capucha *nf* : hood, cowl

capuchina *nf* : nasturtium

capuchino *nm* **1** : Capuchin (monk) **2** : capuchin (monkey) **3** : cappuccino

capullo *nm* **1** : cocoon **2** : bud (of a flower)

caqui *adj & nm* : khaki

cara *nf* **1** : face **2** ASPECTO : look, appearance ⟨¡qué buena cara tiene ese pastel! : that cake looks delicious!⟩ **3** *fam* : nerve, gall **4 ~ a** *or* **de cara a** : facing **5 de cara a** : in view of, in the light of

carabina *nf* : carbine

caracol *nm* **1** : snail **2** CONCHA : conch, seashell **3** : cochlea **4** : ringlet

caracola *nf* : conch
carácter *nm, pl* **caracteres 1** ÍNDOLE : character, kind, nature **2** TEMPERAMENTO : disposition, temperament **3** : letter, symbol ⟨caracteres chinos : Chinese characters⟩
característica *nf* RASGO : trait, feature, characteristic
característico, -ca *adj* : characteristic — **característicamente** *adv*
caracterizar {21} *vt* : to characterize — **caracterización** *nf*
caramba *interj* **1** (*expressing annoyance*) : darn!, heck! **2** (*expressing disgust or surprise*) : jeez!
carámbano *nm* : icicle
carambola *nf* **1** : carom **2** : ruse, trick ⟨por carambola : by a lucky chance⟩
caramelo *nm* **1** : caramel **2** DULCE : candy
caramillo *nm* **1** : pipe, small flute **2** : heap, pile
caraqueño[1], -ña *adj* : of or from Caracas
caraqueño[2], -ña *n* : person from Caracas
carátula *nf* **1** : title page **2** : cover, dust jacket **3** CARETA : mask **4** *Mex* : face, dial (of a clock or watch)
caravana *nf* **1** : caravan **2** : convoy, motorcade **3** REMOLQUE : trailer
caray → **caramba**
carbohidrato *nm* : carbohydrate
carbón *nm, pl* **carbones 1** : coal **2** : charcoal
carbonatado, -da *adj* : carbonated
carbonato *nm* : carbonate
carboncillo *nm* : charcoal
carbonera *nf* : coal cellar, coal bunker (on a ship)
carbonero, -ra *adj* : coal
carbonizar {21} *vt* : to carbonize, to char
carbono *nm* : carbon
carbunco *or* **carbunclo** *nm* : carbuncle
carburador *nm* : carburetor
carburante *nm* : fuel
carca *nmf fam* : old fogy
carcacha *nf fam* : jalopy, wreck
carcaj *nm* : quiver (for arrows)
carcajada *nf* : loud laugh, guffaw ⟨reírse a carcajadas : to roar with laughter⟩
carcajearse *vr* : to roar with laughter, to be in stitches
cárcel *nf* PRISIÓN : jail, prison
carcelero, -ra *n* : jailer
carcinogénico, -ca *adj* : carcinogenic
carcinógeno *nm* CANCERÍGENO : carcinogen
carcinoma *nm* : carcinoma
carcomer *vt* : to eat away at, to consume
carcomido, -da *adj* **1** : worm-eaten **2** : decayed, rotten
cardán *nm, pl* **cardanes** : universal joint
cardar *vt* : to card, to comb
cardenal *nm* **1** : cardinal (in religion) **2** : bruise
cardíaco *or* **cardiaco, -ca** *adj* : cardiac, heart

cárdigan *nm, pl* **-gans** : cardigan
cardinal *adj* : cardinal
cardiología *nf* : cardiology
cardiólogo, -ga *n* : cardiologist
cardiovascular *adj* : cardiovascular
cardo *nm* : thistle
cardumen *nm* : school of fish
carear *vt* : to bring face-to-face
carecer {53} *vi* ~ **de** : to lack ⟨el cheque carecía de fondos : the check lacked funds⟩
carencia *nf* **1** FALTA : lack **2** ESCASEZ : shortage **3** DEFICIENCIA : deficiency
carente *adj* ~ **de** : lacking (in)
carero, -ra *adj fam* : pricey
carestía *nf* **1** : rise in cost ⟨la carestía de la vida : the high cost of living⟩ **2** : dearth, scarcity
careta *nf* MÁSCARA : mask
carey *nm* **1** : hawksbill turtle, sea turtle **2** : tortoiseshell
carga *nf* **1** : loading **2** : freight, load, cargo **3** : burden, responsibility **4** : charge ⟨carga eléctrica : electrical charge⟩ **5** : attack, charge
cargado, -da *adj* **1** : loaded **2** : bogged down, weighted down **3** : close, stuffy **4** : charged ⟨cargado de tensión : charged with tension⟩ **5** FUERTE : strong ⟨café cargado : strong coffee⟩ **6 cargado de hombros** : stoop-shouldered
cargador[1], -dora *n* : longshoreman *m*, longshorewoman *f*
cargador[2] *nm* **1** : magazine (for a firearm) **2** : charger (for batteries)
cargamento *nm* : cargo, load
cargar {52} *vt* **1** : to carry **2** : to load, to fill **3** : to charge — *vi* **1** : to load **2** : to rest (in architecture) **3** ~ **sobre** : to fall upon
cargo *nm* **1** : burden, load **2** : charge ⟨a cargo de : in charge of⟩ **3** : position, office
cargue, etc. → **cargar**
carguero[1], -ra *adj* : freight, cargo ⟨tren carguero : freight train⟩
carguero[2] *nm* : freighter, cargo ship
cariarse *vr* : to decay (of teeth)
caribe *adj* : Caribbean ⟨el mar Caribe : the Caribbean Sea⟩
caribeño, -ña *adj* : Caribbean
caribú *nm* : caribou
caricatura *nf* **1** : caricature **2** : cartoon
caricaturista *nmf* : caricaturist, cartoonist
caricaturizar {21} *vt* : to caricature
caricia *nf* **1** : caress **2 hacer caricias** : to pet, to stroke
caridad *nf* **1** : charity **2** LIMOSNA : alms *pl*
caries *nfs & pl* : cavity (in a tooth)
carillón *nm, pl* **-llones 1** : carillon **2** : glockenspiel
cariño *nm* AFECTO : affection, love
cariñoso, -sa *adj* AFECTUOSO : affectionate, loving — **cariñosamente** *adv*
carioca[1] *adj* : of or from Rio de Janeiro

51

carioca[2] *nmf* : person from Rio de Janeiro

carisma *nf* : charisma

carismático, -ca *adj* : charismatic

carita *adj Mex fam* : cute (said of a man) ⟨tu primo se cree muy carita : your cousin thinks he's gorgeous⟩

caritativo, -va *adj* : charitable

cariz *nm, pl* **carices** : appearance, aspect

carmesí *adj & nm* : crimson

carmín *nm, pl* **carmines** 1 : carmine 2 **carmín de labios** : lipstick

carnada *nf* CEBO : bait

carnal *adj* 1 : carnal 2 **primo carnal** : first cousin

carnaval *nm* : carnival

carnaza *nf* : bait

carne *nf* 1 : meat ⟨carne molida : ground beef⟩ 2 : flesh ⟨carne de gallina : goose bumps⟩

carné → **carnet**

carnero *nm* 1 : ram, sheep 2 : mutton

carnet *nm* 1 : identification card, ID 2 : membership card 3 **carnet de conducir** *Spain* : driver's license

carnicería *nf* 1 : butcher shop 2 MATANZA : slaughter, carnage

carnicero, -ra *n* : butcher

carnívoro[1]**, -ra** *adj* : carnivorous

carnívoro[2] *nm* : carnivore

carnoso, -sa *adj* : fleshy, meaty

caro[1] *adv* : dearly, a lot ⟨pagué caro : I paid a high price⟩

caro[2]**, -ra** *adj* 1 : expensive, dear 2 QUERIDO : dear, beloved

carpa *nf* 1 : carp 2 : big top (of a circus) 3 : tent

carpelo *nm* : carpel

carpeta *nf* : folder, binder, portfolio (of drawings, etc.)

carpetazo *nm* **dar carpetazo a** : to shelve, to defer

carpintería *nf* 1 : carpentry 2 : carpenter's workshop

carpintero, -ra *n* : carpenter

carraspear *vi* : to clear one's throat

carraspera *nf* : hoarseness ⟨tener carraspera : to have a frog in one's throat⟩

carrera *nf* 1 : run, running ⟨a la carrera : at full speed⟩ ⟨de carrera : hastily⟩ 2 : race 3 : course of study 4 : career, profession 5 : run (in baseball)

carreta *nf* : cart, wagon

carrete *nm* 1 BOBINA : reel, spool 2 : roll of film

carretel → **carrete**

carretera *nf* : highway, road ⟨carretera de peaje : turnpike⟩

carretero, -ra *adj* : highway ⟨el sistema carretero nacional : the national highway system⟩

carretilla *nf* 1 : wheelbarrow 2 **carretilla elevadora** : forklift

carril *nm* 1 : lane ⟨carretera de doble carril : two-lane highway⟩ 2 : rail (on a railroad track)

carrillo *nm* : cheek, jowl

carrito *nm* : cart ⟨carrito de compras : shopping cart⟩

carrizo *nm* JUNCO : reed

carro *nm* 1 COCHE : car 2 : cart 3 *Chile, Mex* : coach (of a train) 4 **carro alegórico** : float (in a parade)

carrocería *nf* : bodywork, body (of a vehicle)

carroña *nf* : carrion

carroñero, -ra *n* : scavenger (animal)

carroza *nf* 1 : carriage 2 : float (in a parade)

carruaje *nm* : carriage

carrusel *nm* 1 : merry-go-round 2 : carousel ⟨carrusel de equipaje : luggage carousel⟩

carta *nf* 1 : letter 2 NAIPE : playing card 3 : charter, constitution 4 MENÚ : menu 5 : map, chart 6 **tomar cartas en** : to intervene in

cártamo *nm* : safflower

cartearse *vr* ESCRIBIRSE : to write to one another, to correspond

cartel *nm* : sign, poster

cártel *or* **cartel** *nm* : cartel

cartelera *nf* 1 : billboard 2 : marquee

cartera *nf* 1 BILLETERA : wallet, billfold 2 BOLSO : pocketbook, purse 3 : portfolio ⟨cartera de acciones : stock portfolio⟩

carterista *nmf* : pickpocket

cartero, -ra *n* : letter carrier, mailman *m*

cartilaginoso, -sa *adj* : cartilaginous, gristly

cartílago *nm* : cartilage

cartilla *nf* 1 : primer, reader 2 : booklet ⟨cartilla de ahorros : bankbook⟩

cartografía *nf* : cartography

cartógrafo, -fa *n* : cartographer

cartón *nm, pl* **cartones** 1 : cardboard ⟨cartón madera : fiberboard⟩ 2 : carton

cartucho *nm* : cartridge

cartulina *nf* : poster board, cardboard

carúncula *nf* : wattle (of a bird)

casa *nf* 1 : house, building 2 HOGAR : home 3 : household, family 4 : company, firm 5 **echar la casa por la ventana** : to spare no expense

casaca *nf* : jacket

casado[1]**, -da** *adj* : married

casado[2]**, -da** *n* : married person

casamentero, -ra *n* : matchmaker

casamiento *nm* 1 : marriage 2 BODA : wedding

casar *vt* : to marry — *vi* : to go together, to match up — **casarse** *vr* 1 : to get married 2 ~ **con** : to marry

casateniente *nmf Mex* : landlord, landlady *f*

cascabel[1] *nm* : small bell

cascabel[2] *nf* : rattlesnake

cascada *nf* CATARATA, SALTO : waterfall, cascade

cascajo *nm* 1 : pebble, rock fragment 2 *fam* : piece of junk

cascanueces *nms & pl* : nutcracker

cascar {72} *vt* : to crack (a shell) — **cascarse** *vr* : to crack, to chip

cáscara *nf* **1** : skin, peel, rind, husk **2** : shell (of a nut or egg)

cascarón *nm, pl* **-rones** **1** : eggshell **2** *Mex* : shell filled with confetti

cascarrabias *nmfs & pl fam* : grouch, crab

casco *nm* **1** : helmet **2** : hull **3** : hoof **4** : fragment, shard **5** : center (of a town) **6** *Mex* : empty bottle **7 cascos** *nmpl* : headphones

caserío *nm* **1** : country house **2** : hamlet

casero[1], **-ra** *adj* **1** : domestic, household **2** : homemade

casero[2], **-ra** *n* DUEÑO : landlord *m*, landlady *f*

caseta *nf* : booth, stand, stall ⟨caseta telefónica : telephone booth⟩

casete → **cassette**

casi *adv* **1** : almost, nearly, virtually **2** (*in negative phrases*) : hardly ⟨casi nunca : hardly ever⟩

casilla *nf* **1** : booth **2** : pigeonhole **3** : box (on a form)

casino *nm* **1** : casino **2** : (social) club

caso *nm* **1** : case **2 en caso de** : in case of, in the event of **3 hacer caso de** : to pay attention to, to notice **4 hacer caso omiso de** : to ignore, to take no notice of **5 no venir al caso** : to be beside the point

caspa *nf* : dandruff

casque, etc. → **cascar**

casquete *nm* **1** : skullcap **2 casquete glaciar** : ice cap **3 casquete corto** *Mex* : crew cut

casquillo *nm* : case, casing (of a bullet)

cassette *nmf* : cassette

casta *nf* **1** : caste **2** : lineage, stock ⟨de casta : thoroughbred, purebred⟩ **3 sacar la casta** *Mex* : to come out ahead

castaña *nf* : chestnut

castañetear *vi* : to chatter (of teeth)

castaño[1], **-ña** *adj* : chestnut, brown

castaño[2] *nm* **1** : chestnut tree **2** : chestnut, brown

castañuela *nf* : castanet

castellano[1], **-na** *adj & n* : Castilian

castellano[2] *nm* ESPAÑOL : Spanish, Castilian (language)

castidad *nf* : chastity

castigar {52} *vt* : to punish

castigo *nm* : punishment

castillo *nm* **1** : castle **2 castillo de proa** : forecastle

casto, -ta *adj* : chaste, pure — **castamente** *adv*

castor *nm* : beaver

castración *nf, pl* **-ciones** : castration

castrar *vt* **1** : to castrate, to spay, to neuter, to geld **2** DEBILITAR : to weaken, to debilitate

castrense *adj* : military

casual *adj* **1** FORTUITO : fortuitous, accidental **2** *Mex* : casual (of clothing)

casualidad *nf* **1** : chance **2 por ~** *or* **de ~** : by chance, by any chance

casualmente *adv* : accidentally, by chance

casucha *or* **casuca** *nf* : shanty, hovel

cataclismo *nm* : cataclysm

catacumbas *nfpl* : catacombs

catador, -dora *n* : wine taster

catalán[1], **-lana** *adj & n, mpl* **-lanes** : Catalan

catalán[2] *nm* : Catalan (language)

catálisis *nf* : catalysis

catalítico, -ca *adj* : catalytic

catalizador *nm* **1** : catalyst **2** : catalytic converter

catalogar {52} *vt* : to catalog, to classify

catálogo *nm* : catalog

catamarán *nm, pl* **-ranes** : catamaran

cataplasma *nf* : poultice

catapulta *nf* : catapult

catapultar *vt* : to catapult

catar *vt* **1** : to taste, to sample **2** : to look at, to examine

catarata *nf* **1** CASCADA, SALTO : waterfall **2** : cataract

catarro *nm* RESFRIADO : cold, catarrh

catarsis *nf* : catharsis

catártico, -ca *adj* : cathartic

catástrofe *nf* DESASTRE : catastrophe, disaster

catastrófico, -ca *adj* DESASTROSO : catastrophic, disastrous

catcher *nmf* : catcher (in baseball)

catecismo *nm* : catechism

cátedra *nf* **1** : chair, professorship **2** : subject, class **3 libertad de cátedra** : academic freedom

catedral *nf* : cathedral

catedrático, -ca *n* PROFESOR : professor

categoría *nf* **1** CLASE : category **2** RANGO : rank, standing **3 categoría gramatical** : part of speech **4 de ~** : first-rate, outstanding

categórico, -ca *adj* : categorical, unequivocal — **categóricamente** *adv*

catéter *nm* : catheter

cátodo *nm* : cathode

catolicismo *nm* : Catholicism

católico, -ca *adj & n* : Catholic

catorce *adj & nm* : fourteen

catorceavo *nm* : fourteenth

catre *nm* : cot

catsup *nm* : ketchup

caucásico, -ca *adj & n* : Caucasian

cauce *nm* **1** LECHO : riverbed **2** : means *pl*, channel

caucho *nm* **1** GOMA : rubber **2** : rubber tree **3** *Ven* : tire

caución *nf, pl* **cauciones** FIANZA : bail, security

caudal *nm* **1** : volume of water **2** RIQUEZA : capital, wealth **3** ABUNDANCIA : abundance

caudillaje *nm* : leadership

caudillo *nm* : leader, commander

causa nf **1** MOTIVO : cause, reason, motive ⟨a causa de : because of⟩ **2** IDEAL : cause ⟨morir por una causa : to die for a cause⟩ **3** : lawsuit
causal[1] adj : causal
causal[2] nm : cause, grounds pl
causalidad nf : causality
causante[1] adj ~ **de** : causing, responsible for
causante[2] nmf Mex : taxpayer
causar vt **1** : to cause **2** : to provoke, to arouse ⟨eso me causa gracia : that strikes me as being funny⟩
cáustico, -ca adj : caustic
cautela nf : caution, prudence
cautelar adj : precautionary, preventive
cauteloso, -sa adj : cautious, prudent — **cautelosamente** adv
cauterizar {21} vt : to cauterize
cautivador, -dora adj : captivating
cautivar vt HECHIZAR : to captivate, to charm
cautiverio nm : captivity
cautivo, -va adj & n : captive
cauto, -ta adj : cautious, careful
cavar vt : to dig — vi ~ **en** : to delve into, to probe
caverna nf : cavern, cave
cavernoso, -sa adj **1** : cavernous **2** : deep, resounding
caviar nm : caviar
cavidad nf : cavity
cavilar vi : to ponder, to deliberate
cayado nm : crook, staff, crosier
cayena nf : cayenne pepper
cayó, etc. → **caer**
caza[1] nf **1** CACERÍA : hunt, hunting **2** : game
caza[2] nm : fighter plane
cazador, -dora n **1** : hunter **2 cazador furtivo** : poacher
cazar {21} vt **1** : to hunt **2** : to catch, to bag **3** fam : to land (a job, a spouse) — vi : to go hunting
cazatalentos nmfs & pl : talent scout
cazo nm **1** : saucepan, pot **2** CUCHARÓN : ladle
cazuela nf **1** : pan, saucepan **2** : casserole
cazurro, -ra adj : sullen, surly
CD nm : CD, compact disk
cebada nf : barley
cebar vt **1** : to bait **2** : to feed, to fatten **3** : to prime (a pump, etc.) — **cebarse** vr ~ **en** : to take it out on
cebo nm **1** CARNADA : bait **2** : feed **3** : primer (for firearms)
cebolla nf : onion
cebolleta nf : scallion, green onion
cebollino nm **1** : chive **2** : scallion
cebra nf : zebra
cebú nm, pl **cebús** or **cebúes** : zebu (cattle)
cecear vi : to lisp
ceceo nm : lisp
cecina nf : dried beef, beef jerky
cedazo nm : sieve

ceder vi **1** : to yield, to give way **2** : to diminish, to abate **3** : to give in, to relent — vt : to cede, to hand over
cedro nm : cedar
cédula nf : document, certificate
céfiro nm : zephyr
cegador, -dora adj : blinding
cegar {49} vt **1** : to blind **2** : to block, to stop up — vi : to be blinded, to go blind
cegatón, -tona adj, mpl **-tones** fam : blind as a bat
ceguera nf : blindness
ceiba nf : ceiba, silk-cotton tree
ceja nf **1** : eyebrow ⟨fruncir las cejas : to knit one's brows⟩ **2** : flange, rim
cejar vi : to give in, to back down
celada nf : trap, ambush
celador, -dora n GUARDIA : guard, warden
celda nf : cell (of a jail)
celebración nf, pl **-ciones** : celebration
celebrado, -da adj CÉLEBRE, FAMOSO : famous, celebrated
celebrante nmf OFICIANTE : celebrant
celebrar vt **1** FESTEJAR : to celebrate **2** : to hold (a meeting) **3** : to say (Mass) **4** : to welcome, to be happy about — vi : to be glad — **celebrarse** vr **1** : to be celebrated, to fall **2** : to be held, to take place
célebre adj CELEBRADO, FAMOSO : celebrated, famous
celebridad nf **1** : celebrity **2** FAMA : fame, renown
celeridad nf : celerity, swiftness
celeste[1] adj **1** : celestial **2** : sky blue, azure
celeste[2] nm : sky blue
celestial adj : heavenly, celestial
celibato nm : celibacy
célibe adj & nmf : celibate
cello nm : cello
celo nm **1** : zeal, fervor **2** : heat (of females), rut (of males) **3 celos** nmpl : jealousy ⟨tenerle celos a alguien : to be jealous of someone⟩
celofán nm, pl **-fanes** : cellophane
celosía nf **1** : lattice window **2** : latticework, trellis
celoso, -sa adj **1** : jealous **2** : zealous — **celosamente** adv
celta[1] adj : Celtic
celta[2] nmf : Celt
célula nf : cell
celular adj : cellular
celuloide nm **1** : celluloid **2** : film, cinema
celulosa nf : cellulose
cementar vt : to cement
cementerio nm : cemetery
cemento nm : cement
cena nf : supper, dinner
cenador nm : arbor
cenagal nm : bog, quagmire
cenagoso, -sa adj : swampy
cenar vi : to have dinner, to have supper — vt : to have for dinner or supper

⟨anoche cenamos tamales : we had tamales for supper last night⟩
cencerro *nm* : cowbell
cenicero *nm* : ashtray
ceniciento, -ta *adj* : ashen
cenit *nm* : zenith, peak
ceniza *nf* **1** : ash **2 cenizas** *nfpl* : ashes (of a deceased person)
cenizo, -za *n* : jinx
cenote *nm Mex* : natural deposit of spring water
censar *vt* : to take a census of
censo *nm* : census
censor, -sora *n* : censor, critic
censura *nf* **1** : censorship **2** : censure, criticism
censurable *adj* : reprehensible, blameworthy
censurar *vt* **1** : to censor **2** : to censure, to criticize
centauro *nm* : centaur
centavo *nm* **1** : cent (in English-speaking countries) **2** : unit of currency in various Latin-American countries
centella *nf* **1** : lightning flash **2** : spark
centellear *vi* **1** : to twinkle **2** : to gleam, to sparkle
centelleo *nm* : twinkling, sparkle
centenar *nm* **1** : hundred **2 a centenares** : by the hundreds
centenario[1], -ria *adj & n* : centenarian
centenario[2] *nm* : centennial
centeno *nm* : rye
centésimo[1], -ma *adj* : hundredth
centésimo[2] *nm* : hundredth
centígrado *adj* : centigrade, Celsius
centigramo *nm* : centigram
centímetro *nm* : centimeter
centinela *nmf* : sentinel, sentry
central[1] *adj* **1** : central **2** PRINCIPAL : main, principal
central[2] *nf* **1** : main office, headquarters **2 central camionera** *Mex* : bus terminal
centralita *nf* : switchboard
centralizar {21} *vt* : to centralize — **centralización** *nf*
centrar *vt* **1** : to center **2** : to focus — **centrarse** *vr* ~ **en** : to focus on, to concentrate on
céntrico, -ca *adj* : central
centrífugo, -ga *adj* : centrifugal
centrípeto, -ta *adj* : centripetal
centro[1] *nmf* : center (in sports)
centro[2] *nm* **1** MEDIO : center ⟨centro de atención : center of attention⟩ ⟨centro de gravedad : center of gravity⟩ **2** : downtown **3 centro de mesa** : centerpiece
centroamericano, -na *adj & n* : Central American
ceñido, -da *adj* AJUSTADO : tight, tight-fitting
ceñir {67} *vt* **1** : to encircle, to surround **2** : to hug, to cling to ⟨me ciñe demasiado : it's too tight on me⟩ — **ceñirse** *vr* ~ **a** : to restrict oneself to, to stick to

ceño *nm* **1** : frown, scowl **2 fruncir el ceño** : to frown, to knit one's brows
cepa *nf* **1** : stump (of a tree) **2** : stock (of a vine) **3** LINAJE : ancestry, stock
cepillar *vt* **1** : to brush **2** : to plane (wood) — **cepillarse** *vr*
cepillo *nm* **1** : brush ⟨cepillo de dientes : toothbrush⟩ **2** : plane (for woodworking)
cepo *nm* : trap (for animals)
cera *nf* **1** : wax ⟨cera de abejas : beeswax⟩ **2** : polish
cerámica *nf* **1** : ceramics *pl* **2** : pottery
cerámico, -ca *adj* : ceramic
ceramista *nmf* ALFARERO : potter
cerca[1] *adv* **1** : close, near, nearby **2** ~ **de** : nearly, almost
cerca[2] *nf* **1** : fence **2** : (stone) wall
cercado *nm* : enclosure
cercanía *nf* **1** PROXIMIDAD : proximity, closeness **2 cercanías** *nfpl* : outskirts, suburbs
cercano, -na *adj* : near, close
cercar {72} *vt* **1** : to fence in, to enclose **2** : to surround
cercenar *vt* **1** : to cut off, to amputate **2** : to diminish, to curtail
cerceta *nf* : teal (duck)
cerciorarse *vr* ASEGURARSE ~ **de** : to make sure of, to verify
cerco *nm* **1** : siege **2** : cordon, circle **3** : fence
cerda *nf* **1** : bristle **2** : sow
cerdo *nm* **1** : pig, hog **2 carne de cerdo** : pork
cereal *nm* : cereal — **cereal** *adj*
cerebelo *nm* : cerebellum
cerebral *adj* : cerebral
cerebro *nm* : brain
ceremonia *nf* : ceremony — **ceremonial** *adj*
ceremonioso, -sa *adj* : ceremonious
cereza *nf* : cherry
cerezo *nm* : cherry tree
cerilla *nf* **1** : match **2** : earwax
cerillo *nm* (*in various countries*) : match
cerner {56} *vt* : to sift — **cernerse** *vr* **1** : to hover **2** ~ **sobre** : to loom over, to threaten
cernidor *nm* : sieve
cernir → **cerner**
cero *nm* : zero
ceroso, -sa *adj* : waxy
cerque, etc. → **cercar**
cerquita *adv fam* : very close, very near
cerrado, -da *adj* **1** : closed, shut **2** : thick, broad ⟨tiene un acento cerrado : she has a thick accent⟩ **3** : cloudy, overcast **4** : quiet, reserved **5** : dense, stupid
cerradura *nf* : lock
cerrajería *nf* : locksmith's shop
cerrajero, -ra *n* : locksmith
cerrar {55} *vt* **1** : to close, to shut **2** : to turn off **3** : to bring to an end — *vi* **1** : to close up, to lock up **2** : to close down — **cerrarse** *vr* **1** : to close **2** : to fasten, to button up **3** : to conclude, to end

cerrazón *nf, pl* **-zones** : obstinacy, stubbornness
cerro *nm* COLINA, LOMA : hill
cerrojo *nm* PESTILLO : bolt, latch
certamen *nm, pl* **-támenes** : competition, contest
certero, -ra *adj* : accurate, precise — **certeramente** *adv*
certeza *nf* : certainty
certidumbre *nf* : certainty
certificable *adj* : certifiable
certificación *nf, pl* **-ciones** : certification
certificado[1]**, -da** *adj* **1** : certified **2** : registered (of mail)
certificado[2] *nm* **1** : certificate **2** : registered letter
certificar {72} *vt* **1** : to certify **2** : to register (mail)
cervato *nm* : fawn
cervecera *nf* : brewery
cervecería *nf* **1** : brewery **2** : beer hall, bar
cerveza *nf* : beer ⟨cerveza de barril : draft beer⟩
cervical *adj* : cervical
cerviz *nf, pl* **cervices** : nape of the neck, cervix
cesación *nf, pl* **-ciones** : cessation, suspension
cesante *adj* : laid off, unemployed
cesantía *nf* : unemployment
cesar *vi* : to cease, to stop — *vt* : to dismiss, to lay off
cesárea *nf* : cesarean, C-section
cese *nm* **1** : cessation, stop ⟨cese del fuego : cease-fire⟩ **2** : dismissal
cesio *nm* : cesium
cesión *nf, pl* **cesiones** : transfer, assignment ⟨cesión de bienes : transfer of property⟩
césped *nm* : lawn, grass
cesta *nf* **1** : basket **2** : jai alai racket
cesto *nm* **1** : hamper **2** : basket (in basketball) **3 cesto de (la) basura** : wastebasket
cetrería *nf* : falconry
cetrino, -na *adj* : sallow
cetro *nm* : scepter
chabacano[1]**, -na** *adj* : tacky, tasteless
chabacano[2] *nm Mex* : apricot
chacal *nm* : jackal
cháchara *nf fam* **1** : small talk, chatter **2 chácharas** *nfpl* : trinkets, junk
chacharear *vi fam* : to chatter, to gab
chacra *nf Arg, Chile, Peru* : small farm
chadiano, -na *adj & n* : Chadian
chal *nm* MANTÓN : shawl
chalado[1]**, -da** *adj fam* : crazy, nuts
chalado[2]**, -da** *n* : nut, crazy person
chalán *nm, pl* **chalanes** *Mex* : barge
chalé → chalet
chaleco *nm* : vest
chalet *nm Spain* : house
chalupa *nf* **1** : small boat **2** *Mex* : small stuffed tortilla
chamaco, -ca *n Mex fam* : kid, boy *m*, girl *f*

chamarra *nf* **1** : sheepskin jacket **2** : poncho, blanket
chamba *nf Mex, Peru fam* : job, work
chambear *vi Mex, Peru fam* : to work
chamo, -ma *n Ven fam* **1** : kid, boy *m*, girl *f* **2** : buddy, pal
champaña *or* **champán** *nm* : champagne
champiñón *nm, pl* **-ñones** : mushroom
champú *nm, pl* **-pus** *or* **-púes** : shampoo
champurrado *nm Mex* : hot chocolate thickened with cornstarch
chamuco *nm Mex fam* : devil
chamuscar {72} *vt* : to singe, to scorch — **chamuscarse** *vr*
chamusquina *nf* : scorch
chance *nm* OPORTUNIDAD : chance, opportunity
chancho[1]**, -cha** *adj fam* : dirty, filthy, gross
chancho[2]**, -cha** *n* **1** : pig, hog **2** *fam* : slob
chanchullero, -ra *adj fam* : shady, crooked
chanchullo *nm fam* : shady deal, scam
chancla *nf* **1** : thong sandal, slipper **2** : old shoe
chancleta → chancla
chanclo *nm* **1** : clog **2 chanclos** *nmpl* : overshoes, galoshes, rubbers
chancro *nm* : chancre
changarro *nm Mex* : small shop, stall
chango, -ga *n Mex* : monkey
chantaje *nm* : blackmail
chantajear *vt* : to blackmail
chantajista *nmf* : blackmailer
chanza *nf* **1** : joke, jest **2** *Mex fam* : chance, opportunity
chapa *nf* **1** : sheet, panel, veneer **2** : lock **3** : badge
chapado, -da *adj* **1** : plated **2 chapado a la antigua** : old-fashioned
chapar *vt* **1** : to veneer **2** : to plate (metals)
chaparrón *nm, pl* **-rrones** **1** : downpour **2** : great quantity, torrent
chapeado, -da *adj Col, Mex* : flushed
chapopote *nm Mex* : tar, blacktop
chapotear *vi* : to splash about
chapucero[1]**, -ra** *adj* **1** : crude, shoddy **2** *Mex fam* : dishonest
chapucero[2]**, -ra** *n* **1** : sloppy worker, bungler **2** *Mex fam* : cheat, swindler
chapulín *nm, pl* **-lines** *CA, Mex* : grasshopper, locust
chapuza *nf* **1** : botched job **2** *Mex fam* : fraud, trick ⟨hacer chapuzas : to cheat⟩
chapuzón *nm, pl* **-zones** : dip, swim ⟨darse un chapuzón : to go for a quick dip⟩
chaqueta *nf* : jacket
charada *nf* : charades (game)
charango *nm* : traditional Andean stringed instrument
charca *nf* : pond, pool
charco *nm* : puddle, pool

charcutería *nf* : delicatessen
charla *nf* : chat, talk
charlar *vi* : to chat, to talk
charlatán[1], **-tana** *adj* : talkative, chatty
charlatán[2], **-tana** *n, mpl* **-tanes** 1 : chatterbox 2 FARSANTE : charlatan, phony
charlatanear *vi* : to chatter away
charol *nm* 1 : lacquer, varnish 2 : patent leather 3 : tray
charola *nf Bol, Mex, Peru* : tray
charreada *nf Mex* : charro show, rodeo
charretera *nf* : epaulet
charro[1], **-rra** *adj* 1 : gaudy, tacky 2 *Mex* : pertaining to charros
charro[2], **-rra** *n Mex* : charro (Mexican cowboy or cowgirl)
chascarrillo *nm fam* : joke, funny story
chasco *nm* 1 BROMA : trick, joke 2 DECEPCIÓN, DESILUSIÓN : disillusionment, disappointment
chasis *or* **chasís** *nm* : chassis
chasquear *vt* 1 : to click (the tongue, fingers, etc.) 2 : to snap (a whip)
chasquido *nm* 1 : click (of the tongue or fingers) 2 : snap, crack
chatarra *nf* : scrap metal
chato, -ta *adj* 1 : pug-nosed 2 : flat
chauvinismo *nm* : chauvinism
chauvinista[1] *adj* : chauvinistic
chauvinista[2] *nmf* : chauvinist
chaval, -vala *n fam* : kid, boy *m*, girl *f*
chavo[1], **-va** *adj Mex fam* : young
chavo[2], **-va** *n Mex fam* : kid, boy *m*, girl *f*
chavo[3] *nm fam* : cent, buck ⟨no tengo un chavo : I'm broke⟩
chayote *nm* : chayote (plant, fruit)
checar {72} *vt Mex* : to check, to verify
checo[1], **-ca** *adj & n* : Czech
checo[2] *nm* : Czech (language)
checoslovaco, -ca *adj & n* : Czechoslovakian
chef *nm* : chef
chelín *nm, pl* **chelines** : shilling
cheque[1], **etc.** → **checar**
cheque[2] *nm* 1 : check 2 **cheque de viajero** : traveler's check
chequear *vt* 1 : to check, to verify 2 : to check in (baggage)
chequeo *nm* 1 INSPECCIÓN : check, inspection 2 : checkup, examination
chequera *nf* : checkbook
chévere *adj fam* : great, fantastic
chic *adj & nm* : chic
chica → **chico**
chicano, -na *adj & n* : Chicano *m*, Chicana *f*
chicha *nf* : fermented alcoholic beverage made from corn
chícharo *nm* : pea
chicharra *nf* 1 CIGARRA : cicada 2 : buzzer
chicharrón *nm, pl* **-rrones** 1 : pork rind 2 **darle chicharrón a** *Mex fam* : to get rid of
chichón *nm, pl* **chichones** : bump, swelling

chicle *nm* : chewing gum
chicloso *nm Mex* : taffy
chico[1], **-ca** *adj* 1 : little, small 2 : young
chico[2], **-ca** *n* 1 : child, boy *m*, girl *f* 2 : young man *m*, young woman *f*
chicote *nm* LÁTIGO : whip, lash
chiffon → **chifón**
chiflado[1], **-da** *adj fam* : nuts, crazy
chiflado[2], **-da** *n fam* : crazy person, lunatic
chiflar *vi* : to whistle — *vt* : to whistle at, to boo — **chiflarse** *vr fam* ~ **por** : to be crazy about
chiflido *nm* : whistle, whistling
chiflón *nm, pl* **chiflones** : draft (of air)
chifón *nm, pl* **chifones** : chiffon
chilango[1], **-ga** *adj Mex fam* : of or from Mexico City
chilango[2], **-ga** *n Mex fam* : person from Mexico City
chilaquiles *nmpl Mex* : shredded tortillas in sauce
chile *nm* : chili pepper
chileno, -na *adj & n* : Chilean
chillar *vi* 1 : to squeal, to screech 2 : to scream, to yell 3 : to be gaudy, to clash
chillido *nm* 1 : scream, shout 2 : squeal, screech, cry (of an animal)
chillo *nm PRi* : red snapper
chillón, -llona *adj, mpl* **chillones** 1 : piercing, shrill 2 : loud, gaudy
chilpayate *nmf Mex fam* : child, little kid
chimenea *nf* 1 : chimney 2 : fireplace
chimichurri *nm Arg* : traditional hot sauce
chimpancé *nm* : chimpanzee
china *nf* 1 : pebble, small stone 2 *PRi* : orange
chinchar *vt fam* : to annoy, to pester — **chincharse** *vr fam* : to put up with something, to grin and bear it
chinchayote *nm Mex* : chayote root
chinche[1] *nf* 1 : bedbug 2 *Ven* : ladybug 3 : thumbtack
chinche[2] *nmf fam* : nuisance, pain in the neck
chinchilla *nf* : chinchilla
chino[1], **-na** *adj* 1 : Chinese 2 *Mex* : curly, kinky
chino[2], **-na** *n* : Chinese person
chino[3] *nm* : Chinese (language)
chip *nm, pl* **chips** : chip ⟨chip de memoria : memory chip⟩
chipote *nm Mex fam* : bump (on the head)
chipotle *nm Mex* : type of chili pepper
chipriota *adj & nmf* : Cypriot
chiquear *vt Mex* : to spoil, to indulge
chiquero *nm* POCILGA : pigpen, pigsty
chiquillada *nf* : childish prank
chiquillo[1], **-lla** *adj* : very young, little
chiquillo[2], **-lla** *n* : kid, youngster
chiquito[1], **-ta** *adj* : tiny
chiquito[2], **-ta** *n* : little one, baby
chiribita *nf* 1 : spark 2 **chiribitas** *nfpl* : spots before the eyes
chiribitil *nm* 1 DESVÁN : attic, garret 2 : cubbyhole

chirigota *nf fam* : joke
chirimía *nf* : traditional reed pipe
chirimoya *nf* : cherimoya, custard apple
chiripa *nf* **1** : fluke **2 de ~** : by sheer luck
chirivía *nf* : parsnip
chirona *nf fam* : slammer, jail
chirriar {85} *vi* **1** : to squeak, to creak **2** : to screech — **chirriante** *adj*
chirrido *nm* **1** : squeak, squeaking **2** : screech, screeching
chirrión *nm, pl* **chirriones** *Mex* : whip, lash
chisme *nm* **1** : gossip, tale **2** *Spain fam* : gadget, thingamajig
chismear *vi* : to gossip
chismoso[1], **-sa** *adj* : gossipy, gossiping
chismoso[2], **-sa** *n* **1** : gossiper, gossip **2** *Mex fam* : tattletale
chispa[1] *adj* **1** *Mex fam* : lively, vivacious ⟨un perrito chispa : a frisky puppy⟩ **2** *Spain fam* : tipsy
chispa[2] *nf* **1** : spark **2 echar chispas** : to be furious
chispeante *adj* : sparkling, scintillating
chispear *vi* **1** : to give off sparks **2** : to sparkle
chisporrotear *vi* : to crackle, to sizzle
chiste *nm* **1** : joke, funny story **2 tener chiste** : to be funny **3 tener su chiste** *Mex* : to be tricky
chistoso[1], **-sa** *adj* **1** : funny, humorous **2** : witty
chistoso[2], **-sa** *n* : wit, joker
chivas *nfpl Mex fam* : stuff, odds and ends
chivo[1], **-va** *n* **1** : kid, young goat **2 chivo expiatorio** : scapegoat
chivo[2] *nm* **1** : billy goat **2** : fit of anger
chocante *adj* **1** : shocking **2** : unpleasant, rude
chocar {72} *vi* **1** : to crash, to collide **2** : to clash, to conflict **3** : to be shocking ⟨le chocó : he was shocked⟩ **4** *Mex, Ven fam* : to be unpleasant or obnoxious ⟨me choca tu jefe : I can't stand your boss⟩ — *vt* **1** : to shake (hands) **2** : to clink glasses
chochear *vi* **1** : to be senile **2 ~ por** : to dote on, to be soft on
chochín *nm, pl* **-chines** : wren
chocho, -cha *adj* **1** : senile **2** : doting
choclo *nm* **1** : ear of corn, corncob **2** : corn **3 meter el choclo** *Mex fam* : to make a mistake
chocolate *nm* **1** : chocolate **2** : hot chocolate, cocoa
chofer *or* **chófer** *nm* **1** : chauffeur **2** : driver
choke *nm* : choke (of an automobile)
chole *interj* *Mex fam* **¡ya chole!** : enough!, cut it out!
cholo, -la *adj & n* : mestizo
cholla *nf fam* : head
chollo *nm Spain fam* : bargain
chongo *nm* **1** *Mex* : bun (chignon) **2 chongos** *nmpl Mex* : dessert made with fried bread

choque[1], etc. → **chocar**
choque[2] *nm* **1** : crash, collision **2** : clash, conflict **3** : shock
chorizo *nm* : chorizo, sausage
chorrear *vi* **1** : to drip **2** : to pour out, to gush out
chorrito *nm* : squirt, splash
chorro *nm* **1** : flow, stream, jet **2** *Mex fam* : heap, ton
choteado, -da *adj Mex fam* : worn-out, stale ⟨esa canción está bien choteada : that song's been played to death⟩
chotear *vt* : to make fun of
choteo *nm* : joking around, kidding
chovinismo, chovinista → **chauvinismo, chauvinista**
choza *nf* BARRACA, CABAÑA : hut, shack
chubasco *nm* : downpour, storm
chuchería *nf* : knickknack, trinket
chueco, -ca *adj* **1** : crooked, bent **2** *Chile, Mex fam* : dishonest, shady
chulada *nf Mex, Spain fam* : cute or pretty thing ⟨¡qué chulada de vestido! : what a lovely dress!⟩
chulear *vt Mex fam* : to compliment
chuleta *nf* : cutlet, chop
chulo[1], **-la** *adj* **1** *fam* : cute, pretty **2** *Spain fam* : cocky, arrogant
chulo[2] *nm Spain* : pimp
chupada *nf* **1** : suck, sucking **2** : puff, drag (on a cigarette)
chupado, -da *adj fam* **1** : gaunt, skinny **2** : plastered, drunk
chupaflor *nm* COLIBRÍ : hummingbird
chupamirto *nm Mex* : hummingbird
chupar *vt* **1** : to suck **2** : to absorb **3** : to puff on **4** *fam* : to drink, to guzzle — *vi* **1** : to suckle — **chuparse** *vr* **1** : to waste away **2** *fam* : to put up with **3 ¡chúpate esa!** *fam* : take that!
chupete *nm* **1** : pacifier **2** *Chile, Peru* : lollipop
chupetear *vt* : to suck (at)
chupón *nm, pl* **chupones** **1** : sucker (of a plant) **2** : baby bottle, pacifier
churrasco *nm* **1** : steak **2** : barbecued meat
churro *nm* **1** : fried dough **2** *fam* : botch, mess **3** *fam* : attractive person, looker
chusco, -ca *adj* : funny, amusing
chusma *nf* GENTUZA : riffraff, rabble
chutar *vi* : to shoot (in soccer)
chute *nm* : shot (in soccer)
cianuro *nm* : cyanide
cibernética *nf* : cybernetics
cicatriz *nf, pl* **-trices** : scar
cicatrizarse {21} *vr* : to form a scar, to heal
cíclico, -ca *adj* : cyclical
ciclismo *nm* : bicycling
ciclista *nmf* : bicyclist
ciclo *nm* : cycle
ciclomotor *nm* : moped
ciclón *nm, pl* **ciclones** : cyclone
cicuta *nf* : hemlock
cidra *nf* : citron (fruit)
ciega, ciegue etc. → **cegar**

ciego[1], **-ga** *adj* **1** INVIDENTE : blind **2 a ciegas** : blindly **3 quedarse ciego** : to go blind — **ciegamente** *adv*

ciego[2], **-ga** *n* INVIDENTE : blind person

cielo *nm* **1** : sky **2** : heaven **3** : ceiling

ciempiés *nms & pl* : centipede

cien[1] *adj* **1** : a hundred, hundred ⟨las primeras cien páginas : the first hundred pages⟩ **2 cien por cien** *or* **cien por ciento** : a hundred percent, through and through, wholeheartedly

cien[2] *nm* : one hundred

ciénaga *nf* : swamp, bog

ciencia *nf* **1** : science **2** : learning, knowledge **3 a ciencia cierta** : for a fact, for certain

cieno *nm* : mire, mud, silt

científico[1], **-ca** *adj* : scientific — **científicamente** *adv*

científico[2], **-ca** *n* : scientist

ciento[1] *adj* (*used in compound numbers*) : one hundred ⟨ciento uno : one hundred and one⟩

ciento[2] *nm* **1** : hundred, group of a hundred **2 por** ~ : percent

cierne, etc. → **cerner**

cierra, etc. → **cerrar**

cierre *nm* **1** : closing, closure **2** : fastener, clasp, zipper

cierto, -ta *adj* **1** : true, certain, definite ⟨lo cierto es que . . . : the fact is that . . .⟩ **2** : certain, one ⟨cierto día de verano : one summer day⟩ ⟨bajo ciertas circunstancias : under certain circumstances⟩ **3 por** ~ : in fact, as a matter of fact — **ciertamente** *adv*

ciervo, -va *n* : deer, stag *m*, hind *f*

cifra *nf* **1** : figure, number **2** : quantity, amount **3** CLAVE : code, cipher

cifrar *vt* **1** : to write in code **2** : to place, to pin ⟨cifró su esperanza en la lotería : he pinned his hopes on the lottery⟩ — **cifrarse** *vr* : to amount ⟨la multa se cifra en millares : the fine amounts to thousands⟩

cigarra *nf* CHICHARRA : cicada

cigarrera *nf* : cigarette case

cigarrillo *nm* : cigarette

cigarro *nm* **1** : cigarette **2** PURO : cigar

cigoto *nm* : zygote

cigüeña *nf* : stork

cilantro *nm* : cilantro, coriander

cilíndrico, -ca *adj* : cylindrical

cilindro *nm* : cylinder

cima *nf* CUMBRE : peak, summit, top

cimarrón, -rrona *adj*, *mpl* **-rrones** : untamed, wild

címbalo *nm* : cymbal

cimbel *nm* : decoy

cimbrar *vt* : to shake, to rock — **cimbrarse** *vr* : to sway, to swing

cimentar {55} *vt* **1** : to lay the foundation of, to establish **2** : to strengthen, to cement

cimientos *nmpl* : base, foundation(s)

cinc *nm* : zinc

cincel *nm* : chisel

cincelar *vt* **1** : to chisel **2** : to engrave

cincha *nf* : cinch, girth

cinchar *vt* : to cinch (a horse)

cinco *adj & nm* : five

cincuenta *adj & nm* : fifty

cincuentavo[1], **-va** *adj* : fiftieth

cincuentavo[2] *nm* : fiftieth (fraction)

cine *nm* **1** : cinema, movies *pl* **2** : movie theater

cineasta *nmf* : filmmaker

cinematográfico, -ca *adj* : movie, film, cinematic ⟨la industria cinematográfica : the film industry⟩

cingalés[1], **-lesa** *adj & n* : Sinhalese

cingalés[2] *nm* : Sinhalese (language)

cínico[1], **-ca** *adj* **1** : cynical **2** : shameless, brazen — **cínicamente** *adv*

cínico[2], **-ca** *n* : cynic

cinismo *nm* : cynicism

cinta *nf* **1** : ribbon **2** : tape ⟨cinta métrica : tape measure⟩ **3** : strap, belt ⟨cinta transportadora : conveyor belt⟩

cinto *nm* : strap, belt

cintura *nf* **1** : waist, waistline **2 meter en cintura** *fam* : to bring into line, to discipline

cinturón *nm*, *pl* **-rones** **1** : belt **2 cinturón de seguridad** : seat belt

ciñe, etc. → **ceñir**

ciprés *nm*, *pl* **cipreses** : cypress

circo *nm* : circus

circón *nm*, *pl* **circones** : zircon

circonio *nm* : zirconium

circuitería *nf* : circuitry

circuito *nm* : circuit

circulación *nf*, *pl* **-ciones** **1** : circulation **2** : movement **3** : traffic

circular[1] *vi* **1** : to circulate **2** : to move along **3** : to drive

circular[2] *adj* : circular

circular[3] *nf* : circular, flier

circulatorio, -ria *adj* : circulatory

círculo *nm* **1** : circle **2** : club, group

circuncidar *vt* : to circumcise

circuncisión *nf*, *pl* **-siones** : circumcision

circundar *vt* : to surround — **circundante** *adj*

circunferencia *nf* : circumference

circunflejo, -ja *adj* **acento circunflejo** : circumflex

circunlocución *nf*, *pl* **-ciones** : circumlocution

circunloquio *nm* → **circunlocución**

circunnavegar {52} *vt* : to circumnavigate — **circunnavegación** *nf*

circunscribir {33} *vt* : to circumscribe, to constrict, to limit — **circunscribirse** *vr*

circunscripción *nf*, *pl* **-ciones** **1** : limitation, restriction **2** : constituency

circunscrito *pp* → **circunscribir**

circunspección *nf*, *pl* **-ciones** : circumspection, prudence

circunspecto, -ta *adj* : circumspect, prudent

circunstancia *nf* : circumstance

circunstancial *adj* : circumstantial, incidental

circunstante *nmf* **1** : onlooker, bystander **2 los circunstantes** : those present

circunvalación *nf, pl* **-ciones** : surrounding, encircling ⟨carretera de circunvalación : bypass, beltway⟩

circunvecino, -na *adj* : surrounding, neighboring

cirio *nm* : large candle

cirro *nm* : cirrus (cloud)

cirrosis *nf* : cirrhosis

ciruela *nf* **1** : plum **2 ciruela pasa** : prune

cirugía *nf* : surgery

cirujano, -na *n* : surgeon

cisma *nm* : schism, rift

cisne *nm* : swan

cisterna *nf* : cistern, tank

cita *nf* **1** : quote, quotation **2** : appointment, date

citable *adj* : quotable

citación *nf, pl* **-ciones** EMPLAZAMIENTO : summons, subpoena

citadino[1]**, -na** *adj* : of the city, urban

citadino[2]**, -na** *n* : city dweller

citado, -da *adj* : said, aforementioned

citar *vt* **1** : to quote, to cite **2** : to make an appointment with **3** : to summon (to court), to subpoena — **citarse** *vr* ~ **con** : to arrange to meet (someone)

cítara *nf* : zither

citatorio *nm* : subpoena

citoplasma *nm* : cytoplasm

cítrico[1]**, -ca** *adj* : citric

cítrico[2] *nm* : citrus fruit

ciudad *nf* **1** : city, town **2 ciudad universitaria** : college or university campus **3 ciudad perdida** *Mex* : shantytown

ciudadanía *nf* **1** : citizenship **2** : citizenry, citizens *pl*

ciudadano[1]**, -na** *adj* : civic, city

ciudadano[2]**, -na** *n* **1** NACIONAL : citizen **2** HABITANTE : resident, city dweller

ciudadela *nf* : citadel, fortress

cívico, -ca *adj* **1** : civic **2** : public-spirited

civil[1] *adj* **1** : civil **2** : civilian

civil[2] *nmf* : civilian

civilidad *nf* : civility, courtesy

civilización *nf, pl* **-ciones** : civilization

civilizar {21} *vt* : to civilize

civismo *nm* : community spirit, civic-mindedness, civics

cizaña *nf* : discord, rift

clamar *vi* : to clamor, to raise a protest — *vt* : to cry out for

clamor *nm* : clamor, outcry

clamoroso, -sa *adj* : clamorous, resounding, thunderous

clan *nm* : clan

clandestinidad *nf* : secrecy ⟨en la clandestinidad : underground⟩

clandestino, -na *adj* : clandestine, secret

clara *nf* : egg white

claraboya *nf* : skylight

claramente *adv* : clearly

clarear *v impers* **1** : to clear, to clear up **2** : to get light, to dawn — *vi* : to go gray, to turn white

claridad *nf* **1** NITIDEZ : clarity, clearness **2** : brightness, light

clarificación *nf, pl* **-ciones** ACLARACIÓN : clarification, explanation

clarificar {72} *vt* ACLARAR : to clarify, to explain

clarín *nm, pl* **clarines** : bugle

clarinete *nm* : clarinet

clarividencia *nf* **1** : clairvoyance **2** : perspicacity, discernment

clarividente[1] *adj* **1** : clairvoyant **2** : perspicacious, discerning

clarividente[2] *nmf* : clairvoyant

claro[1] *adv* **1** : clearly ⟨habla más claro : speak more clearly⟩ **2** : of course, surely ⟨¡claro!, ¡claro que sí! : absolutely!, of course!⟩ ⟨claro que entendió : of course she understood⟩

claro[2]**, -ra** *adj* **1** : bright, clear **2** : pale, fair, light **3** : clear, evident

claro[3] *nm* **1** : clearing **2 claro de luna** : moonlight

clase *nf* **1** : class **2** ÍNDOLE, TIPO : sort, kind, type

clasicismo *nm* : classicism

clásico[1]**, -ca** *adj* **1** : classic **2** : classical

clásico[2] *nm* : classic

clasificación *nf, pl* **-ciones** **1** : classification, sorting out **2** : rating **3** CALIFICACIÓN : qualification (in competitions)

clasificado, -da *adj* : classified ⟨aviso clasificado : classified ad⟩

clasificar {72} *vt* **1** : to classify, to sort out **2** : to rate, to rank — *vi* CALIFICAR : to qualify (in competitions) — **clasificarse** *vr*

claudicación *nf, pl* **-ciones** : surrender, abandonment of one's principles

claudicar {72} *vi* : to back down, to abandon one's principles

claustro *nm* : cloister

claustrofobia *nf* : claustrophobia

claustrofóbico, -ca *adj* : claustrophobic

cláusula *nf* : clause

clausura *nf* **1** : closure, closing **2** : closing ceremony **3** : cloister

clausurar *vt* **1** : to close, to bring to a close **2** : to close down

clavadista *nmf* : diver

clavado[1]**, -da** *adj* **1** : nailed, fixed, stuck **2** *fam* : punctual, on the dot **3** *fam* : identical ⟨es clavado a su padre : he's the image of his father⟩

clavado[2] *nm* : dive

clavar *vt* **1** : to nail, to hammer **2** HINCAR : to plunge, to stick **3** : to fix (one's eyes) on — **clavarse** *vr* : to stick oneself (with a sharp object)

clave[1] *adj* : key, essential

clave[2] *nf* **1** CIFRA : code **2** : key ⟨la clave del misterio : the key to the mystery⟩ **3** : clef **4** : keystone

clavel *nm* : carnation

clavelito *nm* : pink (flower)

clavicémbalo *nm* : harpsichord
clavícula *nf* : collarbone
clavija *nf* **1** : plug **2** : peg, pin
clavo *nm* **1** : nail ⟨clavo grande : spike⟩ **2** : clove **3 dar en el clavo** : to hit the nail on the head
claxon *nm, pl* **cláxones** : horn (of an automobile)
clemencia *nf* : clemency, mercy
clemente *adj* : merciful
cleptomanía *nf* : kleptomania
cleptómano, -na *n* : kleptomaniac
clerecía *nf* : ministry, ministers *pl*
clerical *adj* : clerical
clérigo, -ga *n* : cleric, member of the clergy
clero *nm* : clergy
cliché *nm* **1** : cliché **2** : stencil **3** : negative (of a photograph)
cliente, -ta *n* : customer, client
clientela *nf* : clientele, customers *pl*
clima *nm* **1** : climate **2** AMBIENTE : atmosphere, ambience
climático, -ca *adj* : climatic
climatización *nf, pl* **-ciones** : air-conditioning
climatizar {21} *vt* : to air-condition — **climatizado, -da** *adj*
clímax *nm* : climax
clínica *nf* : clinic
clínico, -ca *adj* : clinical — **clínicamente** *adv*
clip *nm, pl* **clips 1** : clip **2** : paper clip
clítoris *nms & pl* : clitoris
cloaca *nf* ALCANTARILLA : sewer
clocar {82} *vi* : to cluck
cloche *nm* CA, Car, Col, Ven : clutch (of an automobile)
clon *nm* : clone
cloqué, etc. → clocar
cloquear *vi* : to cluck
clorar *vt* : to chlorinate — **cloración** *nf*
cloro *nm* : chlorine
clorofila *nf* : chlorophyll
cloroformo *nm* : chloroform
cloruro *nm* : chloride
clóset *nm, pl* **clósets 1** : closet **2** : cupboard
club *nm* : club
clueca, clueque etc. → clocar
coa *nf Mex* : hoe
coacción *nf, pl* **-ciones** : coercion, duress
coaccionar *vt* : to coerce
coactivo, -va *adj* : coercive
coagular *v* : to clot, to coagulate — **coagulación** *nf*
coágulo *nm* : clot
coalición *nf, pl* **-ciones** : coalition
coartada *nf* : alibi
coartar *vt* : to restrict, to limit
cobalto *nm* : cobalt
cobarde[1] *adj* : cowardly
cobarde[2] *nmf* : coward
cobardía *nf* : cowardice
cobaya *nf* : guinea pig
cobertizo *nm* : shed, shelter
cobertor *nm* COLCHA : bedspread, quilt

cobertura *nf* **1** : coverage **2** : cover, collateral
cobija *nf* FRAZADA, MANTA : blanket
cobijar *vt* : to shelter — **cobijarse** *vr* : to take shelter
cobra *nf* : cobra
cobrador, -dora *n* **1** : collector **2** : conductor (of a bus or train)
cobrar *vt* **1** : to charge **2** : to collect, to draw, to earn **3** : to acquire, to gain **4** : to recover, to retrieve **5** : to cash (a check) **6** : to claim, to take (a life) **7** : to shoot (game), to bag — *vi* **1** : to be paid **2 llamar por cobrar** *Mex* : to call collect
cobre *nm* : copper
cobrizo, -za *adj* : coppery
cobro *nm* : collection (of money), cashing (of a check)
coca *nf* **1** : coca **2** *fam* : coke, cocaine
cocaína *nf* : cocaine
cocal *nm* : coca plantation
cocción *nf, pl* **cocciones** : cooking
cocear *vi* : to kick (of an animal)
cocer {14} *vt* **1** COCINAR : to cook **2** HERVIR : to boil
cochambre *nmf fam* : filth, grime
cochambroso, -sa *adj* : filthy, grimy
coche *nm* **1** : car, automobile **2** : coach, carriage **3 coche cama** : sleeping car **4 coche fúnebre** : hearse
cochecito *nm* : baby carriage, stroller
cochera *nf* : garage, carport
cochinada *nf fam* **1** : filthy language **2** : disgusting behavior **3** : dirty trick
cochinillo *nm* : suckling pig, piglet
cochino[1], **-na** *adj* **1** : dirty, filthy, disgusting **2** *fam* : rotten, lousy
cochino[2], **-na** *n* : pig, hog
cocido[1], **-da** *adj* **1** : boiled, cooked **2 bien cocido** : well-done
cocido[2] *nm* ESTOFADO, GUISADO : stew
cociente *nm* : quotient
cocimiento *nm* : cooking, baking
cocina *nf* **1** : kitchen **2** : stove **3** : cuisine, cooking
cocinar *v* : to cook
cocinero, -ra *n* : cook, chef
cocineta *nf Mex* : kitchenette
coco *nm* **1** : coconut **2** *fam* : head **3** *fam* : bogeyman
cocoa *nf* : cocoa, hot chocolate
cocodrilo *nm* : crocodile
cocotero *nm* : coconut palm
coctel *or* **cóctel** *nm* **1** : cocktail **2** : cocktail party
coctelera *nf* : cocktail shaker
codazo *nm* **1 darle un codazo a** : to elbow, to nudge **2 abrirse paso a codazos** : to elbow one's way through
codearse *vr* : to rub elbows, to hobnob
códice *nm* : codex, manuscript
codicia *nf* AVARICIA : avarice, covetousness
codiciar *vt* : to covet
codicilo *nm* : codicil
codicioso, -sa *adj* : avaricious, covetous

codificación *nf, pl* **-ciones 1** : codification **2** : coding, encoding
codificar {72} *vt* **1** : to codify **2** : to code, to encode
código *nm* **1** : code **2 código postal** : zip code **3 código morse** : Morse code
codo[1], **-da** *adj Mex* : cheap, stingy
codo[2], **-da** *n Mex* : tightwad, cheapskate
codo[3] *nm* : elbow
codorniz *nf, pl* **-nices** : quail
coeficiente *nm* **1** : coefficient **2 coeficiente intelectual** : IQ, intelligence quotient
coexistir *vi* : to coexist — **coexistencia** *nf*
cofa *nf* : crow's nest
cofre *nm* **1** BAÚL : trunk, chest **2** *Mex* CAPOTE : hood (of a car)
coger {15} *vt* **1** : to seize, to take hold of **2** : to catch **3** : to pick up **4** : to gather, to pick **5** : to gore — **cogerse** *vr* AGARRARSE : to hold on
cogida *nf* **1** : gathering, harvest **2** : goring
cognición *nf, pl* **-ciones** : cognition
cognitivo, -va *adj* : cognitive
cogollo *nm* **1** : heart (of a vegetable) **2** : bud, bulb **3** : core, crux ⟨el cogollo de la cuestión : the heart of the matter⟩
cogote *nm* : scruff, nape
cohabitar *vi* : to cohabit — **cohabitación** *nf*
cohechar *vt* SOBORNAR : to bribe
cohecho *nm* SOBORNO : bribe, bribery
coherencia *nf* : coherence — **coherente** *adj*
cohesión *nf, pl* **-siones** : cohesion
cohesivo, -va *adj* : cohesive
cohete *nm* : rocket
cohibición *nf, pl* **-ciones 1** : (legal) restraint **2** INHIBICIÓN : inhibition
cohibido, -da *adj* : inhibited, shy
cohibir {62} *vt* : to inhibit, to make self-conscious — **cohibirse** *vr* : to feel shy or embarrassed
cohorte *nf* : cohort
coima *nf Arg, Chile, Peru* : bribe
coimear *vt Arg, Chile, Peru* : to bribe
coincidencia *nf* : coincidence
coincidente *adj* **1** : coincident **2** ACORDE : coinciding
coincidir *vi* **1** : to coincide **2** : to agree
coito *nm* : sexual intercourse, coitus
coja, etc. → **coger**
cojear *vi* **1** : to limp **2** : to wobble, to rock **3 cojear del mismo pie** : to be two of a kind
cojera *nf* : limp
cojín *nm, pl* **cojines** : cushion, throw pillow
cojinete *nm* **1** : bearing, bushing **2 cojinete de bola** : ball bearing
cojo[1], **-ja** *adj* **1** : limping, lame **2** : wobbly **3** : weak, ineffectual
cojo[2], **-ja** *n* : lame person

cojones *nmpl usu considered vulgar* **1** : testicles *pl* **2** : guts *pl*, courage
col *nf* **1** REPOLLO : cabbage **2 col de Bruselas** : Brussels sprout **3 col rizada** : kale
cola *nf* **1** RABO : tail ⟨cola de caballo : ponytail⟩ **2** FILA : line (of people) ⟨hacer cola : to wait in line⟩ **3** : cola, drink **4** : train (of a dress) **5** : tails *pl* (of a tuxedo) **6** PEGAMENTO : glue **7** *fam* : buttocks *pl*, rear end
colaboracionista *nmf* : collaborator, traitor
colaborador, -dora *n* **1** : contributor (to a periodical) **2** : collaborator
colaborar *vi* : to collaborate — **colaboración** *nf*
colación *nf, pl* **-ciones 1** : light meal **2** : comparison, collation ⟨sacar a colación : to bring up, to broach⟩ **3** : conferral (of a degree)
colador *nm* **1** : colander, strainer **2** *PRi* : small coffeepot
colapso *nm* **1** : collapse **2** : standstill
colar {19} *vt* : to strain, to filter — **colarse** *vr* **1** : to sneak in, to cut in line, to gate-crash **2** : to slip up, to make a mistake
colateral[1] *adj* : collateral — **colateralmente** *adv*
colateral[2] *nm* : collateral
colcha *nf* COBERTOR : bedspread, quilt
colchón *nm, pl* **colchones 1** : mattress **2** : cushion, padding, buffer
colchoneta *nf* : mat (for gymnastic sports)
colear *vi* **1** : to wag its tail **2 vivito y coleando** *fam* : alive and kicking
colección *nf, pl* **-ciones** : collection
coleccionar *vt* : to collect, to keep a collection of
coleccionista *nmf* : collector
colecta *nf* : collection (of donations)
colectar *vt* : to collect
colectividad *nf* : community, group
colectivo[1], **-va** *adj* : collective — **colectivamente** *adv*
colectivo[2] *nm* **1** : collective **2** *Arg, Bol, Peru* : city bus
colector[1], **-tora** *n* : collector ⟨colector de impuestos : tax collector⟩
colector[2] *nm* **1** : sewer **2** : manifold (of an engine)
colega *nmf* **1** : colleague **2** HOMÓLOGO : counterpart **3** *fam* : buddy
colegiado[1], **-da** *adj* : collegiate
colegiado[2], **-da** *n* **1** ÁRBITRO : referee **2** : member (of a professional association)
colegial[1], **-giala** *adj* **1** : school, collegiate **2** *Mex fam* : green, inexperienced
colegial[2], **-giala** *n* : schoolboy *m*, schoolgirl *f*
colegiatura *nf Mex* : tuition
colegio *nm* **1** : school **2** : college ⟨colegio electoral : electoral college⟩ **3** : professional association

colegir {28} *vt* **1** JUNTAR : to collect, to gather **2** INFERIR : to infer, to deduce
cólera[1] *nm* : cholera
cólera[2] *nf* FURIA, IRA : anger, rage
colérico, -ca *adj* **1** FURIOSO : angry **2** IRRITABLE : irritable
colesterol *nm* : cholesterol
coleta *nf* **1** : ponytail **2** : pigtail
coletazo *nm* : lash, flick (of a tail)
colgado, -da *adj* **1** : hanging, hanged **2** : pending **3 dejar colgado a** : to disappoint, to let down
colgante[1] *adj* : hanging, dangling
colgante[2] *nm* : pendant, charm (on a bracelet)
colgar {16} *vt* **1** : to hang (up), to put up **2** AHORCAR : to hang (someone) **3** : to hang up (a telephone) **4** *fam* : to fail (an exam) — **colgarse** *vr* **1** : to hang, to be suspended **2** AHORCARSE : to hang oneself **3** : to hang up a telephone
colibrí *nm* CHUPAFLOR : hummingbird
cólico *nm* : colic
coliflor *nf* : cauliflower
colilla *nf* : butt (of a cigarette)
colina *nf* CERRO, LOMA : hill
colindante *adj* CONTIGUO : adjacent, neighboring
colindar *vi* : to adjoin, to be adjacent
coliseo *nm* : coliseum
colisión *nf, pl* **-siones** : collision
colisionar *vi* : to collide
collage *nm* : collage
collar *nm* **1** : collar (for an animal) **2** : necklace ⟨collar de perlas : string of pearls⟩
colmado, -da *adj* : heaping
colmar *vt* **1** : to fill to the brim **2** : to fulfill, to satisfy **3** : to heap, to shower ⟨me colmaron de regalos : they showered me with gifts⟩
colmena *nf* : beehive
colmenar *nm* APIARIO : apiary
colmillo *nm* **1** CANINO : canine (tooth), fang **2** : tusk
colmilludo, -da *adj Mex, PRi* : astute, shrewd, crafty
colmo *nm* : height, extreme, limit ⟨el colmo de la locura : the height of folly⟩ ⟨¡eso es el colmo! : that's the last straw!⟩
colocación *nf, pl* **-ciones 1** : placement, placing **2** : position, job **3** : investment
colocar {72} *vt* **1** PONER : to place, to put **2** : to find a job for **3** : to invest — **colocarse** *vr* **1** SITUARSE : to position oneself **2** : to get a job
colofón *nm, pl* **-fones 1** : ending, finale **2** : colophon
colofonia *nf* : rosin
colombiano, -na *adj & n* : Colombian
colon *nm* : (intestinal) colon
colón *nm, pl* **colones** : Costa Rican and Salvadoran unit of currency
colonia *nf* **1** : colony **2** : cologne **3** *Mex* : residential area, neighborhood
colonial *adj* : colonial

colonización *nf, pl* **-ciones** : colonization
colonizador[1], **-dora** *adj* : colonizing
colonizador[2], **-dora** *n* : colonizer, colonist
colonizar {21} *vt* : to colonize, to settle
colono, -na *n* **1** : settler, colonist **2** : tenant farmer
coloquial *adj* : colloquial
coloquio *nm* **1** : discussion, talk **2** : conference, symposium
color *nm* **1** : color **2** : paint, dye **3 colores** *nmpl* : colored pencils
coloración *nf, pl* **-ciones** : coloring, coloration
colorado[1], **-da** *adj* **1** ROJO : red **2 ponerse colorado** : to blush **3 chiste colorado** *Mex* : off-color joke
colorado[2] *nm* ROJO : red
colorante *nm* : coloring ⟨colorante de alimentos : food coloring⟩
colorear *vt* : to color — *vi* **1** : to redden **2** : to ripen
colorete *nm* : rouge, blusher
colorido *nm* : color, coloring
colorín *nm, pl* **-rines 1** : bright color **2** : goldfinch
colosal *adj* : colossal
coloso *nm* : colossus
coludir *vi* : to be in collusion, to conspire
columna *nf* **1** : column **2 columna vertebral** : spine, backbone
columnata *nf* : colonnade
columnista *nmf* : columnist
columpiar *vt* : to push (on a swing) — **columpiarse** *vr* : to swing
columpio *nm* : swing
colusión *nf, pl* **-siones** : collusion
colza *nf* : rape (plant)
coma[1] *nm* : coma
coma[2] *nf* : comma
comadre *nf* **1** : godmother of one's child **2** : mother of one's godchild **3** *fam* : neighbor, female friend **4** *fam* : gossip
comadrear *vi fam* : to gossip
comadreja *nf* : weasel
comadrona *nf* : midwife
comanche *nmf* : Comanche
comandancia *nf* **1** : command headquarters **2** : command
comandante *nmf* **1** : commander, commanding officer **2** : major
comandar *vt* : to command, to lead
comando *nm* **1** : commando **2** : command (for computers)
comarca *nf* REGIÓN : region
comarcal *adj* REGIONAL : regional, local
comatoso, -sa *adj* : comatose
combar *vt* : to bend, to curve — **combarse** *vr* **1** : to bend, to buckle **2** : to warp, to bulge, to sag
combate *nm* **1** : combat **2** : fight, boxing match
combatiente *nmf* : combatant, fighter
combatir *vt* : to combat, to fight against — *vi* : to fight

combatividad *nf* : fighting spirit
combativo, -va *adj* : combative, spirited
combinación *nf, pl* -ciones 1 : combination 2 : connection (in travel)
combinar *vt* 1 UNIR : to combine, to mix together 2 : to match, to put together — combinarse *vr* : to get together, to conspire
combo *nm* 1 : (musical) band 2 *Chile, Peru* : sledgehammer 3 *Chile, Peru* : punch
combustible¹ *adj* : combustible
combustible² *nm* : fuel
combustión *nf, pl* -tiones : combustion
comedero *nm* : trough, feeder
comedia *nf* : comedy
comediante *nmf* : actor, actress *f*
comedido, -da *adj* MESURADO : moderate, restrained
comediógrafo, -fa *n* : playwright
comedor *nm* : dining room
comején *nm, pl* -jenes : termite
comelón¹, -lona *adj, mpl* -lones *fam* : gluttonous
comelón², -lona *n, pl* -lones *fam* : big eater, glutton
comensal *nmf* : dinner guest
comentador, -dora *n* → comentarista
comentar *vt* 1 : to comment on, to discuss 2 : to mention, to remark
comentario *nm* 1 : comment, remark ⟨sin comentarios : no comment⟩ 2 : commentary
comentarista *nmf* : commentator
comenzar {29} *v* EMPEZAR : to begin, to start
comer¹ *vt* 1 : to eat 2 : to consume, to eat up, to eat into — *vi* 1 : to eat 2 CENAR : to have a meal 3 dar de comer : to feed — comerse *vr* : to eat up
comer² *nm* : eating, dining
comercial *adj & nm* : commercial — comercialmente *adv*
comercializar {21} *vt* 1 : to commercialize 2 : to market
comerciante *nmf* : merchant, dealer
comerciar *vi* : to do business, to trade
comercio *nm* 1 : commerce, trade 2 NEGOCIO : business, place of business
comestible *adj* : edible
comestibles *nmpl* VÍVERES : groceries, food
cometa¹ *nm* : comet
cometa² *nf* : kite
cometer *vt* 1 : to commit 2 cometer un error : to make a mistake
cometido *nm* : assignment, task
comezón *nf, pl* -zones PICAZÓN : itchiness, itching
comible *adj fam* : eatable, edible
comic *or* cómic *nm* : comic strip, comic book
comicastro, -tra *n* : second-rate actor, ham
comicidad *nf* HUMOR : humor, wit
comicios *nmpl* : elections, voting
cómico¹, -ca *adj* : comic, comical

cómico², -ca *n* HUMORISTA : comic, comedian, comedienne *f*
comida *nf* 1 : food 2 : meal 3 : dinner 4 comida basura : junk food 5 comida rápida : fast food
comidilla *nf* : talk, gossip
comienzo *nm* 1 : start, beginning 2 al comienzo : at first 3 dar comienzo : to begin
comillas *nfpl* : quotation marks ⟨entre comillas : in quotes⟩
comilón, -lona → comelón, -lona
comilona *nf fam* : feast
comino *nm* 1 : cumin 2 me vale un comino *fam* : not to matter to someone ⟨no me importa un comino : I couldn't care less⟩
comisaría *nf* : police station
comisario, -ria *n* : commissioner
comisión *nf, pl* -siones 1 : commission, committing 2 : committee 3 : percentage, commission ⟨comisión sobre las ventas : sales commission⟩
comisionado¹, -da *adj* : commissioned, entrusted
comisionado², -da *n* → comisario
comisionar *vt* : to commission
comité *nm* : committee
comitiva *nf* : retinue, entourage
como¹ *adv* 1 : around, about ⟨cuesta como 500 pesos : it costs around 500 pesos⟩ 2 : kind of, like ⟨tengo como mareos : I'm kind of dizzy⟩
como² *conj* 1 : how, as ⟨hazlo como dijiste que lo harías : do it the way you said you would⟩ 2 : since, given that ⟨como estaba lloviendo, no salí : since it was raining, I didn't go out⟩ 3 : if ⟨como lo vuelva a hacer lo arrestarán : if he does that again he'll be arrested⟩ 4 como quiera : in any way
como³ *prep* 1 : like, as ⟨ligero como una pluma : light as a feather⟩ 2 así como : as well as
cómo *adv* : how ⟨¿cómo estás? : how are you?⟩ ⟨¿a cómo están las manzanas? : how much are the apples?⟩ ⟨¿cómo? : excuse me?, what was that?⟩ ⟨¿se puede? ¡cómo no! : may I? please do!⟩
cómoda *nf* : bureau, chest of drawers
comodidad *nf* 1 : comfort 2 : convenience
comodín *nm, pl* -dines 1 : joker, wild card 2 : all-purpose word or thing 3 : pretext, excuse
cómodo, -da *adj* 1 CONFORTABLE : comfortable 2 : convenient — cómodamente *adv*
comodoro *nm* : commodore
comoquiera *adv* 1 : in any way 2 comoquiera que : in whatever way, however ⟨comoquiera que sea eso : however that may be⟩
compa *nm fam* : buddy, pal
compactar *vt* : to compact, to compress
compacto, -ta *adj* : compact

compadecer {53} *vt* : to sympathize with, to feel sorry for — **compadecerse** *vr* **1** ~ **de** : to take pity on, to commiserate with **2** ~ **con** : to fit, to accord (with)

compadre *nm* **1** : godfather of one's child **2** : father of one's godchild **3** *fam* : buddy, pal

compaginar *vt* **1** COORDINAR : to combine, to coordinate **2** : to collate

compañerismo *nm* : comradeship, camaraderie

compañero, -ra *n* : companion, mate, partner

compañía *nf* **1** : company ⟨llegó en compañía de su madre : he arrived with his mother⟩ **2** EMPRESA, FIRMA : firm, company

comparable *adj* : comparable

comparación *nf, pl* **-ciones** : comparison

comparado, -da *adj* : comparative ⟨literatura comparada : comparative literature⟩

comparar *vt* : to compare

comparativo¹, -va *adj* : comparative, relative — **comparativamente** *adv*

comparativo² *nm* : comparative degree or form

comparecencia *nf* **1** : appearance (in court) **2 orden de comparecencia** : subpoena, summons

comparecer {53} *vi* : to appear (in court)

compartimiento *or* **compartimento** *nm* : compartment

compartir *vt* : to share

compás *nm, pl* **-pases 1** : beat, rhythm, time **2** : compass

compasión *nf, pl* **-siones** : compassion, pity

compasivo, -va *adj* : compassionate, sympathetic

compatibilidad *nf* : compatibility

compatible *adj* : compatible

compatriota *nmf* PAISANO : compatriot, fellow countryman

compeler *vt* : to compel

compendiar *vt* : to summarize, to condense

compendio *nm* : summary

compenetración *nf, pl* **-ciones** : rapport, mutual understanding

compenetrarse *vr* **1** : to understand each other **2** ~ **con** : to identify oneself with

compensación *nf, pl* **-ciones** : compensation

compensar *vt* : to compensate for, to make up for — *vi* : to be worth one's while

compensatorio, -ria *adj* : compensatory

competencia *nf* **1** : competition, rivalry **2** : competence

competente *adj* : competent, able — **competentemente** *adv*

competición *nf, pl* **-ciones** : competition

competidor¹, -dora *adj* RIVAL : competing, rival

competidor², -dora *n* RIVAL : competitor, rival

competir {54} *vi* : to compete

competitividad *nf* : competitiveness

competitivo, -va *adj* : competitive — **competitivamente** *adv*

compilar *vt* : to compile — **compilación** *nf*

compinche *nmf fam* **1** : buddy, pal **2** : partner in crime, accomplice

complacencia *nf* : pleasure, satisfaction

complacer {57} *vt* : to please — **complacerse** *vr* ~ **en** : to take pleasure in

complaciente *adj* : obliging, eager to please

complejidad *nf* : complexity

complejo¹, -ja *adj* : complex

complejo² *nm* : complex

complementar *vt* : to complement, to supplement — **complementarse** *vr*

complementario, -ria *adj* : complementary

complemento *nm* **1** : complement, supplement **2** : supplementary pay, allowance

completamente *adv* : completely, totally

completar *vt* TERMINAR : to complete, to finish

completo, -ta *adj* **1** : complete **2** : perfect, absolute **3** : full, detailed

complexión *nf, pl* **-xiones** : (physical) constitution

complicación *nf, pl* **-ciones** : complication

complicado, -da *adj* : complicated

complicar {72} *vt* **1** : to complicate **2** : to involve — **complicarse** *vr*

cómplice *nmf* : accomplice

complicidad *nf* : complicity

complot *nm, pl* **complots** CONFABULACIÓN, CONSPIRACIÓN : conspiracy, plot

componenda *nf* : shady deal, scam

componente *adj* & *nm* : component, constituent

componer {60} *vt* **1** ARREGLAR : to fix, to repair **2** CONSTITUIR : to make up, to compose **3** : to compose, to write **4** : to set (a bone) — **componerse** *vr* **1** : to improve, to get better **2** ~ **de** : to consist of

comportamiento *nm* CONDUCTA : behavior, conduct

comportarse *vr* : to behave, to conduct oneself

composición *nf, pl* **-ciones 1** OBRA : composition, work **2** : makeup, arrangement

compositor, -tora *n* : composer, songwriter

compostura *nf* **1** : composure **2** : mending, repair

compra *nf* **1** : purchase **2 ir de compras** : to go shopping **3 orden de compra** : purchase order

comprador, -dora *n* : buyer, shopper
comprar *vt* : to buy, to purchase
compraventa *nf* : buying and selling
comprender *vt* **1** ENTENDER : to comprehend, to understand **2** ABARCAR : to cover, to include — *vi* : to understand ⟨¡ya comprendo! : now I understand!⟩
comprensible *adj* : understandable — **comprensiblemente** *adv*
comprensión *nf, pl* **-siones 1** : comprehension, understanding, grasp **2** : understanding, sympathy
comprensivo, -va *adj* : understanding
compresa *nf* **1** : compress **2** *or* **compresa higiénica** : sanitary napkin
compresión *nf, pl* **-siones** : compression
compresor *nm* : compressor
comprimido *nm* PÍLDORA, TABLETA : pill, tablet
comprimir *vt* : to compress
comprobable *adj* : verifiable, provable
comprobación *nf, pl* **-ciones** : verification, confirmation
comprobante *nm* **1** : proof ⟨comprobante de identidad : proof of identity⟩ **2** : voucher, receipt ⟨comprobante de ventas : sales slip⟩
comprobar {19} *vt* **1** : to verify, to check **2** : to prove
comprometedor, -dora *adj* : compromising
comprometer *vt* **1** : to compromise **2** : to jeopardize **3** : to commit, to put under obligation — **comprometerse** *vr* **1** : to commit oneself **2** ~ **con** : to get engaged to
comprometido, -da *adj* **1** : compromising, awkward **2** : committed, obliged **3** : engaged (to be married)
compromiso *nm* **1** : obligation, commitment **2** : engagement ⟨anillo de compromiso : engagement ring⟩ **3** : agreement **4** : awkward situation, fix
compuerta *nf* : floodgate
compuesto¹ *pp* → **componer**
compuesto², -ta *adj* **1** : fixed, repaired **2** : compound, composite **3** : decked out, spruced up **4** ~ **de** : made up of, consisting of
compuesto³ *nm* : compound
compulsión *nf, pl* **-siones** : compulsion
compulsivo, -va *adj* **1** : compelling, urgent **2** : compulsive — **compulsivamente** *adv*
compungido, -da *adj* : contrite, remorseful
compungirse {35} *vr* : to feel remorse
compuso, etc. → **componer**
computable *adj* : countable ⟨años computables : years accrued⟩ ⟨ingresos computables : qualifying income⟩
computación *nf, pl* **-ciones** : computing, computers *pl*
computador *nm* → **computadora**
computadora *nf* **1** : computer **2** **computadora portátil** : laptop computer

computar *vt* : to compute, to calculate
computarizar {21} *vt* : to computerize
cómputo *nm* : computation, calculation
comulgar {52} *vi* : to receive Communion
común *adj, pl* **comunes 1** : common **2** **común y corriente** : ordinary, regular **3** **por lo común** : generally, as a rule
comuna *nf* : commune
comunal *adj* : communal
comunicación *nf, pl* **-ciones 1** : communication **2** : access, link **3** : message, report
comunicado *nm* **1** : communiqué **2** **comunicado de prensa** : press release
comunicar {72} *vt* **1** : to communicate, to convey **2** : to notify — **comunicarse** *vr* ~ **con 1** : to contact, to get in touch with **2** : to be connected to
comunicativo, -va *adj* : communicative, talkative
comunidad *nf* : community
comunión *nf, pl* **-niones 1** : communion, sharing **2** : Communion
comunismo *nm* : communism, Communism
comunista *adj & nmf* : communist
comúnmente *adv* : commonly
con *prep* **1** : with ⟨vengo con mi padre : I'm going with my father⟩ ⟨¿con quién hablas? : who are you speaking to?⟩ **2** : in spite of ⟨con todo : in spite of it all⟩ **3** : to, towards ⟨ella es amable con los niños : she is kind to the children⟩ **4** : by ⟨con llegar temprano : by arriving early⟩ **5 con (tal) que** : as long as, so long as
conato *nm* : attempt, effort ⟨conato de robo : attempted robbery⟩
cóncavo, -va *adj* : concave
concebible *adj* : conceivable
concebir {54} *vt* **1** : to conceive **2** : to conceive of, to imagine — *vi* : to conceive, to become pregnant
conceder *vt* **1** : to grant, to bestow **2** : to concede, to admit
concejal, -jala *n* : councilman *m*, councilwoman *f*, alderman *m*, alderwoman *f*
concejo *nm* : council ⟨concejo municipal : town council⟩
concentración *nf, pl* **-ciones** : concentration
concentrado *nm* : concentrate
concentrar *vt* : to concentrate — **concentrarse** *vr*
concéntrico, -ca *adj* : concentric
concepción *nf, pl* **-ciones** : conception
concepto *nm* NOCIÓN : concept, idea, opinion
conceptuar {3} *vt* : to regard, to judge
concernir {17} *vi* : to be of concern
concertar {55} *vt* **1** : to arrange, to set up **2** : to agree on, to settle **3** : to harmonize — *vi* : to be in harmony
concesión *nf, pl* **-siones 1** : concession **2** : awarding, granting
concha *nf* : conch, seashell

conciencia *nf* **1** : conscience **2** : consciousness, awareness
concientizar {21} *vt* : to make aware —
　concientizarse *vr* ~ **de** : to realize, to become aware of
concienzudo, -da *adj* : conscientious
concierto *nm* **1** : concert **2** : agreement **3** : concerto
conciliador[1], **-dora** *adj* : conciliatory
conciliador[2], **-dora** *n* : arbitrator, peacemaker
conciliar *vt* : to conciliate, to reconcile — **conciliación** *nf*
conciliatorio, -ria *adj* → **conciliador**[1]
concilio *nm* : (church) council
conciso, -sa *adj* : concise — **concisión** *nf*
conciudadano, -na *n* : fellow citizen
cónclave *nm* : conclave, private meeting
concluir {41} *vt* **1** TERMINAR : to conclude, to finish **2** DEDUCIR : to deduce, to infer — *vi* : to end, to conclude
conclusión *nf, pl* **-siones** : conclusion
concluyente *adj* : conclusive
concomitante *adj* : concomitant
concordancia *nf* : agreement, accordance
concordar {19} *vi* : to agree, to coincide — *vt* : to reconcile
concordia *nf* : concord, harmony
concretar *vt* **1** : to pinpoint, to specify **2** : to fulfill, to realize — **concretarse** *vr* : to become real, to take shape
concretizar → **concretar**
concreto[1], **-ta** *adj* **1** : concrete, actual **2** : definite, specific ⟨en concreto : specifically⟩ — **concretamente** *adv*
concreto[2] *nm* HORMIGÓN : concrete
concubina *nf* : concubine
concurrencia *nf* **1** : audience, turnout **2** : concurrence
concurrente *adj* : concurrent — **concurrentemente** *adv*
concurrido, -da *adj* : busy, crowded
concurrir *vi* **1** : to converge, to come together **2** : to concur, to agree **3** : to take part, to participate **4** : to attend, to be present ⟨concurrir a una reunión : to attend a meeting⟩ **5** ~ **a** : to contribute to
concursante *nmf* : contestant, competitor
concursar *vt* : to compete in — *vi* : to compete, to participate
concurso *nm* **1** : contest, competition **2** : concurrence, coincidence **3** : crowd, gathering **4** : cooperation, assistance
condado *nm* **1** : county **2** : earldom
conde, -desa *n* : count *m*, earl *m*, countess *f*
condecoración *nf, pl* **-ciones** : decoration, medal
condecorar *vt* : to decorate, to award (a medal)
condena *nf* **1** REPROBACIÓN : disapproval, condemnation **2** SENTENCIA : sentence, conviction

condenable *adj* : reprehensible
condenación *nf, pl* **-ciones** **1** : condemnation **2** : damnation
condenado[1], **-da** *adj* **1** : fated, doomed **2** : convicted, sentenced **3** *fam* : darn, damned
condenado[2], **-da** *n* : convict
condenar *vt* **1** : to condemn **2** : to sentence **3** : to board up, to wall up — **condenarse** *vr* : to be damned
condensación *nf, pl* **-ciones** : condensation
condensar *vt* : to condense
condesa *nf* → **conde**
condescendencia *nf* : condescension
condescender {56} *vi* **1** : to condescend **2** : to agree, to acquiesce
condición *nf, pl* **-ciones** **1** : condition, state **2** : capacity, position **3** **condiciones** *nfpl* : conditions, circumstances ⟨condiciones de vida : living conditions⟩
condicional *adj* : conditional — **condicionalmente** *adv*
condicionamiento *nm* : conditioning
condicionar *vt* **1** : to condition, to determine **2** ~ **a** : to be contingent on, to depend on
condimentar *vt* SAZONAR : to season, to spice
condimento *nm* : condiment, seasoning, spice
condiscípulo, -la *n* : classmate
condolencia *nf* : condolence, sympathy
condolerse {47} *vr* : to sympathize
condominio *nm* : condominium, condo
condón *nm, pl* **condones** : condom
cóndor *nm* : condor
conducción *nf, pl* **-ciones** **1** : conduction (of electricity, etc.) **2** DIRECCIÓN : management, direction
conducir {61} *vt* **1** DIRIGIR, GUIAR : to direct, to lead **2** MANEJAR : to drive (a vehicle) — *vi* **1** : to drive a vehicle **2** ~ **a** : to lead to — **conducirse** *vr* PORTARSE : to behave, to conduct oneself
conducta *nf* COMPORTAMIENTO : conduct, behavior
conducto *nm* : conduit, channel, duct
conductor[1], **-tora** *adj* : conducting, leading
conductor[2], **-tora** *n* : driver
conductor[3] *nm* : conductor (of electricity, etc.)
conectar *vt* : to connect — *vi* ~ **con** : to link up with, to communicate with
conector *nm* : connector
conejera *nf* : rabbit hutch
conejillo *nm* **conejillo de Indias** : guinea pig
conejo, -ja *n* : rabbit
conexión *nf, pl* **-xiones** : connection
confabulación *nf, pl* **-ciones** COMPLOT, CONSPIRACIÓN : plot, conspiracy
confabularse *vr* : to plot, to conspire
confección *nf, pl* **-ciones** **1** : preparation **2** : tailoring, dressmaking
confeccionar *vt* : to make, to produce, to prepare

confederación *nf, pl* **-ciones** : confederation

confederarse *vr* : to confederate, to form a confederation

conferencia *nf* **1** REUNIÓN : conference, meeting **2** : lecture

conferenciante *nmf* : lecturer

conferencista → **conferenciante**

conferir {76} *vt* : to confer, to bestow

confesar {55} *v* : to confess — **confesarse** *vr* : to go to confession

confesión *nf, pl* **-siones 1** : confession **2** : creed, denomination

confesionario *nm* : confessional

confesor *nm* : confessor

confeti *nm* : confetti

confiable *adj* : trustworthy, reliable

confiado, -da *adj* **1** : confident, self-confident **2** : trusting — **confiadamente** *adv*

confianza *nf* **1** : trust ⟨de poca confianza⟩ : untrustworthy⟩ **2** : confidence, self-confidence

confianzudo, -da *adj* : forward, presumptuous

confiar {85} *vi* : to have trust, to be trusting — *vt* **1** : to confide **2** : to entrust — **confiarse** *vr* **1** : to be overconfident **2** ~ **a** : to confide in

confidencia *nf* : confidence, secret

confidencial *adj* : confidential — **confidencialmente** *adv*

confidencialidad *nf* : confidentiality

confidente *nmf* **1** : confidant, confidante *f* **2** : informer

configuración *nf, pl* **-ciones** : configuration, shape

configurar *vt* : to shape, to form

confín *nm, pl* **confines** : boundary, limit

confinamiento *nm* : confinement

confinar *vt* **1** : to confine, to limit **2** : to exile — *vi* ~ **con** : to border on

confirmación *nf, pl* **-ciones** : confirmation

confirmar *vt* : to confirm, to substantiate

confiscación *nf, pl* **-ciones** : confiscation

confiscar {72} *vt* DECOMISAR : to confiscate, to seize

confitado, -da *adj* : candied

confite *nm* : comfit, candy

confitería *nf* **1** DULCERÍA : candy store, confectionery **2** : tearoom, café

confitero, -ra *n* : confectioner

confitura *nf* : preserves, jam

conflagración *nf, pl* **-ciones 1** : conflagration, fire **2** : war

conflictivo, -va *adj* **1** : troubled **2** : controversial

conflicto *nm* : conflict

confluencia *nf* : junction, confluence

confluir {41} *vi* **1** : to converge, to join **2** : to gather, to assemble

conformar *vt* **1** : to form, to create **2** : to constitute, to make up — **conformarse** *vr* **1** RESIGNARSE : to resign

oneself **2** : to comply, to conform **3** ~ **con** : to content oneself with, to be satisfied with

conforme[1] *adj* **1** : content, satisfied **2** ~ **a** : in accordance with

conforme[2] *conj* : as ⟨entreguen sus tareas conforme vayan saliendo : hand in your homework as you leave⟩

conformidad *nf* **1** : agreement, consent **2** : resignation

confort *nm* : comfort

confortable *adj* CÓMODO : comfortable

confortar *vt* CONSOLAR : to comfort, to console

confraternidad *nf* : brotherhood, fraternity

confraternización *nf, pl* **-ciones** : fraternization

confraternizar *vi* : to fraternize

confrontación *nf, pl* **-ciones** : confrontation

confrontar *vt* **1** ENCARAR : to confront **2** : to compare **3** : to bring face-to-face — *vi* : to border — **confrontarse** *vr* ~ **con** : to face up to

confundir *vt* : to confuse, to mix up — **confundirse** *vr* : to make a mistake, to be confused ⟨confundirse de número : to get the wrong number⟩

confusión *nf, pl* **-siones** : confusion

confuso, -sa *adj* **1** : confused, mixed-up **2** : obscure, indistinct

congelación *nf, pl* **-ciones 1** : freezing **2** : frostbite

congelado, -da *adj* HELADO : frozen

congelador *nm* HELADORA : freezer

congelamiento *nm* → **congelación**

congelar *vt* : to freeze — **congelarse** *vr*

congeniar *vi* : to get along (with someone)

congénito, -ta *adj* : congenital

congestión *nf, pl* **-tiones** : congestion

congestionado, -da *adj* : congested

congestionamiento *nm* → **congestión**

congestionarse *vr* **1** : to become flushed **2** : to become congested

conglomerado[1]**, -da** *adj* : conglomerate, mixed

conglomerado[2] *nm* : conglomerate, conglomeration

congoja *nf* ANGUSTIA : anguish, grief

congoleño, -ña *adj & n* : Congolese

congraciarse *vr* : to ingratiate oneself

congratular *vt* FELICITAR : to congratulate

congregación *nf, pl* **-ciones** : congregation, gathering

congregar {52} *vt* : to bring together — **congregarse** *vr* : to congregate, to assemble

congresista *nmf* : congressman *m*, congresswoman *f*

congreso *nm* : congress, conference

congruencia *nf* **1** : congruence **2** COHERENCIA : coherence — **congruente** *adj*

cónico, -ca *adj* : conical, conic

conífera *nf* : conifer

conífero, -ra *adj* : coniferous
conjetura *nf* : conjecture, guess
conjeturar *vt* : to guess, to conjecture
conjugación *nf, pl* **-ciones** : conjugation
conjugar {52} *vt* **1** : to conjugate **2** : to combine
conjunción *nf, pl* **-ciones** : conjunction
conjuntivo, -va *adj* : connective ⟨tejido conjuntivo : connective tissue⟩
conjunto¹, -ta *adj* : joint
conjunto² *nm* **1** : collection, group **2** : ensemble, outfit ⟨conjunto musical : musical ensemble⟩ **3** : whole, entirety ⟨en conjunto : as a whole, altogether⟩
conjurar *vt* **1** : to exorcise **2** : to avert, to ward off — *vi* CONSPIRAR : to conspire, to plot
conjuro *nm* **1** : exorcism **2** : spell
conllevar *vt* **1** : to bear, to suffer **2** IMPLICAR : to entail, to involve
conmemorar *vt* : to commemorate — **conmemoración** *nf*
conmemorativo, -va *adj* : commemorative, memorial
conmigo *pron* : with me ⟨habló conmigo : he talked with me⟩
conminar *vt* AMENAZAR : to threaten, to warn
conmiseración *nf, pl* **-ciones** : pity, commiseration
conmoción *nf, pl* **-ciones** **1** : shock, upheaval **2** *or* **conmoción cerebral** : concussion
conmocionar *vt* : to shake, to shock
conmovedor, -dora *adj* EMOCIONANTE : moving, touching
conmover {47} *vt* **1** EMOCIONAR : to move, to touch **2** : to shake up — **conmoverse** *vr*
conmutador *nm* **1** : switch **2** : switchboard
conmutar *vt* **1** : to commute (a sentence) **2** : to switch, to exchange
connivencia *nf* : connivance
connotación *nf, pl* **-ciones** : connotation
connotar *vt* : to connote, to imply
cono *nm* : cone
conocedor¹, -dora *adj* : knowledgeable
conocedor², -dora *n* : connoisseur, expert
conocer {18} *vt* **1** : to know, to be acquainted with ⟨ya lo conocí : I've already met him⟩ **2** : to meet **3** RECONOCER : to recognize — **conocerse** *vr* **1** : to know each other **2** : to meet **3** : to know oneself
conocido¹, -da *adj* **1** : familiar **2** : well-known, famous
conocido², -da *n* : acquaintance
conocimiento *nm* **1** : knowledge **2** SENTIDO : consciousness
conque *conj* : so, so then, and so ⟨¡ah, conque esas tenemos! : oh, so that's what's going on!⟩
conquista *nf* : conquest
conquistador¹, -dora *adj* : conquering

conquistador², -dora *n* : conqueror
conquistar *vt* : to conquer
consabido, -da *adj* : usual, typical
consagración *nf, pl* **-ciones** : consecration
consagrar *vt* **1** : to consecrate **2** DEDICAR : to dedicate, to devote
consciencia → **conciencia**
consciente *adj* : conscious, aware — **conscientemente** *adv*
conscripción *nf, pl* **-ciones** : conscription, draft
conscripto, -ta *n* : conscript, inductee
consecución *nf, pl* **-ciones** : attainment
consecuencia *nf* **1** : consequence, result ⟨a consecuencia de : as a result of⟩ **2** en ~ : accordingly
consecuente *adj* : consistent — **consecuentemente** *adv*
consecutivo, -va *adj* : consecutive, successive — **consecutivamente** *adv*
conseguir {75} *vt* **1** : to get, to obtain **2** : to achieve, to attain **3** : to manage to ⟨consiguió acabar el trabajo : she managed to finish the job⟩
consejero, -ra *n* : adviser, counselor
consejo *nm* **1** : advice, counsel **2** : council ⟨consejo de guerra : court-martial⟩
consenso *nm* : consensus
consentido, -da *adj* : spoiled, pampered
consentimiento *nm* : consent, permission
consentir {76} *vt* **1** PERMITIR : to consent to, to allow **2** MIMAR : to pamper, to spoil — *vi* ~ **en** : to agree to, to approve of
conserje *nmf* : custodian, janitor, caretaker
conserva *nf* **1** : preserve(s), jam **2** **conservas** *nfpl* : canned goods
conservación *nf, pl* **-ciones** : conservation, preservation
conservacionista *nmf* : conservationist
conservador¹, -dora *adj & n* : conservative
conservador² *nm* : preservative
conservadurismo *nf* : conservatism
conservante *nm* : preservative
conservar *vt* **1** : to preserve **2** GUARDAR : to keep, to conserve
conservatorio *nm* : conservatory
considerable *adj* : considerable — **considerablemente** *adv*
consideración *nf, pl* **-ciones** **1** : consideration **2** : respect **3** de ~ : considerable, important
considerado, -da *adj* **1** : considerate, thoughtful **2** : respected
considerar *vt* **1** : to consider, to think over **2** : to judge, to deem **3** : to treat with respect
consigna *nf* **1** ESLOGAN : slogan **2** : assignment, orders *pl* **3** : checkroom
consignación *nf, pl* **-ciones** **1** : consignment **2** ASIGNACIÓN : allocation
consignar *vt* **1** : to consign **2** : to record, to write down **3** : to assign, to allocate

consigo *pron* : with her, with him, with you, with oneself ⟨se llevó las llaves consigo : she took the keys with her⟩

consiguiente *adj* **1** : resulting, consequent **2 por** ∼ : consequently, as a result

consistencia *nf* : consistency

consistente *adj* **1** : firm, strong, sound **2** : consistent — **consistentemente** *adv*

consistir *vi* **1** ∼ **en** : to consist of **2** ∼ **en** : to lie in, to consist in

consola *nf* : console

consolación *nf, pl* **-ciones** : consolation ⟨premio de consolación : consolation prize⟩

consolar {19} *vt* CONFORTAR : to console, to comfort

consolidar *vt* : to consolidate — **consolidación** *nf*

consomé *nm* CALDO : consommé, clear soup

consonancia *nf* **1** : consonance, harmony **2 en consonancia con** : in accordance with

consonante[1] *adj* : consonant, harmonious

consonante[2] *nf* : consonant

consorcio *nm* : consortium

consorte *nmf* : consort, spouse

conspicuo, -cua *adj* : eminent, famous

conspiración *nf, pl* **-ciones** COMPLOT, CONFABULACIÓN : conspiracy, plot

conspirador, -dora *n* : conspirator

conspirar *vi* CONJURAR : to conspire, to plot

constancia *nf* **1** PRUEBA : proof, certainty **2** : record, evidence ⟨que quede constancia : for the record⟩ **3** : perseverance, constancy

constante[1] *adj* : constant — **constantemente** *adv*

constante[2] *nf* : constant

constar *vi* **1** : to be evident, to be on record ⟨que conste : believe me, have no doubt⟩ **2** ∼ **de** : to consist of

constatación *nf, pl* **-ciones** : confirmation, proof

constatar *vt* **1** : to verify **2** : to state

constelación *nf, pl* **-ciones** : constellation

consternación *nf, pl* **-ciones** : consternation, dismay

consternar *vt* : to dismay, to appall

constipación *nf, pl* **-ciones** : constipation

constipado[1], **-da** *adj* **estar constipado** : to have a cold

constipado[2] *nm* RESFRIADO : cold

constiparse *vr* : to catch a cold

constitución *nf, pl* **-ciones** : constitution — **constitucional** *adj* — **constitucionalmente** *adv*

constitucionalidad *nf* : constitutionality

constituir {41} *vt* **1** FORMAR : to constitute, to make up, to form **2** FUNDAR : to establish, to set up — **constituirse**

vr ∼ **en** : to set oneself up as, to become

constitutivo, -va *adj* : constituent, component

constituyente *adj & nmf* : constituent

constreñir {67} *vt* **1** FORZAR, OBLIGAR : to constrain, to oblige **2** LIMITAR : to restrict, to limit

construcción *nf, pl* **-ciones** : construction, building

constructivo, -va *adj* : constructive — **constructivamente** *adv*

constructor, -tora *n* : builder

constructora *nf* : construction company

construir {41} *vt* : to build, to construct

consuelo *nm* : consolation, comfort

consuetudinario, -ria *adj* **1** : customary, habitual **2 derecho consuetudinario** : common law

cónsul *nmf* : consul — **consular** *adj*

consulado *nm* : consulate

consulta *nf* **1** : consultation **2** : inquiry

consultar *vt* : to consult

consultor[1], **-tora** *adj* : consulting ⟨firma consultora : consulting firm⟩

consultor[2], **-tora** *n* : consultant

consultorio *nm* : office (of a doctor or dentist)

consumación *nf, pl* **-ciones** : consummation

consumado, -da *adj* : consummate, perfect

consumar *vt* **1** : to consummate, to complete **2** : to commit, to carry out

consumible *adj* : consumable

consumición *nf, pl* **-ciones** **1** : consumption **2** : drink (in a restaurant)

consumido, -da *adj* : thin, emaciated

consumidor, -dora *n* : consumer

consumir *vt* : to consume — **consumirse** *vr* : to waste away

consumo *nm* : consumption

contabilidad *nf* **1** : accounting, bookkeeping **2** : accountancy

contabilizar {21} *vt* : to enter, to record (in accounting)

contable[1] *adj* : countable

contable[2] *nmf Spain* : accountant, bookkeeper

contactar *vt* : to contact — *vi* ∼ **con** : to get in touch with, to contact

contacto *nm* : contact

contado[1], **-da** *adj* **1** : counted ⟨tenía los días contados : his days were numbered⟩ **2** : rare, scarce ⟨en contadas ocasiones : on rare occasions⟩

contado[2] *nm* **al contado** : cash ⟨pagar al contado : to pay in cash⟩

contador[1], **-dora** *n* : accountant

contador[2] *nm* : meter ⟨contador de agua : water meter⟩

contaduría *nf* **1** : accounting office **2** CONTABILIDAD : accountancy

contagiar *vt* **1** : to infect **2** : to transmit (a disease) — **contagiarse** *vr* **1** : to be contagious **2** : to become infected

contagio *nm* : contagion, infection

contagioso, -sa *adj* : contagious, catching

contaminación *nf, pl* **-ciones** : contamination, pollution

contaminante *nm* : pollutant, contaminant

contaminar *vt* : to contaminate, to pollute

contar {19} *vt* **1** : to count **2** : to tell **3** : to include — *vi* **1** : to count (up) **2** : to matter, to be of concern ⟨eso no cuenta : that doesn't matter⟩ **3** ~ **con** : to rely on, to count on — **contarse** *vr* ~ **entre** : to be numbered among

contemplación *nf, pl* **-ciones** : contemplation — **contemplativo, -va** *adj*

contemplar *vt* **1** : to contemplate, to ponder **2** : to gaze at, to look at

contemporáneo, -nea *adj* & *n* : contemporary

contención *nf, pl* **-ciones** : containment, holding

contencioso, -sa *adj* : contentious

contender {56} *vi* **1** : to contend, to compete **2** : to fight

contendiente *nmf* : contender

contenedor *nm* **1** : container, receptacle **2** : Dumpster™

contener {80} *vt* **1** : to contain, to hold **2** ATAJAR : to restrain, to hold back — **contenerse** *vr* : to restrain oneself

contenido¹, -da *adj* : restrained, reserved

contenido² *nm* : contents *pl,* content

contentar *vt* : to please, to make happy — **contentarse** *vr* : to be satisfied, to be pleased

contento¹, -ta *adj* : contented, glad, happy

contento² *nm* : joy, happiness

contestación *nf, pl* **-ciones 1** : answer, reply **2** : protest

contestar *vt* RESPONDER : to answer — *vi* **1** RESPONDER : to answer, to reply **2** REPLICAR : to answer back

contexto *nm* : context

contienda *nf* **1** : dispute, conflict **2** : contest, competition

contigo *pron* : with you ⟨voy contigo : I'm going with you⟩

contiguo, -gua *adj* COLINDANTE : contiguous, adjacent

continencia *nf* : continence

continente *nm* : continent — **continental** *adj*

contingencia *nf* : contingency, eventuality

contingente *adj* & *nm* : contingent

continuación *nf, pl* **-ciones 1** : continuation **2 a** ~ : next ⟨lo demás sigue a continuación : the rest follows⟩ **3 a continuación de** : after, following

continuar {3} *v* : to continue

continuidad *nf* : continuity

continuo, -nua *adj* : continuous, steady, constant — **continuamente** *adv*

contonearse *vr* : to sway one's hips

contoneo *nm* : swaying, wiggling (of the hips)

contorno *nm* **1** : outline **2 contornos** *nmpl* : outskirts

contorsión *nf, pl* **-siones** : contortion

contra¹ *nf* **1** *fam* : difficulty, snag **2 llevar la contra a** : to oppose, to contradict

contra² *nm* : con ⟨los pros y los contras : the pros and cons⟩

contra³ *prep* : against

contraalmirante *nm* : rear admiral

contraatacar {72} *v* : to counterattack — **contraataque** *nm*

contrabajo *nm* : double bass

contrabalancear *vt* : to counterbalance — **contrabalanza** *nf*

contrabandear *v* : to smuggle

contrabandista *nmf* : smuggler, black marketeer

contrabando *nm* **1** : smuggling **2** : contraband

contracción *nf, pl* **-ciones** : contraction

contracepción *nf, pl* **-ciones** : contraception

contraceptivo *nm* ANTICONCEPTIVO : contraceptive

contrachapado *nm* : plywood

contracorriente *nf* **1** : crosscurrent **2 ir a contracorriente** : to go against the tide

contractual *adj* : contractual

contradecir {11} *vt* DESMENTIR : to contradict — **contradecirse** *vr* DESDECIRSE : to contradict oneself

contradicción *nf, pl* **-ciones** : contradiction

contradictorio, -ria *adj* : contradictory

contraer {81} *vt* **1** : to contract (a disease) **2** : to establish by contract ⟨contraer matrimonio : to get married⟩ **3** : to tighten, to contract — **contraerse** *vr* : to contract, to tighten up

contrafuerte *nm* : buttress

contragolpe *nm* **1** : counterblow **2** : backlash

contrahecho, -cha *adj* : deformed, hunchbacked

contraindicado, -da *adj* : contraindicated — **contraindicación** *nf*

contralor, -lora *n* : comptroller

contralto *nmf* : contralto

contramaestre *nm* **1** : boatswain **2** : foreman

contramandar *vt* : to countermand

contramano *nm* **a** ~ : the wrong way (on a street)

contramedida *nf* : countermeasure

contraorden *nf* : countermand

contraparte *nf* **1** : counterpart **2 en** ~ : on the other hand

contrapartida *nf* : compensation

contrapelo *nm* **a** ~ : in the wrong direction, against the grain

contrapeso *nm* : counterbalance

contraponer {60} *vt* **1** : to counter, to oppose **2** : to contrast, to compare

contraposición *nf, pl* **-ciones** : comparison

contraproducente *adj* : counterproductive

contrapunto *nm* : counterpoint

contrariar {85} *vt* **1** : to contradict, to oppose **2** : to vex, to annoy

contrariedad *nf* **1** : setback, obstacle **2** : vexation, annoyance

contrario, -ria *adj* **1** : contrary, opposite ⟨al contrario : on the contrary⟩ **2** : conflicting, opposed

contrarrestar *vt* : to counteract

contrarrevolución *nf, pl* **-ciones** : counterrevolution — **contrarrevolucionario, -ria** *adj & n*

contrasentido *nm* : contradiction

contraseña *nf* : password

contrastante *adj* : contrasting

contrastar *vt* **1** : to resist **2** : to check, to confirm — *vi* : to contrast

contraste *nm* : contrast

contratar *vt* **1** : to contract for **2** : to hire, to engage

contratiempo *nm* **1** PERCANCE : mishap, accident **2** DIFICULTAD : setback, difficulty

contratista *nmf* : contractor

contrato *nm* : contract

contravenir {87} *vt* : to contravene, to infringe

contraventana *nf* : shutter

contribución *nf, pl* **-ciones** : contribution

contribuidor, -dora *n* : contributor

contribuir {41} *vt* **1** APORTAR : to contribute **2** : to pay (in taxes) — *vi* **1** : contribute, to help out **2** : to pay taxes

contribuyente[1] *adj* : contributing

contribuyente[2] *nmf* : taxpayer

contrición *nf, pl* **-ciones** : contrition

contrincante *nmf* : rival, opponent

contrito, -ta *adj* : contrite, repentant

control *nm* **1** : control **2** : inspection, check **3** : checkpoint, roadblock

controlador, -dora *n* : controller ⟨controlador aéreo : air traffic controller⟩

controlar *vt* **1** : to control **2** : to monitor, to check

controversia *nf* : controversy

controversial → **controvertido**

controvertido, -da *adj* : controversial

controvertir {76} *vt* : to dispute, to argue about — *vi* : to argue, to debate

contubernio *nm* : conspiracy

contumacia *nf* : obstinacy, stubbornness

contumaz *adj, pl* **-maces** : obstinate, stubbornly disobedient

contundencia *nf* **1** : forcefulness, weight **2** : severity

contundente *adj* **1** : blunt ⟨un objeto contundente : a blunt instrument⟩ **2** : forceful, convincing — **contundentemente** *adv*

contusión *nf, pl* **-siones** : bruise, contusion

contuvo, etc. → **contener**

convalecencia *nf* : convalescence

convalecer {53} *vi* : to convalesce, to recover

convaleciente *adj & nmf* : convalescent

convección *nf, pl* **-ciones** : convection

convencer {86} *vt* : to convince, to persuade — **convencerse** *vr*

convencimiento *nm* : belief, conviction

convención *nf, pl* **-ciones** **1** : convention, conference **2** : pact, agreement **3** : convention, custom

convencional *adj* : conventional — **convencionalmente** *adv*

convencionalismo *nm* : conventionality

conveniencia *nf* **1** : convenience **2** : fitness, suitability, advisability

conveniente *adj* **1** : convenient **2** : suitable, advisable

convenio *nm* PACTO : agreement, pact

convenir {87} *vi* **1** : to be suitable, to be advisable **2** : to agree

convento *nm* **1** : convent **2** : monastery

convergencia *nf* : convergence

convergente *adj* : convergent, converging

converger {15} *vi* **1** : to converge **2** ~ **en** : to concur on

conversación *nf, pl* **-ciones** : conversation

conversador, -dora *n* : conversationalist, talker

conversar *vi* : to converse, to talk

conversión *nf, pl* **-siones** : conversion

converso, -sa *n* : convert

convertible *adj & nm* : convertible

convertidor *nm* : converter

convertir {76} *vt* **1** : to convert **2** : to transform, to change **3** : to exchange (money) — **convertirse** *vr* ~ **en** : to turn into

convexo, -xa *adj* : convex

convicción *nf, pl* **-ciones** : conviction

convicto[1] **, -ta** *adj* : convicted

convicto[2] **, -ta** *n* : convict, prisoner

convidado, -da *n* : guest

convidar *vt* **1** INVITAR : to invite **2** : to offer

convincente *adj* : convincing — **convincentemente** *adv*

convivencia *nf* **1** : coexistence **2** : cohabitation

convivir *vi* **1** : to coexist **2** : to live together

convocación *nf, pl* **-ciones** : convocation

convocar {72} *vt* : to convoke, to call together

convocatoria *nf* : summons, call

convoy *nm* : convoy

convulsión *nf, pl* **-siones** **1** : convulsion **2** : agitation, upheaval

convulsionar *vt* : to shake, to convulse — **convulsionarse** *vr*

convulsivo, -va *adj* : convulsive

conyugal *adj* : conjugal

cónyuge *nmf* : spouse, partner

coñac *nm* : cognac, brandy

cooperación *nf, pl* **-ciones** : cooperation

cooperador, -dora *adj* : cooperative

cooperar *vi* : to cooperate
cooperativa *nf* : cooperative, co-op
cooperativo, -va *adj* : cooperative
cooptar *vt* : to co-opt
coordenada *nf* : coordinate
coordinación *nf, pl* **-ciones** : coordination
coordinador, -dora *n* : coordinator
coordinar *vt* COMPAGINAR : to coordinate, to combine
copa *nf* 1 : wineglass, goblet 2 : drink ⟨irse de copas : to go out drinking⟩ 3 : cup, trophy
copar *vt* 1 : to take ⟨ya está copado el puesto : the job is already taken⟩ 2 : to fill, to crowd
copartícipe *nmf* : joint partner
copete *nm* 1 : tuft (of hair) 2 **estar hasta el copete** : to be completely fed up
copia *nf* 1 : copy 2 : imitation, replica
copiadora *nf* : photocopier
copiar *vt* : to copy
copiloto *nmf* : copilot
copioso, -sa *adj* : copious, abundant
copla *nf* 1 : popular song or ballad 2 : couplet, stanza
copo *nm* 1 : snowflake 2 **copos de avena** : rolled oats 3 **copos de maíz** : cornflakes
copra *nf* : copra
cópula *nf* : copulation
copular *vi* : to copulate
coque *nm* : coke (fuel)
coqueta *nf* : dressing table
coquetear *vi* : to flirt
coqueteo *nm* : flirting, coquetry
coqueto[1], -ta *adj* : flirtatious, coquettish
coqueto[2], -ta *n* : flirt
coraje *nm* 1 VALOR : valor, courage 2 IRA : anger ⟨darle coraje a alguien : to make someone angry⟩
corajudo, -da *adj* : brave
coral[1] *nm* 1 : coral 2 : chorale
coral[2] *nf* : choir
Corán *nm* **el Corán** : the Koran
coraza *nf* 1 : armor, armor plating 2 : shell (of an animal)
corazón *nm, pl* **-zones** 1 : heart ⟨de todo corazón : wholeheartedly⟩ ⟨de buen corazón : kindhearted⟩ 2 : core 3 : darling, sweetheart
corazonada *nf* : hunch, impulse
corbata *nf* : tie, necktie
corcel *nm* : steed, charger
corchete *nm* 1 : hook and eye, clasp 2 : square bracket
corcho *nm* : cork
corcholata *nf Mex* : cap, bottle top
corcovear *vi* : to buck
cordel *nm* : cord, string
cordero *nm* : lamb
cordial[1] *adj* : cordial, affable — **cordialmente** *adv*
cordial[2] *nm* : cordial (liqueur)
cordialidad *nf* : cordiality, warmth
cordillera *nf* : mountain range
córdoba *nf* : Nicaraguan unit of currency

cordón *nm, pl* **cordones** 1 : cord ⟨cordón umbilical : umbilical cord⟩ 2 : cordon
cordura *nf* 1 : sanity 2 : prudence, good judgment
coreano[1], -na *adj & n* : Korean
coreano[2] *nm* : Korean (language)
corear *vt* : to chant, to chorus
coreografía *nf* : choreography
coreografiar {85} *vt* : to choreograph
coreográfico, -ca *adj* : choreographic
coreógrafo, -fa *n* : choreographer
corista *nmf* 1 : chorister 2 : chorus girl *f*
cormorán *nm, pl* **-ranes** : cormorant
cornada *nf* : goring, butt (with the horns)
córnea *nf* : cornea
cornear *vt* : to gore
cornejo *nm* : dogwood (tree)
corneta *nf* : bugle, horn, cornet
cornisa *nf* : cornice
cornudo, -da *adj* : horned
coro *nm* 1 : choir 2 : chorus
corola *nf* : corolla
corolario *nm* : corollary
corona *nf* 1 : crown 2 : wreath, garland 3 : corona (in astronomy)
coronación *nf, pl* **-ciones** : coronation
coronar *vt* 1 : to crown 2 : to reach the top of, to culminate
coronario, -ria *adj* : coronary
coronel, -nela *n* : colonel
coronilla *nf* 1 : crown (of the head) 2 **estar hasta la coronilla** : to be completely fed up
corpiño *nm* 1 : bodice 2 *Arg* : brassiere, bra
corporación *nf, pl* **-ciones** : corporation
corporal *adj* : corporal, bodily
corporativo, -va *adj* : corporate
corpóreo, -rea *adj* : corporeal, physical
corpulencia *nf* : corpulence, stoutness, sturdiness
corpulento, -ta *adj* ROBUSTO : robust, stout, sturdy
corpúsculo *nm* : corpuscle
corral *nm* 1 : farmyard 2 : corral, pen, stockyard 3 *or* **corralito** : playpen
correa *nf* : strap, belt
correcaminos *nms & pl* : roadrunner
corrección *nf, pl* **-ciones** 1 : correction 2 : correctness, propriety 3 : rebuke, reprimand 4 **corrección de pruebas** : proofreading
correccional *nm* REFORMATORIO : reformatory
correctivo, -va *adj* : corrective ⟨lentes correctivos : corrective lenses⟩
correcto, -ta *adj* 1 : correct, right 2 : courteous, polite — **correctamente** *adv*
corrector, -tora *n* : proofreader
corredizo, -za *adj* : sliding ⟨puerta corrediza : sliding door⟩
corredor[1], -dora *n* 1 : runner, racer 2 : agent, broker ⟨corredor de bolsa : stockbroker⟩
corredor[2] *nm* PASILLO : corridor, hallway

correduría *nf* → **corretaje**
corregir {28} *vt* **1** ENMENDAR : to correct, to emend **2** : to reprimand **3 corregir pruebas** : to proofread — **corregirse** *vr* : to reform, to mend one's ways
correlación *nf, pl* **-ciones** : correlation
correo *nm* **1** : mail ⟨correo aéreo : airmail⟩ **2** : post office
correoso, -sa *adj* : leathery, rough
correr *vi* **1** : to run, to race **2** : to rush **3** : to flow — *vt* **1** : to travel over, to cover **2** : to move, to slide, to roll, to draw (curtains) **3 correr un riesgo** : to run a risk — **correrse** *vr* **1** : to move along **2** : to run, to spill over
correspondencia *nf* **1** : correspondence, mail **2** : equivalence **3** : connection, interchange
corresponder *vi* **1** : to correspond **2** : to pertain, to belong **3** : to be appropriate, to fit **4** : to reciprocate — **corresponderse** *vr* : to write to each other
correspondiente *adj* : corresponding, respective
corresponsal *nmf* : correspondent
corretaje *nm* : brokerage
corretear *vi* **1** VAGAR : to loiter, to wander about **2** : to run around, to scamper about — *vt* : to pursue, to chase
corrida *nf* **1** : run, dash **2** : bullfight
corrido¹, -da *adj* **1** : straight, continuous **2** : worldly, experienced
corrido² *nm* : Mexican narrative folk song
corriente¹ *adj* **1** : common, everyday **2** : current, present **3** *Mex* : cheap, trashy **4 perro corriente** *Mex* : mutt
corriente² *nf* **1** : current ⟨corriente alterna : alternating current⟩ ⟨direct current : corriente continua⟩ **2** : draft **3** TENDENCIA : tendency, trend
corrillo *nm* : small group, clique
corro *nm* : ring, circle (of people)
corroboración *nf, pl* **-ciones** : corroboration
corroborar *vt* : to corroborate
corroer {69} *vt* **1** : to corrode **2** : to erode, to wear away
corromper *vt* **1** : to corrupt **2** : to rot — **corromperse** *vr*
corrompido, -da *adj* CORRUPTO : corrupt, rotten
corrosión *nf, pl* **-siones** : corrosion
corrosivo, -va *adj* : corrosive
corrugar {52} *vt* : to corrugate — **corrugación** *nf*
corrupción *nf, pl* **-ciones** **1** : decay **2** : corruption
corruptela *nf* : corruption, abuse of power
corrupto, -ta *adj* CORROMPIDO : corrupt
corsario *nm* : privateer
corsé *nm* : corset
cortada *nf* : cut, gash
cortador, -dora *n* : cutter
cortadora *nf* : cutter, slicer
cortadura *nf* : cut, slash
cortafuegos *nms & pl* **1** : firebreak **2** : firewall (program)

cortante *adj* : cutting, sharp
cortar *vt* **1** : to cut, to slice, to trim **2** : to cut out, to omit **3** : to cut off, to interrupt **4** : to block, to close off **5** : to curdle (milk) — *vi* **1** : to cut **2** : to break up **3** : to hang up (the telephone) — **cortarse** *vr* **1** : to cut oneself ⟨cortarse el pelo : to cut one's hair⟩ **2** : to be cut off **3** : to sour (of milk)
cortauñas *nms & pl* : nail clippers
corte¹ *nm* **1** : cut, cutting ⟨corte de pelo : haircut⟩ **2** : style, fit
corte² *nf* **1** : court ⟨corte suprema : supreme court⟩ **2 hacer la corte a** : to court, to woo
cortejar *vt* GALANTEAR : to court, to woo
cortejo *nm* **1** GALANTEO : courtship **2** : retinue, entourage
cortés *adj* : courteous, polite — **cortésmente** *adv*
cortesano¹, -na *adj* : courtly
cortesano², -na *n* : courtier
cortesía *nf* **1** : courtesy, politeness **2 de** ~ : complimentary, free
corteza *nf* **1** : bark **2** : crust **3** : peel, rind **4** : cortex ⟨corteza cerebral : cerebral cortex⟩
cortijo *nm* : farmhouse
cortina *nf* : curtain
cortisona *nf* : cortisone
corto, -ta *adj* **1** : short (in length or duration) **2** : scarce **3** : timid, shy **4 corto de vista** : nearsighted
cortocircuito *nm* : short circuit
corvejón *nm, pl* **-jones** JARRETE : hock
corvo, -va *adj* : curved, bent
cosa *nf* **1** : thing, object **2** : matter, affair **3 otra cosa** : anything else, something else
cosecha *nf* : harvest, crop
cosechador, -dora *n* : harvester, reaper
cosechadora *nf* : harvester (machine)
cosechar *vt* **1** : to harvest, to reap **2** : to win, to earn, to garner — *vi* : to harvest
coser *vt* **1** : to sew **2** : to stitch up — *vi* : to sew.
cosmético¹, -ca *adj* : cosmetic
cosmético² *nm* : cosmetic
cósmico, -ca *adj* : cosmic
cosmonauta *nmf* : cosmonaut
cosmopolita *adj & nmf* : cosmopolitan
cosmos *nm* : cosmos
cosquillas *nfpl* **1** : tickling **2 hacer cosquillas** : to tickle
cosquilleo *nm* : tickling sensation, tingle
cosquilloso, -sa *adj* : ticklish
costa *nf* **1** : coast, shore **2** : cost ⟨a toda costa : at all costs⟩
costado *nm* **1** : side **2 al costado** : alongside
costar {19} *v* : to cost ⟨¿cuánto cuesta? : how much does it cost?⟩
costarricense *adj & nmf* : Costa Rican
costarriqueño, -ña → **costarricense**
coste → **costo**
costear *vt* : to pay for, to finance

costero, -ra *adj* : coastal, coast

costilla *nf* 1 : rib 2 : chop, cutlet 3 *fam* : better half, wife

costo *nm* 1 : cost, price 2 costo de vida : cost of living

costoso, -sa *adj* : costly, expensive

costra *nf* 1 : crust 2 POSTILLA : scab

costumbre *nf* 1 : custom 2 HÁBITO : habit

costura *nf* 1 : seam 2 : sewing, dressmaking 3 alta costura : haute couture

costurera *nf* : seamstress *f*

cotejar *vt* : to compare, to collate

cotejo *nm* : comparison, collation

cotidiano, -na *adj* : daily, everyday ⟨la vida cotidiana : daily life⟩

cotización *nf, pl* -ciones 1 : market price 2 : quote, estimate

cotizado, -da *adj* : in demand, sought after

cotizar {21} *vt* : to quote, to value — cotizarse *vr* : to be worth

coto *nm* 1 : enclosure, reserve 2 poner coto a : to put a stop to

cotorra *nf* 1 : small parrot 2 *fam* : chatterbox, windbag

cotorrear *vi fam* : to chatter, to gab, to blab

cotorreo *nm fam* : chatter, prattle

coyote *nm* 1 : coyote 2 *Mex fam* : smuggler (of illegal immigrants)

coyuntura *nf* 1 ARTICULACIÓN : joint 2 : occasion, moment

coz *nf, pl* coces : kick (of an animal)

crac *nm, pl* cracs : crash (of the stock market)

cozamos, etc. → cocer

craneal *adj* : cranial

cráneo *nf* : cranium, skull — craneano, -na *adj*

cráter *nm* : crater

crayón *nm, pl* -yones : crayon

creación *nf, pl* -ciones : creation

creador[1], -dora *adj* : creative, creating

creador[2], -dora *n* : creator

crear *vt* 1 : to create, to cause 2 : to originate

creatividad *nf* : creativity

creativo, -va *adj* : creative

crecer {53} *vi* 1 : to grow 2 : to increase

crecida *nf* : flooding, floodwater

crecido, -da *adj* 1 : grown, grown-up 2 : large (of numbers)

creciente *adj* 1 : growing, increasing 2 luna creciente : waxing moon

crecientemente *adv* : increasingly

crecimiento *nm* 1 : growth 2 : increase

credencial *adj* cartas credenciales : credentials

credenciales *nfpl* : documents, documentation, credentials

credibilidad *nf* : credibility

crédito *nm* : credit

credo *nm* : creed, credo

credulidad *nf* : credulity

crédulo, -la *adj* : credulous, gullible

creencia *nf* : belief

creer {20} *v* 1 : to believe 2 : to suppose, to think ⟨creo que sí : I think so⟩

— creerse *vr* 1 : to believe, to think 2 : to regard oneself as ⟨se cree guapísimo : he thinks he's so handsome⟩

creíble *adj* : believable, credible

creído, -da *adj* 1 *fam* : conceited 2 : confident, sure

crema *nf* 1 : cream 2 la crema y nata : the pick of the crop

cremación *nf, pl* -ciones : cremation

cremallera *nf* : zipper

cremar *vt* : to cremate

cremoso, -sa *adj* : creamy

crepa *nf Mex* : crepe (pancake)

crepe *or* crep *nmf* : crepe (pancake)

crepé *nm* 1 → crespón 2 papel crepé : crepe paper

crepitar *vi* : to crackle

crepúsculo *nm* : twilight

crescendo *nm* : crescendo

crespo, -pa *adj* : curly, frizzy

crespón *nm, pl* crespones : crepe (fabric)

cresta *nf* 1 : crest 2 : comb (of a rooster)

creta *nf* : chalk (mineral)

cretino, -na *n* : cretin

creyente *nmf* : believer

creyó, etc. → creer

crezca, etc. → crecer

cría *nf* 1 : breeding, rearing 2 : young 3 : litter

criadero *nm* : hatchery

criado[1], -da *adj* 1 : raised, brought up 2 bien criado : well-bred

criado[2], -da *n* : servant, maid *f*

criador, -dora *n* : breeder

crianza *nf* : upbringing, rearing

criar {85} *vt* 1 : to breed 2 : to bring up, to raise

criatura *nf* 1 : baby, child 2 : creature

criba *nf* : sieve, screen

cribar *vt* : to sift

cric *nm, pl* crics : jack

crimen *nm, pl* crímenes : crime

criminal *adj & nmf* : criminal

crin *nf* 1 : mane 2 : horsehair

criollo[1], -lla *adj* 1 : Creole 2 : native, national ⟨comida criolla : native cuisine⟩

criollo[2], -lla *n* : Creole

criollo[3] *nm* : Creole (language)

cripta *nf* : crypt

críptico, -ca *adj* 1 : cryptic, coded 2 : enigmatic, cryptic

criptón *nm* : krypton

críquet *nm* : cricket (game)

crisálida *nf* : chrysalis, pupa

crisantemo *nm* : chrysanthemum

crisis *nf* 1 : crisis 2 crisis nerviosa : nervous breakdown

crisma *nf fam* : head ⟨romperle la crisma a alguien : to knock someone's block off⟩

crisol *nm* 1 : crucible 2 : melting pot

crispar *vt* 1 : to cause to contract 2 : to irritate, to set on edge ⟨eso me crispa : that gets on my nerves⟩ — crisparse *vr* : to tense up

cristal *nm* **1** VIDRIO : glass, piece of glass **2** : crystal
cristalería *nf* **1** : glassware shop ⟨como chivo en cristalería : like a bull in a china shop⟩ **2** : glassware, crystal
cristalino[1], **-na** *adj* : crystalline, clear
cristalino[2] *nm* : lens (of the eye)
cristalizar {21} *vi* : to crystallize — **cristalización** *nf*
cristiandad *nf* : Christendom
cristianismo *nm* : Christianity
cristiano, -na *adj & n* : Christian
Cristo *nm* : Christ
criterio *nm* **1** : criterion **2** : judgment, sense
crítica *nf* **1** : criticism **2** : review, critique
criticar {72} *vt* : to criticize
crítico[1], **-ca** *adj* : critical — **críticamente** *adv*
crítico[2], **-ca** *n* : critic
criticón[1], **-cona** *adj, mpl* **-cones** *fam* : hypercritical, captious
criticón[2], **-cona** *n, mpl* **-cones** *fam* : faultfinder, critic
croar *vi* : to croak
croata *adj & nmf* : Croatian
crocante *adj* : crunchy
croché *or* **crochet** *nm* : crochet
cromático, -ca *adj* : chromatic
cromo *nm* **1** : chromium, chrome **2** : picture card, sports card
cromosoma *nm* : chromosome
crónica *nf* **1** : news report **2** : chronicle, history
crónico, -ca *adj* : chronic
cronista *nmf* **1** : reporter, newscaster **2** HISTORIADOR : chronicler, historian
cronología *nf* : chronology
cronológico, -ca *adj* : chronological — **cronológicamente** *adv*
cronometrador, -dora *n* : timekeeper
cronometrar *vt* : to time, to clock
cronómetro *nm* : chronometer
croquet *nm* : croquet
croqueta *nf* : croquette
croquis *nm* : rough sketch
cruce[1], **etc.** → **cruzar**
cruce[2] *nm* **1** : crossing, cross **2** : crossroads, intersection ⟨cruce peatonal : crosswalk⟩
crucero *nm* **1** : cruise **2** : cruiser, warship **3** *Mex* : intersection
crucial *adj* : crucial — **crucialmente** *adv*
crucificar {72} *vt* : to crucify
crucifijo *nm* : crucifix
crucifixión *nf, pl* **-fixiones** : crucifixion
crucigrama *nm* : crossword puzzle
crudo[1], **-da** *adj* **1** : raw **2** : crude, harsh
crudo[2] *nm* : crude oil
cruel *adj* : cruel — **cruelmente** *adv*
crueldad *nf* : cruelty
cruento, -ta *adj* : bloody
crujido *nm* **1** : rustling **2** : creaking **3** : crackling (of a fire) **4** : crunching
crujiente *adj* : crunchy, crisp
crujir *vi* **1** : to rustle **2** : to creak, to crack **3** : to crunch

crup *nm* : croup
crustáceo *nm* : crustacean
crutón *nm, pl* **crutones** : crouton
cruz *nf, pl* **cruces** : cross
cruza *nf* : cross (hybrid)
cruzada *nf* : crusade
cruzado[1], **-da** *adj* : crossed ⟨espadas cruzadas : crossed swords⟩
cruzado[2] *nm* **1** : crusader **2** : Brazilian unit of currency
cruzar {21} *vt* **1** : to cross **2** : to exchange (words, greetings) **3** : to cross, to interbreed — **cruzarse** *vr* **1** : to intersect **2** : to meet, to pass each other
cuaderno *nm* LIBRETA : notebook
cuadra *nf* **1** : city block **2** : stable
cuadrado[1], **-da** *adj* : square
cuadrado[2] *nm* : square ⟨elevar al cuadrado : to square (a number)⟩
cuadragésimo[1] *adj* : fortieth, forty-
cuadragésimo[2], **-ma** *n* : fortieth, forty- (in a series)
cuadrante *nm* **1** : quadrant **2** : dial
cuadrar *vi* : to conform, to agree — *vt* : to square — **cuadrarse** *vr* : to stand at attention
cuadriculado *nm* : grid (on a map, etc.)
cuadrilátero *nm* **1** : quadrilateral **2** : ring (in sports)
cuadrilla *nf* : gang, team, group
cuadro *nm* **1** : square ⟨una blusa a cuadros : a checkered blouse⟩ **2** : painting, picture **3** : baseball diamond, infield **4** : panel, board, cadre
cuadrúpedo *nm* : quadruped
cuadruple *adj* : quadruple
cuadruplicar {72} *vt* : to quadruple — **cuadruplicarse** *vr*
cuajada *nf* : curd
cuajar *vi* **1** : to curdle **2** COAGULAR : to clot, to coagulate **3** : to set, to jell **4** : to be accepted ⟨su idea no cuajó : his idea didn't catch on⟩ — *vt* **1** : to curdle **2** ~ **de** : to fill with
cual[1] *prep* : like, as
cual[2] *pron* **1 el cual, la cual, los cuales, las cuales** : who, whom, which ⟨la razón por la cual lo dije : the reason I said it⟩ **2 lo cual** : which ⟨se rió, lo cual me dio rabia : he laughed, which made me mad⟩ **3 cada cual** : everyone, everybody
cuál[1] *adj* : which, what ⟨¿cuáles libros? : which books?⟩
cuál[2] *pron* **1** (*in questions*) : which (one), what (one) ⟨¿cuál es el mejor? : which one is the best?⟩ ⟨¿cuál es tu apellido? : what is your last name?⟩ **2 cuál más, cuál menos** : some more, some less
cualidad *nf* : quality, trait
cualitativo, -va *adj* : qualitative — **cualitativamente** *adv*
cualquier *adj* → **cualquiera**[1]
cualquiera[1] (**cualquier** *before nouns*) *adj, pl* **cualesquiera 1** : any, whichever ⟨cualquier persona : any person⟩ **2** : everyday, ordinary ⟨un hombre cualquiera : an ordinary man⟩

cualquiera[2] *pron, pl* **cualesquiera 1** : anyone, anybody, whoever **2** : whatever, whichever

cuán *adv* : how ⟨¡cuán risible fue todo eso! : how funny it all was!⟩

cuando[1] *conj* **1** : when ⟨cuando llegó : when he arrived⟩ **2** : since, if ⟨cuando lo dices : if you say so⟩ **3 cuando más** : at the most **4 de vez en cuando** : from time to time

cuando[2] *prep* : during, at the time of ⟨cuando la guerra : during the war⟩

cuándo *adv & conj* **1** : when ⟨cuándo llegará? : when will she arrive?⟩ ⟨no sabemos cuándo será : we don't know when it will be⟩ **2** ¿**de cuándo acá?** : since when?, how come?

cuantía *nf* **1** : quantity, extent **2** : significance, import

cuántico, -ca *adj* : quantum ⟨teoría cuántica : quantum theory⟩

cuantioso, -sa *adj* **1** : abundant, considerable **2** : heavy, grave ⟨cuantiosos daños : heavy damage⟩

cuantitativo, -va *adj* : quantitative — **cuantitativamente** *adv*

cuanto[1] *adv* **1** : as much as ⟨come cuanto puedas : eat as much as you can⟩ **2 cuanto antes** : as soon as possible **3 en ∼** : as soon as **4 en cuanto a** : as for, as regards

cuanto[2], **-ta** *adj* : as many, whatever ⟨llévate cuantas flores quieras : take as many flowers as you wish⟩

cuanto[3], **-ta** *pron* : as much as, all that, everything ⟨tengo cuanto deseo : I have all that I want⟩ **2 unos cuantos, unas cuantas** : a few

cuánto[1] *adv* : how much, how many ⟨¿a cuánto están las manzanas? : how much are the apples?⟩ ⟨no sé cuánto desean : I don't know how much they want⟩

cuánto[2], **-ta** *adj* : how much, how many ⟨¿cuántos niños tiene? : how many children do you have?⟩

cuánto[3] *pron* : how much, how many ⟨¿cuántos quieren participar? : how many want to take part?⟩ ⟨¿cuánto cuesta? : how much does it cost?⟩

cuarenta *adj & nm* : forty

cuarentavo[1], **-va** *adj* : fortieth

cuarentavo[2] *nm* : fortieth (fraction)

cuarentena *nf* **1** : group of forty **2** : quarantine

Cuaresma *nf* : Lent

cuartear *vt* **1** : to quarter **2** : to divide up — **cuartearse** *vr* AGRIETARSE : to crack, to split

cuartel *nm* **1** : barracks, headquarters **2** : mercy ⟨una guerra sin cuartel : a merciless war⟩

cuartelazo *nm* : coup d'état

cuarteto *nm* : quartet

cuartilla *nf* : sheet (of paper)

cuarto[1], **-ta** *adj* : fourth

cuarto[2], **-ta** *n* : fourth (in a series)

cuarto[3] *nm* **1** : quarter, fourth ⟨cuarto de galón : quart⟩ **2** HABITACIÓN : room

cuarzo *nm* : quartz

cuate, -ta *n Mex* **1** : twin **2** *fam* : buddy, pal

cuatrero, -ra *n* : rustler

cuatrillizo, -za *n* : quadruplet

cuatro *adj & nm* : four

cuatrocientos[1], **-tas** *adj* : four hundred

cuatrocientos[2] *nms & pl* : four hundred

cuba *nf* BARRIL : cask, barrel

cubano, -na *adj & n* : Cuban

cubertería *nf* : flatware, silverware

cubeta *nf* **1** : keg, cask **2** : bulb (of a thermometer) **3** *Mex* : bucket, pail

cúbico, -ca *adj* : cubic, cubed

cubículo *nm* : cubicle

cubierta *nf* **1** : covering **2** FORRO : cover, jacket (of a book) **3** : deck

cubierto[1] *pp* → **cubrir**

cubierto[2] *nm* **1** : cover, shelter ⟨bajo cubierto : under cover⟩ **2** : table setting **3** : utensil, piece of silverware

cubil *nm* : den, lair

cúbito *nm* : ulna

cubo *nm* **1** : cube **2** BALDE : pail, bucket, can ⟨cubo de basura : garbage can⟩ **3** : hub (of a wheel)

cubrecama *nm* COLCHA : bedspread

cubrir {2} *vt* : to cover — **cubrirse** *vr*

cucaracha *nf* : cockroach, roach

cuchara *nf* : spoon

cucharada *nf* : spoonful

cucharilla *or* **cucharita** *nf* : teaspoon

cucharón *nm, pl* **-rones** : ladle

cuchichear *vi* : to whisper

cuchicheo *nm* : whisper

cuchilla *nf* **1** : kitchen knife, cleaver **2** : blade ⟨cuchilla de afeitar : razor blade⟩ **3** : crest, ridge

cuchillada *nf* : stab, knife wound

cuchillo *nm* : knife

cuclillas *nfpl* **en ∼** : squatting, crouching

cuco[1], **-ca** *adj fam* : pretty, cute

cuco[2] *nm* : cuckoo

cucurucho *nm* : ice-cream cone

cuece, cueza etc. → **cocer**

cuela, etc. → **colar**

cuelga, cuelgue etc. → **colgar**

cuello *nm* **1** : neck **2** : collar (of a shirt) **3 cuello del útero** : cervix

cuenca *nf* **1** : river basin **2** : eye socket

cuenco *nm* : bowl, basin

cuenta[1], **etc.** → **contar**

cuenta[2] *nf* **1** : calculation, count **2** : account **3** : check, bill **4 darse cuenta** : to realize **5 tener en cuenta** : to bear in mind

cuentagotas *nfs & pl* **1** : dropper **2 con ∼** : little by little

cuentista *nmf* **1** : short story writer **2** *fam* : liar, fibber

cuento *nm* **1** : story, tale **2 cuento de hadas** : fairy tale **3 sin ∼** : countless

cuerda *nf* **1** : cord, rope, string **2 cuerdas vocales** : vocal cords **3 darle cuerda a** : to wind up (a clock, a toy, etc.)

cuerdo, -da *adj* : sane, sensible
cuerno *nm* **1** : horn, antler **2** : cusp (of the moon) **3** : horn (musical instrument)
cuero *nm* **1** : leather, hide **2 cuero cabelludo** : scalp
cuerpo *nm* **1** : body **2** : corps
cuervo *nm* : crow, raven
cuesta¹, etc. → *costar*
cuesta² *nf* **1** : slope ⟨cuesta arriba : uphill⟩ **2 a cuestas** : on one's back
cuestión *nf, pl* **-tiones** ASUNTO, TEMA : matter, affair
cuestionable *adj* : questionable, dubious
cuestionar *vt* : to question
cuestionario *nm* **1** : questionnaire **2** : quiz
cueva *nf* : cave
cuidado *nm* **1** : care **2** : worry, concern **3 tener cuidado** : to be careful **4 ¡cuidado!** : watch out!, be careful!
cuidador, -dora *n* : caretaker
cuidadoso, -sa *adj* : careful, attentive — **cuidadosamente** *adv*
cuidar *vt* **1** : to take care of, to look after **2** : to pay attention to — *vi* **1 ~ de** : to look after **2 cuidar de que** : to make sure that — **cuidarse** *vr* : to take care of oneself
culata *nf* : butt (of a gun)
culatazo *nf* : kick, recoil
culebra *nf* SERPIENTE : snake
culi *nmf* : coolie
culinario, -ria *adj* : culinary
culminante *adj* **punto culminante** : peak, high point, climax
culminar *vi* : to culminate — **culminación** *nf*
culo *nm* **1** *fam* : backside, behind **2** : bottom (of a glass)
culpa *nf* **1** : fault, blame ⟨echarle la culpa a alguien : to blame someone⟩ **2** : sin
culpabilidad *nf* : guilt
culpable¹ *adj* : guilty
culpable² *nmf* : culprit, guilty party
culpar *vt* : to blame
cultivado, -da *adj* **1** : cultivated, farmed **2** : cultured
cultivador, -dora *n* : cultivator
cultivar *vt* **1** : to cultivate **2** : to foster
cultivo *nm* **1** : cultivation, farming **2** : crop
culto¹, -ta *adj* : cultured, educated
culto² *nm* **1** : worship **2** : cult
cultura *nf* : culture
cultural *adj* : cultural — **culturalmente** *adv*
cumbre *nf* CIMA : top, peak, summit
cumpleaños *nms & pl* : birthday
cumplido¹, -da *adj* **1** : complete, full **2** : courteous, correct
cumplido² *nm* : compliment, courtesy ⟨por cumplido : out of courtesy⟩ ⟨andarse con cumplidos : to stand on ceremony, to be formal⟩
cumplimentar *vt* **1** : to congratulate **2** : to carry out, to perform

cumplimiento *nm* **1** : completion, fulfillment **2** : performance
cumplir *vt* **1** : to accomplish, to carry out **2** : to comply with, to fulfill **3** : to attain, to reach ⟨su hermana cumple los 21 el viernes : her sister will be 21 on Friday⟩ — *vi* **1** : to expire, to fall due **2** : to fulfill one's obligations ⟨cumplir con el deber : to do one's duty⟩ ⟨cumplir con la palabra : to keep one's word⟩ — **cumplirse** *vr* **1** : to come true, to be fulfilled ⟨se cumplieron sus sueños : her dreams came true⟩ **2** : to run out, to expire
cúmulo *nm* **1** MONTÓN : heap, pile **2** : cumulus
cuna *nf* **1** : cradle **2** : birthplace ⟨Puerto Rico es la cuna de la música salsa : Puerto Rico is the birthplace of salsa music⟩
cundir *vi* **1** : to propagate, to spread ⟨cundió el pánico en el vecindario : panic spread throughout the neighborhood⟩ **2** : to progress, to make headway
cuneta *nf* : ditch (in a road), gutter
cuña *nf* : wedge
cuñado, -da *n* : brother-in-law *m*, sister-in-law *f*
cuño *nm* : die (for stamping)
cuota *nf* **1** : fee, dues **2** : quota, share **3** : installment, payment
cupé *nm* : coupe
cupo¹, etc. → *caber*
cupo² *nm* **1** : quota, share **2** : capacity, room
cupón *nm, pl* **cupones 1** : coupon, voucher **2 cupón federal** : food stamp
cúpula *nf* : dome, cupola
cura¹ *nm* : priest
cura² *nf* **1** CURACIÓN, TRATAMIENTO : cure, treatment **2** : dressing, bandage
curación *nf, pl* **-ciones** CURA, TRATAMIENTO : cure, treatment
curandero, -ra *nm* **1** : witch doctor **2** : quack, charlatan
curar *vt* **1** : to cure, to heal **2** : to treat, to dress **3** CURTIR : to tan **4** : to cure (meat) — *vi* : to get well, to recover — **curarse** *vr*
curativo, -va *adj* : curative, healing
curiosear *vi* **1** : to snoop, to pry **2** : to browse — *vt* : to look over, to check
curiosidad *nf* **1** : curiosity **2** : curio
curioso, -sa *adj* **1** : curious, inquisitive **2** : strange, unusual, odd — **curiosamente** *adv*
currículo → *currículum*
currículum *nm, pl* **-lums 1** : résumé, curriculum vitae **2** : curriculum, course of study
curry ['kurri] *nm, pl* **-rries 1** : curry powder **2** : curry (dish)
cursar *vt* **1** : to attend (school), to take (a course) **2** : to dispatch, to pass on
cursi *adj fam* : affected, pretentious
cursilería *nf* **1** : vulgarity, poor taste **2** : pretentiousness

cursiva *nf* BASTARDILLA : italic type, italics *pl*
curso *nm* **1** : course, direction **2** : school year **3** : course, subject (in school)
cursor *nm* : cursor
curtido, -da *adj* : weather-beaten, leathery (of skin)
curtidor, -dora *n* : tanner
curtiduría *nf* : tannery
curtir *vt* **1** : to tan **2** : to harden, to weather — **curtirse** *vr*
curva *nf* : curve, bend
curvar *vt* : to bend

curvatura *nf* : curvature
curvilíneo, -nea *adj* : curvaceous, shapely
curvo, -va *adj* : curved, bent
cúspide *nf* : zenith, apex, peak
custodia *nf* : custody
custodiar *vt* : to guard, to look after
custodio, -dia *n* : keeper, guardian
cúter *nm* : cutter (boat)
cutícula *nf* : cuticle
cutis *nms & pl* : skin, complexion
cuyo, -ya *adj* **1** : whose, of whom, of which **2 en cuyo caso** : in which case

D

d *nf* : fourth letter of the Spanish alphabet
dable *adj* : feasible, possible
dactilar *adj* **huellas dactilares** : fingerprints
dádiva *nf* : gift, handout
dadivoso, -sa *adj* : generous
dado, -da *adj* **1** : given **2 dado que** : given that, since
dador, -dora *n* : giver, donor
dados *nmpl* : dice
daga *nf* : dagger
dalia *nf* : dahlia
dálmata *nm* : dalmatian
daltónico, -ca *adj* : color-blind
daltonismo *nm* : color blindness
dama *nf* **1** : lady **2 damas** *nfpl* : checkers
damasco *nm* : damask
damisela *nf* : damsel
damnificado, -da *n* : victim (of a disaster)
damnificar {72} *vt* : to damage, to injure
dance, etc. → **danzar**
dandi *nm* : dandy, fop
danés¹, -nesa *adj* : Danish
danés², -nesa *n, mpl* **daneses** : Dane, Danish person
danza *nf* : dance, dancing ⟨danza folklórica : folk dance⟩
danzante, -ta *n* BAILARÍN : dancer
danzar {21} *v* BAILAR : to dance
dañar *vt* **1** : to damage, to spoil **2** : to harm, to hurt — **dañarse** *vr*
dañino, -na *adj* : harmful
daño *nm* **1** : damage **2** : harm, injury **3 hacer daño a** : to harm, to damage **4 daños y perjuicios** : damages
dar {22} *vt* **1** : to give **2** ENTREGAR : to deliver, to hand over **3** : to hit, to strike **4** : to yield, to produce **5** : to perform **6** : to give off, to emit **7** ~ **como** *or* ~ **por** : to regard as, to consider — *vi* **1** ALCANZAR : to suffice, to be enough ⟨no me da para dos pasajes : I don't have enough for two fares⟩ **2** ~ **a** *or* ~ **sobre** : to overlook, to look out on **3** ~ **con** : to run into **4** ~ **con** : to hit upon (an idea) **5 dar de sí** : to give, to stretch — **darse** *vr* **1** : to give in, to

surrender **2** : to occur, to arise **3** : to grow, to come up **4** ~ **con** *or* ~ **contra** : to hit oneself against **5 dárselas de** : to boast about ⟨se las da de muy listo : he thinks he's very smart⟩
dardo *nm* : dart
datar *vt* : to date — *vi* ~ **de** : to date from, to date back to
dátil *nm* : date (fruit)
dato *nm* **1** : fact, piece of information **2 datos** *nmpl* : data, information
dé → **dar**
de *prep* **1** : of ⟨la casa de Pepe : Pepe's house⟩ ⟨un niño de tres años : a three-year-old boy⟩ **2** : from ⟨es de Managua : she's from Managua⟩ ⟨salió del edificio : he left the building⟩ **3** : in, at ⟨a las tres de la mañana : at three in the morning⟩ ⟨salen de noche : they go out at night⟩ **4** : than ⟨más de tres : more than three⟩
deambular *vi* : to wander, to roam
debacle *nf* : debacle
debajo *adv* **1** : underneath, below, on the bottom **2** ~ **de** : under, underneath **3 por** ~ : below, beneath
debate *nm* : debate
debatir *vt* : to debate, to discuss — **debatirse** *vr* : to struggle
debe *nm* : debit column, debit
deber¹ *vt* : to owe — *v aux* **1** : must, have to ⟨debo ir a la oficina : I must go to the office⟩ **2** : should, ought to ⟨deberías buscar trabajo : you ought to look for work⟩ **3** (*expressing probability*) : must ⟨debe ser mexicano : he must be Mexican⟩ — **deberse** *vr* ~ **a** : to be due to
deber² *nm* **1** OBLIGACIÓN : duty, obligation **2 deberes** *nmpl, Spain* : homework
debidamente *adv* : properly, duly
debido, -da *adj* **1** : right, proper, due **2** ~ **a** : due to, owing to
débil *adj* : weak, feeble — **débilmente** *adv*
debilidad *nf* : weakness, debility, feebleness
debilitamiento *nm* : debilitation, weakening

debilitar *vt* : to debilitate, to weaken —
 debilitarse *vr*
debilucho[1], **-cha** *adj* : weak, frail
debilucho[2], **-cha** *n* : weakling
debitar *vt* : to debit
débito *nm* **1** DEUDA : debt **2** : debit
debut [de'but] *nm, pl* **debuts** : debut
debutante[1] *nmf* : beginner, newcomer
debutante[2] *nf* : debutante *f*
debutar *vi* : to debut, to make a debut
década *nf* DECENIO : decade
decadencia *nf* **1** : decadence **2** : decline
decadente *adj* **1** : decadent **2** : declining
decaer {13} *vi* **1** : to decline, to decay,
 to deteriorate **2** FLAQUEAR : to weak-
 en, to flag
decaiga, etc. → **decaer**
decano, -na *n* **1** : dean **2** : senior member
decantar *vt* : to decant
decapitar *vt* : to decapitate, to behead
decayó, etc. → **decaer**
decena *nf* : group of ten
decencia *nf* : decency
decenio *nm* DÉCADA : decade
decente *adj* : decent — **decentemente**
 adv
decepción *nf, pl* **-ciones** : disappointment, letdown
decepcionante *adj* : disappointing
decepcionar *vt* : to disappoint, to let
 down — **decepcionarse** *vr*
deceso *nm* DEFUNCIÓN : death, passing
dechado *nm* **1** : sampler (of embroidery) **2** : model, paragon
decibelio *or* **decibel** *nm* : decibel
decidido, -da *adj* : decisive, determined,
 resolute — **decididamente** *adv*
decidir *vt* **1** : to decide, to determine ⟨no
 he decidido nada : I haven't made a de-
 cision⟩ **2** : to persuade, to decide ⟨su
 padre lo decidió a estudiar : his father
 persuaded him to study⟩ — *vi* : to decide — **decidirse** *vr* : to make up one's
 mind
decimal *adj* : decimal
décimo, -ma *adj* : tenth — **décimo, -ma**
 n
decimoctavo[1], **-va** *adj* : eighteenth
decimoctavo[2], **-va** *n* : eighteenth (in a
 series)
decimocuarto[1], **-ta** *adj* : fourteenth
decimocuarto[2], **-ta** *n* : fourteenth (in a
 series)
decimonoveno[1], **-na** *or* **decimonono,
 -na** *adj* : nineteenth
decimonoveno[2], **-na** *or* **decimonono,
 -na** *n* : nineteenth (in a series)
decimoquinto[1], **-ta** *adj* : fifteenth
decimoquinto[2], **-ta** *n* : fifteenth (in a series)
decimoséptimo[1], **-ma** *adj* : seventeenth
decimoséptimo[2], **-ma** *n* : seventeenth
 (in a series)
decimosexto[1], **-ta** *adj* : sixteenth
decimosexto[2], **-ta** *n* : sixteenth (in a series)

decimotercero[1], **-ra** *adj* : thirteenth
decimotercero[2], **-ra** *n* : thirteenth (in a
 series)
decir[1] {23} *vt* **1** : to say ⟨dice que no
 quiere ir : she says she doesn't want to
 go⟩ **2** : to tell ⟨dime lo que estás pen-
 sando : tell me what you're thinking⟩
 3 : to speak, to talk ⟨no digas tonterías
 : don't talk nonsense⟩ **4** : to call ⟨me
 dicen Rosy : they call me Rosy⟩ **5 es
 decir** : that is to say **6 querer decir** : to
 mean — **decirse** *vr* **1** : to say to oneself **2** : to be said ⟨¿cómo se dice "lápiz"
 en francés? : how do you say "pencil"
 in French?⟩
decir[2] *nm* DICHO : saying, expression
decisión *nf, pl* **-siones** : decision, choice
decisivo, -va *adj* : decisive, conclusive
 — **decisivamente** *adv*
declamar *vi* : to declaim — *vt* : to recite
declaración *nf, pl* **-ciones** **1** : declaration, statement **2** TESTIMONIO : deposition, testimony **3 declaración de
 derechos** : bill of rights **4 declaración
 jurada** : affidavit
declarado, -da *adj* : professed, open —
 declaradamente *adv*
declarar *vt* : to declare, to state — *vi*
 ATESTIGUAR : to testify — **declararse**
 vr **1** : to declare oneself, to make a
 statement **2** : to confess one's love **3**
 : to plead (in court) ⟨declararse inocente : to plead not guilty⟩
declinación *nf, pl* **-ciones** **1** : drop,
 downward trend **2** : declination **3** : de-
 clension (in grammar)
declinar *vt* : to decline, to turn down —
 vi **1** : to draw to a close **2** : to diminish, to decline
declive *nm* **1** DECADENCIA : decline **2**
 : slope, incline
decodificador *nm* : decoder
decolar *vi Chile, Col, Ecua* : to take off
 (of an airplane)
decolorar *vt* : to bleach — **decolorarse**
 vr : to fade
decomisar *vt* CONFISCAR : to seize, to
 confiscate
decomiso *nm* : seizure, confiscation
decoración *nf, pl* **-ciones** **1** : decoration **2** : decor **3** : stage set, scenery
decorado *nm* : stage set, scenery
decorador, -dora *n* : decorator
decorar *vt* ADORNAR : to decorate, to
 adorn
decorativo, -va *adj* : decorative, ornamental
decoro *nm* : decorum, propriety
decoroso, -sa *adj* : decent, proper, respectable
decrecer {53} *vi* : to decrease, to wane,
 to diminish — **decreciente** *adj*
decrecimiento *nm* : decrease, decline
decrépito, -ta *adj* : decrepit
decretar *vt* : to decree, to order
decreto *nm* : decree
decúbito *nm* : horizontal position ⟨en
 decúbito prono : prone⟩ ⟨en decúbito
 supino : supine⟩

dedal *nm* : thimble
dedalera *nf* DIGITAL : foxglove
dedicación *nf, pl* **-ciones** : dedication, devotion
dedicar {72} *vt* CONSAGRAR : to dedicate, to devote — **dedicarse** *vr* ~ **a** : to devote oneself to, to engage in
dedicatoria *nf* : dedication (of a book, song, etc.)
dedo *nm* **1** : finger ⟨dedo meñique : little finger⟩ **2 dedo del pie** : toe
deducción *nf, pl* **-ciones** : deduction
deducible *adj* **1** : deducible, inferable **2** : deductible
deducir {61} *vt* **1** INFERIR : to deduce **2** DESCONTAR : to deduct
defecar {72} *vi* : to defecate — **defecación** *nf*
defecto *nm* **1** : defect, flaw, shortcoming **2 en su defecto** : lacking that, in the absence of that
defectuoso, -sa *adj* : defective, faulty
defender {56} *vt* : to defend, to protect — **defenderse** *vr* **1** : to defend oneself **2** : to get by, to know the basics ⟨su inglés no es perfecto pero se defiende : his English isn't perfect but he gets by⟩
defendible *adj* : defensible, tenable
defensa[1] *nf* : defense
defensa[2] *nmf* : defender, back (in sports)
defensiva *nf* : defensive, defense
defensivo, -va *adj* : defensive — **defensivamente** *adv*
defensor[1]**, -sora** *adj* : defending, defense
defensor[2]**, -sora** *n* **1** : defender, advocate **2** : defense counsel
defeño, -ña *n* : person from the Federal District (Mexico City)
deferencia *nf* : deference
deficiencia *nf* : deficiency, flaw
deficiente *adj* : deficient
déficit *nm, pl* **-cits 1** : deficit **2** : shortage, lack
definición *nf, pl* **-ciones** : definition
definido, -da *adj* : definite, well-defined
definir *vt* **1** : to define **2** : to determine
definitivamente *adv* **1** : finally **2** : permanently, for good **3** : definitely, absolutely
definitivo, -va *adj* **1** : definitive, conclusive **2 en definitiva** : all in all, on the whole **3 en definitiva** *Mex* : permanently, for good
deflación *nf, pl* **-ciones** : deflation
deforestación *nf, pl* **-ciones** : deforestation
deformación *nf, pl* **-ciones 1** : deformation **2** : distortion
deformar *vt* **1** : to deform, to disfigure **2** : to distort — **deformarse** *vr*
deforme *adj* : deformed, misshapen
deformidad *nf* : deformity
defraudación *nf, pl* **-ciones** : fraud
defraudar *vt* **1** ESTAFAR : to defraud, to cheat **2** : to disappoint
defunción *nf, pl* **-ciones** DECESO : death, passing

degeneración *nf, pl* **-ciones 1** : degeneration **2** : degeneracy, depravity
degenerado, -da *adj* DEPRAVADO : degenerate
degenerar *vi* : to degenerate
degenerativo, -va *adj* : degenerative
degollar {19} *vt* **1** : to slit the throat of, to slaughter **2** DECAPITAR : to behead **3** : to ruin, to destroy
degradación *nf, pl* **-ciones 1** : degradation **2** : demotion
degradar *vt* **1** : to degrade, to debase **2** : to demote
degustación *nf, pl* **-ciones** : tasting, sampling
degustar *vt* : to taste
deidad *nf* : deity
deificar {72} *vt* : to idolize, to deify
dejado, -da *adj* **1** : slovenly **2** : careless, lazy
dejar *vt* **1** : to leave **2** ABANDONAR : to abandon, to forsake **3** : to let be, to let go **4** PERMITIR : to allow, to permit — *vi* ~ **de** : to stop, to quit ⟨dejar de fumar : to quit smoking⟩ — **dejarse** *vr* **1** : to let oneself be ⟨se deja insultar : he lets himself be insulted⟩ **2** : to forget, to leave ⟨me dejé las llaves en el carro : I left the keys in the car⟩ **3** : to neglect oneself, to let oneself go **4** : to grow ⟨nos estamos dejando el pelo largo : we're growing our hair long⟩
dejo *nm* **1** : aftertaste **2** : touch, hint **3** : (regional) accent
del (*contraction of* **de** *and* **el**) → **de**
delación *nf, pl* **-ciones** : denunciation, betrayal
delantal *nm* **1** : apron **2** : pinafore
delante *adv* **1** ENFRENTE : ahead, in front **2** ~ **de** : before, in front of
delantera *nf* **1** : front, front part, front row ⟨tomar la delantera : to take the lead⟩ **2** : forward line (in sports)
delantero[1]**, -ra** *adj* **1** : front, forward **2 tracción delantera** : front-wheel drive
delantero[2]**, -ra** *n* : forward (in sports)
delatar *vt* **1** : to betray, to reveal **2** : to denounce, to inform against
delegación *nf, pl* **-ciones** : delegation
delegado, -da *n* : delegate, representative
delegar {52} *vt* : to delegate
deleitar *vt* : to delight, to please — **deleitarse** *vr*
deleite *nm* : delight, pleasure
deletrear *vi* : to spell ⟨¿como se deletrea? : how do you spell it?⟩
deleznable *adj* **1** : brittle, crumbly **2** : slippery **3** : weak, fragile ⟨una excusa deleznable : a weak excuse⟩
delfín *nm, pl* **delfines 1** : dolphin **2** : dauphin, heir apparent
delgadez *nf* : thinness, skinniness
delgado, -da *adj* **1** FLACO : thin, skinny **2** ESBELTO : slender, slim **3** DELICADO : delicate, fine **4** AGUDO : sharp, clever
deliberación *nf, pl* **-ciones** : deliberation

deliberado, -da *adj* : deliberate, intentional — **deliberadamente** *adv*
deliberar *vi* : to deliberate
deliberativo, -va *adj* : deliberative
delicadeza *nf* **1** : delicacy, fineness **2** : gentleness, softness **3** : tact, discretion, consideration
delicado, -da *adj* **1** : delicate, fine **2** : sensitive, frail **3** : difficult, tricky **4** : fussy, hard to please **5** : tactful, considerate
delicia *nf* : delight
delicioso, -sa *adj* **1** RICO : delicious **2** : delightful
delictivo, -va *adj* : criminal
delictuoso, -sa → **delictivo**
delimitación *nf, pl* **-ciones 1** : demarcation **2** : defining, specifying
delimitar *vt* **1** : to demarcate **2** : to define, to specify
delincuencia *nf* : delinquency, crime
delincuente[1] *adj* : delinquent
delincuente[2] *nmf* CRIMINAL : delinquent, criminal
delinear *vt* **1** : to delineate, to outline **2** : to draft, to draw up
delinquir {24} *vi* : to break the law
delirante *adj* : delirious
delirar *vi* **1** DESVARIAR : to be delirious **2** : to rave, to talk nonsense
delirio *nm* **1** DESVARÍO : delirium **2** DISPARATE : nonsense, ravings *pl* ⟨delirios de grandeza : delusions of grandeur⟩ **3** FRENESÍ : mania, frenzy ⟨¡fue el delirio! : it was wild!⟩
delito *nm* : crime, offense
delta *nm* : delta
demacrado, -da *adj* : emaciated, gaunt
demagogia *nf* : demagogy
demagógico, -ca *adj* : demagogic, demagogical
demagogo, -ga *n* : demagogue
demanda *nf* **1** : demand ⟨la oferta y la demanda : supply and demand⟩ **2** : petition, request **3** : lawsuit
demandado, -da *n* : defendant
demandante *nmf* : plaintiff
demandar *vt* **1** : to demand **2** REQUERIR : to call for, to require **3** : to sue, to file a lawsuit against
demarcar {72} *vt* : to demarcate — **demarcación** *nf*
demás[1] *adj* : remaining ⟨acabó las demás tareas : she finished the rest of the chores⟩
demás[2] *pron* **1** lo (la, los, las) demás : the rest, everyone else, everything else ⟨Pepe, Rosa, y los demás : Pepe, Rosa, and everybody else⟩ **2** estar por demás : to be of no use, to be pointless ⟨no estaría por demás : it couldn't hurt, it's worth a try⟩ **3** por demás : extremely **4** por lo demás : otherwise **5** y demás : and so on, et cetera
demasía *nf* en ∼ : excessively, in excess
demasiado[1] *adv* **1** : too ⟨vas demasiado aprisa : you're going too fast⟩ **2** : too

much ⟨estoy comiendo demasiado : I'm eating too much⟩
demasiado[2], **-da** *adj* : too much, too many, excessive
demencia *nf* **1** : dementia **2** LOCURA : madness, insanity
demente[1] *adj* : insane, mad
demente[2] *nmf* : insane person
demeritar *vt* **1** : to detract from **2** : to discredit
demérito *nm* **1** : fault **2** : discredit, disrepute
democracia *nf* : democracy
demócrata[1] *adj* : democratic
demócrata[2] *nmf* : democrat
democrático, -ca *adj* : democratic — **democráticamente** *adv*
democratizar {21} *vt* : to democratize, to make democratic
demografía *nf* : demography
demográfico, -ca *adj* : demographic
demoledor, -dora *adj* : devastating
demoler {47} *vt* DERRIBAR, DERRUMBAR : to demolish, to destroy
demolición *nf, pl* **-ciones** : demolition
demonio *nm* DIABLO : devil, demon
demora *nf* : delay
demorar *vt* **1** RETRASAR : to delay **2** TARDAR : to take, to last ⟨la reparación demorará varios días : the repair will take several days⟩ — *vi* : to delay, to linger — **demorarse** *vr* **1** : to be slow, to take a long time **2** : to take too long
demostración *nf, pl* **-ciones** : demonstration
demostrar {19} *vt* : to demonstrate, to show
demostrativo, -va *adj* : demonstrative
demudar *vt* : to change, to alter — **demudarse** *vr* : to change one's expression
denegación *nf, pl* **-ciones** : denial, refusal
denegar {49} *vt* : to deny, to turn down
denigrante *adj* : degrading, humiliating
denigrar *vt* **1** DIFAMAR : to denigrate, to disparage **2** : to degrade, to humiliate
denodado, -da *adj* : bold, dauntless
denominación *nf, pl* **-ciones 1** : name, designation **2** : denomination (of money)
denominador *nm* : denominator
denominar *vt* : to designate, to name
denostar {19} *vt* : to revile
denotar *vt* : to denote, to show
densidad *nf* : density, thickness
denso, -sa *adj* : dense, thick — **densamente** *adv*
dentado, -da *adj* SERRADO : serrated, jagged
dentadura *nf* **1** : teeth *pl* **2** dentadura postiza : dentures *pl*
dental *adj* : dental
dentellada *nf* **1** : bite **2** : tooth mark
dentera *nf* **1** : envy, jealousy **2** dar dentera : to set one's teeth on edge
dentición *nf, pl* **-ciones 1** : teething **2** : dentition, set of teeth

dentífrico *nm* : toothpaste

dentista *nmf* : dentist

dentro *adv* **1** : in, inside **2** : indoors **3** ~ **de** : within, inside, in **4 dentro de poco** : soon, shortly **5 dentro de todo** : all in all, all things considered **6 por** ~ : inwardly, inside

denuedo *nm* : valor, courage

denuesto *nm* : insult

denuncia *nf* **1** : denunciation, condemnation **2** : police report

denunciante *nmf* : accuser (of a crime)

denunciar *vt* **1** : to denounce, to condemn **2** : to report (to the authorities)

deparar *vt* : to have in store for, to provide with ⟨no sabemos lo que nos depara el destino : we don't know what fate has in store for us⟩

departamental *adj* **1** : departmental **2 tienda departamental** *Mex* : department store

departamento *nm* **1** : department **2** APARTAMENTO : apartment

departir *vi* : to converse

dependencia *nf* **1** : dependence, dependency ⟨dependencia emocional : emotional dependence⟩ ⟨dependencia del alcohol : dependence on alcohol⟩ **2** : agency, branch office

depender *vi* **1** : to depend **2** ~ **de** : to depend on **3** ~ **de** : to be subordinate to

dependiente[1] *adj* : dependent

dependiente[2], **-ta** *n* : clerk, salesperson

deplorable *adj* : deplorable

deplorar *vt* **1** : to deplore **2** LAMENTAR : to regret

deponer {60} *vt* **1** : to depose, to overthrow **2** : to abandon (an attitude or stance) **3 deponer las armas** : to lay down one's arms — *vi* **1** TESTIFICAR : to testify, to make a statement **2** EVACUAR : to defecate

deportación *nf, pl* **-ciones** : deportation

deportar *vt* : to deport

deporte *nm* : sport, sports *pl* ⟨hacer deporte : to engage in sports⟩

deportista[1] *adj* **1** : fond of sports **2** : sporty

deportista[2] *nmf* **1** : sports fan **2** : athlete, sportsman *m*, sportswoman *f*

deportividad *nf Spain* : sportsmanship

deportivo, -va *adj* **1** : sports, sporting ⟨artículos deportivos : sporting goods⟩ **2** : sporty

deposición *nf, pl* **-ciones** **1** : statement, testimony **2** : removal from office

depositante *nmf* : depositor

depositar *vt* **1** : to deposit, to place **2** : to store — **depositarse** *vr* : to settle

depósito *nm* **1** : deposit **2** : warehouse, storehouse

depravación *nf, pl* **-ciones** : depravity

depravado, -da *adj* DEGENERADO : depraved, degenerate

depravar *vt* : to deprave, to corrupt

depreciación *nf, pl* **-ciones** : depreciation

depreciar *vt* : to depreciate, to reduce the value of — **depreciarse** *vr* : to lose value

depredación *nf* SAQUEO : depredation, plunder

depredador[1], **-dora** *adj* : predatory

depredador[2] *nm* **1** : predator **2** SAQUEADOR : plunderer

depresión *nf, pl* **-siones** **1** : depression **2** : hollow, recess **3** : drop, fall **4** : slump, recession

depresivo[1], **-va** *adj* **1** : depressive **2** : depressant

depresivo[2] *nm* : depressant

deprimente *adj* : depressing

deprimir *vt* **1** : to depress **2** : to lower — **deprimirse** *vr* ABATIRSE : to get depressed

depuesto *pp* → **deponer**

depuración *nf, pl* **-ciones** **1** PURIFICACIÓN : purification **2** PURGA : purge **3** : refinement, polish

depurar *vt* **1** PURIFICAR : to purify **2** PURGAR : to purge

depuso, etc. → **deponer**

derecha *nf* **1** : right **2** : right hand, right side **3** : right wing, right (in politics)

derechazo *nm* **1** : pass with the cape on the right hand (in bullfighting) **2** : right (in boxing) **3** : forehand (in tennis)

derechista[1] *adj* : rightist, right-wing

derechista[2] *nmf* : right-winger

derecho[1] *adv* **1** : straight **2** : upright **3** : directly

derecho[2], **-cha** *adj* **1** : right **2** : right-hand **3** RECTO : straight, upright, erect

derecho[3] *nm* **1** : right ⟨derechos humanos : human rights⟩ **2** : law ⟨derecho civil : civil law⟩ **3** : right side (of cloth or clothing)

deriva *nf* **1** : drift **2 a la deriva** : adrift

derivación *nf, pl* **-ciones** **1** : derivation **2** RAMIFICACIÓN : ramification, consequence

derivar *vi* **1** : to drift **2** ~ **de** : to come from, to derive from **3** ~ **en** : to result in — *vt* : to steer, to direct ⟨derivó la discusión hacia la política : he steered the discussion over to politics⟩ — **derivarse** *vr* : to be derived from, to arise from

dermatología *nf* : dermatology

dermatológico, -ca *adj* : dermatological

dermatólogo, -ga *n* : dermatologist

derogación *nf, pl* **-ciones** : abolition, repeal

derogar {52} *vt* ABOLIR : to abolish, to repeal

derramamiento *nm* **1** : spilling, overflowing **2 derramamiento de sangre** : bloodshed

derramar *vt* **1** : to spill **2** : to shed (tears, blood) — **derramarse** *vr* **1** : to spill over **2** : to scatter

derrame *nm* **1** : spilling, shedding **2** : leakage, overflow **3** : discharge, hemorrhage

derrapar *vi* : to skid

derrape *nm* : skid
derredor *nm* **al derredor** *or* **en derredor**
: around, round about
derrengado, -da *adj* **1** : bent, twisted **2**
: exhausted
derretir {54} *vt* : to melt, to thaw — **derretirse** *vr* **1** : to melt, to thaw **2** ~ **por**
fam : to be crazy about
derribar *vt* **1** DEMOLER, DERRUMBAR
: to demolish, to knock down **2** : to
shoot down, to bring down (an airplane) **3** DERROCAR : to overthrow
derribo *nm* **1** : demolition, razing **2**
: shooting down **3** : overthrow
derrocamiento *nm* : overthrow
derrocar {72} *vt* DERRIBAR : to overthrow, to topple
derrochador¹, -dora *adj* : extravagant,
wasteful
derrochador², -dora *n* : spendthrift
derrochar *vt* : to waste, to squander
derroche *nm* : extravagance, waste
derrota *nf* **1** : defeat, rout **2** : course (at
sea)
derrotar *vt* : to defeat
derrotero *nm* RUTA : course
derrotista *adj & nmf* : defeatist
derruir {41} *vt* : to demolish, to tear down
derrumbamiento *nm* : collapse
derrumbar *vt* **1** DEMOLER, DERRIBAR
: to demolish, to knock down **2** DE-
SPEÑAR : to cast down, to topple —
derrumbarse *vr* DESPLOMARSE : to collapse, to break down
derrumbe *nm* **1** DESPLOME : collapse,
fall ⟨el derrumbe del comunismo : the
fall of Communism⟩ **2** : landslide
desabastecimiento *nm* : shortage, scarcity
desabasto *nm Mex* : shortage, scarcity
desabrido, -da *adj* : tasteless, bland
desabrigar {52} *vt* **1** : to undress **2** : to
uncover **3** : to deprive of shelter
desabrochar *vt* : to unbutton, to undo
— **desabrocharse** *vr* : to come undone
desacatar *vt* **1** DESAFIAR : to defy **2**
DESOBEDECER : to disobey
desacato *nm* **1** : disrespect **2** : contempt (of court)
desacelerar *vi* : to decelerate, to slow
down
desacertado, -da *adj* **1** : mistaken **2**
: unwise
desacertar {55} *vi* ERRAR : to err, to be
mistaken
desacierto *nm* ERROR : error, mistake
desaconsejable *adj* : inadvisable
desaconsejado, -da *adj* : ill-advised,
unwise
desacorde *adj* **1** : conflicting **2** : discordant
desacostumbrado, -da *adj* : unaccustomed, unusual
desacreditar *vt* DESPRESTIGIAR : to discredit, to disgrace
desactivar *vt* : to deactivate, to defuse
desacuerdo *nm* : disagreement
desafiante *adj* : defiant

desafiar {85} *vt* RETAR : to defy, to challenge
desafilado, -da *adj* : blunt
desafinado, -da *adj* : out-of-tune, off-
key
desafinarse *vr* : to go out of tune
desafío *nm* **1** RETO : challenge **2** RE-
SISTENCIA : defiance
desafortunado, -da *adj* : unfortunate,
unlucky — **desafortunadamente** *adv*
desafuero *nm* ABUSO : injustice, outrage
desagradable *adj* : unpleasant, disagreeable — **desagradablemente** *adv*
desagradar *vi* : to be unpleasant, to be
disagreeable
desagradecido, -da *adj* : ungrateful
desagrado *nm* **1** : displeasure **2 con** ~
: reluctantly
desagravio *nm* **1** : apology **2** : amends,
reparation
desagregarse {52} *vr* : to break up, to
disintegrate
desaguar {10} *vi* : to drain, to empty
desagüe *nm* **1** : drain **2** : drainage
desahogado, -da *adj* **1** : well-off, comfortable **2** : spacious, roomy
desahogar {52} *vt* **1** : to relieve, to ease
2 : to give vent to — **desahogarse** *vr*
1 : to recover, to feel better **2** : to unburden oneself, to let off steam
desahogo *nm* **1** : relief, outlet **2 con**
~ : comfortably
desahuciar *vt* **1** : to deprive of hope **2**
: to evict — **desahuciarse** *vr* : to lose
all hope
desahucio *nm* : eviction
desairar {5} *vt* : to snub, to rebuff
desaire *nm* : rebuff, snub, slight
desajustar *vt* **1** : to disarrange, to put
out of order **2** : to upset (plans)
desajuste *nm* **1** : maladjustment **2** : imbalance **3** : upset, disruption
desalentador, -dora *adj* : discouraging,
disheartening
desalentar {55} *vt* DESANIMAR : to discourage, to dishearten — **desalen-
tarse** *vr*
desaliento *nm* : discouragement
desaliñado, -da *adj* : slovenly, untidy
desalmado, -da *adj* : heartless, callous
desalojar *vt* **1** : to remove, to clear **2**
EVACUAR : to evacuate, to vacate **3** : to
evict
desalojo *nm* **1** : removal, expulsion **2**
: evacuation **3** : eviction
desamor *nm* **1** FRIALDAD : indifference
2 ENEMISTAD : dislike, enmity
desamparado, -da *adj* DESVALIDO
: helpless, destitute
desamparar *vt* : to abandon, to forsake
desamparo *nm* **1** : abandonment, neglect **2** : helplessness
desamueblado, -da *adj* : unfurnished
desandar {6} *vt* : to go back, to return
to the starting point
desangelado, -da *adj* : dull, lifeless
desangrar *vt* : to bleed, to bleed dry —
desangrarse *vr* **1** : to be bleeding **2**
: to bleed to death

desanimar *vt* DESALENTAR : to discourage, to dishearten — **desanimarse** *vr*
desánimo *nm* DESALIENTO : discouragement, dejection
desanudar *vt* : to untie, to disentangle
desapacible *adj* : unpleasant, disagreeable
desaparecer {53} *vt* : to cause to disappear — *vi* : to disappear, to vanish
desaparecido¹, -da *adj* **1** : late, deceased **2** : missing
desaparecido², -da *n* : missing person
desaparición *nf, pl* **-ciones** : disappearance
desapasionado, -da *adj* : dispassionate, impartial — **desapasionadamente** *adv*
desapego *nm* : coolness, indifference
desapercibido, -da *adj* **1** : unnoticed **2** DESPREVENIDO : unprepared, off guard
desaprobación *nf, pl* **-ciones** : disapproval
desaprobar {19} *vt* REPROBAR : to disapprove of
desaprovechar *vt* MALGASTAR : to waste, to misuse — *vi* : to lose ground, to slip back
desarmador *nm* *Mex* : screwdriver
desarmar *vt* **1** : to disarm **2** DESMONTAR : to disassemble, to take apart
desarme *nm* : disarmament
desarraigado, -da *adj* : rootless
desarraigar {52} *vt* : to uproot, to root out
desarreglado, -da *adj* : untidy, disorganized
desarreglar *vt* **1** : to mess up **2** : to upset, to disrupt
desarreglo *nm* **1** : untidiness **2** : disorder, confusion
desarrollar *vt* : to develop — **desarrollarse** *vr* : to take place
desarrollo *nm* : development
desarticulación *nf, pl* **-ciones** **1** : dislocation **2** : breaking up, dismantling
desarticular *vt* **1** DISLOCAR : to dislocate **2** : to break up, to dismantle
desaseado, -da *adj* **1** : dirty **2** : messy, untidy
desastre *nm* CATÁSTROFE : disaster
desastroso, -sa *adj* : disastrous, catastrophic
desatar *vt* **1** : to undo, to untie **2** : to unleash **3** : to trigger, to precipitate — **desatarse** *vr* : to break out, to erupt
desatascar {72} *vt* : to unblock, to clear
desatención *nf, pl* **-ciones** **1** : absentmindedness, distraction **2** : discourtesy
desatender {56} *vt* **1** : to disregard **2** : to neglect
desatento, -ta *adj* **1** DISTRAÍDO : absentminded **2** GROSERO : discourteous, rude
desatinado, -da *adj* : foolish, silly
desatino *nm* : folly, mistake

desautorizar {21} *vt* : to deprive of authority, to discredit
desavenencia *nf* DISCORDANCIA : disagreement, dispute
desayunar *vi* : to have breakfast — *vt* : to have for breakfast
desayuno *nm* : breakfast
desazón *nf, pl* **-zones** INQUIETUD : uneasiness, anxiety
desbalance *nm* : imbalance
desbancar {72} *vt* : to displace, to oust
desbandada *nf* : scattering, dispersal
desbarajuste *nm* DESORDEN : disarray, disorder, mess
desbaratar *vt* **1** ARRUINAR : to destroy, to ruin **2** DESCOMPONER : to break, to break down — **desbaratarse** *vr* : to fall apart
desbloquear *vt* **1** : to open up, to clear, to break through **2** : to free, to release
desbocado, -da *adj* : unbridled, rampant
desbocarse {72} *vr* : to run away, to bolt
desbordamiento *nm* : overflowing
desbordante *adj* : overflowing, bursting ⟨desbordante de energía : bursting with energy⟩
desbordar *vt* **1** ; to overflow, to spill over **2** : to surpass, to exceed — **desbordarse** *vr*
descabellado, -da *adj* : outlandish, ridiculous
descafeinado, -da *adj* : decaffeinated
descalabrar *vt* : to hit on the head — **descalabrarse** *vr*
descalabro *nm* : setback, misfortune, loss
descalificación *nf, pl* **-ciones** **1** : disqualification **2** : disparaging remark
descalificar {72} *vt* **1** : to disqualify **2** DESACREDITAR : to discredit — **descalificarse** *vr*
descalzarse {21} *vr* : take off one's shoes
descalzo, -za *adj* : barefoot
descansado, -da *adj* **1** : rested, refreshed **2** : restful, peaceful
descansar *vi* : to rest, to relax — *vt* : to rest ⟨descansar la vista : to rest one's eyes⟩
descansillo *nm* : landing (of a staircase)
descanso *nm* **1** : rest, relaxation **2** : break **3** : landing (of a staircase) **4** : intermission
descapotable *adj* & *nm* : convertible
descarado, -da *adj* : brazen, impudent — **descaradamente** *adv*
descarga *nf* **1** : discharge **2** : unloading
descargar {52} *vt* **1** : to discharge **2** : to unload **3** : to release, to free **4** : to take out, to vent (anger, etc.) — **descargarse** *vr* **1** : to unburden oneself **2** : to quit **3** : to lose power
descargo *nm* **1** : unloading **2** : defense ⟨testigo de descargo : witness for the defense⟩
descarnado, -da *adj* : scrawny, gaunt
descaro *nm* : audacity, nerve

descarriado, -da *adj* : lost, gone astray
descarrilar *vi* : to derail — **descarrilarse** *vr*
descartar *vt* : to rule out, to reject — **descartarse** *vr* : to discard
descascarar *vt* : to peel, to shell, to husk — **descascararse** *vr* : to peel off, to chip
descendencia *nf* **1** : descendants *pl* **2** LINAJE : descent, lineage
descendente *adj* : downward, descending
descender {56} *vt* **1** : to descend, to go down **2** BAJAR : to lower, to take down, to let down — *vi* **1** : to descend, to come down **2** : to drop, to fall **3** ~ **de** : to be a descendant of
descendiente *adj & nm* : descendant
descenso *nm* **1** : descent **2** BAJA, CAÍDA : drop, fall
descentralizar {21} *vt* : to decentralize — **descentralizarse** *vr* — **descentralización** *nf*
descifrable *adj* : decipherable
descifrar *vt* : to decipher, to decode
descodificar {72} *vt* : to decode
descolgar {16} *vt* **1** : to take down, to let down **2** : to pick up, to answer (the telephone)
descollar {19} *vi* SOBRESALIR : to stand out, to be outstanding, to excel
descolorarse *vr* : to fade
descolorido, -da *adj* : discolored, faded
descomponer {60} *vt* **1** : to rot, to decompose **2** DESBARATAR : to break, to break down — **descomponerse** *vr* **1** : to break down **2** : to decompose
descomposición *nf, pl* **-ciones 1** : breakdown, decomposition **2** : decay
descompresión *nf* : decompression
descompuesto[1] *pp* → **descomponer**
descompuesto[2], **-ta** *adj* **1** : broken down, out of order **2** : rotten, decomposed
descomunal *adj* **1** ENORME : enormous, huge **2** EXTRAORDINARIO : extraordinary
desconcertante *adj* : disconcerting
desconcertar {55} *vt* : to disconcert — **desconcertarse** *vr*
desconchar *vt* : to chip — **desconcharse** *vr* : to chip off, to peel
desconcierto *nm* : uncertainty, confusion
desconectar *vt* **1** : to disconnect, to switch off **2** : to unplug
desconfiado, -da *adj* : distrustful, suspicious
desconfianza *nf* RECELO : distrust, suspicion
desconfiar {85} *vi* ~ **de** : to distrust, to be suspicious of
descongelar *vt* **1** : to thaw **2** : to defrost **3** : to unfreeze (assets — **descongelarse** *vr*
descongestionante *adj & nm* : decongestant

desconocer {18} *vt* **1** IGNORAR : to be unaware of **2** : to fail to recognize
desconocido[1], **-da** *adj* : unknown, unfamiliar
desconocido[2], **-da** *n* EXTRAÑO : stranger
desconocimiento *nm* : ignorance
desconsiderado, -da *adj* : inconsiderate, thoughtless — **desconsideradamente** *adj*
desconsolado, -da *adj* : disconsolate, heartbroken
desconsuelo *nm* AFLICCIÓN : grief, distress, despair
descontaminar *vt* : to decontaminate — **descontaminación** *nf*
descontar {19} *vt* **1** : to discount, to deduct **2** EXCEPTUAR : to except, to exclude
descontento[1], **-ta** *adj* : discontented, dissatisfied
descontento[2] *nm* : discontent, dissatisfaction
descontrol *nm* : lack of control, disorder, chaos
descontrolarse *vr* : to get out of control, to be out of hand
descorazonado, -da *adj* : disheartened, discouraged
descorazonador, -dora *adj* : disheartening, discouraging
descorrer *vt* : to draw back
descortés *adj, pl* **-teses** : discourteous, rude
descortesía *nf* : discourtesy, rudeness
descrédito *nm* DESPRESTIGIO : discredit
descremado, -da *adj* : nonfat, skim
describir {33} *vt* : to describe
descripción *nf, pl* **-ciones** : description
descriptivo, -va *adj* : descriptive
descrito *pp* → **describir**
descuartizar {21} *vt* **1** : to cut up, to quarter **2** : to tear to pieces
descubierto[1] *pp* → **descubrir**
descubierto[2], **-ta** *adj* **1** : exposed, revealed **2 al descubierto** : out in the open
descubridor, -dora *n* : discoverer, explorer
descubrimiento *nm* : discovery
descubrir {2} *vt* **1** HALLAR : to discover, to find out **2** REVELAR : to uncover, to reveal — **descubrirse** *vr*
descuento *nm* REBAJA : discount
descuidado, -da *adj* **1** : neglectful, careless **2** : neglected, unkempt
descuidar *vt* : to neglect, to overlook — *vi* : to be careless — **descuidarse** *vr* **1** : to be careless, to drop one's guard **2** : to let oneself go
descuido *nm* **1** : carelessness, negligence **2** : slip, oversight
desde *prep* **1** : from **2** : since **3 desde ahora** : from now on **4 desde entonces** : since then **5 desde hace** : for, since (a time) ⟨ha estado nevando desde hace dos días : it's been snowing for

two days⟩ **6 desde luego** : of course **7 desde que** : since, ever since **8 desde ya** : right now, immediately
desdecir {11} *vi* **1** ~ **de** : to be unworthy of **2** ~ **de** : to clash with — **desdecirse** *vr* **1** CONTRADECIRSE : to contradict oneself **2** RETRACTARSE : to go back on one's word
desdén *nm, pl* **desdenes** DESPRECIO : disdain, scorn
desdentado, -da *adj* : toothless
desdeñar *vt* DESPRECIAR : to disdain, to scorn, to despise
desdeñoso, -sa *adj* : disdainful, scornful — **desdeñosamente** *adv*
desdibujar *vt* : to blur — **desdibujarse** *vr*
desdicha *nf* **1** : misery **2** : misfortune
desdichado[1], -da *adj* **1** : unfortunate **2** : miserable, unhappy
desdichado[2], -da *n* : wretch
desdicho *pp* → **desdecir**
desdiga, desdijo etc. → **desdecir**
desdoblar *vt* DESPLEGAR : to unfold
deseable *adj* : desirable
desear *vt* **1** : to wish ⟨te deseo buena suerte : I wish you good luck⟩ **2** QUERER : to want, to desire
desecar {72} *vt* : to dry (flowers, etc.)
desechable *adj* : disposable
desechar *vt* **1** : to discard, to throw away **2** RECHAZAR : to reject
desecho *nm* **1** : reject **2 desechos** *nmpl* RESIDUOS : rubbish, waste
desembarazarse {21} *vr* ~ **de** : to get rid of
desembarcadero *nm* : jetty, landing pier
desembarcar {72} *vi* : to disembark — *vt* : to unload
desembarco *nm* **1** : landing, arrival **2** : unloading
desembarque → **desembarco**
desembocadura *nf* **1** : mouth (of a river) **2** : opening, end (of a street)
desembocar {72} *vi* ~ **en** *or* ~ **a 1** : to flow into, to join **2** : to lead to, to result in
desembolsar *vt* PAGAR : to disburse, to pay out
desembolso *nm* PAGO : disbursement, payment
desempacar {72} *v* : to unpack
desempate *nm* : tiebreaker, play-off
desempeñar *vt* **1** : to play (a role) **2** : to fulfill, to carry out **3** : to redeem (from a pawnshop) — **desempeñarse** *vr* : to function, to act
desempeño *nm* **1** : fulfillment, carrying out **2** : performance
desempleado[1], -da *adj* : unemployed
desempleado[2], -da *n* : unemployed person
desempleo *nm* : unemployment
desempolvar *vt* **1** : to dust off **2** : to resurrect, to revive
desencadenar *vt* **1** : to unchain **2** : to trigger, to unleash — **desencadenarse** *vr*

desencajar *vt* **1** : to dislocate **2** : to disconnect, to disengage
desencantar *vt* : to disenchant, to disillusion — **desencantarse** *vr*
desencanto *nm* : disenchantment, disillusionment
desenchufar *vt* : to disconnect, to unplug
desenfadado, -da *adj* **1** : uninhibited, carefree **2** : confident, self-assured
desenfado *nm* **1** DESENVOLTURA : self-assurance, confidence **2** : naturalness, ease
desenfrenadamente *adv* : wildly, with abandon
desenfrenado, -da *adj* : unbridled, unrestrained
desenfreno *nm* : abandon, unrestraint
desenganchar *vt* : to unhitch, to uncouple
desengañar *vt* : to disillusion, to disenchant — **desengañarse** *vr*
desengaño *nm* : disenchantment, disillusionment
desenlace *nm* : ending, outcome
desenlazar {21} *vt* **1** : to untie **2** : to clear up, to resolve
desenmarañar *vt* : to disentangle, to unravel
desenmascarar *vt* : to unmask, to expose
desenredar *vt* : to untangle, to disentangle
desenrollar *vt* : to unroll, to unwind
desentenderse {56} *vr* **1** ~ **de** : to want nothing to do with, to be uninterested in **2** ~ **de** : to pretend ignorance of
desenterrar {55} *vt* **1** EXHUMAR : to exhume **2** : to unearth, to dig up
desentonar *vi* **1** : to clash, to conflict **2** : to be out of tune, to sing off-key
desentrañar *vt* : to get to the bottom of, to unravel
desenvainar *vt* : to draw, to unsheathe (a sword)
desenvoltura *nf* **1** DESENFADO : confidence, self-assurance **2** ELOCUENCIA : eloquence, fluency
desenvolver {89} *vt* : to unwrap, to open — **desenvolverse** *vr* **1** : to unfold, to develop **2** : to manage, to cope
desenvuelto[1] *pp* → **desenvolver**
desenvuelto[2], -ta *adj* : confident, relaxed, self-assured
deseo *nm* : wish, desire
deseoso, -sa *adj* : eager, anxious
desequilibrar *vt* : to unbalance, to throw off balance — **desequilibrarse** *vr*
desequilibrio *nm* : imbalance
deserción *nf, pl* **-ciones** : desertion, defection
desertar *vi* **1** : to desert, to defect **2** ~ **de** : to abandon, to neglect
desertor, -tora *n* : deserter, defector
desesperación *nf, pl* **-ciones** : desperation, despair

desesperado, -da *adj* : desperate, despairing, hopeless — **desesperadamente** *adv*
desesperanza *nf* : despair, hopelessness
desesperar *vt* : to exasperate — *vi* : to despair, to lose hope — **desesperarse** *vr* : to become exasperated
desestimar *vt* **1** : to reject, to disallow **2** : to have a low opinion of
desfachatez *nf, pl* **-teces** : audacity, nerve, cheek
desfalcador, -dora *n* : embezzler
desfalcar {72} *vt* : to embezzle
desfalco *nm* : embezzlement
desfallecer {53} *vi* **1** : to weaken **2** : to faint
desfallecimiento *nm* **1** : weakness **2** : fainting
desfasado, -da *adj* **1** : out of sync **2** : out of step, behind the times
desfase *nm* : gap, lag ⟨desfase horario : jet lag⟩
desfavorable *adj* : unfavorable, adverse — **desfavorablemente** *adv*
desfavorecido, -da *adj* : underprivileged
desfigurar *vt* **1** : to disfigure, to mar **2** : to distort, to misrepresent
desfiladero *nm* : narrow gorge, defile
desfilar *vi* : to parade, to march
desfile *nm* : parade, procession
desfogar {52} *vt* **1** : to vent **2** *Mex* : to unclog, to unblock — **desfogarse** *vr* : to vent one's feelings, to let off steam
desforestación *nf, pl* **-ciones** : deforestation
desgajar *vt* **1** : to tear off **2** : to break apart — **desgajarse** *vr* : to come apart
desgana *nf* **1** INAPETENCIA : lack of appetite **2** APATÍA : apathy, unwillingness, reluctance
desgano *nm* → **desgana**
desgarbado, -da *adj* : ungainly
desgarrador, -dora *adj* : heartrending, heartbreaking
desgarradura *nf* : tear, rip
desgarrar *vt* **1** : to tear, to rip **2** : to break (one's heart) — **desgarrarse** *vr*
desgarre → **desgarro**
desgarro *nm* : tear
desgarrón *nm, pl* **-rrones** : rip, tear
desgastar *vt* **1** : to use up **2** : to wear away, to wear down
desgaste *nm* : deterioration, wear and tear
desglosar *vt* : to break down, to itemize
desglose *nm* : breakdown, itemization
desgobierno *nm* : anarchy, disorder
desgracia *nf* **1** : misfortune **2** : disgrace **3** por ~ : unfortunately
desgraciadamente *adv* : unfortunately
desgraciado[1], -da *adj* **1** : unfortunate, unlucky **2** : vile, wretched
desgraciado[2], -da *n* : unfortunate person, wretch
desgranar *vt* : to shuck, to shell
deshabitado, -da *adj* : unoccupied, uninhabited

deshacer {40} *vt* **1** : to destroy, to ruin **2** DESATAR : to undo, to untie **3** : to break apart, to crumble **4** : to dissolve, to melt **5** : to break, to cancel — **deshacerse** *vr* **1** : to fall apart, to come undone **2** ~ **de** : to get rid of
deshecho[1] *pp* → **deshacer**
deshecho[2], -cha *adj* **1** : destroyed, ruined **2** : devastated, shattered **3** : undone, untied
desheredado, -da *adj* MARGINADO : dispossessed, destitute
desheredar *vt* : to disinherit
deshicieron, etc. → **deshacer**
deshidratar *vt* : to dehydrate — **deshidratación** *nf*
deshielo *nm* : thaw, thawing
deshilachar *vt* : to fray — **deshilacharse** *vr*
deshizo → **deshacer**
deshonestidad *nf* : dishonesty
deshonesto, -ta *adj* : dishonest
deshonra *nf* : dishonor, disgrace
deshonrar *vt* : to dishonor, to disgrace
deshonroso, -sa *adj* : dishonorable, disgraceful
deshuesar *vt* **1** : to pit (a fruit, etc.) **2** : to bone, to debone
deshumanizar {21} *vt* : to dehumanize — **deshumanización** *nf*
desidia *nf* **1** APATÍA : apathy, indolence **2** NEGLIGENCIA : negligence, sloppiness
desierto[1], -ta *adj* : deserted, uninhabited
desierto[2] *nm* : desert
designación *nf, pl* **-ciones** NOMBRAMIENTO : appointment, naming (to an office, etc.)
designar *vt* NOMBRAR : to designate, to appoint, to name
designio *nm* : plan
desigual *adj* **1** : unequal **2** DISPAREJO : uneven
desigualdad *nf* **1** : inequality **2** : unevenness
desilusión *nf, pl* **-siones** DESENCANTO, DESENGAÑO : disillusionment, disenchantment
desilusionar *vt* DESENCANTAR, DESENGAÑAR : to disillusion, to disenchant — **desilusionarse** *vr*
desinfectante *adj & nm* : disinfectant
desinfectar *vt* : to disinfect — **desinfección** *nf*
desinflar *vt* : to deflate — **desinflarse** *vr*
desinhibido, -da *adj* : uninhibited, unrestrained
desintegración *nf, pl* **-ciones** : disintegration
desintegrar *vt* : to disintegrate, to break up — **desintegrarse** *vr*
desinterés *nm* **1** : lack of interest, indifference **2** : unselfishness
desinteresado, -da *adj* GENEROSO : unselfish
desintoxicar {72} *vt* : to detoxify, to detox

desistir *vi* **1** : to desist, to stop **2** ~ **de** : to give up, to relinquish

deslave *nm Mex* : landslide

desleal *adj* INFIEL : disloyal — **deslealmente** *adv*

deslealtad *nf* : disloyalty

desleír {66} *vt* : to dilute, to dissolve

desligar {52} *vt* **1** : to separate, to undo **2** : to free (from an obligation) — **desligarse** *vr* ~ **de** : to extricate oneself from

deslindar *vt* **1** : to mark the limits of, to demarcate **2** : to define, to clarify

deslinde *nm* : demarcation

desliz *nm, pl* **deslices** : error, mistake, slip ⟨desliz de la lengua : slip of the tongue⟩

deslizar {21} *vt* **1** : to slide, to slip **2** : to slip in — **deslizarse** *vr* **1** : to slide, to glide **2** : to slip away

deslucido, -da *adj* **1** : unimpressive, dull **2** : faded, dingy, tarnished

deslucir {45} *vt* **1** : to spoil **2** : to fade, to dull, to tarnish **3** : to discredit

deslumbrar *vt* : to dazzle — **deslumbrante** *adj*

deslustrado, -da *adj* : dull, lusterless

deslustrar *vt* : to tarnish, to dull

deslustre *nm* : tarnish

desmán *nm, pl* **desmanes 1** : outrage, abuse **2** : misfortune

desmandarse *vr* : to behave badly, to get out of hand

desmantelar *vt* DESMONTAR : to dismantle

desmañado, -da *adj* : clumsy, awkward

desmayado, -da *adj* **1** : fainting, weak **2** : dull, pale

desmayar *vi* : to lose heart, to falter — **desmayarse** *vr* DESVANECERSE : to faint, to swoon

desmayo *nm* **1** : faint, fainting **2 sufrir un desmayo** : to faint

desmedido, -da *adj* DESMESURADO : excessive, undue

desmejorar *vt* : to weaken, to make worse — *vi* : to decline (in health), to get worse

desmembramiento *nm* : dismemberment

desmembrar {55} *vt* **1** : to dismember **2** : to break up

desmemoriado, -da *adj* : absentminded, forgetful

desmentido *nm* : denial

desmentir {76} *vt* **1** NEGAR : to deny, to refute **2** CONTRADECIR : to contradict

desmenuzar {21} *vt* **1** : to break down, to scrutinize **2** : to crumble, to shred — **desmenuzarse** *vr*

desmerecer {53} *vt* : to be unworthy of — *vi* **1** : to decline in value **2** ~ **de** : to compare unfavorably with

desmesurado, -da *adj* DESMEDIDO : excessive, inordinate — **desmesuradamente** *adv*

desmigajar *vt* : to crumble — **desmigajarse** *vr*

desmilitarizado, -da *adj* : demilitarized

desmontar *vt* **1** : to clear, to level off **2** DESMANTELAR : to dismantle, to take apart — *vi* : to dismount

desmonte *nm* : clearing, leveling

desmoralizador, -dora *adj* : demoralizing

desmoralizar {21} *vt* DESALENTAR : to demoralize, to discourage

desmoronamiento *nm* : crumbling, falling apart

desmoronar *vt* : to wear away, to erode — **desmoronarse** *vr* : to crumble, to deteriorate, to fall apart

desmotadora *nf* : gin, cotton gin

desmovilizar {21} *vt* : to demobilize — **desmovilización** *nf*

desnaturalizar {21} *vt* **1** : to denature **2** : to distort, to alter

desnivel *nm* **1** : disparity, difference **2** : unevenness (of a surface)

desnivelado, -da *adj* **1** : uneven **2** : unbalanced

desnudar *vt* **1** : to undress **2** : to strip, to lay bare — **desnudarse** *vr* : to undress, to strip off one's clothing

desnudez *nf, pl* **-deces** : nudity, nakedness

desnudismo → **nudismo**

desnudista → **nudista**

desnudo¹, -da *adj* : nude, naked, bare

desnudo² *nm* : nude

desnutrición *nf, pl* **-ciones** MALNUTRICIÓN : malnutrition, undernourishment

desnutrido, -da *adj* MALNUTRIDO : malnourished, undernourished

desobedecer {53} *v* : to disobey

desobediencia *nf* : disobedience

desobediente *adj*

desocupación *nf, pl* **-ciones** : unemployment

desocupado, -da *adj* **1** : vacant, empty **2** : free, unoccupied **3** : unemployed

desocupar *vt* **1** : to empty **2** : to vacate, to move out of — **desocuparse** *vr* : to leave, to quit (a job)

desodorante *adj & nm* : deodorant

desolación *nf, pl* **-ciones** : desolation

desolado, -da *adj* **1** : desolate **2** : devastated, distressed

desolador, -dora *adj* **1** : devastating **2** : bleak, desolate

desollar *vt* : to skin, to flay

desorbitado, -da *adj* **1** : excessive, exorbitant **2 con los ojos desorbitados** : with eyes popping out of one's head

desorden *nm, pl* **desórdenes 1** DESBARAJUSTE : disorder, mess **2** : disorder, disturbance, upset

desordenado, -da *adj* **1** : untidy, messy **2** : disorderly, unruly

desordenar *vt* : to mess up — **desordenarse** *vr* : to get messed up

desorganización *nf, pl* **-ciones** : disorganization

desorganizar {21} *vt* : to disrupt, to disorganize

desorientación *nf, pl* **-ciones** : disorientation, confusion

desorientar *vt* : to disorient, to mislead, to confuse — **desorientarse** *vr* : to become disoriented, to lose one's way

desovar *vi* : to spawn

despachar *vt* **1** : to complete, to conclude **2** : to deal with, to take care of, to handle **3** : to dispatch, to send off **4** *fam* : to finish off, to kill — **despacharse** *vr fam* : to gulp down, to polish off

despacho *nm* **1** : dispatch, shipment **2** OFICINA : office, study

despacio *adv* LENTAMENTE, LENTO : slowly, slow ⟨¡despacio! : take it easy!, easy does it!⟩

desparasitar *vt* : to worm (an animal), to delouse

desparpajo *nm fam* **1** : self-confidence, nerve **2** *CA* : confusion, muddle

desparramar *vt* **1** : to spill, to splatter **2** : to spread, to scatter

despatarrarse *vr* : to sprawl (out)

despavorido, -da *adj* : terrified, horrified

despecho *nm* **1** : spite **2 a despecho de** : despite, in spite of

despectivo, -va *adj* **1** : contemptuous, disparaging **2** : derogatory, pejorative

despedazar {21} *vt* : to cut to pieces, to tear apart

despedida *nf* **1** : farewell, good-bye **2 despedida de soltera** : bridal shower

despedir {54} *vt* **1** : to see off, to show out **2** : to dismiss, to fire **3** EMITIR : to give off, to emit ⟨despedir un olor : to give off an odor⟩ — **despedirse** *vr* : to take one's leave, to say good-bye

despegado, -da *adj* **1** : separated, detached **2** : cold, distant

despegar {52} *vt* : to remove, to detach — *vi* : to take off, to lift off, to blast off

despegue *nm* : takeoff, liftoff

despeinado, -da *adj* : disheveled, tousled ⟨estoy despeinada : my hair's a mess⟩

despeinarse *vr* **1** : to mess up one's hair **2** : to become disheveled ⟨me despeiné : my hair got messed up⟩

despejado, -da *adj* **1** : clear, fair **2** : alert, clear-headed **3** : uncluttered, unobstructed

despejar *vt* **1** : to clear, to free **2** : to clarify — *vi* **1** : to clear up **2** : to punt (in sports)

despeje *nm* **1** : clearing **2** : punt (in sports)

despellejar *vt* : to skin (an animal)

despenalizar {21} *vt* : to legalize — **despenalización** *nf*

despensa *nf* **1** : pantry, larder **2** PROVISIONES : provisions *pl*, supplies *pl*

despeñar *vt* : to hurl down

despepitar *vt* : to seed, to remove the seeds from

desperdiciar *vt* **1** DESAPROVECHAR, MALGASTAR : to waste **2** : to miss, to miss out on

desperdicio *nm* **1** : waste **2 desperdicios** *nmpl* RESIDUOS : refuse, scraps, rubbish

desperdigar {52} *vt* DISPERSAR : to disperse, to scatter

desperfecto *nm* **1** DEFECTO : flaw, defect **2** : damage

despertador *nm* : alarm clock

despertar {55} *vi* : to awaken, to wake up — *vt* **1** : to arouse, to wake **2** EVOCAR : to elicit, to evoke — **despertarse** *vr* : to wake (oneself) up

despiadado, -da *adj* CRUEL : cruel, merciless, pitiless — **despiadadamente** *adv*

despido *nm* : dismissal, layoff

despierto, -ta *adj* **1** : awake, alert **2** LISTO : clever, sharp ⟨con la mente despierta : with a sharp mind⟩

despilfarrador¹, -dora *adj* : extravagant, wasteful

despilfarrador², -dora *n* : spendthrift, prodigal

despilfarrar *vt* MALGASTAR : to squander, to waste

despilfarro *nm* : extravagance, wastefulness

despintar *vt* : to strip the paint from — **despintarse** *vr* : to fade, to wash off, to peel off

despistado¹, -da *adj* **1** DISTRAÍDO : absentminded, forgetful **2** CONFUSO : confused, bewildered

despistado², -da *n* : scatterbrain, absentminded person

despistar *vt* : to throw off the track, to confuse — **despistarse** *vr*

despiste *nm* **1** : absentmindedness **2** : mistake, slip

desplantador *nm* : garden trowel

desplante *nm* : insolence, rudeness

desplazamiento *nm* **1** : movement, displacement **2** : journey

desplazar {21} *vt* **1** : to replace, to displace **2** TRASLADAR : to move, to shift

desplegar {49} *vt* **1** : to display, to show, to manifest **2** DESDOBLAR : to unfold, to unfurl **3** : to spread (out) **4** : to deploy

despliegue *nm* **1** : display **2** : deployment

desplomarse *vr* **1** : to plummet, to fall **2** DERRUMBARSE : to collapse, to break down

desplome *nm* **1** : fall, drop **2** : collapse

desplumar *vt* : to pluck (a chicken, etc.)

despoblado¹, -da *adj* : uninhabited, deserted

**despoblado² ** *nm* : open country, deserted area

despoblar {19} *vt* : to depopulate

despojar *vt* **1** : to strip, to clear **2** : to divest, to deprive — **despojarse** *vr* **1 ∼ de** : to remove (clothing) **2 ∼ de** : to relinquish, to renounce

despojos *nmpl* **1** : remains, scraps **2** : plunder, spoils

desportilladura *nf* : chip, nick

desportillar *vt* : to chip — **desportillarse** *vr*

desposeer {20} *vt* : to dispossess

déspota *nmf* : despot, tyrant

despotismo *nm* : despotism — **despótico, -ca** *adj*

despotricar {72} *vi* : to rant and rave, to complain excessively

despreciable *adj* **1** : despicable, contemptible **2** : negligible ⟨nada despreciable : not inconsiderable, significant⟩

despreciar *vt* DESDEÑAR, MENOSPRECIAR : to despise, to scorn, to disdain

despreciativo, -va *adj* : scornful, disdainful

desprecio *nm* DESDÉN, MENOSPRECIO : disdain, contempt, scorn

desprender *vt* **1** SOLTAR : to detach, to loosen, to unfasten **2** EMITIR : to emit, to give off — **desprenderse** *vr* **1** : to come off, to come undone **2** : to be inferred, to follow **3** ~ **de** : to part with, to get rid of

desprendido, -da *adj* : generous, unselfish, disinterested

desprendimiento *nm* **1** : detachment **2** GENEROSIDAD : generosity **3** **desprendimiento de tierras** : landslide

despreocupación *nf, pl* **-ciones** : indifference, lack of concern

despreocupado, -da *adj* : carefree, easygoing, unconcerned

desprestigiar *vt* DESACREDITAR : to discredit, to disgrace — **desprestigiarse** *vr* : to lose prestige

desprestigio *nm* DESCRÉDITO : discredit, disrepute

desprevenido, -da *adj* DESAPERCIBIDO : unprepared, off guard, unsuspecting

desproporción *nf, pl* **-ciones** : disproportion, disparity

desproporcionado, -da *adj* : out of proportion

despropósito *nm* : piece of nonsense, absurdity

desprotegido, -da *adj* : unprotected, vulnerable

desprovisto, -ta *adj* ~ **de** : devoid of, lacking in

después *adv* **1** : afterward, later **2** : then, next **3** ~ **de** : after, next after ⟨después de comer : after eating⟩ **4** **después (de) que** : after ⟨después que lo acabé : after I finished it⟩ **5** **después de todo** : after all **6** **poco después** : shortly after, soon thereafter

despuntado, -da *adj* : blunt, dull

despuntar *vt* : to blunt — *vi* **1** : to dawn **2** : to sprout **3** : to excel, to stand out

desquiciar *vt* **1** : to unhinge (a door) **2** : to drive crazy — **desquiciarse** *vr* : to go crazy

desquitarse *vr* **1** : to get even, to retaliate **2** ~ **con** : to take it out on

desquite *nm* : revenge

desregulación *nf, pl* **-ciones** : deregulation

desregular *vt* : to deregulate

desregularización *nf* → **desregulación**

destacadamente *adv* : outstandingly, prominently

destacado, -da *adj* **1** : outstanding, prominent **2** : stationed, posted

destacamento *nm* : detachment (of troops)

destacar {72} *vt* **1** ENFATIZAR, SUBRAYAR : to emphasize, to highlight, to stress **2** : to station, to post — *vi* : to stand out

destajo *nm* **1** : piecework **2 a** ~ : by the item, by the job

destapador *nm* : bottle opener

destapar *vt* **1** : to open, to take the top off **2** DESCUBRIR : to reveal, to uncover **3** : to unblock, to unclog

destape *nm* : uncovering, revealing

destartalado, -da *adj* : dilapidated, tumbledown

destellar *vi* **1** : to sparkle, to flash, to glint **2** : to twinkle

destello *nm* **1** : flash, sparkle, twinkle **2** : glimmer, hint

destemplado, -da *adj* **1** : out of tune **2** : irritable, out of sorts **3** : unpleasant (of weather)

desteñir {67} *vi* : to run, to fade — **desteñirse** *vr* DESCOLORARSE : to fade

desterrado[1], -da *adj* : banished, exiled

desterrado[2], -da *n* : exile

desterrar {55} *vt* **1** EXILIAR : to banish, to exile **2** ERRADICAR : to eradicate, to do away with

destetar *vt* : to wean

destiempo *adv* **a** ~ : at the wrong time

destierro *nm* EXILIO : exile

destilación *nf, pl* **-ciones** : distillation

destilador, -dora *n* : distiller

destilar *vt* **1** : to exude **2** : to distill

destilería *nf* : distillery

destinación *nf, pl* **-ciones** DESTINO : destination

destinado, -da *adj* : destined, bound

destinar *vt* **1** : to appoint, to assign **2** ASIGNAR : to earmark, to allot

destinatario, -ria *n* **1** : addressee **2** : payee

destino *nm* **1** : destiny, fate **2** DESTINACIÓN : destination **3** : use **4** : assignment, post

destitución *nf, pl* **-ciones** : dismissal, removal from office

destituir {41} *vt* : to dismiss, to remove from office

destorcer {14} *vt* : to untwist

destornillador *nm* : screwdriver

destornillar *vt* : to unscrew

destrabar *vt* **1** : to untie, to undo, to ease up **2** : to separate

destreza *nf* HABILIDAD : dexterity, skill

destronar *vt* : to depose, to dethrone

destrozado, -da *adj* **1** : ruined, destroyed **2** : devastated, brokenhearted

destrozar {21} *vt* **1** : to smash, to shatter **2** : to destroy, to wreck — **destrozarse** *vr*
destrozo *nm* **1** DAÑO : damage **2** : havoc, destruction
destrucción *nf, pl* **-ciones** : destruction
destructivo, -va *adj* : destructive
destructor[1], **-tora** *adj* : destructive
destructor[2] *nm* : destroyer (ship)
destruir {41} *vt* : to destroy — **destruirse** *vr*
desubicado, -da *adj* **1** : out of place **2** : confused, disoriented
desunión *nf, pl* **-niones** : disunity
desunir *vt* : to split, to divide
desusado, -da *adj* **1** INSÓLITO : unusual **2** OBSOLETO : obsolete, disused, antiquated
desuso *nm* : disuse, obsolescence ⟨caer en desuso : to fall into disuse⟩
desvaído, -da *adj* **1** : pale, washed-out **2** : vague, blurred
desvainar *vt* : to shell
desvalido, -da *adj* DESAMPARADO : destitute, helpless
desvalijar *vt* **1** : to ransack **2** : to rob
desvalorización *nf, pl* **-ciones** **1** DEVALUACIÓN : devaluation **2** : depreciation
desvalorizar {21} *vt* : to devalue
desván *nm, pl* **desvanes** ÁTICO, BUHARDILLA : attic
desvanecer {53} *vt* **1** DISIPAR : to make disappear, to dispel **2** : to fade, to blur — **desvanecerse** *vr* **1** : to vanish, to disappear **2** : to fade **3** DESMAYARSE : to faint, to swoon
desvanecimiento *nm* **1** : disappearance **2** DESMAYO : faint **3** : fading
desvariar {85} *vi* **1** DELIRAR : to be delirious **2** : to rave, to talk nonsense
desvarío *nm* DELIRIO : delirium
desvelado, -da *adj* : sleepless
desvelar *vt* **1** : to keep awake **2** REVELAR : to reveal, to disclose — **desvelarse** *vr* **1** : to stay awake **2** : to do one's utmost
desvelo *nm* **1** : sleeplessness **2** **desvelos** *nmpl* : efforts, pains
desvencijado, -da *adj* : dilapidated, rickety
desventaja *nf* : disadvantage, drawback
desventajoso, -sa *adj* : disadvantageous, unfavorable
desventura *nf* INFORTUNIO : misfortune
desventurado, -da *adj* : unfortunate, ill-fated
desvergonzado, -da *adj* : shameless, impudent
desvergüenza *nf* : shamelessness, impudence
desvestir {54} *vt* : to undress — **desvestirse** *vr* : to get undressed
desviación *nf, pl* **-ciones** **1** : deviation, departure **2** : detour, diversion
desviar {85} *vt* **1** : to change the course of, to divert **2** : to turn away, to deflect — **desviarse** *vr* **1** : to branch off **2** APARTARSE : to stray
desvinculación *nf, pl* **-ciones** : dissociation
desvincular *vt* ∼ **de** : to separate from, to dissociate from — **desvincularse** *vr*
desvío *nm* **1** : diversion, detour **2** : deviation
desvirtuar {3} *vt* **1** : to impair, to spoil **2** : to detract from **3** : to distort, to misrepresent
detalladamente *adv* : in detail, at great length
detallar *vt* : to detail
detalle *nm* **1** : detail **2 al detalle** : retail
detallista[1] *adj* **1** : meticulous **2** : retail
detallista[2] *nmf* **1** : perfectionist **2** : retailer
detección *nf, pl* **-ciones** : detection
detectar *vt* : to detect — **detectable** *adj*
detective *nmf* : detective
detector *nm* : detector ⟨detector de mentiras : lie detector⟩
detención *nf, pl* **-ciones** **1** ARRESTO : detention, arrest **2** : stop, halt **3** : delay, holdup
detener {80} *vt* **1** ARRESTAR : to arrest, to detain **2** PARAR : to stop, to halt **3** : to keep, to hold back — **detenerse** *vr* **1** : to stop **2** : to delay, to linger
detenidamente *adv* : thoroughly, at length
detenimiento *nm* **con** ∼ : carefully, in detail
detentar *vt* : to hold, to retain
detergente *nm* : detergent
deteriorado, -da *adj* : damaged, worn
deteriorar *vt* ESTROPEAR : to damage, to spoil — **deteriorarse** *vr* **1** : to get damaged, to wear out **2** : to deteriorate, to worsen
deterioro *nm* **1** : deterioration, wear **2** : worsening, decline
determinación *nf, pl* **-ciones** **1** : determination, resolve **2 tomar una determinación** : to make a decision
determinado, -da *adj* **1** : certain, particular **2** : determined, resolute
determinante[1] *adj* : determining, deciding
determinante[2] *nm* : determinant
determinar *vt* **1** : to determine **2** : to cause, to bring about — **determinarse** *vr* : to make up one's mind, to decide
detestar *vt* : to detest — **detestable** *adj*
detonación *nf, pl* **-ciones** : detonation
detonador *nm* : detonator
detonante[1] *adj* : detonating, explosive
detonante[2] *nm* **1** → **detonador 2** : catalyst, cause
detonar *vi* : to detonate, to explode
detractor, -tora *n* : detractor, critic
detrás *adv* **1** : behind **2** ∼ **de** : in back of **3 por** ∼ : from behind
detrimento *nm* : detriment ⟨en detrimento de : to the detriment of⟩
detuvo, etc. → **detener**

deuda *nf* **1** DÉBITO : debt **2 en deuda con** : indebted to
deudo, -da *n* : relative
deudor[1], **-dora** *adj* : indebted
deudor[2], **-dora** *n* : debtor
devaluación *nf, pl* **-ciones** DESVAL-ORIZACIÓN : devaluation
devaluar {3} *vt* : to devalue — **devaluarse** *vr* : to depreciate
devanarse *vr* **devanarse los sesos** : to rack one's brains
devaneo *nm* **1** : flirtation, fling **2** : idle pursuit
devastador, -dora *adj* : devastating
devastar *vt* : to devastate — **devastación** *nf*
devenir {87} *vi* **1** : to come about **2** ~ **en** : to become, to turn into
devoción *nf, pl* **-ciones** : devotion
devolución *nf, pl* **-ciones** REEMBOLSO : return, refund
devolver {89} *vt* **1** : to return, to give back **2** REEMBOLSAR : to refund, to pay back **3** : to vomit, to bring up — *vi* : to vomit, to throw up — **devolverse** *vr* : to return, to come back, to go back
devorar *vt* **1** : to devour **2** : to consume
devoto[1], **-ta** *adj* : devout — **devotamente** *adv*
devoto[2], **-ta** *n* : devotee, admirer
di → **dar, decir**
día *nm* **1** : day ⟨todos los días : every day⟩ **2** : daytime, daylight ⟨de día : by day, in the daytime⟩ ⟨en pleno día : in broad daylight⟩ **3 al día** : up-to-date **4 en su día** : in due time
diabetes *nf* : diabetes
diabético, -ca *adj & n* : diabetic
diablillo *nm* : little devil, imp
diablo *nm* DEMONIO : devil
diablura *nf* **1** : prank **2 diabluras** *nfpl* : mischief
diabólico, -ca *adj* : diabolical, diabolic, devilish
diaconisa *nf* : deaconess
diácono *nm* : deacon
diacrítico, -ca *adj* : diacritic, diacritical
diadema *nf* : diadem, crown
diáfano, -na *adj* : diaphanous
diafragma *nm* : diaphragm
diagnosticar {72} *vt* : to diagnose
diagnóstico[1], **-ca** *adj* : diagnostic
diagnóstico[2] *nm* : diagnosis
diagonal *adj & nf* : diagonal — **diagonalmente** *adv*
diagrama *nm* **1** : diagram **2 diagrama de flujo** ORGANIGRAMA : flowchart
dial *nm* : dial (on a radio, etc.)
dialecto *nm* : dialect
dialogar {52} *vi* : to have a talk, to converse
diálogo *nm* : dialogue
diamante *nm* : diamond
diametral *adj* : diametric, diametrical — **diametralmente** *adv*
diámetro *nm* : diameter
diana *nf* **1** : target, bull's-eye **2** *or* **toque de diana** : reveille

diapositiva *nf* : slide, transparency
diario[1] *adv Mex* : every day, daily
diario[2], **-ria** *adj* : daily, everyday — **diariamente** *adv*
diario[3] *nm* **1** : diary **2** PERIÓDICO : newspaper
diarrea *nf* : diarrhea
diatriba *nf* : diatribe, tirade
dibujante *nmf* **1** : draftsman *m*, draftswoman *f* **2** CARICATURISTA : cartoonist
dibujar *vt* **1** : to draw, to sketch **2** : to portray, to depict
dibujo *nm* **1** : drawing **2** : design, pattern **3 dibujos animados** : (animated) cartoons
dicción *nf, pl* **-ciones** : diction
diccionario *nm* : dictionary
dícese → **decir**
dicha *nf* **1** SUERTE : good luck **2** FELICIDAD : happiness, joy
dicho[1] *pp* → **decir**
dicho[2], **-cha** *adj* : said, aforementioned
dicho[3] *nm* DECIR : saying, proverb
dichoso, -sa *adj* **1** : blessed **2** FELIZ : happy **3** AFORTUNADO : fortunate, lucky
diciembre *nm* : December
diciendo → **decir**
dictado *nm* : dictation
dictador, -dora *n* : dictator
dictadura *nf* : dictatorship
dictamen *nm, pl* **dictámenes** **1** : report **2** : judgment, opinion
dictaminar *vt* : to report — *vi* : to give an opinion, to pass judgment
dictar *vt* **1** : to dictate **2** : to pronounce (a judgment) **3** : to give, to deliver ⟨dictar una conferencia : to give a lecture⟩
dictatorial *adj* : dictatorial
didáctico, -ca *adj* : didactic
diecinueve *adj & nm* : nineteen
diecinueveavo[1], **-va** *adj* : nineteenth
diecinueveavo[2] *nm* : nineteenth (fraction)
dieciocho *adj & nm* : eighteen
dieciochoavo[1], **-va** *or* **dieciochavo, -va** *adj* : eighteenth
dieciochoavo[2] *or* **dieciochavo** *nm* : eighteenth (fraction)
dieciséis *adj & nm* : sixteen
dieciseisavo[1], **-va** *adj* : sixteenth
dieciseisavo[2] *nm* : sixteenth (fraction)
diecisiete *adj & nm* : seventeen
diecisieteavo[1], **-va** *adj* : seventeenth
diecisieteavo[2] *nm* : seventeenth
diente *nm* **1** : tooth ⟨diente canino : eyetooth, canine tooth⟩ **2** : tusk, fang **3** : prong, tine **4 diente de león** : dandelion
dieron, etc. → **dar**
diesel [ˈdisɛl] *nm* : diesel
diestra *nf* : right hand
diestramente *adv* : skillfully, adroitly
diestro[1], **-tra** *adj* **1** : right **2** : skillful, accomplished
diestro[2] *nm* : bullfighter, matador
dieta *nf* : diet

dietética *nf* : dietetics
dietético, -ca *adj* : dietetic
dietista *nmf* : dietitian
diez *adj & nm, pl* **dieces** : ten
difamación *nf, pl* **-ciones** : defamation, slander
difamar *vt* : to defame, to slander
difamatorio, -ria *adj* : slanderous, defamatory, libelous
diferencia *nf* **1** : difference **2 a diferencia de** : unlike, in contrast to
diferenciación *nf, pl* **-ciones** : differentiation
diferenciar *vt* : to differentiate between, to distinguish — **diferenciarse** *vr* : to differ
diferendo *nm* : dispute, conflict
diferente *adj* DISTINTO : different — **diferentemente** *adv*
diferir {76} *vt* DILATAR, POSPONER : to postpone, to put off — *vi* : to differ
difícil *adj* : difficult, hard
difícilmente *adv* **1** : with difficulty **2** : hardly
dificultad *nf* : difficulty
dificultar *vt* : to make difficult, to obstruct
dificultoso, -sa *adj* : difficult, hard
difteria *nf* : diphtheria
difundir *vt* **1** : to diffuse, to spread out **2** : to broadcast, to spread
difunto, -ta *adj & n* FALLECIDO : deceased
difusión *nf, pl* **-siones** **1** : spreading **2** : diffusion (of heat, etc.) **3** : broadcast, broadcasting ⟨los medios de difusión : the media⟩
difuso, -sa *adj* : diffuse, widespread
diga, etc. → **decir**
digerir {76} *vt* : to digest — **digerible** *adj*
digestión *nf, pl* **-tiones** : digestion
digestivo, -va *adj* : digestive
digital[1] *adj* : digital — **digitalmente** *adv*
digital[2] *nf* **1** DEDALERA : foxglove **2** : digitalis
dígito *nm* : digit
dignarse *vr* : to deign, to condescend ⟨no se dignó contestar : he didn't deign to answer⟩
dignatario, -ria *n* : dignitary
dignidad *nf* **1** : dignity **2** : dignitary
dignificar {72} *vt* : to dignify
digno, -na *adj* **1** HONORABLE : honorable **2** : worthy — **dignamente** *adv*
digresión *nf, pl* **-ciones** : digression
dije *nm* : charm (on a bracelet)
dijo, etc. → **decir**
dilación *nf, pl* **-ciones** : delay
dilapidar *vt* : to waste, to squander
dilatar *vt* **1** : to dilate, to widen, to expand **2** DIFERIR, POSPONER : to put off, to postpone — **dilatarse** *vr* **1** : to expand (of gases, metals, etc.) **2** *Mex* : to take long, to be long
dilatorio, -ria *adj* : dilatory, delaying
dilema *nm* : dilemma
diletante *nmf* : dilettante

diligencia *nf* **1** : diligence, care **2** : promptness, speed **3** : action, step **4** : task, errand **5** : stagecoach **6 diligencias** *nfpl* : judicial procedures, formalities
diligente *adj* : diligent — **diligentemente** *adv*
dilucidar *vt* : to elucidate, to clarify
dilución *nf, pl* **-ciones** : dilution
diluir {41} *vt* : to dilute
diluviar *v impers* : to pour (with rain), to pour down
diluvio *nm* **1** : flood **2** : downpour
dimensión *nf, pl* **-siones** : dimension — **dimensional** *adj*
dimensionar *vt* : to measure, to gauge
diminutivo[1], **-va** *adj* : diminutive
diminutivo[2] *nm* : diminutive
diminuto, -ta *adj* : minute, tiny
dimisión *nf, pl* **-siones** : resignation
dimitir *vi* : to resign, to step down
dimos → **dar**
dinámica *nf* : dynamics
dinámico, -ca *adj* : dynamic — **dinámicamente** *adv*
dinamismo *nm* : energy, vigor
dinamita *nf* : dynamite
dinamitar *vt* : to dynamite
dínamo *or* **dinamo** *nm* : dynamo
dinastía *nf* : dynasty
dineral *nm* : fortune, large sum of money
dinero *nm* : money
dinosaurio *nm* : dinosaur
dintel *nm* : lintel
dio, etc. → **dar**
diocesano, -na *adj* : diocesan
diócesis *nfs & pl* : diocese
dios, diosa *n* : god, goddess *f*
Dios *nm* : God
diploma *nm* : diploma
diplomacia *nf* : diplomacy
diplomado[1], **-da** *adj* : qualified, trained
diplomado[2] *nm Mex* : seminar
diplomático[1], **-ca** *adj* : diplomatic — **diplomáticamente** *adv*
diplomático[2], **-ca** *n* : diplomat
diptongo *nm* : diphthong
diputación *nf, pl* **-ciones** : deputation, delegation
diputado, -da *n* : delegate, representative
dique *nm* : dike
dirá, etc. → **decir**
dirección *nf, pl* **-ciones** **1** : address **2** : direction **3** : management, leadership **4** : steering (of an automobile)
direccional[1] *adj* : directional
direccional[2] *nf* : directional, turn signal
directa *nf* : high gear
directamente *adv* : straight, directly
directiva *nf* **1** ORDEN : directive **2** DIRECTORIO, JUNTA : board of directors
directivo[1], **-va** *adj* : executive, managerial
directivo[2], **-va** *n* : executive, director
directo, -ta *adj* **1** : direct, straight, immediate **2 en** ～ : live (in broadcasting)

director, -tora *n* **1** : director, manager, head **2** : conductor (of an orchestra)
directorial *adj* : managing, executive
directorio *nm* **1** : directory **2** DIRECTIVA, JUNTA : board of directors
directriz *nf, pl* **-trices** : guideline
dirigencia *nf* : leaders *pl,* leadership
dirigente[1] *adj* : directing, leading
dirigente[2] *nmf* : director, leader
dirigible *nm* : dirigible, blimp
dirigir {35} *vt* **1** : to direct, to lead **2** : to address **3** : to aim, to point **4** : to conduct (music) — **dirigirse** *vr* ~ **a 1** : to go towards **2** : to speak to, to address
dirimir *vt* **1** : to resolve, to settle **2** : to annul, to dissolve (a marriage)
discapacidad *nf* MINUSVALÍA : disability, handicap
discapacitado[1], **-da** *adj* : disabled, handicapped
discapacitado[2], **-da** *n* : disabled person, handicapped person
discar {72} *v* : to dial
discernimiento *nm* : discernment
discernir {25} *v* : to discern, to distinguish
disciplina *nf* : discipline
disciplinar *vt* : to discipline — **disciplinario, -ria** *adj*
discípulo, -la *n* : disciple, follower
disc jockey [ˌdiskˈjoke, -ˈʤo-] *nmf* : disc jockey
disco *nm* **1** : phonograph record **2** : disc, disk ⟨disco compacto : compact disc⟩ **3** : discus
díscolo, -la *adj* : unruly, disobedient
disconforme *adj* : in disagreement
discontinuidad *nf* : discontinuity
discontinuo, -nua *adj* : discontinuous
discordancia *nf* DESAVENENCIA : conflict, disagreement
discordante *adj* **1** : discordant **2** : conflicting
discordia *nf* : discord
discoteca *nf* **1** : disco, discotheque **2** *CA, Mex* : record store
discreción *nf, pl* **-ciones** : discretion
discrecional *adj* : discretionary
discrepancia *nf* : discrepancy
discrepar *vi* **1** : to disagree **2** : to differ
discreto, -ta *adj* : discreet — **discretamente** *adv*
discriminación *nf, pl* **-ciones** : discrimination
discriminar *vt* **1** : to discriminate against **2** : to distinguish, to differentiate
discriminatorio, -ria *adj* : discriminatory
disculpa *nf* **1** : apology **2** : excuse
disculpable *adj* : excusable
disculpar *vt* **1** : to excuse, to pardon — **disculparse** *vr* : to apologize
discurrir *vi* **1** : to flow **2** : to pass, to go by **3** : to ponder, to reflect
discurso *nm* **1** ORACIÓN : speech, address **2** : discourse, treatise

discusión *nf, pl* **-siones 1** : discussion **2** ALTERCADO, DISPUTA : argument
discutible *adj* : arguable, debatable
discutidor, -dora *adj* : argumentative
discutir *vt* **1** : to discuss **2** : to dispute — *vi* ALTERCAR : to argue, to quarrel
disecar {72} *vt* **1** : to dissect **2** : to stuff (for preservation)
disección *nf, pl* **-ciones** : dissection
diseminación *nf, pl* **-ciones** : dissemination, spreading
diseminar *vt* : to disseminate, to spread
disensión *nf, pl* **-siones** : dissension, disagreement
disentería *nf* : dysentery
disentir {76} *vi* : to dissent, to disagree
diseñador, -dora *n* : designer
diseñar *vt* **1** : to design, to plan **2** : to lay out, to outline
diseño *nm* : design
disentimiento *nm* : dissent
disertación *nf, pl* **-ciones 1** : lecture, talk **2** : dissertation
disertar *vi* : to lecture, to give a talk
disfraz *nm, pl* **disfraces 1** : disguise **2** : costume **3** : front, pretense
disfrazar {21} *vt* **1** : to disguise **2** : to mask, to conceal — **disfrazarse** *vr* : to wear a costume, to be in disguise
disfrutar *vt* : to enjoy — *vi* : to enjoy oneself, to have a good time
disfrute *nm* : enjoyment
disfunción *nf, pl* **-ciones** : dysfunction — **disfuncional** *adj*
disgresión → digresión
disgustar *vt* : to upset, to displease, to make angry — **disgustarse** *vr*
disgusto *nm* **1** : annoyance, displeasure **2** : argument, quarrel **3** : trouble, misfortune
disidencia *nf* : dissidence, dissent
disidente *adj & nmf* : dissident
disímbolo, -la *adj Mex* : dissimilar
disímil *adj* : dissimilar
disimulado, -da *adj* **1** : concealed, disguised **2** : furtive, sly
disimular *vi* : to dissemble, to pretend — *vt* : to conceal, to hide
disimulo *nm* **1** : dissembling, pretense **2** : slyness, furtiveness **3** : tolerance
disipar *vt* **1** : to dissipate, to dispel **2** : to squander — **disiparse** *vr*
diskette [diˈskɛt] *nm* : floppy disk, diskette
dislocar {72} *vt* : to dislocate — **dislocación** *nf*
disminución *nf, pl* **-ciones** : decrease, drop, fall
disminuir {41} *vt* REDUCIR : to reduce, to decrease, to lower — *vi* **1** : to lower **2** : to drop, to fall
disociación *nf, pl* **-ciones** : dissociation
disociar *vt* : to dissociate, to separate
disolución *nf, pl* **-ciones 1** : dissolution, dissolving **2** : breaking up **3** : dissipation
disoluto, -ta *adj* : dissolute, dissipated

disolver {89} *vt* **1** : to dissolve **2** : to break up — **disolverse** *vr*
disonancia *nf* : dissonance — **disonante** *adj*
dispar *adj* **1** : different, disparate **2** DIVERSO : diverse **3** DESIGUAL : inconsistent
disparado, -da *adj* **salir disparado** *fam* : to take off in a hurry, to rush away
disparar *vi* **1** : to shoot, to fire **2** *Mex fam* : to pay — *vt* **1** : to shoot **2** *Mex fam* : to treat to, to buy — **dispararse** *vr* : to shoot up, to skyrocket
disparatado, -da *adj* ABSURDO, RIDÍCULO : absurd, ridiculous, crazy
disparate *nm* : silliness, stupidity ⟨decir disparates : to talk nonsense⟩
disparejo, -ja *adj* DESIGUAL : uneven
disparidad *nf* : disparity
disparo *nm* TIRO : shot
dispendio *nm* : wastefulness, extravagance
dispendioso, -sa *adj* : wasteful, extravagant
dispensa *nf* : dispensation
dispensable *adj* **1** : dispensable **2** : excusable
dispensar *vt* **1** : to dispense, to give, to grant **2** EXCUSAR : to excuse, to forgive **3** EXIMIR : to exempt
dispensario *nm* **1** : dispensary, clinic **2** *Mex* : dispenser
dispersar *vt* DESPERDIGAR : to disperse, to scatter
dispersión *nf, pl* **-siones** : dispersion
disperso, -sa *adj* : dispersed, scattered
displicencia *nf* : indifference, coldness, disdain
displicente *adj* : indifferent, cold, disdainful
disponer {60} *vt* **1** : to arrange, to lay out **2** : to stipulate, to order **3** : to prepare — *vi* ~ **de** : to have at one's disposal — **disponerse** *vr* ~ **a** : to prepare to, to be about to
disponibilidad *nf* : availability
disponible *adj* : available
disposición *nf, pl* **-ciones** **1** : disposition **2** : aptitude, talent **3** : order, arrangement **4** : willingness, readiness **5 última disposición** : last will and testament
dispositivo *nm* **1** APARATO, MECANISMO : device, mechanism **2** : force, detachment
dispuesto[1] *pp* → **disponer**
dispuesto[2]**, -ta** *adj* PREPARADO : ready, prepared, disposed
dispuso, etc. → **disponer**
disputa *nf* ALTERCADO, DISCUSIÓN : dispute, argument
disputar *vi* : to argue, to contend, to vie — *vt* **1** : to dispute, to question — **disputarse** *vr* : to be in competition for ⟨se disputan la corona : they're fighting for the crown⟩
disquera *nf* : record label, recording company

disquete → **diskette**
disquisición *nf, pl* **-ciones** **1** : formal discourse **2 disquisiciones** *nfpl* : digressions
distancia *nf* : distance
distanciamiento *nm* **1** : distancing **2** : rift, estrangement
distanciar *vt* **1** : to space out **2** : to draw apart — **distanciarse** *vr* : to grow apart, to become estranged
distante *adj* **1** : distant, far-off **2** : aloof
distar *vi* ~ **de** : to be far from ⟨dista de ser perfecto : he is far from perfect⟩
diste → **dar**
distender {56} *vt* : to distend, to stretch
distensión *nf, pl* **-siones** : distension
distinción *nf, pl* **-ciones** : distinction
distinguible *adj* : distinguishable
distinguido, -da *adj* : distinguished, refined
distinguir {26} *vt* **1** : to distinguish **2** : to honor — **distinguirse** *vr*
distintivo, -va *adj* : distinctive, distinguishing
distinto, -ta *adj* **1** DIFERENTE : different **2** CLARO : distinct, clear, evident
distorsión *nf, pl* **-siones** : distortion
distorsionar *vt* : to distort
distracción *nf, pl* **-ciones** **1** : distraction, amusement **2** : forgetfulness **3** : oversight
distraer {81} *vt* **1** : to distract **2** ENTRETENER : to entertain, to amuse — **distraerse** *vr* **1** : to get distracted **2** : to amuse oneself
distraídamente *adv* : absentmindedly
distraído[1] *pp* → **distraer**
distraído[2]**, -da** *adj* **1** : distracted, preoccupied **2** DESPISTADO : absentminded
distribución *nf, pl* **-ciones** : distribution
distribuidor, -dora *n* : distributor
distribuir {41} *vt* : to distribute
distributivo, -va *adj* : distributive
distrital *adj* : district, of the district
distrito *nm* : district
distrofia *nf* : dystrophy ⟨distrofia muscular : muscular dystrophy⟩
disturbio *nm* : disturbance
disuadir *vt* : to dissuade, to discourage
disuasión *nf, pl* **-siones** : dissuasion
disuasivo, -va *adj* : deterrent, discouraging
disuasorio, -ria *adj* : discouraging
disuelto *pp* → **disolver**
disyuntiva *nf* : dilemma
DIU [ˈdiu] *nm* (*dispositivo intrauterino*) : IUD, intrauterine device
diurético[1]**, -ca** *adj* : diuretic
diurético[2] *nm* : diuretic
diurno, -na *adj* : day, daytime
diva *nf* → **divo**
divagar {52} *vi* : to digress
diván *nm, pl* **divanes** : divan
divergencia *nf* : divergence, difference
divergente *adj* : divergent, differing
divergir {35} *vi* **1** : to diverge **2** : to differ, to disagree

diversidad *nf* : diversity, variety
diversificación *nf, pl* **-ciones** : diversification
diversificar {72} *vt* : to diversify
diversión *nf, pl* **-siones** ENTRETENIMIENTO : fun, amusement, diversion
diverso, -sa *adj* : diverse, various
divertido, -da *adj* **1** : amusing, funny **2** : entertaining, enjoyable
divertir {76} *vt* ENTRETENER : to amuse, to entertain — **divertirse** *vr* : to have fun, to have a good time
dividendo *nm* : dividend
dividir *vt* **1** : to divide, to split **2** : to distribute, to share out — **dividirse** *vr*
divieso *nm* : boil
divinidad *nf* : divinity
divino, -na *adj* : divine
divisa *nf* **1** : currency **2** LEMA : motto **3** : emblem, insignia
divisar *vt* : to discern, to make out
divisible *adj* : divisible
división *nf, pl* **-siones** : division
divisionismo *nm* : factionalism
divisivo, -va *adj* : divisive
divisor *nm* : denominator
divisorio, -ria *adj* : dividing
divo, -va *n* **1** : prima donna **2** : celebrity, star
divorciado¹, -da *adj* **1** : divorced **2** : split, divided
divorciado², -da *n* : divorcé *m,* divorcée *f*
divorciar *vt* : to divorce — **divorciarse** *vr* : to get a divorce
divorcio *nm* : divorce
divulgación *nf, pl* **-ciones** **1** : spreading, dissemination **2** : popularization
divulgar {52} *vt* **1** : to spread, to circulate **2** REVELAR : to divulge, to reveal **3** : to popularize — **divulgarse** *vr*
dizque *adv* : supposedly, apparently
dobladillar *vt* : to hem
dobladillo *nm* : hem
doblar *vt* **1** : to double **2** PLEGAR : to fold, to bend **3** : to turn ⟨doblar la esquina : to turn the corner⟩ **4** : to dub — *vi* **1** : to turn **2** : to toll, to ring — **doblarse** *vr* **1** : to fold up, to double over **2** : to give in, to yield
doble¹ *adj* : double — **doblemente** *adv*
doble² *nm* **1** : double **2** : toll (of a bell), knell
doble³ *nmf* : stand-in, double
doblegar {52} *vt* **1** : to fold, to crease **2** : to force to yield — **doblegarse** *vr* : to yield, to bow
doblez¹ *nm, pl* **dobleces** : fold, crease
doblez² *nmf* : duplicity, deceitfulness
doce *adj & nm* : twelve
doceavo¹, -va *adj* : twelfth
doceavo² *nm* : twelfth (fraction)
docena *nf* **1** : dozen **2 docena de fraile** : baker's dozen
docencia *nf* : teaching
docente¹ *adj* : educational, teaching
docente² *n* : teacher, lecturer
dócil *adj* : docile — **dócilmente** *adv*

docilidad *nf* : docility
docto, -ta *adj* : learned, erudite
doctor, -tora *n* : doctor
doctorado *nm* : doctorate
doctrina *nf* : doctrine — **doctrinal** *adj*
documentación *nf, pl* **-ciones** : documentation
documental *adj & nm* : documentary
documentar *vt* : to document
documento *nm* : document
dogma *nm* : dogma
dogmático, -ca *adj* : dogmatic
dogmatismo *nm* : dogmatism
dólar *nm* : dollar
dolencia *nf* : ailment, malaise
doler {47} *vi* **1** : to hurt, to ache **2** : to grieve — **dolerse** *vr* **1** : to be distressed **2** : to complain
doliente *nmf* : mourner, bereaved
dolor *nm* **1** : pain, ache ⟨dolor de cabeza : headache⟩ **2** PENA, TRISTEZA : grief, sorrow
dolorido, -da *adj* **1** : sore, aching **2** : hurt, upset
doloroso, -sa *adj* **1** : painful **2** : distressing — **dolorosamente** *adv*
doloso, -sa *adj* : fraudulent — **dolosamente** *adv*
domador, -dora *n* : tamer
domar *vt* : to tame, to break in
domesticado, -da *adj* : domesticated, tame
domesticar {72} *vt* : to domesticate, to tame
doméstico, -ca *adj* : domestic, household
domiciliado, -da *adj* : residing
domiciliario, -ria *adj* **1** : home **2 arresto domiciliario** : house arrest
domiciliarse *vr* RESIDIR : to reside
domicilio *nm* : home, residence ⟨cambio de domicilio : change of address⟩
dominación *nf, pl* **-ciones** : domination
dominancia *nf* : dominance
dominante *adj* **1** : dominant **2** : domineering
dominar *vt* **1** : to dominate **2** : to master, to be proficient at — *vi* : to predominate, to prevail — **dominarse** *vr* : to control oneself
domingo *nm* : Sunday
dominical *adj* : Sunday ⟨periódico dominical : Sunday newspaper⟩
dominicano, -na *adj & n* : Dominican
dominio *nm* **1** : dominion, power **2** : mastery **3** : domain, field
dominó *nm, pl* **-nós** **1** : domino (tile) **2** : dominoes *pl* (game)
domo *nm* : dome
don¹ *nm* **1** : gift, present **2** : talent
don² *nm* **1** : title of courtesy preceding a man's first name **2 don nadie** : nobody, insignificant person
dona *nf Mex* : doughnut, donut
donación *nf, pl* **-ciones** : donation
donador, -dora *n* : donor
donaire *nm* **1** GARBO : grace, poise **2** : witticism

donante *nf* → **donador**
donar *vt* : to donate
donativo *nm* : donation
doncella *nf* : maiden, damsel
doncellez *nf* : maidenhood
donde[1] *conj* : where, in which ⟨el pueblo donde vivo : the town where I live⟩
donde[2] *prep* : over by ⟨lo encontré donde la silla : I found it over by the chair⟩
dónde *adv* : where ⟨¿dónde está su casa? : where is your house?⟩
dondequiera *adv* 1 : anywhere, no matter where 2 **dondequiera que** : wherever, everywhere
doña *nf* : title of courtesy preceding a woman's first name
doquier *adv* **por** ~ : everywhere, all over
dorado[1], **-da** *adj* : gold, golden
dorado[2], **-da** *nm* : gilt
dorar *vt* 1 : to gild 2 : to brown (food)
dormido, -da *adj* 1 : asleep 2 : numb ⟨tiene el pie dormido : her foot's numb, her foot's gone to sleep⟩
dormilón, -lona *n* : sleepyhead, late riser
dormir {27} *vt* : to put to sleep — *vi* : to sleep — **dormirse** *vr* : to fall asleep
dormitar *vi* : to snooze, to doze
dormitorio *nm* 1 : bedroom 2 : dormitory
dorsal[1] *adj* : dorsal
dorsal[2] *nm* : number (worn in sports)
dorso *nm* 1 : back ⟨el dorso de la mano : the back of the hand⟩ 2 *Mex* : backstroke
dos *adj & nm* : two
doscientos[1], **-tas** *adj* : two hundred
doscientos[2] *nms & pl* : two hundred
dosel *nm* : canopy
dosificación *nf, pl* **-ciones** : dosage
dosis *nfs & pl* 1 : dose 2 : amount, quantity
dossier *nm* : dossier
dotación *nf, pl* **-ciones** 1 : endowment, funding 2 : staff, personnel
dotado, -da *adj* 1 : gifted 2 ~ **de** : endowed with, equipped with
dotar *vt* 1 : to provide, to equip 2 : to endow
dote *nf* 1 : dowry 2 **dotes** *nfpl* : talent, gift
doy → **dar**
draga *nf* : dredge
dragado *nm* : dredging
dragar {52} *vt* : to dredge
dragón *nm, pl* **dragones** 1 : dragon 2 : snapdragon
drague, etc. → **dragar**
drama *nm* : drama
dramático, -ca *adj* : dramatic — **dramáticamente** *adv*
dramatizar {21} *vt* : to dramatize — **dramatización** *nf*
dramaturgo, -ga *n* : dramatist, playwright

drástico, -ca *adj* : drastic — **drásticamente** *adv*
drenaje *nm* : drainage
drenar *vt* : to drain
drene *nm Mex* : drain
driblar *vi* : to dribble (in basketball)
drible *nm* : dribble (in basketball)
droga *nf* : drug
drogadicción *nf, pl* **-ciones** : drug addiction
drogadicto, -ta *n* : drug addict
drogar {52} *vt* : to drug — **drogarse** *vr* : to take drugs
drogue, etc. → **drogar**
droguería *nf* FARMACIA : drugstore
dromedario *nm* : dromedary
dual *adj* : dual
dualidad *nf* : duality
dualismo *nm* : dualism
ducha *nf* : shower ⟨darse una ducha : to take a shower⟩
ducharse *vr* : to take a shower
ducho, -cha *adj* : experienced, skilled, expert
dúctil *adj* : ductile
ducto *nm* 1 : duct, shaft 2 : pipeline
duda *nf* : doubt ⟨no cabe duda : there's no doubt about it⟩
dudar *vt* : to doubt — *vi* ~ **en** : to hesitate to ⟨no dudes en pedirme ayuda : don't hesitate to ask me for help⟩
dudoso, -sa *adj* 1 : doubtful 2 : dubious, questionable — **dudosamente** *adv*
duele, etc. → **doler**
duelo *nm* 1 : duel 2 LUTO : mourning
duende *nm* 1 : elf, goblin 2 ENCANTO : magic, charm ⟨una bailarina que tiene duende : a dancer with a certain magic⟩
dueño, -ña *n* 1 : owner, proprietor, proprietress *f* 2 : landlord, landlady *f*
duerme, etc. → **dormir**
dueto *nm* : duet
dulce[1] *adv* : sweetly, softly
dulce[2] *adj* 1 : sweet 2 : mild, gentle, mellow — **dulcemente** *adv*
dulce[3] *nm* : candy, sweet
dulcería *nf* : candy store
dulcificante *nm* : sweetener
dulzura *nf* 1 : sweetness 2 : gentleness, mellowness
duna *nf* : dune
dúo *nm* : duo, duet
duodécimo[1], **-ma** *adj* : twelfth
duodécimo[2], **-ma** *nm* : twelfth (in a series)
dúplex *nms & pl* : duplex apartment
duplicación *nf, pl* **-ciones** : duplication, copying
duplicado *nm* : duplicate, copy
duplicar {72} *vt* 1 : to double 2 : to duplicate, to copy
duplicidad *nf* : duplicity
duque *nm* : duke
duquesa *nf* : duchess
durabilidad *nf* : durability
durable → **duradero**

duración *nf, pl* **-ciones** : duration, length
duradero, -ra *adj* : durable, lasting
duramente *adv* **1** : harshly, severely **2** : hard
durante *prep* : during ⟨durante todo el día : all day long⟩ ⟨trabajó durante tres horas : he worked for three hours⟩
durar *vi* : to last; to endure
durazno *nm* **1** : peach **2** : peach tree

dureza *nf* **1** : hardness, toughness **2** : severity, harshness
durmiente¹ *adj* : sleeping
durmiente² *nmf* : sleeper
durmió, etc. → dormir
duro¹ *adv* : hard ⟨trabajé tan duro : I worked so hard⟩
duro², -ra *adj* **1** : hard, tough **2** : harsh, severe

E

e¹ *nf* : fifth letter of the Spanish alphabet
e² *conj* (used instead of **y** before words beginning with i- or hi-) : and
ebanista *nmf* : cabinetmaker
ebanistería *nf* : cabinetmaking
ébano *nm* : ebony
ebriedad *nf* EMBRIAGUEZ : inebriation, drunkenness
ebrio, -bria *adj* EMBRIAGADO : inebriated, drunk
ebullición *nf, pl* **-ciones** : boiling
eccéntrico → excéntrico
echar *vt* **1** LANZAR : to throw, to cast, to hurl **2** EXPULSAR : to throw out, to expel **3** EMITIR : to emit, give off **4** BROTAR : to sprout, to put forth **5** DESPEDIR : to fire, to dismiss **6** : to put in, to add **7 echar a perder** : to spoil, to ruin **8 echar de menos** : to miss ⟨echan de menos a su madre : they miss their mother⟩ — *vi* **1** : to start off **2** ~ **a** : to begin to — **echarse** *vr* **1** : to throw oneself **2** : to lie down **3** : to put on **4** ~ **a** : to start to **5 echarse a perder** : to go bad, to spoil **6 echárselas de** : to pose as
ecléctico, -ca *adj* : eclectic
eclesiástico¹, -ca *adj* : ecclesiastical, ecclesiastic
eclesiástico² *nm* CLÉRIGO : cleric, clergyman
eclipsar *vt* **1** : to eclipse **2** : to outshine, to surpass
eclipse *nm* : eclipse
eco *nm* : echo
ecografía *nf* : ultrasound scanning
ecología *nf* : ecology
ecológico, -ca *adj* : ecological — **ecológicamente** *adv*
ecologista *nmf* : ecologist, environmentalist
ecólogo, -ga *n* : ecologist
economía *nf* **1** : economy **2** : economics
económicamente *adv* : financially
económico, -ca *adj* : economic, economical
economista *nmf* : economist
economizar {21} *vt* : to save, to economize on — *vi* : to save up, to be frugal
ecosistema *nm* : ecosystem
ecuación *nf, pl* **-ciones** : equation
ecuador *nm* : equator

ecuánime *adj* **1** : even-tempered **2** : impartial
ecuanimidad *nf* **1** : equanimity **2** : impartiality
ecuatorial *adj* : equatorial
ecuatoriano, -na *adj & n* : Ecuadorian
ecuestre *adj* : equestrian
ecuménico, -ca *adj* : ecumenical
eczema *nm* : eczema
edad *nf* **1** : age ⟨¿qué edad tiene? : how old is she?⟩ **2** ÉPOCA, ERA : epoch, era
edema *nm* : edema
Edén *nm, pl* **Edenes** : Eden, paradise
edición *nf, pl* **-ciones** **1** : edition **2** : publication, publishing
edicto *nm* : edict, proclamation
edificación *nf, pl* **-ciones** **1** : edification **2** : construction, building
edificante *adj* : edifying
edificar {72} *vt* **1** : to edify **2** CONSTRUIR : to build, to construct
edificio *nm* : building, edifice
editar *vt* **1** : to edit **2** PUBLICAR : to publish
editor¹, -tora *adj* : publishing ⟨casa editora : publishing house⟩
editor², -tora *n* **1** : editor **2** : publisher
editora *nf* : publisher, publishing company
editorial¹ *adj* **1** : publishing **2** : editorial
editorial² *nm* : editorial
editorial³ *nf* : publishing house
editorializar {21} *vi* : to editorialize
edredón *nm, pl* **-dones** COBERTOR, COLCHA : comforter, eiderdown, quilt
educable *adj* : educable, teachable
educación *nf, pl* **-ciones** **1** ENSEÑANZA : education **2** : manners *pl* — **educacional** *adj*
educado, -da *adj* : polite, well-mannered
educador, -dora *n* : educator
educando, -da *n* ALUMNO, PUPILO : pupil, student
educar {72} *vt* **1** : to educate **2** CRIAR : to bring up, to raise **3** : to train — **educarse** *vr* : to be educated
educativo, -va *adj* : educational
efectista *adj* : dramatic, sensational
efectivamente *adv* : really, actually
efectividad *nf* : effectiveness

efectivo[1], **-va** *adj* **1** : effective **2** : real, actual **3** : permanent, regular (of employment)
efectivo[2] *nm* : cash
efecto *nm* **1** : effect **2 en** ～ : actually, in fact **3 efectos** *nmpl* : goods, property ⟨efectos personales : personal effects⟩
efectuar {3} *vt* : to carry out, to bring about
efervescencia *nf* **1** : effervescence **2** : vivacity, high spirits *pl*
efervescente *adj* **1** : effervescent **2** : vivacious
eficacia *nf* **1** : effectiveness, efficacy **2** : efficiency
eficaz *adj, pl* **-caces 1** : effective **2** EFICIENTE : efficient — **eficazmente** *adv*
eficiencia *nf* : efficiency
eficiente *adj* EFICAZ : efficient — **eficientemente** *adv*
eficientizar {21} *vt Mex* : to streamline, to make more efficient
efigie *nf* : effigy
efímera *nf* : mayfly
efímero, -ra *adj* : ephemeral
efusión *nf, pl* **-siones 1** : effusion **2** : warmth, effusiveness **3 con** ～ : effusively
efusivo, -va *adj* : effusive — **efusivamente** *adv*
egipcio, -cia *adj & n* : Egyptian
eglefino *nm* : haddock
ego *nm* : ego
egocéntrico, -ca *adj* : egocentric, self-centered
egoísmo *nm* : selfishness, egoism
egoísta[1] *adj* : selfish, egoistic
egoísta[2] *nmf* : egoist, selfish person
egotismo *nm* : egotism, conceit
egotista[1] *adj* : egotistic, egotistical, conceited
egotista[2] *nmf* : egotist, conceited person
egresado, -da *n* : graduate
egresar *vi* : to graduate
egreso *nm* **1** : graduation **2 ingresos y egresos** : income and expenditure
eh *interj* **1** : hey! **2** : eh?, huh?
eje *nm* **1** : axle **2** : axis
ejecución *nf, pl* **-ciones** : execution
ejecutante *nmf* : performer
ejecutar *vt* **1** : to execute, to put to death **2** : to carry out, to perform
ejecutivo, -va *adj & n* : executive
ejecutor, -tora *n* : executor
ejemplar[1] *adj* : exemplary, model
ejemplar[2] *nm* **1** : copy (of a book, magazine, etc.) **2** : specimen, example
ejemplificar {72} *vt* : to exemplify, to illustrate
ejemplo *nm* **1** : example **2 por** ～ : for example **3 dar ejemplo** : to set an example
ejercer {86} *vi* ～ **de** : to practice as, to work as — *vt* **1** : to practice **2** : exercise (a right) **3** : to exert
ejercicio *nm* **1** : exercise **2** : practice
ejercitar *vt* **1** : to exercise **2** ADIESTRAR : to drill, to train

ejército *nm* : army
ejidal *adj Mex* : cooperative
ejido *nm* **1** : common land **2** *Mex* : cooperative
ejote *nm Mex* : green bean
el[1] *pron (referring to masculine nouns)* **1** : the one ⟨tengo mi libro y el tuyo : I have my book and yours⟩ ⟨de los cantantes me gusta el de México : I prefer the singer from México⟩ **2 el que** : he who, whoever, the one that ⟨el que vino ayer : the one who came yesterday⟩ ⟨el que trabaja duro estará contento : he who works hard will be happy⟩
el[2], **la** *art, pl* **los, las** : the ⟨los niños están en la casa : the boys are in the house⟩ ⟨me duele el pie : my foot hurts⟩
él *pron* : he, him ⟨él es mi amigo : he's my friend⟩ ⟨hablaremos con él : we will speak with him⟩
elaboración *nf, pl* **-ciones 1** PRODUCCIÓN : production, making **2** : preparation, devising
elaborado, -da *adj* : elaborate
elaborar *vt* **1** : to make, to produce **2** : to devise, to draw up
elasticidad *nf* : elasticity
elástico[1], **-ca** *adj* **1** FLEXIBLE : flexible **2** : elastic
elástico[2] *nm* **1** : elastic (material) **2** : rubber band
elección *nf, pl* **-ciones 1** SELECCIÓN : choice, selection **2** : election
electivo, -va *adj* : elective
electo, -ta *adj* : elect ⟨el presidente electo : the president-elect⟩
elector, -tora *n* : elector, voter
electorado *nm* : electorate
electoral *adj* : electoral, election
electricidad *nf* : electricity
electricista *nmf* : electrician
eléctrico, -ca *adj* : electric, electrical
electrificar {72} *vt* : to electrify — **electrificación** *nf*
electrizar {21} *vt* : to electrify, to thrill — **electrizante** *adj*
electrocardiógrafo *nm* : electrocardiograph
electrocardiograma *nm* : electrocardiogram
electrocutar *vt* : to electrocute — **electrocución** *nf*
electrodo *nm* : electrode
electrodoméstico *nm* : electric appliance
electroimán *nm, pl* **-manes** : electromagnet
electrólisis *nfs & pl* : electrolysis
electrolito *nm* : electrolyte
electromagnético, -ca *adj* : electromagnetic
electromagnetismo *nm* : electromagnetism
electrón *nm, pl* **-trones** : electron
electrónica *nf* : electronics
electrónico, -ca *adj* : electronic — **electrónicamente** *adv*

elefante, -ta *n* : elephant
elegancia *nf* : elegance
elegante *adj* : elegant, smart — **elegantemente** *adv*
elegía *nf* : elegy
elegíaco, -ca *adj* : elegiac
elegibilidad *nf* : eligibility
elegible *adj* : eligible
elegido, -da *adj* 1 : chosen, selected 2 : elected
elegir {28} *vt* 1 ESCOGER, SELECCIONAR : to choose, to select 2 : to elect
elemental *adj* 1 : elementary, basic 2 : fundamental, essential
elemento *nm* : element
elenco *nm* : cast (of actors)
elepé *nm* : long-playing record
elevación *nf, pl* **-ciones** : elevation, height
elevado, -da *adj* 1 : elevated, lofty 2 : high
elevador *nm* ASCENSOR : elevator
elevar *vt* 1 ALZAR : to raise, to lift 2 AUMENTAR : to raise, to increase 3 : to elevate (in a hierarchy), to promote 4 : to present, to submit — **elevarse** *vr* : to rise
elfo *nm* : elf
eliminación *nf, pl* **-ciones** : elimination, removal
eliminar *vt* 1 : to eliminate, to remove 2 : to do in, to kill
elipse *nf* : ellipse
elipsis *nf* : ellipsis
elíptico, -ca *adj* : elliptical, elliptic
elite *or* **élite** *nf* : elite
elixir *or* **elíxir** *nm* : elixir
ella *pron* : she, her ⟨ella es mi amiga : she is my friend⟩ ⟨nos fuimos con ella : we left with her⟩
ello *pron* : it ⟨es por ello que me voy : that's why I'm going⟩
ellos, ellas *pron pl* 1 : they, them 2 **de ellos, de ellas** : theirs
elocución *nf, pl* **-ciones** : elocution
elocuencia *nf* : eloquence
elocuente *adj* : eloquent — **elocuentemente** *adv*
elogiar *vt* ENCOMIAR : to praise
elogio *nm* : praise
elote *nm* 1 *Mex* : corn, maize 2 *CA, Mex* : corncob
elucidación *nf, pl* **-ciones** ESCLARECIMIENTO : elucidation
elucidar *vt* ESCLARECER : to elucidate
eludir *vt* EVADIR : to evade, to avoid, to elude
emanación *nf, pl* **-ciones** : emanation
emanar *vi* ∼ **de** : to emanate from — *vt* : to exude
emancipar *vt* : to emancipate — **emancipación** *nf*
embadurnar *vt* EMBARRAR : to smear, to daub
embajada *nf* : embassy
embajador, -dora *n* : ambassador
embalaje *nm* : packing, packaging
embalar *vt* EMPAQUETAR : to pack

embaldosar *vt* : to tile, to pave with tiles
embalsamar *vt* : to embalm
embalsar *vt* : to dam, to dam up
embalse *nm* : dam, reservoir
embarazada *adj* ENCINTA, PREÑADA : pregnant, expecting
embarazar {21} *vt* 1 : to obstruct, to hamper 2 PREÑAR : to make pregnant
embarazo *nm* : pregnancy
embarazoso, -sa *adj* : embarrassing, awkward
embarcación *nf, pl* **-ciones** : boat, craft
embarcadero *nm* : wharf, pier, jetty
embarcar {72} *vi* : to embark, to board — *vt* : to load
embarco *nm* : embarkation
embargar {52} *vt* 1 : to seize, to impound 2 : to overwhelm
embargo *nm* 1 : seizure 2 : embargo 3 **sin** ∼ : however, nevertheless
embarque *nm* 1 : embarkation 2 : shipment
embarrancar {72} *vi* 1 : to run aground 2 : to get bogged down
embarrar *vt* 1 : to cover with mud 2 EMBADURNAR : to smear
embarullar *vt fam* : to muddle, to confuse — **embarullarse** *vr fam* : to get mixed up
embate *nm* 1 : onslaught 2 : battering (of waves or wind)
embaucador, -dora *n* : swindler, deceiver
embaucar {72} *vt* : to trick, to swindle
embeber *vt* : to absorb, to soak up — *vi* : to shrink
embelesado, -da *adj* : spellbound
embelesar *vt* : to enchant, to captivate
embellecer {53} *vt* : to embellish, to beautify
embellecimiento *nm* : beautification, embellishment
embestida *nf* 1 : charge (of a bull) 2 ARREMETIDA : attack, onslaught
embestir {54} *vt* : to hit, to run into, to charge at — *vi* ARREMETER : to charge, to attack
emblanquecer {53} *vt* BLANQUEAR : to bleach, to whiten — **emblanquecerse** *vr* : to turn white
emblema *nm* : emblem
emblemático, -ca *adj* : emblematic
embolia *nf* : embolism
émbolo *nm* : piston
embolsarse *vr* 1 : to pocket (money) 2 : to collect (payment)
emborracharse *vr* EMBRIAGARSE : to get drunk
emborronar *vt* 1 : to blot, to smudge 2 GARABATEAR : to scribble
emboscada *nf* : ambush
emboscar {72} *vt* : to ambush — **emboscarse** *vr* : to lie in ambush
embotadura *nf* : bluntness, dullness
embotar *vt* 1 : to dull, to blunt 2 : to weaken, to enervate
embotellamiento *nm* ATASCO : traffic jam

embotellar *vt* ENVASAR : to bottle
embragar {52} *vi* : to engage the clutch
embrague *nm* : clutch
embravecerse {53} *vr* **1** : to get furious **2** : to get rough ⟨el mar se embraveció : the sea became tempestuous⟩
embriagado, -da *adj* : inebriated, drunk
embriagador, -dora *adj* : intoxicating
embriagarse {52} *vr* EMBORRACHARSE : to get drunk
embriaguez *nf* EBRIEDAD : drunkenness, inebriation
embrión *nm, pl* **embriones** : embryo
embrionario, -ria *adj* : embryonic
embrollo *nm* ENREDO : imbroglio, confusion
embrujar *vt* HECHIZAR : to bewitch
embrujo *nm* : spell, curse
embudo *nm* : funnel
embuste *nm* **1** MENTIRA : lie, fib **2** ENGAÑO : trick, hoax
embustero[1]**, -ra** *adj* : lying, deceitful
embustero[2]**, -ra** *n* : liar, cheat
embutido *nm* **1** : sausage **2** : inlaid work
embutir *vt* **1** : to cram, to stuff, to jam **2** : to inlay
emergencia *nf* **1** : emergency **2** : emergence
emergente *adj* **1** : emergent **2** : consequent, resultant
emerger {15} *vi* : to emerge, to surface
emético[1]**, -ca** *adj* : emetic
emético[2] *nm* : emetic
emigración *nf, pl* **-ciones** **1** : emigration **2** : migration
emigrante *adj & nmf* : emigrant
emigrar *vi* **1** : to emigrate **2** : to migrate
eminencia *nf* : eminence
eminente *adj* : eminent, distinguished
eminentemente *adv* : basically, essentially
emisario[1]**, -ria** *n* : emissary
emisario[2] *nm* : outlet (of a body of water)
emisión *nf, pl* **-siones** **1** : emission **2** : broadcast **3** : issue ⟨emisión de acciones : stock issue⟩
emisor *nm* TRANSMISOR : television or radio transmitter
emisora *nf* : radio station
emitir *vt* **1** : to emit, to give off **2** : to broadcast **3** : to issue **4** : to cast (a vote)
emoción *nf, pl* **-ciones** : emotion —
emocional *adj* — **emocionalmente** *adv*
emocionado, -da *adj* **1** : moved, affected by emotion **2** ENTUSIASMADO : excited
emocionante *adj* **1** CONMOVEDOR : moving, touching **2** EXCITANTE : exciting, thrilling
emocionar *vt* **1** CONMOVER : to move, to touch **2** : to excite, to thrill — **emocionarse** *vr*
emotivo, -va *adj* : emotional, moving
empacador, -dora *n* : packer

empacar {72} *vt* **1** EMPAQUETAR : to pack **2** : to bale — *vi* : to pack — **empacarse** *vr* **1** : to balk, to refuse to budge **2** *Col, Mex fam* : to eat ravenously, to devour
empachar *vt* **1** ESTORBAR : to obstruct **2** : to give indigestion to **3** DISFRAZAR : to disguise, to mask — **empacharse** *vr* **1** INDIGESTARSE : to get indigestion **2** AVERGONZARSE : to be embarrassed
empacho *nm* **1** INDIGESTIÓN : indigestion **2** VERGÜENZA : embarrassment **3** **no tener empacho en** : to have no qualms about
empadronarse *vr* : to register to vote
empalagar {52} *vt* **1** : to cloy, to surfeit **2** FASTIDIAR : to annoy, to bother
empalagoso, -sa *adj* MELOSO : cloying, excessively sweet
empalar *vt* : to impale
empalizada *nf* : palisade (fence)
empalmar *vt* **1** : to splice, to link **2** : to combine — *vi* : to meet, to converge
empalme *nm* **1** CONEXIÓN : connection, link **2** : junction
empanada *nf* : pie, turnover
empanadilla *nf* : meat or seafood pie
empanar *vt* : to bread
empantanado, -da *adj* : bogged down, delayed
empañar *vt* **1** : to steam up **2** : to tarnish, to sully
empapado, -da *adj* : soggy, sodden
empapar *vt* MOJAR : to soak, to drench — **empaparse** *vr* **1** : to get soaking wet **2** ~ **de** : to absorb, to be imbued with
empapelar *vt* : to wallpaper
empaque *nm fam* **1** : presence, bearing **2** : pomposity **3** DESCARO : impudence, nerve
empaquetar *vt* EMBALAR : to pack, to package — **empaquetarse** *vr fam* : to dress up
emparedado *nm* : sandwich
emparedar *vt* : to wall in, to confine
emparejar *vt* **1** : to pair, to match up **2** : to make even — *vi* : to catch up — **emparejarse** *vr* : to pair up
emparentado, -da *adj* : related
emparentar {55} *vi* : to become related by marriage
emparrillado *nm Mex* : gridiron (in football)
empastar *vt* **1** : to fill (a tooth) **2** : to bind (a book)
empaste *nm* : filling (of a tooth)
empatar *vt* : to tie, to connect — *vi* : to result in a draw, to be tied — **empatarse** *vr Ven* : to hook up, to link together
empate *nm* : draw, tie
empatía *nf* : empathy
empecinado, -da *adj* TERCO : stubborn
empecinarse *vr* OBSTINARSE : to be stubborn, to persist
empedernido, -da *adj* INCORREGIBLE : hardened, inveterate
empedrado *nm* : paving, pavement

empedrar {55} *vt* : to pave (with stones)
empeine *nm* : instep
empellón *nm, pl* **-llones** : shove, push
empelotado, -da *adj* **1** *Mex fam* : madly in love **2** *fam* : stark naked
empeñado, -da *adj* : determined, committed
empeñar *vt* **1** : to pawn **2** : to pledge, to give (one's word) — **empeñarse** *vr* **1** : to insist stubbornly **2** : to make an effort
empeño *nm* **1** : pledge, commitment **2** : insistence **3** ESFUERZO : effort, determination **4** : pawning ⟨casa de empeños : pawnshop⟩
empeoramiento *nm* : worsening, deterioration
empeorar *vi* : to deteriorate, to get worse — *vt* : to make worse
empequeñecer {53} *vi* : to diminish, to become smaller — *vt* : to minimize, to make smaller
emperador *nm* : emperor
emperatriz *nf, pl* **-trices** : empress
empero *conj* : however, nevertheless
empezar {29} *v* COMENZAR : to start, to begin
empinado, -da *adj* : steep
empinar *vt* ELEVAR : to lift, to raise — **empinarse** *vr* : to stand on tiptoe
empírico, -ca *adj* : empirical — **empíricamente** *adv*
emplasto *nm* : poultice, dressing
emplazamiento *nm* **1** : location, site **2** CITACIÓN : summons, subpoena
emplazar {21} *vt* **1** CONVOCAR : to convene, to summon **2** : to subpoena **3** UBICAR : to place, to position
empleado, -da *n* : employee
empleador, -dora *n* PATRÓN : employer
emplear *vt* **1** : to employ **2** USAR : to use — **emplearse** *vr* **1** : to get a job **2** : to occupy oneself
empleo *nm* **1** OCUPACIÓN : employment, occupation, job **2** : use, usage
empobrecer {53} *vt* : to impoverish — *vi* : to become poor — **empobrecerse** *vr*
empobrecimiento *nm* : impoverishment
empollar *vi* : to brood eggs — *vt* : to incubate
empolvado, -da *adj* **1** : dusty **2** : powdered, powdery
empolvar *vt* **1** : to cover with dust **2** : to powder — **empolvarse** *vr* **1** : to gather dust **2** : to powder one's face
emporio *nm* **1** : center, capital, empire ⟨un emporio cultural : a cultural center⟩ ⟨un emporio financiero : a financial empire⟩ **2** : department store
empotrado, -da *adj* : built-in ⟨armarios empotrados : built-in cabinets⟩
empotrar *vt* : to build into, to embed
emprendedor, -dora *adj* : enterprising
emprender *vt* : to undertake, to begin

empresa *nf* **1** COMPAÑÍA, FIRMA : company, corporation, firm **2** : undertaking, venture
empresariado *nm* **1** : business world **2** : management, managers *pl*
empresarial *adj* : business, managerial, corporate
empresario, -ria *n* **1** : manager **2** : businessman *m*, businesswoman *f* **3** : impresario
empréstito *nm* : loan
empujar *vi* : to push, to shove — *vt* **1** : to push **2** PRESIONAR : to spur on, to press
empuje *nm* : impetus, drive
empujón *nm, pl* **-jones** : push, shove
empuñadura *nf* MANGO : hilt, handle
empuñar *vt* **1** ASIR : to grasp **2** empuñar las armas : to take up arms
emú *nm* : emu
emular *vt* IMITAR : to emulate — **emulación** *nf*
emulsión *nf, pl* **-siones** : emulsion
emulsionante *nm* : emulsifier
emulsionar *vt* : to emulsify
en *prep* **1** : in ⟨en el bolsillo : in one's pocket⟩ ⟨en una semana : in a week⟩ **2** : on ⟨en la mesa : on the table⟩ **3** : at ⟨en casa : at home⟩ ⟨en el trabajo : at work⟩ ⟨en ese momento : at that moment⟩
enagua *nf* : petticoat, slip
enajenación *nf, pl* **-ciones** **1** : transfer (of property) **2** : alienation **3** : absentmindedness
enajenado, -da *adj* : out of one's mind
enajenar *vt* **1** : to transfer (property) **2** : to alienate **3** : to enrapture — **enajenarse** *vr* **1** : to become estranged **2** : to go mad
enaltecer {53} *vt* : to praise, to extol
enamorado[1], -da *adj* : in love
enamorado[2], -da *n* : lover, sweetheart
enamoramiento *nm* : infatuation, crush
enamorar *vt* : to enamor, to win the love of — **enamorarse** *vr* : to fall in love
enamoriscarse {72} *vr fam* : to have a crush, to be infatuated
enamorizado, -da *adj* : amorous, passionate
enano[1], -na *adj* : tiny, minute
enano[2], -na *n* : dwarf, midget
enarbolar *vt* **1** : to hoist, to raise **2** : to brandish
enarcar {72} *vt* : to arch, to raise
enardecer {53} *vt* **1** : to arouse (anger, passions) **2** : to stir up, to excite — **enardecerse** *vr*
encabezado *nm Mex* : headline
encabezamiento *nm* **1** : heading **2** : salutation, opening
encabezar {21} *vt* **1** : to head, to lead **2** : to put a heading on
encabritarse *vr* **1** : to rear up **2** *fam* : to get angry
encadenar *vt* **1** : to chain **2** : to connect, to link **3** INMOVILIZAR : to immobilize

encajar *vi* : to fit, to fit together, to fit in — *vt* **1** : to insert, to stick **2** : to take, to cope with ⟨encajó el golpe : he withstood the blow⟩

encaje *nm* **1** : lace **2** : financial reserve

encajonar *vt* **1** : to box, to crate **2** : to cram in

encalar *vt* : to whitewash

encallar *vi* **1** : to run aground **2** : to get stuck

encallecido, -da *adj* : callused

encamar *vt* : to confine to a bed

encaminado, -da *adj* **1** : on the right track **2** ~ **a** : aimed at, designed to

encaminar *vt* **1** : to direct, to channel **2** : to head in the right direction — **encaminarse** *vr* ~ **a** : to head for, to aim at

encandilar *vt* : to dazzle

encanecer {53} *vi* : to gray, to go gray

encantado, -da *adj* **1** : charmed, bewitched **2** : delighted

encantador¹, -dora *adj* : charming, delightful

encantador², -dora *n* : magician

encantamiento *nm* : enchantment, spell

encantar *vt* **1** : to enchant, to bewitch **2** : to charm, to delight ⟨me encanta esta canción : I love this song⟩

encanto *nm* **1** : charm, fascination **2** HECHIZO : spell **3** : delightful person or thing

encañonar *vt* : to point (a gun) at, to hold up

encapotado, -da *adj* : cloudy, overcast

encapotarse *vr* : to cloud over, to become overcast

encaprichado, -da *adj* : infatuated

encaprichamiento *nm* : infatuation

encapuchado, -da *adj* : hooded

encarado, -da *adj* **estar mal encarado** *fam* : to be ugly-looking, to look mean

encaramar *vt* : to raise, to lift up — **encaramarse** *vr* : to perch

encarar *vt* CONFRONTAR : to face, to confront

encarcelación *nf* → **encarcelamiento**

encarcelamiento *nm* : incarceration, imprisonment

encarcelar *vt* : to incarcerate, to imprison

encarecer {53} *vt* **1** : to increase, to raise (price, value) **2** : to beseech, to entreat — **encarecerse** *vr* : to become more expensive

encarecidamente *adv* : insistently, urgently

encarecimiento *nm* : increase, rise (in price)

encargado¹, -da *adj* : in charge

encargado², -da *n* : manager, person in charge

encargar {52} *vt* **1** : to put in charge of **2** : to recommend, to advise **3** : to order, to request — **encargarse** *vr* ~ **de** : to take charge of

encargo *nm* **1** : errand **2** : job assignment **3** : order ⟨hecho de encargo : custom-made, made to order⟩

encariñarse *vr* ~ **con** : to become fond of, to grow attached to

encarnación *nf, pl* **-ciones** : incarnation, embodiment

encarnado¹, -da *adj* **1** : incarnate **2** : flesh-colored **3** : red **4** : ingrown

encarnado² *nm* : red

encarnar *vt* : to incarnate, to embody — **encarnarse una uña** *vr* : to have an ingrown nail

encarnizado, -da *adj* **1** : bloodshot, inflamed **2** : fierce, bloody

encarnizar {21} *vt* : to enrage, to infuriate — **encarnizarse** *vr* : to be brutal, to attack viciously

encarrilar *vt* : to guide, to put on the right track

encasillar *vt* CLASIFICAR : to classify, to pigeonhole, to categorize

encausar *vt* : to prosecute, to charge

encauzar {21} *vt* : to channel, to guide — **encauzarse** *vr*

encebollado, -da *adj* : cooked with onions

encefalitis *nms & pl* : encephalitis

enceguecedor, -dora *n* : blinding

encendedor *nm* : lighter

encender {56} *vi* : to light — *vt* **1** : to light, to set fire to **2** PRENDER : to switch on **3** : to start (a motor) **4** : to arouse, to kindle — **encenderse** *vr* **1** : to get excited **2** : to blush

encendido¹, -da *adj* **1** : burning **2** : flushed **3** : fiery, passionate

encendido² *nm* : ignition

encerado *nm* **1** : waxing, polishing **2** : blackboard

encerar *vt* : to wax, to polish

encerrar {55} *vt* **1** : to lock up, to shut away **2** : to contain, to include **3** : to involve, to entail

encerrona *nf* **1** TRAMPA : trap, setup **2 prepararle una encerrona a alguien** : to set a trap for someone, to set someone up

encestar *vi* : to make a basket (in basketball)

enchapado *nm* : plating, coating (of metal)

encharcamiento *nm* : flood, flooding

encharcar {72} *vt* : to flood, to swamp — **encharcarse** *vr*

enchilada *nf* : enchilada

enchilar *vt Mex* : to season with chili

enchuecar {72} *vt Chile, Mex fam* : to make crooked, to twist

enchufar *vt* **1** : to plug in **2** : to connect, to fit together

enchufe *nm* **1** : connection **2** : plug, socket

encía *nf* : gum (tissue)

encíclica *nf* : encyclical

enciclopedia *nf* : encyclopedia

enciclopédico, -ca *adj* : encyclopedic

encierro *nm* **1** : confinement **2** : enclosure

encima *adv* **1** : on top, above **2** ADEMÁS : as well, besides **3** ~ **de** : on, on top

of, over **4 por encima de** : above, beyond ⟨por encima de la ley : above the law⟩ **5 echarse encima** : to take upon oneself **6 estar encima de** *fam* : to nag, to criticize **7 quitarse de encima** : to get rid of
encina *nf* : evergreen oak
encinta *adj* EMBARAZADA, PREÑADA : pregnant, expecting
enclaustrado, -da *adj* : cloistered, shut away
enclavado, -da *adj* : buried
enclenque *adj* : weak, sickly
encoger {15} *vt* **1** : to shrink, to make smaller **2** : to intimidate — *vi* : to shrink, to contract — **encogerse** *vr* **1** : to shrink **2** : to be intimidated, to cower, to cringe **3 encogerse de hombros** : to shrug (one's shoulders)
encogido, -da *adj* **1** : shriveled, shrunken **2** TÍMIDO : shy, inhibited
encogimiento *nm* **1** : shrinking, shrinkage **2** : shrug **3** TIMIDEZ : shyness
encolar *vt* : to paste, to glue
encolerizar {21} *vt* ENFURECER : to enrage, to infuriate — **encolerizarse** *vr*
encomendar {55} *vt* CONFIAR : to entrust, to commend — **encomendarse** *vr*
encomiable *adj* : commendable, praiseworthy
encomiar *vt* ELOGIAR : to praise, to pay tribute to
encomienda *nf* **1** : charge, mission **2** : royal land grant **3** : parcel
encomio *nm* : praise, eulogy
encomioso, -sa *adj* : eulogistic, laudatory
enconar *vt* **1** : to irritate, to anger **2** : to inflame — **enconarse** *vr* **1** : to become heated **2** : to fester
encono *nm* **1** RENCOR : animosity, rancor **2** : inflammation, infection
encontrado, -da *adj* : contrary, opposing
encontrar {19} *vt* **1** HALLAR : to find **2** : to encounter, to meet — **encontrarse** *vr* **1** REUNIRSE : to meet **2** : to clash, to conflict **3** : to be ⟨su abuelo se encuentra mejor : her grandfather is doing better⟩
encorvar *vt* : to bend, to curve — **encorvarse** *vr* : to hunch over, to stoop
encrespar *vt* **1** : to curl, to ruffle, to ripple **2** : to annoy, to irritate — **encresparse** *vr* **1** : to curl one's hair **2** : to become choppy **3** : to get annoyed
encrucijada *nf* : crossroads
encuadernación *nf, pl* **-ciones** : bookbinding
encuadernar *vt* EMPASTAR : to bind (a book)
encuadrar *vt* **1** ENMARCAR : to frame **2** ENCAJAR : to fit, to insert **3** COMPRENDER : to contain, to include
encubierto *pp* → **encubrir**
encubrimiento *nm* : cover-up
encubrir {2} *vt* : to cover up, to conceal

encuentro *nm* **1** : meeting, encounter **2** : conference, congress
encuerado, -da *adj fam* : naked
encuerar *vt fam* : to undress
encuesta *nf* **1** INVESTIGACIÓN, PESQUISA : inquiry, investigation **2** SONDEO : survey
encuestador, -dora *n* : pollster
encuestar *vt* : to poll, to take a survey of
encumbrado, -da *adj* **1** : lofty, high **2** : eminent, distinguished
encumbrar *vt* **1** : to exalt, to elevate **2** : to extol — **encumbrarse** *vr* : to reach the top
encurtir *vt* ESCABECHAR : to pickle
ende *adv* por ~ : therefore, consequently
endeble *adj* : feeble, weak
endeblez *nf* : weakness, frailty
endémico, -ca *adj* : endemic
endemoniado, -da *adj* : fiendish, diabolical
endentecer {53} *vi* : to teethe
enderezar {21} *vt* **1** : to straighten (out) **2** : to stand on end, to put upright
endeudado, -da *adj* : in debt, indebted
endeudamiento *nm* : indebtedness
endeudarse *vr* **1** : to go into debt **2** : to feel obliged
endiabladamente *adv* : extremely, diabolically
endiablado, -da *adj* **1** : devilish, diabolical **2** : complicated, difficult
endibia *or* **endivia** *nf* : endive
endilgar {52} *vt fam* : to spring, to foist ⟨me endilgó la responsabilidad : he saddled me with the responsibility⟩
endocrino, -na *adj* : endocrine
endogamia *nf* : inbreeding
endosar *vt* : to endorse
endoso *nm* : endorsement
endulzante *nm* : sweetener
endulzar {21} *vt* **1** : to sweeten **2** : to soften, to mellow — **endulzarse** *vr*
endurecer {53} *vt* : to harden, to toughen — **endurecerse** *vr*
enebro *nm* : juniper
eneldo *nm* : dill
enema *nm* : enema
enemigo, -ga *adj & n* : enemy
enemistad *nf* : enmity, hostility
enemistar *vt* : to make enemies of — **enemistarse** *vr* ~ **con** : to fall out with
energía *nf* : energy
enérgico, -ca *adj* **1** : energetic, vigorous **2** : forceful, emphatic — **enérgicamente** *adv*
energúmeno, -na *n fam* : lunatic, crazy person
enero *nm* : January
enervar *vt* **1** : to enervate **2** *fam* : to annoy, to get on one's nerves — **enervante** *adj*
enésimo, -ma *adj* : umpteenth, nth
enfadar *vt* **1** : to annoy, to make angry **2** *Mex fam* : to bore — **enfadarse** *vr* : to get angry, to get annoyed

enfado *nm* : anger, annoyance
enfadoso, -sa *adj* : irritating, annoying
enfardar *vt* : to bale
énfasis *nms & pl* : emphasis
enfático, -ca *adj* : emphatic — **enfáticamente** *adv*
enfatizar {21} *vt* DESTACAR, SUBRAYAR : to emphasize
enfermar *vt* : to make sick — *vi* : to fall ill, to get sick — **enfermarse** *vr*
enfermedad *nf* **1** INDISPOSICIÓN : sickness, illness **2** : disease
enfermería *nf* : infirmary
enfermero, -ra *n* : nurse
enfermizo, -za *adj* : sickly
enfermo¹, -ma *adj* : sick, ill
enfermo², -ma *n* **1** : sick person, invalid **2** PACIENTE : patient
enfilar *vt* **1** : to take, to go along ⟨enfiló la carretera de Montevideo : she went up the road to Montevideo⟩ **2** : to line up, to put in a row **3** : to string, to thread **4** : to aim, to direct — *vi* : to make one's way
enflaquecer {53} *vi* : to lose weight, to become thin — *vt* : to emaciate
enfocar {72} *vt* **1** : to focus (on) **2** : to consider, to look at
enfoque *nm* : focus
enfrascamiento *nm* : immersion, absorption
enfrascarse {72} *vr* ~ **en** : to immerse oneself in, to get caught up in
enfrentamiento *nm* : clash, confrontation
enfrentar *vt* : to confront, to face — **enfrentarse** *vr* **1** ~ **con** : to clash with **2** ~ **a** : to face up to
enfrente *adv* **1** DELANTE : in front **2** : opposite
enfriamiento *nm* **1** CATARRO : chill, cold **2** : cooling off, damper
enfriar {85} *vt* **1** : to chill, to cool **2** : to cool down, to dampen — *vi* : to get cold — **enfriarse** *vr* : to get chilled, to catch a cold
enfundar *vt* : to sheathe, to encase
enfurecer {53} *vt* ENCOLERIZAR : to infuriate — **enfurecerse** *vr* : to fly into a rage
enfurecido, -da *adj* : furious, raging
enfurruñarse *vr fam* : to sulk
engalanar *vt* : to decorate, to deck out — **engalanarse** *vr* : to dress up
enganchar *vt* **1** : to hook, to snag **2** : to attach, to hitch up — **engancharse** *vr* **1** : to get snagged, to get hooked **2** : to enlist
enganche *nm* **1** : hook **2** : coupling, hitch **3** *Mex* : down payment
engañar *vt* **1** EMBAUCAR : to trick, to deceive, to mislead **2** : to cheat on, to be unfaithful to — **engañarse** *vr* **1** : to be mistaken **2** : to deceive oneself
engaño *nm* **1** : deception, trick **2** : fake, feint (in sports)
engañoso, -sa *adj* **1** : deceitful **2** : misleading, deceptive

engarrotarse *vr* : to stiffen up, to go numb
engatusamiento *nm* : cajolery
engatusar *vt* : to coax, to cajole
engendrar *vt* **1** : to beget, to father **2** : to give rise to, to engender
engentarse *vr Mex* : to be in a daze
englobar *vt* : to include, to embrace
engomar *vt* : to glue
engordar *vt* : to fatten, to fatten up — *vi* : to gain weight
engorro *nm* : nuisance, bother
engorroso, -sa *adj* : bothersome
engranaje *nm* : gears *pl*, cogs *pl*
engranar *vt* : to mesh, to engage — *vi* : to mesh gears
engrandecer {53} *vt* **1** : to enlarge **2** : to exaggerate **3** : to exalt
engrandecimiento *nm* **1** : enlargement **2** : exaggeration **3** : exaltation
engrane *nm Mex* : cogwheel
engrapadora *nf* : stapler
engrapar *vt* : to staple
engrasar *vt* : to grease, to lubricate
engrase *nm* : greasing, lubrication
engreído, -da *adj* PRESUMIDO, VANIDOSO : vain, conceited, stuck-up
engreimiento *nm* ARROGANCIA : arrogance, conceit
engreír {66} *vt* ENVANECER : to make vain — **engreírse** *vr* : to become conceited
engrosar {19} *vt* : to enlarge, to increase, to swell — *vi* ENGORDAR : to gain weight
engrudo *nm* : paste
engullir {38} *vt* : to gulp down, to gobble up — **engullirse** *vr*
enharinar *vt* : to flour
enhebrar *vt* ENSARTAR : to string, to thread
enhiesto, -ta *adj* **1** : erect, upright **2** : lofty, towering
enhilar *vt* : to thread (a needle, etc.)
enhorabuena *nf* FELICIDADES : congratulations *pl*
enigma *nm* : enigma, mystery
enigmático, -ca *adj* : enigmatic — **enigmáticamente** *adv*
enjabonar *vt* : to soap up, to lather — **enjabonarse** *vr*
enjaezar {21} *vt* : to harness
enjalbegar {52} *vt* : to whitewash
enjambrar *vi* : to swarm
enjambre *nm* **1** : swarm **2** MUCHEDUMBRE : crowd, mob
enjaular *vt* **1** : to cage **2** *fam* : to jail, to lock up
enjuagar {52} *vt* : to rinse — **enjuagarse** *vr* : to rinse out
enjuague *nm* **1** : rinse **2 enjuague bucal** : mouthwash
enjugar {52} *vt* : to wipe away (tears)
enjuiciar *vt* **1** : to indict, to prosecute **2** JUZGAR : to try
enjundioso, -sa *adj* : substantial, weighty
enjuto, -ta *adj* : lean, gaunt

enlace *nm* **1** : bond, link, connection **2** : liaison
enladrillado *nm* : brick paving
enladrillar *vt* : to pave with bricks
enlatar *vt* ENVASAR : to can
enlazar {21} *v* : to join, to link, to fit together
enlistar *vt* : to list — **enlistarse** *vr* : to enlist
enlodado, -da *adj* BARROSO : muddy
enlodar *vt* **1** : to cover with mud **2** : to stain, to sully — **enlodarse** *vr*
enlodazar → **enlodar**
enloquecedor, -dora *adj* : maddening
enloquecer {53} *vt* ALOCAR : to drive crazy — **enloquecerse** *vr* : to go crazy
enlosado *nm* : flagstone pavement
enlosar *vt* : to pave with flagstone
enlutarse *vr* : to go into mourning
enmaderado *nm* **1** : wood paneling **2** : hardwood floor
enmarañar *vt* **1** : to tangle **2** : to complicate **3** : to confuse, to mix up — **enmarañarse** *vr*
enmarcar {72} *vt* **1** ENCUADRAR : to frame **2** : to provide the setting for
enmascarar *vt* : to mask, to disguise
enmasillar *vt* : to putty, to caulk
enmendar {55} *vt* **1** : to amend **2** CORREGIR : to emend, to correct **3** COMPENSAR : to compensate for — **enmendarse** *vr* : to mend one's ways
enmienda *nf* **1** : amendment **2** : correction, emendation
enmohecerse {53} *vr* **1** : to become moldy **2** OXIDARSE : to rust, to become rusty
enmudecer {53} *vt* : to mute, to silence — *vi* : to fall silent
enmugrar *vt* : to soil, to make dirty — **enmugrarse** *vr* : to get dirty
ennegrecer {53} *vt* : to blacken, to darken — **ennegrecerse** *vr*
ennoblecer {53} *vt* **1** : to ennoble **2** : to embellish
enojadizo, -za *adj* IRRITABLE : irritable, cranky
enojado, -da *adj* **1** : annoyed **2** : angry, mad
enojar *vt* **1** : to anger **2** : to annoy, to upset — **enojarse** *vr*
enojo *nm* **1** CÓLERA : anger **2** : annoyance
enojón, -jona *adj, pl* **-jones** *Chile, Mex fam* : irritable, cranky
enojoso, -sa *adj* FASTIDIOSO, MOLESTOSO : annoying, irritating
enorgullecer {53} *vt* : to make proud — **enorgullecerse** *vr* : to pride oneself
enorme *adj* INMENSO : enormous, huge — **enormemente** *adv*
enormidad *nf* **1** : enormity, seriousness **2** : immensity, hugeness
enraizado, -da *adj* : deep-seated, deeply rooted
enraizar {30} *vi* : to take root
enramada *nf* : arbor, bower
enramar *vt* : to cover with branches

enrarecer {53} *vt* : to rarefy — **enrarecerse** *vr*
enredadera *nf* : climbing plant, vine
enredar *vt* **1** : to tangle up, to entangle **2** : to confuse, to complicate **3** : to involve, to implicate — **enredarse** *vr*
enredo *nm* **1** EMBROLLO : muddle, confusion **2** MARAÑA : tangle
enredoso, -sa *adj* : complicated, tricky
enrejado *nm* **1** : railing **2** : grating, grille **3** : trellis, lattice
enrevesado, -da *adj* : complicated, involved
enriquecer {53} *vt* : to enrich — **enriquecerse** *vr* : to get rich
enriquecido, -da *adj* : enriched
enriquecimiento *nm* : enrichment
enrojecer {53} *vt* : to make red, to redden — **enrojecerse** *vr* : to blush
enrolar *vt* RECLUTAR : to recruit — **enrolarse** *vr* INSCRIBIRSE : to enlist, to sign up
enrollar *vt* : to roll up, to coil — **enrollarse** *vr*
enronquecerse {53} *vr* : to become hoarse
enroscar {72} *vt* TORCER : to twist — **enroscarse** *vr* : to coil, to twine
ensacar {72} *vt* : to bag (up)
ensalada *nf* : salad
ensaladera *nf* : salad bowl
ensalmo *nm* : incantation, spell
ensalzar {21} *vt* **1** : to praise, to extol **2** EXALTAR : to exalt
ensamblaje *nm* : assembly
ensamblar *vt* **1** : to assemble **2** : to join, to fit together
ensanchar *vt* **1** : to widen **2** : to expand, to extend — **ensancharse** *vr*
ensanche *nm* **1** : widening **2** : expansion, development
ensangrentado, -da *adj* : bloody, bloodstained
ensañarse *vr* : to act cruelly, to be merciless
ensartar *vt* **1** ENHEBRAR : to string, to thread **2** : to skewer, to pierce
ensayar *vi* : to rehearse — *vt* **1** : to try out, to test **2** : to assay
ensayista *nmf* : essayist
ensayo *nm* **1** : essay **2** : trial, test **3** : rehearsal **4** : assay (of metals)
enseguida *adv* INMEDIATAMENTE : right away, immediately, at once
ensenada *nf* : cove, inlet
enseña *nf* **1** INSIGNIA : emblem, insignia **2** : standard, banner
enseñanza *nf* **1** EDUCACIÓN : education **2** : teaching
enseñar *vt* **1** : to teach **2** MOSTRAR : to show, to display — **enseñarse** *vr* ~ **a** : to learn to, to get used to
enseres *nmpl* : equipment, furnishings *pl* ⟨enseres domésticos : household goods⟩
ensillar *vt* : to saddle (up)
ensimismado, -da *adj* : absorbed, engrossed

ensimismarse *vr* : to lose oneself in thought

ensoberbecerse {53} *vr* : to become haughty

ensombrecer {53} *vt* : to cast a shadow over, to darken — **ensombrecerse** *vr*

ensoñación *nf, pl* **-ciones** : fantasy

ensopar *vt* **1** : to drench **2** : to dunk, to dip

ensordecedor, -dora *adj* : deafening, thunderous

ensordecer {53} *vt* : to deafen — *vi* : to go deaf

ensuciar *vt* : to soil, to dirty — **ensuciarse** *vr*

ensueño *nm* **1** : daydream, revery **2** FANTASÍA : illusion, fantasy

entablar *vt* **1** : to cover with boards **2** : to initiate, to enter into, to start

entallar *vt* AJUSTAR : to tailor, to fit, to take in — *vi* QUEDAR : to fit

ente *nm* **1** : being, entity **2** : body, organization ⟨ente rector : ruling body⟩ **3** *fam* : eccentric, crackpot

enteco, -ca *adj* : gaunt, frail

entenado, -da *n Mex* : stepchild, stepson *m*, stepdaughter *f*

entender[1] {56} *vt* **1** COMPRENDER : to understand **2** OPINAR : to think, to believe **3** : to mean, to intend **4** DEDUCIR : to infer, to deduce — *vi* **1** : to understand ⟨¡ya entiendo! : now I understand!⟩ **2** ~ **de** : to know about, to be good at **3** ~ **en** : to be in charge of — **entenderse** *vr* **1** : to be understood **2** : to get along well, to understand each other **3** ~ **con** : to deal with

entender[2] *nm* **a mi entender** : in my opinion

entendible *adj* : understandable

entendido[1]**, -da** *adj* **1** : skilled, expert **2 tener entendido** : to understand, to be under the impression ⟨teníamos entendido que vendrías : we were under the impression you would come⟩ **3 darse por entendido** : to go without saying

entendido[2] *nm* : expert, authority, connoisseur

entendimiento *nm* **1** : intellect, mind **2** : understanding, agreement

enterado, -da *adj* : aware, well-informed ⟨estar enterado de : to be privy to⟩

enteramente *adv* : entirely, completely

enterar *vt* INFORMAR : to inform — **enterarse** *vr* INFORMARSE : to find out, to learn

entereza *nf* **1** INTEGRIDAD : integrity **2** FORTALEZA : fortitude **3** FIRMEZA : resolve

enternecedor, -dora *adj* CONMOVEDOR : touching, moving

enternecer {53} *vt* CONMOVER : to move, to touch

entero[1]**, -ra** *adj* **1** : entire, whole **2** : complete, absolute **3** : intact — **enteramente** *adv*

entero[2] *nm* **1** : integer, whole number **2** : point (in finance)

enterramiento *nm* : burial

enterrar {55} *vt* : to bury

entibiar *vt* : to cool (down) — **entibiarse** *vr* : to become lukewarm

entidad *nf* **1** ENTE : entity **2** : body, organization **3** : firm, company **4** : importance, significance

entierro *nm* **1** : burial **2** : funeral

entintar *vt* : to ink

entoldado *nm* : awning

entomología *nf* : entomology

entomólogo, -ga *n* : entomologist

entonación *nf, pl* **-ciones** : intonation

entonar *vi* : to be in tune — *vt* **1** : to intone **2** : to tone up

entonces *adv* **1** : then **2 desde** ~ : since then **3 en aquel entonces** : in those days

entornado, -da *adj* ENTREABIERTO : half-closed, ajar

entornar *vt* ENTREABRIR : to leave ajar

entorno *nm* : surroundings *pl*, environment

entorpecer {53} *vt* **1** : to hinder, to obstruct **2** : to dull — **entorpecerse** *vr* : to dull the senses

entrada *nf* **1** : entrance, entry **2** : ticket, admission **3** : beginning, onset **4** : entrée **5** : cue (in music) **6 entradas** *nfpl* : income ⟨entradas y salidas : income and expenditures⟩ **7 tener entradas** : to have a receding hairline

entrado, -da *adj* **entrado en años** : elderly

entramado *nm* : framework

entrampar *vt* **1** ATRAPAR : to entrap, to ensnare **2** ENGAÑAR : to deceive, to trick

entrante *adj* **1** : next, upcoming ⟨el año entrante : next year⟩ **2** : incoming, new ⟨el presidente entrante : the president elect⟩

entraña *nf* **1** MEOLLO : core, heart, crux **2 entrañas** *nfpl* VÍSCERAS : entrails

entrañable *adj* : close, intimate

entrañar *vt* : to entail, to involve

entrar *vi* **1** : to enter, to go in, to come in **2** : to begin — *vt* **1** : to bring in, to introduce **2** : to access

entre *prep* **1** : between **2** : among

entreabierto[1] *pp* → **entreabrir**

entreabierto[2]**, -ta** *adj* ENTORNADO : half-open, ajar

entreabrir {2} *vt* ENTORNAR : to leave ajar

entreacto *nm* : intermission, interval

entrecano, -na *adj* : grayish, graying

entrecejo *nm* **fruncir el entrecejo** : to knit one's brows

entrecomillar *vt* : to place in quotation marks

entrecortado, -da *adj* **1** : labored, difficult ⟨respiración entrecortada : shortness of breath⟩ **2** : faltering, hesitant ⟨con la voz entrecortada : with a catch in his voice⟩

entrecruzar {21} *vt* ENTRELAZAR : to interweave, to intertwine — **entrecruzarse** *vr*
entredicho *nm* **1** DUDA : doubt, question **2** : prohibition
entrega *nf* **1** : delivery **2** : handing over, surrender **3** : installment ⟨entrega inicial : down payment⟩
entregar {52} *vt* **1** : to deliver **2** DAR : to give, to present **3** : to hand in, to hand over — **entregarse** *vr* **1** : to surrender, to give in **2** : to devote oneself
entrelazar {21} *vt* ENTRECRUZAR : to interweave, to intertwine
entremedias *adv* **1** : in between, halfway **2** : in the meantime
entremés *nm, pl* **-meses 1** APERITIVO : appetizer, hors d'oeuvre **2** : interlude, short play
entremeterse → **entrometerse**
entremetido *nm* → **entrometido**
entremezclar *vt* : to intermingle
entrenador, -dora *n* : trainer, coach
entrenamiento *nm* : training, drill, practice
entrenar *vt* : to train, to drill, to practice — **entrenarse** *vr* : to train, to spar (in boxing)
entreoír {50} *vt* : to hear indistinctly
entrepierna *nf* **1** : inner thigh **2** : crotch **3** : inseam
entrepiso *nm* ENTRESUELO : mezzanine
entresacar {72} *vt* **1** SELECCIONAR : to pick out, to select **2** : to thin out
entresuelo *nm* ENTREPISO : mezzanine
entretanto[1] *adv* : meanwhile
entretanto[2] *nm* **en el entretanto** : in the meantime
entretejer *vt* : to interweave
entretela *nf* : facing (of a garment)
entretener {80} *vt* **1** DIVERTIR : to entertain, to amuse **2** DISTRAER : to distract **3** DEMORAR : to delay, to hold up — **entretenerse** *vr* **1** : to amuse oneself **2** : to dally
entretenido, -da *adj* DIVERTIDO : entertaining, amusing
entretenimiento *nm* **1** : entertainment, pastime **2** DIVERSIÓN : fun, amusement
entrever {88} *vt* **1** : to catch a glimpse of **2** : to make out, to see indistinctly
entreverar *vt* : to mix, to intermingle
entrevero *nm* : confusion, disorder
entrevista *nf* : interview
entrevistador, -dora *n* : interviewer
entrevistar *vt* : to interview — **entrevistarse** *vr* REUNIRSE ~ **con** : to meet with
entristecer {53} *vt* : to sadden
entrometerse *vr* : to interfere, to meddle
entrometido, -da *n* : meddler, busybody
entroncar {72} *vt* RELACIONAR : to establish a relationship between, to connect — *vi* **1** : to be related **2** : to link up, to be connected
entronque *nm* **1** : kinship **2** VÍNCULO : link, connection

entuerto *nm* : wrong, injustice
entumecer {53} *vt* : to make numb, to be numb — **entumecerse** *vr* : to go numb, to fall asleep
entumecido, -da *adj* **1** : numb **2** : stiff (of muscles, joints, etc.)
entumecimiento *nm* : numbness
enturbiar *vt* **1** : to cloud **2** : to confuse — **enturbiarse** *vr*
entusiasmar *vt* : to excite, to fill with enthusiasm — **entusiasmarse** *vr* : to get excited
entusiasmo *nm* : enthusiasm
entusiasta[1] *adj* : enthusiastic
entusiasta[2] *nmf* AFICIONADO : enthusiast
enumerar *vt* : to enumerate — **enumeración** *nf*
enunciación *nf, pl* **-ciones** : enunciation, statement
enunciar *vt* : to enunciate, to state
envainar *vt* : to sheathe
envalentonar *vt* : to make bold, to encourage — **envalentonarse** *vr*
envanecer {53} *vt* ENGREÍR : to make vain — **envanecerse** *vr*
envasar *vt* **1** EMBOTELLAR : to bottle **2** ENLATAR : to can **3** : to pack in a container
envase *nm* **1** : packaging, packing **2** : container **3** LATA : can **4** : empty bottle
envejecer {53} *vt* : to age, to make look old — *vi* : to age, to grow old
envejecido, -da *adj* : aged, old-looking
envejecimiento *nm* : aging
envenenamiento *nm* : poisoning
envenenar *vt* **1** : to poison **2** : to embitter
envergadura *nf* **1** : span, breadth, spread **2** : importance, scope
envés *nm, pl* **enveses** : reverse, opposite side
enviado, -da *n* : envoy, correspondent
enviar {85} *vt* **1** : to send **2** : to ship
envidia *nf* : envy, jealousy
envidiar *vt* : to envy — **envidiable** *adj*
envidioso, -sa *adj* : envious, jealous
envilecer {53} *vt* : to degrade, to debase
envilecimiento *nm* : degradation, debasement
envío *nm* **1** : shipment **2** : remittance
enviudar *vi* : to be widowed, to become a widower
envoltorio *nm* **1** : bundle, package **2** : wrapping, wrapper
envoltura *nf* : wrapper, wrapping
envolver {89} *vt* **1** : to wrap **2** : to envelop, to surround **3** : to entangle, to involve — **envolverse** *vr* **1** : to become involved **2** : to wrap oneself (up)
envuelto *pp* → **envolver**
enyerbar *vt* Mex : to bewitch
enyesar *vt* **1** : to plaster **2** ESCAYOLAR : to put in a plaster cast
enzima *nf* : enzyme
éon *nm, pl* **eones** : aeon
eperlano *nm* : smelt (fish)

épico, -ca *adj* : epic
epicúreo¹, -rea *adj* : epicurean
epicúreo², -rea *n* : epicure
epidemia *nf* : epidemic
epidémico, -ca *adj* : epidemic
epidermis *nf* : epidermis
epifanía *nf* : feast of the Epiphany (January 6th)
epigrama *nm* : epigram
epilepsia *nf* : epilepsy
epiléptico, -ca *adj & n* : epileptic
epílogo *nm* : epilogue
episcopal *adj* : episcopal
episcopaliano, -na *adj & n* : Episcopalian
episódico, -ca *adj* : episodic
episodio *nm* : episode
epístola *nf* : epistle
epitafio *nm* : epitaph
epíteto *nm* : epithet, name
epítome *nm* : summary, abstract
época *nf* **1** EDAD, ERA, PERÍODO : epoch, age, period **2** : time of year, season **3 de ~** : vintage, antique
epopeya *nf* : epic poem
equidad *nf* JUSTICIA : equity, justice, fairness
equilátero, -ra *adj* : equilateral
equilibrado, -da *adj* : well-balanced
equilibrar *vt* : to balance — **equilibrarse** *vr*
equilibrio *nm* **1** : balance, equilibrium ⟨perder el equilibrio : to lose one's balance⟩ ⟨equilibrio político : balance of power⟩ **2** : poise, aplomb
equilibrista *nmf* ACRÓBATA, FUNÁMBULO : acrobat, tightrope walker
equino, -na *adj* : equine
equinoccio *nm* : equinox
equipaje *nm* BAGAJE : baggage, luggage
equipamiento *nm* : equipping, equipment
equipar *vt* : to equip — **equiparse** *vr*
equiparable *adj* : comparable
equiparar *vt* **1** IGUALAR : to put on a same level, to make equal **2** COMPARAR : to compare
equipo *nm* **1** : team, crew **2** : gear, equipment
equitación *nf, pl* **-ciones** : horseback riding, horsemanship
equitativo, -va *adj* JUSTO : equitable, fair, just — **equitativamente** *adv*
equivalencia *nf* : equivalence
equivalente *adj & nm* : equivalent
equivaler {84} *vi* : to be equivalent
equivocación *nf, pl* **-ciones** ERROR : error, mistake
equivocado, -da *adj* : mistaken, wrong — **equivocadamente** *adv*
equivocar {72} *vt* : to mistake, to confuse — **equivocarse** *vr* : to make a mistake, to be wrong
equívoco¹, -ca *adj* AMBIGUO : ambiguous, equivocal
equívoco² *nm* : misunderstanding
era¹, etc. → ser
era² *nf* EDAD, ÉPOCA : era, age

erario *nm* : public treasury
erección *nf, pl* **-ciones** : erection, raising
eremita *nmf* ERMITAÑO : hermit
ergonomía *nf* : ergonomics
erguido, -da *adj* : erect, upright
erguir {31} *vt* : to raise, to lift up — **erguirse** *vr* : to straighten up
erial *nm* : uncultivated land
erigir {35} *vt* : to build, to erect — **erigirse** *vr* ~ **en** : to set oneself up as
erizado, -da *adj* : bristly
erizarse {21} *vr* : to bristle, to stand on end
erizo *nm* **1** : hedgehog **2 erizo de mar** : sea urchin
ermitaño¹, -ña *n* EREMITA : hermit, recluse
ermitaño² *nm* : hermit crab
erogación *nf, pl* **-ciones** : expenditure
erogar {52} *vt* **1** : to pay out **2** : to distribute
erosión *nf, pl* **-siones** : erosion
erosionar *vt* : to erode
erótico, -ca *adj* : erotic
erotismo *nm* : eroticism
errabundo, -da *adj* ERRANTE, VAGABUNDO : wandering
erradicar {72} *vt* : to eradicate — **erradicación** *nf*
errado, -da *adj* : wrong, mistaken
errante *adj* ERRABUNDO, VAGABUNDO : errant, wandering
errar {32} *vt* FALLAR : to miss — *vi* **1** DESACERTAR : to be wrong, to be mistaken **2** VAGAR : to wander
errata *nf* : misprint, error
errático, -ca *adj* : erratic — **erráticamente** *adv*
erróneo, -nea *adj* EQUIVOCADO : erroneous, wrong — **erróneamente** *adv*
error *nm* EQUIVOCACIÓN : error, mistake
eructar *vi* : to belch, to burp
eructo *nm* : belch, burp
erudición *nf, pl* **-ciones** : erudition, learning
erudito¹, -ta *adj* LETRADO : erudite, learned
erudito², -ta *n* : scholar
erupción *nf, pl* **-ciones** **1** : eruption **2** SARPULLIDO : rash
eruptivo, -va *adj* : eruptive
es → ser
esbelto, -ta *adj* DELGADO : slender, slim
esbirro *nm* : henchman
esbozar {21} *vt* BOSQUEJAR : to sketch, to outline
esbozo *nm* **1** : sketch **2** : rough draft
escabechar *vt* **1** ENCURTIR : to pickle **2** *fam* : to kill, to rub out
escabeche *nm* : brine (for pickling)
escabechina *nf* MASACRE : massacre, bloodbath
escabel *nm* : footstool
escabroso, -sa *adj* **1** : rugged, rough **2** : difficult, tough **3** : risqué
escabullirse {38} *vr* : to slip away, to escape

escala *nf* **1** : scale **2** ESCALERA : ladder **3** : stopover

escalada *nf* : ascent, climb

escalador, -dora *n* ALPINISTA : mountain climber

escalafón *nm, pl* **-fones** **1** : list of personnel **2** : salary scale, rank

escalar *vt* : to climb, to scale — *vi* **1** : to go climbing **2** : to escalate

escaldar *vt* : to scald

escalera *nf* **1** : ladder ⟨escalera de tijera : stepladder⟩ **2** : stairs *pl*, staircase **3 escalera mecánica** : escalator

escalfador *nm* : chafing dish

escalfar *vt* : to poach (eggs)

escalinata *nf* : flight of stairs

escalofriante *adj* : horrifying, bloodcurdling

escalofrío *nm* : shiver, chill, shudder

escalón *nm, pl* **-lones** **1** : echelon **2** : step, rung

escalonado, -da *adj* GRADUAL : gradual, staggered

escalonar *vt* **1** : to terrace **2** : to stagger, to alternate

escalpelo *nm* BISTURÍ : scalpel

escama *nf* **1** : scale (of fish or reptiles) **2** : flake (of skin)

escamar *vt* **1** : to scale (fish) **2** : to make suspicious

escamocha *nf Mex* : fruit salad

escamoso, -sa *adj* : scaly

escamotear *vt* **1** : to palm, to conceal **2** *fam* : to lift, to swipe **3** : to hide, to cover up

escandalizar {21} *vt* : to shock, to scandalize — *vi* : to make a fuss — **escandalizarse** *vr* : to be shocked

escándalo *nm* **1** : scandal **2** : scene, commotion

escandaloso, -sa *adj* **1** : shocking, scandalous **2** RUIDOSO : noisy, rowdy **3** : flagrant, outrageous — **escandalosamente** *adv*

escandinavo, -va *adj & n* : Scandinavian

escandir *vt* : to scan (poetry)

escanear *vt* : to scan

escáner *nm* : scanner, scan

escaño *nm* **1** : seat (in a legislative body) **2** BANCO : bench

escapada *nf* HUIDA : flight, escape

escapar *vi* HUIR : to escape, to flee, to run away — **escaparse** *vr* : to escape notice, to leak out

escaparate *nm* **1** : shop window **2** : showcase

escapatoria *nf* **1** : loophole, excuse, pretext ⟨no tener escapatoria : to have no way out⟩ **2** ESCAPADA : escape, flight

escape *nm* **1** FUGA : escape **2** : exhaust (from a vehicle)

escapismo *nm* : escapism

escápula *nf* OMÓPLATO : scapula, shoulder blade

escapulario *nm* : scapular

escarabajo *nm* : beetle

escaramuza *nf* **1** : skirmish **2** : scrimmage

escaramuzar {21} *vi* : to skirmish

escarapela *nf* : rosette (ornament)

escarbar *vt* **1** : to dig, to scratch up **2** : to poke, to pick **3** ~ **en** : to investigate, to pry into

escarcha *nf* **1** : frost **2** *Mex, PRi* : glitter

escarchar *vt* **1** : to frost (a cake) **2** : to candy (fruit)

escardar *vt* **1** : to weed, to hoe **2** : to weed out

escariar *vt* : to ream

escarlata *adj & nf* : scarlet

escarlatina *nf* : scarlet fever

escarmentar {55} *vt* : to punish, to teach a lesson to — *vi* : to learn one's lesson

escarmiento *nm* **1** : lesson, warning **2** CASTIGO : punishment

escarnecer {53} *vt* RIDICULIZAR : to ridicule, to mock

escarnio *nm* : ridicule, mockery

escarola *nf* : escarole

escarpa *nf* : escarpment, steep slope

escarpado, -da *adj* : steep, sheer

escarpia *nf* : hook, spike

escasamente *adv* : scarcely, barely

escasear *vi* : to be scarce, to run short

escasez *nf, pl* **-seces** : shortage, scarcity

escaso, -sa *adj* **1** : scarce, scant **2** ~ **de** : short of

escatimar *vt* : to skimp on, to be sparing with ⟨no escatimar esfuerzos : to spare no effort⟩

escayola *nf* **1** : plaster (for casts) **2** : plaster cast

escayolar *vt* : to put in a plaster cast

escena *nf* **1** : scene **2** : stage

escenario *nm* **1** ESCENA : stage **2** : setting, scene ⟨el escenario del crimen : the scene of the crime⟩

escénico, -ca *adj* **1** : scenic **2** : stage

escenificar {72} *vt* : to stage, to dramatize

escepticismo *nm* : skepticism

escéptico[1], -ca *adj* : skeptical

escéptico[2], -ca *n* : skeptic

escindirse *vr* **1** : to split **2** : to break away

escisión *nf, pl* **-siones** **1** : split, division **2** : excision

esclarecer {53} *vt* **1** ELUCIDAR : to elucidate, to clarify **2** ILUMINAR : to illuminate, to light up

esclarecimiento *nm* ELUCIDACIÓN : elucidation, clarification

esclavitud *nf* : slavery

esclavización *nf, pl* **-ciones** : enslavement

esclavizar {21} *vt* : to enslave

esclavo, -va *n* : slave

esclerosis *nf* **esclerosis múltiple** : multiple sclerosis

esclusa *nf* : floodgate, lock (of a canal)

escoba *nf* : broom

escobilla *nf* : small broom, brush, whisk broom

escobillón *nm, pl* **-llones** : swab

escocer {14} *vi* ARDER : to smart, to sting — **escocerse** *vr* : to be sore

escocés[1], **-cesa** *adj, mpl* **-ceses** 1 : Scottish 2 : tartan, plaid

escocés[2], **-cesa** *n, mpl* **-ceses** : Scottish person, Scot

escocés[3] *nm* 1 : Scots (language) 2 *pl* **-ceses** : Scotch (whiskey)

escofina *nf* : file, rasp

escoger {15} *vt* ELEGIR, SELECCIONAR : to choose, to select

escogido, -da *adj* : choice, select

escolar[1] *adj* : school

escolar[2] *nmf* : student, pupil

escolaridad *nf* : schooling ⟨escolaridad obligatoria : compulsory education⟩

escolarización *nf, pl* **-ciones** : education, schooling

escollo *nm* 1 : reef 2 OBSTÁCULO : obstacle

escolta *nmf* : escort

escoltar *vt* : to escort, to accompany

escombro *nm* 1 : debris, rubbish 2 **escombros** *nmpl* : ruins, rubble

esconder *vt* OCULTAR : to hide, to conceal

escondidas *nfpl* 1 : hide-and-seek 2 a ～ : secretly, in secret

escondimiento *nm* : concealment

escondite *nm* 1 ENCONDRIJO : hiding place 2 ESCONDIDAS : hide-and-seek

escondrijo *nm* ESCONDITE : hiding place

escopeta *nf* : shotgun

escoplear *vt* : to chisel (out)

escoplo *nm* : chisel

escora *nf* : list, heeling

escorar *vi* : to list, to heel (of a boat)

escorbuto *nm* : scurvy

escoria *nf* 1 : slag, dross 2 HEZ : dregs *pl*, scum ⟨la escoria de la sociedad : the dregs of society⟩

Escorpio *or* **Escorpión** *nmf* : Scorpio

escorpión *nm, pl* **-piones** ALACRÁN : scorpion

escote *nm* 1 : low neckline 2 **pagar a escote** : to go dutch

escotilla *nf* : hatch, hatchway

escotillón *nf, pl* **-llones** : trapdoor

escozor *nm* : smarting, stinging

escriba *nm* : scribe

escribano, -na *n* 1 : court clerk 2 NOTARIO : notary public

escribir {33} *v* 1 : to write 2 : to spell — **escribirse** *vr* CARTEARSE : to write to one another, to correspond

escrito[1] *pp* → **escribir**

escrito[2], **-ta** *adj* : written

escrito[3] *nm* 1 : written document 2 **escritos** *nmpl* : writings, works

escritor, -tora *n* : writer

escritorio *nm* : desk

escritorzuelo, -la *n* : hack (writer)

escritura *nf* 1 : writing, handwriting 2 : deed 3 **las Escrituras** : the Scriptures

escroto *nm* : scrotum

escrúpulo *nm* : scruple

escrupuloso, -sa *adj* 1 : scrupulous 2 METICULOSO : exact, meticulous — **escrupulosamente** *adv*

escrutador, -dora *adj* : penetrating, searching

escrutar *vt* ESCUDRIÑAR : to scrutinize, to examine closely

escrutinio *nm* : scrutiny

escuadra *nf* 1 : square (instrument) 2 : fleet, squadron

escuadrilla *nf* : squadron, formation, flight

escuadrón *nm, pl* **-drones** : squadron

escuálido, -da *adj* 1 : skinny, scrawny 2 INMUNDO : filthy, squalid

escuchar *vt* 1 : to listen to 2 : to hear — *vi* : to listen — **escucharse** *vr*

escudar *vt* : to shield — **escudarse** *vr* ～ **en** : to hide behind

escudero *nm* : squire

escudo *nm* 1 : shield 2 **escudo de armas** : coat of arms

escudriñar *vt* 1 ESCRUTAR : to scrutinize 2 : to inquire into, to investigate

escuela *nf* : school

escueto, -ta *adj* 1 : plain, simple 2 : succinct, concise — **escuetamente** *adv*

escuincle, -cla *n Mex fam* : child, kid

esculcar {72} *vt* : to search

esculpir *vt* 1 : to sculpt 2 : to carve, to engrave — *vi* : to sculpt

escultor, -tora *n* : sculptor

escultórico, -ca *adj* : sculptural

escultura *nf* : sculpture

escultural *adj* : statuesque

escupidera *nf* : spittoon, cuspidor

escupir *v* : to spit

escupitajo *nm* : spit

escurridizo, -za *adj* : slippery, elusive

escurridor *nm* 1 : dish rack 2 : colander

escurrir *vt* 1 : to wring out 2 : to drain — *vi* 1 : to drain 2 : to drip, to drip-dry — **escurrirse** *vr* : to slip away

ese, esa *adj, mpl* **esos** : that, those

ése, ésa *pron, mpl* **ésos** : that one, those ones *pl*

esencia *nf* : essence

esencial *adj* : essential — **esencialmente** *adv*

esfera *nf* 1 : sphere 2 : face, dial (of a watch)

esférico[1], **-ca** *adj* : spherical

esférico[2] *nm* : ball (in sports)

esfinge *nf* : sphinx

esforzado, -da *adj* 1 : energetic, vigorous 2 VALIENTE : courageous, brave

esforzar {36} *vt* : to strain — **esforzarse** *vr* : to make an effort

esfuerzo *nm* 1 : effort 2 ÁNIMO, VIGOR : spirit, vigor 3 **sin** ～ : effortlessly

esfumar *vt* : to tone down, to soften — **esfumarse** *vr* 1 : to fade away, to vanish 2 *fam* : to take off, to leave

esgrima *nf* : fencing (sport)

esgrimidor, -dora *n* : fencer

esgrimir *vt* 1 : to brandish, to wield 2 : to use, to resort to — *vi* : to fence

esguince *nm* : sprain, strain (of a muscle)
eslabón *nm, pl* **-bones** : link
eslabonar *vt* : to link, to connect, to join
eslavo[1], **-va** *adj* : Slavic
eslavo[2], **-va** *n* : Slav
eslogan *nm, pl* **-lóganes** : slogan
eslovaco, -ca *adj & n* : Slovakian, Slovak
esloveno, -na *adj & nm* : Slovene, Slovenian
esmaltar *vt* : to enamel
esmalte *nm* 1 : enamel 2 **esmalte de uñas** : nail polish
esmerado, -da *adj* : careful, painstaking
esmeralda *nf* : emerald
esmerarse *vr* : to take great pains, to do one's utmost
esmeril *nm* : emery
esmero *nm* : meticulousness, great care
esmoquin *nm, pl* **-quins** : tuxedo
esnob[1] *adj, pl* **esnobs** : snobbish
esnob[2] *nmf, pl* **esnobs** : snob
esnobismo *nm* : snobbery, snobbishness
eso *pron* (*neuter*) 1 : that ⟨eso no me gusta : I don't like that⟩ 2 **¡eso es!** : that's it!, that's right! 3 **a eso de** : around ⟨a eso de las tres : around three o'clock⟩ 4 **en ~** : at that point, just then
esófago *nm* : esophagus
esos → **ese**
ésos → **ése**
esotérico, -ca *adj* : esoteric — **esotéricamente** *adv*
espabilado, -da *adj* : bright, smart
espabilarse *vr* 1 : to awaken 2 : to get a move on 3 : to get smart, to wise up
espacial *adj* 1 : space 2 : spatial
espaciar *vt* DISTANCIAR : to space out, to spread out
espacio *nm* 1 : space, room 2 : period, length (of time) 3 **espacio exterior** : outer space
espacioso, -sa *adj* : spacious, roomy
espada[1] *nf* 1 : sword 2 **espadas** *nfpl* : spades (in playing cards)
espada[2] *nm* MATADOR, TORERO : bullfighter, matador
espadaña *nf* 1 : belfry 2 : cattail
espadilla *nf* : scull, oar
espagueti *nm or* **espaguetis** *nmpl* : spaghetti
espalda *nf* 1 : back 2 **espaldas** *nfpl* : shoulders, back 3 **por la espalda** : from behind
espaldarazo *nm* 1 : recognition, support 2 : slap on the back
espaldera *nf* : trellis
espantajo *nm* : scarecrow
espantapájaros *nms & pl* : scarecrow
espantar *vt* ASUSTAR : to scare, to frighten — **espantarse** *vr*
espanto *nm* : fright, fear, horror
espantoso, -sa *adj* 1 : frightening, terrifying 2 : frightful, dreadful

español[1], **-ñola** *adj* : Spanish
español[2], **-ñola** *n* : Spaniard
español[3] *nm* CASTELLANO : Spanish (language)
esparadrapo *nm* : adhesive bandage, Band-Aid™
esparcimiento *nm* 1 DIVERSIÓN, RECREO : entertainment, recreation 2 DESCANSO : relaxation 3 DISEMINACIÓN : dissemination, spreading
esparcir {83} *vt* DISPERSAR : to scatter, to spread — **esparcirse** *vr* 1 : to spread out 2 DESCANSARSE : to take it easy 3 DIVERTIRSE : to amuse oneself
espárrago *nm* : asparagus
espartano, -na *adj* : severe, austere
espasmo *nm* : spasm
espasmódico, -ca *adj* : spasmodic
espástico, -ca *adj* : spastic
espátula *nf* : spatula
especia *nf* : spice
especial *adj & nm* : special
especialidad *nf* : specialty
especialista *nmf* : specialist, expert
especialización *nf, pl* **-ciones** : specialization
especializarse {21} *vr* : to specialize
especialmente *adv* : especially, particularly
especie *nf* 1 : species 2 CLASE, TIPO : type, kind, sort
especificación *nf, pl* **-ciones** : specification
especificar {72} *vt* : to specify
específico, -ca *adj* : specific — **específicamente** *adv*
espécimen *nm, pl* **especímenes** : specimen
especioso, -sa *adj* : specious
espectacular *adj* : spectacular — **espectacularmente** *adv*
espectáculo *nm* 1 : spectacle, sight 2 : show, performance
espectador, -dora *n* : spectator, onlooker
espectro *nm* 1 : ghost, specter 2 : spectrum
especulación *nf, pl* **-ciones** : speculation
especulador, -dora *n* : speculator
especular *vi* : to speculate
especulativo, -va *adj* : speculative
espejismo *nm* 1 : mirage 2 : illusion
espejo *nm* : mirror
espejuelos *nmpl* ANTEOJOS : spectacles, glasses
espeluznante *adj* : hair-raising, terrifying
espera *nf* : wait
esperado, -da *adj* : anticipated
esperanza *nf* : hope, expectation
esperanzado, -da *adj* : hopeful
esperanzador, -dora *adj* : encouraging, promising
esperanzar {21} *vt* : to give hope to
esperar *vt* 1 AGUARDAR : to wait for, to await 2 : to expect 3 : to hope ⟨espero poder trabajar : I hope to be able to work⟩ ⟨espero que sí : I hope so⟩ — *vi*

: to wait — **esperarse** *vr* **1** : to expect, to be hoped ⟨como podría esperarse : as would be expected⟩ **2** : to hold on, to hang on ⟨espérate un momento : hold on a minute⟩
esperma *nmf* : sperm
esperpéntico, -ca *adj* GROTESCO : grotesque
esperpento *nm fam* MAMARRACHO : sight, fright ⟨voy hecha un esperpento : I really look a sight⟩
espesante *nm* : thickener
espesar *vt* : to thicken — **espesarse** *vr*
espeso, -sa *adj* : thick, heavy, dense
espesor *nm* : thickness, density
espesura *nf* **1** : thickness **2** : thicket
espetar *vt* **1** : to blurt out **2** : to skewer
espía *nmf* : spy
espiar {85} *vt* : to spy on, to observe — *vi* : to spy
espiga *nf* **1** : ear (of wheat) **2** : spike (of flowers)
espigado, -da *adj* : willowy, slender
espigar {52} *vt* : to glean, to gather — **espigarse** *vr* : to grow quickly, to shoot up
espigón *nm, pl* **-gones** : breakwater
espina *nf* **1** : thorn **2** : spine ⟨espina dorsal : spinal column⟩ **3** : fish bone
espinaca *nf* **1** : spinach (plant) **2** **espinacas** *nfpl* : spinach (food)
espinal *adj* : spinal
espinazo *nm* : backbone
espineta *nf* : spinet
espinilla *nf* **1** BARRO, GRANO : pimple **2** : shin
espino *nm* : hawthorn
espinoso, -sa *adj* **1** : thorny, prickly **2** : bony (of fish) **3** : knotty, difficult
espionaje *nm* : espionage
espiración *nf, pl* **-ciones** : exhalation
espiral *adj & nf* : spiral
espirar *vt* EXHALAR : to breathe out, to give off — *vi* : to exhale
espiritismo *nm* : spiritualism
espiritista *nmf* : spiritualist
espíritu *nm* **1** : spirit **2** ÁNIMO : state of mind, spirits *pl* **3 el Espíritu Santo** : the Holy Ghost
espiritual *adj* : spiritual — **espiritualmente** *adv*
espiritualidad *nf* : spirituality
espita *nf* : spigot, tap
esplendidez *nf, pl* **-deces** ESPLENDOR : magnificence, splendor
espléndido, -da *adj* **1** : splendid, magnificent **2** : generous, lavish — **espléndidamente** *adv*
esplendor *nm* ESPLENDIDEZ : splendor
esplendoroso, -sa *adj* MAGNÍFICO : magnificent, grand
espliego *nm* LAVANDA : lavender
espolear *vt* : to spur on
espoleta *nf* **1** DETONADOR : detonator, fuse **2** : wishbone
espolón *nm, pl* **-lones** : spur (of poultry), fetlock (of a horse)

espolvorear *vt* : to sprinkle, to dust
esponja *nf* **1** : sponge **2 tirar la esponja** : to throw in the towel
esponjado, -da *adj* : spongy
esponjoso, -sa *adj* **1** : spongy **2** : soft, fluffy
esponsales *nmpl* : betrothal, engagement
espontaneidad *nf* : spontaneity
espontáneo, -nea *adj* : spontaneous — **espontáneamente** *adv*
espora *nf* : spore
esporádico, -ca *adj* : sporadic — **esporádicamente** *adv*
esposar *vt* : to handcuff
esposas *nfpl* : handcuffs
esposo, -sa *n* : spouse, wife *f*, husband *m*
esprint *nm* : sprint
esprintar *vi* : to sprint
esprínter *nmf* : sprinter
espuela *nf* : spur
espuerta *nf* : two-handled basket
espulgar {52} *vt* **1** : to delouse **2** : to scrutinize
espuma *nf* **1** : foam **2** : lather **3** : froth, head (on beer)
espumar *vi* : to foam, to froth — *vt* : to skim off
espumoso, -sa *adj* : foamy, frothy
espurio, -ria *adj* : spurious
esputar *v* : to expectorate, to spit
esputo *nm* : spit, sputum
esqueje *nm* : cutting (from a plant)
esquela *nf* **1** : note **2** : notice, announcement
esquelético, -ca *adj* : emaciated, skeletal
esqueleto *nm* **1** : skeleton **2** ARMAZÓN : framework
esquema *nf* BOSQUEJO : outline, sketch, plan
esquemático, -ca *adj* : schematic
esquí *nm* **1** : ski **2 esquí acuático** : water ski, waterskiing
esquiador, -dora *n* : skier
esquiar {85} *vi* : to ski
esquife *nm* : skiff
esquila *nf* **1** CENCERRO : cowbell **2** : shearing
esquilar *vt* TRASQUILAR : to shear
esquimal *adj & nmf* : Eskimo
esquina *nf* : corner
esquinazo *nm* **1** : corner **2 dar esquinazo a** *fam* : to stand up, to give the slip to
esquirla *nf* : splinter (of bone, glass, etc.)
esquirol *nm* ROMPEHUELGAS : strikebreaker, scab
esquisto *nm* : shale
esquivar *vt* **1** EVADIR : to dodge, to evade **2** EVITAR : to avoid
esquivez *nf, pl* **-veces** **1** : aloofness **2** TIMIDEZ : shyness
esquivo, -va *adj* **1** HURAÑO : aloof, unsociable **2** : shy **3** : elusive, evasive
esquizofrenia *nf* : schizophrenia
esquizofrénico, -ca *adj & n* : schizophrenic

esta *adj* → **este**[1]
ésta → **éste**
estabilidad *nf* : stability
estabilización *nf, pl* **-ciones** : stabilization
estabilizador *nm* : stabilizer
estabilizar {21} *vt* : to stabilize — **estabilizarse** *vr*
estable *adj* : stable, steady
establecer {53} *vt* FUNDAR, INSTITUIR : to establish, to found, to set up — **establecerse** *vr* INSTALARSE : to settle, to establish oneself
establecimiento *nm* **1** : establishing **2** : establishment, institution, office
establo *nm* : stable
estaca *nf* : stake, picket, post
estacada *nf* **1** : picket fence **2** : stockade
estacar {72} *vt* **1** : to stake out **2** : to fasten down with stakes — **estacarse** *vr* : to remain rigid
estación *nf, pl* **-ciones** **1** : station ⟨estación de servicio : service station, gas station⟩ **2** : season
estacional *adj* : seasonal
estacionamiento *nm* **1** : parking **2** : parking lot
estacionar *vt* **1** : to place, to station **2** : to park — **estacionarse** *vr* **1** : to park **2** : to remain stationary
estacionario, -ria *adj* **1** : stationary **2** : stable
estada *nf* : stay
estadía *nf* ESTANCIA : stay, sojourn
estadio *nm* **1** : stadium **2** : phase, stage
estadista *nmf* : statesman
estadística *nf* **1** : statistic, figure **2** : statistics
estadístico[1], **-ca** *adj* : statistical — **estadísticamente** *adv*
estadístico[2], **-ca** *n* : statistician
estado *nm* **1** : state **2** : status ⟨estado civil : marital status⟩ **3** CONDICIÓN : condition
estadounidense *adj & nmf* AMERICANO, NORTEAMERICANO : American
estafa *nf* : swindle, fraud
estafador, -dora *n* : cheat, swindler
estafar *vt* DEFRAUDAR : to swindle, to defraud
estalactita *nf* : stalactite
estalagmita *nf* : stalagmite
estallar *vi* **1** REVENTAR : to burst, to explode, to erupt **2** : to break out
estallido *nm* **1** EXPLOSIÓN : explosion **2** : report (of a gun) **3** : outbreak, outburst
estambre *nm* **1** : worsted (fabric) **2** : stamen
estampa *nf* **1** ILUSTRACIÓN, IMAGEN : printed image, illustration **2** ASPECTO : appearance, demeanor
estampado[1], **-da** *adj* : patterned, printed
estampado[2] *nm* : print, pattern
estampar *vt* : to stamp, to print, to engrave

estampida *nf* : stampede
estampilla *nf* **1** : rubber stamp **2** SELLO, TIMBRE : postage stamp
estancado, -da *adj* : stagnant
estancamiento *nm* : stagnation
estancar {72} *vt* **1** : to dam up, to hold back **2** : to bring to a halt, to deadlock — **estancarse** *vr* **1** : to stagnate **2** : to be brought to a standstill, to be deadlocked
estancia *nf* **1** ESTADÍA : stay, sojourn **2** : ranch, farm
estanciero, -ra *n* : rancher, farmer
estanco, -ca *adj* : watertight
estándar *adj & nm* : standard
estandarización *nf, pl* **-ciones** : standardization
estandarizar {21} *vt* : to standardize
estandarte *nm* : standard, banner
estanque *nm* **1** : pool, pond **2** : tank, reservoir
estante *nm* REPISA : shelf
estantería *nf* : shelves *pl*, bookcase
estaño *nm* : tin
estaquilla *nf* **1** : peg **2** ESPIGA : spike
estar {34} *v aux* : to be ⟨estoy aprendiendo inglés : I'm learning English⟩ ⟨está terminado : it's finished⟩ — *vi* **1** (*indicating a state or condition*) : to be ⟨está muy alto : he's so tall, he's gotten very tall⟩ ⟨¿ya estás mejor? : are you feeling better now?⟩ ⟨estoy casado : I'm married⟩ **2** (*indicating location*) : to be ⟨están en la mesa : they're on the table⟩ ⟨estamos en la página 2 : we're on page 2⟩ **3** : to be at home ⟨¿está María? : is Maria in?⟩ **4** : to remain ⟨estaré aquí 5 días : I'll be here for 5 days⟩ **5** : to be ready, to be done ⟨estará para las diez : it will be ready by ten o'clock⟩ **6** : to agree ⟨¿estamos? : are we in agreement?⟩ ⟨estoy contigo : I'm with you⟩ **7** ¿cómo estás? : how are you? **8** ¡está bien! : all right!, that's fine! **9** ~ **a** : to cost **10** ~ **a** : to be ⟨¿a qué día estamos? : what's today's date?⟩ **11** ~ **con** : to have ⟨está con fiebre : she has a fever⟩ **12** ~ **de** : to be ⟨estoy de vacaciones : I'm on vacation⟩ ⟨está de director hoy : he's acting as director today⟩ **13** estar bien (mal) : to be well (sick) **14** ~ **para** : to be in the mood for **15** ~ **por** : to be in favor of **16** ~ **por** : to be about to ⟨está por cerrar : it's on the verge of closing⟩ **17** estar de más : to be unnecessary **18** estar que : to be (in a state or condition) ⟨está que echa chispas : he's hopping mad⟩ — **estarse** *vr* QUEDARSE : to stay, to remain ⟨¡estáte quieto! : be still!⟩
estarcir {83} *vt* : to stencil
estatal *adj* : state, national
estática *nf* : static
estático, -ca *adj* : static
estatizar {21} *vt* : to nationalize — **estatización** *nf*
estatua *nf* : statue

estatuilla *nf* : statuette, figurine
estatura *nf* : height, stature ⟨de mediana estatura : of medium height⟩
estatus *nm* : status, prestige
estatutario, -ria *adj* : statutory
estatuto *nm* : statute
este[1], **esta** *adj, mpl* **estos** : this, these
este[2] *adj* : eastern, east
este[3] *nm* **1** ORIENTE : east **2** : east wind **3 el Este** : the East, the Orient
éste, ésta *pron, mpl* **éstos 1** : this one, these ones *pl* **2** : the latter
estela *nf* **1** : wake (of a ship) **2** RASTRO : trail (of dust, smoke, etc.)
estelar *adj* : stellar
estelarizar {21} *vt Mex* : to star in, to be the star of
esténcil *nm* : stencil
estentóreo, -rea *adj* : loud, thundering
estepa *nf* : steppe
éster *nf* : ester
estera *nf* : mat
estercolero *nm* : dunghill
estéreo *adj & nm* : stereo
estereofónico, -ca *adj* : stereophonic
estereotipado, -da *adj* : stereotyped
estereotipar *vt* : to stereotype
estereotipo *nm* : stereotype
estéril *adj* **1** : sterile, germ-free **2** : infertile, barren **3** : futile, vain
esterilidad *nf* **1** : sterility **2** : infertility
esterilizar {21} *vt* **1** : to sterilize, to disinfect **2** : to sterilize (a person), to spay (an animal) — **esterilización** *nf*
esterlina *adj* : sterling
esternón *nm, pl* **-nones** : sternum
estero *nm* : estuary
estertor *nm* : death rattle
estética *nf* : aesthetics
estético, -ca *adj* : aesthetic — **estéticamente** *adv*
estetoscopio *nm* : stethoscope
estibador, -dora *n* : longshoreman, stevedore
estibar *vt* : to load (freight)
estiércol *nm* : dung, manure
estigma *nm* : stigma
estigmatizar {21} *vt* : to stigmatize, to brand
estilarse *vr* : to be in fashion
estilete *nm* : stiletto
estilista *nmf* : stylist
estilizar {21} *vt* : to stylize
estilo *nm* **1** : style **2** : fashion, manner **3** : stylus
estima *nf* ESTIMACIÓN : esteem, regard
estimable *adj* **1** : considerable **2** : estimable, esteemed
estimación *nf, pl* **-ciones 1** ESTIMA : esteem, regard **2** : estimate
estimado, -da *adj* : esteemed, dear ⟨Estimado señor Ortiz : Dear Mr. Ortiz⟩
estimar *vt* **1** APRECIAR : to esteem, to respect **2** EVALUAR : to estimate, to appraise **3** OPINAR : to consider, to deem
estimulación *nf, pl* **-ciones** : stimulation
estimulante[1] *adj* : stimulating
estimulante[2] *nm* : stimulant

estimular *vt* **1** : to stimulate **2** : to encourage
estímulo *nm* **1** : stimulus **2** INCENTIVO : incentive, encouragement
estío *nm* : summertime
estipendio *nm* **1** : salary **2** : stipend, remuneration
estipular *vt* : to stipulate — **estipulación** *nf*
estirado, -da *adj* **1** : stretched, extended **2** PRESUMIDO : stuck-up, conceited
estiramiento *nm* **1** : stretching **2 estiramiento facial** : face-lift
estirar *vt* : to stretch (out), to extend — **estirarse** *vr*
estirón *nm, pl* **-rones 1** : pull, tug **2 dar un estirón** : to grow quickly, to shoot up
estirpe *nf* LINAJE : lineage, stock
estival *adj* VERANIEGO : summer
esto *pron (neuter)* **1** : this ⟨¿qué es esto? : what is this?⟩ **2 en ~** : at this point **3 por ~** : for this reason
estocada *nf* **1** : final thrust (in bullfighting) **2** : thrust, lunge (in fencing)
estofa *nf* CLASE : class, quality ⟨de baja estofa : low-class, poor-quality⟩
estofado *nm* COCIDO, GUISADO : stew
estofar *vt* GUISAR : to stew
estoicismo *nm* : stoicism
estoico[1], **-ca** *adj* : stoic, stoical
estoico[2], **-ca** *n* : stoic
estola *nf* : stole
estomacal *adj* GÁSTRICO : stomach, gastric
estómago *nm* : stomach
estoniano, -na *adj & n* : Estonian
estonio, -nia *adj & n* : Estonian
estopa *nf* **1** : tow (yarn or cloth) **2** : burlap
estopilla *nf* : cheesecloth
estoque *nm* : rapier, sword
estorbar *vt* OBSTRUIR : to obstruct, to hinder — *vi* : to get in the way
estorbo *nm* **1** : obstacle, hindrance **2** : nuisance
estornino *nm* : starling
estornudar *vi* : to sneeze
estornudo *nm* : sneeze
estos *adj* → **este**[1]
éstos → **éste**
estoy → **estar**
estrabismo *nm* : squint
estrado *nm* **1** : dais, platform, bench (of a judge) **2 estrados** *nmpl* : courts of law
estrafalario, -ria *adj* ESTRAMBÓTICO, EXCÉNTRICO : eccentric, bizarre
estragar {52} *vt* DEVASTAR : to ruin, to devastate
estragón *nm* : tarragon
estragos *nmpl* **1** : ravages, destruction, devastation ⟨los estragos de la guerra : the ravages of war⟩ **2 hacer estragos en** *or* **causar estragos entre** : to play havoc with
estrambótico, -ca *adj* ESTRAFALARIO, EXCÉNTRICO : eccentric, bizarre

estrangulamiento *nm* : strangling, strangulation

estrangular *vt* AHOGAR : to strangle — **estrangulación** *nf*

estratagema *nf* ARTIMAÑA : stratagem, ruse

estratega *nmf* : strategist

estrategia *nf* : strategy

estratégico, -ca *adj* : strategic, tactical — **estratégicamente** *adv*

estratificación *nf, pl* -ciones : stratification

estratificado, -da *adj* : stratified

estrato *nm* : stratum, layer

estratosfera *nf* : stratosphere

estratosférico, -ca *adj* 1 : stratospheric 2 : astronomical, exorbitant

estrechamiento *nm* 1 : narrowing 2 : narrow point 3 : tightening, strengthening (of relations)

estrechar *vt* 1 : to narrow 2 : to tighten, to strengthen (a bond) 3 : to hug, to embrace 4 **estrechar la mano de** : to shake hands with — **estrecharse** *vr*

estrechez *nf, pl* -checes 1 : tightness, narrowness 2 **estrecheces** *nfpl* : financial problems

estrecho¹, -cha *adj* 1 : tight, narrow 2 ÍNTIMO : close — **estrechamente** *adv*

estrecho² *nm* : strait, narrows

estrella *nf* 1 ASTRO : star ⟨estrella fugaz : shooting star⟩ 2 : destiny ⟨tener buena estrella : to be born lucky⟩ 3 : movie star 4 **estrella de mar** : starfish

estrellado, -da *adj* 1 : starry 2 : star-shaped 3 **huevos estrellados** : fried eggs

estrellamiento *nm* : crash, collision

estrellar *vt* : to smash, to crash — **estrellarse** *vr* : to crash, to collide

estrellato *nm* : stardom

estremecedor, -dora *adj* : horrifying

estremecer {53} *vt* : to cause to shake — *vi* : to tremble, to shake — **estremecerse** *vr* : to shudder, to shiver (with emotion)

estremecimiento *nm* : trembling, shaking, shivering

estrenar *vt* 1 : to use for the first time 2 : to premiere, to open — **estrenarse** *vr* : to make one's debut

estreno *nm* DEBUT : debut, premiere

estreñimiento *nm* : constipation

estreñirse {67} *vr* : to be constipated

estrépito *nm* ESTRUENDO : clamor, din

estrepitoso, -sa *adj* : clamorous, noisy — **estrepitosamente** *adv*

estrés *nm, pl* **estreses** : stress

estresante *adj* : stressful

estresar *vt* : to stress, to stress out

estría *nf* : fluting, groove

estribación *nf, pl* -ciones 1 : spur, ridge 2 **estribaciones** *nfpl* : foothills

estribar *vi* FUNDARSE ～ **en** : to be due to, to stem from

estribillo *nm* : refrain, chorus

estribo *nm* 1 : stirrup 2 : abutment, buttress 3 **perder los estribos** : to lose one's temper

estribor *nm* : starboard

estricnina *nf* : strychnine

estricto, -ta *adj* SEVERO : strict, severe — **estrictamente** *adv*

estridente *adj* : strident, shrill, loud — **estridentemente** *adv*

estrofa *nf* : stanza, verse

estrógeno *nm* : estrogen

estropajo *nm* : scouring pad

estropear *vt* 1 ARRUINAR : to ruin, to spoil 2 : to break, to damage — **estropearse** *vr* 1 : to spoil, to go bad 2 : to break down

estropicio *nm* DAÑO : damage, breakage

estructura *nf* : structure, framework

estructuración *nf, pl* -ciones : structuring, structure

estructural *adj* : structural — **estructuralmente** *adv*

estructurar *vt* : to structure, to organize

estruendo *nm* ESTRÉPITO : racket, din, roar

estruendoso, -sa *adj* : resounding, thunderous

estrujar *vt* APRETAR : to press, to squeeze

estuario *nm* : estuary

estuche *nm* : kit, case

estuco *nm* : stucco

estudiado, -da *adj* : affected, mannered

estudiantado *nm* : student body, students *pl*

estudiante *nmf* : student

estudiantil *adj* : student ⟨la vida estudiantil : student life⟩

estudiar *v* : to study

estudio *nm* 1 : study 2 : studio 3 **estudios** *nmpl* : studies, education

estudioso, -sa *adj* : studious

estufa *nf* 1 : stove, heater 2 *Col, Mex* : cooking stove, range

estupefacción *nf, pl* -ciones : stupefaction, astonishment

estupefaciente¹ *adj* : narcotic

estupefaciente² *nm* DROGA, NARCÓTICO : drug, narcotic

estupefacto, -ta *adj* : astonished, stunned

estupendo, -da *adj* MARAVILLOSO : stupendous, marvelous — **estupendamente** *adv*

estupidez *nf, pl* -deces 1 : stupidity 2 : nonsense

estúpido¹, -da *adj* : stupid — **estúpidamente** *adj*

estúpido², -da *n* IDIOTA : idiot, fool

estupor *nm* 1 : stupor 2 : amazement

esturión *nm, pl* -riones : sturgeon

estuvo, etc. → **estar**

etano *nm* : ethane

etanol *nm* : ethanol

etapa *nf* FASE : stage, phase

etcétera¹ : et cetera, and so on

etcétera² *nmf* : et cetera

éter *nm* : ether

etéreo, -rea *adj* : ethereal, heavenly
eternidad *nf* : eternity
eternizar {21} *vt* PERPETUAR : to make eternal, to perpetuate — **eternizarse** *vr* *fam* : to take forever
eterno, -na *adj* : eternal, endless — **eternamente** *adv*
ética *nf* : ethics
ético, -ca *adj* : ethical — **éticamente** *adv*
etimología *nf* : etymology
etimológico, -ca *adj* : etymological
etimólogo, -ga *n* : etymologist
etíope *adj* & *nmf* : Ethiopian
etiqueta *nf* 1 : etiquette 2 : tag, label 3 de ~ : formal, dressy
etiquetar *vt* : to label
étnico, -ca *adj* : ethnic
etnología *nf* : ethnology
etnólogo, -ga *n* : ethnologist
eucalipto *nm* : eucalyptus
Eucaristía *nf* : Eucharist, communion
eucarístico, -ca *adj* : eucharistic
eufemismo *nm* : euphemism
eufemístico, -ca *adj* : euphemistic
eufonía *nf* : euphony
eufónico, -ca *adj* : euphonious
euforia *nf* : euphoria, joyousness
eufórico, -ca *adj* : euphoric, exuberant, joyous — **eufóricamente** *adv*
eunuco *nm* : eunuch
europeo, -pea *adj* & *n* : European
euskera *nm* : Basque (language)
eutanasia *nf* : euthanasia
evacuación *nf, pl* **-ciones** : evacuation
evacuar *vt* 1 : to evacuate, to vacate 2 : to carry out — *vi* : to have a bowel movement
evadir *vt* ELUDIR : to evade, to avoid — **evadirse** *vr* : to escape, to slip away
evaluación *nf, pl* **-ciones** : assessment, evaluation
evaluador, -dora *n* : assessor
evaluar {3} *vt* : to evaluate, to assess, to appraise
evangélico, -ca *adj* : evangelical — **evangélicamente** *adv*
evangelio *nm* : gospel
evangelismo *nm* : evangelism
evangelista *nmf* : evangelist
evangelizador, -dora *n* : evangelist, missionary
evaporación *nf, pl* **-ciones** : evaporation
evaporar *vt* : to evaporate — **evaporarse** *vr* ESFUMARSE : to disappear, to vanish
evasión *nf, pl* **-siones** 1 : escape, flight 2 : evasion, dodge
evasiva *nf* : excuse, pretext
evasivo, -va *adj* : evasive
evento *nm* : event
eventual *adj* 1 : possible 2 : temporary ⟨trabajadores eventuales : temporary workers⟩ — **eventualmente** *adv*
eventualidad *nf* : possibility, eventuality
evidencia *nf* 1 : evidence, proof 2 poner en evidencia : to demonstrate, to make clear

evidenciar *vt* : to demonstrate, to show — **evidenciarse** *vr* : to be evident
evidente *adj* : evident, obvious, clear — **evidentemente** *adv*
eviscerar *vt* : to eviscerate
evitable *adj* : avoidable, preventable
evitar *vt* 1 : to avoid 2 PREVENIR : to prevent 3 ELUDIR : to escape, to elude
evocación *nf, pl* **-ciones** : evocation
evocador, -dora *adj* : evocative
evocar {72} *vt* 1 : to evoke 2 RECORDAR : to recall
evolución *nf, pl* **-ciones** 1 : evolution 2 : development, progress
evolucionar *vi* 1 : to evolve 2 : to change, to develop
evolutivo, -va *adj* : evolutionary
exabrupto *nm* : pointed remark
exacción *nf, pl* **-ciones** : levying, exaction
exacerbar *vt* 1 : to exacerbate, to aggravate 2 : to irritate, to exasperate
exactamente *adv* : exactly
exactitud *nf* PRECISIÓN : accuracy, precision, exactitude
exacto, -ta *adj* PRECISO : accurate, precise, exact
exageración *nf, pl* **-ciones** : exaggeration
exagerado, -da *adj* 1 : exaggerated 2 : excessive — **exageradamente** *adv*
exagerar *v* : to exaggerate
exaltación *nf, pl* **-ciones** 1 : exaltation 2 : excitement, agitation
exaltado[1], -da *adj* : excitable, hotheaded
exaltado[2], -da *n* : hothead
exaltar *vt* 1 ENSALZAR : to exalt, to extol 2 : to excite, to agitate — **exaltarse** *vr* ACALORARSE : to get overexcited
ex–alumno → alumno
examen *nm, pl* **exámenes** 1 : examination, test 2 : consideration, investigation
examinar *vt* 1 : to examine 2 INSPECCIONAR : to inspect — **examinarse** *vr* : to take an exam
exánime *adj* 1 : lifeless 2 : exhausted
exasperante *adj* : exasperating
exasperar *vt* IRRITAR : to exasperate, to irritate — **exasperación** *nf*
excavación *nf, pl* **-ciones** : excavation
excavadora *nf* : excavator
excavar *v* : to excavate, to dig
excedente[1] *adj* 1 : excessive 2 : excess, surplus
excedente[2] *nm* : surplus, excess
exceder *vt* : to exceed, to surpass — **excederse** *vr* : to go too far
excelencia *nf* 1 : excellence 2 : excellency ⟨Su Excelencia : His Excellency⟩
excelente *adj* : excellent — **excelentemente** *adv*
excelso, -sa *adj* : lofty, sublime
excentricidad *nf* : eccentricity
excéntrico, -ca *adj* & *n* : eccentric
excepción *nf, pl* **-ciones** : exception
excepcional *adj* EXTRAORDINARIO : exceptional, extraordinary, rare

excepto *prep* SALVO : except

exceptuar {3} *vt* EXCLUIR : to except, to exclude

excesivo, -va *adj* : excessive — **excesivamente** *adv*

exceso *nm* **1** : excess **2 excesos** *nmpl* : excesses, abuses **3 exceso de velocidad** : speeding

excitabilidad *nf* : excitability

excitación *nf, pl* **-ciones** : excitement

excitante *adj* : exciting

excitar *vt* : to excite, to arouse — **excitarse** *vr*

exclamación *nf, pl* **-ciones** : exclamation

exclamar *v* : to exclaim

excluir {41} *vt* EXCEPTUAR : to exclude, to leave out

exclusión *nf, pl* **-siones** : exclusion

exclusividad *nf* **1** : exclusiveness **2** : exclusive rights *pl*

exclusivista *adj & nmf* : exclusivist

exclusivo, -va *adj* : exclusive — **exclusivamente** *adv*

excomulgar {52} *vt* : to excommunicate

excomunión *nf, pl* **-niones** : excommunication

excreción *nf, pl* **-ciones** : excretion

excremento *nm* : excrement

excretar *vt* : to excrete

exculpar *vt* : to exonerate, to exculpate — **exculpación** *nf*

excursión *nf, pl* **-siones** : excursion, outing

excursionista *nmf* **1** : sightseer, tourist **2** : hiker

excusa *nf* **1** PRETEXTO : excuse **2** DISCULPA : apology

excusado *nm Mex* : toilet

excusar *vt* **1** : to excuse **2** : to exempt — **excusarse** *vr* : to apologize, to send one's regrets

execrable *adj* : detestable, abominable

exención *nf, pl* **-ciones** : exemption

exento, -ta *adj* **1** : exempt, free **2 exento de impuestos** : tax-exempt

exequias *nfpl* FUNERALES : funeral rites

exhalación *nf, pl* **-ciones** **1** : exhalation **2** : shooting star ⟨salió como una exhalación : he took off like a shot⟩

exhalar *vt* ESPIRAR : to exhale, to give off

exhaustivo, -va *adj* : exhaustive — **exhaustivamente** *adv*

exhausto, -ta *adj* AGOTADO : exhausted, worn-out

exhibición *nf, pl* **-ciones** **1** : exhibition, show **2** : showing

exhibir *vt* : to exhibit, to show, to display — **exhibirse** *vr*

exhortación *nf, pl* **-ciones** : exhortation

exhortar *vt* : to exhort

exhumar *vt* DESENTERRAR : to exhume — **exhumación** *nf*

exigencia *nf* : demand, requirement

exigente *adj* : demanding, exacting

exigir {35} *vt* **1** : to demand, to require **2** : to exact, to levy

exiguo, -gua *adj* : meager

exiliado[1], **-da** *adj* : exiled, in exile

exiliado[2], **-da** *n* : exile

exiliar *vt* DESTERRAR : to exile, to banish — **exiliarse** *vr* : to go into exile

exilio *nm* DESTIERRO : exile

eximio, -mia *adj* : distinguished, eminent

eximir *vt* EXONERAR : to exempt

existencia *nf* **1** : existence **2 existencias** *nfpl* MERCANCÍA : goods, stock

existente *adj* **1** : existing, in existence **2** : in stock

existir *vi* : to exist

éxito *nm* **1** TRIUNFO : success, hit **2 tener éxito** : to be successful

exitoso, -sa *adj* : successful — **exitosamente** *adv*

éxodo *nm* : exodus

exoneración *nf, pl* **-ciones** EXENCIÓN : exoneration, exemption

exonerar *vt* **1** EXIMIR : to exempt, to exonerate **2** DESPEDIR : to dismiss

exorbitante *adj* : exorbitant

exorcismo *nm* : exorcism — **exorcista** *nmf*

exorcizar {21} *vt* : to exorcise

exótico, -ca *adj* : exotic

expandir *vt* EXPANSIONAR : to expand — **expandirse** *vr* : to spread

expansión *nf, pl* **-siones** **1** : expansion, spread **2** DIVERSIÓN : recreation, relaxation

expansionar *vt* EXPANDIR : to expand — **expansionarse** *vr* **1** : to expand **2** DIVERTIRSE : to amuse oneself, to relax

expansivo, -va *adj* : expansive

expatriado, -da *adj & n* : expatriate

expatriarse {85} *vr* **1** EMIGRAR : to emigrate **2** : to go into exile

expectación *nf, pl* **-ciones** : expectation, anticipation

expectante *adj* : expectant

expectativa *nf* **1** : expectation, hope **2 expectativas** *nfpl* : prospects

expedición *nf, pl* **-ciones** : expedition

expediente *nm* **1** : expedient, means **2** ARCHIVO : file, dossier, record

expedir {54} *vt* **1** EMITIR : to issue **2** DESPACHAR : to dispatch, to send

expedito, -ta *adj* **1** : free, clear **2** : quick, easy

expeler *vt* : to expel, to eject

expendedor, -dora *n* : dealer, seller

expendio *nm* TIENDA : store, shop

expensas *nfpl* **1** : expenses, costs **2 a expensas de** : at the expense of

experiencia *nf* **1** : experience **2** EXPERIMENTO : experiment

experimentación *nf, pl* **-ciones** : experimentation

experimental *adj* : experimental

experimentar *vi* : to experiment — *vt* **1** : to experiment with, to test out **2** : to experience

experimento *nm* EXPERIENCIA : experiment

experto, -ta *adj & n* : expert
expiación *nf, pl* **-ciones** : expiation, atonement
expiar {85} *vt* : to expiate, to atone for
expiración *nf, pl* **-ciones** VENCIMIENTO : expiration
expirar *vi* 1 FALLECER, MORIR : to pass away, to die 2 : to expire
explanada *nf* : esplanade, promenade
explayar *vt* : to extend — **explayarse** *vr* : to expound, to speak at length
explicable *adj* : explicable, explainable
explicación *nf, pl* **-ciones** : explanation
explicar {72} *vt* : to explain — **explicarse** *vr* : to understand
explicativo, -va *adj* : explanatory
explicitar *vt* : to state explicitly, to specify
explícito, -ta *adj* : explicit — **explícitamente** *adv*
exploración *nf, pl* **-ciones** : exploration
explorador, -dora *n* : explorer, scout
explorar *vt* : to explore — **exploratorio, -ria** *adj*
explosión *nf, pl* **-siones** 1 ESTALLIDO : explosion 2 : outburst ⟨una explosión de ira : an outburst of anger⟩
explosionar *vi* : to explode
explosivo, -va *adj* : explosive
explotación *nf, pl* **-ciones** 1 : exploitation 2 : operation, running
explotar *vt* 1 : to exploit 2 : to operate, to run — *vi* ESTALLAR, REVENTAR : to explode — **explotable** *adj*
exponencial *adj* : exponential — **exponencialmente** *adv*
exponente *nm* : exponent
exponer {60} *vt* 1 : to exhibit, to show, to display 2 : to explain, to present, to set forth 3 : to expose, to risk — *vi* : to exhibit
exportación *nf, pl* **-ciones** 1 : exportation 2 **exportaciones** *nfpl* : exports
exportador, -dora *n* : exporter
exportar *vt* : to export — **exportable** *adj*
exposición *nf, pl* **-ciones** 1 EXHIBICIÓN : exposition, exhibition 2 : exposure 3 : presentation, statement
expositor, -tora *n* 1 : exhibitor 2 : exponent
exprés *nms & pl* 1 : express, express train 2 : espresso
expresamente *adv* : expressly, on purpose
expresar *vt* : to express — **expresarse** *vr*
expresión *nf, pl* **-siones** : expression
expresivo, -va *adj* 1 : expressive 2 CARIÑOSO : affectionate — **expresivamente** *adv*
expreso[1], **-sa** *adj* : express, specific
expreso[2] *nm* : express train, express
exprimidor *nm* : squeezer, juicer
exprimir *vt* 1 : to squeeze 2 : to exploit
expropiar *vt* : to expropriate, to commandeer — **expropiación** *nf*
expuesto[1] *pp* → exponer
expuesto[2], **-ta** *adj* 1 : exposed 2 : hazardous, risky

expulsar *vt* : to expel, to eject
expulsión *nf, pl* **-siones** : expulsion
expurgar {52} *vt* : to expurgate
expuso, etc. → exponer
exquisitez *nf, pl* **-teces** 1 : exquisiteness, refinement 2 : delicacy, special dish
exquisito, -ta *adj* 1 : exquisite 2 : delicious
extasiarse {85} *vr* : to be in ecstasy, to be enraptured
éxtasis *nms & pl* : ecstasy, rapture
extático, -ca *adj* : ecstatic
extemporáneo, -nea *adj* 1 : unseasonable 2 : untimely
extender {56} *vt* 1 : to spread out, to stretch out 2 : to broaden, to expand ⟨extender la influencia : to broaden one's influence⟩ 3 : to draw up (a document), to write out (a check) — **extenderse** *vr* 1 : to spread 2 : to last
extendido, -da *adj* 1 : outstretched 2 : widespread
extensamente *adv* : extensively, at length
extensible *adj* : extensible, extendable
extensión *nf, pl* **-siones** 1 : extension, stretching 2 : expanse, spread 3 : extent, range 4 : length, duration
extensivo, -va *adj* 1 : extensive 2 **hacer extensivo** : to extend
extenso, -sa *adj* 1 : extensive, detailed 2 : spacious, vast
extenuar {3} *vt* : to exhaust, to tire out — **extenuarse** *vr* — **extenuante** *adj*
exterior[1] *adj* 1 : exterior, external 2 : foreign ⟨asuntos exteriores : foreign affairs⟩
exterior[2] *nm* 1 : outside 2 : abroad
exteriorizar {21} *vt* : to express, to reveal
exteriormente *adv* : outwardly
exterminar *vt* : to exterminate — **exterminación** *nf*
exterminio *nm* : extermination
externar *vt* *Mex* : to express, to display
externo, -na *adj* : external, outward
extinción *nf, pl* **-ciones** : extinction
extinguidor *nm* : fire extinguisher
extinguir {26} *vt* 1 APAGAR : to extinguish, to put out 2 : to wipe out — **extinguirse** *vr* 1 APAGARSE : to go out, to fade out 2 : to die out, to become extinct
extinto, -ta *adj* : extinct
extintor *nm* : extinguisher
extirpación *n, pl* **-ciones** : removal, excision
extirpar *vt* : to eradicate, to remove, to excise — **extirparse** *vr*
extorsión *nf, pl* **-siones** 1 : extortion 2 : harm, trouble
extorsionar *vt* : to extort
extra[1] *adv* : extra
extra[2] *adj* 1 : additional, extra 2 : superior, top-quality
extra[3] *nmf* : extra (in movies)

extra[4] *nm* : extra expense ⟨paga extra : bonus⟩
extracción *nf, pl* **-ciones** : extraction
extracto *nm* **1** : extract ⟨extracto de vainilla : vanilla extract⟩ **2** : abstract, summary
extractor *nm* : extractor
extracurricular *adj* : extracurricular
extradición *nf, pl* **-ciones** : extradition
extraditar *vt* : to extradite
extraer {81} *vt* : to extract
extraído *pp* → **extraer**
extrajudicial *adj* : out-of-court
extramatrimonial *adj* : extramarital
extranjerizante *adj* : foreign-sounding, foreign-looking
extranjero[1], **-ra** *adj* : foreign
extranjero[2], **-ra** *n* : foreigner
extranjero[3] *nm* : foreign countries *pl* ⟨viajó al extranjero : he traveled abroad⟩ ⟨trabajan en el extranjero : they work overseas⟩
extrañamente *adv* : strangely, oddly
extrañamiento *nm* ASOMBRO : amazement, surprise, wonder
extrañar *vt* : to miss (someone) — **extrañarse** *vr* : to be surprised
extrañeza *nf* **1** : strangeness, oddness **2** : surprise
extraño[1], **-ña** *adj* **1** RARO : strange, odd **2** EXTRANJERO : foreign
extraño[2], **-ña** *n* DESCONOCIDO : stranger
extraoficial *adj* OFICIOSO : unofficial — **extraoficialmente** *adv*
extraordinario, -ria *adj* EXCEPCIONAL : extraordinary — **extraordinariamente** *adv*
extrasensorial *adj* : extrasensory ⟨percepción extrasensorial : extrasensory perception⟩
extraterrestre *adj & nmf* : extraterrestrial, alien

extravagancia *nf* : extravagance, outlandishness, flamboyance
extravagante *adj* : extravagant, outrageous, flamboyant
extraviar {85} *vt* **1** : to mislead, to lead astray **2** : to misplace, to lose — **extraviarse** *vr* : to get lost, to go astray
extravío *nm* **1** PÉRDIDA : loss, misplacement **2** : misconduct
extremado, -da *adj* : extreme — **extremadamente** *adv*
extremar *vt* : to carry to extremes — **extremarse** *vr* : to do one's utmost
extremidad *nf* **1** : extremity, tip, edge **2 extremidades** *nfpl* : extremities
extremista *adj & nmf* : extremist
extremo[1], **-ma** *adj* **1** : extreme, utmost **2** EXCESIVO : excessive **3 en caso extremo** : as a last resort
extremo[2] *nm* **1** : extreme, end **2 al extremo de** : to the point of **3 en ~** : in the extreme
extrovertido[1], **-da** *adj* : extroverted, outgoing
extrovertido[2], **-da** *n* : extrovert
extrudir *vt* : to extrude
exuberancia *nf* **1** : exuberance **2** : luxuriance, lushness
exuberante *adj* : exuberant, luxuriant — **exuberantemente** *adv*
exudar *vt* : to exude
exultación *nf, pl* **-ciones** : exultation, elation
exultante *adj* : exultant, elated — **exultantemente** *adv*
exultar *vi* : to exult, to rejoice
eyacular *vi* : to ejaculate — **eyaculación** *nf*
eyección *nf, pl* **-ciones** : ejection, expulsion
eyectar *vt* : to eject, to expel — **eyectarse** *vr*

F

f *nf* : sixth letter of the Spanish alphabet
fábrica *nf* FACTORÍA : factory
fabricación *nf, pl* **-ciones** : manufacture
fabricante *nmf* : manufacturer
fabricar {72} *vt* MANUFACTURAR : to manufacture, to make
fabril *adj* INDUSTRIAL : industrial, manufacturing
fábula *nf* **1** : fable **2** : fabrication, fib
fabuloso, -sa *adj* **1** : fabulous, fantastic **2** : mythical, fabled
facción *nf, pl* **facciones 1** : faction **2 facciones** *nfpl* RASGOS : features
faccioso, -sa *adj* : factious
faceta *nf* : facet
facha *nf* : appearance, look ⟨estar hecho una facha : to look a sight⟩
fachada *nf* : facade
facial *adj* : facial

fácil *adj* **1** : easy **2** : likely, probable ⟨es fácil que no pase : it probably won't happen⟩
facilidad *nf* **1** : facility, ease **2 facilidades** *nfpl* : facilities, services **3 facilidades** *nfpl* : opportunities
facilitar *vt* **1** : to facilitate **2** : to provide, to supply
fácilmente *adv* : easily, readily
facsímil *or* **facsimile** *nm* **1** : facsimile, copy **2** : fax
facsimilar *adj* : facsimile
factibilidad *nf* : feasibility
factible *adj* : feasible, practicable
facticio, -cia *adj* : artificial, factitious
factor[1], **-tora** *n* **1** : agent, factor **2** : baggage clerk
factor[2] *nm* ELEMENTO : factor, element
factoría *nf* FÁBRICA : factory
factótum *nm* : factotum

factura *nf* **1** : making, manufacturing **2** : bill, invoice

facturación *nf, pl* **-ciones 1** : invoicing, billing **2** : check-in

facturar *vt* **1** : to bill, to invoice **2** : to register, to check in

facultad *nf* **1** : faculty, ability ⟨facultades mentales : mental faculties⟩ **2** : authority, power **3** : school (of a university) ⟨facultad de derecho : law school⟩

facultar *vt* : to authorize, to empower

facultativo, -va *adj* **1** OPTATIVO : voluntary, optional **2** : medical ⟨informe facultativo : medical report⟩

faena *nf* : task, job, work ⟨faenas domésticas : housework⟩

faenar *vi* **1** : to work, to labor **2** PESCAR : to fish

fagot *nm* : bassoon

faisán *nm, pl* **faisanes** : pheasant

faja *nf* **1** : sash, belt **2** : girdle **3** : strip (of land)

fajar *vt* **1** : to wrap (a sash or girdle) around **2** : to hit, to thrash — **fajarse** *vr* **1** : to put on a sash or girdle **2** : to come to blows

fajín *nm, pl* **-jines** : sash, belt

fajo *nm* : bundle, sheaf ⟨un fajo de billetes : a wad of cash⟩

falacia *nf* : fallacy

falaz, -laza *adj, mpl* **falaces** FALSO : fallacious, false

falda *nf* **1** : skirt ⟨falda escocesa : kilt⟩ **2** REGAZO : lap (of the body) **3** VERTIENTE : side, slope

faldón *nm, pl* **-dones 1** : tail (of a shirt, etc.) **2** : full skirt **3 faldón bautismal** : christening gown

falible *adj* : fallible

fálico, -ca *adj* : phallic

falla *nf* **1** : flaw, defect **2** : (geological) fault **3** : fault, failing

fallar *vi* **1** FRACASAR : to fail, to go wrong **2** : to rule (in a court of law) — *vt* **1** ERRAR : to miss (a target) **2** : to pronounce judgment on

fallecer {53} *vi* MORIR : to pass away, to die

fallecido, -da *adj & n* DIFUNTO : deceased

fallecimiento *nm* : demise, death

fallido, -da *adj* : failed, unsuccessful

fallo *nm* **1** SENTENCIA : sentence, judgment, verdict **2** : error, fault

falo *nm* : phallus, penis

falsamente *adv* : falsely

falsear *vt* **1** : to falsify, to fake **2** : to distort — *vi* **1** CEDER : to give way **2** : to be out of tune

falsedad *nf* **1** : falseness, hypocrisy **2** MENTIRA : falsehood, lie

falsete *nm* : falsetto

falsificación *nf, pl* **-ciones 1** : counterfeit, forgery **2** : falsification

falsificador, -dora *n* : counterfeiter, forger

falsificar {72} *vt* **1** : to counterfeit, to forge **2** : to falsify

falso, -sa *adj* **1** FALAZ : false, untrue **2** : counterfeit, forged

falta *nf* **1** CARENCIA : lack ⟨hacer falta : to be lacking, to be needed⟩ **2** DEFECTO : defect, fault, error **3** : offense, misdemeanor **4** : foul (in basketball), fault (in tennis)

faltar *vi* **1** : to be lacking, to be needed ⟨me falta tiempo : I don't have enough time⟩ **2** : to be absent, to be missing **3** QUEDAR : to remain, to be left ⟨faltan pocos días para la fiesta : the party is just a few days away⟩ **4 ¡no faltaba más!** : don't mention it!, you're welcome!

falto, -ta *adj* ~ **de** : lacking (in), short of

fama *nf* **1** : fame **2** REPUTACIÓN : reputation **3 de mala fama** : disreputable

famélico, -ca *adj* HAMBRIENTO : starving, famished

familia *nf* **1** : family **2 familia política** : in-laws

familiar[1] *adj* **1** CONOCIDO : familiar **2** : familial, family **3** INFORMAL : informal

familiar[2] *nmf* PARIENTE : relation, relative

familiaridad *nf* **1** : familiarity **2** : informality

familiarizarse {21} *vr* ~ **con** : to familiarize oneself with

famoso[1]**, -sa** *adj* CÉLEBRE : famous

famoso[2]**, -sa** *n* : celebrity

fanal *nm* **1** : beacon, signal light **2** *Mex* : headlight

fanático, -ca *adj & n* : fanatic

fanatismo *nm* : fanaticism

fandango *nm* : fandango

fanfarria *nf* **1** : (musical) fanfare **2** : pomp, ceremony

fanfarrón[1]**, -rrona** *adj, mpl* **-rrones** *fam* : bragging, boastful

fanfarrón[2]**, -rrona** *n, mpl* **-rrones** *fam* : braggart

fanfarronada *nf* : boast, bluster

fanfarronear *vi* : to brag, to boast

fango *nm* LODO : mud, mire

fangosidad *nf* : muddiness

fangoso, -sa *adj* LODOSO : muddy

fantasear *vi* : to fantasize, to daydream

fantasía *nf* **1** : fantasy **2** : imagination

fantasioso, -sa *adj* : fanciful

fantasma *nm* : ghost, phantom

fantasmagórico, -ca *adj* : phantasmagoric

fantasmal *adj* : ghostly

fantástico, -ca *adj* **1** : fantastic, imaginary, unreal **2** *fam* : great, fantastic

faquir *nm* : fakir

farándula *nf* : show business, theater

faraón *nm, pl* **faraones** : pharaoh

fardo *nm* **1** : bale **2** : bundle

farfulla *nf* : jabbering

farfullar *v* : to jabber, to gabble

faringe *nf* : pharynx

faríngeo, -gea *adj* : pharyngeal
fariña *nf* : coarse manioc flour
farmacéutico[1], **-ca** *adj* : pharmaceutical
farmacéutico[2], **-ca** *n* : pharmacist
farmacia *nf* : drugstore, pharmacy
fármaco *nm* : medicine, drug
farmacodependencia *nf* : drug addiction
farmacología *nf* : pharmacology
faro *nm* 1 : lighthouse 2 : headlight
farol *nm* 1 : streetlight 2 : lantern, lamp 3 *fam* : bluff 4 *Mex* : headlight
farola *nf* 1 : lamppost 2 : streetlight
farolero, -ra *n fam* : bluffer
farra *nf* : spree, revelry
fárrago *nm* REVOLTIJO : hodgepodge, jumble
farsa *nf* 1 : farce 2 : fake, sham
farsante *nmf* CHARLATÁN : charlatan, fraud, phony
fascículo *nm* : fascicle, part (of a publication)
fascinación *nf, pl* **-ciones** : fascination
fascinante *adj* : fascinating
fascinar *vt* 1 : to fascinate 2 : to charm, to captivate
fascismo *nm* : fascism
fascista *adj & nmf* : fascist
fase *nf* : phase, stage
fastidiar *vt* 1 MOLESTAR : to annoy, to bother, to hassle 2 ABURRIR : to bore — *vi* : to be annoying or bothersome
fastidio *nm* 1 MOLESTIA : annoyance, nuisance, hassle 2 ABURRIMIENTO : boredom
fastidioso, -sa *adj* 1 MOLESTO : annoying, bothersome 2 ABURRIDO : boring
fatal *adj* 1 MORTAL : fatal 2 *fam* : awful, terrible 3 : fateful, unavoidable
fatalidad *nf* 1 : fatality 2 DESGRACIA : misfortune, bad luck
fatalismo *nm* : fatalism
fatalista[1] *adj* : fatalistic
fatalista[2] *nmf* : fatalist
fatalmente *adv* 1 : unavoidably 2 : unfortunately
fatídico, -ca *adj* : fateful, momentous
fatiga *nf* CANSANCIO : fatigue
fatigado, -da *adj* AGOTADO : weary, tired
fatigar {52} *vt* CANSAR : to fatigue, to tire — **fatigarse** *vr* : to wear oneself out
fatigoso, -sa *adj* : fatiguing, tiring
fatuidad *nf* 1 : fatuousness 2 VANIDAD : vanity, conceit
fatuo, -tua *adj* 1 : fatuous 2 PRESUMIDO : vain
fauces *nfpl* : jaws *pl*, maw
faul *nm, pl* **fauls** : foul, foul ball
fauna *nf* : fauna
fausto *nm* : splendor, magnificence
favor *nm* 1 : favor 2 **a favor de** : in favor of 3 **por** ~ : please
favorable *adj* : favorable — **favorablemente** *adv*
favorecedor, -dora *adj* : becoming, flattering
favorecer {53} *vt* 1 : to favor 2 : to look well on, to suit

favorecido, -da *adj* 1 : flattering 2 : fortunate
favoritismo *nm* : favoritism
favorito, -ta *adj & n* : favorite
fax *nm* : fax, facsimile
fayuca *nf Mex* 1 : contraband 2 : black market
fayuquero *nm Mex* : smuggler, black marketeer
faz *nf* 1 : face, countenance ⟨la faz de la tierra : the face of the earth⟩ 2 : side (of coins, fabric, etc.)
fe *nf* 1 : faith 2 : assurance, testimony ⟨dar fe de : to bear witness to⟩ 3 : intention, will ⟨de buena fe : bona fide, in good faith⟩
fealdad *nf* : ugliness
febrero *nm* : February
febril *adj* : feverish — **febrilmente** *adv*
fecal *adj* : fecal
fecha *nf* 1 : date 2 **fecha de caducidad** *or* **fecha de vencimiento** : expiration date 3 **fecha límite** : deadline
fechar *vt* : to date, to put a date on
fechoría *nf* : misdeed
fécula *nf* : starch
fecundar *vt* : to fertilize (an egg) — **fecundación** *nf*
fecundidad *nf* 1 : fecundity, fertility 2 : productiveness
fecundo, -da *adj* FÉRTIL : fertile, fecund
federación *nf, pl* **-ciones** : federation
federal *adj* : federal
federalismo *nm* : federalism
federalista *adj & nmf* : federalist
federar *vt* : to federate
fehaciente *adj* : reliable, irrefutable — **fehacientemente** *adv*
feldespato *nm* : feldspar
felicidad *nf* 1 : happiness 2 **¡felicidades!** : best wishes!, congratulations!, happy birthday!
felicitación *nf, pl* **-ciones** 1 : congratulation ⟨¡felicitaciones! : congratulations!⟩ 2 : greeting card
felicitar *vt* CONGRATULAR : to congratulate — **felicitarse** *vr* ~ **de** : to be glad about
feligrés, -gresa *n, mpl* **-greses** : parishioner
feligresía *nf* : parish
felino, -na *adj & n* : feline
feliz *adj, pl* **felices** 1 : happy 2 **Feliz Navidad** : Merry Christmas
felizmente *adv* 1 : happily 2 : fortunately, luckily
felonía *nf* : felony
felpa *nf* 1 : terry cloth 2 : plush
felpudo *nm* : doormat
femenil *adj* : women's, girls' ⟨futbol femenil : women's soccer⟩
femenino, -na *adj* 1 : feminine 2 : women's ⟨derechos femeninos : women's rights⟩ 3 : female
femineidad *nf* : femininity
feminidad *nf* : femininity
feminismo *nm* : feminism
feminista *adj & nmf* : feminist

femoral *adj* : femoral
fémur *nm* : femur, thighbone
fenecer {53} *vi* **1** : to die, to pass away **2** : to come to an end, to cease
fénix *nm* : phoenix
fenomenal *adj* **1** : phenomenal **2** *fam* : fantastic, terrific — **fenomenalmente** *adv*
fenómeno *nm* **1** : phenomenon **2** : prodigy, genius
feo[1] *adv* : badly, bad
feo[2], **fea** *adj* **1** : ugly **2** : unpleasant, nasty
féretro *nm* ATAÚD : coffin, casket
feria *nf* **1** : fair, market **2** : festival, holiday **3** *Mex* : change (money)
feriado, -da *adj* día feriado : public holiday
ferial *nm* : fairground
fermentar *v* : to ferment — **fermentación** *nf*
fermento *nm* : ferment
ferocidad *nf* : ferocity, fierceness
feroz *adj, pl* **feroces** FIERO : ferocious, fierce — **ferozmente** *adv*
férreo, -rrea *adj* **1** : iron **2** : strong, steely ⟨una voluntad férrea : an iron will⟩ **3** : strict, severe **4** vía férrea : railroad track
ferretería *nf* **1** : hardware store **2** : hardware **3** : foundry, ironworks
férrico, -ca *adj* : ferric
ferrocarril *nm* : railroad, railway
ferrocarrilero → **ferroviario**
ferroso, -sa *adj* : ferrous
ferroviario, -ria *adj* : rail, railroad
ferry *nm, pl* **ferrys** : ferry
fértil *adj* FECUNDO : fertile, fruitful
fertilidad *nf* : fertility
fertilizante[1] *adj* : fertilizing ⟨droga fertilizante : fertility drug⟩
fertilizante[2] *nm* ABONO : fertilizer
fertilizar *vt* ABONAR : to fertilize — **fertilización** *nf*
ferviente *adj* FERVOROSO : fervent
fervor *nm* : fervor, zeal
fervoroso, -sa *adj* FERVIENTE : fervent, zealous
festejar *vt* **1** CELEBRAR : to celebrate **2** AGASAJAR : to entertain, to wine and dine **3** *Mex fam* : to thrash, to beat
festejo *nm* : celebration, festivity
festín *nm, pl* **festines** : banquet, feast
festinar *vt* : to hasten, to hurry up
festival *nm* : festival
festividad *nf* **1** : festivity **2** : (religious) feast, holiday
festivo, -va *adj* **1** : festive **2** día festivo : holiday — **festivamente** *adv*
fetal *adj* : fetal
fetiche *nm* : fetish
fétido, -da *adj* : fetid, foul
feto *nm* : fetus
feudal *adj* : feudal — **feudalismo** *nm*
feudo *nm* **1** : fief **2** : domain, territory
fiabilidad *nf* : reliability, trustworthiness
fiable *adj* : trustworthy, reliable
fiado, -da *adj* : on credit

fiador, -dora *n* : bondsman, guarantor
fiambrería *nf* : delicatessen
fiambres *nfpl* : cold cuts
fianza *nf* **1** CAUCIÓN : bail, bond **2** : surety, deposit
fiar {85} *vt* **1** : to sell on credit **2** : to guarantee — **fiarse** *vr* ~ **de** : to place trust in
fiasco *nm* FRACASO : fiasco, failure
fibra *nf* **1** : fiber **2** fibra de vidrio : fiberglass
fibrilar *vi* : to fibrillate — **fibrilación** *nf*
fibroso, -sa *adj* : fibrous
ficción *nf, pl* **ficciones** **1** : fiction **2** : fabrication, lie
ficha *nf* **1** : index card **2** : file, record **3** : token **4** : domino, checker, counter, poker chip
fichar *vt* **1** : to open a file on **2** : to sign up — *vi* : to punch in, to punch out
fichero *nm* **1** : card file **2** : filing cabinet
ficticio, -cia *adj* : fictitious
fidedigno, -na *adj* FIABLE : reliable, trustworthy
fideicomisario, -ria *n* : trustee
fideicomiso *nm* : trusteeship, trust ⟨guardar en fideicomiso : to hold in trust⟩
fidelidad *nf* : fidelity, faithfulness
fideo *nm* : noodle
fiduciario[1], **-ria** *adj* : fiduciary
fiduciario[2], **-ria** *n* : trustee
fiebre *nf* **1** CALENTURA : fever, temperature ⟨fiebre amarilla : yellow fever⟩ ⟨fiebre palúdica : malaria⟩ **2** : fever, excitement
fiel[1] *adj* **1** : faithful, loyal **2** : accurate — **fielmente** *adv*
fiel[2] *nm* **1** : pointer (of a scale) **2** los **fieles** : the faithful
fieltro *nm* : felt
fiera *nf* **1** : wild animal, beast **2** : fiend, demon ⟨una fiera para el trabajo : a demon for work⟩
fiereza *nf* : fierceness, ferocity
fiero, -ra *adj* FEROZ : fierce, ferocious
fierro *nm* HIERRO : iron
fiesta *nf* **1** : party, fiesta **2** : holiday, feast day
figura *nf* **1** : figure **2** : shape, form **3** figura retórica : figure of speech
figurado, -da *adj* : figurative — **figuradamente** *adv*
figurar *vi* **1** : to figure, to be included ⟨Rivera figura entre los más grandes pintores de México : Rivera is among Mexico's greatest painters⟩ **2** : to be prominent, to stand out — *vt* : to represent ⟨esta línea figura el horizonte : this line represents the horizon⟩ — **figurarse** *vr* : to imagine, to think ⟨¡figúrate el lío en que se metió! : imagine the mess she got into!⟩
fijación *nf, pl* **-ciones** **1** : fixation, obsession **2** : fixing, establishing **3** : fastening, securing
fijador *nm* **1** : fixative **2** : hair spray

fijamente *adv* : fixedly
fijar *vt* **1** : to fasten, to affix **2** ES-TABLECER : to establish, to set up **3** CONCRETAR : to set, to fix ⟨fijar la fecha : to set the date⟩ — **fijarse** *vr* **1** : to settle, to become fixed **2** ~ **en** : to notice, to pay attention to
fijeza *nf* **1** : firmness (of convictions) **2** : persistence, constancy ⟨mirar con fijeza a : to stare at⟩
fijiano, -na *adj & n* : Fijian
fijo, -ja *adj* **1** : fixed, firm, steady **2** PER-MANENTE : permanent
fila *nf* **1** HILERA : line, file ⟨ponerse en fila : to get in line⟩ **2** : rank, row **3 filas** *nfpl* : ranks ⟨cerrar filas : to close ranks⟩
filamento *nm* : filament
filantropía *nf* : philanthropy
filantrópico, -ca *adj* : philanthropic
filántropo, -pa *n* : philanthropist
filatelia *nf* : philately, stamp collecting
filatelista *nmf* : stamp collector, philatelist
fildeador, -dora *n* : fielder
filete *nm* **1** : fillet **2** SOLOMILLO : sirloin **3** : thread (of a screw)
filiación *nf, pl* **-ciones** **1** : affiliation, connection **2** : particulars *pl*, (police) description
filial¹ *adj* : filial
filial² *nf* : affiliate, subsidiary
filibustero *nm* : freebooter, pirate
filigrana *nf* **1** : filigree **2** : watermark (on paper)
filipino, -na *adj & n* : Filipino
filmación *nf, pl* **-ciones** : filming, shooting
filmar *vt* : to film, to shoot
filme *or* **film** *nm* PELÍCULA : film, movie
filmina *nf* : slide, transparency
filo *nm* **1** : cutting edge, blade **2** : edge ⟨al filo del escritorio : at the edge of the desk⟩ ⟨al filo de la medianoche : at the stroke of midnight⟩
filología *nf* : philology
filólogo, -ga *n* : philologist
filón *nm, pl* **filones** **1** : seam, vein (of minerals) **2** *fam* : successful business, gold mine
filoso, -sa *adj* : sharp
filosofar *vi* : to philosophize
filosofía *nf* : philosophy
filosófico, -ca *adj* : philosophic, philosophical — **filosóficamente** *adv*
filósofo, -fa *n* : philosopher
filtración *nf* : seepage, leaking
filtrar *v* : to filter — **filtrarse** *vr* : to seep through, to leak
filtro *nm* : filter
filudo, -da *adj* : sharp
fin *nm* **1** : end **2** : purpose, aim, objective **3 en** ~ : in short **4 fin de semana** : weekend **5 por** ~ : finally, at last
finado, -da *adj & n* DIFUNTO : deceased
final¹ *adj* : final, ultimate — **finalmente** *adv*

final² *nm* : end, conclusion, finale
final³ *nf* : final, play-off
finalidad *nf* **1** : purpose, aim **2** : finality
finalista *nmf* : finalist
finalización *nf* : completion, end
finalizar {21} *v* : to finish, to end
financiación *nf, pl* **-ciones** : financing, funding
financiamiento *nm* → **financiación**
financiar *vt* : to finance, to fund
financiero¹, -ra *adj* : financial
financiero², -ra *n* : financier
financista *nmf* : financier
finanzas *nfpl* : finances, finance ⟨altas finanzas : high finance⟩
finca *nf* **1** : farm, ranch **2** : country house
fineza *nf* FINURA, REFINAMIENTO : refinement
fingido, -da *adj* : false, feigned
fingimiento *nm* : pretense
fingir {35} *v* : to feign, to pretend
finiquitar *vt* **1** : to settle (an account) **2** : to conclude, to bring to an end
finiquito *nm* : settlement (of an account)
finito, -ta *adj* : finite
finja, etc. → **fingir**
finlandés, -desa *adj & n* : Finnish
fino, -na *adj* **1** : fine, excellent **2** : delicate, slender **3** REFINADO : refined **4** : sharp, acute ⟨olfato fino : keen sense of smell⟩ **5** : subtle
finta *nf* : feint
fintar *or* **fintear** *vi* : to feint
finura *nf* **1** : fineness, high quality **2** FINEZA, REFINAMIENTO : refinement
fiordo *nm* : fjord
fique *nm* : sisal
firma *nf* **1** : signature **2** : signing **3** EM-PRESA : firm, company
firmamento *nm* : firmament, sky
firmante *nmf* : signer, signatory
firmar *v* : to sign
firme *adj* **1** : firm, resolute **2** : steady, stable
firmemente *adv* : firmly
firmeza *nf* **1** : firmness, stability **2** : strength, resolve
firuletes *nmpl* : frills, adornments
fiscal¹ *adj* : fiscal — **fiscalmente** *adv*
fiscal² *nmf* : district attorney, prosecutor
fiscalizar {21} *vt* **1** : to audit, to inspect **2** : to oversee **3** : to criticize
fisco *nm* : national treasury, exchequer
fisgar {52} *vt* HUSMEAR : to pry into, to snoop on
fisgón, -gona *n, mpl* **fisgones** : snoop, busybody
fisgonear *vi* : to snoop, to pry
fisgue, etc. → **fisgar**
física *nf* : physics
físico¹, -ca *adj* : physical — **físicamente** *adv*
físico², -ca *n* : physicist
físico³ *nm* : physique, figure
fisiología *nf* : physiology

fisiológico, -ca *adj* : physiological, physiologic
fisiólogo, -ga *n* : physiologist
fisión *nf, pl* **fisiones** : fission — **fisionable** *adj*
fisionomía → **fisonomía**
fisioterapeuta *nmf* : physical therapist
fisioterapia *nf* : physical therapy
fisonomía *nf* : physiognomy, features *pl*
fistol *nm Mex* : tie clip
fisura *nf* : fissure, crevasse
fláccido, -da *or* **flácido, -da** *adj* : flaccid, flabby
flaco, -ca *adj* **1** DELGADO : thin, skinny **2** : feeble, weak ⟨una flaca excusa : a feeble excuse⟩
flagelar *vt* : to flagellate — **flagelación** *nf*
flagelo *nm* **1** : scourge, whip **2** : calamity
flagrante *adj* : flagrant, glaring, blatant — **flagrantemente** *adv*
flama *nf* LLAMA : flame
flamante *adj* **1** : bright, brilliant **2** : brand-new
flamear *vi* **1** LLAMEAR : to flame, to blaze **2** ONDEAR : to flap, to flutter
flamenco¹, -ca *adj* **1** : flamenco **2** : Flemish
flamenco², -ca *n* : Fleming, Flemish person
flamenco³ *nm* **1** : Flemish (language) **2** : flamingo **3** : flamenco (music or dance)
flanco *nm* : flank, side
flanquear *vt* : to flank
flaquear *vi* DECAER : to flag, to weaken
flaqueza *nf* **1** DEBILIDAD : frailty, feebleness **2** : thinness **3** : weakness, failing
flato *nm* : gloom, melancholy
flatulento, -ta *adj* : flatulent — **flatulencia** *nf*
flauta *nf* **1** : flute **2 flauta dulce** : recorder
flautín *nm, pl* **flautines** : piccolo
flautista *nmf* : flute player, flutist
flebitis *nf* : phlebitis
flecha *nf* : arrow
fleco *nm* **1** : bangs *pl* **2** : fringe
flema *nf* : phlegm
flemático, -ca *adj* : phlegmatic, stolid, impassive
flequillo *nm* : bangs *pl*
fletar *vt* **1** : to charter, to hire **2** : to load (freight)
flete *nm* **1** : charter fee **2** : shipping cost **3** : freight, cargo
fletero *nm* : shipper, carrier
flexibilidad *nf* : flexibility
flexibilizar {21} *vt* : to make more flexible
flexible¹ *adj* : flexible
flexible² *nm* **1** : flexible electrical cord **2** : soft hat
flirtear *vi* : to flirt
flojear *vi* **1** DEBILITARSE : to weaken, to flag **2** : to idle, to loaf around

flojedad *nf* : weakness
flojera *nf fam* **1** : lethargy, feeling of weakness **2** : laziness
flojo, -ja *adj* **1** SUELTO : loose, slack **2** : weak, poor ⟨está flojo en las ciencias : he's weak in science⟩ **3** PEREZOSO : lazy
flor *nf* **1** : flower **2 flor de Pascua** : poinsettia
flora *nf* : flora
floración *nf* : flowering ⟨en plena floración : in full bloom⟩
floral *adj* : floral
floreado, -da *adj* : flowered, flowery
florear *vi* FLORECER : to flower, to bloom — *vt* **1** : to adorn with flowers **2** *Mex* : to flatter, to compliment
florecer {53} *vi* **1** : to bloom, to blossom **2** : to flourish, to thrive
floreciente *adj* **1** : flowering **2** PRÓSPERO : flourishing, thriving
florecimiento *nm* : flowering
floreo *nm* : flourish
florería *nf* : flower shop, florist's
florero¹, -ra *n* : florist
florero² *nm* JARRÓN : vase
floresta *nf* **1** : glade, grove **2** BOSQUE : woods
florido, -da *adj* **1** : full of flowers **2** : florid, flowery ⟨escritos floridos : flowery prose⟩
florista *nmf* : florist
floritura *nf* : frill, embellishment
flota *nf* : fleet
flotabilidad *nf* : buoyancy
flotación *nf, pl* **-ciones** : flotation
flotador *nm* **1** : float **2** : life preserver
flotante *adj* : floating, buoyant
flotar *vi* : to float
flote *nm* **a** ~ : afloat
flotilla *nf* : flotilla, fleet
fluctuar {3} *vi* **1** : to fluctuate **2** VACILAR : to vacillate — **fluctuación** *nf* — **fluctuante** *adj*
fluidez *nf* **1** : fluency **2** : fluidity
fluido¹, -da *adj* **1** : flowing **2** : fluent **3** : fluid
fluido² *nm* : fluid
fluir {41} *vi* : to flow
flujo *nm* **1** : flow **2** : discharge
flúor *nm* : fluorine
fluoración *nf, pl* **-ciones** : fluoridation
fluorescencia *nf* : fluorescence — **fluorescente** *adj*
fluorizar {21} *vt* : to fluoridate
fluoruro *nm* : fluoride
fluvial *adj* : fluvial, river
fluye, etc. → **fluir**
fobia *nf* : phobia
foca *nf* : seal (animal)
focal *adj* : focal
focha *nf* : coot
foco *nm* **1** : focus **2** : center, pocket **3** : lightbulb **4** : spotlight **5** : headlight
fofo, -fa *adj* **1** ESPONJOSO : soft, spongy **2** : flabby
fogaje *nm* **1** FUEGO : skin eruption, cold sore **2** BOCHORNO : hot and humid weather

fogata *nf* : bonfire
fogón *nm, pl* **fogones** : bonfire
fogonazo *nm* : flash, explosion
fogonero, -ra *n* : stoker (of a furnace), fireman
fogoso, -sa *adj* ARDIENTE : ardent
foguear *vt* : to inure, to accustom
foja *nf* : sheet (of paper)
folículo *nm* : follicle
folio *nm* : folio, leaf
folklore *nm* : folklore
folklórico, -ca *adj* : folk, traditional
follaje *nm* : foliage
folleto *nm* : pamphlet, leaflet, circular
fomentar *vt* **1** : to foment, to stir up **2** PROMOVER : to promote, to foster
fomento *nm* : promotion, encouragement
fonda *nf* **1** POSADA : inn **2** : small restaurant
fondeado, -da *adj fam* : rich, in the money
fondear *vt* **1** : to sound **2** : to sound out, to examine **3** *Mex* : to fund, to finance — *vi* ANCLAR : to anchor — **fondearse** *vr fam* : to get rich
fondeo *nm* **1** : anchoring **2** *Mex* : funding, financing
fondillos *mpl* : seat, bottom (of clothing)
fondo *nm* **1** : bottom **2** : rear, back, end **3** : depth **4** : background **5** : sea bed **6** : fund ⟨fondo de inversiones : investment fund⟩ **7** *Mex* : slip, petticoat **8 fondos** *nmpl* : funds, resources ⟨cheque sin fondos : bounced check⟩ **9 a ~** : thoroughly, in depth **10 en ~** : abreast
fonema *nm* : phoneme
fonética *nf* : phonetics
fonético, -ca *adj* : phonetic
fontanería *nf* PLOMERÍA : plumbing
fontanero, -ra *n* PLOMERO : plumber
footing [ˈfuˌtɪŋ] *nm* : jogging ⟨hacer footing : to jog⟩
foque *nm* : jib
forajido, -da *n* : bandit, fugitive, outlaw
foráneo, -nea *adj* : foreign, strange
forastero, -ra *n* : stranger, outsider
forcejear *vi* : to struggle
forcejeo *nm* : struggle
fórceps *nms & pl* : forceps *pl*
forense *adj* : forensic, legal
forestal *adj* : forest
forja *nf* FRAGUA : forge
forjar *vt* **1** : to forge **2** : to shape, to create ⟨forjar un compromiso : to hammer out a compromise⟩ **3** : to invent, to concoct
forma *nf* **1** : form, shape **2** MANERA, MODO : manner, way **3** : fitness ⟨estar en forma : to be fit, to be in shape⟩ **4 formas** *nfpl* : appearances, conventions
formación *nf, pl* **-ciones 1** : formation **2** : training ⟨formación profesional : vocational training⟩

formal *adj* **1** : formal **2** : serious, dignified **3** : dependable, reliable
formaldehído *nm* : formaldehyde
formalidad *nf* **1** : formality **2** : seriousness, dignity **3** : dependability, reliability
formalizar {21} *vt* : to formalize, to make official
formalmente *adv* : formally
formar *vt* **1** : to form, to make **2** CONSTITUIR : to constitute, to make up **3** : to train, to educate — **formarse** *vr* **1** DESARROLLARSE : to develop, to take shape **2** EDUCARSE : to be educated
formatear *vt* : to format
formativo, -va *adj* : formative
formato *nm* : format
formidable *adj* **1** : formidable, tremendous **2** *fam* : fantastic, terrific
formón *nm, pl* **formones** : chisel
fórmula *nf* : formula
formulación *nf, pl* **-ciones** : formulation
formular *vt* **1** : to formulate, to draw up **2** : to make, to lodge (a protest or complaint)
formulario *nm* : form ⟨rellenar un formulario : to fill out a form⟩
fornicar {72} *vi* : to fornicate — **fornicación** *nf*
fornido, -da *adj* : well-built, burly, hefty
foro *nm* **1** : forum **2** : public assembly, open discussion
forraje *nm* **1** : forage, fodder **2** : foraging **3** *fam* : hodgepodge
forrajear *vi* : to forage
forrar *vt* **1** : to line (a garment) **2** : to cover (a book)
forro *nm* **1** : lining **2** CUBIERTA : book cover
forsitia *nf* : forsythia
fortachón, -chona *adj, pl* **-chones** *fam* : brawny, strong, tough
fortalecer {53} *vt* : to strengthen, to fortify — **fortalecerse** *vr*
fortalecimiento *nm* **1** : strengthening, fortifying **2** : fortifications
fortaleza *nf* **1** : fortress **2** FUERZA : strength **3** : resolution, fortitude
fortificación *nf, pl* **-ciones** : fortification
fortificar {72} *vt* **1** : to fortify **2** : to strengthen
fortín *nm, pl* **fortines** : small fort
fortuito, -ta *adj* : fortuitous
fortuna *nf* **1** SUERTE : fortune, luck **2** RIQUEZA : wealth, fortune
forzar {36} *vt* **1** OBLIGAR : to force, to compel **2** : to force open **3** : to strain ⟨forzar los ojos : to strain one's eyes⟩
forzosamente *adv* **1** : forcibly, by force **2** : necessarily, inevitably ⟨forzosamente tendrán que pagar : they'll have no choice but to pay⟩
forzoso, -sa *adj* **1** : forced, compulsory **2** : necessary, inevitable
fosa *nf* **1** : ditch, pit ⟨fosa séptica : septic tank⟩ **2** TUMBA : grave **3** : cavity ⟨fosas nasales : nasal cavities, nostrils⟩
fosfato *nm* : phosphate

fosforescencia *nf* : phosphorescence — **fosforescente** *adj*
fósforo *nm* **1** CERILLA : match **2** : phosphorus
fósil[1] *adj* : fossilized, fossil
fósil[2] *nm* : fossil
fosilizarse {21} *vr* : to fossilize, to become fossilized
foso *nm* **1** FOSA, ZANJA : ditch **2** : pit (of a theater) **3** : moat
foto *nf* : photo, picture
fotocopia *nf* : photocopy — **fotocopiar** *vt*
fotocopiadora *nf* COPIADORA : photocopier
fotoeléctrico, -ca *adj* : photoelectric
fotogénico, -ca *adj* : photogenic
fotografía *nf* **1** : photograph **2** : photography
fotografiar {85} *vt* : to photograph
fotográfico, -ca *adj* : photographic — **fotográficamente** *adv*
fotógrafo, -fa *n* : photographer
fotosíntesis *nf* : photosynthesis
fotosintético, -ca *adj* : photosynthetic
fracasado[1], **-da** *adj* : unsuccessful, failed
fracasado[2], **-da** *n* : failure
fracasar *vi* **1** FALLAR : to fail **2** : to fall through
fracaso *nm* FIASCO : failure
fracción *nf, pl* **fracciones** **1** : fraction **2** : part, fragment **3** : faction, splinter group
fraccionamiento *nm* **1** : division, breaking up **2** *Mex* : residential area, housing development
fraccionar *vt* : to divide, to break up
fraccionario, -ria *adj* : fractional
fractura *nf* **1** : fracture **2 fractura complicada** : compound fracture
fracturarse *vr* QUEBRARSE, ROMPERSE : to fracture, to break ⟨fracturarse el brazo : to break one's arm⟩
fragancia *nf* : fragrance, scent
fragante *adj* : fragrant
fragata *nf* : frigate
frágil *adj* **1** : fragile **2** : frail, delicate
fragilidad *nf* **1** : fragility **2** : frailty, delicacy
fragmentar *vt* : to fragment — **fragmentación** *nf*
fragmentario, -ria *adj* : fragmentary, sketchy
fragmento *nm* **1** : fragment, shard **2** : bit, snippet **3** : excerpt, passage
fragor *nm* : clamor, din, roar
fragoroso, -sa *adj* : thunderous, deafening
fragoso, -sa *adj* **1** : rough, uneven **2** : thick, dense
fragua *nf* FORJA : forge
fraguar {10} *vt* **1** : to forge **2** : to conceive, to concoct, to hatch — *vi* : to set, to solidify
fraile *nm* : friar, monk
frambuesa *nf* : raspberry

francamente *adv* **1** : frankly, candidly **2** REALMENTE : really ⟨es francamente admirable : it's really impressive⟩
francés[1], **-cesa** *adj, mpl* **franceses** : French
francés[2], **-cesa** *n, mpl* **franceses** : French person, Frenchman *m*, Frenchwoman *f*
francés[3] *nm* : French (language)
franciscano, -na *adj & n* : Franciscan
francmasón, -sona *n, mpl* **-sones** : Freemason — **francmasonería** *nf*
franco[1], **-ca** *adj* **1** CÁNDIDO : frank, candid **2** PATENTE : clear, obvious **3** : free ⟨franco a bordo : free on board⟩
franco[2] *nm* : franc
francotirador, -dora *n* : sniper
franela *nf* : flannel
franja *nf* **1** : stripe, band **2** : border, fringe
franquear *vt* **1** : to clear **2** ATRAVESAR : to cross, to go through **3** : to pay the postage on
franqueo *nm* : postage
franqueza *nf* : frankness
franquicia *nf* **1** EXENCIÓN : exemption **2** : franchise
frasco *nm* : small bottle, flask, vial
frase *nf* **1** : phrase **2** ORACIÓN : sentence
frasear *vt* : to phrase
fraternal *adj* : fraternal, brotherly
fraternidad *nf* **1** : brotherhood **2** : fraternity
fraternizar {21} *vi* : to fraternize — **fraternización** *nf*
fraterno, -na *adj* : fraternal, brotherly
fratricida *adj* : fratricidal
fratricidio *nm* : fratricide
fraude *nm* : fraud
fraudulento, -ta *adj* : fraudulent — **fraudulentamente** *adv*
fray *nm* : brother (title of a friar) ⟨Fray Bartolomé : Brother Bartholomew⟩
frazada *nf* COBIJA, MANTA : blanket
frecuencia *nf* : frequency
frecuentar *vt* : to frequent, to haunt
frecuente *adj* : frequent — **frecuentemente** *adv*
fregadera *nf fam* : hassle, pain in the neck
fregadero *nm* : kitchen sink
fregado[1], **-da** *adj fam* : annoying, bothersome
fregado[2] *nm* **1** : scrubbing, scouring **2** *fam* : mess, muddle
fregar {49} *vt* **1** : to scrub, to scour, to wash ⟨fregar los trastes : to do the dishes⟩ ⟨fregar el suelo : to scrub the floor⟩ **2** *fam* : to annoy — *vi* **1** : to wash the dishes **2** : to clean, to scrub **3** *fam* : to be annoying
freidera *nf Mex* : frying pan
freír {37} *vt* : to fry — **freírse** *vr*
frenar *vt* **1** : to brake **2** DETENER : to curb, to check — *vi* : to apply the brakes — **frenarse** *vr* : to restrain oneself

frenesí *nm* : frenzy
frenético, -ca *adj* : frantic, frenzied — **frenéticamente** *adv*
freno *nm* **1** : brake **2** : bit (of a bridle) **3** : check, restraint **4 frenos** *nmpl Mex* : braces (for teeth)
frente¹ *nm* **1** : front ⟨al frente de : at the head of⟩ ⟨en frente : in front, opposite⟩ **2** : facade **3** : front line, sphere of activity **4** : front (in meteorology) ⟨frente frío : cold front⟩ **5 hacer frente a** : to face up to, to brave
frente² *nf* **1** : forehead, brow **2 frente a frente** : face to face
fresa *nf* **1** : strawberry **2** : drill (in dentistry)
fresco¹, -ca *adj* **1** : fresh **2** : cool **3** *fam* : insolent, nervy
fresco² *nm* **1** : coolness **2** : fresh air ⟨al fresco : in the open air, outdoors⟩ **3** : fresco
frescor *nm* : cool air ⟨el frescor de la noche : the cool of the evening⟩
frescura *nf* **1** : freshness **2** : coolness **3** : calmness **4** DESCARO : nerve, audacity
fresno *nm* : ash (tree)
freza *nf* : spawn, roe
frezar {21} *vi* DESOVAR : to spawn
friable *adj* : friable
frialdad *nf* **1** : coldness **2** INDIFERENCIA : indifference, unconcern
fríamente *adv* : coldly, indifferently
fricasé *nm* : fricassee
fricción *nf, pl* **fricciones** **1** : friction **2** : rubbing, massage **3** : discord, disagreement ⟨fricción entre los hermanos : friction between the brothers⟩
friccionar *vt* **1** FROTAR : to rub **2** : to massage
friega¹, friegue, etc. → **fregar**
friega² *nf* **1** FRICCIÓN : rubdown, massage **2** : annoyance, bother
frigidez *nf* : (sexual) frigidity
frigorífico *nm Spain* : refrigerator
frijol *nm* : bean ⟨frijoles refritos : refried beans⟩
frío¹, fría *adj* **1** : cold **2** INDIFERENTE : cool, indifferent
frío² *nm* **1** : cold ⟨hace mucho frío esta noche : it's very cold tonight⟩ **2** INDIFERENCIA : coldness, indifference **3 tener frío** : to feel cold ⟨tengo frío : I'm cold⟩ **4 tomar frío** RESFRIARSE : to catch a cold
friolento, -ta *adj* : sensitive to cold
friolera *nf* (*used ironically or humorously*) : trifling amount ⟨una friolera de mil dólares : a mere thousand dollars⟩
friso *nm* : frieze
fritar *vt* : to fry
frito¹ *pp* → **freír**
frito², -ta *adj* **1** : fried **2** *fam* : worn-out, fed up ⟨tener frito a alguien : to get on someone's nerves⟩ **3** *fam* : fast asleep ⟨se quedó frito en el sofá : she fell asleep on the couch⟩
fritura *nf* **1** : frying **2** : fried food

frivolidad *nf* : frivolity
frívolo, -la *adj* : frivolous — **frívolamente** *adv*
fronda *nf* **1** : frond **2 frondas** *nfpl* : foliage
frondoso, -sa *adj* : leafy, luxuriant
frontal *adj* : frontal, head-on ⟨un choque frontal : a head-on collision⟩
frontalmente *adv* : head-on
frontera *nf* : border, frontier
fronterizo, -za *adj* : border, on the border ⟨estados fronterizos : neighboring states⟩
frontispicio *nm* : frontispiece
frotar *vt* **1** : to rub **2** : to strike (a match) — **frotarse** *vr* : to rub (together)
frote *nm* : rubbing, rub
fructífero, -ra *adj* : fruitful, productive
fructificar {72} *vi* **1** : to bear or produce fruit **2** : to be productive
fructuoso, -sa *adj* : fruitful
frugal *adj* : frugal, thrifty — **frugalmente** *adv*
frugalidad *adj* : frugality
frunce *nm* : gather (in cloth), pucker
fruncido *nm* : gathering, shirring
fruncir {83} *vt* **1** : to gather, to shirr **2** **fruncir el ceño** : to knit one's brow, to frown **3 fruncir la boca** : to pucker up, to purse one's lips
frunza, etc. → **fruncir**
frustración *nf, pl* **-ciones** : frustration
frustrado, -da *adj* **1** : frustrated **2** : failed, unsuccessful
frustrante *adj* : frustrating
frustrar *vt* : to frustrate, to thwart — **frustrarse** *vr* FRACASAR : to fail, to come to nothing ⟨se frustraron sus esperanzas : his hopes were dashed⟩
fruta *nf* : fruit
frutal¹ *adj* : fruit, fruit-bearing
frutal² *nm* : fruit tree
frutilla *nf* : South American strawberry
fruto *nm* **1** : fruit, agricultural product ⟨los frutos de la tierra : the fruits of the earth⟩ **2** : result, consequence ⟨los frutos de su trabajo : the fruits of his labor⟩
fucsia *adj & nm* : fuchsia
fue, etc. → **ir, ser**
fuego *nm* **1** : fire **2** : light ⟨¿tienes fuego? : have you got a light?⟩ **3** : flame, burner (on a stove) **4** : ardor, passion **5** FOGAJE : skin eruption, cold sore **6 fuegos artificiales** *nmpl* : fireworks
fuelle *nm* : bellows
fuente *nf* **1** MANANTIAL : spring **2** : fountain **3** ORIGEN : source ⟨fuentes informativas : sources of information⟩ **4** : platter, serving dish
fuera *adv* **1** : outside, out **2** : abroad, away **3** ~ **de** : outside of, out of, beyond **4** ~ **de** : besides, in addition to ⟨fuera de eso : aside from that⟩ **5 fuera de lugar** : out of place, amiss
fuerce, fuerza etc. → **forzar**

fuero *nm* **1** JURISDICCIÓN : jurisdiction **2** : privilege, exemption **3 fuero interno** : conscience, heart of hearts
fuerte[1] *adv* **1** : strongly, tightly, hard **2** : loudly **3** : abundantly
fuerte[2] *adj* **1** : strong **2** : intense ⟨un fuerte dolor : an intense pain⟩ **3** : loud **4** : extreme, excessive
fuerte[3] *nm* **1** : fort, stronghold **2** : forte, strong point
fuerza *nf* **1** : strength, vigor ⟨fuerza de voluntad : willpower⟩ **2** : force ⟨fuerza bruta : brute force⟩ **3** : power, might ⟨fuerza de brazos : manpower⟩ **4**
fuerzas *nfpl* : forces ⟨fuerzas armadas : armed forces⟩ **5 a fuerza de** : by, by dint of
fuetazo *nm* : lash
fuga *nf* **1** HUIDA : flight, escape **2** : fugue **3** : leak ⟨fuga de gas : gas leak⟩
fugarse {52} *vr* **1** : to escape **2** HUIR : to flee, to run away **3** : to elope
fugaz *adj, pl* **fugaces** : brief, fleeting
fugitivo, -va *adj & n* : fugitive
fulana *nf* : hooker, slut
fulano, -na *n* : so-and-so, what's-his-name, what's-her-name ⟨fulano, mengano, y zutano : Tom, Dick, and Harry⟩ ⟨señora fulana de tal : Mrs. so-and-so⟩
fulcro *nm* : fulcrum
fulgor *nm* : brilliance, splendor
fulgurar *vi* : to shine brightly, to gleam, to glow
fulminante *adj* **1** : fulminating, explosive **2** : devastating, terrible ⟨una mirada fulminante : a withering look⟩
fulminar *vt* **1** : to strike with lightning **2** : to strike down ⟨fulminar a alguien con la mirada : to look daggers at someone⟩
fumador, -dora *n* : smoker
fumar *v* : to smoke
fumble *nm* : fumble (in football)
fumblear *vt* : to fumble (in football)
fumigante *nm* : fumigant
fumigar {52} *vt* : to fumigate — **fumigación** *nf*
funámbulo, -la *n* EQUILIBRISTA : tightrope walker
función *nf, pl* **funciones** **1** : function **2** : duty **3** : performance, show
funcional *adj* : functional — **funcionalmente** *adv*
funcionamiento *nm* **1** : functioning **2 en ~** : in operation
funcionar *vi* **1** : to function **2** : to run, to work
funcionario, -ria *n* : civil servant, official
funda *nf* **1** : case, cover, sheath **2** : pillowcase
fundación *nf, pl* **-ciones** : foundation, establishment
fundado, -da *adj* : well-founded, justified
fundador, -dora *n* : founder

fundamental *adj* BÁSICO : fundamental, basic — **fundamentalmente** *adv*
fundamentalismo *nm* : fundamentalism
fundamentalista *nmf* : fundamentalist
fundamentar *vt* **1** : to lay the foundations for **2** : to support, to back up **3** : to base, to found
fundamento *nm* : basis, foundation, groundwork
fundar *vt* **1** ESTABLECER, INSTITUIR : to found, to establish **2** BASAR : to base — **fundarse** *vr* ~ **en** : to be based on, to stem from
fundición *nf, pl* **-ciones** **1** : founding, smelting **2** : foundry
fundir *vt* **1** : to melt down, to smelt **2** : to fuse, to merge **3** : to burn out (a lightbulb) — **fundirse** *vr* **1** : to fuse together, to blend, to merge **2** : to melt, to thaw **3** : to fade (in television or movies)
fúnebre *adj* **1** : funeral, funereal **2** LÚGUBRE : gloomy, mournful
funeral[1] *adj* : funeral, funerary
funeral[2] *nm* **1** : funeral **2 funerales** *nmpl* EXEQUIAS : funeral rites
funeraria *nf* **1** : funeral home, funeral parlor **2 director de funeraria** : funeral director, undertaker
funerario, -ria *adj* : funeral
funesto, -ta *adj* : terrible, disastrous ⟨consecuencias funestas : disastrous consequences⟩
fungicida[1] *adj* : fungicidal
fungicida[2] *nm* : fungicide
fungir {35} *vi* : to act, to function ⟨fungir de asesor : to act as a consultant⟩
fungoso, -sa *adj* : fungous
funja, etc. → **fungir**
furgón *nm, pl* **furgones** **1** : van, truck **2** : freight car, boxcar **3 furgón de cola** : caboose
furgoneta *nf* : van
furia *nf* **1** CÓLERA, IRA : fury, rage **2** : violence, fury ⟨la furia de la tormenta : the fury of the storm⟩
furibundo, -da *adj* : furious
furiosamente *adv* : furiously, frantically
furioso, -sa *adj* **1** AIRADO : furious, irate **2** : intense, violent
furor *nm* **1** : fury, rage **2** : violence (of the elements) **3** : passion, frenzy **4** : enthusiasm ⟨hacer furor : to be all the rage⟩
furtivo, -va *adj* : furtive — **furtivamente** *adv*
furúnculo *nm* DIVIESO : boil
fuselaje *nm* : fuselage
fusible *nm* : (electrical) fuse
fusil *nm* : rifle
fusilar *vt* **1** : to shoot, to execute (by firing squad) **2** *fam* : to plagiarize, to pirate
fusilería *nf* **1** : rifles *pl*, rifle fire **2 descarga de fusilería** : fusillade
fusión *nf, pl* **fusiones** **1** : fusion **2** : union, merger

fusionar *vt* **1** : to fuse **2** : to merge, to amalgamate — **fusionarse** *vr*

fusta *nf* : riding crop

fustigar {52} *vt* **1** AZOTAR : to whip, to lash **2** : to upbraid, to berate

futbol *or* **fútbol** *nm* **1** : soccer **2 futbol americano** : football

futbolista *nmf* : soccer player

futesa *nf* **1** : small thing, trifle **2 futesas** *nfpl* : small talk

fútil *adj* : trifling, trivial

futurista *adj* : futuristic

futuro¹, -ra *adj* : future

futuro² *nm* PORVENIR : future

G

g *nf* : seventh letter of the Spanish alphabet

gabán *nm, pl* **gabanes** : topcoat, overcoat

gabardina *nf* **1** : gabardine **2** : trench coat, raincoat

gabarra *nf* : barge

gabinete *nm* **1** : cabinet (in government) **2** : study, office (in the home) **3** : (professional) office

gablete *nm* : gable

gabonés, -nesa *adj & n, mpl* **-neses** : Gabonese

gacela *nf* : gazelle

gaceta *nf* : gazette, newspaper

gachas *nfpl* : porridge

gacho, -cha *adj* **1** : drooping, turned downward **2** *Mex fam* : nasty, awful **3 ir a gachas** *fam* : to go on all fours

gaélico¹, -ca *adj* : Gaelic

gaélico² *nm* : Gaelic (language)

gafas *nfpl* ANTEOJOS : eyeglasses, glasses

gaita *nf* : bagpipes *pl*

gajes *nmpl* **gajes del oficio** : occupational hazards

gajo *nm* **1** : broken branch (of a tree) **2** : cluster, bunch (of fruit) **3** : segment (of citrus fruit)

gala *nf* **1** : gala ⟨vestido de gala : formal dress⟩ ⟨tener algo a gala : to be proud of something⟩ **2 galas** *nfpl* : finery, attire

galáctico, -ca *adj* : galactic

galán *nm, pl* **galanes 1** : ladies' man, gallant **2** : leading man, hero **3** : boyfriend, suitor

galano, -na *adj* **1** : elegant **2** *Mex* : mottled

galante *adj* : gallant, attentive — **galantemente** *adv*

galantear *vt* **1** CORTEJAR : to court, to woo **2** : to flirt with

galanteo *nm* **1** CORTEJO : courtship **2** : flirtation, flirting

galantería *nf* **1** : gallantry, attentiveness **2** : compliment

galápago *nm* : aquatic turtle

galardón *nm, pl* **-dones** : award, prize

galardonado, -da *adj* : prize-winning

galardonar *vt* : to give an award to

galaxia *nf* : galaxy

galeno *nm fam* : physician, doctor

galeón *nm, pl* **galeones** : galleon

galera *nf* : galley

galería *nf* **1** : gallery, balcony (in a theater) ⟨galería comercial : shopping mall⟩ **2** : corridor, passage

galerón *n, mpl* **-rones** *Mex* : large hall

galés¹, -lesa *adj* : Welsh

galés², -lesa *n, mpl* **galeses 1** : Welshman *m*, Welshwoman *f* **2 los galeses** : the Welsh

galés³ *nm* : Welsh (language)

galgo *nm* : greyhound

galimatías *nms & pl* : gibberish, nonsense

galio *nm* : gallium

gallardete *nm* : pennant, streamer

gallardía *nf* **1** VALENTÍA : bravery **2** APOSTURA : elegance, gracefulness

gallardo, -da *adj* **1** VALIENTE : brave **2** APUESTO : elegant, graceful

gallear *vi* : to show off, to strut around

gallego¹, -ga *adj* **1** : Galician **2** *fam* : Spanish

gallego², -ga *n* **1** : Galician **2** *fam* : Spaniard

galleta *nf* **1** : cookie **2** : cracker

gallina *nf* **1** : hen **2 gallina de Guinea** : guinea fowl

gallinazo *nm* : vulture, buzzard

gallinero *nm* : chicken coop, henhouse

gallito, -ta *adj fam* : cocky, belligerent

gallo *nm* **1** : rooster, cock **2** *fam* : squeak or crack in the voice **3** *Mex* : serenade **4 gallo de pelea** : gamecock

galo¹, -la *adj* **1** : Gaulish **2** : French

galo², -la *n* : Frenchman *m*, Frenchwoman *f*

galocha *nf* : galosh

galón *nm, pl* **galones 1** : gallon **2** : stripe (military insignia)

galopada *nf* : gallop

galopante *adj* : galloping ⟨inflación galopante : galloping inflation⟩

galopar *vi* : to gallop

galope *nm* : gallop

galpón *nm, pl* **galpones** : shed, storehouse

galvanizar {21} *vt* : to galvanize — **galvanización** *nf*

gama *nf* **1** : range, spectrum, gamut **2** → **gamo**

gamba *nf* : large shrimp, prawn

gamberro, -rra *n Spain* : hooligan, troublemaker

gambiano, -na *adj & n* : Gambian

gambito *nm* : gambit (in chess)

gameto *nm* : gamete

gamo, -ma *n* : fallow deer
gamuza *nf* **1** : suede **2** : chamois
gana *nf* **1** : desire, inclination **2 de buena gana** : willingly, readily, gladly **3 de mala gana** : reluctantly, halfheartedly **4 tener ganas de** : to feel like, to be in the mood for ⟨tengo ganas de bailar : I feel like dancing⟩ **5 ponerle ganas a algo** : to put effort into something
ganadería *nf* **1** : cattle raising, stockbreeding **2** : cattle ranch **3** GANADO : cattle *pl*, livestock
ganadero[1], **-ra** *adj* : cattle, ranching
ganadero[2], **-ra** *n* : rancher, stockbreeder
ganado *nm* **1** : cattle *pl*, livestock **2 ganado ovino** : sheep *pl* **3 ganado porcino** : swine *pl*
ganador[1], **-dora** *adj* : winning
ganador[2], **-dora** *n* : winner
ganancia *nf* **1** : profit **2 ganancias** *nfpl* : winnings, gains
ganancioso, -sa *adj* : profitable
ganar *vt* **1** : to win **2** : to gain ⟨ganar tiempo : to buy time⟩ **3** : to earn ⟨ganar dinero : to make money⟩ **4** : to acquire, to obtain — *vi* **1** : to win **2** : to profit ⟨salir ganando : to come out ahead⟩ — **ganarse** *vr* **1** : to gain, to win ⟨ganarse a alguien : to win someone over⟩ **2** : to earn ⟨ganarse la vida : to make a living⟩ **3** : to deserve
gancho *nm* **1** : hook **2** : clothes hanger **3** : hairpin, bobby pin **4** *Col* : safety pin
gandul[1] *nm CA, Car, Col* : pigeon pea
gandul[2], **-dula** *n fam* : idler, lazybones
gandulear *vi* : to idle, to loaf, to lounge about
ganga *nf* : bargain
ganglio *nm* **1** : ganglion **2** : gland
gangrena *nf* : gangrene — **gangrenoso, -sa** *adj*
gángster *nmf, pl* **gángsters** : gangster
gansada *nf* : silly thing, nonsense
ganso, -sa *n* **1** : goose, gander *m* **2** : idiot, fool
gañido *nm* : yelp (of a dog)
gañir {38} *vi* : to yelp
garabatear *v* : to scribble, to scrawl, to doodle
garabato *nm* **1** : doodle **2 garabatos** *nmpl* : scribble, scrawl
garaje *nm* : garage
garante *nmf* : guarantor
garantía *nf* **1** : guarantee, warranty **2** : security ⟨garantía de trabajo : job security⟩
garantizar {21} *vt* : to guarantee
garapiña *nf* : pineapple drink
garapiñar *vt* : to candy
garbanzo *nm* : chickpea, garbanzo
garbo *nm* **1** DONAIRE : grace, poise **2** : jauntiness
garboso, -sa *adj* **1** : graceful **2** : elegant, stylish
garceta *nf* : egret

gardenia *nf* : gardenia
garfio *nm* : hook, gaff, grapnel
gargajo *nm fam* : phlegm
garganta *nf* **1** : throat **2** : neck (of a person or a bottle) **3** : ravine, narrow pass
gargantilla *nf* : choker, necklace
gárgara *nf* **1** : gargle, gargling **2 hacer gárgaras** : to gargle
gargarizar *vi* : to gargle
gárgola *nf* : gargoyle
garita *nf* **1** : cabin, hut **2** : sentry box, lookout post
garoso, -sa *adj Col, Ven* : gluttonous, greedy
garra *nf* **1** : claw **2** : hand, paw **3 garras** *nfpl* : claws, clutches ⟨caer en las garras de alguien : to fall into someone's clutches⟩
garrafa *nf* : decanter, carafe
garrafal *adj* : terrible, monstrous
garrafón *nm, pl* **-fones** : large decanter, large bottle
garrapata *nf* : tick
garrobo *nm CA* : large lizard, iguana
garrocha *nf* **1** PICA : lance, pike **2** : pole ⟨salto con garrocha : pole vault⟩
garrotazo *nm* : blow (with a club)
garrote *nm* **1** : club, stick **2** *Mex* : brake
garúa *nf* : drizzle
garuar {3} *v impers* LLOVIZNAR : to drizzle
garza *nf* : heron
gas *nm* : gas, vapor, fumes *pl* ⟨gas lagrimógeno : tear gas⟩
gasa *nf* : gauze
gasear *vt* **1** : to gas **2** : to aerate (a liquid)
gaseosa *nf* REFRESCO : soda, soft drink
gaseoso, -sa *adj* **1** : gaseous **2** : carbonated, fizzy
gasoducto *nm* : gas pipeline
gasolina *nf* : gasoline, gas
gasolinera *nf* : gas station, service station
gastado, -da *adj* **1** : spent **2** : worn, worn-out
gastador[1], **-dora** *adj* : extravagant, spendthrift
gastador[2], **-dora** *n* : spendthrift
gastar *vt* **1** : to spend **2** CONSUMIR : to consume, to use up **3** : to squander, to waste **4** : to wear ⟨gasta un bigote : he sports a mustache⟩ — **gastarse** *vr* **1** : to spend, to expend **2** : to run down, to wear out
gasto *nm* **1** : expense, expenditure **2** DETERIORO : wear **3 gastos generales** *or* **gastos indirectos** : overhead
gástrico, -ca *adj* : gastric
gastritis *nf* : gastritis
gastronomía *nf* : gastronomy
gastronómico, -ca *adj* : gastronomic
gastrónomo, -ma *n* : gourmet
gatas *adv* **andar a gatas** : to crawl, to go on all fours
gatear *vi* **1** : to crawl **2** : to climb, to clamber (up)

gatillero *nm Mex* : gunman
gatillo *nm* : trigger
gatito, -ta *n* : kitten
gato¹, -ta *n* : cat
gato² *nm* : jack (for an automobile)
gauchada *nf Arg, Uru* : favor, kindness
gaucho *nm* : gaucho
gaveta *nf* **1** CAJÓN : drawer **2** : till
gavilla *nf* **1** : gang, band **2** : sheaf
gaviota *nf* : gull, seagull
gay ['ge, 'gai] *adj* : gay (homosexual)
gaza *nf* : loop
gazapo *nm* **1** : young rabbit **2** : misprint, error
gazmoñería *nf* MOJIGATERÍA : prudery, primness
gazmoño¹, -ña *adj* : prudish, prim
gazmoño², -ña *n* MOJIGATO : prude, prig
gaznate *nm* : throat, gullet
gazpacho *nm* : gazpacho
géiser *or* **géyser** *nm* : geyser
gel *nm* : gel
gelatina *nf* : gelatin
gélido, -da *adj* : icy, freezing cold
gelificarse *vr* : to jell
gema *nf* : gem
gemelo¹, -la *adj & n* MELLIZO : twin
gemelo² *nm* **1** : cuff link **2 gemelos** *nmpl* BINOCULARES : binoculars
gemido *nm* : moan, groan, wail
Géminis *nmf* : Gemini
gemir {54} *vi* : to moan, to groan, to wail
gen *or* **gene** *nm* : gene
gendarme *nmf* POLICÍA : police officer, policeman *m*, policewoman *f*
gendarmería *nf* : police
genealogía *nf* : genealogy
genealógico, -ca *adj* : genealogical
generación *nf, pl* **-ciones 1** : generation ⟨tercera generación : third generation⟩ **2** : generating, creating **3** : class ⟨la generación del '97 : the class of '97⟩
generacional *adj* : generation, generational
generador *nm* : generator
general¹ *adj* **1** : general **2 en ~** *or* **por lo general** : in general, generally
general² *nmf* **1** : general **2 general de división** : major general
generalidad *nf* **1** : generality, generalization **2** : majority
generalización *nf, pl* **-ciones 1** : generalization **2** : escalation, spread
generalizado, -da *adj* : generalized, widespread
generalizar {21} *vi* : to generalize — *vt* : to spread, to spread out — **generalizarse** *vr* : to become widespread
generalmente *adv* : usually, generally
generar *vt* : to generate — **generarse** *vr*
genérico, -ca *adj* : generic
género *nm* **1** : genre, class, kind ⟨el género humano : the human race, mankind⟩ **2** : gender (in grammar) **3 géneros** *nmpl* : goods, commodities
generosidad *nf* : generosity
generoso, -sa *adj* **1** : generous, unselfish **2** : ample — **generosamente** *adv*

genética *nf* : genetics
genético, -ca *adj* : genetic — **genéticamente** *adv*
genetista *nmf* : geneticist
genial *adj* **1** AGRADABLE : genial, pleasant **2** : brilliant ⟨una obra genial : a work of genius⟩ **3** *fam* FORMIDABLE : fantastic, terrific
genialidad *nf* **1** : genius **2** : stroke of genius **3** : eccentricity
genio *nm* **1** : genius **2** : temper, disposition ⟨de mal genio : bad-tempered⟩ **3** : genie
genital *adj* : genital
genitales *nmpl* : genitals, genitalia
genocidio *nm* : genocide
genotipo *nm* : genotype
gente *nf* **1** : people **2** : relatives *pl*, folks *pl* **3 gente menuda** *fam* : children, kids *pl* **4 ser buena gente** : to be nice, to be kind
gentil¹ *adj* **1** AMABLE : kind **2** : gentile
gentil² *nmf* : gentile
gentileza *nf* **1** AMABILIDAD : kindness **2** CORTESÍA : courtesy
gentilicio, -cia *adj* **1** : national, tribal **2** : family
gentío *nm* MUCHEDUMBRE, MULTITUD : crowd, mob
gentuza *nf* CHUSMA : riffraff, rabble
genuflexión *nf, pl* **-xiones 1** : genuflection **2 hacer una genuflexión** : to genuflect
genuino, -na *adj* : genuine — **genuinamente** *adv*
geofísica *nf* : geophysics
geofísico, -ca *adj* : geophysical
geografía *nf* : geography
geográfico, -ca *adj* : geographic, geographical — **geográficamente** *adv*
geógrafo, -fa *n* : geographer
geología *nf* : geology
geológico, -ca *adj* : geologic, geological — **geológicamente** *adv*
geólogo, -ga *n* : geologist
geometría *nf* : geometry
geométrico, -ca *adj* : geometric, geometrical — **geométricamente** *adv*
geopolítica *nf* : geopolitics
geopolítico, -ca *adj* : geopolitical
georgiano, -na *adj & n* : Georgian
geranio *nm* : geranium
gerbo *nm* : gerbil
gerencia *nf* : management, administration
gerencial *adj* : managerial
gerente *nmf* : manager, director
geriatría *nf* : geriatrics
geriátrico, -ca *adj* : geriatric
germanio *nm* : germanium
germano, -na *adj* : Germanic, German
germen *nm, pl* **gérmenes** : germ
germicida *nf* : germicide
germinación *nf, pl* **-ciones** : germination
germinar *vi* : to germinate, to sprout
gerontología *nf* : gerontology
gerundio *nm* : gerund

gesta *nf* : deed, exploit
gestación *nf, pl* **-ciones** : gestation
gesticulación *nf, pl* **-ciones** : gesturing, gesticulation
gesticular *vi* : to gesticulate, to gesture
gestión *nf, pl* **gestiones** **1** TRÁMITE : procedure, step **2** ADMINISTRACIÓN : management **3 gestiones** *nfpl* : negotiations
gestionar *vt* **1** : to negotiate, to work towards **2** ADMINISTRAR : to manage, to handle
gesto *nm* **1** ADEMÁN : gesture **2** : facial expression **3** MUECA : grimace
gestor¹, -tora *adj* : facilitating, negotiating, managing
gestor², -tora *n* : facilitator, manager
géyser → **géiser**
ghanés, -nesa *adj & n, mpl* **ghaneses** : Ghanaian
ghetto → **gueto**
giba *nf* **1** : hump (of an animal) **2** : hunchback (of a person)
gibón *nm, pl* **gibones** : gibbon
giboso¹, -sa *adj* : hunchbacked, humpbacked
giboso², -sa *n* : hunchback, humpback
gigabyte *nm* : gigabyte
gigante¹ *adj* : giant, gigantic
gigante², -ta *n* : giant
gigantesco, -ca *adj* : gigantic, huge
gime, etc. → **gemir**
gimnasia *nf* : gymnastics
gimnasio *nm* : gymnasium, gym
gimnasta *nmf* : gymnast
gimnástico, -ca *adj* : gymnastic
gimotear *vi* LLORIQUEAR : to whine, to whimper
gimoteo *nm* : whimpering
ginebra *nf* : gin
ginecología *nf* : gynecology
ginecológico, -ca *adj* : gynecologic, gynecological
ginecólogo, -ga *n* : gynecologist
ginseng *nm* : ginseng
gira *nf* : tour
giralda *nf* : weather vane
girar *vi* **1** : to turn around, to revolve **2** : to swing around, to swivel — *vt* **1** : to turn, to twist, to rotate **2** : to draft (checks) **3** : to transfer (funds)
girasol *nm* MIRASOL : sunflower
giratorio, -ria *adj* : revolving
giro *nm* **1** VUELTA : turn, rotation **2** : change of direction ⟨giro de 180 grados : U-turn, about-face⟩ **3 giro bancario** : bank draft **4 giro postal** : money order
giroscopio *or* **giróscopo** *nm* : gyroscope
gis *nm Mex* : chalk
gitano, -na *adj & n* : Gypsy
glacial *adj* : glacial, icy — **glacialmente** *adv*
glaciar *nm* : glacier
gladiador *nm* : gladiator
gladiolo *or* **gladíolo** *nm* : gladiolus
glándula *nf* : gland — **glandular** *adj*

glaseado *nm* : glaze, icing
glasear *vt* : to glaze
glaucoma *nm* : glaucoma
glicerina *nf* : glycerin, glycerol
glicinia *nf* : wisteria
global *adj* **1** : global, worldwide **2** : full, comprehensive **3** : total, overall
globalizar {21} *vt* **1** ABARCAR : to include, to encompass **2** : to extend worldwide
globalmente *adv* : globally, as a whole
globo *nm* **1** : globe, sphere **2** : balloon **3 globo ocular** : eyeball
glóbulo *nm* **1** : globule **2** : blood cell, corpuscle
gloria *nf* **1** : glory **2** : fame, renown **3** : delight, enjoyment **4** : star, legend ⟨las glorias del cine : the great names in motion pictures⟩
glorieta *nf* **1** : rotary, traffic circle **2** : bower, arbor
glorificar {72} *vt* ALABAR : to glorify — **glorificación** *nf*
glorioso, -sa *adj* : glorious — **gloriosamente** *adv*
glosa *nf* **1** : gloss **2** : annotation, commentary
glosar *vt* **1** : to gloss **2** : to annotate, to comment on (a text)
glosario *nm* : glossary
glotis *nf* : glottis
glotón¹, -tona *adj, mpl* **glotones** : gluttonous
glotón², -tona *n, mpl* **glotones** : glutton
glotón³ *nm, pl* **glotones** : wolverine
glotonería *nf* GULA : gluttony
glucosa *nf* : glucose
glutinoso, -sa *adj* : glutinous
gnomo [ˈnomo] *nm* : gnome
gobernación *nf, pl* **-ciones** : governing, government
gobernador, -dora *n* : governor
gobernante¹ *adj* : ruling, governing
gobernante² *nmf* : ruler, leader, governor
gobernar {55} *vt* **1** : to govern, to rule **2** : to steer, to sail (a ship) — *vi* **1** : to govern **2** : to steer
gobierno *nm* : government
goce¹, etc. → **gozar**
goce² *nm* **1** PLACER : enjoyment, pleasure **2** : use, possession
gol *nm* : goal (in soccer)
golear *vt* : to rout, to score many goals against (in soccer)
goleta *nf* : schooner
golf *nm* : golf
golfista *nmf* : golfer
golfo *nm* : gulf, bay
golondrina *nf* **1** : swallow (bird) **2 golondrina de mar** : tern
golosina *nf* : sweet, snack
goloso, -sa *adj* : fond of sweets ⟨ser goloso : to have a sweet tooth⟩
golpazo *nm* : heavy blow, bang, thump
golpe *nm* **1** : blow ⟨caerle a golpes a alguien : to give someone a beating⟩ **2** : knock **3 de ~** : suddenly **4 de un**

golpe : all at once, in one fell swoop **5**
golpe de estado : coup, coup d'etat **6**
golpe de suerte : stroke of luck
golpeado, -da *adj* **1** : beaten, hit **2** : bruised (of fruit) **3** : dented
golpear *vt* **1** : to beat (up), to hit **2** : to slam, to bang, to strike — *vi* **1** : to knock (at a door) **2** : to beat ⟨la lluvia golpeaba contra el tejado : the rain beat against the roof⟩ — **golpearse** *vr*
golpetear *v* : to knock, to rattle, to tap
golpeteo *nm* : banging, knocking, tapping
goma *nf* **1** : gum ⟨goma de mascar : chewing gum⟩ **2** CAUCHO : rubber ⟨goma espuma : foam rubber⟩ **3** PEGAMENTO : glue **4** : rubber band **5** *Arg* : tire **6** *or* **goma de borrar** : eraser
gomita *nf* : rubber band
gomoso, -sa *adj* : gummy, sticky
góndola *nf* : gondola
gong *nm* : gong
gonorrea *nf* : gonorrhea
gorda *nf Mex* : thick corn tortilla
gordinflón[1], -flona *adj, mpl* **-flones** *fam* : chubby, pudgy
gordinflón[2], -flona *n, mpl* **-flones** *fam* : chubby person
gordo[1], -da *adj* **1** : fat **2** : thick **3** : fatty, greasy, oily **4** : unpleasant ⟨me cae gorda tu tía : I can't stand your aunt⟩
gordo[2], -da *n* : fat person
gordo[3] *nm* **1** GRASA : fat **2** : jackpot
gordura *nf* : fatness, flab
gorgojo *nm* : weevil
gorgotear *vi* : to gurgle, to bubble
gorgoteo *nm* : gurgle
gorila *nm* : gorilla
gorjear *vi* **1** : to chirp, to tweet, to warble **2** : to gurgle
gorjeo *nm* **1** : chirping, warbling **2** : gurgling
gorra *nf* **1** : bonnet **2** : cap **3 de ~** *fam* : for free, at someone else's expense ⟨vivir de gorra : to sponge, to freeload⟩
gorrear *vt fam* : to bum, to scrounge — *vi fam* : to freeload
gorrero, -ra *n fam* : freeloader, sponger
gorrión *nm, pl* **gorriones** : sparrow
gorro *nm* **1** : cap **2 estar hasta el gorro** : to be fed up
gorrón, -rrona *n, mpl* **gorrones** *fam* : freeloader, scrounger
gorronear *vt fam* : to bum, to scrounge — *vi fam* : to freeload
gota *nf* **1** : drop ⟨una gota de sudor : a bead of sweat⟩ ⟨como dos gotas de agua : like two peas in a pod⟩ ⟨sudar la gota gorda : to sweat buckets, to work very hard⟩ **2** : gout
gotear *v* **1** : to drip **2** : to leak — *v impers* LLOVIZNAR : to drizzle
goteo *nm* : drip, dripping
gotera *nf* **1** : leak **2** : stain (from dripping water)
gotero *nm* : (medicine) dropper
gótico, -ca *adj* : Gothic
gourmet *nmf* : gourmet

gozar {21} *vi* **1** : to enjoy oneself, to have a good time **2 ~ de** : to enjoy, to have, to possess ⟨gozar de buena salud : to enjoy good health⟩ **3 ~ con** : to take delight in
gozne *nm* BISAGRA : hinge
gozo *nm* **1** : joy **2** PLACER : enjoyment, pleasure
gozoso, -sa *adj* : joyful
grabación *nf, pl* **-ciones** : recording
grabado *nm* **1** : engraving **2 grabado al aguafuerte** : etching
grabador, -dora *n* : engraver
grabadora *nf* : tape recorder
grabar *vt* **1** : to engrave **2** : to record, to tape — *vi* **grabar al aguafuerte** : to etch — **grabarse** *vr* **grabársele a alguien en la memoria** : to become engraved on someone's mind
gracia *nf* **1** : grace **2** : favor, kindness **3** : humor, wit ⟨su comentario no me hizo gracia : I wasn't amused by his remark⟩ **4 gracias** *nfpl* : thanks ⟨¡gracias! : thank you!⟩ ⟨dar gracias : to give thanks⟩
grácil *adj* **1** : graceful **2** : delicate, slender, fine
gracilidad *nm* : gracefulness
gracioso, -sa *adj* **1** CHISTOSO : funny, amusing **2** : cute, attractive
grada *nf* **1** : harrow **2** PELDAÑO : step, stair **3 gradas** *nfpl* : bleachers, grandstand
gradación *nf, pl* **-ciones** : gradation, scale
gradar *vt* : to harrow, to hoe
gradería *nf* : tiers *pl*, stands *pl*, rows *pl* (in a theater)
gradiente *nf* : gradient, slope
grado *nm* **1** : degree (in meteorology and mathematics) ⟨grado centígrado : degree centigrade⟩ **2** : extent, level, degree ⟨en grado sumo : greatly, to the highest degree⟩ **3** RANGO : rank **4** : year, class (in education) **5 de buen grado** : willingly, readily
graduable *adj* : adjustable
graduación *nf, pl* **-ciones** **1** : graduation (from a school) **2** GRADO : rank **3** : alcohol content, proof
graduado[1], -da *adj* **1** : graduated **2 lentes graduados** : prescription lenses
graduado[2], -da *n* : graduate
gradual *adj* : gradual — **gradualmente** *adv*
graduar {3} *v* **1** : to regulate, to adjust **2** CALIBRAR : to calibrate, to gauge — **graduarse** *vr* : to graduate (from a school)
graffiti *or* **grafiti** *nmpl* : graffiti *pl*
gráfica *nf* → **gráfico[2]**
gráfico[1], -ca *adj* : graphic — **gráficamente** *adv*
gráfico[2] *nm* **1** : graph, chart **2** : graphic (for a computer, etc.) **3 gráfico de barras** : bar graph
grafismo *nm* : graphics *pl*

grafito *nm* : graphite
gragea *nf* **1** : coated pill or tablet **2**
 grageas *nfpl* : sprinkles, jimmies
grajo *nm* : rook (bird)
grama *nf* : grass
gramática *nf* : grammar
gramatical *adj* : grammatical — **gra-**
 maticalmente *adv*
gramo *nm* : gram
gran → **grande**
grana *nf* : scarlet, deep red
granada *nf* **1** : pomegranate **2** : grenade
 ⟨granada de mano : hand grenade⟩
granadero *nm* **1** : grenadier **2**
 granaderos *nmpl Mex* : riot squad
granadino, -na *adj & n* : Grenadian
granado, -da *adj* **1** DISTINGUIDO : distinguished **2** : choice, select
granate *nm* **1** : garnet **2** : deep red, maroon
grande *adj* (**gran** *before singular nouns*)
 1 : large, big ⟨un libro grande : a big
 book⟩ **2** ALTO : tall **3** NOTABLE : great
 ⟨un gran autor : a great writer⟩ **4** (*indicating intensity*) : great ⟨con gran
 placer : with great pleasure⟩ **5** : old,
 grown-up ⟨hijos grandes : grown chil-
 dren⟩
grandeza *nf* **1** MAGNITUD : greatness,
 size **2** : nobility **3** : generosity, graciousness **4** : grandeur, magnificence
grandilocuencia *nf* : grandiloquence —
 grandilocuente *adj*
grandiosidad *nf* : grandeur
grandioso, -sa *adj* **1** MAGNÍFICO
 : grand, magnificent **2** : grandiose
granel *adv* **1 a** ~ : galore, in great quan-
 tities **2 a** ~ : in bulk ⟨vender a granel
 : to sell in bulk⟩
granero *nm* : barn, granary
granito *nm* : granite
granizada *nf* : hailstorm
granizar {21} *v impers* : to hail
granizo *nm* : hail
granja *nf* : farm
granjear *vt* : to earn, to win —
 granjearse *vr* : to gain, to earn
granjero, -ra *n* : farmer
grano *nm* **1** PARTÍCULA : grain, particle
 ⟨un grano de arena : a grain of sand⟩
 2 : grain (of rice, etc.), bean (of coffee),
 seed **3** : grain (of wood or rock) **4** BAR-
 RO, ESPINILLA : pimple **5 ir al grano**
 : to get to the point
granuja *nmf* PILLUELO : rascal, urchin
granular[1] *vt* : to granulate — **granularse**
 vr : to break out in spots
granular[2] *adj* : granular, grainy
granza *nf* : chaff
grapa *nf* **1** : staple **2** : clamp
grapadora *nf* ENGRAPADORA : stapler
grapar *vt* ENGRAPAR : to staple
grasa *nf* **1** : grease **2** : fat **3** *Mex* : shoe
 polish
grasiento, -ta *adj* : greasy, oily
graso, -sa *adj* **1** : fatty **2** : greasy, oily
grasoso, -sa *adj* GRASIENTO : greasy,
 oily

gratificación *nf, pl* **-ciones 1** SATISFAC-
 CIÓN : gratification **2** : bonus **3** REC-
 OMPENSA : recompense, reward
gratificar {72} *vt* **1** SATISFACER : to satisfy, to gratify **2** RECOMPENSAR : to reward **3** : to give a bonus to
gratinado, -da *adj* : au gratin
gratis[1] *adv* GRATUITAMENTE : free, for
 free, gratis
gratis[2] *adj* GRATUITO : free, gratis
gratitud *nf* : gratitude
grato, -ta *adj* AGRADABLE, PLACEN-
 TERO : pleasant, agreeable — **grata-**
 mente *adv*
gratuitamente *adv* **1** : gratuitously **2**
 GRATIS : free, for free, gratis
gratuito, -ta *adj* **1** : gratuitous, unwarranted **2** GRATIS : free, gratis
grava *nf* : gravel
gravamen *nm, pl* **-vámenes 1** : burden,
 obligation **2** : (property) tax
gravar *vt* **1** : to burden, to encumber **2**
 : to levy (a tax)
grave *adj* **1** : grave, important **2** : serious, somber **3** : serious (of an illness)
gravedad *nf* **1** : gravity ⟨centro de
 gravedad : center of gravity⟩ **2** : seriousness, severity
gravemente *adv* : gravely, seriously
gravilla *nf* : (fine) gravel
gravitación *nf, pl* **-ciones** : gravitation
gravitacional *adj* : gravitational
gravitar *vi* **1** : to gravitate **2** ~ **sobre**
 : to rest on **3** ~ **sobre** : to loom over
gravoso, -sa *adj* **1** ONEROSO : burdensome, onerous **2** : costly
graznar *vi* : to caw, to honk, to quack,
 to squawk
graznido *nm* : cawing, honking, quack-
 ing, squawking
gregario, -ria *adj* : gregarious
gregoriano, -na *adj* : Gregorian
gremial *adj* SINDICAL : union, labor
gremio *nm* SINDICATO : union, guild
greña *nf* **1** : mat, tangle **2 greñas** *nfpl*
 MELENAS : shaggy hair, mop
greñudo, -da *n* HIPPIE, MELENUDO
 : longhair, hippie
grey *nf* : congregation, flock
griego[1]**, -ga** *adj & n* : Greek
griego[2] *nm* : Greek (language)
grieta *nf* : crack, crevice
grifo *nm* **1** : faucet ⟨agua del grifo : tap
 water⟩ **2** : griffin
grillete *nm* : shackle
grillo *nm* **1** : cricket **2 grillos** *nmpl* : fetters, shackles
grima *nf* **1** : disgust, uneasiness **2 dar-**
 le grima a alguien : to get on someone's nerves
gringo, -ga *adj & n* YANQUI : Yankee,
 gringo
gripa *nf Col, Mex* : flu
gripe *nf* : flu
gris *adj* **1** : gray **2** : overcast, cloudy
grisáceo, -cea *adj* : grayish
gritar *v* : to shout, to scream, to cry
gritería *nf* : shouting, clamor

grito *nm* : shout, scream, cry ⟨a grito pelado : at the top of one's voice⟩

groenlandés, -desa *adj & n* : Greenlander

grogui *adj fam* : dazed, groggy

grosella *nf* **1** : currant **2 grosella espinosa** : gooseberry

grosería *nf* **1** : insult, coarse language **2** : rudeness, discourtesy

grosero¹, -ra *adj* **1** : rude, fresh **2** : coarse, vulgar

grosero², -ra *n* : rude person

grosor *nm* : thickness

grosso *adj* **a grosso modo** : roughly, broadly, approximately

grotesco, -ca *adj* : grotesque, hideous

grúa *nf* **1** : crane (machine) **2** : tow truck

gruesa *nf* : gross

grueso¹, -sa *adj* **1** : thick, bulky **2** : heavy, big **3** : heavyset, stout

grueso² *nm* **1** : thickness **2** : main body, mass **3 en ~** : in bulk

grulla *nf* : crane (bird)

grumo *nm* : lump, glob

gruñido *nm* : growl, grunt

gruñir {38} *vi* **1** : to growl, to grunt **2** : to grumble

gruñón¹, -ñona *adj, mpl* **gruñones** *fam* : grumpy, crabby

gruñón², -ñona *n, mpl* **gruñones** *fam* : grumpy person, nag

grupa *nf* : rump, hindquarters *pl*

grupo *nm* : group

gruta *nf* : grotto, cave

guacal *nm Col, Mex, Ven* : crate

guacamayo *nm* : macaw

guacamole *or* **guacamol** *nm* : guacamole

guacamote *nm Mex* : yuca, cassava

guachinango → **huachinango**

guacho, -cha *adj* **1** *Arg, Col, Chile, Peru* : orphaned **2** *Chile, Peru* : odd, unmatched

guadaña *nf* : scythe

guagua *nf* **1** *Arg, Col, Chile, Peru* : baby **2** *Cuba, PRi* : bus

guaira *nf* **1** *CA* : traditional flute **2** *Peru* : smelting furnace

guajiro, -ra *n Cuba* : peasant

guajolote *nm Mex* : turkey

guanábana *nf* : guanabana, soursop (fruit)

guanaco *nm* : guanaco

guandú *nm CA, Car, Col* : pigeon pea

guango, -ga *adj Mex* **1** : loose-fitting, baggy **2** : slack, loose

guano *nm* : guano

guante *nm* **1** : glove ⟨guante de boxeo : boxing glove⟩ **2 arrojarle el guante (a alguien)** : to throw down the gauntlet (to someone)

guantelete *nm* : gauntlet

guapo, -pa *adj* **1** : handsome, good-looking, attractive **2** : elegant, smart **3** *fam* : bold, dashing

guapura *nf fam* : handsomeness, attractiveness, good looks *pl* ⟨¡qué guapura! : what a vision!⟩

guarache → **huarache**

guarachear *vi Cuba, PRi fam* : to go on a spree, to go out on the town

guaraní¹ *adj & nmf* : Guarani

guaraní² *nm* : Guarani (language of Paraguay)

guarda *nmf* **1** GUARDIÁN : security guard **2** : keeper, custodian

guardabarros *nms & pl* : fender, mudguard

guardabosque *nmf* : forest ranger, gamekeeper

guardacostas¹ *nmfs & pl* : coastguardsman

guardacostas² *nms & pl* : coast guard vessel

guardaespaldas *nmfs & pl* : bodyguard

guardafangos *nms & pl* : fender, mudguard

guardameta *nmf* ARQUERO, PORTERO : goalkeeper, goalie

guardapelo *nm* : locket

guardapolvo *nm* **1** : dustcover **2** : duster, housecoat

guardar *vt* **1** : to guard **2** : to maintain, to preserve **3** CONSERVAR : to put away **4** RESERVAR : to save **5** : to keep (a secret or promise) — **guardarse** *vr* **1** ~ **de** : to refrain from **2** ~ **de** : to guard against, to be careful not to

guardarropa *nm* **1** : cloakroom, checkroom **2** ARMARIO : closet, wardrobe

guardería *nf* : nursery, day-care center

guardia¹ *nf* **1** : guard, defense **2** : guard duty, watch **3 en ~** : on guard

guardia² *nmf* **1** : sentry, guardsman, guard **2** : police officer, policeman *m*, policewoman *f*

guardiamarina *nmf* : midshipman

guardián, -diana *n, mpl* **guardianes 1** GUARDA : security guard, watchman **2** : guardian, keeper **3 perro guardián** : watchdog

guarecer {53} *vt* : to shelter, to protect — **guarecerse** *vr* : to take shelter

guarida *nf* **1** : den, lair **2** : hideout

guarismo *nm* : figure, numeral

guarnecer {53} *vt* **1** : to adorn **2** : to garnish **3** : to garrison

guarnición *nf, pl* **-ciones 1** : garnish **2** : garrison **3** : decoration, trimming, setting (of a jewel)

guaro *nm CA* : liquor distilled from sugarcane

guasa *nf fam* **1** : joking, fooling around **2 de ~** : in jest, as a joke

guasón¹, -sona *adj, mpl* **guasones** *fam* : funny, witty

guasón², -sona *n, mpl* **guasones** *fam* : joker, clown

guatemalteco, -ca *adj & n* : Guatemalan

guau *interj* : wow!

guayaba *nf* : guava (fruit)

gubernamental *adj* : governmental

gubernativo, -va → **gubernamental**

gubernatura *nf Mex* : governing body

guepardo *nm* : cheetah

güero, -ra *adj Mex* : blond, fair

guerra *nf* **1** : war ⟨declarar la guerra : to declare war⟩ ⟨guerra sin cuartel : all-out war⟩ **2** : warfare **3** LUCHA : conflict, struggle
guerrear *vi* : to wage war
guerrero[1], **-ra** *adj* **1** : war, fighting **2** : warlike
guerrero[2], **-ra** *n* : warrior
guerrilla *nf* : guerrilla warfare
guerrillero, -ra *adj & n* : guerrilla
gueto *nm* : ghetto
guía[1] *nf* **1** : directory, guidebook **2** ORIENTACIÓN : guidance, direction ⟨la conciencia me sirve como guía : conscience is my guide⟩
guía[2] *nmf* : guide, leader ⟨guía de turismo : tour guide⟩
guiar {85} *vt* **1** : to guide, to lead **2** CONDUCIR : to manage — **guiarse** *vr* : to be guided by, to go by
guija *nf* : pebble
guijarro *nm* : pebble
guillotina *nf* : guillotine — **guillotinar** *vt*
guinda[1] *adj & nm Mex* : burgundy (color)
guinda[2] *nf* : morello (cherry)
guineo *nm Car* : banana
guinga *nf* : gingham
guiñada → **guiño**
guiñar *vi* : to wink
guiño *nm* : wink
guión *nm, pl* **guiones 1** : script, screenplay **2** : hyphen, dash **3** ESTANDARTE : standard, banner
guirnalda *nf* : garland
guisa *nf* **1** : manner, fashion **2 a guisa de** : like, by way of **3 de tal guisa** : in such a way

guisado ESTOFADO *nm* : stew
guisante *nm* : pea
guisar *vt* **1** ESTOFAR : to stew **2** *Spain* : to cook
guiso *nm* **1** : stew **2** : casserole
güisqui → **whisky**
guita *nf* : string, twine
guitarra *nf* : guitar
guitarrista *nmf* : guitarist
gula *nf* GLOTONERÍA : gluttony, greed
gusano *nm* **1** LOMBRIZ : worm, earthworm ⟨gusano de seda : silkworm⟩ **2** : caterpillar, maggot, grub
gustar *vt* **1** : to taste **2** : to like ⟨¿gustan pasar? : would you like to come in?⟩ — *vi* **1** : to be pleasing ⟨me gustan los dulces : I like sweets⟩ ⟨a María le gusta Carlos : Maria is attracted to Carlos⟩ ⟨no me gusta que me griten : I don't like to be yelled at⟩ **2** ~ **de** : to like, to enjoy ⟨no gusta de chismes : she doesn't like gossip⟩ **3 como guste** : as you wish, as you like
gustativo, -va *adj* : taste ⟨papilas gustativas : taste buds⟩
gusto *nm* **1** : flavor, taste **2** : taste, style **3** : pleasure, liking **4** : whim, fancy ⟨a gusto : at will⟩ **5 a** ~ : comfortable, at ease **6 al gusto** : to taste, as one likes **7 mucho gusto** : pleased to meet you
gustosamente *adv* : gladly
gustoso, -sa *adj* **1** : willing, glad ⟨nuestra empresa participará gustosa : our company will be pleased to participate⟩ **2** : zesty, tasty
gutural *adj* : guttural

H

h *nf* : eighth letter of the Spanish alphabet
ha → **haber**
haba *nf* : broad bean
habanero[1], **-ra** *adj* : of or from Havana
habanero[2], **-ra** *n* : native or resident of Havana
haber[1] {39} *v aux* **1** : have, has ⟨no ha llegado el envío : the shipment hasn't arrived⟩ **2** ~ **de** : must ⟨ha de ser tarde : it must be late⟩ — *v impers* **1 hay** : there is, there are ⟨hay dos mensajes : there are two messages⟩ ⟨¿qué hay de nuevo? : what's new?⟩ **2 hay que** : it is necessary ⟨hay que trabajar más rápido : you have to work faster⟩
haber[2] *nm* **1** : assets *pl* **2** : credit, credit side **3 haberes** *nmpl* : salary, income, remuneration
habichuela *nf* **1** : bean, kidney bean **2** : green bean
hábil *adj* **1** : able, skillful **2** : working ⟨días hábiles : working days⟩
habilidad *nf* CAPACIDAD : ability, skill
habilidoso, -sa *adj* : skillful, clever

habilitación *nf, pl* **-ciones 1** : authorization **2** : furnishing, equipping
habilitar *vt* **1** : to enable, to authorize, to empower **2** : to equip, to furnish
hábilmente *adv* : skillfully, expertly
habitable *adj* : habitable, inhabitable
habitación *nf, pl* **-ciones 1** CUARTO : room **2** DORMITORIO : bedroom **3** : habitation, occupancy
habitante *nmf* : inhabitant, resident
habitar *vt* : to inhabit — *vi* : to reside, to dwell
hábitat *nm, pl* **-tats** : habitat
hábito *nm* **1** : habit, custom **2** : habit (of a monk or nun)
habitual *adj* : habitual, customary — **habitualmente** *adv*
habituar {3} *vt* : to accustom, to habituate — **habituarse** *vr* ~ **a** : to get used to, to grow accustomed to
habla *nf* **1** : speech **2** : language, dialect **3 de** ~ : speaking ⟨de habla inglesa : English-speaking⟩
hablado, -da *adj* **1** : spoken **2 mal hablado** : foulmouthed

hablador[1], **-dora** *adj* : talkative
hablador[2], **-dora** *n* : chatterbox
habladuría *nf* 1 : rumor 2 **habladurías** *nfpl* : gossip, scandal
hablante *nmf* : speaker
hablar *vi* 1 : to speak, to talk ⟨hablar en broma : to be joking⟩ 2 ~ **de** : to mention, to talk about 3 **dar que hablar** : to make people talk — *vt* 1 : to speak (a language) 2 : to talk about, to discuss ⟨háblalo con tu jefe : discuss it with your boss⟩ — **hablarse** *vr* 1 : to speak to each other, to be on speaking terms 2 **se habla inglés (etc.)** : English (etc.) spoken
habrá, etc. → **haber**
hacedor, -dora *n* : creator, maker, doer
hacendado, -da *n* : landowner
hacer {40} *vt* 1 : to make 2 : to do, to perform 3 : to force, to oblige ⟨los hice esperar : I made them wait⟩ — *vi* : to act ⟨haces bien : you're doing the right thing⟩ — *v impers* 1 (*referring to weather*) ⟨hacer frío : to be cold⟩ ⟨hace viento : it's windy⟩ 2 **hace** : ago ⟨hace mucho tiempo : a long time ago, for a long time⟩ 3 **no le hace** : it doesn't matter, it makes no difference 4 **hacer falta** : to be necessary, to be needed — **hacerse** *vr* 1 : to become 2 : to pretend, to act, to play ⟨hacerse el tonto : to play dumb⟩ 3 : to seem ⟨el examen se me hizo difícil : the exam seemed difficult to me⟩ 4 : to get, to grow ⟨se hace tarde : it's growing late⟩
hacha *nf* : hatchet, ax
hachazo *nm* : blow, chop (with an ax)
hachís *nm* : hashish
hacia *prep* 1 : toward, towards ⟨hacia abajo : downward⟩ ⟨hacia adelante : forward⟩ 2 : near, around, about ⟨hacia las seis : about six o'clock⟩
hacienda *nf* 1 : estate, ranch, farm 2 : property 3 : livestock 4 **la Hacienda** : department of revenue, tax office
hacinar *vt* 1 : to pile up, to stack 2 : to overcrowd — **hacinarse** *vr* : to crowd together
hada *nf* : fairy
hado *nm* : destiny, fate
haga, etc. → **hacer**
haitiano, -na *adj & n* : Haitian
hala *interj Spain* 1 (*expressing encouragement or disbelief*) : come on! 2 (*expressing surprise*) : wow! 3 (*expressing protest*) : hey!
halagador[1], **-dora** *adj* : flattering
halagador[2], **-dora** *n* : flatterer
halagar {52} *vt* : to flatter, to compliment
halago *nm* : flattery, praise
halagüeño, -ña *adj* 1 : flattering 2 : encouraging, promising
halar *vt CA, Car* → **jalar**
halcón *nm, pl* **halcones** : hawk, falcon
halibut *nm, pl* **-buts** : halibut
hálito *nm* 1 : breath 2 : gentle breeze

hallar *vt* 1 ENCONTRAR : to find 2 DESCUBRIR : to discover, to find out — **hallarse** *vr* 1 : to be situated, to find oneself 2 : to feel ⟨no se halla bien : he doesn't feel comfortable, he feels out of place⟩
hallazgo *nm* 1 : discovery 2 : find ⟨¡es un verdadero hallazgo! : it's a real find!⟩
halo *nm* 1 : halo 2 : aura
halógeno *nm* : halogen
hamaca *nf* : hammock
hambre *nf* 1 : hunger 2 : starvation 3 **tener hambre** : to be hungry 4 **dar hambre** : to make hungry
hambriento, -ta *adj* : hungry, starving
hambruna *nf* : famine
hamburguesa *nf* : hamburger
hampa *nf* : criminal underworld
hampón, -pona *n, mpl* **hampones** : criminal, thug
hámster ['xamster] *nm, pl* **hámsters** : hamster
han → **haber**
handicap *or* **hándicap** ['handi‚kap] *nm, pl* **-caps** : handicap (in sports)
hangar *nm* : hangar
hará, etc. → **hacer**
haragán[1], **-gana** *adj, mpl* **-ganes** : lazy, idle
haragán[2], **-gana** *n, mpl* **-ganes** HOLGAZÁN : slacker, good-for-nothing
haraganear *vi* : to be lazy, to waste one's time
haraganería *nf* : laziness
harapiento, -ta *adj* : ragged, tattered
harapos *nmpl* ANDRAJOS : rags, tatters
hardware ['hard‚wer] *nm* : computer hardware
harén *nm, pl* **harenes** : harem
harina *nf* 1 : flour 2 **harina de maíz** : cornmeal
hartar *vt* 1 : to glut, to satiate 2 FASTIDIAR : to tire, to irritate, to annoy — **hartarse** *vr* : to be weary, to get fed up
harto[1] *adv* : most, extremely, very
harto[2], **-ta** *adj* 1 : full, satiated 2 : fed up
hartura *nf* 1 : surfeit 2 : abundance, plenty
has → **haber**
hasta[1] *adv* : even
hasta[2] *prep* 1 : until, up until ⟨hasta entonces : until then⟩ ⟨¡hasta luego! : see you later!⟩ 2 : as far as ⟨nos fuimos hasta Managua : we went all the way to Managua⟩ 3 : up to ⟨hasta cierto punto : up to a certain point⟩ 4 **hasta que** : until
hastiar {85} *vt* 1 : to make weary, to bore 2 : to disgust, to sicken — **hastiarse** *vr* ~ **de** : to get tired of
hastío *nm* 1 TEDIO : tedium 2 REPUGNANCIA : disgust
hato *nm* 1 : flock, herd 2 : bundle (of possessions)
hawaiano, -na *adj & n* : Hawaiian
hay → **haber**[1]

haya[1], etc. → **haber**
haya[2] *nf* : beech (tree and wood)
hayuco *nm* : beechnut
haz[1] → **hacer**
haz[2] *nm, pl* **haces 1** FARDO : bundle **2** : beam (of light)
haz[3] *nf, pl* **haces 1** : face **2 haz de la tierra** : surface of the earth
hazaña *nf* PROEZA : feat, exploit
hazmerreír *nm fam* : laughingstock
he[1] {39} → **haber**
he[2] *v impers* **he aquí** : here is, here are, behold
hebilla *nf* : buckle, clasp
hebra *nf* : strand, thread
hebreo[1], **-brea** *adj & n* : Hebrew
hebreo[2] *nm* : Hebrew (language)
hecatombe *nf* **1** MATANZA : massacre **2** : disaster
heces → **hez**
hechicería *nf* **1** BRUJERÍA : sorcery, witchcraft **2** : curse, spell
hechicero[1], **-ra** *adj* : bewitching, enchanting
hechicero[2], **-ra** *n* : sorcerer, sorceress *f*
hechizar {21} *vt* **1** EMBRUJAR : to bewitch **2** CAUTIVAR : to charm
hechizo *nm* **1** SORTILEGIO : spell, enchantment **2** ENCANTO : charm, fascination
hecho[1] *pp* → **hacer**
hecho[2], **-cha** *adj* **1** : made, done **2** : ready-to-wear **3** : complete, finished ⟨hecho y derecho : full-fledged⟩
hecho[3] *nm* **1** : fact **2** : event ⟨hechos históricos : historic events⟩ **3** : act, action **4 de ～** : in fact, in reality
hechura *nf* **1** : style **2** : craftsmanship, workmanship **3** : product, creation
hectárea *nf* : hectare
heder {56} *vi* : to stink, to reek
hediondez *nf, pl* **-deces** : stink, stench
hediondo, -da *adj* MALOLIENTE : foul-smelling, stinking
hedor *nm* : stench, stink
hegemonía *nf* **1** : dominance **2** : hegemony (in politics)
helada *nf* : frost (in meteorology)
heladería *nf* : ice-cream parlor, ice-cream stand
helado[1], **-da** *adj* **1** GÉLIDO : icy, freezing cold **2** CONGELADO : frozen
helado[2] *nm* : ice cream
heladora *nf* CONGELADOR : freezer
helar {55} *v* CONGELAR : to freeze — *v impers* : to produce frost ⟨anoche heló : there was frost last night⟩ — **helarse** *vr*
helecho *nm* : fern, bracken
hélice *nf* **1** : spiral, helix **2** : propeller
helicóptero *nm* : helicopter
helio *nm* : helium
helipuerto *nm* : heliport
hembra *adj & nf* : female
hemisférico, -ca *adj* : hemispheric, hemispherical
hemisferio *nm* : hemisphere
hemofilia *nf* : hemophilia

hemofílico, -ca *adj & n* : hemophiliac
hemoglobina *nf* : hemoglobin
hemorragia *nf* **1** : hemorrhage **2 hemorragia nasal** : nosebleed
hemorroides *nfpl* ALMORRANAS : hemorrhoids, piles
hemos → **haber**
henchido, -da *adj* : swollen, bloated
henchir {54} *vt* **1** : to stuff, to fill **2** : to swell, to swell up — **henchirse** *vr* **1** : to stuff oneself **2** LLENARSE : to fill up, to be full
hender {56} *vt* : to cleave, to split
hendidura *nf* : crack, crevice, fissure
henequén *nm, pl* **-quenes** : sisal hemp
heno *nm* : hay
hepatitis *nf* : hepatitis
heráldica *nf* : heraldry
heráldico, -ca *adj* : heraldic
heraldo *nm* : herald
herbario, -ria *adj* : herbal
herbicida *nm* : herbicide, weed killer
herbívoro[1], **-ra** *adj* : herbivorous
herbívoro[2] *nm* : herbivore
herbolario, -ria *n* : herbalist
hercio *nm* : hertz
hercúleo, -lea *adj* : herculean
heredar *vt* : to inherit
heredero, -ra *n* : heir, heiress *f*
hereditario, -ria *adj* : hereditary
hereje *nmf* : heretic
herejía *nf* : heresy
herencia *nf* **1** : inheritance **2** : heritage **3** : heredity
herético, -ca *adj* : heretical
herida *nf* : injury, wound
herido[1], **-da** *adj* **1** : injured, wounded **2** : hurt, offended
herido[2], **-da** *n* : injured person, casualty
herir {76} *vt* **1** : to injure, to wound **2** : to hurt, to offend
hermafrodita *nmf* : hermaphrodite
hermanar *vt* **1** : to unite, to bring together **2** : to match up, to twin (cities)
hermanastro, -tra *n* : half brother *m*, half sister *f*
hermandad *nf* **1** FRATERNIDAD : brotherhood ⟨hermandad de mujeres : sisterhood, sorority⟩ **2** : association
hermano, -na *n* : sibling, brother *m*, sister *f*
hermético, -ca *adj* : hermetic, watertight — **herméticamente** *adv*
hermoso, -sa *adj* BELLO : beautiful, lovely — **hermosamente** *adv*
hermosura *nf* BELLEZA : beauty, loveliness
hernia *nf* : hernia
héroe *nm* : hero
heroicidad *nf* : heroism, heroic deed
heroico, -ca *adj* : heroic — **heroicamente** *adv*
heroína *nf* **1** : heroine **2** : heroin
heroísmo *nm* : heroism
herpes *nms & pl* **1** : herpes **2** : shingles
herradura *nf* : horseshoe
herraje *nm* : ironwork

herramienta *nf* : tool
herrar {55} *vt* : to shoe (a horse)
herrería *nf* : blacksmith's shop
herrero, -ra *n* : blacksmith
herrumbre *nf* ORÍN : rust
herrumbroso, -sa *adj* OXIDADO : rusty
hertzio *nm* : hertz
hervidero *nm* **1** : mass, swarm **2** : hotbed (of crime, etc.)
hervidor *nm* : kettle
hervir {76} *vi* **1** BULLIR : to boil, to bubble **2 ~ de** : to teem with, to be swarming with — *vt* : to boil
hervor *nm* **1** : boiling **2** : fervor, ardor
heterogeneidad *nf* : heterogeneity
heterogéneo, -nea *adj* : heterogeneous
heterosexual *adj & nmf* : heterosexual
heterosexualidad *nf* : heterosexuality
hexágono *nm* : hexagon — **hexagonal** *adj*
hez *nf, pl* **heces 1** ESCORIA : scum, dregs *pl* **2** : sediment, lees *pl* **3 heces** *nfpl* : feces, excrement
hiato *nm* : hiatus
hibernar *vi* : to hibernate — **hibernación** *nf*
híbrido¹, -da *adj* : hybrid
híbrido² *nm* : hybrid
hicieron, etc. → **hacer**
hidalgo, -ga *n* : nobleman *m*, noblewoman *f*
hidrante *nm CA, Col* : hydrant
hidratar *vt* : to moisturize — **hidratante** *adj*
hidrato *nm* **1** : hydrate **2 hidrato de carbono** : carbohydrate
hidráulico, -ca *adj* : hydraulic
hidroavión *nm, pl* **-viones** : seaplane
hidrocarburo *nm* : hydrocarbon
hidroeléctrico, -ca *adj* : hydroelectric
hidrofobia *nf* RABIA : hydrophobia, rabies
hidrófugo, -ga *adj* : water-repellent
hidrógeno *nm* : hydrogen
hidroplano *nm* : hydroplane
hiede, etc. → **heder**
hiedra *nf* **1** : ivy **2 hiedra venenosa** : poison ivy
hiel *nf* **1** BILIS : bile **2** : bitterness
hiela, etc. → **helar**
hielo *nm* **1** : ice **2** : coldness, reserve ⟨romper el hielo : to break the ice⟩
hiena *nf* : hyena
hiende, etc. → **hender**
hierba *nf* **1** : herb **2** : grass **3 mala hierba** : weed
hierbabuena *nf* : mint, spearmint
hiere, etc. → **herir**
hierra, etc. → **herrar**
hierro *nm* **1** : iron ⟨hierro fundido : cast iron⟩ **2** : branding iron
hierve, etc. → **hervir**
hígado *nm* : liver
higiene *nf* : hygiene
higiénico, -ca *adj* : hygienic — **higiénicamente** *adv*
higienista *nmf* : hygienist
higo *nm* **1** : fig **2 higo chumbo** : prickly pear (fruit)

higrómetro *nm* : hygrometer
higuera *nf* : fig tree
hijastro, -tra *n* : stepson *m*, stepdaughter *f*
hijo, -ja *n* **1** : son *m*, daughter *f* **2 hijos** *nmpl* : children, offspring
híjole *interj Mex* : wow!, good grief!
hilacha *nf* **1** : ravel, loose thread **2 mostrar la hilacha** : to show one's true colors
hilado *nm* **1** : spinning **2** HILO : yarn, thread
hilar *vt* **1** : to spin (thread) **2** : to consider, to string together (ideas) — *vi* **1** : to spin **2 hilar delgado** : to split hairs
hilarante *adj* **1** : humorous, hilarious **2 gas hilarante** : laughing gas
hilaridad *nf* : hilarity
hilera *nf* FILA : file, row, line
hilo *nm* **1** : thread ⟨colgar de un hilo : to hang by a thread⟩ ⟨hilo dental : dental floss⟩ **2** LINO : linen **3** : (electric) wire **4** : theme, thread (of a discourse) **5** : trickle (of water, etc.)
hilvanar *vt* **1** : to baste, to tack **2** : to piece together
himnario *nm* : hymnal
himno *nm* **1** : hymn **2 himno nacional** : national anthem
hincapié *nm* **hacer hincapié en** : to emphasize, to stress
hincar {72} *vt* CLAVAR : to stick, to plunge — **hincarse** *vr* **hincarse de rodillas** : to kneel down, to fall to one's knees
hinchado, -da *adj* **1** : swollen, inflated **2** : pompous, overblown
hinchar *vt* **1** INFLAR : to inflate **2** : to exaggerate — **hincharse** *vr* **1** : to swell up **2** : to become conceited, to swell with pride
hinchazón *nf, pl* **-zones** : swelling
hinche, etc. → **henchir**
hindi *nm* : Hindi
hindú *adj & nmf* : Hindu
hinduismo *nm* : Hinduism
hiniesta *nf* : broom (plant)
hinojo *nm* **1** : fennel **2 de hinojos** : on bended knee
hinque, etc. → **hincar**
hipar *vi* : to hiccup
hiperactividad *nf* : hyperactivity
hiperactivo, -va *adj* : hyperactive, overactive
hipérbole *nf* : hyperbole
hiperbólico, -ca *adj* : hyperbolic, exaggerated
hipercrítico, -ca *adj* : hypercritical
hipermetropía *nf* : farsightedness
hipersensibilidad *nf* : hypersensitivity
hipersensible *adj* : hypersensitive
hipertensión *nf, pl* **-siones** : hypertension, high blood pressure
hip-hop [ˌxipˈxop] *nm* : hip-hop (music)
hípico, -ca *adj* : equestrian ⟨concurso hípico : horse show⟩
hipil → **huipil**
hipnosis *nfs & pl* : hypnosis

hipnótico, -ca *adj* : hypnotic
hipnotismo *nm* : hypnotism
hipnotizador[1], **-dora** *adj* **1** : hypnotic **2** : spellbinding, mesmerizing
hipnotizador[2], **-dora** *n* : hypnotist
hipnotizar {21} *vt* : to hypnotize
hipo *nm* : hiccup, hiccups *pl*
hipocampo *nm* : sea horse
hipocondría *nf* : hypochondria
hipocondríaco, -ca *adj & n* : hypochondriac
hipocresía *nf* : hypocrisy
hipócrita[1] *adj* : hypocritical — **hipócritamente** *adv*
hipócrita[2] *nmf* : hypocrite
hipodérmico, -ca *adj* **aguja hipodérmica** : hypodermic needle
hipódromo *nm* : racetrack
hipopótamo *nm* : hippopotamus
hipoteca *nf* : mortgage
hipotecar {72} *vt* **1** : to mortgage **2** : to compromise, to jeopardize
hipotecario, -ria *adj* : mortgage
hipotensión *nf* : low blood pressure
hipotenusa *nf* : hypotenuse
hipótesis *nfs & pl* : hypothesis
hipotético, -ca *adj* : hypothetical — **hipotéticamente** *adv*
hippie *or* **hippy** ['hipi] *nmf, pl* **hippies** [-pis] : hippie
hiriente *adj* : hurtful, offensive
hirió, etc. → herir
hirsuto, -ta *adj* **1** : hirsute, hairy **2** : bristly, wiry
hirviente *adj* : boiling
hirvió, etc. → hervir
hisopo *nm* **1** : hyssop **2** : cotton swab
hispánico, -ca *adj & n* : Hispanic
hispano[1], **-na** *adj* : Hispanic ⟨de habla hispana : Spanish-speaking⟩
hispano[2], **-na** *n* : Hispanic (person)
hispanoamericano[1], **-na** *adj* LATINOAMERICANO : Latin-American
hispanoamericano[2], **-na** *n* LATINOAMERICANO : Latin American
hispanohablante[1] *adj* : Spanish-speaking
hispanohablante[2] *nmf* : Spanish speaker
histerectomía *nf* : hysterectomy
histeria *nf* **1** : hysteria **2** : hysterics
histérico, -ca *adj* : hysterical — **histéricamente** *adv*
histerismo *nm* **1** : hysteria **2** : hysterics
historia *nf* **1** : history **2** NARRACIÓN, RELATO : story
historiador, -dora *n* : historian
historial *nm* **1** : record, document **2** CURRÍCULUM : résumé, curriculum vitae
histórico, -ca *adj* **1** : historical **2** : historic, important — **históricamente** *adv*
historieta *nf* : comic strip
histrionismo *nm* : histrionics, acting
hit ['hit] *nm, pl* **hits 1** ÉXITO : hit, popular song **2** : hit (in baseball)
hito *nm* : milestone, landmark

hizo → hacer
hobby ['hɔbi] *nm, pl* **hobbies** [-bis] : hobby
hocico *nm* : snout, muzzle
hockey ['hɔke, -ki] *nm* : hockey
hogar *nm* **1** : home **2** : hearth, fireplace
hogareño, -ña *adj* **1** : home-loving **2** : domestic, homelike
hogaza *nf* : large loaf (of bread)
hoguera *nf* **1** FOGATA : bonfire **2 morir en la hoguera** : to burn at the stake
hoja *nf* **1** : leaf, petal, blade (of grass) **2** : sheet (of paper), page (of a book) ⟨hoja de cálculo : spreadsheet⟩ **3** FORMULARIO : form ⟨hoja de pedido : order form⟩ **4** : blade (of a knife) ⟨hoja de afeitar : razor blade⟩
hojalata *nf* : tinplate
hojaldre *nm* : puff pastry
hojarasca *nf* : fallen leaves *pl*
hojear *vt* : to leaf through (a book or magazine)
hojuela *nf* **1** : leaflet, young leaf **2** : flake
hola *interj* : hello!, hi!
holandés[1], **-desa** *adj, mpl* **-deses** : Dutch
holandés[2], **-desa** *n, mpl* **-deses** : Dutch person, Dutchman *m*, Dutchwoman *f* ⟨los holandeses : the Dutch⟩
holandés[3] *nm* : Dutch (language)
holgadamente *adv* : comfortably, easily ⟨vivir holgadamente : to be well-off⟩
holgado, -da *adj* **1** : loose, baggy **2** : at ease, comfortable
holganza *nf* : leisure, idleness
holgazán[1], **-zana** *adj, mpl* **-zanes** : lazy
holgazán[2], **-zana** *n, mpl* **-zanes** HARAGÁN : slacker, idler
holgazanear *vi* HARAGANEAR : to laze around, to loaf
holgazanería *nf* PEREZA : idleness, laziness
holgura *nf* **1** : looseness **2** COMODIDAD : comfort, ease
holístico, -ca *adj* : holistic
hollar {19} *vt* : to tread on, to trample
hollín *nm, pl* **hollines** TIZNE : soot
holocausto *nm* : holocaust
holograma *nm* : hologram
hombre *nm* **1** : man ⟨el hombre : man, mankind⟩ **2 hombre de estado** : statesman **3 hombre de negocios** : businessman **4 hombre lobo** : werewolf
hombrera *nf* **1** : shoulder pad **2** : epaulet
hombría *nf* : manliness
hombro *nm* : shoulder ⟨encogerse de hombros : to shrug one's shoulders⟩
hombruno, -na *adj* : mannish
homenaje *nm* : homage, tribute ⟨rendir homenaje a : to pay tribute to⟩
homenajear *vt* : to pay homage to, to honor
homeopatía *nf* : homeopathy
homicida[1] *adj* : homicidal, murderous
homicida[2] *nmf* ASESINO : murderer
homicidio *nm* ASESINATO : homicide, murder

homilía *nf* : homily, sermon
homófono *nm* : homophone
homogeneidad *nf* : homogeneity
homogeneización *nf* : homogenization
homogeneizar {21} *vt* : to homogenize
homogéneo, -nea *adj* : homogeneous
homógrafo *nm* : homograph
homologación *nf, pl* **-ciones** 1 : sanctioning, approval 2 : parity
homologar {52} *vt* 1 : to sanction 2 : to bring into line
homólogo[1], **-ga** *adj* : homologous, equivalent
homólogo[2], **-ga** *n* : counterpart
homónimo[1], **-ma** *n* TOCAYO : namesake
homónimo[2] *nm* : homonym
homosexual *adj & nmf* : homosexual
homosexualidad *nf* : homosexuality
honda *nf* : sling
hondo[1] *adv* : deeply
hondo[2], **-da** *adj* PROFUNDO : deep ⟨en lo más hondo de : in the depths of⟩ — **hondamente** *adv*
hondonada *nf* 1 : hollow, depression 2 : ravine, gorge
hondura *nf* : depth
hondureño, -ña *adj & n* : Honduran
honestidad *nf* 1 : decency, modesty 2 : honesty, uprightness
honesto, -ta *adj* 1 : decent, virtuous 2 : honest, honorable — **honestamente** *adv*
hongo *nm* 1 : fungus 2 : mushroom
honor *nm* 1 : honor ⟨en honor a la verdad : to be quite honest⟩ 2 **honores** *nmpl* : honors ⟨hacer los honores : to do the honors⟩
honorable *adj* HONROSO : honorable — **honorablemente** *adv*
honorario, -ria *adj* : honorary
honorarios *nmpl* : payment, fees (for professional services)
honorífico, -ca *adj* : honorary ⟨mención honorífica : honorable mention⟩
honra *nf* 1 : dignity, self-respect ⟨tener a mucha honra : to take great pride in⟩ 2 : good name, reputation
honradamente *adv* : honestly, decently
honradez *nf, pl* **-deces** : honesty, integrity, probity
honrado, -da *adj* 1 HONESTO : honest, upright 2 : honored
honrar *vt* 1 : to honor 2 : to be a credit to ⟨su generosidad lo honra : his generosity does him credit⟩
honroso, -sa *adj* HONORABLE : honorable — **honrosamente** *adv*
hora *nf* 1 : hour ⟨media hora : half an hour⟩ ⟨a la última hora : at the last minute⟩ ⟨a la hora en punto : on the dot⟩ ⟨horas de oficina : office hours⟩ 2 : time ⟨¿qué hora es? : what time is it?⟩ 3 CITA : appointment
horario *nm* : schedule, timetable, hours *pl* ⟨horario de visita : visiting hours⟩
horca *nf* 1 : gallows *pl* 2 : pitchfork
horcajadas *nfpl* **a ~** : astride, astraddle
horcón *nm, pl* **horcones** : wooden post, prop

horda *nf* : horde
horizontal *adj* : horizontal — **horizontalmente** *adv*
horizonte *nm* : horizon, skyline
horma *nf* 1 : shoe tree 2 : shoemaker's last
hormiga *nf* : ant
hormigón *nm, pl* **-gones** CONCRETO : concrete
hormigonera *nf* : cement mixer
hormigueo *nm* 1 : tingling, pins and needles *pl* 2 : uneasiness
hormiguero *nm* 1 : anthill 2 : swarm (of people)
hormona *nf* : hormone — **hormonal** *adj*
hornacina *nf* : niche, recess
hornada *nf* : batch
hornear *vt* : to bake
hornilla *nf* : burner (of a stove)
horno *nm* 1 : oven ⟨horno crematorio : crematorium⟩ ⟨horno de microondas : microwave oven⟩ 2 : kiln
horóscopo *nm* : horoscope
horqueta *nf* 1 : fork (in a river or road) 2 : crotch (in a tree) 3 : small pitchfork
horquilla *nf* 1 : hairpin, bobby pin 2 : pitchfork
horrendo, -da *adj* : horrendous, horrible
horrible *adj* : horrible, dreadful — **horriblemente** *adv*
horripilante *adj* : horrifying, hair-raising
horripilar *vt* : to horrify, to terrify
horror *nm* : horror, dread
horrorizado, -da *adj* : terrified
horrorizar {21} *vt* : to horrify, to terrify — **horrorizarse** *vr*
horroroso, -sa *adj* 1 : horrifying, terrifying 2 : dreadful, bad
hortaliza *nf* 1 : vegetable 2 **hortalizas** *nfpl* : garden produce
hortera *adj Spain fam* : tacky, gaudy
hortícola *adj* : horticultural
horticultor, -ra *n* : horticulturist
horticultura *nf* : horticulture
hosco, -ca *adj* : sullen, gloomy
hospedaje *nm* : lodging, accommodations *pl*
hospedar *vt* : to provide with lodging, to put up — **hospedarse** *vr* : to stay, to lodge
hospicio *nm* : orphanage
hospital *nm* : hospital
hospitalario, -ria *adj* : hospitable
hospitalidad *nf* : hospitality
hospitalización *nf, pl* **-ciones** : hospitalization
hospitalizar {21} *vt* : to hospitalize — **hospitalizarse** *vr*
hostería *nf* POSADA : inn
hostia *nf* : host, Eucharist
hostigamiento *nm* : harassment
hostigar {52} *vt* ACOSAR, ASEDIAR : to harass, to pester
hostil *adj* : hostile

hostilidad *nf* **1** : hostility, antagonism **2 hostilidades** *nfpl* : (military) hostilities
hostilizar {21} *vt* : to harass
hotel *nm* : hotel
hotelero¹, -ra *adj* : hotel ⟨la industria hotelera : the hotel business⟩
hotelero², -ra *n* : hotel manager, hotelier
hoy *adv* **1** : today ⟨hoy mismo : right now, this very day⟩ **2** : now, nowadays ⟨de hoy en adelante : from now on⟩
hoyo *nm* AGUJERO : hole
hoyuelo *nm* : dimple
hoz *nf, pl* **hoces** : sickle
hozar {21} *vi* : to root (of a pig)
huachinango *nm Mex* : red snapper
huarache *nm* : huarache sandal
hubo, etc. → **haber**
hueco¹, -ca *adj* **1** : hollow, empty **2** : soft, spongy **3** : hollow-sounding, resonant **4** : proud, conceited **5** : superficial
hueco² *nm* **1** : hole, hollow, cavity **2** : gap, space **3** : recess, alcove
huele, etc. → **oler**
huelga *nf* **1** PARO : strike **2 hacer huelga** : to strike, to go on strike
huelguista *nmf* : striker
huella¹, etc. → **hollar**
huella² *nf* **1** : footprint ⟨seguir las huellas de alguien : to follow in someone's footsteps⟩ **2** : mark, impact ⟨dejar huella : to leave one's mark⟩ ⟨sin dejar huella : without a trace⟩ **3 huella digital** *or* **huella dactilar** : fingerprint
huérfano¹, -na *adj* **1** : orphan, orphaned **2** : defenseless **3** ~ **de** : lacking, devoid of
huérfano², -na *n* : orphan
huerta *nf* **1** : large vegetable garden, truck farm **2** : orchard **3** : irrigated land
huerto *nm* **1** : vegetable garden **2** : orchard
hueso *nm* **1** : bone **2** : pit, stone (of a fruit)
huésped¹, -peda *n* INVITADO : guest
huésped² *nm* : host ⟨organismo huésped : host organism⟩
huestes *nfpl* **1** : followers **2** : troops, army
huesudo, -da *adj* : bony
hueva *nf* : roe, spawn
huevo *nm* : egg ⟨huevos revueltos : scrambled eggs⟩
huida *nf* : flight, escape
huidizo, -za *adj* **1** ESCURRIDIZO : elusive, slippery **2** : shy, evasive
huipil *nm CA, Mex* : traditional sleeveless blouse or dress
huir {41} *vi* **1** ESCAPAR : to escape, to flee **2** ~ **de** : to avoid
huiro *nm Chile, Peru* : seaweed
huizache *nm* : huisache, acacia
hule *nm* **1** : oilcloth, oilskin **2** *Mex* : rubber **3 hule espuma** *Mex* : foam rubber
humanidad *nf* **1** : humanity, mankind

2 : humaneness **3 humanidades** *nfpl* : humanities *pl*
humanismo *nm* : humanism
humanista *nmf* : humanist
humanístico, -ca *adj* : humanistic
humanitario, -ria *adj & n* : humanitarian
humano¹, -na *adj* **1** : human **2** BENÉVOLO : humane, benevolent — **humanamente** *adv*
humano² *nm* : human being, human
humareda *nf* : cloud of smoke
humeante *adj* **1** : smoky **2** : smoking, steaming
humear *vi* **1** : to smoke **2** : to steam
humectante¹ *adj* : moisturizing
humectante² *nm* : moisturizer
humedad *nf* **1** : humidity **2** : dampness, moistness
humedecer {53} *vt* **1** : to humidify **2** : to moisten, to dampen
húmedo, -da *adj* **1** : humid **2** : moist, damp
humidificador *nm* : humidifier
humidificar {72} *vt* : to humidify
humildad *nf* **1** : humility **2** : lowliness
humilde *adj* **1** : humble **2** : lowly ⟨gente humilde : poor people⟩
humildemente *adv* : meekly, humbly
humillación *nf, pl* **-ciones** : humiliation
humillante *adj* : humiliating
humillar *vt* : to humiliate — **humillarse** *vr* : to humble oneself ⟨humillarse a hacer algo : to stoop to doing something⟩
humo *nm* **1** : smoke, steam, fumes **2 humos** *nmpl* : airs *pl*, conceit
humor *nm* **1** : humor **2** : mood, temper ⟨está de buen humor : she's in a good mood⟩
humorada *nf* **1** BROMA : joke, witticism **2** : whim, caprice
humorismo *nm* : humor, wit
humorista *nmf* : humorist, comedian, comedienne *f*
humorístico, -ca *adj* : humorous — **humorísticamente** *adv*
humoso, -sa *adj* : smoky, steamy
humus *nm* : humus
hundido, -da *adj* **1** : sunken **2** : depressed
hundimiento *nm* **1** : sinking **2** : collapse, ruin
hundir *vt* **1** : to sink **2** : to destroy, to ruin — **hundirse** *vr* **1** : to sink down **2** : to cave in **3** : to break down, to go to pieces
húngaro¹, -ra *adj & n* : Hungarian
húngaro² *nm* : Hungarian (language)
huracán *nm, pl* **-canes** : hurricane
huraño, -ña *adj* **1** : unsociable, aloof **2** : timid, skittish (of an animal)
hurgar {52} *vt* : to poke, to jab, to rake (a fire) — *vi* ~ **en** : to rummage in, to poke through
hurgue, etc. → **hurgar**
hurón *nm, pl* **hurones** : ferret
huronear *vi* : to pry, to snoop

hurra *interj* : hurrah!, hooray!
hurtadillas *nfpl* **a ~** : stealthily, on the sly
hurtar *vt* ROBAR : to steal
hurto *nm* **1** : theft, robbery **2** : stolen property, loot
husmear *vt* **1** : to follow the scent of, to track **2** : to sniff out, to pry into — *vi* **1** : to pry, to snoop **2** : to sniff around (of an animal)
huso *nm* **1** : spindle **2 huso horario** : time zone
huy *interj* : ow!, ouch!
huye, etc. → **huir**

I

i *nf* : ninth letter of the Spanish alphabet
iba, etc. → **ir**
ibérico, -ca *adj* : Iberian
ibero, -ra *or* **íbero, -ra** *adj & n* : Iberian
iberoamericano, -na *adj* HISPANO-AMERICANO, LATINOAMERICANO : Latin-American
ibis *nfs & pl* : ibis
ice, etc. → **izar**
iceberg *nm, pl* **icebergs** : iceberg
icono *nm* : icon
iconoclasia *nf* : iconoclasm
iconoclasta *nmf* : iconoclast
ictericia *nf* : jaundice
ida *nf* **1** : going, departure **2 ida y vuelta** : round-trip **3 idas y venidas** : comings and goings
idea *nf* **1** : idea, notion **2** : opinion, belief **3** PROPÓSITO : intention
ideal *adj & nm* : ideal — **idealmente** *adv*
idealismo *nm* : idealism
idealista¹ *adj* : idealistic
idealista² *nmf* : idealist
idealizar {21} *vt* : to idealize — **idealización** *nf*
idear *vt* : to devise, to think up
ideario *nm* : ideology
ídem *nm* : idem, the same, ditto
idéntico, -ca *adj* : identical, alike — **idénticamente** *adv*
identidad *nf* : identity
identificable *adj* : identifiable
identificación *nf, pl* **-ciones 1** : identification, identifying **2** : identification document, ID
identificar {72} *vt* : to identify — **identificarse** *vr* **1** : to identify oneself **2 ~ con** : to identify with
ideología *nf* : ideology — **ideológicamente** *adv*
ideológico, -ca *adj* : ideological
idílico, -ca *adj* : idyllic
idilio *nm* : idyll
idioma *nm* : language ⟨el idioma inglés : the English language⟩
idiomático, -ca *adj* : idiomatic — **idiomáticamente** *adv*
idiosincrasia *nf* : idiosyncrasy
idiosincrásico, -ca *adj* : idiosyncratic
idiota¹ *adj* : idiotic, stupid, foolish
idiota² *nmf* : idiot, foolish person
idiotez *nf, pl* **-teces 1** : idiocy **2** : idiotic act or remark ⟨¡no digas idioteces! : don't talk nonsense!⟩
ido *pp* → **ir**

idólatra¹ *adj* : idolatrous
idólatra² *nmf* : idolater
idolatrar *vt* : to idolize
idolatría *nf* : idolatry
ídolo *nm* : idol
idoneidad *nf* : suitability
idóneo, -nea *adj* ADECUADO : suitable, fitting
iglesia *nf* : church
iglú *nm* : igloo
ignición *nf, pl* **-ciones** : ignition
ignífugo, -ga *adj* : fire-resistant, fireproof
ignominia *nf* : ignominy, disgrace
ignominioso, -sa *adj* : ignominious, shameful
ignorancia *nf* : ignorance
ignorante¹ *adj* : ignorant
ignorante² *nmf* : ignorant person, ignoramus
ignorar *vt* **1** : to ignore **2** DESCONOCER : to be unaware of ⟨lo ignoramos por absoluto : we have no idea⟩
ignoto, -ta *adj* : unknown
igual¹ *adv* **1** : in the same way **2 por ~** : equally
igual² *adj* **1** : equal **2** IDÉNTICO : the same, alike **3** : even, smooth **4** SEMEJANTE : similar **5** CONSTANTE : constant
igual³ *nmf* : equal, peer
igualación *nf* **1** : equalization **2** : leveling, smoothing **3** : equating (in mathematics)
igualado, -da *adj* **1** : even (of a score) **2** : level **3** *Mex* : disrespectful
igualar *vt* **1** : to equalize **2** : to tie ⟨igualar el marcador : to even the score⟩
igualdad *nf* **1** : equality **2** UNIFORMIDAD : evenness, uniformity
igualmente *adv* **1** : equally **2** ASIMISMO : likewise
iguana *nf* : iguana
ijada *nf* : flank, loin, side
ijar *nm* → **ijada**
ilegal¹ *adj* : illegal, unlawful — **ilegalmente** *adv*
ilegal² *nmf* *CA, Mex* : illegal alien
ilegalidad *nf* : illegality, unlawfulness
ilegibilidad *nf* : illegibility
ilegible *adj* : illegible — **ilegiblemente** *adv*
ilegitimidad *nf* : illegitimacy
ilegítimo, -ma *adj* : illegitimate, unlawful

ileso, -sa *adj* : uninjured, unharmed

ilícito, -ta *adj* : illicit — **ilícitamente** *adv*

ilimitado, -da *adj* : unlimited

ilógico, -ca *adj* : illogical — **ilógicamente** *adv*

iluminación *nf, pl* **-ciones 1** : illumination **2** ALUMBRADO : lighting

iluminado, -da *adj* : illuminated, lighted

iluminar *vt* **1** : to illuminate, to light (up) **2** : to enlighten

ilusión *nf, pl* **-siones 1** : illusion, delusion **2** ESPERANZA : hope ⟨hacerse ilusiones : to get one's hopes up⟩

ilusionado, -da *adj* ESPERANZADO : hopeful, eager

ilusionar *vt* : to build up hope, to excite — **ilusionarse** *vr* : to get one's hopes up

iluso¹, -sa *adj* : naive, gullible

iluso², -sa *n* SOÑADOR : dreamer, visionary

ilusorio, -ria *adj* ENGAÑOSO : illusory, misleading

ilustración *nf, pl* **-ciones 1** : illustration **2** : erudition, learning ⟨la Ilustración : the Enlightenment⟩

ilustrado, -da *adj* **1** : illustrated **2** DOCTO : learned, erudite

ilustrador, -dora *n* : illustrator

ilustrar *vt* **1** : to illustrate **2** ACLARAR, CLARIFICAR : to explain

ilustrativo, -va *adj* : illustrative

ilustre *adj* : illustrious, eminent

imagen *nf, pl* **imágenes** : image, picture

imaginable *adj* : imaginable, conceivable

imaginación *nf, pl* **-ciones** : imagination

imaginar *vt* : to imagine — **imaginarse** *vr* **1** : to suppose, to imagine **2** : to picture

imaginario, -ria *adj* : imaginary

imaginativo, -va *adj* : imaginative — **imaginativamente** *adv*

imaginería *nf* **1** : imagery **2** : image making (in religion)

imán *nm, pl* **imanes** : magnet

imantar *vt* : to magnetize

imbatible *adj* : unbeatable

imbécil¹ *adj* : stupid, idiotic

imbécil² *nmf* **1** : imbecile **2** *fam* : idiot, dope

imborrable *adj* : indelible

imbuir {41} *vt* : to imbue — **imbuirse** *vr*

imitación *nf, pl* **-ciones 1** : imitation **2** : mimicry, impersonation

imitador¹, -dora *adj* : imitative

imitador², -dora *n* **1** : imitator **2** : mimic

imitar *vt* **1** : to imitate, to copy **2** : to mimic, to impersonate

imitativo, -va *adj* → **imitador¹**

impaciencia *nf* : impatience

impacientar *vt* : to make impatient, to exasperate — **impacientarse** *vr*

impaciente *adj* : impatient — **impacientemente** *adv*

impactado, -da *adj* : shocked, stunned

impactante *adj* **1** : shocking **2** : impressive, powerful

impactar *vt* **1** GOLPEAR : to hit **2** IMPRESIONAR : to impact, to affect — **impactarse** *vr*

impacto *nm* **1** : impact, effect **2** : shock, collision

impagable *adj* **1** : unpayable **2** : priceless

impago *nm* : nonpayment

impalpable *adj* INTANGIBLE : impalpable, intangible

impar¹ *adj* : odd ⟨números impares : odd numbers⟩

impar² *nm* : odd number

imparable *adj* : unstoppable

imparcial *adj* : impartial — **imparcialmente** *adv*

imparcialidad *nf* : impartiality

impartir *vt* : to impart, to give

impasible *adj* : impassive, unmoved — **impasiblemente** *adv*

impasse *nm* : impasse

impávido, -da *adj* : undaunted, unperturbed

impecable *adj* INTACHABLE : impeccable, faultless — **impecablemente** *adv*

impedido, -da *adj* : disabled, crippled

impedimento *nm* **1** : impediment, obstacle **2** : disability

impedir {54} *vt* **1** : to prevent, to block **2** : to impede, to hinder

impeler *vt* **1** : to drive, to propel **2** : to impel

impenetrable *adj* : impenetrable — **impenetrabilidad** *nf*

impenitente *adj* : unrepentant, impenitent

impensable *adj* : unthinkable

impensado, -da *adj* : unforeseen, unexpected

imperante *adj* : prevailing

imperar *vi* **1** : to reign, to rule **2** PREDOMINAR : to prevail

imperativo¹, -va *adj* : imperative

imperativo² *nm* : imperative

imperceptible *adj* : imperceptible — **imperceptiblemente** *adv*

imperdible *nm* *Spain* : safety pin

imperdonable *adj* : unpardonable, unforgivable

imperecedero, -ra *adj* **1** : imperishable **2** INMORTAL : immortal, everlasting

imperfección *nf, pl* **-ciones 1** : imperfection **2** DEFECTO : defect, flaw

imperfecto¹, -ta *adj* : imperfect, flawed

imperfecto² *nm* : imperfect tense

imperial *adj* : imperial

imperialismo *nm* : imperialism

imperialista *adj* & *nmf* : imperialist

impericia *nf* : lack of skill, incompetence

imperio *nm* : empire

imperioso, -sa *adj* **1** : imperious **2** : pressing, urgent — **imperiosamente** *adv*

impermeabilizante *adj* : water-repellent

impermeabilizar {21} *vt* : to waterproof

impermeable¹ *adj* **1** : impervious **2** : impermeable, waterproof

impermeable² *nm* : raincoat

impersonal *adj* : impersonal — **impersonalmente** *adv*
impertinencia *nf* INSOLENCIA : impertinence, insolence
impertinente *adj* **1** INSOLENTE : impertinent, insolent **2** INOPORTUNO : inappropriate, uncalled-for **3** IRRELEVANTE : irrelevant
imperturbable *adj* : imperturbable, impassive, stolid
ímpetu *nm* **1** : impetus, momentum **2** : vigor, energy **3** : force, violence
impetuoso, -sa *adj* : impetuous, impulsive — **impetuosamente** *adv*
impiedad *nf* : impiety
impío, -pía *adj* : impious, ungodly
implacable *adj* : implacable, relentless — **implacablemente** *adv*
implantación *nf, pl* **-ciones 1** : implantation **2** ESTABLECIMIENTO : establishment, introduction
implantado, -da *adj* : well-established
implantar *vt* **1** : to implant **2** ESTABLECER : to establish, to introduce — **implantarse** *vr*
implante *nm* : implant
implementar *vt* : to implement — **implementarse** *vr* — **implementación** *nf*
implemento *nm* : implement, tool
implicación *nf, pl* **-ciones** : implication
implicar {72} *vt* **1** ENREDAR, ENVOLVER : to involve, to implicate **2** : to imply
implícito, -ta *adj* : implied, implicit — **implícitamente** *adv*
implorar *vt* : to implore
implosión *nf, pl* **-siones** : implosion — **implosivo, -va** *adj*
implosionar *vi* : to implode
imponderable *adj & nm* : imponderable
imponente *adj* : imposing, impressive
imponer {60} *vt* **1** : to impose **2** : to confer — *vi* : to be impressive, to command respect — **imponerse** *vr* **1** : to take on (a duty) **2** : to assert oneself **3** : to prevail
imponible *adj* : taxable
impopular *adj* : unpopular — **impopularidad** *nf*
importación *nf, pl* **-ciones 1** : importation **2 importaciones** *nfpl* : imports
importado, -da *adj* : imported
importador[1], -dora *adj* : importing
importador[2], -dora *n* : importer
importancia *nf* : importance
importante *adj* : important — **importantemente** *adv*
importar *vi* : to matter, to be important ⟨no le importa lo que piensen : she doesn't care what they think⟩ — *vt* : to import
importe *nm* **1** : price, cost **2** : sum, amount
importunar *vt* : to bother, to inconvenience — *vi* : to be inconvenient
importuno, -na *adj* **1** : inopportune, inconvenient **2** : bothersome, annoying
imposibilidad *nf* : impossibility

imposibilitado, -da *adj* **1** : disabled, crippled **2 verse imposibilitado** : to be unable (to do something)
imposibilitar *vt* **1** : to make impossible **2** : to disable, to incapacitate — **imposibilitarse** *vr* : to become disabled
imposible *adj* : impossible
imposición *nf, pl* **-ciones 1** : imposition **2** EXIGENCIA : demand, requirement **3** : tax **4** : deposit
impositivo, -va *adj* : tax ⟨tasa impositiva : tax rate⟩
impostor, -tora *n* : impostor
impostura *nf* **1** : fraud, imposture **2** CALUMNIA : slander
impotencia *nf* **1** : impotence, powerlessness **2** : impotence (in medicine)
impotente *adj* **1** : powerless **2** : impotent
impracticable *adj* : impracticable
imprecisión *nf, pl* **-siones 1** : imprecision, vagueness **2** : inaccuracy
impreciso, -sa *adj* **1** : imprecise, vague **2** : inaccurate
impredecible *adj* : unpredictable
impregnar *vt* : to impregnate
imprenta *nf* **1** : printing **2** : printing shop, press
imprescindible *adj* : essential, indispensable
impresentable *adj* : unpresentable, unfit
impresión *nf, pl* **-siones 1** : print, printing **2** : impression, feeling
impresionable *adj* : impressionable
impresionante *adj* : impressive, incredible, amazing — **impresionantemente** *adv*
impresionar *vt* **1** : to impress, to strike **2** : to affect, to move — *vi* : to make an impression — **impresionarse** *vr* : to be affected, to be removed
impresionismo *nm* : impressionism
impresionista[1] *adj* : impressionist, impressionistic
impresionista[2] *nmf* : impressionist
impreso[1] *pp* → **imprimir**
impreso[2], -sa *adj* : printed
impreso[3] *nm* PUBLICACIÓN : printed matter, publication
impresor, -sora *n* : printer
impresora *nf* : (computer) printer
imprevisible *adj* : unforeseeable
imprevisión *nf, pl* **-siones** : lack of foresight, thoughtlessness
imprevisto[1], -ta *adj* : unexpected, unforeseen
imprevisto[2] *nm* : unexpected occurrence, contingency
imprimir {42} *vt* **1** : to print **2** : to imprint, to stamp, to impress
improbabilidad *nf* : improbability
improbable *adj* : improbable, unlikely
improcedente *adj* **1** : inadmissible **2** : inappropriate, improper
improductivo, -va *adj* : unproductive
improperio *nm* : affront, insult
impropiedad *nf* : impropriety

impropio, -pia *adj* **1** : improper, incorrect **2** INADECUADO : unsuitable, inappropriate

improvisación *nf, pl* **-ciones** : improvisation, ad-lib

improvisado, -da *adj* : improvised, ad-lib

improvisar *v* : to improvise, to ad-lib

improviso *adj* **de ~** : all of a sudden, unexpectedly

imprudencia *nf* INDISCRECIÓN : imprudence, indiscretion

imprudente *adj* INDISCRETO : imprudent, indiscreet — **imprudentemente** *adv*

impúdico, -ca *adj* : shameless, indecent

impuesto[1] *pp* → **imponer**

impuesto[2] *nm* : tax

impugnar *vt* : to challenge, to contest

impulsar *vt* : to propel, to drive

impulsividad *nf* : impulsiveness

impulsivo, -va *adj* : impulsive — **impulsivamente** *adv*

impulso *nm* **1** : drive, thrust **2** : impulse, urge

impune *adj* : unpunished

impunemente *adv* : with impunity

impunidad *nf* : impunity

impureza *nf* : impurity

impuro, -ra *adj* : impure

impuso, etc. → **imponer**

imputable *adj* ATRIBUIBLE : attributable

imputación *nf, pl* **-ciones** **1** : attribution, imputation **2** : accusation

imputar *vt* ATRIBUIR : to impute, to attribute

inacabable *adj* : endless

inacabado, -da *adj* INCONCLUSO : unfinished

inaccesibilidad *nf* : inaccessibility

inaccesible *adj* **1** : inaccessible **2** : unattainable

inacción *nf, pl* **-ciones** : inactivity, inaction

inaceptable *adj* : unacceptable

inactividad *nf* : inactivity, idleness

inactivo, -va *adj* : inactive, idle

inadaptado[1], **-da** *adj* : maladjusted

inadaptado[2], **-da** *n* : misfit

inadecuación *nf, pl* **-ciones** : inadequacy

inadecuado, -da *adj* **1** : inadequate **2** IMPROPIO : inappropriate — **inadecuadamente** *adv*

inadmisible *adj* **1** : inadmissible **2** : unacceptable

inadvertencia *nf* : oversight

inadvertidamente *adv* : inadvertently

inadvertido, -da *adj* **1** : unnoticed ⟨pasar inadvertido : to go unnoticed⟩ **2** DESPISTADO, DISTRAÍDO : inattentive, distracted

inagotable *adj* : inexhaustible

inaguantable *adj* INSOPORTABLE : insufferable, unbearable

inalámbrico, -ca *adj* : wireless, cordless

inalcanzable *adj* : unreachable, unattainable

inalienable *adj* : inalienable

inalterable *adj* **1** : unalterable, unchangeable **2** : impassive **3** : colorfast

inamovible *adj* : immovable, fixed

inanición *nf, pl* **-ciones** : starvation

inanimado, -da *adj* : inanimate

inapelable *adj* : indisputable

inapetencia *nf* : lack of appetite

inaplicable *adj* : inapplicable

inapreciable *adj* **1** : imperceptible, negligible **2** : invaluable

inapropiado, -da *adj* : inappropriate, unsuitable

inarticulado, -da *adj* : inarticulate, unintelligible — **inarticuladamente** *adv*

inasequible *adj* : unattainable, inaccessible

inasistencia *nf* AUSENCIA : absence

inatacable *adj* : unassailable, indisputable

inaudible *adj* : inaudible

inaudito, -ta *adj* : unheard-of, unprecedented

inauguración *nf, pl* **-ciones** : inauguration

inaugural *adj* : inaugural, opening

inaugurar *vt* **1** : to inaugurate **2** : to open

inca *adj & nmf* : Inca

incalculable *adj* : incalculable

incalificable *adj* : indescribable

incandescencia *nf* : incandescence — **incandescente** *adj*

incansable *adj* INFATIGABLE : tireless — **incansablemente** *adv*

incapacidad *nf* **1** : inability, incapacity **2** : disability, handicap

incapacitado, -da *adj* **1** : disqualified **2** : disabled, handicapped

incapacitar *vt* **1** : to incapacitate, to disable **2** : to disqualify

incapaz *adj, pl* **-paces** **1** : incapable, unable **2** : incompetent, inept

incautación *nf, pl* **-ciones** : seizure, confiscation

incautar *vt* CONFISCAR : to confiscate, to seize — **incautarse** *vr*

incauto, -ta *adj* : unwary, unsuspecting

incendiar *vt* **1** : to set fire to, to burn (down) — **incendiarse** *vr* : to catch fire

incendiario[1], **-ria** *adj* : incendiary, inflammatory

incendiario[2], **-ria** *n* : arsonist

incendio *nm* **1** : fire **2 incendio premeditado** : arson

incensario *nm* : censer

incentivar *vt* : to encourage, to stimulate

incentivo *nm* : incentive

incertidumbre *nf* : uncertainty, suspense

incesante *adj* : incessant — **incesantemente** *adv*

incesto *nm* : incest

incestuoso, -sa *adj* : incestuous

incidencia *nf* **1** : incident **2** : effect, impact **3 por ~** : by chance, accidentally

incidental *adj* : incidental
incidentalmente *adv* : by chance
incidente *nm* : incident, occurrence
incidir *vi* **1** ~ **en** : to fall into, to enter into ⟨incidimos en el mismo error : we fell into the same mistake⟩ **2** ~ **en** : to affect, to influence, to have a bearing on
incienso *nm* : incense
incierto, -ta *adj* **1** : uncertain **2** : untrue **3** : unsteady, insecure
incineración *nf, pl* **-ciones 1** : incineration **2** : cremation
incinerador *nm* : incinerator
incinerar *vt* **1** : to incinerate **2** : to cremate
incipiente *adj* : incipient
incisión *nf, pl* **-siones** : incision
incisivo¹, -va *adj* : incisive
incisivo² *nm* : incisor
inciso *nm* : digression, aside
incitación *nf, pl* **-ciones** : incitement
incitador¹, -dora *n* : instigator, agitator
incitador², -dora *adj* : provocative
incitante *adj* : provocative
incitar *vt* : to incite, to rouse
incivilizado, -da *adj* : uncivilized
inclemencia *nf* : inclemency, severity
inclemente *adj* : inclement
inclinación *nf, pl* **-ciones 1** PROPENSIÓN : inclination, tendency **2** : incline, slope
inclinado, -da *adj* **1** : sloping **2** : inclined, apt
inclinar *vt* : to tilt, to lean, to incline ⟨inclinar la cabeza : to bow one's head⟩ — **inclinarse** *vr* **1** : to lean, to lean over **2** ~ **a** : to be inclined to
incluir {41} *vt* : to include
inclusión *nf, pl* **-siones** : inclusion
inclusive *adv* : inclusively, up to and including
inclusivo, -va *adj* : inclusive
incluso *adv* **1** AUN : even, in fact ⟨es importante e incluso crucial : it is important and even crucial⟩ **2** : inclusively
incógnita *nf* **1** : unknown quantity (in mathematics) **2** : mystery
incógnito, -ta *adj* **1** : unknown **2 de incógnito** : incognito
incoherencia *nf* : incoherence
incoherente *adj* : incoherent — **incoherentemente** *adv*
incoloro, -ra *adj* : colorless
incombustible *adj* : fireproof
incomible *adj* : inedible
incomodar *vt* **1** : to make uncomfortable **2** : to inconvenience — **incomodarse** *vr* : to put oneself out, to take the trouble
incomodidad *nf* **1** : discomfort, awkwardness **2** MOLESTIA : inconvenience, bother
incómodo, -da *adj* **1** : uncomfortable, awkward **2** INCONVENIENTE : inconvenient
incomparable *adj* : incomparable

incompatibilidad *nf* : incompatibility
incompatible *adj* : incompatible, uncongenial
incompetencia *nf* : incompetence
incompetente *adj & nmf* : incompetent
incompleto, -ta *adj* : incomplete
incomprendido, -da *adj* : misunderstood
incomprensible *adj* : incomprehensible
incomprensión *nf, pl* **-siones** : lack of understanding, incomprehension
incomunicación *nf, pl* **-ciones** : lack of communication
incomunicado, -da *adj* **1** : cut off, isolated **2** : in solitary confinement
inconcebible *adj* : inconceivable, unthinkable — **inconcebiblemente** *adv*
inconcluso, -sa *adj* INACABADO : unfinished
incondicional *adj* : unconditional — **incondicionalmente** *adv*
inconexo, -xa *adj* : unconnected, disconnected
inconfesable *adj* : unspeakable, shameful
inconforme *adj & nmf* : nonconformist
inconformidad *nf* : nonconformity
inconformista *adj & nmf* : nonconformist
inconfundible *adj* : unmistakable, obvious — **inconfundiblemente** *adv*
incongruencia *nf* : incongruity
incongruente *adj* : incongruous
inconmensurable *adj* : vast, immeasurable
inconquistable *adj* : unyielding
inconsciencia *nf* **1** : unconsciousness, unawareness **2** : irresponsibility
inconsciente¹ *adj* **1** : unconscious, unaware **2** : reckless, needless — **inconscientemente** *adv*
inconsciente² *nm* **el inconsciente** : the unconscious
inconsecuente *adj* : inconsistent — **inconsecuencia** *nf*
inconsiderado, -da *adj* : inconsiderate, thoughtless
inconsistencia *nf* : inconsistency
inconsistente *adj* **1** : weak, flimsy **2** : inconsistent, weak (of an argument)
inconsolable *adj* : inconsolable — **inconsolablemente** *adv*
inconstancia *nf* : inconstancy
inconstante *adj* : inconstant, fickle, changeable
inconstitucional *adj* : unconstitutional
inconstitucionalidad *nf* : unconstitutionality
incontable *adj* INNUMERABLE : countless, innumerable
incontenible *adj* : uncontrollable, unstoppable
incontestable *adj* INCUESTIONABLE, INDISCUTIBLE : irrefutable, indisputable
incontinencia *nf* : incontinence — **incontinente** *adj*
incontrolable *adj* : uncontrollable
incontrolado, -da *adj* : uncontrolled, out of control

incontrovertible *adj* : indisputable
inconveniencia *nf* **1** : inconvenience, trouble **2** : unsuitability, inappropriateness **3** : tactless remark
inconveniente[1] *adj* **1** INCÓMODO : inconvenient **2** INAPROPIADO : improper, unsuitable
inconveniente[2] *nm* : obstacle, problem, snag ⟨no tengo inconveniente en hacerlo : I don't mind doing it⟩
incorporación *nf*, *pl* **-ciones** : incorporation
incorporar *vt* **1** : to incorporate **2** : to add, to include — **incorporarse** *vr* **1** : to sit up **2** ~ **a** : to join
incorpóreo, -rea *adj* : incorporeal, bodiless
incorrección *n*, *pl* **-ciones** : impropriety, improper word or action
incorrecto, -ta *adj* : incorrect — **incorrectamente** *adv*
incorregible *adj* : incorrigible — **incorregibilidad** *nf*
incorruptible *adj* : incorruptible
incredulidad *nf* : incredulity, skepticism
incrédulo[1] **, -la** *adj* : incredulous, skeptical
incrédulo[2] **, -la** *n* : skeptic
increíble *adj* : incredible, unbelievable — **increíblemente** *adv*
incrementar *vt* : to increase — **incrementarse** *vr*
incremento *nm* AUMENTO : increase
incriminar *vt* : to incriminate — **incriminación** *nf*
incriminatorio, -ria *adj* : incriminating, incriminatory
incruento, -ta *adj* : bloodless
incrustación *nf*, *pl* **-ciones** : inlay
incrustar *vt* **1** : to embed **2** : to inlay — **incrustarse** *vr* : to become embedded
incubación *nf*, *pl* **-ciones** : incubation
incubadora *nf* : incubator
incubar *v* : to incubate
incuestionable *adj* INCONTESTABLE, INDISCUTIBLE : unquestionable, indisputable — **incuestionablemente** *adv*
inculcar {72} *vt* : to inculcate, to instill
inculpar *vt* ACUSAR : to accuse, to charge
inculto, -ta *adj* **1** : uncultured, ignorant **2** : uncultivated, fallow
incumbencia *nf* : obligation, responsibility
incumbir *vi* (*3rd person only*) ~ **a** : to be incumbent upon, to be of concern to ⟨a mí no me incumbe : it's not my concern⟩
incumplido, -da *adj* : irresponsible, unreliable
incumplimiento *nm* **1** : nonfulfillment, neglect **2 incumplimiento de contrato** : breach of contract
incumplir *vt* : to fail to carry out, to break (a promise, a contract)
incurable *adj* : incurable
incurrir *vi* **1** ~ **en** : to incur ⟨incurrir en gastos : to incur expenses⟩ **2** ~ **en** : to fall into, to commit ⟨incurrió en un error : he made a mistake⟩

incursión *nf*, *pl* **-siones** : incursion, raid
incursionar *vi* **1** : to raid **2** ~ **en** : to go into, to enter ⟨el actor incursionó en el baile : the actor worked in dance for awhile⟩
indagación *nf*, *pl* **-ciones** : investigation, inquiry
indagar {52} *vt* : to inquire into, to investigate
indebido, -da *adj* : improper, undue — **indebidamente** *adv*
indecencia *nf* : indecency, obscenity
indecente *adj* : indecent, obscene
indecible *adj* : indescribable, inexpressible
indecisión *nf*, *pl* **-siones** : indecision
indeciso, -sa *adj* **1** IRRESOLUTO : indecisive **2** : undecided
indeclinable *adj* : unavoidable
indecoro *nm* : impropriety, indecorousness
indecoroso, -sa *adj* : indecorous, unseemly
indefectible *adj* : unfailing, sure
indefendible *adj* : indefensible
indefenso, -sa *adj* : defenseless, helpless
indefinible *adj* : indefinable
indefinido, -da *adj* **1** : undefined, vague **2** INDETERMINADO : indefinite — **indefinidamente** *adv*
indeleble *adj* : indelible — **indeleblemente** *adv*
indelicado, -da *adj* : indelicate, tactless
indemnización *nf*, *pl* **-ciones** **1** : indemnity **2 indemnización por despido** : severance pay
indemnizar {21} *vt* : to indemnify, to compensate
independencia *nf* : independence
independiente *adj* : independent — **independientemente** *adv*
independizarse {21} *vr* : to become independent, to gain independence
indescifrable *adj* : indecipherable
indescriptible *adj* : indescribable — **indescriptiblemente** *adv*
indeseable *adj* & *nmf* : undesirable
indestructible *adj* : indestructible
indeterminación *nf*, *pl* **-ciones** : indeterminacy
indeterminado, -da *adj* **1** INDEFINIDO : indefinite **2** : indeterminate
indexar *vt* INDICIAR : to index (wages, prices, etc.)
indicación *nf*, *pl* **-ciones** **1** : sign, signal **2** : direction, instruction **3** : suggestion, hint
indicado, -da *adj* **1** APROPIADO : appropriate, suitable **2** : specified, indicated ⟨al día indicado : on the specified day⟩
indicador *nm* **1** : gauge, dial, meter **2** : indicator ⟨indicadores económicos : economic indicators⟩
indicar {72} *vt* **1** SEÑALAR : to indicate **2** ENSEÑAR, MOSTRAR : to show
indicativo[1] **, -va** *adj* : indicative
indicativo[2] *nm* : indicative (mood)

índice *nm* **1** : index **2** : index finger, forefinger **3** INDICIO : indication

indiciar *vt* : to index (prices, wages, etc.)

indicio *nm* : indication, sign

indiferencia *nf* : indifference

indiferente *adj* **1** : indifferent, unconcerned **2 ser indiferente** : to be of no concern ⟨me es indiferente : it doesn't matter to me⟩

indígena[1] *adj* : indigenous, native

indígena[2] *nmf* : native

indigencia *nf* MISERIA : poverty, destitution

indigente *adj & nmf* : indigent

indigestarse *vr* **1** EMPACHARSE : to have indigestion **2** *fam* : to nauseate, to disgust ⟨ese tipo se me indigesta : that guy makes me sick⟩

indigestión *nf, pl* **-tiones** EMPACHO : indigestion

indigesto, -ta *adj* : indigestible, difficult to digest

indignación *nf, pl* **-ciones** : indignation

indignado, -da *adj* : indignant

indignante *adj* : outrageous, infuriating

indignar *vt* : to outrage, to infuriate — **indignarse** *vr*

indignidad *nf* : indignity

indigno, -na *adj* : unworthy

índigo *nm* : indigo

indio[1]**, -dia** *adj* **1** : American Indian, Indian, Amerindian **2** : Indian (from India)

indio[2]**, -dia** *n* **1** : American Indian **2** : Indian (from India)

indirecta *nf* **1** : hint, innuendo **2 echar indirectas** *or* **lanzar indirectas** : to drop a hint, to insinuate

indirecto, -ta *adj* : indirect — **indirectamente** *adv*

indisciplina *nf* : indiscipline, unruliness

indisciplinado, -da *adj* : undisciplined, unruly

indiscreción *nf, pl* **-ciones** **1** IMPRUDENCIA : indiscretion **2** : tactless remark

indiscreto, -ta *adj* IMPRUDENTE : indiscreet, imprudent — **indiscretamente** *adv*

indiscriminado, -da *adj* : indiscriminate — **indiscriminadamente** *adv*

indiscutible *adj* INCONTESTABLE, INCUESTIONABLE : indisputable, unquestionable — **indiscutiblemente** *adv*

indispensable *adj* : indispensable — **indispensablemente** *adv*

indisponer {60} *vt* **1** : to spoil, to upset **2** : to make ill — **indisponerse** *vr* **1** : to become ill **2** ∼ **con** : to fall out with

indisposición *nf, pl* **-ciones** : indisposition, illness

indispuesto, -ta *adj* : unwell, indisposed

indistinguible *adj* : indistinguishable

indistintamente *adv* **1** : indistinctly **2** : indiscriminately

indistinto, -ta *adj* : indistinct, vague, faint

individual *adj* : individual — **individualmente** *adv*

individualidad *nf* : individuality

individualismo *nm* : individualism

individualista[1] *adj* : individualistic

individualista[2] *nmf* : individualist

individualizar {21} *vt* : to individualize

individuo *nm* : individual, person

indivisible *adj* : indivisible — **indivisibilidad** *nf*

indocumentado, -da *n* : illegal immigrant

índole *nf* **1** : nature, character **2** CLASE, TIPO : sort, kind

indolencia *nf* : indolence, laziness

indolente *adj* : indolent, lazy

indoloro, -ra *adj* : painless

indomable *adj* **1** : indomitable **2** : unruly, unmanageable

indómito, -ta *adj* : indomitable

indonesio, -sia *adj & n* : Indonesian

inducción *nf, pl* **-ciones** : induction

inducir {61} *vt* **1** : to induce, to cause **2** : to infer, to deduce

inductivo, -va *adj* : inductive

indudable *adj* : unquestionable, beyond doubt

indudablemente *adv* : undoubtedly, unquestionably

indulgencia *nf* **1** : indulgence, leniency **2** : indulgence (in religion)

indulgente *adj* : indulgent, lenient

indultar *vt* : to pardon, to reprieve

indulto *nm* : pardon, reprieve

indumentaria *nf* : clothing, attire

industria *nf* : industry

industrial[1] *adj* : industrial

industrial[2] *nmf* : industrialist, manufacturer

industrialización *nf, pl* **-ciones** : industrialization

industrializar {21} *vt* : to industrialize

industrioso, -sa *adj* : industrious

inédito, -ta *adj* **1** : unpublished **2** : unprecedented

inefable *adj* : ineffable

ineficacia *nf* **1** : inefficiency **2** : ineffectiveness

ineficaz *adj, pl* **-caces** **1** : inefficient **2** : ineffective — **ineficazmente** *adv*

ineficiencia *nf* : inefficiency

ineficiente *adj* : inefficient — **ineficientemente** *adv*

inelegancia *nf* : inelegance — **inelegante** *adj*

inelegible *adj* : ineligible — **inelegibilidad** *nf*

ineludible *adj* : inescapable, unavoidable — **ineludiblemente** *adv*

ineptitud *nf* : ineptitude, incompetence

inepto, -ta *adj* : inept, incompetent

inequidad *nf* : inequity

inequitativo, -va *adj* : inequitable

inequívoco, -ca *adj* : unequivocal, unmistakable — **inequívocamente** *adv*

inercia *nf* **1** : inertia **2** : apathy, passivity **3 por** ∼ : out of habit

inerme *adj* : unarmed, defenseless

inerte *adj* : inert
inescrupuloso, -sa *adj* : unscrupulous
inescrutable *adj* : inscrutable
inesperado, -da *adj* : unexpected — **inesperadamente** *adv*
inestabilidad *nf* : instability, unsteadiness
inestable *adj* : unstable, unsteady
inestimable *adj* : inestimable, invaluable
inevitabilidad *nf* : inevitability
inevitable *adj* : inevitable, unavoidable — **inevitablemente** *adv*
inexactitud *nf* : inaccuracy
inexacto, -ta *adj* : inexact, inaccurate
inexcusable *adj* : inexcusable, unforgivable
inexistencia *nf* : lack, nonexistence
inexistente *adj* : nonexistent
inexorable *adj* : inexorable — **inexorablemente** *adv*
inexperiencia *nf* : inexperience
inexperto, -ta *adj* : inexperienced, unskilled
inexplicable *adj* : inexplicable — **inexplicablemente** *adv*
inexplorado, -da *adj* : unexplored
inexpresable *adj* : inexpressible
inexpresivo, -va *adj* : inexpressive, expressionless
inexpugnable *adj* : impregnable
inextinguible *adj* 1 : inextinguishable 2 : unquenchable
inextricable *adj* : inextricable — **inextricablemente** *adv*
infalibilidad *nf* : infallibility
infalible *adj* : infallible — **infaliblemente** *adv*
infame *adj* 1 : infamous 2 : loathsome, vile ⟨tiempo infame : terrible weather⟩
infamia *nf* : infamy, disgrace
infancia *nf* 1 NIÑEZ : infancy, childhood 2 : children *pl* 3 : beginnings *pl*
infante *nm* 1 : infante, prince 2 : infantryman
infantería *nf* : infantry
infantil *adj* 1 : childish, infantile 2 : child's, children's
infantilismo *nm* 1 : infantilism 2 INMADUREZ : childishness
infarto *nm* : heart attack
infatigable *adj* : indefatigable, tireless — **infatigablemente** *adv*
infección *nf, pl* **-ciones** : infection
infeccioso, -sa *adj* : infectious
infectar *vt* : to infect — **infectarse** *vr*
infecto, -ta *adj* 1 : infected 2 : repulsive, sickening
infecundidad *nf* : infertility
infecundo, -da *adj* : infertile, barren
infelicidad *nf* : unhappiness
infeliz[1] *adj, pl* **-lices** 1 : unhappy 2 : hapless, unfortunate, wretched
infeliz[2] *nmf, pl* **-lices** : wretch
inferencia *nf* : inference
inferior[1] *adj* : inferior, lower
inferior[2] *nmf* : inferior, underling
inferioridad *nf* : inferiority

inferir {76} *vt* 1 DEDUCIR : to infer, to deduce 2 : to cause (harm or injury), to inflict
infernal *adj* : infernal, hellish
infestación *n, pl* **-ciones** : infestation
infestar *vt* 1 : to infest 2 : to overrun, to invade
inficíon *nf, pl* **-ciones** *Mex* : pollution
infidelidad *nf* : unfaithfulness, infidelity
infiel[1] *adj* : unfaithful, disloyal
infiel[2] *nmf* : infidel, heathen
infierno *nm* 1 : hell 2 **el quinto infierno** : the middle of nowhere
infiltrar *vt* : to infiltrate — **infiltrarse** *vr* — **infiltración** *nf*
infinidad *nf* 1 : infinity 2 SINFÍN : great number, huge quantity ⟨una infinidad de veces : countless times⟩
infinitesimal *adj* : infinitesimal
infinitivo *nm* : infinitive
infinito[1] *adv* : infinitely, vastly
infinito[2], **-ta** *adj* 1 : infinite 2 : limitless, endless 3 **hasta lo infinito** : ad infinitum — **infinitamente** *adv*
infinito[3] *nm* : infinity
inflable *adj* : inflatable
inflación *nf, pl* **-ciones** : inflation
inflacionario, -ria *adj* : inflationary
inflacionista → **inflacionario**
inflamable *adj* : flammable
inflamación *nf, pl* **-ciones** : inflammation
inflamar *vt* : to inflame
inflamatorio, -ria *adj* : inflammatory
inflar *vt* HINCHAR : to inflate — **inflarse** *vr* 1 : to swell 2 : to become conceited
inflexibilidad *nf* : inflexibility
inflexible *adj* : inflexible, unyielding
inflexión *nf, pl* **-xiones** : inflection
infligir {35} *vt* : to inflict
influencia *nf* INFLUJO : influence
influenciable *adj* : easily influenced, suggestible
influenciar *vt* : to influence
influenza *nf* : influenza
influir {41} *vt* : to influence — *vi* ~ **en** *or* ~ **sobre** : to have an influence on, to affect
influjo *nm* INFLUENCIA : influence
influyente *adj* : influential
información *nf, pl* **-ciones** 1 : information 2 INFORME : report, inquiry 3 NOTICIAS : news
informado, -da *adj* : informed ⟨bien informado : well-informed⟩
informador, -dora *n* : informer, informant
informal *adj* 1 : unreliable (of persons) 2 : informal, casual — **informalmente** *adv*
informalidad *nf* : informality
informante *nmf* : informant
informar *vt* ENTERAR : to inform — *vi* : to report — **informarse** *vr* ENTERARSE : to get information, to find out
informática *nf* : computer science, computing

informativo[1], **-va** *adj* : informative
informativo[2] *nm* : news program, news
informatización *nf, pl* **-ciones** : computerization
informatizar {21} *vt* : to computerize
informe[1] *adj* AMORFO : shapeless, formless
informe[2] *nm* **1** : report **2** : reference (for employment) **3 informes** *nmpl* : information, data
infortunado, -da *adj* : unfortunate, unlucky
infortunio *nm* **1** DESGRACIA : misfortune **2** CONTRATIEMPO : mishap
infracción *nf, pl* **-ciones** : violation, offense, infraction
infractor, -tora *n* : offender
infraestructura *nf* : infrastructure
infrahumano, -na *adj* : subhuman
infranqueable *adj* **1** : impassable **2** : insurmountable
infrarrojo, -ja *adj* : infrared
infrecuente *adj* : infrequent
infringir {35} *vt* : to infringe, to breach
infructuoso, -sa *adj* : fruitless — **infructuosamente** *adv*
ínfulas *nfpl* **1** : conceit **2 darse ínfulas** : to put on airs
infundado, -da *adj* : unfounded, baseless
infundio *nm* : false story, lie, tall tale ⟨todo eso son infundios : that's a pack of lies⟩
infundir *vt* **1** : to instill **2 infundir ánimo a** : to encourage **3 infundir miedo a** : to intimidate
infusión *nf, pl* **-siones** : infusion
ingeniar *vt* : to devise, to think up — **ingeniarse** *vr* : to manage, to find a way
ingeniería *nf* : engineering
ingeniero, -ra *n* : engineer
ingenio *nm* **1** : ingenuity **2** CHISPA : wit, wits **3** : device, apparatus **4 ingenio azucarero** : sugar refinery
ingenioso, -sa *adj* **1** : ingenious **2** : clever, witty — **ingeniosamente** *adv*
ingente *adj* : huge, enormous
ingenuidad *nf* : naïveté, ingenuousness
ingenuo[1], **-nua** *adj* CÁNDIDO : naive — **ingenuamente** *adv*
ingenuo[2], **-nua** *n* : naive person
ingerencia → **injerencia**
ingerir {76} *vt* : to ingest, to consume
ingestión *nf, pl* **-tiones** : ingestion
ingle *nf* : groin
inglés[1], **-glesa** *adj, mpl* **ingleses** : English
inglés[2], **-glesa** *n, mpl* **ingleses** : Englishman *m*, Englishwoman *f*
inglés[3] *nm* : English (language)
inglete *nm* : miter joint
ingobernable *adj* : ungovernable, lawless
ingratitud *nf* : ingratitude
ingrato[1], **-ta** *adj* **1** : ungrateful **2** : thankless
ingrato[2], **-ta** *n* : ingrate
ingrediente *nm* : ingredient

ingresar *vt* **1** : to admit ⟨ingresaron a Luis al hospital : Luis was admitted into the hospital⟩ **2** : to deposit — *vi* **1** : to enter, to go in **2** ~ **en** : to join, to enroll in
ingreso *nm* **1** : entrance, entry **2** : admission **3 ingresos** *nmpl* : income, earnings *pl*
íngrimo, -ma *adj* : all alone, all by oneself
inhábil *adj* : unskillful, clumsy
inhabilidad *nf* **1** : unskillfulness **2** : unfitness
inhabilitar *vt* **1** : to disqualify, to bar **2** : to disable
inhabitable *adj* : uninhabitable
inhabituado, -da *adj* ~ **a** : unaccustomed to
inhalador *nm* : inhaler
inhalante *nm* : inhalant
inhalar *vt* : to inhale — **inhalación** *nf*
inherente *adj* : inherent
inhibición *nf, pl* **-ciones** COHIBICIÓN : inhibition
inhibir *vt* : to inhibit — **inhibirse** *vr*
inhóspito, -ta *adj* : inhospitable
inhumación *nf, pl* **-ciones** : interment, burial
inhumanidad *nf* : inhumanity
inhumano, -na *adj* : inhuman, cruel, inhumane
inhumar *vt* : to inter, to bury
iniciación *nf, pl* **-ciones** **1** : initiation **2** : introduction
iniciado, -da *n* : initiate
iniciador[1], **-dora** *adj* : initiatory
iniciador[2], **-dora** *n* : initiator, originator
inicial[1] *adj* : initial, original — **inicialmente** *adv*
inicial[2] *nf* : initial (letter)
iniciar *vt* COMENZAR : to initiate, to begin — **iniciarse** *vr*
iniciativa *nf* : initiative
inicio *nm* COMIENZO : beginning
inicuo, -cua *adj* : iniquitous, wicked
inigualado, -da *adj* : unequaled
inimaginable *adj* : unimaginable
inimitable *adj* : inimitable
ininteligible *adj* : unintelligible
ininterrumpido, -da *adj* : uninterrupted, continuous — **ininterrumpidamente** *adv*
iniquidad *nf* : iniquity, wickedness
injerencia *nf* : interference
injerirse {76} *vr* ENTROMETERSE, INMISCUIRSE : to meddle, to interfere
injertar *vt* : to graft
injerto *nm* : graft ⟨injerto de piel : skin graft⟩
injuria *nf* AGRAVIO : affront, insult
injuriar *vt* INSULTAR : to insult, to revile
injurioso, -sa *adj* : insulting, abusive
injusticia *nf* : injustice, unfairness
injustificable *adj* : unjustifiable
injustificadamente *adv* : unjustifiably, unfairly
injustificado, -da *adj* : unjustified, unwarranted

injusto, -ta *adj* : unfair, unjust — **injustamente** *adv*
inmaculado, -da *adj* : immaculate, spotless
inmadurez *nf, pl* **-reces** : immaturity
inmaduro, -ra *adj* **1** : immature **2** : unripe
inmediaciones *nfpl* : environs, surrounding area
inmediatamente *adv* ENSEGUIDA : immediately
inmediatez *nf, pl* **-teces** : immediacy
inmediato, -ta *adj* **1** : immediate **2** CONTIGUO : adjoining **3 de** ~ : immediately, right away **4** ~ **a** : next to, close to
inmejorable *adj* : excellent, unbeatable
inmemorial *adj* : immemorial ⟨tiempos inmemoriales : time immemorial⟩
inmensidad *nf* : immensity, vastness
inmenso, -sa *adj* ENORME : immense, huge, vast — **inmensamente** *adv*
inmensurable *adj* : boundless, immeasurable
inmerecido, -da *adj* : undeserved — **inmerecidamente** *adv*
inmersión *nf, pl* **-siones** : immersion
inmerso, -sa *adj* **1** : immersed **2** : involved, absorbed
inmigración *nf, pl* **-ciones** : immigration
inmigrado, -da *adj & n* : immigrant
inmigrante *adj & nmf* : immigrant
inmigrar *vi* : to immigrate
inminencia *nf* : imminence
inminente *adj* : imminent — **inminentemente** *adv*
inmiscuirse {41} *vr* ENTROMETERSE, INJERIRSE : to meddle, to interfere
inmobiliario, -ria *adj* : real estate, property
inmoderación *n, pl* **-ciones** : immoderation, intemperance
inmoderado, -da *adj* : immoderate, excessive — **inmoderamente** *adv*
inmodestia *nf* : immodesty — **inmodesto, -ta** *adj*
inmolar *vt* : to immolate — **inmolación** *nf*
inmoral *adj* : immoral
inmoralidad *nf* : immorality
inmortal *adj & nmf* : immortal
inmortalidad *nf* : immortality
inmortalizar {21} *vt* : to immortalize
inmotivado, -da *adj* **1** : unmotivated **2** : groundless
inmovible *adj* : immovable, fixed
inmóvil *adj* **1** : still, motionless **2** : steadfast
inmovilidad *nf* : immobility
inmovilizar {21} *vt* : to immobilize
inmueble *nm* : building, property
inmundicia *nf* : dirt, filth, trash
inmundo, -da *adj* : dirty, filthy, nasty
inmune *adj* : immune
inmunidad *nf* : immunity
inmunizar {21} *vt* : to immunize — **inmunización** *nf*
inmunología *nf* : immunology

inmunológico, -ca *adj* : immune ⟨sistema inmunológico : immune system⟩
inmutabilidad *nf* : immutability
inmutable *adj* : immutable, unchangeable
innato, -ta *adj* : innate, inborn
innecesario, -ria *adj* : unnecessary — **innecesariamente** *adv*
innegable *adj* : undeniable
innoble *adj* : ignoble — **innoblemente** *adv*
innovación *nf, pl* **-ciones** : innovation
innovador, -dora *adj* : innovative
innovar *vt* : to introduce — *vi* : to innovate
innumerable *adj* INCONTABLE : innumerable, countless
inobjetable *adj* : indisputable, unobjectionable
inocencia *nf* : innocence
inocente[1] *adj* **1** : innocent **2** INGENUO : naive — **inocentemente** *adv*
inocente[2] *nmf* : innocent person
inocentón[1], -tona *adj, mpl* **-tones** : naive, gullible
inocentón[2], -tona *n, mpl* **-tones** : simpleton, dupe
inocuidad *nf* : harmlessness
inocular *vt* : to inoculate, to vaccinate — **inoculación** *nf*
inocuo, -cua *adj* : innocuous, harmless
inodoro[1], -ra *adj* : odorless
inodoro[2] *nm* : toilet
inofensivo, -va *adj* : inoffensive, harmless
inolvidable *adj* : unforgettable
inoperable *adj* : inoperable
inoperante *adj* : ineffective, inoperative
inopinado, -da *adj* : unexpected — **inopinadamente** *adv*
inoportuno, -na *adj* : untimely, inopportune, inappropriate
inorgánico, -ca *adj* : inorganic
inoxidable *adj* **1** : rustproof **2 acero inoxidable** : stainless steel
inquebrantable *adj* : unshakable, unwavering
inquietante *adj* : disturbing, worrisome
inquietar *vt* PREOCUPAR : to disturb, to upset, to worry — **inquietarse** *vr*
inquieto, -ta *adj* **1** : anxious, uneasy, worried **2** : restless
inquietud *nf* **1** : anxiety, uneasiness, worry **2** AGITACIÓN : restlessness
inquilinato *nm* : tenancy
inquilino, -na *n* : tenant, occupant
inquina *nf* **1** : aversion, dislike **2** : ill will ⟨tener inquina a alguien : to have a grudge against someone⟩
inquirir {4} *vi* : to make inquiries — *vt* : to investigate
inquisición *nf, pl* **-ciones** : investigation, inquiry
inquisidor, -dora *adj* : inquisitive
inquisitivo, -va *adj* : inquisitive, curious — **inquisitivamente** *adv*
insaciable *adj* : insatiable
insalubre *adj* **1** : unhealthy **2** ANTIHIGIÉNICO : unsanitary

insalubridad *nf* : unhealthiness
insalvable *adj* : insuperable, insurmountable
insano, -na *adj* **1** LOCO : insane, mad **2** INSALUBRE : unhealthy
insatisfacción *nf, pl* **-ciones** : dissatisfaction
insatisfactorio *nm* : unsatisfactory
insatisfecho, -cha *adj* **1** : dissatisfied **2** : unsatisfied
inscribir {33} *vt* **1** MATRICULAR : to enroll, to register **2** GRABAR : to engrave — **inscribirse** *vr* : to register, to sign up
inscripción *nf, pl* **-ciones 1** MATRÍCULA : enrollment, registration **2** : inscription
inscrito *pp* → **inscribir**
insecticida[1] *adj* : insecticidal
insecticida[2] *nm* : insecticide
insecto *nm* : insect
inseguridad *nf* **1** : insecurity **2** : lack of safety **3** : uncertainty
inseguro, -ra *adj* **1** : insecure **2** : unsafe **3** : uncertain
inseminar *vt* : to inseminate — **inseminación** *nf*
insensatez *nf, pl* **-teces** : foolishness, stupidity
insensato[1], **-ta** *adj* : foolish, senseless
insensato[2], **-ta** *n* : fool
insensibilidad *nf* : insensitivity
insensible *adj* : insensitive, unfeeling
inseparable *adj* : inseparable — **inseparablemente** *adv*
inserción *nf, pl* **-ciones** : insertion
insertar *vt* : to insert
inservible *adj* INÚTIL : useless, unusable
insidia *nf* **1** : snare, trap **2** : malice
insidioso, -sa *adj* : insidious
insigne *adj* : noted, famous
insignia *nf* ENSEÑA : insignia, emblem, badge
insignificancia *nf* **1** : insignificance **2** NIMIEDAD : trifle, triviality
insignificante *adj* : insignificant
insincero, -ra *adj* : insincere — **insinceridad** *nf*
insinuación *nf, pl* **-ciones** : insinuation, hint
insinuante *adj* : suggestive
insinuar {3} *vt* : to insinuate, to hint at — **insinuarse** *vr* **1** ~ **a** : to make advances to **2** ~ **en** : to worm one's way into
insipidez *nf, pl* **-deces** : insipidness, blandness
insípido, -da *adj* : insipid, bland
insistencia *nf* : insistence
insistente *adj* : insistent — **insistentemente** *adv*
insistir *v* : to insist
insociable *adj* : unsociable
insolación *nf, pl* **-ciones** : sunstroke
insolencia *nf* IMPERTINENCIA : insolence
insolente *adj* IMPERTINENTE : insolent
insólito, -ta *adj* : rare, unusual

insoluble *adj* : insoluble — **insolubilidad** *nf*
insolvencia *nf* : insolvency, bankruptcy
insolvente *adj* : insolvent, bankrupt
insomne *adj & nmf* : insomniac
insomnio *nm* : insomnia
insondable *adj* : fathomless, deep
insonorizado, -da *adj* : soundproof
insoportable *adj* INAGUANTABLE : unbearable, intolerable
insoslayable *adj* : unavoidable, inescapable
insospechado, -da *adj* : unexpected, unforeseen
insostenible *adj* : untenable
inspección *nf, pl* **-ciones** : inspection
inspeccionar *vt* : to inspect
inspector, -tora *n* : inspector
inspiración *nf, pl* **-ciones 1** : inspiration **2** INHALACIÓN : inhalation
inspirador, -dora *adj* : inspiring
inspirar *vt* : to inspire — *vi* INHALAR : to inhale
instalación *nf, pl* **-ciones** : installation
instalar *vt* **1** : to install **2** : to instate — **instalarse** *vr* ESTABLECERSE : to settle, to establish oneself
instancia *nf* **1** : petition, request **2 en última instancia** : as a last resort
instantánea *nf* : snapshot
instantáneo, -nea *adj* : instantaneous — **instantáneamente** *adv*
instante *nm* **1** : instant, moment **2 al instante** : immediately **3 a cada instante** : frequently, all the time **4 por instantes** : constantly, incessantly
instar *vt* APREMIAR : to urge, to press — *vi* URGIR : to be urgent or pressing ⟨insta que vayamos pronto : it is imperative that we leave soon⟩
instauración *nf, pl* **-ciones** : establishment
instaurar *vt* : to establish
instigador, -dora *n* : instigator
instigar {52} *vt* : to instigate, to incite
instintivo, -va *adj* : instinctive — **instintivamente** *adv*
instinto *nm* : instinct
institución *nf, pl* **-ciones** : institution
institucional *adj* : institutional — **institucionalmente** *adv*
institucionalización *nf, pl* **-ciones** : institutionalization
institucionalizar {21} *vt* : to institutionalize
instituir {41} *vt* ESTABLECER, FUNDAR : to institute, to establish, to found
instituto *nm* : institute
institutriz *nf, pl* **-trices** : governess *f*
instrucción *nf, pl* **-ciones 1** EDUCACIÓN : education **2 instrucciones** *nfpl* : instructions, directions
instructivo, -va *adj* : instructive, educational
instructor, -tora *n* : instructor
instruir {41} *vt* **1** ADIESTRAR : to instruct, to train **2** ENSEÑAR : to educate, to teach

instrumentación *nf, pl* **-ciones** : orchestration
instrumental *adj* : instrumental
instrumentar *vt* : to orchestrate
instrumentista *nmf* : instrumentalist
instrumento *nm* : instrument
insubordinado, -da *adj* : insubordinate — **insubordinación** *nf*
insubordinarse *vr* : to rebel
insuficiencia *nf* **1** : insufficiency, inadequacy **2 insuficiencia cardíaca** : heart failure
insuficiente *adj* : insufficient, inadequate — **insuficientemente** *adv*
insufrible *adj* : insufferable
insular *adj* : insular
insularidad *nf* : insularity
insulina *nf* : insulin
insulso, -sa *adj* **1** INSÍPIDO : insipid, bland **2** : dull
insultante *adj* : insulting
insultar *vt* : to insult
insulto *nm* : insult
insumos *nmpl* : supplies ⟨insumos agrícolas : agricultural supplies⟩
insuperable *adj* : insuperable, insurmountable
insurgente *adj & nmf* : insurgent — **insurgencia** *nf*
insurrección *nf, pl* **-ciones** : insurrection, uprising
insustancial *adj* : insubstantial, flimsy
insustituible *adj* : irreplaceable
intachable *adj* : irreproachable, faultless
intacto, -ta *adj* : intact
intangible *adj* IMPALPABLE : intangible, impalpable
integración *nf, pl* **-ciones** : integration
integral *adj* **1** : integral, essential **2 pan integral** : whole grain bread
integrante[1] *adj* : integrating, integral
integrante[2] *nmf* : member
integrar *vt* : to make up, to compose — **integrarse** *vr* : to integrate, to fit in
integridad *nf* **1** RECTITUD : integrity, honesty **2** : wholeness, completeness
integrismo *nm* : fundamentalism
integrista *adj & nmf* : fundamentalist
íntegro, -gra *adj* **1** : honest, upright **2** ENTERO : whole, complete **3** : unabridged
intelecto *nm* : intellect
intelectual *adj & nmf* : intellectual — **intelectualmente** *adv*
intelectualidad *nf* : intelligentsia
inteligencia *nf* : intelligence
inteligente *adj* : intelligent — **inteligentemente** *adv*
inteligible *adj* : intelligible — **inteligibilidad** *nf*
intemperancia *adj* : intemperance, excess
intemperie *nf* **1** : bad weather, elements *pl* **2 a la intemperie** : in the open air, outside
intempestivo, -va *adj* : inopportune, untimely — **intempestivamente** *adv*

intención *nf, pl* **-ciones** : intention, plan
intencionado, -da → **intencional**
intencional *adj* : intentional — **intencionalmente** *adv*
intendencia *nf* : management, administration
intendente *nmf* : quartermaster
intensidad *nf* : intensity
intensificación *nf, pl* **-ciones** : intensification
intensificar {72} *vt* : to intensify — **intensificarse** *vr*
intensivo, -va *adj* : intensive — **intensivamente** *adv*
intenso, -sa *adj* : intense — **intensamente** *adv*
intentar *vt* : to attempt, to try
intento *nm* **1** PROPÓSITO : intent, intention **2** TENTATIVA : attempt, try
interacción *nf, pl* **-ciones** : interaction
interactivo, -va *adj* : interactive
interactuar {3} *vi* : to interact
intercalar *vt* : to intersperse, to insert
intercambiable *adj* : interchangeable
intercambiar *vt* CANJEAR : to exchange, to trade
intercambio *nm* CANJE : exchange, trade
interceder *vi* : to intercede
intercepción *nf, pl* **-ciones** : interception
interceptar *vt* **1** : to intercept, to block **2 interceptar las líneas** : to wiretap
intercesión *nf, pl* **-siones** : intercession
intercomunicación *nf, pl* **-ciones** : intercommunication
interconexión *nf, pl* **-xiones** : interconnection
interconfesional *adj* : interdenominational
interdepartamental *adj* : interdepartmental
interdependencia *nf* : interdependence — **interdependiente** *adj*
interdicción *nf, pl* **-ciones** : interdiction, prohibition
interés *nm, pl* **-reses** : interest
interesado, -da *adj* **1** : interested **2** : selfish, self-seeking
interesante *adj* : interesting
interesar *vt* : to interest — *vi* : to be of interest, to be interesting — **interesarse** *vr*
interestatal *adj* : interstate ⟨autopista interestatal : interstate highway⟩
interestelar *adj* : interstellar
interfase → **interfaz**
interfaz *nf, pl* **-faces** : interface
interferencia *nf* : interference, static
interferir {76} *vi* : to interfere, to meddle — *vt* : to interfere with, to obstruct
intergaláctico, -ca *adj* : intergalactic
intergubernamental *adj* : intergovernmental
interín[1] *or* **ínterin** *adv* : meanwhile
interín[2] *or* **ínterin** *nm, pl* **-rines** : meantime, interim ⟨en el interín : in the meantime⟩

interinamente *adv* : temporarily
interino, -na *adj* : acting, temporary, interim
interior[1] *adj* : interior, inner
interior[2] *nm* **1** : interior, inside **2** : inland region
interiormente *adv* : inwardly
interjección *nf, pl* **-ciones** : interjection
interlocutor, -tora *n* : interlocutor, speaker
interludio *nm* : interlude
intermediario, -ria *adj & n* : intermediary, go-between
intermedio[1], **-dia** *adj* : intermediate
intermedio[2] *nm* **1** : intermission **2 por intermedio de** : by means of
interminable *adj* : interminable, endless — **interminablemente** *adv*
intermisión *nf, pl* **-siones** : intermission, pause
intermitente[1] *adj* **1** : intermittent **2** : flashing, blinking (of a light) — **intermitentemente** *adv*
intermitente[2] *nm* : blinker, turn signal
internacional *adj* : international — **internacionalmente** *adv*
internacionalismo *nm* : internationalism
internacionalizar {21} *vt* : to internacionalize
internado *nm* : boarding school
internar *vt* : to commit, to confine — **internarse** *vr* **1** : to penetrate, to advance into **2 ~ en** : to go into, to enter
internista *nmf* : internist
interno[1], **-na** *adj* : internal — **internamente** *adv*
interno[2], **-na** *n* **1** : intern **2** : inmate, internee
interpelación *nf, pl* **-ciones** : appeal, plea
interpelar *vt* : to question (formally)
interpersonal *adj* : interpersonal
interpolar *vt* : to insert, to interpolate
interponer {60} *vt* : to interpose — **interponerse** *vr* : to intervene
interpretación *nf, pl* **-ciones** : interpretation
interpretar *vt* **1** : to interpret **2** : to play, to perform
interpretativo, -va *adj* : interpretive
intérprete *nmf* **1** TRADUCTOR : interpreter **2** : performer
interpuesto *pp* → **interponer**
interracial *adj* : interracial
interrelación *nf, pl* **-ciones** : interrelationship
interrelacionar *vi* : to interrelate
interrogación *nf, pl* **-ciones** **1** : interrogation, questioning **2 signo de interrogación** : question mark
interrogador, -dora *n* : interrogator, questioner
interrogante[1] *adj* : questioning
interrogante[2] *nm* **1** : question mark **2** : query
interrogar {52} *vt* : to interrogate, to question

interrogativo, -va *adj* : interrogative
interrogatorio *nm* : interrogation, questioning
interrumpir *v* : to interrupt
interrupción *nf, pl* **-ciones** : interruption
interruptor *nm* **1** : (electrical) switch **2** : circuit breaker
intersección *nf, pl* **-ciones** : intersection
intersticio *nm* : interstice — **intersticial** *adj*
interuniversitario, -ria *adj* : intercollegiate
interurbano, -na *adj* **1** : intercity **2** : long-distance ⟨llamadas interurbanas : long-distance calls⟩
intervalo *nm* : interval
intervención *nf, pl* **-ciones** **1** : intervention **2** : audit **3 intervención quirúrgica** : operation
intervencionista *adj & nmf* : interventionist
intervenir {87} *vi* **1** : to take part **2** INTERCEDER : to intervene, to intercede — *vt* **1** : to control, to supervise **2** : to audit **3** : to operate on **4** : to tap (a telephone)
interventor, -tora *n* **1** : inspector **2** : auditor, comptroller
intestado, -da *adj* : intestate
intestinal *adj* : intestinal
intestino *nm* : intestine
intimar *vi* **~ con** : to become friendly with — *vt* : to require, to call on
intimidación *nf, pl* **-ciones** : intimidation
intimidad *nf* **1** : intimacy **2** : privacy, private life
intimidar *vt* ACOBARDAR : to intimidate
íntimo, -ma *adj* **1** : intimate, close **2** PRIVADO : private — **íntimamente** *adv*
intitular *vt* : to entitle, to title
intocable *adj* : untouchable
intolerable *adj* : intolerable, unbearable
intolerancia *nf* : intolerance
intolerante[1] *adj* : intolerant
intolerante[2] *nmf* : intolerant person, bigot
intoxicación *nf, pl* **-ciones** : poisoning
intoxicante *nm* : poison
intoxicar {72} *vt* : to poison
intranquilidad *nf* PREOCUPACIÓN : worry, anxiety
intranquilizar {21} *vt* : to upset, to make uneasy — **intranquilizarse** *vr* : to get worried, to be anxious
intranquilo, -la *adj* PREOCUPADO : uneasy, worried
intransigencia *nf* : intransigence
intransigente *adj* : intransigent, unyielding
intransitable *adj* : impassable
intransitivo, -va *adj* : intransitive
intrascendente *adj* : unimportant, insignificant
intratable *adj* **1** : intractable **2** : awkward **3** : unsociable
intravenoso, -sa *adj* : intravenous

intrepidez *nf* : fearlessness
intrépido, -da *adj* : intrepid, fearless
intriga *nf* : intrigue
intrigante *nmf* : schemer
intrigar {52} *v* : to intrigue — **intrigante** *adj*
intrincado, -da *adj* : intricate, involved
intrínseco, -ca *adj* : intrinsic — **intrínsecamente** *adv*
introducción *nf, pl* **-ciones** : introduction
introducir {61} *vt* **1** : to introduce **2** : to bring in **3** : to insert **4** : to input, to enter — **introducirse** *vr* : to penetrate, to get into
introductorio, -ria *adj* : introductory
intromisión *nf, pl* **-siones** : interference, meddling
introspección *nf, pl* **-ciones** : introspection
introspectivo, -va *adj* : introspective
introvertido[1], -da *adj* : introverted
introvertido[2], -da *n* : introvert
intrusión *nf, pl* **-siones** : intrusion
intruso[1], -sa *adj* : intrusive
intruso[2], -sa *n* : intruder
intuición *nf, pl* **-ciones** : intuition
intuir {41} *vt* : to intuit, to sense
intuitivo, -va *adj* : intuitive — **intuitivamente** *adv*
inundación *nf, pl* **-ciones** : flood, inundation
inundar *vt* : to flood, to inundate
inusitado, -da *adj* : unusual, uncommon — **inusitadamente** *adv*
inusual *adj* : unusual, uncommon — **inusualmente** *adv*
inútil[1] *adj* INSERVIBLE : useless — **inútilmente** *adv*
inútil[2] *nmf* : good-for-nothing
inutilidad *nf* : uselessness
inutilizar {21} *vt* **1** : to make useless **2** INCAPACITAR : to disable, to put out of commission
invadir *vt* : to invade
invalidar *vt* : to nullify, to invalidate
invalidez *nf, pl* **-deces 1** : invalidity **2** : disablement
inválido, -da *adj* & *n* : invalid
invalorable *adj* : invaluable
invariable *adj* : invariable — **invariablemente** *adv*
invasión *nf, pl* **-siones** : invasion
invasivo, -va *adj* : invasive
invasor[1], -sora *adj* : invading
invasor[2], -sora *n* : invader
invectiva *nf* : invective, abuse
invencibilidad *nf* : invincibility
invencible *adj* **1** : invincible **2** : insurmountable
invención *nf, pl* **-ciones 1** INVENTO : invention **2** MENTIRA : fabrication, lie
inventar *vt* **1** : to invent **2** : to fabricate, to make up
inventariar {85} *vt* : to inventory
inventario *nm* : inventory
inventiva *nf* : ingenuity, inventiveness
inventivo, -va *adj* : inventive

invento *nm* INVENCIÓN : invention
inventor, -tora *n* : inventor
invernadero *nm* : greenhouse, hothouse
invernal *adj* : winter, wintry
invernar {55} *vi* **1** : to spend the winter **2** HIBERNAR : to hibernate
inverosímil *adj* : unlikely, far-fetched
inversión *nf, pl* **-siones 1** : inversion **2** : investment
inversionista *nmf* : investor
inverso[1], -sa *adj* **1** : inverse, inverted **2** CONTRARIO : opposite **3 a la inversa** : on the contrary, vice versa **4 en orden inverso** : in reverse order — **inversamente** *adv*
inverso[2] *n* : inverse
inversor, -sora *n* : investor
invertebrado[1], -da *adj* : invertebrate
invertebrado[2] *nm* : invertebrate
invertir {76} *vt* **1** : to invert, to reverse **2** : to invest — *vi* : to make an investment — **invertirse** *vr* : to be reversed
investidura *nf* : investiture, inauguration
investigación *nf, pl* **-ciones 1** ENCUESTA, INDAGACIÓN : investigation, inquiry **2** : research
investigador[1], -dora *adj* : investigative
investigador[2], -dora *n* **1** : investigator **2** : researcher
investigar {52} *vt* **1** INDAGAR : to investigate **2** : to research — *vi* ~ **sobre** : to do research into
investir {54} *vt* **1** : to empower **2** : to swear in, to inaugurate
inveterado, -da *adj* : inveterate, deep-seated
invicto, -ta *adj* : undefeated
invidente[1] *adj* CIEGO : blind, sightless
invidente[2] *nmf* CIEGO : blind person
invierno *nm* : winter, wintertime
inviolable *adj* : inviolable — **inviolabilidad** *nf*
inviolado, -da *adj* : inviolate, pure
invisibilidad *nf* : invisibility
invisible *adj* : invisible — **invisiblemente** *adv*
invitación *nf, pl* **-ciones** : invitation
invitado, -da *n* : guest
invitar *vt* : to invite
invocación *nf, pl* **-ciones** : invocation
invocar {72} *vt* : to invoke, to call on
involucramiento *nm* : involvement
involucrar *vt* : to implicate, to involve — **involucrarse** *vr* : to get involved
involuntario, -ria *adj* : involuntary — **involuntariamente** *adv*
invulnerable *adj* : invulnerable
inyección *nf, pl* **-ciones** : injection, shot
inyectado, -da *adj* **ojos inyectados** : bloodshot eyes
inyectar *vt* : to inject
ion *nm* : ion
iónico, -ca *adj* : ionic
ionizar {21} *vt* : to ionize — **ionización** *nf*
ionosfera *nf* : ionosphere
ir {43} *vi* **1** : to go ⟨ir a pie : to go on foot, to walk⟩ ⟨ir a caballo : to ride

horseback⟩ ⟨ir a casa : to go home⟩ **2**
: to lead, to extend, to stretch ⟨el
camino va de Cali a Bogotá : the road
goes from Cali to Bogotá⟩ **3** FUN-
CIONAR : to work, to function ⟨esta
computadora ya no va : this computer
doesn't work anymore⟩ **4** : to get on,
to get along ⟨¿cómo te va? : how are
you?, how's it going?⟩ ⟨el negocio no
va bien : the business isn't doing well⟩
5 : to suit ⟨ese vestido te va bien : that
dress really suits you⟩ **6** ~ **con** : to be
⟨ir con prisa : to be in a hurry⟩ **7** ~
por : to follow, to go along ⟨fueron por
la costa : they followed the shoreline⟩
8 dejarse ir : to let oneself go **9 ir a
parar** : to end up **10 vamos a ver** : let's
see — *v aux* **1** (*with present participle*)
⟨ir caminando : to walk⟩ ⟨¡voy corriendo! : I'll be right there!⟩ **2** ~ **a** : to
be going to ⟨voy a hacerlo : I'm going
to do it⟩ ⟨el avión va a despegar : the
plane is about to take off⟩ — **irse** *vr* **1**
: to leave, to go ⟨¡vámonos! : let's go!⟩
⟨todo el mundo se fue : everyone left⟩
2 ESCAPARSE : to leak **3** GASTARSE : to
be used up, to be gone
ira *nf* CÓLERA, FURIA : wrath, anger
iracundo, -da *adj* : irate, angry
iraní *adj & nmf* : Iranian
iraquí *adj & nmf* : Iraqi
irascible *adj* : irascible, irritable — **irascibilidad** *nf*
irga, irgue etc. → **erguir**
iridio *nm* : iridium
iridiscencia *nf* : iridescence — **iridiscente** *adj*
iris *nms & pl* **1** : iris **2 arco iris** : rainbow
irlandés[1]**, -desa** *adj, mpl* **-deses** : Irish
irlandés[2]**, -desa** *n, pl* **-deses** : Irish person, Irishman *m*, Irishwoman *f*
irlandés[3] *nm* : Irish (language)
ironía *nf* : irony
irónico, -ca *adj* : ironic, ironical —
irónicamente *adv*
irracional *adj* : irrational — **irracionalmente** *adv*
irracionalidad *nf* : irrationality
irradiación *nf, pl* **-ciones** : irradiation
irradiar *vt* : to radiate, to irradiate
irrazonable *adj* : unreasonable
irreal *adj* : unreal
irrebatible *adj* : unanswerable, irrefutable
irreconciliable *adj* : irreconcilable
irreconocible *adj* : unrecognizable
irrecuperable *adj* : irrecoverable, irretrievable
irredimible *adj* : irredeemable
irreductible *adj* : unyielding
irreemplazable *adj* : irreplaceable
irreflexión *nf, pl* **-xiones** : thoughtlessness, impetuosity
irreflexivo, -va *adj* : rash, unthinking —
irreflexivamente *adv*
irrefrenable *adj* : uncontrollable, unstoppable ⟨un impulso irrefrenable : an
irresistible urge⟩

irrefutable *adj* : irrefutable
irregular *adj* : irregular — **irregularmente** *adv*
irregularidad *nf* : irregularity
irrelevante *adj* : irrelevant — **irrelevancia** *nf*
irreligioso, -sa *adj* : irreligious
irremediable *adj* : incurable — **irreme-
diablemente** *adv*
irreparable *adj* : irreparable
irreprimible *adj* : irrepressible
irreprochable *adj* : irreproachable
irresistible *adj* : irresistible — **irre-
sistiblemente** *adv*
irresolución *nf, pl* **-ciones** : indecision,
hesitation
irresoluto, -ta *adj* INDECISO : undecided
irrespeto *nm* : disrespect
irrespetuoso, -sa *adj* : disrespectful —
irrespetuosamente *adv*
irresponsabilidad *nf* : irresponsibility
irresponsable *adj* : irresponsible — **irr-
esponsablemente** *adv*
irrestricto, -ta *adj* : unrestricted, unconditional
irreverencia *nf* : disrespect
irreverente *adj* : disrespectful
irreversible *adj* : irreversible
irrevocable *adj* : irrevocable — **irrevo-
cablemente** *adv*
irrigar {52} *vt* : to irrigate — **irrigación**
nf
irrisible *adj* : laughable
irrisión *nf, pl* **-siones** : derision, ridicule
irrisorio, -ria *adj* RISIBLE : ridiculous,
ludicrous
irritabilidad *nf* : irritability
irritable *adj* : irritable
irritación *nf, pl* **-ciones** : irritation
irritante *adj* : irritating
irritar *vt* : to irritate — **irritación** *nf*
irrompible *adj* : unbreakable
irrumpir *vi* ~ **en** : to burst into
irrupción *nf, pl* **-ciones** **1** : irruption **2**
: invasion
isla *nf* : island
islámico, -ca *adj* : Islamic, Muslim
islandés[1]**, -desa** *adj, mpl* **-deses** : Icelandic
islandés[2]**, -desa** *n, mpl* **-deses** : Icelander
islandés[3] *nm* : Icelandic (language)
isleño, -ña *n* : islander
islote *nm* : islet
isometría *nfs & pl* : isometrics
isométrico, -ca *adj* : isometric
isósceles *adj* : isosceles ⟨triángulo
isósceles : isosceles triangle⟩
isótopo *nm* : isotope
israelí *adj & nmf* : Israeli
istmo *nm* : isthmus
itacate *nm Mex* : pack, provisions *pl*
italiano[1]**, -na** *adj & n* : Italian
italiano[2] *nm* : Italian (language)
iterbio *nm* : ytterbium
itinerante *adj* AMBULANTE : traveling,
itinerant
itinerario *nm* : itinerary, route

itrio *nm* : yttrium
izar {21} *vt* : to hoist, to raise ⟨izar la bandera : to raise the flag⟩

izquierda *nf* : left
izquierdista *adj & nmf* : leftist
izquierdo, -da *adj* : left

J

j *nf* : tenth letter of the Spanish alphabet
ja *interj* 1 : ha! 2 **ja, ja** : ha-ha!
jabalí *nm* : wild boar
jabalina *nf* : javelin
jabón *nm, pl* **jabones** : soap
jabonar *vt* ENJABONAR : to soap up, to lather — **jabonarse** *vr*
jabonera *nf* : soap dish
jabonoso, -sa *adj* : soapy
jaca *nf* 1 : pony 2 YEGUA : mare
jacal *nm Mex* : shack, hut
jacinto *nm* : hyacinth
jactancia *nf* 1 : boastfulness 2 : boasting, bragging
jactancioso¹, -sa *adj* : boastful
jactancioso², -sa *n* : boaster, braggart
jactarse *vr* : to boast, to brag
jade *nm* : jade
jadear *vi* : to pant, to gasp, to puff — **jadeante** *adj*
jadeo *nm* : panting, gasping, puffing
jaez *nm, pl* **jaeces** 1 : harness 2 : kind, sort, ilk 3 **jaeces** *nmpl* : trappings
jaguar *nm* : jaguar
jai alai *nm* : jai alai
jaiba *nf* CANGREJO : crab
jalapeño *nm Mex* : jalapeño pepper
jalar *vt* 1 : to pull, to tug 2 *fam* : to attract, to draw in ⟨las ideas nuevas lo jalan : new ideas appeal to him⟩ — *vi* 1 : to pull, to pull together 2 *fam* : to hurry up, to get going 3 *Mex fam* : to be in working order ⟨esta máquina no jala : this machine doesn't work⟩
jalbegue *nm* : whitewash
jalea *nf* : jelly
jalear *vt* : to encourage, to urge on
jaleo *nm* 1 *fam* : uproar, ruckus, racket 2 *fam* : confusion, hassle 3 : cheering and clapping (for a dance)
jalón *nm, pl* **jalones** 1 : milestone, landmark 2 TIRÓN : pull, tug
jalonar *vt* : to mark, to stake out
jalonear *vt Mex, Peru fam* : to tug at — *vi* 1 *fam* : to pull, to tug 2 *CA fam* : to haggle
jamaica *nf* : hibiscus
jamaicano, -na → **jamaiquino**
jamaiquino, -na *adj & n* : Jamaican
jamás *adv* 1 NUNCA : never 2 **nunca jamás** *or* **jamás de los jamases** : never ever 3 **para siempre jamás** : for ever and ever
jamba *nf* : jamb
jamelgo *nm* : nag (horse)
jamón *nm, pl* **jamones** : ham
Januká *nmf* : Hanukkah
japonés¹, -nesa *adj & n, mpl* **-neses** : Japanese

japonés² *nm, pl* **-neses** : Japanese (language)
jaque *nm* 1 : check (in chess) ⟨jaque mate : checkmate⟩ 2 **tener en jaque** : to intimidate, to bully
jaqueca *nf* : headache, migraine
jarabe *nm* 1 : syrup 2 : Mexican folk dance
jarana *nf* 1 *fam* : revelry, partying, spree 2 *fam* : joking, fooling around 3 : small guitar
jaranear *vi fam* : to go on a spree, to party
jarcia *nf* 1 : rigging 2 : fishing tackle
jardín *nm, pl* **jardines** 1 : garden 2 **jardín de niños** : kindergarten 3 **los jardines** *nmpl* : the outfield
jardinería *nf* : gardening
jardinero, -ra *n* 1 : gardener 2 : outfielder (in baseball)
jarra *nf* 1 : pitcher, jug 2 : stein, mug 3 **de jarras** *or* **en jarras** : akimbo
jarrete *nm* 1 : back of the knee 2 CORVEJÓN : hock
jarro *nm* 1 : pitcher, jug 2 : mug
jarrón *nm, pl* **jarrones** FLORERO : vase
jaspe *nm* : jasper
jaspeado, -da *adj* 1 VETEADO : streaked, veined 2 : speckled, mottled
jaula *nf* : cage
jauría *nf* : pack of hounds
javanés, -nesa *adj & n* : Javanese
jazmín *nm, pl* **jazmines** : jasmine
jazz ['jas, 'ʤas] *nm* : jazz
jeans ['jins, 'ʤins] *nmpl* : jeans
jeep ['jip, 'ʤip] *nm, pl* **jeeps** : jeep
jefatura *nf* 1 : leadership 2 : headquarters ⟨jefatura de policía : police headquarters⟩
jefe, -fa *n* 1 : chief, head, leader ⟨jefe de bomberos : fire chief⟩ 2 : boss
Jehová *nm* : Jehovah
jején *nm, pl* **jejenes** : gnat, small mosquito
jengibre *nm* : ginger
jeque *nm* : sheikh, sheik
jerarca *nmf* : leader, chief
jerarquía *nf* 1 : hierarchy 2 RANGO : rank
jerárquico, -ca *adj* : hierarchical
jerbo *nm* : gerbil
jerez *nm, pl* **jereces** : sherry
jerga *nf* 1 : jargon, slang 2 : coarse cloth
jerigonza *nf* GALIMATÍAS : mumbo jumbo, gibberish
jeringa *nf* : syringe
jeringar {52} *vt* 1 : to inject 2 *fam* JOROBAR : to annoy, to pester — *vi fam*

JOROBAR : to be annoying, to be a nuisance

jeringuear → **jeringar**

jeringuilla → **jeringa**

jeroglífico *nm* : hieroglyphic

jersey *nm, pl* **jerseys 1** : jersey (fabric) **2** *Spain* : sweater

Jesucristo *nm* : Jesus Christ

jesuita *adj & nm* : Jesuit

Jesús *nm* **1** : Jesus **2 ¡Jesús!** : goodness!, good heavens!

jeta *nf* **1** : snout **2** *fam* : face, mug

jíbaro, -ra *adj* **1** : Jivaro **2** : rustic, rural

jibia *nf* : cuttlefish

jícama *nf* : jicama

jícara *nf Mex* : calabash

jilguero *nm* : European goldfinch

jinete *nmf* : horseman, horsewoman *f*, rider

jinetear *vt* **1** : to ride, to perform (on horseback) **2** DOMAR : to break in (a horse) — *vi* CABALGAR : to ride horseback

jingoísmo [ˌjɪŋgoˈizmo, ˌdʒɪŋ-] *nm* : jingoism

jingoísta *adj* : jingoist, jingoistic

jiote *nm Mex* : rash

jira *nf* : outing, picnic

jirafa *nf* **1** : giraffe **2** : boom microphone

jirón *nm, pl* **jirones** : shred, rag ⟨hecho jirones : in tatters⟩

jitomate *nm Mex* : tomato

jockey [ˈjɔki, ˈdʒɔ-] *nmf, pl* **jockeys** [-kis] : jockey

jocosidad *nf* : humor, jocularity

jocoso, -sa *adj* : playful, jocular — **jocosamente** *adv*

jofaina *nf* : washbowl

jogging [ˈjɔgɪŋ, ˈdʒɔ-] *nm* : jogging

jolgorio *nm* : merrymaking, fun

jonrón *nm, pl* **jonrones** : home run

jordano, -na *adj & n* : Jordanian

jornada *nf* **1** : expedition, day's journey **2 jornada de trabajo** : working day **3 jornadas** *nfpl* : conference, congress

jornal *nm* **1** : day's pay **2 a** ∼ : by the day

jornalero, -ra *n* : day laborer

joroba *nf* **1** GIBA : hump **2** *fam* : nuisance, pain in the neck

jorobado¹, -da *adj* GIBOSO : hunchbacked, humpbacked

jorobado², -da *n* GIBOSO : hunchback, humpback

jorobar *vt fam* JERINGAR : to bother, to annoy — *vi fam* JERINGAR : to be annoying, to be a nuisance

jorongo *nm Mex* : full-length poncho

jota *nf* **1** : jot, bit ⟨no entiendo ni jota : I don't understand a word of it⟩ ⟨no se ve ni jota : you can't see a thing⟩ **2** : jack (in playing cards)

joven¹ *adj, pl* **jóvenes 1** : young **2** : youthful

joven² *nmf, pl* **jóvenes** : young man *m*, young woman *f*, young person

jovial *adj* : jovial, cheerful — **jovialmente** *adv*

jovialidad *nf* : joviality, cheerfulness

joya *nf* **1** : jewel, piece of jewelry **2** : treasure, gem ⟨la nueva empleada es una joya : the new employee is a real gem⟩

joyería *nf* **1** : jewelry store **2** : jewelry **3 joyería de fantasía** : costume jewelry

joyero, -ra *n* : jeweler

juanete *nm* : bunion

jubilación *nf, pl* **-ciones 1** : retirement **2** PENSIÓN : pension

jubilado¹, -da *adj* : retired, in retirement

jubilado², -da *nmf* : retired person, retiree

jubilar *vt* **1** : to retire, to pension off **2** *fam* : to get rid of, to discard — **jubilarse** *vr* : to retire

jubileo *nm* : jubilee

júbilo *nm* : jubilation, joy

jubiloso, -sa *adj* : jubilant, joyous

judaico, -ca *adj* : Judaic, Jewish

judaísmo *nm* : Judaism

judía *nf* **1** : bean **2** *or* **judía verde** : green bean, string bean

judicatura *nf* **1** : judiciary, judges *pl* **2** : office of judge

judicial *adj* : judicial — **judicialmente** *adv*

judío¹, -día *adj* : Jewish

judío², -día *n* : Jewish person, Jew

judo [ˈjuðo, ˈdʒu-] *nm* : judo

juega, juegue, etc. → **jugar**

juego *nm* **1** : play, playing ⟨poner en juego : to bring into play⟩ **2** : game, sport ⟨juego de cartas : card game⟩ ⟨Juegos Olímpicos : Olympic Games⟩ **3** : gaming, gambling ⟨estar en juego : to be at stake⟩ **4** : set ⟨un juego de llaves : a set of keys⟩ **5 hacer juego** : to go together, to match **6 juego de manos** : conjuring trick, sleight of hand

juerga *nf* : partying, binge ⟨irse de juerga : to go on a spree⟩

juerguista *nmf* : reveler, carouser

jueves *nms & pl* : Thursday

juez¹ *nmf, pl* **jueces 1** : judge **2** ÁRBITRO : umpire, referee

juez², jueza *n* → **juez¹**

jugada *nf* **1** : play, move **2** : trick ⟨hacer una mala jugada : to play a dirty trick⟩

jugador, -dora *n* **1** : player **2** : gambler

jugar {44} *vi* **1** : to play ⟨jugar a la pelota : to play ball⟩ **2** APOSTAR : to gamble, to bet **3** : to joke, to kid — *vt* **1** : to play ⟨jugar un papel : to play a role⟩ ⟨jugar una carta : to play a card⟩ **2** : to bet — **jugarse** *vr* **1** : to risk, to gamble away ⟨jugarse la vida : to risk one's life⟩ **2 jugarse el todo por el todo** : to risk everything

jugarreta *nf fam* : prank, dirty trick

juglar *nm* : minstrel

jugo *nm* **1** : juice **2** : substance, essence ⟨sacarle el jugo a algo : to get the most out of something⟩
jugosidad *nf* : juiciness, succulence
jugoso, -sa *adj* : juicy
juguete *nm* : toy
juguetear *vi* **1** : to play, to cavort, to frolic **2** : to toy, to fiddle
juguetería *nf* : toy store
juguetón, -tona *adj, mpl* **-tones** : playful — **juguetonamente** *adv*
juicio *nm* **1** : good judgment, reason, sense **2** : opinion ⟨a mi juicio : in my opinion⟩ **3** : trial ⟨llevar a juicio : to take to court⟩
juicioso, -sa *adj* : judicious, wise — **juiciosamente** *adv*
julio *nm* : July
juncia *nf* : sedge
junco *nm* **1** : reed, rush **2** : junk (boat)
jungla *nf* : jungle
junio *nm* : June
junquillo *nm* : jonquil
junta *nf* **1** : board, committee ⟨junta directiva : board of directors⟩ **2** REUNIÓN : meeting, session **3** : junta **4** : joint, gasket
juntamente *adv* **1** : jointly, together ⟨juntamente con : together with⟩ **2** : at the same time
juntar *vt* **1** UNIR : to unite, to combine, to put together **2** REUNIR : to collect, to gather together, to assemble **3** : to close partway ⟨juntar la puerta : to leave the door ajar⟩ — **juntarse** *vr* **1** : to join together **2** : to socialize, to get together
junto, -ta *adj* **1** UNIDO : joined, united **2** : close, adjacent ⟨colgaron los dos retratos juntos : they hung the two paintings side by side⟩ **3** (*used adverbially*) : together ⟨llegamos juntos : we arrived together⟩ **4** ~ **a** : next to, alongside of **5** ~ **con** : together with, along with
juntura *nf* : joint, coupling
Júpiter *nm* : Jupiter
jura *nf* : oath, pledge ⟨jura de bandera : pledge of allegiance⟩

jurado[1] *nm* : jury
jurado[2], **-da** *n* : juror
juramento *nm* **1** : oath ⟨juramento hipocrático : Hippocratic oath⟩ **2** : swearword, oath
jurar *vt* **1** : to swear ⟨jurar lealtad : to swear loyalty⟩ **2** : to take an oath ⟨el alcalde juró su cargo : the mayor took the oath of office⟩ — *vi* : to curse, to swear
jurídico, -ca *adj* : legal
jurisdicción *nf, pl* **-ciones** : jurisdiction
jurisdiccional *adj* : jurisdictional, territorial
jurisprudencia *nf* : jurisprudence, law
jurista *nmf* : jurist
justa *nf* **1** : joust **2** TORNEO : tournament, competition
justamente *adv* **1** PRECISAMENTE : precisely, exactly **2** : justly, fairly
justar *vi* : to joust
justicia *nf* **1** : justice, fairness ⟨hacerle justicia a : to do justice to⟩ ⟨ser de justicia : to be only fair⟩ **2 la justicia** : the law ⟨tomarse la justicia por su mano : to take the law into one's own hands⟩
justiciero, -ra *adj* : righteous, avenging
justificable *adj* : justifiable
justificación *nf, pl* **-ciones** : justification
justificante *nm* **1** : justification **2** : proof, voucher
justificar {72} *vt* **1** : to justify **2** : to excuse, to vindicate
justo[1] *adv* **1** : justly **2** : right, exactly ⟨justo a tiempo : just in time⟩ **3** : tightly
justo[2], **-ta** *adj* **1** : just, fair **2** : right, exact **3** : tight ⟨estos zapatos me quedan muy justos : these shoes are too tight⟩
justo[3], **-ta** *n* : just person ⟨los justos : the just⟩
juvenil *adj* **1** : juvenile, young, youthful **2** ADOLESCENTE : teenage
juventud *nf* **1** : youth **2** : young people
juzgado *nm* TRIBUNAL : court, tribunal
juzgar {52} *vt* **1** : to try, to judge (a case in court) **2** : to pass judgment on **3** CONSIDERAR : to consider, to deem
juzgue, etc. → **juzgar**

K

k *nf* : eleventh letter of the Spanish alphabet
káiser *nm* : kaiser
kaki → **caqui**
kaleidoscopio → **caleidoscopio**
kamikaze *adj & nm* : kamikaze
kampucheano, -na *adj & n* : Kampuchean
kan *nm* : khan
karaoke *nm* : karaoke
karate *or* **kárate** *nm* : karate
kayac *or* **kayak** *nm, pl* **kayacs** *or* **kayaks** : kayak

keniano, -na *adj & n* : Kenyan
kepí *nm* : kepi
kermesse *or* **kermés** [kɛr'mɛs] *nf, pl* **kermesses** *or* **kermeses** [-'mɛsɛs] : charity fair, bazaar
kerosene *or* **kerosén** *or* **keroseno** *nm* : kerosene, paraffin
kibutz *or* **kibbutz** *nms & pl* : kibbutz
kilo *nm* **1** : kilo, kilogram **2** *fam* : large amount
kilobyte [ˌkilo'bait] *nm* : kilobyte
kilociclo *nm* : kilocycle
kilogramo *nm* : kilogram

kilohertzio *nm* : kilohertz
kilometraje *nm* : distance in kilometers, mileage
kilométrico, -ca *adj fam* : endless, very long
kilómetro *nm* : kilometer
kilovatio *nm* : kilowatt
kimono *nm* : kimono
kinder ['kɪndɛr] → **kindergarten**
kindergarten [ˌkɪndɛr'gartɛn] *nm, pl* **kindergartens** [-tɛns] : kindergarten, nursery school
kinesiología *nf* : physical therapy

kinesiólogo, -ga *n* : physical therapist
kiosco → **quiosco**
kit *nm, pl* **kits** : kit
kiwi ['kiwi] *nm* **1** : kiwi (bird) **2** : kiwifruit
klaxon → **claxon**
knockout [nɔ'kaut] → **nocaut**
koala *nm* : koala bear
kriptón *nm* : krypton
kurdo¹, -da *adj* : Kurdish
kurdo², -da *n* : Kurd
kuwaití [kuˌwai'ti] *adj & nmf* : Kuwaiti

L

l *nf* : twelfth letter of the Spanish alphabet
la¹ *pron* **1** : her, it ⟨llámala hoy : call her today⟩ ⟨sacó la botella y la abrió : he took out the bottle and opened it⟩ **2** (*formal*) : you ⟨no la vi a usted, Señora Díaz : I didn't see you, Mrs. Díaz⟩ **3** : the one ⟨mi casa y la de la puerta roja : my house and the one with the red door⟩ **4 la que** : the one who
la² *art* → **el²**
laberíntico, -ca *adj* : labyrinthine
laberinto *nm* : labyrinth, maze
labia *nf fam* : gift of gab ⟨tu amigo tiene labia : your friend has a way with words⟩
labial *adj* : labial, lip ⟨lápiz labial : lipstick⟩
labio *nm* **1** : lip **2 labio leporino** : harelip
labor *nf* : work, labor
laborable *adj* **1** : arable **2 día laborable** : workday, business day
laboral *adj* : work, labor ⟨costos laborales : labor costs⟩
laborar *vi* : to work
laboratorio *nm* : laboratory, lab
laboriosidad *nf* : industriousness, diligence
laborioso, -sa *adj* **1** : laborious, hard **2** : industrious, hardworking
labrado¹, -da *adj* **1** : cultivated, tilled **2** : carved, wrought
labrado² *nm* : cultivated field
labrador, -dora *n* : farmer
labranza *nf* : farming
labrar *vt* **1** : to carve, to work (metal) **2** : to cultivate, to till **3** : to cause, to bring about
laca *nf* **1** : lacquer, shellac **2** : hair spray **3 laca de uñas** : nail polish
lacayo *nm* : lackey
lace, etc. → **lazar**
lacear *vt* : to lasso
laceración *nf, pl* **-ciones** : laceration
lacerante *adj* : hurtful, wounding
lacerar *vt* **1** : to lacerate, to cut **2** : to hurt, to wound (one's feelings)
lacio, -cia *adj* **1** : limp, lank **2 pelo lacio** : straight hair

lacónico, -ca *adj* : laconic — **lacónicamente** *adv*
lacra *nf* **1** : scar, mark (on the skin) **2** : stigma, blemish
lacrar *vt* : to seal (with wax)
lacrimógeno, -na *adj* **gas lacrimógeno** : tear gas
lacrimoso, -sa *adj* : tearful, moving
lactancia *nf* **1** : lactation **2** : breast-feeding
lactante *nmf* : nursing infant, suckling
lactar *v* : to breast-feed
lácteo, -tea *adj* **1** : dairy **2 Vía Láctea** : Milky Way
láctico, -ca *adj* : lactic
lactosa *nf* : lactose
ladeado, -da *adj* : crooked, tilted, lopsided
ladear *vt* : to tilt, to tip — **ladearse** *vr* : to bend (over)
ladera *nf* : slope, hillside
ladino¹, -na *adj* **1** : cunning, shrewd **2** *CA, Mex* : mestizo
ladino², -na *n* **1** : trickster **2** *CA, Mex* : Spanish-speaking Indian **3** *CA, Mex* : mestizo
lado *nm* **1** : side **2** PARTE : place ⟨miró por todos lados : he looked everywhere⟩ **3 al lado de** : next to, beside **4 de ~** : tilted, sideways ⟨está de lado : it's lying on its side⟩ **5 hacerse a un lado** : to step aside **6 lado a lado** : side by side **7 por otro lado** : on the other hand
ladrar *vi* : to bark
ladrido *nm* : bark (of a dog), barking
ladrillo *nm* **1** : brick **2** AZULEJO : tile
ladrón, -drona *n, mpl* **ladrones** : robber, thief, burglar
lagartija *nf* : small lizard
lagarto *nm* **1** : lizard **2 lagarto de Indias** : alligator
lago *nm* : lake
lágrima *nf* : tear, teardrop
lagrimear *vi* **1** : to water (of eyes) **2** : to weep easily
laguna *nf* **1** : lagoon **2** : lacuna, gap
laicado *nm* : laity
laico¹, -ca *adj* : lay, secular
laico², -ca *n* : layman *m*, laywoman *f*

laja *nf* : slab
lama[1] *nf* : slime, ooze
lama[2] *nm* : lama
lamber *vt* : to lick
lamé *nm* : lamé
lamentable *adj* **1** : unfortunate, lamentable **2** : pitiful, sad
lamentablemente *adv* : unfortunately, regrettably
lamentación *nf, pl* **-ciones** : lamentation, groaning, moaning
lamentar *vt* **1** : to lament **2** : to regret ⟨lo lamento : I'm sorry⟩ — **lamentarse** *vr* : to grumble, to complain
lamento *nm* : lament, groan, cry
lamer *vt* **1** : to lick **2** : to lap against
lamida *nf* : lick
lámina *nf* **1** PLANCHA : sheet, plate **2** : plate, illustration
laminado[1], **-da** *adj* : laminated
laminado[2] *nm* : laminate
laminar *vt* : to laminate — **laminación** *nf*
lámpara *nf* : lamp
lampiño, -ña *adj* : hairless
lamprea *nf* : lamprey
lana *nf* **1** : wool ⟨lana de acero : steel wool⟩ **2** *Mex fam* : money, dough
lance[1], etc. → **lanzar**
lance[2] *nm* **1** INCIDENTE : event, incident **2** RIÑA : quarrel **3** : throw, cast (of a net, etc.) **4** : move, play (in a game), throw (of dice)
lancear *vt* : to spear
lanceta *nf* : lancet
lancha *nf* **1** : small boat, launch **2** lancha motora : motorboat, speedboat
langosta *nf* **1** : lobster **2** : locust
langostino *nm* : prawn, crayfish
languidecer {53} *vi* : to languish
languidez *nf, pl* **-deces** : languor, listlessness
lánguido, -da *adj* : languid, listless — **lánguidamente** *adv*
lanolina *nf* : lanolin
lanudo, -da *adj* : woolly
lanza *nf* : spear, lance
lanzadera *nf* **1** : shuttle (for weaving) **2** lanzadera espacial : space shuttle
lanzado, -da *adj* **1** : impulsive, brazen **2** : forward, determined ⟨ir lanzado : to hurtle along⟩
lanzador, -dora *n* : thrower, pitcher
lanzallamas *nms & pl* : flamethrower
lanzamiento *nm* **1** : throw **2** : pitch (in baseball) **3** : launching, launch
lanzar {21} *vt* **1** : to throw, to hurl **2** : to pitch **3** : to launch — **lanzarse** *vr* : to throw oneself (at, into) **2** ∼ **a** : to embark upon, to undertake
laosiano, -na *adj & n* : Laotian
lapicero *nm* **1** : mechanical pencil **2** *CA, Peru* : ballpoint pen
lápida *nf* : marker, tombstone
lapidar *vt* APEDREAR : to stone
lapidario, -ria *adj & n* : lapidary
lápiz *nm, pl* **lápices** **1** : pencil **2** lápiz de labios *or* lápiz labial : lipstick

lapón, -pona *adj & n, mpl* **lapones** : Lapp
lapso *nm* : lapse, space (of time)
lapsus *nms & pl* : error, slip
laptop *nm, pl* **laptops** : laptop
laquear *vt* : to lacquer, to varnish, to shellac
largamente *adv* **1** : at length, extensively **2** : easily, comfortably **3** : generously
largar {52} *vt* **1** SOLTAR : to let loose, to release **2** AFLOJAR : to loosen, to slacken **3** *fam* : to give, to hand over **4** *fam* : to hurl, to let fly (insults, etc.) — **largarse** *vr fam* : to scram, to beat it
largo[1], **-ga** *adj* **1** : long **2** a lo largo : lengthwise **3** a lo largo de : along **4** a la larga : in the long run
largo[2] *nm* : length ⟨tres metros de largo : three meters long⟩
largometraje *nm* : feature film
largue, etc. → **largar**
larguero *nm* : crossbeam
largueza *nf* : generosity, largesse
larguirucho, -cha *adj fam* : lanky
largura *nf* : length
laringe *nf* : larynx
laringitis *nfs & pl* : laryngitis
larva *nf* : larva — **larval** *adj*
las → **el**[2], **los**[1]
lasaña *nf* : lasagna
lasca *nf* : chip, chipping
lascivia *nf* : lasciviousness, lewdness
lascivo, -va *adj* : lascivious, lewd — **lascivamente** *adv*
láser *nm* : laser
lasitud *nf* : lassitude, weariness
laso, -sa *adj* : languid, weary
lástima *nf* **1** : compassion, pity **2** PENA : shame, pity ⟨¡qué lástima! : what a shame!⟩
lastimadura *nf* : injury, wound
lastimar *vt* **1** DAÑAR, HERIR : to hurt, to injure **2** AGRAVIAR : to offend — **lastimarse** *vr* : to hurt oneself
lastimero, -ra *adj* : pitiful, wretched
lastimoso, -sa *adj* **1** : shameful **2** : pitiful, terrible
lastrar *vt* **1** : to ballast **2** : to burden, to encumber
lastre *nm* **1** : burden **2** : ballast
lata *nf* **1** : tinplate **2** : tin can **3** *fam* : pest, bother, nuisance **4** dar lata *fam* : to bother, to annoy
latencia *nf* : latency
latente *adj* : latent
lateral[1] *adj* **1** : lateral, side **2** : indirect — **lateralmente** *adv*
lateral[2] *nm* : end piece, side
látex *nms & pl* : latex
latido *nm* : beat, throb ⟨latido del corazón : heartbeat⟩
latifundio *nm* : large estate
latigazo *nm* : lash (with a whip)
látigo *nm* AZOTE : whip
latín *nm* : Latin (language)
latino[1], **-na** *adj* **1** : Latin **2** *fam* : Latin-American

latino², -na *n fam* : Latin American
latinoamericano¹, -na *adj* HISPANO-AMERICANO : Latin American
latinoamericano, -na *n* : Latin American
latir *vi* **1** : to beat, to throb **2 latirle a uno** *Mex fam* : to have a hunch ⟨me late que no va a venir : I have a feeling he's not going to come⟩
latitud *nf* **1** : latitude **2** : breadth
lato, -ta *adj* **1** : extended, lengthy **2** : broad (in meaning)
latón *nm, pl* **latones** : brass
latoso¹, -sa *adj fam* : annoying, bothersome
latoso², -sa *n fam* : pest, nuisance
latrocinio *nm* : larceny
laúd *nm* : lute
laudable *adj* : laudable, praiseworthy
laudo *nm* : findings, decision
laureado, -da *adj & n* : laureate
laurear *vt* : to award, to honor
laurel *nm* **1** : laurel **2** : bay leaf **3 dormirse en sus laureles** : to rest on one's laurels
lava *nf* : lava
lavable *adj* : washable
lavabo *nm* **1** LAVAMANOS : sink, washbowl **2** : lavatory, toilet
lavadero *nm* : laundry room
lavado *nm* **1** : laundry, wash **2** : laundering ⟨lavado de dinero : money laundering⟩
lavadora *nf* : washing machine
lavamanos *nms & pl* LAVABO : sink, washbowl
lavanda *nf* ESPLIEGO : lavender
lavandería *nf* : laundry (service)
lavandero, -ra *n* : launderer, laundress *f*
lavaplatos *nms & pl* **1** : dishwasher **2** *Chile, Col, Mex* : kitchen sink
lavar *vt* **1** : to wash, to clean **2** : to launder (money) **3 lavar en seco** : to dry-clean — **lavarse** *vr* **1** : to wash oneself **2 lavarse las manos de** : to wash one's hands of
lavativa *nf* : enema
lavatorio *nm* : lavatory, washroom
lavavajillas *nms & pl* : dishwasher
laxante *adj & nm* : laxative
laxitud *nf* : laxity, slackness
laxo, -xa *adj* : lax, slack
lazada *nf* : bow, loop
lazar {21} *vt* : to rope, to lasso
lazo *nm* **1** VÍNCULO : link, bond **2** : bow, ribbon **3** : lasso, lariat
le *pron* **1** : to her, to him, to it ⟨¿qué le dijiste? : what did you tell him?⟩ **2** : from her, from him, from it ⟨el ladrón le robó la cartera : the thief stole his wallet⟩ **3** : for her, for him, for it ⟨cómprale flores a tu mamá : buy your mom some flowers⟩ **4** *(formal)* : to you, for you ⟨le traje un regalo : I brought you a gift⟩
leal *adj* : loyal, faithful — **lealmente** *adv*
lealtad *nf* : loyalty, allegiance

lebrel *nm* : hound
lección *nf, pl* **lecciones** : lesson
lechada *nf* **1** : whitewash **2** : grout
lechal *adj* : suckling, unweaned ⟨cordero lechal : suckling lamb⟩
leche *nf* **1** : milk ⟨leche en polvo : powdered milk⟩ ⟨leche de magnesia : milk of magnesia⟩ **2** : milky sap
lechera *nf* **1** : milk jug **2** : dairymaid *f*
lechería *nf* : dairy store
lechero¹, -ra *adj* : dairy
lechero², -ra *n* : milkman *m*, milk dealer
lecho *nm* **1** : bed ⟨un lecho de rosas : a bed of roses⟩ ⟨lecho de muerte : deathbed⟩ **2** : riverbed **3** : layer, stratum (in geology)
lechón, -chona *n, mpl* **lechones** : suckling pig
lechoso, -sa *adj* : milky
lechuga *nf* : lettuce
lechuza *nf* BÚHO : owl, barn owl
lectivo, -va *adj* : school ⟨año lectivo : school year⟩
lector¹, -tora *adj* : reading ⟨nivel lector : reading level⟩
lector², -tora *n* : reader
lector³ *nm* : scanner, reader ⟨lector óptico : optical scanner⟩
lectura *nf* **1** : reading **2** : reading matter
leer {20} *v* : to read
legación *nf, pl* **-ciones** : legation
legado *nm* **1** : legacy, bequest **2** : legate, emissary
legajo *nm* : dossier, file
legal *adj* : legal, lawful — **legalmente** *adv*
legalidad *nf* : legality, lawfulness
legalista *adj* : legalistic
legalizar {21} *vt* : to legalize — **legalización** *nf*
legar {52} *vt* **1** : to bequeath, to hand down **2** DELEGAR : to delegate
legendario, -ria *adj* : legendary
legible *adj* : legible
legión *nf, pl* **legiones** : legion
legionario, -ria *n* : legionnaire
legislación *nf* **1** : legislation, lawmaking **2** : laws *pl*, legislation
legislador¹, -dora *adj* : legislative
legislador², -dora *n* : legislator
legislar *vi* : to legislate
legislativo, -va *adj* : legislative
legislatura *nf* **1** : legislature **2** : term of office
legitimar *vt* **1** : to legitimize **2** : to authenticate — **legitimación** *nf*
legitimidad *nf* : legitimacy
legítimo, -ma *adj* **1** : legitimate **2** : genuine, authentic — **legítimamente** *adv*
lego¹, -ga *adj* **1** : secular, lay **2** : uninformed, ignorant
lego², -ga *n* : layperson, layman *m*, laywoman *f*
legua *nf* **1** : league **2 notarse a leguas** : to be very obvious ⟨se notaba a leguas : you could tell from a mile away⟩

legue, etc. → **legar**
legumbre *nf* **1** HORTALIZA : vegetable
  2 : legume
leíble *adj* : readable
leída *nf* : reading, read ⟨de una leída : in
  one reading, at one go⟩
leído[1] *pp* → **leer**
leído[2], **-da** *adj* : well-read
lejanía *nf* : remoteness, distance
lejano, -na *adj* : remote, distant, far
  away
lejía *nf* **1** : lye **2** : bleach
lejos *adv* **1** : far away, distant ⟨a lo lejos
  : in the distance, far off⟩ ⟨desde lejos
  : from a distance⟩ **2** : long ago, a long
  way off ⟨está lejos de los 50 años : he's
  a long way from 50 years old⟩ **3 de ∼**
  : by far ⟨esta decisión fue de lejos la
  más fácil : this decision was by far the
  easiest⟩ **4 ∼ de** : far from ⟨lejos de ser
  reprobado, recibió una nota de B : far
  from failing, he got a B⟩
lelo, -la *adj* : silly, stupid
lema *nm* : motto, slogan
lencería *nf* : lingerie
lengua *nf* **1** : tongue ⟨morderse la
  lengua : to bite one's tongue⟩ **2** IDIOMA
  : language ⟨lengua materna : mother
  tongue, native language⟩ ⟨lengua
  muerta : dead language⟩
lenguado *nm* : sole, flounder
lenguaje *nm* **1** : language, speech **2**
  lenguaje gestual *or* **lenguaje de
  gestos** : sign language **3 lenguaje de
  programación** : programming language
lengüeta *nf* **1** : tongue (of a shoe), tab,
  flap **2** : reed (of a musical instrument)
  3 : barb, point
lengüetada *nf* **beber a lengüetadas** : to
  lap (up)
lenidad *nf* : leniency
lenitivo, -va *adj* : soothing
lente *nmf* **1** : lens ⟨lentes de contacto
  : contact lenses⟩ **2 lentes** *nmpl* AN-
  TEOJOS : eyeglasses ⟨lentes de sol : sun-
  glasses⟩
lenteja *nf* : lentil
lentejuela *nf* : sequin, spangle
lentitud *nf* : slowness
lento[1] *adv* DESPACIO : slowly
lento[2], **-ta** *adj* **1** : slow **2** : slow-witted,
  dull — **lentamente** *adv*
leña *nf* : wood, firewood
leñador, -dora *n* : lumberjack, woodcutter
leñera *nf* : woodshed
leño *nm* : log
leñoso, -sa *adj* : woody
Leo *nmf* : Leo
león, -ona *n, mpl* **leones 1** : lion, lioness
  f **2** (*in various countries*) : puma, cougar
leonado, -da *adj* : tawny
leonino, -na *adj* **1** : leonine **2** : one-
  sided, unfair
leopardo *nm* : leopard
leotardo *nm* MALLA : leotard, tights *pl*
leperada *nf Mex* : obscenity

lépero, -ra *adj Mex* : vulgar, coarse
lepra *nf* : leprosy
leproso[1], **-sa** *adj* : leprous
leproso[2], **-sa** *n* : leper
lerdo, -da *adj* **1** : clumsy **2** : dull, oafish,
  slow-witted
les *pron* **1** : to them ⟨dales una propina
  : give them a tip⟩ **2** : from them ⟨se
  les privó de su herencia : they were de-
  prived of their inheritance⟩ **3** : for
  them ⟨les hice sus tareas : I did their
  homework for them⟩ **4** : to you *pl*, for
  you *pl* ⟨les compré un regalo : I bought
  you all a present⟩
lesbiana *nf* : lesbian — **lesbiano, -na** *adj*
lesbianismo *nm* : lesbianism
lesión *nf, pl* **lesiones** HERIDA : lesion,
  wound, injury ⟨una lesión grave : a serious injury⟩
lesionado, -da *adj* HERIDO : injured,
  wounded
lesionar *vt* : to injure, to wound — **le-
  sionarse** *vr* : to hurt oneself
lesivo, -va *adj* : harmful, damaging
letal *adj* MORTÍFERO : deadly, lethal —
  letalmente *adv*
letanía *nf* **1** : litany **2** *fam* : spiel, song
  and dance
letárgico, -ca *adj* : lethargic
letargo *nm* : lethargy, torpor
letón[1], **-tona** *adj & n, mpl* **letones** : Latvian
letón[2] *nm* : Latvian (language)
letra *nf* **1** : letter **2** CALIGRAFÍA : handwriting, lettering **3** : lyrics *pl* **4 al pie
  de la letra** : word for word, by the book
  5 letras *nfpl* : arts (in education)
letrado[1], **-da** *adj* ERUDITO : learned, erudite
letrado[2], **-da** *n* : attorney-at-law, lawyer
letrero *nm* RÓTULO : sign, notice
letrina *nf* : latrine
letrista *nmf* : lyricist, songwriter
leucemia *nf* : leukemia
leva *nf* : cam
levadizo, -za *adj* **1** : liftable **2 puente
  levadizo** : drawbridge
levadura *nf* **1** : yeast, leavening **2
  levadura en polvo** : baking powder
levantamiento *nm* **1** ALZAMIENTO : uprising **2** : raising, lifting ⟨levantamien-
  to de pesas : weight lifting⟩
levantar *vt* **1** ALZAR : to lift, to raise **2**
  : to put up, to erect **3** : to call off, to
  adjourn **4** : to give rise to, to arouse
  ⟨levantar sospechas : to arouse suspi-
  cion⟩ — **levantarse** *vr* **1** : to rise, to
  stand up **2** : to get out of bed
levar *vt* **levar anclas** : to weigh anchor
leve *adj* **1** : light, slight **2** : trivial, unimportant — **levemente** *adv*
levedad *nf* : lightness
levemente *adv* LIGERAMENTE : lightly,
  softly
leviatán *nm, pl* **-tanes** : leviathan
léxico[1], **-ca** *adj* : lexical
léxico[2] *nm* : lexicon, glossary
lexicografía *nf* : lexicography

lexicográfico, -ca *adj* : lexicographical, lexicographic

lexicógrafo, -fa *n* : lexicographer

ley *nf* **1** : law ⟨fuera de la ley : outside the law⟩ ⟨la ley de gravedad : the law of gravity⟩ **2** : purity (of metals) ⟨oro de ley : pure gold⟩

leyenda *nf* **1** : legend **2** : caption, inscription

leyó, etc. → **leer**

liar {85} *vt* **1** ATAR : to bind, to tie (up) **2** : to roll (a cigarette) **3** : to confuse — **liarse** *vr* : to get mixed up

libanés, -nesa *adj & n, mpl* **-neses** : Lebanese

libar *vt* **1** : to suck (nectar) **2** : to sip, to swig (liquor, etc.)

libelo *nm* **1** : libel, lampoon **2** : petition (in court)

libélula *nf* : dragonfly

liberación *nf, pl* **-ciones** : liberation, deliverance ⟨liberación de la mujer : women's liberation⟩

liberado, -da *adj* **1** : liberated ⟨una mujer liberada : a liberated woman⟩ **2** : freed, delivered

liberal *adj & nmf* : liberal

liberalidad *nf* : generosity, liberality

liberalismo *nm* : liberalism

liberalizar {21} *vt* : to liberalize — **liberalización** *nf*

liberar *vt* : to liberate, to free — **liberarse** *vr* : to get free of

liberiano, -na *adj & n* : Liberian

libertad *nf* **1** : freedom, liberty ⟨tomarse la libertad de : to take the liberty of⟩ **2 libertad bajo fianza** : bail **3 libertad condicional** : parole

libertador[1], -dora *adj* : liberating

libertador[2], -dora *n* : liberator

libertar *vt* LIBRAR : to set free

libertario, -ria *adj & n* : libertarian

libertinaje *nm* : licentiousness, dissipation

libertino[1], -na *adj* : licentious, dissolute

libertino[2], -na *n* : libertine

libidinoso, -sa *adj* : lustful, lewd

libido *nf* : libido

libio, -bia *adj & n* : Libyan

libra *nf* **1** : pound **2 libra esterlina** : pound sterling

Libra *nmf* : Libra

libramiento *nm* **1** : liberating, freeing **2** LIBRANZA : order of payment **3** *Mex* : beltway

libranza *nf* : order of payment

librar *vt* **1** LIBERTAR : to deliver, to set free **2** : to wage ⟨librar batalla : to do battle⟩ **3** : to issue ⟨librar una orden : to issue an order⟩ — **librarse** *vr* ~ **de** : to free oneself from, to get out of

libre[1] *adj* **1** : free ⟨un país libre : a free country⟩ ⟨libre de : free from, exempt from⟩ ⟨libre albedrío : free will⟩ **2** DESOCUPADO : vacant **3 día libre** : day off

libre[2] *nm Mex* : taxi

librea *nf* : livery

librecambio *nm* : free trade

libremente *adv* : freely

librería *nf* : bookstore

librero[1], -ra *n* : bookseller

librero[2] *nm Mex* : bookcase

libresco, -ca *adj* : bookish

libreta *nf* CUADERNO : notebook

libretista *nmf* **1** : librettist **2** : scriptwriter

libreto *nm* : libretto, script

libro *nm* **1** : book ⟨libro de texto : textbook⟩ **2 libros** *nmpl* : books (in bookkeeping), accounts ⟨llevar los libros : to keep the books⟩

licencia *nf* **1** : permission **2** : leave, leave of absence **3** : permit, license ⟨licencia de conducir : driver's license⟩

licenciado, -da *n* **1** : university graduate **2** ABOGADO : lawyer

licenciar *vt* **1** : to license, to permit, to allow **2** : to discharge **3** : to grant a university degree to — **licenciarse** *vr* : to graduate

licenciatura *nf* **1** : college degree **2** : course of study (at a college or university)

licencioso, -sa *adj* : licentious, lewd

liceo *nm* : secondary school, high school

licitación *nf, pl* **-ciones** : bid, bidding

licitar *vt* : to bid on

lícito, -ta *adj* **1** : lawful, licit **2** JUSTO : just, fair

licor *nm* **1** : liquor **2** : liqueur

licorera *nf* : decanter

licuado *nm* BATIDO : milk shake

licuadora *nf* : blender

licuar {3} *vt* : to liquefy — **licuarse** *vr*

lid *nf* **1** : fight, combat **2** : argument, dispute **3 lides** *nfpl* : matters, affairs **4 en buena lid** : fair and square

líder[1] *adj* : leading, foremost

líder[2] *nmf* : leader

liderar *vt* DIRIGIR : to lead, to head

liderato *nm* : leadership, leading

liderazgo → **liderato**

lidiar *vt* : to fight — *vi* BATALLAR, LUCHAR : to struggle, to battle, to wrestle

liebre *nf* : hare

liendre *nf* : nit

lienzo *nm* **1** : linen **2** : canvas, painting **3** : stretch of wall or fencing

liga *nf* **1** ASOCIACIÓN : league **2** GOMITA : rubber band **3** : garter

ligado, -da *adj* : linked, connected

ligadura *nf* **1** ATADURA : tie, bond **2** : ligature

ligamento *nm* : ligament

ligar {52} *vt* : to bind, to tie (up)

ligeramente *adv* **1** : slightly **2** LEVEMENTE : lightly, gently **3** : casually, flippantly

ligereza *nf* **1** : lightness **2** : flippancy **3** : agility

ligero, -ra *adj* **1** : light, lightweight **2** : slight, minor **3** : agile, quick **4** : lighthearted, superficial

lignito *nm* : lignite

ligue, etc. → ligar
lija *nf or* **papel de lija** : sandpaper
lijar *vt* : to sand
lila¹ *adj* : lilac, light purple
lila² *nf* : lilac
lima *nf* **1** : lime (fruit) **2** : file ⟨lima de uñas : nail file⟩
limadora *nf* : polisher
limar *vt* **1** : to file **2** : to polish, to put the final touch on **3** : to smooth over ⟨limar las diferencias : to iron out differences⟩
limbo *nm* **1** : limbo **2** : limb (in botany and astronomy)
limeño¹, -ña *adj* : of or from Lima, Peru
limeño², -ña *n* : person from Lima, Peru
limero *nm* : lime tree
limitación *nf, pl* **-ciones 1** : limitation **2** : limit, restriction ⟨sin limitación : unlimited⟩
limitado, -da *adj* **1** RESTRINGIDO : limited **2** : dull, slow-witted
limitar *vt* RESTRINGIR : to limit, to restrict — *vi* ~ **con** : to border on — **limitarse** *vr* ~ **a** : to limit oneself to
límite *nm* **1** : boundary, border **2** : limit ⟨el límite de mi paciencia : the limit of my patience⟩ ⟨límite de velocidad : speed limit⟩ **3 fecha límite** : deadline
limítrofe *adj* LINDANTE, LINDERO : bordering, adjoining
limo *nm* : slime, mud
limón *nm, pl* **limones 1** : lemon **2** : lemon tree **3 limón verde** *Mex* : lime
limonada *nf* : lemonade
limosna *nf* : alms, charity
limosnear *vi* : to beg (for alms)
limosnero, -ra *n* MENDIGO : beggar
limoso, -sa *adj* : slimy
limpiabotas *nmfs & pl* : bootblack
limpiador¹, -dora *adj* : cleaning
limpiador², -dora *n* : cleaning person, cleaner
limpiamente *adv* : cleanly, honestly, fairly
limpiaparabrisas *nms & pl* : windshield wiper
limpiar *vt* **1** : to clean, to cleanse **2** : to clean up, to remove defects **3** *fam* : to clean out (in a game) **4** *fam* : to swipe, to pinch — *vi* : to clean — **limpiarse** *vr*
limpiavidrios *nmfs & pl Mex* : windshield wiper
límpido, -da *adj* : limpid
limpieza *nf* **1** : cleanliness, tidiness **2** : cleaning **3** HONRADEZ : integrity, honesty **4** DESTREZA : skill, dexterity
limpio¹ *adv* : fairly
limpio², -pia *adj* **1** : clean, neat **2** : honest ⟨un juego limpio : a fair game⟩ **3** : free ⟨limpio de impurezas : pure, free from impurities⟩ **4** : clear, net ⟨ganancia limpia : clear profit⟩
limusina *nf* : limousine
linaje *nm* ABOLENGO : lineage, ancestry
linaza *nf* : linseed
lince *nm* : lynx

linchamiento *nm* : lynching
linchar *vt* : to lynch
lindante *adj* LIMÍTROFE, LINDERO : bordering, adjoining
lindar *vi* **1** ~ **con** : to border, to skirt **2** ~ **con** BORDEAR : to border on, to verge on
linde *nmf* : boundary, limit
lindero¹, -ra *adj* LIMÍTROFE, LINDANTE : bordering, adjoining
lindero² *nm* : boundary, limit
lindeza *nf* **1** : prettiness **2** : clever remark **3 lindezas** *nfpl, (used ironically)* : insults
lindo¹ *adv* **1** : beautifully, wonderfully ⟨canta lindo tu mujer : your wife sings beautifully⟩ **2 de lo lindo** : a lot, a great deal ⟨los zancudos nos picaban de lo lindo : the mosquitoes were biting away at us⟩
lindo², -da *adj* **1** BONITO : pretty, lovely **2** MONO : cute
línea *nf* **1** : line ⟨línea divisoria : dividing line⟩ ⟨línea de banda : sideline⟩ **2** : line, course, position ⟨línea de conducta : course of action⟩ ⟨en líneas generales : in general terms, along general lines⟩ **3** : line, service ⟨línea aérea : airline⟩ ⟨línea telefónica : telephone line⟩
lineal *adj* : linear
linfa *nf* : lymph
linfático, -ca *adj* : lymphatic
lingote *nm* : ingot
lingüista *nmf* : linguist
lingüística *nf* : linguistics
lingüístico, -ca *adj* : linguistic
linimento *nm* : liniment
lino *nm* **1** : linen **2** : flax
linóleo *nm* : linoleum
linterna *nf* **1** : lantern **2** : flashlight
lío *nm fam* **1** : confusion, mess **2** : hassle, trouble, jam ⟨meterse en un lío : to get into a jam⟩ **3** : affair, liaison
liofilizar {21} *vt* : to freeze-dry
lioso, -sa *adj fam* **1** : confusing, muddled **2** : troublemaking
liquen *nm* : lichen
liquidación *nf, pl* **-ciones 1** : liquidation **2** : clearance sale **3** : settlement, payment
liquidar *vt* **1** : to liquefy **2** : to liquidate **3** : to settle, to pay off **4** *fam* : to rub out, to kill
liquidez *nf, pl* **-deces** : liquidity
líquido¹, -da *adj* **1** : liquid, fluid **2** : net ⟨ingresos líquidos : net income⟩
líquido² *nm* **1** : liquid, fluid ⟨líquido de frenos : brake fluid⟩ **2** : ready cash, liquid assets
lira *nf* : lyre
lírica *nf* : lyric poetry
lírico, -ca *adj* : lyric, lyrical
lirio *nm* **1** : iris **2 lirio de los valles** MUGUETE : lily of the valley
lirismo *nm* : lyricism
lirón *nm, pl* **lirones** : dormouse
lisiado¹, -da *adj* : disabled, crippled

lisiado², **-da** *n* : disabled person, cripple
lisiar *vt* : to cripple, to disable — **lisiarse** *vr*
liso, **-sa** *adj* **1** : smooth **2** : flat **3** : straight ⟨pelo liso : straight hair⟩ **4** : plain, unadorned ⟨liso y llano : plain and simple⟩
lisonja *nf* : flattery
lisonjear *vt* ADULAR : to flatter
lista *nf* **1** : list **2** : roster, roll ⟨pasar lista : to take attendance⟩ **3** : stripe, strip **4** : menu
listado¹, **-da** *adj* : striped
listado² *nm* : listing
listar *vt* : to list
listeza *nf* : smartness, alertness
listo, **-ta** *adj* **1** DISPUESTO, PREPARADO : ready ⟨¿estás listo? : are you ready?⟩ **2** : clever, smart
listón *nm, pl* **listones 1** : ribbon **2** : strip (of wood), lath **3** : high bar (in sports)
lisura *nf* : smoothness
litera *nf* : bunk bed, berth
literal *adj* : literal — **literalmente** *adv*
literario, **-ria** *adj* : literary
literato, **-ta** *n* : writer, author
literatura *nf* : literature
litigante *adj & nmf* : litigant
litigar {52} *vi* : to litigate, to be in litigation
litigio *nm* **1** : litigation, lawsuit **2 en ~** : in dispute
litigioso, **-sa** *adj* : litigious
litio *nm* : lithium
litografía *nf* **1** : lithography **2** : lithograph
litógrafo, **-fa** *n* : lithographer
litoral¹ *adj* : coastal
litoral² *nm* : shore, seaboard
litosfera *nf* : lithosphere
litro *nm* : liter
lituano¹, **-na** *adj & n* : Lithuanian
lituano² *nm* : Lithuanian (language)
liturgia *nf* : liturgy
litúrgico, **-ca** *adj* : liturgical — **litúrgicamente** *adv*
liviandad *nf* LIGEREZA : lightness
liviano, **-na** *adj* **1** : light, slight **2** INCONSTANTE : fickle
lividez *nf* PALIDEZ : pallor
lívido, **-da** *adj* **1** AMORATADO : livid **2** PÁLIDO : pallid, extremely pale
living *nm* : living room
llaga *nf* : sore, wound
llama *nf* **1** : flame **2** : llama
llamada *nf* : call ⟨llamada a larga distancia : long-distance call⟩ ⟨llamada al orden : call to order⟩
llamado¹, **-da** *adj* : named, called ⟨una mujer llamada Rosa : a woman called Rosa⟩
llamado² → **llamamiento**
llamador *nm* : door knocker
llamamiento *nm* : call, appeal
llamar *vt* **1** : to name, to call **2** : to call, to summon **3** : to phone, to call up — **llamarse** *vr* : to be called, to be named ⟨¿cómo te llamas? : what's your name?⟩

llamarada *nf* **1** : flare-up, sudden blaze **2** : flushing (of the face)
llamativo, **-va** *adj* : flashy, showy, striking
llameante *adj* : flaming, blazing
llamear *vi* : to flame, to blaze
llana *nf* **1** : trowel **2** → **llano²**
llanamente *adv* : simply, plainly, straightforwardly
llaneza *nf* : simplicity, naturalness
llano¹, **-na** *adj* **1** : even, flat **2** : frank, open **3** LISO : plain, simple
llano² *nm* : plain
llanta *nf* **1** NEUMÁTICO : tire **2** : rim
llantén *nm, pl* **llantenes** : plantain (weed)
llanto *nm* : crying, weeping
llanura *nf* : plain, prairie
llave *nf* **1** : key **2** : faucet **3** INTERRUPTOR : switch **4** : brace (punctuation mark) **5 llave inglesa** : monkey wrench
llavero *nm* : key chain, key ring
llegada *nf* : arrival
llegar {52} *vi* **1** : to arrive, to come **2 ~ a** : to arrive at, to reach, to amount to **3 ~ a** : to manage to ⟨llegó a terminar la novela : she managed to finish the novel⟩ **4 llegar a ser** : to become ⟨llegó a ser un miembro permanente : he became a permanent member⟩
llegue, etc. → **llegar**
llenar *vt* **1** : to fill, to fill up, to fill in **2** : to meet, to fulfill ⟨los regalos no llenaron sus expectativas : the gifts did not meet her expectations⟩ — **llenarse** *vr* : to fill up, to become full
llenito, **-ta** *adj fam* REGORDETE : chubby, plump
lleno¹, **-na** *adj* **1** : full, filled **2 de ~** : completely, fully **3 estar lleno de sí mismo** : to be full of oneself
lleno² *nm* **1** *fam* : plenty, abundance **2** : full house, sellout
llevadero, **-ra** *adj* : bearable
llevar *vt* **1** : to take away, to carry ⟨me gusta, me lo llevo : I like it, I'll take it⟩ **2** : to wear **3** : to take, to lead ⟨llevamos a Pedro al cine : we took Pedro to the movies⟩ **4 llevar a cabo** : to carry out **5 llevar adelante** : to carry on, to keep going — *vi* : to lead ⟨un problema lleva al otro : one problem leads to another⟩ — *v aux* : to have ⟨llevo mucho tiempo buscándolo : I've been looking for it for a long time⟩ ⟨lleva leído medio libro : he's halfway through the book⟩ — **llevarse** *vr* **1** : to take away, to carry off **2** : to get along ⟨siempre nos llevábamos bien : we always got along well⟩
llorar *vi* : to cry, to weep — *vt* : to mourn, to bewail
lloriquear *vi* : to whimper, to whine
lloriqueo *nm* : whimpering, whining
llorón, **-rona** *n, mpl* **llorones** : crybaby, whiner
lloroso, **-sa** *adj* : tearful, sad

llovedizo, -za *adj* : rain ⟨agua llovediza : rainwater⟩

llover {47} *v impers* : to rain ⟨está lloviendo : it's raining⟩ ⟨llover a cántaros : to rain cats and dogs⟩ — *vi* : to rain down, to shower ⟨le llovieron regalos : he was showered with gifts⟩

llovizna *nf* : drizzle, sprinkle

lloviznar *v impers* : to drizzle, to sprinkle

llueve, etc. → **llover**

lluvia *nf* **1** : rain, rainfall **2** : barrage, shower

lluvioso, -sa *adj* : rainy

lo[1] *pron* **1** : him, it ⟨lo vi ayer : I saw him yesterday⟩ ⟨lo entiendo : I understand it⟩ ⟨no lo creo : I don't believe so⟩ **2** (*formal, masculine*) : you ⟨disculpe, señor, no lo oí : excuse me sir, I didn't hear you⟩ **3 lo que** : what, that which ⟨eso es lo que más le gusta : that's what he likes the most⟩

lo[2] *art* **1** : the ⟨lo mejor : the best, the best thing⟩ **2** : how ⟨sé lo bueno que eres : I know how good you are⟩

loa *nf* : praise

loable *adj* : laudable, praiseworthy — **loablemente** *adv*

loar *vt* : to praise, to laud

lobato, -ta *n* : wolf cub

lobby *nm* : lobby, pressure group

lobo, -ba *n* : wolf

lóbrego, -ga *adj* SOMBRÍO : gloomy, dark

lobulado, -da *adj* : lobed

lóbulo *nm* : lobe ⟨lóbulo de la oreja : earlobe⟩

locación *nf, pl* **-ciones 1** : location (in moviemaking) **2** *Mex* : place

local[1] *adj* : local — **localmente** *adv*

local[2] *nm* : premises *pl*

localidad *nf* : town, locality

localización *nf, pl* **-ciones 1** : locating, localization **2** : location

localizar {21} *vt* **1** UBICAR : to locate, to find **2** : to localize — **localizarse** *vr* UBICARSE : to be located ⟨se localiza en el séptimo piso : it is located on the seventh floor⟩

locatario, -ria *n* : tenant

loción *nf, pl* **-ciones** : lotion

lócker *nm, pl* **lóckers** : locker

loco[1], **-ca** *adj* **1** DEMENTE : crazy, insane, mad **2 a lo loco** : wildly, recklessly **3 volverse loco** : to go mad

loco[2], **-ca** *n* **1** : crazy person, lunatic **2 hacerse el loco** : to act the fool

locomoción *nf, pl* **-ciones** : locomotion

locomotor, -tora *adj* : locomotive

locomotora *nf* **1** : locomotive **2** : driving force

locuacidad *nf* : loquacity, talkativeness

locuaz *adj, pl* **locuaces** : loquacious, talkative

locución *nf, pl* **-ciones** : locution, phrase ⟨locución adverbial : adverbial phrase⟩

locura *nf* **1** : insanity, madness **2** : crazy thing, folly

locutor, -tora *n* : announcer

lodazal *nm* : bog, quagmire

lodo *nm* BARRO : mud, mire

lodoso, -sa *adj* : muddy

logaritmo *nm* : logarithm

logia *nf* : lodge ⟨logia masónica : Masonic lodge⟩

lógica *nf* : logic

lógico, -ca *adj* : logical — **lógicamente** *adv*

logística *nf* : logistics *pl*

logístico, -ca *adj* : logistic, logistical

logo → **logotipo**

logotipo *nm* : logo

logrado, -da *adj* : successful, well done

lograr *vt* **1** : to get, to obtain **2** : to achieve, to attain — **lograrse** *vr* : to be successful

logro *nm* : achievement, attainment

loma *nf* : hill, hillock

lombriz *nf, pl* **lombrices** : worm ⟨lombriz de tierra : earthworm, night crawler⟩ ⟨lombriz solitaria : tapeworm⟩ ⟨tener lombrices : to have worms⟩

lomo *nm* **1** : back (of an animal) **2** : loin ⟨lomo de cerdo : pork loin⟩ **3** : spine (of a book) **4** : blunt edge (of a knife)

lona *nf* : canvas

loncha *nf* LONJA, REBANADA : slice

lonche *nm* **1** ALMUERZO : lunch **2** *Mex* : submarine sandwich

lonchería *nf Mex* : luncheonette

londinense[1] *adj* : of or from London

londinense[2] *nmf* : Londoner

longaniza *nf* : spicy pork sausage

longevidad *nf* : longevity

longevo, -va *adj* : long-lived

longitud *nf* **1** LARGO : length ⟨longitud de onda : wavelength⟩ **2** : longitude

longitudinal *adj* : longitudinal

lonja *nf* LONCHA, REBANADA : slice

lontananza *nf* : background ⟨en lontananza : in the distance, far away⟩

lord *nm, pl* **lores** (*title in England*) : lord

loro *nm* : parrot

los[1], **las** *pron* **1** : them ⟨hice galletas y se las di a los nuevos vecinos : I made cookies and gave them to the new neighbors⟩ **2** : you ⟨voy a llevarlos a los dos : I am going to take both of you⟩ **3 los que, las que** : those, who, the ones ⟨los que van a cantar deben venir temprano : those who are singing must come early⟩ **4** (*used with* **haber**) ⟨los hay en varios colores : they come in various colors⟩

los[2] *art* → **el**[2]

losa *nf* : flagstone, paving stone

loseta *nf* BALDOSA : floor tile

lote *nm* **1** : part, share **2** : batch, lot **3** : plot of land, lot

lotería *nf* : lottery

loto *nm* : lotus

loza *nf* **1** : crockery, earthenware **2** : china

lozanía *nf* **1** : healthiness, robustness **2** : luxuriance, lushness

lozano, -na *adj* **1** : robust, healthy-looking ⟨un rostro lozano : a smooth, fresh face⟩ **2** : lush, luxuriant

LSD *nm* : LSD

lubricante[1] *adj* : lubricating

lubricante[2] *nm* : lubricant

lubricar {72} *vt* : to lubricate, to oil — **lubricación** *nf*

lucero *nm* : bright star ⟨lucero del alba : morning star⟩

lucha *nf* **1** : struggle, fight **2** : wrestling

luchador, -dora *n* **1** : fighter **2** : wrestler

luchar *vi* **1** : to fight, to struggle **2** : to wrestle

luchón, -chona *adj, mpl* **luchones** *Mex* : industrious, hardworking

lucidez *nf, pl* **-deces** : lucidity, clarity

lucido, -da *adj* MAGNÍFICO : magnificent, splendid

lúcido, -da *adj* : lucid

luciérnaga *nf* : firefly, glowworm

lucimiento *nm* **1** : brilliance, splendor, sparkle **2** : triumph, success ⟨salir con lucimiento : to succeed with flying colors⟩

lucio *nm* : pike (fish)

lucir {45} *vi* **1** : to shine **2** : to look good, to stand out **3** : to seem, to appear ⟨ahora luce contento : he looks happy now⟩ — *vt* **1** : to wear, to sport **2** : to flaunt, to show off — **lucirse** *vr* **1** : to distinguish oneself, to excel **2** : to show off

lucrarse *vr* : to make a profit

lucrativo, -va *adj* : lucrative, profitable — **lucrativamente** *adv*

lucro *nm* GANANCIA : profit, gain

luctuoso, -sa *adj* : mournful, tragic

luego[1] *adv* **1** DESPUÉS : then, afterwards **2** : later (on) **3** desde ∼ : of course **4** ¡hasta luego! : see you later! **5** luego que : as soon as **6** luego luego *Mex fam* : right away, immediately

luego[2] *conj* : therefore ⟨pienso, luego existo : I think, therefore I am⟩

lugar *nm* **1** : place, position ⟨se llevó el primer lugar en su división : she took first place in her division⟩ **2** ESPACIO : space, room **3** dar lugar a : to give rise to, to lead to **4** en lugar de : instead of **5** lugar común : cliché, platitude **6** tener lugar : to take place

lugareño[1], -ña *adj* : village, rural

lugareño[2], -ña *n* : villager

lugarteniente *nmf* : lieutenant, deputy

lúgubre *adj* : gloomy, lugubrious

lujo *nm* **1** : luxury **2** de ∼ : deluxe

lujoso, -sa *adj* : luxurious

lujuria *nf* : lust, lechery

lujurioso, -sa *adj* : lustful, lecherous

lumbago *nm* : lumbago

lumbar *adj* : lumbar

lumbre *nf* **1** FUEGO : fire **2** : brilliance, splendor **3** poner en la lumbre : to put on the stove, to warm up

lumbrera *nf* **1** : skylight **2** : vent, port **3** : brilliant person, luminary

luminaria *nf* **1** : altar lamp **2** LUMBRERA : luminary, celebrity

luminiscencia *nf* : luminescence — **luminiscente** *adj*

luminosidad *nf* : luminosity, brightness

luminoso, -sa *adj* : shining, luminous

luna *nf* **1** : moon **2** luna de miel : honeymoon

lunar[1] *adj* : lunar

lunar[2] *nm* **1** : mole, beauty spot **2** : defect, blemish **3** : polka dot

lunático, -ca *adj & n* : lunatic

lunes *nms & pl* : Monday

luneta *nf* **1** : lens (of eyeglasses) **2** : windshield (of an automobile) **3** : crescent

lupa *nf* : magnifying glass

lúpulo *nm* : hops (plant)

lustrar *vt* : to shine, to polish

lustre *nm* **1** BRILLO : luster, shine **2** : glory, distinction

lustroso, -sa *adj* BRILLOSO : lustrous, shiny

luto *nm* : mourning ⟨estar de luto : to be in mourning⟩

luz *nf, pl* **luces** **1** : light **2** : lighting **3** *fam* : electricity **4** : window, opening **5** : light, lamp **6** : span, spread (between supports) **7** a la luz de : in light of **8** dar a luz : to give birth **9** traje de luces : matador's costume

luzca, etc. → **lucir**

M

m *nf* : thirteenth letter of the Spanish alphabet

macabro, -bra *adj* : macabre

macaco[1], -ca *adj* : ugly, misshapen

macaco[2], -ca *n* : macaque

macadán *nm, pl* **-danes** : macadam

macana *nf* **1** : club, cudgel **2** *fam* : nonsense, silliness **3** *fam* : lie, fib

macanudo, -da *adj fam* : great, fantastic

macarrón *nm, pl* **-rrones** **1** : macaroon **2** macarrones *nmpl* : macaroni

maceta *nf* **1** : flowerpot **2** : mallet **3** *Mex fam* : head

macetero *nm* **1** : plant stand **2** TIESTO : flowerpot, planter

machacar {72} *vt* **1** : to crush, to grind **2** : to beat, to pound — *vi* : to insist, to go on (about)

machacón, -cona *adj, mpl* **-cones** : insistent, tiresome

machete *nm* : machete

machetear *vt* : to hack with a machete — *vi Mex fam* : to plod, to work tirelessly

machismo *nm* **1** : machismo **2** : male chauvinism

machista *nm* : male chauvinist

macho[1] *adj* **1** : male **2** : macho, virile, tough
macho[2] *nm* **1** : male **2** : he-man
machote *nm* **1** *fam* : tough guy, he-man **2** *CA, Mex* : rough draft, model **3** *Mex* : blank form
machucar {72} *vt* **1** : to pound, to beat, to crush **2** : to bruise
machucón *nm, pl* **-cones 1** MORETÓN : bruise **2** : smashing, pounding
macilento, -ta *adj* : gaunt, wan
macis *nm* : mace (spice)
macizo, -za *adj* **1** : solid ⟨oro macizo : solid gold⟩ **2** : strong, strapping **3** : massive
macrocosmo *nm* : macrocosm
mácula *nf* : blemish, stain
madeja *nf* **1** : skein, hank **2** : tangle (of hair)
madera *nf* **1** : wood **2** : lumber, timber **3 madera dura** *or* **madera noble** : hardwood
maderero, -ra *adj* : timber, lumber
madero *nm* : piece of lumber, plank
madrastra *nf* : stepmother
madrazo *nm Mex fam* : punch, blow ⟨se agarraron a madrazos : they beat each other up⟩
madre *nf* **1** : mother **2 madre política** : mother-in-law **3 la Madre Patria** : the mother country (said of Spain)
madrear *vt Mex fam* : to beat up
madreperla *nf* NÁCAR : mother-of-pearl
madreselva *nf* : honeysuckle
madriguera *nf* : burrow, den, lair
madrileño[1], **-ña** *adj* : of or from Madrid
madrileño[2], **-ña** *n* : person from Madrid
madrina *nf* **1** : godmother **2** : bridesmaid **3** : sponsor
madrugada *nf* **1** : early morning, wee hours **2** ALBA : dawn, daybreak
madrugador, -dora *n* : early riser
madrugar {52} *vi* **1** : to get up early **2** : to get a head start
madurar *v* **1** : to ripen **2** : to mature
madurez *nf, pl* **-reces 1** : maturity **2** : ripeness
maduro, -ra *adj* **1** : mature **2** : ripe
maestría *nf* **1** : mastery, skill **2** : master's degree
maestro[1], **-tra** *adj* **1** : masterly, skilled **2** : chief, main **3** : trained ⟨un elefante maestro : a trained elephant⟩
maestro[2], **-tra** *n* **1** : teacher (in grammar school) **2** : expert, master **3** : maestro
Mafia *nf* : Mafia
mafioso, -sa *n* : mafioso, gangster
magdalena *nf* : bun, muffin
magenta *adj & n* : magenta
magia *nf* : magic
mágico, -ca *adj* : magic, magical — **mágicamente** *adv*
magisterio *nm* **1** : teaching **2** : teachers *pl*, teaching profession
magistrado, -da *n* : magistrate, judge
magistral *adj* **1** : masterful, skillful **2** : magisterial

magistralmente *adv* : masterfully, brilliantly
magistratura *nf* : judgeship, magistracy
magma *nm* : magma
magnanimidad *nf* : magnanimity
magnánimo, -ma *adj* GENEROSO : magnanimous — **magnánimamente** *adv*
magnate *nmf* : magnate, tycoon
magnesia *nf* : magnesia
magnesio *nm* : magnesium
magnético, -ca *adj* : magnetic
magnetismo *nm* : magnetism
magnetizar {21} *vt* : to magnetize
magnetófono *nm* : tape recorder
magnetofónico, -ca *adj* **cinta magnetofónica** : magnetic tape
magnificar {72} *vt* **1** : to magnify **2** EXAGERAR : to exaggerate **3** ENSALZAR : to exalt, to extol, to praise highly
magnificencia *nf* : magnificence, splendor
magnífico, -ca *adj* ESPLENDOROSO : magnificent, splendid — **magníficamente** *adv*
magnitud *nf* : magnitude
magnolia *nf* : magnolia (flower)
magnolio *nm* : magnolia (tree)
mago, -ga *n* **1** : magician **2** : wizard (in folk tales, etc.) **3 los Reyes Magos** : the Magi
magro, -gra *adj* **1** : lean (of meat) **2** : meager
maguey *nm* : maguey
magulladura *nf* MORETÓN : bruise
magullar *vt* : to bruise — **magullarse** *vr*
mahometano[1], **-na** *adj* ISLÁMICO : Islamic, Muslim
mahometano[2], **-na** *n* : Muslim
mahonesa → **mayonesa**
maicena *nf* : cornstarch
mainframe ['mein,freim] *nm* : mainframe
maíz *nm* : corn, maize
maizal *nm* : cornfield
maja *nf* : pestle
majadería *nf* **1** TONTERÍA : stupidity, foolishness **2** *Mex* LEPERADA : insult, obscenity
majadero[1], **-ra** *adj* **1** : foolish, silly **2** *Mex* LÉPERO : crude, vulgar
majadero[2], **-ra** *n* **1** TONTO : fool **2** *Mex* : rude person, boor
majar *vt* : to crush, to mash
majestad *nf* : majesty ⟨Su Majestad : Your Majesty⟩
majestuosamente *adv* : majestically
majestuosidad *nf* : majesty, grandeur
majestuoso, -sa *adj* : majestic, stately
majo, -ja *adj Spain* **1** : nice, likeable **2** GUAPO : attractive, good-looking
mal[1] *adv* **1** : badly, poorly ⟨baila muy mal : he dances very badly⟩ **2** : wrong, incorrectly ⟨me entendió mal : she misunderstood me⟩ **3** : with difficulty, hardly ⟨mal puedo oírte : I can hardly hear you⟩ **4 de mal en peor** : from bad to worse **5 menos mal** : it could have been worse

mal² *adj* → **malo**
mal³ *nm* **1** : evil, wrong **2** DAÑO : harm, damage **3** DESGRACIA : misfortune **4** ENFERMEDAD : illness, sickness
malabar *adj* **juegos malabares** : juggling
malabarista *nmf* : juggler
malaconsejado, -da *adj* : ill-advised
malacostumbrado, -da *adj* CONSENTIDO : spoiled, pampered
malacostumbrar *vt* : to spoil
malagradecido, -da *adj* INGRATO : ungrateful
malaisio → **malasio**
malaquita *nf* : malachite
malaria *nf* PALUDISMO : malaria
malasio, -sia *adj & n* : Malaysian
malauiano, -na *adj & n* : Malawian
malaventura *nf* : misadventure, misfortune
malaventurado, -da *adj* MALHADADO : ill-fated, unfortunate
malayo, -ya *adj & n* : Malay, Malayan
malbaratar *vt* **1** MALGASTAR : to squander **2** : to undersell
malcriado¹, -da *adj* **1** : ill-bred, ill-mannered **2** : spoiled, pampered
malcriado², -da *n* : spoiled brat
maldad *nf* **1** : evil, wickedness **2** : evil deed
maldecir {11} *vt* : to curse, to damn — *vi* **1** : to curse, to swear **2** ~ **de** : to speak ill of, to slander, to defame
maldición *nf, pl* **-ciones** : curse
maldiga, maldijo etc. → **maldecir**
maldito, -ta *adj* **1** : cursed, damned ⟨¡maldita sea! : damn it all!⟩ **2** : wicked
maldoso, -sa *adj Mex* : mischievous
maleable *adj* : malleable
maleante *nmf* : crook, thug
malecón *nm, pl* **-cones** : jetty, breakwater
maleducado, -da *adj* : ill-mannered, rude
maleficio *nm* : curse, hex
maléfico, -ca *adj* : evil, harmful
malentender {56} *vt* : to misunderstand
malentendido *nm* : misunderstanding
malestar *nm* **1** : discomfort **2** IRRITACIÓN : annoyance **3** INQUIETUD : uneasiness, unrest
maleta *nf* : suitcase, bag ⟨haz tus maletas : pack your bags⟩
maletero¹, -ra *n* : porter
maletero² *nm* : trunk (of an automobile)
maletín *nm, pl* **-tines** **1** PORTAFOLIO : briefcase **2** : overnight bag, satchel
malevolencia *nf* : malevolence, wickedness
malévolo, -la *adj* : malevolent, wicked
maleza *nf* **1** : thicket, underbrush **2** : weeds *pl*
malformación *nf, pl* **-ciones** : malformation
malgache *adj & nmf* : Madagascan
malgastar *vt* : to squander (resources), to waste (time, effort)
malhablado, -da *adj* : foul-mouthed

malhadado, -da *adj* MALAVENTURADO : ill-fated
malhechor, -chora *n* : criminal, delinquent, wrongdoer
malherir {76} *vt* : to injure seriously
malhumor *nm* : bad mood, sullenness
malhumorado, -da *adj* : bad-tempered, cross
malicia *nf* **1** : wickedness, malice **2** : mischief, naughtiness **3** : cunning, craftiness
malicioso, -sa *adj* **1** : malicious **2** PÍCARO : mischievous
malignidad *nf* **1** : malignancy **2** MALDAD : evil
maligno, -na *adj* **1** : malignant ⟨un tumor maligno : a malignant tumor⟩ **2** : evil, harmful, malign
malinchismo *nm Mex* : preference for foreign goods or people — **malinchista** *adj*
malintencionado, -da *adj* : malicious, spiteful
malinterpretar *vt* : to misinterpret
malla *nf* **1** : mesh **2** LEOTARDO : leotard, tights *pl* **3** **malla de baño** : bathing suit
mallorquín, -quina *adj & n* : Majorcan
malnutrición *nf, pl* **-ciones** DESNUTRICIÓN : malnutrition
malnutrido, -da *adj* DESNUTRIDO : malnourished, undernourished
malo¹, -la *adj* (**mal** *before masculine singular nouns*) **1** : bad ⟨mala suerte : bad luck⟩ **2** : wicked, naughty **3** : cheap, poor (quality) **4** : harmful ⟨malo para la salud : bad for one's health⟩ **5** (*using the form* **mal**) : unwell ⟨estar mal del corazón : to have heart trouble⟩ **6** **estar de malas** : to be in a bad mood
malo², -la *n* : villain, bad guy (in novels, movies, etc.)
malogrado, -da *adj* : failed, unsuccessful
malograr *vt* **1** : to spoil, to ruin **2** : to waste (an opportunity, time) — **malograrse** *vr* **1** FRACASAR : to fail **2** : to die young
malogro *nm* **1** : untimely death **2** FRACASO : failure
maloliente *adj* HEDIONDO : foul-smelling, smelly
malparado, -da *adj* **salir malparado** *or* **quedar malparado** : to come out of (something) badly, to end up in a bad state
malpensado, -da *adj* : distrustful, suspicious, nasty-minded
malquerencia *nf* AVERSIÓN : ill will, dislike
malquerer {64} *vt* : to dislike
malquiso, etc. → **malquerer**
malsano, -na *adj* : unhealthy
malsonante *adj* : rude, offensive ⟨palabras malsonantes : foul language⟩
malta *nf* : malt
malteada *nf* : malted milk ⟨malteada de chocolate : chocolate malt⟩

maltés, -tesa *adj* & *n, mpl* **malteses** : Maltese

maltratar *vt* **1** : to mistreat, to abuse **2** : to damage, to spoil

maltrato *nm* : mistreatment, abuse

maltrecho, -cha *adj* : battered, damaged

malucho, -cha *adj fam* : sick, under the weather

malva *adj* & *nm* : mauve

malvado¹, -da *adj* : evil, wicked

malvado², -da *n* : evildoer, wicked person

malvavisco *nm* : marshmallow

malvender *vt* : to sell at a loss

malversación *nf, pl* **-ciones** : misappropriation (of funds), embezzlement

malversador, -dora *n* : embezzler

malversar *vt* : to embezzle

malvivir *vi* : to live badly, to just scrape by

mamá *nf fam* : mom, mama

mamar *vi* **1** : to suckle **2 darle de mamar a** : to breast-feed — *vt* **1** : to suckle, to nurse **2** : to learn from childhood, to grow up with — **mamarse** *vr fam* : to get drunk

mamario, -ria *adj* : mammary

mamarracho *nm fam* **1** ESPERPENTO : mess, sight **2** : laughingstock, fool **3** : rubbish, junk

mambo *nm* : mambo

mami *nf fam* : mommy

mamífero¹, -ra *adj* : mammalian

mamífero² *nm* : mammal

mamila *nf* **1** : nipple **2** *Mex* : baby bottle, pacifier

mamografía *nf* : mammogram

mamola *nf* : pat, chuck under the chin

mamotreto *nm fam* **1** : huge book, tome **2** ARMATOSTE : hulk, monstrosity

mampara *nf* BIOMBO : screen, room divider

mamparo *nm* : bulkhead

mampostería *nf* : masonry, stonemasonry

mampostero *nm* : mason, stonemason

mamut *nm, pl* **mamuts** : mammoth

maná *nm* : manna

manada *nf* **1** : flock, herd, pack **2** *fam* : horde, mob ⟨llegaron en manada : they came in droves⟩

manantial *nm* **1** FUENTE : spring **2** : source

manar *vi* **1** : to flow **2** : to abound

manatí *nm* : manatee

mancha *nf* **1** : stain, spot, mark ⟨mancha de sangre : bloodstain⟩ **2** : blemish, blot ⟨una mancha en su reputación : a blemish on his reputation⟩ **3** : patch

manchado, -da *adj* : stained

manchar *vt* **1** ENSUCIAR : to stain, to soil **2** DESHONRAR : to sully, to tarnish — **mancharse** *vr* : to get dirty

mancillar *vt* : to sully, to besmirch

manco, -ca *adj* : one-armed, one-handed

mancomunar *vt* : to combine, to pool — **mancomunarse** *vr* : to unite, to join together

mancomunidad *nf* **1** : commonwealth **2** : association, confederation

mancuernas *nfpl* : cuff links

mancuernillas *nf Mex* : cuff links

mandadero, -ra *n* : errand boy *m*, errand girl *f*, messenger

mandado *nm* **1** : order, command **2** : errand ⟨hacer los mandados : to run errands, to go shopping⟩

mandamás *nmf, pl* **-mases** *fam* : boss, bigwig, honcho

mandamiento *nm* **1** : commandment **2** : command, order, warrant ⟨mandamiento judicial : warrant, court order⟩

mandar *vt* **1** ORDENAR : to command, to order **2** ENVIAR : to send ⟨te manda saludos : he sends you his regards⟩ **3** ECHAR : to hurl, to throw **4** ¿**mande?** *Mex* : yes?, pardon? — *vi* : to be the boss, to be in charge — **mandarse** *vr Mex* : to take liberties, to take advantage

mandarín *nm* : Mandarin

mandarina *nf* : mandarin orange, tangerine

mandatario, -ria *n* **1** : leader (in politics) ⟨primer mandatario : head of state⟩ **2** : agent (in law)

mandato *nm* **1** : term of office **2** : mandate

mandíbula *nf* **1** : jaw **2** : mandible

mandil *nm* **1** DELANTAL : apron **2** : horse blanket

mandilón *nm, pl* **-lones** *fam* : wimp, coward

mandioca *nf* **1** : manioc, cassava **2** : tapioca

mando *nm* **1** : command, leadership **2** : control (for a device) ⟨mando a distancia : remote control⟩ **3 al mando de** : in charge of **4 al mando de** : under the command of

mandolina *nf* : mandolin

mandón, -dona *adj, mpl* **mandones** : bossy, domineering

mandonear *vt fam* MANGONEAR : to boss around

mandrágora *nf* : mandrake

manecilla *nf* : hand (of a clock), pointer

manejable *adj* **1** : manageable **2** : docile, easily led

manejar *vt* **1** CONDUCIR : to drive (a car) **2** OPERAR : to handle, to operate **3** : to manage **4** : to manipulate (a person) — *vi* : to drive — **manejarse** *vr* **1** COMPORTARSE : to behave **2** : to get along, to manage

manejo *nm* **1** : handling, operation **2** : management

manera *nf* **1** MODO : way, manner, fashion **2 de cualquier manera** *or* **de todas maneras** : anyway, anyhow **3 de manera que** : so, in order that **4 de ninguna manera** : by no means, absolutely not **5 manera de ser** : personality, demeanor

manga *nf* **1** : sleeve **2** MANGUERA : hose
manganeso *nm* : manganese
mangle *nm* : mangrove
mango *nm* **1** : hilt, handle **2** : mango
mangonear *vt fam* : to boss around, to bully — *vi* **1** : to be bossy **2** : to loaf, to fool around
mangosta *nf* : mongoose
manguera *nf* : hose
manguito *nm* **1** : muff **2** : sleeve (of a pipe, etc.), hose (of a car)
maní *nm, pl* **maníes** : peanut
manía *nf* **1** OBSESIÓN : mania, obsession **2** : craze, fad **3** : odd habit, peculiarity **4** : dislike, aversion
maníaco¹, -ca *adj* : maniacal
maníaco², -ca *n* : maniac
maniatar *vt* : to tie the hands of, to manacle
maniático¹, -ca *adj* **1** MANÍACO : maniacal **2** : obsessive **3** : fussy, finicky
maniático², -ca *n* **1** MANÍACO : maniac, lunatic **2** : obsessive person, fanatic **3** : eccentric, crank
manicomio *nm* : insane asylum, madhouse
manicura *nf* : manicure
manicuro, -ra *n* : manicurist
manido, -da *adj* : hackneyed, stale, trite
manifestación *nf, pl* **-ciones 1** : manifestation, sign **2** : demonstration, rally
manifestante *nmf* : demonstrator
manifestar {55} *vt* **1** : to demonstrate, to show **2** : to declare — **manifestarse** *vr* **1** : to be or become evident **2** : to state one's position ⟨se han manifestado a favor del acuerdo : they have declared their support for the agreement⟩ **3** : to demonstrate, to rally
manifiesto¹, -ta *adj* : manifest, evident, clear — **manifiestamente** *adv*
manifiesto² *nm* : manifesto
manija *nf* MANGO : handle
manilla → **manecilla**
manillar *nm* : handlebars *pl*
maniobra *nf* : maneuver, stratagem
maniobrar *v* : to maneuver
manipulación *nf, pl* **-ciones** : manipulation
manipulador¹, -dora *adj* : manipulating, manipulative
manipulador², -dora *n* : manipulator
manipular *vt* **1** : to manipulate **2** MANEJAR : to handle
maniquí¹ *nmf, pl* **-quíes** : mannequin, model
maniquí² *nm, pl* **-quíes** : mannequin, dummy
manirroto¹, -ta *adj* : extravagant
manirroto², -ta *n* : spendthrift
manivela *nf* : crank
manjar *nm* : delicacy, special dish
mano¹ *nf* **1** : hand **2** : coat (of paint or varnish) **3 a** ～ : by hand **4 a** ～ *or* **a la mano** : handy, at hand, nearby **5 darse la mano** : to shake hands **6 de la mano** : hand in hand ⟨la política y la economía van de la mano : politics

and economics go hand in hand⟩ **7 de primera mano** : firsthand, at firsthand **8 de segunda mano** : secondhand ⟨ropa de segunda mano : secondhand clothing⟩ **9 mano a mano** : one-on-one **10 mano de obra** : labor, manpower **11 mano de mortero** : pestle **12 echar una mano** : to lend a hand **13 mano negra** *Mex fam* : shady dealings *pl*
mano², -na *n Mex fam* : buddy, pal ⟨¡oye, mano! : hey man!⟩
manojo *nm* PUÑADO : handful, bunch
manopla *nf* **1** : mitten, mitt **2** : brass knuckles *pl*
manosear *vt* **1** : to handle or touch excessively **2** ACARICIAR : to fondle, to caress
manotazo *nm* : slap, smack, swipe
manotear *vi* : to wave one's hands, to gesticulate
mansalva *adv* **a** ～ : at close range
mansarda *nf* BUHARDILLA : attic
mansedumbre *nf* **1** : gentleness, meekness **2** : tameness
mansión *nf, pl* **-siones** : mansion
manso, -sa *adj* **1** : gentle, meek **2** : tame — **mansamente** *adv*
manta *nf* **1** COBIJA, FRAZADA : blanket **2** : poncho **3** *Mex* : coarse cotton fabric
manteca *nf* **1** GRASA : lard, fat **2** : butter
mantecoso, -sa *adj* : buttery
mantel *nm* **1** : tablecloth **2** : altar cloth
mantelería *nf* : table linen
mantener {80} *vt* **1** SUSTENTAR : to support, to feed ⟨mantener uno su familia : to support one's family⟩ **2** CONSERVAR : to keep, to preserve **3** CONTINUAR : to keep up, to sustain ⟨mantener una correspondencia : to keep up a correspondence⟩ **4** AFIRMAR : to maintain, to affirm — **mantenerse** *vr* **1** : to support oneself, to subsist **2 mantenerse firme** : to hold one's ground
mantenimiento *nm* **1** : maintenance, upkeep **2** : sustenance, food **3** : preservation
mantequera *nf* **1** : churn **2** : butter dish
mantequería *nf* **1** : creamery, dairy **2** : grocery store
mantequilla *nf* : butter
mantilla *nf* : mantilla
mantis *nf* **mantis religiosa** : praying mantis
manto *nm* **1** : cloak **2** : mantle (in geology)
mantón *nm, pl* **-tones** CHAL : shawl
mantuvo, etc. → **mantener**
manual¹ *adj* **1** : manual ⟨trabajo manual : manual labor⟩ **2** : handy, manageable — **manualmente** *adv*
manual² *nm* : manual, handbook
manualidades *nfpl* : handicrafts (in schools)
manubrio *nm* **1** : handle, crank **2** : handlebars *pl*

manufactura *nf* **1** FABRICACIÓN : manufacture **2** : manufactured item, product **3** FÁBRICA : factory

manufacturar *vt* FABRICAR : to manufacture

manufacturero[1], **-ra** *adj* : manufacturing

manufacturero[2], **-ra** *n* FABRICANTE : manufacturer

manuscrito[1], **-ta** *adj* : handwritten

manuscrito[2] *nm* : manuscript

manutención *nf, pl* **-ciones** : maintenance, support

manzana *nf* **1** : apple **2** CUADRA : block (enclosed by streets or buildings) **3** *or* **manzana de Adán** : Adam's apple

manzanal *nm* **1** : apple orchard **2** MANZANO : apple tree

manzanar *nm* : apple orchard

manzanilla *nf* **1** : chamomile **2** : chamomile tea

manzano *nm* : apple tree

maña *nf* **1** : dexterity, skill **2** : cunning, guile **3 mañas** *or* **malas mañas** *nfpl* : bad habits, vices

mañana *nf* **1** : morning **2** : tomorrow

mañanero, -ra *adj* MATUTINO : morning ⟨rocío mañanero : morning dew⟩

mañanitas *nfpl Mex* : birthday serenade

mañoso, -sa *adj* **1** HÁBIL : skillful **2** ASTUTO : cunning, crafty **3** : fussy, finicky

mapa *nm* CARTA : map

mapache *nm* : raccoon

mapamundi *nm* : map of the world

maqueta *nf* : model, mock-up

maquillador, -dora *n* : makeup artist

maquillaje *nm* : makeup

maquillarse *vr* : to put on makeup, to make oneself up

máquina *nf* **1** : machine ⟨máquina de coser : sewing machine⟩ ⟨máquina de escribir : typewriter⟩ **2** LOCOMOTORA : engine, locomotive **3** : machine (in politics) **4 a toda máquina** : at full speed

maquinación *nf, pl* **-ciones** : machination, scheme, plot

maquinal *adj* : mechanical, automatic — **maquinalmente** *adv*

maquinar *vt* : to plot, to scheme

maquinaria *nf* **1** : machinery **2** : mechanism, works *pl*

maquinilla *nf* **1** : small machine or device **2** *CA, Car* : typewriter

maquinista *nmf* **1** : machinist **2** : railroad engineer

mar *nmf* **1** : sea ⟨un mar agitado : a rough sea⟩ ⟨hacerse a la mar : to set sail⟩ **2 alta mar** : high seas

maraca *nf* : maraca

maraña *nf* **1** : thicket **2** ENREDO : tangle, mess

marasmo *nm* : paralysis, stagnation

maratón *nm, pl* **-tones** : marathon

maravilla *nf* **1** : wonder, marvel ⟨a las mil maravillas : wonderfully, mar-

velously⟩ ⟨hacer maravillas : to work wonders⟩ **2** : marigold

maravillar *vt* ASOMBRAR : to astonish, to amaze — **maravillarse** *vr* : to be amazed, to marvel

maravilloso, -sa *adj* ESTUPENDO : wonderful, marvelous — **maravillosamente** *adv*

marbete *nm* **1** ETIQUETA : label, tag **2** *PRi* : registration sticker (of a car)

marca *nf* **1** : mark **2** : brand, make **3** : trademark ⟨marca registrada : registered trademark⟩ **4** : record (in sports) ⟨batir la marca : to beat the record⟩

marcado, -da *adj* : marked ⟨un marcado contraste : a marked contrast⟩

marcador *nm* **1** TANTEADOR : scoreboard **2** : marker, felt-tipped pen **3 marcador de libros** : bookmark

marcaje *nm* **1** : scoring (in sports) **2** : guarding (in sports)

marcapasos *nms & pl* : pacemaker

marcar {72} *vt* **1** : to mark **2** : to brand (livestock) **3** : to indicate, to show **4** RESALTAR : to emphasize **5** : to dial (a telephone) **6** : to guard (an opponent) **7** ANOTAR : to score (a goal, a point) — *vi* **1** ANOTAR : to score **2** : to dial

marcha *nf* **1** : march **2** : hike, walk ⟨ir de marcha : to go hiking⟩ **3** : pace, speed ⟨a toda marcha : at top speed⟩ **4** : gear (of an automobile) ⟨marcha atrás : reverse, reverse gear⟩ **5 en ~** : in motion, in gear, under way

marchar *vi* **1** IR : to go, to travel **2** ANDAR : to walk **3** FUNCIONAR : to work, to go **4** : to march — **marcharse** *vr* : to leave

marchitar *vi* : to make wither, to wilt — **marchitarse** *vr* **1** : to wither, to shrivel up, to wilt **2** : to languish, to fade away

marchito, -ta *adj* : withered, faded

marcial *adj* : martial, military

marco *nm* **1** : frame, framework **2** : goalposts *pl* **3** AMBIENTE : setting, atmosphere **4** : mark (unit of currency)

marea *nf* : tide

mareado, -da *adj* **1** : dizzy, lightheaded **2** : queasy, nauseous **3** : seasick

marear *vt* **1** : to make sick ⟨los gases me marearon : the fumes made me sick⟩ **2** : to bother, to annoy — **marearse** *vr* **1** : to get sick, to become nauseated **2** : to feel dizzy **3** : to get tipsy

marejada *nf* **1** : surge, swell (of the sea) **2** : undercurrent, ferment, unrest

maremoto *nm* : tidal wave

mareo *nm* **1** : dizzy spell **2** : nausea **3** : seasickness, motion sickness **4** : annoyance, vexation

marfil *nm* : ivory

margarina *nf* : margarine

margarita *nf* **1** : daisy **2** : margarita (cocktail)

margen[1] *nf, pl* **márgenes** : bank (of a river), side (of a street)

margen² *nm, pl* **márgenes 1** : edge, border **2** : margin ⟨margen de ganancia : profit margin⟩
marginación *nf, pl* **-ciones** : marginalization, exclusion
marginado¹, -da *adj* **1** DESHEREDADO : outcast, alienated, dispossessed **2 clases marginadas** : underclass
marginado², -da *n* : outcast, misfit
marginal *adj* : marginal, fringe
marginalidad *nf* : marginality
marginar *vt* : to ostracize, to exclude
mariachi *nm* : mariachi musician or band
maridaje *nm* : marriage, union
maridar *vt* UNIR : to marry, to unite
marido *nm* ESPOSO : husband
marihuana *or* **mariguana** *or* **marijuana** *nf* : marihuana
marimacho *nmf fam* **1** : mannish woman **2** : tomboy
marimba *nf* : marimba
marina *nf* **1** : coast, coastal area **2** : navy, fleet ⟨marina mercante : merchant marine⟩
marinada *nf* : marinade
marinar *vt* : to marinate
marinero¹, -ra *adj* **1** : seaworthy **2** : sea, marine
marinero² *nm* : sailor
marino¹, -na *adj* : marine, sea
marino² *nm* : sailor, seaman
marioneta *nf* TÍTERE : puppet, marionette
mariposa *nf* **1** : butterfly **2 mariposa nocturna** : moth
mariquita¹ *nf* : ladybug
mariquita² *nm fam* : sissy, wimp
mariscal *nm* **1** : marshal **2 mariscal de campo** : field marshal (in the military), quarterback (in football)
marisco *nm* **1** : shellfish **2 mariscos** *nmpl* : seafood
marisma *nf* : marsh, salt marsh
marital *adj* : marital, married ⟨la vida marital : married life⟩
marítimo, -ma *adj* : maritime, shipping ⟨la industria marítima : the shipping industry⟩
marmita *nf* : (cooking) pot
mármol *nm* : marble
marmóreo, -rea *adj* : marble, marmoreal
marmota *nf* **1** : marmot **2 marmota de América** : woodchuck, groundhog
maroma *nf* **1** : rope **2** : acrobatic stunt **3** *Mex* : somersault
marque, etc. → **marcar**
marqués, -quesa *n, mpl* **marqueses** : marquis *m*, marquess *m*, marquise *f*, marchioness *f*
marquesina *nf* : marquee, canopy
marqueta *nf Mex* : block (of chocolate), lump (of sugar or salt)
marranada *nf* **1** : disgusting thing **2** : dirty trick
marrano¹, -na *adj* : filthy, disgusting
marrano², -na *n* **1** CERDO : pig, hog **2** : dirty pig, slob

marrar *vt* : to miss (a target) — *vi* : to fail, to go wrong
marras *adv* **1** : long ago **2 de ~** : said, aforementioned ⟨el individuo de marras : the individual in question⟩
marrasquino *nm* : maraschino
marrón *adj & nm, pl* **marrones** CASTAÑO : brown
marroquí *adj & nmf, pl* **-quíes** : Moroccan
marsopa *nf* : porpoise
marsupial *nm* : marsupial
marta *nf* **1** : marten **2 marta cebellina** : sable (animal)
Marte *nm* : Mars
martes *nms & pl* : Tuesday
martillar *v* : to hammer
martillazo *nm* : blow with a hammer
martillo *nm* **1** : hammer **2 martillo neumático** : jackhammer
martinete *nm* **1** : heron **2** : pile driver
mártir *nmf* : martyr
martirio *nm* **1** : martyrdom **2** : ordeal, torment
martirizar {21} *vt* **1** : to martyr **2** ATORMENTAR : to torment
marxismo *nm* : Marxism
marxista *adj & nmf* : Marxist
marzo *nm* : March
mas *conj* PERO : but
más¹ *adv* **1** : more ⟨¿hay algo más grande? : is there anything bigger?⟩ **2** : most ⟨Luis es el más alto : Luis is the tallest⟩ **3** : longer ⟨el sabor dura más : the flavor lasts longer⟩ **4** : rather ⟨más querría andar : I would rather walk⟩ **5 a ~** : besides, in addition **6 más allá** : further **7 qué . . . más . . .** : what . . ., what a . . . ⟨¡qué día más bonito! : what a beautiful day!⟩
más² *adj* **1** : more ⟨dáme dos kilos más : give me two more kilos⟩ **2** : most ⟨la que ganó más dinero : the one who earned the most money⟩ **3** : else ⟨¿quién más quiere vino? : who else wants wine?⟩
más³ *n* : plus sign
más⁴ *prep* : plus ⟨tres más dos es igual a cinco : three plus two equals five⟩
más⁵ *pron* **1** : more ⟨¿tienes más? : do you have more?⟩ **2 a lo más** : at most **3 de ~** : extra, excess **4 más o menos** : more or less, approximately **5 por más que** : no matter how much ⟨por más que corras no llegarás a tiempo : no matter how fast you run you won't arrive on time⟩
masa *nf* **1** : mass, volume ⟨masa atómica : atomic mass⟩ ⟨producción en masa : mass production⟩ **2** : dough, batter **3 masas** *nfpl* : people, masses ⟨las masas populares : the common people⟩ **4 masa harina** *Mex* : corn flour (for tortillas, etc.)
masacrar *vt* : to massacre
masacre *nf* : massacre
masaje *nm* : massage
masajear *vt* : to massage

masajista *nmf* : masseur *m*, masseuse *f*
mascar {72} *v* MASTICAR : to chew
máscara *nf* **1** CARETA : mask **2** : appearance, pretense **3 máscara antigás** : gas mask
mascarada *nf* : masquerade
mascarilla *nf* **1** : mask (in medicine) ⟨mascarilla de oxígeno : oxygen mask⟩ **2** : facial mask (in cosmetology)
mascota *nf* : mascot
masculinidad *nf* : masculinity
masculino, -na *adj* **1** : masculine, male **2** : manly **3** : masculine (in grammar)
mascullar *v* : to mumble, to mutter
masificado, -da *adj* : overcrowded
masilla *nf* : putty
masivamente *adv* : en masse
masivo, -va *adj* : mass ⟨comunicación masiva : mass communication⟩
masón *nm, pl* **masones** FRANCMASÓN : Mason, Freemason
masonería *nf* FRANCMASONERÍA : Masonry, Freemasonry
masónico, -ca *adj* : Masonic
masoquismo *nm* : masochism
masoquista[1] *adj* : masochistic
masoquista[2] *nmf* : masochist
masque, etc. → **mascar**
masticar {72} *v* MASCAR : to chew, to masticate
mástil *nm* **1** : mast **2** ASTA : flagpole **3** : neck (of a stringed instrument)
mastín *nm, pl* **mastines** : mastiff
mástique *nm* : putty, filler
mastodonte *nm* : mastodon
masturbación *nf, pl* **-ciones** : masturbation
masturbarse *vr* : to masturbate
mata *nf* **1** ARBUSTO : bush, shrub **2** : plant ⟨mata de tomate : tomato plant⟩ **3** : sprig, tuft **4 mata de pelo** : mop of hair
matadero *nm* : slaughterhouse, abattoir
matado, -da *adj Mex* : strenuous, exhausting
matador *nm* TORERO : matador, bullfighter
matamoscas *nms & pl* : flyswatter
matanza *nf* MASACRE : slaughter, butchering
matar *vt* **1** : to kill **2** : to slaughter, to butcher **3** APAGAR : to extinguish, to put out (fire, light) **4** : to tone down (colors) **5** : to pass, to waste (time) **6** : to trump (in card games) — *vi* : to kill — **matarse** *vr* **1** : to be killed **2** SUICIDARSE : to commit suicide **3** *fam* : to exhaust oneself ⟨se mató tratando de terminarlo : he knocked himself out trying to finish it⟩
matasanos *nms & pl fam* : quack
matasellar *vt* : to cancel (a stamp), to postmark
matasellos *nms & pl* : postmark
matatena *nf Mex* : jacks
mate[1] *adj* : matte, dull
mate[2] *nm* **1** : maté **2 jaque mate** : checkmate ⟨darle mate a *or* darle jaque mate a : to checkmate⟩

matemática → **matemáticas**
matemáticas *nfpl* : mathematics, math
matemático[1]**, -ca** *adj* : mathematical — **matemáticamente** *adv*
matemático[2]**, -ca** *n* : mathematician
materia *nf* **1** : matter ⟨materia gris : gray matter⟩ **2** : material ⟨materia prima : raw material⟩ **3** : (academic) subject **4 en materia de** : on the subject of, concerning
material[1] *adj* **1** : material, physical, real **2 daños materiales** : property damage
material[2] *nm* **1** : material ⟨material de construcción : building material⟩ **2** EQUIPO : equipment, gear
materialismo *nm* : materialism
materialista[1] *adj* : materialistic
materialista[2] *nmf* **1** : materialist **2** *Mex* : truck driver
materializar {21} *vt* : to bring to fruition, to realize — **materializarse** *vr* : to materialize, to come into being
materialmente *adv* **1** : materially, physically ⟨materialmente imposible : physically impossible⟩ **2** : really, absolutely
maternal *adj* : maternal, motherly
maternidad *nf* **1** : maternity, motherhood **2** : maternity hospital, maternity ward
materno, -na *adj* : maternal
matinal *adj* MATUTINO : morning ⟨la pálida luz matinal : the pale morning light⟩
matinée *or* **matiné** *nf* : matinee
matiz *nm, pl* **matices** **1** : hue, shade **2** : nuance
matización *nf, pl* **-ciones** **1** : tinting, toning, shading **2** : clarification (of a statement)
matizar {21} *vt* **1** : to tinge, to tint (colors) **2** : to vary, to modulate (sounds) **3** : to qualify (statements)
matón *nm, pl* **matones** : thug, bully
matorral *nm* **1** : thicket **2** : scrub, scrubland
matraca *nf* **1** : rattle, noisemaker **2 dar la matraca a** : to pester, to nag
matriarca *nf* : matriarch
matriarcado *nm* : matriarchy
matrícula *nf* **1** : list, roll, register **2** INSCRIPCIÓN : registration, enrollment **3** : license plate, registration number
matriculación *nf, pl* **-ciones** : matriculation, registration
matricular *vt* **1** INSCRIBIR : to enroll, to register (a person) **2** : to register (a vehicle) — **matricularse** *vr* : to matriculate
matrimonial *adj* : marital, matrimonial ⟨la vida matrimonial : married life⟩
matrimonio *nm* **1** : marriage, matrimony **2** : married couple
matriz *nf, pl* **matrices** **1** : uterus, womb **2** : original, master copy **3** : main office, headquarters **4** : stub (of a check) **5** : matrix ⟨matriz de puntos : dot matrix⟩

matrona *nf* : matron
matronal *adj* : matronly
matutino¹, -na *adj* : morning ⟨la edición matutina : the morning edition⟩
matutino² *nm* : morning paper
maullar {8} *vi* : to meow
maullido *nm* : meow
mauritano, -na *adj & n* : Mauritanian
mausoleo *nm* : mausoleum
maxilar *nm* : jaw, jawbone
máxima *nf* : maxim
máxime *adv* ESPECIALMENTE : especially, principally
maximizar {21} *vt* : to maximize
máximo¹, -ma *adj* : maximum, greatest, highest
máximo² *nm* **1** : máximum **2 al máximo** : to the utmost **3 como ∼** : at the most, at the latest
maya¹ *adj & nmf* : Mayan
maya² *nmf* : Maya, Mayan
mayo *nm* : May
mayonesa *nf* : mayonnaise
mayor¹ *adj* **1** (*comparative of* **grande**) : bigger, larger, greater, elder, older **2** (*superlative of* **grande**) : biggest, largest, greatest, eldest, oldest **3** : grown-up, mature **4** : main, major **5 mayor de edad** : of (legal) age **6 al por mayor** *or* **por ∼** : wholesale
mayor² *nmf* **1** : major (in the military) **2** : adult
mayoral *nm* CAPATAZ : foreman, overseer
mayordomo *nm* : butler, majordomo
mayoreo *nm* : wholesale
mayores *nmpl* : grown-ups, elders
mayoría *nf* **1** : majority **2 en su mayoría** : on the whole
mayorista¹ *adj* ALMACENISTA : wholesale
mayorista² *nmf* : wholesaler
mayoritariamente *adv* : primarily, chiefly
mayoritario, -ria *adj & n* : majority ⟨un consenso mayoritario : a majority consensus⟩
mayormente *adv* : primarily, chiefly
mayúscula *nf* : capital letter
mayúsculo, -la *adj* **1** : capital, uppercase **2** : huge, terrible ⟨un problema mayúsculo : a huge problem⟩
maza *nf* **1** : mace (weapon) **2** : drumstick **3** *fam* : bore, pest
mazacote *nm* **1** : concrete **2** : lumpy mess (of food) **3** : eyesore, crude work of art
mazapán *nm, pl* **-panes** : marzipan
mazmorra *nf* CALABOZO : dungeon
mazo *nm* **1** : mallet **2** : pestle **3** MANOJO : handful, bunch
mazorca *nf* **1** CHOCLO : cob, ear of corn **2 pelar la mazorca** *Mex fam* : to smile from ear to ear
me *pron* **1** : me ⟨me vieron : they saw me⟩ **2** : to me, for me, from me ⟨dame el libro : give me the book⟩ ⟨me lo compró : he bought it for me⟩ ⟨me robaron la cartera : they stole my pocketbook⟩ **3** : myself, to myself, for myself, from myself ⟨me preparé una buena comida : I cooked myself a good dinner⟩ ⟨me equivoqué : I made a mistake⟩
mecánica *nf* : mechanics
mecánico¹, -ca *adj* : mechanical — **mecánicamente** *adv*
mecánico², -ca *n* **1** : mechanic **2** : technician ⟨mecánico dental : dental technician⟩
mecanismo *nm* : mechanism
mecanización *nf, pl* **-ciones** : mechanization
mecanizar {21} *vt* : to mechanize
mecanografía *nf* : typing
mecanografiar {85} *vt* : to type
mecanógrafo, -fa *n* : typist
mecate *nm CA, Mex, Ven* : rope, twine, cord
mecedor *nm* : glider (seat)
mecedora *nf* : rocking chair
mecenas *nmfs & pl* : patron (of the arts), sponsor
mecenazgo *nm* PATROCINIO : sponsorship, patronage
mecer {86} *vt* **1** : to rock **2** COLUMPIAR : to push (on a swing) — **mecerse** *vr* : to rock, to swing, to sway
mecha *nf* **1** : fuse **2** : wick **3 mechas** *nfpl* : highlights (in hair)
mechero *nm* **1** : burner **2** *Spain* : lighter
mechón *nm, pl* **mechones** : lock (of hair)
medalla *nf* : medal, medallion
medallista *nmf* : medalist
medallón *nm, pl* **-llones** **1** : medallion **2** : locket
media *nf* **1** CALCETÍN : sock **2** : average, mean **3 medias** *nfpl* : stockings, hose, tights **4 a medias** : by halves, half and half, halfway ⟨ir a medias : to go halves⟩ ⟨verdad a medias : half-truth⟩
mediación *nf, pl* **-ciones** : mediation
mediado, -da *adj* **1** : half full, half empty, half over **2** : halfway through ⟨mediada la tarea : halfway through the job⟩
mediador, -dora *n* : mediator
mediados *nmpl* **a mediados de** : halfway through, in the middle of ⟨a mediados del mes : towards the middle of the month, mid-month⟩
medialuna *nf* **1** : crescent **2** : croissant, crescent roll
medianamente *adv* : fairly, moderately
medianero, -ra *adj* **1** : dividing **2** : mediating
medianía *nf* **1** : middle position **2** : mediocre person, mediocrity
mediano, -na *adj* **1** : medium, average ⟨la mediana edad : middle age⟩ **2** : mediocre
medianoche *nf* : midnight
mediante *prep* : through, by means of ⟨Dios mediante : God willing⟩
mediar *vi* **1** : to mediate **2** : to be in the middle, to be halfway through **3** : to elapse, to pass ⟨mediaron cinco años entre el inicio de la guerra y el armisti-

cio : five years passed between the start of the war and the armistice⟩ **4** : to be a consideration ⟨media el hecho de que cuesta mucho : one must take into account that it is costly⟩ **5** : to come up, to happen ⟨medió algo urgente : something pressing came up⟩

mediatizar {21} *vt* : to influence, to interfere with

medicación *nf, pl* **-ciones** : medication, treatment

medicamento *nm* : medication, medicine, drug

medicar {72} *vt* : to medicate — **medicarse** *vr* : to take medicine

medicina *nf* : medicine

medicinal *adj* **1** : medicinal **2** : medicated

medicinar *vt* : to give medication to, to dose

medición *nf, pl* **-ciones** : measuring, measurement

médico[1], **-ca** *adj* : medical ⟨una receta médica : a doctor's prescription⟩

médico[2], **-ca** *n* DOCTOR : doctor, physician

medida *nf* **1** : measurement, measure ⟨hecho a medida : custom-made⟩ **2** : measure, step ⟨tomar medidas : to take steps⟩ **3** : moderation, prudence ⟨sin medida : immoderately⟩ **4** : extent, degree ⟨en gran medida : to a great extent⟩

medidor *nm* : meter, gauge

medieval *adj* : medieval — **medievalista** *nmf*

medievo → **medioevo**

medio[1] *adv* **1** : half ⟨está medio dormida : she's half asleep⟩ **2** : rather, kind of ⟨está medio aburrida esta fiesta : this party is rather boring⟩

medio[2], **-dia** *adj* **1** : half ⟨una media hora : half an hour⟩ ⟨medio hermano : half brother⟩ ⟨a media luz : in the half-light⟩ ⟨son las tres y media : it's half past three, it's three-thirty⟩ **2** : midway, halfway ⟨a medio camino : halfway there⟩ **3** : middle ⟨la clase media : the middle class⟩ **4** : average ⟨la temperatura media : the average temperature⟩

medio[3] *nm* **1** CENTRO : middle, center ⟨en medio de : in the middle of, amid⟩ **2** AMBIENTE : milieu, environment **3** : medium, spiritualist **4** : means *pl*, way ⟨por medio de : by means of⟩ ⟨los medios de comunicación : the media⟩ **5 medios** *nmpl* : means, resources

mediocampista *nmf* : midfielder

mediocre *adj* : mediocre, average

mediocridad *nf* : mediocrity

mediodía *nm* : noon, midday

medioevo *nm* : Middle Ages

medir {54} *vt* **1** : to measure **2** : to weigh, to consider ⟨medir los riesgos : to weigh the risks⟩ — *vi* : to measure — **medirse** *vr* : to be moderate, to exercise restraint

meditabundo, -da *adj* PENSATIVO : pensive, thoughtful

meditación *nf, pl* **-ciones** : meditation, thought

meditar *vi* : to meditate, to think ⟨meditar sobre la vida : to contemplate life⟩ — *vt* **1** : to think over, to consider **2** : to plan, to work out

meditativo, -va *adj* : pensive

mediterráneo, -nea *adj* : Mediterranean

medrar *vi* **1** PROSPERAR : to prosper, to thrive **2** AUMENTAR : to increase, to grow

medro *nm* PROSPERIDAD : prosperity, growth

medroso, -sa *adj* : fainthearted, fearful

médula *nf* **1** : marrow, pith **2 médula espinal** : spinal cord

medular *adj* : fundamental, core ⟨el punto medular : the crux of the matter⟩

medusa *nf* : jellyfish, medusa

megabyte *nm* : megabyte

megáfono *nm* : megaphone

megahercio *nm* : megahertz

megahertzio *nm* : megahertz

megatón *nm, pl* **-tones** : megaton

megavatio *nm* : megawatt

mejicano → **mexicano**

mejilla *nf* : cheek

mejillón *nm, pl* **-llones** : mussel

mejor[1] *adv* **1** : better ⟨Carla cocina mejor que Ana : Carla cooks better than Ann⟩ **2** : best ⟨ella es la que lo hace mejor : she's the one who does it best⟩ **3** : rather ⟨mejor morir que rendirme : I'd rather die than give up⟩ **4** : it's better that ... ⟨mejor te vas : you'd better go⟩ **5 a lo mejor** : maybe, perhaps

mejor[2] *adj* **1** (*comparative of* **bueno**) : better ⟨a falta de algo mejor : for lack of something better⟩ **2** (*comparative of* **bien**) : better ⟨está mucho mejor : he's much better⟩ **3** (*superlative of* **bueno**) : best, the better ⟨mi mejor amigo : my best friend⟩ **4** (*superlative of* **bien**) : best, the better ⟨duermo mejor en un clima seco : I sleep best in a dry climate⟩ **5** PREFERIBLE : preferable, better **6 lo mejor** : the best thing, the best part

mejor[3] *nmf* (*with definite article*) : the better (one), the best (one)

mejora *nf* : improvement

mejoramiento *nm* : improvement

mejorana *nf* : marjoram

mejorar *vt* : to improve, to make better — *vi* : to improve, to get better — **mejorarse** *vr*

mejoría *nf* : improvement, betterment

mejunje *nm* : concoction, brew

melancolía *nf* : melancholy, sadness

melancólico, -ca *adj* : melancholy, sad

melanoma *nm* : melanoma

melaza *nf* : molasses

melena *nf* **1** : mane **2** : long hair **3 melenas** *nfpl* GREÑAS : shaggy hair, mop

melenudo[1], **-da** *adj fam* : longhaired
melenudo[2], **-da** *n* GREÑUDO : longhair, hippie
melindres *nmpl* **1** : affectation, airs *pl* **2** : finickiness
melindroso[1], **-sa** *adj* **1** : affected **2** : fussy, finicky
melindroso[2], **-sa** *n* : finicky person, fussbudget
melisa *nf* : lemon balm
mella *nf* **1** : dent, nick **2 hacer mella en** : to have an effect on, to make an impression on
mellado, -da *adj* **1** : chipped, dented **2** : gap-toothed
mellar *vt* : to dent, to nick
mellizo, -za *adj & n* GEMELO : twin
melocotón *nm, pl* **-tones** : peach
melodía *nf* : melody, tune
melódico, -ca *adj* : melodic
melodioso, -sa *adj* : melodious
melodrama *nm* : melodrama
melodramático, -ca *adj* : melodramatic
melón *nm, pl* **melones** : melon, cantaloupe
meloso, -sa *adj* **1** : honeyed, sweet **2** EMPALAGOSO : cloying, saccharine
membrana *nf* **1** : membrane **2 membrana interdigital** : web, webbing (of a bird's foot) — **membranoso, -sa** *adj*
membresía *nf* : membership, members *pl*
membrete *nm* : letterhead, heading
membrillo *nm* : quince
membrudo, -da *adj* FORNIDO : muscular, well-built
memez *nf, pl* **memeces** : stupid thing
memo, -ma *adj* : silly, stupid
memorabilia *nf* : memorabilia
memorable *adj* : memorable
memorándum *or* **memorando** *nm, pl* **-dums** *or* **-dos** **1** : memorandum, memo **2** : memo book, appointment book
memoria *nf* **1** : memory ⟨de memoria : by heart⟩ ⟨hacer memoria : to try to remember⟩ ⟨traer a la memoria : to call to mind⟩ **2** RECUERDO : remembrance, memory ⟨su memoria perdurará para siempre : his memory will live forever⟩ **3** : report ⟨memoria annual : annual report⟩ **4 memorias** *nfpl* : memoirs
memorizar {21} *vt* : to memorize — **memorización** *nf*
mena *nf* : ore
menaje *nm* : household goods *pl*, furnishings *pl*
mención *nf, pl* **-ciones** : mention
mencionar *vt* : to mention, to refer to
mendaz *adj, pl* **mendaces** : mendacious, lying
mendicidad *nf* : begging
mendigar {52} *vi* : to beg — *vt* : to beg for
mendigo, -ga *n* LIMOSNERO : beggar
mendrugo *nm* : crust (of bread)

menear *vt* **1** : to shake (one's head) **2** : to sway, to wiggle (one's hips) **3** : to wag (a tail) **4** : to stir (a liquid) — **menearse** *vr* **1** : to wiggle one's hips **2** : to fidget
meneo *nm* **1** : movement **2** : shake, toss **3** : swaying, wagging, wiggling **4** : stir, stirring
menester *nm* **1** : activity, occupation, duties *pl* **2 ser menester** : to be necessary ⟨es menester que vengas : you must come⟩
mengano, -na → **fulano**
mengua *nf* **1** : decrease, decline **2** : lack, want **3** : discredit, dishonor
menguar *vt* : to diminish, to lessen — *vi* **1** : to decline, to decrease **2** : to wane — **menguante** *adj*
meningitis *nf* : meningitis
menisco *nm* : meniscus, cartilage
menjurje → **mejunje**
menopausia *nf* : menopause
menor[1] *adj* **1** (*comparative of* **pequeño**) : smaller, lesser, younger **2** (*superlative of* **pequeño**) : smallest, least, youngest **3** : minor **4 al por menor** : retail **5 ser menor de edad** : to be a minor, to be underage
menor[2] *nmf* : minor, juvenile
menos[1] *adv* **1** : less ⟨llueve menos en agosto : it rains less in August⟩ **2** : least ⟨el coche menos caro : the least expensive car⟩ **3 ~ de** : less than, fewer than
menos[2] *adj* **1** : less, fewer ⟨tengo más trabajo y menos tiempo : I have more work and less time⟩ **2** : least, fewest ⟨la clase que tiene menos estudiantes : the class that has the fewest students⟩
menos[3] *prep* **1** SALVO, EXCEPTO : except **2** : minus ⟨quince menos cuatro son once : fifteen minus four is eleven⟩
menos[4] *pron* **1** : less, fewer ⟨no deberías aceptar menos : you shouldn't accept less⟩ **2 al menos** *or* **por lo menos** : at least **3 a menos que** : unless
menoscabar *vt* **1** : to lessen, to diminish **2** : to disgrace, to discredit **3** PERJUDICAR : to harm, to damage
menoscabo *nm* **1** : lessening, diminishing **2** : disgrace, discredit **3** : harm, damage
menospreciar *vt* **1** DESPRECIAR : to scorn, to look down on **2** : to underestimate, to undervalue
menosprecio *nm* DESPRECIO : contempt, scorn
mensaje *nm* : message
mensajero, -ra *n* : messenger
menso, -sa *adj Mex fam* : foolish, stupid
menstrual *adj* : menstrual
menstruar {3} *vi* : to menstruate — **menstruación** *nf*
mensual *adj* : monthly
mensualidad *nf* **1** : monthly payment, installment **2** : monthly salary
mensualmente *adv* : every month, monthly

mensurable *adj* : measurable
menta *nf* **1** : mint, peppermint **2 menta verde** : spearmint
mentado, -da *adj* **1** : aforementioned **2** FAMOSO : renowned, famous
mental *adj* : mental, intellectual — **mentalmente** *adv*
mentalidad *nf* : mentality
mentar {55} *vt* **1** : to mention, to name **2 mentar la madre a** *fam* : to insult, to swear at
mente *nf* : mind ⟨tener en mente : to have in mind⟩
mentecato¹, -ta *adj* : foolish, simple
mentecato², -ta *n* : fool, idiot
mentir {76} *vi* : to lie
mentira *nf* : lie
mentiroso¹, -sa *adj* EMBUSTERO : lying, untruthful
mentiroso², -sa *n* EMBUSTERO : liar
mentís *nm, pl* **mentises** : denial, repudiation ⟨dar el mentís a : to deny, to refute⟩
mentol *nm* : menthol
mentón *nm, pl* **mentones** BARBILLA : chin
mentor *nm* : mentor, counselor
menú *nm, pl* **menús** : menu
menudear *vi* : to occur frequently — *vt* : to do repeatedly
menudencia *nf* **1** : trifle **2 menudencias** *nfpl* : giblets
menudeo *nm* : retail, retailing
menudillos *nmpl* : giblets
menudo¹, -da *adj* **1** : minute, small **2 a ~** FRECUENTEMENTE : often, frequently
menudo² *nm* **1** *Mex* : tripe stew **2 menudos** *nmpl* : giblets
meñique *nm* or **dedo meñique** : little finger, pinkie
meollo *nm* **1** MÉDULA : marrow **2** SESO : brains *pl* **3** ENTRAÑA : essence, core ⟨el meollo del asunto : the heart of the matter⟩
mequetrefe *nm fam* : good-for-nothing
mercachifle *nm* : peddler, hawker
mercadeo *nm* : marketing
mercadería *nf* : merchandise, goods *pl*
mercado *nm* : market ⟨mercado de trabajo *or* mercado laboral : labor market⟩ ⟨mercado de valores *or* mercado bursátil : stock market⟩
mercadotecnia *nf* : marketing
mercancía *nf* : merchandise, goods *pl*
mercante *nmf* : merchant, dealer
mercantil *adj* COMERCIAL : commercial, mercantile
merced *nf* **1** : favor **2 ~ a** : thanks to, due to **3 a merced de** : at the mercy of
mercenario, -ria *adj & n* : mercenary
mercería *nf* : notions store
Mercosur *nm* : economic community consisting of Argentina, Brazil, Paraguay, and Uruguay
mercurio *nm* : mercury
Mercurio *nm* : Mercury (planet)

merecedor, -dora *adj* : deserving, worthy
merecer {53} *vt* : to deserve, to merit — *vi* : to be worthy
merecidamente *adv* : rightfully, deservedly
merecido *nm* : something merited, due ⟨recibieron su merecido : they got their just deserts⟩
merecimiento *nm* : merit, worth
merendar {55} *vi* : to have an afternoon snack — *vt* : to have as an afternoon snack
merendero *nm* **1** : lunchroom, snack bar **2** : picnic area
merengue *nm* **1** : meringue **2** : merengue (dance)
meridiano¹, -na *adj* **1** : midday **2** : crystal clear
meridiano² *nm* : meridian
meridional *adj* SUREÑO : southern
merienda *nf* : afternoon snack, tea
mérito *nm* : merit
meritorio¹, -ria *adj* : deserving, meritorious
meritorio², -ria *n* : intern, trainee
merluza *nf* : hake
merma *nf* **1** : decrease, cut **2** : waste, loss
mermar *vi* : to decrease, to diminish — *vt* : to reduce, to cut down
mermelada *nf* : marmalade, jam
mero¹, -ra *adv Mex fam* **1** : nearly, almost ⟨ya mero me caí : I almost fell⟩ **2** : just, exactly ⟨aquí mero : right here⟩
mero², -ra *adj* **1** : mere, simple **2** *Mex fam* (*used as an intensifier*) : very ⟨en el mero centro : in the very center of town⟩
mero³ *nm* : grouper
merodeador, -dora *n* **1** : marauder **2** : prowler
merodear *vi* **1** : to maraud, to pillage **2** : to prowl around, to skulk
mes *nm* : month
mesa *nf* **1** : table **2** : committee, board
mesada *nf* : allowance, pocket money
mesarse *vr* : to pull at ⟨mesarse los cabellos : to tear one's hair⟩
mesero, -ra *n* CAMARERO : waiter, waitress *f*
meseta *nf* : plateau, tableland
Mesías *nm* : Messiah
mesón *nm, pl* **mesones** : inn
mesonero, -ra *nm* : innkeeper
mestizo¹, -za *adj* **1** : of mixed ancestry **2** HÍBRIDO : hybrid
mestizo², -za *n* : person of mixed ancestry
mesura *nf* **1** MODERACIÓN : moderation, discretion **2** CORTESÍA : courtesy **3** GRAVEDAD : seriousness, dignity
mesurado, -da *adj* COMEDIDO : moderate, restrained
mesurar *vt* : to moderate, to restrain, to temper — **mesurarse** *vr* : to restrain oneself
meta *nf* : goal, objective

metabólico, -ca *adj* : metabolic
metabolismo *nm* : metabolism
metabolizar {21} *vt* : to metabolize
metafísica *nf* : metaphysics
metafísico, -ca *adj* : metaphysical
metáfora *nf* : metaphor
metafórico, -ca *adj* : metaphoric, metaphorical
metal *nm* **1** : metal **2** : brass section (in an orchestra)
metálico, -ca *adj* : metallic, metal
metalistería *nf* : metalworking
metalurgia *nf* : metallurgy
metalúrgico[1], **-ca** *adj* : metallurgical
metalúrgico[2], **-ca** *n* : metallurgist
metamorfosis *nfs & pl* : metamorphosis
metano *nm* : methane
metedura *nf* **metedura de pata** : blunder, faux pas
meteórico, -ca *adj* : meteoric
meteorito *nm* : meteorite
meteoro *nm* : meteor
meteorología *nf* : meteorology
meteorológico, -ca *adj* : meteorologic, meteorological
meteorólogo, -ga *n* : meteorologist
meter *vt* **1** : to put (in) ⟨metieron su dinero en el banco : they put their money in the bank⟩ **2** : to fit, to squeeze ⟨puedes meter dos líneas más en esa página : you can fit two more lines on that page⟩ **3** : to place (in a job) ⟨lo metieron de barrendero : they got him a job as a street sweeper⟩ **4** : to involve ⟨lo metió en un buen lío : she got him in an awful mess⟩ **5** : to make, to cause ⟨meten demasiado ruido : they make too much noise⟩ **6** : to spread (a rumor) **7** : to strike (a blow) **8** : to take up, to take in (clothing) **9 a todo meter** : at top speed — **meterse** *vr* **1** : to get into, to enter **2** *fam* : to meddle ⟨no te metas en lo que no te importa : mind your own business⟩ **3 ~ con** *fam* : to pick a fight with, to provoke ⟨no te metas conmigo : don't mess with me⟩
metiche[1] *adj Mex fam* : nosy
metiche[2] *nmf Mex fam* : busybody
meticulosidad *nf* : thoroughness, meticulousness
meticuloso, -sa *adj* : meticulous, thorough — **meticulosamente** *adv*
metida *nf* **metida de pata** *fam* : blunder, gaffe, blooper
metódico, -ca *adj* : methodical — **metódicamente** *adv*
metodista *adj & nmf* : Methodist
método *nm* : method
metodología *nf* : methodology
metomentodo *nmf fam* : busybody
metraje *nm* : length (of a film) ⟨de largo metraje : feature-length⟩
metralla *nf* : shrapnel
metralleta *nf* : submachine gun
métrico, -ca *adj* **1** : metric **2 cinta métrica** : tape measure
metro *nm* **1** : meter **2** : subway
metrónomo *nm* : metronome

metrópoli *nf or* **metrópolis** *nfs & pl* : metropolis
metropolitano, -na *adj* : metropolitan
mexicanismo *nm* : Mexican word or expression
mexicano, -na *adj & n* : Mexican
mexicoamericano, -na *adj & n* : Mexican-American
meza, etc. → **mecer**
mezcla *nf* **1** : mixing **2** : mixture, blend **3** : mortar (masonry material)
mezclar *vt* **1** : to mix, to blend **2** : to mix up, to muddle **3 INVOLUCRAR** : to involve — **mezclarse** *vr* **1** : to get mixed up (in) **2** : to mix, to mingle (socially)
mezclilla *nf Chile, Mex* : denim ⟨pantalones de mezclilla : jeans⟩
mezcolanza *nf* : jumble, hodgepodge
mezquindad *nf* **1** : meanness, stinginess **2** : petty deed, mean action
mezquino[1], **-na** *adj* **1** : mean, petty **2** : stingy **3** : paltry
mezquino[2] *nm Mex* : wart
mezquita *nf* : mosque
mezquite *nm* : mesquite
mi *adj* : my
mí *pron* **1** : me ⟨es para mí : it's for me⟩ ⟨a mí no me importa : it doesn't matter to me⟩ **2 mí mismo, mí misma** : myself
miasma *nm* : miasma
miau *nm* : meow
mica *nf* : mica
mico *nm* : monkey, long-tailed monkey
micra *nf* : micron
microbio *nm* : microbe, germ
microbiología *nf* : microbiology
microbiológico, -ca *adj* : microbiological
microbús *nm, pl* **-buses** : minibus
microcomputadora *nf* : microcomputer
microcosmos *nms & pl* : microcosm
microficha *nf* : microfiche
microfilm *nm, pl* **-films** : microfilm
micrófono *nm* : microphone
micrómetro *nm* : micrometer
microonda *nf* : microwave
microondas *nms & pl* : microwave, microwave oven
microordenador *nm Spain* : microcomputer
microorganismo *nm* : microorganism
microprocesador *nm* : microprocessor
microscópico, -ca *adj* : microscopic
microscopio *nm* : microscope
mide, etc. → **medir**
miedo *nm* **1 TEMOR** : fear ⟨le tiene miedo al perro : he's scared of the dog⟩ ⟨tenían miedo de hablar : they were afraid to speak⟩ **2 dar miedo** : to frighten
miedoso, -sa *adj* **TEMEROSO** : fearful
miel *nf* : honey
miembro *nm* **1** : member **2 EXTREMIDAD** : limb, extremity
mienta, etc. → **mentar**
miente, etc. → **mentir**

mientras¹ *adv* **1** *or* **mientras tanto** : meanwhile, in the meantime **2 mientras más** : the more ⟨mientras más como, más quiero : the more I eat, the more I want⟩
mientras² *conj* **1** : while, as ⟨roncaba mientras dormía : he snored while he was sleeping⟩ **2** : as long as ⟨luchará mientras pueda : he will fight as long as he is able⟩ **3 mientras que** : while, whereas ⟨él es alto mientras que ella es muy baja : he is tall, whereas she is very short⟩
miércoles *nms & pl* : Wednesday
miga *nf* **1** : crumb **2 hacer buenas (malas) migas con** : to get along well (poorly) with
migaja *nf* **1** : crumb **2 migajas** *nfpl* SOBRAS : leftovers, scraps
migración *nf, pl* **-ciones** : migration
migrante *nmf* : migrant
migraña *nf* : migraine
migratorio, -ria *adj* : migratory
mijo *nm* : millet
mil¹ *adj* : thousand
mil² *nm* : one thousand, a thousand
milagro *nm* : miracle ⟨de milagro : miraculously⟩
milagroso, -sa *adj* : miraculous, marvelous — **milagrosamente** *adv*
milenio *nm* : millennium
milésimo, -ma *adj* : thousandth — **milésimo** *nm*
milicia *nf* **1** : militia **2** : military service
miligramo *nm* : milligram
mililitro *nm* : milliliter
milímetro *nm* : millimeter
militancia *nf* : militancy
militante¹ *adj* : militant
militante² *nmf* : militant, activist
militar¹ *vi* **1** : to serve (in the military) **2** : to be active (in politics)
militar² *adj* : military
militar³ *nmf* SOLDADO : soldier
militarismo *nm* : militarism
militarista *adj & nmf* : militarist
militarizar {21} *vt* : to militarize
milla *nf* : mile
millar *nm* : thousand
millón *nm, pl* **millones** : million
millonario, -ria *n* : millionaire
millonésimo¹, -ma *adj* : millionth
millonésimo² *nm* : millionth
mil millones *nms & pl* : billion
milpa *nf CA, Mex* : cornfield
milpiés *nms & pl* : millipede
mimar *vt* CONSENTIR : to pamper, to spoil
mimbre *nm* : wicker
mimeógrafo *nm* : mimeograph
mímica *nf* **1** : mime, sign language **2** IMITACIÓN : mimicry
mimo *nm* **1** : pampering, indulgence ⟨hacerle mimos a alguien : to pamper someone⟩ **2** : mime
mimoso, -sa *adj* **1** : fussy, finicky **2** : affectionate, clinging
mina *nf* **1** : mine **2** : lead (for pencils)

minar *vt* **1** : to mine **2** DEBILITAR : to undermine
minarete *nm* ALMINAR : minaret
mineral *adj & nm* : mineral
minería *nf* : mining
minero¹, -ra *adj* : mining
minero², -ra *n* : miner, mine worker
miniatura *nf* : miniature
minicomputadora *nf* : minicomputer
minifalda *nf* : miniskirt
minifundio *nm* : small farm
minimizar {21} *vt* : to minimize
mínimo¹, -ma *adj* **1** : minimum ⟨salario mínimo : minimum wage⟩ **2** : least, smallest **3** : very small, minute
mínimo² *nm* **1** : minimum, least amount **2** : modicum, small amount **3 como ~** : at least
minino, -na *n fam* : pussy, pussycat
miniserie *nf* : miniseries
ministerial *adj* : ministerial
ministerio *nm* : ministry, department
ministro, -tra *n* : minister, secretary ⟨primer ministro : prime minister⟩ ⟨Ministro de Defensa : Secretary of Defense⟩
minivan [ˌminiˈban, -ˈvan] *nf, pl* **-vanes** : minivan
minoría *nf* : minority
minorista¹ *adj* : retail
minorista² *nmf* : retailer
minoritario, -ria *adj* : minority
mintió, etc. → **mentir**
minuciosamente *adv* **1** : minutely **2** : in great detail **3** : thoroughly, meticulously
minucioso, -sa *adj* **1** : minute **2** DETALLADO : detailed **3** : thorough, meticulous
minué *nm* : minuet
minúsculo, -la *adj* DIMINUTO : tiny, miniscule
minusvalía *nf* : disability, handicap
minusválido¹, -da *adj* : handicapped, disabled
minusválido², -da *n* : handicapped person
minuta *nf* **1** BORRADOR : rough draft **2** : bill, fee
minutero *nm* : minute hand
minuto *nm* : minute
mío¹, mía *adj* **1** : my, of mine ⟨¡Dios mío! : my God!, good heavens!⟩ ⟨una amiga mía : a friend of mine⟩ **2** : mine ⟨es mío : it's mine⟩
mío², mía *pron* (*with definite article*) : mine, my own ⟨tus zapatos son iguales a los míos : your shoes are just like mine⟩
miope *adj* : nearsighted, myopic
miopía *nf* : myopia, nearsightedness
mira *nf* **1** : sight (of a firearm or instrument) **2** : aim, objective ⟨con miras a : with the intention of, with a view to⟩ ⟨de amplias miras : broad-minded⟩ ⟨poner la mira en : to aim at, to aspire to⟩

mirada *nf* **1** : look, glance, gaze **2** EX-PRESIÓN : look, expression ⟨una mirada de sorpresa : a look of surprise⟩
mirado, -da *adj* **1** : cautious, careful **2** : considerate **3 bien mirado** : well thought of **4 mal mirado** : disliked, disapproved of
mirador *nm* : balcony, lookout, vantage point
miramiento *nm* **1** CONSIDERACIÓN : consideration, respect **2 sin miramientos** : without due consideration, carelessly
mirar *vt* **1** : to look at **2** OBSERVAR : to watch **3** REFLEXIONAR : to consider, to think over — *vi* **1** : to look **2** : to face, to overlook **3 ~ por** : to look after, to look out for — **mirarse** *vr* **1** : to look at oneself **2** : to look at each other
mirasol *nm* GIRASOL : sunflower
miríada *nf* : myriad
mirlo *nm* : blackbird
mirra *nf* : myrrh
mirto *nm* ARRAYÁN : myrtle
misa *nf* : Mass
misantropía *nf* : misanthropy
misantrópico, -ca *adj* : misanthropic
misántropo, -pa *n* : misanthrope
miscelánea *nf* : miscellany
misceláneo, -nea *adj* : miscellaneous
miserable *adj* **1** LASTIMOSO : miserable, wretched **2** : paltry, meager **3** MEZQUINO : stingy, miserly **4** : despicable, vile
miseria *nf* **1** POBREZA : poverty **2** : misery, suffering **3** : pittance, meager amount
misericordia *nf* COMPASIÓN : mercy, compassion
misericordioso, -sa *adj* : merciful
mísero, -ra *adj* **1** : wretched, miserable **2** : stingy **3** : paltry, meager
misil *nm* : missile
misión *nf, pl* **misiones** : mission
misionero, -ra *adj & n* : missionary
misiva *nf* : missive, letter
mismísimo, -ma *adj (used as an intensifier)* : very, selfsame ⟨el mismísimo día : that very same day⟩
mismo[1] *adv (used as an intensifier)* : right, exactly ⟨hazlo ahora mismo : do it right now⟩ ⟨te llamará hoy mismo : he'll definitely call you today⟩
mismo[2]**, -ma** *adj* **1** : same **2** *(used as an intensifier)* : very ⟨en ese mismo momento : at that very moment⟩ **3** : oneself ⟨lo hizo ella misma : she made it herself⟩ **4 por lo mismo** : for that reason
misoginia *nf* : misogyny
misógino *nm* : misogynist
misterio *nm* : mystery
misterioso, -sa *adj* : mysterious — **misteriosamente** *adv*
misticismo *nm* : mysticism
místico[1]**, -ca** *adj* : mystic, mystical
místico[2]**, -ca** *n* : mystic

mitad *nf* **1** : half ⟨mitad y mitad : half and half⟩ **2** MEDIO : middle ⟨a mitad de : halfway through⟩ ⟨por la mitad : in half⟩
mítico, -ca *adj* : mythical, mythic
mitigar {52} *vt* ALIVIAR : to mitigate, to alleviate — **mitigación** *nf*
mitin *nm, pl* **mítines** : (political) meeting, rally
mito *nm* LEYENDA : myth, legend
mitología *nf* : mythology
mitológico, -ca *adj* : mythological
mitosis *nfs & pl* : mitosis
mitra *nf* : miter (bishop's hat)
mixto, -ta *adj* **1** : mixed, joint **2** : co-educational
mixtura *nf* : mixture, blend
mnemónico, -ca *adj* : mnemonic
mobiliario *nm* : furniture
mocasín *nm, pl* **-sines** : moccasin
mocedad *nf* **1** JUVENTUD : youth **2** : youthful prank
mochila *nf* MORRAL : backpack, knapsack
moción *nf, pl* **-ciones** **1** MOVIMIENTO : motion, movement **2** : motion (to a court or assembly)
moco *nm* **1** : mucus **2** *fam* : snot ⟨limpiarse los mocos : to wipe one's (runny) nose⟩
mocoso, -sa *n* : kid, brat
moda *nf* **1** : fashion, style **2 a la moda** *or* **de ~** : in style, fashionable **3 moda pasajera** : fad
modales *nmpl* : manners
modalidad *nf* **1** CLASE : kind, type **2** MANERA : way, manner
modelar *vt* : to model, to mold — **modelarse** *vr* : to model oneself after, to emulate
modelo[1] *adj* : model ⟨una casa modelo : a model home⟩
modelo[2] *nm* : model, example, pattern
modelo[3] *nmf* : model, mannequin
módem *or* **modem** ['moðɛm] *nm* : modem
moderación *nf, pl* **-ciones** MESURA : moderation
moderado, -da *adj & n* : moderate — **moderadamente** *adv*
moderador, -dora *n* : moderator, chair
moderar *vt* **1** TEMPERAR : to temper, to moderate **2** : to curb, to reduce ⟨moderar gastos : to curb spending⟩ **3** PRESIDIR : to chair (a meeting) — **moderarse** *vr* **1** : to restrain oneself **2** : to diminish, to calm down
modernidad *nf* **1** : modernity, modernness **2** : modern age
modernismo *nm* : modernism
modernista[1] *adj* : modernist, modernistic
modernista[2] *nmf* : modernist
modernizar {21} *vt* : to modernize — **modernización** *nf*
moderno, -na *adj* : modern, up-to-date
modestia *nf* : modesty

modesto, -ta *adj* : modest — **modesta-mente** *adv*
modificación *nf, pl* **-ciones** : alteration
modificador¹, -dora *adj* : modifying, moderating
modificador² → **modificante**
modificante *nm* : modifier
modificar {72} *vt* ALTERAR : to modify, to alter, to adapt
modismo *nm* : idiom
modista *nmf* **1** : dressmaker **2** : fashion designer
modo *nm* **1** MANERA : way, manner, mode ⟨de un modo u otro : one way or another⟩ ⟨a mi modo de ver : to my way of thinking⟩ **2** : mood (in grammar) **3** : mode (in music) **4 a modo de** : by way of, in the manner of, like ⟨a modo de ejemplo : by way of example⟩ **5 de cualquier modo** : in any case, anyway **6 de modo que** : so, in such a way that **7 de todos modos** : in any case, anyway **8 en cierto modo** : in a way, to a certain extent
modorra *nf* : drowsiness, lethargy
modular¹ *v* : to modulate — **modulación** *nf*
modular² *adj* : modular
módulo *nm* : module, unit
mofa *nf* **1** : mockery, ridicule **2 hacer mofa de** : to make fun of, to ridicule
mofarse *vr* ~ **de** : to scoff at, to make fun of
mofeta *nf* ZORRILLO : skunk
mofle *nm* CA, Mex : muffler (of a car)
moflete *nm fam* : fat cheek
mofletudo, -da *adj fam* : fat-cheeked, chubby
mohín *nm, pl* **mohines** : grimace, face
mohino, -na *adj* : gloomy, melancholy
moho *nm* **1** : mold, mildew **2** : rust
mohoso, -sa *adj* **1** : moldy **2** : rusty
moisés *nm, pl* **moiseses** : bassinet, cradle
mojado¹, -da *adj* : wet
mojado², -da *n Mex fam* : illegal immigrant
mojar *vt* **1** : to wet, to moisten **2** : to dunk — **mojarse** *vr* : to get wet
mojigatería *nf* **1** : hypocrisy **2** GAZMOÑERÍA : primness, prudery
mojigato¹, -ta *adj* : prudish, prim — **mojigatamente** *adv*
mojigato², -ta *n* : prude, prig
mojón *nm, pl* **mojones** : boundary stone, marker
molar *nm* MUELA : molar
molcajete *nm Mex* : mortar
molde *nm* **1** : mold, form **2 letras de molde** : printing, block lettering
moldear *vt* **1** FORMAR : to mold, to shape **2** : to cast
moldura *nf* : molding
mole¹ *nm Mex* **1** : spicy sauce made with chilies and usually chocolate **2** : meat served with mole sauce
mole² *nf* : mass, bulk
molécula *nf* : molecule — **molecular** *adj*

moler {47} *vt* **1** : to grind, to crush **2** CANSAR : to exhaust, to wear out
molestar *vt* **1** FASTIDIAR : to annoy, to bother **2** : to disturb, to disrupt — *vi* : to be a nuisance — **molestarse** *vr* ~ **en** : to take the trouble to
molestia *nf* **1** FASTIDIO : annoyance, bother, nuisance **2** : trouble ⟨se tomó la molestia de investigar : she took the trouble to investigate⟩ **3** MALESTAR : discomfort
molesto, -ta *adj* **1** ENOJADO : bothered, annoyed **2** FASTIDIOSO : bothersome, annoying
molestoso, -sa *adj* : bothersome, annoying
molido, -da *adj* **1** MACHACADO : ground, crushed **2 estar molido** : to be exhausted
molienda *nf* : milling, grinding
molinero, -ra *n* : miller
molinillo *nm* : grinder, mill ⟨molinillo de café : coffee grinder⟩
molino *nm* **1** : mill **2 molino de viento** : windmill
molla *nf* : soft fleshy part, flesh (of fruit), lean part (of meat)
molleja *nf* : gizzard
molusco *nm* : mollusk
momentáneamente *adv* : momentarily
momentáneo, -nea *adj* **1** : momentary **2** TEMPORARIO : temporary
momento *nm* **1** : moment, instant ⟨espera un momentito : wait just a moment⟩ **2** : time, period of time ⟨momentos difíciles : hard times⟩ **3** : present, moment ⟨los atletas del momento : the athletes of the moment, today's popular athletes⟩ **4** : momentum **5 al momento** : right away, at once **6 de** ~ : at the moment, for the moment **7 de un momento a otro** : any time now **8 por momentos** : at times
momia *nf* : mummy
monaguillo *nm* ACÓLITO : altar boy
monarca *nmf* : monarch
monarquía *nf* : monarchy
monárquico, -ca *n* : monarchist
monasterio *nm* : monastery
monástico, -ca *adj* : monastic
mondadientes *nms & pl* PALILLO : toothpick
mondar *vt* : to peel
mondongo *nm* ENTRAÑAS : innards *pl,* insides *pl,* guts *pl*
moneda *nf* **1** : coin **2** : money, currency
monedero *nm* : change purse
monetario, -ria *adj* : monetary, financial
mongol, -gola *adj & n* : Mongol, Mongolian
monitor¹, -tora *n* : instructor (in sports)
monitor² *nm* : monitor ⟨monitor de televisión : television monitor⟩
monitorear *vt* : to monitor
monja *nf* : nun
monje *nm* : monk
mono¹, -na *adj fam* : lovely, pretty, cute, darling

mono², **-na** *n* : monkey
monóculo *nm* : monocle
monogamia *nf* : monogamy
monógamo, **-ma** *adj* : monogamous
monografía *nf* : monograph
monograma *nm* : monogram
monolingüe *adj* : monolingual
monolítico, **-ca** *adj* : monolithic
monolito *nm* : monolith
monólogo *nm* : monologue
monomanía *nf* : obsession
monopatín *nm, pl* **-tines 1** : scooter **2** : skateboard
monopolio *nm* : monopoly
monopolizar {21} *vt* : to monopolize — **monopolización** *nf*
monosilábico, **-ca** *adj* : monosyllabic
monosílabo *nm* : monosyllable
monoteísmo *nm* : monotheism
monoteísta¹ *adj* : monotheistic
monoteísta² *nmf* : monotheist
monotonía *nf* **1** : monotony **2** : monotone
monótono, **-na** *adj* : monotonous — **monótonamente** *adv*
monóxido *nm* : monoxide ⟨monóxido de carbono : carbon monoxide⟩
monserga *nf* : gibberish, drivel
monstruo *nm* : monster
monstruosidad *nf* : monstrosity
monstruoso, **-sa** *adj* : monstrous — **monstruosamente** *adv*
monta *nf* **1** : sum, total **2** : importance, value ⟨de poca monta : unimportant, insignificant⟩
montaje *nm* **1** : assembling, assembly **2** : montage
montante *nm* : transom, fanlight
montaña *nf* **1** MONTE : mountain **2** **montaña rusa** : roller coaster
montañero, **-ra** *n* : mountaineer, mountain climber
montañoso, **-sa** *adj* : mountainous
montar *vt* **1** : to mount **2** ESTABLECER : to set up, to establish **3** ARMAR : to assemble, to put together **4** : to edit (a film) **5** : to stage, to put on (a show) **6** : to cock (a gun) **7 montar en bicicleta** : to get on a bicycle **8 montar a caballo** CABALGAR : to ride horseback
monte *nm* **1** MONTAÑA : mountain, mount **2** : woodland, scrubland ⟨monte bajo : underbrush⟩ **3** : outskirts (of a town), surrounding country **4 monte de piedad** : pawnshop
montés *adj, pl* **monteses** : wild (of animals or plants)
montículo *nm* **1** : mound, heap **2** : hillock, knoll
monto *nm* : amount, total
montón *nm, pl* **-tones 1** : heap, pile **2** *fam* : ton, load ⟨un montón de preguntas : a ton of questions⟩ ⟨montones de gente : loads of people⟩
montura *nf* **1** : mount (horse) **2** : saddle, tack **3** : setting, mounting (of jewelry) **4** : frame (of glasses)

monumental *adj fam* **1** : tremendous, terrific **2** : massive, huge
monumento *nm* : monument
monzón *nm, pl* **monzones** : monsoon
moño *nm* **1** : bun (chignon) **2** LAZO : bow, knot ⟨corbata de moño : bow tie⟩
moquear *vi* : to snivel
moquillo *nm* : distemper
mora *nf* **1** : blackberry **2** : mulberry
morada *nf* RESIDENCIA : dwelling, abode
morado¹, **-da** *adj* : purple
morado² *nm* : purple
morador, **-dora** *n* : dweller, inhabitant
moral¹ *adj* : moral — **moralmente** *adv*
moral² *nf* **1** MORALIDAD : ethics, morality, morals *pl* **2** ÁNIMO : morale, spirits *pl*
moraleja *nf* : moral (of a story)
moralidad *nf* : morality
moralista¹ *adj* : moralistic
moralista² *nmf* : moralist
morar *vi* : to dwell, to reside
moratoria *nf* : moratorium
mórbido, **-da** *adj* : morbid
morboso, **-sa** *adj* : morbid — **morbosidad** *nf*
morcilla *nf* : blood sausage, blood pudding
mordacidad *nf* : bite, sharpness
mordaz *adj* : caustic, scathing
mordaza *nf* **1** : gag **2** : clamp
mordedura *nf* : bite (of an animal)
morder {47} *v* : to bite
mordida *nf* **1** : bite **2** *CA, Mex* : bribe, payoff
mordisco *nm* : bite, nibble
mordisquear *vt* : to nibble (on), to bite
morena *nf* **1** : moraine **2** : moray (eel)
moreno¹, **-na** *adj* **1** : brunette **2** : dark, dark-skinned
moreno², **-na** *n* **1** : brunette **2** : dark-skinned person
moretón *nm, pl* **-tones** : bruise
morfina *nf* : morphine
morfología *nf* : morphology
morgue *nf* : morgue
moribundo¹, **-da** *adj* : dying, moribund
moribundo², **-da** *n* : dying person
morillo *nm* : andiron
morir {46} *vi* **1** FALLECER : to die **2** APAGARSE : to die out, to go out
mormón, **-mona** *adj & n, pl* **mormones** : Mormon
moro¹, **-ra** *adj* : Moorish
moro², **-ra** *n* **1** : Moor **2** : Muslim
morosidad *nf* **1** : delinquency (in payment) **2** : slowness
moroso, **-sa** *adj* **1** : delinquent, in arrears ⟨cuentas morosas : delinquent accounts⟩ **2** : slow, sluggish
morral *nm* MOCHILA : backpack, knapsack
morralla *nf* **1** : small fish **2** : trash, riffraff **3** *Mex* : small change
morriña *nf* : homesickness
morro *nm* HOCICO : snout

morsa *nf* : walrus
morse *nm* : Morse code
mortaja *nf* SUDARIO : shroud
mortal[1] *adj* **1** : mortal **2** FATAL : fatal, deadly — **mortalmente** *adv*
mortal[2] *nmf* : mortal
mortalidad *nf* : mortality
mortandad *nf* **1** : loss of life, death toll **2** : carnage, slaughter
mortero *nm* : mortar (bowl, cannon, or building material)
mortífero, -ra *adj* LETAL : deadly, fatal
mortificación *nf, pl* **-ciones 1** : mortification **2** TORMENTO : anguish, torment
mortificar {72} *vt* **1** : to mortify **2** TORTURAR : to trouble, to torment — **mortificarse** *vr* : to be mortified, to feel embarrassed
mosaico *nm* : mosaic
mosca *nf* **1** : fly **2 mosca común** : housefly
moscada *adj* **nuez moscada** : nutmeg
moscovita *adj & nmf* : Muscovite
mosquearse *vr* **1** : to become suspicious **2** : to take offense
mosquete *nm* : musket
mosquetero *nm* : musketeer
mosquitero *nm* : mosquito net
mosquito *nm* ZANCUDO : mosquito
mostachón *nm, pl* **-chones** : macaroon
mostaza *nf* : mustard
mostrador *nm* : counter (in a store)
mostrar {19} *vt* **1** : to show **2** EXHIBIR : to exhibit, to display — **mostrarse** *vr* : to show oneself, to appear
mota *nf* **1** : fleck, speck **2** : defect, blemish
mote *nm* SOBRENOMBRE : nickname
moteado, -da *adj* : dotted, spotted, dappled
motel *nm* : motel
motín *nm, pl* **motines 1** : riot **2** : rebellion, mutiny
motivación *nf, pl* **-ciones** : motivation — **motivacional** *adj*
motivar *vt* **1** CAUSAR : to cause **2** IMPULSAR : to motivate
motivo *nm* **1** MÓVIL : motive **2** CAUSA : cause, reason **3** TEMA : theme, motif
moto *nf* : motorcycle, motorbike
motocicleta *nf* : motorcycle
motociclismo *nm* : motorcycling
motociclista *nmf* : motorcyclist
motor[1]**, -ra** *adj* MOTRIZ : motor
motor[2] *nm* **1** : motor, engine **2** : driving force, cause
motorista *nmf* : motorist
motriz *adj, pl* **motrices** : driving
motu proprio *adv* **de motu proprio** [de ꞌmotuꞌproprio] : voluntarily, of one's own accord
mousse [ꞌmus] *nmf* : mousse
mover {47} *vt* **1** TRASLADAR : to move, to shift **2** AGITAR : to shake, to nod (the head) **3** ACCIONAR : to power, to drive **4** INDUCIR : to provoke, to cause **5** : to excite, to stir — **moverse** *vr* **1**

: to move, to move over **2** : to hurry, to get a move on **3** : to get moving, to make an effort
movible *adj* : movable
movida *nf* : move (in a game)
móvil[1] *adj* : mobile
móvil[2] *nm* **1** MOTIVO : motive **2** : mobile
movilidad *nf* : mobility
movilizar {21} *vt* : to mobilize — **movilización** *nf*
movimiento *nm* : movement, motion ⟨movimiento del cuerpo : bodily movement⟩ ⟨movimiento sindicalista : labor movement⟩
mozo[1]**, -za** *adj* : young, youthful
mozo[2]**, -za** *n* **1** JOVEN : young man *m*, young woman *f*, youth **2** : helper, servant **3** *Arg, Chile, Col, Peru* : waiter *m*, waitress *f*
mucamo, -ma *n* : servant, maid *f*
muchacha *nf* : maid
muchacho, -cha *n* **1** : kid, boy *m*, girl *f* **2** JOVEN : young man *m*, young woman *f*
muchedumbre *nf* MULTITUD : crowd, multitude
mucho[1] *adv* **1** : much, a lot ⟨mucho más : much more⟩ ⟨le gusta mucho : he likes it a lot⟩ **2** : long, a long time ⟨tardó mucho en venir : he was a long time getting here⟩ **3 por mucho que** : no matter how much
mucho[2]**, -cha** *adj* **1** : a lot of, many, much ⟨mucha gente : a lot of people⟩ ⟨hace mucho tiempo que no lo veo : I haven't seen him in ages⟩ **2 muchas veces** : often
mucho[3]**, -cha** *pron* **1** : a lot, many, much ⟨hay mucho que hacer : there is a lot to do⟩ ⟨muchas no vinieron : many didn't come⟩ **2 cuando** ∼ *or* **como** ∼ : at most **3 con** ∼ : by far **4 ni mucho menos** : not at all, far from it
mucílago *nm* : mucilage
mucosidad *nf* : mucus
mucoso, -sa *adj* : mucous, slimy
muda *nf* **1** : change ⟨muda de ropa : change of clothes⟩ **2** : molt, molting
mudanza *nf* **1** CAMBIO : change **2** TRASLADO : move, moving
mudar *v* **1** CAMBIAR : to change **2** : to molt, to shed — **mudarse** *vr* **1** TRASLADARSE : to move (one's residence) **2** : to change (clothes)
mudo[1]**, -da** *adj* SILENCIOSO : silent ⟨el cine mudo : silent films⟩ **2** : mute, dumb
mudo[2]**, -da** *n* : mute
mueble *nm* **1** : piece of furniture **2 muebles** *nmpl* : furniture, furnishings
mueblería *nf* : furniture store
mueca *nf* : grimace, face
muela *nf* **1** : tooth, molar ⟨dolor de muelas : toothache⟩ ⟨muela de juicio : wisdom tooth⟩ **2** : millstone **3** : whetstone
muele, etc. → **moler**

muelle[1] *adj* : soft, comfortable, easy
muelle[2] *nm* **1** : wharf, dock **2** RESORTE : spring
muérdago *nm* : mistletoe
muerde, *etc.* → **morder**
muere, *etc.* → **morir**
muerte *nf* : death
muerto[1] *pp* → **morir**
muerto[2], **-ta** *adj* **1** : dead **2** : lifeless, flat, dull **3** ~ **de** : dying of ⟨estoy muerto de hambre : I'm dying of hunger⟩
muerto[3], **-ta** *nm* DIFUNTO : dead person, deceased
muesca *nf* : nick, notch
muestra[1], *etc.* → **mostrar**
muestra[2] *nf* **1** : sample **2** SEÑAL : sign, show ⟨una muestra de respeto : a show of respect⟩ **3** EXPOSICIÓN : exhibition, exposition **4** : pattern, model
mueve, *etc.* → **mover**
mugido *nm* : moo, lowing, bellow
mugir {35} *vi* : to moo, to low, to bellow
mugre *nf* SUCIEDAD : grime, filth
mugriento, **-ta** *adj* : filthy
muguete *nm* : lily of the valley
muja, *etc.* → **mugir**
mujer *nf* **1** : woman **2** ESPOSA : wife
mulato, **-ta** *adj & n* : mulatto
muleta *nf* : crutch
mullido, **-da** *adj* **1** : soft, fluffy **2** : spongy, springy
mulo, **-la** *n* : mule
multa *nf* : fine
multar *vt* : to fine
multicolor *adj* : multicolored
multicultural *adj* : multicultural
multidisciplinario, **-ria** *adj* : multidisciplinary
multifacético, **-ca** *adj* : multifaceted
multifamiliar *adj* : multifamily
multilateral *adj* : multilateral
multimedia *nf* : multimedia
multimillonario, **-ria** *n* : multimillionaire
multinacional *adj* : multinational
múltiple *adj* : multiple
multiplicación *nf, pl* **-ciones** : multiplication
multiplicar {72} *v* **1** : to multiply **2** : to increase — **multiplicarse** *vr* : to multiply, to reproduce
multiplicidad *nf* : multiplicity
múltiplo *nm* : multiple
multitud *nf* MUCHEDUMBRE : crowd, multitude
multiuso, **-sa** *adj* : multipurpose
multivitamínico, **-ca** *adj* : multivitamin
mundano, **-na** *adj* : worldly, earthly
mundial *adj* : world, worldwide
mundialmente *adv* : worldwide, all over the world

mundo *nm* **1** : world **2 todo el mundo** : everyone, everybody
municiones *nfpl* : ammunition, munitions
municipal *adj* : municipal
municipio *nm* **1** : municipality **2** AYUNTAMIENTO : town council
muñeca *nf* **1** : doll **2** MANIQUÍ : mannequin **3** : wrist
muñeco *nm* **1** : doll, boy doll **2** MARIONETA : puppet
muñón *nm, pl* **muñones** : stump (of an arm or leg)
mural *adj & nm* : mural
muralista *nmf* : muralist
muralla *nf* : rampart, wall
murciélago *nm* : bat (animal)
murga *nf* : band of street musicians
murió, *etc.* → **morir**
murmullo *nm* **1** : murmur, murmuring **2** : rustling, rustle ⟨el murmullo de las hojas : the rustling of the leaves⟩
murmurar *vt* **1** : to murmur, to mutter **2** : to whisper (gossip) — *vi* **1** : to murmur **2** CHISMEAR : to gossip
muro *nm* : wall
musa *nf* : muse
musaraña *nf* : shrew
muscular *adj* : muscular
musculatura *nf* : muscles *pl,* musculature
músculo *nm* : muscle
musculoso, **-sa** *adj* : muscular, brawny
muselina *nf* : muslin
museo *nm* : museum
musgo *nm* : moss
musgoso, **-sa** *adj* : mossy
música *nf* : music
musical *adj* : musical — **musicalmente** *adv*
músico[1], **-ca** *adj* : musical
músico[2], **-ca** *n* : musician
musitar *vt* : to mumble, to murmur
muslo *nm* : thigh
musulmán, **-mana** *adj & n, mpl* **-manes** : Muslim
mutación *nf, pl* **-ciones** : mutation
mutante *adj & nm* : mutant
mutar *v* : to mutate
mutilar *vt* : to mutilate — **mutilación** *nf*
mutis *nm* **1** : exit (in theater) **2** : silence
mutual *adj* : mutual
mutuo, **-tua** *adj* : mutual, reciprocal — **mutuamente** *adv*
muy *adv* **1** : very, quite ⟨es muy inteligente : she's very intelligent⟩ ⟨muy bien : very well, fine⟩ ⟨eso es muy americano : that's typically American⟩ **2** : too ⟨es muy grande para él : it's too big for him⟩

N

n *nf* : fourteenth letter of the Spanish alphabet

nabo *nm* : turnip

nácar *nm* MADREPERLA : nacre, mother-of-pearl

nacarado, -da *adj* : pearly

nacer {48} *vi* **1** : to be born ⟨nací en Guatemala : I was born in Guatemala⟩ ⟨no nació ayer : he wasn't born yesterday⟩ **2** : to hatch **3** : to bud, to sprout **4** : to rise, to originate **5 nacer para algo** : to be born to be something **6 volver a nacer** : to have a lucky escape

nacido¹, -da *adj* **1** : born **2 recién nacido** : newborn

nacido², -da *n* **1 los nacidos** : those born (at a particular time) **2 recién nacido** : newborn baby

naciente *adj* **1** : newfound, growing **2** : rising ⟨el sol naciente : the rising sun⟩

nacimiento *nm* **1** : birth **2** : source (of a river) **3** : beginning, origin **4** BELÉN : Nativity scene, crèche

nación *nf, pl* **naciones** : nation, country, people (of a country)

nacional¹ *adj* : national

nacional² *nmf* CIUDADANO : national, citizen

nacionalidad *nf* : nationality

nacionalismo *nm* : nationalism

nacionalista¹ *adj* : nationalist, nationalistic

nacionalista² *nmf* : nationalist

nacionalización *nf, pl* **-ciones 1** : nationalization **2** : naturalization

nacionalizar {21} *vt* **1** : to nationalize **2** : to naturalize (as a citizen) — **nacionalizarse** *vr*

naco, -ca *adj Mex* : trashy, vulgar, common

nada¹ *adv* : not at all, not in the least ⟨no estamos nada cansados : we are not at all tired⟩

nada² *nf* **1** : nothingness **2** : smidgen, bit ⟨una nada le disgusta : the slightest thing upsets him⟩

nada³ *pron* **1** : nothing ⟨no estoy haciendo nada : I'm not doing anything⟩ **2 casi nada** : next to nothing **3 de ~** : you're welcome **4 dentro de nada** : very soon, in no time **5 nada más** : nothing else, nothing more

nadador, -dora *n* : swimmer

nadar *vi* **1** : to swim **2 ~ en** : to be swimming in, to be rolling in — *vt* : to swim

nadería *nf* : small thing, trifle

nadie *pron* : nobody, no one ⟨no vi a nadie : I didn't see anyone⟩

nadir *nm* : nadir

nado *nm* **1** *Mex* : swimming **2 a ~** : swimming ⟨cruzó el río a nado : he swam across the river⟩

nafta *nf* **1** : naphtha **2** (*in various countries*) : gasoline

naftalina *nf* : naphthalene, mothballs *pl*

náhuatl¹ *adj & nmf, pl* **nahuas** : Nahuatl

náhuatl² *nm* : Nahuatl (language)

nailon → **nilón**

naipe *nm* : playing card

nalga *nf* **1** : buttock **2 nalgas** *nfpl* : buttocks, bottom

nalgada *nf* : smack on the bottom, spanking

namibio, -bia *adj & n* : Namibian

nana *nf* **1** : lullaby **2** *fam* : grandma **3** *CA, Col, Mex, Ven* : nanny

nanay *interj fam* : no way!, not likely!

naranja¹ *adj & nm* : orange (color)

naranja² *nf* : orange (fruit)

naranjal *nm* : orange grove

naranjo *nm* : orange tree

narcisismo *nm* : narcissism

narcisista¹ *adj* : narcissistic

narcisista² *nmf* : narcissist

narciso *nm* : narcissus, daffodil

narcótico¹, -ca *adj* : narcotic

narcótico² *nm* : narcotic

narcotizar {21} *vt* : to drug, to dope

narcotraficante *nmf* : drug trafficker

narcotráfico *nm* : drug trafficking

narigón, -gona *adj, mpl* **-gones** : big-nosed

narigudo → **narigón**

nariz *nf, pl* **narices 1** : nose ⟨sonar(se) la nariz : to blow one's nose⟩ **2** : sense of smell

narración *nf, pl* **-ciones** : narration, account

narrador, -dora *n* : narrator

narrar *vt* : to narrate, to tell

narrativa *nf* : narrative, story

narrativo, -va *adj* : narrative

narval *nm* : narwhal

nasa *nf* : creel

nasal *adj* : nasal

nata *nf* **1** : cream ⟨nata batida : whipped cream⟩ **2** : skin (on boiled milk)

natación *nf, pl* **-ciones** : swimming

natal *adj* : native, natal

natalicio *nm* : birthday ⟨el natalicio de George Washington : George Washington's birthday⟩

natalidad *nf* : birthrate

natillas *nfpl* : custard

natividad *nf* : birth, nativity

nativo, -va *adj & n* : native

nato, -ta *adj* : born, natural

natural¹ *adj* **1** : natural **2** : normal ⟨como es natural : naturally, as expected⟩ **3 ~ de** : native of, from **4 de tamaño natural** : life-size

natural² *nm* **1** CARÁCTER : disposition, temperament **2** : native ⟨un natural de Venezuela : a native of Venezuela⟩

naturaleza *nf* **1** : nature ⟨la madre naturaleza : mother nature⟩ **2** ÍNDOLE : nature, disposition, constitution ⟨la naturaleza humana : human nature⟩ **3 naturaleza muerta** : still life

naturalidad *nf* : simplicity, naturalness
naturalismo *nm* : naturalism
naturalista[1] *adj* : naturalistic
naturalista[2] *nmf* : naturalist
naturalización *nf, pl* **-ciones** : naturalization
naturalizar {21} *vt* : to naturalize — **naturalizarse** *vr* NACIONALIZARSE : to become naturalized
naturalmente *adv* **1** : naturally, inherently **2** : of course
naufragar {52} *vi* **1** : to be shipwrecked **2** FRACASAR : to fail, to collapse
naufragio *nm* **1** : shipwreck **2** FRACASO : failure, collapse
náufrago[1], **-ga** *adj* : shipwrecked, castaway
náufrago[2], **-ga** *n* : shipwrecked person, castaway
náusea *nf* **1** : nausea **2 dar náuseas** : to nauseate, to disgust **3 náuseas matutinas** : morning sickness
nauseabundo, -da *adj* : nauseating, sickening
náutica *nf* : navigation
náutico, -ca *adj* : nautical
nautilo *nm* : nautilus
navaja *nf* **1** : pocketknife, penknife ⟨navaja de muelle : switchblade⟩ **2 navaja de afeitar** : straight razor, razor blade
navajo, -ja *adj & n* : Navajo
naval *adj* : naval
nave *nf* **1** : ship ⟨nave capitana : flagship⟩ ⟨nave espacial : spaceship⟩ **2** : nave ⟨nave lateral : aisle⟩ **quemar uno sus naves** : to burn one's bridges
navegabilidad *nf* : navigability
navegable *adj* : navigable
navegación *nf, pl* **-ciones** : navigation
navegante[1] *adj* : sailing, seafaring
navegante[2] *nmf* : navigator
navegar {52} *v* : to navigate, to sail
Navidad *nf* : Christmas, Christmastime ⟨Feliz Navidad : Merry Christmas⟩
navideño, -ña *adj* : Christmas
naviero, -ra *adj* : shipping
náyade *nf* : naiad
nazca, etc. → **nacer**
nazi *adj & nmf* : Nazi
nazismo *nm* : Nazism
nébeda *nf* : catnip
neblina *nf* : light fog, mist
neblinoso, -sa *adj* : misty, foggy
nebulosa *nf* : nebula
nebulosidad *nf* : mistiness, haziness
nebuloso, -sa *adj* **1** : hazy, misty **2** : nebulous, vague
necedad *nf* : stupidity, foolishness ⟨decir necedades : to talk nonsense⟩
necesariamente *adv* : necessarily
necesario, -ria *adj* **1** : necessary **2 si es necesario** : if need be **3 hacerse necesario** : to be required
neceser *nm* : toilet kit, vanity case
necesidad *nf* **1** : need, necessity **2** : poverty, want **3 necesidades** *nfpl* : hardships **4 hacer sus necesidades** : to relieve oneself

necesitado, -da *adj* : needy
necesitar *vt* **1** : to need **2** : to necessitate, to require — *vi* ∼ **de** : to have need of
necio[1], **-cia** *adj* **1** : foolish, silly, dumb **2** *fam* : naughty
necio[2], **-cia** *n* ESTÚPIDO : fool, idiot
necrología *nf* : obituary
necrópolis *nfs & pl* : cemetery
néctar *nm* : nectar
nectarina *nf* : nectarine
neerlandés[1], **-desa** *adj, mpl* **-deses** HOLANDÉS : Dutch
neerlandés[2], **-desa** *n, mpl* **-deses** HOLANDÉS : Dutch person, Dutchman *m*
nefando, -da *adj* : unspeakable, heinous
nefario, -ria *adj* : nefarious
nefasto, -ta *adj* **1** : ill-fated, unlucky **2** : disastrous, terrible
negación *nf, pl* **-ciones** **1** : negation, denial **2** : negative (in grammar)
negar {49} *vt* **1** : to deny **2** REHUSAR : to refuse **3** : to disown — **negarse** *vr* **1** : to refuse **2** : to deny oneself
negativa *nf* **1** : denial **2** : refusal
negativo[1], **-va** *adj* : negative
negativo[2] *nm* : negative (of a photograph)
negligé *nm* : negligee
negligencia *nf* : negligence
negligente *adj* : neglectful, negligent — **negligentemente** *adv*
negociable *adj* : negotiable
negociación *nf, pl* **-ciones** **1** : negotiation **2 negociación colectiva** : collective bargaining
negociador, -dora *n* : negotiator
negociante *nmf* : businessman *m*, businesswoman *f*
negociar *vt* : to negotiate — *vi* : to deal, to do business
negocio *nm* **1** : business, place of business **2** : deal, transaction **3 negocios** *nmpl* : commerce, trade, business
negrero, -ra *n* **1** : slave trader **2** *fam* : slave driver, brutal boss
negrita *nf* : boldface (type)
negro[1], **-gra** *adj* **1** : black, dark **2** BRONCEADO : suntanned **3** : gloomy, awful, desperate ⟨la cosa se está poniendo negra : things are looking bad⟩ **4 mercado negro** : black market
negro[2], **-gra** *n* **1** : dark-skinned person, black person **2** *fam* : darling, dear
negro[3] *nm* : black (color)
negrura *nf* : blackness
negruzco, -ca *adj* : blackish
nene, -na *n* : baby, small child
nenúfar *nm* : water lily
neocelandés → **neozelandés**
neoclasicismo *nm* : neoclassicism
neoclásico, -ca *adj* : neoclassical
neófito, -ta *n* : neophyte, novice
neologismo *nm* : neologism
neón *nm, pl* **neones** : neon
neoyorquino[1], **-na** *adj* : of or from New York

neoyorquino², -na *n* : New Yorker
neozelandés¹, -desa *adj, mpl* **-deses** : of or from New Zealand
neozelandés², -desa *n, mpl* **-deses** : New Zealander
nepalés, -lesa *adj & n, mpl* **-leses** : Nepali
nepotismo *nm* : nepotism
neptunio *nm* : neptunium
Neptuno *nm* : Neptune
nervio *nm* **1** : nerve **2** : tendon, sinew, gristle (in meat) **3** : energy, drive **4** : rib (of a vault) **5 nervios** *nmpl* : nerves ⟨estar mal de los nervios : to be a bundle of nerves⟩ ⟨ataque de nervios : nervous breakdown⟩
nerviosamente *adv* : nervously
nerviosidad → **nerviosismo**
nerviosismo *nf* : nervousness, anxiety
nervioso, -sa *adj* **1** : nervous, nerve ⟨sistema nervioso : nervous system⟩ **2** : high-strung, restless, anxious ⟨ponerse nervioso : to get nervous⟩ **3** : vigorous, energetic
nervudo, -da *adj* : sinewy, wiry
neta *nf Mex fam* : truth ⟨la neta es que me cae mal : the truth is, I don't like her⟩
netamente *adv* : clearly, obviously
neto, -ta *adj* **1** : net ⟨peso neto : net weight⟩ **2** : clear, distinct
neumático¹, -ca *adj* : pneumatic
neumático² *nm* LLANTA : tire
neumonía *nf* PULMONÍA : pneumonia
neural *adj* : neural
neuralgia *nf* : neuralgia
neuritis *nf* : neuritis
neurología *nf* : neurology
neurológico, -ca *adj* : neurological, neurologic
neurólogo, -ga *n* : neurologist
neurosis *nfs & pl* : neurosis
neurótico, -ca *adj & n* : neurotic
neutral *adj* : neutral
neutralidad *nf* : neutrality
neutralizar {21} *vt* : to neutralize — **neutralización** *nf*
neutro, -tra *adj* **1** : neutral **2** : neuter
neutrón *nm, pl* **neutrones** : neutron
nevada *nf* : snowfall
nevado, -da *adj* **1** : snowcapped **2** : snow-white
nevar {55} *v impers* : to snow
nevasca *nf* : snowstorm, blizzard
nevera *nf* REFRIGERADOR : refrigerator
nevería *nf Mex* : ice cream parlor
nevisca *nf* : light snowfall, flurry
nevoso, -sa *adj* : snowy
nexo *nm* VÍNCULO : link, connection, nexus
ni *conj* **1** : neither, nor ⟨afuera no hace ni frío ni calor : it's neither cold nor hot outside⟩ **2 ni que** : not even if, not as if ⟨ni que me pagaran : not even if they paid me⟩ ⟨ni que fuera (yo) su madre : it's not as if I were his mother⟩ **3 ni siquiera** : not even ⟨ni siquiera nos llamaron : they didn't even call us⟩

nicaragüense *adj & nmf* : Nicaraguan
nicho *nm* : niche
nicotina *nf* : nicotine
nido *nm* **1** : nest **2** : hiding place, den
niebla *nf* : fog, mist
niega, niegue etc. → **negar**
nieto, -ta *n* **1** : grandson *m*, granddaughter *f* **2 nietos** *nmpl* : grandchildren
nieva, etc. → **nevar**
nieve *nf* **1** : snow **2** *Cuba, Mex, PRi* : sherbet
nigeriano, -na *adj & n* : Nigerian
nigua *nf* : sand flea, chigger
nihilismo *nm* : nihilism
nilón *or* **nilon** *nm, pl* **nilones** : nylon
nimbo *nm* **1** : halo **2** : nimbus
nimiedad *nf* INSIGNIFICANCIA : trifle, triviality
nimio, -mia *adj* INSIGNIFICANTE : insignificant, trivial
ninfa *nf* : nymph
ningunear *vt Mex fam* : to disrespect
ninguno¹, -na (**ningún** *before masculine singular nouns*) *adj, mpl* **ningunos** : no, none ⟨no es ninguna tonta : she's no fool⟩ ⟨no debe hacerse en ningún momento : that should never be done⟩
ninguno², -na *pron* **1** : neither, none ⟨ninguno de los dos ha vuelto aún : neither one has returned yet⟩ **2** : no one, no other ⟨te quiero más que a ninguna : I love you more than any other⟩
niña *nf* **1** PUPILA : pupil (of the eye) **2 la niña de los ojos** : the apple of one's eye
niñada *nf* **1** : childishness **2** : trifle, silly thing
niñería → **niñada**
niñero, -ra *n* : baby-sitter, nanny
niñez *nf, pl* **niñeces** INFANCIA : childhood
niño, -ña *n* : child, boy *m*, girl *f*
niobio *nm* : niobium
nipón, -pona *adj & n, mpl* **nipones** JAPONÉS : Japanese
níquel *nm* : nickel
nitidez *nf, pl* **-deces** CLARIDAD : clarity, vividness, sharpness
nítido, -da *adj* CLARO : clear, vivid, sharp
nitrato *nm* : nitrate
nítrico, -ca *adj* ácido nítrico : nitric acid
nitrito *nm* : nitrite
nitrógeno *nm* : nitrogen
nitroglicerina *nf* : nitroglycerin
nivel *nm* **1** : level, height ⟨nivel del mar : sea level⟩ **2** : level, standard ⟨nivel de vida : standard of living⟩
nivelar *vt* : to level (out)
nixtamal *nm Mex* : limed corn used for tortillas
no *adv* **1** : no ⟨¿quieres ir al mercado? no, voy más tarde : do you want to go shopping? no, I'm going later⟩ **2** : not ⟨no hagas eso! : don't do that!⟩ ⟨creo que no : I don't think so⟩ **3** : non- ⟨no fumador : non-smoker⟩ **4 ¡como no!** : of course! **5 no bien** : as soon as, no sooner

nobelio *nm* : nobelium
noble[1] *adj* : noble — **noblemente** *adv*
noble[2] *nmf* : nobleman *m*, noblewoman *f*
nobleza *nf* **1** : nobility **2** HONRADEZ : honesty, integrity
nocaut *nm* : knockout, KO
noche *nf* **1** : night, nighttime, evening **2 buenas noches** : good evening, good night **3 de noche** *or* **por la noche** : at night **4 hacerse de noche** : to get dark
Nochebuena *nf* : Christmas Eve
nochecita *nf* : dusk
Nochevieja *nf* : New Year's Eve
noción *nf, pl* **nociones 1** CONCEPTO : notion, concept **2 nociones** *nfpl* : smattering, rudiments *pl*
nocivo, -va *adj* DAÑINO : harmful, noxious
noctámbulo, -la *n* **1** : sleepwalker **2** : night owl
nocturno[1], **-na** *adj* : night, nocturnal
nocturno[2] *nm* : nocturne
nodriza *nf* : wet nurse
nódulo *nm* : nodule
nogal *nm* **1** : walnut tree **2** *Mex* : pecan tree **3 nogal americano** : hickory
nómada[1] *adj* : nomadic
nómada[2] *nmf* : nomad
nomás *adv* : only, just ⟨lo hice nomás porque sí : I did it just because⟩ ⟨nomás de recordarlo me enojo : I get angry just remembering it⟩ ⟨nomás faltan dos semanas para Navidad : there are only two weeks left till Christmas⟩
nombradía *nf* RENOMBRE : fame, renown
nombrado, -da *adj* : famous, well-known
nombramiento *nm* : appointment, nomination
nombrar *vt* **1** : to appoint **2** : to mention, to name
nombre *nm* **1** : name ⟨nombre de pluma : pseudonym, pen name⟩ ⟨en nombre : on behalf of⟩ ⟨sin nombre : nameless⟩ **2** : noun ⟨nombre propio : proper noun⟩ **3** : fame, renown
nomenclatura *nf* : nomenclature
nomeolvides *nmfs & pl* : forget-me-not
nómina *nf* : payroll
nominación *nf, pl* **-ciones** : nomination
nominal *adj* : nominal — **nominalmente** *adv*
nominar *vt* : to nominate
nominativo[1], **-va** *adj* : nominative
nominativo[2] *nm* : nominative (case)
nomo *nm* : gnome
non[1] *adj* IMPAR : odd, not even
non[2] *nm* : odd number
nonagésimo[1], **-ma** *adj* : ninetieth, ninety-
nonagésimo[2], **-ma** *n* : ninetieth, ninety- (in a series)
nono, -na *adj* : ninth — **nono** *nm*
nopal *nm* : nopal, cactus
nopalitos *nmpl* *Mex* : pickled cactus leaves
noquear *vt* : to knock out, to KO

norcoreano, -na *adj & n* : North Korean
nordeste[1] *or* **noreste** *adj* **1** : northeastern **2** : northeasterly
nordeste[2] *or* **noreste** *nm* : northeast
nórdico, -ca *adj & n* **1** ESCANDINAVO : Scandinavian **2** : Norse
noreste → **nordeste**
noria *nf* **1** : waterwheel **2** : Ferris wheel
norirlandés[1], **-desa** *adj, mpl* **-deses** : Northern Irish
norirlandés[2], **-desa** *n, mpl* **-deses** : person from Northern Ireland
norma *nf* **1** : rule, regulation **2** : norm, standard
normal *adj* **1** : normal, usual **2** : standard **3 escuela normal** : teacher-training college
normalidad *nf* : normality, normalcy
normalización *nf, pl* **-ciones** *nf* **1** REGULARIZACIÓN : normalization **2** ESTANDARIZACIÓN : standardization
normalizar {21} *vt* **1** REGULARIZAR : to normalize **2** ESTANDARIZAR : to standardize — **normalizarse** *vr* : to return to normal
normalmente *adv* GENERALMENTE : ordinarily, generally
noroeste[1] *adj* **1** : northwestern **2** : northwesterly
noroeste[2] *nm* : northwest
norte[1] *adj* : north, northern
norte[2] *nm* **1** : north **2** : north wind **3** META : aim, objective
norteamericano, -na *adj & n* **1** : North American **2** AMERICANO, ESTADOUNIDENSE : American, native or inhabitant of the United States
norteño[1], **-ña** *adj* : northern
norteño[2], **-ña** *n* : Northerner
noruego[1], **-ga** *adj & n* : Norwegian
noruego[2] *nm* : Norwegian (language)
nos *pron* **1** : us ⟨nos enviaron a la frontera : they sent us to the border⟩ **2** : ourselves ⟨nos divertimos muchísimo : we enjoyed ourselves a great deal⟩ **3** : each other, one another ⟨nos vimos desde lejos : we saw each other from far away⟩ **4** : to us, for us, from us ⟨nos lo dio : he gave it to us⟩ ⟨nos lo compraron : they bought it from us⟩
nosotros, -tras *pron* **1** : we ⟨nosotros llegamos ayer : we arrived yesterday⟩ **2** : us ⟨ven con nosotros : come with us⟩ **3 nosotros mismos** : ourselves ⟨lo arreglamos nosotros mismos : we fixed it ourselves⟩
nostalgia *nf* **1** : nostalgia, longing **2** : homesickness
nostálgico, -ca *adj* **1** : nostalgic **2** : homesick
nota *nf* **1** : note, message **2** : announcement ⟨nota de prensa : press release⟩ **3** : grade, mark (in school) **4** : characteristic, feature, touch **5** : note (in music) **6** : bill, check (in a restaurant)

notable *adj* **1** : notable, noteworthy **2** : outstanding
notación *nf, pl* **-ciones** : notation
notar *vt* **1** : to notice ⟨hacer notar algo : to point out something⟩ **2** : to tell ⟨la diferencia se nota inmediatamente : you can tell the difference right away⟩ — **notarse** *vr* **1** : to be evident, to show **2** : to feel, to seem
notario, -ria *n* : notary, notary public
noticia *nf* **1** : news item, piece of news **2 noticias** *nfpl* : news
noticiero *nm* : news program, newscast
noticioso, -sa *adj* : news ⟨agencia noticiosa : news agency⟩
notificación *nf, pl* **-ciones** : notification
notificar {72} *vt* : to notify, to inform
notoriedad *nf* **1** : knowledge, obviousness **2** : fame, notoriety
notorio, -ria *adj* **1** OBVIO : obvious, evident **2** CONOCIDO : well-known
novato[1], -ta *adj* : inexperienced, new
novato[2], -ta *n* : beginner, novice
novecientos[1], -tas *adj* : nine hundred
novecientos[2] *nms & pl* : nine hundred
novedad *nf* **1** : newness, novelty **2** : innovation
novedoso, -sa *adj* : original, novel
novel *adj* NOVATO : inexperienced, new
novela *nf* **1** : novel **2** : soap opera
novelar *vt* : to fictionalize, to make a novel out of
novelesco, -ca *adj* **1** : fictional **2** : fantastic, fabulous
novelista *nmf* : novelist
novena *nf* : novena
noveno, -na *adj* : ninth — **noveno, -na** *n*
noventa *adj & nm* : ninety
noventavo[1], -va *adj* : ninetieth
noventavo[2] *nm* : ninetieth (fraction)
noviazgo *nm* **1** : courtship, relationship **2** : engagement, betrothal
novicio, -cia *n* **1** : novice (in religion) **2** PRINCIPIANTE : novice, beginner
noviembre *nm* : November
novilla *nf* : heifer
novillada *nf* : bullfight featuring young bulls
novillero, -ra *n* : apprentice bullfighter
novillo *nm* : young bull
novio, -via *n* **1** : boyfriend *m*, girlfriend *f* **2** PROMETIDO : fiancé *m*, fiancée *f* **3** : bridegroom *m*, bride *f*
novocaína *nf* : novocaine
nubarrón *nm, pl* **-rrones** : storm cloud
nube *nf* **1** : cloud ⟨andar en las nubes : to have one's head in the clouds⟩ ⟨por las nubes : sky-high⟩ **2** : cloud (of dust), swarm (of insects, etc.)
nublado[1], -da *adj* **1** NUBOSO : cloudy, overcast **2** : clouded, dim
nublado[2] *nm* **1** : storm cloud **2** AMENAZA : menace, threat
nublar *vt* **1** : to cloud **2** OSCURECER : to obscure — **nublarse** *vr* : to get cloudy
nubosidad *nf* : cloudiness
nuboso, -sa *adj* NUBLADO : cloudy

nuca *nf* : nape, back of the neck
nuclear *adj* : nuclear
núcleo *nm* **1** : nucleus **2** : center, heart, core
nudillo *nm* : knuckle
nudismo *nm* : nudism
nudista *adj & nmf* : nudist
nudo *nm* **1** : knot ⟨nudo de rizo : square knot⟩ ⟨un nudo en la garganta : a lump in one's throat⟩ **2** : node **3** : junction, hub ⟨nudo de comunicaciones : communication center⟩ **4** : crux, heart (of a problem, etc.)
nudoso, -sa *adj* : knotty, gnarled
nuera *nf* : daughter-in-law
nuestro[1], -tra *adj* : our
nuestro[2], -tra *pron* (*with definite article*) : ours, our own ⟨el nuestro es más grande : ours is bigger⟩ ⟨es de los nuestros : it's one of ours⟩
nuevamente *adv* : again, anew
nuevas *nfpl* : tidings *pl*
nueve *adj & nm* : nine
nuevecito, -ta *adj* : brand-new
nuevo, -va *adj* **1** : new ⟨una casa nueva : a new house⟩ ⟨¿qué hay de nuevo? : what's new?⟩ **2 de ~** : again, once more **3 Nuevo Testamento** : New Testament
nuez *nf, pl* **nueces** **1** : nut **2** : walnut **3** *Mex* : pecan **4 nuez de Adán** : Adam's apple **5 nuez moscada** : nutmeg
nulidad *nf* **1** : nullity **2** : incompetent person ⟨¡es una nulidad! : he's hopeless!⟩
nulo, -la *adj* **1** : null, null and void **2** INEPTO : useless, inept ⟨es nula para la cocina : she's hopeless at cooking⟩
numen *nm* : poetic muse, inspiration
numerable *adj* : countable
numeración *nf, pl* **-ciones** **1** : numbering **2** : numbers *pl*, numerals *pl* ⟨numeración romana : Roman numerals⟩
numerador *nm* : numerator
numeral *adj* : numeral
numerar *vt* : to number
numerario, -ria *adj* : long-standing, permanent ⟨profesor numerario : tenured professor⟩
numérico, -ca *adj* : numerical — **numéricamente** *adv*
número *nm* **1** : number ⟨número impar : odd number⟩ ⟨número ordinal : ordinal number⟩ ⟨número arábico : Arabic numeral⟩ ⟨número quebrado : fraction⟩ **2** : issue (of a publication) **3 sin ~** : countless
numeroso, -sa *adj* : numerous
numismática *nf* : numismatics
nunca *adv* **1** : never, ever ⟨nunca es tarde : it's never too late⟩ ⟨no trabaja casi nunca : he hardly ever works⟩ **2 nunca más** : never again **3 nunca jamás** : never ever
nuncio *nm* : harbinger, herald
nupcial *adj* : nuptial, wedding
nupcias *nfpl* : nuptials *pl*, wedding

nutria *nf* **1** : otter **2** : nutria
nutrición *nf, pl* **-ciones** : nutrition, nourishment
nutrido, -da *adj* **1** : nourished ⟨mal nutrido : undernourished, malnourished⟩ **2** : considerable, abundant ⟨de nutrido : full of, abounding in⟩
nutriente *nm* : nutrient
nutrimento *nm* : nutriment
nutrir *vt* **1** ALIMENTAR : to feed, to nourish **2** : to foster, to provide
nutritivo, -va *adj* : nourishing, nutritious

nylon → **nilón**
ñ *nf* : fifteenth letter of the Spanish alphabet
ñame *nm* : yam
ñandú *nm* : rhea
ñapa *nf* : extra amount ⟨de ñapa : for good measure⟩
ñoñear *vi fam* : to whine
ñoño, -ña *adj fam* : whiny, fussy ⟨no seas tan ñoño : don't be such a wimp⟩
ñoquis *nmpl* : gnocchi *pl*
ñu *nm* : gnu, wildebeest

O

o¹ *nf* : sixteenth letter of the Spanish alphabet
o² *conj* (**u** *before words beginning with o-* *or ho-*) **1** : or ⟨¿vienes con nosotros o te quedas? : are you coming with us or staying?⟩ **2** : either ⟨o vienes con nosotros o te quedas : either you come with us or you stay⟩ **3 o sea** : that is to say, in other words
oasis *nms & pl* : oasis
obcecado, -da *adj* **1** : blinded ⟨obcecado por la ira : blinded by rage⟩ **2** : stubborn, obstinate
obcecar {72} *vt* : to blind (by emotions) — **obcecarse** *vr* : to become stubborn
obedecer {53} *vt* : to obey ⟨obedecer órdenes : to obey orders⟩ ⟨obedece a tus padres : obey your parents⟩ — *vi* **1** : to obey **2** ~ **a** : to respond to **3** ~ **a** : to be due to, to result from
obediencia *nf* : obedience
obediente *adj* : obedient — **obedientemente** *adv*
obelisco *nm* : obelisk
obertura *nf* : overture
obesidad *nf* : obesity
obeso, -sa *adj* : obese
óbice *nm* : obstacle, impediment
obispado *nm* DIÓCESIS : bishopric, diocese
obispo *nm* : bishop
obituario *nm* : obituary
objeción *nf, pl* **-ciones** : objection ⟨ponerle objeciones a algo : to object to something⟩
objetar *v* : to object ⟨no tengo nada que objetar : I have no objections⟩
objetividad *nf* : objectivity
objetivo¹, -va *adj* : objective — **objetivamente** *adv*
objetivo² *nm* **1** META : objective, goal, target **2** : lens
objeto *nm* **1** COSA : object, thing **2** OBJETIVO : objective, purpose ⟨con objeto de : in order to, with the aim of⟩ **3 objeto volador no identificado** : unidentified flying object
objetor, -tora *n* : objector ⟨objetor de conciencia : conscientious objector⟩
oblea *nf* **1** : wafer **2 hecho una oblea** *fam* : skinny as a rail

oblicuo, -cua *adj* : oblique — **oblicuamente** *adv*
obligación *nf, pl* **-ciones** **1** DEBER : obligation, duty **2** : bond, debenture
obligado, -da *adj* **1** : obliged **2** : obligatory, compulsory **3** : customary
obligar {52} *vt* : to force, to require, to oblige — **obligarse** *vr* : to commit oneself, to undertake (to do something)
obligatorio, -ria *adj* : mandatory, required, compulsory
obliterar *vt* : to obliterate, to destroy — **obliteración** *nf*
oblongo, -ga *adj* : oblong
obnubilación *nf, pl* **-ciones** : bewilderment, confusion
obnubilar *vt* : to daze, to bewilder
oboe¹ *nm* : oboe
oboe² *nmf* : oboist
obra *nf* **1** : work ⟨obra de arte : work of art⟩ ⟨obra de teatro : play⟩ ⟨obra de consulta : reference work⟩ **2** : deed ⟨una buena obra : a good deed⟩ **3** : construction work **4 obra maestra** : masterpiece **5 obras públicas** : public works **6 por obra de** : thanks to, because of
obrar *vt* : to work, to produce ⟨obrar milagros : to work miracles⟩ — *vi* **1** : to act, to behave ⟨obrar con cautela : to act with caution⟩ **2 obrar en poder de** : to be in possession of
obrero¹, -ra *adj* : working ⟨la clase obrera : the working class⟩
obrero², -ra *n* : worker, laborer
obscenidad *nf* : obscenity
obsceno, -na *adj* : obscene
obscurecer, obscuridad, obscuro → **oscurecer, oscuridad, oscuro**
obsequiar *vt* REGALAR : to give, to present ⟨lo obsequiaron con una placa : they presented him with a plaque⟩
obsequio *nm* REGALO : gift, present
obsequiosidad *nf* : attentiveness, deference
obsequioso, -sa *adj* : obliging, attentive
observable *adj* : observable
observación *nf, pl* **-ciones** **1** : observation, watching **2** : remark, comment
observador¹, -dora *adj* : observant

observador[2], **-dora** *n* : observer, watcher

observancia *nf* : observance

observante *adj* : observant ⟨los judíos observantes : observant Jews⟩

observar *vt* **1** : to observe, to watch ⟨estábamos observando a los niños : we were watching the children⟩ **2** NOTAR : to notice **3** ACATAR : to obey, to abide by **4** COMENTAR : to remark, to comment

observatorio *nm* : observatory

obsesión *nf, pl* **-siones** : obsession

obsesionar *vt* : to obsess, to preoccupy excessively — **obsesionarse** *vr*

obsesivo, -va *adj* : obsessive

obseso, -sa *adj* : obsessed

obsolescencia *nf* DESUSO : obsolescence — **obsolescente** *adj*

obsoleto, -ta *adj* DESUSADO : obsolete

obstaculizar {21} *vt* IMPEDIR : to obstruct, to hinder

obstáculo *nm* IMPEDIMENTO : obstacle

obstante[1] *conj* **no obstante** : nevertheless, however

obstante[2] *prep* **no obstante** : in spite of, despite ⟨mantuvo su inocencia no obstante la evidencia : he maintained his innocence in spite of the evidence⟩

obstar *v impers* ~ **a** *or* ~ **para** : to hinder, to prevent ⟨eso no obsta para que me vaya : that doesn't prevent me from leaving⟩

obstetra *nmf* TOCÓLOGO : obstetrician

obstetricia *nf* : obstetrics

obstétrico, -ca *adj* : obstetric, obstetrical

obstinación *nf, pl* **-ciones** **1** TERQUEDAD : obstinacy, stubbornness **2** : perseverance, tenacity

obstinado, -da *adj* **1** TERCO : obstinate, stubborn **2** : persistent — **obstinadamente** *adv*

obstinarse *vr* EMPECINARSE : to be obstinate, to be stubborn

obstrucción *nf, pl* **-ciones** : obstruction, blockage

obstruccionismo *nm* : obstructionism, filibustering

obstruccionista *adj* : obstructionist, filibustering

obstructor, -tora *adj* : obstructive

obstruir {41} *vt* BLOQUEAR : to obstruct, to block, to clog — **obstruirse** *vr*

obtención *nf* : obtaining, procurement

obtener {80} *vt* : to obtain, to secure, to get — **obtenible** *adj*

obturador *nm* : shutter (of a camera)

obtuso, -sa *adj* : obtuse

obtuvo, etc. → **obtener**

obús *nm, pl* **obuses** **1** : mortar (weapon) **2** : mortar shell

obviar *vt* : to get around (a difficulty), to avoid

obvio, -via *adj* : obvious — **obviamente** *adv*

oca *nf* : goose

ocasión *nf, pl* **-siones** **1** : occasion, time **2** : opportunity, chance **3** : bargain **4 de** ~ : secondhand **5 aviso de ocasión** *Mex* : classified ad

ocasional *adj* **1** : occasional **2** : chance, fortuitous

ocasionalmente *adv* **1** : occasionally **2** : by chance

ocasionar *vt* CAUSAR : to cause, to occasion

ocaso *nm* **1** ANOCHECER : sunset, sundown **2** DECADENCIA : decline, fall

occidental *adj* : western, occidental

occidente *nm* **1** OESTE, PONIENTE : west **2 el Occidente** : the West

oceánico, -ca *adj* : oceanic

océano *nm* : ocean

oceanografía *nf* : oceanography

oceanográfico, -ca *adj* : oceanographic

ocelote *nm* : ocelot

ochenta *adj & nm* : eighty

ochentavo[1], **-va** *adj* : eightieth

ochentavo[2] *nm* : eightieth (fraction)

ocho *adj & nm* : eight

ochocientos[1], **-tas** *adj* : eight hundred

ochocientos[2] *ms & pl* : eight hundred

ocio *nm* **1** : free time, leisure **2** : idleness

ociosidad *nf* : idleness, inactivity

ocioso, -sa *adj* **1** INACTIVO : idle, inactive **2** INÚTIL : pointless, useless

ocre *nm* : ocher

octágono *nm* : octagon — **octagonal** *adj*

octava *nf* : octave

octavo, -va *adj* : eighth — **octavo, -va** *n*

octeto *nm* **1** : octet **2** : byte

octogésimo[1], **-ma** *adj* : eightieth, eighty-

octogésimo[2], **-ma** *n* : eightieth, eighty- (in a series)

octubre *nm* : October

ocular *adj* **1** : ocular, eye ⟨músculos oculares : eye muscles⟩ **2 testigo ocular** : eyewitness

oculista *nmf* : oculist, ophthalmologist

ocultación *nf, pl* **-ciones** : concealment

ocultar *vt* ESCONDER : to conceal, to hide — **ocultarse** *vr*

oculto, -ta *adj* **1** ESCONDIDO : hidden, concealed **2** : occult

ocupación *nf, pl* **-ciones** **1** : occupation, activity **2** : occupancy **3** EMPLEO : employment, job

ocupacional *adj* : occupational, job-related

ocupado, -da *adj* **1** : busy **2** : taken ⟨este asiento está ocupado : this seat is taken⟩ **3** : occupied ⟨territorios ocupados : occupied territories⟩ **4 señal de ocupado** : busy signal

ocupante *nmf* : occupant

ocupar *vt* **1** : to occupy, to take possession of **2** : to hold (a position) **3** : to employ, to keep busy **4** : to fill (space, time) **5** : to inhabit (a dwelling) **6** : to bother, to concern — **ocuparse** *vr* ~ **de 1** : to be concerned with **2** : to take care of

ocurrencia *nf* **1** : occurrence, event **2** : witticism **3** : bright idea

ocurrente *adj* **1** : witty **2** : clever, sharp

ocurrir *vi* : to occur, to happen — **ocurrirse** *vr* ~ **a** : to occur to, to strike ⟨se me ocurrió una mejor idea : a better idea occurred to me⟩

oda *nf* : ode

odiar *vt* ABOMINAR, ABORRECER : to hate

odio *nm* : hate, hatred

odioso, -sa *adj* ABOMINABLE, ABORRECIBLE : hateful, detestable

odisea *nf* : odyssey

odontología *nf* : dentistry, dental surgery

odontólogo, -ga *n* : dentist, dental surgeon

oeste¹ *adj* **1** : west, western ⟨la región oeste : the western region⟩ **2** : westerly

oeste² *nm* **1** : west, West **2** : west wind

ofender *vt* AGRAVIAR : to offend, to insult — *vi* : to offend, to be insulting — **ofenderse** *vr* : to take offense

ofensa *nf* : offense, insult

ofensiva *nf* : offensive ⟨pasar a la ofensiva : to go on the offensive⟩

ofensivo, -va *adj* : offensive, insulting

ofensor, -sora *n* : offender

oferente *nmf* **1** : supplier **2** FUENTE : source ⟨un oferente no identificado : an unidentified source⟩

oferta *nf* **1** : offer **2** : sale, bargain ⟨las camisas están en oferta : the shirts are on sale⟩ **3 oferta y demanda** : supply and demand

ofertar *vt* OFRECER : to offer

oficial¹ *adj* : official — **oficialmente** *adv*

oficial² *nmf* **1** : officer, police officer, commissioned officer (in the military) **2** : skilled worker

oficializar {21} *vt* : to make official

oficiante *nmf* : celebrant

oficiar *vt* **1** : to inform officially **2** : to officiate at, to celebrate (Mass) — *vi* ~ **de** : to act as

oficina *nf* : office

oficinista *nmf* : office worker

oficio *nm* **1** : trade, profession ⟨es electricista de oficio : he's an electrician by trade⟩ **2** : function, role **3** : official communication **4** : experience ⟨tener oficio : to be experienced⟩ **5** : religious ceremony

oficioso, -sa *adj* **1** EXTRAOFICIAL : unofficial **2** : officious — **oficiosamente** *adv*

ofrecer {53} *vt* **1** : to offer **2** : to provide, to give **3** : to present (an appearance, etc.) — **ofrecerse** *vr* **1** : to offer oneself, to volunteer **2** : to open up, to present itself

ofrecimiento *nm* : offer, offering

ofrenda *nf* : offering

oftalmología *nf* : ophthalmology

oftalmólogo, -ga *n* : ophthalmologist

ofuscación *nf*, *pl* **-ciones** : blindness, confusion

ofuscar {72} *vt* **1** : to blind, to dazzle **2** CONFUNDIR : to bewilder, to confuse — **ofuscarse** *vr* ~ **con** : to be blinded by

ogro *nm* : ogre

ohm *nm*, *pl* **ohms** : ohm

ohmio → **ohm**

oídas *nfpl* **de** ~ : by hearsay

oído *nm* **1** : ear ⟨oído interno : inner ear⟩ **2** : hearing ⟨duro de oído : hard of hearing⟩ **3 tocar de oído** : to play by ear

oiga, etc. → **oír**

oír {50} *vi* : to hear — *vt* **1** : to hear **2** ESCUCHAR : to listen to **3** : to pay attention to, to heed **4** ¡**oye**! *or* ¡**oiga**! : listen!, excuse me!, look here!

ojal *nm* : buttonhole

ojalá *interj* **1** : I hope so!, if only!, God willing! **2** : I hope, I wish, hopefully ⟨¡ojalá que le vaya bien! : I hope things go well for her!⟩ ⟨¡ojalá no llueva! : hopefully it won't rain!⟩

ojeada *nf* : glimpse, glance ⟨echar una ojeada : to have a quick look⟩

ojear *vt* : to eye, to have a look at

ojete *nm* : eyelet

ojiva *nf* : warhead

ojo *nm* **1** : eye **2** : judgment, sharpness ⟨tener buen ojo para : to be a good judge of, to have a good eye for⟩ **3** : hole (in cheese), eye (in a needle), center (of a storm) **4** : span (of a bridge) **5 a ojos vistas** : openly, publicly **6 andar con ojo** : to be careful **7 ojo de agua** *Mex* : spring, source **8** ¡**ojo**! : look out!, pay attention!

ola *nf* **1** : wave **2 ola de calor** : heat wave

oleada *nf* : swell, wave ⟨una oleada de protestas : a wave of protests⟩

oleaje *nm* : waves *pl*, surf

óleo *nm* **1** : oil **2** : oil painting

oleoducto *nm* : oil pipeline

oleoso, -sa *adj* : oily

oler {51} *vt* **1** : to smell **2** INQUIRIR : to pry into, to investigate **3** AVERIGUAR : to smell out, to uncover — *vi* **1** : to smell ⟨huele mal : it smells bad⟩ **2** ~ **a** : to smell like, to smell of ⟨huele a pino : it smells like pine⟩ — **olerse** *vr* : to have a hunch, to suspect

olfatear *vt* **1** : to sniff **2** : to sense, to sniff out

olfativo, -va *adj* : olfactory

olfato *nm* **1** : sense of smell **2** : nose, instinct

oligarquía *nf* : oligarchy

olimpiada *or* **olimpíada** *nf* **1** : Olympiad **2** *or* **olympiadas** *nfpl* : Olympics *pl*

olímpico, -ca *adj* : Olympic

olisquear *vt* : to sniff at

oliva *nf* ACEITUNA : olive ⟨aceite de oliva : olive oil⟩

olivo *nm* : olive tree

olla *nf* **1** : pot ⟨olla de presión : pressure cooker⟩ **2 olla podrida** : Spanish stew

olmeca *adj & nmf* : Olmec
olmo *nm* : elm
olor *nm* : smell, odor
oloroso, -sa *adj* : scented, fragrant
olote *nm Mex* : cob, corncob
olvidadizo, -za *adj* : forgetful, absent-minded
olvidar *vt* **1** : to forget, to forget about ⟨olvida lo que pasó : forget about what happened⟩ **2** : to leave behind ⟨olvidé mi chequera en la casa : I left my checkbook at home⟩ — **olvidarse** *vr* : to forget ⟨se me olvidó mi cuaderno : I forgot my notebook⟩ ⟨se le olvidó llamarme : he forgot to call me⟩
olvido *nm* **1** : forgetfulness **2** : oblivion **3** DESCUIDO : oversight
omaní *adj & nmf* : Omani
ombligo *nm* : navel, belly button
ombudsman *nmfs & pl* : ombudsman
omelette *nmf* : omelet
ominoso, -sa *adj* : ominous — **ominosamente** *adv*
omisión *nf, pl* **-siones** : omission, neglect
omiso, -sa *adj* **1** NEGLIGENTE : neglectful **2 hacer caso omiso de** : to ignore
omitir *vt* **1** : to omit, to leave out **2** : to fail to ⟨omitió dar su nombre : he failed to give his name⟩
ómnibus *n, pl* **-bus** *or* **-buses** : bus, coach
omnipotencia *nf* : omnipotence
omnipotente *adj* TODOPODEROSO : omnipotent, almighty
omnipresencia *nf* : ubiquity, omnipresence
omnipresente *adj* : ubiquitous, omnipresent
omnisciente *adj* : omniscient — **omnisciencia** *nf*
omnívoro, -ra *adj* : omnivorous
omóplato *or* **omoplato** *nm* : shoulder blade
once *adj & nm* : eleven
onceavo[1], -va *adj* : eleventh
onceavo[2] *nm* : eleventh (fraction)
onda *nf* **1** : wave, ripple, undulation ⟨onda sonora : sound wave⟩ **2** : wave (in hair) **3** : scallop (on clothing) **4** *fam* : wavelength, understanding ⟨agarrar la onda : to get the point⟩ ⟨en la onda : on the ball, with it⟩ **5 ¿qué onda?** *fam* : what's happening?, what's up?
ondear *vi* : to ripple, to undulate, to flutter
ondulación *nf, pl* **-ciones** : undulation
ondulado, -da *adj* **1** : wavy ⟨pelo ondulado : wavy hair⟩ **2** : undulating
ondulante *adj* : undulating
ondular *vt* : to wave (hair) — *vi* : to undulate, to ripple
oneroso, -sa *adj* GRAVOSO : onerous, burdensome
ónix *nm* : onyx
onza *nf* : ounce

opacar {72} *vt* **1** : to make opaque or dull **2** : to outshine, to overshadow
opacidad *nf* **1** : opacity **2** : dullness
opaco, -ca *adj* **1** : opaque **2** : dull
ópalo *nm* : opal
opción *nf, pl* **opciones 1** ALTERNATIVA : option, choice **2** : right, chance ⟨tener opción a : to be eligible for⟩
opcional *adj* : optional — **opcionalmente** *adv*
ópera *nf* : opera
operación *nf, pl* **-ciones 1** : operation **2** : transaction, deal
operacional *adj* : operational
operador, -dora *n* **1** : operator **2** : cameraman, projectionist
operante *adj* : operating, working
operar *vt* **1** : to produce, to bring about **2** INTERVENIR : to operate on **3** *Mex* : to operate, to run (a machine) — *vi* **1** : to operate, to function **2** : to deal, to do business — **operarse** *vr* **1** : to come about, to take place **2** : to have an operation
operario, -ria *n* : laborer, worker
operático, -ca → **operístico**
operativo[1], -va *adj* **1** : operating ⟨capacidad operativa : operating capacity⟩ **2** : operative
operativo[2] *nm* : operation ⟨operativo militar : military operation⟩
opereta *nf* : operetta
operístico, -ca *adj* : operatic
opiato *nm* : opiate
opinable *adj* : arguable
opinar *vi* **1** : to think, to have an opinion **2** : to express an opinion **3 opinar bien de** : to think highly of — *vt* : to think ⟨opinamos lo mismo : we're of the same opinion, we're in agreement⟩
opinión *nf, pl* **-niones** : opinion, belief
opio *nm* : opium
oponente *nmf* : opponent
oponer {60} *vt* **1** CONTRAPONER : to oppose, to place against **2 oponer resistencia** : to resist, to put up a fight — **oponerse** *vr* ~ **a** : to object to, to be against
oporto *nm* : port (wine)
oportunamente *adv* **1** : at the right time, opportunely **2** : appropriately
oportunidad *nf* : opportunity, chance
oportunismo *nm* : opportunism
oportunista[1] *adj* : opportunistic
oportunista[2] *nmf* : opportunist
oportuno, -na *adj* **1** : opportune, timely **2** : suitable, appropriate
oposición *nf, pl* **-ciones** : opposition
opositor, -tora *n* ADVERSARIO : opponent
oposum *nm* ZARIGÜEYA : opossum
opresión *nf, pl* **-siones 1** : oppression **2 opresión de pecho** : tightness in the chest
opresivo, -va *adj* : oppressive
opresor[1], -sora *adj* : oppressive
opresor[2], -sora *n* : oppressor

oprimir *vt* **1** : to oppress **2** : to press, to squeeze ⟨oprima el botón : push the button⟩

oprobio *nm* : opprobrium, shame

optar *vi* **1** ~ **por** : to opt for, to choose **2** ~ **a** : to aspire to, to apply for ⟨dos candidatos optan a la presidencia : two candidates are running for president⟩

optativo, -va *adj* FACULTATIVO : optional

óptica *nf* **1** : optics **2** : optician's shop **3** : viewpoint

óptico[1], **-ca** *adj* : optical, optic

óptico[2], **-ca** *n* : optician

optimismo *nm* : optimism

optimista[1] *adj* : optimistic

optimista[2] *nmf* : optimist

óptimo, -ma *adj* : optimum, optimal

optometría *nf* : optometry — **optometrista** *nmf*

opuesto[1] *pp* → **oponer**

opuesto[2] *adj* **1** : opposite, contrary **2** : opposed

opulencia *nf* : opulence — **opulento, -ta** *adj*

opus *nm* : opus

opuso, etc. → **oponer**

ora *conj* : now ⟨los matices eran variados, ora verdes, ora ocres : the hues were varied, now green, now ocher⟩

oración *nf, pl* **-ciones 1** DISCURSO : oration, speech **2** PLEGARIA : prayer **3** FRASE : sentence, clause

oráculo *nm* : oracle

orador, -dora *n* : speaker, orator

oral *adj* : oral — **oralmente** *adv*

órale *interj Mex fam* **1** : sure!, OK! ⟨¿los dos por cinco pesos? ¡órale! : both for five pesos? you've got a deal!⟩ **2** : come on! ⟨¡órale, vámonos! : come on, let's go!⟩

orangután *nm, pl* **-tanes** : orangutan

orar *vi* REZAR : to pray

oratoria *nf* : oratory

oratorio *nm* **1** CAPILLA : oratory, chapel **2** : oratorio

orbe *nm* **1** : orb, sphere **2** GLOBO : globe, world

órbita *nf* **1** : orbit **2** : eye socket **3** ÁMBITO : sphere, field

orbitador *nm* : space shuttle, orbiter

orbital *adj* : orbital

orbitar *v* : to orbit

orden[1] *nm, pl* **órdenes 1** : order ⟨todo está en orden : everything's in order⟩ ⟨por orden cronológico : in chronological order⟩ **2 orden del día** : agenda (at a meeting) **3 orden público** : law and order

orden[2] *nf, pl* **órdenes 1** : order ⟨una orden religiosa : a religious order⟩ ⟨una orden de tacos : an order of tacos⟩ **2 orden de compra** : purchase order **3 estar a la orden del día** : to be the order of the day, to be prevalent

ordenación *nf, pl* **-ciones 1** : ordination **2** : ordering, organizing

ordenadamente *adv* : in an orderly fashion, neatly

ordenado, -da *adj* : orderly, neat

ordenador *nm Spain* : computer

ordenamiento *nm* **1** : ordering, organizing **2** : code (of laws)

ordenanza[1] *nf* REGLAMENTO : ordinance, regulation

ordenanza[2] *nm* : orderly (in the armed forces)

ordenar *vt* **1** MANDAR : to order, to command **2** ARREGLAR : to put in order, to arrange **3** : to ordain (a priest)

ordeñar *vt* : to milk

ordeño *nm* : milking

ordinal *nm* : ordinal (number)

ordinariamente *adv* **1** : usually **2** : coarsely

ordinariez *nf* : coarseness, vulgarity

ordinario, -ria *adj* **1** : ordinary **2** : coarse, common, vulgar **3 de** ~ : usually

orear *vt* : to air

orégano *nm* : oregano

oreja *nf* : ear

orfanato *nm* : orphanage

orfanatorio *nm Mex* : orphanage

orfebre *nmf* : goldsmith, silversmith

orfebrería *nf* : articles of gold or silver

orfelinato *nm* : orphanage

orgánico, -ca *adj* : organic — **orgánicamente** *adv*

organigrama *nm* : organization chart, flowchart

organismo *nm* **1** : organism **2** : agency, organization

organista *nmf* : organist

organización *nf, pl* **-ciones** : organization

organizador[1], **-dora** *adj* : organizing

organizador[2], **-dora** *n* : organizer

organizar {21} *vt* : to organize, to arrange — **organizarse** *vr* : to get organized

organizativo, -va *adj* : organizational

órgano *nm* : organ

orgasmo *nm* : orgasm

orgía *nf* : orgy

orgullo *nm* : pride

orgulloso, -sa *adj* : proud — **orgullosamente** *adv*

orientación *nf, pl* **-ciones 1** : orientation **2** DIRECCIÓN : direction, course **3** GUÍA : guidance, direction

oriental[1] *adj* **1** : eastern **2** : oriental **3** *Arg, Uru* : Uruguayan

oriental[2] *nmf* **1** : Easterner **2** : Oriental **3** *Arg, Uru* : Uruguayan

orientar *vt* **1** : to orient, to position **2** : to guide, to direct — **orientarse** *vr* **1** : to orient oneself, to get one's bearings **2** ~ **hacia** : to turn towards, to lean towards

oriente *nm* **1** : east, East **2 el Oriente** : the Orient

orífice *nmf* : goldsmith

orificio *nm* : orifice, opening

origen *nm, pl* **orígenes 1** : origin **2** : lineage, birth **3 dar origen a** : to give rise to **4 en su origen** : originally

original *adj & nm* : original — **originalmente** *adv*
originalidad *nf* : originality
originar *vt* : to originate, to give rise to — **originarse** *vr* : to originate, to begin
originario, -ria *adj* ~ **de** : native of
originariamente *adv* : originally
orilla *nf* **1** BORDE : border, edge **2** : bank (of a river) **3** : shore
orillar *vt* **1** : to skirt, to go around **2** : to trim, to edge (cloth) **3** : to settle, to wind up **4** *Mex* : to pull over (a vehicle)
orín *nm* **1** HERRUMBRE : rust **2 orines** *nmpl* : urine
orina *nf* : urine
orinación *nf* : urination
orinal *nm* : urinal (vessel)
orinar *vi* : to urinate — **orinarse** *vr* : to wet oneself
oriol *nm* OROPÉNDOLA : oriole
oriundo, -da *adj* ~ **de** : native of
orla *nf* : border, edging
orlar *vt* : to edge, to trim
ornamentación *nf, pl* **-ciones** : ornamentation
ornamental *adj* : ornamental
ornamentar *vt* ADORNAR : to ornament, to adorn
ornamento *nm* : ornament, adornment
ornar *vt* : to adorn, to decorate
ornitología *nf* : ornithology
ornitólogo, -ga *n* : ornithologist
ornitorrinco *nm* : platypus
oro *nm* : gold
orondo, -da *adj* **1** : rounded, potbellied (of a container) **2** *fam* : smug, self-satisfied
oropel *nm* : glitz, glitter, tinsel
oropéndola *nf* : oriole
orquesta *nf* : orchestra — **orquestal** *adj*
orquestar *vt* : to orchestrate — **orquestación** *nf*
orquídea *nf* : orchid
ortiga *nf* : nettle
ortodoncia *nf* : orthodontics
ortodoncista *nmf* : orthodontist
ortodoxia *nf* : orthodoxy
ortodoxo, -xa *adj* : orthodox
ortografía *nf* : orthography, spelling
ortográfico, -ca *adj* : orthographic, spelling
ortopedia *nf* : orthopedics
ortopédico, -ca *adj* : orthopedic
ortopedista *nmf* : orthopedist
oruga *nf* **1** : caterpillar **2** : track (of a tank, etc.)
orzuelo *nm* : sty, stye (in the eye)
os *pron pl* (*objective form of* **vosotros**) *Spain* **1** : you, to you **2** : yourselves, to yourselves **3** : each other, to each other
osa *nf* → **oso**
osadía *nf* **1** VALOR : boldness, daring **2** AUDACIA : audacity, nerve
osado, -da *adj* **1** : bold, daring **2** : audacious, impudent — **osadamente** *adv*

osamenta *nf* : skeletal remains *pl*, bones *pl*
osar *vi* : to dare
oscilación *nf, pl* **-ciones 1** : oscillation **2** : fluctuation **3** : vacillation, wavering
oscilar *vi* **1** BALANCEARSE : to swing, to sway, to oscillate **2** FLUCTUAR : to fluctuate **3** : to vacillate, to waver
oscuramente *adv* : obscurely
oscurecer {53} *vt* **1** : to darken **2** : to obscure, to confuse, to cloud **3 al oscurecer** : at dusk, at nightfall — *v impers* : to grow dark, to get dark — **oscurecerse** *vr* : to darken, to dim
oscuridad *nf* **1** : darkness **2** : obscurity
oscuro, -ra *adj* **1** : dark **2** : obscure **3 a oscuras** : in the dark, in darkness
óseo, ósea *adj* : skeletal, bony
ósmosis *or* **osmosis** *nf* : osmosis
oso, osa *n* **1** : bear **2 Osa Mayor** : Big Dipper **3 Osa Menor** : Little Dipper **4 oso blanco** : polar bear **5 oso hormiguero** : anteater **6 oso de peluche** : teddy bear
ostensible *adj* : ostensible, apparent — **ostensiblemente** *adv*
ostentación *nf, pl* **-ciones** : ostentation, display
ostentar *vt* **1** : to display, to flaunt **2** POSEER : to have, to hold ⟨ostenta el récord mundial : he holds the world record⟩
ostentoso, -sa *adj* : ostentatious, showy — **ostentosamente** *adv*
osteópata *nmf* : osteopath
osteopatía *n* : osteopathy
osteoporosis *nf* : osteoporosis
ostión *nm, pl* **ostiones 1** *Mex* : oyster **2** *Chile* : scallop
ostra *nf* : oyster
ostracismo *nm* : ostracism
otear *vt* : to scan, to survey, to look over
otero *nm* : knoll, hillock
otomana *nf* : ottoman (mueble)
otomano, -na *adj & n* : Ottoman
otoñal *adj* : autumn, autumnal
otoño *nm* : autumn, fall
otorgamiento *nm* : granting, awarding
otorgar {52} *vt* **1** : to grant, to award **2** : to draw up, to frame (a legal document)
otro¹, otra *adj* **1** : other **2** : another ⟨en otro juego, ellos ganaron : in another game, they won⟩ **3 otra vez** : again **4 de otra manera** : otherwise **5 otra parte** : elsewhere **6 en otro tiempo** : once, formerly
otro², otra *pron* **1** : another one ⟨dame otro : give me another⟩ **2** : other one ⟨el uno o el otro : one or the other⟩ **3 los otros, las otras** : the others, the rest ⟨me dio una y se quedó con las otras : he gave me one and kept the rest⟩
ovación *nf, pl* **-ciones** : ovation
ovacionar *vt* : to cheer, to applaud

oval → ovalado
ovalado, -da *adj* : oval
óvalo *nm* : oval
ovárico, -ca *adj* : ovarian
ovario *nm* : ovary
oveja *nf* 1 : sheep, ewe 2 oveja negra : black sheep
overol *nm* : overalls *pl*
ovillar *vt* : to roll into a ball
ovillo *nm* 1 : ball (of yarn) 2 : tangle
ovni *or* OVNI *nm* (objeto volador no identificado) : UFO
ovoide *adj* : ovoid, ovoidal
ovulación *nf, pl* -ciones : ovulation
ovular *vi* : to ovulate
óvulo *nm* : ovum

oxidación *nf, pl* -ciones 1 : oxidation 2 : rusting
oxidado, -da *adj* : rusty
oxidar *vt* 1 : to cause to rust 2 : to oxidize — oxidarse *vr* : to rust, to become rusty
óxido *nm* 1 HERRUMBRE, ORÍN : rust 2 : oxide
oxigenar *vt* 1 : to oxygenate 2 : to bleach (hair)
oxígeno *nm* : oxygen
oxiuro *nm* : pinworm
oye, etc. → oír
oyente *nmf* 1 : listener 2 : auditor, auditing student
ozono *nm* : ozone

P

p *nf* : seventeenth letter of the Spanish alphabet
pabellón *nm, pl* -llones 1 : pavilion 2 : summerhouse, lodge 3 : flag (of a vessel)
pabilo *nm* MECHA : wick
paca *nf* FARDO : bale
pacana *nf* : pecan
pacer {48} *v* : to graze, to pasture
paces → paz
pachanga *nf fam* : party, bash
paciencia *nf* : patience
paciente *adj & nmf* : patient — pacientemente *adv*
pacificación *nf, pl* -ciones : pacification
pacíficamente *adv* : peacefully, peaceably
pacificar {72} *vt* : to pacify, to calm — pacificarse *vr* : to calm down, to abate
pacífico, -ca *adj* : peaceful, pacific
pacifismo *nm* : pacifism
pacifista *adj & nmf* : pacifist
pacotilla *nf de* ~ : shoddy, trashy
pactar *vt* : to agree on — *vi* : to come to an agreement
pacto *nm* CONVENIO : pact, agreement
padecer {53} *vt* : to suffer, to endure — *vi* ADOLECER ~ de : to suffer from
padecimiento *nm* 1 : suffering 2 : ailment, condition
padrastro *nm* 1 : stepfather 2 : hangnail
padre[1] *adj Mex fam* : fantastic, great
padre[2] *nm* 1 : father 2 padres *nmpl* : parents
padrenuestro *nm* : Lord's Prayer, paternoster
padrino *nm* 1 : godfather 2 : best man 3 : sponsor, patron
padrón *nm, pl* padrones : register, roll ⟨padrón municipal : city register⟩
paella *nf* : paella
paga *nf* 1 : payment 2 : pay, wages *pl*
pagadero, -ra *adj* : payable
pagado, -da *adj* 1 : paid 2 pagado de sí mismo : self-satisfied, smug
pagador, -dora *n* : payer

paganismo *nm* : paganism
pagano, -na *adj & n* : pagan
pagar {52} *vt* : to pay, to pay for, to repay — *vi* : to pay
pagaré *nm* VALE : promissory note, IOU
página *nf* : page
pago *nm* 1 : payment 2 en pago de : in return for
pagoda *nf* : pagoda
pague, etc. → pagar
país *nm* 1 NACIÓN : country, nation 2 REGIÓN : region, territory
paisaje *nm* : scenery, landscape
paisano, -na *n* COMPATRIOTA : compatriot, fellow countryman
paja *nf* 1 : straw 2 *fam* : trash, tripe
pajar *nm* : hayloft, haystack
pajarera *nf* : aviary
pájaro *nm* : bird ⟨pájaro cantor : songbird⟩ ⟨pájaro bobo : penguin⟩ ⟨pájaro carpintero : woodpecker⟩
pajita *nf* : (drinking) straw
pajote *nm* : straw, mulch
pala *nf* 1 : shovel, spade 2 : blade (of an oar or a rotor) 3 : paddle, racket
palabra *nf* 1 VOCABLO : word 2 PROMESA : word, promise ⟨un hombre de palabra : a man of his word⟩ 3 HABLA : speech 4 : right to speak ⟨tener la palabra : to have the floor⟩
palabrería *nf* : empty talk
palabrota *nf* : swearword
palacio *nm* 1 : palace, mansion 2 palacio de justicia : courthouse
paladar *nm* 1 : palate 2 GUSTO : taste
paladear *vt* SABOREAR : to savor
paladín *nm, pl* -dines : champion, defender
palanca *nf* 1 : lever, crowbar 2 *fam* : leverage, influence 3 palanca de cambio *or* palanca de velocidad : gearshift
palangana *nf* : washbowl
palanqueta *nf* : jimmy, small crowbar
palco *nm* : box (in a theater or stadium)
palear *vt* 1 : to shovel 2 : to paddle
palenque *nm* 1 ESTACADA : stockade, palisade 2 : arena, ring

paleontología *nf* : paleontology
paleontólogo, -ga *n* : paleontologist
palestino, -na *adj & n* : Palestinian
palestra *nf* : arena ⟨salir a la palestra : to join the fray⟩
paleta *nf* **1** : palette **2** : trowel **3** : spatula **4** : blade, vane **5** : paddle **6** *CA, Mex* : lollipop, Popsicle
paletilla *nf* : shoulder blade
paliar *vt* MITIGAR : to alleviate, to palliate
paliativo¹, -va *adj* : palliative
paliativo² *nm* : palliative
palidecer {53} *vi* : to turn pale
palidez *nf, pl* **-deces** : paleness, pallor
pálido, -da *adj* : pale
palillo *nm* **1** MONDADIENTES : toothpick **2 palillos** *nmpl* : chopsticks **3 palillo de tambor** : drumstick
paliza *nf* : beating, pummeling ⟨darle una paliza a : to beat, to thrash⟩
palma *nf* **1** : palm (of the hand) **2** : palm (tree or leaf) **3 batir palmas** : to clap, to applaud **4 llevarse la palma** *fam* : to take the cake
palmada *nf* **1** : pat **2** : slap **3** : clap
palmarés *nm* : record (of achievements)
palmario, -ria *adj* MANIFIESTO : clear, manifest
palmeado, -da *adj* : webbed
palmear *vt* : to slap on the back — *vi* : to clap, to applaud
palmera *nf* : palm tree
palmo *nm* **1** : span, small amount **2 palmo a palmo** : bit by bit, inch by inch **3 dejar con un palmo de narices** : to disappoint
palmotear *vi* : to applaud
palmoteo *nm* : clapping, applause
palo *nm* **1** : stick, pole, post **2** : shaft, handle ⟨palo de escoba : broomstick⟩ **3** : mast, spar **4** : wood **5** : blow (with a stick) **6** : suit (of cards)
paloma *nf* **1** : pigeon, dove **2 paloma mensajera** : carrier pigeon
palomilla *nf* : moth
palomitas *nfpl* : popcorn
palpable *adj* : palpable, tangible
palpar *vt* : to feel, to touch
palpitación *nf, pl* **-ciones** : palpitation
palpitar *vi* : to palpitate, to throb — **palpitante** *adj*
palta *nf* : avocado
paludismo *nm* MALARIA : malaria
palurdo, -da *n* : boor, yokel, bumpkin
pampa *nf* : pampa
pampeano, -na *adj* : pampean, pampas
pampero → **pampeano**
pan *nm* **1** : bread **2** : loaf of bread **3** : cake, bar ⟨pan de jabón : bar of soap⟩ **4 pan dulce** *CA, Mex* : traditional pastry **5 pan tostado** : toast **6 ser pan comido** *fam* : to be a piece of cake, to be a cinch
pana *nf* : corduroy
panacea *nf* : panacea
panadería *nf* : bakery, bread shop
panadero, -ra *n* : baker

panal *nm* : honeycomb
panameño, -ña *adj & n* : Panamanian
pancarta *nf* : placard, sign
pancita *nf Mex* : tripe
páncreas *nms & pl* : pancreas
panda *nmf* : panda
pandeado, -da *adj* : warped
pandearse *vr* **1** : to warp **2** : to bulge, to sag
pandemonio *or* **pandemónium** *nm* : pandemonium
pandereta *nf* : tambourine
pandero *nm* : tambourine
pandilla *nf* **1** : group, clique **2** : gang
panecito *nm* : roll, bread roll
panegírico¹, -ca *adj* : eulogistic, panegyrical
panegírico² *nm* : eulogy, panegyric
panel *nm* : panel — **panelista** *nmf*
panera *nf* : bread box
panfleto *nm* : pamphlet
pánico *nm* : panic
panorama *nm* **1** VISTA : panorama, view **2** : scene, situation ⟨el panorama nacional : the national scene⟩ **3** PERSPECTIVA : outlook
panorámico, -ca *adj* : panoramic
panqueque *nm* : pancake
pantaletas *nfpl* : panties
pantalla *nf* **1** : screen, monitor **2** : lampshade **3** : fan
pantalón *nm, pl* **-lones 1** : pants *pl*, trousers *pl* **2 pantalones vaqueros** : jeans **3 pantalones de mezclilla** *Chile, Mex* : jeans **4 pantalones de montar** : jodhpurs
pantano *nm* **1** : swamp, marsh, bayou **2** : reservoir **3** : obstacle, difficulty
pantanoso, -sa *adj* **1** : marshy, swampy **2** : difficult, thorny
panteón *nm, pl* **-teones 1** CEMENTERIO : cemetery **2** : pantheon, mausoleum
pantera *nf* : panther
pantimedias *nfpl Mex* : panty hose
pantomima *nf* : pantomime
pantorrilla *nf* : calf (of the leg)
pantufla *nf* ZAPATILLA : slipper
panza *nf* BARRIGA : belly, paunch
panzón, -zona *adj, mpl* **panzones** : potbellied, paunchy
pañal *nm* : diaper
pañería *nf* **1** : cloth, material **2** : fabric store
pañito *nm* : doily
paño *nm* **1** : cloth **2** : rag, dust cloth **3 paño de cocina** : dishcloth **4 paño higiénico** : sanitary napkin
pañuelo *nm* **1** : handkerchief **2** : scarf
papa¹ *nm* : pope
papa² *nf* **1** : potato **2 papa dulce** : sweet potato **3 papas fritas** : potato chips, french fries **4 papas a la francesa** *Mex* : french fries
papá *nm fam* **1** : dad, pop **2 papás** *nmpl* : parents, folks
papada *nf* **1** : double chin, jowl **2** : dewlap
papagayo *nm* LORO : parrot

papal *adj* : papal
papalote *nm Mex* : kite
papaya *nf* : papaya
papel *nm* **1** : paper, piece of paper **2** : role, part **3 papel de estaño** : tinfoil **4 papel de empapelar** *or* **papel pintado** : wallpaper **5 papel higiénico** : toilet paper **6 papel de lija** : sandpaper
papeleo *nm* : paperwork, red tape
papelera *nf* : wastebasket
papelería *nf* : stationery store
papelero, -ra *adj* : paper
papeleta *nf* **1** : ballot **2** : ticket, slip
paperas *nfpl* : mumps
papi *nm fam* : daddy, papa
papilla *nf* **1** : pap, mash **2 hacer papilla** : to beat to a pulp
papiro *nm* : papyrus
paquete *nm* BULTO : package, parcel
paquistaní *adj & nmf* : Pakistani
par[1] *adj* : even (in number)
par[2] *nm* **1** : pair, couple **2** : equal, peer ⟨sin par : matchless, peerless⟩ **3** : par (in golf) **4** : rafter **5 de par en par** : wide open
par[3] *nf* **1** : par ⟨por encima de la par : above par⟩ **2 a la par que** : at the same time as, as well as ⟨interesante a la par que instructivo : both interesting and informative⟩
para *prep* **1** : for ⟨para ti : for you⟩ ⟨alta para su edad : tall for her age⟩ ⟨una cita para el lunes : an appointment for Monday⟩ **2** : to, towards ⟨para la derecha : to the right⟩ ⟨van para el río : they're heading towards the river⟩ **3** : to, in order to ⟨lo hace para molestarte : he does it to annoy you⟩ **4** : around, by (a time) ⟨para mañana estarán listos : they'll be ready by tomorrow⟩ **5 para adelante** : forwards **6 para atrás** : backwards **7 para que** : so, so that, in order that ⟨te lo digo para que sepas : I'm telling you so you'll know⟩
parabién *nm, pl* **-bienes** : congratulations *pl*
parábola *nf* **1** : parable **2** : parabola
parabrisas *nms & pl* : windshield
paracaídas *nms & pl* : parachute
paracaidista *nmf* **1** : parachutist **2** : paratrooper
parachoques *nms & pl* : bumper
parada *nf* **1** : stóp ⟨parada de autobús : bus stop⟩ **2** : catch, save, parry (in sports) **3** DESFILE : parade
paradero *nm* : whereabouts
paradigma *nm* : paradigm
paradisíaco, -ca *or* **paradisiaco, -ca** *adj* : heavenly
parado, -da *adj* **1** : motionless, idle, stopped **2** : standing (up) **3** : confused, bewildered **4 bien (mal) parado** : in good (bad) shape ⟨salió bien parado : it turned out well for him⟩
paradoja *nf* : paradox
paradójico, -ca *adj* : paradoxical
parafernalia *nf* : paraphernalia

parafina *nf* : paraffin
parafrasear *vt* : to paraphrase
paráfrasis *nfs & pl* : paraphrase
paraguas *nms & pl* : umbrella
paraguayo, -ya *adj & n* : Paraguayan
paraíso *nm* **1** : paradise, heaven **2 paraíso fiscal** : tax shelter
paraje *nm* : spot, place
paralelismo *nm* : parallelism, similarity
paralelo[1]**, -la** *adj* : parallel
paralelo[2] *nm* : parallel
paralelogramo *nm* : parallelogram
parálisis *nfs & pl* **1** : paralysis **2** : standstill **3 parálisis cerebral** : cerebral palsy
paralítico, -ca *adj & n* : paralytic
paralizar {21} *vt* **1** : to paralyze **2** : to bring to a standstill — **paralizarse** *vr*
parámetro *nm* : parameter
páramo *nm* : barren plateau, moor
parangón *nm, pl* **-gones 1** : comparison **2 sin ~** : incomparable
paraninfo *nm* : auditorium, assembly hall
paranoia *nf* : paranoia
paranoico, -ca *adj & n* : paranoid
parapeto *nm* : parapet, rampart
parapléjico, -ca *adj & n* : paraplegic
parar *vt* **1** DETENER : to stop **2** : to stand, to prop — *vi* **1** CESAR : to stop **2** : to stay, to put up **3 ir a parar** : to end up, to wind up — **pararse** *vr* **1** : to stop **2** ATASCARSE : to stall (out) **3** : to stand up, to get up
pararrayos *nms & pl* : lightning rod
parasitario, -ria *adj* : parasitic
parasitismo *nm* : parasitism
parásito *nm* : parasite
parasol *nm* SOMBRILLA : parasol
parcela *nf* : parcel, tract of land
parcelar *vt* : to parcel (land)
parchar *vt* : to patch, to patch up
parche *nm* : patch
parcial *adj* : partial — **parcialmente** *adv*
parcialidad *nf* : partiality, bias
parco, -ca *adj* **1** : sparing, frugal **2** : moderate, temperate
pardo, -da *adj* : brownish grey
pardusco → **pardo**
parecer[1] {53} *vi* **1** : to seem, to look, to appear to be ⟨parece bien fácil : it looks very easy⟩ ⟨así parece : so it seems⟩ ⟨pareces una princesa : you look like a princess⟩ **2** : to think, to have an opinion ⟨me parece que sí : I think so⟩ **3** : to like, to be in agreement ⟨si te parece : if you like, if it's all right with you⟩ — **parecerse** *vr* **a** : to resemble
parecer[2] *nm* **1** OPINIÓN : opinion **2** ASPECTO : appearance ⟨al parecer : apparently⟩
parecido, -da *adj* **1** : similar, alike **2 bien parecido** : good-looking
parecido[2] *nm* : resemblance, similarity
pared *nf* : wall
pareja *nf* **1** : couple, pair **2** : partner, mate

parejo, -ja *adj* **1** : even, smooth, level **2** : equal, similar

parentela *nf* : relations *pl*, kinfolk

parentesco *nm* : relationship, kinship

paréntesis *nms & pl* **1** : parenthesis **2** : digression

parentético, -ca *adj* : parenthetic, parenthetical

paria *nmf* : pariah, outcast

paridad *nf* : parity, equality

pariente *nmf* : relative, relation

parir *vi* : to give birth — *vt* : to give birth to, to bear

parking *nm* : parking lot

parlamentar *vi* : to talk, to parley

parlamentario¹, -ria *adj* : parliamentary

parlamentario², -ria *n* : member of parliament

parlamento *nm* **1** : parliament **2** : negotiations *pl*, talks *pl*

parlanchín¹, -china *adj, mpl* **-chines** : chatty, talkative

parlanchín², -china *n, mpl* **-chines** : chatterbox

parlante *nm* ALTOPARLANTE : loudspeaker

parlotear *vi fam* : to gab, to chat, to prattle

parloteo *nm fam* : prattle, chatter

paro *nm* **1** HUELGA : strike **2** : stoppage, stopping **3 paro forzoso** : layoff

parodia *nf* : parody

parodiar *vt* : to parody

paroxismo *nm* **1** : fit, paroxysm **2** : peak, height ⟨llevaral paroxismo : to carry to the extreme⟩

parpadear *vi* **1** : to blink **2** : to flicker

pàrpadeo *nm* **1** : blink, blinking **2** : flickering

párpado *nm* : eyelid

parque *nm* **1** : park **2 parque de atracciones** : amusement park

parquear *vt* : to park — **parquearse** *vr*

parqueo *nm* : parking

parquet *or* **parqué** *nm* : parquet

parquímetro *nm* : parking meter

parra *nf* : vine, grapevine

párrafo *nm* : paragraph

parranda *nf fam* : party, spree

parrilla *nf* **1** : broiler, grill **2** : grate

parrillada *nf* BARBACOA : barbecue

párroco *nm* : parish priest

parroquia *nf* **1** : parish **2** : parish church **3** : customers *pl*, clientele

parroquial *adj* : parochial

parroquiano, -na *nm* **1** : parishioner **2** : customer, patron

parsimonia *nf* **1** : calm **2** : parsimony, thrift

parsimonioso, -sa *adj* **1** : calm, unhurried **2** : parsimonious, thrifty

parte¹ *nm* : report, dispatch

parte² *nf* **1** : part, share **2** : part, place ⟨en alguna parte : somewhere⟩ ⟨por todas partes : everywhere⟩ **3** : party (in negotiations, etc.) **4 de parte de** : on behalf of **5 ¿de parte de quién?** : may I ask who's calling? **6 tomar parte** : to take part

partero, -ra *n* : midwife

partición *nf, pl* **-ciones** : division, sharing

participación *nf, pl* **-ciones** **1** : participation **2** : share, interest **3** : announcement, notice

participante *nmf* **1** : participant **2** : competitor, entrant

participar *vi* **1** : to participate, to take part **2 ~ en** : to have a share in — *vt* : to announce, to notify

partícipe *nmf* : participant

participio *nm* : participle

partícula *nf* : particle

particular¹ *adj* **1** : particular, specific **2** : private, personal **3** : special, unique

particular² *nm* **1** : matter, detail **2** : individual

particularidad *nf* : characteristic, peculiarity

particularizar {21} *vt* **1** : to distinguish, to characterize **2** : to specify

partida *nf* **1** : departure **2** : item, entry **3** : certificate ⟨partida de nacimiento : birth certificate⟩ **4** : game, match, hand **5** : party, group

partidario, -ria *n* : follower, supporter

partido *nm* **1** : (political) party **2** : game, match ⟨partido de futbol : soccer game⟩ **3** APOYO : support, following **4** PROVECHO : profit, advantage ⟨sacar partido de : to profit from⟩

partir *vt* **1** : to cut, to split **2** : to break, to crack **3** : to share (out), to divide — *vi* **1** : to leave, to depart **2 ~ de** : to start from **3 a partir de** : as of, from ⟨a partir de hoy : as of today⟩ — **partirse** *vr* **1** : to smash, to split open **2** : to chap

partisano, -na *adj & n* : partisan

partitura *nf* : (musical) score

parto *nm* **1** : childbirth, delivery, labor ⟨estar de parto : to be in labor⟩ **2** : product, creation, brainchild

parvulario *nm* : nursery school

párvulo, -la *n* : toddler, preschooler

pasa *nf* **1** : raisin **2 pasa de Corinto** : currant

pasable *adj* : passable, tolerable — **pasablemente** *adv*

pasada *nf* **1** : passage, passing **2** : pass, wipe, coat (of paint) **3 de ~** : in passing **4 mala pasada** : dirty trick

pasadizo *nm* : passageway, corridor

pasado¹, -da *adj* **1** : past ⟨el año pasado : last year⟩ ⟨pasado mañana : the day after tomorrow⟩ ⟨pasadas las siete : after seven o'clock⟩ **2** : stale, bad, overripe **3** : old-fashioned, out-of-date **4** : overripe, slightly spoiled

pasado² *nm* : past

pasador *nm* **1** : bolt, latch **2** : barrette **3** *Mex* : bobby pin

pasaje *nm* **1** : ticket (for travel) **2** TARIFA : fare **3** : passageway **4** : passengers *pl*

pasajero¹, -ra *adj* : passing, fleeting

pasajero², -ra *n* : passenger

pasamanos *nms & pl* **1** : handrail **2** : bannister

pasante *nmf* : assistant

pasaporte *nm* : passport

pasar *vi* **1** : to pass, to go by, to come by **2** : to come in, to enter ⟨¿se puede pasar? : may we come in?⟩ **3** : to happen ⟨¿qué pasa? : what's happening?, what's going on?⟩ **4** : to manage, to get by **5** : to be over, to end **6** ~ **de** : to exceed, to go beyond **7** ~ **por** : to pretend to be — *vt* **1** : to pass, to give ⟨¿me pasas la sal? : would you pass me the salt?⟩ **2** : to pass (a test) **3** : to go over, to cross **4** : to spend (time) **5** : to tolerate **6** : to go through, to suffer **7** : to show (a movie, etc.) **8** : to overtake, to pass, to surpass **9** : to pass over, to wipe up **10 pasarlo bien** *or* **pasarla bien** : to have a good time **11 pasarlo mal** *or* **pasarla mal** : to have a bad time, to have a hard time **12 pasar por alto** : to overlook, to omit — **pasarse** *vr* **1** : to move, to pass, to go away **2** : to slip one's mind, to forget **3** : to go too far

pasarela *nf* **1** : gangplank **2** : footbridge **3** : runway, catwalk

pasatiempo *nm* : pastime, hobby

Pascua *nf* **1** : Easter **2** : Passover **3** : Christmas **4 Pascuas** *nfpl* : Christmas season

pase *nm* **1** PERMISO : pass, permit **2 pase de abordar** *Mex* : boarding pass

pasear *vi* : to take a walk, to go for a ride — *vt* **1** : to take for a walk **2** : to parade around, to show off — **pasearse** *vr* : to walk around

paseo *nm* **1** : walk, stroll **2** : ride **3** EXCURSIÓN : outing, trip **4** : avenue, walk **5** *or* **paseo marítimo** : boardwalk

pasiflora *nf* : passionflower

pasillo *nm* CORREDOR : hallway, corridor, aisle

pasión *nf, pl* **pasiones** : passion

pasional *adj* : passionate ⟨crimen pasional : crime of passion⟩

pasionaria → **pasiflora**

pasivo¹, -va *adj* : passive — **pasivamente** *adv*

pasivo² *nm* **1** : liability ⟨activos y pasivos : assets and liabilities⟩ **2** : debit side (of an account)

pasmado, -da *adj* : stunned, flabbergasted

pasmar *vt* : to amaze, to stun — **pasmarse** *vr*

pasmo *nm* **1** : shock, astonishment **2** : wonder, marvel

pasmoso, -sa *adj* : incredible, amazing — **pasmosamente** *adv*

paso¹, -sa *adj* : dried ⟨ciruela pasa : prune⟩

paso² *nm* **1** : passage, passing ⟨de paso : in passing, on the way⟩ **2** : way, path ⟨abrirse paso : to make one's way⟩ **3** : crossing ⟨paso de peatones : crosswalk⟩ ⟨paso a desnivel : underpass⟩ ⟨paso elevado : overpass⟩ **4** : step

⟨paso a paso : step by step⟩ **5** : pace, gait ⟨a buen paso : quickly, at a good rate⟩

pasta *nf* **1** : paste ⟨pasta de dientes *or* pasta dental : toothpaste⟩ **2** : pasta **3** : pastry dough **4 libro en pasta dura** : hardcover book **5 tener pasta de** : to have the makings of

pastar *vi* : to graze — *vt* : to put to pasture

pastel¹ *adj* : pastel

pastel² *nm* **1** : cake ⟨pastel de cumpleaños : birthday cake⟩ **2** : pie, turnover **3** : pastel

pastelería *nf* : pastry shop

pasteurización *nf, pl* **-ciones** : pasteurization

pasteurizar {21} *vt* : to pasteurize

pastilla *nf* **1** COMPRIMIDO, PÍLDORA : pill, tablet **2** : lozenge ⟨pastilla para la tos : cough drop⟩ **3** : cake (of soap), bar (of chocolate)

pastizal *nm* : pasture, grazing land

pasto *nm* **1** : pasture **2** HIERBA : grass, lawn

pastor, -tora *n* **1** : shepherd, shepherdess *f* **2** : minister, pastor

pastoral *adj & nf* : pastoral

pastorear *vt* : to shepherd, to tend

pastorela *nf* **1** : pastoral, pastourelle **2** *Mex* : a traditional Christmas play

pastoso, -sa *adj* **1** : pasty, doughy **2** : smooth, mellow (of sounds)

pata *nf* **1** : paw, leg (of an animal) **2** : foot, leg (of furniture) **3 patas de gallo** : crow's-feet **4 meter la pata** *fam* : to put one's foot in it, to make a blunder

patada *nf* **1** PUNTAPIÉ : kick **2** : stamp (of the foot)

patalear *vi* **1** : to kick **2** : to stamp one's feet

pataleta *nf fam* : tantrum

patán¹ *adj, pl* **patanes** : boorish, crude

patán² *nm, pl* **patanes** : boor, lout

patata *nf Spain* : potato

pateador, -dora *n* : kicker (in sports)

patear *vt* : to kick — *vi* : to stamp one's foot

patentar *vt* : to patent

patente¹ *adj* EVIDENTE : obvious, patent — **patentemente** *adv*

patente² *nf* : patent

paternal *adj* : fatherly, paternal

paternidad *nf* **1** : fatherhood, paternity **2** : parenthood **3** : authorship

paterno, -na *adj* : paternal ⟨abuela paterna : paternal grandmother⟩

patético, -ca *adj* : pathetic, moving

patetismo *nm* : pathos

patíbulo *nm* : gallows, scaffold

patillas *nfpl* : sideburns

patín *nm, pl* **patines** : skate ⟨patín de ruedas : roller skate⟩

patinador, -dora *n* : skater

patinaje *nm* : skating

patinar *vi* **1** : to skate **2** : to skid, to slip **3** *fam* : to slip up, to blunder

patinazo *nm* **1** : skid **2** *fam* : blunder, slipup

patineta *nf* **1** : scooter **2** : skateboard
patinete *nm* : scooter
patio *nm* **1** : courtyard, patio **2 patio de recreo** : playground
patito, -ta *n* : duckling
pato, -ta *n* **1** : duck **2 pato real** : mallard **3 pagar el pato** *fam* : to take the blame
patología *nf* : pathology
patológico, -ca *adj* : pathological
patólogo, -ga *n* : pathologist
patraña *nf* : tall tale, humbug, nonsense
patria *nf* : native land
patriarca *nm* : patriarch — **patriarcal** *adj*
patriarcado *nm* : patriarchy
patrimonio *nm* : patrimony, legacy
patrio, -tria *adj* **1** : native, home ⟨suelo patrio : native soil⟩ **2** : paternal
patriota¹ *adj* : patriotic
patriota² *nmf* : patriot
patriotería *nf* : jingoism, chauvinism
patriotero¹, -ra *adj* : jingoistic, chauvinistic
patriotero², -ra *n* : jingoist, chauvinist
patriótico, -ca *adj* : patriotic
patriotismo *nm* : patriotism
patrocinador, -dora *n* : sponsor, patron
patrocinar *vt* : to sponsor
patrocinio *nm* : sponsorship, patronage
patrón¹, -trona *n, mpl* **patrones 1** JEFE : boss **2** : patron saint
patrón² *nm, pl* **patrones 1** : standard **2** : pattern (in sewing)
patronal *adj* **1** : management, employers' ⟨sindicato patronal : employers' association⟩ **2** : pertaining to a patron saint ⟨fiesta patronal : patron saint's day⟩
patronato *nm* **1** : board, council **2** : foundation, trust
patrono, -na *n* **1** : employer **2** : patron saint
patrulla *nf* **1** : patrol **2** : police car, cruiser
patrullar *v* : to patrol
patrullero *nm* **1** : police car **2** : patrol boat
paulatino, -na *adj* : gradual
paupérrimo, -ma *adj* : destitute, poverty-stricken
pausa *nf* : pause, break
pausado¹ *adv* : slowly, deliberately ⟨habla más pausado : speak more slowly⟩
pausado², -da *adj* : slow, deliberate — **pausadamente** *adv*
pauta *nf* **1** : rule, guideline **2** : lines *pl* (on paper)
pava *nf Arg, Bol, Chile* : kettle
pavimentar *vt* : pave
pavimento *nm* : pavement
pavo, -va *n* **1** : turkey **2 pavo real** : peacock **3 comer pavo** : to be a wallflower
pavón *nm, pl* **pavones** : peacock
pavonearse *vr* : to strut, to swagger
pavoneo *nm* : strut, swagger
pavor *nm* TERROR : dread, terror

pavoroso, -sa *adj* ATERRADOR : dreadful, terrifying
payasada *nf* BUFONADA : antic, buffoonery
payasear *vi* : to clown around
payaso, -sa *n* : clown
paz *nf, pl* **paces 1** : peace **2 dejar en paz** : to leave alone **3 hacer las paces** : to make up, to reconcile
pazca, etc. → **pacer**
PC *nmf* : PC, personal computer
peaje *nm* : toll
peatón *nm, pl* **-tones** : pedestrian
peatonal *adj* : pedestrian
peca *nf* : freckle
pecado *nm* : sin
pecador¹, -dora *adj* : sinful, sinning
pecador², -dora *n* : sinner
pecaminoso, -sa *adj* : sinful
pecar {72} *vi* **1** : to sin **2 ~ de** : to be too much (something) ⟨no pecan de amabilidad : they're not overly friendly⟩
pécari *or* **pecarí** *nm* : peccary
pececillo *nm* : small fish
pecera *nf* : fishbowl, fish tank
pecho *nm* **1** : chest **2** SENO : breast, bosom **3** : heart, courage **4 dar el pecho** : to breast-feed **5 tomar a pecho** : to take to heart
pechuga *nf* : breast (of fowl)
pecoso, -sa *adj* : freckled
pectoral *adj* : pectoral
peculado *nm* : embezzlement
peculiar *adj* **1** CARACTERÍSTICO : particular, characteristic **2** RARO : peculiar, uncommon
peculiaridad *nf* : peculiarity
pecuniario, -ria *adj* : pecuniary
pedagogía *nf* : pedagogy
pedagógico, -ca *adj* : pedagogic, pedagogical
pedagogo, -ga *n* : educator, pedagogue
pedal *nm* : pedal
pedalear *vi* : to pedal
pedante¹ *adj* : pedantic
pedante² *nmf* : pedant
pedantería *nf* : pedantry
pedazo *nm* TROZO : piece, bit, chunk ⟨caerse a pedazos : to fall to pieces⟩ ⟨hacer pedazos : to tear into shreds, to smash to pieces⟩
pedernal *nm* : flint
pedestal *nm* : pedestal
pedestre *adj* : commonplace, pedestrian
pediatra *nmf* : pediatrician
pediatría *nf* : pediatrics
pediátrico, -ca *adj* : pediatric
pedido *nm* **1** : order (of merchandise) **2** : request
pedigrí *nm* : pedigree
pedir {54} *vt* **1** : to ask for, to request ⟨le pedí un préstamo a Claudia : I asked Claudia for a loan⟩ **2** : to order (food, merchandise) **3 pedir disculpas** *or* **pedir perdón** : to apologize — *vi* **1** : to order **2** : to beg

pedrada *nf* **1** : blow (with a rock or stone) ⟨la ventana se quebró de una pedrada : the window was broken by a rock⟩ **2** *fam* : cutting remark, dig
pedregal *nm* : rocky ground
pedregoso, -sa *adj* : rocky, stony
pedrera *nf* CANTERA : quarry
pedrería *nf* : precious stones *pl*, gems *pl*
pegado, -da *adj* **1** : glued, stuck, stuck together **2** ~ **a** : right next to
pegajoso, -sa *adj* **1** : sticky, gluey **2** : catchy ⟨una tonada pegajosa : a catchy tune⟩
pegamento *nm* : adhesive, glue
pegar {52} *vt* **1** : to glue, to stick, to paste **2** : to attach, to sew on **3** : to infect with, to give ⟨me pegó el resfriado : he gave me his cold⟩ **4** GOLPEAR : to hit, to deal, to strike ⟨me pegaron un puntapié : they gave me a kick⟩ **5** : to give (out with) ⟨pegó un grito : she let out a yell⟩ — *vi* **1** : to adhere, to stick **2** ~ **en** : to hit, to strike (against) **3** ~ **con** : to match, to go with — **pegarse** *vr* **1** GOLPEARSE : to hit oneself, to hit each other **2** : to stick, to take hold **3** : to be contagious **4** *fam* : to tag along, to stick around
pegote *nm* **1** : sticky mess **2** *Mex* : sticker, adhesive label
pegue, etc. → **pegar**
peinado *nm* : hairstyle, hairdo
peinador, -dora *n* : hairdresser
peinar *vt* : to comb — **peinarse** *vr*
peine *nm* : comb
peineta *nf* : ornamental comb
peladez *nf, pl* **-deces** *Mex fam* : obscenity, bad language
pelado, -da *adj* **1** : bald, hairless **2** : peeled **3** : bare, barren **4** : broke, penniless **5** *Mex fam* : coarse, crude
pelador *nm* : peeler
pelagra *nf* : pellagra
pelaje *nm* : coat (of an animal), fur
pelar *vt* **1** : to peel, to shell **2** : to skin **3** : to pluck **4** : to remove hair from **5** *fam* : to clean out (of money) — **pelarse** *vr* **1** : to peel **2** *fam* : to get a haircut **3** *Mex fam* : to split, to leave
peldaño *nm* **1** : step, stair **2** : rung
pelea *nf* **1** LUCHA : fight **2** : quarrel
pelear *vi* **1** LUCHAR : to fight **2** DISPUTAR : to quarrel — **pelearse** *vr*
peleón, -ona *adj, mpl* **-ones** *Spain* : quarrelsome, argumentative
peleonero, -ra *adj Mex* : quarrelsome
peletería *nf* **1** : fur shop **2** : fur trade
peletero, -ra *n* : furrier
peliagudo, -da *adj* : tricky, difficult, ticklish
pelícano *nm* : pelican
película *nf* **1** : movie, film **2** : (photographic) film **3** : thin covering, layer
peligrar *vi* : to be in danger
peligro *nm* **1** : danger, peril **2** : risk ⟨correr peligro de : to run the risk of⟩
peligroso, -sa *adj* : dangerous, hazardous

pelirrojo¹, -ja *adj* : red-haired, redheaded
pelirrojo², -ja *n* : redhead
pellejo *nm* **1** : hide, skin **2 salvar el pellejo** : to save one's neck
pellizcar {72} *vt* **1** : to pinch **2** : to nibble on
pellizco *nm* : pinch
pelo *nm* **1** : hair **2** : fur **3** : pile, nap **4 a pelo** : bareback **5 con pelos y señales** : in great detail **6 no tener pelos en la lengua** : to not mince words, to be blunt **7 tomarle el pelo a alguien** : to tease someone, to pull someone's leg
pelón, -lona *adj, mpl* **pelones 1** : bald **2** *fam* : broke **3** *Mex fam* : tough, difficult
pelota *nf* **1** : ball **2** *fam* : head **3 en pelotas** *fam* : naked **4 pelota vasca** : jai alai **5 pasar la pelota** *fam* : to pass the buck
pelotón *nm, pl* **-tones** : squad, detachment
peltre *nm* : pewter
peluca *nf* : wig
peluche *nm* : plush (fabric)
peludo, -da *adj* : hairy, shaggy, bushy
peluquería *nf* **1** : hairdresser's, barber shop **2** : hairdressing
peluquero, -ra *n* : barber, hairdresser
peluquín *nm, pl* **-quines** TUPÉ : hairpiece, toupee
pelusa *nf* : lint, fuzz
pélvico, -ca *adj* : pelvic
pelvis *nfs & pl* : pelvis
pena *nf* **1** CASTIGO : punishment, penalty ⟨pena de muerte : death penalty⟩ **2** AFLICCIÓN : sorrow, grief ⟨morir de pena : to die of a broken heart⟩ ⟨qué pena! : what a shame!, how sad!⟩ **3** DOLOR : pain, suffering **4** DIFICULTAD : difficulty, trouble ⟨a duras penas : with great difficulty⟩ **5** VERGÜENZA : shame, embarrassment **6 valer la pena** : to be worthwhile
penacho *nm* **1** : crest, tuft **2** : plume (of feathers)
penal¹ *adj* : penal
penal² *nm* CÁRCEL : prison, penitentiary
penalidad *nf* **1** : hardship **2** : penalty, punishment
penalizar {21} *vt* : to penalize
penalty *nm* : penalty (in sports)
penar *vt* : to punish, to penalize — *vi* : to suffer, to grieve
pendenciero, -ra *adj* : argumentative, quarrelsome
pender *vi* **1** : to hang **2** : to be pending
pendiente¹ *adj* **1** : pending **2 estar pendiente de** : to be watchful of, to be on the lookout for
pendiente² *nm Spain* : earring
pendiente³ *nf* : slope, incline
pendón *nm, pl* **pendones** : banner
péndulo *nm* : pendulum
pene *nm* : penis

penetración *nf, pl* **-ciones 1** : penetration **2** : insight
penetrante *adj* **1** : penetrating, piercing **2** : sharp, acute **3** : deep (of a wound)
penetrar *vi* **1** : to penetrate, to sink in **2 ~ por** *or* **~ en** : to pierce, to go in, to enter into ⟨el frío penetra por la ventana : the cold comes right in through the window⟩ — *vt* **1** : to penetrate, to permeate **2** : to pierce ⟨el dolor penetró su corazón : sorrow pierced her heart⟩ **3** : to fathom, to understand
penicilina *nf* : penicillin
península *nf* : peninsula — **peninsular** *adj*
penitencia *nf* : penance, penitence
penitenciaría *nf* : penitentiary
penitente *adj & nmf* : penitent
penol *nm* : yardarm
penoso, -sa *adj* **1** : painful, distressing **2** : difficult, arduous **3** : shy, bashful
pensado, -da *adj* **1 bien pensado** : well thought-out **2 en el momento menos pensado** : when least expected **3 poco pensado** : badly thought-out **4 mal pensado** : evil-minded
pensador, -dora *n* : thinker
pensamiento *nm* **1** : thought **2** : thinking **3** : pansy
pensar {55} *vi* **1** : to think **2 ~ en** : to think about — *vt* **1** : to think **2** : to think about **3** : to intend, to plan on — **pensarse** *vr* : to think over
pensativo, -va *adj* : pensive, thoughtful
pensión *nf, pl* **pensiones 1** JUBILACIÓN : pension **2** : boarding house **3 pensión alimenticia** : alimony
pensionado, -da *n* → **pensionista**
pensionista *nmf* **1** JUBILADO : pensioner, retiree **2** : boarder, lodger
pentágono *nm* : pentagon — **pentagonal** *adj*
pentagrama *nm* : staff (in music)
penúltimo, -ma *adj* : next to last, penultimate
penumbra *nf* : semidarkness
penuria *nf* **1** ESCASEZ : shortage, scarcity **2** : poverty
peña *nf* : rock, crag
peñasco *nm* : crag, large rock
peñón → **peñasco**
peón *nm, pl* **peones 1** : laborer, peon **2** : pawn (in chess)
peonía *nf* : peony
peor[1] *adv* **1** (*comparative of* **mal**) : worse ⟨se llevan peor que antes : they get along worse than before⟩ **2** (*superlative of* **mal**) : worst ⟨me fue peor que a nadie : I did the worst of all⟩
peor[2] *adj* **1** (*comparative of* **malo**) : worse ⟨es peor que el original : it's worse than the original⟩ **2** (*superlative of* **malo**) : worst ⟨el peor de todos : the worst of all⟩
pepa *nf* : seed, pit (of a fruit)
pepenador, -dora *n CA, Mex* : scavenger
pepenar *vt CA, Mex* : to scavenge, to scrounge

pepinillo *nm* : pickle, gherkin
pepino *nm* : cucumber
pepita *nf* **1** : seed, pip **2** : nugget **3** *Mex* : dried pumpkin seed
peque, etc. → **pecar**
pequeñez *nf, pl* **-ñeces 1** : smallness **2** : trifle, triviality **3 pequeñez de espíritu** : pettiness
pequeño[1]**, -ña** *adj* **1** : small, little ⟨un libro pequeño : a small book⟩ **2** : young **3** BAJO : short
pequeño[2]**, -ña** *n* : child, little one
pera *nf* : pear
peraltar *vt* : to bank (a road)
perca *nf* : perch (fish)
percal *nm* : percale
percance *nm* : mishap, misfortune
percatarse *vr* **~ de** : to notice, to become aware of
percebe *nm* : barnacle
percepción *nf, pl* **-ciones 1** : perception **2** : idea, notion **3** COBRO : receipt (of payment), collection
perceptible *adj* : perceptible, noticeable — **perceptiblemente** *adv*
percha *nf* **1** : perch **2** : coat hanger **3** : coatrack, coat hook
perchero *nm* : coatrack
percibir *vt* **1** : to perceive, to notice, to sense **2** : to earn, to draw (a salary)
percudido, -da *adj* : grimy
percudir *vt* : to make grimy — **percudirse** *vr*
percusión *nf, pl* **-siones** : percussion
percusor *or* **percutor** *nm* : hammer (of a firearm)
perdedor[1]**, -dora** *adj* : losing
perdedor[2]**, -dora** *n* : loser
perder {56} *vt* **1** : to lose **2** : to miss ⟨perdimos la oportunidad : we missed the opportunity⟩ **3** : to waste (time) — *vi* : to lose — **perderse** *vr* EXTRAVIARSE : to get lost, to stray
perdición *nf, pl* **-ciones** : perdition, damnation
pérdida *nf* **1** : loss **2 pérdida de tiempo** : waste of time
perdidamente *adv* : hopelessly
perdido, -da *adj* **1** : lost **2** : inveterate, incorrigible ⟨es un caso perdido : he's a hopeless case⟩ **3** : in trouble, done for **4 de ~** *Mex fam* : at least
perdigón *nm, pl* **-gones** : shot, pellet
perdiz *nf, pl* **perdices** : partridge
perdón[1] *nm, pl* **perdones** : forgiveness, pardon
perdón[2] *interj* : excuse me!, sorry!
perdonable *adj* : forgivable
perdonar *vt* **1** DISCULPAR : to forgive, to pardon **2** : to exempt, to excuse
perdurable *adj* : lasting
perdurar *vi* : to last, to endure, to survive
perecedero, -ra *adj* : perishable
perecer {53} *vi* : to perish, to die
peregrinación *nf, pl* **-ciones** : pilgrimage
peregrinaje *nm* → **peregrinación**

peregrino[1], **-na** *adj* **1** : unusual, odd **2** MIGRATORIO : migratory
peregrino[2], **-na** *n* : pilgrim
perejil *nm* : parsley
perenne *adj* : perennial
perentorio, **-ria** *adj* **1** : peremptory **2** URGENTE : urgent **3** FIJO : fixed, set
pereza *nf* FLOJERA, HOLGAZANERÍA : laziness, idleness
perezoso[1], **-sa** *adj* FLOJO, HOLGAZÁN : lazy
perezoso[2] *nm* : sloth (animal)
perfección *nf, pl* **-ciones** : perfection
perfeccionamiento *nm* : perfecting, refinement
perfeccionar *vt* : to perfect, to refine
perfeccionismo *nm* : perfectionism
perfeccionista *nmf* : perfectionist
perfecto, **-ta** *adj* : perfect — **perfectamente** *adv*
perfidia *nf* : perfidy, treachery
pérfido, **-da** *adj* : perfidious
perfil *nm* **1** : profile **2 de ~** : sideways, from the side **3 perfiles** *nmpl* RASGOS : features, characteristics
perfilar *vt* : to outline, to define — **perfilarse** *vr* **1** : to be outlined, to be silhouetted **2** : to take shape
perforación *nf, pl* **-ciones** **1** : perforation **2** : drilling
perforadora *nf* **1** : hole punch (for paper) **2** : drill (in mining, etc.)
perforar *vt* **1** : to perforate, to pierce **2** : to drill, to bore
perfumar *vt* : to perfume, to scent — **perfumarse** *vr*
perfume *nm* : perfume, scent
pergamino *nm* : parchment
pérgola *nf* : pergola, arbor
pericia *nf* : skill, expertise
pericial *adj* : expert ⟨testigo pericial : expert witness⟩
perico *nm* COTORRA : small parrot
periferia *nf* : periphery
periférico[1], **-ca** *adj* : peripheral
periférico[2] *nm* **1** *CA, Mex* : beltway **2** : peripheral
perilla *nf* **1** : goatee **2** : pommel (on a saddle) **3** *Col, Mex* : knob, handle **4 perilla de la oreja** : earlobe **5 de perillas** *fam* : handy, just right
perímetro *nm* : perimeter
periódico[1], **-ca** *adj* : periodic — **periódicamente** *adv*
periódico[2] *nm* DIARIO : newspaper
periodismo *nm* : journalism
periodista *nmf* : journalist
periodístico, **-ca** *adj* : journalistic, news
período *or* **periodo** *nm* : period
peripecia *nf* VICISITUD : vicissitude, reversal ⟨las peripecias de su carrera : the ups and downs of her career⟩
periquito *nm* **1** : parakeet **2 periquito australiano** : budgerigar
periscopio *nm* : periscope
perito, **-ta** *adj & n* : expert
perjudicar {72} *vt* : to harm, to be detrimental to

perjudicial *adj* : harmful, detrimental
perjuicio *nm* **1** : harm, damage **2 en perjuicio de** : to the detriment of
perjurar *vi* : to perjure oneself
perjurio *nm* : perjury
perjuro, **-ra** *n* : perjurer
perla *nf* **1** : pearl **2 de perlas** *fam* : wonderfully ⟨me viene de perlas : it suits me just fine⟩
permanecer {53} *vi* **1** QUEDARSE : to remain, to stay **2** SEGUIR : to remain, to continue to be
permanencia *nf* **1** : permanence, continuance **2** ESTANCIA : stay
permanente[1] *adj* **1** : permanent **2** : constant — **permanentemente** *adv*
permanente[2] *nf* : permanent (wave)
permeabilidad *nf* : permeability
permeable *adj* : permeable
permisible *adj* : permissible, allowable
permisividad *nf* : permissiveness
permisivo, **-va** *adj* : permissive
permiso *nm* **1** : permission **2** : permit, license **3** : leave, furlough **4 con ~** : excuse me, pardon me
permitir *vt* : to permit, to allow — **permitirse** *vr*
permuta *nf* : exchange
permutar *vt* INTERCAMBIAR : to exchange
pernicioso, **-sa** *adj* : pernicious, destructive
pernil *nm* **1** : haunch (of an animal) **2** : leg (of meat), ham **3** : trouser leg
perno *nm* : bolt, pin
pernoctar *vi* : to stay overnight, to spend the night
pero[1] *nm* **1** : fault, defect ⟨ponerle peros a : to find fault with⟩ **2** : objection
pero[2] *conj* : but
perogrullada *nf* : truism, platitude, cliché
peroné *nm* : fibula
perorar *vi* : to deliver a speech
perorata *nf* : oration, long-winded speech
peróxido *nm* : peroxide
perpendicular *adj & nf* : perpendicular
perpetrar *vt* : to perpetrate
perpetuar {3} *vt* ETERNIZAR : to perpetuate
perpetuidad *nf* : perpetuity
perpetuo, **-tua** *adj* : perpetual — **perpetuamente** *adv*
perplejidad *nf* : perplexity
perplejo, **-ja** *adj* : perplexed, puzzled
perrada *nf fam* : dirty trick
perrera *nf* : kennel, dog pound
perrero, **-ra** *n* : dogcatcher
perrito, **-ta** *n* CACHORRO : puppy, small dog
perro, **-rra** *n* **1** : dog, bitch *f* **2 perro caliente** : hot dog **3 perro salchicha** : dachshund **4 perro faldero** : lapdog **5 perro cobrador** : retriever
persa[1] *adj & nmf* : Persian
persa[2] *nm* : Persian (language)

persecución *nf, pl* **-ciones 1** : pursuit, chase **2** : persecution
perseguidor, -dora *n* **1** : pursuer **2** : persecutor
perseguir {75} *vt* **1** : to pursue, to chase **2** : to persecute **3** : to pester, to annoy
perseverancia *nf* : perseverance
perseverar *vi* : to persevere
persiana *nf* : blind, venetian blind
persignarse *vr* SANTIGUARSE : to cross oneself, to make the sign of the cross
persistir *vi* : to persist — **persistencia** *nf* — **persistente** *adj*
persona *nf* : person
personaje *nm* **1** : character (in drama or literature) **2** : personage, celebrity
personal¹ *adj* : personal — **personalmente** *adv*
personal² *nm* : personnel, staff
personalidad *nf* : personality
personalizar {21} *vt* : to personalize
personificar {72} *vi* : to personify — **personificación** *nf*
perspectiva *nf* **1** : perspective, view **2** : prospect, outlook
perspicacia *nf* : shrewdness, perspicacity, insight
perspicaz *adj, pl* **-caces** : shrewd, perspicacious
persuadir *vt* : to persuade — **persuadirse** *vr* : to become convinced
persuasión *nf, pl* **-siones** : persuasion
persuasivo, -va *adj* : persuasive
pertenecer {53} *vi* : to belong
perteneciente *adj* ～ **a** : belonging to
pertenencia *nf* **1** : membership **2** : ownership **3 pertenencias** *nfpl* : belongings, possessions
pértiga *nf* GARROCHA : pole ⟨salto de pértiga : pole vault⟩
pertinaz *adj, pl* **-naces 1** OBSTINADO : obstinate **2** PERSISTENTE : persistent
pertinencia *nf* : pertinence, relevance — **pertinente** *adj*
pertrechos *nmpl* : equipment, gear
perturbación *nf, pl* **-ciones** : disturbance, disruption
perturbador, -dora *adj* **1** INQUIETANTE : disturbing, troubling **2** : disruptive
perturbar *vt* **1** : to disturb, to trouble **2** : to disrupt
peruano, -na *adj & n* : Peruvian
perversidad *nf* : perversity, depravity
perversión *nf, pl* **-siones** : perversion
perverso, -sa *adj* : wicked, depraved
pervertido¹, -da *adj* DEPRAVADO : perverted, depraved
pervertido², -da *n* : pervert
pervertir {76} *vt* : to pervert, to corrupt
pesa *nf* **1** : weight **2 levantamiento de pesas** : weightlifting
pesadamente *adv* **1** : heavily **2** : slowly, clumsily
pesadez *nf, pl* **-deces 1** : heaviness **2** : slowness **3** : tediousness
pesadilla *nf* : nightmare

pesado¹, -da *adj* **1** : heavy **2** : slow **3** : irritating, annoying **4** : tedious, boring **5** : tough, difficult
pesado², -da *n fam* : bore, pest
pesadumbre *nf* AFLICCIÓN : grief, sorrow, sadness
pésame *nm* : condolences *pl* ⟨mi más sentido pésame : my heartfelt condolences⟩
pesar¹ *vt* **1** : to weigh **2** EXAMINAR : to consider, to think over — *vi* **1** : to weigh ⟨¿cuánto pesa? : how much does it weigh?⟩ **2** : to be heavy **3** : to weigh heavily, to be a burden ⟨no le pesa : it's not a burden on him⟩ ⟨pesa sobre mi corazón : it weighs upon my heart⟩ **4** INFLUIR : to carry weight, to have bearing **5** (*with personal pronouns*) : to grieve, to sadden ⟨me pesa mucho : I'm very sorry⟩ **6 pese a** : in spite of, despite
pesar² *nm* **1** AFLICCIÓN, PENA : sorrow, grief **2** REMORDIMIENTO : remorse **3 a pesar de** : in spite of, despite
pesaroso, -sa *adj* **1** : sad, mournful **2** ARREPENTIDO : sorry, regretful
pesca *nf* : fishing
pescadería *nf* : fish market
pescado *nm* : fish (as food)
pescador, -dora *n* : fisherman *m*, fisherwoman *f*
pescar {72} *vt* **1** : to fish for **2** : to catch **3** *fam* : to get a hold of, to land — *vi* : to fish, to go fishing
pescuezo *nm* : neck
pesebre *nm* : manger
pesero *nm Mex* : minibus
peseta *nf* : peseta (Spanish unit of currency)
pesimismo *nm* : pessimism
pesimista¹ *adj* : pessimistic
pesimista² *nmf* : pessimist
pésimo, -ma *adj* : dreadful, abominable
peso *nm* **1** : weight, heaviness **2** : burden, responsibility **3** : weight (in sports) **4** BÁSCULA : scales *pl* **5** : peso
pesque, etc. → **pescar**
pesquería *nf* : fishery
pesquero¹, -ra *adj* : fishing ⟨pueblo pesquero : fishing village⟩
pesquero² *nm* : fishing boat
pesquisa *nf* INVESTIGACIÓN : inquiry, investigation
pestaña *nf* **1** : eyelash **2** : flange, rim
pestañear *vi* : to blink
pestañeo *nm* : blink
peste *nf* **1** : plague, pestilence **2** : stench, stink **3** : nuisance, pest
pesticida *nm* : pesticide
pestilencia *nf* **1** : stench, foul odor **2** : pestilence
pestilente *adj* **1** : foul, smelly **2** : pestilent
pestillo *nm* CERROJO : bolt, latch
petaca *nf* **1** *Mex* : suitcase **2 petacas** *nfpl Mex fam* : bottom, behind
pétalo *nm* : petal
petardear *vi* : to backfire

petardeo *nm* : backfiring
petardo *nm* : firecracker
petate *nm Mex* : mat
petición *nf, pl* -ciones : petition, request
peticionar *vt* : to petition
peticionario, -ria *n* : petitioner
petirrojo *nm* : robin
peto *nm* : bib (of clothing)
pétreo, -trea *adj* : stone, stony
petrificar {72} *vt* : to petrify
petróleo *nm* : oil, petroleum
petrolero[1], -ra *adj* : oil ⟨industria petrolera : oil industry⟩
petrolero[2] *nm* : oil tanker
petrolífero, -ra *adj* → petrolero[1]
petulancia *nf* INSOLENCIA : insolence, petulance
petulante *adj* INSOLENTE : insolent, petulant — petulantemente *adv*
petunia *nf* : petunia
peyorativo, -va *adj* : pejorative
pez[1] *nm, pl* peces 1 : fish 2 pez de colores : goldfish 3 pez espada : swordfish 4 pez gordo : big shot
pez[2] *nf, pl* peces : pitch, tar
pezón *nm, pl* pezones : nipple
pezuña *nf* : hoof ⟨pezuña hendida : cloven hoof⟩
pi *nf* : pi
piadoso, -sa *adj* 1 : compassionate, merciful 2 DEVOTO : pious, devout
pianista *nmf* : pianist, piano player
piano *nm* : piano
piar {85} *vi* : to chirp, to cheep, to tweet
pibe, -ba *n Arg, Uru fam* : kid, child
pica *nf* 1 : pike, lance 2 : goad (in bullfighting) 3 : spade (in playing cards)
picada *nf* 1 : bite, sting (of an insect) 2 : sharp descent
picadillo *nm* 1 : minced meat, hash 2 hacer picadillo a : to beat to a pulp
picado, -da *adj* 1 : perforated 2 : minced, chopped 3 : decayed (of teeth) 4 : choppy, rough 5 *fam* : annoyed, miffed
picador *nm* : picador
picadura *nf* 1 : sting, bite 2 : prick, puncture 3 : decay, cavity
picaflor *nm* COLIBRÍ : hummingbird
picana *nf* : goad, prod
picante[1] *adj* 1 : hot, spicy 2 : sharp, cutting 3 : racy, risqué
picante[2] *nm* 1 : spiciness 2 : hot spices *pl*, hot sauce
picaporte *nm* 1 : latch 2 : door handle 3 ALDABA : door knocker
picar {72} *vt* 1 : to sting, to bite 2 : to peck at 3 : to nibble on 4 : to prick, to puncture, to punch (a ticket) 5 : to grind, to chop 6 : to goad, to incite 7 : to pique, to provoke — *vi* 1 : to itch 2 : to sting 3 : to be spicy 4 : to nibble 5 : to take the bait 6 ~ en : to dabble in 7 picar muy alto : to aim too high — picarse *vr* 1 : to get a cavity, to decay 2 : to get annoyed, to take offense
picardía *nf* 1 : cunning, craftiness 2 : prank, dirty trick

picaresco, -ca *adj* 1 : picaresque 2 : rascally, roguish
pícaro[1], -ra *adj* 1 : mischievous 2 : cunning, sly 3 : off-color, risqué
pícaro[2], -ra *n* 1 : rogue, scoundrel 2 : rascal
picazón *nf, pl* -zones COMEZÓN : itch
picea *nf* : spruce (tree)
pichel *nm* : pitcher, jug
pichón, -chona *n, mpl* pichones 1 : young pigeon, squab 2 *Mex fam* : novice, greenhorn
picnic *nm* : picnic
pico *nm* 1 : peak 2 : point, spike 3 : beak, bill 4 : pick, pickax 5 y pico : and a little, and a bit ⟨las siete y pico : a little after seven⟩ ⟨dos metros y pico : a bit over two meters⟩
picor *nm* : itch, irritation
picoso, -sa *adj Mex* : very hot, spicy
picota *nf* 1 : pillory, stock 2 poner a alguien en la picota : to put someone on the spot
picotada *nf* → picotazo
picotazo *nm* : peck (of a bird)
picotear *vt* : to peck — *vi* : to nibble, to pick
pictórico, -ca *adj* : pictorial
picudo, -da *adj* 1 : pointy, sharp 2 ~ para *Mex fam* : clever at, good at
pide, etc. → pedir
pie *nm* 1 : foot ⟨a pie : on foot⟩ ⟨de pie : on one's feet, standing⟩ 2 : base, bottom, stem, foot ⟨pie de la cama : foot of the bed⟩ ⟨pie de una lámpara : base of a lamp⟩ ⟨pie de la escalera : bottom of the stairs⟩ ⟨pie de una copa : stem of a glass⟩ 3 : foot (in measurement) ⟨pie cuadrado : square foot⟩ 4 : cue (in theater) 5 dar pie a : to give cause for, to give rise to 6 en pie de igualdad : on equal footing
piedad *nf* 1 COMPASIÓN : mercy, pity 2 DEVOCIÓN : piety, devotion
piedra *nf* 1 : stone 2 : flint (of a lighter) 3 : hailstone 4 piedra de afilar : whetstone, grindstone 5 piedra angular : cornerstone 6 piedra arenisca : sandstone 7 piedra caliza : limestone 8 piedra imán : lodestone 9 piedra de molino : millstone 10 piedra de toque : touchstone
piel *nf* 1 : skin 2 CUERO : leather, hide ⟨piel de venado : deerskin⟩ 3 : fur, pelt 4 CÁSCARA : peel, skin 5 piel de gallina : goose bumps *pl* ⟨me pone la piel de gallina : it gives me goose bumps⟩
piélago *nm* el piélago : the deep, the ocean
piensa, etc. → pensar
pienso *nm* : feed, fodder
pierde, etc. → perder
pierna *nf* : leg
pieza *nf* 1 ELEMENTO : piece, part, component ⟨vestido de dos piezas : two-piece dress⟩ ⟨pieza de recambio : spare part⟩ ⟨pieza clave : key element⟩ 2 : piece (in chess) 3 OBRA : piece, work

⟨pieza de teatro : play⟩ **4** : room, bedroom

pifia *nf fam* : goof, blunder

pigargo *nm* : osprey

pigmentación *nf, pl* **-ciones** : pigmentation

pigmento *nm* : pigment

pigmeo, -mea *adj & n* : pygmy, Pygmy

pijama *nm* : pajamas *pl*

pila *nf* **1** BATERÍA : battery ⟨pila de linterna : flashlight battery⟩ **2** MONTÓN : pile, heap **3** : sink, basin, font ⟨pila bautismal : baptismal font⟩ ⟨pila para pájaros : birdbath⟩

pilar *nm* **1** : pillar, column **2** : support, mainstay

píldora *nf* PASTILLA : pill

pillaje *nm* : pillage, plunder

pillar *vt* **1** *fam* : to catch ⟨¡cuidado! ¡nos pillarán! : watch out! they'll catch us!⟩ **2** *fam* : to grasp, to catch on ⟨¿no lo pillas? : don't you get it?⟩

pillo¹, -lla *adj* : cunning, crafty

pillo², -lla *n* **1** : rascal, brat **2** : rogue, scoundrel

pilluelo, -la *n* : urchin

pilón *nm, pl* **pilones 1** PILA : basin **2** : pillar, tower (for cables), pylon (of a bridge) **3** *Mex* : extra, lagniappe

pilotar *vt* : to pilot, to drive

pilote *nm* : pile (stake)

pilotear → **pilotar**

piloto *nm* **1** : pilot, driver **2** : pilot light

piltrafa *nf* **1** : poor quality meat **2** : wretch **3** **piltrafas** *nfpl* : food scraps

pimentero *nm* : pepper shaker

pimentón *nm, pl* **-tones 1** : paprika **2** : cayenne pepper

pimienta *nf* **1** : pepper (condiment) **2** **pimienta de Jamaica** : allspice

pimiento *nm* : pepper (fruit) ⟨pimiento verde : green pepper⟩

pináculo *nm* **1** : pinnacle (of a building) **2** : peak, acme

pincel *nm* : paintbrush

pincelada *nf* **1** : brushstroke **2** **últimas pinceladas** : final touches

pinchar *vt* **1** PICAR : to puncture (a tire) **2** : to prick, to stick **3** : to goad, to tease, to needle — *vi* **1** : to be prickly **2** : to get a flat tire **3** *fam* : to get beaten, to lose out — **pincharse** *vr* : to give oneself an injection

pinchazo *nm* **1** : prick, jab **2** : puncture, flat tire

pingüe *adj* **1** : rich, huge (of profits) **2** : lucrative

pingüino *nm* : penguin

pininos *or* **pinitos** *nmpl* : first steps ⟨hacer pininos : to take one's first steps, to toddle⟩

pino *nm* : pine, pine tree

pinta *nf* **1** : dot, spot **2** : pint **3** *fam* : aspect, appearance ⟨las peras tienen buena pinta : the pears look good⟩ **4** **pintas** *nfpl Mex* : graffiti

pintadas *nfpl* : graffiti

pintar *vt* **1** : to paint **2** : to draw, to mark **3** : to describe, to depict — *vi* **1** : to paint, to draw **2** : to look ⟨no pinta bien : it doesn't look good⟩ **3** *fam* : to count ⟨aquí no pinta nada : he has no say here⟩ — **pintarse** *vr* **1** MAQUILLARSE : to put on makeup **2** **pintárselas solo** *fam* : to manage by oneself, to know it all

pintarrajear *vt* : to daub (with paint)

pinto, -ta *adj* : speckled, spotted

pintor, -tora *n* **1** : painter **2** **pintor de brocha gorda** : housepainter, dauber

pintoresco, -ca *adj* : picturesque, quaint

pintura *nf* **1** : paint **2** : painting (art, work of art)

pinza *nf* **1** : clothespin **2** : claw, pincer **3** : pleat, dart **4** **pinzas** *nfpl* : tweezers **5** **pinzas** *nfpl* ALICATES : pliers, pincers

pinzón *nm, pl* **pinzones** : finch

piña *nf* **1** : pineapple **2** : pine cone

piñata *nf* : piñata

piñón *nm, pl* **piñones 1** : pine nut **2** : pinion

pío¹, pía *adj* **1** DEVOTO : pious, devout **2** : piebald, pied, dappled

pío² *nm* : peep, tweet, cheep

piocha *nf* **1** : pickax **2** *Mex* : goatee

piojo *nm* : louse

piojoso, -sa *adj* **1** : lousy **2** : filthy

pionero¹, -ra *adj* : pioneering

pionero², -ra *n* : pioneer

pipa *nf* : pipe (for smoking)

pipián *nm, pl* **pipianes** *Mex* : a spicy sauce or stew

pipiolo, -la *n fam* **1** : greenhorn, novice **2** : kid, youngster

pique¹, *etc.* → **picar**

pique² *nm* **1** : pique, resentment **2** : rivalry, competition **3** **a pique de** : about to, on the verge of **4** **irse a pique** : to sink, to founder

piqueta *nf* : pickax

piquete *nm* **1** : picketers *pl*, picket line **2** : squad, detachment **3** *Mex* : prick, jab

piquetear *vt* **1** : to picket **2** *Mex* : to prick, to jab

pira *nf* : pyre

piragua *nf* : canoe — **piragüista** *nmf*

pirámide *nf* : pyramid

piraña *nf* : piranha

pirata¹ *adj* : bootleg, pirated

pirata² *nmf* **1** : pirate **2** : bootlegger **3** **pirata aéreo** : hijacker

piratear *vt* **1** : to hijack, to commandeer **2** : to bootleg, to pirate

piratería *nf* : piracy, bootlegging

piromanía *nf* : pyromania

pirómano, -na *n* : pyromaniac

piropo *nm* : flirtatious compliment

pirotecnia *nf* : fireworks *pl*, pyrotechnics *pl*

pirotécnico, -ca *adj* : fireworks, pyrotechnic

pírrico, -ca *adj* : Pyrrhic

pirueta *nf* : pirouette

pirulí *nm* : cone-shaped lollipop

pisada *nf* 1 : footstep 2 HUELLA : footprint

pisapapeles *nms & pl* : paperweight

pisar *vt* 1 : to step on, to set foot in 2 : to walk all over, to mistreat — *vi* : to step, to walk, to tread

piscina *nf* 1 : swimming pool 2 : fish pond

Piscis *nmf* : Pisces

piso *nm* 1 PLANTA : floor, story 2 SUELO : floor 3 *Spain* : apartment

pisotear *vt* 1 : to stamp on, to trample 2 PISAR : to walk all over 3 : to flout, to disregard

pisotón *nm, pl* **-tones** : stamp, step ⟨sufrieron empujones y pisotones : they were pushed and stepped on⟩

pista *nf* 1 RASTRO : trail, track ⟨siguen la pista de los sospechosos : they're on the trail of the suspects⟩ 2 : clue 3 CAMINO : road, trail 4 : track, racetrack 5 : ring, arena, rink 6 **pista de aterrizaje** : runway, airstrip 7 **pista de baile** : dance floor

pistacho *nm* : pistachio

pistilo *nm* : pistil

pistola *nf* 1 : pistol, handgun 2 : spray gun

pistolera *nf* : holster

pistolero *nm* : gunman

pistón *nm, pl* **pistones** : piston

pita *nf* 1 : agave 2 : pita fiber 3 : twine

pitar *vi* 1 : to blow a whistle 2 : to whistle, to boo 3 : to beep, to honk, to toot — *vt* : to whistle at, to boo

pitido *nm* 1 : whistle, whistling 2 : beep, honk, toot

pito *nm* 1 SILBATO : whistle 2 **no me importa un pito** *fam* : I don't give a damn

pitón *nm, pl* **pitones** 1 : python 2 : point of a bull's horn

pituitario, -ria *adj* : pituitary

pívot *nmf, pl* **pívots** : center (in basketball)

pivote *nm* : pivot

piyama *nmf* : pajamas *pl*

pizarra *nf* 1 : slate 2 : blackboard 3 : scoreboard

pizarrón *nm, pl* **-rrones** : blackboard, chalkboard

pizca *nf* 1 : pinch ⟨una pizca de canela : a pinch of cinnamon⟩ 2 : speck, trace ⟨ni pizca : not a bit⟩ 3 *Mex* : harvest

pizcar {72} *vt Mex* : to harvest

pizque, etc. → **pizcar**

pizza ['pitsa, 'pisa] *nf* : pizza

pizzería *nf* : pizzeria, pizza parlor

placa *nf* 1 : sheet, plate 2 : plaque, nameplate 3 : plate (in photography) 4 : badge, insignia 5 **placa de matrícula** : license plate, tag 6 **placa dental** : plaque, tartar

placebo *nm* : placebo

placenta *nf* : placenta, afterbirth

placentero, -ra *adj* AGRADABLE, GRATO : pleasant, agreeable

placer¹ {57} *vi* GUSTAR : to be pleasing ⟨hazlo como te plazca : do it however you please⟩

placer² *nm* 1 : pleasure, enjoyment 2 **a ~** : as much as one wants

plácido, -da *adj* TRANQUILO : placid, calm

plaga *nf* 1 : plague, infestation, blight 2 CALAMIDAD : disaster, scourge

plagado, -da *adj* **~ de** : filled with, covered with

plagar {52} *vt* : to plague

plagiar *vt* 1 : to plagiarize 2 SECUESTRAR : to kidnap, to abduct

plagiario, -ria *n* 1 : plagiarist 2 SECUESTRADOR : kidnapper, abductor

plagio *nm* 1 : plagiarism 2 SECUESTRO : kidnapping, abduction

plague, etc. → **plagar**

plan *nm* 1 : plan, strategy, program ⟨plan de inversiones : investment plan⟩ ⟨plan de estudios : curriculum⟩ 2 PLANO : plan, diagram 3 : attitude, intent, purpose ⟨ponte en plan serio : be serious⟩ ⟨estamos en plan de divertirnos : we're looking to have some fun⟩

plana *nf* 1 : page ⟨noticias en primera plana : front-page news⟩ 2 **plana mayor** : staff (in the military)

plancha *nf* 1 : iron, ironing 2 : grill, griddle ⟨a la plancha : grilled⟩ 3 : sheet, plate ⟨plancha para hornear : baking sheet⟩ 4 *fam* : blunder, blooper

planchada *nf* : ironing, pressing

planchado *nm* → **planchada**

planchar *v* : to iron

planchazo *nm fam* : goof, blunder

plancton *nm* : plankton

planeación *nf* → **planeamiento**

planeador *nm* : glider (aircraft)

planeamiento *nm* : plan, planning

planear *vt* : to plan — *vi* : to glide (in the air)

planeo *nm* : gliding, soaring

planeta *nm* : planet

planetario¹, -ria *adj* 1 : planetary 2 : global, worldwide

planetario² *nm* : planetarium

planicie *nf* : plain

planificación *nf* : planning ⟨planificación familiar : family planning⟩

planificar {72} *vt* : to plan

planilla *nf* 1 LISTA : list 2 NÓMINA : payroll 3 TABLA : chart, table 4 *Mex* : slate, ticket (of candidates) 5 **planilla de cálculo** *Arg, Chile* : spreadsheet

plano¹, -na *adj* : flat, level, plane

plano² *nm* 1 PLAN : map, plan 2 : plane (surface) 3 NIVEL : level ⟨en un plano personal : on a personal level⟩ 4 : shot (in photography) 5 **de ~** : flatly, outright, directly ⟨se negó de plano : he flatly refused⟩

planta *nf* 1 : plant ⟨planta de interior : houseplant⟩ 2 FÁBRICA : plant, factory 3 PISO : floor, story 4 : staff, employees *pl* 5 : sole (of the foot)

213

plantación · pluma

plantación *nf, pl* **-ciones 1** : plantation
2 : planting
plantado, -da *adj* **1** : planted **2 dejar
plantado** : to stand up (a date), to dump
(a lover)
plantar *vt* **1** : to plant, to sow ⟨plantar
de flores : to plant with flowers⟩ **2** : to
put in, to place **3** *fam* : to plant, to land
⟨plantar un beso : to plant a kiss⟩ **4**
fam : to leave, to jilt — **plantarse** *vr* **1**
: to stand firm **2** *fam* : to arrive, to
show up **3** *fam* : to balk
planteamiento *nm* **1** : approach, position ⟨el planteamiento feminista : the
feminist viewpoint⟩ **2** : explanation,
exposition **3** : proposal, suggestion,
plan
plantear *vt* **1** : to set forth, to bring up,
to suggest **2** : to establish, to set up **3**
: to create, to pose (a problem) —
plantearse *vr* **1** : to think about **2** : to
arise
plantel *nm* **1** : educational institution **2**
: staff, team
planteo → **planteamiento**
plantilla *nf* **1** : insole **2** : pattern, tem-
plate, stencil **3** *Mex, Spain* : staff, roster of employees
plantío *nm* : field (planted with a crop)
plantón *nm, pl* **plantones 1** : seedling
2 : long wait ⟨darle a alguien un plantón : to stand someone up⟩
plañidero¹, -ra *adj* : mournful
plañidero², -ra *nf* : hired mourner
plañir {38} *v* : to mourn, to lament
plasma *nm* : plasma
plasmar *vt* : to express, to give form to
— **plasmarse** *vr*
plasta *nf* : soft mass, lump
plástica *nf* : modeling, sculpture
plasticidad *nf* : plasticity
plástico¹, -ca *adj* : plastic
plástico² *nm* : plastic
plastificar {72} *vt* : to laminate
plata *nf* **1** : silver **2** : money
plataforma *nf* **1** ESTRADO, TARIMA
: platform, dais **2** : platform (in politics) **3** : springboard, stepping stone **4**
plataforma continental : continental
shelf **5 plataforma de lanzamiento**
: launchpad **6 plataforma petrolífera**
: oil rig (at sea)
platal *nm* : large sum of money, fortune
platanal *nm* : banana plantation
platanero¹, -ra *adj* : banana, banana-
producing
platanero², -ra *n* : banana grower
plátano *nm* **1** : banana **2** : plantain **3**
plátano macho *Mex* : plantain
platea *nf* : orchestra, pit (in a theater)
plateado, -da *adj* **1** : silver, silvery **2**
: silver-plated
plática *nf* **1** : talk, lecture **2** : chat, conversation
platicar {72} *vi* : to talk, to chat — *vt*
Mex : to tell, to say
platija *nf* : flatfish, flounder

platillo *nm* **1** : saucer ⟨platillo volador
: flying saucer⟩ **2** : cymbal **3** *Mex* : dish
⟨platillos típicos : local dishes⟩
platino *nm* : platinum
plato *nm* **1** : plate, dish ⟨lavar los platos
: to do the dishes⟩ **2** : serving, helping
3 : course (of a meal) **4** : dish ⟨plato
típico : typical dish⟩ **5** : home plate (in
baseball) **6 plato hondo** : soup bowl
plató *nm* : set (in the movies)
platónico, -ca *adj* : platonic
playa *nf* : beach, seashore
playera *nf* **1** : canvas sneaker **2** *CA, Mex*
: T-shirt
plaza *nf* **1** : square, plaza **2** : marketplace **3** : room, space, seat (in a vehicle) **4** : post, position **5 plaza fuerte**
: stronghold, fortified city **6 plaza de
toros** : bullring
plazca, etc. → **placer**
plazo *nm* **1** : period, term ⟨un plazo de
cinco días : a period of five days⟩ ⟨a
largo plazo : long-term⟩ **2** ABONO : installment ⟨pagar a plazos : to pay in in-
stallments⟩
pleamar *nf* : high tide
plebe *nf* : common people, masses *pl*
plebeyo¹, -ya *adj* : plebeian
plebeyo², -ya *n* : plebeian, commoner
plegable *adj* : folding, collapsible
plegadizo → **plegable**
plegar {49} *vt* DOBLAR : to fold, to bend
— **plegarse** *vr* : to give in, to yield
plegaria *nf* ORACIÓN : prayer
pleito *nm* **1** : lawsuit **2** : fight, argument, dispute
plenamente *adv* COMPLETAMENTE : fully, completely
plenario, -ria *adj* : plenary, full
plenilunio *nm* : full moon
plenipotenciario, -ria *n* : plenipoten-
tiary
plenitud *nf* : fullness, abundance
pleno, -na *adj* COMPLETO ((*often used as
an intensifier*)) : full, complete ⟨en
pleno uso de sus facultades : in full
command of his faculties⟩ ⟨en plena
noche : in the middle of the night⟩ ⟨en
pleno corazón de la ciudad : right in
the heart of the city⟩
plétora *nf* : plethora
pleuresía *nf* : pleurisy
pliega, pliegue etc. → **plegar**
pliego *nm* **1** HOJA : sheet of paper **2**
: sealed document
pliegue *nm* **1** DOBLEZ : crease, fold **2**
: pleat
plisar *vt* : to pleat
plomada *nf* **1** : plumb line **2** : sinker
plomería *nf* FONTANERÍA : plumbing
plomero, -ra *n* FONTANERO : plumber
plomizo, -za *adj* : leaden
plomo *nm* **1** : lead **2** : plumb line **3**
: fuse **4** *fam* : bore, drag **5 a~** : plumb,
straight
plugo, etc. → **placer**
pluma *nf* **1** : feather **2** : pen **3 pluma
fuente** : fountain pen

plumaje *nm* : plumage
plumero *nm* : feather duster
plumilla *nf* : nib
plumón *nm, pl* **plumones** : down
plumoso, -sa *adj* : feathery, downy
plural *adj & nm* : plural
pluralidad *nf* : plurality
pluralizar {21} *vt* : to pluralize
pluriempleado, -da *adj* : holding more than one job
pluriempleo *nm* : moonlighting
plus *nm* : bonus
plusvalía *nf* : appreciation, capital gain
Plutón *nm* : Pluto
plutocracia *nf* : plutocracy
plutonio *nm* : plutonium
población *nf, pl* **-ciones 1** : population **2** : city, town, village
poblado¹, -da *adj* **1** : inhabited, populated **2** : full, thick ⟨cejas pobladas : bushy eyebrows⟩
poblado² *nm* : village, settlement
poblador, -dora *n* : settler
poblar {19} *vt* **1** : to populate, to inhabit **2** : to settle, to colonize **3** — **de** : to stock with, to plant with — **poblarse** *vr* : to fill up, to become crowded
pobre¹ *adj* **1** : poor, impoverished **2** : unfortunate ⟨¡pobre de mí! : poor me!⟩ **3** : weak, deficient ⟨una dieta pobre : a poor diet⟩
pobre² *nmf* : poor person ⟨los pobres : the poor⟩ ⟨¡pobre! : poor thing!⟩
pobremente *adv* : poorly
pobreza *nf* : poverty
pocilga *nf* CHIQUERO : pigsty, pigpen
pocillo *nm* : small coffee cup, demitasse
poción *nf, pl* **pociones** : potion
poco¹ *adv* **1** : little, not much ⟨poco probable : not very likely⟩ ⟨come poco : he doesn't eat much⟩ **2** : a short time, a while ⟨tardaremos poco : we won't be very long⟩ **3 poco antes** : shortly before **4 poco después** : shortly after
poco², -ca *adj* **1** : little, not much, (a) few ⟨tengo poco dinero : I don't have much money⟩ ⟨en no pocas ocasiones : on more than a few occasions⟩ ⟨poca gente : few people⟩ **2 pocas veces** : rarely
poco³, -ca *pron* **1** : little, few ⟨le falta poco para terminar : he's almost finished⟩ ⟨uno de los pocos que quedan : one of the remaining few⟩ **2 un poco** : a little, a bit ⟨un poco de vino : a little wine⟩ ⟨un poco extraño : a bit strange⟩ **3 a ~** *Mex* (*used to express disbelief*) ⟨¿a poco no se te hizo difícil? : you mean you didn't find it difficult?⟩ **4 de a poco** : little by little **5 hace poco** : not long ago **6 poco a poco** : little by little **7 dentro de poco** : shortly, in a little while **8 por ~** : nearly, almost
podar *vt* : to prune, to trim
poder¹ {58} *v aux* **1** : to be able to, can ⟨no puede hablar : he can't speak⟩ **2** (*expressing possibility*) : might, may ⟨puede llover : it may rain at any mo-

ment⟩ ⟨¿cómo puede ser? : how can that be?⟩ **3** (*expressing permission*) : can, may ⟨¿puedo ir a la fiesta? : can I go to the party?⟩ ⟨¿se puede? : may I come in?⟩ — *vi* **1** : to beat, to defeat ⟨cree que le puede a cualquiera : he thinks he can beat anyone⟩ **2** : to be possible ⟨¿crees que vendrán? — puede (que sí) : do you think they'll come? — maybe⟩ **3 ~ con** : to cope with, to manage ⟨¡no puedo con estos niños! : I can't handle these children!⟩ **4 no poder más** : to have had enough ⟨no puede más : she can't take anymore⟩ **5 no poder menos que** : to not be able to help ⟨no pudo menos que asombrarse : she couldn't help but be amazed⟩
poder² *nm* **1** : control, power ⟨poder adquisitivo : purchasing power⟩ **2** : authority ⟨el poder legislativo : the legislature⟩ **3** : possession ⟨está en mi poder : it's in my hands⟩ **4** : strength, force ⟨poder militar : military might⟩
poderío *nm* **1** : power **2** : wealth, influence
poderoso, -sa *adj* **1** : powerful **2** : wealthy, influential **3** : effective
podiatría *nf* : podiatry
podio *nm* : podium
pódium → **podio**
podología *nf* : podiatry, chiropody
podólogo, -ga *n* : podiatrist, chiropodist
podrá, etc. → **poder**
podredumbre *nf* **1** : decay, rottenness **2** : corruption
podrido, -da *adj* **1** : rotten, decayed **2** : corrupt
podrir → **pudrir**
poema *nm* : poem
poesía *nf* **1** : poetry **2** POEMA : poem
poeta *nmf* : poet
poético, -ca *adj* : poetic, poetical
pogrom *nm* : pogrom
póker *or* **poker** *nm* : poker (card game)
polaco¹, -ca *adj* : Polish
polaco², -ca *n* : Pole, Polish person
polaco³ *nm* : Polish (language)
polar *adj* : polar
polarizar {21} *vt* : to polarize — **polarizarse** *vr* — **polarización** *nf*
polea *nf* : pulley
polémica *nf* CONTROVERSIA : controversy, polemics
polémico, -ca *adj* CONTROVERTIDO : controversial, polemical
polen *nm, pl* **pólenes** : pollen
policía¹ *nf* : police
policía² *nmf* : police officer, policeman *m*, policewoman *f*
policíaco, -ca *or* **policiaco, -ca** *adj* : police ⟨novela policíaca : detective story⟩
policial *adj* : police
poliéster *nm* : polyester
poligamia *nf* : polygamy
polígamo¹, -ma *adj* : polygamous
polígamo², -ma *n* : polygamist
polígono *nm* : polygon — **poligonal** *adj*

poliinsaturado, -da *adj* : polyunsaturated

polilla *nf* : moth

polimerizar {21} *vt* : to polymerize

polímero *nm* : polymer

polinesio, -sia *adj & n* : Polynesian

polinizar {21} *vt* : to pollinate — **polinización** *nf*

polio *nf* : polio

poliomielitis *nf* : poliomyelitis, polio

polisón *nm, pl* **-sones** : bustle (on clothing)

politécnico, -ca *adj* : polytechnic

politeísmo *nm* : polytheism — **politeísta** *adj & nmf*

política *nf* **1** : politics **2** : policy

políticamente *adv* : politically

político¹, -ca *adj* **1** : political **2** : tactful, politic **3** : by marriage ⟨padre político : father-in-law⟩

político², -ca *n* : politician

póliza *nf* : policy ⟨póliza de seguros : insurance policy⟩

polizón *nm, pl* **-zones** : stowaway ⟨viajar de polizón : to stow away⟩

polka *nf* : polka

polla *nf* APUESTA : bet

pollera *nf* **1** : chicken coop **2** : skirt

pollero, -ra *n* **1** : poulterer **2** : poultry farm **3** *Mex fam* COYOTE : smuggler of illegal immigrants

pollito, -ta *n* : chick, young bird, fledgling

pollo, -lla *n* **1** : chicken **2** POLLITO : chick **3** JOVEN : young man *m*, young lady *f*

polluelo *nm* → **pollito**

polo *nm* **1** : pole ⟨el Polo Norte : the North Pole⟩ ⟨polo negativo : negative pole⟩ **2** : polo (sport) **3** : polo shirt **4** : focal point, center **5** **polo opuesto** : exact opposite

polución *nf, pl* **-ciones** CONTAMINACIÓN : pollution

polvareda *nf* **1** : cloud of dust **2** : uproar, fuss

polvera *nf* : compact (for face powder)

polvo *nm* **1** : dust **2** : powder **3** **polvos** *nmpl* : face powder **4** **polvos de hornear** : baking powder **5** **hacer polvo** *fam* : to crush, to shatter ⟨vas a hacer polvo el reloj : you're going to destroy your watch⟩

pólvora *nf* **1** : gunpowder **2** : fireworks *pl*

polvoriento, -ta *adj* : dusty, powdery

polvorín *nm, pl* **-rines** : magazine, storehouse (for explosives)

pomada *nf* : ointment, cream

pomelo *nm* : grapefruit

pómez *nf or* **piedra pómez** : pumice

pomo *nm* **1** : pommel (on a sword) **2** : knob, handle **3** : perfume bottle

pompa *nf* **1** : bubble **2** : pomp, splendor **3** **pompas fúnebres** : funeral

pompón *nm, pl* **pompones** BORLA : pom-pom

pomposidad *nf* **1** : pomp, splendor **2** : pomposity, ostentation

pomposo, -sa *adj* : pompous — **pomposamente** *adv*

pómulo *nm* : cheekbone

pon → **poner**

ponchadura *nf Mex* : puncture, flat (tire)

ponchar *vt* **1** : to strike out (in baseball) **2** *Mex* : to puncture — **poncharse** *vr* **1** *Col, Ven* : to strike out (in baseball) **2** *Mex* : to blow out (of a tire)

ponche *nm* **1** : punch (drink) **2** **ponche de huevo** : eggnog

poncho *nm* : poncho

ponderación *nf, pl* **-ciones** **1** : consideration, deliberation **2** : high praise

ponderar *vt* **1** : to weigh, to consider **2** : to speak highly of

pondrá, etc. → **poner**

ponencia *nf* **1** DISCURSO : paper, presentation, address **2** INFORME : report

ponente *nmf* : speaker, presenter

poner {60} *vt* **1** COLOCAR : to put, to place ⟨pon el libro en la mesa : put the book on the table⟩ **2** AGREGAR, AÑADIR : to put in, to add **3** : to put on (clothes) **4** CONTRIBUIR : to contribute **5** ESCRIBIR : to put in writing ⟨no le puso su nombre : he didn't put his name on it⟩ **6** IMPONER : to set, to impose **7** EXPONER : to put, to expose ⟨lo puso en peligro : she put him in danger⟩ **8** : to prepare, to arrange ⟨poner la mesa : to set the table⟩ **9** : to name ⟨le pusimos Ana : we called her Ana⟩ **10** ESTABLECER : to set up, to establish ⟨puso un restaurante : he opened up a restaurant⟩ **11** INSTALAR : to install, to put in **12** (*with an adjective or adverb*) : to make ⟨siempre lo pones de mal humor : you always put him in a bad mood⟩ **13** : to turn on, to switch on **14** SUPONER : to suppose ⟨pongamos que no viene : supposing he doesn't come⟩ **15** : to lay (eggs) **16** ~ **a** : to start (someone doing something) ⟨lo puse a trabajar : I put him to work⟩ **17** ~ **de** : to place as ⟨la pusieron de directora : they made her director⟩ **18** ~ **en** : to put in (a state or condition) ⟨poner en duda : to call into question⟩ — *vi* **1** : to contribute **2** : to lay eggs — **ponerse** *vr* **1** : to move (into a position) ⟨ponerse de pie : to stand up⟩ **2** : to put on, to wear **3** : to become, to turn ⟨se puso colorado : he turned red⟩ **4** : to set (of the sun or moon)

poni *or* **poney** *nm* : pony

ponga, etc. → **poner**

poniente *nm* **1** OCCIDENTE : west **2** : west wind

ponqué *nm Col, Ven* : cake

pontifical *adj* : pontifical

pontificar {72} *vi* : to pontificate

pontífice *nm* : pontiff, pope

pontón *nm, pl* **pontones** : pontoon

ponzoña *nf* VENENO : poison — **ponzoñoso, -sa** *adj*

popa *nf* **1** : stern **2 a ~** : astern, abaft, aft

popelín *nm, pl* **-lines** : poplin

popelina *nf* : poplin

popote *nm Mex* : (drinking) straw

populachero, -ra *adj* : common, popular, vulgar

populacho *nm* : rabble, masses *pl*

popular *adj* **1** : popular **2** : traditional **3** : colloquial

popularidad *nf* : popularity

popularizar {21} *vt* : to popularize — **popularizarse** *vr*

populista *adj & nmf* : populist — **populismo** *nm*

populoso, -sa *adj* : populous

popurrí *nm* : potpourri

por *prep* **1** : for, during ⟨se quedaron allí por la semana : they stayed there during the week⟩ ⟨por el momento : for now, at the moment⟩ **2** : around, during ⟨por noviembre empieza a nevar : around November it starts to snow⟩ ⟨por la mañana : in the morning⟩ **3** : around (a place) ⟨debe estar por allí : it must be over there⟩ ⟨por todas partes : everywhere⟩ **4** : by, through, along ⟨por la puerta : through the door⟩ ⟨pasé por tu casa : I stopped by your house⟩ ⟨por la costa : along the coast⟩ **5** : for, for the sake of ⟨lo hizo por su madre : he did it for his mother⟩ ⟨¡por Dios! : for heaven's sake!⟩ **6** : because of, on account of ⟨llegué tarde por el tráfico : I arrived late because of the traffic⟩ ⟨dejar por imposible : to give up as impossible⟩ **7** : per ⟨60 millas por hora : 60 miles per hour⟩ ⟨por docena : by the dozen⟩ **8** : for, in exchange for, instead of ⟨su hermana habló por él : his sister spoke on his behalf⟩ **9** : by means of ⟨hablar por teléfono : to talk on the phone⟩ ⟨por escrito : in writing⟩ **10** : as for ⟨por mí : as far as I'm concerned⟩ **11** : times ⟨tres por dos son seis : three times two is six⟩ **12** SEGÚN : from, according to ⟨por lo que dices : judging from what you're telling me⟩ **13** : as, for ⟨por ejemplo : for example⟩ **14** : by ⟨hecho por mi abuela : made by my grandmother⟩ ⟨por correo : by mail⟩ **15** : for, in order to ⟨lucha por ganar su respeto : he struggles to win her respect⟩ **16 estar por** : to be about to **17 por ciento** : percent **18 por favor** : please **19 por lo tanto** : therefore, consequently **20 ¿por qué?** : why? **21 por que → porque 22 por . . . que** : no matter how ⟨por mucho que intente : no matter how hard I try⟩ **23 por sí** *or* **por si acaso** : just in case

porcelana *nf* : china, porcelain

porcentaje *nm* : percentage

porche *nm* : porch

porción *nf, pl* **porciones 1** : portion **2** PARTE : part, share **3** RACIÓN : serving, helping

pordiosear *vi* MENDIGAR : beg

pordiosero, -ra *n* MENDIGO : beggar

porfiado, -da *adj* OBSTINADO, TERCO : obstinate, stubborn — **porfiadamente** *adv*

porfiar {85} *vi* : to insist, to persist

pormenor *nm* DETALLE : detail

pormenorizar {21} *vi* : to go into detail — *vt* : to tell in detail

pornografía *nf* : pornography

pornográfico, -ca *adj* : pornographic

poro *nm* : pore

poroso, -sa *adj* : porous — **porosidad** *nf*

poroto *nm Arg, Chile, Uru* : bean

porque *conj* **1** : because **2** *or* **por que** : in order that

porqué *nm* : reason, cause

porquería *nf* **1** SUCIEDAD : dirt, filth **2** : nastiness, vulgarity **3** : worthless thing, trifle **4** : junk food

porra *nf* **1** : nightstick, club **2** *Mex* : cheer, yell ⟨los aficionados le echaban porras : the fans cheered him on⟩

porrazo *nm* **1** : blow, whack **2 de golpe y porrazo** : suddenly

porrista *nmf* **1** : cheerleader **2** : fan, supporter

portaaviones *nms & pl* : aircraft carrier

portada *nf* **1** : title page **2** : cover **3** : facade, front

portador, -dora *n* : carrier, bearer

portafolio *or* **portafolios** *nm, pl* **-lios 1** MALETÍN : briefcase **2** : portfolio (of investments)

portal *nm* **1** : portal, doorway **2** VESTÍBULO : vestibule, hall

portar *vt* **1** : to carry, to bear **2** : to wear — **portarse** *vr* CONDUCIRSE : to behave ⟨pórtate bien : behave yourself⟩

portátil *adj* : portable

portaviandas *nms & pl* : lunch box

portaviones *nm →* **portaaviones**

portavoz *nmf, pl* **-voces** : spokesperson, spokesman *m*, spokeswoman *f*

portazo *nm* : slam (of a door)

porte *nm* **1** ASPECTO : bearing, demeanor **2** TRANSPORTE : transport, carrying ⟨porte pagado : postage paid⟩

portento *nm* MARAVILLA : marvel, wonder

portentoso, -sa *adj* MARAVILLOSO : marvelous, wonderful

porteño, -ña *adj* : of or from Buenos Aires

portería *nf* **1** ARCO : goal, goalposts *pl* **2** : superintendent's office

portero, -ra *n* **1** ARQUERO : goalkeeper, goalie **2** : doorman *m* **3** : janitor, superintendent

pórtico *nm* : portico

portilla *nf* : porthole

portón *nm, pl* **portones 1** : main door **2** : gate

portugués[1]**, -guesa** *adj & n, mpl* **-gueses** : Portuguese

portugués[2] *nm* : Portuguese (language)

porvenir *nm* FUTURO : future
pos *adv* **en pos de** : in pursuit of
posada *nf* **1** : inn **2** *Mex* : Advent celebration
posadero, -ra *n* : innkeeper
posar *vi* : to pose — *vt* : to place, to lay — **posarse** *vr* **1** : to land, to light, to perch **2** : to settle, to rest
posavasos *nms & pl* : coaster (for drinks)
posdata → postdata
pose *nf* : pose
poseedor, -dora *n* : possessor, holder
poseer {20} *vt* : to possess, to hold, to have
poseído, -da *adj* : possessed
posesión *nf, pl* **-siones** : possession
posesionarse *vr* ~ **de** : to take possession of, to take over
posesivo[1], **-va** *adj* : possessive
posesivo[2] *nm* : possessive case
posguerra *nf* : postwar period
posibilidad *nf* **1** : possibility **2 posibilidades** *nfpl* : means, income
posibilitar *vt* : to make possible, to permit
posible *adj* : possible — **posiblemente** *adv*
posición *nf, pl* **-ciones** **1** : position, place **2** : status, standing **3** : attitude, stance
posicionar *vt* **1** : to position, to place **2** : to establish — **posicionarse** *vr*
positivo[1], **-va** *adj* : positive
positivo[2] *nm* : print (in photography)
poso *nm* **1** : sediment, dregs *pl* **2** : grounds *pl* (of coffee)
posoperatorio, -ria *adj* : postoperative
posponer {60} *vt* **1** : to postpone **2** : to put behind, to subordinate
pospuso, etc. → posponer
posta *nf* : relay race
postal[1] *adj* : postal
postal[2] *nf* : postcard
postdata *nf* : postscript
poste *nm* : post, pole ⟨poste de teléfonos : telephone pole⟩
póster *or* **poster** *nm, pl* **pósters** *or* **posters** : poster, placard
postergación *nf, pl* **-ciones** : postponement, deferring
postergar {52} *vt* **1** : to delay, to postpone **2** : to pass over (an employee)
posteridad *nf* : posterity
posterior *adj* **1** ULTERIOR : later, subsequent **2** TRASERO : back, rear
postgrado *nm* : graduate course
postgraduado, -da *n* : graduate student, postgraduate
postigo *nm* **1** CONTRAVENTANA : shutter **2** : small door, wicket gate
postilla *nf* : scab
postizo, -za *adj* : artificial, false ⟨dentadura postiza : dentures⟩
postnatal *adj* : postnatal
postor, -tora *n* : bidder ⟨mejor postor : highest bidder⟩

postración *nf, pl* **-ciones** **1** : prostration **2** ABATIMIENTO : depression
postrado, -da *adj* **1** : prostrate **2 postrado en cama** : bedridden
potranco, -ca *n* → potro[1]
postrar *vt* DEBILITAR : to debilitate, to weaken — **postrarse** *vr* : to prostrate oneself
postre *nm* : dessert
postrero, -ra *adj* (**postrer** *before masculine singular nouns*) ÚLTIMO : last
postulación *nf, pl* **-ciones** **1** : collection **2** : nomination (of a candidate)
postulado *nm* : postulate, assumption
postulante, -ta *n* **1** : postulant **2** : candidate, applicant
postular *vt* **1** : to postulate **2** : to nominate **3** : to propose — **postularse** *vr* : to run, to be a candidate
póstumo, -ma *adj* : posthumous — **póstumamente** *adv*
postura *nf* **1** : posture, position (of the body) **2** ACTITUD, POSICIÓN : position, stance
potable *adj* : drinkable, potable
potaje *nm* : thick vegetable soup, pottage
potasa *nf* : potash
potasio *nm* : potassium
pote *nm* **1** OLLA : pot **2** : jar, container
potencia *nf* **1** : power ⟨potencias extranjeras : foreign powers⟩ ⟨elevado a la tercera potencia : raised to the third power⟩ **2** : capacity, potency
potencial *adj & nm* : potential
potenciar *vt* : to promote, to foster
potenciómetro *nm* : dimmer, dimmer switch
potentado, -da *n* **1** SOBERANO : potentate, sovereign **2** MAGNATE : tycoon, magnate
potente *adj* **1** : powerful, strong **2** : potent, virile
potestad *nf* **1** AUTORIDAD : authority, jurisdiction **2 patria potestad** : custody, guardianship
potrero *nm* **1** : field, pasture **2** : cattle ranch
potro[1], **-tra** *n* : colt *m*, filly *f*
potro[2] *nm* **1** : rack (for torture) **2** : horse (in gymnastics)
pozo *nm* **1** : well ⟨pozo de petróleo : oil well⟩ **2** : deep pool (in a river) **3** : mine shaft **4** *Arg, Par, Uru* : pothole **5 pozo séptico** : cesspool
pozole *nm Mex* : spicy stew made with pork and hominy
práctica *nf* **1** : practice, experience **2** EJERCICIO : exercising ⟨la práctica de la medicina : the practice of medicine⟩ **3** APLICACIÓN : application, practice ⟨poner en práctica : to put into practice⟩ **4 prácticas** *nfpl* : training
practicable *adj* : practicable, feasible
prácticamente *adv* : practically
practicante[1] *adj* : practicing ⟨católicos practicantes : practicing Catholics⟩

practicante² *nmf* : practicer, practitioner

practicar {72} *vt* **1** : to practice **2** : to perform, to carry out **3** : to exercise (a profession) — *vi* : to practice

práctico, -ca *adj* : practical, useful

pradera *nf* : grassland, prairie

prado *nm* **1** CAMPO : field, meadow **2** : park

pragmático, -ca *adj* : pragmatic — **pragmáticamente** *adv*

pragmatismo *nm* : pragmatism

preámbulo *nm* **1** INTRODUCCIÓN : preamble, introduction **2** RODEO : evasion ⟨gastar preámbulos : to beat around the bush⟩

prebélico, -ca *adj* : antebellum

prebenda *nf* : privilege, perquisite

precalentar {55} *vt* : to preheat

precariedad *nf* : precariousness

precario, -ria *adj* : precarious — **precariamente** *adv*

precaución *nf*, *pl* **-ciones 1** : precaution ⟨medidas de precaución : precautionary measures⟩ **2** PRUDENCIA : caution, care ⟨con precaución : cautiously⟩

precautorio, -ria *adj* : precautionary

precaver *vt* PREVENIR : to prevent, to guard against — **precaverse** *vr* PREVENIRSE : to take precautions, to be on guard

precavido, -da *adj* CAUTELOSO : cautious, prudent

precedencia *nf* : precedence, priority

precedente¹ *adj* : preceding, previous

precedente² *nm* : precedent

preceder *v* : to precede

precepto *nm* : rule, precept

preciado, -da *adj* : esteemed, prized, valuable

preciarse *vr* **1** JACTARSE : to boast, to brag **2** ~ **de** : to pride oneself on

precinto *nm* : seal

precio *nm* **1** : price **2** : cost, sacrifice ⟨a cualquier precio : whatever the cost⟩

preciosidad *nf* : beautiful thing ⟨este vestido es una preciosidad : this dress is lovely⟩

precioso, -sa *adj* **1** HERMOSO : beautiful, exquisite **2** VALIOSO : precious, valuable

precipicio *nm* **1** : precipice **2** RUINA : ruin

precipitación *nf*, *pl* **-ciones 1** PRISA : haste, hurry, rush **2** : precipitation, rain, snow

precipitado, -da *adj* **1** : hasty, sudden **2** : rash — **precipitadamente** *adv*

precipitar *vt* **1** APRESURAR : to hasten, to speed up **2** ARROJAR : to hurl, to throw — **precipitarse** *vr* **1** APRESURARSE : to rush **2** : to act rashly **3** ARROJARSE : to throw oneself

precisamente *adv* JUSTAMENTE : precisely, exactly

precisar *vt* **1** : to specify, to determine exactly **2** NECESITAR : to need, to require — *vi* : to be necessary

precisión *nf*, *pl* **-siones 1** EXACTITUD : precision, accuracy **2** CLARIDAD : clarity (of style, etc.) **3** NECESIDAD : necessity ⟨tener precisión de : to have need of⟩

preciso, -sa *adj* **1** EXACTO : precise **2** : very, exact ⟨en ese preciso instante : at that very instant⟩ **3** NECESARIO : necessary

precocidad *nf* : precocity

precocinar *vt* : to precook

preconcebir {54} *vt* : to preconceive

precondición *nf*, *pl* **-ciones** : precondition

preconizar {21} *vt* **1** : to recommend, to advocate **2** : to extol

precoz *adj*, *pl* **precoces 1** : precocious **2** : early, premature — **precozmente** *adv*

precursor, -sora *n* : forerunner, precursor

predecesor, -sora *n* ANTECESOR : predecessor

predecir {11} *vt* : to foretell, to predict

predestinado, -da *adj* : predestined, fated

predestinar *vt* : to predestine — **predestinación** *nf*

predeterminar *vt* : to predetermine

prédica *nf* SERMÓN : sermon

predicado *nm* : predicate

predicador, -dora *n* : preacher

predicar {72} *v* : to preach

predicción *nf*, *pl* **-ciones 1** : prediction **2** PRONÓSTICO : forecast ⟨predicción del tiempo : weather forecast⟩

prediga, predijo etc. → **predecir**

predilección *nf*, *pl* **-ciones** : predilection, preference

predilecto, -ta *adj* : favorite

predio *nm* : property, piece of land

predisponer {60} *vt* **1** : to predispose, to incline **2** : to prejudice, to bias

predisposición *nf*, *pl* **-ciones 1** : predisposition, tendency **2** : prejudice, bias

predominante *adj* : predominant — **predominantemente** *adv*

predominar *vi* PREVALECER : to predominate, to prevail

predominio *nm* : predominance, prevalence

preeminente *adj* : preeminent — **preeminencia** *nf*

preescolar *adj* & *nm* : preschool

preestreno *nm* : preview

prefabricado, -da *adj* : prefabricated

prefacio *nm* : preface

prefecto *nm* : prefect

preferencia *nf* **1** : preference **2** PRIORIDAD : priority **3 de** ~ : preferably

preferencial *adj* : preferential

preferente *adj* : preferential, special ⟨trato preferente : special treatment⟩

preferentemente *adv* : preferably

preferible *adj* : preferable
preferido, -da *adj & n* : favorite
preferir {76} *vt* : to prefer
prefigurar *vt* : foreshadow, prefigure
prefijo *nm* : prefix
pregonar *vt* **1** : to proclaim, to announce **2** : to hawk (merchandise) **3** : to extol **4** : to reveal, to disclose
pregunta *nf* **1** : question **2 hacer una pregunta** : to ask a question
preguntar *vt* : to ask, to question — *vi* : to ask, to inquire — **preguntarse** *vr* : to wonder
preguntón, -tona *adj, mpl* **-tones** : inquisitive
prehistórico, -ca *adj* : prehistoric
prejuiciado, -da *adj* : prejudiced
prejuicio *nm* : prejudice
prejuzgar {52} *vt* : to prejudge
prelado *nm* : prelate
preliminar *adj & nm* : preliminary
preludio *nm* : prelude
prematrimonial *adj* : premarital
prematuro, -ra *adj* : premature
premeditación *nf, pl* **-ciones** : premeditation
premeditar *vt* : to premeditate, to plan
premenstrual *adj* : premenstrual
premiado, -da *adj* : winning, prizewinning
premiar *vt* **1** : to award a prize to **2** : to reward
premier *nmf* : premier, prime minister
premio *nm* **1** : prize ⟨premio gordo : grand prize, jackpot⟩ **2** : reward **3** : premium
premisa *nf* : premise, basis
premolar *nm* : bicuspid (tooth)
premonición *nf, pl* **-ciones** : premonition
premura *nf* : haste, urgency
prenatal *adj* : prenatal
prenda *nf* **1** : piece of clothing **2** : security, pledge
prendar *vt* **1** : to charm, to captivate **2** : to pawn, to pledge — **prendarse** *vr* **~ de** : to fall in love with
prendedor *nm* : brooch, pin
prender *vt* **1** SUJETAR : to pin, to fasten **2** APRESAR : to catch, to apprehend **3** : to light (a cigarette, a match) **4** : to turn on ⟨prende la luz : turn on the light⟩ **5 prender fuego a** : to set fire to — *vi* **1** : to take root **2** : to catch fire **3** : to catch on
prensa *nf* **1** : printing press **2** : press ⟨conferencia de prensa : press conference⟩
prensar *vt* : to press
prensil *adj* : prehensile
preñado, -da *adj* **1** : pregnant **2 ~ de** : filled with
preñar *vt* EMBARAZAR : to make pregnant
preñez *nf, pl* **preñeces** : pregnancy
preocupación *nf, pl* **-ciones** INQUIETUD : worry, concern
preocupante *adj* : worrisome

preocupar *vt* INQUIETAR : to worry, to concern — **preocuparse** *vr* APURARSE : to worry, to be concerned
preparación *nf, pl* **-ciones** **1** : preparation, readiness **2** : education, training **3** : (medicinal) preparation
preparado¹, -da *adj* **1** : ready, prepared **2** : trained
preparado² *nm* : preparation, mixture
preparar *vt* **1** : to prepare, to make ready **2** : to teach, to train, to coach — **prepararse** *vr*
preparativos *nmpl* : preparations
preparatoria *nf Mex* : high school
preparatoria, -ria *adj* : preparatory
preponderante *adj* : preponderant, predominant — **preponderancia** *nf* — **preponderantemente** *adv*
preposición *nf, pl* **-ciones** : preposition — **preposicional** *adj*
prepotente *adj* : arrogant, domineering, overbearing — **prepotencia** *nf*
prerrogativa *nf* : prerogative, privilege
presa *nf* **1** : capture, seizure ⟨hacer presa de : to seize⟩ **2** : catch, prey ⟨presa de : prey to, seized with⟩ **3** : claw, fang **4** DIQUE : dam **5** : morsel, piece (of food)
presagiar *vt* : to presage, to portend
presagio *nm* : omen, portent
presbiterio *nm* : presbytery, sanctuary (of a church)
presbítero *nm* : presbyter
presciencia *nf* : prescience
prescindible *adj* : expendable, dispensable
prescindir *vi* **1** **~ de** : to do without, to dispense with **2** DESATENDER : to ignore, to disregard **3** OMITIR : to omit, to skip
prescribir {33} *vt* : to prescribe
prescripción *nf, pl* **-ciones** : prescription
prescrito *pp* → **prescribir**
presencia *nf* **1** : presence **2** ASPECTO : appearance
presenciar *vt* : to be present at, to witness
presentable *adj* : presentable
presentación *nf, pl* **-ciones** **1** : presentation **2** : introduction **3** : appearance
presentador, -dora *n* : newscaster, anchorman *m*, anchorwoman *f*
presentar *vt* **1** : to present, to show **2** : to offer, to give **3** : to submit (a document), to launch (a product) **4** : to introduce (a person) — **presentarse** *vr* **1** : to show up, to appear **2** : to arise, to come up **3** : to introduce oneself
presente¹ *adj* **1** : present, in attendance **2** : present, current **3 tener presente** : to keep in mind
presente² *nm* **1** : present (time, tense) **2** : one present ⟨entre los presentes se encontraban ... : those present included ... ⟩
presentimiento *nm* : premonition, hunch, feeling

presentir · primicia

presentir {76} *vt* : to sense, to intuit ⟨presentía lo que iba a pasar : he sensed what was going to happen⟩
preservación *nf, pl* **-ciones** : preservation
preservar *vt* **1** : to preserve **2** : to protect
preservativo *nm* CONDÓN : condom
presidencia *nf* **1** : presidency **2** : chairmanship
presidencial *adj* : presidential
presidente, -ta *n* **1** : president **2** : chair, chairperson **3** : presiding judge
presidiario, -ria *n* : convict, prisoner
presidio *nm* : prison, penitentiary
presidir *vt* **1** MODERAR : to preside over, to chair **2** : to dominate, to rule over
presilla *nf* : eye, loop, fastener
presión *nf, pl* **presiones 1** : pressure **2 presión arterial** : blood pressure
presionar *vt* **1** : to pressure **2** : to press, to push — *vi* : to put on the pressure
preso¹, -sa *adj* : imprisoned
preso², -sa *n* : prisoner
prestado, -da *adj* **1** : borrowed, on loan **2 pedir prestado** : to borrow
prestamista *nmf* : moneylender, pawnbroker
préstamo *nm* : loan
prestar *vt* **1** : to lend, to loan **2** : to render (a service), to give (aid) **3 prestar atención** : to pay attention **4 prestar juramento** : to take an oath — **prestarse** *vr* : to lend oneself ⟨se presta a confusiones : it lends itself to confusion⟩
prestatario, -ria *n* : borrower
presteza *nf* : promptness, speed
prestidigitación *nf, pl* **-ciones** : sleight of hand, prestidigitation
prestidigitador, -dora *n* : conjurer, magician
prestigio *nm* : prestige — **prestigioso, -sa** *adj*
presto¹ *adv* : promptly, at once
presto², -ta *adj* **1** : quick, prompt **2** DISPUESTO, PREPARADO : ready
presumido, -da *adj* VANIDOSO : conceited, vain
presumir *vt* SUPONER : to presume, to suppose — *vi* **1** ALARDEAR : to boast, to show off **2 ~ de** : to consider oneself ⟨presume de inteligente : he thinks he's intelligent⟩
presunción *nf, pl* **-ciones 1** SUPOSICIÓN : presumption, supposition **2** VANIDAD : conceit, vanity
presunto, -ta *adj* : presumed, supposed, alleged — **presuntamente** *adv*
presuntuoso, -sa *adj* : conceited
presuponer {60} *vt* : to presuppose
presupuestal *adj* : budget, budgetary
presupuestar *vi* : to budget — *vt* : to budget for
presupuestario, -ria *adj* : budget, budgetary
presupuesto *nm* **1** : budget, estimate **2** : assumption, supposition

presurizar {21} *vt* : to pressurize
presuroso, -sa *adj* : hasty, quick
pretencioso, -sa *adj* : pretentious
pretender *vt* **1** INTENTAR : to attempt, to try ⟨pretendo estudiar : I'm trying to study⟩ **2** AFIRMAR : to claim ⟨pretende ser pobre : he claims he's poor⟩ **3** : to seek, to aspire to ⟨¿qué pretendes tú? : what are you after?⟩ **4** CORTEJAR : to court **5 pretender que** : to expect ⟨¿pretendes que lo crea? : do you expect me to believe you?⟩
pretendiente¹ *nmf* **1** : candidate, applicant **2** : pretender, claimant (to a throne, etc.)
pretendiente² *nm* : suitor
pretensión *nf, pl* **-siones 1** : intention, hope, plan **2** : pretension ⟨sin pretensiones : unpretentious⟩
pretexto *nm* EXCUSA : pretext, excuse
pretil *nm* : parapet, railing
prevalecer {53} *vi* : to prevail, to triumph
prevaleciente *adj* : prevailing, prevalent
prevalerse {84} *vr* **~ de** : to avail oneself of, to take advantage of
prevención *nf, pl* **-ciones 1** : prevention **2** : preparation, readiness **3** : precautionary measure **4** : prejudice, bias
prevenido, -da *adj* **1** PREPARADO : prepared, ready **2** ADVERTIDO : forewarned **3** CAUTELOSO : cautious
prevenir {87} *vt* **1** : to prevent **2** : to warn — **prevenirse** *vr* **~ contra** *or* **~ de** : to take precautions against
preventivo, -va *adj* : preventive, precautionary
prever {88} *vt* ANTICIPAR : to foresee, to anticipate
previo, -via *adj* **1** : previous, prior **2** : after, upon ⟨previo pago : after paying, upon payment⟩
previsible *adj* : foreseeable
previsión *nf, pl* **-siones 1** : foresight **2** : prediction, forecast **3** : precaution
previsor, -sora *adj* : farsighted, prudent
prieto, -ta *adj* **1** : blackish, dark **2** : dark-skinned, swarthy **3** : tight, compressed
prima *nf* **1** : premium **2** : bonus **3** → **primo**
primacía *nf* **1** : precedence, priority **2** : superiority, supremacy
primado *nm* : primate (bishop)
primario, -ria *adj* : primary
primate *nm* : primate
primavera *nf* **1** : spring (season) **2** PRÍMULA : primrose
primaveral *adj* : spring, springlike
primero¹ *adv* **1** : first **2** : rather, sooner
primero², -ra *adj* (**primer** *before masculine singular nouns*) **1** : first **2** : top, leading **3** : fundamental, basic **4 de primera** : first-rate
primero³, -ra *n* : first
primicia *nf* **1** : first fruits **2** : scoop, exclusive

primigenio, -nia *adj* : original, primary
primitivo, -va *adj* **1** : primitive **2** ORIGINAL : original
primo, -ma *n* : cousin
primogénito, -ta *adj & n* : firstborn
primor *nm* **1** : skill, care **2** : beauty, elegance
primordial *adj* **1** : primordial **2** : basic, fundamental
primoroso, -sa *adj* **1** : exquisite, fine, delicate **2** : skillful
prímula *nf* : primrose
princesa *nf* : princess
principado *nm* : principality
principal[1] *adj* **1** : main, principal **2** : foremost, leading
principal[2] *nm* : capital, principal
príncipe *nm* : prince
principesco, -ca *adj* : princely
principiante[1] *adj* : beginning
principiante[2] *nmf* : beginner, novice
principiar *vt* EMPEZAR : to begin
principio *nm* **1** COMIENZO : beginning **2** : principle **3 al principio** : at first **4 a principios de** : at the beginning of ⟨a principios de agosto : at the beginning of August⟩ **5 en ~** : in principle
pringar {52} *vt* **1** : to dip (in grease) **2** : to soil, to spatter (with grease) — **pringarse** *vr*
pringoso, -sa *adj* : greasy
pringue[1], etc. → pringar
pringue[2] *nm* : grease, drippings *pl*
prior, priora *n* : prior *m*, prioress *f*
priorato *nm* : priory
prioridad *nf* : priority, precedence
prisa *nf* **1** : hurry, rush **2 a ~** *or* **de ~** : quickly, fast **3 a toda prisa** : as fast as possible **4 darse prisa** : to hurry **5 tener prisa** : to be in a hurry
prisión *nf, pl* **prisiones 1** CÁRCEL : prison, jail **2** ENCARCELAMIENTO : imprisonment
prisionero, -ra *n* : prisoner
prisma *nm* : prism
prismáticos *nmpl* : binoculars
prístino, -na *adj* : pristine
privacidad *nf* : privacy
privación *nf, pl* **-ciones 1** : deprivation **2** : privation, want
privado, -da *adj* : private — **privadamente** *adv*
privar *vt* **1** DESPOJAR : to deprive **2** : to stun, to knock out — **privarse** *vr* : to deprive oneself
privativo, -va *adj* : exclusive, particular
privilegiado, -da *adj* : privileged
privilegiar *vt* : to grant a privilege to, to favor
privilegio *nm* : privilege
pro[1] *nm* **1** : pro, advantage ⟨los pros y contras : the pros and cons⟩ **2 en pro de** : for, in favor of
pro[2] *prep* : for, in favor of ⟨grupos pro derechos humanos : groups supporting human rights⟩
proa *nf* : bow, prow
probabilidad *nf* : probability

probable *adj* : probable, likely
probablemente *adv* : probably
probar {19} *vt* **1** : to demonstrate, to prove **2** : to test, to try out **3** : to try on (clothing) **4** : to taste, to sample — *vi* : to try — **probarse** *vr* : to try on (clothing)
probeta *nf* : test tube
probidad *nf* : probity
problema *nm* : problem
problemática *nf* : set of problems ⟨la problemática que debemos enfrentar : the problems we must face⟩
probóscide *nf* : proboscis
problemático, -ca *adj* : problematic
procaz *adj, pl* **procaces 1** : insolent, impudent **2** : indecent
procedencia *nf* : origin, source
procedente *adj* **1** : proper, fitting **2 ~ de** : coming from
proceder *vi* **1** AVANZAR : to proceed **2** : to act, to behave **3** : to be appropriate, to be fitting **4 ~ de** : to originate from, to come from
procedimiento *nm* : procedure, process
prócer *nmf* : eminent person, leader
procesado, -da *n* : accused, defendant
procesador *nm* : processor ⟨procesador de textos : word processor⟩
procesamiento *nm* : processing ⟨procesamiento de datos : data processing⟩
procesar *vt* **1** : to prosecute, to try **2** : to process
procesión *nf, pl* **-siones** : procession
proceso *nm* **1** : process **2** : trial, proceedings *pl*
proclama *nf* : proclamation
proclamación *nf, pl* **-ciones** : proclamation
proclamar *vt* : to proclaim — **proclamarse** *vr*
proclive *adj* **~ a** : inclined to, prone to
proclividad *nf* : proclivity, inclination
procrear *vi* : to procreate — **procreación** *nf*
procurador, -dora *n* ABOGADO : attorney
procurar *vt* **1** INTENTAR : to try, to endeavor **2** CONSEGUIR : to obtain, to procure **3 procurar hacer** : to manage to do
prodigar {52} *vt* : to lavish, to be generous with
prodigio *nm* : wonder, marvel
prodigioso, -sa *adj* : prodigious, marvelous
pródigo[1], **-ga** *adj* **1** : generous, lavish **2** : wasteful, prodigal
pródigo[2], **-ga** *n* : spendthrift, prodigal
producción *nf, pl* **-ciones 1** : production **2 producción en serie** : mass production
producir {61} *vt* **1** : to produce, to make, to manufacture **2** : to cause, to bring about **3** : to bear (interest) — **producirse** *vr* : to take place, to occur
productividad *nf* : productivity
productivo, -va *adj* **1** : productive **2** LUCRATIVO : profitable

producto *nm* **1** : product **2** : proceeds *pl*, yield
productor, -tora *n* : producer
proeza *nf* HAZAÑA : feat, exploit
profanar *vt* : to profane, to desecrate — **profanación** *nf*
profano¹, -na *adj* **1** : profane **2** : worldly, secular
profano², -na *n* : nonspecialist
profecía *nf* : prophecy
proferir {76} *vt* **1** : to utter **2** : to hurl (insults)
profesar *vt* **1** : to profess, to declare **2** : to practice, to exercise
profesión *nf, pl* **-siones** : profession
profesional *adj & nmf* : professional — **profesionalmente** *adv*
profesionalismo *nm* : professionalism
profesionalizar {21} *vt* : to professionalize
profesionista *nmf Mex* : professional
profesor, -sora *n* **1** MAESTRO : teacher **2** : professor
profesorado *nm* **1** : faculty **2** : teaching profession
profeta *nm* : prophet
profético, -ca *adj* : prophetic
profetisa *nf* : prophetess, prophet
profetizar {21} *vt* : to prophesy
prófugo, -ga *adj & n* : fugitive
profundidad *nf* : depth, profundity
profundizar {21} *vt* **1** : to deepen **2** : to study in depth — *vi* ～ **en** : to go deeply into, to study in depth
profundo, -da *adj* **1** HONDO : deep **2** : profound — **profundamente** *adv*
profusión *nf, pl* **-siones** : abundance, profusion
profuso, -sa *adj* : profuse, abundant, extensive
progenie *nf* : progeny, offspring
progenitor, -tora *n* ANTEPASADO : ancestor, progenitor
progesterona *nf* : progesterone
prognóstico *nm* : prognosis
programa *nm* **1** : program **2** : plan **3** **programa de estudios** : curriculum
programable *adj* : programmable
programación *nf, pl* **-ciones** **1** : programming **2** : planning
programador, -dora *n* : programmer
programar *vt* **1** : to schedule, to plan **2** : to program (a computer, etc.)
progresar *vi* : to progress, to make progress
progresista *adj & nmf* : progressive
progresivo, -va *adj* : progressive, gradual
progreso *nm* : progress
prohibición *nf, pl* **-ciones** : ban, prohibition
prohibir {62} *vt* : to prohibit, to ban, to forbid
prohibitivo, -va *adj* : prohibitive
prohijar {5} *vt* ADOPTAR : to adopt
prójimo *nm* : neighbor, fellow man
prole *nf* : offspring, progeny
proletariado *nm* : proletariat, working class

proletario, -ria *adj & n* : proletarian
proliferar *vi* : to proliferate — **proliferación** *nf*
prolífico, -ca *adj* : prolific
prolijo, -ja *adj* : wordy, long-winded
prólogo *nm* : prologue, preface, foreword
prolongación *nf, pl* **-ciones** : extension, lengthening
prolongar {52} *vt* **1** : to prolong **2** : to extend, to lengthen — **prolongarse** *vr* CONTINUAR : to last, to continue
promediar *vt* **1** : to average **2** : to divide in half — *vi* : to be half over
promedio *nm* **1** : average **2** : middle, midpoint
promesa *nf* : promise
prometedor, -dora *adj* : promising, hopeful
prometer *vt* : to promise — *vi* : to show promise — **prometerse** *vr* COMPROMETERSE : to get engaged
prometido¹, -da *adj* : engaged
prometido², -da *n* NOVIO : fiancé *m*, fiancée *f*
prominente *adj* : prominent — **prominencia** *nf*
promiscuo, -cua *adj* : promiscuous — **promiscuidad** *nf*
promisorio, -ria *adj* **1** : promising **2** : promissory
promoción *nf, pl* **-ciones** **1** : promotion **2** : class, year **3** : play-off (in soccer)
promocionar *vt* : to promote — **promocional** *adj*
promontorio *nm* : promontory, headland
promotor, -tora *n* : promoter
promover {47} *vt* **1** : to promote, to advance **2** FOMENTAR : to foster, to encourage **3** PROVOCAR : to provoke, to cause
promulgación *nf, pl* **-ciones** **1** : enactment **2** : proclamation, enactment
promulgar {52} *vt* **1** : to promulgate, to proclaim **2** : to enact (a law or decree)
prono, -na *adj* : prone
pronombre *nm* : pronoun
pronosticar {72} *vt* : to predict, to forecast
pronóstico *nm* **1** PREDICCIÓN : forecast, prediction **2** : prognosis
prontitud *nf* **1** PRESTEZA : promptness, speed **2** **con** ～ : promptly, quickly
pronto¹ *adv* **1** : quickly, promptly **2** : soon **3 de** ～ : suddenly **4 lo más pronto posible** : as soon as possible **5 tan pronto como** : as soon as
pronto², -ta *adj* **1** RÁPIDO : quick, speedy, prompt **2** PREPARADO : ready
pronunciación *nf, pl* **-ciones** : pronunciation
pronunciado, -da *adj* **1** : pronounced, sharp, steep **2** : marked, noticeable
pronunciamiento *nm* **1** : pronouncement **2** : military uprising
pronunciar *vt* **1** : to pronounce, to say **2** : to give, to deliver (a speech) **3 pro-**

nunciar un fallo : to pronounce sentence — **pronunciarse** *vr* : to declare oneself

propagación *nf, pl* **-ciones** : propagation, spreading

propaganda *nf* **1** : propaganda **2** PUBLICIDAD : advertising

propagar {52} *vt* **1** : to propagate **2** : to spread, to disseminate — **propagarse** *vr*

propalar *vt* **1** : to divulge **2** : to spread

propano *nm* : propane

propasarse *vr* : to go too far, to overstep one's bounds

propensión *nf, pl* **-siones** INCLINACIÓN : inclination, propensity

propenso, -sa *adj* : prone, susceptible

propiamente *adv* **1** : properly, correctly **2** : exactly, precisely ⟨propiamente dicho : strictly speaking⟩

propiciar *vt* **1** : to propitiate **2** : to favor, to foster

propicio, -cia *adj* : favorable, propitious

propiedad *nf* **1** : property ⟨propiedad privada : private property⟩ **2** : ownership **3** CUALIDAD : property, quality **4** : suitability, appropriateness

propietario¹, -ria *adj* : proprietary

propietario², -ria *n* DUEÑO : owner, proprietor

propina *nf* : tip, gratuity

propinar *vt* : to give, to strike ⟨propinar una paliza : to give a beating⟩

propio, -pia *adj* **1** : own ⟨su propia casa : his own house⟩ ⟨sus recursos propios : their own resources⟩ **2** APROPIADO : appropriate, suitable **3** CARACTERÍSTICO : characteristic, typical **4** MISMO : oneself ⟨el propio director : the director himself⟩

proponer {60} *vt* **1** : to propose, to suggest **2** : to nominate — **proponerse** *vr* : to intend, to plan, to set out ⟨lo que se propone lo cumple : he does what he sets out to do⟩

proporción *nf, pl* **-ciones** **1** : proportion **2** : ratio (in mathematics) **3** **proporciones** *nfpl* : proportions, size ⟨de grandes proporciones : very large⟩

proporcionado, -da *adj* **1** : proportionate **2** : proportioned ⟨bien proporcionado : well-proportioned⟩ — **proporcionadamente** *adv*

proporcional *adj* : proportional — **proporcionalmente** *adv*

proporcionar *vt* **1** : to provide, to give **2** : to proportion, to adapt

proposición *nf, pl* **-ciones** : proposal, proposition

propósito *nm* **1** INTENCIÓN : purpose, intention **2 a ~** : by the way **3 a ~** : on purpose, intentionally

propuesta *nf* PROPOSICIÓN : proposal

propulsar *vt* **1** IMPULSAR : to propel, to drive **2** PROMOVER : to promote, to encourage

propulsión *nf, pl* **-siones** : propulsion

propulsor *nm* : propellant

propuso, etc. → **proponer**

prorrata *nf* **1** : share, quota **2 a ~** : pro rata, proportionately

prórroga *nf* **1** : extension, deferment **2** : overtime (in sports)

prorrogar {52} *vt* **1** : to extend (a deadline) **2** : to postpone

prorrumpir *vi* : to burst forth, to break out ⟨prorrumpí en lágrimas : I burst into tears⟩

prosa *nf* : prose

prosaico, -ca *adj* : prosaic, mundane

proscribir {33} *v* **1** PROHIBIR : to prohibit, to ban, to proscribe **2** DESTERRAR : to banish, to exile

proscripción *nf, pl* **-ciones** **1** PROHIBICIÓN : ban, proscription **2** DESTIERRO : banishment

proscrito¹ *pp* → **proscribir**

proscrito², -ta *n* **1** DESTERRADO : exile **2** : outlaw

prosecución *nf, pl* **-ciones** **1** : continuation **2** : pursuit

proseguir {75} *vt* **1** CONTINUAR : to continue **2** : to pursue (studies, goals) — *vi* : to continue, to go on

prosélito, -ta *n* : proselyte

prospección *nf, pl* **-ciones** : prospecting, exploration

prospectar *vi* : to prospect

prospecto *nm* : prospectus, leaflet, brochure

prosperar *vi* : to prosper, to thrive

prosperidad *nf* : prosperity

próspero, -ra *adj* : prosperous, flourishing

próstata *nf* : prostate

prostitución *nf, pl* **-ciones** : prostitution

prostituir {41} *vt* : to prostitute — **prostituirse** *vr* : to prostitute oneself

prostituto, -ta *n* : prostitute

protagonista *nmf* **1** : protagonist, main character **2** : leader

protagonizar {21} *vt* : to star in

protección *nf, pl* **-ciones** : protection

protector¹, -tora *adj* : protective

protector², -tora *n* **1** : protector, guardian **2** : patron

protector³ *nm* : protector, guard ⟨chaleco protector : chest protector⟩

protectorado *nm* : protectorate

proteger {15} *vt* : to protect, to defend — **protegerse** *vr*

protegido, -da *n* : protégé

proteína *nf* : protein

prótesis *nfs & pl* : prosthesis

protesta *nf* **1** : protest **2** *Mex* : promise, oath

protestante *adj & nmf* : Protestant

protestantismo *nm* : Protestantism

protestar *vi* : to protest, to object — *vt* **1** : to protest, to object to **2** : to declare, to profess

protocolo *nm* : protocol

protón *nm, pl* **protones** : proton

protoplasma *nm* : protoplasm

prototipo *nm* : prototype

protozoario *or* **protozoo** *nm* : protozoan

protuberancia *nf* : protuberance — **pro-tuberante** *adj*

provecho *nm* : benefit, advantage

provechoso, -sa *adj* BENEFICIOSO : beneficial, profitable, useful — **provechosamente** *adv*

proveedor, -dora *n* : provider, supplier

proveer {63} *vt* : to provide, to supply — **proveerse** *vr* ~ **de** : to obtain, to supply oneself with

provenir {87} *vi* ~ **de** : to come from

provenzal¹ *adj* : Provençal

provenzal² *nmf* : Provençal

provenzal³ *nm* : Provençal (language)

proverbio *nm* REFRÁN : proverb — **proverbial** *adj*

providencia *nf* **1** : providence, foresight **2** : Providence, God **3 providencias** *nfpl* : steps, measures

providencial *adj* : providential

provincia *nf* : province — **provincial** *adj*

provinciano, -na *adj* : provincial, unsophisticated

provisión *nf, pl* **-siones** : provision

provisional *adj* : provisional, temporary

provisionalmente *adv* : provisionally, tentatively

provisorio, -ria *adj* : provisional, temporary

provisto *pp* → **proveer**

provocación *nf, pl* **-ciones** : provocation

provocador¹, -dora *adj* : provocative, provoking

provocador², -dora *n* AGITADOR : agitator

provocar {72} *vt* **1** CAUSAR : to provoke, to cause **2** IRRITAR : to provoke, to pique

provocativo, -va *adj* : provocative

proxeneta *nmf* : pimp *m*

próximamente *adv* : shortly, soon

proximidad *nf* **1** : nearness, proximity **2 proximidades** *nfpl* : vicinity

próximo, -ma *adj* **1** : near, close ⟨la Navidad está próxima : Christmas is almost here⟩ **2** SIGUIENTE : next, following ⟨la próxima semana : the following week⟩

proyección *nf, pl* **-ciones 1** : projection **2** : showing, screening (of a film) **3** : range, influence, diffusion

proyectar *vt* **1** : to plan **2** LANZAR : to throw, to hurl **3** : to project, to cast (light or shadow) **4** : to show, to screen (a film)

proyectil *nm* : projectile, missile

proyecto *nm* **1** : plan, project **2 proyecto de ley** : bill

proyector *nm* **1** : projector **2** : spotlight

prudencia *nf* : prudence, care, discretion

prudente *adj* : prudent, sensible, reasonable

prueba¹, etc. → **probar**

prueba² *nf* **1** : proof, evidence **2** : trial, test **3** : proof (in printing or photography) **4** : event, qualifying round (in sports) **5 a prueba de agua** : waterproof **6 prueba de fuego** : acid test **7 poner a prueba** : to put to the test

prurito *nm* **1** : itching **2** : desire, urge

psicoanálisis *nm* : psychoanalysis — **psicoanalista** *nmf*

psicoanalítico, -ca *adj* : psychoanalytic

psicoanalizar {21} *vt* : to psychoanalyze

psicología *nf* : psychology

psicológico, -ca *adj* : psychological — **psicológicamente** *adv*

psicólogo, -ga *n* : psychologist

psicópata *nmf* : psychopath

psicopático, -ca *adj* : psycopathic

psicosis *nfs & pl* : psychosis

psicosomático, -ca *adj* : psychosomatic

psicoterapeuta *nmf* : psychotherapist

psicoterapia *nf* : psychotherapy

psicótico, -ca *adj & n* : psychotic

psique *nf* : psyche

psiquiatra *nmf* : psychiatrist

psiquiatría *nf* : psychiatry

psiquiátrico¹, -ca *adj* : psychiatric

psiquiátrico² *nm* : mental hospital

psíquico, -ca *adj* : psychic

psiquis *nfs & pl* : psyche

psoriasis *nf* : psoriasis

ptomaína *nf* : ptomaine

púa *nf* **1** : barb ⟨alambre de púas : barbed wire⟩ **2** : tooth (of a comb) **3** : quill, spine

pubertad *nf* : puberty

pubiano → **púbico**

púbico, -ca *adj* : pubic

publicación *nf, pl* **-ciones** : publication

publicar {72} *vt* **1** : to publish **2** DIVULGAR : to divulge, to disclose

publicidad *nf* **1** : publicity **2** : advertising

publicista *nmf* : publicist

publicitar *vt* **1** : to publicize **2** : to advertise

publicitario, -ria *adj* : advertising, publicity ⟨agencia publicitaria : advertising agency⟩

público¹, -ca *adj* : public — **públicamente** *adv*

público² *nm* **1** : public **2** : audience, spectators *pl*

puchero *nm* **1** : pot **2** : stew **3** : pout ⟨hacer pucheros : to pout⟩

pucho *nm* **1** : waste, residue **2** : cigarette butt **3 a puchos** : little by little, bit by bit

púdico, -ca *adj* : chaste, modest

pudiente *adj* **1** : powerful **2** : rich, wealthy

pudín *nm, pl* **pudines** BUDÍN : pudding

pudo, etc. → **poder**

pudor *nm* : modesty, reserve

pudoroso, -sa *adj* : modest, reserved, shy

pudrir {59} *vt* **1** : to rot **2** *fam* : to annoy, to upset — **pudrirse** *vr* **1** : to rot **2** : to languish

pueblerino, -na *adj* : provincial, countrified

puebla, etc. → **poblar**
pueblo *nm* **1** NACIÓN : people **2** : common people **3** ALDEA, POBLADO : town, village
puede, etc. → **poder**
puente *nm* **1** : bridge ⟨puente levadizo : drawbridge⟩ **2** : denture, bridge **3 puente aéreo** : airlift
puerco[1], **-ca** *adj* : dirty, filthy
puerco[2], **-ca** *n* **1** CERDO, MARRANO : pig, hog **2** : pig, dirty or greedy person **3 puerco espín** : porcupine
pueril *adj* : childish, puerile
puerro *nm* : leek
puerta *nf* **1** : door, entrance, gate **2 a puerta cerrada** : behind closed doors
puerto *nm* **1** : port, harbor **2** : mountain pass **3 puerto marítimo** : seaport
puertorriqueño, -ña *adj & n* : Puerto Rican
pues *conj* **1** : since, because, for ⟨no puedo ir, pues no tengo plata : I can't go, since I don't have any money⟩ ⟨lo hace, pues a él le gusta : he does it because he likes to⟩ **2** (*used interjectionally*) : well, then ⟨¡pues claro que sí! : well, of course!⟩ ⟨¡pues no voy! : well then, I'm not going!⟩
puesta *nf* **1** : setting ⟨puesta del sol : sunset⟩ **2** : laying (of eggs) **3 puesta a punto** : tune-up **4 puesta en marcha** : start, starting up
puestero, -ra *n* : seller, vendor
puesto[1] *pp* → **poner**
puesto[2], **-ta** *adj* : dressed ⟨bien puesto : well-dressed⟩
puesto[3] *nm* **1** LUGAR, SITIO : place, position **2** : position, job **3** : kiosk, stand, stall **4 puesto que** : since, given that
pugilato *nm* BOXEO : boxing, pugilism
pugilista *nm* BOXEADOR : boxer, pugilist
pugna *nf* **1** CONFLICTO, LUCHA : conflict, struggle **2 en ~** : at odds, in conflict
pugnar *vi* LUCHAR : to fight, to strive, to struggle
pugnaz *adj* : pugnacious
pujante *adj* : mighty, powerful
pujanza *nf* : strength, vigor ⟨pujanza económica : economic strength⟩
pulcritud *nf* **1** : neatness, tidiness **2** ESMERO : meticulousness
pulcro, -cra *adj* **1** : clean, neat **2** : exquisite, delicate, refined
pulga *nf* **1** : flea **2 tener malas pulgas** : to be bad-tempered
pulgada *nf* : inch
pulgar *nm* **1** : thumb **2** : big toe
pulir *vt* **1** : to polish, to shine **2** REFINAR : to refine, to perfect
pulla *nf* **1** : cutting remark, dig, gibe **2** : obscenity
pulmón *nm, pl* **pulmones** : lung
pulmonar *adj* : pulmonary
pulmonía *nf* NEUMONÍA : pneumonia
pulpa *nf* : pulp, flesh
pulpería *nf* : small grocery store

púlpito *nm* : pulpit
pulpo *nm* : octopus
pulsación *nf, pl* **-ciones 1** : beat, pulsation, throb **2** : keystroke
pulsar *vt* **1** APRETAR : to press, to push **2** : to strike (a key) **3** : to assess — *vi* : to beat, to throb
pulsera *nf* : bracelet
pulso *nm* **1** : pulse ⟨tomarle el pulso a alguien : to take someone's pulse⟩ ⟨tomarle el pulso a la opinión : to sound out opinion⟩ **2** : steadiness (of hand) ⟨dibujo a pulso : freehand sketch⟩
pulular *vi* ABUNDAR : to abound, to swarm ⟨en el río pululan los peces : the river is teeming with fish⟩
pulverizador *nm* **1** : atomizer, spray **2** : spray gun
pulverizar {21} *vt* **1** : to pulverize, to crush **2** : to spray
puma *nf* : cougar, puma
puna *nf* : bleak Andean tableland
punción *nf, pl* **punciones** : puncture
punible *adj* : punishable
punitivo, -va *adj* : punitive
punce, etc. → **punzar**
punta *nf* **1** : tip, end ⟨punta del dedo : fingertip⟩ ⟨en la punta de la lengua : at the tip of one's tongue⟩ **2** : point (of a weapon or pencil) ⟨punta de lanza : spearhead⟩ **3** : point, headland **4** : bunch, lot ⟨una punta de ladrones : a bunch of thieves⟩ **5 a punta de** : by, by dint of
puntada *nf* **1** : stitch (in sewing) **2** PUNZADA : sharp pain, stitch, twinge **3** *Mex* : witticism, quip
puntal *nm* **1** : prop, support **2** : stanchion
puntapié *nm* PATADA : kick
puntazo *nm* CORNADA : wound (from a goring)
puntear *vt* **1** : to pluck (a guitar) **2** : to lead (in sports)
puntería *nf* : aim, marksmanship
puntero *nm* **1** : pointer **2** : leader
puntiagudo, -da *adj* : sharp, pointed
puntilla *nf* **1** : lace edging **2** : dagger (in bullfighting) **3 de puntillas** : on tiptoe
puntilloso, -sa *adj* : punctilious
punto *nm* **1** : dot, point **2** : period (in punctuation) **3** : item, question **4** : spot, place **5** : moment, stage, degree **6** : point (in a score) **7** : stitch **8 en ~** : on the dot, sharp ⟨a las dos en punto : at two o'clock sharp⟩ **9 al punto** : at once **10 a punto fijo** : exactly, certainly **11 dos puntos** : colon **12 hasta cierto punto** : up to a point **13 punto decimal** : decimal point **14 punto de vista** : point of view **15 punto y coma** : semicolon **16 y punto** : period ⟨es el mejor que hay y punto : it's the best there is, period⟩ **17 puntos cardinales** : points of the compass

puntuación *nf, pl* **-ciones 1** : punctuation **2** : scoring, score, grade
puntual *adj* **1** : prompt, punctual **2** : exact, accurate — **puntualmente** *adv*
puntualidad *nf* **1** : promptness, punctuality **2** : exactness, accuracy
puntualizar {21} *vt* **1** : to specify, to state **2** : to point out
puntuar {3} *vt* : to punctuate — *vi* : to score points
punzada *nf* : sharp pain, twinge, stitch
punzante *adj* **1** : sharp **2** CÁUSTICO : biting, caustic
punzar {21} *vt* : to pierce, to puncture
punzón *nm, pl* **punzones 1** : awl **2** : hole punch
puñado *nm* **1** : handful **2 a puñados** : lots of, by the handful
puñal *nm* DAGA : dagger
puñalada *nf* : stab, stab wound
puñetazo *nm* : punch (with the fist)
puño *nm* **1** : fist **2** : handful, fistful **3** : cuff (of a shirt) **4** : handle, hilt
pupila *nf* : pupil (of the eye)
pupilo, -la *n* **1** : pupil, student **2** : ward, charge
pupitre *nm* : writing desk
puré *nm* : purée ⟨puré de papas : mashed potatoes⟩
pureza *nf* : purity
purga *nf* **1** : laxative **2** : purge
purgante *adj & nm* : laxative, purgative
purgar {52} *vt* **1** : to purge, to cleanse **2** : to liquidate (in politics), **3** : to give a laxative to — **purgarse** *vr* **1** : to take a laxative **2** ~ **de** : to purge oneself of
purgatorio *nm* : purgatory
purgue, etc. → **purgar**
purificador *nm* : purifier
purificar {72} *vt* : to purify — **purificación** *nf*
puritano[1], -na *adj* : puritanical, puritan
puritano[2], -na *n* **1** : Puritan **2** : puritan
puro[1] *adv* : sheer, much ⟨de puro terco : out of sheer stubbornness⟩
puro[2], -ra *adj* **1** : pure ⟨aire puro : fresh air⟩ **2** : plain, simple, sheer ⟨por pura curiosidad : from sheer curiosity⟩ **3** : only, just ⟨emplean puras mujeres : they only employ women⟩ **4 pura sangre** : Thoroughbred horse
puro[3] *nm* : cigar
púrpura *nf* : purple
purpúreo, -rea *adj* : purple
purpurina *nf* : glitter (for decoration)
pus *nm* : pus
pusilánime *adj* COBARDE : pusillanimous, cowardly
puso, etc. → **poner**
pústula *nf* : pustule, pimple
puta *nf* : whore, slut
putrefacción *nf, pl* **-ciones** : putrefaction
putrefacto, -ta *adj* **1** PODRIDO : putrid, rotten **2** : decayed
pútrido, -da *adj* : putrid, rotten
puya *nf* **1** : point (of a lance) **2 lanzar una puya** : to gibe, to taunt

Q

q *nf* : eighteenth letter of the Spanish alphabet
que[1] *conj* **1** : that ⟨dice que está listo : he says that he's ready⟩ ⟨espero que lo haga : I hope that he does it⟩ **2** : than ⟨más que nada : more than anything⟩ **3** (*implying permission or desire*) ⟨¡que entre! : send him in!⟩ ⟨¡que se vaya bien! : I wish you well!⟩ **4** (*indicating a reason or cause*) ⟨¡cuidado, que te caes! : be careful, you're about to fall!⟩ ⟨no provoques al perro, que te va a morder : don't provoke the dog or (else) he'll bite⟩ **5 es que** : the thing is that, I'm afraid that **6 yo que tú** : if I were you
que[2] *pron* **1** : who, that ⟨la niña que viene : the girl who is coming⟩ **2** : whom, that ⟨los alumnos que enseñé : the students that I taught⟩ **3** : that, which ⟨el carro que me gusta : the car that I like⟩ **4 el (la, lo, las, los) que** → **el[1], la[1], lo[1], los[1]**
qué[1] *adv* : how, what ⟨¡qué bonito! : how pretty!⟩
qué[2] *adj* : what, which ⟨¿qué hora es? : what time is it?⟩
qué[3] *pron* : what ⟨¿qué quieres? : what do you want?⟩
quebracho *nm* : quebracho (tree)
quebrada *nf* DESFILADERO : ravine, gorge
quebradizo, -za *adj* FRÁGIL : breakable, delicate, fragile
quebrado[1], -da *adj* **1** : bankrupt **2** : rough, uneven **3** ROTO : broken
quebrado[2] *nm* : fraction
quebrantamiento *nm* **1** : breaking **2** : deterioration, weakening
quebrantar *vt* **1** : to break, to split, to crack **2** : to weaken **3** : to violate (a law or contract)
quebranto *nm* **1** : break, breaking **2** AFLICCIÓN : affliction, grief **3** PÉRDIDA : loss
quebrar {55} *vt* **1** ROMPER : to break **2** DOBLAR : to bend, to twist — *vi* **1** : to go bankrupt **2** : to fall out, to break up — **quebrarse** *vr*
queda *nf* : curfew
quedar *vi* **1** PERMANECER : to remain, to stay **2** : to be ⟨quedamos contentos con las mejoras : we were pleased with the improvements⟩ **3** : to be situated ⟨queda muy lejos : it's very far, it's too far away⟩ **4** : to be left ⟨quedan sólo dos alternativas : there are only two options left⟩ **5** : to fit, to suit ⟨estos zap-

atos no me quedan : these shoes don't fit⟩ **6 quedar bien (mal)** : to turn out well (badly) **7** ~ **en** : to agree, to arrange ⟨¿en qué quedamos? : what's the arrangement, then?⟩ — **quedarse** *vr* **1** : to stay ⟨se quedó en casa : she stayed at home⟩ **2** : to keep on ⟨se quedó esperando : he kept on waiting⟩ **3 quedarse atrás** : to stay behind ⟨no quedarse atrás : to be no slouch⟩ **4** ~ **con** : to remain ⟨me quedé con hambre después de comer : I was still hungry after I ate⟩

quedo[1] *adv* : softly, quietly

quedo[2], **-da** *adj* : quiet, still

quehacer *nm* **1** : work **2 quehaceres** *nmpl* : chores

queja *nf* : complaint

quejarse *vr* **1** : to complain **2** : to groan, to moan

quejido *nm* **1** : groan, moan **2** : whine, whimper

quejoso, -sa *adj* : complaining, whining

quejumbroso, -sa *adj* : querulous, whining

quema *nf* **1** FUEGO : fire **2** : burning

quemado, -da *adj* **1** : burned, burnt **2** : annoyed **3** : burned-out

quemador *nm* : burner

quemadura *nf* : burn

quemar *vt* : to burn, to set fire to — *vi* : to be burning hot — **quemarse** *vr*

quemarropa *nf* a ~ : point-blank

quemazón *nf, pl* **-zones 1** : burning **2** : intense heat **3** : itch **4** : cutting remark

quena *nf* : Peruvian reed flute

quepa, etc. → **caber**

querella *nf* **1** : complaint **2** : lawsuit

querellante *nmf* : plaintiff

querellarse *vr* ~ **contra** : to bring suit against, to sue

querer[1] {64} *vt* **1** DESEAR : to want, to desire ⟨quiere ser profesor : he wants to be a teacher⟩ ⟨¿cuánto quieres por esta computadora? : how much do you want for this computer?⟩ **2** : to love, to like, to be fond of ⟨te quiero : I love you⟩ **3** (*indicating a request*) ⟨¿quieres pasarme la leche? : please pass the milk⟩ **4 querer decir** : to mean **5 sin** ~ : unintentionally — *vi* : like, want ⟨si quieras : if you like⟩

querer[2] *nm* : love, affection

querido[1], **-da** *adj* : dear, beloved

querido[2], **-da** *n* : dear, sweetheart

queroseno *nm* : kerosene

querrá, etc. → **querer**

querúbico, -ca *adj* : cherubic

querubín *nm, pl* **-bines** : cherub

quesadilla *nf* : quesadilla

quesería *nf* : cheese shop

queso *nm* : cheese

quetzal *nm* **1** : quetzal (bird) **2** : monetary unit of Guatemala

quicio *nm* **1 estar fuera de quicio** : to be beside oneself **2 sacar de quicio** : to exasperate, to drive crazy

quid *nm* : crux, gist ⟨el quid de la cuestión : the crux of the matter⟩

quiebra[1], **etc.** → **quebrar**

quiebra[2] *nf* **1** : break, crack **2** BANCARROTA : failure, bankruptcy

quien *pron, pl* **quienes 1** : who, whom ⟨no sé quien ganará : I don't know who will win⟩ ⟨las personas con quienes trabajo : the people with whom I work⟩ **2** : whoever, whomever ⟨quien quiere salir que salga : whoever wants to can leave⟩ **3** : anyone, some people ⟨hay quienes no están de acuerdo : some people don't agree⟩

quién *pron, pl* **quiénes 1** : who, whom ⟨¿quién sabe? : who knows?⟩ ⟨¿con quién hablo? : with whom am I speaking?⟩ **2 de** ~ : whose ⟨¿de quién es este libro? : whose book is this?⟩

quienquiera *pron, pl* **quienesquiera** : whoever, whomever

quiere, etc. → **querer**

quieto, -ta *adj* **1** : calm, quiet **2** INMÓVIL : still

quietud *nf* **1** : calm, tranquility **2** INMOVILIDAD : stillness

quijada *nf* : jaw, jawbone

quijotesco, -ca *adj* : quixotic

quilate *nm* : karat

quilla *nf* : keel

quimera *nf* : chimera, illusion

quimérico, -ca *adj* : chimeric, fanciful

química *nf* : chemistry

químico[1], **-ca** *adj* : chemical

químico[2], **-ca** *n* : chemist

quimioterapia *nf* : chemotherapy

quimono *nm* : kimono

quince *adj* & *nm* : fifteen

quinceañero, -ra *n* : fifteen-year-old, teenager

quinceavo[1], **-va** *adj* : fifteenth

quinceavo[2] *nm* : fifteenth (fraction)

quincena *nf* : two week period, fortnight

quincenal *adj* : bimonthly, twice a month

quincuagésimo[1], **-ma** *adj* : fiftieth, fifty-

quincuagésimo[2], **-ma** *n* : fiftieth, fifty- (in a series)

quingombó *nm* : okra

quiniela *nf* : sports lottery

quinientos[1], **-tas** *adj* : five hundred

quinientos[2] *nms* & *pl* : five hundred

quinina *nf* : quinine

quino *nm* : cinchona

quinqué *nm* : oil lamp

quinquenal *adj* : five-year ⟨un plan quinquenal : a five-year plan⟩

quinta *nf* : country house, villa

quintaesencia *nf* : quintessence — **quintaesencial** *adj*

quintal *nm* : hundredweight

quinteto *nm* : quintet

quintillizo, -za *n* : quintuplet

quinto, -ta *adj* : fifth — **quinto, -ta** *n*

quíntuplo, -la *adj* : quintuple, five-fold

quiosco *nm* **1** : kiosk **2** : newsstand **3** **quiosco de música** : bandstand

quirófano *nm* : operating room

quiromancia *nf* : palmistry
quiropráctica *nf* : chiropractic
quiropráctico, -ca *n* : chiropractor
quirúrgico, -ca *adj* : surgical — **quirúrgicamente** *adv*
quiso, etc. → **querer**
quisquilloso[1], -sa *adj* : fastidious, fussy
quisquilloso[2], -sa *n* : fussy person, fussbudget
quiste *nm* : cyst
quitaesmalte *nm* : nail polish remover
quitamanchas *nms & pl* : stain remover

quitanieves *nms & pl* : snowplow
quitar *vt* **1** : to remove, to take away **2** : to take off (clothes). **3** : to get rid of, to relieve — **quitarse** *vr* **1** : to withdraw, to leave **2** : to take off (one's clothes) **3** ~ **de** : to give up (a habit) **4 quitar de encima** : to get rid of
quitasol *nm* : parasol
quiteño[1], -ña *adj* : of or from Quito
quiteño[2], -ña *n* : person from Quito
quizá *or* **quizás** *adv* : maybe, perhaps
quórum *nm, pl* **quórums** : quorum

R

r *nf* : nineteenth letter of the Spanish alphabet
rábano *nm* **1** : radish **2 rábano picante** : horseradish
rabí *nmf, pl* **rabíes** : rabbi
rabia *nf* **1** HIDROFOBIA : rabies, hydrophobia **2** : rage, anger
rabiar *vi* **1** : to rage, to be furious **2** : to be in great pain **3 a** ~ *fam* : like crazy, like mad
rabieta *nf* BERRINCHE : tantrum
rabino, -na *n* : rabbi
rabioso, -sa *adj* **1** : enraged, furious **2** : rabid
rabo *nm* **1** COLA : tail **2 el rabo del ojo** : the corner of one's eye
racha *nf* **1** : gust of wind **2** : run, series, string ⟨racha perdedora : losing streak⟩
racheado, -da *adj* : gusty, windy
racial *adj* : racial
racimo *nm* : bunch, cluster ⟨un racimo de uvas : a bunch of grapes⟩
raciocinio *nm* : reason, reasoning
ración *nf, pl* **raciones** **1** : share, ration **2** PORCIÓN : portion, helping
racional *adj* : rational, reasonable — **racionalmente** *adv*
racionalidad *nf* : rationality
racionalización *nf, pl* **-ciones** : rationalization
racionalizar {21} *vt* **1** : to rationalize **2** : to streamline
racionamiento *nm* : rationing
racionar *vt* : to ration
racismo *nm* : racism
racista *adj & nmf* : racist
radar *nm* : radar
radiación *nf, pl* **-ciones** : radiation, irradiation
radiactividad *nf* : radioactivity
radiactivo, -va *adj* : radioactive
radiador *nm* : radiator
radial *adj* **1** : radial **2** : radio, broadcasting ⟨emisora radial : radio transmitter⟩
radiante *adj* : radiant
radiar *vt* **1** : to radiate **2** : to irradiate **3** : to broadcast (on the radio)
radical[1] *adj* : radical, extreme — **radicalmente** *adv*

radical[2] *nmf* : radical
radicalismo *nm* : radicalism
radicar {72} *vi* **1** : to be found, to lie **2** ARRAIGAR : to take root — **radicarse** *vr* : to settle, to establish oneself
radio[1] *nm* **1** : radius **2** : radium
radio[2] *nmf* : radio
radioactividad *nf* : radioactivity
radioactivo, -va *adj* : radioactive
radioaficionado, -da *n* : ham radio operator
radiodifusión *nf, pl* **-siones** : radio broadcasting
radiodifusora *nf* : radio station
radioemisora *nf* : radio station
radiofaro *nm* : radio beacon
radiofónico, -ca *adj* : radio ⟨estación radiofónica pública : public radio station⟩
radiofrecuencia *nf* : radio frequency
radiografía *nf* : X ray (photograph)
radiografiar {85} *vt* : to x-ray
radiología *nf* : radiology
radiólogo, -ga *n* : radiologist
radón *nm* : radon
raer {65} *vt* RASPAR : to scrape, to scrape off
ráfaga *nf* **1** : gust (of wind) **2** : flash, burst ⟨una ráfaga de luz : a flash of light⟩
raid *nm* CA, Mex fam : lift, ride
raído, -da *adj* : worn, shabby
raiga, etc. → **raer**
raíz *nf, pl* **raíces** **1** : root **2** : origin, source **3 a raíz de** : following, as a result of **4 echar raíces** : to take root
raja *nf* **1** : crack, slit **2** : slice, wedge
rajá *nm* : raja
rajadura *nf* : crack, split
rajar *vt* HENDER : to crack, to split — *vi* **1** *fam* : to chatter **2** *fam* : to boast, to brag — **rajarse** *vr* **1** : to crack, to split open **2** *fam* : to back out
rajatabla *adv* **a** ~ : strictly, to the letter
ralea *nf* : kind, sort, ilk ⟨son de la misma valea : they're two of a kind⟩
ralentí *nm* **dejar al ralentí** : to leave (a motor) idling
rallado, -da *adj* **1** : grated **2 pan rallado** : bread crumbs *pl*
rallador *nm* : grater

rallar *vt* : to grate
ralo, -la *adj* : sparse, thin
RAM *nf* : RAM, random-access memory
rama *nf* : branch
ramaje *nm* : branches *pl*
ramal *nm* **1** : branchline **2** : halter, strap
ramera *nf* : harlot, prostitute
ramificación *nf, pl* **-ciones** : ramification
ramificarse {72} *vr* : to branch out, to divide into branches
ramillete *nm* **1** RAMO : bouquet **2** : select group, cluster
ramo *nm* **1** : branch **2** RAMILLETE : bouquet **3** : division (of science or industry) **4 Domingo de Ramos** : Palm Sunday
rampa *nf* : ramp, incline
rana *nf* **1** : frog **2 rana toro** : bullfrog
ranchera *nf Mex* : traditional folk song
ranchería *nf* : settlement
ranchero, -ra *n* : rancher, farmer
rancho *nm* **1** : ranch, farm **2** : hut **3** : settlement, camp **4** : food, mess (for soldiers, etc.)
rancio, -cia *adj* **1** : aged, mellow (of wine) **2** : ancient, old **3** : rancid
rango *nm* **1** : rank, status **2** : high social standing **3** : pomp, splendor
ranúnculo *nm* : buttercup
ranura *nf* : groove, slot
rap *nm* : rap (music)
rapacidad *nf* : rapacity
rapar *vt* **1** : to crop **2** : to shave
rapaz[1] *adj, pl* **rapaces** : rapacious, predatory
rapaz[2], **-paza** *n, mpl* **rapaces** : youngster, child
rape *nm* : close haircut
rapé *nm* : snuff
rapero, -ra *n* : rapper, rap artist
rapidez *nf* : rapidity, speed
rápido[1] *adv* : quickly, fast ⟨¡manejas tan rápido! : you drive so fast!⟩
rápido[2], **-da** *adj* : rapid, quick — **rápidamente** *adv*
rápido[3] *nm* **1** : express train **2 rápidos** *nmpl* : rapids
rapiña *nf* **1** : plunder, pillage **2 ave de rapiña** : bird of prey
raposa *nf* : vixen (fox)
rapsodia *nf* : rhapsody
raptar *vt* SECUESTRAR : to abduct, to kidnap
rapto *nm* **1** SECUESTRO : kidnapping, abduction **2** ARREBATO : fit, outburst
raptor, -tora *n* SECUESTRADOR : kidnapper
raque *nm* : beachcombing
raquero, -ra *n* : beachcomber
raqueta *nf* **1** : racket (in sports) **2** : snowshoe
raquítico, -ca *adj* **1** : scrawny, weak **2** : measly, skimpy
raquitismo *nm* : rickets
raramente *adv* : seldom, rarely
rareza *nf* **1** : rarity **2** : peculiarity, oddity

raro, -ra *adj* **1** EXTRAÑO : odd, strange, peculiar **2** : unusual, rare **3** : exceptional **4 rara vez** : seldom, rarely
ras *nm* **a ras de** : level with
rasar *vt* **1** : to skim, to graze **2** : to level
rascacielos *nms & pl* : skyscraper
rascar {72} *vt* **1** : to scratch **2** : to scrape — **rascarse** *vr* : to scratch an itch
rasgadura *nf* : tear, rip
rasgar {52} *vt* : to rip, to tear — **rasgarse** *vr*
rasgo *nm* **1** : stroke (of a pen) ⟨a grandes rasgos : in broad outlines⟩ **2** CARACTERÍSTICA : trait, characteristic **3** : gesture, deed **4 rasgos** *nmpl* FACCIONES : features
rasgón *nm, pl* **rasgones** : rip, tear
rasgue, etc. → **rasgar**
rasguear *vt* : to strum
rasguñar *vt* **1** : to scratch **2** : to sketch, to outline
rasguño *nm* **1** : scratch **2** : sketch
raso[1], **-sa** *adj* **1** : level, flat **2 soldado raso** : private (in the army) ⟨los soldados rasos : the ranks⟩
raso[2] *nm* : satin
raspadura *nf* **1** : scratching, scraping **2 raspaduras** *nfpl* : scrapings
raspar *vt* **1** : to scrape **2** : to file down, to smooth — *vi* : to be rough
rasque, etc. → **rascar**
rastra *nf* **1** : harrow **2 a rastras** : by dragging, unwillingly
rastrear *vt* **1** : to track, to trace **2** : to comb, to search **3** : to trawl
rastrero, -ra *adj* **1** : creeping, crawling **2** : vile, despicable
rastrillar *vt* : to rake, to harrow
rastrillo *nm* **1** : rake **2 Mex** : razor
rastro *nm* **1** PISTA : trail, track **2** VESTIGIO : trace, sign
rastrojo *nm* : stubble (of plants)
rasuradora *nf Mex, CA* : electric razor, shaver
rasurar *vt* AFEITAR : to shave — **rasurarse** *vr*
rata[1] *nm fam* : pickpocket, thief
rata[2] *nf* **1** : rat **2** *Col, Pan, Peru* : rate, percentage
ratear *vt* : to pilfer, to steal
ratero, -ra *n* : petty thief
ratificación *nf, pl* **-ciones** : ratification
ratificar {72} *vt* **1** : to ratify **2** : to confirm
rato *nm* **1** : while **2 pasar el rato** : to pass the time **3 a cada rato** : all the time, constantly ⟨les sacaba dinero a cada rato : he was always taking money from them⟩ **4 al poco rato** : later, shortly after
ratón[1], **-tona** *n, mpl* **ratones 1** : mouse **2 ratón de biblioteca** *fam* : bookworm
ratón[2] *nm, pl* **ratones 1** : (computer) mouse **2** *CoRi* : biceps
ratonera *nf* : mousetrap
raudal *nm* **1** : torrent **2 a raudales** : in abundance

raya¹, etc. → **raer**
raya² *nf* **1** : line **2** : stripe **3** : skate, ray **4** : part (in the hair) **5** : crease (in clothing)
rayar *vt* **1** ARAÑAR : to scratch **2** : to scrawl on, to mark up ⟨rayaron las paredes : they covered the walls with graffiti⟩ — *vi* **1** : to scratch **2** AMANECER : to dawn, to break ⟨al rayar el alba : at break of day⟩ **3** ~ **con** : to be adjacent to, to be next to **4** ~ **en** : to border on, to verge on ⟨su respuesta raya en lo ridículo : his answer borders on the ridiculous⟩ — **rayarse** *vr*
rayo *nm* **1** : ray, beam ⟨rayo láser : laser beam⟩ ⟨rayo de gamma : gamma ray⟩ ⟨rayo de sol : sunbeam⟩ **2** RELÁMPAGO : lightning bolt **3** rayo X : X-ray
rayón *nm, pl* **rayones** : rayon
raza *nf* **1** : race ⟨raza humana : human race⟩ **2** : breed, strain **3 de** ~ : thoroughbred, pedigreed
razón *nf, pl* **razones** **1** MOTIVO : reason, motive ⟨en razón de : by reason of, because of⟩ **2** JUSTICIA : rightness, justice ⟨tener razón : to be right⟩ **3** : reasoning, sense ⟨perder la razón : to lose one's mind⟩ **4** : ratio, proportion
razonable *adj* : reasonable — **razonablemente** *adv*
razonado, -da *adj* : itemized, detailed
razonamiento *nm* : reasoning
razonar *v* : to reason, to think
reabastecimiento *nm* : replenishment
reabierto *pp* → **reabrir**
reabrir {2} *vt* : to reopen — **reabrirse** *vr*
reacción *nf, pl* **-ciones** **1** : reaction **2 motor a reacción** : jet engine
reaccionar *vi* : to react, to respond
reaccionario, -ria *adj & n* : reactionary
reacio, -cia *adj* : resistant, opposed
reacondicionar *vt* : to recondition
reactivación *nf, pl* **-ciones** : reactivation, revival
reactivar *vt* : reactivate, revive
reactor *nm* **1** : reactor ⟨reactor nuclear : nuclear reactor⟩ **2** : jet engine **3** : jet airplane, jet
reafirmar *vt* : to reaffirm, to assert, to strengthen
reajustar *vt* : to readjust, to adjust
reajuste *nm* : readjustment ⟨reajuste de precios : price increase⟩
real *adj* **1** : real, true **2** : royal
realce *nm* **1** : embossing, relief **2 dar realce** : to highlight, to bring out
realeza *nf* : royalty
realidad *nf* **1** : reality **2 en** ~ : in truth, actually
realinear *vt* : to realign
realismo *nm* **1** : realism **2** : royalism
realista¹ *adj* **1** : realistic **2** : realist **3** : royalist
realista² *nmf* **1** : realist **2** : royalist
realización *nf, pl* **-ciones** : execution, realization

realizar {21} *vt* **1** : to carry out, to execute **2** : to produce, to direct (a film or play) **3** : to fulfill, to achieve **4** : to realize (a profit) — **realizarse** *vr* **1** : to come true **2** : to fulfill oneself
realmente *adv* : really, in reality
realzar {21} *vt* **1** : to heighten, to raise **2** : to highlight, to enhance
reanimación *nf, pl* **-ciones** : revival, resuscitation
reanimar *vt* **1** : to revive, to restore **2** : to resuscitate — **reanimarse** *vr* : to come around, to recover
reanudación *nf, pl* **-ciones** : resumption, renewal
reanudar *vt* : to resume, to renew — **reanudarse** *vr* : to resume, to continue
reaparecer {53} *vi* **1** : to reappear **2** : to make a comeback
reaparición *nf, pl* **-ciones** : reappearance
reapertura *nf* : reopening
reata *nf* **1** : rope **2** *Mex* : lasso, lariat **3 de** ~ : single file
reavivar *vt* : to revive, to reawaken
rebaja *nf* **1** : reduction **2** DESCUENTO : discount **3 rebajas** *nfpl* : sale
rebajar *vt* **1** : to reduce, to lower ⟨a precios rebajados : at reduced prices, on sale⟩ **2** : to lessen, to diminish **3** : to humiliate — **rebajarse** *vr* **1** : to humble oneself **2 rebajarse a** : to stoop to
rebanada *nf* : slice
rebañar *vt* : to mop up, to sop up
rebaño *nm* **1** : flock **2** : herd
rebasar *vt* **1** : to surpass, to exceed **2** *Mex* : to pass, to overtake
rebatiña *nf* : scramble, fight (over something)
rebatir *vt* REFUTAR : to refute
rebato *nm* **1** : surprise attack **2 tocar a rebato** : to sound the alarm
rebelarse *vr* : to rebel
rebelde¹ *adj* : rebellious, unruly
rebelde² *nmf* **1** : rebel **2** : defaulter
rebeldía *nf* **1** : rebelliousness **2 en** ~ : in default
rebelión *nf, pl* **-liones** : rebellion
rebobinar *vt* : to rewind
reborde *nm* : border, flange, rim
rebosante *adj* : brimming, overflowing ⟨rebosante de salud : brimming with health⟩
rebosar *vi* **1** : to overflow **2** ~ **de** : to abound in, to be bursting with — *vt* : to radiate
rebotar *vi* **1** : to bounce **2** : to ricochet, to rebound
rebote *nm* **1** : bounce **2** : rebound, ricochet
rebozar {21} *vt* : to coat in batter
rebozo *nm* **1** : shawl, wrap **2 sin** ~ : frankly, openly
rebullir {38} *v* : to move, to stir — **rebullirse** *vr*
rebuscado, -da *adj* : affected, pretentious
rebuscar {72} *vi* : to search thoroughly

rebuznar *vi* : to bray
rebuzno *nm* : bray, braying
recabar *vt* **1** : to gather, to obtain, to collect **2 recabar fondos** : to raise money
recado *nm* **1** : message ⟨mandar recado : to send word⟩ **2** *Spain* : errand
recaer {13} *vi* **1** : to relapse **2** ～ **en** *or* ～ **sobre** : to fall on, to fall to
recaída *nf* : relapse
recaiga, etc. → recaer
recalar *vi* : to arrive
recalcar {72} *vt* : to emphasize, to stress
recalcitrante *adj* : recalcitrant
recalentar {55} *vt* **1** : to reheat, to warm up **2** : to overheat
recámara *nf* **1** *Col, Mex, Pan* : bedroom **2** : chamber (of a firearm)
recamarera *nf Mex* : chambermaid
recambio *nm* **1** : spare part **2** : refill (for a pen, etc.)
recapacitar *vi* **1** : to reconsider **2** ～ **en** : to reflect on, to weigh
recapitular *v* : to recapitulate — **recapitulación** *nf*
recargable *adj* : rechargeable
recargado, -da *adj* : overly elaborate or ornate
recargar {52} *vt* **1** : to recharge **2** : to overload
recargo *nm* : surcharge
recatado, -da *adj* MODESTO : modest, demure
recato *nm* PUDOR : modesty
recaudación *nf, pl* **-ciones 1** : collection **2** : earnings *pl*, takings *pl*
recaudador, -dora *n* **recaudador de impuestos** : tax collector
recaudar *vt* : to collect
recaudo *nm* : safe place ⟨a (buen) recaudo : in safe keeping⟩
recayó, etc. → recaer
rece, etc. → rezar
recelo *nm* : distrust, suspicion
receloso, -sa *adj* : distrustful, suspicious
recepción *nf, pl* **-ciones** : reception
recepcionista *nmf* : receptionist
receptáculo *nm* : receptacle
receptividad *nf* : receptivity, receptiveness
receptivo, -va *adj* : receptive
receptor¹, -tora *adj* : receiving
receptor², -tora *n* **1** : recipient **2** : catcher (in baseball), receiver (in football)
receptor³ *nm* : receiver ⟨receptor de televisión : television set⟩
recesión *nf, pl* **-siones** : recession
recesivo, -va *adj* : recessive
receso *nm* : recess, adjournment
receta *nf* **1** : recipe **2** : prescription
recetar *vt* : to prescribe (medications)
rechazar {21} *vt* **1** : to reject **2** : to turn down, to refuse
rechazo *nm* : rejection, refusal
rechifla *nf* : booing, jeering
rechinar *vi* **1** : to squeak **2** : to grind, to gnash ⟨hacer rechinar los dientes : to grind one's teeth⟩

rechoncho, -cha *adj fam* : chubby, squat
recibidor *nm* : vestibule, entrance hall
recibimiento *nm* : reception, welcome
recibir *vt* **1** : to receive, to get **2** : to welcome — *vi* : to receive visitors — **recibirse** *vr* ～ **de** : to qualify as
recibo *nm* : receipt
reciclable *adj* : recyclable
reciclado → reciclaje
reciclaje *nm* **1** : recycling **2** : retraining
reciclar *vt* **1** : to recycle **2** : to retrain
recién *adv* **1** : newly, recently ⟨recién nacido : newborn⟩ ⟨recién casados : newlyweds⟩ ⟨recién llegado : newcomer⟩ **2** : just, only just ⟨recién ahora me acordé : I just now remembered⟩
reciente *adj* : recent — **recientemente** *adv*
recinto *nm* **1** : enclosure **2** : site, premises *pl*
recio¹ *adv* **1** : strongly, hard **2** : loudly, loud
recio², -cia *adj* **1** : severe, harsh **2** : tough, strong
recipiente¹ *nm* : container, receptacle
recipiente² *nmf* : recipient
reciprocar {72} *vi* : to reciprocate
reciprocidad *nf* : reciprocity
recíproco, -ca *adj* : reciprocal, mutual
recitación *nf, pl* **-ciones** : recitation, recital
recital *nm* : recital
recitar *vt* : to recite
reclamación *nf, pl* **-ciones 1** : claim, demand **2** QUEJA : complaint
reclamar *vt* **1** EXIGIR : to demand, to require **2** : to claim — *vi* : to complain
reclamo *nm* **1** : bird call, lure **2** : lure, decoy **3** : inducement, attraction **4** : advertisement **5** : complaint
reclinar *vt* : to rest, to lean — **reclinarse** *vr* : to recline, to lean back
recluir {41} *vt* : to confine, to lock up — **recluirse** *vr* : to shut oneself up, to withdraw
reclusión *nf, pl* **-siones** : imprisonment
recluso, -sa *n* **1** : inmate, prisoner **2** SOLITARIO : recluse
recluta *nmf* : recruit, draftee
reclutamiento *nm* : recruitment, recruiting
reclutar *vt* ENROLAR : to recruit, to enlist
recobrar *vt* : to recover, to regain — **recobrarse** *vr* : to recover, to recuperate
recocer {14} *vt* : to overcook, to cook again
recodo *nm* : bend
recogedor *nm* : dustpan
recoger {15} *vt* **1** : to collect, to gather **2** : to get, to retrieve, to pick up **3** : to clean up, to tidy (up)
recogido, -da *adj* : quiet, secluded
recogimiento *nm* **1** : collecting, gathering **2** : withdrawal **3** : absorption, concentration

recolección *nf, pl* **-ciones 1** : collection ⟨recolección de basura : trash pickup⟩ **2** : harvest

recolectar *vt* **1** : to gather, to collect **2** : to harvest, to pick

recomendable *adj* : advisable, recommended

recomendación *nf, pl* **-ciones** : recommendation

recomendar {55} *vt* **1** : to recommend **2** ACONSEJAR : to advise

recompensa *nf* : reward, recompense

recompensar *vt* **1** PREMIAR : to reward **2** : to compensate

reconciliación *nf, pl* **-ciones** : reconciliation

reconciliar *vt* : to reconcile — **reconciliarse** *vr*

recóndito, -ta *adj* **1** : remote, isolated **2** : hidden, recondite **3 en lo más recóndito de** : in the depths of

reconfortar *vt* : to comfort — **reconfortante** *adj*

reconocer {18} *vt* **1** : to recognize **2** : to admit **3** : to examine

reconocible *adj* : recognizable

reconocido, -da *adj* **1** : recognized, accepted **2** : grateful

reconocimiento *nm* **1** : acknowledgment, recognition, avowal **2** : (medical) examination **3** : reconnaissance

reconquista *nf* : reconquest

reconquistar *vt* **1** : to reconquer, to recapture **2** RECUPERAR : to regain, to recover

reconsiderar *vt* : to reconsider — **reconsideración** *nf*

reconstrucción *nf, pl* **-ciones** : reconstruction

reconstruir {41} *vt* : to rebuild, to reconstruct

reconversión *nf, pl* **-siones** : restructuring

reconvertir {76} *vt* **1** : to restructure **2** : to retrain

recopilación *nf, pl* **-ciones 1** : summary **2** : collection, compilation

recopilar *vt* : to compile, to collect

récord *or* **record** ['rɛkɔr] *nm, pl* **récords** *or* **records** [-kɔrs] : record ⟨record mundial : world record⟩ — **récord** *or* **record** *adj*

recordar {19} *vt* **1** : to recall, to remember **2** : to remind — *vi* **1** ACORDARSE : to remember **2** DESPERTAR : to wake up

recordatorio¹, -ria *adj* : commemorative

recordatorio² *nm* : reminder

recorrer *vt* **1** : to travel through, to tour **2** : to cover (a distance) **3** : to go over, to look over

recorrido *nm* **1** : journey, trip **2** : path, route, course **3** : round (in golf)

recortar *vt* **1** : to cut, to reduce **2** : to cut out **3** : to trim, to cut off **4** : to outline — **recortarse** *vr* : to stand out ⟨los árboles se recortaban en el horizonte : the trees were silhouetted against the horizon⟩

recorte *nm* **1** : cut, reduction **2** : clipping ⟨recortes de periódicos : newspaper clippings⟩

recostar {19} *vt* : to lean, to rest — **recostarse** *vr* : to lie down, recline

recoveco *nm* **1** VUELTA : bend, turn **2** : nook, corner **3 recovecos** *nmpl* : intricacies, ins and outs

recreación *nf, pl* **-ciones 1** : re-creation **2** DIVERSIÓN : recreation, entertainment

recrear *vt* **1** : to re-create **2** : to entertain, to amuse — **recrearse** *vr* : to enjoy oneself

recreativo, -va *adj* : recreational

recreo *nm* **1** DIVERSIÓN : entertainment, amusement **2** : recess, break

recriminación *nf, pl* **-ciones** : reproach, recrimination

recriminar *vt* : to reproach — *vi* : to recriminate — **recriminarse** *vr*

recrudecer {53} *v* : to intensify, to worsen — **recrudecerse** *vr*

rectal *adj* : rectal

rectangular *adj* : rectangular

rectángulo *nm* : rectangle

rectificación *nf, pl* **-ciones** : rectification, correction

rectificar {72} *vt* **1** : to rectify, to correct **2** : to straighten (out)

rectitud *nf* **1** : straightness **2** : honesty, rectitude

recto¹ *adv* : straight

recto², -ta *adj* **1** : straight **2** : upright, honorable **3** : sound

recto³ *nm* : rectum

rector¹, -tora *adj* : governing, managing

rector², -tora *n* : rector

rectoría *nf* : rectory

recubierto *pp* → **recubrir**

recubrir {2} *vt* : to cover, to coat

recuento *nm* : recount, count ⟨un recuento de los votos : a recount of the votes⟩

recuerdo *nm* **1** : memory **2** : souvenir, memento **3 recuerdos** *nmpl* : regards

recular *vi* **1** : to back up **2** REPLEGARSE : to retreat, to fall back **3** RETRACTARSE : to back down

recuperación *nf, pl* **-ciones 1** : recovery, recuperation **2 recuperación de datos** : data retrieval

recuperar *vt* **1** : to recover, to get back, to retrieve **2** : to recuperate **3** : to make up for ⟨recuperar el tiempo perdido : to make up for lost time⟩ — **recuperarse** *vr* ~ **de** : to recover from, to get over

recurrente *adj* : recurrent, recurring

recurrir *vi* **1** ~ **a** : to turn to, to appeal to **2** ~ **a** : to resort to **3** : to appeal (in law)

recurso *nm* **1** : recourse ⟨el último recurso : the last resort⟩ **2** : appeal (in law) **3 recursos** *nmpl* : resources, means ⟨recursos naturales : natural resources⟩

red *nf* **1** : net, mesh **2** : network, system, chain **3** : trap, snare
redacción *nf, pl* **-ciones 1** : writing, composition **2** : editing
redactar *vt* **1** : to write, to draft **2** : to edit
redactor, -tora *n* : editor
redada *nf* **1** : raid **2** : catch, haul
redefinir *vt* : to redefine — **redefinición** *nf*
redención *nf, pl* **-ciones** : redemption
redentor[1]**, -tora** *adj* : redeeming
redentor[2]**, -tora** *n* : redeemer
redescubierto *pp* → **redescubrir**
redescubrir {2} *vt* : to rediscover
redicho, -cha *adj fam* : affected, pretentious
redil *nm* **1** : sheepfold **2 volver al redil** : to return to the fold
redimir *vt* : to redeem, to deliver (from sin)
rediseñar *vt* : to redesign
redistribuir {41} *vt* : to redistribute — **redistribución** *nf*
rédito *nm* : return, yield
redituar {3} *vt* : to produce, to yield
redoblar *vt* : to redouble, to strengthen — **redoblado, -da** *adj*
redoble *nm* : drum roll
redomado, -da *adj* **1** : sly, crafty **2** : utter, out-and-out
redonda *nf* **1** : region, surrounding area **2 a la redonda** ALREDEDOR : around ⟨de diez millas a la redonda : for ten miles around⟩
redondear *vt* : to round off, to round out
redondel *nm* **1** : ring, circle **2** : bullring, arena
redondez *nf* : roundness
redondo, -da *adj* **1** : round ⟨mesa redonda : round table⟩ **2** : great, perfect ⟨un negocio redondo : an excellent deal⟩ **3** : straightforward, flat ⟨un rechazo redondo : a flat refusal⟩ **4** *Mex* : round-trip **5 en ~** : around
reducción *nf, pl* **-ciones** : reduction, decrease
reducido, -da *adj* **1** : reduced, limited **2** : small
reducir {61} *vt* **1** DISMINUIR : to reduce, to decrease, to cut **2** : to subdue **3** : to boil down — **reducirse** *vr* **~ a** : to come down to, to be nothing more than
redundancia *nf* : redundancy
redundante *adj* : redundant
reedición *nf, pl* **-ciones** : reprint
reelegir {28} *vt* : to reelect — **reelección** *nf*
reembolsable *adj* : refundable
reembolsar *vt* **1** : to refund, to reimburse **2** : to repay
reembolso *nm* : refund, reimbursement
reemplazable *adj* : replaceable
reemplazar {21} *vt* : to replace, to substitute
reemplazo *nm* : replacement, substitution
reencarnación *nf, pl* **-ciones** : reincarnation

reencuentro *nm* : reunion
reestablecer {53} *vt* : to reestablish
reestructurar *vt* : to restructure
reexaminar *vt* : to reexamine
refaccionar *vt* : to repair, to renovate
refacciones *nfpl* : repairs, renovations
referencia *nf* **1** : reference **2 hacer referencia a** : to refer to
referendo → **referéndum**
referéndum *nm, pl* **-dums** : referendum
referente *adj* **~ a** : concerning
réferi *or* **referi** ['rɛfɛri] *nmf* : referee
referir {76} *vt* **1** : to relate, to tell **2** : to refer ⟨nos refirió al diccionario : she referred us to the dictionary⟩ — **referirse** *vr* **~ a 1** : to refer to **2 ~ a** : to be concerned, to be in reference to ⟨en lo que se refiere a la educación : as far as education is concerned⟩
refinado[1]**, -da** *adj* : refined
refinado[2] *nm* : refining
refinamiento *nm* **1** : refining **2** FINURA : refinement
refinanciar *vt* : to refinance
refinar *vt* : to refine
refinería *nf* : refinery
reflectante *adj* : reflective, reflecting
reflector[1]**, -tora** *adj* : reflecting
reflector[2] *nm* **1** : spotlight, searchlight **2** : reflector
reflejar *vt* : to reflect — **reflejarse** *vr* : to be reflected ⟨la decepción se refleja en su rostro : the disappointment shows on her face⟩
reflejo *nm* **1** : reflection **2** : reflex **3 reflejos** *nmpl* : highlights, streaks (in hair)
reflexión *nf, pl* **-xiones** : reflection, thought
reflexionar *vi* : to reflect, to think
reflexivo, -va *adj* **1** : reflective, thoughtful **2** : reflexive
reflujo *nm* : ebb, ebb tide
reforma *nf* **1** : reform **2** : alteration, renovation
reformador, -dora *n* : reformer
reformar *vt* **1** : to reform **2** : to change, to alter **3** : to renovate, to repair — **reformarse** *vr* : to mend one's ways
reformatorio *nm* : reformatory
reformular *vt* : to reformulate — **reformulación** *nf*
reforzar {36} *vt* **1** : to reinforce, to strengthen **2** : to encourage, to support
refracción *nf, pl* **-ciones** : refraction
refractar *vt* : to refract — **refractarse** *vr*
refractario, -ria *adj* : refractory, obstinate
refrán *nm, pl* **refranes** ADAGIO : proverb, saying
refregar {49} *vt* : to scrub
refrenar *vt* **1** : to rein in (a horse) **2** : to restrain, to check — **refrenarse** *vr* : to restrain oneself
refrendar *vt* **1** : to countersign, to endorse **2** : to stamp (a passport)
refrescante *adj* : refreshing

refrescar {72} *vt* **1** : to refresh, to cool **2** : to brush up (on) **3 refrescar la memoria** : to refresh one's memory — *vi* : to turn cooler

refresco *nm* : refreshment, soft drink

refriega *nf* : skirmish, scuffle

refrigeración *nf, pl* **-ciones 1** : refrigeration **2** : air-conditioning

refrigerador *nmf* NEVERA : refrigerator

refrigeradora *nf Col, Peru* : refrigerator

refrigerante *nm* : coolant

refrigerar *vt* **1** : to refrigerate **2** : to air-condition

refrigerio *nm* : snack, refreshments *pl*

refrito¹, -ta *adj* : refried

refrito² *nm* : rehash

refuerzo *nm* : reinforcement, support

refugiado, -da *n* : refugee

refugiar *vt* : to shelter — **refugiarse** *vr* ACOGERSE : to take refuge

refugio *nm* : refuge, shelter

refulgencia *nf* : brilliance, splendor

refulgir {35} *vi* : to shine brightly

refundir *vt* **1** : to recast (metals) **2** : to revise, to rewrite

refunfuñar *vi* : to grumble, to groan

refutar *vt* : to refute — **refutación** *nf*

regadera *nf* **1** : watering can **2** : shower head, shower **3** : sprinkler

regaderazo *nm Mex* : shower

regalar *vt* **1** OBSEQUIAR : to present (as a gift), to give away **2** : to regale, to entertain **3** : to flatter, to make a fuss over — **regalarse** *vr* : to pamper oneself

regalía *nf* : royalty, payment

regaliz *nm, pl* **-lices** : licorice

regalo *nm* **1** OBSEQUIO : gift, present **2** : pleasure, comfort **3** : treat

regañadientes *mpl* **a** ~ : reluctantly, unwillingly

regañar *vt* : to scold, to give a talking to — *vi* **1** QUEJARSE : to grumble, to complain **2** REÑIR : to quarrel, to argue

regaño *nm fam* : scolding

regañon, -ñona *adj, mpl* **-ñones** *fam* : grumpy, irritable

regar {49} *vt* **1** : to irrigate **2** : to water **3** : to wash, to hose down **4** : to spill, to scatter

regata *nf* : regatta, yacht race

regate *nm* : dodge, feint

regatear *vt* **1** : to haggle over **2** ESCATIMAR : to skimp on, to be sparing with — *vi* : to bargain, to haggle

regateo *nm* : bargaining, haggling

regatón *nm, pl* **-tones** : ferrule, tip

regazo *nm* : lap (of a person)

regencia *nf* : regency

regenerar *vt* : to regenerate — **regenerarse** *vr* — **regeneración** *nf*

regentar *vt* : to run, to manage

regente *nmf* : regent

regidor, -dora *n* : town councillor

régimen *nm, pl* **regímenes 1** : regime **2** : diet **3** : regimen, rules *pl* ⟨régimen de vida : lifestyle⟩

regimiento *nm* : regiment

regio, -gia *adj* **1** : great, magnificent **2** : regal, royal

región *nf, pl* **regiones** : region, area

regional *adj* : regional — **regionalmente** *adv*

regir {28} *vt* **1** : to rule **2** : to manage, to run **3** : to control, to govern ⟨las costumbres que rigen la conducta : the customs which govern behavior⟩ — *vi* : to apply, to be in force ⟨las leyes rigen en los tres países : the laws apply in all three countries⟩ — **regirse** *vr* ~ **por** : to go by, to be guided by

registrador¹, -dora *adj* **caja registradora** : cash register

registrador², -dora *n* : registrar, recorder

registrar *vt* **1** : to register, to record **2** GRABAR : to record, to tape **3** : to search, to examine — **registrarse** *vr* **1** INSCRIBIRSE : to register **2** OCURRIR : to happen, to occur

registro *nm* **1** : register **2** : registration **3** : registry, record office **4** : range (of a voice or musical instrument) **5** : search

regla *nf* **1** NORMA : rule, regulation **2** : ruler ⟨regla de cálculo : slide rule⟩ **3** MENSTRUACIÓN : period, menstruation

reglamentación *nf, pl* **-ciones 1** : regulation **2** : rules *pl*

reglamentar *vt* : to regulate, to set rules for

reglamentario, -ria *adj* : regulation, official ⟨equipo reglamentario : standard equipment⟩

reglamento *nm* : regulations *pl*, rules *pl* ⟨reglamento de tráfico : traffic regulations⟩

regocijar *vt* : to gladden, to delight — **regocijarse** *vr* : to rejoice

regocijo *nm* : delight, rejoicing

regordete, -ta *adj fam* LLENITO : chubby

regresar *vt* DEVOLVER : to give back — *vi* : to return, to come back, to go back

regresión *nf, pl* **-siones** : regression, return

regresivo, -va *adj* : regressive

regreso *nm* **1** : return **2 estar de regreso** : to be back, to be home

reguero *nm* **1** : irrigation ditch **2** : trail, trace **3 propagarse como reguero de pólvora** : to spread like wildfire

regulable *adj* : adjustable

regulación *nf, pl* **-ciones** : regulation, control

regulador¹, -dora *adj* : regulating, regulatory

regulador² *nm* **1** : regulator, governor **2 regulador de tiro** : damper (in a chimney)

regular¹ *vt* : to regulate, to control

regular² *adj* **1** : regular **2** : fair, OK, so-so **3** : medium, average **4 por lo regular** : in general, generally

regularidad *nf* : regularity

regularización *nf, pl* **-ciones** NORMAL-IZACIÓN : normalization
regularizar {21} *vt* NORMALIZAR : to normalize, to make regular
regularmente *adv* : regularly
regusto *nm* : aftertaste
rehabilitar *vt* 1 : to rehabilitate 2 : to reinstate 3 : renovate, to restore — **rehabilitación** *nf*
rehacer {40} *vt* 1 : to redo 2 : to remake, to repair, to renew — **rehacerse** *vr* 1 : to recover 2 ~ **de** : to get over
rehecho *pp* → **rehacer**
rehén *nm, pl* **rehenes** : hostage
rehicieron, etc. → **rehacer**
rehizo → **rehacer**
rehuir {41} *vt* : to avoid, to shun
rehusar {8} *v* : to refuse
reimprimir *vt* : to reprint
reina *nf* : queen
reinado *nm* : reign
reinante *adj* 1 : reigning 2 : prevailing, current
reinar *vi* 1 : to reign 2 : to prevail
reincidencia *nf* : recidivism, relapse
reincidente *nmf* : backslider, recidivist
reincidir *vi* : to backslide, to retrogress
reincorporar *vt* : to reinstate — **reincorporarse** *vr* ~ **a** : to return to, to rejoin
reiniciar *vt* 1 : to resume, to restart 2 : to reboot (a computer)
reino *nm* : kingdom, realm ⟨reino animal : animal kingdom⟩
reinstalar *vt* 1 : to reinstall 2 : to reinstate
reintegración *nf, pl* **-ciones** 1 : reinstatement, reintegration 2 : refund, reimbursement
reintegrar *vt* 1 : to reintegrate, reinstate 2 : to refund, to reimburse — **reintegrarse** *vr* ~ **a** : to return to, to rejoin
reír {66} *vi* : to laugh — *vt* : to laugh at — **reírse** *vr*
reiteración *nf, pl* **-ciones** : reiteration, repetition
reiterado, -da *adj* : repeated ⟨lo explicó en reiteradas ocasiones : he explained it repeatedly⟩ — **reiteradamente** *adv*
reiterar *vt* : to reiterate, to repeat
reiterativo, -va *adj* : repetitive, repetitious
reivindicación *nf, pl* **-ciones** 1 : demand, claim 2 : vindication
reivindicar {72} *vt* 1 : to vindicate 2 : to demand, to claim 3 : to restore
reja *nf* 1 : grille, grating ⟨entre rejas : behind bars⟩ 2 : plowshare
rejilla *nf* : grille, grate, screen
rejuvenecer {53} *vt* : to rejuvenate — *vi* : to be rejuvenated — **rejuvenecerse** *vr*
rejuvenecimiento *nm* : rejuvenation
relación *nf, pl* **-ciones** 1 : relation, connection, relevance 2 : relationship 3 RELATO : account 4 LISTA : list 5 **con relación a** *or* **en relación con** : in re-

lation to, concerning 6 **relaciones-públicas** : public relations
relacionar *vt* : to relate, to connect — **relacionarse** *vr* ~ **con** : to be connected to, to be linked with
relajación *nf, pl* **-ciones** : relaxation
relajado, -da *adj* 1 : relaxed, loose 2 : dissolute, depraved
relajante *adj* : relaxing
relajar *vt* : to relax, to slacken — *vi* : to be relaxing — **relajarse** *vr*
relajo *nm* 1 : commotion, ruckus 2 : joke, laugh ⟨lo hizo de relajo : he did it for a laugh⟩
relamerse *vr* : to smack one's lips, to lick one's chops
relámpago *nm* : flash of lightning
relampaguear *vi* : to flash
relanzar {21} *vt* : to relaunch
relatar *vt* : to relate, to tell
relatividad *nf* : relativity
relativo, -va *adj* 1 : relative 2 **en lo relativo a** : with regard to, concerning — **relativamente** *adv*
relato *nm* 1 : story, tale 2 : account
releer {20} *vt* : to reread
relegar {52} *vt* 1 : to relegate 2 **relegar al olvido** : to consign to oblivion
relevante *adj* : outstanding, important
relevar *vt* 1 : to relieve, to take over from 2 ~ **de** : to exempt from — **relevarse** *vr* : to take turns
relevo *nm* 1 : relief, replacement 2 : relay ⟨carrera de relevos : relay race⟩
relicario *nm* 1 : reliquary 2 : locket
relieve *nm* 1 : relief, projection ⟨mapa en relieve : relief map⟩ ⟨letras en relieve : embossed letters⟩ 2 : prominence, importance 3 **poner en relieve** : to highlight, to emphasize
religión *nf, pl* **-giones** : religion
religiosamente *adv* : religiously, faithfully
religioso[1], -sa *adj* : religious
religioso[2], -sa *n* : monk *m*, nun *f*
relinchar *vi* : to neigh, to whinny
relincho *nm* : neigh, whinny
reliquia *nf* 1 : relic 2 **reliquia de familia** : family heirloom
rellenar *vt* 1 : to refill 2 : to stuff, to fill 3 : to fill out
relleno[1], -na *adj* : stuffed, filled
relleno[2] *nm* : stuffing, filling
reloj *nm* 1 : clock 2 : watch 3 **reloj de arena** : hourglass 4 **reloj de pulsera** : wristwatch 5 **como un reloj** : like clockwork
relojería *nf* 1 : watchmaker's shop 2 : watchmaking, clockmaking
reluciente *adj* : brilliant, shining
relucir {45} *vi* 1 : to glitter, to shine 2 **salir a relucir** : to come to the surface 3 **sacar a relucir** : to bring up, to mention
relumbrante *adj* : dazzling
relumbrar *vi* : to shine brightly
relumbrón *nm, pl* **-brones** 1 : flash, glare 2 **de** ~ : flashy, showy

remachar *vt* **1** : to rivet **2** : to clinch (a nail) **3** : to stress, to drive home — *vi* : to smash, to spike (a ball)

remache *nm* **1** : rivet **2** : smash, spike (in sports)

remanente *nm* **1** : remainder, balance **2** : surplus

remanso *nm* : pool

remar *vi* **1** : to row, to paddle **2** : to struggle, to toil

remarcar {72} *vt* : to emphasize, to stress

rematado, -da *adj* : utter, complete

rematador, -dora *n* : auctioneer

rematar *vt* **1** : to finish off **2** : to auction — *vi* **1** : to shoot **2** : to end

remate *nm* **1** : shot (in sports) **2** : auction **3** : end, conclusion **4 como ~** : to top it off **5 de ~** : completely, utterly

remecer {86} *vt* : to sway, to swing

remedar *vt* **1** IMITAR : to imitate, to copy **2** : to mimic, to ape

remediar *vt* **1** : to remedy, to repair **2** : to help out, to assist **3** EVITAR : to prevent, to avoid

remedio *nm* **1** : remedy, cure **2** : solution **3** : option ⟨no me quedó más remedio : I had no other choice⟩ ⟨no hay remedio : it can't be helped⟩ **4 poner remedio a** : to put a stop to **5 sin ~** : unavoidable, inevitable

remedo *nm* : imitation

rememorar *vi* : to recall ⟨rememorar los viejos tiempos : to reminisce⟩

remendar {55} *vt* **1** : to mend, to patch, to darn **2** : to correct

remero, -ra *n* : rower

remesa *nf* **1** : remittance **2** : shipment

remezón *nm, pl* **-zones** : mild earthquake, tremor

remiendo *nm* **1** : patch **2** : correction

remilgado, -da *adj* **1** : prim, prudish **2** : affected

remilgo *nm* : primness, affectation

reminiscencia *nf* : reminiscence

remisión *nf, pl* **-siones 1** ENVÍO : sending, delivery **2** : remission **3** : reference, cross-reference

remiso, -sa *adj* **1** : lax, remiss **2** : reluctant

remitente[1] *nm* : return address

remitente[2] *nmf* : sender (of a letter, etc.)

remitir *vt* **1** : to send, to remit **2 ~ a** : to refer to, to direct to ⟨nos remitió al diccionario : he referred us to the dictionary⟩ — *vi* : to subside, to let up

remo *nm* **1** : paddle, oar **2** : rowing (sport)

remoción *nf, pl* **-ciones 1** : removal **2** : dismissal

remodelación *nf, pl* **-ciones 1** : remodeling **2** : reorganization, restructuring

remodelar *vt* **1** : to remodel **2** : to restructure

remojar *vt* **1** : to soak, to steep **2** : to dip, to dunk **3** : to celebrate with a drink

remojo *nm* **1** : soaking, steeping **2 poner en remojo** : to soak, to leave soaking

remolacha *nf* : beet

remolcador *nm* : tugboat

remolcar {72} *vt* : to tow, to haul

remolino *nm* **1** : whirlwind **2** : eddy, whirlpool **3** : crowd, throng **4** : cowlick

remolque *nm* **1** : towing, tow **2** : trailer **3 a ~** : in tow

remontar *vt* **1** : to overcome **2** SUBIR : to go up — **remontarse** *vr* **1** : to soar **2 ~ a** : to date from, to go back to

rémora *nf* : obstacle, hindrance

remorder {47} *vt* INQUIETAR : to trouble, to distress

remordimiento *nm* : remorse

remotamente *adv* : remotely, vaguely

remoto, -ta *adj* **1** : remote, unlikely ⟨hay una posibilidad remota : there is a slim possibility⟩ **2** : distant, far-off

remover {47} *vt* **1** : to stir **2** : to move around, to turn over **3** : to stir up **4** : to remove **5** : to dismiss

remozamiento *nm* : renovation

remozar {21} *vt* **1** : to renew, to brighten up **2** : to redo, to renovate

remuneración *nf, pl* **-ciones** : remuneration, pay

remunerar *vt* : to pay, to remunerate

remunerativo, -va *adj* : remunerative

renacer {48} *vi* : to be reborn, to revive

renacimiento *nm* **1** : rebirth, revival **2 el Renacimiento** : the Renaissance

renacuajo *nm* : tadpole, pollywog

renal *adj* : renal, kidney

rencilla *nf* : quarrel

renco, -ca *adj* : lame

rencor *nm* **1** : rancor, enmity, hostility **2 guardar rencor** : to hold a grudge

rencoroso, -sa *adj* : resentful, rancorous

rendición *nf, pl* **-ciones 1** : surrender, submission **2** : yield, return

rendido, -da *adj* **1** : submissive **2** : worn-out, exhausted **3** : devoted

rendija *nf* GRIETA : crack, split

rendimiento *nm* **1** : performance **2** : yield

rendir {54} *vt* **1** : to render, to give ⟨rendir las gracias : to give thanks⟩ ⟨rendir homenaje a : to pay homage to⟩ **2** : to yield **3** CANSAR : to exhaust — *vi* **1** CUNDIR : to progress, to make headway **2** : to last, to go a long way — **rendirse** *vr* : to surrender, to give up

renegado, -da *n* : renegade

renegar {49} *vi* **1 ~ de** : to renounce, to disown, to give up **2 ~ de** : to complain about — *vt* **1** : to deny vigorously **2** : to abhor, to hate

renegociar *vt* : to renegotiate — **renegociación** *nf*

renglón *nm, pl* **renglones 1** : line (of writing) **2** : merchandise, line (of products)

rengo, -ga *adj* : lame
renguear *vi* : to limp
reno *nm* : reindeer
renombrado, -da *adj* : renowned, famous
renombre *nm* NOMBRADÍA : renown, fame
renovable *adj* : renewable
renovación *nf, pl* **-ciones** 1 : renewal ⟨renovación de un contrato : renewal of a contract⟩ 2 : change, renovation
renovar {19} *vt* 1 : to renew, to restore 2 : to renovate
renquear *vi* : to limp, to hobble
renquera *nf* COJERA : limp, lameness
renta *nf* 1 : income 2 : rent 3 **impuesto sobre la renta** : income tax
rentable *adj* : profitable
rentar *vt* 1 : to produce, to yield 2 ALQUILAR : to rent
renuencia *nf* : reluctance, unwillingness
renuente *adj* : reluctant, unwilling
renuncia *nf* 1 : resignation 2 : renunciation 3 : waiver
renunciar *vi* 1 : to resign 2 ~ **a** : to renounce, to relinquish ⟨renunció al título : herelinquished the title⟩
reñido, -da *adj* 1 : tough, hard-fought 2 : at odds, on bad terms
reñir {67} *vi* 1 : to argue 2 ~ **con** : to fall out with, to go up against — *vt* : to scold, to reprimand
reo, rea *n* 1 : accused, defendant 2 : offender, culprit
reojo *nm* **de** ~ : out of the corner of one's eye ⟨una mirada de reojo : a sidelong glance⟩
reorganizar {21} *vt* : to reorganize — **reorganización** *nf*
repantigarse {52} *vr* : to slouch, to loll about
reparación *nf, pl* **-ciones** 1 : reparation, amends 2 : repair
reparar *vt* 1 : to repair, to fix, to mend 2 : to make amends for 3 : to correct 4 : to restore, to refresh — *vi* 1 ~ **en** : to observe, to take notice of 2 ~ **en** : to consider, to think about
reparo *nm* 1 : repair, restoration 2 : reservation, qualm ⟨no tuvieron reparos en decírmelo : they didn't hesitate to tell me⟩ 3 **poner reparos a** : to find fault with, to object to
repartición *nf, pl* **-ciones** 1 : distribution 2 : department, division
repartidor[1], -dora *adj* : delivery ⟨camión repartidor : delivery truck⟩
repartidor[2], -dora *n* : delivery person, distributor
repartimiento *nm* → **repartición**
repartir *vt* 1 : to allocate 2 DISTRIBUIR : to distribute, to hand out 3 : to spread
reparto *nm* 1 : allocation 2 : distribution 3 : cast (of characters)
repasar *vt* 1 : to pass by again 2 : to review, to go over 3 : to mend
repaso *nm* 1 : review 2 : mending 3 : checkup, overhaul

repatriar {85} *vt* : to repatriate — **repatriación** *nf*
repavimentar *vt* : to resurface
repelente[1] *adj* : repellent, repulsive
repelente[2] *nm* : repellent ⟨repelente de insectos : insect repellent⟩
repeler *vt* 1 : to repel, to resist, to repulse 2 : to reject 3 : to disgust ⟨el sabor me repele : I find the taste repulsive⟩
repensar {55} *v* : to rethink, to reconsider
repente *nm* 1 : sudden movement, start ⟨de repente : suddenly⟩ 2 : fit, outburst ⟨un repente de ira : a fit of anger⟩
repentino, -na *adj* : sudden — **repentinamente** *adv*
repercusión *nf, pl* **-siones** : repercussion
repercutir *vi* 1 : to reverberate, to echo 2 ~ **en** : to have effects on, to have repercussions on
repertorio *nm* : repertoire
repetición *nf, pl* **-ciones** 1 : repetition 2 : rerun, repeat
repetidamente *adv* : repeatedly
repetido, -da *adj* 1 : repeated, numerous 2 **repetidas veces** : repeatedly, time and again
repetir {54} *vt* 1 : to repeat 2 : to have a second helping of — **repetirse** *vr* 1 : to repeat oneself 2 : to recur
repetitivo, -va *adj* : repetitive, repetitious
repicar {72} *vt* : to ring — *vi* : to ring out, to peal
repique *nm* : ringing, pealing
repisa *nf* : shelf, ledge ⟨repisa de chimenea : mantelpiece⟩ ⟨repisa de ventana : windowsill⟩
replantear *vt* : to redefine, to restate — **replantearse** *vr* : to reconsider
replegar {49} *vt* : to fold — **replegarse** *vr* RETIRARSE : to retreat, to withdraw
repleto, -ta *adj* 1 : replete, full 2 ~ **de** : packed with, crammed with
réplica *nf* 1 : reply 2 : replica, reproduction 3 *Chile, Mex* : aftershock
replicación *nf, pl* **-ciones** : replication
replicar {72} *vi* 1 : to reply, to retort 2 : to argue, to answer back
repliegue *nm* 1 : fold 2 : retreat, withdrawal
repollo *nm* COL : cabbage
reponer {60} *vt* 1 : to replace, to put back 2 : to reinstate 3 : to reply — **reponerse** *vr* : to recover
reportaje *nm* : article, story, report
reportar *vt* 1 : to check, to restrain 2 : to bring, to carry, to yield ⟨me reportó numerosos beneficios : it brought me many benefits⟩ 3 : to report — **reportarse** *vr* 1 CONTENERSE : to control oneself 2 PRESENTARSE : to report, to show up
reporte *nm* : report
reportear *vt* : to report on, to cover

reportero, -ra *n* 1 : reporter 2 **reportero gráfico** : photojournalist
reposado, -da *adj* : calm
reposar *vi* 1 : to rest, to repose 2 : to stand, to settle ⟨deje reposar la masa media hora : let the dough stand for half an hour⟩ 3 : to lie, to be buried — **reposarse** *vr* : to settle
reposición *nf, pl* **-ciones** 1 : replacement 2 : reinstatement 3 : revival
repositorio *nm* : repository
reposo *nm* : repose, rest
repostar *vi* 1 : to stock up 2 : to refuel
repostería *nf* 1 : confectioner's shop 2 : pastry-making
repostero, -ra *n* : confectioner
repreguntar *vt* : to cross-examine
repreguntas *nfpl* : cross-examination
reprender *vt* : to reprimand, to scold
reprensible *adj* : reprehensible
represa *nf* : dam
represalia *nf* 1 : reprisal, retaliation 2 **tomar represalias** : to retaliate
represar *vt* : to dam
representación *nf, pl* **-ciones** 1 : representation 2 : performance 3 **en representación de** : on behalf of
representante *nmf* 1 : representative 2 : performer
representar *vt* 1 : to represent, to act for 2 : to perform 3 : to look, to appear as 4 : to symbolize, to stand for 5 : to signify, to mean — **representarse** *vr* : to imagine, to picture
representativo, -va *adj* : representative
represión *nf, pl* **-siones** : repression
represivo, -va *adj* : repressive
reprimenda *nf* : reprimand
reprimir *vt* 1 : to repress 2 : to suppress, to stifle
reprobable *adj* : reprehensible, culpable
reprobación *nf* : disapproval
reprobar {19} *vt* 1 DESAPROBAR : to condemn, to disapprove of 2 : to fail (a course)
reprobatorio, -ria *adj* : disapproving, admonitory
reprochable *adj* : reprehensible, reproachable
reprochar *vt* : to reproach — **reprocharse** *vr*
reproche *nm* : reproach
reproducción *nf, pl* **-ciones** : reproduction
reproducir {61} *vt* : to reproduce — **reproducirse** *vr* 1 : to breed, to reproduce 2 : to recur
reproductor, -tora *adj* : reproductive
reptar *vi* : to crawl, to slither
reptil[1] *adj* : reptilian
reptil[2] *nm* : reptile
república *nf* : republic
republicanismo *nm* : republicanism
republicano, -na *adj & n* : republican
repudiar *vt* : to repudiate — **repudiación** *nf*
repudio *nm* : repudiation
repuesto[1] *pp* → reponer

repuesto[2] *nm* 1 : spare part 2 **de ∼** : spare ⟨rueda de repuesto : spare wheel⟩
repugnancia *nf* : repugnance
repugnante *adj* : repulsive, repugnant, revolting
repugnar *vt* : to cause repugnance, to disgust — **repugnarse** *vr*
repujar *vt* : to emboss
repulsivo, -va *adj* : repulsive
repuntar *vt Arg, Chile* : to round up (cattle) — *vi* : to begin to appear — **repuntarse** *vr* : to fall out, to quarrel
repuso, etc. → reponer
reputación *nf, pl* **-ciones** : reputation
reputar *vt* : to consider, to deem
requerir {76} *vt* 1 : to require, to call for 2 : to summon, to send for
requesón *nm, pl* **-sones** : curd cheese, cottage cheese
réquiem *nm* : requiem
requisa *nf* 1 : requisition 2 : seizure 3 : inspection
requisar *vt* 1 : to requisition 2 : to seize 3 INSPECCIONAR : to inspect
requisito *nm* 1 : requirement 2 **requisito previo** : prerequisite
res *nf* 1 : beast, animal 2 *CA, Mex* : beef 3 **reses** *nfpl* : cattle ⟨60 reses : 60 head of cattle⟩
resabio *nm* 1 VICIO : bad habit, vice 2 DEJO : aftertaste
resaca *nf* 1 : undertow 2 : hangover
resaltar *vi* 1 SOBRESALIR : to stand out 2 **hacer resaltar** : to bring out, to highlight — *vt* : to stress, to emphasize
resarcimiento *nm* 1 : compensation 2 : reimbursement
resarcir {83} *vt* : to compensate, to indemnify — **resarcirse** *vr* ∼ **de** : to make up for
resbaladizo, -za *adj* 1 RESBALOSO : slippery 2 : tricky, ticklish, delicate
resbalar *vi* 1 : to slip, to slide 2 : to slip up, to make a mistake 3 : to skid — **resbalarse** *vr*
resbalón *nm, pl* **-lones** : slip
resbaloso, -sa *adj* : slippery
rescatar *vt* 1 : to rescue, to save 2 : to recover, to get back
rescate *nm* 1 : rescue 2 : recovery 3 : ransom
rescindir *vt* : to rescind, to annul, to cancel
rescisión *nf, pl* **-siones** : annulment, cancellation
rescoldo *nm* : embers *pl*
resecar {72} *vt* : to make dry, to dry up — **resecarse** *vr* : to dry up
reseco, -ca *adj* : dry, dried-up
resentido, -da *adj* : resentful
resentimiento *nm* : resentment
resentirse {76} *vr* 1 : to suffer, to be weakened 2 OFENDERSE : to be upset ⟨se resintió porque la insultaron : she got upset when they insulted her, she resented being insulted⟩ 3 ∼ **de** : to feel the effects of

reseña *nf* **1** : report, summary, review **2** : description

reseñar *vt* **1** : to review **2** DESCRIBIR : to describe

reserva *nf* **1** : reservation **2** : reserve **3** : confidence, privacy ⟨con la mayor reserva : in strictest confidence⟩ **4 de ~** : spare, in reserve **5 reservas** *nfpl* : reservations, doubts

reservación *nf, pl* **-ciones** : reservation

reservado, -da *adj* **1** : reserved, reticent **2** : confidential

reservar *vt* : to reserve — **reservarse** *vr* **1** : to save oneself **2** : to conceal, to keep to oneself

reservorio *nm* : reservoir, reserve

resfriado *nm* CATARRO : cold

resfriar {85} *vt* : to cool — **resfriarse** *vr* **1** : to cool off **2** : to catch a cold

resfrío *nm* : cold

resguardar *vt* : to safeguard, to protect — **resguardarse** *vr*

resguardo *nm* **1** : safeguard, protection **2** : receipt, voucher **3** : border guard, coast guard

residencia *nf* **1** : residence **2** : boarding house

residencial *adj* : residential

residente *adj & nmf* : resident

residir *vi* **1** VIVIR : to reside, to dwell **2 ~ en** : to lie in, to consist of

residual *adj* : residual

residuo *nm* **1** : residue **2** : remainder **3 residuos** *nmpl* : waste ⟨residuos nucleares : nuclear waste⟩

resignación *nf, pl* **-ciones** : resignation

resignar *vt* : to resign — **resignarse** *vr* **~ a** : to resign oneself to

resina *nf* **1** : resin **2 resina epoxídica** : epoxy

resistencia *nf* **1** : resistance **2** AGUANTE : endurance, strength, stamina

resistente *adj* **1** : resistant **2** : strong, tough

resistir *vt* **1** : to stand, to bear, to tolerate **2** : to withstand — *vi* : to resist ⟨resistió hasta el último minuto : he held out until the last minute⟩ — **resistirse** *vr* **~ a** : to be resistant to, to be reluctant

resollar {19} *vi* : to breathe heavily, to wheeze

resolución *nf, pl* **-ciones** **1** : resolution, settlement **2** : decision **3** : determination, resolve

resolver {89} *vt* **1** : to resolve, to settle **2** : to decide — **resolverse** *vr* : to make up one's mind

resonancia *nf* **1** : resonance **2** : impact, repercussions *pl*

resonante *adj* **1** : resonant **2** : tremendous, resounding ⟨un éxito resonante : a resounding success⟩

resonar {19} *vi* : to resound, to ring

resoplar *vi* **1** : to puff, to pant **2** : to snort

resoplo *nm* **1** : puffing, panting **2** : snort

resorte *nm* **1** MUELLE : spring **2** : elasticity **3** : influence, means *pl* ⟨tocar resortes : to pull strings⟩

resortera *nf Mex* : slingshot

respaldar *vt* : to back, to support, to endorse — **respaldarse** *vr* : to lean back

respaldo *nm* **1** : back (of an object) **2** : support, backing

respectar *vt* : to concern, to relate to ⟨por lo que a mí respecta : as far as I'm concerned⟩

respectivo, -va *adj* : respective — **respectivamente** *adv*

respecto *nm* **1 ~ a** : in regard to, concerning **2 al respecto** : on this matter, in this respect

respetable *adj* : respectable — **respetabilidad** *nf*

respetar *vt* : to respect

respeto *nm* **1** : respect, consideration **2 respetos** *nmpl* : respects ⟨presentar sus respetos : to pay one's respects⟩

respetuosidad *nf* : respectfulness

respetuoso, -sa *adj* : respectful — **respetuosamente** *adv*

respingo *nm* : start, jump

respiración *nf, pl* **-ciones** : respiration, breathing

respiradero *nm* : vent, ventilation shaft

respirador *nm* : respirator

respirar *v* : to breathe

respiratorio, -ria *adj* : respiratory

respiro *nm* **1** : breath **2** : respite, break

resplandecer {53} *vi* **1** : to shine **2** : to stand out

resplandeciente *adj* **1** : resplendent, shining **2** : radiant

resplandor *nm* **1** : brightness, brilliance, radiance **2** : flash

responder *vt* : to answer — *vi* **1** : to answer, to reply, to respond **2 ~ a** : to respond to ⟨responder al tratamiento : to respond to treatment⟩ **3 ~ de** : to answer for, to vouch for (something) **4 ~ por** : to vouch for (someone)

responsabilidad *nf* : responsibility

responsable *adj* : responsible — **responsablemente** *adv*

respuesta *nf* : answer, response

resquebrajar *vt* : to split, to crack — **resquebrajarse** *vr*

resquemor *nm* : resentment, bitterness

resquicio *nm* **1** : crack **2** : opportunity, chance **3** : trace ⟨sin un resquicio de remordimiento : without a trace of remorse⟩ **4 resquicio legal** : loophole

resta *nf* SUSTRACCIÓN : subtraction

restablecer {53} *vt* : to reestablish, to restore — **restablecerse** *vr* : to recover

restablecimiento *nm* **1** : reestablishment, restoration **2** : recovery

restallar *vi* : to crack, to crackle, to click

restallido *nm* : crack, crackle

restante *adj* **1** : remaining **2 lo restante, los restantes** : the rest

restañar *vt* : to stanch

restar *vt* **1** : to deduct, to subtract ⟨restar un punto : to deduct a point⟩

2 : to minimize, to play down — *vi* : to remain, to be left

restauración *nf, pl* **-ciones 1** : restoration **2** : catering, food service

restaurante *nm* : restaurant

restaurar *vt* : to restore

restitución *nf, pl* **-ciones** : restitution, return

restituir {41} *vt* : to return, to restore, to reinstate

resto *nm* **1** : rest, remainder **2 restos** *nmpl* : remains ⟨restos de comida : leftovers⟩ ⟨restos arqueológicos : archeological ruins⟩ **3 restos mortales** : mortal remains

restorán *nm, pl* **-ranes** : restaurant

restregadura *nf* : scrub, scrubbing

restregar {49} *vt* **1** : to rub **2** : to scrub — **restregarse** *vr*

restricción *nf, pl* **-ciones** : restriction, limitation

restrictivo, -va *adj* : restrictive

restringido, -da *adj* LIMITADO : limited, restricted

restringir {35} *vt* LIMITAR : to restrict, to limit

restructuración *nf* : restructuring

restructurar *vt* : to restructure

resucitación *nf* : resuscitation ⟨resucitación cardiopulmonar : CPR, cardiopulmonary resuscitation⟩

resucitar *vt* **1** : to resuscitate, to revive, to resurrect **2** : to revitalize

resuello *nm* **1** : puffing, heavy breathing, wheezing **2** : break, breather

resuelto[1] *pp* → **resolver**

resuelto[2]**, -ta** *adj* : determined, resolved, resolute

resulta *nf* **1** : consequence, result **2 a resultas de** *or* **de resultas de** : as a result of

resultado *nm* : result, outcome

resultante *adj & nf* : resultant

resultar *vi* **1** : to work, to work out ⟨mi idea no resultó : my idea didn't work out⟩ **2** : to prove, to turn out to be ⟨resultó bien simpático : he turned out to be very nice⟩ **3** ~ **en** : to lead to, to result in **4** ~ **de** : to be the result of

resumen *nm, pl* **-súmenes 1** : summary, summation **2 en** ~ : in summary, in short

resumidero *nm* : drain

resumir *v* : to summarize, to sum up

resurgimiento *nm* : resurgence

resurgir {35} *vi* : to reappear, to revive

resurrección *nf, pl* **-ciones** : resurrection

retablo *nm* **1** : tableau **2** : altarpiece

retador, -dora *n* : challenger (in sports)

retaguardia *nf* : rear guard

retahíla *nf* : string, series ⟨una retahíla de insultos : a volley of insults⟩

retaliación *nf, pl* **-ciones** : retaliation

retama *nf* : broom (plant)

retar *vt* DESAFIAR : to challenge, to defy

retardante *adj* : retardant

retardar *vt* **1** RETRASAR : to delay, to retard **2** : to postpone

retazo *nm* **1** : remnant, scrap **2** : fragment, piece ⟨retazos de su obra : bits and pieces from his writings⟩

retención *nf, pl* **-ciones 1** : retention **2** : deduction, withholding

retener {80} *vt* **1** : to retain, to keep **2** : to withhold **3** : to detain

retentivo, -va *adj* : retentive

reticencia *nf* **1** : reluctance, reticence **2** : insinuation

reticente *adj* **1** : reluctant, reticent **2** : insinuating, misleading

retina *nf* : retina

retintín *nm, pl* **-tines 1** : jingle, jangle **2 con** ~ : sarcastically

retirada *nf* **1** : retreat ⟨batirse en retirada : to withdraw, to beat a retreat⟩ **2** : withdrawal (of funds) **3** : retirement **4** : refuge, haven

retirado, -da *adj* **1** : remote, distant, far off **2** : secluded, quiet

retirar *vt* **1** : to remove, to take away, to recall **2** : to withdraw, to take out — **retirarse** *vr* **1** REPLEGARSE : to retreat, to withdraw **2** JUBILARSE : to retire

retiro *nm* **1** JUBILACIÓN : retirement **2** : withdrawal, retreat **3** : seclusion

reto *nm* DESAFÍO : challenge, dare

retocar {72} *vt* : to touch up

retoñar *vi* : to sprout

retoño *nm* : sprout, shoot

retoque *nm* : retouching

retorcer {14} *vt* **1** : to twist **2** : to wring — **retorcerse** *vr* **1** : to get twisted, to get tangled up **2** : to squirm, to writhe, to wiggle about

retorcijón *nm, pl* **-jones** : cramp, sharp pain

retorcimiento *nm* **1** : twisting, wringing **2** : deviousness

retórica *nf* : rhetoric

retórico, -ca *adj* : rhetorical — **retóricamente** *adv*

retornar *v* : to return

retorno *nm* : return

retozar {21} *vi* : to frolic, to romp

retozo *nm* : frolicking

retozón, -zona *adj, mpl* **-zones** : playful

retracción *nf, pl* **-ciones** : retraction, withdrawal

retractable *adj* : retractable

retractación *nf, pl* **-ciones** : retraction (of a statement, etc.)

retractarse *vr* **1** : to withdraw, to back down **2** ~ **de** : to take back, to retract

retraer {81} *vt* **1** : to bring back **2** : to dissuade — **retraerse** *vr* **1** RETIRARSE : to withdraw, to retire **2** REFUGIARSE : to take refuge

retraído, -da *adj* : withdrawn, retiring, shy

retraimiento *nm* **1** : shyness, timidity **2** : withdrawal

retrasado, -da *adj* **1** : retarded, mentally slow **2** : behind, in arrears **3**

: backward (of a country) **4** : slow (of a watch)

retrasar *vt* **1** DEMORAR, RETARDAR : to delay, to hold up **2** : to put off, to postpone — **retrasarse** *vr* **1** : to be late **2** : to fall behind

retraso *nm* **1** ATRASO : delay, lateness **2 retraso mental** : mental retardation

retratar *vt* **1** : to portray, to depict **2** : to photograph **3** : to paint a portrait of

retrato *nm* **1** : depiction, portrayal **2** : portrait, photograph

retrete *nm* : restroom, toilet

retribución *nf, pl* **-ciones 1** : pay, payment **2** : reward

retribuir {41} *vt* **1** : to pay **2** : to reward

retroactivo, -va *adj* : retroactive — **retroactivamente** *adv*

retroalimentación *nf, pl* **-ciones** : feedback

retroceder *vi* **1** : to move back, to turn back **2** : to back off, to back down **3** : to recoil (of a firearm)

retroceso *nm* **1** : backward movement **2** : backing down **3** : setback, relapse **4** : recoil

retrógrado, -da *adj* **1** : reactionary **2** : retrograde

retropropulsión *nf* : jet propulsion

retrospectiva *nf* : retrospective, hindsight

retrospectivo, -va *adj* **1** : retrospective **2 mirada retrospectiva** : backward glance

retrovisor *nm* : rearview mirror

retruécano *nm* : pun, play on words

retumbar *vi* **1** : to boom, to thunder **2** : to resound, to reverberate

retumbo *nm* : booming, thundering, roll

retuvo, etc. → **retener**

reubicar {72} *vt* : to relocate — **reubicación** *nf*

reuma *or* **reúma** *nmf* → **reumatismo**

reumático, -ca *adj* : rheumatic

reumatismo *nm* : rheumatism

reunión *nf, pl* **-niones 1** : meeting **2** : gathering, reunion

reunir {68} *vt* **1** : to unite, to join, to bring together **2** : to have, to possess ⟨reunieron los requisitos necesarios : they fulfilled the necessary requirements⟩ **3** : to gather, to collect, to raise (funds) — **reunirse** *vr* : to meet

reutilizable *adj* : reusable

reutilizar {21} *vt* : to recycle, to reuse

revalidar *vt* **1** : to confirm, to ratify **2** : to defend (a title)

revaluar {3} *vt* : to reevaluate — **revaluación** *n*

revancha *nf* **1** DESQUITE : revenge, requital **2** : rematch

revelación *nf, pl* **-ciones** : revelation

revelado *nm* : developing (of film)

revelador¹, -dora *adj* : revealing

revelador² *nm* : developer

revelar *vt* **1** : to reveal, to disclose **2** : to develop (film)

revendedor, -dora *n* **1** : scalper **2** DETALLISTA : retailer

revender *vt* **1** : to resell **2** : to scalp

reventa *nf* **1** : resale **2** : scalping

reventar {55} *vi* **1** ESTALLAR, EXPLOTAR : to burst, to blow up **2** ~ **de** : to be bursting with — *vt* **1** : to burst **2** *fam* : to annoy, to rile

reventón *nm, pl* **-tones 1** : burst, bursting **2** : blowout, flat tire **3** *Mex fam* : bash, party

reverberar *vi* : to reverberate — **reverberación** *nf*

reverdecer {53} *vi* **1** : to grow green again **2** : to revive

reverencia *nf* **1** : reverence **2** : bow, curtsy

reverenciar *vt* : to revere, to venerate

reverendo¹, -da *adj* **1** : reverend **2** *fam* : total, absolute ⟨es un reverendo imbécil : he is a complete idiot⟩

reverendo², -da *n* : reverend

reverente *adj* : reverent

reversa *nf Col, Mex* : reverse (gear)

reversible *adj* : reversible

reversión *nf, pl* **-siones** : reversion

reverso *nm* **1** : back, other side **2 el reverso de la medalla** : the complete opposite

revertir {76} *vi* **1** : to revert, to go back **2** ~ **en** : to result in, to end up as

revés *nm, pl* **reveses 1** : back, wrong side **2** : setback, reversal **3** : backhand (in sports) **4 al revés** : the other way around, upside down, inside out **5 al revés de** : contrary to

revestimiento *nm* : covering, facing (of a building)

revestir {54} *vt* **1** : to coat, to cover, to surface **2** : to conceal, to disguise **3** : to take on, to assume ⟨la reunión revistió gravedad : the meeting took on a serious note⟩

revisar *vt* **1** : to examine, to inspect, to check **2** : to check over, to overhaul (machinery) **3** : to revise

revisión *nf, pl* **-siones 1** : revision **2** : inspection, check

revisor, -sora *n* **1** : inspector **2** : conductor (on a train)

revista *nf* **1** : magazine, journal **2** : revue **3 pasar revista** : to review, to inspect

revistar *vt* : to review, to inspect

revitalizar {21} *vt* : to revitalize — **revitalización** *nf*

revivir *vi* : to revive, to come alive again — *vt* : to relive

revocación *nf, pl* **-ciones** : revocation, repeal

revocar {72} *vt* **1** : to revoke, to repeal **2** : to plaster (a wall)

revolcar {82} *vt* : to knock over, to knock down — **revolcarse** *vr* : to roll around, to wallow

revolcón *nm, pl* **-cones** *fam* : tumble, fall

revolotear *vi* : to flutter around, to flit

revoloteo *nm* : fluttering, flitting

revoltijo *nm* **1** FÁRRAGO : mess, jumble **2** *Mex* : traditional seafood dish
revoltoso, -sa *adj* : unruly, rebellious
revolución *nf, pl* **-ciones** : revolution
revolucionar *vt* : to revolutionize
revolucionario, -ria *adj & n* : revolutionary
revolver {89} *vt* **1** : to move about, to mix, to shake, to stir **2** : to upset (one's stomach) **3** : to mess up, to rummage through ⟨revolver la casa : to turn the house upside down⟩ — **revolverse** *vr* **1** : to toss and turn **2** VOLVERSE : to turn around
revólver *nm* : revolver
revoque *nm* : plaster
revuelo *nm* **1** : fluttering **2** : commotion, stir
revuelta *nf* : uprising, revolt
revuelto¹ *pp* → **revolver**
revuelto², -ta *adj* **1** : choppy, rough ⟨mar revuelto : rough sea⟩ **2** : untidy **3 huevos revueltos** : scrambled eggs
rey *nm* : king
reyerta *nf* : brawl, fight
rezagado, -da *n* : straggler, latecomer
rezagar {52} *vt* **1** : to leave behind **2** : to postpone — **rezagarse** *vr* : to fall behind, to lag
rezar {21} *vi* **1** : to pray **2** : to say ⟨como reza el refrán : as the saying goes⟩ **3** ~ **con** : to concern, to have to do with — *vt* : to say, to recite ⟨rezar un Ave María : to say a Hail Mary⟩
rezo *nm* : prayer, praying
rezongar {52} *vi* : to gripe, to grumble
rezumar *v* : to ooze, to leak
ría¹, etc. → **reír**
ría² *nf* : estuary
riachuelo *nm* ARROYO : brook, stream
riada *nf* : flood
ribera *nf* : bank, shore
ribete *nm* **1** : border, trim **2** : frill, adornment **3 ribetes** *nmpl* : hint, touch ⟨tiene sus ribetes de genio : there's a touch of genius in him⟩
ribetear *vt* : to border, to edge, to trim
ricamente *adv* : richly, splendidly
rice, etc. → **rizar**
rico¹, -ca *adj* **1** : rich, wealthy **2** : fertile **3** : luxurious, valuable **4** : delicious **5** : adorable, lovely **6** : great, wonderful
rico², -ca *n* : rich person
ridiculez *nf, pl* **-leces** : ridiculousness, absurdity
ridiculizar {21} *vt* : to ridicule
ridículo¹, -la *adj* ABSURDO, DISPARATADO : ridiculous, ludicrous — **ridículamente** *adv*
ridículo², -la *n* **1 hacer el ridículo** : to make a fool of oneself **2 poner en ridículo** : to ridicule
ríe, etc. → **reír**
riega, riegue etc. → **regar**
riego *nm* : irrigation
riel *nm* : rail, track

rienda *nf* **1** : rein **2 dar rienda suelta a** : to give free rein to **3 llevar las riendas** : to be in charge **4 tomar las riendas** : to take control
riesgo *nm* : risk
riesgoso, -sa *adj* : risky
rifa *nf* : raffle
rifar *vt* : to raffle — *vi* : to quarrel, to fight
rifle *nm* : rifle
rige, rija etc. → **regir**
rigidez *nf, pl* **-deces** **1** : rigidity, stiffness ⟨rigidez cadavérica : rigor mortis⟩ **2** : inflexibility
rígido, -da *adj* **1** : rigid, stiff **2** : strict — **rígidamente** *adv*
rigor *nm* **1** : rigor, harshness **2** : precision, meticulousness **3 de** ~ : usual ⟨la respuesta de rigor : the standard reply⟩ **4 de** ~ : essential, obligatory **5 en** ~ : strictly speaking, in reality
riguroso, -sa *adj* : rigorous — **rigurosamente** *adv*
rima *nf* **1** : rhyme **2 rimas** *nfpl* : verse, poetry
rimar *vi* : to rhyme
rimbombante *adj* **1** : grandiose, showy **2** : bombastic, pompous
rímel *or* **rimel** *nm* : mascara
rin *nm Col, Mex* : wheel, rim (of a tire)
rincón *nm, pl* **rincones** : corner, nook
rinde, etc. → **rendir**
rinoceronte *nm* : rhinoceros
riña *nf* **1** : fight, brawl **2** : dispute, quarrel
riñe, etc. → **reñir**
riñón *nm, pl* **riñones** : kidney
río¹ → **reír**
río² *nm* **1** : river **2** : torrent, stream ⟨un río de lágrimas : a flood of tears⟩
ripio *nm* **1** : debris, rubble **2** : gravel
riqueza *nf* **1** : wealth, riches *pl* **2** : richness **3 riquezas naturales** : natural resources
risa *nf* **1** : laughter, laugh **2 dar risa** : to make laugh ⟨me dio mucha risa : I found it very funny⟩ **3** *fam* **morirse de la risa** : to die laughing, to crack up
risco *nm* : crag, cliff
risible *adj* IRRISORIO : ludicrous, laughable
risita *nf* : giggle, titter, snicker
risotada *nf* : guffaw
ristra *nf* : string, series *pl*
risueño, -ña *adj* **1** : cheerful, pleasant **2** : promising
rítmico, -ca *adj* : rhythmical, rhythmic — **rítmicamente** *adv*
ritmo *nm* **1** : rhythm **2** : pace, tempo ⟨trabajó a ritmo lento : she worked at a slow pace⟩
rito *nm* : rite, ritual
ritual *adj & nm* : ritual — **ritualmente** *adv*
rival *adj & nmf* COMPETIDOR : rival
rivalidad *nf* : rivalry, competition
rivalizar {21} *vi* ~ **con** : to rival, to compete with

rizado, -da *adj* **1** : curly **2** : ridged **3** : ripply, undulating
rizar {21} *vt* **1** : to curl **2** : to ripple, to ruffle (a surface) **3** : to crumple, to fold — **rizarse** *vr* **1** : to frizz **2** : to ripple
rizo *nm* **1** : curl **2** : loop (in aviation)
robalo *or* **róbalo** *nm* : sea bass
robar *vt* **1** : to steal **2** : to rob, to burglarize **3** SECUESTRAR : to abduct, to kidnap **4** : to captivate — *vi* ~ **en** : to break into
roble *nm* : oak
robo *nm* : robbery, theft
robot *nm, pl* **robots** : robot
robótica *nf* : robotics
robustecer {53} *vt* : to grow stronger, to strengthen
robustez *nf* : sturdiness, robustness
robusto, -ta *adj* : robust, sturdy
roca *nf* : rock, boulder
roce[1], etc. → **rozar**
roce[2] *nm* **1** : rubbing, chafing **2** : brush, graze, touch **3** : close contact, familiarity **4** : friction, disagreement
rociador *nm* : sprinkler
rociar {85} *vt* : to spray, to sprinkle
rocío *nm* **1** : dew **2** : shower, light rain
rock *or* **rock and roll** *nm* : rock, rock and roll
rocola *nf* : jukebox
rocoso, -sa *adj* : rocky
rodada *nf* : track (of a tire), rut
rodado, -da *adj* **1** : wheeled **2** : dappled (of a horse)
rodadura *nf* : rolling, taxiing
rodaja *nf* : round, slice
rodaje *nm* **1** : filming, shooting **2** : breaking in (of a vehicle)
rodamiento *nm* **1** : bearing ⟨rodamiento de bolas : ball bearings⟩ **2** : rolling
rodante *adj* : rolling
rodar {19} *vi* **1** : to roll, to roll down, to roll along ⟨rodé por la escalera : I tumbled down the stairs⟩ ⟨todo rodaba bien : everthing was going along well⟩ **2** GIRAR : to turn, to go around **3** : to move about, to travel ⟨andábamos rodando por todas partes : we drifted along from place to place⟩ — *vt* **1** : to film, to shoot **2** : to break in (a new vehicle)
rodear *vt* **1** : to surround **2** : to round up (cattle) — *vi* **1** : to go around **2** : to beat around the bush — **rodearse** *vr* ~ **de** : to surround oneself with
rodeo *nm* **1** : rodeo, roundup **2** DESVÍO : detour **3** : evasion ⟨andar con rodeos : to beat around the bush⟩ ⟨sin rodeos : without reservations⟩
rodilla *nf* : knee
rodillo *nm* **1** : roller **2** : rolling pin
rododendro *nm* : rhododendron
roedor[1], **-dora** *adj* : gnawing
roedor[2] *nm* : rodent
roer {69} *vt* **1** : to gnaw **2** : to eat away at, to torment
rogar {16} *vt* : to beg, to request — *vi* **1** : to beg, to plead **2** : to pray

roiga, etc. → **roer**
rojez *nf* : redness
rojizo, -za *adj* : reddish
rojo[1], **-ja** *adj* **1** : red **2 ponerse rojo** : to blush
rojo[2] *nm* : red
rol *nm* **1** : role **2** : list, roll
rollo *nm* **1** : roll, coil ⟨un rollo de cinta : a roll of tape⟩ ⟨en rollo : rolled up⟩ **2** *fam* : roll of fat **3** *fam* : boring speech, lecture
romance *nm* **1** : Romance language **2** : ballad **3** : romance **4 en buen romance** : simply stated, simply put
romano, -na *adj & n* : Roman
romanticismo *nm* : romanticism
romántico, -ca *adj* : romantic — **románticamente** *adv*
rombo *nm* : rhombus
romería *nf* **1** : pilgrimage, procession **2** : crowd, gathering
romero[1], **-ra** *n* PEREGRINO : pilgrim
romero[2] *nm* : rosemary
romo, -ma *adj* : blunt, dull
rompecabezas *nms & pl* : puzzle, riddle
rompehielos *nms & pl* : icebreaker (ship)
rompehuelgas *nmfs & pl* ESQUIROL : strikebreaker, scab
rompenueces *nms & pl* : nutcracker
rompeolas *ns & pl* : breakwater, jetty
romper {70} *vt* **1** : to break, to smash **2** : to rip, to tear **3** : to break off (relations), to break (a contract) **4** : to break through, to break down **5** GASTAR : to wear out — *vi* **1** : to break ⟨al romper del día : at the break of day⟩ **2** ~ **a** : to begin to, to burst out with ⟨romper a llorar : to burst into tears⟩ **3** ~ **con** : to break off with
rompope *nm CA, Mex* : drink similar to eggnog
ron *nm* : rum
roncar {72} *vi* **1** : to snore **2** : to roar
ronco, -ca *adj* **1** : hoarse **2** : husky (of the voice) — **roncamente** *adv*
ronda *nf* **1** : beat, patrol **2** : round (of drinks, of negotiations, of a game)
rondar *vt* **1** : to patrol **2** : to hang around ⟨siempre está rondando la calle : he's always hanging around the street⟩ **3** : to be approximately ⟨debe rondar los cincuenta : he must be about 50⟩ — *vi* **1** : to be on patrol **2** : to prowl around, to roam about
ronque, etc. → **roncar**
ronquera *nf* : hoarseness
ronquido *nm* **1** : snore **2** : roar
ronronear *vi* : to purr
ronroneo *nm* : purr, purring
ronzal *nm* : halter (for an animal)
ronzar {21} *v* : to munch, to crunch
roña *nf* **1** : mange **2** : dirt, filth **3** *fam* : stinginess
roñoso, -sa *adj* **1** : mangy **2** : dirty **3** *fam* : stingy
ropa *nf* **1** : clothes *pl*, clothing **2 ropa interior** : underwear

ropaje *nm* : apparel, garments *pl*, regalia
ropero *nm* ARMARIO, CLÓSET : wardrobe, closet
rosa[1] *adj* : rose-colored, pink
rosa[2] *nm* : rose, pink (color)
rosa[3] *nf* : rose (flower)
rosáceo, -cea *adj* : pinkish
rosado[1]**, -da** *adj* **1** : pink **2 vino rosado** : rosé
rosado[2] *nm* : pink (color)
rosal *nm* : rosebush
rosario *nm* **1** : rosary **2** : series ⟨un rosario de islas : a string of islands⟩
rosbif *nm* : roast beef
rosca *nf* **1** : thread (of a screw) ⟨una tapa a rosca : a screw top⟩ **2** : ring, coil
roseta *nf* : rosette
rosquilla *nf* : ring-shaped pastry, doughnut
rostro *nm* : face, countenance
rotación *nf, pl* **-ciones** : rotation
rotar *vt* : to rotate, to turn — *vi* : to turn, to spin
rotativo[1]**, -va** *adj* : rotary
rotativo[2] *nm* : newspaper
rotatorio, -ria *adj* → **rotativo**[1]
roto[1] *pp* → **romper**
roto[2]**, -ta** *adj* **1** : broken **2** : ripped, torn
rotonda *nf* **1** : traffic circle, rotary **2** : rotunda
rotor *nm* : rotor
rótula *nf* : kneecap
rotular *vt* **1** : to head, to entitle **2** : to label
rótulo *nm* **1** : heading, title **2** : label, sign
rotundo, -da *adj* **1** REDONDO : round **2** : categorical, absolute ⟨un éxito rotundo : a resounding success⟩ — **rotundamente** *adv*
rotura *nf* : break, tear, fracture
roya *nf* : plant rust
roya, etc. → **roer**
rozado, -da *adj* GASTADO : worn
rozadura *nf* **1** : scratch, abrasion **2** : rubbed spot, sore
rozar {21} *vt* **1** : to chafe, to rub against **2** : to border on, to touch on **3** : to graze, to touch lightly — **rozarse** *vr* ~ **con** *fam* : to rub shoulders with
ruandés, -desa *adj & n* : Rwandan
ruano, -na *adj* : roan
rubí *nm, pl* **rubíes** : ruby
rubio, -bia *adj & n* : blond
rublo *nm* : ruble
rubor *nm* **1** : flush, blush **2** : rouge, blusher
ruborizarse {21} *vr* : to blush
rubrica *nf* : title, heading
rubricar {72} *vt* **1** : sign with a flourish ⟨firmado y rubricado : signed and sealed⟩ **2** : to endorse, to sanction
rubro *nm* **1** : heading, title **2** : line, area (in business)
rudeza *nf* ASPEREZA : roughness, coarseness

rudimentario, -ria *adj* : rudimentary — **rudimentariamente** *adv*
rudimento *nm* : rudiment, basics *pl*
rudo, -da *adj* **1** : rough, harsh **2** : coarse, unpolished — **rudamente** *adv*
rueda[1]**, etc.** → **rodar**
rueda[2] *nf* **1** : wheel **2** RODAJA : round slice **3** : circle, ring **4 rueda de andar** : treadmill **5 rueda de prensa** : press conference **6 ir sobre ruedas** : to go smoothly
ruedita *nf* : caster (on furniture)
ruedo *nm* **1** : bullring, arena **2** : rotation, turn **3** : hem
ruega, ruegue, etc. → **rogar**
ruego *nm* : request, appeal, plea
rugido *nm* : roar
rugir {35} *vi* : to roar
ruibarbo *nm* : rhubarb
ruido *nm* : noise, sound
ruidoso, -sa *adj* : loud, noisy — **ruidosamente** *adv*
ruin *adj* **1** : base, despicable **2** : mean, stingy
ruina *nf* **1** : ruin, destruction **2** : downfall, collapse **3 ruinas** *nfpl* : ruins, remains
ruinoso, -sa *adj* **1** : run-down, dilapidated **2** : ruinous, disastrous
ruiseñor *nm* : nightingale
ruja, etc. → **rugir**
ruleta *nf* : roulette
rulo *nm* : curler, roller
rumano, -na *n* : Romanian, Rumanian
rumbo *nm* **1** : direction, course ⟨con rumbo a : bound for, heading for⟩ ⟨perder el rumbo : to go off course, to lose one's bearings⟩ ⟨sin rumbo : aimless, aimlessly⟩ **2** : ostentation, pomp **3** : lavishness, generosity
rumiante *adj & nm* : ruminant
rumiar *vt* : to ponder, to mull over — *vi* **1** : to chew the cud **2** : to ruminate, to ponder
rumor *nm* **1** : rumor **2** : murmur
rumorearse *or* **rumorarse** *vr* : to be rumored ⟨se rumorea que se va : rumor has it that she's leaving⟩
rumoroso, -sa *adj* : murmuring, babbling ⟨un arroyo rumoroso : a babbling brook⟩
rupia *nf* : rupee
ruptura *nf* **1** : break **2** : breaking, breach (of a contract) **3** : breaking off, breakup
rural *adj* : rural
ruso[1]**, -sa** *adj & n* : Russian
ruso[2] *nm* : Russian (language)
rústico[1]**, -ca** *adj* : rural, rustic
rústico[2]**, -ca** *n* : rustic, country dweller
ruta *nf* : route
rutina *nf* : routine, habit
rutinario, -ria *adj* : routine, ordinary ⟨visita rutinaria : routine visit⟩ — **rutinariamente** *adv*

S

s *nf* : twentieth letter of the Spanish alphabet

sábado *nm* **1** : Saturday **2** : Sabbath

sábalo *nm* : shad

sabana *nf* : savanna

sábana *nf* : sheet, bedsheet

sabandija *nf* BICHO : bug, small reptile, pesky creature

sabático, -ca *adj* : sabbatical

sabedor, -dora *adj* : aware, informed

sabelotodo *nmf fam* : know-it-all

saber[1] {71} *vt* **1** : to know **2** : to know how to, to be able to ⟨sabe tocar el violín : she can play the violin⟩ **3** : to learn, to find out **4 a** ~ : to wit, namely — *vi* **1** : to know, to suppose **2** : to be informed ⟨supimos del desastre : we heard about the disaster⟩ **3** : to taste ⟨esto no sabe bien : this doesn't taste right⟩ **4** ~ **a** : to taste like ⟨sabe a naranja : it tastes like orange⟩ — **saberse** *vr* : to know ⟨ese chiste no me lo sé : I don't know that joke⟩

saber[2] *nm* : knowledge, learning

sabiamente *adv* : wisely

sabido, -da *adj* : well-known

sabiduría *nf* **1** : wisdom **2** : learning, knowledge

sabiendas *adv* **1 a** ~ : knowingly **2 a sabiendas de que** : knowing full well that

sabio[1]**, -bia** *adj* **1** PRUDENTE : wise, sensible **2** DOCTO : learned

sabio[2]**, -bia** *n* **1** : wise person **2** : savant, learned person

sable *nm* : saber, cutlass

sabor *nm* **1** : flavor, taste **2 sin** ~ : flavorless

saborear *vt* **1** : to taste, to savor **2** : to enjoy, to relish

sabotaje *nm* : sabotage

saboteador, -dora *n* : saboteur

sabotear *vt* : to sabotage

sabrá, etc. → **saber**

sabroso, -sa *adj* **1** RICO : delicious, tasty **2** AGRADABLE : pleasant, nice, lovely

sabueso *nm* **1** : bloodhound **2** *fam* : detective, sleuth

sacacorchos *nms & pl* : corkscrew

sacapuntas *nms & pl* : pencil sharpener

sacar {72} *vt* **1** : to pull out, to take out ⟨saca el pollo del congelador : take the chicken out of the freezer⟩ **2** : to get, to obtain ⟨saqué un 100 en el examen : I got 100 on the exam⟩ **3** : to get out, to extract ⟨le saqué la información : I got the information from him⟩ **4** : to stick out ⟨sacar la lengua : to stick out one's tongue⟩ **5** : to bring out, to introduce ⟨sacar un libro : to publish a book⟩ ⟨sacaron una moda nueva : they introduced a new style⟩ **6** : to take (photos) **7** : to make (copies) — *vi* **1** : to kick off (in soccer or football) **2** : to serve (in sports)

sacarina *nf* : saccharin

sacarosa *nf* : sucrose

sacerdocio *nm* : priesthood

sacerdotal *adj* : priestly

sacerdote, -tisa *n* : priest *m*, priestess *f*

saciar *vt* **1** HARTAR : to sate, to satiate **2** SATISFACER : to satisfy

saciedad *nf* : satiety

saco *nm* **1** : bag, sack **2** : sac **3** : jacket, sport coat

sacramento *nm* : sacrament — **sacramental** *adj*

sacrificar {72} *vt* : to sacrifice — **sacrificarse** *vr* : to sacrifice oneself, to make sacrifices

sacrificio *nm* : sacrifice

sacrilegio *nm* : sacrilege

sacrílego, -ga *adj* : sacrilegious

sacristán *nm, pl* **-tanes** : sexton, sacristan

sacristía *nf* : sacristy, vestry

sacro, -cra *adj* SAGRADO : sacred ⟨arte sacro : sacred art⟩

sacrosanto, -ta *adj* : sacrosanct

sacudida *nf* **1** : shaking **2** : jerk, jolt, shock **3** : shake-up, upheaval

sacudir *vt* **1** : to shake, to beat **2** : to jerk, to jolt **3** : to dust off **4** CONMOVER : to shake up, to shock — **sacudirse** *vr* : to shake off

sacudón *nm, pl* **-dones** : intense jolt or shake-up

sádico[1]**, -ca** *adj* : sadistic

sádico[2]**, -ca** *n* : sadist

sadismo *nm* : sadism

safari *nm* : safari

saga *nf* : saga

sagacidad *nf* : sagacity, shrewdness

sagaz *adj, pl* **sagaces** PERSPICAZ : shrewd, discerning, sagacious

Sagitario *nmf* : Sagittarius, Sagittarian

sagrado, -da *adj* : sacred, holy

sainete *nm* : comedy sketch, one-act farce ⟨este proceso es un sainete : these proceedings are a farce⟩

sajar *vt* : to lance, to cut open

sal[1] → **salir**

sal[2] *nf* **1** : salt **2** *CA, Mex* : misfortune, bad luck

sala *nf* **1** : living room **2** : room, hall ⟨sala de conferencias : lecture hall⟩ ⟨sala de urgencias : emergency room⟩ ⟨sala de baile : ballroom⟩

salado, -da *adj* **1** : salty **2 agua salada** : salt water

salamandra *nf* : salamander

salami *nm* : salami

salar *vt* **1** : to salt **2** : to spoil, to ruin **3** *CoRi, Mex* : to jinx, to bring bad luck

salarial *adj* : salary, salary-related

salario *nm* **1** : salary **2 salario mínimo** : minimum wage

salaz *adj, pl* **salaces** : salacious, lecherous

salchicha *nf* **1** : sausage **2** : frankfurter, wiener

salchichón *nf, pl* **-chones** : a type of deli meat

salchichonería *nf Mex* **1** : delicatessen **2** : cold cuts *pl*

saldar *vt* : to settle, to pay off ⟨saldar una cuenta : to settle an account⟩

saldo *nm* **1** : settlement, payment **2** : balance ⟨saldo de cuenta : account balance⟩ **3** : remainder, leftover merchandise

saldrá, etc. → salir

salero *nm* **1** : saltshaker **2** : wit, charm

salga, etc. → salir

salida *nf* **1** : exit ⟨salida de emergencia : emergency exit⟩ **2** : leaving, departure **3** SOLUCIÓN : way out, solution **4** : start (of a race) **5** OCURRENCIA : wisecrack, joke **6 salida del sol** : sunrise

saliente[1] *adj* **1** : departing, outgoing **2** : projecting **3** DESTACADO : salient, prominent

saliente[2] *nm* **1** : projection, protrusion **2 ventana en saliente** : bay window

salinidad *nf* : salinity, saltiness

salino, -na *adj* : saline ⟨solución salina : saline solution⟩

salir {73} *vi* **1** : to go out, to come out, to get out ⟨salimos todas las noches : we go out every night⟩ ⟨su libro acaba de salir : her book just came out⟩ **2** PARTIR : to leave, to depart **3** APARECER : to appear ⟨salió en todos los diarios : it came out in all the papers⟩ **4** : to project, to stick out **5** : to cost, to come to **6** RESULTAR : to turn out, to prove **7** : to come up, to occur ⟨salga lo que salga : whatever happens⟩ ⟨salió una oportunidad : an opportunity came up⟩ **8 ～ a** : to take after, to look like, to resemble **9 ～ con** : to go out with, to date — **salirse** *vr* **1** : to escape, to get out, to leak out **2** : to come loose, to come off **3 salirse con la suya** : to get one's own way

saliva *nf* : saliva

salivar *vi* : to salivate

salmo *nm* : psalm

salmón[1] *adj* : salmon-colored

salmón[2] *nm, pl* **salmones** : salmon

salmuera *nf* : brine

salobre *adj* : brackish, briny

salón *nm, pl* **salones** **1** : hall, large room ⟨salón de clase : classroom⟩ ⟨salón de baile : ballroom⟩ **2** : salon ⟨salón de belleza : beauty salon⟩ **3** : parlor, sitting room

salpicadera *nf Mex* : fender

salpicadura *nf* : spatter, splash

salpicar {72} *vt* **1** : to spatter, to splash **2** : to sprinkle, to scatter about

salpimentar {55} *vt* **1** : to season (with salt and pepper) **2** : to spice up

salsa *nf* **1** : sauce ⟨salsa picante : hot sauce⟩ ⟨salsa inglesa : Worcestershire sauce⟩ ⟨salsa tártara : tartar sauce⟩ **2**

: gravy **3** : salsa (music) **4 salsa mexicana** : salsa (sauce)

salsero, -ra *n* : salsa musician

saltador, -dora *n* : jumper

saltamontes *nms & pl* : grasshopper

saltar *vi* **1** BRINCAR : to jump, to leap **2** : to bounce **3** : to come off, to pop out **4** : to shatter, to break **5** : to explode, to blow up — *vt* **1** : to jump, to jump over **2** : to skip, to miss — **saltarse** *vr* OMITIR : to skip, to omit ⟨me salté ese capítulo : I skipped that chapter⟩

saltarín, -rina *adj, mpl* **-rines** : leaping, hopping ⟨frijol saltarín : jumping bean⟩

salteado, -da *adj* **1** : sautéed **2** : jumbled up ⟨los episodios se transmitieron salteados : the episodes were broadcast in random order⟩

salteador *nm* : highwayman

saltear *vt* **1** SOFREÍR : to sauté **2** : to skip around, to skip over

saltimbanqui *nmf* : acrobat

salto *nm* **1** BRINCO : jump, leap, skip **2** : jump, dive (in sports) **3** : gap, omission **4 dar saltos** : to jump up and down **5 or salto de agua** CATARATA : waterfall

saltón, -tona *adj, mpl* **saltones** : bulging, protruding

salubre *adj* : healthful, salubrious

salubridad *nf* : healthfulness, health

salud *nf* **1** : health ⟨buena salud : good health⟩ **2 ¡salud!** : bless you! (when someone sneezes) **3 ¡salud!** : cheers!, to your health!

saludable *adj* **1** SALUBRE : healthful **2** SANO : healthy, well

saludar *vt* **1** : to greet, to say hello to **2** : to salute — **saludarse** *vr*

saludo *nm* **1** : greeting, regards *pl* **2** : salute

salutación *nf, pl* **-ciones** : salutation

salva *nf* **1** : salvo, volley **2 salva de aplausos** : round of applause

salvación *nf, pl* **-ciones** **1** : salvation **2** RESCATE : rescue

salvado *nm* : bran

salvador, -dora *n* **1** : savior, rescuer **2 el Salvador** : the Savior

salvadoreño, -ña *adj & n* : Salvadoran, El Salvadoran

salvaguardar *vt* : to safeguard

salvaguardia *or* **salvaguarda** *nf* : safeguard, defense

salvajada *nf* ATROCIDAD : atrocity, act of savagery

salvaje[1] *adj* **1** : wild ⟨animales salvajes : wild animals⟩ **2** : savage, cruel **3** : primitive, uncivilized

salvaje[2] *nmf* : savage

salvajismo *nm* : savagery

salvamento *nm* **1** : rescuing, lifesaving **2** : salvation **3** : refuge

salvar *vt* **1** : to save, to rescue **2** : to cover (a distance) **3** : to get around (an obstacle), to overcome (a difficulty) **4**

: to cross, to jump across **5 salvando** : except for, excluding — **salvarse** *vr* **1** : to survive, to escape **2** : to save one's soul

salvavidas[1] *nms & pl* **1** : life preserver **2 bote salvavidas** : lifeboat

salvavidas[2] *nmf* : lifeguard

salvedad *nf* **1** EXCEPCIÓN : exception **2** : proviso, stipulation

salvia *nf* : sage (plant)

salvo[1], **-va** *adj* **1** : unharmed, sound ⟨sano y salvo : safe and sound⟩ **2 a ~** : safe from danger

salvo[2] *prep* **1** EXCEPTO : except (for), save ⟨todos asistirán salvo Jaime : all will attend except for Jaime⟩ **2 salvo que** : unless ⟨salvo que llueva : unless it rains⟩

salvoconducto *nm* : safe-conduct

samba *nf* : samba

San *adj →* **santo**[1]

sanar *vt* : to heal, to cure — *vi* : to get well, to recover

sanatorio *nm* **1** : sanatorium **2** : clinic, private hospital

sanción *nf, pl* **sanciones** : sanction

sancionar *vt* **1** : to penalize, to impose a sanction on **2** : to sanction, to approve

sancochar *vt* : to parboil

sandalia *nf* : sandal

sándalo *nm* : sandalwood

sandez *nf, pl* **sandeces** ESTUPIDEZ : nonsense, silly thing to say

sandía *nf* : watermelon

sandwich ['sandwit͡ʃ, 'saŋgwit͡ʃ] *nm, pl* **sandwiches** [-dwit͡ʃɛs, -gwi-] EMPAREDADO : sandwich

saneamiento *nm* **1** : cleaning up, sanitation **2** : reorganizing, streamlining

sanear *vt* **1** : to clean up, to sanitize **2** : to reorganize, to streamline

sangrante *adj* **1** : bleeding **2** : flagrant, blatant

sangrar *vi* : to bleed — *vt* : to indent (a paragraph, etc.)

sangre *nf* **1** : blood **2 a sangre fría** : in cold blood **3 a sangre y fuego** : by violent force **4 pura sangre** : thoroughbred

sangría *nf* **1** : bloodletting **2** : sangria (wine punch) **3** : drain, draining ⟨una sangría fiscal : a financial drain⟩ **4** : indentation, indenting

sangriento, -ta *adj* **1** : bloody **2** : cruel

sanguijuela *nf* **1** : leech, bloodsucker **2** : sponger, leech

sanguinario, -ria *adj* : bloodthirsty

sanguíneo, -nea *adj* **1** : blood ⟨vaso sanguíneo : blood vessel⟩ **2** : sanguine, ruddy

sanidad *nf* **1** : health **2** : public health, sanitation

sanitario[1], **-ria** *adj* **1** : sanitary **2** : health ⟨centro sanitario : health center⟩

sanitario[2], **-ria** *n* : sanitation worker

sanitario[3] *nm Col, Mex, Ven* : toilet ⟨los sanitarios : the toilets, the restroom⟩

sano, -na *adj* **1** SALUDABLE : healthy **2** : wholesome **3** : whole, intact

santiaguino, -na *adj* : of or from Santiago, Chile

santiamén *nm* **en un santiamén** : in no time at all

santidad *nf* : holiness, sanctity

santificar {72} *vt* : to sanctify, to consecrate, to hallow

santiguarse {10} *vr* PERSIGNARSE : to cross oneself

santo[1], **-ta** *adj* **1** : holy, saintly ⟨el Santo Padre : the Holy Father⟩ ⟨una vida santa : a saintly life⟩ **2 Santo, Santa** (San *before names of masculine saints except those beginning with D or T*) : Saint ⟨Santa Clara : Saint Claire⟩ ⟨Santo Tomás : Saint Thomas⟩ ⟨San Francisco : Saint Francis⟩

santo[2], **-ta** *n* : saint

santo[3] *nm* **1** : saint's day **2** CUMPLEAÑOS : birthday

santuario *nm* : sanctuary

santurrón, -rrona *adj, mpl* **-rrones** : overly pious, sanctimonious — **santurronamente** *adv*

saña *nf* **1** : fury, rage **2** : viciousness ⟨con saña : viciously⟩

sapo *nm* : toad

saque[1], etc. *→* **sacar**

saque[2] *nm* **1** : kickoff (in soccer or football) **2** : serve, service (in sports)

saqueador, -dora *n* DEPREDADOR : plunderer, looter

saquear *vt* : to sack, to plunder, to loot

saqueo *nm* DEPREDACIÓN : sacking, plunder, looting

sarampión *nm* : measles *pl*

sarape *nm CA, Mex* : serape, blanket

sarcasmo *nm* : sarcasm

sarcástico, -ca *adj* : sarcastic

sarcófago *nm* : sarcophagus

sardina *nf* : sardine

sardónico, -ca *adj* : sardonic

sarga *nf* : serge

sargento *nmf* : sergeant

sarna *nf* : mange

sarnoso, -sa *adj* : mangy

sarpullido *nm* ERUPCIÓN : rash

sarro *nm* **1** : deposit, coating **2** : tartar, plaque

sarta *nf* **1** : string, series (of insults, etc.) **2** : string (of pearls, etc.)

sartén *nmf, pl* **sartenes** **1** : frying pan **2 tener la sartén por el mango** : to call the shots, to be in control

sasafrás *nm* : sassafras

sastre, -tra *n* : tailor

sastrería *nf* **1** : tailoring **2** : tailor's shop

Satanás *or* **Satán** *nm* : Satan, the devil

satánico, -ca *adj* : satanic

satélite *nm* : satellite

satín *or* **satén** *nm, pl* **satines** *or* **satenes** : satin

satinado, -da *adj* : satiny, glossy

sátira *nf* : satire

satírico, -ca *adj* : satirical, satiric

satirizar {21} *vt* : to satirize

sátiro *nm* : satyr

satisfacción *nf, pl* **-ciones** : satisfaction

satisfacer {74} *vt* **1** : to satisfy **2** : to fulfill, to meet **3** : to pay, to settle — **satisfacerse** *vr* **1** : to be satisfied **2** : to take revenge

satisfactorio, -ria *adj* : satisfactory — **satisfactoriamente** *adv*

satisfecho, -cha *adj* : satisfied, content, pleased

saturación *nf, pl* **-ciones** : saturation

saturar *vt* **1** : to saturate, to fill up **2** : to satiate, to surfeit

saturnismo *nm* : lead poisoning

Saturno *nm* : Saturn

sauce *nm* : willow

saúco *nm* : elder (tree)

saudí *or* **saudita** *adj & nmf* : Saudi, Saudi Arabian

sauna *nmf* : sauna

savia *nf* : sap

saxofón *nm, pl* **-fones** : saxophone

sazón[1] *nf, pl* **sazones 1** : flavor, seasoning **2** : ripeness, maturity ⟨en sazón : in season, ripe⟩ **3 a la sazón** : at that time, then

sazón[2] *nmf, pl* **sazones** *Mex* : flavor, seasoning

sazonar *vt* CONDIMENTAR : to season, to spice

scanner *nm* → **escáner**

sé → **saber, ser**

se *pron* **1** : to him, to her, to you, to them ⟨se los daré a ella : I'll give them to her⟩ **2** : each other, one another ⟨se abrazaron : they hugged each other⟩ **3** : himself, herself, itself, yourself, yourselves, themselves ⟨se afeitó antes de salir : he shaved before leaving⟩ **4** (*used in passive constructions*) ⟨se dice que es hermosa : they say she's beautiful⟩ ⟨se habla inglés : English spoken⟩

sea, etc. → **ser**

sebo *nm* **1** : grease, fat **2** : tallow **3** : suet

secado *nm* : drying

secador *nm* : hair dryer

secadora *nf* **1** : dryer, clothes dryer **2** *Mex* : hair dryer

secante *nm* : blotting paper, blotter

secar {72} *v* : to dry — **secarse** *vr* **1** : to get dry **2** : to dry up

sección *nf, pl* **secciones 1** : section ⟨sección transversal : cross section⟩ **2** : department, division

seco, -ca *adj* **1** : dry **2** DISECADO : dried ⟨fruta seca : dried fruit⟩ **3** : thin, lean **4** : curt, brusque **5** : sharp ⟨un golpe seco : a sharp blow⟩ **6 a secas** : simply, just ⟨se llama Chico, a secas : he's just called Chico⟩ **7 en ~** : abruptly, suddenly ⟨frenar en seco : to make a sudden stop⟩

secoya *nf* : sequoia, redwood

secreción *nf, pl* **-ciones** : secretion

secretar *vt* : to secrete

secretaría *nf* **1** : secretariat, administrative department **2** *Mex* : ministry, cabinet office

secretariado *nm* **1** : secretariat **2** : secretarial profession

secretario, -ria *n* : secretary — **secretarial** *adj*

secreto[1]**, -ta** *adj* **1** : secret **2** : secretive — **secretamente** *adv*

secreto[2] *nm* **1** : secret **2** : secrecy

secta *nf* : sect

sectario, -ria *adj & n* : sectarian

sector *nm* : sector

secuaz *nmf, pl* **secuaces** : follower, henchman, underling

secuela *nf* : consequence, sequel ⟨las secuelas de la guerra : the aftermath of the war⟩

secuencia *nf* : sequence

secuestrador, -dora *n* **1** : kidnapper, abductor **2** : hijacker

secuestrar *vt* **1** RAPTAR : to kidnap, to abduct **2** : to hijack, to commandeer **3** CONFISCAR : to confiscate, to seize

secuestro *nm* **1** RAPTO : kidnapping, abduction **2** : hijacking **3** : seizure, confiscation

secular *adj* : secular — **secularismo** *nm* — **secularización** *nf*

secundar *vt* : to support, to second

secundaria *nf* **1** : secondary education, high school **2** *Mex* : junior high school, middle school

secundario, -ria *adj* : secondary

secuoya *nf* : sequoia

sed *nf* **1** : thirst ⟨tener sed : to be thirsty⟩ **2 tener sed de** : to hunger for, to thirst for

seda *nf* : silk

sedación *nf, pl* **-ciones** : sedation

sedal *nm* : fishing line

sedán *nm, pl* **sedanes** : sedan

sedante *adj & nm* CALMANTE : sedative

sedar *vt* : to sedate

sede *nf* **1** : seat, headquarters **2** : venue, site **3 la Santa Sede** : the Holy See

sedentario, -ria *adj* : sedentary

sedición *nf, pl* **-ciones** : sedition — **sedicioso, -sa** *adj*

sediento, -ta *adj* : thirsty, thirsting

sedimentación *nf, pl* **-ciones** : sedimentation

sedimentario, -ria *adj* : sedimentary

sedimento *nm* : sediment

sedoso, -sa *adj* : silky, silken

seducción *nf, pl* **-ciones** : seduction

seducir {61} *vt* **1** : to seduce **2** : to captivate, to charm

seductivo, -va *adj* : seductive

seductor[1]**, -tora** *adj* **1** SEDUCTIVO : seductive **2** ENCANTADOR : charming, alluring

seductor[2]**, -tora** *n* : seducer

segador, -dora *n* : harvester

segar {49} *vt* **1** : to reap, to harvest, to cut **2** : to sever abruptly ⟨una vida segada por la enfermedad : a life cut short by illness⟩

seglar[1] *adj* LAICO : lay, secular

seglar[2] *nm* LAICO : layperson, layman *m*, laywoman *f*

segmentación *nf, pl* **-ciones** : segmentation

segmentado, -da *adj* : segmented

segmento *nm* : segment

segregar {52} *vt* **1** : to segregate **2** SECRETAR : to secrete

seguida *nf* **en ～** : right away, immediately ⟨vuelvo en seguida : I'll be right back⟩

seguidamente *adv* **1** : next, immediately after **2** : without a break, continuously

seguido[1] *adv* **1** RECTO : straight, straight ahead **2** : often, frequently

seguido[2]**, -da** *adj* **1** CONSECUTIVO : consecutive, successive ⟨tres días seguidos : three days in a row⟩ **2** : straight, unbroken **3** **～ por** *or* **～ de** : followed by

seguidor, -dora *n* : follower, supporter

seguimiento *nm* **1** : following, pursuit **2** : continuation **3** : tracking, monitoring

seguir {75} *vt* **1** : to follow ⟨el sol sigue la lluvia : sunshine follows the rain⟩ ⟨seguiré tu consejo : I'll follow your advice⟩ ⟨me siguieron con la mirada : they followed me with their eyes⟩ **2** : to go along, to keep on ⟨seguimos toda la carretera panamericana : we continued along the PanAmerican Highway⟩ ⟨siguió hablando : he kept on talking⟩ ⟨seguir el curso : to stay on course⟩ **3** : to take (a course, a treatment) — *vi* **1** : to go on, to keep going ⟨sigue adelante : keep going, carry on⟩ **2** : to remain, to continue to be ⟨¿todavía sigues aquí? : you're still here?⟩ ⟨sigue con vida : she's still alive⟩ **3** : to follow, to come after ⟨la frase que sigue : the following sentence⟩

según[1] *adv* : it depends ⟨según y como : it all depends on⟩

según[2] *conj* **1** COMO, CONFORME : as, just as ⟨según lo dejé : just as I left it⟩ **2** : depending on how ⟨según se vea : depending on how one sees it⟩

según[3] *prep* **1** : according to ⟨según los rumores : according to the rumors⟩ **2** : depending on ⟨según los resultados : depending on the results⟩

segundo[1]**, -da** *adj* : second ⟨el segundo lugar : second place⟩

segundo[2]**, -da** *n* **1** : second (in a series) **2** : second (person), second-in-command

segundo[3] *nm* : second ⟨sesenta segundos : sixty seconds⟩

seguramente *adv* **1** : for sure, surely **2** : probably

seguridad *nf* **1** : safety, security **2** : (financial) security ⟨seguridad social : Social Security⟩ **3** CERTEZA : certainty, assurance ⟨con toda seguridad : with complete certainty⟩ **4** : confidence, self-confidence

seguro[1] *adv* : certainly, definitely ⟨va a llover, seguro : it's going to rain for sure⟩ ⟨¡seguro que sí! : of course!⟩

seguro[2]**, -ra** *adj* **1** : safe, secure **2** : sure, certain ⟨estoy segura que es él : I'm sure that's him⟩ **3** : reliable, trustworthy **4** : self-assured

seguro[3] *nm* **1** : insurance ⟨seguro de vida : life insurance⟩ **2** : fastener, clasp **3** *Mex* : safety pin

seis *adj & nm* : six

seiscientos[1]**, -tas** *adj* : six hundred

seiscientos[2] *nms & pl* : six hundred

selección *nf, pl* **-ciones** **1** ELECCIÓN : selection, choice **2** **selección natural** : natural selection

seleccionar *vt* ELEGIR : to select, to choose

selectivo, -va *adj* : selective — **selectivamente** *adv*

selecto, -ta *adj* **1** : choice, select **2** EXCLUSIVO : exclusive

selenio *nm* : selenium

sellar *vt* **1** : to seal **2** : to stamp

sello *nm* **1** : seal **2** ESTAMPILLA, TIMBRE : postage stamp **3** : hallmark, characteristic

selva *nf* **1** BOSQUE : woods *pl,* forest ⟨selva húmeda : rain forest⟩ **2** JUNGLA : jungle

selvático, -ca *adj* **1** : forest, jungle ⟨sendero selvático : jungle path⟩ **2** : wild

semáforo *nm* **1** : traffic light **2** : stop signal

semana *nf* : week

semanal *adj* : weekly — **semanalmente** *adv*

semanario *nm* : weekly (publication)

semántica *nf* : semantics

semántico, -ca *adj* : semantic

semblante *nm* **1** : countenance, face **2** : appearance, look

semblanza *nf* : biographical sketch, profile

sembrado *nm* : cultivated field

sembrador, -dora *n* : planter, sower

sembradora *nf* : seeder (machine)

sembrar {55} *vt* **1** : to plant, to sow **2** : to scatter, to strew ⟨sembrar el pánico : to spread panic⟩

semejante[1] *adj* **1** PARECIDO : similar, alike **2** TAL : such ⟨nunca he visto cosa semejante : I have never seen such a thing⟩

semejante[2] *nm* PRÓJIMO : fellowman

semejanza *nf* PARECIDO : similarity, resemblance

semejar *vi* : to resemble, to look like — **semejarse** *vr* : to be similar, to look alike

semen *nm* : semen

semental *nm* : stud (animal) ⟨caballo semental : stallion⟩

semestre *nm* : semester

semicírculo *nm* : semicircle, half circle

semiconductor *nm* : semiconductor

semidiós *nm, pl* **-dioses** : demigod *m*

semifinal *nf* : semifinal

semifinalista[1] *adj* : semifinal

semifinalista[2] *nmf* : semifinalist

semiformal *adj* : semiformal

semilla *nf* : seed

semillero *nm* **1** : seedbed **2** : hotbed, breeding ground

seminario *nm* **1** : seminary **2** : seminar, graduate course

seminarista *nm* : seminarian

semiprecioso, -sa *adj* : semiprecious

semita[1] *adj* : Semitic

semita[2] *nmf* : Semite

sémola *nf* : semolina

sempiterno, -na *adj* ETERNO : eternal, everlasting

senado *nm* : senate

senador, -dora *n* : senator

sencillamente *adv* : simply, plainly

sencillez *nf* : simplicity

sencillo[1]**, -lla** *adj* **1** : simple, easy **2** : plain, unaffected **3** : single

sencillo[2] *nm* **1** : single (recording) **2** : small change (coins) **3** : one-way ticket

senda *nf* CAMINO, SENDERO : path, way

sendero *nm* CAMINO, SENDA : path, way

sendos, -das *adj pl* : each, both ⟨llevaban sendos vestidos nuevos : they were each wearing a new dress⟩

senectud *nf* ANCIANIDAD : old age

senegalés, -lesa *adj & n, mpl* **-leses** : Senegalese

senil *adj* : senile — **senilidad** *nf*

seno *nm* **1** : breast, bosom ⟨los senos : the breasts⟩ ⟨el seno de la familia : the bosom of the family⟩ **2** : sinus **3 seno materno** : womb

sensación *nf, pl* **-ciones 1** IMPRESIÓN : feeling ⟨tener la sensación : to have a feeling⟩ **2** : sensation ⟨causar sensación : to cause a sensation⟩

sensacional *adj* : sensational

sensacionalista *adj* : sensationalistic, lurid

sensatez *nf* **1** : good sense **2 con ~** : sensibly

sensato, -ta *adj* : sensible, sound — **sensatamente** *adv*

sensibilidad *nf* **1** : sensitivity, sensibility **2** SENSACIÓN : feeling

sensibilizar {21} *vt* : to sensitize

sensible *adj* **1** : sensitive **2** APRECIABLE : considerable, significant

sensiblemente *adv* : considerably, significantly

sensiblería *nf* : sentimentality, mush

sensiblero, -ra *adj* : mawkish, sentimental, mushy

sensitivo, -va *adj* **1** : sense ⟨órganos sensitivos : sense organs⟩ **2** : sentient, capable of feeling

sensor *nm* : sensor

sensorial *adj* : sensory

sensual *adj* : sensual, sensuous — **sensualmente** *adv*

sensualidad *nf* : sensuality

sentado, -da *adj* **1** : sitting, seated **2** : established, settled ⟨dar por sentado : to take for granted⟩ ⟨dejar sentado : to make clear⟩ **3** : sensible, steady, judicious

sentar {55} *vt* **1** : to seat, to sit **2** : to establish, to set — *vi* **1** : to suit ⟨ese color te sienta : that color suits you⟩ **2** : to agree with (of food or drink) ⟨las cebollas no me sientan : onions don't agree with me⟩ **3** : to please ⟨le sentó mal el paseo : she didn't enjoy the trip⟩ — **sentarse** *vr* : to sit, to sit down ⟨siéntese, por favor : please have a seat⟩

sentencia *nf* **1** : sentence, judgment **2** : maxim, saying

sentenciar *vt* : to sentence

sentido[1]**, -da** *adj* **1** : heartfelt, sincere ⟨mi más sentido pésame : my sincerest condolences⟩ **2** : touchy, sensitive **3** : offended, hurt

sentido[2] *nm* **1** : sense ⟨sentido común : common sense⟩ ⟨los cinco sentidos : the five senses⟩ ⟨sin sentido : senseless⟩ **2** CONOCIMIENTO : consciousness **3** SIGNIFICADO : meaning, sense ⟨doble sentido : double entendre⟩ **4** : direction ⟨calle de sentido único : one-way street⟩

sentimental[1] *adj* **1** : sentimental **2** : love, romantic ⟨vida sentimental : love life⟩

sentimental[2] *nmf* : sentimentalist

sentimentalismo *nm* : sentimentality, sentimentalism

sentimiento *nm* **1** : feeling, emotion **2** PESAR : regret, sorrow

sentir {76} *vt* **1** : to feel, to experience ⟨no siento nada de dolor : I don't feel any pain⟩ ⟨sentía sed : he was feeling thirsty⟩ ⟨sentir amor : to feel love⟩ **2** PERCIBIR : to perceive, to sense ⟨sentir un ruido : to hear a noise⟩ **3** LAMENTAR : to regret, to feel sorry for ⟨lo siento mucho : I'm very sorry⟩ — *vi* **1** : to have feeling, to feel **2 sin ~** : without noticing, inadvertently — **sentirse** *vr* **1** : to feel ⟨¿te sientes mejor? : are you feeling better?⟩ **2** *Chile, Mex* : to take offense

seña *nf* **1** : sign, signal **2 dar señas de** : to show signs of

señal *nf* **1** : signal **2** : sign ⟨señal de tráfico : traffic sign⟩ **3** INDICIO : indication ⟨en señal de : as a token of⟩ **4** VESTIGIO : trace, vestige **5** : scar, mark **6** : deposit, down payment

señalado, -da *adj* : distinguished, notable

señalador *nm* : marker ⟨señalador de libros : bookmark⟩

señalar *vt* **1** INDICAR : to indicate, to show **2** : to mark **3** : to point out, to stress **4** : to fix, to set — **señalarse** *vr* : to distinguish oneself

señor, -ñora *n* **1** : gentleman *m*, man *m*, lady *f*, woman *f*, wife *f* **2** : Sir *m*, Madam *f* ⟨estimados señores : Dear Sirs⟩ **3** : Mr. *m*, Mrs. *f* **4** : lord *m*, lady *f* ⟨el Señor : the Lord⟩

señoría *nf* **1** : lordship **2 Su Señoría** : Your Honor

señorial *adj* : stately, regal

señorío *nm* 1 : manor, estate 2 : dominion, power 3 : elegance, class
señorita *nf* 1 : young lady, young woman 2 : Miss
señuelo *nm* 1 : decoy 2 : bait
sépalo *nm* : sepal
sepa, etc. → **saber**
separación *nf, pl* **-ciones** 1 : separation, division 2 : gap, space
separadamente *adv* : separately, apart
separado, -da *adj* 1 : separated 2 : separate ⟨vidas separadas : separate lives⟩ 3 **por** ∼ : separately
separar *vt* 1 : to separate, to divide 2 : to split up, to pull apart — **separarse** *vr*
sepelio *nm* : interment, burial
sepia[1] *adj & nm* : sepia
sepia[2] *nf* : cuttlefish
septentrional *adj* : northern
séptico, -ca *adj* : septic
septiembre *nm* : September
séptimo[1], **-ma** *adj* : seventh
séptimo[2] *nm* : seventh
septuagésimo[1], **-ma** *adj* : seventieth
septuagésimo[2] *nm* : seventieth
sepulcral *adj* 1 : sepulchral 2 : dismal, gloomy
sepulcro *nm* TUMBA : tomb, sepulchre
sepultar *vt* ENTERRAR : to bury
sepultura *nf* 1 : burial 2 TUMBA : grave, tomb
seque, etc. → **secar**
sequedad *nf* 1 : dryness 2 : brusqueness, curtness
sequía *nf* : drought
séquito *nm* : retinue, entourage
ser[1] {77} *vi* 1 : to be ⟨él es mi hermano : he is my brother⟩ ⟨Camila es linda : Camila is pretty⟩ 2 : to exist, to live ⟨ser, o no ser : to be or not to be⟩ 3 : to take place, to occur ⟨el concierto es el domingo : the concert is on Sunday⟩ 4 (*used with expressions of time, date, season*) ⟨son las diez : it's ten o'clock⟩ ⟨hoy es el 9 : today's the 9th⟩ 5 : to cost, to come to ⟨¿cuánto es? : how much is it?⟩ 6 (*with the future tense*) : to be able to be ⟨¿será posible? : can it be possible?⟩ 7 ∼ **de** : to come from ⟨somos de Managua : we're from Managua⟩ 8 ∼ **de** : to belong to ⟨ese lápiz es de Juan : that's Juan's pencil⟩ 9 **es que** : the thing is that ⟨es que no lo conozco : it's just that I don't know him⟩ 10 **¡sea!** : agreed!, all right! 11 **sea...sea** : either...or — *v aux* (*used in passive constructions*) : to be ⟨la cuenta ha sido pagada : the bill has been paid⟩ ⟨él fue asesinado : he was murdered⟩
ser[2] *nm* : being ⟨ser humano : human being⟩
seráfico, -ca *adj* : angelic, seraphic
serbio[1], **-bia** *adj & n* : Serb, Serbian
serbio[2] *nm* : Serbian (language)
serbocroata[1] *adj* : Serbo-Croatian
serbocroata[2] *nm* : Serbo-Croatian (language)

serenar *vt* : to calm, to soothe — **serenarse** *vr* CALMARSE : to calm down
serenata *nf* : serenade
serendipia *nf* : serendipity
serenidad *nf* : serenity, calmness
sereno[1], **-na** *adj* 1 SOSEGADO : serene, calm, composed 2 : fair, clear (of weather) 3 : calm, still (of the sea) — **serenamente** *adv*
sereno[2] *nm* : night watchman
seriado, -da *adj* : serial
serial *nm* : serial (on radio or television)
seriamente *adv* : seriously
serie *nf* 1 : series 2 SERIAL : serial 3 **fabricación en serie** : mass production 4 **fuera de serie** : extraordinary, amazing
seriedad *nf* 1 : seriousness, earnestness 2 : gravity, importance
serio, -ria *adj* 1 : serious, earnest 2 : reliable, responsible 3 : important 4 **en** ∼ : seriously, in earnest — **seriamente** *adv*
sermón *nm, pl* **sermones** 1 : sermon 2 *fam* : harangue, lecture
sermonear *vt fam* : to harangue, to lecture
serpentear *vi* : to twist, to wind — **serpenteante** *adj*
serpentina *nf* : paper streamer
serpiente *nf* : serpent, snake
serrado, -da *adj* DENTADO : serrated
serranía *nf* : mountainous area
serrano, -na *adj* : from the mountains
serrar {55} *vt* : to saw
serrín *nm, pl* **serrines** : sawdust
serruchar *vt* : to saw up
serrucho *nm* : saw, handsaw
servicentro *nm Peru* : gas station
servicial *adj* : obliging, helpful
servicio *nm* 1 : service 2 SAQUE : serve (in sports) 3 **servicios** *nmpl* : restroom
servidor, -dora *n* 1 : servant 2 **su seguro servidor** : yours truly (in correspondence)
servidumbre *nf* 1 : servitude 2 : help, servants *pl*
servil *adj* 1 : servile, subservient 2 : menial
servilismo *nm* : servility, subservience
servilleta *nf* : napkin
servir {54} *vt* 1 : to serve, to be of use to 2 : to serve, to wait 3 SURTIR : to fill (an order) — *vi* 1 : to work ⟨mi radio no sirve : my radio isn't working⟩ 2 : to be of use, to be helpful ⟨esa computadora no sirve para nada : that computer's perfectly useless⟩ — **servirse** *vr* 1 : to help oneself to 2 : to be kind enough ⟨sírvase enviarnos un catálogo : please send us a catalog⟩
sésamo *nm* AJONJOLÍ : sesame, sesame seeds *pl*
sesenta *adj & nm* : sixty
sesentavo[1], **-va** *adj* : sixtieth
sesentavo[2] *n* : sixtieth (fraction)
sesgado, -da *adj* 1 : inclined, tilted 2 : slanted, biased

sesgar {52} *vt* **1** : to cut on the bias **2** : to tilt **3** : to bias, to slant

sesgo *nm* : bias

sesgue, etc. → **sesgar**

sesión *nf, pl* **sesiones 1** : session **2** : showing, performance

sesionar *vi* REUNIRSE : to meet, to be in session

seso *nm* **1** : brains, intelligence **2 sesos** *nmpl* : brains (as food)

sesudo, -da *adj* **1** : prudent, sensible **2** : brainy

set *nm, pl* **sets** : set (in tennis)

seta *nf* : mushroom

setecientos¹, -tas *adj* : seven hundred

setecientos² *nms & pl* : seven hundred

setenta *adj & nm* : seventy

setentavo¹, -va *adj* : seventieth

setentavo² *nm* : seventieth

setiembre → **septiembre**

seto *nm* **1** : fence, enclosure **2 seto vivo** : hedge

seudónimo *nm* : pseudonym

severidad *nf* **1** : harshness, severity **2** : strictness

severo, -ra *adj* **1** : harsh, severe **2** ESTRICTO : strict — **severamente** *adv*

sexagésimo¹, -ma *adj* : sixtieth, sixty-

sexagésimo², -ma *n* : sixtieth, sixty- (in a series)

sexismo *nm* : sexism — **sexista** *adj & nmf*

sexo *nm* : sex

sextante *nm* : sextant

sexteto *nm* : sextet

sexto, -ta *adj* : sixth — **sexto, -ta** *n*

sexual *adj* : sexual, sex ⟨educación sexual : sex education⟩ — **sexualmente** *adv*

sexualidad *nf* : sexuality

sexy *adj, pl* **sexy** *or* **sexys** : sexy

shock [ˈʃok, ˈtʃok] *nm* : shock ⟨estado de shock : state of shock⟩

short *nm, pl* **shorts** : shorts *pl*

show *nm, pl* **shows** : show

si *conj* **1** : if ⟨lo haré si me pagan : I'll do it if they pay me⟩ ⟨si lo supiera te lo diría : if I knew it I would tell you⟩ **2** : whether, if ⟨no importa si funciona o no : it doesn't matter whether it works (or not)⟩ **3** (*expressing desire, protest, or surprise*) ⟨si supiera la verdad : if only I knew the truth⟩ ⟨¡si no quiero! : but I don't want to!⟩ **4 si bien** : although ⟨si bien se ha progresado : although progress has been made⟩ **5 si no** : otherwise, or else ⟨si no, no voy : otherwise I won't go⟩

sí¹ *adv* **1** : yes ⟨sí, gracias : yes, please⟩ ⟨creo que sí : I think so⟩ **2 sí que** : indeed, absolutely ⟨esta vez sí que ganaré : this time I'm sure to win⟩ **3 porque sí** *fam* : because, just because ⟨lo hizo porque sí : she did it just because⟩

sí² *nm* : yes ⟨dar el sí : to say yes, to express consent⟩

sí³ *pron* **1 de por sí** *or* **en sí** : by itself, in itself, per se **2 fuera de sí** : beside

oneself **3 para sí (mismo)** : to himself, to herself, for himself, for herself **4 entre ～** : among themselves

siamés, -mesa *adj & n, mpl* **siameses** : Siamese

sibilante *adj & nf* : sibilant

siciliano, -na *adj & n* : Sicilian

sico- → **psico-**

sicomoro *or* **sicómoro** *nm* : sycamore

SIDA *or* **sida** *nm* (*síndrome de inmunodeficiencia adquirida*) : AIDS

siderurgia *nf* : iron and steel industry

siderúrgico, -ca *adj* : steel, iron ⟨la industria siderúrgica : the steel industry⟩

sidra *nf* : hard cider

siega¹, siegue, etc. → **segar**

siega² *nf* **1** : harvesting **2** : harvest time **3** : harvested crop

siembra¹, etc. → **sembrar**

siembra² *nf* **1** : sowing **2** : sowing season **3** SEMBRADO : cultivated field

siempre *adv* **1** : always ⟨siempre tienes hambre : you're always hungry⟩ **2** : still ⟨¿siempre te vas? : are you still going?⟩ **3** *Mex* : after all ⟨siempre no fui : I didn't go after all⟩ **4 siempre que** : whenever, every time ⟨siempre que pasa : every time he walks by⟩ **5 para ～** : forever, for good **6 siempre y cuando** : provided that

sien *nf* : temple (on the forehead)

sienta, etc. → **sentar**

siente, etc. → **sentir**

sierpe *nf* : serpent, snake

sierra¹, etc. → **serrar**

sierra² *nf* **1** : saw ⟨sierra de vaivén : jigsaw⟩ **2** CORDILLERA : mountain range **3** : mountains *pl* ⟨viven en la sierra : they live in the mountains⟩

siervo, -va *n* **1** : slave **2** : serf

siesta *nf* : nap, siesta

siete *adj & nm* : seven

sífilis *nf* : syphilis

sifón *nm, pl* **sifones** : siphon

siga, sigue etc. → **seguir**

sigilo *nm* : secrecy, stealth

sigiloso, -sa *adj* FURTIVO : furtive, stealthy — **sigilosamente** *adv*

sigla *nf* : acronym, abbreviation

siglo *nm* **1** : century **2** : age ⟨el Siglo de Oro : the Golden Age⟩ ⟨hace siglos que no te veo : I haven't seen you in ages⟩ **3** : world, secular life

signar *vt* : to sign (a treaty or agreement)

signatario, -ria *n* : signatory

significación *nf, pl* **-ciones 1** : significance, importance **2** : signification, meaning

significado *nm* **1** : sense, meaning **2** : significance

significante *adj* : significant

significar {72} *vt* **1** : to mean, to signify **2** : to express, to make known — **significarse** *vr* **1** : to draw attention, to become known **2** : to take a stance

significativo, -va *adj* **1** : significant, important **2** : meaningful — **significativamente** *adv*

signo *nm* **1** : sign ⟨signo de igual : equal sign⟩ ⟨un signo de alegría : a sign of happiness⟩ **2** : (punctuation) mark ⟨signo de interrogación : question mark⟩ ⟨signo de admiración : exclamation point⟩ ⟨signo de intercalación : caret⟩
siguiente *adj* : next, following
sílaba *nf* : syllable
silábico, -ca *adj* : syllabic
silbar *v* : to whistle
silbato *nm* PITO : whistle
silbido *nm* : whistle, whistling
silenciador *nm* **1** : muffler (of an automobile) **2** : silencer
silenciar *vt* **1** : to silence **2** : to muffle
silencio *nm* **1** : silence, quiet ⟨¡silencio! : be quiet!⟩ **2** : rest (in music)
silencioso, -sa *adj* : silent, quiet — **silenciosamente** *adv*
sílice *nf* : silica
silicio *nm* : silicon
silla *nf* **1** : chair **2 silla de ruedas** : wheelchair
sillón *nm, pl* **sillones** : armchair, easy chair
silo *nm* : silo
silueta *nf* **1** : silhouette **2** : figure, shape
silvestre *adj* : wild ⟨flor silvestre : wildflower⟩
silvicultor, -tora *n* : forester
silvicultura *nf* : forestry
sima *nf* ABISMO : chasm, abyss
simbólico, -ca *adj* : symbolic — **simbólicamente** *adj*
simbolismo *nm* : symbolism
simbolizar {21} *vt* : to symbolize
símbolo *nm* : symbol
simetría *nf* : symmetry
simétrico, -ca *adj* : symmetrical, symmetric
simiente *nf* : seed
símil *nm* **1** : simile **2** : analogy, comparison
similar *adj* SEMEJANTE : similar, alike
similitud *nf* : similarity, resemblance
simio *nm* : ape
simpatía *nf* **1** : liking, affection ⟨tomarle simpatía a : to take a liking to⟩ **2** : warmth, friendliness **3** : support, solidarity
simpático, -ca *adj* : nice, friendly, likeable
simpatizante *nf* : sympathizer, supporter
simpatizar {21} *vi* **1** : to get along, to hit it off ⟨simpaticé mucho con él : I really liked him⟩ **2** ~ **con** : to sympathize with, to support
simple[1] *adj* **1** SENCILLO : plain, simple, easy **2** : pure, mere ⟨por simple vanidad : out of pure vanity⟩ **3** : simpleminded, foolish
simple[2] *n* : fool, simpleton
simplemente *adv* : simply, merely, just
simpleza *nf* **1** : foolishness, simpleness **2** NECEDAD : nonsense
simplicidad *nf* : simplicity

simplificar {72} *vt* : to simplify — **simplificación** *nf*
simplista *adj* : simplistic
simposio *or* **simposium** *nm* : symposium
simulación *nf, pl* **-ciones** : simulation
simulacro *nm* : imitation, sham ⟨simulacro de juicio : mock trial⟩
simular *vt* **1** : to simulate **2** : to feign, to pretend
simultáneo, -nea *adj* : simultaneous — **simultáneamente** *adv*
sin *prep* **1** : without ⟨sin querer : unintentionally⟩ ⟨sin refinar : unrefined⟩ **2**
sin que : without ⟨lo hicimos sin que él se diera cuenta : we did it without him noticing⟩
sinagoga *nf* : synagogue
sinceridad *nf* : sincerity
sincero, -ra *adj* : sincere, honest, true — **sinceramente** *adv*
síncopa *nf* : syncopation
sincopar *vt* : to syncopate
sincronizar {21} *vt* : to synchronize — **sincronización** *nf*
sindical *adj* GREMIAL : union, labor ⟨representante sindical : union representative⟩
sindicalización *nf, pl* **-ciones** : unionizing, unionization
sindicalizar {21} *vt* : to unionize — **sindicalizarse** *vr* **1** : to form a union **2** : to join a union
sindicar → **sindicalizar**
sindicato *nm* GREMIO : union, guild
síndrome *nm* : syndrome
sinecura *nf* : sinecure
sinfín *nm* : endless number ⟨un sinfín de problemas : no end of problems⟩
sinfonía *nf* : symphony
sinfónica *nf* : symphony orchestra
sinfónico, -ca *adj* : symphonic, symphony
singular[1] *adj* **1** : singular, unique **2** PARTICULAR : peculiar, odd **3** : singular (in grammar) — **singularmente** *adv*
singular[2] *nm* : singular
singularidad *nf* : uniqueness, singularity
singularizar {21} *vt* : to make unique or distinct — **singularizarse** *vr* : to stand out, to distinguish oneself
siniestrado, -da *adj* : damaged, wrecked ⟨zona siniestrada : disaster zone⟩
siniestro[1]**, -tra** *adj* **1** IZQUIERDO : left, left-hand **2** MALVADO : sinister, evil
siniestro[2] *nm* : accident, disaster
sinnúmero → **sinfín**
sino *conj* **1** : but, rather ⟨no será hoy, sino mañana : it won't be today, but tomorrow⟩ **2** EXCEPTO : but, except ⟨no hace sino despertar suspicacias : it does nothing but arouse suspicion⟩
sinónimo[1]**, -ma** *adj* : synonymous
sinónimo[2] *nm* : synonym
sinopsis *nfs & pl* RESUMEN : synopsis, summary
sinrazón *nf, pl* **-zones** : wrong, injustice

sinsabores *nmpl* : woes, troubles
sinsonte *nm* : mockingbird
sintáctico, -ca *adj* : syntactic, syntactical
sintaxis *nfs & pl* : syntax
síntesis *nfs & pl* 1 : synthesis, fusion 2 SINOPSIS : synopsis, summary
sintético, -ca *adj* : synthetic — **sintéticamente** *adv*
sintetizar {21} *vt* 1 : to synthesize 2 RESUMIR : to summarize
sintió, etc. → **sentir**
síntoma *nm* : symptom
sintomático, -ca *adj* : symptomatic
sintonía *nf* 1 : tuning in (of a radio) 2 **en sintonía con** : in tune with, attuned to
sintonizador *nm* : tuner, knob for tuning (of a radio, etc.)
sintonizar {21} *vt* : to tune (in) to — *vi* 1 : to tune in 2 ~ **con** : to be in tune with, to empathize with
sinuosidad *nf* : sinuosity
sinuoso, -sa *adj* 1 : winding, sinuous 2 : devious
sinvergüenza¹ *adj* 1 DESCARADO : shameless, brazen, impudent 2 TRAVIESO : naughty
sinvergüenza² *nmf* 1 : rogue, scoundrel 2 : brat, rascal
sionista *adj & nmf* : Zionist — **sionismo** *nm*
siqui- → **psiqui-**
siquiera *adv* 1 : at least ⟨dame siquiera un poquito : at least give me a little bit⟩ 2 (*in negative constructions*) : not even ⟨ni siquiera nos saludaron : they didn't even say hello to us⟩
sirena *nf* 1 : mermaid 2 : siren ⟨sirena de niebla : foghorn⟩
sirio, -ria *adj & n* : Syrian
sirope *nm* : syrup
sirve, etc. → **servir**
sirviente, -ta *n* : servant, maid *f*
sisal *nm* : sisal
sisear *vi* : to hiss
siseo *nm* : hiss
sísmico, -ca *adj* : seismic
sismo *nm* 1 TERREMOTO : earthquake 2 TEMBLOR : tremor
sismógrafo *nm* : seismograph
sistema *nm* : system
sistemático, -ca *adj* : systematic — **sistemáticamente** *adv*
sistematizar {21} *vt* : to systematize
sistémico, -ca *adj* : systemic
sitiar *vt* ASEDIAR : to besiege
sitio *nm* 1 LUGAR : place, site ⟨vámonos a otro sitio : let's go somewhere else⟩ 2 ESPACIO : room, space ⟨hacer sitio a : to make room for⟩ 3 : siege ⟨estado de sitio : state of siege⟩ 4 *Mex* : taxi stand
situación *nf, pl* **-ciones** : situation
situado, -da *adj* : situated, placed
situar {3} *vt* UBICAR : to situate, to place, to locate — **situarse** *vr* 1 : to be placed, to be located 2 : to make a place for oneself, to do well

sketch *nm* : sketch, skit
slip *nm* : briefs *pl*, underpants *pl*
smog *nm* : smog
smoking *nm* ESMOQUIN : tuxedo
snob → **esnob**
so *prep* : under ⟨so pena de : under penalty of⟩
sobaco *nm* : armpit
sobado, -da *adj* 1 : worn, shabby 2 : well-worn, hackneyed
sobar *vt* 1 : to finger, to handle 2 : to knead 3 : to rub, to massage 4 *fam* : to beat, to pummel
soberanía *nf* : sovereignty
soberano, -na *adj & n* : sovereign
soberbia *nf* 1 ORGULLO : pride, arrogance 2 MAGNIFICENCIA : magnificence
soberbio, -bia *adj* 1 : proud, arrogant 2 : grand, magnificent
sobornable *adv* : venal, bribable
sobornar *vt* : to bribe
soborno *nm* 1 : bribery 2 : bribe
sobra *nf* 1 : excess, surplus 2 **de** ~ : extra, to spare 3 **sobras** *nfpl* : leftovers, scraps
sobrado, -da *adj* : abundant, excessive, more than enough
sobrante¹ *adj* : remaining, superfluous
sobrante² *nm* : remainder, surplus
sobrar *vi* : to be in excess, to be superfluous ⟨más vale que sobre a que falte : it's better to have too much than not enough⟩
sobre¹ *nm* 1 : envelope 2 : packet ⟨sobre de sazón : a packet of seasoning⟩
sobre² *prep* 1 : on, on top of ⟨sobre la mesa : on the table⟩ 2 : over, above 3 : about ⟨¿tiene libros sobre Bolivia? : do you have books on Bolivia?⟩ 4 **sobre todo** : especially, above all
sobrealimentar *vt* : to overfeed
sobrecalentar {55} *vt* : to overheat — **sobrecalentarse** *vr*
sobrecama *nmf* : bedspread
sobrecargar {52} *vt* : to overload, to overburden, to weigh down
sobrecoger {15} *vt* 1 : to surprise, to startle 2 : to scare — **sobrecogerse** *vr*
sobrecubierta *nf* : dust jacket
sobredosis *nfs & pl* : overdose
sobreentender {56} *vt* : to infer, to understand
sobreestimar *vt* : to overestimate, to overrate
sobreexcitado, -da *adj* : overexcited
sobreexponer {60} *vt* : to overexpose
sobregirar *vt* : to overdraw
sobregiro *nm* : overdraft
sobrehumano, -na *adj* : superhuman
sobrellevar *vt* : to endure, to bear
sobremanera *adv* : exceedingly
sobremesa *nf* : after-dinner conversation
sobrenatural *adj* : supernatural
sobrenombre *nm* APODO : nickname
sobrentender → **sobreentender**

sobrepasar *vt* : to exceed, to surpass — **sobrepasarse** *vr* PASARSE : to go too far

sobrepelliz *nf, pl* **-pellices** : surplice

sobrepeso *nm* **1** : excess weight **2** : overweight, obesity

sobrepoblación, sobrepoblado → **superpoblación, superpoblado**

sobreponer {60} *vt* **1** SUPERPONER : to superimpose **2** ANTEPONER : to put first, to give priority to — **sobreponerse** *vr* **1** : to pull oneself together **2** ~ **a** : to overcome

sobreprecio *nm* : surcharge

sobreproducción *nf, pl* **-ciones** : overproduction

sobreproducir {61} *vt* : to overproduce

sobreprotector, -tora *adj* : overprotective

sobreproteger {15} *vt* : to overprotect

sobresaliente[1] *adj* **1** : protruding, projecting **2** : outstanding, noteworthy **3** : significant, salient

sobresaliente[2] *nmf* : understudy

sobresalir {73} *vi* **1** : to protrude, to jut out, to project **2** : to stand out, to excel

sobresaltar *vt* : to startle, to frighten — **sobresaltarse** *vr*

sobresalto *nm* : start, fright

sobresueldo *nm* : bonus, additional pay

sobretasa *nf* : surcharge ⟨sobretasa a la gasolina : gas tax⟩

sobretodo *nm* : overcoat

sobrevalorar *or* **sobrevaluar** {3} *vt* : to overvalue, to overrate

sobrevender *vt* : to oversell

sobrevenir {87} *vi* ACAECER : to take place, to come about ⟨podrían sobrevenir complicaciones : complications could occur⟩

sobrevivencia → **supervivencia**

sobreviviente → **superviviente**

sobrevivir *vi* : to survive — *vt* : to outlive, to outlast

sobrevolar {19} *vt* : to fly over, to overfly

sobriedad *nf* : sobriety, moderation

sobrino, -na *n* : nephew *m*, niece *f*

sobrio, -bria *adj* : sober — **sobriamente** *adv*

socarrón, -rrona *adj, mpl* **-rrones 1** : sly, cunning **2** : sarcastic

socavar *vt* : to undermine

sociabilidad *nf* : sociability

sociable *adj* : sociable

social *adj* : social — **socialmente** *adv*

socialista *adj & nmf* : socialist — **socialismo** *nm*

sociedad *nf* **1** : society **2** : company, enterprise **3 sociedad anónima** : incorporated company

socio, -cia *n* **1** : member **2** : partner

socioeconómico, -ca *adj* : socioeconomic

sociología *nf* : sociology

sociológico, -ca *adj* : sociological — **sociológicamente** *adv*

sociólogo, -ga *n* : sociologist

socorrer *vt* : to assist, to come to the aid of

socorrido, -da *adj* ÚTIL : handy, practical

socorrista *nmf* **1** : rescue worker **2** : lifeguard

socorro *nm* AUXILIO **1** : aid, help ⟨equipo de socorro : rescue team⟩ **2** ¡socorro! : help!

soda *nf* : soda, soda water

sodio *nf* : sodium

soez *adj, pl* **soeces** GROSERO : rude, vulgar — **soezmente** *adv*

sofá *nm* : couch, sofa

sofistería *nf* : sophistry — **sofista** *nmf*

sofisticación *nf, pl* **-ciones** : sophistication

sofisticado, -da *adj* : sophisticated

sofocante *adj* : suffocating, stifling

sofocar {72} *vt* **1** AHOGAR : to suffocate, to smother **2** EXTINGUIR : to extinguish, to put out (a fire) **3** APLASTAR : to crush, to put down ⟨sofocar una rebelión : to crush a rebellion⟩ — **sofocarse** *vr* **1** : to suffocate **2** *fam* : to get upset, to get mad

sofreír {66} *vt* : to sauté

sofrito[1], **-ta** *adj* : sautéed

sofrito[2] *nm* : seasoning sauce

softbol *nm* : softball

software *nm* : software

soga *nf* : rope

soja → **soya**

sojuzgar *vt* : to subdue, to conquer, to subjugate

sol *nm* **1** : sun **2** : Peruvian unit of currency

solamente *adv* SÓLO : only, just

solapa *nf* **1** : lapel (of a jacket) **2** : flap (of an envelope)

solapado, -da *adj* : secret, underhanded

solapar *vt* : to cover up, to keep secret — **solaparse** *vr* : to overlap

solar[1] {19} *vt* : to floor, to tile

solar[2] *adj* : solar, sun

solar[3] *nm* **1** TERRENO : lot, piece of land, site **2** *Cuba, Peru* : tenement building

solariego, -ga *adj* : ancestral

solaz *nm, pl* **solaces 1** CONSUELO : solace, comfort **2** DESCANSO : relaxation, recreation

solazarse {21} *vr* : to relax, to enjoy oneself

soldado *nm* **1** : soldier **2 soldado raso** : private, enlisted man

soldador[1], **-dora** *n* : welder

soldador[2] *nm* : soldering iron

soldadura *nf* **1** : welding **2** : soldering, solder

soldar {19} *vt* **1** : to weld **2** : to solder

soleado, -da *adj* : sunny

soledad *nf* : loneliness, solitude

solemne *adj* : solemn — **solemnemente** *adv*

solemnidad *nf* : solemnity

soler {78} *vi* : to be in the habit of, to tend to ⟨solía tomar café por la tarde : she usually drank coffee in the afternoon⟩ ⟨eso suele ocurrir : that frequently happens⟩

solera *nf* **1** : prop, support **2** : tradition

solicitante *nmf* : applicant

solicitar *vt* **1** : to request, to solicit **2** : to apply for ⟨solicitar empleo : to apply for employment⟩

solícito, -ta *adj* : solicitous, attentive, obliging

solicitud *nf* **1** : solicitude, concern **2** : request **3** : application

solidaridad *nf* : solidarity

solidario, -ria *adj* : supportive, united in support ⟨se declararon solidarios con la nueva ley : they declared their support for the new law⟩ ⟨espíritu solidario : spirit of solidarity⟩

solidarizar {21} *vi* : to be in solidarity ⟨solidarizamos con la huelga : we support the strike⟩

solidez *nf* **1** : solidity, firmness **2** : soundness (of an argument, etc.)

solidificar {72} *vt* : to solidify, to make solid — **solidificarse** *vr* — **solidificación** *nf*

sólido¹, -da *adj* **1** : solid, firm **2** : sturdy, well-made **3** : sound, well-founded — **sólidamente** *adv*

sólido² *nm* : solid

soliloquio *nm* : soliloquy

solista *nmf* : soloist

solitaria *nf* TENIA : tapeworm

solitario¹, -ria *adj* **1** : lonely **2** : lone, solitary **3** DESIERTO : deserted, lonely ⟨una calle solitaria : a deserted street⟩

solitario², -ria *n* : recluse, loner

solitario³ *nm* : solitaire

sollozar {21} *vi* : to sob

sollozo *nm* : sob

solo¹, -la *adj* **1** : alone, by oneself **2** : lonely **3** ÚNICO : only, sole, unique ⟨hay un solo problema : there's only one problem⟩ **4 a solas** : alone

solo² *nm* : solo

sólo *adv* SOLAMENTE : just, only ⟨sólo quieren comer : they just want to eat⟩

solomillo *nm* : sirloin, loin

solsticio *nm* : solstice

soltar {19} *vt* **1** : to let go of, to drop **2** : to release, to set free **3** AFLOJAR : to loosen, to slacken

soltería *nf* : bachelorhood, spinsterhood

soltero¹, -ra *adj* : single, unmarried

soltero², -ra *n* **1** : bachelor *m*, single man *m*, single woman *f* **2 apellido de soltera** : maiden name

soltura *nf* **1** : looseness, slackness **2** : fluency (of language) **3** : agility, ease of movement

soluble *adj* : soluble — **solubilidad** *nf*

solución *nf*, *pl* **-ciones 1** : solution (in a liquid) **2** : answer, solution

solucionar *vt* RESOLVER : to solve, to resolve — **solucionarse** *vr*

solvencia *nf* **1** : solvency **2** : settling, payment (of debts) **3** : reliability ⟨solvencia moral : trustworthiness⟩

solvente¹ *adj* **1** : solvent **2** : reliable, trustworthy

solvente² *nm* : solvent

somalí *adj & nmf* : Somalian

sombra *nf* **1** : shadow **2** : shade **3 sombras** *nfpl* : darkness, shadows *pl* **4 sin sombra de duda** : without a shadow of a doubt

sombreado, -da *adj* **1** : shady **2** : shaded, darkened

sombrear *vt* : to shade

sombrerero, -ra *n* : milliner, hatter

sombrero *nm* **1** : hat **2 sin ~** : bareheaded **3 sombrero hongo** : derby

sombrilla *nf* : parasol, umbrella

sombrío, -bría *adj* LÓBREGO : dark, somber, gloomy — **sombríamente** *adv*

someramente *adv* : cursorily, summarily

somero, -ra *adj* : superficial, cursory, shallow

someter *vt* **1** : to subjugate, to conquer **2** : to subordinate **3** : to subject (to treatment or testing) **4** : to submit, to present — **someterse** *vr* **1** : to submit, to yield **2** : to undergo

sometimiento *nm* **1** : submission, subjection **2** : presentation

somnífero¹, -ra *adj* : soporific

somnífero² *nm* : sleeping pill

somnolencia *nf* : drowsiness, sleepiness

somnoliento, -ta *adj* : drowsy, sleepy

somorgujo *or* **somormujo** *nm* : loon, grebe

somos → **ser¹**

son¹ → **ser**

son² *nm* **1** : sound ⟨al son de la trompeta : at the sound of the trumpet⟩ **2** : news, rumor **3 en son de** : as, in the manner of, by way of ⟨en son de broma : as a joke⟩ ⟨en son de paz : in peace⟩

sonado, -da *adj* : celebrated, famous, much-discussed

sonaja *nf* : rattle

sonajero *nm* : rattle (toy)

sonámbulo, -la *n* : sleepwalker

sonar¹ {19} *vi* **1** : to sound ⟨suena bien : it sounds good⟩ **2** : to ring (bells) **3** : to look or sound familiar ⟨me suena ese nombre : that name rings a bell⟩ **4 ~ a** : to sound like — *vt* **1** : to ring **2** : to blow (a trumpet, a nose) — **sonarse** *vr* : to blow one's nose

sonar² *nm* : sonar

sonata *nf* : sonata

sonda *nf* **1** : sounding line **2** : probe **3** CATÉTER : catheter

sondar *vt* **1** : to sound, to probe (in medicine, drilling, etc.) **2** : to probe, to explore (outer space)

sondear *vt* **1** : to sound **2** : to probe **3** : to sound out, to test (opinions, markets)

sondeo *nm* **1** : sounding, probing **2** : drilling **3** ENCUESTA : survey, poll
soneto *nm* : sonnet
sónico, -ca *adj* : sonic
sonido *nm* : sound
sonoridad *nf* : sonority, resonance
sonoro, -ra *adj* **1** : resonant, sonorous, voiced (in linguistics) **2** : resounding, loud **3 banda sonora** : soundtrack
sonreír {66} *vi* : to smile
sonriente *adj* : smiling
sonrisa *nf* : smile
sonrojar *vt* : to cause to blush — **sonrojarse** *vr* : to blush
sonrojo *nm* RUBOR : blush
sonrosado, -da *adj* : rosy, pink
sonsacar {72} *vt* : to wheedle, to extract
sonsonete *nm* **1** : tapping **2** : drone **3** : mocking tone
soñador[1], -dora *adj* : dreamy
soñador[2], -dora *n* : dreamer
soñar {19} *v* **1** : to dream **2 ~ con** : to dream about **3 soñar despierto** : to daydream
soñoliento, -ta *adj* : sleepy, drowsy
sopa *nf* **1** : soup **2 estar hecho una sopa** : to be soaked to the bone
sopera *nf* : soup tureen
sopesar *vt* : to weigh, to evaluate
soplar *vi* : to blow — *vt* : to blow on, to blow out, to blow off
soplete *nm* : blowtorch
soplido *nm* : puff
soplo *nm* : puff, gust
soplón, -plona *n, mpl* **soplones** *fam* : tattletale, sneak
sopor *nm* SOMNOLENCIA : drowsiness, sleepiness
soporífero, -ra *adj* : soporific
soportable *adj* : bearable, tolerable
soportar *vt* **1** SOSTENER : to support, to hold up **2** RESISTIR : to withstand, to resist **3** AGUANTAR : to bear, to tolerate
soporte *nm* : base, stand, support
soprano *nmf* : soprano
sor *nf* : Sister (religious title)
sorber *vt* **1** : to sip, to suck in **2** : to absorb, to soak up
sorbete *nm* : sherbet
sorbo *nm* **1** : sip, gulp, swallow **2 beber a sorbos** : to sip
sordera *nf* : deafness
sordidez *nf, pl* **-deces** : sordidness, squalor
sórdido, -da *adj* : sordid, dirty, squalid
sordina *nf* : mute (for a musical instrument)
sordo, -da *adj* **1** : deaf **2** : muted, muffled
sordomudo, -da *n* : deaf-mute
sorgo *nm* : sorghum
soriasis *nfs & pl* : psoriasis
sorna *nf* : sarcasm, mocking tone
sorprendente *adj* : surprising — **sorprendentemente** *adv*
sorprender *vt* : to surprise — **sorprenderse** *vr*

sorpresa *nf* : surprise
sorpresivo, -va *adj* **1** : surprising, surprise **2** IMPREVISTO : sudden, unexpected
sortear *vt* **1** RIFAR : to raffle, to draw lots for **2** : to dodge, to avoid
sorteo *nm* : drawing, raffle
sortija *nf* **1** ANILLO : ring **2** : curl, ringlet
sortilegio *nm* **1** HECHIZO : spell, charm **2** HECHICERÍA : sorcery
SOS *nm* : SOS
sosegado, -da *adj* SERENO : calm, tranquil, serene
sosegar {49} *vt* : to calm, to pacify — **sosegarse** *vr*
sosiego *nm* : tranquillity, serenity, calm
soslayar *vt* ESQUIVAR : to dodge, to evade
soslayo *nm* **de ~** : obliquely, sideways ⟨mirar de soslayo : to look askance⟩
soso, -sa *adj* **1** INSÍPIDO : bland, flavorless **2** ABURRIDO : dull, boring
sospecha *nf* : suspicion
sospechar *vt* : to suspect — *vi* : to be suspicious
sospechosamente *adv* : suspiciously
sospechoso[1], -sa *adj* : suspicious, suspect
sospechoso[2], -sa *n* : suspect
sostén *nm, pl* **sostenes 1** APOYO : support **2** : sustenance **3** : brassiere, bra
sostener {80} *vt* **1** : to support, to hold up **2** : to hold ⟨sostenme la puerta : hold the door for me⟩ ⟨sostener una conversación : to hold a conversation⟩ **3** : to sustain, to maintain — **sostenerse** *vr* **1** : to stand, to hold oneself up **2** : to continue, to remain
sostenible *adj* : sustainable, tenable
sostenido[1], -da *adj* **1** : sustained, prolonged **2** : sharp (in music)
sostenido[2] *nm* : sharp (in music)
sostuvo, etc. → sostener
sotana *nf* : cassock
sótano *nm* : basement
sotavento *nm* : lee ⟨a sotavento : leeward⟩
soterrar {55} *vt* **1** : to bury **2** : to conceal, to hide away
soto *nm* : grove, copse
souvenir *nm, pl* **-nirs** RECUERDO : souvenir, memento
soviético, -ca *adj* : Soviet
soy → ser
soya *nf* : soy, soybean
spaghetti → espagueti
sport [ε'spor] *adj* : sport, casual
sprint [ε'sprin, -'sprint] *nm* : sprint — **sprinter** *nmf*
squash [ε'skwaʃ, -'skwatʃ] *nm* : squash (sport)
Sr. *nm* : Mr.
Sra. *nf* : Mrs., Ms.
Srta. *or* **Srita.** *nf* : Miss, Ms.
standard → estándar
stress → estrés
su *adj* **1** : his, her, its, their, one's ⟨su libro : her book⟩ ⟨sus consecuencias

: its consequences⟩ **2** (*formal*) : your ⟨tómese su medicina, señor : take your medicine, sir⟩

suave *adj* **1** BLANDO : soft **2** LISO : smooth **3** : gentle, mild **4** *Mex fam* : great, fantastic

suavemente *adj* : smoothly, gently, softly

suavidad *nf* : softness, smoothness, mellowness

suavizante *nm* : softener, fabric softener

suavizar {21} *vt* **1** : to soften, to smooth out **2** : to tone down — **suavizarse** *vr*

subacuático, -ca *adj* : underwater

subalterno¹, -na *adj* **1** SUBORDINADO : subordinate **2** SECUNDARIO : secondary

subalterno², -na *n* SUBORDINADO : subordinate

subarrendar {55} *vt* : to sublet

subasta *nf* : auction

subastador, -dora *n* : auctioneer

subastar *vt* : to auction, to auction off

subcampeón, -peona *n, mpl* **-peones** : runner-up

subcomité *nm* : subcommittee

subconsciente *adj & nm* : subconscious — **subconscientemente** *adv*

subcontratar *vt* : to subcontract

subcontratista *nmf* : subcontractor

subcultura *nf* : subculture

subdesarrollado, -da *adj* : underdeveloped

subdirector, -tora *n* : assistant manager

súbdito, -ta *n* : subject (of a monarch)

subdividir *vt* : to subdivide

subdivisión *nf, pl* **-siones** : subdivision

subestimar *vt* : to underestimate, to undervalue

subexponer {60} *vt* : to underexpose

subexposición *nf, pl* **-ciones** : underexposure

subgrupo *nm* : subgroup

subibaja *nm* : seesaw

subida *nf* **1** : ascent, climb **2** : rise, increase **3** : slope, hill ⟨ir de subida : to go uphill⟩

subido, -da *adj* **1** : intense, strong ⟨amarillo subido : bright yellow⟩ **2** **subido de tono** : risqué

subir *vt* **1** : to bring up, to take up **2** : to climb, to go up **3** : to raise — *vi* **1** : to go up, to come up **2** : to rise, to increase **3** : to be promoted **4** ~ **a** : to get on, to mount ⟨subir a un tren : to get on a train⟩ — **subirse** *vr* **1** : to climb (up) **2** : to pull up (clothing) **3** **subirse a la cabeza** : to go to one's head

súbito, -ta *adj* **1** REPENTINO : sudden **2 de** ~ : all of a sudden, suddenly — **súbitamente** *adv*

subjetivo, -va *adj* : subjective — **subjetivamente** *adv* — **subjetividad** *nf*

subjuntivo¹, -va *adj* : subjunctive

subjuntivo² *nm* : subjunctive

sublevación *nf, pl* **-ciones** ALZAMIENTO : uprising, rebellion

sublevar *vt* : to incite to rebellion — **sublevarse** *vr* : to rebel, to rise up

sublimar *vt* : to sublimate — **sublimación** *nf*

sublime *adj* : sublime

submarinismo *nm* : scuba diving

submarinista *nmf* : scuba diver

submarino¹, -na *adj* : submarine, undersea

submarino² *nm* : submarine

suboficial *nmf* : noncommissioned officer, petty officer

subordinado, -da *adj & n* : subordinate

subordinar *vt* : to subordinate — **subordinarse** *vr* — **subordinación** *nf*

subproducto *nm* : by-product

subrayar *vt* **1** : to underline, to underscore **2** ENFATIZAR : to highlight, to emphasize

subrepticio, -cia *adj* : surreptitious — **subrepticiamente** *adv*

subsahariano, -na *adj* : sub-Saharan

subsanar *vt* **1** RECTIFICAR : to rectify, to correct **2** : to overlook, to excuse **3** : to make up for

subscribir → **suscribir**

subsecretario, -ria *n* : undersecretary

subsecuente *adj* : subsequent — **subsecuentemente** *adv*

subsidiar *vt* : to subsidize

subsidiaria *nf* : subsidiary

subsidio *nm* : subsidy

subsiguiente *adj* : subsequent

subsistencia *nf* **1** : subsistence **2** : sustenance

subsistir *vi* **1** : to subsist, to live **2** : to endure, to survive

substancia → **sustancia**

subteniente *nmf* : second lieutenant

subterfugio *nm* : subterfuge

subterráneo¹, -nea *adj* : underground, subterranean

subterráneo² *nm* **1** : underground passage, tunnel **2** *Arg, Uru* : subway

subtítulo *nm* : subtitle, subheading

subtotal *nm* : subtotal

suburbano, -na *adj* : suburban

suburbio *nm* **1** : suburb **2** : slum (outside a city)

subvención *nf, pl* **-ciones** : subsidy, grant

subvencionar *vt* : to subsidize

subversivo, -va *adj & n* : subversive — **subversión** *nf*

subvertir {76} *vt* : to subvert

subyacente *adj* : underlying

subyugar {52} *vt* : to subjugate — **subyugación** *nf*

succión *nf, pl* **succiones** : suction

succionar *vt* : to suck up, to draw in

sucedáneo *nm* : substitute ⟨sucedáneo de azúcar : sugar substitute⟩

suceder *vi* **1** OCURRIR : to happen, to occur ⟨¿qué sucede? : what's going on?⟩ ⟨suceda lo que suceda : come what may⟩ **2** ~ **a** : to follow, to succeed ⟨suceder al trono : to succeed to the throne⟩ ⟨a la primavera sucede el verano : summer follows spring⟩

sucesión *nf, pl* **-siones 1** : succession **2** : sequence, series **3** : issue, heirs *pl*
sucesivamente *adv* : successively, consecutively ⟨y así sucesivamente : and so on⟩
sucesivo, -va *adj* : successive ⟨en los días sucesivos : in the days that followed⟩
suceso *nm* **1** : event, happening, occurrence **2** : incident, crime
sucesor, -sora *n* : successor
suciedad *nf* **1** : dirtiness, filthiness **2** MUGRE : dirt, filth
sucinto, -ta *adj* CONCISO : succinct, concise — **sucintamente** *adv*
sucio, -cia *adj* : dirty, filthy
sucre *nm* : Ecuadoran unit of currency
suculento, -ta *adj* : succulent
sucumbir *vi* : to succumb
sucursal *nf* : branch (of a business)
sudadera *nf* : sweatshirt
sudado, -da → **sudoroso**
sudafricano, -na *adj & n* : South African
sudamericano, -na *adj & n* : South American
sudanés, -nesa *adj & n, mpl* **-neses** : Sudanese
sudar *vi* TRANSPIRAR : to sweat, to perspire
sudario *nm* : shroud
sudeste → **sureste**
sudoeste → **suroeste**
sudor *nm* TRANSPIRACIÓN : sweat, perspiration
sudoroso, -sa *adj* : sweaty
sueco[1], -ca *adj* : Swedish
sueco[2], -ca *n* : Swede
sueco[3] *nm* : Swedish (language)
suegro, -gra *n* **1** : father-in-law *m*, mother-in-law *f* **2 suegros** *nmpl* : in-laws
suela *nf* : sole (of a shoe)
suelda, etc. → **soldar**
sueldo *nm* : salary, wage
suele, etc. → **soler**
suelo *nm* **1** : ground ⟨caerse al suelo : to fall down, to hit the ground⟩ **2** : floor, flooring **3** TIERRA : soil, land
suelta, etc. → **soltar**
suelto[1], -ta *adj* : loose, free, unattached
suelto[2] *nm* : loose change
suena, etc. → **sonar**
sueña, etc. → **soñar**
sueño *nm* **1** : dream **2** : sleep ⟨perder el sueño : to lose sleep⟩ **3** : sleepiness ⟨tener sueño : to be sleepy⟩
suero *nm* **1** : serum **2** : whey
suerte *nf* **1** FORTUNA : luck, fortune ⟨tener suerte : to be lucky⟩ ⟨por suerte : luckily⟩ **2** DESTINO : fate, destiny, lot **3** CLASE, GÉNERO : sort, kind ⟨toda suerte de cosas : all kinds of things⟩
suertudo, -da *adj fam* : lucky
suéter *nm* : sweater
suficiencia *nf* **1** : adequacy, sufficiency **2** : competence, fitness **3** : smugness, self-satisfaction
suficiente *adj* **1** BASTANTE : enough, sufficient ⟨tener suficiente : to have

enough⟩ **2** : suitable, fit **3** : smug, complacent
suficientemente *adv* : sufficiently, enough
sufijo *nm* : suffix
suflé *nm* : soufflé
sufragar {52} *vt* **1** AYUDAR : to help out, to support **2** : to defray (costs) — *vi* : to vote
sufragio *nm* : suffrage, vote
sufrido, -da *adj* **1** : long-suffering, patient **2** : sturdy, serviceable (of clothing)
sufrimiento *nm* : suffering
sufrir *vt* **1** : to suffer ⟨sufrir una pérdida : to suffer a loss⟩ **2** : to tolerate, to put up with ⟨ella no lo puede sufrir : she can't stand him⟩ — *vi* : to suffer
sugerencia *nf* : suggestion
sugerir {76} *vt* **1** PROPONER, RECOMENDAR : to suggest, to recommend, to propose **2** : to suggest, to bring to mind
sugestión *nf, pl* **-tiones** : suggestion, prompting ⟨poder de sugestión : power of suggestion⟩
sugestionable *adj* : suggestible, impressionable
sugestionar *vt* : to influence, to sway — **sugestionarse** *vr* ~ **con** : to talk oneself into, to become convinced of
sugestivo, -va *adj* **1** : suggestive **2** : interesting, stimulating
suicida[1] *adj* : suicidal
suicida[2] *nmf* : suicide victim, suicide
suicidarse *vr* : to commit suicide
suicidio *nm* : suicide
suite *nf* : suite
suizo, -za *adj & n* : Swiss
sujeción *nf, pl* **-ciones 1** : holding, fastening **2** : subjection
sujetador *nm* **1** : fastener **2** : holder ⟨sujetador de tazas : cup holder⟩
sujetalibros *nms & pl* : bookend
sujetapapeles *nms & pl* CLIP : paper clip
sujetar *vt* **1** : to hold on to, to steady, to hold down **2** FIJAR : to fasten, to attach **3** DOMINAR : to subdue, to conquer — **sujetarse** *vr* **1** : to hold on, to hang on **2** ~ **a** : to abide by
sujeto[1], -ta *adj* **1** : secure, fastened **2** ~ **a** : subject to
sujeto[2] *nm* **1** INDIVIDUO : individual, character **2** : subject (in grammar)
sulfúrico, -ca *adj* : sulfuric
sulfuro *nm* : sulfur
sultán *nm, pl* **sultanes** : sultan
suma *nf* **1** CANTIDAD : sum, quantity **2** : addition
sumamente *adv* : extremely, exceedingly
sumar *vt* **1** : to add, to add up **2** : to add up to, to total — *vi* : to add up — **sumarse** *vr* ~ **a** : to join
sumario[1], -ria *adj* SUCINTO : succinct, summary — **sumariamente** *adv*
sumario[2] *nm* : summary

sumergir {35} *vt* : to submerge, to immerse, to plunge — **sumergirse** *vr*

sumersión *nf, pl* **-siones** : submersion, immersion

sumidero *nm* : drain, sewer

suministrar *vt* : to supply, to provide

suministro *nm* : supply, provision

sumir *vt* SUMERGIR : to plunge, to immerse, to sink — **sumirse** *vr*

sumisión *nf, pl* **-siones** **1** : submission **2** : submissiveness

sumiso, -sa *adj* : submissive, acquiescent, docile

sumo, -ma *adj* **1** : extreme, great, high ⟨la suma autoridad : the highest authority⟩ **2 a lo sumo** : at the most — **sumamente** *adv*

suntuoso, -sa *adj* : sumptuous, lavish — **suntuosamente** *adv*

supeditar *vt* SUBORDINAR : to subordinate — **supeditación** *nf*

super[1] *or* **súper** *adj fam* : super, great

super[2] *nm* SUPERMERCADO : market, supermarket

superable *adj* : surmountable

superabundancia *nf* : overabundance, superabundance — **superabundante** *adj*

superar *vt* **1** : to surpass, to exceed **2** : to overcome, to surmount — **superarse** *vr* : to improve oneself

superávit *nm, pl* **-vit** *or* **-vits** : surplus

superchería *nf* : trickery, fraud

supercomputadora *nf* : supercomputer

superestructura *nf* : superstructure

superficial *adj* : superficial — **superficialmente** *adv*

superficialidad *nf* : superficiality

superficie *nf* **1** : surface **2** : area ⟨la superficie de un triángulo : the area of a triangle⟩

superfluidad *nf* : superfluity

superfluo, -flua *adj* : superfluous

superintendente *nmf* : supervisor, superintendent

superior[1] *adj* **1** : superior **2** : upper ⟨nivel superior : upper level⟩ **3** : higher ⟨educación superior : higher education⟩ **4 ~ a** : above, higher than, in excess of

superior[2] *nm* : superior

superioridad *nf* : superiority

superlativo[1], **-va** *adj* : superlative

superlativo[2] *nm* : superlative

supermercado *nm* : supermarket

superpoblación *nf, pl* **-ciones** : overpopulation

superpoblado, -da *adj* : overpopulated

superponer {60} *vt* : to superimpose

superpotencia *nf* : superpower

superproducción → **sobreproducción**

supersónico, -ca *adj* : supersonic

superstición *nf, pl* **-ciones** : superstition

supersticioso, -sa *adj* : superstitious

supervisar *vt* : to supervise, to oversee

supervisión *nf, pl* **-siones** : supervision

supervisor, -sora *n* : supervisor, overseer

supervivencia *nf* : survival

superviviente *nmf* : survivor

supino, -na *adj* : supine

suplantar *vt* : to supplant, to replace

suplemental → **suplementario**

suplementario, -ria *adj* : supplementary, additional, extra

suplemento *nm* : supplement

suplencia *nf* : substitution, replacement

suplente *adj & nmf* : substitute ⟨equipo suplente : replacement team⟩

supletorio, -ria *adj* : extra, additional ⟨teléfono supletorio : extension phone⟩ ⟨cama supletoria : spare bed⟩

súplica *nf* : plea, entreaty

suplicar {72} *vt* IMPLORAR, ROGAR : to entreat, to implore, to supplicate

suplicio *nm* TORMENTO : ordeal, torture

suplir *vt* **1** COMPENSAR : to make up for, to compensate for **2** REEMPLAZAR : to replace, to substitute

supo, etc. → **saber**

suponer {60} *vt* **1** PRESUMIR : to suppose, to assume ⟨supongo que sí : I guess so, I suppose so⟩ ⟨se supone que van a llegar mañana : they're supposed to arrive tomorrow⟩ **2** : to imply, to suggest **3** : to involve, to entail ⟨el éxito supone mucho trabajo : success involves a lot of work⟩

suposición *nf, pl* **-ciones** PRESUNCIÓN : supposition, assumption

supositorio *nm* : suppository

supremacía *nf* : supremacy

supremo, -ma *adj* : supreme

supresión *nf, pl* **-siones** **1** : suppression, elimination **2** : deletion

suprimir *vt* **1** : to suppress, to eliminate **2** : to delete

supuestamente *adv* : supposedly, allegedly

supuesto, -ta *adj* **1** : supposed, alleged **2 por ~** : of course, absolutely

supurar *vi* : to ooze, to discharge

supuso, etc. → **suponer**

sur[1] *adj* : southern, southerly, south

sur[2] *nm* **1** : south, South **2** : south wind

surafricano, -na → **sudafricano**

suramericano, -na → **sudamericano**

surcar {72} *vt* **1** : to plow (through) **2** : to groove, to score, to furrow

surco *nm* : groove, furrow, rut

sureño[1], **-ña** *adj* : southern, Southern

sureño[2], **-ña** *n* : Southerner

sureste[1] *adj* **1** : southeast, southeastern **2** : southeasterly

sureste[2] *nm* : southeast, Southeast

surf *nm* : surfing

surfear *vi* : to surf

surfing → **surf**

surfista *nmf* : surfer

surgimiento *nm* : rise, emergence

surgir {35} *vi* : to rise, to arise, to emerge

suroeste[1] *adj* **1** : southwest, southwestern **2** : southwesterly

suroeste[2] *nm* : southwest, Southwest

surtido[1], **-da** *adj* **1** : assorted, varied **2** : stocked, provisioned

surtido[2] *nm* : assortment, selection
surtidor *nm* **1** : jet, spout **2** *Arg, Chile, Spain* : gas pump
surtir *vt* **1** : to supply, to provide ⟨surtir un pedido : to fill an order⟩ **2 surtir efecto** : to have an effect — *vi* : to spout, to spurt up — **surtirse** *vr* : to stock up
susceptible *adj* : susceptible, sensitive — **susceptibilidad** *nf*
suscitar *vt* : to provoke, to give rise to
suscribir {33} *vt* **1** : to sign (a formal document) **2** : to endorse, to sanction — **suscribirse** *vr* ∼ **a** : to subscribe to
suscripción *nf, pl* **-ciones 1** : subscription **2** : endorsement, sanction **3** : signing
suscriptor, -tora *n* : subscriber
susodicho, -cha *adj* : aforementioned, aforesaid
suspender *vt* **1** COLGAR : to suspend, to hang **2** : to suspend, to discontinue **3** : to suspend, to dismiss
suspensión *nf, pl* **-siones** : suspension
suspenso *nm* : suspense
suspicacia *nf* : suspicion, mistrust
suspicaz *adj, pl* **-caces** DESCONFIADO : suspicious, wary
suspirar *vi* : to sigh
suspiro *nm* : sigh
surque, etc. → **surcar**
suscrito *pp* → **suscribir**
sustancia *nf* **1** : substance **2 sin** ∼ : shallow, lacking substance
sustancial *adj* **1** : substantial **2** ESENCIAL, FUNDAMENTAL : essential, fundamental — **sustancialmente** *adv*
sustancioso, -sa *adj* **1** NUTRITIVO : hearty, nutritious **2** : substantial, solid
sustantivo *nm* : noun

sustentación *nf, pl* **-ciones** SOSTÉN : support
sustentar *vt* **1** : to support, to hold up **2** : to sustain, to nourish **3** : to maintain, to hold (an opinion) — **sustentarse** *vr* : to support oneself
sustento *nm* **1** : means of support, livelihood **2** : sustenance, food
sustitución *nf, pl* **-ciones** : replacement, substitution
sustituir {41} *vt* **1** : to replace, to substitute for **2** : to stand in for
sustituto, -ta *n* : substitute, stand-in
susto *nm* : fright, scare
sustracción *nf, pl* **-ciones 1** RESTA : subtraction **2** : theft
sustraer {81} *vt* **1** : to remove, to take away **2** RESTAR : to subtract **3** : to steal — **sustraerse** *vr* ∼ **a** : to avoid, to evade
susurrar *vi* **1** : to whisper **2** : to murmur **3** : to rustle (leaves, etc.) — *vt* : to whisper
susurro *nm* **1** : whisper **2** : murmur **3** : rustle, rustling
sutil *adj* **1** : delicate, thin, fine **2** : subtle
sutileza *nf* **1** : delicacy **2** : subtlety
sutura *nf* : suture
suturar *vt* : to suture
suyo[1]**, -ya** *adj* **1** : his, her, its, theirs ⟨los libros suyos : his books⟩ ⟨un amigo suyo : a friend of hers⟩ ⟨esta casa es suya : this house is theirs⟩ **2** (*formal*) : yours ⟨¿este abrigo es suyo, señor? : is this your coat, sir?⟩
suyo[2]**, -ya** *pron* **1** : his, hers, theirs ⟨mi guitarra y la suya : my guitar and hers⟩ ⟨ellos trajeron las suyas : they brought theirs, they brought their own⟩ **2** (*formal*) : yours ⟨usted olvidó la suya : you forgot yours⟩
switch *nm* : switch

T

t *nf* : twenty-first letter of the Spanish alphabet
taba *nf* : anklebone
tabacalero[1]**, -ra** *adj* : tobacco ⟨industria tabacalera : tobacco industry⟩
tabacalero[2]**, -ra** *n* : tobacco grower
tabaco *nm* : tobacco
tábano *nm* : horsefly
taberna *nf* : tavern, bar
tabernáculo *nm* : tabernacle
tabicar {72} *vt* : to wall up
tabique *nm* : thin wall, partition
tabla *nf* **1** : table, list ⟨tabla de multiplicar : multiplication table⟩ **2** : board, plank, slab ⟨tabla de planchar : ironing board⟩ **3** : plot, strip (of land) **4 tablas** *nfpl* : stage, boards *pl*
tablado *nm* **1** : floor **2** : platform, scaffold **3** : stage
tablero *nm* **1** : bulletin board **2** : board (in games) ⟨tablero de ajedrez : chess-

board⟩ ⟨tablero de damas : checkerboard⟩ **3** PIZARRA : blackboard **4** : switchboard **5 tablero de instrumentos** : dashboard, instrument panel
tableta *nf* **1** COMPRIMIDO, PÍLDORA : tablet, pill **2** : bar (of chocolate)
tabletear *vi* : to rattle, to clack
tableteo *nm* : clack, rattling
tablilla *nf* **1** : small board or tablet **2** : bulletin board **3** : splint
tabloide *nm* : tabloid
tablón *nm, pl* **tablones 1** : plank, beam **2 tablón de anuncios** : bulletin board
tabú[1] *adj* : taboo
tabú[2] *nm, pl* **tabúes** *or* **tabús** : taboo
tabulador *nm* : tabulator
tabular[1] *vt* : to tabulate
tabular[2] *adj* : tabular
taburete *nm* : footstool, stool
tacañería *nf* : miserliness, stinginess

tacaño[1], **-ña** *adj* MEZQUINO : stingy, miserly

tacaño[2], **-ña** *n* : miser, tightwad

tacha *nf* **1** : flaw, blemish, defect **2 poner tacha a** : to find fault with **3 sin ~** : flawless

tachadura *nf* : erasure, correction

tachar *vt* **1** : to cross out, to delete **2 ~ de** : to accuse of, to label as ⟨lo tacharon de mentiroso : they accused him of being a liar⟩

tachón *nm, pl* **tachones** : stud, hobnail

tachonar *vt* : to stud

tachuela *nf* : tack, hobnail, stud

tácito, -ta *adj* : tacit, implicit — **tácitamente** *adv*

taciturno, -na *adj* **1** : taciturn **2** : sullen, gloomy

tacle *nm* : tackle

taclear *vt* : to tackle (in football)

taco *nm* **1** : wad, stopper, plug **2** : pad (of paper) **3** : cleat **4** : heel (of a shoe) **5** : cue (in billiards) **6** : light snack, bite **7** : taco

tacón *nm, pl* **tacones** : heel (of a shoe) ⟨de tacón alto : high-heeled⟩

táctica *nf* : tactic, tactics *pl*

táctico[1], **-ca** *adj* : tactical

táctico[2], **-ca** *n* : tactician

táctil *adj* : tactile

tacto *nm* **1** : touch, touching, feel **2** DELICADEZA : tact

tafetán *nm, pl* **-tanes** : taffeta

tahúr *nm, pl* **tahúres** : gambler

tailandés[1], **-desa** *adj & n, pl* **-deses** : Thai

tailandés[2] *nm* : Thai (language)

taimado, -da *adj* **1** : crafty, sly **2** *Chile* : sullen, sulky

tajada *nf* **1** : slice **2 sacar tajada** *fam* : to get one's share

tajante *adj* **1** : cutting, sharp **2** : decisive, categorical

tajantemente *adj* : emphatically, categorically

tajar *vt* : to cut, to slice

tajo *nm* **1** : cut, slash, gash **2** ESCARPA : steep cliff

tal[1] *adv* **1** : so, in such a way **2 tal como** : just as ⟨tal como lo hice : just the way I did it⟩ **3 con tal que** : provided that, as long as **4 ¿qué tal?** : how are you?, how's it going?

tal[2] *adj* **1** : such, such a **2 tal vez** : maybe, perhaps

tal[3] *pron* **1** : such a one, someone **2** : such a thing, something **3 tal para cual** : two of a kind

tala *nf* : felling (of trees)

taladrar *vt* : to drill

taladro *nm* : drill, auger ⟨taladro eléctrico : power drill⟩

talante *nm* **1** HUMOR : mood, disposition **2** VOLUNTAD : will, willingness

talar *vt* **1** : to cut down, to fell **2** DEVASTAR : to devastate, to destroy

talco *nm* **1** : talc **2** : talcum powder

talego *nm* : sack

talento *nm* : talent, ability

talentoso, -sa *adj* : talented, gifted

talismán *nm, pl* **-manes** AMULETO : talisman, charm

talla *nf* **1** ESTATURA : height **2** : size (in clothing) **3** : stature, status **4** : sculpture, carving

tallar *vt* **1** : to sculpt, to carve **2** : to measure (someone's height) **3** : to deal (cards)

tallarín *nf, pl* **-rines** : noodle

talle *nm* **1** : size **2** : waist, waistline **3** : figure, shape

taller *nm* **1** : shop, workshop **2** : studio (of an artist)

tallo *nm* : stalk, stem ⟨tallo de maíz : cornstalk⟩

talón *nm, pl* **talones** **1** : heel (of the foot) **2** : stub (of a check) **3 talón de Aquiles** : Achilles' heel

talud *nm* : slope, incline

tamal *nm* : tamale

tamaño[1], **-ña** *adj* : such a big ⟨¿crees tamaña mentira? : do you believe such a lie?⟩

tamaño[2] *nm* **1** : size **2 de tamaño natural** : life-size

tamarindo *nm* : tamarind

tambalearse *vr* **1** : to teeter **2** : to totter, to stagger, to sway — **tambaleante** *adj*

tambaleo *nm* : staggering, lurching, swaying

también *adv* : too, as well, also

tambor *nm* : drum

tamborilear *vi* : to drum, to tap

tamborileo *nm* : tapping, drumming

tamiz *nm* : sieve

tamizar {21} *vt* : to sift

tampoco *adv* : neither, not either ⟨ni yo tampoco : me neither⟩

tampón *nm, pl* **tampones** **1** : ink pad **2** : tampon

tam–tam *nm* : tom-tom

tan *adv* **1** : so, so very ⟨no es tan difícil : it is not that difficult⟩ **2 : as** ⟨tan pronto como : as soon as⟩ **3 tan siquiera** : at least, at the least **4 tan sólo** : only, merely

tanda *nf* **1** : turn, shift **2** : batch, lot, series

tándem *nm* **1** : tandem (bicycle) **2** : duo, pair

tangente *adj & nf* : tangent — **tangencial** *adj*

tangible *adj* : tangible

tango *nm* : tango

tanino *nm* : tannin

tanque *nm* **1** : tank, reservoir **2** : tanker, tank (vehicle)

tanteador *nm* MARCADOR : scoreboard

tantear *vt* **1** : to feel, to grope **2** : to size up, to weigh — *vi* **1** : to keep score **2** : to feel one's way

tanteo *nm* **1** : estimate, rough calculation **2** : testing, sizing up **3** : scoring

tanto[1] *adv* **1** : so much ⟨tanto mejor : so much the better⟩ **2** : so long ⟨¿por qué te tardaste tanto? : why did you take so long?⟩

tanto², -ta *adj* **1** : so much, so many, such ⟨no hagas tantas preguntas : don't ask so many questions⟩ ⟨tiene tanto encanto : he has such charm, he's so charming⟩ **2** : as much, as many ⟨come tantos dulces como yo : she .eats as many sweets as I do⟩ **3** : odd, however er many ⟨cuarenta y tantos años : forty-odd years⟩

tanto³ *nm* **1** : certain amount **2** : goal, point (in sports) **3 al tanto** : abreast, in the picture **4 un tanto** : somewhat, rather ⟨un tanto cansado : rather tired⟩

tanto⁴, -ta *pron* **1** : so much, so many ⟨tiene tanto que hacer : she has so much to do⟩ ⟨¡no me des tantos! : don't give me so many!⟩ **2 entre ~** : meanwhile **3 por lo tanto** : therefore

tañer {79} *vt* **1** : to ring (a bell) **2** : to play (a musical instrument)

tañido *nm* **1** CAMPANADA : ring, peal, toll **2** : sound (of an instrument)

tapa *nf* **1** : cover, top, lid **2** *Spain* : bar snack

tapacubos *nms & pl* : hubcap

tapadera *nf* **1** : cover, lid **2** : front, cover (for an organization or person)

tapar *vt* **1** CUBRIR : to cover, to cover up **2** OBSTRUIR : to block, to obstruct — **taparse** *vr*

tapete *nm* **1** : small rug, mat **2** : table cover **3 poner sobre el tapete** : to bring up for discussion

tapia *nf* : (adobe) wall, garden wall

tapiar *vt* **1** : to wall in **2** : to enclose, to block off

tapicería *nf* **1** : upholstery **2** TAPIZ : tapestry

tapicero, -ra *n* : upholsterer

tapioca *nf* : tapioca

tapir *nm* : tapir

tapiz *nm, pl* **tapices** : tapestry

tapizar {21} *vt* **1** : to upholster **2** : to cover, to carpet

tapón *nm, pl* **tapones 1** : cork **2** : bottle cap **3** : plug, stopper

tapujo *nm* **1** : deceit, pretension **2 sin tapujos** : openly, frankly

taquigrafía *nf* : stenography, shorthand

taquigráfico, -ca *adj* : stenographic

taquígrafo, -fa *n* : stenographer

taquilla *nf* **1** : box office, ticket office **2** : earnings *pl*, take

taquillero, -ra *adj* : box-office, popular ⟨un éxito taquillero : a box-office success⟩

tarántula *nf* : tarantula

tararear *vt* : to hum

tardanza *nf* : lateness, delay

tardar *vi* **1** : to delay, to take a long time **2** : to be late **3 a más tardar** : at the latest — *vt* DEMORAR : to take (time) ⟨tarda una hora : it takes an hour⟩

tarde¹ *adv* **1** : late **2 tarde o temprano** : sooner or later

tarde² *nf* **1** : afternoon, evening **2 ¡buenas tardes!** : good afternoon!, good evening! **3 en la tarde** *or* **por la tarde** : in the afternoon, in the evening

tardío, -día *adj* : late, tardy

tardo, -da *adj* : slow

tarea *nf* **1** : task, job **2** : homework

tarifa *nf* **1** : rate ⟨tarifas postales : postal rates⟩ **2** : fare (for transportation) **3** : price list **4** ARANCEL : duty

tarima *nf* PLATAFORMA : dais, platform, stage

tarjeta *nf* : card ⟨tarjeta de crédito : credit card⟩ ⟨tarjeta postal : postcard⟩

tarro *nm* **1** : jar, pot **2** *Arg, Chile* : can, tin

tarta *nf* **1** : tart **2** : cake

tartaleta *nf* : tart

tartamudear *vi* : to stammer, to stutter

tartamudeo *nm* : stutter, stammer

tartán *nm, pl* **tartanes** : tartan, plaid

tártaro *nm* : tartar

tasa *nf* **1** : rate ⟨tasa de desempleo : unemployment rate⟩ **2** : tax, fee **3** : appraisal, valuation

tasación *nf, pl* **-ciones** : appraisal, assessment

tasador, -dora *n* : assessor, appraiser

tasar *vt* **1** VALORAR : to appraise, to value **2** : to set the price of **3** : to ration, to limit

tasca *nf* : cheap bar, dive

tatuaje *nm* : tattoo, tattooing

tatuar {3} *vt* : to tattoo

taurino, -na *adj* : bull, bullfighting

Tauro *nmf* : Taurus

tauromaquia *nf* : (art of) bullfighting

taxi *nm, pl* **taxis** : taxi, taxicab

taxidermia *nf* : taxidermy

taxidermista *nmf* : taxidermist

taxímetro *nm* : taximeter

taxista *nmf* : taxi driver

taza *nf* **1** : cup **2** : cupful **3** : (toilet) bowl **4** : basin (of a fountain)

tazón *nm, pl* **tazones 1** : bowl **2** : large cup, mug

te *pron* **1** : you ⟨te quiero : I love you⟩ **2** : to you, from you ⟨me gustaría dártelo : I would like to give it to you⟩ **3** : yourself, for yourself, to yourself, from yourself ⟨¡cálmate! : calm yourself!⟩ ⟨¿te guardaste uno? : did you keep one for yourself?⟩ **4** : thee

té *nm* **1** : tea **2** : tea party

tea *nf* : torch

teatral *adj* : theatrical — **teatralmente** *adv*

teatro *nm* **1** : theater **2 hacer teatro** : to put on an act, to exaggerate

teca *nf* : teak

techado *nm* **1** : roof **2 bajo techado** : under cover, indoors

techar *vt* : to roof, to shingle

techo *nm* **1** TEJADO : roof **2** : ceiling **3** : upper limit, ceiling

techumbre *nf* : roofing

tecla *nf* **1** : key (of a musical instrument or a machine) **2 dar en la tecla** : to hit the nail on the head

teclado *nm* : keyboard
teclear *vt* : to type in, to enter
técnica *nf* 1 : technique, skill 2 : technology
técnico[1], **-ca** *adj* : technical — **técnicamente** *adv*
técnico[2], **-ca** *n* : technician, expert, engineer
tecnología *nf* : technology
tecnológico, -ca *adj* : technological — **tecnológicamente** *adv*
tecolote *nm Mex* : owl
tedio *nm* : tedium, boredom
tedioso, -sa *adj* : tedious, boring — **tediosamente** *adv*
teja *nf* : tile
tejado *nm* TECHO : roof
tejedor, -dora *n* : weaver
tejer *vt* 1 : to knit, to crochet 2 : to weave 3 FABRICAR : to concoct, to make up, to fabricate
tejido *nm* 1 TELA : fabric, cloth 2 : weave, texture 3 : tissue ⟨tejido muscular : muscle tissue⟩
tejo *nm* 1 : yew 2 : hopscotch (children's game)
tejón *nm, pl* **tejones** : badger
tela *nf* 1 : fabric, cloth, material 2 **tela de araña** : spiderweb 3 **poner en tela de juicio** : to call into question, to doubt
telar *nm* : loom
telaraña *nf* : spiderweb, cobweb
tele *nf fam* : TV, television
telecomunicación *nf, pl* **-ciones** : telecommunication
teleconferencia *nf* : teleconference
teledifusión *nf, pl* **-siones** : television broadcasting
teledirigido, -da *adj* : remote-controlled
telefonear *v* : to telephone, to call
telefónico, -ca *adj* : phone, telephone ⟨llamada telefónica : phone call⟩
telefonista *nmf* : telephone operator
teléfono *nm* 1 : telephone 2 **llamar por teléfono** : to telephone, to make a phone call
telegrafiar {85} *v* : to telegraph
telegráfico, -ca *adj* : telegraphic
telégrafo *nm* : telegraph
telegrama *nm* : telegram
telenovela *nf* : soap opera
telepatía *nf* : telepathy
telepático, -ca *adj* : telepathic — **telepáticamente** *adv*
telescópico, -ca *adj* : telescopic
telescopio *nm* : telescope
telespectador, -dora *n* : television viewer
telesquí *nm, pl* **-squís** : ski lift
televidente *nmf* : television viewer
televisar *vt* : to televise
televisión *nf, pl* **-siones** : television, TV
televisivo, -va *adj* : television ⟨serie televisiva : television series⟩
televisor *nm* : television set
telón *nm, pl* **telones** 1 : curtain (in theater) 2 **telón de fondo** : backdrop, background

tema *nm* 1 ASUNTO : theme, topic, subject 2 MOTIVO : motif, central theme
temario *nm* 1 : set of topics (for study) 2 : agenda
temática *nf* : subject matter
temático, -ca *adj* : thematic
temblar {55} *vi* 1 : to tremble, to shake, to shiver ⟨le temblaban las rodillas : his knees were shaking⟩ 2 : to shudder, to be afraid ⟨tiemblo con sólo pensarlo : I shudder to think of it⟩
temblor *nm* 1 : shaking, trembling 2 : tremor, earthquake
tembloroso, -sa *adj* : tremulous, trembling, shaking ⟨con la voz temblorosa : with a shaky voice⟩
temer *vt* : to fear, to dread — *vi* : to be afraid
temerario, -ria *adj* : reckless, rash — **temerariamente** *adv*
temeridad *nf* 1 : temerity, recklessness, rashness 2 : rash act
temeroso, -sa *adj* MIEDOSO : fearful, frightened
temible *adj* : fearsome, dreadful
temor *nm* MIEDO : fear, dread
témpano *nm* : ice floe
temperamento *nm* : temperament — **temperamental** *adj*
temperancia *nf* : temperance
temperar *vt* MODERAR : to temper, to moderate — *vi* : to have a change of air
temperatura *nf* : temperature
tempestad *nf* 1 : storm, tempest 2 **tempestad de arena** : sandstorm
tempestuoso, -sa *adj* : tempestuous, stormy
templado, -da *adj* 1 : temperate, mild 2 : moderate, restrained 3 : warm, lukewarm 4 VALIENTE : courageous, bold
templanza *nf* 1 : temperance, moderation 2 : mildness (of weather)
templar *vt* 1 : to temper (steel) 2 : to restrain, to moderate 3 : to tune (a musical instrument) 4 : to warm up, to cool down — **templarse** *vr* 1 : to be moderate 2 : to warm up, to cool down
temple *nm* 1 : temper (of steel, etc.) 2 HUMOR : mood ⟨de buen temple : in a good mood⟩ 3 : tuning 4 VALOR : courage
templo *nm* 1 : temple 2 : church, chapel
tempo *nm* : tempo (in music)
temporada *nf* 1 : season, time ⟨temporada de béisbol : baseball season⟩ 2 : period, spell ⟨por temporadas : on and off⟩
temporal[1] *adj* 1 : temporal 2 : temporary
temporal[2] *nm* 1 : storm 2 **capear el temporal** : to weather the storm
temporalmente *adv* : temporarily
temporario, -ria *adj* : temporary — **temporariamente** *adv*
temporero[1], **-ra** *adj* : temporary, seasonal

temporero², -ra *n* : temporary or seasonal worker

temporizador *nm* : timer

tempranero, -ra *adj* **1** : early **2** : early-rising

temprano¹ *adv* : early ⟨lo más temprano posible : as soon as possible⟩

temprano², -na *adj* : early ⟨la parte temprana del siglo : the early part of the century⟩

ten → **tener**

tenacidad *nf* : tenacity, perseverance

tenaz *adj, pl* **tenaces 1** : tenacious, persistent **2** : strong, tough

tenaza *nf, or* **tenazas** *nfpl* **1** : pliers, pincers **2** : tongs **3** : claw (of a crustacean)

tenazmente *adv* : tenaciously

tendedero *nm* : clothesline

tendencia *nf* **1** PROPENSIÓN : tendency, inclination **2** : trend

tendencioso, -sa *adj* : tendentious, biased

tendente → **tendiente**

tender {56} *vt* **1** EXTENDER : to spread out, to lay out **2** : to hang out (clothes) **3** : to lay (cables, etc.) **4** : to set (a trap) — *vi* ~ **a** : to tend to, to have a tendency towards — **tenderse** *vr* : to stretch out, to lie down

tendero, -ra *n* : shopkeeper, storekeeper

tendido *nm* **1** : laying (of cables, etc.) **2** : seats *pl*, section (at a bullfight)

tendiente *adj* ~ **a** : aimed at, designed to

tendón *nm, pl* **tendones** : tendon

tenebrosidad *nf* : darkness, gloom

tendrá, etc. → **tener**

tenebroso, -sa *adj* **1** OSCURO : gloomy, dark **2** SINIESTRO : sinister

tenedor¹, -dora *n* **1** : holder **2 tenedor de libros, tenedora de libros** : bookkeeper

tenedor² *nm* : table fork

tenencia *nf* **1** : possession, holding **2** : tenancy **3** : tenure

tener {80} *vt* **1** : to have ⟨tiene ojos verdes : she has green eyes⟩ ⟨tengo mucho que hacer : I have a lot to do⟩ ⟨tiene veinte años : he's twenty years old⟩ ⟨tiene un metro de largo : it's one meter long⟩ **2** : to hold ⟨ten esto un momento : hold this for a moment⟩ **3** : to feel, to make ⟨tengo frío : I'm cold⟩ ⟨eso nos tiene contentos : that makes us happy⟩ **4** ~ **por** : to think, to consider ⟨me tienes por loco : you think I'm crazy⟩ — *v aux* **1 tener que** : to have to ⟨tengo que salir : I have to leave⟩ ⟨tiene que estar aquí : it has to be here, it must be here⟩ **2** (*with past participle*) ⟨tenía pensado escribirte : I've been thinking of writing to you⟩ — **tenerse** *vr* **1** : to stand up **2** ~ **por** : to consider oneself ⟨me tengo por afortunado : I consider myself lucky⟩

tenería *nf* CURTIDURÍA : tannery

tenga, etc. → **tener**

tenia *nf* SOLITARIA : tapeworm

teniente *nmf* **1** : lieutenant **2 teniente coronel** : lieutenant colonel

tenis *nms & pl* **1** : tennis **2 tenis** *nmpl* : sneakers *pl*

tenista *nmf* : tennis player

tenor *nm* **1** : tenor **2** : tone, sense

tensar *vt* **1** : to tense, to make taut **2** : to draw (a bow) — **tensarse** *vr* : to become tense

tensión *nf, pl* **tensiones 1** : tension, tautness **2** : stress, strain **3 tensión arterial** : blood pressure

tenso, -sa *adj* : tense

tentación *nf, pl* **-ciones** : temptation

tentáculo *nm* : tentacle, feeler

tentador¹, -dora *adj* : tempting

tentador², -dora *n* : tempter, temptress *f*

tentar {55} *vt* **1** TOCAR : to feel, to touch **2** PROBAR : to test, to try **3** ATRAER : to tempt, to entice

tentativa *nf* : attempt, try

tentempié *nm fam* : snack, bite

tenue *adj* **1** : tenuous **2** : faint, weak, dim **3** : light, fine **4** : thin, slender

teñir {67} *vt* **1** : to dye **2** : to stain

teodolito *nm* : theodolite, transit (for surveying)

teología *nf* : theology

teológico, -ca *adj* : theological

teólogo, -ga *n* : theologian

teorema *nm* : theorem

teoría *nf* : theory

teórico¹, -ca *adj* : theoretical — **teóricamente** *adv*

teórico², -ca *n* : theorist

teorizar {21} *vi* : to theorize

tepe *nm* : sod, turf

teponaztle *nm Mex* : traditional drum

tequila *nm* : tequila

terapeuta *nmf* : therapist

terapéutica *nf* : therapeutics

terapéutico, -ca *adj* : therapeutic

terapia *nf* **1** : therapy **2 terapia intensiva** : intensive care

tercer → **tercero**

tercermundista *adj* : third-world

tercero¹, -ra *adj* (**tercer** *before masculine singular nouns*) **1** : third **2 el Tercer Mundo** : the Third World

tercero², -ra *n* : third (in a series)

terceto *nm* **1** : tercet, triplet (in literature) **2** : trio (in music)

terciar *vt* **1** : to place diagonally **2** : to divide into three parts — *vi* **1** : to mediate **2** ~ **en** : to take part in

terciario, -ria *adj* : tertiary

tercio¹, -cia → **tercero**

tercio² *nm* : third ⟨dos tercios : two thirds⟩

terciopelo *nm* : velvet

terco, -ca *adj* OBSTINADO : obstinate, stubborn

tergiversación *nf, pl* **-ciones** : distortion

tergiversar *vt* : to distort, to twist

termal *adj* : thermal, hot

termas *nfpl* : hot springs

térmico, -ca *adj* : thermal, heat ⟨energía térmica : thermal energy⟩

terminación · tiende

266

terminación *nf, pl* **-ciones** : termination, conclusion
terminal[1] *adj* : terminal — **terminalmente** *adv*
terminal[2] *nm* (*in some regions f*) : (electric or electronic) terminal
terminal[3] *nf* (*in some regions m*) : terminal, station
terminante *adj* : final, definitive, categorical — **terminantemente** *adv*
terminar *vt* **1** CONCLUIR : to end, to conclude **2** ACABAR : to complete, to finish off — *vi* **1** : to finish **2** : to stop, to end — **terminarse** *vr* **1** : to run out **2** : to come to an end
término *nm* **1** CONCLUSIÓN : end, conclusion **2** : term, expression **3** : period, term of office **4 término medio** : happy medium **5 términos** *nmpl* : terms, specifications ⟨los términos del acuerdo : the terms of the agreement⟩
terminología *nf* : terminology
termita *nf* : termite
termo *nm* : thermos
termodinámica *nf* : thermodynamics
termómetro *nm* : thermometer
termostato *nm* : thermostat
ternera *nf* : veal
ternero, -ra *n* : calf
terno *nm* **1** : set of three **2** : three-piece suit
ternura *nf* : tenderness
terquedad *nf* OBSTINACIÓN : obstinacy, stubbornness
terracota *nf* : terra-cotta
terraplén *nm, pl* **-plenes** : terrace, embankment
terráqueo, -quea *adj* **1** : earth **2 globo terráqueo** : the earth, globe (of the earth)
terrateniente *nmf* : landowner
terraza *nf* **1** : terrace, veranda **2** : balcony (in a theater) **3** : terrace (in agriculture)
terremoto *nm* : earthquake
terrenal *adj* : worldly, earthly
terreno *nm* **1** : terrain **2** SUELO : earth, ground **3** : plot, tract of land **4 perder terreno** : to lose ground **5 preparar el terreno** : to pave the way
terrestre *adj* : terrestrial
terrible *adj* : terrible, horrible — **terriblemente** *adv*
terrier *nmf* : terrier
territorial *adj* : territorial
territorio *nm* : territory
terrón *nm, pl* **terrones 1** : clod (of earth) **2 terrón de azúcar** : lump of sugar
terror *nm* : terror
terrorífico, -ca *adj* : horrific, terrifying
terrorismo *nm* : terrorism
terrorista *adj & nmf* : terrorist
terroso, -sa *adj* : earthy ⟨colores terrosos : earthy colors⟩
terruño *nm* : native land, homeland
terso, -sa *adj* **1** : smooth **2** : glossy, shiny **3** : polished, flowing (of a style)
tersura *nf* **1** : smoothness **2** : shine

tertulia *nf* : gathering, group ⟨tertulia literaria : literary circle⟩
tesauro *nm* : thesaurus
tesis *nfs & pl* : thesis
tesón *nm* : persistence, tenacity
tesonero, -ra *adj* : persistent, tenacious
tesorería *nf* : treasurer's office
tesorero, -ra *n* : treasurer
tesoro *nm* **1** : treasure **2** : thesaurus
test *nm* : test
testaferro *nm* : figurehead
testamentario[1], **-ria** *adj* : testamentary
testamentario[2], **-ria** *n* ALBACEA : executor, executrix *f*
testamento *nm* : testament, will
testar *vi* : to draw up a will
testarudo, -da *adj* : stubborn, pigheaded
testículo *nm* : testicle
testificar {72} *v* : to testify
testigo *nmf* : witness
testimonial *adj* **1** : testimonial **2** : token
testimoniar *vi* : to testify
testimonio *nm* : testimony, statement
teta *nf* : teat
tétano *or* **tétanos** *nm* : tetanus, lockjaw
tetera *nf* **1** : teapot **2** : teakettle
tetilla *nf* **1** : teat **2** : nipple
tetina *nf* : nipple (on a bottle)
tétrico, -ca *adj* : somber, gloomy
textil *adj & nm* : textile
texto *nm* : text
textual *adj* : literal, exact — **textualmente** *adv*
textura *nf* : texture
tez *nf, pl* **teces** : complexion, coloring
ti *pron* **1** : you ⟨es para ti : it's for you⟩ **2 ti mismo, ti misma** : yourself **3** : thee
tía → **tío**
tiamina *nf* : thiamine
tianguis *nm Mex* : open-air market
tibetano[1], **-na** *adj & n* : Tibetan
tibetano[2] *nm* : Tibetan (language)
tibia *nf* : tibia
tibieza *nf* **1** : tepidness **2** : halfheartedness
tibio, -bia *adj* **1** : lukewarm, tepid **2** : cool, unenthusiastic
tiburón *nm, pl* **-rones 1** : shark **2** : raider (in finance)
tic *nm* **1** : click, tick **2 tic nervioso** : tic
tico, -ca *adj & n fam* : Costa Rican
tictac *nm* **1** : ticking, tick-tock **2 hacer tictac** : to tick
tiembla, etc. → **temblar**
tiempo *nm* **1** : time ⟨justo a tiempo : just in time⟩ ⟨perder tiempo : to waste time⟩ ⟨tiempo libre : spare time⟩ **2** : period, age ⟨en los tiempos que corren : nowadays⟩ **3** : season, moment ⟨antes de tiempo : prematurely⟩ **4** : weather ⟨hace buen tiempo : the weather is fine, it's nice outside⟩ **5** : tempo (in music) **6** : half (in sports) **7** : tense (in grammar)
tienda *nf* **1** : store, shop **2** *or* **tienda de campaña** : tent
tiende, etc. → **tender**

tiene, etc. → **tener**
tienta¹, etc. → **tentar**
tienta² *nf* **andar a tientas** : to feel one's way, to grope around
tiernamente *adv* : tenderly
tierno, -na *adj* **1** : affectionate, tender **2** : tender, young
tierra *nf* **1** : land **2** SUELO : ground, earth **3** : country, homeland, soil **4** **tierra natal** : native land **5 tierras altas** : highlands **6 la Tierra** : the Earth
tieso, -sa *adj* **1** : stiff, rigid **2** : upright, erect
tiesto *nm* **1** : potsherd **2** MACETA : flowerpot
tiesura *nf* : stiffness, rigidity
tifoidea *nf* : typhoid
tifoideo, -dea *adj* : typhoid ⟨fiebre tifoidea : typhoid fever⟩
tifón *nm, pl* **tifones** : typhoon
tifus *nm* : typhus
tigre, -gresa *n* **1** : tiger, tigress *f* **2** : jaguar
tijera *nf* **1** *or* **tijeras** *nfpl* : scissors **2 de ~** : folding ⟨escalera de tijera : stepladder⟩
tijereta *nf* : earwig
tijeretada *nf or* **tijeretazo** *nm* : cut, snip
tildar *vt* **~ de** : to brand as, to call ⟨lo tildaron de traidor : they branded him as a traitor⟩
tilde *nf* **1** : accent mark **2** : tilde (accent over ñ)
tilo *nm* : linden (tree)
timador, -dora *n* : swindler
timar *vt* : to swindle, to cheat
timbal *nm* **1** : kettledrum **2 timbales** *nmpl* : timpani
timbre *nm* **1** : bell ⟨tocar el timbre : to ring the doorbell⟩ **2** : tone, timbre **3** SELLO : seal, stamp **4** *CA, Mex* : postage stamp
timidez *nf* : timidity, shyness
tímido, -da *adj* : timid, shy — **tímidamente** *adv*
timo *nm fam* : swindle, trick, hoax
timón *nm, pl* **timones** : rudder ⟨estar al timón : to beat the helm⟩
timonel *nm* : helmsman, coxswain
timorato, -ta *adj* **1** : timorous **2** : sanctimonious
tímpano *nm* **1** : eardrum **2 tímpanos** *nmpl* : timpani, kettledrums
tina *nf* **1** BAÑERA : tub, bathtub **2** : vat
tinaco *nm Mex* : water tank
tinieblas *nfpl* **1** OSCURIDAD : darkness **2** : ignorance
tino *nm* **1** : good judgment, sense **2** : tact, sensitivity, insight
tinta *nf* : ink
tinte *nm* **1** : dye, coloring **2** : overtone ⟨tintes raciales : racial overtones⟩
tintero *nm* **1** : inkwell **2 quedarse en el tintero** : to remain unsaid
tintinear *vt* : to jingle, to clink, to tinkle
tintineo *nm* : clink, jingle, tinkle
tinto, -ta *adj* **1** : dyed, stained ⟨tinto en sangre : bloodstained⟩ **2** : red (of wine)

tintorería *nf* : dry cleaner (service)
tintura *nf* **1** : dye, tint **2** : tincture ⟨tintura de yodo : tincture of iodine⟩
tiña *nf* : ringworm
tiñe, etc. → **teñir**
tío, tía *n* : uncle *m*, aunt *f*
tiovivo *nm* : merry-go-round
tipi *nm* : tepee
típico, -ca *adj* : typical — **típicamente** *adv*
tipificar {72} *vt* **1** : to classify, to categorize **2** : to typify
tiple *nm* : soprano
tipo¹ *nm* **1** CLASE : type, kind, sort **2** : figure, build, appearance **3** : rate ⟨tipo de interés : interest rate⟩ **4** : (printing) type, typeface **5** : style, model ⟨un vestido tipo 60's : a 60's-style dress⟩
tipo², -pa *n fam* : guy *m*, gal *f*, character
tipografía *nf* : typography, printing
tipográfico, -ca *adj* : typographic, typographical
tipógrafo, -fa *n* : printer, typographer
tique *or* **tiquet** *nm* **1** : ticket **2** : receipt
tira *nf* **1** : strip, strap **2 tira cómica** : comic, comic strip
tirabuzón *nf, pl* **-zones** : corkscrew
tirada *nf* **1** : throw **2** : distance, stretch **3** IMPRESIÓN : printing, issue
tiradero *nm Mex* **1** : dump **2** : mess, clutter
tirador¹ *nm* : handle, knob
tirador², -dora *n* : marksman *m*, markswoman *f*
tiragomas *nms & pl* : slingshot
tiranía *nf* : tyranny
tiránico, -ca *adj* : tyrannical
tiranizar {21} *vt* : to tyrannize
tirano¹, -na *adj* : tyrannical, despotic
tirano², -na *n* : tyrant
tirante¹ *adj* **1** : tense, strained **2** : taut
tirante² *nm* **1** : shoulder strap **2 tirantes** *nmpl* : suspenders
tirantez *nf* **1** : tautness **2** : tension, friction, strain
tirar *vt* **1** : to throw, to hurl, to toss **2** BOTAR : to throw away, to throw out, to waste **3** DERRIBAR : to knock down **4** : to shoot, to fire, to launch **5** : to take (a photo) **6** : to print, to run off — *vi* **1** : to pull, to draw **2** : to shoot **3** : to attract **4** : to get by, to manage ⟨va tirando : he's getting along, he's managing⟩ **5 ~ a** : to tend towards, to be rather ⟨tira a picante : it's a bit spicy⟩ — **tirarse** *vr* **1** : to throw oneself **2** *fam* : to spend (time)
tiritar *vi* : to shiver, to tremble
tiro *nm* **1** BALAZO, DISPARO : shot, gunshot **2** : shot, kick (in sports) **3** : flue **4** : team (of horses, etc.) **5 a ~** : within range **6 al tiro** : right away **7 tiro de gracia** : coup de grace, death blow
tiroideo, -dea *adj* : thyroid
tiroides *nmf* : thyroid, thyroid gland — **tiroides** *adj*

tirolés, -lesa *adj* : Tyrolean
tirón *nm, pl* **tirones 1** : pull, tug, yank **2 de un tirón** : all at once, in one go
tiroteo *nm* **1** : shooting **2** : gunfight, shoot-out
tirria *nf* **tener tirria a** *fam* : to have a grudge against
titánico, -ca *adj* : titanic, huge
titanio *nm* : titanium
títere *nm* : puppet
tití *nm* : marmoset
titilar *vi* : to twinkle, to flicker
titileo *nm* : twinkle, flickering
titiritero, -ra *n* **1** : puppeteer **2** : acrobat
titubear *vi* **1** : to hesitate **2** : to stutter, to stammer — **titubeante** *adj*
titubeo *nm* **1** : hesitation **2** : stammering
titulado, -da *adj* **1** : titled, entitled **2** : qualified
titular[1] *vt* : to title, to entitle — **titularse** *vr* **1** : to be called, to be entitled **2** : to receive a degree
titular[2] *adj* : titular, official
titular[3] *nm* : headline
titular[4] *nmf* **1** : owner, holder **2** : officeholder, incumbent
titularidad *nf* **1** : ownership, title **2** : position, office (with a title) **3** : starting position (in sports)
título *nm* **1** : title **2** : degree, qualification **3** : security, bond **4 a título de** : by way of, in the capacity of
tiza *nf* : chalk
tiznar *vt* : to blacken (with soot, etc.)
tizne *nm* HOLLÍN : soot
tiznón *nm, pl* **tiznones** : stain, smudge
tlapalería *nf Mex* : hardware store
TNT *nm* (*trinitrotolueno*) : TNT
toalla *nf* : towel
toallita *nf* : washcloth
tobillo *nm* : ankle
tobogán *nm, pl* **-ganes 1** : toboggan, sled **2** : slide, chute
tocadiscos *nms & pl* : record player, phonograph
tocado[1]**, -da** *adj* **1** : bad, bruised (of fruit) **2** *fam* : touched, not all there
tocado[2] *nm* : headdress
tocador[1] *nm* **1** : dressing table, vanity table **2 artículos de tocador** : toiletries
tocador[2]**, -dora** *n* : player (of music)
tocante *adj* ~ **a** : with regard to, regarding
tocar {72} *vt* **1** : to touch, to feel, to handle **2** : to touch on, to refer to **3** : to concern, to affect **4** : to play (a musical instrument) — *vi* **1** : to knock, to ring ⟨tocar a la puerta : to rap on the door⟩ **2** ~ **en** : to touch on, to border on ⟨eso toca en lo ridículo : that's almost ludicrous⟩ **3 tocarle a** : to fall to, to be up to, to be one's turn ⟨¿a quién le toca manejar? : whose turn is it to drive?⟩
tocayo, -ya *n* : namesake
tocineta *nf Col, Ven* : bacon
tocino *nm* **1** : bacon **2** : salt pork

tocología *nf* OBSTETRICIA : obstetrics
tocólogo, -ga *n* OBSTETRA : obstetrician
tocón *nm, pl* **tocones** CEPA : stump (of a tree)
todavía *adv* **1** AÚN : still, yet ⟨todavía puedes verlo : you can still see it⟩ **2** : even ⟨todavía más rápido : even faster⟩ **3 todavía no** : not yet
todo[1]**, -da** *adj* **1** : all, whole, entire ⟨con toda sinceridad : with all sincerity⟩ ⟨toda la comunidad : the whole community⟩ **2** : every, each ⟨a todo nivel : at every level⟩ **3** : maximum ⟨a toda velocidad : at top speed⟩ **4 todo el mundo** : everyone, everybody
todo[2] *nm* : whole
todo[3]**, -da** *pron* **1** : everything, all, every bit ⟨lo sabe todo : he knows it all⟩ ⟨es todo un soldado : he's every inch a soldier⟩ **2 todos, -das** *pl* : everybody, everyone, all
todopoderoso, -sa *adj* OMNIPOTENTE : almighty, all-powerful
toga *nf* **1** : toga **2** : gown, robe (for magistrates, etc.)
toldo *nm* : awning, canopy
tolerable *adj* : tolerable — **tolerablemente** *adv*
tolerancia *nf* : tolerance, toleration
tolerante *adj* : tolerant — **tolerantemente** *adv*
tolerar *vt* : to tolerate
tolete *nm* : oarlock
tolva *nf* : hopper (container)
toma *nf* **1** : taking, seizure, capture **2** DOSIS : dose **3** : take, shot **4 toma de corriente** : wall socket, outlet **5 toma y daca** : give-and-take
tomar *vt* **1** : to take ⟨tomé el libro : I took the book⟩ ⟨tomar un taxi : to take a taxi⟩ ⟨tomar una foto : to take a photo⟩ ⟨toma dos años : it takes two years⟩ ⟨tomaron medidas drásticas : they took drastic measures⟩ **2** BEBER : to drink **3** CAPTURAR : to capture, to seize **4 tomar el sol** : to sunbathe **5 tomar tierra** : to land — *vi* : to drink (alcohol) — **tomarse** *vr* **1** : to take ⟨tomarse la molestia de : to take the trouble to⟩ **2** : to drink, to eat, to have
tomate *nm* : tomato
tomillo *nm* : thyme
tomo *nm* : volume, tome
ton *nm* **sin ton ni son** : without rhyme or reason
tonada *nf* **1** : tune, song **2** : accent
tonalidad *nf* : tonality
tonel *nm* BARRICA : barrel, cask
tonelada *nf* : ton
tonelaje *nm* : tonnage
tónica *nf* **1** : tonic (water) **2** : tonic (in music) **3** : trend, tone ⟨dar la tónica : to set the tone⟩
tónico, -ca *adj* : tonic
tónico[2] *nm* : tonic ⟨tónico capilar : hair tonic⟩
tono *nm* **1** : tone ⟨tono muscular : muscle tone⟩ **2** : shade (of colors) **3** : key (in music)

tontamente *adv* : foolishly, stupidly
tontear *vi* **1** : to fool around, to play the fool **2** : to flirt
tontería *nf* **1** : foolishness **2** : stupid remark or action **3 decir tonterías** : to talk nonsense
tonto[1], **-ta** *adj* **1** : dumb, stupid **2** : silly **3 a tontas y a locas** : without thinking, haphazardly
tonto[2], **-ta** *n* : fool, idiot
topacio *nm* : topaz
toparse *vr* ~ **con** : to bump into, to run into, to come across ⟨me topé con algunas dificultades : I ran into some problems⟩
tope *nm* **1** : limit, end ⟨hasta el tope : to the limit, to the brim⟩ **2** : stop, check, buffer ⟨tope de puerta : doorstop⟩ **3** : bump, collision **4** *Mex* : speed bump
tópico[1], **-ca** *adj* **1** : topical, external **2** : trite, commonplace
tópico[2] *nm* **1** : topic, subject **2** : cliché, trite expression
topo *nm* **1** : mole (animal) **2** *fam* : clumsy person, blunderer
topografía *nf* : topography
topográfico, -ca *adj* : topographic, topographical
topógrafo, -fa *n* : topographer
toque[1], etc. → **tocar**
toque[2] *nm* **1** : touch ⟨el último toque : the finishing touch⟩ ⟨un toque de color : a touch of color⟩ **2** : ringing, peal, chime **3** *Mex* : shock, jolt **4 toque de queda** : curfew **5 toque de diana** : reveille
toquetear *vt* : to touch, to handle, to finger
tórax *nm* : thorax
torbellino *nm* : whirlwind
torcedura *nf* **1** : twisting, buckling **2** : sprain
torcer {14} *vt* **1** : to bend, to twist **2** : to sprain **3** : to turn (a corner) **4** : to wring, to wring out **5** : to distort — *vi* : to turn — **torcerse** *vr*
torcido, -da *adj* **1** : twisted, crooked **2** : devious
tordo *nm* ZORZAL : thrush
torear *vt* **1** : to fight (bulls) **2** : to dodge, to sidestep
toreo *nm* : bullfighting
torero, -ra *n* MATADOR : bullfighter, matador
tormenta *nf* **1** : storm ⟨tormenta de nieve : snowstorm⟩ **2** : turmoil, frenzy
tormento *nm* **1** : torment, anguish **2** : torture
tormentoso, -sa *adj* : stormy, turbulent
tornado *nm* : tornado
tornamesa *nmf* : turntable
tornar *vt* **1** : to return, to give back **2** : to make, to render — *vi* : to go back — **tornarse** *vr* : to become, to turn into
tornasol *nm* **1** : reflected light **2** : sunflower **3** : litmus
tornear *vt* : to turn (in carpentry)
torneo *nm* : tournament

tornillo *nm* **1** : screw **2 tornillo de banco** : vise
torniquete *nm* **1** : tourniquet **2** : turnstile
torno *nm* **1** : lathe **2** : winch **3 torno de banco** : vise **4 en torno a** : around, about ⟨en torno a este asunto : about this issue⟩ ⟨en torno suyo : around him⟩
toro *nm* : bull
toronja *nf* : grapefruit
toronjil *nm* : balm, lemon balm
torpe *adj* **1** DESMAÑADO : clumsy, awkward **2** : stupid, dull — **torpemente** *adv*
torpedear *vt* : to torpedo
torpedo *nm* : torpedo
torpeza *nf* **1** : clumsiness, awkwardness **2** : stupidity **3** : blunder
torre *nf* **1** : tower ⟨torre de perforación : oil rig⟩ **2** : turret **3** : rook, castle (in chess)
torrencial *adj* : torrential — **torrencialmente** *adv*
torrente *nm* **1** : torrent **2 torrente sanguíneo** : bloodstream
torreón *nm, pl* **-rreones** : tower (of a castle)
torreta *nf* : turret (of a tank, ship, etc.)
tórrido, -da *adj* : torrid
torsión *nf, pl* **torsiones** : torsion — **torsional** *adj*
torso *nm* : torso, trunk
torta *nf* **1** : torte, cake **2** *Mex* : sandwich
tortazo *nm fam* : blow, wallop
tortilla *nf* **1** : tortilla **2** *or* **tortilla de huevo** : omelet
tórtola *nf* : turtledove
tortuga *nf* **1** : turtle, tortoise **2 tortuga de agua dulce** : terrapin **3 tortuga boba** : loggerhead
tortuoso, -sa *adj* : tortuous, winding
tortura *nf* : torture
torturador, -dora *n* : torturer
torturar *vt* : to torture, to torment
torvo, -va *adj* : grim, stern, baleful
torzamos, etc. → **torcer**
tos *nf* **1** : cough **2 tos ferina** : whooping cough
tosco, -ca *adj* : rough, coarse
toser *vi* : to cough
tosquedad *nf* : crudeness, coarseness, roughness
tostada *nf* **1** : piece of toast **2** : tostada
tostador *nm* **1** : toaster **2** : roaster (for coffee)
tostar {19} *vt* **1** : to toast **2** : to roast (coffee) **3** : to tan — **tostarse** *vr* : to get a tan
tostón *nm, pl* **tostones** *Car* : fried plantain chip
total[1] *adv* : in the end, so ⟨total, que no fui : in short, I didn't go⟩
total[2] *adj & nm* : total — **totalmente** *adv*
totalidad *nf* : totality, whole
totalitario, -ria *adj & n* : totalitarian
totalitarismo *nm* : totalitarianism

totalizar {21} *vt* : total, to add up to
tótem *nm*, *pl* **tótems** : totem
totopo *nm CA, Mex* : tortilla chip
totuma *nf* : calabash
tour ['tur] *nm*, *pl* **tours** : tour, excursion
toxicidad *nf* : toxicity
tóxico[1], **-ca** *adj* : toxic, poisonous
tóxico[2] *nm* : poison
toxicomanía *nf* : drug addiction
toxicómano, -na *n* : drug addict
toxina *nf* : toxin
tozudez *nf* : stubbornness, obstinacy
tozudo, -da *adj* : stubborn, obstinate —
　tozudamente *adv*
traba *nf* **1** : tie, bond **2** : obstacle, hindrance
trabajador[1], **-dora** *adj* : hardworking
trabajador[2], **-dora** *n* : worker
trabajar *vi* **1** : to work ⟨trabaja mucho : he works hard⟩ ⟨trabajo de secretaria : I work as a secretary⟩ **2** : to strive ⟨trabajan por mejores oportunidades : they're striving for better opportunities⟩ **3** : to act, to perform ⟨trabajar en una película : to be in a movie⟩ — *vt* **1** : to work (metal) **2** : to knead **3** : to till **4** : to work on ⟨tienes que trabajar el español : you need to work on your Spanish⟩
trabajo *nm* **1** : work, job **2** LABOR : labor, work ⟨tengo mucho trabajo : I have a lot of work to do⟩ **3** TAREA : task **4** ESFUERZA : effort **5 costar trabajo** : to be difficult **6 tomarse el trabajo** : to take the trouble **7 trabajo en equipo** : teamwork **8 trabajos** *nmpl* : hardships, difficulties
trabajoso, -sa *adj* LABORIOSO : laborious — **trabajosamente** *adv*
trabalenguas *nms & pl* : tongue twister
trabar *vt* **1** : to join, to connect **2** : to impede, to hold back **3** : to strike up (a conversation), to form (a friendship) **4** : to thicken (sauces) — **trabarse** *vr* **1** : to jam **2** : to become entangled **3** : to be tongue-tied, to stammer
trabucar {72} *vt* : to confuse, to mix up
trabuco *nm* : blunderbuss
tracalero, -ra *adj Mex* : dishonest, tricky
tracción *nf* : traction
trace, etc. → **trazar**
tracto *nm* : tract
tractor *nm* : tractor
tradición *nf*, *pl* **-ciones** : tradition
tradicional *adj* : traditional — **tradicionalmente** *adv*
traducción *nf*, *pl* **-ciones** : translation
traducible *adj* : translatable
traducir {61} *vt* **1** : to translate **2** : to convey, to express — **traducirse** *vr* ~ **en** : to result in
traductor, -tora *n* : translator
traer {81} *vt* **1** : to bring ⟨trae una ensalada : bring a salad⟩ **2** CAUSAR : to cause, to bring about ⟨el problema puede traer graves consecuencias : the problem could have serious consequences⟩ **3** : to carry, to have ⟨todos los periódicos traían las mismas noti-

cias : all of the newspapers carried the same news⟩ **4** LLEVAR : to wear — **traerse** *vr* **1** : to bring along **2 traérselas** : to be difficult
traficante *nmf* : dealer, trafficker
traficar {72} *vi* **1** : to trade, to deal **2** ~ **con** : to traffic in
tráfico *nm* **1** : trade **2** : traffic
tragaluz *nf*, *pl* **-luces** : skylight, fanlight
tragar {52} *v* : to swallow — **tragarse** *vr*
tragedia *nf* : tragedy
trágico, -ca *adj* : tragic — **trágicamente** *adv*
trago *nm* **1** : swallow, swig **2** : drink, liquor **3 trago amargo** : hard time
trague, etc. → **tragar**
traición *nf*, *pl* **traiciones** **1** : treason **2** : betrayal, treachery
traicionar *vt* : to betray
traicionero, -ra → **traidor**
traidor[1], **-dora** *adj* : traitorous, treasonous
traidor[2], **-dora** *n* : traitor
traiga, etc. → **traer**
tráiler *or* **trailer** *nm* : trailer
traílla *nf* **1** : leash **2** : harrow
traje *nm* **1** : suit **2** : dress **3** : costume **4 traje de baño** : bathing suit
trajín *nm*, *pl* **trajines** **1** : transport **2** *fam* : hustle and bustle
trajinar *vt* : to transport, to carry — *vi* : to rush around
trajo, etc. → **traer**
trama *nf* **1** : plot **2** : weave, weft (fabric)
tramar *vt* **1** : to plot, to plan **2** : to weave
tramitar *vt* : to transact, to negotiate, to handle
trámite *nm* : procedure, step
tramo *nm* **1** : stretch, section **2** : flight (of stairs)
trampa *nf* **1** : trap **2 hacer trampas** : to cheat
trampear *vt* : to cheat
trampero, -ra *n* : trapper
trampilla *nf* : trapdoor
trampolín *nm*, *pl* **-lines** **1** : diving board **2** : trampoline **3** : springboard ⟨un trampolín al éxito : a springboard to success⟩
tramposo[1], **-sa** *adj* : crooked, cheating
tramposo[2], **-sa** *n* : cheat, swindler
tranca *nf* **1** : stick, club **2** : bar, crossbar
trancar {72} *vt* : to bar (a door or window)
trancazo *nm* GOLPE : blow, hit
trance *nm* **1** : critical juncture, tough time **2** : trance **3 en trance de** : in the process of ⟨en trance de extinción : on the verge of extinction⟩
tranco *nm* **1** : stride **2** UMBRAL : threshold
tranque, etc. → **trancar**
tranquilidad *nf* : tranquility, peace
tranquilizador, -dora *adj* **1** : soothing **2** : reassuring
tranquilizante[1] *adj* **1** : reassuring **2** : tranquilizing

tranquilizante² *nm* : tranquilizer
tranquilizar {21} *vt* CALMAR : to calm down, to soothe ⟨tranquilizar la conciencia : to ease the conscience⟩ — **tranquilizarse** *vr*
tranquilo, -la *adj* CALMO : calm, tranquil ⟨una vida tranquila : a quiet life⟩ — **tranquilamente** *adv*
transacción *nf, pl* **-ciones** : transaction
transar *vi* TRANSIGIR : to give way, to compromise — *vt* : to buy and sell
transatlántico¹, -ca *adj* : transatlantic
transatlántico² *nm* : ocean liner
transbordador *nm* **1** : ferry **2 transbordador espacial** : space shuttle
transbordar *v* : to transfer
transbordo *nm* : transfer
transcendencia → **trascendencia**
transcender → **trascender**
transcribir {33} *vt* : to transcribe
transcrito *pp* → **transcribir**
transcripción *nf, pl* **-ciones** : transcription
transcurrir *vi* : to elapse, to pass
transcurso *nm* : course, progression ⟨en el transcurso de cien años : over the course of a hundred years⟩
transeúnte *nmf* **1** : passerby **2** : transient
transferencia *nf* : transfer, transference
transferir {76} *vt* TRASLADAR : to transfer — **transferible** *adj*
transfigurar *vt* : to transfigure, to transform — **transfiguración** *nf*
transformación *nf, pl* **-ciones** : transformation, conversion
transformador *nm* : transformer
transformar *vt* **1** CONVERTIR : to convert **2** : to transform, to change, to alter — **transformarse** *vr*
transfusión *nf, pl* **-siones** : transfusion
transgredir {1} *vt* : to transgress — **transgresión** *nf*
transgresor, -sora *n* : transgressor
transición *nf, pl* **-ciones** : transition ⟨período de transición : transition period⟩
transido, -da *adj* : overcome, beset ⟨transido de dolor : racked with pain⟩
transigir {35} *vi* **1** : to give in, to compromise **2 ~ con** : to tolerate, to put up with
transistor *nm* : transistor
transitable *adj* : passable
transitar *vi* : to go, to pass, to travel ⟨transitar por la ciudad : to travel through the city⟩
transitivo, -va *adj* : transitive
tránsito *nm* **1** TRÁFICO : traffic ⟨hora de máximo tránsito : rush hour⟩ **2** : transit, passage, movement **3** : death, passing
transitorio, -ria *adj* **1** : transitory **2** : provisional, temporary — **transitoriamente** *adv*
translúcido, -da *adj* : translucent
translucir → **traslucir**
transmisible *adj* : transmissible

transmisión *nf, pl* **-siones** **1** : transmission, broadcast **2** : transfer **3** : transmission (of an automobile)
transmisor *nm* : transmitter
transmitir *vt* **1** : to transmit, to broadcast **2** : to pass on, to transfer — *vi* : to transmit, to broadcast
transparencia *nf* : transparency
transparentar *vt* : to reveal, to betray — **transparentarse** *vr* **1** : to be transparent **2** : to show through
transparente¹ *adj* : transparent — **transparentemente** *adv*
transparente² *nm* : shade, blind
transpiración *nf, pl* **-ciones** SUDOR : perspiration, sweat
transpirado, -da *adj* : sweaty
transpirar *vi* **1** SUDAR : to perspire, to sweat **2** : to transpire
transplantar, transplante → **trasplantar, trasplante**
transponer {60} *vt* **1** : to transpose, to move about **2** TRASPLANTAR : to transplant — **transponerse** *vr* **1** OCULTARSE : to hide **2** PONERSE : to set, to go down (of the sun or moon) **3** DORMITAR : to doze off
transportación *nf, pl* **-ciones** : transportation
transportador *nm* **1** : protractor **2** : conveyor
transportar *vt* **1** : to transport, to carry **2** : to transmit **3** : to transpose (music) — **transportarse** *vr* : to get carried away
transporte *nm* : transport, transportation
transportista *nmf* : hauler, carrier, trucker
transpuso, etc. → **transponer**
transversal *adj* : transverse, cross ⟨corte transversal : cross section⟩
transversalmente *adv* : obliquely
transverso, -sa *adj* : transverse
tranvía *nm* : streetcar, trolley
trapeador *nm* : mop
trapear *vt* : to mop
trapecio *nm* **1** : trapezoid **2** : trapeze
trapezoide *nm* : trapezoid
trapo *nm* **1** : cloth, rag ⟨trapo de polvo : dust cloth⟩ **2 soltar el trapo** : to burst into tears **3 trapos** *nmpl fam* : clothes
tráquea *nf* : trachea, windpipe
traquetear *vi* : to clatter, to jolt
traqueteo *nm* **1** : jolting **2** : clattering, clatter
tras *prep* **1** : after ⟨día tras día : day after day⟩ ⟨uno tras otro : one after another⟩ **2** : behind ⟨tras la puerta : behind the door⟩
trasbordar, trasbordo → **transbordar, transbordo**
trascendencia *nf* **1** : importance, significance **2** : transcendence
trascendental *adj* **1** : transcendental **2** : important, momentous
trascendente *adj* **1** : important, significant **2** : transcendent

trascender {56} *vi* **1** : to leak out, to become known **2** : to spread, to have a wide effect **3** ~ **a** : to smell of ⟨la casa trascendía a flores : the house smelled of flowers⟩ **4** ~ **de** : to transcend, to go beyond — *vt* : to transcend

trasero[1], **-ra** *adj* POSTERIOR : rear, back

trasero[2] *nm* : buttocks

trasfondo *nm* **1** : background, backdrop **2** : undertone, undercurrent

trasformación → **transformación**

trasgo *nm* : goblin, imp

trasgredir → **transgredir**

trasladar *vt* **1** TRANSFERIR : to transfer, to move **2** POSPONER : to postpone **3** TRADUCIR : to translate **4** COPIAR : to copy, to transcribe — **trasladarse** *vr* MUDARSE : to move, to relocate

traslado *nm* : transfer, move **2** : copy

traslapar *vt* : to overlap — **traslaparse** *vr*

traslapo *nm* : overlap

traslúcido, -da → **translúcido**

traslucir {45} *vi* : to reveal, to show — **traslucirse** *vr* : to show through

trasmano *nm* **a** ~ : out of the way, out of reach

trasmisión, trasmitir → **transmisión, transmitir**

trasnochar *vi* : to stay up all night

trasparencia *nf* **trasparente** → **transparencia, transparente**

traspasar *vt* **1** PERFORAR : to pierce, to go through **2** : to go beyond ⟨traspasar los límites : to overstep the limits⟩ **3** ATRAVESAR : to cross, to go across **4** : to sell, to transfer

traspaso *nm* : transfer, sale

traspié *nm* **1** : stumble **2** : blunder

traspiración → **transpiración**

trasplantar *vt* : to transplant

trasplante *nm* : transplant

trasponer → **transponer**

trasportar → **transportar**

trasquilar *vt* ESQUILAR : to shear

traste *nm* **1** : fret (on a guitar) **2** *CA, Mex, PRi* : kitchen utensil ⟨lavar los trastes : to do the dishes⟩ **3 dar al traste con** : to ruin, to destroy **4 irse al traste** : to fall through

trastornar *vt* : to disturb, to upset, to disrupt — **trastornarse** *vr*

trastorno *nm* **1** : disorder ⟨trastorno mental : mental disorder⟩ **2** : disturbance, upset

trastos *nmpl* **1** : implements, utensils **2** *fam* : pieces of junk, stuff

trasunto *nm* : image, likeness

tratable *adj* **1** : friendly, sociable **2** : treatable

tratado *nm* **1** : treatise **2** : treaty

tratamiento *nm* : treatment

tratante *nmf* : dealer, trader

tratar *vi* **1** ~ **con** : to deal with, to have contact with ⟨no trato mucho con los clientes : I don't have much contact with customers⟩ **2** ~ **de** : to try to ⟨estoy tratando de comer : I am trying to

eat⟩ **3** ~ **de** *or* ~ **sobre** : to be about, to concern ⟨el libro trata de las plantas : the book is about plants⟩ **4** ~ **en** : to deal in ⟨trata en herramientas : he deals in tools⟩ — *vt* **1** : to treat ⟨tratan bien a sus empleados : they treat their employees well⟩ **2** : to handle ⟨trató el tema con delicadeza : he handled the subject tactfully⟩ — **tratarse** *vr* ~ **de** : to be about, to concern

trato *nm* **1** : deal, agreement **2** : relationship, dealings *pl* **3** : treatment ⟨malos tratos : ill-treatment⟩

trauma *nm* : trauma

traumático, -ca *adj* : traumatic — **traumáticamente** *adv*

traumatismo *nm* : injury ⟨traumatismo cervical : whiplash⟩

través *nm* **1 a través de** : across, through **2 al través** : crosswise, across **3 de través** : sideways

travesaño *nm* **1** : crossbar **2** : crossbeam, crosspiece, transom (of a window)

travesía *nf* : voyage, crossing (of the sea)

travesura *nf* **1** : prank, mischievous act **2 travesuras** *nfpl* : mischief

travieso, -sa *adj* : mischievous, naughty — **traviesamente** *adv*

trayecto *nm* **1** : journey **2** : route **3** : trajectory, path

trayectoria *nf* : course, path, trajectory

trayendo → **traer**

traza *nf* **1** DISEÑO : design, plan **2** : appearance

trazado *nm* **1** BOSQUEJO : outline, sketch **2** PLAN : plan, layout

trazar {21} *vt* **1** : to trace **2** : to draw up, to devise **3** : to outline, to sketch

trazo *nm* **1** : stroke, line **2** : sketch, outline

trébol *nm* **1** : clover, shamrock **2** : club (playing card)

trece *adj* & *nm* : thirteen

treceavo[1], **-va** *adj* : thirteenth

treceavo[2] *nm* : thirteenth (fraction)

trecho *nm* **1** : stretch, period ⟨de trecho en trecho : at intervals⟩ **2** : distance, space

tregua *nf* **1** : truce **2** : lull, respite **3 sin** ~ : relentless, unrelenting

treinta *adj* & *nm* : thirty

treintavo[1], **-va** *adj* : thirtieth

treintavo[2] *nm* : thirtieth (fraction)

tremendo, -da *adj* **1** : tremendous, enormous **2** : terrible, dreadful **3** *fam* : great, super

trementina *nf* AGUARRÁS : turpentine

trémulo, -la *adj* **1** : trembling, shaky **2** : flickering

tren *nm* **1** : train **2** : set, assembly ⟨tren de aterrizaje : landing gear⟩ **3** : speed, pace ⟨a todo tren : at top speed⟩

trence, etc. → **trenzar**

trenza *nf* : braid, pigtail

trenzar {21} *vt* : to braid — **trenzarse** *vr* : to get involved

trepador, -dora *adj* : climbing ⟨rosal trepador : rambling rose⟩

trepadora *nf* **1** : climbing plant, climber **2** : nuthatch

trepar *vi* **1** : to climb ⟨trepar a un árbol : to climb up a tree⟩ **2** : to creep, to spread (of a plant)

trepidación *nf, pl* **-ciones** : vibration

trepidante *adj* **1** : vibrating **2** : fast, frantic

trepidar *vi* **1** : to shake, to vibrate **2** : to hesitate, to waver

tres *adj & nm* : three

trescientos[1], **-tas** *adj* : three hundred

trescientos[2] *nms & pl* : three hundred

treta *nf* : trick, ruse

tríada *nf* : triad

triángulo *nm* : triangle — **triangular** *adj*

tribal *adj* : tribal

tribu *nf* : tribe

tribulación *nf, pl* **-ciones** : tribulation

tribuna *nf* **1** : dais, platform **2** : stands *pl*, bleachers *pl*, grandstand

tribunal *nm* : court, tribunal

tributar *vt* : to pay, to render — *vi* : to pay taxes

tributario[1], **-ria** *adj* : tax ⟨evasión tributaria : tax evasion⟩

tributario[2] *nm* : tributary

tributo *nm* **1** : tax **2** : tribute

triciclo *nm* : tricycle

tricolor *adj* : tricolor, tricolored

tridente *nm* : trident

tridimensional *adj* : three-dimensional, 3-D

trienal *adj* : triennial

trifulca *nf fam* : row, ruckus

trigésimo[1], **-ma** *adj* : thirtieth, thirty-

trigésimo[2], **-ma** *n* : thirtieth, thirty- (in a series)

trigo *nm* **1** : wheat **2 trigo rubión** : buckwheat

trigonometría *nf* : trigonometry

trigueño, -ña *adj* **1** : light brown (of hair) **2** MORENO : dark, olive-skinned

trillado, -da *adj* : trite, hackneyed

trilladora *nf* : thresher, threshing machine

trillar *vt* : to thresh

trillizo, -za *n* : triplet

trilogía *nf* : trilogy

trimestral *adj* : quarterly — **trimestralmente** *adv*

trinar *vi* **1** : to thrill **2** : to warble

trinchar *vt* : to carve, to cut up

trinchera *nf* **1** : trench, ditch **2** : trench coat

trineo *nm* : sled, sleigh

trinidad *nf* **la Trinidad** : the Trinity

trino *nm* : trill, warble

trinquete *nm* : ratchet

trío *nm* : trio

tripa *nf* **1** INTESTINO : gut, intestine **2 tripas** *nfpl fam* : belly, tummy, insides *pl* ⟨dolerle a uno las tripas : to have a stomach ache⟩

tripartito, -ta *adj* : tripartite

triple *adj & nm* : triple

triplicado, -da *adj* : triplicate

triplicar {72} *vt* : to triple, to treble

trípode *nm* : tripod

tripulación *nf, pl* **-ciones** : crew

tripulante *nmf* : crew member

tripular *vt* : to man

tris *nm* **estar en un tris de** : to be within an inch of, to be very close to

triste *adj* **1** : sad, gloomy ⟨ponerse triste : to become sad⟩ **2** : desolate, dismal ⟨una perspectiva triste : a dismal outlook⟩ **3** : sorry, sorry-looking ⟨la triste verdad : the sorry truth⟩

tristeza *nf* DOLOR : sadness, grief

tristón, -tona *adj, mpl* **-tones** : melancholy, downhearted

tritón *nm, pl* **tritones** : newt

triturar *vt* : to crush, to grind

triunfal *adj* : triumphal, triumphant — **triunfalmente** *adv*

triunfante *adj* : triumphant, victorious

triunfar *vi* : to triumph, to win

triunfo *nm* **1** : triumph, victory **2** ÉXITO : success **3** : trump (in card games)

triunvirato *nm* : triumvirate

trivial *adj* **1** : trivial **2** : trite, commonplace

trivialidad *nf* : triviality

triza *nf* **1** : shred, bit **2 hacer trizas** : to tear into shreds, to smash to pieces

trocar {82} *vt* **1** CAMBIAR : to exchange, to trade **2** CAMBIAR : to change, to alter, to transform **3** CONFUNDIR : to confuse, to mix up

trocha *nf* : path, trail

troce, etc. → **trozar**

trofeo *nm* : trophy

tromba *nf* **1** : whirlwind **2 tromba de agua** : downpour, cloudburst

trombón *nm, pl* **trombones 1** : trombone **2** : trombonist — **trombonista** *nmf*

trombosis *nf* : thrombosis

trompa *nf* **1** : trunk (of an elephant), proboscis (of an insect) **2** : horn ⟨trompa de caza : hunting horn⟩ **3** : tube, duct (in the body)

trompada *nf fam* **1** : punch, blow **2** : bump, collision (of persons)

trompeta *nf* : trumpet

trompetista *nmf* : trumpet player, trumpeter

trompo *nm* : spinning top

tronada *nf* : thunderstorm

tronar {19} *vi* **1** : to thunder, to roar **2** : to be furious, to rage **3** CA, Mex fam : to shoot — *v impers* : to thunder ⟨está tronando : it's thundering⟩

tronchar *vt* **1** : to snap, to break off **2** : to cut off (relations)

tronco *nm* **1** : trunk (of a tree) **2** : log **3** : torso

trono *nm* **1** : throne **2** *fam* : toilet

tropa *nf* **1** : troop, soldiers *pl* **2** : crowd, mob **3** : herd (of livestock)

tropel *nm* : mob, swarm

tropezar {29} *vi* **1** : to trip, to stumble **2** : to slip up, to blunder **3** ~ **con** : to run into, to bump into **4** ~ **con** : to come up against (a problem)

tropezón *nm, pl* **-zones 1** : stumble **2** : mistake, slip

tropical *adj* : tropical

trópico *nm* **1** : tropic ⟨trópico de Cáncer : tropic of Cancer⟩ **2 el trópico** : the tropics

tropiezo *nm* **1** CONTRATIEMPO : snag, setback **2** EQUIVOCACIÓN : mistake, slip

troqué, etc. → trocar

troquel *nm* : die (for stamping)

trotamundos *nmf* : globe-trotter

trotar *vi* **1** : to trot **2** : to jog **3** *fam* : to rush about

trote *nm* **1** : trot **2** *fam* : rush, bustle **3 de** ∼ : durable, for everyday use

trovador, -dora *n* : troubadour

trozar {21} *vt* : to cut up, to dice

trozo *nm* **1** PEDAZO : piece, bit, chunk **2** : passage, extract

trucha *nf* : trout

truco *nm* **1** : trick **2** : knack

truculento, -ta *adj* : horrifying, gruesome

trueca, trueque etc. → trocar

truena, etc. → tronar

trueno *nm* : thunder

trueque *nm* : barter, exchange

trufa *nf* : truffle

truncar {72} *vt* **1** : to truncate, to cut short **2** : to thwart, to frustrate ⟨truncó sus esperanzas : she shattered their hopes⟩

trunco, -ca *adj* **1** : truncated **2** : unfinished, incomplete

trunque, etc. → truncar

tu *adj* **1** : your ⟨tu vestido : your dress⟩ ⟨toma tus vitaminas : take your vitamins⟩ **2** : thy

tú *pron* **1** : you ⟨tú eres mi hijo : you are my son⟩ **2** : thou

tuba *nf* : tuba

tubérculo *nm* : tuber

tuberculosis *nf* : tuberculosis

tuberculoso, -sa *adj* : tuberculous, tubercular

tubería *nf* : pipes *pl*, tubing

tuberoso, -sa *adj* : tuberous

tubo *nm* **1** : tube ⟨tubo de ensayo : test tube⟩ **2** : pipe ⟨tubo de desagüe : drainpipe⟩ **3 tubo digestivo** : alimentary canal

tubular *adj* : tubular

tuerca *nf* : nut ⟨tuercas y tornillos : nuts and bolts⟩

tuerce, etc. → torcer

tuerto, -ta *adj* : one-eyed, blind in one eye

tuerza, etc. → torcer

tuesta, etc. → tostar

tuétano *nm* : marrow

tufo *nm* **1** : fume, vapor **2** *fam* : stench, stink

tugurio *nm* : hovel

tulipán *nm, pl* **-panes** : tulip

tumba *nf* **1** SEPULCRO : tomb **2** FOSA : grave **3** : felling of trees

tumbar *vt* **1** : to knock down **2** : to fell, to cut down — *vi* : to fall down —

tumbarse *vr* ACOSTARSE : to lie down

tumbo *nm* **1** : tumble, fall **2 dar tumbos** : to jolt, to bump around

tumor *nm* : tumor

túmulo *nm* : burial mound

tumulto *nm* **1** ALBOROTO : commotion, tumult **2** MOTÍN : riot **3** MULTITUD : crowd

tumultuoso, -sa *adj* : tumultuous

tuna *nf* : prickly pear (fruit)

tundra *nf* : tundra

tunecino, -na *adj & n* : Tunisian

túnel *nm* : tunnel

tungsteno *nm* : tungsten

túnica *nf* : tunic

tupé *nm* PELUQUÍN : toupee

tupido, -da *adj* **1** DENSO : dense, thick **2** OBSTRUIDO : obstructed, blocked up

turba *nf* **1** : peat **2** : mob, throng

turbación *nf, pl* **-ciones 1** : disturbance **2** : alarm, concern **3** : confusion

turbante *nm* : turban

turbar *vt* **1** : to disturb, to disrupt **2** : to worry, to upset **3** : to confuse

turbina *nf* : turbine

turbio, -bia *adj* **1** : cloudy, murky, turbid **2** : dim, blurred **3** : shady, crooked

turbopropulsor *nm* : turboprop

turborreactor *nm* : turbojet

turbulencia *nf* : turbulence

turbulento, -ta *adj* : turbulent

turco¹, -ca *adj* : Turkish

turco², -ca *n* : Turk

turco³ *nm* : Turkish (language)

turgente *adj* : turgid, swollen

turismo *nm* : tourism, tourist industry

turista *nmf* : tourist, vacationer

turístico, -ca *adj* : tourist, travel

turnar *vi* : to take turns, to alternate

turno *nm* **1** : turn ⟨ya te tocará tu turno : you'll get your turn⟩ **2** : shift, duty ⟨turno de noche : night shift⟩ **3 por turno** : alternately

turón *nm, pl* **turones** : polecat

turquesa *nf* : turquoise

turrón *nm, pl* **turrones** : nougat

tusa *nf* : corn husk

tutear *vt* : to address as *tú*

tutela *nf* **1** : guardianship **2** : tutelage, protection

tuteo *nm* : addressing as *tú*

tutor, -tora *n* **1** : tutor **2** : guardian

tuvo, etc. → tener

tuyo¹, -ya *adj* : yours, of yours ⟨un amigo tuyo : a friend of yours⟩ ⟨¿es tuya esta casa? : is this house yours?⟩

tuyo², -ya *pron* **1** : yours ⟨ése es el tuyo : that one is yours⟩ ⟨trae la tuya : bring your own⟩ **2 los tuyos** : your relations, your friends ⟨¿vendrán los tuyos? : are your folks coming?⟩

tweed [¹twið] *nm* : tweed

U

u[1] *nf* : twenty-second letter of the Spanish alphabet

u[2] *conj* (*used instead of* **o** *before words beginning with* o- *or* ho-) : or

ualabí *nm* : wallaby

uapití *nm* : American elk, wapiti

ubicación *nf, pl* **-ciones** : location, position

ubicar {72} *vt* **1** SITUAR : to place, to put, to position **2** LOCALIZAR : to locate, to find — **ubicarse** *vr* **1** LOCALIZARSE : to be placed, to be located **2** SITUARSE : to position oneself

ubicuidad *nf* OMNIPRESENCIA : ubiquity

ubicuo, -cua *adj* OMNIPRESENTE : ubiquitous

ubre *nf* : udder

ucraniano[1]**, -na** *adj & n* : Ukrainian

ucraniano[2] *nm* : Ukranian (language)

Ud., Uds. → **usted**

ufanarse *vr* **~ de** : to boast about, to pride oneself on

ufano, -na *adj* **1** ORGULLOSO : proud **2** : self-satisfied, smug

ugandés, -desa *adj & n, mpl* **-deses** : Ugandan

ukelele *nm* : ukulele

úlcera *nf* : ulcer — **ulceroso, -sa** *adj*

ulcerar *vt* : to ulcerate — **ulcerarse** *vr* — **ulceración** *nf*

ulceroso, -sa *adj* : ulcerous

ulterior *adj* : later, subsequent — **ulteriormente** *adv*

últimamente *adv* : lately, recently

ultimar *vt* **1** CONCLUIR : to complete, to finish, to finalize **2** MATAR : to kill

ultimátum *nm, pl* **-tums** : ultimatum

último, -ma *adj* **1** : last, final ⟨la última galleta : the last cookie⟩ ⟨en último caso : as a last resort⟩ **2** : last, latest, most recent ⟨su último viaje a España : her last trip to Spain⟩ ⟨en los últimos años : in recent years⟩ **3 por ~** : finally

ultrajar *vt* INSULTAR : to offend, to outrage, to insult

ultraje *nm* INSULTO : outrage, insult

ultramar *nm* **de ~** *or* **en ~** : overseas, abroad

ultranza *nf* **1 a ~** : to the extreme ⟨lo defendió a ultranza : she defended him fiercely⟩ **2 a ~** : extreme, out-and-out ⟨perfeccionismo a ultranza : rabid perfectionism⟩

ultrarrojo, -ja *adj* : infrared

ultravioleta *adj* : ultraviolet

ulular *vi* **1** : to hoot **2** : to howl, to wail

ululato *nm* : hoot (of an owl), wail (of a person)

umbilical *adj* : umbilical ⟨cordón umbilical : umbilical cord⟩

umbral *nm* : threshold, doorstep

un[1] *adj* → **uno**[1]

un[2]**, una** *art, mpl* **unos 1** : a, an **2 unos** *or* **unas** *pl* : some, a few ⟨hace unas se-

manas : a few weeks ago⟩ **3 unos** *or* **unas** *pl* : about, approximately ⟨unos veinte años antes : about twenty years before⟩

unánime *adj* : unanimous — **unánimemente** *adv*

unanimidad *nf* **1** : unanimity **2 por ~** : unanimously

unción *nf, pl* **-ciones** : unction

uncir {83} *vt* : to yoke

undécimo[1]**, -ma** *adj* : eleventh

undécimo[2]**, -ma** *n* : eleventh (in a series)

ungir {35} *vt* : to anoint

ungüento *nm* : ointment, salve

únicamente *adv* : only, solely

unicelular *adj* : unicellular

único[1]**, -ca** *adj* **1** : only, sole **2** : unique, extraordinary

único[2]**, -ca** *n* : only one ⟨los únicos que vinieron : the only ones who showed up⟩

unicornio *nm* : unicorn

unidad *nf* **1** : unity **2** : unit

unidireccional *adj* : unidirectional

unido, -da *adj* **1** : joined, united **2** : close ⟨unos amigos muy unidos : very close friends⟩

unificar {72} *vt* : to unify — **unificación** *nf*

uniformado, -da *adj* : uniformed

uniformar *vt* ESTANDARIZAR : to standardize, to make uniform

uniforme[1] *adj* : uniform — **uniformemente** *adv*

uniforme[2] *nm* : uniform

uniformidad *nf* : uniformity

unilateral *adj* : unilateral — **unilateralmente** *adv*

unión *nf, pl* **uniones 1** : union **2** JUNTURA : joint, coupling

unir *vt* **1** JUNTAR : to unite, to join, to link **2** COMBINAR : to combine, to blend — **unirse** *vr* **1** : to join together **2** : to combine, to mix together **3 ~ a** : to join ⟨se unieron al grupo : they joined the group⟩

unísono *nm* : unison ⟨al unísono : in unison⟩

unitario, -ria *adj* : unitary, unit ⟨precio unitario : unit price⟩

universal *adj* : universal — **universalmente** *adv*

universidad *nf* : university

universitario[1]**, -ria** *adj* : university, college

universitario[2]**, -ria** *n* : university student, college student

universo *nm* : universe

unja, etc. → **ungir**

uno[1]**, una** *adj* (**un** *before masculine singular nouns*) : one ⟨una silla : one chair⟩ ⟨tiene treinta y un años : he's thirty-one years old⟩ ⟨el tomo uno : volume one⟩

uno[2] *nm* : one, number one

uno³, una *pron* **1** : one (number) ⟨uno por uno : one by one⟩ ⟨es la una : it's one o'clock⟩ **2** : one (person or thing) ⟨una es mejor que las otras : one (of them) is better than the others⟩ ⟨hacerlo uno mismo : to do it oneself⟩ **3 unos, unas** *pl* : some (ones), some people **4 uno y otro** : both **5 unos y otros** : all of them **6 el uno al otro** : one another, each other ⟨se enseñaron los unos a los otros : they taught each other⟩

untar *vt* **1** : to anoint **2** : to smear, to grease **3** : to bribe

unza, etc. → **uncir**

uña *nf* **1** : fingernail, toenail **2** : claw, hoof, stinger

uranio *nm* : uranium

Urano *nm* : Uranus

urbanidad *nf* : urbanity, courtesy

urbanización *nf, pl* **-ciones** : housing development, residential area

urbanizar {21} *vt* : to develop (an area)

urbano, -na *adj* **1** : urban **2** CORTÉS : urbane, polite

urbe *nf* : large city, metropolis

urdimbre *nf* : warp (in a loom)

urdu *nm* : Urdu

uretra *nf* : urethra

urgencia *nf* **1** : urgency **2** EMERGENCIA : emergency

urgente *adj* : urgent — **urgentemente** *adv*

urgir {35} *v impers* : to be urgent, to be pressing ⟨me urge localizarlo : I urgently need to find him⟩ ⟨el tiempo urge : time is running out⟩

urinario¹, -ria *adj* : urinary

urinario² *nm* : urinal (place)

urja, etc. → **urgir**

urna *nf* **1** : urn **2** : ballot box ⟨acudir a las urnas : to go to the polls⟩

urogallo *nm* : grouse (bird)

urraca *nf* **1** : magpie **2 urraca de América** : blue jay

urticaria *nf* : hives

uruguayo, -ya *adj & n* : Uruguayan

usado, -da *adj* **1** : used, secondhand **2** : worn, worn-out

usanza *nf* : custom, usage

usar *vt* **1** EMPLEAR, UTILIZAR : to use, to make use of **2** CONSUMIR : to consume, to use (up) **3** LLEVAR : to wear **4 de usar y tirar** : disposable — **usarse** *vr* **1** : to be used **2** : to be in fashion

uso *nm* **1** EMPLEO, UTILIZACIÓN : use ⟨de uso personal : for personal use⟩ ⟨hacer uso de : to make use of⟩ **2** : wear ⟨uso y desgaste : wear and tear⟩ **3** USANZA : custom, usage, habit ⟨al uso de : in the manner of, in the style of⟩

usted *pron* **1** (*formal form of address in most countries; often written as* **Ud.** *or* **Vd.**) : you **2 ustedes** *pl* (*often written as* **Uds.** *or* **Vds.**) : you, all of you

usual *adj* : usual, common, normal ⟨poco usual : not very common⟩ — **usualmente** *adv*

usuario, -ria *n* : user

usura *nf* : usury — **usurario, -ria** *adj*

usurero, -ra *n* : usurer

usurpador, -dora *n* : usurper

usurpar *vt* : to usurp — **usurpación** *nf*

utensilio *nm* : utensil, tool

uterino, -na *adj* : uterine

útero *nm* : uterus, womb

útil *adj* : useful, handy, helpful

útiles *nmpl* : implements, tools

utilidad *nf* **1** : utility, usefulness **2 utilidades** *nfpl* : profits

utilitario, -ria *adj* : utilitarian

utilizable *adj* : usable, fit for use

utilización *nf, pl* **-ciones** : utilization, use

utilizar {21} *vt* : to use, to utilize

útilmente *adv* : usefully

utopía *nf* : utopia

utópico, -ca *adj* : utopian

uva *nf* : grape

uvular *adj* : uvular

V

v *nf* : twenty-third letter of the Spanish alphabet

va → **ir**

vaca *nf* : cow

vacación *nf, pl* **-ciones** **1** : vacation ⟨dos semanas de vacaciones : two weeks of vacation⟩ **2 estar de vacaciones** : to be on vacation **3 irse de vacaciones** : to go on vacation

vacacionar *vi Mex* : to vacation

vacacionista *nmf CA, Mex* : vacationer

vacante¹ *adj* : vacant, empty

vacante² *nf* : vacancy (for a job)

vaciado *nm* : cast, casting ⟨vaciado de yeso : plaster cast⟩

vaciar {85} *vt* **1** : to empty, to empty out, to drain **2** AHUECAR : to hollow out **3** : to cast (in a mold) — *vi* ~ **en** : to flow into, to empty into

vacilación *nf, pl* **-ciones** : hesitation, vacillation

vacilante *adj* **1** : hesitant, unsure **2** : shaky, unsteady **3** : flickering

vacilar *vi* **1** : to hesitate, to vacillate, to waver **2** : to be unsteady, to wobble **3** : to flicker **4** *fam* : to joke, to fool around

vacío¹, -cía *adj* **1** : vacant **2** : empty **3** : meaningless

vacío² *nm* **1** : emptiness, void **2** : space, gap **3** : vacuum **4 hacerle el vacío a alguien** : to ostracize someone, to give someone the cold shoulder

vacuidad *nf* : vacuity, vacuousness

vacuna *nf* : vaccine
vacunación *nf, pl* **-ciones** INOCU-LACIÓN : vaccination, inoculation
vacunar *vt* INOCULAR : to vaccinate, to inoculate
vacuno¹, -na *adj* : bovine ⟨ganado vacuno : beef cattle⟩
vacuno² *nm* : bovine
vacuo, -cua *adj* : empty, shallow, inane
vadear *vt* : to ford, to wade across
vado *nm* : ford
vagabundear *vi* : to wander, to roam about
vagabundo¹, -da *adj* **1** ERRANTE : wandering **2** : stray
vagabundo², -da *n* : vagrant, bum, vagabond
vagamente *adv* : vaguely
vagancia *nf* **1** : vagrancy **2** PEREZA : laziness, idleness
vagar {52} *vi* ERRAR : to roam, to wander
vagina *nf* : vagina — **vaginal** *adj*
vago¹, -ga *adj* **1** : vague **2** PEREZOSO : lazy, idle
vago², -ga *n* **1** : idler, loafer **2** VAGABUNDO : vagrant, bum
vagón *nm, pl* **vagones** : car (of a train)
vague, etc. → **vagar**
vaguear *vi* **1** : to loaf, to lounge around **2** VAGAR : to wander
vaguedad *nf* : vagueness
vahído *nm* : dizzy spell
vaho *nm* **1** : breath **2** : vapor, steam (on glass, etc.)
vaina *nf* **1** : sheath, scabbard **2** : pod (of a pea or bean) **3** *fam* : nuisance, bother
vainilla *nf* : vanilla
vaivén *nm, pl* **vaivenes** **1** : swinging, swaying, rocking **2** : change, fluctuation ⟨los vaivenes de la vida : life's ups and downs⟩
vajilla *nf* : dishes *pl*, set of dishes
valdrá, etc. → **valer**
vale *nm* **1** : voucher **2** PAGARÉ : promissory note, IOU
valedero, -ra *adj* : valid
valentía *nf* : courage, valor
valer {84} *vt* **1** : to be worth ⟨valen una fortuna : they're worth a fortune⟩ ⟨no vale protestar : there's no point in protesting⟩ ⟨valer la pena : to be worth the trouble⟩ **2** : to cost ⟨¿cuánto vale? : how much does it cost?⟩ **3** : to earn, to gain ⟨le valió una reprimenda : it earned him a reprimand⟩ **4** : to protect, to aid ⟨¡válgame Dios! : God help me!⟩ **5** : to be equal to — *vi* **1** : to have value ⟨sus consejos no valen para nada : his advice is worthless⟩ **2** : to be valid, to count ⟨eso no vale! : that doesn't count!⟩ **3 hacerse valer** : to assert oneself **4 más vale** : it's better ⟨más vale que te vayas : you'd better go⟩ — **valerse** *vr* **1** ∼ **de** : to take advantage of **2 valerse solo** *or* **valerse por sí mismo** : to look after oneself **3** *Mex* : to be fair ⟨no se vale : it's not fair⟩

valeroso, -sa *adj* : brave, valiant
valet ['balɛt, -'le] *nm* : jack (in playing cards)
valga, etc. → **valer**
valía *nf* : value, worth
validar *vt* : to validate — **validación** *nf*
validez *nf* : validity
válido, -da *adj* : valid
valiente *adj* **1** : brave, valiant **2** (*used ironically*) : fine, great ⟨¡valiente amiga! : what a fine friend!⟩ — **valientemente** *adv*
valija *nf* : suitcase, valise
valioso, -sa *adj* PRECIOSO : valuable, precious
valla *nf* **1** : fence, barricade **2** : hurdle (in sports) **3** : obstacle, hindrance
vallar *vt* : to fence, to put a fence around
valle *nm* : valley, vale
valor *nm* **1** : value, worth, importance **2** CORAJE : courage, valor **3 valores** *nmpl* : values, principles **4 valores** *nmpl* : securities, bonds **5 sin** ∼ : worthless
valoración *nf, pl* **-ciones** **1** EVALUACIÓN : valuation, appraisal, assessment **2** APRECIACIÓN : appreciation
valorar *vt* **1** EVALUAR : to evaluate, to appraise, to assess **2** APRECIAR : to value, to appreciate
valorizarse {21} *vr* : to appreciate, to increase in value — **valorización** *nf*
vals *nm* : waltz
valsar *vi* : to waltz
valuación *nf, pl* **-ciones** : valuation, appraisal
valuar {3} *vt* : to value, to appraise, to assess
válvula *nf* **1** : valve **2 válvula reguladora** : throttle
vamos → **ir**
vampiro *nm* : vampire
van → **ir**
vanadio *nm* : vanadium
vanagloriarse *vr* : to boast, to brag
vanamente *adv* : vainly, in vain
vandalismo : vandalism
vándalo *nm* : vandal — **vandalismo** *nm*
vanguardia *nf* **1** : vanguard **2** : avante-garde **3 a la vanguardia** : at the forefront
vanidad *nf* : vanity
vanidoso, -sa *adj* PRESUMIDO : vain, conceited
vano, -na *adj* **1** INÚTIL : vain, useless **2** : vain, worthless ⟨vanas promesas : empty promises⟩ **3 en** ∼ : in vain, of no avail
vapor *nm* **1** : vapor, steam **2** : steamer, steamship **3 al vapor** : steamed
vaporizador *nm* : vaporizer
vaporizar {21} *vt* : to vaporize — **vaporizarse** *vr* — **vaporización** *nf*
vaporoso, -sa *adj* **1** : vaporous **2** : sheer, airy
vapulear *vt* : to beat, to thrash
vaquero¹, -ra *adj* : cowboy ⟨pantalón vaquero : jeans⟩

vaquero², -ra *n* : cowboy *m*, cowgirl *f*
vaqueros *nmpl* JEANS : jeans
vaquilla *nf* : heifer
vara *nf* 1 : pole, stick, rod 2 : staff (of office) 3 : lance, pike (in bullfighting) 4 : yardstick 5 **vara de oro** : golden-rod
varado, -da *adj* 1 : beached, aground 2 : stranded
varar *vt* : to beach (a ship), to strand — *vi* : to run aground
variable *adj & nf* : variable — **variabilidad** *nf*
variación *nf, pl* **-ciones** : variation
variado, -da *adj* : varied, diverse
variante *adj & nf* : variant
varianza *nf* : variance
variar {85} *vt* 1 : to change, to alter 2 : to diversify — *vi* 1 : to vary, to change 2 **variar de opinión** : to change one's mind
varicela *nf* : chicken pox
varices *or* **várices** *nfpl* : varicose veins
varicoso, -sa *adj* : varicose
variedad *nf* DIVERSIDAD : variety, diversity
varilla *nf* 1 : rod, bar 2 : spoke (of a wheel) 3 : rib (of an umbrella)
vario, -ria *adj* 1 : varied, diverse 2 : variegated, motley 3 : changeable 4 **varios, varias** *pl* : various, several
variopinto, -ta *adj* : diverse, assorted, motley
varita *nf* : wand ⟨varita mágica : magic wand⟩
varón *nm, pl* **varones** 1 HOMBRE : man, male 2 NIÑO : boy
varonil *adj* 1 : masculine, manly 2 : mannish
vas → **ir**
vasallo *nm* : vassal — **vasallaje** *nm*
vasco¹, -ca *adj & n* : Basque
vasco² *nm* : Basque (language)
vascular *adj* : vascular
vasija *nf* : container, vessel
vaso *nm* 1 : glass, tumbler 2 : glassful 3 : vessel ⟨vaso sanguíneo : blood vessel⟩
vástago *nm* 1 : offspring, descendant 2 : shoot (of a plant)
vastedad *nf* : vastness, immensity
vasto, -ta *adj* : vast, immense
vataje *nm* : wattage
vaticinar *vt* : to predict, to foretell
vaticinio *nm* : prediction, prophecy
vatio *nm* : watt
vaya, etc. → **ir**
Vd., Vds. → **usted**
ve, etc. → **ir, ver**
vea, etc. → **ver**
vecinal *adj* : local
vecindad *nf* 1 : neighborhood, vicinity 2 **casa de vecindad** : tenement
vecindario *nm* 1 : neighborhood, area 2 : residents *pl*
vecino, -na *n* 1 : neighbor 2 : resident, inhabitant
veda *nf* 1 PROHIBICIÓN : prohibition 2 : closed season (for hunting or fishing)

vedar *vt* 1 : to prohibit, to ban 2 IMPEDIR : to impede, to prevent
vega *nf* : fertile lowland
vegetación *nf, pl* **-ciones** 1 : vegetation 2 **vegetaciones** *nfpl* : adenoids
vegetal *adj & nm* : vegetable, plant
vegetar *vi* : to vegetate
vegetarianismo *nm* : vegetarianism
vegetariano, -na *adj & n* : vegetarian
vegetativo, -va *adj* : vegetative
vehemente *adj* : vehement — **vehemencia** *nf*
vehículo *nm* : vehicle — **vehicular** *adj*
veía, etc. → **ver**
veinte *adj & nm* : twenty
veinteavo¹, -va *adj* : twentieth
veinteavo² *nm* : twentieth (fraction)
veintena *nf* : group of twenty, score ⟨una veintena de participantes : about twenty participants⟩
vejación *nf, pl* **-ciones** : ill-treatment, humiliation
vejar *vt* : to mistreat, to ridicule, to harass
vejete *nm* : old fellow, codger
vejez *nf* : old age
vejiga *nf* 1 : bladder 2 AMPOLLA : blister
vela *nf* 1 VIGILIA : wakefulness ⟨pasé la noche en vela : I stayed awake all night⟩ 2 : watch, vigil, wake 3 : candle 4 : sail
velada *nf* : evening party, soirée
velado, -da *adj* 1 : veiled, hidden 2 : blurred 3 : muffled
velador¹, -dora *n* : guard, night watchman
velador² *nm* 1 : candlestick 2 : night table
velar *vt* 1 : to hold a wake over 2 : to watch over, to sit up with 3 : to blur, to expose (a photo) 4 : to veil, to conceal — *vi* 1 : to stay awake 2 ∼ **por** : to watch over, to look after
velatorio *nm* VELORIO : wake (for the dead)
veleidad *nf* 1 : fickleness 2 : whim, caprice
veleidoso, -sa *adj* : fickle, capricious
velero *nm* 1 : sailing ship 2 : sailboat
veleta *nf* : weather vane
vello *nm* 1 : body hair 2 : down, fuzz
vellocino *nm* : fleece
vellón *nm, pl* **vellones** 1 : fleece, sheepskin 2 *PRi* : nickel (coin)
vellosidad *nf* : downiness, hairiness
velloso, -sa *adj* : downy, fluffy, hairy
velo *nm* : veil
velocidad *nf* 1 : speed, velocity ⟨velocidad máxima : speed limit⟩ 2 MARCHA : gear (of an automobile)
velocímetro *nm* : speedometer
velocista *nmf* : sprinter
velorio *nm* VELATORIO : wake (for the dead)
velour *nm* : velour, velours
veloz *adj, pl* **veloces** : fast, quick, swift — **velozmente** *adv*
ven → **venir**

vena *nf* **1** : vein ⟨vena yugular : jugular vein⟩ **2** : vein, seam, lode **3** : grain (of wood) **4** : style ⟨en vena lírica : in a lyrical vein⟩ **5** : strain, touch ⟨una vena de humor : a touch of humor⟩ **6** : mood

venado *nm* **1** : deer **2** : venison

venal *adj* : venal — **venalidad** *nf*

vencedor, -dora *n* : winner, victor

vencejo *nm* : swift (bird)

vencer {86} *vt* **1** DERROTAR : to vanquish, to defeat **2** SUPERAR : to overcome, to surmount — *vi* **1** GANAR : to win, to triumph **2** CADUCAR : to expire ⟨el plazo vence el jueves : the deadline is Thursday⟩ **3** : to fall due, to mature — **vencerse** *vr* **1** DOMINARSE : to control oneself **2** : to break, to collapse

vencido, -da *adj* **1** : defeated **2** : expired **3** : due, payable **4 darse por vencido** : to give up

vencimiento *nm* **1** : defeat **2** : expiration **3** : maturity (of a loan)

venda *nf* : bandage

vendaje *nm* : bandage, dressing

vendar *vt* **1** : to bandage **2 vendar los ojos** : to blindfold

vendaval *nm* : gale, strong wind

vendedor, -dora *n* : salesperson, salesman *m*, saleswoman *f*

vender *vt* **1** : to sell **2** : to sell out, to betray — **venderse** *vr* **1** : to be sold ⟨se vende : for sale⟩ **2** : to sell out

vendetta *nf* : vendetta

vendible *adj* : salable, marketable

vendimia *nf* : grape harvest

vendrá, etc. → venir

veneno *nm* **1** : poison **2** : venom

venenoso, -sa *adj* : poisonous, venomous

venerable *adj* : venerable

veneración *nf, pl* **-ciones** : veneration, reverence

venerar *vt* : to venerate, to revere

venéreo, -rea *adj* : venereal

venero *nm* **1** VENA : seam, lode, vein **2** MANANTIAL : spring **3** FUENTE : origin, source

venezolano, -na *adj & n* : Venezuelan

venga, etc. → venir

vengador, -dora *n* : avenger

venganza *nf* : vengeance, revenge

vengar {52} *vt* : to avenge — **vengarse** *vr* : to get even, to revenge oneself

vengativo, -va *adj* : vindictive, vengeful

vengue, etc. → vengar

venia *nf* **1** PERMISO : permission, leave **2** PERDÓN : pardon **3** : bow (of the head)

venial *adj* : venial

venida *nf* **1** LLEGADA : arrival, coming **2** REGRESO : return **3 idas y venidas** : comings and goings

venidero, -ra *adj* : coming, future

venir {87} *vi* **1** : to come ⟨lo vi venir : I saw him coming⟩ ⟨¡venga! : come on!⟩ **2** : to arrive ⟨vinieron en coche : they came by car⟩ **3** : to come, to originate ⟨sus zapatos vienen de Italia : her shoes

are from Italy⟩ **4** : to come, to be available ⟨viene envuelto en plástico : it comes wrapped in plastic⟩ **5** : to come back, to return **6** : to affect, to overcome ⟨me vino un vahído : a dizzy spell came over me⟩ **7** : to fit ⟨te viene un poco grande : it's a little big for you⟩ **8** (*with the present participle*) : to have been ⟨viene entrenando diariamente : he's been training daily⟩ **9 ~ a** (*with the infinitive*) : to end up, to turn out ⟨viene a ser lo mismo : it comes out the same⟩ **10 que viene** : coming, next ⟨el año que viene : next year⟩ **11 venir bien** : to be suitable, to be just right — **venirse** *vr* **1** : to come, to arrive **2** : to come back **3 venirse abajo** : to fall apart, to collapse

venta *nf* **1** : sale **2 venta al por menor** *or* **venta al detalle** : retail sales

ventaja *nf* **1** : advantage **2** : lead, head start **3 ventajas** *nfpl* : perks, extras

ventajoso, -sa *adj* **1** : advantageous **2** : profitable — **ventajosamente** *adv*

ventana *nf* **1** : window (of a building) **2 ventana de la nariz** : nostril

ventanal *nm* : large window

ventanilla *nf* **1** : window (of a vehicle or airplane) **2** : ticket window, box office

ventero, -ra *n* : innkeeper

ventilación *nf, pl* **-ciones** : ventilation

ventilador *nm* **1** : ventilator **2** : fan

ventilar *vt* **1** : to ventilate, to air out **2** : to air, to discuss **3** : to make public, to reveal — **ventilarse** *vr* : to get some air

ventisca *nf* : snowstorm, blizzard

ventisquero *nm* : snowdrift

ventosear *vi* : to break wind

ventosidad *nf* : wind, flatulence

ventoso, -sa *adj* : windy

ventrículo *nm* : ventricle

ventrílocuo, -cua *n* : ventriloquist

ventriloquia *nf* : ventriloquism

ventura *nf* **1** : fortune, luck, chance **2** : happiness **3 a la ventura** : at random, as it comes

venturoso, -sa *adj* **1** AFORTUNADO : fortunate, lucky **2** : successful

Venus *nm* : Venus

venza, etc. → vencer

ver[1] {88} *vt* **1** : to see ⟨vimos la película : we saw the movie⟩ **2** ENTENDER : to understand ⟨ya lo veo : now I get it⟩ **3** EXAMINAR : to examine, to look into ⟨lo veré : I'll take a look at it⟩ **4** JUZGAR : to see, to judge ⟨a mi manera de ver : to my way of thinking⟩ **5** VISITAR : to meet with, to visit **6** AVERIGUAR : to find out **7 a ver** *or* **vamos a ver** : let's see — *vi* **1** : to see **2** ENTERARSE : to learn, to find out **3** ENTENDER : to understand — **verse** *vr* **1** HALLARSE : to find oneself **2** PARECER : to look, to appear **3** ENCONTRARSE : to see each other, to meet

ver[2] *nm* **1** : looks *pl*, appearance **2** : opinion ⟨a mi ver : in my view⟩

vera *nf* : side ⟨a la vera del camino : alongside the road⟩
veracidad *nf* : truthfulness, veracity
veranda *nf* : veranda
veraneante *nmf* : summer vacationer
veranear *vi* : to spend the summer
veraniego, -ga *adj* 1 ESTIVAL : summer ⟨el sol veraniego : the summer sun⟩ 2 : summery
verano *nm* : summer
veras *nfpl* **de ~** : really, truly
veraz *adj, pl* **veraces** : truthful, veracious
verbal *adj* : verbal — **verbalmente** *adv*
verbalizar {21} *vt* : to verbalize, to express
verbena *nf* 1 FIESTA : festival, fair 2 : verbena, vervain
verbigracia *adv* : for example
verbo *nm* : verb
verborrea *nf* : verbiage
verbosidad *nf* : verbosity, wordiness
verboso, -sa *adj* : verbose, wordy
verdad *nf* 1 : truth 2 **de ~** : really, truly 3 ¿**verdad?** : right?, isn't that so?
verdaderamente *adv* : really, truly
verdadero, -dera *adj* 1 REAL, VERÍDICO : true, real 2 AUTÉNTICO : genuine
verde[1] *adj* 1 : green (in color) 2 : green, unripe 3 : inexperienced, green 4 : dirty, risqué
verde[2] *nm* : green
verdear *vi* : to turn green, to become verdant
verdín *nm, pl* **verdines** : slime, scum
verdor *nm* 1 : greenness 2 : verdure
verdoso, -sa *adj* : greenish
verdugo *nm* 1 : executioner, hangman 2 : tyrant
verdugón *nm, pl* **-gones** : welt, wheal
verdura *nf* : vegetable(s), green(s)
vereda *nf* 1 SENDA : path, trail 2 : sidewalk, pavement
veredicto *nm* : verdict
verga *nf* : spar, yard (of a ship)
vergonzoso, -sa *adj* 1 : disgraceful, shameful 2 : bashful, shy — **vergonzosamente** *adv*
vergüenza *nf* 1 : disgrace, shame 2 : embarrassment 3 : bashfulness, shyness
vericueto *nm* : rough terrain
verídico, -ca *adj* 1 REAL, VERDADERO : true, real 2 VERAZ : truthful
verificación *nf, pl* **-ciones** 1 : verification 2 : testing, checking
verificador, -dora *n* : inspector, tester
verificar {72} *vt* 1 : to verify, to confirm 2 : to test, to check 3 : to carry out, to conduct — **verificarse** *vr* 1 : to take place, to occur 2 : to come true
verja *nf* 1 : rails *pl* (of a fence) 2 : grating, grille 3 : gate
vermut *nm, pl* **vermuts** : vermouth
vernáculo, -la *adj* : vernacular
vernal *adj* : vernal, spring
verosímil *adj* 1 : probable, likely 2 : credible, realistic

verosimilitud *nf* 1 : probability, likeliness 2 : verisimilitude
verraco *nm* : boar
verruga *nf* : wart
versado, -da *adj* **~ en** : versed in, knowledgeable about
versar *vi* **~ sobre** : to deal with, to be about
versátil *adj* 1 : versatile 2 : fickle
versatilidad *nf* 1 : versatility 2 : fickleness
versículo *nm* : verse (in the Bible)
versión *nf, pl* **versiones** 1 : version 2 : translation
verso *nm* : verse
versus *prep* : versus, against
vértebra *nf* : vertebra — **vertebral** *adj*
vertebrado[1]**, -da** *adj* : vertebrate
vertebrado[2] *nm* : vertebrate
vertedero *nm* 1 : garbage dump 2 DESAGÜE : drain, outlet
verter {56} *vt* 1 : to pour 2 : to spill, to shed 3 : to empty out 4 : to express, to voice 5 : to translate, to render — *vi* : to flow
vertical *adj & nf* : vertical — **verticalmente** *adv*
vértice *nm* : vertex, apex
vertido *nm* : spilling, spill
vertiente *nf* 1 : slope 2 : aspect, side, element
vertiginoso, -sa *adj* : vertiginous — **vertiginosamente** *adv*
vértigo *nm* : vertigo, dizziness
vesícula *nf* 1 : vesicle 2 **vesícula biliar** : gallbladder
vesicular *adj* : vesicular
vestíbulo *nm* : vestibule, hall, lobby, foyer
vestido *nm* 1 : dress, costume, clothes *pl* 2 : dress (garment)
vestidor *nm* : dressing room
vestiduras *nfpl* 1 : clothing, raiment, regalia 2 *or* **vestiduras sacerdotales** : vestments
vestigio *nm* : vestige, sign, trace
vestimenta *nf* ROPA : clothing, clothes *pl*
vestir {54} *vt* 1 : to dress, to clothe 2 LLEVAR : to wear 3 ADORNAR : to decorate, to dress up — *vi* 1 : to dress ⟨vestir bien : to dress well⟩ 2 : to look good, to suit the occasion — **vestirse** *vr* 1 : to get dressed 2 **~ de** : to dress up as ⟨se vistieron de soldados : they dressed up as soldiers⟩ 3 **~ de** : to wear, to dress in
vestuario *nm* 1 : wardrobe 2 : dressing room, locker room
veta *nf* 1 : grain (in wood) 2 : vein, seam, lode 3 : trace, streak ⟨una veta de terco : a stubborn streak⟩
vetar *vt* : to veto
veteado, -da *adj* : streaked, veined
veterano, -na *adj & n* : veteran
veterinaria *nf* : veterinary medicine
veterinario[1]**, -ria** *adj* : veterinary
veterinario[2]**, -ria** *n* : veterinarian

veto *nm* : veto
vetusto, -ta *adj* ANTIGUO : ancient, very old
vez *nf, pl* **veces 1** : time, occasion ⟨a la vez : at the same time⟩ ⟨a veces : at times, occasionally⟩ ⟨de vez en cuando : from time to time⟩ **2** (*with numbers*) : time ⟨una vez : once⟩ ⟨de una vez : all at once⟩ ⟨de una vez para siempre : once and for all⟩ ⟨dos veces : twice⟩ **3** : turn ⟨a su vez : in turn⟩ ⟨en vez de : instead of⟩ ⟨hacer las veces de : to act as, to stand in for⟩
vía[1] *nf* **1** RUTA, CAMINO : road, route, way ⟨Vía Láctea : Milky Way⟩ **2** MEDIO : means, way ⟨por vía oficial : through official channels⟩ **3** : track, line (of a railroad) **4** : tract, passage ⟨por vía oral : orally⟩ **5 en vías de** : in the process of ⟨en vías de solución : on the road to a solution⟩ **6 por ~** : by (in transportation) ⟨por vía aérea : by air, airmail⟩
vía[2] *prep* : via
viable *adj* : viable, feasible — **viabilidad** *nf*
viaducto *nm* : viaduct
viajante *mf* : traveling salesman, traveling saleswoman
viajar *vi* : to travel, to journey
viaje *nm* : trip, journey ⟨viaje de negocios : business trip⟩
viajero[1], **-ra** *adj* : traveling
viajero[2], **-ra** *n* **1** : traveler **2** PASAJERO : passenger
vial *adj* : road, traffic
viático *nm* : travel allowance, travel expenses *pl*
víbora *nf* : viper
vibración *nf, pl* **-ciones** : vibration
vibrador *nm* : vibrator
vibrante *adj* **1** : vibrant **2** : vibrating
vibrar *vi* : to vibrate
vibratorio, -ria *adj* : vibratory
vicario, -ria *n* : vicar
vicealmirante *nmf* : vice admiral
vicepresidente, -ta *n* : vice president — **vicepresidencia** *nf*
viceversa *adv* : vice versa, conversely
viciado, -da *adj* : stuffy, close
viciar *vt* **1** : to corrupt **2** : to invalidate **3** FALSEAR : to distort **4** : to pollute, to adulterate
vicio *nm* **1** : vice, depravity **2** : bad habit **3** : defect, blemish
vicioso, -sa *adj* : depraved, corrupt
vicisitud *nf* : vicissitude
víctima *nf* : victim
victimario, -ria *n* ASESINO : killer, murderer
victimizar {21} *vt Arg, Mex* : to victimize
victoria *nf* : victory — **victorioso, -sa** *adj* — **victoriosamente** *adv*
victoriano, -na *adj* : Victorian
vid *nf* : vine, grapevine
vida *nf* **1** : life ⟨la vida cotidiana : everyday life⟩ **2** : life span, lifetime **3** BI-

OGRAFÍA : biography, life **4** : way of life, lifestyle **5** : livelihood ⟨ganarse la vida : to earn one's living⟩ **6** VIVEZA : liveliness **7 media vida** : half-life
vidente *nmf* **1** : psychic, clairvoyant **2** : sighted person
video *or* **vídeo** *nm* : video
videocasete *or* **videocassette** *nm* : videocassette
videocasetera *or* **videocassettera** *nf* : videocassette recorder, VCR
videocinta *nf* : videotape
videograbar *vt* : to videotape
vidriado *nm* : glaze
vidriar *vt* : to glaze (pottery, tile, etc.)
vidriera *nf* **1** : stained-glass window **2** : glass door or window **3** : store window
vidriero, -ra *n* : glazier
vidrio *nm* **1** : glass, piece of glass **2** : windowpane
vidrioso, -sa *adj* **1** : brittle, fragile **2** : slippery **3** : glassy, glazed (of eyes) **4** : touchy, delicate
vieira *nf* **1** : scallop **2** : scallop shell
viejo[1], **-ja** *adj* **1** ANCIANO : old, elderly **2** ANTIGUO : former, longstanding ⟨viejas tradiciones : old traditions⟩ ⟨viejos amigos : old friends⟩ **3** GASTADO : old, worn, worn-out
viejo[2], **-ja** *n* ANCIANO : old man *m*, old woman *f*
viene, etc. → **venir**
viento *nm* **1** : wind **2 hacer viento** : to be windy **3 contra viento y marea** : against all odds **4 viento alisio** : trade wind **5 viento en popa** : splendidly, successfully
vientre *nm* **1** : abdomen, belly **2** : womb **3** : bowels *pl*
viernes *nms & pl* : Friday
vierte, etc. → **verter**
vietnamita[1] *adj & nmf* : Vietnamese
vietnamita[2] *nm* : Vietnamese (language)
viga *nf* **1** : beam, rafter, girder **2 viga voladiza** : cantilever
vigencia *nf* **1** : validity **2** : force, effect ⟨entrar en vigencia : to go into effect⟩
vigente *adj* : valid, in force
vigésimo[1], **-ma** *adj* : twentieth, twenty- ⟨la vigésima segunda edición : the twenty-second edition⟩
vigésimo[2], **-ma** *n* : twentieth, twenty- (in a series)
vigía *nmf* : lookout
vigilancia *nf* : vigilance, watchfulness ⟨bajo vigilancia : under surveillance⟩
vigilante[1] *adj* : vigilant, watchful
vigilante[2] *nmf* : watchman, guard
vigilar *vt* CUIDAR : to look after, to keep an eye on **2** GUARDAR : to watch over, to guard — *vi* **1** : to be watchful **2** : to keep watch
vigilia *nf* **1** VELA : wakefulness **2** : night work **3** : vigil (in religion)
vigor *nm* **1** : vigor, energy, strength **2** VIGENCIA : force, effect
vigorizante *adj* : invigorating

vigorizar {21} *vt* : to strengthen, to invigorate
vigoroso, -sa *adj* : vigorous — **vigorosamente** *adv*
VIH *nm* (virus de *in*munodeficiencia *hu*mana) : HIV
vikingo, -ga *adj & n* : Viking
vil *adj* : vile, despicable
vileza *nf* **1** : vileness **2** : despicable action, villainy
vilipendiar *vt* : to vilify, to revile
villa *nf* **1** : town, village **2** : villa
villancico *nm* : carol, Christmas carol
villano, -na *n* **1** : villain **2** : peasant
vilo *nm* **1 en ~** : in the air **2 en ~** : uncertain, in suspense
vinagre *nm* : vinegar
vinagrera *nf* : cruet (for vinegar)
vinatería *nf* : wine shop
vinculación *nf, pl* **-ciones 1** : linking **2** RELACIÓN : bond, link, connection
vincular *vt* CONECTAR, RELACIONAR : to tie, to link, to connect
vínculo *nm* LAZO : tie, link, bond
vindicación *nf, pl* **-ciones** : vindication
vindicar *vt* **1** : to vindicate **2** : to avenge
vinilo *nm* : vinyl
vino¹, etc. → venir
vino² *nm* : wine
viña *nf* : vineyard
viñedo *nm* : vineyard
vio, etc. → ver
viola *nf* : viola
violación *nf, pl* **-ciones 1** : violation, offense **2** : rape
violador¹, -dora *n* : violator, offender
violador² *nm* : rapist
violar *vt* **1** : to rape **2** : to violate (a law or right) **3** PROFANAR : to desecrate
violencia *nf* : violence
violentamente *adv* : by force, violently
violentar *vt* **1** FORZAR : to break open, to force **2** : to distort (words or ideas) — **violentarse** *vr* : to force oneself
violento, -ta *adj* **1** : violent **2** EMBARAZOSO, INCÓMODO : awkward, embarassing
violeta¹ *adj & nm* : violet (color)
violeta² *nf* : violet (flower)
violín *nm, pl* **-lines** : violin
violinista *nmf* : violinist
violonchelista *nmf* : cellist
violonchelo *nm* : cello, violoncello
VIP *nmf, pl* **VIPs** : VIP
vira *nf* : welt (of a shoe)
virago *nf* : virago, shrew
viraje *nm* **1** : turn, swerve **2** : change
viral *adj* : viral
virar *vi* : to tack, to turn, to veer
virgen¹ *adj* : virgin ⟨lana virgen : virgin wool⟩
virgen² *nmf, pl* **vírgenes** : virgin ⟨la Santísima Virgen : the Blessed Virgin⟩
virginal *adj* : virginal, chaste
virginidad *nf* : virginity
Virgo *nmf* : Virgo
vírico, -ca *adj* : viral
viril *adj* : virile — **virilidad** *nf*

virrey, -rreina *n* : viceroy *m*, vicereine *f*
virtual *adj* : virtual — **virtualmente** *adv*
virtud *nf* **1** : virtue **2 en virtud de** : by virtue of
virtuosismo *nm* : virtuosity
virtuoso¹, -sa *adj* : virtuous — **virtuosamente** *adv*
virtuoso², -sa *n* : virtuoso
viruela *nf* **1** : smallpox **2** : pockmark
virulencia *nf* : virulence
virulento, -ta *adj* : virulent
virus *nm* : virus
viruta *nf* : shaving
visa *nf* : visa
visado *nm Spain* : visa
visaje *nm* : face, grimace ⟨hacer visajes : to make faces⟩
visceral *adj* : visceral
vísceras *nfpl* : viscera, entrails
visconde, -desa *n* : viscount *m*, viscountess *f*
viscosidad *nf* : viscosity
viscoso, -sa *adj* : viscous
visera *nf* : visor
visibilidad *nf* : visibility
visible *adj* : visible — **visiblemente** *adv*
visión *nf, pl* **visiones 1** : vision, eyesight **2** : view, perspective **3** : vision, illusion ⟨ver visiones : to be seeing things⟩
visionario, -ria *adj & n* : visionary
visita *nf* **1** : visit, call **2** : visitor **3 ir de visita** : to go visiting
visitador, -dora *n* : visitor, frequent caller
visitante¹ *adj* : visiting
visitante² *nmf* : visitor
visitar *vt* : to visit
vislumbrar *vt* **1** : to discern, to make out **2** : to begin to see, to have an inkling of
vislumbre *nf* : glimmer, gleam
viso *nm* **1** APARIENCIA : appearance ⟨tener visos de : to seem, to show signs of⟩ **2** DESTELLO : glint, gleam **3** : sheen, iridescence
visón *nm, pl* **visones** : mink
víspera *nf* **1** : eve, day before **2** **vísperas** *nfpl* : vespers
vista *nf* **1** VISIÓN : vision, eyesight **2** MIRADA : look, gaze, glance **3** PANORAMA : view, vista, panorama **4** : hearing (in court) **5 a primera vista** : at first sight **6 en vista de** : in view of **7 hacer la vista gorda** : to turn a blind eye **8 ¡hasta la vista!** : so long!, see you! **9 perder de vista** : to lose sight of **10 punto de vista** : point of view
vistazo *nm* : glance, look
viste, etc. → ver¹, vestir
visto¹ *pp* → **ver**
visto², -ta *adj* **1** : obvious, clear **2** : in view of, considering **3 estar bien visto** : to be approved of **4 estar mal visto** : to be frowned upon **5 por lo visto** : apparently **6 nunca visto** : unheard-of **7 visto que** : since, given that
visto³ *nm* **visto bueno** : approval

vistoso, -sa *adj* : colorful, bright
visual *adj* : visual — **visualmente** *adv*
visualización *nf, pl* **-ciones** : visualization
visualizar {21} *vt* **1** : to visualize **2** : to display (on a screen)
vital *adj* **1** : vital **2** : lively, dynamic
vitalicio, -cia *adj* : life, lifetime
vitalidad *nf* : vitality
vitamina *nf* : vitamin
vitamínico, -ca *adj* : vitamin ⟨complejos vitamínicos : vitamin compounds⟩
vitorear *vt* : to cheer, to acclaim
vitral *nm* : stained-glass window
vítreo, -rea *adj* : vitreous, glassy
vitrina *nf* **1** : showcase, display case **2** : store window
vitriolo *nm* : vitriol
vituperar *vt* : to condemn, to vituperate against
vituperio *nm* : vituperation, censure
viudez *nf* : widowerhood, widowhood
viudo, -da *n* : widower *m*, widow *f*
vivacidad *nf* VIVEZA : vivacity, liveliness
vivamente *adv* **1** : in a lively manner **2** : vividly **3** : strongly, acutely ⟨lo recomendamos vivamente : we strongly recommend it⟩
vivaque *nm* : bivouac
vivaquear *vi* : to bivouac
vivar *vi* : to cheer
vivaz *adj, pl* **vivaces 1** : lively, vivacious **2** : clever, sharp **3** : perennial
víveres *nmpl* : provisions, supplies, food
vivero *nm* **1** : nursery (for plants) **2** : hatchery, fish farm
viveza *nf* **1** VIVACIDAD : liveliness **2** BRILLO : vividness, brightness **3** ASTUCIA : cleverness, sharpness
vívido, -da *adj* : vivid, lively
vividor, -dora *n* : sponger, parasite
vivienda *nf* **1** : housing **2** MORADA : dwelling, home
viviente *adj* : living
vivificar {72} *vt* : to vivify, to give life to
vivir¹ *vi* **1** : to live, to be alive **2** SUBSISTIR : to subsist, to make a living **3** RESIDIR : to reside **4** : to spend one's life ⟨vive para trabajar : she lives to work⟩ **5** ~ **de** : to live on — *vt* **1** : to live ⟨vivir su vida : to live one's life⟩ **2** EXPERIMENTAR : to go through, to experience
vivir² *nm* **1** : life, lifestyle **2 de mal vivir** : disreputable
vivisección *nf, pl* **-ciones** : vivisection
vivo, -va *adj* **1** : alive **2** INTENSO : vivid, bright, intense **3** ANIMADO : lively, vivacious **4** ASTUTO : sharp, clever **5 en** ~ : live ⟨transmisión en vivo : live broadcast⟩ **6 al rojo vivo** : red-hot
vizconde, -desa *n* : viscount *m*, viscountess *f*
vocablo *nm* PALABRA : word
vocabulario *nm* : vocabulary
vocación *nf, pl* **-ciones** : vocation
vocacional *adj* : vocational
vocal¹ *adj* : vocal

vocal² *nmf* : member (of a committee, board, etc.)
vocal³ *nf* : vowel
vocalista *nmf* CANTANTE : singer, vocalist
vocalizar {21} *vi* : to vocalize
vocear *v* : to shout
vocerío *nm* : clamor, shouting
vocero, -ra *n* PORTAVOZ : spokesperson, spokesman *m*, spokeswoman *f*
vociferante *adj* : vociferous
vociferar *vi* GRITAR : to shout, to yell
vodevil *nm* : vaudeville
vodka *nm* : vodka
voladizo¹, -za *adj* : projecting
voladizo² *nm* : projection
volador, -dora *adj* : flying
volando *adv* : quickly, in a hurry
volante¹ *adj* : flying
volante² *nm* **1** : steering wheel **2** FOLLETO : flier, circular **3** : shuttlecock **4** : flywheel **5** : balance wheel (of a watch) **6** : ruffle, flounce
volar {19} *vi* **1** : to fly **2** CORRER : to hurry, to rush ⟨el tiempo vuela : time flies⟩ ⟨pasar volando : to fly past⟩ **3** DIVULGARSE : to spread ⟨unos rumores volaban : rumors were spreading around⟩ **4** DESAPARECER : to disappear ⟨el dinero ya voló : the money's already gone⟩ — *vt* **1** : to blow up, to demolish **2** : to irritate
volátil *adj* : volatile — **volatilidad** *nf*
volatilizar {21} *vt* : to volatize — **volatilizarse** *vr*
volcán *nm, pl* **volcanes** : volcano
volcánico, -ca *adj* : volcanic
volcar {82} *vt* **1** : to upset, to knock over, to turn over **2** : to empty out **3** : to make dizzy **4** : to cause a change of mind in **5** : to irritate — *vi* **1** : to overturn, to tip over **2** : to capsize — **volcarse** *vr* **1** : to overturn **2** : to do one's utmost
volea *nf* : volley (in sports)
volear *vi* : to volley (in sports)
voleibol *nm* : volleyball
voleo *nm* **al voleo** : haphazardly, at random
volframio *nm* : wolfram, tungsten
volición *nf, pl* **-ciones** : volition
volqué, etc. → **volcar**
voltaje *nm* : voltage
voltear *vt* **1** : to turn over, to turn upside down **2** : to reverse, to turn inside out **3** : to turn ⟨voltear la cara : to turn one's head⟩ **4** : to knock down — *vi* **1** : to roll over, to do somersaults **2** : to turn ⟨volteó a la izquierda : he turned left⟩ — **voltearse** *vr* **1** : to turn around **2** : to change one's allegiance
voltereta *nf* : somersault, tumble
voltio *nm* : volt
volubilidad *nf* : fickleness, changeableness
voluble *adj* : fickle, changeable
volumen *nm, pl* **-lúmenes 1** TOMO : volume, book **2** : capacity, size, bulk **3** CANTIDAD : amount ⟨el volumen de

ventas : the volume of sales⟩ **4** : volume, loudness

voluminoso, -sa *adj* : voluminous, massive, bulky

voluntad *nf* **1** : will, volition **2** DESEO : desire, wish **3** INTENCIÓN : intention **4 a voluntad** : at will **5 buena voluntad** : good will **6 mala voluntad** : ill will **7 fuerza de voluntad** : willpower

voluntario[1]**, -ria** *adj* : voluntary — **voluntariamente** *adv*

voluntario[2]**, -ria** *n* : volunteer

voluntarioso, -sa *adj* **1** : stubborn **2** : willing, eager

voluptuosidad *nf* : voluptuousness

voluptuoso, -sa *adj* : voluptuous — **voluptuosamente** *adv*

voluta *nf* : spiral, column (of smoke)

volver {89} *vi* **1** : to return, to come or go back ⟨volver a casa : to return home⟩ **2** : to revert ⟨volver al tema : to get back to the subject⟩ **3 ~ a** : to do again ⟨volvieron a llamar : they called again⟩ **4 volver en sí** : to come to, to regain consciousness — *vt* **1** : to turn, to turn over, to turn inside out **2** : to return, to repay, to restore **3** : to cause, to make ⟨la volvía loca : it was driving her crazy⟩ — **volverse** *vr* **1** : to become ⟨se volvió deprimido : he became depressed⟩ **2** : to turn around

vomitar *vi* : to vomit — *vt* **1** : to vomit **2** : to spew out (lava, etc.)

vómito *nm* **1** : vomiting **2** : vomit

voracidad *nf* : voracity

vorágine *nf* : whirlpool, maelstrom

voraz *adj, pl* **voraces** : voracious — **vorazmente** *adv*

vórtice *nm* **1** : whirlpool, vortex **2** TORBELLINO : whirlwind

vos *pron* (*in some regions of Latin America*) : you

vosear *vt* : to address as *vos*

vosotros, -tras *pron pl Spain* **1** : you, yourselves **2** : ye

votación *nf, pl* **-ciones** : vote, voting

votante *nmf* : voter

votar *vi* : to vote — *vt* : to vote for

votivo, -va *adj* : votive

voto *nm* **1** : vote **2** : vow (in religion) **3 votos** *nmpl* : good wishes

voy → **ir**

voz *nf, pl* **voces** **1** : voice **2** : opinion, say **3** GRITO : shout, yell **4** : sound **5** VOCABLO : word, term **6** : rumor **7 a**

voz en cuello : at the top of one's lungs **8 dar voces** : to shout **9 en voz alta** : aloud, in a loud voice **10 en voz baja** : softly, in a low voice

vudú *nm* : voodoo

vuelco *nm* : upset, overturning ⟨me dio un vuelco el corazón : my heart skipped a beat⟩

vuela, etc. → **volar**

vuelca, vuelque etc. → **volcar**

vuelo *nm* **1** : flight, flying ⟨alzar el vuelo : to take flight⟩ **2** : flight (of an aircraft) ⟨vuelo espacial : space flight⟩ **3** : flare, fullness (of clothing) **4 al vuelo** : on the wing

vuelta *nf* **1** GIRO : turn ⟨se dio la vuelta : he turned around⟩ **2** REVOLUCIÓN : circle, revolution ⟨dio la vuelta al mundo : she went around the world⟩ ⟨las ruedas daban vueltas : the wheels were spinning⟩ **3** : flip, turn ⟨le dio la vuelta : she flipped it over⟩ **4** : bend, curve ⟨a la vuelta de la esquina : around the corner⟩ **5** REGRESO : return ⟨de ida y vuelta : round trip⟩ ⟨a vuelta de correo : return mail⟩ **6** : round, lap (in sports or games) **7** PASEO : walk, drive, ride ⟨dio una vuelta : he went for a walk⟩ **8** DORSO, REVÉS : back, other side ⟨a la vuelta : on the back⟩ **9** : cuff (of pants) **10 darle vueltas** : to think over **11 estar de vuelta** : to be back

vuelto *pp* → **volver**

vuelve, etc. → **volver**

vuestro[1]**, -stra** *adj Spain* : your, of yours ⟨vuestros coches : your cars⟩ ⟨una amiga vuestra : a friend of yours⟩

vuestro[2]**, -stra** *pron Spain,* (*with definite article*) : yours ⟨la vuestra es más grande : yours is bigger⟩ ⟨esos son los vuestros : those are yours⟩

vulcanizar {21} *vt* : to vulcanize

vulgar *adj* **1** : common **2** : vulgar

vulgaridad *nf* : vulgarity

vulgarismo *nm* : vulgarism

vulgarizar {21} *vt* : to vulgarize, to popularize

vulgarmente *adv* : vulgarly, popularly

vulgo *nm* **el vulgo** : the masses, common people

vulnerable *adj* : vulnerable — **vulnerabilidad** *nf*

vulnerar *vt* **1** : to injure, to damage (one's reputation or honor) **2** : to violate, to break (a law or contract)

W

w *nf* : twenty-fourth letter of the Spanish alphabet

wafle *nm* : waffle

waflera *nf* : waffle iron

wapití *nm* : wapiti, elk

whisky *nm, pl* **whiskys** *or* **whiskies** : whiskey

wigwam *nm* : wigwam

X

x *nf* : twenty-fifth letter of the Spanish alphabet
xenofobia *nf* : xenophobia
xenófobo¹, -ba *adj* : xenophobic
xenófobo², -ba *n* : xenophobe
xenón *nm* : xenon
xerocopiar *vt* : to photocopy, to xerox
xilófono *nm* : xylophone

Y

y¹ *nf* : twenty-sixth letter of the Spanish alphabet
y² *conj* (**e** *before words beginning with i- or hi-*) **1** : and ⟨mi hermano y yo : my brother and I⟩ ⟨¿y los demás? : and (what about) the others?⟩ **2** (*used in numbers*) ⟨cincuenta y cinco : fifty-five⟩ **3** *fam* : well ⟨y por supuesto : well, of course⟩
ya¹ *adv* **1** : already ⟨ya terminó : she's finished already⟩ **2** : now, right now ⟨¡hazlo ya! : do it now!⟩ ⟨ya mismo : right away⟩ **3** : later, soon ⟨ya iremos : we'll go later on⟩ **4** : no longer, anymore ⟨ya no fuma : he no longer smokes⟩ **5** (*used for emphasis*) ⟨¡ya lo sé! : I know!⟩ ⟨ya lo creo : of course⟩ **6 no ya** : not only ⟨no ya lloran sino gritan : they're not only crying but screaming⟩ **7 ya que** : now that, since ⟨ya que sabe la verdad : now that she knows the truth⟩
ya² *conj* **ya . . . ya** : whether . . . or, first . . . then ⟨ya le gusta, ya no : first he likes it, then he doesn't⟩
yac *nm* : yak
yacer {90} *vi* : to lie ⟨en esta tumba yacen sus abuelos : his grandparents lie in this grave⟩
yacimiento *nm* : bed, deposit ⟨yacimiento petrolífero : oil field⟩
yaga, etc. → **yacer**
yanqui *adj & nmf* : Yankee
yarda *nf* : yard
yate *nm* : yacht
yaz, yazca, yazga etc. → **yacer**
yedra *nf* : ivy
yegua *nf* : mare
yelmo *nm* : helmet
yema *nf* **1** : bud, shoot **2** : yolk (of an egg) **3 yema del dedo** : fingertip
yemenita *adj & nmf* : Yemenite
yen *nm* : yen (currency)
yendo → **ir**

yerba *nf* **1** *or* **yerba mate** : maté **2** → **hierba**
yerga, yergue etc. → **erguir**
yermo¹, -ma *adj* : barren, deserted
yermo² *nm* : wasteland
yerno *nm* : son-in-law
yerra, etc. → **errar**
yerro *nm* : blunder, mistake
yerto, -ta *adj* : rigid, stiff
yesca *nf* : tinder
yeso *nm* **1** : plaster **2** : gypsum
yo¹ *nm* : ego, self
yo² *pron* **1** : I **2** : me ⟨todos menos yo : everyone except me⟩ ⟨tan bajo como yo : as short as me⟩ **3 soy yo** : it is I, it's me
yodado, -da *adj* : iodized
yodo *nm* : iodine
yoduro *nm* : iodide
yoga *nm* : yoga
yogui *nm* : yogi
yogurt *or* **yogur** *nm* : yogurt
yola *nf* : yawl
yoyo *or* **yoyó** *nm* : yo-yo
yuca *nf* **1** : yucca (plant) **2** : cassava, manioc
yucateco¹, -ca *adj* : of or from the Yucatán
yucateco², -ca *n* : person from the Yucatán
yudo → **judo**
yugo *nm* : yoke
yugoslavo, -va *adj & n* : Yugoslavian
yugular *adj* : jugular ⟨vena yugular : jugular vein⟩
yungas *nfpl Bol, Chile, Peru* : warm tropical valleys
yunque *nm* : anvil
yunta *nf* : yoke, team (of oxen)
yuppy *nmf, pl* **yuppies** : yuppie
yute *nm* : jute
yuxtaponer {60} *vt* : to juxtapose — **yuxtaposición** *nf*

Z

z *nf* : twenty-seventh letter of the Spanish alphabet
zacate *nm CA, Mex* **1** : grass, forage **2** : hay
zafacón *nm, pl* **-cones** *Car* : wastebasket
zafar *vt* : to loosen, to untie — **zafarse** *vr* **1** : to loosen up, to come undone **2** : to get free of
zafio, -fia *adj* : coarse, crude
zafiro *nm* : sapphire
zaga *nf* **1** : defense (in sports) **2 a la zaga** *or* **en ~** : behind, in the rear
zagual *nm* : paddle (of a canoe)

zaguán *nm, pl* **zaguanes** : front hall, vestibule
zaherir {76} *vt* **1** : to criticize sharply **2** : to wound, to mortify
zahones *nmpl* : chaps
zaino, -na *adj* : chestnut (color)
zalamería *nf* : flattery, sweet talk
zalamero[1], **-ra** *adj* : flattering, fawning
zalamero[2], **-ra** *n* : flatterer
zambiano, -na *adj & nmf* : Zambian
zambullida *nf* : dive, plunge
zambullirse {38} *vr* : to dive, to plunge
zanahoria *nf* : carrot
zancada *nf* : stride, step
zancadilla *nf* **1** : trip, stumble **2** *fam* : trick, ruse
zancos *nmpl* : stilts
zancuda *nf* : wading bird
zancudo *nm* MOSQUITO : mosquito
zángano *nm* : drone, male bee
zanja *nf* : ditch, trench
zanjar *vt* ACLARAR : to settle, to clear up, to resolve
zapallo *nm Arg, Chile, Peru, Uru* : pumpkin
zapapico *nm* : pickax
zapata *nf* : brake shoe
zapatería *nf* **1** : shoemaker's, shoe factory **2** : shoe store
zapatero[1], **-ra** *adj* : dry, tough, poorly cooked
zapatero[2], **-ra** *n* : shoemaker, cobbler
zapatilla *nf* **1** PANTUFLA : slipper **2** *or* **zapatilla de deporte** : sneaker
zapato *nm* : shoe
zar, zarina *n* : czar *m*, czarina *f*
zarandear *vt* **1** : to sift, to sieve **2** : to shake, to jostle, to jiggle
zarapito *nm* : curlew
zarcillo *nm* **1** : earring **2** : tendril (of a plant)
zarigüeya *nf* : opossum
zarista *adj & nmf* : czarist
zarpa *nf* : paw
zarpar *vi* : to set sail, to raise anchor
zarza *nf* : bramble, blackberry bush
zarzamora *nf* **1** : blackberry **2** : bramble, blackberry bush

zarzaparrilla *nf* : sarsaparilla
zepelin *nm, pl* **-lines** : zeppelin
zigoto *nm* : zygote
zigzag *nm, pl* **zigzags** *or* **zigzagues** : zigzag
zigzaguear *vi* : to zigzag
zimbabuense *adj & nmf* : Zimbabwean
zinc *nm* : zinc
zinnia *nf* : zinnia
zíper *nm CA, Mex* : zipper
zircón *nm, pl* **zircones** : zircon
zócalo *nm Mex* : main square
zodíaco *or* **zodiaco** *nm* : zodiac — **zodíacal** *adj*
zombi *or* **zombie** *nmf* : zombie
zona *nf* : zone, district, area
zonzo[1], **-za** *adj* : stupid, silly
zonzo[2], **-za** *n* : idiot, nitwit
zoo *nm* : zoo
zoología *nf* : zoology
zoológico[1], **-ca** *adj* : zoological
zoológico[2] *nm* : zoo
zoólogo, -ga *n* : zoologist
zoom *nm* : zoom lens
zopilote *nm CA, Mex* : buzzard
zoquete *nmf fam* : oaf, blockhead
zorrillo *nm* MOFETA : skunk
zorro[1], **-rra** *adj* : sly, crafty
zorro[2], **-rra** *n* **1** : fox, vixen **2** : sly crafty person
zorzal *nm* : thrush
zozobra *nf* : anxiety, worry
zozobrar *vi* : to capsize
zueco *nm* : clog (shoe)
zulú[1] *adj & nmf* : Zulu
zulú[2] *nm* : Zulu (language)
zumaque *nm* : sumac
zumbar *vi* : to buzz, to hum — *vt fam* **1** : to hit, to thrash **2** : to make fun of
zumbido *nm* : buzzing, humming
zumo *nf* JUGO : juice
zurcir {83} *vt* : to darn, to mend
zurdo[1], **-da** *adj* : left-handed
zurdo[2], **-da** *n* : left-handed person
zurza, etc. → **zurcir**
zutano, -na → **fulano**

English–Spanish
Dictionary

A

a[1] ['eɪ] *n, pl* **a's** *or* **as** ['eɪz] : primera letra del alfabeto inglés

a[2] [ə, 'eɪ] *art* (**an** /ən, 'æn] before vowel or silent h) **1** : un *m*, una *f* ⟨a house : una casa⟩ ⟨half an hour : media hora⟩ ⟨what a surprise! : ¡qué sorpresa!⟩ **2** PER : por, a la, al ⟨30 kilometers an hour : 30 kilómetros por hora⟩ ⟨twice a month : dos veces al mes⟩

aardvark ['ard,vark] *n* : oso *m* hormiguero

aback [ə'bæk] *adv* **1** : por sorpresa **2 to be taken aback** : quedarse desconcertado

abacus ['æbəkəs] *n, pl* **abaci** ['æbə,saɪ, -,ki:] *or* **abacuses** : ábaco *m*

abaft [ə'bæft] *adv* : a popa

abalone [,æbə'lo:ni] *n* : abulón *m*, oreja *f* marina

abandon[1] [ə'bændən] *vt* **1** DESERT, FORSAKE : abandonar, desamparar (a alguien), desertar de (algo) **2** GIVE UP, SUSPEND : renunciar a, suspender ⟨he abandoned the search : suspendió la búsqueda⟩ **3** EVACUATE, LEAVE : abandonar, evacuar, dejar ⟨to abandon ship : abandonar el buque⟩ **4 to abandon oneself** : entregarse, abandonarse

abandon[2] *n* : desenfreno *m* ⟨with wild abandon : desenfrenadamente⟩

abandoned [ə'bændənd] *adj* **1** DESERTED : abandonado **2** UNRESTRAINED : desenfrenado, desinhibido

abandonment [ə'bændənmənt] *n* : abandono *m*, desamparo *m*

abase [ə'beɪs] *vt* **abased; abasing** : degradar, humillar, rebajar

abash [ə'bæʃ] *vt* : avergonzar, abochornar

abashed [ə'bæʃt] *adj* : avergonzado

abate [ə'beɪt] *vi* **abated; abating** : amainar, menguar, disminuir

abattoir ['æbə,twar] *n* : matadero *m*

abbess ['æbɪs, -,bɛs, -bəs] *n* : abadesa *f*

abbey ['æbi] *n, pl* **-beys** : abadía *f*

abbot ['æbət] *n* : abad *m*

abbreviate [ə'bri:vi,eɪt] *vt* **-ated; -ating** : abreviar

abbreviation [ə,bri:vi'eɪʃən] *n* : abreviación *f*, abreviatura *f*

ABC's [,eɪ,bi:'si:z] *npl* : abecé *m*

abdicate ['æbdɪ,keɪt] *v* **-cated; -cating** : abdicar

abdication [,æbdɪ'keɪʃən] *n* : abdicación *f*

abdomen ['æbdəmən, æb'do:mən] *n* : abdomen *m*, vientre *m*

abdominal [æb'damənəl] *adj* : abdominal — **abdominally** *adv*

abduct [æb'dʌkt] *vt* : raptar, secuestrar

abduction [æb'dʌkʃən] *n* : rapto *m*, secuestro *m*

abductor [æb'dʌktər] *n* : raptor *m*, -tora *f*; secuestrador *m*, -dora *f*

abed [ə'bɛd] *adv & adj* : en cama

aberrant [æ'bɛrənt, 'æbərənt] *adj* **1** ABNORMAL : anormal, aberrante **2** ATYPICAL : anómalo, atípico

aberration [,æbə'reɪʃən] *n* **1** : aberración *f* **2** DERANGEMENT : perturbación *f* mental

abet [ə'bɛt] *vt* **abetted; abetting** ASSIST : ayudar ⟨to aid and abet : ser cómplice de⟩

abeyance [ə'beɪənts] *n* : desuso *m*, suspensión *f*

abhor [əb'hor, æb-] *vt* **-horred; -horring** : abominar, aborrecer

abhorrence [əb'hɔrənts, æb-] *n* : aborrecimiento *m*, odio *m*

abhorrent [əb'hɔrənt, æb-] *adj* : abominable, aborrecible, odioso

abide [ə'baɪd] *v* **abode** [ə'bo:d] *or* **abided; abiding** *vt* STAND : soportar, tolerar ⟨I can't abide them : no los puedo ver⟩ — *vi* **1** ENDURE : quedar, permanecer **2** DWELL : morar, residir **3 to abide by** : atenerse a

ability [ə'bɪləti] *n, pl* **-ties 1** CAPABILITY : aptitud *f*, capacidad *f*, facultad *f* **2** COMPETENCE : competencia *f* **3** TALENT : talento *m*, don *m*, habilidad *f*

abject ['æb,dʒɛkt, æb'-] *adj* **1** WRETCHED : miserable, desdichado **2** HOPELESS : abatido, desesperado **3** SERVILE : servil ⟨abject flattery : halagos serviles⟩ — **abjectly** *adv*

abjure [æb'dʒʊr] *vt* **-jured; -juring** : abjurar de

ablaze [ə'bleɪz] *adj* **1** BURNING : ardiendo, en llamas **2** RADIANT : resplandeciente, radiante

able ['eɪbəl] *adj* **abler; ablest 1** CAPABLE : capaz, hábil **2** COMPETENT : competente

ablution [ə'blu:ʃən] *n* : ablución *f* ⟨to perform one's ablutions : lavarse⟩

ably ['eɪbəli] *adv* : hábilmente, eficientemente

abnormal [æb'nɔrməl] *adj* : anormal — **abnormally** *adv*

abnormality [,æbnər'mæləti, -nɔr-] *n, pl* **-ties** : anormalidad *f*

aboard[1] [ə'bord] *adv* : a bordo

aboard[2] *prep* : a bordo de

abode[1] → **abide**

abode[2] [ə'bo:d] *n* : morada *f*, residencia *f*, vivienda *f*

abolish [ə'balɪʃ] *vt* : abolir, suprimir

abolition [,æbə'lɪʃən] *n* : abolición *f*, supresión *f*

abominable [ə'bamənəbəl] *adj* DETESTABLE : abominable, aborrecible, espantoso

abominate [ə'bamə,neɪt] *vt* **-nated; -nating** : abominar, aborrecer

abomination [ə,bamə'neɪʃən] *n* : abominación *f*

aboriginal [,æbə'rɪdʒənəl] *adj* : aborigen, indígena

aborigine [,æbə'rɪdʒəni] *n* NATIVE : aborigen *mf*, indígena *mf*

abort [ə'bɔrt] *vt* **1** : abortar (en medicina) **2** CALL OFF : suspender, abandonar — *vi* : abortar, hacerse un aborto

abortion [ə'bɔrʃən] *n* : aborto *m*

abortive [ə'bɔrtɪv] *adj* UNSUCCESSFUL : fracasado, frustrado, malogrado

abound [ə'baund] *vi* **to abound in** : abundar en, estar lleno de

about¹ [ə'baut] *adv* **1** APPROXIMATELY : aproximadamente, casi, más o menos **2** AROUND : por todas partes, alrededor ⟨the children are running about : los niños están corriendo por todas partes⟩ **3 to be about to** : estar a punto de **4 to be up and about** : estar levantado

about² *prep* **1** AROUND : alrededor de **2** CONCERNING : de, acerca de, sobre ⟨he always talks about politics : siempre habla de política⟩

above¹ [ə'bʌv] *adv* **1** OVERHEAD : por encima, arriba **2** : más arriba ⟨as stated above : como se indica más arriba⟩

above² *adj* : anterior, antedicho ⟨for the above reasons : por las razones antedichas⟩

above³ *prep* **1** OVER : encima de, arriba de, sobre **2** : superior a, por encima de ⟨he's above those things : él está por encima de esas cosas⟩ **3** : más de, superior a ⟨he earns above $50,000 : gana más de $50,000⟩ ⟨a number above 10 : un número superior a 10⟩ **4 above all** : sobre todo

aboveboard¹ [ə'bʌv₁bord, -₁bord] *adv* **open and aboveboard** : sin tapujos

aboveboard² *adj* : legítimo, sincero

abrade [ə'breɪd] *vt* **abraded; abrading 1** ERODE : erosionar, corroer **2** SCRAPE : escoriar, raspar

abrasion [ə'breɪʒən] *n* **1** SCRAPE, SCRATCH : raspadura *f*, rasguño *m* **2** EROSION : erosión *f*

abrasive¹ [ə'breɪsɪv] *adj* **1** ROUGH : abrasivo, áspero **2** BRUSQUE, IRRITATING : brusco, irritante

abrasive² *n* : abrasivo *m*

abreast [ə'brest] *adv* **1** : en fondo, al lado ⟨to march three abreast : marchar de tres en fondo⟩ **2 to keep abreast** : mantenerse al día

abridge [ə'brɪdʒ] *vt* **abridged; abridging** : compendiar, resumir

abridgment *or* **abridgement** [ə'brɪdʒmənt] *n* : compendio *m*, resumen *m*

abroad [ə'brɔd] *adv* **1** ABOUT, WIDELY : por todas partes, en todas direcciones ⟨the news spread abroad : la noticia corrió por todas partes⟩ **2** OVERSEAS : en el extranjero, en el exterior

abrogate ['æbrə₁geɪt] *vt* **-gated; -gating** : abrogar

abrupt [ə'brʌpt] *adj* **1** SUDDEN : abrupto, repentino, súbito **2** BRUSQUE, CURT : brusco, cortante — **abruptly** *adv*

abscess ['æb₁ses] *n* : absceso *m*

abscond [æb'skand] *vi* : huir, fugarse

absence ['æbsənts] *n* **1** : ausencia *f* (de una persona) **2** LACK : falta *f*, carencia *f*

absent¹ [æb'sent] *vt* **to absent oneself** : ausentarse

absent² ['æbsənt] *adj* : ausente

absentee [₁æbsən'ti:] *n* : ausente *mf*

absentminded [₁æbsənt'maɪndəd] *adj* : distraído, despistado

absentmindedly [₁æbsənt'maɪndədli] *adv* : distraídamente

absentmindedness [₁æbsənt'maɪndədnəs] *n* : distracción *f*, despiste *m*

absolute ['æbsə₁lu:t, ₁æbsə'lu:t] *adj* **1** COMPLETE, PERFECT : completo, pleno, perfecto **2** UNCONDITIONAL : absoluto, incondicional **3** DEFINITE : categórico, definitivo

absolutely ['æbsə₁lu:tli, ₁æbsə'lu:tli] *adv* **1** COMPLETELY : completamente, absolutamente **2** CERTAINLY : desde luego ⟨do you agree? absolutely! : ¿estás de acuerdo? ¡desde luego!⟩

absolution [₁æbsə'lu:ʃən] *n* : absolución *f*

absolutism ['æbsə₁lu:₁tɪzəm] *n* : absolutismo *m*

absolve [əb'zalv, æb-, -'salv] *vt* **-solved; -solving** : absolver, perdonar

absorb [əb'zɔrb, æb-, -'sɔrb] *vt* **1** : absorber, embeber (un líquido), amortiguar (un golpe, la luz) **2** ENGROSS : absorber **3** ASSIMILATE : asimilar

absorbed [əb'zɔrbd, æb-, -'sɔrbd] *adj* ENGROSSED : absorto, ensimismado

absorbency [əb'zɔrbəntsi, æb-, -'sɔr-] *n* : absorbencia *f*

absorbent [əb'zɔrbənt, æb-, -'sɔr-] *adj* : absorbente

absorbing [əb'zɔrbɪŋ, æb-, -'sɔr-] *adj* : absorbente, fascinante

absorption [əb'zɔrpʃən, æb-, -'sɔrp-] *n* **1** : absorción *f* **2** CONCENTRATION : concentración *f*

abstain [əb'steɪn, æb-] *vi* : abstenerse

abstainer [əb'steɪnər, æb-] *n* : abstemio *m*, -mia *f*

abstemious [æb'sti:miəs] *adj* : abstemio, sobrio — **abstemiously** *adv*

abstention [əb'stɛntʃən, æb-] *n* : abstención *f*

abstinence ['æbstənənts] *n* : abstinencia *f*

abstract¹ [æb'strækt, 'æb₁-] *vt* **1** EXTRACT : abstraer, extraer **2** SUMMARIZE : compendiar, resumir

abstract² *adj* : abstracto — **abstractly** [æb'stræktli, 'æb₁-] *adv*

abstract³ ['æb₁strækt] *n* : resumen *m*, compendio *m*, sumario *m*

abstraction [æb'strækʃən] *n* **1** : abstracción *f*, idea *f* abstracta **2** ABSENTMINDEDNESS : distracción *f*

abstruse [əb'stru:s, æb-] *adj* : abstruso, recóndito — **abstrusely** *adv*

absurd [əb'sərd, -'zərd] *adj* : absurdo, ridículo, disparatado — **absurdly** *adv*

absurdity [əb'sərdəṭi, -'zər-] *n, pl* **-ties 1**
: absurdo *m* **2** NONSENSE : disparate
m, despropósito *m*
abundance [ə'bʌndənts] *n* : abundancia
f
abundant [ə'bʌndənt] *adj* : abundante,
cuantioso, copioso
abundantly [ə'bʌndəntli] *adv* : abundantemente, en abundancia
abuse¹ [ə'bju:z] *vt* **abused; abusing 1**
MISUSE : abusar de **2** MISTREAT : maltratar **3** REVILE : insultar, injuriar,
denostar
abuse² [ə'bju:s] *n* **1** MISUSE : abuso *m*
2 MISTREATMENT : abuso *m*, maltrato
m **3** INSULTS : insultos *mpl*, impro-
perios *mpl* ⟨a string of abuse : una serie
de improperios⟩
abuser [ə'bju:zər] *n* : abusador *m*, -dora
f
abusive [ə'bju:sɪv] *adj* **1** ABUSING : abusivo **2** INSULTING : ofensivo, injurioso,
insultante — **abusively** *adv*
abut [ə'bʌt] *v* **abutted; abutting** *vt* : bordear — *vi* **to abut on** : colindar con
abutment [ə'bʌtmənt] *n* **1** BUTTRESS
: contrafuerte *m*, estribo *m* **2** CLOSE-
NESS : contigüidad *f*
abysmal [ə'bɪzməl] *adj* **1** DEEP : abismal, insondable **2** TERRIBLE : atroz,
desastroso
abysmally [ə'bɪzməli] *adv* : desastrosa-
mente, terriblemente
abyss [ə'bɪs, 'æbɪs] *n* : abismo *m*, sima
f
acacia [ə'keɪʃə] *n* : acacia *f*
academic¹ [ˌækə'dɛmɪk] *adj* **1** : académico **2** THEORETICAL : teórico —
academically [-mɪkli] *adv*
academic² *n* : académico *m*, -ca *f*
academician [ˌækədə'mɪʃən] *n* → **academic**
academy [ə'kædəmi] *n, pl* **-mies** : academia *f*
acanthus [ə'kæntθəs] *n* : acanto *m*
accede [æk'si:d] *vi* **-ceded; -ceding 1**
AGREE : acceder, consentir **2** ASCEND
: subir, acceder ⟨he acceded to the
throne : subió al trono⟩
accelerate [ɪk'sɛlə,reɪt, æk-] *v* **-ated;
-ating** *vt* : acelerar, apresurar — *vi*
: acelerar (dícese de un carro)
acceleration [ɪk,sɛlə'reɪʃən, æk-] *n*
: aceleración *f*
accelerator [ɪk'sɛlə,reɪṭər, æk-] *n* : acelerador *m*
accent¹ ['æk,sɛnt, æk'sɛnt] *vt* : acentuar
accent² ['æk,sɛnt, -sənt] *n* **1** : acento *m*
2 EMPHASIS, STRESS : énfasis *m*, acento *m*
accentuate [ɪk'sɛntʃʊ,eɪt, æk-] *vt* **-ated;
-ating** : acentuar, poner énfasis en
accept [ɪk'sɛpt, æk-] *vt* **1** : aceptar **2** AC-
KNOWLEDGE : admitir, reconocer
acceptability [ɪk,sɛptə'bɪləṭi, æk-] *n*
: aceptabilidad *f*

acceptable [ɪk'sɛptəbəl, æk-] *adj*
: aceptable, admisible — **acceptably**
[-bli] *adv*
acceptance [ɪk'sɛptənts, æk-] *n* : aceptación *f*, aprobación *f*
access¹ ['æk,sɛs] *vt* : obtener acceso a,
entrar a
access² *n* : acceso *m*
accessibility [ɪk,sɛsə'bɪləṭi] *n, pl* **-ties**
: accesibilidad *f*
accessible [ɪk'sɛsəbəl, æk-] *adj* : accesible, asequible
accession [ɪk'sɛʃən, æk-] *n* **1** : ascenso
f, subida *f* (al trono, etc.) **2** ACQUISI-
TION : adquisición *f*
accessory¹ [ɪk'sɛsəri, æk-] *adj* : auxiliar
accessory² *n, pl* **-ries 1** : accesorio *m*,
complemento *m* **2** ACCOMPLICE : cómplice *mf*
accident ['æksədənt] *n* **1** MISHAP : accidente *m* **2** CHANCE : casualidad *f*
accidental [ˌæksə'dɛntəl] *adj* : accidental, casual, imprevisto, fortuito
accidentally [ˌæksə'dɛntəli, -'dɛntli] *adv*
1 BY CHANCE : por casualidad **2** UN-
INTENTIONALLY : sin querer, involuntariamente
acclaim¹ [ə'kleɪm] *vt* : aclamar, elogiar
acclaim² *n* : aclamación *f*, elogio *m*
acclamation [ˌæklə'meɪʃən] *n* : aclamación *f*
acclimate ['æklə,meɪt, ə'klaɪmət] → **acclimatize**
acclimatize [ə'klaɪmə,taɪz] *v* **-tized;
-tizing** *vt* **1** : aclimatar **2 to acclimatize oneself** : aclimatarse
accolade ['ækə,leɪd, -,lɑd] *n* **1** PRAISE
: elogio *m* **2** AWARD : galardón *m*
accommodate [ə'kamə,deɪt] *vt* **-dated;
-dating 1** ADAPT : acomodar, adaptar
2 SATISFY : tener en cuenta, satisfacer
3 HOLD : dar cabida a, tener cabida
para
accommodation [ə,kamə'deɪʃən] *n* **1**
: adaptación *f*, adecuación *f* **2 accommodations** *npl* LODGING : alojamiento *m*, hospedaje *m*
accompaniment   [ə'kʌmpənəmənt,
-'kam-] *n* : acompañamiento *m*
accompanist [ə'kʌmpənɪst, -'kam-] *n*
: acompañante *mf*
accompany [ə'kʌmpəni, -'kam-] *vt*
-nied; -nying : acompañar
accomplice [ə'kampləs, -'kʌm-] *n* : cómplice *mf*
accomplish [ə'kamplɪʃ, -'kʌm-] *vt* : efectuar, realizar, lograr, llevar a cabo
accomplished [ə'kamplɪʃt, -'kʌm-] *adj*
: consumado, logrado
accomplishment   [ə'kamplɪʃmənt,
-'kam-] *n* **1** ACHIEVEMENT : logro *m*,
éxito *m* **2** SKILL : destreza *f*, habilidad
f
accord¹ [ə'kɔrd] *vt* GRANT : conceder,
otorgar — *vi* **to accord with** : concordar con, conformarse con
accord² *n* **1** AGREEMENT : acuerdo *m*,
convenio *m* **2** VOLITION : voluntad *f*

⟨on one's own accord : voluntaria-mente, de motu proprio⟩

accordance [əˈkɔrdənts] *n* **1** ACCORD : acuerdo *m*, conformidad *f* **2 in accordance with** : conforme a, según, de acuerdo con

accordingly [əˈkɔrdɪŋli] *adv* **1** CORRE-SPONDINGLY : en consecuencia **2** CON-SEQUENTLY : por consiguiente, por lo tanto

according to [əˈkɔrdɪŋ] *prep* : según, de acuerdo con, conforme a

accordion [əˈkɔrdiən] *n* : acordeón *m*

accordionist [əˈkɔrdiənɪst] *n* : acorde-onista *mf*

accost [əˈkɔst] *vt* : abordar, dirigirse a

account[1] [əˈkaʊnt] *vt* : considerar, esti-mar ⟨he accounts himself lucky : se considera afortunado⟩ — *vi* **to account for** : dar cuenta de, explicar

account[2] *n* **1** : cuenta *f* ⟨savings account : cuenta de ahorros⟩ **2** EXPLANATION : versión *f*, explicación *f* **3** REPORT : re-lato *m*, informe *m* **4** IMPORTANCE : im-portancia *f* ⟨to be of no account : no tener importancia⟩ **5 on account of** BECAUSE OF : a causa de, debido a, por **6 on no account** : de ninguna manera

accountability [ə,kaʊntəˈbiləti] *n* : re-sponsabilidad *f*

accountable [əˈkaʊntəbəl] *adj* : respon-sable

accountant [əˈkaʊntənt] *n* : contador *m*, -dora *f*; contable *mf Spain*

accounting [əˈkaʊntɪŋ] *n* : contabilidad *f*

accoutrements *or* **accouterments** [ə-ˈkuːtrəmənts, -ˈkuːtər-] *npl* **1** EQUIP-MENT : equipo *m*, avíos *mpl* **2** ACCES-SORIES : accesorios *mpl* **3** TRAPPINGS : símbolos *mpl* ⟨the accoutrements of power : los símbolos del poder⟩

accredit [əˈkrɛdət] *vt* : acreditar, autor-izar

accreditation [ə,krɛdəˈteɪʃən] *n* : acred-itación *f*, homologación *f*

accretion [əˈkriːʃən] *n* **1** : acrecen-tamiento *m* (proceso) **2** : acreción *f*, acrecencia *f* (producto)

accrual [əˈkruːəl] *n* : incremento *m*, acu-mulación *f*

accrue [əˈkruː] *vi* **-crued; -cruing** : acu-mularse, aumentarse

accumulate [əˈkjuːmjə,leɪt] *v* **-lated; -lating** *vt* : acumular, amontonar — *vi* : acumularse, amontonarse

accumulation [ə,kjuːmjəˈleɪʃən] *n* : acu-mulación *f*, amontonamiento *m*

accuracy [ˈækjərəsi] *n* : exactitud *f*, pre-cisión *f*

accurate [ˈækjərət] *adj* : exacto, correc-to, fiel, preciso — **accurately** *adv*

accusation [,ækjəˈzeɪʃən] *n* : acusación *f*

accusatory [əˈkjuːzə,tori] *adj* : acusato-rio

accuse [əˈkjuːz] *vt* **-cused; -cusing** : acusar, delatar, denunciar

accused [əˈkjuːzd] *ns & pl* DEFENDANT : acusado *m*, -da *f*

accuser [əˈkjuːzər] *n* : acusador *m*, -dora *f*

accustom [əˈkʌstəm] *vt* : acostumbrar, habituar

ace [ˈeɪs] *n* : as *m*

acerbic [əˈsərbɪk, æ-] *adj* : acerbo, mor-daz

acetate [ˈæsə,teɪt] *n* : acetato *m*

acetic [əˈsiːtɪk] *adj* : acético

acetone [ˈæsə,toːn] *n* : acetona *f*

acetylene [əˈsɛtələn, -tə,liːn] *n* : aceti-leno *m*

ache[1] [ˈeɪk] *vi* **ached; aching** **1** : doler **2 to ache for** : anhelar, ansiar

ache[2] *n* : dolor *m*

achieve [əˈtʃiːv] *vt* **achieved; achieving** : lograr, alcanzar, conseguir, realizar

achievement [əˈtʃiːvmənt] *n* : logro *m*, éxito *m*, realización *f*

acid[1] [ˈæsəd] *adj* **1** SOUR : ácido, agrio **2** CAUSTIC, SHARP : acerbo, mordaz — **acidly** *adv*

acid[2] *n* : ácido *m*

acidic [əˈsɪdɪk, æ-] *adj* : ácido

acidity [əˈsɪdəti, æ-] *n, pl* **-ties** : acidez *f*

acknowledge [ɪkˈnɑlɪdʒ, æk-] *vt* **-edged; -edging** **1** ADMIT : reconocer, admitir **2** RECOGNIZE : reconocer **3 to ac-knowledge receipt of** : acusar recibo de

acknowledgment [ɪkˈnɑlɪdʒmənt, æk-] *n* **1** RECOGNITION : reconocimiento *m* **2** THANKS : agradecimiento *m*

acme [ˈækmi] *n* : colmo *m*, apogeo *m*, cúspide *f*

acne [ˈækni] *n* : acné *m*

acolyte [ˈækə,laɪt] *n* : acólito *m*

acorn [ˈeɪ,kɔrn, -kərn] *n* : bellota *f*

acoustic [əˈkuːstɪk] *or* **acoustical** [-stɪkəl] *adj* : acústico — **acoustically** *adv*

acoustics [əˈkuːstɪks] *ns & pl* : acústica *f*

acquaint [əˈkweɪnt] *vt* **1** INFORM : en-terar, informar **2** FAMILIARIZE : fa-miliarizar **3 to be acquainted with** : conocer a (una persona), estar al tan-to de (un hecho)

acquaintance [əˈkweɪntənts] *n* **1** KNOWLEDGE : conocimiento *m* **2** : conocido *m*, -da *f* ⟨friends and ac-quaintances : amigos y conocidos⟩

acquiesce [,ækwiˈɛs] *vi* **-esced; -escing** : consentir, conformarse

acquiescence [,ækwiˈɛsənts] *n* : con-sentimiento *m*, aquiescencia *f*

acquire [əˈkwaɪr] *vt* **-quired; -quiring** : adquirir, obtener

acquisition [,ækwəˈzɪʃən] *n* : adquisi-ción *f*

acquisitive [əˈkwɪzətɪv] *adj* : adquisiti-vo, codicioso

acquit [əˈkwɪt] *vt* **-quitted; -quitting** **1** : absolver, exculpar **2 to acquit one-self** : comportarse, defenderse

acquittal [əˈkwɪtəl] *n* : absolución *f*, ex-culpación *f*

acre ['eɪkər] *n* : acre *m*

acreage ['eɪkərɪʤ] *n* : superficie *f* en acres

acrid ['ækrəd] *adj* **1** BITTER : acre **2** CAUSTIC : acre, mordaz — **acridly** *adv*

acrimonious [ˌækrə'moːniəs] *adj* : áspero, cáustico, sarcástico

acrimony ['ækrəˌmoːni] *n, pl* **-nies** : acrimonia *f*

acrobat ['ækrəˌbæt] *n* : acróbata *mf*, saltimbanqui *mf*

acrobatic [ˌækrə'bætɪk] *adj* : acrobático

acrobatics [ˌækrə'bætɪks] *ns & pl* : acrobacia *f*

acronym ['ækrəˌnɪm] *n* : acrónimo *m*

across[1] [ə'krɔs] *adv* **1** CROSSWISE : al través **2** : a través, del otro lado ⟨he's already across : ya está del otro lado⟩ **3** : de ancho ⟨40 feet across : 40 pies de ancho⟩

across[2] *prep* **1** : al otro lado de ⟨across the street : al otro lado de la calle⟩ **2** : a través de ⟨a log across the road : un tronco a través del camino⟩

acrylic [ə'krɪlɪk] *n* : acrílico *m*

act[1] ['ækt] *vi* **1** PERFORM : actuar, interpretar **2** FEIGN, PRETEND : fingir, simular **3** BEHAVE : comportarse **4** FUNCTION : actuar, servir, funcionar **5** : tomar medidas ⟨he acted to save the business : tomó medidas para salvar el negocio⟩ **6 to act as** : servir de, hacer de

act[2] *n* **1** DEED : acto *m*, hecho *m*, acción *f* **2** DECREE : ley *f*, decreto *m* **3** : acto *m* (en una obra de teatro), número *m* (en un espectáculo) **4** PRETENSE : fingimiento *m*

action ['ækʃən] *n* **1** DEED : acción *f*, acto *m*, hecho *m* **2** BEHAVIOR : actuación *f*, comportamiento *m* **3** LAWSUIT : demanda *f* **4** MOVEMENT : movimiento *m* **5** COMBAT : combate *m* **6** PLOT : acción *f*, trama *f* **7** MECHANISM : mecanismo *m*

activate ['æktəˌveɪt] *vt* **-vated; -vating** : activar

activation [ˌæktə'veɪʃən] *n* : activación *f*

active ['æktɪv] *adj* **1** MOVING : activo, en movimiento **2** LIVELY : vigoroso, enérgico **3** : en actividad ⟨an active volcano : un volcán en actividad⟩ **4** OPERATIVE : vigente

actively ['æktɪvli] *adv* : activamente, enérgicamente

activist ['æktɪvɪst] *n* : activista *mf* — **activist** *adj*

activity [æk'tɪvəti] *n, pl* **-ties 1** MOVEMENT : actividad *f*, movimiento *m* **2** VIGOR : vigor *m*, energía *f* **3** OCCUPATION : actividad *f*, ocupación *f*

actor ['æktər] *n* : actor *m*, artista *mf*

actress ['æktrəs] *n* : actriz *f*

actual ['æktʃuəl] *adj* : real, verdadero

actuality [ˌæktʃu'æləti] *n, pl* **-ties** : realidad *f*

actually ['æktʃuəli, -ʃəli] *adv* : realmente, en realidad

actuary ['æktʃuˌeri] *n, pl* **-aries** : actuario *m*, -ria *f* de seguros

acumen [ə'kjuːmən] *n* : perspicacia *f*

acupuncture ['ækjuˌpʌŋktʃər] *n* : acupuntura *f*

acute [ə'kjuːt] *adj* **acuter; acutest 1** SHARP : agudo **2** PERCEPTIVE : perspicaz, sagaz **3** KEEN : fino, muy desarrollado, agudo ⟨an acute sense of smell : un fino olfato⟩ **4** SEVERE : grave **5 acute angle** : ángulo *m* agudo

acutely [ə'kjuːtli] *adv* : intensamente ⟨to be acutely aware : estar perfectamente consciente⟩

acuteness [ə'kjuːtnəs] *n* : agudeza *f*

ad ['æd] → **advertisement**

adage ['ædɪʤ] *n* : adagio *m*, refrán *m*, dicho *m*

adamant ['ædəmənt, -ˌmænt] *adj* : firme, categórico, inflexible — **adamantly** *adv*

Adam's apple ['ædəmz] *n* : nuez *f* de Adán

adapt [ə'dæpt] *vt* : adaptar, ajustar — *vi* : adaptarse

adaptability [əˌdæptə'bɪləti] *n* : adaptabilidad *f*, flexibilidad *f*

adaptable [ə'dæptəbəl] *adj* : adaptable, amoldable

adaptation [ˌæˌdæp'teɪʃən, -dəp-] *n* **1** : adaptación *f*, modificación *f* **2** VERSION : versión *f*

adapter [ə'dæptər] *n* : adaptador *m*

add ['æd] *vt* **1** : añadir, agregar ⟨to add a comment : añadir una observación⟩ **2** : sumar ⟨add these numbers : suma estos números⟩ — *vi* : sumar (en total)

adder ['ædər] *n* : víbora *f*

addict[1] [ə'dɪkt] *vt* : causar adicción en

addict[2] ['ædɪkt] *n* **1** : adicto *m*, -ta *f* **2 drug addict** : drogadicto *m*, -ta *f*; toxicómano *m*, -na *f*

addiction [ə'dɪkʃən] *n* **1** : adicción *f*, dependencia *f* **2 drug addiction** : drogadicción *f*

addictive [ə'dɪktɪv] *adj* : adictivo

addition [ə'dɪʃən] *n* **1** : adición *f*, añadidura *f* **2 in ~** : además, también

additional [ə'dɪʃənəl] *adj* : extra, adicional, de más

additionally [ə'dɪʃənəli] *adv* : además, adicionalmente

additive ['ædətɪv] *n* : aditivo *m*

addle ['ædəl] *vt* **-dled; -dling** : confundir, enturbiar

address[1] [ə'dres] *vt* **1** : dirigirse a, pronunciar un discurso ante ⟨to address a jury : dirigirse a un jurado⟩ **2** : dirigir, ponerle la dirección a ⟨to address a letter : dirigir una carta⟩

address[2] [ə'dres, 'æˌdres] *n* **1** SPEECH : discurso *m*, alocución *f* **2** : dirección *f* (de una residencia, etc.)

addressee [ˌæˌdre'siː, ə-] *n* : destinatario *m*, -ria *f*

adduce [ə-'duːs, 'djuːs] *vt* **-duced; -ducing** : aducir

adenoids ['æd,nɔɪd, -dən,ɔɪd] *npl* : adenoides *fpl*

adept [ə'dɛpt] *adj* : experto, hábil — **adeptly** *adv*

adequacy ['ædɪkwəsi] *n, pl* **-cies** : cantidad *f* suficiente

adequate ['ædɪkwət] *adj* **1** SUFFICIENT : adecuado, suficiente **2** ACCEPTABLE, PASSABLE : adecuado, aceptable

adequately ['ædɪkwətli] *adv* : suficientemente, apropiadamente

adhere [æd'hɪr, əd-] *vi* **-hered; -hering 1** STICK : pegarse, adherirse **2 to adhere to** : adherirse a (una política, etc.), cumplir con (una promesa)

adherence [æd'hɪrənts, əd-] *n* : adhesión *f*, adherencia *f*, observancia *f* (de una ley, etc.)

adherent¹ [æd'hɪrənt, əd-] *adj* : adherente, adhesivo, pegajoso

adherent² *n* : adepto *m*, -ta *f*; partidario *m*, -ria *f*

adhesion [æd'hiːʒən, əd-] *n* : adhesión *f*

adhesive¹ [æd'hiːsɪv, əd-, -zɪv] *adj* : adhesivo

adhesive² *n* : adhesivo *m*, pegamento *m*

adjacent [ə'ʤeɪsənt] *adj* : adyacente, colindante, contiguo

adjective ['æʤɪktɪv] *n* : adjetivo *m* — **adjectival** [,æʤɪk'taɪvəl] *adj*

adjoin [ə'ʤɔɪn] *vt* : lindar con, colindar con

adjoining [ə'ʤɔɪnɪŋ] *adj* : contiguo, colindante

adjourn [ə'ʤərn] *vt* : levantar, suspender ⟨the meeting is adjourned : se levanta la sesión⟩ — *vi* : aplazarse

adjournment [ə'ʤərnmənt] *n* : suspensión *f*, aplazamiento *m*

adjudicate [ə'ʤuːdɪ,keɪt] *vt* **-cated; -cating** : juzgar, arbitrar

adjudication [ə,ʤuːdɪ'keɪʃən] *n* **1** JUDGING : arbitrio *m* (judicial) **2** JUDGMENT : fallo *m*

adjunct ['æ,ʤʌŋkt] *n* : adjunto *m*, complemento *m*

adjust [ə'ʤʌst] *vt* : ajustar, arreglar, regular — *vi* **to adjust to** : adaptarse a

adjustable [ə'ʤʌstəbəl] *adj* : ajustable, regulable, graduable

adjustment [ə'ʤʌstmənt] *n* : ajuste *m*, modificación *f*

ad–lib¹ ['æd'lɪb] *v* **-libbed; -libbing** : improvisar

ad–lib² *adj* : improvisado

administer [æd'mɪnəstər, əd-] *vt* : administrar

administration [æd,mɪnə'streɪʃən, əd-] *n* **1** MANAGING : administración *f*, dirección *f* **2** GOVERNMENT, MANAGEMENT : administración *f*, gobierno *m*

administrative [æd'mɪnə,streɪtɪv, əd-] *adj* : administrativo — **administratively** *adv*

administrator [æd'mɪnə,streɪtər, əd-] *n* : administrador *m*, -dora *f*

admirable ['ædmərəbəl] *adj* : admirable, loable — **admirably** *adv*

admiral ['ædmərəl] *n* : almirante *mf*

admiration [,ædmə'reɪʃən] *n* : admiración *f*

admire [æd'maɪr] *vt* **-mired; -miring** : admirar

admirer [æd'maɪrər] *n* : admirador *m*, -dora *f*

admiring [æd'maɪrɪŋ] *adj* : admirativo, de admiración

admiringly [æd'maɪrɪŋli] *adv* : con admiración

admissible [æd'mɪsəbəl] *adj* : admisible, aceptable

admission [æd'mɪʃən] *n* **1** ADMITTANCE : entrada *f*, admisión *f* **2** ACKNOWLEDGMENT : reconocimiento *m*, admisión *f*

admit [æd'mɪt, əd-] *vt* **-mitted; -mitting 1** : admitir, dejar entrar ⟨the museum admits children : el museo deja entrar a los niños⟩ **2** ACKNOWLEDGE : reconocer, admitir

admittance [æd'mɪtənts, əd-] *n* : admisión *f*, entrada *f*, acceso *m*

admittedly [æd'mɪtədli, əd-] *adv* : la verdad es que, lo cierto es que ⟨admittedly we went too fast : la verdad es que fuimos demasiado de prisa⟩

admonish [æd'manɪʃ, əd-] *vt* : amonestar, reprender

admonition [,ædmə'nɪʃən] *n* : admonición *f*

ado [ə'duː] *n* **1** FUSS : ruido *m*, alboroto *m* **2** TROUBLE : dificultad *f*, lío *m* **3 without further ado** : sin más preámbulos

adobe [ə'doːbi] *n* : adobe *m*

adolescence [,ædəl'ɛsənts] *n* : adolescencia *f*

adolescent¹ [,ædəl'ɛsənt] *adj* : adolescente, de adolescencia

adolescent² *n* : adolescente *mf*

adopt [ə'dapt] *vt* : adoptar

adoption [ə'dapʃən] *n* : adopción *f*

adoptive [ə'daptɪv] *adj* : adoptivo

adorable [ə'dorəbəl] *adj* : adorable, encantador

adorably [ə'dorəbli] *adv* : de manera adorable

adoration [,ædə'reɪʃən] *n* : adoración *f*

adore [ə'dor] *vt* **adored; adoring 1** WORSHIP : adorar **2** LOVE : querer, adorar **3** LIKE : encantarle (algo a uno), gustarle mucho (algo a uno) ⟨I adore your new dress : me encanta tu vestido nuevo⟩

adorn [ə'dorn] *vt* : adornar, ornar, engalanar

adornment [ə'dornmənt] *n* : adorno *m*, decoración *f*

adrenaline [ə'drɛnələn] *n* : adrenalina *f*

adrift [ə'drɪft] *adj & adv* : a la deriva

adroit [ə'drɔɪt] *adj* : diestro, hábil — **adroitly** *adv*

adroitness [ə'drɔɪtnəs] *n* : destreza *f*, habilidad *f*

adult[1] [ə'dʌlt, 'æ,dʌlt] *adj* : adulto
adult[2] *n* : adulto *m*, -ta *f*
adulterate [ə'dʌltə,reɪt] *vt* **-ated; -ating** : adulterar
adulterous [ə'dʌltərəs] *adj* : adúltero
adultery [ə'dʌltəri] *n, pl* **-teries** : adulterio *m*
adulthood [ə'dʌlt,hʊd] *n* : adultez *f*, edad *f* adulta
advance[1] [æd'vænts, əd-] *v* **-vanced; -vancing** *vt* **1** : avanzar, adelantar ⟨to advance troops : avanzar las tropas⟩ **2** PROMOTE : ascender, promover **3** PROPOSE : proponer, presentar **4** : adelantar, anticipar ⟨they advanced me next month's salary : me adelantaron el sueldo del próximo mes⟩ — *vi* **1** PROCEED : avanzar, adelantarse **2** PROGRESS : progresar
advance[2] *adj* : anticipado ⟨advance notice : previo aviso⟩
advance[3] *n* **1** PROGRESSION : avance *m* **2** PROGRESS : adelanto *m*, mejora *f*, progreso *m* **3** RISE : aumento *m*, alza *f* **4** LOAN : anticipo *m*, préstamo *m* **5** in ~ : por adelantado
advanced [æd'væntst, əd-] *adj* **1** DEVELOPED : avanzado, desarrollado **2** PRECOCIOUS : adelantado, precoz **3** HIGHER : superior
advancement [æd'væntsmənt, əd-] *n* **1** FURTHERANCE : fomento *m*, adelantamiento *m*, progreso *m* **2** PROMOTION : ascenso *m*
advantage [əd'væntɪʤ, æd-] *n* **1** SUPERIORITY : ventaja *f*, superioridad *f* **2** GAIN : provecho *m*, partido *m* **3** to take advantage of : aprovecharse de
advantageous [,æd,væn'teɪʤəs, -vən-] *adj* : ventajoso, provechoso — **advantageously** *adv*
advent ['æd,vɛnt] *n* **1** Advent : Adviento *m* **2** ARRIVAL : advenimiento *m*, venida *f*
adventure [æd'vɛnʧər, əd-] *n* : aventura *f*
adventurer [æd'vɛnʧərər, əd-] *n* : aventurero *m*, -ra *f*
adventurous [æd'vɛnʧərəs, əd-] *adj* **1** : intrépido, aventurero ⟨an adventurous traveler : un viajero intrépido⟩ **2** RISKY : arriesgado, aventurado
adverb ['æd,vərb] *n* : adverbio *m* — **adverbial** [æd'vərbiəl] *adj*
adversary ['ædvər,sɛri] *n, pl* **-saries** : adversario *m*, -ria *f*
adverse [æd'vərs, 'æd,] *adj* **1** OPPOSING : opuesto, contrario **2** UNFAVORABLE : adverso, desfavorable — **adversely** *adv*
adversity [æd'vərsəti, əd-] *n, pl* **-ties** : adversidad *f*
advertise ['ædvər,taɪz] *v* **-tised; -tising** *vt* : anunciar, hacerle publicidad a — *vi* : hacer publicidad, hacer propaganda
advertisement ['ædvər,taɪzmənt; æd'vərtəzmənt] *n* : anuncio *m*

advertiser ['ædvər,taɪzər] *n* : anunciante *mf*
advertising ['ædvər,taɪzɪŋ] *n* : publicidad *f*, propaganda *f*
advice [æd'vaɪs] *n* : consejo *m*, recomendación *f* ⟨take my advice : sigue mis consejos⟩
advisability [æd,vaɪzə'bɪləti, əd-] *n* : conveniencia *f*
advisable [æd'vaɪzəbəl, əd-] *adj* : aconsejable, recomendable, conveniente
advise [æd'vaɪz, əd-] *v* **-vised; -vising** *vt* **1** COUNSEL : aconsejar, asesorar **2** RECOMMEND : recomendar **3** INFORM : informar, notificar — *vi* : dar consejo
adviser *or* **advisor** [æd'vaɪzər, əd-] *n* : consejero *m*, -ra *f*; asesor *m*, -sora *f*
advisory [æd'vaɪzəri, əd-] *adj* **1** : consultivo **2 in an advisory capacity** : como asesor
advocacy ['ædvəkəsi] *n* : promoción *f*, apoyo *m*
advocate[1] ['ædvə,keɪt] *vt* **-cated; -cating** : recomendar, abogar por, ser partidario de
advocate[2] ['ædvəkət] *n* : defensor *m*, -sora *f*; partidario *m*, -ria *f*
adze ['ædz] *n* : azuela *f*
aeon ['iːən, 'iː,ɑn] *n* : eón *m*, siglo *m*, eternidad *f*
aerate ['ær,eɪt] *vt* **-ated; -ating** : gasear (un líquido), oxigenar (la sangre)
aerial[1] ['æriəl] *adj* : aéreo
aerial[2] *n* : antena *f*
aerie ['æri, 'ɪri, 'eɪəri] *n* : aguilera *f*
aerobic [,ær'oː,bɪk] *adj* : aerobio, aeróbico ⟨aerobic exercises : ejercicios aeróbicos⟩
aerobics [,ær'oː,bɪks] *ns & pl* : aeróbic *m*
aerodynamic [,æroː,daɪ'næmɪk] *adj* : aerodinámico — **aerodynamically** [-mɪkli] *adv*
aerodynamics [,æroː,daɪ'næmɪks] *n* : aerodinámica *f*
aeronautical [,ærə'nɔtɪkəl] *adj* : aeronáutico
aeronautics [,ærə'nɔtɪks] *n* : aeronáutica *f*
aerosol ['ærə,sɔl] *n* : aerosol *m*
aerospace[1] ['æroː,speɪs] *adj* : aeroespacial
aerospace[2] *n* : espacio *m*
aesthetic [ɛs'θɛtɪk] *adj* : estético — **aesthetically** [-tɪkli] *adv*
aesthetics [ɛs'θɛtɪks] *n* : estética *f*
afar [ə'fɑr] *adv* : lejos, a lo lejos
affability [,æfə'bɪləti] *n* : afabilidad *f*
affable ['æfəbəl] *adj* : afable — **affably** *adv*
affair [ə'fær] *n* **1** MATTER : asunto *m*, cuestión *f*, caso *m* **2** EVENT : ocasión *f*, acontecimiento *m* **3** LIAISON : amorío *m*, aventura *f* **4 business affairs** : negocios *mpl* **5 current affairs** : actualidades *fpl*
affect [ə'fɛkt, æ-] *vt* **1** INFLUENCE, TOUCH : afectar, tocar **2** FEIGN : fingir

affectation [ˌæˌfɛkˈteɪʃən] *n* : afectación *f*

affected [əˈfɛktəd, æ-] *adj* **1** FEIGNED : afectado, fingido **2** MOVED : conmovido

affecting [əˈfɛktɪŋ, æ-] *adj* : conmovedor

affection [əˈfɛkʃən] *n* : afecto *m*, cariño *m*

affectionate [əˈfɛkʃənət] *adj* : afectuoso, cariñoso — **affectionately** *adv*

affidavit [ˌæfəˈdeɪvət, ˈæfəˌ-] *n* : declaración *f* jurada, affidávit *m*

affiliate[1] [əˈfɪliˌeɪt] *v* -**ated**; -**ating** *vt* : afiliar, asociar ⟨to be affiliated with : estar afiliado a⟩

affiliate[2] [əˈfɪliət] *n* : afiliado *m*, -da *f* (persona), filial *f* (organización)

affiliation [əˌfɪliˈeɪʃən] *n* : afiliación *f*, filiación *f*

affinity [əˈfɪnəti] *n, pl* -**ties** : afinidad *f*

affirm [əˈfərm] *vt* : afirmar, aseverar, declarar

affirmation [ˌæfərˈmeɪʃən] *n* : afirmación *f*, aserto *m*, declaración *f*

affirmative[1] [əˈfərmətɪv] *adj* : afirmativo ⟨affirmative action : acción afirmativa⟩

affirmative[2] *n* **1** : afirmativa *f* **2 to answer in the affirmative** : responder afirmativamente, dar una respuesta afirmativa

affix [əˈfɪks] *vt* : fijar, poner, pegar

afflict [əˈflɪkt] *vt* **1** : afligir, aquejar **2 to be afflicted with** : padecer de, sufrir de

affliction [əˈflɪkʃən] *n* **1** TRIBULATION : aflicción *f*, tribulación *f* **2** AILMENT : enfermedad *f*, padecimiento *m*

affluence [ˈæˌfluːənts; æˈfluː-, ə-] *n* : afluencia *f*, abundancia *f*, prosperidad *f*

affluent [ˈæˌfluːənt; æˈfluː-, ə-] *adj* : próspero, adinerado

afford [əˈford] *vt* **1** : tener los recursos para, permitirse el lujo de ⟨I can afford it : puedo permitírmelo, tengo con que comprarlo⟩ **2** PROVIDE : ofrecer, proporcionar, dar

affront[1] [əˈfrʌnt] *vt* : afrentar, insultar, ofender

affront[2] *n* : afrenta *f*, insulto *m*, ofensa *f*

Afghan [ˈæfˌgæn, -gən] *n* : afgano *m*, -na *f* — **Afghan** *adj*

afire [əˈfaɪr] *adj* : ardiendo, en llamas

aflame [əˈfleɪm] *adj* : llameante, en llamas

afloat [əˈfloːt] *adv & adj* : a flote

afoot [əˈfut] *adj* **1** WALKING : a pie, andando **2** UNDER WAY : en marcha ⟨something suspicious is afoot : algo sospechoso se está tramando⟩

aforementioned [əˈforˈmɛntʃ ənd] *adj* : antedicho, susodicho

aforesaid [əˈforˌsɛd] *adj* : antes mencionado, antedicho

afraid [əˈfreɪd] *adj* **1 to be afraid** : tener miedo **2 to be afraid that** : temerse que ⟨I'm afraid not : me temo que no⟩

afresh [əˈfrɛʃ] *adv* **1** : de nuevo, otra vez **2 to start afresh** : volver a empezar

African [ˈæfrɪkən] *n* : africano *m*, -na *f* — **African** *adj*

Afro–American[1] [ˌæfroəˈmɛrɪkən] *adj* : afroamericano *m*, -na *f*

Afro–American[2] *n* : afroamericano

aft [ˈæft] *adv* : a popa

after[1] [ˈæftər] *adv* **1** AFTERWARD : después **2** BEHIND : detrás, atrás

after[2] *adj* : posterior, siguiente ⟨in after years : en los años posteriores⟩

after[3] *conj* : después de, después de que ⟨after we ate : después de que comimos, después de comer⟩

after[4] *prep* **1** FOLLOWING : después de, tras ⟨after Saturday : después del sábado⟩ ⟨day after day : día tras día⟩ **2** BEHIND : tras de, después de ⟨I ran after the dog : corrí tras del perro⟩ **3** CONCERNING : por ⟨they asked after you : preguntaron por ti⟩ **4 after all** : después de todo

aftereffect [ˈæftərɪˌfɛkt] *n* : efecto *m* secundario

afterlife [ˈæftərˌlaɪf] *n* : vida *f* venidera, vida *f* después de la muerte

aftermath [ˈæftərˌmæθ] *n* : consecuencias *fpl*, resultados *mpl*

afternoon [ˌæftərˈnuːn] *n* : tarde *f*

aftertaste [ˈæftərˌteɪst] *n* : resabio *m*, regusto *m*

afterthought [ˈæftərˌθɔt] *n* : ocurrencia *f* tardía, idea *f* tardía

afterward [ˈæftərwərd] *or* **afterwards** [-wərdz] *adv* : después, luego ⟨soon afterward : poco después⟩

again [əˈgɛn, -ˈgɪn] *adv* **1** ANEW, OVER : de nuevo, otra vez **2** BESIDES : además **3 then again** : por otra parte ⟨I may stay, then again I may not : puede ser que me quede, por otra parte, puede que no⟩

against [əˈgɛntst, -ˈgɪntst] *prep* **1** TOUCHING : contra ⟨against the wall : contra la pared⟩ **2** OPPOSING : contra, en contra de ⟨I will vote against the proposal : votaré en contra de la propuesta⟩ ⟨against the grain : a contrapelo⟩

agape [əˈgeɪp] *adj* : boquiabierto

agate [ˈægət] *n* : ágata *f*

age[1] [ˈeɪdʒ] *vi* **aged**; **aging** : envejecer, madurar

age[2] *n* **1** : edad *f* ⟨ten years of age : diez años de edad⟩ ⟨to be of age : ser mayor de edad⟩ **2** PERIOD : era *f*, siglo *m*, época *f* **3 old age** : vejez *f* **4 ages** *npl* : siglos *mpl*, eternidad *f*

aged *adj* **1** [ˈeɪdʒəd, ˈeɪdʒd] OLD : anciano, viejo, vetusto **2** [ˈeɪdʒd] (*indicating a specified age*) ⟨a girl aged 10 : una niña de 10 años de edad⟩

ageless [ˈeɪdʒləs] *adj* **1** YOUTHFUL : eternamente joven **2** TIMELESS : eterno, perenne

agency [ˈeɪdʒəntsi] *n, pl* -**cies** **1** : agencia *f*, oficina *f* ⟨travel agency : agencia de viajes⟩ **2 through the agency of** : a través de, por medio de

agenda [ə'dʒndə] *n* : agenda *f*, orden *m* del día

agent ['eɪdʒənt] *n* **1** MEANS : agente *m*, medio *m*, instrumento *m* **2** REPRESENTATIVE : agente *mf*, representante *mf*

aggravate ['ægrə,veɪt] *vt* **-vated; -vating 1** WORSEN : agravar, empeorar **2** ANNOY : irritar, exasperar

aggravation [,ægrə'veɪʃən] *n* **1** WORSENING : empeoramiento *m* **2** ANNOYANCE : molestia *f*, irritación *f*, exasperación *f*

aggregate¹ ['ægrɪ,geɪt] *vt* **-gated; -gating** : juntar, sumar

aggregate² ['ægrɪgət] *adj* : total, global, conjunto

aggregate³ ['ægrɪgət] *n* **1** CONGLOMERATE : agregado *m*, conglomerado *m* **2** WHOLE : total *m*, conjunto *m*

aggression [ə'grɛʃən] *n* **1** ATTACK : agresión *f* **2** AGGRESSIVENESS : agresividad *f*

aggressive [ə'grɛsɪv] *adj* : agresivo — **aggressively** *adv*

aggressiveness [ə'grɛsɪvnəs] *n* : agresividad *f*

aggressor [ə'grɛsər] *n* : agresor *m*, -sora *f*

aggrieved [ə'gri:vd] *adj* : ofendido, herido

aghast [ə'gæst] *adj* : espantado, aterrado, horrorizado

agile ['ædʒəl] *adj* : ágil

agility [ə'dʒɪləti] *n, pl* **-ties** : agilidad *f*

agitate ['ædʒə,teɪt] *v* **-tated; -tating** *vt* **1** SHAKE : agitar **2** UPSET : inquietar, perturbar — *vi* **to agitate against** : hacer campaña en contra de

agitation [,ædʒə'teɪʃən] *n* : agitación *f*, inquietud *f*

agitator ['ædʒə,teɪtər] *n* : agitador *m*, -dora *f*

agnostic [æg'nɑstɪk] *n* : agnóstico *m*, -ca *f*

ago [ə'go:] *adv* : hace ⟨two years ago : hace dos años⟩ ⟨long ago : hace tiempo, hace mucho tiempo⟩

agog [ə'gɑg] *adj* : ansioso, curioso

agonize ['ægə,naɪz] *vi* **-nized; -nizing** : tormentarse, angustiarse

agonizing ['ægə,naɪzɪŋ] *adj* : angustioso, terrible — **agonizingly** [-zɪŋli] *adv*

agony ['ægəni] *n, pl* **-nies 1** PAIN : dolor *m* **2** ANGUISH : angustia *f*

agrarian [ə'grɛriən] *adj* : agrario

agree [ə'gri:] *v* **agreed; agreeing** *vt* ACKNOWLEDGE : estar de acuerdo ⟨he agreed that I was right : estuvo de acuerdo en que tenía razón⟩ — *vi* **1** CONCUR : estar de acuerdo **2** CONSENT : ponerse de acuerdo **3** TALLY : concordar **4 to agree with** : sentarle bien (a alguien) ⟨this climate agrees with me : este clima me sienta bien⟩

agreeable [ə'gri:əbəl] *adj* **1** PLEASING : agradable, simpático **2** WILLING : dispuesto **3** AGREEING : de acuerdo, conforme

agreeably [ə'gri:əbli] *adv* : agradablemente

agreement [ə'gri:mənt] *n* **1** : acuerdo *m*, conformidad *f* ⟨in agreement with : de acuerdo con⟩ **2** CONTRACT, PACT : acuerdo *m*, pacto *m*, convenio *m* **3** CONCORD, HARMONY : concordia *f*

agriculture ['ægrɪ,kʌltʃər] *n* : agricultura *f* — **agricultural** [,ægrɪ'kʌltʃərəl] *adj*

aground [ə'graʊnd] *adj* : encallado, varado

ahead [ə'hɛd] *adv* **1** : al frente, delante, adelante ⟨he walked ahead : caminó delante⟩ **2** BEFOREHAND : por adelantado, con antelación **3** LEADING : a la delantera **4 to get ahead** : adelantar, progresar

ahead of *prep* **1** : al frente de, delante de, antes de **2 to get ahead of** : adelantarse a

ahoy [ə'hɔɪ] *interj* **ship ahoy!** : ¡barco a la vista!

aid¹ ['eɪd] *vt* : ayudar, auxiliar

aid² *n* **1** HELP : ayuda *f*, asistencia *f* **2** ASSISTANT : asistente *mf*

aide ['eɪd] *n* : ayudante *mf*

AIDS ['eɪdz] *n* : SIDA *m*, sida *m*

ail ['eɪl] *vt* : molestar, afligir — *vi* : sufrir, estar enfermo

aileron ['eɪlə,rɑn] *n* : alerón *m*

ailment ['eɪlmənt] *n* : enfermedad *f*, dolencia *f*, achaque *m*

aim¹ ['eɪm] *vt* **1** : apuntar (un arma), dirigir (una observación) **2** INTEND : proponerse, querer ⟨he aims to do it tonight : se propone hacerlo esta noche⟩ — *vi* **1** POINT : apuntar **2 to aim at** : aspirar a

aim² *n* **1** MARKSMANSHIP : puntería *f* **2** GOAL : propósito *m*, objetivo *m*, fin *m*

aimless ['eɪmləs] *adj* : sin rumbo, sin objeto

aimlessly ['eɪmləsli] *adv* : sin rumbo, sin objeto

air¹ ['ær] *vt* **1** : airear, ventilar ⟨to air out a mattress : airear un colchón⟩ **2** EXPRESS : airear, manifestar, comunicar **3** BROADCAST : transmitir, emitir

air² *n* **1** : aire *m* **2** MELODY : aire *m* **3** APPEARANCE : aire *m*, aspecto *m* **4 airs** *npl* : aires *mpl*, afectación *f* **5 by ∼** : por avión (dícese de una carta), en avión (dícese de una persona) **6 to be on the air** : estar en el aire, estar emitiendo

airborne ['ær,bɔrn] *adj* **1** : aerotransportado ⟨airborne troops : tropas aerotransportadas⟩ **2** FLYING : volando, en el aire

air–condition [,ærkən'dɪʃən] *vt* : climatizar, condicionar con el aire

air conditioner [,ærkən'dɪʃənər] *n* : acondicionador *m* de aire

air–conditioning [ˌærkən'dɪʃənɪŋ] *n* : aire *m* acondicionado

aircraft ['ær₁kræft] *ns & pl* **1** : avión *m*, aeronave *f* **2 aircraft carrier** : portaaviones *m*

airfield ['ær₁fi:ld] *n* : aeródromo *m*, campo *m* de aviación

air force *n* : fuerza *f* aérea

airlift ['ær₁lɪft] *n* : puente *m* aéreo, transporte *m* aéreo

airline ['ær₁laɪn] *n* : aerolínea *f*, línea *f* aérea

airliner ['ær₁laɪnər] *n* : avión *m* de pasajeros

airmail[1] ['ær₁meɪl] *vt* : enviar por vía aérea

airmail[2] *n* : correo *m* aéreo

airman ['ærmən] *n*, *pl* **-men** [-mən, -₁mɛn] **1** AVIATOR : aviador *m*, -dora *f* **2** : soldado *m* de la fuerza aérea

airplane ['ær₁pleɪn] *n* : avión *m*

airport ['ær₁port] *n* : aeropuerto *m*

airship ['ær₁ʃɪp] *n* : dirigible *m*, zepelín *m*

airstrip ['ær₁strɪp] *n* : pista *f* de aterrizaje

airtight ['ær'taɪt] *adj* : hermético, herméticamente cerrado

airwaves ['ær₁weɪvz] *npl* : radio *m*, televisión *f*

airy ['æri] *adj* **airier** [-iər]; **-est 1** DELICATE, LIGHT : delicado, ligero **2** BREEZY : aireado, bien ventilado

aisle ['aɪl] *n* : pasillo *m*, nave *f* lateral (de una iglesia)

ajar [ə'dʒɑr] *adj* : entreabierto, entornado

akimbo [ə'kɪmbo] *adj & adv* : en jarras

akin [ə'kɪn] *adj* **1** RELATED : emparentado **2** SIMILAR : semejante, parecido

alabaster ['ælə₁bæstər] *n* : alabastro *m*

alacrity [ə'lækrəti] *n* : presteza *f*, prontitud *f*

alarm[1] [ə'lɑrm] *vt* **1** WARN : alarmar, alertar **2** FRIGHTEN : asustar

alarm[2] *n* **1** WARNING : alarma *f*, alerta *f* **2** APPREHENSION, FEAR : aprensión *f*, inquietud *f*, temor *m* **3 alarm clock** : despertador *m*

alarming [ə'lɑrmɪŋ] *adj* : alarmante

alas [ə'læs] *interj* : ¡ay!

Albanian [æl'beɪniən] *n* : albanés *m*, -nesa *f* — **Albanian** *adj*

albatross ['ælbə₁trɔs] *n*, *pl* **-tross** *or* **-trosses** : albatros *m*

albeit [ɔl'bi:ət, æl-] *conj* : aunque

albino [æl'baɪno] *n*, *pl* **-nos** : albino *m*, -na *f*

album ['ælbəm] *n* : álbum *m*

albumen [æl'bju:mən] *n* **1** : clara *f* de huevo **2** → **albumin**

albumin [æl'bju:mən] *n* : albúmina *f*

alchemist ['ælkəmɪst] *n* : alquimista *mf*

alchemy ['ælkəmi] *n*, *pl* **-mies** : alquimia *f*

alcohol ['ælkə₁hɔl] *n* **1** ETHANOL : alcohol *m*, etanol *m* **2** LIQUOR : alcohol *m*, bebidas *fpl* alcohólicas

alcoholic[1] [ˌælkə'hɔlɪk] *adj* : alcohólico

alcoholic[2] *n* : alcohólico *m*, -ca *f*

alcoholism ['ælkəhɔ₁lɪzəm] *n* : alcoholismo *m*

alcove ['æl₁ko:v] *n* : nicho *m*, hueco *m*

alderman ['ɔldərmən] *n*, *pl* **-men** [-mən, -₁mɛn] : concejal *mf*

ale ['eɪl] *n* : cerveza *f*

alert[1] [ə'lərt] *vt* : alertar, poner sobre aviso

alert[2] *adj* **1** WATCHFUL : alerta, vigilante **2** QUICK : listo, vivo

alert[3] *n* : alerta *f*, alarma *f*

alertly [ə'lərtli] *adv* : con listeza

alertness [ə'lərtnəs] *n* **1** WATCHFULNESS : vigilancia *f* **2** ASTUTENESS : listeza *f*, viveza *f*

alfalfa [æl'fælfə] *n* : alfalfa *f*

alga ['ælgə] *n*, *pl* **-gae** ['æl₁dʒi:] : alga *f*

algebra ['ældʒəbrə] *n* : álgebra *m*

algebraic [ˌældʒə'breɪk] *adj* : algebraico — **algebraically** [-ɪkli] *adv*

Algerian [æl'dʒɪriən] *n* : argelino *m*, -na *f* — **Algerian** *adj*

algorithm ['ælgə₁rɪðəm] *n* : algoritmo *m*

alias[1] ['eɪliəs] *adv* : alias

alias[2] *n* : alias *m*

alibi[1] ['ælə₁baɪ] *vi* : ofrecer una coartada

alibi[2] *n* **1** : coartada *f* **2** EXCUSE : pretexto *m*, excusa *f*

alien[1] ['eɪliən] *adj* **1** STRANGE : ajeno, extraño **2** FOREIGN : extranjero, foráneo **3** EXTRATERRESTRIAL : extraterrestre

alien[2] *n* **1** FOREIGNER : extranjero *m*, -ra *f*; forastero *m*, -ra *f* **2** EXTRATERRESTRIAL : extraterrestre *mf*

alienate ['eɪliə₁neɪt] *vt* **-ated; -ating 1** ESTRANGE : alienar, enajenar **2 to alienate oneself** : alejarse, distanciarse

alienation [ˌeɪliə'neɪʃən] *n* : alienación *f*, enajenación *f*

alight [ə'laɪt] *vi* **1** DISMOUNT : bajarse, apearse **2** LAND : posarse, aterrizar

align [ə'laɪn] *vt* : alinear

alignment [ə'laɪnmənt] *n* : alineación *f*, alineamiento *m*

alike[1] [ə'laɪk] *adv* : igual, del mismo modo

alike[2] *adj* : igual, semejante, parecido

alimentary [ˌælə'mɛntəri] *adj* **1** : alimenticio **2 alimentary canal** : tubo *m* digestivo

alimony ['ælə₁mo:ni] *n*, *pl* **-nies** : pensión *f* alimenticia

alive [ə'laɪv] *adj* **1** LIVING : vivo, viviente **2** LIVELY : animado, activo **3** ACTIVE : vigente, en uso **4** AWARE : consciente ⟨alive to the danger : consciente del peligro⟩

alkali ['ælkə₁laɪ] *n*, *pl* **-lies** [-₁laɪz] *or* **-lis** [-₁laɪz] : álcali *m*

alkaline ['ælkələn, -₁laɪn] *adj* : alcalino

all[1] ['ɔl] *adv* **1** COMPLETELY : todo, completamente **2** : igual ⟨the score is 14 all : es 14 iguales, están empatados a 14⟩

3 all the better : tanto mejor **4 all the more** : aún más, todavía más

all² *adj* : todo ⟨all the children : todos los niños⟩ ⟨in all likelihood : con toda probabilidad, con la mayor probabilidad⟩

all³ *pron* **1** : todo, -da ⟨they ate it all : lo comieron todo⟩ ⟨that's all : eso es todo⟩ ⟨enough for all : suficiente para todos⟩ **2 all in all** : en general **3 not at all** (*in negative constructions*) : en absoluto, para nada

Allah ['ɑla, ɑ'lɑ] *n* : Alá *m*

all-around [,ɔlə'raʊnd] *adj* : completo, amplio

allay [ə'leɪ] *vt* **1** ALLEVIATE : aliviar, mitigar **2** CALM : aquietar, calmar

allegation [,ælɪ'geɪʃən] *n* : alegato *m*, acusación *f*

allege [ə'lɛdʒ] *vt* **-leged; -leging 1** : alegar, afirmar **2 to be alleged** : decirse, pretenderse ⟨she is alleged to be wealthy : se dice que es adinerada⟩

alleged [ə'lɛdʒd, ə'lɛdʒəd] *adj* : presunto, supuesto

allegedly [ə'lɛdʒədli] *adv* : supuestamente, según se alega

allegiance [ə'li:dʒənts] *n* : lealtad *f*, fidelidad *f*

allegorical [,ælə'gɔrɪkəl] *adj* : alegórico

allegory ['ælə,gori] *n, pl* **-ries** : alegoría *f*

alleluia [,ɑlə'lu:jə, ,æ-] → **hallelujah**

allergen ['ælərdʒən] *n* : alérgeno *m*

allergic [ə'lərdʒɪk] *adj* : alérgico

allergy ['ælərdʒi] *n, pl* **-gies** : alergia *f*

alleviate [ə'li:vi,eɪt] *vt* **-ated; -ating** : aliviar, mitigar, paliar

alleviation [ə,li:vi'eɪʃən] *n* : alivio *m*

alley ['æli] *n, pl* **-leys 1** : callejón *m* **2 bowling alley** : bolera *f*

alliance [ə'laɪənts] *n* : alianza *f*, coalición *f*

alligator ['ælə,geɪtər] *n* : caimán *m*

alliteration [ə,lɪtə'reɪʃən] *n* : aliteración *f*

allocate ['ælə,keɪt] *vt* **-cated; -cating** : asignar, adjudicar

allocation [,ælə'keɪʃən] *n* : asignación *f*, reparto *m*, distribución *f*

allot [ə'lɑt] *vt* **-lotted; -lotting** : repartir, distribuir, asignar

allotment [ə'lɑtmənt] *n* : reparto *m*, asignación *f*, distribución *f*

allow [ə'laʊ] *vt* **1** PERMIT : permitir, dejar **2** ALLOT : conceder, dar **3** ADMIT, CONCEDE : admitir, conceder — *vi* **to allow for** : tener en cuenta

allowable [ə'laʊəbəl] *adj* **1** PERMISSIBLE : permisible, lícito **2** : deducible ⟨allowable expenditure : gasto deducible⟩

allowance [ə'laʊənts] *n* **1** : complemento *m* (para gastos, etc.), mesada *f* (para niños) **2 to make allowance(s)** : tener en cuenta, disculpar

alloy ['æ,lɔɪ] *n* : aleación *f*

all-purpose ['ɔl'pərpəs] *adj* : multiuso ⟨all-purpose flour : harina común⟩

all right¹ *adv* **1** YES : sí, por supuesto **2** WELL : bien ⟨I did all right : me fue bien⟩ **3** DEFINITELY : bien, ciertamente, sin duda ⟨he's sick all right : está bien enfermo⟩

all right² *adj* **1** OK : bien ⟨are you all right? : ¿estás bien?⟩ **2** SATISFACTORY : bien, bueno ⟨your work is all right : tu trabajo es bueno⟩

all-round [,ɔl'raʊnd] → **all-around**

allspice ['ɔlspaɪs] *n* : pimienta *f* de Jamaica

allude [ə'lu:d] *vi* **-luded; -luding** : aludir, referirse

allure¹ [ə'lʊr] *vt* **-lured; -luring** : cautivar, atraer

allure² *n* : atractivo *m*, encanto *m*

allusion [ə'lu:ʒən] *n* : alusión *f*

ally¹ [ə'laɪ, 'æ,laɪ] *vi* **-lied; -lying** : aliarse

ally² ['æ,laɪ, ə'laɪ] *n* : aliado *m*, -da *f*

almanac ['ɔlmə,næk, 'æl-] *n* : almanaque *m*

almighty [ɔl'maɪti] *adj* : omnipotente, todopoderoso

almond ['ɑmənd, 'ɑl-, 'æ-, 'æl-] *n* : almendra *f*

almost ['ɔl,mo:st, ɔl'mo:st] *adv* : casi, prácticamente

alms ['ɑmz, 'ɑlmz, 'ælmz] *ns & pl* : limosna *f*, caridad *f*

aloe ['ælo:] *n* : áloe *m*

aloft [ə'lɔft] *adv* : en alto, en el aire

alone¹ [ə'lo:n] *adv* : sólo, solamente, únicamente

alone² *adj* : solo ⟨they're alone in the house : están solos en la casa⟩

along¹ [ə'lɔŋ] *adv* **1** FORWARD : adelante ⟨farther along : más adelante⟩ ⟨come along! : ¡circulen, por favor!⟩ **2 to bring along** : traer **3 ~ with** : con, junto con **4 all along** : desde el principio

along² *prep* **1** : por, a lo largo de ⟨along the coast : a lo largo de la costa⟩ **2** : en, en el curso de, por ⟨along the way : en el curso del viaje⟩

alongside¹ [ə,lɔŋ'saɪd] *adv* : al costado, al lado

alongside² *or* **alongside of** *prep* : junto a, al lado de

aloof [ə'lu:f] *adj* : distante, reservado

aloofness [ə'lu:fnəs] *n* : reserva *f*, actitud *f* distante

aloud [ə'laʊd] *adv* : en voz alta

alpaca [æl'pækə] *n* : alpaca *f*

alphabet ['ælfə,bɛt] *n* : alfabeto *m*

alphabetical [,ælfə'bɛtɪkəl] *or* **alphabetic** [-'bɛtɪk] *adj* : alfabético — **alphabetically** [-tɪkli] *adv*

alphabetize ['ælfəbə,taɪz] *vt* **-ized; -izing** : alfabetizar, poner en orden alfabético

alpine ['æl,paɪn] *adj* : alpino

already [ɔl'rɛdi] *adv* : ya

also ['ɔl,so:] *adv* : también, además

altar ['ɔltər] *n* : altar *m*

alter ['ɔltər] *vt* : alterar, cambiar, modificar

alteration [ˌɔltəˈreɪʃən] *n* : alteración *f*, cambio *m*, modificación *f*

altercation [ˌɔltərˈkeɪʃən] *n* : altercado *m*, disputa *f*

alternate¹ [ˈɔltərˌneɪt] *v* **-nated; -nating** : alternar

alternate² [ˈɔltərnət] *adj* **1** : alterno ⟨alternate cycles of inflation and depression : ciclos alternos de inflación y depresión⟩ **2** : uno sí y otro no ⟨he cooks on alternate days : cocina un día sí y otro no⟩

alternate³ [ˈɔltərnət] *n* : suplente *mf*, sustituto *m*, -ta *f*

alternately [ˈɔltərnətli] *adv* : alternativemente, por turno

alternating current [ˈɔltərˌneɪtɪŋ] *n* : corriente *f* alterna

alternation [ˌɔltərˈneɪʃən] *n* : alternancia *f*, rotación *f*

alternative¹ [ɔlˈtərnətɪv] *adj* : alternativo

alternative² *n* : alternativa *f*

alternator [ˈɔltərˌneɪtər] *n* : alternador *m*

although [ɔlˈðoː] *conj* : aunque, a pesar de que

altitude [ˈæltəˌtuːd, -ˌtjuːd] *n* : altitud *f*, altura *f*

alto [ˈælˌtoː] *n*, *pl* **-tos** : alto *mf*, contralto *mf*

altogether [ˌɔltəˈgɛðər] *adv* **1** COMPLETELY : completamente, totalmente, del todo **2** ON THE WHOLE : en suma, en general

altruism [ˈæltruˌɪzəm] *n* : altruismo *m*

altruistic [ˌæltruˈɪstɪk] *adj* : altruista — **altruistically** [-tɪkli] *adv*

alum [ˈæləm] *n* : alumbre *m*

aluminum [əˈluːmənəm] *n* : aluminio *m*

alumna [əˈlʌmnə] *n*, *pl* **-nae** [-ˌniː] : ex-alumna *f*

alumnus [əˈlʌmnəs] *n*, *pl* **-ni** [-ˌnaɪ] : ex-alumno *m*

always [ˈɔlwiz, -ˌweɪz] *adv* **1** INVARIABLY : siempre, invariablemente **2** FOREVER : para siempre

am → **be**

amalgam [əˈmælgəm] *n* : amalgama *f*

amalgamate [əˈmælgəˌmeɪt] *vt* **-ated; -ating** : amalgamar, unir, fusionar

amalgamation [əˌmælgəˈmeɪʃən] *n* : fusión *f*, unión *f*

amaryllis [ˌæməˈrɪləs] *n* : amarilis *f*

amass [əˈmæs] *vt* : amasar, acumular

amateur [ˈæmətʃər, -tər, -ˌtʊr, -ˌtjʊr] *n* **1** : amateur *mf* **2** BEGINNER : principiante *mf*; aficionado *m*, -da *f*

amateurish [ˈæməˌtʃərɪʃ, -ˌtər-, -ˌtʊr-, -ˌtjʊr-] *adj* : amateur, inexperto

amaze [əˈmeɪz] *vt* **amazed; amazing** : asombrar, maravillar, pasmar

amazement [əˈmeɪzmənt] *n* : asombro *m*, sorpresa *f*

amazing [əˈmeɪzɪŋ] *adj* : asombroso, sorprendente — **amazingly** [-zɪŋli] *adv*

Amazon [ˈæməˌzɑn] *n* : amazona *f* (en mitología)

Amazonian [ˌæməˈzoːniən] *adj* : amazónico

ambassador [æmˈbæsədər] *n* : embajador *m*, -dora *f*

amber [ˈæmbər] *n* : ámbar *m*

ambergris [ˈæmbərˌgrɪs, -ˌgriːs] *n* : ámbar *m* gris

ambidextrous [ˌæmbɪˈdɛkstrəs] *adj* : ambidextro — **ambidextrously** *adv*

ambience *or* **ambiance** [ˈæmbiənts, ˈæmbiˌɑnts] *n* : ambiente *m*, atmósfera *f*

ambiguity [ˌæmbəˈgjuːəti] *n*, *pl* **-ties** : ambigüedad *f*

ambiguous [æmˈbɪgjuəs] *adj* : ambiguo

ambition [æmˈbɪʃən] *n* : ambición *f*

ambitious [æmˈbɪʃəs] *adj* : ambicioso — **ambitiously** *adv*

ambivalence [æmˈbɪvələnts] *n* : ambivalencia *f*

ambivalent [æmˈbɪvələnt] *adj* : ambivalente

amble¹ [ˈæmbəl] *vi* **-bled; -bling** : ir tranquilamente, pasearse despreocupadamente

amble² *n* : paseo *m* tranquilo

ambulance [ˈæmbjələnts] *n* : ambulancia *f*

ambush¹ [ˈæmˌbʊʃ] *vt* : emboscar

ambush² *n* : emboscada *f*, celada *f*

ameliorate [əˈmiːljəˌreɪt] *v* **-rated; -rating** IMPROVE : mejorar

amelioration [əˌmiːljəˈreɪʃən] *n* : mejora *f*

amen [ˈeɪˈmɛn, ˈɑ-] *interj* : amén

amenable [əˈmiːnəbəl, -ˈmɛ-] *adj* RESPONSIVE : susceptible, receptivo, sensible

amend [əˈmɛnd] *vt* **1** IMPROVE : mejorar, enmendar **2** CORRECT : enmendar, corregir

amendment [əˈmɛndmənt] *n* : enmienda *f*

amends [əˈmɛndz] *ns & pl* : compensación *f*, reparación *f*, desagravio *m*

amenity [əˈmɛnəti, -ˈmiː-] *n*, *pl* **-ties 1** PLEASANTNESS : lo agradable, amenidad *f* **2 amenities** *npl* : servicios *mpl*, comodidades *fpl*

American [əˈmɛrɪkən] *n* : americano *m*, -na *f* — **American** *adj*

American Indian *n* : indio *m* (americano), india *f* (americana)

amethyst [ˈæməθəst] *n* : amatista *f*

amiability [ˌeɪmiːəˈbɪləti] *n* : amabilidad *f*, afabilidad *f*

amiable [ˈeɪmiːəbəl] *adj* : amable, afable — **amiably** [-bli] *adv*

amicable [ˈæmɪkəbəl] *adj* : amigable, amistoso, cordial — **amicably** [-bli] *adv*

amid [əˈmɪd] *or* **amidst** [əˈmɪdst] *prep* : en medio de, entre

amino acid [əˈmiːno] *n* : aminoácido *m*

amiss¹ [əˈmɪs] *adv* : mal, fuera de lugar ⟨to take amiss : tomar a mal, llevar a mal⟩

amiss² *adj* **1** WRONG : malo, inoportuno **2 there's something amiss** : pasa algo, algo anda mal

ammeter [ˈæˌmiːtər] *n* : amperímetro *m*

ammonia [ə'mo:njə] *n* : amoníaco *m*
ammunition [ˌæmjə'nɪʃən] *n* **1** : municiones *fpl* **2** ARGUMENTS : argumentos *mpl*
amnesia [æm'ni:ʒə] *n* : amnesia *f*
amnesty ['æmnəsti] *n, pl* **-ties** : amnistía *f*
amoeba [ə'mi:bə] *n, pl* **-bas** *or* **-bae** [-ˌbi:] : ameba *f*
amoebic [ə'mi:bɪk] *adj* : amébico
amok [ə'mʌk, -'mɑk] *adv* **to run amok** : correr a ciegas, enloquecerse, desbocarse (dícese de la economía, etc.)
among [ə'mʌŋ] *prep* : entre
amoral [eɪ'mɔrəl] *adj* : amoral
amorous ['æmərəs] *adj* **1** PASSIONATE : enamoradizo, apasionado **2** ENAMORED : enamorado **3** LOVING : amoroso, cariñoso
amorously ['æmərəsli] *adv* : con cariño
amorphous [ə'mɔrfəs] *adj* : amorfo, informe
amortize ['æmərˌtaɪz, ə'mɔr-] *vt* **-tized; -tizing** : amortizar
amount¹ [ə'maʊnt] *vi* **to amount to 1** : equivaler a, significar ⟨that amounts to treason : eso equivale a la traición⟩ **2** : ascender (a) ⟨my debts amount to $2000 : mis deudas ascienden a $2000⟩
amount² *n* : cantidad *f*, suma *f*
ampere ['æmˌpɪr] *n* : amperio *m*
ampersand ['æmpərˌsænd] *n* : el signo &
amphetamine [æm'fɛtəˌmi:n] *n* : anfetamina *f*
amphibian [æm'fɪbiən] *n* : anfibio *m*
amphibious [æm'fɪbiəs] *adj* : anfibio
amphitheater ['æmfəˌθi:ətər] *n* : anfiteatro *m*
ample ['æmpəl] *adj* **-pler; -plest 1** LARGE, SPACIOUS : amplio, extenso, grande **2** ABUNDANT : abundante, generoso
amplifier ['æmpləˌfaɪər] *n* : amplificador *m*
amplify ['æmpləˌfaɪ] *vt* **-fied; -fying** : amplificar
amply ['æmpli] *adv* : ampliamente, abundantemente, suficientemente
amputate ['æmpjəˌteɪt] *vt* **-tated; -tating** : amputar
amputation [ˌæmpjə'teɪʃən] *n* : amputación *f*
amuck [ə'mʌk] → amok
amulet ['æmjələt] *n* : amuleto *m*, talismán *m*
amuse [ə'mju:z] *vt* **amused; amusing 1** ENTERTAIN : entretener, distraer **2** : hacer reír, divertir ⟨the joke amused us : la broma nos hizo reír⟩
amusement [ə'mju:zmənt] *n* **1** ENTERTAINMENT : diversión *f*, entretenimiento *m*, pasatiempo *m* **2** LAUGHTER : risa *f*
an *art* → a²
anachronism [ə'nækrəˌnɪzəm] *n* : anacronismo *m*
anachronistic [əˌnækrə'nɪstɪk] *adj* : anacrónico

anaconda [ˌænə'kɑndə] *n* : anaconda *f*
anagram ['ænəˌgræm] *n* : anagrama *m*
anal ['eɪnəl] *adj* : anal
analgesic [ˌænəl'dʒi:zɪk, -sɪk] *n* : analgésico *m*
analog ['ænəˌlɔg] *adj* : analógico
analogical [ˌænə'lɑdʒɪkəl] *adj* : analógico — **analogically** [-kli] *adv*
analogous [ə'næləgəs] *adj* : análogo
analogy [ə'nælədʒi] *n, pl* **-gies** : analogía *f*
analysis [ə'næləsəs] *n, pl* **-yses** [-ˌsi:z] **1** : análisis *m* **2** PSYCHOANALYSIS : psicoanálisis *m*
analyst ['ænəlɪst] *n* **1** : analista *mf* **2** PSYCHOANALYST : psicoanalista *mf*
analytic [ˌænə'lɪtɪk] *or* **analytical** [-tɪkəl] *adj* : analítico — **analytically** [-tɪkli] *adv*
analyze ['ænəˌlaɪz] *vt* **-lyzed; -lyzing** : analizar
anarchic [æ'nɑrkɪk] *adj* : anárquico — **anarchically** [-kɪkli] *adv*
anarchism ['ænərˌkɪzəm, -nɑr-] *n* : anarquismo *m*
anarchist ['ænərkɪst, -nɑr-] *n* : anarquista *mf*
anarchy ['ænərki, -nɑr-] *n* : anarquía *f*
anathema [ə'næθəmə] *n* : anatema *m*
anatomic [ˌænə'tɑmɪk] *or* **anatomical** [-mɪkəl] *adj* : anatómico — **anatomically** [-mɪkli] *adv*
anatomy [ə'nætəmi] *n, pl* **-mies** : anatomía *f*
ancestor ['ænˌsɛstər] *n* : antepasado *m*, -da *f*; antecesor *m*, -sora *f*
ancestral [æn'sɛstrəl] *adj* : ancestral, de los antepasados
ancestry ['ænˌsɛstri] *n* **1** DESCENT : ascendencia *f*, linaje *m*, abolengo *m* **2** ANCESTORS : antepasados *mpl*, -das *fpl*
anchor¹ ['æŋkər] *vt* **1** MOOR : anclar, fondear **2** FASTEN : sujetar, asegurar, fijar
anchor² *n* **1** : ancla *f* **2** : presentador *m*, -dora *f* (en televisión)
anchorage ['æŋkərɪdʒ] *n* : anclaje *m*
anchovy ['ænˌtʃo:vi, æn'tʃo:-] *n, pl* **-vies** *or* **-vy** : anchoa *f*
ancient ['eɪntʃənt] *adj* **1** : antiguo ⟨ancient history : historia antigua⟩ **2** OLD : viejo
ancients ['eɪntʃənts] *npl* : los antiguos *mpl*
and ['ænd] *conj* **1** : y (**e** *before words beginning with* i- *or* hi-) **2** : con ⟨ham and eggs : huevos con jamón⟩ **3** : a ⟨go and see : ve a ver⟩ **4** : de ⟨try and finish it soon : trata de terminarlo pronto⟩
Andalusian [ˌændə'lu:ʒən] *n* : andaluz *m*, -luza *f* — **Andalusian** *adj*
Andean ['ændiən] *adj* : andino
andiron ['ænˌdaɪərn] *n* : morillo *m*
Andorran [æn'dɔrən] *n* : andorrano *m*, -na *f* — **Andorran** *adj*
androgynous [æn'drɑdʒənəs] *adj* : andrógino
anecdotal [ˌænɪk'do:təl] *adj* : anecdótico

anecdote ['ænɪk,do:t] *n* : anécdota *f*
anemia [ə'ni:miə] *n* : anemia *f*
anemic [ə'ni:mɪk] *adj* : anémico
anemone [ə'nɛmənɪ] *n* : anémona *f*
anesthesia [,ænəs'θi:ʒə] *n* : anestesia *f*
anesthetic[1] [,ænəs'θɪk] *adj* : anestésico
anesthetic[2] *n* : anestésico *m*
anesthetist [ə'nɛsθətɪst] *n* : anestesista *mf*
anesthetize [ə'nɛsθə,taɪz] *vt* -tize; -tized : anestesiar
aneurysm ['ænjə,rɪzəm] *n* : aneurisma *mf*
anew [ə'nu:, -'nju:] *adv* : de nuevo, otra vez, nuevamente
angel ['eɪndʒəl] *n* : ángel *m*
angelic [æn'dʒɛlɪk] *or* angelical [-lɪkəl] *adj* : angélico, angelical — angelically [-lɪkli] *adv*
anger[1] ['æŋgər] *vt* : enojar, enfadar
anger[2] *n* : enojo *m*, enfado *m*, ira *f*, cólera *f*, rabia *f*
angina [æn'dʒaɪnə] *n* : angina *f*
angle[1] ['æŋgəl] *v* angled; angling *vt* DIRECT, SLANT : orientar, dirigir — *vi* FISH : pescar (con caña)
angle[2] *n* 1 : ángulo *m* 2 POINT OF VIEW : perspectiva *f*, punto *m* de vista
angler ['æŋglər] *n* : pescador *m*, -dora *f*
Anglican ['æŋglɪkən] *n* : anglicano *m*, -na *f* — Anglican *adj*
Anglo–Saxon[1] [,æŋglo'sæksən] *adj* : anglosajón
Anglo–Saxon[2] *n* : anglosajón *m*, -jona *f*
Angolan [æŋ'go:lən, æn-] *n* : angoleño *m*, -ña *f* — Angolan *adj*
angora [æŋ'gorə, æn-] *n* : angora *f*
angrily ['æŋgrəli] *adv* : furiosamente, con ira
angry ['æŋgri] *adj* -grier; -est : enojado, enfadado, furioso
anguish ['æŋgwɪʃ] *n* : angustia *f*, congoja *f*
anguished ['æŋgwɪʃt] *adj* : angustiado, acongojado
angular ['æŋgjələr] *adj* : angular (dícese de las formas), anguloso (dícese de las caras)
animal ['ænəməl] *n* 1 : animal *m* 2 BRUTE : bruto *m*, -ta *f*
animate[1] ['ænə,meɪt] *vt* -mated; -mating : animar
animate[2] ['ænəmət] *adj* : animado
animated ['ænə,meɪtəd] *adj* 1 LIVELY : animado, vivo, vivaz 2 animated cartoon : dibujos *mpl* animados
animation [,ænə'meɪʃən] *n* : animación *f*
animosity [,ænə'mɑsəti] *n, pl* -ties : animosidad *f*, animadversión *f*
anise ['ænəs] *n* : anís *m*
aniseed ['ænəs,si:d] *n* : anís *m*, semilla *f* de anís
ankle ['æŋkəl] *n* : tobillo *m*
anklebone ['æŋkəl,bo:n] *n* : taba *f*
annals ['ænəlz] *npl* : anales *mpl*, crónica *f*
anneal [ə'ni:l] *vt* 1 TEMPER : templar 2 STRENGTHEN : fortalecer

annex[1] [ə'nɛks, 'æ,nɛks] *vt* : anexar
annex[2] ['æ,nɛks, -nɪks] *n* : anexo *m*, anejo *m*
annexation [,æ,nɛk'seɪʃən] *n* : anexión *f*
annihilate [ə'naɪə,leɪt] *vt* -lated; -lating : aniquilar
annihilation [ə,naɪə'leɪʃən] *n* : aniquilación *f*, aniquilamiento *m*
anniversary [,ænə'vərsəri] *n, pl* -ries : aniversario *m*
annotate ['ænə,teɪt] *vt* -tated; -tating : anotar
annotation [,ænə'teɪʃən] *n* : anotación *f*
announce [ə'naʊnts] *vt* -nounced; -nouncing : anunciar
announcement [ə'naʊntsmənt] *n* : anuncio *m*
announcer [ə'naʊntsər] *n* : anunciador *m*, -dora *f*; comentarista *mf*; locutor *m*, -tora *f*
annoy [ə'nɔɪ] *vt* : molestar, fastidiar, irritar
annoyance [ə'nɔɪənts] *n* 1 IRRITATION : irritación *f*, fastidio *m* 2 NUISANCE : molestia *f*, fastidio *m*
annoying [ə'nɔɪɪŋ] *adj* : molesto, fastidioso, engorroso — annoyingly [-ɪŋli] *adv*
annual[1] ['ænjʊəl] *adj* : anual — annually *adv*
annual[2] *n* 1 : planta *f* anual 2 YEARBOOK : anuario *m*
annuity [ə'nu:əti] *n, pl* -ties : anualidad *f*
annul [ə'nʌl] *vt* anulled; anulling : anular, invalidar
annulment [ə'nʌlmənt] *n* : anulación *f*
anode ['æ,no:d] *n* : ánodo *m*
anoint [ə'nɔɪnt] *vt* : ungir
anomalous [ə'nɑmələs] *adj* : anómalo
anomaly [ə'nɑməli] *n, pl* -lies : anomalía *f*
anonymity [,ænə'nɪməti] *n* : anonimato *m*
anonymous [ə'nɑnəməs] *adj* : anónimo — anonymously *adv*
anorexia [,ænə'rɛksiə] *n* : anorexia *f*
anorexic [,ænə'rɛksɪk] *adj* : anoréxico
another[1] [ə'nʌðər] *adj* : otro
another[2] *pron* : otro, otra
answer[1] ['æntsər] *vt* 1 : contestar (a), responder (a) ⟨to answer the telephone : contestar el teléfono⟩ 2 FULFILL : satisfacer 3 to answer for : ser responsable de, pagar por ⟨she'll answer for that mistake : pagará por ese error⟩ — *vi* : contestar, responder
answer[2] *n* 1 REPLY : respuesta *f*, contestación *f* 2 SOLUTION : solución *f*
answerable ['æntsərəbəl] *adj* : responsable
ant ['ænt] *n* : hormiga *f*
antacid [ænt'æsəd, 'æn,tæ-] *n* : antiácido *m*
antagonism [æn'tægə,nɪzəm] *n* : antagonismo *m*, hostilidad *f*
antagonist [æn'tægənɪst] *n* : antagonista *mf*

antagonistic [æn,tægə'nɪstɪk] *adj* : antagonista, hostil
antagonize [æn'tægə,naɪz] *vt* **-nized; -nizing** : antagonizar
antarctic [ænt'ɑrktɪk, -'ɑrtɪk] *adj* : antártico
antarctic circle *n* : círculo *m* antártico
anteater ['ænt,i:tər] *n* : oso *m* hormiguero
antebellum [,æntɪ'bɛləm] *adj* : prebélico
antecedent¹ [,æntə'si:dənt] *adj* : antecedente, precedente
antecedent² *n* : antecedente *mf*; precursor *m*, -sora *f*
antelope ['æntəl,o:p] *n, pl* **-lope** *or* **-lopes** : antílope *m*
antenna [æn'tɛnə] *n, pl* **-nae** [-,ni:, -,naɪ] *or* **-nas** : antena *f*
anterior [æn'tɪriər] *adj* : anterior
anthem ['ænθəm] *n* : himno *m* ⟨national anthem : himno nacional⟩
anther ['ænθər] *n* : antera *f*
anthill ['ænt,hɪl] *n* : hormiguero *m*
anthology [æn'θalədʒi] *n, pl* **-gies** : antología *f*
anthracite ['ænθrə,saɪt] *n* : antracita *f*
anthropoid¹ ['ænθrə,pɔɪd] *adj* : antropoide
anthropoid² *n* : antropoide *mf*
anthropological [,ænθrəpə'ladʒɪkəl] *adj* : antropológico
anthropologist [,ænθrə'palədʒɪst] *n* : antropólogo *m*, -ga *f*
anthropology [,ænθrə'palədʒi] *n* : antropología *f*
antiabortion [,æntiə'bɔrʃən, ,æntaɪ-] *adj* : antiaborto
antiaircraft [,ænti'ær,kræft, ,æntaɪ-] *adj* : antiaéreo
anti–American [,æntiə'mɛrɪkən, ,æntaɪ-] *adj* : antiamericano
antibiotic¹ [,æntibaɪ'ɑtɪk, ,æntaɪ-, -bi-] *adj* : antibiótico
antibiotic² *n* : antibiótico *m*
antibody ['ænti,badi] *n, pl* **-bodies** : anticuerpo *m*
antic¹ ['æntɪk] *adj* : extravagante, juguetón
antic² *n* : payasada *f*, travesura *f*
anticipate [æn'tɪsə,peɪt] *vt* **-pated; -pating 1** FORESEE : anticipar, prever **2** EXPECT : esperar, contar con
anticipation [æn,tɪsə'peɪʃən] *n* **1** FORESIGHT : previsión *f* **2** EXPECTATION : anticipación *f*, expectación *f*, esperanza *f*
anticipatory [æn'tɪsəpə,tori] *adj* : en anticipación, en previsión
anticlimactic [,æntiklaɪ'mæktɪk] *adj* : anticlimático, decepcionante
anticlimax [,ænti'klaɪ,mæks] *n* : anticlímax *m*
anticommunism [,ænti'kɑmjə,nɪzəm, ,æntaɪ-] *n* : anticomunismo *m*
anticommunist¹ [,ænti'kɑmjənɪst, ,æntaɪ-] *adj* : anticomunista
anticommunist² *n* : anticomunista *mf*

antidemocratic [,ænti,dɛmə'krætɪk, ,æntaɪ-] *adj* : antidemocrático
antidepressant [,æntidi'prɛsənt] *n* : antidepresivo *m* — **antidepressant** *adj*
antidote ['ænti,do:t] *n* : antídoto *m*
antidrug [,ænti'drʌg, ,æntaɪ-; 'ænti,drʌg, 'æntaɪ-] *adj* : antidrogas
antifascist [,ænti'fæʃɪst, ,æntaɪ-] *adj* : antifascista
antifeminist [,ænti'fɛmənɪst, ,æntaɪ-] *adj* : antifeminista
antifreeze ['ænti,fri:z] *n* : anticongelante *m*
antigen ['æntɪdʒən, -,dʒɛn] *n* : antígeno *m*
antihistamine [,ænti'hɪstə,mi:n, -mən] *n* : antihistamínico *m*
anti–imperialism [,æntiɪm'pɪriə,lɪzəm, ,æntaɪ-] *n* : antiimperialismo *m*
anti–imperialist [,æntiɪm'pɪriəlɪst, ,æntaɪ-] *adj* : antiimperialista
anti–inflammatory [,ætiɪn'flæmətori] *adj* : antiinflamatorio
anti–inflationary [,æntiɪn'fleɪʃə,nɛri, ,æntaɪ-] *adj* : antiinflacionario
antimony ['æntə,mo:ni] *n* : antimonio *m*
antipathy [æn'tɪpəθi] *n, pl* **-thies** : antipatía *f*, aversión *f*
antiperspirant [,ænti'pərspərənt, ,æntaɪ-] *n* : antitranspirante *m*
antiquarian¹ [,æntə'kwɛriən] *adj* : antiguo, anticuario ⟨an antiquarian book : un libro antiguo⟩
antiquarian² *n* : anticuario *m*, -ria *f*
antiquary ['æntə,kwɛri] *n* → **antiquarian²**
antiquated ['æntə,kweɪtəd] *adj* : anticuado, pasado de moda
antique¹ [æn'ti:k] *adj* **1** OLD : antiguo, de época ⟨an antique mirror : un espejo antiguo⟩ **2** OLD-FASHIONED : anticuado, pasado de moda
antique² *n* : antigüedad *f*
antiquity [æn'tɪkwəţi] *n, pl* **-ties** : antigüedad
antirevolutionary [,ænti,rɛvə'lu:ʃə,nɛri, ,æntaɪ-] *adj* : antirrevolucionario
anti–Semitic [,æntisə'mɪtɪk, ,æntaɪ-] *adj* : antisemita
anti–Semitism [,ænti'sɛmə,tɪzəm, ,æntaɪ-] *n* : antisemitismo *m*
antiseptic¹ [,æntə'sɛptɪk] *adj* : antiséptico — **antiseptically** [-tɪkli] *adv*
antiseptic² *n* : antiséptico *m*
antismoking [,ænti'smo:kɪŋ, ,æntaɪ-] *adj* : antitabaco
antisocial [,ænti'so:ʃəl, ,æntaɪ-] *adj* **1** : antisocial **2** UNSOCIABLE : poco sociable
antitheft [,ænti'θɛft, ,æntaɪ-] *adj* : antirrobo
antithesis [æn'tɪθəsɪs] *n, pl* **-eses** [-,si:z] : antítesis *f*
antitoxin [,ænti'taksən, ,æntaɪ-] *n* : antitoxina *f*
antitrust [,ænti'trʌst, ,æntaɪ-] *adj* : antimonopolista
antler ['æntlər] *n* : asta *f*, cuerno *m*

antonym ['æntə,nɪm] *n* : antónimo *m*

anus ['eɪnəs] *n* : ano *m*

anvil ['ænvəl, -vɪl] *n* : yunque *m*

anxiety [æŋk'zaɪəti] *n, pl* **-eties** 1 UN-EASINESS : inquietud *f*, preocupación *f*, ansiedad *f* 2 APPREHENSION : ansiedad *f*, angustia *f*

anxious ['æŋkʃəs] *adj* 1 WORRIED : inquieto, preocupado, ansioso 2 WORRISOME : preocupante, inquietante 3 EAGER : ansioso, deseoso

anxiously ['æŋkʃəsli] *adv* : con inquietud, con ansiedad

any[1] ['ɛni] *adv* 1 : algo ⟨is it any better? : ¿está (algo) mejor?⟩ 2 : para nada ⟨it is not any good : no sirve para nada⟩

any[2] *adj* 1 : alguno ⟨is there any doubt? : ¿hay alguna duda?⟩ ⟨call me if you have any questions : llámeme si tiene alguna pregunta⟩ 2 : cualquier ⟨I can answer any question : puedo responder a cualquier pregunta⟩ 3 : todo ⟨in any case : en todo caso⟩ 4 : ningún ⟨he would not accept it under any circumstances : no lo aceptaría bajo ninguna circunstancia⟩

any[3] *pron* 1 : alguno *m*, -na *f* ⟨are there any left? : ¿queda alguno?⟩ 2 : ninguno *m*, -na *f* ⟨I don't want any : no quiero ninguno⟩

anybody ['ɛni,bʌdi, -,ba-] → **anyone**

anyhow ['ɛni,haʊ] *adv* 1 HAPHAZARDLY : de cualquier manera 2 IN ANY CASE : de todos modos, en todo caso

anymore [,ɛni'mor] *adv* 1 : ya, ya más ⟨he doesn't dance anymore : ya no baila más⟩ 2 : todavía ⟨do they sing anymore? : ¿cantan todavía?⟩

anyone ['ɛni,wʌn] *pron* 1 : alguien ⟨is anyone here? : ¿hay alguien aquí?⟩ ⟨if anyone wants to come : si alguno quiere venir⟩ 2 : cualquiera ⟨anyone can play : cualquiera puede jugar⟩ 3 : nadie ⟨I don't want anyone here : no quiero a nadie aquí⟩

anyplace ['ɛni,pleɪs] → **anywhere**

anything ['ɛni,θɪŋ] *pron* 1 : algo, alguna cosa ⟨do you want anything? : ¿quieres algo?, ¿quieres alguna cosa?⟩ 2 : nada ⟨hardly anything : casi nada⟩ 3 : cualquier cosa ⟨I eat anything : como de todo⟩

anytime ['ɛni,taɪm] *adv* : en cualquier momento, a cualquier hora, cuando sea

anyway ['ɛni,weɪ] → **anyhow**

anywhere ['ɛni,hwɛr] *adv* 1 : en algún sitio, en alguna parte ⟨do you see it anywhere? : ¿lo ves en alguna parte?⟩ 2 : en ningún sitio, por ninguna parte ⟨I can't find it anywhere : no puedo encontrarlo por ninguna parte⟩ 3 : en cualquier parte, dondequiera, donde sea ⟨put it anywhere : ponlo dondequiera⟩

aorta [eɪ'ɔrtə] *n, pl* **-tas** *or* **-tae** [-ṭi, -ṭaɪ] : aorta *f*

Apache [ə'pætʃi] *n, pl* **Apache** *or* **Apaches** : apache *mf*

apart [ə'pɑrt] *adv* 1 SEPARATELY : aparte, separadamente 2 ASIDE : aparte, a un lado 3 **to fall apart** : deshacerse, hacerse pedazos 4 **to take apart** : desmontar, desmantelar

apartheid [ə'pɑr,teɪt, -,taɪt] *n* : apartheid *m*

apartment [ə'pɑrtmənt] *n* : apartamento *m*, departamento *m*, piso *m Spain*

apathetic [,æpə'θɛtɪk] *adj* : apático, indiferente — **apathetically** [-tɪkli] *adv*

apathy ['æpəθi] *n* : apatía *f*, indiferencia *f*

ape[1] ['eɪp] *vt* **aped; aping** : imitar, remedar

ape[2] *n* : simio *m*; mono *m*, -na *f*

aperitif [ə,pɛrə'ti:f] *n* : aperitivo *m*

aperture ['æpərtʃər, -,tʃʊr] *n* : abertura *f*, rendija *f*, apertura *f* (en fotografía)

apex ['eɪ,pɛks] *n, pl* **apexes** *or* **apices** ['eɪpə,si:z, 'æ-] : ápice *m*, cúspide *f*, cima *f*

aphid ['eɪfɪd, 'æ-] *n* : áfido *m*

aphorism ['æfə,rɪzəm] *n* : aforismo *m*

aphrodisiac [,æfrə'di:zi,æk, -'dɪ-] *n* : afrodisíaco *m*

apiary ['eɪpi,ɛri] *n, pl* **-aries** : apiario *m*, colmenar *m*

apiece [ə'pi:s] *adv* : cada uno

aplenty [ə'plɛnti] *adj* : en abundancia

aplomb [ə'plɑm, -'plʌm] *n* : aplomo *m*

apocalypse [ə'pɑkə,lɪps] *n* : apocalipsis *m*

apocalyptic [ə,pɑkə'lɪptɪk] *adj* : apocalíptico

apocrypha [ə'pɑkrəfə] *n* : textos *mpl* apócrifos

apocryphal [ə'pɑkrəfəl] *adj* : apócrifo

apologetic [ə,pɑlə'ʤɛtɪk] *adj* : lleno de disculpas

apologetically [ə,pɑlə'ʤɛtɪkli] *adv* : disculpándose, con aire de disculpas

apologize [ə'pɑlə,ʤaɪz] *vi* **-gized; -gizing** : disculparse, pedir perdón

apology [ə'pɑləʤi] *n, pl* **-gies** : disculpa *f*, excusa *f*

apoplectic [,æpə'plɛktɪk] *adj* : apoplético

apoplexy ['æpə,plɛksi] *n* : apoplejía *f*

apostasy [ə'pɑstəsi] *n, pl* **-sies** : apostasía *f*

apostate [ə'pɑs,teɪt] *n* : apóstata *mf*

apostle [ə'pɑsəl] *n* : apóstol *m*

apostolic [,æpə'stɑlɪk] *adj* : apostólico

apostrophe [ə'pɑstrə,fi:] *n* : apóstrofo *m* (ortográfico)

apothecary [ə'pɑθə,kɛri] *n, pl* **-caries** : boticario *m*, -ria *f*

appall [ə'pɔl] *vt* : consternar, horrorizar

apparatus [,æpə'ræṭəs, -'reɪ-] *n, pl* **-tuses** *or* **-tus** : aparato *m*, equipo *m*

apparel [ə'pærəl] *n* : atavío *m*, ropa *f*

apparent [ə'pærənt] *adj* 1 VISIBLE : visible 2 OBVIOUS : claro, evidente, manifiesto 3 SEEMING : aparente, ostensible

apparently [ə'pærəntli] *adv* : aparentemente, al parecer

apparition [ˌæpə'rɪʃən] *n* : aparición *f*, visión *f*

appeal¹ [ə'pi:l] *vt* : apelar ⟨to appeal a decision : apelar contra una decisión⟩ — *vi* **1 to appeal for** : pedir, solicitar **2 to appeal to** : atraer a ⟨that doesn't appeal to me : eso no me atrae⟩

appeal² *n* **1** : apelación *f* (en derecho) **2** PLEA : ruego *m*, súplica *f* **3** ATTRACTION : atracción *f*, atractivo *m*, interés *m*

appear [ə'pɪr] *vi* **1** : aparecer, aparecerse, presentarse ⟨he suddenly appeared : apareció de repente⟩ **2** COME OUT : aparecer, salir, publicarse **3** : comparecer (ante el tribunal), actuar (en el teatro) **4** SEEM : parecer

appearance [ə'pɪrənts] *n* **1** APPEARING : aparición *f*, presentación *f*, comparecencia *f* (ante un tribunal), publicación *f* (de un libro) **2** LOOK : apariencia *f*, aspecto *m*

appease [ə'pi:z] *vt* **-peased; -peasing 1** CALM, PACIFY : aplacar, apaciguar, sosegar **2** SATISFY : satisfacer, mitigar

appeasement [ə'pi:zmənt] *n* : aplacamiento *m*, apaciguamiento *m*

append [ə'pɛnd] *vt* : agregar, añadir, adjuntar

appendage [ə'pɛndɪdʒ] *n* **1** ADDITION : apéndice *m*, añadidura *f* **2** LIMB : miembro *m*, extremidad *f*

appendectomy [ˌæpən'dɛktəmi] *n, pl* **-mies** : apendicectomía *f*

appendicitis [ə,pɛndə'saɪtəs] *n* : apendicitis *f*

appendix [ə'pɛndɪks] *n, pl* **-dixes** *or* **-dices** [-də,si:z] : apéndice *m*

appetite ['æpə,taɪt] *n* **1** CRAVING : apetito *m*, deseo *m*, ganas *fpl* **2** PREFERENCE : gusto *m*, preferencia *f* ⟨the cultural appetites of today : los gustos culturales de hoy⟩

appetizer ['æpə,taɪzər] *n* : aperitivo *m*, entremés *m*, botana *f Mex*, tapa *f Spain*

appetizing ['æpə,taɪzɪŋ] *adj* : apetecible, apetitoso — **appetizingly** [-zɪŋli] *adv*

applaud [ə'plɒd] *v* : aplaudir

applause [ə'plɒz] *n* : aplauso *m*

apple ['æpəl] *n* : manzana *f*

appliance [ə'plaɪənts] *n* **1** : aparato *m* **2 household appliance** : electrodoméstico *m*, aparato *m* electrodoméstico

applicability [ˌæplɪkə'bɪləti, ə,plɪkə-] *n* : aplicabilidad *f*

applicable ['æplɪkəbəl, ə'plɪkə-] *adj* : aplicable, pertinente

applicant ['æplɪkənt] *n* : solicitante *mf*, aspirante *mf*, postulante *mf*; candidato *m*, -ta *f*

application [ˌæplə'keɪʃən] *n* **1** USE : aplicación *f*, empleo *m*, uso *m* **2** DILIGENCE : aplicación *f*, diligencia *f*, dedicación *f* **3** REQUEST : solicitud *f*, petición *f*, demanda *f*

applicator ['æplə,keɪtər] *n* : aplicador *m*

appliqué¹ [ˌæplə'keɪ] *vt* : decorar con apliques

appliqué² *n* : aplique *m*

apply [ə'plaɪ] *v* **-plied; -plying** *vt* **1** : aplicar (una sustancia, los frenos, el conocimiento) **2 to apply oneself** : dedicarse, aplicarse — *vi* **1** : aplicarse, referirse ⟨the rules apply to everyone : las reglas se aplican a todos⟩ **2 to apply for** : solicitar, pedir

appoint [ə'pɔɪnt] *vt* **1** NAME : nombrar, designar **2** FIX, SET : fijar, señalar, designar ⟨to appoint a date : fijar una fecha⟩ **3** EQUIP : equipar ⟨a well-appointed office : una oficina bien equipada⟩

appointee [ə,pɔɪn'ti:, ,æ-] *n* : persona *f* designada

appointment [ə'pɔɪntmənt] *n* **1** APPOINTING : nombramiento *m*, designación *f* **2** ENGAGEMENT : cita *f*, hora *f* **3** POST : puesto *m*

apportion [ə'porʃən] *vt* : distribuir, repartir

apportionment [ə'porʃənmənt] *n* : distribución *f*, repartición *f*, reparto *m*

apposite ['æpəzət] *adj* : apropiado, oportuno, pertinente — **appositely** *adv*

appraisal [ə'preɪzəl] *n* : evaluación *f*, valoración *f*, tasación *f*, apreciación *f*

appraise [ə'preɪz] *vt* **-praised; -praising** : evaluar, valorar, tasar, apreciar

appraiser [ə'preɪzər] *n* : tasador *m*, -dora *f*

appreciable [ə'pri:ʃəbəl, -'prɪʃiə-] *adj* : apreciable, sensible, considerable — **appreciably** [-bli] *adv*

appreciate [ə'pri:ʃi,eɪt, -'prɪ-] *v* **-ated; -ating** *vt* **1** VALUE : apreciar, valorar **2** : agradecer ⟨we appreciate his frankness : agradecemos su franqueza⟩ **3** UNDERSTAND : darse cuenta de, entender — *vi* : apreciarse, valorizarse

appreciation [ə,pri:ʃi'eɪʃən, -,prɪ-] *n* **1** GRATITUDE : agradecimiento *m*, reconocimiento *m* **2** VALUING : apreciación *f*, valoración *f*, estimación *f* ⟨art appreciation : apreciación artística⟩ **3** UNDERSTANDING : comprensión *f*, entendimiento *m*

appreciative [ə'pri:ʃətɪv, -'prɪ-; ə'pri:ʃi,eɪ-] *adj* **1** : apreciativo ⟨an appreciative audience : un público apreciativo⟩ **2** GRATEFUL : agradecido **3** ADMIRING : de admiración

apprehend [ˌæprɪ'hɛnd] *vt* **1** ARREST : aprehender, detener, arrestar **2** DREAD : temer **3** COMPREHEND : comprender, entender

apprehension [ˌæprɪ'hɛntʃən] *n* **1** ARREST : arresto *m*, detención *f*, aprehensión *f* **2** ANXIETY : aprensión *f*, ansiedad *f*, temor *m* **3** UNDERSTANDING : comprensión *f*, percepción *f*

apprehensive [ˌæprɪ'hɛntsɪv] *adj* : aprensivo, inquieto — **apprehensively** *adv*

apprentice[1] [ə'prɛntɪs] *vt* **-ticed; -ticing** : colocar de aprendiz

apprentice[2] *n* : aprendiz *m*, -diza *f*

apprenticeship [ə'prɛntɪs,ʃɪp] *n* : aprendizaje *f*

apprise [ə'praɪz] *vt* **-prised; -prising** : informar, avisar

approach[1] [ə'pro:tʃ] *vt* **1** NEAR : acercarse a **2** APPROXIMATE : aproximarse a **3** : abordar, dirigirse a ⟨I approached my boss with the proposal : me dirigí a mi jefe con la propuesta⟩ **4** TACKLE : abordar, enfocar, considerar — *vi* : acercarse, aproximarse

approach[2] *n* **1** NEARING : acercamiento *m*, aproximación *f* **2** POSITION : enfoque *m*, planteamiento *m* **3** OFFER : propuesta *f*, oferta *f* **4** ACCESS : acceso *m*, vía *f* de acceso

approachable [ə'pro:tʃəbəl] *adj* : accesible, asequible

approbation [,æprə'beɪʃən] *n* : aprobación *f*

appropriate[1] [ə'pro:pri,eɪt] *vt* **-ated; -ating 1** SEIZE : apropiarse de **2** ALLOCATE : destinar, asignar

appropriate[2] [ə'pro:priət] *adj* : apropiado, adecuado, idóneo — **appropriately** *adv*

appropriateness [ə'pro:priətnəs] *n* : idoneidad *f*, propiedad *f*

appropriation [ə,pro:pri'eɪʃən] *n* **1** SEIZURE : apropiación *f* **2** ALLOCATION : asignación *f*

approval [ə'pru:vəl] *n* **1** : aprobación *f*, visto *m* bueno **2 on approval** : a prueba

approve [ə'pru:v] *vt* **-proved; -proving 1** : aprobar, sancionar, darle el visto bueno a **2 to approve of** : consentir en, aprobar ⟨he doesn't approve of smoking : está en contra del tabaco⟩

approximate[1] [ə'praksə,meɪt] *vt* **-mated; -mating** : aproximarse a, acercarse a

approximate[2] [ə'praksəmət] *adj* : aproximado

approximately [ə'praksəmətli] *adv* : aproximadamente, más o menos

approximation [ə,praksə'meɪʃən] *n* : aproximación *f*

appurtenance [ə'pərtənənts] *n* : accesorio *m*

apricot ['æprə,kat, 'eɪ-] *n* : albaricoque *m*, chabacano *m* *Mex*

April ['eɪprəl] *n* : abril *m*

apron ['eɪprən] *n* : delantal *m*, mandil *m*

apropos[1] [,æprə'po:, 'æprə,po:] *adv* : a propósito

apropos[2] *adj* : pertinente, oportuno, acertado

apropos of *prep* : a propósito de

apt ['æpt] *adj* **1** FITTING : apto, apropiado, acertado, oportuno **2** LIABLE : propenso, inclinado **3** CLEVER, QUICK : listo, despierto

aptitude ['æptə,tu:d, -,tju:d] *n* **1** : aptitud *f*, capacidad *f* ⟨aptitude test : prueba de aptitud⟩ **2** TALENT : talento *m*, facilidad *f*

aptly ['æptli] *adv* : acertadamente

aqua ['ækwə, 'a-] *n* : color *m* aguamarina

aquarium [ə'kwæriəm] *n, pl* **-iums** *or* **-ia** [-iə] : acuario *m*

Aquarius [ə'kwæriəs] *n* : Acuario *mf*

aquatic [ə'kwatɪk, -'kwæ-] *adj* : acuático

aqueduct ['ækwə,dʌkt] *n* : acueducto *m*

aqueous ['eɪkwiəs, 'æ-] *adj* : acuoso

aquiline ['ækwə,laɪn, -lən] *adj* : aguileño

Arab[1] ['ærəb] *adj* : árabe

Arab[2] *n* : árabe *mf*

arabesque [,ærə'bɛsk] *n* : arabesco *m*

Arabian[1] [ə'reɪbiən] *adj* : árabe

Arabian[2] *n* → **Arab**[2]

Arabic[1] ['ærəbɪk] *adj* : árabe

Arabic[2] *n* : árabe *m* (idioma)

arable ['ærəbəl] *adj* : arable, cultivable

arbiter ['arbətər] *n* : árbitro *m*, -tra *f*

arbitrary ['arbə,trɛri] *adj* : arbitrario — **arbitrarily** [,arbə'trɛrəli] *adv*

arbitrate ['arbə,treɪt] *v* **-trated; -trating** : arbitrar

arbitration [,arbə'treɪʃən] *n* : arbitraje *m*

arbitrator ['arbə,treɪtər] *n* : árbitro *m*, -tra *f*

arbor ['arbər] *n* : cenador *m*, pérgola *f*

arboreal [ar'boriəl] *adj* : arbóreo

arc[1] ['ark] *vi* **arced; arcing** : formar un arco

arc[2] *n* : arco *m*

arcade [ar'keɪd] *n* **1** ARCHES : arcada *f* **2** MALL : galería *f* comercial

arcane [ar'keɪn] *adj* : arcano, secreto, misterioso

arch[1] ['artʃ] *vt* : arquear, enarcar — *vi* : formar un arco, arquearse

arch[2] *adj* **1** CHIEF : principal **2** MISCHIEVOUS : malicioso, pícaro

arch[3] *n* : arco *m*

archaeological [,arkiə'ladʒɪkəl] *adj* : arqueológico

archaeologist [,arki'aladʒɪst] *n* : arqueólogo *m*, -ga *f*

archaeology *or* **archeology** [,arki'aladʒi] *n* : arqueología *f*

archaic [ar'keɪk] *adj* : arcaico — **archaically** [-ɪkli] *adv*

archangel ['ark,eɪndʒəl] *n* : arcángel *m*

archbishop [artʃ'bɪʃəp] *n* : arzobispo *m*

archdiocese [artʃ'daɪəsəs, -,si:z, -,si:s] *n* : archidiócesis *f*

archer ['artʃər] *n* : arquero *m*, -ra *f*

archery ['artʃəri] *n* : tiro *m* al arco

archetypal [,arkɪ'taɪpəl] *adj* : arquetípico

archetype ['arkɪ,taɪp] *n* : arquetipo *m*

archipelago [,arkə'pɛlə,go:, ,artʃ-] *n, pl* **-goes** *or* **-gos** [-go:z] : archipiélago *m*

architect ['arkə,tɛkt] *n* : arquiteto *m*, -ta *f*

architectural [,arkə'tɛktʃərəl] *adj* : arquitectónico — **architecturally** *adv*

architecture ['arkə,tɛktʃər] *n* : arquitectura *f*

archive ['ar,kaɪv] *n or* **archives** ['ar,kaɪvz] *npl* : archivo *m*

archivist ['arkəvɪst, -ˌkaɪ-] n : archivero m, -ra f; archivista mf

archway ['arˌtʃˌweɪ] n : arco m, pasadizo m abovedado

arctic ['arktɪk, 'art-] adj 1 : ártico ⟨arctic regions : zonas árticas⟩ 2 FRIGID : glacial

arctic circle n : círculo m ártico

ardent ['ardənt] adj 1 PASSIONATE : ardiente, fogoso, apasionado 2 FERVENT : ferviente, fervoroso — **ardently** adv

ardor ['ardər] n : ardor m, pasión f, fervor m

arduous ['ardʒuəs] adj : arduo, duro, riguroso — **arduously** adv

arduousness ['ardʒuəsnəs] n : dureza f, rigor m

are → **be**

area ['æriə] n 1 SURFACE : área f, superficie f 2 REGION : área f, región f, zona f 3 FIELD : área f, terreno m, campo m (de conocimiento)

area code n : código m de la zona, prefijo m Spain

arena [ə'ri:nə] n 1 : arena f, estadio m ⟨sports arena : estadio deportivo⟩ 2 : arena f, ruedo m ⟨the political arena : el ruedo político⟩

Argentine ['ardʒənˌtaɪn, -ˌti:n] or **Argentinean** or **Argentinian** [ˌardʒən'tɪniən] n : argentino m, -na f — **Argentine** or **Argentinean** or **Argentinian** adj

argon ['arˌgan] n : argón m

argot ['argət, -ˌgo:] n : argot m

arguable ['argjuəbəl] adj : discutible

argue ['arˌgju:] v **-gued; -guing** vi 1 REASON : argüir, argumentar, razonar 2 DISPUTE : discutir, pelear(se), alegar — vt 1 SUGGEST : sugerir 2 MAINTAIN : alegar, argüir, sostener 3 DISCUSS : discutir, debatir

argument ['argjəmənt] n 1 REASONING : argumento m, razonamiento m 2 DISCUSSION : discusión f, debate m 3 QUARREL : pelea f, riña f, disputa f

argumentative [ˌargjə'mɛntətɪv] adj : discutidor

argyle ['arˌgaɪl] n : diseño m de rombos

aria ['ariə] n : aria f

arid ['ærəd] adj : árido

aridity [ə'rɪdəti, æ-] n : aridez f

Aries ['ɛri:z, -iˌi:z] n : Aries mf

arise [ə'raɪz] vi **arose** [ə'ro:z]; **arisen** [ə'rɪzən]; **arising** 1 ASCEND : ascender, subir, elevarse 2 ORIGINATE : originarse, surgir, presentarse 3 GET UP : levantarse

aristocracy [ˌærə'stakrəsi] n, pl **-cies** : aristocracia f

aristocrat [ə'rɪstəˌkræt] n : aristócrata mf

aristocratic [əˌrɪstə'krætɪk] adj : aristocrático, noble

arithmetic[1] [ˌæriθ'mɛtɪk] or **arithmetical** [-tɪkəl] adj : aritmético

arithmetic[2] [ə'rɪθməˌtɪk] n : aritmética f

ark ['ark] n : arca f

arm[1] ['arm] vt : armar — vi : armarse

arm[2] n 1 : brazo m (del cuerpo o de un sillón), manga f (de una prenda) 2 BRANCH : rama f, sección f 3 WEAPON : arma f ⟨to take up arms : tomar las armas⟩ 4 → **coat of arms**

armada [ar'madə, -'meɪ-] n : armada f, flota f

armadillo [ˌarmə'dɪlo] n, pl **-los** : armadillo m

armament ['arməmənt] n : armamento m

armchair ['armˌtʃɛr] n : butaca f, sillón m

armed ['armd] adj 1 : armado ⟨armed robbery : robo a mano armada⟩ 2 **armed forces** : fuerzas fpl armadas

Armenian [ar'mi:niən] n : armenio m, -nia f — **Armenian** adj

armistice ['arməstɪs] n : armisticio m

armor ['armər] n : armadura f, coraza f

armored ['armərd] adj : blindado, acorazado

armory ['arməri] n, pl **-mories** : arsenal m (almacén), armería f (museo), fábrica f de armas

armpit ['armˌpɪt] n : axila f, sobaco m

army ['armi] n, pl **-mies** : ejército m (militar) 2 MULTITUDE : legión f, multitud f, ejército m

aroma [ə'ro:mə] n : aroma f

aromatic [ˌærə'mætɪk] adj : aromático

around[1] [ə'raund] adv 1 : de circunferencia ⟨a tree three feet around : un árbol de tres pies de circunferencia⟩ 2 : alrededor, a la redonda ⟨for miles around : por millas a la redonda⟩ ⟨all around : por todos lados, todo alrededor⟩ 3 : por ahí ⟨they're somewhere around : deben estar por ahí⟩ 4 APPROXIMATELY : más o menos, aproximadamente ⟨around 5 o'clock : a eso de las 5⟩ 5 **to turn around** : darse la vuelta, voltearse

around[2] prep 1 SURROUNDING : alrededor de, en torno a 2 THROUGH : por, en ⟨he traveled around Mexico : viajó por México⟩ ⟨around the house : en casa⟩ 3 : a la vuelta de ⟨around the corner : a la vuelta de la esquina⟩ 4 NEAR : alrededor de, cerca de

arousal [ə'rauzəl] n : excitación f

arouse [ə'rauz] vt **aroused; arousing** 1 AWAKE : despertar 2 EXCITE : despertar, suscitar, excitar

arraign [ə'reɪn] vt : hacer comparecer (ante un tribunal)

arraignment [ə'reɪnmənt] n : orden m de comparecencia, acusación f

arrange [ə'reɪndʒ] vt **-ranged; -ranging** 1 ORDER : arreglar, poner en orden, disponer 2 SETTLE : arreglar, fijar, concertar 3 ADAPT : arreglar, adaptar

arrangement [ə'reɪndʒmənt] n 1 ORDER : arreglo m, orden m 2 ARRANGING : disposición f ⟨floral arrangement : arreglo floral⟩ 3 AGREEMENT : arreglo m, acuerdo m, convenio m 4 **arrange-**

ments *npl* : preparativos *mpl*, planes *mpl*

array¹ [ə'reɪ] *vt* 1 ORDER : poner en orden, presentar, formar 2 GARB : vestir, ataviar, engalanar

array² *n* 1 ORDER : orden *m*, formación *f* 2 ATTIRE : atavío *m*, galas *mpl* 3 RANGE, SELECTION : selección *f*, serie *f*, gama *f* ⟨an array of problems : una serie de problemas⟩

arrears [ə'rɪrz] *npl* : atrasos *mpl* ⟨to be in arrears : estar atrasado en los pagos⟩

arrest¹ [ə'rɛst] *vt* 1 APPREHEND : arrestar, detener 2 CHECK, STOP : detener, parar

arrest² *n* 1 APPREHENSION : arresto *m*, detención *f* ⟨under arrest : detenido⟩ 2 STOPPING : paro *m*

arrival [ə'raɪvəl] *n* : llegada *f*, venida *f*, arribo *m*

arrive [ə'raɪv] *vi* -rived; -riving 1 COME : llegar, arribar 2 SUCCEED : triunfar, tener éxito

arrogance ['ærəgənts] *n* : arrogancia *f*, soberbia *f*, altanería *f*, altivez *f*

arrogant ['ærəgənt] *adj* : arrogante, soberbio, altanero, altivo — **arrogantly** *adv*

arrogate ['ærə,geɪt] *vt* -gated; -gating **to arrogate to oneself** : arrogarse

arrow ['æro] *n* : flecha *f*

arrowhead ['æro,hɛd] *n* : punta *f* de flecha

arroyo [ə'rɔɪo] *n* : arroyo *m*

arsenal ['arsənəl] *n* : arsenal *m*

arsenic ['arsənɪk] *n* : arsénico *m*

arson ['arsən] *n* : incendio *m* premeditado

arsonist ['arsənɪst] *n* : incendiario *m*, -ria *f*; pirómano *m*, -na *f*

art ['art] *n* 1 : arte *m* 2 SKILL : destreza *f*, habilidad *f*, maña *f* 3 **arts** *npl* : letras *fpl* (en la educación) 4 **fine arts** : bellas artes *fpl*

arterial [ar'tɪriəl] *adj* : arterial

arteriosclerosis [ar,tɪriosklə'ro:sɪs] *n* : arteriosclerosis *f*

artery ['artəri] *n*, *pl* -teries 1 : arteria *f* 2 THOROUGHFARE : carretera *f* principal, arteria *f*

artesian well [ar'ti:ʒən] *n* : pozo *m* artesiano

artful ['artfəl] *adj* 1 INGENIOUS : ingenioso, diestro 2 CRAFTY : astuto, taimado, ladino, artero — **artfully** *adv*

arthritic [ar'θrɪtɪk] *adj* : artrítico

arthritis [ar'θraɪtəs] *n*, *pl* -tides [ar-'θrɪtə,di:z] : artritis *f*

arthropod ['arθrə,pad] *n* : artrópodo *m*

artichoke ['artə,tʃo:k] *n* : alcachofa *f*

article ['artɪkəl] *n* 1 ITEM : artículo *m*, objeto *m* 2 ESSAY : artículo *m* 3 CLAUSE : artículo *m*, cláusula *f* 4 : artículo *m* ⟨definite article : artículo determinado⟩

articulate¹ [ar'tɪkjə,leɪt] *vt* -lated; -lating 1 UTTER : articular, enunciar, expresar 2 CONNECT : articular (en anatomía)

articulate² [ar'tɪkjələt] *adj* **to be articulate** : poder articular palabras, expresarse bien

articulately [ar'tɪkjələtli] *adv* : elocuentemente, con fluidez

articulateness [ar'tɪkjələtnəs] *n* : elocuencia *f*, fluidez *f*

articulation [ar,tɪkjə'leɪʃən] *n* 1 JOINT : articulación *f* 2 UTTERANCE : articulación *f*, declaración *f* 3 ENUNCIATION : articulación *f*, pronunciación *f*

artifact ['artə,fækt] *n* : artefacto *m*

artifice ['artəfəs] *n* : artificio *m*

artificial [,artə'fɪʃəl] *adj* 1 SYNTHETIC : artificial, sintético 2 FEIGNED : artificial, falso, afectado

artificially [,artə'fɪʃəli] *adv* : artificialmente, con afectación

artillery [ar'tɪləri] *n*, *pl* -leries : artillería *f*

artisan ['artəzən, -sən] *n* : artesano *m*, -na *f*

artist ['artɪst] *n* : artista *mf*

artistic [ar'tɪstɪk] *adj* : artístico — **artistically** [-tɪkli] *adv*

artistry ['artəstri] *n* : maestría *f*, arte *m*

artless ['artləs] *adj* : sencillo, natural, ingenuo, cándido — **artlessly** *adv*

artlessness ['artləsnəs] *n* : ingenuidad *f*, candidez *f*

arty ['arti] *adj* **artier; -est** : pretenciosamente artístico

as¹ ['æz] *adv* 1 : tan, tanto ⟨this one's not as difficult : éste no es tan difícil⟩ 2 : como ⟨some trees, as oak and pine : algunos árboles, como el roble y el pino⟩

as² *conj* 1 LIKE : como, igual que 2 WHEN, WHILE : cuando, mientras, a la vez que 3 BECAUSE : porque 4 THOUGH : aunque, por más que ⟨strange as it may appear : por extraño que parezca⟩ 5 **as is** : tal como está

as³ *prep* 1 : de ⟨I met her as a child : la conocí de pequeña⟩ 2 LIKE : como ⟨behave as a man : compórtate como un hombre⟩

as⁴ *pron* : que ⟨in the same building as my brother : en el mismo edificio que mi hermano⟩

asbestos [æz'bɛstəs, æs-] *n* : asbesto *m*, amianto *m*

ascend [ə'sɛnd] *vi* : ascender, subir — *vt* : subir, subir a, escalar

ascendancy [ə'sɛndəntsi] *n* : ascendiente *m*, predominio *m*

ascendant¹ [ə'sɛndənt] *adj* 1 RISING : ascendente 2 DOMINANT : superior, dominante

ascendant² *n* **to be in the ascendant** : estar en alza, ir ganando predominio

ascension [ə'sɛntʃən] *n* : ascensión *f*

ascent [ə'sɛnt] *n* 1 RISE : ascensión *f*, subida *f*, ascenso *m* 2 SLOPE : cuesta *f*, pendiente *f*

ascertain [,æsər'teɪn] *vt* : determinar, establecer, averiguar

ascertainable [,æsər'teɪnəbəl] *adj* : determinable, averiguable

ascetic[1] [ə'sɛt̮ɪk] *adj* : ascético
ascetic[2] *n* : asceta *mf*
asceticism [ə'sɛt̮ə,sɪzəm] *n* : ascetismo *m*
ascribable [ə'skraɪbəbəl] *adj* : atribuible, imputable
ascribe [ə'skraɪb] *vt* **-cribed; -cribing** : atribuir, imputar
aseptic [eɪ'sɛptɪk] *adj* : aséptico
asexual [,eɪ'sɛkʃʊəl] *adj* : asexual
as for *prep* CONCERNING : en cuanto a, respecto a, para
ash ['æʃ] *n* **1** : ceniza *f* ⟨to reduce to ashes : reducir a cenizas⟩ **2** : fresno *m* (árbol)
ashamed [ə'ʃeɪmd] *adj* : avergonzado, abochornado, apenado — **ashamedly** [ə'ʃeɪmədli] *adv*
ashen ['æʃən] *adj* : lívido, ceniciento, pálido
ashore [ə'ʃor] *adv* **1** : en tierra **2 to go ashore** : desembarcar
ashtray ['æʃ,treɪ] *n* : cenicero *m*
Asian[1] ['eɪʒən, -ʃən] *adj* : asiático
Asian[2] *n* : asiático *m*, -ca *f*
aside [ə'saɪd] *adv* **1** : a un lado ⟨to step aside : hacerse a un lado⟩ **2** : de lado, aparte ⟨jesting aside : bromas aparte⟩ **3 to set aside** : guardar, apartar, reservar
aside from *prep* **1** BESIDES : además de **2** EXCEPT : aparte de, menos
as if *conj* : como si
asinine ['æsən,aɪn] *adj* : necio, estúpido
ask ['æsk] *vt* **1** : preguntar ⟨ask him if he's coming : pregúntale si viene⟩ **2** REQUEST : pedir, solicitar ⟨to ask a favor : pedir un favor⟩ **3** INVITE : invitar — *vi* **1** INQUIRE : preguntar ⟨I asked about her children : pregunté por sus niños⟩ **2** REQUEST : pedir ⟨we asked for help : pedimos ayuda⟩
askance [ə'skænts] *adv* **1** SIDELONG : de reojo, de soslayo **2** SUSPICIOUSLY : con recelo, con desconfianza
askew [ə'skju:] *adj* : torcido, ladeado
asleep [ə'sli:p] *adj* **1** : dormido, durmiendo **2 to fall asleep** : quedarse dormido
as of *prep* : desde, a partir de
asparagus [ə'spærəgəs] *n* : espárrago *m*
aspect ['æ,spɛkt] *n* : aspecto *m*
aspen ['æspən] *n* : álamo *m* temblón
asperity [æ'spɛrət̮i, ə-] *n*, *pl* **-ties** : aspereza *f*
aspersion [ə'spərʒən] *n* : difamación *f*, calumnia *f*
asphalt ['æs,fɔlt] *n* : asfalto *m*
asphyxia [æ'sfɪksiə, ə-] *n* : asfixia *f*
asphyxiate [æ'sfɪksi,eɪt] *v* **-ated; -ating** *vt* : asfixiar — *vi* : asfixiarse
asphyxiation [æ,sfɪksi'eɪʃən] *n* : asfixia *f*
aspirant ['æspərənt, ə'spaɪrənt] *n* : aspirante *mf*, pretendiente *mf*
aspiration [,æspə'reɪʃən] *n* **1** DESIRE : aspiración *f*, anhelo *m*, ambición *f* **2** BREATHING : aspiración *f*

aspire [ə'spaɪr] *vi* **-pired; -piring** : aspirar
aspirin ['æsprən, 'æspə-] *n*, *pl* **aspirin** *or* **aspirins** : aspirina *f*
ass ['æs] *n* **1** : asno *m* **2** IDIOT : imbécil *mf*, idiota *mf*
assail [ə'seɪl] *vt* : atacar, asaltar
assailant [ə'seɪlənt] *n* : asaltante *mf*, atacante *mf*
assassin [ə'sæsən] *n* : asesino *m*, -na *f*
assassinate [ə'sæsən,eɪt] *vt* **-nated; -nating** : asesinar
assassination [ə,sæsən'eɪʃən] *n* : asesinato *m*
assault[1] [ə'sɔlt] *vt* : atacar, asaltar, agredir
assault[2] *n* : ataque *m*, asalto *m*, agresión *f*
assay[1] ['æ,seɪ, 'æ,seɪ] *vt* : ensayar
assay[2] ['æ,seɪ, æ'seɪ] *n* : ensayo *m*
assemble [ə'sɛmbəl] *v* **-bled; -bling** *vt* **1** GATHER : reunir, recoger, juntar **2** CONSTRUCT : ensamblar, montar, construir — *vi* : reunirse, congregarse
assembly [ə'sɛmbli] *n*, *pl* **-blies 1** MEETING : reunión *f* **2** CONSTRUCTING : ensamblaje *m*, montaje *m*
assemblyman [ə'sɛmblimən] *n*, *pl* **-men** [-mən, -,mɛn] : asambleísta *m*
assemblywoman [ə'sɛmbli,wʊmən] *n*, *pl* **-women** [-,wɪmən] : asambleísta *f*
assent[1] [ə'sɛnt] *vi* : asentir, consentir
assent[2] *n* : asentimiento *m*, aprobación *f*
assert [ə'sərt] *vt* **1** AFFIRM : afirmar, aseverar, mantener **2 to assert oneself** : imponerse, hacerse valer
assertion [ə'sərʃən] *n* : afirmación *f*, aseveración *f*, aserto *m*
assertive [ə'sərt̮ɪv] *adj* : firme, enérgico
assertiveness [ə'sərt̮ɪvnəs] *n* : seguridad *f* en sí mismo
assess [ə'sɛs] *vt* **1** IMPOSE : gravar (un impuesto), imponer **2** EVALUATE : evaluar, valorar, aquilatar
assessment [ə'sɛsmənt] *n* : evaluación *f*, valoración *f*
assessor [ə'sɛsər] *n* : evaluador *m*, -dora *f*; tasador *m*, -dora *f*
asset ['æ,sɛt] *n* **1** : ventaja *f*, recurso *m* **2 assets** *npl* : bienes *mpl*, activo *m* ⟨assets and liabilities : activo y pasivo⟩
assiduous [ə'sɪdʒʊəs] *adj* : diligente, aplicado, asiduo — **assiduously** *adv*
assign [ə'saɪn] *vt* **1** APPOINT : designar, nombrar **2** ALLOT : asignar, señalar **3** ATTRIBUTE : atribuir, dar, conceder
assignment [ə'saɪnmənt] *n* **1** TASK : función *f*, tarea *f*, misión *f* **2** HOMEWORK : tarea *f*, asignación *f* PRi, deberes *mpl* Spain **3** APPOINTMENT : nombramiento *m* **4** ALLOCATION : asignación *f*
assimilate [ə'sɪmə,leɪt] *v* **-lated; -lating** *vt* : asimilar — *vi* : adaptarse, integrarse
assimilation [ə,sɪmə'leɪʃən] *n* : asimilación *f*
assist[1] [ə'sɪst] *vt* : asistir, ayudar
assist[2] *n* : asistencia *f*, contribución *f*

assistance [ə'sɪstənts] *n* : asistencia *f*, ayuda *f*, auxilio *m*

assistant [ə'sɪstənt] *n* : ayudante *mf*, asistente *mf*

associate¹ [ə'so:ʃi̯ˌeɪt, -si-] *v* **-ated; -ating** *vt* **1** CONNECT, RELATE : asociar, relacionar **2 to be associated with** : estar relacionado con, estar vinculado a — *vi* **to associate with** : relacionarse con, frecuentar

associate² [ə'so:ʃi̯ət, -siət] *n* : asociado *m*, -da *f*; colega *mf*; socio *m*, -cia *f*

association [ə,so:ʃi̯'eɪʃən, -si-] *n* **1** ORGANIZATION : asociación *f*, sociedad *f* **2** RELATIONSHIP : asociación *f*, relación *f*

as soon as *conj* : en cuanto, tan pronto como

assorted [ə'sɔrtəd] *adj* : surtido

assortment [ə'sɔrtmənt] *n* : surtido *m*, variedad *f*, colección *f*

assuage [ə'sweɪʤ] *vt* **-suaged; -suaging 1** EASE : aliviar, mitigar **2** CALM : calmar, aplacar **3** SATISFY : saciar, satisfacer

assume [ə'su:m] *vt* **-sumed; -suming 1** SUPPOSE : suponer, asumir **2** UNDERTAKE : asumir, encargarse de **3** TAKE ON : adquirir, adoptar, tomar ⟨to assume importance : tomar importancia⟩ **4** FEIGN : adoptar, afectar, simular

assumption [ə'sʌmpʃən] *n* : asunción *f*, presunción *f*

assurance [ə'ʃʊrənts] *n* **1** CERTAINTY : certidumbre *f*, certeza *f* **2** CONFIDENCE : confianza *f*, aplomo *m*, seguridad *f*

assure [ə'ʃʊr] *vt* **-sured; -suring** : asegurar, garantizar ⟨I assure you that I'll do it : te aseguro que lo haré⟩

assured [ə'ʃʊrd] *adj* **1** CERTAIN : seguro, asegurado **2** CONFIDENT : confiado, seguro de sí mismo

aster ['æstər] *n* : aster *m*

asterisk ['æstə,rɪsk] *n* : asterisco *m*

astern [ə'stərn] *adv* **1** BEHIND : detrás, a popa **2** BACKWARDS : hacia atrás

asteroid ['æstə,rɔɪd] *n* : asteroide *m*

asthma ['æzmə] *n* : asma *m*

asthmatic [æz'mætɪk] *adj* : asmático

as though → **as if**

astigmatism [ə'stɪgmə,tɪzəm] *n* : astigmatismo *m*

as to *prep* **1** ABOUT : sobre, acerca de **2** → **according to**

astonish [ə'stɑnɪʃ] *vt* : asombrar, sorprender, pasmar

astonishing [ə'stɑnɪʃɪŋ] *adj* : asombroso, sorprendente, increíble — **astonishingly** *adv*

astonishment [ə'stɑnɪʃmənt] *n* : asombro *m*, estupefacción *f*, sorpresa *f*

astound [ə'staʊnd] *vt* : asombrar, pasmar, dejar estupefacto

astounding [ə'staʊndɪŋ] *adj* : asombroso, pasmoso — **astoundingly** *adv*

astraddle [ə'strædəl] *adv* : a horcajadas

astral ['æstrəl] *adj* : astral

astray [ə'streɪ] *adv & adj* : perdido, extraviado, descarriado

astride [ə'straɪd] *adv* : a horcajadas

astringency [ə'strɪnʤəntsi] *n* : astringencia *f*

astringent¹ [ə'strɪnʤənt] *adj* : astringente

astringent² *n* : astringente *m*

astrologer [ə'strɑləʤər] *n* : astrólogo *m*, -ga *f*

astrological [,æstrə'lɑʤɪkəl] *adj* : astrológico

astrology [ə'strɑləʤi] *n* : astrología *f*

astronaut ['æstrə,nɔt] *n* : astronauta *mf*

astronautic [,æstrə'nɔtɪk] *or* **astronautical** [-tɪkəl] *adj* : astronáutico

astronautics [,æstrə'nɔtɪks] *ns & pl* : astronáutica *f*

astronomer [ə'strɑnəmər] *n* : astrónomo *m*, -ma *f*

astronomical [,æstrə'nɑmɪkəl] *adj* **1** : astronómico **2** ENORMOUS : astronómico, enorme, gigantesco

astronomy [ə'strɑnəmi] *n, pl* **-mies** : astronomía *f*

astute [ə'stu:t, -'stju:t] *adj* : astuto, sagaz, perspicaz — **astutely** *adv*

astuteness [ə'stu:tnəs, -'stju:t-] *n* : astucia *f*, sagacidad *f*, perspicacia *f*

asunder [ə'sʌndər] *adv* : en dos, en pedazos ⟨to tear asunder : hacer pedazos⟩

as well as¹ *conj* : tanto como

as well as² *prep* BESIDES : además de, aparte de

as yet *adv* : aún, todavía

asylum [ə'saɪləm] *n* **1** REFUGE : refugio *m*, santuario *m*, asilo *m* **2 insane asylum** : manicomio *m*

asymmetrical [,eɪsə'mɛtrɪkəl] *or* **asymmetric** [-'mɛtrɪk] *adj* : asimétrico

asymmetry [,eɪ'sɪmətri] *n* : asimetría *f*

at ['æt] *prep* **1** : en ⟨at the top : en lo alto⟩ ⟨at peace : en paz⟩ ⟨at Ann's house : en casa de Ana⟩ **2** : a ⟨at the rear : al fondo⟩ ⟨at 10 o'clock : a las diez⟩ **3** : por ⟨at last : por fin⟩ ⟨to be surprised at something : sorprenderse por algo⟩ **4** : de ⟨he's laughing at you : está riéndose de ti⟩ **5** : para ⟨you're good at this : eres bueno para esto⟩

at all *adv* : en absoluto, para nada

ate → **eat**

atheism ['eɪθi,ɪzəm] *n* : ateísmo *m*

atheist ['eɪθiɪst] *n* : ateo *m*, atea *f*

atheistic [,eɪθi'ɪstɪk] *adj* : ateo

athlete ['æθ,li:t] *n* : atleta *mf*

athletic [æθ'lɛtɪk] *adj* : atlético

athletics [æθ'lɛtɪks] *ns & pl* : atletismo *m*

Atlantic [ət'læntɪk, æt-] *adj* : atlántico

atlas ['ætləs] *n* : atlas *m*

ATM [,eɪ,ti:'ɛm] *n* : cajero *m* automático

atmosphere ['ætmə,sfɪr] *n* **1** AIR : atmósfera *f*, aire *m* **2** AMBIENCE : ambiente *m*, atmósfera *f*, clima *m*

atmospheric [,ætmə'sfɪrɪk, -'sfɛr-] *adj* : atmosférico — **atmospherically** [-ɪkli] *adv*

atoll ['æ,tɔl, 'eɪ-, -,tɑl] n : atolón m
atom ['æṱəm] n 1 : átomo m 2 SPECK : ápice m, pizca f
atomic [ə'tɑmɪk] adj : atómico
atomic bomb n : bomba f atómica
atomizer ['æṱə,maɪzər] n : atomizador m, pulverizador m
atone [ə'to:n] vt **atoned; atoning to atone for** : expiar
atonement [ə'to:nmənt] n : expiación f, desagravio m
atop[1] [ə'tɑp] adj : encima
atop[2] prep : encima de, sobre
atrium ['eɪtriəm] n, pl **atria** [-triə] or **atriums 1** : atrio m **2** : aurícula f (del corazón)
atrocious [ə'tro:ʃəs] adj : atroz — **atrociously** adv
atrocity [ə'trɑsəti] n, pl **-ties** : atrocidad f
atrophy[1] ['ætrəfi] vt **-phied; -phying** : atrofiar
atrophy[2] n, pl **-phies** : atrofia f
attach [ə'tætʃ] vt **1** FASTEN : sujetar, atar, amarrar, pegar **2** JOIN : juntar, adjuntar **3** ATTRIBUTE : dar, atribuir ⟨I attached little importance to it : le di poca importancia⟩ **4** SEIZE : embargar **5 to become attached to someone** : encariñarse con alguien
attaché [,æṱə'ʃeɪ, ,æ,tæ-, ,ṱæ-] n : agregado m, -da f
attachment [ə'tætʃmənt] n **1** ACCESSORY : accesorio m **2** CONNECTION : conexión f, acoplamiento m **3** FONDNESS : apego m, cariño m, afición f
attack[1] [ə'tæk] vt **1** ASSAULT : atacar, asaltar, agredir **2** TACKLE : acometer, combatir, enfrentarse con
attack[2] n **1** : ataque m, asalto m, acometida f ⟨to launch an attack : lanzar un ataque⟩ **2** : ataque m, crisis f ⟨heart attack : ataque cardíaco, infarto⟩ ⟨attack of nerves : crisis nerviosa⟩
attacker [ə'tækər] n : asaltante mf
attain [ə'teɪn] vt **1** ACHIEVE : lograr, conseguir, alcanzar, realizar **2** REACH : alcanzar, llegar a
attainable [ə'teɪnəbəl] adj : alcanzable, realizable, asequible
attainment [ə'teɪnmənt] n : logro m, consecución f, realización f
attempt[1] [ə'tɛmpt] vt : intentar, tratar de
attempt[2] n : intento m, tentativa f
attend [ə'tɛnd] vt **1** : asistir a ⟨to attend a meeting : asistir a una reunión⟩ **2** : atender, ocuparse de, cuidar ⟨to attend a patient : atender a un paciente⟩ **3** HEED : atender a, hacer caso de **4** ACCOMPANY : acompañar
attendance [ə'tɛndənts] n **1** ATTENDING : asistencia f **2** TURNOUT : concurrencia f
attendant[1] [ə'tɛndənt] adj : concomitante, inherente
attendant[2] n : asistente mf, acompañante mf, guarda mf

attention [ə'tɛntʃən] n **1** : atención f **2 to pay attention** : prestar atención, hacer caso **3 to stand at attention** : estar firme
attentive [ə'tɛntɪv] adj : atento — **attentively** adv
attentiveness [ə'tɛntɪvnəs] n **1** THOUGHTFULNESS : cortesía f, consideración f **2** CONCENTRATION : atención f, concentración f
attest [ə'tɛst] vt : atestiguar, dar fe de
attestation [,æ,ts'teɪʃən] n : testimonio m
attic ['æṱɪk] n : ático m, desván m, buhardilla f
attire[1] [ə'taɪr] vt **-tired; -tiring** : ataviar
attire[2] n : atuendo m, atavío m
attitude ['æṱə,tu:d, -,tju:d] n **1** FEELING : actitud f **2** POSTURE : postura f
attorney [ə'tərni] n, pl **-neys** : abogado m, -da f
attract [ə'trækt] vt **1** : atraer **2 to attract attention** : llamar la atención
attraction [ə'trækʃən] n : atracción f, atractivo m
attractive [ə'træktɪv] adj : atractivo, atrayente
attractively [ə'træktɪvli] adv : de manera atractiva, de buen gusto, hermosamente
attractiveness [ə'træktɪvnəs] n : atractivo m
attributable [ə'trɪbjʊṱəbəl] adj : atribuible, imputable
attribute[1] [ə'trɪ,bju:t] vt **-tributed; -tributing** : atribuir
attribute[2] ['ætrə,bju:t] n : atributo m, cualidad f
attribution [,ætrə'bju:ʃən] n : atribución f
attune [ə'tu:n, -'tju:n] vt **-tuned; -tuning 1** ADAPT : adaptar, adecuar **2 to be attuned to** : estar en armonía con
atypical [,eɪ'tɪpɪkəl] adj : atípico
auburn ['ɔbərn] adj : castaño rojizo
auction[1] ['ɔkʃən] vt : subastar, rematar
auction[2] n : subasta f, remate m
auctioneer [,ɔkʃə'nɪr] n : subastador m, -dora f; rematador m, -dora f
audacious [ɔ'deɪʃəs] adj : audaz, atrevido
audacity [ɔ'dæsəti] n, pl **-ties** : audacia f, atrevimiento m, descaro m
audible ['ɔdəbəl] adj : audible — **audibly** [-bli] adv
audience ['ɔdiənts] n **1** INTERVIEW : audiencia f **2** PUBLIC : audiencia f, público m, auditorio m, espectadores mpl
audio[1] ['ɔdi,o:] adj : de sonido, de audio
audio[2] n : audio m
audiovisual [,ɔdio'vɪʒuəl] adj : audiovisual
audit[1] ['ɔdət] vt **1** : auditar (finanzas) **2** : asistir como oyente a (una clase o un curso)
audit[2] n : auditoría f
audition[1] [ɔ'dɪʃən] vi : hacer una audición

audition² *n* : audición *f*

auditor ['ɔdətər] *n* **1** : auditor *m*, -tora *f* (de finanzas) **2** STUDENT : oyente *mf*

auditorium [ˌɔdə'toriəm] *n*, *pl* **-riums** *or* **-ria** [-riə] : auditorio *m*, sala *f*

auditory ['ɔdəˌtori] *adj* : auditivo

auger ['ɔgər] *n* : taladro *m*, barrena *f*

augment [ɔg'mɛnt] *vt* : aumentar, incrementar

augmentation [ˌɔgmən'teiʃən] *n* : aumento *m*, incremento *m*

augur¹ ['ɔgər] *vt* : augurar, presagiar — *vi* **to augur well** : ser de buen agüero

augur² *n* : augur *m*

augury ['ɔgjʊri, -gər-] *n*, *pl* **-ries** : augurio *m*, presagio *m*, agüero *m*

august [ɔ'gʌst] *adj* : augusto

August ['ɔgəst] *n* : agosto *m*

auk ['ɔk] *n* : alca *f*

aunt ['ænt, 'ant] *n* : tía *f*

aura ['ɔrə] *n* : aura *f*

aural ['ɔrəl] *adj* : auditivo

auricle ['ɔrikəl] *n* : aurícula *f*

aurora borealis [ə'rorəˌbori'æləs] *n* : aurora *f* boreal

auspices ['ɔspəsəz, -ˌsiːz] *npl* : auspicios *mpl*

auspicious [ɔ'spiʃəs] *adj* : prometedor, propicio, de buen augurio

austere [ɔ'stir] *adj* : austero, severo, adusto — **austerely** *adv*

austerity [ɔ'stɛrəti] *n*, *pl* **-ties** : austeridad *f*

Australian [ɔ'streiljən] *n* : australiano *m*, -na *f* — **Australian** *adj*

Austrian ['ɔstriən] *n* : austriaco *m*, -ca *f* — **Austrian** *adj*

authentic [ə'θɛntik, ɔ-] *adj* : auténtico, genuino — **authentically** [-tikli] *adv*

authenticate [ə'θɛntiˌkeit, ɔ-] *vt* **-cated; -cating** : autenticar, autentificar

authenticity [ɔˌθɛn'tisəti] *n* : autenticidad *f*

author ['ɔθər] *n* **1** WRITER : escritor *m*, -tora *f*; autor *m*, -tora *f* **2** CREATOR : autor *m*, -tora *f*; creador *m*, -dora *f*; artífice *mf*

authoritarian [ɔˌθɔrə'tɛriən, ə-] *adj* : autoritario

authoritative [ə'θɔrəˌteitiv, ɔ-] *adj* **1** RELIABLE : fidedigno, autorizado **2** DICTATORIAL : autoritario, dictatorial, imperioso

authoritatively [ə'θɔrəˌteitivli, ɔ-] *adv* **1** RELIABLY : con autoridad **2** DICTATORIALLY : de manera autoritaria

authority [ə'θɔrəti, ɔ-] *n*, *pl* **-ties** **1** EXPERT : autoridad *f*; experto *m*, -ta *f* **2** POWER : autoridad *f*, poder *m* **3** AUTHORIZATION : autorización *f*, licencia *f* **4 the authorities** : las autoridades **5 on good authority** : de buena fuente

authorization [ˌɔθərə'zeiʃən] *n* : autorización *f*

authorize ['ɔθəˌraiz] *vt* **-rized; -rizing** : autorizar, facultar

authorship ['ɔθərˌʃip] *n* : autoría *f*

autism ['ɔˌtizəm] *n* : autismo *m*

autistic [ɔ'tistik] *adj* : autista

auto ['ɔto] → **automobile**

autobiographical [ˌɔtoˌbaiə'græfikəl] *adj* : autobiográfico

autobiography [ˌɔtobai'agrəfi] *n*, *pl* **-phies** : autobiografía *f*

autocracy [ɔ'takrəsi] *n*, *pl* **-cies** : autocracia *f*

autocrat ['ɔtəˌkræt] *n* : autócrata *mf*

autocratic [ˌɔtə'krætik] *adj* : autocrático — **autocratically** [-tikli] *adv*

autograph¹ ['ɔtəˌgræf] *vt* : autografiar

autograph² *n* : autógrafo *m*

automaker ['ɔto:ˌmeikər] *n* : fabricante *mf* de autos, automotriz *f*

automate ['ɔtəˌmeit] *vt* **-mated; -mating** : automatizar

automatic [ˌɔtə'mætik] *adj* : automático — **automatically** [-tikli] *adv*

automation [ˌɔtə'meiʃən] *n* : automatización *f*

automaton [ɔ'taməˌtan] *n*, *pl* **-atons** *or* **-ata** [-tə, -ˌta] : autómata *m*

automobile [ˌɔtəmo'biːl, -'moːˌbiːl] *n* : automóvil *m*, auto *m*, carro *m*, coche *m*

automotive [ˌɔtə'moːtiv] *adj* : automotor

autonomous [ɔ'tanəməs] *adj* : autónomo — **autonomously** *adv*

autonomy [ɔ'tanəmi] *n*, *pl* **-mies** : autonomía *f*

autopsy ['ɔˌtapsi, -təp-] *n*, *pl* **-sies** : autopsia *f*

autumn ['ɔtəm] *n* : otoño *m*

autumnal [ɔ'tʌmnəl] *adj* : otoñal

auxiliary¹ [ɔg'ziljəri, -'ziləri] *adj* : auxiliar

auxiliary² *n*, *pl* **-ries** : auxiliar *mf*, ayudante *mf*

avail¹ [ə'veil] *vt* **to avail oneself** : aprovecharse, valerse

avail² *n* **1** : provecho *m*, utilidad *f* **2 to no avail** : en vano **3 to be of no avail** : no servir de nada, ser inútil

availability [əˌveilə'biləti] *n*, *pl* **-ties** : disponibilidad *f*

available [ə'veiləbəl] *adj* : disponible

avalanche ['ævəˌlæntʃ] *n* : avalancha *f*, alud *m*

avarice ['ævərəs] *n* : avaricia *f*, codicia *f*

avaricious [ˌævə'riʃəs] *adj* : avaricioso, codicioso

avenge [ə'vɛndʒ] *vt* **avenged; avenging** : vengar

avenger [ə'vɛndʒər] *n* : vengador *m*, -dora *f*

avenue ['ævəˌnuː, -ˌnjuː] *n* **1** : avenida *f* **2** MEANS : vía *f*, camino *m*

average¹ ['ævridʒ, 'ævə-] *vt* **-aged; -aging** **1** : hacer un promedio de ⟨he averages 8 hours a day : hace un promedio de 8 horas diarias⟩ **2** : calcular el promedio de, promediar (en matemáticas)

average² *adj* **1** MEAN : medio ⟨the average temperature : la temperatura media⟩ **2** ORDINARY : común, ordinario ⟨the average man : el hombre común⟩

average[3] *n* : promedio *m*
averse [ə'vərs] *adj* : reacio, opuesto
aversion [ə'vərʒən] *n* : aversión *f*
avert [ə'vərt] *vt* **1** : apartar, desviar ⟨he averted his eyes from the scene : apartó los ojos de la escena⟩ **2** AVOID, PREVENT : evitar, prevenir
aviary ['eɪvi,ɛri] *n, pl* **-aries** : pajarera *f*
aviation [,eɪvi'eɪʃən] *n* : aviación *f*
aviator ['eɪvi,eɪtər] *n* : aviador *m*, -dora *f*
avid ['ævɪd] *adj* **1** GREEDY : ávido, codicioso **2** ENTHUSIASTIC : ávido, entusiasta, ferviente — **avidly** *adv*
avocado [,ævə'kɑdo, ,ɑvə-] *n, pl* **-dos** : aguacate *m*, palta *f*
avocation [,ævə'keɪʃən] *n* : pasatiempo *m*, afición *f*
avoid [ə'vɔɪd] *vt* **1** SHUN : evitar, eludir **2** FORGO : evitar, abstenerse de ⟨I always avoided gossip : siempre evitaba los chismes⟩ **3** EVADE : evitar ⟨if I can avoid it : si puedo evitarlo⟩
avoidable [ə'vɔɪdəbəl] *adj* : evitable
avoidance [ə'vɔɪdənts] *n* : el evitar
avoirdupois [,ævərdə'pɔɪz] *n* : sistema *m* inglés de pesos y medidas
avow [ə'vaʊ] *vt* : reconocer, confesar
avowal [ə'vaʊəl] *n* : reconocimiento *m*, confesión *f*
await [ə'weɪt] *vt* : esperar
awake[1] [ə'weɪk] *v* **awoke** [ə'wo:k]; **awoken** [ə'wo:kən] *or* **awaked; awaking** : despertar
awake[2] *adj* : despierto
awaken [ə'weɪkən] → **awake**[1]
award[1] [ə'wɔrd] *vt* : otorgar, conceder, conferir
award[2] *n* **1** PRIZE : premio *m*, galardón *m* **2** MEDAL : condecoración *f*
aware [ə'wær] *adj* : consciente ⟨to be aware of : darse cuenta de, estar consciente de⟩
awareness [ə'wærnəs] *n* : conciencia *f*, conocimiento *m*
awash [ə'wɔʃ] *adj* : inundado
away[1] [ə'weɪ] *adv* **1** : de aquí ⟨go away! : ¡fuera de aquí!, ¡vete!⟩ **2** : de distancia ⟨10 miles away : 10 millas de distancia, queda a 10 millas⟩ **3 far away** : lejos, a lo lejos **4 right away** : en segui-

da, ahora mismo **5 to be away** : estar ausente, estar de viaje **6 to give away** : regalar (una posesión), revelar (un secreto) **7 to go away** : irse, largarse **8 to put away** : guardar **9 to turn away** : volver la cara
away[2] *adj* **1** ABSENT : ausente ⟨away for the week : ausente por la semana⟩ **2 away game** : partido *m* que se juega fuera
awe[1] ['ɔ] *vt* **awed; awing** : abrumar, asombrar, impresionar
awe[2] *n* : asombro *m*
awesome ['ɔsəm] *adj* **1** IMPOSING : imponente, formidable **2** AMAZING : asombroso
awestruck ['ɔ,strʌk] *adj* : asombrado
awful ['ɔfəl] *adj* **1** AWESOME : asombroso **2** DREADFUL : horrible, terrible, atroz **3** ENORMOUS : enorme, tremendo ⟨an awful lot of people : muchísima gente, la mar de gente⟩
awfully ['ɔfəli] *adv* **1** EXTREMELY : terriblemente, extremadamente **2** BADLY : muy mal, espantosamente
awhile [ə'hwaɪl] *adv* : un rato, algún tiempo
awkward ['ɔkwərd] *adj* **1** CLUMSY : torpe, desmañado **2** EMBARRASSING : embarazoso, delicado — **awkwardly** *adv*
awkwardness ['ɔkwərdnəs] *n* **1** CLUMSINESS : torpeza *f* **2** INCONVENIENCE : incomodidad *f*
awl ['ɔl] *n* : punzón *m*
awning ['ɔnɪŋ] *n* : toldo *m*
awry [ə'raɪ] *adj* **1** ASKEW : torcido **2 to go awry** : salir mal, fracasar
ax *or* **axe** ['æks] *n* : hacha *m*
axiom ['æksiəm] *n* : axioma *m*
axiomatic [,æksiə'mætɪk] *adj* : axiomático
axis ['æksɪs] *n, pl* **axes** [-,si:z] : eje *m*
axle ['æksəl] *n* : eje *m*
aye[1] ['aɪ] *adv* : sí
aye[2] *n* : sí *m*
azalea [ə'zeɪljə] *n* : azalea *f*
azimuth ['æzəməθ] *n* : azimut *m*, acimut *m*
Aztec ['æz,tɛk] *n* : azteca *mf*
azure[1] ['æʒər] *adj* : azur, celeste
azure[2] *n* : azur *m*

B

b ['bi:] *n, pl* **b's** *or* **bs** ['bi:z] : segunda letra del alfabeto inglés
babble[1] ['bæbəl] *vi* **-bled; -bling 1** PRATTLE : balbucear **2** CHATTER : charlatanear, parlotear *fam* **3** MURMUR : murmurar
babble[2] *n* : balbuceo *m* (de bebé), parloteo *m* (de adultos), murmullo *m* (de voces, de un arroyo)
babe ['beɪb] *n* → **baby**[3]
babel ['beɪbəl, 'bæ-] *n* : babel *f*, caos *m*

baboon [bæ'bu:n] *n* : babuino *m*
baby[1] ['beɪbi] *vt* **-bied; -bying** : mimar, consentir
baby[2] *adj* **1** : de niño ⟨a baby carriage : un cochecito⟩ ⟨baby talk : habla infantil⟩ **2** TINY : pequeño, minúsculo
baby[3] *n, pl* **-bies** : bebé *m*; niño *m*, -ña *f*
babyhood ['beɪbi,hʊd] *n* : niñez *f*, primera infancia *f*
babyish ['beɪbiɪʃ] *adj* : infantil, pueril

baby–sit ['beɪbi,sɪt] *vi* **-sat** [-,sæt]; **-sitting** : cuidar niños, hacer de canguro *Spain*

baby–sitter ['beɪbi,sɪtər] *n* : niñero *m*, -ra *f*; canguro *mf Spain*

baccalaureate [,bækə'lɔriət] *n* : licenciatura *f*

bachelor ['bætʃələr] *n* **1** : soltero *m* **2** : licenciado *m*, -da *f* ⟨bachelor of arts degree : licenciatura en filosofía y letras⟩

bacillus [bə'sɪləs] *n, pl* **-li** [-,laɪ] : bacilo *m*

back¹ ['bæk] *vt* **1** *or* **to back up** SUPPORT : apoyar, respaldar **2** *or* **to back up** REVERSE : darle marcha atrás a (un vehículo) **3** : estar detrás de, formar el fondo de ⟨trees back the garden : unos árboles están detrás del jardín⟩ — *vi* **1** *or* **to back up** : retroceder **2 to back away** : echarse atrás **3 to back down** *or* **to back out** : volverse atrás, echarse para atrás

back² *adv* **1** : atrás, hacia atrás, detrás ⟨to move back : moverse atrás⟩ ⟨back and forth : de acá para allá⟩ **2** AGO : atrás, antes, ya ⟨some years back : unos años atrás, ya unos años⟩ ⟨10 months back : hace diez meses⟩ **3** : de vuelta, de regreso ⟨we're back : estamos de vuelta⟩ ⟨she ran back : volvió corriendo⟩ ⟨to call back : llamar de nuevo⟩

back³ *adj* **1** REAR : de atrás, posterior, trasero **2** OVERDUE : atrasado **3 back pay** : atrasos *mpl*

back⁴ *n* **1** : espalda *f* (de un ser humano), lomo *m* (de un animal) **2** : respaldo *m* (de una silla), espalda *f* (de ropa) **3** REVERSE : reverso *m*, dorso *m*, espalda *f* **4** REAR : fondo *m*, parte *f* de atrás **5** : defensa *mf* (en deportes)

backache ['bæk,eɪk] *n* : dolor *m* de espalda

backbite ['bæk,baɪt] *v* **-bit** [-,bɪt]; **-bitten** [-,bɪtən]; **-biting** *vt* : calumniar, hablar mal de — *vi* : murmurar

backbiter ['bæk,baɪtər] *n* : calumniador *m*, -dora *f*

backbone ['bæk,boːn] *n* **1** : columna *f* vertebral **2** FIRMNESS : firmeza *f*, carácter *m*

backdrop ['bæk,drɑp] *n* : telón *m* de fondo

backer ['bækər] *n* **1** SUPPORTER : partidario *m*, -ria *f* **2** SPONSOR : patrocinador *m*, -dora *f*

backfire¹ ['bæk,faɪr] *vi* **-fired; -firing 1** : petardear (dícese de un automóvil) **2** FAIL : fallar, salir el tiro por la culata

backfire² *n* : petardeo *m*, explosión *f*

background ['bæk,graʊnd] *n* **1** : fondo *m* (de un cuadro, etc.), antecedentes *mpl* (de una situación) **2** EXPERIENCE, TRAINING : experiencia *f* profesional, formación *f*

backhand¹ ['bæk,hænd] *adv* : de revés, con el revés

backhand² *n* : revés *m*

backhanded ['bæk,hændəd] *adj* **1** : dado con el revés, de revés **2** INDIRECT : indirecto, ambiguo

backing ['bækɪŋ] *n* **1** SUPPORT : apoyo *m*, respaldo *m* **2** REINFORCEMENT : refuerzo *m* **3** SUPPORTERS : partidarios *mpl*, -rias *fpl*

backlash ['bæk,læʃ] *n* : reacción *f* violenta

backlog ['bæk,lɔg] *n* : atraso *m*, trabajo *m* acumulado

backpack¹ ['bæk,pæk] *vi* : viajar con mochila

backpack² *n* : mochila *f*

backrest ['bæk,rɛst] *n* : respaldo *m*

backside ['bæk,saɪd] *n* : trasero *m*

backslide ['bæk,slaɪd] *vi* **-slid** [-,slɪd]; **-slid** *or* **-slidden** [-,slɪdən]; **-sliding** : recaer, reincidir

backstage [,bæk'steɪdʒ, 'bæk,-] *adv & adj* : entre bastidores

backtrack ['bæk,træk] *vi* : dar marcha atrás, volverse atrás

backup ['bæk,ʌp] *n* **1** SUPPORT : respaldo *m*, apoyo *m* **2** : copia *f* de seguridad (para computadoras)

backward¹ ['bækwərd] *or* **backwards** [-wərdz] *adv* **1** : hacia atrás **2** : de espaldas ⟨he fell backwards : se cayó de espaldas⟩ **3** : al revés ⟨you're doing it backwards : lo estás haciendo al revés⟩ **4 to bend over backwards** : hacer todo lo posible

backward² *adj* **1** : hacia atrás ⟨a backward glance : una mirada hacia atrás⟩ **2** RETARDED : retrasado **3** SHY : tímido **4** UNDERDEVELOPED : atrasado

backwardness ['bækwərdnəs] *n* : atraso *m* (dícese de una región), retraso *m* (dícese de una persona)

backwoods [,bæk'wʊdz] *npl* : monte *m*, región *f* alejada

bacon ['beɪkən] *n* : tocino *m*, tocineta *f Col, Ven*, bacon *m Spain*

bacterial [bæk'tɪriəl] *adj* : bacteriano

bacteriologist [bæk,tɪri'ɑlədʒɪst] *n* : bacteriólogo *m*, -ga *f*

bacteriology [bæk,tɪri'ɑlədʒi] *n* : bacteriología *f*

bacterium [bæk'tɪriəm] *n, pl* **-ria** [-iə] : bacteria *f*

bad¹ ['bæd] *adv* → **badly**

bad² *adj* **1** : malo **2** ROTTEN : podrido **3** SERIOUS, SEVERE : grave **4** DEFECTIVE : defectuoso ⟨a bad check : un cheque sin fondos⟩ **5** HARMFUL : perjudicial **6** CORRUPT, EVIL : malo, corrompido **7** NAUGHTY : travieso **8 from bad to worse** : de mal en peor **9 too bad!** : ¡qué lástima!

bad³ *n* : lo malo ⟨the good and the bad : lo bueno y lo malo⟩

bade → **bid**

badge ['bædʒ] *n* : insignia *f*, botón *m*, chapa *f*

badger¹ ['bædʒər] *vt* : fastidiar, acosar, importunar

badger[2] *n* : tejón *m*
badly ['bædli] *adv* **1** : mal **2** URGENTLY : mucho, con urgencia **3** SEVERELY : gravemente
badminton ['bæd,mɪntən, -,mɪt-] *n* : bádminton *m*
badness ['bædnəs] *n* : maldad *f*
baffle[1] ['bæfəl] *vt* **-fled; -fling 1** PERPLEX : desconcertar, confundir **2** FRUSTRATE : frustrar
baffle[2] *n* : deflector *m*, bafle *m* (acústico)
bafflement ['bæfəlmənt] *n* : desconcierto *m*, confusión *f*
bag[1] ['bæg] *v* **bagged; bagging** *vi* SAG : formar bolsas — *vt* **1** : ensacar, poner en una bolsa **2** : cobrar (en la caza), cazar
bag[2] *n* **1** : bolsa *f*, saco *m* **2** HANDBAG : cartera *f*, bolso *m*, bolsa *f Mex* **3** SUITCASE : maleta *f*, valija *f*
bagatelle [,bægə'tɛl] *n* : bagatela *f*
bagel ['beigəl] *n* : rosquilla *f* de pan
baggage ['bægɪdʒ] *n* : equipaje *m*
baggy ['bægi] *adj* **-gier; -est** : holgado, ancho
bagpipe ['bæg,paɪp] *n or* **bagpipes** ['bæg,paɪps] *npl* : gaita *f*
bail[1] ['beil] *vt* **1** : achicar (agua de un bote) **2 to bail out** : poner en libertad (de una cárcel) bajo fianza **3 to bail out** EXTRICATE : sacar de apuros
bail[2] *n* : fianza *f*, caución *f*
bailiff ['beiləf] *n* : alguacil *mf*
bailiwick ['beili,wɪk] *n* : dominio *m*
bailout ['beil,aʊt] *n* : rescate *m* (financiero)
bait[1] ['beit] *vt* **1** : cebar (un anzuelo o cepo) **2** HARASS : acosar
bait[2] *n* : cebo *m*, carnada *f*
bake[1] ['beik] *vt* **baked; baking** : hornear, hacer al horno
bake[2] *n* : fiesta con platos hechos al horno
baker ['beikər] *n* : panadero *m*, -ra *f*
baker's dozen *n* : docena *f* de fraile
bakery ['beikəri] *n, pl* **-ries** : panadería *f*
bakeshop ['beik,ʃɑp] *n* : pastelería *f*, panadería *f*
baking powder *n* : levadura *f* en polvo
baking soda → **sodium bicarbonate**
balance[1] ['bæləns] *v* **-anced; -ancing** *vt* **1** : hacer el balance de (una cuenta) ⟨to balance the books : cuadrar las cuentas⟩ **2** EQUALIZE : balancear, equilibrar **3** HARMONIZE : armonizar — *vi* : balancearse
balance[2] *n* **1** SCALES : balanza *f*, báscula *f* **2** COUNTERBALANCE : contrapeso *m* **3** EQUILIBRIUM : equilibrio *m* **4** REMAINDER : balance *m*, resto *m*
balanced ['bælən*t*st] *adj* : equilibrado, balanceado
balcony ['bælkəni] *n, pl* **-nies 1** : balcón *m*, terraza *f* (de un edificio) **2** : galería *f* (de un teatro)

bald ['bɔld] *adj* **1** : calvo, pelado, pelón **2** PLAIN : simple, puro ⟨the bald truth : la pura verdad⟩
balding ['bɔldɪŋ] *adj* : quedándose calvo
baldly ['bɔldli] *adv* : sin reparos, sin rodeos, francamente
baldness ['bɔldnəs] *n* : calvicie *f*
bale[1] ['beil] *vt* **baled; baling** : empacar, hacer balas de
bale[2] *n* : bala *f*, fardo *m*, paca *f*
baleful ['beilfəl] *adj* **1** DEADLY : mortífero **2** SINISTER : siniestro, funesto, torvo ⟨a baleful glance : una mirada torva⟩
balk[1] ['bɔk] *vt* : obstaculizar, impedir — *vi* **1** : plantarse *fam* (dícese de un caballo, etc.) **2 to balk at** : resistirse a, mostrarse reacio a
balk[2] *n* : obstáculo *m*
Balkan ['bɔlkən] *adj* : balcánico
balky ['bɔki] *adj* **balkier; -est** : reacio, obstinado, terco
ball[1] ['bɔl] *vt* : apelotonar, ovillar
ball[2] *n* **1** : pelota *f*, bola *f*, balón *m*, ovillo *m* (de lana) **2** : juego *m* con pelota o bola **3** DANCE : baile *m*, baile *m* de etiqueta
ballad ['bæləd] *n* : romance *m*, balada *f*
balladeer [,bælə'dɪr] *n* : cantante *mf* de baladas
ballast[1] ['bæləst] *vt* : lastrar
ballast[2] *n* : lastre *m*
ball bearing *n* : cojinete *m* de bola
ballerina [,bælə'ri:nə] *n* : bailarina *f*
ballet [bæ'lei, 'bæ,lei] *n* : ballet *m*
ballistic [bə'lɪstɪk] *adj* : balístico
ballistics [bə'lɪstɪks] *ns & pl* : balística *f*
balloon[1] [bə'lu:n] *vi* **1** : viajar en globo **2** SWELL : hincharse, inflarse
balloon[2] *n* : globo *m*
balloonist [bə'lu:nɪst] *n* : aeróstata *mf*
ballot[1] ['bælət] *vi* : votar
ballot[2] *n* **1** : papeleta *f* (de voto) **2** BALLOTING : votación *f* **3** VOTE : voto *m*
ballpoint pen ['bɔl,pɔint] *n* : bolígrafo *m*
ballroom ['bɔl,ru:m, -,rʊm] *n* : sala *f* de baile
ballyhoo ['bæli,hu:] *n* : propaganda *f*, publicidad *f*, bombo *m fam*
balm ['bɑm, 'bɑlm] *n* : bálsamo *m*, ungüento *m*
balmy ['bɑmi, 'bɑl-] *adj* **balmier; -est 1** MILD : templado, agradable **2** SOOTHING : balsámico **3** CRAZY : chiflado *fam*, chalado *fam*
baloney [bə'lo:ni] *n* NONSENSE : tonterías *fpl*, estupideces *fpl*
balsa ['bɔlsə] *n* : balsa *f*
balsam ['bɔlsəm] *n* **1** : bálsamo *m* **2 or balsam fir** : abeto *m* balsámico
Baltic ['bɔltɪk] *adj* : báltico
baluster ['bæləstər] *n* : balaustre *m*
balustrade ['bælə,streid] *n* : balaustrada *f*
bamboo [bæm'bu:] *n* : bambú *m*
bamboozle [bæm'bu:zəl] *vt* **-zled; -zling** : engañar, embaucar

ban[1] ['bæn] *vt* **banned; banning** : prohibir, proscribir

ban[2] *n* : prohibición *f*, proscripción *f*

banal [bə'nɑl, bə'næl, 'beɪnəl] *adj* : banal, trivial

banality [bə'næləti] *n, pl* **-ties** : banalidad *f*, trivialidad *f*

banana [bə'nænə] *n* : banano *m*, plátano *m*, banana *f*, cambur *m* Ven, guineo *m* Car

band[1] ['bænd] *vt* **1** BIND : fajar, atar **2 to band together** : unirse, juntarse

band[2] *n* **1** STRIP : banda *f*, cinta *f* (de un sombrero, etc.) **2** STRIPE : franja *f* **3** : banda *f* (de radiofrecuencia) **4** RING : anillo *m* **5** GROUP : banda *f*, grupo *m*, conjunto *m* ⟨jazz band : conjunto de jazz⟩

bandage[1] ['bændɪdʒ] *vt* **-daged; -daging** : vendar

bandage[2] *n* : vendaje *m*, venda *f*

bandanna *or* **bandana** [bæn'dænə] *n* : pañuelo *m* (de colores)

bandit ['bændət] *n* : bandido *m*, -da *f*; bandolero *m*, -ra *f*

banditry ['bændətri] *n* : bandolerismo *m*, bandidaje *m*

bandstand ['bænd,stænd] *n* : quiosco *m* de música

bandwagon ['bænd,wægən] *n* **1** : carroza *f* de músicos **2 to jump on the bandwagon** : subirse al carro, seguir la moda

bandy[1] ['bændi] *vt* **-died; -dying 1** EXCHANGE : intercambiar **2 to bandy about** : circular, propagar

bandy[2] *adj* : arqueado, torcido ⟨bandy-legged : de piernas arqueadas⟩

bane ['beɪn] *n* **1** POISON : veneno *m* **2** RUIN : ruina *f*, pesadilla *f*

baneful ['beɪnfəl] *adj* : nefasto, funesto

bang[1] ['bæŋ] *vt* **1** STRIKE : golpear, darse ⟨he banged his elbow against the door : se dio con el codo en la puerta⟩ **2** SLAM : cerrar (la puerta) con un portazo — *vi* **1** SLAM : cerrarse de un golpe **2 to bang on** : aporrear, golpear ⟨she was banging on the table : aporreaba la mesa⟩

bang[2] *adv* : directamente, exactamente

bang[3] *n* **1** BLOW : golpe *m*, porrazo *m*, trancazo *m* **2** EXPLOSION : explosión *f*, estallido *m* **3** SLAM : portazo *m* **4 bangs** *npl* : flequillo *m*, fleco *m*

Bangladeshi [,bɑŋglə'deʃi, ,bæŋ-, ,bʌŋ-, -'deɪ-] *n* : bangladesí *mf* — **Bangladeshi** *adj*

bangle ['bæŋgəl] *n* : brazalete *m*, pulsera *f*

banish ['bænɪʃ] *vt* **1** EXILE : desterrar, exiliar **2** EXPEL : expulsar

banishment ['bænɪʃmənt] *n* **1** EXILE : destierro *m*, exilio *m* **2** EXPULSION : expulsión *f*

banister ['bænəstər] *n* **1** BALUSTER : balaustre *m* **2** HANDRAIL : pasamanos *m*, barandilla *f*, barandal *m*

banjo ['bæn,dʒo:] *n, pl* **-jos** : banjo *m*

bank[1] ['bæŋk] *vt* **1** TILT : peraltar (una carretera), ladear (un avión) **2** HEAP : amontonar **3** : cubrir (un fuego) **4** : depositar (dinero en un banco) — *vi* **1** : ladearse (dícese de un avión) **2** : tener una cuenta (en un banco) **3 to bank on** : contar con

bank[2] *n* **1** MASS : montón *m*, montículo *m*, masa *f* **2** : orilla *f*, ribera *f* (de un río) **3** : peralte *m* (de una carretera) **4** : banco *m* ⟨World Bank : Banco Mundial⟩ ⟨banco de sangre : blood bank⟩

bankbook ['bæŋk,bʊk] *n* : libreta *f* bancaria, libreta *f* de ahorros

banker ['bæŋkər] *n* : banquero *m*, -ra *f*

banking ['bæŋkɪŋ] *n* : banca *f*

bankrupt[1] ['bæŋ,krʌpt] *vt* : hacer quebrar, llevar a la quiebra, arruinar

bankrupt[2] *adj* **1** : en bancarrota, en quiebra **2 ~ of** LACKING : carente de, falto de

bankrupt[3] *n* : fallido *m*, -da *f*; quebrado *m*, -da *f*

bankruptcy ['bæŋ,krʌptsi] *n, pl* **-cies** : ruina *f*, quiebra *f*, bancarrota *f*

banner[1] ['bænər] *adj* : excelente

banner[2] *n* : estandarte *m*, bandera *f*

banns ['bænz] *npl* : amonestaciones *fpl*

banquet[1] ['bæŋkwət] *vi* : celebrar un banquete

banquet[2] *n* : banquete *m*

banter[1] ['bæntər] *vi* : bromear, hacer bromas

banter[2] *n* : bromas *fpl*

baptism ['bæp,tɪzəm] *n* : bautismo *m*

baptismal [bæp'tɪzməl] *adj* : bautismal

Baptist ['bæptɪst] *n* : bautista *mf* — **Baptist** *adj*

baptize [bæp'taɪz, 'bæp,taɪz] *vt* **-tized; -tizing** : bautizar

bar[1] ['bɑr] *vt* **barred; barring 1** OBSTRUCT : obstruir, bloquear **2** EXCLUDE : excluir **3** PROHIBIT : prohibir **4** SECURE : atrancar, asegurar ⟨bar the door! : ¡atranca la puerta!⟩

bar[2] *n* **1** : barra *f*, barrote *m* (de una ventana), tranca *f* (de una puerta) **2** BARRIER : barrera *f*, obstáculo *m* **3** LAW : abogacía *f* **4** STRIPE : franja *f* **5** COUNTER : mostrador *m*, barra *f* **6** TAVERN : bar *m*, taberna *f*

bar[3] *prep* : excepto, con excepción de **2 bar none** : sin excepción

barb ['bɑrb] *n* **1** POINT : púa *f*, lengüeta *f* **2** GIBE : pulla *f*

barbarian[1] [bɑr'bæriən] *adj* **1** : bárbaro **2** CRUDE : tosco, bruto

barbarian[2] *n* : bárbaro *m*, -ra *f*

barbaric [bɑr'bærɪk] *adj* **1** PRIMITIVE : primitivo **2** CRUEL : brutal, cruel

barbarity [bɑr'bærəti] *n, pl* **-ties** : barbaridad *f*

barbarous ['bɑrbərəs] *adj* **1** UNCIVILIZED : bárbaro **2** MERCILESS : despiadado, cruel

barbarously ['bɑrbərəsli] *adv* : bárbaramente

barbecue¹ ['bɑrbɪ,kjuː] *vt* **-cued; -cuing** : asar a la parrilla
barbecue² *n* : barbacoa *f*, parrillada *f*
barbed ['bɑrbd] *adj* **1** : con púas ⟨barbed wire : alambre de púas⟩ **2** BITING : mordaz
barber ['bɑrbər] *n* : barbero *m*, -ra *f*
barbiturate [bɑr'bɪtʃərət] *n* : barbitúrico *m*
bard ['bɑrd] *n* : bardo *m*
bare¹ ['bær] *vt* **bared; baring** : desnudar
bare² *adj* **1** NAKED : desnudo **2** EXPOSED : descubierto, sin protección **3** EMPTY : desprovisto, vacío **4** MINIMUM : mero, mínimo ⟨the bare necessities : las necesidades mínimas⟩ **5** PLAIN : puro, sencillo
bareback ['bær,bæk] *or* **barebacked** [-,bækt] *adv & adj* : a pelo
barefaced ['bær,feɪst] *adj* : descarado
barefoot ['bær,fʊt] *or* **barefooted** [-,fʊt̬əd] *adv & adj* : descalzo
bareheaded ['bær'hɛdəd] *adv & adj* : sin sombrero, con la cabeza descubierta
barely ['bærli] *adv* : apenas, por poco
bareness ['bærnəs] *n* : desnudez *f*
bargain¹ ['bɑrgən] *vi* HAGGLE : regatear, negociar — *vt* BARTER : trocar, cambiar
bargain² *n* **1** AGREEMENT : acuerdo *m*, convenio *m* ⟨to strike a bargain : cerrar un trato⟩ **2** : ganga *f* ⟨bargain price : precio de ganga⟩
barge¹ ['bɑrdʒ] *vi* **barged; barging 1** : mover con torpeza **2 to barge in** : entrometerse, interrumpir
barge² *n* : barcaza *f*, gabarra *f*
bar graph *n* : gráfico *m* de barras
baritone ['bærə,toːn] *n* : barítono *m*
barium ['bæriəm] *n* : bario *m*
bark¹ ['bɑrk] *vi* : ladrar — *vt or* **to bark out** : gritar ⟨to bark out an order : dar una orden a gritos⟩
bark² *n* **1** : ladrido *m* (de un perro) **2** : corteza *f* (de un árbol) **3** *or* **barque** : tipo de embarcación con velas de proa y popa
barley ['bɑrli] *n* : cebada *f*
barn ['bɑrn] *n* : granero *m* (para cosechas), establo *m* (para ganado)
barnacle ['bɑrnɪkəl] *n* : percebe *m*
barnyard ['bɑrn,jɑrd] *n* : corral *m*
barometer [bə'rɑmət̬ər] *n* : barómetro *m*
barometric [,bærə'mɛtrɪk] *adj* : barométrico
baron ['bærən] *n* **1** : barón *m* **2** TYCOON : magnate *mf*
baroness ['bærənɪs, -nəs, -,nɛs] *n* : baronesa *f*
baronet [,bærə'nɛt, 'bærənət] *n* : baronet *m*
baronial [bə'roːniəl] *adj* **1** : de barón **2** STATELY : señorial, majestuoso
baroque [bə'roːk, -'rɑk] *adj* : barroco
barracks ['bærəks] *ns & pl* : cuartel *m*
barracuda [,bærə'kuːdə] *n, pl* **-da** *or* **-das** : barracuda *f*

barrage [bə'rɑʒ, -'rɑdʒ] *n* **1** : descarga *f* (de artillería) **2** DELUGE : aluvión *m* ⟨a barrage of questions : un aluvión de preguntas⟩
barred ['bɑrd] *adj* : excluido, prohibido
barrel¹ ['bærəl] *v* **-reled** *or* **-relled; -reling** *or* **-relling** *vt* : embarrilar — *vi* : ir disparado
barrel² *n* **1** : barril *m*, tonel *m* **2** : cañón *m* (de un arma de fuego), cilindro *m* (de una cerradura)
barren ['bærən] *adj* **1** STERILE : estéril (dícese de las plantas o la mujer), árido (dícese del suelo) **2** DESERTED : yermo, desierto
barrette [bɑ'rɛt, bə-] *n* : pasador *m*, broche *m* para el cabello
barricade¹ ['bærə,keɪd, ,bærə'-] *vt* **-caded; -cading** : cerrar con barricadas
barricade² *n* : barricada *f*
barrier ['bæriər] *n* **1** : barrera *f* **2** OBSTACLE : obstáculo *m*, impedimento *m*
barring ['bɑrɪŋ] *prep* : excepto, salvo, a excepción de
barrio ['bɑrio, 'bær-] *n* : barrio *m*
barroom ['bɑr,ruːm, -,rʊm] *n* : bar *m*
barrow ['bær,oː] → **wheelbarrow**
bartender ['bɑr,tɛndər] *n* : camarero *m*, -ra *f*; barman *m*
barter¹ ['bɑrtər] *vt* : cambiar, trocar
barter² *n* : trueque *m*, permuta *f*
basalt [bə'sɔlt, 'beɪ,-] *n* : basalto *m*
base¹ ['beɪs] *vt* **based; basing** : basar, fundamentar, establecer
base² *adj* **baser; basest 1** : de baja ley (dícese de un metal) **2** CONTEMPTIBLE : vil, despreciable
base³ *n, pl* **bases** : base *f*
baseball ['beɪs,bɔl] *n* : beisbol *m*, béisbol *m*
baseless ['beɪsləs] *adj* : infundado
basely ['beɪsli] *adv* : vilmente
basement ['beɪsmənt] *n* : sótano *m*
baseness ['beɪsnəs] *n* : vileza *f*, bajeza *f*
bash¹ ['bæʃ] *vt* : golpear violentamente
bash² *n* **1** BLOW : golpe *m*, porrazo *m*, madrazo *m* *Mex fam* **2** PARTY : fiesta *f*, juerga *f* *fam*
bashful ['bæʃfəl] *adj* : tímido, vergonzoso, penoso
bashfulness ['bæʃfəlnəs] *n* : timidez *f*
basic¹ ['beɪsɪk] *adj* **1** FUNDAMENTAL : básico, fundamental **2** RUDIMENTARY : básico, elemental **3** : básico (en química)
basic² *n* : fundamento *m*, rudimento *m*
basically ['beɪsɪkli] *adv* : fundamentalmente
basil ['beɪzəl, 'bæzəl] *n* : albahaca *f*
basilica [bə'sɪlɪkə] *n* : basílica *f*
basin ['beɪsən] *n* **1** WASHBOWL : palangana *f*, lavamanos *m*, lavabo *m* **2** : cuenca *f* (de un río)
basis ['beɪsəs] *n, pl* **bases** [-,siːz] **1** BASE : base *f*, pilar *m* **2** FOUNDATION : fundamento *m*, base *f* **3 on a weekly basis** : semanalmente

bask ['bæsk] *vi* : disfrutar, deleitarse ⟨to bask in the sun : disfrutar del sol⟩

basket ['bæskət] *n* : cesta *f*, cesto *m*, canasta *f*

basketball ['bæskət,bɔl] *n* : baloncesto *m*, basquetbol *m*

bas–relief [,bɑrɪ'li:f] *n* : bajorrelieve *m*

bass[1] ['bæs] *n, pl* **bass** *or* **basses** : róbalo *m* (pesca)

bass[2] ['beɪs] *n* : bajo *m* (tono, voz, cantante)

bass drum *n* : bombo *m*

basset hound ['bæsət,haʊnd] *n* : basset *m*

bassinet [,bæsə'nɛt] *n* : moisés *m*, cuna *f*

bassist ['beɪsɪst] *n* : bajista *mf*

bassoon [bə'su:n, bæ-] *n* : fagot *m*

bass viol ['beɪs'vaɪəl, -,o:l] → **double bass**

bastard[1] ['bæstərd] *adj* : bastardo

bastard[2] *n* : bastardo *m*, -da *f*

bastardize ['bæstər,daɪz] *vt* **-ized; -izing** DEBASE : degradar, envilecer

baste ['beɪst] *vt* **basted; basting** 1 STITCH : hilvanar 2 : bañar (con su jugo durante la cocción)

bastion ['bæstʃən] *n* : bastión *m*, baluarte *m*

bat[1] ['bæt] *vt* **batted; batting** 1 HIT : batear 2 **without batting an eye** : sin pestañear

bat[2] *n* 1 : murciélago *m* (animal) 2 : bate *m* ⟨baseball bat : bate de beisbol⟩

batch ['bætʃ] *n* : hornada *f*, tanda *f*, grupo *m*, cantidad *f*

bate ['beɪt] *vt* **bated; bating** 1 : aminorar, reducir 2 **with bated breath** : con ansiedad, aguantando la respiración

bath ['bæθ, 'bɑθ] *n, pl* **baths** ['bæðz, 'bæθs, 'bɑðz, 'bɑθs] 1 BATHING : baño *m* ⟨to take a bath : bañarse⟩ 2 : baño *m* (en fotografía, etc.) 3 BATHROOM : baño *m*, cuarto *m* de baño 4 SPA : balneario *m* 5 LOSS : pérdida *f*

bathe ['beɪð] *v* **bathed; bathing** *vt* 1 WASH : bañar, lavar 2 SOAK : poner en remojo 3 FLOOD : inundar ⟨to bathe with light : inundar de luz⟩ — *vi* : bañarse, ducharse

bather ['beɪðər] *n* : bañista *mf*

bathrobe ['bæθ,ro:b] *n* : bata *f* (de baño)

bathroom ['bæθ,ru:m, -,rʊm] *n* : baño *m*, cuarto *m* de baño

bathtub ['bæθ,tʌb] *n* : bañera *f*, tina *f* (de baño)

batiste [bə'ti:st] *n* : batista *f*

baton [bə'tɑn] *n* : batuta *f*, bastón *m*

battalion [bə'tæljən] *n* : batallón *m*

batten ['bætən] *vt* **to batten down the hatches** : cerrar las escotillas

batter[1] ['bætər] *vt* 1 BEAT : aporrear, golpear 2 MISTREAT : maltratar

batter[2] *n* 1 : masa *f* para rebozar 2 HITTER : bateador *m*, -dora *f*

battering ram *n* : ariete *m*

battery ['bætəri] *n, pl* **-teries** 1 : lesiones *fpl* ⟨assault and battery : agresión con

lesiones⟩ 2 ARTILLERY : batería *f* 3 : batería *f*, pila *f* (de electricidad) 4 SERIES : serie *f*

batting ['bætɪŋ] *n* 1 *or* **cotton batting** : algodón *m* en láminas 2 : bateo *m* (en beisbol)

battle[1] ['bætəl] *vi* **-tled; -tling** : luchar, pelear

battle[2] *n* : batalla *f*, lucha *f*, pelea *f*

battle–ax ['bætəl,æks] *n* : hacha *f* de guerra

battlefield ['bætəl,fi:ld] *n* : campo *m* de batalla

battlements ['bætəlmənts] *npl* : almenas *fpl*

battleship ['bætəl,ʃɪp] *n* : acorazado *m*

batty ['bæti] *adj* **-tier; -est** : chiflado *fam*, chalado *fam*

bauble ['bɔbəl] *n* : chuchería *f*, baratija *f*

Bavarian [bə'vɛriən] *n* : bávaro *m*, -ra *f* — **Bavarian** *adj*

bawdiness ['bɔdinəs] *n* : picardía *f*

bawdy ['bɔdi] *adj* **bawdier; -est** : subido de tono, verde, colorado *Mex*

bawl[1] ['bɔl] *vi* : llorar a gritos

bawl[2] *n* : grito *m*, alarido *m*

bawl out *vt* SCOLD : regañar

bay[1] ['beɪ] *vi* HOWL : aullar

bay[2] *adj* : castaño, zaino (dícese de los caballos)

bay[3] *n* 1 : bahía *f* ⟨Bay of Campeche : Bahía de Campeche⟩ 2 *or* **bay horse** : caballo *m* castaño 3 LAUREL : laurel *m* 4 HOWL : aullido *m* 5 : saliente *m* ⟨bay window : ventana en saliente⟩ 6 COMPARTMENT : área *f*, compartimento *m* 7 **at** ∼ : acorralado

bayberry ['beɪ,bɛri] *n, pl* **-ries** : arrayán *m* brabántico

bayonet[1] [,beɪə'nɛt, 'beɪə,nɛt] *vt* **-neted; -neting** : herir *o* matar) con bayoneta

bayonet[2] *n* : bayoneta *f*

bayou ['baɪ,u:, -,o:] *n* : pantano *m*

bazaar [bə'zɑr] *n* 1 : bazar *m* 2 SALE : venta *f* benéfica

bazooka [bə'zu:kə] *n* : bazuca *f*

BB ['bi:bi] *n* : balín *m*

be ['bi:] *v* **was** ['wəz, 'wɑz]; **were** ['wər]; **been** ['bɪn]; **being; am** ['æm]; **is** ['ɪz]; **are** ['ɑr] *vi* 1 (*expressing equality*) : ser ⟨José is a doctor : José es doctor⟩ ⟨I'm Ann's sister : soy la hermana de Ana⟩ 2 (*expressing quality*) : ser ⟨the tree is tall : el árbol es alto⟩ ⟨you're silly! : ¡eres tonto!⟩ 3 (*expressing origin or possession*) : ser ⟨she's from Managua : es de Managua⟩ ⟨it's mine : es mío⟩ 4 (*expressing location*) : estar ⟨my mother is at home : mi madre está en casa⟩ ⟨the cups are on the table : las tazas están en la mesa⟩ 5 (*expressing existence*) : ser, existir ⟨to be or not to be : ser, o no ser⟩ ⟨I think, therefore I am : pienso, luego existo⟩ 6 (*expressing a state of being*) : estar, tener ⟨how are you? : ¿cómo estás?⟩ ⟨I'm cold : tengo frío⟩ ⟨she's 10 years old : tiene 10 años⟩ ⟨they're both sick : están enfermos los dos〉 — *v impers* **1** (*indicating time*) : ser 〈it's eight o'clock : son las ocho〉 〈it's Friday : hoy es viernes〉 **2** (*indicating a condition*) : hacer, estar 〈it's sunny : hace sol〉 〈it's very dark outside : está bien oscuro afuera〉 — *v aux* **1** (*expressing progression*) : estar 〈what are you doing? : ¿qué haces?—estoy trabajando〉 **2** (*expressing occurrence*) : ser 〈it was finished yesterday : fue acabado ayer, se acabó ayer〉 〈it was cooked in the oven : se cocinó en el horno〉 **3** (*expressing possibility*) : poderse 〈can she be trusted? : ¿se puede confiar en ella?〉 **4** (*expressing obligation*) : deber 〈you are to stay here : debes quedarte aquí〉 〈he was to come yesterday : se esperaba que viniese ayer〉

beach[1] [ˈbiːtʃ] *vt* : hacer embarrancar, hacer varar, hacer encallar

beach[2] *n* : playa *f*

beachcomber [ˈbiːtʃˌkoːmər] *n* : raquero *m*, -ra *f*

beachhead [ˈbiːtʃˌhɛd] *n* : cabeza *f* de playa

beacon [ˈbiːkən] *n* : faro *m*

bead[1] [ˈbiːd] *vi* : formarse en gotas

bead[2] *n* **1** : cuenta *f* **2** DROP : gota *f* **3 beads** *npl* NECKLACE : collar *m*

beady [ˈbiːdi] *adj* **beadier; -est 1** : de forma de cuenta **2 beady eyes** : ojos *mpl* pequeños y brillantes

beagle [ˈbiːgəl] *n* : beagle *m*

beak [ˈbiːk] *n* : pico *m*

beaker [ˈbiːkər] *n* **1** CUP : taza *f* alta **2** : vaso *m* de precipitados (en un laboratorio)

beam[1] [ˈbiːm] *vi* **1** SHINE : brillar **2** SMILE : sonreír radiantemente — *vt* BROADCAST : transmitir, emitir

beam[2] *n* **1** : viga *f*, barra *f* **2** RAY : rayo *m*, haz *m* de luz **3** : haz *m* de radiofaro (para guiar pilotos, etc.)

bean [ˈbiːn] *n* **1** : habichuela *f*, frijol *m* **2 broad bean** : haba *f* **3 string bean** : judía *f*

bear[1] [ˈbær] *v* **bore** [ˈbor]; **borne** [ˈbɔrn]; **bearing** *vt* **1** CARRY : llevar, portar **2** : dar a luz a (un niño) **3** PRODUCE : dar (frutas, cosechas) **4** ENDURE, SUPPORT : soportar, resistir, aguantar — *vi* **1** TURN : doblar, dar la vuelta 〈bear right : doble a la derecha〉 **2 to bear up** : resistir

bear[2] *n, pl* **bears** *or* **bear** : oso *m*, osa *f*

bearable [ˈbærəbəl] *adj* : soportable

beard [ˈbɪrd] *n* **1** : barba *f* **2** : arista *f* (de plantas)

bearded [ˈbɪrdəd] *adj* : barbudo, de barba

bearer [ˈbærər] *n* : portador *m*, -dora *f*

bearing [ˈbærɪŋ] *n* **1** CONDUCT, MANNERS : comportamiento *m*, modales *mpl* **2** SUPPORT : soporte *f* **3** SIGNIFICANCE : relación *f*, importancia *f* 〈to have no bearing on : no tener nada que ver con〉 **4** : cojinete *m*, rodamiento *m*

(de una máquina) **5** COURSE, DIRECTION : dirección *f*, rumbo *m* 〈to get one's bearings : orientarse〉

beast [ˈbiːst] *n* **1** : bestia *f*, fiera *f* 〈beast of burden : animal de carga〉 **2** BRUTE : bruto *m*, -ta *f*; bestia *mf*

beastly [ˈbiːstli] *adj* : detestable, repugnante

beat[1] [ˈbiːt] *v* **beat; beaten** [ˈbiːtən] *or* **beat; beating** *vt* **1** STRIKE : golpear, pegar, darle una paliza (a alguien) **2** DEFEAT : vencer, derrotar **3** AVOID : anticiparse a, evitar 〈to beat the crowd : evitar el gentío〉 **4** MASH, WHIP : batir — *vi* THROB : palpitar, latir

beat[2] *adj* EXHAUSTED : derrengado, muy cansado 〈I'm beat! : ¡estoy molido!〉

beat[3] *n* **1** : golpe *m*, redoble *m* (de un tambor), latido *m* (del corazón) **2** RHYTHM : ritmo *m*, tiempo *m*

beater [ˈbiːtər] *n* **1** : batidor *m*, -dora *f* **2** EGGBEATER : batidor *m*

beatific [ˌbiːəˈtɪfɪk] *adj* : beatífico

beatitude [biˈætəˌtuːd] *n* **1** : beatitud *f* **2 the Beatitudes** : las bienaventuranzas

beau [ˈboː] *n, pl* **beaux** *or* **beaus** : pretendiente *m*, galán *m*

beautification [ˌbjuːtəfəˈkeɪʃən] *n* : embellecimiento *m*

beautiful [ˈbjuːtɪfəl] *adj* : hermoso, bello, lindo, precioso

beautifully [ˈbjuːtɪfəli] *adv* **1** ATTRACTIVELY : hermosamente **2** EXCELLENTLY : maravillosamente, excelentemente

beauty [ˈbjuːti] *n, pl* **-ties** : belleza *f*, hermosura *f*, beldad *f*

beauty shop *or* **beauty salon** *n* : salón *m* de belleza

beaver [ˈbiːvər] *n* : castor *m*

because [bɪˈkʌz, -ˈkɔz] *conj* : porque

because of *prep* : por, a causa de, debido a

beck [ˈbɛk] *n* **to be at the beck and call of** : estar a la entera disposición de, estar sometido a la voluntad de

beckon [ˈbɛkən] *vi* **to beckon to someone** : hacerle señas a alguien

become [bɪˈkʌm] *v* **-came** [-ˈkeɪm]; **-come; -coming** *vi* : hacerse, volverse, ponerse 〈he became famous : se hizo famoso〉 〈to become sad : ponerse triste〉 〈to become accustomed to : acostumbrarse a〉 — *vt* **1** BEFIT : ser apropiado para **2** SUIT : favorecer, quedarle bien (a alguien) 〈that dress becomes you : ese vestido te favorece〉

becoming [bɪˈkʌmɪŋ] *adj* **1** SUITABLE : apropiado **2** FLATTERING : favorecedor

bed[1] [ˈbɛd] *v* **bedded; bedding** *vt* : acostar — *vi* : acostarse

bed[2] *n* **1** : cama *f*, lecho *m* **2** : cauce *m* (de un río), fondo *m* (del mar) **3** : arriate *m* (para plantas) **4** LAYER, STRATUM : estrato *m*, capa *f*

bedbug ['bɛd,bʌg] *n* : chinche *f*
bedclothes ['bɛd,kloːðz, -,kloːz] *npl* : ropa *f* de cama, sábanas *fpl*
bedding ['bɛdɪŋ] *n* **1** → **bedclothes 2** : cama *f* (para animales)
bedeck [bɪ'dɛk] *vt* : adornar, engalanar
bedevil [bɪ'dɛvəl] *vt* **-iled** *or* **-illed; -iling** *or* **-illing** : acosar, plagar
bedlam ['bɛdləm] *n* : locura *f*, caos *m*, alboroto *m*
bedraggled [bɪ'drægəld] *adj* : desaliñado, despeinado
bedridden ['bɛd,rɪdən] *adj* : postrado en cama
bedrock ['bɛd,rɑk] *n* : lecho *m* de roca
bedroom ['bɛd,ruːm, -,rʊm] *n* : dormitorio *m*, habitación *f*, pieza *f*, recámara *f Col, Mex, Pan*
bedspread ['bɛd,sprɛd] *n* : cubrecama *m*, colcha *f*, cobertor *m*
bee ['biː] *n* **1** : abeja *f* (insecto) **2** GATHERING : círculo *m*, reunión *f*
beech ['biːtʃ] *n, pl* **beeches** *or* **beech** : haya *f*
beechnut ['biːtʃ,nʌt] *n* : hayuco *m*
beef[1] ['biːf] *vt* **to beef up** : fortalecer, reforzar — *vi* COMPLAIN : quejarse
beef[2] *n, pl* **beefs** ['biːfs] *or* **beeves** ['biːvz] : carne *f* de vaca, carne *f* de res *CA, Mex*
beefsteak ['biːf,steɪk] *n* : filete *m*, bistec *m*
beehive ['biː,haɪv] *n* : colmena *f*
beekeeper ['biː,kiːpər] *n* : apicultor *m*, -tora *f*
beeline ['biː,laɪn] *n* **to make a beeline for** : ir derecho a, ir directo hacia
been → **be**
beep[1] ['biːp] *v* : pitar
beep[2] *n* : pitido *m*
beeper ['biːpər] *n* : busca *m*, buscapersonas *m*
beer ['bɪr] *n* : cerveza *f*
beeswax ['biːz,wæks] *n* : cera *f* de abejas
beet ['biːt] *n* : remolacha *f*, betabel *m Mex*
beetle ['biːtəl] *n* : escarabajo *m*
befall [bɪ'fɔl] *v* **-fell** [-'fɛl]; **-fallen** [-'fɔlən] *vt* : sucederle a, acontecerle a — *vi* : acontecer
befit [bɪ'fɪt] *vt* **-fitted; -fitting** : convenir a, ser apropiado para
before[1] [bɪ'for] *adv* **1** : antes ⟨before and after : antes y después⟩ **2** : anterior ⟨the month before : el mes anterior⟩
before[2] *conj* : antes que ⟨he would die before surrendering : moriría antes que rendirse⟩
before[3] *prep* **1** : antes de ⟨before eating : antes de comer⟩ **2** : delante de, ante ⟨I stood before the house : estaba parada delante de la casa⟩ ⟨before the judge : ante el juez⟩
beforehand [bɪ'for,hænd] *adv* : antes, por adelantado, de antemano, con anticipación
befriend [bɪ'frɛnd] *vt* : hacerse amigo de

befuddle [bɪ'fʌdəl] *vt* **-dled; -dling** : aturdir, ofuscar, confundir
beg ['bɛg] *v* **begged; begging** *vt* : pedir, mendigar, suplicar ⟨I begged him to go : le supliqué que fuera⟩ — *vi* : mendigar, pedir limosna
beget [bɪ'gɛt] *vt* **-got** [-'gɑt]; **-gotten** [-'gɑtən] *or* **-got; -getting** : engendrar
beggar ['bɛgər] *n* : mendigo *m*, -ga *f*; pordiosero *m*, -ra *f*
begin [bɪ'gɪn] *v* **-gan** [-'gæn]; **-gun** [-'gʌn]; **-ginning** *vt* : empezar, comenzar, iniciar — *vi* **1** START : empezar, comenzar, iniciarse **2** ORIGINATE : nacer, originarse **3 to begin with** : en primer lugar, para empezar
beginner [bɪ'gɪnər] *n* : principiante *mf*
beginning [bɪ'gɪnɪŋ] *n* : principio *m*, comienzo *m*
begone [bɪ'gɔn] *interj* : ¡fuera de aquí!
begonia [bɪ'goːnjə] *n* : begonia *f*
begrudge [bɪ'grʌdʒ] *vt* **-grudged; -grudging 1** : dar de mala gana **2** ENVY : envidiar, resentir
beguile [bɪ'gaɪl] *vt* **-guiled; -guiling 1** DECEIVE : engañar **2** AMUSE : divertir, entretener
behalf [bɪ'hæf, -'haf] *n* **1** : favor *m*, beneficio *m*, parte *f* **2 on behalf of** *or* **in behalf of** : de parte de, en nombre de
behave [bɪ'heɪv] *vi* **-haved; -having** : comportarse, portarse
behavior [bɪ'heɪvjər] *n* : comportamiento *m*, conducta *f*
behead [bɪ'hɛd] *vt* : decapitar
behest [bɪ'hɛst] *n* **1** : mandato *m*, orden *f* **2 at the behest of** : a instancia de
behind[1] [bɪ'haɪnd] *adv* : atrás, detrás ⟨to fall behind : quedarse atrás⟩
behind[2] *prep* **1** : atrás de, detrás de, tras ⟨behind the house : detrás de la casa⟩ ⟨one behind another : uno tras otro⟩ **2** : atrasado con, después de ⟨behind schedule : atrasado con el trabajo⟩ ⟨I arrived behind the others : llegué después de los otros⟩ **3** SUPPORTING : en apoyo de, detrás
behind[3] [bɪ'haɪnd, 'biː,haɪnd] *n* : trasero *m*
behold [bɪ'hoːld] *vt* **-held; -holding** : contemplar
beholder [bɪ'hoːldər] *n* : observador *m*, -dora *f*
behoove [bɪ'huːv] *vt* **-hooved; -hooving** : convenirle a, corresponderle a ⟨it behooves us to help him : nos conviene ayudarlo⟩
beige[1] ['beɪʒ] *adj* : beige
beige[2] *n* : beige *m*
being ['biːɪŋ] *n* **1** EXISTENCE : ser *m*, existencia *f* **2** CREATURE : ser *m*, ente *m*
belabor [bɪ'leɪbər] *vt* **to belabor the point** : extenderse sobre el tema
belated [bɪ'leɪtəd] *adj* : tardío, retrasado
belch[1] ['bɛltʃ] *vi* **1** BURP : eructar **2** EXPEL : expulsar, arrojar
belch[2] *n* : eructo *m*

beleaguer [bɪ'li:gər] *vt* **1** BESIEGE : asediar, sitiar **2** HARASS : fastidiar, molestar

belfry ['bɛlfri] *n, pl* **-fries** : campanario *m*

Belgian ['bɛlʤən] *n* : belga *mf* — **Belgian** *adj*

belie [bɪ'laɪ] *vt* **-lied; -lying** **1** MISREPRESENT : falsear, ocultar **2** CONTRADICT : contradecir, desmentir

belief [bə'li:f] *n* **1** TRUST : confianza *f* **2** CONVICTION : creencia *f*, convicción *f* **3** FAITH : fe *f*

believable [bə'li:vəbəl] *adj* : verosímil, creíble

believe [bə'li:v] *v* **-lieved; -lieving** : creer

believer [bə'li:vər] *n* : creyente *mf* **2** : partidario *m*, -ria *f*; entusiasta *mf* ⟨she's a great believer in vitamins : ella es una gran partidaria de las vitaminas⟩

belittle [bɪ'lɪtəl] *vt* **-littled; -littling** **1** DISPARAGE : menospreciar, denigrar, rebajar **2** MINIMIZE : minimizar, quitar importancia a

Belizean [bə'li:ziən] *n* : beliceño *m*, -ña *f* — **Belizean** *adj*

bell¹ ['bɛl] *vt* : ponerle un cascabel a

bell² *n* : campana *f*, cencerro *m* (para una vaca o cabra), cascabel *m* (para un gato), timbre *m* (de teléfono, de la puerta)

belle ['bɛl] *n* : belleza *f*, beldad *f*

bellhop ['bɛl,hɑp] *n* : botones *m*

bellicose ['bɛlɪ,ko:s] *adj* : belicoso *m* — **bellicosity** [,bɛlɪ'kasəti] *n*

belligerence [bə'lɪʤərənts] *n* : agresividad *f*, beligerancia *f*

belligerent¹ [bə'lɪʤərənt] *adj* : agresivo, beligerante

belligerent² *n* : beligerante *mf*

bellow¹ ['bɛ,lo:] *vi* : bramar, mugir — *vt* : gritar

bellow² *n* : bramido *m*, grito *m*

bellows ['bɛ,lo:z] *ns & pl* : fuelle *m*

bellwether ['bɛl,wɛðər] *n* : líder *mf*

belly¹ ['bɛli] *vi* **-lied; -lying** SWELL : hincharse, inflarse

belly² *n, pl* **-lies** : abdomen *m*, vientre *m*, barriga *f*, panza *f*

belong [bɪ'lɔŋ] *vi* **1** : pertenecer (a), ser propiedad (de) ⟨it belongs to her : pertenece a ella, es suyo, es de ella⟩ **2** : ser parte (de), ser miembro (de) ⟨he belongs to the club : es miembro del club⟩ **3** : deber estar, ir ⟨your coat belongs in the closet : tu abrigo va en el ropero⟩

belongings [bɪ'lɔŋɪŋz] *npl* : pertenencias *fpl*, efectos *mpl* personales

beloved¹ [bɪ'lʌvəd, -'lʌvd] *adj* : querido, amado

beloved² *n* : amado *m*, -da *f*; enamorado *m*, -da *f*; amor *m*

below¹ [bɪ'lo:] *adv* : abajo

below² *prep* **1** : abajo de, debajo de ⟨below the window : debajo de la ventana⟩ **2** : por debajo de, bajo ⟨below average : por debajo del promedio⟩ ⟨5 degrees below zero : 5 grados bajo cero⟩

belt¹ ['bɛlt] *vt* **1** : ceñir con un cinturón, ponerle un cinturón a **2** THRASH : darle una paliza a, darle un trancazo a

belt² *n* **1** : cinturón *m*, cinto *m* (para el talle) **2** BAND, STRAP : cinta *f*, correa *f*, banda *f* Mex **3** AREA : frente *m*, zona *f*

beltway ['bɛlt,weɪ] *n* : carretera *f* de circunvalación; periférico *m* CA, Mex; libramiento *m* Mex

bemoan [bɪ'mo:n] *vt* : lamentarse de

bemuse [bɪ'mju:z] *vt* **-mused; -musing** **1** BEWILDER : confundir, desconcertar **2** ENGROSS : absorber

bench ['bɛntʃ] *n* **1** SEAT : banco *m*, escaño *m*, banca *f* **2** : estrado *m* (de un juez) **3** COURT : tribunal *m*

bend¹ ['bɛnd] *v* **bent** ['bnt;]; **bending** *vt* : torcer, doblar, curvar, flexionar — *vi* **1** : torcerse, agacharse ⟨to bend over : inclinarse⟩ **2** TURN : torcer, hacer una curva

bend² *n* **1** TURN : vuelta *f*, recodo *m* **2** CURVE : curva *f*, ángulo *m*, codo *m*

beneath¹ [bɪ'ni:θ] *adv* : bajo, abajo, debajo

beneath² *prep* : bajo de, abajo de, por debajo de

benediction [,bɛnə'dɪkʃən] *n* : bendición *f*

benefactor ['bɛnə,fæktər] *n* : benefactor *m*, -tora *f*

beneficence [bə'nɛfəsənts] *n* : beneficencia *f*

beneficent [bə'nɛfəsənt] *adj* : benéfico, caritativo

beneficial [,bɛnə'fɪʃəl] *adj* : beneficioso, provechoso — **beneficially** *adv*

beneficiary [,bɛnə'fɪʃi,ɛri, -'fɪʃəri] *n, pl* **-ries** : beneficiario *m*, -ria *f*

benefit¹ ['bɛnəfɪt] *vt* : beneficiar — *vi* : beneficiarse

benefit² *n* **1** ADVANTAGE : beneficio *m*, ventaja *f*, provecho *m* **2** AID : asistencia *f*, beneficio *m* **3** : función *f* benéfica (para recaudar fondos)

benevolence [bə'nɛvələnts] *n* : bondad *f*, benevolencia *f*

benevolent [bə'nɛvələnt] *adj* : benévolo, bondadoso — **benevolently** *adv*

Bengali [bɛŋ'gɑli, bɛŋ-] *n* **1** : bengalí *mf* **2** : bengalí *m* (idioma) — **Bengali** *adj*

benign [bɪ'naɪn] *adj* **1** GENTLE, KIND : benévolo, amable **2** FAVORABLE : propicio, favorable **3** MILD : benigno ⟨a benign tumor : un tumor benigno⟩

Beninese [bə,nɪ'ni:z, -,ni:-, -'ni:s; ,bnɪ'-] *n* : beninés *m*, -nesa *f* — **Beninese** *adj*

bent ['bɛnt] *n* : aptitud *f*, inclinación *f*

benumb [bɪ'nʌm] *vt* : entumecer

benzene ['bɛn,zi:n] *n* : benceno *m*

bequeath [bɪ'kwi:θ, -'kwi:ð] *vt* : legar, dejar en testamento

bequest [bɪ'kwɛst] *n* : legado *m*

berate [bɪ'reɪt] *vt* **-rated; -rating** : reprender, regañar

bereaved¹ [bɪ'ri:vd] *adj* : que está de luto, afligido (por la muerte de alguien)

bereaved² *n* **the bereaved** : los deudos del difunto (o de la difunta)
bereavement [bɪˈriːvmənt] *n* **1** SORROW : dolor *m*, pesar *m* **2** LOSS : pérdida *f*
bereft [bɪˈrɛft] *adj* : privado, desprovisto
beret [bəˈreɪ] *n* : boina *f*
beriberi [ˌbɛriˈbɛri] *n* : beriberi *m*
berm [ˈbərm] *n* : arcén *m*
berry [ˈbɛri] *n, pl* **-ries** : baya *f*
berserk [bərˈsərk, -ˈzərk] *adj* **1** : enloquecido **2 to go beserk** : volverse loco
berth¹ [ˈbərθ] *vi* : atracar
berth² *n* **1** DOCK : atracadero *m* **2** ACCOMMODATION : litera *f*, camarote *m* **3** POSITION : trabajo *m*, puesto *m*
beryl [ˈbɛrəl] *n* : berilo *m*
beseech [bɪˈsiːtʃ] *vt* **-seeched** *or* **-sought** [-ˈsɔt]; **-seeching** : suplicar, implorar, rogar
beset [bɪˈsɛt] *vt* **-set; -setting 1** HARASS : acosar **2** SURROUND : rodear
beside [bɪˈsaɪd] *prep* : al lado de, junto a
besides¹ [bɪˈsaɪdz] *adv* **1** ALSO : además, también, aparte **2** MOREOVER : además, por otra parte
besides² *prep* **1** : además de, aparte de ⟨six others besides you : seis otros además de ti⟩ **2** EXCEPT : excepto, fuera de, aparte de
besiege [bɪˈsiːdʒ] *vt* **-sieged; -sieging** : asediar, sitiar, cercar
besmirch [bɪˈsmərtʃ] *vt* : ensuciar, mancillar
best¹ [ˈbɛst] *vt* : superar, ganar a
best² *adv* (*superlative of* **well**) : mejor ⟨as best I can : lo mejor que puedo⟩
best³ *adj* (*superlative of* **good**) : mejor ⟨my best friend : mi mejor amigo⟩
best⁴ *n* **1 the best** : lo mejor, el mejor, la mejor, los mejores, las mejores **2 at ~** : a lo más **3 to do one's best** : hacer todo lo posible
bestial [ˈbɛstʃəl, ˈbiːs-] *adj* **1** : bestial **2** BRUTISH : brutal, salvaje
best man *n* : padrino *m*
bestow [bɪˈstoː] *vt* : conferir, otorgar, conceder
bestowal [bɪˈstoːəl] *n* : concesión *f*, otorgamiento *m*
bet¹ [ˈbɛt] *v* **bet; betting** *vt* : apostar — *vi* **to bet on** : apostarle a
bet² *n* : apuesta *f*
betoken [bɪˈtoːkən] *vt* : denotar, ser indicio de
betray [bɪˈtreɪ] *vt* **1** : traicionar ⟨to betray one's country : traicionar uno a su patria⟩ **2** DIVULGE, REVEAL : delatar, revelar ⟨to betray a secret : revelar un secreto⟩
betrayal [bɪˈtreɪəl] *n* : traición *f*, delación *f*, revelación *f* ⟨betrayal of trust : abuso de confianza⟩
betrothal [bɪˈtroːðəl, -ˈtrɔ-] *n* : esponsales *mpl*, compromiso *m*
betrothed [bɪˈtroːðd, -ˈtrɔθt] *n* FIANCÉ : prometido *m*, -da *f*

better¹ [ˈbɛt̬ər] *vt* **1** IMPROVE : mejorar **2** SURPASS : superar
better² *adv* (*comparative of* **well**) **1** : mejor **2** MORE : más ⟨better than 50 miles : más de 50 millas⟩
better³ *adj* (*comparative of* **good**) **1** : mejor ⟨the weather is better today : hace mejor tiempo hoy⟩ ⟨I was sick, but now I'm better : estuve enfermo, pero ahora estoy mejor⟩ **2** : mayor ⟨the better part of a month : la mayor parte de un mes⟩
better⁴ *n* **1** : el mejor, la mejor ⟨the better of the two : el mejor de los dos⟩ **2 to get the better of** : vencer a, quedar por encima de, superar
betterment [ˈbɛt̬ərmənt] *n* : mejoramiento *m*, mejora *f*
bettor *or* **better** [ˈbɛt̬ər] *n* : apostador *m*, -dora *f*
between¹ [bɪˈtwiːn] *adv* **1** : en medio, por lo medio **2 in ~** : intermedio
between² *prep* : entre
bevel¹ [ˈbɛvəl] *v* **-eled** *or* **-elled; -eling** *or* **-elling** *vt* : biselar — *vi* INCLINE : inclinarse
bevel² *n* : bisel *m*
beverage [ˈbɛvrɪdʒ, ˈbɛvə-] *n* : bebida *f*
bevy [ˈbɛvi] *n, pl* **bevies** : grupo *m* (de personas), bandada *f* (de pájaros)
bewail [bɪˈweɪl] *vt* : lamentarse de, llorar
beware [bɪˈwær] *vi* **to beware of** : tener cuidado con ⟨beware of the dog! : ¡cuidado con el perro!⟩ — *vt* : guardarse de, cuidarse de
bewilder [bɪˈwɪldər] *vt* : desconcertar, dejar perplejo
bewilderment [bɪˈwɪldərmənt] *n* : desconcierto *m*, perplejidad *f*
bewitch [bɪˈwɪtʃ] *vt* **1** : hechizar, embrujar **2** CHARM : cautivar, encantar
bewitchment [bɪˈwɪtʃmənt] *n* : hechizo *m*
beyond¹ [biˈjɑnd] *adv* **1** FARTHER, LATER : más allá, más lejos (en el espacio), más adelante (en el tiempo) **2** MORE : más ⟨$50 and beyond : $50 o más⟩
beyond² *n* **the beyond** : el más allá, lo desconocido
beyond³ *prep* **1** : más allá de ⟨beyond the frontier : más allá de la frontera⟩ **2** : fuera de ⟨beyond one's reach : fuera de su alcance⟩ **3** BESIDES : además de
biannual [ˌbaɪˈænjuəl] *adj* : bianual — **biannually** *adv*
bias¹ [ˈbaɪəs] *vt* **-ased** *or* **-assed; -asing** *or* **-assing 1** : predisponer, sesgar, influir en, afectar **2 to be biased against** : tener prejuicio contra
bias² *n* **1** : sesgo *m*, bies *m* (en la costura) **2** PREJUDICE : prejuicio *m* **3** TENDENCY : inclinación *f*, tendencia *f*
biased [ˈbaɪəst] *adj* : tendencioso, parcial
bib [ˈbɪb] *n* **1** : peto *m* **2** : babero *m* (para niños)
Bible [ˈbaɪbəl] *n* : Biblia *f*
biblical [ˈbɪblɪkəl] *adj* : bíblico

bibliographer [ˌbɪbli'ɑgrəfər] *n* : bibliógrafo *m*, -fa *f*

bibliographic [ˌbɪbliə'græfɪk] *adj* : bibliográfico

bibliography [ˌbɪbli'ɑgrəfi] *n, pl* **-phies** : bibliografía *f*

bicameral [ˌbaɪ'kæmərəl] *adj* : bicameral

bicarbonate [ˌbaɪ'kɑrbənət, -ˌneɪt] *n* : bicarbonato *m*

bicentennial [ˌbaɪsɛn'tɛniəl] *n* : bicentenario *m*

biceps ['baɪˌsɛps] *ns & pl* : bíceps *m*

bicker¹ ['bɪkər] *vi* : pelear, discutir, reñir

bicker² *n* : pelea *f*, riña *f*, discusión *f*

bicuspid [baɪ'kʌspɪd] *n* : premolar *m*, diente *m* bicúspide

bicycle¹ ['baɪsɪkəl, -ˌsɪ-] *vi* **-cled; -cling** : ir en bicicleta

bicycle² *n* : bicicleta *f*

bicycling ['baɪsɪkəlɪŋ] *n* : ciclismo *m*

bicyclist ['baɪsɪkəlɪst] *n* : ciclista *mf*

bid¹ ['bɪd] *vt* **bade** ['bæd, 'beɪd] *or* **bid; bidden** ['bɪdən] *or* **bid; bidding 1** ORDER : pedir, mandar **2** INVITE : invitar **3** SAY : dar, decir ⟨to bid good evening : dar las buenas noches⟩ ⟨to bid farewell to : decir adiós a⟩ **4** : ofrecer (en una subasta), declarar (en juegos de cartas)

bid² *n* **1** OFFER : oferta *f* (en una subasta), declaración *f* (en juegos de cartas) **2** INVITATION : invitación *f* **3** ATTEMPT : intento *m*, tentativa *f*

bidder ['bɪdər] *n* : postor *m*, -tora *f*

bide ['baɪd] *v* **bode** ['bo:d] *or* **bided; bided; biding** *vt* : esperar, aguardar ⟨to bide one's time : esperar el momento oportuno⟩ — *vi* DWELL : morar, vivir

biennial [baɪ'ɛniəl] *adj* : bienal — **biennially** *adv*

bier ['bɪr] *n* **1** STAND : andas *fpl* **2** COFFIN : ataúd *m*, féretro *m*

bifocals ['baɪˌfo:kəlz] *npl* : lentes *mpl* bifocales, bifocales *mpl*

big ['bɪg] *adj* **bigger; biggest 1** LARGE : grande **2** PREGNANT : embarazada **3** IMPORTANT, MAJOR : importante, grande ⟨a big decision : una gran decisión⟩ **4** POPULAR : popular, famoso, conocido

bigamist ['bɪgəmɪst] *n* : bígamo *m*, -ma *f*

bigamous ['bɪgəməs] *adj* : bígamo

bigamy ['bɪgəmi] *n* : bigamia *f*

Big Dipper → **dipper**

bighorn ['bɪgˌhɔrn] *n, pl* **-horn** *or* **-horns** *or* **bighorn sheep** : oveja *f* salvaje de las montañas

bight ['baɪt] *n* : bahía *f*, ensenada *f*, golfo *m*

bigot ['bɪgət] *n* : intolerante *mf*

bigoted ['bɪgətəd] *adj* : intolerante, prejuiciado, fanático

bigotry ['bɪgətri] *n, pl* **-tries** : intolerancia *f*

big shot *n* : pez *m* gordo *fam*, mandamás *mf*

bigwig ['bɪgˌwɪg] → **big shot**

bike ['baɪk] *n* **1** : bicicleta *f*, bici *f fam* **2** : motocicleta *f*, moto *f*

bikini [bə'ki:ni] *n* : bikini *m*

bilateral [baɪ'lætərəl] *adj* : bilateral — **bilaterally** *adv*

bile ['baɪl] *n* **1** : bilis *f* **2** IRRITABILITY : mal genio *m*

bilingual [baɪ'lɪŋgwəl] *adj* : bilingüe

bilious ['bɪliəs] *adj* **1** : bilioso **2** IRRITABLE : bilioso, colérico

bilk ['bɪlk] *vt* : burlar, estafar, defraudar

bill¹ ['bɪl] *vt* : pasarle la cuenta a — *vi* : acariciar ⟨to bill and coo : acariciarse⟩

bill² *n* **1** LAW : proyecto *m* de ley, ley *f* **2** INVOICE : cuenta *f*, factura *f* **3** POSTER : cartel *m* **4** PROGRAM : programa *m* (del teatro) **5** : billete *m* ⟨a five-dollar bill : un billete de cinco dólares⟩ **6** BEAK : pico *m*

billboard ['bɪlˌbɔrd] *n* : cartelera *f*

billet¹ ['bɪlət] *vt* : acuartelar, alojar

billet² *n* : alojamiento *m*

billfold ['bɪlˌfo:ld] *n* : billetera *f*, cartera *f*

billiards ['bɪljərdz] *n* : billar *m*

billion ['bɪljən] *n, pl* **billions** *or* **billion** : mil millones *mpl*

billow¹ ['bɪlo] *vi* : hincharse, inflarse

billow² *n* **1** WAVE : ola *f* **2** CLOUD : nube *f* ⟨a billow of smoke : un nube de humo⟩

billowy ['bɪlowi] *adj* : ondulante

billy goat ['bɪliˌgo:t] *n* : macho *m* cabrío

bin ['bɪn] *n* : cubo *m*, cajón *m*

binary ['baɪnəri, -ˌnɛri] *adj* : binario *m*

bind ['baɪnd] *vt* **bound** ['baʊnd]; **binding 1** TIE : atar, amarrar **2** OBLIGATE : obligar **3** UNITE : aglutinar, ligar, unir **4** BANDAGE : vendar **5** : encuadernar (un libro)

binder ['baɪndər] *n* **1** FOLDER : carpeta *f* **2** : encuadernador *m*, -dora *f* (de libros)

binding ['baɪndɪŋ] *n* **1** : encuadernación *f* (de libros) **2** COVER : cubierta *f*, forro *m*

binge ['bɪndʒ] *n* : juerga *f*, parranda *f fam*

bingo ['bɪŋˌgo:] *n, pl* **-gos** : bingo *m*

binocular [baɪ'nɑkjələr, bə-] *adj* : binocular

binoculars [bə'nɑkjələrz, baɪ-] *npl* : binoculares *mpl*

biochemical¹ [ˌbaɪo'kɛmɪkəl] *adj* : bioquímico

biochemical² *n* : bioquímico *m*

biochemist [ˌbaɪo'kɛmɪst] *n* : bioquímico *m*, -ca *f*

biochemistry [ˌbaɪo'kɛməstri] *n* : bioquímica *f*

biodegradable [ˌbaɪodɪ'greɪdəbəl] *adj* : biodegradable

biodegradation [ˌbaɪodɛgrə'deɪʃən] *n* : biodegradación *f*

biodegrade [ˌbaɪodɪ'greɪd] *vi* **-graded; -grading** : biodegradarse

biodiversity · blacklist

biodiversity [ˌbaɪodəˈvərsəti, -daɪ-] *n, pl*
-ties : bioversidad *f*
biographer [baɪˈɑgrəfər] *n* : biógrafo *m*,
-fa *f*
biographical [ˌbaɪəˈgræfɪkəl] *adj* : biográfico
biography [baɪˈɑgrəfi, bi:-] *n, pl* -phies
: biografía *f*
biologic [ˌbaɪəˈlɑʤɪk] *or* **biological**
[-ʤɪkəl] *adj* : biológico
biologist [baɪˈɑləʤɪst] *n* : biólogo *m*, -ga
f
biology [baɪˈɑləʤi] *n* : biología *f*
biophysical [ˌbaɪoˈfɪzɪkəl] *adj* : biofísico
biophysicist [ˌbaɪoˈfɪzəsɪst] *n* : biofísico
m, -ca *f*
biophysics [ˌbaɪoˈfɪzɪks] *ns & pl* : biofísica *f*
biopsy [ˈbaɪˌɑpsi] *n, pl* -sies : biopsia *f*
biosphere [ˈbaɪəˌsfɪr] *n* : biosfera *f*, biósfera *f*
biotechnology [ˌbaɪotɛkˈnɑləʤi] *n* : biotecnología *f*
biotic [baɪˈɑtɪk] *adj* : biótico
bipartisan [baɪˈpɑrtəzən, -sən] *adj* : bipartidista, de dos partidas
biped [ˈbaɪˌpɛd] *n* : bípedo *m*
birch [ˈbərʧ] *n* : abedul *m*
bird [ˈbərd] *n* : pájaro *m* (pequeño), ave
f (grande)
birdbath [ˈbərd,bæθ, -ˌbɑθ] *n* : pila *f* para
pájaros
bird dog *n* : perro *m*, -rra *f* de caza
bird of prey *n* : ave *f* rapaz, ave *f* de presa
birdseed [ˈbərd,si:d] *n* : alpiste *m*
bird's–eye [ˈbərdz,aɪ] *adj* **1** : visto desde arriba ⟨bird's-eye view : vista aérea⟩
2 CURSORY : rápido, somero
birth [ˈbərθ] *n* **1** : nacimiento *m*, parto
m **2** ORIGIN : origen *m*, nacimiento *m*
birthday [ˈbərθ,deɪ] *n* : cumpleaños *m*,
aniversario *m*
birthmark [ˈbərθ,mɑrk] *n* : mancha *f* de
nacimiento
birthplace [ˈbərθ,pleɪs] *n* : lugar *m* de
nacimiento
birthrate [ˈbərθ,reɪt] *n* : índice *m* de natalidad
birthright [ˈbərθ,raɪt] *n* : derecho *m* de
nacimiento
biscuit [ˈbɪskət] *n* : bizcocho *m*
bisect [ˈbaɪ,sɛkt, ˌbaɪˈ-] *vt* : bisecar
bisexual [ˌbaɪˈsɛkʃuəl] *adj* : bisexual
bishop [ˈbɪʃəp] *n* **1** : obispo *m* **2** : alfil
m (en ajedrez)
bismuth [ˈbɪzməθ] *n* : bismuto *m*
bison [ˈbaɪzən, -sən] *ns & pl* : bisonte *m*
bistro [ˈbi:stro, ˈbɪs-] *n, pl* -tros : bar *m*,
restaurante *m* pequeño
bit [ˈbɪt] *n* **1** FRAGMENT, PIECE : pedazo *m*, trozo *m* ⟨a bit of luck : un poco
de suerte⟩ **2** : freno *m*, bocado *m* (de
una brida) **3** : broca *f* (de un taladro)
4 : bit *m* (de información)
bitch[1] [ˈbɪʧ] *vi* COMPLAIN : quejarse,
reclamar

bitch[2] *n* : perra *f*
bite[1] [ˈbaɪt] *v* **bit** [ˈbɪt]; **bitten** [ˈbɪtən];
biting *vt* **1** : morder **2** STING : picar **3**
PUNCTURE : punzar, pinchar **4** GRIP
: agarrar — *vi* **1** : morder ⟨that dog
bites : ese perro muerde⟩ **2** STING
: picar (dícese de un insecto), cortar
(dícese del viento) **3** : picar ⟨the fish
are biting now : ya están picando los
peces⟩ **4** GRAB : agarrarse
bite[2] *n* **1** BITING : mordisco *m*, dentellada *f* **2** SNACK : bocado *m* ⟨a bite to
eat : algo de comer⟩ **3** : picadura *f* (de
un insecto), mordedura *f* (de un animal) **4** SHARPNESS : mordacidad *f*, penetración *f*
biting *adj* **1** PENETRATING : cortante,
penetrante **2** CAUSTIC : mordaz, sarcástico
bitter [ˈbɪtər] *adj* **1** ACRID : amargo, acre
2 PENETRATING : cortante, penetrante
⟨bitter cold : frío glacial⟩ **3** HARSH
: duro, amargo ⟨to the bitter end : hasta el final⟩ **4** INTENSE, RELENTLESS
: intenso, extremo, implacable ⟨bitter
hatred : odio implacable⟩
bitterly [ˈbɪtərli] *adv* : amargamente
bitterness [ˈbɪtərnəs] *n* : amargura *f*
bittersweet [ˈbɪtər,swi:t] *adj* : agridulce
bivalve [ˈbaɪ,vælv] *n* : bivalvo *m* — **bivalve** *adj*
bivouac[1] [ˈbɪvə,wæk, ˈbɪv,wæk] *vi*
-ouacked; -ouacking : acampar, vivaquear
bivouac[2] *n* : vivaque *m*
bizarre [bəˈzɑr] *adj* : extraño, singular,
estrafalario, estrambótico — **bizarrely**
adv
blab [ˈblæb] *vi* blabbed; blabbing : parlotear *fam*, cotorrear *fam*
black[1] [ˈblæk] *vt* : ennegrecer
black[2] *adj* **1** : negro (color, raza) **2**
SOILED : sucio **3** DARK : oscuro, negro
4 WICKED : malvado, perverso, malo **5**
GLOOMY : negro, sombrío, deprimente
black[3] *n* **1** : negro *m* (color) **2** : negro
m, -gra *f* (persona)
black–and–blue [ˌblækənˈblu:] *adj*
: amoratado
blackball [ˈblæk,bɔl] *vt* **1** OSTRACIZE
: hacerle el vacío a, aislar **2** BOYCOTT
: boicotear
blackberry [ˈblæk,bɛri] *n, pl* -ries : mora
f
blackbird [ˈblæk,bərd] *n* : mirlo *m*
blackboard [ˈblæk,bɔrd] *n* : pizarra *f*,
pizarrón *m*
blacken [ˈblækən] *vt* **1** BLACK : ennegrecer **2** DEFAME : deshonrar,
difamar, manchar
blackhead [ˈblæk,hɛd] *n* : espinilla *f*,
punto *m* negro
black hole *n* : agujero *m* negro
blackjack [ˈblæk,ʤæk] *n* **1** : cachiporra
f (arma) **2** : veintiuna *f* (juego de cartas)
blacklist[1] [ˈblæk,lɪst] *vt* : poner en la lista
negra

blacklist² *n* : lista *f* negra
blackmail¹ ['blæk‚meɪl] *vt* : chantajear, hacer chantaje a
blackmail² *n* : chantaje *m*
blackmailer ['blæk‚meɪlər] *n* : chantajista *mf*
blackout ['blæk‚aʊt] *n* 1 : apagón *m* (de poder eléctrico) 2 FAINT : desmayo *m*, desvanecimiento *m*
black out *vt* : dejar sin luz — *vi* FAINT : perder el conocimiento, desmayarse
blacksmith ['blæk‚smɪθ] *n* : herrero *m*
blacktop ['blæk‚tɑp] *n* : asfalto *m*
bladder ['blædər] *n* : vejiga *f*
blade ['bleɪd] *n* : hoja *f* (de un cuchillo), cuchilla *f* (de un patín), pala *f* (de un remo o una hélice), brizna *f* (de hierba)
blamable ['bleɪməbəl] *adj* : culpable
blame¹ ['bleɪm] *vt* **blamed; blaming** : culpar, echar la culpa a
blame² *n* : culpa *f*
blameless ['bleɪmləs] *adj* : intachable, sin culpa, inocente — **blamelessly** *adv*
blameworthiness ['bleɪm‚wərðinəs] *n* : culpa *f*, culpabilidad *f*
blameworthy ['bleɪm‚wərði] *adj* : culpable, reprochable, censurable
blanch ['blæntʃ] *vt* WHITEN : blanquear — *vi* PALE : palidecer
bland ['blænd] *adj* : soso, insulso, desabrido ⟨a bland smile : una sonrisa insulsa⟩ ⟨a bland diet : una dieta fácil de digerir⟩
blandishments ['blændɪʃmənts] *npl* : lisonjas *fpl*, halagos *mpl*
blandly ['blændli] *adv* : de manera insulsa
blandness ['blændnəs] *n* : lo insulso, lo desabrido
blank¹ ['blæŋk] *vt* OBLITERATE : borrar
blank² *adj* 1 DAZED : perplejo, desconcertado 2 EXPRESSIONLESS : sin expresión, inexpresivo 3 : en blanco (dícese de un papel), liso (dícese de una pared) 4 EMPTY : vacío, en blanco ⟨a blank stare : una mirada vacía⟩ ⟨his mind went blank : se quedó en blanco⟩
blank³ *n* 1 SPACE : espacio *m* en blanco 2 FORM : formulario *m* 3 CARTRIDGE : cartucho *m* de fogueo 4 *or* **blank key** : llave *f* ciega
blanket¹ ['blæŋkət] *vt* : cubrir
blanket² *adj* : global
blanket³ *n* : manta *f*, cobija *f*, frazada *f*
blankly ['blæŋkli] *adv* : sin comprender
blankness ['blæŋknəs] *n* 1 PERPLEXITY : desconcierto *m*, perplejidad *f* 2 EMPTINESS : vacío *m*, vacuidad *f*
blare¹ ['blær] *vi* **blared; blaring** : resonar
blare² *n* : estruendo *m*
blarney ['blɑrni] *n* : labia *f fam*
blasé [blɑ'zeɪ] *adj* : displicente, indiferente
blaspheme [blæs'fiːm, 'blæs‚-] *vi* **-phemed; -pheming** : blasfemar
blasphemer [blæs'fiːmər, 'blæs‚-] *n* : blasfemo *m*, -ma *f*

blasphemous ['blæsfəməs] *adj* : blasfemo
blasphemy ['blæsfəmi] *n, pl* **-mies** : blasfemia *f*
blast¹ ['blæst] *vt* 1 BLOW UP : volar, hacer volar 2 ATTACK : atacar, arremeter contra
blast² *n* 1 GUST : ráfaga *f* 2 EXPLOSION : explosión *f*
blast–off ['blæst‚ɔf] *n* : despegue *m*
blast off *vi* : despegar
blatant ['bleɪtənt] *adj* : descarado — **blatantly** ['bleɪtəntli] *adv*
blaze¹ ['bleɪz] *v* **blazed; blazing** *vi* SHINE : arder, brillar, resplandecer — *vt* MARK : marcar, señalar ⟨to blaze a trail : abrir un camino⟩
blaze² *n* 1 FIRE : fuego *m* 2 BRIGHTNESS : resplandor *m*, brillantez *f* 3 OUTBURST : arranque *m* ⟨a blaze of anger : un arranque de cólera⟩ 4 DISPLAY : alarde *m*, llamarada *f* ⟨a blaze of color : un derroche de color⟩
blazer ['bleɪzər] *n* : chaqueta *f* deportiva, blazer *m*
bleach¹ ['bliːtʃ] *vt* : blanquear, decolorar
bleach² *n* : lejía *f*, blanqueador *m*
bleachers ['bliːtʃərz] *ns & pl* : gradas *fpl*, tribuna *f* descubierta
bleak ['bliːk] *adj* 1 DESOLATE : inhóspito, sombrío, desolado 2 DEPRESSING : deprimente, triste, sombrío
bleakly ['bliːkli] *adv* : sombríamente
bleakness ['bliːknəs] *n* : lo inhóspito, lo sombrío
blear ['blɪr] *adj* : empañado, nublado
bleary ['blɪri] *adj* 1 : adormilado, fatigado 2 **bleary–eyed** : con los ojos nublados
bleat¹ ['bliːt] *vi* : balar
bleat² *n* : balido *m*
bleed ['bliːd] *v* **bled** ['blɛd]; **bleeding** *vi* 1 : sangrar 2 GRIEVE : sufrir, afligirse 3 EXUDE : exudar (dícese de una planta), correrse (dícese de los colores) — *vt* 1 : sangrar (a una persona), purgar (frenos) 2 **to bleed someone dry** : sacarle todo el dinero a alguien
blemish¹ ['blɛmɪʃ] *vt* : manchar, marcar
blemish² *n* : imperfección *f*, mancha *f*, marca *f*
blend¹ ['blɛnd] *vt* 1 MIX : mezclar 2 COMBINE : combinar, aunar
blend² *n* : mezcla *f*, combinación *f*
blender ['blɛndər] *n* : licuadora *f*
bless ['blɛs] *vt* **blessed** ['blɛst]; **blessing** 1 CONSECRATE : bendecir, consagrar 2 : bendecir ⟨may God bless you! : ¡que Dios te bendiga!⟩ 3 **to bless with** : dotar de 4 **to bless oneself** : santiguarse
blessed ['blɛsəd] *or* **blest** ['blɛst] *adj* : bienaventurado, bendito, dichoso
blessedly ['blɛsədli] *adv* : felizmente, alegremente, afortunadamente
blessing ['blɛsɪŋ] *n* 1 : bendición *f* 2 APPROVAL : aprobación *f*, consentimiento *m*

blew → **blow**
blight[1] ['blaɪt] vt : arruinar, infestar
blight[2] n 1 : añublo m 2 PLAGUE : peste f, plaga f 3 DECAY : deterioro m, ruina f
blimp ['blɪmp] n : dirigible m
blind[1] ['blaɪnd] vt 1 : cegar, dejar ciego 2 DAZZLE : deslumbrar
blind[2] adj 1 SIGHTLESS : ciego 2 INSENSITIVE : ciego, insensible, sin razón 3 CLOSED : sin salida ⟨blind alley : callejón sin salida⟩
blind[3] n 1 : persiana f (para una ventana) 2 COVER : escondite m, escondrijo m
blinders ['blaɪndərz] npl : anteojeras fpl
blindfold[1] ['blaɪnd,fo:ld] vt : vendar los ojos
blindfold[2] n : venda f (para los ojos)
blinding ['blaɪndɪŋ] adj : enceguecedor, cegador ⟨with blinding speed : con una rapidez inusitada⟩
blindly ['blaɪndli] adv : a ciegas, ciegamente
blindness ['blaɪndnəs] n : ceguera f
blink[1] ['blɪŋk] vi 1 WINK : pestañear, parpadear 2 : brillar intermitentemente
blink[2] n : pestañeo m, parpadeo m
blinker ['blɪŋkər] n : intermitente m, direccional f
bliss ['blɪs] n 1 HAPPINESS : dicha f, felicidad f absoluta 2 PARADISE : paraíso m
blissful ['blɪsfəl] adj : dichoso, feliz — **blissfully** adv
blister[1] ['blɪstər] vi : ampollarse
blister[2] n : ampolla f (en la piel o una superficie), burbuja f (en una superficie)
blithe ['blaɪθ, 'blaɪð] adj **blither; blithest** 1 CAREFREE : despreocupado 2 CHEERFUL : alegre, risueño — **blithely** adv
blitz[1] ['blɪts] vt 1 BOMBARD : bombardear 2 : atacar con rapidez
blitz[2] n 1 : bombardeo m aéreo 2 CAMPAIGN : ataque m, acometida f
blizzard ['blɪzərd] n : tormenta f de nieve, ventisca f
bloat ['blo:t] vi : hincharse, inflarse
blob ['blɑb] n : gota f, mancha f, borrón m
bloc ['blɑk] n : bloque m
block[1] ['blɑk] vt 1 OBSTRUCT : obstruir, bloquear 2 CLOG : atascar, atorar
block[2] n 1 PIECE : bloque m ⟨building blocks : cubos de construcción⟩ ⟨auction block : plataforma de subastas⟩ ⟨starting block : taco de salida⟩ 2 OBSTRUCTION : obstrucción f, bloqueo m 3 : cuadra f, manzana f (de edificios) ⟨to go around the block : dar la vuelta a la cuadra⟩ 4 BUILDING : edificio m (de apartamentos, oficinas, etc.) 5 GROUP, SERIES : serie f, grupo m ⟨a block of tickets : una serie de entradas⟩ 6 **block and tackle** : aparejo m de poleas

blockade[1] [blɑ'keɪd] vt **-aded; -ading** : bloquear
blockade[2] n : bloqueo m
blockage ['blɑkɪʤ] n : bloqueo m, obstrucción f
blockhead ['blɑk,hɛd] n : bruto m, -ta f; estúpido m, -da f
blond[1] or **blonde** ['blɑnd] adj : rubio, güero Mex, claro (dícese de la madera)
blond[2] or **blonde** n : rubio m, -bia f; güero m, -ra f Mex
blood ['blʌd] n 1 : sangre f 2 LIFEBLOOD : vida f, alma f 3 LINEAGE : linaje m, sangre f
blood bank n : banco m de sangre
bloodcurdling ['blʌd,kərdəlɪŋ] adj : espeluznante, aterrador
blooded ['blʌdəd] adj : de sangre ⟨cold-blooded animal : animal de sangre fría⟩
bloodhound ['blʌd,haʊnd] n : sabueso m
bloodless ['blʌdləs] adj 1 : incruento, sin derramamiento de sangre 2 LIFELESS : desanimado, insípido, sin vida
bloodmobile ['blʌdmo,bi:l] n : unidad f móvil para donantes de sangre
blood pressure n : tensión f, presión f (arterial)
bloodshed ['blʌd,ʃɛd] n : derramamiento m de sangre
bloodshot ['blʌd,ʃɑt] adj : inyectado de sangre
bloodstain ['blʌd,steɪn] n : mancha f de sangre
bloodstained ['blʌd,steɪnd] adj : manchado de sangre
bloodstream ['blʌd,stri:m] n : torrente m sanguíneo, corriente f sanguínea
bloodsucker ['blʌd,sʌkər] n : sanguijuela f
bloodthirsty ['blʌd,θərsti] adj : sanguinario
blood vessel n : vaso m sanguíneo
bloody ['blʌdi] adj **bloodier; -est** : ensangrentado, sangriento
bloom[1] ['blu:m] vi 1 FLOWER : florecer 2 MATURE : madurar
bloom[2] n 1 FLOWER : flor f ⟨to be in bloom : estar en flor⟩ 2 FLOWERING : floración f ⟨in full bloom : en plena floración⟩ 3 : rubor m (de la tez) ⟨in the bloom of youth : en plena juventud, en la flor de la vida⟩
bloomers ['blu:mərz] npl : bombachos mpl
blooper ['blu:pər] n : metedura f de pata fam
blossom[1] ['blɑsəm] vi : florecer, dar flor
blossom[2] n : flor f
blot[1] ['blɑt] vt **blotted; blotting** 1 SPOT : emborronar, borronear 2 DRY : secar
blot[2] n 1 STAIN : mancha f, borrón m 2 BLEMISH : mancha f, tacha f
blotch[1] ['blɑtʃ] vt : emborronar, borronear
blotch[2] n : mancha f, borrón m
blotchy ['blɑtʃi] adj **blotchier; -est** : lleno de manchas

blotter ['blɑtər] *n* : hoja *f* de papel secante, secante *m*

blouse ['blaʊs, 'blaʊz] *n* : blusa *f*

blow[1] ['bloː] *v* **blew** ['bluː]; **blown** ['bloːn]; **blowing** *vi* **1** : soplar, volar ⟨the wind is blowing hard : el viento está soplando con fuerza⟩ ⟨it blew out the door : voló por la puerta⟩ ⟨the window blew shut : se cerró la ventana⟩ **2** SOUND : sonar ⟨the whistle blew : sonó el silbato⟩ **3 to blow out** : fundirse (dícese de un fusible eléctrico), reventarse (dícese de una llanta) **4 to blow off** : dejar plantado (a alguien), flatar a (una cita, etc.) — *vt* **1** : soplar, echar ⟨to blow smoke : echar humo⟩ **2** SOUND : tocar, sonar **3** SHAPE : soplar, dar forma a ⟨to blow glass : soplar vidrio⟩ **4** BUNGLE : echar a perder

blow[2] *n* **1** PUFF : soplo *m*, soplido *m* **2** GALE : vendaval *f* **3** HIT, STROKE : golpe *m* **4** CALAMITY : golpe *m*, desastre *m* **5 to come to blows** : llegar a las manos

blower ['bloːər] *n* FAN : ventilador *m*

blowout ['bloː,aʊt] *n* : reventón *m*

blowtorch ['bloː,tɔrtʃ] *n* : soplete *m*

blow up *vi* EXPLODE : estallar, hacer explosión — *vt* BLAST : volar, hacer volar

blubber[1] ['blʌbər] *vi* : lloriquear

blubber[2] *n* : esperma *f* de ballena

bludgeon ['blʌʤən] *vt* : aporrear

blue[1] ['bluː] *adj* **bluer; bluest 1** : azul **2** MELANCHOLY : melancólico, triste

blue[2] *n* : azul *m*

blueberry ['bluː,bɛri] *n*, *pl* **-ries** : arándano *m*

bluebird ['bluː,bərd] *n* : azulejo *m*

blue cheese *n* : queso *m* azul

blueprint ['bluː,prɪnt] *n* **1** : plano *m*, proyecto *m*, cianotipo *m* **2** PLAN : anteproyecto *m*, programa *m*

blues ['bluːz] *npl* **1** DEPRESSION : depresión *f*, melancolía *f* **2** : blues *m* ⟨to sing the blues : cantar blues⟩

bluff[1] ['blʌf] *vi* : hacer un farol, blofear *Col, Mex*

bluff[2] *adj* **1** STEEP : escarpado **2** FRANK : campechano, franco, directo

bluff[3] *n* **1** : farol *m*, blof *m Col, Mex* **2** CLIFF : acantilado *m*, risco *m*

bluing *or* **blueing** ['bluːɪŋ] *n* : añil *m*, azulete *m*

bluish ['bluːɪʃ] *adj* : azulado

blunder[1] ['blʌndər] *vi* **1** STUMBLE : tropezar, dar traspiés **2** ERR : cometer un error, tropezar, meter la pata *fam*

blunder[2] *n* : error *m*, fallo *m* garrafal, metedura *f* de pata *fam*

blunderbuss ['blʌndər,bʌs] *n* : trabuco *m*

blunt[1] ['blʌnt] *vt* : despuntar (aguja o lápiz), desafilar (cuchillo o tijeras), suavizar (crítica)

blunt[2] *adj* **1** DULL : desafilado, despuntado **2** DIRECT : directo, franco, categórico

bluntly ['blʌntli] *adv* : sin rodeos, francamente, bruscamente

bluntness ['blʌntnəs] *n* **1** DULLNESS : falta *f* de filo, embotadura *f* **2** FRANKNESS : franqueza *f*

blur[1] ['blər] *vt* **blurred; blurring** : desdibujar, hacer borroso

blur[2] *n* **1** SMEAR : mancha *f*, borrón *m* **2** : aspecto *m* borroso ⟨everything was just a blur : todo se volvió borroso⟩

blurb ['blərb] *n* : propaganda *f*, nota *f* publicitaria

blurry ['bləri] *adj* : borroso

blurt ['blərt] *vt* : espetar, decir impulsivamente

blush[1] ['blʌʃ] *vi* : ruborizarse, sonrojarse, hacerse colorado

blush[2] *n* : rubor *m*, sonrojo *m*

bluster[1] ['blʌstər] *vi* **1** BLOW : soplar con fuerza **2** BOAST : fanfarronear, echar bravatas

bluster[2] *n* : fanfarronada *f*, bravatas *fpl*

blustery ['blʌstəri] *adj* : borrascoso, tempestuoso

boa ['boːə] *n* : boa *f*

boar ['bor] *n* : cerdo *m* macho, verraco *m*

board[1] ['bord] *vt* **1** : embarcarse en, subir a bordo de (una nave o un avión), subir a (un tren o carro) **2** LODGE : hospedar, dar hospedaje con comidas a **3 to board up** : cerrar con tablas

board[2] *n* **1** PLANK : tabla *f*, tablón *m* **2** : tablero *m* ⟨chessboard : tablero de ajedrez⟩ **3** MEALS : comida *f* ⟨board and lodging : comida y alojamiento⟩ **4** COMMITTEE, COUNCIL : junta *f*, consejo *m*

boarder ['bordər] *n* LODGER : huésped *m*, -peda *f*

boardinghouse ['bordɪŋ,haʊs] *n* : casa *f* de huéspedes

boarding school *n* : internado *m*

boardwalk ['bord,wɔk] *n* : paseo *m* marítimo

boast[1] ['boːst] *vi* : alardear, presumir, jactarse

boast[2] *n* : jactancia *f*, alarde *m*

boaster ['boːstər] *n* : presumido *m*, -da *f*; fanfarrón *m*, -rrona *f fam*

boastful ['boːstfəl] *adj* : jactancioso, fanfarrón *fam*

boastfully ['boːstfəli] *adv* : de manera jactanciosa

boat[1] ['boːt] *vt* : transportar en barco, poner a bordo

boat[2] *n* : barco *m*, embarcación *f*, bote *m*, barca *f*

boatman ['boːtmən] *n*, *pl* **-men** [-mən, -,mɛn] : barquero *m*

boatswain ['boːsən] *n* : contramaestre *m*

bob[1] ['bɑb] *v* **bobbed; bobbing** *vi* **1** : balancearse, mecerse ⟨to bob up and down : subir y bajar⟩ **2** *or* **to bob up** APPEAR : presentarse, surgir — *vt* **1** : inclinar (la cabeza o el cuerpo) **2** CUT : cortar, recortar ⟨she bobbed her hair : se cortó el pelo⟩

bob² *n* **1** : inclinación *f* (de la cabeza, del cuerpo), sacudida *f* **2** FLOAT : flotador *m*, corcho *m* (de pesca) **3** : pelo *m* corto

bobbin ['bɑbən] *n* : bobina *f*, carrete *m*

bobby pin ['bɑbi,pɪn] *n* : horquilla *f*

bobcat ['bɑb,kæt] *n* : lince *m* rojo

bobolink ['bɑbə,lɪŋk] *n* : tordo *m* arrocero

bobsled ['bɑb,slɛd] *n* : bobsleigh *m*

bobwhite ['bɑb'hwaɪt] *n* : codorniz *m* (del Nuevo Mundo)

bode¹ ['bo:d] *v* **boded; boding** *vt* : presagiar, augurar — *vi* **to bode well** : ser de buen agüero

bode² → **bide**

bodice ['bɑdəs] *n* : corpiño *m*

bodied ['bɑdid] *adj* : de cuerpo ⟨lean-bodied : de cuerpo delgado⟩ ⟨able-bodied : no discapacitado⟩

bodiless ['bɑdiləs, 'bɑdələs] *adj* : incorpóreo

bodily¹ ['bɑdəli] *adv* : en peso ⟨to lift someone bodily : levantar a alguien en peso⟩

bodily² *adj* : corporal, del cuerpo ⟨bodily harm : daños corporales⟩

body ['bɑdi] *n, pl* **bodies 1** : cuerpo *m*, organismo *m* **2** CORPSE : cadáver *m* **3** PERSON : persona *f*, ser *m* humano **4** : nave *f* (de una iglesia), carrocería (de un automóvil), fuselaje *m* (de un avión), casco *m* (de una nave) **5** COLLECTION, MASS : conjunto *m*, grupo *m*, masa *f* ⟨in a body : todos juntos, en masa⟩ **6** ORGANIZATION : organismo *m*, organización *f*

bodyguard ['bɑdi,gɑrd] *n* : guardaespaldas *mf*

bog¹ ['bɑg, 'bɔg] *vt* **bogged; bogging** : empantanar, inundar ⟨to get bogged down : empantanarse⟩

bog² *n* : lodazal *m*, ciénaga *f*, cenagal *m*

bogey ['bʊgi, 'bo:-] *n, pl* **-geys** : terror *m*, coco *m fam*

boggle ['bɑgəl] *vi* **-gled; -gling** : quedarse atónito, quedarse pasmado ⟨the mind boggles! : ¡es increíble!⟩

boggy ['bɑgi, 'bɔ-] *adj* **boggier; -est** : cenagoso

bogus ['bo:gəs] *adj* : falso, fingido, falaz

bohemian [bo:'hi:miən] *n* : bohemio *m*, -mia *f* — **bohemian** *adj*

boil¹ ['bɔɪl] *vi* **1** : hervir **2 to make one's blood boil** : hervirle la sangre a uno — *vt* **1** : hervir, hacer hervir ⟨to boil water : hervir agua⟩ **2** : cocer, hervir ⟨to boil potatoes : cocer papas⟩

boil² *n* **1** BOILING : hervor *m* **2** : furúnculo *m*, divieso *m* (en medicina)

boiler ['bɔɪlər] *n* : caldera *f*

boisterous ['bɔɪstərəs] *adj* : bullicioso, escandaloso — **boisterously** *adv*

bold ['bo:ld] *adj* **1** COURAGEOUS : valiente **2** INSOLENT : insolente, descarado **3** DARING : atrevido, audaz — **boldly** *adv*

boldface ['bo:ld,feɪs] *or* **boldface type** *n* : negrita *f*

boldness ['bo:ldnəs] *n* **1** COURAGE : valor *m*, coraje *m* **2** INSOLENCE : atrevimiento *m*, insolencia *f*, descaro *m* **3** DARING : audacia *f*

bolero [bə'lɛro] *n, pl* **-ros** : bolero *m*

Bolivian [bə'lɪviən] *n* : boliviano *m*, -na *f* — **Bolivian** *adj*

boll ['bo:l] *n* : cápsula *f* (del algodón)

boll weevil *n* : gorgojo *m* del algodón

bologna [bə'lo:ni] *n* : salchicha *f* ahumada

bolster¹ ['bo:lstər] *vt* **-stered; -stering** : reforzar, reafirmar ⟨to bolster morale : levantar la moral⟩

bolster² *n* : cabezal *m*, almohadón *m*

bolt¹ ['bo:lt] *vt* **1** : atornillar, sujetar con pernos ⟨bolted to the floor : sujetado con pernos al suelo⟩ **2** : cerrar con pestillo, echar el cerrojo a ⟨to bolt the door : echar el cerrojo a la puerta⟩ **3 to bolt down** : engullir ⟨she bolted down her dinner : engulló su comida⟩ — *vi* : echar a correr, salir corriendo ⟨he bolted from the room : salió corriendo de la sala⟩

bolt² *n* **1** LATCH : pestillo *m*, cerrojo *m* **2** : tornillo *m*, perno *m* ⟨nuts and bolts : tuercas y tornillos⟩ **3** : rollo *m* ⟨a bolt of cloth : un rollo de tela⟩ **4 lightning bolt** : relámpago *m*, rayo *m*

bomb¹ ['bɑm] *vt* : bombardear

bomb² *n* : bomba *f*

bombard [bɑm'bɑrd, bəm-] *vt* : bombardear

bombardier [,bɑmbə'dɪr] *n* : bombardero *m*, -ra *f*

bombardment [bɑm'bɑrdmənt] *n* : bombardeo *m*

bombast ['bɑm,bæst] *n* : grandilocuencia *f*, ampulosidad *f*

bombastic [bɑm'bæstɪk] *adj* : grandilocuente, ampuloso, bombástico

bomber ['bɑmər] *n* : bombardero *m*

bombproof ['bɑm,pru:f] *adj* : a prueba de bombas

bombshell ['bɑm,ʃɛl] *n* : bomba *f* ⟨a political bombshell : una bomba política⟩

bona fide ['bo:nə,faɪd, 'bɑ-, ,bo:nə'faɪd] *adj* **1** : de buena fe ⟨a bona fide offer : una oferta de buena fe⟩ **2** GENUINE : genuino, auténtico

bonanza [bə'nænzə] *n* : bonanza *f*

bonbon ['bɑn,bɑn] *n* : bombón *m*

bond¹ ['bɑnd] *vt* **1** INSURE : dar fianza a, asegurar **2** STICK : adherir, pegar — *vi* : adherirse, pegarse

bond² *n* **1** LINK, TIE : vínculo *m*, lazo *m* **2** BAIL : fianza *f*, caución *f* **3** : bono *m* ⟨stocks and bonds : acciones y bonos⟩ **4 bonds** *npl* FETTERS : cadenas *fpl*

bondage ['bɑndɪdʒ] *n* : esclavitud *f*

bondholder ['bɑnd,ho:ldər] *n* : tenedor *m*, -dora *f* de bonos

bondsman ['bɑndzmən] *n, pl* **-men** [-mən, -,mn] **1** SLAVE : esclavo *m* **2** SURETY : fiador *m*, -dora *f*

bone¹ ['bo:n] *vt* **boned; boning** : deshuesar

bone² n : hueso m

boneless ['bo:nləs] adj : sin huesos, sin espinas

boner ['bo:nər] n : metedura f de pata, metida f de pata

bonfire ['ban,faɪr] n : hoguera f, fogata f, fogón m

bonito [bə'ni:ṭo] n, pl -tos or -to : bonito m

bonnet ['banət] n : sombrero m (de mujer), gorra f (de niño)

bonus ['bo:nəs] n 1 : prima f, bonificación f (pagado al empleado) 2 ADVANTAGE, BENEFIT : beneficio m, provecho m

bony ['bo:ni] adj bonier; -est : huesudo

boo¹ ['bu:] vt : abuchear

boo² n, pl boos : abucheo m

booby ['bu:bi] n, pl -bies : bobo m, -ba f; tonto m, -ta f

book¹ ['bʊk] vt : reservar ⟨to book a flight : reservar un vuelo⟩

book² n 1 : libro m 2 the Book : la Biblia 3 by the book : según las reglas

bookcase ['bʊk,keɪs] n : estantería f, librero m Mex

bookend ['bʊk,ɛnd] n : sujetalibros m

bookie ['bʊki] → bookmaker

bookish ['bʊkɪʃ] adj : libresco

bookkeeper ['bʊk,ki:pər] n : tenedor m, -dora f de libros; contable mf Spain

bookkeeping ['bʊk,ki:pɪŋ] n : contabilidad f, teneduría f de libros

booklet ['bʊklət] n : folleto m

bookmaker ['bʊk,meɪkər] n : corredor m, -dora f de apuestas

bookmark ['bʊk,mark] n : señalador m de libros, marcador m de libros

bookseller ['bʊk,slər] n : librero m, -ra f

bookshelf ['bʊk,ʃɛlf] n, pl -shelves 1 : estante m 2 bookshelves npl : estantería f

bookstore ['bʊk,stor] n : librería f

bookworm ['bʊk,wərm] n : ratón m de biblioteca fam

boom¹ ['bu:m] vi 1 THUNDER : tronar, resonar 2 FLOURISH, PROSPER : estar en auge, prosperar

boom² n 1 BOOMING : bramido m, estruendo m 2 FLOURISHING : auge m ⟨population boom : auge de población⟩

boomerang ['bu:mə,ræŋ] n : bumerán m

boon¹ ['bu:n] adj boon companion : amigo m, -ga f del alma

boon² n : ayuda f, beneficio m, adelanto m

boondocks ['bu:n,daks] npl : área f rural remota, región f alejada

boor ['bʊr] n : grosero m, -ra f

boorish ['bʊrɪʃ] adj : grosero

boost¹ ['bu:st] vt 1 LIFT : levantar, alzar 2 INCREASE : aumentar, incrementar 3 PROMOTE : promover, fomentar, hacer publicidad por

boost² n 1 THRUST : impulso m, empujón m 2 ENCOURAGEMENT : estímulo m, aliento m 3 INCREASE : aumento m, incremento m

booster ['bu:stər] n 1 SUPPORTER : partidario m, -ria f 2 booster rocket : cohete m propulsor 3 booster shot : vacuna f de refuerzo

boot¹ ['bu:t] vt KICK : dar una patada a, patear

boot² n 1 : bota f, botín m 2 KICK : puntapié m, patada f

bootee or **bootie** ['bu:ṭi] n : botita f, botín m

booth ['bu:θ] n, pl booths ['bu:ðz, 'bu:θs] : cabina f (de teléfono, de votar), caseta f (de información), barraca f (a una feria)

bootlegger ['bu:t,lɛgər] n : contrabandista mf del alcohol

booty ['bu:ṭi] n, pl -ties : botín m

booze ['bu:z] n fam : alcohol m

borax ['bor,æks] n : bórax m

border¹ ['bordər] vt 1 EDGE : ribetear, bordear 2 BOUND : limitar con, lindar con — vi VERGE : rayar, lindar ⟨that borders on absurdity : eso raya en el absurdo⟩

border² n 1 EDGE : borde m, orilla f 2 TRIM : ribete m 3 FRONTIER : frontera f

bore¹ ['bor] vt bored; boring 1 PIERCE : taladrar, perforar ⟨to bore metals : taladrar metales⟩ 2 OPEN : hacer, abrir ⟨to bore a tunnel : abrir un túnel⟩ 3 WEARY : aburrir

bore² → bear¹

bore³ n 1 : pesado m, -da f (persona aburrida) 2 TEDIOUSNESS : pesadez f, lo aburrido 3 DIAMETER : calibre m

boredom ['bordəm] n : aburrimiento m

boring ['borɪŋ] adj : aburrido, pesado

born ['bɔrn] adj 1 : nacido, nato ⟨she's a born singer : es una cantante nata⟩ ⟨he's a born leader : nació para mandar⟩

borne pp → bear¹

boron ['bor,an] n : boro m

borough ['bəro] n : distrito m municipal

borrow ['baro] vt 1 : pedir prestado, tomar prestado 2 APPROPRIATE : apropiarse de, adoptar

borrower ['barəwər] n : prestatario m, -ria f

Bosnian ['baznɪən, 'bɔz-] n : bosnio m, -nia f — Bosnian adj

bosom¹ ['bʊzəm, 'bu:-] adj : íntimo

bosom² n 1 CHEST : pecho m 2 BREAST : pecho m, seno m 3 CLOSENESS : seno m ⟨in the bosom of her family : en el seno de su familia⟩

bosomed ['bʊzəmd, 'bu:-] adj : con busto ⟨big-bosomed : con mucho busto⟩

boss¹ ['bɔs] vt 1 SUPERVISE : dirigir, supervisar 2 to boss around : mandonear fam, mangonear fam

boss² n : jefe m, -fa f; patrón m, -trona f

bossy ['bɔsi] adj bossier; -est : mandón fam, autoritario, dominante

botanist ['bɑtənɪst] *n* : botánico *m*, -ca *f*
botany ['bɑtəni] *n* : botánica *f* — **botanical** [bə'tænɪkəl] *adj*
botch¹ ['bɑtʃ] *vt* : hacer una chapuza de, estropear
botch² *n* : chapuza *f*
both¹ ['bo:θ] *adj* : ambos, los dos, las dos ⟨both books : ambos libros, los dos libros⟩
both² *conj* : tanto como ⟨both Ann and her mother are tall : tanto Ana como su madre son altas⟩
both *pron* : ambos *m*, -bas *f*; los dos, las dos
bother¹ ['bɑðər] *vt* **1** IRK : preocupar ⟨nothing's bothering me : nada me preocupa⟩ ⟨what's bothering him? : ¿qué le pasa?⟩ **2** PESTER : molestar, fastidiar — *vi* **to bother to** : molestarse en, tomar la molestia de
bother² *n* **1** TROUBLE : molestia *f*, problemas *mpl* **2** ANNOYANCE : molestia *f*, fastidio *m*
bothersome ['bɑðərsəm] *adj* : molesto, fastidioso
bottle¹ ['bɑtəl] *vt* **bottled; bottling** : embotellar, envasar
bottle² *n* : botella *f*, frasco *m*
bottleneck ['bɑtəl,nɛk] *n* **1** : cuello *m* de botella (en un camino) **2** : embotellamiento *m*, atasco *m* (de tráfico) **3** OBSTACLE : obstáculo *m*
bottom¹ ['bɑtəm] *adj* : más bajo, inferior, de abajo
bottom² *n* **1** : fondo *m* (de una caja, de una taza, del mar), pie *m* (de una escalera, una página, una montaña), asiento *m* (de una silla), parte *f* de abajo (de una pila) **2** CAUSE : origen *m*, causa *f* ⟨to get to the bottom of : llegar al fondo de⟩ **3** BUTTOCKS : trasero *m*, nalgas *fpl*
bottomless ['bɑtəmləs] *adj* : sin fondo, sin límites
botulism ['bɑtʃə,lɪzəm] *n* : botulismo *m*
boudoir [bə'dwar, bʊ-; 'bu:,-, 'bʊ-] *n* : tocador *m*
bough ['baʊ] *n* : rama *f*
bought → **buy¹**
bouillon ['bu:,jɑn; 'bʊl,jɑn, -jən] *n* : caldo *m*
boulder ['bo:ldər] *n* : canto *m* rodado, roca *f* grande
boulevard ['bʊlə,vard, 'bu:-] *n* : bulevar *m*, boulevard *m*
bounce¹ ['baʊnts] *v* **bounced; bouncing** *vt* : hacer rebotar — *vi* : rebotar
bounce² *n* : rebote *m*
bouncy ['baʊntsi] *adj* **bouncier; -est 1** LIVELY : vivo, exuberante, animado **2** RESILIENT : elástico, flexible **3** : que rebota (dícese de una pelota)
bound¹ ['baʊnd] *vt* : delimitar, rodear — *vi* LEAP : saltar, dar brincos
bound² *adj* **1** OBLIGED : obligado **2** : encuadernado, empastado ⟨a book bound in leather : un libro encuadernado en cuero⟩ **3** DETERMINED : decidido, empeñado **4 to be bound to** : ser seguro que, tener que, no caber duda que ⟨it was bound to happen : tenía que suceder⟩ **5 bound for** : con rumbo a ⟨bound for Chicago : con rumbo a Chicago⟩ ⟨to be homeward bound : ir camino a casa⟩
bound³ *n* **1** LIMIT : límite *m* **2** LEAP : salto *m*, brinco *m*
boundary ['baʊndri, -dəri] *n*, *pl* **-aries** : límite *m*, línea *f* divisoria, linde *mf*
boundless ['baʊndləs] *adj* : sin límites, infinito
bounteous ['baʊntiəs] *adj* **1** GENEROUS : generoso **2** ABUNDANT : copioso, abundante — **bounteously** *adv*
bountiful ['baʊntɪfəl] *adj* **1** GENEROUS, LIBERAL : munificente, pródigo, generoso **2** ABUNDANT : copioso, abundante
bounty ['baʊnti] *n*, *pl* **-ties 1** GENEROSITY : generosidad *f*, munificencia *f* **2** REWARD : recompensa *f*
bouquet [bo:'keɪ, bu:-] *n* **1** : ramo *m*, ramillete *m* **2** FRAGRANCE : bouquet *m*, aroma *m*
bourbon ['bərbən, 'bʊr-] *n* : bourbon *m*, whisky *m* americano
bourgeois¹ ['bʊrʒ,wa, bʊrʒ'wa] *adj* : burgués
bourgeois² *n* : burgués *m*, -guesa *f*
bourgeoisie [,bʊrʒ,wa'zi] *n* : burguesía *f*
bout ['baʊt] *n* **1** : encuentro *m*, combate *m* (en deportes) **2** ATTACK : ataque *m* (de una enfermedad) **3** PERIOD, SPELL : período *m* (de actividad)
boutique [bu:'ti:k] *n* : boutique *f*
bovine¹ ['bo:,vaɪn, -,vi:n] *adj* : bovino, vacuno
bovine² *n* : bovino *m*
bow¹ ['baʊ] *vi* **1** : hacer una reverencia, inclinarse **2** SUBMIT : ceder, resignarse, someterse — *vt* **1** LOWER : inclinar, bajar **2** BEND : doblar
bow² ['baʊ] *n* **1** BOWING : reverencia *f*, inclinación *f* **2** : proa *f* (de un barco)
bow³ ['bo:] *vi* CURVE : arquearse, doblarse
bow⁴ ['bo:] *n* **1** ARCH, CURVE : arco *m*, curva *f* **2** : arco *m* (arma o vara para tocar varios instrumentos de música) **3** : lazo *m*, moño *m* ⟨to tie a bow : hacer un moño⟩
bowels ['baʊəls] *npl* **1** INTESTINES : intestinos *mpl* **2** : entrañas *fpl* ⟨in the bowels of the earth : en las entrañas de la tierra⟩
bower ['baʊər] *n* : enramada *f*
bowl¹ ['bo:l] *vi* : jugar a los bolos
bowl² *n* : tazón *m*, cuenco *m*
bowler ['bo:lər] *n* : jugador *m*, -dora *f* de bolos
bowling ['bo:lɪŋ] *n* : bolos *mpl*
box¹ ['bɑks] *vt* **1** PACK : empaquetar, embalar, encajonar **2** SLAP : bofetear, cachetear — *vi* : boxear

box² *n* **1** CONTAINER : caja *f*, cajón *m* **2** COMPARTMENT : compartimento *m*, palco *m* (en el teatro) **3** SLAP : bofetada *f*, cachetada *f* **4** : boj *m* (planta)

boxcar ['bɑks,kɑr] *n* : vagón *m* de carga, furgón *m*

boxer ['bɑksər] *n* : boxeador *m*, -dora *f*

boxing ['bɑksɪŋ] *n* : boxeo *m*

box office *n* : taquilla *f*, boletería *f*

boxwood ['bɑks,wʊd] *n* : boj *m*

boy ['bɔɪ] *n* **1** : chico *m*, muchacho *m* **2** *or* **little boy** : niño *m*, chico *m* **3** SON : hijo *m*

boycott¹ ['bɔɪ,kɑt] *vt* : boicotear

boycott² *n* : boicot *m*

boyfriend ['bɔɪ,frɛnd] *n* **1** FRIEND : amigo *m* **2** SWEETHEART : novio *m*

boyhood ['bɔɪ,hʊd] *n* : niñez *f*

boyish ['bɔɪɪʃ] *adj* : de niño, juvenil

bra ['brɑ] → **brassiere**

brace¹ ['breɪs] *v* **braced; bracing** *vt* **1** PROP UP, SUPPORT : apuntalar, apoyar, sostener **2** INVIGORATE : vigorizar **3** REINFORCE : reforzar — *vi* **to brace oneself** PREPARE : prepararse

brace² *n* **1** : berbiquí *m* ⟨brace and bit : berbiquí y barrena⟩ **2** CLAMP, REINFORCEMENT : abrazadera *f*, refuerzo *m* **3** : llave *f* (signo de puntuación) **4 braces** *npl* : aparatos *mpl* (de ortodoncia), frenos *mpl Mex*

bracelet ['breɪslət] *n* : brazalete *m*, pulsera *f*

bracken ['brækən] *n* : helecho *m*

bracket¹ ['brækət] *vt* **1** SUPPORT : asegurar, apuntalar **2** : poner entre corchetes **3** CATEGORIZE, GROUP : catalogar, agrupar

bracket² *n* **1** SUPPORT : soporte *m* **2** : corchete *m* (marca de puntuación) **3** CATEGORY, CLASS : clase *f*, categoría *f*

brackish ['brækɪʃ] *adj* : salobre

brad ['bræd] *n* : clavo *m* con cabeza pequeña, clavito *m*

brag¹ ['bræg] *vi* **bragged; bragging** : alardear, fanfarronear, jactarse

brag² *n* : alarde *m*, jactancia *f*, fanfarronada *f*

braggart ['brægərt] *n* : fanfarrón *m*, -rrona *f fam*; jactancioso *m*, -sa *f*

braid¹ ['breɪd] *vt* : trenzar

braid² *n* : trenza *f*

braille ['breɪl] *n* : braille *m*

brain¹ ['breɪn] *vt* : romper la crisma a, aplastar el cráneo a

brain² *n* **1** : cerebro *m* **2 brains** *npl* INTELLECT : inteligencia *f*, sesos *mpl*

brainless ['breɪnləs] *adj* : estúpido, tonto

brainstorm ['breɪn,stɔrm] *n* : idea *f* brillante, idea *f* genial

brainy ['breɪni] *adj* **brainier; -est** : inteligente, listo

braise ['breɪz] *vt* **braised; braising** : cocer a fuego lento, estofar

brake¹ ['breɪk] *v* **braked; braking** : frenar

brake² *n* : freno *m*

bramble ['bræmbəl] *n* : zarza *f*, zarzamora *f*

bran ['bræn] *n* : salvado *m*

branch¹ ['bræntʃ] *vi* **1** : echar ramas (dícese de una planta) **2** DIVERGE : ramificarse, separarse

branch² *n* **1** : rama *f* (de una planta) **2** EXTENSION : ramal *m* (de un camino, un ferrocarril, un río), rama *f* (de una familia o un campo de estudiar), sucursal *f* (de una empresa), agencia *f* (del gobierno)

brand¹ ['brænd] *vt* **1** : marcar (ganado) **2** LABEL : tachar, tildar ⟨they branded him as a liar : lo tacharon de mentiroso⟩

brand² *n* **1** : marca *f* (de ganado) **2** STIGMA : estigma *m* **3** MAKE : marca *f* ⟨brand name : marca de fábrica⟩

brandish ['brændɪʃ] *vt* : blandir

brand–new ['brænd'nu:, -'nju:] *adj* : nuevo, flamante

brandy ['brændi] *n, pl* **-dies** : brandy *m*

brash ['bræʃ] *adj* **1** IMPULSIVE : impulsivo, impetuoso **2** BRAZEN : excesivamente desenvuelto, descarado

brass ['bræs] *n* **1** : latón *m* **2** GALL, NERVE : descaro *m*, cara *f fam* **3** OFFICERS : mandamases *mpl fam*

brassiere [brə'zɪr, brɑ-] *n* : sostén *m*, brasier *m Col, Mex*

brassy ['bræsi] *adj* **brassier; -est** : dorado

brat ['bræt] *n* : mocoso *m*, -sa *f*; niño *m* mimado, niña *f* mimada

bravado [brə'vɑdo] *n, pl* **-does** *or* **-dos** : bravuconadas *fpl*, bravatas *fpl*

brave¹ ['breɪv] *vt* **braved; braving** : afrontar, hacer frente a

brave² *adj* **braver; bravest** : valiente, valeroso — **bravely** *adv*

brave³ *n* : guerrero *m* indio

bravery ['breɪvəri] *n* : valor *m*, valentía *f*

bravo ['brɑ,vo:] *n, pl* **-vos** : bravo *m*

brawl¹ ['brɔl] *vi* : pelearse, pegarse

brawl² *n* : pelea *f*, reyerta *f*

brawn ['brɔn] *n* : fuerza *f* muscular

brawny ['brɔni] *adj* **brawnier; -est** : musculoso

bray¹ ['breɪ] *vi* : rebuznar

bray² *n* : rebuzno *m*

brazen ['breɪzən] *adj* **1** : de latón **2** BOLD : descarado, directo

brazenly ['breɪzənli] *adv* : descaradamente, insolentemente

brazenness ['breɪzənnəs] *n* : descaro *m*, atrevimiento *m*

brazier ['breɪʒər] *n* : brasero *m*

Brazilian [brə'zɪljən] *n* : brasileño *m*, -ña *f* — **Brazilian** *adj*

Brazil nut [brə'zɪl,nʌt] *n* : nuez *f* de Brasil

breach¹ ['bri:tʃ] *vt* **1** PENETRATE : abrir una brecha en, penetrar **2** VIOLATE : infringir, violar

breach² *n* **1** VIOLATION : infracción *f*, violación *f* ⟨breach of trust : abuso de confianza⟩ **2** GAP, OPENING : brecha *f*

bread[1] ['brɛd] *vt* : empanar
bread[2] *n* : pan *m*
breadth ['brɛtθ] *n* : ancho *m*, anchura *f*
breadwinner ['brɛd,wɪnər] *n* : sostén *m* de la familia
break[1] ['breɪk] *v* **broke** ['bro:k]; **broken** ['bro:kən]; **breaking** *vt* **1** SMASH : romper, quebrar **2** VIOLATE : infringir, violar, romper **3** SURPASS : batir, superar **4** CRUSH, RUIN : arruinar, deshacer, destrozar ⟨to break one's spirit : quebrantar su espíritu⟩ **5** : dar, comunicar ⟨to break the news : dar las noticias⟩ **6** INTERRUPT : cortar, interrumpir — *vi* **1** : romperse, quebrarse ⟨my calculator broke : se me rompió la calculadora⟩ **2** DISPERSE : dispersarse, despejarse **3** : estallar (dícese de una tormenta), romper (dícese del día) **4** CHANGE : cambiar (dícese del tiempo o de la voz) **5** DECREASE : bajar ⟨my fever broke : me bajó la fiebre⟩ **6** : divulgarse, revelarse ⟨the news broke : la noticia se divulgó⟩ **7 to break into** : forzar, abrir **8 to break out of** : escaparse de **9 to break through** : penetrar
break[2] *n* **1** : ruptura *f*, rotura *f*, fractura *f* (de un hueso), claro *m* (entre las nubes), cambio *m* (del tiempo) **2** CHANCE : oportunidad *f* ⟨a lucky break : un golpe de suerte⟩ **3** REST : descanso *m* ⟨to take a break : tomar(se) un descanso⟩
breakable ['breɪkəbəl] *adj* : quebradizo, frágil
breakage ['breɪkɪdʒ] *n* **1** BREAKING : rotura *f* **2** DAMAGE : destrozos *mpl*, daños *mpl*
breakdown ['breɪk,daʊn] *n* **1** : avería *f* (de máquinas), interrupción *f* (de comunicaciones), fracaso *m* (de negociaciones) **2** ANALYSIS : análisis *m*, desglose *m* **3** *or* **nervous breakdown** : crisis *f* nerviosa
break down *vi* **1** : estropearse, descomponerse ⟨the machine broke down : la máquina se descompuso⟩ **2** FAIL : fracasar **3** CRY : echarse a llorar — *vt* **1** DESTROY : derribar, echar abajo **2** OVERCOME : vencer (la resistencia), disipar (sospechas) **3** ANALYZE : analizar, descomponer
breaker ['breɪkər] *n* **1** WAVE : ola *f* grande **2** : interruptor *m* automático (de electricidad)
breakfast[1] ['brɛkfəst] *vi* : desayunar
breakfast[2] *n* : desayuno *m*
breakneck ['breɪk,nɛk] *adj* **at breakneck speed** : a una velocidad vertiginosa
break out *vi* **1** : salirse ⟨she broke out in spots : le salieron granos⟩ **2** ERUPT : estallar (dícese de una guerra, la violencia, etc.) **3** ESCAPE : fugarse, escaparse
breakup ['breɪk,əp] *n* **1** DIVISION : desintegración *f* **2** : ruptura *f*

break up *vt* **1** DIVIDE : dividir **2** : disolver (una muchedumbre, una pelea, etc.) — *vi* **1** BREAK : romperse **2** SEPARATE : deshacerse, separarse ⟨I broke up with him : terminé con él⟩
breast ['brɛst] *n* **1** : pecho *m*, seno *m* (de una mujer) **2** CHEST : pecho *m*
breastbone ['brɛst,bo:n] *n* : esternón *m*
breast–feed ['brɛst,fi:d] *vt* **-fed** [-,fɛd]; **-feeding** : amamantar, darle de mamar (a un niño)
breath ['brɛθ] *n* **1** BREATHING : aliento *m* ⟨to hold one's breath : aguantar la respiración⟩ **2** BREEZE : soplo *m* ⟨a breath of fresh air : un soplo de aire fresco⟩
breathe ['bri:ð] *v* **breathed**; **breathing** *vi* **1** : respirar **2** LIVE : vivir, respirar — *vt* **1** : respirar, aspirar ⟨to breathe fresh air : respirar el aire fresco⟩ **2** UTTER : decir ⟨I won't breathe a word of this : no diré nada de esto⟩
breathless ['brɛθləs] *adj* : sin aliento, jadeante
breathlessly ['brɛθləsli] *adv* : entrecortadamente, jadeando
breathlessness ['brɛθləsnəs] *n* : dificultad *f* al respirar
breathtaking ['brɛθ,teɪkɪŋ] *adj* IMPRESSIVE : impresionante, imponente
breeches ['brɪtʃəz, 'bri:-] *npl* : pantalones *mpl*, calzones *mpl*, bombachos *mpl*
breed[1] ['bri:d] *v* **bred** ['brɛd]; **breeding** *vt* **1** : criar (animales) **2** ENGENDER : engendrar, producir ⟨familiarity breeds contempt : la confianza hace perder el respeto⟩ **3** RAISE, REAR : criar, educar — *vi* REPRODUCE : reproducirse
breed[2] *n* **1** : variedad *f* (de plantas), raza *f* (de animales) **2** CLASS : clase *f*, tipo *m*
breeder ['bri:dər] *n* : criador *m*, -dora *f* (de animales); cultivador *m*, -dora *f* (de plantas)
breeze[1] ['bri:z] *vi* **breezed**; **breezing** : pasar con ligereza ⟨to breeze in : entrar como si nada⟩
breeze[2] *n* : brisa *f*, soplo *m* (de aire)
breezy ['bri:zi] *adj* **breezier**; **-est 1** AIRY, WINDY : aireado, ventoso **2** LIVELY : animado, alegre **3** NONCHALANT : despreocupado
brethren → **brother**
brevity ['brɛvəti] *n*, *pl* **-ties** : brevedad *f*, concisión *f*
brew[1] ['bru:] *vt* **1** : fabricar, elaborar (cerveza) **2** FOMENT : tramar, maquinar, fomentar — *vi* **1** : fabricar cerveza **2** : amenazar ⟨a storm is brewing : una tormenta amenaza⟩
brew[2] *n* **1** BEER : cerveza *f* **2** POTION : brebaje *m*
brewer ['bru:ər] *n* : cervecero *m*, -ra *f*
brewery ['bru:əri, 'bruri] *n*, *pl* **-eries** : cervecería *f*
briar ['braɪər] → **brier**

bribe¹ ['braɪb] *vt* **bribed; bribing** : sobornar, cohechar, coimear *Arg, Chile, Peru*

bribe² *n* : soborno *m*, cohecho *m*, coima *f Arg, Chile, Peru*, mordida *f CA, Mex*

bribery ['braɪbəri] *n, pl* **-eries** : soborno *m*, cohecho *m*, coima *f*, mordida *f CA, Mex*

bric-a-brac ['brɪkə,bræk] *npl* : baratijas *fpl*, chucherías *fpl*

brick¹ ['brɪk] *vt* **to brick up** : tabicar, tapiar

brick² *n* : ladrillo *m*

bricklayer ['brɪk,leɪər] *n* : albañil *mf*

bricklaying ['brɪk,leɪɪŋ] *n* : albañilería *f*

bridal ['braɪdəl] *adj* : nupcial, de novia

bride ['braɪd] *n* : novia *f*

bridegroom ['braɪd,gru:m] *n* : novio *m*

bridesmaid ['braɪdz,meɪd] *n* : dama *f* de honor

bridge¹ ['brɪʤ] *vt* **bridged; bridging 1** : tender un puente sobre **2 to bridge the gap** : salvar las diferencias

bridge² *n* **1** : puente *m* **2** : caballete *m* (de la nariz) **3** : puente *m* de mando (de un barco) **4** DENTURE : puente *m* (dental) **5** : bridge *m* (juego de naipes)

bridle¹ ['braɪdəl] *v* **-dled; -dling** *vt* **1** : embridar (un caballo) **2** RESTRAIN : refrenar, dominar, contener — *vi* **to bridle at** : molestarse por, picarse por

bridle² *n* : brida *f*

brief¹ ['bri:f] *vt* : dar órdenes a, instruir

brief² *adj* : breve, sucinto, conciso

brief³ *n* **1** : resumen *m*, sumario *m* **2 briefs** *npl* : calzoncillos *mpl*

briefcase ['bri:f,keɪs] *n* : portafolio *m*, maletín *m*

briefly ['bri:fli] *adv* : brevemente, por poco tiempo ⟨to speak briefly : discursar en pocas palabras⟩

brier ['braɪər] *n* **1** BRAMBLE : zarza *f*, rosal *m* silvestre **2** HEATH : brezo *m* veteado

brig ['brɪg] *n* **1** : bergantín *m* (barco) **2** : calabozo *m* (en un barco)

brigade [brɪ'geɪd] *n* : brigada *f*

brigadier general [,brɪgə'dɪr] *n* : general *m* de brigada

brigand ['brɪgənd] *n* : bandolero *m*, -ra *f*; forajido *m*, -da *f*

bright ['braɪt] *adj* **1** : brillante (dícese del sol, de los ojos), vivo (dícese de un color), claro, fuerte **2** CHEERFUL : alegre, animado ⟨bright and early : muy temprano⟩ **3** INTELLIGENT : listo, inteligente ⟨a bright idea : una idea luminosa⟩

brighten ['braɪtən] *vt* **1** ILLUMINATE : iluminar **2** ENLIVEN : alegrar, animar — *vi* **1** : hacerse más brillante **2 to brighten up** : animarse, alegrarse, mejorar

brightly ['braɪtli] *adv* : vivamente, intensamente, alegremente

brightness ['braɪtnəs] *n* **1** LUMINOSITY : luminosidad *f*, brillantez *f*, resplandor *m*, brillo *m* **2** CHEERFULNESS : alegría *f*, ánimo *m*

brilliance ['brɪljənts] *n* **1** BRIGHTNESS : resplandor *m*, fulgor *m*, brillo *m*, brillantez *f* **2** INTELLIGENCE : inteligencia *f*, brillantez *f*

brilliancy ['brɪljəntsi] → **brilliance**

brilliant ['brɪljənt] *adj* : brillante

brilliantly ['brɪljəntli] *adv* : brillantemente, con brillantez

brim¹ ['brɪm] *vi* **brimmed; brimming 1** *or* **to brim over** : desbordarse, rebosar **2 to brim with tears** : llenarse de lágrimas

brim² *n* **1** : ala *f* (de un sombrero) **2** : borde *m* (de una taza o un vaso)

brimful ['brɪm'fʊl] *adj* : lleno hasta el borde, repleto, rebosante

brimless ['brɪmləs] *adj* : sin ala

brimstone ['brɪm,sto:n] *n* : azufre *m*

brindled ['brɪndəld] *adj* : manchado, pinto

brine ['braɪn] *n* **1** : salmuera *f*, escabeche *m* (para encurtir) **2** OCEAN : océano *m*, mar *m*

bring ['brɪŋ] *vt* **brought** ['brɔt]; **bringing 1** CARRY : traer ⟨bring me some coffee : tráigame un café⟩ **2** PRODUCE : traer, producir, conseguir ⟨his efforts will bring him success : sus esfuerzos le conseguirán el éxito⟩ **3** PERSUADE : convencer, persuadir **4** YIELD : rendir, alcanzar, venderse por ⟨to bring a good price : alcanzar un precio alto⟩ **5 to bring to an end** : terminar (con) **6 to bring to light** : sacar a la luz

bring about *vt* : ocasionar, provocar, determinar

bring forth *vt* PRODUCE : producir

bring out *vt* : sacar, publicar (un libro, etc.)

bring to *vt* REVIVE : resucitar

bring up *vt* **1** REAR : criar **2** MENTION : sacar, mencionar

brininess ['braɪninəs] *n* : salinidad *f*

brink ['brɪŋk] *n* : borde *m*

briny ['braɪni] *adj* **brinier; -est** : salobre

briquette *or* **briquet** [brɪ'kɛt] *n* : briqueta *f*

brisk ['brɪsk] *adj* **1** LIVELY : rápido, enérgico, brioso **2** INVIGORATING : fresco, estimulante

brisket ['brɪskət] *n* : falda *f*

briskly ['brɪskli] *adv* : rápidamente, enérgicamente, con brío

briskness ['brɪsknəs] *n* : brío *m*, rapidez *f*

bristle¹ ['brɪsəl] *vi* **-tled; -tling 1** : erizarse, ponerse de punta **2** : enfurecerse, enojarse ⟨she bristled at the suggestion : se enfureció ante tal sugerencia⟩ **3** : estar plagado, estar repleto ⟨a city bristling with tourists : una ciudad repleta de turistas⟩

bristle² *n* : cerda *f* (de un animal), pelo *m* (de una planta)

bristly ['brɪsəli] *adj* **bristlier; -est** : áspero y erizado

British¹ ['brɪtɪʃ] *adj* : británico

British² *n* **the British** *npl* : los británicos

brittle ['brɪtəl] *adj* **-tler; -tlest** : frágil, quebradizo
brittleness ['brɪtəlnəs] *n* : fragilidad *f*
broach ['broːʧ] *vt* BRING UP : mencionar, abordar, sacar
broad ['brɔd] *adj* **1** WIDE : ancho **2** SPACIOUS : amplio, extenso **3** FULL : pleno ⟨in broad daylight : en pleno día⟩ **4** OBVIOUS : claro, evidente **5** TOLERANT : tolerante, liberal **6** GENERAL : general **7** ESSENTIAL : principal, esencial ⟨the broad outline : los rasgos esenciales⟩
broadcast¹ ['brɔd,kæst] *vt* **-cast; -casting 1** SCATTER : esparcir, diseminar **2** CIRCULATE, SPREAD : divulgar, difundir, propagar **3** TRANSMIT : transmitir, emitir
broadcast² *n* **1** TRANSMISSION : transmisión *f*, emisión *f* **2** PROGRAM : programa *m*, emisión *f*
broadcaster ['brɔd,kæstər] *n* : presentador *m*, -dora *f*; locutor *m*, -tora *f*
broadcloth ['brɔd,klɔθ] *n* : paño *m* fino
broaden ['brɔdən] *vt* : ampliar, ensanchar — *vi* : ampliarse, ensancharse
broadloom ['brɔd,luːm] *adj* : tejido en telar ancho
broadly ['brɔdli] *adv* **1** GENERALLY : en general, aproximadamente **2** WIDELY : extensivamente
broad-minded ['brɔd'maɪndəd] *adj* : tolerante, de amplias miras
broad-mindedness [brɔd'maɪndədnəs] *n* : tolerancia *f*
broadside ['brɔd,saɪd] *n* **1** VOLLEY : andanada *f* **2** ATTACK : ataque *m*, invectiva *f*, andanada *f*
brocade [bro'keɪd] *n* : brocado *m*
broccoli ['brɑkəli] *n* : brócoli *m*, brécol *m*
brochure [bro'ʃʊr] *n* : folleto *m*
brogue ['broːg] *n* : acento *m* irlandés
broil¹ ['brɔɪl] *vt* : asar a la parrilla
broil² *n* : asado *m*
broiler ['brɔɪlər] *n* **1** GRILL : parrilla *f* **2** : pollo *m* para asar
broke¹ ['broːk] → **break¹**
broke² *adj* : pelado, arruinado ⟨to go broke : arruinarse, quebrar⟩
broken ['broːkən] *adj* **1** DAMAGED, SHATTERED : roto, quebrado, fracturado **2** IRREGULAR, UNEVEN : accidentado, irregular, recortado **3** VIOLATED : roto, quebrantado **4** INTERRUPTED : interrumpido, descontinuo **5** CRUSHED : abatido, quebrantado ⟨a broken man : un hombre destrozado⟩ **6** IMPERFECT : mal ⟨to speak broken English : hablar el inglés con dificultad⟩
brokenhearted [,broːkən'hɑrtəd] *adj* : descorazonado, desconsolado
broker¹ ['broːkər] *vt* : hacer corretaje de
broker² *n* **1** : agente *mf*; corredor *m*, -dora *f* **2** → **stockbroker**
brokerage ['broːkərɪʤ] *n* : corretaje *m*, agencia *f* de corredores

bromine ['broː,miːn] *n* : bromo *m*
bronchitis [brɑn'kaɪtəs, brɑŋ-] *n* : bronquitis *f*
bronze¹ ['brɑnz] *vt* **bronzed; bronzing** : broncear
bronze² *n* : bronce *m*
brooch ['broːʧ, 'bruːʧ] *n* : broche *m*, prendedor *m*
brood¹ ['bruːd] *vt* **1** INCUBATE : empollar, incubar **2** PONDER : sopesar, considerar — *vi* **1** INCUBATE : empollar **2** REFLECT : rumiar, reflexionar **3** WORRY : ponerse melancólico, inquietarse
brood² *adj* : de cría
brood³ *n* : nidada *f* (de pájaros), camada *f* (de mamíferos)
brooder ['bruːdər] *n* **1** THINKER : pensador *m*, -dora *f* **2** INCUBATOR : incubadora *f*
brook¹ ['brʊk] *vt* TOLERATE : tolerar, admitir
brook² *n* : arroyo *m*
broom ['bruːm, 'brʊm] *n* **1** : retama *f*, hiniesta *f* **2** : escoba *f* (para barrer)
broomstick ['bruːm,stɪk, 'brʊm-] *n* : palo *m* de escoba
broth ['brɔθ] *n, pl* **broths** ['brɔθs, 'brɔðz] : caldo *m*
brothel ['brɑθəl, 'brɔ-] *n* : burdel *m*
brother ['brʌðər] *n, pl* **brothers** *also* **brethren** ['brɔðrən, -ðərn] **1** : hermano *m* **2** KINSMAN : pariente *m*, familiar *m*
brotherhood ['brʌðər,hʊd] *n* **1** FELLOWSHIP : fraternidad *f* **2** ASSOCIATION : hermandad *f*
brother-in-law ['brʌðərɪn,lɔ] *n, pl* **brothers-in-law** : cuñado *m*
brotherly ['brʌðərli] *adj* : fraternal
brought → **bring**
brow ['braʊ] *n* **1** EYEBROW : ceja *f* **2** FOREHEAD : frente *f* **3** : cima *f* ⟨the brow of a hill : la cima de una colina⟩
browbeat ['braʊ,biːt] *vt* **-beat; -beaten** [-,biːtən] *or* **-beat; -beating** : intimidar
brown¹ ['braʊn] *vt* **1** : dorar (en cocina) **2** TAN : broncear — *vi* **1** : dorarse (en cocina) **2** TAN : broncearse
brown² *adj* : marrón, café, castaño (dícese del pelo), moreno (dícese de la piel)
brown³ *n* : marrón *m*, café *m*
brownish ['braʊnɪʃ] *adj* : pardo
browse ['braʊz] *vi* **browsed; browsing 1** GRAZE : pacer **2** LOOK : mirar, echar un vistazo
bruin ['bruːɪn] *n* BEAR : oso *m*
bruise¹ ['bruːz] *vt* **bruised; bruising 1** : contusionar, machucar, magullar (a una persona) **2** DAMAGE : magullar, dañar (frutas) **3** CRUSH : majar **4** HURT : herir (los sentimientos)
bruise² *n* : moretón *m*, cardenal *m*, magulladura *f* (dícese de frutas)
brunch ['brʌnʧ] *n* : combinación *f* de desayuno y almuerzo
brunet¹ *or* **brunette** [bruː'nɛt] *adj* : moreno
brunet² *or* **brunette** *n* : moreno *m*, -na *f*

brunt ['brʌnt] *n* **to bear the brunt of** : llevar el peso de, aguantar el mayor impacto de

brush¹ ['brʌʃ] *vt* **1** : cepillar ⟨to brush one's teeth : cepillarse uno los dientes⟩ **2** SWEEP : barrer, quitar con un cepillo **3** GRAZE : rozar **4 to brush off** DISREGARD : hacer caso omiso de, ignorar — *vi* **to brush up on** : repasar, refrescar, dar un repaso a

brush² *n* **1** *or* **brushwood** ['brʌʃ,wʊd] : broza *f* **2** SCRUB, UNDERBRUSH : maleza *f* **3** : cepillo *m*, pincel *m* (de artista), brocha *f* (de pintor) **4** TOUCH : roce *m* **5** SKIRMISH : escaramuza *f*

brush–off ['brʌʃ,ɔf] *n* **to give the brush–off to** : dar calabazas a

brusque ['brʌsk] *adj* : brusco — **brusquely** *adv*

brussels sprout ['brʌsəlz,spraʊt] *n* : col *f* de Bruselas

brutal ['bru:t̬əl] *adj* : brutal, cruel, salvaje — **brutally** *adv*

brutality [bru:'tæləti] *n, pl* **-ties** : brutalidad *f*

brutalize ['bru:t̬əl,aɪz] *vt* **-ized; -izing** : brutalizar, maltratar

brute¹ ['bru:t] *adj* : bruto ⟨brute force : fuerza bruta⟩

brute² *n* **1** BEAST : bestia *f*, animal *m* **2** : bruto *m*, -ta *f*; bestia *mf* (persona)

brutish ['bru:t̬ɪʃ] *adj* **1** : de animal **2** CRUEL : brutal, salvaje **3** STUPID : bruto, estúpido

bubble¹ ['bʌbəl] *vi* **-bled; -bling** : burbujear ⟨to bubble over with joy : rebosar de alegría⟩

bubble² *n* : burbuja *f*

bubbly ['bʌbəli] *adj* **bubblier; -est 1** BUBBLING : burbujeante **2** LIVELY : vivaz, lleno de vida

bubonic plague [bu:'bɑnɪk, 'bju:-] *n* : peste *f* bubónica

buccaneer [,bʌkə'nɪr] *n* : bucanero *m*

buck¹ ['bʌk] *vi* **1** : corcovear (dícese de un caballo o un burro) **2** JOLT : dar sacudidas **3 to buck against** : resistirse a, rebelarse contra **4 to buck up** : animarse, levantar el ánimo — *vt* OPPOSE : oponerse a, ir en contra de

buck² *n, pl* **buck** *or* **bucks 1** : animal *m* macho, ciervo *m* (macho) **2** DOLLAR : dólar *m* **3 to pass the buck** *fam* : pasar la pelota *fam*

bucket ['bʌkət] *n* : balde *m*, cubo *m*, cubeta *f Mex*

bucketful ['bʌkət,fʊl] *n* : balde *m* lleno

buckle¹ ['bʌkəl] *v* **-led; -ling** *vt* **1** FASTEN : abrochar **2** BEND, TWIST : combar, torcer — *vi* **1** BEND, TWIST : combarse, torcerse, doblarse (dícese de las rodillas) **2 to buckle down** : ponerse a trabajar con esmero **3 to buckle up** : abrocharse

buckle² *n* **1** : hebilla *f* **2** TWISTING : torcedura *f*

buckshot ['bʌk,ʃɑt] *n* : perdigón *m*

buckskin ['bʌk,skɪn] *n* : gamuza *f*

bucktooth ['bʌk,tu:θ] *n* : diente *m* saliente, diente *m* salido

buckwheat ['bʌk,hwi:t] *n* : trigo *m* rubión, alforfón *m*

bucolic [bju:'kɑlɪk] *adj* : bucólico

bud¹ ['bʌd] *v* **budded; budding** *vt* GRAFT : injertar — *vi* : brotar, hacer brotes

bud² *n* : brote *m*, yema *f*, capullo *m* (de una flor)

Buddhism ['bu:,dɪzəm, 'bʊ-] *n* : budismo *m*

Buddhist ['bu:dɪst, 'bʊ-] *n* : budista *mf* — **Buddhist** *adj*

buddy ['bʌdi] *n, pl* **-dies** : amigo *m*, -ga *f*; compinche *mf fam*; cuate *m*, -ta *f Mex fam*

budge ['bʌdʒ] *vi* **budged; budging 1** MOVE : moverse, desplazarse **2** YIELD : ceder

budget¹ ['bʌdʒət] *vt* : presupuestar (gastos), asignar (dinero) — *vi* : presupuestar, planear el presupuesto

budget² *n* : presupuesto

budgetary ['bʌdʒə,tɛri] *adj* : presupuestario

buff¹ ['bʌf] *vt* POLISH : pulir, sacar brillo a, lustrar

buff² *adj* : beige, amarillento

buff³ *n* **1** : beige *m*, amarillento *m* **2** ENTHUSIAST : aficionado *m*, -da *f*; entusiasta *mf*

buffalo ['bʌfə,lo:] *n, pl* **-lo** *or* **-loes 1** : búfalo *m* **2** BISON : bisonte *m*

buffer ['bʌfər] *n* **1** BARRIER : barrera *f* ⟨buffer state : estado tapón⟩ **2** SHOCK ABSORBER : amortiguador *m*

buffet¹ ['bʌfət] *vt* : golpear, zarandear, sacudir

buffet² *n* BLOW : golpe *m*

buffet³ [,bʌ'feɪ, ,bu:-] *n* **1** : bufete *m*, bufé *m* (comida) **2** SIDEBOARD : aparador *m*

buffoon [,bʌ'fu:n] *n* : bufón *m*, -fona *f*; payaso *m*, -sa *f*

buffoonery [,bʌ'fu:nəri] *n, pl* **-eries** : bufonada *f*, payasada *f*

bug¹ ['bʌg] *vt* **bugged; bugging 1** PESTER : fastidiar, molestar **2** : ocultar micrófonos en

bug² *n* **1** INSECT : bicho *m*, insecto *m* **2** DEFECT : defecto *m*, falla *f*, problema *m* **3** GERM : microbio *m*, virus *m* **4** MICROPHONE : micrófono *m*

bugaboo ['bʌgə,bu:] → **bogey**

bugbear ['bʌg,bær] *n* : pesadilla *f*, coco *m*

buggy ['bʌgi] *n, pl* **-gies** : calesa *f* (tirada por caballos), cochecito *m* (para niños)

bugle ['bju:gəl] *n* : clarín *m*, corneta *f*

bugler ['bju:gələr] *n* : corneta *mf*

build¹ ['bɪld] *v* **built** ['bɪlt]; **building** *vt* **1** CONSTRUCT : construir, edificar, ensamblar, levantar **2** DEVELOP : desarrollar, elaborar, forjar **3** INCREASE : incrementar, aumentar — *vi* **to build up** : aumentar, intensificar

build² *n* PHYSIQUE : físico *m*, complexión *f*

builder ['bɪldər] *n* : constructor *m*, -tora *f*; contratista *mf*

building ['bɪldɪŋ] *n* **1** EDIFICE : edificio *m* **2** CONSTRUCTION : construcción *f*

built-in ['bɪlt'ɪn] *adj* **1** : empotrado ⟨built-in cabinets : armarios empotrados⟩ **2** INHERENT : incorporado, intrínseco

bulb ['bʌlb] *n* **1** : bulbo *m* (de una planta), cabeza *f* (de ajo), cubeta *f* (de un termómetro) **2** LIGHTBULB : bombilla *f*, foco *m*, bombillo *m* CA, Col, Ven

bulbous ['bʌlbəs] *adj* : bulboso

Bulgarian [bʌl'gærɪən, bʊl-] *n* **1** : búlgaro *m*, -ra *f* **2** : búlgaro *m* (idioma) — **Bulgarian** *adj*

bulge[1] ['bʌldʒ] *vi* **bulged; bulging** : abultar, sobresalir

bulge[2] *n* : bulto *m*, protuberancia *f*

bulk[1] ['bʌlk] *vt* : hinchar — *vi* EXPAND, SWELL : ampliarse, hincharse

bulk[2] *n* **1** SIZE, VOLUME : volumen *m*, tamaño *m* **2** FIBER : fibra *f* **3** MASS : mole *f* **4 the bulk of** : la mayor parte de **5 in ～** : en grandes cantidades

bulkhead ['bʌlk‚hɛd] *n* : mamparo *m*

bulky ['bʌlki] *adj* **bulkier; -est** : voluminoso, grande

bull[1] ['bʊl] *adj* : macho

bull[2] *n* **1** : toro *m*, macho *m* (de ciertas especies) **2** : bula *f* (papal) **3** DECREE : decreto *m*, edicto *m*

bulldog ['bʊl‚dɔg] *n* : bulldog *m*

bulldoze ['bʊl‚do:z] *vt* **-dozed; -dozing 1** LEVEL : nivelar (el terreno), derribar (un edificio) **2** FORCE : forzar ⟨he bulldozed his way through : se abrió paso a codazos⟩

bulldozer ['bʊl‚do:zər] *n* : bulldozer *m*

bullet ['bʊlət] *n* : bala *f*

bulletin ['bʊlətən, -lətən] *n* **1** NOTICE : comunicado *m*, anuncio *m*, boletín *m* **2** NEWSLETTER : boletín *m* (informativo)

bulletin board *n* : tablón *m* de anuncios

bulletproof ['bʊlət‚pru:f] *adj* : antibalas, a prueba de balas

bullfight ['bʊl‚faɪt] *n* : corrida *f* (de toros)

bullfighter ['bʊl‚faɪtər] *n* : torero *m*, -ra *f*; matador *m*

bullfrog ['bʊl‚frɔg] *n* : rana *f* toro

bullheaded ['bʊl'hɛdəd] *adj* : testarudo

bullion ['bʊljən] *n* : oro *m* en lingotes, plata *f* en lingotes

bullock ['bʊlək] *n* **1** STEER : buey *m*, toro *m* castrado **2** : toro *m* joven, novillo *m*

bull's-eye ['bʊlz‚aɪ] *n, pl* **bull's-eyes** : diana *f*, blanco *m*

bully[1] ['bʊli] *vt* **-lied; -lying** : intimidar, amedrentar, mangonear

bully[2] *n, pl* **-lies** : matón *m*; bravucón *m*, -cona *f*

bulrush ['bʊl‚rʌʃ] *n* : especie *f* de junco

bulwark ['bʊl‚wərk, -‚wɔrk; 'bʌl‚wərk] *n* : baluarte *m*, bastión *f*

bum[1] ['bʌm] *v* **bummed; bumming** *vi* **to bum around** : vagabundear, vagar — *vt* : gorronear *fam*, sablear *fam*

bum[2] *adj* : inútil, malo ⟨a bum rap : una acusación falsa⟩

bum[3] *n* **1** LOAFER : vago *m*, -ga *f* **2** HOBO, TRAMP : vagabundo *m*, -da *f*

bumblebee ['bʌmbəl‚bi:] *n* : abejorro *m*

bump[1] ['bʌmp] *vt* : chocar contra, golpear contra, dar ⟨to bump one's head : darse (un golpe) en la cabeza⟩ — *vi* **to bump into** MEET : encontrarse con, tropezarse con

bump[2] *n* **1** BULGE : bulto *m*, protuberancia *f* **2** IMPACT : golpe *m*, choque *m* **3** JOLT : sacudida *f*

bumper[1] ['bʌmpər] *adj* : extraordinario, récord ⟨a bumper crop : una cosecha abundante⟩

bumper[2] *n* : parachoques *mpl*

bumpkin ['bʌmpkən] *n* : palurdo *m*, -da *f*

bumpy ['bʌmpi] *adj* **bumpier; -est** : desigual, lleno de baches (dícese de un camino), agitado (dícese de un vuelo en avión)

bun ['bʌn] *n* : bollo *m*

bunch[1] ['bʌntʃ] *vt* : agrupar, amontonar — *vi* **to bunch up** : amontonarse, agruparse, fruncirse (dícese de una tela)

bunch[2] *n* : grupo *m*, montón *m*, ramo *m* (de flores)

bundle[1] ['bʌndəl] *vt* **-dled; -dling** : liar, atar

bundle[2] *n* **1** : fardo *m*, atado *m*, bulto *m*, haz *m* (de palos) **2** PARCEL : paquete *m* **3** LOAD : montón *m* ⟨a bundle of money : un montón de dinero⟩

bungalow ['bʌngə‚lo:] *n* : tipo de casa de un solo piso

bungle[1] ['bʌngəl] *vt* **-gled; -gling** : echar a perder, malograr

bungle[2] *n* : chapuza *f*, desatino *m*

bungler ['bʌngələr] *n* : chapucero *m*, -ra *f*; inepto *m*, -ta *f*

bunion ['bʌnjən] *n* : juanete *m*

bunk[1] ['bʌŋk] *vi* : dormir (en una litera)

bunk[2] *n* **1** *or* **bunk bed** : litera *f* **2** NONSENSE : tonterías *fpl*, bobadas *fpl*

bunker ['bʌŋkər] *n* **1** : carbonera *f* (en un barco) **2** SHELTER : búnker *m*

bunny ['bʌni] *n, pl* **-nies** : conejo *m*, -ja *f*

buoy[1] ['bu:i, 'bɔɪ] *vt* **to buoy up 1** : mantener a flote **2** CHEER, HEARTEN : animar, levantar el ánimo a

buoy[2] *n* : boya *f*

buoyancy ['bɔɪəntsi, 'bu:jən-] *n* **1** : flotabilidad *f* **2** OPTIMISM : confianza *f*, optimismo *m*

buoyant ['bɔɪənt, 'bu:jənt] *adj* : boyante, flotante

bur *or* **burr** ['bər] *n* : abrojo *m* (de una planta)

burden[1] ['bərdən] *vt* : cargar, oprimir

burden[2] *n* : carga *f*, peso *m*

burdensome ['bərdənsəm] *adj* : oneroso

burdock ['bər‚dɑk] *n* : bardana *f*

bureau ['bjʊro] *n* **1** CHEST OF DRAWERS : cómoda *f* **2** DEPARTMENT : departamento *m* (del gobierno) **3** AGENCY

: agencia *f* ⟨travel bureau : agencia de viajes⟩

bureaucracy [bjʊ'rɑkrəsi] *n*, *pl* **-cies** : burocracia *f*

bureaucrat ['bjʊrə,kræt] *n* : burócrata *mf*

bureaucratic [,bjʊrə'kræ̣tɪk] *adj* : burocrático

burgeon ['bərdʒən] *vi* : florecer, retoñar, crecer

burglar ['bərglər] *n* : ladrón *m*, -drona *f*

burglarize ['bərglə,raɪz] *vt* **-ized; -izing** : robar

burglary ['bərgləri] *n*, *pl* **-glaries** : robo *m*

burgle ['bərgəl] *vt* **-gled; -gling** : robar

burgundy ['bərgəndi] *n*, *pl* **-dies** : borgoña *m*, vino *m* de Borgoña

burial ['beriəl] *n* : entierro *m*, sepelio *m*

burlap ['bər,læp] *n* : arpillera *f*

burlesque[1] [bər'lesk] *vt* **-lesqued; -lesquing** : parodiar

burlesque[2] *n* **1** PARODY : parodia *f* **2** REVUE : revista *f* (musical)

burly ['bərli] *adj* **-lier; -liest** : fornido, corpulento, musculoso

Burmese [,bər'mi:z, -'mi:s] *n* : birmano *m*, -na *f* — **Burmese** *adj*

burn[1] ['bərn] *v* **burned** ['bərnd, 'bərnt] *or* **burnt** ['bərnt]; **burning** *vt* **1** : quemar, incendiar ⟨to burn a building : incendiar un edificio⟩ ⟨I burned my hand : me quemé la mano⟩ **2** CONSUME : usar, gastar, consumir — *vi* **1** : arder (dícese de un fuego o un edificio), quemarse (dícese de la comida, etc.) **2** : estar prendido, estar encendido ⟨we left the lights burning : dejamos las luces encendidas⟩ **3 to burn out** : consumirse, apagarse **4 to burn with** : arder de ⟨he was burning with jealousy : ardía de celos⟩

burn[2] *n* : quemadura *f*

burner ['bərnər] *n* : quemador *m*

burnish ['bərnɪʃ] *vt* : bruñir

burp[1] ['bərp] *vi* : eructar — *vt* : hacer eructar

burp[2] *n* : eructo *m*

burr → **bur**

burro ['bəro, 'bʊr-] *n*, *pl* **-os** : burro *m*

burrow[1] ['bəro] *vi* **1** : cavar, hacer una madriguera **2 to burrow into** : hurgar en — *vt* : cavar, excavar

burrow[2] *n* : madriguera *f*, conejera *f* (de un conejo)

bursar ['bərsər] *n* : administrador *m*, -dora *f*

bursitis [bər'saɪtəs] *n* : bursitis *f*

burst[1] ['bərst] *v* **burst; bursting** *vi* **1** : reventarse (dícese de una llanta o un globo), estallar (dícese de obuses o fuegos artificiales), romperse (dícese de un dique) **2 to burst in** : irrumpir en **3 to burst into** : empezar a, echar a ⟨to burst into tears : echarse a llorar⟩ — *vt* : reventar

burst[2] *n* **1** EXPLOSION : estallido *m*, explosión *f*, reventón *m* (de una llanta) **2** OUTBURST : arranque *m* (de actividad,

de velocidad), arrebato *m* (de ira), salva *f* (de aplausos)

Burundian [bʊ'ru:ndiən, -'rʊn-] *n* : burundés *m*, -desa *f* — **Burundian** *adj*

bury ['beri] *vt* **buried; burying 1** INTER : enterrar, sepultar **2** HIDE : esconder, ocultar **3 to bury oneself in** : enfrascarse en

bus[1] ['bʌs] *v* **bused** *or* **bussed** ['bʌst]; **busing** *or* **bussing** ['bʌsɪŋ] *vt* : transportar en autobús — *vi* : viajar en autobús

bus[2] *n* : autobús *m*, bus *m*, camión *m* *Mex*, colectivo *m* *Arg, Bol, Peru*

busboy ['bʌs,bɔɪ] *n* : ayudante *mf* de camarero

bush ['bʊʃ] *n* **1** SHRUB : arbusto *m*, mata *f* **2** THICKET : maleza *f*, matorral *m*

bushel ['bʊʃəl] *n* : medida *f* de áridos igual a 35.24 litros

bushing ['bʊʃɪŋ] *n* : cojinete *m*

bushy ['bʊʃi] *adj* **bushier; -est** : espeso, poblado ⟨bushy eyebrows : cejas pobladas⟩

busily ['bɪzəli] *adv* : afanosamente, diligentemente

business ['bɪznəs, -nəz] *n* **1** OCCUPATION : ocupación *f*, oficio *m* **2** DUTY, MISSION : misión *f*, deber *m*, responsabilidad *f* **3** ESTABLISHMENT, FIRM : empresa *f*, firma *f*, negocio *m*, comercio *m* **4** COMMERCE : negocios *mpl*, comercio *m* **5** AFFAIR, MATTER : asunto *m*, cuestión *f*, cosa *f* ⟨it's none of your business : no es asunto tuyo⟩

businessman ['bɪznəs,mæn, -nəz] *n*, *pl* **-men** [-mən, -,mɛn] : empresario *m*, hombre *m* de negocios

businesswoman ['bɪznəs,wʊmən, -nəz-] *n*, *pl* **-women** [-,wɪmən] : empresaria *f*, mujer *f* de negocios

bust[1] ['bʌst] *vt* **1** BREAK, SMASH : romper, estropear, destrozar **2** TAME : domar, amansar (un caballo) — *vi* : romperse, estropearse

bust[2] *n* **1** : busto *m* (en la escultura) **2** BREASTS : pecho *m*, senos *mpl*, busto *m*

bustle[1] ['bʌsəl] *vi* **-tled; -tling to bustle about** : ir y venir, trajinar, ajetrearse

bustle[2] *n* **1** *or* **hustle and bustle** : bullicio *m*, ajetreo *m* **2** : polisón *m* (en la ropa feminina)

busy[1] ['bɪzi] *vt* **busied; busying to busy oneself with** : ocuparse con, ponerse a, entretenerse con

busy[2] *adj* **busier; -est 1** OCCUPIED : ocupado, atareado ⟨he's busy working : está ocupado en su trabajo⟩ ⟨the telephone was busy : el teléfono estaba ocupado⟩ **2** BUSTLING : concurrido, animado ⟨a busy street : una calle concurrida, una calle con mucho tránsito⟩

busybody ['bɪzi,bɑdi] *n*, *pl* **-bodies** : entrometido *m*, -da *f*; metiche *mf fam*; metomentodo *mf*

but[1] ['bʌt] *conj* **1** THAT : que ⟨there is no doubt but he is lazy : no cabe duda

que sea perezoso⟩ **2** WITHOUT : sin que
3 NEVERTHELESS : pero, no obstante,
sin embargo ⟨I called her but she did-
n't answer : la llamé pero no contestó⟩
4 YET : pero ⟨he was poor but proud
: era pobre pero orgulloso⟩
but² *prep* EXCEPT : excepto, menos
⟨everyone but Carlos : todos menos
Carlos⟩ ⟨the last but one : el penúlti-
mo⟩
butcher¹ [ˈbʊtʃər] *vt* **1** SLAUGHTER
: matar (animales) **2** KILL : matar, asesinar, masacrar **3** BOTCH : estropear,
hacer una chapuza
butcher² *n* **1** : carnicero *m*, -ra *f* **2**
KILLER : asesino *m*, -na *f* **3** BUNGLER
: chapucero *m*, -ra *f*
butler [ˈbʌtlər] *n* : mayordomo *m*
butt¹ [ˈbʌt] *vt* **1** : embestir (con los cuernos), darle un cabezazo a **2** ABUT : colindar con, bordear — *vi* **to butt in 1**
INTERRUPT : interrumpir **2** MEDDLE
: entrometerse, meterse
butt² *n* **1** BUTTING : embestida *f* (de cuernos), cabezazo *m* **2** TARGET : blanco
m ⟨the butt of their jokes : el blanco
de sus bromas⟩ **3** BOTTOM, END : extremo *m*, culata *f* (de un rifle), colilla *f*
(de un cigarrillo)
butte [ˈbjuːt] *n* : colina *f* empinada y aislada
butter¹ [ˈbʌtər] *vt* **1** : untar con mantequilla **2 to butter up** : halagar
butter² *n* : mantequilla *f*
buttercup [ˈbʌtərˌkʌp] *n* : ranúnculo *m*
butterfat [ˈbʌtərˌfæt] *n* : grasa *f* de la
leche
butterfly [ˈbʌtərˌflaɪ] *n, pl* **-flies** : mariposa *f*
buttermilk [ˈbʌtərˌmɪlk] *n* : suero *m* de
la leche
butternut [ˈbʌtərˌnʌt] *n* : nogal *m* ceniciento (árbol)
butterscotch [ˈbʌtərˌskɑtʃ] *n* : caramelo
m duro hecho con mantequilla
buttery [ˈbʌtəri] *adj* : mantecoso
buttocks [ˈbʌtəks, -ˌtɑks] *npl* : nalgas *fpl*,
trasero *m*
button¹ [ˈbʌtən] *vt* : abrochar, abotonar
— *vi* : abrocharse, abotonarse
button² *n* : botón *m*
buttonhole¹ [ˈbʌtənˌhoːl] *vt* **-holed;
-holing** : acorralar
buttonhole² *n* : ojal *m*
buttress¹ [ˈbʌtrəs] *vt* : apoyar, reforzar
buttress² *n* **1** : contrafuerte *m* (en la arquitectura) **2** SUPPORT : apoyo *m*,
sostén *m*

buxom [ˈbʌksəm] *adj* : con mucho busto, con mucho pecho
buy¹ [ˈbaɪ] *vt* **bought** [ˈbɔt]; **buying**
: comprar
buy² *n* BARGAIN : compra *f*, ganga *f*
buyer [ˈbaɪər] *n* : comprador *m*, -dora *f*
buzz¹ [ˈbʌz] *vi* : zumbar (dícese de un insecto), sonar (dícese de un teléfono o
un despertador)
buzz² *n* **1** : zumbido *m* (de insectos) **2**
: murmullo *m*, rumor *m* (de voces)
buzzard [ˈbʌzərd] *n* VULTURE : buitre *m*,
zopilote *m* CA, Mex
buzzer [ˈbʌzər] *n* : timbre *m*, chicharra *f*
buzzword [ˈbʌzˌwərd] *n* : palabra *f* de
moda
by¹ [ˈbaɪ] *adv* **1** NEAR : cerca ⟨he lives
close by : vive muy cerca⟩ **2 to stop
by** : pasar por casa, hacer una visita **3
to go by** : pasar ⟨they rushed by
: pasaron corriendo⟩ **4 to put by**
: reservar, poner a un lado **5 by and
by** : poco después, dentro de poco **6
by and large** : en general
by² *prep* **1** NEAR : cerca de, al lado de,
junto a **2** VIA : por ⟨she left by the door
: salió por la puerta⟩ **3** PAST : por, por
delante de ⟨they walked by him
: pasaron por delante de él⟩ **4** DURING
: de, durante ⟨by night : de noche⟩ **5**
(in expressions of time) : para ⟨we'll be
there by ten : estaremos allí para las
diez⟩ ⟨by then : para entonces⟩ **6** *(indicating cause or agent)* : por, de, a
⟨built by the Romans : construido por
los romanos⟩ ⟨a book by Borges : un
libro de Borges⟩ ⟨made by hand : hecho a mano⟩
by and by *adv* : dentro de poco
bygone¹ [ˈbaɪˌgɔn] *adj* : pasado
bygone² *n* **let bygones be bygones** : lo
pasado, pasado está
bylaw *or* **byelaw** [ˈbaɪˌlɔ] *n* : norma *f*,
reglamento *m*
by-line [ˈbaɪˌlaɪn] *n* : data *f*
bypass¹ [ˈbaɪˌpæs] *vt* : evitar
bypass² *n* **1** BELTWAY : carretera *f* de
circunvalación **2** DETOUR : desvío *m*
by-product [ˈbaɪˌprɑdəkt] *n* : subproducto *m*, producto *m* derivado
bystander [ˈbaɪˌstændər] *n* : espectador
m, -dora *f*
byte [ˈbaɪt] *n* : byte *m*
byway [ˈbaɪˌweɪ] *n* : camino *m* (apartado), carretera *f* secundaria
byword [ˈbaɪˌwərd] *n* **1** PROVERB
: proverbio *m*, refrán *m* **2 to be a byword for** : estar sinónimo de

butcher¹ ['bʊtʃər] *vt* **1** SLAUGHTER : matar (animales) **2** KILL : matar, asesinar, masacrar **3** BOTCH : estropear, hacer una chapuza

butcher² *n* **1** : carnicero *m*, -ra *f* **2** KILLER : asesino *m*, -na *f* **3** BUNGLER : chapucero *m*, -ra

butler ['bʌtlər] *n* : mayordomo *m*

butt¹ ['bʌt] *vt* **1** : embestir (con los cuernos), darle un cabezazo a **2** ABUT : colindar con, bordear — *vi* **to butt in 1** INTERRUPT : interrumpir **2** MEDDLE : entrometerse, meterse

butt² *n* **1** BUTTING : embestida *f* (de cuernos), cabezazo *m* **2** TARGET : blanco *m* ⟨the butt of their jokes : el blanco de sus bromas⟩ **3** BOTTOM, END : extremo *m*, culata *f* (de un rifle), colilla *f* (de un cigarrillo)

butte ['bju:t] *n* : colina *f* empinada y aislada

butter¹ ['bʌtər] *vt* : untar con mantequilla *f* **2 to butter up** : halagar

butter² *n* : mantequilla *f*

buttercup ['bʌtər,kʌp] *n* : ranúnculo *m*

butterfat ['bʌtər,fæt] *n* : grasa *f* de la leche

butterfly ['bʌtər,flaɪ] *n, pl* **-flies** : mariposa *f*

buttermilk ['bʌtər,mɪlk] *n* : suero *m* de la leche

butternut ['bʌtər,nʌt] *n* : nogal *m* ceniciento (árbol)

butterscotch ['bʌtər,skɑtʃ] *n* : caramelo *m* duro hecho con mantequilla

buttery ['bʌtəri] *adj* : mantecoso

buttocks ['bʌtəks, -taks] *npl* : nalgas *fpl*, trasero *m*

button¹ ['bʌtən] *vt* : abrochar, abotonar — *vi* : abrocharse, abotonarse

button² *n* : botón *m*

buttonhole¹ ['bʌtən,hoːl] *vt* **-holed; -holing** : acorralar

buttonhole² *n* : ojal *m*

buttress¹ ['bʌtrəs] *vt* : apoyar, reforzar

buttress² *n* **1** : contrafuerte *m* (en la arquitectura) **2** SUPPORT : apoyo *m*, sostén *m*

buxom ['bʌksəm] *adj* : con mucho busto, con mucho pecho

buy¹ ['baɪ] *vt* **bought** ['bɔt]; **buying** : comprar

buy² *n* BARGAIN : compra *f*, ganga *f*

buyer ['baɪər] *n* : comprador *m*, -dora *f*

buzz¹ ['bʌz] *vi* : zumbar (dícese de un insecto), sonar (dícese de un teléfono o un despertador)

buzz² *n* **1** : zumbido *m* (de insectos) **2** : murmullo *m*, rumor *m* (de voces)

buzzard ['bʌzərd] *n* VULTURE : buitre *m*, zopilote *m* (CA, Mex

buzzer ['bʌzər] *n* : timbre *m*, chicharra *f*

buzzword ['bʌz,wərd] *n* : palabra *f* de moda

by¹ ['baɪ] *adv* **1** NEAR : cerca ⟨he lives close by : vive muy cerca⟩ **2 to stop by** : pasar por casa, hacer una visita **3 to go by** : pasar ⟨they rushed by : pasaron corriendo⟩ **4 to put by** : reservar, poner a un lado **5 by and by** : poco después, dentro de poco **6 by and large** : en general

by² *prep* **1** NEAR : cerca de, al lado de, junto a **2** VIA : por ⟨she left by the door : salió por la puerta⟩ **3** PAST : por, por delante de ⟨they walked by him : pasaron por delante de él⟩ **4** DURING : de, durante ⟨by night : de noche⟩ **5** (in expressions of time) : para ⟨we'll be there by ten : estaremos allí para las diez⟩ ⟨by then : para entonces⟩ **6** (indicating cause or agent) : por, de, a ⟨built by the Romans : construido por los romanos⟩ ⟨a book by Borges : un libro de Borges⟩ ⟨made by hand : hecho a mano⟩

by and by *adv* : dentro de poco

bygone¹ ['baɪ,gɔn] *adj* : pasado

bygone² *n* **let bygones be bygones** : lo pasado, pasado está

bylaw *or* **byelaw** ['baɪ,lɔ] *n* : norma *f*, reglamento *m*

by-line ['baɪ,laɪn] *n* : data *f*

bypass¹ ['baɪ,pæs] *vt* : evitar

bypass² *n* **1** BELTWAY : carretera *f* de circunvalación **2** DETOUR : desvío *m*

by-product ['baɪ,prɑdəkt] *n* : subproducto *m*, producto *m* derivado

bystander ['baɪ,stændər] *n* : espectador *m*, -dora *f*

byte ['baɪt] *n* : byte *m*

byway ['baɪ,weɪ] *n* : camino *m* (apartado), carretera *f* secundaria

byword ['baɪ,wərd] *n* **1** PROVERB : proverbio *m*, refrán *m* **2 to be a byword for** : estar sinónimo de

bureau f : agencia de viajes>

bureaucracy [bjʊ'rɑkrəsi] *n*, *pl* **-cies** : burocracia *f*

bureaucrat ['bjʊrə,kræt] *n* : burócrata *mf*

bureaucratic [,bjʊrə'krætɪk] *adj* : burocrático

burgeon ['bərdʒən] *vi* : florecer, retoñar, crecer

burglar ['bərglər] *n* : ladrón *m*, -drona *f*

burglarize ['bərglə,raɪz] *vt* **-ized, -izing** : robar

burglary ['bərgləri] *n*, *pl* **-glaries** : robo *m*

burgle ['bərgəl] *vt* **-gled; -gling** : robar *m*

burgundy ['bərgəndi] *n*, *pl* **-dies** : borgoña *m*, vino *m* de Borgoña

burial ['bɛriəl] *n* : entierro *m*, sepelio *m*

burlap ['bər,læp] *n* : arpillera *f*

burlesque [bər'lɛsk] *vt* **-lesqued; -lesquing** : parodiar

burlesque² *n* **1** PARODY : parodia *f* **2** REVUE : revista *f* (musical)

burly ['bərli] *adj* **-lier; -liest** : fornido, corpulento, musculoso

Burmese [,bər'miz, -'mis] *n* : birmano *m*, -na *f* — **Burmese** *adj*

burn¹ ['bərn] *v* **burned** ['bərnd, 'bərnt] *or* **burnt** ['bərnt]; **burning** *vt* **1** : quemar, incendiar <to burn a building : incendiar un edificio> <I burned my hand : me quemé la mano> **2** CONSUME : usar, gastar, consumir — *vi* **1** : arder (dícese de un fuego o un edificio), quemarse (dícese de la comida, etc), **2** : estar prendido, estar encendido <we left the lights burning : dejamos las luces encendidas> **3 to burn out** : consumirse, apagarse **4 to burn with** : arder de <he was burning with jealousy : ardía de celos>

burn² *n* : quemadura *f*

burner ['bərnər] *n* : quemador *m*

burnish ['bərnɪʃ] *vt* : bruñir

burp¹ ['bərp] *vi* : eructar — *vt* : hacer eructar

burp² *n* : eructo *m*

burro ['bəro, 'bʊr-] *n*, *pl* **-os** : burro *m* → **bur**

burrow¹ ['bəro] *vt* **1** : cavar, hacer una madriguera **2 to burrow into** : hurgar en — *vt* : cavar, excavar

burrow² *n* : madriguera *f*, conejera *f* (de un conejo)

bursar ['bərsər] *n* : administrador *m*, -dora *f*

bursitis [bər'saɪtəs] *n* : bursitis *f*

burst¹ ['bərst] *v* **burst; bursting** *vi* **1** : reventarse (dícese de una llanta o un globo), estallar (dícese de obuses o fuegos artificiales), romperse (dícese de un dique) **2 to burst in** : irrumpir en **3 to burst into** : empezar a, echar a <to burst into tears : echarse a llorar> — *vt* : reventar

burst² *n* **1** EXPLOSION : estallido *m*, explosión *f*, reventón *m* (de una llanta) **2** OUTBURST : arranque *m* (de actividad, de velocidad), arrebato *m* (de ira), salva *f* (de aplausos),

Burundian [bʊ'rʌndiən] *n* : burundés *m*, -desa *f* — **Burundian** *adj*

bury ['bɛri] *vt* **buried; burying 1** INTER : enterrar, sepultar **2** HIDE : esconder, ocultar **3 to bury oneself in** : enfrascarse en

bus¹ ['bəs] *v* **bused** *or* **bussed; busing** *or* **bussing** *vt* : transportar en autobús — *vi* : viajar en autobús

bus² *n* : autobús *m*, bus *m*, camión *m* (*Mex*), colectivo *m* (*Arg, Bol, Peru*)

busboy ['bʌs,bɔɪ] *n* : ayudante *mf* de camarero

bush ['bʊʃ] *n* **1** SHRUB : arbusto *m*, mata *f* **2** THICKET : maleza *f*, matorral *m*

bushel ['bʊʃəl] *n* : medida de áridos igual a 35.24 litros

bushy ['bʊʃi] *adj* **bushier; -est** : espeso, poblado <bushy eyebrows : cejas pobladas>

busily ['bɪzəli] *adv* : afanosamente, diligentemente

business ['bɪznəs, -nəz] *n* **1** OCCUPATION : ocupación *f*, oficio *m* **2** DUTY, MISSION : misión *f*, deber *m*, responsabilidad *f* **3** ESTABLISHMENT, FIRM : empresa *f*, firma *f*, negocio *m*, comercio *m* **4** COMMERCE : negocios *mpl*, comercio *m* **5** AFFAIR, MATTER : asunto *m*, cuestión *f*, cosa *f* <it's none of your business : no es asunto tuyo>

businessman ['bɪznəs,mæn, -nəz-] *n*, *pl* **-men** [-mɛn, -,mɛn] : empresario *m*, hombre *m* de negocios

businesswoman ['bɪznəs,wʊmən, -nəz-] *n*, *pl* **-women** [-,wɪmən] : empresaria *f*, mujer *f* de negocios

bust¹ ['bəst] *vt* **1** BREAK, SMASH : romper, estropear, destrozar **2** TAME : domar, amansar (un caballo) — *vi* : romperse, estropearse

bust² *n* **1** : busto *m* (en la escultura) **2** BREASTS : pecho *m*, senos *mpl*, busto *m*

bustle¹ ['bʌsəl] *vi* **-tled; -tling to bustle about** : ir y venir, trajinar, ajetrearse

bustle² *n* **1** *or* **hustle and bustle** : bullicio *m*, ajetreo *m* **2** : polisón *m* (en la ropa femenina)

busy¹ ['bɪzi] *vt* **busied; busying to busy oneself with** : ocuparse con, ponerse a, entretenerse con

busy² *adj* **busier; -est 1** OCCUPIED : ocupado, atareado <he's busy working : está ocupado en su trabajo> <the telephone was busy : el teléfono estaba ocupado> **2** BUSTLING : concurrido, animado <a busy street : una calle concurrida, una calle con mucho tránsito>

busybody ['bɪzi,bɑdi] *n*, *pl* **-bodies** : entrometido *m*, -da *f*; metiche *mf* *fam*; metomentodo *mf*

but¹ ['bət] *conj* **1** THAT : que <there is no doubt but he is lazy : no cabe duda

C

c ['si:] *n*, *pl* **c's** *or* **cs** : tercera letra del alfabeto inglés

cab ['kæb] *n* **1** TAXI : taxi *m* **2** : cabina *f* (de un camión o una locomotora) **3** CARRIAGE : coche *m* de caballos

cabal [kə'bɑl, -'bæl] *n* **1** INTRIGUE, PLOT : conspiración *f*, complot *m*, intriga *f* **2** : grupo *m* de conspiradores

cabaret [ˌkæbə'reɪ] *n* : cabaret *m*

cabbage ['kæbɪʤ] *n* : col *f*, repollo *m*

cabbie *or* **cabby** ['kæbi] *n* : taxista *mf*

cabin ['kæbən] *n* **1** HUT : cabaña *f*, choza *f*, barraca *f* **2** STATEROOM : camarote *m* **3** : cabina *f* (de un automóvil o avión)

cabinet ['kæbnət] *n* **1** CUPBOARD : armario *m* **2** : gabinete *m*, consejo *m* de ministros **3** medicine cabinet : botiquín *m*

cabinetmaker ['kæbnətˌmeɪkər] *n* : ebanista *mf*

cabinetmaking ['kæbnətˌmeɪkɪŋ] *n* : ebanistería *f*

cable¹ ['keɪbəl] *vt* **-bled; -bling** : enviar un cable, telegrafiar

cable² *n* **1** : cable *m* (para colgar o sostener algo) **2** : cable *m* eléctrico **3** → **cablegram**

cablegram ['keɪbəlˌgræm] *n* : telegrama *m*, cable *m*

caboose [kə'bu:s] *n* : furgón *m* de cola, cabús *m Mex*

cabstand ['kæbˌstænd] *n* : parada *f* de taxis

cacao [kə'kau, -'keɪo] *n*, *pl* **cacaos** : cacao *m*

cache¹ ['kæʃ] *vt* **cached; caching** : esconder, guardar en un escondrijo

cache² *n* **1** : escondite *m*, escondrijo *m* ⟨cache of weapons : escondite de armas⟩ **2** : cache *m* ⟨cache memory : memoria cache⟩

cachet [kæ'ʃeɪ] *n* : caché *m*, prestigio *m*

cackle¹ ['kækəl] *vi* **-led; -ling 1** CLUCK : cacarear **2** : reírse o carcajearse estridentemente ⟨he was cackling with delight : estaba carcajeándose de gusto⟩

cackle² *n* **1** : cacareo *m* (de una polla) **2** LAUGH : risa *f* estridente

cacophony [kæ'kɑfəni, -'kɔ-] *n*, *pl* **-nies** : cacofonía *f*

cactus ['kæktəs] *n*, *pl* **cacti** [-ˌtaɪ] *or* **-tuses** : cacto *m*, cactus *m*

cadaver [kə'dævər] *n* : cadáver *m*

cadaverous [kə'dævərəs] *adj* : cadavérico

caddie¹ *or* **caddy** ['kædi] *vi* **caddied; caddying** : trabajar de caddie, hacer de caddie

caddie² *or* **caddy** *n*, *pl* **-dies** : caddie *mf*

caddy ['kædi] *n*, *pl* **-dies** : cajita *f* para té

cadence ['keɪdənts] *n* : cadencia *f*, ritmo *m*

cadenced ['keɪdəntst] *adj* : cadencioso, rítmico

cadet [kə'dɛt] *n* : cadete *mf*

cadmium ['kædmiəm] *n* : cadmio *m*

cadre ['kæˌdreɪ, 'kɑ-, -ˌdri:] *n* : cuadro *m* (de expertos)

café [kæ'feɪ, kə-] *n* : café *m*, cafetería *f*

cafeteria [ˌkæfə'tɪriə] *n* : cafetería *f*, restaurante *m* de autoservicio

caffeine [kæ'fi:n] *n* : cafeína *f*

cage¹ ['keɪʤ] *vt* **caged; caging** : enjaular

cage² *n* : jaula *f*

cagey ['keɪʤi] *adj* **-gier; -est 1** CAUTIOUS : cauteloso, reservado **2** SHREWD : astuto, vivo — **cagily** [-ʤəli] *adv*

caisson ['keɪˌsɑn, -sən] *n* **1** : cajón *m* de municiones **2** : cajón *m* hidráulico

cajole [kə'ʤo:l] *vt* **-joled; -joling** : engatusar

cajolery [kə'ʤo:ləri] *n* : engatusamiento *m*

cake¹ ['keɪk] *v* **caked; caking** *vt* : cubrir ⟨caked with mud : cubierto de barro⟩ — *vi* : endurecerse

cake² *n* **1** : torta *f*, bizcocho *m*, pastel *m* **2** : pastilla *f* (de jabón) **3 to take the cake** : llevarse la palma, ser el colmo

calabash ['kælə,bæʃ] *n* : calabaza *f*

calamari [ˌkɑlə'mɑri] *ns & pl* : calamares *mpl*

calamine ['kælə,maɪn] *n* : calamina *f* ⟨calamine lotion : loción de calamina⟩

calamitous [kə'læmətəs] *adj* : desastroso, catastrófico, calamitoso — **calamitously** *adv*

calamity [kə'læməti] *n*, *pl* **-ties** : desastre *m*, desgracia *f*, calamidad *f*

calcium ['kælsiəm] *n* : calcio *m*

calcium carbonate ['kɑrbə,neɪt, -nət] *n* : carbonato *m* de calcio

calculable ['kælkjələbəl] *adj* : calculable, computable

calculate ['kælkjə,leɪt] *v* **-lated; -lating** *vt* **1** COMPUTE : calcular, computar **2** ESTIMATE : calcular, creer **3** INTEND : planear, tener la intención de ⟨I calculated on spending $100 : planeaba gastar $100⟩ — *vi* : calcular, hacer cálculos

calculated ['kælkjə,leɪtəd] *adj* **1** ESTIMATED : calculado **2** DELIBERATE : intencional, premeditado, deliberado

calculating ['kælkjə,leɪtɪŋ] *adj* SHREWD : calculador, astuto

calculation [ˌkælkjə'leɪʃən] *n* : cálculo *m*

calculator ['kælkjə,leɪtər] *n* : calculadora *f*

calculus ['kælkjələs] *n*, *pl* **-li** [-,laɪ] **1** : cálculo *m* ⟨differential calculus : cálculo diferencial⟩ **2** TARTAR : sarro *m* (dental)

caldron ['kɔldrən] → **cauldron**

calendar ['kæləndər] *n* **1** : calendario *m* **2** SCHEDULE : calendario *m*, programa *m*, agenda *f*

calf ['kæf, 'kaf] *n, pl* **calves** ['kævz, 'kavz] **1** : becerro *m*, -rra *f*; ternero *m*, -ra *f* (de vacunos) **2** : cría *f* (de otros mamíferos) **3** : pantorrilla *f* (de la pierna)

calfskin ['kæf,skɪn] *n* : piel *f* de becerro

caliber *or* **calibre** ['kæləbər] *n* **1** : calibre *m* ⟨a .38 caliber gun : una pistola de calibre .38⟩ **2** ABILITY : calibre *m*, valor *m*, capacidad *f*

calibrate ['kælə,breɪt] *vt* -**brated; -brating** : calibrar (armas), graduar (termómetros)

calibration [,kælə'breɪʃən] *n* : calibrado *m*, calibración *f*

calico ['kælɪ,ko:] *n, pl* -**coes** *or* -**cos 1** : calicó *m*, percal *m* **2** *or* **calico cat** : gato *m* manchado

calipers ['kæləpərz] *npl* : calibrador *m*

caliph *or* **calif** ['keɪləf, 'kæ-] *n* : califa *m*

calisthenics [,kæləs'θenɪks] *ns & pl* : calistenia *f*

calk ['kɔk] → **caulk**

call[1] ['kɔl] *vi* **1** CRY, SHOUT : gritar, vociferar **2** VISIT : hacer (una) visita, visitar **3 to call for** : exigir, requerir, necesitar ⟨it calls for patience : requiere mucha paciencia⟩ — *vt* **1** SUMMON : llamar, convocar **2** TELEPHONE : llamar por teléfono, telefonear **3** NAME : llamar, apodar

call[2] *n* **1** SHOUT : grito *m*, llamada *f* **2** : grito *m* (de un animal), reclamo *m* (de un pájaro) **3** SUMMONS : llamada *f* **4** DEMAND : llamado *m*, petición *f* **5** VISIT : visita *f* **6** DECISION : decisión *f* (en deportes) **7** *or* **telephone call** : llamada *f* (telefónica)

call down *vt* REPRIMAND : reprender, reñir

caller ['kɔlər] *n* **1** VISITOR : visita *f* **2** : persona *f* que llama (por teléfono)

calligraphy [kə'lɪɡrəfi] *n, pl* -**phies** : caligrafía *f*

calling ['kɔlɪŋ] *n* : vocación *f*, profesión *f*

calliope [kə'laɪə,pi:, 'kæli,o:p] *n* : órgano *m* de vapor

call off *vt* CANCEL : cancelar, suspender

callous[1] ['kæləs] *vt* : encallecer

callous[2] *adj* **1** CALLUSED : calloso, encallecido **2** UNFEELING : insensible, desalmado, cruel

callously ['kæləsli] *adv* : cruelmente, insensiblemente

callousness ['kæləsnəs] *n* : insensibilidad *f*, crueldad *f*

callow ['kælo] *adj* : inexperto, inmaduro

callus ['kæləs] *n* : callo *m*

callused ['kæləst] *adj* : encallecido, calloso

calm[1] ['kam, 'kalm] *vt* : tranquilizar, calmar, sosegar — *vi* : tranquilizarse, calmarse ⟨calm down! : ¡tranquilízate!⟩

calm[2] *adj* **1** TRANQUIL : calmo, tranquilo, sereno, ecuánime **2** STILL : en calma (dícese del mar), sin viento (dícese del aire)

calm[3] *n* : tranquilidad *f*, calma *f*

calmly ['kamli, 'kalm-] *adv* : con calma, tranquilamente

calmness ['kamnəs, 'kalm-] *n* : calma *f*, tranquilidad *f*

caloric [kə'lɔrɪk] *adj* : calórico (dícese de los alimentos), calorífico (dícese de la energía)

calorie ['kæləri] *n* : caloría *f*

calumniate [kə'lʌmni,eɪt] *vt* -**ated; -ating** : calumniar, difamar

calumny ['kæləmni] *n, pl* -**nies** : calumnia *f*, difamación *f*

calve ['kæv, 'kav] *vi* **calved; calving** : parir (dícese de los mamíferos)

calves → **calf**

calypso [kə'lɪp,so:] *n, pl* -**sos** : calipso *m*

calyx ['keɪlɪks, 'kæ-] *n, pl* -**lyxes** *or* -**lyces** [-lə,si:z] : cáliz *m*

cam ['kæm] *n* : leva *f*

camaraderie [,kam'radəri, ,kæm-; ,kamə'ra-] *n* : compañerismo *m*, camaradería *f*

Cambodian [kæm'bo:diən] *n* : camboyano *m*, -na *f* — **Cambodian** *adj*

came → **come**

camel ['kæməl] *n* : camello *m*

camellia [kə'mi:ljə] *n* : camelia *f*

cameo ['kæmi,o:] *n, pl* -**eos 1** : camafeo *m* **2** *or* **cameo performance** : actuación *f* especial

camera ['kæmrə, 'kæmərə] *n* : cámara *f*, máquina *f* fotográfica

Cameroonian [,kæmə'ru:niən] *n* : camerunés *m*, -nesa *f*

camouflage[1] ['kæmə,flaʒ, -,flaʤ] *vt* -**flaged; -flaging** : camuflajear, camuflar

camouflage[2] *n* : camuflaje *m*

camp[1] ['kæmp] *vi* : acampar, ir de camping

camp[2] *n* **1** : campamento *m* **2** FACTION : campo *m*, bando *m* ⟨in the same camp : del mismo bando⟩ **3 to pitch camp** : acampar, poner el campamento **4 to break camp** : levantar el campamento

campaign[1] [kæm'peɪn] *vi* : hacer (una) campaña

campaign[2] *n* : campaña *f*

campanile [,kæmpə'ni:,li:, -'ni:l] *n, pl* -**niles** *or* -**nili** [-'ni:,li:] : campanario *m*

camper ['kæmpər] *n* **1** : campista *mf* (persona) **2** : cámper *m* (vehículo)

campground ['kæmp,graʊnd] *n* : campamento *m*, camping *m*

camphor ['kæmpfər] *n* : alcanfor *m*

campsite ['kæmp,saɪt] *n* : campamento *m*, camping *m*

campus ['kæmpəs] *n* : campus *m*, recinto *m* universitario

can[1] ['kæn] *v aux, past* **could** ['kʊd]; *present s & pl* **can 1** : poder ⟨could you help me? : ¿podría ayudarme?⟩ **2** : saber ⟨she can't drive yet : todavía no sabe manejar⟩ **3** MAY : tener permiso para ⟨can I sit down? : ¿puedo sentarme?⟩ **4** : poder ⟨it can't be! : ¡no puede ser!⟩ ⟨where can they be? : ¿dónde estarán?⟩

can² ['kæn] *vt* **canned; canning 1** : enlatar, envasar ⟨to can tomatoes : enlatar tomates⟩ **2** DISMISS, FIRE : despedir, echar

can³ *n* : lata *f*, envase *m*, cubo *m* ⟨a can of beer : una lata de cerveza⟩ ⟨garbage can : cubo de basura⟩

Canadian [kə'neɪdiən] *n* : canadiense *mf* — **Canadian** *adj*

canal [kə'næl] *n* **1** : canal *m*, tubo *m* ⟨alimentary canal : tubo digestivo⟩ **2** : canal *m* ⟨Panama Canal : Canal de Panamá⟩

canapé ['kænəpi, -ˌpeɪ] *n* : canapé *m*

canary [kə'nɛri] *n, pl* **-naries** : canario *m*

cancel ['kæntsəl] *vt* **-celed** *or* **-celled; -celing** *or* **-celling** : cancelar

cancellation [ˌkæntsə'leɪʃən] *n* : cancelación *f*

cancer ['kæntsər] *n* : cáncer *m*

Cancer *n* : Cáncer *mf*

cancerous ['kæntsərəs] *adj* : canceroso

candelabrum [ˌkændə'labrəm, -'læ-] *or* **candelabra** [-brə] *n, pl* **-bra** *or* **-bras** : candelabro *m*

candid ['kændɪd] *adj* **1** FRANK : franco, sincero, abierto **2** : natural, espontáneo (en la fotografía)

candidacy ['kændədəsi] *n, pl* **-cies** : candidatura *f*

candidate ['kændəˌdeɪt, -dət] *n* : candidato *m*, -ta *f*

candidly ['kændɪdli] *adv* : con franqueza

candied ['kændid] *adj* : confitado

candle ['kændəl] *n* : vela *f*, candela *f*, cirio *m* (ceremonial)

candlestick ['kændəlˌstɪk] *n* : candelero *m*

candor ['kændər] *n* : franqueza *f*

candy ['kændi] *n, pl* **-dies** : dulce *m*, caramelo *m*

cane¹ ['keɪn] *vt* **caned; caning 1** : tapizar (muebles) con mimbre **2** FLOG : azotar con una vara

cane² *n* **1** : bastón *m* (para andar), vara *f* (para castigar) **2** REED : caña *f*, mimbre *m* (para muebles)

canine¹ ['keɪˌnaɪn] *adj* : canino

canine² *n* **1** DOG : canino *m*; perro *m*, -rra *f* **2** *or* **canine tooth** : colmillo *m*, diente *m* canino

canister ['kænəstər] *n* : lata *f*, bote *m*

canker ['kæŋkər] *n* : úlcera *f* bucal

cannery ['kænəri] *n, pl* **-ries** : fábrica *f* de conservas

cannibal ['kænəbəl] *n* : caníbal *mf*; antropófago *m*, -ga *f*

cannibalism ['kænəbəˌlɪzəm] *n* : canibalismo *m*, antropofagia *f*

cannibalize ['kænəbəˌlaɪz] *vt* **-ized; -izing** : canibalizar

cannily ['kænəli] *adv* : astutamente, sagazmente

cannon ['kænən] *n, pl* **-nons** *or* **-non** : cañón *m*

cannot (can not) ['kænˌat, kə'nat] → **can¹**

canny ['kæni] *adj* **-nier; -est** SHREWD : astuto, sagaz

canoe¹ [kə'nu:] *vt* **-noed; -noeing** : ir en canoa

canoe² *n* : canoa *f*, piragua *f*

canon ['kænən] *n* **1** : canon *m* ⟨canon law : derecho canónico⟩ **2** WORKS : canon *m* ⟨the canon of American literature : el canon de la literatura americana⟩ **3** : canónigo *m* (de una catedral) **4** STANDARD : canon *m*, norma *f*

canonical [kə'nanɪkəl] *adj* : canónico

canonize ['kænəˌnaɪz] *vt* **-ized; -izing** : canonizar

canopy ['kænəpi] *n, pl* **-pies** : dosel *m*, toldo *m*

cant¹ ['kænt] *vt* TILT : ladear, inclinar — *vi* **1** SLANT : ladearse, inclinarse, escorar (dícese de un barco) **2** : hablar insinceramente

cant² *n* **1** SLANT : plano *m* inclinado **2** JARGON : jerga *f* **3** : palabras *fpl* insinceras

can't ['kænt, 'kant] (*contraction of* **can not**) → **can¹**

cantaloupe ['kæntəlˌo:p] *n* : melón *m*, cantalupo *m*

cantankerous [kæn'tæŋkərəs] *adj* : irritable, irascible — **cantankerously** *adv*

cantankerousness [kæn'tæŋkərəsnəs] *n* : irritabilidad *f*, irascibilidad *f*

cantata [kən'tatə] *n* : cantata *f*

canteen [kæn'ti:n] *n* **1** FLASK : cantimplora *f* **2** CAFETERIA : cantina *f*, comedor *m* **3** : club *m* para actividades sociales y recreativas

canter¹ ['kæntər] *vi* : ir a medio galope

canter² *n* : medio galope *m*

cantilever ['kæntəˌlivər, -ˌlevər] *n* **1** : viga *f* voladiza **2 cantilever bridge** : puente *m* voladizo

canto ['kænˌto:] *n, pl* **-tos** : canto *m*

canton ['kæntən, -ˌtan] *n* : cantón *m*

Cantonese [ˌkæntən'i:z, -'i:s] *n* **1** : cantonés *m*, -nesa *f* **2** : cantonés *m* (idioma) — **Cantonese** *adj*

cantor ['kæntər] *n* : solista *mf*

canvas ['kænvəs] *n* **1** : lona *f* **2** SAILS : velas *fpl* (de un barco) **3** : lienzo *m*, tela *f* (de pintar) **4** PAINTING : pintura *f*, óleo *m*, cuadro *m*

canvass¹ ['kænvəs] *vt* **1** SOLICIT : solicitar votos o pedidos de, hacer campaña entre **2** SOUND OUT : sondear (opiniones, etc.)

canvass² *n* SURVEY : sondeo *m*, encuesta *f*

canyon ['kænjən] *n* : cañón *m*

cap¹ ['kæp] *vt* **capped; capping 1** COVER : tapar (un recipiente), enfundar (un diente), cubrir (una montaña) **2** CLIMAX : coronar, ser el punto culminante de ⟨to cap it all off : para colmo⟩ **3** LIMIT : limitar, poner un tope a

cap² *n* **1** : gorra *f*, gorro *m*, cachucha *f* *Mex* ⟨baseball cap : gorra de béisbol⟩

2 COVER, TOP : tapa *f*, tapón *m* (de botellas), corcholata *f Mex* 3 LIMIT : tope *m*, límite *m*

capability [ˌkeɪpəˈbɪləti] *n, pl* **-ties** : capacidad *f*, habilidad *f*, competencia *f*

capable [ˈkeɪpəbəl] *adj* : competente, capaz, hábil — **capably** [-bli] *adv*

capacious [kəˈpeɪʃəs] *adj* : amplio, espacioso, de gran capacidad

capacity[1] [kəˈpæsəti] *adj* : completo, total ⟨a capacity crowd : un lleno completo⟩

capacity[2] *n, pl* **-ties** 1 ROOM, SPACE : capacidad *f*, cabida *f*, espacio *m* 2 CAPABILITY : habilidad *f*, competencia *f* 3 FUNCTION, ROLE : calidad *f*, función *f* ⟨in his capacity as ambassador : en su calidad de embajador⟩

cape [ˈkeɪp] *n* 1 : capa *f* 2 : cabo *m* ⟨Cape Horn : el Cabo de Hornos⟩

caper[1] [ˈkeɪpər] *vi* : dar saltos, correr y brincar

caper[2] *n* 1 : alcaparra *f* ⟨olives and capers : aceitunas y alcaparras⟩ 2 ANTIC, PRANK : broma *f*, travesura *f* 3 LEAP : brinco *m*, salto *m*

Cape Verdean [ˈkeɪpˈvərdiən] *n* : caboverdiano *m*, -na *f* — **Cape Verdean** *adj*

capful [ˈkæpˌfʊl] *n* : tapa *f*, tapita *f*

capillary[1] [ˈkæpəˌlɛri] *adj* : capilar

capillary[2] *n, pl* **-ries** : capilar *m*

capital[1] [ˈkæpətəl] *adj* 1 : capital ⟨capital punishment : pena capital⟩ 2 : mayúsculo (dícese de las letras) 3 : de capital ⟨capital assets : activo fijo⟩ ⟨capital gain : ganancia de capital, plusvalía⟩ 4 EXCELLENT : excelente, estupendo

capital[2] *n* 1 *or* **capital city** : capital *f*, sede *f* del gobierno 2 WEALTH : capital *m* 3 *or* **capital letter** : mayúscula *f* 4 : capitel *m* (de una columna)

capitalism [ˈkæpətəlˌɪzəm] *n* : capitalismo *m*

capitalist[1] [ˈkæpətəlɪst] *or* **capitalistic** [ˌkæpətəlˈɪstɪk] *adj* : capitalista

capitalist[2] *n* : capitalista *mf*

capitalization [ˌkæpətələˈzeɪʃən] *n* : capitalización *f*

capitalize [ˈkæpətəlˌaɪz] *v* **-ized; -izing** *vt* 1 FINANCE : capitalizar, financiar 2 : escribir con mayúscula — *vi* **to capitalize on** : sacar partido de, aprovechar

capitol [ˈkæpətəl] *n* : capitolio *m*

capitulate [kəˈpɪtʃəˌleɪt] *vi* **-lated; -lating** : capitular

capitulation [kəˌpɪtʃəˈleɪʃən] *n* : capitulación *f*

capon [ˈkeɪˌpɑn, -pən] *n* : capón *m*

cappuccino [ˌkɑpəˈtʃiːnoː] *n* : capuchino *m* (café)

caprice [kəˈpriːs] *n* : capricho *m*, antojo *m*

capricious [kəˈprɪʃəs, -ˈpriː-] *adj* : caprichoso — **capriciously** *adv*

Capricorn [ˈkæprɪˌkɔrn] *n* : Capricornio *mf*

capsize [ˈkæpˌsaɪz, kæpˈsaɪz] *v* **-sized; -sizing** *vi* : volcar, volcarse — *vt* : hacer volcar

capstan [ˈkæpstən, -ˌstæn] *n* : cabrestante *m*

capsule [ˈkæpsəl, -ˌsuːl] *n* 1 : cápsula *f* (en la farmacéutica y botánica) 2 **space capsule** : cápsula *f* espacial

captain[1] [ˈkæptən] *vt* : capitanear

captain[2] *n* 1 : capitán *m*, -tana *f* 2 HEADWAITER : jefe *m*, -fa *f* de comedor 3 **captain of industry** : magnate *mf*

caption[1] [ˈkæpʃən] *vt* : ponerle una leyenda a (una ilustración), titular (un artículo), subtitular (una película)

caption[2] *n* 1 HEADING : titular *m*, encabezamiento *m* 2 : leyenda *f* (al pie de una ilustración) 3 SUBTITLE : subtítulo *m*

captivate [ˈkæptəˌveɪt] *vt* **-vated; -vating** CHARM : cautivar, hechizar, encantar

captivating [ˈkæptəˌveɪtɪŋ] *adj* : cautivador, hechicero, encantador

captive[1] [ˈkæptɪv] *adj* : cautivo

captive[2] *n* : cautivo *m*, -va *f*

captivity [kæpˈtɪvəti] *n* : cautiverio *m*

captor [ˈkæptər] *n* : captor *m*, -tora *f*

capture[1] [ˈkæpʃər] *vt* **-tured; -turing** 1 SEIZE : capturar, apresar 2 CATCH : capturar ⟨to capture one's interest : captar el interés de uno⟩

capture[2] *n* : captura *f*, apresamiento *m*

car [ˈkɑr] *n* 1 AUTOMOBILE : automóvil *m*, coche *m*, carro *m* 2 : vagón *m*, coche *m* (de un tren) 3 : cabina *f* (de un ascensor)

carafe [kəˈræf, -ˈrɑf] *n* : garrafa *f*

caramel [ˈkɑrməl; ˈkærəməl, -ˌmɛl] *n* 1 : caramelo *m*, azúcar *f* quemada 2 *or* **caramel candy** : caramelo *m*, dulce *m* de leche

carat [ˈkærət] *n* : quilate *m*

caravan [ˈkærəˌvæn] *n* : caravana *f*

caraway [ˈkærəˌweɪ] *n* : alcaravea *f*

carbine [ˈkɑrˌbaɪn, -ˌbiːn] *n* : carabina *f*

carbohydrate [ˌkɑrboˈhaɪˌdreɪt, -drət] *n* : carbohidrato *m*, hidrato *m* de carbono

carbon [ˈkɑrbən] *n* 1 : carbono *m* 2 → **carbon paper** 3 → **carbon copy**

carbonated [ˈkɑrbəˌneɪtəd] *adj* : carbonatado (dícese del agua), gaseoso (dícese de las bebidas)

carbon copy *n* 1 : copia *f* al carbón 2 DUPLICATE : duplicado *m*, copia *f* exacta

carbon paper *n* : papel *m* carbón

carbuncle [ˈkɑrˌbʌŋkəl] *n* : carbunco *m*

carburetor [ˈkɑrbəˌreɪtər, -bjə-] *n* : carburador *m*

carcass [ˈkɑrkəs] *n* : cuerpo *m* (de un animal muerto)

carcinogen [kɑrˈsɪnədʒən, ˈkɑrsənəˌdʒɛn] *n* : carcinógeno *m*, cancerígeno *m*

carcinogenic [ˌkɑrsənoˈdʒɛnɪk] *adj* : carcinogénico

carcinoma [ˌkɑrsəˈnoːmə] *n* : carcinoma *m*

card¹ ['kɑrd] *vt* : cardar (fibras)
card² *n* **1** : carta *f*, naipe *m* ⟨to play cards : jugar a las cartas⟩ ⟨a deck of cards : una baraja⟩ **2** : tarjeta *f* ⟨birthday card : tarjeta de cumpleaños⟩ ⟨business card : tarjeta (de visita)⟩
cardboard ['kɑrd,bord] *n* : cartón *m*, cartulina *f*
cardiac ['kɑrdi,æk] *adj* : cardíaco, cardiaco
cardigan ['kɑrdɪgən] *n* : cárdigan *m*, chaqueta *f* de punto
cardinal¹ ['kɑrdənəl] *adj* FUNDAMENTAL : cardinal, fundamental
cardinal² *n* : cardenal *m*
cardinal number *n* : número *m* cardinal
cardinal point *n* : punto *m* cardinal
cardiologist [,kɑrdi'ɑləʤɪst] *n* : cardiólogo *m*, -ga *f*
cardiology [,kɑrdi'ɑləʤi] *n* : cardiología *f*
cardiovascular [,kɑrdio'væskjələr] *adj* : cardiovascular
care¹ ['kær] *v* cared; caring *vi* **1** : importarle a uno ⟨they don't care : no les importa⟩ **2** : preocuparse, inquietarse ⟨she cares about the poor : se preocupa por los pobres⟩ **3 to care for** TEND : cuidar (de), atender, encargarse de **4 to care for** CHERISH : querer, sentir cariño por **5 to care for** LIKE : gustarle (algo a uno) ⟨I don't care for your attitude : tu actitud no me agrada⟩ — *vt* WISH : desear, querer ⟨if you care to go : si deseas ir⟩
care² *n* **1** ANXIETY : inquietud *f*, preocupación *f* **2** CAREFULNESS : cuidado *m*, atención *f* ⟨handle with care : manejar con cuidado⟩ **3** CHARGE : cargo *m*, cuidado *m* **4 to take care of** : cuidar (de), atender, encargarse de
careen [kə'ri:n] *vi* **1** SWAY : oscilar, balancearse **2** CAREER : ir a toda velocidad
career¹ [kə'rɪr] *vi* : ir a toda velocidad
career² *n* VOCATION : vocación *f*, profesión *f*, carrera *f*
carefree ['kær,fri:, ,kær'-] *adj* : despreocupado
careful ['kærfəl] *adj* **1** CAUTIOUS : cuidadoso, cauteloso **2** PAINSTAKING : cuidadoso, esmerado, meticuloso
carefully ['kærfəli] *adv* : con cuidado, cuidadosamente
carefulness ['kærfəlnəs] *n* **1** CAUTION : cuidado *m*, cautela *f* **2** METICULOUSNESS : esmero *m*, meticulosidad *f*
caregiver ['kær,gɪvər] *n* : persona *f* que cuida a niños o enfermos
careless ['kærləs] *adj* : descuidado, negligente — **carelessly** *adv*
carelessness ['kærləsnəs] *n* : descuido *m*, negligencia *f*
caress¹ [kə'rɛs] *vt* : acariciar
caress² *n* : caricia *f*
caret ['kærət] *n* : signo *m* de intercalación
caretaker ['kɛr,teɪkər] *n* : conserje *mf*; velador *m*, -dora *f*

cargo ['kɑr,go:] *n*, *pl* **-goes** *or* **-gos** : cargamento *m*, carga *f*
Caribbean [kærə'bi:ən, kə'rɪbiən] *adj* : caribeño ⟨the Caribbean Sea : el mar Caribe⟩
caribou ['kærə,bu:] *n*, *pl* **-bou** *or* **-bous** : caribú *m*
caricature¹ ['kærɪkə,tʃur] *vt* **-tured; -turing** : caricaturizar
caricature² *n* : caricatura *f*
caricaturist ['kærɪkə,tʃurɪst] *n* : caricaturista *mf*
caries ['kær,i:z] *ns & pl* : caries *f*
carillon ['kærə,lɑn] *n* : carillón *m*
carmine ['kɑrmən, -,maɪn] *n* : carmín *m*
carnage ['kɑrnɪʤ] *n* : matanza *f*, carnicería *f*
carnal ['kɑrnəl] *adj* : carnal
carnation [kɑr'neɪʃən] *n* : clavel *m*
carnival ['kɑrnəvəl] *n* : carnaval *m*, feria *f*
carnivore ['kɑrnə,vor] *n* : carnívoro *m*
carnivorous [kɑr'nɪvərəs] *adj* : carnívoro
carol¹ ['kærəl] *vi* **-oled** *or* **-olled; -oling** *or* **-olling** : cantar villancicos
carol² *n* : villancico *m*
caroler *or* **caroller** ['kærələr] *n* : persona *f* que canta villancicos
carom¹ ['kærəm] *vi* **1** REBOUND : rebotar ⟨the bullet caromed off the wall : la bala rebotó contra el muro⟩ **2** : hacer carambola (en billar)
carom² *n* : carambola *f*
carouse [kə'rauz] *vt* **-roused; -rousing** : irse de parranda, irse de juerga
carousel *or* **carrousel** [,kærə'sɛl, 'kærə,-] *n* : carrusel *m*, tiovivo *m*
carouser [kə'rauzər] *n* : juerguista *mf*
carp¹ ['kɑrp] *vi* **1** COMPLAIN : quejarse **2 to carp at** : criticar
carp² *n*, *pl* **carp** *or* **carps** : carpa *f*
carpel ['kɑrpəl] *n* : carpelo *m*
carpenter ['kɑrpəntər] *n* : carpintero *m*, -ra *f*
carpentry ['kɑrpəntri] *n* : carpintería *f*
carpet¹ ['kɑrpət] *vt* : alfombrar
carpet² *n* : alfombra *f*
carpeting ['kɑrpətɪŋ] *n* : alfombrado *m*
carport ['kɑr,port] *n* : cochera *f*, garaje *m* abierto
carriage ['kærɪʤ] *n* **1** TRANSPORT : transporte *m* **2** POSTURE : porte *m*, postura *f* **3 horse-drawn carriage** : carruaje *m*, coche *m* **4 baby carriage** : cochecito *m*
carrier ['kæriər] *n* **1** : transportista *mf*, empresa *f* de transportes **2** : portador *m*, -dora *f* (de una enfermedad) **3 aircraft carrier** : portaaviones *m*
carrier pigeon : paloma *f* mensajera
carrion ['kæriən] *n* : carroña *f*
carrot ['kærət] *n* : zanahoria *f*
carry ['kæri] *v* **-ried; -rying** *vt* **1** TRANSPORT : llevar, cargar, transportar (cargamento), conducir (electricidad), portar (un virus) ⟨to carry a bag : cargar una bolsa⟩ ⟨to carry money : llevar dinero encima, traer dinero consi-

go〉 **2** BEAR : soportar, aguantar, resistir (peso) **3** STOCK : vender, tener en abasto **4** ENTAIL : llevar, implicar, acarrear **5** WIN : ganar (una elección o competición), aprobar (una moción) **6 to carry oneself** : portarse, comportarse 〈he carried himself honorably : se comportó dignamente〉 — *vi* : oírse, proyectarse 〈her voice carries well : su voz se puede oír desde lejos〉

carryall ['kæri,ɔl] *n* : bolsa *f* de viaje

carry away *vt* **to get carried away** : exaltarse, entusiasmarse

carry on *vt* CONDUCT : realizar, ejercer, mantener 〈to carry on research : realizar investigaciones〉 〈to carry on a correspondence : mantener una correspondencia〉 — *vi* **1** : portarse de manera escandalosa o inapropiada 〈it's embarrassing how he carries on : su manera de comportarse da vergüenza〉 **2** CONTINUE : seguir, continuar

carry out *vt* **1** PERFORM : llevar a cabo, realizar **2** FULFILL : cumplir

cart[1] ['kɑrt] *vt* : acarrear, llevar

cart[2] *n* : carreta *f*, carro *m*

cartel [kɑr'tɛl] *n* : cártel *m*

cartilage ['kɑrtǝlɪʤ] *n* : cartílago *m*

cartilaginous [,kɑrtǝl'æʤǝnǝs] *adj* : cartilaginoso

cartographer [kɑr'tɑgrǝfǝr] *n* : cartógrafo *m*, -fa *f*

cartography [kɑr'tɑgrǝfi] *n* : cartografía *f*

carton ['kɑrtǝn] *n* : caja *f* de cartón

cartoon [kɑr'tu:n] *n* **1** : chiste *m* (gráfico), caricatura *f* 〈a political cartoon : un chiste político〉 **2** COMIC STRIP : tira *f* cómica, historieta *f* **3** *or* animated cartoon : dibujo *m* animado

cartoonist [kɑr'tu:nɪst] *n* : caricaturista *mf*, dibujante *mf* (de chistes)

cartridge ['kɑrtrɪʤ] *n* : cartucho *m*

carve ['kɑrv] *vt* **carved; carving 1** : tallar (madera), esculpir (piedra), grabar 〈he carved his name in the bark : grabó su nombre en la corteza〉 **2** SLICE : cortar, trinchar (carne)

cascade[1] [kæs'keɪd] *vi* **-caded; -cading** : caer en cascada

cascade[2] *n* : cascada *f*, salto *m* de agua

case[1] ['keɪs] *vt* **cased; casing 1** BOX, PACK : embalar, encajonar **2** INSPECT : observar, inspeccionar (antes de cometer un delito)

case[2] *n* **1** : caso *m* 〈an unusual case : un caso insólito〉 〈ablative case : caso ablativo〉 〈a case of the flu : un caso de gripe〉 **2** BOX : caja *f* **3** CONTAINER : funda *f*, estuche *m* **4 in any case** : de todos modos, en cualquier caso **5 in case** : como precaución 〈just in case : por si acaso〉 **6 in case of** : en caso de

casement ['keɪsmǝnt] *n* : ventana *f* con bisagras

cash[1] ['kæʃ] *vt* : convertir en efectivo, cobrar, cambiar (un cheque)

cash[2] *n* : efectivo *m*, dinero *m* en efectivo

cashew ['kæ,ʃu:, kǝ'ʃu:] *n* : anacardo *m*

cashier[1] [kæ'ʃɪr] *vt* : destituir, despedir

cashier[2] *n* : cajero *m*, -ra *f*

cashmere ['kæʒ,mɪr, 'kæʃ-] *n* : cachemir *m*

casino [kǝ'si:,no:] *n, pl* **-nos** : casino *m*

cask ['kæsk] *n* : tonel *m*, barrica *f*, barril *m*

casket ['kæskǝt] *n* COFFIN : ataúd *m*, féretro *m*

cassava [kǝ'sɑvǝ] *n* : mandioca *f*, yuca *f*

casserole ['kæsǝ,ro:l] *n* **1** : cazuela *f* **2** : guiso *m*, guisado *m* 〈tuna casserole : guiso de atún〉

cassette [kǝ'sɛt, kæ-] *n* : cassette *mf*

cassock ['kæsǝk] *n* : sotana *f*

cast[1] ['kæst] *vt* **cast; casting 1** THROW : tirar, echar, arrojar 〈the die is cast : la suerte está echada〉 **2** : depositar (un voto) **3** : asignar (papeles en una obra de teatro) **4** MOLD : moldear, fundir, vaciar **5 to cast off** ABANDON : desamparar, abandonar

cast[2] *n* **1** THROW : lance *m*, lanzamiento *m* **2** APPEARANCE : aspecto *m*, forma *f* **3** : elenco *m*, reparto *m* (de una obra de teatro) **4 plaster cast** : molde *m* de yeso, escayola *f*

castanets [,kæstǝ'nɛts] *npl* : castañuelas *fpl*

castaway[1] ['kæstǝ,weɪ] *adj* : náufrago

castaway[2] *n* : náufrago *m*, -ga *f*

caste ['kæst] *n* : casta *f*

caster ['kæstǝr] *n* : ruedita *f* (de un mueble)

castigate ['kæstǝ,geɪt] *vt* **-gated; -gating** : castigar severamente, censurar, reprobar

Castilian [kæ'stɪljǝn] *n* **1** : castellano *m*, -na *f* **2** : castellano *m* (idioma) — **Castilian** *adj*

cast iron *n* : hierro *m* fundido

castle ['kæsǝl] *n* **1** : castillo *m* **2** : torre *f* (en ajedrez)

cast–off ['kæst,ɔf] *adj* : desechado

castoff ['kæst,ɔf] *n* : desecho *m*

castrate ['kæs,treɪt] *vt* **-trated; -trating** : castrar

castration [kæ'streɪʃǝn] *n* : castración *f*

casual ['kæʒuǝl] *adj* **1** FORTUITOUS : casual, fortuito **2** INDIFFERENT : indiferente, despreocupado **3** INFORMAL : informal — **casually** ['kæʒuǝli, 'kæʒǝli] *adv*

casualness ['kæʒuǝlnǝs] *n* **1** FORTUITOUSNESS : casualidad *f* **2** INDIFFERENCE : indiferencia *f*, despreocupación *f* **3** INFORMALITY : informalidad *f*

casualty ['kæʒuǝlti, 'kæʒǝl-] *n, pl* **-ties 1** ACCIDENT : accidente *m* serio, desastre *m* **2** VICTIM : víctima *f*; baja *f*; herido *m*, -da *f*

cat ['kæt] *n* : gato *m*, -ta *f*

cataclysm ['kætǝ,klɪzǝm] *n* : cataclismo *m*

cataclysmal [ˌkætəˈklɪzməl] or cataclysmic [ˌkætəˈklɪzmɪk] adj : catastrófico

catacombs [ˈkætəˌkoːmz] npl : catacumbas fpl

Catalan [ˈkætələn, -ˌlæn] n 1 : catalán m, catalana f 2 : catalán m (idioma) — Catalan adj

catalog¹ or catalogue [ˈkætəˌlɔg] vt -loged or -logued; -loging or -loguing : catalogar

catalog² n : catálogo m

catalyst [ˈkætələst] n : catalizador m

catalytic [ˌkætəlˈɪtɪk] adj : catalítico

catamaran [ˌkætəməˈræn, ˈkætəməˌræn] n : catamarán m

catapult¹ [ˈkætəˌpʌlt, -ˌpʊlt] vt : catapultar

catapult² n : catapulta f

cataract [ˈkætəˌrækt] n : catarata f

catarrh [kəˈtɑr] n : catarro m

catastrophe [kəˈtæstrəˌfiː] n : catástrofe f

catastrophic [ˌkætəˈstrɑfɪk] adj : catastrófico — catastrophically [-fɪkli] adv

catcall [ˈkætˌkɔl] n : rechifla f, abucheo m

catch¹ [ˈkætʃ, ˈkɛtʃ] v caught [ˈkɔt]; catching vt 1 CAPTURE, TRAP : capturar, agarrar, atrapar, coger 2 : agarrar, pillar fam, tomar de sorpresa ⟨they caught him red-handed : lo pillaron con las manos en la masa⟩ 3 GRASP : agarrar, captar 4 ENTANGLE : enganchar, enredar 5 : tomar (un tren, etc.) 6 : contagiarse de ⟨to catch a cold : contagiarse de un resfriado, resfriarse⟩ — vi 1 GRASP : agarrar 2 HOOK : engancharse 3 IGNITE : prender, agarrar

catch² n 1 CATCHING : captura f, atrapada f, parada f (de una pelota) 2 : redada f (de pescado), presa f (de caza) ⟨he's a good catch : es un buen partido⟩ 3 LATCH : pestillo m, pasador m 4 DIFFICULTY, TRICK : problema m, trampa f, truco m

catcher [ˈkætʃər, ˈkɛ-] n : catcher mf; receptor m, -tora f (en béisbol)

catching [ˈkætʃɪŋ, ˈkɛ-] adj : contagioso

catchup [ˈkætʃəp, ˈkɛ-] → ketchup

catchword [ˈkætʃˌwərd, ˈkɛtʃ-] n : eslogan m, lema m

catchy [ˈkætʃi, ˈkɛ-] adj catchier; -est : pegajoso ⟨a catchy song : una canción pegajosa⟩

catechism [ˈkætəˌkɪzəm] n : catecismo m

categorical [ˌkætəˈgɔrɪkəl] adj : categórico, absoluto, rotundo — categorically [-kli] adv

categorize [ˈkætɪgəˌraɪz] vt -rized; -rizing : clasificar, catalogar

category [ˈkætəˌgɔri] n, pl -ries : categoría f, género m, clase f

cater [ˈkeɪtər] vi 1 : proveer alimentos (para fiestas, bodas, etc.) 2 to cater to : atender a ⟨to cater to all tastes : atender a todos los gustos⟩

catercorner¹ [ˈkætiˌkɔrnər, ˈkætə-, ˈkɪti-] or cater–cornered [-ˌkɔrnərd] adv : diagonalmente, en diagonal

catercorner² or cater–cornered adj : diagonal

caterer [ˈkeɪtərər] n : proveedor m, -dora f de comida

caterpillar [ˈkætərˌpɪlər] n : oruga f

catfish [ˈkætˌfɪʃ] n : bagre m

catgut [ˈkætˌgʌt] n : cuerda f de tripa

catharsis [kəˈθɑrsɪs] n, pl catharses [-ˌsiːz] : catarsis f

cathartic¹ [kəˈθɑrtɪk] adj : catártico

cathartic² n : purgante m

cathedral [kəˈθiːdrəl] n : catedral f

catheter [ˈkæθətər] n : catéter m, sonda f

cathode [ˈkæˌθoːd] n : cátodo m

catholic [ˈkæθəlɪk] adj 1 BROAD, UNIVERSAL : liberal, universal 2 Catholic : católico

Catholic n : católico m, -ca f

Catholicism [kəˈθɑləˌsɪzəm] n : catolicismo m

catlike [ˈkætˌlaɪk] adj : gatuno, felino

catnap¹ [ˈkætˌnæp] vi -napped; -napping : tomarse una siestecita

catnap² n : siesta f breve, siestecita f

catnip [ˈkætˌnɪp] n : nébeda f

catsup [ˈkɛtʃəp, ˈkætsəp] → ketchup

cattail [ˈkætˌteɪl] n : espadaña f, anea f

cattiness [ˈkætinəs] n : malicia f

cattle [ˈkætəl] npl : ganado m, reses fpl

cattleman [ˈkætəlmən, -ˌmæn] n, pl -men [-mən, -ˌmɛn] : ganadero m

catty [ˈkæti] adj -tier; -est : malicioso, malintencionado

catwalk [ˈkætˌwɔk] n : pasarela f

Caucasian¹ [kɔˈkeɪʒən] adj : caucásico

Caucasian² n : caucásico m, -ca f

caucus [ˈkɔkəs] n : junta f de políticos

caught → catch

cauldron [ˈkɔldrən] n : caldera f

cauliflower [ˈkɑlɪˌflaʊər, ˈkɔ-] n : coliflor f

caulk¹ [ˈkɔk] vt : calafatear (un barco), enmasillar (una grieta)

caulk² n : masilla f

causal [ˈkɔzəl] adj : causal

causality [kɔˈzæləti] n : causalidad f

cause¹ [ˈkɔz] vt caused; causing : causar, provocar, ocasionar

cause² n 1 ORIGIN : causa f, origen m 2 REASON : causa f, razón f, motivo m 3 LAWSUIT : litigio m, pleito m 4 MOVEMENT : causa f, movimiento m

causeless [ˈkɔzləs] adj : sin causa

causeway [ˈkɔzˌweɪ] n : camino m elevado

caustic [ˈkɔstɪk] adj 1 CORROSIVE : cáustico, corrosivo 2 BITING : mordaz, sarcástico

cauterize [ˈkɔtəˌraɪz] vt -ized; -izing : cauterizar

caution¹ [ˈkɔʃən] vt : advertir

caution² n 1 WARNING : advertencia f, aviso m 2 CARE, PRUDENCE : precaución f, cuidado m, cautela f

cautionary ['kɔʃə,nɛri] *adv* : admonitorio ⟨cautionary tale : cuento moral⟩

cautious ['kɔʃəs] *adj* : cauteloso, cuidadoso, precavido

cautiously ['kɔʃəsli] *adv* : cautelosamente, con precaución

cautiousness ['kɔʃəsnəs] *n* : cautela *f*, precaución *f*

cavalcade [,kævəl'keɪd, 'kævəl,-] *n* **1** : cabalgata *f* **2** SERIES : serie *f*

cavalier[1] [,kævə'lɪr] *adj* : altivo, desdeñoso — **cavalierly** *adv*

cavalier[2] *n* : caballero *m*

cavalry ['kævəlri] *n, pl* **-ries** : caballería *f*

cave[1] ['keɪv] *vi* **caved; caving** *or* **to cave in** : derrumbarse

cave[2] *n* : cueva *f*

cavern ['kævərn] *n* : caverna *f*

cavernous ['kævərnəs] *adj* : cavernoso — **cavernously** *adv*

caviar *or* **caviare** ['kævi,ɑr, 'kɑ-] *n* : caviar *m*

cavity ['kævəti] *n, pl* **-ties 1** HOLE : cavidad *f*, hueco *m* **2** CARIES : caries *f*

cavort [kə'vɔrt] *vi* : brincar, hacer cabriolas

caw[1] ['kɔ] *vi* : graznar

caw[2] *n* : graznido *m*

cayenne pepper [,kaɪ'ɛn, ,keɪ-] *n* : pimienta *f* cayena, pimentón *m*

CD [,si:'di:] *n* : CD *m*, disco *m* compacto

CD–ROM [,si:,di:'ram] *n* : CD-ROM *m*

cease ['si:s] *v* **ceased; ceasing** *vt* : dejar de ⟨they ceased bickering : dejaron de discutir⟩ — *vi* : cesar, pasarse

ceaseless ['si:sləs] *adj* : incesante, continuo

cedar ['si:dər] *n* : cedro *m*

cede ['si:d] *vt* **ceded; ceding** : ceder, conceder

ceiling ['si:lɪŋ] *n* **1** : techo *m*, cielo *m* raso **2** LIMIT : límite *m*, tope *m*

celebrant ['sɛləbrənt] *n* : celebrante *mf*, oficiante *mf*

celebrate ['sɛlə,breɪt] *v* **-brated; -brating** *vt* **1** : celebrar, oficiar ⟨to celebrate Mass : celebrar la misa⟩ **2** : celebrar, festejar ⟨we're celebrating our anniversary : estamos celebrando nuestro aniversario⟩ **3** EXTOL : alabar, ensalzar, exaltar — *vi* : estar de fiesta, divertirse

celebrated ['sɛlə,breɪtəd] *adj* : célebre, famoso, renombrado

celebration [,sɛlə'breɪʃən] *n* : celebración *f*, festejos *mpl*

celebrity [sə'lɛbrəti] *n, pl* **-ties 1** RENOWN : fama *f*, renombre *m*, celebridad *f* **2** PERSONALITY : celebridad *f*, personaje *m*

celery ['sɛləri] *n, pl* **-eries** : apio *m*

celestial [sə'lɛstʃəl, -'lstiəl] *adj* **1** : celeste **2** HEAVENLY : celestial, paradisiaco

celibacy ['sɛləbəsi] *n* : celibato *m*

celibate[1] ['sɛləbət] *adj* : célibe

celibate[2] *n* : célibe *mf*

cell ['sɛl] *n* **1** : célula *f* (de un organismo) **2** : celda *f* (en una cárcel, etc.) **3** : elemento *m* (de una pila)

cellar ['sɛlər] *n* **1** BASEMENT : sótano *m* **2** : bodega *f* (de vinos)

cellist ['tʃɛlɪst] *n* : violonchelista *mf*

cello ['tʃɛ,lo:] *n, pl* **-los** : violonchelo *m*

cellophane ['sɛlə,feɪn] *n* : celofán *m*

cell phone *n* : teléfono *m* celular

cellular ['sɛljələr] *adj* : celular

celluloid ['sɛljə,lɔɪd] *n* : celuloide

cellulose ['sɛljə,lo:s] *n* : celulosa *f*

Celsius ['sɛlsiəs] *adj* : centígrado ⟨100 degrees Celsius : 100 grados centígrados⟩

Celt ['kɛlt, 'sɛlt] *n* : celta *mf*

Celtic[1] ['kɛltɪk, 'sɛl-] *adj* : celta

Celtic[2] *n* : celta *m*

cement[1] [sɪ'mɛnt] *vi* : unir o cubrir algo con cemento, cementar

cement[2] *n* **1** : cemento *m* **2** GLUE : pegamento *m*

cemetery ['sɛmə,tɛri] *n, pl* **-teries** : cementerio *m*, panteón *m*

censer ['sɛntsər] *n* : incensario *m*

censor[1] ['sɛntsər] *vt* : censurar

censor[2] *n* : censor *m*, -sora *f*

censorious [sɛn'soriəs] *adj* : de censura, crítico

censorship ['sɛntsər,ʃɪp] *n* : censura *f*

censure[1] ['sɛntʃər] *vt* **-sured; -suring** : censurar, criticar, reprobar — **censurable** [-tʃərəbəl] *adj*

censure[2] *n* : censura *f*, reproche *m* oficial

census ['sɛntsəs] *n* : censo *m*

cent ['sɛnt] *n* : centavo *m*

centaur ['sɛn,tɔr] *n* : centauro *m*

centennial[1] [sɛn'tɛniəl] *adj* : del centenario

centennial[2] *n* : centenario *m*

center[1] ['sɛntər] *vt* **1** : centrar **2** CONCENTRATE : concentrar, fijar, enfocar — *vi* : centrarse, enfocarse

center[2] *n* **1** : centro *m* ⟨center of gravity : centro de gravedad⟩ **2** : centro *mf* (en el futbol americano), pívot *mf* (en basquetbol)

centerpiece ['sɛntər,pi:s] *n* : centro *m* de mesa

centigrade ['sɛntə,greɪd, 'san-] *adj* : centígrado

centigram ['sɛntə,græm, 'san-] *n* : centigramo *m*

centimeter ['sɛntə,mi:ṭər, 'san-] *n* : centímetro *m*

centipede ['sɛntə,pi:d] *n* : ciempiés *m*

central ['sɛntrəl] *adj* **1** : céntrico, central ⟨in a central location : en un lugar céntrico⟩ **2** MAIN, PRINCIPAL : central, fundamental, principal

Central American[1] *adj* : centroamericano

Central American[2] *n* : centroamericano *m*, -na *f*

centralization [,sɛntrələ'zeɪʃən] *n* : centralización *f*

centralize ['sɛntrə,laɪz] *vt* **-ized; -izing** : centralizar

centrally ['sɛntrəli] *adv* **1 centrally heated** : con calefacción central **2 centrally located** : céntrico, en un lugar céntrico

centre ['sɛntər] → **center**

centrifugal [sɛn'trɪfjəgəl, -'trɪfɪ-] *adj* : centrífugo

centrifugal force *n* : fuerza *f* centrífuga

century ['sɛntʃəri] *n*, *pl* **-ries** : siglo *m*

ceramic[1] [sə'ræmɪk] *adj* : de cerámica

ceramic[2] *n* **1** : objeto *m* de cerámica, cerámica *f* **2 ceramics** *npl* : cerámica *f*

cereal[1] ['sɪriəl] *adj* : cereal

cereal[2] *n* : cereal *m*

cerebellum [ˌsɛrə'bɛləm] *n*, *pl* **-bellums** *or* **-bella** [-'bɛlə] : cerebelo *m*

cerebral [sə'riːbrəl, 'sɛrə-] *adj* : cerebral

cerebral palsy *n* : parálisis *f* cerebral

cerebrum [sə'riːbrəm, 'sɛrə-] *n*, *pl* **-brums** *or* **-bra** [-brə] : cerebro *m*

ceremonial[1] [ˌsɛrə'moːniəl] *adj* : ceremonial

ceremonial[2] *n* : ceremonial *m*

ceremonious [ˌsɛrə'moːniəs] *adj* **1** FORMAL : ceremonioso, formal **2** CEREMONIAL : ceremonial

ceremony ['sɛrəˌmoːni] *n*, *pl* **-nies** : ceremonia *f*

cerise [sə'riːs] *n* : rojo *m* cereza

certain[1] ['sərtən] *adj* **1** DEFINITE : cierto, determinado ⟨a certain percentage : un porcentaje determinado⟩ **2** TRUE : cierto, con certeza ⟨I don't know for certain : no sé exactamente⟩ **3** : cierto, alguno ⟨it has a certain charm : tiene cierta gracia⟩ **4** INEVITABLE : seguro, inevitable **5** ASSURED : seguro, asegurado ⟨she's certain to do well : seguro que le irá bien⟩

certain[2] *pron* : ciertos *pl*, algunos *pl* ⟨certain of my friends : algunos de mis amigos⟩

certainly ['sərtənli] *adv* **1** DEFINITELY : ciertamente, seguramente **2** OF COURSE : por supuesto

certainty ['sərtənti] *n*, *pl* **-ties** : certeza *f*, certidumbre *f*, seguridad *f*

certifiable [ˌsərtə'faɪəbəl] *adj* : certificable

certificate [sər'tɪfɪkət] *n* : certificado *m*, acta *f* ⟨birth certificate : acta de nacimiento⟩

certification [ˌsərtəfə'keɪʃən] *n* : certificación *f*

certify ['sərtəˌfaɪ] *vt* **-fied; -fying 1** VERIFY : certificar, verificar, confirmar **2** ENDORSE : endosar, aprobar oficialmente

certitude ['sərtəˌtuːd, -ˌtjuːd] *n* : certeza *f*, certidumbre *f*

cervical ['sərvɪkəl] *adj* **1** : cervical (dícese del cuello) **2** : del cuello del útero

cervix ['sərvɪks] *n*, *pl* **-vices** [-və-ˌsiːz] *or* **-vixes 1** NECK : cerviz *f* **2** *or* **uterine cervix** : cuello *m* del útero

cesarean[1] [sɪ'zæriən] *adj* : cesáreo

cesarean[2] *n* : cesárea *f*

cesium ['siːziəm] *n* : cesio *m*

cessation [s'seɪʃən] *n* : cesación *f*, cese *m*

cesspool ['sɛsˌpuːl] *n* : pozo *m* séptico

Chadian ['tʃædiən] *n* : chadiano *m*, -na *f* — **Chadian** *adj*

chafe ['tʃeɪf] *v* **chafed; chafing** *vi* : enojarse, irritarse — *vt* : rozar

chaff ['tʃæf] *n* **1** : barcia *f*, granzas *fpl* **2 to separate the wheat from the chaff** : separar el grano de la paja

chafing dish ['tʃeɪfɪŋˌdɪʃ] *n* : escalfador *m*

chagrin[1] [ʃə'grɪn] *vt* : desilusionar, avergonzar

chagrin[2] *n* : desilusión *f*, disgusto *m*

chain[1] ['tʃeɪn] *vt* : encadenar

chain[2] *n* **1** : cadena *f* ⟨steel chain : cadena de acero⟩ ⟨restaurant chain : cadena de restaurantes⟩ **2** SERIES : serie *f* ⟨chain of events : serie de eventos⟩ **3 chains** *npl* FETTERS : grillos *mpl*

chair[1] ['tʃɛr] *vt* : presidir, moderar

chair[2] *n* **1** : silla *f* **2** CHAIRMANSHIP : presidencia *f* **3** → **chairman, chairwoman**

chairman ['tʃɛrmən] *n*, *pl* **-men** [-mən, -ˌmɛn] : presidente *m*

chairmanship ['tʃɛrmənˌʃɪp] *n* : presidencia *f*

chairwoman ['tʃɛrˌwumən] *n*, *pl* **-women** [-ˌwɪmən] : presidenta *f*

chaise longue ['ʃeɪz'lɔŋ] *n*, *pl* **chaise longues** [-lɔŋ, -'lɔŋz] : chaise longue *f*

chalet [ʃæ'leɪ] *n* : chalet *m*, chalé *m*

chalice ['tʃælɪs] *n* : cáliz *m*

chalk[1] ['tʃɔk] *vt* : escribir con tiza

chalk[2] *n* **1** LIMESTONE : creta *f*, caliza *f* **2** : tiza *f*, gis *m Mex* (para escribir)

chalkboard ['tʃɔkˌbɔrd] → **blackboard**

chalk up *vt* **1** ASCRIBE : atribuir, adscribir **2** SCORE : apuntarse, anotarse (una victoria, etc.)

chalky ['tʃɔki] *adj* **chalkier; -est 1** : calcáreo **2** PALE : pálido **3** POWDERY : polvoriento

challenge[1] ['tʃælɪndʒ] *vt* **-lenged; -lenging 1** DISPUTE : disputar, cuestionar, poner en duda **2** DARE : desafiar, retar **3** STIMULATE : estimular, incentivar

challenge[2] *n* : reto *m*, desafío *m*

challenger ['tʃælɪndʒər] *n* : retador *m*, -dora *f*; contendiente *mf*

chamber ['tʃeɪmbər] *n* **1** ROOM : cámara *f*, sala *f* ⟨the senate chamber : la cámara del senado⟩ **2** : recámara *f* (de un arma de fuego), cámara *f* (de combustión) **3** : cámara *f* ⟨chamber of commerce : cámara de comercio⟩ **4 chambers** *npl or* **judge's chambers** : despacho *m* del juez

chambermaid ['tʃeɪmbərˌmeɪd] *n* : camarera *f*

chamber music *n* : música *f* de cámara

chameleon [kə'miːljən, -liən] *n* : camaleón *m*

chamois [ˈʃæmi] *n, pl* **chamois** [-mi, -miz] : gamuza *f*

champ[1] [ˈtʃæmp, ˈtʃɑmp] *vi* **1** : masticar ruidosamente **2 to champ at the bit** : impacientarse, comerle a uno la impaciencia

champ[2] [ˈtʃæmp] *n* : campeón *m*, -peona *f*

champagne [ʃæmˈpeɪn] *n* : champaña *m*, champán *m*

champion[1] [ˈtʃæmpiən] *vt* : defender, luchar por (una causa)

champion[2] *n* **1** ADVOCATE, DEFENDER : paladín *m*; campeón *m*, -peona *f*; defensor *m*, -sora *f* **2** WINNER : campeón *m*, -peona *f* ⟨world champion : campeón mundial⟩

championship [ˈtʃæmpiənˌʃɪp] *n* : campeonato *m*

chance[1] [ˈtʃænts] *v* **chanced; chancing** *vi* **1** HAPPEN : ocurrir por casualidad **2 to chance upon** : encontrar por casualidad — *vt* RISK : arriesgar

chance[2] *adj* : fortuito, casual ⟨a chance encounter : un encuentro casual⟩

chance[3] *n* **1** FATE, LUCK : azar *m*, suerte *f*, fortuna *f* **2** OPPORTUNITY : oportunidad *f*, ocasión *f* **3** PROBABILITY : probabilidad *f*, posibilidad *f* **4** RISK : riesgo *m* **5** : boleto *m* (de una rifa o lotería) **6 by chance** : por casualidad

chancellor [ˈtʃæntsələr] *n* **1** : canciller *m* **2** : rector *m*, -tora *f* (de una universidad)

chancre [ˈʃæŋkər] *n* : chancro *m*

chancy [ˈtʃæntsi] *adj* **chancier; -est** : riesgoso, arriesgado

chandelier [ˌʃændəˈlɪr] *n* : araña *f* de luces

change[1] [ˈtʃeɪndʒ] *v* **changed; changing** *vt* **1** ALTER : cambiar, alterar, modificar **2** EXCHANGE : cambiar de, intercambiar ⟨to change places : cambiar de sitio⟩ — *vi* **1** VARY : cambiar, variar, transformarse ⟨you haven't changed : no has cambiado⟩ **2** *or* **to change clothes** : cambiarse (de ropa)

change[2] *n* **1** ALTERATION : cambio *m* **2** : cambio *m*, vuelto *m* ⟨two dollars change : dos dólares de vuelto⟩ **3** COINS : cambio *m*, monedas *fpl*

changeable [ˈtʃeɪndʒəbəl] *adj* : cambiante, variable

changeless [ˈtʃeɪndʒləs] *adj* : invariable, constante

changer [ˈtʃeɪndʒər] *n* **1** : cambiador *m* ⟨record changer : cambiador de discos⟩ **2** *or* **money changer** : cambista *mf* (de dinero)

channel[1] [ˈtʃænəl] *vt* **-neled** *or* **-nelled; -neling** *or* **-nelling** : encauzar, canalizar

channel[2] *n* **1** RIVERBED : cauce *m* **2** STRAIT : canal *m*, estrecho *m* ⟨English Channel : Canal de la Mancha⟩ **3** COURSE, MEANS : vía *f*, conducto *m* ⟨the usual channels : las vías normales⟩ **4** : canal *m* (de televisión)

chant[1] [ˈtʃænt] *v* : salmodiar, cantar

chant[2] *n* **1** : salmodia *f* **2** **Gregorian chant** : canto *m* gregoriano

Chanukah [ˈxɑnəkə, ˈhɑ-] → **Hanukkah**

chaos [ˈkeɪˌɑs] *n* : caos *m*

chaotic [keɪˈɑtɪk] *adj* : caótico — **chaotically** [-tɪkli] *adv*

chap[1] [ˈtʃæp] *vi* **chapped; chapping** : partirse, agrietarse

chap[2] *n* FELLOW : tipo *m*, hombre *m*

chapel [ˈtʃæpəl] *n* : capilla *f*

chaperon *or* **chaperone** [ˈʃæpəˌroːn] *vt* **-oned; -oning** : ir de chaperón, acompañar

chaperon[2] *or* **chaperone** *n* : chaperón *m*, -rona *f*; acompañante *mf*

chaplain [ˈtʃæplɪn] *n* : capellán *m*

chapter [ˈtʃæptər] *n* **1** : capítulo *m* (de un libro) **2** BRANCH : sección *f*, división *f* (de una organización)

char [ˈtʃɑr] *vt* **charred; charring 1** BURN : carbonizar **2** SCORCH : chamuscar

character [ˈkærɪktər] *n* **1** LETTER, SYMBOL : carácter *m* ⟨Chinese characters : caracteres chinos⟩ **2** DISPOSITION : carácter *m*, personalidad *f* ⟨of good character : de buena reputación⟩ **3** : tipo *m*, personaje *m* peculiar ⟨he's quite a character! : ¡él es algo serio!⟩ **4** : personaje *m* (ficticio)

characteristic[1] [ˌkærɪktəˈrɪstɪk] *adj* : característico, típico — **characteristically** [-tɪkli] *adv*

characteristic[2] *n* : característica *f*

characterization [ˌkærɪktərəˈzeɪʃən] *n* : caracterización *f*

characterize [ˈkærɪktəˌraɪz] *vt* **-ized; -izing** : caracterizar

charades [ʃəˈreɪdz] *ns & pl* : charada *f*

charcoal [ˈtʃɑrˌkoːl] *n* : carbón *m*

chard [ˈtʃɑrd] → **Swiss chard**

charge[1] [ˈtʃɑrdʒ] *v* **charged; charging** *vt* **1** : cargar ⟨to charge the batteries : cargar las pilas⟩ **2** ENTRUST : encomendar, encargar **3** COMMAND : ordenar, mandar **4** ACCUSE : acusar ⟨charged with robbery : acusado de robo⟩ **5** : cargar a una cuenta, comprar a crédito — *vi* **1** : cargar (contra el enemigo) ⟨charge! : ¡a la carga!⟩ **2** : cobrar ⟨they charge too much : cobran demasiado⟩

charge[2] *n* **1** : carga *f* (eléctrica) **2** BURDEN : carga *f*, peso *m* **3** RESPONSIBILITY : cargo *m*, responsabilidad *f* ⟨to take charge of : hacerse cargo de⟩ **4** ACCUSATION : cargo *m*, acusación *f* **5** COST : costo *m*, cargo *m*, precio *m* **6** ATTACK : carga *f*, ataque *m*

charge card → **credit card**

chargeable [ˈtʃɑrdʒəbəl] *adj* **1** : acusable, perseguible (dícese de un delito) **2 ~ to** : a cargo de (una cuenta)

charger [ˈtʃɑrdʒər] *n* : corcel *m*, caballo *m* (de guerra)

chariot [ˈtʃæriət] *n* : carro *m* (de guerra)

charisma [kəˈrɪzmə] *n* : carisma *m*

charismatic [ˌkærəzˈmætɪk] *adj* : carismático

charitable ['tʃærətəbəl] *adj* **1** GENER-
OUS : caritativo ⟨a charitable organization : una organización benéfica⟩ **2**
KIND, UNDERSTANDING : generoso,
benévolo, comprensivo — **charitably**
[-bli] *adv*
charitableness ['tʃærətəbəlnəs] *n* : caridad *f*
charity ['tʃærəti] *n, pl* **-ties 1** GENEROS-
ITY : caridad *f* **2** ALMS : caridad *f*,
limosna *f* **3** : organización *f* benéfica,
obra *f* de beneficencia
charlatan ['ʃarlətən] *n* : charlatán *m*,
-tana *f*; farsante *mf*
charley horse ['tʃarli‚hɔrs] *n* : calambre
m
charm[1] ['tʃarm] *vt* : encantar, cautivar,
fascinar
charm[2] *n* **1** AMULET : amuleto *m*, talismán *m* **2** ATTRACTION : encanto *m*,
atractivo *m* ⟨it has a certain charm
: tiene cierto atractivo⟩ **3** : dije *m*, colgante *m* ⟨charm bracelet : pulsera de
dijes⟩
charmer ['tʃarmər] *n* : persona *f* encantadora
charming ['tʃarmɪŋ] *adj* : encantador,
fascinante
chart[1] ['tʃart] *vt* **1** : trazar un mapa de,
hacer un gráfico de **2** PLAN : trazar,
planear ⟨to chart a course : trazar un
derrotero⟩
chart[2] *n* **1** MAP : carta *f*, mapa *m* **2** DI-
AGRAM : gráfico *m*, cuadro *m*, tabla *f*
charter[1] ['tʃartər] *vt* **1** : establecer los estatutos de (una organización) **2** RENT
: alquilar, fletar
charter[2] *n* **1** STATUTES : estatutos *mpl*
2 CONSTITUTION : carta *f*, constitución
f
chartreuse [ʃar'truːz, -'truːs] *n* : color *m*
verde-amarillo intenso
chary ['tʃæri] *adj* **charier; -est 1** WARY
: cauteloso, precavido **2** SPARING : parco
chase[1] ['tʃeɪs] *vt* **chased; chasing 1**
PURSUE : perseguir, ir a la caza de **2**
DRIVE : ahuyentar, echar ⟨he chased
the dog from the garden : ahuyentó al
perro del jardín⟩ **3** : grabar (metales)
chase[2] *n* **1** PURSUIT : persecución *f*,
caza *f* **2 the chase** HUNTING : caza *f*
chaser ['tʃeɪsər] *n* **1** PURSUER : perseguidor *m*, -dora *f* **2** : bebida *f* que se
toma después de un trago de licor
chasm ['kæzəm] *n* : abismo *m*, sima *f*
chassis ['tʃæsi, 'ʃæsi] *n, pl* **chassis** [-siz]
: chasis *m*, armazón *m*
chaste ['tʃeɪst] *adj* **chaster; -est 1** : casto **2** MODEST : modesto, puro **3** AUS-
TERE : austero, sobrio
chastely ['tʃeɪstli] *adv* : castamente
chasten ['tʃeɪsən] *vt* : castigar, sancionar
chasteness ['tʃeɪstnəs] *n* **1** MODESTY
: modestia *f*, castidad *f* **2** AUSTERITY
: sobriedad *f*, austeridad *f*

chastise ['tʃæs‚taɪz, tʃæs'-] *vt* **-tised;
-tising 1** REPRIMAND : reprender, corregir, reprobar **2** PUNISH : castigar
chastisement ['tʃæs‚taɪzmənt, tʃæs'taɪz-
‚ 'tʃæstəz-] *n* : castigo *m*, corrección *f*
chastity ['tʃæstəti] *n* : castidad *f*, decencia *f*, modestia *f*
chat[1] ['tʃæt] *vi* **chatted; chatting** : charlar, platicar
chat[2] *n* : charla *f*, plática *f*
château [ʃæ'toː] *n, pl* **-teaus** [-'toːz] *or*
-teaux [-'toː, -'toːz] : mansión *f*
campestre
chattel ['tʃætəl] *n* : bienes *fpl* muebles,
enseres *mpl*
chatter[1] ['tʃætər] *vi* **1** : castañetear
(dícese de los dientes) **2** GAB : parlotear
fam, cotorrear *fam*
chatter[2] *n* **1** CHATTERING : castañeteo
m (de dientes) **2** GABBING : parloteo
m fam, cotorreo *m fam*, cháchara *f fam*
chatterbox ['tʃætər‚baks] *n* : parlanchín
m, -china *f*; charlatán *m*, -tana *f*;
hablador *m*, -dora *f*
chatty ['tʃæti] *adj* **chattier; chattiest 1**
TALKATIVE : parlanchín, charlatán **2**
CONVERSATIONAL : familiar, conversador ⟨a chatty letter : una carta llena
de noticias⟩
chauffeur[1] ['ʃoːfər, ʃo'fər] *vi* : trabajar
de chofer privado — *vt* : hacer de
chofer para
chauffeur[2] *n* : chofer *m* privado
chauvinism ['ʃoːvə‚nɪzəm] *n* : chauvinismo *m*, patriotería *f*
chauvinist ['ʃoːvənɪst] *n* : chauvinista
mf; patriotero *m*, -ra *f*
chauvinistic [‚ʃoːvə'nɪstɪk] *adj* : chauvinista, patriotero
cheap[1] ['tʃiːp] *adv* : barato ⟨to sell cheap
: vender barato⟩
cheap[2] *adj* **1** INEXPENSIVE : barato,
económico **2** SHODDY : barato, mal hecho **3** STINGY : tacaño, agarrado *fam*,
codo *Mex*
cheapen ['tʃiːpən] *vt* : degradar, rebajar
cheaply ['tʃiːpli] *adv* : barato, a precio
bajo
cheapness ['tʃiːpnəs] *n* **1** : baratura *f*,
precio *m* bajo **2** STINGINESS : tacañería
f
cheapskate ['tʃiːp‚skeɪt] *n* : tacaño *m*,
-ña *f*; codo *m*, -da *f Mex*
cheat[1] ['tʃiːt] *vt* : defraudar, estafar, engañar — *vi* : hacer trampa
cheat[2] *n* **1** CHEATING : engaño *m*,
fraude *m*, trampa *f* **2** → **cheater**
cheater ['tʃiːtər] *n* : estafador *m*, -dora *f*;
tramposo *m*, -sa *f*
check[1] ['tʃek] *vt* **1** HALT : frenar, parar,
detener **2** RESTRAIN : refrenar, contener, reprimir **3** VERIFY : verificar,
comprobar **4** INSPECT : revisar,
chequear, inspeccionar **5** MARK : marcar, señalar **6** : chequear, facturar
(maletas, equipaje) **7** CHECKER : marcar con cuadros **8 to check in** : registrarse en un hotel **9 to check out** : irse
de un hotel

check² *n* **1** HALT : detención *f* súbita, parada *f* **2** RESTRAINT : control *m*, freno *m* **3** INSPECTION : inspección *f*, verificación *f*, chequeo *m* **4** : cheque *m* ⟨to pay by check : pagar con cheque⟩ **5** VOUCHER : resguardo *m*, comprobante *m* **6** BILL : cuenta *f* (en un restaurante) **7** SQUARE : cuadro *m* **8** MARK : marca *f* **9** : jaque *m* (en ajedrez)

checkbook ['tʃɛk,bʊk] *n* : chequera *f*

checker¹ ['tʃɛkər] *vt* : marcar con cuadros

checker² *n* **1** : pieza *f* (en el juego de damas) **2** : verificador *m*, -dora *f* **3** CASHIER : cajero *m*, -ra *f*

checkerboard ['tʃɛkər,bord] *n* : tablero *m* de damas

checkers ['tʃɛkərz] *n* : damas *fpl*

checkmate¹ ['tʃɛk,meɪt] *vt* **-mated; -mating 1** : dar jaque mate a (en ajedrez) **2** THWART : frustrar, arruinar

checkmate² *n* : jaque mate *m*

checkout ['tʃɛk,aʊt] *n or* **checkout counter** : caja *f*

checkpoint ['tʃɛk,pɔɪnt] *n* : puesto *m* de control

checkup ['tʃɛk,ʌp] *n* : examen *m* médico, chequeo *m*

cheddar ['tʃɛdər] *n* : queso *m* Cheddar

cheek ['tʃiːk] *n* **1** : mejilla *f*, cachete *m* **2** IMPUDENCE : insolencia *f*, descaro *m*

cheekbone ['tʃiːk,boːn] *n* : pómulo *m*

cheeky ['tʃiːki] *adj* **cheekier; -est** : descarado, insolente, atrevido

cheep¹ ['tʃiːp] *vi* : piar

cheep² *n* : pío *m*

cheer¹ ['tʃɪr] *vt* **1** ENCOURAGE : alentar, animar **2** GLADDEN : alegrar, levantar el ánimo a **3** ACCLAIM : aclamar, vitorear, echar porras a

cheer² *n* **1** CHEERFULNESS : alegría *f*, buen humor *m*, jovialidad *f* **2** APPLAUSE : aclamación *f*, ovación *f*, aplausos *mpl* ⟨three cheers for the chief! : ¡viva el jefe!⟩ **3 cheers!** : ¡salud!

cheerful ['tʃɪrfəl] *adj* : alegre, de buen humor

cheerfully ['tʃɪrfəli] *adv* : alegremente, jovialmente

cheerfulness ['tʃɪrfəlnəs] *n* : buen humor *m*, alegría *f*

cheerily ['tʃɪrəli] *adv* : alegremente

cheeriness ['tʃɪrinəs] *n* : buen humor *m*, alegría *f*

cheerleader ['tʃɪr,liːdər] *n* : porrista *mf*

cheerless ['tʃɪrləs] *adj* BLEAK : triste, sombrío

cheerlessly ['tʃɪrləsli] *adv* : desanimadamente

cheery ['tʃɪri] *adj* **cheerier; -est** : alegre, de buen humor

cheese ['tʃiːz] *n* : queso *m*

cheesecloth ['tʃiːz,klɔθ] *n* : estopilla *f*

cheesy ['tʃiːzi] *adj* **cheesier; -est 1** : a queso **2** : que contiene queso **3** CHEAP : barato, de mala calidad

cheetah ['tʃiːtə] *n* : guepardo *m*

chef ['ʃɛf] *n* : chef *m*

chemical¹ ['kɛmɪkəl] *adj* : químico — **chemically** [-mɪkli] *adv*

chemical² *n* : sustancia *f* química

chemise [ʃə'miːz] *n* **1** : camiseta *f*, prenda *f* interior de una pieza **2** : vestido *m* holgado

chemist ['kɛmɪst] *n* : químico *m*, -ca *f*

chemistry ['kɛmɪstri] *n, pl* **-tries** : química *f*

chemotherapy [,kiːmo'θɛrəpi, ,kɛmo-] *n, pl* **-pies** : quimioterapia *f*

chenille [ʃə'niːl] *n* : felpilla *f*

cherish ['tʃɛrɪʃ] *vt* **1** VALUE : apreciar, valorar **2** HARBOR : abrigar, albergar

cherry ['tʃɛri] *n, pl* **-ries 1** : cereza *f* (fruta) **2** : cerezo *m* (árbol)

cherub ['tʃɛrəb] *n* **1** *pl* **-ubim** ['tʃɛrə,bɪm, 'tʃɛrjə-]** ANGEL : ángel *m*, querubín *m* **2** *pl* **-ubs** : niño *m* regordete, niña *f* regordeta

cherubic [tʃə'ruːbɪk] *adj* : querúbico, angelical

chess ['tʃɛs] *n* : ajedrez *m*

chessboard ['tʃɛs,bord] *n* : tablero *m* de ajedrez

chessman ['tʃɛsmən, -,mæn] *n, pl* **-men** [-mən, -,mɛn] : pieza *f* de ajedrez

chest ['tʃɛst] *n* **1** : cofre *m*, baúl *m* **2** : pecho *m* ⟨chest pains : dolores de pecho⟩

chestnut ['tʃɛst,nʌt] *n* **1** : castaña *f* (fruto) **2** : castaño *m* (árbol)

chest of drawers *n* : cómoda *f*

chevron ['ʃɛvrən] *n* : galón *m* (de un oficial militar)

chew¹ ['tʃuː] *vt* : masticar, mascar

chew² *n* : algo que se masca (como tabaco)

chewable ['tʃuːəbəl] *adj* : masticable

chewing gum *n* : goma *f* de mascar, chicle *m*

chewy ['tʃuːi] *adj* **chewier; -est 1** : fibroso (dícese de las carnes o los vegetales) **2** : pegajoso, chicloso (dícese de los dulces)

chic¹ ['ʃiːk] *adj* : chic, elegante, de moda

chic² *n* : chic *m*, elegancia *f*

Chicano [tʃɪ'kano] *n* : chicano *m*, -na *f* — **Chicano** *adj*

chick ['tʃɪk] *n* : pollito *m*, -ta *f*; polluelo *m*, -la *f*

chicken ['tʃɪkən] *n* **1** FOWL : pollo *m* **2** COWARD : cobarde *mf*

chickenhearted ['tʃɪkən,hɑrtəd] *n* : miedoso, cobarde

chicken pox *n* : varicela *f*

chickpea ['tʃɪk,piː] *n* : garbanzo *m*

chicle ['tʃɪkəl] *n* : chicle *m* (resina)

chicory ['tʃɪkəri] *n, pl* **-ries 1** : endibia *f* (para ensaladas) **2** : achicoria *f* (aditivo de café)

chide ['tʃaɪd] *vt* **chid** ['tʃɪd] *or* **chided; chid** *or* **chidden** ['tʃɪdən] *or* **chided; chiding** ['tʃaɪdɪŋ] : regañar, reprender

chief¹ ['tʃiːf] *adj* : principal, capital ⟨chief negotiator : negociador en jefe⟩ — **chiefly** *adv*

chief² *n* : jefe *m*, -fa *f*

chieftain ['ʧiːftən] *n* : jefe *m*, -fa *f* (de una tribu)
chiffon [ʃɪ'fɑn, 'ʃɪˌ-] *n* : chifón *m*
chigger ['ʧɪgər] *n* : nigua *f*
chignon ['ʃiːnˌjɑn, -ˌjɔn] *n* : moño *m*, chongo *m Mex*
chilblain ['ʧɪlˌbleɪn] *n* : sabañón *m*
child ['ʧaɪld] *n*, *pl* **children** ['ʧɪldrən] **1** BABY, YOUNGSTER : niño *m*, -ña *f*; criatura *f* **2** OFFSPRING : hijo *m*, -ja *f*; progenie *f*
childbearing[1] ['ʧaɪlˌbɛrɪŋ] *adj* : relativo al parto ⟨of childbearing age : en edad fértil⟩
childbearing[2] → **childbirth**
childbirth ['ʧaɪldˌbərθ] *n* : parto *m*
childhood ['ʧaɪldˌhʊd] *n* : infancia *f*, niñez *f*
childish ['ʧaɪldɪʃ] *adj* : infantil, inmaduro — **childishly** *adv*
childishness ['ʧaɪldɪʃnəs] *n* : infantilismo *m*, inmadurez *f*
childless ['ʧaɪldləs] *adj* : sin hijos
childlike ['ʧaɪldˌlaɪk] *adj* : infantil, inocente ⟨a childlike imagination : una imaginación infantil⟩
childproof ['ʧaɪldˌpruːf] *adj* : a prueba de niños
Chilean ['ʧɪliən, ʧɪ'leɪən] *n* : chileno *m*, -na *f* — **Chilean** *adj*
chili *or* **chile** *or* **chilli** ['ʧɪli] *n*, *pl* **chilies** *or* **chiles** *or* **chillies 1** *or* **chili pepper** : chile *m*, ají *m* **2** : chile *m* con carne
chill[1] ['ʧɪl] *v* : enfriar
chill[2] *adj* : frío, gélido ⟨a chill wind : un viento frío⟩
chill[3] *n* **1** CHILLINESS : fresco *m*, frío *m* **2** SHIVER : escalofrío *m* **3** DAMPER : enfriamiento *m*, frío *m* ⟨to cast a chill over : enfriar⟩
chilliness ['ʧɪlinəs] *n* : frío *m*, fresco *m*
chilly ['ʧɪli] *adj* **chillier; -est** : frío ⟨it's chilly tonight : hace frío esta noche⟩
chime[1] ['ʧaɪm] *v* **chimed; chiming** *vt* : hacer sonar (una campana) — *vi* : sonar una campana, dar campanadas
chime[2] *n* **1** BELLS : juego *m* de campanitas sintonizadas, carillón *m* **2** PEAL : tañido *m*, campanada *f*
chime in *vi* : meterse en una conversación
chimera *or* **chimaera** [kaɪ'mɪrə, kə-] *n* : quimera *f*
chimney ['ʧɪmni] *n*, *pl* **-neys** : chimenea *f*
chimney sweep *n* : deshollinador *m*, -dora *f*
chimp ['ʧɪmp, 'ʃɪmp] → **chimpanzee**
chimpanzee [ˌʧɪmˌpæn'ziː, ˌʃɪm-; ʧɪm'pænzi, ʃɪm-] *n* : chimpancé *m*
chin ['ʧɪn] *n* : barbilla *f*, mentón *m*, barba *f*
china ['ʧaɪnə] *n* **1** PORCELAIN : porcelana *f*, loza *f* **2** CROCKERY, TABLEWARE : loza *f*, vajilla *f*
chinchilla [ʧɪn'ʧɪlə] *n* : chinchilla *f*
Chinese ['ʧaɪ'niːz, -'niːs] *n* **1** : chino *m*, -na *f* **2** : chino *m* (idioma) — **Chinese** *adj*

chink ['ʧɪŋk] *n* : grieta *f*, abertura *f*
chintz ['ʧɪnts] *n* : chintz *m*, chinz *m*
chip[1] ['ʧɪp] *v* **chipped; chipping** *vt* : desportillar, desconchar, astillar (madera) — *vi* : desportillarse, desconcharse, descascararse (dícese de la pintura, etc.)
chip[2] *n* **1** : astilla *f* (de madera o vidrio), lasca *f* (de piedra) ⟨he's a chip off the old block : de tal palo, tal astilla⟩ **2** : bocado *m* pequeño (en rodajas o rebanadas) ⟨tortilla chips : totopos, tortillitas tostadas⟩ **3** : ficha *f* (de póker, etc.) **4** NICK : desportilladura *f*, mella *f* **5** : chip *m* ⟨memory chip : chip de memoria⟩
chip in *v* CONTRIBUTE : contribuir
chipmunk ['ʧɪpˌmʌŋk] *n* : ardilla *f* listada
chipper ['ʧɪpər] *adj* : alegre y vivaz
chiropodist [kə'rɑpədɪst, ʃə-] *n* : podólogo *m*, -ga *f*
chiropody [kə'rɑpədi, ʃə-] *n* : podología *f*
chiropractic ['kaɪrəˌpræktɪk] *n* : quiropráctica *f*
chiropractor ['kaɪrəˌpræktər] *n* : quiropráctico *m*, -ca *f*
chirp[1] ['ʧərp] *vi* : gorjear (dícese de los pájaros), chirriar (dícese de los grillos)
chirp[2] *n* : gorjeo *m* (de un pájaro), chirrido *m* (de un grillo)
chisel[1] ['ʧɪzəl] *vt* **-eled** *or* **-elled; -eling** *or* **-elling 1** : cincelar, tallar, labrar **2** CHEAT : estafar, defraudar
chisel[2] *n* : cincel *m* (para piedras y metales), escoplo *m* (para madera), formón *m*
chiseler ['ʧɪzələr] *n* SWINDLER : estafador *m*, -dora *f*; fraude *mf*
chit ['ʧɪt] *n* : resguardo *m*, recibo *m*
chitchat ['ʧɪtˌʧæt] *n* : cotorreo *m*, charla *f*
chivalric [ʃə'vælrɪk] → **chivalrous**
chivalrous ['ʃɪvəlrəs] *adj* **1** KNIGHTLY : caballeresco, relativo a la caballería **2** GENTLEMANLY : caballeroso, honesto, cortés
chivalrousness ['ʃɪvəlrəsnəs] *n* : caballerosidad *f*, cortesía *f*
chivalry ['ʃɪvəlri] *n*, *pl* **-ries 1** KNIGHTHOOD : caballería *f* **2** CHIVALROUSNESS : caballerosidad *f*, nobleza *f*, cortesía *f*
chive ['ʧaɪv] *n* : cebollino *m*
chloride ['klorˌaɪd] *n* : cloruro *m*
chlorinate ['klorəˌneɪt] *vt* **-nated; -nating** : clorar
chlorination [ˌklorə'neɪʃən] *n* : cloración *f*
chlorine ['klorˌiːn] *n* : cloro *m*
chloroform ['klorəˌfɔrm] *n* : cloroformo *m*
chlorophyll ['klorəˌfɪl] *n* : clorofila *f*
chock–full ['ʧɑk'fʊl, 'ʧʌk-] *adj* : colmado, repleto
chocolate ['ʧɑkələt, 'ʧɔk-] *n* **1** : chocolate *m* **2** BONBON : bombón *m* **3** : color *m* chocolate, marrón *m*

choice[1] ['tʃɔɪs] *adj* **choicer; -est** : selecto, escogido, de primera calidad

choice[2] *n* **1** CHOOSING : elección *f*, selección *f* **2** OPTION : elección *f*, opción *f* ⟨I have no choice : no tengo alternativa⟩ **3** PREFERENCE : preferencia *f*, elección *f* **4** VARIETY : surtido *m*, selección *f* ⟨a wide choice : un gran surtido⟩

choir ['kwaɪr] *n* : coro *m*

choirboy ['kwaɪr,bɔɪ] *n* : niño *m* de coro

choke[1] ['tʃo:k] *v* **choked; choking** *vt* **1** ASPHYXIATE, STRANGLE : sofocar, asfixiar, ahogar, estrangular **2** BLOCK : tapar, obstruir — *vi* **1** SUFFOCATE : asfixiarse, sofocarse, ahogarse, atragantarse (con comida) **2** CLOG : taparse, obstruirse

choke[2] *n* **1** CHOKING : estrangulación *f* **2** : choke *m* (de un motor)

choker ['tʃo:kər] *n* : gargantilla *f*

cholera ['kɑlərə] *n* : cólera *m*

cholesterol [kə'lɛstə,rɔl] *n* : colesterol *m*

choose ['tʃu:z] *v* **chose** ['tʃo:z]; **chosen** ['tʃo:zən]; **choosing** *vt* **1** SELECT : escoger, elegir ⟨choose only one : escoja sólo uno⟩ **2** DECIDE : decidir ⟨he chose to leave : decidió irse⟩ **3** PREFER : preferir ⟨which one do you choose? : ¿cuál prefiere?⟩ — *vi* : escoger ⟨much to choose from : mucho de donde escoger⟩

choosy *or* **choosey** ['tʃu:zi] *adj* **choosier; -est** : exigente, remilgado

chop[1] ['tʃɑp] *vt* **chopped; chopping 1** MINCE : picar, cortar, moler (carne) **2 to chop down** : cortar, talar (un árbol)

chop[2] *n* **1** CUT : hachazo *m* (con una hacha), tajo *m* (con una cuchilla) **2** BLOW : golpe *m* (penetrante) ⟨karate chop : golpe de karate⟩ **3** : chuleta *f* ⟨pork chops : chuletas de cerdo⟩

chopper ['tʃɑpər] → **helicopter**

choppy ['tʃɑpi] *adj* **choppier; -est 1** : agitado, picado (dícese del mar) **2** DISCONNECTED : incoherente, inconexo

chops ['tʃɑps] *npl* **1** : quijada *f*, mandíbula *f*, boca *f* (de una persona) **2 to lick one's chops** : relamerse

chopsticks ['tʃɑp,stɪks] *npl* : palillos *mpl*

choral ['korəl] *adj* : coral

chorale [kə'ræl, -'rɑl] *n* **1** : coral *f* (composición musical vocal) **2** CHOIR, CHORUS : coral *f*, coro *m*

chord ['kɔrd] *n* **1** : acorde *m* (en música) **2** : cuerda *f* (en anatomía o geometría)

chore ['tʃor] *n* **1** TASK : tarea *f* rutinaria **2** BOTHER, NUISANCE : lata *f fam*, fastidio *m* **3 chores** *npl* WORK : quehaceres *mpl*, faenas *fpl*

choreograph ['koriə,græf] *vt* : coreografiar

choreographer [,kori'ɑgrəfər] *n* : coreógrafo *m*, -fa *f*

choreographic [,koriə'græfɪk] *adj* : coreográfico

choreography [,kori'ɑgrəfi] *n, pl* **-phies** : coreografía *f*

chorister ['korəstər] *n* : corista *mf*

chortle[1] ['tʃɔrtəl] *vi* **-tled; -tling** : reírse (con satisfacción o júbilo)

chortle[2] *n* : risa *f* (de satisfacción o júbilo)

chorus[1] ['korəs] *vt* : corear

chorus[2] *n* **1** : coro *m* (grupo o composición musical) **2** REFRAIN : coro *m*, estribillo *m*

chose → **choose**

chosen ['tʃo:zən] *adj* : elegido, selecto

chow ['tʃaʊ] *n* **1** FOOD : comida *f* **2** : chow-chow *m* (perro)

chowder ['tʃaʊdər] *n* : sopa *f* de pescado

Christ ['kraɪst] *n* **1** : Cristo *m* **2 for Christ's sake** : ¡por Dios!

christen ['krɪsən] *vt* **1** BAPTIZE : bautizar **2** NAME : bautizar con el nombre de

Christendom ['krɪsəndəm] *n* : cristiandad *f*

christening ['krɪsənɪŋ] *n* : bautismo *m*, bautizo *m*

Christian[1] ['krɪstʃən] *adj* : cristiano

Christian[2] *n* : cristiano *m*, -na *f*

Christianity [,krɪstʃi'ænəti, ,krɪs'tʃæ-] *n* : cristianismo *m*

Christian name *n* : nombre *m* de pila

Christmas ['krɪsməs] *n* : Navidad *f* ⟨Christmas season : las Navidades⟩

chromatic [kro'mætɪk] *adj* : cromático ⟨chromatic scale : escala cromática⟩

chrome ['kro:m] *n* : cromo *m* (metal)

chromium ['kro:miəm] *n* : cromo *m* (elemento)

chromosome ['kro:mə,so:m, -,zo:m] *n* : cromosoma *m*

chronic ['krɑnɪk] *adj* : crónico — **chronically** [-nɪkli] *adv*

chronicle[1] ['krɑnɪkəl] *vt* **-cled; -cling** : escribir (una crónica o historia)

chronicle[2] *n* : crónica *f*, historia *f*

chronicler ['krɑnɪklər] *n* : historiador *m*, -dora *f*; cronista *mf*

chronological [,krɑnəl'ɑdʒɪkəl] *adj* : cronológico — **chronologically** [-kli] *adv*

chronology [krə'nɑlədʒi] *n, pl* **-gies** : cronología *f*

chronometer [krə'nɑmətər] *n* : cronómetro *m*

chrysalis ['krɪsələs] *n, pl* **chrysalides** [krɪ'sælə,di:z] *or* **chrysalises** : crisálida *f*

chrysanthemum [krɪ'sæntθəməm] *n* : crisantemo *m*

chubbiness ['tʃʌbinəs] *n* : gordura *f*

chubby ['tʃʌbi] *adj* **-bier; -est** : gordito, regordete, rechoncho

chuck[1] ['tʃʌk] *vt* **1** TOSS : tirar, lanzar, aventar *Col, Mex* **2 to chuck under the chin** : hacer la mamola

chuck[2] *n* **1** PAT : mamola *f*, palmada *f* **2** TOSS : lanzamiento *m* **3** *or* **chuck steak** : corte *m* de carne de res

chuckle[1] ['tʃʌkəl] *vi* **-led; -ling** : reírse entre dientes

chuckle[2] *n* : risita *f*, risa *f* ahogada

chug[1] [ˈtʃʌg] *vi* **chugged; chugging** : resoplar, traquetear

chug[2] *n* : resoplido *m*, traqueteo *m*

chum[1] [ˈtʃʌm] *vi* **chummed; chumming** : ser camaradas, ser cuates *Mex fam*

chum[2] *n* : amigo *m*, -ga *f*; camarada *mf*; compinche *mf fam*

chummy [ˈtʃʌmi] *adj* **-mier; -est** : amistoso ⟨they're very chummy : son muy amigos⟩

chump [ˈtʃʌmp] *n* : tonto *m*, -ta *f*; idiota *mf*

chunk [ˈtʃʌnk] *n* **1** PIECE : cacho *m*, pedazo *m*, trozo *m* **2** : cantidad *f* grande ⟨a chunk of money : mucho dinero⟩

chunky [ˈtʃʌnki] *adj* **chunkier; -est 1** STOCKY : fornido, robusto **2** : que contiene pedazos

church [ˈtʃərtʃ] *n* **1** : iglesia *f* ⟨to go to church : ir a la iglesia⟩ **2** CHRISTIANS : iglesia *f*, conjunto *m* de fieles cristianos **3** DENOMINATION : confesión *f*, secta *f* **4** CONGREGATION : feligreses *mpl*, fieles *mpl*

churchgoer [ˈtʃərtʃˌgoːər] *n* : practicante *mf*

churchyard [ˈtʃərtʃˌjard] *n* : cementerio *m* (junto a una iglesia)

churn[1] [ˈtʃərn] *vt* **1** : batir (crema), hacer (mantequilla) **2** : agitar con fuerza, revolver — *vi* : agitarse, arremolinarse

churn[2] *n* : mantequera *f*

chute [ˈʃuːt] *n* : conducto *m* inclinado, vertedero *m* (para basuras)

chutney [ˈtʃʌtni] *n, pl* **-neys** : chutney *m*

chutzpah [ˈhʊtspə, ˈxʊt-, -ˌspɑ] *n* : descaro *m*, frescura *f*, cara *f fam*

cicada [səˈkeɪdə, -ˈkɑ-] *n* : cigarra *f*, chicharra *f*

cider [ˈsaɪdər] *n* **1** : jugo *m* (de manzana, etc.) **2 hard cider** : sidra *f*

cigar [sɪˈgɑr] *n* : puro *m*, cigarro *m*

cigarette [ˌsɪgəˈrɛt, ˈsɪgəˌrɛt] *n* : cigarrillo *m*, cigarro *m*

cilantro [sɪˈlɑntroː, -ˈlæn-] *n* : cilantro *m*

cinch[1] [ˈsɪntʃ] *vt* **1** : cinchar (un caballo) **2** ASSURE : asegurar

cinch[2] *n* **1** : cincha *f* (para caballos) **2** : algo fácil o seguro ⟨it's a cinch : es bien fácil, es pan comido⟩

cinchona [sɪŋˈkoːnə] *n* : quino *m*

cinder [ˈsɪndər] *n* **1** EMBER : brasa *f*, ascua *f* **2 cinders** *npl* ASHES : cenizas *fpl*

cinema [ˈsɪnəmə] *n* : cine *m*

cinematic [ˌsɪnəˈmæt̬ɪk] *adj* : cinematográfico

cinnamon [ˈsɪnəmən] *n* : canela *f*

cipher [ˈsaɪfər] *n* **1** ZERO : cero *m* **2** CODE : cifra *f*, clave *f*

circa [ˈsərkə] *prep* : alrededor de, hacia ⟨circa 1800 : hacia el año 1800⟩

circle[1] [ˈsərkəl] *v* **-cled; -cling** *vt* **1** : encerrar en un círculo, poner un círculo alrededor de **2** : girar alrededor de, dar vueltas a ⟨we circled the building twice : le dimos vueltas al edificio dos veces⟩ — *vi* : dar vueltas

circle[2] *n* **1** : círculo *m* **2** CYCLE : ciclo *m* ⟨to come full circle : volver al punto de partida⟩ **3** GROUP : círculo *m*, grupo *m* (social)

circuit [ˈsərkət] *n* **1** BOUNDARY : circuito *m*, perímetro *m* (de una zona o un territorio) **2** TOUR : circuito *m*, recorrido *m*, tour *m* **3** : circuito *m* (eléctrico) ⟨a short circuit : un cortocircuito⟩

circuitous [ˌsərˈkjuːət̬əs] *adj* : sinuoso, tortuoso

circuitry [ˈsərkətri] *n, pl* **-ries** : sistema *m* de circuitos

circular[1] [ˈsərkjələr] *adj* ROUND : circular, redondo

circular[2] *n* : circular *f*

circulate [ˈsərkjəˌleɪt] *v* **-lated; -lating** *vi* : circular — *vt* **1** : circular (noticias, etc.) **2** DISSEMINATE : hacer circular, divulgar

circulation [ˌsərkjəˈleɪʃən] *n* : circulación *f*

circulatory [ˈsərkjələˌtori] *adj* : circulatorio

circumcise [ˈsərkəmˌsaɪz] *vt* **-cised; -cising** : circuncidar

circumcision [ˌsərkəmˈsɪʒən, ˈsərkəmˌ-] *n* : circuncisión *f*

circumference [sərˈkʌmpfrən̩ts] *n* : circunferencia *f*

circumflex [ˈsərkəmˌflɛks] *n* : acento *m* circunflejo

circumlocution [ˌsərkəmloˈkjuːʃən] *n* : circunlocución *f*

circumnavigate [ˌsərkəmˈnævəˌgeɪt] *vt* **-gated; -gating** : circunnavegar

circumscribe [ˈsərkəmˌskraɪb] *vt* **-scribed; -scribing 1** : circunscribir, trazar una figura alrededor de **2** LIMIT : circunscribir, limitar

circumspect [ˈsərkəmˌspɛkt] *adj* : circunspecto, prudente, cauto

circumspection [ˌsərkəmˈspɛkʃən] *n* : circunspección *f*, cautela *f*

circumstance [ˈsərkəmˌstæn̩ts] *n* **1** EVENT : circunstancia *f*, acontecimiento *m* **2 circumstances** *npl* SITUATION : circunstancias *fpl*, situación *f* ⟨under the circumstances : dadas las circunstancias⟩ ⟨under no circumstances : de ninguna manera, bajo ningún concepto⟩ **3 circumstances** *npl* : situación *f* económica

circumstantial [ˌsərkəmˈstænʃəl] *adj* : circunstancial

circumvent [ˌsərkəmˈvɛnt] *vt* : evadir, burlar (una ley o regla), sortear (una responsabilidad o dificultad)

circumvention [ˌsərkəmˈvɛnʃən] *n* : evasión *f*

circus [ˈsərkəs] *n* : circo *m*

cirrhosis [səˈroːsɪs] *n, pl* **-rhoses** [-ˈroːˌsiːz] : cirrosis *f*

cirrus [ˈsɪrəs] *n, pl* **-ri** [ˈsɪrˌaɪ] : cirro *m*

cistern [ˈsɪstərn] *n* : cisterna *f*, aljibe *m*

citadel [ˈsɪt̬ədəl, -ˌdɛl] *n* FORTRESS : ciudadela *f*, fortaleza *f*

citation [saɪ'teɪʃən] *n* **1** SUMMONS : emplazamiento *m*, citación *f*, convocatoria *f* (judicial) **2** QUOTATION : cita *f* **3** COMMENDATION : elogio *m*, mención *f* (de honor)

cite ['saɪt] *vt* **cited; citing 1** ARRAIGN, SUBPOENA : emplazar, citar, hacer comparecer (ante un tribunal) **2** QUOTE : citar **3** COMMEND : elogiar, honrar (oficialmente)

citizen ['sɪt̬əzən] *n* : ciudadano *m*, -na *f*

citizenry ['sɪt̬əzənri] *n, pl* **-ries** : ciudadanía *f*, conjunto *m* de ciudadanos

citizenship ['sɪt̬əzən,ʃɪp] *n* : ciudadanía *f* ⟨Nicaraguan citizenship : ciudadanía nicaragüense⟩

citron ['sɪtrən] *n* : cidra *f*

citrus ['sɪtrəs] *n, pl* **-rus** *or* **-ruses** : cítrico *m*

city ['sɪt̬i] *n, pl* **cities** : ciudad *f*

civic ['sɪvɪk] *adj* : cívico

civics ['sɪvɪks] *ns & pl* : civismo *m*

civil ['sɪvəl] *adj* **1** : civil ⟨civil law : derecho civil⟩ **2** POLITE : cortés

civilian [sə'vɪljən] *n* : civil *mf* ⟨soldiers and civilians : soldados y civiles⟩

civility [sə'vɪlət̬i] *n, pl* **-ties** : cortesía *f*, educación *f*

civilization [,sɪvələ'zeɪʃən] *n* : civilización *f*

civilize ['sɪvə,laɪz] *vt* **-lized; -lizing** : civilizar — **civilized** *adj*

civil liberties *npl* : derechos *mpl* civiles

civilly ['sɪvəli] *adv* : cortésmente

civil rights *npl* : derechos *mpl* civiles

civil service *n* : administración *f* pública

civil war *n* : guerra *f* civil

clack¹ ['klæk] *vi* : tabletear

clack² *n* : tableteo *m*

clad ['klæd] *adj* **1** CLOTHED : vestido **2** COVERED : cubierto

claim¹ ['kleɪm] *vt* **1** DEMAND : reclamar, reivindicar ⟨she claimed her rights : reclamó sus derechos⟩ **2** MAINTAIN : afirmar, sostener ⟨they claim it's theirs : sostienen que es suyo⟩

claim² *n* **1** DEMAND : demanda *f*, reclamación *f* **2** DECLARATION : declaración *f*, afirmación *f* **3** **to stake a claim** : reclamar, reivindicar

claimant ['kleɪmənt] *n* : demandante *mf* (ante un juez), pretendiente *mf* (al trono, etc.)

clairvoyance [klær'vɔɪən*t*s] *n* : clarividencia *f*

clairvoyant¹ [klær'vɔɪənt] *adj* : clarividente

clairvoyant² *n* : clarividente *mf*

clam ['klæm] *n* : almeja *f*

clamber ['klæmbər] *vi* : treparse o subirse torpemente

clammy ['klæmi] *adj* **-mier; -est** : húmedo y algo frío

clamor¹ ['klæmər] *vi* : gritar, clamar

clamor² *n* : clamor *m*

clamorous ['klæmərəs] *adj* : clamoroso, ruidoso, estrepitoso

clamp¹ ['klæmp] *vt* : sujetar con abrazaderas

clamp² *n* : abrazadera *f*

clan ['klæn] *n* : clan *m*

clandestine [klæn'dɛstɪn] *adj* : clandestino, secreto

clang¹ ['klæŋ] *vi* : hacer resonar (dícese de un objeto metálico)

clang² *n* : ruido *m* metálico fuerte

clangor ['klæŋər, -gər] *n* : estruendo *m* metálico

clank¹ ['klæŋk] *vi* : producir un ruido metálico seco

clank² *n* : ruido *m* metálico seco

clannish ['klænɪʃ] *adj* : exclusivista

clap¹ ['klæp] *v* **clapped; clapping** *vt* **1** SLAP, STRIKE : golpear ruidosamente, dar una palmada ⟨to clap one's hands : batir palmas, dar palmadas⟩ **2** APPLAUD : aplaudir — *vi* APPLAUD : aplaudir

clap² *n* **1** SLAP : palmada *f*, golpecito *m* **2** NOISE : ruido *m* seco ⟨a clap of thunder : un trueno⟩

clapboard ['klæbərd, 'klæp,bord] *n* : tabla *f* de madera (para revestir muros)

clapper ['klæpər] *n* : badajo *m* (de una campana)

clarification [,klærəfə'keɪʃən] *n* : clarificación *f*

clarify ['klærə,faɪ] *vt* **-fied; -fying 1** EXPLAIN : aclarar **2** : clarificar (un líquido)

clarinet [,klærə'nɛt] *n* : clarinete *m*

clarion ['klæriən] *adj* : claro y sonoro

clarity ['klærət̬i] *n* : claridad *f*, nitidez *f*

clash¹ ['klæʃ] *vi* **1** : sonar, chocarse ⟨the cymbals clashed : los platillos sonaron⟩ **2** : chocar, enfrentarse ⟨the students clashed with the police : los estudiantes se enfrentaron con la policía⟩ **3** CONFLICT : estar en conflicto, oponerse **4** : desentonar (dícese de los colores), coincidir (dícese de los datos)

clash² *n* **1** : ruido *m* (producido por un choque) **2** CONFLICT, CONFRONTATION : enfrentamiento *m*, conflicto *m*, choque *m* **3** : desentono *m* (de colores), coincidencia *f* (de datos)

clasp¹ ['klæsp] *vt* **1** FASTEN : sujetar, abrochar **2** EMBRACE, GRASP : agarrar, sujetar, abrazar

clasp² *n* **1** FASTENING : broche *m*, cierre *m* **2** EMBRACE, SQUEEZE : apretón *m*, abrazo *m*

class¹ ['klæs] *vt* : clasificar, catalogar

class² *n* **1** KIND, TYPE : clase *f*, tipo *m*, especie *f* **2** : clase *f*, rango *m* social ⟨the working class : la clase obrera⟩ **3** LESSON : clase *f*, curso *m* ⟨English class : clase de inglés⟩ **4** : conjunto *m* de estudiantes, clase *f* ⟨the class of '97 : la promoción del 97⟩

classic¹ ['klæsɪk] *adj* : clásico

classic² *n* : clásico *m*, obra *f* clásica

classical ['klæsɪkəl] *adj* : clásico — **classically** [-kli] *adv*

classicism ['klæsə,sɪzəm] *n* : clasicismo *m*

classification [,klæsəfə'keɪʃən] *n* : clasificación *f*

classified ['klæsə,faɪd] *adj* **1** : clasificado ⟨classified ads : avisos clasificados⟩ **2** RESTRICTED : confidencial, secreto ⟨classified documents : documentos secretos⟩

classify ['klæsə,faɪ] *vt* **-fied; -fying** : clasificar, catalogar

classless ['klæsləs] *adj* : sin clases

classmate ['klæs,meɪt] *n* : compañero *m*, -ra *f* de clase

classroom ['klæs,ru:m] *n* : aula *f*, salón *m* de clase

clatter[1] ['klætər] *vi* : traquetear, hacer ruido

clatter[2] *n* : traqueteo *m*, ruido *m*, estrépito *m*

clause ['klɔz] *n* : cláusula *f*

claustrophobia [,klɔstrə'fo:biə] *n* : claustrofobia *f*

claustrophobic [,klɔstrə'fo:bɪk] *adj* : claustrofóbico

clavicle ['klævɪkəl] *n* : clavícula *f*

claw[1] ['klɔ] *v* : arañar

claw[2] *n* : garra *f*, uña *f* (de un gato), pinza *f* (de un crustáceo)

clay ['kleɪ] *n* : arcilla *f*, barro *m*

clayey ['kleɪi] *adj* : arcilloso

clean[1] ['kli:n] *vt* : limpiar, lavar, asear

clean[2] *adv* : limpio, limpiamente ⟨to play clean : jugar limpio⟩

clean[3] *adj* **1** : limpio **2** UNADULTERATED : puro **3** IRREPROACHABLE : intachable, sin mancha ⟨to have a clean record : no tener antecedentes penales⟩ **4** DECENT : decente **5** COMPLETE : completo, absoluto ⟨a clean break with the past : un corte radical con el pasado⟩

cleaner ['kli:nər] *n* **1** : limpiador *m*, -dora *f* **2** : producto *m* de limpieza **3** DRY CLEANER : tintorería *f* (servicio)

cleanliness ['klɛnlinəs] *n* : limpieza *f*, aseo *m*

cleanly[1] ['kli:nli] *adv* : limpiamente, con limpieza

cleanly[2] ['klɛnli] *adj* **-lier; -est** : limpio, pulcro

cleanness ['kli:nnəs] *n* : limpieza *f*

cleanse ['klɛnz] *vt* **cleansed; cleansing** : limpiar, purificar

cleanser ['klɛnzər] *n* : limpiador *m*, purificador *m*

clear[1] ['klɪr] *vt* **1** CLARIFY : aclarar, clarificar (un líquido) **2** : despejar (una superficie), desatascar (un tubo), desmontar (una selva) ⟨to clear the table : levantar la mesa⟩ ⟨to clear one's throat : carraspear, aclararse la voz⟩ **3** EXONERATE : absolver, limpiar el nombre de **4** EARN : ganar, sacar (una ganancia de) **5** : pasar sin tocar ⟨he cleared the hurdle : saltó por encima de la valla⟩ **6 to clear up** RESOLVE : aclarar, resolver, esclarecer — *vi* **1**

DISPERSE : irse, despejarse, disiparse **2** : ser compensado (dícese de un cheque) **3 to clear up** : despejar (dícese del tiempo), mejorarse (dícese de una enfermedad)

clear[2] *adv* : claro, claramente

clear[3] *adj* **1** BRIGHT : claro, lúcido **2** FAIR : claro, despejado **3** TRANSPARENT : transparente, translúcido **4** EVIDENT, UNMISTAKABLE : evidente, claro, obvio **5** CERTAIN : seguro **6** UNOBSTRUCTED : despejado, libre

clear[4] *n* **1 in the clear** : inocente, libre de toda sospecha **2 in the clear** SAFE : fuera de peligro

clearance ['klɪrənts] *n* **1** CLEARING : despeje *m* **2** SPACE : espacio *m* (libre), margen *m* **3** AUTHORIZATION : autorización *f*, despacho *m* (de la aduana)

clearing ['klɪrɪŋ] *n* : claro *m* (de un bosque)

clearly ['klɪrli] *adv* **1** DISTINCTLY : claramente, directamente **2** OBVIOUSLY : obviamente, evidentemente

cleat ['kli:t] *n* **1** : taco *m* **2 cleats** *npl* : zapatos *mpl* deportivos (con tacos)

cleavage ['kli:vɪʤ] *n* **1** CLEFT : hendidura *f*, raja *f* **2** : escote *m* (del busto)

cleave[1] ['kli:v] *vi* **cleaved** ['kli:vd] *or* **clove** ['klo:v]; **cleaving** ADHERE : adherirse, unirse

cleave[2] *vt* **cleaved; cleaving** SPLIT : hender, dividir, partir

cleaver ['kli:vər] *n* : cuchilla *f* de carnicero

clef ['klɛf] *n* : clave *f*

cleft ['klɛft] *n* : hendidura *f*, raja *f*, grieta *f*

clemency ['klɛməntsi] *n* : clemencia *f*

clement ['klɛmənt] *adj* **1** MERCIFUL : clemente, piadoso **2** MILD : clemente, apacible

clench ['klɛntʃ] *vt* **1** CLUTCH : agarrar **2** TIGHTEN : apretar (el puño, los dientes)

clergy ['klərʤi] *n, pl* **-gies** : clero *m*

clergyman ['klərʤimən] *n, pl* **-men** [-mən, -,mɛn] : clérigo *m*

cleric ['klɛrɪk] *n* : clérigo *m*, -ga *f*

clerical ['klɛrɪkəl] *adj* **1** : clerical ⟨a clerical collar : un alzacuello⟩ **2** : de oficina ⟨clerical staff : personal de oficina⟩

clerk[1] ['klərk, *Brit* 'klɑrk] *vi* : trabajar de oficinista, trabajar de dependiente

clerk[2] *n* **1** : funcionario *m*, -ria *f* (de una oficina gubernamental) **2** : oficinista *mf*, empleado *m*, -da *f* de oficina **3** SALESPERSON : dependiente *m*, -ta *f*

clever ['klɛvər] *adj* **1** SKILLFUL : ingenioso, hábil **2** SMART : listo, inteligente, astuto

cleverly ['klɛvərli] *adv* **1** SKILLFULLY : ingeniosamente, hábilmente **2** INTELLIGENTLY : inteligentemente

cleverness ['klɛvərnəs] *n* **1** SKILL : ingenio *m*, habilidad *f* **2** INTELLIGENCE : inteligencia *f*

clew ['klu:] → **clue**
cliché [kli'ʃeɪ] *n* : cliché *m*, tópico *m*
click¹ ['klɪk] *vt* **1** : chasquear (los dedos, etc.) ⟨to click one's heels : dar un taconazo⟩ **2** : hacer clic en (un botón, etc.) — *vi* **1** : hacer clic **2** SNAP : chasquear **3** SUCCEED : tener éxito **4** GET ALONG : congeniar, llevarse bien
click² *n* : chasquido *m* (de los dedos, etc.), clic *m* (de un botón, etc.)
client ['klaɪənt] *n* : cliente *m*, -ta *f*
clientele [ˌklaɪən'tɛl, ˌkli:-] *n* : clientéla *f*
cliff ['klɪf] *n* : acantilado *m*, precipicio *m*, risco *m*
climate ['klaɪmət] *n* : clima *m*
climatic [klaɪ'mætɪk, klə-] *adj* : climático
climax¹ ['klaɪˌmæks] *vi* : llegar al punto culminante, culminar — *vt* : ser el punto culminante de
climax² *n* : clímax *m*, punto *m* culminante
climb¹ ['klaɪm] *vt* : escalar, trepar a, subir a ⟨to climb a mountain : escalar una montaña⟩ — *vi* **1** RISE : subir, ascender ⟨prices are climbing : los precios están subiendo⟩ **2** : subirse, treparse ⟨to climb up a tree : treparse a un árbol⟩
climb² *n* : ascenso *m*, subida *f*
climber ['klaɪmər] *n* **1** : escalador *m*, -dora *f* ⟨a mountain climber : un alpinista⟩ **2** : trepadora *f* (planta)
clinch¹ ['klɪntʃ] *vt* **1** FASTEN, SECURE : remachar (un clavo), afianzar, abrochar **2** SETTLE : decidir, cerrar ⟨to clinch the title : ganar el título⟩
clinch² *n* : abrazo *m*, clinch *m* (en el boxeo)
clincher ['klɪntʃər] *n* : argumento *m* decisivo
cling ['klɪŋ] *vi* **clung** ['klʌŋ]; **clinging 1** STICK : adherirse, pegarse **2** : aferrarse, agarrarse ⟨he clung to the railing : se aferró a la barandilla⟩
clinic ['klɪnɪk] *n* : clínica *f*
clinical ['klɪnɪkəl] *adj* : clínico — **clinically** [-kli] *adv*
clink¹ ['klɪŋk] *vi* : tintinear
clink² *n* : tintineo *m*
clip¹ ['klɪp] *vt* **clipped; clipping 1** CUT : cortar, recortar **2** HIT : golpear, dar un puñetazo a **3** FASTEN : sujetar (con un clip)
clip² *n* **1** → **clippers 2** BLOW : golpe *m*, puñetazo *m* **3** PACE : paso *m* rápido **4** FASTENER : clip *m* ⟨a paper clip : un sujetapapeles⟩
clipper ['klɪpər] *n* **1** : clíper *m* (buque de vela) **2 clippers** *npl* : tijeras *fpl* ⟨nail clippers : cortauñas⟩
clique ['kli:k, 'klɪk] *n* : grupo *m* exclusivo, camarilla *f* (de políticos)
clitoris ['klɪtərəs, klɪ'tɔrəs] *n, pl* **clitorides** [-'tɔrəˌdi:z] : clítoris *m*
cloak¹ ['klo:k] *vt* : encubrir, envolver (en un manto de)

cloak² *n* : capa *f*, capote *m*, manto *m* ⟨under the cloak of darkness : al amparo de la oscuridad⟩
clobber ['klɑbər] *vt* : dar una paliza a
clock¹ ['klɑk] *vt* : cronometrar
clock² *n* **1** : reloj *m* (de pared), cronómetro *m* (en deportes o competencias) **2 around the clock** : las veinticuatro horas
clockwise ['klɑkˌwaɪz] *adv & adj* : en la dirección de las manecillas del reloj
clockwork ['klɑkˌwərk] *n* : mecanismo *m* de relojería
clod ['klɑd] *n* **1** : terrón *m* **2** OAF : zoquete *mf*
clog¹ ['klɑg] *v* **clogged; clogging** *vt* **1** HINDER : estorbar, impedir **2** BLOCK : atascar, tapar — *vi* : atascarse, taparse
clog² *n* **1** OBSTACLE : traba *f*, impedimento *m*, estorbo *m* **2** : zueco *m* (zapato)
cloister¹ ['klɔɪstər] *vt* : enclaustrar
cloister² *n* : claustro *m*
clone ['klo:n] *n* **1** : clon *m* (de un organismo) **2** COPY : copia *f*, reproducción *f*
close¹ ['klo:z] *v* **closed; closing** *vt* : cerrar — *vi* **1** : cerrarse, cerrar **2** TERMINATE : concluirse, terminar **3 to close in** APPROACH : acercarse, aproximarse
close² ['klo:s] *adv* : cerca, de cerca
close³ *adj* **closer; closest 1** CONFINING : restrictivo, estrecho **2** SECRETIVE : reservado **3** STRICT : estricto, detallado **4** STUFFY : cargado, bochornoso (dícese del tiempo) **5** TIGHT : apretado, entallado, ceñido ⟨it's a close fit : es muy apretado⟩ **6** NEAR : cercano, próximo **7** INTIMATE : íntimo ⟨close friends : amigos íntimos⟩ **8** ACCURATE : fiel, exacto **9** : reñido ⟨a close election : una elección muy reñida⟩
close⁴ ['klo:z] *n* : fin *m*, final *m*, conclusión *f*
closely ['klo:sli] *adv* : cerca, de cerca
closeness ['klo:snəs] *n* **1** NEARNESS : cercanía *f*, proximidad *f* **2** INTIMACY : intimidad *f*
closet¹ ['klɑzət] *vt* **to be closeted with** : estar encerrado con
closet² *n* : armario *m*, guardarropa *f*, clóset *m*
closure ['klo:ʒər] *n* **1** CLOSING, END : cierre *m*, clausura *f*, fin *m* **2** FASTENER : cierre *m*
clot¹ ['klɑt] *v* **clotted; clotting** *vt* : coagular, cuajar — *vi* : cuajarse, coagularse
clot² *n* : coágulo *m*
cloth ['klɔθ] *n, pl* **cloths** ['klɔðz, 'klɔθs] **1** FABRIC : tela *f* **2** RAG : trapo *m* **3** TABLECLOTH : mantel *m*
clothe ['klo:ð] *vt* **clothed** *or* **clad** ['klæd]; **clothing** DRESS : vestir, arropar, ataviar
clothes ['klo:z, 'klo:ðz] *npl* **1** CLOTHING : ropa *f* **2** BEDCLOTHES : ropa *f* de cama
clothespin ['klo:zˌpɪn] *n* : pinza *f* (para la ropa)

clothing ['kloːðɪŋ] *n* : ropa *f*, indumentaria *f*

cloud¹ ['klaʊd] *vt* : nublar, oscurecer — *vi* **to cloud over** : nublarse

cloud² *n* : nube *f*

cloudburst ['klaʊd,bərst] *n* : chaparrón *m*, aguacero *m*

cloudless ['klaʊdləs] *adj* : despejado, claro

cloudy ['klaʊdi] *adj* **cloudier; -est** : nublado, nuboso

clout¹ ['klaʊt] *vt* : bofetear, dar un tortazo a

clout² *n* **1** BLOW : golpe *m*, tortazo *m fam* **2** INFLUENCE : influencia *f*, palanca *f fam*

clove¹ ['kloːv] *n* **1** : diente *m* (de ajo) **2** : clavo *m* (especia)

clove² → **cleave**

cloven hoof ['kloːvən] *n* : pezuña *f* hendida

clover ['kloːvər] *n* : trébol *m*

cloverleaf ['kloːvər,liːf] *n, pl* **-leafs** *or* **-leaves** [-,liːvz] : intersección *f* en trébol

clown¹ ['klaʊn] *vi* : payasear, bromear ⟨stop clowning around : déjate de payasadas⟩

clown² *n* : payaso *m*, -sa *f*

clownish ['klaʊnɪʃ] *adj* **1** : de payaso **2** BOORISH : grosero — **clownishly** *adv*

cloying ['klɔɪɪŋ] *adj* : empalagoso, meloso

club¹ ['klʌb] *vt* **clubbed; clubbing** : aporrear, dar garrotazos a

club² *n* **1** CUDGEL : garrote *m*, porra *f* **2** : palo *m* ⟨golf club : palo de golf⟩ **3** : trébol *m* (naipe) **4** ASSOCIATION : club *m*

clubfoot ['klʌb,fʊt] *n, pl* **-feet** : pie *m* deforme

clubhouse ['klʌb,haʊs] *n* : sede *f* de un club

cluck¹ ['klʌk] *vi* : cloquear, cacarear

cluck² *n* : cloqueo *m*, cacareo *m*

clue¹ ['kluː] *vt* **clued; clueing** *or* **cluing** *or* **to clue in** : dar una pista a, informar

clue² *n* : pista *f*, indicio *m*

clump¹ ['klʌmp] *vi* **1** : caminar con pisadas fuertes **2** LUMP : agruparse, aglutinarse — *vt* : amontonar

clump² *n* **1** : grupo *m* (de arbustos o árboles), terrón *m* (de tierra) **2** : pisada *f* fuerte

clumsily ['klʌmzəli] *adv* : torpemente, sin gracia

clumsiness ['klʌmzinəs] *n* : torpeza *f*

clumsy ['klʌmzi] *adj* **-sier; -est 1** AWKWARD : torpe, desmañado **2** TACTLESS : carente de tacto, poco delicado

clung → **cling**

clunky ['klʌŋki] *adj* : torpe, poco elegante

cluster¹ ['klʌstər] *vt* : agrupar, juntar — *vi* : agruparse, apiñarse, arracimarse

cluster² *n* : grupo *m*, conjunto *m*, racimo *m* (de uvas)

clutch¹ ['klʌtʃ] *vt* : agarrar, asir — *vi* **to clutch at** : tratar de agarrar

clutch² *n* **1** GRASP, GRIP : agarre *m*, apretón *m* **2** : embrague *m*, clutch *m* (de una máquina) **3** **clutches** *npl* : garras *fpl* ⟨he fell into their clutches : cayó en sus garras⟩

clutter¹ ['klʌtər] *vt* : atiborrar o atestar de cosas, llenar desordenadamente

clutter² *n* : desorden *m*, revoltijo *m*

coach¹ ['koːtʃ] *vt* : entrenar (atletas, artistas), preparar (alumnos)

coach² *n* **1** CARRIAGE : coche *m*, carruaje *m*, carroza *f* **2** : vagón *m* de pasajeros (de un tren) **3** BUS : autobús *m*, ómnibus *m* **4** : pasaje *m* aéreo de segunda clase **5** TRAINER : entrenador *m*, -dora *f*

coagulate [ko'ægjə,leɪt] *v* **-lated; -lating** *vt* : coagular, cuajar — *vi* : coagularse, cuajarse

coal ['koːl] *n* **1** EMBER : ascua *f*, brasa *f* **2** : carbón *m* ⟨a coal mine : una mina de carbón⟩

coalesce [,koːə'lɛs] *vi* **-alesced; -alescing** : unirse

coalition [,koːə'lɪʃən] *n* : coalición *f*

coarse ['kors] *adj* **coarser; -est 1** : grueso (dícese de la arena o la sal), basto (dícese de las telas), áspero (dícese de la piel) **2** CRUDE, ROUGH : basto, tosco, ordinario **3** VULGAR : grosero — **coarsely** *adv*

coarsen ['korsən] *vt* : hacer áspero o basto — *vi* : volverse áspero o basto

coarseness ['korsnəs] *n* : aspereza *f*, tosquedad *f*

coast¹ ['koːst] *vi* : deslizarse, rodar sin impulso

coast² *n* : costa *f*, litoral *m*

coastal ['koːstəl] *adj* : costero

coaster ['koːstər] *n* : posavasos *m*

coast guard *n* : guardia *f* costera, guardacostas *mpl*

coastline ['koːst,laɪn] *n* : costa *f*

coat¹ ['koːt] *vt* : cubrir, revestir, bañar (en un líquido)

coat² *n* **1** : abrigo *m* ⟨a sport coat : una chaqueta, un saco⟩ **2** : pelaje *m* (de animales) **3** LAYER : capa *f*, mano *f* (de pintura)

coating ['koːtɪŋ] *n* : capa *f*

coat of arms *n* : escudo *m* de armas

coax ['koːks] *vt* : engatusar, persuadir

cob ['kab] → **corncob**

cobalt ['koː,bɔlt] *n* : cobalto *m*

cobble ['kabəl] *vt* **cobbled; cobbling 1** : fabricar o remendar (zapatos) **2 to cobble together** : improvisar, hacer apresuradamente

cobbler ['kablər] *n* **1** SHOEMAKER : zapatero *m*, -ra *f* **2 fruit cobbler** : tarta *f* de fruta

cobblestone ['kabəl,stoːn] *n* : adoquín *m*

cobra ['koːbrə] *n* : cobra *f*

cobweb ['kab,wɛb] *n* : telaraña *f*

coca ['koːkə] *n* : coca *f*

cocaine [ko:'keɪn, 'ko:ˌkeɪn] n : cocaína f

cock¹ ['kɑk] vt 1 : ladear ⟨to cock one's head : ladear la cabeza⟩ 2 : montar, amartillar (un arma de fuego)

cock² n 1 ROOSTER : gallo m 2 FAUCET : grifo m, llave f 3 : martillo m (de un arma de fuego)

cockatoo ['kɑkəˌtu:] n, pl -toos : cacatúa f

cockeyed ['kɑkˌaɪd] adj 1 ASKEW : ladeado, torcido, chueco 2 ABSURD : disparatado, absurdo

cockfight ['kɑkˌfaɪt] n : pelea f de gallos

cockiness ['kɑkinəs] n : arrogancia f

cockle ['kɑkəl] n : berberecho m

cockpit ['kɑkˌpɪt] n : cabina f

cockroach ['kɑkˌro:ʧ] n : cucaracha f

cocktail ['kɑkˌteɪl] n 1 : coctel m, cóctel m 2 APPETIZER : aperitivo m

cocky ['kɑki] adj cockier; -est : creído, engreído

cocoa ['ko:ˌko:] n 1 CACAO : cacao m 2 : cocoa f, chocolate m (bebida)

coconut ['ko:kəˌnʌt] n : coco m

cocoon [kə'ku:n] n : capullo m

cod ['kɑd] n, pl cod : bacalao m

coddle ['kɑdəl] vt -dled; -dling : mimar, consentir

code ['ko:d] n 1 : código m ⟨civil code : código civil⟩ 2 : código m, clave f ⟨secret code : clave secreta⟩

codeine ['ko:ˌdi:n] n : codeína f

codex ['ko:ˌdɛks] n, pl -dexes [-ˌdɛksəz] or -dices [-dəˌsi:z] : códice m

codger ['kɑʤər] n : viejo m, vejete m

codify ['kɑdəˌfaɪ, 'ko:-] vt -fied; -fying : codificar

coeducation [ˌko:ˌɛʤə'keɪʃən] n : coeducación f, enseñanza f mixta

coeducational [ˌko:ˌɛʤə'keɪʃənəl] adj : mixto

coefficient [ˌko:ə'fɪʃənt] n : coeficiente m

coerce [ko'ərs] vt -erced; -ercing : coaccionar, forzar, obligar

coercion [ko'ərʒən, -ʃən] n : coacción f

coercive [ko'ərsɪv] adj : coactivo

coexist [ˌko:ɪg'zɪst] vi : coexistir

coexistence [ˌko:ɪg'zɪstənts] n : coexistencia f

coffee ['kɔfi] n : café m

coffeepot ['kɔfiˌpɑt] n : cafetera f

coffee table n : mesa f de centro

coffer ['kɔfər] n : cofre m

coffin ['kɔfən] n : ataúd m, féretro m

cog ['kɑg] n : diente m (de una rueda dentada)

cogent ['ko:ʤənt] adj : convincente, persuasivo

cogitate ['kɑʤəˌteɪt] vi -tated; -tating : reflexionar, meditar, discurrir

cogitation [ˌkɑʤə'teɪʃən] n : reflexión f, meditación f

cognac ['ko:nˌjæk] n : coñac m

cognate ['kɑgˌneɪt] adj : relacionado, afín

cognition [kɑg'nɪʃən] n : cognición f

cognitive ['kɑgnətɪv] adj : cognitivo

cogwheel ['kɑgˌʍi:l] n : rueda f dentada

cohabit [ˌko:'hæbət] vi : cohabitar

cohere [ko'hɪr] vi -hered; -hering 1 ADHERE : adherirse, pegarse 2 : ser coherente o congruente

coherence [ko'hɪrənts] n : coherencia f, congruencia f

coherent [ko'hɪrənt] adj : coherente, congruente — coherently adv

cohesion [ko'hi:ʒən] n : cohesión f

cohesive [ko:'hi:sɪv, -zɪv] adj : cohesivo

cohort ['ko:ˌhɔrt] n 1 : cohorte f (de soldados) 2 COMPANION : compañero m, -ra f; colega mf

coiffure [kwa'fjʊr] n : peinado m

coil¹ ['kɔɪl] vt : enrollar — vi : enrollarse, enroscarse

coil² n : rollo m (de cuerda, etc.), espiral f (de humo)

coin¹ ['kɔɪn] vt 1 MINT : acuñar (moneda) 2 INVENT : acuñar, crear, inventar ⟨to coin a phrase : como se suele decir⟩

coin² n : moneda f

coincide [ˌko:ɪn'saɪd, 'ko:ɪnˌsaɪd] vi -cided; -ciding : coincidir

coincidence [ko'ɪntsədənts] n : coincidencia f, casualidad f ⟨what a coincidence! : ¡qué casualidad!⟩

coincident [ko'ɪntsədənt] adj : coincidente, concurrente

coincidental [koˌɪntsə'dɛntəl] adj : casual, accidental, fortuito

coitus ['ko:ətəs] n : coito m

coke ['ko:k] n : coque m

colander ['kɑləndər, 'kʌ-] n : colador m

cold¹ ['ko:ld] adj : frío ⟨it's cold out : hace frío⟩ ⟨a cold reception : una fría recepción⟩ ⟨in cold blood : a sangre fría⟩

cold² n 1 : frío m ⟨to feel the cold : sentir frío⟩ 2 : resfriado m, catarro m ⟨to catch a cold : resfriarse⟩

cold–blooded ['ko:ld'blʌdəd] adj 1 CRUEL : cruel, despiadado 2 : de sangre fría (dícese de los reptiles, etc.)

coldly ['ko:ldli] adv : fríamente, con frialdad

coldness ['ko:ldnəs] n : frialdad f (de una persona o una actitud), frío m (de la temperatura)

coleslaw ['ko:lˌslɔ] n : ensalada f de col

colic ['kɑlɪk] n : cólico m

coliseum [ˌkɑlə'si:əm] n : coliseo m, arena f

collaborate [kə'læbəˌreɪt] vi -rated; -rating : colaborar

collaboration [kəˌlæbə'reɪʃən] n : colaboración f

collaborator [kə'læbəˌreɪtər] n 1 COLLEAGUE : colaborador m, -dora f 2 TRAITOR : colaboracionista mf

collage [kə'lɑʒ] n : collage m

collapse¹ [kə'læps] vi -lapsed; -lapsing 1 : derrumbarse, desplomarse, hundirse ⟨the building collapsed : el edificio se derrumbó⟩ **2** FALL : desplomarse, caerse ⟨he collapsed on the bed : se desplomó en la cama⟩ ⟨to collapse with laughter : morirse de risa⟩ **3** FAIL : fracasar, quebrar, arruinarse **4** FOLD : plegarse

collapse² *n* **1** FALL : derrumbe *m*, desplome *m* **2** BREAKDOWN, FAILURE : fracaso *m*, colapso *m* (físico), quiebra *f* (económica)

collapsible [kə'læpsəbəl] *adj* : plegable

collar¹ ['kɑlər] *vt* : agarrar, atrapar

collar² *n* : cuello *m*

collarbone ['kɑlər,boːn] *n* : clavícula *f*

collate [kə'leɪt; 'kɑ,leɪt, 'koː-] *vt* **-lated; -lating 1** COMPARE : cotejar, comparar **2** : ordenar, recopilar (páginas)

collateral¹ [kə'læt̬ərəl] *adj* : colateral

collateral² *n* : garantía *f*, fianza *f*, prenda *f*

colleague ['kɑ,liːg] *n* : colega *mf*; compañero *m*, -ra *f*

collect¹ [kə'lɛkt] *vt* **1** GATHER : recopilar, reunir, recoger ⟨she collected her thoughts : puso en orden sus ideas⟩ **2** : coleccionar, juntar ⟨to collect stamps : coleccionar timbres⟩ **3** : cobrar (una deuda), recaudar (un impuesto) **4** DRAW : cobrar, percibir (un sueldo, etc.) — *vi* **1** ACCUMULATE : acumularse, juntarse **2** CONGREGATE : congregarse, reunirse

collect² *adv* & *adj* : por cobrar, a cobro revertido

collectible *or* **collectable** [kə'lɛktəbəl] *adj* : coleccionable

collection [kə'lɛkʃən] *n* **1** COLLECTING : colecta *f* (de contribuciones), cobro *m* (de deudas), recaudación *f* (de impuestos) **2** GROUP : colección *f* (de objetos), grupo *m* (de personas)

collective¹ [kə'lɛktɪv] *adj* : colectivo — **collectively** *adv*

collective² *n* : colectivo *m*

collector [kə'lɛktər] *n* **1** : coleccionista *mf* (de objetos) **2** : cobrador *m*, -dora *f* (de deudas)

college ['kɑlɪdʒ] *n* **1** : universidad *f* **2** : colegio *m* (de electores o profesionales)

collegiate [kə'liːdʒət] *adj* : universitario

collide [kə'laɪd] *vi* **-lided; -liding** : chocar, colisionar, estrellarse

collie ['kɑli] *n* : collie *mf*

collision [kə'lɪʒən] *n* : choque *m*, colisión *f*

colloquial [kə'loːkwiəl] *adj* : coloquial

colloquialism [kə'loːkwiə,lɪzəm] *n* : expresión *f* coloquial

collusion [kə'luː ʒən] *n* : colusión *f*

cologne [kə'loːn] *n* : colonia *f*

Colombian [kə'lʌmbiən] *n* : colombiano *m*, -na *f* — **Colombian** *adj*

colon¹ ['koːlən] *n*, *pl* **colons** *or* **cola** [-lə] : colon *m* (de los intestinos)

colon² *n*, *pl* **colons** : dos puntos *mpl* (signo ortográfico)

colonel ['kərnəl] *n* : coronel *m*

colonial¹ [kə'loːniəl] *adj* : colonial

colonial² *n* : colono *m*, -na *f*

colonist ['kɑlənɪst] *n* : colono *m*, -na *f*; colonizador *m*, -dora *f*

colonization [,kɑlənə'zeɪʃən] *n* : colonización *f*

colonize ['kɑlə,naɪz] *vt* **-nized; -nizing 1** : establecer una colonia en **2** SETTLE : colonizar

colonnade [,kɑlə'neɪd] *n* : columnata *f*

colony ['kɑləni] *n*, *pl* **-nies** : colonia *f*

color¹ ['kʌlər] *vt* **1** : colorear, pintar **2** INFLUENCE : influir en, influenciar — *vi* BLUSH : sonrojarse, ruborizarse

color² *n* **1** : color *m* ⟨primary colors : colores primarios⟩ **2** INTEREST, VIVIDNESS : color *m*, colorido *m* ⟨local color : color local⟩

coloration [kələ'reɪʃən] *n* : coloración *f*

color-blind ['kʌlər,blaɪnd] *adj* : daltónico

color blindness *n* : daltonismo *m*

colored ['kʌlərd] *adj* **1** : de color (dícese de los objetos) **2** : de color, negro (dícese de las personas)

colorfast ['kʌlər,fæst] *adj* : que no se destiñe

colorful ['kʌlərfəl] *adj* **1** : lleno de colorido, de colores vivos **2** PICTURESQUE, STRIKING : pintoresco, llamativo

coloring ['kələrɪŋ] *n* **1** : color *m*, colorido *m* **2 food coloring** : colorante *m*

colorless ['kʌlərləs] *adj* **1** : incoloro, sin color **2** DULL : soso, aburrido

colossal [kə'lɑsəl] *adj* : colosal

colossus [kə'lɑsəs] *n*, *pl* **-si** [-,saɪ] : coloso *m*

colt ['koːlt] *n* : potro *m*, potranco *m*

column ['kɑləm] *n* : columna *f*

columnist ['kɑləmnɪst, -ləmɪst] *n* : columnista *mf*

coma ['koːmə] *n* : coma *m*, estado *m* de coma

Comanche [kə'mæntʃi] *n* : comanche *mf* — **Comanche** *adj*

comatose ['koːmə,toːs, 'kɑ-] *adj* : comatoso, en estado de coma

comb¹ ['koːm] *vt* **1** : peinar (el pelo) **2** SEARCH : peinar, rastrear, registrar a fondo

comb² *n* **1** : peine *m* **2** : cresta *f* (de un gallo)

combat¹ [kəm'bæt, 'kɑm,bæt] *vt* **-bated** *or* **-batted; -bating** *or* **-batting** : combatir, luchar contra

combat² ['kɑm,bæt] *n* : combate *m*, lucha *f*

combatant [kəm'bæt̬ənt] *n* : combatiente *mf*

combative [kəm'bæt̬ɪv] *adj* : combativo

combination [,kɑmbə'neɪʃən] *n* : combinación *f*

combine¹ [kəm'baɪn] *v* **-bined; -bining** *vt* : combinar, aunar — *vi* : combinarse, mezclarse

combine² ['kɑm,baɪn] *n* **1** ALLIANCE : alianza *f* comercial o política **2** HARVESTER : cosechadora *f*

combustible [kəm'bʌstəbəl] *adj* : inflamable, combustible

combustion [kəm'bʌstʃən] *n* : combustión *f*

come ['kʌm] *vi* **came** ['keɪm]; **come**; **coming 1** APPROACH : venir, aproximarse ⟨here they come : acá vienen⟩ **2** ARRIVE : venir, llegar, alcanzar ⟨they came yesterday : vinieron ayer⟩ **3** ORIGINATE : venir, provenir ⟨this wine comes from France : este vino viene de Francia⟩ **4** AMOUNT : llegar, ascender ⟨the investment came to two million : la inversión llegó a dos millones⟩ **5 to come clean** : confesar, desahogar la conciencia **6 to come into** ACQUIRE : adquirir ⟨to come into a fortune : heredar una fortuna⟩ **7 to come off** SUCCEED : tener éxito, ser un éxito **8 to come out** : salir, aparecer, publicarse **9 to come to** REVIVE : recobrar el conocimiento, volver en sí **10 to come to pass** HAPPEN : acontecer **11 to come to terms** : llegar a un acuerdo

comeback ['kʌm,bæk] *n* **1** RETORT : réplica *f*, respuesta *f* **2** RETURN : retorno *m*, regreso *m* ⟨the champion announced his comeback : el campeón anunció su regreso⟩

come back *vi* **1** RETORT : replicar, contestar **2** RETURN : volver ⟨come back here! : ¡vuelve acá!⟩ ⟨that style's coming back : ese estilo está volviendo⟩

comedian [kə'mi:diən] *n* : cómico *m*, -ca *f*; humorista *mf*

comedienne [kə,mi:di'ɛn] *n* : cómica *f*, humorista *f*

comedy ['kɑmədi] *n, pl* **-dies** : comedia *f*

comely ['kʌmli] *adj* **-lier; -est** : bello, bonito

comet ['kɑmət] *n* : cometa *m*

comfort¹ ['kʌmpfərt] *vt* **1** CHEER : confortar, alentar **2** CONSOLE : consolar

comfort² *n* **1** CONSOLATION : consuelo *m* **2** WELL-BEING : confort *m*, bienestar *m* **3** CONVENIENCE : comodidad *f* ⟨the comforts of home : las comodidades del hogar⟩

comfortable ['kʌmpfərtəbəl, 'kʌmpftə-] *adj* : cómodo, confortable — **comfortably** ['kʌmpfərtəbli, 'kʌmpftə-] *adv*

comforter ['kʌmpfərtər] *n* QUILT : edredón *m*, cobertor *m*

comic¹ ['kɑmɪk] *adj* : cómico, humorístico

comic² *n* **1** COMEDIAN : cómico *m*, -ca *f*; humorista *mf* **2** *or* **comic book** : historieta *f*, cómic *m*

comical ['kɑmɪkəl] *adj* : cómico, gracioso, chistoso

comic strip *n* : tira *f* cómica, historieta *f*

coming ['kʌmɪŋ] *adj* : siguiente, próximo, que viene

comma ['kɑmə] *n* : coma *f*

command¹ [kə'mænd] *vt* **1** ORDER : ordenar, mandar **2** CONTROL, DIRECT : comandar, tener el mando de — *vi* **1** : dar órdenes **2** GOVERN : estar al mando *m*, gobernar

command² *n* **1** CONTROL, LEADERSHIP : mando *m*, control *m*, dirección *f* **2** ORDER : orden *f*, mandato *m* **3** MASTERY : maestría *f*, destreza *f*, dominio *m* **4** : tropa *f* asignada a un comandante

commandant ['kɑmən,dɑnt, -,dænt] *n* : comandante *mf*

commandeer [,kɑmən'dɪr] *vt* : piratear, secuestrar (un vehículo, etc.)

commander [kə'mændər] *n* : comandante *mf*

commandment [kə'mændmənt] *n* : mandamiento *m*, orden *f* ⟨the Ten Commandments : los diez mandamientos⟩

commando [kə'mændo:] *n* : comando *m*

commemorate [kə'mɛmə,reɪt] *vt* **-rated; -rating** : conmemorar

commemoration [kə,mɛmə'reɪʃən] *n* : conmemoración *f*

commemorative [kə'mɛmrətɪv, -'mɛmə,reɪtɪv] *adj* : conmemorativo

commence [kə'mɛnʦ] *v* **-menced; -mencing** *vt* : iniciar, comenzar — *vi* : iniciarse, comenzar

commencement [kə'mɛnʦmənt] *n* **1** BEGINNING : inicio *m*, comienzo *m* **2** : ceremonia *f* de graduación

commend [kə'mɛnd] *vt* **1** ENTRUST : encomendar **2** RECOMMEND : recomendar **3** PRAISE : elogiar, alabar

commendable [kə'mɛndəbəl] *adj* : loable, meritorio, encomiable

commendation [,kɑmən'deɪʃən, -,mɛn-] *n* : elogio *m*, encomio *m*

commensurate [kə'mɛnʦərət, -'mɛntʃurət] *adj* : proporcionado ⟨commensurate with : en proporción a⟩

comment¹ ['kɑ,mɛnt] *vi* **1** : hacer comentarios **2 to comment on** : comentar, hacer observaciones sobre

comment² *n* : comentario *m*, observación *f*

commentary ['kɑmən,tɛri] *n, pl* **-taries** : comentario *m*, crónica *f* (deportiva)

commentator ['kɑmən,teɪtər] *n* : comentarista *mf*, cronista *mf* (de deportes)

commerce ['kɑmərs] *n* : comercio *m*

commercial¹ [kə'mərʃəl] *adj* : comercial — **commercially** *adv*

commercial² *n* : comercial *m*

commercialize [kə'mərʃə,laɪz] *vt* **-ized; -izing** : comercializar

commiserate [kə'mɪzə,reɪt] *vi* **-ated; -ating** : compadecerse, consolarse

commiseration [kə,mɪzə'reɪʃən] *n* : conmiseración *f*

commission¹ [kə'mɪʃən] *vt* **1** : nombrar (un oficial) **2** : comisionar, encargar ⟨to commission a painting : encargar una pintura⟩

commission² n **1** : nombramiento m (al grado de oficial) **2** COMMITTEE : comisión f, comité m **3** COMMITTING : comisión f, realización f (de un acto) **4** PERCENTAGE : comisión f ⟨sales commissions : comisiones de venta⟩

commissioned officer n : oficial mf

commissioner [kə'mɪʃənər] n **1** : comisionado m, -da f; miembro m de una comisión **2** : comisario m, -ria f (de policía, etc.)

commit [kə'mɪt] vt **-mitted; -mitting 1** ENTRUST : encomendar, confiar **2** CONFINE : internar (en un hospital), encarcelar (en una prisión) **3** PERPETRATE : cometer ⟨to commit a crime : cometer un crimen⟩ **4 to commit oneself** : comprometerse

commitment [kə'mɪtmənt] n **1** RESPONSIBILITY : compromiso m, responsabilidad f **2** DEDICATION : dedicación f, devoción f ⟨commitment to the cause : devoción a la causa⟩

committee [kə'mɪti] n : comité m

commodious [kə'mo:diəs] adj SPACIOUS : amplio, espacioso

commodity [kə'madəti] n, pl **-ties** : artículo m de comercio, mercancía f, mercadería f

commodore ['kamə‚dor] n : comodoro m

common¹ ['kamən] adj **1** PUBLIC : común, público ⟨the common good : el bien común⟩ **2** SHARED : común ⟨a common interest : un interés común⟩ **3** GENERAL : común, general ⟨it's common knowledge : todo el mundo lo sabe⟩ **4** ORDINARY : ordinario, común y corriente ⟨the common man : el hombre medio, el hombre de la calle⟩

common² n **1** : tierra f comunal **2 in ∼** : en común

common cold n : resfriado m común

common denominator n : denominador m común

commoner ['kamənər] n : plebeyo m, -ya f

commonly ['kamənli] adv **1** FREQUENTLY : comúnmente, frecuentemente **2** USUALLY : normalmente

common noun n : nombre m común

commonplace¹ ['kamən‚pleɪs] adj : común, ordinario

commonplace² n : cliché m, tópico m

common sense n : sentido m común

commonwealth ['kamən‚wɛlθ] n : entidad f política ⟨the British Commonwealth : la Mancomunidad Británica⟩

commotion [kə'mo:ʃən] n **1** RUCKUS : alboroto m, jaleo m, escándalo m **2** STIR, UPSET : revuelo m, conmoción f

communal [kə'mju:nəl] adj : comunal

commune¹ [kə'mju:n] vi **-muned; -muning** : estar en comunión

commune² ['ka‚mju:n, kə'mju:n] n : comuna f

communicable [kə'mju:nɪkəbəl] adj CONTAGIOUS : transmisible, contagioso

communicate [kə'mju:nə‚keɪt] v **-cated; -cating** vt **1** CONVEY : comunicar, expresar, hacer saber **2** TRANSMIT : transmitir (una enfermedad), contagiar — vi : comunicarse, expresarse

communication [kə‚mju:nə'keɪʃən] n : comunicación f

communicative [kə'mju:nɪ‚keɪţɪv, -kəţɪv] adj : comunicativo

communion [kə'mju:njən] n **1** SHARING : comunión f **2 Communion** : comunión f, eucaristía f

communiqué [kə'mju:nə‚keɪ, -‚mju:nə-'keɪ] n : comunicado m

communism or **Communism** ['kamjə‚nɪzəm] n : comunismo m

communist¹ or **Communist** ['kamjə‚nɪst] adj : comunista ⟨the Communist Party : el Partido Comunista⟩

communist² or **Communist** n : comunista mf

communistic or **Communistic** [‚kamjə-'nɪstɪk] adj : comunista

community [kə'mju:nəti] n, pl **-ties** : comunidad f

commute [kə'mju:t] v **-muted; -muting** vt REDUCE : conmutar, reducir (una sentencia) — vi : viajar de la residencia al trabajo

commuter [kə'mju:ţər] n : persona f que viaja diariamente al trabajo

compact¹ [kəm'pækt, 'kam‚pækt] vt : compactar, consolidar, comprimir

compact² [kəm'pækt, 'kam‚pækt] adj **1** DENSE, SOLID : compacto, macizo, denso **2** CONCISE : breve, conciso

compact³ ['kam‚pækt] n **1** AGREEMENT : acuerdo m, pacto m **2** : polvera f, estuche m de maquillaje **3** or **compact car** : auto m compacto

compact disc ['kam‚pækt'dɪsk] n : disco m compacto, compact disc m

compactly [kəm'pæktli, 'kam‚pækt-] adv **1** DENSELY : densamente, macizamente **2** CONCISELY : concisamente, brevemente

companion [kəm'pænjən] n **1** COMRADE : compañero m, -ra f; acompañante mf **2** MATE : pareja f (de un zapato, etc.)

companionable [kəm'pænjənəbəl] adj : sociable, amigable

companionship [kəm'pænjən‚ʃɪp] n : compañerismo m, camaradería f

company ['kʌmpəni] n, pl **-nies 1** FIRM : compañía f, empresa f **2** GROUP : compañía f (de actores o soldados) **3** GUESTS : visita f ⟨we have company : tenemos visita⟩

comparable ['kampərəbəl] adj : comparable, parecido

comparative¹ [kəm'pærəţɪv] adj RELATIVE : comparativo, relativo — **comparatively** adv

comparative² n : comparativo m

compare¹ [kəm'pær] v -pared; -paring vt : comparar — vi to compare with : poder comparar con, tener comparación con

compare² n : comparación f ⟨beyond compare : sin igual, sin par⟩

comparison [kəm'pærəsən] n : comparación f

compartment [kəm'pɑrtmənt] n : compartimiento m, compartimiento m

compass ['kʌmpəs, 'kɑm-] n 1 RANGE, SCOPE : alcance m, extensión f, límites mpl 2 : compás m (para trazar circunferencias) 3 : compás m, brújula f ⟨the points of the compass : los puntos cardinales⟩

compassion [kəm'pæʃən] n : compasión f, piedad f, misericordia f

compassionate [kəm'pæʃənət] adj : compasivo

compatibility [kəm,pætə'bɪləti] n : compatibilidad f

compatible [kəm'pætəbəl] adj : compatible, afín

compatriot [kəm'peɪtriət, -'pæ-] n : compatriota mf; paisano m, -na f

compel [kəm'pɛl] vt -pelled; -pelling : obligar, compeler

compelling [kəm'pɛlɪŋ] adj 1 FORCEFUL : fuerte 2 ENGAGING : absorbente 3 PERSUASIVE : persuasivo, convincente

compendium [kəm'pɛndiəm] n, pl -diums or -dia [-diə] : compendio m

compensate ['kɑmpən,seɪt] vi -sated; -sating vi to compensate for : compensar — vt : indemnizar, compensar

compensation [,kɑmpən'seɪʃən] n : compensación f, indemnización f

compensatory [kəm'pɛntsə,tori] adj : compensatorio

compete [kəm'pi:t] vi -peted; -peting : competir, contender, rivalizar

competence ['kɑmpətənts] n : competencia f, aptitud f

competency ['kɑmpətəntsi] → competence

competent ['kɑmpətənt] adj : competente, capaz

competition [,kɑmpə'tɪʃən] n : competencia f, concurso m

competitive [kəm'pɛtətɪv] adj : competitivo

competitor [kəm'pɛtətər] n : competidor m, -dora f

compilation [,kɑmpə'leɪʃən] n : recopilación f, compilación f

compile [kəm'paɪl] vt -piled; -piling : compilar, recopilar

complacency [kəm'pleɪsəntsi] n : satisfacción f consigo mismo, suficiencia f

complacent [kəm'pleɪsənt] adj : satisfecho de sí mismo, suficiente

complain [kəm'pleɪn] vi 1 GRIPE : quejarse, regañar, rezongar 2 PROTEST : reclamar, protestar

complaint [kəm'pleɪnt] n 1 GRIPE : queja f 2 AILMENT : afección f, dolencia f

3 ACCUSATION : reclamo m, acusación f

complement¹ ['kɑmplə,mɛnt] vt : complementar

complement² ['kɑmpləmənt] n : complemento m

complementary [,kɑmplə'mɛntəri] adj : complementario

complete¹ [kəm'pli:t] vt -pleted; -pleting 1 : completar, hacer entero ⟨this piece completes the collection : esta pieza completa la colección⟩ 2 FINISH : completar, acabar, terminar ⟨she completed her studies : completó sus estudios⟩

complete² adj -pleter; -est 1 WHOLE : completo, entero, íntegro 2 FINISHED : terminado, acabado 3 TOTAL : completo, total, absoluto

completely [kəm'pli:tli] adv : completamente, totalmente

completion [kəm'pli:ʃən] n : finalización f, cumplimiento m

complex¹ [kɑm'plɛks, kəm-; 'kɑm,plɛks] adj : complejo, complicado

complex² ['kɑm,plɛks] n : complejo m

complexion [kəm'plɛkʃən] n : cutis m, tez f ⟨of dark complexion : de tez morena⟩

complexity [kəm'plɛksəti, kɑm-] n, pl -ties : complejidad f

compliance [kəm'plaɪənts] n : conformidad f ⟨in compliance with the law : conforme a la ley⟩

compliant [kəm'plaɪənt] adj : dócil, sumiso

complicate ['kɑmplə,keɪt] vt -cated; -cating : complicar

complicated ['kɑmplə,keɪt̬əd] adj : complicado

complication [,kɑmplə'keɪʃən] n : complicación f

complicity [kəm'plɪsəti] n, pl -ties : complicidad f

compliment¹ ['kɑmplə,mɛnt] vt : halagar, florear Mex

compliment² ['kɑmpləmənt] n 1 : halago m, cumplido m 2 compliments npl : saludos mpl ⟨give them my compliments : déles saludos de mi parte⟩

complimentary [,kɑmplə'mɛntəri] adj 1 FLATTERING : halagador, halagüeño 2 FREE : de cortesía, gratis

comply [kəm'plaɪ] vi -plied; -plying : cumplir, acceder, obedecer

component¹ [kəm'po:nənt, 'kɑm-,po:-] adj : componente

component² n : componente m, elemento m, pieza f

compose [kəm'po:z] vt -posed; -posing 1 : componer, crear ⟨to compose a melody : componer una melodía⟩ 2 CALM : calmar, serenar ⟨to compose oneself : serenarse⟩ 3 CONSTITUTE : constar, componer ⟨to be composed of : constar de⟩ 4 : componer (un texto a imprimirse)

composer [kəm'po:zər] n : compositor m, -tora f

composite[1] [kam'pazət, kəm-; 'kampəzət] *adj* : compuesto (de varias partes)

composite[2] *n* : compuesto *m*, mezcla *f*

composition [ˌkampə'zıʃən] *n* 1 MAKE-UP : composición *f* 2 ESSAY : ensayo *m*, trabajo *m*

compost ['kam.po:st] *n* : abono *m* vegetal

composure [kəm'po:ʒər] *n* : compostura *f*, serenidad *f*

compound[1] [kam'paʊnd, kəm-; 'kam.paʊnd] *vt* 1 COMBINE, COMPOSE : combinar, componer 2 AUGMENT : agravar, aumentar ⟨to compound a problem : agravar un problema⟩

compound[2] ['kam.paʊnd; kam'paʊnd, kəm-] *adj* : compuesto ⟨compound interest : interés compuesto⟩

compound[3] ['kam.paʊnd] *n* 1 MIXTURE : compuesto *m*, mezcla *f* 2 ENCLOSURE : recinto *m* (de residencias, etc.)

compound fracture *n* : fractura *f* complicada

comprehend [ˌkamprı'hɛnd] *vt* 1 UNDERSTAND : comprender, entender 2 INCLUDE : comprender, incluir, abarcar

comprehensible [ˌkamprı'hɛntsəbəl] *adj* : comprensible

comprehension [ˌkamprı'hɛntʃən] *n* : comprensión *f*

comprehensive [ˌkamprı'hɛntsıv] *adj* 1 INCLUSIVE : inclusivo, exhaustivo 2 BROAD : extenso, amplio

compress[1] [kəm'prɛs] *vt* : comprimir

compress[2] ['kam.prɛs] *n* : compresa *f*

compression [kəm'prɛʃən] *n* : compresión *f*

compressor [kəm'prɛsər] *n* : compresor *m*

comprise [kəm'praız] *vt* -prised; -prising 1 INCLUDE : comprender, incluir 2 : componerse de, constar de ⟨the installation comprises several buildings : la instalación está compuesta de varios edificios⟩

compromise[1] ['kamprə.maız] *v* -mised; -mising *vi* : transigir, avenirse — *vt* JEOPARDIZE : comprometer, poner en peligro

compromise[2] *n* : acuerdo *m* mutuo, compromiso *m*

comptroller [kən'tro:lər, 'kamp-.tro:-] *n* : contralor *m*, -lora *f*; interventor *m*, -tora *f*

compulsion [kəm'pʌlʃən] *n* 1 COERCION : coacción *f* 2 URGE : compulsión *f*, impulso *m*

compulsive [kəm'pʌlsıv] *adj* : compulsivo

compulsory [kəm'pʌlsəri] *adj* : obligatorio

compunction [kəm'pʌŋkʃən] *n* 1 QUALM : reparo *m*, escrúpulo *m* 2 REMORSE : remordimiento *m*

computation [ˌkampjʊ'teıʃən] *n* : cálculo *m*, cómputo *m*

compute [kəm'pju:t] *vt* -puted; -puting : computar, calcular

computer [kəm'pju:tər] *n* : computadora *f*, computador *m*, ordenador *m* *Spain*

computerize [kəm'pju:tə.raız] *vt* -ized; -izing : computarizar, informatizar

comrade ['kam.ræd] *n* : camarada *mf*; compañero *m*, -ra *f*

con[1] ['kan] *vt* **conned; conning** SWINDLE : estafar, timar

con[2] *adv* : contra

con[3] *n* : contra *m* ⟨the pros and cons : los pros y los contras⟩

concave [kan'keıv, 'kan.keıv] *adj* : cóncavo

conceal [kən'si:l] *vt* : esconder, ocultar, disimular

concealment [kən'si:lmənt] *n* : escondimiento *m*, ocultación *f*

concede [kən'si:d] *vt* -ceded; -ceding 1 ALLOW, GRANT : conceder 2 ADMIT : conceder, reconocer ⟨to concede defeat : reconocer la derrota⟩

conceit [kən'si:t] *n* : engreimiento *m*, presunción *f*

conceited [kən'si:t̬əd] *adj* : presumido, engreído, presuntuoso

conceivable [kən'si:vəbəl] *adj* : concebible, imaginable

conceivably [kən'si:vəbli] *adv* : posiblemente, de manera concebible

conceive [kən'si:v] *v* -ceived; -ceiving *vi* : concebir, embarazarse — *vt* IMAGINE : concebir, imaginar

concentrate[1] ['kantsən.treıt] *v* -trated; -trating *vt* : concentrar — *vi* : concentrarse

concentrate[2] *n* : concentrado *m*

concentration [ˌkantsən'treıʃən] *n* : concentración *f*

concentric [kən'sɛntrık] *adj* : concéntrico

concept ['kan.spt] *n* : concepto *m*, idea *f*

conception [kən'sɛpʃən] *n* 1 : concepción *f* (de un bebé) 2 IDEA : concepto *m*, idea *f*

concern[1] [kən'sərn] *vt* 1 : tratarse de, tener que ver con ⟨the novel concerns a sailor : la novela se trata de un marinero⟩ 2 INVOLVE : concernir, incumbir a, afectar ⟨that does not concern me : eso no me incumbe⟩

concern[2] *n* 1 AFFAIR : asunto *m* 2 WORRY : inquietud *f*, preocupación *f* 3 BUSINESS : negocio *m*

concerned [kən'sərnd] *adj* 1 ANXIOUS : preocupado, ansioso 2 INTERESTED, INVOLVED : interesado, afectado

concerning [kən'sərnıŋ] *prep* REGARDING : con respecto a, acerca de, sobre

concert ['kan.sərt] *n* 1 AGREEMENT : concierto *m*, acuerdo *m* 2 : concierto *m* (musical)

concerted [kən'sərt̬əd] *adj* : concertado, coordinado ⟨to make a concerted effort : coordinar los esfuerzos⟩

concertina [ˌkantsər'ti:nə] *n* : concertina *f*

concerto [kən'tʃɛrto:] *n, pl* **-ti** [-ti, -,ti:] *or* **-tos** : concierto *m* ⟨violin concerto : concierto para violín⟩

concession [kən'sɛʃən] *n* : concesión *f*

conch ['kaŋk, 'kantʃ] *n, pl* **conchs** ['kaŋks] *or* **conches** ['kantʃəz] : caracol *m* (animal), caracola *f* (concha)

conciliatory [kən'sɪliə,tori] *adj* : conciliador, conciliatorio

concise [kən'saɪs] *adj* : conciso, breve — **concisely** *adv*

conclave ['kan,kleɪv] *n* : cónclave *m*

conclude [kən'klu:d] *v* **-cluded; -cluding** *vt* **1** END : concluir, finalizar ⟨to conclude a meeting : concluir una reunión⟩ **2** DECIDE : concluir, llegar a la conclusión de — *vi* END : concluir, terminar

conclusion [kən'klu:ʒən] *n* **1** INFERENCE : conclusión *f* **2** END : fin *m*, final *m*

conclusive [kən'klu:sɪv] *adj* : concluyente, decisivo — **conclusively** *adv*

concoct [kən'kakt, kan-] *vt* **1** PREPARE : preparar, confeccionar **2** DEVISE : inventar, tramar

concoction [kən'kakʃən] *n* : invención *f*, mejunje *m*, brebaje *m*

concomitant [kən'kamətənt] *adj* : concomitante

concord ['kan,kord, 'kaŋ-] *n* **1** HARMONY : concordia *f*, armonía *f* **2** AGREEMENT : acuerdo *m*

concordance [kən'kordənts] *n* : concordancia *f*

concourse ['kan,kors] *n* : explanada *f*, salón *m* (para pasajeros)

concrete¹ [kan'kri:t, 'kan,kri:t] *adj* **1** REAL : concreto ⟨concrete objects : objetos concretos⟩ **2** SPECIFIC : determinado, específico **3** : de concreto, de hormigón ⟨concrete walls : paredes de concreto⟩

concrete² ['kan,kri:t, kan'kri:t] *n* : concreto *m*, hormigón *m*

concur [kən'kər] *vi* **concurred; concurring** **1** COINCIDE : concurrir, coincidir **2** AGREE : concurrir, estar de acuerdo

concurrent [kən'kərənt] *adj* : concurrente, simultáneo

concussion [kən'kʌʃən] *n* : conmoción *f* cerebral

condemn [kən'dɛm] *vt* **1** CENSURE : condenar, reprobar, censurar **2** : declarar insalubre (alimentos), declarar ruinoso (un edificio) **3** SENTENCE : condenar ⟨condemned to death : condenado a muerte⟩

condemnation [,kan,dɛm'neɪʃən] *n* : condena *f*, reprobación *f*

condensation [,kan,dɛn'seɪʃən, -dən-] *n* : condensación *f*

condense [kən'dɛnts] *v* **-densed; -densing** *vt* **1** ABRIDGE : condensar, resumir **2** : condensar (vapor, etc.) — *vi* : condensarse

condescend [,kandı'sɛnd] *vi* **1** DEIGN : condescender, dignarse **2 to condescend to someone** : tratar a alguien con condescendencia

condescension [,kandı'sɛntʃən] *n* : condescendencia *f*

condiment ['kandəmənt] *n* : condimento *m*

condition¹ [kən'dɪʃən] *vt* **1** DETERMINE : condicionar, determinar **2** : acondicionar (el pelo o el aire), poner en forma (el cuerpo)

condition² *n* **1** STIPULATION : condición *f*, estipulación *f* ⟨on the condition that : a condición de que⟩ **2** STATE : condición *f*, estado *m* ⟨in poor condition : en malas condiciones⟩ **3 conditions** *npl* : condiciones *fpl*, situación *f* ⟨working conditions : condiciones del trabajo⟩

conditional [kən'dɪʃənəl] *adj* : condicional — **conditionally** *adv*

conditioner [kən'dɪʃənər] *n* : acondicionador *m*

condo ['kando:] → **condominium**

condolence [kən'do:lənts] *n* **1** SYMPATHY : condolencia *f* **2 condolences** *npl* : pésame *m*

condom ['kandəm] *n* : condón *m*

condominium [,kandə'mɪniəm] *n, pl* **-ums** : condominio *m*

condone [kən'do:n] *vt* **-doned; -doning** : aprobar, perdonar, tolerar

condor ['kandər, -,dor] *n* : cóndor *m*

conducive [kən'du:sɪv, -'dju:-] *adj* : propicio, favorable

conduct¹ [kən'dʌkt] *vt* **1** GUIDE : guiar, conducir ⟨to conduct a tour : guiar una visita⟩ **2** DIRECT : conducir, dirigir ⟨to conduct an orchestra : dirigir una orquesta⟩ **3** CARRY OUT : realizar, llevar a cabo ⟨to conduct an investigation : llevar a cabo una investigación⟩ **4** TRANSMIT : conducir, transmitir (calor, electricidad, etc.) **5 to conduct oneself** BEHAVE : conducirse, comportarse

conduct² ['kan,dʌkt] *n* **1** MANAGEMENT : conducción *f*, dirección *f*, manejo *m* ⟨the conduct of foreign affairs : la conducción de asuntos exteriores⟩ **2** BEHAVIOR : conducta *f*, comportamiento *m*

conduction [kən'dʌkʃən] *n* : conducción *f*

conductivity [,kan,dʌk'tɪvəti] *n, pl* **-ties** : conductividad *f*

conductor [kən'dʌktər] *n* **1** : conductor *m*, -tora *f*; revisor *m*, -sora *f* (en un tren); cobrador *m*, -dora *f* (en un bus); director *m*, -tora *f* (de una orquesta) **2** : conductor *m* (de electricidad, etc.)

conduit ['kan,du:ət, -,dju:-] *n* : conducto *m*, canal *m*, vía *f*

cone ['ko:n] *n* **1** : piña *f* (fruto de las coníferas) **2** : cono *m* (en geometría) **3 ice-cream cone** : cono *m*, barquillo *m*, cucurucho *m*

confection [kən'fɛkʃən] *n* : dulce *m*

confectioner [kən'fɛkʃənər] *n* : confitero *m*, -ra *f*

confederacy [kən'fɛdərəsi] *n, pl* **-cies** : confederación *f*

confederate¹ [kən'fɛdə,reɪt] *v* **-ated; -ating** *vt* : unir, confederar — *vi* : confederarse, aliarse

confederate² [kən'fɛdərət] *adj* : confederado

confederate³ *n* : cómplice *mf*; aliado *m*, -da *f*

confederation [kən,fɛdə'reɪʃən] *n* : confederación *f*, alianza *f*

confer [kən'fər] *v* **-ferred; -ferring** *vt* : conferir, otorgar — *vi* **to confer with** : consultar

conference ['kɑnfrənts, -fərənts] *n* : conferencia *f* ⟨press conference : conferencia de prensa⟩

confess [kən'fɛs] *vt* : confesar — *vi* 1 : confesar ⟨the prisoner confessed : el detenido confesó⟩ 2 : confesarse (en religión)

confession [kən'fɛʃən] *n* : confesión *f*

confessional [kən'fɛʃənəl] *n* : confesionario *m*

confessor [kən'fɛsər] *n* : confesor *m*

confetti [kən'fɛti] *n* : confeti *m*

confidant ['kɑnfə,dɑnt, -,dænt] *n* : confidente *mf*

confide [kən'faɪd] *v* **-fided; -fiding** : confiar

confidence ['kɑnfədənts] *n* 1 TRUST : confianza *f* 2 SELF-ASSURANCE : confianza *f* en sí mismo, seguridad *f* en sí mismo 3 SECRET : confidencia *f*, secreto *m*

confident ['kɑnfədənt] *adj* 1 SURE : seguro 2 SELF-ASSURED : confiado, seguro de sí mismo

confidential [,kɑnfə'dɛntʃəl] *adj* : confidencial — **confidentially** [,kɑnfə'dɛntʃəli] *adv*

confidently ['kɑnfədəntli] *adv* : con seguridad, con confianza

configuration [kən,fɪgjə'reɪʃən] *n* : configuración *f*

confine [kən'faɪn] *vt* **-fined; -fining** 1 LIMIT : confinar, restringir, limitar 2 IMPRISON : recluir, encarcelar, encerrar

confinement [kən'faɪnmənt] *n* : confinamiento *m*, reclusión *f*, encierro *m*

confines ['kɑn,faɪnz] *npl* : límites *mpl*, confines *mpl*

confirm [kən'fərm] *vt* 1 RATIFY : ratificar 2 VERIFY : confirmar, verificar 3 : confirmar (en religión)

confirmation [,kɑnfər'meɪʃən] *n* : confirmación *f*

confiscate ['kɑnfə,skeɪt] *vt* **-cated; -cating** : confiscar, incautar, decomisar

confiscation [,kɑnfə'skeɪʃən] *n* : confiscación *f*, incautación *f*, decomiso *m*

conflagration [,kɑnflə'greɪʃən] *n* : conflagración *f*

conflict¹ [kən'flɪkt] *vi* : estar en conflicto, oponerse

conflict² ['kɑn,flɪkt] *n* : conflicto *m* ⟨to be in conflict : estar en desacuerdo⟩

confluence ['kɑn,flu:ənts, kən'flu:ənts] *n* : confluencia *f*

conform [kən'fɔrm] *vi* 1 ACCORD, COMPLY : ajustarse, adaptarse, conformarse ⟨it conforms with our standards : se ajusta a nuestras normas⟩ 2 CORRESPOND : corresponder, encajar ⟨to conform to the truth : corresponder a la verdad⟩

conformity [kən'fɔrməti] *n, pl* **-ties** : conformidad *f*

confound [kən'faʊnd, kɑn-] *vt* : confundir, desconcertar

confront [kən'frʌnt] *vt* : afrontar, enfrentarse a, encarar

confrontation [,kɑnfrən'teɪʃən] *n* : enfrentamiento *m*, confrontación *f*

confuse [kən'fju:z] *vt* **-fused; -fusing** 1 PUZZLE : confundir, enturbiar 2 COMPLICATE : confundir, enredar, complicar ⟨to confuse the issue : complicar las cosas⟩

confusing [kən'fju:zɪŋ] *adj* : complicado, que confunde

confusion [kən'fju:ʒən] *n* 1 PERPLEXITY : confusión *f* 2 MESS, TURMOIL : confusión *f*, embrollo *m*, lío *m fam*

congeal [kən'dʒi:l] *vi* 1 FREEZE : congelarse 2 COAGULATE, CURDLE : coagularse, cuajarse

congenial [kən'dʒi:niəl] *adj* : agradable, simpático

congenital [kən'dʒɛnətəl] *adj* : congénito

congest [kən'dʒɛst] *vt* 1 : congestionar (en la medicina) 2 OVERCROWD : abarrotar, atestar, congestionar (el tráfico) — *vi* : congestionarse

congestion [kən'dʒɛstʃən] *n* : congestión *f*

conglomerate¹ [kən'glɑmərət] *adj* : conglomerado

conglomerate² [kən'glɑmərət] *n* : conglomerado *m*

conglomeration [kən,glɑmə'reɪʃən] *n* : conglomerado *m*, acumulación *f*

Congolese [,kɑŋgə'li:z, -'li:s] *n* : congoleño *m*, -ña *f* — **Congolese** *adj*

congratulate [kən'grædʒə,leɪt, -'grætʃə-] *vt* **-lated; -lating** : felicitar

congratulation [kən,grædʒə'leɪʃən, -,grætʃə-] *n* : felicitación *f* ⟨congratulations! : ¡felicidades!, ¡enhorabuena!⟩

congregate ['kɑŋgrɪ,geɪt] *v* **-gated; -gating** *vt* : congregar, reunir — *vi* : congregarse, reunirse

congregation [,kɑŋgrɪ'geɪʃən] *n* 1 GATHERING : congregación *f*, fieles *mpl* (a un servicio religioso) 2 PARISHIONERS : feligreses *mpl*

congress ['kɑŋgrəs] *n* : congreso *m*

congressional [kən'grɛʃənəl, kɑn-] *adj* : del congreso

congressman ['kɑŋgrəsmən] *n, pl* **-men** [-mən, -,mɛn] : congresista *m*, diputado *m*

congresswoman ['kɑŋgrəs,wʊmən] *n*, *pl* **-women** [-,wɪmən] : congresista *f*, diputada *f*

congruence [kən'gru:ənts, 'kɑŋgru-ənts] *n* : congruencia *f*

congruent [kən'gru:ənt, 'kɑŋgruənt] *adj* : congruente

conic ['kɑnɪk] → **conical**

conical ['kɑnɪkəl] *adj* : cónico

conifer ['kɑnəfər, 'ko:-] *n* : conífera *f*

coniferous [ko:'nɪfərəs, kə-] *adj* : conífero

conjecture¹ [kən'dʒɛktʃər] *v* **-tured; -turing** : conjeturar

conjecture² *n* : conjetura *f*, presunción *f*

conjugal ['kɑndʒɪgəl, kən'dʒu:-] *adj* : conyugal

conjugate ['kɑndʒə,geɪt] *vt* **-gated; -gating** : conjugar

conjugation [,kɑndʒə'geɪʃən] *n* : conjugación *f*

conjunction [kən'dʒʌŋkʃən] *n* : conjunción *f* ⟨in conjunction with : en combinación con⟩

conjure ['kɑndʒər, 'kʌn-] *v* **-jured; -juring** *vt* 1 ENTREAT : rogar, suplicar 2 to conjure up : hacer aparecer (apariciones), evocar (memorias, etc.) — *vi* : practicar la magia

conjurer *or* **conjuror** ['kɑndʒərər, 'kʌn-] *n* : mago *m*, -ga *f*; prestidigitador *m*, -dora *f*

connect [kə'nɛkt] *vi* : conectar, enlazar, empalmar, comunicarse — *vt* 1 JOIN, LINK : conectar, unir, juntar, vincular 2 RELATE : relacionar, asociar (ideas)

connection [kə'nɛkʃən] *n* : conexión *f*, enlace *m* ⟨professional connections : relaciones profesionales⟩

connective [kə'nɛktɪv] *adj* : conectivo, conjuntivo ⟨connective tissue : tejido conjuntivo⟩

connector [kə'nɛktər] *n* : conector *m*

connivance [kə'naɪvənts] *n* : connivencia *f*, complicidad *f*

connive [kə'naɪv] *vi* **-nived; -niving** CONSPIRE, PLOT : actuar en connivencia, confabularse, conspirar

connoisseur [,kɑnə'sər, -'sʊr] *n* : conocedor *m*, -dora *f*; entendido *m*, -da *f*

connotation [,kɑnə'teɪʃən] *n* : connotación *f*

connote [kə'no:t] *vt* **-noted; -noting** : connotar

conquer ['kɑŋkər] *vt* : conquistar, vencer

conqueror ['kɑŋkərər] *n* : conquistador *m*, -dora *f*

conquest ['kɑn,kwɛst, 'kɑŋ-] *n* : conquista *f*

conscience ['kɑntʃənts] *n* : conciencia *f*, consciencia *f* ⟨to have a clear conscience : tener la conciencia limpia⟩

conscientious [,kɑntʃi'ɛntʃəs] *adj* : concienzudo — **conscientiously** *adv*

conscious ['kɑntʃəs] *adj* 1 AWARE : consciente ⟨to become conscious of : darse

cuenta de⟩ 2 ALERT, AWAKE : consciente 3 INTENTIONAL : intencional, deliberado

consciously ['kɑntʃəsli] *adv* INTENTIONALLY : intencionalmente, deliberadamente, a propósito

consciousness ['kɑntʃəsnəs] *n* 1 AWARENESS : conciencia *f*, consciencia *f* 2 : conocimiento *m* ⟨to lose consciousness : perder el conocimiento⟩

conscript¹ [kən'skrɪpt] *vt* : reclutar, alistar, enrolar

conscript² ['kɑn,skrɪpt] *n* : conscripto *m*, -ta *f*; recluta *mf*

consecrate ['kɑntsə,kreɪt] *vt* **-crated; -crating** : consagrar

consecration [,kɑntsə'kreɪʃən] *n* : consagración *f*, dedicación *f*

consecutive [kən'sɛkjətɪv] *adj* : consecutivo, seguido ⟨on five consecutive days : cinco días seguidos⟩

consecutively [kən'sɛkjətɪvli] *adv* : consecutivamente

consensus [kən'sɛntsəs] *n* : consenso *m*

consent¹ [kən'sɛnt] *vi* 1 AGREE : acceder, ponerse de acuerdo 2 to consent to do something : consentir en hacer algo

consent² *n* : consentimiento *m*, permiso *m* ⟨by common consent : de común acuerdo⟩

consequence ['kɑntsə,kwɛnts, -kwənts] *n* 1 RESULT : consecuencia *f*, secuela *f* 2 IMPORTANCE : importancia *f*, trascendencia *f*

consequent ['kɑntsəkwənt, -,kwɛnt] *adj* : consiguiente

consequential [,kɑntsə'kwɛntʃəl] *adj* 1 CONSEQUENT : consiguiente 2 IMPORTANT : importante, trascendente, trascendental

consequently ['kɑntsəkwəntli, -,kwɛnt-] *adv* : por consiguiente, por ende, por lo tanto

conservation [,kɑntsər'veɪʃən] *n* : conservación *f*, protección *f*

conservationist [,kɑntsər'veɪʃənɪst] *n* : conservacionista *mf*

conservatism [kən'sərvə,tɪzəm] *n* : conservadurismo *m*

conservative¹ [kən'sərvətɪv] *adj* 1 : conservador 2 CAUTIOUS : moderado, cauteloso ⟨a conservative estimate : un cálculo moderado⟩

conservative² *n* : conservador *m*, -dora *f*

conservatory [kən'sərvə,tori] *n*, *pl* **-ries** : conservatorio *m*

conserve¹ [kən'sərv] *vt* **-served; -serving** : conservar, preservar

conserve² ['kɑn,sərv] *n* PRESERVES : confitura *f*

consider [kən'sɪdər] *vt* 1 CONTEMPLATE : considerar, pensar en ⟨we'd considered attending : habíamos pensado en asistir⟩ 2 : considerar, tener en cuenta ⟨consider the consequences : considera las consecuencias⟩ 3 JUDGE, REGARD : considerar, estimar

considerable [kən'sɪdərəbəl] *adj* : considerable — **considerably** [-bli] *adv*
considerate [kən'sɪdərət] *adj* : considerado, atento
consideration [kən₁sɪdə'reɪʃən] *n* : consideración *f* ⟨to take into consideration : tener en cuenta⟩
considering [kən'sɪdərɪŋ] *prep* : teniendo en cuenta, visto
consign [kən'saɪn] *vt* **1** COMMIT, ENTRUST : confiar, encomendar **2** TRANSFER : consignar, transferir **3** SEND : consignar, enviar (mercancía)
consignment [kən'saɪnmənt] *n* **1** : envío *m*, remesa *f* **2 on ~** : en consignación
consist [kən'sɪst] *vi* **1** LIE : consistir ⟨success consists in hard work : el éxito consiste en trabajar duro⟩ **2** : constar, componerse ⟨the set consists of 5 pieces : el juego se compone de 5 piezas⟩
consistency [kən'sɪstəntsi] *n, pl* **-cies 1** : consistencia *f* (de una mezcla o sustancia) **2** COHERENCE : coherencia *f* **3** UNIFORMITY : regularidad *f*, uniformidad *f*
consistent [kən'sɪstənt] *adj* **1** COMPATIBLE : compatible, coincidente ⟨consistent with policy : coincidente con la política⟩ **2** UNIFORM : uniforme, constante, regular — **consistently** [kən'sɪstəntli] *adv*
consolation [₁kɑntsə'leɪʃə n] *n* **1** : consuelo *m* **2 consolation prize** : premio *m* de consolación
console¹ [kən'so:l] *vt* **-soled; -soling** : consolar
console² ['kɑn₁so:l] *n* : consola *f*
consolidate [kən'sɑlə₁deɪt] *vt* **-dated; -dating** : consolidar, unir
consolidation [kən₁sɑlə'deɪʃən] *n* : consolidación *f*
consommé [₁kɑntsə'meɪ] *n* : consomé *m*
consonant ['kɑntsənənt] *n* : consonante *m*
consort¹ [kən'sɔrt] *vi* : asociarse, relacionarse, tener trato ⟨to consort with criminals : tener trato con criminales⟩
consort² ['kɑn₁sɔrt] *n* : consorte *mf*
consortium [kən'sɔrʃəm] *n, pl* **-tia** [-ʃə] or **-tiums** [-ʃəmz] : consorcio *m*
conspicuous [kən'spɪkjuəs] *adj* **1** OBVIOUS : visible, evidente **2** STRIKING : llamativo
conspicuously [kən'spɪkjuəsli] *adv* : de manera llamativa
conspiracy [kən'spɪrəsi] *n, pl* **-cies** : conspiración *f*, complot *m*, confabulación *f*
conspirator [kən'spɪrətər] *n* : conspirador *m*, -dora *f*
conspire [kən'spaɪr] *vi* **-spired; -spiring** : conspirar, confabularse
constable ['kɑntstəbəl, 'kʌntstə-] *n* : agente *mf* de policía (en un pueblo)
constancy ['kɑntstəntsi] *n, pl* **-cies** : constancia *f*

constant¹ ['kɑntstənt] *adj* **1** FAITHFUL : leal, fiel **2** INVARIABLE : constante, invariable **3** CONTINUAL : constante, continuo
constant² *n* : constante *f*
constantly ['kɑntstəntli] *adv* : constantemente, continuamente
constellation [₁kɑntstə'leɪʃən] *n* : constelación *f*
consternation [₁kɑntstər'neɪʃən] *n* : consternación *f*
constipate ['kɑntstə₁peɪt] *vt* **-pated; -pating** : estreñir
constipation ['kɑntstə'peɪʃən] *n* : estreñimiento *m*, constipación *f* (de vientre)
constituency [kən'stɪtʃuəntsi] *n, pl* **-cies 1** : distrito *m* electoral **2** : residentes *mpl* de un distrito electoral
constituent¹ [kən'stɪtʃuənt] *adj* **1** COMPONENT : constituyente, componente **2** : constituyente, constitutivo ⟨a constituent assembly : una asamblea constituyente⟩
constituent² *n* **1** COMPONENT : componente *m* **2** ELECTOR, VOTER : elector *m*, -tora *f*; votante *mf*
constitute ['kɑntstə₁tu:t, -₁tju:t] *vt* **-tuted; -tuting 1** ESTABLISH : constituir, establecer **2** COMPOSE, FORM : constituir, componer
constitution [₁kɑntstə'tu:ʃən, -'tju:-] *n* : constitución *f*
constitutional [₁kɑntstə'tu:ʃənəl, -'tju:-] *adj* : constitucional
constitutionality [₁kɑntstə₁tu:ʃə'næləti, -₁tju:-] *n* : constitucionalidad *f*
constrain [kən'streɪn] *vt* **1** COMPEL : constreñir, obligar **2** CONFINE : constreñir, limitar, restringir **3** RESTRAIN : contener, refrenar
constraint [kən'streɪnt] *n* : restricción *f*, limitación *f*
constrict [kən'strɪkt] *vt* : estrechar, apretar, comprimir
constriction [kən'strɪkʃən] *n* : estrechamiento *m*, compresión *f*
construct [kən'strʌkt] *vt* : construir
construction [kən'strʌkʃən] *n* : construcción *f*
constructive [kən'strʌktɪv] *adj* : constructivo
construe [kən'stru:] *vt* **-strued; -struing** : interpretar
consul ['kɑntsəl] *n* : cónsul *mf*
consular ['kɑntsələr] *adj* : consular
consulate ['kɑntsələt] *n* : consulado *m*
consult [kən'sʌlt] *vt* : consultar — *vi* **to consult with** : consultar con, solicitar la opinión de
consultant [kən'sʌltənt] *n* : consultor *m*, -tora *f*; asesor *m*, -sora *f*
consultation [₁kɑntsəl'teɪʃən] *n* : consulta *f*
consumable [kən'su:məbəl] *adj* : consumible
consume [kən'su:m] *vt* **-sumed; -suming** : consumir, usar, gastar

consumer [kən'su:mər] *n* : consumidor *m*, -dora *f*

consummate¹ ['kɑntsə,meɪt] *vt* **-mated; -mating** : consumar

consummate² [kən'sʌmət, 'kɑntsə-mət] *adj* : consumado, perfecto

consummation [,kɑntsə'meɪʃən] *n* : consumación *f*

consumption [kən'sʌmpʃən] *n* **1** USE : consumo *m*, uso *m* ⟨consumption of electricity : consumo de electricidad⟩ **2** TUBERCULOSIS : tisis *f*, consunción *f*

contact¹ ['kɑn,tækt, kən'-] *vt* : ponerse en contacto con, contactar (con)

contact² ['kɑn,tækt] *n* **1** TOUCHING : contacto *m* ⟨to come into contact with : entrar en contacto con⟩ **2** TOUCH : contacto *m*, comunicación *f* ⟨to lose contact with : perder contacto con⟩ **3** CONNECTION : contacto *m* (en negocios) **4** → **contact lens**

contact lens ['kɑn,tækt'lenz] *n* : lente *mf* de contacto, pupilente *m Mex*

contagion [kən'teɪdʒən] *n* : contagio *m*

contagious [kən'teɪdʒəs] *adj* : contagioso

contain [kən'teɪn] *vt* **1** : contener **2 to contain oneself** : contenerse

container [kən'teɪnər] *n* : recipiente *m*, envase *m*

containment [kən'teɪnmənt] *n* : contención *f*

contaminant [kən'tæmənənt] *n* : contaminante *m*

contaminate [kən'tæmə,neɪt] *vt* **-nated; -nating** : contaminar

contamination [kən,tæmə'neɪʃən] *n* : contaminación *f*

contemplate ['kɑntəm,pleɪt] *v* **-plated; -plating** *vt* **1** VIEW : contemplar **2** PONDER : contemplar, considerar **3** CONSIDER, PROPOSE : proponerse, proyectar, pensar en ⟨to contemplate a trip : pensar en viajar⟩ — *vi* MEDITATE : meditar

contemplation [,kɑntəm'pleɪʃən] *n* : contemplación *f*

contemplative [kən'templətɪv, 'kɑntəm,pleɪtɪv] *adj* : contemplativo

contemporaneous [kən,tempə'reɪniəs] *adj* → **contemporary¹**

contemporary¹ [kən'tempə,reri] *adj* : contemporáneo

contemporary² *n, pl* **-raries** : contemporáneo *m*, -nea *f*

contempt [kən'tempt] *n* **1** DISDAIN : desprecio *m*, desdén *m* ⟨to hold in contempt : despreciar⟩ **2** : desacato *m* (ante un tribunal)

contemptible [kən'temptəbəl] *adj* : despreciable, vil

contemptuous [kən'temptʃuəs] *adj* : despectivo, despreciativo, desdeñoso

contemptuously [kən'temptʃuəsli] *adv* : despectivamente, con desprecio

contend [kən'tend] *vi* **1** STRUGGLE : luchar, lidiar, contender ⟨to contend with a problem : lidiar con un proble-

ma⟩ **2** COMPETE : competir ⟨to contend for a position : competir por un puesto⟩ — *vt* **1** ARGUE, MAINTAIN : argüir, sostener, afirmar ⟨he contended that he was right : afirmó que tenía razón⟩ **2** CONTEST : protestar contra (una decisión, etc.), disputar

contender [kən'tendər] *n* : contendiente *mf*; aspirante *mf*; competidor *m*, -dora *f*

content¹ [kən'tent] *vt* SATISFY : contentar, satisfacer

content² *adj* : conforme, contento, satisfecho

content³ *n* CONTENTMENT : contento *m*, satisfacción *f* ⟨to one's heart's content : hasta quedar satisfecho, a más no poder⟩

content⁴ ['kɑn,tent] *n* **1** MEANING : contenido *m*, significado *m* **2** PROPORTION : contenido *m*, proporción *f* ⟨fat content : contenido de grasa⟩ **3 contents** *npl* : contenido *m*, sumario *m* (de un libro) ⟨table of contents : índice de materias⟩

contented [kən'tentəd] *adj* : conforme, satisfecho ⟨a contented smile : una sonrisa de satisfacción⟩

contentedly [kən'tentədli] *adv* : con satisfacción

contention [kən'tenʃən] *n* **1** DISPUTE : disputa *f*, discusión *f* **2** COMPETITION : competencia *f*, contienda *f* **3** OPINION : argumento *m*, opinión *f*

contentious [kən'tenʃəs] *adj* : disputador, pugnaz, combativo

contentment [kən'tentmənt] *n* : satisfacción *f*, contento *m*

contest¹ [kən'test] *vt* : disputar, cuestionar, impugnar ⟨to contest a will : impugnar un testamento⟩

contest² ['kɑn,test] *n* **1** STRUGGLE : lucha *f*, contienda *f* **2** GAME : concurso *m*, competencia *f*

contestable [kən'testəbəl] *adj* : discutible, cuestionable

contestant [kən'testənt] *n* : concursante *mf*; competidor *m*, -dora *f*

context ['kɑn,tekst] *n* : contexto *m*

contiguous [kən'tɪgjuəs] *adj* : contiguo

continence ['kɑntənənts] *n* : continencia *f*

continent¹ ['kɑntənənt] *adj* : continente

continent² *n* : continente *m* — **continental** [,kɑntən'entəl] *adj*

contingency [kən'tɪndʒəntsi] *n, pl* **-cies** : contingencia *f*, eventualidad *f*

contingent¹ [kən'tɪndʒənt] *adj* **1** POSSIBLE : contingente, eventual **2** ACCIDENTAL : fortuito, accidental **3 to be contingent on** : depender de, estar sujeto a

contingent² *n* : contingente *m*

continual [kən'tɪnjuəl] *adj* : continuo, constante — **continually** [kən-'tɪnjuəli, -'tɪnjəli] *adv*

continuance [kən'tɪnjuənts] *n* **1** CONTINUATION : continuación *f* **2** DURA-

TION : duración *f* **3** : aplazamiento *m* (de un proceso)

continuation [kən,tɪnjʊ'eɪʃən] *n* : continuación *f*, prolongación *f*

continue [kən'tɪnju:] *v* **-tinued; -tinuing** *vi* **1** CARRY ON : continuar, seguir, proseguir ⟨please continue : continúe, por favor⟩ **2** ENDURE, LAST : continuar, prolongarse, durar **3** RESUME : continuar, reanudarse — *vt* **1** : continuar, seguir ⟨she continued writing : continuó escribiendo⟩ **2** RESUME : continuar, reanudar **3** EXTEND, PROLONG : continuar, prolongar

continuity [,kɑntə-'nu:əṭi, -'nju:-] *n, pl* **-ties** : continuidad *f*

continuous [kən'tɪnjuəs] *adj* : continuo — **continuously** *adv*

contort [kən'tɔrt] *vt* : torcer, retorcer, contraer (el rostro) — *vi* : contraerse, demudarse

contortion [kən'tɔrʃən] *n* : contorsión *f*

contour ['kɑn,tʊr] *n* **1** OUTLINE : contorno *m* **2 contours** *npl* SHAPE : forma *f*, curvas *fpl* **3 contour map** : mapa *m* topográfico

contraband ['kɑntrə,bænd] *n* : contrabando *m*

contraception [,kɑntrə'sɛpʃən] *n* : anticoncepción *f*, contracepción *f*

contraceptive¹ [,kɑntrə'sɛptɪv] *adj* : anticonceptivo, contraceptivo

contraceptive² *n* : anticonceptivo *m*, contraceptivo *m*

contract¹ [kən'trækt, 1 *usu* 'kɑn-,trækt] *vt* **1** : contratar (servicios profesionales) **2** : contraer (una enfermedad, una deuda) **3** TIGHTEN : contraer (un músculo) **4** SHORTEN : contraer (una palabra) — *vi* : contraerse, reducirse

contract² ['kɑn,trækt] *n* : contrato *m*

contraction [kən'trækʃən] *n* : contracción *f*

contractor ['kɑn,træktər, kən'træk-] *n* : contratista *mf*

contractual [kən'trækʧʊəl] *adj* : contractual — **contractually** *adv*

contradict [,kɑntrə'dɪkt] *vt* : contradecir, desmentir

contradiction [,kɑntrə'dɪkʃən] *n* : contradicción *f*

contradictory [,kɑntrə'dɪktəri] *adj* : contradictorio

contralto [kən'træl,to:] *n, pl* **-tos** : contralto *m* (voz), contralto *mf* (vocalista)

contraption [kən'træpʃən] *n* DEVICE : aparato *m*, artefacto *m*

contrary¹ ['kɑn,treri, 2 *often* kən-'treri] *adj* **1** OPPOSITE : contrario, opuesto **2** BALKY, STUBBORN : terco, testarudo **3 contrary to** : al contrario de, en contra de ⟨contrary to the facts : en contra de los hechos⟩

contrary² ['kɑn,treri] *n, pl* **-traries 1** OPPOSITE : lo contrario, lo opuesto **2 on the contrary** : al contrario, todo lo contrario

contrast¹ [kən'træst] *vi* DIFFER : contrastar, diferir — *vt* COMPARE : contrastar, comparar

contrast² ['kɑn,træst] *n* : contraste *m*

contravene [,kɑntrə'vi:n] *vt* **-vened; -vening** : contravenir, infringir

contribute [kən'trɪbjət] *v* **-uted; -uting** *vt* : contribuir, aportar (dinero, bienes, etc.) — *vi* : contribuir

contribution [,kɑntrə'bju:ʃən] *n* : contribución *f*

contributor [kən'trɪbjəṭər] *n* : contribuidor *m*, -dora *f*; colaborador *m*, -dora *f* (en periodismo)

contrite ['kɑn,traɪt, kən'traɪt] *adj* REPENTANT : contrito, arrepentido

contrition [kən'trɪʃən] *n* : contrición *f*, arrepentimiento *m*

contrivance [kən'traɪvənts] *n* **1** DEVICE : aparato *m*, artefacto *m* **2** SCHEME : artimaña *f*, treta *f*, ardid *m*

contrive [kən'traɪv] *vt* **-trived; -triving 1** DEVISE : idear, ingeniar, maquinar **2** MANAGE : lograr, ingeniárselas para ⟨she contrived a way out of the mess : se las ingenió para salir del enredo⟩

control¹ [kən'tro:l] *vt* **-trolled; -trolling** : controlar, dominar

control² *n* **1** : control *m*, dominio *m*, mando *m* ⟨to be under control : estar bajo control⟩ **2** RESTRAINT : control *m*, limitación *f* ⟨birth control : control natal⟩ **3** : control *m*, dispositivo *m* de mando ⟨remote control : control remoto⟩

controllable [kən'tro:ləbəl] *adj* : controlable

controller [kən'tro:lər, 'kɑn,-] *n* **1** → **comptroller 2** : controlador *m*, -dora *f* ⟨air traffic controller : controlador aéreo⟩

controversial [,kɑntrə'vərʃəl, -siəl] *adj* : controvertido ⟨a controversial decision : una decisión controvertida⟩

controversy ['kɑntrə,vərsi] *n, pl* **-sies** : controversia *f*

controvert ['kɑntrə,vərt, ,kɑntrə'-] *vt* : controvertir, contradecir

contusion [kən'tu:ʒən, -tju:-] *n* BRUISE : contusión *f*, moretón *m*

conundrum [kə'nʌndrəm] *n* RIDDLE : acertijo *m*, adivinanza *f*

convalesce [,kɑnvə'lɛs] *vi* **-lesced; -lescing** : convalecer

convalescence [,kɑnvə'lɛsənts] *n* : convalecencia *f*

convalescent¹ [,kɑnvə'lɛsənt] *adj* : convaleciente

convalescent² *n* : convaleciente *mf*

convection [kən'vɛkʃən] *n* : convección *f*

convene [kən'vi:n] *v* **-vened; -vening** *vt* : convocar — *vi* : reunirse

convenience [kən'vi:njənts] *n* **1** : conveniencia *f* ⟨at your convenience : cuando le resulte conveniente⟩ **2** AMENITY : comodidad *f* ⟨modern conveniences : comodidades modernas⟩

convenience store *n* : tienda *f* de conveniencia

convenient [kən'vi:njənt] *adj* : conveniente, cómodo — **conveniently** *adv*

convent ['kɑnvənt, -ˌvɛnt] *n* : convento *m*

convention [kən'vɛntʃən] *n* **1** PACT : convención *f*, convenio *m*, pacto *m* ⟨the Geneva Convention : la Convención de Ginebra⟩ **2** MEETING : convención *f*, congreso *m* **3** CUSTOM : convención *f*, convencionalismo *m*

conventional [kən'vɛntʃənəl] *adj* : convencional — **conventionally** *adv*

converge [kən'vərdʒ] *vi* **-verged; -verging** : converger, convergir

convergence [kən'vərdʒənts] *n* : convergencia *f*

convergent [kən'vərdʒənt] *adj* : convergente

conversant [kən'vərsənt] *adj* **conversant with** : versado con, experto en

conversation [ˌkɑnvər'seɪʃən] *n* : conversación *f*

conversational [ˌkɑnvər'seɪʃənəl] *adj* : familiar ⟨a conversational style : un estilo familiar⟩

converse¹ [kən'vərs] *vi* **-versed; -versing** : conversar

converse² [kən'vərs, 'kɑnˌvərs] *adj* : contrario, opuesto, inverso

conversely [kən'vərsli, 'kɑnˌvərs-] *adv* : a la inversa

conversion [kən'vərʒən] *n* **1** CHANGE : conversión *f*, transformación *f*, cambio *m* **2** : conversión *f* (a una religión)

convert¹ [kən'vərt] *vt* **1** : convertir (a una religión o un partido) **2** CHANGE : convertir, cambiar — *vi* : convertirse

convert² ['kɑnˌvərt] *n* : converso *m*, -sa *f*

converter *or* **convertor** [kən'vərtər] *n* : convertidor *m*

convertible¹ [kən'vərtəbəl] *adj* : convertible

convertible² *n* : convertible *m*, descapotable *m*

convex [kɑn'vɛks, 'kɑnˌ-, kən'-] *adj* : convexo

convey [kən'veɪ] *vt* **1** TRANSPORT : transportar, conducir **2** TRANSMIT : transmitir, comunicar, expresar (noticias, ideas, etc.)

conveyance [kən'veɪənts] *n* **1** TRANSPORT : transporte *m*, transportación *f* **2** COMMUNICATION : transmisión *f*, comunicación *f* **3** TRANSFER : transferencia *f*, traspaso *m* (de una propiedad)

conveyor [kən'veɪər] *n* : transportador *m*, -dora *f* ⟨conveyor belt : cinta transportadora⟩

convict¹ [kən'vɪkt] *vt* : declarar culpable

convict² ['kɑnˌvɪkt] *n* : preso *m*, -sa *f*; presidiario *m*, -ria *f*; recluso *m*, -sa *f*

conviction [kən'vɪkʃən] *n* **1** : condena *f* (de un acusado) **2** BELIEF : convicción *f*, creencia *f*

convince [kən'vɪnts] *vt* **-vinced; -vincing** : convencer

convincing [kən'vɪntsɪŋ] *adj* : convincente, persuasivo

convincingly [kən'vɪntsɪŋli] *adv* : de forma convincente

convivial [kən'vɪvjəl, -'vɪviəl] *adj* : jovial, festivo, alegre

conviviality [kənˌvɪvi'æləti] *n, pl* **-ties** : jovialidad *f*

convoke [kən'voːk] *vt* **-voked; -voking** : convocar

convoluted ['kɑnvəˌluːtəd] *adj* : intrincado, complicado

convoy ['kɑnˌvɔɪ] *n* : convoy *m*

convulse [kən'vʌls] *v* **-vulsed; -vulsing** *vt* : convulsionar ⟨convulsed with laughter : muerto de risa⟩ — *vi* : sufrir convulsiones

convulsion [kən'vʌlʃən] *n* : convulsión *f*

convulsive [kən'vʌlsɪv] *adj* : convulsivo — **convulsively** *adv*

coo¹ ['kuː] *vi* : arrullar

coo² *n* : arrullo *m* (de una paloma)

cook¹ ['kʊk] *vi* : cocinar — *vt* **1** : preparar (comida) **2 to cook up** CONCOCT : inventar, tramar

cook² *n* : cocinero *m*, -ra *f*

cookbook ['kʊkˌbʊk] *n* : libro *m* de cocina

cookery ['kʊkəri] *n, pl* **-eries** : cocina *f*

cookie *or* **cooky** ['kʊki] *n, pl* **-ies** : galleta *f* (dulce)

cooking ['kʊkɪŋ] *n* **1** COOKERY : cocina *f* **2** : cocción *f*, cocimiento *m* ⟨cooking time : tiempo de cocción⟩

cookout ['kʊkˌaʊt] *n* : comida *f* al aire libre

cool¹ ['kuːl] *vt* : refrescar, enfriar — *vi* **1** : refrescarse, enfriarse ⟨the pie is cooling : el pastel se está enfriando⟩ **2** : calmarse, tranquilizarse ⟨his anger cooled : su ira se calmó⟩

cool² *adj* **1** : fresco, frío ⟨cool weather : tiempo fresco⟩ **2** CALM : tranquilo, sereno **3** ALOOF : frío, distante

cool³ *n* **1** : fresco *m* ⟨the cool of the evening : el fresco de la tarde⟩ **2** COMPOSURE : calma *f*, serenidad *f*

coolant ['kuːlənt] *n* : refrigerante *m*

cooler ['kuːlər] *n* : nevera *f* portátil

coolie ['kuːli] *n* : culi *m*

coolly ['kuːlli] *adv* **1** CALMLY : con calma, tranquilamente **2** COLDLY : fríamente, con frialdad

coolness ['kuːlnəs] *n* **1** : frescura *f*, frescor *m* ⟨the coolness of the night : el frescor de la noche⟩ **2** CALMNESS : tranquilidad *f*, serenidad *f* **3** COLDNESS, INDIFFERENCE : frialdad *f*, indiferencia *f*

coop¹ ['kuːp, 'kʊp] *vt or* **to coop up** : encerrar ⟨cooped up in the house : encerrado en la casa⟩

coop² *n* : gallinero *m*

co–op ['koːˌɑp] *n* → **cooperative²**

cooperate [koˈɑpəˌreɪt] *vi* **-ated; -ating** : cooperar, colaborar

cooperation [ko͜ɑpə'reɪʃən] n : cooperación f, colaboración f

cooperative[1] [ko'ɑpərət̬ɪv, -'ɑpə͜reɪt̬ɪv] adj : cooperativo

cooperative[2] [ko'ɑpərət̬ɪv] n : cooperativa f

co-opt [ko'ɑpt] vt 1 : nombrar como miembro, cooptar 2 APPROPRIATE : apropiarse de

coordinate[1] [ko'ɔrdən͜eɪt] v -nated; -nating vt : coordinar — vi : coordinarse, combinar, acordar

coordinate[2] [ko'ɔrdənət] adj 1 COORDINATED : coordinado 2 EQUAL : igual, semejante

coordinate[3] [ko'ɔrdənət] n : coordenada f

coordination [ko͜ɔrdən'eɪʃən] n : coordinación f

coordinator [ko'ɔrdən͜eɪt̬ər] n : coordinador m, -dora f

cop ['kɑp] → police officer

cope ['ko:p] vi coped; coping 1 : arreglárselas 2 to cope with : hacer frente a, poder con ⟨I can't cope with all this! : ¡no puedo con todo esto!⟩

copier ['kɑpiər] n : copiadora f, fotocopiadora f

copilot ['ko͜ːpaɪlət] n : copiloto m

copious ['ko:piəs] adj : copioso, abundante — **copiously** adv

copiousness ['ko:piəsnəs] n : abundancia f

copper ['kɑpər] n : cobre m

coppery ['kɑpəri] adj : cobrizo

copra ['ko:prə, 'kɑ-] n : copra f

copse ['kɑps] n THICKET : soto m, matorral m

copulate ['kɑpjə͜leɪt] vi -lated; -lating : copular

copulation [͜kɑpjə'leɪʃən] n : cópula f, relaciones fpl sexuales

copy[1] ['kɑpi] vt copied; copying 1 DUPLICATE : hacer una copia de, duplicar, reproducir 2 IMITATE : copiar, imitar

copy[2] n, pl **copies** 1 : copia f, duplicado m (de un documento), reproducción f (de una obra de arte) 2 : ejemplar m (de un libro), número m (de una revista) 3 TEXT : manuscrito m, texto m

copyright[1] ['kɑpi͜raɪt] vt : registrar los derechos de

copyright[2] n : derechos mpl de autor

coral[1] ['kɔrəl] adj : de coral ⟨a coral reef : un arrecife de coral⟩

coral[2] n : coral m

coral snake n : serpiente f de coral

cord ['kɔrd] n 1 ROPE, STRING : cuerda f, cordón m, cordel m 2 : cuerda f, cordón m, médula f (en la anatomía) ⟨vocal cords : cuerdas vocales⟩ 3 : cuerda f ⟨a cord of firewood : una cuerda de leña⟩ 4 or electric cord : cable m eléctrico

cordial[1] ['kɔrdʒəl] adj : cordial — **cordially** adv

cordial[2] n : cordial m

cordiality [͜kɔrdʒi'æləti] n : cordialidad f

cordless ['kɔrdləs] adj : inalámbrico

cordon[1] ['kɔrdən] vt to cordon off : acordonar

cordon[2] n : cordón m

corduroy ['kɔrdə͜rɔɪ] n 1 : pana f 2 **corduroys** npl : pantalones mpl de pana

core[1] ['kor] vt cored; coring : quitar el corazón a (una fruta)

core[2] n 1 : corazón m, centro m (de algunas frutas) 2 CENTER : núcleo m, centro m 3 ESSENCE : núcleo m, meollo m ⟨to the core : hasta la médula⟩

coriander ['kori͜ændər] n : cilantro m

cork[1] ['kɔrk] vt : ponerle un corcho a

cork[2] n : corcho m

corkscrew ['kɔrk͜skru:] n : tirabuzón m, sacacorchos m

cormorant ['kɔrmərənt, -͜rænt] n : cormorán m

corn[1] ['kɔrn] vt : conservar en salmuera ⟨corned beef : carne en conserva⟩

corn[2] n 1 GRAIN : grano m 2 : maíz m, elote m Mex ⟨corn tortillas : tortillas de maíz⟩ 3 : callo m ⟨corn plaster : emplasto para callos⟩

corncob ['kɔrn͜kɑb] n : mazorca f (de maíz), choclo m, elote m CA, Mex

cornea ['kɔrniə] n : córnea f

corner[1] ['kɔrnər] vt 1 TRAP : acorralar, arrinconar 2 MONOPOLIZE : monopolizar, acaparar (un mercado) — vi : tomar una curva, doblar una esquina (en un automóvil)

corner[2] n 1 ANGLE : rincón m, esquina f, ángulo m ⟨the corner of a room : el rincón de una sala⟩ ⟨all corners of the world : todos los rincones del mundo⟩ ⟨to cut corners : atajar, economizar esfuerzos⟩ 2 INTERSECTION : esquina f 3 IMPASSE, PREDICAMENT : aprieto m, impasse m ⟨to be backed into a corner : estar acorralado⟩

cornerstone ['kɔrnər͜sto:n] n : piedra f angular

cornet [kɔr'nɛt] n : corneta f

cornfield ['kɔrn͜fi:ld] n : maizal m; milpa f CA, Mex

cornice ['kɔrnɪs] n : cornisa f

cornmeal ['kɔrn͜mi:l] n : harina f de maíz

cornstalk ['kɔrn͜stɔk] n : tallo m del maíz

cornstarch ['kɔrn͜stɑrtʃ] n : maicena f, almidón m de maíz

cornucopia [͜kɔrnə'ko:piə, -njə-] n : cornucopia f

corolla [kə'rɑlə] n : corola f

corollary ['kɔrə͜lɛri] n, pl -laries : corolario m

corona [kə'ro:nə] n : corona f (del sol)

coronary[1] ['kɔrə͜nɛri] adj : coronario

coronary[2] n, pl -naries 1 : trombosis f coronaria 2 HEART ATTACK : infarto m, ataque m al corazón

coronation [͜kɔrə'neɪʃən] n : coronación f

coroner ['kɔrənər] *n* : médico *m* forense

corporal[1] ['kɔrpərəl] *adj* : corporal ⟨corporal punishment : castigos corporales⟩

corporal[2] *n* : cabo *m*

corporate ['kɔrpərət] *adj* : corporativo, empresarial

corporation [ˌkɔrpə'reɪʃən] *n* : sociedad *f* anónima, corporación *f*, empresa *f*

corporeal [kɔr'pɔriəl] *adj* **1** PHYSICAL : corpóreo **2** MATERIAL : material, tangible — **corporeally** *adv*

corps ['kor] *n*, *pl* **corps** ['korz] : cuerpo *m* ⟨medical corps : cuerpo médico⟩ ⟨diplomatic corps : cuerpo diplomático⟩

corpse ['kɔrps] *n* : cadáver *m*

corpulence ['kɔrpjələnts] *n* : obesidad *f*, gordura *f*

corpulent ['kɔrpjələnt] *adj* : obeso, gordo

corpuscle ['kɔr,pʌsəl] *n* : corpúsculo *m*, glóbulo *m* (sanguíneo)

corral[1] [kə'ræl] *vt* **-ralled; -ralling** : acorralar, encorralar (ganado)

corral[2] *n* : corral *m*

correct[1] [kə'rɛkt] *vt* **1** RECTIFY : corregir, rectificar **2** REPRIMAND : corregir, reprender

correct[2] *adj* **1** ACCURATE, RIGHT : correcto, exacto ⟨to be correct : estar en lo cierto⟩ **2** PROPER : correcto, apropiado

correction [kə'rɛkʃən] *n* : corrección *f*

corrective [kə'rɛktɪv] *adj* : correctivo

correctly [kə'rɛktli] *adv* : correctamente

correctness [kə'rɛk(t)nəs] *n* **1** ACCURACY : exactitud *f* **2** PROPRIETY : corrección *f*

correlate ['kɔrə,leɪt] *vt* **-lated; -lating** : relacionar, poner en correlación

correlation [ˌkɔrə'leɪʃən] *n* : correlación *f*

correspond [ˌkɔrə'spɑnd] *vi* **1** MATCH : corresponder, concordar, coincidir **2** WRITE : corresponderse, escribirse

correspondence [ˌkɔrə'spɑndənts] *n* : correspondencia *f*

correspondent [ˌkɔrə'spɑndənt] *n* : corresponsal *mf*

corresponding [kɔrə'spɑndɪŋ, kɑr-] *adj* : correspondiente

correspondingly [ˌkɔrə'spɑndɪŋli] *adv* : en consecuencia, de la misma manera

corridor ['kɔrədər, -ˌdɔr] *n* : corredor *m*, pasillo *m*

corroborate [kə'rɑbə,reɪt] *vt* **-rated; -rating** : corroborar

corroboration [kə,rɑbə'reɪʃən] *n* : corroboración *f*

corrode [kə'ro:d] *v* **-roded; -roding** *vt* : corroer — *vi* : corroerse

corrosion [kə'ro:ʒən] *n* : corrosión *f*

corrosive [kə'ro:sɪv] *adj* : corrosivo

corrugate ['kɔrə,geɪt] *vt* **-gated; -gating** : ondular, acanalar, corrugar

corrugated ['kɔrə,geɪtəd] *adj* : ondulado, acanalado ⟨corrugated cardboard : cartón ondulado⟩

corrupt[1] [kə'rʌpt] *vt* **1** PERVERT : corromper, pervertir, degradar (información) **2** BRIBE : sobornar

corrupt[2] *adj* : corrupto, corrompido

corruptible [kə'rʌptəbəl] *adj* : corruptible

corruption [kə'rʌpʃən] *n* : corrupción *f*

corsage [kɔr'sɑʒ, -'sɑʤ] *n* : ramillete *m* que se lleva como adorno

corset ['kɔrsət] *n* : corsé *m*

cortex ['kɔr,tɛks] *n*, *pl* **-tices** ['kɔrtə,si:z] *or* **-texes** : corteza *f* ⟨cerebral cortex : corteza cerebral⟩

cortisone ['kɔrtə,so:n, -zo:n] *n* : cortisona *f*

cosmetic[1] [kaz'mɛtɪk] *adj* : cosmético

cosmetic[2] *n* : cosmético *m*

cosmic ['kazmɪk] *adj* **1** : cósmico ⟨cosmic ray : rayo cósmico⟩ **2** VAST : grandioso, inmenso, vasto

cosmonaut ['kazmə,nɔt] *n* : cosmonauta *mf*

cosmopolitan[1] [ˌkazmə'pɑlətən] *adj* : cosmopolita

cosmopolitan[2] *n* : cosmopolita *mf*

cosmos ['kazməs, -ˌmo:s, -ˌmas] *n* : cosmos *m*, universo *m*

cost[1] ['kɔst] *v* **cost; costing** *vt* : costar ⟨how much does it cost? : ¿cuánto cuesta?, ¿cuánto vale?⟩ — *vi* : costar ⟨these cost more : éstos cuestan más⟩

cost[2] *n* : costo *m*, precio *m*, coste *m* ⟨cost of living : costo de vida⟩ ⟨victory at all costs : victoria a toda costa⟩

Costa Rican[1] [ˌkastə'ri:kən] *adj* : costarricense

Costa Rican[2] *n* : costarricense *mf*

costly ['kɔstli] *adj* : costoso, caro

costume ['kas,tu:m, -ˌtju:m] *n* **1** : traje *m* ⟨national costume : traje típico⟩ **2** : disfraz *m* ⟨costume party : fiesta de disfraces⟩ **3** OUTFIT : vestimenta *f*, traje *m*, conjunto *m*

cosy ['ko:zi] → **cozy**

cot ['kat] *n* : catre *m*

coterie ['ko:tə,ri, ˌko:tə'-] *n* : tertulia *f*, círculo *m* (social)

cottage ['katɪʤ] *n* : casita *f* (de campo)

cottage cheese *n* : requesón *m*

cotton ['katən] *n* : algodón *m*

cottonmouth ['katən,mauθ] → **moccasin**

cottonseed ['katən,si:d] *n* : semilla *f* de algodón

cotton swab → **swab**

cottontail ['katən,teɪl] *n* : conejo *m* de cola blanca

couch[1] ['kauʧ] *vt* : expresar, formular ⟨couched in strong language : expresado en lenguaje enérgico⟩

couch[2] *n* SOFA : sofá *m*

couch potato *n* : haragán *m*, -gana *f*; vago *m*, -ga *f*

cougar ['ku:gər] *n* : puma *m*

cough[1] ['kɔf] *vi* : toser

cough² *n* : tos *f*

could ['kʊd] → **can**

council ['kaʊntsəl] *n* **1** : concejo *m* ⟨city council : concejo municipal, ayuntamiento⟩ **2** MEETING : concejo *m*, junta *f* **3** BOARD : consejo *m* **4** : concilio *m* (eclesiástico)

councillor *or* **councilor** ['kaʊntsələr] *n* : concejal *m*, -jala *f*

councilman ['kaʊntsəlmən] *n, pl* **-men** [-mən, -ˌmen] : concejal *m*

councilwoman ['kaʊntsəlˌwʊmən] *n, pl* **-women** [-ˌwɪmən] : concejala *f*

counsel¹ ['kaʊntsəl] *v* **-seled** *or* **-selled; -seling** *or* **-selling** *vt* ADVISE : aconsejar, asesorar, recomendar — *vi* CONSULT : consultar

counsel² *n* **1** ADVICE : consejo *m*, recomendación *f* **2** CONSULTATION : consulta *f* **3** **counsel** *ns & pl* LAWYER : abogado *m*, -da *f*

counselor *or* **counsellor** ['kaʊntsələr] *n* : consejero *m*, -ra *f*; consultor *m*, -tora *f*; asesor *m*, -sora *f*

count¹ ['kaʊnt] *vt* : contar, enumerar — *vi* **1** : contar ⟨to count out loud : contar en voz alta⟩ **2** MATTER : contar, valer, importar ⟨that's what counts : eso es lo que cuenta⟩ **3** **to count on** : contar con

count² *n* **1** COMPUTATION : cómputo *m*, recuento *m*, cuenta *f* ⟨to lose count : perder la cuenta⟩ **2** CHARGE : cargo *m* ⟨two counts of robbery : dos cargos de robo⟩ **3** : conde *m* (noble)

countable ['kaʊntəbəl] *adj* : numerable

countdown ['kaʊntˌdaʊn] *n* : cuenta *f* atrás

countenance¹ ['kaʊntənənts] *vt* **-nanced; -nancing** : permitir, tolerar

countenance² *n* FACE : semblante *m*, rostro *m*

counter¹ ['kaʊntər] *vt* **1** → **counteract** **2** OPPOSE : oponerse a, resistir — *vi* RETALIATE : responder, contraatacar

counter² *adv* **counter to** : contrario a, en contra de

counter³ *adj* : contrario, opuesto

counter⁴ *n* **1** PIECE : ficha *f* (de un juego) **2** : mostrador *m* (de un negocio), ventanilla *f* (en un banco) **3** : contador *m* (aparato) **4** COUNTERBALANCE : fuerza *f* opuesta, contrapeso *m*

counteract [ˌkaʊntər'ækt] *vt* : contrarrestar

counterattack ['kaʊntərəˌtæk] *n* : contraataque *m*

counterbalance¹ [ˌkaʊntər'bælənts] *vt* **-anced; -ancing** : contrapesar

counterbalance² ['kaʊntərˌbælənts] *n* : contrapeso *m*

counterclockwise [ˌkaʊntər'klɑkˌwaɪz] *adv & adj* : en el sentido opuesto al de las manecillas del reloj

counterfeit¹ ['kaʊntərˌfɪt] *vt* **1** : falsificar (dinero) **2** PRETEND : fingir, aparentar

counterfeit² *adj* : falso, inauténtico

counterfeit³ *n* : falsificación *f*

counterfeiter ['kaʊntərˌfɪtər] *n* : falsificador *m*, -dora *f*

countermand ['kaʊntərˌmænd, ˌkaʊntər'-] *vt* : contramandar

countermeasure ['kaʊntərˌmɛʒər] *n* : contramedida *f*

counterpart ['kaʊntərˌpɑrt] *n* : homólogo *m*, contraparte *f Mex*

counterpoint ['kaʊntərˌpɔɪnt] *n* : contrapunto *m*

counterproductive [ˌkaʊntərprə'dʌktɪv] *adj* : contraproducente

counterrevolution [ˌkaʊntərˌrɛvə'lu:ʃən] *n* : contrarrevolución *f*

counterrevolutionary¹ [ˌkaʊntərˌrɛvə'lu:ʃənˌɛri] *adj* : contrarrevolucionario

counterrevolutionary² *n, pl* **-ries** : contrarrevolucionario *m*, -ria *f*

countersign ['kaʊntərˌsaɪn] *n* : contraseña *f*

countess ['kaʊntɪs] *n* : condesa *f*

countless ['kaʊntləs] *adj* : incontable, innumerable

country¹ ['kʌntri] *adj* : campestre, rural

country² *n, pl* **-tries** **1** NATION : país *m*, nación *f*, patria *f* ⟨country of origin : país de origen⟩ ⟨love of one's country : amor a la patria⟩ **2** : campo *m* ⟨they left the city for the country : se fueron de la ciudad al campo⟩

countryman ['kʌntrimən] *n, pl* **-men** [-mən, -ˌmen] : compatriota *mf*; paisano *m*, -na *f*

countryside ['kʌntriˌsaɪd] *n* : campo *m*, campiña *f*

county ['kaʊnti] *n, pl* **-ties** : condado *m*

coup ['ku:] *n, pl* **coups** ['ku:z] **1** : golpe *m* maestro **2** *or* **coup d'etat** : golpe *m* (de estado), cuartelazo *m*

coupe ['ku:p] *n* : cupé *m*

couple¹ ['kʌpəl] *vt* **-pled; -pling** : acoplar, enganchar, conectar

couple² *n* **1** PAIR : par *m* ⟨a couple of hours : un par de horas, unas dos horas⟩ **2** : pareja *f* ⟨a young couple : una pareja joven⟩

coupling ['kʌplɪŋ] *n* : acoplamiento *m*

coupon ['ku:ˌpɑn, 'kju:-] *n* : cupón *m*

courage ['kərɪdʒ] *n* : valor *m*, valentía *f*, coraje *m*

courageous [kə'reɪdʒəs] *adj* : valiente, valeroso

courier ['kʊriər, 'kəriər] *n* : mensajero *m*, -ra *f*

course¹ ['kors] *vi* **coursed; coursing** : correr (a toda velocidad)

course² *n* **1** PROGRESS : curso *m*, transcurso *m* ⟨to run its course : seguir su curso⟩ **2** DIRECTION : rumbo *m* (de un avión), derrota *f*, derrotero *m* (de un barco) **3** PATH, WAY : camino *m*, vía *f* ⟨course of action : línea de conducta⟩ **4** : plato *m* (de una cena) ⟨the main course : el plato principal⟩ **5** : curso *m* (académico) **6** **of course** : desde luego, por supuesto ⟨yes, of course! : ¡claro que sí!⟩

court¹ [ˈkort] *vt* WOO : cortejar, galantear
court² *n* **1** PALACE : palacio *m* **2** RETINUE : corte *f*, séquito *m* **3** COURTYARD : patio *m* **4** : cancha *f* (de tenis, baloncesto, etc.) **5** TRIBUNAL : corte *f*, tribunal *m* ⟨the Supreme Court : la Corte Suprema⟩
courteous [ˈkərtiəs] *adj* : cortés, atento, educado — **courteously** *adv*
courtesan [ˈkortəzən, ˈkər-] *n* : cortesana *f*
courtesy [ˈkərtəsi] *n, pl* **-sies** : cortesía *f*
courthouse [ˈkort‚haʊs] *n* : palacio *m* de justicia, juzgado *m*
courtier [ˈkortiər, ˈkortjər] *n* : cortesano *m*, -na *f*
courtly [ˈkortli] *adj* **-lier; -est** : distinguido, elegante, cortés
court–martial¹ [ˈkort‚marʃəl] *vt* : someter a consejo de guerra
court–martial² *n, pl* **courts–martial** [ˈkorts‚marʃəl] : consejo *m* de guerra
court order *n* : mandamiento *m* judicial
courtroom [ˈkort‚ruːm] *n* : tribunal *m*, corte *f*
courtship [ˈkort‚ʃɪp] *n* : cortejo *m*, noviazgo *m*
courtyard [ˈkort‚jard] *n* : patio *m*
cousin [ˈkʌzən] *n* : primo *m*, -ma *f*
couture [kuːˈtʊr] *n* : industria *f* de la moda ⟨haute couture : alta costura⟩
cove [ˈkoːv] *n* : ensenada *f*, cala *f*
covenant [ˈkʌvənənt] *n* : pacto *m*, contrato *m*
cover¹ [ˈkʌvər] *vt* **1** : cubrir, tapar ⟨cover your head : tápate la cabeza⟩ ⟨covered with mud : cubierto de lodo⟩ **2** HIDE, PROTECT : encubrir, proteger **3** TREAT : tratar **4** INSURE : asegurar, cubrir
cover² *n* **1** SHELTER : cubierta *f*, abrigo *m*, refugio *m* ⟨to take cover : ponerse a cubierto⟩ ⟨under cover of darkness : al amparo de la oscuridad⟩ **2** LID, TOP : cubierta *f*, tapa *f* **3** : cubierta *f* (de un libro), portada *f* (de una revista) **4** **covers** *npl* BEDCLOTHES : ropa *f* de cama, cobijas *fpl*, mantas *fpl*
coverage [ˈkʌvərɪdʒ] *n* : cobertura *f*
coverlet [ˈkʌvərlət] *n* : cobertor *m*
covert¹ [ˈkoː‚vərt, ˈkʌvərt] *adj* : encubierto, secreto ⟨covert operations : operaciones encubiertas⟩
covert² [ˈkʌvərt, ˈkoː-] *n* THICKET : espesura *f*, maleza *f*
cover–up [ˈkʌvər‚ʌp] *n* : encubrimiento *m* (de algo ilícito)
covet [ˈkʌvət] *vt* : codiciar
covetous [ˈkʌvətəs] *adj* : codicioso
covey [ˈkʌvi] *n, pl* **-eys 1** : bandada *f* pequeña (de codornices, etc.) **2** GROUP : grupo *m*
cow¹ [ˈkaʊ] *vt* : intimidar, acobardar
cow² *n* : vaca *f*, hembra *f* (de ciertas especies)
coward [ˈkaʊərd] *n* : cobarde *mf*

cowardice [ˈkaʊərdɪs] *n* : cobardía *f*
cowardly [ˈkaʊərdli] *adj* : cobarde
cowboy [ˈkaʊ‚bɔɪ] *n* : vaquero *m*, cowboy *m*
cower [ˈkaʊər] *vi* : encogerse (de miedo), acobardarse
cowgirl [ˈkaʊ‚gərl] *n* : vaquera *f*
cowherd [ˈkaʊ‚hərd] *n* : vaquero *m*, -ra *f*
cowhide [ˈkaʊ‚haɪd] *n* : cuero *m*, piel *f* de vaca
cowl [ˈkaʊl] *n* : capucha *f* (de un monje)
cowlick [ˈkaʊ‚lɪk] *n* : remolino *m*
cowpuncher [ˈkaʊ‚pʌntʃər] → **cowboy**
cowslip [ˈkaʊ‚slɪp] *n* : prímula *f*, primavera *f*
coxswain [ˈkaksən, -‚sweɪn] *n* : timonel *m*
coy [ˈkɔɪ] *adj* **1** SHY : tímido, cohibido **2** COQUETTISH : coqueto
coyote [kaɪˈoːt̬i, ˈkaɪ‚oːt] *n, pl* **coyotes** *or* **coyote** : coyote *m*
cozy [ˈkoːzi] *adj* **-zier; -est** : acogedor, cómodo
CPU [‚siː‚piːˈjuː] *n* (central processing unit) : CPU *f*
crab [ˈkræb] *n* : cangrejo *m*, jaiba *f*
crabby [ˈkræbi] *adj* **-bier; -est** : gruñón, malhumorado
crabgrass [ˈkræb‚græs] *n* : garranchuelo *m*
crack¹ [ˈkræk] *vi* **1** : chasquear, restallar ⟨the whip cracked : el látigo restalló⟩ **2** SPLIT : rajarse, resquebrajarse, agrietarse **3** : quebrarse (dícese de la voz) — *vt* **1** : restallar, chasquear (un látigo, etc.) **2** SPLIT : rajar, agrietar, resquebrajar **3** BREAK : romper (un huevo), cascar (nueces), forzar (una caja fuerte) **4** SOLVE : resolver, descifrar (un código)
crack² *adj* FIRST-RATE : buenísimo, de primera
crack³ *n* **1** : chasquido *m*, restallido *m*, estallido *m* (de un arma de fuego), crujido *m* (de huesos) ⟨a crack of thunder : un trueno⟩ **2** WISECRACK : chiste *m*, ocurrencia *f*, salida *f* **3** CREVICE : raja *f*, grieta *f*, fisura *f* **4** BLOW : golpe *m* **5** ATTEMPT : intento *m*
crackdown [ˈkræk‚daʊn] *n* : medidas *fpl* enérgicas
crack down *vt* : tomar medidas enérgicas
cracker [ˈkrækər] *n* : galleta *f* (de soda, etc.)
crackle¹ [ˈkrækəl] *vi* **-led; -ling** : crepitar, chisporrotear
crackle² *n* : crujido *m*, chisporroteo *m*
crackpot [ˈkræk‚pat] *n* : excéntrico *m*, -ca *f*; chiflado *m*, -da *f*
crack–up [ˈkræk‚ʌp] *n* **1** CRASH : choque *m*, estrellamiento *m* **2** BREAKDOWN : crisis *f* nerviosa
crack up *vt* **1** : estrellar (un vehículo) **2** : hacer reír **3** : elogiar ⟨it isn't all that it's cracked up to be : no es tan bueno como se dice⟩ — *vi* **1** : estrellarse **2** LAUGH : echarse a reír

cradle¹ [ˈkreɪdəl] *vt* **-dled; -dling** : acunar, mecer (a un niño)
cradle² *n* : cuna *f*
craft [ˈkræft] *n* **1** TRADE : oficio *m* ⟨the craft of carpentry : el oficio de carpintero⟩ **2** CRAFTSMANSHIP, SKILL : arte *m*, artesanía *f*, destreza *f* **3** CRAFTINESS : astucia *f*, maña *f* **4** *pl usually* **craft** BOAT : barco *m*, embarcación *f* **5** *pl usually* **craft** AIRCRAFT : avión *m*, aeronave *f*
craftiness [ˈkræftinəs] *n* : astucia *f*, maña *f*
craftsman [ˈkræftsmən] *n, pl* **-men** [-mən, -ˌmɛn] : artesano *m*, -na *f*
craftsmanship [ˈkræftsmənˌʃɪp] *n* : artesanía *f*, destreza *f*
crafty [ˈkræfti] *adj* **craftier; -est** : astuto, taimado
crag [ˈkræg] *n* : peñasco *m*
craggy [ˈkrægi] *adj* **-gier; -est** : peñascoso
cram [ˈkræm] *v* **crammed; cramming** *vt* **1** JAM : embutir, meter **2** STUFF : atiborrar, abarrotar ⟨crammed with people : atiborrado de gente⟩ — *vi* : estudiar a última hora, memorizar (para un examen)
cramp¹ [ˈkræmp] *vt* **1** : dar calambre en **2** RESTRICT : limitar, restringir, entorpecer ⟨to cramp someone's style : cortarle el vuelo a alguien⟩ — *vi or* **to cramp up** : acalambrarse
cramp² *n* **1** SPASM : calambre *m*, espasmo *m* (de los músculos) **2** **cramps** *npl* : retorcijones *mpl* ⟨stomach cramps : retorcijones de estómago⟩
cranberry [ˈkrænˌbɛri] *n, pl* **-berries** : arándano *m* (rojo y agrio)
crane¹ [ˈkreɪn] *vt* **craned; craning** : estirar ⟨to crane one's neck : estirar el cuello⟩
crane² *n* **1** : grulla *f* (ave) **2** : grúa *f* (máquina)
cranial [ˈkreɪniəl] *adj* : craneal, craneano
cranium [ˈkreɪniəm] *n, pl* **-niums** *or* **-nia** [-niə] : cráneo *m*
crank¹ [ˈkræŋk] *vt or* **to crank up** : arrancar (con una manivela)
crank² *n* **1** : manivela *f*, manubrio *m* **2** ECCENTRIC : excéntrico *m*, -ca *f*
cranky [ˈkræŋki] *adj* **crankier; -est** : irritable, malhumorado, enojadizo
cranny [ˈkræni] *n, pl* **-nies** : grieta *f* ⟨every nook and cranny : todos los rincones⟩
crash¹ [ˈkræʃ] *vi* **1** SMASH : caerse con estrépito, estrellarse **2** COLLIDE : estrellarse, chocar **3** BOOM, RESOUND : retumbar, resonar — *vt* **1** SMASH : estrellar **2 to crash a party** : colarse en una fiesta **3 to crash one's car** : tener un accidente
crash² *n* **1** DIN : estrépito *m* **2** COLLISION : choque *m*, colisión *f* ⟨car crash : accidente automovilístico⟩ **3** FAILURE : quiebra *f* (de un negocio), crac *m* (de la bolsa)

crass [ˈkræs] *adj* : grosero, de mal gusto
crate¹ [ˈkreɪt] *vt* **crated; crating** : empacar en un cajón
crate² *n* : cajón *m* (de madera)
crater [ˈkreɪtər] *n* : cráter *m*
cravat [krəˈvæt] *n* : corbata *f*
crave [ˈkreɪv] *vt* **craved; craving** : ansiar, apetecer, tener muchas ganas de
craven [ˈkreɪvən] *adj* : cobarde, pusilánime
craving [ˈkreɪvɪŋ] *n* : ansia *f*, antojo *m*, deseo *m*
crawfish [ˈkrɔˌfɪʃ] → **crayfish**
crawl¹ [ˈkrɔl] *vi* **1** CREEP : arrastrarse, gatear (dícese de un bebé) **2** TEEM : estar plagado
crawl² *n* : paso *m* lento
crayfish [ˈkreɪˌfɪʃ] *n* **1** : ástaco *m* (de agua dulce) **2** : langostino *m* (de mar)
crayon [ˈkreɪˌɑn, -ən] *n* : crayón *m*
craze [ˈkreɪz] *n* : moda *f* pasajera, manía *f*
crazed [ˈkreɪzd] *adj* : enloquecido
crazily [ˈkreɪzəli] *adv* : locamente, erráticamente, insensatamente
craziness [ˈkreɪzinəs] *n* : locura *f*, demencia *f*
crazy [ˈkreɪzi] *adj* **-zier; -est 1** INSANE : loco, demente ⟨to go crazy : volverse loco⟩ **2** ABSURD, FOOLISH : loco, insensato, absurdo **3 like crazy** : como loco **4 to be crazy about** : estar loco por
creak¹ [ˈkriːk] *vi* : chirriar, rechinar, crujir
creak² *n* : chirrido *m*, crujido *m*
creaky [ˈkriːki] *adj* **creakier; -est** : chirriante, que cruje
cream¹ [ˈkriːm] *vt* **1** BEAT, MIX : batir, mezclar (azúcar y mantequilla, etc.) **2** : preparar (alimentos) con crema
cream² *n* **1** : crema *f* (de leche) **2** LOTION : crema *f*, loción *f* **3** ELITE : crema *f*, elite *f* ⟨the cream of the crop : la crema y nata, lo mejor⟩
creamery [ˈkriːməri] *n, pl* **-eries** : fábrica *f* de productos lácteos
creamy [ˈkriːmi] *adj* **creamier; -est** : cremoso
crease¹ [ˈkriːs] *vt* **creased; creasing 1** : plegar, poner una raya en (pantalones) **2** WRINKLE : arrugar
crease² *n* : pliegue *m*, doblez *m*, raya *f* (de pantalones)
create [kriˈeɪt] *vt* **-ated; -ating** : crear, hacer
creation [kriˈeɪʃən] *n* : creación *f*
creative [kriˈeɪtɪv] *adj* : creativo, original ⟨creative people : personas creativas⟩ ⟨a creative work : un obra original⟩
creatively [kriˈeɪtɪvli] *adv* : creativamente, con originalidad
creativity [ˌkriːeɪˈtɪvəti] *n* : creatividad *f*
creator [kriˈeɪtər] *n* : creador *m*, -dora *f*
creature [ˈkriːtʃər] *n* : ser *m* viviente, criatura *f*, animal *m*

credence ['kri:dənts] *n* : crédito *m*

credentials [krɪ'dentʃəlz] *npl* : referencias *fpl* oficiales, cartas *fpl* credenciales

credibility [ˌkrɛdə'bɪləti] *n* : credibilidad *f*

credible ['krɛdəbəl] *adj* : creíble

credit[1] ['krɛdɪt] *vt* **1** BELIEVE : creer, dar crédito a **2** : ingresar, abonar ⟨to credit $100 to an account : ingresar $100 en (una) cuenta⟩ **3** ATTRIBUTE : atribuir ⟨they credit the invention to him : a él se le atribuye el invento⟩

credit[2] *n* **1** : saldo *m* positivo, saldo *m* a favor (de una cuenta) **2** : crédito *m* ⟨to buy on credit : comprar a crédito⟩ ⟨credit card : tarjeta de crédito⟩ **3** CREDENCE : crédito *m* ⟨I gave credit to everything he said : di crédito a todo lo que dijo⟩ **4** RECOGNITION : reconocimiento *m* **5** : orgullo *m*, honor *m* ⟨she's a credit to the school : ella es el orgullo de la escuela⟩

creditable ['krɛdɪtəbəl] *adj* : encomiable — **creditably** [-bli] *adv*

credit card *n* : tarjeta de crédito

creditor ['krɛdɪtər] *n* : acreedor *m*, -dora *f*

credo ['kri:do:, 'kreɪ-] *n* : credo *m*

credulity [krɪ'du:ləti, -'dju:-] *n* : credulidad *f*

credulous ['krɛdʒələs] *adj* : crédulo

creed ['kri:d] *n* : credo *m*

creek ['kri:k, 'krɪk] *n* : arroyo *m*, riachuelo *m*

creel ['kri:l] *n* : nasa *f*, cesta *f* (de pescador)

creep[1] ['kri:p] *vi* **crept** ['krɛpt]; **creeping** **1** CRAWL : arrastrarse, gatear **2** : moverse lentamente o sigilosamente ⟨he crept out of the house : salió sigilosamente de la casa⟩ **3** SPREAD : trepar (dícese de una planta)

creep[2] *n* **1** CRAWL : paso *m* lento **2** : asqueroso *m*, -sa *f* **3** **creeps** *npl* : escalofríos *mpl* ⟨that gives me the creeps : eso me da escalofríos⟩

creeper ['kri:pər] *n* : planta *f* trepadora, trepadora *f*

creepy ['kri:pi] *adj* **1** SPOOKY : espeluznante **2** UNPLEASANT : asqueroso

cremate ['kri:ˌmeɪt] *vt* **-mated; -mating** : cremar

cremation [krɪ'meɪʃən] *n* : cremación *f*

Creole ['kri:ˌo:l] *n* **1** : criollo *m*, criolla *f* **2** : criollo *m* (idioma) — **Creole** *adj*

creosote ['kri:əˌso:t] *n* : creosota *f*

crepe *or* **crêpe** ['kreɪp] *n* **1** : crespón *m* (tela) **2** PANCAKE : crepe *mf*, crepa *f* Mex

crescendo [krɪ'ʃɛnˌdo:] *n, pl* **-dos** *or* **-does** : crescendo *m*

crescent ['krɛsənt] *n* : creciente *m*

crest ['krɛst] *n* **1** : cresta *f*, penacho *m* (de un ave) **2** PEAK, TOP : cresta *f* (de una ola), cima *f* (de una colina) **3** : emblema *m* (en un escudo de armas)

crestfallen ['krɛstˌfɔlən] *adj* : alicaído, abatido

cretin ['kri:tən] *n* : cretino *m*, -na *f*

crevasse [krɪ'væs] *n* : grieta *f*, fisura *f*

crevice ['krɛvɪs] *n* : grieta *f*, hendidura *f*

crew ['kru:] *n* **1** : tripulación *f* (de una nave) **2** TEAM : equipo *m* (de trabajadores o atletas)

crib ['krɪb] *n* **1** MANGER : pesebre *m* **2** GRANARY : granero *m* **3** : cuna *f* (de un bebé)

crick ['krɪk] *n* : calambre *m*, espasmo *m* muscular

cricket ['krɪkət] *n* **1** : grillo *m* (insecto) **2** : críquet *m* (juego)

crime ['kraɪm] *n* **1** : crimen *m*, delito *m* ⟨to commit a crime : cometer un delito⟩ **2** : crimen *m*, delincuencia *f* ⟨organized crime : crimen organizado⟩

criminal[1] ['krɪmənəl] *adj* : criminal

criminal[2] *n* : criminal *mf*, delincuente *mf*

crimp ['krɪmp] *vt* : ondular, rizar (el pelo), arrugar (una tela, etc.)

crimson ['krɪmzən] *n* : carmesí *m*

cringe ['krɪndʒ] *vi* **cringed; cringing** : encogerse

crinkle[1] ['krɪŋkəl] *v* **-kled; -kling** *vt* : arrugar — *vi* : arrugarse

crinkle[2] *n* : arruga *f*

crinkly ['krɪŋkəli] *adj* : arrugado

cripple[1] ['krɪpəl] *vt* **-pled; -pling** **1** DISABLE : lisiar, dejar inválido **2** INCAPACITATE : inutilizar, incapacitar

cripple[2] *n* : lisiado *m*, -da *f*

crisis ['kraɪsɪs] *n, pl* **crises** [-ˌsi:z] : crisis *f*

crisp[1] ['krɪsp] *vt* : tostar, hacer crujiente

crisp[2] *adj* **1** CRUNCHY : crujiente, crocante **2** FIRM, FRESH : firme, fresco ⟨crisp lettuce : lechuga fresca⟩ **3** LIVELY : vivaz, alegre ⟨a crisp tempo : un ritmo alegre⟩ **4** INVIGORATING : fresco, vigorizante ⟨the crisp autumn air : el fresco aire otoñal⟩ — **crisply** *adv*

crisp[3] *n* : postre *m* de fruta (con pedacitos de masa dulce por encima)

crispy ['krɪspi] *adj* **crispier; -est** : crujiente ⟨crispy potato chips : papitas crujientes⟩

crisscross ['krɪsˌkrɔs] *vt* : entrecruzar

criterion [kraɪ'tɪriən] *n, pl* **-ria** [-iə] : criterio *m*

critic ['krɪtɪk] *n* **1** : crítico *m*, -ca *f* (de las artes) **2** FAULTFINDER : detractor *m*, -tora *f*; criticón *m*, -cona *f*

critical ['krɪtɪkəl] *adj* : crítico

critically ['krɪtɪkli] *adv* : críticamente ⟨critically ill : gravemente enfermo⟩

criticism ['krɪtəˌsɪzəm] *n* : crítica *f*

criticize ['krɪtəˌsaɪz] *vt* **-cized; -cizing** **1** EVALUATE, JUDGE : criticar, analizar, evaluar **2** CENSURE : criticar, reprobar

critique [krɪ'ti:k] *n* : crítica *f*, evaluación *f*

croak[1] ['kro:k] *vi* : croar

croak[2] *n* : croar *m*, canto *m* (de la rana)

Croatian [kro'eɪʃən] *n* : croata *mf* — **Croatian** *adj*

crochet[1] [kroːˈʃeɪ] *v* : tejer al croché
crochet[2] *n* : croché *m*, crochet *m*
crock [ˈkrɑk] *n* : vasija *f* de barro
crockery [ˈkrɑkəri] *n* : vajilla *f* (de barro)
crocodile [ˈkrɑkəˌdaɪl] *n* : cocodrilo *m*
crocus [ˈkroːkəs] *n, pl* **-cuses** : azafrán *m*
croissant [krəˈsɑnt] *n* : croissant *m*
crone [ˈkroːn] *n* : vieja *f* arpía, vieja *f* bruja
crony [ˈkroːni] *n, pl* **-nies** : amigote *m* *fam*; compinche *mf* *fam*
crook[1] [ˈkrʊk] *vt* : doblar (el brazo o el dedo)
crook[2] *n* **1** STAFF : cayado *m* (de pastor), báculo *m* (de obispo) **2** THIEF : ratero *m*, -ra *f*; ladrón *m*, -drona *f*
crooked [ˈkrʊkəd] *adj* **1** BENT : chueco, torcido **2** DISHONEST : deshonesto
crookedness [ˈkrʊkədnəs] *n* **1** : lo torcido, lo chueco **2** DISHONESTY : falta *f* de honradez
croon [ˈkruːn] *v* : cantar suavemente
crop[1] [ˈkrɑp] *v* **cropped; cropping** *vt* TRIM : recortar, cortar — *vi* **to crop up** : aparecer, surgir ⟨these problems keep cropping up : estos problemas no cesan de surgir⟩
crop[2] *n* **1** : buche *m* (de un ave o insecto) **2** WHIP : fusta *f* (de jinete) **3** HARVEST : cosecha *f*, cultivo *m*
croquet [ˌkroːˈkeɪ] *n* : croquet *m*
croquette [ˌkroːˈkɛt] *n* : croqueta *f*
cross[1] [ˈkrɔs] *vt* **1** : cruzar, atravesar ⟨to cross the street : cruzar la calle⟩ ⟨several canals cross the city : varios canales atraviesan la ciudad⟩ **2** CANCEL : tachar, cancelar ⟨he crossed his name off the list : tachó su nombre de la planilla⟩ **3** INTERBREED : cruzar (en genética)
cross[2] *adj* **1** : que atraviesa ⟨cross ventilation : ventilación que atraviesa un cuarto⟩ **2** CONTRARY : contrario, opuesto ⟨cross purposes : objetivos opuestos⟩ **3** ANGRY : enojado, de mal humor
cross[3] *n* **1** : cruz *f* ⟨the sign of the cross : la señal de la cruz⟩ **2** : cruza *f* (en biología)
crossbones [ˈkrɔsˌboːnz] *npl* **1** : huesos *mpl* cruzados **2** → **skull**
crossbow [ˈkrɔsˌboː] *n* : ballesta *f*
crossbreed [ˈkrɔsˌbriːd] *vt* **-bred** [-ˌbrɛd]; **-breeding** : cruzar
crosscurrent [ˈkrɔsˌkərənt] *n* : contracorriente *f*
cross-examination [ˌkrɔsɪɡˌzæməˈneɪʃən] *n* : repreguntas *fpl*, interrogatorio *m*
cross-examine [ˌkrɔsɪɡˈzæmən] *vt* **-ined; -ining** : repreguntar
cross-eyed [ˈkrɔsˌaɪd] *adj* : bizco
crossing [ˈkrɔsɪŋ] *n* **1** INTERSECTION : cruce *m*, paso *m* ⟨pedestrian crossing : paso de peatones⟩ **2** VOYAGE : travesía *f* (del mar)

crossly [ˈkrɔsli] *adv* : con enojo, con enfado
cross-reference [ˌkrɔsˈrefrənts, -ˈrefərənts] *n* : referencia *f*, remisión *f*
crossroads [ˈkrɔsˌroːdz] *n* : cruce *m*, encrucijada *f*, crucero *m Mex*
cross section *n* **1** SECTION : corte *m* transversal **2** SAMPLE : muestra *f* representativa ⟨a cross section of the population : una muestra representativa de la población⟩
crosswalk [ˈkrɔsˌwɔk] *n* : cruce *m* peatonal, paso *m* de peatones
crossways [ˈkrɔsˌweɪz] → **crosswise**
crosswise[1] [ˈkrɔsˌwaɪz] *adv* : transversalmente, diagonalmente
crosswise[2] *adj* : transversal, diagonal
crossword puzzle [ˈkrɔsˌwərd] *n* : crucigrama *m*
crotch [ˈkrɑtʃ] *n* : entrepierna *f*
crotchety [ˈkrɑtʃəti] *adj* CRANKY : malhumorado, irritable, enojadizo
crouch [ˈkraʊtʃ] *vi* : agacharse, ponerse de cuclillas
croup [ˈkruːp] *n* : crup *m*
crouton [ˈkruːˌtɑn] *n* : crutón *m*
crow[1] [ˈkroː] *vi* **1** : cacarear, cantar (como un cuervo) **2** BRAG : alardear, presumir
crow[2] *n* **1** : cuervo *m* (ave) **2** : cantar *m* (del gallo)
crowbar [ˈkroːˌbɑr] *n* : palanca *f*
crowd[1] [ˈkraʊd] *vi* : aglomerarse, amontonarse — *vt* : atestar, atiborrar, llenar
crowd[2] *n* : multitud *f*, muchedumbre *f*, gentío *m*
crown[1] [ˈkraʊn] *vt* : coronar
crown[2] *n* : corona *f*
crow's nest *n* : cofa *f*
crucial [ˈkruːʃəl] *adj* : crucial, decisivo
crucible [ˈkruːsəbəl] *n* : crisol *m*
crucifix [ˈkruːsəˌfɪks] *n* : crucifijo *m*
crucifixion [ˌkruːsəˈfɪkʃən] *n* : crucifixión *f*
crucify [ˈkruːsəˌfaɪ] *vt* **-fied; -fying** : crucificar
crude [ˈkruːd] *adj* **cruder; -est 1** RAW, UNREFINED : crudo, sin refinar ⟨crude oil : petróleo crudo⟩ **2** VULGAR : grosero, de mal gusto **3** ROUGH : tosco, burdo, rudo
crudely [ˈkruːdli] *adv* **1** VULGARLY : groseramente **2** ROUGHLY : burdamente, de manera rudimentaria
crudity [ˈkruːdəti] *n, pl* **-ties 1** VULGARITY : grosería *f* **2** COARSENESS, ROUGHNESS : tosquedad *f*, rudeza *f*
cruel [ˈkruːəl] *adj* **-eler** *or* **-eller; -elest** *or* **-ellest** : cruel
cruelly [ˈkruːəli] *adv* : cruelmente
cruelty [ˈkruːəlti] *n, pl* **-ties** : crueldad *f*
cruet [ˈkruːɪt] *n* : vinagrera *f*, aceitera *f*
cruise[1] [ˈkruːz] *vi* **cruised; cruising 1** : hacer un crucero **2** : navegar o conducir a una velocidad constante ⟨cruising speed : velocidad de crucero⟩
cruise[2] *n* : crucero *m*

cruiser ['kru:zər] *n* **1** WARSHIP : crucero *m*, buque *m* de guerra **2** : patrulla *f* (de policía)

crumb ['krʌm] *n* : miga *f*, migaja *f*

crumble ['krʌmbəl] *v* **-bled; -bling** *vt* : desmigajar, desmenuzar — *vi* : desmigajarse, desmoronarse, desmenuzarse

crumbly ['krʌmbli] *adj* : que se desmenuza fácilmente, friable

crumple ['krʌmpəl] *v* **-pled; -pling** *vt* RUMPLE : arrugar — *vi* **1** WRINKLE : arrugarse **2** COLLAPSE : desplomarse

crunch[1] ['krʌntʃ] *vt* **1** : ronzar (con los dientes) **2** : hacer crujir (con los pies, etc.) — *vi* : crujir

crunch[2] *n* : crujido *m*

crunchy ['krʌntʃi] *adj* **crunchier; -est** : crujiente

crusade[1] [kru:'seɪd] *vi* **-saded; -sading** : hacer una campaña (a favor de o contra algo)

crusade[2] *n* **1** : campaña *f* (de reforma, etc.) **2 Crusade** : cruzada *f*

crusader [kru:'seɪdər] *n* **1** : cruzado *m* (en la Edad Media) **2** : campeón *m*, -peona *f* (de una causa)

crush[1] ['krʌʃ] *vt* **1** SQUASH : aplastar, apachurrar **2** GRIND, PULVERIZE : triturar, machacar **3** SUPPRESS : aplastar, suprimir

crush[2] *n* **1** CROWD, MOB : gentío *m*, multitud *f*, aglomeración *f* **2** INFATUATION : enamoramiento *m*

crushing ['krʌʃɪŋ] *adj* : aplastante, abrumador

crust ['krʌst] *n* **1** : corteza *f*, costra *f* (de pan) **2** : tapa *f* de masa, pasta *f* (de un pastel) **3** LAYER : capa *f*, corteza *f* ⟨the earth's crust : la corteza terrestre⟩

crustacean [ˌkrʌs'teɪʃən] *n* : crustáceo *m*

crusty ['krʌsti] *adj* **crustier; -est 1** : de corteza dura **2** CROSS, GRUMPY : enojado, malhumorado

crutch ['krʌtʃ] *n* : muleta *f*

crux ['krʌks, 'krʊks] *n, pl* **cruxes** : quid *m*, esencia *f*, meollo *m* ⟨the crux of the problem : el quid del problema⟩

cry[1] ['kraɪ] *vi* **cried; crying 1** SHOUT : gritar ⟨they cried for more : a gritos pidieron más⟩ **2** WEEP : llorar

cry[2] *n, pl* **cries 1** SHOUT : grito *m* **2** WEEPING : llanto *m* **3** : chillido *m* (de un animal)

crybaby ['kraɪˌbeɪbi] *n, pl* **-bies** : llorón *m*, -rona *f*

crypt ['krɪpt] *n* : cripta *f*

cryptic ['krɪptɪk] *adj* : enigmático, críptico

crystal ['krɪstəl] *n* : cristal *m*

crystalline ['krɪstəlɪn] *adj* : cristalino

crystallize ['krɪstəˌlaɪz] *v* **-lized; -lizing** *vt* : cristalizar, materializar ⟨to crystallize one's thoughts : cristalizar uno sus pensamientos⟩ — *vi* : cristalizarse

cub ['kʌb] *n* : cachorro *m*

Cuban ['kju:bən] *n* : cubano *m*, -na *f* — **Cuban** *adj*

cubbyhole ['kʌbiˌho:l] *n* : chiribitil *m*

cube[1] ['kju:b] *vt* **cubed; cubing 1** : elevar (un número) al cubo **2** : cortar en cubos

cube[2] *n* **1** : cubo *m* **2 ice cube** : cubito *m* de hielo **3 sugar cube** : terrón *m* de azúcar

cubic ['kju:bɪk] *adj* : cúbico

cubicle ['kju:bɪkəl] *n* : cubículo *m*

cuckoo[1] ['ku:ˌku:, 'kʊ-] *adj* : loco, chiflado

cuckoo[2] *n, pl* **-oos** : cuco *m*, cuclillo *m*

cucumber ['kju:ˌkʌmbər] *n* : pepino *m*

cud ['kʌd] *n* **to chew the cud** : rumiar

cuddle ['kʌdəl] *v* **-dled; -dling** *vi* : abrazarse tiernamente, acurrucarse — *vt* : abrazar

cudgel[1] ['kʌdʒəl] *vt* **-geled** *or* **-gelled; -geling** *or* **-gelling** : apalear, aporrear

cudgel[2] *n* : garrote *m*, porra *f*

cue[1] ['kju:] *vt* **cued; cuing** *or* **cueing** : darle el pie a, darle la señal a

cue[2] *n* **1** SIGNAL : señal *f*, pie *m* (en teatro), entrada *f* (en música) **2** : taco *m* (de billar)

cuff[1] ['kʌf] *vt* : bofetear, cachetear

cuff[2] *n* **1** : puño *m* (de una camisa), vuelta *f* (de pantalones) **2** SLAP : bofetada *f*, cachetada *f* **3 cuffs** *npl* HANDCUFFS : esposas *fpl*

cuisine [kwɪ'zi:n] *n* : cocina *f* ⟨Mexican cuisine : la cocina mexicana⟩

culinary ['kʌləˌneri, 'kju:lə-] *adj* : culinario

cull ['kʌl] *vt* : seleccionar, entresacar

culminate ['kʌlməˌneɪt] *vi* **-nated; -nating** : culminar

culmination [ˌkʌlmə'neɪʃən] *n* : culminación *f*, punto *m* culminante

culpable ['kʌlpəbəl] *adj* : culpable

culprit ['kʌlprɪt] *n* : culpable *mf*

cult ['kʌlt] *n* : culto *m*

cultivate ['kʌltəˌveɪt] *vt* **-vated; -vating 1** TILL : cultivar, labrar **2** FOSTER : cultivar, fomentar **3** REFINE : cultivar, refinar ⟨to cultivate the mind : cultivar la mente⟩

cultivation [ˌkʌltə'veɪʃən] *n* **1** : cultivo *m* ⟨under cultivation : en cultivo⟩ **2** CULTURE, REFINEMENT : cultura *f*, refinamiento *m*

cultural ['kʌltʃərəl] *adj* : cultural — **culturally** *adv*

culture ['kʌltʃər] *n* **1** CULTIVATION : cultivo *m* **2** REFINEMENT : cultura *f*, educación *f*, refinamiento *m* **3** CIVILIZATION : cultura *f*, civilización *f* ⟨the Incan culture : la cultura inca⟩

cultured ['kʌltʃərd] *adj* **1** EDUCATED, REFINED : culto, educado, refinado **2** : de cultivo, cultivado ⟨cultured pearls : perlas de cultivo⟩

culvert ['kʌlvərt] *n* : alcantarilla *f*

cumbersome ['kʌmbərsəm] *adj* : torpe y pesado, difícil de manejar

cumin ['kʌmən] *n* : comino *m*

cumulative ['kju:mjələtɪv, -ˌleɪtɪv] *adj* : acumulativo

cumulus ['kju:mjələs] *n, pl* **-li** [-ˌlaɪ, -ˌli:] : cúmulo *m*

cunning[1] ['kʌnɪŋ] *adj* **1** CRAFTY : astuto, taimado **2** CLEVER : ingenioso, hábil **3** CUTE : mono, gracioso, lindo

cunning[2] *n* **1** SKILL : habilidad *f* **2** CRAFTINESS : astucia *f*, maña *f*

cup[1] ['kʌp] *vt* **cupped; cupping** : ahuecar (las manos)

cup[2] *n* **1** : taza *f* ⟨a cup of coffee : una taza de café⟩ **2** CUPFUL : taza *f* **3** : media pinta *f* (unidad de medida) **4** GOBLET : copa *f* **5** TROPHY : copa *f*, trofeo *m*

cupboard ['kʌbərd] *n* : alacena *f*, armario *m*

cupcake ['kʌpˌkeɪk] *n* : pastelito *m*

cupful ['kʌpˌfʊl] *n* : taza *f*

cupola ['kju:pələ, -ˌloː] *n* : cúpula *f*

cur ['kər] *n* : perro *m* callejero, perro *m* corriente *Mex*

curate ['kjʊrət] *n* : cura *m*, párroco *m*

curator ['kjʊrˌeɪtər, kjʊ'reɪtər] *n* : conservador *m*, -dora *f* (de un museo); director *m*, -tora *f* (de un zoológico)

curb[1] ['kərb] *vt* : refrenar, restringir, controlar

curb[2] *n* **1** RESTRAINT : freno *m*, control *m* **2** : borde *m* de la acera

curd ['kərd] *n* : cuajada *f*

curdle ['kərdəl] *v* **-dled; -dling** *vi* : cuajarse — *vt* : cuajar ⟨to curdle one's blood : helarle la sangre a uno⟩

cure[1] ['kjʊr] *vt* **cured; curing** **1** HEAL : curar, sanar **2** REMEDY : remediar **3** PROCESS : curar (alimentos, etc.)

cure[2] *n* **1** RECOVERY : curación *f*, recuperación *f* **2** REMEDY : cura *f*, remedio *m*

curfew ['kərˌfju:] *n* : toque *m* de queda

curio ['kjʊriˌoː] *n, pl* **-rios** : curiosidad *f*, objeto *m* curioso

curiosity [ˌkjʊri'ɑsəti] *n, pl* **-ties** : curiosidad *f*

curious ['kjʊriəs] *adj* **1** INQUISITIVE : curioso **2** STRANGE : curioso, raro

curl[1] ['kərl] *vt* **1** : rizar, ondular (el pelo) **2** COIL : enrollar **3** TWIST : torcer ⟨to curl one's lip : hacer una mueca⟩ — *vi* **1** : rizarse, ondularse **2 to curl up** : acurrucarse (con un libro, etc.)

curl[2] *n* **1** RINGLET : rizo *m* **2** COIL : espiral *f*, rosca *f*

curler ['kərlər] *n* : rulo *m*

curlew ['kərˌlu:, 'kərlˌju:] *n, pl* **-lews** or **-lew** : zarapito *m*

curly ['kərli] *adj* **curlier; -est** : rizado, crespo

currant ['kərənt] *n* **1** : grosella *f* (fruta) **2** RAISIN : pasa *f* de Corinto

currency ['kərəntsi] *n, pl* **-cies** **1** PREVALENCE, USE : uso *m*, aceptación *f*, difusión *f* ⟨to be in currency : estar en uso⟩ **2** MONEY : moneda *f*, dinero *m*

current[1] ['kərənt] *adj* **1** PRESENT : actual ⟨current events : actualidades⟩ **2** PREVALENT : corriente, común — **currently** *adv*

current[2] *n* : corriente *f*

curriculum [kə'rɪkjələm] *n, pl* **-la** [-lə] : currículum *m*, currículo *m*, programa *m* de estudio

curriculum vitae ['vi:ˌtaɪ, 'vaɪti] *n, pl* **curricula vitae** : currículum *m*, currículo *m*

curry[1] ['kəri] *vt* **-ried; -rying** **1** GROOM : almohazar (un caballo) **2** : condimentar con curry **3 to curry favor** : congraciarse (con alguien)

curry[2] *n, pl* **-ries** : curry *m*

curse[1] ['kərs] *v* **cursed; cursing** *vt* **1** DAMN : maldecir **2** INSULT : injuriar, insultar, decir malas palabras a **3** AFFLICT : afligir — *vi* : maldecir, decir malas palabras

curse[2] *n* **1** : maldición *f* ⟨to put a curse on someone : echarle una maldición a alguien⟩ **2** AFFLICTION : maldición *f*, aflicción *f*, cruz *f*

cursor ['kərsər] *n* : cursor *m*

cursory ['kərsəri] *adj* : rápido, superficial, somero

curt ['kərt] *adj* : cortante, brusco, seco — **curtly** *adv*

curtail [kər'teɪl] *vt* : acortar, limitar, restringir

curtailment [kər'teɪlmənt] *n* : restricción *f*, limitación *f*

curtain ['kərtən] *n* : cortina *f* (de una ventana), telón *m* (en un teatro)

curtness ['kərtnəs] *n* : brusquedad *f*, sequedad *f*

curtsy[1] or **curtsey** ['kərtsi] *vt* **-sied** or **-seyed; -sying** or **-seying** : hacer una reverencia

curtsy[2] or **curtsey** *n, pl* **-sies** or **-seys** : reverencia *f*

curvature ['kərvəˌtʃʊr] *n* : curvatura *f*

curve[1] ['kərv] *v* **curved; curving** *vi* : torcerse, describir una curva — *vt* : encorvar

curve[2] *n* : curva *f*

cushion[1] ['kʊʃən] *vt* **1** : poner cojines o almohadones a **2** SOFTEN : amortiguar, mitigar, suavizar ⟨to cushion a blow : amortiguar un golpe⟩

cushion[2] *n* **1** : cojín *m*, almohadón *m* **2** PROTECTION : colchón *m*, protección *f*

cusp ['kʌsp] *n* : cúspide *f* (de un diente), cuerno *m* (de la luna)

cuspid ['kʌspɪd] *n* : diente *m* canino, colmillo *m*

custard ['kʌstərd] *n* : natillas *fpl*

custodian [ˌkʌ'stoːdiən] *n* : custodio *m*, -dia *f*; guardián, -diana *f*

custody ['kʌstədi] *n, pl* **-dies** : custodia *f*, cuidado *m* ⟨to be in custody : estar detenido⟩

custom[1] ['kʌstəm] *adj* : a la medida, a la orden

custom[2] *n* **1** : costumbre *f*, tradición *f* **2 customs** *npl* : aduana *f*

customarily [ˌkʌstə'mɛrəli] *adv* : habitualmente, normalmente, de costumbre

customary ['kʌstə‚mɛri] *adj* **1** TRADI-
TIONAL : tradicional **2** USUAL : habitual, de costumbre
customer ['kʌstəmər] *n* : cliente *m*, -ta *f*
custom–made ['kʌstəm'meɪd] *adj* : hecho a la medida
cut¹ ['kʌt] *v* **cut; cutting** *vt* **1** : cortar ⟨to
cut paper : cortar papel⟩ **2** : cortarse
⟨to cut one's finger : cortarse uno el
dedo⟩ **3** TRIM : cortar, recortar ⟨to
have one's hair cut : cortarse el pelo⟩
4 INTERSECT : cruzar, atravesar **5**
SHORTEN : acortar, abreviar **6** REDUCE
: reducir, rebajar ⟨to cut prices : rebajar los precios⟩ **7 to cut one's teeth**
: salirle los dientes a uno — *vi* **1** : cortar, cortarse **2 to cut in** : entrometerse
cut² *n* **1** : corte *m* ⟨a cut of meat : un
corte de carne⟩ **2** SLASH : tajo *m*, corte
m, cortadura *f* **3** REDUCTION : rebaja
f, reducción *f* ⟨a cut in the rates : una
rebaja en las tarifas⟩
cute ['kjuːt] *adj* **cuter; -est** : mono *fam*,
lindo
cuticle ['kjuːtɪkəl] *n* : cutícula *f*
cutlass ['kʌtləs] *n* : alfanje *m*
cutlery ['kʌtləri] *n* : cubiertos *mpl*
cutlet ['kʌtlət] *n* : chuleta *f*
cutter ['kʌtər] *n* **1** : cortadora *f* (implemento) **2** : cortador *m*, -dora *f* (persona) **3** : cúter *m* (embarcación)
cutthroat ['kʌt‚θroːt] *adj* : despiadado,
desalmado ⟨cutthroat competition
: competencia feroz⟩
cutting¹ ['kʌtɪŋ] *adj* **1** : cortante ⟨a cutting wind : un viento cortante⟩ **2** CAUS-
TIC : mordaz

cutting² *n* : esqueje *m* (de una planta)
cuttlefish ['kʌtəl‚fɪʃ] *n, pl* **-fish** *or*
-fishes : jibia *f*, sepia *f*
cyanide ['saɪə‚naɪd, -nɪd] *n* : cianuro *m*
cycle¹ ['saɪkəl] *vi* **-cled; -cling** : andar en
bicicleta, ir en bicicleta
cycle² *n* **1** : ciclo *m* ⟨life cycle : ciclo de
vida, ciclo vital⟩ **2** BICYCLE : bicicleta
f **3** MOTORCYCLE : motocicleta *f*
cyclic ['saɪklɪk, 'sɪ-] *or* **cyclical** [-klɪkəl]
adj : cíclico
cyclist ['saɪklɪst] *n* : ciclista *mf*
cyclone ['saɪ‚kloːn] *n* **1** : ciclón *m* **2**
TORNADO : tornado *m*
cyclopedia *or* **cyclopaedia** [‚saɪklə-
'piːdiə] → **encyclopedia**
cylinder ['sɪləndər] *n* : cilindro *m*
cylindrical [sə'lɪndrɪkəl] *adj* : cilíndrico
cymbal ['sɪmbəl] *n* : platillo *m*, címbalo
m
cynic ['sɪnɪk] *n* : cínico *m*, -ca *f*
cynical ['sɪnɪkəl] *adj* : cínico
cynicism ['sɪnə‚sɪzəm] *n* : cinismo *m*
cypress ['saɪprəs] *n* : ciprés *m*
Cypriot ['sɪpriət, -‚ɑt] *n* : chipriota *mf* —
Cypriot *adj*
cyst ['sɪst] *n* : quiste *m*
cytoplasm ['saɪtə‚plæzəm] *n* : citoplasma *m*
czar ['zɑr, 'sɑr] *n* : zar *m*
czarina [zɑ'riːnə, sɑ-] *n* : zarina *f*
Czech ['tʃɛk] *n* **1** : checo *m*, -ca *f* **2**
: checo *m* (idioma) — **Czech** *adj*
Czechoslovak [‚tʃɛko'sloː‚vɑk, -‚væk] *or*
Czechoslovakian [-sloː'vɑkiən, -'væ-] *n*
: checoslovaco *m*, -ca *f* — **Czechoslovak** *or* **Czechoslovakian** *adj*

D

d ['diː] *n, pl* **d's** *or* **ds** ['diːz] : cuarta
letra del alfabeto inglés
dab¹ ['dæb] *vt* **dabbed; dabbing** : darle
toques ligeros a, aplicar suavemente
dab² *n* **1** BIT : toque *m*, pizca *f*, poco *m*
⟨a dab of ointment : un toque de
ungüento⟩ **2** PAT : toque *m* ligero,
golpecito *m*
dabble ['dæbəl] *v* **-bled; -bling** *vt* SPAT-
TER : salpicar — *vi* **1** SPLASH
: chapotear **2** TRIFLE : jugar, interesarse superficialmente
dabbler ['dæbələr] *n* : diletante *mf*
dachshund ['dɑks‚hʊnt, -‚hʊnd; 'dɑk-
sənt, -sənd] *n* : perro *m* salchicha
dad ['dæd] *n* : papá *m fam*
daddy ['dædi] *n, pl* **-dies** : papi *m fam*
daffodil ['dæfə‚dɪl] *n* : narciso *m*
daft ['dæft] *adj* : tonto, bobo
dagger ['dægər] *n* : daga *f*, puñal *m*
dahlia ['dæljə, 'dɑl-, 'deɪl-] *n* : dalia *f*
daily¹ ['deɪli] *adv* : a diario, diariamente
daily² *adj* : diario, cotidiano
daily³ *n, pl* **-lies** : diario *m*, periódico *m*
daintily ['deɪntəli] *adv* : delicadamente,
con delicadeza

daintiness ['deɪntinəs] *n* : delicadeza *f*,
finura *f*
dainty¹ ['deɪnti] *adj* **-tier; -est 1** DELI-
CATE : delicado **2** FASTIDIOUS : remilgado, melindroso **3** DELICIOUS : exquisito, sabroso
dainty² *n, pl* **-ties** DELICACY : exquisitez
f, manjar *m*
dairy ['dæri] *n, pl* **-ies 1** *or* **dairy store**
: lechería *f* **2** *or* **dairy farm** : granja *f*
lechera
dairymaid ['dæri‚meɪd] *n* : lechera *f*
dairyman ['dærimən, -‚mæn] *n, pl* **-men**
[-mən, -‚mɛn] : lechero *m*
dais ['deɪəs] *n* : tarima *f*, estrado *m*
daisy ['deɪzi] *n, pl* **-sies** : margarita *f*
dale ['deɪl] *n* : valle *m*
dally ['dæli] *vi* **-lied; -lying 1** TRIFLE
: juguetear **2** DAWDLE : entretenerse,
perder tiempo
dalmatian [dæl'meɪʃən, dɔl-] *n* : dálmata *m*
dam¹ ['dæm] *vt* **dammed; damming**
: represar, embalsar
dam² *n* **1** : represa *f*, dique *m* **2** : madre
f (de animales domésticos)

damage[1] ['dæmɪʤ] *vt* **-aged; -aging** : dañar (un objeto o una máquina), perjudicar (la salud o una reputación)
damage[2] *n* **1** : daño *m*, perjuicio *m* **2** **damages** *npl* : daños y perjuicios *mpl*
damaging ['dæməʤɪŋ] *adj* : perjudicial
damask ['dæməsk] *n* : damasco *m*
dame ['deɪm] *n* LADY : dama *f*, señora *f*
damn[1] ['dæm] *vt* **1** CONDEMN : condenar **2** CURSE : maldecir
damn[2] *or* **damned** ['dæmd] *adj* : condenado *fam*, maldito *fam*
damn[3] *n* : pito *m*, bledo *m*, comino *m* ⟨it's not worth a damn : no vale un pito⟩ ⟨I don't give a damn : me importa un comino⟩
damnable ['dæmnəbəl] *adj* : condenable, detestable
damnation [dæm'neɪʃən] *n* : condenación *f*
damned[1] ['dæmd] *adv* VERY : muy
damned[2] *adj* **1** → **damnable 2** REMARKABLE : extraordinario
damp[1] ['dæmp] *vt* → **dampen**
damp[2] *adj* : húmedo
damp[3] *n* MOISTURE : humedad *f*
dampen ['dæmpən] *vt* **1** MOISTEN : humedecer **2** DISCOURAGE : desalentar, desanimar
damper ['dæmpər] *n* **1** : regulador *m* de tiro (de una chimenea) **2** : sordina *f* (de un piano) **3 to put a damper on** : desanimar, apagar (el entusiasmo), enfriar
dampness ['dæmpnəs] *n* : humedad *f*
damsel ['dæmzəl] *n* : damisela *f*
dance[1] ['dænʦ] *v* **danced; dancing** : bailar
dance[2] *n* : baile *m*
dancer ['dænʦər] *n* : bailarín *m*, -rina *f*
dandelion ['dændəl,aɪən] *n* : diente *m* de león
dandruff ['dændrəf] *n* : caspa *f*
dandy[1] ['dændi] *adj* **-dier; -est** : excelente, magnífico, macanudo *fam*
dandy[2] *n*, *pl* **-dies 1** FOP : dandi *m* **2** : algo *m* excelente ⟨this new program is a dandy : este programa nuevo es algo excelente⟩
Dane ['deɪn] *n* : danés *m*, -nesa *f*
danger ['deɪnʤər] *n* : peligro *m*
dangerous ['deɪnʤərəs] *adj* : peligroso
dangle ['dæŋgəl] *v* **-gled; -gling** *vi* HANG : colgar, pender — *vt* **1** SWING : hacer oscilar **2** PROFFER : ofrecer (como incentivo) **3 to keep someone dangling** : dejar a alguien en suspenso
Danish[1] ['deɪnɪʃ] *adj* : danés
Danish[2] *n* : danés *m* (idioma)
dank ['dæŋk] *adj* : frío y húmedo
dapper ['dæpər] *adj* : pulcro, atildado
dappled ['dæpəld] *adj* : moteado ⟨a dappled horse : un caballo rodado⟩
dare[1] ['dær] *v* **dared; daring** *vi* : osar, atreverse ⟨how dare you! : ¡cómo te atreves!⟩ — *vt* **1** CHALLENGE : desafiar, retar **2 to dare to do something** : atreverse a hacer algo, osar hacer algo

dare[2] *n* : desafío *m*, reto *m*
daredevil ['dær,dɛvəl] *n* : persona *f* temeraria
daring[1] ['dærɪŋ] *adj* : osado, atrevido, audaz
daring[2] *n* : arrojo *m*, coraje *m*, audacia *f*
dark ['dɑrk] *adj* **1** : oscuro (dícese del ambiente o de los colores), moreno (dícese del pelo o de la piel) **2** SOMBER : sombrío, triste
darken ['dɑrkən] *vt* **1** DIM : oscurecer **2** SADDEN : entristecer — *vi* : ensombrecerse, nublarse
darkly ['dɑrkli] *adv* **1** DIMLY : oscuramente **2** GLOOMILY : tristemente **3** MYSTERIOUSLY : misteriosamente, enigmáticamente
darkness ['dɑrknəs] *n* : oscuridad *f*, tinieblas *f*
darling[1] ['dɑrlɪŋ] *adj* **1** BELOVED : querido, amado **2** CHARMING : encantador, mono *fam*
darling[2] *n* **1** BELOVED : querido *m*, -da *f*; amado *m*, -da *f*; cariño *m*, -ña *f* **2** FAVORITE : preferido *m*, -da *f*; favorito *m*, -ta *f*
darn[1] ['dɑrn] *vt* : zurcir
darn[2] *n* **1** : zurcido *m* **2** → **damn**[3]
dart[1] ['dɑrt] *vt* THROW : lanzar, tirar — *vi* DASH : lanzarse, precipitarse
dart[2] *n* **1** : dardo *m* **2 darts** *npl* : juego *m* de dardos
dash[1] ['dæʃ] *vt* **1** SMASH : romper, estrellar **2** HURL : arrojar, lanzar **3** SPLASH : salpicar **4** FRUSTRATE : frustrar **5 to dash off** : hacer (algo) rápidamente — *vi* **1** SMASH : romperse, estrellarse **2** DART : lanzarse, irse apresuradamente
dash[2] *n* **1** BURST, SPLASH : arranque *m*, salpicadura *f* (de aguas) **2** : guión *m* largo (signo de puntuación) **3** DROP : gota *f*, pizca *f* **4** VERVE : brío *m* **5** RACE : carrera *f* ⟨a 100-meter dash : una carrera de 100 metros⟩ **6 to make a dash for it** : precipitarse (hacia), echarse a correr **7** → **dashboard**
dashboard ['dæʃ,bord] *n* : tablero *m* de instrumentos
dashing ['dæʃɪŋ] *adj* : gallardo, apuesto
data ['deɪtə, 'dæ-, 'dɑ-] *ns & pl* : datos *mpl*, información *f*
database ['deɪtə,beɪs, 'dæ-, 'dɑ-] *n* : base *f* de datos
date[1] ['deɪt] *v* **dated; dating** *vt* **1** : fechar (una carta, etc.), datar (un objeto) ⟨it was dated June 9 : estaba fechada el 9 de junio⟩ **2** : salir con ⟨she's dating my brother : sale con mi hermano⟩ — *vi* : datar
date[2] *n* **1** : fecha *f* ⟨to date : hasta la fecha⟩ **2** EPOCH, PERIOD : época *f*, período *m* **3** APPOINTMENT : cita *f* **4** COMPANION : acompañante *mf* **5** : dátil *m* (fruta)
dated ['deɪtəd] *adj* OUT-OF-DATE : anticuado, pasado de moda

datum ['deɪt̬əm, 'dæ-, 'dɑ-] *n, pl* **-ta** [-t̬ə] *or* **-tums** : dato *m*

daub¹ ['dɔb] *vt* : embadurnar

daub² *n* : mancha *f*

daughter ['dɔt̬ər] *n* : hija *f*

daughter–in–law ['dɔt̬ərɪn,lɔ] *n, pl* **daughters–in–law** : nuera *f*, hija *f* política

daunt ['dɔnt] *vt* : amilanar, acobardar, intimidar

dauntless ['dɔntləs] *adj* : intrépido, impávido

davenport ['dævən,pɔrt] *n* : sofá *m*

dawdle ['dɔdəl] *vi* **-dled; -dling 1** DALLY : demorarse, entretenerse, perder tiempo **2** LOITER : vagar, holgazanear, haraganear

dawn¹ ['dɔn] *vi* **1** : amanecer, alborear, despuntar ⟨Saturday dawned clear and bright : el sábado amaneció claro y luminoso⟩ **2 to dawn on** : hacerse obvio ⟨it dawned on me that she was right : me di cuenta de que tenía razón⟩

dawn² *n* **1** DAYBREAK : amanecer *m*, alba *f* **2** BEGINNING : albor *m*, comienzo *m* ⟨the dawn of history : los albores de la historia⟩ **3 from dawn to dusk** : de sol a sol

day ['deɪ] *n* **1** : día *m* **2** DATE : fecha *f* **3** TIME : día *m*, tiempo *m* ⟨in olden days : intaño⟩ **4** WORKDAY : jornada *f* laboral

daybreak ['deɪ,breɪk] *n* : alba *f*, amanecer *m*

day care *n* : servicio *m* de guardería infantil

daydream¹ ['deɪ,driːm] *vi* : soñar despierto, fantasear

daydream² *n* : ensueño *m*, ensoñación *f*, fantasía *f*

daylight ['deɪ,laɪt] *n* **1** : luz *f* del día ⟨in broad daylight : a plena luz del día⟩ **2** → **daybreak 3** → **daytime**

daylight saving time *n* : hora *f* de verano

daytime ['deɪ,taɪm] *n* : horas *fpl* diurnas, día *m*

daze¹ ['deɪz] *vt* **dazed; dazing 1** STUN : aturdir **2** DAZZLE : deslumbrar, ofuscar

daze² *n* **1** : aturdimiento *m* **2 in a daze** : aturdido, atontado

dazzle¹ ['dæzəl] *vt* **-zled; -zling** : deslumbrar, ofuscar

dazzle² *n* : resplandor *m*, brillo *m*

DDT [,diː,diː'tiː] *n* : DDT *m*

deacon ['diːkən] *n* : diácono *m*

dead¹ ['dɛd] *adv* **1** ABRUPTLY : repentinamente, súbitamente ⟨to stop dead : parar en seco⟩ **2** ABSOLUTELY : absolutamente ⟨I'm dead certain : estoy absolutamente seguro⟩ **3** DIRECTLY : justo ⟨dead ahead : justo adelante⟩

dead² *adj* **1** LIFELESS : muerto **2** NUMB : entumecido **3** INDIFFERENT : indiferente, frío **4** INACTIVE : inactivo ⟨a dead volcano : un volcán inactivo⟩ **5** : desconectado (dícese del teléfono),

descargado (dícese de una batería) **6** EXHAUSTED : agotado, derrengado, muerto **7** OBSOLETE : obsoleto, muerto ⟨a dead language : una lengua muerta⟩ **8** EXACT : exacto ⟨in the dead center : justo en el blanco⟩

dead³ *n* **1 the dead** : los muertos **2 in the dead of night** : a las altas horas de la noche **3 in the dead of winter** : en pleno invierno

deadbeat ['dɛd,biːt] *n* **1** LOAFER : vago *m*, -ga *f*; holgazán *m*, -zana *f* **2** FREELOADER : gorrón *m*, -rrona *f fam*; gorrero *m*, -ra *f fam*

deaden ['dɛdən] *vt* **1** : atenuar (un dolor), entorpecer (sensaciones) **2** DULL : deslustrar **3** DISPIRIT : desanimar **4** MUFFLE : amortiguar, reducir (sonidos)

dead–end ['dɛd'ɛnd] *adj* **1** : sin salida ⟨dead-end street : calle sin salida⟩ **2** : sin futuro ⟨a dead-end job : un trabajo sin porvenir⟩

dead end *n* : callejón *m* sin salida

dead heat *n* : empate *m*

deadline ['dɛd,laɪn] *n* : fecha *f* límite, fecha *f* tope, plazo *m* (determinado)

deadlock¹ ['dɛd,lɑk] *vt* : estancar — *vi* : estancarse, llegar a punto muerto

deadlock² *n* : punto *m* muerto, impasse *m*

deadly¹ ['dɛdli] *adv* : extremadamente, sumamente ⟨deadly serious : muy en serio⟩

deadly² *adj* **-lier; -est 1** LETHAL : mortal, letal, mortífero **2** ACCURATE : certero, preciso ⟨a deadly aim : una puntería infalible⟩ **3** CAPITAL : capital ⟨the seven deadly sins : los siete pecados capitales⟩ **4** DULL : funesto, aburrido **5** EXTREME : extremo, absoluto ⟨a deadly calm : una calma absoluta⟩

deadpan¹ ['dɛd,pæn] *adv* : de manera inexpresiva, sin expresión

deadpan² *adj* : inexpresivo, impasible

deaf ['dɛf] *adj* : sordo

deafen ['dɛfən] *vt* **-ened; -ening** : ensordecer

deafening ['dɛfənɪŋ] *adj* : ensordecedor

deaf–mute ['dɛf'mjuːt] *n* : sordomudo *m*, -da *f*

deafness ['dɛfnəs] *n* : sordera *f*

deal¹ ['diːl] *v* **dealt; dealing** *vt* **1** APPORTION : repartir ⟨to deal justice : repartir la justicia⟩ **2** DISTRIBUTE : repartir, dar (naipes) **3** DELIVER : asestar, propinar ⟨to deal a blow : asestar un golpe⟩ — *vi* **1** : dar, repartir (en juegos de naipes) **2 to deal in** : comerciar en, traficar con (drogas) **3 to deal with** CONCERN : tratar de, tener que ver con ⟨the book deals with poverty : el libro trata de la pobreza⟩ **4 to deal with** HANDLE : tratar (con), encargarse de **5 to deal with** TREAT : tratar ⟨the judge dealt with him severely : el juez lo trató con severidad⟩ **6 to deal with** ACCEPT : aceptar (una situación o desgracia)

deal² *n* **1** : reparto *m* (de naipes) **2** AGREEMENT, TRANSACTION : trato *m*, acuerdo *m*, transacción *f* **3** TREATMENT : trato *m* ⟨he got a raw deal : le hicieron una injusticia⟩ **4** BARGAIN : ganga *f*, oferta *f* **5 a good deal** *or* **a great deal** : mucho, una gran cantidad

dealer ['di:lər] *n* : comerciante *mf*, traficante *mf*

dealership ['di:lər‚ʃɪp] *n* : concesión *f*

dealings ['di:lɪŋz] *npl* **1** : relaciones *fpl* (personales) **2** TRANSACTIONS : negocios *mpl*, transacciones *fpl*

dean ['di:n] *n* **1** : deán *m* (del clero) **2** : decano *m*, -na *f* (de una facultad o profesión)

dear¹ ['dɪr] *adj* **1** ESTEEMED, LOVED : querido, estimado ⟨a dear friend : un amigo querido⟩ ⟨Dear Sir : Estimado Señor⟩ **2** COSTLY : caro, costoso

dear² *n* : querido *m*, -da *f*; amado *m*, -da *f*

dearly ['dɪrli] *adv* **1** : mucho ⟨I love them dearly : los quiero mucho⟩ **2** : caro ⟨to pay dearly : pagar caro⟩

dearth ['dərθ] *n* : escasez *f*, carestía *f*

death ['dɛθ] *n* **1** : muerte *f*, fallecimiento *m* ⟨to be the death of : matar⟩ **2** FATALITY : víctima *f* (mortal); muerto *m*, -ta *f* **3** END : fin *m* ⟨the death of civilization : el fin de la civilización⟩

deathbed ['dɛθ‚bɛd] *n* : lecho *m* de muerte

deathblow ['dɛθ‚blo:] *n* : golpe *m* mortal

deathless ['dɛθləs] *adj* : eterno, inmortal

deathly ['dɛθli] *adj* : de muerte, sepulcral (dícese del silencio), cadavérico (dícese de la palidez)

debacle [dɪ'bɑkəl, -'bæ-] *n* : desastre *m*, debacle *m*, fiasco *m*

debar [di'bɑr] *vt* **-barred; -barring** : excluir, prohibir

debase [di'beɪs] *vt* **-based; -basing** : degradar, envilecer

debasement [di'beɪsmənt] *n* : degradación *f*, envilecimiento *m*

debatable [di'beɪtəbəl] *adj* : discutible

debate¹ [di'beɪt] *vt* **-bated; -bating** : debatir, discutir

debate² *n* : debate *m*, discusión *f*

debauch [di'bɔtʃ] *vt* : pervertir, corromper

debauchery [di'bɔtʃəri] *n, pl* **-eries** : libertinaje *m*, disipación *f*, intemperancia *f*

debilitate [di'bɪlə‚teɪt] *vt* **-tated; -tating** : debilitar

debility [di'bɪləti] *n, pl* **-ties** : debilidad *f*

debit¹ ['dɛbɪt] *vt* : adeudar, cargar, debitar

debit² *n* : débito *m*, cargo *m*, debe *m*

debonair [‚dɛbə'nær] *adj* : elegante y desenvuelto, apuesto

debris [də'bri:, deɪ-; 'deɪ‚bri:] *n, pl* **-bris** [-'bri:z, -‚bri:z] **1** RUBBLE, RUINS : escombros *mpl*, ruinas *fpl*, restos *mpl* **2** RUBBISH : basura *f*, deshechos *mpl*

debt ['dɛt] *n* **1** : deuda *f* ⟨to pay a debt : saldar una deuda⟩ **2** INDEBTEDNESS : endeudamiento *m*

debtor ['dɛtər] *n* : deudor *m*, -dora *f*

debunk [di'bʌŋk] *vt* DISCREDIT : desacreditar, desprestigiar

debut¹ [deɪ'bju:, 'deɪ‚bju:] *vi* : debutar

debut² *n* **1** : debut *m* (de un actor), estreno *m* (de una obra) **2** : debut *m*, presentación *f* (en sociedad)

debutante ['dɛbju‚tɑnt] *n* : debutante *f*

decade ['dɛ‚keɪd, dɛ'keɪd] *n* : década *f*

decadence ['dɛkədən/s] *n* : decadencia *f*

decadent ['dɛkədənt] *adj* : decadente

decaf¹ ['di:‚kæf] → **decaffeinated**

decaf² *n* : café *m* descafeinado

decaffeinated [di'kæfə‚neɪtəd] *adj* : descafeinado

decal ['di:‚kæl, di'kæl] *n* : calcomanía *f*

decamp [di'kæmp] *vi* : irse, largarse *fam*

decant [di'kænt] *vt* : decantar

decanter [di'kæntər] *n* : licorera *f*, garrafa *f*

decapitate [di'kæpə‚teɪt] *vt* **-tated; -tating** : decapitar

decay¹ [di'keɪ] *vi* **1** DECOMPOSE : descomponerse, pudrirse **2** DETERIORATE : deteriorarse **3** : cariarse (dícese de los dientes)

decay² *n* **1** DECOMPOSITION : descomposición *f* **2** DECLINE, DETERIORATION : decadencia *f*, deterioro *m* **3** : caries *f* (de los dientes)

decease¹ [di'si:s] *vi* **-ceased; -ceasing** : morir, fallecer

decease² *n* : fallecimiento *m*, defunción *f*, deceso *m*

deceit [di'si:t] *n* **1** DECEPTION : engaño *m* **2** DISHONESTY : deshonestidad *f*

deceitful [di'si:tfəl] *adj* : falso, embustero, engañoso, mentiroso

deceitfully [di'si:tfəli] *adv* : con engaño, con falsedad

deceitfulness [di'si:tfəlnəs] *n* : falsedad *f*, engaño *m*

deceive [di'si:v] *vt* **-ceived; -ceiving** : engañar, burlar

deceiver [di'si:vər] *n* : impostor *m*, -tora *f*

decelerate [di'sɛlə‚reɪt] *vi* **-ated; -ating** : reducir la velocidad, desacelerar

December [di'sɛmbər] *n* : diciembre *m*

decency ['di:sənsi] *n, pl* **-cies** : decencia *f*, decoro *m*

decent ['di:sənt] *adj* **1** CORRECT, PROPER : decente, decoroso, correcto **2** CLOTHED : vestido, presentable **3** MODEST : púdico, modesto **4** ADEQUATE : decente, adecuado ⟨decent wages : paga adecuada⟩

decently ['di:səntli] *adv* : decentemente

decentralize [di'sɛntrə‚laɪz] *v* **-lized [-‚laɪzd]; -lizing** [-‚laɪzɪŋ] *vt* : descentralizar — *vi* : descentralizarse

deception [di'sɛpʃən] *n* : engaño *m*

deceptive [dɪ'sɛptɪv] *adj* : engañoso, falaz — **deceptively** *adv*

decibel ['dɛsəbəl, -ˌbɛl] *n* : decibelio *m*

decide [dɪ'saɪd] *v* -cided; -ciding *vt* 1 CONCLUDE : decidir, llegar a la conclusión de ⟨he decided what to do : decidió qué iba a hacer⟩ 2 DETERMINE : decidir, determinar ⟨one blow decided the fight : un solo golpe determinó la pelea⟩ 3 CONVINCE : decidir ⟨her pleas decided me to help : sus súplicas me decidieron a ayudarla⟩ 4 RESOLVE : resolver — *vi* : decidirse

decided [dɪ'saɪdəd] *adj* 1 UNQUESTIONABLE : indudable 2 RESOLUTE : decidido, resuelto — **decidedly** *adv*

deciduous [dɪ'sɪdʒuəs] *adj* : caduco, de hoja caduca

decimal[1] ['dɛsəməl] *adj* : decimal

decimal[2] *n* : número *m* decimal

decipher [dɪ'saɪfər] *vt* : descifrar — **decipherable** [-əbəl] *adj*

decision [dɪ'sɪʒən] *n* : decisión *f*, determinación *f* ⟨to make a decision : tomar una decisión⟩

decisive [dɪ'saɪsɪv] *adj* 1 DECIDING : decisivo ⟨the decisive vote : el voto decisivo⟩ 2 CONCLUSIVE : decisivo, concluyente, contundente ⟨a decisive victory : una victoria contundente⟩ 3 RESOLUTE : decidido, resuelto, firme

decisively [dɪ'saɪsɪvli] *adv* : con decisión, de manera decisiva

decisiveness [dɪ'saɪsɪvnəs] *n* 1 FORCEFULNESS : contundencia *f* 2 RESOLUTION : firmeza *f*, decisión *f*, determinación *f*

deck[1] ['dɛk] *vt* 1 FLOOR : tumbar, derribar ⟨she decked him with one blow : lo tumbó de un solo golpe⟩ 2 to deck out : adornar, engalanar

deck[2] *n* 1 : cubierta *f* (de un barco) 2 *or* **deck of cards** : baraja *f* (de naipes)

declaim [dɪ'kleɪm] *v* : declamar

declaration [ˌdɛklə'reɪʃən] *n* : declaración *f*, pronunciamiento *m* (oficial)

declare [dɪ'klær] *vt* -clared; -claring : declarar, manifestar ⟨to declare war : declarar la guerra⟩ ⟨they declared their support : manifestaron su apoyo⟩

decline[1] [dɪ'klaɪn] *v* -clined; -clining *vi* 1 DESCEND : descender 2 DETERIORATE : deteriorarse, decaer ⟨her health is declining : su salud se está deteriorando⟩ 3 DECREASE : disminuir, decrecer, decaer 4 REFUSE : rehusar — *vt* 1 INFLECT : declinar 2 REFUSE, TURN DOWN : declinar, rehusar

decline[2] *n* 1 DETERIORATION : decadencia *f*, deterioro *m* 2 DECREASE : disminución *f*, descenso *m* 3 SLOPE : declive *m*, pendiente *f*

decode [dɪ'ko:d] *vt* -coded; -coding : descifrar (un mensaje), descodificar (una señal)

decoder [dɪ'ko:dər] *n* : descodificador *m*

decompose [ˌdi:kəm'po:z] *v* -posed; -posing *vt* 1 BREAK DOWN : descomponer 2 ROT : descomponer, pudrir — *vi* : descomponerse, pudrirse

decomposition [ˌdi:ˌkɑmpə'zɪʃən] *n* : descomposición *f*

decongestant [ˌdi:kən'dʒɛstənt] *n* : descongestionante *m*

decor *or* **décor** [deɪ'kor, 'deɪˌkor] *n* : decoración *f*

decorate ['dɛkəˌreɪt] *vt* -rated; -rating 1 ADORN : decorar, adornar 2 : condecorar ⟨he was decorated for bravery : lo condecoraron por valor⟩

decoration [ˌdɛkə'reɪʃən] *n* 1 ADORNMENT : decoración *f*, adorno *m* 2 : condecoración *f* (de honor)

decorative ['dɛkərətɪv, -ˌreɪ-] *adj* : decorativo, ornamental, de adorno

decorator ['dɛkəˌreɪtər] *n* : decorador *m*, -dora *f*

decorum [dɪ'korəm] *n* : decoro *m*

decoy[1] ['di:ˌkɔɪ, dɪ'-] *vt* : atraer (con señuelo)

decoy[2] *n* : señuelo *m*, reclamo *m*, cimbel *m*

decrease[1] [dɪ'kri:s] *v* -creased; -creasing *vi* : decrecer, disminuir, bajar — *vt* : reducir, disminuir

decrease[2] ['di:ˌkri:s] *n* : disminución *f*, descenso *m*, bajada *f*

decree[1] [dɪ'kri:] *vt* -creed; -creeing : decretar

decree[2] *n* : decreto *m*

decrepit [dɪ'krɛpɪt] *adj* 1 FEEBLE : decrépito, débil 2 DILAPIDATED : deteriorado, ruinoso

decry [dɪ'kraɪ] *vt* -cried; -crying : censurar, criticar

dedicate ['dɛdɪˌkeɪt] *vt* -cated; -cating 1 : dedicar ⟨she dedicated the book to Carlos : le dedicó el libro a Carlos⟩ 2 : consagrar, dedicar ⟨to dedicate one's life : consagrar uno su vida⟩

dedication [ˌdɛdɪ'keɪʃən] *n* 1 DEVOTION : dedicación *f*, devoción *f* 2 : dedicatoria *f* (de un libro, una canción, etc.) 3 CONSECRATION : dedicación *f*

deduce [dɪ'du:s, -'dju:s] *vt* -duced; -ducing : deducir, inferir

deduct [dɪ'dʌkt] *vt* : deducir, descontar, restar

deductible [dɪ'dʌktəbəl] *adj* : deducible

deduction [dɪ'dʌkʃən] *n* : deducción *f*

deed[1] ['di:d] *vt* : ceder, transferir

deed[2] *n* 1 ACT : acto *m*, acción *f*, hecho *m* ⟨a good deed : una buena acción⟩ 2 FEAT : hazaña *f*, proeza *f* 3 TITLE : escritura *f*, título *m*

deem ['di:m] *vt* : considerar, juzgar

deep[1] ['di:p] *adv* : hondo, profundamente ⟨to dig deep : cavar hondo⟩

deep[2] *adj* 1 : hondo, profundo ⟨the deep end : la parte honda⟩ ⟨a deep wound : una herida profunda⟩ 2 WIDE : ancho 3 INTENSE : profundo, intenso 4 DARK : intenso, subido ⟨deep red : rojo subido⟩ 5 LOW : profundo ⟨a deep tone

: un tono profundo⟩ **6** ABSORBED : absorto ⟨deep in thought : absorto en la meditación⟩

deep³ *n* **1 the deep** : lo profundo, el piélago **2 the deep of night** : lo más profundo de la noche

deepen ['di:pən] *vt* **1** : ahondar, profundizar **2** INTENSIFY : intensificar — *vi* **1** : hacerse más profundo **2** INTENSIFY : intensificarse

deeply ['di:pli] *adv* : hondo, profundamente ⟨I'm deeply sorry : lo siento sinceramente⟩

deep–seated ['di:p'si:t̬əd] *adj* : profundamente arraigado, enraizado

deer ['dır] *ns & pl* : ciervo *m*, venado *m*

deerskin ['dır,skın] *n* : piel *f* de venado

deface [di'feıs] *vt* **-faced; -facing** MAR : desfigurar

defacement [di'feısmənt] *n* : desfiguración *f*

defamation [,dɛfə'meıʃən] *n* : difamación *f*

defamatory [di'fæmə,tori] *adj* : difamatorio

defame [di'feım] *vt* **-famed; -faming** : difamar, calumniar

default¹ [di'fɔlt, 'di:,fɔlt] *vi* **1** : no cumplir (con una obligación), no pagar **2** : no presentarse (en un tribunal)

default² *n* **1** NEGLECT : omisión *f*, negligencia *f* **2** NONPAYMENT : impago *m*, falta *f* de pago **3 to win by default** : ganar por abandono

defaulter [di'fɔltər] *n* : moroso *m*, -sa *f*; rebelde *mf* (en un tribunal)

defeat¹ [di'fi:t] *vt* **1** FRUSTRATE : frustrar **2** BEAT : vencer, derrotar

defeat² *n* : derrota *f*, rechazo *m* (de legislación), fracaso *m* (de planes, etc.)

defecate ['dɛfı,keıt] *vi* **-cated; -cating** : defecar

defect¹ [di'fɛkt] *vi* : desertar

defect² ['di:,fɛkt, di'fɛkt] *n* : defecto *m*

defection [di'fɛkʃən] *n* : deserción *f*, defección *f*

defective [di'fɛktıv] *adj* **1** FAULTY : defectuoso **2** DEFICIENT : deficiente

defector [di'fɛktər] *n* : desertor *m*, -tora *f*

defend [di'fɛnd] *vt* : defender

defendant [di'fɛndənt] *n* : acusado *m*, -da *f*; demandado *m*, -da *f*

defender [di'fɛndər] *n* **1** ADVOCATE : defensor *m*, -sora *f* **2** : defensa *mf* (en deportes)

defense [di'fɛnts, 'di:,fɛnts] *n* : defensa *f*

defenseless [di'fɛntsləs] *adj* : indefenso

defensive¹ [di'fɛntsıv] *adj* : defensivo

defensive² *n* **on the defensive** : a la defensiva

defer [di'fər] *v* **-ferred; -ferring** *vt* POSTPONE : diferir, aplazar, posponer — *vi* **to defer to** : deferir a

deference ['dɛfərənts] *n* : deferencia *f*

deferential [,dɛfə'rɛntʃəl] *adj* : respetuoso

deferment [di'fərmənt] *n* : aplazamiento *m*

defiance [di'faıənts] *n* : desafío *m*

defiant [di'faıənt] *adj* : desafiante, insolente

deficiency [di'fıʃəntsi] *n*, *pl* **-cies** : deficiencia *f*, carencia *f*

deficient [di'fıʃənt] *adj* : deficiente, carente

deficit ['dɛfəsıt] *n* : déficit *m*

defile [di'faıl] *vt* **-filed; -filing 1** DIRTY : ensuciar, manchar **2** CORRUPT : corromper **3** DESECRATE, PROFANE : profanar **4** DISHONOR : deshonrar

defilement [di'faılmənt] *n* **1** DESECRATION : profanación *f* **2** CORRUPTION : corrupción *f* **3** CONTAMINATION : contaminación *f*

define [di'faın] *vt* **-fined; -fining 1** BOUND : delimitar, demarcar **2** CLARIFY : aclarar, definir **3** : definir ⟨to define a word : definir una palabra⟩

definite ['dɛfənıt] *adj* **1** CERTAIN : definido, determinado **2** CLEAR : claro, explícito **3** UNQUESTIONABLE : seguro, incuestionable

definite article *n* : artículo *m* definido

definitely ['dɛfənıtli] *adv* **1** DOUBTLESSLY : indudablemente, sin duda **2** DEFINITIVELY : definitivamente, seguramente

definition [,dɛfə'nıʃən] *n* : definición *f*

definitive [di'fınət̬ıv] *adj* **1** CONCLUSIVE : definitivo, decisivo **2** AUTHORITATIVE : de autoridad, autorizado

deflate [di'fleıt] *v* **-flated; -flating** *vt* **1** : desinflar (una llanta, etc.) **2** REDUCE : rebajar ⟨to deflate one's ego : bajarle los humos a uno⟩ — *vi* : desinflarse

deflation [di'fleıʃən] *n* **1** : desinflación *f* (de una llanta, etc.) **2** : deflación *f* (económica)

deflect [di'flɛkt] *vt* : desviar — *vi* : desviarse

defoliant [di'fo:liənt] *n* : defoliante *m*

deforestation [di,fɔrə'steıʃən] *n* : deforestación *f*, desforestación *f*

deform [di'fɔrm] *vt* : deformar

deformation [,di:,fɔr'meıʃən] *n* : deformación *f*

deformed [di'fɔrmd] *adj* : deforme

deformity [di'fɔrmət̬i] *n*, *pl* **-ties** : deformidad *f*

defraud [di'frɔd] *vt* : estafar, defraudar

defray [di'freı] *vt* : sufragar, costear

defrost [di'frɔst] *vt* : descongelar, deshelar — *vi* : descongelarse, deshelarse

deft ['dɛft] *adj* : hábil, diestro — **deftly** *adv*

defunct [di'fʌŋkt] *adj* **1** DECEASED : difunto, fallecido **2** EXTINCT : extinto, fenecido

defuse [di'fju:z] *vt* : desactivar ⟨to defuse the situation : reducir las tensiones⟩

defy [di'faı] *vt* **-fied; -fying 1** CHALLENGE : desafiar, retar **2** DISOBEY : desobedecer **3** RESIST : resistir, hacer imposible, hacer inútil

degenerate¹ [di'dʒenə,reɪt] *vi* **-ated; -ating** : degenerar
degenerate² [di'dʒenərət] *adj* : degenerado
degeneration [di,dʒenə'reɪʃən] *n* : degeneración *f*
degenerative [di'dʒenərətɪv] *adj* : degenerative
degradation [,degrə'deɪʃən] *n* : degradación *f*
degrade [di'greɪd] *vt* **-graded; -grading** **1** : degradar, envilecer **2 to degrade oneself** : rebajarse
degrading [di'greɪdɪŋ] *adj* : degradante
degree [di'gri:] *n* **1** EXTENT : grado *m* ⟨a third degree burn : una quemadura de tercer grado⟩ **2** : título *m* (de enseñanza superior) **3** : grado *m* (de un círculo, de la temperatura) **4 by degrees** : gradualmente, poco a poco
dehydrate [di'haɪ,dreɪt] *v* **-drated; -drating** *vt* : deshidratar — *vi* : deshidratarse
dehydration [,di:haɪ'dreɪʃən] *n* : deshidratación *f*
deice [,di:'aɪs] *vt* **-iced; -icing** : deshelar, descongelar
deify ['di:ə,faɪ, 'deɪ-] *vt* **-fied; -fying** : deificar
deign ['deɪn] *vi* : dignarse, condescender
deity ['di:əti, 'deɪ-] *n, pl* **-ties 1 the Deity** : Dios *m* **2** GOD, GODDESS : deidad *f*; dios *m*, diosa *f*
dejected [di'dʒektəd] *adj* : abatido, desalentado, desanimado
dejection [di'dʒekʃən] *n* : abatimiento *m*, desaliento *m*, desánimo *m*
delay¹ [di'leɪ] *vt* **1** POSTPONE : posponer, postergar **2** HOLD UP : retrasar, demorar — *vi* : tardar, demorar
delay² *n* **1** LATENESS : tardanza *f* **2** HOLDUP : demora *f*, retraso *m*
delectable [di'lektəbəl] *adj* **1** DELICIOUS : delicioso, exquisito **2** DELIGHTFUL : encantador
delegate¹ ['deli,geɪt] *v* **-gated; -gating** : delegar
delegate² ['deligət, -,geɪt] *n* : delegado *m*, -da *f*
delegation [,deli'geɪʃən] *n* : delegación *f*
delete [di'li:t] *vt* **-leted; -leting** : suprimir, tachar, eliminar
deletion [di'li:ʃən] *n* : supresión *f*, tachadura *f*, eliminación *f*
deli ['deli] → delicatessen
deliberate¹ [di'libə,reɪt] *v* **-ated; -ating** *vt* : deliberar sobre, reflexionar sobre, considerar — *vi* : deliberar
deliberate² [di'libərət] *adj* **1** CONSIDERED : reflexionado, premeditado **2** INTENTIONAL : deliberado, intencional **3** SLOW : lento, pausado
deliberately [di'libərətli] *adv* **1** INTENTIONALLY : adrede, a propósito **2** SLOWLY : pausadamente, lentamente
deliberation [di,libə'reɪʃən] *n* **1** CONSIDERATION : deliberación *f*, consideración *f* **2** SLOWNESS : lentitud *f*

delicacy ['delikəsi] *n, pl* **-cies 1** : manjar *m*, exquisitez *f* ⟨caviar is a real delicacy : el caviar es un verdadero manjar⟩ **2** FINENESS : delicadeza *f* **3** FRAGILITY : fragilidad *f*
delicate ['delikət] *adj* **1** SUBTLE : delicado ⟨a delicate fragrance : una fragancia delicada⟩ **2** DAINTY : delicado, primoroso, fino **3** FRAGILE : frágil **4** SENSITIVE : delicado ⟨a delicate matter : un asunto delicado⟩
delicately ['delikətli] *adv* : delicadamente, con delicadeza
delicatessen [,delikə'tesən] *n* : charcutería *f*, fiambrería *f*, salchichonería *f* *Mex*
delicious [di'liʃəs] *adj* : delicioso, exquisito, rico — **deliciously** *adv*
delight¹ [di'laɪt] *vt* : deleitar, encantar — *vi* **to delight in** : deleitarse con, complacerse en
delight² *n* **1** JOY : placer *m*, deleite *m*, gozo *m* **2** : encanto *m* ⟨your garden is a delight : su jardín es un encanto⟩
delightful [di'laɪtfəl] *adj* : delicioso, encantador
delightfully [di'laɪtfəli] *adv* : de manera encantadora, de maravilla
delineate [di'lini,eɪt] *vt* **-eated; -eating** : delinear, trazar, bosquejar
delinquency [di'liŋkwəntsi] *n, pl* **-cies** : delincuencia *f*
delinquent¹ [di'liŋkwənt] *adj* **1** : delincuente **2** OVERDUE : vencido y sin pagar, moroso
delinquent² *n* : delincuente *mf* ⟨juvenile delinquent : delincuente juvenil⟩
delirious [di'liriəs] *adj* : delirante ⟨delirious with joy : loco de alegría⟩
delirium [di'liriəm] *n* : delirio *m*, desvarío *m*
deliver [di'livər] *vt* **1** FREE : liberar, librar **2** DISTRIBUTE, HAND : entregar, repartir **3** : asistir en el parto de (un niño) **4** : pronunciar ⟨to deliver a speech : pronunciar un discurso⟩ **5** PROJECT : despachar, lanzar ⟨he delivered a fast ball : lanzó una pelota rápida⟩ **6** DEAL : propinar, asestar ⟨to deliver a blow : asestar un golpe⟩
deliverance [di'livərənts] *n* : liberación *f*, rescate *m*, salvación *f*
deliverer [di'livərər] *n* RESCUER : libertador *m*, -dora *f*; salvador *m*, -dora *f*
delivery [di'livəri] *n, pl* **-eries 1** LIBERATION : liberación *f* **2** : entrega *f*, reparto *m* ⟨cash on delivery : entrega contra reembolso⟩ ⟨home delivery : servicio a domicilio⟩ **3** CHILDBIRTH : parto *m*, alumbramiento *m* **4** SPEECH : expresión *f* oral, modo *m* de hablar **5** THROW : lanzamiento *m*
dell ['del] *n* : hondonada *f*, valle *m* pequeño
delta ['deltə] *n* : delta *m*
delude [di'lu:d] *vt* **-luded; -luding 1** : engañar **2 to delude oneself** : engañarse

deluge[1] ['dɛl,ju:ʤ, -,ju:ʒ] *vt* **-uged; -uging 1** FLOOD : inundar **2** OVERWHELM : abrumar ⟨deluged with requests : abrumado de pedidos⟩

deluge[2] *n* **1** FLOOD : inundación *f* **2** DOWNPOUR : aguacero *m* **3** BARRAGE : aluvión *m*

delusion [di'lu:ʒən] *n* **1** : ilusión *f* (falsa) **2 delusions of grandeur** : delirios *mpl* de grandeza

deluxe [di'lʌks, -'lʊks] *adj* : de lujo

delve ['dɛlv] *vi* **delved; delving 1** DIG : escarbar **2 to delve into** PROBE : cavar en, ahondar en

demagogue ['dɛmə,gɑg] *n* : demagogo *m*, demagoga *f*

demand[1] [di'mænd] *vt* : demandar, exigir, reclamar

demand[2] *n* **1** REQUEST : petición *f*, pedido *m*, demanda *f* ⟨by popular demand : a petición del público⟩ **2** CLAIM : reclamación *f*, exigencia *f* **3** MARKET : demanda *f* ⟨supply and demand : la oferta y la demanda⟩

demanding [di'mændɪŋ] *adj* : exigente

demarcation [,di:,mɑr'keɪʃən] *n* : demarcación *f*, deslinde *m*

demean [di'mi:n] *vt* : degradar, rebajar

demeanor [di'mi:nər] *n* : comportamiento *m*, conducta *f*

demented [di'mɛntəd] *adj* : demente, loco

dementia [di'mɛntʃə] *n* : demencia *f*

demerit [di'mɛrət] *n* : demérito *m*

demigod ['dɛmi,gɑd, -,gɔd] *n* : semidiós *m*

demise [dɪ'maɪz] *n* **1** DEATH : fallecimiento *m*, deceso *m* **2** END : hundimiento *m*, desaparición *f* (de una institución, etc.)

demitasse ['dɛmi,tæs, -,tɑs] *n* : taza *f* pequeña (de café)

demobilization [di,mo:bələ'zeɪʃən] *n* : desmovilización *f*

demobilize [di'mo:bə,laɪz] *vt* **-lized; -lizing** : desmovilizar

democracy [di'mɑkrəsi] *n, pl* **-cies** : democracia *f*

democrat ['dɛmə,kræt] *n* : demócrata *mf*

democratic [,dɛmə'krætɪk] *adj* : democrático — **democratically** [-tɪkli] *adv*

demographic [dɛmə'græfɪk] *adj* : demográfico

demolish [di'mɑlɪʃ] *vt* **1** RAZE : demoler, derribar, arrasar **2** DESTROY : destruir, destrozar

demolition [,dɛmə'lɪʃən, ,di:-] *n* : demolición *f*, derribo *m*

demon ['di:mən] *n* : demonio *m*, diablo *m*

demonstrably [di'mɑntstrəbli] *adv* : manifiestamente, claramente

demonstrate ['dɛmən,streɪt] *vt* **-strated; -strating 1** SHOW : demostrar **2** PROVE : probar, demostrar **3** EXPLAIN : explicar, ilustrar

demonstration [,dɛmən'streɪʃən] *n* **1** SHOW : muestra *f*, demostración *f* **2** RALLY : manifestación *f*

demonstrative [di'mɑntstrətɪv] *adj* **1** EFFUSIVE : efusivo, expresivo, demostrativo **2** : demostrativo (en lingüística) ⟨demonstrative pronoun : pronombre demostrativo⟩

demonstrator ['dɛmən,streɪtər] *n* **1** : demostrador *m*, -dora *f* (de productos) **2** PROTESTER : manifestante *mf*

demoralize [di'mɔrə,laɪz] *vt* **-ized; -izing** : desmoralizar

demote [di'mo:t] *vt* **-moted; -moting** : degradar, bajar de categoría

demotion [di'mo:ʃən] *n* : degradación *f*, descenso *m* de categoría

demur [di'mər] *vi* **-murred; -murring 1** OBJECT : oponerse **2 to demur at** : ponerle objeciones a (algo)

demure [di'mjʊr] *adj* : recatado, modesto — **demurely** *adv*

den ['dɛn] *n* **1** LAIR : cubil *m*, madriguera *f* **2** HIDEOUT : guarida *f* **3** STUDY : estudio *m*, gabinete *m*

denature [di'neɪtʃər] *vt* **-tured; -turing** : desnaturalizar

denial [di'naɪəl] *n* **1** REFUSAL : rechazo *m*, denegación *f*, negativa *f* **2** REPUDIATION : negación *f* (de una creencia, etc.), rechazo *m*

denigrate ['dɛni,greɪt] *vt* **-grated; -grating** : denigrar

denim ['dɛnəm] *n* **1** : tela *f* vaquera, mezclilla *f Chile, Mex* **2 denims** *npl* → **jeans**

denizen ['dɛnəzən] *n* : habitante *mf*; morador *m*, -dora *f*

denomination [dɪ,nɑmə'neɪʃən] *n* **1** FAITH : confesión *f*, fe *f* **2** VALUE : denominación *f*, valor *m* (de una moneda)

denominator [dɪ'nɑmə,neɪtər] *n* : denominador *m*

denote [di'no:t] *vt* **-noted; -noting 1** INDICATE, MARK : indicar, denotar, señalar **2** MEAN : significar

denouement [,deɪ,nu:'mɑ] *n* : desenlace *m*

denounce [di'naʊnts] *vt* **-nounced; -nouncing 1** CENSURE : denunciar, censurar **2** ACCUSE : denunciar, acusar, delatar

dense ['dɛnts] *adj* **denser; -est 1** THICK : espeso, denso ⟨dense vegetation : vegetación densa⟩ ⟨a dense fog : una niebla espesa⟩ **2** STUPID : estúpido, burro *fam*

densely ['dɛntsli] *adv* **1** THICKLY : densamente **2** STUPIDLY : torpemente

denseness ['dɛntsnəs] *n* **1** → **density 2** STUPIDITY : estupidez *f*

density ['dɛntsəti] *n, pl* **-ties** : densidad *f*

dent[1] ['dɛnt] *vt* : abollar, mellar

dent[2] *n* : abolladura *f*, mella *f*

dental ['dɛntəl] *adj* : dental

dental floss *n* : hilo *m* dental

dentifrice ['dɛntəfrɪs] *n* : dentífrico *m*, pasta *f* de dientes

dentist ['dɛntɪst] *n* : dentista *mf*

dentistry ['dɛntɪstri] *n* : odontología *f*

dentures ['dɛntʃərz] *npl* : dentadura *f* postiza

denude [dɪ'nu:d, -'nju:d] *vt* **-nuded; -nuding** STRIP : desnudar, despojar

denunciation [dɪ,nʌntsi'eɪʃən] *n* : denuncia *f*, acusación *f*

deny [dɪ'naɪ] *vt* **-nied; -nying 1** REFUTE : desmentir, negar **2** DISOWN, REPUDIATE : negar, renegar de **3** REFUSE : denegar **4 to deny oneself** : privarse, sacrificarse

deodorant [di'o:dərənt] *n* : desodorante *m*

deodorize [di'o:də,raɪz] *vt* **-ized; -izing** : desodorizar

depart [dɪ'part] *vt* : salirse de — *vi* **1** LEAVE : salir, partir, irse **2** DIE : morir

department [dɪ'partmənt] *n* **1** DIVISION : sección *f* (de una tienda, una organización, etc.), departamento *m* (de una empresa, una universidad, etc.), ministerio *m* (del gobierno) **2** PROVINCE, SPHERE : esfera *f*, campo *m*, competencia *f*

departmental [di,part'mɛntəl, ,di:-] *adj* : departamental

department store *n* : grandes almacenes *mpl*

departure [dɪ'partʃər] *n* **1** LEAVING : salida *f*, partida *f* **2** DEVIATION : desviación *f*

depend [dɪ'pɛnd] *vi* **1** RELY : contar (con), confiar (en) ⟨depend on me! : ¡cuenta conmigo!⟩ **2 to depend on** : depender de ⟨success depends on hard work : el éxito depende de trabajar duro⟩ **3 that depends** : según, eso depende

dependable [dɪ'pɛndəbəl] *adj* : responsable, digno de confianza, fiable

dependence [dɪ'pɛndənts] *n* : dependencia *f*

dependency [dɪ'pɛndəntsi] *n, pl* **-cies 1** → **dependence 2** : posesión *f* (de una unidad política)

dependent[1] [dɪ'pɛndənt] *adj* : dependiente

dependent[2] *n* : persona *f* a cargo de alguien

depict [dɪ'pɪkt] *vt* **1** PORTRAY : representar **2** DESCRIBE : describir

depiction [dɪ'pɪkʃən] *n* : representación *f*, descripción *f*

deplete [dɪ'pli:t] *vt* **-pleted; -pleting 1** EXHAUST : agotar **2** REDUCE : reducir

depletion [dɪ'pli:ʃən] *n* **1** EXHAUSTION : agotamiento *m* **2** REDUCTION : reducción *f*, disminución *f*

deplorable [dɪ'plorəbəl] *adj* **1** CONTEMPTIBLE : deplorable, despreciable **2** LAMENTABLE : lamentable

deplore [dɪ'plor] *vt* **-plored; -ploring 1** REGRET : deplorar, lamentar **2** CONDEMN : condenar, deplorar

deploy [dɪ'plɔɪ] *vt* : desplegar

deployment [dɪ'plɔɪmənt] *n* : despliegue *m*

deport [dɪ'port] *vt* **1** EXPEL : deportar, expulsar (de un país) **2 to deport oneself** BEHAVE : comportarse

deportation [,di:,por'teɪʃən] *n* : deportación *f*

depose [dɪ'po:z] *vt* **-posed; -posing** : deponer

deposit[1] [dɪ'pazət] *vt* **-ited; -iting** : depositar

deposit[2] *n* **1** : depósito *m* (en el banco) **2** DOWN PAYMENT : entrega *f* inicial **3** : depósito *m*, yacimiento *m* (en geología)

deposition [,dɛpə'zɪʃən] *n* TESTIMONY : deposición *f*

depositor [dɪ'pazətər] *n* : depositante *mf*

depository [dɪ'pazə,tori] *n, pl* **-ries** : almacén *m*, depósito *m*

depot [*in sense 1 usu* 'dɛ,po:, *2 usu* 'di:-] *n* **1** STOREHOUSE : almacén *m*, depósito *m* **2** STATION, TERMINAL : terminal *mf*, estación *f* (de autobuses, ferrocarriles, etc.)

deprave [dɪ'preɪv] *vt* **-praved; -praving** : depravar, pervertir

depraved [dɪ'preɪvd] *adj* : depravado, degenerado

depravity [dɪ'prævəti] *n, pl* **-ties** : depravación *f*

depreciate [dɪ'pri:ʃi,eɪt] *v* **-ated; -ating** *vt* **1** DEVALUE : depreciar, devaluar **2** DISPARAGE : menospreciar, despreciar — *vi* : depreciarse, devaluarse

depreciation [dɪ,pri:ʃi'eɪʃən] *n* : depreciación *f*, devaluación *f*

depress [dɪ'prɛs] *vt* **1** PRESS, PUSH : apretar, presionar, pulsar **2** REDUCE : reducir, hacer bajar (precios, ventas, etc.) **3** SADDEN : deprimir, abatir, entristecer **4** DEVALUE : depreciar

depressant[1] [dɪ'prɛsənt] *adj* : depresivo

depressant[2] *n* : depresivo *m*

depressed [dɪ'prɛst] *adj* **1** DEJECTED : deprimido, abatido **2** : deprimido, en crisis (dícese de la economía)

depressing [dɪ'prɛsɪŋ] *adj* : deprimente, triste

depression [dɪ'prɛʃən] *n* **1** DESPONDENCY : depresión *f*, abatimiento *m* **2** : depresión (en una superficie) **3** RECESSION : depresión *f* económica, crisis *f*

deprivation [,dɛprə'veɪʃən] *n* : privación *f*

deprive [dɪ'praɪv] *vt* **-prived; -priving** : privar

depth ['dɛpθ] *n, pl* **depths** ['dɛpθs, 'dɛps] : profundidad *f*, fondo *m* ⟨to study in depth : estudiar a fondo⟩ ⟨in the depths of winter : en pleno invierno⟩

deputize ['dɛpju,taɪz] *vt* **-tized; -tizing** : nombrar como segundo

deputy ['dɛpjʊti] *n, pl* **-ties** : suplente *mf*, sustituto *m*, -ta *f*

derail [dɪ'reɪl] *v* : descarrilar

derailment [di'reɪlmənt] *n* : descarrilamiento *m*

derange [di'reɪndʒ] *vt* -ranged; -ranging 1 DISARRANGE : desarreglar, desordenar 2 DISTURB, UPSET : trastornar, perturbar 3 MADDEN : enloquecer, volver loco

derangement [di'reɪndʒmənt] *n* 1 DISTURBANCE, UPSET : trastorno *m* 2 INSANITY : locura *f*, perturbación *f* mental

derby ['dərbi] *n*, *pl* -bies 1 : derby *m* ⟨the Kentucky Derby : el Derby de Kentucky⟩ 2 : sombrero *m* hongo

deregulate [di'rɛgjʊˌleɪt] *vt* -lated; -lating : desregular

deregulation [diˌrɛgjʊ'leɪʃən] *n* : desregulación *f*

derelict¹ ['dɛrəˌlɪkt] *adj* 1 ABANDONED : abandonado, en ruinas 2 REMISS : negligente, remiso

derelict² *n* 1 : propiedad *f* abandonada 2 VAGRANT : vagabundo *m*, -da *f*

deride [di'raɪd] *vt* -rided; -riding : ridiculizar, burlarse de

derision [di'rɪʒən] *n* : escarnio *m*, irrisión *f*, mofa *f*

derisive [di'raɪsɪv] *adj* : burlón

derivation [ˌdɛrə'veɪʃən] *n* : derivación *f*

derivative¹ [di'rɪvətɪv] *adj* 1 DERIVED : derivado 2 BANAL : carente de originalidad, banal

derivative² *n* : derivado *m*

derive [di'raɪv] *v* -rived; -riving *vt* 1 OBTAIN : obtener, sacar 2 DEDUCE : deducir, inferir — *vi* : provenir, derivar, proceder

dermatologist [ˌdərmə'talədʒɪst] *n* : dermatólogo *m*, -ga *f*

dermatology [ˌdərmə'talədʒi] *n* : dermatología *f*

derogatory [di'ragəˌtori] *adj* : despectivo, despreciativo

derrick ['dɛrɪk] *n* 1 CRANE : grúa *f* 2 : torre *f* de perforación (sobre un pozo de petróleo)

descend [di'sɛnd] *vt* : descender, bajar — *vi* 1 : descender, bajar ⟨he descended from the platform : descendió del estrado⟩. 2 DERIVE : descender, provenir 3 STOOP : rebajarse ⟨I descended to his level : me rebajé a su nivel⟩ 4 to descend upon : caer sobre, invadir

descendant¹ [di'sɛndənt] *adj* : descendente

descendant² *n* : descendiente *mf*

descent [di'sɛnt] *n* 1 : bajada *f*, descenso *m* ⟨the descent from the mountain : el descenso de la montaña⟩ 2 ANCESTRY : ascendencia *f*, linaje *f* 3 SLOPE : pendiente *f*, cuesta *f* 4 FALL : caída *f* 5 ATTACK : incursión *f*, ataque *m*

describe [di'skraɪb] *vt* -scribed; -scribing : describir

description [di'skrɪpʃən] *n* : descripción *f*

descriptive [di'skrɪptɪv] *adj* : descriptivo ⟨descriptive adjective : adjetivo calificativo⟩

desecrate ['dɛsɪˌkreɪt] *vt* -crated; -crating : profanar

desecration [ˌdɛsɪ'kreɪʃən] *n* : profanación *f*

desegregate [di'sɛgrəˌgeɪt] *vt* -gated; -gating : eliminar la segregación racial de

desegregation [diˌsɛgrə'geɪʃən] *n* : eliminación *f* de la segregación racial

desert¹ [di'zərt] *vt* : abandonar (una persona o un lugar), desertar de (una causa, etc.) — *vi* : desertar

desert² ['dɛzərt] *adj* : desierto ⟨a desert island : una isla desierta⟩

desert³ *n* 1 ['dɛzərt] : desierto *m* (en geografía) 2 [di'zərt] → deserts

deserter [di'zərtər] *n* : desertor *m*, -tora *f*

desertion [di'zərʃən] *n* : abandono *m*, deserción *f* (militar)

deserts [di'zərts] *npl* : merecido *m* ⟨to get one's just deserts : llevarse uno su merecido⟩

deserve [di'zərv] *vt* -served; -serving : merecer, ser digno de

deserving [di'zərvɪŋ] *adj* : meritorio ⟨deserving of : digno de⟩

desiccate ['dɛsɪˌkeɪt] *vt* -cated; -cating : desecar, deshidratar

design¹ [di'zaɪn] *vt* 1 DEVISE : diseñar, concebir, idear 2 PLAN : proyectar 3 SKETCH : trazar, bosquejar

design² *n* 1 PLAN, SCHEME : plan *m*, proyecto *m* ⟨by design : a propósito, intencionalmente⟩ 2 SKETCH : diseño *m*, bosquejo *m* 3 PATTERN, STYLE : diseño *m*, estilo *m* 4 designs *npl* INTENTIONS : propósitos *mpl*, designios *mpl*

designate ['dɛzɪgˌneɪt] *vt* -nated; -nating 1 INDICATE, SPECIFY : indicar, especificar 2 APPOINT : nombrar, designar

designation [ˌdɛzɪg'neɪʃən] *n* 1 NAMING : designación *f* 2 NAME : denominación *f*, nombre *m* 3 APPOINTMENT : designación *f*, nombramiento *m*

designer [di'zaɪnər] *n* : diseñador *m*, -dora *f*

desirability [diˌzaɪrə'bɪləti] *n*, *pl* -ties 1 ADVISABILITY : conveniencia *f* 2 ATTRACTIVENESS : atractivo *m*

desirable [di'zaɪrəbəl] *adj* 1 ADVISABLE : conveniente, aconsejable 2 ATTRACTIVE : deseable, atractivo

desire¹ [di'zaɪr] *vt* -sired; -siring 1 WANT : desear 2 REQUEST : rogar, solicitar

desire² *n* : deseo *m*, anhelo *m*, ansia *m*

desist [di'sɪst, -'zɪst] *vi* to desist from : desistir de, abstenerse de

desk ['dɛsk] *n* : escritorio *m*, pupitre *m* (en la escuela)

desktop ['dɛskˌtap] *adj* : de escritorio

desolate¹ ['dɛsəˌleɪt, -zə-] *vt* -lated; -lating : devastar, desolar

desolate² ['dɛsələt, -zə-] *adj* **1** BARREN : desolado, desierto, yermo **2** DISCONSOLATE : desconsolado, desolado

desolation [ˌdɛsə'leɪʃən, -zə-] *n* : desolación *f*

despair¹ [di'spær] *vi* : desesperar, perder las esperanzas

despair² *n* : desesperación *f*, desesperanza *f*

desperate ['dɛspərət] *adj* **1** HOPELESS : desesperado, sin esperanzas **2** RASH : desesperado, precipitado **3** SERIOUS, URGENT : grave, urgente, apremiante ⟨a desperate need : una necesidad apremiante⟩

desperately ['dɛspərətli] *adv* : desesperadamente, urgentemente

desperation [ˌdɛspə'reɪʃən] *n* : desesperación *f*

despicable [di'spɪkəbəl, 'dɛspɪ-] *adj* : vil, despreciable, infame

despise [di'spaɪz] *vt* **-spised; -spising** : despreciar

despite [də'spaɪt] *prep* : a pesar de, aún con

despoil [di'spɔɪl] *vt* : saquear

despondency [di'spɑndənsi] *n* : desaliento *m*, desánimo *m*, depresión *f*

despondent [di'spɑndənt] *adj* : desalentado, desanimado

despot ['dɛspət, -ˌpɑt] *n* : déspota *mf*; tirano *m*, -na *f*

despotic [dɛs'pɑtɪk] *adj* : despótico

despotism ['dɛspəˌtɪzəm] *n* : despotismo *m*

dessert [di'zərt] *n* : postre *m*

destination [ˌdɛstə'neɪʃən] *n* : destino *m*, destinación *f*

destined ['dɛstənd] *adj* **1** FATED : predestinado **2** BOUND : destinado, con destino (a), con rumbo (a)

destiny ['dɛstəni] *n, pl* **-nies** : destino *m*

destitute ['dɛstəˌtuːt, -ˌtjuːt] *adj* **1** LACKING : carente, desprovisto **2** POOR : indigente, en miseria

destitution [ˌdɛstə'tuːʃən, -'tjuː-] *n* : indigencia *f*, miseria *f*

destroy [di'strɔɪ] *vt* **1** KILL : matar **2** DEMOLISH : destruir, destrozar

destroyer [di'strɔɪər] *n* : destructor *m* (buque)

destructible [di'strʌktəbəl] *adj* : destructible

destruction [di'strʌkʃən] *n* : destrucción *f*, ruina *f*

destructive [di'strʌktɪv] *adj* : destructor, destructivo

desultory ['dɛsəlˌtori] *adj* **1** AIMLESS : sin rumbo, sin objeto **2** DISCONNECTED : inconexo

detach [di'tætʃ] *vt* : separar, quitar, desprender

detached [di'tætʃt] *adj* **1** SEPARATE : separado, suelto **2** ALOOF : distante, indiferente **3** IMPARTIAL : imparcial, objetivo

detachment [di'tætʃmənt] *n* **1** SEPARATION : separación *f* **2** DETAIL : desta-

camento *m* (de tropas) **3** ALOOFNESS : reserva *f*, indiferencia *f* **4** IMPARTIALITY : imparcialidad *f*

detail¹ [di'teɪl, 'di:ˌteɪl] *vt* : detallar, exponer en detalle

detail² *n* **1** : detalle *m*, pormenor *m* **2** : destacamento *m* (de tropas)

detailed [di'teɪld, 'di:ˌteɪld] *adj* : detallado, minucioso

detain [di'teɪn] *vt* **1** HOLD : detener **2** DELAY : entretener, demorar, retrasar

detect [di'tɛkt] *vt* : detectar, descubrir

detection [di'tɛkʃən] *n* : descubrimiento *m*

detective [di'tɛktɪv] *n* : detective *mf* ⟨private detective : detective privado⟩

detector [di'tɛktər] *n* : detector *m*

detention [di'tɛnʃən] *n* : detención *m*

deter [di'tər] *vt* **-terred; -terring** : disuadir, impedir

detergent [di'tərdʒənt] *n* : detergente *m*

deteriorate [di'tɪriəˌreɪt] *vi* **-rated; -rating** : deteriorarse, empeorar

deterioration [diˌtɪriə'reɪʃən] *n* : deterioro *m*, empeoramiento *m*

determinant¹ [di'tərmənənt] *adj* : determinante

determinant² *n* **1** : factor *m* determinante **2** : determinante *m* (en matemáticas)

determination [diˌtərmə'neɪʃən] *n* **1** DECISION : determinación *f*, decisión *f* **2** RESOLUTION : resolución *f*, determinación *f* ⟨with grim determination : con una firme resolución⟩

determine [di'tərmən] *vt* **-mined; -mining** **1** ESTABLISH : determinar, establecer **2** SETTLE : decidir **3** FIND OUT : averiguar **4** BRING ABOUT : determinar

determined [di'tərmənd] *adj* RESOLUTE : decidido, resuelto

deterrent [di'tərənt] *n* : medida *f* disuasiva

detest [di'tɛst] *vt* : detestar, odiar, aborrecer

detestable [di'tɛstəbəl] *adj* : detestable, odioso, aborrecible

dethrone [di'θroːn] *vt* **-throned; -throning** : destronar

detonate ['dɛtənˌeɪt] *v* **-nated; -nating** *vt* : hacer detonar — *vi* : detonar, estallar

detonation [ˌdɛtə'neɪʃən] *n* : detonación *f*

detour¹ ['di:ˌtʊr, di'tʊr] *vi* : desviarse

detour² *n* : desvío *m*, rodeo *m*

detract [di'trækt] *vi* **to detract from** : restarle valor a, quitarle méritos a

detractor [di'træktər] *n* : detractor *m*, -tora *f*

detriment ['dɛtrəmənt] *n* : detrimento *m*, perjuicio *m*

detrimental [ˌdɛtrə'mɛntəl] *adj* : perjudicial — **detrimentally** *adv*

devaluation [diˌvæljʊ'eɪʃən] *n* : devaluación *f*

devalue [di'vælˌjuː] *vt* **-ued; -uing** : devaluar, depreciar

devastate ['dɛvə,steɪt] vt **-tated; -tating** : devastar, arrasar, asolar

devastation [,dɛvə'steɪʃən] n : devastación f, estragos mpl

develop [di'vɛləp] vt **1** FORM, MAKE : desarrollar, elaborar, formar **2** : revelar (en fotografía) **3** FOSTER : desarrollar, fomentar **4** EXPLOIT : explotar (recursos), urbanizar (un área) **5** ACQUIRE : adquirir ⟨to develop an interest : adquirir un interés⟩ **6** CONTRACT : contraer (una enfermedad) — vi **1** GROW : desarrollarse **2** ARISE : aparecer, surgir

developed [di'vɛləpt] adj : avanzado, desarrollado

developer [di'vɛləpər] n **1** : inmobiliaria f, urbanizadora f **2** : revelador m (en fotografía)

development [di'vɛləpmənt] n **1** : desarrollo m ⟨physical development : desarrollo físico⟩ **2** : urbanización f (de un área), explotación f (de recursos), creación f (de inventos) **3** EVENT : acontecimiento m, suceso m ⟨to await developments : esperar acontecimientos⟩

deviant ['di:viənt] adj : desviado, anormal

deviate ['di:vi,eɪt] v **-ated; -ating** vi : desviarse, apartarse — vt : desviar

deviation [,di:vi'eɪʃən] n : desviación f

device [di'vaɪs] n **1** MECHANISM : dispositivo m, aparato m, mecanismo m **2** EMBLEM : emblema m

devil[1] ['dɛvəl] vt **-iled** or **-illed; -iling** or **-illing** **1** : sazonar con picante y especias **2** PESTER : molestar

devil[2] n **1** SATAN : el diablo, Satanás m **2** DEMON : diablo m, demonio m **3** FIEND : persona f diabólica; malvado m, -da f

devilish ['dɛvəlɪʃ] adj : diabólico

devilry ['dɛvəlri] n, pl **-ries** : diabluras fpl, travesuras fpl

devious ['di:viəs] adj **1** CRAFTY : taimado, artero **2** WINDING : tortuoso, sinuoso

devise [di'vaɪz] vt **-vised; -vising** **1** INVENT : idear, concebir, inventar **2** PLOT : tramar

devoid [di'vɔɪd] adj ∼ **of** : carente de, desprovisto de

devote [di'vo:t] vt **-voted; -voting** **1** DEDICATE : consagrar, dedicar ⟨to devote one's life : dedicar uno su vida⟩ **2** **to devote oneself** : dedicarse

devoted [di'vo:ţəd] adj **1** FAITHFUL : leal, fiel **2 to be devoted to someone** : tenerle mucho cariño a alguien

devotee [,dɛvə'ti:, -'teɪ] n : devoto m, -ta f

devotion [di'vo:ʃən] n **1** DEDICATION : dedicación f, devoción f **2 devotions** PRAYERS : oraciones fpl, devociones fpl

devour [di'vauər] vt : devorar

devout [di'vaut] adj **1** PIOUS : devoto, piadoso **2** EARNEST, SINCERE : sincero, ferviente — **devoutly** adv

devoutness [di'vautnəs] n : devoción f, piedad f

dew ['du:, 'dju:] n : rocío m

dewlap ['du:,læp, 'dju-] n : papada f

dew point n : punto m de condensación

dewy ['du:i, 'dju:i] adj **dewier; -est** : cubierto de rocío

dexterity [dɛk'stɛrəţi] n, pl **-ties** : destreza f, habilidad f

dexterous ['dɛkstrəs] adj : diestro, hábil

dexterously ['dɛkstrəsli] adv : con destreza, con habilidad, hábilmente

dextrose ['dɛk,stro:s] n : dextrosa f

diabetes [,daɪə'bi:ţiz] n : diabetes f

diabetic[1] [,daɪə'bɛţɪk] adj : diabético

diabetic[2] n : diabético m, -ca f

diabolic [,daɪə'bɑlɪk] or **diabolical** [-lɪkəl] adj : diabólico, satánico

diacritical mark [,daɪə'krɪţɪkəl] n : signo m diacrítico

diadem ['daɪə,dɛm, -dəm] n : diadema f

diagnose ['daɪɪg,no:s, ,daɪɪg'no:s] vt **-nosed; -nosing** : diagnosticar

diagnosis [,daɪɪg'no:sɪs] n, pl **-noses** [-'no:,si:z] : diagnóstico m

diagnostic [,daɪɪg'nɑstɪk] adj : diagnóstico

diagonal[1] [daɪ'ægənəl] adj : diagonal, en diagonal

diagonal[2] n : diagonal f

diagonally [daɪ'ægənəli] adv : diagonalmente, en diagonal

diagram[1] ['daɪə,græm] vt **-gramed** or **-grammed; -graming** or **-gramming** : hacer un diagrama de

diagram[2] n : diagrama m, gráfico m, esquema m

dial[1] ['daɪl] v **dialed** or **dialled; dialing** or **dialling** : marcar, discar

dial[2] n : esfera f (de un reloj), dial m (de un radio), disco m (de un teléfono)

dialect ['daɪə,lɛkt] n : dialecto m

dialogue ['daɪə,lɔg] n : diálogo m

diameter [daɪ'æməţər] n : diámetro m

diamond ['daɪmənd, 'daɪə-] n **1** : diamante m, brillante m ⟨a diamond necklace : un collar de brillantes⟩ **2** : rombo m, forma f de rombo **3** : diamante m (en naipes) **4** INFIELD : cuadro m, diamante m (en béisbol)

diaper ['daɪpər, 'daɪə-] n : pañal m

diaphragm ['daɪə,fræm] n : diafragma m

diarrhea [,daɪə'ri:ə] n : diarrea f

diary ['daɪəri] n, pl **-ries** : diario m

diatribe ['daɪə,traɪb] n : diatriba f

dice[1] ['daɪs] vt **diced; dicing** : cortar en cubos

dice[2] ns & pl **1** → **die**[2] **2** : dados mpl (juego)

dicker ['dɪkər] vt : regatear

dictate[1] ['dɪk,teɪt, dɪk'teɪt] v **-tated; -tating** vt **1** : dictar ⟨to dictate a letter : dictar una carta⟩ **2** ORDER : mandar, ordenar — vi : dar órdenes

dictate² ['dɪk,teɪt] n 1 : mandato m, orden f 2 **dictates** npl : dictados mpl ⟨the dictates of conscience : los dictados de la conciencia⟩

dictation [dɪk'teɪʃən] n : dictado m

dictator ['dɪk,teɪtər] n : dictador m, -dora f

dictatorial [,dɪktə'toriəl] adj : dictatorial — **dictatorially** adv

dictatorship [dɪk'teɪtər,ʃɪp, 'dɪk,-] n : dictadura f

diction ['dɪkʃən] n 1 : lenguaje m, estilo m 2 ENUNCIATION : dicción f, articulación f

dictionary ['dɪkʃə,nɛri] n, pl **-naries** : diccionario m

did → **do**

didactic [daɪ'dæktɪk] adj : didáctico

die¹ ['daɪ] vi **died** ['daɪd]; **dying** ['daɪɪŋ] 1 : morir 2 CEASE : morir, morirse ⟨a dying civilization : una civilización moribunda⟩ 3 STOP : apagarse, dejar de funcionar ⟨the motor died : el motor se apagó⟩ 4 **to die down** SUBSIDE : amainar, disminuir 5 **to die out** : extinguirse 6 **to be dying for** or **to be dying to** : morirse por ⟨I'm dying to leave : me muero por irme⟩

die² ['daɪ] n, pl **dice** ['daɪs] : dado m

die³ n, pl **dies** ['daɪz] 1 STAMP : troquel m, cuño m 2 MOLD : matriz f, molde m

diesel ['di:zəl, -səl] n : diesel m

diet¹ ['daɪət] vi : ponerse a régimen, hacer dieta

diet² n : régimen m, dieta f

dietary ['daɪə,tɛri] adj : alimenticio, dietético

dietitian or **dietician** [,daɪə'tɪʃən] n : dietista mf

differ ['dɪfər] vi **-ferred**; **-ferring** 1 : diferir, diferenciarse 2 VARY : variar 3 DISAGREE : discrepar, diferir, no estar de acuerdo

difference ['dɪfrənts, 'dɪfərənts] n : diferencia f

different ['dɪfrənt, 'dɪfərənt] adj : distinto, diferente

differentiate [,dɪfə'rɛntʃi,eɪt] v **-ated**; **-ating** vt 1 : hacer diferente 2 DISTINGUISH : distinguir, diferenciar — vi : distinguir

differentiation [,dɪfə,rɛntʃi'eɪʃən] n : diferenciación f

differently ['dɪfrəntli, 'dɪfərənt-] adv : de otra manera, de otro modo, distintamente

difficult ['dɪfɪ,kʌlt] adj : difícil

difficulty ['dɪfɪ,kʌlti] n, pl **-ties** 1 : dificultad f 2 PROBLEM : problema f, dificultad f

diffidence ['dɪfədənts] n 1 SHYNESS : retraimiento m, timidez f, apocamiento m 2 RETICENCE : reticencia f

diffident ['dɪfədənt] adj 1 SHY : tímido, apocado, inseguro 2 RESERVED : reservado

diffuse¹ [dɪ'fju:z] v **-fused**; **-fusing** vt : difundir, esparcir — vi : difundirse, esparcirse

diffuse² [dɪ'fju:s] adj 1 WORDY : prolijo, verboso 2 WIDESPREAD : difuso

diffusion [dɪ'fju:ʒən] n : difusión f

dig¹ ['dɪg] v **dug** ['dʌg]; **digging** vt 1 : cavar, excavar ⟨to dig a hole : cavar un hoyo⟩ 2 EXTRACT : sacar ⟨to dig up potatoes : sacar papas del suelo⟩ 3 POKE, THRUST : clavar, hincar ⟨he dug me in the ribs : me dio un codazo en las costillas⟩ 4 **to dig up** DISCOVER : descubrir, sacar a luz — vi : cavar, excavar

dig² n 1 POKE : codazo m 2 GIBE : pulla f 3 EXCAVATION : excavación f

digest¹ [daɪ'dʒɛst, dɪ-] vt 1 ASSIMILATE : digerir, asimilar 2 : digerir (comida) 3 SUMMARIZE : compendiar, resumir

digest² ['daɪ,dʒɛst] n : compendio m, resumen m

digestible [daɪ'dʒɛstəbəl, dɪ-] adj : digerible

digestion [daɪ'dʒɛstʃən, dɪ-] n : digestión f

digestive [daɪ'dʒɛstɪv, dɪ-] adj : digestivo ⟨the digestive system : el sistema digestivo⟩

digit ['dɪdʒət] n 1 NUMERAL : dígito m, número m 2 FINGER, TOE : dedo m

digital ['dɪdʒətəl] adj : digital — **digitally** adv

dignified ['dɪgnə,faɪd] adj : digno, decoroso

dignify ['dɪgnə,faɪ] vt **-fied**; **-fying** : dignificar, honrar

dignitary ['dɪgnə,tɛri] n, pl **-taries** : dignatario m, -ria f

dignity ['dɪgnəti] n, pl **-ties** : dignidad f

digress [daɪ'grɛs, də-] vi : desviarse del tema, divagar

digression [daɪ'grɛʃən, də-] n : digresión f

dike or **dyke** ['daɪk] n : dique m

dilapidated [də'læpə,deɪtəd] adj : ruinoso, desvencijado, destartalado

dilapidation [də,læpə'deɪʃən] n : deterioro m, estado m ruinoso

dilate [daɪ'leɪt, 'daɪ,leɪt] v **-lated**; **-lating** vt : dilatar — vi : dilatarse

dilemma [dɪ'lɛmə] n : dilema m

dilettante ['dɪlə,tɑnt, -,tænt] n, pl **-tantes** [-,tɑnts, -,tænts] or **-tanti** [,dɪlə'tɑnti, -'tæn-] : diletante mf

diligence ['dɪlədʒənts] n : diligencia f, aplicación f

diligent ['dɪlədʒənt] adj : diligente ⟨a diligent search : una búsqueda minuciosa⟩ — **diligently** adv

dill ['dɪl] n : eneldo m

dillydally ['dɪli,dæli] vi **-lied**; **lying** : demorarse, perder tiempo

dilute [daɪ'lu:t, də-] vt **-luted**; **-luting** : diluir, aguar

dilution [daɪ'lu:ʃən, də-] n : dilución f

dim¹ ['dɪm] v **dimmed**; **dimming** vt : atenuar (la luz), nublar (la vista), bo-

rrar (la memoria), opacar (una superficie) — *vi* : oscurecerse, apagarse

dim² *adj* **dimmer; dimmest 1** FAINT : oscuro, tenue (dícese de la luz), nublado
(dícese de la vista), borrado (dícese de
la memoria) **2** DULL : deslustrado **3**
STUPID : tonto, torpe

dime ['daɪm] *n* : moneda *f* de diez centavos

dimension [də'mɛntʃən, daɪ-] *n* **1** : dimensión *f* **2 dimensions** *npl* EXTENT,
SCOPE : dimensiones *fpl*, extensión *f*,
medida *f*

diminish [də'mɪnɪʃ] *vt* LESSEN : disminuir, reducir, amainar — *vi* DWIN-
DLE, WANE : menguar, reducirse

diminutive [də'mɪnjʊtɪv] *adj* : diminutivo, minúsculo

dimly ['dɪmli] *adv* : indistintamente, débilmente

dimmer ['dɪmər] *n* : potenciómetro *m*,
conmutador *m* de luces (en automóviles)

dimness ['dɪmnəs] *n* : oscuridad *f*, debilidad *f* (de la vista), imprecisión *f* (de
la memoria)

dimple ['dɪmpəl] *n* : hoyuelo *m*

din ['dɪn] *n* : estrépito *m*, estruendo *m*

dine ['daɪn] *vi* **dined; dining** : cenar

diner ['daɪnər] *n* **1** : comensal *mf* (persona) **2** : vagón *m* restaurante (en un
tren) **3** : cafetería *f*, restaurante *m*
barato

dinghy ['dɪŋi, 'dɪŋgi, 'dɪŋki] *n, pl* **-ghies**
: bote *m*

dinginess ['dɪndʒinəs] *n* **1** DIRTINESS
: suciedad *f* **2** SHABBINESS : lo gastado, lo deslucido

dingy ['dɪndʒi] *adj* **-gier; -est 1** DIRTY
: sucio **2** SHABBY : gastado, deslucido

dinner ['dɪnər] *n* : cena *f*, comida *f*

dinosaur ['daɪnəˌsɔr] *n* : dinosaurio *m*

dint ['dɪnt] *n* **by dint of** : a fuerza de

diocese ['daɪəsəs, -ˌsiːz, -ˌsiːs] *n, pl*
-ceses ['daɪəsəsəz] : diócesis *f*

dip¹ ['dɪp] *v* **dipped; dipping** *vt* **1** DUNK,
PLUNGE : sumergir, mojar, meter **2** LA-
DLE : servir con cucharón **3** LOWER
: bajar, arriar (una bandera) — *vi* **1**
DESCEND, DROP : bajar en picada, de-
scender **2** SLOPE : bajar, inclinarse

dip² *n* **1** SWIM : chapuzón *m* **2** DROP
: descenso *m*, caída *f* **3** SLOPE : cuesta
f, declive *m* **4** SAUCE : salsa *f*

diphtheria [dɪf'θɪriə] *n* : difteria *f*

diphthong ['dɪfˌθɔŋ] *n* : diptongo *m*

diploma [də'ploːmə] *n, pl* **-mas** : diploma *m*

diplomacy [də'ploːməsi] *n* **1** : diplomacia *f* **2** TACT : tacto *m*, discreción *f*

diplomat ['dɪpləˌmæt] *n* **1** : diplomático
m, -ca *f* (en relaciones internacionales)
2 : persona *f* diplomática

diplomatic [ˌdɪplə'mætɪk] *adj* : diplomático ⟨diplomatic immunity : inmunidad diplomática⟩

dipper ['dɪpər] *n* **1** LADLE : cucharón *m*,
cazo *m* **2 Big Dipper** : Osa *f* Mayor **3**
Little Dipper : Osa *f* Menor

dire ['daɪr] *adj* **direr; direst 1** HORRIBLE
: espantoso, terrible, horrendo **2** EX-
TREME : extremo ⟨dire poverty : pobreza extrema⟩

direct¹ [də'rɛkt, daɪ-] *vt* **1** ADDRESS : dirigir, mandar **2** AIM, POINT : dirigir **3**
GUIDE : indicarle el camino (a alguien),
orientar **4** MANAGE : dirigir ⟨to direct
a film : dirigir una película⟩ **5** COM-
MAND : ordenar, mandar

direct² *adv* : directamente

direct³ *adj* **1** STRAIGHT : directo **2**
FRANK : franco

direct current *n* : corriente *f* continua

direction [də'rɛkʃən, daɪ-] *n* **1** SUPER-
VISION : dirección *f* **2** INSTRUCTION,
ORDER : instrucción *f*, orden *f* **3**
COURSE : dirección *f*, rumbo *m* ⟨to
change direction : cambiar de direc-
ción⟩ **4 to ask directions** : pedir indi-
caciones

directional [də'rɛkʃənəl, daɪ-] *adj* : direccional

directive [də'rɛktɪv, daɪ-] *n* : directiva *f*

directly [də'rɛktli, daɪ-] *adv* **1** STRAIGHT
: directamente ⟨directly north : directamente al norte⟩ **2** FRANKLY : francamente **3** EXACTLY : exactamente,
justo ⟨directly opposite : justo en-
frente⟩ **4** IMMEDIATELY : en seguida,
inmediatamente

directness [də'rɛktnəs, daɪ-] *n* : franqueza *f*

director [də'rɛktər, daɪ-] *n* **1** : director
m, -tora *f* **2 board of directors** : junta
f directiva, directorio *m*

directory [də'rɛktəri, daɪ-] *n, pl* **-ries**
: guía *f*, directorio *m* ⟨telephone directory : directorio telefónico⟩

dirge ['dərdʒ] *n* : canto *m* fúnebre

dirigible ['dɪrədʒəbəl, də'rɪdʒə-] *n* : dirigible *m*, zepelín *m*

dirt ['dərt] *n* **1** FILTH : suciedad *f*, mugre *f*, porquería *f* **2** SOIL : tierra *f*

dirtiness ['dərtinəs] *n* : suciedad *f*

dirty¹ ['dərti] *vt* **dirtied; dirtying** : ensuciar, manchar

dirty² *adj* **dirtier; -est 1** SOILED,
STAINED : sucio, manchado **2** DIS-
HONEST : sucio, deshonesto ⟨a dirty
player : un jugador tramposo⟩ ⟨a dirty
trick : una mala pasada⟩ **3** INDECENT
: indecente, cochino ⟨a dirty joke : un
chiste verde⟩

disability [ˌdɪsə'bɪləti] *n, pl* **-ties** : minusvalía *f*, discapacidad *f*, invalidez *f*

disable [dɪs'eɪbəl] *vt* **-abled; -abling** : dejar inválido, inutilizar, incapacitar

disabled [dɪs'eɪbəld] *adj* : minusválido,
discapacitado

disabuse [ˌdɪsə'bjuːz] *vt* **-bused;
-busing** : desengañar, sacar del error

disadvantage [ˌdɪsəd'væntɪdʒ] *n* : desventaja *f*

disadvantageous [ˌdɪsˌædˌvæn'teɪdʒəs]
adj : desventajoso, desfavorable

disagree · discouragement

disagree [‚dısə'gri:] vi **1** DIFFER : discrepar, no coincidir **2** DISSENT : disentir, discrepar, no estar de acuerdo
disagreeable [‚dısə'gri:əbəl] adj : desagradable
disagreement [‚dısə'gri:mənt] n **1** : desacuerdo m **2** DISCREPANCY : discrepancia f **3** ARGUMENT : discusión f, altercado m, disputa f
disappear [‚dısə'pır] vi : desaparecer, desvanecerse ⟨to disappear from view : perderse de vista⟩
disappearance [‚dısə'pırənts] n : desaparición f
disappoint [‚dısə'pɔınt] vt : decepcionar, defraudar, fallar
disappointing [‚dısə'pɔıntıŋ] adj : decepcionante
disappointment [‚dısə'pɔıntmənt] n : decepción f, desilusión f, chasco m
disapproval [‚dısə'pru:vəl] n : desaprobación f
disapprove [‚dısə'pru:v] vi **-proved; -proving** : desaprobar, estar en contra
disapprovingly [‚dısə'pru:vıŋli] adv : con desaprobación
disarm [dıs'arm] vt : desarmar
disarmament [dıs'arməmənt] n : desarme m ⟨nuclear disarmament : desarme nuclear⟩
disarrange [‚dısə'reındʒ] vt **-ranged; -ranging** : desarreglar, desordenar
disarray [‚dısə'reı] n : desorden m, confusión f, desorganización f
disaster [dı'zæstər] n : desastre m, catástrofe f
disastrous [dı'zæstrəs] adj : desastroso
disband [dıs'bænd] vt : disolver — vi : disolverse, dispersarse
disbar [dıs'bar] vt **-barred; -barring** : prohibir de ejercer la abogacía
disbelief [‚dısbı'li:f] n : incredulidad f
disbelieve [‚dısbı'li:v] v **-lieved; -lieving** : no creer, dudar
disburse [dıs'bərs] vt **-bursed; -bursing** : desembolsar
disbursement [dıs'bərsmənt] n : desembolso m
disc → disk
discard [dıs'kard, 'dıs‚kard] vt : desechar, deshacerse de, botar — vi : descartarse (en juegos de naipes)
discern [dı'sərn, -'zərn] vt : discernir, distinguir, percibir
discernible [dı'sərnəbəl, -'zər-] adj : perceptible, visible
discernment [dı'sərnmənt, -'zərn-] n : discernimiento m, criterio m
discharge¹ [dıs'tʃardʒ, 'dıs‚-] v **-charged; -charging 1** UNLOAD : descargar (carga), desembarcar (pasajeros) **2** SHOOT : descargar, disparar **3** FREE : liberar, poner en libertad **4** DISMISS : despedir **5** EMIT : despedir (humo, etc.), descargar (electricidad) **6** : cumplir con (una obligación), saldar (una deuda) — vi **1** : descargarse (dícese de una batería) **2** OOZE : supurar

discharge² ['dıs‚tʃardʒ, dıs'-] n **1** EMISSION : descarga f (de electricidad), emisión f (de gases) **2** DISMISSAL : despido m (del empleo), baja f (del ejército) **3** SECRETION : secreción f
disciple [dı'saıpəl] n : discípulo m, -la f
discipline¹ ['dısəplən] vt **-plined; -plining 1** PUNISH : castigar, sancionar (a los empleados) **2** CONTROL : disciplinar **3 to discipline oneself** : disciplinarse
discipline² n **1** FIELD : disciplina f, campo m **2** TRAINING : disciplina f **3** PUNISHMENT : castigo m **4** SELF-CONTROL : dominio m de sí mismo
disc jockey n : disc jockey mf
disclaim [dıs'kleım] vt DENY : negar
disclose [dıs'klo:z] vt **-closed; -closing** : revelar, poner en evidencia
disclosure [dıs'klo:ʒər] n : revelación f
disco ['dısko:] n **1 → discotheque 2** or **disco music** : disco f, música f disco
discolor [dıs'kʌlər] vt **1** BLEACH : decolorar **2** FADE : desteñir **3** STAIN : manchar — vi : decolorarse, desteñirse
discoloration [dıs‚kʌlə'reıʃən] n **1** FADING : decoloración f **2** STAIN : mancha f
discomfort [dıs'kʌmfərt] n **1** PAIN : molestia f, malestar m **2** UNEASINESS : inquietud f
disconcert [‚dıskən'sərt] vt : desconcertar
disconcerting [‚dıskən'sərtıŋ] adj : desconcertante
disconnect [‚dıskə'nɛkt] vt : desconectar
disconnected [‚dıskə'nɛktəd] adj : inconexo
disconsolate [dıs'kantsələt] adj : desconsolado
discontent [‚dıskən'tɛnt] n : descontento m
discontented [‚dıskən'tɛntəd] adj : descontento
discontinue [‚dıskən'tın‚ju:] vt **-ued; -uing** : suspender, descontinuar
discontinuity [dıs‚kantə'nu:əti, -'nju:-] n, pl **-ties** : discontinuidad f
discontinuous [‚dıskən'tınjəwəs] adj : discontinuo
discord ['dıs‚kɔrd] n **1** STRIFE : discordia f, discordancia f **2** : disonancia f (en música)
discordant [dıs'kɔrdənt] adj : discordante, discorde — **discordantly** adv
discotheque ['dıskə‚tɛk, ‚dıskə'tɛk] n : discoteca f
discount¹ ['dıs‚kaunt, dıs'-] vt **1** REDUCE : descontar, rebajar (precios) **2** DISREGARD : descartar, ignorar
discount² ['dıs‚kaunt] n : descuento m, rebaja f
discourage [dıs'kərıdʒ] vt **-aged; -aging 1** DISHEARTEN : desalentar, desanimar **2** DISSUADE : disuadir
discouragement [dıs'kərıdʒmənt] n : desánimo m, desaliento m

discouraging [dɪs'kərədʒɪŋ] *adj* : desalentador

discourse¹ [dɪs'kors] *vi* -coursed; -coursing : disertar, conversar

discourse² ['dɪs,kors] *n* 1 TALK : conversación *f* 2 SPEECH, TREATISE : discurso *m*, tratado *m*

discourteous [dɪs'kərt̬iəs] *adj* : descortés — **discourteously** *adv*

discourtesy [dɪs'kərt̬əsi] *n, pl* -sies : descortesía *f*

discover [dɪs'kʌvər] *vt* : descubrir

discoverer [dɪs'kʌvərər] *n* : descubridor *m*, -dora *f*

discovery [dɪs'kʌvəri] *n, pl* -ries : descubrimiento *m*

discredit¹ [dɪs'krɛdət] *vt* 1 DISBELIEVE : no creer, dudar 2 : desacreditar, desprestigiar, poner en duda ⟨they discredited his research : desacreditaron sus investigaciones⟩

discredit² *n* 1 DISREPUTE : descrédito *m*, desprestigio *m* 2 DOUBT : duda *f*

discreet [dɪs'kri:t] *adj* : discreto — **discreetly** *adv*

discrepancy [dɪs'krepəntsi] *n, pl* -cies : discrepancia *f*

discretion [dɪs'krɛʃən] *n* 1 CIRCUMSPECTION : discreción *f*, circunspección *f* 2 JUDGMENT : discernimiento *m*, criterio *m*

discretionary [dɪs'krɛʃə,nɛri] *adj* : discrecional

discriminate [dɪs'krɪmə,neɪt] *v* -nated; -nating *vt* DISTINGUISH : distinguir, discriminar, diferenciar — *vi* : discriminar ⟨to discriminate against women : discriminar a las mujeres⟩

discrimination [dɪs,krɪmə'neɪʃən] *n* 1 PREJUDICE : discriminación *f* 2 DISCERNMENT : discernimiento *m*

discriminatory [dɪs'krɪmənə,tori] *adj* : discriminatorio

discus ['dɪskəs] *n, pl* -cuses [-kəsəz] : disco *m*

discuss [dɪs'kʌs] *vt* : hablar de, discutir, tratar (de)

discussion [dɪs'kʌʃən] *n* : discusión *f*, debate *m*, conversación *f*

disdain¹ [dɪs'deɪn] *vt* : desdeñar, despreciar ⟨they disdained to reply : no se dignaron a responder⟩

disdain² *n* : desdén *m*

disdainful [dɪs'deɪnfəl] *adj* : desdeñoso — **disdainfully** *adv*

disease [dɪ'zi:z] *n* : enfermedad *f*, mal *m*, dolencia *f*

diseased [dɪ'zi:zd] *adj* : enfermo

disembark [,dɪsɪm'bark] *v* : desembarcar

disembarkation [dɪs,ɛm,bar'keɪʃən] *n* : desembarco *m*, desembarque *m*

disembodied [,dɪsɪm'badid] *adj* : incorpóreo

disenchant [,dɪsɪn'tʃænt] *vt* : desilusionar, desencantar, desengañar

disenchantment [,dɪsɪn'tʃæntmənt] *n* : desencanto *m*, desilusión *f*

disengage [,dɪsɪn'geɪdʒ] *vt* -gaged; -gaging 1 : soltar, desconectar (un mecanismo) 2 **to disengage the clutch** : desembragar

disentangle [,dɪsɪn'tæŋgəl] *vt* -gled; -gling UNTANGLE : desenredar, desenmarañar

disfavor [dɪs'feɪvər] *n* : desaprobación *f*

disfigure [dɪs'fɪgjər] *vt* -ured; -uring : desfigurar (a una persona), afear (un edificio, un área)

disfigurement [dɪs'fɪgjərmənt] *n* : desfiguración *f*, afeamiento *m*

disfranchise [dɪs'fræn,tʃaɪz] *vt* -chised; -chising : privar del derecho a votar

disgrace¹ [dɪ'skreɪs] *vt* -graced; -gracing : deshonrar

disgrace² *n* 1 DISHONOR : desgracia *f*, deshonra *f* 2 SHAME : vergüenza *f* ⟨he's a disgrace to his family : es una vergüenza para su familia⟩

disgraceful [dɪ'skreɪsfəl] *adj* : vergonzoso, deshonroso, ignominioso

disgracefully [dɪ'skreɪsfəli] *adv* : vergonzosamente

disgruntle [dɪs'grʌntəl] *vt* -tled; -tling : enfadar, contrariar

disguise¹ [dɪs'kaɪz] *vt* -guised; -guising 1 : disfrazar, enmascarar (el aspecto) 2 CONCEAL : encubrir, disimular

disguise² *n* : disfraz *m*

disgust¹ [dɪ'skʌst] *vt* : darle asco (a alguien), asquear, repugnar ⟨that disgusts me : eso me da asco⟩

disgust² *n* : asco *m*, repugnancia *f*

disgusting [dɪ'skʌstɪŋ] *adj* : asqueroso, repugnante — **disgustingly** *adv*

dish¹ ['dɪʃ] *vt* SERVE : servir

dish² *n* 1 : plato *m* ⟨the national dish : el plato nacional⟩ 2 PLATE : plato *m* ⟨to wash the dishes : lavar los platos⟩ 3 **serving dish** : fuente *f*

dishcloth ['dɪʃ,klɔth] *n* : paño *m* de cocina (para secar), trapo *m* de fregar (para lavar)

dishearten [dɪs'hart̬ən] *vt* : desanimar, desalentar

dishevel [dɪ'ʃɛvəl] *vt* -eled *or* -elled; -eling *or* -elling : desarreglar, despeinar (el pelo)

disheveled *or* **dishevelled** [dɪ'ʃɛvəld] *adj* : despeinado (dícese del pelo), desarreglado, desaliñado

dishonest [dɪ'sanəst] *adj* : deshonesto, fraudulento — **dishonestly** *adv*

dishonesty [dɪ'sanəsti] *n, pl* -ties : deshonestidad *f*, falta *f* de honradez

dishonor¹ [dɪ'sanər] *vt* : deshonrar

dishonor² *n* : deshonra *f*

dishonorable [dɪ'sanərəbəl] *adj* : deshonroso — **dishonorably** [-bli] *adv*

dishrag ['dɪʃ,ræg] → **dishcloth**

dishwasher ['dɪʃ,wɔʃər] *n* : lavaplatos *m*, lavavajillas *m*

disillusion [,dɪsə'lu:ʒən] *vt* : desilusionar, desencantar, desengañar

disillusionment [,dɪsə'lu:ʒənmənt] *n* : desilusión *f*, desencanto *m*

disinclination [dɪs,ɪnklə'neɪʃən, -,ɪŋ-] n
: aversión f

disinclined [,dɪsɪn'klaɪnd] adv : poco
dispuesto

disinfect [,dɪsɪn'fɛkt] vt : desinfectar

disinfectant¹ [,dɪsɪn'fɛktənt] adj : desinfectante

disinfectant² n : desinfectante m

disinherit [,dɪsɪn'hɛrət] vt : desheredar

disintegrate [dɪs'ɪntə,greɪt] v **-grated;**
-grating vt : desintegrar, deshacer — vi
: desintegrarse, deshacerse

disintegration [dɪs,ɪntə'greɪʃən] n : desintegración f

disinterested [dɪs'ɪntərəstəd, -,rɛs-] adj
1 INDIFFERENT : indiferente **2** IMPAR-
TIAL : imparcial, desinteresado

disinterestedness [dɪs'ɪntərəstədnəs,
-,rɛs-] n : desinterés m

disjointed [dɪs'dʒɔɪntəd] adj : inconexo,
incoherente

disk or **disc** ['dɪsk] n : disco m

disk drive n : unidad f de disco

diskette [,dɪs'kɛt] n : diskette m, disquete m

dislike¹ [dɪs'laɪk] vt **-liked; -liking** : tenerle aversión a (algo), tenerle antipatía
(a alguien), no gustarle (algo a uno)

dislike² n : aversión f, antipatía f

dislocate ['dɪslo,keɪt, dɪs'lo:-] vt **-cated;**
-cating : dislocar

dislocation [,dɪslo'keɪʃən] n : dislocación f

dislodge [dɪs'lɑdʒ] vt **-lodged; -lodging**
: sacar, desalojar, desplazar

disloyal [dɪs'lɔɪəl] adj : desleal

disloyalty [dɪs'lɔɪəlti] n, pl **-ties** : deslealtad f

dismal ['dɪzməl] adj **1** GLOOMY : sombrío, lúgubre, tétrico **2** DEPRESSING
: deprimente, triste

dismantle [dɪs'mæntəl] vt **-tled; -tling**
: desmantelar, desmontar, desarmar

dismay¹ [dɪs'meɪ] vt : consternar

dismay² n : consternación f

dismember [dɪs'mɛmbər] vt : desmembrar

dismiss [dɪs'mɪs] vt **1** : dejar salir, dar-
le permiso (a alguien) para retirarse **2**
DISCHARGE : despedir, destituir **3** RE-
JECT : descartar, desechar, rechazar

dismissal [dɪs'mɪsəl] n **1** : permiso m
para retirarse **2** DISCHARGE : despido
m (de un empleado), destitución f (de
un funcionario) **3** REJECTION : rechazo m

dismount [dɪs'maʊnt] vi : desmontar,
bajarse, apearse

disobedience [,dɪsə'bi:diənts] n : desobediencia f — **disobedient** [-ənt] adj

disobey [,dɪsə'beɪ] v : desobedecer

disorder¹ [dɪs'ɔrdər] vt : desordenar, desarreglar

disorder² n **1** DISARRAY : desorden m
2 UNREST : disturbios mpl, desórdenes
mpl **3** AILMENT : afección f, indisposición f, dolencia f

disorderly [dɪs'ɔrdərli] adj **1** UNTIDY
: desordenado, desarreglado **2** UN-
RULY : indisciplinado, alborotado **3**
disorderly conduct : conducta f escandalosa

disorganization [dɪs,ɔrgənə'zeɪʃən] n
: desorganización f

disorganize [dɪs'ɔrgə,naɪz] vt **-nized;**
-nizing : desorganizar

disorient [dɪs'ori,ɛnt] vt : desorientar

disown [dɪs'o:n] vt : renegar de, repudiar

disparage [dɪs'pærɪdʒ] vt **-aged; -aging**
: menospreciar, denigrar

disparagement [dɪs'pærɪdʒmənt] n
: menosprecio m

disparate ['dɪspərət, dɪs'pærət] adj : dispar, diferente

disparity [dɪs'pærəti] n, pl **-ties** : disparidad f

dispassionate [dɪs'pæʃənət] adj : desapasionado, imparcial — **dispas-
sionately** adv

dispatch¹ [dɪs'pætʃ] vt **1** SEND : despachar, enviar **2** KILL : despachar, matar
3 HANDLE : despachar

dispatch² n **1** SENDING : envío m,
despacho m **2** MESSAGE : despacho m,
reportaje m (de un periodista), parte m
(en el ejército) **3** PROMPTNESS : prontitud f, rapidez f

dispel [dɪs'pɛl] vt **-pelled; -pelling** : disipar, desvanecer

dispensable [dɪ'spɛntsəbəl] adj : prescindible

dispensation [,dɪspɛn'seɪʃən] n EXEMP-
TION : exención m, dispensa f

dispense [dɪs'pɛnts] v **-pensed; -pens-
ing** vt **1** DISTRIBUTE : repartir, distribuir, dar **2** ADMINISTER, BESTOW
: administrar (justicia), conceder (fa-
vores, etc.) **3** : preparar y despachar
(medicamentos) — vi **to dispense with**
: prescindir de

dispenser [dɪs'pɛntsər] n : dispensador
m, distribuidor m automático

dispersal [dɪs'pərsəl] n : dispersión f

disperse [dɪs'pərs] v **-persed; -persing**
vt : dispersar, diseminar — vi : dispersarse

dispersion [dɪ'spərʒən] n : dispersión f

dispirit [dɪ'spɪrət] vt : desalentar, desanimar

displace [dɪs'pleɪs] vt **-placed; -placing**
1 : desplazar (un líquido, etc.) **2** RE-
PLACE : reemplazar

displacement [dɪs'pleɪsmənt] n **1** : desplazamiento m (de personas) **2** RE-
PLACEMENT : sustitución f, reemplazo
m

display¹ [dɪs'pleɪ] vt : exponer, exhibir,
mostrar

display² n **1** : muestra f, exposición f,
alarde m **2** : visualizador m (de una
computadora)

displease [dɪs'pli:z] vt **-pleased; -pleas-
ing** : desagradar a, disgustar, contrariar

displeasure [dɪs'plɛʒər] *n* : desagrado *m*
disposable [dɪs'po:zəbəl] *adj* 1 : desechable ⟨disposable diapers : pañales
desechables⟩ 2 AVAILABLE : disponible
disposal [dɪs'po:zəl] *n* 1 PLACEMENT
: disposición *f*, colocación *f* 2 RE-
MOVAL : eliminación *f* 3 **to have at
one's disposal** : disponer de, tener a
su disposición
dispose [dɪs'po:z] *v* **-posed; -posing** *vt*
1 ARRANGE : disponer, colocar 2 IN-
CLINE : predisponer — *vi* 1 **to dispose
of** DISCARD : desechar, deshacerse de
2 **to dispose of** HANDLE : despachar
disposition [ˌdɪspə'zɪʃən] *n* 1 AR-
RANGEMENT : disposición *f* 2 TEN-
DENCY : predisposición *f*, inclinación *f*
3 TEMPERAMENT : temperamento *m*,
carácter *m*
dispossess [ˌdɪspə'zɛs] *vt* : deposeer
disproportion [ˌdɪsprə'porʃən] *n* : desproporción *f*
disproportionate [ˌdɪsprə'porʃənət] *adj*
: desproporcionado — **disproportion-
ately** *adv*
disprove [dɪs'pru:v] *vt* **-proved; -prov-
ing** : rebatir, refutar
disputable [dɪs'pju:təbəl, 'dɪspjutəbəl]
adj : disputable, discutible
dispute[1] [dɪs'pju:t] *v* **-puted; -puting** *vt*
1 QUESTION : discutir, cuestionar 2 OP-
POSE : combatir, resistir — *vi* ARGUE,
DEBATE : discutir
dispute[2] *n* 1 DEBATE : debate *m*, discusión *f* 2 QUARREL : disputa *f*, discusión *f*
disqualification [dɪsˌkwɑləfə'keɪʃən] *n*
: descalificación *f*
disqualify [dɪs'kwɑlə,faɪ] *vt* **-fied; -fying**
: descalificar, inhabilitar
disquiet[1] [dɪs'kwaɪət] *vt* : inquietar
disquiet[2] *n* : ansiedad *f*, inquietud *f*
disregard[1] [ˌdɪsrɪ'gɑrd] *vt* : ignorar, no
prestar atención a
disregard[2] *n* : indiferencia *f*
disrepair [ˌdɪsrɪ'pær] *n* : mal estado *m*
disreputable [dɪs'rɛpjutəbəl] *adj* : de
mala fama (dícese de una persona o un
lugar), vergonzoso (dícese de la conducta)
disreputably [dɪs'rɛpjutəbli] *adv* : vergonzosamente
disrepute [ˌdɪsrɪ'pju:t] *n* : descrédito *m*,
mala fama *f*, deshonra *f*
disrespect [ˌdɪsrɪ'spɛkt] *n* : falta *f* de respeto
disrespectful [ˌdɪsrɪ'spɛktfəl] *adj* : irrespetuoso — **disrespectfully** *adv*
disrobe [dɪs'ro:b] *v* **-robed; -robing** *vt*
: desvestir, desnudar — *vi* : desvestirse,
desnudarse
disrupt [dɪs'rʌpt] *vt* : trastornar, perturbar
disruption [dɪs'rʌpʃən] *n* : trastorno *m*
disruptive [dɪs'rʌptɪv] *adj* : perjudicial,
perturbador — **disruptively** *adv*
dissatisfaction [dɪsˌsætəs'fækʃən] *n*
: descontento *m*, insatisfacción *f*

dissatisfied [dɪs'sætəsˌfaɪd] *adj* : descontento, insatisfecho
dissatisfy [dɪs'sætəsˌfaɪ] *vt* **-fied; -fying**
: no contentar, no satisfacer
dissect [dɪ'sɛkt] *vt* : disecar
dissection [dɪ'sɛkʃən] *n* : disección *f*
dissemble [dɪ'sɛmbəl] *v* **-bled; -bling** *vt*
HIDE : ocultar, disimular — *vi* PRE-
TEND : fingir, disimular
disseminate [dɪ'sɛməˌneɪt] *vt* **-nated;
-nating** : diseminar, difundir, divulgar
dissemination [dɪˌsɛmə'neɪʃən] *n* : diseminación *f*, difusión *f*
dissension [dɪ'sɛntʃən] *n* : disensión *f*,
desacuerdo *m*
dissent[1] [dɪ'sɛnt] *vi* : disentir
dissent[2] *n* : disentimiento *m*, disensión
f
dissertation [ˌdɪsər'teɪʃən] *n* 1 DIS-
COURSE : disertación *f*, discurso *m* 2
THESIS : tesis *f*
disservice [dɪs'sərvɪs] *n* : perjuicio *m*
dissident[1] ['dɪsədənt] *adj* : disidente
dissident[2] *n* : disidente *mf*
dissimilar [dɪ'sɪmələr] *adj* : distinto,
diferente, disímil
dissipate ['dɪsəˌpeɪt] *vt* **-pated; -pating**
1 DISPERSE : disipar, dispersar 2
SQUANDER : malgastar, desperdiciar,
derrochar, disipar
dissipation [ˌdɪsə'peɪʃən] *n* : disipación
f, libertinaje *m*
dissociate [dɪ'so:ʃiˌeɪt, -si-] *v* **-ated**
[-ˌeɪtəd]; **-ating** [-ˌeɪtɪŋ] *vt* : disociar ⟨to
disassociate oneself : disociarse⟩ — *vi*
: disociarse
dissociation [dɪˌso:ʃi'eɪʃən, -si-] *n* : disociación *f*
dissolute ['dɪsəˌlu:t] *adj* : disoluto
dissolution [ˌdɪsə'lu:ʃən] *n* : disolución
f
dissolve [dɪ'zɑlv] *v* **-solved; -solving** *vt*
: disolver — *vi* : disolverse
dissonance ['dɪsənənts] *n* : disonancia *f*
dissuade [dɪ'sweɪd] *vt* **-suaded; -suad-
ing** : disuadir
distance[1] ['dɪstənts] *vt* **-tanced** [-təntst];
-tancing [-təntsɪŋ] **to distance oneself**
: distanciarse
distance[2] *n* 1 : distancia *f* ⟨the distance
between two points : la distancia entre
dos puntos⟩ ⟨in the distance : a lo lejos⟩
2 RESERVE : actitud *f* distante, reserva
f ⟨to keep one's distance : guardar las
distancias⟩
distant ['dɪstənt] *adj* 1 FAR : distante, lejano 2 REMOTE : distante, lejano, remoto 3 ALOOF : distante, frío
distantly ['dɪstəntli] *adv* 1 LOOSELY
: aproximadamente, vagamente 2
COLDLY : fríamente, con frialdad
distaste [dɪs'teɪst] *n* : desagrado *m*, aversión *f*
distasteful [dɪs'teɪstfəl] *adj* : desagradable, de mal gusto
distemper [dɪs'tɛmpər] *n* : moquillo *m*
distend [dɪs'tɛnd] *vt* : dilatar, hinchar —
vi : dilatarse, hincharse

distill [dɪ'stɪl] *vt* : destilar
distillation [ˌdɪstə'leɪʃən] *n* : destilación *f*
distiller [dɪ'stɪlər] *n* : destilador *m*, -dora *f*
distillery [dɪ'stɪləri] *n*, *pl* **-ries** [-riz] : destilería *f*
distinct [dɪ'stɪŋkt] *adj* **1** DIFFERENT : distinto, diferente **2** CLEAR, UNMISTAKABLE : marcado, claro, evidente ⟨a distinct possibility : una clara posibilidad⟩
distinction [dɪ'stɪŋkʃən] *n* **1** DIFFERENTIATION : distinción *f* **2** DIFFERENCE : diferencia *f* **3** EXCELLENCE : distinción *f*, excelencia *f* ⟨a writer of distinction : un escritor destacado⟩
distinctive [dɪ'stɪŋktɪv] *adj* : distintivo, característico — **distinctively** *adv*
distinctiveness [dɪ'stɪŋktɪvnəs] *n* : peculiaridad *f*
distinctly [dɪ'stɪŋktli] *adv* : claramente, con claridad
distinguish [dɪs'tɪŋgwɪʃ] *vt* **1** DIFFERENTIATE : distinguir, diferenciar **2** DISCERN : distinguir ⟨he distinguished the sound of the piano : distinguió el sonido del piano⟩ **3** to distinguish oneself : señalarse, distinguirse — *vi* DISCRIMINATE : distinguir
distinguishable [dɪs'tɪŋgwɪʃəbəl] *adj* : distinguible
distinguished [dɪs'tɪŋgwɪʃt] *adj* : distinguido
distort [dɪ'stɔrt] *vt* **1** MISREPRESENT : distorsionar, tergiversar **2** DEFORM : distorsionar, deformar
distortion [dɪ'stɔrʃən] *n* : distorsión *f*, deformación *f*, tergiversación *f*
distract [dɪ'strækt] *vt* : distraer, entretener
distracted [dɪ'stræktəd] *adj* : distraído
distraction [dɪ'strækʃən] *n* **1** INTERRUPTION : distracción *f*, interrupción *f* **2** CONFUSION : confusión *f* **3** AMUSEMENT : diversión *f*, entretenimiento *m*, distracción *f*
distraught [dɪ'strɔt] *adj* : afligido, turbado
distress[1] [dɪ'strɛs] *vt* : afligir, darle pena (a alguien), hacer sufrir
distress[2] *n* **1** SORROW : dolor *m*, angustia *f*, aflicción *f* **2** PAIN : dolor *m* **3** in ~ : en peligro
distressful [dɪ'strɛsfəl] *adj* : doloroso, penoso
distribute [dɪ'strɪˌbjuːt, -bjʊt] *vt* **-uted; -uting** : distribuir, repartir
distribution [ˌdɪstrə'bjuːʃən] *n* : distribución *f*, reparto *m*
distributive [dɪ'strɪbjʊtɪv] *adj* : distributivo
distributor [dɪ'strɪbjʊtər] *n* : distribuidor *m*, -dora *f*
district ['dɪsˌtrɪkt] *n* **1** REGION : región *f*, zona *f*, barrio *m* (de una ciudad) **2** : distrito *m* (zona política)
distrust[1] [dɪs'trʌst] *vt* : desconfiar de

distrust[2] *n* : desconfianza *f*, recelo *m*
distrustful [dɪs'trʌstfəl] *adj* : desconfiado, receloso, suspicaz
disturb [dɪ'stərb] *vt* **1** BOTHER : molestar, perturbar ⟨sorry to disturb you : perdone la molestia⟩ **2** DISARRANGE : desordenar **3** WORRY : inquietar, preocupar **4** to disturb the peace : alterar el orden público
disturbance [dɪ'stərbənts] *n* **1** COMMOTION : alboroto *m*, disturbio *m* **2** INTERRUPTION : interrupción *f*
disuse [dɪs'juːs] *n* : desuso *m*
ditch[1] ['dɪtʃ] *vt* **1** : cavar zanjas en **2** DISCARD : deshacerse de, botar
ditch[2] *n* : zanja *f*, fosa *f*, cuneta *f* (en una carretera)
dither ['dɪðər] *n* **to be in a dither** : estar nervioso, ponerse como loco
ditto ['dɪtoː] *n*, *pl* **-tos** **1** : lo mismo, ídem *m* **2** **ditto marks** : comillas *fpl*
ditty ['dɪti] *n*, *pl* **-ties** : canción *f* corta y simple
diurnal [daɪ'ərnəl] *adj* **1** DAILY : diario, cotidiano **2** : diurno ⟨a diurnal animal : un animal diurno⟩
divan ['daɪˌvæn, dɪ'-] *n* : diván *m*
dive[1] ['daɪv] *vi* **dived** *or* **dove** ['doːv]; **dived; diving 1** PLUNGE : tirarse al agua, zambullirse, dar un clavado **2** SUBMERGE : sumergirse **3** DROP : bajar en picada (dícese de un avión), caer en picada
dive[2] *n* **1** PLUNGE : zambullida *f*, clavado *m* (en el agua) **2** DESCENT : descenso *m* en picada **3** BAR, JOINT : antro *m*
diver ['daɪvər] *n* : saltador *m*, -dora *f*; clavadista *mf*
diverge [də'vərdʒ, daɪ-] *vi* **-verged; -verging 1** SEPARATE : divergir, separarse **2** DIFFER : divergir, discrepar
divergence [də'vərdʒənts, daɪ-] *n* : divergencia *f* — **divergent** [-ənt] *adj*
diverse [daɪ'vərs, də-, 'daɪˌvərs] *adj* : diverso, variado
diversification [daɪˌvərsəfə'keɪʃən, də-] *n* : diversificación *f*
diversify [daɪ'vərsəˌfaɪ, də-] *vt* **-fied; -fying** : diversificar, variar
diversion [daɪ'vərʒən, də-] *n* **1** DEVIATION : desviación *f* **2** AMUSEMENT, DISTRACTION : diversión *f*, distracción *f*, entretenimiento *m*
diversity [daɪ'vərsəti, də-] *n*, *pl* **-ties** : diversidad *f*
divert [də'vərt, daɪ-] *vt* **1** DEFLECT : desviar **2** DISTRACT : distraer **3** AMUSE : divertir, entretener
divest [daɪ'vɛst, də-] *vt* **1** UNDRESS : desnudar, desvestir **2** **to divest of** : despojar de
divide [də'vaɪd] *v* **-vided; -viding** *vt* **1** HALVE : dividir, partir por la mitad **2** SHARE : repartir, dividir **3** : dividir (números) — *vi* : dividirse, dividir (en matemáticas)

dividend ['dɪvə‚dɛnd, -dənd] *n* **1** : dividendo *m* (en finanzas) **2** BONUS : benefício *m*, provecho *m* **3** : dividendo *m* (en matemáticas)

divider [dɪ'vaɪdər] *n* **1** : separador *m* (para ficheros, etc.) **2** *or* **room divider** : mampara *f*, biombo *m*

divination [‚dɪvə'neɪʃən] *n* : adivinación *f*

divine[1] [də'vaɪn] *adj* **-viner; -est** **1** : divino **2** SUPERB : divino, espléndido — **divinely** *adv*

divine[2] *n* : clérigo *m*, eclesiástico *m*

divinity [də'vɪnəti] *n, pl* **-ties** : divinidad *f*

divisible [dɪ'vɪzəbəl] *adj* : divisible

division [dɪ'vɪʒən] *n* **1** DISTRIBUTION : división *f*, reparto *m* ⟨division of labor : distribución del trabajo⟩ **2** PART : división *f*, sección *f* **3** : división *f* (en matemáticas)

divisive [də'vaɪsɪv] *adj* : divisivo

divisor [dɪ'vaɪzər] *n* : divisor *m*

divorce[1] [də'vors] *v* **-vorced; -vorcing** *vt* : divorciar — *vi* : divorciarse

divorce[2] *n* : divorcio *m*

divorcé [dɪ‚vor'seɪ, -'si:; -'vor‚-] *n* : divorciado *m*

divorcée [dɪ‚vor'seɪ, -'si:; -'vor‚-] *n* : divorciada *f*

divulge [də'vʌlʤ, daɪ-] *vt* **-vulged; -vulging** : revelar, divulgar

dizzily ['dɪzəli] *adv* : vertiginosamente

dizziness ['dɪzinəs] *n* : mareo *m*, vahído *m*, vértigo *m*

dizzy ['dɪzi] *adj* **dizzier; -est** **1** : mareado ⟨I feel dizzy : estoy mareado⟩ **2** : vertiginoso ⟨a dizzy speed : una velocidad vertiginosa⟩

DNA [‚di:‚ɛn'eɪ] *n* : ADN *m*

do ['du:] *v* **did** ['dɪd]; **done** ['dʌn]; **doing; does** ['dʌz] *vt* **1** CARRY OUT, PERFORM : hacer, realizar, llevar a cabo ⟨she did her best : hizo todo lo posible⟩ **2** PREPARE : preparar, hacer ⟨do your homework : haz tu tarea⟩ **3** ARRANGE : arreglar, peinar (el pelo) **4 to do in** RUIN : estropear, arruinar **5 to do in** KILL : matar, liquidar *fam* — *vi* **1** : hacer ⟨you did well : hiciste bien⟩ **2** FARE : estar, ir, andar ⟨how are you doing? : ¿cómo estás?, ¿cómo te va?⟩ **3** FINISH : terminar ⟨now I'm done : ya terminé⟩ **4** SERVE : servir, ser suficiente, alcanzar ⟨this will do for now : esto servirá por el momento⟩ **5 to do away with** ABOLISH : abolir, suprimir **6 to do away with** KILL : eliminar, matar **7 to do by** TREAT : tratar ⟨he does well by her : él la trata bien⟩ — *v aux* **1** (*used in interrogative sentences and negative statements*) ⟨do you know her? : ¿la conoces?⟩ ⟨I don't like that : a mí no me gusta eso⟩ **2** (*used for emphasis*) ⟨I do hope you'll come : espero que vengas⟩ **3** (*used as a substitute verb to avoid repetition*) ⟨do you speak English? yes, I do : ¿habla inglés? sí⟩

docile ['dɑsəl] *adj* : dócil, sumiso

dock[1] ['dɑk] *vt* **1** CUT : cortar **2** : descontar dinero de (un sueldo) — *vi* ANCHOR, LAND : fondear, atracar

dock[2] *n* **1** PIER : atracadero *m* **2** WHARF : muelle *m* **3** : banquillo *m* de los acusados (en un tribunal)

doctor[1] ['dɑktər] *vt* **1** TREAT : tratar, curar **2** ALTER : adulterar, alterar, falsificar (un documento)

doctor[2] *n* **1** : doctor *m*, -tora *f* ⟨Doctor of Philosophy : doctor en filosofía⟩ **2** PHYSICIAN : médico *m*, -ca *f*; doctor *m*, -tora *f*

doctorate ['dɑktərət] *n* : doctorado *m*

doctrine ['dɑktrɪn] *n* : doctrina *f*

document[1] ['dɑkju‚mɛnt] *vt* : documentar

document[2] ['dɑkjumənt] *n* : documento *m*

documentary[1] [‚dɑkju'mɛntəri] *adj* : documental

documentary[2] *n, pl* **-ries** : documental *m*

documentation [‚dɑkjumən'teɪʃən] *n* : documentación *f*

dodge[1] ['dɑʤ] *v* **dodged; dodging** *vt* : esquivar, eludir, evadir (impuestos) — *vi* : echarse a un lado

dodge[2] *n* **1** RUSE : truco *m*, treta *f*, artimaña *f* **2** EVASION : regate *m*, evasión *f*

dodo ['do:‚do:] *n, pl* **-does** *or* **-dos** : dodo *m*

doe ['do:] *n, pl* **does** *or* **doe** : gama *f*, cierva *f*

doer ['du:ər] *n* : hacedor *m*, -dora *f*

does → **do**

doff ['dɑf, 'dɔf] *vt* : quitarse ⟨to doff one's hat : quitarse el sombrero⟩

dog[1] ['dɔg, 'dɑg] *vt* **dogged; dogging** : seguir de cerca, perseguir, acosar ⟨to dog someone's footsteps : seguir los pasos de alguien⟩ ⟨dogged by bad luck : perseguido por la mala suerte⟩

dog[2] *n* : perro *m*, -rra *f*

dogcatcher ['dɔg‚kætʃər] *n* : perrero *m*, -ra *f*

dog-eared ['dɔg‚ɪrd] *adj* : con las esquinas dobladas

dogged ['dɔgəd] *adj* : tenaz, terco, obstinado

doggy ['dɔgi] *n, pl* **doggies** : perrito *m*, -ta *f*

doghouse ['dɔg‚haʊs] *n* : casita *f* de perro

dogma ['dɔgmə] *n* : dogma *m*

dogmatic [dɔg'mætɪk] *adj* : dogmático

dogmatism ['dɔgmə‚tɪzəm] *n* : dogmatismo *m*

dogwood ['dɔg‚wʊd] *n* : cornejo *m*

doily ['dɔɪli] *n, pl* **-lies** : pañito *m*

doings ['du:ɪŋz] *npl* : eventos *mpl*, actividades *fpl*

doldrums ['do:ldrəmz, 'dɑl-] *npl* **1** : zona *f* de las calmas ecuatoriales **2 to be in the doldrums** : estar abatido (dícese de una persona), estar estancado (dícese de una empresa)

dole ['do:l] *n* **1** ALMS : distribución *f* a los necesitados, limosna *f* **2** : subsidios *mpl* de desempleo

doleful ['do:lfəl] *adj* : triste, lúgubre

dolefully ['do:lfəli] *adv* : con pesar, de manera triste

dole out *vt* **doled out; doling out** : repartir

doll ['dɑl, 'dɔl] *n* : muñeco *m*, -ca *f*

dollar ['dɑlər] *n* : dólar *m*

dolly ['dɑli] *n, pl* **-lies** **1** → **doll** **2** : plataforma *f* rodante

dolphin ['dɑlfən, 'dɔl-] *n* : delfín *m*

dolt ['do:lt] *n* : imbécil *mf*; tonto *m*, -ta *f*

domain [do'meɪn, də-] *n* **1** TERRITORY : dominio *m*, territorio *m* **2** FIELD : campo *m*, esfera *f*, ámbito *m* ⟨the domain of art : el ámbito de las artes⟩

dome ['do:m] *n* : cúpula *f*, bóveda *f*

domestic[1] [də'mɛstɪk] *adj* **1** HOUSEHOLD : doméstico, casero **2** : nacional, interno ⟨domestic policy : política interna⟩ **3** TAME : domesticado

domestic[2] *n* : empleado *m* doméstico, empleada *f* doméstica

domestically [də'mɛstɪkli] *adv* : domésticamente

domesticate [də'mɛstɪˌkeɪt] *vt* **-cated; -cating** : domesticar

domicile ['dɑməˌsaɪl, 'do:-; 'dɑməsɪl] *n* : domicilio *m*

dominance ['dɑmənənts] *n* : dominio *m*, dominación *f*

dominant ['dɑmənənt] *adj* : dominante

dominate ['dɑməˌneɪt] *v* **-nated; -nating** : dominar

domination [ˌdɑmə'neɪʃən] *n* : dominación *f*

domineer [ˌdɑmə'nɪr] *vt* : dominar sobre, avasallar, tiranizar

Dominican [də'mɪnɪkən] *n* : dominicano *m*, -na *f* — **Dominican** *adj*

dominion [də'mɪnjən] *n* **1** POWER : dominio *m* **2** DOMAIN, TERRITORY : dominio *m*, territorio *m*

domino ['dɑməˌno:] *n, pl* **-noes** *or* **-nos** **1** : dominó *m* **2 dominoes** *npl* : dominó *m* (juego)

don ['dɑn] *vt* **donned; donning** : ponerse

donate ['do:ˌneɪt, do:'-] *vt* **-nated; -nating** : donar, hacer un donativo de

donation [do:'neɪʃən] *n* : donación *f*, donativo *m*

done[1] ['dʌn] → **do**

done[2] *adj* **1** FINISHED : terminado, acabado, concluido **2** COOKED : cocinado

donkey ['dɑŋki, 'dʌŋ-] *n, pl* **-keys** : burro *m*, asno *m*

donor ['do:nər] *n* : donante *mf*; donador *m*, -dora *f*

don't ['do:nt] (*contraction* of **do not**) → **do**

doodle[1] ['du:dəl] *v* **-dled; -dling** : garabatear

doodle[2] *n* : garabato *m*

doom[1] ['du:m] *vt* : condenar

doom[2] *n* **1** JUDGMENT : sentencia *f*, condena *f* **2** DEATH : muerte *f* **3** FATE : destino *m* **4** RUIN : perdición *f*, ruina *f*

door ['dor] *n* : puerta *f*

doorbell ['dor,bɛl] *n* : timbre *m*

doorknob ['dor,nɑb] *n* : pomo *m*, perilla *f*

doorman ['dormən] *n, pl* **-men** [-mən, -,mɛn] : portero *m*

doormat ['dor,mæt] : felpudo *m*

doorstep ['dor,stɛp] *n* : umbral *m*

doorway ['dor,weɪ] *n* : entrada *f*, portal *m*

dope[1] ['do:p] *vt* **doped; doping** : drogar, narcotizar

dope[2] *n* **1** DRUG : droga *f*, estupefaciente *m*, narcótico *m* **2** IDIOT : idiota *mf*; tonto *m*, -ta *f* **3** INFORMATION : información *f*

dormant ['dɔrmənt] *adj* : inactivo, latente

dormer ['dɔrmər] *n* : buhardilla *f*

dormitory ['dɔrmə,tori] *n, pl* **-ries** : dormitorio *m*, residencia *f* de estudiantes

dormouse ['dɔr,maʊs] *n* : lirón *m*

dorsal ['dɔrsəl] *adj* : dorsal — **dorsally** *adv*

dory ['dori] *n, pl* **-ries** : bote *m* de fondo plano

dosage ['do:sɪdʒ] *n* : dosis *f*

dose[1] ['do:s] *vt* **dosed; dosing** : medicinar

dose[2] *n* : dosis *f*

dossier ['dɔs,jeɪ, 'dɑs-] *n* : dossier *m*

dot[1] ['dɑt] *vt* **dotted; dotting** **1** : poner el punto sobre (una letra) **2** SCATTER : esparcir, salpicar

dot[2] *n* : punto *m* ⟨at six on the dot : a las seis en punto⟩ ⟨dots and dashes : puntos y rayas⟩

dote ['do:t] *vi* **doted; doting** : chochear

double[1] ['dʌbəl] *v* **-bled; -bling** *vt* **1** : doblar, duplicar (una cantidad), redoblar (esfuerzos) **2** FOLD : doblar, plegar **3 to double one's fist** : apretar el puño — *vi* **1** : doblarse, duplicarse **2 to double over** : retorcerse

double[2] *adj* : doble — **doubly** *adv*

double[3] *n* : doble *mf*

double bass *n* : contrabajo *m*

double–cross [ˌdʌbəl'krɔs] *vt* : traicionar

double–crosser [ˌdʌbəl'krɔsər] *n* : traidor *m*, -dora *f*

double–jointed [ˌdʌbəl'dʒɔɪntəd] *adj* : con articulaciones dobles

double–talk ['dʌbəl,tɔk] *n* : ambigüedades *fpl*, lenguaje *m* con doble sentido

doubt[1] ['daʊt] *vt* **1** QUESTION : dudar de, cuestionar **2** DISTRUST : desconfiar de **3** : dudar, creer poco probable ⟨I doubt it very much : lo dudo mucho⟩

doubt[2] *n* **1** UNCERTAINTY : duda *f*, incertidumbre *f* **2** DISTRUST : desconfianza *f* **3** SKEPTICISM : duda *f*, escepticismo *m*

doubtful ['daʊtfəl] *adj* **1** QUESTIONABLE : dudoso **2** UNCERTAIN : dudoso, incierto

doubtfully ['daʊtfəli] *adv* : dudosamente, sin estar convencido

doubtless ['daʊtləs] *or* **doubtlessly** *adv* : sin duda

douche¹ ['duːʃ] *vt* **douched; douching** : irrigar

douche² *n* : ducha *f*, irrigación *f*

dough ['doː] *n* : masa *f*

doughnut *or* **donut** ['doːˌnʌt] *n* : rosquilla *f*, dona *f* *Mex*

doughty ['daʊti] *adj* **-tier; -est** : fuerte, valiente

dour ['daʊər, 'dʊr] *adj* **1** STERN : severo, adusto **2** SULLEN : hosco, taciturno — **dourly** *adv*

douse ['daʊs, 'daʊz] *vt* **doused; dousing 1** DRENCH : empapar, mojar **2** EXTINGUISH : extinguir, apagar

dove¹ ['doːv] → dive

dove² ['dʌv] *n* : paloma *f*

dovetail ['dʌvˌteɪl] *vi* : encajar, enlazar

dowdy ['daʊdi] *adj* **dowdier; -est** : sin gracia, poco elegante

dowel ['daʊəl] *n* : clavija *f*

down¹ ['daʊn] *vt* **1** FELL : tumbar, derribar, abatir **2** DEFEAT : derrotar

down² *adv* **1** DOWNWARD : hacia abajo **2 to lie down** : acostarse, echarse **3 to put down (money)** : pagar un depósito (de dinero) **4 to sit down** : sentarse **5 to take down, to write down** : apuntar, anotar

down³ *adj* **1** DESCENDING : de bajada ⟨the down elevator : el ascensor de bajada⟩ **2** REDUCED : reducido, rebajado ⟨attendance is down : la concurrencia ha disminuido⟩ **3** DOWNCAST : abatido, deprimido

down⁴ *n* **1** : plumón *m* **2** : down *m* (en deportes) **3 ups and downs** : altibajos *mpl*

down⁵ *prep* **1** : (hacia) abajo ⟨down the mountain : montaña abajo⟩ ⟨I walked down the stairs : bajé por la escalera⟩ **2** ALONG : por, a lo largo de ⟨we ran down the beach : corrimos por la playa⟩ **3** : a través de ⟨down the years : a través de los años⟩

downcast ['daʊnˌkæst] *adj* **1** SAD : triste, abatido **2 with downcast eyes** : con los ojos bajos, con los ojos mirando al suelo

downfall ['daʊnˌfɔl] *n* : ruina *f*, perdición *f*

downgrade¹ ['daʊnˌgreɪd] *vt* **-graded; -grading** : bajar de categoría

downgrade² *n* : bajada *f*

downhearted ['daʊnˌhɑrtəd] *adj* : desanimado, descorazonado

downhill ['daʊn'hɪl] *adv & adj* : cuesta abajo

download¹ ['daʊnˌloːd] *vt* : descargar (un archivo)

download² *n* : descarga *f* (de archivos, etc.)

down payment *n* : entrega *f* inicial

downplay ['daʊnˌpleɪ] *vt* : minimizar

downpour ['daʊnˌpor] *n* : aguacero *m*, chaparrón *m*

downright¹ ['daʊnˌraɪt] *adv* THOROUGHLY : absolutamente, completamente

downright² *adj* : patente, manifiesto, absoluto ⟨a downright refusal : un rechazo categórico⟩

downside ['daʊnˌsaɪd] *n* : desventaja *f*

downstairs¹ ['daʊn'stærz] *adv* : abajo

downstairs² ['daʊnˌstærz] *adj* : del piso de abajo

downstairs³ ['daʊn'stærz, -ˌstærz] *n* : planta *f* baja

downstream ['daʊn'striːm] *adv* : río abajo

down–to–earth [ˌdaʊntu'ərth] *adj* : práctico, realista

downtown¹ [ˌdaʊn'taʊn] *adv* : hacia el centro, al centro, en el centro (de la ciudad)

downtown² *adj* : del centro (de la ciudad) ⟨downtown Chicago : el centro de Chicago⟩

downtown³ [ˌdaʊn'taʊn, 'daʊnˌtaʊn] *n* : centro *m* (de la ciudad)

downtrodden ['daʊnˌtrɑdən] *adj* : oprimido

downward ['daʊnwərd] *or* **downwards** [-wərdz] *adv & adj* : hacia abajo

downwind ['daʊn'wɪnd] *adv & adj* : en la dirección del viento

downy ['daʊni] *adj* **downier; -est 1** : cubierto de plumón, plumoso **2** VELVETY : aterciopelado, velloso

dowry ['daʊri] *n, pl* **-ries** : dote *f*

doze¹ ['doːz] *vi* **dozed; dozing** : dormitar

doze² *n* : sueño *m* ligero, cabezada *f*

dozen ['dʌzən] *n, pl* **dozens** *or* **dozen** : docena *f*

drab ['dræb] *adj* **drabber; drabbest 1** BROWNISH : pardo **2** DULL, LACKLUSTER : monótono, gris, deslustrado

draft¹ ['dræft, 'draft] *vt* **1** CONSCRIPT : reclutar **2** COMPOSE, SKETCH : hacer el borrador de, redactar

draft² *adj* **1** : de barril ⟨draft beer : cerveza de barril⟩ **2** : de tiro ⟨draft horses : caballos de tiro⟩

draft³ *n* **1** HAULAGE : tiro *m* **2** DRINK, GULP : trago *m* **3** OUTLINE, SKETCH : bosquejo *m*, borrador *m*, versión *f* **4** : corriente *f* de aire, chiflón *m*, tiro *m* (de una chimenea) **5** CONSCRIPTION : conscripción *f* **6 bank draft** : giro *m* bancario, letra *f* de cambio

draftee [dræf'tiː] *n* : recluta *mf*

draftsman ['dræftsmən] *n, pl* **-men** [-mən, -ˌmɛn] : dibujante *mf*

drafty ['dræfti] *adj* **draftier; -est** : con corrientes de aire

drag¹ ['dræg] *v* **dragged; dragging** *vt* **1** HAUL : arrastrar, jalar **2** DREDGE : dragar — *vi* **1** TRAIL : arrastrarse **2** LAG : rezagarse **3** : hacerse pesado, hacerse largo ⟨the day dragged on : el día se hizo largo⟩

drag² *n* **1** RESISTANCE : resistencia *f* (aerodinámica) **2** HINDRANCE : traba *f*, estorbo *m* **3** BORE : pesadez *f*, plomo *m fam*

dragnet ['dræg,nɛt] *n* **1** : red *f* barredera (en pesca) **2** : operativo *m* policial de captura

dragon ['drægən] *n* : dragón *m*

dragonfly ['drægən,flaɪ] *n, pl* **-flies** : libélula *f*

drain¹ ['dreɪn] *vt* **1** EMPTY : vaciar, drenar **2** EXHAUST : agotar, consumir — *vi* **1** : escurrir, escurrirse ⟨the dishes are draining : los platos están escurriéndose⟩ **2** EMPTY : desaguar **3 to drain away** : irse agotando

drain² *n* **1** : desagüe *m* **2** SEWER : alcantarilla *f* **3** GRATING : sumidero *m*, resumidero *m*, rejilla *f* **4** EXHAUSTION : agotamiento *m*, disminución *f* (de energía, etc.) ⟨to be a drain on : agotar, consumir⟩ **5 to throw down the drain** : tirar por la ventana

drainage ['dreɪnɪdʒ] *n* : desagüe *m*, drenaje *m*

drainpipe ['dreɪn,paɪp] *n* : tubo *m* de desagüe, caño *m*

drake ['dreɪk] *n* : pato *m* (macho)

drama ['drɑmə, 'dræ-] *n* **1** THEATER : drama *m*, teatro *m* **2** PLAY : obra *f* de teatro, drama *m*

dramatic [drə'mætɪk] *adj* : dramático — **dramatically** [-tɪkli] *adv*

dramatist ['dræmətɪst, 'drɑ-] *n* : dramaturgo *m*, -ga *f*

dramatization [,dræmətə'zeɪʃən, ,drɑ-] *n* : dramatización *f*

dramatize ['dræmə,taɪz, 'drɑ-] *vt* **-tized; -tizing** : dramatizar

drank → **drink**

drape¹ ['dreɪp] *vt* **draped; draping 1** COVER : cubrir (con tela) **2** HANG : drapear, disponer los pliegues de

drape² *n* **1** HANG : caída *f* **2 drapes** *npl* : cortinas *fpl*

drapery ['dreɪpəri] *n, pl* **-eries 1** CLOTH : pañería *f*, tela *f* para cortinas **2 draperies** *npl* : cortinas *fpl*

drastic ['dræstɪk] *adj* **1** HARSH, SEVERE : drástico, severo **2** EXTREME : radical, excepcional — **drastically** [-tɪkli] *adv*

draught ['dræft, 'draft] *n* → **draft³**

draughty ['drafti] → **drafty**

draw¹ ['drɔ] *v* **drew** ['dru:]; **drawn** ['drɔn]; **drawing** *vt* **1** PULL : tirar de, jalar, correr (cortinas) **2** ATTRACT : atraer **3** PROVOKE : provocar, suscitar **4** INHALE : aspirar ⟨to draw breath : respirar⟩ **5** EXTRACT : sacar, extraer **6** TAKE : sacar ⟨to draw a number : sacar un número⟩ **7** COLLECT : cobrar, percibir (un sueldo, etc.) **8** BEND : tensar (un arco) **9** TIE : empatar (en deportes) **10** SKETCH : dibujar, trazar **11** FORMULATE : sacar, formular, llegar a ⟨to draw a conclusion : llegar a

una conclusión⟩ **12 to draw out** : hacer hablar (sobre algo), hacer salir de sí mismo **13 to draw up** DRAFT : redactar — *vi* **1** SKETCH : dibujar **2** TUG : tirar, jalar **3 to draw near** : acercarse **4 to draw to a close** : terminar, finalizar **5 to draw up** STOP : parar

draw² *n* **1** DRAWING, RAFFLE : sorteo *m* **2** TIE : empate *m* **3** ATTRACTION : atracción *f* **4** PUFF : chupada *f* (de un cigarrillo, etc.)

drawback ['drɔ,bæk] *n* : desventaja *f*, inconveniente *m*

drawbridge ['drɔ,brɪdʒ] *n* : puente *m* levadizo

drawer ['drɔr, 'drɔər] *n* **1** ILLUSTRATOR : dibujante *mf* **2** : gaveta *f*, cajón *m* (en un mueble) **3 drawers** *npl* UNDERPANTS : calzones *mpl*

drawing ['drɔɪŋ] *n* **1** LOTTERY : sorteo *m*, lotería *f* **2** SKETCH : dibujo *m*, bosquejo *m*

drawl¹ ['drɔl] *vi* : hablar arrastrando las palabras

drawl² *n* : habla *f* lenta y con vocales prolongadas

dread¹ ['drɛd] *vt* : tenerle pavor a, temer

dread² *adj* : pavoroso, aterrado

dread³ *n* : pavor *m*, temor *m*

dreadful ['drɛdfəl] *adj* **1** DREAD : pavoroso **2** TERRIBLE : espantoso, atroz, terrible — **dreadfully** *adv*

dream¹ ['dri:m] *v* **dreamed** ['drɛmpt, 'dri:md] *or* **dreamt** ['drɛmpt]; **dreaming** *vi* **1** : soñar ⟨to dream about : soñar con⟩ **2** FANTASIZE : fantasear — *vt* **1** : soñar **2** IMAGINE : imaginarse **3 to dream up** : inventar, idear

dream² *n* **1** : sueño *m*, ensueño *m* **2 bad dream** NIGHTMARE : pesadilla *f*

dreamer ['dri:mər] *n* : soñador *m*, -dora *f*

dreamlike ['dri:m,laɪk] *adj* : de ensueño

dreamy ['dri:mi] *adj* **dreamier; -est 1** DISTRACTED : soñador, distraído **2** DREAMLIKE : de ensueño **3** MARVELOUS : maravilloso

drearily ['drɪrəli] *adv* : sombríamente

dreary ['drɪri] *adj* **-rier; -est** : deprimente, lóbrego, sombrío

dredge¹ ['drɛdʒ] *vt* **dredged; dredging 1** DIG : dragar **2** COAT : espolvorear, enharinar

dredge² *n* : draga *f*

dredger ['drɛdʒər] *n* : draga *f*

dregs ['drɛgz] *npl* **1** LEES : posos *mpl*, heces *fpl* (de un líquido) **2** : heces *fpl*, escoria *f* ⟨the dregs of society : la escoria de la sociedad⟩

drench ['drɛntʃ] *vt* : empapar, mojar, calar

dress¹ ['drɛs] *vt* **1** CLOTHE : vestir **2** DECORATE : decorar, adornar **3** : preparar (pollo o pescado), aliñar (ensalada) **4** : curar, vendar (una herida) **5** FERTILIZE : abonar (la tierra) — *vi* **1** : vestirse **2 to dress up** : ataviarse, engalanarse, ponerse de etiqueta

dress² *n* **1** APPAREL : indumentaria *f*, ropa *f* **2** : vestido *m*, traje *m* (de mujer)

dresser ['drɛsər] *n* : cómoda *f* con espejo

dressing ['drɛsɪŋ] *n* **1** : vestirse *m* **2** : aderezo *m*, aliño *m* (de ensalada), relleno *m* (de pollo) **3** BANDAGE : vendaje *m*, gasa *f*

dressmaker ['drɛs,meɪkər] *n* : modista *mf*

dressmaking ['drɛs,meɪkɪŋ] *n* : costura *f*

dressy ['drɛsi] *adj* **dressier; -est** : de mucho vestir, elegante

drew → **draw**

dribble¹ ['drɪbəl] *vi* **-bled; -bling 1** DRIP : gotear **2** DROOL : babear **3** : driblar (en basquetbol)

dribble² *n* **1** TRICKLE : goteo *m*, hilo *m* **2** DROOL : baba *f* **3** : drible *m* (en basquetbol)

drier → **dry²**, **dryer**

driest *adj* → **dry²**

drift¹ ['drɪft] *vi* **1** : dejarse llevar por la corriente, ir a la deriva (dícese de un bote), ir sin rumbo (dícese de una persona) **2** ACCUMULATE : amontonarse, acumularse, apilarse

drift² *n* **1** DRIFTING : deriva *f* **2** HEAP, MASS : montón *m* (de arena, etc.), ventisquero *m* (de nieve) **3** MEANING : sentido *m*

drifter ['drɪftər] *n* : vagabundo *m*, -da *f*

driftwood ['drɪft,wʊd] *n* : madera *f* flotante

drill¹ ['drɪl] *vt* **1** BORE : perforar, taladrar **2** INSTRUCT : instruir por repetición — *vi* **1** TRAIN : entrenarse **2 to drill for oil** : perforar en busca de petróleo

drill² *n* **1** : taladro *m*, barrena *f* **2** EXERCISE, PRACTICE : ejercicio *m*, instrucción *f*

drily → **dryly**

drink¹ ['drɪŋk] *v* **drank** ['dræŋk]; **drunk** ['drʌŋk] *or* **drank; drinking** *vt* **1** IMBIBE : beber, tomar **2 to drink up** ABSORB : absorber — *vi* **1** : beber **2** : beber alcohol, tomar

drink² *n* **1** : bebida *f* **2** : bebida *f* alcohólica

drinkable ['drɪŋkəbəl] *adj* : potable

drinker ['drɪŋkər] *n* : bebedor *m*, -dora *f*

drip¹ ['drɪp] *vi* **dripped; dripping** : gotear, chorrear

drip² *n* **1** DROP : gota *f* **2** DRIPPING : goteo *m*

drive¹ ['draɪv] *v* **drove** ['droːv]; **driven** ['drɪvən]; **driving** *vt* **1** IMPEL : impeler, impulsar **2** OPERATE : guiar, conducir, manejar (un vehículo) **3** COMPEL : obligar, forzar **4** : clavar, hincar ⟨to drive a stake : clavar una estaca⟩ **5** *or* **to drive away** : ahuyentar, echar **6 to drive crazy** : volver loco — *vi* : manejar, conducir ⟨do you know how to drive? : ¿sabes manejar?⟩

drive² *n* **1** RIDE : paseo *m* en coche **2** CAMPAIGN : campaña *f* ⟨fund-raising drive : campaña para recaudar fondos⟩ **3** DRIVEWAY : camino *m* de entrada, entrada *f* **4** TRANSMISSION : transmisión *f* ⟨front-wheel drive : tracción delantera⟩ **5** ENERGY : dinamismo *m*, energía *f* **6** INSTINCT, NEED : instinto *m*, necesidad *f* básica **7** → **disk drive**

drivel ['drɪvəl] *n* : tontería *f*, estupidez *f*

driver ['draɪvər] *n* : conductor *m*, -tora *f*; chofer *m*

driveway ['draɪv,weɪ] *n* : camino *m* de entrada, entrada *f* (para coches)

drizzle¹ ['drɪzəl] *vi* **-zled; -zling** : lloviznar, garuar

drizzle² *n* : llovizna *f*, garúa *f*

droll ['droːl] *adj* : cómico, gracioso, chistoso — **drolly** *adv*

dromedary ['drɑmə,dɛri] *n*, *pl* **-daries** : dromedario *m*

drone¹ ['droːn] *vi* **droned; droning 1** BUZZ : zumbar **2** MURMUR : hablar con monotonía, murmurar

drone² *n* **1** : zángano *m* (abeja) **2** FREELOADER : gorrón *m*, -rrona *f fam*; parásito *m*, -ta *f* **3** BUZZ, HUM : zumbido *m*, murmullo *m*

drool¹ ['druːl] *vi* : babear

drool² *n* : baba *f*

droop ['druːp] *vi* **1** HANG : inclinarse (dícese de la cabeza), encorvarse (dícese de los escombros), marchitarse (dícese de las flores) **2** FLAG : decaer, flaquear ⟨his spirits drooped : se desanimó⟩

droop² *n* : inclinación *f*, caída *f*

drop¹ ['drɑp] *v* **dropped; dropping** *vt* **1** : dejar caer, soltar ⟨she dropped the glass : se le cayó el vaso⟩ ⟨to drop a hint : dejar caer una indirecta⟩ **2** SEND : mandar ⟨drop me a line : mándame unas líneas⟩ **3** ABANDON : abandonar, dejar ⟨to drop the subject : cambiar de tema⟩ **4** LOWER : bajar ⟨he dropped his voice : bajó la voz⟩ **5** OMIT : omitir **6 to drop off** : dejar — *vi* **1** DRIP : gotear **2** FALL : caer(se) **3** DECREASE, DESCEND : bajar, descender ⟨the wind dropped : amainó el viento⟩ **4 to drop back** *or* **to drop behind** : rezagarse, quedarse atrás **5 to drop by** *or* **to drop in** : pasar

drop² *n* **1** : gota *f* (de líquido) **2** DECLINE : caída *f*, bajada *f*, descenso *m* **3** INCLINE : caída *f*, pendiente *f* ⟨a 20-foot drop : una caída de 20 pies⟩ **4** SWEET : pastilla *f*, dulce *m* **5 drops** *npl* : gotas *fpl* (de medicina)

droplet ['drɑplət] *n* : gotita *f*

dropper ['drɑpər] *n* : gotero *m*, cuentagotas *m*

dross ['drɑs, 'drɔs] *n* : escoria *f*

drought ['draʊt] *n* : sequía *f*

drove¹ → **drive**

drove² ['droːv] *n* : multitud *f*, gentío *m*, manada *f* (de ganado) ⟨in droves : en manada⟩

drown ['draʊn] *vt* **1** : ahogar **2** INUN-DATE : anegar, inundar **3 to drown out** : ahogar — *vi* : ahogarse

drowse[1] ['draʊz] *vi* **drowsed; drowsing** DOZE : dormitar

drowse[2] *n* : sueño *m* ligero, cabezada *f*

drowsiness ['draʊzinəs] *n* : somnolencia *f*, adormecimiento *m*

drowsy ['draʊzi] *adj* **drowsier; -est** : somnoliento, soñoliento

drub ['drʌb] *vt* **drubbed; drubbing 1** BEAT, THRASH : golpear, apalear **2** DEFEAT : derrotar por completo

drudge[1] ['drʌdʒ] *vi* **drudged; drudging** : trabajar como esclavo, trabajar duro

drudge[2] *n* : esclavo *m*, -va *f* del trabajo

drudgery ['drʌdʒəri] *n, pl* **-eries** : trabajo *m* pesado

drug[1] ['drʌg] *vt* **drugged; drugging** : drogar, narcotizar

drug[2] *n* **1** MEDICATION : droga *f*, medicina *f*, medicamento *m* **2** NARCOTIC : narcótico *m*, estupefaciente *m*, droga *f*

druggist ['drʌgist] *n* : farmacéutico *m*, -ca *f*

drugstore ['drʌg,stor] *n* : farmacia *f*, botica *f*, droguería *f*

drum[1] ['drʌm] *v* **drummed; drumming** *vt* : meter a fuerza ⟨he drummed it into my head : me lo metió en la cabeza a fuerza⟩ — *vi* : tocar el tambor

drum[2] *n* **1** : tambor *m* **2** : bidón *m* ⟨oil drum : bidón de petróleo⟩

drummer ['drʌmər] *n* : baterista *mf*

drumstick ['drʌm,stik] *n* **1** : palillo *m* (de tambor), baqueta *f* **2** : muslo *m* de pollo

drunk[1] *pp* → **drink**[1]

drunk[2] ['drʌŋk] *adj* : borracho, embriagado, ebrio

drunk[3] *n* : borracho *m*, -cha *f*

drunkard ['drʌŋkərd] *n* : borracho *m*, -cha *f*

drunken ['drʌŋkən] *adj* : borracho, ebrio ⟨drunken driver : conductor ebrio⟩ ⟨drunken brawl : pleito de borrachos⟩

drunkenly ['drʌŋkənli] *adv* : como un borracho

drunkenness ['drʌŋkənnəs] *n* : borrachera *f*, embriaguez *f*, ebriedad *f*

dry[1] ['draɪ] *v* **dried; drying** *vt* : secar — *vi* : secarse

dry[2] *adj* **drier; driest** **1** : seco **2** THIRSTY : sediento **3** : donde la venta de bebidas alcohólicas está prohibida ⟨a dry county : un condado seco⟩ **4** DULL : aburrido, árido **5** : seco (dícese del vino), brut (dícese de la champaña)

dry–clean ['draɪ,kli:n] *v* : limpiar en seco

dry cleaner *n* : tintorería *f* (servicio)

dry cleaning *n* : limpieza *f* en seco

dryer ['draɪər] *n* **1 hair dryer** : secador *m* **2 clothes dryer** : secadora *f*

dry goods *npl* : artículos *mpl* de confección

dry ice *n* : hielo *m* seco

dryly ['draɪli] *adv* : secamente

dryness ['draɪnəs] *n* : sequedad *f*, aridez *f*

dual ['du:əl, 'dju:-] *adj* : doble

dualism ['du:ə,lɪzəm] *n* : dualismo *m*

dub ['dʌb] *vt* **dubbed; dubbing 1** CALL : apodar **2** : doblar (una película), mezclar (una grabación)

dubious ['du:biəs, 'dju:-] *adj* **1** UNCERTAIN : dudoso, indeciso **2** QUESTIONABLE : sospechoso, dudoso, discutible

dubiously ['du:biəsli, 'dju:-] *adv* **1** UNCERTAINLY : dudosamente, con desconfianza **2** SUSPICIOUSLY : de modo sospechoso, con recelo

duchess ['dʌtʃəs] *n* : duquesa *f*

duck[1] ['dʌk] *vt* **1** LOWER : agachar, bajar (la cabeza) **2** PLUNGE : zambullir **3** EVADE : eludir, evadir — *vi* **to duck down** : agacharse

duck[2] *n, pl* **duck** *or* **ducks** : pato *m*, -ta *f*

duckling ['dʌklɪŋ] *n* : patito *m*, -ta *f*

duct ['dʌkt] *n* : conducto *m*

ductile ['dʌktəl] *adj* : dúctil

dude ['du:d, 'dju:d] *n* **1** DANDY : dandi *m*, dandy *m* **2** GUY : tipo *m*

due[1] ['du:, 'dju:] *adv* : justo a, derecho hacia ⟨due north : derecho hacia el norte⟩

due[2] *adj* **1** PAYABLE : pagadero, sin pagar **2** APPROPRIATE : debido, apropiado ⟨after due consideration : con las debidas consideraciones⟩ **3** EXPECTED : esperado ⟨the train is due soon : esperamos el tren muy pronto, el tren debe llegar pronto⟩ **4 due to** : debido a, por

due[3] *n* **1 to give someone his (her) due** : darle a alguien su merecido **2 dues** *npl* : cuota *f*

duel[1] ['du:əl, 'dju:-] *vi* : batirse en duelo

duel[2] *n* : duelo *m*

duet [du'ɛt, dju-] *n* : dúo *m*

due to *prep* : debido a

dug → **dig**

dugout ['dʌg,aʊt] *n* **1** CANOE : piragua *f* **2** SHELTER : refugio *m* subterráneo

duke ['du:k, 'dju:k] *n* : duque *m*

dull[1] ['dʌl] *vt* **1** DIM : opacar, quitar el brillo a, deslustrar **2** BLUNT : embotar (un filo), entorpecer (los sentidos), aliviar (el dolor), amortiguar (sonidos)

dull[2] *adj* **1** STUPID : torpe, lerdo, lento **2** BLUNT : desafilado, despuntado **3** LACKLUSTER : sin brillo, deslustrado **4** BORING : aburrido, soso, pesado — **dully** *adv*

dullness ['dʌlnəs] *n* **1** STUPIDITY : estupidez *f* **2** : embotamiento *m* (de los sentidos) **3** MONOTONY : monotonía *f*, insipidez *f* **4** : falta *f* de brillo **5** BLUNTNESS : falta *f* de filo, embotadura *f*

duly ['du:li, 'dju:-] *adv* PROPERLY : debidamente, a su debido tiempo

dumb ['dʌm] *adj* **1** MUTE : mudo **2** STUPID : estúpido, tonto, bobo — **dumbly** *adv*

dumbbell ['dʌm,bɛl] *n* **1** WEIGHT : pesa *f* **2** : estúpido *m*, -da *f*
dumbfound *or* **dumfound** [,dʌm-'faʊnd] *vt* : dejar atónito, dejar sin habla
dummy ['dʌmi] *n, pl* **-mies 1** SHAM : imitación *f*, sustituto *m* **2** PUPPET : muñeco *m* **3** MANNEQUIN : maniquí *m* **4** IDIOT : tonto *m*, -ta *f*; idiota *mf*
dump¹ ['dʌmp] *vt* : descargar, verter
dump² *n* **1** : vertedero *m*, tiradero *m* *Mex* **2 down in the dumps** : triste, deprimido
dumpling ['dʌmplɪŋ] *n* : bola *f* de masa hervida
dumpy ['dʌmpi] *adj* **dumpier; -est** : rechoncho, regordete
dun¹ ['dʌn] *vt* **dunned; dunning** : apremiar (a un deudor)
dun² *adj* : pardo (color)
dunce ['dʌnts] *n* : estúpido *m*, -da *f*; burro *m*, -rra *f fam*
dune ['du:n, 'dju:n] *n* : duna *f*
dung ['dʌŋ] *n* **1** FECES : excrementos *mpl* **2** MANURE : estiércol *m*
dungaree [,dʌŋgə'ri:] *n* **1** DENIM : tela *f* vaquera, mezclilla *f Chile, Mex* **2 dungarees** *npl* : pantalones *mpl* de trabajo hechos de tela vaquera
dungeon ['dʌndʒən] *n* : mazmorra *f*, calabozo *m*
dunk ['dʌŋk] *vt* : mojar, ensopar
duo ['du:o:, 'dju:-] *n, pl* **duos** : dúo *m*, par *m*
dupe¹ ['du:p, dju:p] *vt* **duped; duping** : engañar, embaucar
dupe² *n* : inocentón *m*, -tona *f*; simple *mf*
duplex¹ ['du:,plɛks, 'dju:-] *adj* : doble
duplex² *n* : casa *f* de dos viviendas, dúplex *m*
duplicate¹ ['du:plɪ,keɪt, 'dju:-] *vt* **-cated; -cating** COPY : duplicar, hacer copias de **2** REPEAT : repetir, reproducir
duplicate² ['du:plɪkət, 'dju:-] *adj* : duplicado ⟨a duplicate invoice : una factura por duplicado⟩
duplicate³ ['du:plɪkət, 'dju:-] *n* : duplicado *m*, copia *f*
duplication [,du:plɪ'keɪʃən, ,dju:-] *n* **1** DUPLICATING : duplicación *f*, repetición *f* (de esfuerzos) **2** DUPLICATE : copia *f*, duplicado *m*
duplicity [dʊ'plɪsəti, ,dju:-] *n, pl* **-ties** : duplicidad *f*
durability [,dʊrə'bɪləti, ,djʊr-] *n* : durabilidad *f* (de un producto) permanencia *f*
durable ['dʊrəbəl, 'djʊr-] *adj* : duradero *f*
duration [dʊ'reɪʃən, dju-] *n* : duración *f*
duress [dʊ'rɛs, dju-] *n* : coacción *f*

during ['dʊrɪŋ, 'djʊr-] *prep* : durante
dusk ['dʌsk] *n* : anochecer *m*, crepúsculo *m*
dusky ['dʌski] *adj* **duskier; -est** : oscuro (dícese de los colores)
dust¹ ['dʌst] *vt* **1** : quitar el polvo de **2** SPRINKLE : espolvorear
dust² *n* : polvo *m*
duster ['dʌstər] *n* **1** *or* **dust cloth** : trapo *m* de polvo **2** HOUSECOAT : guardapolvo *m* **3 feather duster** : plumero *m*
dustpan ['dʌst,pæn] *n* : recogedor *m*
dusty ['dʌsti] *adj* **dustier; -est** : cubierto de polvo, polvoriento
Dutch¹ ['dʌtʃ] *adj* : holandés
Dutch² *n* **1** : holandés *m* (idioma) **2 the Dutch** *npl* : los holandeses
Dutch treat *n* : invitación o pago a escote
dutiful ['du:tɪfəl, 'dju:-] *adj* : motivado por sus deberes, responsable
duty ['du:ti, 'dju:-] *n, pl* **-ties 1** OBLIGATION : deber *m*, obligación *f*, responsabilidad *f* **2** TAX : impuesto *m*, arancel *m*
DVD [,di:,vi:'di:] *n* : DVD *m*
dwarf¹ ['dwɔrf] *vt* **1** STUNT : arrestar el crecimiento de **2** : hacer parecer pequeño
dwarf² *n, pl* **dwarfs** ['dwɔrfs] *or* **dwarves** ['dwɔrvz] : enano *m*, -na *f*
dwell ['dwɛl] *vi* **dwelled** *or* **dwelt** ['dwɛlt]; **dwelling 1** RESIDE : residir, morar, vivir **2 to dwell on** : pensar demasiado en, insistir en
dweller ['dwɛlər] *n* : habitante *mf*
dwelling ['dwɛlɪŋ] *n* : morada *f*, vivienda *f*, residencia *f*
dwindle ['dwɪndəl] *vi* **-dled; -dling** : menguar, reducirse, disminuir
dye¹ ['daɪ] *vt* **dyed; dyeing** : teñir
dye² *n* : tintura *f*, tinte *m*
dying → **die**
dyke → **dike**
dynamic [daɪ'næmɪk] *adj* : dinámico
dynamics [daɪ'næmɪks] *npl* : dinámica *f*
dynamite¹ ['daɪnə,maɪt] *vt* **-mited; -miting** : dinamitar
dynamite² *n* : dinamita *f*
dynamo ['daɪnə,mo:] *n, pl* **-mos** : dínamo *m*, generador *m* de electricidad
dynasty ['daɪnəsti, -,næs-] *n, pl* **-ties** : dinastía *f*
dysentery ['dɪsən,tɛri] *n, pl* **-teries** : disentería *f*
dysfunction [dɪs'fʌŋkʃən] *n* : disfunción *f*
dystrophy ['dɪstrəfi] *n, pl* **-phies 1** : distrofia *f* **2** → **muscular dystrophy**

E

e ['i:] *n, pl* **e's** *or* **es** ['i:z] : quinta letra del alfabeto inglés

each¹ ['i:tʃ] *adv* : cada uno, por persona ⟨they cost $10 each : costaron $10 cada uno⟩

each² *adj* : cada ⟨each student : cada estudiante⟩ ⟨each and every one : todos sin excepción⟩

each³ *pron* **1** : cada uno *m*, cada una *f* ⟨each of us : cada uno de nosotros⟩ **2 each other** : el uno al otro, mutuamente ⟨we are helping each other : nos ayudamos el uno al otro⟩ ⟨they love each other : se aman⟩

eager ['i:gər] *adj* **1** ENTHUSIASTIC : entusiasta, ávido, deseoso **2** ANXIOUS : ansioso, impaciente

eagerly ['i:gərli] *adv* : con entusiasmo, ansiosamente

eagerness ['i:gərnəs] *n* : entusiasmo *m*, deseo *m*, impaciencia *f*

eagle ['i:gəl] *n* : águila *f*

ear ['ɪr] *n* **1** : oído *m*, oreja *f* ⟨inner ear : oído interno⟩ ⟨big ears : orejas grandes⟩ **2 ear of corn** : mazorca *f*, choclo *m*

earache ['ɪr,eɪk] *n* : dolor *m* de oído

eardrum ['ɪr,drʌm] *n* : tímpano *m*

earl ['ərl] *n* : conde *m*

earlobe ['ɪr,lo:b] *n* : lóbulo *m* de la oreja, perilla *f* de la oreja

early¹ ['ərli] *adv* **earlier; -est** : temprano, pronto ⟨he arrived early : llegó temprano⟩ ⟨as early as possible : lo más pronto posible, cuanto antes⟩ ⟨ten minutes early : diez minutos de adelanto⟩

early² *adj* **earlier; -est 1** (*referring to a beginning*) : primero ⟨the early stages : las primeras etapas⟩ ⟨in early May : a principios de mayo⟩ **2** (*referring to antiquity*) : primitivo, antiguo ⟨early man : el hombre primitivo⟩ ⟨early painting : la pintura antigua⟩ **3** (*referring to a designated time*) : temprano, antes de la hora, prematuro ⟨he was early : llegó temprano⟩ ⟨early fruit : frutas tempraneras⟩ ⟨an early death : una muerte prematura⟩

earmark ['ɪr,mɑrk] *vt* : destinar ⟨earmarked funds : fondos destinados⟩

earn ['ərn] *vt* **1** : ganar ⟨to earn money : ganar dinero⟩ **2** DESERVE : ganarse, merecer

earnest¹ ['ərnəst] *adj* : serio, sincero

earnest² *n* **in ~** : en serio, de verdad ⟨we began in earnest : empezamos de verdad⟩

earnestly ['ərnəstli] *adv* **1** SERIOUSLY : con seriedad, en serio **2** FERVENTLY : de todo corazón

earnestness ['ərnəstnəs] *n* : seriedad *f*, sinceridad *f*

earnings ['ərnɪnz] *npl* : ingresos *mpl*, ganancias *fpl*, utilidades *fpl*

earphone ['ɪr,fo:n] *n* : audífono *m*

earring ['ɪr,rɪn] *n* : zarcillo *m*, arete *m*, aro *m Arg, Chile, Uru*, pendiente *m Spain*

earshot ['ɪr,ʃɑt] *n* : alcance *m* del oído

earth ['ərθ] *n* **1** LAND, SOIL : tierra *f*, suelo *m* **2 the Earth** : la Tierra

earthen ['ərθən, -ðən] *adj* : de tierra, de barro

earthenware ['ərθən,wær, -ðən-] *n* : loza *f*, vajillas *fpl* de barro

earthly ['ərθli] *adj* : terrenal, mundano

earthquake ['ərθ,kweɪk] *n* : terremoto *m*, temblor *m*

earthworm ['ərθ,wərm] *n* : lombriz *f* (de tierra)

earthy ['ərθi] *adj* **earthier; -est 1** : terroso ⟨earthy colors : colores terrosos⟩ **2** DOWN-TO-EARTH : realista, práctico, llano **3** COARSE, CRUDE : basto, grosero, tosco ⟨earthy jokes : chistes groseros⟩

earwax ['ɪr,wæks] *n* → **wax²**

earwig ['ɪr,wɪg] *n* : tijereta *f*

ease¹ ['i:z] *v* **eased; easing** *vt* **1** ALLEVIATE : aliviar, calmar, hacer disminuir **2** LOOSEN, RELAX : aflojar (una cuerda), relajar (restricciones), descargar (tensiones) **3** FACILITATE : facilitar — *vi* : calmarse, relajarse

ease² *n* **1** CALM, RELIEF : tranquilidad *f*, comodidad *f*, desahogo *m* **2** FACILITY : facilidad *f* **3 at ~** : relajado, cómodo ⟨to put someone at ease : tranquilizar a alguien⟩

easel ['i:zəl] *n* : caballete *m*

easily ['i:zəli] *adv* **1** : fácilmente, con facilidad **2** UNQUESTIONABLY : con mucho, de lejos

easiness ['i:zinəs] *n* : facilidad *f*, soltura *f*

east¹ ['i:st] *adv* : al este

east² *adj* : este, del este, oriental ⟨east winds : vientos del este⟩

east³ *n* **1** : este *m* **2 the East** : el Oriente

Easter ['i:stər] *n* : Pascua *f* (de Resurrección)

easterly ['i:stərli] *adv & adj* : del este

eastern ['i:stərn] *adj* **1** : Oriental, del Este ⟨Eastern Europe : Europa del Este⟩ **2** : oriental, este

Easterner ['i:stərnər] *n* : habitante *mf* del este

eastward ['i:stwərd] *adv & adj* : hacia el este

easy ['i:zi] *adj* **easier; -est 1** : fácil **2** LENIENT : indulgente

easygoing [,i:zi'go:ɪn] *adj* : acomodaticio, tolerante, poco exigente

eat ['i:t] *v* **ate** ['eɪt]; **eaten** ['i:tən]; **eating** *vt* **1** : comer **2** CONSUME : consumir, gastar, devorar ⟨expenses ate up profits : los gastos devoraron las ganancias⟩ **3** CORRODE : corroer — *vi* **1** : comer **2 to eat away at** *or* **to eat into** : comerse **3 to eat out** : comer fuera

eatable[1] [ˈiːt̬əbəl] *adj* : comestible, comible *fam*

eatable[2] *n* **1** : algo para comer **2 eatables** *npl* : comestibles *mpl*, alimentos *mpl*

eater [ˈiːt̬ər] *n* : comedor *m*, -dora *f*

eaves [ˈiːvz] *npl* : alero *m*

eavesdrop [ˈiːvzˌdrɑp] *vi* **-dropped; -dropping** : escuchar a escondidas

eavesdropper [ˈiːvzˌdrɑpər] *n* : persona *f* que escucha a escondidas

ebb[1] [ˈɛb] *vi* **1** : bajar, menguar (dícese de la marea) **2** DECLINE : decaer, disminuir

ebb[2] *n* **1** : reflujo *m* (de una marea) **2** DECLINE : decadencia *f*, declive *m*, disminución *f*

ebony[1] [ˈɛbəni] *adj* **1** : de ébano **2** BLACK : de color ébano, negro

ebony[2] *n, pl* **-nies** : ébano *m*

ebullience [ɪˈbʊljənts, -ˈbʌl-] *n* : efervescencia *f*, vivacidad *f*

ebullient [ɪˈbʊljənt, -ˈbʌl-] *adj* : efervescente, vivaz

eccentric[1] [ɪkˈsɛntrɪk] *adj* **1** : excéntrico ⟨an eccentric wheel : una rueda excéntrica⟩ **2** ODD, SINGULAR : excéntrico, extraño, raro — **eccentrically** [-trɪkli] *adv*

eccentric[2] *n* : excéntrico *m*, -ca *f*

eccentricity [ˌkˌsɛnˈtrɪsəti] *n, pl* **-ties** : excentricidad *f*

ecclesiastic [ɪˌkliːziˈæstɪk] *n* : eclesiástico *m*, clérigo *m*

ecclesiastical [ɪˌkliːziˈæstɪkəl] *or* **ecclesiastic** *adj* : eclesiástico — **ecclesiastically** *adv*

echelon [ˈɛʃəˌlɑn] *n* **1** : escalón *m* (de tropas o aviones) **2** LEVEL : nivel *m*, esfera *f*, estrato *m*

echo[1] [ˈɛˌkoː] *v* **echoed; echoing** *vi* : hacer eco, resonar — *vt* : repetir

echo[2] *n, pl* **echoes** : eco *m*

éclair [eɪˈklær, i-] *n* : pastel *m* relleno de crema

eclectic [ɛˈklɛktɪk, ɪ-] *adj* : ecléctico

eclipse[1] [ɪˈklɪps] *vt* **eclipsed; eclipsing** : eclipsar

eclipse[2] *n* : eclipse *m*

ecological [ˌiːkəˈlɑdʒɪkəl, ˌɛkə-] *adj* : ecológico — **ecologically** *adv*

ecologist [iˈkɑlədʒɪst, ɛ-] *n* : ecólogo *m*, -ga *f*

ecology [iˈkɑlədʒi, ɛ-] *n, pl* **-gies** : ecología *f*

economic [ˌiːkəˈnɑmɪk, ˌɛkə-] *adj* : económico

economical [ˌiːkəˈnɑmɪkəl, ˌɛkə-] *adj* : económico — **economically** *adv*

economics [ˌiːkəˈnɑmɪks, ˌɛkə-] *n* : economía *f*

economist [iˈkɑnəmɪst] *n* : economista *mf*

economize [iˈkɑnəˌmaɪz] *v* **-mized; -mizing** : economizar, ahorrar

economy [iˈkɑnəmi] *n, pl* **-mies 1** : economía *f*, sistema *m* económico **2** THRIFT : economía *f*, ahorro *m*

ecosystem [ˈiːkoˌsɪstəm] *n* : ecosistema *m*

ecru [ˈɛˌkruː, ˈeɪ-] *n* : color *m* crudo

ecstasy [ˈɛkstəsi] *n, pl* **-sies** : éxtasis *m*

ecstatic [ɛkˈstæt̬ɪk, ɪk-] *adj* : extático

ecstatically [ɛkˈstæt̬ɪkli, ɪk-] *adv* : con éxtasis, con gran entusiasmo

Ecuadoran [ˌɛkwəˈdorən] *or* **Ecuadorean** *or* **Ecuadorian** [-ˈdoriən] *n* : ecuatoriano *m*, -na *f* — **Ecuadorean** *or* **Ecuadorian** *adj*

ecumenical [ˌɛkjʊˈmnɪkəl] *adj* : ecuménico

eczema [ɪɡˈziːmə, ˈɛɡzəmə, ˈɛksə-] *n* : eczema *m*

eddy[1] [ˈɛdi] *vi* **eddied; eddying** : arremolinarse, hacer remolinos

eddy[2] *n, pl* **-dies** : remolino *m*

edema [ɪˈdiːmə] *n* : edema *m*

Eden [ˈiːdən] *n* : Edén *m*

edge[1] [ˈɛdʒ] *v* **edged; edging** *vt* **1** BORDER : bordear, ribetear, orlar **2** SHARPEN : afilar, aguzar **3** *or* **to edge one's way** : avanzar poco a poco **4 to edge out** : derrotar por muy poco — *vi* ADVANCE : ir avanzando (poco a poco)

edge[2] *n* **1** : filo *m* (de un cuchillo) **2** BORDER : borde *m*, orilla *f*, margen *m* **3** ADVANTAGE : ventaja *f*

edger [ˈɛdʒər] *n* : cortabordes *m*

edgewise [ˈɛdʒˌwaɪz] *adv* SIDEWAYS : de lado, de canto

edginess [ˈɛdʒinəs] *n* : tensión *f*, nerviosismo *m*

edgy [ˈɛdʒi] *adj* **edgier; -est** : tenso, nervioso

edible [ˈɛdəbəl] *adj* : comestible

edict [ˈiːˌdɪkt] *n* : edicto *m*, mandato *m*, orden *f*

edification [ˌɛdəfəˈkeɪʃən] *n* : edificación *f*, instrucción *f*

edifice [ˈɛdəfɪs] *n* : edificio *m*

edify [ˈɛdəˌfaɪ] *vt* **-fied; -fying** : edificar

edit [ˈɛdɪt] *vt* **1** : editar, redactar, corregir **2** *or* **to edit out** DELETE : recortar, cortar

edition [ɪˈdɪʃən] *n* : edición *f*

editor [ˈɛdɪt̬ər] *n* : editor *m*, -tora *f*; redactor *m*, -tora *f*

editorial[1] [ˌɛdɪˈtoriəl] *adj* **1** : de redacción **2** : editorial ⟨an editorial comment : un comentario editorial⟩

editorial[2] *n* : editorial *m*

editorship [ˈɛdɪt̬ərˌʃɪp] *n* : dirección *f*

educable [ˈɛdʒəkəbəl] *adj* : educable

educate [ˈɛdʒəˌkeɪt] *vt* **-cated; -cating 1** TEACH : educar, enseñar **2** INSTRUCT : formar, educar, instruir **3** INFORM : informar, concientizar

education [ˌɛdʒəˈkeɪʃən] *n* : educación *f*

educational [ˌɛdʒəˈkeɪʃənəl] *adj* **1** : docente, de enseñanza ⟨an educational institution : una institución docente⟩ **2** PEDAGOGICAL : pedagógico **3** INSTRUCTIONAL : educativo, instructivo

educator [ˈɛdʒəˌkeɪt̬ər] *n* : educador *m*, -dora *f*

eel [ˈiːl] *n* : anguila *f*

eerie ['ɪri] *adj* **-rier; -est 1** SPOOKY : que da miedo, espeluznante **2** GHOSTLY : fantasmagórico

eerily ['ɪrəli] *adv* : de manera extraña y misteriosa

efface [ɪ'feɪs, -] *vt* **-faced; -facing** : borrar

effect[1] [ɪ'fɛkt] *vt* **1** CARRY OUT : efectuar, llevar a cabo **2** ACHIEVE : lograr, realizar

effect[2] *n* **1** RESULT : efecto *m*, resultado *m*, consecuencia *f* ⟨to no effect : sin resultado⟩ **2** MEANING : sentido *m* ⟨something to that effect : algo por el estilo⟩ **3** INFLUENCE : efecto *m*, influencia *f* **4 effects** *npl* BELONGINGS : efectos *mpl*, pertenencias *fpl* **5 to go into effect** : entrar en vigor **6 in ~** REALLY : en realidad, efectivamente

effective [ɪ'fɛktɪv] *adj* **1** EFFECTUAL : efectivo, eficaz **2** OPERATIVE : vigente — **effectively** *adv*

effectiveness [ɪ'fɛktɪvnəs] *n* : eficacia *f*, efectividad *f*

effectual [ɪ'fɛktʃuəl] *adj* : eficaz, efectivo — **effectually** *adv*

effeminate [ə'fɛmənət] *adj* : afeminado

effervesce [ˌɛfər'vɛs] *vi* **-vesced; -vescing 1** : estar en efervescencia, burbujear (dícese de líquidos) **2** : estar eufórico, estar muy animado (dícese de las personas)

effervescence [ˌɛfər'vɛsənts] *n* **1** : efervescencia *f* **2** LIVELINESS : vivacidad *f*

effervescent [ˌɛfər'vɛsənt] *adj* **1** : efervescente **2** LIVELY, VIVACIOUS : vivaz, animado

effete [ɛ'fi:t, ɪ-] *adj* **1** WORN-OUT : desgastado, agotado **2** DECADENT : decadente **3** EFFEMINATE : afeminado

efficacious [ˌɛfə'keɪʃəs] *adj* : eficaz, efectivo

efficacy ['ɛfɪkəsi] *n, pl* **-cies** : eficacia *f*

efficiency [ɪ'fɪʃəntsi] *n, pl* **-cies** : eficiencia *f*

efficient [ɪ'fɪʃənt] *adj* : eficiente — **efficiently** *adv*

effigy ['ɛfədʒi] *n, pl* **-gies** : efigie *f*

effluent ['ɛˌfluːənt, ɛ'fluː-] *n* : efluente *m* — **effluent** *adj*

effort ['ɛfərt] *n* **1** EXERTION : esfuerzo *m* **2** ATTEMPT : tentativa *f*, intento *m* ⟨it's not worth the effort : no vale la pena⟩

effortless ['ɛfərtləs] *adj* : fácil, sin esfuerzo

effortlessly ['ɛfərtləsli] *adv* : sin esfuerzo, fácilmente

effrontery [ɪ'frʌntəri] *n, pl* **-teries** : insolencia *f*, desfachatez *f*, descaro *m*

effusion [ɪ'fjuːʒən, ɛ-] *n* : efusión *f*

effusive [ɪ'fjuːsɪv, ɛ-] *adj* : efusivo — **effusively** *adv*

egg[1] ['ɛg] *vt* **to egg on** : incitar, azuzar, provocar

egg[2] *n* **1** : huevo *m* **2** OVUM : óvulo *m*

eggbeater ['ɛgˌbiːtər] *n* : batidor *m* (de huevos)

eggnog ['ɛgˌnɑg] *n* : ponche *m* de huevo, rompope *m* CA, Mex

eggplant ['ɛgˌplænt] *n* : berenjena *f*

eggshell ['ɛgˌʃl] *n* : cascarón *m*

ego ['iːˌgoː] *n, pl* **egos 1** SELF-ESTEEM : amor *m* propio **2** SELF : ego *m*, yo *m*

egocentric [ˌiːgo'sɛntrɪk] *adj* : egocéntrico

egoism ['iːgoˌwɪzəm] *n* : egoísmo *m*

egoist ['iːgowɪst] *n* : egoísta *mf*

egoistic [ˌiːgo'wɪstɪk] *adj* : egoísta

egotism ['iːgəˌtɪzəm] *n* : egotismo *m*

egotist ['iːgətɪst] *n* : egotista *mf*

egotistic [ˌiːgə'tɪstɪk] *or* **egotistical** [-'tɪstɪkəl] *adj* : egotista — **egotistically** *adv*

egregious [ɪ'griːdʒəs] *adj* : atroz, flagrante, mayúsculo — **egregiously** *adv*

egress ['iːˌgrɛs] *n* : salida *f*

egret ['iːˌgrət, -ˌgrɛt] *n* : garceta *f*

Egyptian [ɪ'dʒɪpʃən] *n* **1** : egipcio *m*, -cia *f* **2** : egipcio *m* (idioma) — **Egyptian** *adj*

eiderdown ['aɪdərˌdaʊn] *n* **1** : plumón *m* **2** COMFORTER : edredón *m*

eight[1] ['eɪt] *adj* : ocho

eight[2] *n* : ocho *m*

eight hundred[1] *adj* : ochocientos

eight hundred[2] *n* : ochocientos *m*

eighteen[1] [eɪt'tiːn] *adj* : dieciocho

eighteen[2] *n* : dieciocho *m*

eighteenth[1] [eɪt'tiːnθ] *adj* : decimoctavo

eighteenth[2] *n* **1** : decimoctavo *m*, -va *f* (en una serie) **2** : dieciochoavo *m*, dieciochoava parte *f*

eighth[1] ['eɪtθ] *adj* : octavo

eighth[2] *n* **1** : octavo *m*, -va *f* (en una serie) **2** : octavo *m*, octava parte *f*

eightieth[1] ['eɪtiəθ] *adj* : octogésimo

eightieth[2] *n* **1** : octogésimo *m*, -ma *f* (en una serie) **2** : ochentavo *m*, ochentava parte *f*

eighty[1] ['eɪti] *adj* : ochenta

eighty[2] *n, pl* **eighties 1** : ochenta *m* **2 the eighties** : los ochenta *mpl*

either[1] ['iːðər, 'aɪ-] *adj* **1** : cualquiera (de los dos) ⟨we can watch either movie : podemos ver cualquiera de las dos películas⟩ **2** : ninguno de los dos ⟨she wasn't in either room : no estaba en ninguna de las dos salas⟩ **3** EACH : cada ⟨on either side of the street : a cada lado de la calle⟩

either[2] *pron* **1** : cualquiera *mf* (de los dos) ⟨either is fine : cualquiera de los dos está bien⟩ **2** : ninguno *m*, -na *f* (de los dos) ⟨I don't like either : no me gusta ninguno⟩ **3** : algún *m*, alguna *f* ⟨is either of you interested? : ¿está alguno de ustedes (dos) interesado?⟩

either[3] *conj* **1** : o, u ⟨either David or Daniel could go : puede ir (o) David o Daniel⟩ **2** : ni ⟨we won't watch either this movie or the other : no veremos ni esta película ni la otra⟩

ejaculate [i'dʒækjəˌleɪt] *v* **-lated; -lating** *vt* **1** : eyacular **2** EXCLAIM : exclamar — *vi* : eyacular

ejaculation [i͵ʤækjə'leɪʃən] *n* **1** : eyaculación *f* (en fisiología) **2** EXCLAMATION : exclamación *f*

eject [i'ʤɛkt] *vt* : expulsar, expeler

ejection [i'ʤɛkʃən] *n* : expulsión *f*

eke ['i:k] *vt* **eked; eking** *or* **to eke out** : ganar a duras penas

elaborate[1] [i'læbə͵reɪt] *v* **-rated; -rating** *vt* : elaborar, idear, desarrollar — *vi* **to elaborate on** : ampliar, entrar en detalles

elaborate[2] [i'læbərət] *adj* **1** DETAILED : detallado, minucioso, elaborado **2** COMPLICATED : complicado, intrincado, elaborado — **elaborately** *adv*

elaboration [i͵læbə'reɪʃən] *n* : elaboración *f*

elapse [i'læps] *vi* **elapsed; elapsing** : transcurrir, pasar

elastic[1] [i'læstɪk] *adj* : elástico

elastic[2] *n* **1** : elástico *m* **2** RUBBER BAND : goma *f*, gomita *f*, elástico *m*, liga *f*

elasticity [i͵læs'tɪsəti, ͵iː͵læs-] *n, pl* **-ties** : elasticidad *f*

elate [i'leɪt] *vt* **elated; elating** : alborozar, regocijar

elation [i'leɪʃən] *n* : euforia *f*, júbilo *m*, alborozo *m*

elbow[1] ['ɛl͵boː] *vt* : darle un codazo a

elbow[2] *n* : codo *m*

elder[1] ['ɛldər] *adj* : mayor

elder[2] *n* **1 to be someone's elder** : ser mayor que alguien **2** : anciano *m*, -na *f* (de un pueblo o una tribu) **3** : miembro *m* del consejo (en varias religiones)

elderberry ['ɛldər͵bɛri] *n, pl* **-berries** : baya *f* de saúco (fruta), saúco *m* (árbol)

elderly ['ɛldərli] *adj* : mayor, de edad, anciano

eldest ['ɛldəst] *adj* : mayor, de más edad

elect[1] [i'lɛkt] *vt* : elegir

elect[2] *adj* : electo ⟨the president-elect : el presidente electo⟩

elect[3] *npl* **the elect** : los elegidos *mpl*

election [i'lɛkʃən] *n* : elección *f*

elective[1] [i'lɛktɪv] *adj* **1** : electivo **2** OPTIONAL : facultativo, optativo

elective[2] *n* : asignatura *f* electiva

elector [i'lɛktər] *n* : elector *m*, -tora *f*

electoral [i'lɛktərəl] *adj* : electoral

electorate [i'lɛktərət] *n* : electorado *m*

electric [i'lɛktrɪk] *adj* **1** *or* **electrical** [-trɪkəl] : eléctrico **2** THRILLING : electrizante, emocionante

electrician [i͵lɛk'trɪʃən] *n* : electricista *mf*

electricity [i͵lɛk'trɪsəti] *n, pl* **-ties** **1** : electricidad *f* **2** CURRENT : corriente *m* eléctrica

electrification [i͵lɛktrəfə'keɪʃən] *n* : electrificación *f*

electrify [i'lɛktrə͵faɪ] *vt* **-fied; -fying 1** : electrificar **2** THRILL : electrizar, emocionar

electrocardiogram [i͵lɛktro'kɑrdiə͵græm] *n* : electrocardiograma *m*

electrocardiograph [i͵lɛktro'kɑrdiə͵græf] *n* : electrocardiógrafo *m*

electrocute [i'lɛktrə͵kju:t] *vt* **-cuted; -cuting** : electrocutar

electrocution [i͵lɛktrə'kju:ʃən] *n* : electrocución *f*

electrode [i'lɛk͵troːd] *n* : electrodo *m*

electrolysis [i͵lɛk'trɑləsɪs] *n* : electrólisis *f*

electrolyte [i'lɛktrə͵laɪt] *n* : electrolito *m*

electromagnet [i͵lɛktro'mægnət] *n* : electroimán *m*

electromagnetic [i͵lɛktromæg'nɛtɪk] *adj* : electromagnético — **electromagnetically** [-țikli] *adv*

electromagnetism [i͵lɛktro'mægnə͵tɪzəm] *n* : electromagnetismo *m*

electron [i'lɛk͵trɑn] *n* : electrón *m*

electronic [i͵lɛk'trɑnɪk] *adj* : electrónico — **electronically** [-nɪkli] *adv*

electronic mail *n* : correo *m* electrónico

electronics [i͵lɛk'trɑnɪks] *n* : electrónica *f*

electroplate [i'lɛktrə͵pleɪt] *vt* **-plated; plating** : galvanizar mediante electrólisis

elegance ['ɛligənts] *n* : elegancia *f*

elegant ['ɛligənt] *adj* : elegante — **elegantly** *adv*

elegy ['ɛləʤi] *n, pl* **-gies** : elegía *f*

element ['ɛləmənt] *n* **1** COMPONENT : elemento *m*, factor *m* **2** : elemento *m* (en la química) **3** MILIEU : elemento *m*, medio *m* ⟨to be in one's element : estar en su elemento⟩ **4 elements** *npl* RUDIMENTS : elementos *mpl*, rudimentos *mpl*, bases *fpl* **5 the elements** WEATHER : los elementos *mpl*

elemental [͵ɛlə'mɛntəl] *adj* **1** BASIC : elemental, primario **2** : elemental (dícese de los elementos químicos)

elementary [͵ɛlə'mɛntri] *adj* **1** SIMPLE : elemental, simple, fundamental **2** : de enseñanza primaria

elementary school *n* : escuela *f* primaria

elephant ['ɛləfənt] *n* : elefante *m*, -ta *f*

elevate ['ɛlə͵veɪt] *vt* **-vated; -vating 1** RAISE : elevar, levantar, alzar **2** EXALT, PROMOTE : elevar, exaltar, ascender **3** ELATE : alborozar, regocijar

elevation [͵ɛlə'veɪʃən] *n* **1** : elevación *f* **2** ALTITUDE : altura *f*, altitud *f* **3** PROMOTION : ascenso *m*

elevator ['ɛlə͵veɪtər] *n* : ascensor *m*, elevador *m*

eleven[1] [ɪ'lɛvən] *adj* : once

eleven[2] *n* : once *m*

eleventh[1] [ɪlɛvəntθ] *adj* : undécimo

eleventh[2] *n* **1** : undécimo *m*, -ma *f* (en una serie) **2** : onceavo *m*, onceava parte *f*

elf ['ɛlf] *n, pl* **elves** ['ɛlvz] : elfo *m*, geniecillo *m*, duende *m*

elfin ['ɛlfən] *adj* **1** : de elfo, menudo **2** ENCHANTING, MAGIC : mágico, encantador

elfish ['ɛlfɪʃ] *adj* **1** : de elfo **2** MISCHIEVOUS : travieso

elicit [ɪ'lɪsət] *vt* : provocar

eligibility [ˌɛləʤə'bɪləti] *n, pl* **-ties** : elegibilidad *f*
eligible ['ɛləʤəbəl] *adj* **1** QUALIFIED : elegible **2** SUITABLE : idóneo
eliminate [ɪ'lɪmə,neɪt] *vt* **-nated; -nating** : eliminar
elimination [ɪ,lɪmə'neɪʃən] *n* : eliminación *f*
elite [eɪ'liːt, i-] *n* : elite *f*
elixir [i'lɪksər] *n* : elixir *m*
elk ['ɛlk] *n* : alce *m* (de Europa), uapití *m* (de América)
ellipse [ɪ'lɪps, -] *n* : elipse *f*
ellipsis [ɪ'lɪpsəs, -] *n, pl* **-lipses** [-,siːz] **1** : elipsis *f* **2** : puntos *mpl* suspensivos (en la puntuación)
elliptical [ɪ'lɪptɪkəl, -] *or* **elliptic** [-tɪk] *adj* : elíptico
elm ['ɛlm] *n* : olmo *m*
elocution [ˌɛlə'kjuːʃən] *n* : elocución *f*
elongate [i'lɔŋ,geɪt] *vt* **-gated; -gating** : alargar
elongation [ˌiː,lɔŋ'geɪʃən] *n* : alargamiento *m*
elope [i'loːp] *vi* **eloped; eloping** : fugarse
elopement [i'loːpmənt] *n* : fuga *f*
eloquence ['ɛləkwənts] *n* : elocuencia *f*
eloquent ['ɛləkwənt] *adj* : elocuente —
eloquently *adv*
El Salvadoran [ˌɛl,sælvə'dorən] *n* : salvadoreño *m*, -ña *f* — **El Salvadoran** *adj*
else[1] ['ɛls] *adv* **1** DIFFERENTLY : de otro modo, de otra manera ⟨how else? : ¿de qué otro modo?⟩ **2** ELSEWHERE : de otro sitio, de otro lugar ⟨where else? : ¿en qué otro sitio?⟩ **3 or else** OTHERWISE : si no, de lo contrario
else[2] *adj* **1** OTHER : otro ⟨anyone else : cualquier otro⟩ ⟨everyone else : todos los demás⟩ ⟨nobody else : ningún otro, nadie más⟩ ⟨somebody else : otra persona⟩ **2** MORE : más ⟨nothing else : nada más⟩ ⟨what else? : ¿qué más?⟩
elsewhere ['ɛls,ʰwer] *adv* : en otra parte, en otro sitio, en otro lugar
elucidate [i'luːsə,deɪt] *vt* **-dated; -dating** : dilucidar, elucidar, esclarecer
elucidation [i,luːsə'deɪʃən] *n* : elucidación *f*, esclarecimiento *m*
elude [i'luːd] *vt* **eluded; eluding** : eludir, evadir
elusive [i'luːsɪv] *adj* **1** EVASIVE : evasivo, esquivo **2** SLIPPERY : huidizo, escurridizo **3** FLEETING, INTANGIBLE : impalpable, fugaz
elusively [i'luːsɪvli] *adv* : de manera esquiva
elves → **elf**
emaciate [i'meɪʃi,eɪt] *vt* **-ated; -ating** : enflaquecer
emaciation [i,meɪsi'eɪʃən, -ʃi-] *n* : enflaquecimiento *m*, escualidez *f*, delgadez *f* extrema
e—mail ['iː,meɪl] *n* : e-mail *m*
emanate ['ɛmə,neɪt] *v* **-nated; -nating** *vi* : emanar, provenir, proceder — *vt* : emanar

emanation [ˌɛmə'neɪʃən] *n* : emanación *f*
emancipate [i'mæntsə,peɪt] *vt* **-pated; -pating** : emancipar
emancipation [i,mæntsə'peɪʃən] *n* : emancipación *f*
emasculate [i'mæskjə,leɪt] *vt* **-lated; -lating** **1** CASTRATE : castrar, emascular **2** WEAKEN : debilitar
embalm [ɪm'bɑm, ɛm-, -'bɑlm] *vt* : embalsamar
embankment [ɪm'bæŋkmənt, ɛm-] *n* : terraplén *m*, muro *m* de contención
embargo[1] [ɪm'bɑrgo, ɛm-] *vt* **-goed; -going** : imponer un embargo sobre
embargo[2] *n, pl* **-goes** : embargo *m*
embark [ɪm'bɑrk, ɛm-] *vt* : embarcar — *vi* **1** : embarcarse **2 to embark on** START : emprender, embarcarse en
embarkation [ˌɛm,bɑr'keɪʃən] *n* : embarque *m*, embarco *m*
embarrass [ɪm'bærəs, ɛm-] *vt* : avergonzar, abochornar
embarrassing [ɪm'bærəsɪŋ, ɛm-] *adj* : embarazoso, violento
embarrassment [ɪm'bærəsmənt, ɛm-] *n* : vergüenza *f*, pena *f*
embassy ['ɛmbəsi] *n, pl* **-sies** : embajada *f*
embed [ɪm'bɛd, ɛm-] *vt* **-bedded; -bedding** : incrustar, empotrar, grabar (en la memoria)
embellish [ɪm'bɛlɪʃ, ɛm-] *vt* : adornar, embellecer
embellishment [ɪm'bɛlɪʃmənt, ɛm-] *n* : adorno *m*
ember ['ɛmbər] *n* : ascua *f*, brasa *f*
embezzle [ɪm'bɛzəl, ɛm-] *vt* **-zled; -zling** : desfalcar, malversar
embezzlement [ɪm'bɛzəlmənt, ɛm-] *n* : desfalco *m*, malversación *f*
embezzler [ɪm'bɛzələr, ɛm-] *n* : desfalcador *m*, -dora *f*; malversador *m*, -dora *f*
embitter [ɪm'bɪtər, ɛm-] *vt* : amargar
emblem ['ɛmbləm] *n* : emblema *m*, símbolo *m*
emblematic [ˌɛmblə'mætɪk] *adj* : emblemático, simbólico
embodiment [ɪm'bɑdɪmənt, ɛm-] *n* : encarnación *f*, personificación *f*
embody [ɪm'bɑdi, ɛm-] *vt* **-bodied; -bodying** : encarnar, personificar
emboss [ɪm'bɑs, ɛm-, -'bɔs] *vt* : repujar, grabar en relieve
embrace[1] [ɪm'breɪs, ɛm-] *vt* **-braced; -bracing** **1** HUG : abrazar **2** ADOPT, TAKE ON : adoptar, aceptar **3** INCLUDE : abarcar, incluir
embrace[2] *n* : abrazo *m*
embroider [ɪm'brɔɪdər, ɛm-] *vt* : bordar (una tela), adornar (una historia)
embroidery [ɪm'brɔɪdəri, ɛm-] *n, pl* **-deries** : bordado *m*
embroil [ɪm'brɔɪl, ɛm-] *vt* : embrollar, enredar
embryo ['ɛmbri,oː] *n, pl* **embryos** : embrión *m*

embryonic [ˌɛmbri'ɑnɪk] *adj* : embrionario

emend [i'mɛnd] *vt* : enmendar, corregir

emendation [ˌi:ˌmɛn'deɪʃən] *n* : enmienda *f*

emerald[1] ['ɛmrəld, 'ɛmə-] *adj* : verde esmeralda

emerald[2] *n* : esmeralda *f*

emerge [i'mərʤ] *vi* **emerged; emerging** : emerger, salir, aparecer, surgir

emergence [i'mərʤənʦ] *n* : aparición *f*, surgimiento *m*

emergency [i'mərʤənʦi] *n, pl* **-cies** : emergencia *f*

emergent [i'mərʤənt] *adj* : emergente

emery ['ɛməri] *n, pl* **-eries** : esmeril *m*

emetic[1] [i'mɛtɪk] *adj* : vomitivo, emético

emetic[2] *n* : vomitivo *m*, emético *m*

emigrant ['ɛmɪɡrənt] *n* : emigrante *mf*

emigrate ['ɛməˌɡreɪt] *vi* **-grated; -grating** : emigrar

emigration [ˌɛmə'ɡreɪʃən] *n* : emigración *f*

eminence ['ɛmənənʦ] *n* **1** PROMINENCE : eminencia *f*, prestigio *m*, renombre *m* **2** DIGNITARY : eminencia *f*; dignatario *m*, -ria *f* ⟨Your Eminence : Su Eminencia⟩

eminent ['ɛmənənt] *adj* : eminente, ilustre

eminently ['ɛmənəntli] *adv* : sumamente

emissary ['ɛməˌsɛri] *n, pl* **-saries** : emisario *m*, -ria *f*

emission [i'mɪʃən] *n* : emisión *f*

emit [i'mɪt] *vt* **emitted; emitting** : emitir, despedir, producir

emote [i'mo:t] *vi* **emoted; emoting** : exteriorizar las emociones

emotion [i'mo:ʃən] *n* : emoción *f*, sentimiento *m*

emotional [i'mo:ʃənəl] *adj* **1** : emocional, afectivo ⟨an emotional reaction : una reacción emocional⟩ **2** MOVING : emocionante, emotivo, conmovedor

emotionally [i'mo:ʃənəli] *adv* : emocionalmente

empathy ['ɛmpəθi] *n* : empatía *f*

emperor ['ɛmpərər] *n* : emperador *m*

emphasis ['ɛmfəsɪs] *n, pl* **-phases** [-ˌsi:z] : énfasis *m*, hincapié *m*

emphasize ['ɛmfəˌsaɪz] *vt* **-sized; -sizing** : enfatizar, destacar, subrayar, hacer hincapié en

emphatic [ɪm'fætɪk, ɛm-] *adj* : enfático, enérgico, categórico — **emphatically** [-ɪkli] *adv*

empire ['ɛmˌpaɪr] *n* : imperio *m*

empirical [ɪm'pɪrɪkəl, ɛm-] *adj* : empírico — **empirically** [-ɪkli] *adv*

employ[1] [ɪm'plɔɪ, ɛm-] *vt* **1** USE : usar, utilizar **2** HIRE : contratar, emplear **3** OCCUPY : ocupar, dedicar, emplear

employ[2] [ɪm'plɔɪ, ɛm-; 'ɪmˌ-, 'ɛmˌ-] *n* **1** : puesto *m*, cargo *m*, ocupación *f* **2 to be in the employ of** : estar al servicio de, trabajar para

employee [ɪmˌplɔɪ'i:, ɛm-, -'plɔɪˌi:] *n* : empleado *m*, -da *f*

employer [ɪm'plɔɪər, ɛm-] *n* : patrón *m*, -trona *f*; empleador *m*, -dora *f*

employment [ɪm'plɔɪmənt, ɛm-] *n* : trabajo *m*, empleo *m*

empower [ɪm'paʊər, ɛm-] *vt* : facultar, autorizar, conferirle poder a

empowerment [ɪm'paʊərmənt, ɛm-] *n* : autorización *f*

empress ['ɛmprəs] *n* : emperatriz *f*

emptiness ['ɛmptinəs] *n* : vacío *m*, vacuidad *f*

empty[1] ['ɛmpti] *v* **-tied; -tying** *vt* : vaciar — *vi* : desaguar (dícese de un río)

empty[2] *adj* **emptier; -est 1** : vacío **2** VACANT : desocupado, libre **3** MEANINGLESS : vacío, hueco, vano

empty–handed [ˌɛmpti'hændəd] *adj* : con las manos vacías

empty–headed [ˌɛmpti'hɛdəd] *adj* : cabeza hueca, tonto

emu ['i:ˌmju:] *n* : emú *m*

emulate ['ɛmjəˌleɪt] *vt* **-lated; -lating** : emular

emulation [ˌɛmjə'leɪʃən] *n* : emulación *f*

emulsifier [ɪ'mʌlsəˌfaɪər] *n* : emulsionante *m*

emulsify [ɪ'mʌlsəˌfaɪ] *vt* **-fied; -fying** : emulsionar

emulsion [ɪ'mʌlʃən] *n* : emulsión *f*

enable [ɪ'neɪbəl, ɛ-] *vt* **-abled; -abling 1** EMPOWER : habilitar, autorizar, facultar **2** PERMIT : hacer posible, posibilitar, permitir

enact [ɪ'nækt, ɛ-] *vt* **1** : promulgar (un ley o decreto) **2** : representar (un papel en el teatro)

enactment [ɪ'næktmənt, ɛ-] *n* : promulgación *f*

enamel[1] [ɪ'næməl] *vt* **-eled** *or* **-elled; -eling** *or* **-elling** : esmaltar

enamel[2] *n* : esmalte *m*

enamor [ɪ'næmər] *vt* **1** : enamorar **2 to be enamored of** : estar enamorado de (una persona), estar entusiasmado con (algo)

encamp [ɪn'kæmp, ɛn-] *vi* : acampar

encampment [ɪn'kæmpmənt, ɛn-] *n* : campamento *m*

encase [ɪn'keɪs, ɛn-] *vt* **-cased; -casing** : encerrar, revestir

encephalitis [ɪnˌsfə'laɪtəs, ɛn-] *n, pl* **-litides** ['lɪtəˌdi:z] : encefalitis *f*

enchant [ɪn'tʃænt, ɛn-] *vt* **1** BEWITCH : hechizar, encantar, embrujar **2** CHARM, FASCINATE : cautivar, fascinar, encantar

enchanting [ɪn'tʃæntɪŋ, ɛn-] *adj* : encantador

enchanter [ɪn'tʃæntər, ɛn-] *n* SORCERER : mago *m*, encantador *m*

enchantment [ɪn'tʃæntmənt, ɛn-] *n* **1** SPELL : encanto *m*, hechizo *m* **2** CHARM : encanto *m*

enchantress [ɪn'tʃæntrəs, ɛn-] *n* **1** SORCERESS : maga *f*, hechicera *f* **2** CHARMER : mujer *f* cautivadora

encircle [ɪn'sərkəl, ɛn-] *vt* **-cled; -cling** : rodear, ceñir, cercar

enclose [ɪn'klo:z, ɛn-] *vt* **-closed;
-closing 1** SURROUND : encerrar, cercar, rodear **2** INCLUDE : incluir, adjuntar, acompañar ⟨please find enclosed : le enviamos adjunto⟩

enclosure [ɪn'klo:ʒər, ɛn-] *n* **1** ENCLOSING : encierro *m* **2** : cercado *m* (de terreno), recinto *m* ⟨an enclosure for the press : un recinto para la prensa⟩ **3** ADJUNCT : anexo *m* (con una carta), documento *m* adjunto

encode [ɪn'ko:d, ɛn-] *vt* : cifrar (mensajes, etc.), codificar (en informática)

encompass [ɪn'kʌmpəs, ɛn-, -'kɑm-] *vt* **1** SURROUND : circundar, rodear **2** INCLUDE : abarcar, comprender

encore ['ɑn,kor] *n* : bis *m*, repetición *f*

encounter[1] [ɪn'kauntər, ɛn-] *vt* **1** MEET : encontrar, encontrarse con, toparse con, tropezar con **2** FIGHT : combatir, luchar contra

encounter[2] *n* : encuentro *m*

encourage [ɪn'kərɪʤ, ɛn-] *vt* **-aged;
-aging 1** HEARTEN, INSPIRE : animar, alentar **2** FOSTER : fomentar, promover

encouragement [ɪn'kərɪʤmənt, ɛn-] *n* : ánimo *m*, aliento *m*

encouraging [ɪn'kərəʤɪŋ, ɛn-] *adj* : alentador, esperanzador

encroach [ɪn'kro:ʧ, ɛn-] *vi* **to encroach on** : invadir, abusar (derechos), quitar (tiempo)

encroachment [ɪn'kro:ʧmənt, ɛn-] *n* : invasión *f*, usurpación *f*

encrust [ɪn'krʌst, ɛn-] *vt* **1** : recubrir con una costra **2** INLAY : incrustar ⟨encrusted with gems : incrustado de gemas⟩

encumber [ɪn'kʌmbər, ɛn-] *vt* **1** BLOCK : obstruir, estorbar **2** BURDEN : cargar, gravar

encumbrance [ɪn'kʌmbrənts, ɛn-] *n* : estorbo *m*, carga *f*, gravamen *m*

encyclopedia [ɪn,saɪklə'pi:diə, ɛn-] *n* : enciclopedia *f*

encyclopedic [ɪn,saɪklə'pi:dɪk, ɛn-] *adj* : enciclopédico

end[1] ['ɛnd] *vt* **1** STOP : terminar, poner fin a **2** CONCLUDE : concluir, terminar — *vi* : terminar(se), acabar, concluir(se)

end[2] *n* **1** EXTREMITY : extremo *m*, final *m*, punta *f* **2** CONCLUSION : fin *m*, final *m* **3** AIM : fin *m*

endanger [ɪn'deɪnʤər, ɛn-] *vt* : poner en peligro

endear [ɪn'dɪr, ɛn-] *vt* **to endear oneself to** : ganarse la simpatía de, granjearse el cariño de

endearment [ɪn'dɪrmənt, ɛn-] *n* : expresión *f* de cariño

endeavor[1] [ɪn'dɛvər, ɛn-] *vt* : intentar, esforzarse por ⟨he endeavored to improve his work : intentó por mejorar su trabajo⟩

endeavor[2] *n* : intento *m*, esfuerzo *m*

endemic [ɛn'dɛmɪk, ɪn-] *adj* : endémico

ending ['ɛndɪŋ] *n* **1** CONCLUSION : final *m*, desenlace *m* **2** SUFFIX : sufijo *m*, terminación *f*

endive ['ɛn,daɪv, ,ɑn'di:v] *n* : endibia *f*, endivia *f*

endless ['ɛndləs] *adj* **1** INTERMINABLE : interminable, inacabable, sin fin **2** INNUMERABLE : innumerable, incontable

endlessly ['ɛndləsli] *adv* : interminablemente, eternamente, sin parar

endocrine ['ɛndəkrən, -,kraɪn, -,kri:n] *adj* : endocrino

endorse [ɪn'dɔrs, ɛn-] *vt* **-dorsed;
-dorsing 1** SIGN : endosar, firmar **2** APPROVE : aprobar, sancionar

endorsement [ɪn'dɔrsmənt, ɛn-] *n* **1** SIGNATURE : endoso *m*, firma *f* **2** APPROVAL : aprobación *f*, aval *m*

endow [ɪn'dau, ɛn-] *vt* : dotar

endowment [ɪn'daumənt, ɛn-] *n* **1** FUNDING : dotación *f* **2** DONATION : donación *f*, legado *m* **3** ATTRIBUTE, GIFT : atributo *m*, dotes *fpl*

endurable [ɪn'durəbəl, ɛn-, -'djur-] *adj* : tolerable, soportable

endurance [ɪn'durənts, ɛn-, -'djur-] *n* : resistencia *f*, aguante *m*

endure [ɪn'dur, ɛn-, -'djur] *v* **-dured;
-during** *vt* **1** BEAR : resistir, soportar, aguantar **2** TOLERATE : tolerar, soportar — *vi* LAST : durar, perdurar

enema ['ɛnəmə] *n* : enema *m*, lavativa *f*

enemy ['ɛnəmi] *n, pl* **-mies** : enemigo *m*, -ga *f*

energetic [,ɛnər'ʤɛtɪk] *adj* : enérgico, vigoroso — **energetically** [-tɪkli] *adv*

energize ['ɛnər,ʤaɪz] *vt* **-gized; -gizing
1** ACTIVATE : activar **2** INVIGORATE : vigorizar

energy ['ɛnərʤi] *n, pl* **-gies 1** VITALITY : energía *f*, vitalidad *f* **2** EFFORT : esfuerzo *m*, energías *fpl* **3** POWER : energía *f* ⟨atomic energy : energía atómica⟩

enervate ['ɛnər,veɪt] *vt* **-vated; -vating** : enervar, debilitar

enfold [ɪn'fo:ld, ɛn-] *vt* : envolver

enforce [ɪn'fors, ɛn-] *vt* **-forced; -forcing
1** : hacer respetar, hacer cumplir (una ley, etc.) **2** IMPOSE : imponer ⟨to enforce obedience : imponer la obediencia⟩

enforcement [ɪn'forsmənt, ɛn-] *n* : imposición *f*

enfranchise [ɪn'fræn,ʧaɪz, ɛn-] *vt* **-chised; -chising** : conceder el voto a

enfranchisement [ɪn'fræn,ʧaɪzmənt, ɛn-] *n* : concesión *f* del voto

engage [ɪn'geɪʤ, ɛn-] *v* **-gaged; -gaging**
vt **1** ATTRACT : captar, atraer, llamar ⟨to engage one's attention : captar la atención⟩ **2** MESH : engranar ⟨to engage the clutch : embragar⟩ **3** COMMIT : comprometer ⟨to get engaged : comprometerse⟩ **4** HIRE : contratar **5** : entablar combate con (un enemigo)

— *vi* **1** PARTICIPATE : participar **2 to engage in combat** : entrar en combate

engagement [ɪn'geɪʤmənt, ɛn-] *n* **1** APPOINTMENT : cita *f*, hora *f* **2** BETROTHAL : compromiso *m*

engaging [ɪn'geɪʤɪŋ, ɛn-] *adj* : atractivo, encantador, interesante

engender [ɪn'ʤɛndər, ɛn-] *vt* **-dered; -dering** : engendrar

engine ['ɛnʤən] *n* **1** MOTOR : motor *m* **2** LOCOMOTIVE : locomotora *f*, máquina *f*

engineer¹ [ˌɛnʤə'nɪr] *vt* **1** : diseñar, construir (un sistema, un mecanismo, etc.) **2** CONTRIVE : maquinar, tramar, fraguar

engineer² *n* **1** : ingeniero *m*, -ra *f* **2** : maquinista *mf* (de locomotoras)

engineering [ˌɛnʤə'nɪrɪŋ] *n* : ingeniería *f*

English¹ ['ɪŋglɪʃ, 'ɪŋlɪʃ] *adj* : inglés

English² *n* **1** : inglés *m* (idioma) **2 the English** : los ingleses

Englishman ['ɪŋglɪʃmən, 'ɪŋlɪʃ-] *n, pl* **-men** [-mən, -ˌmɛn] : inglés *m*

Englishwoman ['ɪŋglɪʃˌwʊmən, 'ɪŋlɪʃ-] *n, pl* **-women** [-ˌwɪmən] : inglesa *f*

engrave [ɪn'greɪv, ɛn-] *vt* **-graved; -graving** : grabar

engraver [ɪn'greɪvər, ɛn-] *n* : grabador *m*, -dora *f*

engraving [ɪn'greɪvɪŋ, ɛn-] *n* : grabado *m*

engross [ɪn'groːs, ɛn-] *vt* : absorber

engrossed [ɪn'groːst, ɛn-] *adj* : absorto

engrossing [ɪn'groːsɪŋ, ɛn-] *adj* : fascinante, absorbente

engulf [ɪn'gʌlf, ɛn-] *vt* : envolver, sepultar

enhance [ɪn'hænts, ɛn-] *vt* **-hanced; -hancing** : realzar, aumentar, mejorar

enhancement [ɪn'hæntsmənt, ɛn-] *n* : mejora *f*, realce *m*, aumento *m*

enigma [ɪ'nɪgmə] *n* : enigma *m*

enigmatic [ˌɛnɪg'mætɪk, ˌiːnɪg-] *adj* : enigmático — **enigmatically** [-ˌtɪkli] *adv*

enjoin [ɪn'ʤɔɪn, ɛn-] *vt* **1** COMMAND : ordenar, imponer **2** FORBID : prohibir, vedar

enjoy [ɪn'ʤɔɪ, ɛn-] *vt* **1** : disfrutar, gozar de ⟨did you enjoy the book? : ¿te gustó el libro?⟩ ⟨to enjoy good health : gozar de buena salud⟩ **2 to enjoy oneself** : divertirse, pasarlo bien

enjoyable [ɪn'ʤɔɪəbəl, ɛn-] *adj* : agradable, placentero, divertido

enjoyment [ɪn'ʤɔɪmənt, ɛn-] *n* : placer *m*, goce *m*, disfrute *m*, deleite *m*

enlarge [ɪn'lɑrʤ, ɛn-] *v* **-larged; -larging** *vt* : extender, agrandar, ampliar — *vi* **1** : ampliarse **2 to enlarge upon** : extenderse sobre, entrar en detalles sobre

enlargement [ɪn'lɑrʤmənt, ɛn-] *n* : expansión *f*, ampliación *f* (dícese de fotografías)

enlarger [ɪn'lɑrʤər, ɛn-] *n* : ampliadora *f*

enlighten [ɪn'laɪtən, ɛn-] *vt* : iluminar, aclarar

enlightenment [ɪn'laɪtənmənt, ɛn-] *n* **1** : ilustración *f* ⟨the Enlightenment : la Ilustración⟩ **2** CLARIFICATION : aclaración *f*

enlist [ɪn'lɪst, ɛn-] *vt* **1** ENROLL : alistar, reclutar **2** SECURE : conseguir ⟨to enlist the support of : conseguir el apoyo de⟩ — *vi* : alistarse

enlisted man [ɪn'lɪstəd, ɛn-] *n* : soldado *m* raso

enlistment [ɪn'lɪstmənt, ɛn-] *n* : alistamiento *m*, reclutamiento *m*

enliven [ɪn'laɪvən, ɛn-] *vt* : animar, alegrar, darle vida a

enmity ['ɛnməti] *n, pl* **-ties** : enemistad *f*, animadversión *f*

ennoble [ɪ'noːbəl, ɛ-] *vt* **-bled; -bling** : ennoblecer

ennui [ˌɑn'wiː] *n* : hastío *m*, tedio *m*, fastidio *m*, aburrimiento *m*

enormity [ɪ'nɔrməti] *n, pl* **-ties 1** ATROCITY : atrocidad *f*, barbaridad *f* **2** IMMENSITY : enormidad *f*, inmensidad *f*

enormous [ɪ'nɔrməs] *adj* : enorme, inmenso, tremendo — **enormously** *adv*

enough¹ [ɪ'nʌf] *adv* **1** : bastante, suficientemente **2 fair enough!** : ¡está bien!, ¡de acuerdo! **3 strangely enough** : por extraño que parezca **4 sure enough** : en efecto, sin duda alguna **5 well enough** : muy bien, bastante bien

enough² *adj* : bastante, suficiente ⟨do we have enough chairs? : ¿tenemos suficientes sillas?⟩

enough³ *pron* : (lo) suficiente, (lo) bastante ⟨enough to eat : lo suficiente para comer⟩ ⟨it's not enough : no basta⟩ ⟨I've had enough! : ¡estoy harto!, ¡está bueno ya!⟩

enquire [ɪn'kwaɪr, ɛn-] **enquiry** ['ɪnˌkwaɪri, 'ɛn-, -kwəri; ɪn'kwaɪri, ɛn'-] → **inquire, inquiry**

enrage [ɪn'reɪʤ, ɛn-] *vt* **-raged; -raging** : enfurecer, encolerizar

enraged [ɪn'reɪʤd, ɛn-] *adj* : enfurecido, furioso

enrich [ɪn'rɪʧ, ɛn-] *vt* : enriquecer

enrichment [ɪn'rɪʧmənt, ɛn-] *n* : enriquecimiento *m*

enroll *or* **enrol** [ɪn'roːl, ɛn-] *v* **-rolled; -rolling** *vt* : matricular, inscribir — *vi* : matricularse, inscribirse

enrollment [ɪn'roːlmənt, ɛn-] *n* : matrícula *f*, inscripción *f*

en route [ɑ'ruːt, ɛn'raʊt] *adv* : de camino, por el camino

ensconce [ɪn'skɑnts, ɛn-] *vt* **-sconced; -sconcing** : acomodar, instalar, establecer cómodamente

ensemble [ɑn'sɑmbəl] *n* : conjunto *m*

enshrine [ɪn'ʃraɪn, ɛn-] *vt* **-shrined; -shrining** : conservar religiosamente, preservar

ensign ['ɛnʦən, 'ɛnˌsaɪn] *n* **1** FLAG : enseña *f*, pabellón *m* **2** : alférez *mf* (de fragata)

enslave [ɪnˈsleɪv, ɛn-] *vt* **-slaved; -slaving** : esclavizar

enslavement [ɪnˈsleɪvmənt, ɛn-] *n* : esclavización *f*

ensnare [ɪnˈsnær, ɛn-] *vt* **-snared; -snaring** : atrapar

ensue [ɪnˈsuː, ɛn-] *vi* **-sued; -suing** : seguir, resultar

ensure [ɪnˈʃʊr, ɛn-] *vt* **-sured; -suring** : asegurar, garantizar

entail [ɪnˈteɪl, ɛn-] *vt* : implicar, suponer, conllevar

entangle [ɪnˈtæŋɡəl, ɛn-] *vt* **-gled; -gling** : enredar

entanglement [ɪnˈtæŋɡəlmənt, ɛn-] *n* : enredo *m*

enter [ˈɛntər] *vt* **1** : entrar en, entrar a **2** BEGIN : entrar en, comenzar, iniciar **3** RECORD : anotar, inscribir, dar entrada a ⟨to enter data : introducir datos⟩ **4** JOIN : entrar en, alistarse en, hacerse socio de — *vi* **1** : entrar **2 to enter into** : entrar en, firmar (un acuerdo), entablar (negociaciones, etc.)

enterprise [ˈɛntərˌpraɪz] *n* **1** UNDERTAKING : empresa *f* **2** BUSINESS : empresa *f*, firma *f* **3** INITIATIVE : iniciativa *f*, empuje *m*

enterprising [ˈɛntərˌpraɪzɪŋ] *adj* : emprendedor

entertain [ˌɛntərˈteɪn] *vt* **1** : recibir, agasajar ⟨to entertain guests : tener invitados⟩ **2** CONSIDER : considerar, contemplar **3** AMUSE : entretener, divertir

entertainer [ˌɛntərˈteɪnər] *n* : artista *mf*

entertaining [ˌɛntərˈteɪnɪŋ] *adj* : entretenido, divertido

entertainment [ˌɛntərˈteɪnmənt] *n* : entretenimiento *m*, diversión *f*

enthrall *or* **enthral** [ɪnˈθrɔl, ɛn-] *vt* **-thralled; -thralling** : cautivar, embelesar

enthuse [ɪnˈθuiz, ɛn-] *v* **-thused; -thusing** *vt* **1** EXCITE : entusiasmar **2** : decir con entusiasmo — *vi* **to enthuse over** : hablar con entusiasmo sobre

enthusiasm [ɪnˈθuːziˌæzəm, ɛn-, -ˈθjuː-] *n* : entusiasmo *m*

enthusiast [ɪnˈθuːziˌæst, ɛn-, -ˈθjuː-, -əst] *n* : entusiasta *mf*; aficionado *m*, -da *f*

enthusiastic [ɪnˌθuːziˈæstɪk, ɛn-, -ˌθjuː-] *adj* : entusiasta, aficionado

enthusiastically [ɪnˌθuːziˈæstɪkli, ɛn-, -ˌθjuː-] *adv* : con entusiasmo

entice [ɪnˈtaɪs, ɛn-] *vt* **-ticed; -ticing** : atraer, tentar

enticement [ɪnˈtaɪsmənt, ɛn-] *n* : tentación *f*, atracción *f*, señuelo *m*

entire [ɪnˈtaɪr, ɛn-] *adj* : entero, completo

entirely [ɪnˈtaɪrli, ɛn-] *adv* : completamente, totalmente

entirety [ɪnˈtaɪrti, ɛn-, -ˈtaɪrəti] *n, pl* **-ties** : totalidad *f*

entitle [ɪnˈtaɪtəl, ɛn-] *vt* **-tled; -tling 1** NAME : titular, intitular **2** : dar derecho a ⟨it entitles you to enter free : le da derecho a entrar gratis⟩ **3 to be entitled to** : tener derecho a

entitlement [ɪnˈtaɪtəlmənt, ɛn-] *n* RIGHT : derecho *m*

entity [ˈɛntəti] *n, pl* **-ties** : entidad *f*, ente *m*

entomologist [ˌɛntəˈmɑlədʒɪst] *n* : entomólogo *m*, -ga *f*

entomology [ˌɛntəˈmɑlədʒi] *n* : entomología *f*

entourage [ˌɑntʊˈrɑʒ] *n* : séquito *m*

entrails [ˈɛnˌtreɪlz, -trəlz] *npl* : entrañas *fpl*, vísceras *fpl*

entrance[1] [ɪnˈtrænts, ɛn-] *vt* **-tranced; -trancing** : encantar, embelesar, fascinar

entrance[2] [ˈɛntrənts] *n* **1** ENTERING : entrada *f* ⟨to make an entrance : entrar en escena⟩ **2** ENTRY : entrada *f*, puerta *f* **3** ADMISSION : entrada *f*, ingreso *m* ⟨entrance examination : examen de ingreso⟩

entrant [ˈɛntrənt] *n* : candidato *m*, -ta *f* (en un examen); participante *mf* (en un concurso)

entrap [ɪnˈtræp, ɛn-] *vt* **-trapped; -trapping** : atrapar, entrampar, hacer caer en una trampa

entrapment [ɪnˈtræpmənt, ɛn-] *n* : captura *f*

entreat [ɪnˈtriːt, ɛn-] *vt* : suplicar, rogar

entreaty [ɪnˈtriːti, ɛn-] *n, pl* **-treaties** : ruego *m*, súplica *f*

entrée *or* **entree** [ˈɑnˌtreɪ, ˌɑnˈ-] *n* : plato *m* principal

entrench [ɪnˈtrɛnʃ, ɛn-] *vt* **1** FORTIFY : atrincherar (una posición militar) **2** : consolidar, afianzar ⟨firmly entrenched in his job : afianzado en su puesto⟩

entrepreneur [ˌɑntrəprəˈnər, -ˈnjʊr] *n* : empresario *m*, -ria *f*

entrust [ɪnˈtrʌst, ɛn-] *vt* : confiar, encomendar

entry [ˈɛntri] *n, pl* **-tries 1** ENTRANCE : entrada *f* **2** NOTATION : entrada *f*, anotación *f*

entwine [ɪnˈtwaɪn, ɛn-] *vt* **-twined; -twining** : entrelazar, entretejer, entrecruzar

enumerate [ɪˈnuːməˌreɪt, ɛ-, -ˈnjuː-] *vt* **-ated; -ating 1** LIST : enumerar **2** COUNT : contar, enumerar

enumeration [ɪˌnuːməˈreɪʃən, ɛ-, -ˌnjuː-] *n* : enumeración *f*, lista *f*

enunciate [iˈnʌntsiˌeɪt, ɛ-] *vt* **-ated; -ating 1** STATE : enunciar, decir **2** PRONOUNCE : articular, pronunciar

enunciation [iˌnʌntsiˈeɪʃən, ɛ-] *n* **1** STATEMENT : enunciación *f*, declaración *f* **2** ARTICULATION : articulación *f*, pronunciación *f*, dicción *f*

envelop [ɪnˈvləp, ɛn-] *vt* : envolver, cubrir

envelope [ˈɛnvəˌloːp, ˈɑn-] *n* : sobre *m*

enviable [ˈɛnviəbəl] *adj* : envidiable

envious [ˈɛnviəs] *adj* : envidioso — **enviously** *adv*

environment [ɪn'vaɪrənmənt, ɛn-, -'vaɪərn-] *n* : medio *m* (ambiente), ambiente *m*, entorno *m*

environmental [ɪn,vaɪrən'mɛntəl, ɛn-, -,vaɪərn-] *adj* : ambiental

environmentalist [ɪn,vaɪrən'mɛntəlɪst, ɛn-, -,vaɪərn-] *n* : ecologista *mf*

environs [ɪn'vaɪrənz, ɛn-, -'vaɪərnz] *npl* : alrededores *mpl*, entorno *m*, inmediaciones *fpl*

envisage [ɪn'vɪzɪʤ, ɛn-] *vt* **-aged; -aging** **1** IMAGINE : imaginarse, concebir **2** FORESEE : prever

envision [ɪn'vɪʒən, ɛn-] *vt* : imaginar

envoy ['ɛn,vɔɪ, 'ɑn-] *n* : enviado *m*, -da *f*

envy[1] ['ɛnvi] *vt* **-vied; -vying** : envidiar

envy[2] *n, pl* **envies** : envidia *f*

enzyme ['ɛn,zaɪm] *n* : enzima *f*

eon ['i:ən, i:,ɑn] → **aeon**

epaulet [,pə'lɛt] *n* : charretera *f*

ephemeral [ɪ'fɛmərəl, -'fi:-] *adj* : efímero, fugaz

epic[1] ['ɛpɪk] *adj* : épico

epic[2] *n* : poema *m* épico, epopeya *f*

epicure ['ɛpɪ,kjʊr] *n* : epicúreo *m*, -rea *f*; gastrónomo *m*, -ma *f*

epicurean [,ɛpɪkjʊ'ri:ən, -'kjʊriən] *adj* : epicúreo

epidemic[1] [,ɛpə'dɛmɪk] *adj* : epidémico

epidemic[2] *n* : epidemia *f*

epidermis [,ɛpə'dərməs] *n* : epidermis *f*

epigram ['ɛpə,græm] *n* : epigrama *m*

epilepsy ['ɛpə,lɛpsi] *n, pl* **-sies** : epilepsia *f*

epileptic[1] [,ɛpə'lɛptɪk] *adj* : epiléptico

epileptic[2] *n* : epiléptico *m*, -ca *f*

epilogue ['ɛpə,lɔg, -,lɑg] *n* : epílogo *m*

epiphany [ɪ'pɪfəni] *n, pl* **-nies** **1** **Epiphany** : Epifanía *f* **2 to have an epiphany** : tener una revelación

episcopal [ɪ'pɪskəpəl] *adj* : episcopal

Episcopalian [ɪ,pɪskə'peɪljən] *n* : episcopalista *mf*; episcopaliano *m*, -na *f*

episode ['ɛpə,so:d] *n* : episodio *m*

episodic [,ɛpə'sɑdɪk] *adj* : episódico

epistle [ɪ'pɪsəl] *n* : epístola *f*, carta *f*

epitaph ['ɛpə,tæf] *n* : epitafio *m*

epithet ['ɛpə,θɛt, -θət] *n* : epíteto *m*

epitome [ɪ'pɪtəmi] *n* **1** SUMMARY : epítome *m*, resumen *m* **2** EMBODIMENT : personificación *f*

epitomize [ɪ'pɪtə,maɪz] *vt* **-mized; -mizing** **1** SUMMARIZE : resumir **2** EMBODY : ser la personificación de, personificar

epoch ['ɛpək, 'ɛ,pɑk, 'i:,pɑk] *n* : época *f*, era *f*

epoxy [ɪ'pɑksi] *n, pl* **epoxies** : resina *f* epoxídica

equable ['ɛkwəbəl, 'i:-] *adj* **1** CALM, STEADY : ecuánime **2** UNIFORM : estable (dícese de la temperatura), constante (dícese del clima), uniforme

equably ['ɛkwəbli, 'i:-] *adv* : con ecuanimidad

equal[1] ['i:kwəl] *vt* **equaled** *or* **equalled; equaling** *or* **equalling** **1** : ser igual a

⟨two plus three equals five : dos más tres es igual a cinco⟩ **2** MATCH : igualar

equal[2] *adj* **1** SAME : igual **2** ADEQUATE : adecuado, capaz

equal[3] *n* : igual *mf*

equality [ɪ'kwɑləti] *n, pl* **-ties** : igualdad *f*

equalize ['i:kwə,laɪz] *vt* **-ized; -izing** : igualar, equiparar

equally ['i:kwəli] *adv* : igualmente, por igual

equanimity [,i:kwə'nɪməti, ,ɛ-] *n, pl* **-ties** : ecuanimidad *f*

equate [ɪ'kweɪt] *vt* **equated; equating** : equiparar, identificar

equation [ɪ'kweɪʒən] *n* : ecuación *f*

equator [ɪ'kweɪtər] *n* : ecuador *m*

equatorial [,i:kwə'toriəl, ,ɛ-] *adj* : ecuatorial

equestrian[1] [ɪ'kwɛstriən, ɛ-] *adj* : ecuestre

equestrian[2] *n* : jinete *mf*, caballista *mf*

equilateral [,i:kwə'lætərəl, ,ɛ-] *adj* : equilátero

equilibrium [,i:kwə'lɪbriəm, ,ɛ-] *n, pl* **-riums** *or* **-ria** [-briə] : equilibrio *m*

equine ['i:,kwaɪn, 'ɛ-] *adj* : equino, hípico

equinox ['i:kwə,nɑks, 'ɛ-] *n* : equinoccio *m*

equip [ɪ'kwɪp] *vt* **equipped; equipping** **1** FURNISH : equipar **2** PREPARE : preparar

equipment [ɪ'kwɪpmənt] *n* : equipo *m*

equitable ['ɛkwətəbəl] *adj* : equitativo, justo, imparcial

equity ['ɛkwəti] *n, pl* **-ties** **1** FAIRNESS : equidad *f*, imparcialidad *f* **2** VALUE : valor *m* líquido

equivalence [ɪ'kwɪvələnts] *n* : equivalencia *f*

equivalent[1] [ɪ'kwɪvələnt] *adj* : equivalente

equivalent[2] *n* : equivalente *m*

equivocal [ɪ'kwɪvəkəl] *adj* **1** AMBIGUOUS : equívoco, ambiguo **2** QUESTIONABLE : incierto, dudoso, sospechoso

equivocate [ɪ'kwɪvə,keɪt] *vi* **-cated; -cating** : usar lenguaje equívoco, andarse con evasivas

equivocation [ɪ'kwɪvə'keɪʃən] *n* : evasiva *f*, subterfugio *m*

era ['ɪrə, 'ɛrə, 'i:rə] *n* : era *f*, época *f*

eradicate [ɪ'rædə,keɪt] *vt* **-cated; -cating** : erradicar

erase [ɪ'reɪs] *vt* **erased; erasing** : borrar

eraser [ɪ'reɪsər] *n* : goma *f* de borrar, borrador *m*

erasure [ɪ'reɪʃər] *n* : tachadura *f*

ere[1] ['ɛr] *conj* : antes de que

ere[2] *prep* **1** : antes de **2 ere long** : dentro de poco

erect[1] [ɪ'rɛkt] *vt* **1** CONSTRUCT : erigir, construir **2** RAISE : levantar **3** ESTABLISH : establecer

erect[2] *adj* : erguido, derecho, erecto

erection [ɪ'rɛkʃən] *n* **1** : erección *f* (en fisiología) **2** BUILDING : construcción *f*

ergonomics [ˌərgə'nɑmɪks] *npl* : ergonomía *f*

ermine ['ərmən] *n* : armiño *m*

erode [ɪ'ro:d] *vt* **eroded; eroding** : erosionar (el suelo), corroer (metales)

erosion [ɪ'ro:ʒən] *n* : erosión *f*, corrosión *f*

erotic [ɪ'rɑtɪk] *adj* : erótico — **erotically** [-tɪkli] *adv*

eroticism [ɪ'rɑtəˌsɪzəm] *n* : erotismo *m*

err ['ɛr, 'ər] *vi* : cometer un error, equivocarse, errar

errand ['ɛrənd] *n* : mandado *m*, encargo *m*, recado *m* *Spain* ⟨an errand of mercy : una misión de caridad⟩

errant ['ɛrənt] *adj* **1** WANDERING : errante **2** ASTRAY : descarriado

erratic [ɪ'rætɪk] *adj* **1** INCONSISTENT : errático, irregular, inconsistente **2** ECCENTRIC : excéntrico, raro

erratically [ɪ'rætɪkli] *adv* : erráticamente, de manera irregular

erroneous [ɪ'ro:niəs, ɛ-] *adj* : erróneo — **erroneously** *adv*

error ['ɛrər] *n* : error *m*, equivocación *f* ⟨to be in error : estar equivocado⟩

ersatz ['ɛrˌsɑts, 'ərˌsæts] *adj* : artificial, sustituto

erstwhile ['ərstˌʰwaɪl] *adj* : antiguo

erudite ['ɛrəˌdaɪt, 'ɛrjʊ-] *adj* : erudito, letrado

erudition [ˌɛrə'dɪʃən, ˌɛrjʊ-] *n* : erudición *f*

erupt [ɪ'rʌpt] *vi* **1** : hacer erupción (dícese de un volcán o un sarpullido) **2** : estallar (dícese de la cólera o la violencia)

eruption [ɪ'rʌpʃən] *n* : erupción *f*, estallido *m*

eruptive [ɪ'rʌptɪv] *adj* : eruptivo

escalate ['ɛskəˌleɪt] *v* **-lated; -lating** *vt* : intensificar (un conflicto), aumentar (precios) — *vi* : intensificarse, aumentarse

escalation [ˌɛskə'leɪʃən] *n* : intensificación *f*, escalada *f*, aumento *m*, subida *f*

escalator ['ɛskəˌleɪtər] *n* : escalera *f* mecánica

escapade ['ɛskəˌpeɪd] *n* : aventura *f*

escape¹ [ɪ'skeɪp, ɛ-] *v* **-caped; -caping** *vt* : escaparse de, librarse de, evitar — *vi* : escaparse, fugarse, huir

escape² *n* **1** FLIGHT : fuga *f*, huida *f*, escapada *f* **2** LEAKAGE : escape *m*, fuga *f* **3** : escapatoria *f*, evasión *f* ⟨to have no escape : no tener escapatoria⟩ ⟨escape from reality : evasión de la realidad⟩

escapee [ɪˌskeɪ'pi:, ˌɛ-] *n* : fugitivo *m*, -va *f*

escarole ['ɛskəˌro:l] *n* : escarola *f*

escarpment [ɪs'kɑrpmənt, ɛs-] *n* : escarpa *f*, escarpadura *f*

eschew [ɛ'ʃu:, ɪs'tʃu:] *vt* : evitar, rehuir, abstenerse de

escort¹ [ɪ'skɔrt, ɛ-] *vt* **1** : escoltar ⟨to escort a ship : escoltar un barco⟩ **2** ACCOMPANY : acompañar

escort² ['ɛsˌkɔrt] *n* **1** : escolta *f* ⟨armed escort : escolta armada⟩ **2** COMPANION : acompañante *mf*; compañero *m*, -ra *f*

escrow ['ɛsˌkro:] *n* **in escrow** : en depósito, en custodia de un tercero

Eskimo ['ɛskəˌmo:] *n* **1** : esquimal *mf* **2** : esquimal *m* (idioma) — **Eskimo** *adj*

esophagus [ɪ'sɑfəgəs, i:-] *n, pl* **-gi** [-ˌgaɪ, -ˌdʒaɪ] : esófago *m*

esoteric [ˌɛsə'tɛrɪk] *adj* : esotérico, hermético

especially [ɪ'spɛʃəli] *adv* : especialmente, particularmente

espionage ['ɛspiəˌnɑʒ, -ˌnɑdʒ] *n* : espionaje *m*

espouse [ɪ'spaʊz, ɛ-] *vt* **espoused; espousing** **1** MARRY : casarse con **2** ADOPT, ADVOCATE : apoyar, adherirse a, adoptar

espresso ['ɛspreˌso:] *n, pl* **-sos** : café *m* exprés

essay¹ ['ɛseɪ, 'ɛ,seɪ] *vt* : intentar, tratar

essay² ['ɛ,seɪ] *n* **1** COMPOSITION : ensayo *m*, trabajo *m* **2** ATTEMPT : intento *m*

essayist ['ɛ,seɪɪst] *n* : ensayista *mf*

essence ['ɛsənts] *n* **1** CORE : esencia *f*, núcleo *m*, meollo *m* ⟨in essence : esencialmente⟩ **2** EXTRACT : esencia *f*, extracto *m* **3** PERFUME : esencia *f*, perfume *m*

essential¹ [ɪ'sɛntʃəl] *adj* : esencial, imprescindible, fundamental — **essentially** *adv*

essential² *n* : elemento *m* esencial, lo imprescindible

establish [ɪ'stæblɪʃ, ɛ-] *vt* **1** FOUND : establecer, fundar **2** SET UP : establecer, instaurar, instituir **3** PROVE : demostrar, probar

establishment [ɪ'stæblɪʃmənt, ɛ-] *n* **1** ESTABLISHING : establecimiento *m*, fundación *f*, instauración *f* **2** BUSINESS : negocio *m*, establecimiento *m* **3** **the Establishment** : la clase dirigente

estate [ɪ'steɪt, ɛ-] *n* **1** POSSESSIONS : bienes *mpl*, propiedad *f*, patrimonio *m* **2** PROPERTY : hacienda *f*, finca *f*, propiedad *f*

esteem¹ [ɪ'sti:m, ɛ-] *vt* : estimar, apreciar

esteem² *n* : estima *f*, aprecio *m*

ester ['ɛstər] *n* : éster *m*

esthetic [ɛs'θɛtɪk] → **aesthetic**

estimable ['ɛstəməbəl] *adj* : estimable

estimate¹ ['ɛstəˌmeɪt] *vt* **-mated; -mating** : calcular, estimar

estimate² ['ɛstəmət] *n* **1** : cálculo *m* aproximado ⟨to make an estimate : hacer un cálculo⟩ **2** ASSESSMENT : valoración *f*, estimación *f*

estimation [ˌɛstə'meɪʃən] *n* **1** JUDGMENT : juicio *m*, opinión *f* ⟨in my estimation : en mi opinión, según mis cálculos⟩ **2** ESTEEM : estima *f*, aprecio *m*

estimator [ˈɛstəˌmeɪtər] *n* : tasador *m*, -dora *f*
Estonian [ɛˈstoːniən] *n* : estonio *m*, -nia *f* — **Estonian** *adj*
estrange [ɪˈstreɪndʒ, ɛ-] *vt* **-tranged; -tranging** : enajenar, apartar, alejar
estrangement [ɪˈstreɪndʒmənt, ɛ-] *n* : alejamiento *m*, distanciamiento *m*
estrogen [ˈɛstrədʒən] *n* : estrógeno *m*
estrus [ˈɛstrəs] *n* : celo *m*
estuary [ˈɛstʃuˌwɛri] *n*, *pl* **-aries** : estuario *m*, -ría *f*
et cetera [ɛtˈsɛtərə, -ˈsɛtrə] : etcétera
etch [ˈɛtʃ] *v* : grabar al aguafuerte
etching [ˈɛtʃɪŋ] *n* : aguafuerte *m*, grabado *m* al aguafuerte
eternal [ɪˈtərnəl, iː-] *adj* **1** EVERLASTING : eterno **2** INTERMINABLE : constante, incesante
eternally [ɪˈtərnəli, iː-] *adv* : eternamente, para siempre
eternity [ɪˈtərnəti, iː-] *n*, *pl* **-ties** : eternidad *f*
ethane [ˈɛˌθeɪn] *n* : etano *m*
ethanol [ˈɛθəˌnɔl, -ˌnoːl] *n* : etanol *m*
ether [ˈiːθər] *n* : éter *m*
ethereal [ɪˈθɪriəl, iː-] *adj* **1** CELESTIAL : etéreo, celeste **2** DELICATE : delicado
ethical [ˈɛθɪkəl] *adj* : ético — **ethically** *adv*
ethics [ˈɛθɪks] *ns & pl* **1** : ética *f* **2** MORALITY : ética *f*, moral *f*, moralidad *f*
Ethiopian [ˌiːθiˈoːpiən] *n* : etíope *mf* — **Ethiopian** *adj*
ethnic [ˈɛθnɪk] *adj* : étnico
ethnologist [ɛθˈnɑlədʒɪst] *n* : etnólogo *m*, -ga *f*
ethnology [ɛθˈnɑlədʒi] *n* : etnología *f*
etiquette [ˈɛtɪkət, -ˌkɛt] *n* : etiqueta *f*, protocolo *m*
etymological [ˌɛtəməˈlɑdʒɪkəl] *adj* : etimológico
etymology [ˌɛtəˈmɑlədʒi] *n*, *pl* **-gies** : etimología *f*
eucalyptus [ˌjuːkəˈlɪptəs] *n*, *pl* **-ti** [-ˌtaɪ] *or* **-tuses** [-təsəz] : eucalipto *m*
Eucharist [ˈjuːkərɪst] *n* : Eucaristía *f*
eulogize [ˈjuːləˌdʒaɪz] *vt* **-gized; -gizing** : elogiar, encomiar
eulogy [ˈjuːlədʒi] *n*, *pl* **-gies** : elogio *m*, encomio *m*, panegírico *m*
eunuch [ˈjuːnək] *n* : eunuco *m*
euphemism [ˈjuːfəˌmɪzəm] *n* : eufemismo *m*
euphemistic [ˌjuːfəˈmɪstɪk] *adj* : eufemístico
euphony [ˈjuːfəni] *n*, *pl* **-nies** : eufonía *f*
euphoria [jʊˈforiə] *n* : euforia *f*
euphoric [jʊˈforɪk] *adj* : eufórico
European [ˌjʊrəˈpiːən] *n* : europeo *m*, europea *f* — **European** *adj*
euthanasia [ˌjuːθəˈneɪʒə, -ʒiə] *n* : eutanasia *f*
evacuate [ɪˈvækjuˌeɪt] *v* **-ated; -ating** *vt* VACATE : evacuar, desalojar — *vi* WITHDRAW : retirarse

evacuation [ɪˌvækjuˈeɪʃən] *n* : evacuación *f*, desalojo *m*
evade [ɪˈveɪd] *vt* **evaded; evading** : evadir, eludir, esquivar
evaluate [ɪˈvæljuˌeɪt] *vt* **-ated; -ating** : evaluar, valorar, tasar
evaluation [ɪˌvæljuˈeɪʃən] *n* : evaluación *f*, valoración *f*, tasación *f*
evangelical [ˌiːˌvænˈdʒɛlɪkəl, ˌɛvən-] *adj* : evangélico
evangelist [ɪˈvændʒəlɪst] *n* **1** : evangelista *m* **2** PREACHER : predicador *m*, -dora *f*
evaporate [ɪˈvæpəˌreɪt] *vi* **-rated; -rating** **1** VAPORIZE : evaporarse **2** VANISH : evaporarse, desvanecerse, esfumarse
evaporation [ɪˌvæpəˈreɪʃən] *n* : evaporación *f*
evasion [ɪˈveɪʒən] *n* : evasión *f*
evasive [ɪˈveɪsɪv] *adj* : evasivo
evasiveness [ɪˈveɪsɪvnəs] *n* : carácter *m* evasivo
eve [ˈiːv] *n* **1** : víspera *f* ⟨on the eve of the festivities : en vísperas de las festividades⟩ **2** → **evening**
even[1] [ˈiːvən] *vt* **1** LEVEL : allanar, nivelar, emparejar **2** EQUALIZE : igualar, equilibrar — *vi* **to even out** : nivelarse, emparejarse
even[2] *adv* **1** : hasta, incluso ⟨even a child can do it : hasta un niño puede hacerlo⟩ ⟨he looked content, even happy : se le veía satisfecho, incluso feliz⟩ **2** (*in negative constructions*) : ni siquiera ⟨he didn't even try : ni siquiera lo intentó⟩ **3** (*in comparisons*) : aún, todavía ⟨even better : aún mejor, todavía mejor⟩ **4 even if** : aunque **5 even so** : aun así **6 even though** : aun cuando, a pesar de que
even[3] *adj* **1** SMOOTH : uniforme, liso, parejo **2** FLAT : plano, llano **3** EQUAL : igual, igualado ⟨an even score : un marcador igualado⟩ **4** REGULAR : regular, constante ⟨an even pace : un ritmo constante⟩ **5** EXACT : exacto, justo **6** : par ⟨even number : número par⟩ **7 to be even** : estar en paz, estar a mano **8 to get even** : desquitarse, vengarse
evening [ˈiːvnɪŋ] *n* : tarde *f*, noche *f* ⟨in the evening : por la noche⟩
evenly [ˈiːvənli] *adv* **1** UNIFORMLY : de modo uniforme, de manera constante **2** FAIRLY : igualmente, equitativamente
evenness [ˈiːvənnəs] *n* : uniformidad *f*, igualdad *f*, regularidad *f*
event [ɪˈvɛnt] *n* **1** : acontecimiento *m*, suceso *m*, prueba *f* (en deportes) **2 in the event that** : en caso de que
eventful [ɪˈvɛntfəl] *adj* : lleno de incidentes, memorable
eventual [ɪˈvɛntʃuəl] *adj* : final, consiguiente
eventuality [ɪˌvɛntʃuˈæləti] *n*, *pl* **-ties** : eventualidad *f*
eventually [ɪˈvɛntʃuəli] *adv* : al fin, con el tiempo, algún día

ever [ˈɛvər] *adv* **1** ALWAYS : siempre ⟨as ever : como siempre⟩ ⟨ever since : desde entonces⟩ **2** (*in questions*) : alguna vez, algún día ⟨have you ever been to Mexico? : ¿has estado en México alguna vez?⟩ **3** (*in negative constructions*) : nunca ⟨doesn't he ever work? : ¿es que nunca trabaja?⟩ ⟨nobody ever helps me : nadie nunca me ayuda⟩ **4** (*in comparisons*) : nunca ⟨better than ever : mejor que nunca⟩ **5** (*as intensifier*) ⟨I'm ever so happy! : ¡estoy tan y tan feliz!⟩ ⟨he looks ever so angry : parece estar muy enojado⟩

evergreen¹ [ˈɛvərˌgriːn] *adj* : de hoja perenne

evergreen² *n* : planta *f* de hoja perenne

everlasting [ˌɛvərˈlæstɪŋ] *adj* : eterno, perpetuo, imperecedero

evermore [ˌɛvərˈmor] *adv* : eternamente

every [ˈɛvri] *adj* **1** EACH : cada ⟨every time : cada vez⟩ ⟨every other house : cada dos casas⟩ **2** ALL : todo ⟨every month : todos los meses⟩ ⟨every woman : toda mujer, todas las mujeres⟩ **3** COMPLETE : pleno, entero ⟨to have every confidence : tener plena confianza⟩

everybody [ˈɛvriˌbʌdi, -ˌbɑ-] *pron* : todos *mpl*, -das *fpl*; todo el mundo

everyday [ˌɛvriˈdei, ˈɛvriˌ-] *adj* : cotidiano, diario, corriente ⟨everyday clothes : ropa de todos los días⟩

everyone [ˈɛvriˌwʌn] → **everybody**

everything [ˈɛvriˌθɪŋ] *pron* : todo

everywhere [ˈɛvriˌhwɛr] *adv* : en todas partes, por todas partes, dondequiera ⟨I looked everywhere : busqué en todas partes⟩ ⟨everywhere we go : dondequiera que vayamos⟩

evict [ɪˈvɪkt] *vt* : desalojar, desahuciar

eviction [ɪˈvɪkʃən] *n* : desalojo *m*, desahucio *m*

evidence [ˈɛvədənts] *n* **1** INDICATION : indicio *m*, señal *m* ⟨to be in evidence : estar a la vista⟩ **2** PROOF : evidencia *f*, prueba *f* **3** TESTIMONY : testimonio *m*, declaración *f* ⟨to give evidence : declarar como testigo, prestar declaración⟩

evident [ˈɛvidənt] *adj* : evidente, patente, manifiesto

evidently [ˈɛvidəntli, ˌɛviˈdɛntli] *adv* **1** CLEARLY : claramente, obviamente **2** APPARENTLY : aparentemente, evidentemente, al parecer

evil¹ [ˈiːvəl, -vɪl] *adj* **eviler** *or* **eviller**; **evilest** *or* **evillest** **1** WICKED : malvado, malo, maligno **2** HARMFUL : nocivo, dañino, pernicioso **3** UNPLEASANT : desagradable ⟨an evil odor : un olor horrible⟩

evil² *n* **1** WICKEDNESS : mal *m*, maldad *f* **2** MISFORTUNE : desgracia *f*, mal *m*

evildoer [ˌiːvəlˈduːər, ˌiːvɪl-] *n* : malvado *m*, -da *f*

evince [ɪˈvɪnts] *vt* **evinced**; **evincing** : mostrar, manifestar, revelar

eviscerate [ɪˈvɪsəˌreit] *vt* **-ated**; **-ating** : eviscerar, destripar (un pollo, etc.)

evocation [ˌiːvoˈkeiʃən, ˌɛ-] *n* : evocación *f*

evocative [iˈvɑkətɪv] *adj* : evocador

evoke [iˈvoːk] *vt* **evoked**; **evoking** : evocar, provocar

evolution [ˌɛvəˈluːʃən, ˌiː-] *n* : evolución *f*, desarrollo *m*

evolutionary [ˌɛvəˈluːʃəˌnɛri, ˌiː-] *adj* : evolutivo

evolve [iˈvɑlv] *vi* **evolved**; **evolving** : evolucionar, desarrollarse

ewe [ˈjuː] *n* : oveja *f*

exacerbate [ɪgˈzæsərˌbeit] *vt* **-bated**; **-bating** : exacerbar

exact¹ [ɪgˈzækt, ɛ-] *vt* : exigir, imponer, arrancar

exact² *adj* : exacto, preciso — **exactly** *adv*

exacting [ɪˈzæktɪŋ, ɛg-] *adj* : exigente, riguroso

exactitude [ɪgˈzæktəˌtuːd, ɛg-, -ˌtjuːd] *n* : exactitud *f*, precisión *f*

exaggerate [ɪgˈzædʒəˌreit, ɛg-] *v* **-ated**; **-ating** : exagerar

exaggerated [ɪgˈzædʒəˌreitəd, ɛg-] *adj* : exagerado — **exaggeratedly** *adv*

exaggeration [ɪgˌzædʒəˈreiʃən, ɛg-] *n* : exageración *f*

exalt [ɪgˈzɔlt, ɛg-] *vt* : exaltar, ensalzar, glorificar

exaltation [ˌɛgˌzɔlˈteiʃən, ˌɛkˌsɔl-] *n* : exaltación *f*

exam [ɪgˈzæm, ɛg-] → **examination**

examination [ɪgˌzæməˈneiʃən, ɛg-] *n* **1** TEST : examen *m* **2** INSPECTION : inspección *f*, revisión *f* **3** INVESTIGATION : examen *m*, estudio *m*

examine [ɪgˈzæmən, ɛg-] *vt* **-ined**; **-ining** **1** TEST : examinar **2** INSPECT : inspeccionar, revisar **3** STUDY : examinar

example [ɪgˈzæmpəl, ɛg-] *n* : ejemplo *m* ⟨for example : por ejemplo⟩ ⟨to set an example : dar ejemplo⟩

exasperate [ɪgˈzæspəˌreit, ɛg-] *vt* **-ated**; **-ating** : exasperar, sacar de quicio

exasperation [ɪgˌzæspəˈreiʃən, ɛg-] *n* : exasperación *f*

excavate [ˈɛkskəˌveit] *vt* **-vated**; **-vating** : excavar

excavation [ˌɛkskəˈveiʃən] *n* : excavación *f*

exceed [ɪkˈsiːd, ɛk-] *vt* **1** SURPASS : exceder, rebasar, sobrepasar **2** : exceder de, sobrepasar ⟨not exceeding two months : que no exceda de dos meses⟩

exceedingly [ɪkˈsiːdɪŋli, ɛk-] *adv* : extremadamente, sumamente

excel [ɪkˈsɛl, ɛk-] *v* **-celled**; **-celling** *vi* : sobresalir, descollar, lucirse — *vt* : superar

excellence [ˈɛksələnts] *n* : excelencia *f*

excellency [ˈɛksələntsi] *n, pl* **-cies** : excelencia *f* ⟨His Excellency : Su Excelencia⟩

excellent [ˈɛksələnt] *adj* : excelente, sobresaliente — **excellently** *adv*

except¹ [ɪk'sɛpt] *vt* : exceptuar, excluir

except² *conj* : pero, si no fuera por

except³ *prep* : excepto, menos, salvo ⟨everyone except Carlos : todos menos Carlos⟩

exception [ɪk'sɛpʃən] *n* **1** : excepción *f* **2 to take exception to** : ofenderse por, objetar a

exceptional [ɪk'sɛpʃənəl] *adj* : excepcional, extraordinario — **exceptionally** *adv*

excerpt¹ [ɛk'sərpt, ɛg'zərpt, 'ɛkₜ-, 'gₜ-] *vt* : escoger, seleccionar

excerpt² ['ɛkₜsərpt, 'ɛgₜzərpt] *n* : pasaje *m*, selección *f*

excess¹ ['ɛkₜsɛs, ɪk'sɛs] *adj* **1** : excesivo, de sobra **2 excess baggage** : exceso *m* de equipaje

excess² [ɪk'sɛs, 'ɛkₜsɛs] *n* **1** SUPERFLUITY : exceso *m*, superfluidad *f* ⟨an excess of energy : un exceso de energía⟩ **2** SURPLUS : excedente *m*, sobrante *m* ⟨in excess of : superior a⟩

excessive [ɪk'sɛsɪv, ɛk-] *adj* : excesivo, exagerado, desmesurado — **excessively** *adv*

exchange¹ [ɪks'tʃeɪndʒ, ɛks-; 'ɛksₜtʃeɪndʒ] *vt* **-changed; -changing** : cambiar, intercambiar, canjear

exchange² *n* **1** : cambio *m*, intercambio *m*, canje *m* **2 stock exchange** : bolsa *f* (de valores)

exchangeable [ɪks'tʃeɪndʒəbəl, ɛks-] *adj* : canjeable

excise¹ [ɪk'saɪz, ɛk-] *vt* **-cised; -cising** : extirpar

excise² ['ɛkₜsaɪz] *n* **excise tax** : impuesto *m* interno, impuesto *m* sobre el consumo

excision [ɪk'sɪʒən, ɛk-] *n* : extirpación *f*, excisión *f*

excitability [ɪkₜsaɪtə'bɪləti, ɛk-] *n* : excitabilidad *f*

excitable [ɪk'saɪtəbəl, ɛk-] *adj* : excitable

excitation [ₜɛkₜsaɪ'teɪʃən] *n* : excitación *f*

excite [ɪk'saɪt, ɛk-] *vt* **-cited; -citing 1** AROUSE, STIMULATE : excitar, mover, estimular **2** ANIMATE : entusiasmar, animar **3** EVOKE, PROVOKE : provocar, despertar, suscitar ⟨to excite curiosity : despertar la curiosidad⟩

excited [ɪk'saɪtəd, ɛk-] *adj* **1** STIMULATED : excitado, estimulado **2** ENTHUSIASTIC : entusiasmado, emocionado

excitedly [ɪk'saɪtədli, ɛk-] *adv* : con excitación, con entusiasmo

excitement [ɪk'saɪtmənt, ɛk-] *n* **1** ENTHUSIASM : entusiasmo *m*, emoción *f* **2** AGITATION : agitación *f*, alboroto *m*, conmoción *f* **3** AROUSAL : excitación *f*

exciting [ɪk'saɪtɪŋ, ɛk-] *adj* **1** : emocionante **2** AROUSING : excitante

exclaim [ɪks'kleɪm, ɛk-] *v* : exclamar

exclamation [ₜɛksklə'meɪʃən] *n* : exclamación *f*

exclamation point *n* : signo *m* de admiración

exclamatory [ɪks'klæməₜtori, ɛks-] *adj* : exclamativo

exclude [ɪks'kluːd, ɛks-] *vt* **-cluded; -cluding 1** BAR : excluir, descartar, no admitir **2** EXPEL : expeler, expulsar

exclusion [ɪks'kluːʒən, ɛks-] *n* : exclusión *f*

exclusive¹ [ɪks'kluːsɪv, ɛks-] *adj* **1** SOLE : exclusivo, único **2** SELECT : exclusivo, selecto

exclusive² *n* : exclusiva *f*

exclusively [ɪks'kluːsɪvli, ɛks-] *adv* : exclusivamente, únicamente

exclusiveness [ɪks'kluːsɪvnəs, ɛks-] *n* : exclusividad *f*

excommunicate [ₜɛkskə'mjuːnəₜkeɪt] *vt* **-cated; -cating** : excomulgar

excommunication [ₜɛkskəₜmjuːnə'keɪʃən] *n* : excomunión *f*

excrement ['ɛkskrəmənt] *n* : excremento *m*

excrete [ɪk'skriːt, ɛk-] *vt* **-creted; -creting** : excretar

excretion [ɪk'skriːʃən, ɛk-] *n* : excreción *f*

excruciating [ɪk'skruːʃiₜeɪtɪŋ, ɛk-] *adj* : insoportable, atroz, terrible — **excruciatingly** *adv*

exculpate ['ɛkskəlₜpeɪt] *vt* **-pated; -pating** : exculpar

excursion [ɪk'skərʒən, ɛk-] *n* **1** OUTING : excursión *f*, paseo *m* **2** DIGRESSION : digresión *f*

excuse¹ [ɪk'skjuːz, ɛk-] *vt* **-cused; -cusing 1** PARDON : disculpar, perdonar ⟨excuse me : con permiso, perdóneme, perdón⟩ **2** EXEMPT : eximir, disculpar **3** JUSTIFY : excusar, justificar

excuse² [ɪk'skjuːs, ɛk-] *n* **1** JUSTIFICATION : excusa *f*, justificación *f* **2** PRETEXT : pretexto *m* **3 to make one's excuses to someone** : pedirle disculpas a alguien

execute ['ɛksɪₜkjuːt] *vt* **-cuted; -cuting 1** CARRY OUT : ejecutar, llevar a cabo, desempeñar **2** ENFORCE : ejecutar, cumplir (un testamento, etc.) **3** KILL : ejecutar, ajusticiar

execution [ₜɛksɪ'kjuːʃən] *n* **1** PERFORMANCE : ejecución *f*, desempeño *m* **2** IMPLEMENTATION : cumplimiento *m* **3** : ejecución *f* (por un delito)

executioner [ₜɛksɪ'kjuːʃənər] *n* : verdugo *m*

executive¹ [ɪg'zɛkjətɪv, ɛg-] *adj* : ejecutivo

executive² *n* : ejecutivo *m*, -va *f*

executor [ɪg'zɛkjətər, ɛg-] *n* : albacea *m*, testamentario *m*

executrix [ɪg'zɛkjəₜtrɪks, ɛg-] *n, pl* **executrices** [-ₜzɛkjə'traɪₜsiːz] *or* **executrixes** [-'zɛkjəₜtrɪksəz] : albacea *f*, testamentaria *f*

exemplary [ɪg'zɛmpləri, ɛg-] *adj* : ejemplar

exemplify [ɪg'zɛmpləₜfaɪ, ɛg-] *vt* **-fied; -fying** : ejemplificar, ilustrar, demostrar

exempt[1] [ɪg'zɛmpt, ɛg-] *vt* : eximir, dispensar, exonerar

exempt[2] *adj* : exento, eximido

exemption [ɪg'zɛmpʃən, ɛg-] *n* : exención *f*

exercise[1] ['ɛksər,saɪz] *v* **-cised; -cising** *vt* **1** : ejercitar (el cuerpo) **2** USE : ejercer, hacer uso de — *vi* : hacer ejercicio

exercise[2] *n* **1** : ejercicio *m* **2 exercises** *npl* WORKOUT : ejercicios *mpl* físicos **3 exercises** *npl* CEREMONY : ceremonia *f*

exert [ɪg'zərt, ɛg-] *vt* **1** : ejercer, emplear **2 to exert oneself** : esforzarse

exertion [ɪg'zərʃən, ɛg-] *n* **1** USE : ejercicio *m* (de autoridad, etc.), uso *m* (de fuerza, etc.) **2** EFFORT : esfuerzo *m*, empeño *m*

exhalation [,ɛksə'leɪʃən, ,ɛkshə-] *n* : exhalación *f*, espiración *f*

exhale [ɛks'heɪl] *v* **-haled; -haling** *vt* **1** : exhalar, espirar **2** EMIT : exhalar, despedir, emitir — *vi* : espirar

exhaust[1] [ɪg'zɔst, ɛg-] *vt* **1** DEPLETE : agotar **2** TIRE : cansar, fatigar, agotar **3** EMPTY : vaciar

exhaust[2] *n* **1 exhaust fumes** : gases *mpl* de escape **2 exhaust pipe** : tubo *m* de escape **3 exhaust system** : sistema *m* de escape

exhausted [ɪg'zɔstəd, ɛg-] *adj* : agotado, derrengado

exhausting [ɪg'zɔstɪŋ, ɛg-] *adj* : extenuante, agotador

exhaustion [ɪg'zɔstʃən, ɛg-] *n* : agotamiento *m*

exhaustive [ɪg'zɔstɪv, ɛg-] *adj* : exhaustivo

exhibit[1] [ɪg'zɪbət, ɛg-] *vt* **1** DISPLAY : exhibir, exponer **2** PRODUCE, SHOW : mostrar, presentar

exhibit[2] *n* **1** OBJECT : objeto *m* expuesto **2** EXHIBITION : exposición*f*, exhibición *f* **3** EVIDENCE : prueba *f* instrumental

exhibition [,ɛksə'bɪʃən] *n* **1** : exposición *f*, exhibición *f* **2 to make an exhibition of oneself** : dar el espectáculo, hacer el ridículo

exhibitor [ɪg'zɪbətər] *n* : expositor *m*, -tora *f*

exhilarate [ɪg'zɪlə,reɪt, ɛg-] *vt* **-rated; -rating** : alegrar, levantar el ánimo de

exhilaration [ɪg,zɪlə'reɪʃən, ɛg-] *n* : alegría *f*, regocijo *m*, júbilo *m*

exhort [ɪg'zɔrt, ɛg-] *vt* : exhortar

exhortation [,ɛk,sɔr'teɪʃən, -sər-; ,ɛg-,zɔr-] *n* : exhortación *f*

exhumation [,ɛksju'meɪʃən, -hju-; ,ɛgzu-, -zju-] *n* : exhumación *f*

exhume [ɪg'zu:m, -'zju:m; ɪks'ju:m, -'hju:m] *vt* **-humed; -huming** : exhumar, desenterrar

exigencies ['ɛksɪdʒəntsiz, ɪg'zɪdʒən,si:z] *npl* : exigencias *fpl*

exile[1] ['ɛg,zaɪl, 'ɛk,saɪl] *vt* **exiled; exiling** : exiliar, desterrar

exile[2] *n* **1** BANISHMENT : exilio *m*, destierro *m* **2** OUTCAST : exiliado *m*, -da *f*; desterrado *m*, -da *f*

exist [ɪg'zɪst, ɛg-] *vi* **1** BE : existir **2** LIVE : subsistir, vivir

existence [ɪg'zɪstənts, ɛg-] *n* : existencia *f*

existent [ɪg'zɪstənt, ɛg-] *adj* : existente

existing [ɪg'zɪstɪŋ] *adj* : existente

exit[1] ['ɛgzət, 'ɛksət] *vi* : salir, hacer mutis (en el teatro) — *vt* : salir de

exit[2] *n* **1** DEPARTURE : salida *f*, partida *f* **2** EGRESS : salida *f* ⟨emergency exit : salida de emergencia⟩

exodus ['ɛksədəs] *n* : éxodo *m*

exonerate [ɪg'zɑnə,reɪt, ɛg-] *vt* **-ated; -ating** : exonerar, disculpar, absolver

exoneration [ɪg,zɑnə'reɪʃən, ɛg-] *n* : exoneración *f*

exorbitant [ɪg'zɔrbətənt, ɛg-] *adj* : exorbitante, excesivo

exorcise ['ɛk,sɔr,saɪz, -sər-] *vt* **-cised; -cising** : exorcizar

exorcism ['ɛksər,sɪzəm] *n* : exorcismo *m*

exotic[1] [ɪg'zɑtɪk, ɛg-] *adj* : exótico — **exotically** [-ɪkli] *adv*

exotic[2] *n* : planta *f* exótica

expand [ɪk'spænd, ɛk-] *vt* **1** ENLARGE : expandir, dilatar, aumentar, ampliar **2** EXTEND : extender — *vi* **1** ENLARGE : ampliarse, extenderse **2** : expandirse, dilatarse (dícese de los metales, gases, etc.)

expanse [ɪk'spænts, ɛk-] *n* : extensión *f*

expansion [ɪk'spænʃən, ɛk-] *n* **1** ENLARGEMENT : expansión *f*, ampliación *f* **2** EXPANSE : extensión *f*

expansive [ɪk'spæntsɪv, ɛk-] *adj* **1** : expansivo **2** OUTGOING : expansivo, comunicativo **3** AMPLE : ancho, amplio — **expansively** *adv*

expansiveness [ɪk'spæntsɪvnəs, ɛk-] *n* : expansibilidad *f*

expatriate[1] [ɛks'peɪtri,eɪt] *vt* **-ated; -ating** : expatriar

expatriate[2] [ɛks'peɪtriət, -,eɪt] *adj* : expatriado

expatriate[3] [ɛks'peɪtriət, -,eɪt] *n* : expatriado *m*, -da *f*

expect [ɪk'spkt, ɛk-] *vt* **1** SUPPOSE : suponer, imaginarse **2** ANTICIPATE : esperar **3** COUNT ON, REQUIRE : contar con, esperar — *vi* **to be expecting** : estar embarazada

expectancy [ɪk'spktəntsi, ɛk-] *n, pl* **-cies** : expectativa *f*, esperanza *f*

expectant [ɪk'spktənt, ɛk-] *adj* **1** ANTICIPATING : expectante **2** EXPECTING : futuro ⟨expectant mother : futura madre⟩

expectantly [ɪk'spktəntli, ɛk-] *adv* : con expectación

expectation [,ɛk,spk'teɪʃən] *n* **1** ANTICIPATION : expectación *f* **2** EXPECTANCY : expectativa *f*

expedient[1] [ɪk'spi:diənt, ɛk-] *adj* : conveniente, oportuno

expedient[2] *n* : expediente *m*, recurso *m*

expedite ['ɛkspə,daɪt] *vt* **-dited; -diting**
1 FACILITATE : facilitar, dar curso a **2**
HASTEN : acelerar

expedition [,ɛkspə'dɪʃən] *n* : expedición
f

expeditious [,ɛkspə'dɪʃəs] *adj* : pronto,
rápido

expel [ɪk'spɛl, ɛk-] *vt* **-pelled; -pelling**
: expulsar, expeler

expend [ɪk'spɛnd, ɛk-] *vt* **1** DISBURSE
: gastar, desembolsar **2** CONSUME
: consumir, agotar

expendable [ɪk'spɛndəbəl, ɛk-] *adj* : prescindible

expenditure [ɪk'spɛndɪtʃər, ɛk-, -,tʃʊr] *n*
: gasto *m*

expense [ɪk'spɛnts, ɛk-] *n* **1** COST : gasto *m* **2 expenses** *npl* : gastos *mpl*, expensas *fpl* **3 at the expense of** : a expensas de

expensive [ɪk'spɛntsɪv, ɛk-] *adj* : costoso, caro — **expensively** *adv*

experience¹ [ɪk'spɪriənts, ɛk-] *vt* **-enced;**
-encing : experimentar (sentimientos),
tener (dificultades), sufrir (una pérdida)

experience² *n* : experiencia *f*

experienced [ɪk'spɪriəntst, ɛk-] *adj* : con
experiencia, experimentado

experiment¹ [ɪk'spɛrəmənt, ɛk-, -'spɪr-]
vi : experimentar, hacer experimentos

experiment² *n* : experimento *m*

experimental [ɪk,spɛrə'mntəl, ɛk-,
-,spɪr-] *adj* : experimental — **experi-**
mentally *adv*

experimentation [ɪk,spɛrəmən'teɪʃən,
ɛk-, -,spɪr-] *n* : experimentación *f*

expert¹ ['ɛk,spərt, ɪk'spərt] *adj* : experto, de experto, pericial (dícese de un
testigo) — **expertly** *adv*

expert² ['ɛk,spərt] *n* : experto *m*, -ta *f*;
perito *m*, -ta *f*; especialista *mf*

expertise [,ɛkspər'tiːz] *n* : pericia *f*, competencia *f*

expiate ['ɛkspi,eɪt] *vt* **-ated; -ating** : expiar

expiation [,ɛkspi'eɪʃən] *n* : expiación *f*

expiration [,ɛkspə'reɪʃən] *n* **1** EXHALA-
TION : exhalación *f*, espiración *f* **2**
DEATH : muerte *f* **3** TERMINATION
: vencimiento *m*, caducidad *f*

expire [ɪk'spaɪr, ɛk-] *vi* **-pired; -piring 1**
EXHALE : espirar **2** DIE : expirar, morir
3 TERMINATE : caducar, vencer

explain [ɪk'spleɪn, ɛk-] *vt* : explicar

explanation [,ɛksplə'neɪʃən] *n* : explicación *f*

explanatory [ɪk'splænə,tori, ɛk-] *adj*
: explicativo, aclaratorio

expletive ['ɛksplətɪv] *n* : improperio *m*,
palabrota *f fam*, grosería *f*

explicable [ɛk'splɪkəbəl, 'ɛkspli-] *adj*
: explicable

explicit [ɪk'splɪsət, ɛk-] *adj* : explícito,
claro, categórico, rotundo — **explicit-**
ly *adv*

explicitness [ɪk'splɪsətnəs, ɛk-] *n* : claridad *f*, carácter *m* explícito

explode [ɪk'sploːd, ɛk-] *v* **-ploded;**
-ploding *vt* **1** BURST : hacer explosionar, hacer explotar **2** REFUTE : rebatir, refutar, desmentir — *vi* **1** BURST
: explotar, estallar, reventar **2** SKY-
ROCKET : dispararse

exploit¹ [ɪk'splɔɪt, ɛk-] *vt* : explotar,
aprovecharse de

exploit² ['ɛk,splɔɪt] *n* : hazaña *f*, proeza
f

exploitation [,ɛk,splɔɪ'teɪʃən] *n* : explotación *f*

exploration [,ɛksplə'reɪʃən] *n* : exploración *f*

exploratory [ɪk'splorə,tori, ɛk-] *adj* : exploratorio

explore [ɪk'splor, ɛk-] *vt* **-plored;**
-ploring : explorar, investigar, examinar

explorer [ɪk'splorər, ɛk-] *n* : explorador
m, -dora *f*

explosion [ɪk'splo:ʒən, ɛk-] *n* : explosión
f, estallido *m*

explosive¹ [ɪk'splo:sɪv, ɛk-] *adj* : explosivo, fulminante — **explosively** *adv*

explosive² *n* : explosivo *m*

exponent [ɪk'spo:nənt, 'ɛk,spo:-] *n* **1**
: exponente *m* **2** ADVOCATE : defensor
m, -sora *f*; partidario *m*, -ria *f*

exponential [,ɛkspə'nɛntʃəl] *adj* : exponencial — **exponentially** *adv*

export¹ [ɛk'sport, 'ɛk,sport] *vt* : exportar

export² ['ɛk,sport] *n* **1** : artículo *m* de
exportación **2** → **exportation**

exportation [,ɛk,spor'teɪʃən] *n* : exportación *f*

exporter [ɛk'sportər, 'ɛk,spor-] *n* : exportador *m*, -dora *f*

expose [ɪk'spo:z, ɛk-] *vt* **-posed;**
-posing 1 : exponer (al peligro, a los
elementos, a una enfermedad) **2** : exponer (una película a la luz) **3** DIS-
CLOSE : descubrir, revelar, poner en evidencia **4** UNMASK : desenmascarar

exposé *or* **expose** [,ɛkspo'zeɪ] *n* : exposición *f* (de hechos), revelación *f* (de
un escándalo)

exposed [ɪk'spo:zd, ɛk-] *adj* : descubierto, sin protección

exposition [,ɛkspə'zɪʃən] *n* : exposición
f

exposure [ɪk'spo:ʒər, ɛk-] *n* **1** : exposición *f* **2** CONTACT : exposición *f*, experiencia *f*, contacto *m* **3** UNMASKING
: desenmascaramiento *m* **4** ORIENTA-
TION : orientación *f* ⟨a room with a
northern exposure : una sala orienta-
da al norte⟩

expound [ɪk'spaund, ɛk-] *vt* : exponer,
explicar — *vi* : hacer comentarios de-
tallados

express¹ [ɪk'sprɛs, ɛk-] *vt* **1** SAY : expresar, comunicar **2** SHOW : expresar,
manifestar, externar *Mex* **3** SQUEEZE
: exprimir ⟨to express the juice from a
lemon : exprimir el jugo de un limón⟩

express² *adv* : por correo exprés, por
correo urgente

express[3] *adj* **1** EXPLICIT : expreso, manifiesto **2** SPECIFIC : específico ⟨for that express purpose : con ese fin específico⟩ **3** RAPID : expreso, rápido

express[4] *n* **1** : correo *m* exprés, correo *m* urgente **2** : expreso *m* (tren)

expression [ɪk'sprɛʃən, ɛk-] *n* **1** UTTERANCE : expresión *f* ⟨freedom of expression : libertad de expresión⟩ **2** : expresión *f* (en la matemática) **3** PHRASE : frase *f*, expresión *f* **4** LOOK : expresión *f*, cara *f*, gesto *m* ⟨with a sad expression : con un gesto de tristeza⟩

expressionless [ɪk'sprɛʃənləs, ɛk-] *adj* : inexpresivo

expressive [ɪk'sprɛsɪv, ɛk-] *adj* : expresivo

expressway [ɪk'sprɛs,weɪ, ɛk-] *n* : autopista *f*

expulsion [ɪk'spʌlʃən, ɛk-] *n* : expulsión *f*

expurgate ['ɛkspər,geɪt] *vt* -gated; -gating : expurgar

exquisite [ɛk'skwɪzət, 'ɛk,skwɪ-] *adj* **1** FINE : exquisito, delicado, primoroso **2** INTENSE : intenso, extremo

extant ['ɛkstənt, ɛk'stænt] *adj* : existente

extemporaneous [ɛk,stɛmpə'reɪniəs] *adj* : improvisado — **extemporaneously** *adv*

extend [ɪk'stɛnd, ɛk-] *vt* **1** STRETCH : extender, tender **2** PROLONG : prolongar, prorrogar **3** ENLARGE : agrandar, ampliar, aumentar **4** PROFFER : extender, dar, ofrecer — *vi* : extenderse

extended [ɪk'stɛndəd, ɛk-] *adj* LENGTHY : prolongado, largo

extension [ɪk'stɛntʃən, ɛk-] *n* **1** EXTENDING : extensión *f*, ampliación *f*, prórroga *f*, prolongación *f* **2** ANNEX : ampliación *f*, anexo *m* **3** : extensión *f* (de teléfono)

extensive [ɪk'stɛntsɪv, ɛk-] *adj* : extenso, vasto, amplio — **extensively** *adv*

extent [ɪk'stɛnt, ɛk-] *n* **1** SIZE : extensión *f*, magnitud *f* **2** DEGREE, SCOPE : alcance *m*, grado *m* ⟨to a certain extent : hasta cierto punto⟩

extenuate [ɪk'stɛnjə,weɪt] *vt* -ated; -ating : atenuar, aminorar, mitigar ⟨extenuating circumstances : circunstancias atenuantes⟩

extenuation [ɪk,stɛnjə'weɪʃən, ɛk-] *n* : atenuación *f*, aminoración *f*

exterior[1] [ɛk'stɪriər] *adj* : exterior

exterior[2] *n* : exterior *m*

exterminate [ɪk'stərmə,neɪt, ɛk-] *vt* -nated; -nating : exterminar

extermination [ɪk,stərmə'neɪʃən, ɛk-] *n* : exterminación *f*, exterminio *m*

exterminator [ɪk'stərmə,neɪtər, ɛk-] *n* : exterminador *m*, -dora *f*

external [ɪk'stərnəl, ɛk-] *adj* : externo, exterior — **externally** *adv*

extinct [ɪk'stɪŋkt, ɛk-] *adj* : extinto

extinction [ɪk'stɪŋkʃən, ɛk-] *n* : extinción *f*

extinguish [ɪk'stɪŋgwɪʃ, ɛk-] *vt* : extinguir, apagar

extinguisher [ɪk'stɪŋgwɪʃər, ɛk-] *n* : extinguidor *m*, extintor *m*

extirpate ['ɛkstər,peɪt] *vt* -pated; -pating : extirpar, exterminar

extol [ɪk'stoːl, ɛk-] *vt* -tolled; -tolling : exaltar, ensalzar, alabar

extort [ɪk'stɔrt, ɛk-] *vt* : extorsionar

extortion [ɪk'stɔrʃən, ɛk-] *n* : extorsión *f*

extra[1] ['ɛkstrə] *adv* : extra, más, extremadamente, super ⟨extra special : super especial⟩

extra[2] *adj* **1** ADDITIONAL : adicional, suplementario, de más **2** SUPERIOR : superior

extra[3] *n* : extra *m*

extract[1] [ɪk'strækt, ɛk-] *vt* : extraer, sacar

extract[2] ['ɛk,strækt] *n* **1** EXCERPT : pasaje *m*, selección *f*, trozo *m* **2** : extracto *m* ⟨vanilla extract : extracto de vainilla⟩

extraction [ɪk'strækʃən, ɛk-] *n* : extracción *f*

extractor [ɪk'stræktər, ɛk-] *n* : extractor *m*

extracurricular [,ɛkstrəkə'rɪkjələr] *adj* : extracurricular

extradite ['ɛkstrə,daɪt] *vt* -dited; -diting : extraditar

extradition [,ɛkstrə'dɪʃən] *n* : extradición *f*

extramarital [,ɛkstrə'mærətəl] *adj* : extramatrimonial

extraneous [ɛk'streɪniəs] *adj* **1** OUTSIDE : extrínseco, externo **2** SUPERFLUOUS : superfluo, ajeno — **extraneously** *adv*

extraordinary [ɪk'strɔrdən,ɛri, ,ɛkstrə-'ɔrd-] *adj* : extraordinario, excepcional — **extraordinarily** [ɪk,strɔrdən'ɛrəli, ,kstrə,ord-] *adv*

extrasensory [,ɛkstrə'sɛntsəri] *adj* : extrasensorial

extraterrestrial[1] [,ɛkstrətə'rɛstriəl] *adj* : extraterrestre

extraterrestrial[2] *n* : extraterrestre *mf*

extravagance [ɪk'strævɪgənts, ɛk-] *n* **1** EXCESS : exceso *m*, extravagancia *f* **2** WASTEFULNESS : derroche *m*, despilfarro *m* **3** LUXURY : lujo *m*

extravagant [ɪk'strævɪgənt, ɛk-] *adj* **1** EXCESSIVE : excesivo, extravagante **2** WASTEFUL : despilfarrador, derrochador, gastador **3** EXORBITANT : costoso, exorbitante

extravagantly [ɪk'strævɪgəntli, ɛk-] *adv* **1** LAVISHLY : a lo grande **2** EXCESSIVELY : exageradamente, desmesuradamente

extravaganza [ɪk,strævə'gænzə, ɛk-] *n* : gran espectáculo *m*

extreme[1] [ɪk'striːm, ɛk-] *adj* **1** UTMOST : extremo, sumo ⟨of extreme importance : de suma importancia⟩ **2** INTENSE : intenso, extremado ⟨extreme cold : frío extremado⟩ **3** EXCESSIVE : excesivo, extremo ⟨extreme views : opiniones extremas⟩ ⟨extreme measures : medidas excepcionales, medidas drásticas⟩ **4** OUTERMOST : extremo ⟨the extreme north : el norte extremo⟩

extreme² *n* **1** : extremo *m* **2 in the extreme** : en extremo, en sumo grado

extremely [ɪk'striːmli, ɛk-] *adv* : sumamente, extremadamente, terriblemente

extremist [ɪk'striːmɪst, ɛk-] *n* : extremista *mf* — **extremist** *adj*

extremity [ɪk'strɛməţi, ɛk-] *n, pl* **-ties 1** EXTREME : extremo *m* **2 extremities** *npl* LIMBS : extremidades *fpl*

extricate ['ɛkstrə,keɪt] *vt* **-cated; -cating** : librar, sacar

extrinsic [ɪk'strɪnzɪk, -'strɪntsɪk] *adj* : extrínseco

extrovert ['ɛkstrə,vərt] *n* : extrovertido *m*, -da *f*

extroverted ['ɛkstrə,vərţəd] *adj* : extrovertido

extrude [ɪk'struːd, ɛk-] *vt* **-truded; -truding** : extrudir, expulsar

exuberance [ɪg'zuːbərənts, ɛg-] *n* **1** JOYOUSNESS : euforia *f*, exaltación *f* **2** VIGOR : exuberancia *f*, vigor *m*

exuberant [ɪg'zuːbərənt, ɛg-] *adj* **1** JOYOUS : eufórico **2** LUSH : exuberante — **exuberantly** *adv*

exude [ɪg'zuːd, ɛg-] *vi* **-uded; -uding 1** OOZE : rezumar, exudar **2** EMANATE : emanar, irradiar

exult [ɪg'zʌlt, ɛg-] *vi* : exultar, regocijarse

exultant [ɪg'zʌltənt, ɛg-] *adj* : exultante, jubiloso — **exultantly** *adv*

exultation [,ɛksəl'teɪʃən, ,ɛgzəl-] *n* : exultación *f*, júbilo *m*, alborozo *m*

eye¹ ['aɪ] *vt* **eyed; eyeing** *or* **eying** : mirar, observar

eye² *n* **1** : ojo *m* **2** VISION : visión *f*, vista *f*, ojo *m* ⟨a good eye for bargains : un buen ojo para las gangas⟩ **3** GLANCE : mirada *f*, ojeada *f* **4** ATTENTION : atención *f* ⟨to catch one's eye : llamar la atención⟩ **5** POINT OF VIEW : punto *m* de vista ⟨in the eyes of the law : según la ley⟩ **6** : ojo *m* (de una aguja, una papa, una tormenta)

eyeball ['aɪ,bɔl] *n* : globo *m* ocular

eyebrow ['aɪ,braʊ] *n* : ceja *f*

eyedropper ['aɪ,drɑpər] *n* : cuentagotas *f*

eyeglasses ['aɪ,glæsəz] *npl* : anteojos *mpl*, lentes *mpl*, espejuelos *mpl*, gafas *fpl*

eyelash ['aɪ,læʃ] *n* : pestaña *f*

eyelet ['aɪlət] *n* : ojete *m*

eyelid ['aɪ,lɪd] *n* : párpado *m*

eye–opener ['aɪ,oːpənər] *n* : revelación *f*, sorpresa *f*

eye–opening ['aɪ,oːpənɪŋ] *adj* : revelador

eyepiece ['aɪ,piːs] *n* : ocular *m*

eyesight ['aɪ,saɪt] *n* : vista *f*, visión *f*

eyesore ['aɪ,sor] *n* : monstruosidad *f*, adefesio *m*

eyestrain ['aɪ,streɪn] *n* : fatiga *f* visual, vista *f* cansada

eyetooth ['aɪ,tuː,θ] *n* : colmillo *m*

eyewitness ['aɪ'wɪtnəs] *n* : testigo *mf* ocular, testigo *mf* presencial

eyrie ['aɪri] → **aerie**

F

f ['ɛf] *n, pl* **f's** *or* **fs** ['ɛfs] : sexta letra del alfabeto inglés

fable ['feɪbəl] *n* : fábula *f*

fabled ['feɪbəld] *adj* : legendario, fabuloso

fabric ['fæbrɪk] *n* **1** MATERIAL : tela *f*, tejido *m* **2** STRUCTURE : estructura *f* ⟨the fabric of society : la estructura de la sociedad⟩

fabricate ['fæbrɪ,keɪt] *vt* **-cated; -cating 1** CONSTRUCT, MANUFACTURE : construir, fabricar **2** INVENT : inventar (excusas o mentiras)

fabrication [,fæbrɪ'keɪʃən] *n* **1** LIE : mentira *f*, invención *f* **2** MANUFACTURE : fabricación *f*

fabulous ['fæbjələs] *adj* **1** LEGENDARY : fabuloso, legendario **2** INCREDIBLE : increíble, fabuloso ⟨fabulous wealth : riqueza fabulosa⟩ **3** WONDERFUL : magnífico, estupendo, fabuloso — **fabulously** *adv*

facade [fə'sɑd] *n* : fachada *f*

face¹ ['feɪs] *v* **faced; facing** *vt* **1** LINE : recubrir (una superficie), forrar (ropa) **2** CONFRONT : enfrentarse a, afrontar, hacer frente a ⟨to face the music : afrontar las consecuencias⟩ ⟨to face the facts : aceptar la realidad⟩ **3** : estar de cara a, estar enfrente de ⟨she's facing her brother : está de cara a su hermano⟩ **4** OVERLOOK : dar a — *vi* : mirar (hacia), estar orientado (a)

face² *n* **1** : cara *f*, rostro *m* ⟨he told me to my face : me lo dijo a la cara⟩ **2** EXPRESSION : cara *f*, expresión *f* ⟨to pull a long face : poner mala cara⟩ **3** GRIMACE : mueca *f* ⟨to make faces : hacer muecas⟩ **4** APPEARANCE : fisonomía *f*, aspecto *m* ⟨the face of society : la fisonomía de la sociedad⟩ **5** EFFRONTERY : desfachatez *f* **6** PRESTIGE : prestigio *m* ⟨to lose face : desprestigiarse⟩ **7** FRONT, SIDE : cara *f* (de una moneda), esfera *f* (de un reloj), fachada *f* (de un edificio), pared *f* (de una montaña) **8** SURFACE : superficie *f*, faz *f* (de la tierra), cara *f* (de la luna) **9 in the face of** DESPITE : en medio de, en visto de, ante

facedown ['feɪs,daʊn] *adv* : boca abajo

faceless ['feɪsləs] *adj* ANONYMOUS : anónimo

face–lift ['feɪs,lɪft] *n* **1** : estiramiento *m*

facial **2** RENOVATION : renovación *f*, remozamiento *m*

facet ['fæsət] *n* **1** : faceta *f* (de una piedra) **2** ASPECT : faceta *f*, aspecto *m*

facetious [fə'si:ʃəs] *adj* : gracioso, burlón, bromista

facetiously [fə'si:ʃəsli] *adv* : en tono de burla

facetiousness [fə'si:ʃəsnəs] *n* : jocosidad *f*

face-to-face *adv & adj* : cara a cara

faceup ['feɪs'ʌp] *adv* : boca arriba

face value *n* : valor *m* nominal

facial[1] ['feɪʃəl] *adj* : de la cara, facial

facial[2] *n* : tratamiento *m* facial, limpieza *f* de cutis

facile ['fæsəl] *adj* SUPERFICIAL : superficial, simplista

facilitate [fə'sɪlə,teɪt] *vt* **-tated; -tating** : facilitar

facility [fə'sɪləti] *n, pl* **-ties 1** EASE : facilidad *f* **2** CENTER, COMPLEX : centro *m*, complejo *m* **3 facilities** *npl* AMENITIES : comodidades *fpl*, servicios *mpl*

facing ['feɪsɪŋ] *n* **1** LINING : entretela *f* (de una prenda) **2** : revestimiento *m* (de un edificio)

facsimile [fæk'sɪməli] *n* : facsímile *m*, facsímil *m*

fact ['fækt] *n* **1** : hecho *m* ⟨as a matter of fact : de hecho⟩ **2** INFORMATION : información *f*, datos *mpl* ⟨facts and figures : datos y cifras⟩ **3** REALITY : realidad *f* ⟨in fact : en realidad⟩

faction ['fækʃən] *n* : facción *m*, bando *m*

factional ['fækʃənəl] *adj* : entre facciones

factious ['fækʃəs] *adj* : faccioso, contencioso

factitious [fæk'tɪʃəs] *adj* : artificial, facticio

factor ['fæktər] *n* : factor *m*

factory ['fæktəri] *n, pl* **-ries** : fábrica *f*

factual ['fæktʃuəl] *adj* : basado en hechos, objetivo

factually ['fæktʃuəli] *adv* : en cuanto a los hechos

faculty ['fækəlti] *n, pl* **-ties 1** : facultad *f* ⟨the faculty of sight : las facultades visuales, el sentido de la vista⟩ **2** APTITUDE : aptitud *f*, facilidad *f* **3** TEACHERS : cuerpo *m* docente

fad ['fæd] *n* : moda *f* pasajera, manía *f*

fade ['feɪd] *v* **faded; fading** *vi* **1** WITHER : debilitarse (dícese de las personas), marchitarse (dícese de las flores y las plantas) **2** DISCOLOR : desteñirse, decolorarse **3** DIM : apagarse (dícese de la luz), perderse (dícese de los sonidos), fundirse (dícese de las imágenes) **4** VANISH : desvanecerse, decaer — *vt* DISCOLOR : desteñir

fag ['fæg] *vt* **fagged; fagging** EXHAUST : cansar, fatigar

fagot *or* faggot ['fægət] *n* : haz *m* de leña

Fahrenheit ['færən,haɪt] *adj* : Fahrenheit

fail[1] ['feɪl] *vi* **1** WEAKEN : fallar, deteriorarse **2** STOP : fallar, detenerse ⟨his heart failed : le falló el corazón⟩ **3** : fracasar, fallar ⟨her plan failed : su plan fracasó⟩ ⟨the crops failed : se perdió la cosecha⟩ **4** : quebrar ⟨a business about to fail : una empresa a punto de quebrar⟩ **5 to fail in** : faltar a, no cumplir con ⟨to fail in one's duties : faltar a sus deberes⟩ — *vt* **1** FLUNK : reprobar (un examen) **2** : fallar ⟨words fail me : las palabras me fallan, no encuentro palabras⟩ **3** DISAPPOINT : fallar, decepcionar ⟨don't fail me! : ¡no me falles!⟩

fail[2] *n* : fracaso *m*

failing ['feɪlɪŋ] *n* : defecto *m*

failure ['feɪljər] *n* **1** : fracaso *m*, malogro *m* ⟨crop failure : pérdida de la cosecha⟩ ⟨heart failure : insuficiencia cardíaca⟩ ⟨engine failure : falla mecánica⟩ **2** BANKRUPTCY : bancarrota *f*, quiebra *f* **3** : fracaso *m* (persona) ⟨he was a failure as a manager : como gerente, fue un fracaso⟩

faint[1] ['feɪnt] *vi* : desmayarse

faint[2] *adj* **1** COWARDLY, TIMID : cobarde, tímido **2** DIZZY : mareado ⟨faint with hunger : desfallecido de hambre⟩ **3** SLIGHT : leve, ligero, vago ⟨I haven't the faintest idea : no tengo la más mínima idea⟩ **4** INDISTINCT : tenue, indistinto, apenas perceptible

faint[3] *n* : desmayo *m*

fainthearted ['feɪnt'hɑrtəd] *adj* : cobarde, pusilánime

faintly ['feɪntli] *adv* : débilmente, ligeramente, levemente

faintness ['feɪntnəs] *n* **1** INDISTINCTNESS : lo débil, falta *f* de claridad **2** FAINTING : desmayo *m*, desfallecimiento *m*

fair[1] ['fær] *adj* **1** ATTRACTIVE, BEAUTIFUL : bello, hermoso, atractivo **2** (*relating to weather*) : bueno, despejado ⟨fair weather : tiempo despejado⟩ **3** JUST : justo, imparcial **4** ALLOWABLE : permisible **5** BLOND, LIGHT : rubio (dícese del pelo), blanco (dícese de la tez) **6** ADEQUATE : bastante, adecuado ⟨fair to middling : mediano, regular⟩ **7 fair game** : presa *f* fácil **8 to play fair** : jugar limpio

fair[2] *n* : feria *f*

fairground ['fær,graʊnd] *n* : parque *m* de diversiones

fairly ['færli] *adv* **1** IMPARTIALLY : imparcialmente, limpiamente, equitativamente **2** QUITE : bastante **3** MODERATELY : medianamente

fairness ['færnəs] *n* **1** IMPARTIALITY : imparcialidad *f*, justicia *f* **2** LIGHTNESS : blancura *f* (de la piel), lo rubio (del pelo)

fairy ['færi] *n, pl* **fairies 1** : hada *f* **2 fairy tale** : cuento *m* de hadas

fairyland ['færi,lænd] *n* **1** : país *m* de las hadas **2** : lugar *m* encantador

faith ['feɪθ] *n, pl* **faiths** ['feɪθs, 'feɪðz] **1** BELIEF : fe *f* **2** ALLEGIANCE : lealtad *f* **3** CONFIDENCE, TRUST : confianza *f*, fe *f* **4** RELIGION : religión *f*

faithful ['feɪθfəl] *adj* : fiel — **faithfully** *adv*

faithfulness ['feɪθfəlnəs] *n* : fidelidad *f*

faithless ['feɪθləs] *adj* **1** DISLOYAL : desleal **2** : infiel (en la religión) — **faithlessly** *adv*

faithlessness ['feɪθləsnəs] *n* : deslealtad *f*

fake¹ ['feɪk] *v* **faked; faking** *vt* **1** FALSIFY : falsificar, falsear **2** FEIGN : fingir — *vi* **1** PRETEND : fingir **2** : hacer un engaño, hacer una finta (en deportes)

fake² *adj* : falso, fingido, postizo

fake³ *n* **1** IMITATION : imitación *f*, falsificación *f* **2** IMPOSTOR : impostor *m*, -tora *f*; charlatán *m*, -tana *f*; farsante *mf* **3** FEINT : engaño *m*, finta *f* (en deportes)

faker ['feɪkər] *n* : impostor *m*, -tora *f*; charlatán *m*, -tana *f*; farsante *mf*

fakir [fə'kɪr, 'feɪkər] *n* : faquir *m*

falcon ['fælkən, 'fɔl-] *n* : halcón *m*

falconry ['fælkənri, 'fɔl-] *n* : cetrería *f*

fall¹ ['fɔl] *vi* **fell** ['fɛl], **fallen** ['fɔlən]; **falling 1** : caer, caerse ⟨to fall out of bed : caer de la cama⟩ ⟨to fall down : caerse⟩ **2** HANG : caer **3** DESCEND : caer (dícese de la lluvia o de la noche), bajar (dícese de los precios), descender (dícese de la temperatura) **4** : caer (a un enemigo), rendirse ⟨the city fell : la ciudad se rindió⟩ **5** OCCUR : caer ⟨Christmas falls on a Friday : la Navidad cae en viernes⟩ **6 to fall asleep** : dormirse, quedarse dormido **7 to fall from grace** SIN : perder la gracia **8 to fall sick** : caer enfermo, enfermarse **9 to fall through** : fracasar, caer en la nada **10 to fall to** : tocar a, corresponder a ⟨the task fell to him : le tocó hacerlo⟩

fall² *n* **1** TUMBLE : caída *f* ⟨to break one's fall : frenar uno su caída⟩ ⟨a fall of three feet : una caída de tres pies⟩ **2** FALLING : derrumbe *m* (de rocas), aguacero *m* (de lluvia), nevada *f* (de nieve), bajada *f* (de precios), disminución *f* (de cantidades) **3** AUTUMN : otoño *m* **4** DOWNFALL : caída *f*, ruina *f* **5 falls** *npl* WATERFALL : cascada *f*, catarata *f*

fallacious [fə'leɪʃəs] *adj* : erróneo, engañoso, falaz

fallacy ['fæləsi] *n, pl* **-cies** : falacia *f*

fall back *vi* **1** RETREAT : retirarse, replegarse **2 to fall back on** : recurrir a

fall guy *n* SCAPEGOAT : chivo *m* expiatorio

fallible ['fæləbəl] *adj* : falible

fallout ['fɔl,aʊt] *n* **1** : lluvia *f* radioactiva **2** CONSEQUENCES : secuelas *fpl*, consecuencias *fpl*

fallow¹ ['fælo] *vt* : barbechar

fallow² *adj* **to lie fallow** : estar en barbecho

fallow³ *n* : barbecho *m*

false ['fɔls] *adj* **falser; falsest 1** UNTRUE : falso **2** ERRONEOUS : erróneo, equivocado **3** FAKE : falso, postizo **4** UNFAITHFUL : infiel **5** FRAUDULENT : fraudulento ⟨under false pretenses : por fraude⟩

falsehood ['fɔls,hʊd] *n* : mentira *f*, falsedad *f*

falsely ['fɔlsli] *adv* : falsamente, con falsedad

falseness ['fɔlsnəs] *n* : falsedad *f*

falsetto [fɔl'sɛto:] *n, pl* **-tos** : falsete *m*

falsification [,fɔlsəfə'keɪʃən] *n* : falsificación *f*, falseamiento *m*

falsify ['fɔlsə,faɪ] *vt* **-fied; fying** : falsificar, falsear

falsity ['fɔlsəti] *n, pl* **-ties** : falsedad *f*

falter ['fɔltər] *vi* **-tered; -tering 1** TOTTER : tambalearse **2** STAMMER : titubear, tartamudear **3** WAVER : vacilar

faltering ['fɔltərɪŋ] *adj* : titubeante, vacilante

fame ['feɪm] *n* : fama *f*

famed ['feɪmd] *adj* : famoso, célebre, afamado

familial [fə'mɪljəl, -liəl] *adj* : familiar

familiar¹ [fə'mɪljər] *adj* **1** KNOWN : familiar, conocido ⟨to be familiar with : estar familiarizado con⟩ **2** INFORMAL : familiar, informal **3** INTIMATE : íntimo, de confianza **4** FORWARD : confianzudo, atrevido — **familiarly** *adv*

familiar² *n* : espíritu *m* guardián

familiarity [fə,mɪli'ærəti, -,mɪl'jær-] *n, pl* **-ties 1** KNOWLEDGE : conocimiento *m*, familiaridad *f* **2** INFORMALITY, INTIMACY : confianza *f*, familiaridad *f* **3** FORWARDNESS : exceso *m* de confianza, descaro *m*

familiarize [fə'mɪljə,raɪz] *vt* **-ized; -izing 1** : familiarizar **2 to familiarize oneself** : familiarizarse

family ['fæmli, 'fæmə-] *n, pl* **-lies** : familia *f*

family room *n* : living *m*, sala *f* (informal)

family tree *n* : árbol *m* genealógico

famine ['fæmən] *n* : hambre *f*, hambruna *f*

famish ['fæmɪʃ] *vi* **to be famished** : estar famélico, estar hambriento, morir de hambre *fam*

famous ['feɪməs] *adj* : famoso

famously ['feɪməsli] *adv* **to get on famously** : llevarse de maravilla

fan¹ ['fæn] *vt* **fanned; fanning 1** : abanicar (a una persona), avivar (un fuego) **2** STIMULATE : avivar, estimular

fan² *n* **1** : ventilador *m*, abanico *m* **2** ADMIRER, ENTHUSIAST : aficionado *m*, -da *f*; entusiasta *mf*; admirador *m*, -dora *f*

fanatic¹ [fə'næṭɪk] *or* **fanatical** [-ṭɪ-kəl] *adj* : fanático

fanatic² *n* : fanático *m*, -ca *f*

fanaticism [fə'næt̬ə,sɪzəm] *n* : fanatismo *m*

fanciful ['fæntsɪfəl] *adj* **1** CAPRICIOUS : caprichoso, fantástico, extravagante **2** IMAGINATIVE : imaginativo — **fancifully** *adv*

fancy¹ ['fæntsi] *vt* **-cied; -cying 1** IMAGINE : imaginarse, figurarse ⟨fancy that! : ¡figúrate!, ¡imagínate!⟩ **2** CRAVE : apetecer, tener ganas de

fancy² *adj* **-cier; -est 1** ELABORATE : elaborado **2** LUXURIOUS : lujoso, elegante — **fancily** ['fæntsəli] *adv*

fancy³ *n, pl* **-cies 1** LIKING : gusto *m*, afición *f* **2** WHIM : antojo *m*, capricho *m* **3** IMAGINATION : fantasía *f*, imaginación *f*

fandango [fæn'dæŋgo] *n, pl* **-gos** : fandango *m*

fanfare ['fæn,fær] *n* : fanfarria *f*

fang ['fæŋ] *n* : colmillo *m* (de un animal), diente *m* (de una serpiente)

fanlight ['fæn,laɪt] *n* : tragaluz *m*

fantasia [fæn'teɪʒə, -ziə; ˌfæntə-'zi:ə] *n* : fantasía *f*

fantasize ['fæntə,saɪz] *vi* **-sized; -sizing** : fantasear

fantastic [fæn'tæstɪk] *adj* **1** UNBELIEVABLE : fantástico, increíble, extraño **2** ENORMOUS : fabuloso, inmenso ⟨fantastic sums : sumas fabulosas⟩ **3** WONDERFUL : estupendo, fantástico, bárbaro *fam*, macanudo *fam* — **fantastically** [-tɪkli] *adv*

fantasy ['fæntəsi] *n, pl* **-sies** : fantasía *f*

far¹ ['far] *adv* **farther** ['farðər] *or* **further** ['fər-]; **farthest** *or* **furthest** [-ðəst] **1** : lejos ⟨far from here : lejos de aquí⟩ ⟨to go far : llegar lejos⟩ ⟨as far as Chicago : hasta Chicago⟩ ⟨far away : a lo lejos⟩ **2** MUCH : muy, mucho ⟨far bigger : mucho más grande⟩ ⟨far superior : muy superior⟩ ⟨it's by far the best : es con mucho el mejor⟩ **3** (*expressing degree or extent*) ⟨the results are far off : salieron muy inexactos los resultados⟩ ⟨to go so far as : decir tanto como⟩ ⟨to go far enough : tener el alcance necesario⟩ **4** (*expressing progress*) ⟨the work is far advanced : el trabajo está muy avanzado⟩ ⟨to take (something) too far : llevar (algo) demasiado lejos⟩ **5 far and wide** : por todas partes **6 far from it!** : ¡todo lo contrario! **7 so far** : hasta ahora, todavía

far² *adj* **farther** *or* **further; farthest** *or* **furthest 1** REMOTE : lejano, remoto ⟨the Far East : el Lejano Oriente, el Extremo Oriente⟩ ⟨a far country : un país lejano⟩ **2** LONG : largo ⟨a far journey : un viaje largo⟩ **3** EXTREME : extremo ⟨the far right : la extrema derecha⟩ ⟨at the far end of the room : en el otro extremo de la sala⟩

faraway ['farə,weɪ] *adj* : remoto, lejano

farce ['fars] *n* : farsa *f*

farcical ['farsɪkəl] *adj* : absurdo, ridículo

fare¹ ['fær] *vi* **fared; faring** : ir, salir ⟨how did you fare? : ¿cómo te fue?⟩

fare² *n* **1** : pasaje *m*, billete *m*, boleto *m* ⟨half fare : medio pasaje⟩ **2** FOOD : comida *f*

farewell¹ ['fær'wɛl] *adj* : de despedida

farewell² *n* : despedida *f*

far–fetched ['far'fɛtʃt] *adj* : improbable, exagerado

farina [fə'ri:nə] *n* : harina *f*

farm¹ ['farm] *vt* **1** : cultivar, labrar **2** : criar (animales) — *vi* : ser agricultor

farm² *n* : granja *f*, hacienda *f*, finca *f*, estancia *f*

farmer ['farmər] *n* : agricultor *m*, granjero *m*

farmhand ['farm,hænd] *n* : peón *m*

farmhouse ['farm,haʊs] *n* : granja *f*, vivienda *f* del granjero, casa *f* de hacienda

farming ['farmɪŋ] *n* : labranza *f*, cultivo *m*, crianza *f* (de animales)

farmland ['farm,lænd] *n* : tierras *fpl* de labranza

farmyard ['farm,jard] *n* : corral *m*

far–off ['far,ɔf, -'ɔf] *adj* : remoto, distante, lejano

far–reaching ['far'ri:tʃɪŋ] *adj* : de gran alcance

farsighted ['far,saɪt̬əd] *adj* **1** : hipermétrope **2** JUDICIOUS : con visión de futuro, previsor, precavido

farsightedness ['far,saɪt̬ədnəs] *n* **1** : hipermetropía *f* **2** PRUDENCE : previsión *f*

farther¹ ['farðər] *adv* **1** AHEAD : más lejos (en el espacio), más adelante (en el tiempo) **2** MORE : más

farther² *adj* : más lejano, más remoto

farthermost ['farðər,mo:st] *adj* : (el) más lejano

farthest¹ ['farðəst] *adv* **1** : lo más lejos ⟨I jumped farthest : salté lo más lejos⟩ **2** : lo más avanzado ⟨he progressed farthest : progresó al punto más avanzado⟩ **3** : más ⟨the farthest developed plan : el plan más desarrollado⟩

farthest² *adj* : más lejano

fascicle ['fæsɪkəl] *n* : fascículo *m*

fascinate ['fæsən,eɪt] *vt* **-nated; -nating** : fascinar, cautivar

fascinating ['fæsən,eɪt̬ɪŋ] *adj* : fascinante

fascination [ˌfæsən'eɪʃən] *n* : fascinación *f*

fascism ['fæʃ,ɪzəm] *n* : fascismo *m*

fascist¹ ['fæʃɪst] *adj* : fascista

fascist² *n* : fascista *mf*

fashion¹ ['fæʃən] *vt* : formar, moldear

fashion² *n* **1** MANNER : manera *f*, modo *m* **2** CUSTOM : costumbre *f* **3** STYLE : moda *f*

fashionable ['fæʃənəbəl] *adj* : de moda, chic

fashionably ['fæʃənəbli] *adv* : a la moda

fast¹ ['fæst] *vi* : ayunar

fast² *adv* **1** SECURELY : firmemente, seguramente ⟨to hold fast : agarrarse bien⟩ **2** RAPIDLY : rápidamente, rápido, de prisa **3 to run fast** : ir adelantado (dícese de un reloj) **4** SOUNDLY : profundamente ⟨fast asleep : profundamente dormido⟩

fast³ *adj* **1** SECURE : firme, seguro ⟨to make fast : amarrar (un barco)⟩ **2** FAITHFUL : leal ⟨fast friends : amigos leales⟩ **3** RAPID : rápido, veloz **4** : adelantado ⟨my watch is fast : tengo el reloj adelantado⟩ **5** DEEP : profundo ⟨a fast sleep : un sueño profundo⟩ **6** COLORFAST : inalterable, que no destiñe **7** DISSOLUTE : extravagante, disipado, disoluto

fast⁴ *n* : ayuno *m*

fasten ['fæsən] *vt* **1** ATTACH : sujetar, atar **2** FIX : fijar ⟨to fasten one's eyes on : fijar los ojos en⟩ **3** SECURE : abrochar (ropa o cinturones), atar (cordones), cerrar (una maleta) — *vi* : abrocharse, cerrar

fastener ['fæsənər] *n* : cierre *m*, sujetador *m*

fastening ['fæsənɪŋ] *n* : cierre *m*, sujetador *m*

fast food *n* : comida *f* rápida

fastidious [fæs'tɪdiəs] *adj* : quisquilloso, exigente — **fastidiously** *adv*

fat¹ ['fæt] *adj* **fatter; fattest 1** OBESE : gordo, obeso **2** THICK : grueso

fat² *n* : grasa *f*

fatal ['feɪt̬əl] *adj* **1** DEADLY : mortal **2** ILL-FATED : malhadado, fatal **3** MOMENTOUS : fatídico

fatalism ['feɪt̬əl,ɪzəm] *n* : fatalismo *m*

fatalist ['feɪt̬əlɪst] *n* : fatalista *mf*

fatalistic [,feɪt̬əl'ɪstɪk] *adj* : fatalista

fatality [feɪ'tæləti, fə-] *n, pl* **-ties** : víctima *f* mortal

fatally ['feɪt̬əli] *adv* : mortalmente

fate ['feɪt] *n* **1** DESTINY : destino *m* **2** END, LOT : final *m*, suerte *f*

fated ['feɪt̬əd] *adj* : predestinado

fateful ['feɪtfəl] *adj* **1** MOMENTOUS : fatídico, aciago **2** PROPHETIC : profético — **fatefully** *adv*

father¹ ['fɑðər] *vt* : engendrar

father² *n* **1** : padre *m* ⟨my father and my mother : mi padre y mi madre⟩ ⟨Father Smith : el padre Smith⟩ **2 the Father** GOD : el Padre, Dios *m*

fatherhood ['fɑðər,hʊd] *n* : paternidad *f*

father-in-law ['fɑðərɪn,lɔ] *n, pl* **fathers-in-law** : suegro *m*

fatherland ['fɑðər,lænd] *n* : patria *f*

fatherless ['fɑðərləs] *adj* : huérfano de padre, sin padre

fatherly ['fɑðərli] *adj* : paternal

fathom¹ ['fæðəm] *vt* UNDERSTAND : entender, comprender

fathom² *n* : braza *f*

fatigue¹ [fə'tiːg] *vt* **-tigued; -tiguing** : fatigar, cansar

fatigue² *n* : fatiga *f*

fatness ['fætnəs] *n* : gordura *f* (de una persona o un animal), grosor *m* (de un objeto)

fatten ['fæt̬ən] *vt* : engordar, cebar

fatty ['fæt̬i] *adj* **fattier; -est** : graso, grasoso, adiposo (dícese de los tejidos)

fatuous ['fætʃuəs] *adj* : necio, fatuo — **fatuously** *adv*

faucet ['fɔsət] *n* : llave *f*, canilla *f Arg, Uru*, grifo *m*

fault¹ ['fɔlt] *vt* : encontrar defectos a

fault² *n* **1** SHORTCOMING : defecto *m*, falta *f* **2** DEFECT : falta *f*, defecto *m*, falla *f* **3** BLAME : culpa *f* **4** FRACTURE : falla *f* (geológica)

faultfinder ['fɔlt,faɪndər] *n* : criticón *m*, -cona *f*

faultfinding ['fɔlt,faɪndɪŋ] *n* : crítica *f*

faultless ['fɔltləs] *adj* : sin culpa, sin imperfecciones, impecable

faultlessly ['fɔltləsli] *adv* : impecablemente, perfectamente

faulty ['fɔlti] *adj* **faultier; -est** : defectuoso, imperfecto — **faultily** ['fɔltəli] *adv*

fauna ['fɔnə] *n* : fauna *f*

faux ['foː] *adj* : de imitación

faux pas [,foː'pɑ] *n, pl* **faux pas** [*same or* -'pɑz] : metedura *f* de pata *fam*

favor¹ ['feɪvər] *vt* **1** SUPPORT : estar a favor de, ser partidario de, apoyar **2** OBLIGE : hacerle un favor a **3** PREFER : preferir **4** RESEMBLE : parecerse a, salir a

favor² *n* : favor *m* ⟨in favor of : a favor de⟩ ⟨an error in his favor : un error a su favor⟩

favorable ['feɪvərəbəl] *adj* : favorable, propicio

favorably ['feɪvərəbli] *adv* : favorablemente, bien

favorite¹ ['feɪvərət] *adj* : favorito, preferido

favorite² *n* : favorito *m*, -ta *f*; preferido *m*, -da *f*

favoritism ['feɪvərə,tɪzəm] *n* : favoritismo *m*

fawn¹ ['fɔn] *vi* : adular, lisonjear

fawn² *n* : cervato *m*

fax ['fæks] *n* : facsímil *m*, facsímile *m*

faze ['feɪz] *vt* **fazed; fazing** : desconcertar, perturbar

fear¹ ['fɪr] *vt* : temer, tener miedo de — *vi* : temer

fear² *n* : miedo *m*, temor *m* ⟨for fear of : por temor a⟩

fearful ['fɪrfəl] *adj* **1** FRIGHTENING : espantoso, aterrador, horrible **2** FRIGHTENED : temeroso, miedoso

fearfully ['fɪrfəli] *adv* **1** EXTREMELY : extremadamente, terriblemente **2** TIMIDLY : con temor

fearless ['fɪrləs] *adj* : intrépido, impávido

fearlessly ['fɪrləsli] *adv* : sin temor

fearlessness ['fɪrləsnəs] *n* : intrepidez *f*, impavidez *f*

fearsome ['fɪrsəm] *adj* : aterrador

feasibility [,fiːzə'bɪləti] *n* : viabilidad *f*, factibilidad *f*

feasible ['fiːzəbəl] *adj* : viable, factible, realizable

feast · feminist

feast¹ ['fiːst] *vi* : banquetear — *vt* **1** : agasajar, festejar **2 to feast one's eyes on** : regalarse la vista con

feast² *n* **1** BANQUET : banquete *m*, festín *m* **2** FESTIVAL : fiesta *f*

feat ['fiːt] *n* : proeza *f*, hazaña *f*

feather¹ ['fɛðər] *vt* **1** : emplumar **2 to feather one's nest** : hacer su agosto

feather² *n* **1** : pluma *f* **2 a feather in one's cap** : un triunfo personal

feathered ['fɛðərd] *adj* : con plumas

feathery ['fɛðəri] *adj* **1** DOWNY : plumoso **2** LIGHT : liviano

feature¹ ['fiːtʃər] *v* **-tured; -turing** *vt* **1** IMAGINE : imaginarse **2** PRESENT : presentar — *vi* : figurar

feature² *n* **1** CHARACTERISTIC : característica *f*, rasgo *m* **2** : largometraje *m* (en el cine), artículo *m* (en un periódico), documental *m* (en la televisión) **3 features** *npl* : rasgos *mpl*, facciones *fpl* ⟨delicate features : facciones delicadas⟩

February ['fɛbjuˌri, 'fɛbu-, 'fbru-] *n* : febrero *m*

fecal ['fiːkəl] *adj* : fecal

feces ['fiːˌsiːz] *npl* : heces *fpl*, excrementos *mpl*

feckless ['fɛkləs] *adj* : irresponsable

fecund ['fɛkənd, 'fiː-] *adj* : fecundo

fecundity [fɪ'kʌndəti, fɛ-] *n* : fecundidad *f*

federal ['fɛdrəl, -dərəl] *adj* : federal

federalism ['fɛdrəˌlɪzəm, -dərə-] *n* : federalismo *m*

federalist¹ ['fɛdrəlɪst, -dərə-] *adj* : federalista

federalist² *n* : federalista *mf*

federate ['fɛdəˌreɪt] *vt* **-ated; -ating** : federar

federation [ˌfɛdə'reɪʃən] *n* : federación *f*

fedora [fɪ'dorə] *n* : sombrero *m* flexible de fieltro

fed up *adj* : harto

fee ['fiː] *n* **1** : honorarios *mpl* (a un médico, un abogado, etc.) **2 entrance fee** : entrada *f*

feeble ['fiːbəl] *adj* **-bler; -blest 1** WEAK : débil, endeble **2** INEFFECTIVE : flojo, pobre, poco convincente

feebleminded [ˌfiːbəl'maɪndəd] *adj* **1** : débil mental **2** FOOLISH, STUPID : imbécil, tonto

feebleness ['fiːbəlnəs] *n* : debilidad *f*

feebly ['fiːbli] *adv* : débilmente

feed¹ ['fiːd] *v* **fed** ['fɛd]; **feeding** *vt* **1** : dar de comer a, nutrir, alimentar (a una persona) **2** : alimentar (un fuego o una máquina), proveer (información), introducir (datos) — *vi* : comer, alimentarse

feed² *n* **1** NOURISHMENT : alimento *m* **2** FODDER : pienso *m*

feedback ['fiːdˌbæk] *n* **1** : realimentación *f* (electrónica) **2** RESPONSE : reacción *f*

feeder ['fiːdər] *n* : comedero *m* (para animales)

feel¹ ['fiːl] *v* **felt** ['fɛlt]; **feeling** *vi* **1** : sentirse, encontrarse ⟨I feel tired : me siento cansada⟩ ⟨he feels hungry : tiene hambre⟩ ⟨she feels like a fool : se siente como una idiota⟩ ⟨to feel like doing something : tener ganas de hacer algo⟩ **2** SEEM : parecer ⟨it feels like spring : parece primavera⟩ **3** THINK : parecerse, opinar, pensar ⟨how does he feel about that? : ¿qué opina él de eso?⟩ — *vt* **1** TOUCH : tocar, palpar **2** SENSE : sentir ⟨to feel the cold : sentir el frío⟩ **3** CONSIDER : sentir, creer, considerar ⟨to feel (it) necessary : creer necesario⟩

feel² *n* **1** SENSATION, TOUCH : sensación *f*, tacto *m* **2** ATMOSPHERE : ambiente *m*, atmósfera *f* **3 to have a feel for** : tener un talento especial para

feeler ['fiːlər] *n* : antena *f*, tentáculo *m*

feeling ['fiːlɪŋ] *n* **1** SENSATION : sensación *f*, sensibilidad *f* **2** EMOTION : sentimiento *m* **3** OPINION : opinión *f* **4 feelings** *npl* SENSIBILITIES : sentimientos *mpl* ⟨to hurt someone's feelings : herir los sentimientos de alguien⟩

feet → foot

feign ['feɪn] *vt* : simular, aparentar, fingir

feint¹ ['feɪnt] *vi* : fintar, fintear

feint² *n* : finta *f*

feldspar ['fɛldˌspar] *n* : feldespato *m*

felicitate [fɪ'lɪsəˌteɪt] *vt* **-tated; -tating** : felicitar, congratular

felicitation [fɪˌlɪsə'teɪʃən] *n* : felicitación *f*

felicitous [fɪ'lɪsətəs] *adj* : acertado, oportuno

feline¹ ['fiːˌlaɪn] *adj* : felino

feline² *n* : felino *m*, -na *f*

fell¹ ['fɛl] *vt* : talar (un árbol), derribar (a una persona)

fell² → fall

fellow ['fɛˌloː] *n* **1** COMPANION : compañero *m*, -ra *f*; camarada *mf* **2** ASSOCIATE : socio *m*, -cia *f* **3** MAN : tipo *m*, hombre *m*

fellowman [ˌfɛlo'mæn] *n*, *pl* **-men** : prójimo *m*, semejante *m*

fellowship ['fɛloˌʃɪp] *n* **1** COMPANIONSHIP : camaradería *f*, compañerismo *m* **2** ASSOCIATION : fraternidad *f* **3** GRANT : beca *f* (de investigación)

felon ['fɛlən] *n* : malhechor *m*, -chora *f*; criminal *mf*

felonious [fə'loːniəs] *adj* : criminal

felony ['fɛləni] *n*, *pl* **-nies** : delito *m* grave

felt¹ ['fɛlt] *n* : fieltro *m*

felt² → feel

female¹ ['fiːˌmeɪl] *adj* : femenino

female² *n* **1** : hembra *f* (de animal) **2** WOMAN : mujer *f*

feminine ['fɛmənən] *adj* : femenino

femininity [ˌfɛmə'nɪnəti] *n* : feminidad *f*, feminiedad *f*

feminism ['fɛməˌnɪzəm] *n* : feminismo *m*

feminist¹ ['fɛmənɪst] *adj* : feminista

feminist² *n* : feminista *mf*

femoral ['fɛmərəl] *adj* : femoral
femur ['fi:mər] *n, pl* **femurs** *or* **femora** ['fɛmərə] : fémur *m*
fence[1] ['fɛnts] *v* **fenced; fencing** *vt* : vallar, cercar — *vi* : hacer esgrima
fence[2] *n* : cerca *f*, valla *f*, cerco *m*
fencer ['fɛntsər] *n* : esgrimista *mf*; esgrimidor *m*, -dora *f*
fencing ['fɛntsɪŋ] *n* **1** : esgrima *m* (deporte) **2** : materiales *mpl* para cercas **3** ENCLOSURE : cercado *m*
fend ['fɛnd] *vt* **to fend off** : rechazar (un enemigo), parar (un golpe), eludir (una pregunta) — *vi* **to fend for oneself** : arreglárselas sólo, valerse por sí mismo
fender ['fɛndər] *n* : guardabarros *mpl*, salpicadera *f Mex*
fennel ['fɛnəl] *n* : hinojo *m*
ferment[1] [fər'mɛnt] *v* : fermentar
ferment[2] ['fər,mɛnt] *n* **1** : fermento *m* (en la química) **2** TURMOIL : agitación *f*, conmoción *f*
fermentation [,fərmən'teɪʃən, -,mɛn-] *n* : fermentación *f*
fern ['fərn] *n* : helecho *m*
ferocious [fə'roːʃəs] *adj* : feroz — **ferociously** *adv*
ferociousness [fə'roːʃəsnəs] *n* : ferocidad *f*
ferocity [fə'rɑsəti] *n* : ferocidad *f*
ferret[1] ['fɛrət] *vi* SNOOP : hurgar, husmear — *vt* **to ferret out** : descubrir
ferret[2] *n* : hurón *m*
ferric ['fɛrɪk] *or* **ferrous** ['fɛrəs] *adj* : férrico
Ferris wheel ['fɛrɪs] *n* : noria *f*
ferry[1] ['fɛri] *vt* **-ried; -rying** : llevar, transportar
ferry[2] *n, pl* **-ries** : transbordador *m*, ferry *m*
ferryboat ['fɛri,boːt] *n* : transbordador *m*, ferry *m*
fertile ['fərtəl] *adj* : fértil, fecundo
fertility [fər'tɪləti] *n* : fertilidad *f*
fertilization [,fərtələ'zeɪʃən] *n* : fertilización *f* (del suelo), fecundación (de un huevo)
fertilize ['fərtəl,aɪz] *vt* **-ized; -izing 1** : fecundar (un huevo) **2** : fertilizar, abonar (el suelo)
fertilizer ['fərtəl,aɪzər] *n* : fertilizante *m*, abono *m*
fervent ['fərvənt] *adj* : ferviente, fervoroso, ardiente — **fervently** *adv*
fervid ['fərvɪd] *adj* : ardiente, apasionado — **fervidly** *adv*
fervor ['fərvər] *n* : fervor *m*, ardor *m*
fester ['fɛstər] *vi* : enconarse, supurar
festival ['fɛstəvəl] *n* : fiesta *f*, festividad *f*, festival *m*
festive ['fɛstɪv] *adj* : festivo — **festively** *adv*
festivity [fɛs'tɪvəti] *n, pl* **-ties** : festividad *f*, celebración *f*
festoon[1] [fɛs'tu:n] *vt* : adornar, engalanar
festoon[2] *n* GARLAND : guirnalda *f*
fetal ['fi:təl] *adj* : fetal

fetch ['fɛtʃ] *vt* **1** BRING : traer, recoger, ir a buscar **2** REALIZE : realizar, venderse por ⟨the jewelry fetched $10,000 : las joyas se vendieron por $10,000⟩
fetching ['fɛtʃɪŋ] *adj* : atractivo, encantador
fête[1] ['feɪt, 'fɛt] *vt* **fêted; fêting** : festejar, agasajar
fête[2] *n* : fiesta *f*
fetid ['fɛtəd] *adj* : fétido
fetish ['fɛtɪʃ] *n* : fetiche *m*
fetlock ['fɛt,lɑk] *n* : espolón *m*
fetter ['fɛtər] *vt* : encadenar, poner grillos a
fetters ['fɛtərz] *npl* : grillos *mpl*, grilletes *mpl*, cadenas *fpl*
fettle ['fɛtəl] *n* **in fine fettle** : en buena forma, en plena forma
fetus ['fi:təs] *n* : feto *m*
feud[1] ['fju:d] *vi* : pelear, contender
feud[2] *n* : contienda *f*, enemistad *f* (heredada)
feudal ['fju:dəl] *adj* : feudal
feudalism ['fju:dəl,ɪzəm] *n* : feudalismo *m*
fever ['fi:vər] *n* : fiebre *f*, calentura *f*
feverish ['fi:vərɪʃ] *adj* **1** : afiebrado, con fiebre, febril **2** FRANTIC : febril, frenético
few[1] ['fju:] *adj* : pocos ⟨with few exceptions : con pocas excepciones⟩ ⟨a few times : varias veces⟩
few[2] *pron* **1** : pocos ⟨few (of them) were ready : pocos estaban listos⟩ **2 a few** : algunos, unos cuantos **3 few and far between** : contados
fewer ['fju:ər] *pron* : menos ⟨the fewer the better : cuantos menos mejor⟩
fez ['fɛz] *n, pl* **fezzes** : fez *m*
fiancé [,fi:,ɑn'seɪ, ,fi:'ɑn,seɪ] *n* : prometido *m*, novio *m*
fiancée [,fi:,ɑn'seɪ, ,fi:'ɑn,seɪ] *n* : prometida *f*, novia *f*
fiasco [fi'æs,ko:] *n, pl* **-coes** : fiasco *m*, fracaso *m*
fiat ['fi:,ɑt, -,æt, -ət; 'faɪət, -,æt] *n* : decreto *m*, orden *m*
fib[1] ['fɪb] *vi* **fibbed; fibbing** : decir mentirillas
fib[2] *n* : mentirilla *f*, bola *f fam*
fibber ['fɪbər] *n* : mentirosillo *m*, -lla *f*; cuentista *mf fam*
fiber *or* **fibre** ['faɪbər] *n* : fibra *f*
fiberboard ['faɪbər,bord] *n* : cartón *m* madera
fiberglass ['faɪbər,glæs] *n* : fibra *f* de vidrio
fibrillate ['fɪbrə,leɪt, 'faɪ-] *vi* **-lated; -lating** : fibrilar
fibrillation [,fɪbrə'leɪʃən, ,faɪ-] *n* : fibrilación *f*
fibrous ['faɪbrəs] *adj* : fibroso
fibula ['fɪbjələ] *n, pl* **-lae** [-,li:, -,laɪ] *or* **-las** : peroné *m*
fickle ['fɪkəl] *adj* : inconstante, voluble, veleidoso
fickleness ['fɪkəlnəs] *n* : volubilidad *f*, inconstancia *f*, veleidad *f*

fiction ['fɪkʃən] *n* : ficción *f*
fictional ['fɪkʃənəl] *adj* : ficticio
fictitious [fɪk'tɪʃəs] *adj* **1** IMAGINARY : ficticio, imaginario **2** FALSE : falso, ficticio
fiddle¹ ['fɪdəl] *vi* **-dled; -dling 1** : tocar el violín **2 to fiddle with** : juguetear con, toquetear
fiddle² *n* : violín *m*
fiddler ['fɪdlər, 'fɪdələr] *n* : violinista *mf*
fiddlesticks ['fɪdəl‚stɪks] *interj* : ¡tonterías!
fidelity [fə'dɛləti, faɪ-] *n, pl* **-ties** : fidelidad *f*
fidget¹ ['fɪdʒət] *vi* **1** : moverse, estarse inquieto **2 to fidget with** : juguetear con
fidget² *n* **1** : persona *f* inquieta **2 fidgets** *npl* RESTLESSNESS : inquietud *f*
fidgety ['fɪdʒəti] *adj* : inquieto
fiduciary¹ [fə'du:ʃi‚ɛri, -'dju:-, -ʃəri] *adj* : fiduciario
fiduciary² *n, pl* **-ries** : fiduciario *m*, -ria *f*
field¹ ['fi:ld] *vt* : interceptar y devolver (una pelota), presentar (un candidato), sortear (una pregunta)
field² *adj* : de campaña, de campo ⟨field hospital : hospital de campaña⟩ ⟨field goal : gol de campo⟩ ⟨field trip : viaje de estudio⟩
field³ *n* **1** : campo *m* (de cosechas, de batalla, de magnetismo) **2** : campo *m*, cancha *f* (en deportes) **3** : campo *m* (de trabajo), esfera *f* (de actividades)
fielder ['fi:ldər] *n* : jugador *m*, -dora *f* de campo; fildeador *m*, -dora *f*
field glasses *n* : binoculares *mpl*, gemelos *mpl*
fiend ['fi:nd] *n* **1** DEMON : demonio *m* **2** EVILDOER : persona *f* maligna; malvado *m*, -da *f* **3** FANATIC : fanático *m*, -ca *f*
fiendish ['fi:ndɪʃ] *adj* : diabólico — **fiendishly** *adv*
fierce ['fɪrs] *adj* **fiercer; -est 1** FEROCIOUS : fiero, feroz **2** HEATED : acalorado **3** INTENSE : intenso, violento, fuerte — **fiercely** *adv*
fierceness ['fɪrsnəs] *n* **1** FEROCITY : ferocidad *f*, fiereza *f* **2** INTENSITY : intensidad *f*, violencia *f*
fieriness ['faɪərinəs] *n* : pasión *f*, ardor *m*
fiery ['faɪəri] *adj* **fierier; -est 1** BURNING : ardiente, llameante **2** GLOWING : encendido **3** PASSIONATE : acalorado, ardiente, fogoso
fiesta [fi'ɛstə] *n* : fiesta *f*
fife ['faɪf] *n* : pífano *m*
fifteen¹ [fɪf'ti:n] *adj* : quince
fifteen² *n* : quince *m*
fifteenth¹ [fɪf'ti:nθ] *adj* : decimoquinto
fifteenth² *n* **1** : decimoquinto *m*, -ta *f* (en una serie) **2** : quinceavo *m*, quinceava parte *f*
fifth¹ ['fɪfθ] *adj* : quinto

fifth² *n* **1** : quinto *m*, -ta *f* (en una serie) **2** : quinto *m*, quinta parte *f* **3** : quinta *f* (en la música)
fiftieth¹ ['fɪftiəθ] *adj* : quincuagésimo
fiftieth² *n* **1** : quincuagésimo *m*, -ma *f* (en una serie) **2** : cincuentavo *m*, cincuentava parte *f*
fifty¹ ['fɪfti] *adj* : cincuenta
fifty² *n, pl* **-ties** : cincuenta *m*
fifty–fifty¹ [‚fɪfti'fɪfti] *adv* : a medias, mitad y mitad
fifty–fifty² *adj* **to have a fifty–fifty chance** : tener un cincuenta por ciento de posibilidades
fig ['fɪg] *n* : higo *m*
fight¹ ['faɪt] *v* **fought** ['fɔt]; **fighting** *vi* : luchar, combatir, pelear — *vt* : luchar contra, combatir contra
fight² *n* **1** COMBAT : lucha *f*, pelea *f*, combate *m* **2** MATCH : pelea *f*, combate *m* (en boxeo) **3** QUARREL : disputa *f*, pelea *f*, pleito *m*
fighter ['faɪtər] *n* **1** COMBATANT : luchador *m*, -dora *f*; combatiente *mf* **2** BOXER : boxeador *m*, -dora *f*
figment ['fɪgmənt] *n* **figment of the imagination** : producto *m* de la imaginación
figurative ['fɪgjərəţɪv, -gə-] *adj* : figurado, metafórico
figuratively ['fɪgjərəţɪvli, -gə-] *adv* : en sentido figurado, de manera metafórica
figure¹ ['fɪgjər, -gər] *v* **-ured; -uring** *vt* **1** CALCULATE : calcular **2** ESTIMATE : figurarse, calcular ⟨he figured it was possible : se figuró que era posible⟩ — *vi* **1** FEATURE, STAND OUT : figurar, destacar **2 that figures!** : ¡obvio!, ¡no me extraña nada!
figure² *n* **1** DIGIT : número *m*, cifra *f* **2** PRICE : precio *m*, cifra *f* **3** PERSONAGE : figura *f*, personaje *m* **4** : figura *f*, tipo *m*, físico *m* ⟨to have a good figure : tener buen tipo, tener un buen físico⟩ **5** DESIGN, OUTLINE : figura *f* **6 figures** *npl* : aritmética *f*
figurehead ['fɪgjər‚hɛd, -gər-] *n* : testaferro *m*, líder *mf* sin poder
figure of speech *n* : figura *f* retórica, figura *f* de hablar
figure out *vt* **1** UNDERSTAND : entender **2** RESOLVE : resolver (un problema, etc.)
figurine [‚fɪgjə'ri:n] *n* : estatuilla *f*
Fijian ['fi:dʒiən, fɪ'ji:ən] *n* : fijiano *m*, -na *f* — **Fijian** *adj*
filament ['fɪləmənt] *n* : filamento *m*
filbert ['fɪlbərt] *n* : avellana *f*
filch ['fɪltʃ] *vt* : hurtar, birlar *fam*
file¹ ['faɪl] *v* **filed; filing** *vt* **1** CLASSIFY : clasificar **2** : archivar (documentos) **3** SUBMIT : presentar ⟨to file charges : presentar cargos⟩ **4** SMOOTH : limar — *vi* : desfilar, entrar (o salir) en fila
file² *n* **1** : lima *f* ⟨nail file : lima de uñas⟩ **2** DOCUMENTS : archivo *m* **3** LINE : fila *f*

filial ['fɪliəl, 'fɪljəl] *adj* : filial
filibuster¹ ['fɪlə,bʌstər] *vi* : practicar el obstruccionismo
filibuster² *n* : obstruccionismo *m*
filibusterer ['fɪlə,bʌstərər] *n* : obstruccionista *mf*
filigree ['fɪlə,gri:] *n* : filigrana *f*
Filipino [,fɪlə'pi:no:] *n* : filipino *m*, -na *f* — **Filipino** *adj*
fill¹ ['fɪl] *vt* **1** : llenar, ocupar ⟨to fill a cup : llenar una taza⟩ ⟨to fill a room : ocupar una sala⟩ **2** STUFF : rellenar **3** PLUG : tapar, rellenar, empastar (un diente) **4** SATISFY : cumplir con, satisfacer **5** *or* **to fill out** : llenar, re- llenar ⟨to fill out a form : rellenar un formulario⟩
fill² *n* **1** FILLING, STUFFING : relleno *m* **2 to eat one's fill** : comer lo suficiente **3 to have one's fill of** : estar harto de
filler¹ ['fɪlər] *n* : relleno *m*
fillet¹ ['fɪlət, fɪ'leɪ, 'fɪ,leɪ] *vt* : cortar en filetes
fillet² *n* : filete *m*
fill in *vt* INFORM : informar, poner al corriente — *vi* **to fill in for** : reemplazar a
filling ['fɪlɪŋ] *n* **1** : relleno *m* **2** : empaste *m* (de un diente)
filling station → **gas station**
filly ['fɪli] *n, pl* **-lies** : potra *f*, potranca *f*
film¹ ['fɪlm] *vt* : filmar — *vi* : rodar
film² *n* **1** COATING : capa *f*, película *f* **2** : película *f* (fotográfica) **3** MOVIE : película *f*, filme *m*
filmmaker ['fɪlm,meɪkər] *n* : cineasta *mf*
filmy ['fɪlmi] *adj* **filmier; -est 1** GAUZY : diáfano, vaporoso **2** : cubierto de una película
filter¹ ['fɪltər] *vt* : filtrar
filter² *n* : filtro *m*
filth ['fɪlθ] *n* : mugre *f*, porquería *f*, roña *f*
filthiness ['fɪlθinəs] *n* : suciedad *f*
filthy ['fɪlθi] *adj* **filthier; -est 1** DIRTY : mugriento, sucio **2** OBSCENE : obsceno, indecente
filtration [fɪl'treɪʃən] *n* : filtración *f*
fin ['fɪn] *n* **1** : aleta *f* **2** : alerón *m* (de un automóvil o un avión)
finagle [fə'neɪgəl] *vt* **-gled; -gling** : arreglárselas para conseguir
final¹ ['faɪnəl] *adj* **1** DEFINITIVE : definitivo, final, inapelable **2** ULTIMATE : final **3** LAST : último, final
final² *n* **1** : final *f* (en deportes) **2 finals** *npl* : exámenes *mpl* finales
finale [fɪ'næli, -'nɑ-] *n* : final *m* ⟨grand finale : final triunfal⟩
finalist ['faɪnəlɪst] *n* : finalista *mf*
finality [faɪ'næləṭi, fə-] *n, pl* **-ties** : finalidad *f*
finalize ['faɪnəl,aɪz] *vt* **-ized; -izing** : finalizar
finally ['faɪnəli] *adv* **1** LASTLY : por último, finalmente **2** EVENTUALLY : por fin, al final **3** DEFINITIVELY : definitivamente

finance¹ [fə'nænts, 'faɪ,nænts] *vt* **-nanced; -nancing** : financiar
finance² *n* **1** : finanzas *fpl* **2 finances** *npl* RESOURCES : recursos *mpl* financieros
financial [fə'næntʃəl, faɪ-] *adj* : financiero, económico
financially [fə'næntʃəli, faɪ-] *adv* : económicamente
financier [,fɪnən'sɪr, ,faɪ,næn-] *n* : financiero *m*, -ra *f*; financista *mf*
financing [fə'næntsɪŋ, 'fæɪ,næntsɪŋ] *n* : financiación *f*, financiamiento *m*
finch ['fɪntʃ] *n* : pinzón *m*
find¹ ['faɪnd] *vt* **found** ['faʊnd]; **finding 1** LOCATE : encontrar, hallar ⟨I can't find it : no lo encuentro⟩ ⟨to find one's way : encontrar el camino, orientarse⟩ **2** DISCOVER, REALIZE : descubrir, darse cuenta de ⟨he found it difficult : descubrió que era difícil⟩ **3** DECLARE : declarar, hallar ⟨they found him guilty : lo declararon culpable⟩
find² *n* : hallazgo *m*
finder ['faɪndər] *n* : descubridor *m*, -dora *f*
finding ['faɪndɪŋ] *n* **1** FIND : hallazgo *m* **2 findings** *npl* : conclusiones *fpl*
find out *vt* DISCOVER : descubrir, averiguar — *vi* LEARN : enterarse
fine¹ ['faɪn] *vt* **fined; fining** : multar
fine² *adj* **finer; -est 1** PURE : puro (dícese del oro y de la plata) **2** THIN : fino, delgado **3** : fino ⟨fine sand : arena fina⟩ **4** SMALL : pequeño, minúsculo ⟨fine print : letras minúsculas⟩ **5** SUBTLE : sutil, delicado **6** EXCELLENT : excelente, magnífico, selecto **7** FAIR : bueno ⟨it's a fine day : hace buen tiempo⟩ **8** EXQUISITE : exquisito, delicado, fino **9 fine arts** : bellas artes *fpl*
fine³ *n* : multa *f*
finely ['faɪnli] *adv* **1** EXCELLENTLY : con arte **2** ELEGANTLY : elegantemente **3** PRECISELY : con precisión **4 to chop finely** : picar muy fino, picar en trozos pequeños
fineness ['faɪnnəs] *n* **1** EXCELLENCE : excelencia *f* **2** ELEGANCE : elegancia *f*, refinamiento *m* **3** DELICACY : delicadeza *f*, lo fino **4** PRECISION : precisión *f* **5** SUBTLETY : sutileza *f* **6** PURITY : ley *f* (de oro y plata)
finery ['faɪnəri] *n* : galas *fpl*, adornos *mpl*
finesse¹ [fə'nɛs] *vt* **-nessed; -nessing** : ingeniar
finesse² *n* **1** REFINEMENT : refinamiento *m*, finura *f* **2** TACT : delicadeza *f*, tacto *m*, diplomacia *f* **3** CRAFTINESS : astucia *f*
finger¹ ['fɪŋgər] *vt* **1** HANDLE : tocar, toquetear **2** ACCUSE : acusar, delatar
finger² *n* : dedo *m*
fingerling ['fɪŋgərlɪŋ] *n* : pez *m* pequeño y joven
fingernail ['fɪŋgər,neɪl] *n* : uña *f*
fingerprint¹ ['fɪŋgər,prɪnt] *vt* : tomar las huellas digitales a

fingerprint² *n* : huella *f* digital
fingertip ['fɪŋgər,tɪp] *n* : punta *f* del dedo, yema *f* del dedo
finicky ['fɪnɪki] *adj* : maniático, melindroso, mañoso
finish¹ ['fɪnɪʃ] *vt* **1** COMPLETE : acabar, terminar **2** : aplicar un acabado a (muebles, etc.)
finish² *n* **1** END : fin *m*, final *m* **2** REFINEMENT : refinamiento *m* **3** : acabado *m* ⟨a glossy finish : un acabado brillante⟩
finite ['faɪ,naɪt] *adj* : finito
fink ['fɪŋk] *n* : mequetrefe *mf fam*
Finn ['fɪn] *n* : finlandés *m*, -desa *f*
Finnish¹ ['fɪnɪʃ] *adj* : finlandés
Finnish² *n* : finlandés *m* (idioma)
fiord [fiˈɔrd] → **fjord**
fir ['fər] *n* : abeto *m*
fire¹ ['faɪr] *vt* **fired; firing 1** IGNITE, KINDLE : encender **2** ENLIVEN : animar, avivar **3** DISMISS : despedir **4** SHOOT : disparar **5** BAKE : cocer (cerámica)
fire² *n* **1** : fuego *m* **2** BURNING : incendio *m* ⟨fire alarm : alarma contra incendios⟩ ⟨to be on fire : estar en llamas⟩ **3** ENTHUSIASM : ardor *m*, entusiasmo *m* **4** SHOOTING : disparos *mpl*, fuego *m*
firearm ['faɪr,arm] *n* : arma *f* de fuego
fireball ['faɪr,bɔl] *n* **1** : bola *f* de fuego **2** METEOR : bólido *m*
firebreak ['faɪr,breɪk] *n* : cortafuegos *m*
firebug ['faɪr,bʌg] *n* : pirómano *m*, -na *f*; incendiario *m*, -ria *f*
firecracker ['faɪr,krækər] *n* : petardo *m*
fire escape *n* : escalera *f* de incendios
firefighter ['faɪr,faɪtər] *n* : bombero *m*, -ra *f*
firefly ['faɪr,flaɪ] *n, pl* **-flies** : luciérnaga *f*
fireman ['faɪrmən] *n, pl* **-men** [-mən, -,mɛn] **1** FIREFIGHTER : bombero *m*, -ra *f* **2** STOKER : fogonero *m*, -ra *f*
fireplace ['faɪr,pleɪs] *n* : hogar *m*, chimenea *f*
fireproof¹ ['faɪr,pru:f] *vt* : hacer incombustible
fireproof² *adj* : incombustible, ignífugo
fireside¹ ['faɪr,saɪd] *adj* : informal ⟨fireside chat : charla informal⟩
fireside² *n* **1** HEARTH : chimenea *f*, hogar *m* **2** HOME : hogar *m*, casa *f*
firewall ['faɪr,wɔl] *n* : cortafuegos *m*
firewood ['faɪr,wʊd] *n* : leña *f*
fireworks ['faɪr,wərks] *npl* : fuegos *mpl* artificiales, pirotecnia *f*
firm¹ ['fərm] *vt or* **to firm up** : endurecer
firm² *adj* **1** VIGOROUS : fuerte, vigoroso **2** SOLID, UNYIELDING : firme, duro, sólido **3** UNCHANGING : firme, inalterable **4** RESOLUTE : firme, resuelto
firm³ *n* : empresa *f*, firma *f*, compañía *f*
firmament ['fərməmənt] *n* : firmamento *m*
firmly ['fərmli] *adv* : firmemente
firmness ['fərmnəs] *n* : firmeza *f*
first¹ ['fərst] *adv* **1** : primero ⟨finish your homework first : primero termina tu tarea⟩ ⟨first and foremost : ante todo⟩ ⟨first of all : en primer lugar⟩ **2** : por primera vez ⟨I saw it first in Boston : lo vi por primera vez en Boston⟩
first² *adj* **1** : primero ⟨the first time : la primera vez⟩ ⟨at first sight : a primera vista⟩ ⟨in the first place : en primer lugar⟩ ⟨the first ten applicants : los diez primeros candidatos⟩ **2** FOREMOST : principal, primero ⟨first tenor : tenor principal⟩
first³ *n* **1** : primero *m*, -ra *f* **2** *or* **first gear** : primera *f* **3 at ~** : al principio
first aid *n* : primeros auxilios *mpl*
first-class¹ ['fərst'klæs] *adv* : en primera ⟨to travel first-class : viajar en primera⟩
first-class² *adj* : de primera
first class *n* : primera clase *f*
firsthand¹ ['fərst'hænd] *adv* : directamente
firsthand² *adj* : de primera mano
first lieutenant *n* : teniente *mf*; teniente primero *m*, teniente primera *f*
firstly ['fərstli] *adv* : primeramente, principalmente, en primer lugar
first-rate¹ ['fərst'reɪt] *adv* : muy bien
first-rate² *adj* : de primera, de primera clase
first sergeant *n* : sargento *mf*
firth ['fərθ] *n* : estuario *m*
fiscal ['fɪskəl] *adj* : fiscal — **fiscally** *adv*
fish¹ ['fɪʃ] *vi* **1** : pescar **2 to fish for** SEEK : buscar, rebuscar ⟨to fish for compliments : andar a la caza de cumplidos⟩ — *vt* : pescar
fish² *n, pl* **fish** *or* **fishes** : pez *m* (vivo), pescado *m* (para comer)
fisherman ['fɪʃərmən] *n, pl* **-men** [-mən, -,mɛn] : pescador *m*, -dora *f*
fishery ['fɪʃəri] *n, pl* **-eries 1** → **fishing 2** : zona *f* pesquera, pesquería *f*
fishhook ['fɪʃ,hʊk] *n* : anzuelo *m*
fishing ['fɪʃɪŋ] *n* : pesca *f*, industria *f* pesquera
fishing pole *n* : caña *f* de pescar
fish market *n* : pescadería *f*
fishy ['fɪʃi] *adj* **fishier; -est 1** : a pescado ⟨a fishy taste : un sabor a pescado⟩ **2** QUESTIONABLE : dudoso, sospechoso ⟨there's something fishy going on : aquí hay gato encerrado⟩
fission ['fɪʃən, -ʒən] *n* : fisión *f*
fissure ['fɪʃər] *n* : fisura *f*, hendidura *f*
fist ['fɪst] *n* : puño *m*
fistful ['fɪst,fʊl] *n* : puñado *m*
fisticuffs ['fɪstɪ,kʌfs] *npl* : lucha *f* a puñetazos
fit¹ ['fɪt] *v* **fitted; fitting** *vt* **1** MATCH : corresponder a, coincidir con ⟨the punishment fits the crime : el castigo corresponde al crimen⟩ **2** : quedar ⟨the dress doesn't fit me : el vestido no me queda⟩ **3** GO : caber, encajar en ⟨her key fits the lock : su llave encaja en la cerradura⟩ **4** INSERT, INSTALL : poner, colocar **5** ADAPT : adecuar, ajustar, adaptar **6** *or* **to fit out** EQUIP : equipar

— *vi* **1** : quedar, entallar ⟨these pants don't fit : estos pantalones no me quedan⟩ **2** CONFORM : encajar, cuadrar **3 to fit in** : encajar, estar integrado

fit² *adj* **fitter; fittest 1** SUITABLE : adecuado, apropiado, conveniente **2** QUALIFIED : calificado, competente **3** HEALTHY : sano, en forma

fit³ *n* **1** ATTACK : ataque *m*, acceso *m*, arranque *m* **2 to be a good fit** : quedar bien **3 to be a tight fit** : ser muy entallado (de ropa), estar apretado (de espacios)

fitful ['fitfəl] *adj* : irregular, intermitente — **fitfully** *adv*

fitness ['fitnəs] *n* **1** HEALTH : salud *f*, buena forma *f* (física) **2** SUITABILITY : idoneidad *f*

fitting¹ ['fitiŋ] *adj* : adecuado, apropiado

fitting² *n* : accesorio *m*

five¹ ['faiv] *adj* : cinco

five² *n* : cinco *m*

five hundred¹ *adj* : quinientos

five hundred² *n* : quinientos *m*

fix¹ ['fiks] *vt* **1** ATTACH, SECURE : sujetar, asegurar, fijar **2** ESTABLISH : fijar, concretar, establecer **3** REPAIR : arreglar, reparar **4** PREPARE : preparar ⟨to fix dinner : preparar la cena⟩ **5** : arreglar, amañar ⟨to fix a race : arreglar una carrera⟩ **6** RIVET : fijar (los ojos, la mirada, etc.)

fix² *n* **1** PREDICAMENT : aprieto *m*, apuro *m* **2** : posición *f* ⟨to get a fix on : establecer la posición de⟩

fixate ['fik,seit] *vi* **-ated; -ating** : obsesionarse

fixation [fik'seiʃən] *n* : fijación *f*, obsesión *f*

fixed ['fikst] *adj* **1** STATIONARY : estacionario, inmóvil **2** UNCHANGING : fijo, inalterable **3** INTENT : fijo ⟨a fixed stare : una mirada fija⟩ **4 to be comfortably fixed** : estar en posición acomodada

fixedly ['fiksədli] *adv* : fijamente

fixedness ['fiksədnəs, 'fikst-] *n* : rigidez *f*

fixture ['fikstʃər] *n* **1** : parte *f* integrante, elemento *m* fijo **2 fixtures** *npl* : instalaciones *fpl* (de una casa)

fizz¹ ['fiz] *vi* : burbujear

fizz² *n* : efervescencia *f*, burbujeo *m*

fizzle¹ ['fizəl] *vi* **-zled; -zling 1** FIZZ : burbujear **2** FAIL : fracasar

fizzle² *n* : fracaso *m*, fiasco *m*

fjord [fi'ord] *n* : fiordo *m*

flab ['flæb] *n* : gordura *f*

flabbergast ['flæbər,gæst] *vt* : asombrar, pasmar, dejar atónito

flabby ['flæbi] *adj* **-bier; -est** : blando, fofo, aguado *CA, Col, Mex*

flaccid ['flæksəd, 'flæsəd] *adj* : fláccido

flag¹ ['flæg] *vi* **flagged; flagging 1** : hacer señales con banderas **2** WEAKEN : flaquear, desfallecer

flag² *n* : bandera *f*, pabellón *m*, estandarte *m*

flagon ['flægən] *n* : jarra *f* grande

flagpole ['flæg,po:l] *n* : asta *f*, mástil *m*

flagrant ['fleigrənt] *adj* : flagrante — **flagrantly** *adv*

flagship ['flæg,ʃip] *n* : buque *m* insignia

flagstone ['flæg,stæf] → **flagpole**
['flæg,sto:n] *n* : losa *f*, piedra *f*

flail¹ ['fle...] : sacudir, *vt* **1** : trillar (grano) **2**

flail² *n* : ma... (los brazos)

flair ['flær] *n* :...

flak ['flæk] *ns & m*, facilidad *f* **2** CRITICISM : c... fuego *m* antiaéreo

flake¹ ['fleik] *vi* fi...s *fpl* menuzarse, pelars... **flaking** : desmenuzarse

flake² *n* : copo *m* (... ese de la piel) (de la piel), astilla *f* (...e), escama *f*

flamboyance [flæm'bɔ...dera) agancia *f*, rimbombanci...

flamboyant [flæm'bɔiənt] : extravante, extravagante, rimbo...

flame¹ ['fleim] *vi* **flamed;** ...uber- BLAZE : arder, llamear **2** GL... lar, encenderse

flame² *n* BLAZE : llama *f* ⟨to bu... flames : estallar en llamas⟩ ⟨to ... in flame : incendiarse⟩

flamethrower ['fleim,θro:ər] *n* : lanz... lamas *m*

flamingo [flə'miŋgo] *n, pl* **-gos** : flamenco *m*

flammable ['flæməbəl] *adj* : inflamable, flamable

flange ['flændʒ] *n* : reborde *m*, pestaña *f*

flank¹ ['flæŋk] *vt* **1** : flanquear (para defender o atacar) **2** BORDER, LINE : bordear

flank² *n* : ijada *f* (de un animal), costado *m* (de una persona), falda *f* (de una colina), flanco *m* (de un cuerpo de soldados)

flannel ['flænəl] *n* : franela *f*

flap¹ ['flæp] *v* **flapped; flapping** *vi* **1** : aletear ⟨the bird was flapping (its wings) : el pájaro aleteaba⟩ **2** FLUTTER : ondear, agitarse — *vt* : batir, agitar

flap² *n* **1** FLAPPING : aleteo *m*, aletazo *m* (de alas) **2** : soplada *f* (de un sobre), hoja *f* (de una mesa), faldón *m* (de una chaqueta)

flapjack ['flæp,dʒæk] → **pancake**

flare¹ ['flær] *vi* **flared; flaring 1** FLAME, SHINE : llamear, brillar **2 to flare up** : estallar, explotar (de cólera)

flare² *n* **1** FLASH : destello *m* **2** SIGNAL : (luz *f* de) bengala *f* **3 solar flare** : erupción *f* solar

flash¹ ['flæʃ] *vi* **1** SHINE, SPARKLE : destellar, brillar, relampaguear **2** : pasar como un relámpago ⟨an idea flashed through my mind : una idea me cruzó la mente como un relámpago⟩ — *vt* : despedir, lanzar (una luz), transmitir (un mensaje)

flash² *adj* SUDDEN : repentino

flash³ *n* **1** : destello *m* (de luz), fogonazo *m* (de una explosión) **2 flash of lightning** : relámpago *m* **3 in a flash** : de repente, de un abrir y cerrar los ojos

flashback ['flæʃ,bæk] *n* : flashback *m*

flashiness ['flæʃinəs] *n* : ostentación *f*

flashlight ['flæʃ,laɪt] *n* : linterna *f*, llama-

flashy ['flæʃi] *adj* **flashier; -est** : llamativo, ostentoso

flask ['flæsk] *n* : frasco *m*

flat¹ ['flæt] *vt* **flatted; flatting** **1** FLATTEN : aplanar, achatar **2** : bajar de tono (en música)

flat² *adv* **1** EXACTLY : exactamente ⟨in ten minutes flat⟩ : diez minutos exactos⟩ **2** : desafinado, demasiado bajo (en la música)

flat³ *adj* **flatter; flattest** **1** EVEN, LEVEL : plano, llano **2** SMOOTH : liso **3** DEFINITE : categórico, rotundo, explícito ⟨a flat refusal : una negativa categórica⟩ **4** DULL : aburrido, soso, monótono ⟨to sing flat : cantar desafinado⟩ **5** DEFLATED : pinchado, ponchado *Mex* **6** : (en música) ⟨to sing flat : cantar desafinado⟩

flat⁴ *n* **1** PLAIN : llano *m*, terreno *m* llano **2** : bemol *m* (en la música) **3** APARTMENT : apartamento *m*, departamento *m* *or* **flat tire** : pinchazo *m*, ponchadura *f* *Mex*

flatbed ['flæt,bɛd] *n* : camión *m* de plataforma

flatcar ['flæt,kɑr] *n* : vagón *m* abierto

flatfish ['flæt,fɪʃ] *n* : platija *f*

flat–footed ['flæt,fʊtəd, ,flæt'-] *adj* : de pies planos

flatly ['flætli] *adv* DEFINITELY : categóricamente, rotundamente

flatness ['flætnəs] *n* **1** EVENNESS : lo llano, lisura *f*, uniformidad *f* **2** DULLNESS : monotonía *f*

flat–out ['flæt'aʊt] *adj* **1** : frenético, a toda máquina ⟨a flat-out effort : un esfuerzo frenético⟩ **2** CATEGORICAL : descarado, rotundo, categórico

flatten ['flætən] *vt* : aplanar, achatar

flatter ['flætər] *vt* **1** OVERPRAISE : adular **2** COMPLIMENT : halagar **3** : favorecer ⟨the photo flatters you : la foto te favorece⟩

flatterer ['flætərər] *n* : adulador *m*, -dora *f*

flattering ['flætərɪŋ] *adj* **1** COMPLIMENTARY : halagador **2** BECOMING : favorecedor

flattery ['flætəri] *n, pl* **-ries** : halagos *mpl*

flatulence ['flætʃələnts] *n* : flatulencia *f*, ventosidad *f*

flatulent ['flætʃələnt] *adj* : flatulento

flatware ['flæt,wær] *n* : cubertería *f*, cubiertos *mpl*

flaunt¹ ['flɔnt] *vt* : alardear, hacer alarde de

flaunt² *n* : alarde *m*, ostentación *f*

flavor¹ ['fleɪvər] *vt* : dar sabor a, sazonar

flavor² *n* **1** : gusto *m*, sabor *m* **2** FLAVORING : sazón *f*, condimento *m*

flavorful ['fleɪvərfəl] *adj* : sabroso

flavoring ['fleɪvərɪŋ] *n* : condimento *m*, sazón *f*

flavorless ['fleɪvərləs] *adj* : sin sabor

flaw ['flɔ] *n* : falla *f*, defecto *m*, imperfección *f*

flawed ['flɔd] *adj* : imperfecto, con defectos

flawless ['flɔləs] *adj* : impecable, perfecto — **flawlessly** *adv*

flax ['flæks] *n* : lino *m*

flaxen ['flæksən] *adj* : rubio, blondo (dícese del pelo)

flay ['fleɪ] *vt* **1** SKIN : desollar, despellejar **2** VILIFY : criticar con dureza, vilipendiar

flea ['fli:] *n* : pulga *f*

fleck¹ ['flɛk] *vt* : salpicar

fleck² *n* : mota *f*, pinta *f*

fledgling ['flɛdʒlɪŋ] *n* : polluelo *m*, pollito *m*

flee ['fli:] *v* **fled** ['flɛd]; **fleeing** *vi* : huir, escapar(se) — *vt* : huir de

fleece¹ ['fli:s] *vt* **fleeced; fleecing** **1** SHEAR : esquilar, trasquilar **2** SWINDLE : estafar, defraudar

fleece² *n* : lana *f*, vellón *m*

fleet¹ ['fli:t] *vi* : moverse con rapidez

fleet² *adj* SWIFT : rápido, veloz

fleet³ *n* : flota *f*

fleet admiral *n* : almirante *mf*

fleeting ['fli:tɪŋ] *adj* : fugaz, breve

flesh ['flɛʃ] *n* **1** : carne *f* (de seres humanos y animales) **2** : pulpa *f* (de frutas)

flesh out *vt* : desarrollar, darle cuerpo a

fleshy ['flɛʃi] *adj* **fleshier; -est** : gordo (dícese de las personas), carnoso (dícese de la fruta)

flew → fly

flex ['flɛks] *vt* : doblar, flexionar

flexibility [,flɛksə'bɪləti] *n, pl* **-ties** : flexibilidad *f*, elasticidad *f*

flexible ['flɛksəbəl] *adj* : flexible — **flexibly** [-bli] *adv*

flick¹ ['flɪk] *vt* : dar un capirotazo a (con el dedo) ⟨to flick a switch : darle al interruptor⟩ — *vi* **1** FLIT : revolotear **2 to flick through** : hojear (un libro)

flick² *n* : coletazo *m* (de una cola), capirotazo *m* (de un dedo)

flicker¹ ['flɪkər] *vi* **1** FLUTTER : revolotear, aletear **2** BLINK, TWINKLE : parpadear, titilar

flicker² *n* **1** : parpadeo *m*, titileo *m* **2** HINT, TRACE : indicio *m*, rastro *m* ⟨a flicker of hope : un rayo de esperanza⟩

flier ['flaɪər] *n* **1** AVIATOR : aviador *m*, -dora *f* **2** CIRCULAR : folleto *m* publicitario, circular *f*

flight ['flaɪt] *n* **1** : vuelo *m* (de aves o aviones), trayectoria *f* **2** TRIP : vuelo *m* **3** FLOCK, SQUADRON : bandada *f* (de pájaros), escuadrilla *f* (de aviones) **4** ESCAPE : huida *f*, fuga *f* **5 flight of fancy** : ilusiones *fpl*, fantasía *f* **6 flight of stairs** : tramo *m*

flight attendant *n* : auxiliar *mf* de vuelo

flightless ['flaɪtləs] *adj* : no volador

flighty ['flaɪţi] *adj* **flightier; -est** : caprichoso, frívolo

flimsy [flɪmzi] *adj* **flimsier; -est 1** LIGHT, THIN : ligero, fino **2** WEAK : endeble, poco sólido **3** IMPLAUSIBLE : pobre, flojo, poco convincente ⟨a flimsy excuse : una excusa floja⟩

flinch ['flɪntʃ] *vi* **1** WINCE : estremecerse **2** RECOIL : recular, retroceder

fling¹ ['flɪŋ] *vt* **flung** ['flʌŋ]; **flinging 1** THROW : lanzar, tirar, arrojar **2 to fling oneself** : lanzarse, tirarse, precipitarse

fling² *n* **1** THROW : lanzamiento *m* **2** ATTEMPT : intento *m* **3** AFFAIR : aventura *f* **4** BINGE : juerga *f*

flint ['flɪnt] *n* : pedernal *m*

flinty ['flɪnti] *adj* **flintier; -est 1** : de pedernal **2** STERN, UNYIELDING : severo, inflexible

flip¹ ['flɪp] *v* **flipped; flipping** *vt* **1** TOSS : tirar ⟨to flip a coin : echar a cara o cruz⟩ **2** OVERTURN : dar la vuelta a, voltear — *vi* **1** : moverse bruscamente **2 to flip through** : hojear (un libro)

flip² *adj* : insolente, descarado

flip³ *n* **1** FLICK : capirotazo *m*, golpe *m* ligero **2** SOMERSAULT : voltereta *f*

flip–flop ['flɪp,flɑp] *n* **1** REVERSAL : giro *m* radical **2** THONG : chancla *f*, chancleta *f*

flippancy ['flɪpənsi] *n*, *pl* **-cies** : ligereza *f*, falta *f* de seriedad

flippant ['flɪpənt] *adj* : ligero, frívolo, poco serio

flipper ['flɪpər] *n* : aleta *f*

flirt¹ ['flərt] *vi* **1** : coquetear, flirtear **2** TRIFLE : jugar ⟨to flirt with death : jugar con la muerte⟩

flirt² *n* : coqueto *m*, -ta *f*

flirtation [,flər'teɪʃən] *n* : devaneo *m*, coqueteo *m*

flirtatious [,flər'teɪʃəs] *adj* : insinuante, coqueto

flit ['flɪt] *vi* **flitted; flitting 1** : revolotear **2 to flit about** : ir y venir rápidamente

float¹ ['flo:t] *vi* **1** : flotar **2** WANDER : vagar, errar — *vt* **1** : poner a flote, hacer flotar (un barco) **2** LAUNCH : hacer flotar (una empresa) **3** ISSUE : emitir (acciones en la bolsa)

float² *n* **1** : flotador *m*, corcho *m* (para pescar) **2** BUOY : boya *f* **3** : carroza *f* (en un desfile)

floating ['flo:ţɪŋ] *adj* : flotante

flock¹ ['flɑk] *vi* **1** : moverse en rebaño **2** CONGREGATE : congregarse, reunirse

flock² *n* : rebaño *m* (de ovejas), bandada *f* (de pájaros)

floe ['flo:] *n* : témpano *m* de hielo

flog ['flɑg] *vt* **flogged; flogging** : azotar, fustigar

flood¹ ['flʌd] *vt* : inundar, anegar

flood² *n* **1** INUNDATION : inundación *f* **2** TORRENT : avalancha *f*, diluvio *m*, torrente *m* ⟨a flood of tears : un mar de lágrimas⟩

floodlight ['flʌd,laɪt] *n* : foco *m*

floodwater ['flʌd,wɔţər] *n* : crecida *f*, creciente *f*

floor¹ ['flor] *vt* **1** : solar, poner suelo a (una casa o una sala) **2** KNOCK DOWN : derribar, echar al suelo **3** NONPLUS : desconcertar, confundir, dejar perplejo

floor² *n* **1** : suelo *m*, piso *m* ⟨dance floor : pista de baile⟩ **2** STORY : piso *m*, planta *f* ⟨ground floor : planta baja⟩ ⟨second floor : primer piso⟩ **3** : mínimo *m* (de sueldos, precios, etc.)

floorboard ['flor,bord] *n* : tabla *f* del suelo, suelo *m*, piso *m*

flooring ['florɪŋ] *n* : entarimado *m*

flop¹ ['flɑp] *vi* **flopped; flopping 1** FLAP : golpearse, agitarse **2** COLLAPSE : dejarse caer, desplomarse **3** FAIL : fracasar

flop² *n* **1** FAILURE : fracaso *m* **2 to take a flop** : caerse

floppy ['flɑpi] *adj* **-pier; -est 1** : blando, flexible **2 floppy disk** : diskette *m*, disquete *m*

flora ['florə] *n* : flora *f*

floral ['florəl] *adj* : floral, floreado

florid ['florɪd] *adj* **1** FLOWERY : florido **2** REDDISH : rojizo

florist ['florɪst] *n* : florista *mf*

floss¹ ['flɔs] *vi* : limpiarse los dientes con hilo dental

floss² *n* **1** : hilo *m* de seda (de bordar) **2** → **dental floss**

flotation [flo'teɪʃən] *n* : flotación *f*

flotilla [flo'tɪlə] *n* : flotilla *f*

flotsam ['flɑtsəm] *n* **1** : restos *mpl* flotantes (en el mar) **2 flotsam and jetsam** : desechos *mpl*, restos *mpl*

flounce¹ ['flaʊnts] *vi* **flounced; flouncing** : moverse haciendo aspavientos ⟨she flounced into the room : entró en la sala haciendo aspavientos⟩

flounce² *n* **1** RUFFLE : volante *m* **2** FLOURISH : aspaviento *m*

flounder¹ ['flaʊndər] *vi* **1** STRUGGLE : forcejear **2** STUMBLE : no saber qué hacer o decir, perder el hilo (en un discurso)

flounder² *n*, *pl* **flounder** *or* **flounders** : platija *f*

flour¹ ['flaʊər] *vt* : enharinar

flour² *n* : harina *f*

flourish¹ ['flərɪʃ] *vi* THRIVE : florecer, prosperar, crecer (dícese de las plantas) — *vt* BRANDISH : blandir

flourish² *n* : floritura *f*, floreo *m*

flourishing ['flərɪʃɪŋ] *adj* : floreciente, próspero

flout ['flaʊt] *vt* : desacatar, burlarse de

flow¹ ['flo:] *vi* **1** COURSE : fluir, manar, correr **2** CIRCULATE : circular, correr ⟨traffic is flowing smoothly : el tránsito está circulando con fluidez⟩

flow² *n* **1** FLOWING : flujo *m*, circulación *f* **2** STREAM : corriente *f*, chorro *m*

flower¹ ['flaʊər] *vi* : florecer, florear

flower² *n* : flor *f*

flowered ['flaʊərd] *adj* : florido, floreado

floweriness ['flaʊərinəs] *n* : floritura *f*

flowering¹ ['flaʊərɪŋ] *adj* : floreciente

flowering² *n* : floración *f*, florecimiento *m*

flowerpot ['flaʊər,pɑt] *n* : maceta *f*, tiesto *m*, macetero *m*

flowery ['flaʊəri] *adj* **1** : florido **2** FLOWERED : floreado, de flores

flowing ['floːɪŋ] *adj* : fluido, corriente

flown → **fly**

flu ['fluː] *n* : gripe *f*, gripa *f Col, Mex*

fluctuate ['flʌktʃʊ,eɪt] *vi* **-ated; -ating** : fluctuar

fluctuation [,flʌktʃʊ'eɪʃən] *n* : fluctuación *f*

flue ['fluː] *n* : tiro *m*, salida *f* de humos

fluency ['fluːəntsi] *n* : fluidez *f*, soltura *f*

fluent ['fluːənt] *adj* : fluido

fluently ['fluːəntli] *adv* : con soltura, con fluidez

fluff¹ ['flʌf] *vt* **1** : mullir ⟨to fluff up the pillows : mullir las almohadas⟩ **2** BUNGLE : echar a perder, equivocarse

fluff² *n* **1** FUZZ : pelusa *f* **2** DOWN : plumón *m*

fluffy ['flʌfi] *adj* **fluffier; -est 1** DOWNY : lleno de pelusa, velloso **2** SPONGY : esponjoso

fluid¹ ['fluːɪd] *adj* : fluido

fluid² *n* : fluido *m*, líquido *m*

fluidity [flu'ɪdəti] *n* : fluidez *f*

fluid ounce *n* : onza *f* líquida (29.57 mililitros)

fluke ['fluːk] *n* : golpe *m* de suerte, chiripa *f*, casualidad *f*

flung → **fling**

flunk ['flʌŋk] *vt* FAIL : reprobar — *vi* : salir reprobando

fluorescence [,flʊr'ɛsənts, ,flɔr-] *n* : fluorescencia *f*

fluorescent [,flʊr'ɛsənt, ,flɔr-] *adj* : fluorescente

fluoridate ['flɔrə,deɪt, 'flʊr-] *vt* **-dated; -dating** : fluorizar

fluoridation [,flɔrə'deɪʃən, ,flʊr-] *n* : fluorización *f*, fluoración *f*

fluoride ['flɔr,aɪd, 'flʊr-] *n* : fluoruro *m*

fluorine ['flʊr,iːn] *n* : flúor *m*

fluorocarbon [,flʊro'karbən, ,flʊr-] *n* : fluorocarbono *m*

flurry ['flɔri] *n, pl* **-ries 1** GUST : ráfaga *f* **2** SNOWFALL : nevisca *f* **3** BUSTLE : frenesí *m*, bullicio *m* **4** BARRAGE : aluvión *m*, oleada *f* ⟨a flurry of questions : un aluvión de preguntas⟩

flush¹ ['flʌʃ] *vt* **1** : limpiar con agua ⟨to flush the toilet : jalar la cadena⟩ **2** RAISE : hacer salir, levantar (en la caza) — *vi* BLUSH : ruborizarse, sonrojarse

flush² *adv* : al mismo nivel, a ras

flush³ *adj* **1** *or* **flushed** ['flʌʃt] : colorado, rojo, encendido (dícese de la cara) **2** FILLED : lleno a rebosar **3** ABUNDANT : copioso, abundante **4** AFFLUENT : adinerado **5** ALIGNED, SMOOTH : alineado, liso **6 flush against** : pegado a, contra

flush⁴ *n* **1** FLOW, JET : chorro *m*, flujo *m* rápido **2** SURGE : arrebato *m*, arranque *m* ⟨a flush of anger : un arrebato de cólera⟩ **3** BLUSH : rubor *m*, sonrojo *m* **4** GLOW : resplandor *m*, flor *f* ⟨the flush of youth : la flor de la juventud⟩ ⟨in the flush of victory : en la euforia del triunfo⟩

fluster¹ ['flʌstər] *vt* : poner nervioso, aturdir

fluster² *n* : agitación *f*, confusión *f*

flute ['fluːt] *n* : flauta *f*

fluted ['fluːtəd] *adj* **1** GROOVED : estriado, acanalado **2** WAVY : ondulado

fluting ['fluːtɪŋ] *n* : estrías *fpl*

flutist ['fluːtɪst] *n* : flautista *mf*

flutter¹ ['flʌtər] *vi* **1** : revolotear (dícese de un pájaro), ondear (dícese de una bandera), palpitar con fuerza (dícese del corazón) **2 to flutter about** : ir y venir, revolotear — *vt* : sacudir, batir

flutter² *n* **1** FLUTTERING : revoloteo *m*, aleteo *m* **2** COMMOTION, STIR : revuelo *m*, agitación *f*

flux ['flʌks] *n* **1** : flujo *m* (en física y medicina) **2** CHANGE : cambio *m* ⟨to be in a state of flux : estar cambiando continuamente⟩

fly¹ ['flaɪ] *v* **flew** ['fluː]; **flown** ['floːn]; **flying 1** : volar (dícese de los pájaros, etc.) **2** TRAVEL : volar (dícese de los aviones), ir en avión (dícese de los pasajeros) **3** FLOAT : flotar, ondear **4** FLEE : huir, escapar **5** RUSH : correr, irse volando **6** PASS : pasar (volando) ⟨how time flies! : ¡cómo pasa el tiempo!⟩ **7 to fly open** : abrir de golpe — *vt* : pilotar (un avión), hacer volar (una cometa)

fly² *n, pl* **flies 1** : mosca *f* ⟨to drop like flies : caer como moscas⟩ **2** : braugeta *f* (de pantalones, etc.)

flyer → **flier**

flying saucer *n* : platillo *m* volador

flypaper ['flaɪ,peɪpər] *n* : papel *m* matamoscas

flyspeck ['flaɪ,spɛk] *n* **1** : excremento *m* de mosca **2** SPECK : motita *f*, puntito *m*

flyswatter ['flaɪ,swɑtər] *n* : matamoscas *m*

flywheel ['flaɪ,ʍiːl] *n* : volante *m*

foal¹ ['foːl] *vi* : parir

foal² *n* : potro *m*, -tra *f*

foam¹ ['foːm] *vi* : hacer espuma

foam² *n* : espuma *f*

foamy ['foːmi] *adj* **foamier; -est** : espumoso

focal ['foːkəl] *adj* **1** : focal, central **2 focal point** : foco *m*, punto *m* de referencia

fo'c'sle ['foːksəl] → **forecastle**

focus¹ ['fo:kəs] *v* -cused *or* -cussed; -cusing *or* -cussing *vt* **1** : enfocar (un instrumento) **2** CONCENTRATE : concentrar, centrar — *vi* : enfocar, fijar la vista

focus² *n, pl* -ci ['fo:ˌsaɪ, -ˌkaɪ] **1** : foco *m* ⟨to be in focus : estar enfocado⟩ **2** FOCUSING : enfoque *m* **3** CENTER : centro *m*, foco *m*

fodder ['fɑdər] *n* : pienso *m*, forraje *m*

foe ['fo:] *n* : enemigo *m*, -ga *f*

fog¹ ['fɔg, 'fɑg] *v* **fogged; fogging** *vt* : empañar — *vi* **to fog up** : empañarse

fog² *n* : niebla *f*, neblina *f*

foggy ['fɔgi, 'fɑ-] *adj* **foggier; -est** : nebuloso, brumoso

foghorn ['fɔgˌhɔrn, 'fɑg-] *n* : sirena *f* de niebla

fogy ['fo:gi] *n, pl* -gies : carca *mf fam*, persona *f* chapada a la antigua

foible ['fɔɪbəl] *n* : flaqueza *f*, debilidad *f*

foil¹ ['fɔɪl] *vt* : frustrar, hacer fracasar

foil² *n* **1** : lámina *f* de metal, papel *m* de aluminio **2** CONTRAST : contraste *m*, complemento *m* **3** SWORD : florete *m* (en esgrima)

foist ['fɔɪst] *vt* : encajar, endilgar *fam*, colocar

fold¹ ['fo:ld] *vt* **1** BEND : doblar, plegar **2** CLASP : cruzar (brazos), enlazar (manos), plegar (alas) **3** EMBRACE : estrechar, abrazar **4 to fold in** : incorporar ⟨fold in the cream : incorpore la crema⟩ — *vi* **1** FAIL : fracasar **2 to fold up** : doblarse, plegarse

fold² *n* **1** SHEEPFOLD : redil *m* (para ovejas) **2** FLOCK : rebaño *m* ⟨to return to the fold : volver al redil⟩ **3** CREASE : pliegue *m*, doblez *m*

folder ['fo:ldər] *n* **1** CIRCULAR : circular *f*, folleto *m* **2** BINDER : carpeta *f*

foliage ['fo:liɪdʒ, -lɪdʒ] *n* : follaje *m*

folio ['fo:liˌo:] *n, pl* -lios : folio *m*

folk¹ ['fo:k] *adj* : popular, folklórico ⟨folk customs : costumbres populares⟩ ⟨folk dance : danza folklórica⟩

folk² *n, pl* **folk** *or* **folks** **1** PEOPLE : gente *f* **2 folks** *npl* : familia *f*, padres *mpl*

folklore ['fo:kˌlor] *n* : folclore *m*

folklorist ['fo:kˌlorɪst] *n* : folklorista *mf*

folksy ['fo:ksi] *adj* **folksier; -est** : campechano

follicle ['fɑlɪkəl] *n* : folículo *m*

follow ['fɑlo] *vt* **1** : seguir ⟨follow the guide : siga al guía⟩ ⟨she followed the road : siguió el camino, continuó por el camino⟩ **2** PURSUE : perseguir, seguir **3** OBEY : seguir, cumplir, observar **4** UNDERSTAND : entender — *vi* **1** : seguir **2** UNDERSTAND : entender **3 it follows that . . .** : se deduce que . . .

follower ['fɑloər] *n* : seguidor *m*, -dora *f*

following¹ ['fɑloɪŋ] *adj* NEXT : siguiente

following² *n* FOLLOWERS : seguidores *mpl*

following³ *prep* AFTER : después de

follow through *vi* **to follow through with** : continuar con, realizar

follow up *vt* : seguir (una sugerencia, etc.), investigar (una huella)

folly ['fɑli] *n, pl* -lies : locura *f*, desatino *m*

foment [fo'mɛnt] *vt* : fomentar

fond ['fɑnd] *adj* **1** LOVING : cariñoso, tierno **2** PARTIAL : aficionado **3** FERVENT : ferviente, fervoroso

fondle ['fɑndəl] *vt* -dled; -dling : acariciar

fondly ['fɑndli] *adv* : cariñosamente, afectuosamente

fondness ['fɑndnəs] *n* **1** LOVE : cariño *m* **2** LIKING : afición *f*

fondue [fɑn'du:, -'dju:] *n* : fondue *f*

font ['fɑnt] *n* **1** *or* **baptismal font** : pila *f* bautismal **2** FOUNTAIN : fuente *f*

food ['fu:d] *n* : comida *f*, alimento *m*

food chain *n* : cadena *f* alimenticia

foodstuffs ['fu:dˌstʌfs] *npl* : comestibles *mpl*

fool¹ ['fu:l] *vi* **1** JOKE : bromear, hacer el tonto **2** TOY : jugar, juguetear ⟨don't fool with the computer : no juegues con la computadora⟩ **3 to fool around** : perder el tiempo ⟨he fools around instead of working : pierde el tiempo en vez de trabajar⟩ — *vt* DECEIVE : engañar, burlar

fool² *n* **1** IDIOT : idiota *mf*; tonto *m*, -ta *f*; bobo *m*, -ba *f* **2** JESTER : bufón *m*, -fona *f*

foolhardiness ['fu:lˌhɑrdinəs] *n* : imprudencia *f*

foolhardy ['fu:lˌhɑrdi] *adj* RASH : imprudente, temerario, precipitado

foolish ['fu:lɪʃ] *adj* **1** STUPID : insensato, estúpido **2** SILLY : idiota, tonto

foolishly ['fu:lɪʃli] *adv* : tontamente

foolishness ['fu:lɪʃnəs] *n* : insensatez *f*, estupidez *f*, tontería *f*

foolproof ['fu:lˌpru:f] *adj* : infalible

foot ['fʊt] *n, pl* **feet** ['fi:t] : pie *m*

footage ['fʊtɪdʒ] *n* : medida *f* en pies, metraje *m* (en el cine)

football ['fʊtˌbɔl] *n* : futbol *m* americano, fútbol *m* americano

footbridge ['fʊtˌbrɪdʒ] *n* : pasarela *f*, puente *m* peatonal

foothills ['fʊtˌhɪlz] *npl* : estribaciones *fpl*

foothold ['fʊtˌho:ld] *n* **1** : punto *m* de apoyo **2 to gain a foothold** : afianzarse en una posición

footing ['fʊtɪŋ] *n* **1** BALANCE : equilibrio *m* **2** FOOTHOLD : punto *m* de apoyo **3** BASIS : base *f* ⟨on an equal footing : en igualdad⟩

footlights ['fʊtˌlaɪts] *npl* : candilejas *fpl*

footlocker ['fʊtˌlɑkər] *n* : baúl *m* pequeño, cofre *m*

footloose ['fʊtˌlu:s] *adj* : libre y sin compromiso

footman ['fʊtmən] *n, pl* -men [-mən, -ˌmɛn] : lacayo *m*

footnote ['fʊtˌno:t] *n* : nota *f* al pie de la página

footpath ['fʊtˌpæθ] *n* : sendero *m*, senda *f*, vereda *f*

footprint ['fʊt,prɪnt] *n* : huella *f*
footrace ['fʊt,reɪs] *n* : carrera *f* pedestre
footrest ['fʊt,rɛst] *n* : apoyapiés *m*, reposapiés *m*
footstep ['fʊt,stɛp] *n* **1** STEP : paso *m* **2** FOOTPRINT : huella *f*
footstool ['fʊt,stu;l] *n* : taburete *m*, escabel *m*
footwear ['fʊt,wær] *n* : calzado *m*
footwork ['fʊt,wərk] *n* : juego *m* de piernas, juego *m* de pies
fop ['fɑp] *n* : petimetre *m*, dandi *m*
for[1] ['fɔr] *conj* : puesto que, porque
for[2] *prep* **1** (*indicating purpose*) : para, de ⟨clothes for children : ropa para niños⟩ ⟨it's time for dinner : es la hora de comer⟩ **2** BECAUSE OF : por ⟨for fear of : por miedo de⟩ **3** (*indicating a recipient*) : para, por ⟨a gift for you : un regalo para ti⟩ **4** (*indicating support*) : por ⟨he fought for his country : luchó por su patria⟩ **5** (*indicating a goal*) : por, para ⟨a cure for cancer : una cura para el cáncer⟩ ⟨for your own good : por tu propio bien⟩ **6** (*indicating correspondence or exchange*) : por, para ⟨I bought it for $5 : lo compré por $5⟩ ⟨a lot of trouble for nothing : mucha molestia para nada⟩ **7** AS FOR : para, con respecto a **8** (*indicating duration*) : durante, por ⟨he's going for two years : se va por dos años⟩ ⟨I spoke for ten minutes : hablé (durante) diez minutos⟩ ⟨she has known it for three months : lo sabe desde hace tres meses⟩
forage[1] ['fɔrɪʤ] *v* **-aged; -aging** *vi* : hurgar (en busca de alimento) — *vt* : buscar (provisiones)
forage[2] *n* : forraje *m*
foray ['fɔr,eɪ] *n* : incursión *f*
forbear[1] [fɔr'bær] *vi* **-bore** [-'bor]; **-borne** [-'born]; **-bearing** **1** ABSTAIN : abstenerse **2** : tener paciencia
forbear[2] → **forbear**
forbearance [fɔr'bærənts] *n* **1** ABSTAINING : abstención *f* **2** PATIENCE : paciencia *f*
forbid [fər'bɪd] *vt* **-bade** [-'bæd, -'beɪd]; **-bidden** [-'bɪdən]; **-bidding** **1** PROHIBIT : prohibir **2** PREVENT : impedir
forbidding [fər'bɪdɪŋ] *adj* **1** IMPOSING : imponente **2** DISAGREEABLE : desagradable, ingrato **3** GRIM : severo
force[1] ['fors] *vt* **forced; forcing** **1** COMPEL : obligar, forzar **2** : forzar ⟨to force open the window : forzar la ventana⟩ ⟨to force a lock : forzar una cerradura⟩ **3** IMPOSE : imponer, obligar
force[2] *n* **1** : fuerza *f* **2** by force : por la fuerza **3** in force : en vigor, en vigencia
forced ['forst] *adj* : forzado, forzoso
forceful ['forsfəl] *adj* : fuerte, energético, contundente
forcefully ['forsfəli] *adv* : con energía, con fuerza
forcefulness ['forsfəlnəs] *n* : contundencia *f*, fuerza *f*

forceps ['fɔrsəps, -,sɛps] *ns & pl* : fórceps *m*
forcible ['forsəbəl] *adj* **1** FORCED : forzoso **2** CONVINCING : contundente, convincente — **forcibly** [-bli] *adv*
ford[1] ['ford] *vt* : vadear
ford[2] *n* : vado *m*
fore[1] ['for] *adv* **1** FORWARD : hacia adelante **2 fore and aft** : de popa a proa
fore[2] *adj* **1** FORWARD : delantero, de adelante **2** FORMER : anterior
fore[3] *n* **1** : frente *m*, delantera *f* **2 to come to the fore** : empezar a destacar, saltar a primera plana
fore-and-aft ['forən'æft, -ənd-] *adj* : longitudinal
forearm ['for,ɑrm] *n* : antebrazo *m*
forebear ['for,bær] *n* : antepasado *m*, -da *f*
foreboding [for'bo:dɪŋ] *n* : premonición *f*, presentimiento *m*
forecast[1] ['for,kæst] *vt* **-cast; -casting** : pronosticar, predecir
forecast[2] *n* : predicción *f*, pronóstico *m*
forecastle ['fo:ksəl] *n* : castillo *m* de proa
foreclose [for'klo:z] *vt* **-closed; -closing** : ejecutar (una hipoteca)
forefather ['for,fɑðər] *n* : antepasado *m*, ancestro *m*
forefinger ['for,fɪŋgər] *n* : índice *m*, dedo *m* índice
forefoot ['for,fʊt] *n* : pata *f* delantera
forefront ['for,frʌnt] *n* : frente *m*, vanguardia *f* ⟨in the forefront : a la vanguardia⟩
forego [for'go:] *vt* **-went; -gone; -going** **1** PRECEDE : preceder **2** → **forgo**
foregoing [for'go:ɪŋ] *adj* : precedente, anterior
foregone [for'gɔn] *adj* : previsto ⟨a foregone conclusion : un resultado inevitable⟩
foreground ['for,graʊnd] *n* : primer plano *m*
forehand[1] ['for,hænd] *adj* : directo, derecho
forehand[2] *n* : golpe *m* del derecho
forehead ['forəd, 'for,hɛd] *n* : frente *f*
foreign ['fɔrən] *adj* **1** : extranjero, exterior ⟨foreign countries : países extranjeros⟩ ⟨foreign trade : comercio exterior⟩ **2** ALIEN : ajeno, extraño ⟨foreign to their nature : ajeno a su carácter⟩ ⟨a foreign body : un cuerpo extraño⟩
foreigner ['fɔrənər] *n* : extranjero *m*, -ra *f*
foreknowledge [for'nɑlɪʤ] *n* : conocimiento *m* previo
foreleg ['for,lɛg] *n* : pata *f* delantera
foreman ['formən] *n, pl* **-men** [-mən, -,mɛn] : capataz *mf* ⟨foreman of the jury : presidente del jurado⟩
foremost[1] ['for,mo:st] *adv* : en primer lugar
foremost[2] *adj* : más importante, principal, grande
forenoon ['for,nu:n] *n* : mañana *m*

forensic [fə'rɛn*ts*ɪk] *adj* **1** RHETORICAL : retórico, de argumentación **2** : forense ⟨forensic medicine : medicina forense⟩

foreordain [ˌforɔr'deɪn] *vt* : predestinar, predeterminar

forequarter ['for,kwɔrtər] *n* : cuarto *m* delantero

forerunner ['for,rʌnər] *n* : precursor *m*, -sora *f*

foresee [for'si:] *vt* **-saw; -seen; -seeing** : prever

foreseeable [for'si:əbəl] *adj* : previsible ⟨in the foreseeable future : en el futuro inmediato⟩

foreshadow [for'ʃædo:] *vt* : anunciar, prefigurar

foresight ['for,saɪt] *n* : previsión *f*

foresighted ['for,saɪtəd] *adj* : previsto

forest ['fɔrəst] *n* : bosque *m* (en zonas templadas), selva *f* (en zonas tropicales)

forestall [for'stɔl] *vt* **1** PREVENT : prevenir, impedir **2** PREEMPT : adelantarse a

forested ['fɔrəstəd] *adj* : arbolado

forester ['fɔrəstər] *n* : silvicultor *m*, -tora *f*

forestland ['fɔrəst,lænd] *n* : zona *f* boscosa

forest ranger → **ranger**

forestry ['fɔrəstri] *n* : silvicultura *f*, ingeniería *f* forestal

foreswear → **forswear**

foretaste[1] ['for,teɪst] *vt* **-tasted; -tasting** : anticipar

foretaste[2] *n* : anticipo *m*

foretell [for'tɛl] *vt* **-told; -telling** : predecir, pronosticar, profetizar

forethought ['for,θɔt] *n* : previsión *f*, reflexión *f* previa

forever [for'ɛvər] *adv* **1** PERPETUALLY : para siempre, eternamente **2** CONTINUALLY : siempre, constantemente

forevermore [for,ɛvər'mor] *adv* : por siempre jamás

forewarn [for'wɔrn] *vt* : prevenir, advertir

foreword ['forwərd] *n* : prólogo *m*

forfeit[1] ['fɔrfət] *vt* : perder el derecho a

forfeit[2] *n* **1** FINE, PENALTY : multa *f* **2** : prenda *f* (en un juego)

forge[1] ['fordʒ] *v* **forged; forging** *vt* **1** : forjar (metal o un plan) **2** COUNTERFEIT : falsificar — *vi* **to forge ahead** : avanzar, seguir adelante

forge[2] *n* : forja *f*

forger ['fordʒər] *n* : falsificador *m*, -dora *f*

forgery ['fordʒəri] *n, pl* **-eries** : falsificación *f*

forget [fər'gɛt] *v* **-got** [-'gɑt]; **-gotten** [-'gɑtən] *or* **-got; -getting** *vt* : olvidar — *vi* **to forget about** : olvidarse de, no acordarse de

forgetful [fər'gɛtfəl] *adj* : olvidadizo

forget–me–not [fər'gɛtmi,nɑt] *n* : nomeolvides *mf*

forgettable [fər'gɛtəbəl] *adj* : poco memorable

forgivable [fər'gɪvəbəl] *adj* : perdonable

forgive [fər'gɪv] *vt* **-gave** [-'geɪv]; **-given** [-'gɪvən]; **-giving** : perdonar

forgiveness [fər'gɪvnəs] *n* : perdón *m*

forgiving [fər'gɪvɪŋ] *adj* : indulgente, comprensivo, clemente

forgo *or* **forego** [for'go:] *vt* **-went; -gone; -going** : privarse de, renunciar a

fork[1] ['fɔrk] *vi* : ramificarse, bifurcarse — *vt* **1** : levantar (con un tenedor, una horca, etc.) **2 to fork over** : desembolsar

fork[2] *n* **1** : tenedor *m* (utensilio de cocina) **2** PITCHFORK : horca *f*, horquilla *f* **3** : bifurcación *f* (de un río o camino), horqueta *f* (de un árbol)

forked ['fɔrkt, 'fɔrkəd] *adj* : bífido, ahorquillado

forklift ['fɔrk,lɪft] *n* : carretilla *f* elevadora

forlorn [for'lɔrn] *adj* **1** DESOLATE : abandonado, desolado, desamparado **2** SAD : triste **3** DESPERATE : desesperado

forlornly [for'lɔrnli] *adv* **1** SADLY : con tristeza **2** HALFHEARTEDLY : sin ánimo

form[1] ['fɔrm] *vt* **1** FASHION, MAKE : formar **2** DEVELOP : moldear, desarrollar **3** CONSTITUTE : constituir, formar **4** ACQUIRE : adquirir (un hábito), formar (una idea) — *vi* : tomar forma, formarse

form[2] *n* **1** SHAPE : forma *f*, figura *f* **2** MANNER : manera *f*, forma *f* **3** DOCUMENT : formulario *m* **4** : forma *f* ⟨in good form : en buena forma⟩ ⟨true to form : en forma consecuente⟩ **5** MOLD : molde *m* **6** KIND, VARIETY : clase *f*, tipo *m* **7** : forma *f* (en gramática) ⟨plural forms : formas plurales⟩

formal[1] ['fɔrməl] *adj* **1** CEREMONIOUS : formal, de etiqueta, ceremonioso **2** OFFICIAL : formal, oficial, de forma

formal[2] *n* **1** BALL : baile *m* formal, baile *m* de etiqueta **2** *or* **formal dress** : traje *m* de etiqueta

formaldehyde [fɔr'mældə,haɪd] *n* : formaldehído *m*

formality [fɔr'mæləti] *n, pl* **-ties** : formalidad *f*

formalize ['fɔrmə,laɪz] *vt* **-ized; -izing** : formalizar

formally ['fɔrməli] *adv* : formalmente

format[1] ['fɔr,mæt] *vt* **-matted; -matting** : formatear

format[2] *n* : formato *m*

formation [fɔr'meɪʃən] *n* **1** FORMING : formación *f* **2** SHAPE : forma *f* **3 in formation** : en formación

formative ['fɔrmətɪv] *adj* : formativo

former ['fɔrmər] *adj* **1** PREVIOUS : antiguo, anterior ⟨the former president : el antiguo presidente⟩ **2** : primero (de dos)

formerly ['fɔrmərli] *adv* : anteriormente, antes

formidable ['fɔrmədəbəl, fɔr'mɪdə-] *adj*
: formidable — **formidably** *adv*
formless ['fɔrmləs] *adj* : informe, amorfo
formula ['fɔrmjələ] *n, pl* **-las** *or* **-lae** [-ˌliː, -ˌlaɪ] **1** : fórmula *f* **2 baby formula**
: preparado *m* para biberón
formulate ['fɔrmjəˌleɪt] *vt* **-lated; -lating**
: formular, hacer
formulation [ˌfɔrmjə'leɪʃən] *n* : formulación *f*
fornicate ['fɔrnəˌkeɪt] *vi* **-cated; -cating**
: fornicar
fornication [ˌfɔrnə'keɪʃən] *n* : fornicación *f*
forsake [fər'seɪk] *vt* **-sook** [-'sʊk];
-saken [-'seɪkən]; **-saking 1** ABANDON
: abandonar, desamparar **2** RELINQUISH : renunciar a
forswear [fɔr'swær] *v* **-swore; -sworn;
-swearing** *vt* RENOUNCE : renunciar a
— *vi* : perjurar
forsythia [fər'sɪθiə] *n* : forsitia *f*
fort ['fɔrt] *n* **1** STRONGHOLD : fuerte *m*,
fortaleza *f*, fortín *m* **2** BASE : base *f* militar
forte ['fɔrt, 'fɔrˌteɪ] *n* : fuerte *m*
forth ['fɔrθ] *adv* **1** : adelante ⟨from this
day forth : de hoy en adelante⟩ **2 and
so forth** : etcétera
forthcoming [forθ'kʌmɪŋ, 'forθˌ-] *adj* **1**
COMING : próximo **2** DIRECT, OPEN
: directo, franco, comunicativo
forthright ['forθˌraɪt] *adj* : directo, franco — **forthrightly** *adv*
forthrightness ['forθˌraɪtnəs] *n* : franqueza *f*
forthwith [forθ'wɪθ, -'wɪð] *adv* : inmediatamente, en el acto, enseguida
fortieth[1] ['fortiəθ] *adj* : cuadragésimo
fortieth[2] *n* **1** : cuadragésimo *m*, -ma *f*
(en una serie) **2** : cuarentavo *m*,
cuarentava parte *f*
fortification [ˌfortəfə'keɪʃən] *n* : fortificación *f*
fortify ['fortəˌfaɪ] *vt* **-fied; -fying** : fortificar
fortitude ['fortəˌtuːd, -ˌtjuːd] *n* : fortaleza
f, valor *m*
fortnight ['fortˌnaɪt] *n* : quince días *mpl*,
dos semanas *fpl*
fortnightly[1] ['fortˌnaɪtli] *adv* : cada
quince días
fortnightly[2] *adj* : quincenal
fortress ['fortrəs] *n* : fortaleza *f*
fortuitous [for'tuːətəs, -'tjuː-] *adj* : fortuito, accidental
fortunate ['fortʃənət] *adj* : afortunado
fortunately ['fortʃənətli] *adv* : afortunadamente, con suerte
fortune ['fortʃən] *n* **1** : fortuna *f* ⟨to seek
one's fortune : buscar uno su fortuna⟩
2 LUCK : suerte *f*, fortuna *f* **3** DESTINY,
FUTURE : destino *m*, buenaventura *f* **4**
: dineral *m*, platal *m* ⟨she spent a fortune : se gastó un dineral⟩
fortune–teller ['fortʃənˌtɛlər] *n* : adivino
m, -na *f*

fortune–telling ['fortʃənˌtɛlɪŋ] *n* : adivinación *f*
forty[1] ['forti] *adj* : cuarenta
forty[2] *n, pl* **forties** : cuarenta *m*
forum ['forəm] *n, pl* **-rums** : foro *m*
forward[1] ['forwərd] *vt* **1** PROMOTE : promover, adelantar, fomentar **2** SEND
: remitir, enviar
forward[2] *adv* **1** : adelante, hacia adelante ⟨to go forward : irse adelante⟩ **2
from this day forward** : de aquí en adelante
forward[3] *adj* **1** : hacia adelante, delantero **2** BRASH : atrevido, descarado
forward[4] *n* : delantero *m*, -ra *f* (en deportes)
forwarder ['forwərdər] *n* : agencia *f* de
transportes, agente *mf* expedidor
forwardness ['forwərdnəs] *n* : atrevimiento *m*, descaro *m*
forwards ['forwərdz] *adv* → **forward[2]**
fossil[1] ['fɑsəl] *adj* : fósil
fossil[2] *n* : fósil *m*
fossilize ['fɑsəˌlaɪz] *vt* **-ized; -izing** : fosilizar — *vi* : fosilizarse
foster[1] ['fɔstər] *vt* : promover, fomentar
foster[2] *adj* : adoptivo ⟨foster child : niño
adoptivo⟩
fought → **fight**
foul[1] ['faʊl] *vi* : cometer faltas (en deportes) — *vt* **1** DIRTY, POLLUTE : contaminar, ensuciar **2** TANGLE : enredar
foul[2] *adv* **1** → **foully 2** : contra las reglas
foul[3] *adj* **1** REPULSIVE : asqueroso, repugnante **2** CLOGGED : atascado, obstruido **3** TANGLED : enredado **4** OBSCENE : obsceno **5** BAD : malo ⟨foul
weather : mal tiempo⟩ **6** : antirreglamentario (en deportes)
foul[4] *n* : falta *f*, faul *m*
foully ['faʊli] *adv* : asquerosamente
foulmouthed ['faʊlˌmæʊːðd, -ˌmaʊθt]
adj : malhablado
foulness ['faʊlnəs] *n* **1** DIRTINESS : suciedad *f* **2** INCLEMENCY : inclemencia
f **3** OBSCENITY : obscenidad *f*, grosería
f
foul play *n* : actos *mpl* criminales
foul–up ['faʊlˌʌp] *n* : lío *m*, confusión *f*,
desastre *m*
foul up *vt* SPOIL : estropear, arruinar —
vi BUNGLE : echar todo a perder
found[1] → **find**
found[2] ['faʊnd] *vt* : fundar, establecer
foundation [faʊn'deɪʃən] *n* **1** FOUNDING : fundación *f* **2** BASIS : fundamento
m, base *f* **3** INSTITUTION : fundación *f*
4 : cimientos *mpl* (de un edificio)
founder[1] ['faʊndər] *vi* SINK : hundirse,
irse a pique
founder[2] *n* : fundador *m*, -dora *f*
founding ['faʊndɪŋ] *adj* : fundador ⟨the
founding fathers : los fundadores⟩
foundling ['faʊndlɪŋ] *n* : expósito *m*, -ta
f
foundry ['faʊndri] *n, pl* **-dries** : fundición *f*

fount ['faʊnt] *n* SOURCE : fuente *f*, origen *m*

fountain ['faʊntən] *n* **1** SPRING : fuente *f*, manantial *m* **2** SOURCE : fuente *f*, origen *m* **3** JET : chorro *m* (de agua), surtidor *m*

fountain pen *n* : pluma *f* fuente

four[1] ['for] *adj* : cuatro

four[2] *n* **1** : cuatro *m* **2 on all fours** : a gatas

fourfold ['for,fo:ld, -'fo:ld] *adj* : cuadruple

four hundred[1] *adj* : cuatrocientos

four hundred[2] *n* : cuatrocientos *m*

fourscore ['for'skor] *adj* EIGHTY : ochenta *m*

fourteen[1] [for'ti:n] *adj* : catorce

fourteen[2] *n* : catorce *m*

fourteenth[1] [for'ti:nθ] *adj* : decimocuarto

fourteenth[2] *n* **1** : decimocuarto *m*, -ta *f* (en una serie) **2** : catorceavo *m*, catorceava parte *f*

fourth[1] ['forθ] *adj* : cuarto

fourth[2] *n* **1** : cuarto *m*, -ta *f* (en una serie) **2** : cuarto *m*, cuarta parte *f*

fowl ['faʊl] *n, pl* **fowl** *or* **fowls** **1** BIRD : ave *f* **2** CHICKEN : pollo *m*

fox[1] ['fɑks] *vt* **1** TRICK : engañar **2** BAFFLE : confundir

fox[2] *n, pl* **foxes** : zorro *m*, -ra *f*

foxglove ['fɑks,glʌv] *n* : dedalera *f*, digital *f*

foxhole ['fɑks,ho:l] *n* : hoyo *m* para atrincherarse, trinchera *f* individual

foxy ['fɑksi] *adj* **foxier; -est** SHREWD : astuto

foyer ['fɔɪər, 'fɔɪ,jeɪ] *n* : vestíbulo *m*

fracas ['freɪkəs, 'fræ-] *n, pl* **-cases** [-kəsəz] : altercado *m*, pelea *f*, reyerta *f*

fraction ['frækʃən] *n* **1** : fracción *f*, quebrado *m* **2** PORTION : porción *f*, parte *f*

fractional ['frækʃənəl] *adj* **1** : fraccionario **2** TINY : minúsculo, mínimo, insignificante

fractious ['frækʃəs] *adj* **1** UNRULY : rebelde **2** IRRITABLE : malhumorado, irritable

fracture[1] ['fræktʃər] *vt* **-tured; -turing** : fracturar

fracture[2] *n* **1** : fractura *f* (de un hueso) **2** CRACK : fisura *f*, grieta *f*, falla *f* (geológica)

fragile ['frædʒəl, -,dʒaɪl] *adj* : frágil

fragility [frə'dʒɪləti] *n, pl* **-ties** : fragilidad *f*

fragment[1] ['fræg,mɛnt] *vt* : fragmentar — *vi* : fragmentarse, hacerse añicos

fragment[2] ['frægmənt] *n* : fragmento *m*, trozo *m*, pedazo *m*

fragmentary ['frægmən,tɛri] *adj* : fragmentario, incompleto

fragmentation [,frægmən'teɪʃən, -,mn-] *n* : fragmentación *f*

fragrance ['freɪgrənts] *n* : fragancia *f*, aroma *m*

fragrant ['freɪgrənt] *adj* : fragante, aromático — **fragrantly** *adv*

frail ['freɪl] *adj* : débil, delicado

frailty ['freɪlti] *n, pl* **-ties** : debilidad *f*, flaqueza *f*

frame[1] ['freɪm] *vt* **framed; framing** **1** FORMULATE : formular, elaborar **2** BORDER : enmarcar, encuadrar **3** INCRIMINATE : incriminar

frame[2] *n* **1** BODY : cuerpo *m* **2** : armazón *f* (de un edificio, un barco, o un avión), bastidor *m* (de un automóvil), cuadro *m* (de una bicicleta), marco *m* (de un cuadro, una ventana, una puerta, etc.) **3 frames** *npl* : armazón *mf*, montura *f* (para anteojos) **4 frame of mind** : estado *m* de ánimo

framework ['freɪm,wərk] *n* **1** SKELETON, STRUCTURE : armazón *f*, estructura *f* **2** BASIS : marco *m*

franc ['fræŋk] *n* : franco *m*

franchise ['fræn,tʃaɪz] *n* **1** LICENSE : licencia *f* exclusiva, concesión *f* (en comercio) **2** SUFFRAGE : sufragio *m*

franchisee [,fræn,tʃa'zi:, -tʃə-] *n* : concesionario *m*, -ria *f*

Franciscan [fræn'sɪskən] *n* : franciscano *m*, -na *f* — **Franciscan** *adj*

frank[1] ['fræŋk] *vt* : franquear

frank[2] *adj* : franco, sincero, cándido — **frankly** *adv*

frank[3] *n* : franqueo *m* (de correo)

frankfurter ['fræŋkfərtər, -,fər-] *or* **frankfurt** [-fərt] *n* : salchicha *f* (de Frankfurt, de Viena), perro *m* caliente

frankincense ['fræŋkən,sɛnts] *n* : incienso *m*

frankness ['fræŋknəs] *n* : franqueza *f*, sinceridad *f*, candidez *f*

frantic ['fræntɪk] *adj* : frenético, desesperado — **frantically** *adv*

fraternal [frə'tərnəl] *adj* : fraterno, fraternal

fraternity [frə'tərnəti] *n, pl* **-ties** : fraternidad *f*

fraternization [,frætərnə'zeɪʃən] *n* : fraternización *f*, confraternización *f*

fraternize ['frætər,naɪz] *vt* **-nized; -nizing** : fraternizar, confraternizar

fratricidal [,frætrə'saɪdəl] *adj* : fratricida

fratricide ['frætrə,saɪd] *n* : fratricidio *m*

fraud ['frɔd] *n* **1** DECEPTION, SWINDLE : fraude *m*, estafa *f*, engaño *m* **2** IMPOSTOR : impostor *m*, -tora *f*; farsante *mf*

fraudulent ['frɔdʒələnt] *adj* : fraudulento — **fraudulently** *adv*

fraught ['frɔt] *adj* **fraught with** : lleno de, cargado de

fray[1] ['freɪ] *vt* **1** WEAR : desgastar, deshilachar **2** IRRITATE : crispar, irritar (los nervios) — *vi* : desgastarse, deshilacharse

fray[2] *n* : pelea *f* ⟨to join the fray : salir a la palestra⟩ ⟨to return to the fray : volver a la carga⟩

frazzle · fridge

frazzle¹ ['fræzəl] *vt* **-zled; -zling 1** FRAY : desgastar, deshilachar **2** EXHAUST : agotar, fatigar

frazzle² *n* EXHAUSTION : agotamiento *m*

freak ['fri:k] *n* **1** ODDITY : ejemplar *m* anormal, fenómeno *m*, rareza *f* **2** ENTHUSIAST : entusiasta *mf*

freakish ['fri:kɪʃ] *adj* : extraño, estrafalario, raro

freak out *vi* : ponerse como loco — *vt* : darle un ataque (a alguien)

freckle¹ ['frɛkəl] *vi* **-led; -ling** : cubrirse de pecas

freckle² *n* : peca *f*

free¹ ['fri:] *vt* **freed; freeing 1** LIBERATE : libertar, liberar, poner en libertad **2** RELIEVE, RID : librar, eximir **3** RELEASE, UNTIE : desatar, soltar **4** UNCLOG : desatascar, destapar

free² *adv* **1** FREELY : libremente **2** GRATIS : gratuitamente, gratis

free³ *adj* **freer; freest 1** : libre ⟨free as a bird : libre como un pájaro⟩ **2** EXEMPT : libre ⟨tax-free : libre de impuestos⟩ **3** GRATIS : gratuito, gratis **4** VOLUNTARY : espontáneo, voluntario, libre **5** UNOCCUPIED : desocupado, libre **6** LOOSE : suelto

freebooter ['fri:,bu:tər] *n* : pirata *mf*

freeborn ['fri:'bɔrn] *adj* : nacido libre

freedom ['fri:dəm] *n* : libertad *f*

free-for-all ['fri:fər,ɔl] *n* : pelea *f*, batalla *f* campal

freelance¹ ['fri:,lænts] *vi* **-lanced; -lancing** : trabajar por cuenta propia

freelance² *adj* : por cuenta propia, independiente

freeload ['fri:,lo:d] *vi* : gorronear *fam*, gorrear *fam*

freeloader ['fri:,lo:dər] *n* : gorrón *m*, -rrona *f*; gorrero *m*, -ra *f*; vividor *m*, -dora *f*

freely ['fri:li] *adv* **1** FREE : libremente **2** GRATIS : gratis, gratuitamente

freestanding ['fri:'stændɪŋ] *adj* : de pie, no empotrado, independiente

freeway ['fri:,weɪ] *n* : autopista *f*

freewill ['fri:,wɪl] *adj* : de propia voluntad

free will *n* : libre albedrío *m*, propia voluntad *f*

freeze¹ ['fri:z] *v* **froze** ['fro:z]; **frozen** ['fro:zən]; **freezing** *vi* **1** : congelarse, helarse ⟨the water froze in the lake : el agua se congeló en el lago⟩ ⟨my blood froze : se me heló la sangre⟩ ⟨I'm freezing : me estoy helando⟩ **2** STOP : quedarse inmóvil — *vt* : helar, congelar (líquidos), congelar (alimentos, precios, activos)

freeze² *n* **1** FROST : helada *f* **2** FREEZING : congelación *f*, congelamiento *m*

freeze-dried ['fri:z'draɪd] *adj* : liofilizado

freeze-dry ['fri:z'draɪ] *vt* **-dried; -drying** : liofilizar

freezer ['fri:zər] *n* : congelador *m*

freezing ['fri:zɪŋ] *adj* : helando ⟨it's freezing! : ¡hace un frío espantoso!⟩

freezing point *n* : punto *m* de congelación

freight¹ ['freɪt] *vt* : enviar como carga

freight² *n* **1** SHIPPING, TRANSPORT : transporte *m*, porte *m*, flete *m* **2** GOODS : mercancías *fpl*, carga *f*

freighter ['freɪtər] *n* : carguero *m*, buque *m* de carga

French¹ ['frɛntʃ] *adj* : francés

French² *n* **1** : francés *m* (idioma) **2 the French** *npl* : los franceses

french fries ['frɛntʃ,fraɪz] *npl* : papas *fpl* fritas

Frenchman ['frɛntʃmən] *n, pl* **-men** [-mən, -,mɛn] : francés *m*

Frenchwoman ['frɛntʃ,wumən] *n, pl* **-women** [-,wɪmən] : francesa *f*

frenetic [frɪ'nɛtɪk] *adj* : frenético — **frenetically** [-tɪkli] *adv*

frenzied ['frɛnzid] *adj* : frenético

frenzy ['frɛnzi] *n, pl* **-zies** : frenesí *m*

frequency ['fri:kwəntsi] *n, pl* **-cies** : frecuencia *f*

frequent¹ [fri'kwɛnt, 'fri:,kwɛnt] *vt* : frecuentar

frequent² ['fri:kwənt] *adj* : frecuente — **frequently** *adv*

fresco ['frɛs,ko:] *n, pl* **-coes** : fresco *m*

fresh ['frɛʃ] *adj* **1** : dulce ⟨freshwater : agua dulce⟩ **2** PURE : puro **3** : fresco ⟨fresh fruits : frutas frescas⟩ **4** CLEAN, NEW : limpio, nuevo ⟨fresh clothes : ropa limpia⟩ ⟨fresh evidence : evidencia nueva⟩ **5** REFRESHED : fresco, descansado **6** IMPERTINENT : descarado, impertinente

freshen ['frɛʃən] *vt* : refrescar, arreglar — *vi* **to freshen up** : arreglarse, lavarse

freshet ['frɛʃət] *n* : arroyo *m* desbordado

freshly ['frɛʃli] *adv* : recientemente, recién

freshman ['frɛʃmən] *n, pl* **-men** [-mən, -,mɛn] : estudiante *mf* de primer año universitario

freshness ['frɛʃnəs] *n* : frescura *f*

freshwater ['frɛʃ,wɔtər] *n* : agua *f* dulce

fret¹ ['frɛt] *vi* **fretted; fretting** : preocuparse, inquietarse

fret² *n* **1** VEXATION : irritación *f*, molestia *f* **2** WORRY : preocupación *f* **3** : traste *m* (de un instrumento musical)

fretful ['frɛtfəl] *adj* : fastidioso, quejoso, neurótico

fretfully ['frɛtfəli] *adv* : ansiosamente, fastidiosamente, inquieto

fretfulness ['frɛtfəlnəs] *n* : inquietud *f*, irritabilidad *f*

friable ['fraɪəbəl] *adj* : friable, pulverizable

friar ['fraɪər] *n* : fraile *m*

fricassee¹ ['frɪkə,si:, ,frɪkə'si:] *vt* **-seed; -seeing** : cocinar al fricasé

fricassee² *n* : fricasé *m*

friction ['frɪkʃən] *n* **1** RUBBING : fricción *f* **2** CONFLICT : fricción *f*, roce *m*

Friday ['fraɪ,deɪ, -di] *n* : viernes *m*

fridge ['frɪʤ] → **refrigerator**

friend ['frɛnd] *n* : amigo *m*, -ga *f*
friendless ['frɛndləs] *adj* : sin amigos
friendliness ['frɛndlinəs] *n* : simpatía *f*, amabilidad *f*
friendly ['frɛndli] *adj* **-lier; -est 1** : simpático, amable, de amigo ⟨a friendly child : un niño simpático⟩ ⟨friendly advice : consejo de amigo⟩ **2** : agradable, acogedor ⟨a friendly atmosphere : un ambiente agradable⟩ **3** GOOD-NATURED : amigable, amistoso ⟨friendly competition : competencia amistosa⟩
friendship ['frɛnd,ʃɪp] *n* : amistad *f*
frieze ['fri:z] *n* : friso *m*
frigate ['frɪgət] *n* : fragata *f*
fright ['fraɪt] *n* : miedo *m*, susto *m*
frighten ['fraɪtən] *vt* : asustar, espantar
frightened ['fraɪtənd] *adj* : asustado, temeroso
frightening ['fraɪtənɪŋ] *adj* : espantoso, aterrador
frightful ['fraɪtfəl] *adj* **1** → frightening **2** TREMENDOUS : espantoso, tremendo
frightfully ['fraɪtfəli] *adv* : terriblemente, tremendamente
frigid ['frɪdʒɪd] *adj* : glacial, extremadamente frío
frigidity [frɪ'dʒɪdəti] *n* **1** COLDNESS : frialdad *f* **2** : frigidez *f* (sexual)
frill ['frɪl] *n* **1** RUFFLE : volante *m* **2** EMBELLISHMENT : floritura *f*, adorno *m*
frilly ['frɪli] *adj* **frillier; -est 1** RUFFLY : con volantes **2** OVERDONE : recargado
fringe¹ ['frɪndʒ] *vt* **fringed; fringing** : orlar, bordear
fringe² *n* **1** BORDER : fleco *m*, orla *f* **2** EDGE : periferia *f*, margen *m* **3 fringe benefits** : incentivos *mpl*, extras *mpl*
frisk ['frɪsk] *vi* FROLIC : retozar, juguetear — *vt* SEARCH : cachear, registrar
friskiness ['frɪskinəs] *n* : vivacidad *f*
frisky ['frɪski] *adj* **friskier; -est** : retozón, juguetón
fritter¹ ['frɪtər] *vt* : desperdiciar, malgastar ⟨I frittered away the money : malgasté el dinero⟩
fritter² *n* : buñuelo *m*
frivolity [frɪ'vɑləti] *n*, *pl* **-ties** : frivolidad *f*
frivolous ['frɪvələs] *adj* : frívolo, de poca importancia
frivolously ['frɪvələsli] *adv* : frívolamente, a la ligera
frizz¹ ['frɪz] *vi* : rizarse, encresparse, ponerse chino *Mex*
frizz² *n* : rizos *mpl* muy apretados
frizzy ['frɪzi] *adj* **frizzier; -est** : rizado, crespo, chino *Mex*
fro ['fro:] *adv* **to and fro** : de aquí para allá, de un lado para otro
frock ['frɑk] *n* DRESS : vestido *m*
frog ['frɔg, 'frɑg] *n* **1** : rana *f* **2** FASTENER : alamar *m* **3 to have a frog in one's throat** : tener carraspera
frogman ['frɔg,mæn, 'frɑg-, -mən] *n*, *pl* **-men** [-mən, -,mɛn] : hombre *m* rana, submarinista *mf*

frolic¹ ['frɑlɪk] *vi* **-icked; -icking** : retozar, juguetear
frolic² *n* FUN : diversión *f*
frolicsome ['frɑlɪksəm] *adj* : juguetón
from ['frʌm, 'frɑm] *prep* **1** (*indicating a starting point*) : desde, de, a partir de ⟨from Cali to Bogota : de Cali a Bogotá⟩ ⟨where are you from? : ¿de dónde eres?⟩ ⟨from that time onward : desde entonces⟩ ⟨from tomorrow : a partir de mañana⟩ **2** (*indicating a source or sender*) : de ⟨a letter from my friend : una carta de mi amiga⟩ ⟨a quote from Shakespeare : una cita de Shakespeare⟩ **3** (*indicating distance*) : de ⟨10 feet from the entrance : a 10 pies de la entrada⟩ **4** (*indicating a cause*) : de ⟨red from crying : rojos de llorar⟩ ⟨he died from the cold : murió del frío⟩ **5** OFF, OUT OF : de ⟨she took it from the drawer : lo sacó del cajón⟩ **6** (*with adverbs or adverbial phrases*) : de, desde ⟨from above : desde arriba⟩ ⟨from among : de entre⟩
frond ['frɑnd] *n* : fronda *f*, hoja *f*
front¹ ['frʌnt] *vi* **1** FACE : dar, estar orientado ⟨the house fronts north : la casa da al norte⟩ **2** : servir de pantalla ⟨he fronts for his boss : sirve de pantalla para su jefe⟩
front² *adj* : delantero, de adelante, primero ⟨the front row : la primera fila⟩
front³ *n* **1** : frente *m*, parte *f* de adelante, delantera *f* ⟨the front of the class : el frente de la clase⟩ ⟨at the front of the train : en la parte delantera del tren⟩ **2** AREA, ZONE : frente *m*, zona *f* ⟨the Eastern front : el frente oriental⟩ ⟨on the educational front : en el frente de la enseñanza⟩ **3** FACADE : fachada *f* (de un edificio o una persona) **4** : frente *m* (en meteorología)
frontage ['frʌntɪdʒ] *n* : fachada *f*, frente *m*
frontal ['frʌntəl] *adj* : frontal, de frente
frontier [ˌfrʌn'tɪr] *n* : frontera *f*
frontiersman [ˌfrʌn'tɪrzmən] *n*, *pl* **-men** [-mən, -,mɛn] : hombre *m* de la frontera
frontispiece ['frʌntəs,pi:s] *n* : frontispicio *m*
frost¹ ['frɔst] *vt* **1** FREEZE : helar **2** ICE : escarchar (pasteles)
frost² *n* **1** : helada *f* (en meteorología) **2** : escarcha *f* ⟨frost on the window : escarcha en la ventana⟩
frostbite ['frɔst,baɪt] *n* : congelación *f*
frostbitten ['frɔst,bɪtən] *adj* : congelado (dícese de una persona), quemado (dícese de una planta)
frosting ['frɔstɪŋ] *n* ICING : glaseado *m*, betún *m Mex*
frosty ['frɔsti] *adj* **frostier; -est 1** CHILLY : helado, frío **2** COOL, UNFRIENDLY : frío, glacial
froth ['frɔθ] *n*, *pl* **froths** ['frɔθs, 'frɔðz] : espuma *f*

frothy ['frɔθi] *adj* **frothier; -est** : espumoso

frown[1] ['fraʊn] *vi* **1** : fruncir el ceño, fruncir el entrecejo **2 to frown at** : mirar (algo) con ceño, mirar (a alguien) con ceño

frown[2] *n* : ceño *m* (fruncido)

frowsy *or* **frowzy** ['fraʊzi] *adj* **frowsier** *or* **frowzier; -est** : desaliñado, desaseado

froze → **freeze**

frozen → **freeze**

frugal ['fru:gəl] *adj* : frugal, ahorrativo, parco — **frugally** *adv*

frugality [fru'gæləti] *n* : frugalidad *f*

fruit[1] ['fru:t] *vi* : dar fruto

fruit[2] *n* **1** : fruta *f* (término genérico), fruto *m* (término particular) **2 fruits** *npl* REWARDS : frutos *mpl* ⟨the fruits of his labor : los frutos de su trabajo⟩

fruitcake ['fru:t,keɪk] *n* : pastel *m* de frutas

fruitful ['fru:tfəl] *adj* : fructífero, provechoso

fruition [fru'ɪʃən] *n* **1** : cumplimiento *m*, realización *f* **2 to bring to fruition** : realizar

fruitless ['fru:tləs] *adj* : infructuoso, inútil — **fruitlessly** *adv*

fruity ['fru:ti] *adj* **fruitier; -est** : (con sabor) a fruta

frumpy ['frʌmpi] *adj* **frumpier; -est** : anticuado y sin atractivo

frustrate ['frʌs,treɪt] *vt* **-trated; -trating** : frustrar

frustrating ['frʌs,treɪtɪŋ] *adj* : frustrante — **frustratingly** *adv*

frustration [,frʌs'treɪʃən] *n* : frustración *f*

fry[1] ['fraɪ] *vt* **fried; frying** : freír

fry[2] *n, pl* **fries 1** : fritura *f*, plato *m* frito **2** : fiesta *f* en que se sirven frituras **3** *pl* **fry** : alevín *m* (pez)

frying pan *n* : sartén *mf*

fuchsia ['fju:ʃə] *n* **1** : fucsia *f* (planta) **2** : fucsia *m* (color)

fuddle ['fʌdəl] *vt* **-dled; -dling** : confundir, atontar

fuddy–duddy ['fʌdi,dʌdi] *n, pl* **-dies** : persona *f* chapada a la antigua, carca *mf*

fudge[1] ['fʌdʒ] *vt* **fudged; fudging 1** FALSIFY : amañar, falsificar **2** DODGE : esquivar

fudge[2] *n* : dulce *m* blando de chocolate y leche

fuel[1] ['fju:əl] *vt* **-eled** *or* **-elled; -eling** *or* **-elling 1** : abastecer de combustible **2** STIMULATE : estimular

fuel[2] *n* : combustible *m*, carburante *m* (para motores)

fugitive[1] ['fju:dʒətɪv] *adj* **1** RUNAWAY : fugitivo **2** FLEETING : efímero, pasajero, fugaz

fugitive[2] *n* : fugitivo *m*, -va *f*

fugue ['fju:g] *n* : fuga *f*

fulcrum ['fʊlkrəm, 'fʌl-] *n, pl* **-crums** *or* **-cra** [-krə] : fulcro *m*

fulfill *or* **fulfil** [fʊl'fɪl] *vt* **-filled; -filling 1** PERFORM : cumplir con, realizar, llevar a cabo **2** SATISFY : satisfacer

fulfillment [fʊl'fɪlmənt] *n* **1** PERFORMANCE : cumplimiento *m*, ejecución *f* **2** SATISFACTION : satisfacción *f*, realización *f*

full[1] ['fʊl, 'fʌl] *adv* **1** VERY : muy ⟨full well : muy bien, perfectamente⟩ **2** ENTIRELY : completamente ⟨she swung full around : giró completamente⟩ **3** DIRECTLY : de lleno, directamente ⟨he looked me full in the face : me miró directamente a la cara⟩

full[2] *adj* **1** FILLED : lleno **2** COMPLETE : completo, detallado **3** MAXIMUM : todo, pleno ⟨at full speed : a toda velocidad⟩ ⟨in full bloom : en plena flor⟩ **4** PLUMP : redondo, llenito *fam*, regordete *fam* ⟨a full face : una cara redonda⟩ ⟨a full figure : un cuerpo llenito⟩ **5** AMPLE : amplio ⟨a full skirt : una falda amplia⟩

full[3] *n* **1 to pay in full** : pagar en su totalidad **2 to the full** : al máximo

full–fledged ['fʊl'flɛdʒd] *adj* : hecho y derecho

fullness ['fʊlnəs] *n* **1** ABUNDANCE : plenitud *f*, abundancia *f* **2** : amplitud *f* (de una falda)

fully ['fʊli] *adv* **1** COMPLETELY : completamente, totalmente **2** : al menos, por lo menos ⟨fully half of them : al menos la mitad de ellos⟩

fulsome ['fʊlsəm] *adj* : excesivo, exagerado, efusivo

fumble[1] ['fʌmbəl] *v* **-bled; -bling** *vt* **1** : dejar caer, fumblear **2 to fumble one's way** : ir a tientas — *vi* **1** GROPE : hurgar, tantear **2 to fumble with** : manejar con torpeza

fumble[2] *n* : fumble *m* (en futbol americano)

fume[1] ['fju:m] *vi* **fumed; fuming 1** SMOKE : echar humo, humear **2** : estar furioso

fume[2] *n* : gas *m*, humo *m*, vapor *m*

fumigate ['fju:mə,geɪt] *vt* **-gated; -gating** : fumigar

fumigation [,fju:mə'geɪʃən] *n* : fumigación *m*

fun[1] ['fʌn] *adj* : divertido, entretenido

fun[2] *n* **1** AMUSEMENT : diversión *f*, entretenimiento *m* **2** ENJOYMENT : disfrute *m* **3 to have fun** : divertirse **4 to make fun of** : reírse de, burlarse de

function[1] ['fʌŋkʃən] *vi* : funcionar, desempeñarse, servir

function[2] *n* **1** PURPOSE : función *f* **2** GATHERING : reunión *f* social, recepción *f* **3** CEREMONY : ceremonia *f*, acto *m*

functional ['fʌŋkʃənəl] *adj* : funcional — **functionally** *adv*

functionary ['fʌŋkʃə,nɛri] *n, pl* **-aries** : funcionario *m*, -ria *f*

fund[1] ['fʌnd] *vt* : financiar

fund² *n* **1** SUPPLY : reserva *f*, cúmulo *m* **2** : fondo *m* ⟨investment fund : fondo de inversiones⟩ **3** funds *npl* RESOURCES : fondos *mpl*

fundamental¹ [ˌfʌndəˈmɛntəl] *adj* **1** BASIC : fundamental, básico **2** PRINCIPAL : esencial, principal **3** INNATE : innato, intrínseco

fundamental² *n* : fundamento *m*

fundamentalism [ˌfʌndəˈmɛntəlˌɪzəm] *n* : integrismo *m*, fundamentalismo *m*

fundamentalist [ˌfʌndəˈmɛntəlɪst] *n* : integrista *mf*, fundamentalista *mf* — **fundamentalist** *adj*

fundamentally [ˌfʌndəˈmɛntəli] *adv* : fundamentalmente, básicamente

funding [ˈfʌndɪŋ] *n* : financiación *f*

fund–raiser [ˈfʌndˌreɪzər] *n* : función *f* para recaudar fondos

funeral¹ [ˈfju:nərəl] *adj* **1** : funeral, funerario, fúnebre ⟨funeral procession : cortejo fúnebre⟩ **2 funeral home** : funeraria *f*

funeral² *n* : funeral *m*, funerales *mpl*

funereal [fju:ˈnɪriəl] *adj* : fúnebre

fungal [ˈfʌŋgəl] *adj* : de hongos, micótico

fungicidal [ˌfʌndʒəˈsaɪdəl, ˌfʌŋgə-] *adj* : fungicida

fungicide [ˈfʌndʒəˌsaɪd, ˈfʌŋgə-] *n* : fungicida *m*

fungous [ˈfʌŋgəs] *adj* : fungoso

fungus [ˈfʌŋgəs] *n, pl* **fungi** [ˈfʌnˌdʒaɪ, ˈfʌnˌgaɪ] : hongo *m*

funk [ˈfʌŋk] *n* **1** FEAR : miedo *m* **2** DEPRESSION : depresión *f*

funky [ˈfʌŋki] *adj* **funkier; -est** ODD, QUAINT : raro, extraño, original

funnel¹ [ˈfʌnəl] *vt* **-neled; -neling** CHANNEL : canalizar, encauzar

funnel² *n* **1** : embudo *m* **2** SMOKESTACK : chimenea *f* (de un barco o vapor)

funnies [ˈfʌniz] *npl* : tiras *fpl* cómicas

funny [ˈfʌni] *adj* **funnier; -est** **1** AMUSING : divertido, cómico **2** STRANGE : extraño, raro

fur¹ [ˈfər] *adj* : de piel

fur² *n* **1** : pelaje *m*, piel *f* **2** : prenda *f* de piel

furbish [ˈfərbɪʃ] *vt* : pulir, limpiar

furious [ˈfjʊriəs] *adj* **1** ANGRY : furioso **2** FRANTIC : violento, frenético, vertiginoso (dícese de la velocidad)

furiously [ˈfjʊriəsli] *adv* **1** ANGRILY : furiosamente **2** FRANTICALLY : frenéticamente

furlong [ˈfərˌlɔŋ] *n* : estadio *m* (201.2 m)

furlough¹ [ˈfərˌlo:] *vt* : dar permiso a, dar licencia a

furlough² *n* LEAVE : permiso *m*, licencia *f*

furnace [ˈfərnəs] *n* : horno *m*

furnish [ˈfərnɪʃ] *vt* **1** SUPPLY : proveer, suministrar **2** : amueblar ⟨furnished apartment : departamento amueblado⟩

furnishings [ˈfərnɪʃɪŋz] *npl* **1** ACCESSORIES : accesorios *mpl* **2** FURNITURE : muebles *mpl*, mobiliario *m*

furniture [ˈfərnɪtʃər] *n* : muebles *mpl*, mobiliario *m*

furor [ˈfjʊrˌɔr, -ər] *n* **1** RAGE : furia *f*, rabia *f* **2** UPROAR : escándalo *m*, jaleo *m*, alboroto *m*

furrier [ˈfəriər] *n* : peletero *m*, -ra *f*

furrow¹ [ˈfəro:] *vt* **1** : surcar **2 to furrow one's brow** : fruncir el ceño

furrow² *n* **1** GROOVE : surco *m* **2** WRINKLE : arruga *f*, surco *m*

furry [ˈfəri] *adj* **furrier; -est** : peludo (dícese de un animal), peluche (dícese de un objeto)

further¹ [ˈfərðər] *vt* : promover, fomentar

further² *adv* **1** FARTHER : más lejos, más adelante **2** MOREOVER : además **3** MORE : más ⟨I'll consider it further in the morning : lo consideraré más en la mañana⟩

further³ *adj* **1** FARTHER : más lejano **2** ADDITIONAL : adicional, más

furtherance [ˈfərðərənts] *n* : promoción *f*, fomento *m*, adelantamiento *m*

furthermore [ˈfərðərˌmor] *adv* : además

furthermost [ˈfərðərˌmo:st] *adj* : más lejano, más distante

furthest [ˈfərðəst] → **farthest¹, farthest²**

furtive [ˈfərtɪv] *adj* : furtivo, sigiloso — **furtively** *adv*

furtiveness [ˈfərtɪvnəs] *n* STEALTH : sigilo *m*

fury [ˈfjʊri] *n, pl* **-ries** **1** RAGE : furia *f*, ira *f* **2** VIOLENCE : furia *f*, furor *m*

fuse¹ [ˈfju:z] *or* **fuze** *vt* **fused** *or* **fuzed; fusing** *or* **fuzing** : equipar con un fusible

fuse² *v* **fused; fusing** *vt* **1** SMELT : fundir **2** MERGE : fusionar, fundir — *vi* : fundirse, fusionarse

fuse³ *n* : fusible *m*

fuselage [ˈfju:sə,lɑʒ, -zə-] *n* : fuselaje *m*

fusillade [ˈfju:səˌlɑd, -ˌleɪd, ˌfju:səˈ-, -zə-] *n* : descarga *f* de fusilería

fusion [ˈfju:ʒən] *n* : fusión *f*

fuss¹ [ˈfʌs] *vi* **1** WORRY : preocuparse **2 to fuss with** : juguetear con, toquetear **3 to fuss over** : mimar

fuss² *n* **1** COMMOTION : alboroto *m*, escándalo *m* **2** ATTENTION : atenciones *fpl* **3** COMPLAINT : quejas *fpl*

fussbudget [ˈfʌsˌbʌdʒət] *n* : quisquilloso *m*, -sa *f*; melindroso *m*, -sa *f*

fussiness [ˈfʌsinəs] *n* **1** IRRITABILITY : irritabilidad *f* **2** ORNATENESS : lo recargado **3** METICULOUSNESS : meticulosidad *f*

fussy [ˈfʌsi] *adj* **fussier; -est** **1** IRRITABLE : irritable, nervioso **2** OVERELABORATE : recargado **3** METICULOUS : meticuloso **4** FASTIDIOUS : quisquilloso, exigente

futile [ˈfju:təl, ˈfju:ˌtaɪl] *adj* : inútil, vano

futility [fju:ˈtɪləti] *n, pl* **-ties** : inutilidad *f*

future¹ [ˈfju:tʃər] *adj* : futuro

future² *n* : futuro *m*

futuristic [ˌfju:tʃəˈrɪstɪk] *adj* : futurista

fuze → **fuse¹**

fuzz ['fʌz] *n* : pelusa *f*
fuzziness ['fʌzinəs] *n* **1** DOWNINESS : vellosidad *f* **2** INDISTINCTNESS : falta *f* de claridad

fuzzy ['fʌzi] *adj* **fuzzier; -est 1** FLUFFY, FURRY : con pelusa, peludo **2** INDISTINCT : indistinto ⟨a fuzzy image : una imagen borrosa⟩

G

g ['ʤi:] *n, pl* **g's** *or* **gs** ['ʤi:z] : séptima letra del alfabeto inglés
gab[1] ['gæb] *vi* **gabbed; gabbing** : charlar, cotorrear *fam*, parlotear *fam*
gab[2] *n* CHATTER : cotorreo *m fam*, parloteo *m fam*
gabardine ['gæbər,di:n] *n* : gabardina *f*
gabby ['gæbi] *adj* **gabbier; -est** : hablador, parlanchín
gable ['geɪbəl] *n* : hastial *m*, aguilón *m*
Gabonese [,gæbə'ni:z, -'ni:s] *n* : gabonés *m*, -nesa *f* — **Gabonese** *adj*
gad ['gæd] *vi* **gadded; gadding** WANDER : deambular, vagar, callejear
gadfly ['gæd,flaɪ] *n, pl* **-flies 1** : tábano *m* (insecto) **2** FAULTFINDER : criticón *m*, -cona *f fam*
gadget ['gæʤət] *n* : artilugio *m*, aparato *m*
gadgetry ['gæʤətri] *n* : artilugios *mpl*, aparatos *mpl*
Gaelic ['geɪlɪk, 'gæ] *n* : gaélico *m* (idioma) — **Gaelic** *adj*
gaff ['gæf] *n* **1** : garfio *m* **2** → **gaffe**
gaffe ['gæf] *n* : metedura *f* de pata *fam*
gag[1] ['gæg] *v* **gagged; gagging** *vt* : amordazar ⟨to tie up and gag : atar y amordazar⟩ — *vi* **1** CHOKE : atragantarse **2** RETCH : hacer arcadas
gag[2] *n* **1** : mordaza *f* (para la boca) **2** JOKE : chiste *m*
gage → **gauge**
gaggle ['gægəl] *n* : bandada *f*, manada *f* (de gansos)
gaiety ['geɪəti] *n, pl* **-eties 1** MERRYMAKING : juerga *f* **2** MERRIMENT : alegría *f*, regocijo *m*
gaily ['geɪli] *adv* : alegremente
gain[1] ['geɪn] *vt* **1** ACQUIRE, OBTAIN : ganar, obtener, adquirir, conseguir ⟨to gain knowledge : adquirir conocimientos⟩ ⟨to gain a victory : obtener una victoria⟩ **2** REACH : alcanzar, llegar a **3** INCREASE : ganar, aumentar ⟨to gain weight : aumentar de peso⟩ **4** : adelantarse, ganar ⟨the watch gains two minutes a day : el reloj se adelanta dos minutos por día⟩ — *vi* **1** PROFIT : beneficiarse **2** INCREASE : aumentar
gain[2] *n* **1** PROFIT : beneficio *m*, ganancia *f*, lucro *m*, provecho *m* **2** INCREASE : aumento *m*
gainful ['geɪnfəl] *adj* : lucrativo, beneficioso, provechoso ⟨gainful employment : trabajo remunerado⟩
gait ['geɪt] *n* : paso *m*, andar *m*, manera *f* de caminar
gal ['gæl] *n* : muchacha *f*
gala[1] ['geɪlə, 'gæ-, 'gɑ-] *adj* : de gala

gala[2] *n* : gala *f*, fiesta *f*
galactic [gə'læktɪk] *adj* : galáctico
galaxy ['gæləksi] *n, pl* **-axies** : galaxia *f*
gale ['geɪl] *n* **1** WIND : vendaval *f*, viento *m* fuerte **2** **gales of laughter** : carcajadas *fpl*
gall[1] ['gɔl] *vt* **1** CHAFE : rozar **2** IRRITATE, VEX : irritar, molestar
gall[2] *n* **1** BILE : bilis *f*, hiel *f* **2** INSOLENCE : audacia *f*, insolencia *f*, descaro *m* **3** SORE : rozadura *f* (de un caballo) **4** : agalla *f* (de una planta)
gallant ['gælənt] *adj* **1** BRAVE : valiente, gallardo **2** CHIVALROUS, POLITE : galante, cortés
gallantry ['gæləntri] *n, pl* **-ries** : galantería *f*, caballerosidad *f*
gallbladder ['gɔl,blædər] *n* : vesícula *f* biliar
galleon ['gæljən] *n* : galeón *m*
gallery ['gæləri] *n, pl* **-leries 1** BALCONY : galería *f* (para espectadores) **2** CORRIDOR : pasillo *m*, galería *f*, corredor *m* **3** : galería *f* (para exposiciones)
galley ['gæli] *n, pl* **-leys** : galera *f*
gallium ['gæliəm] *n* : galio *m*
gallivant ['gælə,vænt] *vi* : callejear
gallon ['gælən] *n* : galón *m*
gallop[1] ['gæləp] *vi* : galopar
gallop[2] *n* : galope *m*
gallows ['gæ,lo:z] *n, pl* **-lows** *or* **-lowses** [-,lo:zəz] : horca *f*
gallstone ['gɔl,sto:n] *n* : cálculo *m* biliar
galore [gə'lor] *adj* : en abundancia ⟨bargains galore : muchísimas gangas⟩
galoshes [gə'lɑʃəz] *npl* : galochas *fpl*, chanclos *mpl*
galvanize ['gælvən,aɪz] *vt* **-nized; -nizing 1** STIMULATE : estimular, excitar, impulsar **2** : galvanizar (metales)
Gambian ['gæmbiən] *n* : gambiano *m*, -na *f* — **Gambian** *adj*
gambit ['gæmbɪt] *n* **1** : gambito *m* (en ajedrez) **2** STRATAGEM : estratagema *f*, táctica *f*
gamble[1] ['gæmbəl] *v* **-bled; -bling** *vi* : jugar, arriesgarse — *vt* **1** BET, WAGER : apostar, jugarse **2** RISK : arriesgar
gamble[2] *n* **1** BET : apuesta *f* **2** RISK : riesgo *m*
gambler ['gæmbələr] *n* : jugador *m*, -dora *f*
gambling ['gæmbəlɪŋ] *n* : juego *m*
gambol ['gæmbəl] *vi* **-boled** *or* **-bolled; -boling** *or* **-bolling** FROLIC : retozar, juguetear
game[1] ['geɪm] *adj* **1** READY : listo, dispuesto ⟨we're game for anything : es-

tamos listos para lo que sea⟩ **2** LAME : cojo

game² *n* **1** AMUSEMENT : juego *m*, diversión *f* **2** CONTEST : juego *m*, partido *m*, concurso *m* **3** : caza *f* ⟨big game : caza mayor⟩

gamecock ['geɪm,kɑk] *n* : gallo *m* de pelea

gamekeeper ['geɪm,ki:pər] *n* : guardabosque *mf*

gamely ['geɪmli] *adv* : animosamente

gamma ray ['gæmə] *n* : rayo *m* gamma

gamut ['gæmət] *n* : gama *f*, espectro *m* ⟨to run the gamut : pasar por toda la gama⟩

gamy *or* **gamey** ['geɪmi] *adj* **gamier; -est** : con sabor de animal de caza, fuerte

gander ['gændər] *n* **1** : ganso *m* (animal) **2** GLANCE : mirada *f*, vistazo *m*, ojeada *f*

gang¹ ['gæŋ] *vi* **to gang up** : agruparse, unirse

gang² *n* : banda *f*, pandilla *f*

gangling ['gæŋglɪŋ] *adj* LANKY : larguirucho *fam*

ganglion ['gæŋgliən] *n*, *pl* **-glia** [-gliə] : ganglio *m*

gangplank ['gæŋ,plæŋk] *n* : pasarela *f*

gangrene ['gæŋ,gri:n, 'gæn-; gæŋ'-, gæn'-] *n* : gangrena *f*

gangrenous ['gæŋgrənəs] *adj* : gangrenoso

gangster ['gæŋstər] *n* : gángster *mf*

gangway ['gæŋ,weɪ] *n* **1** : pasarela *f* **2 gangway!** : ¡abran paso!

gap ['gæp] *n* **1** BREACH, OPENING : espacio *m*, brecha *f*, abertura *f* **2** GORGE : desfiladero *m*, barranco *m* **3** : laguna *f* ⟨a gap in my education : una laguna en mi educación⟩ **4** INTERVAL : pausa *f*, intervalo *m* **5** DISPARITY : brecha *f*, disparidad *f*

gape¹ ['geɪp] *vi* **gaped; gaping 1** OPEN : abrirse, estar abierto **2** STARE : mirar fijamente con la boca abierta, mirar boquiabierto

gape² *n* **1** OPENING : abertura *f*, brecha *f* **2** STARE : mirada *f* boquiabierta

garage¹ [gə'rɑʒ, -'rɑdʒ] *vt* **-raged; -raging** : dejar en un garaje

garage² *n* : garaje *m*, cochera *f*

garb¹ ['gɑrb] *vt* : vestir, ataviar

garb² *n* : vestimenta *f*, atuendo *f*

garbage ['gɑrbɪdʒ] *n* : basura *f*, desechos *mpl*

garbageman ['gɑrbɪdʒmən] *n*, *pl* **-men** [-mən, -,mɛn] : basurero *m*

garble ['gɑrbəl] *vt* **-bled; -bling** : tergiversar, distorsionar

garbled ['gɑrbəld] *adj* : incoherente, incomprensible

garden¹ ['gɑrdən] *vi* : trabajar en el jardín

garden² *n* : jardín *m*

gardener ['gɑrdənər] *n* : jardinero *m*, -ra *f*

gardenia [gɑr'di:njə] *n* : gardenia *f*

gardening ['gɑrdənɪŋ] *n* : jardinería *f*

gargantuan [gɑr'gæntʃuən] *adj* : gigantesco, colosal

gargle¹ ['gɑrgəl] *vi* **-gled; -gling** : hacer gárgaras, gargarizar

gargle² *n* : gárgara *f*

gargoyle ['gɑr,gɔɪl] *n* : gárgola *f*

garish ['gærɪʃ] *adj* GAUDY : llamativo, chillón, charro — **garishly** *adv*

garland¹ ['gɑrlənd] *vt* : adornar con guirnaldas

garland² *n* : guirnalda *f*

garlic ['gɑrlɪk] *n* : ajo *m*

garment ['gɑrmənt] *n* : prenda *f*

garner ['gɑrnər] *vt* : recoger, cosechar

garnet ['gɑrnət] *n* : granate *m*

garnish¹ ['gɑrnɪʃ] *vt* : aderezar, guarnecer

garnish² *n* : aderezo *m*, guarnición *f*

garret ['gærət] *n* : buhardilla *f*, desván *m*

garrison¹ ['gærəsən] *vt* **1** QUARTER : acuartelar (tropas) **2** OCCUPY : guarnecer, ocupar (con tropas)

garrison² *n* **1** : guarnición *f* (ciudad) **2** FORT : fortaleza *f*, poste *m* militar

garrulous ['gærələs] *adj* : charlatán, parlanchín, garlero *Col fam*

garter ['gɑrtər] *n* : liga *f*

gas¹ ['gæs] *v* **gassed; gassing** *vt* : gasear — *vi* **to gas up** : llenar el tanque con gasolina

gas² *n*, *pl* **gases** ['gæsəz] **1** : gas *m* ⟨tear gas : gas lacrimógeno⟩ **2** GASOLINE : gasolina *f*

gaseous ['gæʃəs, 'gæsiəs] *adj* : gaseoso

gash¹ ['gæʃ] *vt* : hacer un tajo en, cortar

gash² *n* : cuchillada *f*, tajo *m*

gasket ['gæskət] *n* : junta *f*

gas mask *n* : máscara *f* antigás

gasoline ['gæsə,li:n, ,gæsə'-] *n* : gasolina *f*, nafta *f*

gasp¹ ['gæsp] *vi* **1** : boquear ⟨to gasp with surprise : gritar de asombro⟩ **2** PANT : jadear, respirar con dificultad

gasp² *n* **1** : boqueada *f* ⟨a gasp of surprise : un grito sofocado⟩ **2** PANTING : jadeo *m*

gas station *n* : estación *f* de servicio, gasolinera *f*

gastric ['gæstrɪk] *adj* : gástrico ⟨gastric juice : jugo gástrico⟩

gastronomic [,gæstrə'nɑmɪk] *adj* : gastronómico

gastronomy [gæs'trɑnəmi] *n* : gastronomía *f*

gate ['geɪt] *n* : portón *m*, verja *f*, puerta *f*

gatekeeper ['geɪt,ki:pər] *n* : guarda *mf*; guardián *m*, -diana *f*

gateway ['geɪt,weɪ] *n* : puerta *f* (de acceso), entrada *f*

gather ['gæðər] *vt* **1** ASSEMBLE : juntar, recoger, reunir **2** HARVEST : recoger, cosechar **3** : fruncir (una tela) **4** INFER : deducir, suponer

gathering ['gæðərɪŋ] *n* : reunión *f*

gauche ['goːʃ] *adj* : torpe, falto de tacto

gaudy ['gɔdi] *adj* **gaudier; -est** : chillón, llamativo

gauge[1] ['geɪʤ] *vt* **gauged; gauging 1** MEASURE : medir **2** ESTIMATE, JUDGE : estimar, evaluar, juzgar

gauge[2] *n* **1** : indicador *m* ⟨pressure gauge : indicador de presión⟩ **2** CALIBER : calibre *m* **3** INDICATION : indicio *m*, muestra *f*

gaunt ['gɔnt] *adj* : demacrado, enjuto, descarnado

gauntlet ['gɔntlət] *n* : guante *m* ⟨to run the gauntlet of : exponerse a⟩

gauze ['gɔz] *n* : gasa *f*

gauzy ['gɔzi] *adj* **gauzier; -est** : diáfano, vaporoso

gave → **give**

gavel ['gævəl] *n* : martillo *m* (de un juez, un subastador, etc.)

gawk ['gɔk] *vi* GAPE : mirar boquiabierto

gawky ['gɔki] *adj* **gawkier; -est** : desmañado, torpe, desgarbado

gay ['geɪ] *adj* **1** MERRY : alegre **2** BRIGHT, COLORFUL : vistoso, vivo **3** HOMOSEXUAL : homosexual

gaze[1] ['geɪz] *vi* **gazed; gazing** : mirar (fijamente)

gaze[2] *n* : mirada *f* (fija)

gazelle [gə'zɛl] *n* : gacela *f*

gazette [gə'zɛt] *n* : gaceta *f*

gazetteer [ˌgæzə'tɪr] *n* : diccionario *m* geográfico

gear[1] ['gɪr] *vt* ADAPT, ORIENT : adaptar, ajustar, orientar ⟨a book geared to children : un libro adaptado a los niños⟩ — *vi* **to gear up** : prepararse

gear[2] *n* **1** CLOTHING : ropa *f* **2** BELONGINGS : efectos *mpl* personales **3** EQUIPMENT, TOOLS : equipo *m*, aparejo *m*, herramientas *fpl* ⟨fishing gear : aparejo de pescar⟩ ⟨landing gear : tren de aterrizaje⟩ **4** COGWHEEL : rueda *f* dentada **5** : marcha *f*, velocidad *f* (de un vehículo) ⟨to put in gear : poner en marcha⟩ ⟨to change gear(s) : cambiar de velocidad⟩

gearshift ['gɪrˌʃɪft] *n* : palanca *f* de cambio, palanca *f* de velocidad

geek ['gi:k] *n fam* : intelectual *mf*

geese → **goose**

Geiger counter ['gaɪgərˌkaʊntər] *n* : contador *m* Geiger

gel ['ʤɛl] *n* : gel *m*

gelatin ['ʤɛlətən] *n* : gelatina *f*

gem ['ʤɛm] *n* : joya *f*, gema *f*, alhaja *f*

Gemini ['ʤɛməˌnaɪ] *n* : Géminis *mf*

gemstone ['ʤɛmˌstoːn] *n* : piedra *f* (semipreciosa o preciosa), gema *f*

gender ['ʤɛndər] *n* **1** SEX : sexo *m* **2** : género *m* (en la gramática)

gene ['ʤi:n] *n* : gen *m*, gene *m*

genealogical [ˌʤi:niə'lɑʤɪkəl] *adj* : genealógico

genealogy [ˌʤi:ni'ɑləʤi, ˌʤɛ-, -'æ-] *n, pl* **-gies** : genealogía *f*

genera → **genus**

general[1] ['ʤɛnrəl, 'ʤɛnə-] *adj* : general ⟨in general : en general, por lo general⟩

general[2] *n* : general *mf*

generality [ˌʤɛnə'ræləti] *n, pl* **-ties** : generalidad *f*

generalization [ˌʤɛnrələ'zeɪʃən, ˌʤɛnərə-] *n* : generalización *f*

generalize ['ʤɛnrəˌlaɪz, 'ʤɛnərə-] *v* **-ized; -izing** : generalizar

generally ['ʤɛnrəli, 'ʤɛnərə-] *adv* : generalmente, por lo general, en general

generate ['ʤɛnəˌreɪt] *vt* **-ated; -ating** : generar, producir

generation [ˌʤɛnə'reɪʃən] *n* : generación *f*

generator ['ʤɛnəˌreɪtər] *n* : generador *m*

generic [ʤə'nɛrɪk] *adj* : genérico

generosity [ˌʤɛnə'rɑsəti] *n, pl* **-ties** : generosidad *f*

generous ['ʤɛnərəs] *adj* **1** OPENHANDED : generoso, dadivoso, desprendido **2** ABUNDANT, AMPLE : abundante, amplio, generoso — **generously** *adv*

genetic [ʤə'nɛtɪk] *adj* : genético — **genetically** [-tɪkli] *adv*

geneticist [ʤə'nɛtəsɪst] *n* : genetista *mf*

genetics [ʤə'nɛtɪks] *n* : genética *f*

genial ['ʤi:niəl] *adj* GRACIOUS : simpático, cordial, afable — **genially** *adv*

geniality [ˌʤi:ni'æləti] *n* : simpatía *f*, afabilidad *f*

genie ['ʤi:ni] *n* : genio *m*

genital ['ʤɛnətəl] *adj* : genital

genitals ['ʤɛnətəlz] *npl* : genitales *mpl*

genius ['ʤi:njəs] *n* : genio *m*

genocide ['ʤɛnəˌsaɪd] *n* : genocidio *m*

genre ['ʒɑnrə, 'ʒɑr] *n* : género *m*

genteel [ʤɛn'ti:l] *adj* : cortés, fino, refinado

gentile[1] ['ʤɛnˌtaɪl] *adj* : gentil

gentile[2] *n* : gentil *mf*

gentility [ʤɛn'tɪləti] *n, pl* **-ties 1** : nobleza *f* (de nacimiento) **2** POLITENESS, REFINEMENT : cortesía *f*, refinamiento *m*

gentle ['ʤɛntəl] *adj* **-tler; -tlest 1** NOBLE : bien nacido, noble **2** DOCILE : dócil, manso **3** KINDLY : bondadoso, amable **4** MILD : suave, apacible ⟨a gentle breeze : una brisa suave⟩ **5** SOFT : suave (dícese de un sonido), ligero (dícese del tacto) **6** MODERATE : moderado, gradual ⟨a gentle slope : una cuesta gradual⟩

gentleman ['ʤɛntəlmən] *n, pl* **-men** [-mən, -ˌmɛn] : caballero *m*, señor *m*

gentlemanly ['ʤɛntəlmənli] *adj* : caballeroso

gentleness ['ʤɛntəlnəs] *n* : delicadeza *f*, suavidad *f*, ternura *f*

gentlewoman ['ʤɛntəlˌwʊmən] *n, pl* **-women** [-ˌwɪmən] : dama *f*, señora *f*

gently ['ʤɛntli] *adv* **1** CAREFULLY, SOFTLY : con cuidado, suavemente, ligeramente **2** KINDLY : amablemente, con delicadeza

gentry ['ʤɛntri] *n, pl* **-tries** : aristocracia *f*
genuflect ['ʤɛnjʊˌflɛkt] *vi* : doblar la rodilla, hacer una genuflexión
genuflection [ˌʤɛnjʊ'flɛkʃən] *n* : genuflexión *f*
genuine ['ʤɛnjuwən] *adj* **1** AUTHENTIC, REAL : genuino, verdadero, auténtico **2** SINCERE : sincero — **genuinely** *adv*
genus ['ʤiːnəs] *n, pl* **genera** ['ʤɛ-nərə] : género *m*
geographer [ʤi'ɑgrəfər] *n* : geógrafo *m*, -fa *f*
geographical [ˌʤiː'ə'græfɪkəl] *or* **geographic** [-fɪk] *adj* : geográfico — **geographically** [-fɪkli] *adv*
geography [ʤi'ɑgrəfi] *n, pl* **-phies** : geografía *f*
geologic [ˌʤiː'ə'lɑʤɪk] *or* **geological** [-ʤɪkəl] *adj* : geológico — **geologically** [-ʤɪkli] *adv*
geologist [ʤi'ɑləʤɪst] *n* : geólogo *m*, -ga *f*
geology [ʤi'ɑləʤi] *n* : geología *f*
geometric [ˌʤiː'ə'mɛtrɪk] *or* **geometrical** [-trɪkəl] *adj* : geométrico
geometry [ʤi'ɑmətri] *n, pl* **-tries** : geometría *f*
geopolitical [ˌʤiː'opə'lɪtɪkəl] *adj* : geopolítico
Georgian ['ʤɔrʤən] *n* **1** : georgiano *m* (idioma) **2** : georgiano *m*, -na *f* — **Georgian** *adj*
geranium [ʤə'reɪniəm] *n* : geranio *m*
gerbil ['ʤərbəl] *n* : jerbo *m*, gerbo *m*
geriatric [ˌʤɛri'ætrɪk] *adj* : geriátrico
geriatrics [ˌʤɛri'ætrɪks] *n* : geriatría *f*
germ ['ʤərm] *n* **1** MICROORGANISM : microbio *m*, germen *m* **2** BEGINNING : germen *m*, principio *m* ⟨the germ of a plan : el germen de un plan⟩
German ['ʤərmən] *n* **1** : alemán *m*, -mana *f* **2** : alemán *m* (idioma) — **German** *adj*
germane [ʤər'meɪn] *adj* : relevante, pertinente
Germanic[1] [ʤər'mænɪk] *adj* : germánico, germano
Germanic[2] *n* : germánico *m* (idioma)
germanium [ʤər'meɪniəm] *n* : germanio *m*
germ cell *n* : célula *f* germen
germicide ['ʤərməˌsaɪd] *n* : germicida *m*
germinate ['ʤərməˌneɪt] *v* **-nated; -nating** *vi* : germinar — *vt* : hacer germinar
germination [ˌʤərmə'neɪʃən] *n* : germinación *f*
gerund ['ʤɛrənd] *n* : gerundio *m*
gestation [ʤɛ'steɪʃən] *n* : gestación *f*
gesture[1] ['ʤɛstʃər] *vi* **-tured; -turing** : gesticular, hacer gestos
gesture[2] *n* **1** : gesto *m*, ademán *m* **2** SIGN, TOKEN : gesto *m*, señal *f* ⟨a gesture of friendship : una señal de amistad⟩

get ['gɛt] *v* **got** ['gɑt]; **got** *or* **gotten** ['gɑtən]; **getting** *vt* **1** OBTAIN : conseguir, obtener, adquirir **2** RECEIVE : recibir ⟨to get a letter : recibir una carta⟩ **3** EARN : ganar ⟨he gets $10 an hour : gana $10 por hora⟩ **4** FETCH : traer ⟨get me my book : tráigame el libro⟩ **5** CATCH : tomar (un tren, etc.), agarrar (una pelota, una persona, etc.) **6** CONTRACT : contagiarse de, contraer ⟨she got the measles : le dio el sarampión⟩ **7** PREPARE : preparar (una comida) **8** PERSUADE : persuadir, mandar a hacer ⟨I got him to agree : logré convencerlo⟩ **9** (*to cause to be*) : ⟨to get one's hair cut : cortarse el pelo⟩ **10** UNDERSTAND : entender ⟨now I get it! : ¡ya entiendo!⟩ **11 to have got** : tener ⟨I've got a headache : tengo un dolor de cabeza⟩ **12 to have got to** : tener que ⟨you've got to come : tienes que venir⟩ — *vi* **1** BECOME : ponerse, volverse, hacerse ⟨to get angry : ponerse furioso, enojarse⟩ **2** GO, MOVE : ir, avanzar ⟨he didn't get far : no avanzó mucho⟩ **3** ARRIVE : llegar ⟨to get home : llegar a casa⟩ **4 to get to be** : llegar a ser ⟨she got to be the director : llegó a ser directora⟩ **5 to get ahead** : adelantarse, progresar **6 to get along** : llevarse bien (con alguien), congeniar **7 to get by** MANAGE : arreglárselas **8 to get over** OVERCOME : superar, consolarse de **9 to get together** MEET : reunirse **10 to get up** : levantarse
getaway ['gɛtəˌweɪ] *n* ESCAPE : fuga *f*, huida *f*, escapada *f*
geyser ['gaɪzər] *n* : géiser *m*
Ghanaian ['gɑniən, 'gæ-] *n* : ghanés *m*, -nesa *f* — **Ghanaian** *adj*
ghastly ['gæstli] *adj* **-lier; -est 1** HORRIBLE : horrible, espantoso **2** PALE : pálido, cadavérico
gherkin ['gərkən] *n* : pepinillo *m*
ghetto ['gɛtoː] *n, pl* **-tos** *or* **-toes** : gueto *m*
ghost ['goːst] *n* **1** : fantasma *f*, espectro *m* **2 the Holy Ghost** : el Espíritu Santo
ghostly ['goːstli] *adv* : fantasmal
ghoul ['guːl] *n* **1** : demonio *m* necrófago **2** : persona *f* de gustos macabros
GI [ˌʤiː'aɪ] *n, pl* **GI's** *or* **GIs** : soldado *m* estadounidense
giant[1] ['ʤaɪənt] *adj* : gigante, gigantesco, enorme
giant[2] *n* : gigante *m*, -ta *f*
gibberish ['ʤɪbərɪʃ] *n* : galimatías *m*, jerigonza *f*
gibbon ['gɪbən] *n* : gibón *m*
gibe[1] ['ʤaɪb] *vi* **gibed; gibing** : mofarse, burlarse
gibe[2] *n* : pulla *f*, burla *f*, mofa *f*
giblets ['ʤɪbləts] *npl* : menudos *mpl*, menudencias *fpl*
giddiness ['gɪdinəs] *n* **1** DIZZINESS : vértigo *m*, mareo *m* **2** SILLINESS : frivolidad *f*, estupidez *f*

giddy ['gɪdi] *adj* **-dier; -est 1** DIZZY : mareado, vertiginoso **2** FRIVOLOUS, SILLY : frívolo, tonto

gift ['gɪft] *n* **1** TALENT : don *m*, talento *m*, dotes *fpl* **2** PRESENT : regalo *m*, obsequio *m*

gifted ['gɪftəd] *adj* TALENTED : talentoso

gig ['gɪg] *vi* : trabajo *m* (de duración limitada) ⟨to play a gig : tocar en un concierto⟩

gigabyte ['dʒɪgə,baɪt, 'gɪ-] *n* : gigabyte *m*

gigantic [dʒaɪ'gæntɪk] *adj* : gigantesco, enorme, colosal

giggle¹ ['gɪgəl] *vi* **-gled; -gling** : reírse tontamente

giggle² *n* : risita *f*, risa *f* tonta

gild ['gɪld] *vt* **gilded** *or* **gilt** ['gɪlt]; **gilding** : dorar

gill ['gɪl] *n* : agalla *f*, branquia *f*

gilt¹ ['gɪlt] *adj* : dorado

gilt² *n* : dorado *m*

gimlet ['gɪmlət] *n* **1** : barrena *f* (herramienta) **2** : bebida *f* de vodka o ginebra y limón

gimmick ['gɪmɪk] *n* **1** GADGET : artilugio *m* **2** CATCH : engaño *m*, trampa *f* **3** SCHEME, TRICK : ardid *m*, truco *m*

gin ['dʒɪn] *n* **1** : desmotadora *f* (de algodón) **2** : ginebra *f* (bebida alcohólica)

ginger ['dʒɪndʒər] *n* : jengibre *m*

ginger ale *n* : ginger ale *m*, gaseosa *f* de jengibre

gingerbread ['dʒɪndʒər,brɛd] *n* : pan *m* de jengibre

gingerly ['dʒɪndʒərli] *adv* : con cuidado, cautelosamente

gingham ['gɪnəm] *n* : guinga *f*

ginseng ['dʒɪn,sɪn, -,sɛn] *n* : ginseng *m*

giraffe [dʒə'ræf] *n* : jirafa *f*

gird ['gərd] *vt* **girded** *or* **girt** ['gərt]; **girding 1** BIND : ceñir, atar **2** ENCIRCLE : rodear **3 to gird oneself** : prepararse

girder ['gərdər] *n* : viga *f*

girdle¹ ['gərdəl] *vt* **-dled; -dling 1** GIRD : ceñir, atar **2** SURROUND : rodear, circundar

girdle² *n* : faja *f*

girl ['gərl] *n* **1** : chica *f*, muchacha *f* **2** *or* **little girl** : niña *f*, chica *f* **3** SWEETHEART : novia *f* **4** DAUGHTER : hija *f*

girlfriend ['gərl,frɛnd] *n* : novia *f*, amiga *f*

girlhood ['gərl,hʊd] *n* : niñez *f*, juventud *f* (de una muchacha)

girlish ['gərlɪʃ] *adj* : de niña

girth ['gərθ] *n* **1** : circunferencia *f* (de un árbol, etc.), cintura *f* (de una persona) **2** CINCH : cincha *f* (para caballos, etc.)

gist ['dʒɪst] *n* : quid *m*, meollo *m*

give¹ ['gɪv] *v* **gave** ['geɪv]; **given** ['gɪvən]; **giving** *vt* **1** HAND, PRESENT : dar, regalar, obsequiar ⟨give it to me : dámelo⟩ ⟨they gave him a gold watch : le regalaron un reloj de oro⟩ **2** PAY : dar, pagar ⟨I'll give you $10 for this one : te daré $10 por éste⟩ **3** UTTER : dar, pronunciar ⟨to give a shout : dar un grito⟩ ⟨to give a speech : pronunciar un discurso⟩ ⟨to give a verdict : dictar sentencia⟩ **4** PROVIDE : dar ⟨to give one's word : dar uno su palabra⟩ ⟨to give a party : dar una fiesta⟩ **5** CAUSE : dar, causar, ocasionar ⟨to give trouble : causar problemas⟩ ⟨to give someone to understand : darle a entender a alguien⟩ **6** GRANT : dar, otorgar ⟨to give permission : dar permiso⟩ — *vi* **1** : hacer regalos **2** YIELD : ceder, romperse ⟨it gave under the weight of the crowd : cedió bajo el peso de la muchedumbre⟩ **3 to give in** *or* **to give up** SURRENDER : rendirse, entregarse **4 to give out** : agotarse, acabarse ⟨the supplies gave out : las provisiones se agotaron⟩

give² *n* FLEXIBILITY : flexibilidad *f*, elasticidad *f*

giveaway ['gɪvə,weɪ] *n* **1** : revelación *f* involuntaria **2** GIFT : regalo *m*, obsequio *m*

given ['gɪvən] *adj* **1** INCLINED : dado, inclinado ⟨he's given to quarreling : es muy dado a discutir⟩ **2** SPECIFIC : dado, determinado ⟨at a given time : en un momento dado⟩

given name *n* : nombre *m* de pila

give up *vt* : dejar, renunciar a, abandonar ⟨to give up smoking : dejar de fumar⟩

gizzard ['gɪzərd] *n* : molleja *f*

glacial ['gleɪʃəl] *adj* : glacial — **glacially** *adv*

glacier ['gleɪʃər] *n* : glaciar *m*

glad ['glæd] *adj* **gladder; gladdest 1** PLEASED : alegre, contento ⟨she was glad I came : se alegró de que haya venido⟩ ⟨glad to meet you! : ¡mucho gusto!⟩ **2** HAPPY, PLEASING : feliz, agradable ⟨glad tidings : buenas nuevas⟩ **3** WILLING : dispuesto, gustoso ⟨I'll be glad to do it : lo haré con mucho gusto⟩

gladden ['glædən] *vt* : alegrar

glade ['gleɪd] *n* : claro *m*

gladiator ['glædi,eɪt̬ər] *n* : gladiador *m*

gladiolus [,glædi'o:ləs] *n, pl* **-li** [-li, -,laɪ] : gladiolo *m*, gladíolo *m*

gladly ['glædli] *adv* : con mucho gusto

gladness ['glædnəs] *n* : alegría *f*, gozo *m*

glamor *or* **glamour** ['glæmər] *n* : atractivo *m*, hechizo *m*, encanto *m*

glamorous ['glæmərəs] *adj* : atractivo, encantador

glance¹ ['glænts] *vi* **glanced; glancing 1** RICOCHET : rebotar ⟨it glanced off the wall : rebotó en la pared⟩ **2 to glance at** : mirar, echar un vistazo a **3 to glance away** : apartar los ojos

glance² *n* : mirada *f*, vistazo *m*, ojeada *f*

gland ['glænd] *n* : glándula *f*

glandular ['glændʒʊlər] *adj* : glandular

glare¹ ['glær] *vi* **glared; glaring 1** SHINE : brillar, relumbrar **2** STARE : mirar con ira, lanzar una mirada feroz

glare[2] *n* **1** BRIGHTNESS : resplandor *m*, luz *f* deslumbrante **2** : mirada *f* feroz

glaring ['glærɪŋ] *adj* **1** BRIGHT : deslumbrante, brillante **2** FLAGRANT, OBVIOUS : flagrante, manifiesto ⟨a glaring error : un error que salta a la vista⟩

glass ['glæs] *n* **1** : vidrio *m*, cristal *m* ⟨stained glass : vidrio de color⟩ **2** : vaso *m* ⟨a glass of milk : un vaso de leche⟩ **3 glasses** *npl* SPECTACLES : gafas *fpl*, anteojos *mpl*, lentes *mpl*, espejuelos *mpl*

glassblowing ['glæs,blo:ɪŋ] *n* : soplado *m* del vidrio

glassful ['glæs,fʊl] *n* : vaso *m*, copa *f*

glassware ['glæs,wær] *n* : cristalería *f*

glassy ['glæsi] *adj* **glassier; -est 1** VITREOUS : vítreo **2** : vidrioso ⟨glassy eyes : ojos vidriosos⟩

glaucoma [glaʊ'ko:mə, glɔ-] *n* : glaucoma *m*

glaze[1] ['gleɪz] *vt* **glazed; glazing 1** : ponerle vidrios a (una ventana, etc.) **2** : vidriar (cerámica) **3** : glasear (papel, verduras, etc.)

glaze[2] *n* : vidriado *m*, glaseado *m*, barniz *m*

glazier ['gleɪʒər] *n* : vidriero *m*, -ra *f*

gleam[1] ['gli:m] *vi* : brillar, destellar, relucir

gleam[2] *n* **1** LIGHT : luz *f* (oscura) **2** GLINT : destello *m* **3** GLIMMER : rayo *m*, vislumbre *f* ⟨a gleam of hope : un rayo de esperanza⟩

glean ['gli:n] *vt* : recoger, espigar

glee ['gli:] *n* : alegría *f*, júbilo *m*, regocijo *m*

gleeful ['gli:fəl] *adj* : lleno de alegría

glen ['glɛn] *n* : cañada *f*

glib ['glɪb] *adj* **glibber; glibbest 1** : simplista ⟨a glib reply : una respuesta simplista⟩ **2** : con mucha labia (dícese de una persona)

glibly ['glɪbli] *adv* : con mucha labia

glide[1] ['glaɪd] *vi* **glided; gliding** : deslizarse (en una superficie), planear (en el aire)

glide[2] *n* : planeo *m*

glider ['glaɪdər] *n* **1** : planeador *m* (aeronave) **2** : mecedor *m* (tipo de columpio)

glimmer[1] ['glɪmər] *vi* : brillar con luz trémula

glimmer[2] *n* **1** : luz *f* trémula, luz *f* tenue **2** GLEAM : rayo *m*, vislumbre *f* ⟨a glimmer of understanding : un rayo de entendimiento⟩

glimpse[1] ['glɪmps] *vt* **glimpsed; glimpsing** : vislumbrar, entrever

glimpse[2] *n* : mirada *f* breve ⟨to catch a glimpse of : alcanzar a ver, vislumbrar⟩

glint[1] ['glɪnt] *vi* GLEAM, SPARKLE : destellar, fulgurar

glint[2] *n* **1** SPARKLE : destello *m*, centelleo *m* **2 to have a glint in one's eye** : chispearle los ojos a uno

glisten[1] ['glɪsən] *vi* : brillar, centellear

glisten[2] *n* : brillo *m*, centelleo *m*

glitch ['glɪtʃ] *n* **1** MALFUNCTION : mal funcionamiento *m* **2** SNAG : problema *m*, complicación *f*

glitter[1] ['glɪtər] *vi* **1** SPARKLE : destellar, relucir, brillar **2** FLASH : relampaguear ⟨his eyes glittered in anger : le relampagueaban los ojos de ira⟩

glitter[2] *n* **1** BRIGHTNESS : brillo *m* **2** : purpurina *f* (para decoración)

glitz ['glɪts] *n* : oropel *m*

gloat ['glo:t] *vi* **to gloat over** : regodearse en

glob ['glɑb] *n* : plasta *f*, masa *f*, grumo *m*

global ['glo:bəl] *adj* **1** SPHERICAL : esférico **2** WORLDWIDE : global, mundial — **globally** *adv*

globe ['glo:b] *n* **1** SPHERE : esfera *f*, globo *m* **2** EARTH : globo *m*, Tierra *f* **3** : globo *m* terráqueo (modelo de la Tierra)

globe–trotter ['glo:b,trɑtər] *n* : trotamundos *mf*

globular ['glɑbjʊlər] *adj* : globular

globule ['glɑ,bju:l] *n* : glóbulo *m*

gloom ['glu:m] *n* **1** DARKNESS : penumbra *f*, oscuridad *f* **2** MELANCHOLY : melancolía *f*, tristeza *f*

gloomily ['glu:məli] *adv* : tristemente

gloomy ['glu:mi] *adj* **gloomier; -est 1** DARK : oscuro, tenebroso ⟨gloomy weather : tiempo gris⟩ **2** MELANCHOLY : melancólico **3** PESSIMISTIC : pesimista **4** DEPRESSING : deprimente, lúgubre

glorification [,glorəfə'keɪʃən] *n* : glorificación *f*

glorify ['glorə,faɪ] *vt* **-fied; -fying** : glorificar

glorious ['gloriəs] *adj* **1** ILLUSTRIOUS : glorioso, ilustre **2** MAGNIFICENT : magnífico, espléndido, maravilloso — **gloriously** *adv*

glory[1] ['glori] *vi* **-ried; -rying** EXULT : exultar, regocijarse

glory[2] *n, pl* **-ries 1** RENOWN : gloria *f*, fama *f*, honor *m* **2** PRAISE : gloria *f* ⟨glory to God : gloria a Dios⟩ **3** MAGNIFICENCE : magnificencia *f*, esplendor *m*, gloria *f* **4 to be in one's glory** : estar uno en su gloria

gloss[1] ['glɔs, 'glɑs] *vt* **1** EXPLAIN : glosar, explicar **2** POLISH : lustrar, pulir **3 to gloss over** : quitarle importancia a, minimizar

gloss[2] *n* **1** SHINE : lustre *m*, brillo *m* **2** EXPLANATION : glosa *f*, explicación *f* breve **3** → **glossary**

glossary ['glɔsəri, 'glɑ-] *n, pl* **-ries** : glosario *m*

glossy ['glɔsi, 'glɑ-] *adj* **glossier; -est** : brillante, lustroso, satinado (dícese del papel)

glove ['glʌv] *n* : guante *m*

glow[1] ['glo:] *vi* **1** SHINE : brillar, resplandecer **2** BRIM : rebosar ⟨to glow with health : rebosar de salud⟩

glow² *n* **1** BRIGHTNESS : resplandor *m*, brillo *m*, luminosidad *f* **2** FEELING : sensación *f* (de bienestar), oleada *f* (de sentimiento) **3** INCANDESCENCE : incandescencia *f*

glower ['glaʋər] *vi* : fruncir el ceño

glowworm ['glo:ˌwərm] *n* : luciérnaga *f*

glucose ['glu:ˌko:s] *n* : glucosa *f*

glue¹ ['glu:] *vt* **glued; gluing** *or* **glueing** : pegar, encolar

glue² *n* : pegamento *m*, cola *f*

gluey ['glu:i] *adj* **gluier; -est** : pegajoso

glum ['glʌm] *adj* **glummer; glummest** **1** SULLEN : hosco, sombrío **2** DREARY, GLOOMY : sombrío, triste, melancólico

glut¹ ['glʌt] *vt* **glutted; glutting 1** SATIATE : saciar, hartar **2** : inundar (el mercado)

glut² *n* : exceso *m*, superabundancia *f*

glutinous ['glu:tənəs] *adj* STICKY : pegajoso, glutinoso

glutton ['glʌtən] *n* : glotón *m*, -tona *f*

gluttonous ['glʌtənəs] *adj* : glotón

gluttony ['glʌtəni] *n, pl* **-tonies** : glotonería *f*, gula *f*

gnarled ['nɑrld] *adj* **1** KNOTTY : nudoso **2** TWISTED : retorcido

gnash ['næʃ] *vt* : hacer rechinar (los dientes)

gnat ['næt] *n* : jején *m*

gnaw ['nɔ] *vt* : roer

gnome ['no:m] *n* : gnomo *m*

gnu ['nu:, 'nju:] *n, pl* **gnu** *or* **gnus** : ñu *m*

go¹ ['go:] *v* **went** ['wɛnt]; **gone** ['gɔn, 'gɑn]; **going; goes** ['go:z] *vi* **1** PROCEED : ir ⟨to go slow : ir despacio⟩ ⟨to go shopping : ir de compras⟩ **2** LEAVE : irse, marcharse, salir ⟨let's go! : ¡vámonos!⟩ ⟨the train went on time : el tren salió a tiempo⟩ **3** DISAPPEAR : desaparecer, pasarse, irse ⟨her fear is gone : se le ha pasado el miedo⟩ ⟨my pen is gone! : ¡mi pluma desapareció!⟩ **4** EXTEND : ir, extenderse, llegar ⟨this road goes to the river : este camino se extiende hasta el río⟩ ⟨to go from top to bottom : ir de arriba abajo⟩ **5** FUNCTION : funcionar, marchar ⟨the car won't go : el coche no funciona⟩ ⟨to get something going : poner algo en marcha⟩ **6** SELL : venderse ⟨it goes for $15 : se vende por $15⟩ **7** PROGRESS : ir, andar, seguir ⟨my exam went well : me fue bien en el examen⟩ ⟨how did the meeting go? : ¿qué tal la reunión?⟩ **8** BECOME : volverse, quedarse ⟨he's going crazy : está volviéndose loco⟩ ⟨the tire went flat : la llanta se desinfló⟩ **9** FIT : caber ⟨it will go through the door : cabe por la puerta⟩ **10** anything goes! : ¡todo vale! **11 to go** : faltar ⟨only 10 days to go : faltan sólo 10 días⟩ **12 to go back on** : faltar una a (su promesa) **13 to go bad** SPOIL : estropearse, echarse a perder **14 to go for** : interesarse uno en, gustarle a uno (algo, alguien) ⟨I don't go for that : eso

no me interesa⟩ **15 to go off** EXPLODE : estallar **16 to go with** MATCH : armonizar con, hacer juego con — *v aux* **to be going to** : ir a ⟨I'm going to write a letter : voy a escribir una carta⟩ ⟨it's not going to last : no va a durar⟩

go² *n, pl* **goes 1** ATTEMPT : intento *m* ⟨to have a go at : intentar, probar⟩ **2** SUCCESS : éxito *m* **3** ENERGY : energía *f*, empuje *m* ⟨to be on the go : no parar, no descansar⟩

goad¹ ['go:d] *vt* : aguijonear (un animal), incitar (a una persona)

goad² *n* : aguijón *m*

goal ['go:l] *n* **1** : gol *m* (en deportes) ⟨to score a goal : anotar un gol⟩ **2** *or* **goalposts** : portería *f* **3** AIM, OBJECTIVE : meta *m*, objetivo *m*

goalie ['go:li] → **goalkeeper**

goalkeeper ['go:lˌki:pər] *n* : portero *m*, -ra *f*; guardameta *mf*; arquero *m*, -ra *f*

goaltender ['go:lˌtɛndər] → **goalkeeper**

goat ['go:t] *n* **1** : cabra *f* (hembra) **2** billy goat : macho *m* cabrío, chivo *m*

goatee [go:'ti:] *n* : barbita *f* de chivo, piocha *f Mex*

goatskin ['go:tˌskɪn] *n* : piel *f* de cabra

gob ['gɑb] *n* : masa *f*, grumo *m*

gobble ['gɑbəl] *v* **-bled; -bling** *vt* **to gobble up** : tragar, engullir — *vi* : hacer ruidos de pavo

gobbledygook ['gɑbəldiˌgʊk, -ˌgu:k] *n* GIBBERISH : jerigonza *f*

go-between ['go:bɪˌtwi:n] *n* : intermediario *m*, -ria *f*; mediador *m*, -dora *f*

goblet ['gɑblət] *n* : copa *f*

goblin ['gɑblən] *n* : duende *m*, trasgo *m*

god ['gɑd, 'gɔd] *n* **1** : dios *m* **2** God : Dios *m*

godchild ['gɑdˌtʃaɪld, 'gɔd-] *n, pl* **-children** : ahijado *m*, -da *f*

goddess ['gɑdəs, 'gɔ-] *n* : diosa *f*

godfather ['gɑdˌfɑðər, 'gɔd-] *n* : padrino *m*

godless ['gɑdləs, 'gɔd-] *adj* : ateo

godlike ['gɑdˌlaɪk, 'gɔd-] *adj* : divino

godly ['gɑdli, 'gɔd-] *adj* **-lier; -est 1** DIVINE : divino **2** DEVOUT, PIOUS : piadoso, devoto, beato

godmother ['gɑdˌmʌðər, 'gɔd-] *n* : madrina *f*

godparents ['gɑdˌpærənts, 'gɔd-] *npl* : padrinos *mpl*

godsend ['gɑdˌsɛnd, 'gɔd-] *n* : bendición *f*, regalo *m* divino

goes → **go**

go-getter ['go:ˌgɛtər] *n* : persona *f* ambiciosa, buscavidas *mf fam*

goggle ['gɑgəl] *vi* **-gled; -gling** : mirar con ojos desorbitados

goggles ['gɑgəlz] *npl* : gafas *fpl* (protectoras), anteojos *mpl*

goings-on [ˌgo:ɪŋz'ɑn, -'ɔn] *npl* : sucesos *mpl*, ocurrencias *fpl*

goiter ['gɔɪtər] *n* : bocio *m*

gold ['go:ld] *n* : oro *m*

golden ['go:ldən] *adj* **1** : (hecho) de oro **2** : dorado, de color oro ⟨golden hair

: pelo rubio⟩ **3** FLOURISHING, PROSPEROUS : dorado, próspero ⟨golden years : años dorados⟩ **4** FAVORABLE : favorable, excelente ⟨a golden opportunity : una excelente oportunidad⟩

goldenrod ['go:ldən,rɑd] *n* : vara *f* de oro

golden rule *n* : regla *f* de oro

goldfinch ['go:ld,fɪntʃ] *n* : jilguero *m*

goldfish ['go:ld,fɪʃ] *n* : pez *m* de colores

goldsmith ['go:ld,smɪθ] *n* : orífice *mf*, orfebre *mf*

golf[1] ['gɑlf, 'gɔlf] *vi* : jugar (al) golf

golf[2] *n* : golf *m*

golfer ['gɑlfər, 'gɔl-] *n* : golfista *mf*

gondola ['gɑndələ, gɑn'do:lə] *n* : góndola *f*

gone ['gɔn] *adj* **1** DEAD : muerto **2** PAST : pasado, ido **3** LOST : perdido, desaparecido **4 to be far gone** : estar muy avanzado **5 to be gone on** : estar loco por

goner ['gɔnər] *n* **to be a goner** : estar en las últimas

gong ['gɔŋ, 'gɑŋ] *n* : gong *m*

gonorrhea [,gɑnə'ri:ə] *n* : gonorrea *f*

good[1] ['gʊd] *adv* **1** (*used as an intensifier*) : bien ⟨a good strong rope : una cuerda bien fuerte⟩ **2** WELL : bien

good[2] *adj* **better** ['bɛtər]; **best** ['bɛst] **1** PLEASANT : bueno, agradable ⟨good news : buenas noticias⟩ ⟨to have a good time : divertirse⟩ **2** BENEFICIAL : bueno, beneficioso ⟨good for a cold : beneficioso para los resfriados⟩ ⟨it's good for you : es bueno para uno⟩ **3** FULL : completo, entero ⟨a good hour : una hora entera⟩ **4** CONSIDERABLE : bueno, bastante ⟨a good many people : muchísima gente, un buen número de gente⟩ **5** ATTRACTIVE, DESIRABLE : bueno, bien ⟨a good salary : un buen sueldo⟩ ⟨to look good : quedar bien⟩ **6** KIND, VIRTUOUS : bueno, amable ⟨she's a good person : es buena gente⟩ ⟨that's good of you! : ¡qué amable!⟩ ⟨good deeds : buenas obras⟩ **7** SKILLED : bueno, hábil ⟨to be good at : tener facilidad para⟩ **8** SOUND : bueno, sensato ⟨good advice : buenos consejos⟩ **9** (*in greetings*) : bueno ⟨good morning : buenos días⟩ ⟨good afternoon (evening) : buenas tardes⟩ ⟨good night : buenas noches⟩

good[3] *n* **1** RIGHT : bien *m* ⟨to do good : hacer el bien⟩ **2** GOODNESS : bondad *f* **3** BENEFIT : bien *m*, provecho *m* ⟨it's for your own good : es por tu propio bien⟩ **4 goods** *npl* PROPERTY : efectos *mpl* personales, posesiones *fpl* **5 goods** *npl* WARES : mercancía *f*, mercadería *f*, artículos *mpl* **6 for ~** : para siempre

good–bye *or* **good–by** [gʊd'baɪ] *n* : adiós *m*

good–for–nothing ['gʊdfər,nʌθɪŋ] *n* : inútil *mf*; haragán *m*, -gana *f*; holgazán *m*, -zana *f*

Good Friday *n* : Viernes *m* Santo

good–hearted ['gʊd'hɑrtəd] *adj* : bondadoso, benévolo, de buen corazón

good–looking ['gʊd'lʊkɪŋ] *adj* : bello, bonito, guapo

goodly ['gʊdli] *adj* **-lier; -est** : considerable, importante ⟨a goodly number : un número considerable⟩

good–natured ['gʊd'neɪtʃərd] *adj* : amigable, amistoso, bonachón *fam*

goodness ['gʊdnəs] *n* **1** : bondad *f* **2 thank goodness!** : ¡gracias a Dios!, ¡menos mal!

good–tempered ['gʊd'tɛmpərd] *adj* : de buen genio

goodwill [,gʊd'wɪl] *n* **1** BENEVOLENCE : benevolencia *f*, buena voluntad *f* **2** : buen nombre *m* (de comercios), renombre *m* comercial

goody ['gʊdi] *n, pl* **goodies** : cosa *f* rica para comer, golosina *f*

gooey ['gu:i] *adj* **gooier; gooiest** : pegajoso

goof[1] ['gu:f] *vi* **1 to goof off** : holgazanear **2 to goof around** : hacer tonterías **3 to goof up** BLUNDER : cometer un error

goof[2] *n* **1** : bobo *m*, -ba *f*; tonto *m*, -ta *f* **2** BLUNDER : error *m*, planchazo *m fam*

goofy ['gu:fi] *adj* **goofier; -est** SILLY : tonto, bobo

goose ['gu:s] *n, pl* **geese** ['gi:s] : ganso *m*, -sa *f*; ánsar *m*; oca *f*

gooseberry ['gu:s,bɛri:, 'gu:z-] *n, pl* **-berries** : grosella *f* espinosa

goose bumps *npl* : carne *f* de gallina

gooseflesh ['gu:s,flɛʃ] → **goose bumps**

goose pimples → **goose bumps**

gopher ['go:fər] *n* : taltuza *f*

gore[1] ['gor] *vt* **gored; goring** : cornear

gore[2] *n* BLOOD : sangre *f*

gorge[1] ['gɔrdʒ] *vt* **gorged; gorging 1** SATIATE : saciar, hartar **2 to gorge oneself** : hartarse, atiborrarse, atracarse *fam*

gorge[2] *n* RAVINE : desfiladero *m*

gorgeous ['gɔrdʒəs] *adj* : hermoso, espléndido, magnífico

gorilla [gə'rɪlə] *n* : gorila *m*

gory ['gori] *adj* **gorier; -est** BLOODY : sangriento

gosling ['gɑzlɪŋ, 'gɔz-] *n* : ansarino *m*

gospel ['gɑspəl] *n* **1** *or* **Gospel** : evangelio *m* ⟨the four Gospels : los cuatro evangelios⟩ **2 the gospel truth** : el evangelio, la pura verdad

gossamer ['gɑsəmər, 'gɑzə-] *adj* : tenue, sutil ⟨gossamer wings : alas tenues⟩

gossip[1] ['gɑsɪp] *vi* : chismear, contar chismes

gossip[2] *n* **1** : chismoso *m*, -sa *f* (persona) **2** RUMOR : chisme *m*, rumor *m*

gossipy ['gɑsɪpi] *adj* : chismoso

got → **get**

Gothic ['gɑθɪk] *adj* : gótico

gotten → **get**

gouge[1] ['gaʊdʒ] *vt* **gouged; gouging 1** : excavar, escoplear (con una gubia) **2** SWINDLE : estafar, extorsionar

gouge² *n* **1** CHISEL : gubia *f*, formón *m* **2** GROOVE : ranura *f*, hoyo *m* (hecho por un formón)

goulash ['guː₁lɑʃ, -₁læʃ] *n* : estofado *m*, guiso *m* al estilo húngaro

gourd ['gord, 'gurd] *n* : calabaza *f*

gourmand ['gur₁mɑnd] *n* **1** GLUTTON : glotón *m*, -tona *f* **2** → gourmet

gourmet ['gur₁meɪ, gur'meɪ] *n* : gourmet *mf*; gastrónomo *m*, -ma *f*

gout ['gaut] *n* : gota *f*

govern ['gʌvərn] *vt* **1** RULE : gobernar **2** CONTROL, DETERMINE : determinar, controlar, guiar **3** RESTRAIN : dominar (las emociones, etc.) — *vi* : gobernar

governess ['gʌvərnəs] *n* : institutriz *f*

government ['gʌvərmənt] *n* : gobierno *m*

governmental [₁gʌvər'mɛntəl] *adj* : gubernamental, gubernativo

governor ['gʌvənər, 'gʌvərnər] *n* **1** : gobernador *m*, - dora *f* (de un estado, etc.) **2** : regulador *m* (de una máquina)

governorship ['gʌvənər₁ʃɪp, 'gʌvərnər-] *n* : cargo *m* de gobernador

gown ['gaun] *n* **1** : vestido *m* ⟨evening gown : traje de fiesta⟩ **2** : toga *f* (de magistrados, clérigos, etc.)

grab¹ ['græb] *v* **grabbed; grabbing** *vt* SNATCH : agarrar, arrebatar — *vi* : agarrarse

grab² *n* **1 to make a grab for** : tratar de agarrar **2 up for grabs** : disponible, libre

grace¹ ['greɪs] *vt* **graced; gracing 1** HONOR : honrar **2** ADORN : adornar, embellecer

grace² *n* **1** : gracia *f* ⟨by the grace of God : por la gracia de Dios⟩ **2** BLESSING : bendición *f* (de la mesa) **3** RESPITE : plazo *m*, gracia *f* ⟨a five days' grace (period) : un plazo de cinco días⟩ **4** GRACIOUSNESS : gentileza *f*, cortesía *f* **5** ELEGANCE : elegancia *f*, gracia *f* **6 to be in the good graces of** : estar en buenas relaciones con **7 with good grace** : de buena gana

graceful ['greɪsfəl] *adj* : lleno de gracia, garboso, grácil

gracefully ['greɪsfəli] *adv* : con gracia, con garbo

gracefulness ['greɪsfəlnəs] *n* : gracilidad *f*, apostura *f*, gallardía *f*

graceless ['greɪsləs] *adj* **1** DISCOURTEOUS : descortés **2** CLUMSY, INELEGANT : torpe, desgarbado, poco elegante

gracious ['greɪʃəs] *adj* : cortés, gentil, cordial

graciously ['greɪʃəsli] *adv* : gentilmente

graciousness ['greɪʃəsnəs] *n* : gentileza *f*

gradation [greɪ'deɪʃən, grə-] *n* : gradación *f*

grade¹ ['greɪd] *vt* **graded; grading 1** SORT : clasificar **2** LEVEL : nivelar **3** : calificar (exámenes, alumnos)

grade² *n* **1** QUALITY : categoría *f*, calidad *f* **2** RANK : grado *m*, rango *m* (mil-

itar) **3** YEAR : grado *m*, curso *m*, año *m* ⟨sixth grade : el sexto grado⟩ **4** MARK : nota *f*, calificación *f* (en educación) **5** SLOPE : cuesta *f*, pendiente *f*, gradiente *f*

grade school → **elementary school**

gradient ['greɪdiənt] *n* : gradiente *f*

gradual ['grædʒuəl] *adj* : gradual, paulatino

gradually ['grædʒuəli, 'grædʒəli] *adv* : gradualmente, poco a poco

graduate¹ ['grædʒu₁eɪt] *v* **-ated; -ating** *vi* : graduarse, licenciarse — *vt* : graduar ⟨a graduated thermometer : un termómetro graduado⟩

graduate² ['grædʒuət] *adj* : de postgrado ⟨graduate course : curso de postgrado⟩

graduate³ *n* **1** : licenciado *m*, -da *f*; graduado *m*, -da *f* (de la universidad) **2** : bachiller *mf* (de la escuela secundaria)

graduate student *n* : postgraduado *m*, -da *f*

graduation [₁grædʒu'eɪʃən] *n* : graduación *f*

graffiti [grə'fiːṭi, græ-] *npl* : pintadas *fpl*, graffiti *mpl*

graft¹ ['græft] *vt* : injertar

graft² *n* **1** : injerto *m* ⟨skin graft : injerto cutáneo⟩ **2** CORRUPTION : soborno *m* (político), ganancia *f* ilegal

grain ['greɪn] *n* **1** : grano *m* ⟨a grain of corn : un grano de maíz⟩ ⟨like a grain of sand : como grano de arena⟩ **2** CEREALS : cereales *mpl* **3** : veta *f*, vena *f*, grano *m* (de madera) **4** SPECK, TRACE : pizca *f*, ápice *m* ⟨a grain of truth : una pizca de verdad⟩ **5** grano *m* (unidad de peso)

gram ['græm] *n* : gramo *m*

grammar ['græmər] *n* : gramática *f*

grammar school → **elementary school**

grammatical [grə'mæṭɪkəl] *adj* : gramatical — **grammatically** [-kli] *adv*

granary ['greɪnəri, 'græ-] *n*, *pl* **-ries** : granero *m*

grand ['grænd] *adj* **1** FOREMOST : grande **2** IMPRESSIVE : impresionante, magnífico ⟨a grand view : una vista magnífica⟩ **3** LAVISH : grandioso, suntuoso, lujoso ⟨to live in a grand manner : vivir a lo grande⟩ **4** FABULOUS : fabuloso, magnífico ⟨to have a grand time : pasarlo estupendamente, pasarlo en grande⟩ **5 grand total** : total *m*, suma *f* total

grandchild ['grænd₁tʃaɪld] *n*, *pl* **-children** : nieto *m*, -ta *f*

granddaughter ['grænd₁dɔṭər] *n* : nieta *f*

grandeur ['grændʒər] *n* : grandiosidad *f*, esplendor *m*

grandfather ['grænd₁fɑðər] *n* : abuelo *m*

grandiose ['grændi₁oːs, ₁grændi'-] *adj* **1** IMPOSING : imponente, grandioso **2** POMPOUS : pomposo, presuntuoso

grandma ['græn₁mɑ, -₁mɔ] *n* : abuelita *f*, nana *f*

grandmother ['grænd,mʌðər] *n* : abuela *f*

grandpa ['græm,pɑ, -,pɔ] *n* : abuelito *m*

grandparents ['grænd,pærənts] *npl* : abuelos *mpl*

grandson ['grænd,sʌn] *n* : nieto *m*

grandstand ['grænd,stænd] *n* : tribuna *f*

granite ['grænɪt] *n* : granito *m*

grant[1] ['grænt] *vt* **1** ALLOW : conceder ⟨to grant a request : conceder una petición⟩ **2** BESTOW : conceder, dar, otorgar ⟨to grant a favor : otorgar un favor⟩ **3** ADMIT : reconocer, admitir ⟨I'll grant that he's clever : reconozco que es listo⟩ **4 to take for granted** : dar (algo) por sentado

grant[2] *n* **1** GRANTING : concesión *f*, otorgamiento *m* **2** SCHOLARSHIP : beca *f* **3** SUBSIDY : subvención *f*

granular ['grænjʊlər] *adj* : granular

granulated ['grænjʊ,leɪt̬əd] *adj* : granulado

grape ['greɪp] *n* : uva *f*

grapefruit ['greɪp,fru:t] *n* : toronja *f*, pomelo *m*

grapevine ['greɪp,vaɪn] *n* **1** : vid *f*, parra *f* **2 through the grapevine** : por vías secretas ⟨I heard it through the grapevine : me lo contaron⟩

graph ['græf] *n* : gráfica *f*, gráfico *m*

graphic ['græfɪk] *adj* **1** VIVID : vívido, gráfico **2 graphic arts** : artes gráficas

graphically ['græfɪkli] *adv* : gráficamente

graphite ['græ,faɪt] *n* : grafito *m*

grapnel ['græpnəl] *n* : rezón *m*

grapple ['græpəl] *v* **-pled; -pling** *vt* GRIP : agarrar (con un garfio) — *vi* STRUGGLE : forcejear, luchar (con un problema, etc.)

grasp[1] ['græsp] *vt* **1** GRIP, SEIZE : agarrar, asir **2** COMPREHEND : entender, comprender — *vi* **to grasp at** : aprovechar

grasp[2] *n* **1** GRIP : agarre *m* **2** CONTROL : control *m*, garras *fpl* **3** REACH : alcance *m* ⟨within your grasp : a su alcance⟩ **4** UNDERSTANDING : comprensión *f*, entendimiento *m*

grass ['græs] *n* **1** : hierba *f* (planta) **2** PASTURE : pasto *m*, zacate *m* CA, Mex **3** LAWN : césped *m*, pasto *m*

grasshopper ['græs,hɑpər] *n* : saltamontes *m*

grassland ['græs,lænd] *n* : pradera *f*

grassy ['græsi] *adj* **grassier; -est** : cubierto de hierba

grate[1] ['greɪt] *v* **grated; -ing** *vt* **1** : rallar (en cocina) **2** SCRAPE : rascar **3 to grate one's teeth** : hacer rechinar los dientes — *vi* **1** RASP, SQUEAK : chirriar **2** IRRITATE : irritar ⟨to grate on one's nerves : crisparle los nervios a uno⟩

grate[2] *n* **1** : parrilla *f* (para cocinar) **2** GRATING : reja *f*, rejilla *f*, verja *f* (en una ventana)

grateful ['greɪtfəl] *adj* : agradecido

gratefully ['greɪtfəli] *adv* : con agradecimiento

gratefulness ['greɪtfəlnəs] *n* : gratitud *f*, agradecimiento *m*

grater ['greɪt̬ər] *n* : rallador *m*

gratification [,grætəfə'keɪʃən] *n* : gratificación *f*

gratify ['grætə,faɪ] *vt* **-fied; -fying 1** PLEASE : complacer **2** SATISFY : satisfacer, gratificar

grating ['greɪt̬ɪŋ] *n* : reja *f*, rejilla *f*

gratis[1] ['græt̬əs, 'greɪ-] *adv* : gratis, gratuitamente

gratis[2] *adj* : gratis, gratuito

gratitude ['græt̬ə,tu:d, -,tju:d] *n* : gratitud *f*, agradecimiento *m*

gratuitous [grə'tu:ət̬əs] *adj* : gratuito

gratuity [grə'tu:ət̬i] *n, pl* **-ities** TIP : propina *f*

grave[1] ['greɪv] *adj* **graver; -est 1** IMPORTANT : grave, de mucha gravedad **2** SERIOUS, SOLEMN : grave, serio

grave[2] *n* : tumba *f*, sepultura *f*

gravel ['grævəl] *n* : grava *f*, gravilla *f*

gravelly ['grævəli] *adj* **1** : de grava **2** HARSH : áspero (dícese de la voz)

gravely ['greɪvli] *adv* : gravemente

gravestone ['greɪv,sto:n] *n* : lápida *f*

graveyard ['greɪv,jɑrd] *n* CEMETERY : cementerio *m*, panteón *m*, camposanto *m*

gravitate ['grævə,teɪt] *vi* **-tated; -tating** : gravitar

gravitation [,grævə'teɪʃən] *n* : gravitación *f*

gravitational [,grævə'teɪʃənəl] *adj* : gravitacional

gravity ['grævət̬i] *n, pl* **-ties 1** SERIOUSNESS : gravedad *f*, seriedad *f* **2** : gravedad *f* ⟨the law of gravity : la ley de la gravedad⟩

gravy ['greɪvi] *n, pl* **-vies** : salsa *f* (preparada con el jugo de la carne asada)

gray[1] ['greɪ] *vt* : hacer gris — *vi* : encanecer, ponerse gris

gray[2] *adj* **1** : gris (dícese del color) **2** : cano, canoso ⟨gray hair : pelo canoso⟩ ⟨to go gray : volverse cano⟩ **3** DISMAL, GLOOMY : gris, triste

gray[3] *n* : gris *m*

grayish ['greɪɪʃ] *adj* : grisáceo

graze ['greɪz] *v* **grazed; grazing** *vi* : pastar, pacer — *vt* **1** : pastorear (ganado) **2** BRUSH : rozar **3** SCRATCH : raspar

grease[1] ['gri:s, 'gri:z] *vt* **greased; greasing** : engrasar, lubricar

grease[2] ['gri:s] *n* : grasa *f*

greasy ['gri:si, -zi] *adj* **greasier; -est 1** : grasiento **2** OILY : graso, grasoso

great ['greɪt] *adj* **1** LARGE : grande ⟨a great mountain : una montaña grande⟩ ⟨a great crowd : una gran muchedumbre⟩ **2** INTENSE : intenso, fuerte, grande ⟨great pain : gran dolor⟩ **3** EMINENT : grande, eminente, distinguido ⟨a great poet : un gran poeta⟩ **4** EXCELLENT, TERRIFIC : excelente, estu-

pendo, fabuloso ⟨to have a great time
: pasarlo en grande⟩ **5 a great while**
: mucho tiempo
great–aunt [ˌgreɪt'ænt, -'ant] *n* : tía *f*
abuela
greater ['greɪt̬ər] (*comparative* of **great**)
: mayor
greatest ['greɪt̬əst] (*superlative* of **great**)
: el mayor, la mayor
great–grandchild [ˌgreɪt'grænd-ˌt͡ʃaɪld]
n, pl **-children** [-ˌt͡ʃɪldrən] : bisnieto *m*,
-ta *f*
great–grandfather [ˌgreɪt'grænd-ˌfɑðər]
n : bisabuelo *m*
great–grandmother [ˌgreɪt'grænd-
ˌmʌðər] *n* : bisabuela *f*
greatly ['greɪtli] *adv* **1** MUCH : mucho,
sumamente ⟨to be greatly improved
: haber mejorado mucho⟩ **2** VERY
: muy ⟨greatly superior : muy superi-
or⟩
greatness ['greɪtnəs] *n* : grandeza *f*
great–uncle [ˌgreɪt'ʌŋkəl] *n* : tío *m* abuelo
grebe ['gri:b] *n* : somorgujo *m*
greed ['gri:d] *n* **1** AVARICE : avaricia *f*,
codicia *f* **2** GLUTTONY : glotonería *f*,
gula *f*
greedily ['gri:dəli] *adv* : con avaricia,
con gula
greediness ['gri:dinəs] → **greed**
greedy ['gri:di] *adj* **greedier; -est** **1**
AVARICIOUS : codicioso, avaricioso **2**
GLUTTONOUS : glotón
Greek ['gri:k] *n* **1** : griego *m*, -ga *f* **2**
: griego *m* (idioma) — **Greek** *adj*
green[1] ['gri:n] *adj* **1** : verde (dícese del
color) **2** UNRIPE : verde, inmaduro **3**
INEXPERIENCED : verde, novato
green[2] *n* **1** : verde *m* **2 greens** *npl* VEG-
ETABLES : verduras *fpl*
greenery ['gri:nəri] *n, pl* **-eries** : plantas
fpl verdes, vegetación *f*
greenhorn ['gri:nˌhorn] *n* : novato *m*, -ta
f
greenhouse ['gri:nˌhaʊs] *n* : invernadero *m*
greenhouse effect : efecto *m* invernadero
greenish ['gri:nɪʃ] *adj* : verdoso
Greenlander ['gri:nləndər, -ˌlæn-] *n*
: groenlandés *m*, -desa *f*
greenness ['gri:nnəs] *n* **1** : verdor *m* **2**
INEXPERIENCE : inexperiencia *f*
green thumb *n* **to have a green thumb**
: tener buena mano para las plantas
greet ['gri:t] *vt* **1** : saludar ⟨to greet a
friend : saludar a un amigo⟩ **2** : acoger,
recibir ⟨they greeted him with boos : lo
recibieron con abucheos⟩
greeting ['gri:tɪŋ] *n* **1** : saludo *m* **2**
greetings *npl* REGARDS : saludos *mpl*,
recuerdos *mpl*
gregarious [grɪ'gæriəs] *adj* : gregario
(dícese de los animales), sociable
(dícese de las personas) — **gregari-
ously** *adv*
gregariousness [grɪ'gæriəsnəs] *n* : sociabilidad *f*

gremlin ['grɛmlən] *n* : duende *m*
grenade [grə'neɪd] *n* : granada *f*
Grenadian [grə'neɪdiən] *n* : granadino
m, -na *f* — **Grenadian** *adj*
grew → **grow**
grey → **gray**
greyhound ['greɪˌhaʊnd] *n* : galgo *m*
grid ['grɪd] *n* **1** GRATING : rejilla *f* **2** NET-
WORK : red *f* (de electricidad, etc.) **3**
: cuadriculado *m* (de un mapa)
griddle ['grɪdəl] *n* : plancha *f*
griddle cake → **pancake**
gridiron ['grɪdˌaɪərn] *n* **1** GRILL : parrilla *f* **2** : campo *m* de futbol americano
gridlock ['grɪdˌlɑk] *n* : atasco *m* completo (de una red de calles)
grief ['gri:f] *n* **1** SORROW : dolor *m*, pena
f **2** ANNOYANCE, TROUBLE : proble-
mas *mpl*, molestia *f*
grievance ['gri:vənts] *n* COMPLAINT
: queja *f*
grieve ['gri:v] *v* **grieved; grieving** *vt* DIS-
TRESS : afligir, entristecer, apenar — *vi*
1 : sufrir, afligirse **2 to grieve for** *or* **to
grieve over** : llorar, lamentar
grievous ['gri:vəs] *adj* **1** OPPRESSIVE
: gravoso, opresivo, severo **2** GRAVE,
SERIOUS : grave, severo, doloroso
grievously ['gri:vəsli] *adv* : gravemente,
de gravedad
grill[1] ['grɪl] *vt* **1** : asar (a la parrilla) **2**
INTERROGATE : interrogar
grill[2] *n* **1** : parrilla *f* (para cocinar) **2**
: parrillada *f* (comida) **3** RESTAURANT
: grill *m*
grille *or* **grill** ['grɪl] *n* : reja *f*, enrejado *m*
grim ['grɪm] *adj* **grimmer; grimmest** **1**
CRUEL : cruel, feroz **2** STERN : adusto, severo ⟨a grim expression : un gesto
severo⟩ **3** GLOOMY : sombrío, deprimente **4** SINISTER : macabro, siniestro
5 UNYIELDING : inflexible, persistente
⟨with grim determination : con una
voluntad de hierro⟩
grimace[1] ['grɪməs, grɪ'meɪs] *vi* **-maced;
-macing** : hacer muecas
grimace[2] *n* : mueca *f*
grime ['graɪm] *n* : mugre *f*, suciedad *f*
grimly ['grɪmli] *adv* **1** STERNLY : severamente **2** RESOLUTELY : inexorablemente
grimy ['graɪmi] *adj* **grimier; -est** : mugriento, sucio
grin[1] ['grɪn] *vi* **grinned; grinning** : sonreír abiertamente
grin[2] *n* : sonrisa *f* abierta
grind[1] ['graɪnd] *v* **ground** ['graʊnd];
grinding *vt* **1** CRUSH : moler,
machacar, triturar **2** SHARPEN : afilar
3 POLISH : pulir, esmerilar (lentes, es-
pejos) **4 to grind one's teeth** : rechi-
narle los dientes a uno **5 to grind down**
OPPRESS : oprimir, agobiar — *vi* **1**
: funcionar con dificultad, rechinar ⟨to
grind to a halt : pararse poco a poco,
llegar a un punto muerto⟩ **2** STUDY
: estudiar mucho

grind² *n* : trabajo *m* pesado ⟨the daily grind : la rutina diaria⟩

grinder ['graɪndər] *n* : molinillo *m* ⟨coffee grinder : molinillo de café⟩

grindstone ['graɪnd,sto:n] *n* : piedra *m* de afilar

grip¹ ['grɪp] *vt* **gripped; gripping 1** GRASP : agarrar, asir **2** HOLD, INTEREST : captar el interés de

grip² *n* **1** GRASP : agarre *m*, asidero *m* ⟨to have a firm grip on something : agarrarse bien de algo⟩ **2** CONTROL, HOLD : control *m*, dominio *m* ⟨to lose one's grip on : perder el control de⟩ ⟨inflation tightened its grip on the economy : la inflación se afianzó en su dominio de la economía⟩ **3** UNDERSTANDING : comprensión *f*, entendimiento *m* ⟨to come to grips with : llegar a entender⟩ **4** HANDLE : asidero *m*, empuñadura *f* (de un arma)

gripe¹ ['graɪp] *v* **griped; griping** *vt* IRRITATE, VEX : irritar, fastidiar, molestar — *vi* COMPLAIN : quejarse, rezongar

gripe² *n* : queja *f*

grippe ['grɪp] *n* : influenza *f*, gripe *f*, gripa *f* Col, Mex

grisly ['grɪzli] *adj* **-lier; -est** : horripilante, horroroso, truculento

grist ['grɪst] *n* : molienda *f* ⟨it's all grist for the mill : todo ayuda, todo es provechoso⟩

gristle ['grɪsəl] *n* : cartílago *m*

gristly ['grɪsli] *adj* **-tlier; -est** : cartilaginoso

grit¹ ['grɪt] *vt* **gritted; gritting** : hacer rechinar (los dientes, etc.)

grit² *n* **1** SAND : arena *f* **2** GRAVEL : grava *f* **3** COURAGE : valor *m*, coraje *m* **4** **grits** *npl* : sémola *f* de maíz

gritty ['grɪti] *adj* **-tier; -est 1** : arenoso ⟨a gritty surface : una superficie arenosa⟩ **2** PLUCKY : valiente

grizzled ['grɪzəld] *adj* : entrecano

grizzly bear ['grɪzli] *n* : oso *m* pardo

groan¹ ['gro:n] *vi* **1** MOAN : gemir, quejarse **2** CREAK : crujir

groan² *n* **1** MOAN : gemido *m*, quejido *m* **2** CREAK : crujido *m*

grocer ['gro:sər] *n* : tendero *m*, -ra *f*

grocery ['gro:səri, -ʃəri] *n, pl* **-ceries 1** *or* **grocery store** : tienda *f* de comestibles, tienda *f* de abarrotes **2** **groceries** *npl* : comestibles *mpl*, abarrotes *mpl*

groggy ['grɑgi] *adj* **-gier; -est** : atontado, grogui, tambaleante

groin ['grɔɪn] *n* : ingle *f*

grommet ['grɑmət, 'grʌ-] *n* : arandela *f*

groom¹ ['gru:m, 'grʊm] *vt* **1** : cepillar, almohazar (un animal) **2** : arreglar, cuidar ⟨well-groomed : bien arreglado⟩ **3** PREPARE : preparar

groom² *n* **1** : mozo *m*, -za *f* de cuadra **2** BRIDEGROOM : novio *m*

groove¹ ['gru:v] *vt* **grooved; grooving** : acanalar, hacer ranuras en, surcar

groove² *n* **1** FURROW, SLOT : ranura *f*, surco *m* **2** RUT : rutina *f*

grope ['gro:p] *v* **groped; groping** *vi* : andar a tientas, tantear ⟨he groped for the switch : buscó el interruptor a tientas⟩ — *vt* **to grope one's way** : avanzar a tientas

gross¹ ['gro:s] *vt* : tener entrada bruta de, recaudar en bruto

gross² *adj* **1** FLAGRANT : flagrante, grave ⟨a gross error : un error flagrante⟩ ⟨a gross injustice : una injusticia grave⟩ **2** FAT : muy gordo, obeso **3** : bruto ⟨gross national product : producto nacional bruto⟩ **4** COARSE, VULGAR : grosero, basto

gross³ *n* **1** *pl* **gross** : gruesa *f* (12 docenas) **2** *or* **gross income** : ingresos *mpl* brutos

grossly ['gro:sli] *adv* **1** EXTREMELY : extremadamente ⟨grossly unfair : totalmente injusto⟩ **2** CRUDELY : groseramente

grotesque [gro:'tɛsk] *adj* : grotesco

grotesquely [gro:'tɛskli] *adv* : de forma grotesca

grotto ['grɑto:] *n, pl* **-toes** : gruta *f*

grouch¹ ['graʊtʃ] *vi* : refunfuñar, rezongar

grouch² *n* **1** COMPLAINT : queja *f* **2** GRUMBLER : gruñón *m*, -ñona *f*; cascarrabias *mf fam*

grouchy ['graʊtʃi] *adj* **grouchier; -est** : malhumorado, gruñón

ground¹ ['graʊnd] *vt* **1** BASE : fundar, basar **2** INSTRUCT : enseñar los conocimientos básicos a ⟨to be well grounded in : ser muy entendido en⟩ **3** : conectar a tierra (un aparato eléctrico) **4** : varar, hacer encallar (un barco) **5** : restringir (un avión o un piloto) a la tierra

ground² *n* **1** EARTH, SOIL : suelo *m*, tierra *f* ⟨to dig (in) the ground : cavar la tierra⟩ ⟨to fall to the ground : caerse al suelo⟩ **2** LAND, TERRAIN : terreno *m* ⟨hilly ground : terreno alto⟩ ⟨to lose ground : perder terreno⟩ **3** BASIS, REASON : razón *f*, motivo *m* ⟨grounds for complaint : motivos de queja⟩ **4** BACKGROUND : fondo *m* **5** FIELD : campo *m*, plaza *f* ⟨parade ground : plaza de armas⟩ **6** : tierra *f* (para electricidad) **7** **grounds** *npl* PREMISES : recinto *m*, terreno *m* **8** **grounds** *npl* DREGS : posos *mpl* (de café)

ground³ → **grind**

groundhog ['graʊnd,hɔg] *n* : marmota *f* (de América)

groundless ['graʊndləs] *adj* : infundado

groundwork ['graʊnd,wərk] *n* **1** FOUNDATION : fundamento *m*, base *f* **2** PREPARATION : trabajo *m* preparatorio

group¹ ['gru:p] *vt* : agrupar

group² *n* : grupo *m*, agrupación *f*, conjunto *m*, compañía *f*

grouper ['gru:pər] *n* : mero *m*

grouse¹ ['graʊs] *vi* **groused; grousing** : quejarse, rezongar, refunfuñar

grouse² *n, pl* **grouse** *or* **grouses** : urogallo *m* (ave)

grout ['graʊt] *n* : lechada *f*

grove ['groːv] *n* : bosquecillo *m*, arboleda *f*, soto *m*

grovel ['grɑvəl, 'grʌ-] *vi* **-eled** *or* **-elled; -eling** *or* **-elling 1** CRAWL : arrastrarse **2** : humillarse, postrarse ⟨to grovel before someone : postrarse ante alguien⟩

grow ['groː] *v* **grew** ['gruː]; **grown** ['groːn]; **growing** *vi* **1** : crecer ⟨palm trees grow on the islands : las palmas crecen en las islas⟩ ⟨my hair grows very fast : mi pelo crece muy rápido⟩ **2** DEVELOP, MATURE : desarrollarse, madurar **3** INCREASE : crecer, aumentar **4** BECOME : hacerse, volverse, ponerse ⟨she was growing angry : se estaba poniendo furiosa⟩ ⟨to grow dark : oscurecerse⟩ **5 to grow up** : hacerse mayor ⟨grow up! : ¡no seas niño!⟩ — *vt* **1** CULTIVATE, RAISE : cultivar **2** : dejar crecer ⟨to grow one's hair : dejarse crecer el pelo⟩

grower ['groːər] *n* : cultivador *m*, -dora *f*

growl¹ ['graʊl] *vi* : gruñir (dícese de un animal), refunfuñar (dícese de una persona)

growl² *n* : gruñido *m*

grown–up¹ ['groːn,ʌp] *adj* : adulto, mayor

grown–up² *n* : adulto *m*, -ta *f*; persona *f* mayor

growth ['groːθ] *n* **1** : crecimiento *m* ⟨to stunt one's growth : detener el crecimiento⟩ **2** INCREASE : aumento *m*, crecimiento *m*, expansión *f* **3** DEVELOPMENT : desarrollo *m* ⟨economic growth : desarrollo económico⟩ ⟨a five days' growth of beard : una barba de cinco días⟩ **4** LUMP, TUMOR : bulto *m*, tumor *m*

grub¹ ['grʌb] *vi* **grubbed; grubbing 1** DIG : escarbar **2** RUMMAGE : hurgar, buscar **3** DRUDGE : trabajar duro

grub² *n* **1** : larva *f* ⟨beetle grub : larva del escarabajo⟩ **2** DRUDGE : esclavo *m*, -va *f* del trabajo **3** FOOD : comida *f*

grubby ['grʌbi] *adj* **grubbier; -est** : mugriento, sucio

grudge¹ ['grʌʤ] *vt* **grudged; grudging** : resentir, envidiar

grudge² *n* : rencor *m*, resentimiento *m* ⟨to hold a grudge : guardar rencor⟩

grueling *or* **gruelling** ['gruːlɪŋ, 'gruːə-] *adj* : extenuante, agotador, duro

gruesome ['gruːsəm] *adj* : horripilante, truculento, horroroso

gruff ['grʌf] *adj* **1** BRUSQUE : brusco ⟨a gruff reply : una respuesta brusca⟩ **2** HOARSE : ronco — **gruffly** *adv*

grumble¹ ['grʌmbəl] *vi* **-bled; -bling 1** COMPLAIN : refunfuñar, rezongar, quejarse **2** RUMBLE : hacer un ruido sordo, retumbar (dícese del trueno)

grumble² *n* **1** COMPLAINT : queja *f* **2** RUMBLE : ruido *m* sordo, estruendo *m*

grumbler ['grʌmbələr] *n* : gruñón *m*, -ñona *f*

grumpy ['grʌmpi] *adj* **grumpier; -est** : malhumorado, gruñón

grungy ['grʌnʤi] *adj* : sucio

grunt¹ ['grʌnt] *vi* : gruñir

grunt² *n* : gruñido *m*

guacamole [,gwɑkə'moːli] *n* : guacamole *m*, guacamol *m*

guarantee¹ [,gærən'tiː] *vt* **-teed; -teeing 1** PROMISE : asegurar, prometer **2** : poner bajo garantía, garantizar (un producto o servicio)

guarantee² *n* **1** PROMISE : garantía *f*, promesa *f* ⟨lifetime guarantee : garantía de por vida⟩ **2** → **guarantor**

guarantor [,gærən'tɔr] *n* : garante *mf*; fiador *m*, -dora *f*

guaranty [,gærən'tiː] → **guarantee**

guard¹ ['gɑrd] *vt* **1** DEFEND, PROTECT : defender, proteger **2** : guardar, vigilar, custodiar ⟨to guard the frontier : vigilar la frontera⟩ ⟨she guarded my secret well : guardó bien mi secreto⟩ — *vi* **to guard against** : protegerse contra, evitar

guard² *n* **1** WATCHMAN : guarda *mf* ⟨security guard : guarda de seguridad⟩ **2** VIGILANCE : guardia *f*, vigilancia *f* ⟨to be on guard : estar en guardia⟩ ⟨to let one's guard down : bajar la guardia⟩ **3** SAFEGUARD : salvaguardia *f*, dispositivo *m* de seguridad (en una máquina) **4** PRECAUTION : precaución *f*, protección *f*

guardhouse ['gɑrd,haʊs] *n* : cuartel *m* de la guardia

guardian ['gɑrdiən] *n* **1** PROTECTOR : guardián *m*, -diana *f*; custodio *m*, -dia *f* **2** : tutor *m*, -tora *f* (de un niño)

guardianship ['gɑrdiən,ʃɪp] *n* : custodia *f*, tutela *f*

Guatemalan [,gwɑtə'mɑlən] *n* : guatemalteco *m*, -ca *f* — **Guatemalan** *adj*

guava ['gwɑvə] *n* : guayaba *f*

gubernatorial [,guː'bənə'toriːəl, ,gjuː-] *adj* : del gobernador

guerrilla *or* **guerilla** [gə'rɪlə] *n* : guerrillero *m*, -ra *f*

guess¹ ['gɛs] *vt* **1** CONJECTURE : adivinar, conjeturar ⟨guess what happened! : ¡adivina lo que pasó!⟩ **2** SUPPOSE : pensar, creer, suponer ⟨I guess so : supongo que sí⟩ **3** : adivinar correctamente, acertar ⟨to guess the answer : acertar la respuesta⟩ — *vi* : adivinar

guess² *n* : conjetura *f*, suposición *f*

guesswork ['gɛs,wərk] *n* : suposiciones *fpl*, conjeturas *fpl*

guest ['gɛst] *n* : huésped *mf*; invitado *m*, -da *f*

guffaw¹ [gə'fɔ] *vi* : reírse a carcajadas, carcajearse *fam*

guffaw² [gə'fɔ, 'gʌ,fɔ] *n* : carcajada *f*, risotada *f*

guidance ['gaɪdənts] *n* : orientación *f*, consejos *mpl*

guide¹ ['gaɪd] *vt* **guided; guiding 1** DIRECT, LEAD : guiar, dirigir, conducir **2** ADVISE, COUNSEL : aconsejar, orientar

guide² *n* : guía *f*

guidebook ['gaɪd,bʊk] *n* : guía *f* (para viajeros)

guideline ['gaɪd,laɪn] *n* : pauta *f*, directriz *f*

guild ['gɪld] *n* : gremio *m*, sindicato *m*, asociación *f*

guile ['gaɪl] *n* : astucia *f*, engaño *m*

guileless ['gaɪlləs] *adj* : inocente, cándido, sin malicia

guillotine¹ ['gɪlə,tiːn, 'giːjə,-] *vt* **-tined; -tining** : guillotinar

guillotine² *n* : guillotina *f*

guilt ['gɪlt] *n* : culpa *f*, culpabilidad *f*

guilty ['gɪlti] *adj* **guiltier; -est** : culpable

guinea fowl ['gɪni] *n* : gallina *f* de Guinea

guinea pig *n* : conejillo *m* de Indias, cobaya *f*

guise ['gaɪz] *n* : apariencia *f*, aspecto *m*, forma *f*

guitar [gə'tɑr, gɪ-] *n* : guitarra *f*

guitarist [gə'tɑrɪst, gɪ-] *n* : guitarrista *mf*

gulch ['gʌltʃ] *n* : barranco *m*, quebrada *f*

gulf ['gʌlf] *n* **1** : golfo *m* ⟨the Gulf of Mexico : el Golfo de México⟩ **2** GAP : brecha *f* ⟨the gulf between generations : la brecha entre las generaciones⟩ **3** CHASM : abismo *m*

gull ['gʌl] *n* : gaviota *f*

gullet ['gʌlət] *n* : garganta *f*

gullible ['gʌlɪbəl] *adj* : crédulo

gully ['gʌli] *n, pl* **-lies** : barranco *m*, hondonada *f*

gulp¹ ['gʌlp] *vt* **1** : engullir, tragar ⟨he gulped down the whiskey : engulló el whisky⟩ **2** SUPPRESS : suprimir, reprimir, tragar ⟨to gulp down a sob : reprimir un sollozo⟩ — *vi* : tragar saliva, tener un nudo en la garganta

gulp² *n* : trago *m*

gum ['gʌm] *n* **1** CHEWING GUM : goma *f* de mascar, chicle *m* **2 gums** *npl* : encías *fpl*

gumbo ['gʌm,boː] *n* : sopa *f* de quingombó

gumdrop ['gʌm,drɑp] *n* : pastilla *f* de goma

gummy ['gʌmi] *adj* **gummier; -est** : gomoso

gumption ['gʌmpʃən] *n* : iniciativa *f*, agallas *fpl fam*

gun¹ ['gʌn] *vt* **gunned; gunning 1** *or* **to gun down** : matar a tiros, asesinar **2** : acelerar (rápidamente) ⟨to gun the engine : acelerar el motor⟩

gun² *n* **1** CANNON : cañón *m* **2** FIREARM : arma *f* de fuego **3** SPRAY GUN : pistola *f* **4 to jump the gun** : adelantarse, salir antes de tiempo

gunboat ['gʌn,boːt] *n* : cañonero *m*

gunfight ['gʌn,faɪt] *n* : tiroteo *m*, balacera *f*

gunfire ['gʌn,faɪr] *n* : disparos *mpl*

gunman ['gʌnmən] *n, pl* **-men** [-mən, -,mɛn] : pistolero *m*, gatillero *m Mex*

gunner ['gʌnər] *n* : artillero *m*, -ra *f*

gunnysack ['gʌni,sæk] *n* : saco *m* de yute

gunpowder ['gʌn,paʊdər] *n* : pólvora *f*

gunshot ['gʌn,ʃɑt] *n* : disparo *m*, tiro *m*, balazo *m*

gunwale ['gʌnəl] *n* : borda *f*

guppy ['gʌpi] *n, pl* **-pies** : lebistes *m*

gurgle¹ ['gərgəl] *vi* **-gled; -gling 1** : borbotar, gorgotear (dícese de un líquido) **2** : gorjear (dícese de un niño)

gurgle² *n* **1** : borboteo *m*, gorgoteo *m* (de un líquido) **2** : gorjeo *m* (de un niño)

gush ['gʌʃ] *vi* **1** SPOUT : surgir, salir a chorros, chorrear **2** : hablar con entusiasmo efusivo ⟨she gushed with praise : se deshizo en elogios⟩

gust ['gʌst] *n* : ráfaga *f*, racha *f*

gusto ['gʌs,toː] *n, pl* **gustoes** : entusiasmo *m* ⟨with gusto : con deleite, con ganas⟩

gusty ['gʌsti] *adj* **gustier; -est** : racheado

gut¹ ['gʌt] *vt* **gutted; gutting 1** EVISCERATE : destripar (un pollo, etc.), limpiar (un pescado) **2** : destruir el interior de (un edificio)

gut² *n* **1** INTESTINE : intestino *m* **2 guts** *npl* INNARDS : tripas *fpl fam*, entrañas *fpl* **3 guts** *npl* COURAGE : valentía *f*, agallas *fpl*

gutter ['gʌtər] *n* **1** : canal *mf*, canaleta *f* (de un techo) **2** : cuneta *f*, arroyo *m* (de una calle)

guttural ['gʌtərəl] *adj* : gutural

guy ['gaɪ] *n* **1** *or* **guyline** : cuerda *f* tensora, cable *m* **2** FELLOW : tipo *m*, hombre *m*

guzzle ['gʌzəl] *vt* **-zled; -zling** : chupar, tragarse

gym ['dʒɪm] → **gymnasium**

gymnasium [dʒɪm'neɪziəm, -ʒəm] *n, pl* **-siums** *or* **-sia** [-ziːə, -ʒə] : gimnasio *m*

gymnast ['dʒɪmnəst, -,næst] *n* : gimnasta *mf*

gymnastic [dʒɪm'næstɪk] *adj* : gimnástico

gymnastics [dʒɪm'næstɪks] *ns & pl* : gimnasia *f*

gynecologist [,gaɪnə'kɑlədʒɪst, ,dʒɪnə-] *n* : ginecólogo *m*, -ga *f*

gynecology [,gaɪnə'kɑlədʒi, ,dʒɪnə-] *n* : ginecología *f*

gyp¹ ['dʒɪp] *vt* **gypped; gypping** : estafar, timar

gyp² *n* **1** SWINDLER : estafador *m*, -dora *f* **2** FRAUD, SWINDLE : estafa *f*, timo *m fam*

gypsum ['dʒɪpsəm] *n* : yeso *m*

Gypsy ['dʒɪpsi] *n, pl* **-sies** : gitano *m*, -na *f*

gyrate ['dʒaɪ,reɪt] *vi* **-rated; -rating** : girar, rotar

gyration [dʒaɪ'reɪʃən] *n* : giro *m*, rotación *f*

gyroscope ['dʒaɪrə,skoːp] *n* : giroscopio *m*, giróscopo *m*

H

h ['eɪtʃ] *n, pl* **h's** *or* **hs** ['eɪtʃəz] : octava letra del alfabeto inglés

ha ['hɑ] *interj* : ¡ja!

haberdashery ['hæbər,dæʃəri] *n, pl* **-eries** : tienda *f* de ropa para caballeros

habit ['hæbɪt] *n* **1** CUSTOM : hábito *m*, costumbre *f* **2** : hábito *m* (de un monje o una religiosa) **3** ADDICTION : dependencia *f*, adicción *f*

habitable ['hæbɪtəbəl] *adj* : habitable

habitat ['hæbɪ,tæt] *n* : hábitat *m*

habitation [,hæbɪ'teɪʃən] *n* **1** OCCUPANCY : habitación *f* **2** RESIDENCE : residencia *f*, morada *f*

habit–forming ['hæbɪt,fɔrmɪŋ] *adj* : que crea dependencia

habitual [hə'bɪtʃuəl] *adj* **1** CUSTOMARY : habitual, acostumbrado **2** INVETERATE : incorregible, empedernido — **habitually** *adv*

habituate [hə'bɪtʃu,eɪt] *vt* **-ated; -ating** : habituar, acostumbrar

hack¹ ['hæk] *vt* : cortar, tajear (a hachazos, etc.) ⟨to hack one's way : abrirse paso⟩ — *vi* **1** : hacer tajos **2** COUGH : toser

hack² *n* **1** CHOP : hachazo *m*, tajo *m* **2** HORSE : caballo *m* de alquiler **3** WRITER : escritor *m*, -tora *f* a sueldo; escritorzuelo *m*, -la *f* **4** COUGH : tos *f* seca

hackles ['hækəlz] *npl* **1** : pluma *f* erizada (de un ave), pelo *m* erizado (de un perro, etc.) **2 to get one's hackles up** : ponerse furioso

hackney ['hækni] *n, pl* **-neys** : caballo *m* de silla, caballo *m* de tiro

hackneyed ['hæknid] *adj* TRITE : trillado, gastado

hacksaw ['hæk,sɔ] *n* : sierra *f* para metales

had → **have**

haddock ['hædək] *ns & pl* : eglefino *m*

hadn't ['hædənt] (*contraction of* **had not**) → **have**

haft ['hæft] *n* : mango *m*, empuñadura *f*

hag ['hæg] *n* **1** WITCH : bruja *f*, hechicera *f* **2** CRONE : vieja *f* fea

haggard ['hægərd] *adj* : demacrado, macilento — **haggardly** *adv*

haggle ['hægəl] *vi* **-gled; -gling** : regatear

ha–ha [,hɑ'hɑ, 'hɑ'hɑ] *interj* : ¡ja, ja!

hail¹ ['heɪl] *vt* **1** GREET : saludar **2** SUMMON : llamar ⟨to hail a taxi : llamar un taxi⟩ — *vi* : granizar (en meteorología)

hail² *n* **1** : granizo *m* **2** BARRAGE : aluvión *m*, lluvia *f*

hail³ *interj* : ¡salve!

hailstone ['heɪl,sto:n] *n* : granizo *m*, piedra *f* de granizo

hailstorm ['heɪl,stɔrm] *n* : granizada *f*

hair ['hær] *n* **1** : pelo *m*, cabello *m* ⟨to get one's hair cut : cortarse el pelo⟩ **2** : vello *m* (en las piernas, etc.)

hairbreadth ['hær,brɛdθ] *or* **hairsbreadth** ['hærz-] *n* **by a hairbreadth** : por un pelo

hairbrush ['hær,brʌʃ] *n* : cepillo *m* (para el pelo)

haircut ['hær,kʌt] *n* : corte *m* de pelo

hairdo ['hær,du:] *n, pl* **-dos** : peinado *m*

hairdresser ['hær,drɛsər] *n* : peluquero *m*, -ra *f*

hairiness ['hærinəs] *n* : vellosidad *f*

hairless ['hærləs] *adj* : sin pelo, calvo, pelón

hairline ['hær,laɪn] *n* **1** : línea *f* delgada **2** : nacimiento *m* del pelo ⟨to have a receding hairline : tener entradas⟩

hairpin ['hær,pɪn] *n* : horquilla *f*

hair–raising ['hær,reɪzɪŋ] *adj* : espeluznante

hair spray *n* : laca *f*, fijador *m* (para el pelo)

hairstyle ['hær,staɪl] *n* : peinado *m*

hairy ['hæri] *adj* **hairier; -est** : peludo, velludo

Haitian ['heɪʃən, 'heɪtiən] *n* : haitiano *m*, -na *f* — **Haitian** *adj*

hake ['heɪk] *n* : merluza *f*

hale¹ ['heɪl] *vt* **haled; haling** : arrastrar, halar ⟨to hale to court : arrastrar al tribunal⟩

hale² *adj* : saludable, robusto

half¹ ['hæf, 'haf] *adv* : medio, a medias ⟨half cooked : medio cocido⟩

half² *adj* : medio, a medias ⟨a half hour : una media hora⟩ ⟨a half truth : una verdad a medias⟩

half³ *n, pl* **halves** ['hævz, 'havz] **1** : mitad *f* ⟨half of my friends : la mitad de mis amigos⟩ ⟨in half : por la mitad⟩ **2** : tiempo *m* (en deportes)

half brother *n* : medio hermano *m*, hermanastro *m*

halfhearted ['hæf'hɑrʈəd] *adj* : sin ánimo, poco entusiasta

halfheartedly ['hæf'hɑrʈədli] *adv* : con poco entusiasmo, sin ánimo

half–life ['hæf,laɪf] *n, pl* **half–lives** : media vida *f*

half sister *n* : media hermana *f*, hermanastra *f*

halfway¹ ['hæf'weɪ] *adv* : a medio camino, a mitad de camino

halfway² *adj* : medio, intermedio ⟨a halfway point : un punto intermedio⟩

half–wit ['hæf,wɪt] *n* : tonto *m*, -ta *f*; imbécil *mf*

half–witted ['hæf,wɪʈəd] *adj* : estúpido

halibut ['hælɪbət] *ns & pl* : halibut *m*

hall ['hɔl] *n* **1** BUILDING : residencia *f* estudiantil, facultad *f* (de una universidad) **2** VESTIBULE : entrada *f*, vestíbulo *m*, zaguán *m* **3** CORRIDOR : corredor *m*, pasillo *m* **4** AUDITORIUM : sala *f*, salón *m* ⟨concert hall : sala de conciertos⟩ **5 city hall** : ayuntamiento *m*

hallelujah [,hælə'lu:jə, ,hɑ-] *interj* : ¡aleluya!

hallmark ['hɔl,mɑrk] *n* : sello *m* (distintivo)

hallow ['hæ,lo:] *vt* : santificar, consagrar

hallowed ['hæ,lo:d, 'hæ,lo:əd, 'hɑ,lo:d] *adj* : sagrado

Halloween [,hælə'wi:n, ,hɑ-] *n* : víspera *f* de Todos los Santos

hallucinate [hæ'lu:sən,eɪt] *vi* -nated; -nating : alucinar

hallucination [hə,lu:sən'eɪʃən] *n* : alucinación *f*

hallucinatory [hə'lu:sənə,tori] *adj* : alucinante

hallucinogen [hə'lu:sənədʒən] *n* : alucinógeno *m*

hallucinogenic [hə,lu:sənə'dʒɛnɪk] *adj* : alucinógeno

hallway ['hɔl,weɪ] *n* 1 ENTRANCE : entrada *f* 2 CORRIDOR : corredor *m*, pasillo *m*

halo ['heɪ,lo:] *n*, *pl* -los *or* -loes : aureola *f*, halo *m*

halt[1] ['hɔlt] *vi* : detenerse, pararse — *vt* 1 STOP : detener, parar (a una persona) 2 INTERRUPT : interrumpir (una actividad)

halt[2] *n* 1 : alto *m*, parada *f* 2 to come to a halt : pararse, detenerse

halter ['hɔltər] *n* 1 : cabestro *m*, ronzal *m* (para un animal) 2 : blusa *f* sin espalda

halting ['hɔltɪŋ] *adj* HESITANT : vacilante, titubeante — haltingly *adv*

halve ['hæv, 'hav] *vt* halved; halving 1 DIVIDE : partir por la mitad 2 REDUCE : reducir a la mitad

halves → half

ham ['hæm] *n* 1 : jamón *m* 2 *or* ham actor : comicastro *m*, -tra *f* 3 *or* ham radio operator : radioaficionado *m*, -da *f* 4 hams *npl* HAUNCHES : ancas *fpl*

hamburger ['hæm,bərgər] *or* hamburg [-,bərg] *n* 1 : carne *f* molida 2 : hamburguesa *f* (emparedado)

hamlet ['hæmlət] *n* VILLAGE : aldea *f*, poblado *m*

hammer[1] ['hæmər] *vt* 1 STRIKE : clavar, golpear 2 NAIL : clavar, martillar 3 to hammer out NEGOTIATE : elaborar, negociar, llegar a — *vi* : martillar, golpear

hammer[2] *n* 1 : martillo *m* 2 : percusor *m*, percutor *m* (de un arma de fuego)

hammock ['hæmək] *n* : hamaca *f*

hamper[1] ['hæmpər] *vt* : obstaculizar, dificultar

hamper[2] *n* : cesto *m*, canasta *f*

hamster ['hæmpstər] *n* : hámster *m*

hamstring ['hæm,strɪŋ] *vt* -strung [-,strʌŋ]; -stringing 1 : cortarle el tendón del corvejón a (un animal) 2 INCAPACITATE : incapacitar, inutilizar

hand[1] ['hænd] *vt* : pasar, dar, entregar

hand[2] *n* 1 : mano *f* ⟨made by hand : hecho a mano⟩ 2 POINTER : manecilla *f*, aguja *f* (de un reloj o instrumento) 3 SIDE : lado *m* ⟨on the other hand : por otro lado⟩ 4 HANDWRITING : letra *f*, escritura *f* 5 APPLAUSE : aplauso *m* 6 : mano *f*, cartas *fpl* (en juegos de naipes)

7 WORKER : obrero *m*, -ra *f*; trabajador *m*, -dora *f* 8 to ask for someone's hand (in marriage) : pedir la mano de alguien 9 to lend a hand : echar una mano

handbag ['hænd,bæg] *n* : cartera *f*, bolso *m*, bolsa *f Mex*

handball ['hænd,bɔl] *n* : frontón *m*, pelota *f*

handbill ['hænd,bɪl] *n* : folleto *m*, volante *m*

handbook ['hænd,bʊk] *n* : manual *m*

handcuff ['hænd,kʌf] *vt* : esposar, ponerle esposas (a alguien)

handcuffs ['hænd,kʌfs] *npl* : esposas *fpl*

handful ['hænd,fʊl] *n* : puñado *m*

handgun ['hænd,gʌn] *n* : pistola *f*, revólver *m*

handheld ['hænd,hɛld] *adj* : de mano

handicap[1] ['hændi,kæp] *vt* -capped; -capping 1 : asignar un handicap a (en deportes) 2 HAMPER : obstaculizar, poner en desventaja

handicap[2] *n* 1 DISABILITY : minusvalía *f*, discapacidad *f* 2 DISADVANTAGE : desventaja *f*, handicap *m* (en deportes)

handicapped ['hændi,kæpt] *adj* DISABLED : minusválido, discapacitado

handicraft ['hændi,kræft] *n* : artesanía *f*

handily ['hændəli] *adv* EASILY : fácilmente, con facilidad

handiwork ['hændi,wərk] *n* 1 WORK : trabajo *m* 2 CRAFTS : artesanías *fpl*

handkerchief ['hæŋkərtʃəf, -,tʃi:f] *n*, *pl* -chiefs : pañuelo *m*

handle[1] ['hændəl] *v* -dled; -dling *vt* 1 TOUCH : tocar 2 MANAGE : tratar, manejar, despachar 3 SELL : comerciar con, vender — *vi* : responder, conducirse (dícese de un vehículo)

handle[2] *n* : asa *m*, asidero *m*, mango *m* (de un cuchillo, etc.), pomo *m* (de una puerta), tirador *m* (de un cajón)

handlebars ['hændəl,bɑrz] *npl* : manubrio *m*, manillar *m*

handler ['hændələr] *n* : cuidador *m*, -dora *f*

handling ['hændəlɪŋ] *n* 1 MANAGEMENT : manejo *m* 2 TOUCHING : manoseo *m* 3 shipping and handling : porte *m*, transporte *m*

handmade ['hænd,meɪd] *adj* : hecho a mano

hand—me—downs ['hændmi,daʊnz] *npl* : ropa *f* usada

handout ['hænd,aʊt] *n* 1 AID : dádiva *f*, limosna *f* 2 LEAFLET : folleto *m*

handpick ['hænd'pɪk] *vt* : seleccionar con cuidado

handrail ['hænd,ɹeɪl] *n* : pasamanos *m*, barandilla *f*, barandal *m*

handsaw ['hænd,sɔ] *n* : serrucho *m*

hands down *adv* 1 EASILY : con facilidad 2 UNQUESTIONABLY : con mucho, de lejos

handshake ['hænd,ʃeɪk] *n* : apretón *m* de manos

handsome ['hæn*t*səm] *adj* **-somer; -est**
1 ATTRACTIVE : apuesto, guapo, atractivo **2** GENEROUS : generoso **3** SIZ-
ABLE : considerable
handsomely ['hæn*t*səmli] *adv* **1** ELE-
GANTLY : elegantemente **2** GENER-
OUSLY : con generosidad
handspring ['hænd,sprɪŋ] *n* : voltereta *f*
handstand ['hænd,stænd] *n* **to do a**
handstand : pararse de manos
hand-to-hand ['hæn*d*tə'hænd] *adj*
: cuerpo a cuerpo
handwriting ['hænd,raɪṭɪŋ] *n* : letra *f*, escritura *f*
handwritten ['hænd,rɪtən] *adj* : escrito a
mano
handy ['hændi] *adj* **handier; -est 1**
NEARBY : a mano, cercano **2** USEFUL
: útil, práctico **3** DEXTEROUS : hábil
hang[1] ['hæŋ] *v* **hung** ['hʌŋ]; **hanging** *vt*
1 SUSPEND : colgar, tender, suspender
2 *past tense often* **hanged** EXECUTE
: colgar, ahorcar **3 to hang one's head**
: bajar la cabeza — *vi* **1** FALL : caer
(dícese de las telas y la ropa) **2** DAN-
GLE : colgar **3** HOVER : flotar, sostenerse en el aire **4** : ser ahorcado **5**
DROOP : inclinarse **6 to hang up** : colgar ⟨he hung up on me : me colgó⟩
hang[2] *n* **1** DRAPE : caída *f* **2 to get the**
hang of something : agarrarle la onda
a algo
hangar ['hæŋər, 'hæŋgər] *n* : hangar *m*
hanger ['hæŋər] *n* : percha *f*, gancho *m*
(para ropa)
hangman ['hæŋmən] *n, pl* **-men** [-mən,
-,mɛn] : verdugo *m*
hangnail ['hæŋ,neɪl] *n* : padrastro *m*
hangout ['hæŋ,aʊt] *n* : lugar *m* popular,
sitio *m* muy frecuentado
hangover ['hæŋ,oːvər] *n* : resaca *f*
hank ['hæŋk] *n* : madeja *f*
hanker ['hæŋkər] *vi* **to hanker for** : tener ansias de, tener ganas de
hankering ['hæŋkərɪŋ] *n* : ansia *f*, anhelo *m*
hansom ['hæn*t*səm] *n* : coche *m* de caballos
Hanukkah ['xɑnəkə, 'hɑ-] *n* : Januká,
Hanukkah
haphazard [hæp'hæzərd] *adj* : casual,
fortuito, al azar — **haphazardly** *adv*
hapless ['hæpləs] *adj* UNFORTUNATE
: desafortunado, desventurado — **hap-
lessly** *adv*
happen ['hæpən] *vi* **1** OCCUR : pasar,
ocurrir, suceder, tener lugar **2** BEFALL
: pasar, acontecer ⟨what happened to
her? : ¿qué le ha pasado?⟩ **3** CHANCE
: resultar, ocurrir por casualidad ⟨it
happened that I wasn't home : resulta
que estaba fuera de casa⟩ ⟨he happens
to be right : da la casualidad de que
tiene razón⟩
happening ['hæpənɪŋ] *n* : suceso *m*,
acontecimiento *m*
happiness ['hæpinəs] *n* : felicidad *f*,
dicha *f*

happy ['hæpi] *adj* **-pier; -est 1** JOYFUL
: feliz, contento, alegre **2** FORTUNATE
: afortunado, feliz — **happily** [-pəli] *adv*
happy-go-lucky ['hæpigoː'lʌki] *adj*
: despreocupado
harangue[1] [hə'ræŋ] *vt* **-rangued; -ran-
guing** : arengar
harangue[2] *n* : arenga *f*
harass [hə'ræs, 'hærəs] *vt* **1** BESIEGE,
HOUND : acosar, asediar, hostigar **2**
ANNOY : molestar
harassment [hə'ræsmənt, 'hærəsmənt]
n : acoso *m*, hostigamiento *m* ⟨sexual
harrassment : acoso sexual⟩
harbinger ['hɑrbɪnʤər] *n* **1** HERALD
: heraldo *m*, precursor *m* **2** OMEN : presagio *m*
harbor[1] ['hɑrbər] *vt* **1** SHELTER : dar
refugio a, albergar **2** CHERISH, KEEP
: abrigar, guardar, albergar ⟨to harbor
doubts : guardar dudas⟩
harbor[2] *n* **1** REFUGE : refugio *m* **2** PORT
: puerto *m*
hard[1] ['hɑrd] *adv* **1** FORCEFULLY
: fuerte, con fuerza ⟨the wind blew
hard : el viento sopló fuerte⟩ **2** STREN-
UOUSLY : duro, mucho ⟨to work hard
: trabajar duro⟩ **3 to take something**
hard : tomarse algo muy mal, estar muy
afectado por algo
hard[2] *adj* **1** FIRM, SOLID : duro, firme,
sólido **2** DIFFICULT : difícil, arduo **3**
SEVERE : severo, duro ⟨a hard winter
: un invierno severo⟩ **4** UNFEELING
: insensible, duro **5** DILIGENT : diligente ⟨to be a hard worker : ser muy
trabajador⟩ **6 hard liquor** : bebidas *fpl*
fuertes **7 hard water** : agua *f* dura
hardcover ['hɑrd,kʌvər] *adj* : de pasta
dura, de tapa dura
hard disk *n* : disco *m* duro
hard drive → **hard disk**
harden ['hɑrdən] *vt* : endurecer
hardheaded [,hɑrd'hɛdəd] *adj* **1** STUB-
BORN : testarudo, terco **2** REALISTIC
: realista, práctico — **hardheadedly**
adv
hard-hearted [,hɑrd'hɑrtəd] *adj* : despiadado, insensible — **hard-hearted-
ly** *adv*
hard-heartedness [,hɑrd'hɑrtədnəs] *n*
: dureza *f* de corazón
hardly ['hɑrdli] *adv* **1** SCARCELY : apenas, casi ⟨I hardly knew her : apenas
la conocía⟩ ⟨hardly ever : casi nunca⟩
2 NOT : difícilmente, poco, no ⟨they
can hardly blame me! : ¡difícilmente
pueden echarme la culpa!⟩ ⟨it's hardly likely : es poco probable⟩
hardness ['hɑrdnəs] *n* **1** FIRMNESS
: dureza *f* **2** DIFFICULTY : dificultad *f*
3 SEVERITY : severidad *f*
hardship ['hɑrd,ʃɪp] *n* : dificultad *f*, privación *f*
hardware ['hɑrd,wær] *n* **1** TOOLS : ferretería *f* **2** : hardware *m* (de una computadora)
hardwood ['hɑrd,wʊd] *n* : madera *f* dura,
madera *f* noble

hardworking ['hɑrd'wərkɪŋ] *adj* : trabajador

hardy ['hɑrdi] *adj* **-dier; -est** : fuerte, robusto, resistente (dícese de las plantas) — **hardily** [-dəli] *adv*

hare ['hær] *n, pl* **hare** *or* **hares** : liebre *f*

harebrained ['hær,breɪnd] *adj* : estúpido, absurdo, disparatado

harelip ['hær,lɪp] *n* : labio *m* leporino

harem ['hærəm] *n* : harén *m*

hark ['hɑrk] *vi* 1 (*used only in the imperative*) LISTEN : escuchar 2 **hark back** RETURN : volver 3 **hark back** RECALL : recordar

harlequin ['hɑrlɪkən, -kwən] *n* : arlequín *m*

harm[1] ['hɑrm] *vt* : hacerle daño a, perjudicar

harm[2] *n* : daño *m*, perjuicio *m*

harmful ['hɑrmfəl] *adj* : dañino, perjudicial — **harmfully** *adv*

harmless ['hɑrmləs] *adj* : inofensivo, inocuo — **harmlessly** *adv*

harmlessness ['hɑrmləsnəs] *n* : inocuidad *f*

harmonic [hɑr'mɑnɪk] *adj* : armónico — **harmonically** [-nɪkli] *adv*

harmonica [hɑr'mɑnɪkə] *n* : armónica *f*

harmonious [hɑr'mo:niəs] *adj* : armonioso — **harmoniously** *adv*

harmonize ['hɑrmə,naɪz] *v* **-nized; -nizing** : armonizar

harmony ['hɑrməni] *n, pl* **-nies** : armonía *f*

harness[1] ['hɑrnəs] *vt* 1 : enjaezar (un animal) 2 UTILIZE : utilizar, aprovechar

harness[2] *n* : arreos *mpl*, guarniciones *fpl*, arnés *m*

harp[1] ['hɑrp] *vi* **to harp on** : insistir sobre, machacar sobre

harp[2] *n* : arpa *m*

harpist ['hɑrpɪst] *n* : arpista *mf*

harpoon[1] [hɑr'pu:n] *vt* : arponear

harpoon[2] *n* : arpón *m*

harpsichord ['hɑrpsɪ,kɔrd] *n* : clavicémbalo *m*

harrow[1] ['hær,o:] *vt* 1 CULTIVATE : gradar, labrar (la tierra) 2 TORMENT : atormentar

harrow[2] *n* : grada *f*, rastra *f*

harry ['hæri] *vt* **-ried; -rying** HARASS : acosar, hostigar

harsh ['hɑrʃ] *adj* 1 ROUGH : áspero 2 SEVERE : duro, severo 3 : discordante (dícese de los sonidos) — **harshly** *adv*

harshness ['hɑrʃnəs] *n* 1 ROUGHNESS : aspereza *f* 2 SEVERITY : dureza *f*, severidad *f*

harvest[1] ['hɑrvəst] *v* : cosechar

harvest[2] *n* 1 HARVESTING : siega *f*, recolección *f* 2 CROP : cosecha *f*

harvester ['hɑrvəstər] *n* : segador *m*, -dora *f*; cosechadora *f* (máquina)

has → **have**

hash[1] ['hæʃ] *vt* 1 MINCE : picar 2 **to hash over** DISCUSS : discutir, repasar

hash[2] *n* 1 : picadillo *m* (comida) 2 JUMBLE : revoltijo *m*, fárrago *m*

hasn't ['hæzənt] (*contraction of* **has not**) → **has**

hasp ['hæsp] *n* : picaporte *m*, pestillo *m*

hassle[1] ['hæsəl] *vt* **-sled; -sling** : fastidiar, molestar

hassle[2] *n* 1 ARGUMENT : discusión *f*, disputa *f*, bronca *f* 2 FIGHT : pelea *f*, riña *f* 3 BOTHER, TROUBLE : problemas *mpl*, lío *m*

hassock ['hæsək] *n* 1 CUSHION : almohadón *m*, cojín *m* 2 FOOTSTOOL : escabel *m*

haste ['heɪst] *n* 1 : prisa *f*, apuro *m* 2 **to make haste** : darse prisa, apurarse

hasten ['heɪsən] *vt* : acelerar, precipitar — *vi* : apresurarse, apurarse

hasty ['heɪsti] *adj* **hastier; -est** 1 HURRIED, QUICK : rápido, apresurado, apurado 2 RASH : precipitado — **hastily** [-təli] *adv*

hat ['hæt] *n* : sombrero *m*

hatch[1] ['hætʃ] *vt* 1 : incubar, empollar (huevos) 2 DEVISE : idear, tramar — *vi* : salir del cascarón

hatch[2] *n* : escotilla *f*

hatchery ['hætʃəri] *n, pl* **-ries** : criadero *m*

hatchet ['hætʃət] *n* : hacha *f*

hatchway ['hætʃ,weɪ] *n* : escotilla *f*

hate[1] ['heɪt] *vt* **hated; hating** : odiar, aborrecer, detestar

hate[2] *n* : odio *m*

hateful ['heɪtfəl] *adj* : odioso, aborrecible, detestable — **hatefully** *adv*

hatred ['heɪtrəd] *n* : odio *m*

hatter ['hætər] *n* : sombrerero *m*, -ra *f*

haughtiness ['hɔtinəs] *n* : altanería *f*, altivez *f*

haughty ['hɔti] *adj* **-tier; -est** : altanero, altivo — **haughtily** [-təli] *adv*

haul[1] ['hɔl] *vt* 1 DRAG, PULL : arrastrar, jalar 2 TRANSPORT : transportar

haul[2] *n* 1 PULL : tirón *m*, jalón *m* 2 CATCH : redada *f* 3 JOURNEY : viaje *m*, trayecto *m* ⟨it's a long haul : es un trayecto largo⟩

haulage ['hɔlɪdʒ] *n* : transporte *m*, tiro *m*

hauler ['hɔlər] *n* : transportista *mf*

haunch ['hɔntʃ] *n* 1 HIP : cadera *f* 2 **haunches** *npl* HINDQUARTERS : ancas *fpl*, cuartos *mpl* traseros

haunt[1] ['hɔnt] *vt* 1 : aparecer en (dícese de un fantasma) 2 FREQUENT : frecuentar, rondar 3 PREOCCUPY : perseguir, obsesionar

haunt[2] *n* : guarida *f* (de animales o ladrones), lugar *m* predilecto

haunting ['hɔntɪŋ] *adj* : obsesionante, evocador — **hauntingly** *adv*

haute ['o:t] *adj* 1 : de moda, de categoría 2 **haute couture** [,o:tku'tur] : alta costura *f* 3 **haute cuisine** [,o:tkwɪ'zi:n] : alta cocina *f*

have ['hæv, *in sense 3 as an auxiliary verb usu* 'hæf] *v* **had** ['hæd]; **having; has** ['hæz, *in sense 3 as an auxiliary verb usu* 'hæs] *vt* 1 POSSESS : tener ⟨do you have

change? : ¿tienes cambio?⟩ **2** EXPERI-
ENCE, UNDERGO : tener, experimentar, sufrir ⟨I have a toothache : tengo
un dolor de muelas⟩ **3** INCLUDE : tener, incluir ⟨April has 30 days : abril
tiene 30 días⟩ **4** CONSUME : comer,
tomar **5** RECEIVE : tener, recibir ⟨he
had my permission : tenía mi permiso⟩
6 ALLOW : permitir, dejar ⟨I won't have
it! : ¡no lo permitiré!⟩ **7** HOLD : hacer
⟨to have a party : dar una fiesta⟩ ⟨to
have a meeting : convocar una re-
unión⟩ **8** HOLD : tener ⟨he had me in
his power : me tenía en su poder⟩ **9**
BEAR : tener (niños) **10** (*indicating
causation*) ⟨she had a dress made
: mandó hacer un vestido⟩ ⟨to have
one's hair cut : cortarse el pelo⟩ — *v
aux* **1** : haber ⟨she has been very busy
: ha estado muy ocupada⟩ ⟨I've lived
here three years : hace tres años que
vivo aquí⟩ **2** (*used in tags*) ⟨you've finished, haven't you? : ha terminado,
¿no?⟩ **3 to have to** : deber, tener que
⟨we have to leave : tenemos que salir⟩
haven ['heɪvən] *n* : refugio *m*
havoc ['hævək] *n* **1** DESTRUCTION : estragos *mpl*, destrucción *f* **2** CHAOS,
DISORDER : desorden *m*, caos *m*
Hawaiian¹ [hə'waɪən] *adj* : hawaiano
Hawaiian² *n* : hawaiano *m*, -na *f*
hawk¹ ['hɔk] *vt* : pregonar, vender (mercancías) en la calle
hawk² *n* : halcón *m*
hawker ['hɔkər] *n* : vendedor *m*, -dora *f*
ambulante
hawthorn ['hɔ,θɔrn] *n* : espino *m*
hay ['heɪ] *n* : heno *m*
hay fever *n* : fiebre *f* del heno
hayloft ['heɪ,lɔft] *n* : pajar *m*
hayseed ['heɪ,si:d] *n* : palurdo *m*, -da *f*
haystack ['heɪ,stæk] *n* : almiar *m*
haywire ['heɪ,waɪr] *adj* : descompuesto,
desbaratado ⟨to go haywire : estro-
pearse⟩
hazard¹ ['hæzərd] *vt* : arriesgar, aventurar
hazard² *n* **1** DANGER : peligro *m*, riesgo *m* **2** CHANCE : azar *m*
hazardous ['hæzərdəs] *adj* : arriesgado,
peligroso
haze¹ ['heɪz] *vt* **hazed; hazing** : abrumar, acosar
haze² *n* : bruma *f*, neblina *f*
hazel ['heɪzəl] *n* **1** : avellano *m* (árbol)
2 : color *m* avellana
hazelnut ['heɪzəl,nʌt] *n* : avellana *f*
haziness ['heɪzinəs] *n* **1** MISTINESS
: nebulosidad *f* **2** VAGUENESS
: vaguedad *f*
hazy ['heɪzi] *adj* **hazier; -est 1** MISTY
: brumoso, neblinoso, nebuloso **2**
VAGUE : vago, confuso
he ['hi:] *pron* : él
head¹ ['hɛd] *vt* **1** LEAD : encabezar **2**
DIRECT : dirigir — *vi* : dirigirse
head² *adj* MAIN : principal ⟨the head office : la oficina central, la sede⟩

head³ *n* **1** : cabeza *f* ⟨from head to foot
: de pies a cabeza⟩ **2** MIND : mente *f*,
cabeza *f* **3** TIP, TOP : cabeza *f* (de un
clavo, un martillo, etc.), cabecera *f* (de
una mesa o un río), punta *f* (de una
flecha), flor *m* (de un repollo, etc.), encabezamiento *m* (de una carta, etc.),
espuma *f* (de cerveza) **4** DIRECTOR,
LEADER : director *m*, -tora *f*; jefe *m*, -fa
f; cabeza *f* (de una familia) **5** : cara *f*
(de una moneda) ⟨heads or tails : cara
o cruz⟩ **6** : cabeza *f* ⟨500 head of cattle : 500 cabezas de ganado⟩ ⟨$10 a
head : $10 por cabeza⟩ **7 to come to
a head** : llegar a un punto crítico
headache ['hɛd,eɪk] *n* : dolor *m* de
cabeza, jaqueca *f*
headband ['hɛd,bænd] *n* : cinta *f* del
pelo
headdress ['hɛd,drɛs] *n* : tocado *m*
headfirst ['hɛd'fərst] *adv* : de cabeza
headgear ['hɛd,gɪr] *n* : gorro *m*, casco
m, sombrero *m*
heading ['hɛdɪŋ] *n* **1** DIRECTION : dirección *f* **2** TITLE : encabezamiento *m*,
título *m* **3** : membrete *m* (de una carta)
headland ['hɛdlənd, -,lænd] *n* : cabo *m*
headlight ['hɛd,laɪt] *n* : faro *m*, foco *m*,
farol *m Mex*
headline ['hɛd,laɪn] *n* : titular *m*
headlong¹ ['hɛd'lɔŋ] *adv* **1** HEADFIRST
: de cabeza **2** HASTILY : precipitadamente
headlong² ['hɛd,lɔŋ] *adj* : precipitado
headmaster ['hɛd,mæstər] *n* : director
m
headmistress ['hɛd,mɪstrəs, -'mɪs-] *n*
: directora *f*
head–on ['hɛd'ɑn, -'ɔn] *adv & adj* : de
frente
headphones ['hɛd,fo:nz] *npl* : audífonos
mpl, cascos *mpl*
headquarters ['hɛd,kwɔrtərz] *ns & pl* **1**
SEAT : oficina *f* central, sede *f* **2** : cuartel *m* general (de los militares)
headrest ['hɛd,rɛst] *n* : apoyacabezas *m*
headship ['hɛd,ʃɪp] *n* : dirección *f*
head start *n* : ventaja *f*
headstone ['hɛd,sto:n] *n* : lápida *f*
headstrong ['hɛd'strɔŋ] *adj* : testarudo,
obstinado, empecinado
headwaiter ['hɛd'weɪtər] *n* : jefe *m*, -fa *f*
de comedor
headwaters ['hɛd,wɔtərz, -,wɑ-] *npl*
: cabecera *f*
headway ['hɛd,weɪ] *n* : progreso *m* ⟨to
make headway against : avanzar con-
tra⟩
heady ['hɛdi] *adj* **headier; -est 1** IN-
TOXICATING : embriagador, excitante
2 SHREWD : astuto, sagaz
heal ['hi:l] *vt* : curar, sanar — *vi* **1** : sanar, curarse **2 to heal up** : cicatrizarse
healer ['hi:lər] *n* **1** : curandero *m*, -dera
f **2** : curador *m*, -dora *f* (cosa)
health ['hɛlθ] *n* : salud *f*

healthful ['hɛlθfəl] *adj* : saludable, salubre — **healthfully** *adv*

healthy ['hɛlθi] *adj* **healthier; -est** : sano, bien — **healthily** [-θəli] *adv*

heap[1] ['hi:p] *vt* **1** PILE : amontonar, apilar **2** SHOWER : colmar

heap[2] *n* : montón *m*, pila *f*

hear ['hɪr] *v* **heard** ['hərd]; **hearing** *vt* **1** : oír ⟨do you hear me? : ¿me oyes?⟩ **2** HEED : oír, prestar atención a **3** LEARN : oír, enterarse de — *vi* **1** : oír ⟨to hear about : oír hablar de⟩ **2 to hear from** : tener noticias de

hearing ['hɪrɪŋ] *n* **1** : oído *m* ⟨hard of hearing : duro de oído⟩ **2** : vista *f* (en un tribunal) **3** ATTENTION : consideración *f*, oportunidad *f* de expresarse **4** EARSHOT : alcance *m* del oído

hearing aid *n* : audífono *m*

hearken ['harkən] *vt* : escuchar

hearsay ['hɪr,seɪ] *n* : rumores *mpl*

hearse ['hərs] *n* : coche *m* fúnebre

heart ['hart] *n* **1** : corazón *m* **2** CENTER, CORE : corazón *m*, centro *m* ⟨the heart of the matter : el meollo del asunto⟩ **3** FEELINGS : corazón *m*, sentimientos *mpl* ⟨a broken heart : un corazón destrozado⟩ ⟨to have a good heart : tener buen corazón⟩ ⟨to take something to heart : tomarse algo a pecho⟩ **4** COURAGE : valor *m*, corazón *m* ⟨to take heart : animarse, cobrar ánimos⟩ **5 hearts** *npl* : corazones *mpl* (en juegos de naipes) **6 by heart** : de memoria

heartache ['hart,eɪk] *n* : pena *f*, angustia *f*

heart attack *n* : infarto *m*, ataque *m* al corazón

heartbeat ['hart,bi:t] *n* : latido *m* (del corazón)

heartbreak ['hart,breɪk] *n* : congoja *f*, angustia *f*

heartbreaking ['hart,breɪkɪŋ] *adj* : desgarrador, que parte el corazón

heartbroken ['hart,bro:kən] *adj* : desconsolado, destrozado

heartburn ['hart,bərn] *n* : acidez *f* estomacal

hearten ['hartən] *vt* : alentar, animar

heartfelt ['hart,fɛlt] *adj* : sentido

hearth ['harθ] *n* : hogar *m*, chimenea *f*

heartily ['hartəli] *adv* **1** ENTHUSIASTICALLY : de buena gana, con entusiasmo **2** TOTALLY : totalmente, completamente

heartless ['hartləs] *adj* : desalmado, despiadado, cruel

heartsick ['hart,sɪk] *adj* : abatido, desconsolado

heartstrings ['hart,strɪŋz] *npl* : fibras *fpl* del corazón

heartwarming ['hart,wɔrmɪŋ] *adj* : conmovedor, emocionante

hearty ['harti] *adj* **heartier; -est 1** CORDIAL, WARM : cordial, caluroso **2** STRONG : fuerte ⟨to have a hearty appetite : ser de buen comer⟩ **3** SUBSTANTIAL : abundante, sustancioso ⟨a hearty breakfast : un desayuno abundante⟩

heat[1] ['hi:t] *vt* : calentar

heat[2] *n* **1** WARMTH : calor *m* **2** HEATING : calefacción *f* **3** EXCITEMENT : calor *m*, entusiasmo *m* ⟨in the heat of the moment : en el calor del momento⟩ **4** ESTRUS : celo *m*

heated ['hi:təd] *adj* **1** WARMED : calentado **2** IMPASSIONED : acalorado, apasionado

heater ['hi:tər] *n* : calentador *m*, estufa *f*, calefactor *m*

heath ['hi:θ] *n* **1** MOOR : brezal *m*, páramo *m* **2** HEATHER : brezo *m*

heathen[1] ['hi:ðən] *adj* : pagano

heathen[2] *n, pl* **-thens** *or* **-then** : pagano *m*, -na *f*; infiel *mf*

heather ['hɛðər] *n* : brezo *m*

heave[1] ['hi:v] *v* **heaved** *or* **hove** ['ho:v]; **heaving** *vt* **1** LIFT, RAISE : levantar con esfuerzo **2** HURL : lanzar, tirar **3 to heave a sigh** : echar un suspiro, suspirar — *vi* **1** : subir y bajar, palpitar (dícese del pecho) **2 to heave up** RISE : levantarse

heave[2] *n* **1** EFFORT : gran esfuerzo *m* (para levantar algo) **2** THROW : lanzamiento *m*

heaven ['hɛvən] *n* **1** : cielo *m* ⟨for heaven's sake : por Dios⟩ **2 heavens** *npl* SKY : cielo *m* ⟨the heavens opened up : empezó a llover a cántaros⟩

heavenly ['hɛvənli] *adj* **1** : celestial, celeste **2** DELIGHTFUL : divino, encantador

heavily ['hɛvəli] *adv* **1** : pesadamente, con mucho peso **2** LABORIOUSLY : trabajosamente, penosamente **3** : mucho

heaviness ['hɛvinəs] *n* : peso *m*, pesadez *f*

heavy ['hɛvi] *adj* **heavier; -est 1** WEIGHTY : pesado **2** DENSE, THICK : denso, espeso, grueso **3** BURDENSOME : oneroso, gravoso **4** PROFOUND : profundo **5** SLUGGISH : lento, tardo **6** STOUT : corpulento **7** SEVERE : severo, duro, fuerte

heavy–duty ['hɛvi'du:ti, -'dju:-] *adj* : muy resistente, fuerte

heavyweight ['hɛvi,weɪt] *n* : peso *m* pesado (en deportes)

Hebrew[1] ['hi:,bru:] *adj* : hebreo

Hebrew[2] *n* **1** : hebreo *m*, -brea *f* **2** : hebreo *m* (idioma)

heck ['hɛk] *n* : ¡caramba!, ¡caray! ⟨a heck of a lot : un montón⟩ ⟨what the heck is ... ? : ¿que diablos es ... ?⟩

heckle ['hɛkəl] *vt* **-led; -ling** : interrumpir (a un orador)

hectare ['hɛk,tær] *n* : hectárea *f*

hectic ['hɛktɪk] *adj* : agitado, ajetreado — **hectically** [-tɪkli] *adv*

he'd ['hi:d] (*contraction* of **he had** *or* **he would**) → **have, would**

hedge[1] ['hɛdʒ] *v* **hedged; hedging** *vt* **1** : cercar con un seto **2 to hedge one's bet** : cubrirse — *vi* **1** : dar rodeos, con-

testar con evasivas **2 to hedge against** : cubrirse contra, protegerse contra
hedge² n **1** : seto m vivo **2** SAFEGUARD : salvaguardia f, protección f
hedgehog ['hɛdʒ,hɔg, -hɑg] n : erizo m
heed¹ ['hi:d] vt : prestar atención a, hacer caso de
heed² n : atención f
heedless ['hi:dləs] adj : descuidado, despreocupado, inconsciente ⟨to be heedless of : hacer caso omiso de⟩ — **heedlessly** adv
heel¹ ['hi:l] vi : inclinarse
heel² n : talón m (del pie), tacón m (de calzado)
heft ['hɛft] vt : sopesar
hefty ['hɛfti] adj **heftier; -est** : robusto, fornido, pesado
hegemony [hɪ'dʒɛməni] n, pl **-nies** : hegemonía f
heifer ['hɛfər] n : novilla f
height ['haɪt] n **1** PEAK : cumbre f, cima f, punto m alto ⟨at the height of her career : en la cumbre de su carrera⟩ ⟨the height of stupidity : el colmo de la estupidez⟩ **2** TALLNESS : estatura f (de una persona), altura f (de un objeto) **3** ALTITUDE : altura f
heighten ['haɪtən] vt **1** : hacer más alto **2** INTENSIFY : aumentar, intensificar — vi : aumentarse, intensificarse
heinous ['heɪnəs] adj : atroz, abominable, nefando
heir ['ær] n : heredero m, -ra f
heiress ['ærəs] n : heredera f
heirloom ['ær,lu:m] n : reliquia f de familia
held → **hold**
helicopter ['hɛlə,kɑptər] n : helicóptero m
helium ['hi:liəm] n : helio m
helix ['hi:lɪks] n, pl **helices** ['hɛlə,si:z, 'hi:-] or **helixes** ['hi:lɪksəz] : hélice f
hell ['hɛl] n : infierno m
he'll ['hi:l, 'hɪl] (contraction of **he shall** or **he will**) → **shall, will**
hellish ['hɛlɪʃ] adj : horroroso, infernal
hello [hə'lo:, hɛ-] interj : ¡hola!
helm ['hɛlm] n **1** : timón m **2 to take the helm** : tomar el mando
helmet ['hɛlmət] n : casco m
help¹ ['hɛlp] vt **1** AID, ASSIST : ayudar, auxiliar, socorrer, asistir **2** ALLEVIATE : aliviar **3** SERVE : servir ⟨help yourself! : ¡sírvete!⟩ **4** AVOID : evitar ⟨it can't be helped : no lo podemos evitar, no hay más remedio⟩ ⟨I couldn't help smiling : no pude menos que sonreír⟩
help² n **1** ASSISTANCE : ayuda f ⟨help! : ¡socorro!, ¡auxilio!⟩ **2** STAFF : personal m (en una oficina), servicio m doméstico
helper ['hɛlpər] n : ayudante mf
helpful ['hɛlpfəl] adj **1** OBLIGING : servicial, amable, atento **2** USEFUL : útil, práctico — **helpfully** adv
helpfulness ['hɛlpfəlnəs] n **1** KINDNESS : bondad f, amabilidad f **2** USEFULNESS : utilidad f

helping ['hɛlpɪŋ] n : porción f
helpless ['hɛlpləs] adj **1** POWERLESS : incapaz, impotente **2** DEFENSELESS : indefenso
helplessly ['hɛlpləsli] adv : en vano, inútilmente
helplessness ['hɛlpləsnəs] n POWERLESSNESS : incapacidad f, impotencia f
helter–skelter [,hɛltər'skɛltər] adv : atropelladamente, precipitadamente
hem¹ ['hɛm] vt **hemmed; hemming 1** : dobladillar **2 to hem in** : encerrar
hem² n : dobladillo m, bastilla f
hemisphere ['hɛmə,sfɪr] n : hemisferio m
hemispheric [,hɛmə'sfɪrɪk, -'sfr-] or **hemispherical** [-ɪkəl] adj : hemisférico
hemlock ['hɛm,lɑk] n : cicuta f
hemoglobin ['hi:mə,glo:bən] n : hemoglobina f
hemophilia [,hi:mə'fɪliə] n : hemofilia f
hemorrhage¹ ['hɛmərɪdʒ] vi **-rhaged; -rhaging** : sufrir una hemorragia
hemorrhage² n : hemorragia f
hemorrhoids ['hɛmə,rɔɪdz, 'hɛm-,rɔɪdz] npl : hemorroides fpl, almorranas fpl
hemp ['hɛmp] n : cáñamo m
hen ['hɛn] n : gallina f
hence ['hɛnts] adv **1** : de aquí, de ahí ⟨10 years hence : de aquí a 10 años⟩ ⟨a dog bit me, hence my dislike of animals : un perro me mordió, de ahí mi aversión a los animales⟩ **2** THEREFORE : por lo tanto, por consiguiente
henceforth ['hɛnts,forθ, ,hɛnts'-] adv : de ahora en adelante
henchman ['hɛntʃmən] n, pl **-men** [-mən, -,mɛn] : secuaz mf, esbirro m
henpeck ['hɛn,pɛk] vt : dominar (al marido)
hepatitis [,hɛpə'taɪtəs] n, pl **-titides** [-'tɪtə,di:z] : hepatitis f
her¹ ['hər] adj : su, sus, de ella ⟨her house : su casa, la casa de ella⟩
her² ['hər, ər] pron **1** (used as direct object) : la ⟨I saw her yesterday : la vi ayer⟩ **2** (used as indirect object) : le, se ⟨he gave her the book : le dio el libro⟩ ⟨he sent it to her : se lo mandó⟩ **3** (used as object of a preposition) : ella ⟨we did it for her : lo hicimos por ella⟩ ⟨taller than her : más alto que ella⟩
herald¹ ['hɛrəld] vt ANNOUNCE : anunciar, proclamar
herald² n **1** MESSENGER : heraldo m **2** HARBINGER : precursor m
heraldic [hɛ'rældɪk, hə-] adj : heráldico
heraldry ['hɛrəldri] n, pl **-ries** : heráldica f
herb ['ərb, 'hərb] n : hierba f
herbal ['ərbəl, 'hər-] adj : herbario
herbicide ['ərbə,saɪd, 'hər-] n : herbicida m
herbivore ['ərbə,vor, 'hər-] n : herbívoro m
herbivorous [,ər'bɪvərəs, ,hər-] adj : herbívoro
herculean [,hərkjə'li:ən, ,hər'kju:-liən] adj : hercúleo, sobrehumano

herd[1] [ˈhərd] *vt* : reunir en manada, conducir en manada — *vi* : ir en manada (dícese de los animales), apiñarse (dícese de la gente)

herd[2] *n* : manada *f*

herder [ˈhərdər] → **herdsman**

herdsman [ˈhərdzmən] *n, pl* **-men** [-mən, -ˌmɛn] : vaquero *m* (de ganado), pastor *m* (de ovejas)

here [ˈhɪr] *adv* 1 : aquí, acá ⟨come here! : ¡ven acá!⟩ ⟨right here : aquí mismo⟩ 2 NOW : en este momento, ahora, ya ⟨here he comes : ya viene⟩ ⟨here it's three o'clock (already) : ahora son las tres⟩ 3 : en este punto ⟨here we agree : estamos de acuerdo en este punto⟩ 4 **here you are!** : ¡toma!

hereabouts [ˈhɪrəˌbaʊts] *or* **hereabout** [-ˌbaʊt] *adv* : por aquí (cerca)

hereafter[1] [hɪrˈæftər] *adv* 1 : de aquí en adelante, a continuación 2 : en el futuro

hereafter[2] *n* **the hereafter** : el más allá

hereby [hɪrˈbaɪ] *adv* : por este medio

hereditary [həˈrɛdəˌtɛri] *adj* : hereditario

heredity [həˈrɛdəti] *n* : herencia *f*

herein [hɪrˈɪn] *adv* : aquí

hereof [hɪrˈʌn] *adv* : de aquí

hereon [hɪrˈɑn, -ˈɔn] *adv* : sobre esto

heresy [ˈhɛrəsi] *n, pl* **-sies** : herejía *f*

heretic [ˈhɛrəˌtɪk] *n* : hereje *mf*

heretical [həˈrɛtɪkəl] *adj* : herético

hereto [hɪrˈtuː] *adv* : a esto

heretofore [ˈhɪrtəˌfor] *adv* HITHERTO : hasta ahora

hereunder [hɪrˈʌndər] *adv* : a continuación, abajo

hereupon [hɪrəˈpɑn, -ˈpɔn] *adv* : con esto, en ese momento

herewith [hɪrˈwɪθ] *adv* : adjunto

heritage [ˈhɛrətɪdʒ] *n* : patrimonio *m* (nacional)

hermaphrodite [hərˈmæfrəˌdaɪt] *n* : hermafrodita *mf*

hermetic [hərˈmɛtɪk] *adj* : hermético — **hermetically** [-tɪkli] *adv*

hermit [ˈhərmət] *n* : ermitaño *m*, -ña *f*; eremita *mf*

hernia [ˈhərniə] *n, pl* **-nias** *or* **-niae** [-niˌiː, -niˌaɪ] : hernia *f*

hero [ˈhiːˌroː, ˈhɪrˌoː] *n, pl* **-roes** 1 : héroe *m* 2 PROTAGONIST : protagonista *mf*

heroic [hɪˈroːɪk] *adj* : heroico — **heroically** [-ɪkli] *adv*

heroics [hɪˈroːɪks] *npl* : actos *mpl* heroicos

heroin [ˈhɛroən] *n* : heroína *f*

heroine [ˈhɛroən] *n* 1 : heroína *f* 2 PROTAGONIST : protagonista *f*

heroism [ˈhɛroˌɪzəm] *n* : heroísmo *m*

heron [ˈhɛrən] *n* : garza *f*

herpes [ˈhərˌpiːz] *n* : herpes *m*

herring [ˈhɛrɪŋ] *n, pl* **-ring** *or* **-rings** : arenque *m*

hers [ˈhərz] *pron* : suyo, -ya; suyos, -yas; de ella ⟨these shoes are hers : estos zapatos son suyos⟩ ⟨hers are bigger : los de ella son más grandes⟩

herself [hərˈsɪf] *pron* 1 (*used reflexively*) : se ⟨she dressed herself : se vistió⟩ 2 (*used emphatically*) : ella misma ⟨she fixed it herself : lo arregló ella misma, lo arregló por sí sola⟩

hertz [ˈhərts, ˈhrts] *ns & pl* : hercio *m*

he's [ˈhiːz] (*contraction of* **he is** *or* **he has**) → **be, have**

hesitancy [ˈhɛzətənˌtsi] *n, pl* **-cies** : vacilación *f*, titubeo *m*, indecisión *f*

hesitant [ˈhɛzətənt] *adj* : titubeante, vacilante — **hesitantly** *adv*

hesitate [ˈhɛzəˌteɪt] *vi* **-tated; -tating** : vacilar, titubear

hesitation [ˌhɛzəˈteɪʃən] *n* : vacilación *f*, indecisión *f*, titubeo *m*

heterogeneous [ˌhɛtərəˈdʒiːniəs, -njəs] *adj* : heterogéneo

heterosexual[1] [ˌhɛtəroˈskʃʊəl] *adj* : heterosexual

heterosexual[2] *n* : heterosexual *mf*

heterosexuality [ˌhɛtəroˌskʃʊˈæləti] *n* : heterosexualidad *f*

hew [ˈhjuː] *v* **hewed; hewed** *or* **hewn** [ˈhjuːn]; **hewing** *vt* 1 CUT : cortar, talar (árboles) 2 SHAPE : labrar, tallar — *vi* CONFORM : conformarse, ceñirse

hex[1] [ˈhɛks] *vt* : hacerle un maleficio (a alguien)

hex[2] *n* : maleficio *m*

hexagon [ˈhɛksəˌɡɑn] *n* : hexágono *m*

hexagonal [hɛkˈsæɡənəl] *adj* : hexagonal

hey [ˈheɪ] *interj* : ¡eh!, ¡oye!

heyday [ˈheɪˌdeɪ] *n* : auge *m*, apogeo *m*

hi [ˈhaɪ] *interj* : ¡hola!

hiatus [haɪˈeɪtəs] *n* 1 : hiato *m* 2 PAUSE : pausa *f*

hibernate [ˈhaɪbərˌneɪt] *vi* **-nated; -nating** : hibernar, invernar

hibernation [ˌhaɪbərˈneɪʃən] *n* : hibernación *f*

hiccup[1] [ˈhɪkəp] *vi* **-cuped; -cuping** : hipar, tener hipo

hiccup[2] *n* : hipo *m* ⟨to have the hiccups : tener hipo⟩

hick [ˈhɪk] *n* BUMPKIN : palurdo *m*, -da *f*

hickory [ˈhɪkəri] *n, pl* **-ries** : nogal *m* americano

hidden [ˈhɪdən] *adj* : oculto

hide[1] [ˈhaɪd] *v* **hid** [ˈhɪd]; **hidden** [ˈhɪdən] *or* **hid; hiding** *vt* 1 CONCEAL : esconder 2 : ocultar ⟨to hide one's motives : ocultar uno sus motivos⟩ 3 SCREEN : tapar, no dejar ver — *vi* : esconderse

hide[2] *n* : piel *f*, cuero *m* ⟨to save one's hide : salvar el pellejo⟩

hide–and–seek [ˈhaɪdəndˈsiːk] *n* **to play hide–and–seek** : jugar a las escondidas

hidebound [ˈhaɪdˌbaʊnd] *adj* : rígido, conservador

hideous [ˈhɪdiəs] *adj* : horrible, horroroso, espantoso — **hideously** *adv*

hideout [ˈhaɪdˌaʊt] *n* : guarida *f*, escondrijo *m*

hierarchical [ˌhaɪəˈrɑrkɪkəl] *adj* : jerárquico

hierarchy ['haɪə,rɑrki] *n, pl* **-chies** : jerarquía *f*

hieroglyphic [,haɪərə'glɪfɪk] *n* : jeroglífico *m*

hi–fi ['haɪ'faɪ] *n* **1** → **high fidelity 2** : equipo *m* de alta fidelidad

high[1] ['haɪ] *adv* : alto

high[2] *adj* **1** TALL : alto ⟨a high wall : una pared alta⟩ **2** ELEVATED : alto, elevado ⟨high prices : precios elevados⟩ ⟨high blood pressure : presión alta⟩ **3** GREAT, IMPORTANT : grande, importante, alto ⟨a high number : un número grande⟩ ⟨high society : alta sociedad⟩ ⟨high hopes : grandes esperanzas⟩ **4** : alto (en música) **5** INTOXICATED : borracho, drogado

high[3] *n* **1** : récord *m*, punto *m* máximo ⟨to reach an all-time high : batir el récord⟩ **2** : zona *f* de alta presión (en meteorología) **3** *or* **high gear** : directa *f* **4 on high** : en las alturas

highbrow ['haɪ,braʊ] *n* : intelectual *mf*

higher ['haɪər] *adj* : superior

high fidelity *n* : alta fidelidad *f*

high–flown ['haɪ'flo:n] *adj* : altisonante

high–handed ['haɪ'hændəd] *adj* : arbitrario

highlands ['haɪləndz] *npl* : tierras *fpl* altas, altiplano *m*

highlight[1] ['haɪ,laɪt] *vt* **1** EMPHASIZE : destacar, poner en relieve, subrayar **2** : ser el punto culminante de

highlight[2] *n* : punto *m* culminante

highly ['haɪli] *adv* **1** VERY : muy, sumamente **2** FAVORABLY : muy bien ⟨to speak highly of : hablar muy bien de⟩ ⟨to think highly of : tener en mucho a⟩

highness ['haɪnəs] *n* **1** HEIGHT : altura *f* **2 Highness** : Alteza *f* ⟨Your Royal Highness : Su Alteza Real⟩

high–pitched ['haɪ'pɪtʃt] *adj* : agudo

high–rise ['haɪ,raɪz] *adj* : alto, de muchas plantas

high school *n* : escuela *f* superior, escuela *f* secundaria

high seas *npl* : alta mar *f*

high–spirited ['haɪ'spɪrətəd] *adj* : vivaz, muy animado, brioso

high–strung [,haɪ'strʌn] *adj* : nervioso, excitable

highway ['haɪ,weɪ] *n* : carretera *f*

highwayman ['haɪ,weɪmən] *n, pl* **-men** [-mən, -,mɛn] : salteador *m* (de caminos), bandido *m*

hijack[1] ['haɪ,dʒæk] *vt* : secuestrar

hijack[2] *n* : secuestro *m*

hijacker ['haɪ,dʒækər] *n* : secuestrador *m*, -dora *f*

hike[1] ['haɪk] *v* **hiked; hiking** *vi* : hacer una caminata — *vt* RAISE : subir

hike[2] *n* **1** : caminata *f*, excursión *f* **2** INCREASE : subida *f* (de precios)

hiker ['haɪkər] *n* : excursionista *mf*

hilarious [hɪ'læriəs, haɪ'-] *adj* : muy divertido, hilarante

hilarity [hɪ'lærəti, haɪ'-] *n* : hilaridad *f*

hill ['hɪl] *n* **1** : colina *f*, cerro *m* **2** SLOPE : cuesta *f*, pendiente *f*

hillbilly ['hɪl,bɪli] *n, pl* **-lies** : palurdo *m*, -da *f* (de las montañas)

hillock ['hɪlək] *n* : loma *f*, altozano *m*, otero *m*

hillside ['hɪl,saɪd] *n* : ladera *f*, cuesta *f*

hilltop ['hɪl,tɑp] *n* : cima *f*, cumbre *f*

hilly ['hɪli] *adj* **hillier; -est** : montañoso, accidentada

hilt ['hɪlt] *n* : puño *m*, empuñadura *f*

him ['hɪm, əm] *pron* **1** (*used as direct object*) : lo ⟨I found him : lo encontré⟩ **2** (*used as indirect object*) : le, se ⟨we gave him a present : le dimos un regalo⟩ ⟨I sent it to him : se lo mandé⟩ **3** (*used as object of a preposition*) : él ⟨she was thinking of him : pensaba en él⟩ ⟨younger than him : más joven que él⟩

himself [hɪm'sɛlf] *pron* **1** (*used reflexively*) : se ⟨he washed himself : se lavó⟩ **2** (*used emphatically*) : él mismo ⟨he did it himself : lo hizo él mismo, lo hizo por sí solo⟩

hind[1] ['haɪnd] *adj* : trasero, posterior ⟨hind legs : patas traseras⟩

hind[2] *n* : cierva *f*

hinder ['hɪndər] *vt* : dificultar, impedir, estorbar

Hindi ['hɪndi:] *n* : hindi *m*

hindquarters ['haɪnd,kwɔrtərz] *npl* : cuartos *mpl* traseros

hindrance ['hɪndrənts] *n* : estorbo *m*, obstáculo *m*, impedimento *m*

hindsight ['haɪnd,saɪt] *n* : retrospectiva *f* ⟨with the benefit of hindsight : en retrospectiva, con la perspectiva que da la experiencia⟩

Hindu[1] ['hɪn,du:] *adj* : hindú

Hindu[2] *n* : hindú *mf*

Hinduism ['hɪndu:,ɪzəm] *n* : hinduismo *m*

hinge[1] ['hɪndʒ] *v* **hinged; hinging** *vt* : unir con bisagras — *vi* **to hinge on** : depender de

hinge[2] *n* : bisagra *f*, gozne *m*

hint[1] ['hɪnt] *vt* : insinuar, dar a entender — *vi* : soltar indirectas

hint[2] *n* **1** INSINUATION : insinuación *f*, indirecta *f* **2** TIP : consejo *m*, sugerencia *f* **3** TRACE : pizca *f*, indicio *m*

hinterland ['hɪntər,lænd, -lənd] *n* : interior *m* (de un país)

hip ['hɪp] *n* : cadera *f*

hip–hop ['hɪp,hɑp] *n* : hip-hop *m*

hippie ['hɪpi] *n* : hippie *mf*, hippy *mf*

hippopotamus [,hɪpə'pɑtəməs] *n, pl* **-muses** *or* **-mi** [-,maɪ] : hipopótamo *m*

hippo ['hɪpo:] *n, pl* **hippos** → **hippopotamus**

hire[1] ['haɪr] *vt* **hired; hiring 1** EMPLOY : contratar, emplear **2** RENT : alquilar, arrendar

hire[2] *n* **1** RENT : alquiler *m* ⟨for hire : se alquila⟩ **2** WAGES : paga *f*, sueldo *m* **3** EMPLOYEE : empleado *m*, -da *f*

his[1] ['hɪz, ɪz] *adj* : su, sus, de él ⟨his hat : su sombrero, el sombrero de él⟩

his[2] *pron* : suyo, -ya; suyos, suyas; de él ⟨the decision is his : la decisión es suya⟩ ⟨it's his, not hers : es de él, no de ella⟩

Hispanic[1] [hɪ'spænɪk] *adj* : hispano, hispánico

Hispanic[2] *n* : hispano *m*, -na *f*; hispánico *m*, -ca *f*

hiss[1] ['hɪs] *vi* : sisear, silbar — *vt* : decir entre dientes

hiss[2] *n* : siseo *m*, silbido *m*

historian [hɪ'stɔriən] *n* : historiador *m*, -dora *f*

historic [hɪ'stɔrɪk] *or* **historical** [-ɪkəl] *adj* : histórico — **historically** [-ɪkli] *adv*

history ['hɪstəri] *n, pl* **-ries** 1 : historia *f* 2 RECORD : historial *m*

histrionics [ˌhɪstri'ɑnɪks] *ns & pl* : histrionismo *m*

hit[1] ['hɪt] *v* **hit; hitting** *vt* 1 STRIKE : golpear, pegar, batear (una pelota) ⟨he hit the dog : le pegó al perro⟩ 2 : chocar contra, dar con, dar en (el blanco) ⟨the car hit a tree : el coche chocó contra un árbol⟩ 3 AFFECT : afectar ⟨the news hit us hard : la noticia nos afectó mucho⟩ 4 ENCOUNTER : tropezar con, toparse con ⟨to hit a snag : tropezar con un obstáculo⟩ 5 REACH : llegar a, alcanzar ⟨the price hit $10 a pound : el precio alcanzó los $10 dólares por libra⟩ ⟨to hit town : llegar a la ciudad⟩ ⟨to hit the headlines : ser noticia⟩ 6 **to hit on** *or* **to hit upon** : dar con — *vi* : golpear

hit[2] *n* 1 BLOW : golpe *m* 2 : impacto *m* (de un arma) 3 SUCCESS : éxito *m*

hitch[1] ['hɪtʃ] *vt* 1 : mover con sacudidas 2 ATTACH : enganchar, atar, amarrar 3 → **hitchhike** 4 **to hitch up** : subirse (los pantalones, etc.)

hitch[2] *n* 1 JERK : tirón *m*, jalón *m* 2 OBSTACLE : obstáculo *m*, impedimento *m*, tropiezo *m*

hitchhike ['hɪtʃˌhaɪk] *vi* **-hiked; -hiking** : hacer autostop, ir de aventón *Col, Mex fam*

hitchhiker ['hɪtʃˌhaɪkər] *n* : autostopista *mf*

hither ['hɪðər] *adv* : acá, por aquí

hitherto ['hɪðərˌtuː, ˌhɪðər'-] *adv* : hasta ahora

hitter ['hɪtər] *n* BATTER : bateador *m*, -dora *f*

HIV [ˌɛɪtʃˌaɪ'viː] *n* (*h*uman *i*mmunodeficiency *v*irus) : VIH *m*, virus *m* del sida

hive ['haɪv] *n* 1 : colmena *f* 2 SWARM : enjambre *m* 3 : lugar *m* muy activo ⟨a hive of activity : un hervidero de actividad⟩

hives ['haɪvz] *ns & pl* : urticaria *f*

hoard[1] ['hɔrd] *vt* : acumular, atesorar

hoard[2] *n* : tesoro *m*, reserva *f*, provisión *f*

hoarfrost ['hɔrˌfrɔst] *n* : escarcha *f*

hoarse ['hɔrs] *adj* **hoarser; -est** : ronco — **hoarsely** *adv*

hoarseness ['hɔrsnəs] *n* : ronquera *f*

hoary ['hɔri] *adj* **hoarier; -est** 1 : cano, canoso 2 OLD : vetusto, antiguo

hoax[1] ['hoːks] *vt* : engañar, embaucar, bromear

hoax[2] *n* : engaño *m*, broma *f*

hobble[1] ['hɑbəl] *v* **-bled; -bling** *vi* LIMP : cojear, renguear — *vt* : manear (un animal)

hobble[2] *n* 1 LIMP : cojera *f*, rengo *m* 2 : maniota *f* (para un animal)

hobby ['hɑbi] *n, pl* **-bies** : pasatiempo *m*, afición *f*

hobgoblin ['hɑbˌgɑblən] *n* : duende *m*

hobnail ['hɑbˌneɪl] *n* : tachuela *f*

hobnob ['hɑbˌnɑb] *vi* **-nobbed; -nobbing** : codearse

hobo ['hoːˌboː] *n, pl* **-boes** : vagabundo *m*, -da *f*

hock[1] ['hɑk] *vt* PAWN : empeñar

hock[2] *n* **in hock** : empeñado

hockey ['hɑki] *n* : hockey *m*

hodgepodge ['hɑdʒˌpɑdʒ] *n* : mezcolanza *f*

hoe[1] ['hoː] *vt* **hoed; hoeing** : azadonar

hoe[2] *n* : azada *f*, azadón *m*

hog[1] ['hɔg, 'hɑg] *vt* **hogged; hogging** : acaparar, monopolizar

hog[2] *n* 1 PIG : cerdo *m*, -da *f* 2 GLUTTON : glotón *m*, -tona *f*

hogshead ['hɔgzˌhɛd, 'hɑgz-] *n* : tonel *m*

hoist[1] ['hɔɪst] *vt* : levantar, alzar, izar (una bandera, una vela)

hoist[2] *n* : grúa *f*

hold[1] ['hoːld] *v* **held** ['hɛld]; **holding** *vt* 1 POSSESS : tener ⟨to hold office : ocupar un puesto⟩ 2 RESTRAIN : detener, controlar ⟨to hold one's temper : controlar su mal genio⟩ 3 CLASP, GRASP : agarrar, coger ⟨to hold hands : agarrarse de la mano⟩ 4 : sujetar, mantener fijo ⟨hold this nail for me : sujétame este clavo⟩ 5 CONTAIN : contener, dar cabida a 6 SUPPORT : aguantar, sostener 7 REGARD : considerar, tener ⟨he held me responsible : me consideró responsable⟩ 8 CONDUCT : celebrar (una reunión), realizar (un evento), mantener (una conversación) — *vi* 1 : aguantar, resistir ⟨the rope will hold : la cuerda resistirá⟩ 2 : ser válido, valer ⟨my offer still holds : mi oferta todavía es válida⟩ 3 **to hold forth** : perorar, arengar 4 **to hold to** : mantenerse firme en 5 **to hold with** : estar de acuerdo con

hold[2] *n* 1 GRIP : agarre *m*, llave *f* (en deportes) 2 CONTROL : control *m*, dominio *m* ⟨to get hold of oneself : controlarse⟩ 3 DELAY : demora *f* ⟨to put on hold : suspender temporalmente⟩ 4 : bodega *f* (en un barco o un avión) 5 **to get hold of** : conseguir, localizar

holder ['hoːldər] *n* : poseedor *m*, -dora *f*; titular *mf*

holdings ['hoːldɪŋz] *npl* : propiedades *fpl*

hold out *vi* 1 LAST : aguantar, durar 2 RESIST : resistir

holdup ['hoːldˌʌp] *n* 1 ROBBERY : atraco *m* 2 DELAY : retraso *m*, demora *f*

hold up *vt* 1 ROB : robarle (a alguien), atracar, asaltar 2 DELAY : retrasar

hole ['hoːl] *n* : agujero *m*, hoyo *m*

holiday ['hɑlə‚deɪ] *n* **1** : día *m* feriado, fiesta *f* **2** VACATION : vacaciones *fpl*
holiness ['ho:linəs] *n* **1** : santidad *f* **2 His Holiness** : Su Santidad
holistic [ho:'lɪstɪk] *adj* : holístico
holler[1] ['hɑlər] *vi* : gritar, chillar
holler[2] *n* : grito *m*, chillido *m*
hollow[1] ['hɑ‚lo:] *vt or* **to hollow out** : ahuecar
hollow[2] *adj* **-lower; -est 1** : hueco, hundido (dícese de las mejillas, etc.), cavernoso (dícese de un sonido) **2** EMPTY, FALSE : vacío, falso
hollow[3] *n* **1** CAVITY : hueco *m*, depresión *f*, cavidad *f* **2** VALLEY : hondonada *f*, valle *m*
hollowness ['hɑ‚lo:nəs] *n* **1** HOLLOW : hueco *m*, cavidad *f* **2** FALSENESS : falsedad *f* **3** EMPTINESS : vacuidad *f*
holly ['hɑli] *n, pl* **-lies** : acebo *m*
hollyhock ['hɑli‚hɑk] *n* : malvarrosa *f*
holocaust ['hɑlə‚kɔst, 'ho:-, 'hɔ-] *n* : holocausto *m*
hologram ['ho:lə‚græm, 'hɑ-] *n* : holograma *m*
holster ['ho:lstər] *n* : pistolera *f*
holy ['ho:li] *adj* **-lier; -est** : santo, sagrado
Holy Ghost → Holy Spirit
Holy Spirit *n* **the Holy Spirit** : el Espíritu Santo
homage ['ɑmɪʤ, 'hɑ-] *n* : homenaje *m*
home ['ho:m] *n* **1** : casa *f*, hogar *m*, domicilio *m* ⟨to feel at home : sentirse en casa⟩ **2** INSTITUTION : residencia *f*, asilo *m*
homecoming ['ho:m‚kʌmɪŋ] *n* : regreso *m* (a casa)
homegrown ['ho:m'gro:n] *adj* **1** : de cosecha propia **2** LOCAL : local
homeland ['ho:m‚lænd] *n* : patria *f*, tierra *f* natal, terruño *m*
homeless ['ho:mləs] *adj* : sin hogar, sin techo
homely ['ho:mli] *adj* **-lier; -est 1** DOMESTIC : casero, hogareño **2** UGLY : feo, poco atractivo
homemade ['ho:m'meɪd] *adj* : casero, hecho en casa
homemaker ['ho:m‚meɪkər] *n* : ama *f* de casa, persona *f* que se ocupa de la casa
home plate *n* : base *f* del bateador
home run *n* : jonrón *m*
homesick ['ho:m‚sɪk] *adj* : nostálgico ⟨to be homesick : echar de menos a la familia⟩
homesickness ['ho:m‚sɪknəs] *n* : nostalgia *f*, morriña *f*
homespun ['ho:m‚spʌn] *adj* : simple, sencillo
homestead ['ho:m‚stɛd] *n* : estancia *f*, hacienda *f*
homeward[1] ['ho:mwərd] *or* **homewards** [-wərdz] *adv* : de vuelta a casa, hacia casa
homeward[2] *adj* : de vuelta, de regreso
homework ['ho:m‚wərk] *n* : tarea *f*, deberes *mpl Spain*, asignación *f PRi*

homey ['ho:mi] *adj* **homier; -est** : hogareño
homicidal [‚hɑmə'saɪdəl, ‚ho:-] *adj* : homicida
homicide ['hɑmə‚saɪd, 'ho:-] *n* : homicidio *m*
hominy ['hɑməni] *n* : maíz *m* descascarillado
homogeneity [‚ho:məʤə'ni:əti, -'neɪ-] *n, pl* **-ties** : homogeneidad *f*
homogeneous [‚ho:mə'ʤi:niəs, -njəs] *adj* : homogéneo — **homogeneously** *adv*
homogenize [ho:'mɑʤə‚naɪz, hə-] *vt* **-nized; -nizing** : homogeneizar
homograph ['hɑmə‚græf, 'ho:-] *n* : homógrafo *m*
homologous [ho:'mɑləgəs, hə-] *adj* : homólogo
homonym ['hɑmə‚nɪm, 'ho:-] *n* : homónimo *m*
homophone ['hɑmə‚fo:n, 'ho:-] *n* : homófono *m*
homosexual[1] [‚ho:mə'sɛkʃuəl] *adj* : homosexual
homosexual[2] *n* : homosexual *mf*
homosexuality [‚ho:mə‚sɛkʃu'æləti] *n* : homosexualidad *f*
honcho ['hɑn‚tʃo:] *n* : pez *m* gordo ⟨the head honcho : el jefe⟩
Honduran [hɑn'dʊrən, -'djʊr-] *n* : hondureño *m*, -ña *f* — **Honduran** *adj*
hone ['ho:n] *vt* **honed; honing** : afilar
honest ['ɑnəst] *adj* : honesto, honrado — **honestly** *adv*
honesty ['ɑnəsti] *n, pl* **-ties** : honestidad *f*, honradez *f*
honey ['hʌni] *n, pl* **-eys** : miel *f*
honeybee ['hʌni‚bi:] *n* : abeja *f*
honeycomb ['hʌni‚ko:m] *n* : panal *m*
honeymoon[1] ['hʌni‚mu:n] *vi* : pasar la luna de miel
honeymoon[2] *n* : luna *f* de miel
honeysuckle ['hʌni‚sʌkəl] *n* : madreselva *f*
honk[1] ['hɑŋk, 'hɔŋk] *vi* **1** : graznar (dícese del ganso) **2** : tocar la bocina (dícese de un vehículo), pitar
honk[2] *n* : graznido *m* (del ganso), bocinazo *m* (de un vehículo)
honor[1] ['ɑnər] *vt* **1** RESPECT : honrar **2** : cumplir con ⟨to honor one's word : cumplir con su palabra⟩ **3** : aceptar (un cheque, etc.)
honor[2] *n* **1** : honor *m* ⟨in honor of : en honor de⟩ **2 honors** *npl* AWARDS : honores *mpl*, condecoraciones *fpl* **3 Your Honor** : Su Señoría
honorable ['ɑnərəbəl] *adj* : honorable, honroso — **honorably** [-bli] *adv*
honorary ['ɑnə‚rɛri] *adj* : honorario
hood ['hʊd] *n* **1** : capucha *f* **2** : capó *m*, bonete *m Car* (de un automóvil)
hooded ['hʊdəd] *adj* : encapuchado
hoodlum ['hʊdləm, 'hu:d-] *n* THUG : maleante *mf*, matón *m*
hoodwink ['hʊd‚wɪŋk] *vt* : engañar

hoof ['hʊf, 'huːf] *n, pl* **hooves** ['hʊvz, 'huːvz] *or* **hoofs** : pezuña *f*, casco *m*
hoofed ['hʊft, 'huːft] *adj* : ungulado
hook[1] ['hʊk] *vt* : enganchar — *vi* : abrocharse, engancharse
hook[2] *n* : gancho *m*, percha *f*
hooked ['hʊkt] *adj* **1** : en forma de gancho **2 to be hooked on** : estar enganchado a
hooker ['hʊkər] *n* : prostituta *f*, fulana *f fam*
hookworm ['hʊk,wərm] *n* : anquilostoma *m*
hooligan ['huːlɪgən] *n* : gamberro *m*, -rra *f*
hoop ['huːp] *n* : aro *m*
hooray [hʊ'reɪ] → **hurrah**
hoot[1] ['huːt] *vi* **1** SHOUT : gritar ⟨to hoot with laughter : morirse de risa, reírse a carcajadas⟩ **2** : ulular (dícese de un búho), tocar la bocina (dícese de un vehículo), silbar (dícese de un tren o un barco)
hoot[2] *n* **1** : ululato *m* (de un búho), silbido *m* (de un tren), bocinazo *m* (de un vehículo) **2** GUFFAW : carcajada *f*, risotada *f* **3 I don't give a hoot** : me vale un comino, me importa un pito
hop[1] ['hɑp] *vi* **hopped; hopping** : brincar, saltar
hop[2] *n* **1** LEAP : salto *m*, brinco *m* **2** FLIGHT : vuelo *m* corto **3** : lúpulo *m* (planta)
hope[1] ['hoːp] *v* **hoped; hoping** *vi* : esperar — *vt* : esperar que ⟨we hope she comes : esperamos que venga⟩ ⟨I hope not : espero que no⟩
hope[2] *n* : esperanza *f*
hopeful ['hoːpfəl] *adj* : esperanzado — **hopefully** *adv*
hopeless ['hoːpləs] *adj* **1** DESPAIRING : desesperado **2** IMPOSSIBLE : imposible ⟨a hopeless case : un caso perdido⟩
hopelessly ['hoːpləsli] *adv* **1** : sin esperanzas, desesperadamente **2** COMPLETELY : totalmente, completamente **3** IMPOSSIBLY : imposiblemente
hopelessness ['hoːpləsnəs] *n* : desesperanza *f*
hopper ['hɑpər] *n* : tolva *f*
hopscotch ['hɑp,skɑtʃ] *n* : tejo *m*
horde ['hord] *n* : horda *f*, multitud *f*
horizon [hə'raɪzən] *n* : horizonte *m*
horizontal [,hɔrə'zɑntəl] *adj* : horizontal — **horizontally** *adv*
hormone ['hɔr,moːn] *n* : hormona *f* — **hormonal** [hɔr'moːnəl] *adj*
horn ['hɔrn] *n* **1** : cuerno *m* (de un toro, una vaca, etc.) **2** : cuerno *m*, trompa *f* (instrumento musical) **3** : bocina *f*, claxon *m* (de un vehículo)
horned ['hɔrnd, 'hɔrnəd] *adj* : cornudo, astado, con cuernos
hornet ['hɔrnət] *n* : avispón *m*
horny ['hɔrni] *adj* **hornier; -est 1** CALLOUS : calloso **2** LUSTFUL *fam* : caliente *fam*
horoscope ['hɔrə,skoːp] *n* : horóscopo *m*

horrendous [hɔ'rɛndəs] *adj* : horrendo, horroroso, atroz
horrible ['hɔrəbəl] *adj* : horrible, espantoso, horroroso — **horribly** [-bli] *adv*
horrid ['hɔrɪd] *adj* : horroroso, horrible — **horridly** *adv*
horrific [hɔ'rɪfɪk] *adj* : terrorífico, horroroso
horrify ['hɔrə,faɪ] *vt* **-fied; -fying** : horrorizar
horrifying ['hɔrə,faɪɪŋ] *adj* : horripilante, horroroso
horror ['hɔrər] *n* : horror *m*
hors d'oeuvre [ɔr'dərv] *n, pl* **hors d'oeuvres** [-'dərvz] : entremés *m*
horse ['hɔrs] *n* : caballo *m*
horseback ['hɔrs,bæk] *n* **on ∼** : a caballo
horse chestnut *n* : castaña *f* de Indias
horsefly ['hɔrs,flaɪ] *n, pl* **-flies** : tábano *m*
horsehair ['hɔrs,hær] *n* : crin *f*
horseman ['hɔrsmən] *n, pl* **-men** [-mən, -,mɛn] : jinete *m*, caballista *m*
horsemanship ['hɔrsmən,ʃɪp] *n* : equitación *f*
horseplay ['hɔrs,pleɪ] *n* : payasadas *fpl*
horsepower ['hɔrs,paʊər] *n* : caballo *m* de fuerza
horseradish ['hɔrs,rædɪʃ] *n* : rábano *m* picante
horseshoe ['hɔrs,ʃuː] *n* : herradura *f*
horsewhip ['hɔrs,ʰwɪp] *vt* **-whipped; -whipping** : azotar, darle fuetazos (a alguien)
horsewoman ['hɔrs,wʊmən] *n, pl* **-women** [-,wɪmən] : amazona *f*, jinete *f*, caballista *f*
horsey *or* **horsy** ['hɔrsi] *adj* **horsier; -est** : relacionado a los caballos, caballar
horticultural [,hɔrtə'kʌltʃərəl] *adj* : hortícola
horticulture ['hɔrtə,kʌltʃər] *n* : horticultura *f*
hose[1] ['hoːz] *vt* **hosed; hosing** : regar o lavar con manguera
hose[2] *n* **1** *pl* **hose** SOCKS : calcetines *mpl*, medias *fpl* **2** *pl* **hose** STOCKINGS : medias *fpl* **3** *pl* **hoses** : manguera *f*, manga *f*
hosiery ['hoːʒəri, 'hoːzə-] *n* : calcetería *f*, medias *fpl*
hospice ['hɑspəs] *n* : hospicio *m*
hospitable [hɑ'spɪtəbəl, 'hɑs,pɪ-] *adj* : hospitalario — **hospitably** [-bli] *adv*
hospital ['hɑs,pɪtəl] *n* : hospital *m*
hospitality [,hɑspə'tæləti] *n, pl* **-ties** : hospitalidad *f*
hospitalization [,hɑs,pɪtələ'zeɪʃən] *n* : hospitalización *f*
hospitalize ['hɑs,pɪtəl,aɪz] *vt* **-ized; -izing** : hospitalizar
host[1] ['hoːst] *vt* : presentar (un programa de televisión, etc.)
host[2] *n* **1** : anfitrión *m*, -triona *f* (en la casa, a un evento); presentador *m*, -dora *f* (de un programa de televisión, etc.) **2** *or* **host organism** : huésped *m*

3 TROOPS : huestes *fpl* 4 MULTITUDE : multitud *f* ⟨for a host of reasons : por muchas razones⟩ 5 EUCHARIST : hostia *f*, Eucaristía *f*

hostage ['hɑstɪʤ] *n* : rehén *m*

hostel ['hɑstəl] *n* : albergue *m* juvenil

hostess ['ho:stɪs] *n* : anfitriona *f* (en la casa), presentadora *f* (de un programa)

hostile ['hɑstəl, -,taɪl] *adj* : hostil — **hostilely** *adv*

hostility [hɑs'tɪləti] *n*, *pl* **-ties** : hostilidad *f*

hot ['hɑt] *adj* **hotter; hottest** 1 : caliente, cálido, caluroso ⟨hot water : agua caliente⟩ ⟨a hot climate : un clima cálido⟩ ⟨a hot day : un día caluroso⟩ 2 ARDENT, FIERY : ardiente, acalorado ⟨to have a hot temper : tener mal genio⟩ 3 SPICY : picante 4 FRESH : reciente, nuevo ⟨hot news : noticias de última hora⟩ 5 EAGER : ávido 6 STOLEN : robado

hot air *n* : palabrería *f*

hotbed ['hɑt,bɛd] *n* 1 : semillero *m* (de plantas) 2 : hervidero *m*, semillero *m* (de crimen, etc.)

hot dog *n* : perro *m* caliente

hotel [ho:'tɛl] *n* : hotel *m*

hothead ['hɑt,hɛd] *n* : exaltado *m*, -da *f*

hotheaded ['hɑt'hɛdəd] *adj* : exaltado

hothouse ['hɑt,haʊs] *n* : invernadero *m*

hot plate *n* : placa *f* (de cocina)

hot rod *n* : coche *m* con motor modificado

hot water *n* **to get into hot water** : meterse en un lío

hound¹ ['haʊnd] *vt* : acosar, perseguir

hound² *n* : perro *m* (de caza)

hour ['aʊər] *n* : hora *f*

hourglass ['aʊər,glæs] *n* : reloj *m* de arena

hourly ['aʊərli] *adv & adj* : cada hora, por hora

house¹ ['haʊz] *vt* **housed; housing** : albergar, alojar, hospedar

house² ['haʊs] *n*, *pl* **houses** ['haʊzəz, -səz] 1 HOME : casa *f* 2 : cámara *f* (del gobierno) 3 BUSINESS : casa *f*, empresa *f*

houseboat ['haʊs,bo:t] *n* : casa *f* flotante

housebroken ['haʊs,bro:kən] *adj* : enseñado

housefly ['haʊs,flaɪ] *n*, *pl* **-flies** : mosca *f* común

household¹ ['haʊs,ho:ld] *adj* 1 DOMESTIC : doméstico, de la casa 2 FAMILIAR : conocido por todos

household² *n* : casa *f*, familia *f*

householder ['haʊs,ho:ldər] *n* : dueño *m*, -ña *f* de casa

housekeeper ['haʊs,ki:pər] *n* : ama *f* de llaves

housekeeping ['haʊs,ki:pɪŋ] *n* : gobierno *m* de la casa, quehaceres *mpl* domésticos

housemaid ['haʊs,meɪd] *n* : criada *f*, mucama *f*, muchacha *f*, sirvienta *f*

housewarming ['haʊs,wɔrmɪŋ] *n* : fiesta *f* de estreno de una casa

housewife ['haʊs,waɪf] *n*, *pl* **-wives** : ama *f* de casa

housework ['haʊs,wərk] *n* : faenas *fpl* domésticas, quehaceres *mpl* domésticos

housing ['haʊzɪŋ] *n* 1 HOUSES : vivienda *f* 2 COVERING : caja *f* protectora

hove → **heave**

hovel ['hʌvəl, 'hɑ-] *n* : casucha *f*, tugurio *m*

hover ['hʌvər, 'hɑ-] *vi* 1 : cernerse, sostenerse en el aire 2 **to hover about** : rondar

how ['haʊ] *adv* 1 : cómo ⟨how are you? : ¿cómo estás?⟩ ⟨I don't know how to fix it : no se cómo arreglarlo⟩ 2 : qué ⟨how beautiful! : ¡qué bonito!⟩ 3 : cuánto ⟨how old are you? : ¿cuántos años tienes?⟩ 4 **how about . . . ?** : ¿qué te parece . . . ?

however¹ [haʊ'ɛvər] *adv* 1 : por mucho que, por más que ⟨however hot it is : por mucho calor que haga⟩ 2 NEVERTHELESS : sin embargo, no obstante

however² *conj* : comoquiera que, de cualquier manera que

howl¹ ['haʊl] *vi* : aullar

howl² *n* : aullido *m*, alarido *m*

hub ['hʌb] *n* 1 CENTER : centro *m* 2 : cubo *m* (de una rueda)

hubbub ['hʌ,bʌb] *n* : algarabía *f*, alboroto *m*, jaleo *m*

hubcap ['hʌb,kæp] *n* : tapacubos *m*

huckster ['hʌkstər] *n* : buhonero *m*, -ra *f*; vendedor *m*, -dora *f* ambulante

huddle¹ ['hʌdəl] *vi* **-dled; -dling** 1 : apiñarse, amontonarse 2 **to huddle together** : acurrucarse

huddle² *n* : grupo *m* (cerrado) ⟨to go into a huddle : conferenciar en secreto⟩

hue ['hju:] *n* : color *m*, tono *m*

huff ['hʌf] *n* : enojo *m*, enfado *m* ⟨to be in a huff : estar enojado⟩

huffy ['hʌfi] *adj* **huffier; -est** : enojado, enfadado

hug¹ ['hʌg] *vt* **hugged; hugging** 1 EMBRACE : abrazar 2 : ir pegado a ⟨the road hugs the river : el camino está pegado al río⟩

hug² *n* : abrazo *m*

huge ['hju:ʤ] *adj* **huger; hugest** : inmenso, enorme — **hugely** *adv*

hulk ['hʌlk] *n* 1 : persona *f* fornida 2 : casco *m* (barco), armatoste *m* (edificio, etc.)

hulking ['hʌlkɪŋ] *adj* : grandote *fam*, pesado

hull¹ ['hʌl] *vt* : pelar

hull² *n* 1 HUSK : cáscara *f* 2 : casco *m* (de un barco, un avión, etc.)

hullabaloo ['hʌləbə,lu:] *n*, *pl* **-loos** : alboroto *m*, jaleo *m*

hum¹ ['hʌm] *v* **hummed; humming** *vi* 1 BUZZ : zumbar 2 : estar muy activo, moverse ⟨to hum with activity : bullir de actividad⟩ — *vt* : tararear (una melodía)

hum² *n* : zumbido *m*, murmullo *m*
human¹ ['hju:mən, 'ju:-] *adj* : humano
— **humanly** *adv*
human² *n* : ser *m* humano
humane [hju:'meɪn, ju:-] *adj* : humano,
humanitario — **humanely** *adv*
humanism ['hju:mə,nɪzəm, 'ju:-] *n* : humanismo *m*
humanist¹ ['hju:mənɪst, 'ju:-] *n* : humanista *mf*
humanist² *or* **humanistic** [,hju:mə-
'nɪstɪk, ,ju:-] *adj* : humanístico
humanitarian¹ [hju:,mænə'triən, ju:-]
adj : humanitario
humanitarian² *n* : humanitario *m*, -ria *f*
humanity [hju:'mænəṭi, ju:-] *n, pl* **-ties**
: humanidad *f*
humankind ['hju:mən'kaɪnd, 'ju:-] *n*
: género *m* humano
humble¹ ['hʌmbəl] *vt* **-bled; -bling** 1
: humillar **2 to humble oneself** : humillarse
humble² *adj* **-bler; -blest** : humilde,
modesto — **humbly** ['hʌmbli] *adv*
humbug ['hʌm,bʌg] *n* 1 FRAUD : charlatán *m*, -tana *f*; farsante *mf* 2 NON-
SENSE : patrañas *fpl*, tonterías *fpl*
humdrum ['hʌm,drʌm] *adj* : monótono,
rutinario
humid ['hju:məd, 'ju:-] *adj* : húmedo
humidifier [hju:'mɪdə,faɪər, ju:-] *n* : humidificador *m*
humidify [hju:'mɪdə,faɪ, ju:-] *vt* **-fied;
-fying** : humidificar
humidity [hju:'mɪdəṭi, ju:-] *n, pl* **-ties**
: humedad *f*
humiliate [hju:'mɪli,eɪt, ju:-] *vt* **-ated;
-ating** : humillar
humiliating [hju:'mɪli,eɪtɪŋ, ju:-] *adj*
: humillante
humiliation [hju:,mɪli'eɪʃən, ju:-] *n* : humillación *f*
humility [hju:'mɪləṭi, ju:-] *n* : humildad
f
hummingbird ['hʌmɪŋ,bərd] *n* : colibrí
m, picaflor *m*
hummock ['hʌmək] *n* : montículo *m*
humor¹ ['hju:mər, 'ju:-] *vt* : seguir el humor a, complacer
humor² *n* : humor *m*
humorist ['hju:mərɪst, 'ju:-] *n* : humorista *mf*
humorless ['hju:mərləs, 'ju:-] *adj* : sin
sentido del humor ⟨a humorless smile
: una sonrisa forzada⟩
humorous ['hju:mərəs, 'ju:-] *adj* : humorístico, cómico — **humorously** *adv*
hump ['hʌmp] *n* : joroba *f*, giba *f*
humpback ['hʌmp,bæk] *n* 1 HUMP
: joroba *f*, giba *f* 2 HUNCHBACK
: jorobado *m*, -da *f*; giboso *m*, -sa *f*
humpbacked ['hʌmp,bækt] *adj*
: jorobado, giboso
humus ['hju:məs, 'ju:-] *n* : humus *m*
hunch¹ ['hʌntʃ] *vt* : encorvar — *vi or* **to
hunch up** : encorvarse
hunch² *n* PREMONITION : presentimiento *m*

hunchback ['hʌntʃ,bæk] *n* 1 HUMP
: joroba *f*, giba *f* 2 HUMPBACK : jorobado *m*, -da *f*; giboso *m*, -sa *f*
hunchbacked ['hʌntʃ,bækt] *adj* : jorobado, giboso
hundred¹ ['hʌndrəd] *adj* : cien, ciento
hundred² *n, pl* **-dreds** *or* **-dred** : ciento
m
hundredth¹ ['hʌndrədθ] *adj* : centésimo
hundredth² *n* 1 : centésimo *m*, -ma *f* (en
una serie) 2 : centésimo *m*, centésima
parte *f*
hung → **hang**
Hungarian [hʌŋ'gæriən] *n* 1 : húngaro
m, -ra *f* 2 : húngaro *m* (idioma) — **Hungarian** *adj*
hunger¹ ['hʌŋgər] *vi* 1 : tener hambre
2 **to hunger for** : ansiar, anhelar
hunger² *n* : hambre *m*
hungrily ['hʌŋgrəli] *adv* : ávidamente
hungry ['hʌŋgri] *adj* **-grier; -est** 1
: hambriento **2 to be hungry** : tener
hambre
hunk ['hʌŋk] *n* : trozo *m*, pedazo *m*
hunt¹ ['hʌnt] *vt* 1 PURSUE : cazar **2 to
hunt for** : buscar
hunt² *n* 1 PURSUIT : caza *f*, cacería *f* 2
SEARCH : búsqueda *f*, busca *f*
hunter ['hʌntər] *n* : cazador *m*, -dora *f*
hunting ['hʌntɪŋ] *n* : caza *f* ⟨to go hunting : ir de caza⟩
hurdle¹ ['hərdəl] *vt* **-dled; -dling** : saltar,
salvar (un obstáculo)
hurdle² *n* : valla *f* (en deportes), obstáculo *m*
hurl ['hərl] *vt* : arrojar, tirar, lanzar
hurrah [hʊ'rɑ, -'rɔ] *interj* : ¡hurra!
hurricane ['hərə,keɪn] *n* : huracán *m*
hurried ['hərid] *adj* : apresurado, precipitado
hurriedly ['hərədli] *adv* : apresuradamente, de prisa
hurry¹ ['həri] *v* **-ried; -rying** *vi* : apurarse,
darse prisa, apresurarse — *vt* : apurar,
darle prisa (a alguien)
hurry² *n* : prisa *f*, apuro *f*
hurt¹ ['hərt] *v* **hurt; hurting** *vt* 1 INJURE
: hacer daño a, herir, lastimar ⟨to hurt
oneself : hacerse daño⟩ 2 DISTRESS,
OFFEND : hacer sufrir, ofender, herir
— *vi* : doler ⟨my foot hurts : me duele
el pie⟩
hurt² *n* 1 INJURY : herida *f* 2 DISTRESS,
PAIN : dolor *m*, pena *f*
hurtful ['hərtfəl] *adj* : hiriente, doloroso
hurtle ['hərtəl] *vi* **-tled; -tling** : lanzarse,
precipitarse
husband¹ ['hʌzbənd] *vt* : economizar,
bien administrar
husband² *n* : esposo *m*, marido *m*
husbandry ['hʌzbəndri] *n* 1 MANAGE-
MENT, THRIFT : economía *f*, buena administración *f* 2 AGRICULTURE : agricultura *f* ⟨animal husbandry : cría de
animales⟩
hush¹ ['hʌʃ] *vt* 1 SILENCE : hacer callar,
acallar 2 CALM : calmar, apaciguar
hush² *n* : silencio *m*

hush–hush ['hʌʃˌhʌʃ, ˌhʌʃ'hʌʃ] *adj* : muy secreto, confidencial
husk[1] ['hʌsk] *vt* : descascarar
husk[2] *n* : cáscara *f*
huskily ['hʌskəli] *adv* : con voz ronca
husky[1] ['hʌski] *adj* **-kier; -est 1** HOARSE : ronco **2** BURLY : fornido
husky[2] *n, pl* **-kies** : perro *m*, -rra *f* esquimal
hustle[1] ['həsəl] *v* **-tled; -tling** *vt* : darle prisa (a alguien), apurar ⟨they hustled me in : me hicieron entrar a empujones⟩ — *vi* : apurarse, ajetrearse
hustle[2] *n* BUSTLE : ajetreo *m*
hut ['hʌt] *n* : cabaña *f*, choza *f*, barraca *f*
hutch ['hʌtʃ] *n* **1** CUPBOARD : alacena *f* **2 rabbit hutch** : conejera *f*
hyacinth ['haɪəˌsɪnθ] *n* : jacinto *m*
hybrid[1] ['haɪbrɪd] *adj* : híbrido
hybrid[2] *n* : híbrido *m*
hydrant ['haɪdrənt] *n* : boca *f* de riego, hidrante *m CA, Col* ⟨fire hydrant : boca de incendios⟩
hydraulic [haɪ'drɔlɪk] *adj* : hidráulico — **hydraulically** *adv*
hydrocarbon [ˌhaɪdro'kɑrbən] *n* : hidrocarburo *m*
hydrochloric acid [ˌhaɪdro'klorɪk] *n* : ácido *m* clorhídrico
hydroelectric [ˌhaɪdroɪ'lɛktrɪk] *adj* : hidroeléctrico
hydrogen ['haɪdrədʒən] *n* : hidrógeno *m*
hydrogen bomb *n* : bomba *f* de hidrógeno
hydrogen peroxide *n* : agua *f* oxigenada, peróxido *m* de hidrógeno
hydrophobia [ˌhaɪdrə'fo:biə] *n* : hidrofobia *f*, rabia *f*
hydroplane ['haɪdrəˌpleɪn] *n* : hidroplano *m*
hyena [haɪ'i:nə] *n* : hiena *f*
hygiene ['haɪˌdʒi:n] *n* : higiene *f*
hygienic [haɪ'dʒɛnɪk, -'dʒi:-; ˌhaɪ-dʒi'nɪk] *adj* : higiénico — **hygienically** [-nɪkli] *adv*
hygienist [haɪ'dʒi:nɪst, -'dʒɛ-; 'haɪ-ˌdʒi:-] *n* : higienista *mf*
hygrometer [haɪ'grɑmətər] *n* : higrómetro *m*
hymn ['hɪm] *n* : himno *m*

hymnal ['hɪmnəl] *n* : himnario *m*
hype ['haɪp] *n* : bombo *m* publicitario
hyperactive [ˌhaɪpər'æktɪv] *adj* : hiperactivo
hyperactivity [ˌhaɪpərˌæk'tɪvəti] *n, pl* **-ties** : hiperactividad *f*
hyperbole [haɪ'pərbəli] *n* : hipérbole *f*
hyperbolic [ˌhaɪpər'balɪk] *adj* : hiperbólico
hypercritical [ˌhaɪpər'krɪtəkəl] *adj* : hipercrítico
hypersensitivity [ˌhaɪpərˌsɛntsə'tɪ-vəti] *n* : hipersensibilidad *f*
hypertension ['haɪpərˌtɛntʃən] *n* : hipertensión *f*
hyphen ['haɪfən] *n* : guión *m*
hyphenate ['haɪfənˌeɪt] *vt* **-ated; -ating** : escribir con guión
hypnosis [hɪp'no:sɪs] *n, pl* **-noses** [-ˌsi:z] : hipnosis *f*
hypnotic [hɪp'nɑtɪk] *adj* : hipnótico, hipnotizador
hypnotism ['hɪpnəˌtɪzəm] *n* : hipnotismo *m*
hypnotize ['hɪpnəˌtaɪz] *vt* **-tized; -tizing** : hipnotizar
hypochondria [ˌhaɪpə'kandriə] *n* : hipocondría *f*
hypochondriac [ˌhaɪpə'kandriˌæk] *n* : hipocondríaco *m*, -ca *f*
hypocrisy [hɪp'akrəsi] *n, pl* **-sies** : hipocresía *f*
hypocrite ['hɪpəˌkrɪt] *n* : hipócrita *mf*
hypocritical [ˌhɪpə'krɪtɪkəl] *adj* : hipócrita
hypodermic[1] [ˌhaɪpə'dərmɪk] *adj* : hipodérmico
hypodermic[2] *n* : aguja *f* hipodérmica
hypotenuse [haɪ'pɑtənˌu:s, -ˌu:z, -ˌju:s, -ju:z] *n* : hipotenusa *f*
hypothesis [haɪ'pɑθəsɪs] *n, pl* **-eses** [-ˌsi:z] : hipótesis *f*
hypothetical [ˌhaɪpə'θɛtɪkəl] *adj* : hipotético — **hypothetically** [-tɪkli] *adv*
hysteria [hɪs'tɛriə, -tɪr-] *n* : histeria *f*, histerismo *m*
hysterical [hɪs'tɛrɪkəl] *adj* : histérico — **hysterically** [-ɪkli] *adv*
hysterics [hɪs'tɛrɪks] *n* : histeria *f*, histerismo *m*

I

i ['aɪ] *n, pl* **i's** *or* **is** ['aɪz] : novena letra del alfabeto inglés
I ['aɪ] *pron* : yo
Iberian [aɪ'bɪriən] *adj* : ibérico
ibis ['aɪbəs] *n, pl* **ibis** *or* **ibises** : ibis *f*
ice[1] ['aɪs] *v* **iced; icing** *vt* **1** FREEZE : congelar, helar **2** CHILL : enfriar **3 to ice a cake** : escarchar un pastel — *vi* : helarse, congelarse
ice[2] *n* **1** : hielo *m* **2** SHERBET : sorbete *m*, nieve *f Cuba, Mex, PRi*

iceberg ['aɪsˌbərg] *n* : iceberg *m*
icebox ['aɪsˌbaks] → **refrigerator**
icebreaker ['aɪsˌbreɪkər] *n* : rompehielos *m*
ice cap *n* : casquete *m* glaciar
ice–cold ['aɪs'ko:ld] *adj* : helado
ice cream *n* : helado *m*, mantecado *m PRi*
Icelander ['aɪsˌlændər, -lən-] *n* : islandés *m*, -desa *f*
Icelandic[1] [aɪs'lændɪk] *adj* : islandés

Icelandic² *n* : islandés *m* (idioma)
ice–skate ['aɪsˌskeɪt] *vi* **-skated; -skating** : patinar
ice skater *n* : patinador *m*, -dora *f*
ichthyology [ˌɪkthiˈɑləʤi] *n* : ictiología *f*
icicle ['aɪˌsɪkəl] *n* : carámbano *m*
icily ['aɪsəli] *adv* : fríamente, con frialdad ⟨he stared at me icily : me fijó la mirada con mucha frialdad⟩
icing ['aɪsɪŋ] *n* : glaseado *m*, betún *m* Mex
icon ['aɪˌkɑn, -kən] *n* : icono *m*
iconoclasm [aɪˈkɑnəˌklæzəm] *n* : iconoclasia *f*
iconoclast [aɪˈkɑnəˌklæst] *n* : iconoclasta *mf*
icy ['aɪsi] *adj* **icier; -est** **1** : cubierto de hielo ⟨an icy road : una carretera cubierta de hielo⟩ **2** FREEZING : helado, gélido, glacial **3** ALOOF : frío, distante
id ['ɪd] *n* : id *m*
I'd ['aɪd] (*contraction of* **I should** *or* **I would**) → **should, would**
idea [aɪˈdiːə] *n* : idea *f*
ideal¹ [aɪˈdiːəl] *adj* : ideal
ideal² *n* : ideal *m*
idealism [aɪˈdiːəˌlɪzəm] *n* : idealismo *m*
idealist [aɪˈdiːəlɪst] *n* : idealista *mf*
idealistic [aɪˌdiːəˈlɪstɪk] *adj* : idealista
idealistically [aɪˌdiːəˈlɪstɪkli] *adv* : con idealismo
idealization [aɪˌdiːəlɪˈzeɪʃən] *n* : idealización *f*
idealize [aɪˈdiːəˌlaɪz] *vt* **-ized; -izing** : idealizar
ideally [aɪˈdiːəli] *adv* : perfectamente
identical [aɪˈdɛntɪkəl] *adj* : idéntico — **identically** [-tɪkli] *adv*
identifiable [aɪˌdɛntəˈfaɪəbəl] *adj* : identificable
identification [aɪˌdɛntəfəˈkeɪʃən] *n* **1** : identificación *f* **2 identification card** : carnet *m*, cédula *f* de identidad, identificación *f*
identify [aɪˈdɛntəˌfaɪ] *v* **-fied; -fying** *vt* : identificar — *vi* **to identify with** : identificarse con
identity [aɪˈdɛntəti] *n, pl* **-ties** : identidad *f*
ideological [ˌaɪdiəˈlɑʤɪkəl, ˌɪ-] *adj* : ideológico — **ideologically** [-ʤɪkli] *adv*
ideology [ˌaɪdiˈɑləʤi, ˌɪ-] *n, pl* **-gies** : ideología *f*
idiocy ['ɪdiəsi] *n, pl* **-cies** **1** : idiotez *f* **2** NONSENSE : estupidez *f*, tontería *f*
idiom ['ɪdiəm] *n* **1** LANGUAGE : lenguaje *m* **2** EXPRESSION : modismo *m*, expresión *f* idiomática
idiomatic [ˌɪdiəˈmætɪk] *adj* : idiomático
idiosyncrasy [ˌɪdioˈsɪŋkrəsi] *n, pl* **-sies** : idiosincrasia *f*
idiosyncratic [ˌɪdiosɪnˈkrætɪk] *adj* : idiosincrásico — **idiosyncratically** [-tɪkli] *adv*
idiot ['ɪdiət] *n* **1** : idiota *mf* (en medicina) **2** FOOL : idiota *mf*; tonto *m*, -ta *f*; imbécil *mf fam*

idiotic [ˌɪdiˈɑtɪk] *adj* : estúpido, idiota
idiotically [ˌɪdiˈɑtɪkli] *adv* : estúpidamente
idle¹ ['aɪdəl] *v* **idled; idling** *vi* **1** LOAF : holgazanear, flojear, haraganear **2** : andar al ralentí (dícese de un automóvil), marchar en vacío (dícese de una máquina) — *vt* : dejar sin trabajo
idle² *adj* **idler; idlest** **1** VAIN : frívolo, vano, infundado ⟨idle curiosity : pura curiosidad⟩ **2** INACTIVE : inactivo, parado, desocupado **3** LAZY : holgazán, haragán, perezoso
idleness ['aɪdəlnəs] *n* **1** INACTIVITY : inactividad *f*, ociosidad *f* **2** LAZINESS : holgazanería *f*, flojera *f*, pereza *f*
idler ['aɪdələr] *n* : haragán *m*, -gana *f*; holgazán *m*, -zana *f*
idly ['aɪdəli] *adv* : ociosamente
idol ['aɪdəl] *n* : ídolo *m*
idolater *or* **idolator** [aɪˈdɑlətər] *n* : idólatra *mf*
idolatrous [aɪˈdɑlətrəs] *adj* : idólatra
idolatry [aɪˈdɑlətri] *n, pl* **-tries** : idolatría *f*
idolize ['aɪdəˌlaɪz] *vt* **-ized; -izing** : idolatrar
idyll ['aɪdəl] *n* : idilio *m*
idyllic [aɪˈdɪlɪk] *adj* : idílico
if ['ɪf] *conj* **1** : si ⟨I would do it if I could : lo haría si pudiera⟩ ⟨if so : si es así⟩ ⟨as if : como si⟩ ⟨if I were you : yo que tú⟩ **2** WHETHER : si ⟨I don't know if they're ready : no sé si están listos⟩ **3** THOUGH : aunque, si bien ⟨it's pretty, if somewhat old-fashioned : es lindo aunque algo anticuado⟩
igloo ['ɪˌgluː] *n, pl* **-loos** : iglú *m*
ignite [ɪgˈnaɪt] *v* **-nited; -niting** *vt* : prenderle fuego a, encender — *vi* : prender, encenderse
ignition [ɪgˈnɪʃən] *n* **1** IGNITING : ignición *f*, encendido *m* **2** *or* **ignition switch** : encendido *m*, arranque *m* ⟨to turn on the ignition : arrancar el motor⟩
ignoble [ɪgˈnoːbəl] *adj* : innoble — **ignobly** *adv*
ignominious [ˌɪgnəˈmɪniəs] *adj* : ignominioso, deshonroso — **ignominiously** *adv*
ignominy ['ɪgnəˌmɪni] *n, pl* **-nies** : ignominia *f*
ignoramus [ˌɪgnəˈreɪməs] *n* : ignorante *mf*; bestia *mf*; bruto *m*, -ta *f*
ignorance ['ɪgnərənts] *n* : ignorancia *f*
ignorant ['ɪgnərənt] *adj* **1** : ignorante **2 to be ignorant of** : no ser consciente de, desconocer, ignorar
ignorantly ['ɪgnərəntli] *adv* : ignorantemente, con ignorancia
ignore [ɪgˈnor] *vt* **-nored; -noring** : ignorar, hacer caso omiso de, no hacer caso de
iguana [ɪˈgwɑnə] *n* : iguana *f*, garrobo *f* CA
ilk ['ɪlk] *n* : tipo *m*, clase *f*, índole *f*
ill¹ ['ɪl] *adv* **worse** ['wərs]; **worst** ['wərst] : mal ⟨to speak ill of : hablar mal de⟩

⟨he can ill afford to fail : mal puede permitirse el lujo de fracasar⟩
ill² adj worse; worst 1 SICK : enfermo **2** BAD : malo ⟨ill luck : mala suerte⟩
ill³ n 1 EVIL : mal *m* **2** MISFORTUNE : mal *m*, desgracia *f* **3** AILMENT : enfermedad *f*
I'll ['aɪl] (*contraction of* **I shall** *or* **I will**) → **shall, will**
illegal [ɪl'li:ɡəl] *adj* : ilegal — **illegally** *adv*
illegality [ɪli'ɡæləti] *n* : ilegalidad *f*
illegibility [ɪl,lɛdʒə'bɪləti] *n, pl* **-ties** : ilegibilidad *f*
illegible [ɪl'lɛdʒəbəl] *adj* : ilegible — **illegibly** [-bli] *adv*
illegitimacy [,ɪli'dʒɪtəməsi] *n* : ilegitimidad *f*
illegitimate [,ɪli'dʒɪtəmət] *adj* **1** BASTARD : ilegítimo, bastardo **2** UNLAWFUL : ilegítimo, ilegal — **illegitimately** *adv*
ill–fated ['ɪl'feɪtəd] *adj* : malhadado, infortunado, desventurado
illicit [ɪl'lɪsət] *adj* : ilícito — **illicitly** *adv*
illiteracy [ɪl'lɪtərəsi] *n, pl* **-cies** : analfabetismo *m*
illiterate¹ [ɪl'lɪtərət] *adj* : analfabeto
illiterate² *n* : analfabeto *m*, -ta *f*
ill–mannered [,ɪl'manərd] *adj* : descortés, maleducado
ill–natured [,ɪl'neɪtʃərd] *adj* : desagradable, de mal genio
ill–naturedly [,ɪl'neɪtʃərdli] *adv* : desagradablemente
illness ['ɪlnəs] *n* : enfermedad *f*
illogical [ɪl'lɑdʒɪkəl] *adj* : ilógico — **illogically** [-kli] *adv*
ill–tempered [,ɪl'tempərd] → **ill–natured**
ill–treat [,ɪl'tri:t] *vt* : maltratar
ill–treatment [,ɪl'tri:tmənt] *n* : maltrato *m*
illuminate [ɪ'lu:mə,neɪt] *vt* **-nated; -nating 1** : iluminar, alumbrar **2** ELUCIDATE : esclarecer, elucidar
illumination [ɪ,lu:mə'neɪʃən] *n* **1** LIGHTING : iluminación *f*, luz *f* **2** ELUCIDATION : esclarecimiento *m*, elucidación *f*
ill–use ['ɪl'ju:z] → **ill–treat**
illusion [ɪ'lu:ʒən] *n* : ilusión *f*
illusory [ɪ'lu:səri, -zəri] *adj* : engañoso, ilusorio
illustrate ['ɪləs,treɪt] *v* **-trated; -trating** : ilustrar
illustration [,ɪlə'streɪʃən] *n* **1** PICTURE : ilustración *f* **2** EXAMPLE : ejemplo *m*, ilustración *f*
illustrative [ɪ'lʌstrətɪv, 'ɪlə,streɪtɪv] *adj* : ilustrativo — **illustratively** *adv*
illustrator ['ɪlə,streɪtər] *n* : ilustrador *m*, -dora *f*; dibujante *mf*
illustrious [ɪ'lʌstriəs] *adj* : ilustre, eminente, glorioso
illustriousness [ɪ'lʌstriəsnəs] *n* : eminencia *f*, prestigio *m*
ill will *n* : animosidad *f*, malquerencia *f*, mala voluntad *f*

I'm ['aɪm] (*contraction of* **I am**) → **be**
image¹ ['ɪmɪdʒ] *vt* **-aged; -aging** : imaginar, crear una imagen de
image² *n* : imagen *f*
imagery ['ɪmɪdʒri] *n, pl* **-eries 1** IMAGES : imágenes *fpl* **2** : imaginería *f* (en el arte)
imaginable [ɪ'mædʒənəbəl] *adj* : imaginable — **imaginably** [-bli] *adv*
imaginary [ɪ'mædʒə,nɛri] *adj* : imaginario
imagination [ɪ,mædʒə'neɪʃən] *n* : imaginación *f*
imaginative [ɪ'mædʒənətɪv, -ə,neɪtɪv] *adj* : imaginativo — **imaginatively** *adv*
imagine [ɪ'mædʒən] *vt* **-ined; -ining** : imaginar(se)
imbalance [ɪm'bælənts] *n* : desajuste *m*, desbalance *m*, desequilibrio *m*
imbecile¹ ['ɪmbəsəl, -,sɪl] *or* **imbecilic** [,ɪmbə'sɪlɪk] *adj* : imbécil, estúpido
imbecile² *n* **1** : imbécil *mf* (en medicina) **2** FOOL : idiota *mf*; imbécil *mf fam*; estúpido *m*, -da *f*
imbecility [,ɪmbə'sɪləti] *n, pl* **-ties** : imbecilidad *f*
imbibe [ɪm'baɪb] *v* **-bibed; -bibing** *vt* **1** DRINK : beber **2** ABSORB : absorber, embeber — *vi* : beber
imbue [ɪm'bju:] *vt* **-bued; -buing** : imbuir
imitate ['ɪmə,teɪt] *vt* **-tated; -tating** : imitar, remedar
imitation¹ [,ɪmə'teɪʃən] *adj* : de imitación, artificial
imitation² *n* : imitación *f*
imitative ['ɪmə,teɪtɪv] *adj* : imitativo, imitador, poco original
imitator ['ɪmə,teɪtər] *n* : imitador *m*, -dora *f*
immaculate [ɪ'mækjələt] *adj* **1** PURE : inmaculado, puro **2** FLAWLESS : impecable, intachable — **immaculately** *adv*
immaterial [,ɪmə'tɪriəl] *adj* **1** INCORPOREAL : incorpóreo **2** UNIMPORTANT : irrelevante, sin importancia
immature [,ɪmə'tʃʊr, -'tjʊr, -'tʊr] *adj* : inmaduro, verde (dícese de la fruta)
immaturity [,ɪmə'tʃʊrəti, -'tjʊr-, -'tʊr-] *n, pl* **-ties** : inmadurez *f*, falta *f* de madurez
immeasurable [ɪ'mɛʒərəbəl] *adj* : inconmensurable, incalculable — **immeasurably** [-bli] *adv*
immediacy [ɪ'mi:diəsi] *n* : inmediatez *f*
immediate [ɪ'mi:diət] *adj* **1** INSTANT : inmediato, instantáneo ⟨immediate relief : alivio instantáneo⟩ **2** DIRECT : inmediato, directo ⟨the immediate cause of death : la causa directa de la muerte⟩ **3** URGENT : urgente, apremiante **4** CLOSE : cercano, próximo, inmediato ⟨her immediate family : sus familiares más cercanos⟩ ⟨in the immediate vicinity : en los alrededores, en las inmediaciones⟩
immediately [ɪ'mi:diətli] *adv* : inmediatamente, enseguida

immemorial [ˌɪməˈmoriəl] *adj* : inmemorial

immense [ɪˈmɛnts] *adj* : inmenso, enorme — **immensely** *adv*

immensity [ɪˈmɛntsəti] *n, pl* **-ties** : inmensidad *f*

immerse [ɪˈmərs] *vt* **-mersed; -mersing** 1 SUBMERGE : sumergir 2 **to immerse oneself in** : enfrascarse en

immersion [ɪˈmərʒən] *n* 1 : inmersión *f* (en un líquido) 2 : enfrascamiento *m* (en una actividad)

immigrant [ˈɪmɪɡrənt] *n* : inmigrante *mf*

immigrate [ˈɪməˌɡreɪt] *vi* **-grated; -grating** : inmigrar

immigration [ˌɪməˈɡreɪʃən] *n* : inmigración *f*

imminence [ˈɪmənənts] *n* : inminencia *f*

imminent [ˈɪmənənt] *adj* : inminente — **imminently** *adv*

immobile [ɪmˈoːbəl] *adj* 1 FIXED, IMMOVABLE : inmovible, fijo 2 MOTIONLESS : inmóvil

immobility [ˌɪmoˈbɪləti] *n, pl* **-ties** : inmovilidad *f*

immobilize [ɪˈmoːbəˌlaɪz] *vt* **-lized; -lizing** : inmovilizar, paralizar

immoderate [ɪˈmɑdərət] *adj* : inmoderado, desmesurado, desmedido, excesivo — **immoderately** *adv*

immodest [ɪˈmɑdəst] *adj* 1 INDECENT : inmodesto, indecente, impúdico 2 CONCEITED : inmodesto, presuntuoso, engreído — **immodestly** *adv*

immodesty [ɪˈmɑdəsti] *n* : inmodestia *f*

immoral [ɪˈmɔrəl] *adj* : inmoral

immorality [ˌɪməˈræləti, ˌɪmə-] *n, pl* **-ties** : inmoralidad *f*

immorally [ɪˈmɔrəli] *adv* : de manera inmoral

immortal[1] [ɪˈmɔrtəl] *adj* : inmortal

immortal[2] *n* : inmortal *mf*

immortality [ˌɪˌmɔrˈtæləti] *n* : inmortalidad *f*

immortalize [ɪˈmɔrtəlˌaɪz] *vt* **-ized; -izing** : inmortalizar

immovable [ɪˈmuːvəbəl] *adj* 1 FIXED : fijo, inmovible 2 UNYIELDING : inflexible

immune [ɪˈmjuːn] *adj* 1 : inmune ⟨immune to smallpox : inmune a la viruela⟩ 2 EXEMPT : exento, inmune

immune system *n* : sistema *m* inmunológico

immunity [ɪˈmjuːnəti] *n, pl* **-ties** 1 : inmunidad *f* 2 EXEMPTION : exención *f*

immunization [ˌɪmjʊnəˈzeɪʃən] *n* : inmunización *f*

immunize [ˈɪmjʊˌnaɪz] *vt* **-nized; -nizing** : inmunizar

immunology [ˌɪmjʊˈnɑlʤi] *n* : inmunología *f*

immutable [ɪˈmjuːtəbəl] *adj* : inmutable

imp [ˈɪmp] *n* RASCAL : diablillo *m*; pillo *m*, -lla *f*

impact[1] [ɪmˈpækt] *vt* 1 STRIKE : chocar con, impactar 2 AFFECT : afectar, impactar, impresionar — *vi* 1 STRIKE : hacer impacto, golpear 2 **to impact on** : tener un impacto sobre

impact[2] [ˈɪmˌpækt] *n* 1 COLLISION : impacto *m*, choque *m*, colisión *f* 2 EFFECT : efecto *m*, impacto *m*, consecuencias *fpl*

impacted [ɪmˈpæktəd] *adj* : impactado, incrustado (dícese de los dientes)

impair [ɪmˈpær] *vt* : perjudicar, dañar, afectar

impairment [ɪmˈpærmənt] *n* : perjuicio *m*, daño *m*

impala [ɪmˈpɑlə, -ˈpæ-] *n, pl* **impalas** *or* **impala** : impala *m*

impale [ɪmˈpeɪl] *vt* **-paled; -paling** : empalar

impanel [ɪmˈpænəl] *vt* **-eled** *or* **-elled; eling** *or* **-elling** : elegir (un jurado)

impart [ɪmˈpɑrt] *vt* 1 CONVEY : impartir, dar, conferir 2 DISCLOSE : revelar, divulgar

impartial [ɪmˈpɑrʃəl] *adj* : imparcial — **impartially** *adv*

impartiality [ɪmˌpɑrʃiˈæləti] *n, pl* **-ties** : imparcialidad *f*

impassable [ɪmˈpæsəbəl] *adj* : infranqueable, intransitable — **impassably** [-bli] *adv*

impasse [ˈɪmˌpæs] *n* 1 DEADLOCK : impasse *m*, punto *m* muerto 2 DEAD END : callejón *m* sin salida

impassioned [ɪmˈpæʃənd] *adj* : apasionado, vehemente

impassive [ɪmˈpæsɪv] *adj* : impasible, indiferente

impassively [ɪmˈpæsɪvli] *adv* : impasiblemente, sin emoción

impatience [ɪmˈpeɪʃənts] *n* : impaciencia *f*

impatient [ɪmˈpeɪʃənt] *adj* : impaciente — **impatiently** *adv*

impeach [ɪmˈpiːʧ] *vt* : destituir (a un funcionario) de su cargo

impeachment [ɪmˈpiːʧmənt] *n* 1 ACCUSATION : acusación *f* 2 DISMISSAL : destitución *f*

impeccable [ɪmˈpɛkəbəl] *adj* : impecable — **impeccably** [-bli] *adv*

impecunious [ˌɪmpɪˈkjuːniəs] *adj* : falto de dinero

impede [ɪmˈpiːd] *vt* **-peded; -peding** : impedir, dificultar, obstaculizar

impediment [ɪmˈpɛdəmənt] *n* 1 HINDRANCE : impedimento *m*, obstáculo *m* 2 **speech impediment** : defecto *m* del habla

impel [ɪmˈpɛl] *vt* **-pelled; -pelling** : impeler

impend [ɪmˈpɛnd] *vi* : ser inminente

impenetrable [ɪmˈpɛnətrəbəl] *adj* 1 : impenetrable ⟨an impenetrable forest : una selva impenetrable⟩ 2 INSCRUTABLE : incomprensible, inescrutable, impenetrable — **impenetrably** [-bli] *adv*

impenitent [ɪmˈpɛnətənt] *adj* : impenitente

imperative¹ [ɪm'pɛrətɪv] *adj* **1** AUTHOR-
ITATIVE : imperativo, imperioso **2**
NECESSARY : imprescindible — **im-
peratively** *adv*
imperative² *n* : imperativo *m*
imperceptible [ˌɪmpər'sɛptəbəl] *adj* : imperceptible — **imperceptibly** [-bli] *adv*
imperfect [ɪm'pərfɪkt] *adj* : imperfecto,
defectuoso — **imperfectly** *adv*
imperfection [ˌɪmˌpər'fkʃən] *n* : imperfección *f*, defecto *m*
imperial [ɪm'pɪriəl] *adj* **1** : imperial **2**
SOVEREIGN : soberano **3** IMPERIOUS
: imperioso, señorial
imperialism [ɪm'pɪriəˌlɪzəm] *n* : imperialismo *m*
imperialist¹ [ɪm'pɪriəlɪst] *adj* : imperialista
imperialist² *n* : imperialista *mf*
imperialistic [ɪmˌpɪri:ə'lɪstɪk] *adj* : imperialista
imperil [ɪm'pɛrəl] *vt* **-iled** *or* **-illed; -iling**
or **-illing** : poner en peligro
imperious [ɪm'pɪriəs] *adj* : imperioso —
imperiously *adv*
imperishable [ɪm'pɛrɪʃəbəl] *adj* : imperecedero
impermanent [ɪm'pərmənənt] *adj*
: pasajero, inestable, efímero — **im-
permanently** *adv*
impermeable [ɪm'pərmiəbəl] *adj* : impermeable
impersonal [ɪm'pərsənəl] *adj* : impersonal — **impersonally** *adv*
impersonate [ɪm'pərsənˌeɪt] *vt* **-ated;
-ating** : hacerse pasar por, imitar
impersonation [ɪmˌpərsən'eɪʃən] *n* : imitación *f*
impersonator [ɪm'pərsənˌeɪtər] *n* : imitador *m*, -dora *f*
impertinence [ɪm'pərtənənts] *n* : impertinencia *f*
impertinent [ɪm'pərtənənt] *adj* **1** IR-
RELEVANT : impertinente, irrelevante
2 INSOLENT : impertinente, insolente
impertinently [ɪm'pərtənəntli] *adv* : con
impertinencia, impertinentemente
imperturbable [ˌɪmpər'tərbəbəl] *adj*
: imperturbable
impervious [ɪm'pərviəs] *adj* **1** IMPENE-
TRABLE : impermeable **2** INSENSITIVE
: insensible ⟨impervious to criticism
: insensible a la crítica⟩
impetuosity [ɪmˌpɛtʃu'asəti] *n, pl* **-ties**
: impetuosidad *f*
impetuous [ɪm'pɛtʃuəs] *adj* : impetuoso,
impulsivo
impetuously [ɪm'pɛtʃuəsli] *adv* : de manera impulsiva, impetuosamente
impetus ['ɪmpətəs] *n* : ímpetu *m*, impulso *m*
impiety [ɪm'paɪəti] *n, pl* **-ties** : impiedad
f
impinge [ɪm'pɪndʒ] *vi* **-pinged; -pinging**
1 to impinge on AFFECT : afectar a, incidir en **2 to impinge on** VIOLATE : violar, vulnerar
impious ['ɪmpiəs, ɪm'paɪəs] *adj* : impío,
irreverente

impish ['ɪmpɪʃ] *adj* MISCHIEVOUS : pícaro, travieso
impishly ['ɪmpɪʃli] *adv* : con picardía
implacable [ɪm'plækəbəl] *adj* : implacable — **implacably** [-bli] *adv*
implant¹ [ɪm'plænt] *vt* **1** INCULCATE, IN-
STILL : inculcar, implantar **2** INSERT
: implantar, insertar
implant² ['ɪmˌplænt] *n* : implante *m* (de
pelo), injerto *m* (de piel)
implantation [ˌɪmˌplæn'teɪʃən] *n* : implantación *f*
implausibility [ɪmˌplɔzə'bɪləti] *n, pl* **-ties**
: inverosimilitud *f*
implausible [ɪm'plɔzəbəl] *adj* : inverosímil, poco convincente
implement¹ ['ɪmpləˌmnt] *vt* : poner en
práctica, implementar
implement² ['ɪmpləmənt] *n* : utensilio *m*,
instrumento *m*, implemento *m*
implementation [ˌɪmpləmən'teɪʃən] *n*
: implementación *f*, ejecución *f*, cumplimiento *m*
implicate ['ɪmpləˌkeɪt] *vt* **-cated; -cating**
: implicar, involucrar
implication [ˌɪmplə'keɪʃən] *n* **1** CONSE-
QUENCE : implicación *f*, consecuencia
f **2** INFERENCE : insinuación *f*, inferencia *f*
implicit [ɪm'plɪsət] *adj* **1** IMPLIED : implícito, tácito **2** ABSOLUTE : absoluto,
completo ⟨implicit faith : fe ciega⟩ —
implicitly *adv*
implied [ɪm'plaɪd] *adj* : implícito, tácito
implode [ɪm'plo:d] *vi* **-ploded; -ploding**
: implosionar
implore [ɪm'plor] *vt* **-plored; -ploring**
: implorar, suplicar
implosion [ɪm'plo:ʒən] *n* : implosión *f*
imply [ɪm'plaɪ] *vt* **-plied; -plying** **1** SUG-
GEST : insinuar, dar a entender **2** IN-
VOLVE : implicar, suponer ⟨rights imply obligations : los derechos implican
unas obligaciones⟩
impolite [ˌɪmpə'laɪt] *adj* : descortés,
maleducado
impoliteness [ˌɪmpə'laɪtnəs] *n* : descortesía *f*, falta *f* de educación
impolitic [ɪm'palə,tɪk] *adj* : imprudente,
poco político
imponderable¹ [ɪm'pandərəbəl] *adj*
: imponderable
imponderable² *n* : imponderable *m*
import¹ [ɪm'port] *vt* **1** SIGNIFY : significar **2** : importar ⟨to import foreign
cars : importar autos extranjeros⟩
import² ['ɪmˌport] *n* **1** SIGNIFICANCE
: importancia *f*, significación *f* **2** → **importation**
importance [ɪm'portənts] *n* : importancia *f*
important [ɪm'portənt] *adj* : importante
importantly [ɪm'portəntli] *adv* **1** : con
importancia **2 more importantly** : lo
que es más importante
importation [ˌɪmˌpor'teɪʃən] *n* : importación *f*
importer [ɪm'portər] *n* : importador *m*,
-dora *f*

importunate [ɪm'pɔrtʃənət] *adj* : importuno, insistente

importune [ˌɪmpər'tu:n, -'tju:n; ɪm'pɔrtʃən] *vt* **-tuned; -tuning** : importunar, implorar

impose [ɪm'po:z] *v* **-posed; -posing** *vt* : imponer ⟨to impose a tax : imponer un impuesto⟩ — *vi* **to impose on** : abusar de, molestar ⟨to impose on her kindness : abusar de su bondad⟩

imposing [ɪm'po:zɪŋ] *adj* : imponente, impresionante

imposition [ˌɪmpə'zɪʃən] *n* : imposición *f*

impossibility [ɪmˌpɑsə'bɪləti] *n, pl* **-ties** : imposibilidad *f*

impossible [ɪm'pɑsəbəl] *adj* **1** : imposible ⟨an impossible task : una tarea imposible⟩ ⟨to make life impossible for : hacerle la vida imposible a⟩ **2** UNACCEPTABLE : inaceptable

impossibly [ɪm'pɑsəbli] *adv* : imposiblemente, increíblemente

impostor *or* **imposter** [ɪm'pɑstər] *n* : impostor *m*, -tora *f*

impotence ['ɪmpətənts] *n* : impotencia *f*

impotency ['ɪmpətəntsi] → **impotence**

impotent ['ɪmpətənt] *adj* : impotente

impound [ɪm'paʊnd] *vt* : incautar, embargar, confiscar

impoverish [ɪm'pɑvərɪʃ] *vt* : empobrecer

impoverishment [ɪm'pɑvərɪʃmənt] *n* : empobrecimiento *m*

impracticable [ɪm'præktɪkəbəl] *adj* : impracticable

impractical [ɪm'præktɪkəl] *adj* : poco práctico

imprecise [ˌɪmprɪ'saɪs] *adj* : impreciso

imprecisely [ˌɪmprɪ'saɪsli] *adv* : con imprecisión

impreciseness [ˌɪmprɪ'saɪsnəs] → **imprecision**

imprecision [ˌɪmprɪ'sɪʒən] *n* : imprecisión *f*, falta de precisión *f*

impregnable [ɪm'pregnəbəl] *adj* : inexpugnable, impenetrable, inconquistable

impregnate [ɪm'preg,neɪt] *vt* **-nated; -nating 1** FERTILIZE : fecundar **2** PERMEATE, SATURATE : impregnar, empapar, saturar

impresario [ˌɪmprə'sɑri,o, -'sær-] *n, pl* **-rios** : empresario *m*, -ria *f*

impress [ɪm'pres] *vt* **1** IMPRINT : imprimir, estampar **2** : impresionar, causar impresión a ⟨I was not impressed : no me hizo buena impresión⟩ **3 to impress (something) on someone** : recalcarle (algo) a alguien — *vi* : impresionar, hacer una impresión

impression [ɪm'preʃən] *n* **1** IMPRINT : marca *f*, huella *f*, molde *m* (de los dientes) **2** EFFECT : impresión *f*, efecto *m*, impacto *m* **3** PRINTING : impresión *f* **4** NOTION : impresión *f*, noción *f*

impressionable [ɪm'preʃənəbəl] *adj* : impresionable

impressionism [ɪm'preʃə,nɪzəm] *n* : impresionismo *m*

impressionist [ɪm'preʃənɪst] *n* : impresionista *mf* — **impressionist** *adj*

impressive [ɪm'presɪv] *adj* : impresionante — **impressively** *adv*

impressiveness [ɪm'presɪvnəs] *n* : calidad de ser impresionante

imprint[1] [ɪm'prɪnt, 'ɪm,-] *vt* : imprimir, estampar

imprint[2] ['ɪm,prɪnt] *n* : marca *f*, huella *f*

imprison [ɪm'prɪzən] *vt* **1** JAIL : encarcelar, aprisionar **2** CONFINE : recluir, encerrar

imprisonment [ɪm'prɪzənmənt] *n* : encarcelamiento *m*

improbability [ɪmˌprɑbə'bɪləti] *n, pl* **-ties** : improbabilidad *f*, inverosimilitud *f*

improbable [ɪm'prɑbəbəl] *adj* : improbable, inverosímil

impromptu[1] [ɪm'prɑmp,tu:, -,tju:] *adv* : sin preparación, espontáneamente

impromptu[2] *adj* : espontáneo, improvisado

impromptu[3] *n* : improvisación *f*

improper [ɪm'prɑpər] *adj* **1** INCORRECT : incorrecto, impropio **2** INDECOROUS : indecoroso

improperly [ɪm'prɑpərli] *adv* : incorrectamente, indebidamente

impropriety [ˌɪmprə'praɪəti] *n, pl* **-eties 1** INDECOROUSNESS : indecoro *m*, falta *f* de decoro **2** ERROR : impropiedad *f*, incorrección *f*

improve [ɪm'pru:v] *v* **-proved; -proving** : mejorar

improvement [ɪm'pru:vmənt] *n* : mejoramiento *m*, mejora *f*

improvidence [ɪm'prɑvədənts] *n* : imprevisión *f*

improvisation [ɪmˌprɑvə'zeɪʃən, ˌɪmprəvə-] *n* : improvisación *f*

improvise ['ɪmprə,vaɪz] *v* **-vised; -vising** : improvisar

imprudence [ɪm'pru:dənts] *n* : imprudencia *f*, indiscreción *f*

imprudent [ɪm'pru:dənt] *adj* : imprudente, indiscreto

impudence ['ɪmpjədənts] *n* : insolencia *f*, descaro *m*

impudent ['ɪmpjədənt] *adj* : insolente, descarado — **impudently** *adv*

impugn [ɪm'pju:n] *vt* : impugnar

impulse ['ɪm,pʌls] *n* **1** : impulso *m* **2 on impulse** : sin reflexionar

impulsive [ɪm'pʌlsɪv] *adj* : impulsivo — **impulsively** *adv*

impulsiveness [ɪm'pʌlsɪvnəs] *n* : impulsividad *f*

impunity [ɪm'pju:nəti] *n* **1** : impunidad *f* **2 with impunity** : impunemente

impure [ɪm'pjʊr] *adj* **1** : impuro ⟨impure thoughts : pensamientos impuros⟩ **2** CONTAMINATED : con impurezas, impuro

impurity [ɪm'pjʊrəti] *n, pl* **-ties** : impureza *f*

impute [ɪm'pjuːt] *vt* **-puted; -puting** AT-TRIBUTE : imputar, atribuir

in¹ ['ɪn] *adv* **1** INSIDE : dentro, adentro ⟨let's go in : vamos adentro⟩ **2** HAR-VESTED : recogido ⟨the crops are in : las cosechas ya están recogidas⟩ **3 to be in** : estar ⟨is Linda in? : ¿está Linda?⟩ **4 to be in** : estar en poder ⟨the Democrats are in : los demócratas están en el poder⟩ **5 to be in for** : ser objeto de, estar a punto de ⟨they're in for a treat : los van a agasajar⟩ ⟨he's in for a surprise : se va a llevar una sorpresa⟩ **6 to be in on** : participar en, tomar parte en

in² *adj* **1** INSIDE : interior ⟨the in part : la parte interior⟩ **2** FASHIONABLE : de moda

in³ *prep* **1** (*indicating location or position*) ⟨in the lake : en el lago⟩ ⟨a pain in the leg : un dolor en la pierna⟩ ⟨in the sun : al sol⟩ ⟨in the rain : bajo la lluvia⟩ ⟨the best restaurant in Buenos Aires : el mejor restaurante de Buenos Aires⟩ **2** INTO : en, a ⟨he broke it in pieces : lo rompió en pedazos⟩ ⟨she went in the house : se metió a la casa⟩ **3** DURING : por, durante ⟨in the afternoon : por la tarde⟩ **4** WITHIN : dentro de ⟨I'll be back in a week : vuelvo dentro de una semana⟩ **5** (*indicating manner*) : en, con, de ⟨in Spanish : en español⟩ ⟨written in pencil : escrito con lápiz⟩ ⟨in this way : de esta manera⟩ **6** (*indicating states or circumstances*) ⟨to be in luck : tener suerte⟩ ⟨to be in love : estar enamorado⟩ ⟨to be in a hurry : tener prisa⟩ **7** (*indicating purpose*) : en ⟨in reply : en respuesta, como réplica⟩

in⁴ *n* **ins and outs** : pormenores *mpl*

inability [ˌɪnə'bɪləti] *n, pl* **-ties** : incapacidad *f*

inaccessibility [ˌɪnɪkˌsɛsə'bɪləti] *n, pl* **-ties** : inaccesibilidad *f*

inaccessible [ˌɪnɪk'sɛsəbəl] *adj* : inaccesible

inaccuracy [ɪn'ækjərəsi] *n, pl* **-cies 1** : inexactitud *f* **2** MISTAKE : error *m*

inaccurate [ɪn'ækjərət] *n* : inexacto, erróneo, incorrecto

inaccurately [ɪn'ækjərətli] *adv* : incorrectamente, con inexactitud

inaction [ɪn'ækʃən] *n* : inactividad *f*, inacción *f*

inactive [ɪn'æktɪv] *adj* : inactivo

inactivity [ˌɪnˌæk'tɪvəti] *n, pl* **-ties** : inactividad *f*, ociosidad *f*

inadequacy [ɪn'ædɪkwəsi] *n, pl* **-cies 1** INSUFFICIENCY : insuficiencia *f* **2** INCOMPETENCE : ineptitud *f*, incompetencia *f*

inadequate [ɪn'ædɪkwət] *adj* **1** INSUFFICIENT : insuficiente, inadecuado **2** INCOMPETENT : inepto, incompetente

inadmissible [ˌɪnæd'mɪsəbəl] *adj* : inadmisible

inadvertent [ˌɪnəd'vərtənt] *adj* : inadvertido, involuntario — **inadvertently** *adv*

inadvisable [ˌɪnæd'vaɪzəbəl] *adj* : desaconsejable

inalienable [ɪn'eɪljənəbəl, -'eɪliənə-] *adj* : inalienable

inane [ɪ'neɪn] *adj* **inaner; -est** : estúpido, idiota, necio

inanimate [ɪn'ænəmət] *adj* : inanimado, exánime

inanity [ɪ'nænəti] *n, pl* **-ties 1** STUPIDITY : estupidez *f* **2** NONSENSE : idiotez *f*, disparate *m*

inapplicable [ɪn'æplɪkəbəl, ˌɪnə-'plɪkəbəl] *adj* IRRELEVANT : inaplicable, irrelevante

inappreciable [ˌɪnə'priːʃəbəl] *adj* : inapreciable, imperceptible

inappropriate [ˌɪnə'proːpriət] *adj* : inapropiado, inadecuado, impropio

inappropriateness [ˌɪnə'proːpriətnəs] *n* : lo inapropiado, impropiedad *f*

inapt [ɪn'æpt] *adj* **1** UNSUITABLE : inadecuado, inapropiado **2** INEPT : inepto

inarticulate [ˌɪnɑr'tɪkjələt] *adj* : inarticulado, incapaz de expresarse

inarticulately [ˌɪnɑr'tɪkjələtli] *adv* : inarticuladamente

inasmuch as [ˌɪnæz'mʌtʃæz] *conj* : ya que, dado que, puesto que

inattention [ˌɪnə'tɛntʃən] *n* : falta *f* de atención, distracción *f*

inattentive [ˌɪnə'tɛntɪv] *adj* : distraído, despistado

inattentively [ˌɪnə'tɛntɪvli] *adv* : distraídamente, sin prestar atención

inaudible [ɪn'ɔdəbəl] *adj* : inaudible

inaudibly [ɪn'ɔdəbli] *adv* : de forma inaudible

inaugural¹ [ɪ'nɔgjərəl, -gərəl] *adj* : inaugural, de investidura

inaugural² *n* **1** *or* **inaugural address** : discurso *m* de investidura **2** INAUGURATION : investidura *f* (de una persona)

inaugurate [ɪ'nɔgjə,reɪt, -gə-] *vt* **-rated; -rating 1** BEGIN : inaugurar **2** INDUCT : investir ⟨to inaugurate the president : investir al presidente⟩

inauguration [ɪˌnɔgjə'reɪʃən, -gə-] *n* **1** : inauguración *f* (de un edificio, un sistema, etc.) **2** : investidura *f* (de una persona)

inauspicious [ˌɪnɔ'spɪʃəs] *adj* : desfavorable, poco propicio

inborn ['ɪnˌbɔrn] *adj* **1** CONGENITAL, INNATE : innato, congénito **2** HEREDITARY : hereditario

inbred ['ɪnˌbrɛd] *adj* **1** : engendrado por endogamia **2** INNATE : innato

inbreed ['ɪnˌbriːd] *vt* **-bred; -breeding** : engendrar por endogamia

inbreeding ['ɪnˌbriːdɪŋ] *n* : endogamia *f*

Inca ['ɪŋkə] *n* : inca *mf*

incalculable [ɪn'kælkjələbəl] *adj* : incalculable — **incalculably** [-bli] *adv*

incandescence [ˌɪnkən'dɛsənts] *n* : incandescencia *f*

incandescent [ˌɪnkən'dɛsənt] *adj* **1** : incandescente **2** BRILLIANT : brillante

incantation [ˌɪnˌkæn'teɪʃən] *n* : conjuro *m*, ensalmo *m*

incapable [ɪn'keɪpəbəl] *adj* : incapaz

incapacitate [ˌɪnkə'pæsə,teɪt] *vt* **-tated; -tating** : incapacitar

incapacity [ˌɪnkə'pæsəti] *n, pl* **-ties** : incapacidad *f*

incarcerate [ɪn'kɑrsə,reɪt] *vt* **-ated; -ating** : encarcelar

incarceration [ɪnˌkɑrsə'reɪʃən] *n* : encarcelamiento *m*, encarcelación *f*

incarnate[1] [ɪn'kɑr,neɪt] *vt* **-nated; -nating** : encarnar

incarnate[2] [ɪn'kɑrnət, -ˌneɪt] *adj* : encarnado

incarnation [ˌɪnˌkɑr'neɪʃən] *n* : encarnación *f*

incendiary[1] [ɪn'sɛndi,ri] *adj* : incendiario

incendiary[2] *n, pl* **-aries** : incendiario *m*, -ria *f*; pirómano *m*, -na *f*

incense[1] [ɪn'sɛnts] *vt* **-censed; -censing** : indignar, enfadar, enfurecer

incense[2] ['ɪnˌsɛnts] *n* : incienso *m*

incentive [ɪn'sɛntɪv] *n* : incentivo *m*, aliciente *m*, motivación *f*, acicate *m*

inception [ɪn'sɛpʃən] *n* : comienzo *m*, principio *m*

incessant [ɪn'sɛsənt] *adj* : incesante, continuo — **incessantly** *adv*

incest ['ɪnˌsɛst] *n* : incesto *m*

incestuous [ɪn'sɛstʃʊəs] *adj* : incestuoso

inch[1] ['ɪntʃ] *v* : avanzar poco a poco

inch[2] *n* **1** : pulgada *f* **2 every inch** : absoluto, seguro ⟨every inch a winner : un seguro ganador⟩ **3 within an inch of** : a punto de

incidence ['ɪntsədənts] *n* **1** FREQUENCY : frecuencia *f*, índice *m* ⟨a high incidence of crime : un alto índice de crímenes⟩ **2 angle of incidence** : ángulo *m* de incidencia

incident[1] ['ɪntsədənt] *adj* : incidente

incident[2] *n* : incidente *m*, incidencia *f*, episodio *m* (en una obra de ficción)

incidental[1] [ˌɪntsə'dɛntəl] *adj* **1** SECONDARY : incidental, secundario **2** ACCIDENTAL : casual, fortuito

incidental[2] *n* **1** : algo incidental **2 incidentals** *npl* : imprevistos *mpl*

incidentally [ˌɪntsə'dɛntəli, -'dɛntli] *adv* **1** BY CHANCE : incidentalmente, casualmente **2** BY THE WAY : a propósito, por cierto

incinerate [ɪn'sɪnə,reɪt] *vt* **-ated; -ating** : incinerar

incinerator [ɪn'sɪnə,reɪtər] *n* : incinerador *m*

incipient [ɪn'sɪpiənt] *adj* : incipiente, naciente

incise [ɪn'saɪz] *vt* **-cised; -cising** **1** ENGRAVE : grabar, cincelar, inscribir **2** : hacer una incisión en

incision [ɪn'sɪʒən] *n* : incisión *f*

incisive [ɪn'saɪsɪv] *adj* : incisivo, penetrante

incisively [ɪn'saɪsɪvli] *adv* : con agudeza

incisor [ɪn'saɪzər] *n* : incisivo *m*

incite [ɪn'saɪt] *vt* **-cited; -citing** : incitar, instigar

incitement [ɪn'saɪtmənt] *n* : incitación *f*

inclemency [ɪn'klɛməntsi] *n, pl* **-cies** : inclemencia *f*

inclement [ɪn'klɛmənt] *adj* : inclemente, tormentoso

inclination [ˌɪnklə'neɪʃən] *n* **1** PROPENSITY : inclinación *f*, tendencia *f* **2** DESIRE : deseo *m*, ganas *fpl* **3** BOW : inclinación *f*

incline[1] [ɪn'klaɪn] *v* **-clined; -clining** *vi* **1** SLOPE : inclinarse **2** TEND : inclinarse, tender ⟨he is inclined to be late : tiende a llegar tarde⟩ — *vt* **1** LOWER : inclinar, bajar ⟨to incline one's head : bajar la cabeza⟩ **2** SLANT : inclinar **3** PREDISPOSE : predisponer

incline[2] ['ɪnˌklaɪn] *n* : inclinación *f*, pendiente *f*

inclined [ɪn'klaɪnd] *adj* **1** SLOPING : inclinado **2** PRONE : prono, dispuesto, dado

inclose, inclosure → **enclose, enclosure**

include [ɪn'kluːd] *vt* **-cluded; -cluding** : incluir, comprender

inclusion [ɪn'kluːʒən] *n* : inclusión *f*

inclusive [ɪn'kluːsɪv] *adj* : inclusivo

incognito [ˌɪnˌkɑg'niːˌto, ɪn'kɑgnə-ˌto:] *adv & adj* : de incógnito

incoherence [ˌɪnko'hɪrənts, -'hɛr-] *n* : incoherencia *f*

incoherent [ˌɪnko'hɪrənt, -'hɛr-] *adj* : incoherente — **incoherently** *adv*

incombustible [ˌɪnkəm'bʌstəbəl] *adj* : incombustible

income ['ɪnˌkʌm] *n* : ingresos *mpl*, entradas *fpl*

income tax *n* : impuesto *m* sobre la renta

incoming ['ɪnˌkʌmɪŋ] *adj* **1** ARRIVING : que se recibe (dícese del correo), que llega (dícese de las personas), ascendente (dícese de la marea) **2** NEW : nuevo, entrante ⟨the incoming president : el nuevo presidente⟩ ⟨the incoming year : el año entrante⟩

incommunicado [ˌɪnkəˌmjuːnə'kɑdo] *adj* : incomunicado

incomparable [ɪn'kɑmpərəbəl] *adj* : incomparable, sin igual

incompatible [ˌɪnkəm'pætəbəl] *adj* : incompatible

incompetence [ɪn'kɑmpətənts] *n* : incompetencia *f*, impericia *f*, ineptitud *f*

incompetent [ɪn'kɑmpətənt] *adj* : incompetente, inepto, incapaz

incomplete [ˌɪnkəm'pliːt] *adj* : incompleto — **incompletely** *adv*

incomprehensible [ˌɪnˌkɑmpri'hɛntsəbəl] *adj* : incomprensible

inconceivable [ˌɪnkən'siːvəbəl] *adj* **1** INCOMPREHENSIBLE : incomprensible **2** UNBELIEVABLE : inconcebible, increíble

inconceivably [ˌɪnkənˈsiːvəbli] *adv* : inconcebiblemente, increíblemente

inconclusive [ˌɪnkənˈkluːsɪv] *adj* : inconcluyente, no decisivo

incongruity [ˌɪnkənˈgruːəti, -ˌkɑn-] *n, pl* **-ties** : incongruencia *f*

incongruous [ɪnˈkɑŋgruəs] *adj* : incongruente, inapropiado, fuera de lugar

incongruously [ɪnˈkɑŋgruəsli] *adv* : de manera incongruente, inapropiadamente

inconsequential [ˌɪnˌkɑnsəˈkwɛntʃəl] *adj* : intrascendente, de poco importancia

inconsiderable [ˌɪnkənˈsɪdərəbəl] *adj* : insignificante

inconsiderate [ˌɪnkənˈsɪdərət] *adj* : desconsiderado, sin consideración — **inconsiderately** *adv*

inconsistency [ˌɪnkənˈsɪstəntsi] *n, pl* **-cies** : inconsecuencia *f*, inconsistencia *f*

inconsistent [ˌɪnkənˈsɪstənt] *adj* : inconsecuente, inconsistente

inconsolable [ˌɪnkənˈsoːləbəl] *adj* : inconsolable — **inconsolably** [-bli] *adv*

inconspicuous [ˌɪnkənˈspɪkjuəs] *adj* : discreto, no conspicuo, que no llama la atención

inconspicuously [ˌɪnkənˈspɪkjuəsli] *adv* : discretamente, sin llamar la atención

incontestable [ˌɪnkənˈtɛstəbəl] *adj* : incontestable, indiscutible — **incontestably** [-bli] *adv*

incontinence [ɪnˈkɑntənənts] *n* : incontinencia *f*

incontinent [ɪnˈkɑntənənt] *adj* : incontinente

inconvenience[1] [ˌɪnkənˈviːnjənts] *vt* **-nienced; -niencing** : importunar, incomodar, molestar

inconvenience[2] *n* : incomodidad *f*, molestia *f*

inconvenient [ˌɪnkənˈviːnjənt] *adj* : inconveniente, importuno, incómodo — **inconveniently** *adv*

incorporate [ɪnˈkɔrpəˌreɪt] *vt* **-rated; -rating 1** INCLUDE : incorporar, incluir **2** : incorporar, constituir en sociedad (dícese de un negocio)

incorporation [ɪnˌkɔrpəˈreɪʃən] *n* : incorporación *f*

incorporeal [ˌɪnˌkɔrˈporiəl] *adj* : incorpóreo

incorrect [ˌɪnkəˈrɛkt] *adj* **1** INACCURATE : incorrecto **2** WRONG : equivocado, erróneo **3** IMPROPER : impropio — **incorrectly** *adv*

incorrigible [ɪnˈkɔrədʒəbəl] *adj* : incorregible

incorruptible [ˌɪnkəˈrʌptəbəl] *adj* : incorruptible

increase[1] [ɪnˈkriːs, ˈɪnˌkriːs] *v* **-creased; -creasing** *vi* GROW : aumentar, crecer, subir (dícese de los precios) — *vt* AUGMENT : aumentar, acrecentar

increase[2] [ˈɪnˌkriːs, ɪnˈkriːs] *n* : aumento *m*, incremento *m*, subida *f* (de precios)

increasing [ɪnˈkriːsɪŋ, ˈɪnˌkriːsɪŋ] *adj* : creciente

increasingly [ɪnˈkriːsɪŋli] *adv* : cada vez más

incredible [ɪnˈkrɛdəbəl] *adj* : increíble — **incredibly** [-bli] *adv*

incredulity [ˌɪnkrɪˈduːləti, -ˈdjuː-] *n* : incredulidad *f*

incredulous [ɪnˈkrɛdʒələs] *adj* : incrédulo, escéptico

incredulously [ɪnˈkrɛdʒələsli] *adv* : con incredulidad

increment [ˈɪŋkrəmənt, ˈɪn-] *n* : incremento *m*, aumento *m*

incremental [ˌɪŋkrəˈmɛntəl, ˌɪn-] *adj* : de incremento

incriminate [ɪnˈkrɪməˌneɪt] *vt* **-nated; -nating** : incriminar

incrimination [ɪnˌkrɪməˈneɪʃən] *n* : incriminación *f*

incriminatory [ɪnˈkrɪmənəˌtori] *adj* : incriminatorio

incubate [ˈɪŋkjʊˌbeɪt, ˈɪn-] *v* **-bated; -bating** *vt* : incubar, empollar — *vi* : incubar(se), empollar

incubation [ˌɪŋkjʊˈbeɪʃən, ˌɪn-] *n* : incubación *f*

incubator [ˈɪŋkjʊˌbeɪtər, ˈɪn-] *n* : incubadora *f*

inculcate [ɪnˈkʌl,keɪt, ˈɪn,kʌl-] *vt* **-cated; -cating** : inculcar

incumbency [ɪnˈkʌmbəntsi] *n, pl* **-cies 1** OBLIGATION : incumbencia *f* **2** : mandato *m* (en la política)

incumbent[1] [ɪnˈkʌmbənt] *adj* : obligatorio

incumbent[2] *n* : titular *mf*

incur [ɪnˈkər] *vt* **incurred; incurring** : provocar (al enojo), incurrir en (gastos, obligaciones)

incurable [ɪnˈkjʊrəbəl] *adj* : incurable, sin remedio

incursion [ɪnˈkərʒən] *n* : incursión *f*

indebted [ɪnˈdɛtəd] *adj* **1** : endeudado **2 to be indebted to** : estar en deuda con, estarle agradecido a

indebtedness [ɪnˈdɛtədnəs] *n* : endeudamiento *m*

indecency [ɪnˈdiːsəntsi] *n, pl* **-cies** : indecencia *f*

indecent [ɪnˈdiːsənt] *adj* : indecente — **indecently** *adv*

indecipherable [ˌɪndɪˈsaɪfərəbəl] *adj* : indescifrable

indecision [ˌɪndɪˈsɪʒən] *n* : indecisión *f*, irresolución *f*

indecisive [ˌɪndɪˈsaɪsɪv] *adj* **1** INCONCLUSIVE : indeciso, que no es decisivo **2** IRRESOLUTE : indeciso, irresoluto, vacilante **3** INDEFINITE : indefinido — **indecisively** *adv*

indecorous [ɪnˈdɛkərəs, ˌɪndɪˈkorəs] *adj* : indecoroso — **indecorously** *adv*

indecorousness [ɪnˈdkərəsnəs, ˌɪndɪˈkorəs-] *n* : indecoro *m*

indeed [ɪnˈdiːd] *adv* **1** TRULY : verdaderamente, de veras **2** (*used as intensifier*) ⟨thank you very much indeed

: muchísimas gracias⟩ **3** OF COURSE : claro, por supuesto

indefatigable [ˌɪndɪ'fætɪgəbəl] *adj* : incansable, infatigable — **indefatigably** [-bli] *adv*

indefensible [ˌɪndɪ'fɛntsəbəl] *adj* **1** VULNERABLE : indefendible, vulnerable **2** INEXCUSABLE : inexcusable

indefinable [ˌɪndɪ'faɪnəbəl] *adj* : indefinible

indefinite [ɪn'dɛfənət] *adj* **1** : indefinido, indeterminado ⟨indefinite pronouns : pronombres indefinidos⟩ **2** VAGUE : vago, impreciso

indefinitely [ɪn'dɛfənətli] *adv* : indefinidamente, por un tiempo indefinido

indelible [ɪn'dɛləbəl] *adj* : indeleble, imborrable — **indelibly** [-bli] *adv*

indelicacy [ɪn'dɛləkəsi] *n* : falta *f* de delicadeza

indelicate [ɪn'dɛlɪkət] *adj* **1** IMPROPER : indelicado, indecoroso **2** TACTLESS : indiscreto, falto de tacto

indemnify [ɪn'dɛmnəˌfaɪ] *vt* **-fied; -fying 1** INSURE : asegurar **2** COMPENSATE : indemnizar, compensar

indemnity [ɪn'dɛmnəti] *n, pl* **-ties 1** INSURANCE : indemnidad *f* **2** COMPENSATION : indemnización *f*

indent [ɪn'dɛnt] *vt* : sangrar (un párrafo)

indentation [ˌɪnˌdɛn'teɪʃən] *n* **1** NOTCH : muesca *f*, mella *f* **2** INDENTING : sangría *f* (de un párrafo)

indenture[1] [ɪn'dɛnʧər] *vt* **-tured; -turing** : ligar por contrato

indenture[2] *n* : contrato de aprendizaje

independence [ˌɪndə'pɛndənts] *n* : independencia *f*

Independence Day *n* : día *m* de la Independencia (4 de julio en los EE.UU.)

independent[1] [ˌɪndə'pɛndənt] *adj* : independiente — **independently** *adv*

independent[2] *n* : independiente *mf*

indescribable [ˌɪndɪ'skraɪbəbəl] *adj* : indescriptible, incalificable — **indescribably** [-bli] *adv*

indestructibility [ˌɪndɪˌstrʌktəˈbɪləti] *n* : indestructibilidad *f*

indestructible [ˌɪndɪ'strʌktəbəl] *adj* : indestructible

indeterminate [ˌɪndɪ'tərmənət] *adj* **1** VAGUE : vago, impreciso, indeterminado **2** INDEFINITE : indeterminado, indefinido

index[1] ['ɪnˌdɛks] *vt* **1** : ponerle un índice a (un libro o una revista) **2** : incluir en un índice ⟨all proper names are indexed : todos los nombres propios están incluidos en el índice⟩ **3** INDICATE : indicar, señalar **4** REGULATE : indexar, indiciar ⟨to index prices : indiciar los precios⟩

index[2] *n, pl* **-dexes** *or* **-dices** ['ɪndəˌsiːz] **1** : índice *m* (de un libro, de precios) **2** INDICATION : indicio *m*, índice *m*, señal *f* ⟨an index of her character : una señal de su carácter⟩

index finger *n* FOREFINGER : dedo *m* índice

Indian ['ɪndiən] *n* **1** : indio *m*, -dia *f* **2** → American Indian — **Indian** *adj*

indicate ['ɪndəˌkeɪt] *vt* **-cated; -cating 1** POINT OUT : indicar, señalar **2** SHOW, SUGGEST : ser indicio de, ser señal de **3** EXPRESS : expresar, señalar **4** REGISTER : marcar, poner (una medida, etc.)

indication [ˌɪndə'keɪʃən] *n* : indicio *m*, señal *f*

indicative [ɪn'dɪkətɪv] *adj* : indicativo

indicator ['ɪndəˌkeɪtər] *n* : indicador *m*

indict [ɪn'daɪt] *vt* : acusar, procesar (por un crimen)

indictment [ɪn'daɪtmənt] *n* : acusación *f*

indifference [ɪn'dɪfrənts, -'dɪfə-] *n* : indiferencia *f*

indifferent [ɪn'dɪfrənt, -'dɪfə-] *adj* **1** UNCONCERNED : indiferente **2** MEDIOCRE : mediocre

indifferently [ɪn'dɪfrəntli, -'dɪfə-] *adv* **1** : con indiferencia, indiferentemente **2** SO-SO : de modo regular, más o menos

indigence ['ɪndɪʤənts] *n* : indigencia *f*

indigenous [ɪn'dɪʤənəs] *adj* : indígena, nativo

indigent ['ɪndɪʤənt] *adj* : indigente, pobre

indigestible [ˌɪndaɪ'ʤɛstəbəl, -dɪ-] *adj* : difícil de digerir

indigestion [ˌɪndaɪ'ʤɛsʧən, -dɪ-] *n* : indigestión *f*, empacho *m*

indignant [ɪn'dɪgnənt] *adj* : indignado

indignantly [ɪn'dɪgnəntli] *adv* : con indignación

indignation [ˌɪndɪg'neɪʃən] *n* : indignación *f*

indignity [ɪn'dɪgnəti] *n, pl* **-ties** : indignidad *f*

indigo ['ɪndɪˌgoː] *n, pl* **-gos** *or* **-goes** : añil *m*, índigo *m*

indirect [ˌɪndə'rɛkt, -daɪ-] *adj* : indirecto — **indirectly** *adv*

indiscernible [ˌɪndɪ'sərnəbəl, -'zər-] *adj* : imperceptible

indiscreet [ˌɪndɪ'skriːt] *adj* : indiscreto, imprudente — **indiscreetly** *adv*

indiscretion [ˌɪndɪ'skrɛʃən] *n* : indiscreción *f*, imprudencia *f*

indiscriminate [ˌɪndɪ'skrɪmənət] *adj* : indiscriminado

indiscriminately [ˌɪndɪ'skrɪmənətli] *adv* : sin discriminación, sin discernimiento

indispensable [ˌɪndɪ'spɛntsəbəl] *adj* : indispensable, necesario, imprescindible — **indispensably** [-bli] *adv*

indisposed [ˌɪndɪ'spoːzd] *adj* **1** ILL : indispuesto, enfermo **2** AVERSE, DISINCLINED : opuesto, reacio ⟨to be indisposed toward working : no tener ganas de trabajar⟩

indisputable [ˌɪndɪ'spjuːtəbəl, ɪn'dɪspjuːtə-] *adj* : indiscutible, incuestionable, incontestable — **indisputably** [-bli] *adv*

indistinct · inestimable

484

indistinct [ˌɪndɪ'stɪŋkt] *adj* : indistinto — **indistinctly** *adv*

indistinctness [ˌɪndɪ'stɪŋktnəs] *n* : falta *f* de claridad

indistinguishable [ˌɪndɪ'stɪŋgwɪʃəbəl] *adj* : indistinguible

individual[1] [ˌɪndə'vɪʤʊəl] *adj* **1** PERSONAL : individual, personal ⟨individual traits : características personales⟩ **2** SEPARATE : individual, separado **3** PARTICULAR : particular, propio

individual[2] *n* : individuo *m*

individualism [ˌɪndə'vɪʤəwəˌlɪzəm] *n* : individualismo *m*

individualist [ˌɪndə'vɪʤʊəlɪst] *n* : individualista *mf*

individuality [ˌɪndəˌvɪʤʊ'æləti] *n, pl* **-ties** : individualidad *f*

individually [ˌɪndə'vɪʤʊəli, -ʤəli] *adv* : individualmente

indivisible [ˌɪndɪ'vɪzəbəl] *adj* : indivisible

indoctrinate [ɪn'dɑktrəˌneɪt] *vt* **-nated; -nating 1** TEACH : enseñar, instruir **2** PROPAGANDIZE : adoctrinar

indoctrination [ɪnˌdɑktrə'neɪʃən] *n* : adoctrinamiento *m*

indolence ['ɪndələnts] *n* : indolencia *f*

indolent ['ɪndələnt] *adj* : indolente

indomitable [ɪn'dɑmətəbəl] *adj* : invencible, indomable, indómito — **indomitably** [-bli] *adv*

Indonesian [ˌɪndo'niːʒən, -ʃən] *n* : indonesio *m*, -sia *f* — **Indonesian** *adj*

indoor ['ɪn'dor] *adj* : interior (dícese de las plantas), para estar en casa (dícese de la ropa), cubierto (dícese de las piscinas, etc.), bajo techo (dícese de los deportes)

indoors ['ɪn'dorz] *adv* : adentro, dentro

indubitable [ɪn'duːbəṭəbəl, -'djuː-] *adj* : indudable, incuestionable, indiscutible

indubitably [ɪn'duːbəṭəbli, -'djuː-] *adv* : indudablemente

induce [ɪn'duːs, -'djuːs] *vt* **-duced; -ducing 1** PERSUADE : persuadir, inducir **2** CAUSE : inducir, provocar ⟨to induce labor : provocar un parto⟩

inducement [ɪn'duːsmənt, -'djuːs-] *n* **1** INCENTIVE : incentivo *m*, aliciente *m* **2** : inducción *f*, provocación *f* (de un parto)

induct [ɪn'dʌkt] *vt* **1** INSTALL : instalar, investir **2** ADMIT : admitir (como miembro) **3** CONSCRIPT : reclutar (al servicio militar)

inductee [ˌɪnˌdʌk'tiː] *n* : recluta *mf*, conscripto *m*, -ta *f*

induction [ɪn'dʌkʃən] *n* **1** INTRODUCTION : iniciación *f*, introducción *f* **2** : inducción *f* (en la lógica o la electricidad)

inductive [ɪn'dʌktɪv] *adj* : inductivo

indulge [ɪn'dʌlʤ] *v* **-dulged; -dulging** *vt* **1** GRATIFY : gratificar, satisfacer **2** SPOIL : consentir, mimar — *vi* **to indulge in** : permitirse

indulgence [ɪn'dʌlʤənts] *n* **1** SATISFYING : satisfacción *f*, gratificación *f* **2** HUMORING : complacencia *f*, indulgencia *f* **3** SPOILING : consentimiento *m* **4** : indulgencia *f* (en la religión)

indulgent [ɪn'dʌlʤənt] *adj* : indulgente, consentido — **indulgently** *adv*

industrial [ɪn'dʌstriəl] *adj* : industrial — **industrially** *adv*

industrialist [ɪn'dʌstriəlɪst] *n* : industrial *mf*

industrialization [ɪnˌdʌstriələ'zeɪ-ʃən] *n* : industrialización *f*

industrialize [ɪn'dʌstriəˌlaɪz] *vt* **-ized; -izing** : industrializar

industrious [ɪn'dʌstriəs] *adj* : diligente, industrioso, trabajador

industriously [ɪn'dʌstriəsli] *adv* : con diligencia, con aplicación

industriousness [ɪn'dʌstriəsnəs] *n* : diligencia *f*, aplicación *f*

industry ['ɪndəstri] *n, pl* **-tries 1** DILIGENCE : diligencia *f*, aplicación *f* **2** : industria *f* ⟨the steel industry : la industria siderúrgica⟩

inebriated [ɪ'niːbriˌeɪṭəd] *adj* : ebrio, embriagado

inebriation [ɪˌniːbri'eɪʃən] *n* : ebriedad *f*, embriaguez *f*

ineffable [ɪn'ɛfəbəl] *adj* : inefable — **ineffably** [-bli] *adv*

ineffective [ˌɪnɪ'fɛktɪv] *adj* **1** INEFFECTUAL : ineficaz, inútil **2** INCAPABLE : incompetente, ineficiente, incapaz

ineffectively [ˌɪnɪ'fɛktɪvli] *adv* : ineficazmente, infructuosamente

ineffectual [ˌɪnɪ'fɛktʃʊəl] *adj* : inútil, ineficaz — **ineffectually** *adv*

inefficiency [ˌɪnɪ'fɪʃəntsi] *n, pl* **-cies** : ineficiencia *f*, ineficacia *f*

inefficient [ˌɪnɪ'fɪʃənt] *adj* **1** : ineficiente, ineficaz **2** INCAPABLE, INCOMPETENT : incompetente, incapaz — **inefficiently** *adv*

inelegance [ɪn'ɛləgənts] *n* : inelegancia *f*

inelegant [ɪn'ɛləgənt] *adj* : inelegante, poco elegante

ineligibility [ɪnˌɛləʤə'bɪləti] *n* : inelegibilidad *f*

ineligible [ɪn'ɛləʤəbəl] *adj* : inelegible

inept [ɪ'nɛpt] *adj* : inepto ⟨inept at : incapaz para⟩

ineptitude [ɪ'nɛptəˌtuːd, -ˌtjuːd] *n* : ineptitud *f*, incompetencia *f*, incapacidad *f*

inequality [ˌɪnɪ'kwɑləti] *n, pl* **-ties** : desigualdad *f*

inert [ɪ'nərt] *adj* **1** INACTIVE : inerte, inactivo **2** SLUGGISH : lento

inertia [ɪ'nərʃə] *n* : inercia *f*

inescapable [ˌɪnɪ'skeɪpəbəl] *adj* : inevitable, ineludible — **inescapably** [-bli] *adv*

inessential [ˌɪnɪ'sɛntʃəl] *adj* : que no es esencial, innecesario

inestimable [ɪn'ɛstəməbəl] *adj* : inestimable, inapreciable

inevitability [ɪnˌɛvətəˈbɪləṭi] *n, pl* **-ties** : inevitabilidad *f*

inevitable [ɪnˈɛvətəbəl] *adj* : inevitable — **inevitably** [-bli] *adv*

inexact [ˌɪnɪɡˈzækt] *adj* : inexacto

inexactly [ˌɪnɪɡˈzæktli] *adv* : sin exactitud

inexcusable [ˌɪnɪkˈskju:zəbəl] *adj* : inexcusable, imperdonable — **inexcusably** [-bli] *adv*

inexhaustible [ˌɪnɪɡˈzɔstəbəl] *adj* **1** INDEFATIGABLE : infatigable, incansable **2** ENDLESS : inagotable — **inexhaustibly** [-bli] *adv*

inexorable [ɪnˈɛksərəbəl] *adj* : inexorable — **inexorably** [-bli] *adv*

inexpensive [ˌɪnɪkˈspɛntsɪv] *adj* : barato, económico

inexperience [ˌɪnɪkˈspɪriənts] *n* : inexperiencia *f*

inexperienced [ˌɪnɪkˈspɪriəntst] *adj* : inexperto, novato

inexplicable [ˌɪnɪkˈsplɪkəbəl] *adj* : inexplicable — **inexplicably** [-bli] *adv*

inexpressible [ˌɪnɪkˈsprɛsəbəl] *adj* : inexpresable, inefable

inextricable [ˌɪnɪkˈstrɪkəbəl, ɪˈnɛk-ˌstrɪ-] *adj* : inextricable — **inextricably** [-bli] *adv*

infallibility [ɪnˌfæləˈbɪləṭi] *n* : infalibilidad *f*

infallible [ɪnˈfæləbəl] *adj* : infalible — **infallibly** [-bli] *adv*

infamous [ˈɪnfəməs] *adj* : infame — **infamously** *adv*

infamy [ˈɪnfəmi] *n, pl* **-mies** : infamia *f*

infancy [ˈɪnfəntsi] *n, pl* **-cies** : infancia *f*

infant [ˈɪnfənt] *n* : bebé *m*; niño *m*, -ña *f*

infantile [ˈɪnfənˌtaɪl, -təl, -ˌti:l] *adj* : infantil, pueril

infantile paralysis → **poliomyelitis**

infantry [ˈɪnfəntri] *n, pl* **-tries** : infantería *f*

infatuated [ɪnˈfætʃuˌeɪṭəd] *adj* **to be infatuated with** : estar encaprichado con

infatuation [ɪnˌfætʃuˈeɪʃən] *n* : encaprichamiento *m*, enamoramiento *m*

infect [ɪnˈfɛkt] *vt* : infectar, contagiar

infection [ɪnˈfɛkʃən] *n* : infección *f*, contagio *m*

infectious [ɪnˈfɛkʃəs] *adj* : infeccioso, contagioso

infer [ɪnˈfər] *vt* **inferred; inferring 1** DEDUCE : deducir, inferir **2** SURMISE : concluir, suponer, tener entendido **3** IMPLY : sugerir, insinuar

inference [ˈɪnfərənts] *n* : deducción *f*, inferencia *f*, conclusión *f*

inferior[1] [ɪnˈfɪriər] *adj* : inferior, malo

inferior[2] *n* : inferior *mf*

inferiority [ɪnˌfɪriˈɔrəṭi] *n, pl* **-ties** : inferioridad *f* ⟨inferiority complex : complejo de inferioridad⟩

infernal [ɪnˈfərnəl] *adj* **1** : infernal ⟨infernal fires : fuegos infernales⟩ **2** DIABOLICAL : infernal, diabólico **3** DAMNABLE : maldito, condenado

inferno [ɪnˈfərˌno:] *n, pl* **-nos** : infierno *m*

infertile [ɪnˈfərṭəl, -ˌtaɪl] *adj* : estéril, infecundo

infertility [ˌɪnfərˈtɪləṭi] *n* : esterilidad *f*, infecundidad *f*

infest [ɪnˈfɛst] *vt* : infestar, plagar

infestation [ˌɪnˌfɛsˈteɪʃən] *n* : infestación *f*, plaga *f*

infidel [ˈɪnfədəl, -ˌdɛl] *n* : infiel *mf*

infidelity [ˌɪnfəˈdɛləṭi, -faɪ-] *n, pl* **-ties 1** UNFAITHFULNESS : infidelidad *f* **2** DISLOYALTY : deslealtad *f*

infield [ˈɪnˌfi:ld] *n* : cuadro *m*, diamante *m*

infiltrate [ɪnˈfɪlˌtreɪt, ˈɪnfɪl-] *v* **-trated; -trating** *vt* : infiltrar — *vi* : infiltrarse

infiltration [ˌɪnfɪlˈtreɪʃən] *n* : infiltración *f*

infinite [ˈɪnfənət] *adj* **1** LIMITLESS : infinito, sin límites **2** VAST : infinito, vasto, extenso

infinitely [ˈɪnfənətli] *adv* : infinitamente

infinitesimal [ˌɪnˌfɪnəˈtɛsəməl] *adj* : infinitésimo, infinitesimal — **infinitesimally** *adv*

infinitive [ɪnˈfɪnəṭɪv] *n* : infinitivo *m*

infinity [ɪnˈfɪnəṭi] *n, pl* **-ties 1** : infinito *m* (en matemáticas, etc.) **2** : infinidad *f* ⟨an infinity of stars : una infinidad de estrellas⟩

infirm [ɪnˈfərm] *adj* **1** FEEBLE : enfermizo, endeble **2** INSECURE : inseguro

infirmary [ɪnˈfərməri] *n, pl* **-ries** : enfermería *f*, hospital *m*

infirmity [ɪnˈfərməṭi] *n, pl* **-ties 1** FRAILTY : debilidad *f*, endeblez *f* **2** AILMENT : enfermedad *f*, dolencia *f* ⟨the infirmities of age : los achaques de la vejez⟩

inflame [ɪnˈfleɪm] *v* **-flamed; -flaming** *vt* **1** KINDLE : inflamar, encender **2** : inflamar (una herida) **3** STIR UP : encender, provocar, inflamar — *vi* : inflamarse

inflammable [ɪnˈflæməbəl] *adj* **1** FLAMMABLE : inflamable **2** IRASCIBLE : irascible, explosivo

inflammation [ˌɪnfləˈmeɪʃən] *n* : inflamación *f*

inflammatory [ɪnˈflæməˌtori] *adj* : inflamatorio, incendiario

inflatable [ɪnˈfleɪṭəbəl] *adj* : inflable

inflate [ɪnˈfleɪt] *vt* **-flated; -flating** : inflar, hinchar

inflation [ɪnˈfleɪʃən] *n* : inflación *f*

inflationary [ɪnˈfleɪʃəˌnɛri] *adj* : inflacionario, inflacionista

inflect [ɪnˈflɛkt] *vt* **1** CONJUGATE, DECLINE : conjugar, declinar **2** MODULATE : modular (la voz)

inflection [ɪnˈflɛkʃən] *n* : inflexión *f*

inflexibility [ɪnˌflɛksəˈbɪləṭi] *n, pl* **-ties** : inflexibilidad *f*

inflexible [ɪnˈflɛksɪbəl] *adj* : inflexible

inflict [ɪnˈflɪkt] *vt* **1** : infligir, causar, imponer **2 to inflict oneself on** : imponer uno su presencia (a alguien)

infliction [ɪnˈflɪkʃən] *n* : imposición *f*

influence¹ ['ɪn,flu:ənts, ɪn'flu:ənts] *vt* -enced; -encing : influenciar, influir en

influence² *n* **1** : influencia *f*, influjo *m* ⟨to exert influence over : ejercer influencia sobre⟩ ⟨the influence of gravity : el influjo de la gravedad⟩ **2 under the influence** : bajo la influencia del alcohol, embriagado

influential [,ɪnflu'ɛnʧəl] *adj* : influyente

influenza [,ɪnflu'ɛnzə] *n* : gripe *f*, influenza *f*, gripa *f Col, Mex*

influx ['ɪn,flʌks] *n* : afluencia *f* (de gente), entrada *f* (de mercancías), llegada *f* (de ideas)

inform [ɪn'fɔrm] *vt* : informar, notificar, avisar — *vi* **to inform on** : delatar, denunciar

informal [ɪn'fɔrməl] *adj* **1** UNCEREMONIOUS : sin ceremonia, sin etiqueta **2** CASUAL : informal, familiar (dícese del lenguaje) **3** UNOFFICIAL : extraoficial

informality [,ɪnfɔr'mæləti, -fər-] *n, pl* -ties : informalidad *f*, familiaridad *f*, falta *f* de ceremonia

informally [ɪn'fɔrməli] *adv* : sin ceremonias, de manera informal, informalmente

informant [ɪn'fɔrmənt] *n* : informante *mf*; informador *m*, -dora *f*

information [,ɪnfər'meɪʃən] *n* : información *f*

informative [ɪn'fɔrmətɪv] *adj* : informativo, instructivo

informer [ɪn'fɔrmər] *n* : informante *mf*; informador *m*, -dora *f*

infraction [ɪn'frækʃən] *n* : infracción *f*, violación *f*, transgresión *f*

infrared [,ɪnfrə'rɛd] *adj* : infrarrojo

infrastructure ['ɪnfrə,strʌktʃər] *n* : infraestructura *f*

infrequent [ɪn'fri:kwənt] *adj* : infrecuente, raro

infrequently [ɪn'fri:kwəntli] *adv* : raramente, con poca frecuencia

infringe [ɪn'frɪnʤ] *v* -fringed; -fringing *vt* : infringir, violar — *vi* **to infringe on** : abusar de, violar

infringement [ɪn'frɪnʤmənt] *n* **1** VIOLATION : violación *f* (de la ley), incumplimiento *m* (de un contrato) **2** ENCROACHMENT : usurpación *f* (de derechos, etc.)

infuriate [ɪn'fjʊri,eɪt] *vt* -ated; -ating : enfurecer, poner furioso

infuriating [ɪn'fjʊri,eɪtɪŋ] *adj* : indignante, exasperante

infuse [ɪn'fju:z] *vt* -fused; -fusing **1** INSTILL : infundir **2** STEEP : hacer una infusión de

infusion [ɪn'fju:ʒən] *n* : infusión *f*

ingenious [ɪn'ʤi:njəs] *adj* : ingenioso — **ingeniously** *adv*

ingenue *or* **ingénue** ['ɑnʤə,nu:, 'æn-; 'æʒə-, -'ɑ-] *n* : ingenua *f*

ingenuity [,ɪnʤə'nu:əti, -'nju:-] *n, pl* -ities : ingenio

ingenuous [ɪn'ʤɛnjʊəs] *adj* **1** FRANK : cándido, franco **2** NAIVE : ingenuo — **ingenuously** *adv*

ingenuousness [ɪn'ʤɛnjʊəsnəs] *n* **1** FRANKNESS : candidez *f*, candor *m* **2** NAÏVETÉ : ingenuidad *f*

ingest [ɪn'ʤɛst] *vt* : ingerir

ingestion [ɪn'ʤɛstʃən] *n* : ingestión *f*

inglorious [ɪn'gloriəs] *adj* : deshonroso, ignominioso

ingot ['ɪŋgət] *n* : lingote *m*

ingrained [ɪn'greɪnd] *adj* : arraigado

ingrate ['ɪn,greɪt] *n* : ingrato *m*, -ta *f*

ingratiate [ɪn'greɪʃi,eɪt] *vt* -ated; -ating : conseguir la benevolencia de ⟨to ingratiate oneself with someone : congraciarse con alguien⟩

ingratiating [ɪn'greɪʃi,eɪtɪŋ] *adj* : halagador, zalamero, obsequioso

ingratitude [ɪn'grætə,tu:d, -,tju:d] *n* : ingratitud *f*

ingredient [ɪn'gri:diənt] *n* : ingrediente *m*, componente *m*

ingrown ['ɪn,gro:n] *adj* **1** : crecido hacia adentro **2 ingrown toenail** : uña *f* encarnada

inhabit [ɪn'hæbət] *vt* : vivir en, habitar, ocupar

inhabitable [ɪn'hæbətəbəl] *adj* : habitable

inhabitant [ɪn'hæbətənt] *n* : habitante *mf*

inhalant [ɪn'heɪlənt] *n* : inhalante *m*

inhalation [,ɪnhə'leɪʃən, ,ɪnə-] *n* : inhalación *f*

inhale [ɪn'heɪl] *v* -haled; -haling *vt* : inhalar, aspirar — *vi* : inspirar

inhaler [ɪn'heɪlər] *n* : inhalador *m*

inhere [ɪn'hɪr] *vi* -hered; -hering : ser inherente

inherent [ɪn'hɪrənt, -'hɛr-] *adj* : inherente, intrínseco — **inherently** *adv*

inherit [ɪn'hɛrət] *vt* : heredar

inheritance [ɪn'hɛrətənts] *n* : herencia *f*

inheritor [ɪn'hɛrətər] *n* : heredero *m*, -da *f*

inhibit [ɪn'hɪbət] *vt* IMPEDE : inhibir, impedir

inhibition [,ɪnhə'bɪʃən, ,ɪnə-] *n* : inhibición *f*, cohibición *f*

inhuman [ɪn'hju:mən, -'ju:-] *adj* : inhumano, cruel — **inhumanly** *adv*

inhumane [,ɪnhju'meɪn, -ju-] *adj* INHUMAN : inhumano, cruel

inhumanity [,ɪnhju'mænəti, -ju-] *n, pl* -ties : inhumanidad *f*, crueldad *f*

inimical [ɪ'nɪmɪkəl] *adj* **1** UNFAVORABLE : adverso, desfavorable **2** HOSTILE : hostil — **inimically** *adv*

inimitable [ɪ'nɪmətəbəl] *adj* : inimitable

iniquitous [ɪ'nɪkwətəs] *adj* : inicuo, malvado

iniquity [ɪ'nɪkwəti] *n, pl* -ties : iniquidad *f*

initial¹ [ɪ'nɪʃəl] *vt* -tialed *or* -tialled; -tialing *or* -tialling : poner las iniciales a, firmar con las iniciales

initial² *adj* : inicial, primero — **initially** *adv*

initial³ *n* : inicial *f*
initiate¹ [ɪˈnɪʃiˌeɪt] *vt* **-ated; -ating 1** BE-GIN : comenzar, iniciar **2** INDUCT : instruir **3** INTRODUCE : introducir, instruir
initiate² [ɪˈnɪʃiət] *n* : iniciado *m*, -da *f*
initiation [ɪˌnɪʃiˈeɪʃən] *n* : iniciación *f*
initiative [ɪˈnɪʃətɪv] *n* : iniciativa *f*
initiatory [ɪˈnɪʃiəˌtori] *adj* **1** INTRODUCTORY : introductorio **2** : de iniciación ⟨initiatory rites : ritos de iniciación⟩
inject [ɪnˈʤɛkt] *vt* : inyectar
injection [ɪnˈʤɛkʃən] *n* : inyección *f*
injudicious [ˌɪnʤʊˈdɪʃəs] *adj* : imprudente, indiscreto, poco juicioso
injunction [ɪnˈʤʌŋkʃən] *n* **1** ORDER : orden *f*, mandato *m* **2** COURT ORDER : mandamiento *m* judicial
injure [ˈɪnʤər] *vt* **-jured; -juring 1** WOUND : herir, lesionar **2** HURT : lastimar, dañar, herir **3 to injure oneself** : hacerse daño
injurious [ɪnˈʤʊriəs] *adj* : perjudicial ⟨injurious to one's health : perjudicial a la salud⟩
injury [ˈɪnʤəri] *n, pl* **-ries 1** WRONG : mal *m*, injusticia *f* **2** DAMAGE, HARM : herida *f*, daño *m*, perjuicio *m*
injustice [ɪnˈʤʌstəs] *n* : injusticia *f*
ink¹ [ɪŋk] *vt* : entintar
ink² *n* : tinta *f*
inkling [ˈɪŋklɪŋ] *n* : presentimiento *m*, indicio *m*, sospecha *f*
inkwell [ˈɪŋkˌwɛl] *n* : tintero *m*
inky [ˈɪŋki] *adj* **1** : manchado de tinta **2** BLACK : negro, impenetrable ⟨inky darkness : negra oscuridad⟩
inland¹ [ˈɪnˌlænd, -lənd] *adv* : hacia el interior, tierra adentro
inland² *adj* : interior
inland³ *n* : interior *m*
in–law [ˈɪnˌlɔ] *n* **1** : pariente *m* político **2 in–laws** *npl* : suegros *mpl*
inlay¹ [ɪnˈleɪ, ˈɪnˌleɪ] *vt* **-laid** [-ˈleɪd, -ˌleɪd]; **-laying** : incrustar, taracear
inlay² [ˈɪnˌleɪ] *n* **1** : incrustación *f* **2** : empaste *m* (de un diente)
inlet [ˈɪnˌlɛt, -lət] *n* : cala *f*, ensenada *f*
inmate [ˈɪnˌmeɪt] *n* : paciente *mf* (en un hospital); preso *m*, -sa *f* (en una prisión); interno *m*, -na *f* (en un asilo)
in memoriam [ˌɪnməˈmoriəm] *prep* : en memoria de
inmost [ˈɪnˌmoːst] → **innermost**
inn [ɪn] *n* **1** : posada *f*, hostería *f*, fonda *f* **2** TAVERN : taberna *f*
innards [ˈɪnərdz] *npl* : entrañas *fpl*, tripas *fpl fam*
innate [ɪˈneɪt] *adj* **1** INBORN : innato **2** INHERENT : inherente
inner [ˈɪnər] *adj* : interior, interno
innermost [ˈɪnərˌmoːst] *adj* : más íntimo, más profundo
innersole [ˈɪnərˈsoːl] → **insole**
inning [ˈɪnɪŋ] *n* : entrada *f*
innkeeper [ˈɪnˌkiːpər] *n* : posadero *m*, -ra *f*
innocence [ˈɪnəsənts] *n* : inocencia *f*

innocent¹ [ˈɪnəsənt] *adj* : inocente — **innocently** *adv*
innocent² *n* : inocente *mf*
innocuous [ɪˈnɑkjəwəs] *adj* **1** HARMLESS : inocuo **2** INOFFENSIVE : inofensivo
innovate [ˈɪnəˌveɪt] *vi* **-vated; -vating** : innovar
innovation [ˌɪnəˈveɪʃən] *n* : innovación *f*, novedad *f*
innovative [ˈɪnəˌveɪtɪv] *adj* : innovador
innovator [ˈɪnəˌveɪtər] *n* : innovador *m*, -dora *f*
innuendo [ˌɪnjuˈɛndo] *n, pl* **-dos** *or* **-does** : insinuación *f*, indirecta *f*
innumerable [ɪˈnuːmərəbəl, -ˈnjuː-] *adj* : innumerable
inoculate [ɪˈnɑkjəˌleɪt] *vt* **-lated; -lating** : inocular
inoculation [ɪˌnɑkjəˈleɪʃən] *n* : inoculación *f*
inoffensive [ˌɪnəˈfɛntsɪv] *adj* : inofensivo
inoperable [ɪnˈɑpərəbəl] *adj* : inoperable
inoperative [ɪnˈɑpərətɪv, -ˌreɪ-] *adj* : inoperante
inopportune [ɪnˌɑpərˈtuːn, -ˈtjuːn] *adj* : inoportuno — **inopportunely** *adv*
inordinate [ɪnˈɔrdənət] *adj* : excesivo, inmoderado, desmesurado — **inordinately** *adv*
inorganic [ˌɪnˌɔrˈgænɪk] *adj* : inorgánico
inpatient [ˈɪnˌpeɪʃənt] *n* : paciente *mf* hospitalizado
input¹ [ˈɪnˌpʊt] *vt* **inputted** *or* **input; inputting** : entrar (datos, información)
input² *n* **1** CONTRIBUTION : aportación *f*, contribución *f* **2** ENTRY : entrada *f* (de datos) **3** ADVICE, OPINION : consejos *mpl*, opinión *f*
inquest [ˈɪnˌkwɛst] *n* INQUIRY, INVESTIGATION : investigación *f*, averiguación *f*, pesquisa *f* (judicial)
inquire [ɪnˈkwaɪr] *v* **-quired; -quiring** *vt* : preguntar, informarse de, inquirir ⟨he inquired how to get in : preguntó como entrar⟩ — *vi* **1** ASK : preguntar, informarse ⟨to inquire about : informarse sobre⟩ ⟨to inquire after (someone) : preguntar por (alguien)⟩ **2 to inquire into** INVESTIGATE : investigar, inquirir sobre
inquiringly [ɪnˈkwaɪrɪŋli] *adv* : inquisitivamente
inquiry [ˈɪnˌkwaɪri, ɪnˈkwaɪri; ˈɪnkwəri, ˈɪŋ-] *n, pl* **-ries 1** QUESTION : pregunta *f* ⟨to make inquiries about : pedir información sobre⟩ **2** INVESTIGATION : investigación *f*, inquisición *f*, pesquisa *f*
inquisition [ˌɪnkwəˈzɪʃən, ˌɪŋ-] *n* **1** : inquisición *f*, interrogatorio *m*, investigación *f* **2 the Inquisition** : la Inquisición *f*
inquisitive [ɪnˈkwɪzətɪv] *adj* : inquisidor, inquisitivo, curioso — **inquisitively** *adv*

inquisitiveness [ɪn'kwɪzətɪvnəs] *n* : curiosidad *f*

inquisitor [ɪn'kwɪzətər] *n* : inquisidor *m*, -dora *f*; interrogador *m*, -dora *f*

inroad ['ɪn,ro:d] *n* **1** ENCROACHMENT, INVASION : invasión *f*, incursión *f* **2 to make inroads into** : ocupar parte de (un tiempo), agotar parte de (ahorros, recursos), invadir (un territorio)

insane [ɪn'seɪn] *adj* **1** MAD : loco, demente ⟨to go insane : volverse loco⟩ **2** ABSURD : absurdo, insensato ⟨an insane scheme : un proyecto insensato⟩

insanely [ɪn'seɪnli] *adv* : como un loco ⟨insanely suspicious : loco de recelo⟩

insanity [ɪn'sænəti] *n, pl* **-ties 1** MADNESS : locura *f* **2** FOLLY : locura *f*, insensatez *f*

insatiable [ɪn'seɪʃəbəl] *adj* : insaciable — **insatiably** [-bli] *adv*

inscribe [ɪn'skraɪb] *vt* **-scribed; -scribing 1** ENGRAVE : inscribir, grabar **2** ENROLL : inscribir **3** DEDICATE : dedicar (un libro)

inscription [ɪn'skrɪpʃən] *n* : inscripción *f* (en un monumento), dedicación *f* (en un libro), leyenda *f* (de una ilustración, etc.)

inscrutable [ɪn'skru:təbəl] *adj* : inescrutable, misterioso — **inscrutably** [-bli] *adv*

inseam ['ɪn,si:m] *n* : entrepierna *f*

insect ['ɪn,sɛkt] *n* : insecto *m*

insecticidal [ɪn,sɛktə'saɪdəl] *adj* : insecticida

insecticide [ɪn'sɛktə,saɪd] *n* : insecticida *m*

insecure [,ɪnsɪ'kjʊr] *adj* : inseguro, poco seguro — **insecurely** *adv*

insecurely [,ɪnsɪ'kjʊrli] *adv* : inseguramente

insecurity [,ɪnsɪ'kjʊrəti] *n, pl* **-ties** : inseguridad *f*

inseminate [ɪn'sɛmə,neɪt] *vt* **-nated; -nating** : inseminar

insemination [ɪn,sɛmə'neɪʃən] *n* : inseminación *f*

insensibility [ɪn,sɛntsə'bɪləti] *n, pl* **-ties** : insensibilidad *f*

insensible [ɪn'sɛntsəbəl] *adj* **1** UNCONSCIOUS : inconsciente, sin conocimiento **2** NUMB : insensible, entumecido **3** UNAWARE : inconsciente

insensitive [ɪn'sɛntsətɪv] *adj* : insensible

insensitivity [ɪn,sɛntsə'tɪvəti] *n, pl* **-ties** : insensibilidad *f*

inseparable [ɪn'sɛpərəbəl] *adj* : inseparable

insert[1] [ɪn'sərt] *vt* **1** : insertar, introducir, poner, meter ⟨insert your key in the lock : mete tu llave en la cerradura⟩ **2** INTERPOLATE : interpolar, intercalar

insert[2] ['ɪn,sərt] *n* : inserción *f*, hoja *f* insertada (en una revista, etc.)

insertion [ɪn'sərʃən] *n* : inserción *f*

inset ['ɪn,sɛt] *n* : página *f* intercalada (en un libro), entredós *m* (de encaje en la ropa)

inshore[1] ['ɪn'ʃor] *adv* : hacia la costa

inshore[2] *adj* : cercano a la costa, costero ⟨inshore fishing : pesca costera⟩

inside[1] [ɪn'saɪd, 'ɪn,saɪd] *adv* : adentro, dentro ⟨to run inside : correr para adentro⟩ ⟨inside and out : por dentro y por fuera⟩

inside[2] *adj* **1** : interior, de adentro, de dentro ⟨the inside lane : el carril interior⟩ **2** : confidencial ⟨inside information : información confidencial⟩

inside[3] *n* **1** : interior *m*, parte *f* de adentro **2 insides** *npl* BELLY, GUTS : tripas *fpl fam* **3 inside out** : al revés

inside[4] *prep* **1** INTO : al interior de **2** WITHIN : dentro de **3** (*referring to time*) : en menos de ⟨inside an hour : en menos de una hora⟩

inside of *prep* INSIDE : dentro de

insider [ɪn'saɪdər] *n* : persona *f* enterada

insidious [ɪn'sɪdiəs] *adj* : insidioso — **insidiously** *adv*

insidiousness [ɪn'sɪdiəsnəs] *n* : insidia *f*

insight ['ɪn,saɪt] *n* : perspicacia *f*, penetración *f*

insightful [ɪn'saɪtfəl] *adj* : perspicaz

insignia [ɪn'sɪgniə] *or* **insigne** [-,ni:] *n, pl* **-nia** *or* **-nias** : insignia *f*, enseña *f*

insignificance [,ɪnsɪg'nɪfɪkənts] *n* : insignificancia *f*

insignificant [,ɪnsɪg'nɪfɪkənt] *adj* : insignificante

insincere [,ɪnsɪn'sɪr] *adj* : insincero, poco sincero

insincerely [,ɪnsɪn'sɪrli] *adv* : con poca sinceridad

insincerity [,ɪnsɪn'sɛrəti, -'sɪr-] *n, pl* **-ties** : insinceridad *f*

insinuate [ɪn'sɪnju,eɪt] *vt* **-ated; -ating** : insinuar

insinuation [ɪn,sɪnju'eɪʃən] *n* : insinuación *f*

insipid [ɪn'sɪpəd] *adj* : insípido

insist [ɪn'sɪst] *v* : insistir

insistence [ɪn'sɪstənts] *n* : insistencia *f*

insistent [ɪn'sɪstənt] *adj* : insistente — **insistently** *adv*

insofar as [,ɪnso'fɑræz] *conj* : en la medida en que, en tanto que, en cuanto a

insole ['ɪn,so:l] *n* : plantilla *f*

insolence ['ɪntsələnts] *n* : insolencia *f*

insolent ['ɪntsələnt] *adj* : insolente

insolubility [ɪn,saljə'bɪləti] *n* : insolubilidad *f*

insoluble [ɪn'saljəbəl] *adj* : insoluble

insolvency [ɪn'salvəntsi] *n, pl* **-cies** : insolvencia *f*

insolvent [ɪn'salvənt] *adj* : insolvente

insomnia [ɪn'samniə] *n* : insomnio *m*

insomuch as [,ɪnso'mʌtʃæz] → **inasmuch as**

insomuch that *conj* SO : así que, de manera que

inspect [ɪn'spɛkt] *vt* : inspeccionar, examinar, revisar

inspection [ɪn'spɛkʃən] *n* : inspección *f*, examen *m*, revisión *f*, revista *f* (de tropas)

inspector [ɪn'spɛktər] *n* : inspector *m*, -tora *f*

inspiration [ˌɪntspə'reɪʃən] *n* : inspiración *f*

inspirational [ˌɪntspə'reɪʃənəl] *adj* : inspirador

inspire [ɪn'spaɪr] *v* **-spired; -spiring** *vt* **1** INHALE : inhalar, aspirar **2** STIMULATE : estimular, animar, inspirar **3** INSTILL : inspirar, infundir — *vi* : inspirar

instability [ˌɪntstə'bɪləti] *n*, *pl* **-ties** : inestabilidad *f*

install [ɪn'stɔl] *vt* **-stalled; -stalling 1** : instalar ⟨to install the new president : instalar el presidente nuevo⟩ ⟨to install a fan : montar un abanico⟩ **2 to install oneself** : instalarse

installation [ˌɪntstə'leɪʃən] *n* : instalación *f*

installment [ɪn'stɔlmənt] *n* **1** : plazo *m*, cuota *f* ⟨to pay in four installments : pagar a cuatro plazos⟩ **2** : entrega *f* (de una publicación o telenovela) **3** INSTALLATION : instalación *f*

instance ['ɪntstənts] *n* **1** INSTIGATION : instancia *f* **2** EXAMPLE : ejemplo *m* ⟨for instance : por ejemplo⟩ **3** OCCASION : instancia *f*, caso *m*, ocasión *f* ⟨he prefers, in this instance, to remain anonymous : en este caso prefiere quedarse anónimo⟩

instant¹ ['ɪntstənt] *adj* **1** IMMEDIATE : inmediato, instantáneo ⟨an instant reply : una respuesta inmediata⟩ **2** : instantáneo ⟨instant coffee : café instantáneo⟩

instant² *n* : momento *m*, instante *m*

instantaneous [ˌɪntstən'teɪniəs] *adj* : instantáneo

instantaneously [ˌɪntstən'teɪniəsli] *adv* : instantáneamente, al instante

instantly ['ɪntstəntli] *adv* : al instante, instantáneamente

instead [ɪn'stɛd] *adv* **1** : en cambio, en lugar de eso, en su lugar ⟨Dad was going, but Mom went instead : papá iba a ir, pero mamá fue en su lugar⟩ **2** RATHER : al contrario

instead of *prep* : en vez de, en lugar de

instep ['ɪnˌstɛp] *n* : empeine *m*

instigate ['ɪntstəˌgeɪt] *vt* **-gated; -gating** INCITE, PROVOKE : instigar, incitar, provocar, fomentar

instigation [ˌɪntstə'geɪʃən] *n* : instancia *f*, incitación *f*

instigator ['ɪntstəˌgeɪtər] *n* : instigador *m*, -dora *f*; incitador *m*, -dora *f*

instill [ɪn'stɪl] *vt* **-stilled; -stilling** : inculcar, infundir

instinct ['ɪnˌstɪŋkt] *n* **1** TALENT : instinto *m*, don *m* ⟨an instinct for the right word : un don para escoger la palabra apropiada⟩ **2** : instinto *m* ⟨maternal instincts : instintos maternales⟩

instinctive [ɪn'stɪŋktɪv] *adj* : instintivo

instinctively [ɪn'stɪŋktɪvli] *adv* : instintivamente, por instinto

instinctual [ɪn'stɪŋktʃuəl] *adj* : instintivo

institute¹ ['ɪntstəˌtuːt, -ˌtjuːt] *vt* **-tuted; -tuting 1** ESTABLISH : establecer, instituir, fundar **2** INITIATE : iniciar, empezar, entablar

institute² *n* : instituto *m*

institution [ˌɪntstə'tuːʃən, -'tjuː-] *n* **1** ESTABLISHING : institución *f*, establecimiento *m* **2** CUSTOM : institución *f*, tradición *f* ⟨the institution of marriage : la institución del matrimonio⟩ **3** ORGANIZATION : institución *f*, organismo *m* **4** ASYLUM : asilo *m*

institutional [ˌɪntstə'tuːʃənəl, -'tjuː-] *adj* : institucional

institutionalize [ˌɪntstə'tuːʃənəˌlaɪz, -'tjuː-] *vt* **-ized; -izing 1** : institucionalizar ⟨institutionalized values : valores institucionalizados⟩ **2** : internar ⟨institutionalized orphans : huérfanos internados⟩

instruct [ɪn'strʌkt] *vt* **1** TEACH, TRAIN : instruir, adiestrar, enseñar **2** COMMAND : mandar, ordenar, dar instrucciones a

instruction [ɪn'strʌkʃən] *n* **1** TEACHING : instrucción *f*, enseñanza *f* **2** COMMAND : orden *f*, instrucción *f* **3** **instructions** *npl* DIRECTIONS : instrucciones *fpl*, modo *m* de empleo

instructional [ɪn'strʌkʃənəl] *adj* : instructivo, educativo

instructive [ɪn'strʌktɪv] *adj* : instructivo

instructor [ɪn'strʌktər] *n* : instructor *m*, -tora *f*

instrument ['ɪntstrəmənt] *n* : instrumento *m*

instrumental [ˌɪntstrə'mɛntəl] *adj* : instrumental

instrumentalist [ˌɪntstrə'mɛntəlɪst] *n* : instrumentista *mf*

insubordinate [ˌɪnsə'bɔrdənət] *adj* : insubordinado

insubordination [ˌɪnsəˌbɔrdən'eɪʃən] *n* : insubordinación *f*

insubstantial [ˌɪnsəb'stæntʃəl] *adj* : insustancial, poco nutritivo (dícese de una comida), poco sólido (dícese de una estructura o un argumento)

insufferable [ɪn'sʌfərəbəl] *adj* UNBEARABLE : insufrible, intolerable, inaguantable, insoportable — **insufferably** [-bli] *adv*

insufficiency [ˌɪnsə'fɪʃəntsi] *n*, *pl* **-cies** : insuficiencia *f*

insufficient [ˌɪnsə'fɪʃənt] *adj* : insuficiente — **insufficiently** *adv*

insular ['ɪntsʊlər, -sjʊ-] *adj* **1** : isleño (dícese de la gente), insular (dícese del clima) ⟨insular residents : residentes de la isla⟩ **2** NARROW-MINDED : de miras estrechas

insularity [ˌɪntsʊ'lærəti, -sjʊ-] *n* : insularidad *f*

insulate ['ɪntsəˌleɪt] *vt* **-lated; -lating** : aislar

insulation [ˌɪntsə'leɪʃən] *n* : aislamiento *m*

insulator ['ɪntsəˌleɪtər] *n* : aislador *m* (pieza), aislante *m* (material)

insulin ['ɪntsələn] *n* : insulina *f*
insult[1] [ɪn'sʌlt] *vt* : insultar, ofender, injuriar
insult[2] ['ɪn,sʌlt] *n* : insulto *m*, injuria *f*, agravio *m*
insulting [ɪn'sʌltɪŋ] *adj* : ofensivo, injurioso, insultante
insultingly [ɪn'sʌltɪŋli] *adv* : ofensivamente, de manera insultante
insuperable [ɪn'su:pərəbəl] *adj* : insuperable — **insuperably** [-bli] *adv*
insurable [ɪn'ʃurəbəl] *adj* : asegurable
insurance [ɪn'ʃurənts, 'ɪn,ʃur-] *n* : seguro *m* ⟨life insurance : seguro de vida⟩ ⟨insurance company : compañía de seguros⟩
insure [ɪn'ʃur] *vt* **-sured; -suring 1** UNDERWRITE : asegurar **2** ENSURE : asegurar, garantizar
insured [ɪn'ʃurd] *n* : asegurado *m*, -da *f*
insurer [ɪn'ʃurər] *n* : asegurador *m*, -dora *f*
insurgent[1] [ɪn'sərdʒənt] *adj* : insurgente
insurgent[2] *n* : insurgente *mf*
insurmountable [,ɪnsər'mauntəbəl] *adj* : insuperable, insalvable — **insurmountably** [-bli] *adv*
insurrection [,ɪnsə'rɛkʃən] *n* : insurrección *f*, levantamiento *m*, alzamiento *m*
intact [ɪn'tækt] *adj* : intacto
intake ['ɪn,teɪk] *n* **1** OPENING : entrada *f*, toma *f* ⟨fuel intake : toma de combustible⟩ **2** : entrada *f* (de agua o aire), consumo *m* (de sustancias nutritivas) **3 intake of breath** : inhalación *f*
intangible [ɪn'tændʒəbəl] *adj* : intangible, impalpable — **intangibly** [-bli] *adv*
integer ['ɪntɪdʒər] *n* : entero *m*
integral ['ɪntɪgrəl] *adj* : integral, esencial
integrate ['ɪntə,greɪt] *v* **-grated; -grating** *vt* **1** UNITE : integrar, unir **2** DESEGREGATE : eliminar la segregación de — *vi* : integrarse
integration [,ɪntə'greɪʃən] *n* : integración *f*
integrity [ɪn'tɛgrəti] *n* : integridad *f*
intellect ['ɪntəl,ɛkt] *n* : intelecto *m*, inteligencia *f*, capacidad *f* intelectual
intellectual[1] [,ɪntə'lɛktʃuəl] *adj* : intelectual — **intellectually** *adv*
intellectual[2] *n* : intelectual *mf*
intellectualism [,ɪntə'lɛktʃuə,lɪzəm] *n* : intelectualismo *m*
intelligence [ɪn'tɛlədʒənts] *n* **1** : inteligencia *f* **2** INFORMATION, NEWS : inteligencia *f*, información *f*, noticias *fpl*
intelligent [ɪn'tɛlədʒənt] *adj* : inteligente — **intelligently** *adv*
intelligentsia [ɪn,tɛlə'dʒɛntsiə, -'gɛn-] *ns & pl* : intelectualidad *f*
intelligibility [ɪn,tɛlədʒə'bɪləti] *n* : inteligibilidad *f*
intelligible [ɪn'tɛlədʒəbəl] *adj* : inteligible, comprensible — **intelligibly** [-bli] *adv*
intemperance [ɪn'tɛmpərənts] *n* : inmoderación *f*, intemperancia *f*

intemperate [ɪn'tɛmpərət] *adj* : excesivo, inmoderado, desmedido
intend [ɪn'tɛnd] *vt* **1** MEAN : querer decir ⟨that's not what I intended : eso no es lo que quería decir⟩ **2** PLAN : tener planeado, proyectar, proponerse ⟨I intend to finish by Thursday : me propongo acabar para el jueves⟩
intended [ɪn'tɛndəd] *adj* **1** PLANNED : previsto, proyectado **2** INTENTIONAL : intencional, deliberado
intense [ɪn'tɛnts] *adj* **1** EXTREME : intenso, extremo ⟨intense pain : dolor intenso⟩ **2** : profundo, intenso ⟨to my intense relief : para mi alivio profundo⟩ ⟨intense enthusiasm : entusiasmo ardiente⟩
intensely [ɪn'tɛntsli] *adv* : sumamente, profundamente, intensamente
intensification [ɪn,tɛntsəfə'keɪʃən] *n* : intensificación *f*
intensify [ɪn'tɛntsə,faɪ] *v* **-fied; -fying** *vt* **1** STRENGTHEN : intensificar, redoblar ⟨to intensify one's efforts : redoblar uno sus esfuerzos⟩ **2** SHARPEN : intensificar, agudizar (dolor, ansiedad) — *vi* : intensificarse, hacerse más intenso
intensity [ɪn'tɛntsəti] *n, pl* **-ties** : intensidad *f*
intensive [ɪn'tɛntsɪv] *adj* : intensivo — **intensively** *adv*
intent[1] [ɪn'tɛnt] *adj* **1** FIXED : concentrado, fijo ⟨an intent stare : una mirada fija⟩ **2 intent on** *or* **intent upon** : resuelto a, atento a
intent[2] *n* **1** PURPOSE : intención *f*, propósito *m* **2 for all intents and purposes** : a todos los efectos, prácticamente
intention [ɪn'tɛntʃən] *n* : intención *f*, propósito *m*
intentional [ɪn'tɛntʃənəl] *adj* : intencional, deliberado
intentionally [ɪn'tɛntʃənəli] *adv* : a propósito, adrede
intently [ɪn'tɛntli] *adv* : atentamente, fijamente
inter [ɪn'tər] *vt* **-terred; -terring** : enterrar, inhumar
interact [,ɪntər'ækt] *vi* : interactuar, actuar recíprocamente, relacionarse
interaction [,ɪntər'ækʃən] *n* : interacción *f*, interrelación *f*
interactive [,ɪntər'æktɪv] *adj* : interactivo
interbreed [,ɪntər'bri:d] *v* **-bred** [-'brɛd]; **-breeding** *vt* : cruzar — *vi* : cruzarse
intercalate [ɪn'tərkə,leɪt] *vt* **-lated; -lating** : intercalar
intercede [,ɪntər'si:d] *vi* **-ceded; -ceding** : interceder
intercept [,ɪntər'sɛpt] *vt* : interceptar
interception [,ɪntər'sɛpʃən] *n* : intercepción *f*
intercession [,ɪntər'sɛʃən] *n* : intercesión *f*

interchange[1] [ˌɪntərˈtʃeɪndʒ] *vt*
 -changed; -changing : intercambiar
interchange[2] [ˈɪntərˌtʃeɪndʒ] *n* **1** EX-
 CHANGE : intercambio *m*, cambio *m* **2**
 JUNCTION : empalme *m*, enlace *m* de
 carreteras
interchangeable [ˌɪntərˈtʃeɪndʒəbəl] *adj*
 : intercambiable
intercity [ˈɪntərˈsɪti] *adj* : interurbano
intercollegiate [ˌɪntərkəˈliːdʒət, -dʒiət]
 adj : interuniversitario
interconnect [ˌɪntərkəˈnɛkt] *vt* **1**
 : conectar, interconectar (en tecnología) **2** RELATE : interrelacionar —
 vi **1** : conectar **2** : interrelacionarse
intercontinental [ˌɪntərˌkɑntənˈnɛtəl]
 adj : intercontinental
intercourse [ˈɪntərˌkors] *n* **1** RELATIONS
 : relaciones *fpl*, trato *m* **2** COPULATION
 : acto *m* sexual, relaciones *fpl* sexuales,
 coito *m*
interdenominational [ˌɪntərdɪˌnɑmə-
 ˈneɪʃənəl] *adj* : interconfesional
interdepartmental [ˌɪntərdɪˌpɑrt-
 ˈmɛntəl, -ˌdiː-] *adj* : interdepartamental
interdependence [ˌɪntərdɪˈpɛndənts] *n*
 : interdependencia *f*
interdependent [ˌɪntərdɪˈpɛndənt] *adj*
 : interdependiente
interdict [ˌɪntərˈdɪkt] *vt* **1** PROHIBIT
 : prohibir **2** : cortar (las líneas de comunicación o provisión del enemigo)
interest[1] [ˈɪntrəst, -təˌrɛst] *vt* : interesar
interest[2] *n* **1** SHARE, STAKE : interés *m*,
 participación *f* **2** BENEFIT : provecho
 m, beneficio *m*, interés *m* ⟨in the public interest : en el interés público⟩ **3**
 CHARGE : interés *m*, cargo *m* ⟨com-
 pound interest : interés compuesto⟩ **4**
 CURIOSITY : interés *m*, curiosidad *f* **5**
 COLOR : color *m*, interés *m* ⟨places of
 local interest : lugares de color local⟩
 6 HOBBY : afición *f*
interesting [ˈɪntrəstɪŋ, -təˌrɛstɪŋ] *adj* : interesante — **interestingly** *adv*
interface [ˈɪntərˌfeɪs] *n* **1** : punto *m* de
 contacto ⟨oil-water interface : punto
 de contacto entre el agua y el aceite⟩
 2 : interfaz *f* (de una computadora), interfase *f*
interfere [ˌɪntərˈfɪr] *vi* **-fered; -fering** **1**
 INTERPOSE : interponerse, hacer interferencia ⟨to interfere with a play : obstruir una jugada⟩ **2** MEDDLE : entrometerse, interferir, intervenir **3 to
 interfere with** DISRUPT : afectar (una
 actividad), interferir (la radiotrans-
 misión) **4 to interfere with** TOUCH : tocar ⟨someone interfered with my papers : alguien tocó mis papeles⟩
interference [ˌɪntərˈfɪrənts] *n* : interferencia *f*, intromisión *f*
intergalactic [ˌɪntərɡəˈlæktɪk] *adj* : intergaláctico
intergovernmental [ˌɪntərˌɡʌvər-ˈmɛntəl,
 -vərn-] *adj* : intergubernamental
interim[1] [ˈɪntərəm] *adj* : interino, provisional

interim[2] *n* **1** : interín *m*, intervalo *m* **2**
 in the interim : en el interín, mientras
 tanto
interior[1] [ɪnˈtɪriər] *adj* : interior
interior[2] *n* : interior *m*
interject [ˌɪntərˈdʒɛkt] *vt* : interponer,
 agregar
interjection [ˌɪntərˈdʒɛkʃən] *n* **1** : interjección *f* (en lingüística) **2** EXCLAMA-
 TION : exclamación *f* **3** INTERPOSI-
 TION, INTERRUPTION : interposición *f*,
 interrupción *f*
interlace [ˌɪntərˈleɪs] *vt* **-laced; -lacing** **1**
 INTERWEAVE : entrelazar **2** INTER-
 SPERSE : intercalar
interlock [ˌɪntərˈlɑk] *vt* **1** UNITE : trabar,
 unir **2** ENGAGE, MESH : engranar — *vi*
 : entrelazarse, trabarse
interloper [ˌɪntərˈloːpər] *n* **1** INTRUDER
 : intruso *m*, -sa *f* **2** MEDDLER : entrometido *m*, -da *f*
interlude [ˈɪntərˌluːd] *n* **1** INTERVAL : intervalo *m*, intermedio *m* (en el teatro)
 2 : interludio *m* (en música)
intermarriage [ˌɪntərˈmærɪdʒ] *n* **1** : matrimonio *m* mixto (entre miembros de
 distintas razas o religiones) **2** : matrimonio *m* entre miembros del mismo
 grupo
intermarry [ˌɪntərˈmæri] *vi* **-married;
 -marrying** **1** : casarse (con miembros
 de otros grupos) **2** : casarse entre sí
 (con miembros del mismo grupo)
intermediary[1] [ˌɪntərˈmiːdiˌɛri] *adj* : intermediario
intermediary[2] *n, pl* **-aries** : intermediario *m*, -ria *f*
intermediate[1] [ˌɪntərˈmiːdiət] *adj* : intermedio
intermediate[2] *n* GO-BETWEEN : intermediario *m*, -ria *f*; mediador *m*, -dora *f*
interment [ɪnˈtərmənt] *n* : entierro *m*
interminable [ɪnˈtərmənəbəl] *adj* : interminable, constante — **interminably**
 [-bli] *adv*
intermingle [ˌɪntərˈmɪŋɡəl] *vt* **-mingled;
 -mingling** : entremezclar, mezclar —
 vi : entremezclarse
intermission [ˌɪntərˈmɪʃən] *n* : intermisión *f*, intervalo *m*, intermedio *m*
intermittent [ˌɪntərˈmɪtənt] *adj* : intermitente — **intermittently** *adv*
intermix [ˌɪntərˈmɪks] *vt* : entremezclar
intern[1] [ˈɪnˌtərn, ɪnˈtərn] *vt* : confinar
 (durante la guerra) — *vi* : servir de interno, hacer las prácticas
intern[2] [ˈɪnˌtərn] *n* : interno *m*, -na *f*
internal [ɪnˈtərnəl] *adj* : interno, interi-
 or ⟨internal bleeding : hemorragia in-
 terna⟩ ⟨internal affairs : asuntos inte-
 riores, asuntos domésticos⟩ —
 internally *adv*
international [ˌɪntərˈnæʃənəl] *adj* : internacional — **internationally** *adv*
internationalize [ˌɪntərˈnæʃənəˌlaɪz] *vt*
 -ized; -izing : internacionalizar
internee [ˌɪnˌtərˈniː] *n* : interno *m*, -na *f*
Internet [ˈɪntərˌnɛt] *n* : Internet *mf*

internist ['ɪn,tərnɪst] *n* : internista *mf*
interpersonal [,ɪntər'pərsənəl] *adj* : interpersonal
interplay ['ɪntər,pleɪ] *n* : interacción *f*, juego *m*
interpolate [ɪn'tərpə,leɪt] *vt* **-lated; -lating** : interpolar
interpose [,ɪntər'po:z] *v* **-posed; -posing** *vt* : interponer, interrumpir con — *vi* : interponerse
interposition [,ɪntərpə'zɪʃən] *n* : interposición *f*
interpret [ɪn'tərprət] *vt* : interpretar
interpretation [ɪn,tərprə'teɪʃən] *n* : interpretación *f*
interpretative [ɪn'tərprə,teɪtɪv] *adj* : interpretativo
interpreter [ɪn'tərprətər] *n* : intérprete *mf*
interpretive [ɪn'tərprətɪv] *adj* : interpretativo
interracial [,ɪntər'reɪʃəl] *adj* : interracial
interrelate [,ɪntərɪ'leɪt] *v* **-related; -relating** : interrelacionar
interrelationship [,ɪntərɪ'leɪʃən,ʃɪp] *n* : interrelación *f*
interrogate [ɪn'tɛrə,geɪt] *vt* **-gated; -gating** : interrogar, someter a un interrogatorio
interrogation [ɪn,tɛrə'geɪʃən] *n* : interrogación *f*
interrogative[1] [,ɪntə'rɑɡətɪv] *adj* : interrogativo
interrogative[2] *n* : interrogativo *m*
interrogator [ɪn'tɛrə,geɪtər] *n* : interrogador *m*, -dora *f*
interrogatory [,ɪntə'rɑɡə,tɔri] *adj* → **interrogative**[1]
interrupt [,ɪntə'rʌpt] *v* : interrumpir
interruption [,ɪntə'rʌpʃən] *n* : interrupción *f*
intersect [,ɪntər'sɛkt] *vt* : cruzar, cortar — *vi* : cruzarse (dícese de los caminos), intersectarse (dícese de las líneas o figuras), cortarse
intersection [,ɪntər'sɛkʃən] *n* : intersección *f*, cruce *m*
intersperse [,ɪntər'spərs] *vt* **-spersed; -spersing** : intercalar, entremezclar
interstate [,ɪntər'steɪt] *adj* : interestatal
interstellar [,ɪntər'stɛlər] *adj* : interestelar
interstice [ɪn'tərstəs] *n, pl* **-stices** [-stə,si:z, -stəsəz] : intersticio *m*
intertwine [,ɪntər'twaɪn] *vi* **-twined; -twining** : entrelazarse
interval ['ɪntərvəl] *n* : intervalo *m*
intervene [,ɪntər'vi:n] *vi* **-vened; -vening 1** ELAPSE : transcurrir, pasar ⟨the intervening years : los años intermediarios⟩ **2** INTERCEDE : intervenir, interceder, mediar
intervention [,ɪntər'vɛntʃən] *n* : intervención *f*
interview[1] ['ɪntər,vju:] *vt* : entrevistar — *vi* : hacer entrevistas
interview[2] *n* : entrevista *f*
interviewer ['ɪntər,vju:ər] *n* : entrevistador *m*, -dora *f*

interweave [,ɪntər'wi:v] *v* **-wove** [-'wo:v]; **-woven** [-'wo:vən]; **-weaving** *vt* : entretejer, entrelazar — *vi* INTERTWINE : entrelazarse, entretejerse
interwoven [,ɪntər'wo:vən] *adj* : entretejido
intestate [ɪn'tɛs,teɪt, -tət] *adj* : intestado
intestinal [ɪn'tɛstənəl] *adj* : intestinal
intestine [ɪn'tɛstən] *n* **1** : intestino *m* **2 small intestine** : intestino *m* delgado **3 large intestine** : intestino *m* grueso
intimacy ['ɪntəməsi] *n, pl* **-cies 1** CLOSENESS : intimidad *f* **2** FAMILIARITY : familiaridad *f*
intimate[1] ['ɪntə,meɪt] *vt* **-mated; -mating** : insinuar, dar a entender
intimate[2] ['ɪntəmət] *adj* **1** CLOSE : íntimo, de confianza ⟨intimate friends : amigos íntimos⟩ **2** PRIVATE : íntimo, privado ⟨intimate clubs : clubes íntimos⟩ **3** INNERMOST, SECRET : íntimo, secreto ⟨intimate fantasies : fantasías secretas⟩
intimate[3] *n* : amigo *m* íntimo, amiga *f* íntima
intimidate [ɪn'tɪmə,deɪt] *vt* **-dated; -dating** : intimidar
intimidation [ɪn,tɪmə'deɪʃən] *n* : intimidación *f*
into ['ɪn,tu:] *prep* **1** (*indicating motion*) : en, a, contra, dentro de ⟨she got into bed : se metió en la cama⟩ ⟨to get into a plane : subir a un avión⟩ ⟨he crashed into the wall : chocó contra la pared⟩ ⟨looking into the sun : mirando al sol⟩ **2** (*indicating state or condition*) : a, en ⟨to burst into tears : echarse a llorar⟩ ⟨the water turned into ice : el agua se convirtió en hielo⟩ ⟨to translate into English : traducir al inglés⟩ **3** (*indicating time*) ⟨far into the night : hasta bien entrada la noche⟩ ⟨he's well into his eighties : tiene los ochenta bien cumplidos⟩ **4** (*in mathematics*) ⟨3 into 12 is 4 : 12 dividido por 3 es 4⟩
intolerable [ɪn'tɑlərəbəl] *adj* : intolerable — **intolerably** [-bli] *adv*
intolerance [ɪn'tɑlərənts] *n* : intolerancia *f*
intolerant [ɪn'tɑlərənt] *adj* : intolerante
intonation [,ɪnto'neɪʃən] *n* : entonación *f*
intone [ɪn'to:n] *vt* **-toned; -toning** : entonar
intoxicant [ɪn'tɑksɪkənt] *n* : bebida *f* alcohólica
intoxicate [ɪn'tɑksə,keɪt] *vt* **-cated; -cating** : emborrachar, embriagar
intoxicated [ɪn'tɑksə,keɪtəd] *adj* : borracho, embriagado
intoxicating [ɪn'tɑksə,keɪtɪŋ] *adj* : embriagador
intoxication [ɪn,tɑksə'keɪʃən] *n* : embriaguez *f*
intractable [ɪn'træktəbəl] *adj* : obstinado, intratable
intramural [,ɪntrə'mjʊrəl] *adj* : interno, dentro de la universidad

intransigence [ɪnˈtrænʦədʒənts, -ˈtrænzə-] *n* : intransigencia *f*

intransigent [ɪnˈtrænʦədʒənt, -ˈtrænzə-] *adj* : intransigente

intransitive [ɪnˈtrænʦətɪv, -ˈtrænzə-] *adj* : intransitivo

intravenous [ˌɪntrəˈviːnəs] *adj* : intravenoso — **intravenously** *adv*

intrepid [ɪnˈtrɛpəd] *adj* : intrépido

intricacy [ˈɪntrɪkəsi] *n, pl* **-cies** : complejidad *f*, lo intrincado

intricate [ˈɪntrɪkət] *adj* : intrincado, complicado — **intricately** *adv*

intrigue¹ [ɪnˈtriːg] *v* **-trigued; -triguing** : intrigar

intrigue² [ˈɪnˌtriːg, ɪnˈtriːg] *n* : intriga *f*

intriguing [ɪnˈtriːgɪŋ] *adj* : intrigante, fascinante

intrinsic [ɪnˈtrɪnzɪk, -ˈtrɪnʦɪk] *adj* : intrínseco, esencial — **intrinsically** [-zɪkli, -sɪ-] *adv*

introduce [ˌɪntrəˈduːs, -ˈdjuːs] *vt* **-duced; -ducing 1** : presentar ⟨let me introduce my father : permítame presentar a mi padre⟩ **2** : introducir (algo nuevo), lanzar (un producto), presentar (una ley), proponer (una idea o un tema)

introduction [ˌɪntrəˈdʌkʃən] *n* : introducción *f*, presentación *f*

introductory [ˌɪntrəˈdʌktəri] *adj* : introductorio, preliminar, de introducción

introspection [ˌɪntrəˈspɛkʃən] *n* : introspección *f*

introspective [ˌɪntrəˈspɛktɪv] *adj* : introspectivo — **introspectively** *adv*

introvert [ˈɪntrəˌvərt] *n* : introvertido *m*, -da *f*

introverted [ˈɪntrəˌvərtəd] *adj* : introvertido

intrude [ɪnˈtruːd] *v* **-truded; -truding** *vi* **1** INTERFERE : inmiscuirse, entrometerse **2** DISTURB, INTERRUPT : molestar, estorbar, interrumpir — *vt* : introducir por fuerza

intruder [ɪnˈtruːdər] *n* : intruso *m*, -sa *f*

intrusion [ɪnˈtruːʒən] *n* : intrusión *f*

intrusive [ɪnˈtruːsɪv] *adj* : intruso

intuit [ɪnˈtuːɪt, -ˈtjuː-] *vt* : intuir

intuition [ˌɪntuˈɪʃən, -tju-] *n* : intuición *f*

intuitive [ɪnˈtuːətɪv, -ˈtjuː-] *adj* : intuitivo — **intuitively** *adv*

inundate [ˈɪnənˌdeɪt] *vt* **-dated; -dating** : inundar

inundation [ˌɪnənˈdeɪʃən] *n* : inundación *f*

inure [ɪˈnʊr, -ˈnjʊr] *vt* **-ured; -uring** : acostumbrar, habituar

invade [ɪnˈveɪd] *vt* **-vaded; -vading** : invadir

invader [ɪnˈveɪdər] *n* : invasor *m*, -sora *f*

invalid¹ [ɪnˈvæləd] *adj* : inválido, nulo

invalid² [ˈɪnvələd] *adj* : inválido, discapacitado

invalid³ [ˈɪnvələd] *n* : inválido *m*, -da *f*

invalidate [ɪnˈvæləˌdeɪt] *vt* **-dated; -dating** : invalidar

invalidity [ˌɪnvəˈlɪdəti] *n, pl* **-ties** : invalidez *f*, falta de validez *f*

invaluable [ɪnˈvæljəbəl, -ˈvæljʊ-] *adj* : invalorable, inestimable, inapreciable

invariable [ɪnˈværiəbəl] *adj* : invariable, constante — **invariably** [-bli] *adv*

invasion [ɪnˈveɪʒən] *n* : invasión *f*

invasive [ɪnˈveɪsɪv] *adj* : invasivo

invective [ɪnˈvɛktɪv] *n* : invectiva *f*, improperio *m*, vituperio *m*

inveigh [ɪnˈveɪ] *vi* **to inveigh against** : arremeter contra, lanzar invectivas contra

inveigle [ɪnˈveɪgəl, -ˈviː-] *vt* **-gled; -gling** : engatusar, embaucar, persuadir con engaños

invent [ɪnˈvɛnt] *vt* : inventar

invention [ɪnˈvɛnʧən] *n* : invención *f*, invento *m*

inventive [ɪnˈvɛntɪv] *adj* : inventivo

inventiveness [ɪnˈvɛntɪvnəs] *n* : ingenio *m*, inventiva *f*

inventor [ɪnˈvɛntər] *n* : inventor *m*, -tora *f*

inventory¹ [ˈɪnvənˌtɔri] *vt* **-ried; -rying** : inventariar

inventory² *n, pl* **-ries 1** LIST : inventario *m* **2** STOCK : existencias *fpl*

inverse¹ [ɪnˈvərs, ˈɪnˌvərs] *adj* : inverso — **inversely** *adv*

inverse² *n* : inverso *m*

inversion [ɪnˈvərʒən] *n* : inversión *f*

invert [ɪnˈvərt] *vt* : invertir

invertebrate¹ [ɪnˈvərtəbrət, -ˌbreɪt] *adj* : invertebrado

invertebrate² *n* : invertebrado *m*

invest [ɪnˈvɛst] *vt* **1** AUTHORIZE : investir, autorizar **2** CONFER : conferir **3** : invertir, dedicar ⟨he invested his savings in stocks : invirtió sus ahorros en acciones⟩ ⟨to invest one's time : dedicar uno su tiempo⟩

investigate [ɪnˈvɛstəˌgeɪt] *v* **-gated; -gating** : investigar

investigation [ɪnˌvɛstəˈgeɪʃən] *n* : investigación *f*, estudio *m*

investigative [ɪnˈvɛstəˌgeɪtɪv] *adj* : investigador

investigator [ɪnˈvɛstəˌgeɪtər] *n* : investigador *m*, -dora *f*

investiture [ɪnˈvɛstəˌʧʊr, -ˌʧər] *n* : investidura *f*

investment [ɪnˈvɛstmənt] *n* : inversión *f*

investor [ɪnˈvɛstər] *n* : inversor *m*, -sora *f*; inversionista *mf*

inveterate [ɪnˈvɛtərət] *adj* **1** DEEP-SEATED : inveterado, enraizado **2** HABITUAL : empedernido, incorregible

invidious [ɪnˈvɪdiəs] *adj* **1** OBNOXIOUS : repugnante, odioso **2** UNJUST : injusto — **invidiously** *adv*

invigorate [ɪnˈvɪgəˌreɪt] *vt* **-rated; -rating** : vigorizar, animar

invigorating [ɪnˈvɪgəˌreɪtɪŋ] *adj* : vigorizante, estimulante

invigoration [ɪnˌvɪgəˈreɪʃən] *n* : animación *f*

invincibility [ɪnˌvɪnʦəˈbɪləti] *n* : invencibilidad *f*

invincible [ɪn'vɪntsəbəl] *adj* : invencible — **invincibly** [-bli] *adv*

inviolable [ɪn'vaɪələbəl] *adj* : inviolable

inviolate [ɪn'vaɪələt] *adj* : inviolado, puro

invisibility [ɪn,vɪzə'bɪləti] *n* : invisibilidad *f*

invisible [ɪn'vɪzəbəl] *adj* : invisible — **invisibly** [-bli] *adv*

invitation [,ɪnvə'teɪʃən] *n* : invitación *f*

invite [ɪn'vaɪt] *vt* **-vited; -viting 1** ATTRACT : atraer, tentar ⟨a book that invites interest : un libro que atrae el interés⟩ **2** PROVOKE : provocar, buscar ⟨to invite trouble : buscarse problemas⟩ **3** ASK : invitar ⟨we invited them for dinner : los invitamos acenar⟩ **4** SOLICIT : solicitar, buscar (preguntas, comentarios, etc.)

inviting [ɪn'vaɪtɪŋ] *adj* : atractivo, atrayente

invocation [,ɪnvə'keɪʃən] *n* : invocación *f*

invoice[1] ['ɪn,vɔɪs] *vt* **-voiced; -voicing** : facturar

invoice[2] *n* : factura *f*

invoke [ɪn'vo:k] *vt* **-voked; -voking 1** : invocar, apelar a ⟨she invoked our aid : apeló a nuestra ayuda⟩ **2** CITE : invocar, citar ⟨to invoke a precedent : invocar un precedente⟩ **3** CONJURE UP : hacer aparecer, invocar

involuntary [ɪn'vɑlən,teri] *adj* : involuntario — **involuntarily** [ɪn-,vɑlən'trəli] *adv*

involve [ɪn'vɑlv] *vt* **-volved; -volving 1** ENGAGE : ocupar (con una tarea, etc.) **2** IMPLICATE : involucrar, enredar, implicar ⟨to be involved in a crime : estar involucrado en un crimen⟩ **3** CONCERN : concernir, afectar **4** CONNECT : conectar, relacionar **5** ENTAIL, INCLUDE : suponer, incluir, consistir en ⟨what does the job involve? : ¿en qué consiste el trabajo?⟩ **6 to be involved with someone** : tener una relación (amorosa) con alguien

involved [ɪn'vɑlvd] *adj* **1** COMPLEX, INTRICATE : complicado, complejo **2** CONCERNED : interesado, afectado

involvement [ɪn'vɑlvmənt] *n* **1** PARTICIPATION : participación *f*, complicidad *f* **2** RELATIONSHIP : relación *f*

invulnerable [ɪn'vʌlnərəbəl] *adj* : invulnerable

inward[1] ['ɪnwərd] *or* **inwards** [-wərdz] *adv* : hacia adentro, hacia el interior

inward[2] *adj* INSIDE : interior, interno

inwardly ['ɪnwərdli] *adv* **1** MENTALLY, SPIRITUALLY : por dentro **2** INTERNALLY : internamente, interiormente **3** PRIVATELY : para sus adentros, para sí

iodide ['aɪə,daɪd] *n* : yoduro *m*

iodine ['aɪə,daɪn, -dən] *n* : yodo *m*, tintura *f* de yodo

iodize ['aɪə,daɪz] *vt* **-dized; -dizing** : yodar

ion ['aɪən, 'aɪ,ɑn] *n* : ion *m*

ionic [aɪ'ɑnɪk] *adj* : iónico

ionize ['aɪə,naɪz] *v* **ionized; ionizing** : ionizar

ionosphere [aɪ'ɑnə,sfɪr] *n* : ionosfera *f*

iota [aɪ'o:tə] *n* : pizca *f*, ápice *m*

IOU [,aɪ,o:'ju:] *n* : pagaré *m*, vale *m*

IPA [,aɪ,pi:'eɪ] *n* International Phonetic Alphabet : AFI *m*

IQ [,aɪ'kju:] *n* (intelligence quotient) : CI *m*, coeficiente *m* intelectual

Iranian [ɪ'reɪniən, -'ræ-, -'rɑ-; aɪ'-] *n* : iraní *mf* — **Iranian** *adj*

Iraqi [ɪ'rɑki:] *n* : iraquí *mf* — **Iraqi** *adj*

irascibility [ɪ,ræsə'bɪləti] *n* : irascibilidad *f*

irascible [ɪ'ræsəbəl] *adj* : irascible

irate [aɪ'reɪt] *adj* : furioso, airado, iracundo — **irately** *adv*

ire ['aɪr] *n* : ira *f*, cólera *f*

iridescence [,ɪrə'dɛsənts] *n* : iridiscencia *f*

iridescent [,ɪrə'dɛsənt] *adj* : iridiscente

iridium [ɪ'rɪdiəm] *n* : iridio *m*

iris ['aɪrəs] *n, pl* **irises** *or* **irides** ['aɪrə-,di:z, 'ɪr-] **1** : iris *m* (del ojo) **2** : lirio *m* (planta)

Irish[1] ['aɪrɪʃ] *adj* : irlandés

Irish[2] **1** : irlandés *m* (idioma) **2 the Irish** *npl* : los irlandeses

Irishman ['aɪrɪʃmən] *n, pl* **-men** : irlandés *m*

Irishwoman ['aɪrɪʃ,wʊmən] *n, pl* **-women** : irlandesa *f*

irk ['ərk] *vt* : fastidiar, irritar, preocupar

irksome ['ərksəm] *adj* : irritante, fastidioso — **irksomely** *adv*

iron[1] ['aɪərn] *v* : planchar

iron[2] *n* **1** : hierro *m*, fierro *m* ⟨a will of iron : una voluntad de hierro, una voluntad férrea⟩ **2** : plancha *f* (para planchar la ropa)

ironclad ['aɪərn'klæd] *adj* **1** : acorazado, blindado **2** STRICT : riguroso, estricto

ironic [aɪ'rɑnɪk] *or* **ironical** [-nɪkəl] *adj* : irónico — **ironically** [-kli] *adv*

ironing ['aɪərnɪŋ] *n* **1** PRESSING : planchada *f* **2** : ropa *f* para planchar

ironing board *n* : tabla *f* (de planchar)

ironwork ['aɪərn,wərk] *n* **1** : obra *f* de hierro **2 ironworks** *npl* : fundición *f*

ironworker ['aɪərn,wərkər] *n* : fundidor *m*, -dora *f*

irony ['aɪrəni] *n, pl* **-nies** : ironía *f*

irradiate [ɪ'reɪdi,eɪt] *vt* **-ated; -ating** : irradiar, radiar

irradiation [ɪ,reɪdi'eɪʃən] *n* : irradiación *f*, radiación *f*

irrational [ɪ'ræʃənəl] *adj* : irracional — **irrationally** *adv*

irrationality [ɪ,ræʃə'næləti] *n, pl* **-ties** : irracionalidad *f*

irreconcilable [ɪ,rɛkən'saɪləbəl] *adj* : irreconciliable

irrecoverable [,ɪrɪ'kʌvərəbəl] *adj* : irrecuperable — **irrecoverably** [-bli] *adv*

irredeemable [ˌɪrɪˈdiːməbəl] *adj* **1** : irredimible (dícese de un bono) **2** HOPELESS : irremediable, irreparable

irreducible [ˌɪrɪˈduːsəbəl, -ˈdjuː-] *adj* : irreducible — **irreducibly** [-bli] *adv*

irrefutable [ˌɪrɪˈfjuːt̬əbəl, ɪrˈrɛfjə-] *adj* : irrefutable

irregular[1] [ɪˈrɛgjələr] *adj* : irregular — **irregularly** *adv*

irregular[2] *n* **1** : soldado *m* irregular **2** **irregulars** *npl* : artículos *mpl* defectuosos

irregularity [ˌɪˌrɛgjəˈlærət̬i] *n, pl* **-ties** : irregularidad *f*

irrelevance [ɪˈrɛləvən̪ts] *n* : irrelevancia *f*

irrelevant [ɪˈrɛləvənt] *adj* : irrelevante

irreligious [ˌɪrɪˈlɪdʒəs] *adj* : irreligioso

irreparable [ɪˈrɛpərəbəl] *adj* : irreparable

irreplaceable [ˌɪrɪˈpleɪsəbəl] *adj* : irreemplazable, insustituible

irrepressible [ˌɪrɪˈprɛsəbəl] *adj* : incontenible, incontrolable

irreproachable [ɪrɪˈproːtʃəbəl] *adj* : irreprochable, intachable

irresistible [ˌɪrɪˈzɪstəbəl] *adj* : irresistible — **irresistibly** [-bli] *adv*

irresolute [ɪˈrɛzəˌluːt] *adj* : irresoluto, indeciso

irresolutely [ɪˈrɛzəˌluːtli, -ˌrzəˈluːt-] *adv* : de manera indecisa

irresolution [ɪˌrɛzəˈluːʃən] *n* : irresolución *f*

irrespective of [ˌɪrɪˈspɛktɪvəv] *prep* : sin tomar en consideración, sin tener en cuenta

irresponsibility [ˌɪrɪˌspanʦəˈbɪlət̬i] *n, pl* **-ties** : irresponsabilidad *f*, falta *f* de responsabilidad

irresponsible [ˌɪrɪˈspan̪tsəbəl] *adj* : irresponsable — **irresponsibly** [-bli] *adv*

irretrievable [ˌɪrɪˈtriːvəbəl] *adj* IRRECOVERABLE : irrecuperable

irreverence [ɪˈrɛvərən̪ts] *n* : irreverencia *f*, falta *f* de respeto

irreverent [ɪˈrɛvərənt] *adj* : irreverente, irrespetuoso

irreversible [ˌɪrɪˈvərsəbəl] *adj* : irreversible

irrevocable [ɪˈrɛvəkəbəl] *adj* : irrevocable — **irrevocably** [-bli] *adv*

irrigate [ˈɪrəˌgeɪt] *vt* **-gated; -gating** : irrigar, regar

irrigation [ˌɪrəˈgeɪʃən] *n* : irrigación *f*, riego *m*

irritability [ˌɪrət̬əˈbɪlət̬i] *n, pl* **-ties** : irritabilidad *f*

irritable [ˈɪrət̬əbəl] *adj* : irritable, colérico

irritably [ˈɪrət̬əbli] *adv* : con irritación

irritant[1] [ˈɪrət̬ənt] *adj* : irritante

irritant[2] *n* : agente *m* irritante

irritate [ˈɪrəˌteɪt] *vt* **-tated; -tating** **1** ANNOY : irritar, molestar **2** : irritar (en medicina)

irritating [ˈɪrəˌteɪt̬ɪŋ] *adj* : irritante

irritatingly [ˈɪrəˌteɪt̬ɪŋli] *adv* : de modo irritante, fastidiosamente

irritation [ˌɪrəˈteɪʃən] *n* : irritación *f*

is → **be**

Islam [ɪsˈlɑm, ɪz-, -ˈlæm; ˈɪsˌlɑm, ˈɪz-, -ˌlæm] *n* : el Islam

Islamic [ɪsˈlɑmɪk, ɪz-, -ˈlæ-] *adj* : islámico

island [ˈaɪlənd] *n* : isla *f*

islander [ˈaɪləndər] *n* : isleño *m*, -ña *f*

isle [ˈaɪl] *n* : isla *f*, islote *m*

islet [ˈaɪlət] *n* : islote *m*

isolate [ˈaɪsəˌleɪt] *vt* **-lated; -lating** : aislar

isolated [ˈaɪsəˌleɪt̬əd] *adj* : aislado, solo

isolation [ˌaɪsəˈleɪʃən] *n* : aislamiento *m*

isometric [ˌaɪsəˈmɛtrɪk] *adj* : isométrico

isometrics [ˌaɪsəˈmetrɪks] *ns & pl* : isometría *f*

isosceles [aɪˈsɑsəˌliːz] *adj* : isósceles

isotope [ˈaɪsəˌtoːp] *n* : isótopo *m*

Israeli [ɪzˈreɪli] *n* : israelí *mf* — **Israeli** *adj*

issue[1] [ˈɪˌʃuː] *v* **-sued; -suing** *vi* **1** EMERGE : emerger, salir, fluir **2** DESCEND : descender (dícese de los padres o antepasados específicos) **3** EMANATE, RESULT : emanar, surgir, resultar — *vt* **1** EMIT : emitir **2** DISTRIBUTE : emitir, distribuir ⟨to issue a new stamp : emitir un sello nuevo⟩ **3** PUBLISH : publicar

issue[2] *n* **1** EMERGENCE, FLOW : emergencia *f*, flujo *m* **2** PROGENY : descendencia *f*, progenie *f* **3** OUTCOME, RESULT : desenlace *m*, resultado *m*, consecuencia *f* **4** MATTER, QUESTION : asunto *m*, cuestión *f* **5** PUBLICATION : publicación *f*, distribución *f*, emisión *f* **6** : número *m* (de un periódico o una revista)

isthmus [ˈɪsməs] *n* : istmo *m*

it [ˈɪt] *pron* **1** (*as subject; generally omitted*) : él, ella, ello ⟨it's a big building : es un edificio grande⟩ ⟨who was it? : ¿quién era?⟩ **2** (*as indirect object*) : le ⟨I'll give it some water : voy a darle agua⟩ **3** (*as direct object*) : lo, la ⟨give it to me : dámelo⟩ **4** (*as object of a preposition; generally omitted*) : él, ella, ello ⟨behind it : detrás, detrás de él⟩ **5** (*in impersonal constructions*) ⟨it's raining : está lloviendo⟩ ⟨it's 8 o'clock : son las ocho⟩ **6** (*as the implied subject or object of a verb*) ⟨it is necessary to study : es necesario estudiar⟩ ⟨to give it all one's got : dar lo mejor de sí⟩

Italian [ɪˈtæliən, aɪ-] *n* **1** : italiano *m*, -na *f* **2** : italiano *m* (idioma) — **Italian** *adj*

italic[1] [ɪˈtælɪk, aɪ-] *adj* : en cursiva, en bastardilla

italic[2] *n* : cursiva *f*, bastardilla *f*

italicize [ɪˈtæləˌsaɪz, aɪ-] *vt* **-cized; -cizing** : poner en cursiva

itch[1] [ˈɪtʃ] *vi* **1** : picar ⟨her arm itched : le pica el brazo⟩ **2** : morirse ⟨they were itching to go outside : se morían por salir⟩ — *vt* : dar picazón, hacer picar

itch² *n* **1** ITCHING : picazón *f*, picor *m*, comezón *f* **2** RASH : sarpullido *m*, erupción *f* **3** DESIRE : ansia *f*, deseo *m*

itchy ['ɪtʃi] *adj* **itchier; -est** : que pica, que da comezón

it'd ['ɪtəd] (*contraction of* **it had** *or* **it would**) → **have, would**

item ['aɪtəm] *n* **1** OBJECT : artículo *m*, pieza *f* ⟨item of clothing : prenda de vestir⟩ **2** : punto *m* (en una agenda), número *m* (en el teatro), ítem *m* (en un documento) **3** news item : noticia *f*

itemize ['aɪtə,maɪz] *vt* **-ized; -izing** : detallar, enumerar, listar

itinerant [aɪ'tɪnərənt] *adj* : itinerante, ambulante

itinerary [aɪ'tɪnə,rɛri] *n, pl* **-aries** : itinerario *m*

it'll ['ɪtəl] (*contraction of* **it shall** *or* **it will**) → **shall, will**

its ['ɪts] *adj* : su, sus ⟨its kennel : su perrera⟩ ⟨a city and its inhabitants : una ciudad y sus habitantes⟩

it's ['ɪts] (*contraction of* **it is** *or* **it has**) → **be, have**

itself [ɪt'sɛlf] *pron* **1** (*used reflexively*) : se ⟨the cat gave itself a bath : el gato se bañó⟩ **2** (*used for emphasis*) : (él) mismo, (ella) misma, sí (mismo), solo ⟨he is courtesy itself : es la misma cortesía⟩ ⟨in and of itself : por sí mismo⟩ ⟨it opened by itself : se abrió solo⟩

IUD [,aɪ,ju:'di:] *n* intrauterine *d*evice : DIU *m*, dispositivo *m* intrauterino

I've ['aɪv] (*contraction of* **I have**) → **have**

ivory ['aɪvəri] *n, pl* **-ries 1** : marfil *m* **2** : color *m* de marfil

ivy ['aɪvi] *n, pl* **ivies 1** : hiedra *f*, yedra *f* **2** → **poison ivy**

J

j ['dʒeɪ] *n, pl* **j's** *or* **js** ['dʒeɪz] : décima letra del alfabeto inglés

jab¹ ['dʒæb] *v* **jabbed; jabbing** *vt* **1** PUNCTURE : clavar, pinchar **2** POKE : dar, golpear (con la punta de algo) ⟨he jabbed me in the ribs : me dio un codazo en las costillas⟩ — *vi* **to jab at** : dar, golpear

jab² *n* **1** PRICK : pinchazo *m* **2** POKE : golpe *m* abrupto

jabber¹ ['dʒæbər] *v* : farfullar

jabber² *n* : galimatías *m*, farfulla *f*

jack¹ ['dʒæk] *vt* **to jack up 1** : levantar (con un gato) **2** INCREASE : subir, aumentar

jack² *n* **1** : gato *m*, cric *m* ⟨hydraulic jack : gato hidráulico⟩ **2** FLAG : pabellón *m* **3** SOCKET : enchufe *m* hembra **4** : jota *f*, valet *m* ⟨jack of hearts : jota de corazones⟩ **5 jacks** *npl* : cantillos *mpl*

jackal ['dʒækəl] *n* : chacal *m*

jackass ['dʒæk,æs] *n* : asno *m*, burro *m*

jacket ['dʒækət] *n* **1** : chaqueta *f* **2** COVER : sobrecubierta *f* (de un libro), carátula *f* (de un disco)

jackhammer ['dʒæk,hæmər] *n* : martillo *m* neumático

jack–in–the–box ['dʒækɪndə,baks] *n* : caja *f* de sorpresa

jackknife¹ ['dʒæk,naɪf] *vi* **-knifed; -knifing** : doblarse como una navaja, plegarse

jackknife² *n* : navaja *f*

jack–of–all–trades *n* : persona *f* que sabe un poco de todo, persona *f* de muchos oficios

jack–o'–lantern ['dʒækə,læntərn] *n* : linterna *f* hecha de una calabaza

jackpot ['dʒæk,pat] *n* **1** : primer premio *m*, gordo *m* **2 to hit the jackpot** : sacarse la lotería, sacarse el gordo

jackrabbit ['dʒæk,ræbət] *n* : liebre *f* grande de Norteamérica

jade ['dʒeɪd] *n* : jade *m*

jaded ['dʒeɪdəd] *adj* **1** TIRED : agotado **2** BORED : hastiado

jagged ['dʒægəd] *adj* : dentado, mellado

jaguar ['dʒæg,war, 'dʒægju,war] *n* : jaguar *m*

jai alai ['haɪ,laɪ] *n* : jai alai *m*, pelota *f* vasca

jail¹ ['dʒeɪl] *vt* : encarcelar

jail² *n* : cárcel *f*

jailbreak ['dʒeɪl,breɪk] *n* : fuga *f*, huida *f* (de la cárcel)

jailer *or* **jailor** ['dʒeɪlər] *n* : carcelero *m*, -ra *f*

jalapeño [,halə'peɪnjo, ,hæ-, -'pi:no] *n* : jalapeño *m*

jalopy [dʒə'lapi] *n, pl* **-lopies** : cacharro *m fam*, carro *m* destartalado

jalousie ['dʒæləsi] *n* : celosía *f*

jam¹ ['dʒæm] *v* **jammed; jamming** *vt* **1** CRAM : apiñar, embutir **2** BLOCK : atascar, atorar **3 to jam on the brakes** : frenar en seco — *vi* STICK : atascarse, atrancarse

jam² *n* **1** *or* **traffic jam** : atasco *m*, embotellamiento *m* (de tráfico) **2** PREDICAMENT : lío *m*, aprieto *m*, apuro *m* **3** : mermelada *f* ⟨strawberry jam : mermelada de fresa⟩

Jamaican [dʒə'meɪkən] *n* : jamaiquino *m*, -na *f*; jamaicano *m*, -na *f* — **Jamaican** *adj*

jamb ['dʒæm] *n* : jamba *f*

jamboree [,dʒæmbə'ri:] *n* : fiesta *f* grande

jangle¹ ['dʒæŋgəl] *v* **-gled; -gling** *vi* : hacer un ruido metálico — *vt* **1** : hacer sonar **2 to jangle one's nerves** : irritar, crispar

jangle² *n* : ruido *m* metálico

janitor ['dʒænətər] *n* : portero *m*, -ra *f*; conserje *mf*

January ['dʒænju,ɛri] *n* : enero *m*

Japanese [,dʒæpə'ni:z, -'ni:s] *n* **1**

: japonés *m*, -nesa *f* **2** : japonés *m* (idioma) — **Japanese** *adj*

jar¹ ['dʒɑr] *v* **jarred; jarring** *vi* **1** GRATE : chirriar **2** CLASH : desentonar **3** SHAKE : sacudirse **4 to jar on** : crispar, enervar — *vt* JOLT : sacudir

jar² *n* **1** GRATING : chirrido *m* **2** JOLT : vibración *f*, sacudida *f* **3** : tarro *m*, bote *m*, pote *m* ⟨a jar of honey : un tarro de miel⟩

jargon ['dʒɑrgən] *n* : jerga *f*

jasmine ['dʒæzmən] *n* : jazmín *m*

jasper ['dʒæspər] *n* : jaspe *m*

jaundice ['dʒɔndɪs] *n* : ictericia *f*

jaundiced ['dʒɔndɪst] *adj* **1** : ictérico **2** EMBITTERED, RESENTFUL : amargado, resentido, negativo ⟨with a jaundiced eye : con una actitud de cinismo⟩

jaunt ['dʒɔnt] *n* : excursión *f*, paseo *m*

jauntily ['dʒɔntəli] *adv* : animadamente

jauntiness ['dʒɔntinəs] *n* : animación *f*, vivacidad *f*

jaunty ['dʒɔnti] *adj* **-tier; -est 1** SPRIGHTLY : animado, alegre **2** RAKISH : desenvuelto, desenfadado

Javanese [ˌdʒævə'niːz, ˌdʒɑ-, -'niːs] *n* **1** : javanés *m* (idioma) **2** : javanés *m*, -nesa *f* — **Javanese** *adj*

javelin ['dʒævələn] *n* : jabalina *f*

jaw¹ ['dʒɔ] *vi* GAB : cotorrear *fam*, parlotear *fam*

jaw² *n* **1** : mandíbula *f*, quijada *f* **2** : mordaza *f* (de una herramienta) **3 the jaws of death** : las garras *f* de la muerte

jawbone ['dʒɔ,boːn] *n* : mandíbula *f*

jay ['dʒeɪ] *n* : arrendajo *m*, chara *f Mex*, azulejo *m Mex*

jaybird ['dʒeɪ,bərd] → **jay**

jaywalk ['dʒeɪ,wɔk] *vi* : cruzar la calle sin prudencia

jaywalker ['dʒeɪ,wɔkər] *n* : peatón *m* imprudente

jazz¹ ['dʒæz] *vt* **to jazz up** : animar, alegrar

jazz² *n* : jazz *m*

jazzy ['dʒæzi] *adj* **jazzier; -est 1** : con ritmo de jazz **2** FLASHY, SHOWY : llamativo, ostentoso

jealous ['dʒɛləs] *adj* : celoso, envidioso — **jealously** *adv*

jealousy ['dʒɛləsi] *n* : celos *mpl*, envidia *f*

jeans ['dʒiːnz] *npl* : jeans *mpl*, vaqueros *mpl*

jeep ['dʒiːp] *n* : jeep *m*

jeer¹ ['dʒɪr] *vi* **1** BOO : abuchear **2** SCOFF : mofarse, burlarse — *vt* RIDICULE : mofarse de, burlarse de

jeer² *n* **1** : abucheo *m* **2** TAUNT : mofa *f*, burla *f*

Jehovah [dʒɪ'hoːvə] *n* : Jehová *m*

jell ['dʒɛl] *vi* **1** SET : gelificarse, cuajar **2** FORM : cuajar, formarse (una idea, etc.)

jelly¹ ['dʒɛli] *v* **jellied; jellying** *vi* **1** JELL : gelificarse, cuajar **2** : hacer jalea — *vt* : gelificar

jelly² *n*, *pl* **-lies 1** : jalea *f* **2** GELATIN : gelatina *f*

jellyfish ['dʒɛli,fɪʃ] *n* : medusa *f*

jeopardize ['dʒɛpər,daɪz] *vt* **-dized; -dizing** : arriesgar, poner en peligro

jeopardy ['dʒɛpərdi] *n* : peligro *m*, riesgo *m*

jerk¹ ['dʒərk] *vt* **1** JOLT : sacudir **2** TUG, YANK : darle un tirón a — *vi* JOLT : dar sacudidas ⟨the train jerked along : el tren iba moviéndose a sacudidas⟩

jerk² *n* **1** TUG : tirón *m*, jalón *m* **2** JOLT : sacudida *f* brusca **3** FOOL : estúpido *m*, -da *f*; idiota *mf*

jerkin ['dʒərkən] *n* : chaqueta *f* sin mangas, chaleco *m*

jerky ['dʒərki] *adj* **jerkier; -est 1** : espasmódico (dícese de los movimientos) **2** CHOPPY : inconexo (dícese de la prosa) — **jerkily** [-kəli] *adv*

jerry–built ['dʒɛri,bɪlt] *adj* : mal construido, chapucero

jersey ['dʒərzi] *n*, *pl* **-seys** : jersey *m*

jest¹ ['dʒɛst] *vi* : bromear

jest² *n* : broma *f*, chiste *m*

jester ['dʒɛstər] *n* : bufón *m*, -fona *f*

Jesuit ['dʒɛzuət] *n* : jesuita *m* — **Jesuit** *adj*

Jesus ['dʒiːzəs, -zəz] *n* **1** : Jesús *m* **2 Jesus Christ** : Jesucristo *m* **3 Jesus (Christ)!** *fam* : ¡por Dios!

jet¹ ['dʒɛt] *v* **jetted; jetting** *vt* SPOUT : arrojar a chorros — *vi* **1** GUSH : salir a chorros, chorrear **2** FLY : viajar en avión, volar

jet² *n* **1** STREAM : chorro *m* **2** *or* **jet airplane** : avión *m* a reacción, reactor *m* **3** : azabache *m* (mineral) **4 jet engine** : reactor *m*, motor *m* a reacción **5 jet lag** : desajuste *m* de horario (debido a un vuelo largo)

jet–propelled *adj* : a reacción

jetsam ['dʒɛtsəm] *n* **flotsam and jetsam** : restos *mpl*, desechos *mpl*

jettison ['dʒɛtəsən] *vt* **1** : echar al mar **2** DISCARD : desechar, deshacerse de

jetty ['dʒɛti] *n*, *pl* **-ties 1** PIER, WHARF : desembarcadero *m*, muelle *m* **2** BREAKWATER : malecón *m*, rompeolas *m*

Jew ['dʒuː] *n* : judío *m*, -día *f*

jewel ['dʒuːəl] *n* **1** : joya *f*, alhaja *f* **2** GEM : piedra *f* preciosa, gema *f* **3** : rubí *m* (de un reloj) **4** TREASURE : joya *f*, tesoro *m*

jeweler *or* **jeweller** ['dʒuːələr] *n* : joyero *m*, -ra *f*

jewelry ['dʒuːəlri] *n* : joyas *fpl*, alhajas *fpl*

Jewish ['dʒuːɪʃ] *adj* : judío

jib ['dʒɪb] *n* : foque *m* (de un barco)

jibe ['dʒaɪb] *vi* **jibed; jibing** AGREE : concordar

jiffy ['dʒɪfi] *n*, *pl* **-fies** : santiamén *m*, segundo *m*, momento *m*

jig¹ ['dʒɪg] *vi* **jigged; jigging** : bailar la giga

jig² *n* **1** : giga *f* **2 the jig is up** : se acabó la fiesta

jigger ['dʒɪgər] *n* : medida de 1 a 2 onzas (para licores)

jiggle¹ ['dʒɪgəl] v -gled; -gling vt : agitar o sacudir ligeramente — vi : agitarse, vibrar

jiggle² n : sacudida f, vibración f

jigsaw ['dʒɪg,sɔ] n 1 : sierra f de vaivén 2 **jigsaw puzzle** : rompecabezas m

jilt ['dʒɪlt] vt : dejar plantado, dar calabazas a

jimmy¹ ['dʒɪmi] vt -mied; -mying : forzar con una palanqueta

jimmy² n, pl -mies : palanqueta f

jingle¹ ['dʒɪŋgəl] v -gled; -gling vi : tintinear — vt : hacer sonar

jingle² n 1 TINKLE : tintineo m, retintín m 2 : canción f rimada

jingoism ['dʒɪŋgo,ɪzəm] n : jingoísmo m, patriotería f

jingoistic [,dʒɪŋgo'ɪstɪk] or **jingoist** ['dʒɪŋgoɪst] adj : jingoísta, patriotero

jinx¹ ['dʒɪŋks] vt : traer mala suerte a, salar CoRi, Mex

jinx² n 1 : cenizo m, -za f 2 **to put a jinx on** : echarle el mal de ojo a

jitters ['dʒɪtərz] npl : nervios mpl ⟨he got the jitters : se puso nervioso⟩

jittery ['dʒɪtəri] adj : nervioso

job ['dʒab] n 1 : trabajo m ⟨he did odd jobs for her : le hizo algunos trabajos⟩ 2 CHORE, TASK : tarea f, quehacer m 3 EMPLOYMENT : trabajo m, empleo m, puesto m

jobber ['dʒabər] n MIDDLEMAN : intermediario m, -ria f

jock ['dʒak] n : deportista mf, atleta mf

jockey¹ ['dʒaki] v -eyed; -eying vt 1 MANIPULATE : manipular 2 MANEUVER : maniobrar — vi **to jockey for position** : maniobrar para conseguir algo

jockey² n, pl -eys : jockey mf

jocose [dʒo'ko:s] adj : jocoso

jocular ['dʒakjulər] adj : jocoso — **jocularly** adv

jocularity [,dʒakju'lærəti] n : jocosidad f

jodhpurs ['dʒadpərz] npl : pantalones mpl de montar

jog¹ ['dʒag] v jogged; jogging vt 1 NUDGE : dar, empujar, codear 2 **to jog one's memory** : refrescar la memoria — vi 1 RUN : correr despacio, trotar, hacer footing (como ejercicio) 2 TRUDGE : andar a trote corto

jog² n 1 PUSH, SHAKE : empujoncito m, sacudida f leve 2 TROT : trote m corto, footing m (en deportes) 3 TWIST : recodo m, vuelta f, curva f

jogger ['dʒagər] n : persona f que hace footing

join ['dʒɔɪn] vt 1 CONNECT, LINK : unir, juntar ⟨to join in marriage : unir en matrimonio⟩ 2 ADJOIN : lindar con, colindar con 3 MEET : reunirse con, encontrarse con ⟨we joined them for lunch : nos reunimos con ellos para almorzar⟩ 4 : hacerse socio de (una organización), afiliarse a (un partido), entrar en (una empresa) — vi 1 UNITE : unirse 2 MERGE : empalmar (dícese de las carreteras), confluir (dícese de

los ríos) 3 **to join up** : hacerse socio, enrolarse

joiner ['dʒɔɪnər] n 1 CARPENTER : carpintero m, -ra f 2 : persona f que se une a varios grupos

joint¹ ['dʒɔɪnt] adj : conjunto, colectivo, mutuo ⟨a joint effort : un esfuerzo conjunto⟩ — **jointly** adv

joint² n 1 : articulación f, coyuntura f ⟨out of joint : dislocado⟩ 2 ROAST : asado m 3 JUNCTURE : juntura f, unión f 4 DIVE : antro m, tasca f

joist ['dʒɔɪst] n : viga f

joke¹ ['dʒo:k] vi joked; joking : bromear

joke² n 1 STORY : chiste m 2 PRANK : broma f

joker ['dʒo:kər] n 1 PRANKSTER : bromista mf 2 : comodín m (en los naipes)

jokingly ['dʒo:kɪŋli] adv : en broma

jollity ['dʒaləti] n, pl -ties MERRIMENT : alegría f, regocijo m

jolly ['dʒali] adj -lier; -est : alegre, jovial

jolt¹ ['dʒo:lt] vi JERK : dar tumbos, dar sacudidas — vt : sacudir

jolt² n 1 JERK : sacudida f brusca 2 SHOCK : golpe m (emocional)

jonquil ['dʒankwɪl] n : junquillo m

Jordanian [dʒɔr'deɪniən] n : jordano m, -na f — **Jordanian** adj

josh ['dʒaʃ] vt TEASE : tomarle el pelo (a alguien) — vi JOKE : bromear

jostle ['dʒasəl] v -tled; -tling vi 1 SHOVE : empujar, dar empellones 2 CONTEND : competir — vt 1 SHOVE : empujar 2 **to jostle one's way** : abrirse paso a empellones

jot¹ ['dʒat] vt jotted; jotting : anotar, apuntar ⟨jot it down : apúntalo⟩

jot² n BIT : ápice m, jota f, pizca f

jounce¹ ['dʒaʊnts] v jounced; jouncing vt JOLT : sacudir — vi : dar tumbos, dar sacudidas

jounce² n JOLT : sacudida f, tumbo m

journal ['dʒərnəl] n 1 DIARY : diario m 2 PERIODICAL : revista f, publicación f periódica 3 NEWSPAPER : periódico m, diario m

journalism ['dʒərnəl,ɪzəm] n : periodismo m

journalist ['dʒərnəlɪst] n : periodista mf

journalistic [,dʒərnəl'ɪstɪk] adj : periodístico

journey¹ ['dʒərni] vi -neyed; -neying : viajar

journey² n, pl -neys : viaje m

journeyman ['dʒərnimən] n, pl -men [-mən, -,mn] : oficial m

joust¹ ['dʒaʊst] vi : justar

joust² n : justa f

jovial ['dʒo:viəl] adj : jovial — **jovially** adv

joviality [,dʒo:vi'æləti] n : jovialidad f

jowl ['dʒaʊl] n 1 JAW : mandíbula f 2 CHEEK : mejilla f, cachete m

joy ['dʒɔɪ] n 1 HAPPINESS : gozo m, alegría f, felicidad f 2 DELIGHT : placer m, deleite m ⟨the child is a real joy : el niño es un verdadero placer⟩

joyful ['dʒɔɪfəl] *adj* : gozoso, alegre, feliz — **joyfully** *adv*

joyless ['dʒɔɪləs] *adj* : sin alegría, triste

joyous ['dʒɔɪəs] *adj* : alegre, feliz, eufórico — **joyously** *adv*

joyousness ['dʒɔɪəsnəs] *n* : alegría *f*, felicidad *f*, euforia *f*

joyride ['dʒɔɪˌraɪd] *n* : paseo *m* temerario e irresponsable (en coche)

joystick ['dʒɔɪˌstɪk] *n* : joystick *m*

jubilant ['dʒu:bələnt] *adj* : jubiloso, alborozado — **jubilantly** *adv*

jubilation [ˌdʒu:bə'leɪʃən] *n* : júbilo *m*

jubilee ['dʒu:bəˌli:] *n* **1** : quincuagésimo aniversario *m* **2** CELEBRATION : celebración *f*, festejos *mpl*

Judaic [dʒu'deɪɪk] *adj* : judaico

Judaism ['dʒu:dəˌɪzəm, 'dʒu:di-, 'dʒu:-ˌdeɪ-] *n* : judaísmo *m*

judge¹ ['dʒʌdʒ] *vt* **judged; judging 1** ASSESS : evaluar, juzgar **2** DEEM : juzgar, considerar **3** TRY : juzgar (ante el tribunal) **4 judging by** : a juzgar por

judge² *n* **1** : juez *mf*, jueza *f* **2 to be a good judge of** : saber juzgar a, entender mucho de

judgment *or* **judgement** ['dʒʌdʒ-mənt] *n* **1** RULING : fallo *m*, sentencia *f* **2** OPINION : opinión *f* **3** DISCERNMENT : juicio *m*, discernimiento *m*

judgmental [ˌdʒʌdʒ'mntəl] *adj* : crítico — **judgmentally** *adv*

judicature ['dʒu:dɪkəˌtʃʊr] *n* : judicatura *f*

judicial [dʒu'dɪʃəl] *adj* : judicial — **judicially** *adv*

judiciary¹ [dʒu'dɪʃiˌri, -'dɪʃəri] *adj* : judicial

judiciary² *n* **1** JUDICATURE : judicatura *f* **2** : poder *m* judicial

judicious [dʒu'dɪʃəs] *adj* SOUND, WISE : juicioso, sensato — **judiciously** *adv*

judo ['dʒu:ˌdo:] *n* : judo *m*

jug ['dʒʌg] *n* **1** : jarra *f*, jarro *m*, cántaro *m* **2** JAIL : cárcel *f*, chirona *f fam*

juggernaut ['dʒʌgərˌnɔt] *n* : gigante *m*, fuerza *f* irresistible ⟨a political juggernaut : un gigante político⟩

juggle ['dʒʌgəl] *v* **-gled; -gling** *vt* **1** : hacer juegos malabares con **2** MANIPULATE : manipular, jugar con — *vi* : hacer juegos malabares

juggler ['dʒʌgələr] *n* : malabarista *mf*

jugular ['dʒʌgjʊlər] *adj* : yugular ⟨jugular vein : vena yugular⟩

juice ['dʒu:s] *n* **1** : jugo *m* (de carne, de frutas) *m*, zumo *m* (de frutas) **2** ELECTRICITY : electricidad *f*, luz *f*

juicer ['dʒu:sər] *n* : exprimidor *m*

juiciness ['dʒu:sinəs] *n* : jugosidad *f*

juicy ['dʒu:si] *adj* **juicier; -est 1** SUCCULENT : jugoso, suculento **2** PROFITABLE : jugoso, lucrativo **3** RACY : picante

jukebox ['dʒu:kˌbɑks] *n* : rocola *f*, máquina *f* de discos

julep ['dʒu:ləp] *n* : bebida *f* hecha con whisky americano y menta

July [dʒu'laɪ] *n* : julio *m*

jumble¹ ['dʒʌmbəl] *vt* **-bled; -bling** : mezclar, revolver

jumble² *n* : revoltijo *m*, fárrago *m*, embrollo *m*

jumbo¹ ['dʒʌmˌbo:] *adj* : gigante, enorme, de tamaño extra grande

jumbo² *n, pl* **-bos** : coloso *m*, cosa *f* de tamaño extra grande

jump¹ ['dʒʌmp] *vi* **1** LEAP : saltar, brincar **2** START : levantarse de un salto, sobresaltarse **3** MOVE, SHIFT : moverse, pasar ⟨to jump from job to job : pasar de un empleo a otro⟩ **4** INCREASE, RISE : dar un salto, aumentarse de golpe, subir bruscamente **5** BUSTLE : animarse, ajetrearse **6 to jump to conclusions** : sacar conclusiones precipitadas — *vt* **1** : saltar ⟨to jump a fence : saltar una valla⟩ **2** SKIP : saltarse **3** ATTACK : atacar, asaltar **4 to jump the gun** : precipitarse

jump² *n* **1** LEAP : salto *m* **2** START : sobresalto *m*, respingo *m* **3** INCREASE : subida *f* brusca, aumento *m* **4** ADVANTAGE : ventaja *f* ⟨we got the jump on them : les llevamos la ventaja⟩

jumper ['dʒʌmpər] *n* **1** : saltador *m*, -dora *f* (en deportes) **2** : jumper *m*, vestido *m* sin mangas

jumpy ['dʒʌmpi] *adj* **jumpier; -est** : asustadizo, nervioso

junction ['dʒʌŋkʃən] *n* **1** JOINING : unión *f* **2** : cruce *m* (de calles), empalme *m* (de un ferrocarril), confluencia *f* (de ríos)

juncture ['dʒʌŋktʃər] *n* **1** UNION : juntura *f*, unión *f* **2** MOMENT, POINT : coyuntura *f* ⟨at this juncture : en esta coyuntura, en este momento⟩

June ['dʒu:n] *n* : junio *m*

jungle ['dʒʌŋgəl] *n* : jungla *f*, selva *f*

junior¹ ['dʒu:njər] *adj* **1** YOUNGER : más joven ⟨John Smith, Junior : John Smith, hijo⟩ **2** SUBORDINATE : subordinado, subalterno

junior² *n* **1** : persona *f* de menor edad ⟨she's my junior : es menor que yo⟩ **2** SUBORDINATE : subalterno *m*, -na *f*; subordinado *m*, -da *f* **3** : estudiante *mf* de penúltimo año

juniper ['dʒu:nəpər] *n* : enebro *m*

junk¹ ['dʒʌŋk] *vt* : echar a la basura

junk² *n* **1** RUBBISH : desechos *mpl*, desperdicios *mpl* **2** STUFF : trastos *mpl fam*, cachivaches *mpl fam* **3 piece of junk** : cacharro *m*, porquería *f*

junket ['dʒʌŋkət] *n* : viaje *m* (pagado con dinero público)

junta ['hʊntə, 'dʒʌn-, 'hʌn-] *n* : junta *f* militar

Jupiter ['dʒu:pətər] *n* : Júpiter *m*

jurisdiction [ˌdʒʊrəs'dɪkʃən] *n* : jurisdicción *f*

jurisprudence [ˌdʒʊrəs'pru:dəns] *n* : jurisprudencia *f*

jurist ['dʒʊrɪst] *n* : jurista *mf*; magistrado *m*, -da *f*

juror ['dʒʊrər] *n* : jurado *m*, -da *f*
jury ['dʒʊri] *n, pl* **-ries** : jurado *m*
just¹ ['dʒʌst] *adv* **1** EXACTLY : justo, precisamente, exactamente **2** POSSIBLY : posiblemente ⟨it just might work : tal vez resulte⟩ **3** BARELY : justo, apenas ⟨just in time : justo a tiempo⟩ **4** ONLY : sólo, solamente, nada más ⟨just us : sólo nosotros⟩ **5** QUITE : muy, simplemente ⟨it's just horrible! : ¡qué horrible!⟩ **6 to have just (done something)** : acabar de (hacer algo) ⟨he just called : acaba de llamar⟩
just² *adj* : justo — **justly** *adv*
justice ['dʒʌstɪs] *n* **1** : justicia *f* **2** JUDGE : juez *mf*, jueza *f*

justification [,dʒʌstəfə'keɪʃən] *n* : justificación *f*
justify ['dʒʌstə,faɪ] *vt* **-fied; -fying** : justificar — **justifiable** [,dʒʌstə-'faɪəbəl] *adj*
jut ['dʒʌt] *vi* **jutted; jutting** : sobresalir
jute ['dʒuːt] *n* : yute *m*
juvenile¹ ['dʒuːvə,naɪl, -vənəl] *adj* **1** : juvenil ⟨juvenile delinquent : delincuente juvenil⟩ ⟨juvenile court : tribunal de menores⟩ **2** CHILDISH : infantil
juvenile² *n* : menor *mf*
juxtapose ['dʒʌkstə,poːz] *vt* **-posed; -posing** : yuxtaponer
juxtaposition [,dʒʌkstəpə'zɪʃən] *n* : yuxtaposición *f*

K

k ['keɪ] *n, pl* **k's** *or* **ks** ['keɪz] : undécima letra del alfabeto inglés
kaiser ['kaɪzər] *n* : káiser *m*
kale ['keɪl] *n* : col *f* rizada
kaleidoscope [kə'laɪdə,skoːp] *n* : calidoscopio *m*
kamikaze [,kɑmɪ'kɑzi] *n* : kamikaze *m* — **kamikaze** *adj*
kangaroo [,kæŋgə'ruː] *n, pl* **-roos** : canguro *m*
kaolin ['keɪələn] *n* : caolín *m*
karaoke [,kæri'oːki] *n* : karaoke *m*
karat ['kærət] *n* : quilate *m*
karate [kə'rɑti] *n* : karate *m*
katydid ['keɪti,dɪd] *n* : saltamontes *m*
kayak ['kaɪ,æk] *n* : kayac *m*, kayak *m*
keel¹ ['kiːl] *vi* **to keel over** : volcar (dícese de un barco), desplomarse (dícese de una persona)
keel² *n* : quilla *f*
keen ['kiːn] *adj* **1** SHARP : afilado, filoso ⟨a keen blade : una hoja afilada⟩ **2** PENETRATING : cortante, penetrante ⟨a keen wind : un viento cortante⟩ **3** ENTHUSIASTIC : entusiasta **4** ACUTE : agudo, fino ⟨keen hearing : oído fino⟩ ⟨keen intelligence : inteligencia aguda⟩
keenly ['kiːnli] *adv* **1** ENTHUSIASTICALLY : con entusiasmo **2** INTENSELY : vivamente, profundamente ⟨keenly aware of : muy consciente de⟩
keenness ['kiːnnəs] *n* **1** SHARPNESS : lo afilado, lo filoso **2** ENTHUSIASM : entusiasmo *m* **3** ACUTENESS : agudeza *f*
keep¹ ['kiːp] *v* **kept** ['kɛpt]; **keeping** *vt* **1** : cumplir (la palabra a uno), acudir a (una cita) **2** OBSERVE : observar (una fiesta) **3** GUARD : guardar, cuidar **4** CONTINUE : mantener ⟨to keep silence : mantener silencio⟩ **5** SUPPORT : mantener (una familia) **6** RAISE : criar (animales) **7** : llevar, escribir (un diario, etc.) **8** RETAIN : guardar, conservar, quedarse con **9** STORE : guardar **10** DETAIN : hacer quedar, detener **11** PRESERVE : guardar ⟨to keep a secret : guardar un secreto⟩ — *vi* **1** : conser-

varse (dícese de los alimentos) **2** CONTINUE : seguir, no dejar ⟨he keeps on pestering us : no deja de molestarnos⟩ **3 to keep from** : abstenerse de ⟨I couldn't keep from laughing : no podía contener la risa⟩
keep² *n* **1** TOWER : torreón *m* (de un castillo), torre *f* del homenaje **2** SUSTENANCE : manutención *f*, sustento *m* **3 for keeps** : para siempre
keeper ['kiːpər] *n* **1** : guarda *mf* (en un zoológico); conservador *m*, -dora *f* (en un museo) **2** GAMEKEEPER : guardabosque *mf*
keeping ['kiːpɪŋ] *n* **1** CONFORMITY : conformidad *f*, acuerdo *m* ⟨in keeping with : de acuerdo con⟩ **2** CARE : cuidado *m* ⟨in the keeping of : al cuidado de⟩
keepsake ['kiːp,seɪk] *n* : recuerdo *m*
keep up *vt* CONTINUE, MAINTAIN : mantener, seguir con — *vi* **1** : mantenerse al corriente ⟨he kept up with the news : se mantenía al tanto de las noticias⟩ **2** CONTINUE : continuar **3 to keep up with someone** : mantener contacto con alguien
keg ['kɛg] *n* : barril *m*
kelp ['kɛlp] *n* : alga *f* marina
ken ['kɛn] *n* **1** SIGHT : vista *f*, alcance *m* de la vista **2** UNDERSTANDING : comprensión *f*, alcance *m* del conocimiento ⟨it's beyond his ken : no lo puede entender⟩
kennel ['kɛnəl] *n* : caseta *f* para perros, perrera *f*
Kenyan ['kɛnjən, 'kiːn-] *n* : keniano *m*, -na *f* — **Kenyan** *adj*
kept → keep
kerchief ['kərtʃəf, -,tʃiːf] *n* : pañuelo *m*
kernel ['kərnəl] *n* **1** : almendra *f* (de semillas y nueces) **2** : grano *m* (de cereales) **3** CORE : meollo *m* ⟨a kernel of truth : un fondo de verdad⟩
kerosene *or* **kerosine** ['kɛrə,siːn, ,kɛrə'-] *n* : queroseno *m*, kerosén *m*, kerosene *m*

ketchup ['kɛʧəp, 'kæ-] *n* : salsa *f* catsup
kettle ['kɛtəl] *n* **1** : hervidor *m*, pava *f*
  Arg, Bol, Chile **2** → **teakettle**
kettledrum ['kɛtəl,drʌm] *n* : timbal *m*
key[1] ['ki:] *vt* **1** ATTUNE : adaptar, adecuar **2 to key up** : poner nervioso, inquietar
key[2] *adj* : clave, fundamental
key[3] *n* **1** : llave *f* **2** SOLUTION : clave *f*, soluciones *fpl* **3** : tecla *f* (de un piano o una máquina) **4** : tono *m*, tonalidad *f* (en la música) **5** ISLET, REEF : cayo *m*, islote *m*
keyboard ['ki:,bord] *n* : teclado *m*
keyhole ['ki:,ho:l] *n* : bocallave *f*, ojo *m* (de una cerradura)
keynote[1] ['ki:,no:t] *vt* -**noted**; -**noting 1** : establecer la tónica de (en música) **2** : pronunciar el discurso principal de
keynote[2] *n* **1** : tónica *f* (en música) **2** : idea *f* fundamental
keystone ['ki:,sto:n] *n* : clave *f*, dovela *f*
keystroke ['ki:,stro:k] *n* : pulsación *f* (de tecla)
khaki ['kæki, 'kɑ-] *n* : caqui *m*
khan ['kɑn, 'kæn] *n* : kan *m*
kibbutz [kə'bʊts, -'bu:ts] *n, pl* -**butzim** [-,bʊt'si:m, -,bu:t-] : kibutz *m*
kibitz ['kɪbɪts] *vi* : dar consejos molestos
kibitzer ['kɪbɪtsər, kɪ'bɪt-] *n* : persona *f* que da consejos molestos
kick[1] ['kɪk] *vi* **1** : dar patadas (dícese de una persona), cocear (dícese de un animal) **2** PROTEST : patalear, protestar **3** RECOIL : dar un culatazo (dícese de un arma de fuego) — *vt* : patear, darle una patada (a alguien)
kick[2] *n* **1** : patada *f*, puntapié *m*, coz *f* (de un animal) **2** RECOIL : culatazo *m* (de un arma de fuego) **3** : fuerza *f* ⟨a drink with a kick : una bebida fuerte⟩
kicker ['kɪkər] *n* : pateador *m*, -dora *f* (en deportes)
kickoff ['kɪk,ɔf] *n* : saque *m* (inicial)
kick off *vi* **1** : hacer el saque inicial (en deportes) **2** BEGIN : empezar — *vt* : empezar
kid[1] ['kɪd] *v* **kidded**; **kidding** *vt* **1** FOOL : engañar **2** TEASE : tomarle el pelo (a alguien) — *vi* JOKE : bromear ⟨I'm only kidding : lo digo en broma⟩
kid[2] *n* **1** : chivo *m*, -va *f*; cabrito *m*, -ta *f* **2** CHILD : chico *m*, -ca *f*; niño *m*, -ña *f*
kidder ['kɪdər] *n* : bromista *mf*
kiddingly ['kɪdɪŋli] *adv* : en broma
kidnap ['kɪd,næp] *vt* -**napped** *or* -**naped** [-,næpt]; -**napping** *or* -**naping** [-,næpɪŋ] : secuestrar, raptar
kidnapper *or* **kidnaper** ['kɪd,næpər] *n* : secuestrador *m*, -dora *f*; raptor *m*, -tora *f*
kidnapping ['kɪd,næpɪŋ] *n* : secuestro *m*
kidney ['kɪdni] *n, pl* -**neys** : riñón *m*
kidney bean *n* : frijol *m*
kill[1] ['kɪl] *vt* **1** : matar **2** END : acabar con, poner fin a **3 to kill time** : matar el tiempo

kill[2] *n* **1** KILLING : matanza *f* **2** PREY : presa *f*
killer ['kɪlər] *n* : asesino *m*, -na *f*
killjoy ['kɪl,ʤɔɪ] *n* : aguafiestas *mf*
kiln ['kɪl, 'kɪln] *n* : horno *m*
kilo ['ki:,lo:] *n, pl* -**los** : kilo *m*
kilobyte ['kɪlə,baɪt] *n* : kilobyte *m*
kilocycle ['kɪlə,saɪkəl] *n* : kilociclo *m*
kilogram ['kɪlə,græm, 'ki:-] *n* : kilogramo *m*
kilohertz ['kɪlə,hərts] *n* : kilohertzio *m*
kilometer [kɪ'lɑmətər, 'kɪlə,mi:-] *n* : kilómetro *m*
kilowatt ['kɪlə,wɑt] *n* : kilovatio *m*
kilt ['kɪlt] *n* : falda *f* escocesa
kilter ['kɪltər] *n* **1** ORDER : buen estado *m* **2 out of kilter** : descompuesto, estropeado
kimono [kə'mo:no, -nə] *n, pl* -**nos** : kimono *m*, quimono *m*
kin ['kɪn] *n* : familiares *mpl*, parientes *mpl*
kind[1] ['kaɪnd] *adj* : amable, bondadoso, benévolo
kind[2] *n* **1** ESSENCE : esencia *f* ⟨a difference in degree, not in kind : una diferencia cuantitativa y no cualitativa⟩ **2** CATEGORY : especie *f*, género *m* **3** TYPE : clase *f*, tipo *m*, índole *f*
kindergarten ['kɪndər,gɑrtən, -dən] *n* : kinder *m*, kindergarten *m*, jardín *m* de infantes, jardín *m* de niños *Mex*
kindhearted [,kaɪnd'hɑrtəd] *adj* : bondadoso, de buen corazón
kindle ['kɪndəl] *v* -**dled**; -**dling** *vt* **1** IGNITE : encender **2** AROUSE : despertar, suscitar — *vi* : encenderse
kindliness ['kaɪndlinəs] *n* : bondad *f*
kindling ['kɪndlɪŋ, 'kɪndlən] *n* : astillas *fpl*, leña *f*
kindly[1] ['kaɪndli] *adv* **1** AMIABLY : amablemente, bondadosamente **2** COURTEOUSLY : cortésmente, con cortesía ⟨we kindly ask you not smoke : les rogamos que no fumen⟩ **3** PLEASE : por favor **4 to take kindly to** : aceptar de buena gana
kindly[2] *adj* -**lier**; -**est** : bondadoso, amable
kindness ['kaɪndnəs] *n* : bondad *f*
kind of *adv* SOMEWHAT : un tanto, algo
kindred[1] ['kɪndrəd] *adj* SIMILAR : similar, afín ⟨kindred spirits : almas gemelas⟩
kindred[2] *n* **1** FAMILY : familia *f*, parentela *f* **2** → **kin**
kinfolk ['kɪn,fo:k] *or* **kinfolks** [-,fo:ks] *npl* → **kin**
king ['kɪŋ] *n* : rey *m*
kingdom ['kɪŋdəm] *n* : reino *m*
kingfisher ['kɪŋ,fɪʃər] *n* : martín *m* pescador
kingly ['kɪŋli] *adj* -**lier**; -**est** : regio, real
king-size ['kɪŋ,saɪz] *or* **king-sized** [-,saɪzd] *adj* : de tamaño muy grande, extra largo (dícese de cigarrillos)
kink ['kɪŋk] *n* **1** : rizo *m* (en el pelo), vuelta *f* (en una cuerda) **2** CRAMP

: calambre *m* ⟨to have a kink in the neck : tener tortícolis⟩

kinky ['kɪŋki] *adj* **-kier; -est** : rizado (dícese del pelo), enroscado (dícese de una cuerda)

kinship ['kɪn,ʃɪp] *n* : parentesco *m*

kinsman ['kɪnzmən] *n, pl* **-men** [-mən, -,mɛn] : familiar *m*, pariente *m*

kinswoman ['kɪnz,wʊmən] *n, pl* **-women** [-,wɪmən] : familiar *f*, pariente *f*

kiosk ['ki:,ɑsk] *n* : quiosco *m*

kipper ['kɪpər] *n* : arenque *m* ahumado

kiss¹ ['kɪs] *vt* : besar — *vi* : besarse

kiss² *n* : beso *m*

kit ['kɪt] *n* **1** SET : juego *m*, kit *m* **2** CASE : estuche *m*, caja *f* **3 first–aid kit** : botiquín *m* **4 tool kit** : caja *f* de herramientas **5 travel kit** : neceser *m*

kitchen ['kɪtʃən] *n* : cocina *f*

kite ['kaɪt] *n* **1** : milano *m* (ave) **2** : cometa *f*, papalote *m Mex* ⟨to fly a kite : hacer volar una cometa⟩

kith ['kɪθ] *n* : amigos *mpl* ⟨kith and kin : amigos y parientes⟩

kitten ['kɪtən] *n* : gatito *m*, -ta *f*

kitty ['kɪti] *n, pl* **-ties 1** FUND, POOL : bote *m*, fondo *m* común **2** CAT : gato *m*, gatito *m*

kitty–corner ['kɪti,kɔrnər] *or* **kitty–cornered** [-nərd] → **catercorner**

kiwi ['ki:,wi:] *n* : kiwi *m*

kleptomania [,klɛptə'meɪniə] *n* : cleptomanía *f*

kleptomaniac [,klɛptə'meɪni,æk] *n* : cleptómano *m*, -na *f*

knack ['næk] *n* : maña *f*, facilidad *f*

knapsack ['næp,sæk] *n* : mochila *f*, morral *m*

knave ['neɪv] *n* : bellaco *m*, pícaro *m*

knead ['ni:d] *vt* **1** : amasar, sobar **2** MASSAGE : masajear

knee ['ni:] *n* : rodilla *f*

kneecap ['ni:,kæp] *n* : rótula *f*

kneel ['ni:l] *vi* **knelt** ['nɛlt] *or* **kneeled** ['ni:ld]; **kneeling** : arrodillarse, ponerse de rodillas

knell ['nɛl] *n* : doble *m*, toque *m* ⟨death knell : toque de difuntos⟩

knew → **know**

knickers ['nɪkərz] *npl* : pantalones *mpl* bombachos de media pierna

knickknack ['nɪk,næk] *n* : chuchería *f*, baratija *f*

knife¹ ['naɪf] *vt* **knifed** ['naɪft]; **knifing** : acuchillar, apuñalar

knife² *n, pl* **knives** ['naɪvz] : cuchillo *m*

knight¹ ['naɪt] *vt* : conceder el título de *Sir* a

knight² *n* **1** : caballero *m* ⟨knight errant : caballero andante⟩ **2** : caballo *m* (en ajedrez) **3** : uno que tiene el título de *Sir*

knighthood ['naɪt,hʊd] *n* **1** : caballería *f* **2** : título *m* de *Sir*

knightly ['naɪtli] *adj* : caballeresco

knit¹ ['nɪt] *v* **knit** *or* **knitted** ['nɪtəd]; **knitting** *vt* **1** UNITE : unir, enlazar **2** : tejer ⟨to knit a sweater : tejer un suéter⟩ **3**

to knit one's brows : fruncir el ceño — *vi* **1** : tejer **2** : soldarse (dícese de los huesos)

knit² *n* : prenda *f* tejida

knitter ['nɪtər] *n* : tejedor *m*, -dora *f*

knob ['nɑb] *n* **1** LUMP : bulto *m*, protuberancia *f* **2** HANDLE : perilla *f*, tirador *m*, botón *m*

knobbed ['nɑbd] *adj* **1** KNOTTY : nudoso **2** : que tiene perilla o botón

knobby ['nɑbi] *adj* **knobbier; -est 1** KNOTTY : nudoso **2 knobby knees** : rodillas *fpl* huesudas

knock¹ ['nɑk] *vt* **1** HIT, RAP : golpear, golpetear **2** : hacer chocar ⟨they knocked heads : se dieron en la cabeza⟩ **3** CRITICIZE : criticar — *vi* **1** RAP : dar un golpe, llamar (a la puerta) **2** COLLIDE : darse, chocar

knock² *n* : golpe *m*, llamada *f* (a la puerta), golpeteo *m* (de un motor)

knock down *vt* : derribar, echar al suelo

knocker ['nɑkər] *n* : aldaba *f*, llamador *m*

knock–kneed ['nɑk'ni:d] *adj* : patizambo

knockout ['nɑk,aʊt] *n* : nocaut *m*, knockout *m* (en deportes)

knock out *vt* : dejar sin sentido, poner fuera de combate (en el boxeo)

knoll ['no:l] *n* : loma *f*, otero *m*, montículo *m*

knot¹ ['nɑt] *v* **knotted; knotting** *vt* : anudar — *vi* : anudarse

knot² *n* **1** : nudo *m* (en cordel o madera), nódulo *m* (en los músculos) **2** CLUSTER : grupo *m* **3** : nudo *m* (unidad de velocidad)

knotty ['nɑti] *adj* **-tier; -est 1** GNARLED : nudoso **2** COMPLEX : espinoso, enredado, complejo

know ['no:] *v* **knew** ['nu:, 'nju:]; **known** ['no:n]; **knowing** *vt* **1** : saber ⟨he knows the answer : sabe la respuesta⟩ **2** : conocer (a una persona, un lugar) ⟨do you know Julia? : ¿conoces a Julia?⟩ **3** RECOGNIZE : reconocer **4** DISCERN, DISTINGUISH : distinguir, discernir **5 to know how to** : saber ⟨I don't know how to dance : no sé bailar⟩ — *vi* : saber

knowable ['no:əbəl] *adj* : conocible

knowing ['no:ɪŋ] *adj* **1** KNOWLEDGEABLE : informado ⟨a knowing look : una mirada de complicidad⟩ **2** ASTUTE : astuto **3** DELIBERATE : deliberado, intencional

knowingly ['no:ɪŋli] *adv* **1** : con complicidad ⟨she smiled knowingly : sonrió con una mirada de complicidad⟩ **2** DELIBERATELY : a sabiendas, adrede, a propósito

know–it–all ['no:ɪt,ɔl] *n* : sabelotodo *mf fam*

knowledge ['nɑlɪdʒ] *n* **1** AWARENESS : conocimiento *m* **2** LEARNING : conocimientos *mpl*, saber *m*

knowledgeable ['nɑlɪdʒəbəl] *adj* : informado, entendido, enterado

known ['noːn] *adj* : conocido, familiar
knuckle ['nʌkəl] *n* : nudillo *m*
koala [koˈwalə] *n* : koala *m*
kohlrabi [ˌkoːlˈrɑbi, -ˈræ-] *n, pl* **-bies** : colinabo *m*
Koran [kəˈrɑn, -ˈræn] *n* **the Koran** : el Corán
Korean [kəˈriːən] *n* **1** : coreano *m*, -na *f* **2** : coreano *m* (idioma) — **Korean** *adj*
kosher ['koːʃər] *adj* : aprobado por la ley judía

kowtow [ˌkaʊˈtaʊ, ˈkaʊˌtaʊ] *vi* **to kowtow to** : humillarse ante, doblegarse ante
krypton ['krɪpˌtɑn] *n* : criptón *m*
kudos ['kjuːˌdɑs, 'kuː-, -ˌdoːz] *n* : fama *f*, renombre *m*
kumquat ['kʌmˌkwɑt] *n* : naranjita *f* china
Kurd ['kʊrd, 'kərd] *n* : kurdo *m*, -da *f*
Kurdish ['kʊrdɪʃ, 'kər-] *adj* : kurdo
Kuwaiti [kʊˈweɪti] *n* : kuwaití *mf* — **Kuwaiti** *adj*

L

l ['ɛl] *n, pl* **l's** *or* **ls** ['ɛlz] : duodécima letra del alfabeto inglés
lab ['læb] → **laboratory**
label[1] ['leɪbəl] *vt* **-beled** *or* **-belled; -beling** *or* **-belling** **1** : etiquetar, poner etiqueta a **2** BRAND, CATEGORIZE : calificar, tildar, tachar ⟨they labeled him as a fraud : lo calificaron de farsante⟩
label[2] *n* **1** : etiqueta *f*, rótulo *m* **2** DESCRIPTION : calificación *f*, descripción *f* **3** BRAND : marca *f*
labial ['leɪbiəl] *adj* : labial
labor[1] ['leɪbər] *vi* **1** WORK : trabajar **2** STRUGGLE : avanzar penosamente (dícese de una persona), funcionar con dificultad (dícese de un motor) **3 to labor under a delusion** : hacerse ilusiones, tener una falsa impresión — *vt* BELABOR : insistir en, extenderse sobre
labor[2] *n* **1** EFFORT, WORK : trabajo *m*, esfuerzos *mpl* **2** : parto *m* ⟨to be in labor : estar de parto⟩ **3** TASK : tarea *f*, labor *m* **4** WORKERS : mano *f* de obra
laboratory ['læbrəˌtori, ləˈbɔrə-] *n, pl* **-ries** : laboratorio *m*
Labor Day *n* : Día *m* del Trabajo
laborer ['leɪbərər] *n* : peón *m*; trabajador *m*, -dora *f*
laborious [ləˈboriəs] *adj* : laborioso, difícil
laboriously [ləˈboriəsli] *adv* : laboriosamente, trabajosamente
labor union → **union**
labyrinth ['læbəˌrɪnθ] *n* : laberinto *m*
lace[1] ['leɪs] *vt* **laced; lacing** **1** TIE : acordonar, atar los cordones de **2** : adornar de encaje ⟨I laced the dress in white : adorné el vestido de encaje blanco⟩ **3** SPIKE : echar licor a
lace[2] *n* **1** : encaje *m* **2** SHOELACE : cordón *m* (de zapatos), agujeta *f Mex*
lacerate ['læsəˌreɪt] *vt* **-ated; -ating** : lacerar
laceration [ˌlæsəˈreɪʃən] *n* : laceración *f*
lack[1] ['læk] *vt* : carecer de, no tener ⟨she lacks patience : carece de paciencia⟩ — *vi* : faltar ⟨they lack for nothing : no les falta nada⟩
lack[2] *n* : falta *f*, carencia *f*
lackadaisical [ˌlækəˈdeɪzɪkəl] *adj*

: apático, indiferente, lánguido — **lackadaisically** [-kli] *adv*
lackey ['læki] *n, pl* **-eys** **1** FOOTMAN : lacayo *m* **2** TOADY : adulador *m*, -dora *f*
lackluster ['lækˌlʌstər] *adj* **1** DULL : sin brillo, apagado, deslustrado **2** MEDIOCRE : deslucido, mediocre
laconic [ləˈkɑnɪk] *adj* : lacónico — **laconically** [-nɪkli] *adv*
lacquer[1] ['lækər] *vt* : laquear, pintar con laca
lacquer[2] *n* : laca *f*
lacrosse [ləˈkrɔs] *n* : lacrosse *f*
lactic acid ['læktɪk] *n* : ácido *m* láctico
lacuna [ləˈkuːnə, -ˈkjuː-] *n, pl* **-nae** [-ˌniː, -ˌnaɪ] *or* **-nas** : laguna *f*
lacy ['leɪsi] *adj* **lacier; -est** : de encaje, como de encaje
lad ['læd] *n* : muchacho *m*, niño *m*
ladder ['lædər] *n* : escalera *f*
laden ['leɪdən] *adj* : cargado
ladle[1] ['leɪdəl] *vt* **-dled; -dling** : servir con cucharón
ladle[2] *n* : cucharón *m*, cazo *m*
lady ['leɪdi] *n, pl* **-dies** **1** : señora *f*, dama *f* **2** WOMAN : mujer *f*
ladybird ['leɪdiˌbərd] → **ladybug**
ladybug ['leɪdiˌbʌg] *n* : mariquita *f*
lag[1] ['læg] *vi* **lagged; lagging** : quedarse atrás, retrasarse, rezagarse
lag[2] *n* **1** DELAY : retraso *m*, demora *f* **2** INTERVAL : lapso *m*, intervalo *m*
lager ['lɑgər] *n* : cerveza *f* rubia
laggard[1] ['lægərd] *adj* : retardado, retrasado
laggard[2] *n* : rezagado *m*, -da *f*
lagoon [ləˈguːn] *n* : laguna *f*
laid → **lay**[1]
laid-back ['leɪdˈbæk] *adj* : tranquilo, relajado
lain *pp* → **lie**[1]
lair ['lær] *n* : guarida *f*, madriguera *f*
laissez-faire [ˌlɛˌseɪˈfær, ˌleɪˌzeɪ-] *n* : liberalismo *m* económico
laity ['leɪəti] *n* **the laity** : los laicos, el laicado
lake ['leɪk] *n* : lago *m*
lama ['lɑmə] *n* : lama *m*
lamb ['læm] *n* **1** : cordero *m*, borrego *m* (animal) **2** : carne *f* de cordero

lambaste [læm'beɪst] *or* **lambast**
[-'bæst] *vt* **-basted; -basting 1** BEAT,
THRASH : golpear, azotar, darle una
paliza (a alguien) **2** CENSURE : arremeter contra, censurar
lame[1] [leɪm] *vt* **lamed; laming** : lisiar,
hacer cojo
lame[2] *adj* **lamer; lamest 1** : cojo, renco, rengo **2** WEAK : pobre, débil, poco
convincente ⟨a lame excuse : una excusa débil⟩
lamé [lɑ'meɪ, læ-] *n* : lamé *m*
lame duck *n* : persona *f* sin poder ⟨a
lame-duck President : un presidente
saliente⟩
lamely ['leɪmli] *adv* : sin convicción
lameness ['leɪmnəs] *n* **1** : cojera *f*, renquera *f* **2** : falta *f* de convicción, debilidad *f*, pobreza *f* ⟨the lameness of her
response : la pobreza de su respuesta⟩
lament[1] [lə'mɛnt] *vt* **1** MOURN : llorar,
llorar por **2** DEPLORE : lamentar, deplorar — *vi* : llorar
lament[2] *n* : lamento *m*
lamentable ['læməntəbəl, lə'mɛntə-] *adj*
: lamentable, deplorable — **lamenta-
bly** [-bli] *adv*
lamentation [ˌlæmən'teɪʃən] *n* : lamentación *f*, lamento *m*
laminate[1] ['læmə.neɪt] *vt* **-nated; -nating**
: laminar
laminate[2] ['læmənət] *n* : laminado *m*
laminated ['læmə.neɪt̬əd] *adj* : laminado
lamp ['læmp] *n* : lámpara *f*
lampoon[1] [læm'puːn] *vt* : satirizar
lampoon[2] *n* : sátira *f*
lamprey ['læmpri] *n*, *pl* **-preys** : lamprea *f*
lance[1] ['lænts] *vt* **lanced; lancing** : abrir
con lanceta, sajar
lance[2] *n* : lanza *f*
lance corporal *n* : cabo *m* interino, soldado *m* de primera clase
lancet ['læntsət] *n* : lanceta *f*
land[1] ['lænd] *vt* **1** : desembarcar
(pasajeros de un barco), hacer aterrizar
(un avión) **2** CATCH : pescar, sacar (un
pez) del agua **3** GAIN, SECURE : conseguir, ganar ⟨to land a job : conseguir
empleo⟩ **4** DELIVER : dar, asestar ⟨he
landed a punch : asestó un puñetazo⟩
— *vi* **1** : aterrizar, tomar tierra, atracar
⟨the plane just landed : el avión acaba
de aterrizar⟩ ⟨the ship landed an hour
ago : el barco atracó hace una hora⟩ **2**
ALIGHT : posarse, aterrizar ⟨to land on
one's feet : caer de pie⟩
land[2] *n* **1** GROUND : tierra *f* ⟨dry land
: tierra firme⟩ **2** TERRAIN : terreno *m*
3 NATION : país *m*, nación *f* **4** DOMAIN
: mundo *m*, dominio *m* ⟨the land of
dreams : el mundo de los sueños⟩
landfill ['lænd.fɪl] *n* : vertedero *m* (de basuras)
landing ['lændɪŋ] *n* **1** : aterrizaje *m* (de
aviones), desembarco *m* (de barcos) **2**
: descansillo *m* (de una escalera)
landing field *n* : campo *m* de aterrizaje

landing strip → **airstrip**
landlady ['lænd.leɪdi] *n*, *pl* **-dies** : casera
f, dueña *f*, arrendadora *f*
landless ['lændləs] *adj* : sin tierra
landlocked ['lænd.lɑkt] *adj* : sin salida
al mar
landlord ['lænd.lɔrd] *n* : dueño *m*, casero
m, arrendador *m*
landlubber ['lænd.lʌbər] *n* : marinero *m*
de agua dulce
landmark ['lænd.mɑrk] *n* **1** : señal *f* (ge-
ográfica), punto *m* de referencia **2**
MILESTONE : hito *m* ⟨a landmark in our
history : un hito en nuestra historia⟩ **3**
MONUMENT : monumento *m* histórico
landowner ['lænd.oːnər] *n* : hacendado
m, -da *f*; terrateniente *mf*
landscape[1] ['lænd.skeɪp] *vt* **-scaped;
-scaping** : ajardinar
landscape[2] *n* : paisaje *m*
landslide ['lænd.slaɪd] *n* **1** : desprendimiento *m* de tierras, derrumbe *m* **2**
landslide victory : victoria *f* arroll-
adora
landward ['lændwərd] *adv* : en dirección
de la tierra, hacia tierra
lane ['leɪn] *n* **1** PATH, WAY : camino *m*,
sendero *m* **2** : carril *m* (de una carretera)
language ['læŋgwɪdʒ] *n* **1** : idioma *m*,
lengua *f* ⟨the English language : el idioma inglés⟩ **2** : lenguaje *m* ⟨body language : lenguaje corporal⟩
languid ['læŋgwɪd] *adj* : lánguido — **lan-
guidly** *adv*
languish ['læŋgwɪʃ] *vi* **1** WEAKEN : languidecer, debilitarse **2** PINE : consumirse, suspirar (por) ⟨to languish for
love : suspirar por el amor⟩ ⟨he lan-
guished in prison : estuvo pudriéndose
en la cárcel⟩
languor ['læŋgər] *n* : languidez *f*
languorous ['læŋgərəs] *adj* : lánguido
— **languorously** *adv*
lank ['læŋk] *adj* **1** THIN : delgado,
larguirucho *fam* **2** LIMP : lacio
lanky ['læŋki] *adj* **lankier; -est** : delgado, larguirucho *fam*
lanolin ['lænələn] *n* : lanolina *f*
lantern ['læntərn] *n* : linterna *f*, farol *m*
Laotian [leɪ'oːʃən, 'lauʃən] *n* : laosiano
m, -na *f* — **Laotian** *adj*
lap[1] ['læp] *v* **lapped; lapping** *vt* **1** FOLD
: plegar, doblar **2** WRAP : envolver **3**
: lamer, besar ⟨waves were lapping the
shore : las olas lamían la orilla⟩ **4 to
lap up** : beber a lengüetadas (como un
gato) — *vi* OVERLAP : traslaparse
lap[2] *n* **1** : falda *f*, regazo *m* (del cuerpo)
2 OVERLAP : traslapo *m* **3** : vuelta *f* (en
deportes) **4** STAGE : etapa *f* (de un viaje)
lapdog ['læp.dɔg] *n* : perro *m* faldero
lapel [lə'pɛl] *n* : solapa *f*
lapp ['læp] *n* : lapón *m*, -pona *f* — **Lapp**
adj
lapse[1] ['læps] *vi* **lapsed; lapsing 1** FALL,
SLIP : caer ⟨to lapse into bad habits
: caer en malos hábitos⟩ ⟨to lapse into

unconsciousness : perder el conocimiento⟩ ⟨to lapse into silence : quedarse callado⟩ 2 FADE : decaer, desvanecerse ⟨her dedication lapsed : su dedicación se desvaneció⟩ 3 CEASE : cancelarse, perderse 4 ELAPSE : transcurrir, pasar 5 EXPIRE : caducar

lapse² n 1 SLIP : lapsus m, desliz m, falla f ⟨a lapse of memory : una falla de memoria⟩ 2 INTERVAL : lapso m, intervalo m, período m 3 EXPIRATION : caducidad f

laptop¹ ['læp‚tɑp] adj : portátil, laptop

laptop² n : laptop m

larboard ['lɑrbərd] n : babor m

larcenous ['lɑrsənəs] adj : de robo

larceny ['lɑrsəni] n, pl **-nies** : robo m, hurto m

larch ['lɑrtʃ] n : alerce f

lard ['lɑrd] n : manteca f de cerdo

larder ['lɑrdər] n : despensa f, alacena f

large ['lɑrdʒ] adj **larger; largest** 1 BIG : grande 2 COMPREHENSIVE : amplio, extenso 3 **by and large** : por lo general

largely ['lɑrdʒli] adv : en gran parte, en su mayoría

largeness ['lɑrdʒnəs] n : lo grande

largesse or **largess** [lɑr'ʒɛs, -'dʒɛs] n : generosidad f, largueza f

lariat ['læriət] n : lazo m

lark ['lɑrk] n 1 FUN : diversión f ⟨what a lark! : ¡qué divertido!⟩ 2 : alondra f (pájaro)

larva ['lɑrvə] n, pl **-vae** [-‚viː, -‚vaɪ] : larva f — **larval** [-vəl] adj

laryngitis [‚lærən'dʒaɪtəs] n : laringitis f

larynx ['lærɪŋks] n, pl **-rynges** [lə'rɪn‚dʒiːz] or **-ynxes** ['lærɪŋksəz] : laringe f

lasagna [lə'zɑnjə] n : lasaña f

lascivious [lə'sɪviəs] adj : lascivo

lasciviousness [lə'sɪviəsnəs] n : lascivia f, lujuria f

laser ['leɪzər] n : láser m

laser disc n : disco m láser

lash¹ ['læʃ] vt 1 WHIP : azotar 2 BIND : atar, amarrar

lash² n 1 WHIP : látigo m 2 STROKE : latigazo m 3 EYELASH : pestaña f

lass ['læs] or **lassie** ['læsi] n : muchacha f, chica f

lassitude ['læsə‚tuːd, -‚tjuːd] n : lasitud f

lasso¹ ['læ‚soː, læ'suː] vt : lazar

lasso² n, pl **-sos** or **-soes** : lazo m, reata f Mex

last¹ ['læst] vi 1 CONTINUE : durar ⟨how long will it last? : ¿cuánto durará?⟩ 2 ENDURE : aguantar, durar 3 SURVIVE : durar, sobrevivir 4 SUFFICE : durar, bastar — vt 1 : durar ⟨it will last a lifetime : durará toda la vida⟩ 2 **to last out** : aguantar

last² adv 1 : en último lugar, al último ⟨we came in last : llegamos en último lugar⟩ 2 : por última vez, la última vez ⟨I saw him last in Bogota : lo vi por última vez en Bogotá⟩ 3 FINALLY : por último, en conclusión

last³ adj 1 FINAL : último, final 2 PREVIOUS : pasado ⟨last year : el año pasado⟩

last⁴ n 1 : el último, la última, lo último ⟨at last : por fin, al fin, finalmente⟩ 2 : horma f (de zapatero)

lasting ['læstɪŋ] adj : perdurable, duradero, estable

lastly ['læstli] adv : por último, finalmente

latch¹ ['lætʃ] vt : cerrar con picaporte

latch² n : picaporte m, pestillo m, pasador m

late¹ ['leɪt] adv **later; latest** 1 : tarde ⟨to arrive late : llegar tarde⟩ ⟨to sleep late : dormir hasta tarde⟩ 2 : a última hora, a finales ⟨late in the month : a finales del mes⟩ 3 RECENTLY : recién, últimamente ⟨as late as last year : todavía en el año pasado⟩

late² adj **later; latest** 1 TARDY : tardío, de retraso ⟨to be late : llegar tarde⟩ 2 : avanzado ⟨because of the late hour : a causa de la hora avanzada⟩ 3 DECEASED : difunto, fallecido 4 RECENT : reciente, último ⟨our late quarrel : nuestra última pelea⟩

latecomer ['leɪt‚kʌmər] n : rezagado m, -da f

lately ['leɪtli] adv : recientemente, últimamente

lateness ['leɪtnəs] n 1 DELAY : retraso m, atraso m, tardanza f 2 : lo avanzado (de la hora)

latent ['leɪtənt] adj : latente — **latently** adv

lateral ['lætərəl] adj : lateral — **laterally** adv

latex ['leɪ‚tɛks] n, pl **-tices** ['leɪtə‚siːz, 'lætə-] or **-texes** : látex m

lath ['læθ, 'læð] n, pl **laths** or **lath** : listón m

lathe ['leɪð] n : torno m

lather¹ ['læðər] vt : enjabonar — vi : espumar, hacer espuma

lather² n 1 : espuma f (de jabón) 2 : sudor m (de caballo) 3 **to get into a lather** : ponerse histérico

Latin¹ adj : latino

Latin² n 1 : latín m (idioma) 2 → **Latin American**

Latin–American ['lætənə'mrikən] adj : latinoamericano

Latin American n : latinoamericano m, -na f

latitude ['lætə‚tuːd, -‚tjuːd] n : latitud f

latrine [lə'triːn] n : letrina f

latte ['lɑ‚teɪ] n : café m con leche

latter¹ ['lætər] adj 1 SECOND : segundo 2 LAST : último

latter² pron **the latter** : éste, ésta, éstos pl, éstas pl

lattice ['lætəs] n : enrejado m, celosía f

Latvian ['lætviən] n : letón m, -tona f — **Latvian** adj

laud¹ ['lɔd] vt : alabar, loar

laud² n : alabanza f, loa f

laudable ['lɔdəbəl] *adj* : loable — **laud-ably** [-bli] *adv*

laugh¹ ['læf] *vi* : reír, reírse

laugh² *n* **1** LAUGHTER : risa *f* **2** JOKE : chiste *m*, broma *f* ⟨he did it for a laugh : lo hizo en broma, lo hizo para divertirse⟩

laughable ['læfəbəl] *adj* : risible, de risa

laughingstock ['læfɪŋˌstɑk] *n* : hazmerreír *m*

laughter ['læftər] *n* : risa *f*, risas *fpl*

launch¹ ['lɔntʃ] *vt* **1** HURL : lanzar **2** : botar (un barco) **3** START : iniciar, empezar

launch² *n* **1** : lancha *f* (bote) **2** LAUNCHING : lanzamiento *m*

launder ['lɔndər] *vt* **1** : lavar y planchar (ropa) **2** : blanquear, lavar (dinero)

launderer ['lɔndərər] *n* : lavandero *m*, -ra *f*

laundress ['lɔndrəs] *n* : lavandera *f*

laundry ['lɔndri] *n, pl* **laundries 1** : ropa *f* sucia, ropa *f* para lavar ⟨to do the laundry : lavar la ropa⟩ **2** : lavandería *f* (servicio de lavar)

laureate ['lɔriət] *n* : laureado *m*, -da *f* ⟨poet laureate : poeta laureado⟩

laurel ['lɔrəl] *n* **1** : laurel *m* (planta) **2** **laurels** *npl* : laureles *mpl* ⟨to rest on one's laurels : dormirse uno en sus laureles⟩

lava ['lɑvə, 'læ-] *n* : lava *f*

lavatory ['lævəˌtori] *n, pl* **-ries** : baño *m*, cuarto *m* de baño

lavender ['lævəndər] *n* : lavanda *f*, espliego *m*

lavish¹ ['lævɪʃ] *vt* : prodigar (a), colmar (de)

lavish² *adj* **1** EXTRAVAGANT : pródigo, generoso, derrochador **2** ABUNDANT : abundante **3** LUXURIOUS : lujoso, espléndido

lavishly ['lævɪʃli] *adv* : con generosidad, espléndidamente ⟨to live lavishly : vivir a lo grande⟩

lavishness ['lævɪʃnəs] *n* : generosidad *f*, esplendidez *f*

law ['lɔ] *n* **1** : ley *f* ⟨to break the law : violar la ley⟩ **2** : derecho *m* ⟨criminal law : derecho criminal⟩ **3** : abogacía *f* ⟨to practice law : ejercer la abogacía⟩

law–abiding ['lɔəˌbaɪdɪŋ] *adj* : observante de la ley

lawbreaker ['lɔˌbreɪkər] *n* : infractor *m*, -tora *f* de la ley

lawful ['lɔfəl] *adj* : legal, legítimo, lícito — **lawfully** *adv*

lawgiver ['lɔˌgɪvər] *n* : legislador *m*, -dora *f*

lawless ['lɔləs] *adj* : anárquico, ingobernable — **lawlessly** *adv*

lawlessness ['lɔləsnəs] *n* : anarquía *f*, desorden *m*

lawmaker ['lɔˌmeɪkər] *n* : legislador *m*, -dora *f*

lawman ['lɔmən] *n, pl* **-men** [-mən, -ˌmɛn] : agente *m* del orden

lawn ['lɔn] *n* : césped *m*, pasto *m*

lawn mower *n* : cortadora *f* de césped

lawsuit ['lɔˌsuːt] *n* : pleito *m*, litigio *m*, demanda *f*

lawyer ['lɔɪər, 'lɔjər] *n* : abogado *m*, -da *f*

lax ['læks] *adj* : laxo, relajado — **laxly** *adv*

laxative ['læksətɪv] *n* : laxante *m*

laxity ['læksəti] *n* : relajación *f*, descuido *m*, falta *f* de rigor

lay¹ ['leɪ] *vt* **laid** ['leɪd]; **laying 1** PLACE, PUT : poner, colocar ⟨she laid it on the table : lo puso en la mesa⟩ ⟨to lay eggs : poner huevos⟩ **2** : hacer ⟨to lay a bet : hacer una apuesta⟩ **3** IMPOSE : imponer ⟨to lay a tax : imponer un impuesto⟩ ⟨to lay the blame on : echarle la culpa a⟩ **4 to lay out** PRESENT : presentar, exponer ⟨he laid out his plan : presentó su proyecto⟩ **5 to lay out** DESIGN : diseñar (el trazado de)

lay² → **lie**¹

lay³ *adj* SECULAR : laico, lego

lay⁴ *n* **1** : disposición *f*, configuración *f* ⟨the lay of the land : la configuración del terreno⟩ **2** BALLAD : romance *m*, balada *f*

layer ['leɪər] *n* **1** : capa *f* (de pintura, etc.), estrato *m* (de roca) **2** : gallina *f* ponedora

layman ['leɪmən] *n, pl* **-men** [-mən, -ˌmɛn] : laico *m*, lego *m*

layoff ['leɪˌɔf] *n* : despido *m*

lay off *vt* : despedir

layout ['leɪˌaʊt] *n* : disposición *f*, distribución *f* (de una casa, etc.), trazado *m* (de una ciudad)

lay up *vt* **1** STORE : guardar, almacenar **2 to be laid up** : estar enfermo, tener que guardar cama

laywoman ['leɪˌwʊmən] *n, pl* **-women** [-ˌwɪmən] : laica *f*, lega *f*

laziness ['leɪzinəs] *n* : pereza *f*, flojera *f*

lazy ['leɪzi] *adj* **-zier; -est** : perezoso, holgazán — **lazily** ['leɪzəli] *adv*

leach ['liːtʃ] *vt* : filtrar

lead¹ ['liːd] *vt* **led** ['lɛd]; **leading 1** GUIDE : conducir, llevar, guiar **2** DIRECT : dirigir **3** HEAD : encabezar, ir al frente de **4 to lead to** : resultar en, llevar a ⟨it only leads to trouble : sólo resulta en problemas⟩

lead² *n* : delantera *f*, primer lugar *m* ⟨to take the lead : tomar la delantera⟩

lead³ ['lɛd] *n* **1** : plomo *m* (metal) **2** : mina *f* (de lápiz) **3 lead poisoning** : saturnismo *m*

leaden ['lɛdən] *adj* **1** : plomizo ⟨a leaden sky : un ciel plomizo⟩ **2** HEAVY : pesado

leader ['liːdər] *n* : jefe *m*, -fa *f*; líder *mf*; dirigente *mf*; gobernante *mf*

leadership ['liːdərˌʃɪp] *n* : mando *m*, dirección *f*

leaf¹ ['liːf] *vi* **1** : echar hojas (dícese de un árbol) **2 to leaf through** : hojear (un libro)

leaf² *n, pl* **leaves** ['li:vz] **1** : hoja *f* (de plantas o libros) **2 to turn over a new leaf** : hacer borrón y cuenta nueva
leafless ['li:fləs] *adj* : sin hojas, pelado
leaflet ['li:flət] *n* : folleto *m*
leafy ['li:fi] *adj* **leafier; -est** : frondoso
league¹ ['li:g] *v* **leagued; leaguing** *vt* : aliar, unir — *vi* : aliarse, unirse
league² *n* **1** : legua *f* (medida de distancia) **2** ASSOCIATION : alianza *f*, sociedad *f*, liga *f*
leak¹ ['li:k] *vt* **1** : perder, dejar escapar (un líquido o un gas) **2** : filtrar (información) — *vi* **1** : gotear, escaparse, fugarse (dícese de un líquido o un gas) **2** : hacer agua (dícese de un bote) **3** : filtrarse, divulgarse (dícese de información)
leak² *n* **1** HOLE : agujero *m* (en recipientes), gotera *f* (en un tejado) **2** ESCAPE : fuga *f*, escape *m* **3** : filtración *f* (de información)
leakage ['li:kɪdʒ] *n* : escape *m*, fuga *f*
leaky ['li:ki] *adj* **leakier; -est** : agujereado (dícese de un recipiente), que hace agua (dícese de un bote), con goteras (dícese de un tejado)
lean¹ ['li:n] *vi* **1** BEND : inclinarse, ladearse **2** RECLINE : reclinarse **3** RELY : apoyarse (en), depender (de) **4** INCLINE, TEND : inclinarse, tender — *vt* : apoyar
lean² *adj* **1** THIN : delgado, flaco **2** : sin grasa, magro (dícese de la carne)
leanness ['li:nnəs] *n* : delgadez *f*
lean–to ['li:n,tu:] *n* : cobertizo *m*
leap¹ ['li:p] *vi* **leaped** ['li:pt, 'lɛpt] *or* **leapt; leaping** : saltar, brincar
leap² *n* : salto *m*, brinco *m*
leap year *n* : año *m* bisiesto
learn ['lərn] *vt* **1** : aprender ⟨to learn to sing : aprender a cantar⟩ **2** MEMORIZE : aprender de memoria **3** DISCOVER : saber, enterarse de — *vi* **1** : aprender ⟨to learn from experience : aprender por experiencia⟩ **2** FIND OUT : enterarse, saber
learned ['lərnəd] *adj* : erudito
learner ['lərnər] *n* : principiante *mf*, estudiante *mf*
learning ['lərnɪŋ] *n* : erudición *f*, saber *m*
lease¹ ['li:s] *vt* **leased; leasing** : arrendar
lease² *n* : contrato *m* de arrendamiento
leash¹ ['li:ʃ] *vt* : atraillar (un animal)
leash² *n* : traílla *f*
least¹ ['li:st] *adv* : menos ⟨when least expected : cuando menos se espera⟩
least² *adj* (*superlative of* **little**) : menor, más mínimo
least³ *n* **1** : lo menos ⟨at least : por lo menos⟩ **2 to say the least** : por no decir más
leather ['lɛðər] *n* : cuero *m*
leathery ['lɛðəri] *adj* : curtido (dícese de la piel), correoso (dícese de la carne)

leave¹ ['li:v] *v* **left** ['lɛft]; **leaving** *vt* **1** BEQUEATH : dejar, legar **2** DEPART : dejar, salir(se) de **3** ABANDON : abandonar, dejar **4** FORGET : dejar, olvidarse de ⟨I left the books at the library : dejé los libros en la biblioteca⟩ **5 to be left** : quedar ⟨it's all I have left : es todo lo que me queda⟩ **6 to be left over** : sobrar **7 to leave out** : omitir, excluir — *vi* : irse, salir, partir, marcharse ⟨she left yesterday morning : se fue ayer por la mañana⟩
leave² *n* **1** PERMISSION : permiso *m* ⟨by your leave : con su permiso⟩ **2** *or* **leave of absence** : permiso *m*, licencia *f* ⟨maternity leave : licencia por maternidad⟩ **3 to take one's leave** : despedirse
leaven ['lɛvən] *n* : levadura *f*
leaves → leaf²
leaving ['li:vɪŋ] *n* **1** : salida *f*, partida *f* **2 leavings** *npl* : restos *mpl*, sobras *fpl*
Lebanese [,lɛbə'ni:z, -'ni:s] *n* : libanés *m*, -nesa *f* — **Lebanese** *adj*
lecherous ['lɛtʃərəs] *adj* : lascivo, libidinoso — **lecherously** *adv*
lechery ['lɛtʃəri] *n* : lascivia *f*, lujuria *f*
lecture¹ ['lɛktʃər] *v* **-tured; -turing** *vi* : dar clase, dictar clase, dar una conferencia — *vt* SCOLD : sermonear, echar una reprimenda a, regañar
lecture² *n* **1** : conferencia *f* **2** REPRIMAND : reprimenda *f*
lecturer ['lɛktʃərər] *n* **1** SPEAKER : conferenciante *mf* **2** TEACHER : profesor *m*, -sora *f*
led → lead¹
ledge ['lɛdʒ] *n* : repisa *f* (de una pared), antepecho *m* (de una ventana), saliente *m* (de una montaña)
ledger ['lɛdʒər] *n* : libro *m* mayor, libro *m* de contabilidad
lee¹ ['li:] *adj* : de sotavento
lee² *n* : sotavento *m*
leech ['li:tʃ] *n* : sanguijuela *f*
leek ['li:k] *n* : puerro *m*
leer¹ ['lɪr] *vi* : mirar con lascivia
leer² *n* : mirada *f* lasciva
leery ['lɪri] *adj* : receloso
lees ['li:z] *npl* : posos *mpl*, heces *fpl*
leeward¹ ['li:wərd, 'lu:ərd] *adj* : de sotavento
leeward² *n* : sotavento *m*
leeway ['li:,weɪ] *n* : libertad *f*, margen *m*
left¹ ['lɛft] *adv* : hacia la izquierda
left² → leave¹
left³ *adj* : izquierdo
left⁴ *n* : izquierda *f* ⟨on the left : a la izquierda⟩
left–hand ['lɛft'hand] *adj* **1** : de la izquierda **2 → left–handed**
left–handed ['lɛft'handəd] *adj* **1** : zurdo (dícese de una persona) **2** : con doble sentido ⟨a left-handed compliment : un cumplido a medias⟩
leftist ['lɛftɪst] *n* : izquierdista *mf* — **leftist** *adj*
leftover ['lɛft,o:vər] *adj* : sobrante, que sobra

leftovers ['lɛft,o:vərz] *npl* : restos *mpl*, sobras *fpl*

left wing *n* **the left wing** : la izquierda

left–winger ['lɛft'wɪŋər] *n* : izquierdista *mf*

leg ['lɛg] *n* **1** : pierna *f* (de una persona, de carne, de ropa), pata *f* (de un animal, de muebles) **2** STAGE : etapa *f* (de un viaje), vuelta *f* (de una carrera)

legacy ['lɛgəsi] *n, pl* **-cies** : legado *m*, herencia *f*

legal ['li:gəl] *adj* **1** : legal, jurídico ⟨legal advisor : asesor jurídico⟩ ⟨the legal profession : la abogacía⟩ **2** LAWFUL : legítimo, legal

legalistic [,li:gə'lɪstɪk] *adj* : legalista

legality [li'gæləti] *n, pl* **-ties** : legalidad *f*

legalize ['li:gə,laɪz] *vt* **-ized; -izing** : legalizar

legally ['li:gəli] *adv* : legalmente

legate ['lɛgət] *n* : legado *m*

legation [lɪ'geɪʃən] *n* : legación *f*

legend ['lɛdʒənd] *n* **1** STORY : leyenda *f* **2** INSCRIPTION : leyenda *f*, inscripción *f* **3** : signos *mpl* convencionales (en un mapa)

legendary ['lɛdʒən,dɛri] *adj* : legendario

legerdemain [,lɛdʒərdə'meɪn] → **sleight of hand**

leggings ['lɛgɪnz, 'lɛgənz] *npl* : mallas *fpl*

legibility [,lɛdʒə'bɪləti] *n* : legibilidad *f*

legible ['lɛdʒəbəl] *adj* : legible

legibly ['lɛdʒəbli] *adv* : de manera legible

legion ['li:dʒən] *n* : legión *f*

legionnaire [,li:dʒə'nær] *n* : legionario *m*, -ria *f*

legislate ['lɛdʒəs,leɪt] *vi* **-lated; -lating** : legislar

legislation [,lɛdʒəs'leɪʃən] *n* : legislación *f*

legislative ['lɛdʒəs,leɪtɪv] *adj* : legislativo, legislador

legislator ['lɛdʒəs,leɪtər] *n* : legislador *m*, -dora *f*

legislature ['lɛdʒəs,leɪtʃər] *n* : asamblea *f* legislativa

legitimacy [lɪ'dʒɪtəməsi] *n* : legitimidad *f*

legitimate [lɪ'dʒɪtəmət] *adj* **1** VALID : legítimo, válido, justificado **2** LAWFUL : legítimo, legal

legitimately [lɪ'dʒɪtəmətli] *adv* : legítimamente

legitimize [lɪ'dʒɪtə,maɪz] *vt* **-mized; -mizing** : legitimar, hacer legítimo

legume ['lɛ,gju:m, lɪ'gju:m] *n* : legumbre *f*

leisure ['li:ʒər, 'lɛ-] *n* **1** : ocio *m*, tiempo *m* libre ⟨a life of leisure : una vida de ocio⟩ **2 to take one's leisure** : reposar **3 at your leisure** : cuando te venga bien, cuando tengas tiempo

leisurely ['li:ʒərli, 'lɛ-] *adj & adv* : lento, sin prisas

lemming ['lɛmɪn] *n* : lemming *m*

lemon ['lɛmən] *n* : limón *m*

lemonade [,lɛmə'neɪd] *n* : limonada *f*

lemony ['lɛməni] *adj* : a limón

lend ['lɛnd] *vt* **lent** ['lɛnt]; **lending 1** : prestar ⟨to lend money : prestar dinero⟩ **2** GIVE : dar ⟨it lends force to his criticism : da fuerza a su crítica⟩ **3 to lend oneself to** : prestarse a

length ['lɛŋkθ] *n* **1** : longitud *f*, largo *m* ⟨10 feet in length : 10 pies de largo⟩ **2** DURATION : duración *f* **3** : trozo *m* (de madera), corte *m* (de tela) **4 to go to any lengths** : hacer todo lo posible **5 at ～** : extensamente ⟨to speak at length : hablar largo y tendido⟩

lengthen ['lɛŋkθən] *vt* **1** : alargar ⟨can they lengthen the dress? : ¿se puede alargar el vestido?⟩ **2** EXTEND, PROLONG : prolongar, extender — *vi* : alargarse, crecer ⟨the days are lengthening : los días están creciendo⟩

lengthways ['lɛŋkθ,weɪz] → **lengthwise**

lengthwise ['lɛŋkθ,waɪz] *adv* : a lo largo, longitudinalmente

lengthy ['lɛŋkθi] *adj* **lengthier; -est 1** OVERLONG : largo y pesado **2** EXTENDED : prolongado, largo

leniency ['li:niəntsi] *n, pl* **-cies** : lenidad *f*, indulgencia *f*

lenient ['li:niənt] *adj* : indulgente, poco severo

leniently ['li:niəntli] *adv* : con lenidad, con indulgencia

lens ['lɛnz] *n* **1** : cristalino *m* (del ojo) **2** : lente *mf* (de un instrumento o una cámara) **3** → **contact lens**

lent → **lend**

Lent ['lɛnt] *n* : Cuaresma *f*

lentil ['lɛntəl] *n* : lenteja *f*

Leo ['li:o:] *n* : Leo *mf*

leopard ['lɛpərd] *n* : leopardo *m*

leotard ['li:ə,tɑrd] *n* : leotardo *m*, malla *f*

leper ['lɛpər] *n* : leproso *m*, -sa *f*

leprechaun ['lɛprə,kɑn] *n* : duende *m* (irlandés)

leprosy ['lɛprəsi] *n* : lepra *f* — **leprous** ['lɛprəs] *adj*

lesbian[1] ['lɛzbiən] *adj* : lesbiano

lesbian[2] *n* : lesbiana *f*

lesbianism ['lɛzbiə,nɪzəm] *n* : lesbianismo *m*

lesion ['li:ʒən] *n* : lesión *f*

less[1] ['lɛs] *adv* (*comparative of* **little**[1]) : menos ⟨the less you know, the better : cuanto menos sepas, mejor⟩ ⟨less and less : cada vez menos⟩

less[2] *adj* (*comparative of* **little**[2]) : menos ⟨less than three : menos de tres⟩ ⟨less money : menos dinero⟩ ⟨nothing less than perfection : nada menos que la perfección⟩

less[3] *pron* : menos ⟨I'm earning less : estoy ganando menos⟩

less[4] *prep* : menos ⟨one month less two days : un mes menos dos días⟩

lessee [lɛ'si:] *n* : arrendatario *m*, -ria *f*

lessen ['lɛsən] *vt* : disminuir, reducir — *vi* : disminuir, reducirse

lesser ['lɛsər] *adj* : menor ⟨to a lesser degree : en menor grado⟩
lesson ['lɛsən] *n* **1** CLASS : clase *f*, curso *m* **2** : lección *f* ⟨the lessons of history : las lecciones de la historia⟩
lessor ['lɛˌsɔr, lˈsɔr] *n* : arrendador *m*, -dora *f*
lest ['lɛst] *conj* : para (que) no ⟨lest we forget : para que no olvidemos⟩
let ['lɛt] *vt* **let; letting 1** ALLOW : dejar, permitir ⟨let me see it : déjame verlo⟩ **2** MAKE : hacer ⟨let me know : házmelo saber, avísame⟩ ⟨let them wait : que esperen, haz que esperen⟩ **3** RENT : alquilar **4** (*used in the first person plural imperative*) ⟨let's go! : ¡vamos!, ¡vámonos!⟩ ⟨let us pray : oremos⟩ **5 to let down** DISAPPOINT : fallar **6 to let off** FORGIVE : perdonar **7 to let out** REVEAL : revelar **8 to let up** ABATE : amainar, disminuir ⟨the pace never lets up : el ritmo nunca disminuye⟩
letdown *n* : chasco *m*, decepción *f*
lethal ['li:θəl] *adj* : letal — **lethally** *adv*
lethargic [lɪˈθɑrʤɪk] *adj* : letárgico
lethargy ['lɛθərʤi] *n* : letargo *m*
let on *vi* **1** ADMIT : reconocer ⟨don't let on! : ¡no digas nada!⟩ **2** PRETEND : fingir
let's ['lɛts] (*contraction of* **let us**) → **let**
letter[1] ['lɛt̬ər] *vt* : marcar con letras, inscribir letras en
letter[2] *n* **1** : letra *f* (del alfabeto) **2** : carta *f* ⟨a letter to my mother : una carta a mi madre⟩ **3 letters** *npl* ARTS : letras *fpl* **4 to the letter** : al pie de la letra
lettering ['lɛt̬ərɪŋ] *n* : letra *f*
lettuce ['lɛt̬əs] *n* : lechuga *f*
leukemia [luːˈkiːmiə] *n* : leucemia *f*
levee ['lɛvi] *n* : dique *m*
level[1] ['lɛvəl] *vt* **-eled** *or* **-elled; -eling** *or* **-elling 1** FLATTEN : nivelar, aplanar **2** AIM : apuntar (una pistola), dirigir (una acusación) **3** RAZE : rasar, arrasar
level[2] *adj* **1** EVEN : llano, plano, parejo **2** CALM : tranquilo ⟨to keep a level head : no perder la cabeza⟩
level[3] *n* : nivel *m*
leveler ['lɛvələr] *n* : nivelador *m*, -dora *f*
levelheaded ['lɛvəlˌhɛdəd] *adj* : sensato, equilibrado
levelly ['lɛvəli] *adv* CALMLY : con ecuanimidad *f*, con calma
levelness ['lɛvəlnəs] *n* : uniformidad *f*
lever ['lɛvər, 'liː-] *n* : palanca *f*
leverage ['lɛvərɪʤ, 'li:-] *n* **1** : apalancamiento *m* (en física) **2** INFLUENCE : influencia *f*, palanca *f* *fam*
leviathan [lɪˈvaɪəθən] *n* : leviatán *m*, gigante *m*
levity ['lɛvət̬i] *n* : ligereza *f*, frivolidad *f*
levy[1] ['lɛvi] *vt* **levied; levying 1** IMPOSE : imponer, exigir, gravar (un impuesto) **2** COLLECT : recaudar (un impuesto)
levy[2] *n, pl* **levies** : impuesto *m*, gravamen *m*
lewd ['lu:d] *adj* : lascivo — **lewdly** *adv*
lewdness ['lu:dnəs] *n* : lascivia *f*

lexical ['lɛksikəl] *adj* : léxico
lexicographer [ˌlɛksəˈkɑgrəfər] *n* : lexicógrafo *m*, -fa *f*
lexicographical [ˌlɛksəkoˈgræfɪkəl] *or* **lexicographic** [-ˈgræfɪk] *adj* : lexicográfico
lexicography [ˌlɛksəˈkɑgrəfi] *n* : lexicografía *f*
lexicon ['lɛksɪˌkɑn] *n, pl* **-ica** [-kə] *or* **-icons** : léxico *m*, lexicón *m*
liability [ˌlaɪəˈbɪlət̬i] *n, pl* **-ties 1** RESPONSIBILITY : responsabilidad *f* **2** SUSCEPTIBILITY : propensión *f* **3** DRAWBACK : desventaja *f* **4 liabilities** *npl* DEBTS : deudas *fpl*, pasivo *m*
liable ['laɪəbəl] *adj* **1** RESPONSIBLE : responsable **2** SUSCEPTIBLE : propenso **3** PROBABLE : probable ⟨it's liable to happen : es probable que suceda⟩
liaison ['liːəˌzɑn, liˈeɪ-] *n* **1** CONNECTION : enlace *m*, relación *f* **2** AFFAIR : amorío *m*, aventura *f*
liar ['laɪər] *n* : mentiroso *m*, -sa *f*; embustero *m*, -ra *f*
libel[1] ['laɪbəl] *vt* **-beled** *or* **-belled; -beling** *or* **-belling** : difamar, calumniar
libel[2] *n* : difamación *f*, calumnia *f*
libeler ['laɪbələr] *n* : difamador *m*, -dora *f*; calumniador *m*, -dora *f*; libelista *mf*
libelous *or* **libellous** ['laɪbələs] *adj* : difamatorio, calumnioso, injurioso
liberal[1] ['lɪbrəl, 'lɪbərəl] *adj* **1** TOLERANT : liberal, tolerante **2** GENEROUS : generoso **3** ABUNDANT : abundante **4 liberal arts** : humanidades *fpl*, artes *fpl* liberales
liberal[2] *n* : liberal *mf*
liberalism ['lɪbrəˌlɪzəm, 'lɪbərə-] *n* : liberalismo *m*
liberality [ˌlɪbəˈrælət̬i] *n, pl* **-ties** : liberalidad *f*, generosidad *f*
liberalize ['lɪbrəˌlaɪz, 'lɪbərə-] *vt* **-ized; -izing** : liberalizar
liberally ['lɪbrəli, 'lɪbərə-] *adv* **1** GENEROUSLY : generosamente **2** ABUNDANTLY : abundantemente **3** FREELY : libremente
liberate ['lɪbəˌreɪt] *vt* **-ated; -ating** : liberar, libertar
liberation [ˌlɪbəˈreɪʃən] *n* : liberación *f*
liberator ['lɪbəˌreɪt̬ər] *n* : libertador *m*, -dora *f*
Liberian [laɪˈbɪriən] *n* : liberiano *m*, -na *f* — **Liberian** *adj*
libertine ['lɪbərˌti:n] *n* : libertino *m*, -na *f*
liberty ['lɪbərt̬i] *n, pl* **-ties 1** : libertad *f* **2 to take the liberty of** : tomarse la libertad de **3 to take liberties with** : tomarse confianzas con, tomarse libertades con
libido [ləˈbi:doː, -ˈbaɪ-] *n, pl* **-dos** : libido *f* — **libidinous** [ləˈbɪdənəs] *adj*
Libra ['li:brə] *n* : Libra *mf*
librarian [laɪˈbrɛriən] *n* : bibliotecario *m*, -ria *f*
library ['laɪˌbrɛri] *n, pl* **-braries** : biblioteca *f*

librettist [lɪˈbrɛtɪst] *n* : libretista *mf*
libretto [lɪˈbrɛto] *n, pl* **-tos** *or* **-ti** [-ţiː] : libreto *m*
Libyan [ˈlɪbiən] *n* : libio *m*, -bia *f* — **Libyan** *adj*
lice → **louse**
license[1] [ˈlaɪsənts] *vt* **licensed; licensing** : licenciar, autorizar, dar permiso a
license[2] *or* **licence** *n* **1** PERMISSION : licencia *f*, permiso *m* **2** PERMIT : licencia *f*, carnet *m Spain* ⟨driver's license : licencia de conducir⟩ **3** FREEDOM : libertad *f* **4** LICENTIOUSNESS : libertinaje *m*
licentious [laɪˈsɛntʃəs] *adj* : licencioso, disoluto — **licentiously** *adv*
licentiousness [laɪˈsɛntʃəsnəs] *n* : libertinaje *m*
lichen [ˈlaɪkən] *n* : liquen *m*
licit [ˈlɪsət] *adj* : lícito
lick[1] [ˈlɪk] *vt* **1** : lamer **2** BEAT : darle una paliza (a alguien)
lick[2] *n* **1** : lamida *f*, lengüetada *f* ⟨a lick of paint : una mano de pintura⟩ **2** BIT : pizca *f*, ápice *m* **3 a lick and a promise** : una lavada a la carrera
licorice [ˈlɪkərɪʃ, -rəs] *n* : regaliz *m*, dulce *m* de regaliz
lid [ˈlɪd] *n* **1** COVER : tapa *f* **2** EYELID : párpado *m*
lie[1] [ˈlaɪ] *vi* **lay** [ˈleɪ]; **lain** [ˈleɪn]; **lying** [ˈlaɪɪŋ] **1** : acostarse, echarse ⟨I lay down : me acosté⟩ **2** : estar, estar situado, encontrarse ⟨the book lay on the table : el libro estaba en la mesa⟩ ⟨the city lies to the south : la ciudad se encuentra al sur⟩ **3** CONSIST : consistir **4 to lie in** : residir en ⟨the power lies in the people : el poder reside en el pueblo⟩
lie[2] *vi* **lied; lying** [ˈlaɪɪŋ] : mentir
lie[3] *n* **1** UNTRUTH : mentira *f* ⟨to tell lies : decir mentiras⟩ **2** POSITION : posición *f*
liege [ˈliːdʒ] *n* : señor *m* feudal
lien [ˈliːn, ˈliːən] *n* : derecho *m* de retención
lieutenant [luˈtɛnənt] *n* : teniente *mf*
lieutenant colonel *n* : teniente *mf* coronel
lieutenant commander *n* : capitán *m*, -tana *f* de corbeta
lieutenant general *n* : teniente *mf* general
life [ˈlaɪf] *n, pl* **lives** [ˈlaɪvz] **1** : vida *f* ⟨plant life : la vida vegetal⟩ **2** EXISTENCE : vida *f*, existencia *f* **3** BIOGRAPHY : biografía *f*, vida *f* **4** DURATION : duración *f*, vida *f* **5** LIVELINESS : vivacidad *f*, animación *f*
lifeblood [ˈlaɪfˌblʌd] *n* : parte *f* vital, sustento *m*
lifeboat [ˈlaɪfˌboːt] *n* : bote *m* salvavidas
lifeguard [ˈlaɪfˌgɑrd] *n* : socorrista *mf*, salvavidas *mf*
lifeless [ˈlaɪfləs] *adj* : sin vida, muerto
lifelike [ˈlaɪfˌlaɪk] *adj* : que parece vivo, natural, verosímil

lifelong [ˈlaɪfˈlɔŋ] *adj* : de toda la vida ⟨a lifelong friend : un amigo de toda la vida⟩
life preserver *n* : salvavidas *m*
lifesaver [ˈlaɪfˌseɪvər] *n* **1** : salvación *f* **2** → **lifeguard**
lifesaving [ˈlaɪfˌseɪvɪŋ] *n* : socorrismo *m*
lifestyle [ˈlaɪfˌstaɪl] *n* : estilo *m* de vida
lifetime [ˈlaɪfˌtaɪm] *n* : vida *f*, curso *m* de la vida
lift[1] [ˈlɪft] *vt* **1** RAISE : levantar, alzar, subir **2** END : levantar ⟨to lift a ban : levantar una prohibición⟩ — *vi* **1** RISE : levantarse, alzarse **2** CLEAR UP : despejar ⟨the fog lifted : se disipó la niebla⟩
lift[2] *n* **1** LIFTING : levantamiento *m*, alzamiento *m* **2** BOOST : impulso *m*, estímulo *m* **3 to give someone a lift** : llevar en coche a alguien
liftoff [ˈlɪftˌɔf] *n* : despegue *m*
ligament [ˈlɪgəmənt] *n* : ligamento *m*
ligature [ˈlɪgəˌtʃur, -tʃər] *n* : ligadura *f*
light[1] [ˈlaɪt] *v* **lit** [ˈlɪt] *or* **lighted; lighting** *vt* **1** ILLUMINATE : iluminar, alumbrar **2** IGNITE : encender, prenderle fuego a — *vi* : encenderse, prender
light[2] *vi* **lighted** *or* **lit** [ˈlɪt]; **lighting 1** LAND, SETTLE : posarse **2** DISMOUNT : bajarse, apearse
light[3] [ˈlaɪt] *adv* **1** LIGHTLY : suavemente, ligeramente **2 to travel light** : viajar con poco equipaje
light[4] *adj* **1** LIGHTWEIGHT : ligero, liviano, poco pesado **2** EASY : fácil, ligero, liviano ⟨light reading : lectura fácil⟩ ⟨light work : trabajo liviano⟩ **3** GENTLE, MILD : fino, suave, leve ⟨a light breeze : una brisa suave⟩ ⟨a light rain : una lluvia fina⟩ **4** FRIVOLOUS : de poca importancia, superficial **5** BRIGHT : bien iluminado, claro **6** PALE : claro (dícese de los colores), rubio (dícese del pelo)
light[5] *n* **1** ILLUMINATION : luz *f* **2** DAYLIGHT : luz *f* del día **3** DAWN : amanecer *m*, madrugada *f* **4** LAMP : lámpara *f* ⟨to turn on off the light : apagar la luz⟩ **5** ASPECT : aspecto *m* ⟨in a new light : con otros ojos⟩ ⟨in the light of : en vista de, a la luz de⟩ **6** MATCH : fósforo *m*, cerillo *m* **7 to bring to light** : sacar a (la) luz
lightbulb [ˈlaɪtˌbʌlb] *n* : bombilla *f*, foco *m*, bombillo *m CA, Col, Ven*
lighten [ˈlaɪtən] *vt* **1** ILLUMINATE : iluminar, dar más luz a **2** : aclararse (el pelo) **3** : aligerar (una carga, etc.) **4** RELIEVE : aliviar **5** GLADDEN : alegrar ⟨it lightened his heart : alegró su corazón⟩
lighter [ˈlaɪtər] *n* : encendedor *m*
lighthearted [ˈlaɪtˈhɑrtəd] *adj* : alegre, despreocupado, desenfadado — **lightheartedly** *adv*
lightheartedness [ˈlaɪtˈhɑrtədnəs] *n* : desenfado *m*, alegría *f*
lighthouse [ˈlaɪtˌhaʊs] *n* : faro *m*

lighting ['laɪtɪŋ] *n* : iluminación *f*
lightly ['laɪtli] *adv* **1** GENTLY : suavemente **2** SLIGHTLY : ligeramente **3** FRIVOLOUSLY : a la ligera **4 to let off lightly** : tratar con indulgencia
lightness ['laɪtnəs] *n* **1** BRIGHTNESS : luminosidad *f*, claridad *f* **2** GENTLENESS : ligereza *f*, suavidad *f*, delicadeza *f* **3** : ligereza *f*, liviandad *f* (de peso)
lightning ['laɪtnɪŋ] *n* : relámpago *m*, rayo *m*
lightning bug → firefly
lightproof ['laɪt,pru:f] *adj* : impenetrable por la luz, opaco
lightweight ['laɪt'weɪt] *adj* : ligero, liviano, de poco peso
light-year ['laɪt,jɪr] *n* : año *m* luz
lignite ['lɪg,naɪt] *n* : lignito *m*
likable *or* **likeable** ['laɪkəbəl] *adj* : simpático, agradable
like¹ ['laɪk] *v* **liked; liking** *vt* **1** : agradar, gustarle (algo a uno) ⟨he likes rice : le gusta el arroz⟩ ⟨she doesn't like flowers : a ella no le gustan las flores⟩ ⟨I like you : me caes bien⟩ **2** WANT : querer, desear ⟨I'd like a hamburger : quiero una hamburguesa⟩ ⟨he would like more help : le gustaría tener más ayuda⟩ — *vi* : querer ⟨do as you like : haz lo que quieras⟩
like² *adj* : parecido, semejante, similar
like³ *n* **1** PREFERENCE : preferencia *f*, gusto *m* **2 the like** : cosa *f* parecida, cosas *fpl* por el estilo ⟨I've never seen the like : nunca he visto cosa parecida⟩
like⁴ *conj* **1** AS IF : como si ⟨they looked at me like I was crazy : se me quedaron mirando como si estuviera loca⟩ **2** AS : como, igual que ⟨she doesn't love you like I do : ella no te quiere como yo⟩
like⁵ *prep* **1** : como, parecido a ⟨she acts like my mother : se comporta como mi madre⟩ ⟨he looks like me : se parece a mí⟩ **2** : propio de, típico de ⟨that's just like her : eso es muy típico de ella⟩ **3** : como ⟨animals like cows : animales como vacas⟩ **4 like this, like that** : así ⟨do it like that : hazlo así⟩
likelihood ['laɪkli,hʊd] *n* : probabilidad *f* ⟨in all likelihood : con toda probabilidad⟩
likely¹ ['laɪkli] *adv* : probablemente ⟨most likely he's sick : lo más probable es que esté enfermo⟩ ⟨they're likely to come : es probable que vengan⟩
likely² *adj* **-lier; -est 1** PROBABLE : probable ⟨to be likely to : ser muy probable que⟩ **2** SUITABLE : apropiado, adecuado **3** BELIEVABLE : verosímil, creíble **4** PROMISING : prometedor
liken ['laɪkən] *vt* : comparar
likeness ['laɪknəs] *n* **1** SIMILARITY : semejanza *f*, parecido *m* **2** PORTRAIT : retrato *m*
likewise ['laɪk,waɪz] *adv* **1** SIMILARLY : de la misma manera, asimismo **2** ALSO : también, además, asimismo

liking ['laɪkɪŋ] *n* **1** FONDNESS : afición *f* (por una cosa), simpatía *f* (por una persona) **2** TASTE : gusto *m* ⟨is it to your liking? : ¿te gusta?⟩
lilac ['laɪlək, -,læk, -,lɑk] *n* : lila *f*
lilt ['lɪlt] *n* : cadencia *f*, ritmo *m* alegre
lily ['lɪli] *n, pl* **lilies 1** : lirio *m*, azucena *f* **2 lily of the valley** : lirio *m* de los valles, muguete *m*
lima bean ['laɪmə] *n* : frijol *m* de media luna
limb ['lɪm] *n* **1** APPENDAGE : miembro *m*, extremidad *f* **2** BRANCH : rama *f*
limber¹ ['lɪmbər] *vi or* **to limber up** : calentarse, prepararse
limber² *adj* : ágil (dícese de las personas), flexible (dícese de los objetos)
limbo ['lɪm,bo:] *n, pl* **-bos 1** : limbo *m* (en la religión) **2** OBLIVION : olvido *m* ⟨the project is in limbo : el proyecto ha caído en el olvido⟩
lime ['laɪm] *n* **1** : cal *f* (óxido) **2** : lima *f* (fruta), limón *m* verde *Mex*
limelight ['laɪm,laɪt] *n* **to be in the limelight** : ser el centro de atención, estar en el candelero
limerick ['lɪmərɪk] *n* : poema *m* jocoso de cinco versos
limestone ['laɪm,sto:n] *n* : piedra *f* caliza, caliza *f*
limit¹ ['lɪmət] *vt* : limitar, restringir
limit² *n* **1** MAXIMUM : límite *m*, máximo *m* ⟨speed limit : límite de velocidad⟩ **2 limits** *npl* : límites *mpl*, confines *mpl* ⟨city limits : límites de la ciudad⟩ **3 that's the limit!** : ¡eso es el colmo!
limitation [,lɪmə'teɪʃən] *n* : limitación *f*, restricción *f*
limited ['lɪmətəd] *adj* : limitado, restringido
limitless ['lɪmətləs] *adj* : ilimitado, sin límites
limousine ['lɪmə,zi:n, ,lɪmə'-] *n* : limusina *f*
limp¹ ['lɪmp] *vi* : cojear
limp² *adj* **1** FLACCID : flácido **2** LANK : lacio (dícese del pelo) **3** WEAK : débil ⟨to feel limp : sentirse desfallecer, sentirse sin fuerzas⟩
limp³ *n* : cojera *f*
limpid ['lɪmpəd] *adj* : límpido, claro
limply ['lɪmpli] *adv* : sin fuerzas
limpness ['lɪmpnəs] *n* : flaccidez *f*, debilidad *f*
linden ['lɪndən] *n* : tilo *m*
line¹ ['laɪn] *v* **lined; lining** *vt* **1** : forrar, cubrir ⟨to line a dress : forrar un vestido⟩ ⟨to line the walls : cubrir las paredes⟩ **2** MARK : rayar, trazar líneas en **3** BORDER : bordear **4** ALIGN : alinear — *vi* **to line up** : ponerse in fila, hacer cola
line² *n* **1** CORD, ROPE : cuerda *f* **2** WIRE : cable *m* ⟨power line : cable eléctrico⟩ **3** : línea *f* (de teléfono) **4** ROW : fila *f*, hilera *f* **5** NOTE : nota *f*, líneas *fpl* ⟨drop me a line : mándame unas líneas⟩ **6** COURSE : línea *f* ⟨line of inquiry : línea

de investigación⟩ **7** AGREEMENT : conformidad *f* ⟨to be in line with : ser conforme a⟩ ⟨to fall into line : estar de acuerdo⟩ **8** OCCUPATION : ocupación *f*, rama *f*, especialidad *f* **9** LIMIT : línea *f*, límite *m* ⟨dividing line : línea divisoria⟩ ⟨to draw the line : fijar límites⟩ **10** SERVICE : línea *f* ⟨bus line : línea de autobuses⟩ **11** MARK : línea *f*, arruga *f* (de la cara)

lineage ['lɪniɪʤ] *n* : linaje *m*, abolengo *m*

lineal ['lɪniəl] *adj* : en línea directa

lineaments ['lɪniəmənts] *npl* : facciones *fpl* (de la cara), rasgos *mpl*

linear ['lɪniər] *adj* : lineal

linen ['lɪnən] *n* : lino *m*

liner ['laɪnər] *n* **1** LINING : forro *m* **2** SHIP : buque *m*, transatlántico *m*

lineup ['laɪn,əp] *n* **1** : fila *f* de sospechosos **2** : formación *f* (en deportes) **3** ALIGNMENT : alineación *f*

linger ['lɪŋgər] *vi* **1** TARRY : quedarse, entretenerse, rezagarse **2** PERSIST : persistir, sobrevivir

lingerie [,lɑnʤə'reɪ, ,lænʒə'ri:] *n* : ropa *f* íntima femenina, lencería *f*

lingo ['lɪŋgo] *n, pl* **-goes 1** LANGUAGE : idioma *m* **2** JARGON : jerga *f*

linguist ['lɪŋgwɪst] *n* : lingüista *mf*

linguistic [lɪŋ'gwɪstɪk] *adj* : lingüístico

linguistics [lɪŋ'gwɪstɪks] *n* : lingüística *f*

liniment ['lɪnəmənt] *n* : linimento *m*

lining ['laɪnɪŋ] *n* : forro *m*

link¹ ['lɪŋk] *vt* : unir, enlazar, conectar — *vi* **to link up** : unirse, conectar

link² *n* **1** : eslabón *m* (de una cadena) **2** BOND : conexión *f*, lazo *m*, vínculo *m*

linkage ['lɪŋkɪʤ] *n* : conexión *f*, unión *f*, enlace *m*

linoleum [lə'no:liəm] *n* : linóleo *m*

linseed oil ['lɪn,si:d] *n* : aceite *m* de linaza

lint ['lɪnt] *n* : pelusa *f*

lintel ['lɪntəl] *n* : dintel *m*

lion ['laɪən] *n* : león *m*

lioness ['laɪənɪs] *n* : leona *f*

lionize ['laɪə,naɪz] *vt* **-ized; -izing** : tratar a una persona como muy importante

lip ['lɪp] *n* **1** : labio *m* **2** EDGE, RIM : pico *m* (de una jarra), borde *m* (de una taza)

lipreading ['lɪp,ri:dɪŋ] *n* : lectura *f* de los labios

lipstick ['lɪp,stɪk] *n* : lápiz *m* de labios, barra *f* de labios

liquefy ['lɪkwə,faɪ] *v* **-fied; -fying** *vt* : licuar — *vi* : licuarse

liqueur [lɪ'kʊr, -'kər, -'kjʊr] *n* : licor *m*

liquid¹ ['lɪkwəd] *adj* : líquido

liquid² *n* : líquido *m*

liquidate ['lɪkwə,deɪt] *vt* **-dated; -dating** : liquidar

liquidation [,lɪkwə'deɪʃən] *n* : liquidación *f*

liquidity [lɪk'wɪdəti] *n* : liquidez *f*

liquor ['lɪkər] *n* : alcohol *m*, bebidas *fpl* alcohólicas, licor *m*

lisp¹ ['lɪsp] *vi* : cecear

lisp² *n* : ceceo *m*

lissome ['lɪsəm] *adj* **1** FLEXIBLE : flexible **2** LITHE : ágil y grácil

list¹ ['lɪst] *vt* **1** ENUMERATE : hacer una lista de, enumerar **2** INCLUDE : poner en una lista, incluir — *vi* : escorar (dícese de un barco)

list² *n* **1** ENUMERATION : lista *f* **2** SLANT : escora *f*, inclinación *f*

listen ['lɪsən] *vi* **1** : escuchar, oír **2 to listen to** HEED : prestar atención a, hacer caso de, escuchar **3 to listen to reason** : atender a razones

listener ['lɪsənər] *n* : oyente *mf*, persona *f* que sabe escuchar

listless ['lɪstləs] *adj* : lánguido, apático — **listlessly** *adv*

listlessness ['lɪstləsnəs] *n* : apatía *f*, languidez *f*, desgana *f*

lit ['lɪt] → **light**

litany ['lɪtəni] *n, pl* **-nies** : letanía *f*

liter ['li:tər] *n* : litro *m*

literacy ['lɪtərəsi] *n* : alfabetismo *m*

literal ['lɪtərəl] *adj* : literal — **literally** *adv*

literary ['lɪtə,rri] *adj* : literario

literate ['lɪtərət] *adj* : alfabetizado

literature ['lɪtərə,tʃʊr, -'tʃər] *n* : literatura *f*

lithe ['laɪð, 'laɪθ] *adj* : ágil y grácil

lithesome ['laɪðsəm, 'laɪθ-] → **lissome**

lithium ['lɪθiəm] *n* : litio *m*

lithograph ['lɪθə,græf] *n* : litografía *f*

lithographer [lɪ'θɑgrəfər, 'lɪθə-,græfər] *n* : litógrafo *m*, -fa *f*

lithography [lɪ'θɑgrəfi] *n* : litografía *f*

lithosphere ['lɪθə,sfɪr] *n* : litosfera *f*

Lithuanian [,lɪθə'weɪniən] *n* **1** : lituano *m* (idioma) **2** : lituano *m*, -na *f* — **Lithuanian** *adj*

litigant ['lɪtɪgənt] *n* : litigante *mf*

litigate ['lɪtə,geɪt] *vi* **-gated; -gating** : litigar

litigation [,lɪtə'geɪʃən] *n* : litigio *m*

litmus paper ['lɪtməs] *n* : papel *m* de tornasol

litter¹ ['lɪtər] *vt* : tirar basura en, ensuciar — *vi* : tirar basura

litter² *n* **1** : camada *f*, cría *f* ⟨a litter of kittens : una cría de gatitos⟩ **2** STRETCHER : camilla *f* **3** RUBBISH : basura *f* **4** : arena *f* higiénica (para gatos)

little¹ ['lɪtəl] *adv* **less** ['lɛs]; **least** ['li:st] **1** : poco ⟨she sings very little : canta muy poco⟩ **2 little did I know that . . .** : no tenía la menor idea de que . . . **3 as little as possible** : lo menos posible

little² *adj* **littler** *or* **less** ['lɛs] *or* **lesser** ['lɛsər]; **littlest** *or* **least** ['li:st] **1** SMALL : pequeño **2** : poco ⟨they speak little Spanish : hablan poco español⟩ ⟨little by little : poco a poco⟩ **3** TRIVIAL : sin importancia, trivial

little³ *n* **1** : poco *m* ⟨little has changed : poco ha cambiado⟩ **2 a little** : un poco, algo ⟨it's a little surprising : es algo sorprendente⟩

Little Dipper → **dipper**

liturgical [lə'tərʤɪkəl] *adj* : litúrgico — **liturgically** [-kli] *adv*

liturgy [ˈlɪtərdʒi] *n, pl* **-gies** : liturgia *f*
livable [ˈlɪvəbəl] *adj* : habitable
live[1] [ˈlɪv] *vi* **lived; living 1** EXIST : vivir ⟨as long as I live : mientras viva⟩ ⟨to live from day to day : vivir al día⟩ **2** : llevar una vida, vivir ⟨he lived simply : llevó una vida sencilla⟩ **3** SUBSIST : mantenerse, vivir **4** RESIDE : vivir, residir
live[2] [ˈlaɪv] *adj* **1** LIVING : vivo **2** BURNING : encendido ⟨a live coal : una brasa⟩ **3** : con corriente ⟨live wires : cables con corriente⟩ **4** : cargado, sin estallar ⟨a live bomb : una bomba sin estallar⟩ **5** CURRENT : de actualidad ⟨a live issue : un asunto de actualidad⟩ **6** : en vivo, en directo ⟨a live interview : una entrevista en vivo⟩
livelihood [ˈlaɪvliˌhʊd] *n* : sustento *m*, vida *f*, medio *m* de vida
liveliness [ˈlaɪvlinəs] *n* : animación *f*, vivacidad *f*
livelong [ˈlɪvˈlɔŋ] *adj* : entero, completo
lively [ˈlaɪvli] *adj* **-lier; -est** : animado, vivaz, vivo, enérgico
liven [ˈlaɪvən] *vt* : animar — *vi* : animarse
liver [ˈlɪvər] *n* : hígado *m*
livery [ˈlɪvəri] *n, pl* **-eries** : librea *f*
lives → **life**
livestock [ˈlaɪvˌstɑk] *n* : ganado *m*
live wire *n* : persona *f* vivaz y muy activa
livid [ˈlɪvəd] *adj* **1** BLACK-AND-BLUE : amoratado **2** PALE : lívido **3** ENRAGED : furioso
living[1] [ˈlɪvɪŋ] *adj* : vivo
living[2] *n* **to make a living** : ganarse la vida
living room *n* : living *m*, sala *f* de estar
lizard [ˈlɪzərd] *n* : lagarto *m*
llama [ˈlɑmə, ˈjɑ-] *n* : llama *f*
load[1] [ˈloːd] *vt* : cargar, embarcar
load[2] *n* **1** CARGO : carga *f* **2** WEIGHT : peso *m* **3** BURDEN : carga *f*, peso *m* **4 loads** *npl* : montón *m*, pila *f*, cantidad *f* ⟨loads of work : un montón de trabajo⟩
loaf[1] [ˈloːf] *vi* : holgazanear, flojear, haraganear
loaf[2] *n, pl* **loaves** [ˈloːvz] **1** : pan *m*, pan *m* de molde, barra *f* de pan **2 meat loaf** : pan *m* de carne
loafer [ˈloːfər] *n* : holgazán *m*, -zana *f*; haragán *m*, -gana *f*; vago *m*, -ga *f*
loam [ˈloːm] *n* : marga *f*, suelo *m*
loan[1] [ˈloːn] *vt* : prestar
loan[2] *n* : préstamo *m*, empréstito *m* (del banco)
loath [ˈloːθ, ˈloːð] *adj* : poco dispuesto ⟨I am loath to say it : me resisto a decirlo⟩
loathe [ˈloːð] *vt* **loathed; loathing** : odiar, aborrecer
loathing [ˈloːðɪŋ] *n* : aversión *f*, odio *m*, aborrecimiento *m*
loathsome [ˈloːθsəm, ˈloːð-] *adj* : odioso, repugnante
lob[1] [ˈlɑb] *vt* **lobbed; lobbing** : hacerle un globo (a otro jugador)

lob[2] *n* : globo *m* (en deportes)
lobby[1] [ˈlɑbi] *v* **-bied; -bying** *vt* : presionar, ejercer presión sobre — *vi* **to lobby for** : presionar para (lograr algo)
lobby[2] *n, pl* **-bies 1** FOYER : vestíbulo *m* **2** LOBBYISTS : grupo *m* de presión, lobby *m*
lobbyist [ˈlɑbiɪst] *n* : miembro *m* de un lobby
lobe [ˈloːb] *n* : lóbulo *m*
lobed [ˈloːbd] *adj* : lobulado
lobotomy [ləˈbɑtəmi, lo-] *n, pl* **-mies** : lobotomía *f*
lobster [ˈlɑbstər] *n* : langosta *f*
local[1] [ˈloːkəl] *adj* : local
local[2] *n* **1** : anestesia *f* local **2 the locals** : los vecinos del lugar, los habitantes
locale [loˈkæl] *n* : lugar *m*, escenario *m*
locality [loˈkæləti] *n, pl* **-ties** : localidad *f*
localize [ˈloːkəˌlaɪz] *vt* **-ized; -izing** : localizar
locally [ˈloːkəli] *adv* : en la localidad, en la zona
locate [ˈloːˌkeɪt, loˈkeɪt] *v* **-cated; -cating** *vt* **1** POSITION : situar, ubicar **2** FIND : localizar, ubicar — *vi* SETTLE : establecerse
location [loˈkeɪʃən] *n* **1** POSITION : posición *f*, emplazamiento *m*, ubicación *f* **2** PLACE : lugar *m*, sitio *m*
lock[1] [ˈlɑk] *vt* **1** FASTEN : cerrar **2** CONFINE : encerrar ⟨they locked me in the room : me encerraron en la sala⟩ **3** IMMOBILIZE : bloquear (una rueda) — *vi* **1** : cerrarse (dícese de una puerta) **2** : trabarse, bloquearse (dícese de una rueda)
lock[2] *n* **1** : mechón *m* (de pelo) **2** FASTENER : cerradura *f*, cerrojo *m*, chapa *f* **3** : esclusa *f* (de un canal)
locker [ˈlɑkər] *n* : armario *m*, cajón *m* con llave, lócker *m*
locket [ˈlɑkət] *n* : medallón *m*, guardapelo *m*, relicario *m*
lockjaw [ˈlɑkˌjɔ] *n* : tétano *m*
lockout [ˈlɑkˌaʊt] *n* : cierre *m* patronal, lockout *m*
locksmith [ˈlɑkˌsmɪθ] *n* : cerrajero *m*, -ra *f*
lockup [ˈlɑkˌʌp] *n* JAIL : cárcel *f*
locomotion [ˌloːkəˈmoːʃən] *n* : locomoción *f*
locomotive[1] [ˌloːkəˈmoːtɪv] *adj* : locomotor
locomotive[2] *n* : locomotora *f*
locust [ˈloːkəst] *n* **1** : langosta *f*, chapulín *m* CA, Mex **2** CICADA : cigarra *f*, chicharra *f* **3** : acacia *f* blanca (árbol)
locution [loˈkjuːʃən] *n* : locución *f*
lode [ˈloːd] *n* : veta *f*, vena *f*, filón *m*
lodestar [ˈloːdˌstɑr] *n* : estrella *f* polar
lodestone [ˈloːdˌstoːn] *n* : piedra *f* imán
lodge[1] [ˈlɑdʒ] *v* **lodged; lodging** *vt* **1** HOUSE : hospedar, alojar **2** FILE : presentar ⟨to lodge a complaint : presentar una demanda⟩ — *vi* **1** : posarse, meterse ⟨the bullet lodged in the door

: la bala se incrustó en la puerta⟩ **2** STAY : hospedarse, alojarse

lodge² n **1** : pabellón m, casa f de campo ⟨hunting lodge : refugio de caza⟩ **2** : madriguera f (de un castor) **3** : logia f ⟨Masonic lodge : logia masónica⟩

lodger ['lɑʤər] n : inquilino m, -na f; huésped m, -peda f

lodging ['lɑʤɪŋ] n **1** : alojamiento m **2 lodgings** npl ROOMS : habitaciones fpl

loft ['lɔft] n **1** ATTIC : desván m, ático m, buhardilla f **2** : loft m (en un depósito comercial) **3** HAYLOFT : pajar m **4** : galería f ⟨choir loft : galería del coro⟩

loftily ['lɔftəli] adv : altaneramente, con altivez

loftiness ['lɔftinəs] n **1** NOBILITY : nobleza f **2** ARROGANCE : altanería f, arrogancia f **3** HEIGHT : altura f, elevación f

lofty ['lɔfti] adj **loftier; -est 1** NOBLE : noble, elevado **2** HAUGHTY : altivo, arrogante, altanero **3** HIGH : majestuoso, elevado

log¹ ['lɔg, 'lɑg] vi **logged; logging 1** : talar (árboles) **2** RECORD : registrar, anotar **3 to log on** : entrar (al sistema) **4 to log off** : salir (del sistema)

log² n **1** : tronco m, leño m **2** RECORD : diario m

logarithm ['lɔgə,rɪðəm, 'lɑ-] n : logaritmo m

logger ['lɔgər, 'lɑ-] n : leñador m, -dora f

loggerhead ['lɔgər,hɛd, 'lɑ-] n **1** : tortuga f boba **2 to be at loggerheads** : estar en pugna, estar en desacuerdo

logic ['lɑʤɪk] n : lógica f — **logical** ['lɑʤɪkəl] adj — **logically** [-kli] adv

logistic [lə'ʤɪstɪk, lo-] adj : logístico

logistics [lə'ʤɪstɪks, lo-] ns & pl : logística f

logo ['lo:,go:] n, pl **logos** [-,go:z] : logotipo m

loin ['lɔɪn] n **1** : lomo m ⟨pork loin : lomo de cerdo⟩ **2 loins** npl : lomos mpl ⟨to gird one's loins : prepararse para la lucha⟩

loiter ['lɔɪtər] vi : vagar, perder el tiempo

loll ['lɑl] vi **1** SLOUCH : repantigarse **2** IDLE : holgazanear, hacer el vago

lollipop or **lollypop** ['lɑli,pɑp] n : dulce m en palito, chupete m Chile, Peru, paleta f CA, Mex

lone ['lo:n] adj **1** SOLITARY : solitario **2** ONLY : único

loneliness ['lo:nlinəs] n : soledad f

lonely ['lo:nli] adj **-lier; -est 1** SOLITARY : solitario, aislado **2** LONESOME : solo ⟨to feel lonely : sentirse muy solo⟩

loner ['lo:nər] n : solitario m, -ria f; recluso m, -sa f

lonesome ['lo:nsəm] adj : solo, solitario

long¹ ['lɔŋ] vi **1 to long for** : añorar, desear, anhelar **2 to long to** : anhelar, estar deseando ⟨they longed to see her : estaban deseando verla, tenían muchas ganas de verla⟩

long² adv **1** : mucho, mucho tiempo ⟨it didn't take long : no llevó mucho tiempo⟩ ⟨will it last long? : ¿va a durar mucho?⟩ **2 all day long** : todo el día **3 as long as** or **so long as** : mientras, con tal que **4 long before** : mucho antes **5 so long!** : ¡hasta luego!, ¡adiós!

long³ adj **longer** ['lɔŋgər]; **longest** ['lɔŋgəst] **1** (indicating length)) : largo ⟨the dress is too long : el vestido es demasiado largo⟩ ⟨a long way from : bastante lejos de⟩ ⟨in the long run : a la larga⟩ **2** (indicating time)) : largo, prolongado ⟨a long illness : una enfermedad prolongada⟩ ⟨a long walk : un paseo largo⟩ ⟨at long last : por fin⟩ **3 to be long on** : estar cargado de

long⁴ n **1 before long** : dentro de poco **2 the long and the short** : lo esencial, lo fundamental

longevity [lɑn'ʤɛvəti] n : longevidad f

longhand ['lɔŋ,hænd] n : escritura f a mano, escritura f cursiva

longhorn ['lɔŋ,hɔrn] n : longhorn mf

longing [lɔŋɪŋ] n : vivo deseo m, ansia f, anhelo m

longingly [lɔŋɪŋli] adv : ansiosamente, con ansia

longitude ['lɑnʤə,tu:d, -,tju:d] n : longitud f

longitudinal [,lɑnʤə'tu:dənəl, -'tju:-] adj : longitudinal — **longitudinally** adv

long-lived ['lɔŋ'lɪvd, -'laɪvd] adj : longevo

longshoreman ['lɔŋ'ʃormən] n, pl **-men** [-mən, -,mɛn] : estibador m, -dora f

long-standing ['lɔŋ'stændɪŋ] adj : de larga data

long-suffering ['lɔŋ'sʌfərɪŋ] adj : paciente, sufrido

look¹ ['lʊk] vi **1** GLANCE : mirar ⟨to look out the window : mirar por la ventana⟩ **2** INVESTIGATE : buscar, mirar ⟨look in the closet : busca en el closet⟩ ⟨look before you leap : mira lo que haces⟩ **3** SEEM : parecer ⟨he looks happy : parece estar contento⟩ ⟨I look like my mother : me parezco a mi madre⟩ **4 to look after** : cuidar, cuidar de **5 to look for** EXPECT : esperar **6 to look for** SEEK : buscar — vt : mirar

look² n **1** GLANCE : mirada f **2** EXPRESSION : cara f ⟨a look of disapproval : una cara de desaprobación⟩ **3** ASPECT : aspecto m, apariencia f, aire m **4 looks** npl : belleza f

lookout ['lʊk,aʊt] n **1** : centinela mf, vigía mf **2 to be on the lookout for** : estar al acecho de, andar a la caza de

loom¹ ['lu:m] vi **1** : aparecer, surgir ⟨the city loomed up in the distance : la ciudad surgió en la distancia⟩ **2** IMPEND : amenazar, ser inminente **3 to loom large** : cobrar mucha importancia

loom² n : telar m

loon ['lu:n] n : somorgujo m, somormujo m

loony or **looney** ['lu:ni] adj **-nier; -est** : loco, chiflado fam

loop¹ ['lu:p] *vt* **1** : hacer lazadas con **2 to loop around** : pasar alrededor de — *vi* **1** : rizar el rizo (dícese de un avión) **2** : serpentear (dícese de una carretera)
loop² *n* **1** : lazada *f* (en hilo o cuerda) **2** BEND : curva *f* **3** CIRCUIT : circuito *m* cerrado **4** : rizo *m* (en la aviación) ⟨to loop the loop : rizar el rizo⟩
loophole ['lu:p,ho:l] *n* : escapatoria *f*, pretexto *m*
loose¹ ['lu:s] *vt* **loosed; loosing 1** RELEASE : poner en libertad, soltar **2** UNTIE : deshacer, desatar **3** DISCHARGE, UNLEASH : descargar, desatar
loose² → **loosely**
loose³ *adj* **looser; -est 1** INSECURE : flojo, suelto, poco seguro ⟨a loose tooth : un diente flojo⟩ **2** ROOMY : suelto, holgado ⟨loose clothing : ropa holgada⟩ **3** OPEN : suelto, abierto ⟨loose soil : suelo suelto⟩ ⟨a loose weave : una tejida abierta⟩ **4** FREE : suelto ⟨to break loose : soltarse⟩ **5** SLACK : flojo, flexible **6** APPROXIMATE : libre, aproximado ⟨a loose translation : una traducción aproximada⟩
loosely ['lu:sli] *adv* **1** : sin apretar **2** ROUGHLY : aproximadamente, más o menos
loosen ['lu:sən] *vt* : aflojar
loose-leaf ['lu:s'li:f] *adj* : de hojas sueltas
looseness ['lu:snəs] *n* **1** : aflojamiento *m*, holgura *f* (de ropa) **2** IMPRECISION : imprecisión *f*
loot¹ ['lu:t] *vt* : saquear, robar
loot² *n* : botín *m*
looter ['lu:ṭər] *n* : saqueador *m*, -dora *f*
lop ['lɑp] *vt* **lopped; lopping** : cortar, podar
lope¹ ['lo:p] *vi* **loped; loping** : correr a paso largo
lope² *n* : paso *m* largo
lopsided ['lɑp,saɪdəd] *adj* **1** CROOKED : torcido, chueco, ladeado **2** ASYMETRICAL : asimétrico
loquacious [lo'kweɪʃəs] *adj* : locuaz
lord ['lɔrd] *n* **1** : señor *m*, noble *m* **2** : lord *m* (en la Gran Bretaña) **3 the Lord** : el Señor **4 good Lord!** : ¡Dios mío!
lordly ['lɔrdli] *adj* **-lier; -est** HAUGHTY : arrogante, altanero
lordship ['lɔrd,ʃɪp] *n* : señoría *f*
Lord's Supper *n* : Eucaristía *f*
lore ['lor] *n* : saber *m* popular, tradición *f*
lose ['lu:z] *v* **lost** ['lɔst]; **losing** ['lu:-zɪŋ] *vt* **1** : perder ⟨I lost my umbrella : perdí mi paraguas⟩ ⟨to lose blood : perder sangre⟩ ⟨to lose one's voice : quedarse fónico⟩ ⟨to have nothing to lose : no tener nada que perder⟩ ⟨to lose no time : no perder tiempo⟩ ⟨to lose weight : perder peso, adelgazar⟩ ⟨to lose one's temper : perder los estribos, enojarse, enfadarse⟩ ⟨to lose sight of : perder de vista⟩ **2** : costar, hacer perder ⟨the errors lost him his job : los errores le

costaron su empleo⟩ **3** : atrasar ⟨my watch loses 5 minutes a day : mi reloj atrasa 5 minutos por día⟩ **4 to lose oneself** : perderse, ensimismarse — *vi* **1** : perder ⟨we lost to the other team : perdimos contra el otro equipo⟩ **2** : atrasarse ⟨the clock loses time : el reloj se atrasa⟩
loser ['lu:zər] *n* : perdedor *m*, -dora *f*
loss ['lɔs] *n* **1** LOSING : pérdida *f* ⟨loss of memory : pérdida de memoria⟩ ⟨to sell at a loss : vender con pérdida⟩ ⟨to be at a loss to : no saber como⟩ **2** DEFEAT : derrota *f*, juego *m* perdido **3 losses** *npl* DEATHS : muertos *mpl*
lost ['lɔst] *adj* **1** : perdido ⟨a lost cause : una causa perdida⟩ ⟨lost in thought : absorto⟩ **2 to get lost** : perderse **3 to make up for lost time** : recuperar el tiempo perdido
lot ['lɑt] *n* **1** DRAWING : sorteo *m* ⟨by lot : por sorteo⟩ **2** SHARE : parte *f*, porción *f* **3** FATE : suerte *f* **4** LAND, PLOT : terreno *m*, solar *m*, lote *m*, parcela *f* ⟨parking lot : estacionamiento⟩ **5 a lot of** *or* **lots of** : mucho, un montón de, bastante ⟨lots of books : un montón de libros, muchos libros⟩ ⟨a lot of people : mucha gente⟩
loth ['lo:θ, 'lo:ð] → **loath**
lotion ['lo:ʃən] *n* : loción *f*
lottery ['lɑṭəri] *n, pl* **-teries** : lotería *f*
lotus ['lo:ṭəs] *n* : loto *m*
loud¹ ['laʊd] *adv* : alto, fuerte ⟨out loud : en voz alta⟩
loud² *adj* **1** : alto, fuerte ⟨a loud voice : una voz alta⟩ **2** NOISY : ruidoso ⟨a loud party : una fiesta ruidosa⟩ **3** FLASHY : llamativo, chillón
loudly ['laʊdli] *adv* : alto, fuerte, en voz alta
loudness ['laʊdnəs] *n* : volumen *m*, fuerza *f* (del ruido)
loudspeaker ['laʊd,spi:kər] *n* : altavoz *m*, altoparlante *m*
lounge¹ ['laʊnʤ] *vi* **lounged; lounging** : holgazanear, gandulear
lounge² *n* : salón *m*, sala *f* de estar
louse ['laʊs] *n, pl* **lice** ['laɪs] : piojo *m*
lousy ['laʊzi] *adj* **lousier; -est 1** : piojoso, lleno de piojos **2** BAD : pésimo, muy malo
lout ['laʊt] *n* : bruto *m*, patán *m*
louver *or* **louvre** ['lu:vər] *n* : persiana *f*, listón *m* de persiana
lovable ['lʌvəbəl] *adj* : adorable, amoroso, encantador
love¹ ['lʌv] *v* **loved; loving** *vt* **1** : querer, amar ⟨I love you : te quiero⟩ **2** ENJOY : encantarle a alguien, ser (muy) aficionado a, gustarle mucho a uno (algo) ⟨she loves flowers : le encantan las flores⟩ ⟨he loves golf : es muy aficionado al golf⟩ ⟨I'd love to go with you : me gustaría mucho acompañarte⟩ — *vi* : querer, amar
love² *n* **1** : amor *m*, cariño *m* ⟨to be in love with : estar enamorado de⟩ ⟨to fall

in love with : enamorarse de⟩ **2** EN-THUSIASM, INTEREST : amor *m*, afición *m*, gusto *m* ⟨love of music : afición a la música⟩ **3** BELOVED : amor *m*; amado *m*, -da *f*; enamorado *m*, -da *f*
loveless ['lʌvləs] *adj* : sin amor
loveliness ['lʌvlinəs] *n* : belleza *f*, hermosura *f*
lovelorn ['lʌv,lɔrn] *adj* : herido de amor, perdidamente enamorado
lovely ['lʌvli] *adj* **-lier; -est** : hermoso, bello, lindo, precioso
lover ['lʌvər] *n* : amante *mf* (de personas); aficionado *m*, -da *f* (a alguna actividad)
loving ['lʌvɪŋ] *adj* : amoroso, cariñoso
lovingly ['lʌvɪŋli] *adv* : cariñosamente
low[1] ['lo:] *vi* : mugir
low[2] *adv* : bajo, profundo ⟨to aim low : apuntar bajo⟩ ⟨to lie low : mantenerse escondido⟩ ⟨to turn the lights down low : bajar las luces⟩
low[3] *adj* **lower** ['lo:ər]; **-est 1** : bajo ⟨a low building : un edificio bajo⟩ ⟨a low bow : una profunda reverencia⟩ **2** SOFT : bajo, suave ⟨in a low voice : en voz baja⟩ **3** SHALLOW : bajo, poco profundo **4** HUMBLE : humilde, modesto **5** DEPRESSED : deprimido, bajo de moral **6** INFERIOR : bajo, inferior **7** UNFAVORABLE : mal ⟨to have a low opinion of him : tener un mal concepto de él⟩ **8 to be low on** : tener poco de, estar escaso de
low[4] *n* **1** : punto *m* bajo ⟨to reach an all-time low : estar más bajo que nunca⟩ **2** *or* **low gear** : primera velocidad *f* **3** : mugido *m* (de una vaca)
lowbrow ['lo:,brau] *n* : persona *f* inculta
lower[1] ['lo:ər] *vt* **1** DROP : bajar ⟨to lower one's voice : bajar la voz⟩ **2** : arriar, bajar ⟨to lower the flag : arriar la bandera⟩ **3** REDUCE : reducir, bajar **4 to lower oneself** : rebajarse
lower[2] ['lo:ər] *adj* : inferior, más bajo, de abajo
lowland ['lo:lənd, -,lænd] *n* : tierras *fpl* bajas
lowly ['lo:li] *adj* **-lier; -est** : humilde, modesto
loyal ['lɔɪəl] *adj* : leal, fiel — **loyally** *adv*
loyalist ['lɔɪəlɪst] *n* : partidario *m*, -ria *f* del régimen
loyalty ['lɔɪəlti] *n, pl* **-ties** : lealtad *f*, fidelidad *f*
lozenge ['lazəndʒ] *n* : pastilla *f*
LSD [,ɛl,ɛs'di:] *n* : LSD *m*
lubricant ['lu:brɪkənt] *n* : lubricante *m*
lubricate ['lu:brɪ,keɪt] *vt* **-cated; -cating** : lubricar — **lubrication** [,lu:brɪ'keɪʃən] *n*
lucid ['lu:səd] *adj* : lúcido, claro — **lucidly** *adv*
lucidity [lu:'sɪdəti] *n* : lucidez *f*
luck ['lʌk] *n* **1** : suerte *f* **2 to have bad luck** : tener mala suerte **3 good luck!** : ¡(buena) suerte!
luckily ['lʌkəli] *adv* : afortunadamente, por suerte

luckless ['lʌkləs] *adj* : desafortunado
lucky ['lʌki] *adj* **luckier; -est 1** : afortunado, que tiene suerte ⟨a lucky woman : una mujer afortunada⟩ **2** FORTUITOUS : fortuito, de suerte **3** OPPORTUNE : oportuno **4** : de (la) suerte ⟨lucky number : número de la suerte⟩
lucrative ['lu:krətɪv] *adj* : lucrativo, provechoso — **lucratively** *adv*
ludicrous ['lu:dəkrəs] *adj* : ridículo, absurdo — **ludicrously** *adv*
ludicrousness ['lu:dəkrəsnəs] *n* : ridiculez *f*, absurdo *m*
lug ['lʌg] *vt* **lugged; lugging** : arrastrar, transportar con dificultad
luggage ['lʌgɪdʒ] *n* : equipaje *m*
lugubrious [lʊ'gu:briəs] *adj* : lúgubre — **lugubriously** *adv*
lukewarm ['lu:k'wɔrm] *adj* **1** TEPID : tibio **2** HALFHEARTED : poco entusiasta
lull[1] ['lʌl] *vt* **1** CALM, SOOTHE : calmar, sosegar **2 to lull to sleep** : arrullar, adormecer
lull[2] *n* : calma *f*, pausa *f*
lullaby ['lʌlə,baɪ] *n, pl* **-bies** : canción *f* de cuna, arrullo *m*, nana *f*
lumber[1] ['lʌmbər] *vt* : aserrar (madera) — *vi* : moverse pesadamente
lumber[2] *n* : madera *f*
lumberjack ['lʌmbər,dʒæk] *n* : leñador *m*, -dora *f*
lumberyard ['lʌmbər,jard] *n* : almacén *m* de maderas
luminary ['lu:mə,nɛri] *n, pl* **-naries** : lumbrera *f*, luminaria *f*
luminescence [,lu:mə'nɛsənts] *n* : luminiscencia *f* — **luminescent** [-'nɛsənt] *adj*
luminosity [,lu:mə'nasəti] *n, pl* **-ties** : luminosidad *f*
luminous ['lu:mənəs] *adj* : luminoso — **luminously** *adv*
lump[1] ['lʌmp] *vt or* **to lump together** : juntar, agrupar, amontonar — *vi* CLUMP : agruparse, aglutinarse
lump[2] *n* **1** GLOB : grumo *m* **2** PIECE : pedazo *m*, trozo *m*, terrón *m* ⟨a lump of coal : un trozo de carbón⟩ ⟨a lump of sugar : un terrón de azúcar⟩ **3** SWELLING : bulto *m*, hinchazón *f*, protuberancia *f* **4 to have a lump in one's throat** : tener un nudo en la garganta
lumpy ['lʌmpi] *adj* **lumpier; -est 1** : lleno de grumos (dícese de una salsa) **2** UNEVEN : desigual, disparejo
lunacy ['lu:nəsi] *n, pl* **-cies** : locura *f*
lunar ['lu:nər] *adj* : lunar
lunatic[1] ['lu:nə,tɪk] *adj* : lunático, loco
lunatic[2] *n* : loco *m*, -ca *f*
lunch[1] ['lʌntʃ] *vi* : almorzar, comer
lunch[2] *n* : almuerzo *m*, comida *f*, lonche *m*
luncheon ['lʌntʃən] *n* **1** : comida *f*, almuerzo *m* **2 luncheon meat** : fiambres *fpl*

lung ['lʌŋ] *n* : pulmón *m*
lunge¹ ['lʌndʒ] *vi* **lunged; lunging 1**
THRUST : atacar (en la esgrima) **2 to
lunge forward** : arremeter, lanzarse
lunge² *n* **1** : arremetida *f*, embestida *f* **2**
: estocada *f* (en la esgrima)
lurch¹ ['lərtʃ] *vi* **1** PITCH : cabecear, dar
bandazos, dar sacudidas **2** STAGGER
: tambalearse
lurch² *n* **1** : sacudida *f*, bandazo *m* (de
un vehículo) **2** : tambaleo *m* (de una
persona)
lure¹ ['lʊr] *vt* **lured; luring** : atraer
lure² *n* **1** ATTRACTION : atractivo *m* **2**
ENTICEMENT : señuelo *m*, aliciente
m **3** BAIT : cebo *m* artificial (en la
pesca)
lurid ['lʊrəd] *adj* **1** GRUESOME : espeluznante, horripilante **2** SENSA-
TIONAL : sensacionalista, chocante **3**
GAUDY : chillón
lurk ['lərk] *vi* : estar al acecho
luscious ['lʌʃəs] *adj* **1** DELICIOUS : delicioso, exquisito **2** SEDUCTIVE : seductor, cautivador
lush ['lʌʃ] *adj* **1** LUXURIANT : exuberante, lozano **2** LUXURIOUS : suntuoso,
lujoso
lust¹ ['lʌst] *vi* **to lust after** : desear (a una
persona), codiciar (riquezas, etc.)
lust² *n* **1** LASCIVIOUSNESS : lujuria *f*, lascivia *f* **2** CRAVING : deseo *m*, ansia *f*,
anhelo *m*
luster *or* **lustre** ['lʌstər] *n* **1** GLOSS,

SHEEN : lustre *m*, brillo *m* **2** SPLEN-
DOR : lustre *m*, esplendor *m*
lusterless ['lʌstərləs] *adj* : deslustrado,
sin brillo
lustful ['lʌstfəl] *adj* : lujurioso, lascivo,
lleno de deseo
lustrous ['lʌstrəs] *adj* : brillante, brilloso, lustroso
lusty ['lʌsti] *adj* **lustier; -est** : fuerte, robusto, vigoroso — **lustily** ['lʌstəli] *adv*
lute ['luːt] *n* : laúd *m*
luxuriant [ˌlʌg'ʒʊriənt, ˌlʌk'ʃʊr-] *adj* **1**
: exuberante, lozano (dícese de las
plantas) **2** : abundante y hermoso
(dícese del pelo) — **luxuriantly** *adv*
luxuriate [ˌlʌg'ʒʊriˌeɪt, ˌlʌk'ʃʊr-] *vi*
-ated; -ating 1 : disfrutar **2 to luxuriate in** : deleitarse con
luxurious [ˌlʌg'ʒʊriəs, ˌlʌk'ʃʊr-] *adj* : lujoso, suntuoso — **luxuriously** *adv*
luxury ['lʌkʃəri, 'lʌgʒə-] *n, pl* **-ries** : lujo
m
lye ['laɪ] *n* : lejía *f*
lying → **lie¹, lie²**
lymph ['lɪmpf] *n* : linfa *f*
lymphatic [lɪm'fætɪk] *adj* : linfático
lynch ['lɪntʃ] *vt* : linchar
lynx ['lɪŋks] *n, pl* **lynx** *or* **lynxes** : lince
m
lyre ['laɪr] *n* : lira *f*
lyric¹ ['lɪrɪk] *adj* : lírico
lyric² *n* **1** : poema *m* lírico **2 lyrics** *npl*
: letra *f* (de una canción)
lyrical ['lɪrɪkəl] *adj* : lírico, elocuente

M

m ['ɛm] *n, pl* **m's** *or* **ms** ['ɛmz] : deci-
motercera letra del alfabeto inglés
ma'am ['mæm] → **madam**
macabre [mə'kɑb, -'kɑbər, -'kɑbrə] *adj*
: macabro
macadam [mə'kædəm] *n* : macadán *m*
macaroni [ˌmækə'roːni] *n* : macarrones
mpl
macaroon [ˌmækə'ruːn] *n* : macarrón *m*,
mostachón *m*
macaw [mə'kɔ] *n* : guacamayo *m*
mace ['meɪs] *n* **1** : maza *f* (arma o símbolo) **2** : macis *f* (especia)
machete [mə'ʃɛti] *n* : machete *m*
machination [ˌmækə'neɪʃən, ˌmæʃə-] *n*
: maquinación *f*, intriga *f*
machine¹ [mə'ʃiːn] *vt* **-chined; -chining**
: trabajar a máquina
machine² *n* **1** : máquina *f* ⟨machine
shop : taller de máquinas⟩ ⟨machine
language : lenguaje de la máquina⟩ **2**
: aparato *m*, maquinaria *f* (en política)
machine gun *n* : ametralladora *f*
machinery [mə'ʃiːnəri] *n, pl* **-eries 1**
: maquinaria *f* **2** WORKS : mecanismo
m
machinist [mə'ʃiːnɪst] *n* : maquinista *mf*
machismo [mɑ'tʃiːzmoː] *n* : machismo
m, masculinidad *f*

macho ['mɑtʃoː] *adj* : machote, macho
mackerel ['mækərəl] *n, pl* **-el** *or* **-els** : caballa *f*
mackinaw ['mækəˌnɔ] *n* : chaqueta *f* escocesa de lana
mad ['mæd] *adj* **madder; maddest 1** IN-
SANE : loco, demente **2** RABID : rabioso **3** FOOLISH : tonto, insensato **4**
ANGRY : enojado, furioso **5** CRAZY
: loco ⟨I'm mad about you : estoy loco
por ti⟩
Madagascan [ˌmædə'gæskən] *n* : malgache *mf* — **Madagascan** *adj*
madam ['mædəm] *n, pl* **mesdames**
[meɪ'dɑm, -'dæm] : señora *f*
madcap¹ ['mædˌkæp] *adj* ZANY : alocado, disparatado
madcap² *n* : alocado *m*, -da *f*
madden ['mædən] *vt* : enloquecer, enfurecer
maddening ['mædənɪŋ] *adj* : enloquecedor, exasperante ⟨I find it maddening : me saca de quicio⟩
made → **make¹**
madhouse ['mædˌhaʊs] *n* : manicomio
m ⟨the office was a madhouse : la oficina parecía una casa de locos⟩
madly ['mædli] *adv* : como un loco, locamente

madman ['mæd,mæn, -mən] *n, pl* **-men** [-mən, -,mɛn] : loco *m*, demente *m*
madness ['mædnəs] *n* : locura *f*, demencia *f*
madwoman ['mæd,wʊmən] *n, pl* **-women** [-,wɪmən] : loca *f*, demente *f*
maelstrom ['meɪlstrəm] *n* : remolino *m*, vorágine *f*
maestro ['maɪ,stroː] *n, pl* **-stros** *or* **-stri** [-,striː] : maestro *m*
Mafia ['mɑfiə] *n* : Mafia *f*
magazine ['mægə,ziːn] *n* **1** STOREHOUSE : almacén *m*, polvorín *m* (de explosivos) **2** PERIODICAL : revista *f* **3** : cargador *m* (de un arma de fuego)
magenta [mə'dʒɛntə] *n* : magenta *f*, color *m* magenta
maggot ['mægət] *n* : gusano *m*
magic¹ ['mædʒɪk] *or* **magical** ['mædʒɪkəl] *adj* : mágico
magic² *n* : magia *f*
magically ['mædʒɪkli] *adv* : mágicamente ⟨they magically appeared : aparecieron como por arte de magia⟩
magician [mə'dʒɪʃən] *n* **1** SORCERER : mago *m*, -ga *f* **2** CONJURER : prestidigitador *m*, -dora *f*; mago *m*, -ga *f*
magistrate ['mædʒə,streɪt] *n* : magistrado *m*, -da *f*
magma ['mægmə] *n* : magma *m*
magnanimity [,mægnə'nɪməti] *n, pl* **-ties** : magnanimidad *f*
magnanimous [mæg'nænəməs] *adj* : magnánimo, generoso — **magnanimously** *adv*
magnate ['mæg,neɪt, -nət] *n* : magnate *mf*
magnesium [mæg'niːziəm, -ʒəm] *n* : magnesio *m*
magnet ['mægnət] *n* : imán *m*
magnetic [mæg'nɛtɪk] *adj* : magnético — **magnetically** [-t̬ɪkli] *adv*
magnetic field *n* : campo *m* magnético
magnetism ['mægnə,tɪzəm] *n* : magnetismo *m*
magnetize ['mægnə,taɪz] *vt* **-tized; -tizing 1** : magnetizar, imantar **2** ATTRACT : magnetizar, atraer
magnification [,mægnəfə'keɪʃən] *n* : aumento *m*, ampliación *f*
magnificence [mæg'nɪfəsənts] *n* : magnificencia *f*
magnificent [mæg'nɪfəsənt] *adj* : magnífico — **magnificently** *adv*
magnify ['mægnə,faɪ] *vt* **-fied; -fying 1** ENLARGE : ampliar **2** EXAGGERATE : magnificar, exagerar
magnifying glass *n* : lupa *f*
magnitude ['mægnə,tuːd, -,tjuːd] *n* **1** GREATNESS : magnitud *f*, grandeza *f* **2** QUANTITY : cantidad *f* **3** IMPORTANCE : magnitud *f*, envergadura *f*
magnolia [mæg'noːljə] *n* : magnolia *f* (flor), magnolio *m* (árbol)
magpie ['mæg,paɪ] *n* : urraca *f*
mahogany [mə'hɑgəni] *n, pl* **-nies** : caoba *f*

maid ['meɪd] *n* **1** MAIDEN : doncella *f* **2** *or* **maidservant** ['meɪd,sərvənt] : sirvienta *f*, muchacha *f*, mucama *f*, criada *f*
maiden¹ ['meɪdən] *adj* **1** UNMARRIED : soltera **2** FIRST : primero ⟨maiden voyage : primera travesía⟩
maiden² *n* : doncella *f*
maidenhood ['meɪdən,hʊd] *n* : doncellez *f*
maiden name *n* : nombre *m* de soltera
mail¹ ['meɪl] *vt* : enviar por correo, echar al correo
mail² *n* **1** : correo *m* ⟨airmail : correo aéreo⟩ **2** : malla *f* ⟨coat of mail : cota de malla⟩
mailbox ['meɪl,bɑks] *n* : buzón *m*
mailman ['meɪl,mæn, -mən] *n, pl* **-men** [-mən, -,mn] : cartero *m*
maim ['meɪm] *vt* : mutilar, desfigurar, lisiar
main¹ ['meɪn] *adj* : principal, central ⟨the main office : la oficina central⟩
main² *n* **1** HIGH SEAS : alta mar *f* **2** : tubería *f* principal (de agua o gas), cable *m* principal (de un circuito) **3** with **might and main** : con todas sus fuerzas
mainframe ['meɪn,freɪm] *n* : mainframe *m*, computadora *f* central
mainland ['meɪn,lænd, -lənd] *n* : continente *m*
mainly ['meɪnli] *adv* **1** PRINCIPALLY : principalmente, en primer lugar **2** MOSTLY : principalmente, en la mayor parte
mainstay ['meɪn,steɪ] *n* : pilar *m*, sostén *m* principal
mainstream¹ ['meɪn,striːm] *adj* : dominante, corriente, convencional
mainstream² *n* : corriente *f* principal
maintain [meɪn'teɪn] *vt* **1** SERVICE : dar mantenimiento a (una máquina) **2** PRESERVE : mantener, conservar ⟨to maintain silence : guardar silencio⟩ **3** SUPPORT : mantener, sostener **4** ASSERT : mantener, sostener, afirmar
maintenance ['meɪntənənts] *n* : mantenimiento *m*
maize ['meɪz] *n* : maíz *m*
majestic [mə'dʒɛstɪk] *adj* : majestuoso — **majestically** [-t̬ɪkli] *adv*
majesty ['mædʒəsti] *n, pl* **-ties 1** : majestad *f* ⟨Your Majesty : su Majestad⟩ **2** SPLENDOR : majestuosidad *f*, esplendor *m*
major¹ ['meɪdʒər] *vi* **-jored; -joring** : especializarse
major² *adj* **1** GREATER : mayor **2** NOTEWORTHY : mayor, notable **3** SERIOUS : grave **4** : mayor (en la música)
major³ *n* **1** : mayor *mf*, comandante *mf* (en las fuerzas armadas) **2** : especialidad *f* (universitaria)
Majorcan [mɑ'dʒɔrkən, mə-, -'jɔr-] *n* : mallorquín *m*, -quina *f* — **Majorcan** *adj*
major general *n* : general *mf* de división

majority [mə'dʒɔrəti] *n, pl* **-ties** 1 ADULTHOOD : mayoría *f* de edad 2 : mayoría *f*, mayor parte *f* ⟨the vast majority : la inmensa mayoría⟩

make¹ ['meɪk] *v* **made** ['meɪd;]; **making** *vt* 1 CREATE : hacer ⟨to make noise : hacer ruido⟩ 2 FASHION, MANUFACTURE : hacer, fabricar ⟨she made a dress : hizo un vestido⟩ 3 DEVISE, FORM : desarrollar, elaborar, formar 4 CONSTITUTE : hacer, constituir ⟨made of stone : hecho de piedra⟩ 5 PREPARE : hacer, preparar 6 RENDER : hacer, poner ⟨it makes him nervous : lo pone nervioso⟩ ⟨to make someone happy : hacer feliz a alguien⟩ ⟨it made me sad : me dio pena⟩ 7 PERFORM : hacer ⟨to make a gesture : hacer un gesto⟩ 8 COMPEL : hacer, forzar, obligar 9 EARN : ganar ⟨to make a living : ganarse la vida⟩ — *vi* 1 HEAD : ir, dirigirse ⟨we made for home : nos fuimos a casa⟩ 2 **to make do** : arreglárselas 3 **to make good** REPAY : pagar 4 **to make good** SUCCEED : tener éxito

make² *n* BRAND : marca *f*

make–believe¹ [ˌmeɪkbə'li:v] *adj* : imaginario

make–believe² *n* : fantasía *f*, invención *f* ⟨a world of make-believe : un mundo de ensueño⟩

make out *vt* 1 WRITE : hacer (un cheque) 2 DISCERN : distinguir, divisar 3 UNDERSTAND : comprender, entender — *vi* : arreglárselas ⟨how did you make out? : ¿qué tal te fue?⟩

maker ['meɪkər] *n* : fabricante *mf*

makeshift ['meɪkˌʃɪft] *adj* : provisional, improvisado

makeup ['meɪkˌʌp] *n* 1 COMPOSITION : composición *f* 2 CHARACTER : carácter *m*, temperamento *m* 3 COSMETICS : maquillaje *m*

make up *vt* 1 INVENT : inventar 2 : recuperar ⟨she made up the time : recuperó las horas perdidas⟩ — *vi* RECONCILE : hacer las paces, reconciliarse

making ['meɪkɪŋ] *n* 1 : creación *f*, producción *f* ⟨in the making : en ciernes⟩ 2 **to have the makings of** : tener madera de (dícese de personas), tener los ingredientes para

maladjusted [ˌmælə'dʒʌstəd] *adj* : inadaptado

malady ['mælədi] *n, pl* **-dies** : dolencia *f*, enfermedad *f*, mal *m*

malaise [mə'leɪz, mæ-] *n* : malestar *m*

malapropism ['mælə,prɑ,pɪzəm] *n* : uso *m* incorrecto y cómico de una palabra

malaria [mə'lɛriə] *n* : malaria *f*, paludismo *m*

malarkey [mə'lɑrki] *n* : tonterías *fpl*, estupideces *fpl*

Malawian [mə'lɑwiən] *n* : malauiano *m*, -na *f* — **Malawian** *adj*

Malay [mə'leɪ, 'meɪˌleɪ] *n* 1 *or* **Malayan** [mə'leɪən, meɪ-; 'meɪˌleɪən] : malayo *m*,

-ya *f* 2 : malayo *m* (idioma) — **Malay** *or* **Malayan** *adj*

Malaysian [mə'leɪʒən, -ʃən] *n* : malasio *m*, -sia *f*; malaisio *m*, -sia *f* — **Malaysian** *adj*

male¹ ['meɪl] *adj* 1 : macho 2 MASCULINE : masculino

male² *n* : macho *m* (de animales o plantas), varón *m* (de personas)

malefactor ['mælə,fæktər] *n* : malhechor *m*, -chora *f*

maleness ['meɪlnəs] *n* : masculinidad *f*

malevolence [mə'lɛvələnts] *n* : malevolencia *f*

malevolent [mə'lɛvələnt] *adj* : malévolo

malformation [ˌmælfɔr'meɪʃən] *n* : malformación *f*

malformed [mæl'fɔrmd] *adj* : mal formado, deforme

malfunction¹ [mæl'fʌŋkʃən] *vi* : funcionar mal

malfunction² *n* : mal funcionamiento *m*

malice ['mælɪs] *n* 1 : malicia *f*, malevolencia *f* 2 **with malice aforethought** : con premeditación

malicious [mə'lɪʃəs] *adj* : malicioso, malévolo — **maliciously** *adv*

malign¹ [mə'laɪn] *vt* : calumniar, difamar

malign² *adj* : maligno

malignancy [mə'lɪgnəntsi] *n, pl* **-cies** : malignidad *f*

malignant [mə'lɪgnənt] *adj* : maligno

malinger [mə'lɪŋgər] *vi* : fingirse enfermo

malingerer [mə'lɪŋgərər] *n* : uno que se finge enfermo

mall ['mɔl] *n* 1 PROMENADE : alameda *f*, paseo *m* (arbolado) 2 : centro *m* comercial ⟨shopping mall : galería comercial⟩

mallard ['mælərd] *n, pl* **-lard** *or* **-lards** : pato *m* real, ánade *mf* real

malleable ['mæliəbəl] *adj* : maleable

mallet ['mælət] *n* : mazo *m*

malnourished [mæl'nərɪʃt] *adj* : desnutrido, malnutrido

malnutrition [ˌmælnu'trɪʃən, -nju-] *n* : desnutrición *f*, malnutrición *f*

malodorous [mæl'o:dərəs] *adj* : maloliente

malpractice [ˌmæl'præktəs] *n* : mala práctica *f*, negligencia *f*

malt ['mɔlt] *n* : malta *f*

maltreat [mæl'tri:t] *vt* : maltratar

mama *or* **mamma** ['mɑmə] *n* : mamá *f*

mammal ['mæməl] *n* : mamífero *m*

mammalian [mə'meɪliən, mæ-] *adj* : mamífero

mammary ['mæməri] *adj* 1 : mamario 2 **mammary gland** : glándula mamaria

mammogram ['mæmə,græm] *n* : mamografía *f*

mammoth¹ ['mæməθ] *adj* : colosal, gigantesco

mammoth² *n* : mamut *m*

man¹ ['mæn] *vt* **manned; manning** : tripular (un barco o avión), encargarse de (un servicio)

man² n, pl **men** ['mɛn] **1** PERSON : hombre m, persona f **2** MALE : hombre m **3** MANKIND : humanidad f

manacles ['mænɪkəlz] npl HANDCUFFS : esposas fpl

manage ['mænɪʤ] v **-aged; -aging** vt **1** HANDLE : controlar, manejar **2** DIRECT : administrar, dirigir **3** CONTRIVE : lograr, ingeniárselas para — vi COPE : arreglárselas

manageable ['mænɪʤəbəl] adj : manejable

management ['mænɪʤmənt] n **1** DIRECTION : administración f, gestión f, dirección f **2** HANDLING : manejo m **3** MANAGERS : dirección f, gerencia f

manager ['mænɪʤər] n : director m, -tora f; gerente mf; administrador m, -dora f

managerial [ˌmænə'ʤɪriəl] adj : directivo, gerencial

mandarin ['mændərən] n **1** : mandarín m **2** or **mandarin orange** : mandarina f

mandate ['mæn,deɪt] n : mandato m

mandatory ['mændə,tori] adj : obligatorio

mandible ['mændəbəl] n : mandíbula f

mandolin [ˌmændə'lɪn, 'mændələn] n : mandolina f

mane ['meɪn] n : crin f (de un caballo), melena f (de un león o una persona)

maneuver¹ [mə'nu:vər, -'nju:-] vt **1** PLACE, POSITION : maniobrar, posicionar, colocar **2** MANIPULATE : manipular, maniobrar — vi : maniobrar

maneuver² n : maniobra f

manfully ['mænfəli] adj : valientemente

manganese ['mæŋgə,ni:z, -,ni:s] n : manganeso m

mange ['meɪnʤ] n : sarna f

manger ['meɪnʤər] n : pesebre m

mangle ['mæŋgəl] vt **-gled; -gling 1** CRUSH, DESTROY : aplastar, despedazar, destrozar **2** MUTILATE : mutilar ⟨to mangle a text : mutilar un texto⟩

mango ['mæŋ,go:] n, pl **-goes** : mango m

mangrove ['mæn,gro:v, 'mæŋ-] n : mangle m

mangy ['meɪnʤi] adj **mangier; -est 1** : sarnoso **2** SHABBY : gastado

manhandle ['mæn,hændəl] vt **-dled; -dling** : maltratar, tratar con poco cuidado

manhole ['mæn,ho:l] n : boca f de alcantarilla

manhood ['mæn,hʊd] n **1** : madurez f (de un hombre) **2** COURAGE, MANLINESS : hombría f, valor m **3** MEN : hombres mpl

manhunt ['mæn,hʌnt] n : búsqueda f (de un criminal)

mania ['meɪniə, -njə] n : manía f

maniac ['meɪni,æk] n : maníaco m, -ca f; maniático m, -ca f

maniacal [mə'naɪəkəl] adj : maníaco, maniaco

manicure¹ ['mænə,kjʊr] vt **-cured; -curing 1** : hacer la manicura a **2** TRIM : recortar

manicure² n : manicura f

manicurist ['mænə,kjʊrɪst] n : manicuro m, -ra f

manifest¹ ['mænə,fɛst] vt : manifestar

manifest² adj : manifiesto, patente — **manifestly** adv

manifestation [ˌmænəfə'steɪʃən] n : manifestación f

manifesto [ˌmænə'fɛs,to:] n, pl **-tos** or **-toes** : manifiesto m

manifold¹ ['mænə,fo:ld] adj : diverso, variado

manifold² n : colector m (de escape)

manipulate [mə'nɪpjə,leɪt] vt **-lated; -lating** : manipular

manipulation [mə,nɪpjə'leɪʃən] n : manipulación f

manipulative [mə'nɪpjə,leɪtɪv, -lətɪv] adj : manipulador

mankind ['mæn'kaɪnd, ,kaɪnd] n : género m humano, humanidad f

manliness ['mænlinəs] n : hombría f, masculinidad f

manly ['mænli] adj **-lier; -est** : varonil, viril

man–made ['mæn'meɪd] adj : artificial ⟨man-made fabrics : telas sintéticas⟩

manna ['mænə] n : maná m

mannequin ['mænɪkən] n **1** DUMMY : maniquí m **2** MODEL : modelo mf

manner ['mænər] n **1** KIND, SORT : tipo m, clase f **2** WAY : manera f, modo m **3** STYLE : estilo m (artístico) **4 manners** npl CUSTOMS : costumbres fpl ⟨Victorian manners : costumbres victorianas⟩ **5 manners** npl ETIQUETTE : modales mpl, educación f, etiqueta f ⟨good manners : buenos modales⟩

mannered ['mænərd] adj **1** AFFECTED, ARTIFICIAL : amanerado, afectado **2 well–mannered** : educado, cortés **3** → **ill–mannered**

mannerism ['mænə,rɪzəm] n : peculiaridad f, gesto m particular

mannerly ['mænərli] adj : cortés, bien educado

mannish ['mænɪʃ] adj : masculino, hombruno

man–of–war [ˌmænə'wɔr, -əv'wɔr] n, pl **men–of–war** [ˌmɛn-] WARSHIP : buque m de guerra

manor ['mænər] n **1** : casa f solariega, casa f señorial **2** ESTATE : señorío m

manpower ['mæn,paʊər] n : personal m, mano f de obra

mansion ['mænʧən] n : mansión f

manslaughter ['mæn,slɔtər] n : homicidio m sin premeditación

mantel ['mæntəl] n : repisa f de chimenea

mantelpiece ['mæntəl,pi:s] → **mantel**

mantis ['mæntəs] n, pl **-tises** or **-tes** ['mæn,ti:z] : mantis f religiosa

mantle ['mæntəl] n : manto m

manual[1] ['mænjʊəl] *adj* : manual —
manually *adv*
manual[2] *n* : manual *m*
manufacture[1] [ˌmænjəˈfæktʃər] *vt*
-**tured; -turing** : fabricar, manufacturar, confeccionar (ropa), elaborar
(comestibles)
manufacture[2] *n* : manufactura *f*, fabricación *f*, confección *f* (de ropa), elaboración *f* (de comestibles)
manufacturer [ˌmænjəˈfæktʃərər] *n*
: fabricante *m*; manufacturero *m*, -ra *f*
manure [məˈnʊr, -ˈnjʊr] *n* : estiércol *m*
manuscript ['mænjəˌskrɪpt] *n* : manuscrito *m*
many[1] ['mɛni] *adj* **more** ['mor]; **most**
['moːst] : muchos
many[2] *pron* : muchos *pl*, -chas *pl*
map[1] ['mæp] *vt* **mapped; mapping 1**
: trazar el mapa de **2** PLAN : planear,
proyectar ⟨to map out a program
: planear un programa⟩
map[2] *n* : mapa *m*
maple ['meɪpəl] *n* : arce *m*
mar ['mɑr] *vt* **marred; marring 1** SPOIL
: estropear, echar a perder **2** DEFACE
: desfigurar
maraschino [ˌmærəˈskiːnoː, -ˈʃiː-] *n, pl*
-**nos** : cereza *f* al marrasquino
marathon ['mærəˌθɑn] *n* **1** RACE
: maratón *m* **2** CONTEST : competencia *f* de resistencia
maraud [məˈrɑd] *vi* : merodear
marauder [məˈrɑdər] *n* : merodeador *m*,
-dora *f*
marble ['mɑrbəl] *n* **1** : mármol *m* **2**
: canica *f* ⟨to play marbles : jugar a las
canicas⟩
march[1] ['mɑrtʃ] *vi* **1** : marchar, desfilar
⟨they marched past the grandstand
: desfilaron ante la tribuna⟩ **2** : caminar con resolución ⟨she marched right
up to him : se le acercó sin vacilación⟩
march[2] *n* **1** MARCHING : marcha *f* **2** PAS-
SAGE : paso *m* (del tiempo) **3**
PROGRESS : avance *m*, progreso *m* **4**
: marcha *f* (en música)
March ['mɑrtʃ] *n* : marzo *m*
marchioness ['mɑrʃənɪs] *n* : marquesa
f
Mardi Gras ['mɑrdiˌɡrɑ] *n* : martes *m* de
Carnaval
mare ['mær] *n* : yegua *f*
margarine ['mɑrdʒərən] *n* : margarina *f*
margin ['mɑrdʒən] *n* : margen *m*
marginal ['mɑrdʒənəl] *adj* **1** : marginal
2 MINIMAL : mínimo — **marginally** *adv*
marigold ['mærəˌɡoːld] *n* : maravilla *f*,
caléndula *f*
marijuana [ˌmærəˈhwɑnə] *n* : marihuana *f*
marina [məˈriːnə] *n* : puerto *m* deportivo
marinade [ˌmærəˈnɑd] *n* : adobo *m*,
marinada *f*
marinate ['mærəˌneɪt] *vt* -**nated; -nating**
: marinar

marine[1] [məˈriːn] *adj* **1** : marino ⟨ma-
rine life : vida marina⟩ **2** NAUTICAL
: náutico, marítimo **3** : de la infantería
de marina
marine[2] *n* : soldado *m* de marina
mariner ['mærɪnər] *n* : marinero *m*,
marino *m*
marionette [ˌmæriəˈnɛt] *n* : marioneta *f*,
títere *m*
marital ['mærətəl] *adj* **1** : matrimonial
2 marital status : estado *m* civil
maritime ['mærəˌtaɪm] *adj* : marítimo
marjoram ['mɑrdʒərəm] *n* : mejorana *f*
mark[1] ['mɑrk] *vt* **1** : marcar **2** CHAR-
ACTERIZE : caracterizar **3** SIGNAL
: señalar **4** NOTICE : prestar atención
a, hacer caso de **5 to mark off** : demarcar, delimitar
mark[2] *n* **1** TARGET : blanco *m* **2** : marca *f*, señal *f* ⟨put a mark where you left
off : pon una señal donde terminaste⟩
3 INDICATION : señal *f*, indicio *m* **4**
GRADE : nota *f* **5** IMPRINT : huella *f*,
marca *f* **6** BLEMISH : marca *f*, imperfección *f*
marked ['mɑrkt] *adj* : marcado, notable
— **markedly** ['mɑrkədli] *adv*
marker ['mɑrkər] *n* : marcador *m*
market[1] ['mɑrkət] *vt* : poner en venta,
comercializar
market[2] *n* **1** MARKETPLACE : mercado
m ⟨the open market : el mercado libre⟩
2 DEMAND : demanda *f*, mercado *m* **3**
STORE : tienda *f* **4** → **stock market**
marketable ['mɑrkətəbəl] *adj* : vendible
marketing ['mɑrkətɪŋ] *n* : mercadotecnia *f*, mercadeo *m*
marketplace ['mɑrkətˌpleɪs] *n* : mercado *m*
marksman ['mɑrksmən] *n, pl* -**men**
[-mən, -ˌmn] : tirador *m*
marksmanship ['mɑrksmənˌʃɪp] *n*
: puntería *f*
marlin ['mɑrlɪn] *n* : marlín *m*
marmalade ['mɑrməˌleɪd] *n* : mermelada *f*
marmoset ['mɑrməˌsɛt] *n* : tití *m*
marmot ['mɑrmət] *n* : marmota *f*
maroon[1] [məˈruːn] *vt* : abandonar, aislar
maroon[2] *n* : rojo *m* oscuro, granate *m*
marquee [mɑrˈkiː] *n* : marquesina *f*
marquess ['mɑrkwɪs] *or* **marquis**
['mɑrkwɪs, mɑrˈkiː] *n, pl* -**quesses** *or*
-**quises** [-ˈkiːz, -ˈkiːzəz] *or* -**quis** [-ˈkiː,
-ˈkiːz] : marqués *m*
marquise [mɑrˈkiːz] → **marchioness**
marriage ['mærɪdʒ] *n* **1** : matrimonio *m*
2 WEDDING : casamiento *m*, boda *f*
marriageable ['mærɪdʒəbəl] *adj* **of marriageable age** : de edad de casarse
married ['mærid] *adj* **1** : casado **2 to get
married** : casarse
marrow ['mæroː] *n* : médula *f*, tuétano
m
marry ['mæri] *vt* -**ried; -rying 1** : casar
⟨the priest married them : el cura los
casó⟩ **2** : casarse con ⟨she married
John : se casó con John⟩

Mars ['mɑrz] n : Marte m
marsh ['mɑrʃ] n 1 : pantano m 2 salt
marsh : marisma f
marshal¹ ['mɑrʃəl] vt -shaled or
-shalled; -shaling or -shalling 1 : poner en orden, reunir 2 USHER : conducir
marshal² n 1 : maestro m de ceremonias 2 : mariscal m (en el ejército); jefe
m, -fa f (de la policía, de los bomberos,
etc.)
marshmallow ['mɑrʃˌmɛloː, -ˌmælo:] n
: malvavisco m
marshy ['mɑrʃi] adj marshier; -est
: pantanoso
marsupial [mɑr'su:piəl] n : marsupial m
mart ['mɑrt] n MARKET : mercado m
marten ['mɑrtən] n, pl -ten or -tens
: marta f
martial ['mɑrʃəl] adj : marcial
martin ['mɑrtən] n 1 SWALLOW : golondrina f 2 SWIFT : vencejo m
martyr¹ ['mɑrtər] vt : martirizar
martyr² n : mártir mf
martyrdom ['mɑrtərdəm] n : martirio m
marvel¹ ['mɑrvəl] vi -veled or -velled;
-veling or -velling : maravillarse
marvel² n : maravilla f
marvelous ['mɑrvələs] or marvellous
adj : maravilloso — marvelously adv
Marxism ['mɑrkˌsɪzəm] n : marxismo m
Marxist¹ ['mɑrksɪst] adj : marxista
Marxist² n : marxista mf
mascara [mæs'kærə] n : rímel m, rimel
m
mascot ['mæsˌkɑt, -kət] n : mascota f
masculine ['mæskjələn] adj : masculino
masculinity [ˌmæskjə'lɪnəti] n : masculinidad f
mash¹ ['mæʃ] vt 1 : hacer puré de (papas, etc.) 2 CRUSH : aplastar, majar
mash² n 1 FEED : afrecho m 2 : malta
f (para hacer bebidas alcohólicas) 3
PASTE, PULP : papilla f, pasta f
mask¹ ['mæsk] vt 1 CONCEAL, DISGUISE
: enmascarar, ocultar 2 COVER
: cubrir, tapar
mask² n : máscara f, careta f, mascarilla f (de un cirujano o dentista)
masochism ['mæsəˌkɪzəm, 'mæzə-] n
: masoquismo m
masochist ['mæsəˌkɪst, 'mæzə-] n : masoquista mf
masochistic [ˌmæsə'kɪstɪk, ˌmæzə-] adj
: masoquista
mason ['meɪsən] n 1 BRICKLAYER : albañil mf 2 or stonemason ['stoːnˌ-]
: mampostero m, cantero m
masonry ['meɪsənri] n, pl -ries 1 BRICK-
LAYING : albañería f 2 or stonemasonry ['stoːnˌ-] : mampostería f
masquerade¹ [ˌmæskə'reɪd] vi -aded;
-ading 1 : disfrazarse (de), hacerse
pasar (por) 2 : asistir a una mascarada
masquerade² n 1 : mascarada f, baile
m de disfraces 2 FACADE : farsa f,
fachada f
mass¹ ['mæs] vi : concentrarse, juntarse
en masa — vt : concentrar

mass² n 1 : masa f ⟨atomic mass : masa
atómica⟩ 2 BULK : mole f, volumen m
3 MULTITUDE : cantidad f, montón m
(de cosas), multitud f (de gente) 4 the
masses : las masas, el pueblo, el populacho
Mass ['mæs] n : misa f
massacre¹ ['mæsɪkər] vt -cred; -cring
: masacrar
massacre² n : masacre f
massage¹ [mə'sɑʒ, -'sɑʤ] vt -saged;
-saging : masajear
massage² n : masaje m
masseur [mæ'sər] n : masajista m
masseuse [mæ'søz, -'su:z] n : masajista
f
massive ['mæsɪv] adj 1 BULKY : voluminoso, macizo 2 HUGE : masivo,
enorme — massively adv
mast ['mæst] n : mástil m, palo m
master¹ ['mæstər] vt 1 SUBDUE : dominar 2 : llegar a dominar ⟨she mastered
French : llegó a dominar el francés⟩
master² n 1 TEACHER : maestro m, profesor m 2 EXPERT : experto m, -ta f;
maestro m, -tra f 3 : amo m (de animales o esclavos), señor m (de la casa)
4 master's degree : maestría f
masterful ['mæstərfəl] adj 1 IMPERIOUS
: autoritario, imperioso, dominante 2
SKILLFUL : magistral — masterfully
adv
masterly ['mæstərli] adj : magistral
mastermind ['mæstərˌmaɪnd] n : cerebro m, artífice mf
masterpiece ['mæstərˌpi:s] n : obra f
maestra
masterwork ['mæstərˌwərk] → masterpiece
mastery ['mæstəri] n 1 DOMINION : dominio m, autoridad f 2 SUPERIORITY
: superioridad f 3 EXPERTISE : maestría
f
masticate ['mæstəˌkeɪt] v -cated; -cat-
ing : masticar
mastiff ['mæstɪf] n : mastín m
mastodon ['mæstəˌdɑn] n : mastodonte
m
masturbate ['mæstərˌbeɪt] v -bated; bating vi : masturbarse — vt : masturbar
masturbation [ˌmæstər'beɪʃən] n : masturbación f
mat¹ ['mæt] v matted; matting vt TAN-
GLE : enmarañar — vi : enmarañarse
mat² n 1 : estera f 2 TANGLE : maraña
f 3 PAD : colchoneta f (de gimnasia) 4
or matt or matte ['mæt] FRAME : marco m (de cartón)
mat³ → matte
matador ['mætəˌdɔr] n : matador m
match¹ ['mæʧ] vt 1 PIT : enfrentar,
oponer 2 EQUAL, FIT : igualar, corresponder a, coincidir con 3 : combinar
con, hacer juego con ⟨her shoes match
her dress : sus zapatos hacen juego con
su vestido⟩ — vi 1 CORRESPOND : concordar, coincidir 2 : hacer juego ⟨with
a tie to match : con una corbata que
hace juego⟩

match² *n* **1** EQUAL : igual *mf* ⟨he's no match for her : no puede competir con ella⟩ **2** FIGHT, GAME : partido *m*, combate *m* (en boxeo) **3** MARRIAGE : matrimonio *m*, casamiento *m* **4** : fósforo *m*, cerilla *f*, cerillo *m* *in various countries*⟩ ⟨he lit a match : encendió un fósforo⟩ **5 to be a good match** : hacer buena pareja (dícese de las personas), hacer juego (dícese de la ropa)

matchless ['mætʃləs] *adj* : sin igual, sin par

matchmaker ['mætʃˌmeɪkər] *n* : casamentero *m*, -ra *f*

mate¹ ['meɪt] *v* **mated; mating** *vi* **1** FIT : encajar **2** PAIR : emparejarse **3** (*relating to animals*) : aparearse, copular — *vt* : aparear, acoplar (animales)

mate² *n* **1** COMPANION : compañero *m*, -ra *f*; camarada *mf* **2** : macho *m*, hembra *f* (de animales) **3** : oficial *mf* (de un barco) ⟨first mate : primer oficial⟩ **4** : compañero *m*, -ra *f*; pareja *f* (de un zapato, etc.)

material¹ [mə'tɪriəl] *adj* **1** PHYSICAL : material, físico ⟨the material world : el mundo material⟩ ⟨material needs : necesidades materiales⟩ **2** IMPORTANT : importante, esencial **3 material evidence** : prueba *f* sustancial

material² *n* **1** : material *m* **2** CLOTH : tejido *m*, tela *f*

materialism [mə'tɪriəˌlɪzəm] *n* : materialismo *m*

materialist [mə'tɪriəlɪst] *n* : materialista *mf*

materialistic [məˌtɪriə'lɪstɪk] *adj* : materialista

materialize [mə'tɪriəˌlaɪz] *v* **-ized; -izing** *vt* : materializar, hacer aparecer — *vi* : materializarse, aparecer

maternal [mə'tərnəl] *adj* MOTHERLY : maternal — **maternally** *adv*

maternity¹ [mə'tərnəti] *adj* : de maternidad ⟨maternity clothes : ropa de futura mamá⟩ ⟨maternity leave : licencia por maternidad⟩

maternity² *n, pl* **-ties** : maternidad *f*

math ['mæθ] → **mathematics**

mathematical [ˌmæθə'mætɪkəl] *adj* : matemático — **mathematically** *adv*

mathematician [ˌmæθəmə'tɪʃən] *n* : matemático *m*, -ca *f*

mathematics [ˌmæθə'mætɪks] *ns & pl* : matemáticas *fpl*, matemática *f*

matinee *or* **matinée** [ˌmætən'eɪ] *n* : matiné *f*

matriarch ['meɪtriˌɑrk] *n* : matriarca *f*

matriarchy ['meɪtriˌɑrki] *n, pl* **-chies** : matriarcado *m*

matriculate [mə'trɪkjəˌleɪt] *v* **-lated; -lating** *vt* : matricular — *vi* : matricularse

matriculation [məˌtrɪkjə'leɪʃən] *n* : matrícula *f*, matriculación *f*

matrimony ['mætrəˌmoːni] *n* : matrimonio *m* — **matrimonial** [ˌmætrə'moːniəl] *adj*

matrix ['meɪtrɪks] *n, pl* **-trices** ['meɪtrəˌsiːz, 'mæ-] *or* **-trixes** ['meɪtrɪksəz] : matriz *f*

matron ['meɪtrən] *n* : matrona *f*

matronly ['meɪtrənli] *adj* : de matrona, matronal

matte ['mæt] *adj* : mate, de acabado mate

matter¹ ['mætər] *vi* : importar ⟨it doesn't matter : no importa⟩

matter² *n* **1** QUESTION : asunto *m*, cuestión *f* ⟨a matter of taste : una cuestión de gusto⟩ **2** SUBSTANCE : materia *f*, sustancia *f* **3 matters** *npl* CIRCUMSTANCES : situación *f*, cosas *fpl* ⟨to make matters worse : para colmo de males⟩ **4 to be the matter** : pasar ⟨what's the matter? : ¿qué pasa?⟩ **5 as a matter of fact** : en efecto, en realidad **6 for that matter** : de hecho **7 no matter how much** : por mucho que

matter–of–fact ['mætərəv'fækt] *adj* : práctico, realista

mattress ['mætrəs] *n* : colchón *m*

mature¹ [mə'tʊr, -'tjʊr, -'tʃʊr] *vi* **-tured; -turing** **1** : madurar **2** : vencer ⟨when does the loan mature? : ¿cuándo vence el préstamo?⟩

mature² *adj* **-turer; -est** **1** : maduro **2** DUE : vencido

maturity [mə'tʊrəti, -'tjʊr-, -'tʃʊr-] *n* : madurez *f*

maudlin ['mɔdlɪn] *adj* : sensiblero

maul¹ ['mɔl] *vt* **1** BEAT : golpear, pegar **2** MANGLE : mutilar **3** MANHANDLE : maltratar

maul² *n* MALLET : mazo *m*

Mauritanian [ˌmɔrə'teɪniən] *n* : mauritano *m*, -na *f* — **Mauritanian** *adj*

mausoleum [ˌmɔsə'liːəm, ˌmɔzə-] *n, pl* **-leums** *or* **-lea** [-'liːə] : mausoleo *m*

mauve ['moːv, 'mɔv] *n* : malva *m*

maven *or* **mavin** ['meɪvən] *n* EXPERT : experto *m*, -ta *f*

maverick ['mævrɪk, 'mævə-] *n* **1** : ternero *m* sin marcar **2** NONCONFORMIST : inconformista *mf*, disidente *mf*

mawkish ['mɔkɪʃ] *adj* : sensiblero

maxim ['mæksəm] *n* : máxima *f*

maximize ['mæksəˌmaɪz] *vt* **-mized; -mizing** : maximizar, llevar al máximo

maximum¹ ['mæksəməm] *adj* : máximo

maximum² *n, pl* **-ma** ['mæksəmə] *or* **-mums** : máximo *m*

may ['meɪ] *v aux, past* **might** ['maɪt] *present s & pl* **may 1** (*expressing permission*) : poder ⟨you may go : puedes ir⟩ **2** (*expressing possibility or probability*) : poder ⟨you may be right : puede que tengas razón⟩ ⟨it may happen occasionally : puede pasar de vez en cuando⟩ **3** (*expressing desires, intentions, or contingencies*) ⟨may the best man win : que gane el mejor⟩ ⟨I laugh that I may not weep : me río para no llorar⟩ ⟨come what may : pase lo que pase⟩

May ['meɪ] *n* : mayo *m*

Maya ['maɪə] *or* **Mayan** ['maɪən] *n* : maya *mf* — **Maya** *or* **Mayan** *adj*

maybe ['meɪbi] *adv* PERHAPS : quizás, tal vez

mayfly ['meɪˌflaɪ] *n, pl* **-flies** : efímera *f*

mayhem ['meɪˌhɛm, 'meɪəm] *n* **1** MUTILATION : mutilación *f* **2** DEVASTATION : estragos *mpl*

mayonnaise ['meɪəˌneɪz] *n* : mayonesa *f*

mayor ['meɪər, 'mɛr] *n* : alcalde *m*, -desa *f*

mayoral ['meɪərəl, 'mɛrəl] *adj* : de alcalde

maze ['meɪz] *n* : laberinto *m*

me ['mi:] *pron* **1** : me ⟨she called me : me llamó⟩ ⟨give it to me : dámelo⟩ **2** (*after a preposition*) : mí ⟨for me : para mí⟩ ⟨with me : conmigo⟩ **3** (*after conjunctions and verbs*) : yo ⟨it's me : soy yo⟩ ⟨as big as me : tan grande como yo⟩ **4** (*emphatic use*) : yo ⟨me, too! : ¡yo también!⟩ ⟨who, me? : ¿quién, yo?⟩

meadow ['mɛdo:] *n* : prado *m*, pradera *f*

meadowland ['mɛdoˌlænd] *n* : pradera *f*

meadowlark ['mɛdoˌlɑrk] *n* : pájaro *m* cantor con el pecho amarillo

meager *or* **meagre** ['mi:gər] *adj* **1** THIN : magro, flaco **2** POOR, SCANTY : exiguo, escaso, pobre

meagerly ['mi:gərli] *adv* : pobremente

meagerness ['mi:gərnəs] *n* : escasez *f*, pobreza *f*

meal ['mi:l] *n* **1** : comida *f* ⟨a hearty meal : una comida sustanciosa⟩ **2** : harina *f* (de maíz, etc.)

mealtime ['mi:lˌtaɪm] *n* : hora *f* de comer

mean¹ ['mi:n] *vt* **meant** ['mɛnt]; **meaning 1** INTEND : querer, pensar, tener la intención de ⟨I didn't mean to do it : lo hice sin querer⟩ ⟨what do you mean to do? : ¿qué piensas hacer?⟩ **2** SIGNIFY : querer decir, significar ⟨what does that mean? : ¿qué quiere decir eso?⟩ **3** : importar ⟨health means everything : lo que más importa es la salud⟩

mean² *adj* **1** HUMBLE : humilde **2** NEGLIGIBLE : despreciable ⟨it's no mean feat : no es poca cosa⟩ **3** STINGY : mezquino, tacaño **4** CRUEL : malo, cruel ⟨to be mean to someone : tratar mal a alguien⟩ **5** AVERAGE, MEDIAN : medio

mean³ *n* **1** MIDPOINT : término *m* medio **2** AVERAGE : promedio *m*, media *f* aritmética **3 means** *npl* WAY : medio *m*, manera *f*, vía *f* **4 means** *npl* RESOURCES : medios *mpl*, recursos *mpl* **5 by all means** : por supuesto, cómo no **6 by means of** : por medio de **7 by no means** : de ninguna manera, de ningún modo

meander [mi'ændər] *vi* **-dered; -dering 1** WIND : serpentear **2** WANDER : vagar, andar sin rumbo fijo

meaning ['mi:nɪŋ] *n* **1** : significado *m*, sentido *m* ⟨double meaning : doble sentido⟩ **2** INTENT : intención *f*, propósito *m*

meaningful ['mi:nɪŋfəl] *adj* : significativo — **meaningfully** *adv*

meaningless ['mi:nɪŋləs] *adj* : sin sentido

meanness ['mi:nnəs] *n* **1** CRUELTY : crueldad *f*, mezquindad *f* **2** STINGINESS : tacañería *f*

meantime¹ ['mi:nˌtaɪm] *adv* → **meanwhile¹**

meantime² *n* **1** : interín *m* **2 in the meantime** : entretanto, mientras tanto

meanwhile¹ ['mi:nˌhwaɪl] *adv* : entretanto, mientras tanto

meanwhile² *n* → **meantime²**

measles ['mi:zəlz] *ns & pl* : sarampión *m*

measly ['mi:zli] *adj* **-slier; -est** : miserable, mezquino

measurable ['mɛʒərəbəl, 'meɪ-] *adj* : mensurable — **measurably** [-bli] *adv*

measure¹ ['mɛʒər, 'meɪ-] *v* **-sured; -suring** : medir ⟨he measured the table : midió la mesa⟩ ⟨it measures 15 feet tall : mide 15 pies de altura⟩

measure² *n* **1** AMOUNT : medida *f*, cantidad *f* ⟨in large measure : en gran medida⟩ ⟨a full measure : una cantidad exacta⟩ ⟨a measure of proficiency : una cierta competencia⟩ ⟨for good measure : de ñapa, por añadidura⟩ **2** DIMENSIONS, SIZE : medida *f*, tamaño *m* **3** RULER : regla *f* ⟨tape measure : cinta métrica⟩ **4** MEASUREMENT : medida *f* ⟨cubic measure : medida de capacidad⟩ **5** MEASURING : medición *f* **6 measures** *npl* : medidas *fpl* ⟨security measures : medidas de seguridad⟩

measureless ['mɛʒərləs, 'meɪ-] *adj* : inmensurable

measurement ['mɛʒərmənt, 'meɪ-] *n* **1** MEASURING : medición *f* **2** DIMENSION : medida *f*

measure up *vi* **to measure up to** : estar a la altura de

meat ['mi:t] *n* **1** FOOD : comida *f* **2** : carne *f* ⟨meat and fish : carne y pescado⟩ **3** SUBSTANCE : sustancia *f*, esencia *f* ⟨the meat of the story : la sustancia del cuento⟩

meatball ['mi:tˌbɔl] *n* : albóndiga *f*

meaty ['mi:ti] *adj* **meatier; -est** : con mucha carne, carnoso

mechanic [mɪ'kænɪk] *n* : mecánico *m*, -ca *f*

mechanical [mɪ'kænɪkəl] *adj* : mecánico — **mechanically** *adv*

mechanics [mɪ'kænɪks] *ns & pl* **1** : mecánica *f* ⟨fluid mechanics : la mecánica de fluidos⟩ **2** MECHANISMS : mecanismos *mpl*, aspectos *mpl* prácticos

mechanism ['mɛkəˌnɪzəm] *n* : mecanismo *m*

mechanization [ˌmɛkənə'zeɪʃən] *n* : mecanización *f*

mechanize ['mɛkə,naɪz] *vt* **-nized; -nizing** : mecanizar

medal ['mɛdəl] *n* : medalla *f*, condecoración *f*

medalist ['mɛdəlɪst] *or* **medallist** *n* : medallista *mf*

medallion [mə'dæljən] *n* : medallón *m*

meddle ['mɛdəl] *vi* **-dled; -dling** : meterse, entrometerse

meddler ['mɛdələr] *n* : entrometido *m*, -da *f*

meddlesome ['mɛdəlsəm] *adj* : entrometido

media ['mi:diə] *npl* : medios *mpl* de comunicación

median¹ ['mi:diən] *adj* : medio

median² *n* : valor *m* medio

mediate ['mi:di,eɪt] *vi* **-ated; -ating** : mediar

mediation [,mi:di'eɪʃən] *n* : mediación *f*

mediator ['mi:di,eɪtər] *n* : mediador *m*, -dora *f*

medical ['mɛdɪkəl] *adj* : médico

medicate ['mɛdə,keɪt] *vt* **-cated; -cating** : medicar ⟨medicated powder : polvos medicinales⟩

medication [,mɛdə'keɪʃən] *n* **1** TREATMENT : tratamiento *m*, medicación *f* **2** MEDICINE : medicamento *m* ⟨to be on medication : estar medicado⟩

medicinal [mə'dɪsənəl] *adj* : medicinal

medicine ['mɛdəsən] *n* **1** MEDICATION : medicina *f*, medicamento *m* **2** : medicina *f* ⟨he's studying medicine : estudia medicina⟩

medicine man *n* : hechicero *m*

medieval *or* **mediaeval** [mɪ'di:vəl, ,mi:-, ,m-, -di'i:vəl] *adj* : medieval

mediocre [,mi:di'o:kər] *adj* : mediocre

mediocrity [,mi:di'ɑkrəti] *n, pl* **-ties** : mediocridad *f*

meditate ['mɛdə,teɪt] *vi* **-tated; -tating** : meditar

meditation [,mɛdə'teɪʃən] *n* : meditación *f*

meditative ['mɛdə,teɪtɪv] *adj* : meditabundo

medium¹ ['mi:diəm] *adj* : mediano ⟨of medium height : de estatura mediana, de estatura regular⟩

medium² *n, pl* **-diums** *or* **-dia** ['mi:-diə] **1** MEAN : punto *m* medio, término *m* medio ⟨happy medium : justo medio⟩ **2** MEANS : medio *m* **3** SUBSTANCE : medio *m*, sustancia *f* ⟨a viscous medium : un medio viscoso⟩ **4** : medio *m* de comunicación **5** : medio *m* (artístico)

medley ['mɛdli] *n, pl* **-leys** : popurrí *m* (de canciones)

meek ['mi:k] *adj* **1** LONG-SUFFERING : paciente, sufrido **2** SUBMISSIVE : sumiso, dócil, manso

meekly ['mi:kli] *adv* : dócilmente

meekness ['mi:knəs] *n* : mansedumbre *f*, docilidad *f*

meet¹ ['mi:t] *v* **met** ['mɛt]; **meeting** *vt* **1** ENCOUNTER : encontrarse con **2** JOIN : unirse con **3** CONFRONT : enfrentarse a **4** SATISFY : satisfacer, cumplir con ⟨to meet costs : pagar los gastos⟩ **5** : conocer ⟨I met his sister : conocí a su hermana⟩ — *vi* ASSEMBLE : reunirse, congregarse

meet² *n* : encuentro *m*

meeting ['mi:tɪŋ] *n* **1** : reunión *f* ⟨to open the meeting : abrir la sesión⟩ **2** ENCOUNTER : encuentro *m* **3** : entrevista *f* (formal)

meetinghouse ['mi:tɪŋ,haʊs] *n* : iglesia *f* (de ciertas confesiones protestantes)

megabyte ['mɛgə,baɪt] *n* : megabyte *m*

megahertz ['mɛgə,hərts, -,hrts] *n* : megahercio *m*

megaphone ['mɛgə,fo:n] *n* : megáfono *m*

melancholy¹ ['mɛlən,kɑli] *adj* : melancólico, triste, sombrío

melancholy² *n, pl* **-cholies** : melancolía *f*

melanoma [,mɛlə'no:mə] *n, pl* **-mas** : melanoma *m*

meld ['mɛld] *vt* : fusionar, unir — *vi* : fusionarse, unirse

melee ['meɪ,leɪ, meɪ'leɪ] *n* BRAWL : reyerta *f*, riña *f*, pelea *f*

meliorate ['mi:ljə,reɪt, 'mi:liə-] → **ameliorate**

mellow¹ ['mɛlo:] *vt* : suavizar, endulzar — *vi* : suavizarse, endulzarse

mellow² *adj* **1** RIPE : maduro **2** MILD : apacible ⟨a mellow character : un carácter apacible⟩ ⟨mellow wines : vinos añejos⟩ **3** : suave, dulce ⟨mellow colors : colores suaves⟩ ⟨mellow tones : tonos dulces⟩

mellowness ['mɛlonəs] *n* : suavidad *f*, dulzura *f*

melodic [mə'lɑdɪk] *adj* : melódico — **melodically** [-dɪkli] *adv*

melodious [mə'lo:diəs] *adj* : melodioso — **melodiously** *adv*

melodiousness [mə'lo:diəsnəs] *n* : calidad *f* de melódico

melodrama ['mɛlə,drɑmə, -,dræ-] *n* : melodrama *m*

melodramatic [,mɛlədrə'mætɪk] *adj* : melodramático — **melodramatically** [-tɪkli] *adv*

melody ['mɛlədi] *n, pl* **-dies** : melodía *f*, tonada *f*

melon ['mɛlən] *n* : melón *m*

melt ['mɛlt] *vt* **1** : derretir, disolver **2** SOFTEN : ablandar ⟨it melted his heart : ablandó su corazón⟩ — *vi* **1** : derretirse, disolverse **2** SOFTEN : ablandarse **3** DISAPPEAR : desvanecerse, esfumarse ⟨the clouds melted away : las nubes se desvanecieron⟩

melting point *n* : punto *m* de fusión

member ['mɛmbər] *n* **1** LIMB : miembro *m* **2** : miembro *m* (de un grupo); socio *m*, -cia *f* (de un club) **3** PART : miembro *m*, parte *f*

membership ['mɛmbər,ʃɪp] *n* **1** : membresía *f* ⟨application for membership

: solicitud de entrada⟩ 2 MEMBERS
: membresía *f*, miembros *mpl*, socios
mpl

membrane [ˈmɛmˌbreɪn] *n* : membrana
f — **membranous** [ˈmɛmbrə-nəs] *adj*

memento [mɪˈmɛnˌtoː] *n*, *pl* **-tos** *or* **-toes**
: recuerdo *m*

memo [ˈmɛmoː] *n*, *pl* **memos** : memorándum *m*

memoirs [ˈmɛmˌwɑrz] *npl* : memorias
fpl, autobiografía *f*

memorabilia [ˌmɛmərəˈbiliə, -ˈbɪljə] *npl*
1 : objetos *mpl* de interés histórico 2
MEMENTOS : recuerdos *mpl*

memorable [ˈmɛmərəbəl] *adj* : memorable, notable — **memorably** [-bli] *adv*

memorandum [ˌmɛməˈrændəm] *n*, *pl*
-dums *or* **-da** [-də] : memorándum *m*

memorial[1] [məˈmoriəl] *adj* : conmemorativo

memorial[2] *n* : monumento *m* conmemorativo

Memorial Day *n* : el último lunes de
mayo (observado en Estados Unidos
como día feriado para conmemorar a
los caídos en guerra)

memorialize [məˈmoriəˌlaɪz] *vt* **-ized**;
-izing COMMEMORATE : conmemorar

memorization [ˌmɛmərəˈzeɪʃən] *n*
: memorización *f*

memorize [ˈmɛməˌraɪz] *vt* **-rized**; **-rizing**
: memorizar, aprender de memoria

memory [ˈmɛmri, ˈmɛmə-] *n*, *pl* **-ries** 1
: memoria *f* ⟨he has a good memory
: tiene buena memoria⟩ 2 RECOLLEC-
TION : recuerdo *m* 3 COMMEMORA-
TION : memoria *f*, conmemoración *f*

men → **man**[2]

menace[1] [ˈmɛnəs] *vt* **-aced**; **-acing** 1
THREATEN : amenazar 2 ENDANGER
: poner en peligro

menace[2] *n* : amenaza *f*

menacing [ˈmɛnəsɪŋ] *adj* : amenazador,
amenazante

menagerie [məˈnædʒəri, -ˈnæʒəri] *n*
: colección *f* de animales salvajes

mend[1] [ˈmɛnd] *vt* 1 CORRECT : enmendar, corregir ⟨to mend one's ways
: enmendarse⟩ 2 REPAIR : remendar,
arreglar, reparar — *vi* HEAL : curarse

mend[2] *n* : remiendo *m*

mendicant [ˈmɛndɪkənt] *n* BEGGAR
: mendigo *m*, -ga *f*

menhaden [mɛnˈheɪdən, mən-] *ns* & *pl*
: pez *m* de la misma familia que los
arenques

menial[1] [ˈmiːniəl] *adj* : servil, bajo

menial[2] *n* : sirviente *m*, -ta *f*

meningitis [ˌmɛnənˈdʒaɪtəs] *n*, *pl*
-gitides [-ˈdʒɪtəˌdiːz] : meningitis *f*

menopause [ˈmɛnəˌpɔz] *n* : menopausia
f

menorah [məˈnorə] *n* : candelabro *m*
(usado en los oficios religiosos judíos)

menstrual [ˈmɛntstruəl] *adj* : menstrual

menstruate [ˈmɛntstruˌeɪt] *vi* **-ated**; **-at-
ing** : menstruar

menstruation [ˌmɛntstruˈeɪʃən] *n* : menstruación *f*

mental [ˈmɛntəl] *adj* : mental ⟨mental
hospital : hospital psiquiátrico⟩ —
mentally *adv*

mentality [mɛnˈtæləti] *n*, *pl* **-ties** : mentalidad *f*

menthol [ˈmɛnˌθɔl, -ˌθoːl] *n* : mentol *m*

mentholated [ˌmɛntθəˌleɪtəd] *adj* : men-
tolado

mention[1] [ˈmɛntʃən] *vt* : mencionar,
mentar, referirse a ⟨don't mention it!
: ¡de nada!, ¡no hay de qué!⟩

mention[2] *n* : mención *f*

mentor [ˈmɛnˌtɔr, ˈmɛntər] *n* : mentor *m*

menu [ˈmɛnˌjuː] *n* 1 : menú *m*, carta *f*
(en un restaurante) 2 : menú *m* (de
computadoras)

meow[1] [miˈaʊ] *vi* : maullar

meow[2] *n* : maullido *m*, miau *m*

mercantile [ˈmɔrkənˌtiːl, -ˌtaɪl] *adj* : mercantil

mercenary[1] [ˈmɔrsənɛˌri] *adj* : mercenario

mercenary[2] *n*, *pl* **-naries** : mercenario
m, -ria *f*

merchandise [ˈmɔrtʃənˌdaɪz, -ˌdaɪs] *n*
: mercancía *f*, mercadería *f*

merchandiser [ˈmɔrtʃənˌdaɪzər] *n* : comerciante *mf*; vendedor *m*, -dora *f*

merchant [ˈmɔrtʃənt] *n* : comerciante *mf*

merchant marine *n* : marina *f* mercante

merciful [ˈmɔrsɪfəl] *adj* : misericordioso,
clemente

mercifully [ˈmɔrsɪfli] *adv* 1 : con misericordia, con compasión 2 FORTU-
NATELY : afortunadamente

merciless [ˈmɔrsɪləs] *adj* : despiadado —
mercilessly *adv*

mercurial [ˌmɔrˈkjuriəl] *adj* TEMPERA-
MENTAL : temperamental, volátil

mercury [ˈmɔrkjəri] *n*, *pl* **-ries** : mercurio *m*

Mercury *n* : Mercurio *m*

mercy [ˈmɔrsi] *n*, *pl* **-cies** 1 CLEMENCY
: misericordia *f*, clemencia *f* 2 BLESS-
ING : bendición *f*

mere [ˈmɪr] *adj*, *superlative* **merest**
: mero, simple

merely [ˈmɪrli] *adv* : solamente, simplemente

merge [ˈmɔrdʒ] *v* **merged**; **merging** *vi*
: unirse, fusionarse (dícese de las com-
pañías), confluir (dícese de los ríos, las
calles, etc.) — *vt* : unir, fusionar, combinar

merger [ˈmɔrdʒər] *n* : unión *f*, fusión *f*

meridian [məˈrɪdiən] *n* : meridiano *m*

meringue [məˈræŋ] *n* : merengue *m*

merino [məˈriːno] *n*, *pl* **-nos** 1 : merino
m, -na *f* 2 *or* **merino wool** : lana *f* merino

merit[1] [ˈmɛrət] *vt* : merecer, ser digno de

merit[2] *n* : mérito *m*, valor *m*

meritorious [ˌmɛrəˈtoriəs] *adj* : meritorio

mermaid [ˈmɔrˌmeɪd] *n* : sirena *f*

merriment [ˈmɛrɪmənt] *n* : alegría *f*, júbilo *m*, regocijo *m*

merry ['mɛri] *adj* **-rier; -est** : alegre —
merrily ['mɛrəli] *adv*
merry–go–round ['mɛrigo,raʊnd] *n*
: carrusel *m*, tiovivo *m*
merrymaker ['mɛri,meɪkər] *n* : juerguista *mf*
merrymaking ['mɛri,meɪkɪŋ] *n* : juerga
f
mesa ['meɪsə] *n* : mesa *f*
mesdames → **madam, Mrs.**
mesh[1] ['mɛʃ] *vi* **1** ENGAGE : engranar
(dícese de las piezas mecánicas) **2** TAN-
GLE : enredarse **3** COORDINATE : coordinarse, combinar
mesh[2] *n* **1** : malla *f* ⟨wire mesh : malla
metálica⟩ **2** NETWORK : red *f* **3** MESH-
ING : engranaje *m* ⟨in mesh : engrana-
do⟩
mesmerize ['mɛzmə,raɪz] *vt* **-ized;
-izing 1** HYPNOTIZE : hipnotizar **2**
FASCINATE : cautivar, embelesar, fascinar
mess[1] ['mɛs] *vt* **1** SOIL : ensuciar **2 to
mess up** DISARRANGE : desordenar,
desarreglar **3 to mess up** BUNGLE
: echar a perder — *vi* **1** PUTTER : entretenerse **2** INTERFERE : meterse, entrometerse ⟨don't mess with me : no te
metas conmigo⟩
mess[2] *n* **1** : rancho *m* (para soldados,
etc.) **2** DISORDER : desorden *m* ⟨your
room is a mess : tienes el cuarto hecho
un desastre⟩ **3** CONFUSION, TURMOIL
: confusión *f*, embrollo *m*, lío *m fam*
message ['mɛsɪʤ] *n* : mensaje *m*, recado *m*
messenger ['mɛsənʤər] *n* : mensajero
m, -ra *f*
Messiah [mə'saɪə] *n* : Mesías *m*
Messrs. → **Mr.**
messy ['mɛsi] *adj* **messier; -est** UNTIDY
: desordenado, sucio
met → **meet**
metabolic [,mɛtə'bɑlɪk] *adj* : metabólico
metabolism [mə'tæbə,lɪzəm] *n* : metabolismo *m*
metabolize [mə'tæbə,laɪz] *vt* **-lized;
-lizing** : metabolizar
metal ['mɛtəl] *n* : metal *m*
metallic [mə'tælɪk] *adj* : metálico
metallurgical [,mɛtəl'ərʤɪkəl] *adj* : metalúrgico
metallurgy ['mɛtəl,ərʤi] *n* : metalurgia
f
metalwork ['mɛtəl,wərk] *n* : objeto *m* de
metal
metalworking ['mɛtəl,wərkɪŋ] *n* : metalistería *f*
metamorphosis [,mɛtə'mɔrfəsɪs] *n, pl*
-phoses [-,siz] : metamorfosis *f*
metaphor ['mɛtə,fɔr, -fər] *n* : metáfora
f
metaphoric [,mɛtə'fɔrɪk] *or* **metaphorical** [-ɪkəl] *adj* : metafórico
metaphysical [,mɛtə'fɪzəkəl] *adj*
: metafísico
metaphysics [,mɛtə'fɪzɪks] *n* : metafísica *f*

mete ['mi:t] *vt* **meted; meting** ALLOT
: repartir, distribuir ⟨to mete out punishment : imponer castigos⟩
meteor ['mi:tiər, -ti:,ɔr] *n* : meteoro *m*
meteoric [,mi:ti'ɔrɪk] *adj* : meteórico
meteorite ['mi:tiə,raɪt] *n* : meteorito *m*
meteorologic [,mi:ti,ɔrə'lɑʤɪk] *or* **meteorological** [-'lɑʤɪkəl] *adj* : meteorológico
meteorologist [,mi:tiə'rɑləʤɪst] *n* : meteorólogo *m*, -ga *f*
meteorology [,mi:tiə'rɑləʤi] *n* : meteorología *f*
meter ['mi:tər] *n* **1** : metro *m* ⟨it measures 2 meters : mide 2 metros⟩ **2** : contador *m*, medidor *m* (de electricidad,
etc.) ⟨parking meter : parquímetro⟩ **3**
: metro *m* (en literatura o música)
methane ['mɛ,θeɪn] *n* : metano *m*
method ['mɛθəd] *n* : método *m*
methodical [mə'θɑdɪkəl] *adj* : metódico
— **methodically** *adv*
Methodist ['mɛθədɪst] *n* : metodista *mf*
— **Methodist** *adj*
methodology [,mɛθə'dɑləʤi] *n, pl* **-gies**
: metodología *f*
meticulous [mə'tɪkjələs] *adj* : meticuloso — **meticulously** *adv*
meticulousness [mə'tɪkjələsnəs] *n*
: meticulosidad *f*
metric ['mɛtrɪk] *or* **metrical** [-trɪkəl] *adj*
: métrico
metric system *n* : sistema *m* métrico
metronome ['mɛtrə,no:m] *n*
: metrónomo *m*
metropolis [mə'trɑpələs] *n* : metrópoli
f, metrópolis *f*
metropolitan [,mɛtrə'pɑlətən] *adj* : metropolitano
mettle ['mɛtəl] *n* : temple *m*, valor *m* ⟨on
one's mettle : dispuesto a mostrar su
valía⟩
Mexican ['mɛksɪkən] *n* : mexicano *m*,
-na *f* — **Mexican** *adj*
mezzanine ['mɛzə,ni:n, ,mɛzə'ni:n] *n* **1**
: entrepiso *m*, entresuelo *m* **2** : primer
piso *m* (de un teatro)
miasma [maɪ'æzmə] *n* : miasma *m*
mica ['maɪkə] *n* : mica *f*
mice → **mouse**
micro ['maɪkro] *adj* : muy pequeño, microscópico
microbe ['maɪ,kro:b] *n* : microbio *m*
microbiology [,maɪkrobaɪ'ɑləʤi] *n* : microbiología *f*
microchip ['maɪkro,ʧɪp] *n* : microchip
m
microcomputer ['maɪkrokəm,pju:tər] *n*
: microcomputadora *f*
microcosm ['maɪkro,kɑzəm] *n* : micro-
cosmo *m*
microfilm ['maɪkro,fɪlm] *n* : microfilm
m
micrometer [maɪ'krɑmətər] *n* : micrómetro *m*
micron ['maɪ,krɑn] *n* : micrón *m*
microorganism [,maɪkro'ɔrgə,nɪzəm] *n*
: microorganismo *m*, microbio *m*

microphone ['maɪkrə,fo:n] *n* : micrófono *m*

microprocessor ['maɪkro,prɑ,ssər] *n* : microprocesador *m*

microscope ['maɪkrə,sko:p] *n* : microscopio *m*

microscopic [,maɪkrə'skɑpɪk] *adj* : microscópico

microscopy [maɪ'krɑskəpi] *n* : microscopía *f*

microwave ['maɪkrə,weɪv] *n* **1** : microonda *f* **2** *or* **microwave oven** : microondas *m*

mid ['mɪd] *adj* : medio ⟨mid morning : a media mañana⟩ ⟨in mid-August : a mediados de agosto⟩ ⟨in mid ocean : en alta mar⟩

midair ['mɪd'ær] *n* **in ~** : en el aire ⟨to catch in midair : agarrar al vuelo⟩

midday ['mɪd'deɪ] *n* NOON : mediodía *m*

middle¹ ['mɪdəl] *adj* **1** CENTRAL : medio, del medio, de en medio **2** INTERMEDIATE : intermedio, mediano ⟨middle age : la mediana edad⟩

middle² *n* **1** CENTER : medio *m*, centro *m* ⟨fold it down the middle : dóblalo por la mitad⟩ **2 in the middle of** : en medio de (un espacio), a mitad de (una actividad) ⟨in the middle of the month : a mediados del mes⟩

Middle Ages *npl* : Edad *f* Media

middle class *n* : clase *f* media

middleman ['mɪdəl,mæn] *n, pl* **-men** [-mən, -,mɛn] : intermediario *m*, -ria *f*

middling ['mɪdlɪŋ, -lən] *adj* **1** MEDIUM, MIDDLE : mediano **2** MEDIOCRE : mediocre, regular

midfielder ['mɪd,fi:ldər] *n* : mediocampista *mf*

midge ['mɪdʒ] *n* : mosca *f* pequeña

midget ['mɪdʒət] *n* **1** : enano *m*, -na *f* (persona) **2** : cosa *f* diminuta

midland ['mɪdlənd, -,lænd] *n* : región *f* central (de un país)

midnight ['mɪd,naɪt] *n* : medianoche *f*

midpoint ['mɪd,pɔɪnt] *n* : punto *m* medio, término *m* medio

midriff ['mɪd,rɪf] *n* : diafragma *m*

midshipman ['mɪd,ʃɪpmən, ,mɪd'ʃɪp-] *n, pl* **-men** [-mən, -,mɛn] : guardiamarina *m*

midst¹ ['mɪdst] *n* : medio *m* ⟨in our midst : entre nosotros⟩ ⟨in the midst of : en medio de⟩

midst² *prep* : entre

midstream ['mɪd'stri:m, -,stri:m] *n* : medio *m* de la corriente ⟨in the midstream of his career : en medio de su carrera⟩

midsummer ['mɪd'sʌmər, -,sʌ-] *n* : pleno verano *m*

midtown ['mɪd,taʊn] *n* : centro *m* (de una ciudad)

midway ['mɪd,weɪ] *adv* HALFWAY : a mitad de camino

midweek ['mɪd,wi:k] *n* : medio *m* de la semana ⟨in midweek : a media semana⟩

midwife ['mɪd,waɪf] *n, pl* **-wives** [-,waɪvz] : partera *f*, comadrona *f*

midwinter ['mɪd'wɪntər, -,win-] *n* : pleno invierno *m*

midyear ['mɪd,jɪr] *n* : medio *m* del año ⟨at midyear : a mediados del año⟩

mien ['mi:n] *n* : aspecto *m*, porte *m*, semblante *m*

miff ['mɪf] *vt* : ofender

might¹ ['maɪt] (*used to express permission or possibility or as a polite alternative to* **may**) → **may** ⟨it might be true : podría ser verdad⟩ ⟨might I speak with Sarah? : ¿se puede hablar con Sarah?⟩

might² *n* : fuerza *f*, poder *m*

mightily ['maɪtəli] *adv* : con mucha fuerza, poderosamente

mighty¹ ['maɪti] *adv* VERY : muy ⟨mighty good : muy bueno, buenísimo⟩

mighty² *adj* **mightier; -est 1** POWERFUL : poderoso, potente **2** GREAT : grande, imponente

migraine ['maɪ,greɪn] *n* : jaqueca *f*, migraña *f*

migrant ['maɪgrənt] *n* : trabajador *m*, -dora *f* ambulante

migrate ['maɪ,greɪt] *vi* **-grated; -grating** : emigrar

migration [maɪ'greɪʃən] *n* : migración *f*

migratory ['maɪgrə,tori] *adj* : migratorio

mild ['maɪld] *adj* **1** GENTLE : apacible, suave ⟨a mild disposition : un temperamento suave⟩ **2** LIGHT : leve, ligero ⟨a mild punishment : un castigo leve, un castigo poco severo⟩ **3** TEMPERATE : templado (dícese del clima) — **mildly** *adv*

mildew¹ ['mɪl,du:, -,dju:] *vi* : enmohecerse

mildew² *n* : moho *m*

mildness ['maɪldnəs] *n* : apacibilidad *f*, suavidad *f*

mile ['maɪl] *n* : milla *f*

mileage ['maɪlɪdʒ] *n* **1** ALLOWANCE : viáticos *mpl* (pagados por milla recorrida) **2** : distancia *f* recorrida (en millas), kilometraje *m*

milestone ['maɪl,sto:n] *n* LANDMARK : hito *m*, jalón *m* ⟨a milestone in his life : un hito en su vida⟩

milieu [mi:l'ju:, -'jø] *n, pl* **-lieus** *or* **-lieux** [-'ju:z, -'jø] SURROUNDINGS : entorno *m*, medio *m*, ambiente *m*

militant¹ ['mɪlətənt] *adj* : militante, combativo

militant² *n* : militante *mf*

militarism ['mɪlətə,rɪzəm] *n* : militarismo *m*

militaristic [,mɪlətə'rɪstɪk] *adj* : militarista

military¹ ['mɪlə,teri] *adj* : militar

military² *n* **the military** : las fuerzas armadas

militia [mə'lɪʃə] *n* : milicia *f*

milk¹ ['mɪlk] *vt* **1** : ordeñar (una vaca, etc.) **2** EXPLOIT : explotar

milk² *n* : leche *f*
milkman ['mɪlk,mæn, -mən] *n, pl* **-men** [-mən, -,mɛn] : lechero *m*
milk shake *n* : batido *m*, licuado *m*
milkweed ['mɪlk,wi:d] *n* : algodoncillo *m*
milky ['mɪlki] *adj* **milkier; -est** : lechoso
Milky Way *n* : Vía *f* Láctea
mill¹ ['mɪl] *vt* : moler (granos), fresar (metales), acordonar (monedas) — *vi* **to mill about** : arremolinarse
mill² *n* **1** : molino *m* (para moler granos) **2** FACTORY : fábrica *f* ⟨textile mill : fábrica textil⟩ **3** GRINDER : molinillo *m*
millennium [mə'lɛniəm] *n, pl* **-nia** [-niə] *or* **-niums** : milenio *m*
miller ['mɪlər] *n* : molinero *m*, -ra *f*
millet ['mɪlət] *n* : mijo *m*
milligram ['mɪlə,græm] *n* : miligramo *m*
milliliter ['mɪlə,li:tər] *n* : mililitro *m*
millimeter ['mɪlə,mi:tər] *n* : milímetro *m*
milliner ['mɪlənər] *n* : sombrerero *m*, -ra *f* (de señoras)
millinery ['mɪlə,nɛri] *n* : sombreros *mpl* de señora
million¹ ['mɪljən] *adj* **a million** : un millón de
million² *n, pl* **millions** *or* **million** : millón *m*
millionaire [,mɪljə'nær, 'mɪljə,nær] *n* : millonario *m*, -ria *f*
millionth¹ ['mɪljənθ] *adj* : millonésimo
millionth² *n* : millonésimo *m*
millipede ['mɪlə,pi:d] *n* : milpiés *m*
millstone ['mɪl,sto:n] *n* : rueda *f* de molino, muela *f*
mime¹ ['maɪm] *v* **mimed; miming** *vt* MIMIC : imitar, remedar — *vi* PANTOMIME : hacer la mímica
mime² *n* **1** : mimo *mf* **2** PANTOMIME : pantomima *f*
mimeograph ['mɪmiə,græf] *n* : mimeógrafo *m*
mimic¹ ['mɪmɪk] *vt* **-icked; -icking** : imitar, remedar
mimic² *n* : imitador *m*, -dora *f*
mimicry ['mɪmɪkri] *n, pl* **-ries** : mímica *f*, imitación *f*
minaret [,mɪnə'rɛt] *n* : alminar *m*, minarete *m*
mince ['mɪnts] *v* **minced; mincing** *vt* **1** CHOP : picar, moler (carne) **2 not to mince one's words** : no tener uno pelos en la lengua — *vi* : caminar de manera afectada
mincemeat ['mɪnts,mi:t] *n* : mezcla *f* de fruta picada, sebo, y especias
mind¹ ['maɪnd] *vt* **1** TEND : cuidar, atender ⟨mind the children : cuida a los niños⟩ **2** OBEY : obedecer **3** : preocuparse por, sentirse molestado por ⟨I don't mind his jokes : sus bromas no me molestan⟩ **4** : tener cuidado con ⟨mind the ladder! : ¡cuidado con la escalera!⟩ — *vi* **1** OBEY : obedecer **2** CARE : importarle a uno ⟨I don't mind : no me importa, me es igual⟩
mind² *n* **1** MEMORY : memoria *f*, recuerdo *m* ⟨keep it in mind : téngalo en

cuenta⟩ **2** : mente *f* ⟨the mind and the body : la mente y el cuerpo⟩ **3** INTENTION : intención *f*, propósito *m* ⟨to have a mind to do something : tener intención de hacer algo⟩ **4** : razón *f* ⟨he's out of his mind : está loco⟩ **5** OPINION : opinión *f* ⟨to change one's mind : cambiar de opinión⟩ **6** INTELLECT : capacidad *f* intelectual
minded ['maɪndəd] *adj* **1** (*used in combination*) ⟨narrow-minded : de mentalidad cerrada⟩ ⟨health-minded : preocupado por la salud⟩ **2** INCLINED : inclinado
mindful ['maɪndfəl] *adj* AWARE : consciente — **mindfully** *adv*
mindless ['maɪndləs] *adj* **1** SENSELESS : estúpido, sin sentido ⟨mindless violence : violencia sin sentido⟩ **2** HEEDLESS : inconsciente
mindlessly ['maɪndləsli] *adv* **1** SENSELESSLY : sin sentido **2** HEEDLESSLY : inconscientemente
mine¹ ['maɪn] *vt* **mined; mining 1** : extraer (oro, etc.) **2** : minar (con artefactos explosivos)
mine² *n* : mina *f* ⟨gold mine : mina de oro⟩
mine³ *pron* : mío, mía ⟨that one's mine : ése es el mío⟩ ⟨some friends of mine : unos amigos míos⟩
minefield ['maɪn,fi:ld] *n* : campo *m* de minas
miner ['maɪnər] *n* : minero *m*, -ra *f*
mineral ['mɪnərəl] *n* : mineral *m* — **mineral** *adj*
mineralogy [,mɪnə'rɑləʤi, -'ræ-] *n* : mineralogía *f*
mingle ['mɪŋgəl] *v* **-gled; -gling** *vt* MIX : mezclar — *vi* **1** MIX : mezclarse **2** CIRCULATE : circular
miniature¹ ['mɪniə,tʃʊr, 'mɪni,tʃʊr, -'tʃər] *adj* : en miniatura, diminuto
miniature² *n* : miniatura *f*
minibus ['mɪni,bʌs] *n* : microbús *m*, pesera *f Mex*
minicomputer ['mɪnikəm,pju:tər] *n* : minicomputadora *f*
minimal ['mɪnəməl] *adj* : mínimo
minimally ['mɪnəməli] *adv* : en grado mínimo
minimize ['mɪnə,maɪz] *vt* **-mized; -mizing** : minimizar
minimum¹ ['mɪnəməm] *adj* : mínimo
minimum² *n, pl* **-ma** ['mɪnəmə] *or* **-mums** : mínimo *m*
miniseries ['mɪni,sɪri:z] *n* : miniserie *f*
miniskirt ['mɪni,skərt] *n* : minifalda *f*
minister¹ ['mɪnəstər] *vi* **to minister to** : cuidar (de), atender a
minister² *n* **1** : pastor *m*, -tora *f* (de una iglesia) **2** : ministro *m*, -tra *f* (en política)
ministerial [,mɪnə'stɪriəl] *adj* : ministerial
ministry ['mɪnəstri] *n, pl* **-tries 1** : ministerio *m* (en política) **2** : sacerdocio *m* (en el catolicismo), clerecía *f* (en el protestantismo)

minivan ['mɪni,væn] *n* : minivan *f*
mink ['mɪŋk] *n, pl* **mink** *or* **minks** : visón *m*
minnow ['mɪno:] *n, pl* **-nows** : pececillo *m* de agua dulce
minor[1] ['maɪnər] *adj* : menor
minor[2] *n* 1 : menor *mf* (de edad) 2 : asignatura *f* secundaria (de estudios)
minority [mə'nɔrəti, maɪ-] *n, pl* **-ties** : minoría *f*
minstrel ['mɪntstrəl] *n* : juglar *m*, trovador *m* (en el medioevo)
mint[1] ['mɪnt] *vt* : acuñar
mint[2] *adj* : sin usar ⟨in mint condition : como nuevo⟩
mint[3] *n* 1 : menta *f* ⟨mint tea : té de menta⟩ 2 : pastilla *f* de menta 3 : casa *f* de la moneda ⟨the U.S. Mint : la casa de la moneda de los EE.UU.⟩ 4 FORTUNE : dineral *m*, fortuna *f*
minuet [,mɪnju'ɛt] *n* : minué *m*
minus[1] ['maɪnəs] *n* 1 : cantidad *f* negativa 2 **minus sign** : signo *m* de menos
minus[2] *prep* 1 : menos ⟨four minus two : cuatro menos dos⟩ 2 WITHOUT : sin ⟨minus his hat : sin su sombrero⟩
minuscule *or* **miniscule** ['mɪnəs,kju:l, mɪ'nʌs-] *adj* : minúsculo
minute[1] [maɪ'nu:t, mɪ-, -'nju:t] *adj* **-nuter; -est** 1 TINY : diminuto, minúsculo 2 DETAILED : minucioso
minute[2] ['mɪnət] *n* 1 : minuto *m* ⟨ten minutes late : diez minutos de retraso⟩ 2 MOMENT : momento *m* 3 **minutes** *npl* : actas *fpl* (de una reunión)
minutely [maɪ'nu:tli, mɪ-, -'nju:t-] *adv* : minuciosamente
miracle ['mɪrɪkəl] *n* : milagro *m*
miraculous [mə'rækjələs] *adj* : milagroso — **miraculously** *adv*
mirage [mɪ'rɑʒ, *chiefly Brit* 'mɪr,ɑʒ] *n* : espejismo *m*
mire[1] ['maɪr] *vi* **mired; miring** : atascarse
mire[2] *n* 1 MUD : barro *m*, lodo *m* 2 : atolladero *m* ⟨stuck in a mire of debt : agobiado por la deuda⟩
mirror[1] ['mɪrər] *vt* : reflejar
mirror[2] *n* : espejo *m*
mirth ['mərθ] *n* : alegría *f*, regocijo *m*
mirthful ['mərθfəl] *adj* : alegre, regocijado
misadventure [,mɪsəd'vɛntʃər] *n* : malaventura *f*, desventura *f*
misanthrope ['mɪsən,θro:p] *n* : misántropo *m*, -pa *f*
misanthropic [,mɪsən'θrɑpɪk] *adj* : misantrópico
misanthropy [mɪ'sænθrəpi] *n* : misantropía *f*
misapprehend [,mɪs,æprə'hɛnd] *vt* : entender mal
misapprehension [,mɪs,æprə'hɛntʃən] *n* : malentendido *m*
misappropriate [,mɪsə'pro:pri,eɪt] *vt* **-ated; -ating** : malversar
misbegotten [,mɪsbi'gɑtən] *adj* 1 ILLEGITIMATE : ilegítimo 2 : mal concebido ⟨misbegotten laws : leyes mal concebidas⟩

misbehave [,mɪsbi'heɪv] *vi* **-haved; -having** : portarse mal
misbehavior [,mɪsbi'heɪvjər] *n* : mala conducta *f*
miscalculate [mɪs'kælkjə,leɪt] *v* **-lated; -lating** : calcular mal
miscalculation [mɪs,kælkjə'leɪʃən] *n* : error *m* de cálculo, mal cálculo *m*
miscarriage [,mɪs'kærɪʤ, 'mɪs,kærɪʤ] *n* 1 : aborto *m* 2 FAILURE : fracaso *m*, malogro *m* ⟨a miscarriage of justice : una injusticia, un error judicial⟩
miscarry [,mɪs'kæri, 'mɪs,kæri] *vi* **-ried; -rying** 1 ABORT : abortar 2 FAIL : malograrse, fracasar
miscellaneous [,mɪsə'leɪniəs] *adj* : misceláneo
miscellany ['mɪsə,leɪni] *n, pl* **-nies** : miscelánea *f*
mischance [mɪs'ʧænts] *n* : desgracia *f*, infortunio *m*, mala suerte *f*
mischief ['mɪsʧəf] *n* : diabluras *fpl*, travesuras *fpl*
mischievous ['mɪsʧəvəs] *adj* : travieso, pícaro
mischievously ['mɪsʧəvəsli] *adv* : de manera traviesa
misconception [,mɪskən'sɛpʃən] *n* : concepto *m* erróneo, idea *f* falsa
misconduct [mɪs'kɑndəkt] *n* : mala conducta *f*
misconstrue [,mɪskən'stru:] *vt* **-strued; -struing** : malinterpretar
misdeed [mɪs'di:d] *n* : fechoría *f*
misdemeanor [,mɪsdɪ'mi:nər] *n* : delito *m* menor
miser ['maɪzər] *n* : avaro *m*, -ra *f*; tacaño *m*, -ña *f*
miserable ['mɪzərəbəl] *adj* 1 UNHAPPY : triste, desdichado 2 WRETCHED : miserable, desgraciado ⟨a miserable hut : una choza miserable⟩ 3 UNPLEASANT : desagradable, malo ⟨miserable weather : tiempo malísimo⟩ 4 CONTEMPTIBLE : despreciable, mísero ⟨for a miserable $10 : por unos míseros diez dólares⟩
miserably ['mɪzərəbli] *adv* 1 SADLY : tristemente 2 WRETCHEDLY : miserablemente, lamentablemente 3 UNFORTUNATELY : desgraciadamente
miserly ['maɪzərli] *adj* : avaro, tacaño
misery ['mɪzəri] *n, pl* **-eries** : miseria *f*, sufrimiento *m*
misfire [mɪs'faɪr] *vi* **-fired; -firing** : fallar
misfit ['mɪs,fɪt] *n* : inadaptado *m*, -da *f*
misfortune [mɪs'fɔrʧən] *n* : desgracia *f*, desventura *f*, infortunio *m*
misgiving [mɪs'gɪvɪŋ] *n* : duda *f*, recelo *m*
misguided [mɪs'gaɪdəd] *adj* : desacertado, equivocado, mal informado
mishap ['mɪs,hæp] *n* : contratiempo *m*, percance *m*, accidente *m*
misinform [,mɪsɪn'fɔrm] *vt* : informar mal
misinterpret [,mɪsɪn'tərprət] *vt* : malinterpretar

misinterpretation [ˌmɪsɪnˌtərprəˈteɪ-ʃən] *n* : mala interpretación *f*, malentendido *m*

misjudge [mɪsˈʤʌʤ] *vt* **-judged; -judging** : juzgar mal

mislay [mɪsˈleɪ] *vt* **-laid** [-leɪd]; **-laying** : extraviar, perder

mislead [mɪsˈliːd] *vt* **-led** [-ˈlɛd]; **-leading** : engañar

misleading [mɪsˈliːdɪŋ] *adj* : engañoso

mismanage [mɪsˈmænɪʤ] *vt* **-aged; -aging** : administrar mal

mismanagement [mɪsˈmænɪʤmənt] *n* : mala administración *f*

misnomer [mɪsˈnoːmər] *n* : nombre *m* inapropiado

misogynist [mɪˈsɑʤənɪst] *n* : misógino *m*

misogyny [məˈsɑʤəni] *n* : misoginia *f*

misplace [mɪsˈpleɪs] *vt* **-placed; -placing** : extraviar, perder

misprint [ˈmɪsˌprɪnt, mɪsˈ-] *n* : errata *f*, error *m* de imprenta

mispronounce [ˌmɪsprəˈnaʊnts] *vt* **-nounced; -nouncing** : pronunciar mal

mispronunciation [ˌmɪsprəˌnʌntsiˈeɪʃən] *n* : pronunciación *f* incorrecta

misquote [mɪsˈkwoːt] *vt* **-quoted; -quoting** : citar incorrectamente

misread [mɪsˈriːd] *vt* **-read; -reading 1** : leer mal ⟨she misread the sentence : leyó mal la frase⟩ **2** MISUNDERSTAND : malinterpretar ⟨they misread his intention : malinterpretaron su intención⟩

misrepresent [ˌmɪsˌrprɪˈzɛnt] *vt* : distorsionar, falsear, tergiversar

misrule[1] [mɪsˈruːl] *vt* **-ruled; -ruling** : gobernar mal

misrule[2] *n* : mal gobierno *m*

miss[1] [ˈmɪs] *vt* **1** : errar, faltar ⟨to miss the target : no dar en el blanco⟩ **2** : no encontrar, perder ⟨they missed each other : no se encontraron⟩ ⟨I missed the plane : perdí el avión⟩ **3** : echar de menos, extrañar ⟨we miss him a lot : lo echamos mucho de menos⟩ **4** OVERLOOK : pasar por alto, perder (una oportunidad, etc.) **5** AVOID : evitar ⟨they just missed hitting the tree : por muy poco chocan contra el árbol⟩ **6** OMIT : saltarse ⟨he missed breakfast : se saltó el desayuno⟩

miss[2] *n* **1** : fallo *m* (de un tiro, etc.) **2** FAILURE : fracaso *m* **3** : señorita *f* ⟨Miss Jones called us : nos llamó la señorita Jones⟩ ⟨excuse me, miss : perdone, señorita⟩

missal [ˈmɪsəl] *n* : misal *m*

misshapen [mɪsˈʃeɪpən] *adj* : deforme

missile [ˈmɪsəl] *n* **1** : misil *m* ⟨guided missile : misil guiado⟩ **2** PROJECTILE : proyectil *m*

missing [ˈmɪsɪŋ] *adj* **1** ABSENT : ausente ⟨who's missing? : ¿quién falta?⟩ **2** LOST : perdido, desaparecido ⟨missing persons : los desaparecidos⟩

mission [ˈmɪʃən] *n* **1** : misión *f* (mandada por una iglesia) **2** DELEGATION : misión *f*, delegación *f*, embajada *f* **3** TASK : misión *f*

missionary[1] [ˈmɪʃəˌnɛri] *adj* : misionero

missionary[2] *n, pl* **-aries** : misionero *m*, -ra *f*

missive [ˈmɪsɪv] *n* : misiva *f*

misspell [mɪsˈspɛl] *vt* : escribir mal

misspelling [mɪsˈspɛlɪŋ] *n* : falta *f* de ortografía

misstep [ˈmɪsˌstɛp] *n* : traspié *m*, tropezón *m*

mist [ˈmɪst] *n* **1** HAZE : neblina *f*, niebla *f* **2** SPRAY : rocío *m*

mistake[1] [mɪˈsteɪk] *vt* **-took** [-ˈstʊk]; **-taken** [-ˈsteɪkən]; **-taking 1** MISINTERPRET : malinterpretar **2** CONFUSE : confundir ⟨he mistook her for Clara : la confundió con Clara⟩

mistake[2] *n* **1** MISUNDERSTANDING : malentendido *m*, confusión *f* **2** ERROR : error *m* ⟨I made a mistake : me equivoqué, cometí un error⟩

mistaken [mɪˈsteɪkən] *adj* WRONG : equivocado — **mistakenly** *adv*

mister [ˈmɪstər] *n* : señor *m* ⟨watch out, mister : cuidado, señor⟩

mistiness [ˈmɪstinəs] *n* : nebulosidad *f*

mistletoe [ˈmɪsəlˌtoː] *n* : muérdago *m*

mistreat [mɪsˈtriːt] *vt* : maltratar

mistreatment [mɪsˈtriːtmənt] *n* : maltrato *m*, abuso *m*

mistress [ˈmɪstrəs] *n* **1** : dueña *f*, señora *f* (de una casa) **2** LOVER : amante *f*

mistrust[1] [mɪsˈtrʌst] *vt* : desconfiar de

mistrust[2] *n* : desconfianza *f*

mistrustful [mɪsˈtrʌstfəl] *adj* : desconfiado

misty [ˈmɪsti] *adj* **mistier; -est 1** : nebuloso, nebuloso **2** TEARFUL : lloroso

misunderstand [ˌmɪsˌʌndərˈstænd] *vt* **-stood** [-ˈstʊd]; **-standing 1** : entender mal **2** MISINTERPRET : malinterpretar ⟨don't misunderstand me : no me malinterpretes⟩

misunderstanding [ˌmɪsˌʌndərˈstændɪŋ] *n* **1** MISINTERPRETATION : malentendido *m* **2** DISAGREEMENT, QUARREL : disputa *f*, discusión *f*

misuse[1] [mɪsˈjuːz] *vt* **-used; -using 1** : emplear mal **2** ABUSE, MISTREAT : abusar de, maltratar

misuse[2] [mɪsˈjuːs] *n* **1** : mal empleo *m*, mal uso *m* **2** WASTE : derroche *m*, despilfarro *m* **3** ABUSE : abuso *m*

mite [ˈmaɪt] *n* **1** : ácaro *m* **2** BIT : poco *m* ⟨a mite tired : un poquito cansado⟩

miter *or* mitre [ˈmaɪtər] *n* **1** : mitra *f* (de un obispo) **2** *or* **miter joint** : inglete *m*

mitigate [ˈmɪtəˌɡeɪt] *vt* **-gated; -gating** : mitigar, aliviar

mitigation [ˌmɪtəˈɡeɪʃən] *n* : mitigación *f*, alivio *m*

mitosis [maɪˈtoːsɪs] *n, pl* **-toses** [-ˌsiːz] : mitosis *f*

mitt [ˈmɪt] *n* : manopla *f*, guante *m* (de béisbol)

mitten ['mɪtən] *n* : manopla *f*, mitón *m*

mix¹ ['mɪks] *vt* **1** COMBINE : mezclar **2** STIR : remover, revolver **3 to mix up** CONFUSE : confundir — *vi* : mezclarse

mix² *n* : mezcla *f*

mixer ['mɪksər] *n* **1** : batidora *f* (de la cocina) **2 cement mixer** : hormigonera *f*

mixture ['mɪkstʃər] *n* : mezcla *f*

mix–up ['mɪks,ʌp] *n* CONFUSION : confusión *f*, lío *m fam*

mnemonic [nɪ'manɪk] *adj* : mnemónico

moan¹ ['mo:n] *vi* : gemir

moan² *n* : gemido *m*

moat ['mo:t] *n* : foso *m*

mob¹ ['mab] *vt* **mobbed; mobbing 1** ATTACK : atacar en masa **2** HOUND : acosar, rodear

mob² *n* **1** THRONG : multitud *f*, turba *f*, muchedumbre *f* **2** GANG : pandilla *f*

mobile¹ ['mo:bəl, -,bi:l, -,baɪl] *adj* : móvil ⟨mobile home : caravana, casa rodante⟩

mobile² ['mo,bi:l] *n* : móvil *m*

mobility [mo'bɪləti] *n* : movilidad *f*

mobilize ['mo:bə,laɪz] *vt* **-lized; -lizing** : movilizar

moccasin ['makəsən] *n* **1** : mocasín *m* **2** *or* **water moccasin** : serpiente *f* venenosa de Norteamérica

mocha ['mo:kə] *n* **1** : mezcla *f* de café y chocolate **2** : color *m* chocolate

mock¹ ['mak, 'mɔk] *vt* **1** RIDICULE : burlarse de, mofarse de **2** MIMIC : imitar, remedar (de manera burlona)

mock² *adj* **1** SIMULATED : simulado **2** PHONY : falso

mockery ['makəri, 'mɔ-] *n, pl* **-eries 1** JEER, TAUNT : burla *f*, mofa *f* ⟨to make a mockery of : burlarse de⟩ **2** FAKE : imitación *f* (burlona)

mockingbird ['makɪŋ,bərd, 'mɔ-] *n* : sinsonte *m*

mode ['mo:d] *n* **1** FORM : modo *m*, forma *f* **2** MANNER : modo *m*, manera *f*, estilo *m* **3** FASHION : moda *f*

model¹ ['madəl] *v* **-eled** *or* **-elled; -eling** *or* **-elling** *vt* SHAPE : modelar — *vi* : trabajar de modelo

model² *adj* **1** EXEMPLARY : modelo, ejemplar ⟨a model student : un estudiante modelo⟩ **2** MINIATURE : en miniatura

model³ *n* **1** PATTERN : modelo *m* **2** MINIATURE : modelo *m*, miniatura *f* **3** EXAMPLE : modelo *m*, ejemplo *m* **4** MANNEQUIN : modelo *mf* **5** DESIGN : modelo *m* ⟨the '97 model : el modelo '97⟩

modem ['mo:dəm, -,dɛm] *n* : módem *m*

moderate¹ ['madə,reɪt] *v* **-ated; -ating** *vt* : moderar, temperar — *vi* **1** CALM : moderarse, calmarse **2** : fungir como moderador (en un debate, etc.)

moderate² ['madərət] *adj* : moderado

moderate³ ['madərət] *n* : moderado *m*, -da *f*

moderately ['madərətli] *adv* **1** : con moderación **2** FAIRLY : medianamente

moderation [,madə'reɪʃən] *n* : moderación *f*

moderator ['madə,reɪtər] *n* : moderador *m*, -dora *f*

modern ['madərn] *adj* : moderno

modernism ['madər,nɪzəm] *n* : modernismo *m*

modernist ['madərnɪst] *n* : modernista *mf* — **modernist** *adj*

modernity [mə'dərnəti] *n* : modernidad *f*

modernization [,madərnə'zeɪʃən] *n* : modernización *f*

modernize ['madər,naɪz] *v* **-ized; -izing** *vt* : modernizar — *vi* : modernizarse

modest ['madəst] *adj* **1** HUMBLE : modesto **2** DEMURE : recatado, pudoroso **3** MODERATE : modesto, moderado — **modestly** *adv*

modesty ['madəsti] *n* : modestia *f*

modicum ['madɪkəm] *n* : mínimo *m*, pizca *f*

modification [,madəfə'keɪʃən] *n* : modificación *f*

modifier ['madə,faɪər] *n* : modificante *m*, modificador *m*

modify ['madə,faɪ] *vt* **-fied; -fying** : modificar, calificar (en gramática)

modish ['mo:dɪʃ] *adj* STYLISH : a la moda, de moda

modular ['madʒələr] *adj* : modular

modulate ['madʒə,leɪt] *vt* **-lated; -lating** : modular

modulation [,madʒə'leɪʃən] *n* : modulación *f*

module ['ma,dʒu:l] *n* : módulo *m*

mogul ['mo:gəl] *n* : magnate *mf*; potentado *m*, -da *f*

mohair ['mo:,hær] *n* : mohair *m*

moist ['mɔɪst] *adj* : húmedo

moisten ['mɔɪsən] *vt* : humedecer

moistness ['mɔɪstnəs] *n* : humedad *f*

moisture ['mɔɪstʃər] *n* : humedad *f*

moisturize ['mɔɪstʃə,raɪz] *vt* **-ized; -izing** : humedecer (el aire), humectar (la piel)

moisturizer ['mɔɪtʃə,raɪzər] *n* : crema *f* hidratante, crema *f* humectante

molar ['mo:lər] *n* : muela *f*, molar *m*

molasses [mə'læsəz] *n* : melaza *f*

mold¹ ['mo:ld] *vt* : moldear, formar (carácter, etc.) — *vi* : enmohecerse ⟨the bread will mold : el pan se enmohecerá⟩

mold² *n* **1** *or* **leaf mold** : mantillo *m* **2** FORM : molde *m* ⟨to break the mold : romper el molde⟩ **3** FUNGUS : moho *m*

molder ['mo:ldər] *vi* CRUMBLE : desmoronarse

molding ['mo:ldɪŋ] *n* : moldura *f* (en arquitectura)

moldy ['mo:ldi] *adj* **moldier; -est** : mohoso

mole ['mo:l] *n* **1** : lunar *m* (en la piel) **2** : topo *m* (animal)

molecule ['mɑlɪ,kju:l] *n* : molécula *f* — **molecular** [mə'lekjələr] *adj*
molehill ['mo:l,hɪl] *n* : topera *f*
molest [mə'lest] *vt* **1** ANNOY, DISTURB : molestar **2** : abusar (sexualmente)
mollify ['mɑlə,faɪ] *vt* **-fied; -fying** : apaciguar, aplacar
mollusk *or* **mollusc** ['mɑləsk] *n* : molusco *m*
mollycoddle ['mɑli,kɑdəl] *vt* **-dled; -dling** PAMPER : consentir, mimar
molt ['mo:lt] *vi* : mudar, hacer la muda
molten ['mo:ltən] *adj* : fundido
mom ['mɑm, 'mʌm] *n* : mamá *f*
moment ['mo:mənt] *n* **1** INSTANT : momento *m* ⟨one moment, please : un momento, por favor⟩ **2** TIME : momento *m* ⟨at the moment : de momento, actualmente⟩ ⟨from that moment : desde entonces⟩ **3** IMPORTANCE : importancia *f* ⟨of great moment : de gran importancia⟩
momentarily [,mo:mən'terəli] *adv* **1** : momentáneamente **2** SOON : dentro de poco, pronto
momentary ['mo:mən,teri] *adj* : momentáneo
momentous [mo'mentəs] *adj* : de suma importancia, fatídico
momentum [mo'mentəm] *n, pl* **-ta** [-tə] *or* **-tums** **1** : momento *m* (en física) **2** IMPETUS : ímpetu *m*, impulso *m*
mommy ['mɑmi, 'mʌ-] *n* : mami *f*
monarch ['mɑ,nɑrk, -nərk] *n* : monarca *mf*
monarchism ['mɑ,nɑr,kɪzəm, -nər-] *n* : monarquismo *m*
monarchist ['mɑ,nɑrkɪst, -nər-] *n* : monárquico *m*, -ca *f*
monarchy ['mɑ,nɑrki, -nər-] *n, pl* **-chies** : monarquía *f*
monastery ['mɑnə,steri] *n, pl* **-teries** : monasterio *m*
monastic [mə'næstɪk] *adj* : monástico — **monastically** [-tɪkli] *adv*
Monday ['mʌn,deɪ, -di] *n* : lunes *m*
monetary ['mɑnə,teri, 'mʌnə-] *adj* : monetario
money ['mʌni] *n, pl* **-eys** *or* **-ies** ['mʌniz] : dinero *m*, plata *f*
moneyed ['mʌnid] *adj* : adinerado
moneylender ['mʌni,lendər] *n* : prestamista *mf*
money order *n* : giro *m* postal
Mongol ['mɑŋgəl, -,go:l] → **Mongolian**
Mongolian [mɑn'go:liən, mɑŋ-] *n* : mongol *m*, -gola *f* — **Mongolian** *adj*
mongoose ['mɑn,gu:s, 'mɑŋ-] *n, pl* **-gooses** : mangosta *f*
mongrel ['mɑŋgrəl, 'mʌŋ-] *n* **1** : perro *m* mestizo, perro *m* corriente *Mex* **2** HYBRID : híbrido *m*
monitor[1] ['mɑnətər] *vt* : controlar, monitorear
monitor[2] *n* **1** : ayudante *mf* (en una escuela) **2** : monitor *m* (de una computadora, etc.)
monk ['mʌŋk] *n* : monje *m*

monkey[1] ['mʌŋki] *vi* **-keyed; -keying 1** to monkey around : hacer payasadas, payasear **2** to monkey with : juguetear con
monkey[2] *n, pl* **-keys** : mono *m*, -na *f*
monkeyshines ['mʌŋki,ʃaɪnz] *npl* PRANKS : picardías *fpl*, travesuras *fpl*
monkey wrench *n* : llave *f* inglesa
monocle ['mɑnɪkəl] *n* : monóculo *m*
monogamous [mə'nɑgəməs] *adj* : monógamo
monogamy [mə'nɑgəmi] *n* : monogamia *f*
monogram[1] ['mɑnə,græm] *vt* **-grammed; -gramming** : marcar con monograma ⟨monogrammed towels : toallas con monograma⟩
monogram[2] *n* : monograma *m*
monograph ['mɑnə,græf] *n* : monografía *f*
monolingual [,mɑnə'lɪŋwəl] *adj* : monolingüe
monolith ['mɑnə,lɪθ] *n* : monolito *m*
monolithic [,mɑnə'lɪθɪk] *adj* : monolítico
monologue ['mɑnə,lɔg] *n* : monólogo *m*
monoplane ['mɑnə,pleɪn] *n* : monoplano *m*
monopolize [mə'nɑpə,laɪz] *vt* **-lized; -lizing** : monopolizar
monopoly [mə'nɑpəli] *n, pl* **-lies** : monopolio *m*
monosyllabic [,mɑnosə'læbɪk] *adj* : monosilábico
monosyllable ['mɑno,sɪləbəl] *n* : monosílabo *m*
monotheism ['mɑnoθi:,ɪzəm] *n* : monoteísmo *m*
monotheistic [,mɑnoθi:'ɪstɪk] *adj* : monoteísta
monotone ['mɑnə,to:n] *n* : voz *f* monótona
monotonous [mə'nɑtənəs] *adj* : monótono — **monotonously** *adv*
monotony [mə'nɑtəni] *n* : monotonía *f*, uniformidad *f*
monoxide [mə'nɑk,saɪd] *n* : monóxido *m*
monsoon [mɑn'su:n] *n* : monzón *m*
monster ['mɑnstər] *n* : monstruo *m*
monstrosity [mɑn'strɑsəti] *n, pl* **-ties** : monstruosidad *f*
monstrous ['mɑnstrəs] *adj* : monstruoso — **monstrously** *adv*
montage [mɑn'tɑʒ] *n* : montaje *m*
month ['mʌnθ] *n* : mes *m*
monthly[1] ['mʌnθli] *adv* : mensualmente
monthly[2] *adj* : mensual
monthly[3] *n, pl* **-lies** : publicación *f* mensual
monument ['mɑnjəmənt] *n* : monumento *m*
monumental [,mɑnjə'mentəl] *adj* : monumental — **monumentally** *adv*
moo[1] ['mu:] *vi* : mugir
moo[2] *n* : mugido *m*
mood ['mu:d] *n* : humor *m* ⟨to be in a good mood : estar de buen humor⟩ ⟨to

be in the mood for : tener ganas de⟩ ⟨to be in no mood for : no estar para⟩
moodiness ['muːdinəs] *n* **1** SADNESS : melancolía *f*, tristeza *f* **2** : cambios *mpl* de humor, carácter *m* temperamental
moody ['muːdi] *adj* **moodier; -est 1** GLOOMY : melancólico, deprimido **2** TEMPERAMENTAL : temperamental, de humor variable
moon ['muːn] *n* : luna *f*
moonbeam ['muːnˌbiːm] *n* : rayo *m* de luna
moonlight[1] ['muːnˌlaɪt] *vi* : estar pluriempleado
moonlight[2] *n* : claro *m* de luna, luz *f* de la luna
moonlit ['muːnˌlɪt] *adj* : iluminado por la luna ⟨a moonlit night : una noche de luna⟩
moonshine ['muːnˌʃaɪn] *n* **1** MOONLIGHT : luz *f* de la luna **2** NONSENSE : disparates *mpl*, tonterías *fpl* **3** : whisky *m* destilado ilegalmente
moor[1] ['mʊr, 'mɔr] *vt* : amarrar
moor[2] *n* : brezal *m*, páramo *m*
Moor ['mʊr] *n* : moro *m*, -ra *f*
mooring ['mʊrɪŋ, 'mɔr-] *n* DOCK : atracadero *m*
Moorish ['mʊrɪʃ] *adj* : moro
moose ['muːs] *ns & pl* : alce *m* (norteamericano)
moot ['muːt] *adj* DEBATABLE : discutible
mop[1] ['mɑp] *vt* **mopped; mopping** : trapear
mop[2] *n* : trapeador *m*
mope ['moːp] *vi* **moped; moping** : andar deprimido, quedar abatido
moped ['moːˌped] *n* : ciclomotor *m*
moraine [mə'reɪn] *n* : morena *f*
moral[1] ['mɔrəl] *adj* : moral ⟨moral judgment : juicio moral⟩ ⟨moral support : apoyo moral⟩ — **morally** *adv*
moral[2] *n* **1** : moraleja *f* (de un cuento, etc.) **2 morals** *npl* : moral *f*, moralidad *f*
morale [mə'ræl] *n* : moral *f*
moralist ['mɔrəlɪst] *n* : moralista *mf*
moralistic [ˌmɔrə'lɪstɪk] *adj* : moralista
morality [mə'ræləti] *n, pl* **-ties** : moralidad *f*
morass [mə'ræs] *n* **1** SWAMP : ciénaga *f*, pantano *m* **2** CONFUSION, MESS : lío *m fam*, embrollo *m*
moratorium [ˌmɔrə'toriəm] *n, pl* **-riums** *or* **-ria** [-iə] : moratoria *f*
moray ['mɔrˌeɪ, mə'reɪ] *n* : morena *f*
morbid ['mɔrbɪd] *adj* **1** : mórbido, morboso (en medicina) **2** GRUESOME : morboso, horripilante
morbidity [mɔr'bɪdəti] *n, pl* **-ties** : morbosidad *f*
more[1] ['mor] *adv* : más ⟨what more can I say? : ¿qué más puedo decir?⟩ ⟨more important : más importante⟩ ⟨once more : una vez más⟩
more[2] *adj* : más ⟨nothing more than that : nada más que eso⟩ ⟨more work : más trabajo⟩

more[3] *n* : más *m* ⟨the more you eat, the more you want : cuanto más comes, tanto más quieres⟩
more[4] *pron* : más ⟨more were found : se encontraron más⟩
moreover [mor'oːvər] *adv* : además
mores ['mɔrˌeɪz, -iːz] *npl* CUSTOMS : costumbres *fpl*, tradiciones *fpl*
morgue ['mɔrg] *n* : morgue *f*
moribund ['mɔrəˌbʌnd] *adj* : moribundo
Mormon ['mɔrmən] *n* : mormón *m*, -mona *f* — **Mormon** *adj*
morn ['mɔrn] → **morning**
morning ['mɔrnɪŋ] *n* : mañana *f* ⟨good morning! : ¡buenos días!⟩
Moroccan [mə'rɑkən] *n* : marroquí *mf* — **Moroccan** *adj*
moron ['morˌɑn] *n* **1** : retrasado *m*, -da *f* mental **2** DUNCE : estúpido *m*, -da *f*; tonto *m*, -ta *f*
morose [mə'roːs] *adj* : hosco, sombrío — **morosely** *adv*
moroseness [mə'roːsnəs] *n* : malhumor *m*
morphine ['mɔrˌfiːn] *n* : morfina *f*
morphology [mɔr'fɑlədʒi] *n, pl* **-gies** : morfología *f*
morrow ['mɑroː] *n* : día *m* siguiente
Morse code ['mɔrs] *n* : código *m* morse
morsel ['mɔrsəl] *n* **1** BITE : bocado *m* **2** FRAGMENT : pedazo *m*
mortal[1] ['mɔrt̬əl] *adj* : mortal ⟨mortal blow : golpe mortal⟩ ⟨mortal fear : miedo mortal⟩ — **mortally** *adv*
mortal[2] *n* : mortal *mf*
mortality [mɔr'tæləti] *n* : mortalidad *f*
mortar ['mɔrtər] *n* **1** : mortero *m*, molcajete *m Mex* ⟨mortar and pestle : mortero y maja⟩ **2** : mortero *m* ⟨mortar shell : granada de mortero⟩ **3** CEMENT : mortero *m*, argamasa *f*
mortgage[1] ['mɔrgɪdʒ] *vt* **-gaged; -gaging** : hipotecar
mortgage[2] *n* : hipoteca *f*
mortification [ˌmɔrt̬əfə'keɪʃən] *n* **1** : mortificación *f* **2** HUMILIATION : humillación *f*, vergüenza *f*
mortify ['mɔrt̬əˌfaɪ] *vt* **-fied; -fying 1** : mortificar (en religión) **2** HUMILIATE : humillar, avergonzar
mortuary ['mɔrtʃəˌweri] *n, pl* **-aries** FUNERAL HOME : funeraria *f*
mosaic [moː'zeɪɪk] *n* : mosaico *m*
Moslem ['mɑzləm] → **Muslim**
mosque ['mɑsk] *n* : mezquita *f*
mosquito [mə'skiːt̬oː] *n, pl* **-toes** : mosquito *m*, zancudo *m*
moss ['mɔs] *n* : musgo *m*
mossy ['mɔsi] *adj* **-ier; -est** : musgoso
most[1] ['moːst] *adv* : más ⟨the most interesting book : el libro más interesante⟩
most[2] *adj* **1** : la mayoría de, la mayor parte de ⟨most people : la mayoría de la gente⟩ **2** GREATEST : más (dícese de los números), mayor (dícese de las cantidades) ⟨the most ability : la mayor capacidad⟩

most³ *n* : más *m*, máximo *m* ⟨the most I can do : lo más que puedo hacer⟩ ⟨three weeks at the most : tres semanas como máximo⟩

most⁴ *pron* : la mayoría, la mayor parte ⟨most will go : la mayoría irá⟩

mostly ['mo:stli] *adv* MAINLY : en su mayor parte, principalmente

mote ['mo:t] *n* SPECK : mota *f*

motel [mo'tɛl] *n* : motel *m*

moth ['mɔθ] *n* : palomilla *f*, polilla *f*

mother¹ ['mʌðər] *vt* **1** BEAR : dar a luz a **2** PROTECT : cuidar de, proteger

mother² *n* : madre *f*

motherhood ['mʌðər,hʊd] *n* : maternidad *f*

mother–in–law ['mʌðərɪn,lɔ] *n, pl* **mothers–in–law** : suegra *f*

motherland ['mʌðər,lænd] *n* : patria *f*

motherly ['mʌðərli] *adj* : maternal

mother–of–pearl [,mʌðərəv'pərl] *n* : nácar *m*, madreperla *f*

motif [mo'ti:f] *n* : motivo *m*

motion¹ ['mo:ʃən] *vt* : hacerle señas (a alguien) ⟨she motioned us to come in : nos hizo señas para que entráramos⟩

motion² *n* **1** MOVEMENT : movimiento *m* ⟨to set in motion : poner en marcha⟩ **2** PROPOSAL : moción *f* ⟨to second a motion : apoyar una moción⟩

motionless ['mo:ʃənləs] *adj* : inmóvil, quieto

motion picture *n* MOVIE : película *f*

motivate ['mo:tə,veɪt] *vt* **-vated; -vating** : motivar, mover, inducir

motivation [,mo:tə'veɪʃən] *n* : motivación *f*

motive¹ ['mo:tɪv] *adj* : motor ⟨motive power : fuerza motriz⟩

motive² *n* : motivo *m*, móvil *m*

motley ['mɑtli] *adj* : abigarrado, variopinto

motor¹ ['mo:tər] *vi* : viajar en coche

motor² *n* : motor *m*

motorbike ['mo:tər,baɪk] *n* : motocicleta *f* (pequeña), moto *f*

motorboat ['mo:tər,bo:t] *n* : bote *m* a motor, lancha *f* motora

motorcar ['mo:tər,kɑr] *n* : automóvil *m*

motorcycle ['mo:tər,saɪkəl] *n* : motocicleta *f*

motorcyclist ['mo:tər,saɪkəlɪst] *n* : motociclista *mf*

motorist ['mo:tərɪst] *n* : automovilista *mf*, motorista *mf*

mottle ['mɑtəl] *vt* **-tled; -tling** : manchar, motear ⟨mottled skin : piel manchada⟩ ⟨a mottled surface : una superficie moteada⟩

motto ['mɑto:] *n, pl* **-toes** : lema *m*

mould ['mo:ld] → **mold**

mound ['maʊnd] *n* **1** PILE : montón *m* **2** KNOLL : montículo *m* **3** **burial mound** : túmulo *m*

mount¹ ['maʊnt] *vt* **1** : montar a (un caballo), montar en (una bicicleta), subir a **2** : montar (artillería, etc.) — *vi* INCREASE : aumentar

mount² *n* **1** SUPPORT : soporte *m* **2** HORSE : caballería *f*, montura *f* **3** MOUNTAIN : monte *m*, montaña *f*

mountain ['maʊntən] *n* : montaña *f*

mountaineer [,maʊntən'ɪr] *n* : alpinista *mf*; montañero *m*, -ra *f*

mountaineering [,maʊntən'ɪrɪŋ] *n* : alpinismo *m*

mountainous ['maʊntənəs] *adj* : montañoso

mountaintop ['maʊntən,tɑp] *n* : cima *f*, cumbre *f*

mourn ['morn] *vt* : llorar (por), lamentar ⟨to mourn the death of : llorar la muerte de⟩ — *vi* : llorar, estar de luto

mourner ['mornər] *n* : doliente *mf*

mournful ['mornfəl] *adj* **1** SORROWFUL : lloroso, plañidero, triste **2** GLOOMY : deprimente, entristecedor — **mournfully** *adv*

mourning ['mornɪŋ] *n* : duelo *m*, luto *m*

mouse ['maʊs] *n, pl* **mice** ['maɪs] **1** : ratón *m*, -tona *f* **2** : ratón *m* (de una computadora)

mousetrap ['maʊs,træp] *n* : ratonera *f*

mousse ['mu:s] *n* : mousse *mf*

moustache ['mʌ,stæʃ, mə'stæʃ] → **mustache**

mouth¹ ['maʊð] *vt* **1** : decir con poca sinceridad, repetir sin comprensión **2** : articular en silencio ⟨she mouthed the words : formó las palabras con los labios⟩

mouth² ['maʊθ] *n* : boca *f* (de una persona o un animal), entrada *f* (de un túnel), desembocadura *f* (de un río)

mouthful ['maʊθ,fʊl] *n* : bocado *m* (de comida), bocanada *f* (de líquido o humo)

mouthpiece ['maʊθ,pi:s] *n* : boquilla *f* (de un instrumento musical)

mouthwash ['maʊθ,wɔʃ, -,wɑʃ] *n* : enjuague *m* bucal

movable ['mu:vəbəl] *or* **moveable** *adj* : movible, móvil

move¹ ['mu:v] *v* **moved; moving** *vi* **1** GO : ir **2** RELOCATE : mudarse, trasladarse **3** STIR : moverse ⟨don't move! : ¡no te muevas!⟩ **4** ACT : actuar — *vt* **1** : mover ⟨move it over there : ponlo allí⟩ ⟨he kept moving his feet : no dejaba de mover los pies⟩ **2** INDUCE, PERSUADE : inducir, persuadir, mover **3** TOUCH : conmover ⟨it moved him to tears : lo hizo llorar⟩ **4** PROPOSE : proponer

move² *n* **1** MOVEMENT : movimiento *m* **2** RELOCATION : mudanza *f* (de casa), traslado *m* **3** STEP : paso *m* ⟨a good move : un paso acertado⟩

movement ['mu:vmənt] *n* : movimiento *m*

mover ['mu:vər] *n* : persona *f* que hace mudanzas

movie ['mu:vi] *n* **1** : película *f* **2** **movies** *npl* : cine *m*

moving ['mu:vɪŋ] *adj* **1** : en movimiento ⟨a moving target : un blanco móvil⟩

2 TOUCHING : conmovedor, emocionante

mow[1] ['mo:] vt **mowed; mowed** or **mown** ['mo:n]; **mowing** : cortar (la hierba)

mow[2] ['maʊ] n : pajar m

mower ['mo:ər] → **lawn mower**

Mr. ['mɪstər] n, pl **Messrs.** ['mɛsərz] : señor m

Mrs. ['mɪsəz, -səs, esp South 'mɪzəz, -zəs] n, pl **Mesdames** [meɪ'dɑm, -'dæm] : señora f

Ms. ['mɪz] n : señora f, señorita f

much[1] ['mʌtʃ] adv **more** ['mor]; **most** ['mo:st] : mucho ⟨I'm much happier : estoy mucho más contenta⟩ ⟨she talks as much as I do : habla tanto como yo⟩

much[2] adj **more; most** : mucho ⟨it has much validity : tiene mucha validez⟩ ⟨too much time : demasiado tiempo⟩

much[3] pron : mucho, -cha ⟨I don't need much : no necesito mucho⟩

mucilage ['mju:səlɪdʒ] n : mucílago m

muck ['mʌk] n **1** MANURE : estiércol m **2** DIRT, FILTH : mugre f, suciedad f **3** MIRE, MUD : barro m, fango m, lodo m

mucous ['mju:kəs] adj : mucoso ⟨mucous membrane : membrana mucosa⟩

mucus ['mju:kəs] n : mucosidad f

mud ['mʌd] n : barro m, fango m, lodo m

muddle[1] ['mʌdəl] v **-dled; -dling** vt **1** CONFUSE : confundir **2** BUNGLE : echar a perder, malograr — vi : andar confundido ⟨to muddle through : arreglárselas⟩

muddle[2] n : confusión f, embrollo m, lío m

muddleheaded [,mʌdəl'hɛdəd, 'mʌdəl,-] adj CONFUSED : confuso, despistado

muddy[1] ['mʌdi] vt **-died; -dying** : llenar de barro

muddy[2] adj **-dier; -est** : barroso, fangoso, lodoso, enlodado ⟨you're all muddy : estás cubierto de barro⟩

muff[1] ['mʌf] vt BUNGLE : echar a perder, fallar (un tiro, etc.)

muff[2] n : manguito m

muffin ['mʌfən] n : magdalena f, mantecada f Mex

muffle ['mʌfəl] vt **-fled; -fling 1** ENVELOP : cubrir, tapar **2** DEADEN : amortiguar (un sonido)

muffler ['mʌflər] n **1** SCARF : bufanda f **2** : silenciador m, mofle m CA, Mex (de un automóvil)

mug[1] ['mʌg] v **mugged; mugging** vi : posar (con afectación), hacer muecas ⟨mugging for the camera : haciendo muecas para la cámara⟩ — vt ASSAULT : asaltar, atracar

mug[2] n CUP : tazón m

mugger ['mʌgər] n : atracador m, -dora f

mugginess ['mʌginəs] n : bochorno m

muggy ['mʌgi] adj **-gier; -est** : bochornoso

mulatto [mʊ'lɑto, -'læ-] n, pl **-toes** or **-tos** : mulato m, -ta f

mulberry ['mʌl,bɛri] n, pl **-ries** : morera f (árbol), mora f (fruta)

mulch[1] ['mʌltʃ] vt : cubrir con pajote

mulch[2] n : pajote m

mule ['mju:l] n **1** : mula f **2** : obstinado m, -da f; terco m, -ca f

mulish ['mju:lɪʃ] adj : obstinado, terco

mull ['mʌl] vt **to mull over** : reflexionar sobre

mullet ['mʌlət] n, pl **-let** or **-lets** : mújol m, múgil m

multicolored [,mʌlti'kʌlərd, ,mʌltaɪ-] adj : multicolor, abigarrado

multicultural [,mʌlti'kʌltʃərəl] adj : multicultural

multifaceted [,mʌlti'fæsətəd, ,mʌltaɪ-] adj : multifacético

multifamily [,mʌlti'fæmli, ,mʌltaɪ-] adj : multifamiliar

multifarious [,mʌltə'færiəs] adj DIVERSE : diverso, variado

multilateral [,mʌlti'lætərəl, ,mʌltaɪ-] adj : multilateral

multimedia [,mʌlti'mi:diə, ,mʌltaɪ-] : multimedia

multimillionaire [,mʌlti,mɪljə'nær, ,mʌltaɪ-, -'mɪljə,nær] adj : multimillonario

multinational [,mʌlti'næʃənəl, ,mʌltaɪ-] adj : multinacional

multiple[1] ['mʌltəpəl] adj : múltiple

multiple[2] n : múltiplo m

multiple sclerosis [sklə'ro:sɪs] n : esclerosis f múltiple

multiplication [,mʌltəplə'keɪʃən] n : multiplicación f

multiplicity [,mʌltə'plɪsəti] n, pl **-ties** : multiplicidad f

multiplier ['mʌltə,plaɪər] n : multiplicador m (en matemáticas)

multiply ['mʌltə,plaɪ] v **-plied; -plying** vt : multiplicar — vi : multiplicarse

multipurpose [,mʌlti'pərpəs, ,mʌltaɪ-] adj : multiuso

multitude ['mʌltə,tu:d, -,tju:d] n **1** CROWD : multitud f, muchedumbre f **2** HOST : multitud f, gran cantidad f ⟨a multitude of ideas : numerosas ideas⟩

multivitamin [,mʌlti'vaɪtəmən, ,mʌltaɪ-] adj : multivitamínico

mum[1] ['mʌm] adj SILENT : callado

mum[2] n → **chrysanthemum**

mumble[1] ['mʌmbəl] v **-bled; -bling** vt : mascullar, musitar — vi : mascullar, hablar entre dientes, murmurar

mumble[2] n **to speak in a mumble** : hablar entre dientes

mummy ['mʌmi] n, pl **-mies** : momia f

mumps ['mʌmps] ns & pl : paperas fpl

munch ['mʌntʃ] v : mascar, masticar

mundane [,mʌn'deɪn, 'mʌn,-] adj **1** EARTHLY, WORLDLY : mundano, terrenal **2** COMMONPLACE : rutinario, ordinario

municipal [mju'nɪsəpəl] adj : municipal

municipality [mju,nɪsə'pæləti] n, pl **-ties** : municipio m

munitions [mju'nɪʃənz] npl : municiones fpl

mural¹ ['mjʊrəl] *adj* : mural

mural² ['mjʊrəlɪst] *n* : mural *m*

murder¹ ['mərdər] *vt* : asesinar, matar — *vi* : matar

murder² *n* : asesinato *m*, homicidio *m*

murderer ['mərdərər] *n* : asesino *m*, -na *f*; homicida *mf*

murderess ['mərdərɪs, -də‚rɛs, -dərəs] *n* : asesina *f*, homicida *f*

murderous ['mərdərəs] *adj* : asesino, homicida

murk ['mərk] *n* DARKNESS : oscuridad *f*, tinieblas *fpl*

murkiness ['mərkinəs] *n* : oscuridad *f*, tenebrosidad *f*

murky ['mərki] *adj* **-kier; -est** : oscuro, tenebroso

murmur¹ ['mərmər] *vi* **1** DRONE : murmurar **2** GRUMBLE : refunfuñar, regañar, rezongar — *vt* MUMBLE : murmurar

murmur² *n* **1** COMPLAINT : queja *f* **2** DRONE : murmullo *m*, rumor *m*

muscle¹ ['mʌsəl] *vi* **-cled; -cling** : meterse ⟨to muscle in on : meterse por la fuerza en, entrometerse en⟩

muscle² *n* **1** : músculo *m* **2** STRENGTH : fuerza *f*

muscular ['mʌskjələr] *adj* **1** : muscular ⟨muscular tissue : tejido muscular⟩ **2** BRAWNY : musculoso

muscular dystrophy *n* : distrofia *f* muscular

musculature ['mʌskjələ‚tʃʊr, -tʃər] *n* : musculatura *f*

muse¹ ['mjuːz] *vi* **mused; musing** PONDER, REFLECT : cavilar, meditar, reflexionar

muse² *n* : musa *f*

museum [mjʊ'ziːəm] *n* : museo *m*

mush ['mʌʃ] *n* **1** : gachas *fpl* (de maíz) **2** SENTIMENTALITY : sensiblería *f*

mushroom¹ ['mʌʃ‚ruːm, -‚rʊm] *vi* GROW, MULTIPLY : crecer rápidamente, multiplicarse

mushroom² *n* : hongo *m*, champiñón *m*, seta *f*

mushy ['mʌʃi] *adj* **mushier; -est 1** SOFT : blando **2** MAWKISH : sensiblero

music ['mjuːzɪk] *n* : música *f*

musical¹ ['mjuːzɪkəl] *adj* : musical, de música — **musically** *adv*

musical² *n* : comedia *f* musical

music box *n* : cajita *f* de música

musician [mjʊ'zɪʃən] *n* : músico *m*, -ca *f*

musk ['mʌsk] *n* : almizcle *m*

musket ['mʌskət] *n* : mosquete *m*

musketeer [‚mʌskə'tɪr] *n* : mosquetero *m*

muskrat ['mʌsk‚ræt] *n, pl* **-rat** *or* **-rats** : rata *f* almizclera

Muslim¹ ['mʌzləm, 'mʊs-, 'mʊz-] *adj* : musulmán

Muslim² *n* : musulmán *m*, -mana *f*

muslin ['mʌzlən] *n* : muselina *f*

muss¹ ['mʌs] *vt* : desordenar, despeinar (el pelo)

muss² *n* : desorden *m*

mussel ['mʌsəl] *n* : mejillón *m*

must¹ ['mʌst] *v aux* **1** (*expressing obligation or necessity*) : deber, tener que ⟨you must stop : debes parar⟩ ⟨we must obey : tenemos que obedecer⟩ **2** (*expressing probability*) : deber (de), haber de ⟨you must be tired : debes de estar cansado⟩ ⟨it must be late : ha de ser tarde⟩

must² *n* : necesidad *f* ⟨exercise is a must : el ejercicio es imprescindible⟩

mustache ['mʌ‚stæʃ, mʌ'stæʃ] *n* : bigote *m*, bigotes *mpl*

mustang ['mʌ‚stæŋ] *n* : mustang *m*

mustard ['mʌstərd] *n* : mostaza *f*

muster¹ ['mʌstər] *vt* **1** ASSEMBLE : reunir **2 to muster up** : armarse de, cobrar (valor, fuerzas, etc.)

muster² *n* **1** INSPECTION : revista *f* (de tropas) ⟨it didn't pass muster : no resistió un examen minucioso⟩ **2** COLLECTION : colección *f*

mustiness ['mʌstinəs] *n* : lo mohoso

musty ['mʌsti] *adj* **mustier; -est** : mohoso, que huele a moho, que huele a encerrado

mutant¹ ['mjuːtənt] *adj* : mutante

mutant² *n* : mutante *m*

mutate ['mjuː‚teɪt] *vi* **-tated; -tating 1** : mutar (genéticamente) **2** CHANGE : transformarse

mutation [mjuː'teɪʃən] *n* : mutación *f* (genética)

mute¹ ['mjuːt] *vt* **muted; muting** MUFFLE : amortiguar, ponerle sordina a (un instrumento musical)

mute² *adj* **muter; mutest** : mudo — **mutely** *adv*

mute³ *n* **1** : mudo *m*, -da *f* (persona) **2** : sordina *f* (para un instrumento musical)

mutilate ['mjuːtə‚leɪt] *vt* **-lated; -lating** : mutilar

mutilation [‚mjuːtə'leɪʃən] *n* : mutilación *f*

mutineer [‚mjuːtən'ɪr] *n* : amotinado *m*, -da *f*

mutinous ['mjuːtənəs] *adj* : amotinado

mutiny¹ ['mjuːtəni] *vi* **-nied; -nying** : amotinarse

mutiny² *n, pl* **-nies** : amotinamiento *m*, motín *m*

mutt ['mʌt] *n* MONGREL : perro *m* mestizo, perro *m* corriente *Mex*

mutter ['mʌtər] *vi* **1** MUMBLE : mascullar, hablar entre dientes, murmurar **2** GRUMBLE : refunfuñar, regañar, rezongar

mutton ['mʌtən] *n* : carne *f* de carnero

mutual ['mjuːtʃʊəl] *adj* **1** : mutuo ⟨mutual respect : respeto mutuo⟩ **2** COMMON : común ⟨a mutual friend : un amigo común⟩

mutually ['mjuːtʃʊəli, -tʃəli] *adv* **1** : mutuamente ⟨mutually beneficial : mutuamente beneficioso⟩ **2** JOINTLY : conjuntamente

muzzle[1] ['mʌzəl] *vt* **-zled; -zling** : ponerle un bozal a (un animal), amordazar
muzzle[2] *n* **1** SNOUT : hocico *m* **2** : bozal *m* (para un perro, etc.) **3** : boca *f* (de un arma de fuego)
my[1] ['maɪ] *adj* : mi ⟨my parents : mis padres⟩
my[2] *interj* : ¡caramba!, ¡Dios mío!
myopia [maɪ'o:piə] *n* : miopía *f*
myopic [maɪ'o:pɪk, -'ɑ-] *adj* : miope
myriad[1] ['mɪriəd] *adj* INNUMERABLE : innumerable
myriad[2] *n* : miríada *f*
myrrh ['mər] *n* : mirra *f*
myrtle ['mərt̬əl] *n* : mirto *m*, arrayán *m*
myself [maɪ'sɛlf] *pron* **1** (*used reflexively*) : me ⟨I washed myself : me lavé⟩ **2** (*used for emphasis*) : yo mismo, yo misma ⟨I did it myself : lo hice yo mismo⟩
mysterious [mɪ'stɪriəs] *adj* : misterioso — **mysteriously** *adv*

mysteriousness [mɪ'stɪriəsnəs] *n* : lo misterioso
mystery ['mɪstəri] *n, pl* **-teries** : misterio *m*
mystic[1] ['mɪstɪk] *adj* : místico
mystic[2] *n* : místico *m*, -ca *f*
mystical ['mɪstɪkəl] *adj* : místico — **mystically** *adv*
mysticism ['mɪstə,sɪzəm] *n* : misticismo *m*
mystify ['mɪstə,faɪ] *vt* **-fied; -fying** : dejar perplejo, confundir
mystique [mɪ'sti:k] *n* : aura *f* de misterio
myth ['mɪθ] *n* : mito *m*
mythic ['mɪθɪk] *adj* : mítico
mythical ['mɪθɪkəl] *adj* : mítico
mythological [ˌmɪθə'lɑdʒɪkəl] *adj* : mitológico
mythology [mɪ'θɑlədʒi] *n, pl* **-gies** : mitología *f*

N

n ['ɛn] *n, pl* **n's** *or* **ns** ['ɛnz] : decimocuarta letra del alfabeto inglés
nab ['næb] *vt* **nabbed; nabbing** : prender, pillar *fam*, pescar *fam*
nadir ['neɪdər, 'neɪ,dɪr] *n* : nadir *m*, punto *m* más bajo
nag[1] ['næg] *v* **nagged; nagging** *vi* **1** COMPLAIN : quejarse, rezongar **2 to nag at** HASSLE : molestar, darle (la) lata (a alguien) — *vt* **1** PESTER : molestar, fastidiar **2** SCOLD : regañar, estarle encima a *fam*
nag[2] *n* **1** GRUMBLER : gruñón *m*, -ñona *f* **2** HORSE : jamelgo *m*
naiad ['neɪəd, 'naɪ-, -ˌæd] *n, pl* **-iads** *or* **-iades** [-əˌdi:z] : náyade *f*
nail[1] ['neɪl] *vt* : clavar, sujetar con clavos
nail[2] *n* **1** FINGERNAIL : uña *f* ⟨nail file : lima (de uñas)⟩ ⟨nail polish : laca de uñas⟩ **2** : clavo *m* ⟨to hit the nail on the head : dar en el clavo⟩
naive *or* **naïve** [nɑ'i:v] *adj* **-iver; -est 1** INGENUOUS : ingenuo, cándido **2** GULLIBLE : crédulo
naively [nɑ'i:vli] *adv* : ingenuamente
naiveté [ˌnɑˌi:və'teɪ, nɑ'i:vəˌ-] *n* : ingenuidad *f*
naked ['neɪkəd] *adj* **1** UNCLOTHED : desnudo **2** UNCOVERED : desenvainado (dícese de una espada), pelado (dícese de los árboles), expuesto al aire (dícese de una llama) **3** OBVIOUS, PLAIN : manifiesto, puro, desnudo ⟨the naked truth : la pura verdad⟩ **4 to the naked eye** : a simple vista
nakedly ['neɪkədli] *adv* : manifiestamente
nakedness ['neɪkədnəs] *n* : desnudez *f*
name[1] ['neɪm] *vt* **named; naming 1** CALL : llamar, bautizar, ponerle nombre a **2** MENTION : mentar, mencionar, dar el nombre de ⟨they have named a

suspect : han dado el nombre de un sospechoso⟩ **3** APPOINT : nombrar **4 to name a price** : fijar un precio
name[2] *adj* **1** KNOWN : de nombre ⟨name brand : marca conocida⟩ **2** PROMINENT : de renombre, de prestigio
name[3] *n* **1** : nombre *m* ⟨what is your name? : ¿cómo se llama?⟩ **2** SURNAME : apellido *m* **3** EPITHET : epíteto *m* ⟨to call somebody names : llamar a alguien de todo⟩ **4** REPUTATION : fama *f*, reputación *f* ⟨to make a name for oneself : darse a conocer, hacerse famoso⟩
nameless ['neɪmləs] *adj* **1** ANONYMOUS : anónimo **2** INDESCRIBABLE : indecible, indescriptible
namelessly ['neɪmləsli] *adv* : anónimamente
namely ['neɪmli] *adv* : a saber
namesake ['neɪmˌseɪk] *n* : tocayo *m*, -ya *f*; homónimo *m*, -ma *f*
Namibian [nə'mɪbiən] *n* : namibio *m*, -bia *f* — **Namibian** *adj*
nanny ['næni] *n, pl* **nannies** : niñera *f*; nana *f CA, Col, Mex, Ven*
nap[1] ['næp] *vi* **napped; napping 1** : dormir, dormir la siesta **2 to be caught napping** : estar desprevenido
nap[2] *n* **1** SLEEP : siesta *f* ⟨to take a nap : echarse una siesta⟩ **2** FUZZ, PILE : pelo *m*, pelusa *f* (de telas)
nape ['neɪp, 'næp] *n* : nuca *f*, cerviz *f*, cogote *m*
naphtha ['næfθə] *n* : nafta *f*
napkin ['næpkən] *n* : servilleta *f*
narcissism ['nɑrsəˌsɪzəm] *n* : narcisismo *m*
narcissist ['nɑrsəsɪst] *n* : narcisista *mf*
narcissistic [ˌnɑrsə'sɪstɪk] *adj* : narcisista
narcissus [nɑr'sɪsəs] *n, pl* **-cissus** *or*

-cissuses or **-cissi** [-'sɪ,saɪ, -,si:] : narciso m

narcotic¹ [nɑr'kɑṭɪk] adj : narcótico

narcotic² n : narcótico m, estupefaciente m

narrate ['nær,eɪt] vt **-rated; -rating** : narrar, relatar

narration [næ'reɪʃən] n : narración f

narrative¹ ['nærəṭɪv] adj : narrativo

narrative² n : narración f, narrativa f, relato m

narrator ['nær,eɪṭər] n : narrador m, -dora f

narrow¹ ['nær,o:] vi : estrecharse, angostarse ⟨the river narrowed : el río se estrechó⟩ — vt **1** : estrechar, angostar **2** LIMIT : restringir, limitar ⟨to narrow the search : limitar la búsqueda⟩

narrow² adj **1** : estrecho, angosto **2** LIMITED : estricto, limitado ⟨in the narrowest sense of the word : en el sentido más estricto de la palabra⟩ **3 to have a narrow escape** : escapar por un pelo

narrowly ['næroli] adv **1** BARELY : por poco **2** CLOSELY : de cerca

narrow–minded [,næro'maɪndəd] adj : de miras estrechas

narrowness ['næronəs] n : estrechez f

narrows ['næro:z] npl STRAIT : estrecho m

narwhal ['nɑr,hwɑl, 'nɑrwəl] n : narval m

nasal ['neɪzəl] adj : nasal, gangoso ⟨a nasal voice : una voz gangosa⟩

nasally ['neɪzəli] adv **1** : por la nariz **2** : con voz gangosa

nastily ['næstəli] adv : con maldad, cruelmente

nastiness ['næstinəs] n : porquería f

nasturtium [nə'stərʃəm, næ-] n : capuchina f

nasty ['næsti] adj **-tier; -est 1** FILTHY : sucio, mugriento **2** OBSCENE : obsceno **3** MEAN, SPITEFUL : malo, malicioso **4** UNPLEASANT : desagradable, feo **5** REPUGNANT : asqueroso, repugnante ⟨a nasty smell : un olor asqueroso⟩

natal ['neɪṭəl] adj : natal

nation ['neɪʃən] n : nación f

national¹ ['næʃənəl] adj : nacional

national² n : ciudadano m, -na f; nacional mf

nationalism ['næʃənə,lɪzəm] n : nacionalismo m

nationalist¹ ['næʃənəlɪst] adj : nacionalista

nationalist² n : nacionalista mf

nationalistic [,næʃənə'lɪstɪk] adj : nacionalista

nationality [,næʃə'næləṭi] n, pl **-ties** : nacionalidad f

nationalization [,næʃənələ'zeɪʃən] n : nacionalización f

nationalize ['næʃənə,laɪz] vt **-ized; -izing** : nacionalizar

nationally ['næʃənəli] adv : a escala nacional, a nivel nacional

nationwide ['neɪʃən'waɪd] adj : en toda la nación, por todo el país

native¹ ['neɪṭɪv] adj **1** INNATE : innato **2** : natal ⟨her native city : su ciudad natal⟩ **3** INDIGENOUS : indígena, autóctono

native² n **1** ABORIGINE : nativo m, -va f; indígena mf **2** : natural m ⟨he's a native of Mexico : es natural de México⟩

Native American → **American Indian**

nativity [nə'tɪvəṭi, neɪ-] n, pl **-ties 1** BIRTH : navidad f **2 the Nativity** : la Natividad, la Navidad

natty ['næṭi] adj **-tier; -est** : elegante, garboso

natural¹ ['næt͡ʃərəl] adj **1** : natural, de la naturaleza ⟨natural woodlands : bosques naturales⟩ ⟨natural childbirth : parto natural⟩ **2** INNATE : innato, natural **3** UNAFFECTED : natural, sin afectación **4** LIFELIKE : natural, vivo

natural² n **to be a natural** : tener un talento innato (para algo)

natural gas n : gas m natural

natural history n : historia f natural

naturalism ['næt͡ʃərə,lɪzəm] n : naturalismo m

naturalist ['næt͡ʃərəlɪst] n : naturalista mf — **naturalist** adj

naturalistic [,næt͡ʃərə'lɪstɪk] adj : naturalista

naturalization [,næt͡ʃərələ'zeɪʃən] n : naturalización f

naturalize ['næt͡ʃərə,laɪz] vt **-ized; -izing** : naturalizar

naturally ['næt͡ʃərəli] adv **1** INHERENTLY : naturalmente, intrínsecamente **2** UNAFFECTEDLY : de manera natural **3** OF COURSE : por supuesto, naturalmente

naturalness ['næt͡ʃərəlnəs] n : naturalidad f

natural science n : ciencias fpl naturales

nature ['neɪṭər] n **1** : naturaleza f ⟨the laws of nature : las leyes de la naturaleza⟩ **2** KIND, SORT : índole f, clase f ⟨things of this nature : cosas de esta índole⟩ **3** DISPOSITION : carácter m, natural m, naturaleza f ⟨it is his nature to be friendly : es de natural simpático⟩ ⟨human nature : la naturaleza humana⟩

naught ['nɔt] n **1** : nada f ⟨to come to naught : reducirse a nada, fracasar⟩ **2** ZERO : cero m

naughtily ['nɔṭəli] adv : traviesamente, con malicia

naughtiness ['nɔṭinəs] n : mala conducta f, travesuras fpl, malicia f

naughty ['nɔṭi] adj **-tier; -est 1** MISCHIEVOUS : travieso, pícaro **2** RISQUÉ : picante, subido de tono

nausea ['nɔziə, 'nɔʃə] n **1** SICKNESS : náuseas fpl **2** DISGUST : asco m

nauseate ['nɔzi,eɪt, -ʒi-, -si-, -ʃi-] vt **-ated; -ating 1** SICKEN : darle náuseas (a alguien) **2** DISGUST : asquear, darle asco (a alguien)

nauseating *adj* : nauseabundo, repugnante

nauseatingly ['nɔzi‚eɪtɪŋli, -ʒi-, -si-, -ʃi-] *adv* : hasta el punto de dar asco ⟨nauseatingly sweet : tan dulce que da asco⟩

nauseous ['nɔʃəs, -ziəs] *adj* **1** SICK : mareado, con náuseas **2** SICKENING : nauseabundo

nautical ['nɔtɪkəl] *adj* : náutico

nautilus ['nɔtələs] *n, pl* **-luses** *or* **-li** [-‚laɪ, -‚li:] : nautilo *m*

Navajo ['nævə‚ho:, 'nɑ-] *n* : navajo *m*, -ja *f* — **Navajo** *adj*

naval ['neɪvəl] *adj* : naval

nave ['neɪv] *n* : nave *f*

navel ['neɪvəl] *n* : ombligo *m*

navigability [‚nævɪgə'bɪləti] *n* : navegabilidad *f*

navigable ['nævɪgəbəl] *adj* : navegable

navigate ['nævə‚geɪt] *v* **-gated; -gating** *vi* : navegar — *vt* **1** STEER : gobernar (un barco), pilotar (un avión) **2** : navegar por (un río, etc.)

navigation [‚nævə'geɪʃən] *n* : navegación *f*

navigator ['nævə‚geɪtər] *n* : navegante *mf*

navy ['neɪvi] *n, pl* **-vies 1** FLEET : flota *f* **2** : marina *f* de guerra, armada *f* ⟨the United States Navy : la armada de los Estados Unidos⟩ **3** *or* **navy blue** : azul *m* marino

nay[1] ['neɪ] *adv* : no

nay[2] *n* : no *m*, voto *m* en contra

Nazi ['nɑtsi, 'næt-] *n* : nazi *mf*

Nazism ['nɑt‚sɪzəm, 'næt-] *or* **Naziism** ['nɑtsi‚izəm, 'næt-] *n* : nazismo *m*

Neanderthal man [ni'ændər‚θɔl, -‚tɔl] *n* : hombre *m* de Neanderthal

near[1] ['nɪr] *vt* **1** : acercarse a ⟨the ship is nearing port : el barco se está acercando al puerto⟩ **2** : estar a punto de ⟨she is nearing graduation : está a punto de graduarse⟩

near[2] *adv* **1** CLOSE : cerca ⟨my family lives quite near : mi familia vive muy cerca⟩ **2** NEARLY : casi ⟨I came near to finishing : casi terminé⟩

near[3] *adj* **1** CLOSE : cercano, próximo **2** SIMILAR : parecido, semejante

near[4] *prep* : cerca de

nearby[1] [nɪr'baɪ, 'nɪr‚baɪ] *adv* : cerca

nearby[2] *adj* : cercano

nearly ['nɪrli] *adv* **1** ALMOST : casi ⟨nearly asleep : casi dormido⟩ **2** **not nearly** : ni con mucho, ni mucho menos ⟨it was not nearly so bad as I had expected : no fue ni con mucho tan malo como esperaba⟩

nearness ['nɪrnəs] *n* : proximidad *f*

nearsighted ['nɪr‚saɪtəd] *adj* : miope, corto de vista

nearsightedly ['nɪr‚saɪtədli] *adv* : con miopía

nearsightedness ['nɪr‚saɪtədnəs] *n* : miopía *f*

neat ['ni:t] *adj* **1** CLEAN, ORDERLY : ordenado, pulcro, limpio **2** UNDILUTED : solo, sin diluir **3** SIMPLE, TASTEFUL : sencillo y de buen gusto **4** CLEVER : hábil, ingenioso ⟨a neat trick : un truco ingenioso⟩

neatly ['ni:tli] *adv* **1** TIDILY : ordenadamente **2** CLEVERLY : ingeniosamente

neatness ['ni:tnəs] *n* : pulcritud *f*, limpieza *f*, orden *m*

nebula ['nɛbjulə] *n, pl* **-lae** [-‚li:, -‚laɪ] : nebulosa *f*

nebulous ['nɛbjuləs] *adj* : nebuloso, vago

necessarily [‚nɛsə'sɛrəli] *adv* : necesariamente, forzosamente

necessary[1] ['nɛsə‚sɛri] *adj* **1** INEVITABLE : inevitable **2** COMPULSORY : necesario, obligatorio **3** ESSENTIAL : imprescindible, preciso, necesario

necessary[2] *n, pl* **-saries** : lo esencial, lo necesario

necessitate [nɪ'sɛsə‚teɪt] *vt* **-tated; -tating** : necesitar, requerir

necessity [nɪ'sɛsəti] *n, pl* **-ties 1** NEED : necesidad *f* **2** REQUIREMENT : requisito *m* indispensable **3** POVERTY : indigencia *f*, necesidad *f* **4** INEVITABILITY : inevitabilidad *f*

neck[1] ['nɛk] *vi* : besuquearse

neck[2] *n* **1** : cuello *m* (de una persona), pescuezo *m* (de un animal) **2** COLLAR : cuello *m* **3** : cuello *m* (de una botella), mástil *m* (de una guitarra)

neckerchief ['nɛkərtʃəf, -‚tʃi:f] *n, pl* **-chiefs** [-tʃəfs, -‚tʃi:fs] : pañuelo *m* (para el cuello), mascada *f Mex*

necklace ['nɛkləs] *n* : collar *m*

neckline ['nɛk‚laɪn] *n* : escote *m*

necktie ['nɛk‚taɪ] *n* : corbata *f*

nectar ['nɛktər] *n* : néctar *m*

nectarine [‚nɛktə'ri:n] *n* : nectarina *f*

née *or* **nee** ['neɪ] *adj* : de soltera ⟨Mrs. Smith, née Whitman : la señora Smith, de soltera Whitman⟩

need[1] ['ni:d] *vt* **1** : necesitar ⟨I need your help : necesito su ayuda⟩ ⟨I need money : me falta dinero⟩ **2** REQUIRE : requerir, exigir ⟨that job needs patience : ese trabajo exige paciencia⟩ **3 to need to** : tener que ⟨he needs to study : tiene que estudiar⟩ ⟨they need to be scolded : hay que reprenderlos⟩ — *v aux* **1** MUST : tener que, deber ⟨need you shout? : ¿tienes que gritar?⟩ **2 to be needed** : hacer falta ⟨you needn't worry : no hace falta que te preocupes, no hay por qué preocuparse⟩

need[2] *n* **1** NECESSITY : necesidad *f* ⟨in case of need : en caso de necesidad⟩ **2** LACK : falta *f* ⟨the need for better training : la falta de mejor capacitación⟩ ⟨to be in need : necesitar⟩ **3** POVERTY : necesidad *f*, indigencia *f* **4 needs** *npl* : requisitos *mpl*, carencias *fpl*

needful ['ni:dfəl] *adj* : necesario

needle[1] ['ni:dəl] *vt* **-dled; -dling** : pinchar

needle[2] *n* **1** : aguja *f* ⟨to thread a needle : enhebrar una aguja⟩ ⟨knitting

needle : aguja de tejer⟩ **2** POINTER : aguja *f*, indicador *m*

needlepoint [ˈniːdəlˌpoint] *n* **1** LACE : encaje *m* de mano **2** EMBROIDERY : bordado *m* en cañamazo

needless [ˈniːdləs] *adj* : innecesario

needlessly [ˈniːdləsli] *adv* : sin ninguna necesidad, innecesariamente

needlework [ˈniːdəlˌwərk] *n* : bordado *m*

needn't [ˈniːdənt] (*contraction of* **need not**) → **need**

needy¹ [ˈniːdi] *adj* **needier; -est** : necesitado

needy² *n* **the needy** : los necesitados *mpl*

nefarious [nɪˈfæriəs] *adj* : nefario, nefando, infame

negate [nɪˈgeɪt] *vt* **-gated; -gating 1** DENY : negar **2** NULLIFY : invalidar, anular

negation [nɪˈgeɪʃən] *n* : negación *f*

negative¹ [ˈnɛgətɪv] *adj* : negativo

negative² *n* **1** : negación *f* (en lingüística) **2** : negativa *f* ⟨to answer in the negative : contestar con una negativa⟩ **3** : término *m* negativo (en matemáticas) **4** : negativo *m*, imagen *f* en negativo (en fotografía)

negatively [ˈnɛgətɪvli] *adv* : negativamente

neglect¹ [nɪˈglɛkt] *vt* **1** : desatender, descuidar ⟨to neglect one's health : descuidar la salud⟩ **2** : no cumplir con, faltar a ⟨to neglect one's obligations : faltar uno a sus obligaciones⟩ ⟨he neglected to tell me : omitió decírmelo⟩

neglect² *n* **1** : negligencia *f*, descuido *m*, incumplimiento *m* ⟨through neglect : por negligencia⟩ ⟨neglect of duty : incumplimiento del deber⟩ **2 in a state of neglect** : abandonado, descuidado

neglectful [nɪˈglɛktfəl] *adj* : descuidado *m*

negligee [ˌnɛgləˈʒeɪ] *n* : negligé *m*

negligence [ˈnɛglɪdʒənts] *n* : descuido *m*, negligencia *f*

negligent [ˈnɛglɪdʒənt] *adj* : negligente, descuidado — **negligently** *adv*

negligible [ˈnɛglɪdʒəbəl] *adj* : insignificante, despreciable

negotiable [nɪˈgoːʃəbəl, -ʃiə-] *adj* : negociable

negotiate [nɪˈgoːʃiˌeɪt] *v* **-ated; -ating** *vi* : negociar — *vt* **1** : negociar, gestionar ⟨to negotiate a treaty : negociar un trato⟩ **2** : salvar, franquear ⟨they negotiated the obstacles : salvaron los obstáculos⟩ ⟨to negotiate a turn : tomar una curva⟩

negotiation [nɪˌgoːʃiˈeɪʃən, -siˈeɪ-] *n* : negociación *f*

negotiator [nɪˈgoːʃiˌeɪtər, -siˌeɪ-] *n* : negociador *m*, -dora *f*

Negro [ˈniːˌgroː] *n, pl* **-groes** : negro *m*, -gra *f*

neigh¹ [ˈneɪ] *vi* : relinchar

neigh² *n* : relincho *m*

neighbor¹ [ˈneɪbər] *vt* : ser vecino de, estar junto a ⟨her house neighbors mine : su casa está junto a la mía⟩ — *vi* : estar cercano, lindar, colindar ⟨her land neighbors on mine : sus tierras lindan con las mías⟩

neighbor² *n* **1** : vecino *m*, -na *f* **2 love thy neighbor** : ama a tu prójimo

neighborhood [ˈneɪbərˌhʊd] *n* **1** : barrio *m*, vecindad *f*, vecindario *m* **2 in the neighborhood of** : alrededor de, cerca de

neighborly [ˈneɪbərli] *adv* : amable, de buena vecindad

neither¹ [ˈniːðər, ˈnaɪ-] *adj* : ninguno (de los dos)

neither² *conj* **1** : ni ⟨neither asleep nor awake : ni dormido ni despierto⟩ **2** NOR : ni (tampoco) ⟨I'm not asleep— neither am I : no estoy dormido—ni yo tampoco⟩

neither³ *pron* : ninguno

nemesis [ˈnɛməsɪs] *n, pl* **-eses** [-ˌsiːz] **1** RIVAL : rival *mf* **2** RETRIBUTION : justo castigo *m*

Neoclassical [ˌniːoˈklæsɪkəl] *adj* : neoclásico

neologism [niˈɑləˌdʒɪzəm] *n* : neologismo *m*

neon¹ [ˈniːˌɑn] *adj* : de neón ⟨neon sign : letrero de neón⟩

neon² *n* : neón *m*

neophyte [ˈniːəˌfaɪt] *n* : neófito *m*, -ta *f*

Nepali [nəˈpɔli, -ˈpɑ-, -ˈpæ-] *n* : nepalés *m*, -lesa *f* — **Nepali** *adj*

nephew [ˈnɛˌfjuː, *chiefly British* ˈnɛˌvjuː] *n* : sobrino *m*

nepotism [ˈnɛpəˌtɪzəm] *n* : nepotismo *m*

Neptune [ˈnɛpˌtuːn, -ˌtjuːn] *n* : Neptuno *m*

nerd [ˈnərd] *n* : ganso *m*, -sa *f*

nerve [ˈnərv] *n* **1** : nervio *m* **2** COURAGE : coraje *m*, valor *m*, fuerza *f* de la voluntad ⟨to lose one's nerve : perder el valor⟩ **3** AUDACITY, GALL : atrevimiento *m*, descaro *m* ⟨of all the nerve! : ¡qué descaro!⟩ **4 nerves** *npl* : nervios *mpl* ⟨a fit of nerves : un ataque de nervios⟩

nervous [ˈnərvəs] *adj* **1** : nervioso ⟨the nervous system : el sistema nervioso⟩ **2** EXCITABLE : nervioso, excitable ⟨to get nervous : excitarse, ponerse nervioso⟩ **3** FEARFUL : miedoso, temeroso

nervously [ˈnərvəsli] *adv* : nerviosamente

nervousness [ˈnərvəsnəs] *n* : nerviosismo *m*, nerviosidad *f*, ansiedad *f*

nervy [ˈnərvi] *adj* **nervier; -est 1** COURAGEOUS : valiente **2** IMPUDENT : atrevido, descarado, fresco *fam* **3** NERVOUS : nervioso

nest¹ [ˈnɛst] *vi* : anidar

nest² *n* **1** : nido *m* (de un ave), avispero *m* (de una avispa), madriguera *f* (de un animal) **2** REFUGE : nido *m*, refugio *m* **3** SET : juego *m* ⟨a nest of tables : un juego de mesitas⟩

nestle [ˈnɛsəl] *vi* **-tled; -tling** : acurrucarse, arrimarse cómodamente

net¹ ['nɛt] *vt* **netted; netting 1** CATCH : pescar, atrapar con una red **2** CLEAR : ganar neto ⟨they netted $5000 : ganaron $5000 netos⟩ **3** YIELD : producir neto

net² *adj* : neto ⟨net weight : peso neto⟩ ⟨net gain : ganancia neta⟩

net³ *n* : red *f*, malla *f*

nether ['nɛðər] *adj* **1** : inferior, más bajo **2 the nether regions** : el infierno

nettle¹ ['nɛt̬əl] *vt* **-tled; -tling** : irritar, provocar, molestar

nettle² *n* : ortiga *f*

network ['nɛt̬,wərk] *n* **1** SYSTEM : red *f* **2** CHAIN : cadena *f* ⟨a network of supermarkets : una cadena de supermercados⟩

neural ['nʊrəl, 'njʊr-] *adj* : neural

neuralgia [nʊ'rældʒə, njʊ-] *n* : neuralgia *f*

neuritis [nʊ'raɪt̬əs, njʊ-] *n, pl* **-ritides** [-'rɪt̬ə,diːz] *or* **-ritises** : neuritis *f*

neurological [,nʊrə'ladʒɪkəl, ,njʊr-] *or* **neurologic** [,nʊrə'ladʒɪk, ,njʊr-] *adj* : neurológico

neurologist [nʊ'ralədʒɪst, njʊ-] *n* : neurólogo *m*, -ga *f*

neurology [nʊ'ralədʒi, njʊ-] *n* : neurología *f*

neurosis [nʊ'roːsɪs, njʊ-] *n, pl* **-roses** [-,siːz] : neurosis *f*

neurotic¹ [nʊ'rat̬ɪk, njʊ-] *adj* : neurótico

neurotic² *n* : neurótico *m*, -ca *f*

neuter¹ ['nuːt̬ər, 'njuː-] *vt* : castrar

neuter² *adj* : neutro

neutral¹ ['nuːtrəl, 'njuː-] *adj* **1** IMPARTIAL : neutral, imparcial ⟨to remain neutral : permanecer neutral⟩ **2** : neutro ⟨a neutral color : un color neutro⟩ **3** : neutro (en la química o la electricidad)

neutral² *n* : punto *m* muerto (de un automóvil)

neutrality [nuː'trælət̬i, njuː-] *n* : neutralidad *f*

neutralization [,nuːtrələ'zeɪʃən, ,njuː-] *n* : neutralización *f*

neutralize ['nuːtrə,laɪz, 'njuː-] *vt* **-ized; -izing** : neutralizar

neutron ['nuː,tran, 'njuː-] *n* : neutrón *m*

never ['nɛvər] *adv* **1** : nunca, jamás ⟨he never studies : nunca estudia⟩ **2 never again** : nunca más, nunca jamás **3 never mind** : no importa

nevermore [,nɛvər'mor] *adv* : nunca más

nevertheless [,nɛvərðə'lɛs] *adv* : sin embargo, no obstante

new ['nuː, 'njuː] *adj* **1** : nuevo ⟨a new dress : un vestido nuevo⟩ **2** RECENT : nuevo, reciente ⟨what's new? : ¿qué hay de nuevo?⟩ ⟨a new arrival : un recién llegado⟩ **3** DIFFERENT : nuevo, distinto ⟨this problem is new : este problema es distinto⟩ ⟨new ideas : ideas nuevas⟩ **4 like new** : como nuevo

newborn ['nuː,bɔrn, 'njuː-] *adj* : recién nacido

newcomer ['nuː,kʌmər, 'njuː-] *n* : recién llegado *m*, recién llegada *f*

newfangled ['nuː'fæŋɡəld, 'njuː-] *adj* : novedoso

newfound ['nuː'faʊnd, 'njuː-] *adj* : recién descubierto

newly ['nuːli, 'njuː-] *adv* : recién, recientemente

newlywed ['nuːli,wɛd, 'njuː-] *n* : recién casado *m*, -da *f*

new moon *n* : luna *f* nueva

newness ['nuːnəs, 'njuː-] *n* : novedad *f*

news ['nuːz, 'njuːz] *n* : noticias *fpl*

newscast ['nuːz,kæst, 'njuːz-] *n* : noticiero *m*, informativo *m*

newscaster ['nuːz,kæstər, 'njuːz-] *n* : presentador *m*, -dora *f*; locutor *m*, -tora *f*

newsletter ['nuːz,lɛt̬ər, 'njuːz-] *n* : boletín *m* informativo

newsman ['nuːzmən, 'njuːz-, -,mæn] *n, pl* **-men** [-mən, -,mɛn] : periodista *m*, reportero *m*

newspaper ['nuːz,peɪpər, 'njuːz-] *n* : periódico *m*, diario *m*

newspaperman ['nuːz,peɪpər,mæn, 'njuːz-] *n, pl* **-men** [-mən, -,mɛn] **1** REPORTER : periodista *m*, reportero *m* **2** : dueño *m* de un periódico

newsprint ['nuːz,prɪnt, 'njuːz-] *n* : papel *m* de prensa

newsstand ['nuːz,stænd, 'njuːz-] *n* : quiosco *m*, puesto *m* de periódicos

newswoman ['nuːz,wʊmən, 'njuːz-] *n, pl* **-women** [-,wɪmən] : periodista *f*, reportera *f*

newsworthy ['nuːz,wərði, 'njuːz-] *adj* : de interés periodístico

newsy ['nuːzi, 'njuː-] *adj* **newsier; -est** : lleno de noticias

newt ['nuːt, 'njuːt] *n* : tritón *m*

New Testament *n* : Nuevo Testamento *m*

New Year *n* : Año *m* Nuevo

New Year's Day *n* : día *m* del Año Nuevo

New Yorker [nuː'jɔrkər, njuː-] *n* : neoyorquino *m*, -na *f*

New Zealander [nuː'ziːləndər, njuː-] *n* : neozelandés *m*, -desa *f*

next¹ ['nɛkst] *adv* **1** AFTERWARD : después, luego ⟨what will you do next? : ¿qué harás después?⟩ **2** NOW : después, ahora, entonces ⟨next I will sing a song : ahora voy a cantar una canción⟩ **3** : la próxima vez ⟨when next we meet : la próxima vez que nos encontremos⟩

next² *adj* **1** ADJACENT : contiguo, de al lado **2** COMING : que viene, próximo ⟨next Friday : el viernes que viene⟩ **3** FOLLOWING : siguiente ⟨the next year : el año siguiente⟩

next–door ['nɛkst'dor] *adj* : de al lado

next to¹ *adv* ALMOST : casi, prácticamente ⟨next to impossible : casi imposible⟩

next to[2] *prep* : junto a, al lado de
nexus ['nɛksəs] *n* : nexo *m*
nib ['nɪb] *n* : plumilla *f*
nibble[1] ['nɪbəl] *v* **-bled; -bling** *vt* : pellizcar, mordisquear, picar — *vi* : picar
nibble[2] *n* : mordisco *m*
Nicaraguan [ˌnɪkə'rɑgwən] *n* : nicaragüense *mf* — **Nicaraguan** *adj*
nice ['naɪs] *adj* **nicer; nicest 1** REFINED : pulido, refinado **2** SUBTLE : fino, sutil **3** PLEASING : agradable, bueno, lindo ⟨nice weather : buen tiempo⟩ **4** RESPECTABLE : bueno, decente **5 nice and** : bien, muy ⟨nice and hot : bien caliente⟩ ⟨nice and slow : despacito⟩
nicely ['naɪsli] *adv* **1** KINDLY : amablemente **2** POLITELY : con buenos modales **3** ATTRACTIVELY : de buen gusto
niceness ['naɪsnəs] *n* : simpatía *f*, amabilidad *f*
nicety ['naɪsəti] *n, pl* **-ties 1** DETAIL, SUBTLETY : sutileza *f*, detalle *m* **2 niceties** *npl* : lujos *mpl*, detalles *mpl*
niche ['nɪtʃ] *n* **1** RECESS : nicho *m*, hornacina *f* **2** : nicho *m*, hueco *m* ⟨to make a niche for oneself : hacerse un hueco, encontrarse una buena posición⟩
nick[1] ['nɪk] *vt* : cortar, hacer una muesca en
nick[2] *n* **1** CUT : corte *m*, muesca *f* **2 in the nick of time** : en el momento crítico, justo a tiempo
nickel ['nɪkəl] *n* **1** : níquel *m* **2** : moneda *f* de cinco centavos
nickname[1] ['nɪkˌneɪm] *vt* **-named; -naming** : apodar
nickname[2] *n* : apodo *m*, mote *m*, sobrenombre *m*
nicotine ['nɪkəˌtiːn] *n* : nicotina *f*
niece ['niːs] *n* : sobrina *f*
Nigerian [naɪ'dʒɪriən] *n* : nigeriano *m*, -na *f* — **Nigerian** *adj*
niggardly ['nɪgərdli] *adj* : mezquino, tacaño
niggling ['nɪgəlɪŋ] *adj* **1** PETTY : insignificante **2** PERSISTENT : constante, persistente ⟨a niggling doubt : una duda constante⟩
nigh[1] ['naɪ] *adv* **1** NEARLY : casi **2 to draw nigh** : acercarse, avecinarse
nigh[2] *adj* : cercano, próximo
night[1] ['naɪt] *adj* : nocturno, de la noche ⟨the night sky : el cielo nocturno⟩ ⟨night shift : turno de la noche⟩
night[2] *n* **1** EVENING : noche *f* ⟨at night : de noche⟩ ⟨last night : anoche⟩ ⟨tomorrow night : mañana por la noche⟩ **2** DARKNESS : noche *f*, oscuridad *f* ⟨night fell : cayó la noche⟩
nightclothes ['naɪtˌkloːðz, -ˌkloːz] *npl* : ropa *f* de dormir
nightclub ['naɪtˌklʌb] *n* : cabaret *m*, club *m* nocturno
night crawler ['naɪtˌkrɔlər] *n* EARTHWORM : lombriz *f* (de tierra)
nightfall ['naɪtˌfɔl] *n* : anochecer *m*
nightgown ['naɪtˌgaʊn] *n* : camisón *m* (de noche)

nightingale ['naɪtənˌgeɪl, 'naɪtɪŋ-] *n* : ruiseñor *m*
nightly[1] ['naɪtli] *adv* : cada noche, todas las noches
nightly[2] *adj* : de todas las noches
nightmare ['naɪtˌmær] *n* : pesadilla *f*
nightmarish ['naɪtˌmærɪʃ] *adj* : de pesadilla
night owl *n* : noctámbulo *m*, -la *f*
nightshade ['naɪtˌʃeɪd] *n* : hierba *f* mora
nightshirt ['naɪtˌʃərt] *n* : camisa *f* de dormir
nightstick ['naɪtˌstɪk] *n* : porra *f*
nighttime ['naɪtˌtaɪm] *n* : noche *f*
nihilism ['naɪəˌlɪzəm] *n* : nihilismo *m*
nil ['nɪl] *n* : nada *f*, cero *m*
nimble ['nɪmbəl] *adj* **-bler; -blest 1** AGILE : ágil **2** CLEVER : hábil, ingenioso
nimbleness ['nɪmbəlnəs] *n* : agilidad *f*
nimbly ['nɪmbli] *adv* : con agilidad, ágilmente
nincompoop ['nɪnkəmˌpuːp, 'nɪŋ-] *n* FOOL : tonto *m*, -ta *f*; bobo *m*, -ba *f*
nine[1] ['naɪn] *adj* **1** : nueve **2 nine times out of ten** : casi siempre
nine[2] *n* : nueve *m*
nine hundred[1] *adj* : novecientos
nine hundred[2] *n* : novecientos *m*
ninepins ['naɪnˌpɪnz] *n* : bolos *mpl*
nineteen[1] [naɪn'tiːn] *adj* : diecinueve
nineteen[2] *n* : diecinueve *m*
nineteenth[1] [naɪn'tiːnθ] *adj* : decimonoveno, decimonono ⟨the nineteenth century : el siglo diecinueve⟩
nineteenth[2] *n* **1** : decimonoveno *m*, -na *f*; decimonono *m*, -na *f* (en una serie) **2** : diecinueveavo *m*, diecinueveava parte *f*
ninetieth[1] ['naɪntiəθ] *adj* : nonagésimo
ninetieth[2] *n* **1** : nonagésimo *m*, -ma *f* (en una serie) **2** : noventavo *m*, noventava parte *f*
ninety[1] ['naɪnti] *adj* : noventa
ninety[2] *n, pl* **-ties** : noventa *m*
ninth[1] ['naɪnθ] *adj* : noveno
ninth[2] *n* **1** : noveno *m*, -na *f* (en una serie) **2** : noveno *m*, novena parte *f*
ninny ['nɪni] *n, pl* **ninnies** FOOL : tonto *m*, -ta *f*; bobo *m*, -ba *f*
nip[1] ['nɪp] *vt* **nipped; nipping 1** PINCH : pellizcar **2** BITE : morder, mordisquear **3 to nip in the bud** : cortar de raíz
nip[2] *n* **1** TANG : sabor *m* fuerte **2** PINCH : pellizco *m* **3** NIBBLE : mordisco *m* **4** SWALLOW : trago *m*, traguito *m* **5 there's a nip in the air** : hace fresco
nipple ['nɪpəl] *n* : pezón *m* (de una mujer), tetilla *f* (de un hombre)
nippy ['nɪpi] *adj* **-pier; -est 1** SHARP : fuerte, picante **2** CHILLY : frío ⟨it's nippy today : hoy hace frío⟩
nit ['nɪt] *n* : liendre *f*
nitrate ['naɪˌtreɪt] *n* : nitrato *m*
nitric acid ['naɪtrɪk] *n* : ácido *m* nítrico
nitrite ['naɪˌtraɪt] *n* : nitrito *m*
nitrogen ['naɪtrədʒən] *n* : nitrógeno *m*
nitroglycerin *or* **nitroglycerine** [ˌnaɪtro-'glɪsərən] *n* : nitroglicerina *f*

nitwit ['nɪt,wɪt] *n* : zonzo *m*, -za *f*; bobo *m*, -ba *f*

no¹ ['no:] *adv* : no ⟨are you leaving? — no : ¿te vas?—no⟩ ⟨no less than : no menos de⟩ ⟨to say no : decir que no⟩ ⟨like it or no : quieras o no quieras⟩

no² *adj* 1 : ninguno ⟨it's no trouble : no es ningún problema⟩ ⟨she has no money : no tiene dinero⟩ 2 (*indicating a small amount*) ⟨we'll be there in no time : llegamos dentro de poco, no tardamos nada⟩ 3 (*expressing a negation*) ⟨he's no liar : no es mentiroso⟩

no³ *n, pl* **noes** *or* **nos** ['no:z] 1 DENIAL : no *m* ⟨I won't take no for an answer : no aceptaré un no por respuesta⟩ 2 : vota *f* en contra ⟨the noes have it : se ha rechazado la moción⟩

nobility [no'bɪləti] *n* : nobleza *f*

noble¹ ['no:bəl] *adj* **-bler; -blest** 1 ILLUSTRIOUS : noble, glorioso 2 ARISTOCRATIC : noble 3 STATELY : majestuoso, magnífico 4 LOFTY : noble, elevado ⟨noble sentiments : sentimientos elevados⟩

noble² *n* : noble *mf*, aristócrata *mf*

nobleman ['no:bəlmən] *n, pl* **-men** [-mən, -,mɛn] : noble *m*, aristócrata *m*

nobleness ['no:bəlnəs] *n* : nobleza *f*

noblewoman ['no:bəl,wʊmən] *n, pl* **-women** [-,wɪmən] : noble *f*, aristócrata *f*

nobly ['no:bli] *adv* : noblemente

nobody¹ ['no:bədi, -,badi] *n, pl* **-bodies** : don nadie *m* ⟨he's a mere nobody : es un don nadie⟩

nobody² *pron* : nadie

nocturnal [nak'tərnəl] *adj* : nocturno

nocturne ['nak,tərn] *n* : nocturno *m*

nod¹ ['nad] *v* **nodded; nodding** *vi* 1 : saludar con la cabeza, asentir con la cabeza 2 **to nod off** : dormirse, quedarse dormido — *vt* : inclinar (la cabeza) ⟨to nod one's head in agreement : asentir con la cabeza⟩

nod² *n* : saludo *m* con la cabeza, señal *m* con la cabeza, señal *m* de asentimiento

node ['no:d] *n* : nudo *m* (de una planta)

nodule ['na,dʒu:l] *n* : nódulo *m*

noel [no'ɛl] *n* 1 CAROL : villancico *m* de Navidad 2 **Noel** CHRISTMAS : Navidad *f*

noes → **no³**

noise¹ ['nɔɪz] *vt* **noised; noising** : rumorear, publicar

noise² *n* : ruido *m*

noiseless ['nɔɪzləs] *adj* : silencioso, sin ruido

noiselessly ['nɔɪzləsli] *adv* : silenciosamente

noisemaker ['nɔɪz,meɪkər] *n* : matraca *f*

noisiness ['nɔɪzinəs] *n* : ruido *m*

noisome ['nɔɪsəm] *adj* : maloliente, fétido

noisy ['nɔɪzi] *adj* **noisier; -est** : ruidoso — **noisily** ['nɔɪzəli] *adv*

nomad¹ ['no:,mæd] → **nomadic**

nomad² *n* : nómada *mf*

nomadic [no'mædɪk] *adj* : nómada

nomenclature ['no:mən,kleɪtʃər] *n* : nomenclatura *f*

nominal ['namənəl] *adj* 1 : nominal ⟨the nominal head of his party : el jefe nominal de su partido⟩ 2 TRIFLING : insignificante

nominally ['namənəli] *adv* : sólo de nombre, nominalmente

nominate ['namə,neɪt] *vt* **-nated; -nating** 1 PROPOSE : proponer (como candidato), nominar 2 APPOINT : nombrar

nomination [,namə'neɪʃən] *n* 1 PROPOSAL : propuesta *f*, postulación *f* 2 APPOINTMENT : nombramiento *m*

nominative¹ ['namənətɪv] *adj* : nominativo

nominative² *n or* **nominative case** : nominativo *m*

nominee [,namə'ni:] *n* : candidato *m*, -ta *f*

nonaddictive [,nanə'dɪktɪv] *adj* : que no crea dependencia

nonalcoholic [,nan,ælkə'hɔlɪk] *adj* : sin alcohol, no alcohólico

nonaligned [,nanə'laɪnd] *adj* : no alineado

nonbeliever [,nanbə'li:vər] *n* : no creyente *mf*

nonbreakable [,nan'breɪkəbəl] *adj* : irrompible

nonce ['nanʦ] *n* **for the nonce** : por el momento

nonchalance [,nanʃə'lanʦ] *n* : indiferencia *f*, despreocupación *f*

nonchalant [,nanʃə'lant] *adj* : indiferente, despreocupado, impasible

nonchalantly [,nanʃə'lantli] *adv* : con aire despreocupado, con indiferencia

noncombatant [,nankəm'bætənt, -'kambə-] *n* : no combatiente *mf*

noncommissioned officer [,nankə'mɪʃənd] *n* : suboficial *mf*

noncommittal [,nankə'mɪtəl] *adj* : evasivo, que no se compromete

nonconductor [,nankən'dʌktər] *n* : aislante *m*

nonconformist [,nankən'fɔrmɪst] *n* : inconformista *mf*, inconforme *mf*

nonconformity [,nankən'fɔrməti] *n* : inconformidad *f*, no conformidad *f*

noncontagious [,nankən'teɪdʒəs] *adj* : no contagioso

nondenominational [,nandɪ,namə'neɪʃənəl] *adj* : no sectario

nondescript [,nandɪ'skrɪpt] *adj* : anodino, soso

nondiscriminatory [,nandɪ'skrɪmənə,tori] *adj* : no discriminatorio

nondrinker [,nan'drɪŋkər] *n* : abstemio *m*, -mia *f*

none¹ ['nʌn] *adv* : de ninguna manera, de ningún modo, nada ⟨he was none too happy : no se sintió nada contento⟩ ⟨I'm none the worse for it : no estoy peor por ello⟩ ⟨none too soon : a buena hora⟩

none² *pron* : ninguno, ninguna
nonentity [ˌnɑn'ɛntəˌti] *n, pl* **-ties** : persona *f* insignificante, nulidad *f*
nonessential [ˌnɑnɪ'sɛntʃəl] *adj* : secundario, no esencial
nonessentials [ˌnɑnɪ'sɛntʃəlz] *npl* : cosas *fpl* secundarias, cosas *fpl* accesorias
nonetheless [ˌnʌnðə'lɛs] *adv* : sin embargo, no obstante
nonexistence [ˌnɑnɪg'zɪstənts] *n* : inexistencia *f*
nonexistent [ˌnɑnɪg'zɪstənt] *adj* : inexistente
nonfat [ˌnɑn'fæt] *adj* : sin grasa
nonfattening [ˌnɑn'fætənɪŋ] *adj* : que no engorda
nonfiction [ˌnɑn'fɪkʃən] *n* : no ficción *f*
nonflammable [ˌnɑn'flæməbəl] *adj* : no inflamable
nonintervention [ˌnɑnˌɪntər'vɛntʃən] *n* : no intervención *f*
nonmalignant [ˌnɑnmə'lɪgnənt] *adj* : no maligno, benigno
nonnegotiable [ˌnɑnnɪ'go:ʃəbəl, -ʃiə-] *adj* : no negociable
nonpareil¹ [ˌnɑnpə'rɛl] *adj* : sin parangón, sin par
nonpareil² *n* : persona *f* sin igual, cosa *f* sin par
nonpartisan [ˌnɑn'pɑrtəzən, -sən] *adj* : imparcial
nonpaying [ˌnɑn'peɪɪŋ] *adj* : que no paga
nonpayment [ˌnɑn'peɪmənt] *n* : impago *m*, falta *f* de pago
nonperson [ˌnɑn'pərsən] *n* : persona *f* sin derechos
nonplus [ˌnɑn'plʌs] *vt* **-plussed;** **-plussing** : confundir, desconcertar, dejar perplejo
nonprescription [ˌnɑnprɪ'skrɪpʃən] *adj* : disponible sin receta del médico
nonproductive [ˌnɑnprə'dʌktɪv] *adj* : improductivo
nonprofit [ˌnɑn'prɑfət] *adj* : sin fines lucrativos
nonproliferation [ˌnɑnprəˌlɪfə'reɪʃən] *adj* : no proliferación
nonresident [ˌnɑn'rezədənt, -ˌdɛnt] *n* : no residente *mf*
nonscheduled [ˌnɑn'skɛˌdʒu:ld] *adj* : no programado, no regular
nonsectarian [ˌnɑnˌsɛk'tæriən] *adj* : no sectario
nonsense ['nɑnˌsɛnts, 'nɑntsənts] *n* : tonterías *fpl*, disparates *mpl*
nonsensical [nɑn'sɛntsɪkəl] *adj* ABSURD : absurdo, disparatado — **nonsensically** [-kli] *adv*
nonsmoker [ˌnɑn'smo:kər] *n* : no fumador *m*, -dora *f*; persona *f* que no fuma
nonstandard [ˌnɑn'stændərd] *adj* : no regular, no estándar
nonstick [ˌnɑn'stɪk] *adj* : antiadherente
nonstop¹ [ˌnɑn'stɑp] *adv* : sin parar ⟨he talked nonstop : habló sin parar⟩
nonstop² *adj* : directo, sin escalas ⟨nonstop flight : vuelo directo⟩

nonsupport [ˌnɑnsə'pɔrt] *n* : falta *f* de manutención
nontaxable [ˌnɑn'tæksəbəl] *adj* : exento de impuestos
nontoxic [ˌnɑn'tɑksɪk] *adj* : no tóxico
nonviolence [ˌnɑn'vaɪlənts, -'vaɪə-] *n* : no violencia *f*
nonviolent [ˌnɑn'vaɪlənt, -'vaɪə-] *adj* : pacífico, no violento
noodle ['nu:dəl] *n* : fideo *m*, tallarín *m*
nook ['nʊk] *n* : rincón *m*, recoveco *m*, escondrijo *m* ⟨in every nook and cranny : en todos los rincones⟩
noon ['nu:n] *n* : mediodía *m*
noonday ['nu:nˌdeɪ] *n* : mediodía *m* ⟨the noonday sun : el sol de mediodía⟩
no one *pron* NOBODY : nadie
noontime ['nu:nˌtaɪm] *n* : mediodía *m*
noose ['nu:s] *n* **1** LASSO : lazo *m* **2 hangman's noose** : dogal *m*, soga *f*
nor ['nɔr] *conj* : ni ⟨neither good nor bad : ni bueno ni malo⟩ ⟨nor I! : ¡ni yo tampoco!⟩
Nordic ['nɔrdɪk] *adj* : nórdico
norm ['nɔrm] *n* **1** STANDARD : norma *f*, modelo *m* **2** CUSTOM, RULE : regla *f* general, lo normal
normal ['nɔrməl] *adj* : normal — **normally** *adv*
normalcy ['nɔrməlsi] *n* : normalidad *f*
normality [nɔr'mæləti] *n* : normalidad *f*
normalize ['nɔrməˌlaɪz] *vt* : normalizar
Norse ['nɔrs] *adj* : nórdico
north¹ ['nɔrθ] *adv* : al norte
north² *adj* : norte, del norte ⟨the north coast : la costa del norte⟩
north³ *n* **1** : norte *m* **2 the North** : el Norte *m*
North American *n* : norteamericano *m*, -na *f* — **North American** *adj*
northbound ['nɔrθˌbaʊnd] *adv* : con rumbo al norte
northeast¹ [nɔrθ'i:st] *adv* : hacia el nordeste
northeast² *adj* : nordeste, del nordeste
northeast³ *n* : nordeste *m*, noreste *m*
northeasterly¹ [nɔrθ'i:stərli] *adv* : hacia el nordeste
northeasterly² *adj* : nordeste, del nordeste
northeastern [nɔrθ'i:stərn] *adj* : nordeste, del nordeste
northerly¹ ['nɔrðərli] *adv* : hacia el norte
northerly² *adj* : del norte ⟨a northerly wind : un viento del norte⟩
northern ['nɔrðərn] *adj* : norte, norteño, septentrional
Northerner ['nɔrðərnər] *n* : norteño *m*, -ña *f*
northern lights → aurora borealis
North Pole : Polo *m* Norte
North Star *n* : estrella *f* polar
northward ['nɔrθwərd] *adv & adj* : hacia el norte
northwest¹ [nɔrθ'wɛst] *adv* : hacia el noroeste
northwest² *adj* : del noroeste
northwest³ *n* : noroeste *m*

northwesterly[1] [nɔrθ'wɛstərli] *adv* : hacia el noroeste

northwesterly[2] *adj* : del noroeste

northwestern [nɔrθ'wɛstərn] *adj* : noroeste, del noroeste

Norwegian [nɔr'wiːʤən] *n* **1** : noruego *m*, -ga *f* **2** : noruego *m* (idioma) — **Norwegian** *adj*

nose[1] ['noːz] *v* **nosed; nosing** *vt* **1** SMELL : olfatear **2** : empujar con el hocico ⟨the dog nosed open the bag : el perro abrió el saco con el hocico⟩ **3** EDGE, MOVE : mover poco a poco — *vi* **1** PRY : entrometerse, meter las narices **2** EDGE : avanzar poco a poco

nose[2] *n* **1** : nariz *f* (de una persona), hocico *m* (de un animal) ⟨to blow one's nose : sonarse las narices⟩ **2** SMELL : olfato *m*, sentido *m* del olfato **3** FRONT : parte *f* delantera, nariz *f* (de un avión), proa *f* (de un barco) **4 to follow one's nose** : dejarse guiar por el instinto

nosebleed ['noːz,bliːd] *n* : hemorragia *f* nasal

nosedive ['noːz,daɪv] *n* **1** : descenso *m* en picada (de un avión) **2** : caída *f* súbita (de precios, etc.)

nose–dive ['noːz,daɪv] *vi* : descender en picada, caer en picada

nostalgia [nɑ'stælʤə, nə-] *n* : nostalgia *f*

nostalgic [nɑ'stælʤɪk, nə-] *adj* : nostálgico

nostril ['nɑstrəl] *n* : ventana *f* de la nariz

nostrum ['nɑstrəm] *n* : panacea *f*

nosy *or* **nosey** ['noːzi] *adj* **nosier; -est** : entrometido

not ['nɑt] *adv* **1** (*used to form a negative*) : no ⟨she is not tired : no está cansada⟩ ⟨not to say something would be wrong : no decir nada sería injusto⟩ **2** (*used to replace a negative clause*) : no ⟨are we going or not? : ¿vamos a ir o no?⟩ ⟨of course not! : ¡claro que no!⟩

notable[1] ['noːtəbəl] *adj* **1** NOTEWORTHY : notable, de notar **2** DISTINGUISHED, PROMINENT : distinguido, destacado

notable[2] *n* : persona *f* importante, personaje *m*

notably ['noːtəbli] *adv* : notablemente, particularmente

notarize ['noːtə,raɪz] *vt* **-rized; -rizing** : autenticar, autorizar

notary public ['noːtəri] *n, pl* **-ries public** *or* **-ry publics** : notario *m*, -ria *f*; escribano *m*, -na *f*

notation [noː'teɪʃən] *n* **1** NOTE : anotación *f*, nota *f* **2** : notación *f* ⟨musical notation : notación musical⟩

notch[1] ['nɑtʃ] *vt* : hacer una muesca en, cortar

notch[2] *n* : muesca *f*, corte *m*

note[1] ['noːt] *vt* **noted; noting 1** NOTICE : notar, observar, tomar nota de **2** RECORD : anotar, apuntar

note[2] *n* **1** : nota *f* (musical) **2** COMMENT : nota *f*, comentario *m* **3** LETTER : nota *f*, cartita *f* **4** PROMINENCE : prestigio *m* ⟨a musician of note : un músico destacado⟩ **5** ATTENTION : atención *f* ⟨to take note of : prestar atención a⟩

notebook ['noːt,bʊk] *n* **1** : libreta *f*, cuaderno *m* **2** : notebook *m* (computadora)

noted ['noːtəd] *adj* EMINENT : renombrado, eminente, celebrado

noteworthy ['noːt,wərði] *adj* : notable, de notar, de interés

nothing[1] ['nʌθɪŋ] *adv* **1** : de ninguna manera ⟨nothing daunted, we carried on : sin amilanarnos, seguimos adelante⟩ **2 nothing like** : no . . . en nada ⟨he's nothing like his brother : no se parece en nada a su hermano⟩

nothing[2] *n* **1** NOTHINGNESS : nada *f* **2** ZERO : cero *m* **3** : persona *f* de poca importancia, cero *m* **4** TRIFLE : nimiedad *f*

nothing[3] *pron* : nada ⟨there's nothing better : no hay nada mejor⟩ ⟨nothing else : nada más⟩ ⟨nothing but : solamente⟩ ⟨they mean nothing to me : ellos me son indiferentes⟩

nothingness ['nʌθɪŋnəs] *n* **1** VOID : vacío *m*, nada *f* **2** NONEXISTENCE : inexistencia *f* **3** TRIFLE : nimiedad *f*

notice[1] ['noːtɪs] *vt* **-ticed; -ticing** : notar, observar, advertir, darse cuenta de

notice[2] *n* **1** NOTIFICATION : aviso *m*, notificación *f* **2** ATTENTION : atención *f* ⟨to take notice of : prestar atención a⟩

noticeable ['noːtɪsəbəl] *adj* : evidente, perceptible — **noticeably** [-bli] *adv*

notification [,noːtəfə'keɪʃən] *n* : notificación *f*, aviso *m*

notify ['noːtə,faɪ] *vt* **-fied; -fying** : notificar, avisar

notion ['noːʃən] *n* **1** IDEA : idea *f*, noción *f* **2** WHIM : capricho *m*, antojo *m* **3 notions** *npl* : artículos *mpl* de mercería

notoriety [,noːtə'raɪəti] *n* : mala fama *f*, notoriedad *f*

notorious [noː'toːriəs] *adj* : de mala fama, célebre, bien conocido

notwithstanding[1] [,nɑtwɪθ'stændɪŋ, -wɪð-] *adv* NEVERTHELESS : no obstante, sin embargo

notwithstanding[2] *conj* : a pesar de que

notwithstanding[3] *prep* : a pesar de, no obstante

nougat ['nuːgət] *n* : turrón *m*

nought ['nɔt, 'nɑt] → **naught**

noun ['naʊn] *n* : nombre *m*, sustantivo *m*

nourish ['nərɪʃ] *vt* **1** FEED : alimentar, nutrir, sustentar **2** FOSTER : fomentar, alentar

nourishing ['nərɪʃɪŋ] *adj* : alimenticio, nutritivo

nourishment ['nərɪʃmənt] *n* : nutrición *f*, alimento *m*, sustento *m*

novel[1] ['nɑvəl] *adj* : original, novedoso

novel² *n* : novela *f*
novelist ['nɑvəlɪst] *n* : novelista *mf*
novelty ['nɑvəlti] *n, pl* **-ties 1** : novedad *f* **2 novelties** *npl* TRINKETS : baratijas *fpl*, chucherías *fpl*
November [no'vɛmbər] *n* : noviembre *m*
novice ['nɑvɪs] *n* : novato *m*, -ta *f*; principiante *mf*; novicio *m*, -cia *f*
now¹ ['naʊ] *adv* **1** PRESENTLY : ahora, ya, actualmente ⟨from now on : de ahora en adelante⟩ ⟨long before now : ya hace tiempo⟩ ⟨now and then : de vez en cuando⟩ **2** IMMEDIATELY : ahora (mismo), inmediatamente ⟨do it right now! : ¡hazlo ahora mismo!⟩ **3** THEN : ya, entonces ⟨now they were ready : ya estaban listos⟩ **4** (*used to introduce a statement, a question, a command, or a transition*) ⟨now hear this! : ¡presten atención!⟩ ⟨now what do you think of that? : ¿qué piensas de eso?⟩
now² *n* (*indicating the present time*) ⟨until now : hasta ahora⟩ ⟨by now : ya⟩ ⟨ten years from now : dentro de 10 años⟩
now³ *conj* **now that** : ahora que, ya que
nowadays ['naʊəˌdeɪz] *adv* : hoy en día, actualmente, en la actualidad
nowhere¹ ['noːˌʍwer] *adv* **1** : en ninguna parte, a ningún lado ⟨nowhere to be found : en ninguna parte, por ningún lado⟩ ⟨you're going nowhere : no estás yendo a ningún lado, no estás yendo a ninguna parte⟩ **2 nowhere near** : ni con mucho, nada cerca ⟨it's nowhere near here : no está nada cerca de aquí⟩
nowhere² *n* **1** : ninguna parte *f* **2 out of nowhere** : de la nada
noxious ['nɑkʃəs] *adj* : nocivo, dañino, tóxico
nozzle ['nɑzəl] *n* : boca *f*
nuance ['nuːˌɑnts, 'njuː-] *n* : matiz *m*
nub ['nʌb] *n* **1** KNOB, LUMP : protuberancia *f*, nudo *m* **2** GIST : quid *m*, meollo *m*
nuclear ['nuːkliər, 'njuː-] *adj* : nuclear
nucleus ['nuːkliəs, 'njuː-] *n, pl* **-clei** [-kliˌaɪ] : núcleo *m*
nude¹ ['nuːd, 'njuːd] *adj* **nuder; nudest** : desnudo
nude² *n* : desnudo *m*
nudge¹ ['nʌdʒ] *vt* **nudged; nudging** : darle con el codo (a alguien)
nudge² *n* : toque *m* que se da con el codo
nudism ['nuːˌdɪzəm, 'njuː-] *n* : nudismo *m*
nudist ['nuːdɪst, 'njuː-] *n* : nudista *mf*
nudity ['nuːdəti, 'njuː-] *n* : desnudez *f*
nugget ['nʌgət] *n* : pepita *f*
nuisance ['nuːsənts, 'njuː-] *n* **1** BOTHER : fastidio *m*, molestia *f*, lata *f* **2** PEST : pesado *m*, -da *f fam*
null ['nʌl] *adj* : nulo ⟨null and void : nulo y sin efecto⟩
nullify ['nʌləˌfaɪ] *vt* **-fied; -fying** : invalidar, anular
nullity ['nʌləti] *n, pl* **-ties** : nulidad *f*
numb¹ ['nʌm] *vt* : entumecer, adormecer

numb² *adj* : entumecido, dormido ⟨numb with fear : paralizado de miedo⟩
number¹ ['nʌmbər] *vt* **1** COUNT, INCLUDE : contar, incluir **2** : numerar ⟨number the pages : numera las páginas⟩ **3** TOTAL : ascender a, sumar
number² *n* **1** : número *m* ⟨in round numbers : en números redondos⟩ ⟨telephone number : número de teléfono⟩ **2 a number of** : varios, unos pocos, unos cuantos
numberless ['nʌmbərləs] *adj* : innumerable, sin número
numbness ['nʌmnəs] *n* : entumecimiento *m*
numeral ['nuːmərəl, 'njuː-] *n* : número *m* ⟨Roman numeral : número romano⟩
numerator ['nuːməˌreɪtər, 'njuː-] *n* : numerador *m*
numeric [nʊ'mɛrɪk, njʊ-] *adj* : numérico
numerical [nʊ'mɛrɪkəl, njʊ-] *adj* : numérico — **numerically** [-kli] *adv*
numerous ['nuːmərəs, 'njuː-] *adj* : numeroso
numismatics [ˌnuːməz'mætɪks, ˌnjuː-] *n* : numismática *f*
numskull ['nʌmˌskʌl] *n* : tonto *m*, -ta *f*; mentecato *m*, -ta *f*; zoquete *m fam*
nun ['nʌn] *n* : monja *f*
nuptial ['nʌpʃəl] *adj* : nupcial
nuptials ['nʌpʃəlz] *npl* WEDDING : nupcias *fpl*, boda *f*
nurse¹ ['nərs] *vt* **nursed; nursing 1** SUCKLE : amamantar **2** : cuidar (de), atender ⟨to nurse the sick : cuidar a los enfermos⟩ ⟨to nurse a cold : curarse de un resfriado⟩
nurse² *n* **1** : enfermero *m*, -ra *f* **2** → **nursemaid**
nursemaid ['nərsˌmeɪd] *n* : niñera *f*
nursery ['nərsəri] *n, pl* **-eries 1** *or* **day nursery** : guardería *f* **2** : vivero *m* (de plantas)
nursing home *n* : hogar *m* de ancianos, clínica *f* de reposo
nurture¹ ['nərtʃər] *vt* **-tured; -turing 1** FEED, NOURISH : nutrir, alimentar **2** EDUCATE : criar, educar **3** FOSTER : alimentar, fomentar
nurture² *n* **1** UPBRINGING : crianza *f*, educación *f* **2** FOOD : alimento *m*
nut ['nʌt] *n* **1** : nuez *f* **2** : tuerca *f* ⟨nuts and bolts : tuercas y tornillos⟩ **3** LUNATIC : loco *m*, -ca *f*; chiflado *m*, -da *f fam* **4** ENTHUSIAST : fanático *m*, -ca *f*; entusiasta *mf*
nutcracker ['nʌtˌkrækər] *n* : cascanueces *m*
nuthatch ['nʌtˌhætʃ] *n* : trepador *m*
nutmeg ['nʌtˌmɛg] *n* : nuez *f* moscada
nutrient ['nuːtriənt, 'njuː-] *n* : nutriente *m*, alimento *m* nutritivo
nutriment ['nuːtrəmənt, 'njuː-] *n* : nutrimento *m*
nutrition [nʊ'trɪʃən, njʊ-] *n* : nutrición *f*
nutritional [nʊ'trɪʃənəl, njʊ-] *adj* : alimenticio
nutritious [nʊ'trɪʃəs, njʊ-] *adj* : nutritivo, alimenticio

nuts ['nʌts] *adj* **1** FANATICAL : fanático **2** CRAZY : loco, chiflado *fam*

nutshell ['nʌt,ʃɛl] *n* **1** : cáscara *f* de nuez **2 in a nutshell** : en pocas palabras

nutty ['nʌt̬i] *adj* **-tier; -tiest** : loco, chiflado *fam*

nuzzle ['nʌzəl] *v* **-zled; -zling** *vi* NESTLE : acurrucarse, arrimarse — *vt* : acariciar con el hocico

nylon ['nai,lɑn] *n* **1** : nilón *m* **2 nylons** *npl* : medias *fpl* de nilón

nymph ['nimpf] *n* : ninfa *f*

O

o ['o:] *n, pl* **o's** *or* **os** ['o:z] **1** : decimoquinta letra del alfabeto inglés **2** ZERO : cero *m*

O ['o:] → **oh**

oaf ['o:f] *n* : zoquete *m*; bruto *m*, -ta *f*

oafish ['o:fiʃ] *adj* : torpe, lerdo

oak ['o:k] *n, pl* **oaks** *or* **oak** : roble *m*

oaken ['o:kən] *adj* : de roble

oar ['or] *n* : remo *m*

oarlock ['or,lɑk] *n* : tolete *m*, escálamo *m*

oasis [o'eisis] *n, pl* **oases** [-,si:z] : oasis *m*

oat ['o:t] *n* : avena *f*

oath ['o:θ] *n, pl* **oaths** ['o:ðz, 'o:θs] **1** : juramento *m* ⟨to take an oath : prestar juramento⟩ **2** SWEARWORD : mala palabra *f*, palabrota *f*

oatmeal ['o:t,mi:l] *n* : avena *f* ⟨instant oatmeal : avena instantánea⟩

obdurate ['ɑbdʊrət, -dju-] *adj* : inflexible, firme, obstinado

obedience [o'bi:diənts] *n* : obediencia *f*

obedient [o'bi:diənt] *adj* : obediente — **obediently** *adv*

obelisk ['ɑbə,lisk] *n* : obelisco *m*

obese [o'bi:s] *adj* : obeso

obesity [o'bi:səti] *n* : obesidad *f*

obey [o'bei] *v* **obeyed; obeying** : obedecer ⟨to obey the law : cumplir la ley⟩

obfuscate ['ɑbfə,skeit] *vt* **-cated; -cating** : ofuscar, confundir

obituary [ə'bitʃu,ɛri] *n, pl* **-aries** : obituario *m*, necrología *f*

object¹ [əb'dʒɛkt] *vt* : objetar — *vi* : oponerse, poner reparos, hacer objeciones

object² ['ɑbdʒikt] *n* **1** : objeto *m* **2** OBJECTIVE, PURPOSE : objetivo *m*, propósito *m* **3** : complemento *m* (en gramática)

objection [əb'dʒɛkʃən] *n* : objeción *f*

objectionable [əb'dʒɛkʃənəbəl] *adj* : ofensivo, indeseable — **objectionably** [-bli] *adv*

objective¹ [əb'dʒɛktiv] *adj* **1** IMPARTIAL : objetivo, imparcial **2** : de complemento, directo (en gramática)

objective² *n* **1** : objetivo *m* **2** *or* **objective case** : acusativo *m*

objectively [əb'dʒɛktivli] *adv* : objetivamente

objectivity [,ɑb,dʒɛk'tivəti] *n, pl* **-ties** : objetividad *f*

obligate ['ɑblə,geit] *vt* **-gated; -gating** : obligar

obligation [,ɑblə'geiʃən] *n* : obligación *f*

obligatory [ə'bligə,tori] *adj* : obligatorio

oblige [ə'blaidʒ] *vt* **obliged; obliging 1** COMPEL : obligar **2** : hacerle un favor (a alguien), complacer ⟨to oblige a friend : hacerle un favor a un amigo⟩ **3 to be much obliged** : estar muy agradecido

obliging [ə'blaidʒiŋ] *adj* : servicial, complaciente — **obligingly** *adv*

oblique [o'bli:k] *adj* **1** SLANTING : oblicuo **2** INDIRECT : indirecto — **obliquely** *adv*

obliterate [ə'blit̬ə,reit] *vt* **-ated; -ating 1** ERASE : obliterar, borrar **2** DESTROY : destruir, eliminar

obliteration [ə,blit̬ə'reiʃən] *n* : obliteración *f*

oblivion [ə'bliviən] *n* : olvido *m*

oblivious [ə'bliviəs] *adj* : inconsciente — **obliviously** *adv*

oblong¹ ['ɑ,blɔŋ] *adj* : oblongo

oblong² *n* : figura *f* oblonga, rectángulo *m*

obnoxious [ɑb'nɑkʃəs, əb-] *adj* : repugnante, odioso — **obnoxiously** *adv*

oboe ['o:,bo:] *n* : oboe *m*

oboist ['o,boist] *n* : oboe *mf*

obscene [ɑb'si:n, əb-] *adj* : obsceno, indecente — **obscenely** *adv*

obscenity [ɑb'sɛnət̬i, əb-] *n, pl* **-ties** : obscenidad *f*

obscure¹ [ɑb'skjʊr, əb-] *vt* **-scured; -scuring 1** CLOUD, DIM : oscurecer, nublar **2** HIDE : ocultar

obscure² *adj* **1** DIM : oscuro **2** REMOTE, SECLUDED : recóndito **3** VAGUE : oscuro, confuso, vago **4** UNKNOWN : desconocido ⟨an obscure poet : un poeta desconocido⟩ — **obscurely** *adv*

obscurity [ɑb'skjʊrət̬i, əb-] *n, pl* **-ties** : oscuridad *f*

obsequious [əb'si:kwiəs] *adj* : servil, excesivamente atento

observable [əb'zərvəbəl] *adj* : observable, perceptible

observance [əb'zərvənts] *n* **1** FULFILLMENT : observancia *f*, cumplimiento *m* **2** PRACTICE : práctica *f*

observant [əb'zərvənt] *adj* : observador

observation [,ɑbsər'veiʃən, -zər-] *n* : observación *f*

observatory [əb'zərvə,tori] *n, pl* **-ries** : observatorio *m*

observe [əb'zərv] *v* **-served; -serving** *vt* **1** OBEY : observar, obedecer **2** CELEBRATE : celebrar, guardar (una práctica religiosa) **3** WATCH : observar, mi-

rar **4** REMARK : observar, comentar —
vi LOOK : mirar
observer [ab'zərvər] *n* : observador *m*,
-dora *f*
obsess [əb'sɛs] *vt* : obsesionar
obsession [ab'sɛʃən, əb-] *n* : obsesión *f*
obsessive [ab'sɛsɪv, əb-] *adj* : obsesivo
— **obsessively** *adv*
obsolescence [ˌabsə'lɛsənts] *n* : obsolescencia *f*
obsolescent [ˌabsə'lɛsənt] *adj* : obsolescente ⟨to become obsolescent : caer
en desuso⟩
obsolete [ˌabsə'li:t, 'absəˌ-] *adj* : obsoleto, anticuado
obstacle ['abstɪkəl] *n* : obstáculo *m*, impedimento *m*
obstetric [əb'stɛtrɪk] *or* **obstetrical**
[-trɪkəl] *adj* : obstétrico
obstetrician [ˌabstə'trɪʃən] *n* : obstetra
mf; tocólogo *m*, -ga *f*
obstetrics [əb'stɛtrɪks] *ns & pl* : obstetricia *f*, tocología *f*
obstinacy ['abstənəsi] *n*, *pl* -**cies** : obstinación *f*, terquedad *f*
obstinate ['abstənət] *adj* : obstinado,
terco — **obstinately** *adv*
obstreperous [əb'strɛpərəs] *adj* **1**
CLAMOROUS : ruidoso, clamoroso **2**
UNRULY : rebelde, indisciplinado
obstruct [əb'strʌkt] *vt* : obstruir, bloquear
obstruction [əb'strʌkʃən] *n* : obstrucción *f*, bloqueo *m*
obstructive [əb'strʌktɪv] *adj* : obstructor
obtain [əb'teɪn] *vt* : obtener, conseguir
— *vi* PREVAIL : imperar, prevalecer
obtainable [əb'teɪnəbəl] *adj* : obtenible,
asequible
obtrude [əb'tru:d] *v* -**truded; -truding** *vt*
1 EXTRUDE : expulsar **2** IMPOSE : imponer — *vi* INTRUDE : inmiscuirse, entrometerse
obtrusive [əb'tru:sɪv] *adj* **1** IMPERTI-
NENT, MEDDLESOME : impertinente,
entrometido **2** PROTRUDING : prominente
obtuse [ab'tu:s, əb-, -'tju:s] *adj* : obtuso, torpe
obtuse angle *n* : ángulo obtuso
obviate ['abviˌeɪt] *vt* -**ated; -ating** : obviar, evitar
obvious ['abviəs] *adj* : obvio, evidente,
manifiesto
obviously ['abviəsli] *adv* **1** CLEARLY
: obviamente, evidentemente **2** OF
COURSE : claro, por supuesto
occasion[1] [ə'keɪʒən] *vt* : ocasionar,
causar
occasion[2] *n* **1** OPPORTUNITY : oportunidad *f*, ocasión *f* **2** CAUSE : motivo *m*,
razón *f* **3** INSTANCE : ocasión *f* **4**
EVENT : ocasión *f*, acontecimiento *m*
5 on ~ : de vez en cuando, ocasionalmente
occasional [ə'keɪʒənəl] *adj* : ocasional
occasionally [ə'keɪʒənəli] *adv* : de vez
en cuando, ocasionalmente

occidental [ˌaksə'dɛntəl] *adj* : oeste, del
oeste, occidental
occult[1] [ə'kʌlt, 'aˌkʌlt] *adj* **1** HIDDEN,
SECRET : oculto, secreto **2** ARCANE
: arcano, esotérico
occult[2] *n* **the occult** : las ciencias ocul-
tas
occupancy ['akjəpəntsi] *n*, *pl* -**cies**
: ocupación *f*, habitación *f*
occupant ['akjəpənt] *n* : ocupante *mf*
occupation [ˌakjə'peɪʃən] *n* : ocupación
f, profesión *f*, oficio *m*
occupational [ˌakjə'peɪʃənəl] *adj* : ocupacional
occupy ['akjəˌpaɪ] *vt* -**pied; -pying** : ocupar
occur [ə'kər] *vi* **occurred; occurring 1**
EXIST : encontrarse, existir **2** HAPPEN
: ocurrir, acontecer, suceder, tener lugar **3** : ocurrirse ⟨it occurred to him
that . . . : se le ocurrió que . . . ⟩
occurrence [ə'kərənts] *n* : acontecimiento *m*, suceso *m*, ocurrencia *f*
ocean ['o:ʃən] *n* : océano *m*
oceanic [ˌo:ʃi'ænɪk] *adj* : oceánico
oceanography [ˌo:ʃə'nagrəfi] *n*
: oceanografía *f*
ocelot ['asəˌlat, 'o:-] *n* : ocelote *m*
ocher *or* **ochre** ['o:kər] *n* : ocre *m*
o'clock [ə'klak] *adv* (*used in telling time*)
⟨it's ten o'clock : son las diez⟩ ⟨at six
o'clock : a las seis⟩
octagon ['aktəˌgan] *n* : octágono *m*
octagonal [ak'tægənəl] *adj* : octagonal
octave ['aktɪv] *n* : octava *f*
October [ak'to:bər] *n* : octubre *m*
octopus ['aktəˌpʊs, -pəs] *n*, *pl* -**puses** *or*
-**pi** [-ˌpaɪ] : pulpo *m*
ocular ['akjələr] *adj* : ocular
oculist ['akjəlɪst] *n* **1** OPHTHALMOLO-
GIST : oftalmólogo *m*, -ga *f*; oculista *mf*
2 OPTOMETRIST : optometrista *mf*
odd ['ad] *adj* **1** : sin pareja, suelto ⟨an
odd sock : un calcetín sin pareja⟩ **2**
UNEVEN : impar ⟨odd numbers
: números impares⟩ **3** : y pico, y tantos ⟨forty odd years ago : hace cuarenta
y pico años⟩ **4** : alguno, uno que otro
⟨odd jobs : algunos trabajos⟩ **5**
STRANGE : extraño, raro
oddball ['adˌbɔl] *n* : excéntrico *m*, -ca *f*;
persona *f* rara
oddity ['adəti] *n*, *pl* -**ties** : rareza *f*, cosa
f rara
oddly ['adli] *adv* : de manera extraña
oddness ['adnəs] *n* : rareza *f*, excentricidad *f*
odds ['adz] *npl* **1** CHANCES : probabili-
dades *fpl* **2** : puntos *mpl* de ventaja (de
una apuesta) **3 to be at odds** : estar en
desacuerdo
odds and ends *npl* : costillas *fpl*, cosas
fpl sueltas, cachivaches *mpl*
ode ['o:d] *n* : oda *f*
odious ['o:diəs] *adj* : odioso — **odious-
ly** *adv*
odor ['o:dər] *n* : olor *m*
odorless ['o:dərləs] *adj* : inodoro, sin
olor

odorous ['o:dərəs] *adj* : oloroso
odyssey ['adəsi] *n, pl* **-seys** : odisea *f*
o'er ['or] → **over**
of ['ʌv, 'ɑv] *prep* **1** FROM : de ⟨a man of the city : un hombre de la ciudad⟩ **2** (*indicating character or background*) : de ⟨a woman of great ability : una mujer de gran capacidad⟩ **3** (*indicating cause*) : de ⟨he died of the flu : murió de la gripe⟩ **4** BY : de ⟨the works of Shakespeare : las obras de Shakespeare⟩ **5** (*indicating contents, material, or quantity*) : de ⟨a house of wood : una casa de madera⟩ ⟨a glass of water : un vaso de agua⟩ **6** (*indicating belonging or connection*) : de ⟨the front of the house : el frente de la casa⟩ **7** ABOUT : sobre, de ⟨tales of the West : los cuentos del Oeste⟩ **8** (*indicating a particular example*) : de ⟨the city of Caracas : la ciudad de Caracas⟩ **9** FOR : por, a ⟨love of country : amor por la patria⟩ **10** (*indicating time or date*) ⟨five minutes of ten : las diez menos cinco⟩ ⟨the eighth of April : el ocho de abril⟩
off¹ ['ɔf] *adv* **1** (*indicating change of position or state*) ⟨to march off : marcharse⟩ ⟨he dozed off : se puso a dormir⟩ **2** (*indicating distance in space or time*) ⟨some miles off : a varias millas⟩ ⟨the holiday is three weeks off : faltan tres semanas para la fiesta⟩ **3** (*indicating removal*) ⟨the knob came off : se le cayó el pomo⟩ **4** (*indicating termination*) ⟨shut the television off : apaga la televisión⟩ **5** (*indicating suspension of work*) ⟨to take a day off : tomarse un día de descanso⟩ **6 off and on** : de vez en cuando
off² *adj* **1** FARTHER : más remoto, distante ⟨the off side of the building : el lado distante del edificio⟩ **2** STARTED : empezado ⟨to be off on a spree : irse de juerga⟩ **3** OUT : apagado ⟨the light is off : la luz está apagada⟩ **4** CANCELED : cancelado, suspendido **5** INCORRECT : erróneo, incorrecto **6** REMOTE : remoto, lejano ⟨an off chance : una posibilidad remota⟩ **7** FREE : libre ⟨I'm off today : hoy estoy libre⟩ **8 to be well off** : vivir con desahogo, tener bastante dinero
off³ *prep* **1** (*indicating physical separation*) : de ⟨she took it off the table : lo tomó de la mesa⟩ ⟨a shop off the main street : una tienda al lado de la calle principal⟩ **2** : a la costa de, a expensas de ⟨he lives off his sister : vive a expensas de su hermana⟩ **3** (*indicating the suspension of an activity*) ⟨to be off duty : estar libre⟩ ⟨he's off liquor : ha dejado el alcohol⟩ **4** BELOW : por debajo de ⟨he's off his game : está por debajo de su juego normal⟩
offal ['ɔfəl] *n* **1** RUBBISH, WASTE : desechos *mpl*, desperdicios *mpl* **2** VISCERA : vísceras *fpl*, asaduras *fpl*

offend [ə'fɛnd] *vt* **1** VIOLATE : violar, atentar contra **2** HURT : ofender ⟨to be easily offended : ser muy susceptible⟩
offender [ə'fɛndər] *n* : delincuente *mf*; infractor *m*, -tora *f*
offense *or* **offence** [ə'fɛnts, 'ɔ,fɛnts] *n* **1** INSULT : ofensa *f*, injuria *f*, agravio *m* ⟨to take offense : ofenderse⟩ **2** ASSAULT : ataque *m* **3** : ofensiva *f* (en deportes) **4** CRIME, INFRACTION : infracción *f*, delito *m*
offensive¹ [ə'fɛntsɪv, 'ɔ,fɛnt-] *adj* : ofensivo — **offensively** *adv*
offensive² *n* : ofensiva *f*
offer¹ ['ɔfər] *vt* **1** : ofrecer ⟨they offered him the job : le ofrecieron el puesto⟩ **2** PROPOSE : proponer, sugerir **3** SHOW : ofrecer, mostrar ⟨to offer resistance : ofrecer resistencia⟩
offer² *n* : oferta *f*, ofrecimiento *m*, propuesta *f*
offering ['ɔfərɪŋ] *n* : ofrenda *f*
offhand¹ ['ɔf'hænd] *adv* : sin preparación, sin pensarlo
offhand² *adj* **1** IMPROMPTU : improvisado **2** ABRUPT : brusco
office ['ɔfəs] *n* **1** : cargo *m* ⟨to run for office : presentarse como candidato⟩ **2** : oficina *f*, despacho *m*, gabinete *m* (en la casa) ⟨office hours : horas de oficina⟩
officeholder ['ɔfəs,ho:ldər] *n* : titular *mf*
officer ['ɔfəsər] *n* **1** *or* **police officer** : policía *mf*, agente *mf* de policía **2** OFFICIAL : oficial *mf*; funcionario *m*, -ria *f*; director *m*, -tora *f* (en una empresa) **3** COMMISSIONED OFFICER : oficial *mf*
official¹ [ə'fɪʃəl] *adj* : oficial — **officially** *adv*
official² *n* : funcionario *m*, -ria *f*; oficial *mf*
officiate [ə'fɪʃi,eɪt] *v* **-ated; -ating** *vi* **1** : arbitrar (en deportes) **2 to officiate at** : oficiar, celebrar — *vt* : arbitrar
officious [ə'fɪʃəs] *adj* : oficioso
offing ['ɔfɪŋ] *n* **in the offing** : en perspectiva
offset ['ɔf,sɛt] *vt* **-set; -setting** : compensar
offshoot ['ɔf,ʃuːt] *n* **1** OUTGROWTH : producto *m*, resultado *m* **2** BRANCH, SHOOT : retoño *m*, rama *f*, vástago *m* (de una planta)
offshore¹ ['ɔf'ʃor] *adv* : a una distancia de la costa
offshore² *adj* **1** : de (la) tierra ⟨an offshore wind : un viento que sopla de tierra⟩ **2** : (de) costa afuera, cercano a la costa ⟨an offshore island : una isla costera⟩
offspring ['ɔf,sprɪŋ] *ns & pl* **1** YOUNG : crías *fpl* (de los animales) **2** PROGENY : prole *f*, progenie *f*
off–white ['ɔf'hwaɪt] *adj* : blancuzco
often ['ɔfən, 'ɔftən] *adv* : muchas veces, a menudo, seguido

oftentimes ['ɔfən͵taɪmz, 'ɔftən-] *or* **ofttimes** ['ɔft͵taɪmz] *or* **often**
ogle ['o:gəl] *vt* **ogled; ogling** : comerse con los ojos, quedarse mirando a
ogre ['o:gər] *n* : ogro *m*
oh ['o:] *interj* : ¡oh!, ¡ah!, ¡ay! ⟨oh, of course : ah, por supuesto⟩ ⟨oh no! : ¡ay no!⟩ ⟨oh really? : ¿de veras?⟩
ohm ['o:m] *n* : ohm *m*, ohmio *m*
oil¹ ['ɔɪl] *vt* : lubricar, engrasar, aceitar
oil² *n* **1** : aceite *m* **2** PETROLEUM : petróleo *m* **3** *or* **oil painting** : óleo *m*, pintura *f* al óleo **4** *or* **oil paint(s)** : óleo *m*
oilcloth ['ɔɪl͵klɔθ] *n* : hule *m*
oiliness ['ɔɪlinəs] *n* : lo aceitoso
oilskin ['ɔɪl͵skɪn] *n* **1** : hule *m* **2 oilskins** *npl* : impermeable *m*
oily ['ɔɪli] *adj* **oilier; -est** : aceitoso, grasiento, grasoso ⟨oily fingers : dedos grasientos⟩
ointment ['ɔɪntmənt] *n* : ungüento *m*, pomada *f*
OK¹ [͵o:'keɪ] *vt* **OK'd** *or* **okayed** [͵o:'keɪd]; **OK'ing** *or* **okaying** APPROVE, AUTHORIZE : dar el visto bueno a, autorizar, aprobar
OK² *or* **okay** [͵o:'keɪ] *adv* **1** WELL : bien **2** YES : sí, por supuesto
OK³ *adj* : bien ⟨he's OK : está bien⟩ ⟨it's OK with me : estoy de acuerdo⟩
OK⁴ *n* : autorización *f*, visto *m* bueno
okra ['o:krə, *South also* -kri] *n* : quingombó *m*
old¹ ['o:ld] *adj* **1** ANCIENT : antiguo ⟨old civilizations : civilizaciones antiguas⟩ **2** FAMILIAR : viejo ⟨old friends : viejos amigos⟩ ⟨the same old story : el mismo cuento⟩ **3** (*indicating a certain age*) ⟨he's ten years old : tiene diez años (de edad)⟩ **4** AGED : viejo, anciano ⟨an old woman : una anciana⟩ **5** FORMER : antiguo ⟨her old neighborhood : su antiguo barrio⟩ **6** WORN-OUT : viejo, gastado
old² *n* **1 the old** : los viejos, los ancianos **2 in the days of old** : antaño, en los tiempos antiguos
olden ['o:ldən] *adj* : de antaño, de antigüedad
old–fashioned ['o:ld'fæʃənd] *adj* : anticuado, pasado de moda
old maid *n* **1** SPINSTER : soltera *f* **2** FUSSBUDGET : maniático *m*, -ca *f*; melindroso *m*, -sa *f*
Old Testament *n* : Antiguo Testamento *m*
old–time ['o:ld'taɪm] *adj* : antiguo
old–timer ['o:ld'taɪmər] *n* **1** VETERAN : veterano *m*, -na *f* **2** *or* **oldster** : anciano *m*, -na *f*
old–world ['o:ld'wərld] *adj* : pintoresco (de antaño)
oleander ['o:li͵ændər] *n* : adelfa *f*
oleomargarine [͵o:lio'marʤərən] → **margarine**
olfactory [ɑl'fæktəri, ol-] *adj* : olfativo
oligarchy ['ɑlə͵gɑrki, 'o:lə-] *n, pl* **-chies** : oligarquía *f*

olive ['ɑlɪv, -ləv] *n* **1** : aceituna *f*, oliva *f* (fruta) **2** : olivo *m* (árbol) **3** *or* **olive green** : color *m* aceituna, verde *m* oliva
Olmec ['ɑl͵mɛk, 'o:l-] *n* : olmeca *mf* — **Olmec** *adj*
Olympic [ə'lɪmpɪk, o-] *adj* : olímpico
Olympic Games *npl* : Juegos *mpl* Olímpicos
Olympics [ə'lɪmpɪks, o-] *npl* : olimpiadas *fpl*
Omani [o'mɑni, -'mæ-] *n* : omaní *mf* — **Omani** *adj*
ombudsman ['ɑm͵bʊdzmən, ɑm-'bʊdz-] *n, pl* **-men** [-mən, -͵mɛn] : ombudsman *m*
omelet *or* **omelette** ['ɑmlət, 'ɑmə-] *n* : omelette *mf*, tortilla *f* (de huevo)
omen ['o:mən] *n* : presagio *m*, augurio *m*, agüero *m*
ominous ['ɑmənəs] *adj* : ominoso, agorero, de mal agüero
ominously ['ɑmənəsli] *adv* : de manera amenazadora
omission [o'mɪʃən] *n* : omisión *f*
omit [o'mɪt] *vt* **omitted; omitting 1** LEAVE OUT : omitir, excluir **2** NEGLECT : omitir ⟨they omitted to tell us : omitieron decírnoslo⟩
omnipotence [ɑm'nɪpətənts] *n* : omnipotencia *f* — **omnipotent** [ɑm-'nɪpətənt] *adj*
omnipresent [͵ɑmnɪ'prɛzənt] *adj* : omnipresente
omniscient [ɑm'nɪʃənt] *adj* : omnisciente
omnivorous [ɑm'nɪvərəs] *adj* **1** : omnívoro **2** AVID : ávido, voraz
on¹ ['ɑn, 'ɔn] *adv* **1** (*indicating contact with a surface*) ⟨put the top on : pon la tapa⟩ ⟨he has a hat on : lleva un sombrero puesto⟩ **2** (*indicating forward movement*) ⟨from that moment on : a partir de ese momento⟩ ⟨farther on : más adelante⟩ **3** (*indicating operation or an operating position*) ⟨turn the light on : prende la luz⟩
on² *adj* **1** (*being in operation*) ⟨the radio is on : el radio está prendido⟩ **2** (*taking place*) ⟨the game is on : el juego ha comenzado⟩ **3 to be on to** : estar enterado de
on³ *prep* **1** (*indicating position*) : en, sobre, encima de ⟨on the table : en (sobre, encima de) la mesa⟩ ⟨shadows on the wall : sombras en la pared⟩ ⟨on horseback : a caballo⟩ **2** AT, TO : a ⟨on the right : a la derecha⟩ **3** ABOARD, IN : en, a ⟨on the plane : en el avión⟩ ⟨he got on the train : subió al tren⟩ **4** (*indicating time*) ⟨she worked on Saturdays : trabajaba los sábados⟩ ⟨every hour on the hour : a la hora en punto⟩ **5** (*indicating means or agency*) : por ⟨he cut himself on a can : se cortó con una lata⟩ ⟨to talk on the telephone : hablar por teléfono⟩ **6** (*indicating a state or process*) : en ⟨on fire : en llamas⟩ ⟨on the increase : en aumen-

to⟩ 7 (*indicating connection or membership*) **:** en ⟨on a committee : en una comisión⟩ **8** (*indicating an activity*) ⟨on vacation : de vacaciones⟩ ⟨on a diet : a dieta⟩ **9** ABOUT, CONCERNING **:** sobre ⟨a book on insects : un libro sobre insectos⟩ ⟨reflect on that : reflexiona sobre eso⟩

once¹ ['wʌnts] *adv* **1 :** una vez ⟨once a month : una vez al mes⟩ ⟨once and for all : de una vez por todas⟩ **2** EVER : alguna vez **3** FORMERLY : antes, anteriormente

once² *adj* FORMER : antiguo

once³ *n* **1 :** una vez ∼ SIMULTANEOUSLY : al mismo tiempo, simultáneamente **3 at** ∼ IMMEDIATELY : inmediatamente, en seguida

once⁴ *conj* **:** una vez que, tan pronto como

once–over [ˌwʌnts'oːvər, 'wʌnts̩-] *n* **to give someone the once–over :** echarle un vistazo a alguien

oncoming ['ɑnˌkʌmɪŋ, 'ɔn-] *adj* **:** que viene

one¹ ['wʌn] *adj* **1** (*being a single unit*) **:** un, una ⟨he only wants one apple : sólo quiere una manzana⟩ **2** (*being a particular one*) **:** un, una ⟨he arrived early one morning : llegó temprano una mañana⟩ **3** (*being the same*) **:** mismo, misma ⟨they're all members of one team : todos son miembros del mismo equipo⟩ ⟨one and the same thing : la misma cosa⟩ **4** SOME **:** alguno, alguna, un, una ⟨I'll see you again one day : algún día te veré otra vez⟩ ⟨at one time or another : en una u otra ocasión⟩

one² *n* **1 :** uno *m* (número) **2** (*indicating the first of a set or series*) ⟨from day one : desde el primer momento⟩ **3** (*indicating a single person or thing*) ⟨the one (girl) on the right : la de la derecha⟩ ⟨he has the one but needs the other : tiene uno pero necesita el otro⟩

one³ *pron* **1 :** uno, una ⟨one of his friends : una de sus amigas⟩ ⟨one never knows : uno nunca sabe, nunca se sabe⟩ ⟨to cut one's finger : cortarse el dedo⟩ **2 one and all :** todos, todo el mundo **3 one another :** el uno al otro, se ⟨they loved one another : se amaban⟩ **4 that one :** aquél, aquella **5 which one? :** ¿cuál?

one–on–one [wʌnɔn'wʌn, -ɑn-] *adj* **:** uno a uno — **one–on–one** *adv*

onerous ['ɑnərəs, 'oːnə-] *adj* **:** oneroso, gravoso

oneself [ˌwʌn'sɛlf] *pron* **1** (*used reflexively or for emphasis*) **:** se, sí mismo, uno mismo ⟨to control oneself : controlarse⟩ ⟨to talk to oneself : hablarse a sí mismo⟩ ⟨to do it oneself : hacérselo uno mismo⟩ **2 by** ∼ **:** solo

one–sided ['wʌn'saɪdəd] *adj* **1 :** de un solo lado **2** LOPSIDED **:** asimétrico **3** BIASED **:** parcial, tendencioso **4** UNILATERAL **:** unilateral

onetime ['wʌn'taɪm] *adj* FORMER **:** antiguo

one–way ['wʌn'weɪ] *adj* **1 :** de sentido único, de una sola dirección ⟨a one-way street : una calle de sentido único⟩ **2 :** de ida, sencillo ⟨a one-way ticket : un boleto de ida⟩

ongoing ['ɑnˌgoːɪŋ] *adj* **1** CONTINUING **:** en curso, corriente **2** DEVELOPING **:** en desarrollo

onion ['ʌnjən] *n* **:** cebolla *f*

online ['ɔn'laɪn, 'ɑn-] *adj* **:** en línea

onlooker ['ɔnˌlʊkər, 'ɑn-] *n* **:** espectador *m*, -dora *f*, circunstante *mf*

only¹ ['oːnli] *adv* **1** MERELY **:** sólo, solamente, nomás ⟨for only two dollars : por tan sólo dos dólares⟩ ⟨only once : sólo una vez, no más de una vez⟩ ⟨I only did it to help : lo hice por ayudar nomás⟩ **2** SOLELY **:** únicamente, sólo, solamente ⟨only he knows it : solamente él lo sabe⟩ **3** (*indicating a result*) ⟨it will only cause him problems : no hará más que crearle problemas⟩ **4 if only :** ojalá, por lo menos ⟨if only it were true! : ¡ojalá sea cierto!⟩ ⟨if he could only dance : si por lo menos pudiera bailar⟩

only² *adj* **:** único ⟨an only child : un hijo único⟩ ⟨the only chance : la única oportunidad⟩

only³ *conj* BUT **:** pero ⟨I would go, only I'm sick : iría, pero estoy enfermo⟩

onset ['ɑnˌsɛt] *n* **:** comienzo *m*, llegada *f*

onslaught ['ɑnˌslɔt, 'ɔn-] *n* **:** arremetida *f*, embestida *f*, embate *m*

onto ['ɑnˌtuː, 'ɔn-] *prep* **:** sobre

onus ['oːnəs] *n* **:** responsabilidad *f*, carga *f*

onward¹ ['ɑnwərd, 'ɔn-] *or* **onwards** *adv* FORWARD **:** adelante, hacia adelante

onward² *adj* **:** hacia adelante

onyx ['ɑnɪks] *n* **:** ónix *m*

ooze¹ ['uːz] *v* **oozed; oozing** *vi* **:** rezumar — *vt* **1 :** rezumar **2** EXUDE **:** irradiar, rebosar ⟨to ooze confidence : irradiar confianza⟩

ooze² *n* SLIME **:** cieno *m*, limo *m*

opacity [oˈpæsəti] *n, pl* **-ties :** opacidad *f*

opal ['oːpəl] *n* **:** ópalo *m*

opaque [oˈpeɪk] *adj* **1 :** opaco **2** UNCLEAR **:** poco claro

open¹ ['oːpən] *vt* **1 :** abrir ⟨open the door : abre la puerta⟩ **2** UNCOVER **:** destapar **3** UNFOLD **:** desplegar, abrir **4** CLEAR **:** abrir (un camino, etc.) **5** INAUGURATE **:** abrir (una tienda), inaugurar (una exposición, etc.) **6** INITIATE **:** iniciar, entablar, abrir ⟨to open the meeting : abrir la sesión⟩ ⟨to open a discussion : entablar un debate⟩ — *vi* **1 :** abrirse **2** BEGIN **:** empezar, comenzar

open² *adj* **1 :** abierto ⟨an open window : una ventana abierta⟩ **2** FRANK **:** abierto, franco, directo **3** UNCOV-

ERED : descubierto, abierto **4** EXTENDED : extendido, abierto ⟨with open arms : con los brazos abiertos⟩ **5** UNRESTRICTED : libre, abierto **6** UNDECIDED : pendiente, por decidir, sin resolver ⟨an open question : una cuestión pendiente⟩ **7** AVAILABLE : vacante, libre ⟨the job is open : el puesto está vacante⟩

open³ *n* **in the open 1** OUTDOORS : al aire libre **2** KNOWN : conocido, sacado a la luz

open–air ['o:pən'ær] *adj* OUTDOOR : al aire libre

open–and–shut ['o:pənənd'ʃʌt] *adj* : claro, evidente ⟨an open-and-shut case : un caso muy claro⟩

opener ['o:pənər] *n* : destapador *m*, abrelatas *m*, abridor *m*

openhanded [ˌo:pən'hændəd] *adj* : generoso, liberal

openhearted [ˌo:pən'hɑrtəd] *adj* **1** FRANK : franco, sincero **2** : generoso, de gran corazón

opening ['o:pənɪŋ] *n* **1** BEGINNING : comienzo *m*, principio *m*, apertura *f* **2** APERTURE : abertura *f*, brecha *f*, claro *m* (en el bosque) **3** OPPORTUNITY : oportunidad *f*

openly ['o:pənli] *adv* **1** FRANKLY : abiertamente, francamente **2** PUBLICLY : públicamente, declaradamente

openness ['o:pənnəs] *n* : franqueza *f*

opera ['ɑprə, 'ɑpərə] *n* **1** : ópera *f* **2** → opus

opera glasses *npl* : gemelos *mpl* de teatro

operate ['ɑpəˌreɪt] *v* -ated; -ating *vi* **1** ACT, FUNCTION : operar, funcionar, actuar **2** to operate on (someone) : operar a (alguien) — *vt* **1** WORK : operar, manejar, hacer funcionar (una máquina) **2** MANAGE : manejar, administrar (un negocio)

operatic [ˌɑpə'rætɪk] *adj* : operístico

operation [ˌɑpə'reɪʃən] *n* **1** FUNCTIONING : funcionamiento *m* **2** USE : uso *m*, manejo *m* (de máquinas) **3** SURGERY : operación *f*, intervención *f* quirúrgica

operational [ˌɑpə'reɪʃənəl] *adj* : operacional, de operación

operative ['ɑpərətɪv, -ˌreɪ-] *adj* **1** OPERATING : vigente, en vigor **2** WORKING : operativo **3** SURGICAL : quirúrgico

operator ['ɑpəˌreɪtər] *n* : operador *m*, -dora *f*

operetta [ˌɑpə'rɛtə] *n* : opereta *f*

ophthalmologist [ˌɑf,θæl'mɑlədʒɪst, -θə'mɑ-] *n* : oftalmólogo *m*, -ga *f*

ophthalmology [ˌɑf,θæl'mɑlədʒi, -θə'mɑ-] *n* : oftalmología *f*

opiate ['o:piət, -piˌeɪt] *n* : opiato *m*

opinion [ə'pɪnjən] *n* : opinión *f*

opinionated [ə'pɪnjəˌneɪtəd] *adj* : testarudo, dogmático

opium ['o:piəm] *n* : opio *m*

opossum [ə'pɑsəm] *n* : zarigüeya *f*, oposum *m*

opponent [ə'po:nənt] *n* : oponente *mf*; opositor *m*, -tora *f*; contrincante *mf* (en deportes)

opportune [ˌɑpər'tu:n, -'tju:n] *adj* : oportuno — **opportunely** *adv*

opportunist [ˌɑpər'tu:nɪst, -'tju:-] *n* : oportunista *mf*

opportunistic [ˌɑpərtu'nɪstɪk, -tju-] *adj* : oportunista *mf*

opportunity [ˌɑpər'tu:nəti, -'tju:-] *n, pl* **-ties** : oportunidad *f*, ocasión *f*, chance *m*, posibilidades *fpl*

oppose [ə'po:z] *vt* **-posed; -posing 1** : ir en contra de, oponerse a ⟨good opposes evil : el bien se opone al mal⟩ **2** COMBAT : luchar contra, combatir, resistir

opposite¹ ['ɑpəzət] *adv* : enfrente

opposite² *adj* **1** FACING : de enfrente ⟨the opposite side : el lado de enfrente⟩ **2** CONTRARY : opuesto, contrario ⟨in opposite directions : en direcciones contrarias⟩ ⟨the opposite sex : el sexo opuesto, el otro sexo⟩

opposite³ *n* : lo contrario, lo opuesto

opposite⁴ *prep* : enfrente de, frente a

opposition [ˌɑpə'zɪʃən] *n* **1** : oposición *f*, resistencia *f* **2 in opposition to** AGAINST : en contra de

oppress [ə'prɛs] *vt* **1** PERSECUTE : oprimir, perseguir **2** BURDEN : oprimir, agobiar

oppression [ə'prɛʃən] *n* : opresión *f*

oppressive [ə'prɛsɪv] *adj* **1** HARSH : opresivo, severo **2** STIFLING : agobiante, sofocante ⟨oppressive heat : calor sofocante⟩

oppressor [ə'prɛsər] *n* : opresor *m*, -sora *f*

opprobrium [ə'pro:briəm] *n* : oprobio *m*

opt ['ɑpt] *vi* : optar

optic ['ɑptɪk] *or* **optical** [-tɪkəl] *adj* : óptico

optical disk *n* : disco *m* óptico

optician [ɑp'tɪʃən] *n* : óptico *m*, -ca *f*

optics ['ɑptɪks] *npl* : óptica *f*

optimal ['ɑptəməl] *adj* : óptimo

optimism ['ɑptəˌmɪzəm] *n* : optimismo *m*

optimist ['ɑptəmɪst] *n* : optimista *mf*

optimistic [ˌɑptə'mɪstɪk] *adj* : optimista

optimistically [ˌɑptə'mɪstɪkli] *adv* : con optimismo, positivamente

optimum¹ ['ɑptəməm] *adj* → **optimal**

optimum² *n, pl* **-ma** ['ɑptəmə] : lo óptimo, lo ideal

option ['ɑpʃən] *n* : opción *f* ⟨she has no option : no tiene más remedio⟩

optional ['ɑpʃənəl] *adj* : facultativo, optativo

optometrist [ɑp'tɑmətrɪst] *n* : optometrista *mf*

optometry [ɑp'tɑmətri] *n* : optometría *f*

opulence ['ɑpjələnts] *n* : opulencia *f*

opulent ['ɑpjələnt] *adj* : opulento

opus ['o:pəs] *n, pl* **opera** ['o:pərə, 'ɑpə-] : opus *m*, obra *f* (de música)

or ['ɔr] *conj* **1** (*indicating an alternative*) : o (**u** *before words beginning with* o *or* ho) ⟨coffee or tea : café o té⟩ ⟨one day

or another : un día u otro⟩ **2** (*following a negative*) : ni ⟨he didn't have his keys or his wallet : no llevaba ni sus llaves ni su billetera⟩
oracle [ˈɔrəkəl] *n* : oráculo *m*
oral [ˈɔrəl] *adj* : oral — **orally** *adv*
orange [ˈɔrɪndʒ] *n* **1** : naranja *f*, china *f* PRi (fruto) **2** : naranja *m* (color), color *m* de china PRi
orangeade [ˌɔrɪndʒˈeɪd] *n* : naranjada *f*
orangutan [əˈræŋəˌtæŋ, -ˈræŋgə-, -ˌtæn] *n* : orangután *m*
oration [əˈreɪʃən] *n* : oración *f*, discurso *m*
orator [ˈɔrətər] *n* : orador *m*, -dora *f*
oratorio [ˌɔrəˈtoriˌoː] *n, pl* **-rios** : oratorio *m*
oratory [ˈɔrəˌtori] *n, pl* **-ries** : oratoria *f*
orb [ˈɔrb] *n* : orbe *m*
orbit[1] [ˈɔrbət] *vt* **1** CIRCLE : girar alrededor de, orbitar **2** : poner en órbita (un satélite, etc.) — *vi* : orbitar
orbit[2] *n* : órbita *f*
orbital [ˈɔrbətəl] *adj* : orbital
orchard [ˈɔrtʃərd] *n* : huerto *m*
orchestra [ˈɔrkəstrə] *n* : orquesta *f*
orchestral [ɔrˈkɛstrəl] *adj* : orquestal
orchestrate [ˈɔrkəˌstreɪt] *vt* **-trated; -trating** **1** : orquestar, instrumentar (en música) **2** ORGANIZE : arreglar, organizar
orchestration [ˌɔrkəˈstreɪʃən] *n* : orquestación *f*
orchid [ˈɔrkɪd] *n* : orquídea *f*
ordain [ɔrˈdeɪn] *vt* **1** : ordenar (en religión) **2** DECREE : decretar, ordenar
ordeal [ɔrˈdiːl, ˈɔrˌdiːl] *n* : prueba *f* dura, experiencia *f* terrible
order[1] [ˈɔrdər] *vt* **1** ORGANIZE : arreglar, ordenar, poner en orden **2** COMMAND : ordenar, mandar **3** REQUEST : pedir, encargar ⟨to order a meal : pedir algo de comer⟩ — *vi* : hacer un pedido
order[2] *n* **1** : orden *f* ⟨a religious order : una orden religiosa⟩ **2** COMMAND : orden *f*, mandato *m* ⟨to give an order : dar una orden⟩ **3** REQUEST : orden *f*, pedido *m* ⟨purchase order : orden de compra⟩ **4** ARRANGEMENT : orden *m* ⟨in chronological order : por orden cronológico⟩ **5** DISCIPLINE : orden *m* ⟨law and order : el orden público⟩ **6 in order to** : para **7 out of order** : descompuesto, averiado **8 orders** *npl or* **holy orders** : órdenes *fpl* sagradas
orderliness [ˈɔrdərlinəs] *n* : orden *m*
orderly[1] [ˈɔrdərli] *adj* **1** METHODICAL : ordenado, metódico **2** PEACEFUL : pacífico, disciplinado
orderly[2] *n, pl* **-lies** **1** : ordenanza *m* (en el ejército) **2** : camillero *m* (en un hospital)
ordinal [ˈɔrdənəl] *n or* **ordinal number** : ordinal *m*, número *m* ordinal
ordinance [ˈɔrdənənts] *n* : ordenanza *f*, reglamento *m*
ordinarily [ˌɔrdənˈɛrəli] *adv* : ordinariamente, por lo general

ordinary [ˈɔrdənˌɛri] *adj* **1** NORMAL, USUAL : normal, usual **2** AVERAGE : común y corriente, normal **3** MEDIOCRE : mediocre, ordinario
ordination [ˌɔrdənˈeɪʃən] *n* : ordenación *f*
ordnance [ˈɔrdnənts] *n* : artillería *f*
ore [ˈor] *n* : mineral *m* (metalífero), mena *f*
oregano [əˈregəˌnoː] *n* : orégano *m*
organ [ˈɔrgən] *n* **1** : órgano *m* (instrumento) **2** : órgano *m* (del cuerpo) **3** PERIODICAL : publicación *f* periódica, órgano *m*
organic [ɔrˈgænɪk] *adj* : orgánico — **organically** *adv*
organism [ˈɔrgəˌnɪzəm] *n* : organismo *m*
organist [ˈɔrgənɪst] *n* : organista *mf*
organization [ˌɔrgənəˈzeɪʃən] *n* **1** ORGANIZING : organización *f* **2** BODY : organización *f*, organismo *m*
organizational [ˌɔrgənəˈzeɪʃənəl] *adj* : organizativo
organize [ˈɔrgəˌnaɪz] *vt* **-nized; -nizing** : organizar, arreglar, poner en orden
organizer [ˈɔrgəˌnaɪzər] *n* : organizador *m*, -dora *f*
orgasm [ˈɔrˌgæzəm] *n* : orgasmo *m*
orgy [ˈɔrdʒi] *n, pl* **-gies** : orgía *f*
orient [ˈoriˌent] *vt* : orientar
Orient *n* **the Orient** : el Oriente
oriental [ˌoriˈentəl] *adj* : del Oriente, oriental
Oriental *n* : oriental *mf*
orientation [ˌoriənˈteɪʃən] *n* : orientación *f*
orifice [ˈɔrəfəs] *n* : orificio *m*
origin [ˈɔrədʒən] *n* **1** ANCESTRY : origen *m*, ascendencia *f* **2** SOURCE : origen *m*, raíz *f*, fuente *f*
original[1] [əˈrɪdʒənəl] *adj* : original
original[2] *n* : original *m*
originality [əˌrɪdʒəˈnæləti] *n* : originalidad *f*
originally [əˈrɪdʒənəli] *adv* **1** AT FIRST : al principio, originariamente **2** CREATIVELY : originalmente, con originalidad
originate [əˈrɪdʒəˌneɪt] *v* **-nated; -nating** *vt* : originar, iniciar, crear — *vi* **1** BEGIN : originarse, empezar **2** COME : provenir, proceder, derivarse
originator [əˈrɪdʒəˌneɪtər] *n* : creador *m*, -dora *f*; inventor *m*, -tora *f*
oriole [ˈoriˌoːl, -iəl] *n* : oropéndola *f*
ornament[1] [ˈɔrnəmənt] *vt* : adornar, decorar, ornamentar
ornament[2] *n* : ornamento *m*, adorno *m*, decoración *f*
ornamental [ˌɔrnəˈmɛntəl] *adj* : ornamental, de adorno, decorativo
ornamentation [ˌɔrnəmənˈteɪʃən, -mɛn-] *n* : ornamentación *f*
ornate [ɔrˈneɪt] *adj* : elaborado, recargado
ornery [ˈɔrnəri, ˈɑrnəri] *adj* **ornerier; -est** : de mal genio, malhumorado
ornithologist [ˌɔrnəˈθɑlədʒɪst] *n* : ornitólogo *m*, -ga *f*

ornithology [ˌɔrnəˈθɑlədʒi] *n, pl* **-gies** : ornitología *f*

orphan[1] [ˈɔrfən] *vt* : dejar huérfano

orphan[2] *n* : huérfano *m*, -na *f*

orphanage [ˈɔrfənɪdʒ] *n* : orfelinato *m*, orfanato *m*

orthodontics [ˌɔrθəˈdɑntɪks] *n* : ortodoncia *f*

orthodontist [ˌɔrθəˈdɑntɪst] *n* : ortodoncista *mf*

orthodox [ˈɔrθəˌdɑks] *adj* : ortodoxo

orthodoxy [ˈɔrθəˌdɑksi] *n, pl* **-doxies** : ortodoxia *f*

orthographic [ˌɔrθəˈgræfɪk] *adj* : ortográfico

orthography [ɔrˈθɑgrəfi] *n, pl* **-phies** SPELLING : ortografía *f*

orthopedic [ˌɔrθəˈpiːdɪk] *adj* : ortopédico

orthopedics [ˌɔrθəˈpiːdɪks] *ns & pl* : ortopedia *f*

orthopedist [ˌɔrθəˈpiːdɪst] *n* : ortopedista *mf*

oscillate [ˈɑsəˌleɪt] *vi* **-lated; -lating** : oscilar

oscillation [ˌɑsəˈleɪʃən] *n* : oscilación *f*

osmosis [ɑzˈmoːsɪs, ɑs-] *n* : ósmosis *f*, osmosis *f*

osprey [ˈɑspri, -ˌpreɪ] *n* : pigargo *m*

ostensible [ɑˈstɛnʦəbəl] *adj* APPARENT : aparente, ostensible — **ostensibly** [-bli] *adv*

ostentation [ˌɑstənˈteɪʃən] *n* : ostentación *f*, boato *m*

ostentatious [ˌɑstənˈteɪʃəs] *adj* : ostentoso — **ostentatiously** *adv*

osteopath [ˈɑstiəˌpæθ] *n* : osteópata *f*

osteopathy [ˌɑstiˈɑpəθi] *n* : osteopatía *f*

osteoporosis [ˌɑstiopəˈroːsɪs] *n, pl* **-roses** [-ˌsiːz] : osteoporosis *f*

ostracism [ˈɑstrəˌsɪzəm] *n* : ostracismo *m*

ostracize [ˈɑstrəˌsaɪz] *vt* **-cized; -cizing** : condenar al ostracismo, marginar, aislar

ostrich [ˈɑstrɪʧ, ˈɔs-] *n* : avestruz *m*

other[1] [ˈʌðər] *adv* **other than** : aparte de, fuera de

other[2] *adj* : otro ⟨the other boys : los otros muchachos⟩ ⟨smarter than other people : más inteligente que los demás⟩ ⟨on the other hand : por otra parte, por otro lado⟩ ⟨every other day : cada dos días⟩

other[3] *pron* : otro, otra ⟨one in front of the other : uno tras otro⟩ ⟨myself and three others : yo y tres otros, yo y tres más⟩ ⟨somewhere or other : en alguna parte⟩

otherwise[1] [ˈʌðərˌwaɪz] *adv* **1** DIFFERENTLY : de otro modo, de manera distinta ⟨he could not act otherwise : no pudo actuar de manera distinta⟩ **2** : eso aparte, por lo demás ⟨I'm dizzy, but otherwise I'm fine : estoy mareado pero, por lo demás, estoy bien⟩ **3** OR ELSE : de lo contrario, si no ⟨do what I tell you, otherwise you'll be sorry : haz lo que te digo, de lo contrario, te arrepentirás⟩

otherwise[2] *adj* : diferente, distinto ⟨the facts are otherwise : la realidad es diferente⟩

otter [ˈɑtər] *n* : nutria *f*

Ottoman [ˈɑtəmən] *n* **1** : otomano *m*, -na *f* **2** : otomana *f* (mueble) — **Ottoman** *adj*

ouch [ˈaʊʧ] *interj* : ¡ay!, ¡huy!

ought [ˈɔt] *v aux* : deber ⟨you ought to take care of yourself : deberías cuidarte⟩

oughtn't [ˈɔtənt] (*contraction of* **ought not**) → **ought**

ounce [ˈaʊnʦ] *n* : onza *f*

our [ˈɑr, ˈaʊr] *adj* : nuestro

ours [ˈaʊrz, ˈɑrz] *pron* : nuestro, nuestra ⟨a cousin of ours : un primo nuestro⟩

ourselves [ɑrˈsɛlvz, aʊr-] *pron* **1** (*used reflexively*) : nos, nosotros ⟨we amused ourselves : nos divertimos⟩ ⟨we were always thinking of ourselves : siempre pensábamos en nosotros⟩ **2** (*used for emphasis*) : nosotros mismos, nosotras mismas ⟨we did it ourselves : lo hicimos nosotros mismos⟩

oust [ˈaʊst] *vt* : desbancar, expulsar

ouster [ˈaʊstər] *n* : expulsión *f* (de un país, etc.), destitución *f* (de un puesto)

out[1] [ˈaʊt] *vi* : revelarse, hacerse conocido

out[2] *adv* **1** (*indicating direction or movement*) : para afuera ⟨she opened the door and looked out : abrió la puerta y miró para afuera⟩ **2** (*indicating a location away from home or work*) : fuera, afuera ⟨to eat out : comer afuera⟩ **3** (*indicating loss of control or possession*) ⟨they let the secret out : sacaron el secreto a la luz⟩ **4** (*indicating completion or discontinuance*) ⟨his money ran out : se le acabó el dinero⟩ ⟨to turn out the light : apagar la luz⟩ **5** OUTSIDE : fuera, afuera ⟨out in the garden : afuera en el jardín⟩ **6** ALOUD : en voz alta, en alto ⟨to cry out : gritar⟩

out[3] *adj* **1** EXTERNAL : externo, exterior **2** OUTLYING : alejado, distante ⟨the out islands : las islas distantes⟩ **3** ABSENT : ausente **4** UNFASHIONABLE : fuera de moda **5** EXTINGUISHED : apagado

out[4] *prep* **1** (*used to indicate an outward movement*) : por ⟨I looked out the window : miré por la ventana⟩ ⟨she ran out the door : corrió por la puerta⟩ **2** → **out of**

out–and–out [ˈaʊtənˈaʊt] *adj* UTTER : redomado, absoluto

outboard motor [ˈaʊtˌbord] *n* : motor *m* fuera de borde

outbound [ˈaʊtˌbaʊnd] *adj* : que sale, de salida

outbreak [ˈaʊtˌbreɪk] *n* : brote *m* (de una enfermedad), comienzo *m* (de guerra), ola *f* (de violencia), erupción *f* (de granos)

outbuilding ['aʊt,bɪldɪŋ] *n* : edificio *m* anexo

outburst ['aʊt,bərst] *n* : arranque *m*, arrebato *m*

outcast ['aʊt,kæst] *n* : marginado *m*, -da *f*; paria *mf*

outcome ['aʊt,kʌm] *n* : resultado *m*, desenlace *m*, consecuencia *f*

outcrop ['aʊt,krɑp] *n* : afloramiento *m*

outcry ['aʊt,kraɪ] *n, pl* **-cries** : clamor *m*, protesta *f*

outdated [,aʊt'deɪtəd] *adj* : anticuado, fuera de moda

outdistance [,aʊt'dɪstənts] *vt* **-tanced; -tancing** : aventajar, dejar atrás

outdo [,aʊt'du:] *vt* **-did** [-'dɪd]; **-done** [-'dʌn]; **-doing; -does** [-'dʌz] : superar

outdoor ['aʊt'dor] *adj* : al aire libre ⟨outdoor sports : deportes al aire libre⟩ ⟨outdoor clothing : ropa de calle⟩

outdoors[1] ['aʊt'dorz] *adv* : afuera, al aire libre

outdoors[2] *n* : aire *m* libre

outer ['aʊtər] *adj* **1** : exterior, externo **2 outer space** : espacio *m* exterior

outermost ['aʊtər,mo:st] *adj* : más remoto, más exterior, extremo

outfield ['aʊt,fi:ld] *n* **the outfield** : los jardines

outfielder ['aʊt,fi:ldər] *n* : jardinero *m*, -ra *f*

outfit[1] ['aʊt,fɪt] *vt* **-fitted; -fitting** EQUIP : equipar

outfit[2] *n* **1** EQUIPMENT : equipo *m* **2** COSTUME, ENSEMBLE : traje *m*, conjunto *m* **3** GROUP : conjunto *m*

outgo ['aʊt,go:] *n, pl* **outgoes** : gasto *m*

outgoing ['aʊt,go:ɪŋ] *adj* **1** OUTBOUND : que sale **2** DEPARTING : saliente ⟨an outgoing president : un presidente saliente⟩ **3** EXTROVERTED : extrovertido, expansivo

outgrow [,aʊt'gro:] *vt* **-grew** [-'gru:]; **-grown** [-'gro:n]; **-growing 1** : crecer más que ⟨that tree outgrew all the others : ese árbol creció más que todos los otros⟩ **2 to outgrow one's clothes** : quedarle pequeña la ropa a uno

outgrowth ['aʊt,gro:θ] *n* **1** OFFSHOOT : brote *m*, vástago *m* (de una planta) **2** CONSEQUENCE : consecuencia *f*, producto *m*, resultado *m*

outing ['aʊtɪŋ] *n* : excursión *f*

outlandish [aʊt'lændɪʃ] *adj* : descabellado, muy extraño

outlast [,aʊt'læst] *vt* : durar más que

outlaw[1] ['aʊt,lɔ] *vt* : hacerse ilegal, declarar fuera de la ley, prohibir

outlaw[2] *n* : bandido *m*, -da *f*; bandolero *m*, -ra *f*; forajido *m*, -da *f*

outlay ['aʊt,leɪ] *n* : gasto *m*, desembolso *m*

outlet ['aʊt,lɛt, -lət] *n* **1** EXIT : salida *f*, escape *m* ⟨electrical outlet : toma de corriente⟩ **2** RELIEF : desahogo *m* **3** MARKET : mercado *m*, salida *f*

outline[1] ['aʊt,laɪn] *vt* **-lined; -lining 1** SKETCH : diseñar, esbozar, bosquejar **2** DEFINE, EXPLAIN : perfilar, delinear, explicar ⟨she outlined our responsibilities : delineó nuestras responsabilidades⟩

outline[2] *n* **1** PROFILE : perfil *m*, silueta *f*, contorno *m* **2** SKETCH : bosquejo *m*, boceto *m* **3** SUMMARY : esquema *m*, resumen *m*, sinopsis *m* ⟨an outline of world history : un esquema de la historia mundial⟩

outlive [,aʊt'lɪv] *vt* **-lived; -living** : sobrevivir a

outlook ['aʊt,lʊk] *n* **1** VIEW : vista *f*, panorama *f* **2** POINT OF VIEW : punto *m* de vista **3** PROSPECTS : perspectivas *fpl*

outlying ['aʊt,laɪɪŋ] *adj* : alejado, distante, remoto ⟨the outlying areas : las afueras⟩

outmoded [,aʊt'mo:dəd] *adj* : pasado de moda, anticuado

outnumber [,aʊt'nʌmbər] *vt* : superar en número a, ser más numeroso de

out of *prep* **1** (*indicating direction or movement from within*) : de, por ⟨we ran out of the house : salimos corriendo de la casa⟩ ⟨to look out of the window : mirar por la ventana⟩ **2** (*being beyond the limits of*) ⟨out of control : fuera de control⟩ ⟨to be out of sight : desaparecer de vista⟩ **3** OF : de ⟨one out of four : uno de cada cuatro⟩ **4** (*indicating absence or loss*) : sin ⟨out of money : sin dinero⟩ ⟨we're out of matches : nos hemos quedado sin fósforos⟩ **5** BECAUSE OF : por ⟨out of curiosity : por curiosidad⟩ **6** FROM : de ⟨made out of plastic : hecho de plástico⟩

out–of–date [,aʊtəv'deɪt] *adj* : anticuado, obsoleto, pasado de moda

out–of–door [,aʊtəv'dor] *or* **out–of–doors** [-'dorz] → **outdoor**

out–of–doors *n* → **outdoors**[2]

outpatient ['aʊt,peɪʃənt] *n* : paciente *m* externo, paciente *f* externa

outpost ['aʊt,po:st] *n* : puesto *m* avanzado

output[1] ['aʊt,pʊt] *vt* **-putted** *or* **-put; -putting** : producir

output[2] *n* : producción *f* (de una fábrica), rendimiento *m* (de una máquina), productividad *f* (de una persona)

outrage[1] ['aʊt,reɪʤ] *vt* **-raged; -raging 1** INSULT : ultrajar, injuriar **2** INFURIATE : indignar, enfurecer

outrage[2] *n* **1** ATROCITY : atropello *m*, atrocidad *f*, atentado *m* **2** SCANDAL : escándalo *m* **3** ANGER : ira *f*, furia *f*

outrageous [,aʊt'reɪʤəs] *adj* **1** SCANDALOUS : escandaloso, ofensivo, atroz **2** UNCONVENTIONAL : poco convencional, extravagante **3** EXORBITANT : exorbitante, excesivo (dícese de los precios, etc.)

outright[1] [,aʊt'raɪt] *adv* **1** COMPLETELY : por completo, totalmente ⟨to sell outright : vender por completo⟩ ⟨he refused it outright : lo rechazó rotunda-

mente> 2 DIRECTLY : directamente, sin
reserva 3 INSTANTLY : al instante, en
el acto
outright² ['aʊt,raɪt] *adj* **1** COMPLETE
: completo, absoluto, categórico <an
outright lie : una mentira absoluta> **2**
: sin reservas <an outright gift : un regalo sin reservas>
outset ['aʊt,sɛt] *n* : comienzo *m*, principio *m*
outshine [,aʊt'ʃaɪn] *vt* **-shone** [-'ʃo:n,
-'ʃɑn] *or* **-shined; -shining** : eclipsar
outside¹ [,aʊt'saɪd, 'aʊt,-] *adv* : fuera,
afuera
outside² *adj* **1** : exterior, externo <the
outside edge : el borde exterior> <out-
side influences : influencias externas>
2 REMOTE : remoto <an outside chance
: una posibilidad remota>
outside³ *n* **1** EXTERIOR : parte *f* de
afuera, exterior *m* **2** MOST : máximo
m <three weeks at the outside : tres semanas como máximo> **3 from the outside** : desde afuera, desde fuera
outside⁴ *prep* : fuera de, afuera de <out-
side my window : fuera de mi ventana>
<outside regular hours : fuera del ho-
rario normal> <outside the law : afuera
de la ley>
outside of *prep* **1** → **outside⁴ 2** → **besides²**
outsider [,aʊt'saɪdər] *n* : forastero *m*, -ra
f
outskirts ['aʊt,skərts] *npl* : afueras *fpl*,
alrededores *mpl*
outsmart [,aʊt'smɑrt] → **outwit**
outspoken [,aʊt'spo:kən] *adj* : franco,
directo
outstanding [,aʊt'stændɪŋ] *adj* **1** UN-
PAID : pendiente **2** NOTABLE : destacado, notable, excepcional, sobresaliente
outstandingly [,aʊt'stændɪŋli] *adv* : excepcionalmente
outstretched [,aʊt'strɛtʃt] *adj* : extendido
outstrip [,aʊt'strɪp] *vt* **-stripped** *or* **-stript**
[-'strɪpt]; **-stripping 1** : aventajar, de-
jar atrás <he outstripped the other runners : aventajó a los otros corredores>
2 SURPASS : aventajar, sobrepasar
outward¹ ['aʊtwərd] *or* **outwards**
[-wərdz] *adv* : hacia afuera, hacia el exterior
outward² *adj* **1** : hacia afuera <an outward flow : un flujo hacia afuera> **2**
: externo <outward beauty : belleza ex-
terna>
outwardly ['aʊtwərdli] *adv* **1** EXTER-
NALLY : exteriormente **2** APPARENTLY
: aparentemente <outwardly friendly
: aparentemente simpático>
outwit [,aʊt'wɪt] *vt* **-witted; -witting** : ser
más listo que
ova → **ovum**
oval¹ ['o:vəl] *adj* : ovalado, oval
oval² *n* : óvalo *m*
ovarian [o'væriən] *adj* : ovárico

ovary ['o:vəri] *n, pl* **-ries** : ovario *m*
ovation [o'veɪʃən] *n* : ovación *f*
oven ['ʌvən] *n* : horno *m*
over¹ ['o:vər] *adv* **1** (*indicating movement across*) <he flew over to London
: voló a Londres> <come on over! : ¡ven
acá!> **2** (*indicating an additional
amount*) <the show ran 10 minutes over
: el espectáculo terminó 10 minutos de
tarde> **3** ABOVE, OVERHEAD : por encima **4** AGAIN : otra vez, de nuevo <over
and over : una y otra vez> <to start over
: volver a empezar> **5 all over** EVERY-
WHERE : por todas partes **6 to fall over**
: caerse **7 to turn over** : poner boca
abajo, voltear
over² *adj* **1** HIGHER, UPPER : superior
2 REMAINING : sobrante, que sobra **3**
ENDED : terminado, acabado <the
work is over : el trabajo está termina-
do>
over³ *prep* **1** ABOVE : encima de, arriba
de, sobre <over the fireplace : encima
de la chimenea> <the hawk flew over
the hills : el halcón voló sobre los ce-
rros> **2** : más de <over $50 : más de
$50> **3** ALONG : por, sobre <to glide
over the ice : deslizarse sobre el hielo>
4 (*indicating motion through a place or
thing*) <they showed me over the house
: me mostraron la casa> **5** ACROSS : por
encima de, sobre <he jumped over the
ditch : saltó por encima de la zanja> **6**
UPON : sobre <a cape over my shoulders : una capa sobre los hombros> **7**
ON : por <to speak over the telephone
: hablar por teléfono> **8** DURING : en,
durante <over the past 25 years : durante los últimos 25 años> **9** BECAUSE
OF : por <they fought over the money
: se pelearon por el dinero>
overabundance [,o:vərə'bʌndənts] *n*
: superabundancia *f*
overabundant [,o:vərə'bʌndənt] *adj*
: superabundante
overactive [,o:vər'æktɪv] *adj* : hiperactivo
overall [,o:vər'ɔl] *adj* : total, global, de
conjunto
overalls ['o:vər,ɔlz] *npl* : overol *m*
overawe [,o:vər'ɔ] *vt* **-awed; -awing** : intimidar, impresionar
overbearing [,o:vər'bærɪŋ] *adj* : dominante, imperioso, prepotente
overblown [,o:vər'blo:n] *adj* **1** INFLAT-
ED : inflado, exagerado **2** BOMBASTIC
: grandilocuente, rimbombante
overboard ['o:vər,bord] *adv* : por la borda, al agua
overburden [,o:vər'bərdən] *vt* : sobrecargar, agobiar
overcast ['o:vər,kæst] *adj* CLOUDY
: nublado
overcharge [,o:vər'tʃɑrdʒ] *vt* **-charged;
-charging** : cobrarle de más (a alguien)
overcoat ['o:vər,ko:t] *n* : abrigo *m*
overcome [,o:vər'kʌm] *v* **-came**
[-'keɪm]; **-come; -coming** *vt* **1** CON-

QUER : vencer, derrotar, superar **2**
OVERWHELM : abrumar, agobiar — *vi*
: vencer
overconfidence [ˌoːvərˈkɑnfədənts] *n*
: exceso *m* de confianza
overconfident [ˌoːvərˈkɑnfədənt] *adj*
: demasiado confiado
overcook [ˌoːvərˈkʊk] *vt* : recocer, cocer
demasiado
overcrowded [ˌoːvərˈkraʊdəd] *adj* **1**
PACKED : abarrotado, atestado de
gente **2** OVERPOPULATED : superpoblado
overdo [ˌoːvərˈduː] *vt* **-did** [-ˈdɪd]; **-done**
[-ˈdʌn]; **-doing**; **-does** [-ˈdʌz] **1** : hacer demasiado **2** EXAGGERATE : ex-
agerar **3** OVERCOOK : recocer
overdose [ˈoːvərˌdoːs] *n* : sobredosis *f*
overdraft [ˈoːvərˌdræft] *n* : sobregiro *m*,
descubierto *m*
overdraw [ˌoːvərˈdrɔ] *vt* **-drew** [-ˈdruː];
-drawn [-ˈdrɔn]; **-drawing 1** : sobregirar ⟨my account is overdrawn : tengo
la cuenta en descubierto⟩ **2** EXAG-
GERATE : exagerar
overdue [ˌoːvərˈduː] *adj* **1** UNPAID : vencido y sin pagar **2** TARDY : de retraso,
tardío
overeat [ˌoːvərˈiːt] *vi* **-ate** [-ˈeɪt]; **-eaten**
[-ˈiːtən]; **-eating** : comer demasiado
overelaborate [ˌoːvərɪˈlæbərət] *adj* : recargado
overestimate [ˌoːvərˈɛstəˌmeɪt] *vt*
-mated; **-mating** : sobreestimar
overexcited [ˌoːvərɪkˈsaɪtəd] *adj* : sobreexcitado
overexpose [ˌoːvərɪkˈspoːz] *vt* **-posed**;
-posing : sobreexponer
overfeed [ˌoːvərˈfiːd] *vt* **-fed** [-ˈfɛd];
-feeding : sobrealimentar
overflow[1] [ˌoːvərˈfloː] *vt* **1** : desbordar **2**
INUNDATE : inundar — *vi* : desbor-
darse, rebosar
overflow[2] [ˈoːvərˌfloː] *n* **1** : derrame *m*,
desbordamiento *m* (de un río) **2** SUR-
PLUS : exceso *m*, excedente *m*
overfly [ˌoːvərˈflaɪ] *vt* **-flew** [-ˈfluː];
-flown [-ˈfloːn]; **-flying** : sobrevolar
overgrown [ˌoːvərˈgroːn] *adj* **1** : cubierto ⟨overgrown with weeds : cubierto de malas hierbas⟩ **2** : demasiado grande
overhand[1] [ˈoːvərˌhænd] *adv* : por encima de la cabeza
overhand[2] *adj* : por lo alto (tirada)
overhang[1] [ˌoːvərˈhæŋ] *v* **-hung** [-ˈhʌŋ];
-hanging *vt* **1** : sobresalir por encima
de **2** THREATEN : amenazar — *vi* : sobresalir
overhang[2] [ˈoːvərˌhæŋ] *n* : saliente *mf*
overhaul [ˌoːvərˈhɔl] *vt* **1** : revisar ⟨to
overhaul an engine : revisar un motor⟩
2 OVERTAKE : adelantar
overhead[1] [ˌoːvərˈhɛd] *adv* : por encima,
arriba, por lo alto
overhead[2] [ˈoːvərˌhɛd] *adj* : de arriba
overhead[3] [ˈoːvərˌhɛd] *n* : gastos *mpl*
generales

overhear [ˌoːvərˈhɪr] *vt* **-heard**; **-hearing**
: oír por casualidad
overheat [ˌoːvərˈhiːt] *vt* : recalentar, sobrecalentar, calentar demasiado
overjoyed [ˌoːvərˈdʒɔɪd] *adj* : rebosante
de alegría
overkill [ˈoːvərˌkɪl] *n* : exceso *m*, excedente *m*
overland[1] [ˈoːvərˌlænd, -lənd] *adv* : por
tierra
overland[2] *adj* : terrestre, por tierra
overlap[1] [ˌoːvərˈlæp] *v* **-lapped**; **-lapping**
vt : traslapar — *vi* : traslaparse, solaparse
overlap[2] [ˈoːvərˌlæp] *n* : traslapo *m*
overlay[1] [ˌoːvərˈleɪ] *vt* **-laid** [-ˈleɪd];
-laying : recubrir, revestir
overlay[2] [ˈoːvərˌleɪ] *n* : revestimiento *m*
overload [ˌoːvərˈloːd] *vt* : sobrecargar
overlong [ˌoːvərˈlɔŋ] *adj* : excesivamente largo, largo y pesado
overlook [ˌoːvərˈlʊk] *vt* **1** INSPECT : inspeccionar, revisar **2** : tener vista a, dar
a ⟨a house overlooking the valley : una
casa que tiene vista al valle⟩ **3** MISS
: pasar por alto **4** EXCUSE : dejar pasar,
disculpar
overly [ˈoːvərli] *adv* : demasiado
overnight[1] [ˌoːvərˈnaɪt] *adv* **1** : por la
noche, durante la noche **2** : de la noche
a la mañana ⟨we can't do it overnight
: no podemos hacerlo de la noche a la
mañana⟩
overnight[2] [ˈoːvərˌnaɪt] *adj* **1** : de noche
⟨an overnight stay : una estancia de
una noche⟩ ⟨an overnight bag : una
bolsa de viaje⟩ **2** SUDDEN : repentino
overpass [ˈoːvərˌpæs] *n* : paso *m* elevado, paso *m* a desnivel *Mex*
overpopulated [ˌoːvərˈpɑpjəˌleɪtəd] *adj*
: sobrepoblado
overpower [ˌoːvərˈpaʊər] *vt* **1** CON-
QUER, SUBDUE : vencer, superar **2**
OVERWHELM : abrumar, agobiar
⟨overpowered by the heat : sofocado
por el calor⟩
overpraise [ˌoːvərˈpreɪz] *vt* **-praised**;
-praising : adular
overrate [ˌoːvərˈreɪt] *vt* **-rated**; **-rating**
: sobrevalorar, sobrevaluar
override [ˌoːvərˈraɪd] *vt* **-rode** [-ˈroːd];
-ridden [-ˈrɪdən]; **-riding 1** : predominar sobre, contar más que ⟨hunger
overrode our manners : el hambre pre-
dominó sobre los modales⟩ **2** ANNUL
: anular, invalidar ⟨to override a veto
: anular un veto⟩
overrule [ˌoːvərˈruːl] *vt* **-ruled**; **-ruling**
: anular (una decisión), desautorizar
(una persona), denegar (un pedido)
overrun [ˌoːvərˈrʌn] *v* **-ran** [-ˈræn];
-running *vt* **1** INVADE : invadir **2** IN-
FEST : infestar, plagar **3** EXCEED : exceder, rebasar — *vi* : rebasar el tiempo previsto
overseas[1] [ˌoːvərˈsiːz] *adv* : en el extranjero ⟨to travel overseas : viajar al
extranjero⟩

overseas² ['oːvər₁siːz] *adj* : extranjero, exterior

oversee [₁oːvər'siː] *vt* **-saw** [-'sɔ]; **-seen** [-'siːn]; **-seeing** SUPERVISE : supervisar

overseer ['oːvər₁siːər] *n* : supervisor *m*, -sora *f*; capataz *mf*

overshadow [₁oːvər'ʃæ₁doː] *vt* **1** DARKEN : oscurecer, ensombrecer **2** ECLIPSE, OUTSHINE : eclipsar

overshoe ['oːvər₁ʃuː] *n* : chanclo *m*

overshoot [₁oːvər'ʃuːt] *vt* **-shot** [-'ʃɑt]; **-shooting** : pasarse de ⟨to overshoot the mark : pasarse de la raya⟩

oversight ['oːvər₁saɪt] *n* : descuido *m*, inadvertencia *f*

oversleep [₁oːvər'sliːp] *vi* **-slept** [-'slɛpt]; **-sleeping** : no despertarse a tiempo, quedarse dormido

overspread [₁oːvər'sprɛd] *vt* **-spread**; **-spreading** : extenderse sobre

overstaffed [₁oːvər'stæft] *adj* : con exceso de personal

overstate [₁oːvər'steɪt] *vt* **-stated**; **-stating** EXAGGERATE : exagerar

overstatement [₁oːvər'steɪtmənt] *n* : exageración *f*

overstep [₁oːvər'stɛp] *vt* **-stepped**; **-stepping** EXCEED : sobrepasar, traspasar, exceder

overt [oː'vərt, 'oː₁vərt] *adj* : evidente, manifiesto, patente

overtake [₁oːvər'teɪk] *vt* **-took** [-'tʊk]; **-taken** [-'teɪkən]; **-taking** : pasar, adelantar, rebasar *Mex*

overthrow¹ [₁oːvər'θroː] *vt* **-threw** [-'θruː]; **-thrown** [-'θroːn]; **-throwing 1** OVERTURN : dar la vuelta a, volcar **2** DEFEAT, TOPPLE : derrocar, derribar, deponer

overthrow² ['oːvər₁θroː] *n* : derrocamiento *m*, caída *f*

overtime ['oːvər₁taɪm] *n* **1** : horas *fpl* extras (de trabajo) **2** : prórroga *f* (en deportes)

overtly [oː'vərtli, 'oː₁vərt-] *adv* OPENLY : abiertamente

overtone ['oːvər₁toːn] *n* **1** : armónico *m* (en música) **2** HINT, SUGGESTION : tinte *m*, insinuación *f*

overture ['oːvər₁tʃʊr, -tʃər] *n* **1** PROPOSAL : propuesta *f* **2** : obertura *f* (en música)

overturn [₁oːvər'tərn] *vt* **1** UPSET : dar la vuelta a, volcar **2** NULLIFY : anular, invalidar — *vi* TURN OVER : volcar, dar un vuelco

overuse [₁oːvər'juːz] *vt* **-used**; **-using** : abusar de

overview ['oːvər₁vjuː] *n* : resumen *m*, visión *f* general

overweening [₁oːvər'wiːnɪŋ] *adj* **1** ARROGANT : arrogante, soberbio **2** IMMODERATE : desmesurado

overweight [₁oːvər'weɪt] *adj* : demasiado gordo, demasiado pesado

overwhelm [₁oːvər'hwɛlm] *vt* **1** CRUSH, DEFEAT : aplastar, arrollar **2** SUBMERGE : inundar, sumergir **3** OVERPOWER : abrumar, agobiar ⟨overwhelmed by remorse : abrumado de remordimiento⟩

overwhelming [₁oːvər'hwɛlmɪŋ] *adj* **1** CRUSHING : abrumador, apabullante **2** SWEEPING : arrollador, aplastante ⟨an overwhelming majority : una mayoría aplastante⟩

overwork [₁oːvər'wərk] *vt* **1** : hacer trabajar demasiado **2** OVERUSE : abusar de — *vi* : trabajar demasiado

overwrought [₁oːvər'rɔt] *adj* : alterado, sobreexcitado

ovoid ['oː₁vɔɪd] *or* **ovoidal** [oː'vɔɪdəl] *adj* : ovoide

ovulate ['ɑvjə₁leɪt, 'oː-] *vi* **-lated**; **-lating** : ovular

ovulation [₁ɑvjə'leɪʃən, ₁oː-] *n* : ovulación *f*

ovum ['oːvəm] *n, pl* **ova** [-və] : óvulo *m*

owe ['oː] *vt* **owed**; **owing** : deber ⟨you owe me $10 : me debes $10⟩ ⟨he owes his wealth to his father : le debe su riqueza a su padre⟩

owing to *prep* : debido a

owl ['aʊl] *n* : búho *m*, lechuza *f*, tecolote *m Mex*

own¹ ['oːn] *vt* **1** POSSESS : poseer, tener, ser dueño de **2** ADMIT : reconocer, admitir — *vi* **to own up** : reconocer (algo), admitir (algo)

own² *adj* : propio, personal, particular ⟨his own car : su propio coche⟩

own³ *pron* **my; (your, his/her, our, their); own** : el mío, la mía; el tuyo, la tuya; el suyo, la suya; el nuestro, la nuestra ⟨to each his own : cada uno a lo suyo⟩ ⟨money of my own : mi propio dinero⟩ ⟨to be on one's own : estar solo⟩

owner ['oːnər] *n* : dueño *m*, -ña *f*; propietario *m*, -ria *f*

ownership ['oːnər₁ʃɪp] *n* : propiedad *f*

ox ['ɑks] *n, pl* **oxen** ['ɑksən] : buey *m*

oxidation [₁ɑksə'deɪʃən] *n* : oxidación *f*

oxide ['ɑk₁saɪd] *n* : óxido *m*

oxidize ['ɑksə₁daɪz] *vt* **-dized**; **-dizing** : oxidar

oxygen ['ɑksɪʤən] *n* : oxígeno *m*

oyster ['ɔɪstər] *n* : ostra *f*, ostión *m Mex*

ozone ['oː₁zoːn] *n* : ozono *m*

P

p ['piː] *n, pl* **p's** *or* **ps** ['piːz] : decimosexta letra del alfabeto inglés
pace[1] ['peɪs] *v* **paced; pacing** *vi* : caminar, ir y venir — *vt* **1** : caminar por ⟨she paced the floor : caminaba de un lado a otro del cuarto⟩ **2 to pace a runner** : marcarle el ritmo a un corredor
pace[2] *n* **1** STEP : paso *m* **2** RATE : paso *m*, ritmo *m* ⟨to set the pace : marcar el paso, marcar la pauta⟩
pacemaker ['peɪs,meɪkər] *n* : marcapasos *m*
pacific [pə'sɪfɪk] *adj* : pacífico
pacifier ['pæsə,faɪər] *n* : chupete *m*, chupón *m*, mamila *f Mex*
pacifism ['pæsə,fɪzəm] *n* : pacifismo *m*
pacifist ['pæsəfɪst] *n* : pacifista *mf*
pacify ['pæsə,faɪ] *vt* **-fied; -fying 1** SOOTHE : apaciguar, pacificar **2** : pacificar (un país, una región, etc.)
pack[1] ['pæk] *vt* **1** PACKAGE : empaquetar, embalar, envasar **2** : empacar, meter (en una maleta) ⟨to pack one's bag : hacer la maleta⟩ **3** FILL : llenar, abarrotar ⟨a packed theater : un teatro abarrotado⟩ **4 to pack off** SEND : mandar — *vi* : empacar, hacer las maletas
pack[2] *n* **1** BUNDLE : bulto *m*, fardo *m* **2** BACKPACK : mochila *f* **3** PACKAGE : paquete *m*, cajetilla *f* (de cigarrillos, etc.) **4** : manada *f* (de lobos, etc.), jauría *f* (de perros) ⟨a pack of thieves : una pandilla de ladrones⟩
package[1] ['pækɪʤ] *vt* **-aged; -aging** : empaquetar, embalar
package[2] *n* : paquete *m*, bulto *m*
packaging ['pækɪʤɪŋ] *n* **1** : embalaje *m* **2** WRAPPING : envoltorio *m*
packer ['pækər] *n* : empacador *m*, -dora *f*
packet ['pækət] *n* : paquete *m*
packing ['pækɪŋ] *n* : embalaje *m*
pact ['pækt] *n* : pacto *m*, acuerdo *m*
pad[1] ['pæd] *vt* **padded; padding 1** FILL, STUFF : rellenar, acolchar (una silla, una pared) **2** : meter paja en, rellenar ⟨to pad a speech : rellenar un discurso⟩
pad[2] *n* **1** CUSHION : almohadilla *f* ⟨a shoulder pad : una hombrera⟩ **2** TABLET : bloc *m* (de papel) **3** *or* **lily pad** : hoja *f* grande (de un nenúfar) **4 ink pad** : tampón *m* **5 launching pad** : plataforma *f* (de lanzamiento)
padding ['pædɪŋ] *n* **1** FILLING : relleno *m* **2** : paja *f* (en un discurso, etc.)
paddle[1] ['pædəl] *v* **-dled; -dling** *vt* **1** : hacer avanzar (una canoa) con canalete **2** HIT : azotar, darle nalgadas a (con una pala o paleta) — *vi* **1** : remar (en una canoa) **2** SPLASH : chapotear, mojarse los pies
paddle[2] *n* **1** : canalete *m*, zagual *m* (de una canoa, etc.) **2** : pala *f*, paleta *f* (en deportes)

paddock ['pædək] *n* **1** PASTURE : potrero *m* **2** : paddock *m*, cercado *m* (en un hipódromo)
paddy ['pædi] *n, pl* **-dies** : arrozal *m*
padlock[1] ['pæd,lɑk] *vt* : cerrar con candado
padlock[2] *n* : candado *m*
pagan[1] ['peɪgən] *adj* : pagano
pagan[2] *n* : pagano *m*, -na *f*
paganism ['peɪgən,ɪzəm] *n* : paganismo *m*
page[1] ['peɪʤ] *vt* **paged; paging** : llamar por altavoz
page[2] *n* **1** BELLHOP : botones *m* **2** : página *f* (de un libro, etc.)
pageant ['pæʤənt] *n* **1** SPECTACLE : espectáculo *m* **2** PROCESSION : desfile *m*
pageantry ['pæʤəntri] *n* : pompa *f*, fausto *m*
pager ['peɪʤər] *n* BEEPER : buscapersonas *m*
pagoda [pə'goːdə] *n* : pagoda *f*
paid → **pay**
pail ['peɪl] *n* : balde *m*, cubo *m*, cubeta *f Mex*
pailful ['peɪl,fʊl] *n* : balde *m*, cubo *m*, cubeta *f Mex*
pain[1] ['peɪn] *vt* : doler
pain[2] *n* **1** PENALTY : pena *f* ⟨under pain of death : so pena de muerte⟩ **2** SUFFERING : dolor *m*, malestar *m*, pena *f* (mental) **3 pains** *npl* EFFORT : esmero *m*, esfuerzo *m* ⟨to take pains : esmerarse⟩
painful ['peɪnfəl] *adj* : doloroso — **painfully** *adv*
painkiller ['peɪn,kɪlər] *n* : analgésico *m*
painless ['peɪnləs] *adj* : indoloro, sin dolor
painlessly ['peɪnləsli] *adv* : sin dolor
painstaking ['peɪn,steɪkɪŋ] *adj* : esmerado, cuidadoso, meticuloso — **painstakingly** *adv*
paint[1] ['peɪnt] *v* : pintar
paint[2] *n* : pintura *f*
paintbrush ['peɪnt,brʌʃ] *n* : pincel *m* (de un artista), brocha *f* (para pintar casas, etc.)
painter ['peɪntər] *n* : pintor *m*, -tora *f*
painting ['peɪntɪŋ] *n* : pintura *f*
pair[1] ['pær] *vt* : emparejar, poner en parejas — *vi* : emparejarse
pair[2] *n* : par *m* (de objetos), pareja *f* (de personas o animales) ⟨a pair of scissors : unas tijeras⟩
pajamas [pə'ʤaməz, -'ʤæ-] *npl* : pijama *m*, piyama *m*
Pakistani [,pækɪ'stæni, ,pɑkɪ'stɑni] *n* : paquistaní *mf* — **Pakistani** *adj*
pal ['pæl] *n* : amigo *m*, -ga *f*; compinche *mf fam*; chamo *m*, -ma *f Ven fam*; cuate *m*, -ta *f Mex*
palace ['pæləs] *n* : palacio *m*
palatable ['pælətəbəl] *adj* : sabroso
palate ['pælət] *n* **1** : paladar *m* (de la boca) **2** TASTE : paladar *m*, gusto *m*

palatial [pə'leɪʃəl] *adj* : suntuoso, espléndido

palaver [pə'lævər, -'lɑ-] *n* : palabrería *f*

pale¹ ['peɪl] *v* **paled; paling** *vi* : palidecer — *vt* : hacer pálido

pale² *adj* **paler; palest** 1 : pálido ⟨to turn pale : palidecer, ponerse pálido⟩ 2 : claro (dícese de los colores)

paleness ['peɪlnəs] *n* : palidez *f*

paleontologist [ˌpeɪliˌɑn'tɑlədʒɪst] *n* : paleontólogo *m*, -ga *f*

paleontology [ˌpeɪliˌɑn'tɑlədʒi] *n* : paleontología *f*

Palestinian [ˌpælə'stɪniən] *n* : palestino *m*, -na *f* — **Palestinian** *adj*

palette ['pælət] *n* : paleta *f* (para mezclar pigmentos)

palisade [ˌpælə'seɪd] *n* 1 FENCE : empalizada *f*, estacada *f* 2 CLIFFS : acantilado *m*

pall¹ ['pɔl] *vi* : perder su sabor, dejar de gustar

pall² *n* 1 : paño *m* mortuorio (sobre un ataúd) 2 COVER : cortina *f* (de humo, etc.) 3 **to cast a pall over** : ensombrecer

pallbearer ['pɔlˌbɛrər] *n* : portador *m*, -dora *f* del féretro

pallet ['pælət] *n* 1 BED : camastro *m* 2 PLATFORM : plataforma *f* de carga

palliative ['pæliˌeɪtɪv, 'pæljətɪv] *adj* : paliativo

pallid ['pæləd] *adj* : pálido

pallor ['pælər] *n* : palidez *f*

palm¹ ['pɑm, 'pɑlm] *vt* 1 CONCEAL : escamotear (un naipe, etc.) 2 **to palm off** : encajar, endilgar *fam* ⟨he palmed it off on me : me lo endilgó⟩

palm² *n* 1 *or* **palm tree** : palmera *f* 2 : palma *f* (de la mano)

Palm Sunday *n* : Domingo *m* de Ramos

palomino [ˌpælə'miːˌnoː] *n*, *pl* **-nos** : caballo *m* de color dorado

palpable ['pælpəbəl] *adj* : palpable — **palpably** [-bli] *adv*

palpitate ['pælpəˌteɪt] *vi* **-tated; -tating** : palpitar

palpitation [ˌpælpə'teɪʃən] *n* : palpitación *f*

palsy ['pɔlzi] *n*, *pl* **-sies** 1 : parálisis *f* 2 → **cerebral palsy**

paltry ['pɔltri] *adj* **-trier; -est** : mísero, mezquino, insignificante ⟨a paltry excuse : una mala excusa⟩

pampas ['pæmpəz, 'pɑmpəs] *npl* : pampa *f*

pamper ['pæmpər] *vt* : mimar, consentir, chiquear *Mex*

pamphlet ['pæmpflət] *n* : panfleto *m*, folleto *m*

pan¹ ['pæn] *vt* **panned; panning** CRITICIZE : poner por los suelos — *vi* **to pan for gold** : cribar el oro con batea, lavar oro

pan² *n* 1 : cacerola *f*, cazuela *f* 2 **frying pan** : sartén *mf*, freidera *f Mex*

panacea [ˌpænə'siːə] *n* : panacea *f*

Panamanian [ˌpænə'meɪniən] *n* : panameño *m*, -ña *f* — **Panamanian** *adj*

pancake ['pænˌkeɪk] *n* : panqueque *m*

pancreas ['pæŋkriəs, 'pæn-] *n* : páncreas *m*

panda ['pændə] *n* : panda *mf*

pandemonium [ˌpændə'moːniəm] *n* : pandemonio *m*, pandemónium *m*

pander ['pændər] *vi* **to pander to** : satisfacer, complacer (a alguien) ⟨to pander to popular taste : satisfacer el gusto popular⟩

pane ['peɪn] *n* : cristal *m*, vidrio *m*

panel¹ ['pænəl] *vt* **-eled** *or* **-elled; -eling** *or* **-elling** : adornar con paneles

panel² *n* 1 : lista *f* de nombres (de un jurado, etc.) 2 GROUP : panel *m*, grupo *m* ⟨discussion panel : panel de discusión⟩ 3 : panel *m* (de una pared, etc.) 4 **instrument panel** : tablero *m* de instrumentos

paneling ['pænəlɪŋ] *n* : paneles *mpl*

pang ['pæŋ] *n* : puntada *f*, punzada *f*

panic¹ ['pænɪk] *v* **-icked; -icking** *vt* : llenar de pánico — *vi* : ser presa de pánico

panic² *n* : pánico *m*

panicky ['pænɪki] *adj* : presa de pánico

panorama [ˌpænə'ræmə, -'rɑ-] *n* : panorama *m*

panoramic [ˌpænə'ræmɪk, -'rɑ-] *adj* : panorámico

pansy ['pænzi] *n*, *pl* **-sies** : pensamiento *m*

pant¹ ['pænt] *vi* : jadear, resoplar

pant² *n* : jadeo *m*, resoplo *m*

pantaloons [ˌpæntə'luːnz] → **pants**

pantheon ['pænˌθiˌɑn, -ən] *n* : panteón *m*

panther ['pænθər] *n* : pantera *f*

panties ['pæntiz] *npl* : calzones *mpl*; pantaletas *fpl Mex*, *Ven*; bragas *fpl Spain*

pantomime¹ ['pæntəˌmaɪm] *v* **-mimed; -miming** *vt* : representar mediante la pantomima — *vi* : hacer la mímica

pantomime² *n* : pantomima *f*

pantry ['pæntri] *n*, *pl* **-tries** : despensa *f*

pants ['pænts] *npl* 1 TROUSERS : pantalón *m*, pantalones *mpl* 2 → **panties**

panty hose ['pænti] *ns & pl* : medias *fpl*, panties *mfpl*, pantimedias *fpl Mex*

pap ['pæp] *n* : papilla *f* (para bebés, etc.)

papa ['pɑpə] *n* : papá *m*

papal ['peɪpəl] *adj* : papal

papaya [pə'paɪə] *n* : papaya *f* (fruta)

paper¹ ['peɪpər] *vt* WALLPAPER : empapelar

paper² *adj* : de papel

paper³ *n* 1 : papel *m* ⟨a piece of paper : un papel⟩ 2 DOCUMENT : papel *m*, documento *m* 3 NEWSPAPER : periódico *m*, diario *m*

paperback ['peɪpərˌbæk] *n* : libro *m* en rústica

paper clip *n* : clip *m*, sujetapapeles *m*

paperweight ['peɪpərˌweɪt] *n* : pisapapeles *m*

paperwork ['peɪpər,wərk] *n* : papeleo *m*
papery ['peɪpəri] *adj* : parecido al papel
papier—mâché [,peɪpərmə'ʃeɪ, ,pæ-,pjeɪmæ'ʃeɪ] *n* : papel *m* maché
papoose [pæ'puːs, pə-] *n* : niño *m*, -ña *f* de los indios norteamericanos
paprika [pə'priːkə, pæ-] *n* : pimentón *m*, paprika *f*
papyrus [pə'paɪrəs] *n, pl* **-ruses** *or* **-ri** [-ri, -,raɪ] : papiro *m*
par ['pɑr] *n* **1** VALUE : valor *m* (nominal), par *f* ⟨below par : debajo de la par⟩ **2** EQUALITY : igualdad *f* ⟨to be on a par with : estar al mismo nivel que⟩ **3** : par *m* (en golf)
parable ['pærəbəl] *n* : parábola *f*
parabola [pə'ræbələ] *n* : parábola *f* (en matemáticas)
parachute[1] ['pærə,ʃuːt] *vi* **-chuted; -chuting** : lanzarse en paracaídas
parachute[2] *n* : paracaídas *m*
parachutist ['pærə,ʃuːtɪst] *n* : paracaidista *mf*
parade[1] [pə'reɪd] *vi* **-raded; -rading 1** MARCH : desfilar **2** SHOW OFF : pavonearse, lucirse
parade[2] *n* **1** PROCESSION : desfile *m* **2** DISPLAY : alarde *m*
paradigm ['pærə,daɪm] *n* : paradigma *m*
paradise ['pærə,daɪs, -,daɪz] *n* : paraíso *m*
paradox ['pærə,dɑks] *n* : paradoja *f*
paradoxical [,pærə'dɑksɪkəl] *adj* : paradójico — **paradoxically** *adv*
paraffin ['pærəfən] *n* : parafina *f*
paragon ['pærə,gɑn, -gən] *n* : dechado *m*
paragraph[1] ['pærə,græf] *vt* : dividir en párrafos
paragraph[2] *n* : párrafo *m*, acápite *m*
Paraguayan [,pærə'gwaɪən, -'gweɪ-] *n* : paraguayo *m*, -ya *f* — **Paraguayan** *adj*
parakeet ['pærə,kiːt] *n* : periquito *m*
paralegal [,pærə'liːgəl] *n* : asistente *mf* de abogado
parallel[1] ['pærə,lɛl, -ləl] *vt* **1** MATCH, RESEMBLE : ser paralelo a, ser análogo a, corresponder con **2** : extenderse en línea paralela con ⟨the road parallels the river : el camino se extiende a lo largo del río⟩
parallel[2] *adj* : paralelo
parallel[3] *n* **1** : línea *f* paralela, superficie *f* paralela **2** : paralelo *m* (en geografía) **3** SIMILARITY : paralelismo *m*, semejanza *f*
parallelogram [,pærə'lɛlə,græm] *n* : paralelogramo *m*
paralysis [pə'ræləsəs] *n, pl* **-yses** [-,siːz] : parálisis *f*
paralyze ['pærə,laɪz] *vt* **-lyzed; -lyzing** : paralizar
parameter [pə'ræmətər] *n* : parámetro *m*
paramount ['pærə,maʊnt] *adj* : supremo ⟨of paramount importance : de suma importancia⟩
paranoia [,pærə'nɔɪə] *n* : paranoia *f*

paranoid ['pærə,nɔɪd] *adj* : paranoico
parapet ['pærəpət, -,pɛt] *n* : parapeto *m*
paraphernalia [,pærəfə'neɪljə, -fər-] *ns & pl* : parafernalia *f*
paraphrase[1] ['pærə,freɪz] *vt* **-phrased; -phrasing** : parafrasear
paraphrase[2] *n* : paráfrasis *f*
paraplegic[1] [,pærə'pliːdʒɪk] *adj* : parapléjico
paraplegic[2] *n* : parapléjico *m*, -ca *f*
parasite ['pærə,saɪt] *n* : parásito *m*
parasitic [,pærə'sɪtɪk] *adj* : parasitario
parasol ['pærə,sɔl] *n* : sombrilla *f*, quitasol *m*, parasol *m*
paratrooper ['pærə,truːpər] *n* : paracaidista *mf* (militar)
parboil ['pɑr,bɔɪl] *vt* : sancochar, cocer a medias
parcel[1] ['pɑrsəl] *vt* **-celed** *or* **-celled; -celing** *or* **-celling** *or* **to parcel out** : repartir, parcelar (tierras)
parcel[2] *n* **1** LOT : parcela *f*, lote *m* **2** PACKAGE : paquete *m*, bulto *m*
parch ['pɑrtʃ] *vt* : resecar
parchment ['pɑrtʃmənt] *n* : pergamino *m*
pardon[1] ['pɑrdən] *vt* **1** FORGIVE : perdonar, disculpar ⟨pardon me! : ¡perdone!, ¡disculpe la molestia!⟩ **2** REPRIEVE : indultar (a un delincuente)
pardon[2] *n* **1** FORGIVENESS : perdón *m* **2** REPRIEVE : indulto *m*
pardonable ['pɑrdənəbəl] *adj* : perdonable, disculpable
pare ['pær] *vt* **pared; paring 1** PEEL : pelar **2** TRIM : recortar **3** REDUCE : reducir ⟨he pared it (down) to 50 pages : lo redujo a 50 páginas⟩
parent ['pærənt] *n* **1** : madre *f*, padre *m* **2 parents** *npl* : padres *mpl*
parentage ['pærəntɪdʒ] *n* : linaje *m*, abolengo *m*, origen *m*
parental [pə'rɛntəl] *adj* : de los padres
parenthesis [pə'rɛnθəsɪs] *n, pl* **-theses** [-,siːz] : paréntesis *m*
parenthetic [,pærən'θɛtɪk] *or* **parenthetical** [-,tɪkəl] *adj* : parentético — **parenthetically** [-tɪkli] *adv*
parenthood ['pærənt,hʊd] *n* : paternidad *f*
parfait [pɑr'feɪ] *n* : postre *m* elaborado con frutas y helado
pariah [pə'raɪə] *n* : paria *mf*
parish ['pærɪʃ] *n* : parroquia *f*
parishioner [pə'rɪʃənər] *n* : feligrés *m*, -gresa *f*
parity ['pærəti] *n, pl* **-ties** : paridad *f*
park[1] ['pɑrk] *vt* : estacionar, parquear, aparcar *Spain* — *vi* : estacionarse, parquearse, aparcar *Spain*
park[2] *n* : parque *m*
parka ['pɑrkə] *n* : parka *f*
parking ['pɑrkɪŋ] *n* : estacionamiento *m*, aparcamiento *m* *Spain*
parkway ['pɑrk,weɪ] *n* : carretera *f* ajardinada, bulevar *m*
parley[1] ['pɑrli] *vi* : parlamentar, negociar

parley² *n, pl* **-leys** : negociación *f*, parlamento *m*

parliament [**'**pɑrləmənt, **'**pɑrljə-] *n* : parlamento *m*

parliamentary [ˌpɑrlə**'**mentəri, ˌpɑrljə-] *adj* : parlamentario

parlor [**'**pɑrlər] *n* **1** : sala *f*, salón *m* (en una casa) **2** : salón *m* ⟨beauty parlor : salón de belleza⟩ **3 funeral parlor** : funeraria *f*

parochial [pə**'**roːkiəl] *adj* **1** : parroquial **2** PROVINCIAL : pueblerino, de miras estrechas

parody¹ [**'**pærədi] *vt* **-died; -dying** : parodiar

parody² *n, pl* **-dies** : parodia *f*

parole [pə**'**roːl] *n* : libertad *f* condicional

paroxysm [**'**pærəkˌsɪzəm, pə**'**rɑk-] *n* : paroxismo *m*

parquet [**'**pɑrˌkeɪ, pɑr**'**keɪ] *n* : parquet *m*, parqué *m*

parrakeet → **parakeet**

parrot [**'**pærət] *n* : loro *m*, papagayo *m*

parry¹ [**'**pæri] *v* **-ried; -rying** *vi* : parar un golpe — *vt* EVADE : esquivar (una pregunta, etc.)

parry² *n, pl* **-ries** : parada *f*

parsimonious [ˌpɑrsə**'**moːniəs] *adj* : tacaño, mezquino

parsley [**'**pɑrsli] *n* : perejil *m*

parsnip [**'**pɑrsnɪp] *n* : chirivía *f*

parson [**'**pɑrsən] *n* : pastor *m*, -tora *f*; clérigo *m*

parsonage [**'**pɑrsənɪdʒ] *n* : rectoría *f*, casa *f* del párroco

part¹ [**'**pɑrt] *vi* **1** SEPARATE : separarse, despedirse ⟨we should part as friends : debemos separarnos amistosamente⟩ **2** OPEN : abrirse ⟨the curtains parted : las cortinas se abrieron⟩ **3 to part with** : deshacerse de — *vt* **1** SEPARATE : separar **2 to part one's hair** : hacerse la raya, peinarse con raya

part² *n* **1** SECTION, SEGMENT : parte *f*, sección *f* **2** PIECE : pieza *f* (de una máquina, etc.) **3** ROLE : papel *m* **4** : raya *f* (del pelo)

partake [pɑr**'**teɪk, pər-] *vi* **-took** [-**'**tʊk]; **-taken** [-**'**teɪkən]; **-taking 1 to partake of** CONSUME : comer, beber, tomar **2 to partake in** : participar en (una actividad, etc.)

partial [**'**pɑrʃəl] *adj* **1** BIASED : parcial, tendencioso **2** INCOMPLETE : parcial, incompleto **3 to be partial to** : ser aficionado a

partiality [ˌpɑrʃi**'**æləti] *n, pl* **-ties** : parcialidad *f*

partially [**'**pɑrʃəli] *adv* : parcialmente

participant [pər**'**tɪsəpənt, pɑr-] *n* : participante *mf*

participate [pər**'**tɪsəˌpeɪt, pɑr-] *vi* **-pated; -pating** : participar

participation [pərˌtɪsə**'**peɪʃən, pɑr-] *n* : participación *f*

participle [**'**pɑrtəˌsɪpəl] *n* : participio *m*

particle [**'**pɑrtɪkəl] *n* : partícula *f*

particular¹ [pər**'**tɪkjələr] *adj* **1** SPECIFIC : particular, en particular ⟨this partic-

ular person : esta persona en particular⟩ **2** SPECIAL : particular, especial ⟨with particular emphasis : con un énfasis especial⟩ **3** FUSSY : exigente, maniático ⟨to be very particular : ser muy especial⟩ ⟨I'm not particular : me da igual⟩

particular² *n* **1** DETAIL : detalle *m*, sentido *m* **2 in particular** : en particular, en especial

particularly [pər**'**tɪkjələrli] *adv* **1** ESPECIALLY : particularmente, especialmente **2** SPECIFICALLY : específicamente, en especial

partisan [**'**pɑrtəzən, -sən] *n* **1** ADHERENT : partidario *m*, -ria *f* **2** GUERRILLA : partisano *m*, -na *f*; guerrillero *m*, -ra *f*

partition¹ [pər**'**tɪʃən, pɑr-] *vt* : dividir ⟨to partition off (a room) : dividir (una habitación) con un tabique⟩

partition² *n* **1** DISTRIBUTION : partición *f*, división *f*, reparto *m* **2** DIVIDER : tabique *m*, mampara *f*, biombo *m*

partly [**'**pɑrtli] *adv* : en parte, parcialmente

partner [**'**pɑrtnər] *n* **1** COMPANION : compañero *m*, -ra *f* **2** : pareja *f* (en un juego, etc.) ⟨dancing partner : pareja de baile⟩ **3** SPOUSE : cónyuge *mf* **4** *or* **business partner** : socio *m*, -cia *f*; asociado *m*, -da *f*

partnership [**'**pɑrtnərˌʃɪp] *n* **1** ASSOCIATION : asociación *f*, compañerismo *m* **2** : sociedad *f* (de negociantes) ⟨to form a partnership : asociarse⟩

part of speech : categoría *f* gramatical

partridge [**'**pɑrtrɪdʒ] *n, pl* **-tridge** *or* **-tridges** : perdiz *f*

party [**'**pɑrti] *n, pl* **-ties 1** : partido *m* (político) **2** PARTICIPANT : parte *f*, participante *mf* **3** GROUP : grupo *m* (de personas) **4** GATHERING : fiesta *f* ⟨to throw a party : dar una fiesta⟩

parvenu [**'**pɑrvəˌnuː, -ˌnjuː] *n* : advenedizo *m*, -za *f*

pass¹ [**'**pæs] *vi* **1** : pasar, cruzarse ⟨a car passed by : pasó un coche⟩ ⟨we passed in the hallway : nos cruzamos en el pasillo⟩ **2** CEASE : pasarse ⟨the pain passed : se pasó el dolor⟩ **3** ELAPSE : pasar, transcurrir **4** PROCEED : pasar ⟨let me pass : déjame pasar⟩ **5** HAPPEN : pasar, ocurrir **6** : pasar, aprobar (en un examen) **7** RULE : fallar ⟨the jury passed on the case : el jurado falló en el caso⟩ **8** *or* **to pass down** : pasar ⟨the throne passed to his son : el trono pasó a su hijo⟩ **9 to let pass** OVERLOOK : pasar por alto **10 to pass as** : pasar por **11 to pass away** *or* **to pass on** DIE : fallecer, morir — *vt* **1** : pasar por ⟨they passed the house : pasaron por la casa⟩ **2** OVERTAKE : pasar, adelantar **3** SPEND : pasar (tiempo) **4** HAND : pasar ⟨pass me the salt : pásame la sal⟩ **5** : aprobar (un examen, una ley)

pass² *n* **1** CROSSING, GAP : paso *m*, desfiladero *m*, puerto *m* ⟨mountain pass : puerto de montaña⟩ **2** PERMIT : pase *m*, permiso *m* **3** : pase *m* (en deportes) **4** SITUATION : situación *f* (difícil) ⟨things have come to a pretty pass! : ¡hasta dónde hemos llegado!⟩

passable ['pæsəbəl] *adj* **1** ADEQUATE : adecuado, pasable **2** : transitable (dícese de un camino, etc.)

passably ['pæsəbli] *adv* : pasablemente

passage ['pæsɪʤ] *n* **1** PASSING : paso *m* ⟨the passage of time : el paso del tiempo⟩ **2** PASSAGEWAY : pasillo *m* (dentro de un edificio), pasaje *m* (entre edificios) **3** VOYAGE : travesía *f* (por el mar), viaje *m* ⟨to grant safe passage : dar un salvoconducto⟩ **4** SECTION : pasaje *m* (en música o literatura)

passageway ['pæsɪʤ,weɪ] *n* : pasillo *m*, pasadizo *m*, corredor *m*

passbook ['pæs,bʊk] *n* BANKBOOK : libreta *f* de ahorros

passé [pæ'seɪ] *adj* : pasado de moda

passenger ['pæsənʤər] *n* : pasajero *m*, -ra *f*

passerby [,pæsər'baɪ, 'pæsər,-] *n, pl* **passersby** : transeúnte *mf*

passing ['pæsɪŋ] *n* DEATH : fallecimiento *m*

passion ['pæʃən] *n* : pasión *f*, ardor *m*

passionate ['pæʃənət] *adj* **1** IRASCIBLE : irascible, iracundo **2** ARDENT : apasionado, ardiente, ferviente, fogoso

passionately ['pæʃənətli] *adv* : apasionadamente, fervientemente, con pasión

passive¹ ['pæsɪv] *adj* : pasivo — **passively** *adv*

passive² *n* : voz *f* pasiva (en gramática)

passivity [pæ'sɪvəti] *n* : pasividad *f*

Passover ['pæs,oːvər] *n* : Pascua *f* (en el judaísmo)

passport ['pæs,pɔrt] *n* : pasaporte *m*

password ['pæs,wərd] *n* : contraseña *f*

past¹ ['pæst] *adv* : por delante ⟨he drove past : pasamos en coche⟩

past² *adj* **1** AGO : hace ⟨10 years past : hace 10 años⟩ **2** LAST : último ⟨the past few months : los últimos meses⟩ **3** BYGONE : pasado ⟨in past times : en tiempos pasados⟩ **4** : pasado (en gramática)

past³ *n* : pasado *m*

past⁴ *prep* **1** BY : por, por delante de ⟨he ran past the house : pasó por la casa corriendo⟩ **2** BEYOND : más allá de ⟨just past the corner : un poco más allá de la esquina⟩ ⟨we went past the exit : pasamos la salida⟩ **3** AFTER : después de ⟨past noon : después del mediodía⟩ ⟨half past two : las dos y media⟩

pasta ['pɑstə, 'pæs-] *n* : pasta *f*

paste¹ ['peɪst] *vt* **pasted; pasting** : pegar (con engrudo)

paste² *n* **1** : pasta *f* ⟨tomato paste : pasta de tomate⟩ **2** : engrudo *m* (para pegar)

pasteboard ['peɪst,bɔrd] *n* : cartón *m*, cartulina *f*

pastel [pæ'stɛl] *n* : pastel *m* — **pastel** *adj*

pasteurization [,pæstʃərə'zeɪʃən, ,pæstjə-] *n* : pasteurización *f*

pasteurize ['pæstʃə,raɪz, 'pæstjə-] *vt* **-ized; -izing** : pasteurizar

pastime ['pæs,taɪm] *n* : pasatiempo *m*

pastor ['pæstər] *n* : pastor *m*, -tora *f*

pastoral ['pæstərəl] *adj* : pastoral

past participle *n* : participio *m* pasado

pastry ['peɪstri] *n, pl* **-ries** **1** DOUGH : pasta *f*, masa *f* **2 pastries** *npl* : pasteles *mpl*

pasture¹ ['pæstʃər] *v* **-tured; -turing** *vi* GRAZE : pacer, pastar — *vt* : apacentar, pastar

pasture² *n* : pastizal *m*, potrero *m*, pasto *m*

pasty ['peɪsti] *adj* **pastier; -est** **1** : pastoso (en consistencia) **2** PALLID : pálido

pat¹ ['pæt] *vt* **patted; patting** : dar palmaditas a, tocar

pat² *adv* : de memoria ⟨to have down pat : saberse de memoria⟩

pat³ *adj* **1** APT : apto, apropiado **2** GLIB : fácil **3** UNYIELDING : firme ⟨to stand pat : mantenerse firme⟩

pat⁴ *n* **1** TAP : golpecito *m*, palmadita *f* ⟨a pat on the back : una palmadita en la espalda⟩ **2** CARESS : caricia *f* **3** : porción *f* ⟨a pat of butter : una porción de mantequilla⟩

patch¹ ['pætʃ] *vt* **1** MEND, REPAIR : remendar, parchar, ponerle un parche a **2 to patch together** IMPROVISE : confeccionar, improvisar **3 to patch up** : arreglar ⟨they patched things up : hicieron las paces⟩

patch² *n* **1** : parche *m*, remiendo *m* (para la ropa) ⟨eye patch : parche para el ojo⟩ **2** PIECE : mancha *f*, trozo *m* ⟨a patch of sky : un trozo de cielo⟩ **3** PLOT : parcela *f*, terreno *m* ⟨cabbage patch : parcela de repollos⟩

patchwork ['pætʃ,wərk] *n* : labor *f* de retazos

patchy ['pætʃi] *adj* **patchier; -est** **1** IRREGULAR : irregular, desigual **2** INCOMPLETE : parcial, incompleto

patent¹ ['pætənt] *vt* : patentar

patent² ['pætənt, 'peɪt-] *adj* **1** OBVIOUS : patente, evidente **2** ['pæt-] PATENTED : patentado

patent³ ['pætənt] *n* : patente *f*

patently ['pætəntli] *adv* : patentemente, evidentemente

paternal [pə'tərnəl] *adj* **1** FATHERLY : paternal **2** : paterno ⟨paternal grandfather : abuelo paterno⟩

paternity [pə'tərnəti] *n* : paternidad *f*

path ['pæθ, 'pɑθ] *n* **1** TRACK, TRAIL : camino *m*, sendero *m*, senda *f* **2** COURSE, ROUTE : recorrido *m*, trayecto *m*, trayectoria *f*

pathetic [pə'θɛtɪk] *adj* : patético — **pathetically** [-tɪkli] *adv*

pathological [,pæθə'lɑʤɪkəl] *adj* : patológico

pathologist [pə'θɑlədʒɪst] *n* : patólogo *m*, -ga *f*

pathology [pə'θɑlədʒi] *n, pl* **-gies** : patología *f*

pathos ['peɪˌθɑs, 'pæ-, -ˌθɔs] *n* : patetismo *m*

pathway ['pæθˌweɪ] *n* : camino *m*, sendero *m*, senda *f*, vereda *f*

patience ['peɪʃənts] *n* : paciencia *f*

patient¹ ['peɪʃənt] *adj* : paciente — **patiently** *adv*

patient² *n* : paciente *mf*

patio ['pætiˌoː] *n, pl* **-tios** : patio *m*

patriarch ['peɪtriˌɑrk] *n* : patriarca *m*

patriarchy ['peɪtriˌɑrki] *n, pl* **-chies** : patriarcado *m*

patrimony ['pætrəˌmoːni] *n, pl* **-nies** : patrimonio *m*

patriot ['peɪtriət] *n* : patriota *mf*

patriotic [ˌpeɪtri'ɑtɪk] *adj* : patriótico — **patriotically** *adv*

patriotism ['peɪtriəˌtɪzəm] *n* : patriotismo *m*

patrol¹ [pə'troːl] *v* **-trolled; -trolling** : patrullar

patrol² *n* : patrulla *f*

patrolman [pə'troːlmən] *n, pl* **-men** [-mən, -ˌmɛn] : policía *mf*, guardia *mf*

patron ['peɪtrən] *n* **1** SPONSOR : patrocinador *m*, -dora *f* **2** CUSTOMER : cliente *m*, -ta *f* **3** *or* **patron saint** : patrono *m*, -na *f*

patronage ['peɪtrənɪdʒ, 'pæ-] *n* **1** SPONSORSHIP : patrocinio *m* **2** CLIENTELE : clientela *f* **3** : influencia *f* (política)

patronize ['peɪtrəˌnaɪz, 'pæ-] *vt* **-ized; -izing 1** SPONSOR : patrocinar **2** : ser cliente de (un negocio) **3** : tratar con condescendencia

patter¹ ['pætər] *vi* **1** TAP : golpetear, tamborilear (dícese de la lluvia) **2 to patter about** : corretear (con pasos ligeros)

patter² *n* **1** TAPPING : golpeteo *m*, tamborileo *m* (de la lluvia), correteo *m* (de pies) **2** CHATTER : palabrería *f*, parloteo *m fam*

pattern¹ ['pætərn] *vt* **1** BASE : basar (en un modelo) **2 to pattern after** : hacer imitación de

pattern² *n* **1** MODEL : modelo *m*, patrón *m* (de costura) **2** DESIGN : diseño *m*, dibujo *m*, estampado *m* (de tela) **3** NORM, STANDARD : pauta *f*, norma *f*, patrón *m*

patty ['pæti] *n, pl* **-ties** : porción *f* de carne picada (u otro alimento) en forma de ruedita ⟨a hamburger patty : una hamburguesa⟩

paucity ['pɔsəti] *n* : escasez *f*

paunch ['pɔntʃ] *n* : panza *f*, barriga *f*

pauper ['pɔpər] *n* : pobre *mf*, indigente *mf*

pause¹ ['pɔz] *vi* **paused; pausing** : hacer una pausa, pararse (brevemente)

pause² *n* : pausa *f*

pave ['peɪv] *vt* **paved; paving** : pavimentar ⟨to pave with stones : empedrar⟩

pavement ['peɪvmənt] *n* : pavimento *m*, empedrado *m*

pavilion [pə'vɪljən] *n* : pabellón *m*

paving ['peɪvɪŋ] → **pavement**

paw¹ ['pɔ] *vt* : tocar, manosear, sobar

paw² *n* : pata *f*, garra *f*, zarpa *f*

pawn¹ ['pɔn] *vt* : empeñar, prendar

pawn² *n* **1** PLEDGE, SECURITY : prenda *f* **2** PAWNING : empeño *m* **3** : peón *m* (en ajedrez)

pawnbroker ['pɔnˌbroːkər] *n* : prestamista *mf*

pawnshop ['pɔnˌʃɑp] *n* : casa *f* de empeños, monte *m* de piedad

pay¹ ['peɪ] *v* **paid** ['peɪd]; **paying** *vt* **1** : pagar (una cuenta, a un empleado, etc.) **2 to pay attention** : poner atención, prestar atención, hacer caso **3 to pay back** : pagar, devolver ⟨she paid them back : les devolvió el dinero⟩ ⟨I'll pay you back for what you did! : ¡me las pagarás!⟩ **4 to pay off** SETTLE : saldar, cancelar (una deuda, etc.) **5 to pay one's respects** : presentar uno sus respetos **6 to pay a visit** : hacer una visita — *vi* : valer la pena ⟨crime doesn't pay : no hay crimen sin castigo⟩

pay² *n* : paga *f*

payable ['peɪəbəl] *adj* DUE : pagadero

paycheck ['peɪˌtʃɛk] *n* : sueldo *m*, cheque *m* del sueldo

payee [peɪ'iː] *n* : beneficiario *m*, -ria *f* (de un cheque, etc.)

payment ['peɪmənt] *n* **1** : pago *m* **2** INSTALLMENT : plazo *m*, cuota *f* **3** REWARD : recompensa *f*

payoff ['peɪˌɔf] *n* **1** REWARD : recompensa *f* **2** PROFIT : ganancia *f* **3** BRIBE : soborno *m*

payroll ['peɪˌroːl] *n* : nómina *f*

PC [ˌpiː'siː] *n, pl* **PCs** *or* **PC's** : PC *mf*, computadora *f* personal

pea ['piː] *n* : chícharo *m*, guisante *m*, arveja *f*

peace ['piːs] *n* **1** : paz *f* ⟨peace treaty : tratado de paz⟩ ⟨peace and tranquility : paz y tranquilidad⟩ **2** ORDER : orden *m* (público)

peaceable ['piːsəbəl] *adj* : pacífico — **peaceably** [-bli] *adv*

peaceful ['piːsfəl] *adj* **1** PEACEABLE : pacífico **2** CALM, QUIET : tranquilo, sosegado — **peacefully** *adv*

peacemaker ['piːsˌmeɪkər] *n* : conciliador *m*, -dora *f*; mediador *m*, -dora *f*

peach ['piːtʃ] *n* : durazno *m*, melocotón *m*

peacock ['piːˌkɑk] *n* : pavo *m* real

peak¹ ['piːk] *vi* : alcanzar su nivel máximo

peak² *adj* : máximo

peak³ *n* **1** POINT : punta *f* **2** CREST, SUMMIT : cima *f*, cumbre *f* **3** APEX : cúspide *f*, apogeo *m*, nivel *m* máximo

peaked ['piːkəd] *adj* SICKLY : pálido

peal¹ ['piːl] *vi* : repicar

peal² *n* : repique *m*, tañido *m* (de campanada) ⟨peals of laughter : carcajadas⟩

peanut ['pi:ˌnʌt] *n* : maní *m*, cacahuate *m Mex*, cacahuete *m Spain*

pear ['pær] *n* : pera *f*

pearl ['pərl] *n* : perla *f*

pearly ['pərli] *adj* **pearlier; -est** : nacarado

peasant ['pɛzənt] *n* : campesino *m*, -na *f*

peat ['pi:t] *n* : turba *f*

pebble ['pɛbəl] *n* : guijarro *m*, piedrecita *f*, piedrita *f*

pecan [pɪ'kɑn, -'kæn, 'pi:ˌkæn] *n* : pacana *f*, nuez *f Mex*

peccadillo [ˌpɛkə'dɪlo] *n*, *pl* **-loes** *or* **-los** : pecadillo *m*

peccary ['pɛkəri] *n*, *pl* **-ries** : pécari *m*, pecarí *m*

peck[1] ['pɛk] *vt* : picar, picotear

peck[2] *n* **1** : medida *f* de áridos equivalente a 8.810 litros **2** : picotazo *m* (de un pájaro) ⟨a peck on the cheek : un besito en la mejilla⟩

pectoral ['pɛktərəl] *adj* : pectoral

peculiar [pɪ'kju:ljər] *adj* **1** DISTINCTIVE : propio, peculiar, característico ⟨peculiar to this area : propio de esta zona⟩ **2** STRANGE : extraño, raro — **peculiarly** *adv*

peculiarity [pɪˌkju:l'jærəti, -ˌkju:li'ær-] *n*, *pl* **-ties 1** DISTINCTIVENESS : peculiaridad *f* **2** ODDITY, QUIRK : rareza *f*, idiosincrasia *f*, excentricidad *f*

pecuniary [pɪ'kju:niˌɛri] *adj* : pecuniario

pedagogical [ˌpɛdə'gɑdʒɪkəl, -'go:-] *adj* : pedagógico

pedagogy ['pɛdəˌgo:dʒi, -ˌgɑ-] *n* : pedagogía *f*

pedal[1] ['pɛdəl] *v* **-aled** *or* **-alled; -aling** *or* **-alling** *vi* : pedalear — *vt* : darle a los pedales de

pedal[2] *n* : pedal *m*

pedant ['pɛdənt] *n* : pedante *mf*

pedantic [pɪ'dæntɪk] *adj* : pedante

pedantry ['pɛdəntri] *n*, *pl* **-ries** : pedantería *f*

peddle ['pɛdəl] *vt* **-dled; -dling** : vender (en las calles)

peddler ['pɛdlər] *n* : vendedor *m*, -dora *f* ambulante; mercachifle *m*

pedestal ['pɛdəstəl] *n* : pedestal *m*

pedestrian[1] [pə'dɛstriən] *adj* **1** COMMONPLACE : pedestre, ordinario *m* **2** : de peatón, peatonal ⟨pedestrian crossing : paso de peatones⟩

pedestrian[2] *n* : peatón *m*, -tona *f*

pediatric [ˌpi:di'ætrɪk] *adj* : pediátrico

pediatrician [ˌpi:diə'trɪʃən] *n* : pediatra *mf*

pediatrics [ˌpi:di'ætrɪks] *ns & pl* : pediatría *f*

pedigree ['pɛdəˌgri:] *n* **1** FAMILY TREE : árbol *m* genealógico **2** LINEAGE : pedigrí *m* (de un animal), linaje *m* (de una persona)

peek[1] ['pi:k] *vi* **1** PEEP : espiar, mirar furtivamente **2** GLANCE : echar un vistazo

peek[2] *n* **1** : miradita *f* (furtiva) **2** GLANCE : vistazo *m*, ojeada *f*

peel[1] ['pi:l] *vt* **1** : pelar (fruta, etc.) **2** *or* **to peel away** : quitar — *vi* : pelarse (dícese de la piel), desconcharse (dícese de la pintura)

peel[2] *n* : cáscara *f*

peep[1] ['pi:p] *vi* **1** PEEK : espiar, mirar furtivamente **2** CHEEP : piar **3** **to peep out** SHOW : asomarse

peep[2] *n* **1** CHEEP : pío *m* (de un pajarito) **2** GLANCE : vistazo *m*, ojeada *f*

peer[1] ['pɪr] *vi* : mirar detenidamente, mirar con atención

peer[2] *n* **1** EQUAL : par *m*, igual *mf* **2** NOBLE : noble *mf*

peerage ['pɪrɪdʒ] *n* : nobleza *f*

peerless ['pɪrləs] *adj* : sin par, incomparable

peeve[1] ['pi:v] *vt* **peeved; peeving** : fastidiar, irritar, molestar

peeve[2] *n* : queja *f*

peevish ['pi:vɪʃ] *adj* : quejoso, fastidioso — **peevishly** *adv*

peevishness ['pi:vɪʃnəs] *n* : irritabilidad *f*

peg[1] ['pɛg] *vt* **pegged; pegging 1** PLUG : tapar (con una clavija) **2** FASTEN, FIX : sujetar (con estaquillas) **3** **to peg out** MARK : marcar (con estaquillas)

peg[2] *n* : estaquilla *f* (para clavar), clavija *f* (para tapar)

pejorative [pɪ'dʒɔrətɪv] *adj* : peyorativo — **pejoratively** *adv*

pelican ['pɛlɪkən] *n* : pelícano *m*

pellagra [pə'lægrə, -'leɪ-] *n* : pelagra *f*

pellet ['pɛlət] *n* **1** BALL : bolita *f* ⟨food pellet : bolita de comida⟩ **2** SHOT : perdigón *m*

pell–mell ['pɛl'mɛl] *adv* : desordenadamente, atropelladamente

pelt[1] ['pɛlt] *vt* **1** THROW : lanzar, tirar (algo a alguien) **2** **to pelt with stones** : apedrear — *vi* BEAT : golpear con fuerza ⟨the rain was pelting down : llovía a cántaros⟩

pelt[2] *n* : piel *f*, pellejo *m*

pelvic ['pɛlvɪk] *adj* : pélvico

pelvis ['pɛlvɪs] *n*, *pl* **-vises** *or* **-ves** ['pɛlˌvi:z] : pelvis *f*

pen[1] ['pɛn] *vt* **penned; penning 1** *or* **pen in** : encerrar (animales) **2** WRITE : escribir

pen[2] *n* **1** CORRAL : corral *m*, redil *m* (para ovejas) **2** : pluma *f* ⟨fountain pen : pluma fuente⟩ ⟨ballpoint pen : bolígrafo⟩

penal ['pi:nəl] *adj* : penal

penalize ['pi:nəlˌaɪz, 'pɛn-] *vt* **-ized; -izing** : penalizar, sancionar, penar

penalty ['pɛnəlti] *n*, *pl* **-ties 1** PUNISHMENT : pena *f*, castigo *m* **2** DISADVANTAGE : desventaja *f*, castigo *m*, penalty *m* (en deportes) **3** FINE : multa *f*

penance ['pɛnənts] *n* : penitencia *f*

pence → penny

penchant ['pɛntʃənt] *n* : inclinación *f*, afición *f*

pencil¹ ['pɛntsəl] *vt* **-ciled** *or* **-cilled; -ciling** *or* **-cilling** : escribir con lápiz, dibujar con lápiz
pencil² *n* : lápiz *m*
pendant ['pɛndənt] *n* : colgante *m*
pending¹ ['pɛndɪŋ] *adj* : pendiente
pending² *prep* **1** DURING : durante **2** AWAITING : en espera de
pendulum ['pɛndʒələm, -djʊləm] *n* : péndulo *m*
penetrate ['pɛnə,treɪt] *vt* **-trated; -trating** : penetrar
penetrating ['pɛnə,treɪtɪŋ] *adj* : penetrante, cortante
penetration [,pɛnə'treɪʃən] *n* : penetración *f*
penguin ['pɛŋgwɪn, 'pɛn-] *n* : pingüino *m*
penicillin [,pɛnə'sɪlən] *n* : penicilina *f*
peninsula [pə'nɪntsələ, -'nɪntʃʊlə] *n* : península *f*
penis ['piːnəs] *n, pl* **-nes** [-,niːz] *or* **-nises** : pene *m*
penitence ['pɛnətənts] *n* : arrepentimiento *m*, penitencia *f*
penitent¹ ['pɛnətənt] *adj* : arrepentido, penitente
penitent² *n* : penitente *mf*
penitentiary [,pɛnə'tɛntʃəri] *n, pl* **-ries** : penitenciaría *f*, prisión *m*, presidio *m*
penmanship ['pɛnmən,ʃɪp] *n* : escritura *f*, caligrafía *f*
pen name *n* : seudónimo *m*
pennant ['pɛnənt] *n* : gallardete *m* (de un barco), banderín *m*
penniless ['pɛniləs] *adj* : sin un centavo
penny ['pɛni] *n, pl* **-nies** *or* **pence** ['pɛnts] **1** : penique *m* (del Reino Unido) **2** *pl* **-nies** CENT : centavo *m* (de los Estados Unidos)
pension¹ ['pɛntʃən] *vt or* **to pension off** : jubilar
pension² *n* : pensión *m*, jubilación *f*
pensive ['pɛntsɪv] *adj* : pensativo, meditabundo — **pensively** *adv*
pent ['pɛnt] *adj* : encerrado ⟨pent-up feelings : emociones reprimidas⟩
pentagon ['pɛntə,gɑn] *n* : pentágono *m*
pentagonal [pɛn'tægənəl] *adj* : pentagonal
penthouse ['pɛnt,haʊs] *n* : ático *m*, penthouse *m*
penultimate [pɪ'nʌltəmət] *adj* : penúltimo
penury ['pɛnjəri] *n* : penuria *f*, miseria *f*
peon ['piː,ɑn, -ən] *n, pl* **-ons** *or* **-ones** [peɪ'oːniːz] : peón *m*
peony ['piːəni] *n, pl* **-nies** : peonía *f*
people¹ ['piːpəl] *vt* **-pled; -pling** : poblar
people² *ns & pl* **1** **people** *npl* : gente *f*, personas *fpl* ⟨people like him : él le cae bien a la gente⟩ ⟨many people : mucha gente, muchas personas⟩ **2** *pl* **peoples** : pueblo *m* ⟨the Cuban people : el pueblo cubano⟩
pep¹ ['pɛp] *vt* **pepped; pepping** *or* **to pep up** : animar
pep² *n* : energía *f*, vigor *m*

pepper¹ ['pɛpər] *vt* **1** : añadir pimienta a **2** RIDDLE : acribillar (a balazos) **3** SPRINKLE : salpicar ⟨peppered with quotations : salpicado de citas⟩
pepper² *n* **1** : pimienta *f* (condimento) **2** : pimiento *m*, pimentón *m* (fruta) **3** → **chili**
peppermint ['pɛpər,mɪnt] *n* : menta *f*
peppery ['pɛpəri] *adj* : picante
peppy ['pɛpi] *adj* **peppier; -est** : lleno de energía, vivaz
peptic ['pɛptɪk] *adj* **peptic ulcer** : úlcera *f* estomacal
per ['pər] *prep* **1** : por ⟨miles per hour : millas por hora⟩ **2** ACCORDING TO : según ⟨per his specifications : según sus especificaciones⟩
per annum [pər'ænəm] *adv* : al año, por año
percale [,pər'keɪl, 'pər-,; ,pər'kæl] *n* : percal *m*
per capita [pər'kæpɪtə] *adv & adj* : per cápita
perceive [pər'siːv] *vt* **-ceived; -ceiving** **1** REALIZE : percatarse de, concientizarse de, darse cuenta de **2** NOTE : percibir, notar
percent¹ [pər'sɛnt] *adv* : por ciento
percent² *n, pl* **-cent** *or* **-cents** **1** : por ciento ⟨10 percent of the population : el 10 por ciento de la población⟩ **2** → **percentage**
percentage [pər'sɛntɪdʒ] *n* : porcentaje *m*
perceptible [pər'sɛptəbəl] *adj* : perceptible — **perceptibly** [-bli] *adv*
perception [pər'sɛpʃən] *n* **1** : percepción *f* ⟨color perception : la percepción de los colores⟩ **2** INSIGHT : perspicacia *f* **3** IDEA : idea *f*, imagen *f*
perceptive [pər'sɛptɪv] *adj* : perspicaz
perceptively [pər'sɛptɪvli] *adv* : con perspicacia
perch¹ ['pərtʃ] *vi* **1** ROOST : posarse **2** SIT : sentarse (en un sitio elevado) — *vt* PLACE : posar, colocar
perch² *n* **1** ROOST : percha *f* (para los pájaros) **2** *pl* **perch** *or* **perches** : perca *f* (pez)
percolate ['pərkə,leɪt] *vi* **-lated; -lating** : colarse, filtrarse ⟨percolated coffee : café filtrado⟩
percolator ['pərkə,leɪtər] *n* : cafetera *f* de filtro
percussion [pər'kʌʃən] *n* **1** STRIKING : percusión *f* **2** *or* **percussion instruments** : instrumentos *mpl* de percusión
peremptory [pə'rɛmptəri] *adj* : perentorio
perennial¹ [pə'rɛniəl] *adj* **1** : perenne, vivaz ⟨perennial flowers : flores perennes⟩ **2** RECURRENT : perenne, continuo ⟨a perennial problem : un problema eterno⟩
perennial² *n* : planta *f* perenne, planta *f* vivaz
perfect¹ [pər'fɛkt] *vt* : perfeccionar

perfect² ['pərfɪkt] *adj* : perfecto — **perfectly** *adv*

perfection [pər'fɛkʃən] *n* : perfección *f*

perfectionist [pər'fɛkʃənɪst] *n* : perfeccionista *mf*

perfidious [pər'fɪdiəs] *adj* : pérfido

perforate ['pərfə,reɪt] *vt* **-rated; -rating** : perforar

perforation [,pərfə'reɪʃən] *n* : perforación *f*

perform [pər'fɔrm] *vt* **1** CARRY OUT : realizar, hacer, desempeñar **2** PRESENT : representar, dar (una obra teatral, etc.) — *vi* : actuar (en una obra teatral), cantar (en una ópera, etc.), tocar (en un concierto, etc.), bailar (en un ballet, etc.)

performance [pər'fɔrmənts] *n* **1** EXECUTION : ejecución *f*, realización *f*, desempeño *m*, rendimiento *m* **2** INTERPRETATION : interpretación *f* ⟨his performance of Hamlet : su interpretación de Hamlet⟩ **3** PRESENTATION : representación *f* (de una obra teatral), función *f*

performer [pər'fɔrmər] *n* : artista *mf*; actor *m*, -triz *f*; intérprete *mf* (de música)

perfume¹ [pər'fju:m, 'pər,-] *vt* **-fumed; -fuming** : perfumar

perfume² ['pər,fju:m, pər'-] *n* : perfume *m*

perfunctory [pər'fʌŋktəri] *adj* : mecánico, superficial, somero

perhaps [pər'hæps] *adv* : tal vez, quizá, quizás

peril ['pɛrəl] *n* : peligro *m*

perilous ['pɛrələs] *adj* : peligroso — **perilously** *adv*

perimeter [pə'rɪmətər] *n* : perímetro *m*

period ['pɪriəd] *n* **1** : punto *m* (en puntuación) **2** : período *m* ⟨a two-hour period : un período de dos horas⟩ **3** STAGE : época *f* (histórica), fase *f*, etapa *f*

periodic [,pɪri'adɪk] *or* **periodical** [-dɪkəl] *adj* : periódico — **periodically** [-dɪkli] *adv*

periodical [,pɪri'adɪkəl] *n* : publicación *f* periódica, revista *f*

peripheral [pə'rɪfərəl] *adj* : periférico

periphery [pə'rɪfəri] *n, pl* **-eries** : periferia *f*

periscope ['pɛrə,sko:p] *n* : periscopio *m*

perish ['pɛrɪʃ] *vi* DIE : perecer, morirse

perishable¹ ['pɛrɪʃəbəl] *adj* : perecedero

perishable² *n* : producto *m* perecedero

perjure ['pərdʒər] *vt* **-jured; -juring** (*used in law*) **to perjure oneself** : perjurar, perjurarse

perjury ['pərdʒəri] *n* : perjurio *m*

perk¹ ['pərk] *vt* **1** : levantar (las orejas, etc.) **2** *or* **to perk up** FRESHEN : arreglar — *vi* **to perk up** : animarse, reanimarse

perk² *n* : extra *m*

perky ['pərki] *adj* **perkier; -est** : animado, alegre, lleno de vida

permanence ['pərmənənts] *n* : permanencia *f*

permanent¹ ['pərmənənt] *adj* : permanente — **permanently** *adv*

permanent² *n* : permanente *f*

permeability [,pərmiə'bɪləti] *n* : permeabilidad *f*

permeable ['pərmiəbəl] *adj* : permeable

permeate ['pərmi,eɪt] *v* **-ated; -ating** *vt* **1** PENETRATE : penetrar, impregnar **2** PERVADE : penetrar, difundirse por — *vi* : penetrar

permissible [pər'mɪsəbəl] *adj* : permisible, lícito

permission [pər'mɪʃən] *n* : permiso *m*

permissive [pər'mɪsɪv] *adj* : permisivo

permit¹ [pər'mɪt] *vt* **-mitted; -mitting** : permitir, dejar ⟨weather permitting : si el tiempo lo permite⟩

permit² ['pər,mɪt, pər'-] *n* : permiso *m*, licencia *f*

pernicious [pər'nɪʃəs] *adj* : pernicioso

peroxide [pə'rak,saɪd] *n* **1** : peróxido *m* **2** → hydrogen peroxide

perpendicular¹ [,pərpən'dɪkjələr] *adj* **1** VERTICAL : vertical **2** : perpendicular ⟨perpendicular lines : líneas perpendiculares⟩ — **perpendicularly** *adv*

perpendicular² *n* : perpendicular *f*

perpetrate ['pərpə,treɪt] *vt* **-trated; -trating** : perpetrar, cometer (un delito)

perpetrator ['pərpə,treɪtər] *n* : autor *m*, -tora *f* (de un delito)

perpetual [pər'pɛtʃuəl] *adj* **1** EVERLASTING : perpetuo, eterno **2** CONTINUAL : perpetuo, continuo, constante

perpetually [pər'pɛtʃuəli, -tʃəli] *adv* : para siempre, eternamente

perpetuate [pər'pɛtʃu,eɪt] *vt* **-ated; -ating** : perpetuar

perpetuity [,pərpə'tu:əti, -'tju:-] *n, pl* **-ties** : perpetuidad *f*

perplex [pər'plɛks] *vt* : dejar perplejo, confundir

perplexed [pər'plɛkst] *adj* : perplejo

perplexity [pər'plɛksəti] *n, pl* **-ties** : perplejidad *f*, confusión *f*

persecute ['pərsɪ,kju:t] *vt* **-cuted; -cuting** : perseguir

persecution [,pərsɪ'kju:ʃən] *n* : persecución *f*

perseverance [,pərsə'vɪrənts] *n* : perseverancia *f*

persevere [,pərsə'vɪr] *vi* **-vered; -vering** : perseverar

Persian ['pərʒən] *n* **1** : persa *mf* **2** : persa *m* (idioma) — **Persian** *adj*

persist [pər'sɪst] *vi* : persistir

persistence [pər'sɪstənts] *n* **1** CONTINUATION : persistencia *f* **2** TENACITY : perseverancia *f*, tenacidad *f*

persistent [pər'sɪstənt] *adj* : persistente — **persistently** *adv*

person ['pərsən] *n* **1** HUMAN, INDIVIDUAL : persona *f*, individuo *m*, ser *m* humano **2** : persona *f* (en gramática) **3** **in person** : en persona

personable ['pərsənəbəl] *adj* : agradable

personage ['pərsənɪdʒ] *n* : personaje *m*

personal ['pərsənəl] *adj* **1** OWN, PRIVATE : personal, particular, privado ⟨for personal reasons : por razones personales⟩ **2** : en persona ⟨to make a personal appearance : presentarse en persona, hacerse acto de presencia⟩ **3** : íntimo, personal ⟨personal hygiene : higiene personal⟩ **4** INDISCREET, PRYING : indiscreto, personal

personal computer *n* : computadora *f* personal, ordenador *m* personal *Spain*

personal digital assistant *n* : asistente *m* personal digital

personality [ˌpərsən'æləṭi] *n*, *pl* **-ties 1** DISPOSITION : personalidad *f*, temperamento *m* **2** CELEBRITY : personalidad *f*, personaje *m*, celebridad *f*

personalize ['pərsənə.laɪz] *vt* **-ized; -izing** : personalizar

personally ['pərsənəli] *adv* **1** : personalmente, en persona ⟨I'll do it personally : lo haré personalmente⟩ **2** : como persona ⟨personally she's very amiable : como persona es muy amable⟩ **3** : personalmente ⟨personally, I don't believe it : yo, personalmente, no me lo creo⟩

personification [pərˌsɑnəfə'keɪʃən] *n* : personificación *f*

personify [pər'sɑnəˌfaɪ] *vt* **-fied; -fying** : personificar

personnel [ˌpərsən'ɛl] *n* : personal *m*

perspective [pər'spɛktɪv] *n* : perspectiva *f*

perspicacious [ˌpərspə'keɪʃəs] *adj* : perspicaz

perspiration [ˌpərspə'reɪʃən] *n* : transpiración *f*, sudor *m*

perspire [pər'spaɪr] *vi* **-spired; -spiring** : transpirar, sudar

persuade [pər'sweɪd] *vt* **-suaded; -suading** : persuadir, convencer

persuasion [pər'sweɪʒən] *n* : persuasión *f*

persuasive [pər'sweɪsɪv, -zɪv] *adj* : persuasivo — **persuasively** *adv*

persuasiveness [pər'sweɪsɪvnəs, -zɪv-] *n* : persuasión *f*

pert ['pərt] *adj* **1** SAUCY : descarado, impertinente **2** JAUNTY : alegre, animado ⟨a pert little hat : un sombrero coqueto⟩

pertain [pər'teɪn] *vi* **1** BELONG : pertenecer (a) **2** RELATE : estar relacionado (con)

pertinence ['pərtənənts] *n* : pertinencia *f*

pertinent ['pərtənənt] *adj* : pertinente

perturb [pər'tərb] *vt* : perturbar

perusal [pə'ru:zəl] *n* : lectura *f* cuidadosa

peruse [pə'ru:z] *vt* **-rused; -rusing 1** READ : leer con cuidado **2** SCAN : recorrer con la vista ⟨he perused the newspaper : echó un vistazo al periódico⟩

Peruvian [pə'ru:viən] *n* : peruano *m*, -na *f* — **Peruvian** *adj*

pervade [pər'veɪd] *vt* **-vaded; -vading** : penetrar, difundirse por

pervasive [pər'veɪsɪv, -zɪv] *adj* : penetrante

perverse [pər'vərs] *adj* **1** CORRUPT : perverso, corrompido **2** STUBBORN : obstinado, porfiado, terco (sin razón) — **perversely** *adv*

perversion [pər'vərʒən] *n* : perversión *f*

perversity [pər'vərsəṭi] *n*, *pl* **-ties 1** CORRUPTION : corrupción *f* **2** STUBBORNNESS : obstinación *f*, terquedad *f*

pervert[1] [pər'vərt] *vt* **1** DISTORT : pervertir, distorsionar **2** CORRUPT : pervertir, corromper

pervert[2] ['pər.vərt] *n* : pervertido *m*, -da *f*

pesky ['pɛski] *adj* : molestoso, molesto

peso ['peɪ.so:] *n*, *pl* **-sos** : peso *m*

pessimism ['pɛsə.mɪzəm] *n* : pesimismo *m*

pessimist ['pɛsəmɪst] *n* : pesimista *mf*

pessimistic [ˌpɛsə'mɪstɪk] *adj* : pesimista

pest ['pɛst] *n* **1** NUISANCE : peste *f*; latoso *m*, -sa *f fam* ⟨to be a pest : dar (la) lata⟩ **2** : insecto *m* nocivo, animal *m* nocivo ⟨the squirrels were pests : las ardillas eran una plaga⟩

pester ['pɛstər] *vt* **-tered; -tering** : molestar, fastidiar

pesticide ['pɛstə.saɪd] *n* : pesticida *m*

pestilence ['pɛstələnts] *n* : pestilencia *f*, peste *f*

pestle ['pɛsəl, 'pɛstəl] *n* : mano *f* de mortero, mazo *m*, maja *f*

pet[1] ['pɛt] *vt* **petted; petting** : acariciar

pet[2] *n* **1** : animal *m* doméstico **2** FAVORITE : favorito *m*, -ta *f*

petal ['pɛṭəl] *n* : pétalo *m*

petite [pə'ti:t] *adj* : pequeña, menuda, chiquita

petition[1] [pə'tɪʃən] *vt* : peticionar

petition[2] *n* : petición *f*

petitioner [pə'tɪʃənər] *n* : peticionario *m*, -ria *f*

petrify ['pɛtrə.faɪ] *vt* **-fied; -fying** : petrificar

petroleum [pə'tro:liəm] *n* : petróleo *m*

petticoat ['pɛṭi.ko:t] *n* : enagua *f*, fondo *m Mex*

pettiness ['pɛṭinəs] *n* **1** INSIGNIFICANCE : insignificancia *f* **2** MEANNESS : mezquindad *f*

petty ['pɛṭi] *adj* **-tier; -est 1** MINOR : menor ⟨petty cash : dinero para gastos menores⟩ **2** INSIGNIFICANT : insignificante, trivial, nimio **3** MEAN : mezquino

petty officer *n* : suboficial *mf*

petulance ['pɛtʃələnts] *n* : irritabilidad *f*, mal genio *m*

petulant ['pɛtʃələnt] *adj* : irritable, de mal genio

petunia [pɪ'tu:njə, -'tju:-] *n* : petunia *f*

pew ['pju:] *n* : banco *m* (de iglesia)

pewter ['pju:ʈər] n : peltre m
pH [,pi:'eɪʧ] n : pH m
phallic ['fælɪk] adj : fálico
phallus ['fæləs] n, pl -li ['fæ,laɪ] or -luses : falo m
phantasy ['fæntəsi] → fantasy
phantom ['fæntəm] n : fantasma m
pharaoh ['fɛr,o:, 'feɪ,ro:] n : faraón m
pharmaceutical [,farmə'su:ʈɪkəl] adj : farmacéutico
pharmacist ['farməsɪst] n : farmacéutico m, -ca f
pharmacology [,farmə'kalədʒi] n : farmacología f
pharmacy ['farməsi] n, pl -cies : farmacia f
pharynx ['færɪŋks] n, pl pharynges [fə'rɪn,dʒi:z] : faringe f
phase[1] ['feɪz] vt phased; phasing 1 SYNCHRONIZE : sincronizar, poner en fase 2 STAGGER : escalonar 3 to phase in : introducir progresivamente 4 to phase out : retirar progresivamente, dejar de producir
phase[2] n 1 : fase f (de la luna, etc.) 2 STAGE : fase f, etapa f
pheasant ['fɛzənt] n, pl -ant or -ants : faisán m
phenomenal [fɪ'namənəl] adj : extraordinario, excepcional
phenomenon [fɪ'namə,nan, -nən] n, pl -na [-nə] or -nons 1 : fenómeno m 2 pl -nons PRODIGY : fenómeno m, prodigio m
philanthropic [,fɪlən'θrɑpɪk] adj : filantrópico
philanthropist [fə'lænʈθrəpɪst] n : filántropo m, -pa f
philanthropy [fə'lænʈθrəpi] n, pl -pies : filantropía f
philately [fə'læʈəli] n : filatelia f
philodendron [,fɪlə'dɛndrən] n, pl -drons or -dra [-drə] : arácea f
philosopher [fə'lasəfər] n : filósofo m, -fa f
philosophic [,fɪlə'safɪk] or philosophical [-fɪkəl] adj : filosófico — philosophically [-kli] adv
philosophize [fə'lasə,faɪz] vi -phized; -phizing : filosofar
philosophy [fə'lasəfi] n, pl -phies : filosofía f
phlebitis [flɪ'baɪʈəs] n : flebitis f
phlegm ['flɛm] n : flema f
phlox ['flaks] n, pl phlox or phloxes : polemonio m
phobia ['fo:biə] n : fobia f
phoenix ['fi:nɪks] n : fénix m
phone[1] ['fo:n] v → telephone[1]
phone[2] n → telephone[2]
phoneme ['fo:,ni:m] n : fonema m
phonetic [fə'nɛʈɪk] adj : fonético
phonetics [fə'nɛʈɪks] n : fonética f
phonics ['fanɪks] n : método m fonético de aprender a leer
phonograph ['fo:nə,græf] n : fonógrafo m, tocadiscos m
phony[1] or phoney ['fo:ni] adj -nier; -est : falso

phony[2] or phoney n, pl -nies : farsante mf; charlatán m, -tana f
phosphate ['fas,feɪt] n : fosfato m
phosphorescence [,fasfə'rɛsənʦ] n : fosforescencia f
phosphorescent [,fasfə'rɛsənt] adj : fosforescente — phosphorescently adv
phosphorus ['fasfərəs] n : fósforo m
photo ['fo:to:] n, pl -tos : foto f
photocopier ['fo:to,kapiər] n : fotocopiadora f
photocopy[1] ['fo:to,kapi] vt -copied; -copying : fotocopiar
photocopy[2] n, pl -copies : fotocopia f
photoelectric [,fo:toɪ'lɛktrɪk] adj : fotoeléctrico
photogenic [,fo:tə'dʒɛnɪk] adj : fotogénico
photograph[1] ['fo:tə,græf] vt : fotografiar
photograph[2] n : fotografía f, foto f ⟨to take a photograph of : tomarle una fotografía a, tomar una fotografía de⟩
photographer [fə'tagrəfər] n : fotógrafo m, -fa f
photographic [,fo:tə'græfɪk] adj : fotográfico — photographically [-fɪkli] adv
photography [fə'tagrəfi] n : fotografía f
photosynthesis [,fo:to'sɪnθəsɪs] n : fotosíntesis f
photosynthetic [,fo:tosɪn'θɛʈɪk] adj : fotosintético, de fotosíntesis
phrase[1] ['freɪz] vt phrased; phrasing : expresar
phrase[2] n : frase f, locución f ⟨to coin a phrase : para decirlo así⟩
phylum ['faɪləm] n, pl -la [-lə] : phylum m
physical[1] ['fɪzɪkəl] adj 1 : físico ⟨physical laws : leyes físicas⟩ 2 MATERIAL : material, físico 3 BODILY : físico, corpóreo — physically [-kli] adv
physical[2] n CHECKUP : chequeo m, reconocimiento m médico
physician [fə'zɪʃən] n : médico m, -ca f
physicist ['fɪzəsɪst] n : físico m, -ca f
physics ['fɪzɪks] ns & pl : física f
physiognomy [,fɪzi'agnəmi] n, pl -mies : fisonomía f
physiological ['fɪziə'ladʒɪkəl] or physiologic [-dʒɪk] adj : fisiológico
physiologist [,fɪzi'alədʒɪst] n : fisiólogo m, -ga f
physiology [,fɪzi'alədʒi] n : fisiología f
physique [fə'zi:k] n : físico m
pi ['paɪ] n, pl pis ['paɪz] : pi f
pianist [pi'ænɪst, 'pi:ənɪst] n : pianista mf
piano [pi'æno:] n, pl -anos : piano m
piazza [pi'æzə, -'atsə] n, pl -zas or -ze [-'at,seɪ] : plaza f
picaresque [,pɪkə'rɛsk, ,pi:-] adj : picaresco
picayune [,pɪki'ju:n] adj : trivial, nimio, insignificante
piccolo ['pɪkə,lo:] n, pl -los : flautín m
pick[1] ['pɪk] vt 1 : picar, labrar (con un pico) ⟨he picked the hard soil : picó la

tierra dura〉 **2** : quitar, sacar (poco a poco) 〈to pick meat off the bones : quitar pedazos de carne de los huesos〉 **3** : recoger, arrancar (frutas, flores, etc.) **4** SELECT : escoger, elegir **5** PROVOKE : provocar 〈to pick a quarrel : buscar pleito, buscar pelea〉 **6 to pick a lock** : forzar una cerradura **7 to pick someone's pocket** : robarle algo del bolsillo de alguien 〈someone picked my pocket! : ¡me robaron la cartera del bolsillo!〉 — *vi* **1** NIBBLE : picar, picotear **2 to pick and choose** : ser exigente **3 to pick at** : tocar, rascarse (una herida, etc.) **4 to pick on** TEASE : mofarse de, atormentar

pick² *n* **1** CHOICE : selección *f* **2** BEST : lo mejor 〈the pick of the crop : la crema y nata〉 **3** → **pickax**

pickax ['pɪk,æks] *n* : pico *m*, zapapico *m*, piqueta *f*

pickerel ['pɪkərəl] *n*, *pl* **-el** *or* **-els** : lucio *m* pequeño

picket¹ ['pɪkət] *v* : piquetear

picket² *n* **1** STAKE : estaca *f* **2** STRIKER : huelguista *mf*, integrante *mf* de un piquete

pickle¹ ['pɪkəl] *vt* **-led; -ling** : encurtir, escabechar

pickle² *n* **1** BRINE : escabeche *m* **2** GHERKIN : pepinillo *m* (encurtido) **3** JAM, TROUBLE : lío *m*, apuro *m*

pickpocket ['pɪk,pakət] *n* : carterista *mf*

pickup ['pɪk,əp] *n* **1** IMPROVEMENT : mejora *f* **2** *or* **pickup truck** : camioneta *f*

pick up *vt* **1** LIFT : levantar **2** TIDY : arreglar, ordenar — *vi* IMPROVE : mejorar

picnic¹ ['pɪk,nɪk] *vi* **-nicked; -nicking** : ir de picnic

picnic² *n* : picnic *m*

pictorial [pɪk'toriəl] *adj* : pictórico

picture¹ ['pɪktʃər] *vt* **-tured; -turing 1** DEPICT : representar **2** IMAGINE : imaginarse 〈can you picture it? : ¿te lo puedes imaginar?〉

picture² *n* **1** : cuadro *m* (pintado o dibujado), ilustración *f*, fotografía *f* **2** DESCRIPTION : descripción *f* **3** IMAGE : imagen *f* 〈he's the picture of his father : es la viva imagen de su padre〉 **4** MOVIE : película *f*

picturesque [,pɪktʃə'rɛsk] *adj* : pintoresco

pie ['paɪ] *n* : pastel *m* (con fruta o carne), empanada *f* (con carne)

piebald ['paɪ,bɔld] *adj* : picazo, pío

piece¹ ['pi:s] *vt* **pieced; piecing 1** PATCH : parchar, arreglar **2 to piece together** : construir pieza por pieza

piece² *n* **1** FRAGMENT : trozo *m*, pedazo *m* **2** COMPONENT : pieza *f* 〈a three-piece suit : un traje de tres piezas〉 **3** UNIT : pieza *f* 〈a piece of fruit : una (pieza de) fruta〉 **4** WORK : obra *f*, pieza *f* (de música, etc.) **5** (*in board games*) : ficha *f*, pieza *f*, figura *f* (en ajedrez)

piecemeal¹ ['pi:s,mi:l] *adv* : poco a poco, por partes

piecemeal² *adj* : hecho poco a poco, poco sistemático

pied ['paɪd] *adj* : pío

pier ['pɪr] *n* **1** : pila *f* (de un puente) **2** WHARF : muelle *m*, atracadero *m*, embarcadero *m* **3** PILLAR : pilar *m*

pierce ['pɪrs] *vt* **pierced; piercing 1** PENETRATE : atravesar, traspasar, penetrar (en) 〈the bullet pierced his leg : la bala le atravesó la pierna〉 〈to pierce one's heart : traspasarle el corazón a uno〉 **2** PERFORATE : perforar, agujerear (las orejas, etc.) **3 to pierce the silence** : desgarrar el silencio

piety ['paɪəti] *n*, *pl* **-eties** : piedad *f*

pig ['pɪg] *n* **1** HOG, SWINE : cerdo *m*, -da *f*; puerco *m*, -ca *f* **2** SLOB : persona *f* desaliñada; cerdo *m*, -da *f* **3** GLUTTON : glotón *m*, -tona *f* **4** *or* **pig iron** : lingote *m* de hierro

pigeon ['pɪdʒən] *n* : paloma *f*

pigeonhole ['pɪdʒən,ho:l] *n* : casilla *f*

pigeon–toed ['pɪdʒən,to:d] *adj* : patituerto

piggish ['pɪgɪʃ] *adj* **1** GREEDY : glotón **2** DIRTY : cochino, sucio

piggyback ['pɪgi,bæk] *adv & adj* : a cuestas

pigheaded ['pɪg,hɛdəd] *adj* : terco, obstinado

piglet ['pɪglət] *n* : cochinillo *m*; lechón *m*, -chona *f*

pigment ['pɪgmənt] *n* : pigmento *m*

pigmentation [,pɪgmən'teɪʃən] *n* : pigmentación *f*

pigmy → **pygmy**

pigpen ['pɪg,pɛn] *n* : chiquero *m*, pocilga *f*

pigsty ['pɪg,staɪ] → **pigpen**

pigtail ['pɪg,teɪl] *n* : coleta *f*, trenza *f*

pike ['paɪk] *n*, *pl* **pike** *or* **pikes 1** : lucio *m* (pez) **2** LANCE : pica *f* **3** → **turnpike**

pile¹ ['paɪl] *v* **piled; piling** *vt* : amontonar, apilar — *vi* **to pile up** : amontonarse, acumularse

pile² *n* **1** STAKE : pilote *m* **2** HEAP : montón *m*, pila *f* **3** NAP : pelo *m* (de telas)

piles ['paɪlz] *npl* HEMORRHOIDS : hemorroides *fpl*, almorranas *fpl*

pilfer ['pɪlfər] *vt* : robar (cosas pequeñas), ratear

pilgrim ['pɪlgrəm] *n* : peregrino *m*, -na *f*

pilgrimage ['pɪlgrəmɪdʒ] *n* : peregrinación *f*

pill ['pɪl] *n* : pastilla *f*, píldora *f*

pillage¹ ['pɪlɪdʒ] *vt* **-laged; -laging** : saquear

pillage² *n* : saqueo *m*

pillar ['pɪlər] *n* : pilar *m*, columna *f*

pillory ['pɪləri] *n*, *pl* **-ries** : picota *f*

pillow ['pɪ,lo:] *n* : almohada *f*

pillowcase ['pɪ,lo:,keɪs] *n* : funda *f*

pilot¹ ['paɪlət] *vt* : pilotar, pilotear

pilot² *n* : piloto *mf*

pilot light *n* : piloto *m*

pimento [pə'mɛn,to:] → **pimiento**

pimiento [pə'mɛn,to:, -'mjɛn-] *n, pl* **-tos** : pimiento *m* morrón

pimp ['pɪmp] *n* : proxeneta *m*

pimple ['pɪmpəl] *n* : grano *m*

pimply ['pɪmpəli] *adj* **-plier; -est** : cubierto de granos

pin¹ ['pɪn] *vt* **pinned; pinning 1** FASTEN : prender, sujetar (con alfileres) **2** HOLD, IMMOBILIZE : inmovilizar, sujetar **3 to pin one's hopes on** : poner sus esperanzas en

pin² *n* **1** : alfiler *m* ⟨safety pin : alfiler de gancho⟩ ⟨a bobby pin : una horquilla⟩ **2** BROOCH : alfiler *m*, broche *m*, prendedor *m* **3** *or* **bowling pin** : bolo *m*

pinafore ['pɪnə,for] *n* : delantal *m*

pincer ['pɪntsər] *n* **1** CLAW : pinza *f* (de una langosta, etc.) **2 pincers** *npl* : pinzas *fpl*, tenazas *fpl*, tenaza *f*

pinch¹ ['pɪntʃ] *vt* **1** : pellizcar ⟨she pinched my cheek : me pellizcó el cachete⟩ **2** STEAL : robar — *vi* : apretar ⟨my shoes pinch : me aprietan los zapatos⟩

pinch² *n* **1** EMERGENCY : emergencia *f* ⟨in a pinch : en caso necesario⟩ **2** PAIN : dolor *m*, tormento *m* **3** SQUEEZE : pellizco *m* (con los dedos) **4** BIT : pizca *f*, pellizco *m* ⟨a pinch of cinnamon : una pizca de canela⟩

pinch hitter *n* **1** SUBSTITUTE : sustituto *m*, -ta *f* **2** : bateador *m* emergente (en beisbol)

pincushion ['pɪn,kuʃən] *n* : acerico *m*, alfiletero *m*

pine¹ ['paɪn] *vi* **pined; pining 1 to pine away** : languidecer, consumirse **2 to pine for** : añorar, suspirar por

pine² *n* **1** : pino *m* (árbol) **2** : madera *f* de pino

pineapple ['paɪn,æpəl] *n* : piña *f*, ananá *m*, ananás *m*

ping–pong ['pɪŋ,paŋ, -,pɔŋ] *n* : pingpong *m*

pinion¹ ['pɪnjən] *vt* : sujetar los brazos de, inmovilizar

pinion² *n* : piñón *m*

pink¹ ['pɪŋk] *adj* : rosa, rosado

pink² *n* **1** : clavelito *m* (flor) **2** : rosa *m*, rosado *m* (color) **3 to be in the pink** : estar en plena forma, rebosar de salud

pinkeye ['pɪŋk,aɪ] *n* : conjuntivitis *f* aguda

pinkish ['pɪŋkɪʃ] *adj* : rosáceo

pinnacle ['pɪnɪkəl] *n* **1** : pináculo *m* (de un edificio) **2** PEAK : cima *f*, cumbre *f* (de una montaña) **3** ACME : pináculo *m*, cúspide *f*, apogeo *m*

pinpoint ['pɪn,pɔɪnt] *vt* : precisar, localizar con precisión

pint ['paɪnt] *n* : pinta *f*

pinto ['pɪn,to:] *n, pl* **pintos** : caballo *m* pinto

pinworm ['pɪn,wərm] *n* : oxiuro *m*

pioneer¹ [,paɪə'nɪr] *vt* : promover, iniciar, introducir

pioneer² *n* : pionero *m*, -ra *f*

pious ['paɪəs] *adj* **1** DEVOUT : piadoso, devoto **2** SANCTIMONIOUS : beato

piously ['paɪəsli] *adv* **1** DEVOUTLY : piadosamente **2** SANCTIMONIOUSLY : santurronamente

pipe¹ ['paɪp] *v* **piped; piping** *vi* : hablar en voz chillona — *vt* **1** PLAY : tocar (el caramillo o la flauta) **2** : conducir por tuberías ⟨to pipe water : transportar el agua por tubería⟩

pipe² *n* **1** : caramillo *m* (instrumento musical) **2** BAGPIPE : gaita *f* **3** : tubo *m*, caño *m* ⟨gas pipes : tubería de gas⟩ **4** : pipa *f* (para fumar)

pipeline ['paɪp,laɪn] *n* **1** : conducto *m*, oleoducto *m* (para petróleo), gasoducto *m* (para gas) **2** CONDUIT : vía *f* (de información, etc.)

piper ['paɪpər] *n* : músico *m*, -ca *f* que toca el caramillo o la gaita

piping ['paɪpɪŋ] *n* **1** : música *f* del caramillo o de la gaita **2** TRIM : cordoncillo *m*, ribete *m* con cordón

piquant ['pi:kənt, 'pɪkwənt] *adj* **1** SPICY : picante **2** INTRIGUING : intrigante, estimulante

pique¹ ['pi:k] *vt* **piqued; piquing 1** IRRITATE : picar, irritar **2** AROUSE : despertar (la curiosidad, etc.)

pique² *n* : pique *m*, resentimiento *m*

piracy ['paɪrəsi] *n, pl* **-cies** : piratería *f*

piranha [pə'ranə, -'ranjə, -'rænjə] *n* : piraña *f*

pirate¹ ['paɪrət] *n* : pirata *mf*

pirate² *vt* **-rated; -rating** : piratear (software, etc.)

pirouette [,pɪrə'wɛt] *n* : pirueta *f*

pis → pi

Pisces ['paɪ,si:z, 'pɪ-; 'pɪs,keɪs] *n* : Piscis *mf*

pistachio [pə'stæʃi,o:, -'sta-] *n, pl* **-chios** : pistacho *m*

pistil ['pɪstəl] *n* : pistilo *m*

pistol ['pɪstəl] *n* : pistola *f*

piston ['pɪstən] *n* : pistón *m*, émbolo *m*

pit¹ ['pɪt] *v* **pitted; pitting** *vt* **1** : marcar de hoyos, picar (una superficie) **2** : deshuesar (una fruta) **3 to pit against** : enfrentar a, oponer a — *vi* : quedar marcado

pit² *n* **1** HOLE : fosa *f*, hoyo *m* ⟨a bottomless pit : un pozo sin fondo⟩ **2** MINE : mina *f* **3** : foso *m* ⟨orchestra pit : foso orquestal⟩ **4** POCKMARK : marca *f* (en la cara), cicatriz *f* de viruela **5** STONE : hueso *m*, pepa *f* (de una fruta) **6 pit of the stomach** : boca *f* del estómago

pitch¹ ['pɪtʃ] *vt* **1** SET UP : montar, armar (una tienda) **2** THROW : lanzar, arrojar **3** ADJUST, SET : dar el tono de (un discurso, un instrumento musical) — *vi* **1** *or* **pitch forward** FALL : caerse **2** LURCH : cabecear (dícese de un barco o un avión), dar bandazos

pitch² *n* **1** LURCHING : cabezada *f*, cabeceo *m* (de un barco o un avión) **2** SLOPE : (grado de) inclinación *f*, pendiente *f* **3** : tono *m* (en música) ⟨perfect pitch : oído absoluto⟩ **4** THROW : lanzamiento *m* **5** DEGREE : grado *m*, nivel *m*, punto *m* ⟨the excitement reached a high pitch : la excitación llegó a un punto culminante⟩ **6** *or* **sales pitch** : presentación *f* (de un vendedor) **7** TAR : pez *f*, brea *f*

pitcher ['pɪtʃər] *n* **1** JUG : jarra *f*, jarro *m*, cántaro *m*, pichel *m* **2** : lanzador *m*, -dora *f* (en béisbol, etc.)

pitchfork ['pɪtʃ,fɔrk] *n* : horquilla *f*, horca *f*

piteous ['pɪtiəs] *adj* : lastimoso, lastimero — **piteously** *adv*

pitfall ['pɪt,fɔl] *n* : peligro *m* (poco obvio), dificultad *f*

pith ['pɪθ] *n* **1** : médula *f* (de una planta) **2** CORE : meollo *m*, entraña *f*

pithy ['pɪθi] *adj* **pithier; -est** : conciso y sustancioso ⟨pithy comments : comentarios sucintos⟩

pitiable ['pɪtiəbəl] → **pitiful**

pitiful ['pɪtɪfəl] *adj* **1** LAMENTABLE : lastimero, lastimoso, lamentable **2** CONTEMPTIBLE : despreciable, lamentable — **pitifully** [-fli] *adv*

pitiless ['pɪtɪləs] *adj* : despiadado — **pitilessly** *adv*

pittance ['pɪtənts] *n* : miseria *f*

pituitary [pə'tuː:ə,teri, -'tjuː-] *adj* : pituitario

pity[1] ['pɪti] *vt* **pitied; pitying** : compadecer, compadecerse de

pity[2] *n, pl* **pities 1** COMPASSION : compasión *f*, piedad *f* **2** SHAME : lástima *f*, pena *f* ⟨what a pity! : ¡qué lástima!⟩

pivot[1] ['pɪvət] *vi* **1** : girar sobre un eje **2 to pivot on** : girar sobre, depender de

pivot[2] *n* : pivote *m*

pivotal ['pɪvətəl] *adj* : fundamental, central

pixie *or* **pixy** ['pɪksi] *n, pl* **pixies** : elfo *m*, hada *f*

pizza ['piːtsə] *n* : pizza *f*

pizzazz *or* **pizazz** [pə'zæz] *n* **1** GLAMOR : encanto *m* **2** VITALITY : animación *f*, vitalidad *f*

placard ['plækərd, -,kɑrd] *n* POSTER : cartel *m*, póster *m*, afiche *m*

placate ['pleɪ,keɪt, 'plæ-] *vt* **-cated; -cating** : aplacar, apaciguar

place[1] ['pleɪs] *vt* **placed; placing 1** PUT, SET : poner, colocar **2** SITUATE : situar, ubicar, emplazar ⟨to be well placed : estar bien situado⟩ ⟨to place in a job : colocar en un trabajo⟩ **3** IDENTIFY, RECALL : identificar, ubicar, recordar ⟨I can't place him : no lo ubico⟩ **4 to place an order** : hacer un pedido

place[2] *n* **1** SPACE : sitio *m*, lugar *m* ⟨there's no place to sit : no hay sitio para sentarse⟩ **2** LOCATION, SPOT : lugar *m*, sitio *m*, parte *f* ⟨place of work : lugar de trabajo⟩ ⟨our summer place : nuestra casa de verano⟩ ⟨all over the place : por todas partes⟩ **3** RANK : lugar *m*, puesto *m* ⟨he took first place : ganó el primer lugar⟩ **4** POSITION : lugar *m* ⟨everything in its place : todo en

su debido lugar⟩ ⟨to feel out of place : sentirse fuera de lugar⟩ **5** SEAT : asiento *m*, cubierto *m* (a la mesa) **6** JOB : puesto *m* **7** ROLE : papel *m*, lugar *m* ⟨to change places : cambiarse los papeles⟩ **8 to take place** : tener lugar **9 to take the place of** : sustituir a

placebo [plə'siː:,boː] *n, pl* **-bos** : placebo *m*

placement ['pleɪsmənt] *n* : colocación *f*

placenta [plə'sɛntə] *n, pl* **-tas** *or* **-tae** [-ti, -,taɪ] : placenta *f*

placid ['plæsəd] *adj* : plácido, tranquilo — **placidly** *adv*

plagiarism ['pleɪdʒə,rɪzəm] *n* : plagio *m*

plagiarist ['pleɪdʒərɪst] *n* : plagiario *m*, -ria *f*

plagiarize ['pleɪdʒə,raɪz] *vt* **-rized; -rizing** : plagiar

plague[1] ['pleɪg] *vt* **plagued; plaguing 1** AFFLICT : plagar, afligir **2** HARASS : acosar, atormentar

plague[2] *n* **1** : plaga *f* (de insectos, etc.) **2** : peste *f* (en medicina)

plaid[1] ['plæd] *adj* : escocés, de cuadros ⟨a plaid skirt : una falda escocesa⟩

plaid[2] *n* TARTAN : tela *f* escocesa, tartán *m*

plain[1] ['pleɪn] *adj* **1** SIMPLE, UNADORNED : liso, sencillo, sin adornos **2** CLEAR : claro ⟨in plain language : en palabras claras⟩ **3** FRANK : franco, puro ⟨the plain truth : la pura verdad⟩ **4** HOMELY : ordinario, poco atractivo **5 in plain sight** : a la vista de todos

plain[2] *n* : llanura *f*, llano *m*, planicie *f*

plainly ['pleɪnli] *adv* **1** CLEARLY : claramente **2** FRANKLY : francamente, con franqueza **3** SIMPLY : sencillamente

plaintiff ['pleɪntɪf] *n* : demandante *mf*

plaintive ['pleɪntɪv] *adj* MOURNFUL : lastimero, plañidero

plait[1] ['pleɪt, 'plæt] *vt* **1** PLEAT : plisar **2** BRAID : trenzar

plait[2] *n* **1** PLEAT : pliegue *m* **2** BRAID : trenza *f*

plan[1] ['plæn] *v* **planned; planning** *vt* **1** : planear, proyectar, planificar ⟨to plan a trip : planear un viaje⟩ ⟨to plan a city : planificar una ciudad⟩ **2** INTEND : tener planeado, proyectar — *vi* : hacer planes

plan[2] *n* **1** DIAGRAM : plano *m*, esquema *m* **2** SCHEME : plan *m*, proyecto *m*, programa *m* ⟨to draw up a plan : elaborar un proyecto⟩

plane[1] ['pleɪn] *vt* **planed; planing** : cepillar (madera)

plane[2] *adj* : plano

plane[3] *n* **1** : plano *m* (en matemáticas, etc.) **2** LEVEL : nivel *m* **3** : cepillo *m* (de carpintero) **4** → **airplane**

planet ['plænət] *n* : planeta *f*

planetarium [,plænə'teriəm] *n, pl* **-iums** *or* **-ia** [-iə] : planetario *m*

planetary ['plænə,teri] *adj* : planetario

plank ['plæŋk] *n* **1** BOARD : tablón *m*, tabla *f* **2** : artículo *m*, punto *m* (de una plataforma política)

plankton ['plæŋktən] *n* : plancton *m*
plant¹ ['plænt] *vt* **1** : plantar, sembrar (semillas) ⟨planted with flowers : plantado de flores⟩ **2** PLACE : plantar, colocar ⟨to plant an idea : inculcar una idea⟩
plant² *n* **1** : planta *f* ⟨leafy plants : plantas frondosas⟩ **2** FACTORY : planta *f*, fábrica *f* ⟨hydroelectric plant : planta hidroeléctrica⟩ **3** MACHINERY : maquinaria *f*, equipo *m*
plantain ['plæntən] *n* **1** : llantén *m* (mala hierba) **2** : plátano *m*, plátano *m* macho *Mex* (fruta)
plantation [plæn'teɪʃən] *n* : plantación *f*, hacienda *f* ⟨a coffee plantation : un cafetal⟩
planter ['plæntər] *n* **1** : hacendado *m*, -da *f* (de una hacienda) **2** FLOWERPOT : tiesto *m*, maceta *f*
plaque ['plæk] *n* **1** TABLET : placa *f* **2** : placa *f* (dental)
plasma ['plæzmə] *n* : plasma *m*
plaster¹ ['plæstər] *vt* **1** : enyesar, revocar (con yeso) **2** COVER : cubrir, llenar ⟨a wall plastered with notices : una pared cubierta de avisos⟩
plaster² *n* **1** : yeso *m*, revoque *m* (para paredes, etc.) **2** : escayola *f*, yeso *m* (en medicina) **3 plaster of Paris** ['pærɪs] : yeso *m* mate
plaster cast *n* : vaciado *m* de yeso
plasterer ['plæstərər] *n* : revocador *m*, -dora *f*
plastic¹ ['plæstɪk] *adj* **1** : de plástico **2** PLIABLE : plástico, flexible **3 plastic surgery** : cirugía *f* plástica
plastic² *n* : plástico *m*
plasticity [plæ'stɪsəti] *n*, *pl* **-ties** : plasticidad *f*
plate¹ ['pleɪt] *vt* **plated; plating** : chapar (en metal)
plate² *n* **1** PLAQUE, SHEET : placa *f* ⟨a steel plate : una placa de acero⟩ **2** UTENSILS : vajilla *f* (de metal) ⟨silver plate : vajilla de plata⟩ **3** DISH : plato *m* **4** DENTURES : dentadura *f* postiza **5** ILLUSTRATION : lámina *f* (en un libro) **6 license plate** : matrícula *f*, placa *f* de matrícula
plateau [plæ'to:] *n*, *pl* **-teaus** *or* **-teaux** [-'to:z] : meseta *f*
platform ['plæt,fɔrm] *n* **1** STAGE : plataforma *f*, estrado *m*, tribuna *f* **2** : andén *m* (de una estación de ferrocarril) **3 political platform** : plataforma *f* política, programa *m* electoral
plating ['pleɪtɪŋ] *n* **1** : enchapado *m* **2 silver plating** : plateado *m*
platinum ['plætənəm] *n* : platino *m*
platitude ['plæṭə,tu:d, -,tju:d] *n* : lugar *m* común, perogrullada *f*
platonic [plə'tɑnɪk] *adj* : platónico
platoon [plə'tu:n] *n* : sección *f* (en el ejército)
platter ['plæṭər] *n* : fuente *f*
platypus ['plæṭɪpəs, -,pus] *n*, *pl* **platypuses** *or* **platypi** [-,paɪ, -,pi:] : ornitorrinco *m*

plausibility [,plɔzə'bɪləṭi] *n*, *pl* **-ties** : credibilidad *f*, verosimilitud *f*
plausible ['plɔzəbəl] *adj* : creíble, convincente, verosímil — **plausibly** [-bli] *adv*
play¹ ['pleɪ] *vi* **1** : jugar ⟨to play with a doll : jugar con una muñeca⟩ ⟨to play with an idea : darle vueltas a una idea⟩ **2** FIDDLE, TOY : jugar, juguetear ⟨don't play with your food : no juegues con la comida⟩ **3** : tocar ⟨to play in a band : tocar en un grupo⟩ **4** : actuar (en una obra de teatro) — *vt* **1** : jugar (un deporte, etc.), jugar a (un juego), jugar contra (un contrincante) **2** : tocar (música o un instrumento) **3** PERFORM : interpretar, hacer el papel de (un carácter), representar (una obra de teatro) ⟨she plays the lead : hace el papel principal⟩ **4 to play back** : poner (una grabación) **5 to play down** : minimizar **6 to play up** : resaltar
play² *n* **1** GAME, RECREATION : juego *m* ⟨children at play : niños jugando⟩ ⟨a play on words : un juego de palabras⟩ **2** ACTION : juego *m* ⟨the ball is in play : la pelota está en juego⟩ ⟨to bring into play : poner en juego⟩ **3** DRAMA : obra *f* de teatro, pieza *f* (de teatro) **4** MOVEMENT : juego *m* (de la luz, una brisa, etc.) **5** SLACK : juego *m* ⟨there's not enough play in the wheel : la rueda no da lo suficiente⟩
playacting ['pleɪ,æktɪŋ] *n* : actuación *f*, teatro *m*
player ['pleɪər] *n* **1** : jugador *m*, -dora *f* (en un juego) **2** ACTOR : actor *m*, actriz *f* **3** MUSICIAN : músico *m*, -ca *f*
playful ['pleɪfəl] *adj* **1** FROLICSOME : juguetón **2** JOCULAR : jocoso — **playfully** *adv*
playfulness ['pleɪfəlnəs] *n* : lo juguetón, jocosidad *f*, alegría *f*
playground ['pleɪ,graʊnd] *n* : patio *m* de recreo, jardín *m* para jugar
playhouse ['pleɪ,haʊs] *n* **1** THEATER : teatro *m* **2** : casita *f* de juguete
playing card *n* : naipe *m*, carta *f*
playmate ['pleɪ,meɪt] *n* : compañero *m*, -ra *f* de juego
play-off ['pleɪ,ɔf] *n* : desempate *m*
playpen ['pleɪ,pɛn] *n* : corral *m* (para niños)
plaything ['pleɪ,θɪŋ] *n* : juguete *m*
playwright ['pleɪ,raɪt] *n* : dramaturgo *m*, -ga *f*
plaza ['plæzə, 'plɑ-] *n* **1** SQUARE : plaza *f* **2 shopping plaza** MALL : centro *m* comercial
plea ['pli:] *n* **1** : acto *m* de declararse ⟨he entered a plea of guilty : se declaró culpable⟩ **2** APPEAL : ruego *m*, súplica *f*
plead ['pli:d] *v* **pleaded** *or* **pled** ['plɛd]; **pleading** *vi* **1** : declararse (culpable o inocente) **2 to plead for** : suplicar, implorar — *vt* **1** : alegar, pretextar ⟨he pleaded illness : pretextó la enfermedad⟩ **2 to plead a case** : defender un caso

pleasant ['plɛzənt] *adj* : agradable, grato, bueno — **pleasantly** *adv*

pleasantness ['plɛzəntnəs] *n* : lo agradable, amenidad *f*

pleasantries ['plɛzəntriz] *npl* : cumplidos *mpl*, cortesías *fpl* ⟨to exchange pleasantries : intercambiar cumplidos⟩

please¹ ['pli:z] *v* **pleased; pleasing** *vt* **1** GRATIFY : complacer ⟨please yourself! : ¡cómo quieras!⟩ **2** SATISFY : contentar, satisfacer — *vi* **1** SATISFY : complacer, agradar ⟨anxious to please : deseoso de complacer⟩ **2** LIKE : querer ⟨do as you please : haz lo que quieras, haz lo que te parezca⟩

please² *adv* : por favor

pleased ['pli:zd] *adj* : contento, satisfecho, alegre

pleasing ['pli:zɪŋ] *adj* : agradable — **pleasingly** *adv*

pleasurable ['plɛʒərəbəl] *adj* PLEASANT : agradable

pleasure ['plɛʒər] *n* **1** WISH : deseo *m*, voluntad *f* ⟨at your pleasure : cuando guste⟩ **2** ENJOYMENT : placer *m*, disfrute *m*, goce *m* ⟨with pleasure : con mucho gusto⟩ **3** : placer *m*, gusto *m* ⟨it's a pleasure to be here : me da gusto estar aquí⟩ ⟨the pleasures of reading : los placeres de leer⟩

pleat¹ ['pli:t] *vt* : plisar

pleat² *n* : pliegue *m*

plebeian [plɪ'bi:ən] *adj* : ordinario, plebeyo

pledge¹ ['plɛdʒ] *vt* **pledged; pledging 1** PAWN : empeñar, prendar **2** PROMISE : prometer, jurar

pledge² *n* **1** SECURITY : garantía *f*, prenda *f* **2** PROMISE : promesa *f*

plenteous ['plɛntiəs] *adj* : copioso, abundante

plentiful ['plɛntɪfəl] *adj* : abundante — **plentifully** [-fli] *adv*

plenty ['plɛnti] *n* : abundancia *f* ⟨plenty of time : tiempo de sobra⟩ ⟨plenty of visitors : muchos visitantes⟩

plethora ['plɛθərə] *n* : plétora *f*

pleurisy ['plʊrəsi] *n* : pleuresía *f*

pliable ['plaɪəbəl] *adj* : flexible, maleable

pliant ['plaɪənt] → **pliable**

pliers ['plaɪərz] *npl* : alicates *mpl*, pinzas *fpl*

plight ['plaɪt] *n* : situación *f* difícil, apuro *m*

plod ['plɑd] *vi* **plodded; plodding 1** TRUDGE : caminar pesadamente y lentamente **2** DRUDGE : trabajar laboriosamente

plot¹ ['plɑt] *v* **plotted; plotting** *vt* **1** DEVISE : tramar **2** to plot out : trazar, determinar (una posición, etc.) — *vi* CONSPIRE : conspirar

plot² *n* **1** LOT : terreno *m*, parcela *f*, lote *m* **2** STORY : argumento *m* (en el teatro), trama *f* (en un libro, etc.) **3** CONSPIRACY, INTRIGUE : complot *m*, intriga *f*

plotter ['plɑtər] *n* : conspirador *m*, -dora *f*; intrigante *mf*

plow¹ *or* **plough** ['plaʊ] *vt* **1** : arar (la tierra) **2 to plow the seas** : surcar los mares

plow² *or* **plough** *n* **1** : arado *m* **2** → **snowplow**

plowshare ['plaʊˌʃɛr] *n* : reja *f* del arado

ploy ['plɔɪ] *n* : estratagema *f*, maniobra *f*

pluck¹ ['plʌk] *vt* **1** PICK : arrancar **2** : desplumar (un pollo, etc.) — *vi* **to pluck at** : tirar de

pluck² *n* **1** TUG : tirón *m* **2** COURAGE, SPIRIT : valor *m*, ánimo *m*

plucky ['plʌki] *adj* **pluckier; -est** : valiente, animoso

plug¹ ['plʌg] *vt* **plugged; plugging 1** BLOCK : tapar **2** PROMOTE : hacerle publicidad a, promocionar **3 to plug in** : enchufar

plug² *n* **1** STOPPER : tapón *m* **2** : enchufe *m* (eléctrico) **3** ADVERTISEMENT : publicidad *f*, propaganda *f*

plum ['plʌm] *n* **1** : ciruela *f* (fruta) **2** : color *m* ciruela **3** PRIZE : premio *m*, algo muy atractivo

plumage ['plu:mɪdʒ] *n* : plumaje *m*

plumb¹ ['plʌm] *vt* **1** : aplomar ⟨to plumb a wall : aplomar una pared⟩ **2** SOUND : sondear, sondar

plumb² *adv* **1** VERTICALLY : a plomo, verticalmente **2** EXACTLY : justo, exactamente **3** COMPLETELY : completamente, absolutamente ⟨plumb crazy : loco de remate⟩

plumb³ *adj* : a plomo

plumb⁴ *n or* **plumb line** : plomada *f*

plumber ['plʌmər] *n* : plomero *m*, -ra *f*; fontanero *m*, -ra *f*

plumbing ['plʌmɪŋ] *n* **1** : plomería *f*, fontanería *f* (trabajo del plomero) **2** PIPES : cañería *f*, tubería *f*

plume ['plu:m] *n* **1** FEATHER : pluma *f* **2** TUFT : penacho *m* (en un sombrero, etc.)

plumed ['plu:md] *adj* : con plumas ⟨white-plumed birds : aves de plumaje blanco⟩

plummet ['plʌmət] *vi* : caer en picada, desplomarse

plump¹ ['plʌmp] *vi or* **to plump down** : dejarse caer (pesadamente)

plump² *adv* **1** STRAIGHT : a plomo **2** DIRECTLY : directamente, sin rodeos ⟨he ran plump into the door : dio de cara con la puerta⟩

plump³ *adj* : llenito *fam*, regordete *fam*, rechoncho *fam*

plumpness ['plʌmpnəs] *n* : gordura *f*

plunder¹ ['plʌndər] *vi* : saquear, robar

plunder² *n* : botín *m*

plunderer ['plʌndərər] *n* : saqueador *m*, -dora *f*

plunge¹ ['plʌndʒ] *v* **plunged; plunging** *vt* **1** IMMERSE : sumergir **2** THRUST : hundir, clavar — *vi* **1** DIVE : zambullirse (en el agua) **2** : meterse precipitadamente o violentamente ⟨they plunged into war : se enfrascaron en una guerra⟩ ⟨he plunged into depression : cayó en la depresión⟩ 3 DESCEND : descender en picada ⟨the road plunges dizzily : la calle desciende vertiginosamente⟩

plunge² *n* 1 DIVE : zambullida *f* 2 DROP : descenso *m* abrupto ⟨the plunge in prices : el desplome de los precios⟩

plural¹ ['plʊrəl] *adj* : plural

plural² *n* : plural *m*

plurality [plʊ'ræləti] *n, pl* **-ties** : pluralidad *f*

pluralize ['plʊrə,laɪz] *vt* **-ized; -izing** : pluralizar

plus¹ ['plʌs] *adj* 1 POSITIVE : positivo ⟨a plus factor : un factor positivo⟩ 2 *(indicating a quantity in addition)* ⟨a grade of C plus : una calificación entre C y B⟩ ⟨a salary of $30,000 plus : un sueldo de más de $30,000⟩

plus² *n* 1 *or* **plus sign** : más *m*, signo *m* de más 2 ADVANTAGE : ventaja *f*

plus³ *prep* : más (en matemáticas)

plus⁴ *conj* AND : y

plush¹ ['plʌʃ] *adj* 1 : afelpado 2 LUXURIOUS : lujoso

plush² *n* : felpa *f*, peluche *m*

plushy ['plʌʃi] *adj* **plushier; -est** : lujoso

Pluto ['plu:ţo:] *n* : Plutón *m*

plutocracy [plu:'tɑkrəsi] *n, pl* **-cies** : plutocracia *f*

plutonium [plu:'to:niəm] *n* : plutonio *m*

ply¹ ['plaɪ] *v* **plied; plying** *vt* 1 USE, WIELD : manejar ⟨to ply an ax : manejar un hacha⟩ 2 PRACTICE : ejercer ⟨to ply a trade : ejercer un oficio⟩ 3 **to ply with questions** : acosar con preguntas

ply² *n, pl* **plies** 1 LAYER : chapa *f* (de madera), capa *f* (de papel) 2 STRAND : cabo *m* (de hilo, etc.)

plywood ['plaɪ,wʊd] *n* : contrachapado *m*

pneumatic [nʊ'mætɪk, njʊ-] *adj* : neumático

pneumonia [nʊ'mo:njə, njʊ-] *n* : pulmonía *f*, neumonía *f*

poach ['po:tʃ] *vt* 1 : cocer a fuego lento ⟨to poach an egg : escalfar un huevo⟩ 2 **to poach game** : cazar ilegalmente — *vi* : cazar ilegalmente

poacher ['po:tʃər] *n* : cazador *m* furtivo, cazadora *f* furtiva

pock ['pɑk] *n* 1 PUSTULE : pústula *f* 2 → pockmark

pocket¹ ['pɑkət] *vt* 1 : meterse en el bolsillo ⟨he pocketed the pen : se metió la pluma en el bolsillo⟩ 2 STEAL : embolsarse

pocket² *n* 1 : bolsillo *m*, bolsa *f Mex* ⟨a coat pocket : el bolsillo de un abrigo⟩ ⟨air pockets : bolsas de aire⟩ 2 CENTER : foco *m*, centro *m* ⟨a pocket of resistance : un foco de resistencia⟩

pocketbook ['pɑkət,bʊk] *n* 1 PURSE : cartera *f*, bolso *m*, bolsa *f Mex* 2 MEANS : recursos *mpl*

pocketknife ['pɑkət,naɪf] *n, pl* **-knives** : navaja *f*

pocket–size ['pɑkət'saɪz] *adj* : de bolsillo

pockmark ['pɑk,mɑrk] *n* : cicatriz *f* de viruela, viruela *f*

pod ['pɑd] *n* : vaina *f* ⟨pea pod : vaina de guisantes⟩

podiatrist [pə'daɪətrɪst, po-] *n* : podólogo *m*, -ga *f*

podiatry [pə'daɪətri, po-] *n* : podología *f*, podiatría *f*

podium ['po:diəm] *n, pl* **-diums** *or* **-dia** [-diə] : podio *m*, estrado *m*, tarima *f*

poem ['po:əm] *n* : poema *m*, poesía *f*.

poet ['po:ət] *n* : poeta *mf*

poetic [po'ɛtɪk] *or* **poetical** [-tɪkəl] *adj* : poético

poetry ['po:ətri] *n* : poesía *f*

pogrom ['po:grəm, pə'grɑm, 'pɑgrəm] *n* : pogrom *m*

poignancy ['pɔɪnjənʦi] *n, pl* **-cies** : lo conmovedor

poignant ['pɔɪnjənt] *adj* 1 PAINFUL : penoso, doloroso ⟨poignant grief : profundo dolor⟩ 2 TOUCHING : conmovedor, emocionante

poinsettia [pɔɪn'sɛtiə, -'sɛtə] *n* : flor *f* de Nochebuena

point¹ ['pɔɪnt] *vt* 1 SHARPEN : afilar (la punta de) 2 INDICATE : señalar, indicar ⟨to point the way : señalar el camino⟩ 3 AIM : apuntar 4 **to point out** : señalar, indicar — *vi* 1 **to point at** : señalar (con el dedo) 2 **to point to** INDICATE : señalar, indicar

point² *n* 1 ITEM : punto *m* ⟨the main points : los puntos principales⟩ 2 QUALITY : cualidad *f* ⟨her good points : sus buenas cualidades⟩ ⟨it's not his strong point : no es su (punto) fuerte⟩ 3 *(indicating a chief idea or meaning)* ⟨it's beside the point : no viene al caso⟩ ⟨to get to the point : ir al grano⟩ ⟨to stick to the point : no salirse del tema⟩ 4 PURPOSE : fin *m*, propósito *m* ⟨there's no point to it : no vale la pena, no sirve para nada⟩ 5 PLACE : punto *m*, lugar *m* ⟨points of interest : puntos interesantes⟩ 6 : punto *m* (en una escala) ⟨boiling point : punto de ebullición⟩ 7 MOMENT : momento *m*, coyuntura *f* ⟨at this point : en este momento⟩ 8 TIP : punta *f* 9 HEADLAND : punta *f*, cabo *m* 10 PERIOD : punto *m* (marca de puntuación) 11 UNIT : punto *m* ⟨he scored 15 points : ganó 15 puntos⟩ ⟨shares fell 10 points : las acciones bajaron 10 enteros⟩ 12 **compass points** : puntos *mpl* cardinales 13 **decimal point** : punto *m* decimal, coma *f*

point–blank¹ ['pɔɪnt'blæŋk] *adv* 1 : a quemarropa ⟨to shoot point-blank : disparar a quemarropa⟩ 2 BLUNTLY, DIRECTLY : a bocajarro, sin rodeos, francamente

point–blank² *adj* 1 : a quemarropa ⟨point-blank shots : disparos a quemarropa⟩ 2 BLUNT, DIRECT : directo, franco

pointed ['pɔɪntəd] *adj* **1** POINTY : puntiagudo **2** PERTINENT : atinado **3** CONSPICUOUS : marcado, manifiesto
pointedly ['pɔɪntədli] *adv* : intencionadamente, directamente
pointer ['pɔɪntər] *n* **1** STICK : puntero *m* (para maestros, etc.) **2** INDICATOR, NEEDLE : indicador *m*, aguja *f* **3** : perro *m* de muestra **4** HINT, TIP : consejo *m*
pointless ['pɔɪntləs] *adj* : inútil, ocioso, vano ⟨it's pointless to continue : no tiene sentido continuar⟩
point of view *n* : perspectiva *f*, punto *m* de vista
pointy ['pɔɪnti] *adj* : puntiagudo
poise¹ ['pɔɪz] *vt* **poised; poising** BALANCE : equilibrar, balancear
poise² *n* : aplomo *m*, compostura *f*
poison¹ ['pɔɪzən] *vt* **1** : envenenar, intoxicar **2** CORRUPT : corromper
poison² *n* : veneno *m*
poison ivy *n* : hiedra *f* venenosa
poisonous ['pɔɪzənəs] *adj* : venenoso, tóxico, ponzoñoso
poke¹ ['po:k] *v* **poked; poking** *vt* **1** JAB : golpear (con la punta de algo), dar ⟨he poked me with his finger : me dio con el dedo⟩ **2** THRUST : introducir, asomar ⟨I poked my head out the window : asomé la cabeza por la ventana⟩ — *vi* **1 to poke around** RUMMAGE : hurgar **2 to poke along** DAWDLE : demorarse, entretenerse
poke² *n* : golpe *m* abrupto (con la punta de algo)
poker ['po:kər] *n* **1** : atizador *m* (para el fuego) **2** : póker *m*, poker *m* (juego de naipes)
polar ['po:lər] *adj* : polar
polar bear *n* : oso *m* blanco
Polaris [po'lærɪs, -'lɑr-] → **North Star**
polarize ['po:lə,raɪz] *vt* **-ized; -izing** : polarizar
pole ['po:l] *n* **1** : palo *m*, poste *m*, vara *f* ⟨telephone pole : poste de teléfonos⟩ **2** : polo *m* ⟨the South Pole : el Polo Sur⟩ **3** : polo *m* (eléctrico o magnético)
Pole ['po:l] *n* : polaco *m*, -ca *f*
polecat ['po:l,kæt] *n, pl* **polecats** or **polecat 1** : turón *m* (de Europa) **2** SKUNK : mofeta *f*, zorrillo *m*
polemical [po'lɛmɪkəl] *adj* : polémico
polemics [po'lɛmɪks] *ns & pl* : polémica *f*
polestar ['po:l,stɑr] → **North Star**
police¹ [po'li:s] *vt* **-liced; -licing** : mantener el orden en ⟨to police the streets : patrullar las calles⟩
police² *ns & pl* **1** : policía *f* (organización) **2** POLICE OFFICERS : policías *mfpl*
policeman [po'li:smən] *n, pl* **-men** [-mən, -,mɛn] : policía *m*
police officer *n* : policía *mf*, agente *mf* de policía

policewoman [po'li:s,wʊmən] *n, pl* **-women** [-,wɪmən] : policía *f*, mujer *f* policía
policy ['po:ləsi] *n, pl* **-cies 1** : política *f* ⟨foreign policy : política exterior⟩ **2** or **insurance policy** : póliza *f* de seguros, seguro *m*
polio¹ ['po:li,o:] *adj* : de polio ⟨polio vaccine : vacuna contra la polio⟩
polio² *n* → **poliomyelitis**
poliomyelitis [,po:li,o:,maɪə'laɪtəs] *n* : poliomielitis *f*, polio *f*
polish¹ ['pɑlɪʃ] *vt* **1** : pulir, lustrar, sacar brillo a ⟨to polish one's nails : pintarse las uñas⟩ **2** REFINE : pulir, perfeccionar
polish² *n* **1** LUSTER : brillo *m*, lustre *m* **2** REFINEMENT : refinamiento *m* **3** : betún *m* (para zapatos), cera *f* (para suelos y muebles), esmalte *m* (para las uñas)
Polish¹ ['po:lɪʃ] *adj* : polaco
Polish² *n* : polaco *m* (idioma)
polite [po'laɪt] *adj* **-liter; -est** : cortés, correcto, educado
politely [po'laɪtli] *adv* : cortésmente, correctamente, con buenos modales
politeness [po'laɪtnəs] *n* : cortesía *f*
politic ['pɑlə,tɪk] *adj* : diplomático, prudente
political [po'lɪtɪkəl] *adj* : político — **politically** [-tɪkli] *adv*
politician [,pɑlə'tɪʃən] *n* : político *m*, -ca
politics ['pɑlə,tɪks] *ns & pl* : política *f*
polka ['po:lkə, 'po:kə] *n* : polka *f*
polka dot ['po:kə,dɑt] *n* : lunar *m* (en un diseño)
poll¹ ['po:l] *vt* **1** : obtener (votos) ⟨she polled over 1000 votes : obtuvo más de 1000 votos⟩ **2** CANVASS : encuestar, sondear — *vi* : obtener votos
poll² *n* **1** SURVEY : encuesta *f*, sondeo *m* **2 polls** *npl* : urnas *fpl* ⟨to go to the polls : acudir a las urnas, ir a votar⟩
pollen ['pɑlən] *n* : polen *m*
pollinate ['pɑlə,neɪt] *vt* **-nated; -nating** : polinizar
pollination [,pɑlə'neɪʃən] *n* : polinización *f*
pollster ['po:lstər] *n* : encuestador *m*, -dora *f*
pollutant [po'lu:tənt] *n* : contaminante *m*
pollute [po'lu:t] *vt* **-luted; -luting** : contaminar
pollution [po'lu:ʃən] *n* : contaminación *f*
pollywog or **polliwog** ['pɑli,wɔg] *n* TADPOLE : renacuajo *m*
polo ['po:,lo:] *n* : polo *m*
poltergeist ['po:ltər,gaɪst] *n* : poltergeist *m*, fantasma *m* travieso
polyester ['pɑli,ɛstər, ,pɑli'-] *n* : poliéster *m*
polygamous [po'lɪgəməs] *adj* : polígamo
polygamy [po'lɪgəmi] *n* : poligamia *f*
polygon ['pɑli,gɑn] *n* : polígono *m*

polymer ['pɑləmər] *n* : polímero *m*
Polynesian [,pɑlə'ni:ʒən, -ʃən] *n* : polinesio *m*, -sia *f* — **Polynesian** *adj*
polyunsaturated [,pɑli,ʌn'sætʃə-,reɪtəd] *adj* : poliinsaturado
pomegranate ['pɑmə,grænət, 'pɑm-,grænət] *n* : granada *f* (fruta)
pommel[1] ['pʌməl] *vt* → **pummel**
pommel[2] ['pʌməl, 'pɑ-] *n* 1 : pomo *m* (de una espada) 2 : perilla *f* (de una silla de montar)
pomp ['pɑmp] *n* 1 SPLENDOR : pompa *f*, esplendor *m* 2 OSTENTATION : boato *m*, ostentación *f*
pom–pom ['pɑm,pɑm] *n* : borla *f*, pompón *m*
pomposity [pɑm'pɑsəti] *n, pl* **-ties** : pomposidad *f*
pompous ['pɑmpəs] *adj* : pomposo — **pompously** *adv*
poncho ['pɑn,tʃo:] *n, pl* **-chos** : poncho *m*
pond ['pɑnd] *n* : charca *f* (natural), estanque *m* (artificial)
ponder ['pɑndər] *vt* : reflexionar, considerar — *vi* **to ponder over** : reflexionar sobre, sopesar
ponderous ['pɑndərəs] *adj* : pesado
pontiff ['pɑntɪf] *n* POPE : pontífice *m*
pontificate [pɑn'tɪfə,keɪt] *vi* **-cated; -cating** : pontificar
pontoon [pɑn'tu:n] *n* : pontón *m*
pony ['po:ni] *n, pl* **-nies** : poni *m*, poney *m*, jaca *f*
ponytail ['po:ni,teɪl] *n* : cola *f* de caballo, coleta *f*
poodle ['pu:dəl] *n* : caniche *m*
pool[1] ['pu:l] *vt* : mancomunar, hacer un fondo común de
pool[2] *n* 1 : charca *f* ⟨a swimming pool : una piscina⟩ 2 PUDDLE : charco *m* 3 RESERVE, SUPPLY : fondo *m* común (de recursos), reserva *f* 4 : billar *m* (juego)
poor ['pur, 'por] *adj* 1 : pobre ⟨poor people : los pobres⟩ 2 SCANTY : pobre, escaso ⟨poor attendance : baja asistencia⟩ 3 UNFORTUNATE : pobre ⟨poor thing! : ¡pobrecito!⟩ 4 BAD : malo ⟨to be in poor health : estar mal de salud⟩
poorly ['purli, 'por-] *adv* : mal
pop[1] ['pɑp] *v* **popped; popping** *vi* 1 BURST : reventarse, estallar 2 : ir, venir, o aparecer abruptamente ⟨he popped into the house : se metió en la casa⟩ ⟨a menu pops up : aparece un menú⟩ 3 **to pop out** PROTRUDE : salirse, saltarse ⟨my eyes popped out of my head : se me saltaban los ojos⟩ — *vt* 1 BURST : reventar 2 : hacer o meter abruptamente ⟨he popped it into his mouth : se lo metió en la boca⟩
pop[2] *adj* : popular ⟨pop music : música popular⟩
pop[3] *n* 1 : estallido *m* pequeño (de un globo, etc.) 2 SODA : refresco *m*, gaseosa *f*
popcorn ['pɑp,kɔrn] *n* : palomitas *fpl* (de maíz)

pope ['po:p] *n* : papa *m* ⟨Pope John : el Papa Juan⟩
poplar ['pɑplər] *n* : álamo *m*
poplin ['pɑplɪn] *n* : popelín *m*, popelina *f*
poppy ['pɑpi] *n, pl* **-pies** : amapola *f*
populace ['pɑpjələs] *n* 1 MASSES : pueblo *m* 2 POPULATION : población *f*
popular ['pɑpjələr] *adj* 1 : popular ⟨the popular vote : el voto popular⟩ 2 COMMON : generalizado, común ⟨popular beliefs : creencias generalizadas⟩ 3 : popular, de gran popularidad ⟨a popular singer : un cantante popular⟩
popularity [,pɑpjə'lærəti] *n* : popularidad *f*
popularize ['pɑpjələ,raɪz] *vt* **-ized; -izing** : popularizar
popularly ['pɑpjələrli] *adv* : popularmente, vulgarmente
populate ['pɑpjə,leɪt] *vt* **-lated; -lating** : poblar
population [,pɑpjə'leɪʃən] *n* : población *f*
populist ['pɑpjəlɪst] *n* : populista *mf* — **populist** *adj*
populous ['pɑpjələs] *adj* : populoso
porcelain ['pɔrsələn] *n* : porcelana *f*
porch ['pɔrtʃ] *n* : porche *m*
porcupine ['pɔrkjə,paɪn] *n* : puerco *m* espín
pore[1] ['por] *vi* **pored; poring** 1 GAZE : mirar (con atención) 2 **to pore over** : leer detenidamente, estudiar
pore[2] *n* : poro *m*
pork ['pork] *n* : carne *f* de cerdo, carne *f* de puerco
pornographic [,pɔrnə'græfɪk] *adj* : pornográfico
pornography [pɔr'nɑgrəfi] *n* : pornografía *f*
porous ['porəs] *adj* : poroso
porpoise ['pɔrpəs] *n* 1 : marsopa *f* 2 DOLPHIN : delfín *m*
porridge ['pɔrɪdʒ] *n* : sopa *f* espesa de harina, gachas *fpl*
port[1] ['port] *adj* : de babor ⟨on the port side : a babor⟩
port[2] *n* 1 HARBOR : puerto *m* 2 ORIFICE : orificio *m* (de una válvula, etc.) 3 : puerto *m* (de una computadora) 4 PORTHOLE : portilla *f* 5 *or* **port side** : babor *m* (de un barco) 6 : oporto *m* (vino)
portable ['portəbəl] *adj* : portátil
portal ['portəl] *n* : portal *m*
portend [por'tɛnd] *vt* : presagiar, augurar
portent ['por,tɛnt] *n* : presagio *m*, augurio *m*
portentous [por'tɛntəs] *adj* : profético, que presagia
porter ['portər] *n* : maletero *m*, mozo *m* (de estación)
portfolio [port'fo:li,o] *n, pl* **-lios** 1 FOLDER : cartera *f* (para llevar papeles), carpeta *f* 2 : cartera *f* (diplomáti-

ca) **3 investment portfolio** : cartera de inversiones

porthole ['pɔrtˌhoːl] *n* : portilla *f* (de un barco), ventanilla *f* (de un avión)

portico ['pɔrtˌiˌko] *n, pl* **-coes** *or* **-cos** : pórtico *m*

portion[1] ['pɔrʃən] *vt* DISTRIBUTE : repartir

portion[2] *n* PART, SHARE : porción *f*, parte *f*

portly ['pɔrtli] *adj* **-lier; -est** : corpulento

portrait ['pɔrtrət, -ˌtreɪt] *n* : retrato *m*

portray [pɔr'treɪ] *vt* **1** DEPICT : representar, retratar **2** DESCRIBE : describir **3** PLAY : interpretar (un personaje)

portrayal [pɔr'treɪəl] *n* **1** REPRESENTATION : representación *f* **2** PORTRAIT : retrato *m*

Portuguese [ˌpɔrtʃə'giːz, -'giːs] *n* **1** : portugués *m*, -guesa *f* (persona) **2** : portugués *m* (idioma) — **Portuguese** *adj*

pose[1] ['poːz] *v* **posed; posing** *vt* PRESENT : plantear (una pregunta, etc.), representar (una amenaza) — *vi* **1** : posar (para una foto, etc.) **2 to pose as** : hacerse pasar por

pose[2] *n* **1** : pose *f* ⟨to strike a pose : asumir una pose⟩ **2** PRETENSE : pose *f*, afectación *f*

posh ['pɑʃ] *adj* : elegante, de lujo

position[1] [pə'zɪʃən] *vt* : colocar, situar, ubicar

position[2] *n* **1** APPROACH, STANCE : posición *f*, postura *f*, planteamiento *m* **2** LOCATION : posición *f*, ubicación *f* **3** STATUS : posición *f* (en una jerarquía) **4** JOB : puesto *m*

positive ['pɑzətɪv] *adj* **1** DEFINITE : incuestionable, inequívoco ⟨positive evidence : pruebas irrefutables⟩ **2** CONFIDENT : seguro **3** : positivo (en gramática, matemáticas, y física) **4** AFFIRMATIVE : positivo, afirmativo ⟨a positive response : una respuesta positiva⟩

positively ['pɑzətɪvli] *adv* **1** FAVORABLY : favorablemente **2** OPTIMISTICALLY : positivamente **3** DEFINITELY : definitivamente, en forma concluyente **4** (*used for emphasis*) : realmente, verdaderamente ⟨it's positively awful! : ¡es verdaderamente malo!⟩

possess [pə'zɛs] *vt* **1** HAVE, OWN : poseer, tener **2** SEIZE : apoderarse de ⟨he was possessed by fear : el miedo se apoderó de él⟩

possession [pə'zɛʃən] *n* **1** POSSESSING : posesión *f* **2** : posesión *f* (por un demonio, etc.) **3 possessions** *npl* PROPERTY : bienes *mpl*, propiedad *f*

possessive[1] [pə'zɛsɪv] *adj* **1** : posesivo (en gramática) **2** JEALOUS : posesivo, celoso

possessive[2] *n or* **possessive case** : posesivo *m*

possessor [pə'zɛsər] *n* : poseedor *m*, -dora *f*

possibility [ˌpɑsə'bɪləṭi] *n, pl* **-ties** : posibilidad *f*

possible ['pɑsəbəl] *adj* : posible

possibly ['pɑsəbli] *adv* **1** CONCEIVABLY : posiblemente ⟨it can't possibly be true! : ¡no puede ser!⟩ **2** PERHAPS : quizás, posiblemente

possum ['pɑsəm] → **opossum**

post[1] ['poːst] *vt* **1** MAIL : echar al correo, mandar por correo **2** ANNOUNCE : anunciar ⟨they've posted the grades : han anunciado las notas⟩ **3** AFFIX : fijar, poner (noticias, etc.) **4** STATION : apostar **5 to keep (someone) posted** : tener al corriente (a alguien)

post[2] *n* **1** POLE : poste *m*, palo *m* **2** STATION : puesto *m* **3** CAMP : puesto *m* (militar) **4** JOB, POSITION : puesto *m*, empleo *m*, cargo *m*

postage ['poːstɪdʒ] *n* : franqueo *m*

postal ['poːstəl] *adj* : postal

postcard ['poːstˌkɑrd] *n* : postal *f*, tarjeta *f* postal

poster ['poːstər] *n* : póster *m*, cartel *m*, afiche *m*

posterior[1] [pɑ'stɪriər, po-] *adj* : posterior

posterior[2] *n* BUTTOCKS : trasero *m*, nalgas *fpl*, asentaderas *fpl*

posterity [pɑ'stɛrəṭi] *n* : posteridad *f*

postgraduate[1] [ˌpoːst'grædʒuət] *adj* : de postgrado

postgraduate[2] *n* : postgraduado *m*, -da *f*

posthaste ['poːst'heɪst] *adv* : a toda prisa

posthumous ['pɑstʃəməs] *adj* : póstumo — **posthumously** *adv*

postman ['poːstˌstmən, -ˌmæn] → **mailman**

postmark[1] ['poːstˌmɑrk] *vt* : matasellar

postmark[2] *n* : matasellos *m*

postmaster ['poːstˌmæstər] *n* : administrador *m*, -dora *f* de correos

postmodern [ˌpoːst'mɑdərn] *adj* : posmoderno

postmortem [ˌpoːst'mɔrṭəm] *n* : autopsia *f*

postnatal [ˌpoːst'neɪṭəl] *adj* : postnatal ⟨postnatal depression : depresión posparto⟩

post office *n* : correo *m*, oficina *f* de correos

postoperative [ˌpoːst'ɑpərəṭɪv, -ˌreɪ-] *adj* : posoperatorio

postpaid [ˌpoːst'peɪd] *adv* : con franqueo pagado

postpone [ˌpoːst'poːn] *vt* **-poned; -poning** : postergar, aplazar, posponer

postponement [ˌpoːst'poːnmənt] *n* : postergación *f*, aplazamiento *m*

postscript ['poːstˌskrɪpt] *n* : postdata *f*, posdata *f*

postulate ['pɑstʃəˌleɪt] *vt* **-lated; -lating** : postular

posture[1] ['pɑstʃər] *vi* **-tured; -turing** : posar, asumir una pose

posture[2] *n* : postura *f*

postwar [ˌpoːst'wɔr] *adj* : de (la) posguerra

posy ['po:zi] *n, pl* **-sies 1** FLOWER : flor *f* **2** BOUQUET : ramo *m*, ramillete *m*

pot¹ ['pɑt] *vt* **potted; potting** : plantar (en una maceta)

pot² *n* **1** : olla *f* (de cocina) **2 pots and pans** : cacharros *mpl*

potable ['po:təbəl] *adj* : potable

potash ['pɑt,æʃ] *n* : potasa *f*

potassium [pə'tæsiəm] *n* : potasio *m*

potato [pə'teɪto] *n, pl* **-toes** : papa *f*, patata *f Spain*

potato chips *npl* : papas *fpl* fritas (de bolsa)

potbellied ['pɑt,bɛlid] *adj* : panzón, barrigón *fam*

potbelly ['pɑt,bɛli] *n* : panza *f*, barriga *f*

potency ['po:tənsi] *n, pl* **-cies 1** POWER : fuerza *f*, potencia *f* **2** EFFECTIVENESS : eficacia *f*

potent ['po:tənt] *adj* **1** POWERFUL : potente, poderoso **2** EFFECTIVE : eficaz ⟨a potent medicine : una medicina bien fuerte⟩

potential¹ [pə'tɛntʃəl] *adj* : potencial, posible

potential² *n* **1** : potencial *m* ⟨growth potential : potencial de crecimiento⟩ ⟨a child with potential : un niño que promete⟩ **2** : potencial *m* (eléctrico) — **potentially** *adv*

potful ['pɑt,fʊl] *n* : contenido *m* de una olla ⟨a potful of water : una olla de agua⟩

pothole ['pɑt,ho:l] *n* : bache *m*

potion ['po:ʃən] *n* : brebaje *m*, poción *f*

potluck ['pɑt,lʌk] *n* **to take potluck** : tomar lo que haya

potpourri [,po:pu'ri:] *n* : popurrí *m*

potshot ['pɑt,ʃɑt] *n* **1** : tiro *m* al azar ⟨to take potshots at : disparar al azar a⟩ **2** CRITICISM : crítica *f* (hecha al azar)

potter ['pɑtər] *n* : alfarero *m*, -ra *f*

pottery ['pɑtəri] *n, pl* **-teries** : cerámica *f*

pouch ['paʊtʃ] *n* **1** BAG : bolsa *f* pequeña **2** : bolsa *f* (de un animal)

poultice ['po:ltəs] *n* : emplasto *m*, cataplasma *f*

poultry ['po:ltri] *n* : aves *fpl* de corral

pounce ['paʊnts] *vi* **pounced; pouncing** : abalanzarse

pound¹ ['paʊnd] *vt* **1** CRUSH : machacar, machucar, majar **2** BEAT : golpear, machacar ⟨she pounded the lessons into them : les machacaba las lecciones⟩ ⟨he pounded home his point : les hizo entender su razonamiento⟩ — *vi* **1** BEAT : palpitar (dícese del corazón) **2** RESOUND : retumbar, resonar **3** : andar con paso pesado ⟨we pounded through the mud : caminamos pesadamente por el barro⟩

pound² *n* **1** : libra *f* (unidad de peso) **2** : libra *f* (unidad monetaria) **3 dog pound** : perrera *f*

pour ['por] *vt* **1** : echar, verter, servir (bebidas) ⟨pour it into a pot : viértalo en una olla⟩ **2** : proveer con abundancia ⟨they poured money into it : le invirtieron mucho dinero⟩ **3 to pour out** : dar salida a ⟨he poured out his feelings to her : se desahogó con ella⟩ — *vi* **1** FLOW : manar, fluir, salir ⟨blood was pouring from the wound : la sangre le salía de la herida⟩ **2 it's pouring (outside)** : está lloviendo a cántaros

pout¹ ['paʊt] *vi* : hacer pucheros

pout² *n* : puchero *m*

poverty ['pɑvərti] *n* : pobreza *f*, indigencia *f*

powder¹ ['paʊdər] *vt* **1** : empolvar ⟨to powder one's face : empolvarse la cara⟩ **2** PULVERIZE : pulverizar

powder² *n* : polvo *m*, polvos *mpl*

powdery ['paʊdəri] *adj* : polvoriento, como polvo

power¹ ['paʊər] *vt* : impulsar, propulsar

power² *n* **1** AUTHORITY : poder *m*, autoridad *f* ⟨executive powers : poderes ejecutivos⟩ **2** ABILITY : capacidad *f*, poder *m* **3** : potencia *f* (política) ⟨foreign powers : potencias extranjeras⟩ **4** STRENGTH : fuerza *f* **5** : potencia *f* (en física y matemáticas)

powerful ['paʊərfəl] *adj* : poderoso, potente — **powerfully** *adv*

powerhouse ['paʊər,haʊs] *n* : persona *f* dinámica

powerless ['paʊərləs] *adj* : impotente

power plant *n* : central *f* eléctrica

powwow ['paʊ,waʊ] *n* : conferencia *f*

pox ['pɑks] *n, pl* **pox** *or* **poxes 1** CHICKEN POX : varicela *f* **2** SYPHILIS : sífilis *f*

practicable ['præktɪkəbəl] *adj* : practicable, viable, factible

practical ['præktɪkəl] *adj* : práctico

practicality [,præktɪ'kæləti] *n, pl* **-ties** : factibilidad *f*, viabilidad *f*

practical joke *n* : broma *f* (pesada)

practically ['præktɪkli] *adv* **1** : de manera práctica **2** ALMOST : casi, prácticamente

practice¹ *or* **practise** ['præktəs] *vt* **-ticed** *or* **-tised; -ticing** *or* **-tising 1** : practicar ⟨he practiced his German on us : practicó el alemán con nosotros⟩ ⟨to practice politeness : practicar la cortesía⟩ **2** : ejercer ⟨to practice medicine : ejercer la medicina⟩

practice² *n* **1** USE : práctica *f* ⟨to put into practice : poner en práctica⟩ **2** CUSTOM : costumbre *f* ⟨it's a common practice here : por aquí se acostumbra hacerlo⟩ **3** TRAINING : práctica *f* **4** : ejercicio *m* (de una profesión)

practitioner [præk'tɪʃənər] *n* **1** : profesional *mf* **2 general practitioner** : médico *m*, -ca *f*

pragmatic [præg'mætɪk] *adj* : pragmático — **pragmatically** *adv*

pragmatism ['prægmə,tɪzəm] *n* : pragmatismo

prairie ['prɛri] *n* : pradera *f*, llanura *f*

praise[1] ['preɪz] *vt* **praised; praising** : elogiar, alabar ⟨to praise God : alabar a Dios⟩

praise[2] *n* : elogio *m*, alabanza *f*

praiseworthy ['preɪz,wərði] *adj* : digno de alabanza, loable

prance[1] ['prænʦ] *vi* **pranced; prancing** 1 : hacer cabriolas, cabriolar ⟨a prancing horse : un caballo haciendo cabriolas⟩ 2 SWAGGER : pavonearse

prance[2] *n* : cabriola *f*

prank ['præŋk] *n* : broma *f*, travesura *f*

prankster ['præŋkstər] *n* : bromista *mf*

prattle[1] ['prætəl] *vt* **-tled; -tling** : parlotear *fam*, cotorrear *fam*, balbucear (como un niño)

prattle[2] *n* : parloteo *m fam*, cotorreo *m fam*, cháchara *f fam*

prawn ['prɔn] *n* : langostino *m*, camarón *m*, gamba *f*

pray ['preɪ] *vt* ENTREAT : rogar, suplicar — *vi* : rezar

prayer ['prɛr] *n* 1 : plegaria *f*, oración *f* ⟨to say one's prayers : orar, rezar⟩ 2 PRAYING : rezo *m*, oración *f* ⟨to kneel in prayer : arrodillarse para rezar⟩

praying mantis → **mantis**

preach ['priːʧ] *vi* : predicar — *vt* ADVOCATE : abogar por ⟨to preach cooperation : promover la cooperación⟩

preacher ['priːʧər] *n* 1 : predicador *m*, -dora *f* 2 MINISTER : pastor *m*, -tora *f*

preamble ['priː,æmbəl] *n* : preámbulo *m*

prearrange [,priːə'reɪnʤ] *vt* **-ranged; -ranging** : arreglar de antemano

precarious [prɪ'kæriəs] *adj* : precario — **precariously** *adv*

precariousness [prɪ'kæriəsnəs] *n* : precariedad *f*

precaution [prɪ'kɔʃən] *n* : precaución *f*

precautionary [prɪ'kɔʃə,neri] *adj* : preventivo, cautelar, precautorio

precede [prɪ'siːd] *v* **-ceded; -ceding** : preceder a

precedence ['prɛsədənʦ, prɪ'siːdənʦ] *n* : precedencia *f*

precedent ['prɛsədənt] *n* : precedente *m*

precept ['priː,sɛpt] *n* : precepto *m*

precinct ['priː,sɪŋkt] *n* 1 DISTRICT : distrito *m* (policial, electoral, etc.) 2 **precincts** *npl* PREMISES : recinto *m*, predio *m*, límites *mpl* (de una ciudad)

precious ['prɛʃəs] *adj* 1 : precioso ⟨precious gems : piedras preciosas⟩ 2 DEAR : querido 3 AFFECTED : afectado

precipice ['prɛsəpəs] *n* : precipicio *m*

precipitate [prɪ'sɪpə,teɪt] *v* **-tated; -tating** *vt* 1 HASTEN, PROVOKE : precipitar, provocar 2 HURL : arrojar 3 : precipitar (en química) — *vi* : precipitarse (en química), condensarse (en meteorología)

precipitation [prɪ,sɪpə'teɪʃən] *n* 1 HASTE : precipitación *f*, prisa *f* 2 : precipitaciones *fpl* (en meteorología)

precipitous [prɪ'sɪpəʦs] *adj* 1 HASTY, RASH : precipitado 2 STEEP : escarpado, empinado ⟨a precipitous drop : una caída vertiginosa⟩

précis [preɪ'siː] *n, pl* **précis** [-'siːz] : resumen *m*

precise [prɪ'saɪs] *adj* 1 DEFINITE : preciso, explícito 2 EXACT : exacto, preciso ⟨precise calculations : cálculos precisos⟩ — **precisely** *adv*

preciseness [prɪ'saɪsnəs] *n* : precisión *f*, exactitud *f*

precision [prɪ'sɪʒən] *n* : precisión *f*

preclude [prɪ'kluːd] *vt* **-cluded; -cluding** : evitar, impedir, excluir (una posibilidad, etc.)

precocious [prɪ'koːʃəs] *adj* : precoz — **precociously** *adv*

precocity [prɪ'kɑsəti] *n* : precocidad *f*

preconceive [,priːkən'siːv] *vt* **-ceived; -ceiving** : preconcebir

preconception [,priːkən'spʃən] *n* : idea *f* preconcebida

precondition [,priːkən'dɪʃən] *n* : precondición *f*, condición *f* previa

precook [,priː'kʊk] *vt* : precocinar

precursor [prɪ'kərsər] *n* : precursor *m*, -sora *f*

predator ['prɛdətər] *n* : depredador *m*, -dora *f*

predatory ['prɛdə,tori] *adj* : depredador

predecessor ['prɛdə,sɛsər, 'priː-] *n* : antecesor *m*, -sora *f*; predecesor *m*, -sora *f*

predestination [pri,dɛstə'neɪʃən] *n* : predestinación *f*

predestine [prɪ'dɛstən] *vt* **-tined; -tining** : predestinar

predetermine [,priːdɪ'tərmən] *vt* **-mined; -mining** : predeterminar

predicament [prɪ'dɪkəmənt] *n* : apuro *m*, aprieto *m*

predicate[1] ['prɛdə,keɪt] *vt* **-cated; -cating** 1 AFFIRM : afirmar, aseverar 2 **to be predicated on** : estar basado en

predicate[2] ['prɛdɪkət] *n* : predicado *m*

predict [prɪ'dɪkt] *vt* : pronosticar, predecir

predictable [prɪ'dɪktəbəl] *adj* : previsible — **predictably** [-bli] *adv*

prediction [prɪ'dɪkʃən] *n* : pronóstico *m*, predicción *f*

predilection [,prɛdəl'ɛkʃən, ,priː-] *n* : predilección *f*

predispose [,priːdɪ'spoːz] *vt* **-posed; -posing** : predisponer

predisposition [,priː,dɪspə'zɪʃən] *n* : predisposición *f*

predominance [prɪ'dɑmənənʦ] *n* : predominio *m*

predominant [prɪ'dɑmənənt] *adj* : predominante — **predominantly** *adv*

predominate [prɪ'dɑmə,neɪt] *vi* **-nated; -nating** 1 : predominar (en cantidad) 2 PREVAIL : prevalecer

preeminence [prɪ'ɛmənənʦ] *n* : preeminencia *f*

preeminent [prɪ'ɛmənənt] *adj* : preeminente

preeminently [prɪ'ɛmənəntli] *adv* : especialmente

preempt [pri'ɛmpt] vt 1 APPROPRIATE : apoderarse de, apropiarse de 2 : reemplazar (un programa de televisión, etc.) 3 FORESTALL : adelantarse a (un ataque, etc.)

preen ['pri:n] vt : arreglarse (el pelo, las plumas, etc.)

prefabricated [ˌpri:'fæbrəˌkeɪtəd] adj : prefabricado

preface ['prɛfəs] n : prefacio m, prólogo m

prefatory ['prɛfəˌtori] adj : preliminar

prefer [pri'fər] vt -ferred; -ferring 1 : preferir ⟨I prefer coffee : prefiero café⟩ 2 to prefer charges against : presentar cargos contra

preferable ['prɛfərəbəl] adj : preferible

preferably ['prɛfərəbli] adv : preferentemente, de preferencia

preference ['prɛfrənts, 'prɛfər-] n : preferencia f, gusto m

preferential [ˌprɛfə'rɛntʃəl] adj : preferencial, preferente

prefigure [pri'fɪɡjər] vt -ured; -uring FORESHADOW : prefigurar, anunciar

prefix ['pri:ˌfɪks] n : prefijo m

pregnancy ['prɛɡnəntsi] n, pl -cies : embarazo m, preñez f

pregnant ['prɛɡnənt] adj 1 : embarazada (dícese de una mujer), preñada (dícese de un animal) 2 MEANINGFUL : significativo

preheat [ˌpri:'hi:t] vt : precalentar

prehensile [pri'hɛntsəl, -'hɛnˌsaɪl] adj : prensil

prehistoric [ˌpri:hɪs'tɔrɪk] or **prehistorical** [-ɪkəl] adj : prehistórico

prejudge [ˌpri:'dʒʌdʒ] vt -judged; -judging : prejuzgar

prejudice[1] ['prɛdʒədəs] vt -diced; -dicing 1 DAMAGE : perjudicar 2 BIAS : predisponer, influir en

prejudice[2] n 1 DAMAGE : perjuicio m (en derecho) 2 BIAS : prejuicio m

prelate ['prɛlət] n : prelado m

preliminary[1] [pri'lɪməˌnɛri] adj : preliminar

preliminary[2] n, pl -naries 1 : preámbulo m, preludio m 2 preliminaries npl : preliminares mpl

prelude ['prɛˌlu:d, 'prɛlˌju:d; 'preɪˌlu:d, 'pri:-] n : preludio m

premarital [ˌpri:'mærətəl] adj : prematrimonial

premature [ˌpri:mə'tur, -'tjur, -'tʃur] adj : prematuro — **prematurely** adv

premeditate [pri'mɛdəˌteɪt] vt -tated; -tating : premeditar

premeditation [priˌmɛdə'teɪʃən] n : premeditación f

premenstrual [pri'mɛntstruəl] adj : premenstrual

premier[1] [pri'mɪr, -'mjɪr; 'pri:miər] adj : principal

premier[2] n PRIME MINISTER : primer ministro m, primera ministra f

premiere[1] [prɪ'mjɛr, -'mɪr] vt -miered; -miering : estrenar

premiere[2] n : estreno m

premise ['prɛmɪs] n 1 : premisa f ⟨the premise of his arguments : la premisa de sus argumentos⟩ 2 premises npl : recinto m, local m

premium ['pri:miəm] n 1 BONUS : prima f 2 SURCHARGE : recargo m ⟨to sell at a premium : vender (algo) muy caro⟩ 3 insurance premium : prima f (de seguros) 4 to set a premium on : darle un gran valor (a algo)

premonition [ˌpri:mə'nɪʃən, ˌprɛmə-] n : presentimiento m, premonición f

prenatal [ˌpri:'neɪtəl] adj : prenatal

preoccupation [priˌakjə'peɪʃən] n : preocupación f

preoccupied [pri'akjəˌpaɪd] adj : abstraído, ensimismado, preocupado

preoccupy [pri'akjəˌpaɪ] vt -pied; -pying : preocupar

preparation [ˌprɛpə'reɪʃən] n 1 PREPARING : preparación f 2 MIXTURE : preparado m ⟨a preparation for burns : un preparado para quemaduras⟩ 3 preparations npl ARRANGEMENTS : preparativos mpl

preparatory [pri'pærəˌtori] adj : preparatorio

prepare [pri'pær] v -pared; -paring vt : preparar — vi : prepararse

prepay [ˌpri:'peɪ] vt -paid; -paying : pagar por adelantado

preponderance [pri'pandərənts] n : preponderancia f

preponderant [pri'pandərənt] adj : preponderante — **preponderantly** adv

preposition [ˌprɛpə'zɪʃən] n : preposición f

prepositional [ˌprɛpə'zɪʃənəl] adj : preposicional

prepossessing [ˌpri:pə'zɛsɪŋ] adj : atractivo, agradable

preposterous [pri'pastərəs] adj : absurdo, ridículo

prerequisite[1] [pri'rɛkwəzət] adj : necesario, esencial

prerequisite[2] n : condición f necesario, requisito m previo

prerogative [pri'ragəṭɪv] n : prerrogativa f

presage ['prɛsɪdʒ, pri'seɪdʒ] vt -saged; -saging : presagiar

preschool ['pri:ˌsku:l] adj : preescolar ⟨preschool students : estudiantes de preescolar⟩

prescribe [pri'skraɪb] vt -scribed; -scribing 1 ORDAIN : prescribir, ordenar 2 : recetar (medicinas, etc.)

prescription [pri'skrɪpʃən] n : receta f

presence ['prɛzənts] n : presencia f

present[1] [pri'zɛnt] vt 1 INTRODUCE : presentar ⟨to present oneself : presentarse⟩ 2 : presentar (una obra de teatro, etc.) 3 GIVE : entregar (un regalo, etc.), regalar, obsequiar 4 SHOW : presentar, ofrecer ⟨it presents a lovely view : ofrece una vista muy linda⟩

present[2] ['prɛzənt] adj 1 : actual ⟨present conditions : condiciones actuales⟩

2 : presente ⟨all the students were present : todos los estudiantes estaban presentes⟩

present³ ['prɛzənt] *n* **1** GIFT : regalo *m*, obsequio *m* **2** : presente *m* ⟨at present : en este momento⟩ **3** *or* **present tense** : presente *m*

presentable [pri'zɛntəbəl] *adj* : presentable

presentation [ˌpriːˌzɛn'teɪʃən, ˌprɛzən-] *n* : presentación *f* ⟨presentation ceremony : ceremonia de entrega⟩

presentiment [pri'zɛntəmənt] *n* : presentimiento *m*, premonición *f*

presently ['prɛzəntli] *adv* **1** SOON : pronto, dentro de poco **2** NOW : actualmente, ahora

present participle *n* : participio *m* presente, participio *m* activo

preservation [ˌprɛzər'veɪʃən] *n* : conservación *f*, preservación *f*

preservative [pri'zərvəṭɪv] *n* : conservante *m*

preserve¹ [pri'zərv] *vt* **-served; -serving 1** PROTECT : proteger, preservar **2** : conservar (los alimentos, etc.) **3** MAINTAIN : conservar, mantener

preserve² *n* **1** *or* **preserves** *npl* : conserva *f* ⟨peach preserves : duraznos en conserva⟩ **2** : coto *m* ⟨game preserve : coto de caza⟩

preside [pri'zaɪd] *vi* **-sided; -siding 1 to preside over** : presidir ⟨he presided over the meeting : presidió la reunión⟩ **2 to preside over** : supervisar ⟨she presides over the department : dirige el departamento⟩

presidency ['prɛzədəntsi] *n, pl* **-cies** : presidencia *f*

president ['prɛzədənt] *n* : presidente *m*, -ta *f*

presidential [ˌprɛzə'dɛntʃəl] *adj* : presidencial

press¹ ['prɛs] *vt* **1** PUSH : apretar **2** SQUEEZE : apretar, prensar (frutas, flores, etc.) **3** IRON : planchar (ropa) **4** URGE : instar, apremiar ⟨he pressed me to come : insistió en que viniera⟩ — *vi* **1** PUSH : apretar ⟨press hard : aprieta con fuerza⟩ **2** CROWD : apiñarse **3** : abrirse paso ⟨I pressed through the crowd : me abrí paso entre el gentío⟩ **4** URGE : presionar

press² *n* **1** CROWD : multitud *f* **2** : imprenta *f*, prensa *f* ⟨to go to press : entrar en prensa⟩ **3** URGENCY : urgencia *f*, prisa *f* **4** PRINTER, PUBLISHER : imprenta *f*, editorial *f* **5 the press** : la prensa ⟨freedom of the press : libertad de prensa⟩

pressing ['prɛsɪŋ] *adj* URGENT : urgente

pressure¹ ['prɛʃər] *vt* **-sured; -suring** : presionar, apremiar

pressure² *n* **1** : presión *f* ⟨to be under pressure : estar bajo presión⟩ **2** → **blood pressure**

pressurize ['prɛʃəˌraɪz] *vt* **-ized; -izing** : presurizar

prestige [prɛ'stiːʒ, -'stiːdʒ] *n* : prestigio *m*

prestigious [prɛ'stɪdʒəs] *adj* : prestigioso

presto ['prɛsˌtoː] *adv* : de pronto

presumably [pri'zuːməbli] *adv* : es de suponer, supuestamente ⟨presumably, he's guilty : supone que es culpable⟩

presume [pri'zuːm] *vt* **-sumed; -suming 1** ASSUME, SUPPOSE : suponer, asumir, presumir **2 to presume to** : atreverse a, osar

presumption [pri'zʌmpʃən] *n* **1** AUDACITY : atrevimiento *m*, osadía *f* **2** ASSUMPTION : presunción *f*, suposición *f*

presumptuous [pri'zʌmptʃuəs] *adj* : descarado, atrevido

presuppose [ˌpriːsə'poːz] *vt* **-posed; -posing** : presuponer

pretend [pri'tɛnd] *vt* **1** CLAIM : pretender **2** FEIGN : fingir, simular — *vi* : fingir

pretender [pri'tɛndər] *n* : pretendiente *mf* (al trono, etc.)

pretense *or* **pretence** ['priːˌtɛnts, pri'tɛnts] *n* **1** CLAIM : afirmación *f* (falsa), pretensión *f* **2** FEIGNING : fingimiento *m*, simulación *f* ⟨to make a pretense of doing something : fingir hacer algo⟩ ⟨a pretense of order : una apariencia de orden⟩ **3** PRETEXT : pretexto *m* ⟨under false pretenses : con pretextos falsos, de manera fraudulenta⟩

pretension [pri'tɛntʃən] *n* **1** CLAIM : pretensión *f*, afirmación *f* **2** ASPIRATION : aspiración *f*, ambición *f* **3** PRETENTIOUSNESS : pretensiones *fpl*, presunción *f*

pretentious [pri'tɛntʃəs] *adj* : pretencioso

pretentiousness [pri'tɛntʃəsnəs] *n* : presunción *f*, pretensiones *fpl*

pretext ['priːˌtɛkst] *n* : pretexto *m*, excusa *f*

prettily ['prɪṭəli] *adv* : atractivamente

prettiness ['prɪṭinəs] *n* : lindeza *f*

pretty¹ ['prɪṭi] *adv* : bastante, bien ⟨it's pretty obvious : está bien claro⟩ ⟨it's pretty much the same : es más o menos igual⟩

pretty² *adj* **-tier; -est** : bonito, lindo, guapo ⟨a pretty girl : una muchacha guapa⟩ ⟨what a pretty dress! : ¡qué vestido más lindo!⟩

pretzel ['prɛtsəl] *n* : galleta *f* salada (en forma de nudo)

prevail [pri'veɪl] *vi* **1** TRIUMPH : prevalecer **2** PREDOMINATE : predominar **3 to prevail upon** : persuadir, convencer ⟨I prevailed upon her to sing : la convencí para que cantara⟩

prevailing [pri'veɪlɪŋ] *adj* : imperante, prevaleciente

prevalence ['prɛvələnts] *n* : preponderancia *f*, predominio *m*

prevalent ['prɛvələnt] *adj* **1** COMMON : común y corriente, general **2** WIDESPREAD : extendido

prevaricate [pri'værə‚keɪt] *vi* **-cated; -cating** LIE : mentir
prevarication [pri‚værə'keɪʃən] *n* : mentira *f*
prevent [pri'vɛnt] *vt* **1** AVOID : prevenir, evitar ⟨steps to prevent war : medidas para evitar la guerra⟩ **2** HINDER : impedir
preventable [pri'vɛntəbəl] *adj* : evitable
preventative [pri'vɛntətɪv] → **preventive**
prevention [pri'vɛnʃən] *n* : prevención *f*
preventive [pri'vɛntɪv] *adj* : preventivo
preview ['pri:‚vju] *n* : preestreno *m*
previous ['pri:viəs] *adj* : previo, anterior ⟨previous knowledge : conocimientos previos⟩ ⟨the previous day : el día anterior⟩ ⟨in the previous year : en el año pasado⟩
previously ['pri:viəsli] *adv* : antes
prewar [‚pri:'wɔr] *adj* : de antes de la guerra
prey ['preɪ] *n, pl* **preys** : presa *f*
prey on *vt* **1** : cazar, alimentarse de ⟨it preys on fish : se alimenta de peces⟩ **2 to prey on one's mind** : hacer presa en alguien, atormentar a alguien
price¹ ['praɪs] *vt* **priced; pricing** : poner un precio a
price² *n* : precio *m* ⟨peace at any price : la paz a toda costa⟩
priceless ['praɪsləs] *adj* : inestimable, inapreciable
pricey ['praɪsi] *adj* : caro
prick¹ ['prɪk] *vt* **1** : pinchar **2 to prick up one's ears** : levantar las orejas — *vi* : pinchar
prick² *n* **1** STAB : pinchazo *m* ⟨a prick of conscience : un remordimiento⟩ **2** → **pricker**
pricker ['prɪkər] *n* THORN : espina *f*
prickle¹ ['prɪkəl] *vi* **-led; -ling** : sentir un cosquilleo, tener un hormigueo
prickle² *n* **1** : espina *f* (de una planta) **2** TINGLE : cosquilleo *m*, hormigueo *m*
prickly ['prɪkəli] *adj* **1** THORNY : espinoso **2** : que pica ⟨a prickly sensation : un hormigueo⟩
prickly pear *n* : tuna *f*
pride¹ ['praɪd] *vt* **prided; priding** : estar orgulloso de ⟨to pride oneself on : preciarse de, enorgullecerse de⟩
pride² *n* : orgullo *m*
priest ['pri:st] *n* : sacerdote *m*, cura *m*
priestess ['pri:stɪs] *n* : sacerdotisa *f*
priesthood ['pri:st‚hʊd] *n* : sacerdocio *m*
priestly ['pri:stli] *adj* : sacerdotal
prig ['prɪg] *n* : mojigato *m*, -ta *f*; gazmoño *m*, -ña *f*
prim ['prɪm] *adj* **primmer; primmest 1** PRISSY : remilgado **2** PRUDISH : mojigato, gazmoño
primarily [praɪ'mɛrəli] *adv* : principalmente, fundamentalmente
primary¹ ['praɪ‚mɛri, 'praɪməri] *adj* **1** FIRST : primario **2** PRINCIPAL : principal **3** BASIC : fundamental

primary² *n, pl* **-ries** : elección *f* primaria
primary color *n* : color *m* primario
primary school → **elementary school**
primate *n* **1** ['praɪ‚meɪt, -mət] : primado *m* (obispo) **2** [-‚meɪt] : primate *m* (animal)
prime¹ ['praɪm] *vt* **primed; priming 1** : cebar ⟨to prime a pump : cebar una bomba⟩ **2** PREPARE : preparar (una superficie para pintar) **3** COACH : preparar (a un testigo, etc.)
prime² *adj* **1** CHIEF, MAIN : principal, primero **2** EXCELLENT : de primera (categoría), excelente
prime³ *n* **the prime of one's life** : la flor de la vida
prime minister *n* : primer ministro *m*, primera ministra *f*
primer¹ ['prɪmər] *n* **1** READER : cartilla *f* **2** MANUAL : manual *m*
primer² ['praɪmər] *n* **1** : cebo *m* (para explosivos) **2** : base *f* (de pintura)
prime time *n* : horas *fpl* de mayor audiencia
primeval [praɪ'mi:vəl] *adj* : primitivo, primigenio
primitive ['prɪmətɪv] *adj* : primitivo
primly ['prɪmli] *adv* : mojigatamente
primness ['prɪmnəs] *n* : mojigatería *f*, gazmoñería *f*
primordial [praɪ'mɔrdiəl] *adj* : primordial, fundamental
primp ['prɪmp] *vi* : arreglarse, acicalarse
primrose ['prɪm‚ro:z] *n* : primavera *f*, prímula *f*
prince ['prɪnts] *n* : príncipe *m*
princely ['prɪntsli] *adj* : principesco
princess ['prɪntsəs, 'prɪn‚sɛs] *n* : princesa *f*
principal¹ ['prɪntsəpəl] *adj* : principal — **principally** *adv*
principal² *n* **1** PROTAGONIST : protagonista *mf* **2** : director *m*, -tora *f* (de una escuela) **3** CAPITAL : principal *m*, capital *m* (en finanzas)
principality [‚prɪntsə'pæləti] *n, pl* **-ties** : principado *m*
principle ['prɪntsəpəl] *n* : principio *m*
print¹ ['prɪnt] *vt* : imprimir (libros, etc.) — *vi* : escribir con letra de molde
print² *n* **1** IMPRESSION : marca *f*, huella *f*, impresión *f* **2** : texto *m* impreso ⟨to be out of print : estar agotado⟩ **3** LETTERING : letra *f* **4** ENGRAVING : grabado *m* **5** : copia *f* (en fotografía) **6** : estampado *m* (de tela)
printer ['prɪntər] *n* **1** : impresor *m*, -sora *f* (persona) **2** : impresora *f* (máquina)
printing ['prɪntɪŋ] *n* **1** : impresión *f* (acto) ⟨the third printing : la tercera tirada⟩ **2** : imprenta *f* (profesión) **3** LETTERING : letras *fpl* de molde
printing press *n* : prensa *f*
print out *vt* : imprimir (de una computadora)
printout ['prɪnt‚aʊt] *n* : copia *f* impresa (de una computadora)
prior ['praɪər] *adj* **1** : previo **2 prior to** : antes de

priority [praɪˈɔrəti] *n, pl* **-ties** : prioridad *f*

priory [ˈpraɪəri] *n, pl* **-ries** : priorato *m*

prism [ˈprɪzəm] *n* : prisma *m*

prison [ˈprɪzən] *n* : prisión *f*, cárcel *f*

prisoner [ˈprɪzənər] *n* : preso *m*, -sa *f*; recluso *m*, -sa *f* ⟨prisoner of war : prisionero de guerra⟩

prissy [ˈprɪsi] *adj* **-sier; -est** : remilgado, melindroso

pristine [ˈprɪsˌtiːn, prɪsˈ-] *adj* : puro, prístino

privacy [ˈpraɪvəsi] *n, pl* **-cies** : privacidad *f*

private[1] [ˈpraɪvət] *adj* **1** PERSONAL : privado, particular ⟨private property : propiedad privada⟩ **2** INDEPENDENT : privado, independiente ⟨private studies : estudios privados⟩ **3** SECRET : secreto **4** SECLUDED : aislado, privado — **privately** *adv*

private[2] *n* : soldado *m* raso

privateer [ˌpraɪvəˈtɪr] *n* : corsario *m*

privation [praɪˈveɪʃən] *n* : privación *f*

privilege [ˈprɪvlɪʤ, ˈprɪvə-] *n* : privilegio *m*

privileged [ˈprɪvlɪʤd, ˈprɪvə-] *adj* : privilegiado

privy[1] [ˈprɪvi] *adj* **to be privy to** : estar enterado de

privy[2] *n, pl* **privies** : excusado *m*, retrete *m* (exterior)

prize[1] [ˈpraɪz] *vt* **prized; prizing** : valorar, apreciar

prize[2] *adj* **1** : premiado ⟨a prize stallion : un semental premiado⟩ **2** OUTSTANDING : de primera, excepcional

prize[3] *n* **1** AWARD : premio *m* ⟨third prize : el tercer premio⟩ **2** : joya *f*, tesoro *m* ⟨he's a real prize : es un tesoro⟩

prizefighter [ˈpraɪzˌfaɪtər] *n* : boxeador *m*, -dora *f* profesional

prizewinning [ˈpraɪzˌwɪnɪŋ] *adj* : premiado

pro[1] [ˈproː] *adv* : a favor

pro[2] *adj* → **professional**[1]

pro[3] *n* **1** : pro *m* ⟨the pros and cons : los pros y los contras⟩ **2** → **professional**[2]

probability [ˌprɑbəˈbɪləti] *n, pl* **-ties** : probabilidad *f*

probable [ˈprɑbəbəl] *adj* : probable — **probably** [-bli] *adv*

probate[1] [ˈproːˌbeɪt] *vt* **-bated; -bating** : autenticar (un testamento)

probate[2] *n* : autenticación *f* (de un testamento)

probation [proˈbeɪʃən] *n* **1** : período *m* de prueba (para un empleado, etc.) **2** : libertad *f* condicional (para un preso)

probationary [proˈbeɪʃəˌnɛri] *adj* : de prueba

probe[1] [ˈproːb] *vt* **probed; probing 1** : sondar (en medicina y tecnología) **2** INVESTIGATE : investigar, sondear

probe[2] *n* **1** : sonda *f* (en medicina, etc.) ⟨space probe : sonda espacial⟩ **2** INVESTIGATION : investigación *f*, sondeo *m*

probity [ˈproːbəti] *n* : probidad *f*

problem[1] [ˈprɑbləm] *adj* : difícil

problem[2] *n* : problema *m*

problematic [ˌprɑbləˈmætɪk] *or* **problematical** [-tɪkəl] *adj* : problemático

proboscis [prəˈbɑsɪs] *n, pl* **-cises** *also* **-cides** [-səˌdiːz] : probóscide *f*

procedural [prəˈsiːʤərəl] *adj* : de procedimiento

procedure [prəˈsiːʤər] *n* : procedimiento *m* ⟨administrative procedures : trámites administrativos⟩

proceed [proˈsiːd] *vi* **1** : proceder ⟨to proceed to do something : proceder a hacer algo⟩ **2** CONTINUE : continuar, proseguir, seguir ⟨he proceeded to the next phase : pasó a la segunda fase⟩ **3** ADVANCE : avanzar ⟨as the conference proceeded : mientras seguía avanzando la conferencia⟩ ⟨the road proceeds south : la calle sigue hacia el sur⟩

proceeding [proˈsiːdɪŋ] *n* **1** PROCEDURE : procedimiento *m* **2 proceedings** *npl* EVENTS : acontecimientos *mpl* **3 proceedings** *npl* MINUTES : actas *fpl* (de una reunión, etc.)

proceeds [ˈproːˌsiːdz] *npl* : ganancias *fpl*

process[1] [ˈprɑˌsɛs, ˈproː-] *vt* : procesar, tratar

process[2] *n, pl* **-cesses** [ˈprɑˌsɛsəz, ˈproː-, -səz, -səˌsiːz] **1** : proceso *m* ⟨the process of elimination : el proceso de eliminación⟩ **2** METHOD : proceso *m*, método *m* ⟨manufacturing processes : procesos industriales⟩ **3** : acción *f* judicial ⟨due process of law : el debido proceso (de la ley)⟩ **4** SUMMONS : citación *f* **5** PROJECTION : protuberancia *f* (anatómica) **6 in the process of** : en vías de ⟨in the process of repair : en reparaciones⟩

procession [prəˈsɛʃən] *n* : procesión *f*, desfile *m* ⟨a funeral procession : un cortejo fúnebre⟩

processional [prəˈsɛʃənəl] *n* : himno *m* para una procesión

processor [ˈprɑˌsɛsər, ˈproː-, -səsər] *n* **1** : procesador *m* (de una computadora) **2 food processor** : procesador *m* de alimentos

proclaim [proˈkleɪm] *vt* : proclamar

proclamation [ˌprɑkləˈmeɪʃən] *n* : proclamación *f*

proclivity [proˈklɪvəti] *n, pl* **-ties** : proclividad *f*

procrastinate [prəˈkræstəˌneɪt] *vi* **-nated; -nating** : demorar, aplazar las responsabilidades

procrastination [prəˌkræstəˈneɪʃən] *n* : aplazamiento *m*, demora *f*, dilación *f*

procreate [ˈproːkriˌeɪt] *vi* **-ated; -ating** : procrear

procreation [ˌproːkriˈeɪʃən] *n* : procreación *f*

proctor[1] [ˈprɑktər] *vt* : supervisar (un examen)

proctor[2] *n* : supervisor *m*, -sora *f* (de un examen)

procure [prə'kjʊr] *vt* **-cured; -curing 1**
OBTAIN : procurar, obtener **2** BRING
ABOUT : provocar, lograr, conseguir
procurement [prə'kjʊrmənt] *n* : obtención *f*
prod¹ ['prɑd] *vt* **prodded; prodding 1**
JAB, POKE : pinchar, golpear (con la
punta de algo) **2** GOAD : incitar, estimular
prod² *n* **1** JAB, POKE : golpe *m* (con la
punta de algo), pinchazo *m* **2** STIMU-
LUS : estímulo *m* **3 cattle prod** : picana
f, aguijón *m*
prodigal¹ ['prɑdɪgəl] *adj* SPENDTHRIFT
: pródigo, despilfarrador, derrochador
prodigal² *n* : pródigo *m*, -ga *f*; derrochador *m*, -dora *f*
prodigious [prə'dɪdʒəs] *adj* **1** MAR-
VELOUS : prodigioso, maravilloso **2**
HUGE : enorme, vasto ⟨prodigious
sums : muchísimo dinero⟩ — **prodi-
giously** *adv*
prodigy ['prɑdədʒi] *n, pl* **-gies** : prodigio
m ⟨child prodigy : niño prodigio⟩
produce¹ [prə'du:s, -'dju:s] *vt* **-duced;
-ducing 1** EXHIBIT : presentar,
mostrar **2** YIELD : producir **3** CAUSE
: producir, causar **4** CREATE : producir
⟨to produce a poem : escribir un poe-
ma⟩ **5** : poner en escena (una obra de
teatro), producir (una película)
produce² ['prɑ,du:s, 'pro:-, -,dju:s] *n*
· : productos *mpl* agrícolas
producer [prə'du:sər, -'dju:-] *n* : productor *m*, -tora *f*
product ['prɑ,dʌkt] *n* : producto *m*
production [prə'dʌkʃən] *n* : producción
f
productive [prə'dʌktɪv] *adj* : productivo
productivity [,pro:,dʌk'tɪvəti, ,prɑ-] *n*
: productividad *f*
profane¹ [pro'feɪn] *vt* **-faned; -faning**
: profanar
profane² *adj* **1** SECULAR : profano **2** IR-
REVERENT : irreverente, impío
profanity [pro'fænəti] *n, pl* **-ties 1** IR-
REVERENCE : irreverencia *f*, impiedad
f **2** : blasfemias *fpl*, obscenidades *fpl*
⟨don't use profanity : no digas blas-
femias⟩
profess [prə'fɛs] *vt* **1** DECLARE : declarar, manifestar **2** CLAIM : pretender
3 : profesar (una religión, etc.)
professedly [prə'fɛsədli] *adv* **1** OPENLY
: declaradamente **2** ALLEGEDLY
: supuestamente
profession [prə'fɛʃən] *n* : profesión *f*
professional¹ [prə'fɛʃənəl] *adj* : profesional — **professionally** *adv*
professional² *n* : profesional *mf*
professionalism [prə'fɛʃənə,lizəm] *n*
: profesionalismo *m*
professor [prə'fɛsər] *n* : profesor *m* (universitario), profesora *f* (universitaria);
catedrático *m*, -ca *f*
proffer ['prɑfər] *vt* **-fered; -fering** : ofrecer, dar

proficiency [prə'fɪʃəntsi] *n* : competencia *f*, capacidad *f*
proficient [prə'fɪʃənt] *adj* : competente,
experto — **proficiently** *adv*
profile ['pro:,faɪl] *n* : perfil *m* ⟨a portrait
in profile : un retrato de perfil⟩ ⟨to
keep a low profile : no llamar la atención, hacerse pasar desapercibido⟩
profit¹ ['prɑfət] *vi* : sacar provecho (de),
beneficiarse (de)
profit² *n* **1** ADVANTAGE : provecho *m*,
partido *m*, beneficio *m* **2** GAIN : beneficio *m*, utilidad *f*, ganancia *f* ⟨to make
a profit : sacar beneficios⟩
profitable ['prɑfətəbəl] *adj* : rentable, lucrativo — **profitably** [-bli] *adv*
profitless ['prɑfətləs] *adj* : infructuoso,
inútil
profligate ['prɑflɪgət, -,geɪt] *adj* **1** DIS-
SOLUTE : disoluto, licencioso **2** SPEND-
THRIFT : despilfarrador, derrochador,
pródigo
profound [prə'faʊnd] *adj* : profundo
profoundly [prə'faʊndli] *adv* : profundamente, en profundidad
profundity [prə'fʌndəti] *n, pl* **-ties** : profundidad *f*
profuse [prə'fju:s] *adj* **1** COPIOUS : profuso, copioso **2** LAVISH : pródigo —
profusely *adv*
profusion [prə'fju:ʒən] *n* : abundancia *f*,
profusión *f*
progenitor [pro'dʒɛnətər] *n* : progenitor
m, -tora *f*
progeny ['prɑdʒəni] *n, pl* **-nies** : progenie *f*
progesterone [pro'dʒɛstə,ro:n] *n* : progesterona *f*
prognosis [prɑg'no:sɪs] *n, pl* **-noses**
[-,si:z] : pronóstico *m* (médico)
program¹ ['pro:,græm, -grəm] *vt*
-grammed *or* **-gramed; -gramming** *or*
-graming : programar
program² *n* : programa *m*
programmable ['pro:,græməbəl] *adj*
: programable
programmer ['pro:,græmər] *n* : programador *m*, -dora *f*
programming ['pro:,græmɪŋ] *n* : programación *f*
progress¹ [prə'grɛs] *vi* **1** PROCEED
: progresar, adelantar **2** IMPROVE
: mejorar
progress² ['prɑgrəs, -,grɛs] *n* **1** AD-
VANCE : progreso *m*, adelanto *m*,
avance *m* ⟨to make progress : hacer
progresos⟩ **2** BETTERMENT : mejora *f*,
mejoramiento *m*
progression [prə'grɛʃən] *n* **1** ADVANCE
: avance *m* **2** SEQUENCE : desarrollo
m (de eventos)
progressive [prə'grɛsɪv] *adj* **1** : progresista ⟨a progressive society : una sociedad progresista⟩ **2** : progresivo ⟨a
progressive disease : una enfermedad
progresiva⟩ **3** *or* **Progressive** : progresista (en política) **4** : progresivo (en
gramática)

progressively [prə'grɛsɪvli] *adv* : progresivamente, poco a poco
prohibit [pro'hɪbət] *vt* : prohibir
prohibition [ˌproːə'bɪʃən, ˌproːhə-] *n* : prohibición *f*
prohibitive [pro'hɪbəṭɪv] *adj* : prohibitivo
project[1] [prə'dʒɛkt] *vt* **1** PLAN : proyectar, planear **2** : proyectar (imágenes, misiles, etc.) — *vi* PROTRUDE : sobresalir, salir
project[2] ['prɑˌdʒɛkt, -dʒɪkt] *n* : proyecto *m*, trabajo *m* (de un estudiante) ⟨research project : proyecto de investigación⟩
projectile [prə'dʒɛktəl, -ˌtaɪl] *n* : proyectil *m*
projection [prə'dʒɛkʃən] *n* **1** PLAN : plan *m*, proyección *f* **2** : proyección *f* (de imágenes, misiles, etc.) **3** PROTRUSION : saliente *m*
projector [prə'dʒɛktər] *n* : proyector *m*
proletarian[1] [ˌproːlə'tɛriən] *adj* : proletario
proletarian[2] *n* : proletario *m*, -ria *f*
proletariat [ˌproːlə'tɛriət] *n* : proletariado *m*
proliferate [prə'lɪfəˌreɪt] *vi* **-ated; -ating** : proliferar
proliferation [prəˌlɪfə'reɪʃən] *n* : proliferación *f*
prolific [prə'lɪfɪk] *adj* : prolífico
prologue ['proːˌlɔg] *n* : prólogo *m*
prolong [prə'lɔŋ] *vt* : prolongar
prolongation [ˌproːˌlɔŋ'geɪʃən] *n* : prolongación *f*
prom ['prɑm] *n* : baile *m* formal (de un colegio)
promenade[1] [ˌprɑmə'neɪd, -'nɑd] *vi* **-naded; -nading** : pasear, pasearse, dar un paseo
promenade[2] *n* : paseo *m*
prominence ['prɑmənənts] *n* **1** PROJECTION : prominencia *f* **2** EMINENCE : eminencia *f*, prestigio *m*
prominent ['prɑmənənt] *adj* **1** OUTSTANDING : prominente, destacado **2** PROJECTING : prominente, saliente
prominently ['prɑmənəntli] *adv* : destacadamente, prominentemente
promiscuity [ˌprɑmɪs'kjuːəṭi] *n, pl* **-ties** : promiscuidad *f*
promiscuous [prə'mɪskjuəs] *adj* : promiscuo — **promiscuously** *adv*
promise[1] ['prɑməs] *v* **-ised; -ising** : prometer
promise[2] *n* **1** : promesa *f* ⟨he kept his promise : cumplió su promesa⟩ **2 to show promise** : prometer
promising ['prɑməsɪŋ] *adj* : prometedor
promissory ['prɑməˌsori] *adj* : que promete ⟨a promissory note : un pagaré⟩
promontory ['prɑmənˌtori] *n, pl* **-ries** : promontorio *m*
promote [prə'moːt] *vt* **-moted; -moting 1** : ascender (a un alumno o un empleado) **2** ADVERTISE : promocionar,

hacerle publicidad a **3** FURTHER : promover, fomentar
promoter [prə'moːṭər] *n* : promotor *m*, -tora *f*; empresario *m*, -ria *f* (en deportes)
promotion [prə'moːʃən] *n* **1** : ascenso *m* (de un alumno o un empleado) **2** FURTHERING : promoción *f*, fomento *m* **3** ADVERTISING : publicidad *f*, propaganda *f*
promotional [prə'moːʃənəl] *adj* : promocional
prompt[1] ['prɑmpt] *vt* **1** INDUCE : provocar (una cosa), inducir (a una persona) ⟨curiosity prompted me to ask you : la curiosidad me indujo a preguntarle⟩ **2** : apuntar (a un actor, etc.)
prompt[2] *adj* : pronto, rápido ⟨prompt payment : pago puntual⟩
prompter ['prɑmptər] *n* : apuntador *m*, -dora *f* (en teatro)
promptly ['prɑmptli] *adv* : inmediatamente, rápidamente
promptness ['prɑmptnəs] *n* : prontitud *f*, rapidez *f*
promulgate ['prɑməlˌgeɪt] *vt* **-gated; -gating** : promulgar
prone ['proːn] *adj* **1** LIABLE : propenso, proclive ⟨accident-prone : propenso a los accidentes⟩ **2** : boca abajo, decúbito prono ⟨in a prone position : en decúbito prono⟩
prong ['prɔŋ] *n* : punta *f*, diente *m*
pronoun ['proːˌnaʊn] *n* : pronombre *m*
pronounce [prə'naʊnts] *vt* **-nounced; -nouncing 1** : pronunciar ⟨how do you pronounce your name? : ¿cómo se pronuncia su nombre?⟩ **2** DECLARE : declarar **3 to pronounce sentence** : dictar sentencia, pronunciar un fallo
pronounced [prə'naʊntst] *adj* MARKED : pronunciado, marcado
pronouncement [prə'naʊntsmənt] *n* : declaración *f*
pronunciation [prəˌnʌntsi'eɪʃən] *n* : pronunciación *f*
proof[1] ['pruːf] *adj* : a prueba ⟨proof against tampering : a prueba de manipulación⟩
proof[2] *n* : prueba *f*
proofread ['pruːfˌriːd] *v* **-read; -reading** *vt* : corregir — *vi* : corregir pruebas
proofreader ['pruːfˌriːdər] *n* : corrector *m*, -tora *f* (de pruebas)
prop[1] ['prɑp] *vt* **propped; propping 1 to prop against** : apoyar contra **2 to prop up** SUPPORT : apoyar, apuntalar, sostener **3 to prop up** SUSTAIN : alentar (a alguien), darle ánimo (a alguien)
prop[2] *n* **1** SUPPORT : puntal *m*, apoyo *m*, soporte *m* **2** : accesorio *m* (en teatro)
propaganda [ˌprɑpə'gændə, ˌproː-] *n* : propaganda *f*
propagandize [ˌprɑpə'gænˌdaɪz, ˌproː-] *v* **-dized; -dizing** *vt* : someter a propaganda — *vi* : hacer propaganda

propagate ['prɑpə,geɪt] v **-gated; -gating** vi : propagarse — vt : propagar

propagation [,prɑpə'geɪʃən] n : propagación f

propane ['pro:,peɪn] n : propano m

propel [prə'pɛl] vt **-pelled; -pelling** : impulsar, propulsar, impeler

propellant or **propellent** [prə'pɛlənt] n : propulsor m

propeller [prə'pɛlər] n : hélice f

propensity [prə'pɛntsəti] n, pl **-ties** : propensión f, tendencia f, inclinación f

proper ['prɑpər] adj **1** RIGHT, SUITABLE : apropiado, adecuado **2** : propio, mismo ⟨the city proper : la propia ciudad⟩ **3** CORRECT : correcto **4** GENTEEL : fino, refinado, cortés **5** OWN, SPECIAL : propio ⟨proper name : nombre propio⟩ — **properly** adv

property ['prɑpərti] n, pl **-ties 1** CHARACTERISTIC : característica f, propiedad f **2** POSSESSIONS : propiedad f **3** BUILDING : inmueble m **4** LAND, LOT : terreno m, lote m, parcela f **5** PROP : accesorio m (en teatro)

prophecy ['prɑfəsi] n, pl **-cies** : profecía f, vaticinio m

prophesy ['prɑfə,saɪ] v **-sied; -sying** vt **1** FORETELL : profetizar (como profeta) **2** PREDICT : profetizar, predecir, vaticinar — vi : hacer profecías

prophet ['prɑfət] n : profeta m, profetisa f

prophetic [prə'fɛtɪk] or **prophetical** [-tɪkəl] adj : profético — **prophetically** [-tɪkli] adv

propitiate [pro'pɪʃi,eɪt] vt **-ated; -ating** : propiciar

propitious [prə'pɪʃəs] adj : propicio

proponent [prə'po:nənt] n : defensor m, -sora f; partidario m, -ria f

proportion[1] [prə'porʃən] vt : proporcionar ⟨well-proportioned : de buenas proporciones⟩

proportion[2] n **1** RATIO : proporción f **2** SYMMETRY : proporción f, simetría f ⟨out of proportion : desproporcionado⟩ **3** SHARE : parte f **4 proportions** npl SIZE : dimensiones fpl

proportional [prə'porʃənəl] adj : proporcional — **proportionally** adv

proportionate [prə'porʃənət] adj : proporcional — **proportionately** adv

proposal [prə'po:zəl] n **1** PROPOSITION : propuesta f, proposición f ⟨marriage proposal : propuesta de matrimonio⟩ **2** PLAN : proyecto m, propuesta f

propose [prə'po:z] v **-posed; -posing** vi : proponer matrimonio — vt **1** INTEND : pensar, proponerse **2** SUGGEST : proponer

proposition [,prɑpə'zɪʃən] n **1** PROPOSAL : proposición f, propuesta f **2** STATEMENT : proposición f

propound [prə'paʊnd] vt : proponer, exponer

proprietary [prə'praɪə,tɛri] adj : propietario, patentado

proprietor [prə'praɪətər] n : propietario m, -ria f

propriety [prə'praɪəti] n, pl **-eties 1** DECORUM : decencia f, decoro m **2 proprieties** npl CONVENTIONS : convenciones fpl, cánones mpl sociales

propulsion [prə'pʌlʃən] n : propulsión f

prosaic [pro'zeɪk] adj : prosaico

proscribe [pro'skraɪb] vt **-scribed; -scribing** : proscribir

prose ['pro:z] n : prosa f

prosecute ['prɑsɪ,kju:t] vt **-cuted; -cuting 1** CARRY OUT : llevar a cabo **2** : procesar, enjuiciar ⟨prosecuted for fraud : procesado por fraude⟩

prosecution [,prɑsɪ'kju:ʃən] n **1** : procesamiento m ⟨the prosecution of forgers : el procesamiento de falsificadores⟩ **2** PROSECUTORS : acusación f ⟨witness for the prosecution : testigo de cargo⟩

prosecutor ['prɑsɪ,kju:tər] n : acusador m, -dora f; fiscal mf

prospect[1] ['prɑ,spɛkt] vi : prospectar (el terreno) ⟨to prospect for gold : buscar oro⟩

prospect[2] n **1** VISTA : vista f, panorama m **2** POSSIBILITY : posibilidad f **3** OUTLOOK : perspectiva f **4** : posible cliente m, -ta f ⟨a salesman looking for prospects : un vendedor buscando nuevos clientes⟩

prospective [prə'spɛktɪv, 'prɑ,spɛk-] adj **1** EXPECTANT : futuro ⟨prospective mother : futura madre⟩ **2** POTENTIAL : potencial, posible ⟨prospective employee : posible empleado⟩

prospector ['prɑ,spɛktər, prə'spɛk-] n : prospector m, -tora f; explorador m, -dora f

prospectus [prə'spɛktəs] n : prospecto m

prosper ['prɑspər] vi : prosperar

prosperity [prɑ'spɛrəti] n : prosperidad f

prosperous ['prɑspərəs] adj : próspero

prostate ['prɑ,steɪt] n : próstata f

prosthesis [prɑs'θi:sɪs, 'prɑsθə-] n, pl **-theses** [-,si:z] : prótesis f

prostitute[1] ['prɑstə,tu:t, -,tju:t] vt **-tuted; -tuting 1** : prostituir **2 to prostitute oneself** : prostituirse

prostitute[2] n : prostituto m, -ta f

prostitution [,prɑstə'tu:ʃən, -'tju:-] n : prostitución f

prostrate[1] ['prɑ,streɪt] vt **-trated; -trating 1** : postrar **2 to prostrate oneself** : postrarse

prostrate[2] adj : postrado

prostration [prɑ'streɪʃən] n : postración f

protagonist [pro'tægənɪst] n : protagonista mf

protect [prə'tɛkt] vt : proteger

protection [prə'tɛkʃən] n : protección f

protective [prə'tɛktɪv] adj : protector

protector [prə'tɛktər] n **1** : protector m, -tora f (persona) **2** GUARD : protector m (aparato)

protectorate [prə'tɛktərət] *n* : protectorado *m*

protégé ['pro:tə,ʒeɪ] *n* : protegido *m*, -da *f*

protein ['pro:,ti:n] *n* : proteína *f*

protest[1] ['pro'tɛst] *vt* **1** ASSERT : afirmar, declarar **2** : protestar ⟨they protested the decision : protestaron (por) la decisión⟩ — *vi* **to protest against** : protestar contra

protest[2] ['pro:,tɛst] *n* **1** DEMONSTRATION : manifestación *f* (de protesta) ⟨a public protest : una manifestación pública⟩ **2** COMPLAINT : queja *f*, protesta *f*

Protestant ['prɑtəstənt] *n* : protestante *mf*

Protestantism ['prɑtəstən,tɪzəm] *n* : protestantismo *m*

protocol ['pro:tə,kɔl] *n* : protocolo *m*

proton ['pro:,tɑn] *n* : protón *m*

protoplasm ['pro:tə,plæzəm] *n* : protoplasma *m*

prototype ['pro:tə,taɪp] *n* : prototipo *m*

protozoan [,pro:tə'zo:ən] *n* : protozoario *m*, protozoo *m*

protract [pro'trækt] *vt* : prolongar

protractor [pro'træktər] *n* : transportador *m* (instrumento)

protrude [pro'tru:d] *vi* -truded; -truding : salir, sobresalir

protrusion [pro'tru:ʒən] *n* : protuberancia *f*, saliente *m*

protuberance [pro'tu:bərənts, -'tju:-] *n* : protuberancia *f*

proud ['praʊd] *adj* **1** HAUGHTY : altanero, orgulloso, arrogante **2** : orgulloso ⟨she was proud of her work : estaba orgullosa de su trabajo⟩ ⟨too proud to beg : demasiado orgulloso para rogar⟩ **3** GLORIOUS : glorioso — **proudly** *adv*

prove ['pru:v] *v* **proved; proved** *or* **proven** ['pru:vən]; **proving** *vt* **1** TEST : probar **2** DEMONSTRATE : probar, demostrar — *vi* : resultar ⟨it proved effective : resultó efectivo⟩

Provençal [,pro:vɑn'sɑl, ,prɑvən-] *n* **1** : provenzal *mf* **2** : provenzal *m* (idioma) — **Provençal** *adj*

proverb ['prɑ,vərb] *n* : proverbio *m*, refrán *m*

proverbial [prə'vərbiəl] *adj* : proverbial

provide [prə'vaɪd] *v* -vided; -viding **1** STIPULATE : estipular **2 to provide with** : proveer de, proporcionar — *vi* **1** : proveer ⟨the Lord will provide : el Señor proveerá⟩ **2 to provide for** SUPPORT : mantener **3 to provide for** ANTICIPATE : hacer previsiones para, prever

provided [prə'vaɪdəd] *or* **provided that** *conj* : con tal (de) que, siempre que

providence ['prɑvədənts] *n* **1** PRUDENCE : previsión *f*, prudencia *f* **2** *or* **Providence** : providencia *f* ⟨divine providence : la Divina Providencia⟩ **3 Providence** GOD : Providencia *f*

provident ['prɑvədənt] *adj* **1** PRUDENT : previsor, prudente **2** FRUGAL : frugal, ahorrativo

providential [,prɑvə'dɛntʃəl] *adj* : providencial

provider [prə'vaɪdər] *n* **1** PURVEYOR : proveedor *m*, -dora *f* **2** BREADWINNER : sostén *m* (económico)

providing that → provided

province ['prɑvɪnts] *n* **1** : provincia *f* (de un país) ⟨to live in the provinces : vivir en las provincias⟩ **2** FIELD, SPHERE : campo *m*, competencia *f* ⟨it's not in my province : no es de mi competencia⟩

provincial [prə'vɪntʃəl] *adj* **1** : provincial ⟨provincial government : gobierno provincial⟩ **2** : provinciano, pueblerino ⟨a provincial mentality : una mentalidad provinciana⟩

provision[1] [prə'vɪʒən] *vt* : aprovisionar, abastecer

provision[2] *n* **1** PROVIDING : provisión *f*, suministro *m* **2** STIPULATION : condición *f*, salvedad *f*, estipulación *f* **3 provisions** *npl* : despensa *f*, víveres *mpl*, provisiones *fpl*

provisional [prə'vɪʒənəl] *adj* : provisional, provisorio — **provisionally** *adv*

proviso [prə'vaɪ,zo:] *n*, *pl* **-sos** *or* **-soes** : condición *f*, salvedad *f*, estipulación *f*

provocation [,prɑvə'keɪʃən] *n* : provocación *f*

provocative [prə'vɑkətɪv] *adj* : provocador, provocativo ⟨a provocative article : un artículo que hace pensar⟩

provoke [prə'vo:k] *vt* -voked; -voking : provocar

prow ['praʊ] *n* : proa *f*

prowess ['praʊəs] *n* **1** VALOR : valor *m*, valentía *f* **2** SKILL : habilidad *f*, destreza *f*

prowl ['praʊl] *vi* : merodear, rondar — *vt* : rondar por

prowler ['praʊlər] *n* : merodeador *m*, -dora *f*

proximity [prɑk'sɪməti] *n* : proximidad *f*

proxy ['prɑksi] *n*, *pl* **proxies 1** : poder *m* (de actuar en nombre de alguien) ⟨by proxy : por poder⟩ **2** AGENT : apoderado *m*, -da *f*; representante *mf*

prude ['pru:d] *n* : mojigato *m*, -ta *f*; gazmoño *m*, -ña *f*

prudence ['pru:dənts] *n* **1** SHREWDNESS : prudencia *f*, sagacidad *f* **2** CAUTION : prudencia *f*, cautela *f* **3** THRIFTINESS : frugalidad *f*

prudent ['pru:dənt] *adj* **1** SHREWD : prudente, sagaz **2** CAUTIOUS, FARSIGHTED : prudente, previsor, precavido **3** THRIFTY : frugal, ahorrativo — **prudently** *adv*

prudery ['pru:dəri] *n*, *pl* **-eries** : mojigatería *f*, gazmoñería *f*

prudish ['pru:dɪʃ] *adj* : mojigato, gazmoño

prune¹ [ˈpruːn] *vt* **pruned; pruning** : podar (arbustos, etc.), acortar (un texto), recortar (gastos, etc.)

prune² *n* : ciruela *f* pasa

prurient [ˈprʊriənt] *adj* : lascivo

pry [ˈpraɪ] *v* **pried; prying** *vi* : curiosear, huronear ⟨to pry into other people's business : meterse uno en lo que no le importa⟩ — *vt or* **to pry open** : abrir (con una palanca), apalancar

psalm [ˈsɑm, ˈsɑlm] *n* : salmo *m*

pseudonym [ˈsuːdə̩nɪm] *n* : seudónimo *m*

psoriasis [səˈraɪəsɪs] *n* : soriasis *f*, psoriasis *f*

psyche [ˈsaɪki] *n* : psique *f*, psiquis *f*

psychedelic¹ [ˌsaɪkəˈdɛlɪk] *adj* : psicodélico

psychedelic² *n* : droga *f* psicodélica

psychiatric [ˌsaɪkiˈætrɪk] *adj* : psiquiátrico, siquiátrico

psychiatrist [səˈkaɪətrɪst, saɪ-] *n* : psiquiatra *mf*, siquiatra *mf*

psychiatry [səˈkaɪətri, saɪ-] *n* : psiquiatría *f*, siquiatría *f*

psychic¹ [ˈsaɪkɪk] *adj* **1** : psíquico, síquico (en psicología) **2** CLAIRVOYANT : clarividente

psychic² *n* : vidente *mf*, clarividente *mf*

psychoanalysis [ˌsaɪkoəˈnæləsɪs] *n, pl* **-yses** : psicoanálisis *m*, sicoanálisis *m*

psychoanalyst [ˌsaɪkoˈænəlɪst] *n* : psicoanalista *mf*, sicoanalista *mf*

psychoanalytic [ˌsaɪkoˌænəlˈɪtɪk] *adj* : psicoanalítico, sicoanalítico

psychoanalyze [ˌsaɪkoˈænəl̩aɪz] *vt* **-lyzed; -lyzing** : psicoanalizar, sicoanalizar

psychological [ˌsaɪkəˈlɑʤɪkəl] *adj* : psicológico, sicológico — **psychologically** *adv*

psychologist [saɪˈkɑləʤɪst] *n* : psicólogo *m*, -ga *f*; sicólogo *m*, -ga *f*

psychology [saɪˈkɑləʤi] *n, pl* **-gies** : psicología *f*, sicología *f*

psychopath [ˈsaɪkə̩pæθ] *n* : psicópata *mf*, sicópata *mf*

psychopathic [ˌsaɪkəˈpæθɪk] *adj* : psicopático, sicopático

psychosis [saɪˈkoːsɪs] *n, pl* **-choses** [-ˈkoːˌsiːz] : psicosis *f*, sicosis *f*

psychosomatic [ˌsaɪkəsəˈmætɪk] *adj* : psicosomático, sicosomático

psychotherapist [ˌsaɪkoˈθɛrəpɪst] *n* : psicoterapeuta *mf*, sicoterapeuta *mf*

psychotherapy [ˌsaɪkoˈθɛrəpi] *n, pl* **-pies** : psicoterapia *f*, sicoterapia *f*

psychotic¹ [saɪˈkɑtɪk] *adj* : psicótico, sicótico

psychotic² *n* : psicótico *m*, -ca *f*; sicótico *m*, -ca *f*

puberty [ˈpjuːbərti] *n* : pubertad *f*

pubic [ˈpjuːbɪk] *adj* : pubiano, púbico

public¹ [ˈpʌblɪk] *adj* : público — **publicly** *adv*

public² *n* : público *m*

publication [ˌpʌbləˈkeɪʃən] *n* : publicación *f*

publicist [ˈpʌbləsɪst] *n* : publicista *mf*

publicity [pəˈblɪsəti] *n* : publicidad *f*

publicize [ˈpʌblə̩saɪz] *vt* **-cized; -cizing** : publicitar

public school *n* : escuela *f* pública

publish [ˈpʌblɪʃ] *vt* : publicar

publisher [ˈpʌblɪʃər] *n* : casa *f* editorial (compañía); editor *m*, -tora *f* (persona)

publishing [ˈpʌblɪʃɪŋ] *n* : industria *f* editorial

pucker¹ [ˈpʌkər] *vt* : fruncir, arrugar — *vi* : arrugarse

pucker² *n* : arruga *f*, frunce *m*, fruncido *m*

pudding [ˈpʊdɪŋ] *n* : budín *m*, pudín *m*

puddle [ˈpʌdəl] *n* : charco *m*

pudgy [ˈpʌʤi] *adj* **pudgier; -est** : regordete *fam*, rechoncho *fam*, gordinflón *fam*

puerile [ˈpjʊrəl] *adj* : pueril

Puerto Rican¹ [ˌpwɛrtəˈriːkən, ˌpɔrtə-] *adj* : puertorriqueño

Puerto Rican² *n* : puertorriqueño *m*, -ña *f*

puff¹ [ˈpʌf] *vi* **1** BLOW : soplar **2** PANT : resoplar, jadear **3 to puff up** SWELL : hincharse — *vt* **1** BLOW : soplar ⟨to puff out smoke : echar humo⟩ **2** INFLATE : inflar, hinchar ⟨to puff out one's cheeks : inflar las mejillas⟩

puff² *n* **1** GUST : soplo *m*, ráfaga *f*, bocanada *f* (de humo) **2** DRAW : chupada *f* (a un cigarrillo) **3** SWELLING : hinchazón *f* **4 cream puff** : pastelito *m* de crema **5 powder puff** : borla *f*

puffy [ˈpʌfi] *adj* **puffier; -est 1** SWOLLEN : hinchado, inflado **2** SPONGY : esponjoso, suave

pug [ˈpʌg] *n* **1** : doguillo *m* (perro) **2** *or* **pug nose** : nariz *f* achatada

pugnacious [ˌpʌgˈneɪʃəs] *adj* : pugnaz, agresivo

puke [ˈpjuːk] *vi* **puked; puking** : vomitar, devolver

pull¹ [ˈpʊl, ˈpʌl] *vt* **1** DRAW, TUG : tirar de, jalar **2** EXTRACT : sacar, extraer ⟨to pull teeth : sacar muelas⟩ ⟨to pull a gun on : amenazar a (alguien) con pistola⟩ **3** TEAR : desgarrarse (un músculo, etc.) **4 to pull down** : bajar, echar abajo, derribar (un edificio) **5 to pull in** ATTRACT : atraer (una muchedumbre, etc.) ⟨to pull in votes : conseguir votos⟩ **6 to pull off** REMOVE : sacar, quitar **7 to pull oneself together** : calmarse, tranquilizarse **8 to pull up** RAISE : levantar, subir — *vi* **1** DRAW, TUG : tirar, jalar **2** (*indicating movement in a specific direction*) ⟨they pulled in front of us : se nos metieron delante⟩ ⟨to pull to a stop : pararse⟩ **3 to pull through** RECOVER : recobrarse, reponerse **4 to pull together** COOPERATE : trabajar juntos, cooperar

pull² *n* **1** TUG : tirón *m*, jalón *m* ⟨he gave it a pull : le dio un tirón⟩ **2** ATTRACTION : atracción *f*, fuerza *f* ⟨the pull of gravity : la fuerza de la gravedad⟩ **3**

INFLUENCE : influencia *f* **4** HANDLE : tirador *m* (de un cajón, etc.) **5** bell pull : cuerda *f*

pullet ['pʊlət] *n* : polla *f*, gallina *f* (joven)

pulley ['pʊli] *n, pl* **-leys** : polea *f*

pullover ['pʊl,o:vər] *n* : suéter *m*

pulmonary ['pʊlmə,nɛri, 'pʌl-] *adj* : pulmonar

pulp ['pʌlp] *n* **1** : pulpa *f* (de una fruta, etc.) **2** MASH : papilla *f*, pasta *f* ⟨wood pulp : pasta de papel, pulpa de papel⟩ ⟨to beat to a pulp : hacer papilla (a alguien)⟩ **3** : pulpa *f* (de los dientes)

pulpit ['pʊl,pɪt] *n* : púlpito *m*

pulsate ['pʌl,seɪt] *vi* **-sated; -sating 1** BEAT : latir, palpitar **2** VIBRATE : vibrar

pulsation [,pʌl'seɪʃən] *n* : pulsación *f*

pulse ['pʌls] *n* : pulso *m*

pulverize ['pʌlvə,raɪz] *vt* **-ized; -izing** : pulverizar

puma ['pu:mə, 'pju:-] *n* : puma *m*; león *m*, leona *f* (in various countries)

pumice ['pʌməs] *n* : piedra *f* pómez

pummel ['pʌməl] *vt* **-meled; -meling** : aporrear, apalear

pump[1] ['pʌmp] *vt* **1** : bombear ⟨to pump water : bombear agua⟩ ⟨to pump (up) a tire : inflar una llanta⟩ **2** : mover (una manivela, un pedal, etc.) de arriba abajo ⟨to pump someone's hand : darle un fuerte apretón de manos (a alguien)⟩ **3 to pump out** : sacar, vaciar (con una bomba)

pump[2] *n* **1** : bomba *f* ⟨water pump : bomba de agua⟩ **2** SHOE : zapato *m* de tacón

pumpernickel ['pʌmpər,nɪkəl] *n* : pan *m* negro de centeno

pumpkin ['pʌmpkɪn, 'pʌŋkən] *n* : calabaza *f*, zapallo *m Arg, Chile, Peru, Uru*

pun[1] ['pʌn] *vi* **punned; punning** : hacer juegos de palabras

pun[2] *n* : juego *m* de palabras, albur *m Mex*

punch[1] ['pʌntʃ] *vt* **1** HIT : darle un puñetazo (a alguien), golpear ⟨she punched him in the nose : le dio un puñetazo en la nariz⟩ **2** PERFORATE : perforar (papel, etc.), picar (un boleto)

punch[2] *n* **1** : perforadora *f* ⟨paper punch : perforadora de papel⟩ **2** BLOW : golpe *m*, puñetazo *m* **3** : ponche *m* ⟨fruit punch : ponche de frutas⟩

punctilious [pəŋk'tɪliəs] *adj* : puntilloso

punctual ['pʌŋktʃʊəl] *adj* : puntual

punctuality [,pʌŋktʃʊ'æləti] *n* : puntualidad *f*

punctually ['pʌŋktʃʊəli] *adv* : puntualmente, a tiempo

punctuate ['pʌŋktʃʊ,eɪt] *vt* **-ated; -ating** : puntuar

punctuation [,pʌŋktʃʊ'eɪʃən] *n* : puntuación *f*

puncture[1] ['pʌŋktʃər] *vt* **-tured; -turing** : pinchar, punzar, perforar, ponchar *Mex*

puncture[2] *n* : pinchazo *m*, ponchadura *f Mex*

pundit ['pʌndɪt] *n* : experto *m*, -ta *f*

pungency ['pʌndʒəntsi] *n* : acritud *f*, acrimonia *f*

pungent ['pʌndʒənt] *adj* : acre

punish ['pʌnɪʃ] *vt* : castigar

punishable ['pʌnɪʃəbəl] *adj* : punible

punishment ['pʌnɪʃmənt] *n* : castigo *m*

punitive ['pju:nətɪv] *adj* : punitivo

punt[1] ['pʌnt] *vt* : impulsar (un barco) con una pértiga — *vi* : despejar (en deportes)

punt[2] *n* **1** : batea *f* (barco) **2** : patada *f* de despeje (en deportes)

puny ['pju:ni] *adj* **-nier; -est** : enclenque, endeble

pup ['pʌp] *n* : cachorro *m*, -rra *f* (de un perro); cría *f* (de otros animales)

pupa ['pju:pə] *n, pl* **-pae** [-pi, -,paɪ] *or* **-pas** : crisálida *f*, pupa *f*

pupil ['pju:pəl] *n* **1** : alumno *m*, -na *f* (de colegio) **2** : pupila *f* (del ojo)

puppet ['pʌpət] *n* : títere *m*, marioneta *f*

puppy ['pʌpi] *n, pl* **-pies** : cachorro *m*, -rra *f*

purchase[1] ['pərtʃəs] *vt* **-chased; -chasing** : comprar

purchase[2] *n* **1** PURCHASING : compra *f*, adquisición *f* **2** : compra *f* ⟨last-minute purchases : compras de última hora⟩ **3** GRIP : agarre *m*, asidero *m* ⟨she got a firm purchase on the wheel : se agarró bien del volante⟩

purchase order *n* : orden *f* de compra

pure ['pjur] *adj* **purer; purest** : puro

puree[1] [pju'reɪ, -'ri:] *vt* **-reed; -reeing** : hacer un puré con

puree[2] *n* : puré *m*

purely ['pjurli] *adv* **1** WHOLLY : puramente, completamente ⟨purely by chance : por pura casualidad⟩ **2** SIMPLY : sencillamente, meramente

purgative ['pərgətɪv] *n* : purgante *m*

purgatory ['pərgə,tori] *n, pl* **-ries** : purgatorio *m*

purge[1] ['pərdʒ] *vt* **purged; purging** : purgar

purge[2] *n* : purga *f*

purification [,pjurəfə'keɪʃən] *n* : purificación *f*

purify ['pjurə,faɪ] *vt* **-fied; -fying** : purificar

puritan ['pjurətən] *n* : puritano *m*, -na *f* — **puritan** *adj*

puritanical [,pjurə'tænɪkəl] *adj* : puritano

purity ['pjurəti] *n* : pureza *f*

purl[1] ['pərl] *v* : tejer al revés, tejer del revés

purl[2] *n* : punto *m* del revés

purloin [pər'lɔɪn, 'pər,lɔɪn] *vt* : hurtar, robar

purple ['pərpəl] *n* : morado *m*, color *m* púrpura

purport [pər'port] *vt* : pretender ⟨to purport to be : pretender ser⟩

purpose ['pərpəs] *n* **1** INTENTION : propósito *m*, intención *f* ⟨on purpose

: a propósito, adrede⟩ **2** FUNCTION : función *f* **3** RESOLUTION : resolución *f*, determinación *f*

purposeful ['pərpəsfəl] *adj* : determinado, decidido, resuelto

purposefully ['pərpəsfəli] *adv* : decididamente, resueltamente

purposely ['pərpəsli] *adv* : intencionadamente, a propósito, adrede

purr¹ ['pər] *vi* : ronronear

purr² *n* : ronroneo *m*

purse¹ ['pərs] *vt* **pursed; pursing** : fruncir ⟨to purse one's lips : fruncir la boca⟩

purse² *n* **1** HANDBAG : cartera *f*, bolso *m*, bolsa *f Mex* ⟨a change purse : un monedero⟩ **2** FUNDS : fondos *mpl* **3** PRIZE : premio *m*

pursue [pər'su:] *vt* **-sued; -suing 1** CHASE : perseguir **2** SEEK : buscar, tratar de encontrar ⟨to pursue pleasure : buscar el placer⟩ **3** FOLLOW : seguir ⟨the road pursues a northerly course : el camino sigue hacia el norte⟩ **4** : dedicarse a ⟨to pursue a hobby : dedicarse a un pasatiempo⟩

pursuer [pər'su:ər] *n* : perseguidor *m*, -dora *f*

pursuit [pər'su:t] *n* **1** CHASE : persecución *f* **2** SEARCH : búsqueda *f*, busca *f* **3** ACTIVITY : actividad *f*, pasatiempo *m*

purveyor [pər'veɪər] *n* : proveedor *m*, -dora *f*

pus ['pʌs] *n* : pus *m*

push¹ ['puʃ] *vt* **1** SHOVE : empujar **2** PRESS : apretar, pulsar ⟨push that button : aprieta ese botón⟩ **3** PRESSURE, URGE : presionar **4 to push around** BULLY : intimidar, mangonear — *vi* **1** SHOVE : empujar **2** INSIST : insistir, presionar **3 to push off** LEAVE : marcharse, irse, largarse *fam* **4 to push on** PROCEED : seguir

push² *n* **1** SHOVE : empujón *m* **2** DRIVE : empuje *m*, energía *f*, dinamismo *m* **3** EFFORT : esfuerzo *m*

push–button ['puʃ'bʌtən] *adj* : de botones

pushcart ['puʃ,kɑrt] *n* : carretilla *f* de mano

pushy ['puʃi] *adj* **pushier; -est** : mandón, prepotente

pussy ['pusi] *n, pl* **pussies** : gatito *m*, -ta *f*; minino *m*, -na *f*

pussy willow *n* : sauce *m* blanco

pustule ['pʌs,tʃu:l] *n* : pústula *f*

put ['put] *v* **put; putting** *vt* **1** PLACE : poner, colocar ⟨put it on the table : ponlo en la mesa⟩ **2** INSERT : meter **3** (*indicating causation of a state or feeling*) : poner ⟨it put her in a good mood : la puso de buen humor⟩ ⟨to put into effect : poner en práctica⟩ **4** IMPOSE : imponer ⟨they put a tax on it : lo gravaron con un impuesto⟩ **5** SUBJECT : someter, poner ⟨to put to the test : poner a prueba⟩ ⟨to put to death : ejecutar⟩ **6** EXPRESS : expresar, decir ⟨he put it

simply : lo dijo sencillamente⟩ **7** APPLY : aplicar ⟨to put one's mind to something : proponerse hacer algo⟩ **8** SET : poner ⟨I put him to work : lo puse a trabajar⟩ **9** ATTACH : dar ⟨to put a high value on : dar gran valor a⟩ **10** PRESENT : presentar, exponer ⟨to put a question to someone : hacer una pregunta a alguien⟩ — *vi* **1 to put to sea** : hacerse a la mar **2 to put up with** : aguantar, soportar

put away *vt* **1** KEEP : guardar **2** *or* **to put aside** : dejar a un lado

put by *vt* SAVE : ahorrar

put down *vt* **1** SUPPRESS : aplastar, suprimir **2** ATTRIBUTE : atribuir ⟨she put it down to luck : lo atribuyó a la suerte⟩

put in *vi* : presentarse ⟨I've put in for the position : me presenté para el puesto⟩ — *vt* DEVOTE : dedicar (unas horas, etc.)

put off *vt* DEFER : aplazar, posponer

put on *vt* **1** ASSUME : afectar, adoptar **2** PRODUCE : presentar (una obra de teatro, etc.) **3** WEAR : ponerse

put out *vt* INCONVENIENCE : importunar, incomodar

putrefy ['pju:trə,faɪ] *v* **-fied; -fying** *vt* : pudrir — *vi* : pudrirse

putrid ['pju:trɪd] *adj* : putrefacto, pútrido

putter ['pʌtər] *vi or* **to putter around** : entretenerse

putty¹ ['pʌti] *vt* **-tied; -tying** : poner masilla en

putty² *n, pl* **-ties** : masilla *f*

put up *vt* **1** LODGE : alojar **2** CONTRIBUTE : contribuir, pagar

puzzle¹ ['pʌzəl] *vt* **-zled; -zling 1** CONFUSE : confundir, dejar perplejo **2 to puzzle out** : dar vueltas a, tratar de resolver

puzzle² *n* **1** : rompecabezas *m* ⟨a crossword puzzle : un crucigrama⟩ **2** MYSTERY : misterio *m*, enigma *m*

puzzlement ['pʌzəlmənt] *n* : desconcierto *m*, perplejidad *f*

pygmy¹ ['pɪgmi] *adj* : enano, pigmeo

pygmy² *n, pl* **-mies 1** DWARF : enano *m*, -na *f* **2 Pygmy** : pigmeo *m*, -mea *f*

pylon ['paɪ,lɑn, -lən] *n* **1** : torre *f* de conducta eléctrica **2** : pilón *m* (de un puente)

pyramid ['pɪrə,mɪd] *n* : pirámide *f*

pyre ['paɪr] *n* : pira *f*

pyromania [,paɪro'meɪniə] *n* : piromanía *f*

pyromaniac [,paɪro'meɪni,æk] *n* : pirómano *m*, -na *f*

pyrotechnics [,paɪrə'tɛknɪks] *npl* **1** FIREWORKS : fuegos *mpl* artificiales **2** DISPLAY, SHOW : espectáculo *m*, muestra *f* de virtuosismo ⟨computer pyrotechnics : efectos especiales hechos por computadora⟩

python ['paɪ,θɑn, -θən] *n* : pitón *f*, serpiente *f* pitón

Q

q ['kju:] *n, pl* **q's** *or* **qs** ['kju:z] : decimoséptima letra del alfabeto inglés
quack[1] ['kwæk] *vi* : graznar
quack[2] *n* **1** : graznido *m* (de pato) **2** CHARLATAN : curandero *m*, -ra *f*; matasanos *m fam*
quadrangle ['kwɑ,dræŋgəl] *n* **1** COURTYARD : patio *m* interior **2** → **quadrilateral**
quadrant ['kwɑdrənt] *n* : cuadrante *m*
quadrilateral [,kwɑdrə'lætərəl] *n* : cuadrilátero *m*
quadruped ['kwɑdrə,pɛd] *n* : cuadrúpedo *m*
quadruple [kwɑ'dru:pəl, -'drʌ-; 'kwɑdrə-] *v* **-pled; -pling** *vt* : cuadruplicar — *vi* : cuadruplicarse
quadruplet [kwɑ'dru:plət, -'drʌ-; 'kwɑdrə-] *n* : cuatrillizo *m*, -za *f*
quagmire ['kwæg,maɪr, 'kwɑg-] *n* **1** : lodazal *m*, barrizal *m* **2** PREDICAMENT : atolladero *m*
quail[1] ['kweɪl] *vi* : encogerse, acobardarse
quail[2] *n, pl* **quail** *or* **quails** : codorniz *f*
quaint ['kweɪnt] *adj* **1** ODD : extraño, curioso **2** PICTURESQUE : pintoresco — **quaintly** *adv*
quaintness ['kweɪntnəs] *n* : rareza *f*, lo curioso
quake[1] ['kweɪk] *vi* **quaked; quaking** : temblar
quake[2] *n* : temblor *m*, terremoto *m*
qualification [,kwɑləfə'keɪʃən] *n* **1** LIMITATION, RESERVATION : reserva *f*, limitación *f* ⟨without qualification : sin reservas⟩ **2** REQUIREMENT : requisito *m* **3** **qualifications** *npl* ABILITY : aptitud *f*, capacidad *f*
qualified ['kwɑlə,faɪd] *adj* : competente, capacitado
qualifier ['kwɑlə,faɪər] *n* **1** : clasificado *m*, -da *f* (en deportes) **2** : calificativo *m* (en gramática)
qualify ['kwɑlə,faɪ] *v* **-fied; -fying** *vt* **1** : matizar ⟨to qualify a statement : matizar una declaración⟩ **2** MODIFY : calificar (en gramática) **3** : habilitar ⟨the certificate qualified her to teach : el certificado la habilitó para enseñar⟩ — *vi* **1** : obtener el título, recibirse ⟨to qualify as an engineer : recibirse de ingeniero⟩ **2** : clasificarse (en deportes)
quality ['kwɑləti] *n, pl* **-ties 1** NATURE : carácter *m* **2** ATTRIBUTE : cualidad *f* **3** GRADE : calidad *f* ⟨of good quality : de buena calidad⟩
qualm ['kwɑm, 'kwɑlm, 'kwɔm] *n* **1** MISGIVING : duda *f*, aprensión *f* **2** RESERVATION, SCRUPLE : escrúpulo *m*, reparo *m*
quandary ['kwɑndri] *n, pl* **-ries** : dilema *m*
quantitative ['kwɑntə,teɪtɪv] *adj* : cuantitativo
quantity ['kwɑntəti] *n, pl* **-ties** : cantidad *f*

quantum[1] ['kwɑntəm] *n* : cuanto *m* (en física)
quantum[2] *adj* : cuántico
quantum theory ['kwɑntəm] *n* : teoría *f* cuántica
quarantine[1] ['kwɔrən,ti:n] *vt* **-tined; -tining** : poner en cuarentena
quarantine[2] *n* : cuarentena *f*
quarrel[1] ['kwɔrəl] *vi* **-reled** *or* **-relled; -reling** *or* **-relling** : pelearse, reñir, discutir
quarrel[2] *n* : pelea *f*, riña *f*, disputa *f*
quarrelsome ['kwɔrəlsəm] *adj* : pendenciero, discutidor
quarry[1] ['kwɔri] *vt* **quarried; quarrying 1** EXTRACT : extraer, sacar ⟨to quarry marble : extraer mármol⟩ **2** EXCAVATE : excavar ⟨to quarry a hill : excavar un cerro⟩
quarry[2] *n, pl* **quarries 1** PREY : presa *f* **2** *or* **stone quarry** : cantera *f*
quart ['kwɔrt] *n* : cuarto *m* de galón
quarter[1] ['kwɔrtər] *vt* **1** : dividir en cuatro partes **2** LODGE : alojar, acuartelar (tropas)
quarter[2] *n* **1** : cuarto *m*, cuarta parte *f* ⟨a foot and a quarter : un pie y cuarto⟩ ⟨a quarter after three : las tres y cuarto⟩ **2** : moneda *f* de 25 centavos, cuarto *m* de dólar **3** DISTRICT : barrio *m* ⟨business quarter : barrio comercial⟩ **4** PLACE : parte *f* ⟨from all quarters : de todas partes⟩ ⟨at close quarters : de muy cerca⟩ **5** MERCY : clemencia *f*, cuartel *m* ⟨to give no quarter : no dar cuartel⟩ **6 quarters** *npl* LODGING : alojamiento *m*, cuartel *m* (militar)
quarterback ['kwɔrtər,bæk] *n* : mariscal *m* de campo
quarterly[1] ['kwɔrtərli] *adv* : cada tres meses, trimestralmente
quarterly[2] *adj* : trimestral
quarterly[3] *n, pl* **-lies** : publicación *f* trimestral
quartermaster ['kwɔrtər,mæstər] *n* : intendente *mf*
quartet [kwɔr'tɛt] *n* : cuarteto *m*
quartz ['kwɔrts] *n* : cuarzo *m*
quash ['kwɑʃ, 'kwɔʃ] *vt* **1** ANNUL : anular **2** QUELL : sofocar, aplastar
quaver[1] ['kweɪvər] *vi* **1** SHAKE : temblar ⟨her voice was quavering : le temblaba la voz⟩ **2** TRILL : trinar
quaver[2] *n* : temblor *m* (de la voz)
quay ['ki:, 'keɪ, 'kweɪ] *n* : muelle *m*
queasiness ['kwi:zinəs] *n* : mareo *m*, náusea *f*
queasy ['kwi:zi] *adj* **-sier; -est** : mareado
queen ['kwi:n] *n* : reina *f*
queenly ['kwi:nli] *adj* **-lier; -est** : de reina, regio
queer ['kwɪr] *adj* : extraño, raro, curioso — **queerly** *adv*
quell ['kwl] *vt* : aplastar, sofocar

quench ['kwɛntʃ] *vt* **1** EXTINGUISH : apagar, sofocar **2** SATISFY : saciar, satisfacer (la sed)

querulous ['kwɛrələs, 'kwɛrjələs, 'kwɪr-] *adj* : quejumbroso, quejoso — **querulously** *adv*

query[1] ['kwɪri, 'kwɛr-] *vt* **-ried; -rying 1** ASK : preguntar, interrogar ⟨we queried the professor : preguntamos al profesor⟩ **2** QUESTION : cuestionar, poner en duda ⟨to query a matter : cuestionar un asunto⟩

query[2] *n, pl* **-ries 1** QUESTION : pregunta *f* **2** DOUBT : duda *f*

quest[1] ['kwɛst] *v* : buscar

quest[2] *n* : búsqueda *f*

question[1] ['kwɛstʃən] *vt* **1** ASK : preguntar **2** DOUBT : poner en duda, cuestionar **3** INTERROGATE : interrogar — *vi* INQUIRE : inquirir, preguntar

question[2] *n* **1** QUERY : pregunta *f* **2** ISSUE : asunto *m*, problema *f*, cuestión *f* **3** POSSIBILITY : posibilidad *f* ⟨it's out of the question : es indiscutible⟩ **4** DOUBT : duda *f* ⟨to call into question : poner en duda⟩

questionable ['kwɛstʃənəbəl] *adj* : dudoso, discutible, cuestionable ⟨questionable results : resultados discutibles⟩ ⟨questionable motives : motivos sospechosos⟩

questioner ['kwɛstʃənər] *n* : interrogador *m*, -dora *f*

question mark *n* : signo *m* de interrogación

questionnaire [ˌkwɛstʃəˈnær] *n* : cuestionario *m*

queue[1] ['kju:] *vi* **queued; queuing** *or* **queueing** : hacer cola

queue[2] *n* **1** PIGTAIL : coleta *f*, trenza *f* **2** LINE : cola *f*, fila *f*

quibble[1] ['kwɪbəl] *vi* **-bled; -bling** : quejarse por nimiedades, andar con sutilezas

quibble[2] *n* : objeción *f* de poca monta, queja *f* insignificante

quick[1] ['kwɪk] *adv* : rápidamente

quick[2] *adj* **1** RAPID : rápido **2** ALERT, CLEVER : listo, vivo, agudo **3 a quick temper** : un genio vivo

quick[3] *n* **1** FLESH : carne *f* viva **2 to cut someone to the quick** : herir a alguien en lo más vivo

quicken ['kwɪkən] *vt* **1** REVIVE : resucitar **2** AROUSE : estimular, despertar **3** HASTEN : acelerar ⟨she quickened her pace : aceleró el paso⟩

quickly ['kwɪkli] *adv* : rápidamente, rápido, de prisa

quickness ['kwɪknəs] *n* : rapidez *f*

quicksand ['kwɪkˌsænd] *n* : arena *f* movediza

quicksilver ['kwɪkˌsɪlvər] *n* : mercurio *m*, azogue *m*

quick–tempered ['kwɪk'tɛmpərd] *adj* : irascible, de genio vivo

quick–witted ['kwɪk'wɪtəd] *adj* : agudo

quiet[1] ['kwaɪət] *vt* **1** SILENCE : hacer callar, acallar **2** CALM : calmar, tranquilizar — *vi* **to quiet down** : calmarse, tranquilizarse

quiet[2] *adv* : silenciosamente ⟨a quiet-running engine : un motor silencioso⟩

quiet[3] *adj* **1** CALM : tranquilo, calmoso **2** MILD : sosegado, suave ⟨a quiet disposition : un temperamento sosegado⟩ **3** SILENT : silencioso **4** UNOBTRUSIVE : discreto **5** SECLUDED : aislado ⟨a quiet nook : un rincón aislado⟩ — **quietly** *adv*

quiet[4] *n* **1** CALM : calma *f*, tranquilidad *f* **2** SILENCE : silencio *m*

quietness ['kwaɪətnəs] *n* : suavidad *f*, tranquilidad *f*, quietud *f*

quietude ['kwaɪəˌtu:d, -ˌtju:d] *n* : quietud *f*, reposo *m*

quill ['kwɪl] *n* **1** SPINE : púa *f* (de un puerco espín) **2** : pluma *f* (para escribir)

quilt[1] ['kwɪlt] *vt* : acolchar

quilt[2] *n* : colcha *f*, edredón *m*

quince ['kwɪnts] *n* : membrillo *m*

quinine ['kwaɪˌnaɪn] *n* : quinina *f*

quintessence [kwɪn'tɛsənts] *n* : quintaesencia *f*

quintet [kwɪn'tɛt] *n* : quinteto *m*

quintuple [kwɪn'tu:pəl, -'tju:-, -'tʌ-; 'kwɪntə-] *adj* : quíntuplo

quintuplet [kwɪn'tʌplət, -'tu:-, -'tju:-; 'kwɪntə-] *n* : quintillizo *m*, -za *f*

quip[1] ['kwɪp] *vi* **quipped; quipping** : bromear

quip[2] *n* : ocurrencia *f*, salida *f*

quirk ['kwərk] *n* : peculiaridad *f*, rareza *f* ⟨a quirk of fate : un capricho del destino⟩

quirky ['kwərki] *adj* **-kier; -est** : peculiar, raro

quit ['kwɪt] *v* **quit; quitting** *vt* : dejar, abandonar ⟨to quit smoking : dejar de fumar⟩ — *vi* **1** STOP : parar **2** RESIGN : dimitir, renunciar

quite ['kwaɪt] *adv* **1** COMPLETELY : completamente, totalmente **2** RATHER : bastante ⟨quite near : bastante cerca⟩

quits ['kwɪts] *adj* **to call it quits** : quedar en paz

quitter ['kwɪtər] *n* : derrotista *mf*

quiver[1] ['kwɪvər] *vi* : temblar, estremecerse, vibrar

quiver[2] *n* **1** : carcaj *m*, aljaba *f* (para flechas) **2** TREMBLING : temblor *m*, estremecimiento *m*

quixotic [kwɪk'sɑtɪk] *adj* : quijotesco

quiz[1] ['kwɪz] *vt* **quizzed; quizzing** : interrogar, hacer una prueba a (en el colegio)

quiz[2] *n, pl* **quizzes** : examen *m* corto, prueba *f*

quizzical ['kwɪzɪkəl] *adj* **1** TEASING : burlón **2** CURIOUS : curioso, interrogativo

quorum ['kworəm] *n* : quórum *m*

quota ['kwo:t̯ə] *n* : cuota *f*, cupo *m*
quotable ['kwo:t̯əbəl] *adj* : citable
quotation [kwo'teɪʃən] *n* **1** CITATION
: cita *f* **2** ESTIMATE : presupuesto *m*,
estimación *f* **3** PRICE : cotización *f*
quotation marks *npl* : comillas *fpl*

quote¹ ['kwo:t] *vt* **quoted; quoting 1**
CITE : citar **2** VALUE : cotizar (en finanzas)
quote² *n* **1** → quotation **2** quotes *npl*
→ quotation marks
quotient ['kwo:ʃənt] *n* : cociente *m*

R

r ['ɑr] *n, pl* **r's** *or* **rs** ['ɑrz] : decimoctava
letra del alfabeto inglés
rabbi ['ræ͵baɪ] *n* : rabino *m*, -na *f*
rabbit ['ræbət] *n, pl* **-bit** *or* **-bits** : conejo *m*, -ja *f*
rabble ['ræbəl] *n* **1** MASSES : populacho
m **2** RIFFRAFF : chusma *f*, gentuza *f*
rabid ['ræbɪd] *adj* **1** : rabioso, afectado
con la rabia **2** FURIOUS : furioso **3**
FANATIC : fanático
rabies ['reɪbi:z] *ns & pl* : rabia *f*
raccoon [ræ'ku:n] *n, pl* **-coon** *or* **-coons**
: mapache *m*
race¹ ['reɪs] *vi* **raced; racing 1** : correr,
competir (en una carrera) **2** RUSH : ir
a toda prisa, ir corriendo
race² *n* **1** CURRENT : corriente *f* (de
agua) **2** : carrera *f* ⟨dog race : carrera
de perros⟩ ⟨the presidential race : la
carrera presidencial⟩ **3** : raza *f* ⟨the
black race : la raza negra⟩ ⟨the human
race : el género humano⟩
racecourse ['reɪs͵kors] *n* : pista *f* (de carreras)
racehorse ['reɪs͵hors] *n* : caballo *m* de
carreras
racer ['reɪsər] *n* : corredor *m*, -dora *f*
racetrack ['reɪs͵træk] *n* : pista *f* (de carreras)
racial ['reɪʃəl] *adj* : racial — **racially** *adv*
racism ['reɪ͵sɪzəm] *n* : racismo *m*
racist ['reɪsɪst] *n* : racista *mf*
rack¹ ['ræk] *vt* **1** : atormentar ⟨racked
with pain : atormentado por el dolor⟩
2 to rack one's brains : devanarse los
sesos
rack² *n* **1** SHELF, STAND : estante *m* ⟨a
luggage rack : un portaequipajes⟩ ⟨a
coatrack : un perchero, una percha⟩ **2**
: potro *m* (instrumento de la tortura)
racket ['rækət] *n* **1** : raqueta *f* (en deportes) **2** DIN : estruendo *m*, bulla *f*,
jaleo *m fam* **3** SWINDLE : estafa *f*, timo
m fam
racketeer [͵rækə'tɪr] *n* : estafador *m*,
-dora *f*
raconteur [͵ræ͵kɑn'tər] *n* : anecdotista
mf
racy ['reɪsi] *adj* **racier; -est** : subido de
tono, picante
radar ['reɪ͵dɑr] *n* : radar *m*
radial ['reɪdiəl] *adj* : radial
radiance ['reɪdiənts] *n* : resplandor *m*
radiant ['reɪdiənt] *adj* : radiante — **ra-
diantly** *adv*
radiate ['reɪdi͵eɪt] *v* **-ated; -ating** *vt* : irradiar, emitir ⟨to radiate heat : irradi-

ar el calor⟩ ⟨to radiate happiness : rebosar de alegría⟩ — *vi* **1** : irradiar **2**
SPREAD : salir, extenderse ⟨to radiate
(out) from the center : salir del centro⟩
radiation [͵reɪdi'eɪʃən] *n* : radiación *f*
radiator ['reɪdi͵eɪt̯ər] *n* : radiador *m*
radical¹ ['rædɪkəl] *adj* : radical — **radi-
cally** [-kli] *adv*
radical² *n* : radical *mf*
radicalism ['rædɪkə͵lɪzəm] *n* : radicalismo *m*
radii → radius
radio¹ ['reɪdi͵o:] *v* : llamar por radio,
transmitir por radio
radio² *n, pl* **-dios** : radio *m* (aparato), radio *f* (emisora, radiodifusión)
radioactive ['reɪdio'æktɪv] *adj* : radiactivo, radioactivo
radioactivity [͵reɪdio͵æk'tɪvət̯i] *n, pl*
-ties : radiactividad *f*, radioactividad *f*
radiologist [͵reɪdi'ɑləʤɪst] *n* : radiólogo
m, -ga *f*
radiology [͵reɪdi'ɑləʤi] *n* : radiología *f*
radish ['rædɪʃ] *n* : rábano *m*
radium ['reɪdiəm] *n* : radio *m*
radius ['reɪdiəs] *n, pl* **radii** [-di͵aɪ] : radio
m
radon ['reɪ͵dɑn] *n* : radón *m*
raffle¹ ['ræfəl] *vt* **-fled; -fling** : rifar,
sortear
raffle² *n* : rifa *f*, sorteo *m*
raft ['ræft] *n* **1** : balsa *f* ⟨rubber rafts
: balsas de goma⟩ **2** LOT, SLEW : montón *m* ⟨a raft of documents : un montón de documentos⟩
rafter ['ræftər] *n* : par *m*, viga *f*
rag ['ræg] *n* **1** CLOTH : trapo *m* **2 rags**
npl TATTERS : harapos *mpl*, andrajos
mpl
ragamuffin ['rægə͵mʌfən] *n* : pilluelo *m*,
-la *f*
rage¹ ['reɪʤ] *vi* **raged; raging 1** : estar
furioso, rabiar ⟨to fly into a rage : en-
furecerse⟩ **2** : bramar, hacer estragos
⟨the wind was raging : el viento bram-
aba⟩ ⟨flu raged through the school : la
gripe hizo estragos por el colegio⟩
rage² *n* **1** ANGER : furia *f*, ira *f*, cólera *f*
2 FAD : moda *f*, furor *m*
ragged ['rægəd] *adj* **1** UNEVEN : irregular, desigual **2** TORN : hecho jirones
3 TATTERED : andrajoso, harapiento
ragout [ræ'gu:] *n* : ragú *m*, estofado *m*
ragtime ['ræg͵taɪm] *n* : ragtime *m*
ragweed ['ræg͵wi:d] *n* : ambrosía *f*
raid¹ ['reɪd] *vt* **1** : invadir, hacer una incursión en ⟨raided by enemy troops

: invadido por tropas enemigas⟩ 2
: asaltar, atracar ⟨the gang raided the
warehouse : la pandilla asaltó el al-
macén⟩ 3 : allanar, hacer una redada
en ⟨police raided the house : la policía
allanó la vivienda⟩

raid² *n* 1 : invasión *f* (militar) 2 : asalto
m (por delincuentes) 3 : redada *f*, allanamiento *m* (por la policía)

raider ['reɪdər] *n* 1 ATTACKER : asaltante
mf; invasor *m*, -sora *f* 2 **corporate
raider** : tiburón *m*

rail¹ ['reɪl] *vi* 1 **to rail against** REVILE
: denostar contra 2 **to rail at** SCOLD
: regañar, reprender

rail² *n* 1 BAR : barra *f*, barrera *f* 2
HANDRAIL : pasamanos *m*, barandilla
f 3 TRACK : riel *m* (para ferrocarriles)
4 RAILROAD : ferrocarril *m*

railing ['reɪlɪŋ] *n* 1 : baranda *f* (de un
balcón, etc.) 2 RAILS : verja *f*

raillery ['reɪləri] *n, pl* **-leries** : bromas *fpl*

railroad ['reɪl,roːd] *n* : ferrocarril *m*

railway ['reɪl,weɪ] → **railroad**

raiment ['reɪmənt] *n* : vestiduras *fpl*

rain¹ ['reɪn] *vi* 1 : llover ⟨it's raining : está
lloviendo⟩ 2 **to rain down** SHOWER
: llover ⟨insults rained down on him : le
llovieron los insultos⟩

rain² *n* : lluvia *f*

rainbow ['reɪn,boː] *n* : arco *m* iris

raincoat ['reɪn,koːt] *n* : impermeable *m*

raindrop ['reɪn,drɑp] *n* : gota *f* de lluvia

rainfall ['reɪn,fɔl] *n* : lluvia *f*, precipitación *f*

rainstorm ['reɪn,stɔrm] *n* : temporal *m*
(de lluvia)

rainwater ['reɪn,wɔtər] *n* : agua *f* de lluvia

rainy ['reɪni] *adj* **rainier; -est** : lluvioso

raise¹ ['reɪz] *vt* **raised; raising** 1 LIFT
: levantar, subir, alzar ⟨to raise one's
spirits : levantarle el ánimo a alguien⟩
2 ERECT : levantar, erigir 3 COLLECT
: recaudar ⟨to raise money : recaudar
dinero⟩ 4 REAR : criar ⟨to raise one's
children : criar uno a sus niños⟩ 5
GROW : cultivar 6 INCREASE : aumentar, subir 7 PROMOTE : ascender 8
PROVOKE : provocar ⟨it raised a laugh
: provocó una risa⟩ 9 BRING UP : sacar
(temas, objeciones, etc.)

raise² *n* : aumento *m*

raisin ['reɪzən] *n* : pasa *f*

raja *or* **rajah** ['rɑdʒə, -,dʒɑ, -,ʒɑ] *n* : rajá
m

rake¹ ['reɪk] *v* **raked; raking** *vt* 1 : rastrillar ⟨to rake leaves : rastrillar las ho-
jas⟩ 2 SWEEP : barrer ⟨raked with gunfire : barrido con metralla⟩ — *vi* **to rake
through** : revolver, hurgar en

rake² *n* 1 : rastrillo *m* 2 LIBERTINE : libertino *m*, -na *f*; calavera *m*

rakish ['reɪkɪʃ] *adj* 1 JAUNTY : desenvuelto, desenfadado 2 DISSOLUTE
: libertino, disoluto

rally¹ ['ræli] *v* **-lied; -lying** *vi* 1 MEET,
UNITE : reunirse, congregarse 2 RE-

COVER : recuperarse — *vt* 1 ASSEMBLE
: reunir (tropas, etc.) 2 RECOVER : recobrar (la fuerza, el ánimo, etc.)

rally² *n, pl* **-lies** : reunión *f*, mitin *m*, manifestación *f*

ram¹ ['ræm] *v* **rammed; ramming** *vt* 1
DRIVE : hincar, clavar ⟨he rammed it
into the ground : lo hincó en la tierra⟩
2 SMASH : estrellar, embestir — *vi* COL-
LIDE : chocar (contra), estrellarse

ram² *n* 1 : carnero *m* (animal) 2 **battering ram** : ariete *m*

RAM ['ræm] *n* : RAM *f*

ramble¹ ['ræmbəl] *vi* **-bled; -bling** 1
WANDER : pasear, deambular 2 **to ram-
ble on** : divagar, perder el hilo 3
SPREAD : trepar (dícese de una planta)

ramble² *n* : paseo *m*, excursión *f*

rambler ['ræmblər] *n* 1 WALKER : excursionista *mf* 2 ROSE : rosa *f* trepadora

rambunctious [ræm'bʌŋkʃəs] *adj* UN-
RULY : alborotado

ramification [,ræməfə'keɪʃən] *n* : ramificación *f*

ramify ['ræmə,faɪ] *vi* **-fied; -fying** : ramificarse

ramp ['ræmp] *n* : rampa *f*

rampage¹ ['ræm,peɪdʒ, ræm'peɪdʒ] *vi*
-paged; -paging : andar arrasando
todo, correr destrozando

rampage² ['ræm,peɪdʒ] *n* : alboroto *m*,
frenesí *m* (de violencia)

rampant ['ræmpənt] *adj* : desenfrenado

rampart ['ræm,pɑrt] *n* : terraplén *m*, muralla *f*

ramrod ['ræm,rɑd] *n* : baqueta *f*

ramshackle ['ræm,ʃækəl] *adj* : destartalado

ran → **run**

ranch ['ræntʃ] *n* 1 : hacienda *f*, rancho
m, finca *f* ganadera 2 FARM : granja *f*
⟨fruit ranch : granja de frutas⟩

rancher ['ræntʃər] *n* : estanciero *m*, -ra
f; ranchero *m*, -ra *f*

rancid ['ræntsɪd] *adj* : rancio

rancor ['ræŋkər] *n* : rencor *m*

random ['rændəm] *adj* 1 : fortuito,
aleatorio 2 **at ∼** : al azar — **randomly** *adv*

rang → **ring**

range¹ ['reɪndʒ] *v* **ranged; ranging** *vt*
ARRANGE : alinear, ordenar, arreglar
— *vi* 1 ROAM : deambular ⟨to range
through the town : deambular por el
pueblo⟩ 2 EXTEND : extenderse ⟨the
results range widely : los resultados se
extienden mucho⟩ 3 VARY : variar
⟨discounts range from 20% to 40% : los
descuentos varían entre 20% y 40%⟩

range² *n* 1 ROW : fila *f*, hilera *f* ⟨a mountain range : una cordillera⟩ 2 GRASS-
LAND : pradera *f*, pampa *f* 3 STOVE
: cocina *f* 4 VARIETY : variedad *f*, gama
f 5 SPHERE : ámbito *m*, esfera *f*, campo *m* 6 REACH : registro *m* (de la voz),
alcance *m* (de un arma de fuego) 7
shooting range : campo *m* de tiro

ranger ['reɪndʒər] *n or* **forest ranger** : guardabosque *mf*

rangy ['reɪndʒi] *adj* **rangier; -est** : alto y delgado

rank¹ ['ræŋk] *vt* **1** RANGE : alinear, ordenar, poner en fila **2** CLASSIFY : clasificar — *vi* **1 to rank above** : ser superior a **2 to rank among** : encontrarse entre, figurar entre

rank² *adj* **1** LUXURIANT : lozano, exuberante (dícese de una planta) **2** SMELLY : fétido, maloliente **3** OUTRIGHT : completo, absoluto ⟨a rank injustice : una injusticia manifiesta⟩

rank³ *n* **1** LINE, ROW : fila *f* ⟨to close ranks : cerrar filas⟩ **2** GRADE, POSITION : grado *m*, rango *m* (militar) ⟨to pull rank : abusar de su autoridad⟩ **3** CLASS : categoría *f*, clase *f* **4 ranks** *npl* : soldados *mpl* rasos

rank and file *n* **1** RANKS : soldados *mpl* rasos **2** : bases *fpl* (de un partido, etc.)

rankle ['ræŋkəl] *v* **-kled; -kling** *vi* : doler — *vt* : irritar, herir

ransack ['ræn,sæk] *vt* : revolver, desvalijar, registrar de arriba abajo

ransom¹ ['ræntsəm] *vt* : rescatar, pagar un rescate por

ransom² *n* : rescate *m*

rant ['rænt] *vi or* **to rant and rave** : despotricar, desvariar

rap¹ ['ræp] *v* **rapped; rapping** *vt* **1** KNOCK : golpetear, dar un golpe en **2** CRITICIZE : criticar — *vi* **1** CHAT : charlar, cotorrear *fam* **2** KNOCK : dar un golpe

rap² *n* **1** BLOW, KNOCK : golpe *m*, golpecito *m* **2** CHAT : charla *f* **3** *or* **rap music** : rap *m* **4 to take the rap** : pagar el pato *fam*

rapacious [rə'peɪʃəs] *adj* **1** GREEDY : avaricioso, codicioso **2** PREDATORY : rapaz, de rapiña **3** RAVENOUS : voraz

rape¹ ['reɪp] *vt* **raped; raping** : violar

rape² *n* **1** : colza *f* (planta) **2** : violación *f* (de una persona)

rapid ['ræpɪd] *adj* : rápido — **rapidly** *adv*

rapidity [rə'pɪdəti] *n* : rapidez *f*

rapids ['ræpɪdz] *npl* : rápidos *mpl*

rapier ['reɪpiər] *n* : estoque *m*

rapist ['reɪpɪst] *n* : violador *m*, -dora *f*

rapper ['ræpər] *n* : cantante *mf* de rap; rapero *m*, -ra *f*

rapport [ræ'por] *n* : relación *f* armoniosa, entendimiento *m*

rapt ['ræpt] *adj* : absorto, embelesado

rapture ['ræptʃər] *n* : éxtasis *m*

rapturous ['ræptʃərəs] *adj* : extasiado, embelesado

rare ['rær] *adj* **rarer; rarest 1** RAREFIED : enrarecido **2** FINE : excelente, excepcional ⟨a rare talent : un talento excepcional⟩ **3** UNCOMMON : raro, poco común **4** : poco cocido (dícese de la carne)

rarefy ['rærə,faɪ] *vt* **-fied; -fying** : rarificar, enrarecer

rarely ['rærli] *adv* SELDOM : pocas veces, rara vez

raring ['rærən, -ɪŋ] *adj* : lleno de entusiasmo, con muchas ganas

rarity ['rærəti] *n, pl* **-ties** : rareza *f*

rascal ['ræskəl] *n* : pillo *m*, -lla *f*; pícaro *m*, -ra *f*

rash¹ ['ræʃ] *adj* : imprudente, precipitado — **rashly** *adv*

rash² *n* : sarpullido *m*, erupción *f*

rashness ['ræʃnəs] *n* : precipitación *f*, impetuosidad *f*

rasp¹ ['ræsp] *vt* **1** SCRAPE : raspar, escofinar **2 to rasp out** : decir en voz áspera

rasp² *n* : escofina *f*

raspberry ['ræz,bɛri] *n, pl* **-ries** : frambuesa *f*

rat ['ræt] *n* : rata *f*

ratchet ['rætʃət] *n* : trinquete *m*

rate¹ ['reɪt] *vt* **rated; rating 1** CONSIDER, REGARD : considerar, estimar **2** DESERVE : merecer

rate² *n* **1** PACE, SPEED : velocidad *f*, ritmo *m* ⟨at this rate : a este paso⟩ **2** : índice *m*, tasa *f* ⟨birth rate : índice de natalidad⟩ ⟨interest rate : tasa de interés⟩ **3** CHARGE, PRICE : precio *m*, tarifa *f*

rather ['ræðər, 'rʌ-, 'rɑ-] *adv* **1** (*indicating preference*) ⟨she would rather stay in the house : preferiría quedarse en casa⟩ ⟨I'd rather not : mejor que no⟩ **2** (*indicating preciseness*) ⟨my father, or rather my stepfather : mi padre, o mejor dicho mi padrastro⟩ **3** INSTEAD : sino que, más que, al contrario ⟨I'm not pleased; rather I'm disappointed : no estoy satisfecho, sino desilusionado⟩ **4** SOMEWHAT : algo, un tanto ⟨rather strange : un poco extraño⟩ **5** QUITE : bastante ⟨rather difficult : bastante difícil⟩

ratification [,rætəfə'keɪʃən] *n* : ratificación *f*

ratify ['rætə,faɪ] *vt* **-fied; -fying** : ratificar

rating ['reɪtɪŋ] *n* **1** STANDING : clasificación *f*, posición *f* **2 ratings** *npl* : índice *m* de audiencia

ratio ['reɪʃio] *n, pl* **-tios** : proporción *f*, relación *f*

ration¹ ['ræʃən, 'reɪʃən] *vt* : racionar

ration² *n* **1** : ración *f* **2 rations** *npl* PROVISIONS : víveres *mpl*

rational ['ræʃənəl] *adj* : racional, razonable, lógico — **rationally** *adv*

rationale [,ræʃə'næl] *n* **1** EXPLANATION : explicación *f* **2** BASIS : base *f*, razones *fpl*

rationality [,ræʃə'næləti] *n, pl* **-ties** : racionalidad *f*

rationalization [,ræʃənələ'zeɪʃən] *n* : racionalización *f*

rationalize ['ræʃənə,laɪz] *vt* **-ized; -izing** : racionalizar

rattle¹ ['rætəl] *v* **-tled; -tling** *vi* **1** CLATTER : traquetear, hacer ruido **2 to rattle on** CHATTER : parlotear *fam* — *vt*

1 : hacer sonar, agitar ⟨the wind rattled the door : el viento sacudió la puerta⟩ **2** DISCONCERT, WORRY : desconcertar, poner nervioso **3 to rattle off** : despachar, recitar, decir de corrido

rattle² n **1** CLATTER : traqueteo m, ruido m **2** or **baby's rattle** : sonajero m **3** : cascabel m (de una culebra)

rattler ['ræt̮ələr] → **rattlesnake**

rattlesnake ['ræt̮əl,sneɪk] n : serpiente f de cascabel

ratty ['ræt̮i] adj **rattier; -est** : raído, andrajoso

raucous ['rɔkəs] adj **1** HOARSE : ronco **2** BOISTEROUS : escandaloso, bullicioso — **raucously** adv

ravage¹ ['rævɪʤ] vt **-aged; -aging** : devastar, arrasar, hacer estragos

ravage² n : destrozo m, destrucción f ⟨the ravages of war : los estragos de la guerra⟩

rave ['reɪv] vi **raved; raving 1** : delirar, desvariar ⟨to rave like a maniac : desvariar como un loco⟩ **2 to rave about** : hablar con entusiasmo sobre, entusiasmarse por

ravel ['rævəl] v **-eled** or **-elled; -eling** or **-elling** vt UNRAVEL : desenredar, desenmarañar — vi FRAY : deshilacharse

raven ['reɪvən] n : cuervo m

ravenous ['rævənəs] adj : hambriento, voraz — **ravenously** adv

ravine [rə'viːn] n : barranco m, quebrada f

ravish ['rævɪʃ] vt **1** PLUNDER : saquear **2** ENCHANT : embelesar, cautivar, encantar

raw ['rɔ] adj **rawer; rawest 1** UNCOOKED : crudo **2** UNTREATED : sin tratar, sin refinar, puro ⟨raw data : datos en bruto⟩ ⟨raw materials : materias primas⟩ **3** INEXPERIENCED : novato, inexperto **4** OPEN : abierto, en carne viva ⟨a raw sore : una llaga abierta⟩ **5** : frío y húmedo ⟨a raw day : un día crudo⟩ **6** UNFAIR : injusto ⟨a raw deal : un trato injusto, una injusticia⟩

rawhide ['rɔ,haɪd] n : cuero m sin curtir

ray ['reɪ] n **1** : rayo m (de la luz, etc.) ⟨a ray of hope : un resquicio de esperanza⟩ **2** : raya f (pez)

rayon ['reɪ,ɑn] n : rayón m

raze ['reɪz] vt **razed; razing** : arrasar, demoler

razor ['reɪzər] n **1** or **straight razor** : navaja f (de afeitar) **2** or **safety razor** : maquinilla f de afeitar, rastrillo m Mex **3** SHAVER : afeitadora f, rasuradora f

reach¹ ['riːʧ] vt **1** EXTEND : extender, alargar ⟨to reach out one's hand : extender la mano⟩ **2** : alcanzar ⟨I couldn't reach the apple : no pude alcanzar la manzana⟩ **3** : llegar a, llegar hasta ⟨the shadow reached the wall : la sombra llegó hasta la pared⟩ **4** CONTACT : contactar, ponerse en contacto con — vi **1** or **to reach out** : extender la mano **2** STRETCH : extenderse **3 to**

reach for : tratar de agarrar

reach² n : alcance m, extensión f

react [ri'ækt] vi : reaccionar

reaction [ri'ækʃən] n : reacción f

reactionary¹ [ri'ækʃə,nɛri] adj : reaccionario

reactionary² n, pl **-ries** : reaccionario m, -ria f

reactor [ri'æktər] n : reactor m ⟨nuclear reactor : reactor nuclear⟩

read¹ ['riːd] v **read** ['rɛd]; **reading** vt **1** : leer ⟨to read a story : leer un cuento⟩ **2** INTERPRET : interpretar ⟨it can be read two ways : se puede interpretar de dos maneras⟩ **3** : decir, poner ⟨the sign read "No smoking" : el letrero decía "No Fumar"⟩ **4** : marcar ⟨the thermometer reads 70° : el termómetro marca 70°⟩ — vi **1** : leer ⟨he can read : sabe leer⟩ **2** SAY : decir ⟨the list reads as follows : la lista dice lo siguiente⟩

read² n **to be a good read** : ser una lectura amena

readable ['riːdəbəl] adj : legible — **readably** [-bli] adv

reader ['riːdər] n : lector m, -tora f

readily ['rɛdəli] adv **1** WILLINGLY : de buena gana, con gusto **2** EASILY : fácilmente, con facilidad

readiness ['rɛdinəs] n **1** WILLINGNESS : buena disposición f **2 to be in readiness** : estar preparado

reading ['riːdɪŋ] n : lectura f

readjust [,riːə'ʤʌst] vt : reajustar — vi : volverse a adaptar

readjustment [,riːə'ʤʌstmənt] n : reajuste m

ready¹ ['rɛdi] vt **readied; readying** : preparar

ready² adj **readier; -est 1** PREPARED : listo, preparado **2** WILLING : dispuesto **3** : a punto de ⟨ready to cry : a punto de llorar⟩ **4** AVAILABLE : disponible ⟨ready cash : efectivo⟩ **5** QUICK : vivo, agudo ⟨a ready wit : un ingenio agudo⟩

ready–made ['rɛdi'meɪd] adj : preparado, confeccionado

reaffirm [,riːə'fərm] vt : reafirmar

real¹ ['riːl] adv VERY : muy ⟨we had a real good time : lo pasamos muy bien⟩

real² adj **1** : inmobiliario ⟨real property : bien inmueble, bien raíz⟩ **2** GENUINE : auténtico, genuino **3** ACTUAL, TRUE : real, verdadero ⟨a real friend : un verdadero amigo⟩ **4 for real** SERIOUSLY : de veras, de verdad

real estate n : propiedad f inmobiliaria, bienes mpl raíces

realign [,riːə'laɪn] vt : realinear

realignment [,riːə'laɪnmənt] n : realineamiento m

realism ['riːə,lɪzəm] n : realismo m

realist ['riːəlɪst] n : realista mf

realistic [,riːə'lɪstɪk] adj : realista

realistically [,riːə'lɪstɪkli] adv : de manera realista

reality [ri'æləṭi] *n, pl* **-ties** : realidad *f*
realizable [ˌriːəˈlaɪzəbəl] *adj* : realizable, alcanzable
realization [ˌriːələˈzeɪʃən] *n* : realización *f*
realize [ˈriːəˌlaɪz] *vt* **-ized; -izing 1** AC-COMPLISH : realizar, llevar a cabo **2** GAIN : obtener, realizar, sacar ⟨to realize a profit : realizar beneficios⟩ **3** UNDERSTAND : darse cuenta de, saber
really [ˈrɪli, ˈriː-] *adv* **1** ACTUALLY : de verdad, en realidad **2** TRULY : verdaderamente, realmente **3** FRANKLY : francamente, en serio
realm [ˈrɛlm] *n* **1** KINGDOM : reino *m* **2** SPHERE : esfera *f*, campo *m*
ream¹ [ˈriːm] *vt* : escariar
ream² *n* **1** : resma *f* (de papel) **2 reams** *npl* LOADS : montones *mpl*
reap [ˈriːp] *v* : cosechar
reaper [ˈriːpər] *n* **1** : cosechador *m*, -dora *f* (persona) **2** : cosechadora *f* (máquina)
reappear [ˌriːəˈpɪr] *vi* : reaparecer
reappearance [ˌriːəˈpɪrənts] *n* : reaparición *f*
rear¹ [ˈrɪr] *vt* **1** LIFT, RAISE : levantar **2** BREED, BRING UP : criar — *vi or* **to rear up** : encabritarse
rear² *adj* : trasero, posterior, de atrás
rear³ *n* **1** BACK : parte *f* de atrás ⟨to bring up the rear : cerrar la marcha⟩ **2** *or* **rear end** : trasero *m*
rear admiral *n* : contraalmirante *mf*
rearrange [ˌriːəˈreɪndʒ] *vt* **-ranged; -ranging** : colocar de otra manera, volver a arreglar, reorganizar
rearview mirror [ˈrɪrˌvjuː-] *n* : retrovisor *m*
reason¹ [ˈriːzən] *vt* THINK : pensar — *vi* : razonar ⟨I can't reason with her : no puedo razonar con ella⟩
reason² *n* **1** CAUSE, GROUND : razón *f*, motivo *m* ⟨the reason for his trip : el motivo de su viaje⟩ ⟨for this reason : por esta razón, por lo cual⟩ ⟨the reason why : la razón por la cual, el porqué⟩ **2** SENSE : razón *f* ⟨to lose one's reason : perder los sesos⟩ ⟨to listen to reason : avenirse a razones⟩
reasonable [ˈriːzənəbəl] *adj* **1** SENSIBLE : razonable **2** INEXPENSIVE : barato, económico
reasonably [ˈriːzənəbli] *adv* **1** SENSIBLY : razonablemente **2** FAIRLY : bastante
reasoning [ˈriːzənɪŋ] *n* : razonamiento *m*, raciocinio *m*, argumentos *mpl*
reassess [ˌriːəˈsɛs] *vt* : revaluar, reconsiderar
reassurance [ˌriːəˈʃʊrənts] *n* : consuelo *m*, palabras *fpl* alentadoras
reassure [ˌriːəˈʃʊr] *vt* **-sured; -suring** : tranquilizar
reassuring [ˌriːəˈʃʊrɪŋ] *adj* : tranquilizador
reawaken [ˌriːəˈweɪkən] *vt* : volver a despertar, reavivar
rebate [ˈriːˌbeɪt] *n* : reembolso *m*, devolución *f*

rebel¹ [rɪˈbɛl] *vi* **-belled; -belling** : rebelarse, sublevarse
rebel² [ˈrɛbəl] *adj* : rebelde
rebel³ [ˈrɛbəl] *n* : rebelde *mf*
rebellion [rɪˈbɛljən] *n* : rebelión *f*
rebellious [rɪˈbɛljəs] *adj* : rebelde
rebelliousness [rɪˈbɛljəsnəs] *n* : rebeldía *f*
rebirth [ˌriːˈbərθ] *n* : renacimiento *m*
reboot [riˈbuːt] *vt* : reiniciar (una computadora)
reborn [riˈbɔrn] *adj* **to be reborn** : renacer
rebound¹ [ˈriːˌbaʊnd, ˌriːˈbaʊnd] *vi* : rebotar
rebound² [ˈriːˌbaʊnd] *n* : rebote *m*
rebuff¹ [rɪˈbʌf] *vt* : desairar, rechazar
rebuff² *n* : desaire *m*, rechazo *m*
rebuild [ˌriːˈbɪld] *vt* **-built** [-ˈbɪlt]; **-building** : reconstruir
rebuke¹ [rɪˈbjuːk] *vt* **-buked; -buking** : reprender, regañar
rebuke² *n* : reprimenda *f*, reproche *m*
rebut [riˈbʌt] *vt* **-butted; -butting** : rebatir, refutar
rebuttal [riˈbʌṭəl] *n* : refutación *f*
recalcitrant [riˈkælsətrənt] *adj* : recalcitrante
recall¹ [riˈkɔl] *vt* **1** : llamar, retirar ⟨recalled to active duty : llamado al servicio activo⟩ **2** REMEMBER : recordar, acordarse de **3** REVOKE : revocar
recall² [riˈkɔl, ˈriːˌkɔl] *n* **1** : retirada *f* (de personas o mercancías) **2** MEMORY : memoria *f* ⟨to have total recall : poder recordar todo⟩
recant [riˈkænt] *vt* : retractarse de — *vi* : retractarse, renegar
recapitulate [ˌriːkəˈpɪtʃəˌleɪt] *v* **-lated; -lating** : resumir, recapitular
recapture [ˌriːˈkæptʃər] *vt* **-tured; -turing 1** REGAIN : volver a tomar, reconquistar **2** RELIVE : revivir (la juventud, etc.)
recast [riˈkæst] *vt* **-cast; -casting 1** : refundir (metales) **2** REWRITE : refundir, modificar
recede [riˈsiːd] *vi* **-ceded; -ceding 1** WITHDRAW : retirarse, retroceder **2** FADE : desvanecerse, alejarse **3** SLANT : inclinarse **4 to have a receding hairline** : tener entradas
receipt [riˈsiːt] *n* **1** : recibo *m* **2 receipts** *npl* : ingresos *mpl*, entradas *fpl*
receivable [riˈsiːvəbəl] *adj* **accounts receivable** : cuentas por cobrar
receive [riˈsiːv] *vt* **-ceived; -ceiving 1** GET : recibir ⟨to receive a letter : recibir una carta⟩ ⟨to receive a blow : recibir un golpe⟩ **2** WELCOME : acoger, recibir ⟨to receive guests : tener invitados⟩ **3** : recibir, captar (señales de radio)
receiver [riˈsiːvər] *n* **1** : receptor *m*, -tora *f* (en futbol americano) **2** : receptor *m* (de radio o televisión) **3 telephone receiver** : auricular *m*
recent [ˈriːsənt] *adj* : reciente — **recently** *adv*

receptacle [ri'sɛptɪkəl] *n* : receptáculo *m*, recipiente *m*

reception [ri'sɛpʃən] *n* : recepción *f*

receptionist [ri'sɛpʃənɪst] *n* : recepcionista *mf*

receptive [ri'sɛptɪv] *adj* : receptivo

receptivity [ˌriːˌsɛp'tɪvəti] *n* : receptividad *f*

recess¹ ['riːˌsɛs, rɪ'sɛs] *vt* **1** : poner en un hueco ⟨recessed lighting : iluminación empotrada⟩ **2** ADJOURN : suspender, levantar

recess² *n* **1** ALCOVE : hueco *m*, nicho *m* **2** BREAK : receso *m*, descanso *m*, recreo *m* (en el colegio)

recession [ri'sɛʃən] *n* : recesión *f*, depresión *f* económica

recessive [ri'sɛsɪv] *adj* : recesivo

recharge [ˌriː'tʃɑrdʒ] *vt* **-charged; -charging** : recargar

rechargeable [ˌriː'tʃɑrdʒəbəl] *adj* : recargable

recipe ['rɛsəˌpiː] *n* : receta *f*

recipient [ri'sɪpiənt] *n* : recipiente *mf*

reciprocal [ri'sɪprəkəl] *adj* : recíproco

reciprocate [ri'sɪprəˌkeɪt] *vi* **-cated; -cating** : recíprocar

reciprocity [ˌrɛsə'prɑsəti] *n, pl* **-ties** : reciprocidad *f*

recital [ri'saɪtəl] *n* **1** PERFORMANCE : recital *m* **2** ENUMERATION : relato *m*, enumeración *f*

recitation [ˌrɛsə'teɪʃən] *n* : recitación *f*

recite [ri'saɪt] *vt* **-cited; -citing 1** : recitar (un poema, etc.) **2** RECOUNT : narrar, relatar, enumerar

reckless ['rɛkləs] *adj* : imprudente, temerario — **recklessly** *adv*

recklessness ['rɛkləsnəs] *n* : imprudencia *f*, temeridad *f*

reckon ['rɛkən] *vt* **1** CALCULATE : calcular, contar **2** CONSIDER : considerar

reckoning ['rɛkənɪŋ] *n* **1** CALCULATION : cálculo *m* **2** SETTLEMENT : ajuste *m* de cuentas ⟨day of reckoning : día del juicio final⟩

reclaim [ri'kleɪm] *vt* **1** : ganar, sanear ⟨to reclaim marshy land : sanear las tierras pantanosas⟩ **2** RECOVER : recobrar, reciclar ⟨to reclaim old tires : reciclar llantas desechadas⟩ **3** REGAIN : reclamar, recuperar ⟨to reclaim one's rights : reclamar uno sus derechos⟩

recline [ri'klaɪn] *vi* **-clined; -clining 1** LEAN : reclinarse **2** REPOSE : recostarse

recluse ['rɛˌkluːs, ri'kluːs] *n* : solitario *m*, -ria *f*

recognition [ˌrɛkɪg'nɪʃən] *n* : reconocimiento *m*

recognizable ['rɛkəgˌnaɪzəbəl] *adj* : reconocible

recognize ['rɛkɪgˌnaɪz] *vt* **-nized; -nizing** : reconocer

recoil¹ [ri'kɔɪl] *vi* : retroceder, dar un culatazo

recoil² ['riːˌkɔɪl, ri'-] *n* : retroceso *m*, culatazo *m*

recollect [ˌrɛkə'lɛkt] *v* : recordar

recollection [ˌrɛkə'lɛkʃən] *n* : recuerdo *m*

recommend [ˌrɛkə'mɛnd] *vt* **1** : recomendar ⟨she recommended the medicine : recomendó la medicina⟩ **2** ADVISE, COUNSEL : aconsejar, recomendar

recommendation [ˌrɛkəmən'deɪʃən] *n* : recomendación *f*

recompense¹ ['rɛkəmˌpɛnts] *vt* **-pensed; -pensing** : indemnizar, recompensar

recompense² *n* : indemnización *f*, compensación *f*

reconcile ['rɛkənˌsaɪl] *v* **-ciled; -ciling** *vt* **1** : reconciliar (personas), conciliar (ideas, etc.) **2 to reconcile oneself to** : resignarse a — *vi* MAKE UP : reconciliarse, hacer las paces

reconciliation [ˌrɛkənˌsɪli'eɪʃən] *n* : reconciliación *f* (con personas), conciliación *f* (con ideas, etc.)

recondite ['rɛkənˌdaɪt, ri'kən-] *adj* : recóndito, abstruso

recondition [ˌriːkən'dɪʃən] *vt* : reacondicionar

reconnaissance [ri'kɑnəzənts, -sənts] *n* : reconocimiento *m*

reconnoiter *or* **reconnoitre** [ˌriːkə-'nɔɪtər, ˌrɛkə-] *v* **-tered** *or* **-tred; -tering** *or* **-tring** *vt* : reconocer — *vi* : hacer un reconocimiento

reconsider [ˌriːkən'sɪdər] *vt* : reconsiderar, repensar

reconsideration [ˌriːkənˌsɪdə'reɪʃən] *n* : reconsideración *f*

reconstruct [ˌriːkən'strʌkt] *vt* : reconstruir

reconstruction [ˌriːkən'strʌkʃən] *n* : reconstrucción *f*

record¹ [ri'kɔrd] *vt* **1** WRITE DOWN : anotar, apuntar **2** REGISTER : registrar, hacer constar **3** INDICATE : marcar (una temperatura, etc.) **4** TAPE : grabar

record² ['rɛkərd] *n* **1** DOCUMENT : registro *m*, documento *m* oficial **2** HISTORY : historial *m* ⟨a good academic record : un buen historial académico⟩ ⟨criminal record : antecedentes penales⟩ **3** : récord *m* ⟨the world record : el récord mundial⟩ **4** : disco *m* (de música, etc.) ⟨to make a record : grabar un disco⟩

recorder [ri'kɔrdər] *n* **1** : flauta *f* dulce (instrumento de viento) **2 tape recorder** : grabadora *f*

recording [ri'kɔrdɪŋ] *n* : grabación *f*

recount¹ [ri'kaʊnt] *vt* **1** NARRATE : narrar, relatar **2** : volver a contar (votos, etc.)

recount² ['riːˌkaʊnt, ˌri'-] *n* : recuento *m*

recoup [ri'kuːp] *vt* : recuperar, recobrar

recourse ['riːˌkors, ri'-] *n* : recurso *m* ⟨to have recourse to : recurrir a⟩

recover [ri'kʌvər] *vt* REGAIN : recobrar — *vi* RECUPERATE : recuperarse

recovery [ri'kʌvəri] *n, pl* **-eries** : recuperación *f*
re–create [ˌri:kri'eɪt] *vt* **-ated; -ating** : recrear
recreation [ˌrɛkri'eɪʃən] *n* : recreo *m*, esparcimiento *m*, diversión *f*
recreational [ˌrɛkri'eɪʃənəl] *adj* : recreativo, de recreo
recrimination [rɪˌkrɪmə'neɪʃən] *n* : recriminación *f*
recruit[1] [ri'kru:t] *vt* : reclutar
recruit[2] *n* : recluta *mf*
recruitment [ri'kru:tmənt] *n* : reclutamiento *m*, alistamiento *m*
rectal ['rɛktəl] *adj* : rectal
rectangle ['rɛkˌtæŋɡəl] *n* : rectángulo *m*
rectangular [rɛk'tæŋɡjələr] *adj* : rectangular
rectify ['rɛktəˌfaɪ] *vt* **-fied; -fying** : rectificar
rectitude ['rɛktəˌtu:d, -ˌtju:d] *n* : rectitud *f*
rector ['rɛktər] *n* : rector *m*, -tora *f*
rectory ['rɛktəri] *n, pl* **-ries** : rectoría *f*
rectum ['rɛktəm] *n, pl* **-tums** *or* **-ta** [-tə] : recto *m*
recuperate [ri'ku:pəˌreɪt, -'kju:-] *v* **-ated; -ating** *vt* : recuperar — *vi* : recuperarse, restablecerse
recuperation [riˌku:pə'reɪʃən, -ˌkju:-] *n* : recuperación *f*
recur [ri'kər] *vi* **-curred; -curring** : volver a ocurrir, volver a producirse, repetirse
recurrence [ri'kərənts] *n* : repetición *f*, reaparición *f*
recurrent [ri'kərənt] *adj* : recurrente, que se repite
recyclable [ri'saɪkələbəl] *adj* : reciclable
recycle [ri'saɪkəl] *vt* **-cled; -cling** : reciclar
recycling [ri'saɪkəlɪŋ] *n* : reciclaje *m*
red[1] ['rɛd] *adj* **1** : rojo, colorado ⟨to be red in the face : ponerse colorado⟩ ⟨to have red hair : ser pelirrojo⟩ **2** COMMUNIST : rojo, comunista
red[2] *n* **1** : rojo *m*, colorado *m* **2 Red** COMMUNIST : comunista *mf*
red blood cell *n* : glóbulo *m* rojo
red–blooded ['rɛd'blʌdəd] *adj* : vigoroso
redcap ['rɛdˌkæp] → **porter**
redden ['rɛdən] *vt* : enrojecer — *vi* BLUSH : enrojecerse, ruborizarse
reddish ['rɛdɪʃ] *adj* : rojizo
redecorate [ˌri:'dɛkəˌreɪt] *vt* **-rated; -rating** : renovar, pintar de nuevo
redeem [ri'di:m] *vt* **1** RESCUE, SAVE : rescatar, salvar **2** : desempeñar ⟨she redeemed it from the pawnshop : lo desempeñó de la casa de empeños⟩ **3** : redimir (en religión) **4** : canjear, vender ⟨to redeem coupons : canjear cupones⟩
redeemer [ri'di:mər] *n* : redentor *m*, -tora *f*
redefine [ˌri:dɪ'faɪn] *vt* : redefinir
redemption [ri'dɛmpʃən] *n* : redención *f*

redesign [ˌri:di'zaɪn] *vt* : rediseñar
red–handed ['rɛd'hændəd] *adj* : con las manos en la masa
redhead ['rɛdˌhɛd] *n* : pelirrojo *m*, -ja *f*
red–hot ['rɛd'hɑt] *adj* **1** : al rojo vivo, candente **2** CURRENT : de candente actualidad **3** POPULAR : de gran popularidad
rediscover [ˌri:di'skʌvər] *vt* : redescubrir
redistribute [ˌri:di'strɪˌbju:t] *vt* **-uted; -uting** : redistribuir
red–letter ['rɛd'lɛtər] *adj* **red–letter day** : día *m* memorable
redness ['rɛdnəs] *n* : rojez *f*
redo [ˌri:'du:] *vt* **-did** [-dɪd]; **-done** [-'dʌn]; **-doing 1** : hacer de nuevo **2** → **redecorate**
redolence ['rɛdələnts] *n* : fragancia *f*
redolent ['rɛdələnt] *adj* **1** FRAGRANT : fragante, oloroso **2** SUGGESTIVE : evocador
redouble [ri'dʌbəl] *vt* **-bled; -bling** : redoblar, intensificar (esfuerzos, etc.)
redoubtable [r'dautəbəl] *adj* : temible
redress [ri'drɛs] *vt* : reparar, remediar, enmendar
red snapper *n* : pargo *m*, huachinango *m Mex*
red tape *n* : papeleo *m*
reduce [ri'du:s, -'dju:s] *v* **-duced; -ducing** *vt* **1** LESSEN : reducir, disminuir, rebajar (precios) **2** DEMOTE : bajar de categoría, degradar **3 to be reduced to** : verse rebajado a, verse forzado a **4 to reduce someone to tears** : hacer llorar a alguien — *vi* SLIM : adelgazar
reduction [ri'dʌkʃən] *n* : reducción *f*, rebaja *f*
redundancy [ri'dʌndəntsi] *n, pl* **-cies 1** : superfluidad *f* **2** REPETITION : redundancia *f*
redundant [ri'dʌndənt] *adj* : superfluo, redundante
redwood ['rɛdˌwʊd] *n* : secoya *f*
reed ['ri:d] *n* **1** : caña *f*, carrizo *m*, junco *m* **2** : lengüeta *f* (para instrumentos de viento)
reef ['ri:f] *n* : arrecife *m*, escollo *m*
reek[1] ['ri:k] *vi* : apestar
reek[2] *n* : hedor *m*
reel[1] ['ri:l] *vt* **1 to reel in** : enrollar, sacar (un pez) del agua **2 to reel off** : recitar de un tirón — *vi* **1** SPIN, WHIRL : girar, dar vueltas **2** STAGGER : tambalearse
reel[2] *n* **1** : carrete *m* (de pescar etc.), rollo *m* (de fotos) **2** : baile *m* escocés **3** STAGGER : tambaleo *m*
reelect [ˌri:ɪ'lɛkt] *vt* : reelegir
reenact [ˌri:ɪ'nækt] *vt* : representar de nuevo, reconstruir
reenter [ˌri:'ɛntər] *vt* : volver a entrar
reestablish [ˌri:ɪ'stæblɪʃ] *vt* : restablecer
reevaluate [ˌri:ɪ'væljuˌeɪt] *vt* **-ated; -ating** : revaluar
reevaluation [ˌri:ɪˌvælju'eɪʃən] *n* : revaluación *f*

reexamine [ˌriːɪgˈzæmən, -g-] vt **-ined; -ining** : volver a examinar, reexaminar

refer [rɪˈfər] v **-ferred; -ferring** vt DIRECT, SEND : remitir, enviar ⟨to refer a patient to a specialist : enviar a un paciente a un especialista⟩ — vi **to refer to** MENTION : referirse a, aludir a

referee¹ [ˌrɛfəˈriː] v **-eed; -eeing** : arbitrar

referee² n : árbitro m, -tra f; réferi mf

reference [ˈrɛfrənts, ˈrɛfə-] n **1** ALLUSION : referencia f, alusión f ⟨to make reference to : hacer referencia a⟩ **2** CONSULTATION : consulta f ⟨for future reference : para futuras consultas⟩ **3** or **reference book** : libro m de consulta **4** TESTIMONIAL : informe m, referencia f, recomendación f

referendum [ˌrɛfəˈrɛndəm] n, pl **-da** [-də] or **-dums** : referéndum m

refill¹ [ˌriːˈfɪl] vt : rellenar

refill² [ˈriːˌfɪl] n : recambio m

refinance [ˌriːˈfaɪˌnænts] vt **-nanced; -nancing** : refinanciar

refine [rɪˈfaɪn] vt **-fined; -fining 1** : refinar (azúcar, petróleo, etc.) **2** PERFECT : perfeccionar, pulir

refined [rɪˈfaɪnd] adj **1** : refinado (dícese del azúcar, etc.) **2** CULTURED : culto, educado, refinado

refinement [rɪˈfaɪnmənt] n : refinamiento m, fineza f, finura f

refinery [rɪˈfaɪnəri] n, pl **-eries** : refinería f

reflect [rɪˈflɛkt] vt **1** : reflejar ⟨to reflect light : reflejar la luz⟩ ⟨happiness is reflected in her face : la felicidad se refleja en su cara⟩ **2 to reflect that** : pensar que, considerar que — vi **1 to reflect on** : reflexionar sobre **2 to reflect badly on** : desacreditar, perjudicar

reflection [rɪˈflɛkʃən] n **1** : reflexión f, reflejo m (de la luz, de imágenes, etc.) **2** THOUGHT : reflexión f, meditación f

reflective [rɪˈflɛktɪv] adj **1** THOUGHTFUL : reflexivo, pensativo **2** : reflectante (en física)

reflector [rɪˈflɛktər] n : reflector m

reflex [ˈriːˌflɛks] n : reflejo m

reflexive [rɪˈflɛksɪv] adj : reflexivo ⟨a reflexive verb : un verbo reflexivo⟩

reform¹ [rɪˈfɔrm] vt : reformar — vi : reformarse

reform² n : reforma f

reformation [ˌrɛfərˈmeɪʃən] n : reforma f ⟨the Reformation : la Reforma⟩

reformatory [rɪˈfɔrməˌtori] n, pl **-ries** : reformatorio m

reformer [rɪˈfɔrmər] n : reformador m, -dora f

refract [rɪˈfrækt] vt : refractar — vi : refractarse

refraction [rɪˈfrækʃən] n : refracción f

refractory [rɪˈfræktəri] adj OBSTINATE : refractario, obstinado

refrain¹ [rɪˈfreɪn] vi **to refrain from** : abstenerse de

refrain² n : estribillo m (en música)

refresh [rɪˈfrɛʃ] vt : refrescar ⟨to refresh one's memory : refrescarle la memoria a uno⟩

refreshing [rɪˈfrɛʃɪŋ] adj : refrescante ⟨a refreshing sleep : un sueño reparador⟩

refreshment [rɪˈfrɛʃmənt] n **1** : refresco m **2 refreshments** npl : refrigerio m

refrigerate [rɪˈfrɪdʒəˌreɪt] vt **-ated; -ating** : refrigerar

refrigeration [rɪˌfrɪdʒəˈreɪʃən] n : refrigeración f

refrigerator [rɪˈfrɪdʒəˌreɪtər] n : refrigerador m, -dora f, nevera f

refuel [riːˈfjuːəl] v **-eled** or **-elled; -eling** or **-elling** vi : repostar — vt : llenar de combustible

refuge [ˈrɛˌfjuːdʒ] n : refugio m

refugee [ˌrɛfjʊˈdʒiː] n : refugiado m, -da f

refund¹ [rɪˈfʌnd, ˈriːˌfʌnd] vt : reembolsar, devolver

refund² [ˈriːˌfʌnd] n : reembolso m, devolución f

refundable [rɪˈfʌndəbəl] adj : reembolsable

refurbish [rɪˈfərbɪʃ] vt : renovar, restaurar

refusal [rɪˈfjuːzəl] n : negativa f, rechazo m, denegación f (de una petición)

refuse¹ [rɪˈfjuːz] vt **-fused; -fusing 1** REJECT : rechazar, rehusar **2** DENY : negar, rehusar, denegar ⟨to refuse permission : negar el permiso⟩ **3 to refuse to** : negarse a

refuse² [ˈrɛˌfjuːs, -ˌfjuːz] n : basura f, desechos mpl, desperdicios mpl

refutation [ˌrɛfjʊˈteɪʃən] n : refutación f

refute [rɪˈfjuːt] vt **-futed; -futing 1** DENY : desmentir, negar **2** DISPROVE : refutar, rebatir

regain [riːˈgeɪn] vt **1** RECOVER : recuperar, recobrar **2** REACH : alcanzar ⟨to regain the shore : llegar a la tierra⟩

regal [ˈriːgəl] adj : real, regio

regale [rɪˈgeɪl] vt **-galed; -galing 1** ENTERTAIN : agasajar, entretener **2** AMUSE, DELIGHT : deleitar, divertir

regalia [rɪˈgeɪljə] npl : ropaje m, vestiduras fpl, adornos mpl

regard¹ [rɪˈgɑrd] vt **1** OBSERVE : observar, mirar **2** HEED : tener en cuenta, hacer caso de **3** CONSIDER : considerar **4** RESPECT : respetar ⟨highly regarded : muy estimado⟩ **5 as regards** : en cuanto a, en lo que se refiere a

regard² n **1** CONSIDERATION : consideración f **2** ESTEEM : respeto m, estima f **3** PARTICULAR : aspecto m, sentido m ⟨in this regard : en este sentido⟩ **4 regards** npl : saludos mpl, recuerdos mpl **5 with regard to** : con relación a, con respecto a

regarding [rɪˈgɑrdɪŋ] prep : con respecto a, en cuanto a

regardless [rɪˈgɑrdləs] adv : a pesar de todo

regardless of *prep* : a pesar de, sin tener en cuenta ⟨regardless of our mistakes : a pesar de nuestros errores⟩ ⟨regardless of age : sin tener en cuenta la edad⟩

regenerate [ri'ʤɛnə,reɪt] *v* **-ated; -ating** *vt* : regenerar — *vi* : regenerarse

regeneration [ri,ʤɛnə'reɪʃən] *n* : regeneración *f*

regent ['ri:ʤənt] *n* **1** RULER : regente *mf* **2** : miembro *m* de la junta directiva (de una universidad, etc.)

regime [reɪ'ʒi:m, rɪ-] *n* : régimen *m*

regimen ['rɛʤəmən] *n* : régimen *m*

regiment[1] ['rɛʤə,mɛnt] *vt* : reglamentar

regiment[2] ['rɛʤəmənt] *n* : regimiento *m*

region ['ri:ʤən] *n* **1** : región *f* **2 in the region of** : alrededor de

regional ['ri:ʤənəl] *adj* : regional — **regionally** *adv*

register[1] ['rɛʤəstər] *vt* **1** RECORD : registrar, inscribir **2** INDICATE : marcar (temperatura, medidas, etc.) **3** REVEAL : manifestar, acusar ⟨to register surprise : acusar sorpresa⟩ **4** : certificar (correo) — *vi* ENROLL : inscribirse, matricularse

register[2] *n* : registro *m*

registrar ['rɛʤə,strɑr] *n* : registrador *m*, -dora *f* oficial

registration [,rɛʤə'streɪʃən] *n* **1** REGISTERING : inscripción *f*, matriculación *f*, registro *m* **2 or registration number** : matrícula *f*, número *m* de matrícula

registry ['rɛʤəstri] *n*, *pl* **-tries** : registro *m*

regress [ri'grɛs] *vi* : retroceder

regression [ri'grɛʃən] *n* : retroceso *m*, regresión *f*

regressive [ri'grɛsɪv] *adj* : regresivo

regret[1] [ri'grɛt] *vt* **-gretted; -gretting** : arrepentirse de, lamentar ⟨he regrets nothing : no se arrepiente de nada⟩ ⟨I regret to tell you : lamento decirle⟩

regret[2] *n* **1** REMORSE : arrepentimiento *m*, remordimientos *mpl* **2** SADNESS : pesar *m*, dolor *m* **3 regrets** *npl* : excusas *fpl* ⟨to send one's regrets : excusarse⟩

regretful [ri'grɛtfəl] *adj* : arrepentido, pesaroso

regretfully [ri'grɛtfəli] *adv* : con pesar

regrettable [ri'grɛtəbəl] *adj* : lamentable — **regrettably** [-bli] *adv*

regular[1] ['rɛgjələr] *adj* **1** NORMAL : regular, normal, usual **2** STEADY : uniforme, regular ⟨a regular pace : un paso regular⟩ **3** CUSTOMARY, HABITUAL : habitual, de costumbre

regular[2] *n* : cliente *mf* habitual

regularity [,rɛgjə'lærəti] *n*, *pl* **-ties** : regularidad *f*

regularly ['rɛgjələrli] *adv* : regularmente, con regularidad

regulate ['rɛgjə,leɪt] *vt* **-lated; -lating** : regular

regulation [,rɛgjə'leɪʃən] *n* **1** REGULATING : regulación *f* **2** RULE : regla *f*,

reglamento *m*, norma *f* ⟨safety regulations : reglas de seguridad⟩

regulator ['rɛgjə,leɪtər] *n* **1** : regulador *m* (mecanismo) **2** : persona *f* que regula

regulatory ['rɛgjələ,tori] *adj* : regulador

regurgitate [ri'gərʤə,teɪt] *v* **-tated; -tating** : regurgitar, vomitar

rehabilitate [,ri:hə'bɪlə,teɪt, ,ri:ə-] *vt* **-tated; -tating** : rehabilitar

rehabilitation [,ri:hə,bɪlə'teɪʃən, ,ri:ə-] *n* : rehabilitación *f*

rehearsal [ri'hərsəl] *n* : ensayo *m*

rehearse [ri'hərs] *v* **-hearsed; -hearsing** : ensayar

reheat [,ri:'hi:t] *vt* : recalentar

reign[1] ['reɪn] *vi* **1** RULE : reinar **2** PREVAIL : reinar, predominar ⟨the reigning champion : el actual campeón⟩

reign[2] *n* : reinado *m*

reimburse [,ri:əm'bərs] *vt* **-bursed; -bursing** : reembolsar

reimbursement [,ri:əm'bərsmənt] *n* : reembolso *m*

rein[1] ['reɪn] *vt* : refrenar (un caballo)

rein[2] *n* **1** : rienda *f* ⟨to give free rein to : dar rienda suelta a⟩ **2** CHECK : control *m* ⟨to keep a tight rein on : llevar un estricto control de⟩

reincarnation [,ri:ɪn,kɑr'neɪʃən] *n* : reencarnación *f*

reindeer ['reɪn,dɪr] *n* : reno *m*

reinforce [,ri:ən'fors] *vt* **-forced; -forcing** : reforzar

reinforcement [,ri:ən'forsmənt] *n* : refuerzo *m*

reinstate [,ri:ən'steɪt] *vt* **-stated; -stating 1** : reintegrar, restituir (una persona) **2** RESTORE : restablecer (un servicio, etc.)

reinstatement [,ri:ən'steɪtmənt] *n* : reintegración *f*, restitución *f*, restablecimiento *m*

reiterate [ri'ɪtə,reɪt] *vt* **-ated; -ating** : reiterar, repetir

reiteration [ri,ɪtə'reɪʃən] *n* : reiteración *f*, repetición *f*

reject[1] [ri'ʤɛkt] *vt* : rechazar

reject[2] ['ri:,ʤɛkt] *n* : desecho *m* (cosa), persona *f* rechazada

rejection [ri'ʤɛkʃən] *n* : rechazo *m*

rejoice [ri'ʤɔɪs] *vi* **-joiced; -joicing** : alegrarse, regocijarse

rejoin [,ri:'ʤɔɪn] *vt* **1** : reincorporarse a, reintegrarse a ⟨he rejoined the firm : se reincorporó a la firma⟩ **2** [ri'-] REPLY, RETORT : replicar

rejoinder [ri'ʤɔɪndər] *n* : réplica *f*

rejuvenate [ri'ʤu:və,neɪt] *vt* **-nated; -nating** : rejuvenecer

rejuvenation [ri,ʤu:və'neɪʃən] *n* : rejuvenecimiento *m*

rekindle [,ri:'kɪndəl] *vt* **-dled; -dling** : reavivar

relapse[1] [ri'læps] *vi* **-lapsed; -lapsing** : recaer, volver a caer

relapse[2] ['ri:,læps, ri'læps] *n* : recaída *f*

relate [ri'leɪt] *v* **-lated; -lating** *vt* **1** TELL : relatar, contar **2** ASSOCIATE : relacionar, asociar ⟨to relate crime to poverty : relacionar la delincuencia a la pobreza⟩ — *vi* **1** CONNECT : conectar, estar relacionado (con) **2** INTERACT : relacionarse (con), llevarse bien (con) **3 to relate to** UNDERSTAND : identificarse con, simpatizar con

related [ri'leɪtəd] *adj* : emparentado ⟨to be related to : ser pariente de⟩

relation [ri'leɪʃən] *n* **1** NARRATION : relato *m*, narración *f* **2** RELATIVE : pariente *mf*, familiar *mf* **3** RELATIONSHIP : relación *f* ⟨in relation to : en relación con, con relación a⟩ **4 relations** *npl* : relaciones *fpl* ⟨public relations : relaciones públicas⟩

relationship [ri'leɪʃən‚ʃɪp] *n* **1** CONNECTION : relación *f* **2** KINSHIP : parentesco *m*

relative[1] ['rɛlətɪv] *adj* : relativo — **relatively** *adv*

relative[2] *n* : pariente *mf*, familiar *mf*

relativism ['rɛlətɪ‚vɪzəm] *n* : relativismo *m*

relativity [‚rɛlə'tɪvəṭi] *n, pl* **-ties** : relatividad *f*

relax [ri'læks] *vt* : relajar, aflojar — *vi* : relajarse

relaxation [‚ri:‚læk'seɪʃən] *n* **1** RELAXING : relajación *f*, aflojamiento *m* **2** DIVERSION : esparcimiento *m*, distracción *f*

relaxing [ri'læksɪŋ] *adj* : relajante

relay[1] ['ri:‚leɪ, ri'leɪ] *vt* **-layed; -laying** : transmitir

relay[2] ['ri:‚leɪ] *n* **1** : relevo *m* **2** *or* **relay race** : carrera de relevos

release[1] [ri'li:s] *vt* **-leased; -leasing** **1** FREE : liberar, poner en libertad **2** LOOSEN : soltar, aflojar ⟨to release the brake : soltar el freno⟩ **3** RELINQUISH : renunciar a, ceder **4** ISSUE : publicar (un libro), estrenar (una película), sacar (un disco)

release[2] *n* **1** LIBERATION : liberación *f*, puesta *f* en libertad **2** RELINQUISHMENT : cesión *f* (de propiedad, etc.) **3** ISSUE : estreno *m* (de una película), puesta *f* en venta (de un disco), publicación *f* (de un libro) **4** ESCAPE : escape *m*, fuga *f* (de un gas)

relegate ['rɛlə‚geɪt] *vt* **-gated; -gating** : relegar

relent [ri'lɛnt] *vi* : ablandarse, ceder

relentless [ri'lɛntləs] *adj* : implacable, sin tregua

relentlessly [ri'lɛntləsli] *adv* : implacablemente

relevance ['rɛləvənts] *n* : pertinencia *f*, relación *f*

relevant ['rɛləvənt] *adj* : pertinente — **relevantly** *adv*

reliability [ri‚laɪə'bɪləṭi] *n, pl* **-ties 1** : fiabilidad *f*, seguridad *f* (de una cosa) **2** : formalidad *f*, seriedad *f* (de una persona)

reliable [ri'laɪəbəl] *adj* : confiable, fiable, fidedigno, seguro

reliably [ri'laɪəbli] *adv* : sin fallar ⟨to be reliably informed : saber (algo) de fuentes fidedignas⟩

reliance [ri'laɪənts] *n* **1** DEPENDENCE : dependencia *f* **2** CONFIDENCE : confianza *f*

reliant [ri'laɪənt] *adj* : dependiente

relic ['rɛlɪk] *n* **1** : reliquia *f* **2** VESTIGE : vestigio *m*

relief [ri'li:f] *n* **1** : alivio *m*, desahogo *m* ⟨relief from pain : alivio del dolor⟩ **2** AID, WELFARE : ayuda *f* (benéfica), asistencia *f* social **3** : relieve *m* (en la escultura) ⟨relief map : mapa en relieve⟩ **4** REPLACEMENT : relevo *m*

relieve [ri'li:v] *vt* **-lieved; -lieving 1** ALLEVIATE : aliviar, mitigar ⟨to feel relieved : sentirse aliviado⟩ **2** FREE : liberar, eximir ⟨to relieve someone of responsibility for : eximir a alguien de la responsabilidad de⟩ **3** REPLACE : relevar (a un centinela, etc.) **4** BREAK : romper ⟨to relieve the monotony : romper la monotonía⟩

religion [ri'lɪʤən] *n* : religión *f*

religious [ri'lɪʤəs] *adj* : religioso — **religiously** *adv*

relinquish [ri'lɪŋkwɪʃ, -'lɪn-] *vt* **1** GIVE UP : renunciar a, abandonar **2** RELEASE : soltar

relish[1] ['rɛlɪʃ] *vt* : saborear (comida), disfrutar con (una idea, una perspectiva, etc.)

relish[2] *n* **1** ENJOYMENT : gusto *m*, deleite *m* **2** : salsa *f* (condimento)

relive [‚ri:'lɪv] *vt* **-lived; -living** : revivir

relocate [‚ri:'lo:‚keɪt, ‚ri:lo'keɪt] *v* **-cated; -cating** *vt* : reubicar, trasladar — *vi* : trasladarse

relocation [‚ri:lo'keɪʃən] *n* : reubicación *f*, traslado *m*

reluctance [ri'lʌktənts] *n* : renuencia *f*, reticencia *f*, desgana *f*

reluctant [ri'lʌktənt] *adj* : renuente, reacio, reticente

reluctantly [ri'lʌktəntli] *adv* : a regañadientes

rely [ri'laɪ] *vi* **-lied; -lying 1** DEPEND : depender (de), contar (con) **2** TRUST : confiar (en)

remain [ri'meɪn] *vi* **1** : quedar ⟨very little remains : queda muy poco⟩ ⟨the remaining 10 minutes : los 10 minutos que quedan⟩ **2** STAY : quedarse, permanecer **3** CONTINUE : continuar, seguir ⟨to remain the same : continuar siendo igual⟩ **4 to remain to** : quedar por ⟨to remain to be done : quedar por hacer⟩ ⟨it remains to be seen : está por ver⟩

remainder [ri'meɪndər] *n* : resto *m*, remanente *m*

remains [ri'meɪnz] *npl* : restos *mpl* ⟨mortal remains : restos mortales⟩

remake[1] [ri'meɪk] *vt* **-made; -making 1** TRANSFORM : rehacer **2** : hacer una nueva versión de (una película, etc.)

remake² ['ri:ˌmeɪk] *n* : nueva versión *f*
remark¹ [ri'mɑrk] *vt* **1** NOTICE : observar **2** SAY : comentar, observar — *vi* **to remark on** : hacer observaciones sobre
remark² *n* : comentario *m*, observación *f*
remarkable [ri'mɑrkəbəl] *adj* : extraordinario, notable — **remarkably** [-bli] *adv*
rematch ['ri:ˌmætʃ] *n* : revancha *f*
remedial [ri'mi:diəl] *adj* : correctivo ⟨remedial classes : clases para alumnos atrasados⟩
remedy¹ ['rɛmədi] *vt* **-died; -dying** : remediar
remedy² *n*, *pl* **-dies** : remedio *m*, medicamento *m*
remember [ri'mɛmbər] *vt* **1** RECOLLECT : acordarse de, recordar **2** : no olvidar ⟨remember my words : no olvides mis palabras⟩ ⟨to remember to : acordarse de⟩ **3** : dar saludos, dar recuerdos ⟨remember me to her : dale saludos de mi parte⟩ **4** COMMEMORATE : recordar, conmemorar
remembrance [ri'mɛmbrənts] *n* **1** RECOLLECTION : recuerdo *m* ⟨in remembrance of : en conmemoración de⟩ **2** MEMENTO : recuerdo *m*
remind [ri'maɪnd] *vt* : recordar ⟨remind me to do it : recuérdame que lo haga⟩ ⟨she reminds me of Clara : me recuerda de Clara⟩
reminder [ri'maɪndər] *n* : recuerdo *m*
reminisce [ˌrɛmə'nɪs] *vi* **-nisced; -niscing** : rememorar los viejos tiempos
reminiscence [ˌrɛmə'nɪsənts] *n* : recuerdo *m*, reminiscencia *f*
reminiscent [ˌrɛmə'nɪsənt] *adj* **1** NOSTALGIC : reminiscente, nostálgico **2** SUGGESTIVE : evocador, que recuerda — **reminiscently** *adv*
remiss [ri'mɪs] *adj* : negligente, descuidado, remiso
remission [ri'mɪʃən] *n* : remisión *f*
remit [ri'mɪt] *vt* **-mitted; -mitting 1** PARDON : perdonar **2** SEND : remitir, enviar (dinero)
remittance [ri'mɪtənts] *n* : remesa *f*
remnant ['rɛmnənt] *n* : restos *mpl*, vestigio *m*
remodel [ri'mɑdəl] *vt* **-eled** *or* **-elled; -eling** *or* **-elling** : remodelar, reformar
remonstrate [ri'mɑnˌstreɪt] *vi* **-strated; -strating** : protestar ⟨to remonstrate with someone : quejarse a alguien⟩
remorse [ri'mɔrs] *n* : remordimiento *m*
remorseful [ri'mɔrsfəl] *adj* : arrepentido, lleno de remordimiento
remorseless [ri'mɔrsləs] *adj* **1** PITILESS : despiadado **2** RELENTLESS : implacable
remote [ri'mo:t] *adj* **-moter; -est 1** FAR-OFF : lejano, remoto ⟨remote countries : países remotos⟩ ⟨in the remote past : en el pasado lejano⟩ **2** SECLUDED : recóndito **3** : a distancia, remoto ⟨re-

mote control : control remoto⟩ **4** SLIGHT : remoto **5** ALOOF : distante
remotely [ri'mo:tli] *adv* **1** SLIGHTLY : remotamente **2** DISTANTLY : en un lugar remoto, muy lejos
remoteness [ri'mo:tnəs] *n* : lejanía *f*
removable [ri'mu:vəbəl] *adj* : removible
removal [ri'mu:vəl] *n* : separación *f*, extracción *f*, supresión *f* (en algo escrito), eliminación *f* (de problemas, etc.)
remove [ri'mu:v] *vt* **-moved; -moving 1** : quitar, quitarse ⟨remove the lid : quite la tapa⟩ ⟨to remove one's hat : quitarse el sombrero⟩ **2** EXTRACT : sacar, extraer ⟨to remove the contents of : sacar el contenido de⟩ **3** ELIMINATE : eliminar, disipar
remunerate [ri'mju:nəˌreɪt] *vt* **-ated; -ating** : remunerar
remuneration [riˌmju:nə'reɪʃən] *n* : remuneración *f*
remunerative [ri'mju:nərətɪv, -ˌreɪ-] *adj* : remunerativo
renaissance [ˌrɛnə'sɑnts, -'zɑnts; 'rɛnəˌ-] *n* : renacimiento *m* ⟨the Renaissance : el Renacimiento⟩
renal ['ri:nəl] *adj* : renal
rename [ˌri:'neɪm] *vt* **-named; -naming** : ponerle un nombre nuevo a
rend ['rɛnd] *vt* **rent** ['rɛnt]; **rending** : desgarrar
render ['rɛndər] *vt* **1** : derretir ⟨to render lard : derretir la manteca⟩ **2** GIVE : prestar, dar ⟨to render aid : prestar ayuda⟩ **3** MAKE : hacer, volver, dejar ⟨it rendered him helpless : lo dejó incapacitado⟩ **4** TRANSLATE : traducir, verter ⟨to render into English : traducir al inglés⟩
rendezvous ['rɑndɪˌvu:, -deɪ-] *ns & pl* : encuentro *m*, cita *f*
rendition [rɛn'dɪʃən] *n* : interpretación *f*
renegade ['rɛnɪˌgeɪd] *n* : renegado *m*, -da *f*
renege [ri'nɪg, -'nɛg] *vi* **-neged; -neging** : no cumplir con (una promesa, etc.)
renew [ri'nu:, -'nju:] *vt* **1** REVIVE : renovar, reavivar ⟨to renew the sentiments of youth : renovar los sentimientos de la juventud⟩ **2** RESUME : reanudar **3** EXTEND : renovar ⟨to renew a subscription : renovar una suscripción⟩
renewable [ri'nu:əbəl, -'nju:-] *adj* : renovable
renewal [ri'nu:əl, -'nju:-] *n* : renovación *f*
renounce [ri'naʊnts] *vt* **-nounced; -nouncing** : renunciar a
renovate ['rɛnəˌveɪt] *vt* **-vated; -vating** : restaurar, renovar
renovation [ˌrɛnə'veɪʃən] *n* : restauración *f*, renovación *f*
renown [ri'naʊn] *n* : renombre *m*, fama *f*, celebridad *f*
renowned [ri'naʊnd] *adj* : renombrado, célebre, famoso
rent¹ ['rɛnt] *vt* : rentar, alquilar

rent² *n* **1** : renta *f*, alquiler *m* ⟨for rent : se alquila⟩ **2** RIP : rasgadura *f*
rental¹ [ˈrɛntəl] *adj* RENT : de alquiler
rental² *n* : alquiler *m*
renter [ˈrɛntər] *n* : arrendatario *m*, -ria *f*
renunciation [ri,nʌntsiˈeɪʃən] *n* : renuncia *f*
reopen [,riːˈoːpən] *vt* : volver a abrir
reorganization [,riːˌɔrgənəˈzeɪʃən] *n* : reorganización *f*
reorganize [,riːˈɔrgənˌaɪz] *vt* **-nized; -nizing** : reorganizar
repair¹ [riˈpær] *vt* : reparar, arreglar, refaccionar
repair² *n* **1** : reparación *f*, arreglo *m* **2** CONDITION : estado *m* ⟨in bad repair : en mal estado⟩
reparation [,rɛpəˈreɪʃən] *n* **1** AMENDS : reparación *f* **2 reparations** *npl* COMPENSATION : indemnización *f*
repartee [,rɛpərˈtiː, -,pɑr-, -ˈteɪ] *n* : intercambio *m* de réplicas ingeniosas
repast [riˈpæst, ˈriːˌpæst] *n* : comida *f*
repatriate [riˈpeɪtriˌeɪt] *vt* **-ated; -ating** : repatriar
repay [riˈpeɪ] *vt* **-paid; -paying** : pagar, devolver, reembolsar
repeal¹ [riˈpiːl] *vt* : abrogar, revocar
repeal² *n* : abrogación *f*, revocación *f*
repeat¹ [riˈpiːt] *vt* : repetir
repeat² *n* : repetición *f*
repeatedly [riˈpiːţədli] *adv* : repetidamente, repetidas veces
repel [riˈpɛl] *vt* **-pelled; -pelling 1** REPULSE : repeler (un enemigo, etc.) **2** RESIST : repeler **3** REJECT : rechazar, repeler **4** DISGUST : repugnar, darle asco (a alguien)
repellent *or* **repellant** [riˈpɛlənt] *n* : repelente *m*
repent [riˈpɛnt] *vi* : arrepentirse
repentance [riˈpɛntənts] *n* : arrepentimiento *m*
repentant [riˈpɛntənt] *adj* : arrepentido
repercussion [,riːpərˈkʌʃən, ,rɛpər-] *n* : repercusión *f*
repertoire [ˈrɛpərˌtwɑr] *n* : repertorio *m*
repertory [ˈrɛpərˌtori] *n, pl* **-ries** : repertorio *m*
repetition [,rɛpəˈtɪʃən] *n* : repetición *f*
repetitious [,rɛpəˈtɪʃəs] *adj* : repetitivo, reiterativo — **repetitiously** *adv*
repetitive [riˈpɛţətɪv] *adj* : repetitivo, reiterativo
replace [riˈpleɪs] *vt* **-placed; -placing 1** : volver a poner ⟨replace it in the drawer : vuelve a ponerlo en el cajón⟩ **2** SUBSTITUTE : reemplazar, sustituir **3** : reponer ⟨to replace the worn carpet : reponer la alfombra raída⟩
replaceable [riˈpleɪsəbəl] *adj* : reemplazable
replacement [riˈpleɪsmənt] *n* **1** SUBSTITUTION : reemplazo *m*, sustitución *f* **2** SUBSTITUTE : sustituto *m*, -ta *f*; suplente *mf* (persona) **3 replacement part** : repuesto *m*, pieza *f* de recambio
replenish [riˈplɛnɪʃ] *vt* : rellenar, llenar de nuevo

replenishment [riˈplɛnɪʃmənt] *n* : reabastecimiento *m*
replete [riˈpliːt] *adj* : repleto, lleno
replica [ˈrɛplɪkə] *n* : réplica *f*, reproducción *f*
replicate [ˈrɛpləˌkeɪt] *v* **-cated; -cating** *vt* : duplicar, repetir — *vi* : duplicarse
replication [,rɛpləˈkeɪʃən] *n* **1** REPRODUCTION : reproducción *f* **2** REPETITION : repetición *f* **3** : replicación *f* (celular)
reply¹ [riˈplaɪ] *vi* **-plied; -plying** : contestar, responder
reply² *n, pl* **-plies** : respuesta *f*, contestación *f*
report¹ [riˈport] *vt* **1** ANNOUNCE : relatar, anunciar **2** : dar parte de, informar de, reportar ⟨he reported an accident : dio parte de un accidente⟩ ⟨to report a crime : denunciar un delito⟩ **3** : informar acerca de (en un periódico, la televisión, etc.) — *vi* **1** : hacer un informe, informar **2 to report for duty** : presentarse, reportarse
report² *n* **1** RUMOR : rumor *m* **2** REPUTATION : reputación *f* ⟨people of evil report : personas de mala fama⟩ **3** ACCOUNT : informe *m*, reportaje *m* (en un periódico, etc.) **4** BANG : estallido *m* (de un arma de fuego)
report card *n* : boletín *m* de calificaciones, boletín *m* de notas
reportedly [riˈportədli] *adv* : según se dice, según se informa
reporter [riˈportər] *n* : periodista *mf*; reportero *m*, -ra *f*
repose¹ [riˈpoːz] *vi* **-posed; -posing** : reposar, descansar
repose² *n* **1** : reposo *m*, descanso *m* **2** CALM : calma *f*, tranquilidad *f*
repository [riˈpɑzəˌtori] *n, pl* **-ries** : depósito *m*
repossess [,riːpəˈzɛs] *vt* : recuperar, recobrar la posesión de
reprehensible [,rɛpriˈhɛntsəbəl] *adj* : reprensible — **reprehensibly** *adv*
represent [,rɛprɪˈzɛnt] *vt* **1** SYMBOLIZE : representar ⟨the flag represents our country : la bandera representa a nuestro país⟩ **2** : representar, ser un resentante de ⟨an attorney who represents his client : un abogado que representa su cliente⟩ **3** PORTRAY : presentar ⟨he represents himself as a friend : se presenta como amigo⟩
representation [,rɛprɪˌzɛnˈteɪʃən, -zən-] *n* : representación *f*
representative¹ [,rɛprɪˈzɛntətɪv] *adj* : representativo
representative² *n* **1** : representante *mf* **2** : diputado *m*, -da *f* (en la política)
repress [riˈprɛs] *vt* : reprimir
repression [riˈprɛʃən] *n* : represión *f*
repressive [riˈprɛsɪv] *adj* : represivo
reprieve¹ [riˈpriːv] *vt* **-prieved; -prieving** : indultar
reprieve² *n* : indulto *m*
reprimand¹ [ˈrɛprəˌmænd] *vt* : reprender

reprimand[2] *n* : reprimenda *f*
reprint[1] [ri'prɪnt] *vt* : reimprimir
reprint[2] ['ri:‚prɪnt, ri'prɪnt] *n* : reedición *f*
reprisal [ri'praɪzəl] *n* : represalia *f*
reproach[1] [ri'pro:tʃ] *vt* : reprochar
reproach[2] *n* **1** DISGRACE : deshonra *f* **2** REBUKE : reproche *m*, recriminación *f*
reproachful [ri'pro:tʃfəl] *adj* : de reproche
reproduce [‚ri:prə'du:s, -'dju:s] *v* **-duced; -ducing** *vt* : reproducir — *vi* BREED : reproducirse
reproduction [‚ri:prə'dʌkʃən] *n* : reproducción *f*
reproductive [‚ri:prə'dʌktɪv] *adj* : reproductor
reproof [ri'pru:f] *n* : reprobación *f*, reprimenda *f*, reproche *m*
reprove [ri'pru:v] *vt* **-proved; -proving** : reprender, censurar
reptile ['rɛp‚taɪl] *n* : reptil *m*
republic [ri'pʌblɪk] *n* : república *f*
republican[1] [ri'pʌblɪkən] *adj* : republicano
republican[2] *n* : republicano *m*, -na *f*
repudiate [ri'pju:di‚eɪt] *vt* **-ated; -ating** **1** REJECT : rechazar **2** DISOWN : repudiar, renegar de
repudiation [ri‚pju:di'eɪʃən] *n* : rechazo *m*, repudio *m*
repugnance [ri'pʌgnənts] *n* : repugnancia *f*
repugnant [ri'pʌgnənt] *adj* : repugnante, asqueroso
repulse[1] [ri'pʌls] *vt* **-pulsed; -pulsing** **1** REPEL : repeler **2** REBUFF : desairar, rechazar
repulse[2] *n* : rechazo *m*
repulsive [ri'pʌlsɪv] *adj* : repulsivo, repugnante, asqueroso — **repulsively** *adv*
reputable ['rɛpjətəbəl] *adj* : acreditado, de buena reputación
reputation [‚rɛpjə'teɪʃən] *n* : reputación *f*, fama *f*
repute [ri'pju:t] *n* : reputación *f*, fama *f*
reputed [ri'pju:təd] *adj* : reputado, supuesto ⟨she's reputed to be the best : tiene fama de ser la mejor⟩
reputedly [ri'pju:tədli] *adv* : supuestamente, según se dice
request[1] [ri'kwɛst] *vt* : pedir, solicitar, rogar ⟨to request assistance : solicitar asistencia, pedir ayuda⟩ ⟨I requested him to do it : le pedí que lo hiciera⟩
request[2] *n* : petición *f*, solicitud *f*, pedido *m*
requiem ['rɛkwiəm, 'reɪ-] *n* : réquiem *m*
require [ri'kwaɪr] *vt* **-quired; -quiring 1** CALL FOR, DEMAND : requerir, exigir ⟨if required : si se requiere⟩ ⟨to require that something be done : exigir que algo se haga⟩ **2** NEED : necesitar, requerir
requirement [ri'kwaɪrmənt] *n* **1** NECESSITY : necesidad *f* **2** DEMAND : requisito *m*, demanda *f*

requisite[1] ['rɛkwəzɪt] *adj* : esencial, necesario
requisite[2] *n* : requisito *m*, necesidad *f*
requisition[1] [‚rɛkwə'zɪʃən] *vt* : requisar
requisition[2] *n* : requisición *f*, requisa *f*
reread [‚ri:'ri:d] *vt* **-read; -reading** : releer
reroute [‚ri:'ru:t, -'raʊt] *vt* **-routed; -routing** : desviar
rerun[1] [ri:'rʌn] *vt* **-ran; -run; -running** : reponer (un programa televisivo)
rerun[2] ['ri:‚rʌn] *n* **1** : reposición *f* (de un programa televisivo) **2** REPEAT : repetición *f*
resale ['ri:‚seɪl, ‚ri:'seɪl] *n* : reventa *f* ⟨resale price : precio de venta⟩
rescind [ri'sɪnd] *vt* **1** CANCEL : rescindir, cancelar **2** REPEAL : abrogar, revocar
rescue[1] ['rɛs‚kju:] *vt* **-cued; -cuing** : rescatar, salvar
rescue[2] *n* : rescate *m*
rescuer ['rɛskjuər] *n* : salvador *m*, -dora *f*
research[1] [ri'sərtʃ, 'ri:‚sərtʃ] *v* : investigar
research[2] *n* : investigación *f*
researcher [ri'sərtʃər, 'ri:‚-] *n* : investigador *m*, -dora *f*
resemblance [ri'zɛmbləns] *n* : semejanza *f*, parecido *m*
resemble [ri'zɛmbəl] *vt* **-sembled; -sembling** : parecerse a, asemejarse a
resent [ri'zɛnt] *vt* : resentirse de, ofenderse por
resentful [ri'zɛntfəl] *adj* : resentido, rencoroso — **resentfully** *adv*
resentment [ri'zɛntmənt] *n* : resentimiento *m*
reservation [‚rɛzər'veɪʃən] *n* **1** : reservación *f*, reserva *f* ⟨to make a reservation : hacer una reservación⟩ **2** DOUBT, MISGIVING : reserva *f*, duda *f* ⟨without reservations : sin reservas⟩ **3** : reserva *f* (de indios americanos)
reserve[1] [ri'zərv] *vt* **-served; -serving** : reservar
reserve[2] *n* **1** STOCK : reserva *f* ⟨to keep in reserve : guardar en reserva⟩ **2** RESTRAINT : reserva *f*, moderación *f* **3 reserves** *npl* : reservas *fpl* (militares)
reserved [ri'zərvd] *adj* : reservado
reservoir ['rɛzər‚vwɑr, -‚vwɔr, -‚vɔr] *n* : embalse *m*
reset [‚ri:'sɛt] *vt* **-set; -setting** : reajustar, poner en hora (un reloj), reiniciar (una computadora)
reside [ri'zaɪd] *vi* **-sided; -siding 1** DWELL : residir **2** LIE : radicar, residir ⟨the power resides in the presidency : el poder radica en la presidencia⟩
residence ['rɛzədənts] *n* : residencia *f*
resident[1] ['rɛzədənt] *adj* : residente
resident[2] *n* : residente *mf*
residential [‚rɛzə'dɛntʃəl] *adj* : residencial
residual [ri'zɪdʒuəl] *adj* : residual
residue ['rɛzə‚du:, -‚dju:] *n* : residuo *m*, resto *m*

resign [ri'zaɪn] vt **1** QUIT : dimitir, renunciar **2 to resign oneself** : aguantarse, resignarse

resignation [ˌrɛzɪg'neɪʃən] n : resignación f

resignedly [ri'zaɪnədli] adv : con resignación

resilience [ri'zɪljənts] n **1** : capacidad f de recuperación, adaptabilidad f **2** ELASTICITY : elasticidad f

resiliency [ri'zɪljəntsi] → **resilience**

resilient [ri'zɪljənt] adj **1** STRONG : resistente, fuerte **2** ELASTIC : elástico

resin ['rɛzən] n : resina f

resist [ri'zɪst] vt **1** WITHSTAND : resistir ⟨to resist heat : resistir el calor⟩ **2** OPPOSE : oponerse a

resistance [ri'zɪstənts] n : resistencia f

resistant [ri'zɪstənt] adj : resistente

resolute ['rɛzəˌluːt] adj : firme, resuelto, decidido

resolutely ['rɛzəˌluːtli, ˌrzə'-] adv : resueltamente, firmemente

resolution [ˌrɛzə'luːʃən] n **1** SOLUTION : solución f **2** RESOLVE : resolución f, determinación f **3** DECISION : propósito m, decisión f ⟨New Year's resolutions : propósitos para el Año Nuevo⟩ **4** MOTION, PROPOSAL : moción f, resolución f (legislativa)

resolve¹ [ri'zɑlv] vt **-solved; -solving 1** SOLVE : resolver, solucionar **2** DECIDE : resolver ⟨she resolved to get more sleep : resolvió dormir más⟩

resolve² n : resolución f, determinación f

resonance ['rɛzənənts] n : resonancia f

resonant ['rɛzənənt] adj : resonante, retumbante

resort¹ [ri'zɔrt] vi **to resort to** : recurrir ⟨to resort to force : recurrir a la fuerza⟩

resort² n **1** RECOURSE : recurso m ⟨as a last resort : como último recurso⟩ **2** HANGOUT : lugar m popular, lugar m muy frecuentado **3** : lugar m de vacaciones ⟨tourist resort : centro turístico⟩

resound [ri'zaʊnd] vi : retumbar, resonar

resounding [ri'zaʊndɪŋ] adj **1** RESONANT : retumbante, resonante **2** ABSOLUTE, CATEGORICAL : rotundo, tremendo ⟨a resounding success : un éxito rotundo⟩

resource ['riːˌsors, ri'sors] n **1** RESOURCEFULNESS : ingenio m, recursos mpl **2 resources** npl : recursos mpl ⟨natural resources : recursos naturales⟩ **3 resources** npl MEANS : recursos mpl, medios mpl, fondos mpl

resourceful [ri'sorsfəl, -'zors-] adj : ingenioso

resourcefulness [ri'sorsfəlnəs, -'zors-] n : ingenio m, recursos mpl, inventiva f

respect¹ [ri'spɛkt] vt : respetar, estimar

respect² n **1** REFERENCE : relación f, respeto m ⟨with respect to : en lo que respecta a⟩ **2** ESTEEM : respeto m, es-

tima f **3** DETAIL, PARTICULAR : detalle m, sentido m, respeto m ⟨in some respects : en algunos sentidos⟩ **4 respects** npl : respetos mpl ⟨to pay one's respects : presentar uno susrespetos⟩

respectability [riˌspɛktə'bɪləti] n : respetabilidad f

respectable [ri'spɛktəbəl] adj **1** PROPER : respetable, decente **2** CONSIDERABLE : considerable, respetable ⟨a respectable amount : una cantidad respetable⟩ — **respectably** [-bli] adv

respectful [ri'spɛktfəl] adj : respetuoso — **respectfully** adv

respectfulness [ri'spɛktfəlnəs] n : respetuosidad f

respective [ri'spɛktɪv] adj : respectivo ⟨their respective homes : sus casas respectivas⟩ — **respectively** adv

respiration [ˌrɛspə'reɪʃən] n : respiración f

respirator ['rɛspəˌreɪtər] n : respirador m

respiratory ['rɛspərəˌtori, ri'spaɪrə-] adj : respiratorio

respite ['rɛspɪt, ri'spaɪt] n : respiro m, tregua f

resplendent [ri'splɛndənt] adj : resplandeciente — **resplendently** adv

respond [ri'spɑnd] vi **1** ANSWER : contestar, responder **2** REACT : responder, reaccionar ⟨to respond to treatment : responder al tratamiento⟩

response [ri'spɑnts] n : respuesta f

responsibility [riˌspɑntsə'bɪləti] n, pl **-ties** : responsabilidad f

responsible [ri'spɑntsəbəl] adj : responsable — **responsibly** [-bli] adv

responsive [ri'spɑntsɪv] adj **1** ANSWERING : que responde **2** SENSITIVE : sensible, receptivo

responsiveness [ri'spɑntsɪvnəs] n : receptividad f, sensibilidad f

rest¹ ['rɛst] vi **1** REPOSE : reposar, descansar **2** RELAX : quedarse tranquilo **3** STOP : pararse, detenerse **4** DEPEND : basarse (en), descansar (sobre), depender (de) ⟨the decision rests with her : la decisión pesa sobre ella⟩ **5 to rest on** : apoyarse en, descansar sobre ⟨to rest on one's arm : apoyarse en el brazo⟩ — vt **1** RELAX : descansar **2** SUPPORT : apoyar **3 to rest one's eyes on** : fijar la mirada en

rest² n **1** RELAXATION, REPOSE : reposo m, descanso m **2** SUPPORT : soporte m, apoyo m **3** : silencio m (en música) **4** REMAINDER : resto m **5 to come to rest** : pararse

restart [ri'stɑrt] vt **1** : volver a empezar **2** RESUME : reanudar **3** : volver a arrancar (un motor), reiniciar (una computadora) — vi **1** : reanudarse **2** : volver a arrancar

restatement [ˌri'steɪtmənt] n : repetición f

restaurant ['rɛstəˌrɑnt, -rənt] n : restaurante m

restful ['rɛstfəl] *adj* **1** RELAXING : relajante **2** PEACEFUL : tranquilo, sosegado

restitution [ˌrɛstə'tuːʃən, -'tjuː-] *n* : restitución *f*

restive ['rɛstɪv] *adj* : inquieto, nervioso

restless ['rɛstləs] *adj* **1** FIDGETY : inquieto, agitado **2** IMPATIENT : impaciente **3** SLEEPLESS : desvelado ⟨a restless night : una noche en blanco⟩

restlessly ['rɛstləsli] *adv* : nerviosamente

restlessness ['rɛstləsnəs] *n* : inquietud *f*, agitación *f*

restoration [ˌrɛstə'reɪʃən] *n* : restauración *f*, restablecimiento *m*

restore [ri'stor] *vt* **-stored; -storing 1** RETURN : volver **2** REESTABLISH : restablecer **3** REPAIR : restaurar

restrain [ri'streɪn] *vt* **1** : refrenar, contener **2 to restrain oneself** : contenerse

restrained [ri'streɪnd] *adj* : comedido, templado, contenido

restraint [ri'streɪnt] *n* **1** RESTRICTION : restricción *f*, limitación *f*, control *m* **2** CONFINEMENT : encierro *m* **3** RESERVE : reserva *f*, control *m* de sí mismo

restrict [ri'strɪkt] *vt* : restringir, limitar, constreñir

restricted [ri'strɪktəd] *adj* **1** LIMITED : limitado, restringido **2** CLASSIFIED : secreto, confidencial

restriction [ri'strɪkʃən] *n* : restricción *f*

restrictive [ri'strɪktɪv] *adj* : restrictivo — **restrictively** *adv*

rest room *n* : servicios *mpl*, baño *m*

restructure [ri'strʌktʃər] *vt* **-tured; -turing** : reestructurar

result¹ [ri'zʌlt] *vi* : resultar ⟨to result in : resultar en, tener por resultado⟩

result² *n* : resultado *m*, consecuencia *f* ⟨as a result of : como consecuencia de⟩

resultant [ri'zʌltənt] *adj* : resultante

resume [ri'zuːm] *v* **-sumed; -suming** *vt* : reanudar — *vi* : reanudarse

résumé *or* **resume** *or* **resumé** ['rɛzəˌmeɪ, ˌrɛzə'-] *n* **1** SUMMARY : resumen *m* **2** CURRICULUM VITAE : currículum *m*, currículo *m*

resumption [ri'zʌmpʃən] *n* : reanudación *f*

resurface [ˌriː'sərfəs] *v* **-faced; -facing** *vt* : pavimentar (una carretera) de nuevo — *vi* : volver a salir en la superficie

resurgence [ri'sərdʒənts] *n* : resurgimiento *m*

resurrect [ˌrɛzə'rɛkt] *vt* : resucitar, desempolvar

resurrection [ˌrɛzə'rɛkʃən] *n* : resurrección *f*

resuscitate [ri'sʌsəˌteɪt] *vt* **-tated; -tating** : resucitar, revivir

resuscitation [riˌsʌsə'teɪʃən] *n* : reanimación *f*, resucitación *f*

retail¹ ['riːˌteɪl] *vt* : vender al por menor, vender al detalle

retail² *adv* : al por menor, al detalle

retail³ *adj* : detallista, minorista

retail⁴ *n* : venta *f* al detalle, venta *f* al por menor

retailer ['riːˌteɪlər] *n* : detallista *mf*, minorista *mf*

retain [ri'teɪn] *vt* : retener, conservar, guardar

retainer [ri'teɪnər] *n* **1** SERVANT : criado *m*, -da *f* **2** ADVANCE : anticipo *m*

retaliate [ri'tæliˌeɪt] *vi* **-ated; -ating** : responder, contraatacar, tomar represalias

retaliation [riˌtæli'eɪʃən] *n* : represalia *f*, retaliación *f*

retard [ri'tard] *vt* : retardar, retrasar

retardation [ˌriːˌtar'deɪʃən] *n* **1** : retardación *f* **2** *or* **mental retardation** : retraso *m* mental

retarded [ri'tardəd] *adj* : retrasado

retch ['rɛtʃ] *vi* : hacer arcadas

retention [ri'tɛntʃən] *n* : retención *f*

retentive [ri'tɛntɪv] *adj* : retentivo

rethink [riː'θɪŋk] *vt* **-thought; -thinking** : reconsiderar, repensar

reticence ['rɛtəsənts] *n* : reticencia *f*

reticent ['rɛtəsənt] *adj* : reticente

retina ['rɛtənə] *n, pl* **-nas** *or* **-nae** [-əni, -ənˌaɪ] : retina *f*

retinue ['rɛtənˌuː, -ˌjuː] *n* : séquito *m*, comitiva *f*, cortejo *m*

retire [ri'taɪr] *vi* **-tired; -tiring 1** RETREAT, WITHDRAW : retirarse, retraerse **2** : retirarse, jubilarse (de su trabajo) **3** : acostarse, irse a dormir

retiree [riˌtaɪ'riː] *n* : jubilado *m*, -da *f*

retirement [ri'taɪrmənt] *n* : jubilación *f*

retiring [ri'taɪrɪŋ] *adj* SHY : retraído

retort¹ [ri'tort] *vt* : replicar

retort² *n* : réplica *f*

retrace [ˌriː'treɪs] *vt* **-traced; -tracing** : volver sobre, desandar ⟨to retrace one's steps : volver uno sobre sus pasos⟩

retract [ri'trækt] *vt* **1** TAKE BACK, WITHDRAW : retirar, retractarse de **2** : retraer (las garras) — *vi* : retractarse

retractable [ri'træktəbəl] *adj* : retractable

retrain [ˌriː'treɪn] *vt* : reciclar, reconvertir

retreat¹ [ri'triːt] *vi* : retirarse

retreat² *n* **1** WITHDRAWAL : retirada *f*, repliegue *m*, retiro *m* ⟨to beat a retreat : batirse en retirada⟩ **2** REFUGE : retiro *m*, refugio *m*

retrench [ri'trɛntʃ] *vt* : reducir (gastos) — *vi* : economizar

retribution [ˌrɛtrə'bjuːʃən] *n* PUNISHMENT : castigo *m*, pena *f* merecida

retrieval [ri'triːvəl] *n* : recuperación *f* ⟨beyond retrieval : irrecuperable⟩ ⟨data retrieval : recuperación de datos⟩

retrieve [ri'triːv] *vt* **-trieved; -trieving 1** : cobrar ⟨to retrieve game : cobrar la caza⟩ **2** RECOVER : recuperar

retriever [ri'triːvər] *n* : perro *m* cobrador

retroactive [ˌrɛtroˈæktɪv] *adj* : retroactivo — **retroactively** *adv*

retrograde [ˈrɛtrəˌɡreɪd] *adj* : retrógrado

retrospect [ˈrɛtrəˌspɛkt] *n* **in retrospect** : mirando hacia atrás, retrospectivamente

retrospective [ˌrɛtrəˈspɛktɪv] *adj* : retrospectivo

return¹ [rɪˈtərn] *vi* **1** : volver, regresar ⟨to return home : regresar a casa⟩ **2** REAPPEAR : reaparecer, resurgir **3** ANSWER : responder — *vt* **1** REPLACE, RESTORE : devolver, volver (a poner), restituir ⟨to return something to its place : volver a poner algo en su lugar⟩ **2** YIELD : producir, redituar, rendir **3** REPAY : pagar, devolver ⟨to return a compliment : devolver un cumplido⟩

return² *adj* : de vuelta

return³ *n* **1** RETURNING : regreso *m*, vuelta *f*, retorno *m* **2** *or* **tax return** : declaración *f* de impuestos **3** YIELD : rédito *m*, rendimiento *m*, ganancia *f* **4 returns** *npl* DATA, RESULTS : resultados *mpl*, datos *mpl*

reunion [riˈjuːnjən] *n* : reunión *f*, reencuentro *m*

reunite [ˌriːjuˈnaɪt] *v* **-nited; -niting** *vt* : (volver a) reunir — *vi* : (volver a) reunirse

reusable [riˈjuːzəbəl] *adj* : reutilizable

reuse [riˈjuːz] *vt* **-used; -using** : reutilizar, usar de nuevo

revamp [ˌriˈvæmp] *vt* : renovar

reveal [rɪˈviːl] *vt* **1** DIVULGE : revelar, divulgar ⟨to reveal a secret : revelar un secreto⟩ **2** SHOW : manifestar, mostrar, dejar ver

revealing [rɪˈviːlɪŋ] *adj* : revelador

reveille [ˈrɛvəli] *n* : toque *m* de diana

revel¹ [ˈrɛvəl] *vi* **-eled** *or* **-elled; -eling** *or* **-elling 1** CAROUSE : ir de juerga **2 to revel in** : deleitarse en

revel² *n* : juerga *f*, parranda *f fam*

revelation [ˌrɛvəˈleɪʃən] *n* : revelación *f*

reveler *or* **reveller** [ˈrɛvələr] *n* : juerguista *mf*

revelry [ˈrɛvəlri] *n, pl* **-ries** : juerga *f*, parranda *f fam*, jarana *f fam*

revenge¹ [rɪˈvɛnʤ] *vt* **-venged; -venging** : vengar ⟨to revenge oneself on : vengarse de⟩

revenge² *n* : venganza *f*

revenue [ˈrɛvəˌnuː, -ˌnjuː] *n* : ingresos *mpl*, rentas *fpl*

reverberate [rɪˈvərbəˌreɪt] *vi* **-ated; -ating** : reverberar

reverberation [rɪˌvərbəˈreɪʃən] *n* : reverberación *f*

revere [rɪˈvɪr] *vt* **-vered; -vering** : reverenciar, venerar

reverence [ˈrɛvərənʦ] *n* : reverencia *f*, veneración *f*

reverend [ˈrɛvərənd] *adj* : reverendo ⟨the Reverend John Chapin : el reverendo John Chapin⟩

reverent [ˈrɛvərənt] *adj* : reverente — **reverently** *adv*

reverie [ˈrɛvəri] *n, pl* **-eries** : ensueño *m*

reversal [ˈrɛvərsəl] *n* **1** INVERSION : inversión *f* (del orden normal) **2** CHANGE : cambio *m* total **3** SETBACK : revés *m*, contratiempo *m*

reverse¹ [rɪˈvərs] *v* **-versed; -versing** *vt* **1** INVERT : invertir **2** CHANGE : cambiar totalmente **3** ANNUL : anular, revocar — *vi* : dar marcha atrás

reverse² *adj* **1** : inverso ⟨in reverse order : en orden inverso⟩ ⟨the reverse side : el reverso⟩ **2** OPPOSITE : contrario, opuesto

reverse³ *n* **1** OPPOSITE : lo contrario, lo opuesto **2** SETBACK : revés *m*, contratiempo *m* **3** BACK : reverso *m*, dorso *m*, revés *m* **4** *or* **reverse gear** : marcha *f* atrás, reversa *f Col, Mex*

reversible [rɪˈvərsəbəl] *adj* : reversible

reversion [rɪˈvərʒən] *n* : reversión *f*, vuelta *f*

revert [rɪˈvərt] *vi* : revertir

review¹ [rɪˈvjuː] *vt* **1** REEXAMINE : volver a examinar, repasar (una lección) **2** CRITICIZE : reseñar, hacer una crítica de **3** EXAMINE : examinar, analizar ⟨to review one's life : examinar su vida⟩ **4 to review the troops** : pasar revista a las tropas

review² *n* **1** INSPECTION : revista *f* (de tropas) **2** ANALYSIS, OVERVIEW : resumen *m*, análisis *m* ⟨a review of current affairs : un análisis de las actualidades⟩ **3** CRITICISM : reseña *f*, crítica *f* (de un libro, etc.) **4** : repaso *m* (para un examen) **5** REVUE : revista *f* (musical)

reviewer [rɪˈvjuːər] *n* : crítico *m*, -ca *f*

revile [rɪˈvaɪl] *vt* **-viled; -viling** : injuriar, denostar

revise [rɪˈvaɪz] *vt* **-vised; -vising** : revisar, corregir, refundir ⟨to revise a dictionary : corregir un diccionario⟩

revision [rɪˈvɪʒən] *n* : revisión *f*

revival [rɪˈvaɪvəl] *n* **1** : renacimiento *m* (de ideas, etc.), restablecimiento *m* (de costumbres, etc.), reactivación *f* (de la economía) **2** : reanimación *f*, resucitación *f* (en medicina) **3** *or* **revival meeting** : asamblea *f* evangelista

revive [rɪˈvaɪv] *v* **-vived; -viving** *vt* **1** REAWAKEN : reavivar, reanimar, reactivar (la economía), resucitar (a un paciente) **2** REESTABLISH : restablecer — *vi* **1** : renacer, reanimarse, reactivarse **2** COME TO : recobrar el sentido, volver en sí

revoke [rɪˈvoːk] *vt* **-voked; -voking** : revocar

revolt¹ [rɪˈvoːlt] *vi* **1** REBEL : rebelarse, sublevarse **2 to revolt at** : sentir repugnancia por — *vt* DISGUST : darle asco (a alguien), repugnar

revolt² *n* REBELLION : rebelión *f*, revuelta *f*, sublevación *f*

revolting [rɪˈvoːltɪŋ] *adj* : asqueroso, repugnante

revolution [ˌrɛvəˈluːʃən] *n* : revolución *f*
revolutionary[1] [ˌrɛvəˈluːʃəneˌri] *adj* : revolucionario
revolutionary[2] *n, pl* **-aries** : revolucionario *m*, -ria *f*
revolutionize [ˌrɛvəˈluːʃənˌaɪz] *vt* **-ized; -izing** : cambiar radicalmente, revolucionar
revolve [riˈvɑlv] *v* **-volved; -volving** *vt* ROTATE : hacer girar — *vi* **1** ROTATE : girar ⟨to revolve around : girar alrededor de⟩ **2 to revolve in one's mind** : darle vueltas en la cabeza a alguien
revolver [riˈvɑlvər] *n* : revólver *m*
revue [riˈvjuː] *n* : revista *f* (musical)
revulsion [riˈvʌlʃən] *n* : repugnancia *f*
reward[1] [riˈwɔrd] *vt* : recompensar, premiar
reward[2] *n* : recompensa *f*
rewrite [ˌriːˈraɪt] *vt* **-wrote; -written; -writing** : escribir de nuevo, volver a escribir
rhapsody [ˈræpsədi] *n, pl* **-dies 1** : elogio *m* excesivo ⟨to go into rhapsodies over : extasiarse por⟩ **2** : rapsodia *f* (en música)
rhetoric [ˈrɛtərɪk] *n* : retórica *f*
rhetorical [rɪˈtɔrɪkəl] *adj* : retórico
rheumatic [rʊˈmætɪk] *adj* : reumático
rheumatism [ˈruːməˌtɪzəm, ˈrʊ-] *n* : reumatismo *m*
rhinestone [ˈraɪnˌstoːn] *n* : diamante *m* de imitación
rhino [ˈraɪˌnoː] *n, pl* **rhino** *or* **rhinos** → **rhinoceros**
rhinoceros [raɪˈnɑsərəs] *n, pl* **-eroses** *or* **-eros** *or* **-eri** [-ˌraɪ] : rinoceronte *m*
rhododendron [ˌroːdəˈdɛndrən] *n* : rododendro *m*
rhombus [ˈrɑmbəs] *n, pl* **-buses** *or* **-bi** [-ˌbaɪ, -bi] : rombo *m*
rhubarb [ˈruːˌbɑrb] *n* : ruibarbo *m*
rhyme[1] [ˈraɪm] *vi* **rhymed; rhyming** : rimar
rhyme[2] *n* **1** : rima *f* **2** VERSE : verso *m* (en rima)
rhythm [ˈrɪðəm] *n* : ritmo *m*
rhythmic [ˈrɪðmɪk] *or* **rhythmical** [-mɪkəl] *adj* : rítmico — **rhythmically** [-mɪkli] *adv*
rib[1] [ˈrɪb] *vt* **ribbed; ribbing 1** : hacer en canalé ⟨a ribbed sweater : un suéter en canalé⟩ **2** TEASE : tomarle el pelo (a alguien)
rib[2] *n* **1** : costilla *f* (de una persona o un animal) **2** : nervio *m* (de una bóveda o una hoja), varilla *f* (de un paraguas), canalé *m* (de una prenda tejida)
ribald [ˈrɪbəld] *adj* : escabroso, procaz
ribbon [ˈrɪbən] *n* **1** : cinta *f* **2 to tear to ribbons** : hacer jirones
rice [ˈraɪs] *n* : arroz *m*
rich [ˈrɪtʃ] *adj* **1** WEALTHY : rico **2** SUMPTUOUS : suntuoso, lujoso **3** : pesado ⟨rich foods : comida pesada⟩ **4** ABUNDANT : abundante **5** : vivo, intenso ⟨rich colors : colores vivos⟩ **6** FERTILE : fértil, rico

riches [ˈrɪtʃəz] *npl* : riquezas *fpl*
richly [ˈrɪtʃli] *adv* **1** SUMPTUOUSLY : suntuosamente, ricamente **2** ABUNDANTLY : abundantemente **3 richly deserved** : bien merecido
richness [ˈrɪtʃnəs] *n* : riqueza *f*
rickets [ˈrɪkəts] *n* : raquitismo *m*
rickety [ˈrɪkəti] *adj* : desvencijado, destartalado
ricksha *or* **rickshaw** [ˈrɪkˌʃɔ] *n* : cochecillo *m* tirado por un hombre
ricochet[1] [ˈrɪkəˌʃeɪ] *vi* **-cheted** [-ˌʃeɪd] *or* **-chetted** [-ˌʃɛtəd]; **-cheting** [-ˌʃeɪɪŋ] *or* **-chetting** [-ˌʃɛtɪŋ] : rebotar
ricochet[2] *n* : rebote *m*
rid [ˈrɪd] *vt* **rid; ridding 1** FREE : librar ⟨to rid the city of thieves : librar la ciudad de ladrones⟩ **2 to rid oneself of** : desembarazarse de
riddance [ˈrɪdənts] *n* : libramiento *m* ⟨good riddance! : ¡adiós y buen viaje!, ¡vete con viento fresco!⟩
riddle[1] [ˈrɪdəl] *vt* **-dled; -dling** : acribillar ⟨riddled with bullets : acribillado a balazos⟩ ⟨riddled with errors : lleno de errores⟩
riddle[2] *n* : acertijo *m*, adivinanza *f*
ride[1] [ˈraɪd] *v* **rode** [ˈroːd]; **ridden** [ˈrɪdən]; **riding** *vt* **1** : montar, ir, andar ⟨to ride a horse : montar a caballo⟩ ⟨to ride a bicycle : montar en bicicleta, andar en bicicleta⟩ ⟨to ride the bus : ir en autobús⟩ **2** TRAVERSE : recorrer ⟨he rode 5 miles : recorrió 5 millas⟩ **3** TEASE : burlarse de, ridiculizar **4** CARRY : llevar **5** WEATHER : capear ⟨they rode out the storm : capearon el temporal⟩ **6 to ride the waves** : surcar los mares — *vi* **1** : montar a caballo, cabalgar **2** TRAVEL : ir, viajar (en coche, en bicicleta, etc.) **3** RUN : andar, marchar ⟨the car rides well : el coche anda bien⟩ **4 to ride at anchor** : estar fondeado **5 to let things ride** : dejar pasar las cosas
ride[2] *n* **1** : paseo *m*, vuelta *f* (en coche, en bicicleta, a caballo) ⟨to go for a ride : dar una vuelta⟩ ⟨to give someone a ride : llevar en coche a alguien⟩ **2** : aparato *m* (en un parque de diversiones)
rider [ˈraɪdər] *n* **1** : jinete *mf* ⟨the rider fell off his horse : el jinete se cayó de su caballo⟩ **2** CYCLIST : ciclista *mf* **3** MOTORCYCLIST : motociclista *mf* **4** CLAUSE : cláusula *f* añadida
ridge [ˈrɪdʒ] *n* **1** CHAIN : cadena *f* (de montañas o cerros) **2** : caballete *m* (de un techo), cresta *f* (de una ola o una montaña), cordoncillo *m* (de telas)
ridicule[1] [ˈrɪdəˌkjuːl] *vt* **-culed; -culing** : burlarse de, mofarse de, ridiculizar
ridicule[2] *n* : burlas *fpl*
ridiculous [rəˈdɪkjələs] *adj* : ridículo, absurdo
ridiculously [rəˈdɪkjələsli] *adv* : de forma ridícula
rife [ˈraɪf] *adj* : abundante, común ⟨to be rife with : estar plagado de⟩

riffraff ['rɪf,ræf] *n* : chusma *f*, gentuza *f*
rifle[1] ['raɪfəl] *v* **-fled; -fling** *vt* RANSACK : desvalijar, saquear — *vi* **to rifle through** : revolver
rifle[2] *n* : rifle *m*, fusil *m*
rift ['rɪft] *n* **1** FISSURE : grieta *f*, fisura *f* **2** BREAK : ruptura *f* (entre personas), división *f* (dentro de un grupo)
rig[1] ['rɪg] *vt* **rigged; rigging 1** : aparejar (un barco) **2** EQUIP : equipar **3** FIX : amañar (una elección, etc.) **4 to rig up** CONSTRUCT : construir, erigir **5 to rig oneself out as** : vestirse de
rig[2] *n* **1** : aparejo *m* (de un barco) **2** *or* **oil rig** : torre *f* de perforación, plataforma *f* petrolífera
rigging ['rɪgɪŋ, -gən] *n* : jarcia *f*, aparejo *m*
right[1] ['raɪt] *vt* **1** FIX, RESTORE : reparar ⟨to right the economy : reparar la economía⟩ **2** STRAIGHTEN : enderezar
right[2] *adv* **1** : bien ⟨to live right : vivir bien⟩ **2** PRECISELY : precisamente, justo ⟨right in the middle : justo en medio⟩ **3** DIRECTLY, STRAIGHT : derecho, directamente ⟨he went right home : fue derecho a casa⟩ **4** IMMEDIATELY : inmediatamente ⟨right after lunch : inmediatamente después del almuerzo⟩ **5** COMPLETELY : completamente ⟨he felt right at home : se sintió completamente cómodo⟩ **6** : a la derecha ⟨to look left and right : mirar a la izquierda y a la derecha⟩
right[3] *adj* **1** UPRIGHT : bueno, honrado ⟨right conduct : conducta honrada⟩ **2** CORRECT : correcto ⟨the right answer : la respuesta correcta⟩ **3** APPROPRIATE : apropiado, adecuado, debido ⟨the right man for the job : el hombre perfecto para el trabajo⟩ **4** STRAIGHT : recto ⟨a right line : una línea recta⟩ **5** : derecho ⟨the right hand : la mano derecha⟩ **6** SOUND : bien ⟨he's not in his right mind : no está bien de la cabeza⟩
right[4] *n* **1** GOOD : bien *m* ⟨to do right : hacer el bien⟩ **2** : derecha *f* ⟨on the right : a la derecha⟩ **3** *or* **right hand** : mano *f* derecha **4** ENTITLEMENT : derecho *m* ⟨the right to vote : el derecho a votar⟩ ⟨women's rights : los derechos de la mujer⟩ **5 the Right** : la derecha (en la política)
right angle *n* : ángulo *m* recto
right-angled ['raɪt'æŋgəld] *or* **right-angle** [-gəl] *adj* **1** : en ángulo recto **2 right-angled triangle** : triángulo *m* rectángulo
righteous ['raɪtʃəs] *adj* : recto, honrado — **righteously** *adv*
righteousness ['raɪtʃəsnəs] *n* : rectitud *f*, honradez *f*
rightful ['raɪtfəl] *adj* **1** JUST : justo **2** LAWFUL : legítimo — **rightfully** *adv*
right-hand ['raɪt'hænd] *adj* **1** : situado a la derecha **2** RIGHT-HANDED : para

la mano derecha, con la mano derecha **3 right-hand man** : brazo *m* derecho
right-handed ['raɪt'hændəd] *adj* **1** : diestro ⟨a right-handed pitcher : un lanzador diestro⟩ **2** : para la mano derecha, con la mano derecha **3** CLOCKWISE : en la dirección de las manecillas del reloj
rightly ['raɪtli] *adv* **1** JUSTLY : justamente, con razón **2** PROPERLY : debidamente, apropiadamente **3** CORRECTLY : correctamente
right-of-way ['raɪtə'weɪ, -əv-] *n*, *pl* **rights-of-way 1** : preferencia *f* (del tráfico) **2** ACCESS : derecho *m* de paso
rightward ['raɪtwərd] *adj* : a la derecha, hacia la derecha
right-wing ['raɪt'wɪŋ] *adj* : derechista
right wing *n* **the right wing** : la derecha
right-winger ['raɪt'wɪŋər] *n* : derechista *mf*
rigid ['rɪdʒɪd] *adj* : rígido — **rigidly** *adv*
rigidity [rɪ'dʒɪdəti] *n*, *pl* **-ties** : rigidez *f*
rigmarole ['rɪgmə,roːl, 'rɪgə-] *n* **1** NONSENSE : galimatías *m*, disparates *mpl* **2** PROCEDURES : trámites *mpl*
rigor ['rɪgər] *n* : rigor *m*
rigor mortis [,rɪgər'mortəs] *n* : rigidez *f* cadavérica
rigorous ['rɪgərəs] *adj* : riguroso — **rigorously** *adv*
rile ['raɪl] *vt* **riled; riling** : irritar
rill ['rɪl] *n* : riachuelo *m*
rim ['rɪm] *n* **1** EDGE : borde *m* **2** : llanta *f*, rin *m* *Col, Mex* (de una rueda) **3** FRAME : montura *f* (de anteojos)
rime ['raɪm] *n* : escarcha *f*
rind ['raɪnd] *n* : corteza *f*
ring[1] ['rɪŋ] *v* **rang** ['ræŋ]; **rung** ['rʌŋ]; **ringing** *vi* **1** : sonar ⟨the doorbell rang : el timbre sonó⟩ ⟨to ring for : llamar⟩ **2** RESOUND : resonar **3** SEEM : parecer ⟨to ring true : parecer cierto⟩ — *vt* **1** : tocar, hacer sonar (un timbre, una alarma, etc.) **2** SURROUND : cercar, rodear
ring[2] *n* **1** : anillo *m*, sortija *f* ⟨wedding ring : anillo de matrimonio⟩ **2** BAND : aro *m*, anillo *m* ⟨piston ring : aro de émbolo⟩ **3** CIRCLE : círculo *m* **4** ARENA : arena *f*, ruedo *m* ⟨a boxing ring : un cuadrilátero, un ring⟩ **5** GANG : banda *f* (de ladrones, etc.) **6** SOUND : timbre *m*, sonido *m* **7** CALL : llamada *f* (por teléfono)
ringer ['rɪŋər] *n* **to be a dead ringer for** : ser un vivo retrato de
ringleader ['rɪŋ,liːdər] *n* : cabecilla *mf*
ringlet ['rɪŋlət] *n* : sortija *f*, rizo *m*
ringworm ['rɪŋ,wərm] *n* : tiña *f*
rink ['rɪŋk] *n* : pista *f* ⟨skating rink : pista de patinaje⟩
rinse[1] ['rɪnts] *vt* **rinsed; rinsing** : enjuagar ⟨to rinse out one's mouth : enjuagarse la boca⟩
rinse[2] *n* : enjuague *m*
riot[1] ['raɪət] *vi* : amotinarse
riot[2] *n* : motín *m*, tumulto *m*, alboroto *m*

rioter ['raɪətər] *n* : alborotador *m*, -dora *f*

riotous ['raɪətəs] *adj* **1** UNRULY, WILD : desenfrenado, alborotado **2** ABUNDANT : abundante

rip[1] ['rɪp] *v* **ripped; ripping** *vt* : rasgar, arrancar, desgarrar — *vi* : rasgarse, desgarrarse

rip[2] *n* : rasgón *m*, desgarrón *m*

ripe ['raɪp] *adj* **riper; ripest 1** MATURE : maduro ⟨ripe fruit : fruta madura⟩ **2** READY : listo, preparado

ripen ['raɪpən] *v* : madurar

ripeness ['raɪpnəs] *n* : madurez *f*

rip–off ['rɪp,ɔf] *n* **1** THEFT : robo *m* **2** SWINDLE : estafa *f*, timo *m fam*

rip off *vt* **1** : rasgar, arrancar, desgarrar **2** SWINDLE *fam* : estafar, tifar

ripple[1] ['rɪpəl] *v* **-pled; -pling** *vi* : rizarse, ondear, ondular — *vt* : rizar

ripple[2] *n* : onda *f*, ondulación *f*

rise[1] ['raɪz] *vi* **rose** ['ro:z]; **risen** ['rɪz-ən]; **rising 1** GET UP : levantarse ⟨to rise to one's feet : ponerse de pie⟩ **2** : elevarse, alzarse ⟨the mountains rose to the west : las montañas se elevaron al oeste⟩ **3** : salir (dícese del sol y de la luna) **4** : subir (dícese de las aguas, del humo, etc.) ⟨the river rose : las aguas subieron de nivel⟩ **5** INCREASE : aumentar, subir **6** ORIGINATE : nacer, proceder **7 to rise in rank** : ascender **8 to rise up** REBEL : sublevarse, rebelarse

rise[2] *n* **1** ASCENT : ascensión *f*, subida *f* **2** ORIGIN : origen *m* **3** ELEVATION : elevación *f* **4** INCREASE : subida *f*, aumento *m*, alzamiento *m* **5** SLOPE : pendiente *f*, cuesta *f*

riser ['raɪzər] *n* **1** : contrahuella *f* (de una escalera) **2 early riser** : madrugador *m*, -dora *f* **3 late riser** : dormilón *m*, -lona *f*

risk[1] ['rɪsk] *vt* : arriesgar

risk[2] *n* : riesgo *m*, peligro *m* ⟨at risk : en peligro⟩ ⟨at your own risk : por su cuenta y riesgo⟩

risky ['rɪski] *adj* **riskier; -est** : arriesgado, peligroso, riesgoso

risqué [rɪ'skeɪ] *adj* : escabroso, picante, subido de tono

rite ['raɪt] *n* : rito *m*

ritual[1] ['rɪtʃuəl] *adj* : ritual — **ritually** *adv*

ritual[2] *n* : ritual *m*

rival[1] ['raɪvəl] *vt* **-valed** *or* **-valled; -valing** *or* **-valling** : rivalizar con, competir con

rival[2] *adj* : competidor, rival

rival[3] *n* : rival *mf*; competidor *m*, -dora *f*

rivalry ['raɪvəlri] *n*, *pl* **-ries** : rivalidad *f*, competencia *f*

river ['rɪvər] *n* : río *m*

riverbank ['rɪvər,bæŋk] *n* : ribera *f*, orilla *f*

riverbed ['rɪvər,bɛd] *n* : cauce *m*, lecho *m*

riverside ['rɪvər,saɪd] *n* : ribera *f*, orilla *f*

rivet[1] ['rɪvət] *vt* **1** : remachar **2** FIX : fijar (los ojos, etc.) **3** FASCINATE : fascinar, cautivar

rivet[2] *n* : remache *m*

rivulet ['rɪvjələt] *n* : arroyo *m*, riachuelo *m* ⟨rivulets of sweat : gotas de sudor⟩

roach ['ro:tʃ] → **cockroach**

road ['ro:d] *n* **1** : carretera *f*, calle *f*, camino *m* **2** PATH : camino *m*, sendero *m*, vía *f* ⟨on the road to a solution : en vías de una solución⟩

roadblock ['ro:d,blɑk] *n* : control *m*

roadrunner ['ro:d,rʌnər] *n* : correcaminos *m*

roadside ['ro:d,saɪd] *n* : borde *m* de la carretera

roadway ['ro:d,weɪ] *n* : carretera *f*, calzada *f*

roam ['ro:m] *vi* : vagar, deambular, errar — *vt* : vagar por

roan[1] ['ro:n] *adj* : ruano

roan[2] *n* : caballo *m* ruano

roar[1] ['ror] *vi* : rugir, bramar ⟨to roar with laughter : reírse a carcajadas⟩ — *vt* : decir a gritos

roar[2] *n* **1** : rugido *m*, bramido *m* (de un animal) **2** DIN : clamor *m* (de gente), fragor *m* (del trueno), estruendo *m* (del tráfico, etc.)

roast[1] ['ro:st] *vt* : asar (carne, papas), tostar (café, nueces) — *vi* : asarse

roast[2] *adj* : asado ⟨roast chicken : pollo asado⟩ **2 roast beef** : rosbif *m*

roast[3] *n* : asado *m*

rob ['rɑb] *v* **robbed; robbing** *vt* **1** STEAL : robar **2** DEPRIVE : privar, quitar — *vi* : robar

robber ['rɑbər] *n* : ladrón *m*, -drona *f*

robbery ['rɑbəri] *n*, *pl* **-beries** : robo *m*

robe[1] ['ro:b] *vt* **robed; robing** : vestirse

robe[2] *n* **1** : toga *f* (de magistrados, etc.), sotana *f* (de eclesiásticos) ⟨robe of office : traje de ceremonias⟩ **2** BATHROBE : bata *f*

robin ['rɑbən] *n* : petirrojo *m*

robot ['ro:,bɑt, -bət] *n* : robot *m*

robotic [ro'bɑtɪk] *adj* : robótico, robotizado

robotics [ro'bɑtɪks] *ns & pl* : robótica *f*

robust [ro'bʌst, 'ro:,bʌst] *adj* : robusto, fuerte — **robustly** *adv*

rock[1] ['rɑk] *vt* **1** : acunar (a un niño), mecer (una cuna) **2** SHAKE : sacudir — *vi* SWAY : mecerse, balancearse

rock[2] *adj* : de rock

rock[3] *n* **1** ROCKING : balanceo *m* **2** *or* **rock music** : rock *m*, música *f* rock **3** : roca *f* (substancia) **4** STONE : piedra *f*

rock and roll *n* : rock and roll *m*

rocker ['rɑkər] *n* **1** : balancín *m* **2** *or* **rocking chair** : mecedora *f*, balancín *m* **3 to be off one's rocker** : estar chiflado, estar loco

rocket[1] ['rɑkət] *vi* : dispararse, subir rápidamente

rocket[2] *n* : cohete *m*

rocking horse *n* : caballito *m* (de balancín)
rock salt *n* : sal *f* gema
rocky ['rɑki] *adj* **rockier; -est 1** : rocoso, pedregoso **2** UNSTEADY : inestable
rod ['rɑd] *n* **1** BAR : barra *f*, varilla *f*, vara *f* (de madera) ⟨a fishing rod : una caña (de pescar)⟩ **2** : medida *f* de longitud equivalente a 5.03 metros (5 yardas)
rode → **ride**[1]
rodent ['ro:dənt] *n* : roedor *m*
rodeo ['ro:di‚o:, ro'dei‚o:] *n, pl* **-deos** : rodeo *m*
roe ['ro:] *n* : hueva *f*
rogue ['ro:g] *n* SCOUNDREL : pícaro *m*, -ra *f*; pillo *m*, -lla *f*
roguish ['ro:gɪʃ] *adj* : pícaro, travieso
role ['ro:l] *n* : papel *m*, función *f*, rol *m*
roll[1] ['ro:l] *vt* **1** : hacer rodar ⟨to roll the ball : hacer rodar la pelota⟩ ⟨to roll one's eyes : poner los ojos en blanco⟩ **2** : liar (un cigarrillo) **3** *or* **to roll up** : enrollar ⟨to roll (oneself) up into a ball : hacerse una bola⟩ **4** FLATTEN : estirar (masa), laminar (metales), pasar el rodillo por (el césped) **5 to roll up one's sleeves** : arremangarse — *vi* **1** : rodar ⟨the ball kept on rolling : la pelota siguió rodando⟩ **2** SWAY : balancearse ⟨the ship rolled in the waves : el barco se balanceó en las olas⟩ **3** REVERBERATE, SOUND : tronar (dícese del trueno), redoblar (dícese de un tambor) **4 to roll along** PROCEED : ponerse en marcha **5 to roll around** : revolcarse **6 to roll by** : pasar **7 to roll over** : dar una vuelta
roll[2] *n* **1** LIST : lista *f* ⟨to call the roll : pasar lista⟩ ⟨to have on the roll : tener inscrito⟩ **2** *or* **bread roll** : panecillo *m*, bolillo *m Mex* **3** : rollo *m* (de papel, de tela, etc.) ⟨a roll of film : un carrete⟩ ⟨a roll of bills : un fajo⟩ **4** : redoble *m* (de tambores), retumbo *m* (del trueno, etc.) **5** ROLLING, SWAYING : balanceo *m*
roller ['ro:lər] *n* **1** : rodillo *m* **2** CURLER : rulo *m*
roller coaster ['ro:lər‚ko:stər] *n* : montaña *f* rusa
roller-skate ['ro:lər‚skeɪt] *vi* **-skated; -skating** : patinar (sobre ruedas)
roller skate *n* : patín *m* (de ruedas)
rollicking ['rɑlɪkɪŋ] *adj* : animado, alegre
rolling pin *n* : rodillo *m*
Roman[1] ['ro:mən] *adj* : romano
Roman[2] *n* : romano *m*, -na *f*
Roman Catholic *n* : católico *m*, -ca *f* — **Roman Catholic** *adj*
Roman Catholicism *n* : catolicismo *m*
romance[1] [ro'mænts, 'ro:‚mænts] *vi* **-manced; -mancing** FANTASIZE : fantasear
romance[2] *n* **1** : romance *m*, novela *f* de caballerías **2** : novela *f* de amor, novela *f* romántica **3** AFFAIR : romance *m*, amorío *m*

Romanian [rʊ'meɪniən, ro-] *n* **1** : rumano *m*, -na *f* **2** : rumano *m* (idioma) — **Romanian** *adj*
Roman numeral *n* : número *m* romano
romantic [ro'mæntɪk] *adj* : romántico — **romantically** [-tɪkli] *adv*
romp[1] ['rɑmp] *vi* FROLIC : retozar, juguetear
romp[2] *n* : retozo *m*
roof[1] ['ru:f, 'rʊf] *vt* : techar
roof[2] *n, pl* **roofs** ['ru:fs, 'rʊfs; 'ru:vz, 'rʊvz] **1** : techo *m*, tejado *m*, techado *m* **2 roof of the mouth** : paladar *m*
roofing ['ru:fɪŋ, 'rʊfɪŋ] *n* : techumbre *f*
rooftop ['ru:f‚tɑp, 'rʊf-] *n* ROOF : tejado *m*
rook[1] ['rʊk] *vt* CHEAT : defraudar, estafar, timar
rook[2] *n* **1** : grajo *m* (ave) **2** : torre *f* (en ajedrez)
rookie ['rʊki] *n* : novato *m*, -ta *f*
room[1] ['ru:m, 'rʊm] *vi* LODGE : alojarse, hospedarse
room[2] *n* **1** SPACE : espacio *m*, sitio *m*, lugar *m* ⟨to make room for : hacer lugar para⟩ **2** : cuarto *m*, habitación *f* (en una casa), sala *f* (para reuniones, etc.) **3** BEDROOM : dormitorio *m*, habitación *f*, pieza *f* **4** (*indicating possibility or opportunity*) ⟨room for improvement : posibilidad de mejorar⟩ ⟨there's no room for error : no hay lugar para errores⟩
roomer ['ru:mər, 'rʊmər] *n* : inquilino *m*, -na *f*
rooming house *n* : pensión *f*
roommate ['ru:m‚meɪt, 'rʊm-] *n* : compañero *m*, -ra *f* de cuarto
roomy ['ru:mi, 'rʊmi] *adj* **roomier; -est 1** SPACIOUS : espacioso, amplio **2** LOOSE : suelto, holgado ⟨a roomy blouse : una blusa holgada⟩
roost[1] ['ru:st] *vi* : posarse, dormir (en una percha)
roost[2] *n* : percha *f*
rooster ['ru:stər, 'rʊs-] *n* : gallo *m*
root[1] ['ru:t, 'rʊt] *vi* **1** : arraigar ⟨the plant rooted easily : la planta arraigó con facilidad⟩ ⟨deeply rooted traditions : tradiciones profundamente arraigadas⟩ **2** : hozar (dícese de los cerdos) ⟨to root around in : hurgar en⟩ **3 to root for** : apoyar a, alentar — *vt* **to root out** *or* **to root up** : desarraigar (plantas), extirpar (problemas, etc.)
root[2] *n* **1** : raíz *f* (de una planta) **2** ORIGIN : origen *m*, raíz *f* **3** CORE : centro *m*, núcleo *m* ⟨to get to the root of the matter : ir al centro del asunto⟩
rootless ['ru:tləs, 'rʊt-] *adj* : desarraigado
rope[1] ['ro:p] *vt* **roped; roping 1** TIE : amarrar, atar **2** LASSO : lazar **3 to rope off** : acordonar
rope[2] *n* : soga *f*, cuerda *f*
rosary ['ro:zəri] *n, pl* **-ries** : rosario *m*
rose[1] → **rise**[1]
rose[2] ['ro:z] *adj* : rosa, color de rosa

rose[3] *n* **1** : rosal *m* (planta), rosa *f* (flor) **2** : rosa *m* (color)

rosebush ['ro:z,buʃ] *n* : rosal *m*

rosemary ['ro:z,mɛri] *n, pl* **-maries** : romero *m*

rosette [ro'zɛt] *n* : escarapela *f* (hecho de cintas), roseta *f* (en arquitectura)

Rosh Hashanah [,raʃha'ʃanə, ,ro:ʃ-] *n* : el Año Nuevo judío

rosin ['razən] *n* : colofonia *f*

roster ['rastər] *n* : lista *f*

rostrum ['rastrəm] *n, pl* **-trums** *or* **-tra** [-trə] : tribuna *f*, estrado *m*

rosy ['ro:zi] *adj* **rosier; -est** **1** : sonrosado, de color rosa **2** PROMISING : prometedor, halagüeño

rot[1] ['rat] *v* **rotted; rotting** *vi* : pudrirse, descomponerse — *vt* : pudrir, descomponer

rot[2] *n* : putrefacción *f*, descomposición *f*, podredumbre *f*

rotary[1] ['ro:ṭəri] *adj* : rotativo, rotatorio

rotary[2] *n, pl* **-ries** **1** : máquina *f* rotativa **2** TRAFFIC CIRCLE : rotonda *f*, glorieta *f*

rotate ['ro:,teɪt] *v* **-tated; -tating** *vi* REVOLVE : girar, rotar — *vt* **1** TURN : hacer girar, darle vueltas a **2** ALTERNATE : alternar

rotation [ro'teɪʃən] *n* : rotación *f*

rote ['ro:t] *n* **to learn by rote** : aprender de memoria

rotor ['ro:ṭər] *n* : rotor *m*

rotten ['ratən] *adj* **1** PUTRID : podrido, putrefacto **2** CORRUPT : corrompido **3** BAD : malo ⟨a rotten day : un día malísimo⟩

rottenness ['ratənnəs] *n* : podredumbre *f*

rotund [ro'tʌnd] *adj* **1** ROUNDED : redondeado **2** PLUMP : regordete *fam*, llenito *fam*

rouge ['ru:ʒ, 'ru:dʒ] *n* : colorete *m*

rough[1] ['rʌf] *vt* **1** ROUGHEN : poner áspero **2 to rough out** SKETCH : esbozar, bosquejar **3 to rough up** BEAT : darle una paliza (a alguien) **4 to rough it** : vivir sin comodidades

rough[2] *adj* **1** COARSE : áspero, basto **2** UNEVEN : desigual, escabroso, accidentado (dícese del terreno) **3** : agitado (dícese del mar), tempestuoso (dícese del tiempo), violento (dícese del viento) **4** VIOLENT : violento, brutal ⟨a rough neighborhood : un barrio peligroso⟩ **5** DIFFICULT : duro, difícil **6** CRUDE : rudo, tosco, burdo ⟨a rough cottage : una casita tosca⟩ ⟨a rough draft : un borrador⟩ ⟨a rough sketch : un bosquejo⟩ **7** APPROXIMATE : aproximado ⟨a rough idea : una idea aproximada⟩

rough[3] *n* **1 the rough** : el rough (en golf) **2 in the rough** : en borrador

roughage ['rʌfɪdʒ] *n* : fibra *f*

roughen ['rʌfən] *vt* : poner áspero — *vi* : ponerse áspero

roughly ['rʌfli] *adv* **1** : bruscamente ⟨to treat roughly : maltratar⟩ **2** CRUDELY : burdamente **3** APPROXIMATELY : aproximadamente, más o menos

roughneck ['rʌf,nɛk] *n* : matón *m*

roughness ['rʌfnəs] *n* : rudeza *f*, aspereza *f*

roulette [ru:'lɛt] *n* : ruleta *f*

round[1] ['raʊnd] *vt* **1** : redondear ⟨she rounded the edges : redondeó los bordes⟩ **2** TURN : doblar ⟨to round the corner : dar la vuelta a la esquina⟩ **3 to round off** : redondear (un número) **4 to round off** *or* **to round out** COMPLETE : rematar, terminar **5 to round up** GATHER : reunir

round[2] *adv* → **around**[1]

round[3] *adj* **1** : redondo ⟨a round table : una mesa redonda⟩ ⟨in round numbers : en números redondos⟩ ⟨round shoulders : espaldas cargadas⟩ **2 round trip** : viaje *m* de ida y vuelta

round[4] *n* **1** CIRCLE : círculo *m* **2** SERIES : serie *f*, sucesión *f* ⟨a round of talks : una ronda de negociaciones⟩ ⟨the daily round : la rutina cotidiana⟩ **3** : asalto *m* (en boxeo), recorrido *m* (en golf), vuelta *f* (en varios juegos) **4** : salva *f* (de aplausos) **5 round of drinks** : ronda *f* **6 round of ammunition** : disparo *m*, cartucho *m* **7 rounds** *npl* : recorridos *mpl* (de un cartero), rondas *fpl* (de un vigilante), visitas *fpl* (de un médico) ⟨to make the rounds : hacer visitas⟩

round[5] *prep* → **around**[2]

roundabout ['raʊndə,baʊt] *adj* : indirecto ⟨to speak in a roundabout way : hablar con rodeos⟩

roundly ['raʊndli] *adv* **1** THOROUGHLY : completamente **2** BLUNTLY : francamente, rotundamente **3** VIGOROUSLY : con vigor

roundness ['raʊndnəs] *n* : redondez *f*

roundup ['raʊnd,ʌp] *n* **1** : rodeo *m* (de animales), redada *f* (de delincuentes, etc.) **2** SUMMARY : resumen *m*

round up *vt* **1** : rodear (ganado), reunir (personas) **2** SUMMARIZE : hacer un resumen de

roundworm ['raʊnd,wərm] *n* : lombriz *f* intestinal

rouse ['raʊz] *vt* **roused; rousing** **1** AWAKE : despertar **2** EXCITE : excitar ⟨it roused him to fury : lo enfureció⟩

rout[1] ['raʊt] *vt* **1** DEFEAT : derrotar, aplastar **2 to rout out** : hacer salir

rout[2] *n* **1** DISPERSAL : desbandada *f*, dispersión *f* **2** DEFEAT : derrota *f* aplastante

route[1] ['ru:t, 'raʊt] *vt* **routed; routing** : dirigir, enviar, encaminar

route[2] *n* : camino *m*, ruta *f*, recorrido *m*

routine[1] [ru:'ti:n] *adj* : rutinario — **routinely** *adv*

routine[2] *n* : rutina *f*

rove ['ro:v] *v* **roved; roving** *vi* : vagar, errar — *vt* : errar por

rover ['ro:vər] *n* : vagabundo *m*, -da *f*

row¹ ['ro:] *vt* **1** : avanzar a remo ⟨to row a boat : remar⟩ **2** : llevar a remo ⟨he rowed me to shore : me llevó hasta la orilla⟩ — *vi* : remar

row² ['raʊ] *n* **1** : paseo *m* en barca ⟨to go for a row : salir a remar⟩ **2** LINE, RANK : fila *f*, hilera *f* **3** SERIES : serie *f* ⟨three days in a row : tres días seguidos⟩ **4** RACKET : estruendo *m*, bulla *f* **5** QUARREL : pelea *f*, riña *f*

rowboat ['ro:ˌbo:t] *n* : bote *m* de remos

rowdiness ['raʊdinəs] *n* : bulla *f*

rowdy¹ ['raʊdi] *adj* **-dier; -est** : escandaloso, alborotador

rowdy² *n, pl* **-dies** : alborotador *m*, -dora *f*

rower ['ro:ər] *n* : remero *m*, -ra *f*

royal¹ ['rɔɪəl] *adj* : real — **royally** *adv*

royal² *n* : persona de linaje real, miembro de la familia real

royalty ['rɔɪəlti] *n, pl* **-ties** **1** : realeza *f* (posición) **2** : miembros *mpl* de la familia real **3 royalties** *npl* : derechos *mpl* de autor

rub¹ ['rʌb] *v* **rubbed; rubbing** *vt* **1** : frotar, restregar ⟨to rub one's hands together : frotarse las manos⟩ **2** MASSAGE : friccionar, masajear **3** CHAFE : rozar **4** POLISH : frotar, pulir **5** SCRUB : fregar **6 to rub elbows with** : codearse con **7 to rub someone the wrong way** : sacar de quicio a alguien, caerle mal a alguien — *vi* **to rub against** : rozar

rub² *n* **1** RUBBING : frotamiento *m*, fricción *f* **2** DIFFICULTY : problema *m*

rubber ['rʌbər] *n* **1** : goma *f*, caucho *m*, hule *m Mex* **2 rubbers** *npl* OVERSHOES : chanclos *mpl*

rubber band *n* : goma *f* (elástica), gomita *f*

rubber–stamp ['rʌbər'stæmp] *vt* **1** APPROVE : aprobar, autorizar **2** STAMP : sellar

rubber stamp *n* : sello *m* (de goma)

rubbery ['rʌbəri] *adj* : gomoso

rubbish ['rʌbɪʃ] *n* : basura *f*, desechos *mpl*, desperdicios *mpl*

rubble ['rʌbəl] *n* : escombros *mpl*, ripio *m*

ruble ['ru:bəl] *n* : rublo *m*

ruby ['ru:bi] *n, pl* **-bies** **1** : rubí *m* (gema) **2** : color *m* de rubí

rudder ['rʌdər] *n* : timón *m*

ruddy ['rʌdi] *adj* **-dier; -est** : rubicundo (dícese de la cara, etc.), rojizo (dícese del cielo)

rude ['ru:d] *adj* **ruder; rudest** **1** CRUDE : tosco, rústico **2** IMPOLITE : grosero, descortés, maleducado **3** ABRUPT : brusco ⟨a rude awakening : una sorpresa desagradable⟩

rudely ['ru:dli] *adv* : groseramente

rudeness ['ru:dnəs] *n* **1** IMPOLITENESS : grosería *f*, descortesía *f*, falta *f* de educación **2** ROUGHNESS : tosquedad *f* **3** SUDDENNESS : brusquedad *f*

rudiment ['ru:dəmənt] *n* : rudimento *m*, noción *f* básica ⟨the rudiments of Spanish : los rudimentos del español⟩

rudimentary [ˌru:də'mɛntəri] *adj* : rudimentario, básico

rue ['ru:] *vt* **rued; ruing** : lamentar, arrepentirse de

rueful ['ru:fəl] *adj* **1** PITIFUL : lastimoso **2** REGRETFUL : arrepentido, pesaroso

ruffian ['rʌfiən] *n* : matón *m*

ruffle¹ ['rʌfəl] *vt* **-fled; -fling** **1** AGITATE : agitar, rizar (agua) **2** RUMPLE : arrugar (ropa), despeinar (pelo) **3** ERECT : erizar (plumas) **4** VEX : alterar, irritar, perturbar **5** : fruncir volantes en (tela)

ruffle² *n* FLOUNCE : volante *m*

ruffly ['rʌfəli] *adj* : con volantes

rug ['rʌg] *n* : alfombra *f*, tapete *m*

rugged ['rʌgəd] *adj* **1** ROUGH, UNEVEN : accidentado, escabroso ⟨rugged mountains : montañas accidentadas⟩ **2** HARSH : duro, severo **3** ROBUST, STURDY : robusto, fuerte

ruin¹ ['ru:ən] *vt* **1** DESTROY : destruir, arruinar **2** BANKRUPT : arruinar, hacer quebrar

ruin² *n* **1** : ruina *f* ⟨to fall into ruin : caer en ruinas⟩ **2** : ruina *f*, perdición *f* ⟨to be the ruin of : ser la perdición de⟩ **3 ruins** *npl* : ruinas *fpl*, restos *mpl* ⟨the ruins of the ancient temple : las ruinas del templo antiguo⟩

ruinous ['ru:ənəs] *adj* : ruinoso

rule¹ ['ru:l] *v* **ruled; ruling** *vt* **1** CONTROL, GOVERN : gobernar (un país), controlar (las emociones) **2** DECIDE : decidir, fallar ⟨the judge ruled that . . . : el juez falló que . . . ⟩ **3** DRAW : trazar con una regla — *vi* **1** GOVERN : gobernar, reinar **2** PREVAIL : prevalecer, imperar **3 to rule against** : fallar en contra de

rule² *n* **1** REGULATION : regla *f*, norma *f* **2** CUSTOM, HABIT : regla *f* general ⟨as a rule : por lo general⟩ **3** GOVERNMENT : gobierno *m*, dominio *m* **4** RULER : regla *f* (para medir)

ruler ['ru:lər] *n* **1** LEADER, SOVEREIGN : gobernante *mf*; soberano *m*, -na *f* **2** : regla *f* (para medir)

ruling ['ru:lɪŋ] *n* : resolución *f*, fallo *m*

rum ['rʌm] *n* : ron *m*

Rumanian [rʊ'meɪniən] → **Romanian**

rumble¹ ['rʌmbəl] *vi* **-bled; -bling** : retumbar, hacer ruidos (dícese del estómago)

rumble² *n* : estruendo *m*, ruido *m* sordo, retumbo *m*

ruminant¹ ['ru:mənənt] *adj* : rumiante

ruminant² *n* : rumiante *m*

ruminate ['ru:məˌneɪt] *vi* **-nated; -nating** **1** : rumiar (en zoología) **2** REFLECT : reflexionar, rumiar

rummage ['rʌmɪdʒ] *v* **-maged; -maging** *vi* : hurgar — *vt* RANSACK : revolver ⟨they rummaged the attic : revolvieron el ático⟩

rummy ['rʌmi] *n* : rummy *m* (juego de naipes)

rumor[1] ['ru:mər] *vt* : rumorear ⟨it is rumored that . . . : se rumorea que . . ., se dice que . . . ⟩

rumor[2] *n* : rumor *m*

rump ['rʌmp] *n* **1** : ancas *fpl*, grupa *f* (de un animal) **2** : cadera *f* ⟨rump steak : filete de cadera⟩

rumple ['rʌmpəl] *vt* **-pled; -pling** : arrugar (ropa, etc.), despeinar (pelo)

rumpus ['rʌmpəs] *n* : lío *m*, jaleo *m fam*

run[1] ['rʌn] *v* **ran** ['ræn]; **run; running** *vi* **1** : correr ⟨she ran to catch the bus : corrió para alcanzar el autobús⟩ ⟨run and fetch the doctor : corre a buscar al médico⟩ **2** : circular, correr ⟨the train runs between Detroit and Chicago : el tren circula entre Detroit y Chicago⟩ ⟨to run on time : ser puntual⟩ **3** FUNCTION : funcionar, ir ⟨the engine runs on gasoline : el motor funciona con gasolina⟩ ⟨to run smoothly : ir bien⟩ **4** FLOW : correr, ir **5** LAST : durar ⟨the movie runs for two hours : la película dura dos horas⟩ ⟨the contract runs for three years : el contrato es válido por tres años⟩ **6** : desteñir, despintar (dícese de los colores) **7** EXTEND : correr, extenderse **8 to run for office** : postularse, presentarse — *vt* **1** : correr ⟨to run 10 miles : correr 10 millas⟩ ⟨to run errands : hacer los mandados⟩ ⟨to run out of town : hacer salir del pueblo⟩ **2** PASS : pasar **3** DRIVE : llevar en coche **4** OPERATE : hacer funcionar (un motor, etc.) **5** : echar ⟨to run water : echar agua⟩ **6** MANAGE : dirigir, llevar (un negocio, etc.) **7** EXTEND : tender (un cable, etc.) **8 to run a risk** : correr un riesgo

run[2] *n* **1** : carrera *f* ⟨at a run : a la carrera, corriendo⟩ ⟨to go for a run : ir a correr⟩ **2** TRIP : vuelta *f*, paseo *m* (en coche), viaje *m* (en avión) **3** SERIES : serie *f* ⟨a run of disappointments : una serie de desilusiones⟩ ⟨in the long run : a la larga⟩ ⟨in the short run : a corto plazo⟩ **4** DEMAND : gran demanda *f* ⟨a run on the banks : una corrida bancaria⟩ **5** (*used for theatrical productions and films*) ⟨to have a long run : mantenerse mucho tiempo en la cartelera⟩ **6** TYPE : tipo *m* ⟨the average run of students : el tipo más común de estudiante⟩ **7** : carrera *f* (en béisbol) **8** : carrera *f* (en una media) **9 to have the run of** : tener libre acceso de (una casa, etc.) **10 ski run** : pista *f* (de esquí)

runaway[1] ['rʌnə,weɪ] *adj* **1** FUGITIVE : fugitivo **2** UNCONTROLLABLE : incontrolable, fuera de control ⟨runaway inflation : inflación desenfrenada⟩ ⟨a runaway success : un éxito aplastante⟩

runaway[2] *n* : fugitivo *m*, -va *f*

rundown ['rʌn,daʊn] *n* SUMMARY : resumen *m*

run–down ['rʌn'daʊn] *adj* **1** DILAPIDATED : ruinoso, destartalado **2** SICKLY, TIRED : cansado, débil

rung[1] *pp* → **ring**[1]

rung[2] ['rʌŋ] *n* : peldaño *m*, escalón *m*

run–in ['rʌn,ɪn] *n* : disputa *f*, altercado *m*

runner ['rʌnər] *n* **1** RACER : corredor *m*, -dora *f* **2** MESSENGER : mensajero *m*, -ra *f* **3** TRACK : riel *m* (de un cajón, etc.) **4** : patín *m* (de un trineo), cuchilla *f* (de un patín) **5** : estolón *m* (planta)

runner–up [,rʌnər'ʌp] *n*, *pl* **runners–up** : subcampeón *m*, -peona *f*

running ['rʌnɪŋ] *adj* **1** FLOWING : corriente ⟨running water : agua corriente⟩ **2** CONTINUOUS : continuo ⟨a running battle : una lucha continua⟩ **3** CONSECUTIVE : seguido ⟨six days running : por seis días seguidos⟩

runny ['rʌni] *adj* **-nier; -est 1** WATERY : caldoso **2 to have a runny nose** : moquear

run over *vt* : atropellar — *vi* OVERFLOW : rebosar

runt ['rʌnt] *n* : animal *m* pequeño ⟨the runt of the litter : el más pequeño de la camada⟩

runway ['rʌn,weɪ] *n* : pista *f* de aterrizaje

rupee [ru:'pi:, 'ru:,-] *n* : rupia *f*

rupture[1] ['rʌptʃər] *v* **-tured; -turing** *vt* **1** BREAK, BURST : romper, reventar **2** : causar una hernia en — *vi* : reventarse

rupture[2] *n* **1** BREAK : ruptura *f* **2** HERNIA : hernia *f*

rural ['rʊrəl] *adj* : rural, campestre

ruse ['ru:s, 'ru:z] *n* : treta *f*, ardid *m*, estratagema *f*

rush[1] ['rʌʃ] *vi* : correr, ir de prisa ⟨to rush around : correr de un lado a otro⟩ ⟨to rush off : irse corriendo⟩ — *vt* **1** HURRY : apresurar, apurar **2** ATTACK : abalanzarse sobre, asaltar

rush[2] *adj* : urgente

rush[3] *n* **1** HASTE : prisa *f*, apuro *m* **2** SURGE : ráfaga *f* (de aire), torrente *m* (de aguas), avalancha *f* (de gente) **3** DEMAND : demanda *f* ⟨a rush on sugar : una gran demanda para el azúcar⟩ **4** : carga *f* (en futbol americano) **5** : junco *m* (planta)

russet ['rʌsət] *n* : color *m* rojizo

Russian ['rʌʃən] *n* **1** : ruso *m*, -sa *f* **2** : ruso *m* (idioma) — **Russian** *adj*

rust[1] ['rʌst] *vi* : oxidarse — *vt* : oxidar

rust[2] *n* **1** : herrumbre *f*, orín *m*, óxido *m* (en los metales) **2** : roya *f* (en las plantas)

rustic[1] ['rʌstɪk] *adj* : rústico, campestre — **rustically** [-tɪkli] *adv*

rustic[2] *n* : rústico *m*, -ca *f*; campesino *m*, -na *f*

rustle[1] ['rʌsəl] *v* **-tled; -tling** *vt* **1** : hacer susurrar, hacer crujir ⟨to rustle a newspaper : hacer crujir un periódico⟩ **2** STEAL : robar (ganado) — *vi* : susurrar, crujir

rustle² *n* : murmullo *m*, susurro *m*, crujido *m*

rustler ['rʌsələr] *n* : ladrón *m*, -drona *f* de ganado

rusty ['rʌsti] *adj* **rustier; -est** : oxidado, herrumbroso

rut ['rʌt] *n* **1** GROOVE, TRACK : rodada *f*, surco *m* **2 to be in a rut** : ser esclavo de la rutina

ruthless ['ruːθləs] *adj* : despiadado, cruel — **ruthlessly** *adv*

ruthlessness ['ruːθləsnəs] *n* : crueldad *f*, falta *f* de piedad

Rwandan [ru'andən] *n* : ruandés *m*, -desa *f* — **Rwandan** *adj*

rye ['raɪ] *n* **1** : centeno *m* **2** *or* **rye whiskey** : whisky *m* de centeno

S

s ['ɛs] *n*, *pl* **s's** *or* **ss** ['ɛsəz] : decimonovena letra del alfabeto inglés

Sabbath ['sæbəθ] *n* **1** : sábado *m* (en el judaísmo) **2** : domingo *m* (en el cristianismo)

saber ['seɪbər] *n* : sable *m*

sable ['seɪbəl] *n* **1** BLACK : negro *m* **2** : marta *f* cebellina (animal)

sabotage¹ ['sæbə,taʒ] *vt* **-taged; -taging** : sabotear

sabotage² *n* : sabotaje *m*

sac ['sæk] *n* : saco *m* (anatómico)

saccharin ['sækərən] *n* : sacarina *f*

saccharine ['sækərən, -,riːn, -,raɪn] *adj* : meloso, empalagoso

sachet [sæ'ʃeɪ] *n* : bolsita *f* (perfumada)

sack¹ ['sæk] *vt* **1** FIRE : echar (del trabajo), despedir **2** PLUNDER : saquear

sack² *n* BAG : saco *m*

sacrament ['sækrəmənt] *n* : sacramento *m*

sacramental [,sækrə'mɛntəl] *adj* : sacramental

sacred ['seɪkrəd] *adj* **1** RELIGIOUS : sagrado, sacro ⟨sacred texts : textos sagrados⟩ **2** HOLY : sagrado **3 sacred to** : consagrado a

sacrifice¹ ['sækrə,faɪs] *vt* **-ficed; -ficing 1** : sacrificar **2 to sacrifice oneself** : sacrificarse

sacrifice² *n* : sacrificio *m*

sacrilege ['sækrəlɪdʒ] *n* : sacrilegio *m*

sacrilegious [,sækrə'lɪdʒəs, -'liː-] *adj* : sacrílego

sacrosanct ['sækro,sæŋkt] *adj* : sacrosanto

sad ['sæd] *adj* **sadder; saddest** : triste — **sadly** *adv*

sadden ['sædən] *vt* : entristecer

saddle¹ ['sædəl] *vt* **-dled; -dling** : ensillar

saddle² *n* : silla *f* (de montar)

sadism ['seɪ,dɪzəm, 'sæ-] *n* : sadismo *m*

sadist ['seɪdɪst, 'sæ-] *n* : sádico *m*, -ca *f*

sadistic [sə'dɪstɪk] *adj* : sádico — **sadistically** [-tɪkli] *adv*

sadness ['sædnəs] *n* : tristeza *f*

safari [sə'fari, -'fær-] *n* : safari *m*

safe¹ ['seɪf] *adj* **safer; safest 1** UNHARMED : ileso ⟨safe and sound : sano y salvo⟩ **2** SECURE : seguro **3 to be on the safe side** : para mayor seguridad **4 to play it safe** : ir a la segura

safe² *n* : caja *f* fuerte

safeguard¹ ['seɪf,gard] *vt* : salvaguardar, proteger

safeguard² *n* : salvaguarda *f*, protección *f*

safekeeping ['seɪf'kiːpɪŋ] *n* : custodia *f*, protección *f* ⟨to put into safekeeping : poner en buen recaudo⟩

safely ['seɪfli] *adv* **1** UNHARMED : sin incidentes, sin novedades ⟨they landed safely : aterrizaron sin novedades⟩ **2** SECURELY : con toda seguridad, sin peligro

safety ['seɪfti] *n*, *pl* **-ties** : seguridad *f*

safety belt *n* : cinturón *m* de seguridad

safety pin *n* : alfiler *m* de gancho, alfiler *m* de seguridad, imperdible *m* *Spain*

saffron ['sæfrən] *n* : azafrán *m*

sag¹ ['sæg] *vi* **sagged; sagging 1** DROOP, SINK : combarse, hundirse, inclinarse **2** : colgar, caer ⟨his jowls sagged : le colgaban las mejillas⟩ **3** FLAG : flaquear, decaer ⟨his spirits sagged : se le flaqueó el ánimo⟩

sag² *n* : combadura *f*

saga ['sagə, 'sæ-] *n* : saga *f*

sagacious [sə'geɪʃəs] *adj* : sagaz

sage¹ ['seɪdʒ] *adj* **sager; -est** : sabio — **sagely** *adv*

sage² *n* **1** : sabio *m*, -bia *f* **2** : salvia *f* (planta)

sagebrush ['seɪdʒ,brʌʃ] *n* : artemisa *f*

Sagittarius [,sædʒə'tɛriəs] *n* : Sagitario *mf*

said → **say**

sail¹ ['seɪl] *vi* **1** : navegar (en un barco) **2** : ir fácilmente ⟨we sailed right in : entramos sin ningún problema⟩ — *vt* **1** : gobernar (un barco) **2 to sail the seas** : cruzar los mares

sail² *n* **1** : vela *f* (de un barco) **2** : viaje *m* en velero ⟨to go for a sail : salir a navegar⟩

sailboat ['seɪl,boːt] *n* : velero *m*, barco *m* de vela

sailfish ['seɪl,fɪʃ] *n* : pez *m* vela

sailor ['seɪlər] *n* : marinero *m*

saint ['seɪnt, *before a name* ,seɪnt *or* sənt] *n* : santo *m*, -ta *f* ⟨Saint Francis : San Francisco⟩ ⟨Saint Rose : Santa Rosa⟩

saintliness ['seɪntlinəs] *n* : santidad *f*

saintly ['seɪntli] *adj* **saintlier; -est** : santo

sake ['seɪk] *n* **1** BENEFIT : bien *m* ⟨for the children's sake : por el bien de los niños⟩ **2** (*indicating an end or a purpose*) ⟨art for art's sake : el arte por el arte⟩ ⟨let's say, for argument's sake, that he's wrong : pongamos que está equivocado⟩ **3 for goodness' sake!** : ¡por (el amor de) Dios!

salable *or* **saleable** ['seɪləbəl] *adj* : vendible

salacious [sə'leɪʃəs] *adj* : salaz — **salaciously** *adv*

salad ['sæləd] *n* : ensalada *f*

salamander ['sælə,mændər] *n* : salamandra *f*

salami [sə'lɑmi] *n* : salami *m*

salary ['sæləri] *n, pl* **-ries** : sueldo *m*

sale ['seɪl] *n* **1** SELLING : venta *f* **2** : liquidación *f*, rebajas *fpl* ⟨on sale : de rebaja⟩ **3 sales** *npl* : ventas *fpl* ⟨to work in sales : trabajar en ventas⟩

salesman ['seɪlzmən] *n, pl* **-men** [-mən, -,mɛn] **1** : vendedor *m*, dependiente *m* (en una tienda) **2 traveling salesman** : viajante *m*, representante *m*

salesperson ['seɪlz,pərsən] *n* : vendedor *m*, -dora *f*; dependiente *m*, -ta *f* (en una tienda)

saleswoman ['seɪlz,wʊmən] *n, pl* **-women** [-,wɪmən] **1** : vendedora *f*, dependienta *f* (en una tienda) **2 traveling saleswoman** : viajante *f*, representante *f*

salient ['seɪljənt] *adj* : saliente, sobresaliente

saline ['seɪ,liːn, -,laɪn] *adj* : salino

saliva [sə'laɪvə] *n* : saliva *f*

salivary ['sælə,vɛri] *adj* : salival ⟨salivary gland : glándula salival⟩

salivate ['sælə,veɪt] *vi* **-vated; -vating** : salivar

sallow ['sælo:] *adj* : amarillento, cetrino

sally[1] ['sæli] *vi* **-lied; -lying** SET OUT : salir, hacer una salida

sally[2] *n, pl* **-lies 1** : salida *f* (militar), misión *f* **2** QUIP : salida *f*, ocurrencia *f*

salmon ['sæmən] *ns & pl* **1** : salmón *m* (pez) **2** : color *m* salmón

salon [sə'lɑn, 'sæ,lɑn, sæ'lɔ̃] *n* : salón *m* ⟨beauty salon : salón de belleza⟩

saloon [sə'luːn] *n* **1** HALL : salón *m* (en un barco) **2** BARROOM : bar *m*

salsa ['sɔlsə, 'sɑl-] *n* : salsa *f* mexicana, salsa *f* picante

salt[1] ['sɔlt] *vt* : salar, echarle sal a

salt[2] *adj* : salado

salt[3] *n* : sal *f*

saltwater ['sɔlt,wɔtər, -,wɑ-] *adj* : de agua salada

salty ['sɔlti] *adj* **saltier; -est** : salado

salubrious [sə'luːbriəs] *adj* : salubre

salutary ['sæljə,tɛri] *adj* : saludable, salubre

salutation [,sæljə'teɪʃən] *n* : saludo *m*, salutación *f*

salute[1] [sə'luːt] *v* **-luted; -luting** *vt* **1** : saludar (con gestos o ceremonias) **2** ACCLAIM : reconocer, aclamar — *vi* : hacer un saludo

salute[2] *n* **1** : saludo *m* (gesto), salva *f* (de cañonazos) **2** TRIBUTE : reconocimiento *m*, homenaje *m*

Salvadoran [,sælvə'dorən] → **El Salvadoran**

salvage[1] ['sælvɪʤ] *vt* **-vaged; -vaging** : salvar, rescatar

salvage[2] *n* **1** SALVAGING : salvamento *m*, rescate *m* **2** : objetos *mpl* salvados

salvation [sæl'veɪʃən] *n* : salvación *f*

salve[1] ['sæv, 'sav] *vt* **salved; salving** : calmar, apaciguar ⟨to salve one's conscience : aliviarse la conciencia⟩

salve[2] *n* : ungüento *m*

salvo ['sæl,vo:] *n, pl* **-vos** *or* **-voes** : salva *f*

same[1] ['seɪm] *adj* : mismo, igual ⟨the results are the same : los resultados son iguales⟩ ⟨he said the same thing as you : dijo lo mismo que tú⟩

same[2] *pron* : mismo ⟨it's all the same to me : me da lo mismo⟩ ⟨the same to you! : ¡igualmente!⟩

sameness ['seɪmnəs] *n* **1** SIMILARITY : identidad *f*, semejanza *f* **2** MONOTONY : monotonía *f*

sample[1] ['sæmpəl] *vt* **-pled; -pling** : probar

sample[2] *n* : muestra *f*, prueba *f*

sampler ['sæmplər] *n* **1** : dechado *m* (de bordado) **2** COLLECTION : colección *f* **3** ASSORTMENT : surtido *m*

sanatorium [,sænə'toriəm] *n, pl* **-riums** *or* **-ria** [-iə] : sanatorio *m*

sanctify ['sæŋktə,faɪ] *vt* **-fied; -fying** : santificar

sanctimonious [,sæŋktə'mo:niəs] *adj* : beato, santurrón

sanction[1] ['sæŋkʃən] *vt* : sancionar, aprobar

sanction[2] *n* **1** AUTHORIZATION : sanción *f*, autorización *f* **2 sanctions** *npl* : sanciones *fpl* ⟨to impose sanctions on : imponer sanciones a⟩

sanctity ['sæŋktəṭi] *n, pl* **-ties** : santidad *f*

sanctuary ['sæŋktʃu,ɛri] *n, pl* **-aries 1** : presbiterio *m* (en una iglesia) **2** REFUGE : refugio *m*, asilo *m*

sand[1] ['sænd] *vt* : lijar (madera)

sand[2] *n* : arena *f*

sandal ['sændəl] *n* : sandalia *f*

sandbank ['sænd,bæŋk] *n* : banco *m* de arena

sandpaper *n* : papel *m* de lija

sandpiper ['sænd,paɪpər] *n* : andarríos *m*

sandstone ['sænd,sto:n] *n* : arenisca *f*

sandstorm ['sænd,stɔrm] *n* : tormenta *f* de arena

sandwich[1] ['sænd,wɪtʃ] *vt* : intercalar, encajonar, meter (entre dos cosas)

sandwich[2] *n* : sandwich *m*, emparedado *m*, bocadillo *m* Spain

sandy ['sændi] *adj* **sandier; -est** : arenoso

sane ['seɪn] *adj* **saner; sanest 1** : cuerdo **2** SENSIBLE : sensato, razonable

sang → **sing**
sanguine ['sæŋgwən] *adj* **1** RUDDY : sanguíneo, rubicundo **2** HOPEFUL : optimista
sanitarium [,sænə'tɛriəm] *n, pl* **-iums** *or* **-ia** [-iə] → **sanatorium**
sanitary ['sænəteri] *adj* **1** : sanitario ⟨sanitary measures : medidas sanitarias⟩ **2** HYGIENIC : higiénico **3** **sanitary napkin** : compresa *f*, paño *m* higiénico
sanitation [,sænə'teiʃən] *n* : sanidad *f*
sanitize ['sænə,taiz] *vt* **-tized; -tizing 1** : desinfectar **2** EXPURGATE : expurgar
sanity ['sænəti] *n* : cordura *f*, razón *f* ⟨to lose one's sanity : perder el juicio⟩
sank → **sink**
Santa Claus ['sæntə,klɔz] *n* : Papá Noel, San Nicolás
sap[1] ['sæp] *vt* **sapped; sapping 1** UNDERMINE : socavar **2** WEAKEN : minar, debilitar
sap[2] *n* **1** : savia *f* (de una planta) **2** SUCKER : inocentón *m*, -tona *f*
sapling ['sæpliŋ] *n* : árbol *m* joven
sapphire ['sæ,fair] *n* : zafiro *m*
sarcasm ['sɑr,kæzəm] *n* : sarcasmo *m*
sarcastic [sɑr'kæstik] *adj* : sarcástico — **sarcastically** [-tikli] *adv*
sarcophagus [sɑr'kɑfəgəs] *n, pl* **-gi** [-,gai, -,dʒai] : sarcófago *m*
sardine [sɑr'di:n] *n* : sardina *f*
sardonic [sɑr'dɑnik] *adj* : sardónico — **sardonically** [-nikli] *adv*
sarsaparilla [,sæspə'rilə, ,sɑrs-] *n* : zarzaparrilla *f*
sash ['sæʃ] *n* **1** : faja *f* (de un vestido), fajín *m* (de un uniforme) **2** *pl* **sash** : marco *m* (de una ventana)
sassafras ['sæsə,fræs] *n* : sasafrás *m*
sassy ['sæsi] *adj* **sassier; -est** → **saucy**
sat → **sit**
Satan ['seitən] *n* : Satanás *m*, Satán *m*
satanic [sə'tænik, sei-] *adj* : satánico — **satanically** [-nikli] *adv*
satchel ['sætʃəl] *n* : cartera *f*, saco *m*
sate ['seit] *vt* **sated; sating** : saciar
satellite ['sætə,lait] *n* : satélite *m* ⟨spy satellite : satélite espía⟩
satiate ['seiʃi,eit] *vt* **-ated; -ating** : saciar, hartar
satin ['sætən] *n* : raso *m*, satín *m*, satén *m*
satire ['sæ,tair] *n* : sátira *f*
satiric [sə'tirik] *or* **satirical** [-ikəl] *adj* : satírico
satirize ['sætə,raiz] *vt* **-rized; -rizing** : satirizar
satisfaction [,sætəs'fækʃən] *n* : satisfacción *f*
satisfactory [,sætəs'fæktəri] *adj* : satisfactorio, bueno — **satisfactorily** [-rəli] *adv*
satisfy ['sætəs,fai] *v* **-fied; -fying** *vt* **1** PLEASE : satisfacer, contentar **2** CONVINCE : convencer **3** FULFILL : satisfacer, cumplir con, llenar **4** SETTLE : pagar, saldar (una cuenta) — *vi* SUFFICE : bastar

saturate ['sætʃə,reit] *vt* **-rated; -rating 1** SOAK : empapar **2** FILL : saturar
saturation [,sætʃə'reiʃən] *n* : saturación *f*
Saturday ['sætər,dei, -di] *n* : sábado *m*
Saturn ['sætərn] *n* : Saturno *m*
satyr ['seitər, 'sæ-] *n* : sátiro *m*
sauce ['sɔs] *n* : salsa *f*
saucepan ['sɔs,pæn] *n* : cacerola *f*, cazo *m*, cazuela *f*
saucer ['sɔsər] *n* : platillo *m*
sauciness ['sɔsinəs] *n* : descaro *m*, frescura *f*
saucy ['sɔsi] *adj* **saucier; -est** IMPUDENT : descarado, fresco *fam* — **saucily** *adv*
Saudi ['saudi, 'sɔ-] → **Saudi Arabian**
Saudi Arabian *n* : saudita *mf*, saudí *mf* — **Saudi Arabian** *adj*
sauna ['sɔnə, 'saunə] *n* : sauna *mf*
saunter ['sɔntər, 'sɑn-] *vi* : pasear, parsearse
sausage ['sɔsidʒ] *n* : salchicha *f*, embutido *m*
sauté [sɔ'tei, so:-] *vt* **-téed** *or* **-téd; -téing** : saltear, sofreír
savage[1] ['sævidʒ] *adj* : salvaje, feroz — **savagely** *adv*
savage[2] *n* : salvaje *mf*
savagery ['sævidʒri, -dʒəri] *n, pl* **-ries 1** FEROCITY : ferocidad *f* **2** WILDNESS : salvajismo *m*
savanna [sə'vænə] *n* : sabana *f*
save[1] ['seiv] *vt* **saved; saving 1** RESCUE : salvar, rescatar **2** PRESERVE : preservar, conservar **3** KEEP : guardar, ahorrar (dinero), almacenar (alimentos) **4** : guardar (en informática)
save[2] *prep* EXCEPT : salvo, excepto, menos
savior ['seivjər] *n* **1** : salvador *m*, -dora *f* **2 the Savior** : el Salvador *m*
savor[1] ['seivər] *vt* : saborear
savor[2] *n* : sabor *m*
savory ['seivəri] *adj* : sabroso
saw[1] → **see**
saw[2] ['sɔ] *vt* **sawed; sawed** *or* **sawn** ['sɔn]; **sawing** : serrar, cortar (con sierra)
saw[3] *n* : sierra *f*
sawdust ['sɔ,dʌst] *n* : aserrín *m*, serrín *m*
sawhorse ['sɔ,hɔrs] *n* : caballete *m*, burro *m* (en carpintería)
sawmill ['sɔ,mil] *n* : aserradero *m*
saxophone ['sæksə,fo:n] *n* : saxofón *m*
say[1] ['sei] *v* **said** ['sɛd]; **saying; says** ['sɛz] *vt* **1** EXPRESS, UTTER : decir, expresar ⟨to say no : decir que no⟩ ⟨that goes without saying : ni que decir tiene⟩ ⟨no sooner said than done : dicho y hecho⟩ ⟨to say again : repetir⟩ ⟨to say one's prayers : rezar⟩ **2** INDICATE : marcar, poner ⟨my watch says three o'clock : mi reloj marca las tres⟩ ⟨what does the sign say? : ¿qué pone el letrero?⟩ **3** ALLEGE : decir ⟨it's said that she's pretty : se dice que es bonita⟩ — *vi* : decir

say² *n, pl* **says** ['seɪz] : voz *f*, opinión *f* ⟨to have no say : no tener ni voz ni voto⟩ ⟨to have one's say : dar uno su opinión⟩

saying ['seɪɪŋ] *n* : dicho *m*, refrán *m*

scab ['skæb] *n* **1** : costra *f*, postilla *f* (en una herida) **2** STRIKEBREAKER : rompehuelgas *mf*, esquirol *mf*

scabbard ['skæbərd] *n* : vaina *f* (de una espada), funda *f* (de un puñal, etc.)

scabby ['skæbi] *adj* **scabbier; -est** : lleno de costras

scaffold ['skæfəld, -ˌfoːld] *n* **1** *or* **scaffolding** : andamio *m* (para obreros, etc.) **2** : patíbulo *m*, cadalso *m* (para ejecuciones)

scald ['skɔld] *vt* **1** BURN : escaldar **2** HEAT : calentar (hasta el punto de ebullición)

scale¹ ['skeɪl] *v* **scaled; scaling** *vt* **1** : escamar (un pescado) **2** CLIMB : escalar (un muro, etc.) **3 to scale down** : reducir — *vi* WEIGH : pesar ⟨he scaled in at 200 pounds : pesó 200 libras⟩

scale² *n* **1** *or* **scales** : balanza *f*, báscula *f* (para pesar) **2** : escama *f* (de un pez, etc.) **3** EXTENT : escala *f*, proporción *f* ⟨wage scale : escala salarial⟩ **4** : escala *f* (en música, en cartografía, etc.) ⟨to draw to scale : dibujar a escala⟩

scallion ['skæljən] *n* : cebollino *m*, cebolleta *f*

scallop ['skaləp, 'skæ-] *n* **1** : vieira *f* (molusco) **2** : festón *m* (decoración)

scalp¹ ['skælp] *vt* : arrancar la cabellera a

scalp² *n* : cuero *m* cabelludo

scalpel ['skælpəl] *n* : bisturí *m*, escalpelo *m*

scaly ['skeɪli] *adj* **scalier; -est** : escamoso

scam ['skæm] *n* : estafa *f*, timo *m fam*, chanchullo *m fam*

scamp ['skæmp] *n* : bribón *m*, -bona *f*; granuja *mf*; travieso *m*, -sa *f*

scamper ['skæmpər] *vi* : corretear

scan¹ ['skæn] *vt* **scanned; scanning 1** : escandir (versos) **2** SCRUTINIZE : escudriñar, escrutar ⟨to scan the horizon : escudriñar el horizonte⟩ **3** PERUSE : echarle un vistazo a (un periódico, etc.) **4** EXPLORE : explorar (con radar), hacer un escáner de (en ecografía) **5** : escanear (una imagen)

scan² *n* **1** : ecografía *f*, examen *m* ultrasónico (en medicina) **2** : imagen *f* escaneada (en una computadora)

scandal ['skændəl] *n* **1** DISGRACE, OUTRAGE : escándalo *m* **2** GOSSIP : habladurías *fpl*, chismes *mpl*

scandalize ['skændəlˌaɪz] *vt* **-ized; -izing** : escandalizar

scandalous ['skændələs] *adj* : de escándalo

Scandinavian¹ [ˌskændəˈneɪviən] *adj* : escandinavo

Scandinavian² *n* : escandinavo *m*, -va *f*

scanner ['skænər] *n* : escáner *m*, scanner *m*

scant ['skænt] *adj* : escaso

scanty ['skænti] *adj* **scantier; -est** : exiguo, escaso ⟨a scanty meal : una comida insuficiente⟩ — **scantily** [-təli] *adv*

scapegoat ['skeɪpˌgoːt] *n* : chivo *m* expiatorio, cabeza *f* de turco

scapula ['skæpjələ] *n, pl* **-lae** [-ˌliː, -ˌlaɪ] *or* **-las** → **shoulder blade**

scar¹ ['skɑr] *v* **scarred; scarring** *vt* : dejar una cicatriz en — *vi* : cicatrizar

scar² *n* : cicatriz *f*, marca *f*

scarab ['skærəb] *n* : escarabajo *m*

scarce ['skɛrs] *adj* **scarcer; -est** : escaso

scarcely ['skɛrsli] *adv* **1** BARELY : apenas **2** : ni mucho menos, ni nada que se le parezca ⟨he's scarcely an expert : ciertamente no es experto⟩

scarcity ['skɛrsəti] *n, pl* **-ties** : escasez *f*

scare¹ ['skɛr] *vt* **scared; scaring** : asustar, espantar

scare² *n* **1** FRIGHT : susto *m*, sobresalto *m* **2** ALARM : pánico *m*

scarecrow ['skɛrˌkroː] *n* : espantapájaros *m*, espantajo *m*

scarf ['skɑrf] *n, pl* **scarves** ['skɑrvz] *or* **scarfs 1** MUFFLER : bufanda *f* **2** KERCHIEF : pañuelo *m*

scarlet ['skɑrlət] *n* : escarlata *f* — **scarlet** *adj*

scarlet fever *n* : escarlatina *f*

scary ['skɛri] *adj* **scarier; -est** : espantoso, pavoroso

scathing ['skeɪðɪŋ] *adj* : mordaz, cáustico

scatter ['skæt̬ər] *vt* : esparcir, desparramar — *vi* DISPERSE : dispersarse

scavenge ['skævəndʒ] *v* **-venged; -venging** *vt* : rescatar (de la basura), pepenar *CA, Mex* — *vi* : rebuscar, hurgar en la basura ⟨to scavenge for food : andar buscando comida⟩

scavenger ['skævəndʒər] *n* **1** : persona *f* que rebusca en las basuras; pepenador *m*, -dora *f CA, Mex* **2** : carroñero *m*, -ra *f* (animal)

scenario [səˈnæriˌoː, -ˈnɑr-] *n, pl* **-ios 1** PLOT : argumento *m* (en teatro), guión *m* (en cine) **2** SITUATION : situación *f* hipotética ⟨in the worst-case scenario : en el peor de los casos⟩

scene ['siːn] *n* **1** : escena *f* (en una obra de teatro) **2** SCENERY : decorado *m* (en el teatro) **3** VIEW : escena *f* **4** LOCALE : escenario *m* **5** COMMOTION, FUSS : escándalo *m*, escena *f* ⟨to make a scene : armar un escándalo⟩

scenery ['siːnəri] *n, pl* **-eries 1** : decorado *m* (en el teatro) **2** LANDSCAPE : paisaje *m*

scenic ['siːnɪk] *adj* : pintoresco

scent¹ ['sɛnt] *vt* **1** SMELL : oler, olfatear **2** PERFUME : perfumar **3** SENSE : sentir, percibir

scent² *n* **1** ODOR : olor *m*, aroma *m* **2** : olfato *m* ⟨a dog with a keen scent : un perro con un buen olfato〉 **3** PERFUME : perfume *m*

scented ['sɛntəd] *adj* : perfumado

scepter ['sɛptər] *n* : cetro *m*

sceptic ['skɛptɪk] → **skeptic**

schedule[1] ['skɛˌʤuːl, -ʤəl, *esp Brit* 'ʃɛdˌjuːl] *vt* **-uled; -uling** : planear, programar

schedule[2] *n* **1** PLAN : programa *m*, plan *m* 〈on schedule : según lo previsto〉 〈behind schedule : atrasado, con retraso〉 **2** TIMETABLE : horario *m*

scheme[1] ['skiːm] *vi* **schemed; scheming** : intrigar, conspirar

scheme[2] *n* **1** PLAN : plan *m*, proyecto *m* **2** PLOT, TRICK : intriga *f*, ardid *m* **3** FRAMEWORK : esquema *f* 〈a color scheme : una combinación de colores〉

schemer ['skiːmər] *n* : intrigante *mf*

schism ['sɪzəm, 'skɪ-] *n* : cisma *m*

schizophrenia [ˌskɪtsə'friːniə, ˌskɪzə-, -'frɛ-] *n* : esquizofrenia *f*

schizophrenic [ˌskɪtsə'frɛnɪk, ˌskɪzə-] *n* : esquizofrénico *m*, -ca *f* — **schizophrenic** *adj*

scholar ['skɑlər] *n* **1** STUDENT : escolar *mf*; alumno *m*, -na *f* **2** EXPERT : especialista *mf*

scholarly ['skɑlərli] *adj* : erudito

scholarship ['skɑlərˌʃɪp] *n* **1** LEARNING : erudición *f* **2** GRANT : beca *f*

scholastic [skə'læstɪk] *adj* : académico

school[1] ['skuːl] *vt* : instruir, enseñar

school[2] *n* **1** : escuela *f*, colegio *m* (institución) **2** : estudiantes *mfpl* y profesores *mpl* (de una escuela) **3** : escuela *f* (en pintura, etc.) 〈the Flemish school : la escuela flamenca〉 **4 school of fish** : banco *m*, cardumen *m*

schoolboy ['skuːlˌbɔɪ] *n* : escolar *m*, colegial *m*

schoolgirl ['skuːlˌɡərl] *n* : escolar *f*, colegiala *f*

schoolhouse ['skuːlˌhaʊs] *n* : escuela *f*

schoolmate ['skuːlˌmeɪt] *n* : compañero *m*, -ra *f* de escuela

schoolroom ['skuːlˌruːm, -ˌrʊm] → **classroom**

schoolteacher ['skuːlˌtiːtʃər] *n* : maestro *m*, -tra *f*; profesor *m*, -sora *f*

schoolwork ['skuːlˌwərk] *n* : trabajo *m* escolar

schooner ['skuːnər] *n* : goleta *f*

science ['saɪənts] *n* : ciencia *f*

science fiction *n* : ciencia ficción *f*

scientific [ˌsaɪən'tɪfɪk] *adj* : científico — **scientifically** [-fɪkli] *adv*

scientist ['saɪəntɪst] *n* : científico *m*, -ca *f*

scintillating ['sɪntəˌleɪtɪŋ] *adj* : chispeante, brillante

scissors ['sɪzərz] *npl* : tijeras *fpl*

sclerosis [sklə'roːsəs] *n, pl* **-roses** : esclerosis *f*

scoff ['skɑf] *vi* **to scoff at** : burlarse de, mofarse de

scold ['skoːld] *vt* : regañar, reprender, reñir

scoop[1] ['skuːp] *vt* **1** : sacar (con pala o cucharón) **2 to scoop out** HOLLOW : vaciar, ahuecar

scoop[2] *n* : pala *f* (para harina, etc.), cucharón *m* (para helado, etc.)

scoot ['skuːt] *vi* : ir rápidamente 〈she scooted around the corner : volvió la esquina a toda prisa〉

scooter ['skuːtər] *n* : patineta *f*, monopatín *m*, patinete *m*

scope ['skoːp] *n* **1** RANGE : alcance *m*, ámbito *m*, extensión *f* **2** OPPORTUNITY : posibilidades *fpl*, libertad *f*

scorch ['skɔrtʃ] *vt* : chamuscar, quemar

score[1] ['skor] *v* **scored; scoring** *vt* **1** RECORD : anotar **2** MARK, SCRATCH : marcar, rayar **3** : marcar, meter (en deportes) **4** GAIN : ganar, apuntarse **5** GRADE : calificar (exámenes, etc.) **6** : instrumentar, orquestar (música) — *vi* **1** : marcar (en deportes) **2** : obtener una puntuación (en un examen)

score[2] *n, pl* **scores 1** *or pl* **score** TWENTY : veintena *f* **2** LINE, SCRATCH : línea *f*, marca *f* **3** : resultado *m* (en deportes) 〈what's the score? : ¿cómo va el marcador?〉 **4** GRADE, POINTS : calificación *f* (en un examen), puntuación *f* (en un concurso) **5** ACCOUNT : cuenta *f* 〈to settle a score : ajustar una cuenta〉 〈on that score : a ese respecto〉 **6** : partitura *f* (musical)

scorn[1] ['skɔrn] *vt* : despreciar, menospreciar, desdeñar

scorn[2] *n* : desprecio *m*, menosprecio *m*, desdén *m*

scornful ['skɔrnfəl] *adj* : desdeñoso, despreciativo — **scornfully** *adv*

Scorpio ['skɔrpiˌoː] *n* : Escorpio *mf*, Escorpión *mf*

scorpion ['skɔrpiən] *n* : alacrán *m*, escorpión *m*

Scot ['skɑt] *n* : escocés *m*, -cesa *f*

Scotch[1] ['skɑtʃ] *adj* → **Scottish**[1]

Scotch[2] *npl* **the Scotch** : los escoceses

scot–free ['skɑt'friː] *adj* **to get off scot–free** : salir impune, quedar sin castigo

Scots ['skɑts] *n* : escocés *m* (idioma)

Scottish[1] ['skɑtɪʃ] *adj* : escocés

Scottish[2] *n* → **Scots**

scoundrel ['skaʊndrəl] *n* : sinvergüenza *mf*; bellaco *m*, -ca *f*

scour ['skaʊər] *vt* **1** EXAMINE, SEARCH : registrar (un área), revisar (documentos, etc.) **2** SCRUB : fregar, restregar

scourge[1] ['skərʤ] *vt* **scourged; scourging** : azotar

scourge[2] *n* : azote *m*

scout[1] ['skaʊt] *vi* **1** RECONNOITER : reconocer **2 to scout around for** : explorar en busca de

scout[2] *n* **1** : explorador *m*, -dora *f* **2** *or* **talent scout** : cazatalentos *mf*

scow ['skaʊ] *n* : barcaza *f*, gabarra *f*

scowl[1] ['skaʊl] *vi* : fruncir el ceño

scowl[2] *n* : ceño *m* fruncido

scram ['skræm] *vi* **scrammed; scram-ming** : largarse

scramble[1] ['skræmbəl] *v* **-bled; -bling** *vi* **1** : trepar, gatear (con torpeza) ⟨he scrambled over the fence : se trepó a la cerca con dificultad⟩ **2** STRUGGLE : pelearse (por) ⟨they scrambled for seats : se pelearon por los asientos⟩ — *vt* **1** JUMBLE : mezclar **2 to scramble eggs** : hacer huevos revueltos

scramble[2] *n* : rebatiña *f*, pelea *f*

scrap[1] ['skræp] *v* **scrapped; scrapping** *vt* DISCARD : desechar — *vi* FIGHT : pelearse

scrap[2] *n* **1** FRAGMENT : pedazo *m*, trozo *m* **2** FIGHT : pelea *f* **3** *or* **scrap metal** : chatarra *f* **4 scraps** *npl* LEFTOVERS : restos *mpl*, sobras *fpl*

scrapbook ['skræp,bʊk] *n* : álbum *m* de recortes

scrape[1] ['skreɪp] *v* **scraped; scraping** *vt* **1** GRAZE, SCRATCH : rozar, rascar ⟨to scrape one's knee : rasparse la rodilla⟩ **2** CLEAN : raspar ⟨to scrape carrots : raspar zanahorias⟩ **3 to scrape off** : raspar (pintura, etc.) **4 to scrape up** *or* **to scrape together** : juntar, reunir poco a poco — *vi* **1** RUB : rozar **2 to scrape by** : arreglárselas, ir tirando

scrape[2] *n* **1** SCRAPING : raspadura *f* **2** SCRATCH : rasguño *m* **3** PREDICAMENT : apuro *m*, aprieto *m*

scratch[1] ['skrætʃ] *vt* **1** : arañar, rasguñar ⟨to scratch an itch : rascarse⟩ **2** MARK : rayar, marcar **3 to scratch out** : tachar

scratch[2] *n* **1** : rasguño *m*, arañazo *m* (en la piel), rayón *m* (en un mueble, etc.) **2** : sonido *m* rasposo ⟨I heard a scratch at the door : oí como que raspaban a la puerta⟩

scratchy ['skrætʃi] *adj* **scratchier; -est** : áspero, que pica ⟨a scratchy sweater : un suéter que pica⟩

scrawl[1] ['skrɔl] *v* : garabatear

scrawl[2] *n* : garabato *m*

scrawny ['skrɔni] *adj* **scrawnier; -est** : flaco, escuálido

scream[1] ['skri:m] *vi* : chillar, gritar

scream[2] *n* : chillido *m*, grito *m*

screech[1] ['skri:tʃ] *vi* : chillar (dícese de las personas o de los animales), chirriar (dícese de los frenos, etc.)

screech[2] *n* **1** : chillido *m*, grito *m* (de una persona o un animal) **2** : chirrido *m* (de frenos, etc.)

screen[1] ['skri:n] *vt* **1** SHIELD : proteger **2** CONCEAL : tapar, ocultar **3** EXAMINE : someter a una revisión, hacerle un chequeo (a un paciente) **4** SIEVE : cribar

screen[2] *n* **1** PARTITION : biombo *m*, pantalla *f* **2** SIEVE : criba *f* **3** : pantalla *f* (de un televisor, una computadora, etc.) **4** MOVIES : cine *m* **5** *or* **window screen** : ventana *f* de tela metálica

screenplay ['skri:n,pleɪ] *n* SCRIPT : guión *m*

screw[1] ['skru:] *vt* : atornillar — *vi* **1 to screw in** : atornillarse **2 to screw up** *fam* : meter la pata

screw[2] *n* **1** : tornillo *m* (para fijar algo) **2** TWIST : vuelta *f* **3** PROPELLER : hélice *f*

screwdriver ['skru:,draɪvər] *n* : destornillador *m*, desarmador *m* Mex

scribble[1] ['skrɪbəl] *v* **-bled; -bling** : garabatear

scribble[2] *n* : garabato *m*

scribe ['skraɪb] *n* : escriba *m*

scrimmage ['skrɪmɪdʒ] *n* : escaramuza *f*

scrimp ['skrɪmp] *vi* **1 to scrimp on** : escatimar **2 to scrimp and save** : hacer economías

script ['skrɪpt] *n* **1** HANDWRITING : letra *f*, escritura *f* **2** : guión *m* (de una película, etc.)

scriptural ['skrɪptʃərəl] *adj* : bíblico

scripture ['skrɪptʃər] *n* **1** : escritos *mpl* sagrados (de una religión) **2 the Scriptures** *npl* : las Sagradas Escrituras

scriptwriter ['skrɪpt,raɪtər] *n* : guionista *mf*, libretista *mf*

scroll ['skro:l] *n* **1** : rollo *m* (de pergamino, etc.) **2** : voluta *f* (adorno en arquitectura)

scrotum ['skro:təm] *n*, *pl* **scrota** [-tə] *or* **scrotums** : escroto *m*

scrounge ['skraʊndʒ] *v* **scrounged; scrounging** *vt* **1** BUM : gorrear *fam*, sablear *fam* (dinero) **2 to scrounge around for** : buscar, andar a la busca de — *vi* **to scrounge off someone** : vivir a costa de alguien

scrub[1] ['skrʌb] *vt* **scrubbed; scrubbing** : restregar, fregar

scrub[2] *n* **1** THICKET, UNDERBRUSH : maleza *f*, matorral *m*, matorrales *mpl* **2** SCRUBBING : fregado *m*, restregadura *f*

scrubby ['skrʌbi] *adj* **-bier; -est 1** STUNTED : achaparrado **2** : cubierto de maleza

scruff ['skrʌf] *n* **by the scruff of the neck** : por el cogote, por el pescuezo

scrumptious ['skrʌmpʃəs] *adj* : delicioso, muy rico

scruple ['skru:pəl] *n* : escrúpulo *m*

scrupulous ['skru:pjələs] *adj* : escrupuloso — **scrupulously** *adv*

scrutinize ['skru:tən,aɪz] *vt* **-nized; -nizing** : escrutar, escudriñar

scrutiny ['skru:təni] *n*, *pl* **-nies** : escrutinio *m*, inspección *f*

scuba ['sku:bə] *n* **1** *or* **scuba gear** : equipo *m* de submarinismo **2 scuba diver** : submarinista *mf* **3 scuba diving** : submarinismo *m*

scuff ['skʌf] *vt* : rayar, raspar ⟨to scuff one's feet : arrastrar los pies⟩

scuffle[1] ['skʌfəl] *vi* **-fled; -fling 1** TUSSLE : pelearse **2** SHUFFLE : caminar arrastrando los pies

scuffle[2] *n* **1** TUSSLE : refriega *f*, pelea *f* **2** SHUFFLE : arrastre *m* de los pies

scull[1] ['skʌl] *vi* : remar (con espadilla)

scull² *n* OAR : espadilla *f*

sculpt ['skʌlpt] *v* : esculpir

sculptor ['skʌlptər] *n* : escultor *m*, -tora *f*

scuptural ['skʌlptʃərəl] *adj* : escultórico

sculpture¹ ['skʌlptʃər] *vt* **-tured; -turing** : esculpir

sculpture² *n* : escultura *f*

scum ['skʌm] *n* **1** FROTH : espuma *f*, nata *f* **2** : verdín *m* (encima de un líquido)

scurrilous ['skərələs] *adj* : difamatorio, calumnioso, injurioso

scurry ['skəri] *vi* **-ried; -rying** : corretear

scurvy ['skərvi] *n* : escorbuto *m*

scuttle¹ ['skʌtəl] *v* **-tled; -tling** *vt* : hundir (un barco) — *vi* SCAMPER : corretear

scuttle² *n* : cubo *m* (para carbón)

scythe ['saɪð] *n* : guadaña *f*

sea¹ ['si:] *adj* : del mar

sea² *n* **1** : mar *mf* ⟨the Black Sea : el Mar Negro⟩ ⟨on the high seas : en alta mar⟩ ⟨heavy seas : mar gruesa, mar agitada⟩ **2** MASS : mar *m*, multitud *f* ⟨a sea of faces : un mar de rostros⟩

seabird ['si:,bərd] *n* : ave *f* marina

seaboard ['si:,bord] *n* : litoral *m*

seacoast ['si:,ko:st] *n* : costa *f*, litoral *m*

seafarer ['si:,færər] *n* : marinero *m*

seafaring¹ ['si:,færɪŋ] *adj* : marinero

seafaring² *n* : navegación *f*

seafood ['si:,fu:d] *n* : mariscos *mpl*

seagull ['si:,gʌl] *n* : gaviota *f*

sea horse ['si:,hɔrs] *n* : hipocampo *m*, caballito *m* de mar

seal¹ ['si:l] *vt* **1** CLOSE : sellar, cerrar ⟨to seal a letter : cerrar una carta⟩ ⟨to seal an agreement : sellar un acuerdo⟩ **2 to seal up** : tapar, rellenar (una grieta, etc.)

seal² *n* **1** : foca *f* (animal) **2** : sello *m* ⟨seal of approval : sello de aprobación⟩ **3** CLOSURE : cierre *m*, precinto *m*

sea level *n* : nivel *m* del mar

sea lion *n* : león *m* marino

sealskin ['si:l,skɪn] *n* : piel *f* de foca

seam¹ ['si:m] *vt* **1** STITCH : unir con costuras **2** MARK : marcar

seam² *n* **1** STITCHING : costura *f* **2** LODE, VEIN : veta *f*, filón *m*

seaman ['si:mən] *n*, *pl* **-men** [-mən, -,mɛn] **1** SAILOR : marinero *m* **2** : marino *m* (en la armada)

seamless ['si:mləs] *adj* **1** : sin costuras, de una pieza **2** : perfecto ⟨a seamless transition : una transición fluida⟩

seamstress ['si:mpstrəs] *n* : costurera *f*

seamy ['si:mi] *adj* **seamier; -est** : sórdido

séance ['seɪ,ɑn/s] *n* : sesión *f* de espiritismo

seaplane ['si:,pleɪn] *n* : hidroavión *m*

seaport ['si:,port] *n* : puerto *m* marítimo

sear ['sɪr] *vt* **1** PARCH, WITHER : secar, resecar **2** SCORCH : chamuscar, quemar

search¹ ['sərtʃ] *vt* : registrar (un edificio, un área), cachear (a una persona), buscar en — *vi* **to search for** : buscar

search² *n* : búsqueda *f*, registro *m* (de un edificio, etc.), cacheo *m* (de una persona)

searchlight ['sərtʃ,laɪt] *n* : reflector *m*

seashell ['si:,ʃɛl] *n* : concha *f* (marina)

seashore ['si:,ʃor] *n* : orilla *f* del mar

seasick ['si:,sɪk] *adj* : mareado ⟨to get seasick : marearse⟩

seasickness ['si:,sɪknəs] *n* : mareo *m*

seaside → seacoast

season¹ ['si:zən] *vt* **1** FLAVOR, SPICE : sazonar, condimentar **2** CURE : curar, secar ⟨seasoned wood : madera seca⟩ ⟨a seasoned veteran : un veterano avezado⟩

season² *n* **1** : estación *f* (del año) **2** : temporada *f* (en deportes, etc.) ⟨baseball season : temporada de beisbol⟩

seasonable ['si:zənəbəl] *adj* **1** : propio de la estación (dícese del tiempo, de las temperaturas, etc.) **2** TIMELY : oportuno

seasonal ['si:zənəl] *adj* : estacional — **seasonally** *adv*

seasoning ['si:zənɪŋ] *n* : condimento *m*, sazón *f*

seat¹ ['si:t] *vt* **1** SIT : sentar ⟨please be seated : siéntense, por favor⟩ **2** HOLD : tener cabida para ⟨the stadium seats 40,000 : el estadio tiene 40,000 asientos⟩

seat² *n* **1** : asiento *m*, plaza *f* (en un vehículo) ⟨take a seat : tome asiento⟩ **2** BOTTOM : fondillos *mpl* (de la ropa), trasero *m* (del cuerpo) **3** : sede *f* (de un gobierno, etc.)

seat belt *n* : cinturón *m* de seguridad

sea urchin *n* : erizo *m* de mar

seawall ['si:,wɑl] *n* : rompeolas *m*, dique *m* marítimo

seawater ['si:,wɔtər, -,wɑ-] *n* : agua *f* de mar

seaweed ['si:,wi:d] *n* : alga *f* marina

seaworthy ['si:,wərði] *adj* : en condiciones de navegar

secede [sɪ'si:d] *vi* **-ceded; -ceding** : separarse (de una nación, etc.)

seclude [sɪ'klu:d] *vt* **-cluded; -cluding** : aislar

seclusion [sɪ'klu:ʒən] *n* : aislamiento *m*

second¹ ['sɛkənd] *vt* : secundar, apoyar (una moción)

second² *or* **secondly** ['sɛkəndli] *adv* : en segundo lugar

second³ *adj* : segundo

second⁴ *n* **1** : segundo *m*, -da *f* (en una serie) **2** : segundo *m*, ayudante *m* (en deportes) **3** MOMENT : segundo *m*, momento *m*

secondary ['sɛkən,dri] *adj* : secundario

secondhand ['sɛkənd'hænd] *adj* : de segunda mano

second lieutenant *n* : alférez *mf*, subteniente *mf*

second–rate ['sɛkənd'reɪt] *adj* : mediocre, de segunda categoría

secrecy ['si:krəsi] *n, pl* **-cies** : secreto *m*
secret¹ ['si:krət] *adj* : secreto — **secretly** *adv*
secret² *n* : secreto *m*
secretarial [ˌsɛkrə'triəl] *adj* : de secretario, de oficina
secretariat [ˌsɛkrə'triət] *n* : secretaría *f*, secretariado *m*
secretary ['sɛkrəˌtri] *n, pl* **-taries** **1** : secretario *m*, -ria *f* (en una oficina, etc.) **2** : ministro *m*, -tra *f*; secretario *m*, -ria *f* ⟨Secretary of State : Secretario de Estado⟩
secrete [sɪ'kri:t] *vt* **-creted; -creting** **1** : secretar, segregar (en fisiología) **2** HIDE : ocultar
secretion [sɪ'kri:ʃən] *n* : secreción *f*
secretive ['si:krətɪv, sɪ'kri:tɪv] *adj* : reservado, callado, secreto
sect ['sɛkt] *n* : secta *f*
sectarian [sɛk'triən] *adj* : sectario
section ['sɛkʃən] *n* : sección *f*, parte *f* (de un mueble, etc.), sector *m* (de la población), barrio *m* (de una ciudad)
sectional ['sɛkʃənəl] *adj* **1** : en sección, en corte ⟨a sectional diagram : un gráfico en corte⟩ **2** FACTIONAL : de grupo, entre facciones **3** : modular ⟨sectional furniture : muebles modulares⟩
sector ['sɛktər] *n* : sector *m*
secular ['sɛkjələr] *adj* **1** : secular, laico ⟨secular life : la vida secular⟩ **2** : seglar (dícese de los sacerdotes, etc.)
secure¹ [sɪ'kjʊr] *vt* **-cured; -curing** **1** FASTEN : asegurar (una puerta, etc.), sujetar **2** GET : conseguir
secure² *adj* **-curer; -est** : seguro — **securely** *adv*
security [sɪ'kjʊrəti] *n, pl* **-ties** **1** SAFETY : seguridad *f* **2** GUARANTEE : garantía *f* **3** **securities** *npl* : valores *mpl*
sedan [sɪ'dæn] *n* **1** *or* **sedan chair** : silla *f* de manos **2** : sedán *m* (automóvil)
sedate¹ [sɪ'deɪt] *vt* **-dated; -dating** : sedar
sedate² *adj* : sosegado — **sedately** *adv*
sedation [sɪ'deɪʃən] *n* : sedación *f*
sedative¹ ['sɛdətɪv] *adj* : sedante
sedative² *n* : sedante *m*, calmante *m*
sedentary ['sɛdənˌtɛri] *adj* : sedentario
sedge ['sɛdʒ] *n* : juncia *f*
sediment ['sɛdəmənt] *n* : sedimento *m* (geológico), poso *m* (en un líquido)
sedimentary [ˌsɛdə'mɛntəri] *adj* : sedimentario
sedition [sɪ'dɪʃən] *n* : sedición *f*
seditious [sɪ'dɪʃəs] *adj* : sedicioso
seduce [sɪ'du:s, -'dju:s] *vt* **-duced; -ducing** : seducir
seduction [sɪ'dʌkʃən] *n* : seducción *f*
seductive [sɪ'dʌktɪv] *adj* : seductor, seductivo
see¹ ['si:] *v* **saw** ['sɔ]; **seen** ['si:n]; **seeing** *vt* **1** : ver ⟨I saw a dog : vi un perro⟩ ⟨see you later! : ¡hasta luego!⟩ **2** EXPERIENCE : ver, conocer **3** UNDERSTAND : ver, entender **4** ENSURE : asegurarse ⟨see that it's correct : asegúrese

de que sea correcto⟩ **5** ACCOMPANY : acompañar **6 to see off** : despedir, despedirse de — *vi* **1** : ver ⟨seeing is believing : ver para creer⟩ **2** UNDERSTAND : entender, ver ⟨now I see! : ¡ya entiendo!⟩ **3** CONSIDER : ver ⟨let's see : vamos a ver⟩ **4 to see to** : ocuparse de
see² *n* : sede *f* ⟨the Holy See : la Santa Sede⟩
seed¹ ['si:d] *vt* **1** SOW : sembrar **2** : despepitar, quitarle las semillas a
seed² *n, pl* **seed** *or* **seeds** **1** : semilla *f*, pepita *f* (de una fruta) **2** SOURCE : germen *m*, semilla *f*
seedless ['si:dləs] *adj* : sin semillas
seedling ['si:dlɪŋ] *n* : plantón *m*
seedpod ['si:dˌpɑd] → **pod**
seedy ['si:di] *adj* **seedier; -est** **1** : lleno de semillas **2** SHABBY : raído (dícese de la ropa) **3** RUN-DOWN : ruinoso (dícese de los edificios, etc.), sórdido
seek ['si:k] *v* **sought** ['sɔt]; **seeking** *vt* **1** : buscar ⟨to seek an answer : buscar una solución⟩ **2** REQUEST : solicitar, pedir **3 to seek to** : tratar de, intentar de — *vi* SEARCH : buscar
seem ['si:m] *vi* : parecer
seeming ['si:mɪŋ] *adj* : aparente, ostensible
seemingly ['si:mɪŋli] *adv* : aparentemente, según parece
seemly ['si:mli] *adj* **seemlier; -est** : apropiado, decoroso
seep ['si:p] *vi* : filtrarse
seer ['si:ər] *n* : vidente *mf*, clarividente *mf*
seesaw¹ ['si:ˌsɔ] *vi* **1** : jugar en un subibaja **2** VACILLATE : vacilar, oscilar
seesaw² *n* : balancín *m*, subibaja *m*
seethe ['si:ð] *vi* **seethed; seething** **1** : bullir, hervir **2 to seethe with anger** : rabiar, estar furioso
segment ['sɛgmənt] *n* : segmento *m*
segmented ['sɛgˌmɛntəd, sɛg'mɛn-] *adj* : segmentado
segregate ['sɛgrɪˌgeɪt] *vt* **-gated; -gating** : segregar
segregation [ˌsɛgrɪ'geɪʃən] *n* : segregación *f*
seismic ['saɪzmɪk, 'saɪs-] *adj* : sísmico
seize ['si:z] *v* **seized; seizing** *vt* **1** CAPTURE : capturar, tomar, apoderarse de **2** ARREST : detener **3** CLUTCH, GRAB : agarrar, coger, aprovechar (una oportunidad) **4 to be seized with** : estar sobrecogido por — *vi or* **to seize up** : agarrotarse
seizure ['si:ʒər] *n* **1** CAPTURE : toma *f*, captura *f* **2** ARREST : detención *f* **3** : ataque *m* ⟨an epileptic seizure : un ataque epiléptico⟩
seldom ['sɛldəm] *adv* : pocas veces, rara vez, casi nunca
select¹ [sə'lɛkt] *vt* : escoger, elegir, seleccionar (a un candidato, etc.)
select² *adj* : selecto
selection [sə'lɛkʃən] *n* : selección *f*, elección *f*

selective [sə'lɛktɪv] *adj* : selectivo
selenium [sə'li:niəm] *n* : selenio *m*
self ['sɛlf] *n, pl* **selves** ['sɛlvz] **1** : ser *m*, persona *f* ⟨the self : el yo⟩ ⟨with his whole self : con todo su ser⟩ ⟨her own self : su propia persona⟩ **2** SIDE : lado (de la personalidad) ⟨his better self : su lado bueno⟩
self–addressed [ˌsɛlfə'drst] *adj* : con la dirección del remitente ⟨include a self-addressed envelope : incluya un sobre con su nombre y dirección⟩
self–appointed [ˌsɛlfə'pɔɪntəd] *adj* : autoproclamado, autonombrado
self–assurance [ˌsɛlfə'ʃurənts] *n* : seguridad *f* en sí mismo
self–assured [ˌsɛlfə'ʃurd] *adj* : seguro de sí mismo
self–centered [ˌsɛlf'sɛntərd] *adj* : egocéntrico
self–confidence [ˌsɛlf'kɑnfədənts] *n* : confianza *f* en sí mismo
self–confident [ˌsɛlf'kɑnfədənt] *adj* : seguro de sí mismo
self–conscious [ˌsɛlf'kɑntʃəs] *adj* : cohibido, tímido
self–consciously [ˌsɛlf'kɑntʃəsli] *adv* : de manera cohibida
self–consciousness [ˌsɛlf'kɑntʃəsnəs] *n* : vergüenza *f*, timidez *f*
self–contained [ˌsɛlfkən'teɪnd] *adj* **1** INDEPENDENT : independiente **2** RESERVED : reservado
self–control [ˌsɛlfkən'troːl] *n* : autocontrol *m*, control *m* de sí mismo
self–defense [ˌsɛlfdɪ'fɛnts] *n* : defensa *f* propia, defensa *f* personal ⟨to act in self-defense : actuar en defensa propia⟩ ⟨self-defense class : clase de defensa personal⟩
self–denial [ˌsɛlfdɪ'naɪəl] *n* : abnegación *f*
self–destructive [ˌsɛlfdɪ'strʌktɪv] *adj* : autodestructivo
self–determination [ˌsɛlfdɪˌtərmə'neɪʃən] *n* : autodeterminación *f*
self–discipline [ˌsɛlf'dɪsəplən] *n* : autodisciplina *f*
self–employed [ˌsɛlfɪm'plɔɪd] *adj* : que trabaja por cuenta propia, autónomo
self–esteem [ˌsɛlfɪ'stiːm] *n* : autoestima *f*, amor *m* propio
self–evident [ˌsɛlf'ɛvədənt] *adj* : evidente, manifiesto
self–explanatory [ˌsɛlfɪk'splænəˌtori] *adj* : fácil de entender, evidente
self–expression [ˌsɛlfɪk'sprʃən] *n* : expresión *f* personal
self–government [ˌsɛlf'gʌvərmənt, -vərn-] *n* : autogobierno *m*
self–help [ˌsɛlf'hɛlp] *n* : autoayuda *f*
self–important [ˌsɛlfɪm'pɔrtənt] *adj* **1** VAIN : vanidoso, presumido **2** ARROGANT : arrogante
self–indulgent [ˌsɛlfɪn'dʌldʒənt] *adj* : que se permite excesos
self–inflicted [ˌsɛlfɪn'flɪktəd] *adj* : autoinfligido

self–interest [ˌsɛlf'ɪntrəst, -tə,rst] *n* : interés *m* personal
selfish ['sɛlfɪʃ] *adj* : egoísta
selfishly ['sɛlfɪʃli] *adv* : de manera egoísta
selfishness ['sɛlfɪʃnəs] *n* : egoísmo *m*
selfless ['sɛlfləs] *adj* UNSELFISH : desinteresado
self–made [ˌsɛlf'meɪd] *adj* : próspero gracias a sus propios esfuerzos
self–pity [ˌsɛlf'pɪti] *n, pl* **-ties** : autocompasión *f*
self–portrait [ˌsɛlf'portrət] *n* : autorretrato *m*
self–propelled [ˌsɛlfpro'pɛld] *adj* : autopropulsado
self–reliance [ˌsɛlfri'laɪənts] *n* : independencia *f*, autosuficiencia *f*
self–respect [ˌsɛlfri'spɛkt] *n* : autoestima *f*, amor *m* propio
self–restraint [ˌsɛlfri'streɪnt] *n* : autocontrol *m*, moderación *f*
self–righteous [ˌsɛlf'raɪtʃəs] *adj* : santurrón, moralista
self–sacrifice [ˌsɛlf'sækrəˌfaɪs] *n* : abnegación *f*
selfsame ['sɛlfˌseɪm] *adj* : mismo
self–service [ˌsɛlf'sərvɪs] *adj* **1** : de autoservicio **2** **self-service restaurant** : autoservicio *m*
self–sufficiency [ˌsɛlfsə'fɪʃəntsi] *n* : autosuficiencia *f*
self–sufficient [ˌsɛlfsə'fɪʃənt] *adj* : autosuficiente
self–taught [ˌsɛlf'tɔt] *adj* : autodidacta
sell ['sɛl] *v* **sold** ['soːld]; **selling** *vt* : vender — *vi* : venderse
seller ['sɛlər] *n* : vendedor *m*, -dora *f*
selves → **self**
semantic [sɪ'mæntɪk] *adj* : semántico
semantics [sɪ'mæntɪks] *ns & pl* : semántica *f*
semaphore ['sɛməˌfor] *n* : semáforo *m*
semblance ['sɛmblənts] *n* : apariencia *f*
semen ['siːmən] *n* : semen *m*
semester [sə'mɛstər] *n* : semestre *m*
semicolon ['sɛmiˌkoːlən, 'sɛˌmaɪ-] *n* : punto y coma *m*
semiconductor ['sɛmikənˌdʌktər, 'sɛˌmaɪ-] *n* : semiconductor *m*
semifinal ['sɛmiˌfaɪnəl, 'sɛˌmaɪ-] *n* : semifinal *f*
seminar ['sɛməˌnar] *n* : seminario *m*
seminary ['sɛməˌnɛri] *n, pl* **-naries** : seminario *m*
Semitic [sə'mɪtɪk] *adj* : semita
senate ['sɛnət] *n* : senado *m*
senator ['sɛnətər] *n* : senador *m*, -dora *f*
send ['sɛnd] *vt* **sent** ['sɛnt]; **sending** **1** : mandar, enviar ⟨to send a letter : mandar una carta⟩ ⟨to send word : avisar, mandar decir⟩ **2** PROPEL : mandar, lanzar ⟨he sent it into left field : lo mandó al jardín izquierdo⟩ ⟨to send up dust : alzar polvo⟩ **3** **to send into a rage** : poner furioso
sender ['sɛndər] *n* : remitente *mf* (de una carta, etc.)

Senegalese [ˌsɛnəgəˈliːz, -ˈliːs] n : senegalés m, -lesa f — **Senegalese** adj
senile [ˈsiːˌnaɪl] adj : senil
senility [sɪˈnɪləţi] n : senilidad f
senior¹ [ˈsiːnjər] adj **1** ELDER : mayor ⟨John Doe, Senior : John Doe, padre⟩ **2** : superior (en rango), más antiguo (en años de servicio) ⟨a senior official : un alto oficial⟩
senior² n **1** : superior m (en rango) **2 to be someone's senior** : ser mayor que alguien ⟨she's two years my senior : me lleva dos años⟩
senior citizen n : persona f de la tercera edad
seniority [ˌsiːˈnjɔrəţi] n : antigüedad f (en años de servicio)
sensation [sɛnˈseɪʃən] n : sensación f
sensational [sɛnˈseɪʃənəl] adj : que causa sensación ⟨sensational stories : historias sensacionalistas⟩
sense¹ [ˈsɛnts] vt **sensed; sensing** : sentir ⟨he sensed danger : se dio cuenta del peligro⟩
sense² n **1** MEANING : sentido m, significado m **2** : sentido m ⟨the sense of smell : el sentido del olfato⟩ **3 to make sense** : tener sentido
senseless [ˈsɛntsləs] adj **1** MEANINGLESS : sin sentido, sin razón **2** UNCONSCIOUS : inconsciente
senselessly [ˈsɛntsləsli] adv : sin sentido
sensibility [ˌsɛntsəˈbɪləţi] n, pl -**ties** : sensibilidad f
sensible [ˈsɛntsəbəl] adj **1** PERCEPTIBLE : sensible, perceptible **2** AWARE : consciente **3** REASONABLE : sensato ⟨a sensible man : un hombre sensato⟩ ⟨sensible shoes : zapatos prácticos⟩ — **sensibly** [-bli] adv
sensibleness [ˈsɛntsəbəlnəs] n : sensatez f, solidez f
sensitive [ˈsɛntsəţɪv] adj **1** : sensible, delicado ⟨sensitive skin : piel sensible⟩ **2** IMPRESSIONABLE : sensible, impresionable **3** TOUCHY : susceptible
sensitiveness [ˈsɛntsəţɪvnəs] → **sensitivity**
sensitivity [ˌsɛntsəˈtɪvəţi] n, pl -**ties** : sensibilidad f
sensitize [ˈsɛntsəˌtaɪz] vt -**tized; -tizing** : sensibilizar
sensor [ˈsɛnˌsɔr, ˈsɛntsər] n : sensor m
sensory [ˈsɛntsəri] adj : sensorial
sensual [ˈsɛntʃuəl] adj : sensual — **sensually** adv
sensuality [ˌsɛntʃəˈwæləţi] n, pl -**ties** : sensualidad f
sensuous [ˈsɛntʃuəs] adj : sensual
sent → **send**
sentence¹ [ˈsɛntənts, -ˌənz] vt -**tenced; -tencing** : sentenciar
sentence² n **1** JUDGMENT : sentencia f **2** : oración f, frase f (en gramática)
sentiment [ˈsɛntəmənt] n **1** BELIEF : opinión f **2** FEELING : sentimiento m **3** → **sentimentality**

sentimental [ˌsɛntəˈmɛntəl] adj : sentimental
sentimentality [ˌsɛntəˌmɛnˈtæləţi] n, pl -**ties** : sentimentalismo m, sensiblería f
sentinel [ˈsɛntənəl] n : centinela mf, guardia mf
sentry [ˈsɛntri] n, pl -**tries** : centinela mf
sepal [ˈsiːpəl, ˈsɛ-] n : sépalo m
separable [ˈsɛpərəbəl] adj : separable
separate¹ [ˈsɛpəˌreɪt] v -**rated; -rating** vt **1** DETACH, SEVER : separar **2** DISTINGUISH : diferenciar, distinguir — vi PART : separarse
separate² [ˈsɛprət, ˈsɛpə-] adj **1** INDIVIDUAL : separado, aparte ⟨a separate state : un estado separado⟩ ⟨in a separate envelope : en un sobre aparte⟩ **2** DISTINCT : distinto
separately [ˈsɛprətli, ˈsɛpə-] adv : por separado, separadamente, aparte
separation [ˌsɛpəˈreɪʃən] n : separación f
sepia [ˈsiːpiə] n : color m sepia
September [sɛpˈtɛmbər] n : septiembre m, setiembre m
septic [ˈsɛptɪk] adj : séptico ⟨septic tank : fosa séptica⟩
sepulchre [ˈsɛpəlkər] n : sepulcro m
sequel [ˈsiːkwəl] n **1** CONSEQUENCE : secuela f, consecuencia f **2** : continuación f (de una película, etc.)
sequence [ˈsiːkwənts] n **1** SERIES : serie f, sucesión f, secuencia f (matemática o musical) **2** ORDER : orden m
sequester [sɪˈkwɛstər] vt : aislar
sequin [ˈsiːkwən] n : lentejuela f
sequoia [sɪˈkwɔɪə] n : secoya f, secuoya f
sera → **serum**
Serb [ˈsərb] or **Serbian** [ˈsərbiən] n **1** : serbio m, -bia f **2** : serbio m (idioma) — **Serb** or **Serbian** adj
Serbo–Croatian [ˌsərbokroˈeɪʃən] n : serbocroata m (idioma) — **Serbo–Croatian** adj
serenade¹ [ˌsɛrəˈneɪd] vt -**naded; -nading** : darle una serenata (a alguien)
serenade² n : serenata f
serene [səˈriːn] adj : sereno — **serenely** adv
serenity [səˈrɛnəţi] n : serenidad f
serf [ˈsərf] n : siervo m, -va f
serge [ˈsərdʒ] n : sarga f
sergeant [ˈsɑrdʒənt] n : sargento mf
serial¹ [ˈsɪriəl] adj : seriado
serial² n : serie f, serial m (de radio o televisión), publicación f por entregas
serially [ˈsɪriəli] adv : en serie
series [ˈsɪrˌiːz] n, pl **series** : serie f, sucesión f
serious [ˈsɪriəs] adj **1** SOBER : serio **2** DEDICATED, EARNEST : serio, dedicado ⟨to be serious about something : tomar algo en serio⟩ **3** GRAVE : serio, grave ⟨serious problems : problemas graves⟩
seriously [ˈsɪriəsli] adv **1** EARNESTLY : seriamente, con seriedad, en serio **2** SEVERELY : gravemente

seriousness ['sɪriəsnəs] *n* : seriedad *f*, gravedad *f*

sermon ['sərmən] *n* : sermón *m*

serpent ['sərpənt] *n* : serpiente *f*

serrated [sə'reɪt̬əd, 'sɛrˌeɪt̬əd] *adj* : dentado, serrado

serum ['sɪrəm] *n*, *pl* **serums** *or* **sera** ['sɪrə] : suero *m*

servant ['sərvənt] *n* : criado *m*, -da *f*; sirviente *m*, -ta *f*

serve ['sərv] *v* **served; serving** *vi* 1 : servir ⟨to serve in the navy : servir en la armada⟩ ⟨to serve on a jury : ser miembro de un jurado⟩ 2 DO, FUNCTION : servir ⟨to serve as : servir de, servir como⟩ 3 : sacar (en deportes) — *vt* 1 : servir ⟨to serve God : servir a Dios⟩ 2 HELP : servir ⟨it serves no purpose : no sirve para nada⟩ 3 : servir (comida o bebida) ⟨dinner is served : la cena está servida⟩ 4 SUPPLY : abastecer 5 CARRY OUT : cumplir, hacer ⟨to serve time : servir una pena⟩ 6 **to serve a summons** : entregar una citación

server ['sərvər] *n* 1 : camarero *m*, -ra *f*; mesero *m*, -ra *f* (en un restaurante) 2 *or* **serving dish** : fuente *f* (para servir comida) 3 : servidor *m* (en informática)

service¹ ['sərvəs] *vt* **-viced; -vicing** 1 MAINTAIN : darle mantenimiento a (una máquina), revisar 2 REPAIR : arreglar, reparar

service² *n* 1 HELP, USE : servicio *m* ⟨to do someone a service : hacerle un servicio a alguien⟩ ⟨at your service : a sus órdenes⟩ ⟨to be out of service : no funcionar⟩ 2 CEREMONY : oficio *m* (religioso) 3 DEPARTMENT, SYSTEM : servicio *m* ⟨social services : servicios sociales⟩ ⟨train service : servicio de trenes⟩ 4 SET : juego *m*, servicio *m* ⟨tea service : juego de té⟩ 5 MAINTENANCE : mantenimiento *m*, revisión *f*, servicio *m* 6 : saque *m* (en deportes) 7 **armed services** : fuerzas *fpl* armadas

serviceable ['sərvəsəbəl] *adj* 1 USEFUL : útil 2 DURABLE : duradero

serviceman ['sərvəsˌmæn, -mən, -mən] *n*, *pl* **-men** [-mən, -ˌmɛn] : militar *m*

service station → **gas station**

servicewoman ['sərvəsˌwʊmən] *n*, *pl* **-women** [-ˌwɪmən] : militar *f*

servile ['sərvəl, -ˌvaɪl] *adj* : servil

serving ['sərvɪŋ] *n* HELPING : porción *f*, ración *f*

servitude ['sərvəˌtuːd, -ˌtjuːd] *n* : servidumbre *f*

sesame ['sɛsəmi] *n* : ajonjolí *m*, sésamo *m*

session ['sɛʃən] *n* : sesión *f*

set¹ ['sɛt] *v* **set; setting** *vt* 1 SEAT : sentar 2 *or* **set down** PLACE : poner, colocar 3 ARRANGE : fijar, establecer ⟨to set the date : poner la fecha⟩ ⟨he set the agenda : estableció la agenda⟩ 4 ADJUST : poner (un reloj, etc.) 5 (*indicating the causing of a certain condition*) ⟨to set fire to : prenderle fuego a⟩ ⟨she

set it free : lo soltó⟩ 6 MAKE, START : poner, hacer ⟨I set them working : los puse a trabajar⟩ — *vi* 1 SOLIDIFY : fraguar (dícese del cemento, etc.), cuajar (dícese de la gelatina, etc.) 2 : ponerse (dícese del sol o de la luna)

set² *adj* 1 ESTABLISHED, FIXED : fijo, establecido 2 RIGID : inflexible ⟨to be set in one's ways : tener costumbres muy arraigadas⟩ 3 READY : listo, preparado

set³ *n* 1 COLLECTION : juego *m* ⟨a set of dishes : un juego de platos, una vajilla⟩ ⟨a tool set : una caja de herramientas⟩ 2 *or* **stage set** : decorado *m* (en el teatro), plató *m* (en el cine) 3 APPARATUS : aparato *m* ⟨a television set : un televisor⟩ 4 : conjunto *m* (en matemáticas)

setback ['sɛtˌbæk] *n* : revés *m*, contratiempo *m*

set in *vi* BEGIN : comenzar, empezar

set off *vt* 1 PROVOKE : provocar 2 EXPLODE : hacer estallar (una bomba, etc.) — *vi* *or* **to set forth** : salir

set out *vi* : salir (de viaje) — *vt* INTEND : proponerse

settee [sɛ'tiː] *n* : sofá *m*

setter ['sɛt̬ər] *n* : setter *mf* ⟨Irish setter : setter irlandés⟩

setting ['sɛt̬ɪŋ] *n* 1 : posición *f*, ajuste *m* (de un control) 2 : engaste *m*, montura *f* (de una gema) 3 SCENE : escenario *m* (de una novela, etc.) 4 SURROUNDINGS : ambiente *m*, entorno *m*, marco *m*

settle ['sɛt̬əl] *v* **settled; settling** *vi* 1 ALIGHT, LAND : posarse (dícese de las aves), depositarse (dícese del polvo) 2 SINK : asentarse (dícese de los edificios) ⟨he settled into the chair : se arrellanó en la silla⟩ 3 : instalarse (en una casa), establecerse (en una ciudad o región) 4 **to settle down** : calmarse, tranquilizarse ⟨settle down! : ¡tranquilízate!, ¡cálmate!⟩ 5 **to settle down** : sentar cabeza, hacerse sensato ⟨to marry and settle down : casarse y sentar cabeza⟩ — *vt* 1 ARRANGE, DECIDE : fijar, decidir, acordar (planes, etc.) 2 RESOLVE : resolver, solucionar ⟨to settle an argument : resolver una discusión⟩ 3 PAY : pagar ⟨to settle an account : saldar una cuenta⟩ 4 CALM : calmar (los nervios), asentar (el estómago) 5 COLONIZE : colonizar 6 **to settle oneself** : acomodarse, hacerse cómodo

settlement ['sɛt̬əlmənt] *n* 1 PAYMENT : pago *m*, liquidación *f* 2 COLONY : asentamiento *m* 3 RESOLUTION : acuerdo *m*

settler ['sɛt̬ələr] *n* : poblador *m*, -dora *f*; colono *m*, -na *f*

setup ['sɛt̬ˌʌp] *n* 1 ASSEMBLY : montaje *m*, ensamblaje *m* 2 ARRANGEMENT : disposición *f* 3 PREPARATION : preparación *f* 4 TRAP, TRICK : encerrona *f*

set up *vt* **1** ASSEMBLE : montar, armar **2** ERECT : levantar, erigir **3** ESTABLISH : establecer, fundar, montar (un negocio) **4** CAUSE : armar ⟨they set up a clamor : armaron un alboroto⟩

seven[1] ['sɛvən] *adj* : siete

seven[2] *n* : siete *m*

seven hundred[1] *adj* : setecientos

seven hundred[2] *n* : setecientos *m*

seventeen[1] [ˌsɛvən'tiːn] *adj* : diecisiete

seventeen[2] *n* : diecisiete *m*

seventeenth[1] [ˌsɛvən'tiːnθ] *adj* : decimoséptimo

seventeenth[2] *n* **1** : decimoséptimo *m*, -ma *f* (en una serie) **2** : diecisieteavo *m*, diecisieteava parte *f*

seventh[1] ['sɛvənθ] *adj* : séptimo

seventh[2] *n* **1** : séptimo *m*, -ma *f* (en una serie) **2** : séptimo *m*, séptima parte *f*

seventieth[1] ['sɛvəntiəθ] *adj* : septuagésimo

seventieth[2] *n* **1** : septuagésimo *m*, -ma *f* (en una serie) **2** : setentavo *m*, setentava parte *f*, septuagésima parte *f*

seventy[1] ['sɛvənti] *adj* : setenta

seventy[2] *n, pl* **-ties** : setenta *m*

sever ['sɛvər] *vt* **-ered; -ering** : cortar, romper

several[1] ['sɛvrəl, 'sɛvə-] *adj* **1** DISTINCT : distinto **2** SOME : varios ⟨several weeks : varias semanas⟩

several[2] *pron* : varios, varias

severance ['sɛvrənts, sɛvə-] *n* **1** : ruptura *f* (de relaciones, etc.) **2 severance pay** : indemnización *f* (por despido)

severe [sə'vɪr] *adj* **severer; -est 1** STRICT : severo **2** AUSTERE : sobrio, austero **3** SERIOUS : grave ⟨a severe wound : una herida grave⟩ ⟨severe aches : dolores fuertes⟩ **4** DIFFICULT : duro, difícil — **severely** *adv*

severity [sə'vrəti] *n* **1** HARSHNESS : severidad *f* **2** AUSTERITY : sobriedad *f*, austeridad *f* **3** SERIOUSNESS : gravedad *f* (de una herida, etc.)

sew ['soː] *v* **sewed; sewn** ['soːn] *or* **sewed; sewing** : coser

sewage ['suːɪdʒ] *n* : aguas *fpl* negras, aguas *fpl* residuales

sewer[1] ['soːər] *n* : uno que cose

sewer[2] ['suːər] *n* : alcantarilla *f*, cloaca *f*

sewing ['soːɪŋ] *n* : costura *f*

sex ['sɛks] *n* **1** : sexo *m* ⟨the opposite sex : el sexo opuesto⟩ **2** COPULATION : relaciones *fpl* sexuales

sexism ['sɛkˌsɪzəm] *n* : sexismo *m*

sexist[1] ['sɛksɪst] *adj* : sexista

sexist[2] *n* : sexista *mf*

sextant ['sɛkstənt] *n* : sextante *m*

sextet [sɛk'stɛt] *n* : sexteto *m*

sexton ['sɛkstən] *n* : sacristán *m*

sexual ['sɛkʃʊəl] *adj* : sexual — **sexually** *adv*

sexuality [ˌsɛkʃʊ'æləti] *n* : sexualidad *f*

sexy ['sɛksi] *adj* **sexier; -est** : sexy

shabbily ['ʃæbəli] *adv* **1** : pobremente ⟨shabbily dressed : pobremente vestido⟩ **2** UNFAIRLY : mal, injustamente

shabbiness ['ʃæbinəs] *n* **1** : lo gastado (de ropa, etc.) **2** : lo mal vestido (de personas) **3** UNFAIRNESS : injusticia *f*

shabby ['ʃæbi] *adj* **shabbier; -est 1** : gastado (dícese de la ropa, etc.) **2** : mal vestido (dícese de las personas) **3** UNFAIR : malo, injusto ⟨shabby treatment : mal trato⟩

shack ['ʃæk] *n* : choza *f*, rancho *m*

shackle[1] ['ʃækəl] *vt* **-led; -ling** : ponerle grilletes (a alguien)

shackle[2] *n* : grillete *m*

shad ['ʃæd] *n* : sábalo *m*

shade[1] ['ʃeɪd] *v* **shaded; shading** *vt* **1** SHELTER : proteger (del sol o de la luz) **2** *or* **to shade in** : matizar los colores de — *vi* : convertirse gradualmente ⟨his irritation shaded into rage : su irritación iba convirtiéndose en furia⟩

shade[2] *n* **1** : sombra *f* ⟨to give shade : dar sombra⟩ **2** : tono *m* (de un color) **3** NUANCE : matiz *m* **4** : pantalla *f* (de una lámpara), persiana *f* (de una ventana)

shadow[1] ['ʃædoː] *vt* **1** DARKEN : ensombrecer **2** TRAIL : seguir de cerca, seguirle la pista (a alguien)

shadow[2] *n* **1** : sombra *f* **2** DARKNESS : oscuridad *f* **3** TRACE : sombra *f*, atisbo *m*, indicio *m* ⟨without a shadow of a doubt : sin sombra de duda, sin lugar a dudas⟩ **4 to cast a shadow over** : ensombrecer

shadowy ['ʃædowi] *adj* **1** INDISTINCT : vago, indistinto **2** DARK : oscuro

shady ['ʃeɪdi] *adj* **shadier; -est 1** : sombreado (dícese de un lugar), que da sombra (dícese de un árbol) **2** DISREPUTABLE : sospechoso (dícese de una persona), turbio (dícese de un negocio, etc.)

shaft ['ʃæft] *n* **1** : asta *f* (de una lanza), astil *m* (de una flecha), mango *m* (de una herramienta) **2** *or* **mine shaft** : pozo *m*

shaggy ['ʃægi] *adj* **shaggier; -est 1** HAIRY : peludo ⟨a shaggy dog : un perro peludo⟩ **2** UNKEMPT : enmarañado, despeinado (dícese del pelo, de las barbas, etc.)

shake[1] ['ʃeɪk] *v* **shook** ['ʃʊk]; **shaken** ['ʃeɪkən]; **shaking** *vt* **1** : sacudir, agitar, hacer temblar ⟨he shook his head : negó con la cabeza⟩ **2** WEAKEN : debilitar, hacer flaquear ⟨it shook her faith : debilitó su confianza⟩ **3** UPSET : afectar, alterar **4 to shake hands with someone** : darle la mano a alguien, estrecharle la mano a alguien — *vi* : temblar, sacudirse

shake[2] *n* : sacudida *f*, apretón *m* (de manos)

shaker ['ʃeɪkər] *n* **1 salt shaker** : salero *m* **2 pepper shaker** : pimentero *m* **3 cocktail shaker** : coctelera *f*

shake–up ['ʃeɪkˌʌp] *n* : reorganización *f*

shakily ['ʃeɪkəli] *adv* : temblorosamente

shaky [ˈʃeɪki] *adj* **shakier; -est 1** SHAK-
ING : tembloroso **2** UNSTABLE : poco
firme, inestable **3** PRECARIOUS : precario, incierto **4** QUESTIONABLE : dudoso, cuestionable ⟨shaky arguments
: argumentos discutibles⟩

shale [ˈʃeɪl] *n* : esquisto *m*

shall [ˈʃæl] *v aux, past* **should** [ˈʃʊd] *present* s & *pl* **shall 1** (*used to express a
command*) ⟨you shall do as I say : harás
lo que te digo⟩ **2** (*used to express futu-
rity*) ⟨we shall see : ya veremos⟩ ⟨when
shall we expect you? : ¿cuándo te
podemos esperar?⟩ **3** (*used to express
determination*) ⟨you shall have the
money : tendrás el dinero⟩ **4** (*used to
express a condition*) ⟨if he should die
: si muriera⟩ ⟨if they should call, tell
me : si llaman, dímelo⟩ **5** (*used to express obligation*) ⟨he should have said
it : debería haberlo dicho⟩ **6** (*used to
express probability*) ⟨they should arrive
soon : deben (de) llegar pronto⟩ ⟨why
should he lie? : ¿porqué ha de mentir?⟩

shallow [ˈʃælo:] *adj* **1** : poco profundo
(dícese del agua, etc.) **2** SUPERFICIAL
: superficial

shallows [ˈʃælo:z] *npl* : bajío *m*, bajos
mpl

sham¹ [ˈʃæm] *v* **shammed; shamming**
: fingir

sham² *adj* : falso, fingido

sham³ *n* **1** FAKE, PRETENSE : farsa *f*,
simulación *f*, imitación *f* **2** FAKER : impostor *m*, -tora *f*; farsante *mf*

shamble [ˈʃæmbəl] *vi* **-bled; -bling**
: caminar arrastrando los pies

shambles [ˈʃæmbəlz] *ns* & *pl* : caos *m*,
desorden *m*, confusión *f*

shame¹ [ˈʃeɪm] *vt* **shamed; shaming 1**
: avergonzar ⟨he was shamed by their
words : sus palabras le dieron vergüen-
za⟩ **2** DISGRACE : deshonrar

shame² *n* **1** : vergüenza *f* ⟨to have no
shame : no tener vergüenza⟩ **2** DIS-
GRACE : vergüenza *f*, deshonra *f* **3** PITY
: lástima *f*, pena *f* ⟨what a shame! : ¡qué
pena!⟩

shamefaced [ˈʃeɪmˌfeɪst] *adj* : avergonzado

shameful [ˈʃeɪmfəl] *adj* : vergonzoso —
shamefully *adv*

shameless [ˈʃeɪmləs] *adj* : descarado,
desvergonzado — **shamelessly** *adv*

shampoo¹ [ʃæmˈpu:] *vt* : lavar (el pelo)

shampoo² *n, pl* **-poos** : champú *m*

shamrock [ˈʃæmˌrɑk] *n* : trébol *m*

shank [ˈʃæŋk] *n* : parte *f* baja de la pierna

shan't [ˈʃænt] (*contraction of* **shall not**)
→ **shall**

shanty [ˈʃænti] *n, pl* **-ties** : choza *f*, rancho *m*

shape¹ [ˈʃeɪp] *v* **shaped; shaping** *vt* **1**
: dar forma a, modelar (arcilla, etc.),
tallar (madera, piedra), formar (carácter) ⟨to be shaped like : tener forma
de⟩ **2** DETERMINE : decidir, determi-

nar — *vi or* **to shape up** : tomar forma

shape² *n* **1** : forma *f*, figura *f* ⟨in the
shape of a circle : en forma de círcu-
lo⟩ **2** CONDITION : estado *m*, condiciones *fpl*, forma *f* (física) ⟨to get in
shape : ponerse en forma⟩

shapeless [ˈʃeɪpləs] *adj* : informe

shapely [ˈʃeɪpli] *adj* **shapelier; -est**
: curvilíneo, bien proporcionado

shard [ˈʃɑrd] *n* : fragmento *m*, casco *m*
(de cerámica, etc.)

share¹ [ˈʃɛr] *v* **shared; sharing** *vt* **1** AP-
PORTION : dividir, repartir **2** : compartir ⟨they share a room : comparten
una habitación⟩ — *vi* : compartir

share² *n* **1** PORTION : parte *f*, porción *f*
⟨one's fair share : lo que le corresponde
a uno⟩ **2** : acción *f* (en una compañía)
⟨to hold shares : tener acciones⟩

sharecropper [ˈʃɛrˌkrɑpər] *n* : aparcero
m, -ra *f*

shareholder [ˈʃɛrˌhoːldər] *n* : accionista
mf

shark [ˈʃɑrk] *n* : tiburón *m*

sharp¹ [ˈʃɑrp] *adv* : en punto ⟨at two
o'clock sharp : a las dos en punto⟩

sharp² *adj* **1** : afilado, filoso ⟨a sharp
knife : un cuchillo afilado⟩ **2** PENE-
TRATING : cortante, fuerte **3** CLEVER
: agudo, listo, perspicaz **4** ACUTE : agudo ⟨sharp eyesight : vista aguda⟩ **5**
HARSH, SEVERE : duro, severo, agudo
⟨a sharp rebuke : una reprimenda mor-
daz⟩ **6** STRONG : fuerte ⟨sharp cheese
: queso fuerte⟩ **7** ABRUPT : brusco, repentino **8** DISTINCT : nítido, definido
⟨a sharp image : una imagen bien
definida⟩ **9** ANGULAR : anguloso
(dícese de la cara) **10** : sostenido (en
música)

sharp³ *n* : sostenido *m* (en música)

sharpen [ˈʃɑrpən] *vt* : afilar, aguzar ⟨to
sharpen a pencil : sacarle punta a un
lápiz⟩ ⟨to sharpen one's wits : aguzar
el ingenio⟩

sharpener [ˈʃɑrpənər] *n* : afilador *m*
(para cuchillos, etc.), sacapuntas *m*
(para lápices)

sharply [ˈʃɑrpli] *adv* **1** ABRUPTLY : bruscamente **2** DISTINCTLY : claramente,
marcadamente

sharpness [ˈʃɑrpnəs] *n* **1** : lo afilado (de
un cuchillo, etc.) **2** ACUTENESS
: agudeza *f* (de los sentidos o de la
mente) **3** INTENSITY : intensidad *f*,
agudeza *f* (de dolores, etc.) **4** HARSH-
NESS : dureza *f*, severidad *f* **5** ABRUPT-
NESS : brusquedad *f* **6** CLARITY : nitidez *f*

sharpshooter [ˈʃɑrpˌʃuːtər] *n* : tirador
m, -dora *f* de primera

shatter [ˈʃætər] *vt* **1** : hacer añicos ⟨to
shatter the silence : romper el silencio⟩
2 to be shattered by : quedar destrozado por — *vi* : hacerse añicos,
romperse en pedazos

shave[1] ['ʃeɪv] *v* **shaved; shaved** *or* **shaven** ['ʃeɪvən]; **shaving** *vt* **1** : afeitar, rasurar ⟨she shaved her legs : se rasuró las piernas⟩ ⟨they shaved (off) his beard : le afeitaron la barba⟩ **2** SLICE : cortar (en pedazos finos) — *vi* : afeitarse, rasurarse

shave[2] *n* : afeitada *f*, rasurada *f*

shaver ['ʃeɪvər] *n* : afeitadora *f*, máquina *f* de afeitar, rasuradora *f*

shawl ['ʃɔl] *n* : chal *m*, mantón *m*, rebozo *m*

she ['ʃi:] *pron* : ella

sheaf ['ʃi:f] *n*, *pl* **sheaves** ['ʃi:vz] : gavilla *f* (de cereales), haz *m* (de flechas), fajo *m* (de papeles)

shear ['ʃɪr] *vt* **sheared; sheared** *or* **shorn** ['ʃɔrn]; **shearing 1** : esquilar, trasquilar ⟨to shear sheep : trasquilar ovejas⟩ **2** CUT : cortar (el pelo, etc.)

shears ['ʃɪrz] *npl* : tijeras *fpl* (grandes)

sheath ['ʃi:θ] *n*, *pl* **sheaths** ['ʃi:ðz, 'ʃi:θs] : funda *f*, vaina *f*

sheathe ['ʃi:ð] *vt* **sheathed; sheathing** : envainar, enfundar

shed[1] ['ʃɛd] *vt* **shed; shedding 1** : derramar (sangre o lágrimas) **2** EMIT : emitir (luz) ⟨to shed light on : aclarar⟩ **3** DISCARD : mudar (la piel, etc.) ⟨to shed one's clothes : quitarse uno la ropa⟩

shed[2] *n* : cobertizo *m*

she'd ['ʃi:d] (*contraction of* **she had** *or* **she would**) → **have, would**

sheen ['ʃi:n] *n* : brillo *m*, lustre *m*

sheep ['ʃi:p] *ns & pl* : oveja *f*

sheepfold ['ʃi:p,fo:ld] *n* : redil *m*

sheepish ['ʃi:pɪʃ] *adj* : avergonzado

sheepskin ['ʃi:p,skɪn] *n* : piel *f* de oveja, piel *f* de borrego

sheer[1] ['ʃɪr] *adv* **1** COMPLETELY : completamente, totalmente **2** VERTICALLY : verticalmente

sheer[2] *adj* **1** TRANSPARENT : vaporoso, transparente **2** ABSOLUTE, UTTER : puro ⟨by sheer luck : por pura suerte⟩ **3** STEEP : escarpado, vertical

sheet ['ʃi:t] *n* **1** *or* **bedsheet** ['bɛd-,ʃi:t] : sábana *f* **2** : hoja *f* (de papel) **3** : capa *f* (de hielo, etc.) **4** : lámina *f*, placa *f* (de vidrio, metal, etc.), plancha *f* (de metal, madera, etc.) ⟨baking sheet : placa de horno⟩

sheikh *or* **sheik** ['ʃi:k, 'ʃeɪk] *n* : jeque *m*

shelf ['ʃɛlf] *n*, *pl* **shelves** ['ʃɛlvz] **1** : estante *m*, anaquel *m* (en una pared) **2** : banco *m*, arrecife *m* (en geología) ⟨continental shelf : plataforma continental⟩

shell[1] ['ʃɛl] *vt* **1** : desvainar (chícharos), pelar (nueces, etc.) **2** BOMBARD : bombardear

shell[2] *n* **1** SEASHELL : concha *f* **2** : cáscara *f* (de huevos, nueces, etc.), vaina *f* (de chícharos, etc.), caparazón *m* (de crustáceos, tortugas, etc.) **3** : cartucho *m*, casquillo *m* ⟨a .45 caliber shell : un cartucho calibre .45⟩ **4** *or* **racing shell** : bote *m* (para hacer regatas de remos)

she'll ['ʃi:l, 'ʃɪl] (*contraction of* **she shall** *or* **she will**) → **shall, will**

shellac[1] [ʃə'læk] *vt* **-lacked; -lacking 1** : laquear (madera, etc.) **2** DEFEAT : darle una paliza (a alguien), derrotar

shellac[2] *n* : laca *f*

shellfish ['ʃɛl,fɪʃ] *n* : marisco *m*

shelter[1] ['ʃɛltər] *vt* **1** PROTECT : proteger, abrigar **2** HARBOR : dar refugio a, albergar

shelter[2] *n* : refugio *m*, abrigo *m* ⟨to take shelter : refugiarse⟩

shelve ['ʃɛlv] *vt* **shelved; shelving 1** : poner en estantes **2** DEFER : dar carpetazo a

shenanigans [ʃə'nænɪgənz] *npl* **1** TRICKERY : artimañas *fpl* **2** MISCHIEF : travesuras *fpl*

shepherd[1] ['ʃɛpərd] *vt* **1** : cuidar (ovejas, etc.) **2** GUIDE : conducir, guiar

shepherd[2] *n* : pastor *m*

shepherdess ['ʃɛpərdəs] *n* : pastora *f*

sherbet ['ʃərbət] *or* **sherbert** [-bərt] *n* : sorbete *m*, nieve *f* Cuba, Mex, PRi

sheriff ['ʃerɪf] *n* : sheriff *mf*

sherry ['ʃeri] *n*, *pl* **-ries** : jerez *m*

she's ['ʃi:z] (*contraction of* **she is** *or* **she has**) → **be, have**

shield[1] ['ʃi:ld] *vt* **1** PROTECT : proteger **2** CONCEAL : ocultar ⟨to shield one's eyes : taparse los ojos⟩

shield[2] *n* **1** : escudo *m* (armadura) **2** PROTECTION : protección *f*, blindaje *m* (de un cable)

shier, shiest → **shy**

shift[1] ['ʃɪft] *vt* **1** CHANGE : cambiar ⟨to shift gears : cambiar de velocidad⟩ **2** MOVE : mover **3** TRANSFER : transferir ⟨to shift the blame : echarle la culpa (a otro)⟩ — *vi* **1** CHANGE : cambiar **2** MOVE : moverse **3 to shift for oneself** : arreglárselas solo

shift[2] *n* **1** CHANGE, TRANSFER : cambio *m* ⟨a shift in priorities : un cambio de prioridades⟩ **2** : turno *m* ⟨night shift : turno de noche⟩ **3** DRESS : vestido *m* (suelto) **4** → **gearshift**

shiftless ['ʃɪftləs] *adj* : perezoso, vago, holgazán

shifty ['ʃɪfti] *adj* **shiftier; -est** : taimado, artero ⟨a shifty look : una mirada huidiza⟩

shilling ['ʃɪlɪŋ] *n* : chelín *m*

shimmer ['ʃɪmər] *vi* GLIMMER : brillar con luz trémula

shin[1] ['ʃɪn] *vi* **shinned; shinning** : trepar, subir ⟨she shinned up the pole : subió al poste⟩

shin[2] *n* : espinilla *f*, canilla *f*

shine[1] ['ʃaɪn] *v* **shone** ['ʃo:n] *or* **shined; shining** *vi* **1** : brillar, relucir ⟨the stars were shining : las estrellas brillaban⟩ **2** EXCEL : brillar, lucirse — *vt* **1** : alumbrar ⟨he shined the flashlight at it : lo alumbró con la linterna⟩ **2** POLISH : sacarle brillo a, lustrar

shine[2] *n* : brillo *m*, lustre *m*

shingle[1] ['ʃɪŋgəl] *vt* **-gled; -gling** : techar

shingle² *n* : tablilla *f* (para techar)
shingles ['ʃɪŋgəlz] *npl* : herpes *m*
shinny ['ʃɪni] *vi* -**nied**; -**nying** → **shin¹**
shiny ['ʃaɪni] *adj* **shinier**; -**est** : brillante
ship¹ ['ʃɪp] *vt* **shipped**; **shipping 1** LOAD : embarcar (en un barco) **2** SEND : transportar (en barco), enviar ⟨to ship by air : enviar por avión⟩
ship² *n* **1** : barco *m*, buque *m* **2** → **spaceship**
shipboard ['ʃɪp,bord] *n* **on ~** : a bordo
shipbuilder ['ʃɪp,bɪldər] *n* : constructor *m*, -tora *f* naval
shipment ['ʃɪpmənt] *n* **1** SHIPPING : transporte *m*, embarque *m* **2** : envío *m*, remesa *f* ⟨a shipment of medicine : un envío de medicina⟩
shipping ['ʃɪpɪŋ] *n* **1** SHIPS : barcos *mpl*, embarcaciones *fpl* **2** TRANSPORTATION : transporte *m* (de mercancías)
shipshape ['ʃɪp'ʃeɪp] *adj* : ordenado
shipwreck¹ ['ʃɪp,rɛk] *vt* **to be shipwrecked** : naufragar
shipwreck² *n* : naufragio *m*
shipyard ['ʃɪp,jard] *n* : astillero *m*
shirk ['ʃərk] *vt* : eludir, rehuir ⟨to shirk one's responsibilities : esquivar uno sus responsabilidades⟩
shirt ['ʃərt] *n* : camisa *f*
shiver¹ ['ʃɪvər] *vi* **1** : tiritar (de frío) **2** TREMBLE : estremecerse, temblar
shiver² *n* : escalofrío *m*, estremecimiento *m*
shoal ['ʃoːl] *n* : banco *m*, bajío *m*
shock¹ ['ʃɑk] *vt* **1** UPSET : conmover, conmocionar **2** STARTLE : asustar, sobresaltar **3** SCANDALIZE : escandalizar **4** : darle una descarga eléctrica a
shock² *n* **1** COLLISION, JOLT : choque *m*, sacudida *f* **2** UPSET : conmoción *f*, golpe *m* emocional **3** : shock *m* (en medicina) **4** *or* **electric shock** : descarga *f* eléctrica **5** SHEAVES : gavillas *fpl* **6 shock of hair** : mata *f* de pelo
shock absorber *n* : amortiguador *m*
shocking ['ʃɑkɪŋ] *adj* **1** : chocante **2 shocking pink** : rosa *m* estridente
shoddy ['ʃɑdi] *adj* **shoddier**; -**est** : de mala calidad ⟨a shoddy piece of work : un trabajo chapucero⟩
shoe¹ ['ʃuː] *vt* **shod** ['ʃɑd]; **shoeing** : herrar (un caballo)
shoe² *n* **1** : zapato *m* ⟨the shoe industry : la industria del calzado⟩ **2** HORSESHOE : herradura *f* **3 brake shoe** : zapata *f*
shoelace ['ʃuː,leɪs] *n* : cordón *m* (de zapatos)
shoemaker ['ʃuː,meɪkər] *n* : zapatero *m*, -ra *f*
shone → **shine**
shook → **shake**
shoot¹ ['ʃuːt] *v* **shot** ['ʃɑt]; **shooting** *vt* **1** : disparar, tirar ⟨to shoot a bullet : tirar una bala⟩ **2** : pegarle un tiro a, darle un balazo a ⟨he shot her : le pegó un tiro⟩ ⟨they shot and killed him : lo mataron a balazos⟩ **3** THROW : lanzar

(una pelota, etc.), echar (una mirada) **4** PHOTOGRAPH : fotografiar **5** FILM : filmar — *vi* **1** : disparar (con un arma de fuego) **2** DART : ir rápidamente ⟨it shot past : pasó como una bala⟩
shoot² *n* : brote *m*, retoño *m*, vástago *m*
shooting star *n* : estrella *f* fugaz
shop¹ ['ʃɑp] *vi* **shopped**; **shopping** : hacer compras ⟨to go shopping : ir de compras⟩
shop² *n* **1** WORKSHOP : taller *m* **2** STORE : tienda *f*
shopkeeper ['ʃɑp,kiːpər] *n* : tendero *m*, -ra *f*
shoplift ['ʃɑp,lɪft] *vi* : hurtar mercancía (de una tienda) — *vt* : hurtar (de una tienda)
shoplifter ['ʃɑp,lɪftər] *n* : ladrón *m*, -drona *f* (que roba en una tienda)
shopper ['ʃɑpər] *n* : comprador *m*, -dora *f*
shore¹ ['ʃor] *vt* **shored**; **shoring** : apuntalar ⟨they shored up the wall : apuntalaron la pared⟩
shore² *n* **1** : orilla *f* (del mar, etc.) **2** PROP : puntal *m*
shoreline ['ʃor,laɪn] *n* : orilla *f*
shorn → **shear**
short¹ ['ʃort] *adv* **1** ABRUPTLY : repentinamente, súbitamente ⟨the car stopped short : el carro se paró en seco⟩ **2 to fall short** : no alcanzar, quedarse corto
short² *adj* **1** : corto (de medida), bajo (de estatura) **2** BRIEF : corto ⟨short and sweet : corto y bueno⟩ ⟨a short time ago : hace poco⟩ **3** CURT : brusco, cortante, seco **4** : corto (de tiempo, de dinero) ⟨I'm one dollar short : me falta un dólar⟩
short³ *n* **1 shorts** *npl* : shorts *mpl*, pantalones *mpl* cortos **2** → **short circuit**
shortage ['ʃortɪdʒ] *n* : falta *f*, escasez *f*, carencia *f*
shortcake ['ʃort,keɪk] *n* : tarta *f* de fruta
shortchange ['ʃort'tʃeɪndʒ] *vt* -**changed**; -**changing** : darle mal el cambio (a alguien)
short circuit *n* : cortocircuito *m*, corto *m* (eléctrico)
shortcoming ['ʃort,kʌmɪŋ] *n* : defecto *m*
shortcut ['ʃort,kʌt] *n* **1** : atajo *m* ⟨to take a shortcut : cortar camino⟩ **2** : alternativa *f* fácil, método *m* rápido
shorten ['ʃortən] *vt* : acortar — *vi* : acortarse
shorthand ['ʃort,hænd] *n* : taquigrafía *f*
short–lived ['ʃort'lɪvd, -'laɪvd] *adj* : efímero
shortly ['ʃortli] *adv* **1** BRIEFLY : brevemente ⟨to put it shortly : para decirlo en pocas palabras⟩ **2** SOON : dentro de poco
shortness ['ʃortnəs] *n* **1** : lo corto ⟨shortness of stature : estatura baja⟩ **2** BREVITY : brevedad *f* **3** CURTNESS : brusquedad *f* **4** SHORTAGE : falta *f*, escasez *f*, carencia *f*

shortsighted ['ʃɔrtˌsaɪtəd] → **near-sighted**

shot ['ʃɑt] *n* **1** : disparo *m*, tiro *m* ⟨to fire a shot : disparar⟩ **2** PELLETS : perdigones *mpl* **3** : tiro *m* (en deportes) **4** ATTEMPT : intento *m*, tentativa *f* ⟨to have a shot at : hacer un intento por⟩ **5** RANGE : alcance *m* ⟨a long shot : una posibilidad remota⟩ **6** PHOTOGRAPH : foto *f* **7** INJECTION : inyección *f* **8** : trago *m* (de licor)

shotgun ['ʃɑtˌgʌn] *n* : escopeta *f*

should → **shall**

shoulder¹ ['ʃoːldər] *vt* **1** JOSTLE : empujar (con el hombro) **2** : ponerse al hombro (una mochila, etc.) **3** : cargar con (la responsabilidad, etc.)

shoulder² *n* **1** : hombro *m* ⟨to shrug one's shoulders : encogerse los hombros⟩ **2** : arcén *m* (de una carretera)

shoulder blade *n* : omóplato *m*, omoplato *m*, escápula *f*

shouldn't ['ʃʊdənt] (*contraction of* should not) → **shall**

shout¹ ['ʃaʊt] *v* : gritar, vocear

shout² *n* : grito *m*

shove¹ ['ʃʌv] *v* **shoved; shoving** : empujar bruscamente

shove² *n* : empujón *m*, empellón *m*

shovel¹ ['ʃʌvəl] *vt* **-veled** *or* **-velled; -veling** *or* **-velling** **1** : mover con (una) pala ⟨they shoveled the dirt out : sacaron la tierra con palas⟩ **2** DIG : cavar (con una pala)

shovel² *n* : pala *f*

show¹ ['ʃoː] *v* **showed; shown** ['ʃoːn] *or* **showed; showing** *vt* **1** DISPLAY : mostrar, enseñar **2** REVEAL : demostrar, manifestar, revelar ⟨he showed himself to be a coward : se reveló como cobarde⟩ **3** TEACH : enseñar **4** PROVE : demostrar, probar **5** CONDUCT, DIRECT : llevar, acompañar ⟨to show someone the way : indicarle el camino a alguien⟩ **6** : proyectar (una película), dar (un programa de televisión) — *vi* **1** : notarse, verse ⟨the stain doesn't show : la mancha no se ve⟩ **2** APPEAR : aparecer, dejarse ver

show² *n* **1** : demostración *f* ⟨a show of force : una demostración de fuerza⟩ **2** EXHIBITION : exposición *f*, exhibición *f* ⟨flower show : exposición de flores⟩ ⟨to be on show : estar expuesto⟩ **3** : espectáculo *m* (teatral), programa *m* (de televisión, etc.) ⟨to go to a show : ir al teatro⟩

showcase ['ʃoːˌkeɪs] *n* : vitrina *f*

showdown ['ʃoːˌdaʊn] *n* : confrontación *f* (decisiva)

shower¹ ['ʃaʊər] *vt* **1** SPRAY : regar, mojar **2** HEAP : colmar ⟨they showered him with gifts : lo colmaron de regalos, le llovieron los regalos⟩ — *vi* **1** BATHE : ducharse, darse una ducha **2** RAIN : llover

shower² *n* **1** : chaparrón *m*, chubasco *m* ⟨a chance of showers : una posibil-

idad de chaparrones⟩ **2** : ducha *f* ⟨to take a shower : ducharse⟩ **3** PARTY : fiesta *f* ⟨a bridal shower : una despedida de soltera⟩

show off *vt* : hacer alarde de, ostentar — *vi* : lucirse

show up *vi* APPEAR : aparecer — *vt* EXPOSE : revelar

showy ['ʃoːi] *adj* **showier; -est** : llamativo, ostentoso — **showily** *adv*

shrank → **shrink**

shrapnel ['ʃræpnəl] *ns & pl* : metralla *f*

shred¹ ['ʃred] *vt* **shredded; shredding** : hacer trizas, desmenuzar (con las manos), triturar (con una máquina) ⟨to shred vegetables : cortar verduras en tiras⟩

shred² *n* **1** STRIP : tira *f*, jirón *m* (de tela) **2** BIT : pizca *f* ⟨not a shred of evidence : ni la mínima prueba⟩

shrew ['ʃruː] *n* **1** : musaraña *f* (animal) **2** : mujer *f* regañona, arpía *f*

shrewd ['ʃruːd] *adj* : astuto, inteligente, sagaz — **shrewdly** *adv*

shrewdness ['ʃruːdnəs] *n* : astucia *f*

shriek¹ ['ʃriːk] *vi* : chillar, gritar

shriek² *n* : chillido *m*, alarido *m*, grito *m*

shrill ['ʃrɪl] *adj* : agudo, estridente

shrilly ['ʃrɪli] *adv* : agudamente

shrimp ['ʃrɪmp] *n* : camarón *m*, langostino *m*

shrine ['ʃraɪn] *n* **1** TOMB : sepulcro *m* (de un santo) **2** SANCTUARY : lugar *m* sagrado, santuario *m*

shrink ['ʃrɪŋk] *vi* **shrank** ['ʃræŋk] *or* **shrunk** ['ʃrʌŋk]; **shrunk** *or* **shrunken** ['ʃrʌŋkən]; **shrinking** **1** RECOIL : retroceder ⟨he shrank back : se echó para atrás⟩ **2** : encogerse (dícese de la ropa)

shrinkage ['ʃrɪŋkɪdʒ] *n* : encogimiento *m* (de ropa, etc.), contracción *f*, reducción *f*

shrivel ['ʃrɪvəl] *vi* **-veled** *or* **-velled; -veling** *or* **-velling** : arrugarse, marchitarse

shroud¹ ['ʃraʊd] *vt* : envolver

shroud² *n* **1** : sudario *m*, mortaja *f* **2** VEIL : velo *m* ⟨wrapped in a shroud of mystery : envuelto en un aura de misterio⟩

shrub ['ʃrʌb] *n* : arbusto *m*, mata *f*

shrubbery ['ʃrʌbəri] *n*, *pl* **-beries** : arbustos *mpl*, matas *fpl*

shrug ['ʃrʌg] *vi* **shrugged; shrugging** : encogerse de hombros

shrunk → **shrink**

shuck¹ ['ʃʌk] *vt* : pelar (mazorcas, etc.), abrir (almejas, etc.)

shuck² *n* **1** HUSK : cascarilla *f*, cáscara *f* (de una nuez, etc.), hojas *fpl* (de una mazorca) **2** SHELL : concha *f* (de una almeja, etc.)

shudder¹ ['ʃʌdər] *vi* : estremecerse

shudder² *n* : estremecimiento *m*, escalofrío *m*

shuffle¹ ['ʃʌfəl] *v* **-fled; -fling** *vt* MIX : mezclar, revolver, barajar (naipes) — *vi* : caminar arrastrando los pies

shuffle² *n* **1** : acto *m* de revolver ⟨each player gets a shuffle : a cada jugador le toca barajar⟩ **2** JUMBLE : revoltijo *m* **3** : arrastramiento *m* de los pies

shun [' ʃʌn] *vi* shunned; shunning : evitar, esquivar, eludir

shunt [' ʃʌnt] *vt* : desviar, cambiar de vía (un tren)

shut [' ʃʌt] *v* shut; shutting *vt* **1** CLOSE : cerrar ⟨shut the lid : tápalo⟩ **2 to shut out** EXCLUDE : excluir, dejar fuera a (personas), no dejar que entre (luz, ruido, etc.) **3 to shut up** CONFINE : encerrar — *vi* : cerrarse ⟨the factory shut down : la fábrica cerró suspuertas⟩

shut–in [' ʃʌt,ɪn] *n* : inválido *m*, -da *f* (que no puede salir de casa)

shutter [' ʃʌtər] *n* **1** : contraventana *f*, postigo *m* (de una ventana o puerta) **2** : obturador *m* (de una cámara)

shuttle¹ [' ʃʌtəl] *v* -tled; -tling *vt* : transportar ⟨she shuttled him back and forth : lo llevaba de acá para allá⟩ — *vi* : ir y venir

shuttle² *n* **1** : lanzadera *f* (para tejer) **2** : vehículo *m* que hace recorridos cortos **3** → space shuttle

shuttlecock [' ʃʌtəl,kɑk] *n* : volante *m*

shut up *vi* : callarse ⟨shut up! : ¡cállate (la boca)!⟩

shy¹ [' ʃaɪ] *vi* shied; shying : retroceder, asustarse

shy² *adj* shier *or* shyer [' ʃaɪər]; shiest *or* shyest [' ʃaɪəst] **1** TIMID : tímido *m* WARY : cauteloso ⟨he's not shy about asking : no vacila en preguntar⟩ **3** SHORT : corto (de dinero, etc.) ⟨I'm two dollars shy : me faltan dos dólares⟩

shyly [' ʃaɪli] *adv* : tímidamente

shyness [' ʃaɪnəs] *n* : timidez *f*

Siamese¹ [,saɪə'mi:z, -'mi:s-] *adj* : siamés ⟨Siamese twins : hermanos siameses⟩

Siamese² *n* **1** : siamés *m*, -mesa *f* **2** : siamés *m* (idioma) **3** *or* Siamese cat : gato *m* siamés

sibling [' sɪblɪŋ] *n* : hermano *m*, hermana *f*

Sicilian [sə'sɪljən] *n* : siciliano *m*, -na *f* — **Sicilian** *adj*

sick [' sɪk] *adj* **1** : enfermo **2** NAUSEOUS : mareado, con náuseas ⟨to get sick : vomitar⟩ **3** : para uso de enfermos ⟨sick day : día de permiso (por enfermedad)⟩

sickbed [' sɪk,bɛd] *n* : lecho *m* de enfermo

sicken [' sɪkən] *vt* **1** : poner enfermo **2** REVOLT : darle asco (a alguien) — *vi* : enfermar(se), caer enfermo

sickening [' sɪkənɪŋ] *adj* : asqueroso, repugnante, nauseabundo

sickle [' sɪkəl] *n* : hoz *f*

sickly [' sɪkli] *adj* sicklier; -est **1** : enfermizo **2** → sickening

sickness [' sɪknəs] *n* **1** : enfermedad *f* **2** NAUSEA : náuseas *fpl*

side [' saɪd] *n* **1** : lado *m*, costado *m* (de una persona), ijada *f* (de un animal) **2** : lado *m*, cara *f* (de una moneda, etc.) **3** : lado *m*, parte *f* ⟨he's on my side : está de mi parte⟩ ⟨to take sides : tomar partido⟩

sideboard [' saɪd,bord] *n* : aparador *m*

sideburns [' saɪd,bərnz] *npl* : patillas *fpl*

sided [' saɪdəd] *adj* : que tiene lados ⟨one-sided : de un lado⟩

side effect *n* : efecto *m* secundario

sideline [' saɪd,laɪn] *n* **1** : línea *f* de banda (en deportes) **2** : actividad *f* suplementaria (en negocios) **3 to be on the sidelines** : estar al margen

sidelong [' saɪd,lɔŋ] *adj* : de reojo, de soslayo

sideshow [' saɪd,ʃo:] *n* : espectáculo *m* secundario, atracción *f* secundaria

sidestep [' saɪd,stɛp] *v* -stepped; -stepping *vi* : dar un paso hacia un lado — *vt* AVOID : esquivar, eludir

sidetrack [' saɪd,træk] *vt* : desviar (una conversación, etc.), distraer (a una persona)

sidewalk [' saɪd,wɔk] *n* : acera *f*, vereda *f*, andén *m CA, Col*, banqueta *f Mex*

sideways¹ [' saɪd,weɪz] *adv* **1** : hacia un lado ⟨it leaned sideways : se inclinaba hacia un lado⟩ **2** : de lado, de costado ⟨lie sideways : acuéstese de costado⟩

sideways² *adj* : hacia un lado ⟨a sideways glance : una mirada de reojo⟩

siding [' saɪdɪŋ] *n* **1** : apartadero *m* (para trenes) **2** : revestimiento *m* exterior (de un edificio)

sidle [' saɪdəl] *vi* -dled; -dling : moverse furtivamente

siege [' si:dʒ, 'si:ʒ] *n* : sitio *m* ⟨to be under siege : estar sitiado⟩

siesta [si:'ɛstə] *n* : siesta *f*

sieve [' sɪv] *n* : tamiz *m*, cedazo *m*, criba *f* (en mineralogía)

sift [' sɪft] *vt* **1** : tamizar, cerner ⟨sift the flour : tamice la harina⟩ **2** *or* to sift through : examinar cuidadosamente, pasar por el tamiz

sifter [' sɪftər] *n* : tamiz *m*, cedazo *m*

sigh¹ [' saɪ] *vi* : suspirar

sigh² *n* : suspiro *m*

sight¹ [' saɪt] *vt* : ver (a una persona), divisar (la tierra, un barco)

sight² *n* **1** : vista *f* (facultad) ⟨out of sight : fuera de vista⟩ **2** : algo visto ⟨it's a familiar sight : se ve con frecuencia⟩ ⟨she's a sight for sore eyes : da gusto verla⟩ **3** : lugar *m* de interés (para turistas, etc.) **4** : mira *f* (de un rifle, etc.) **5** GLIMPSE : mirada *f* breve ⟨I caught sight of her : la divisé, alcancé a verla⟩

sighting [' saɪtɪŋ] *n* : avistamiento *m*

sightless [' saɪtləs] *adj* : invidente, ciego

sightseer [' saɪt,si:ər] *n* : turista *mf*

sign¹ [' saɪn] *vt* **1** : firmar ⟨to sign a check : firmar un cheque⟩ **2** *or* to sign on HIRE : contratar (a un empleado), fichar (a un jugador) — *vi* **1** : hacer una seña ⟨she signed for him to stop : le hizo una seña para que se parara⟩ **2** : comunicarse por señas

sign² *n* **1** SYMBOL : símbolo *m*, signo *m* ⟨minus sign : signo de menos⟩ **2** GESTURE : seña *f*, señal *f*, gesto *m* **3** : letrero *m*, cartel *m* ⟨neon sign : letrero de neón⟩ **4** TRACE : señal *f*, indicio *m*

signal¹ ['sıgnəl] *vt* **-naled** *or* **-nalled; -naling** *or* **-nalling 1** : hacerle señas (a alguien) ⟨she signaled me to leave : me hizo señas para que saliera⟩ **2** INDICATE : señalar, indicar — *vi* : hacer señas, comunicar por señas

signal² *adj* NOTABLE : señalado, notable

signal³ *n* : señal *f*

signature ['sıgnə,tʃur] *n* : firma *f*

signet ['sıgnət] *n* : sello *m*

significance [sıg'nıfıkənts] *n* **1** MEANING : significado *m* **2** IMPORTANCE : importancia *f*

significant [sıg'nıfıkənt] *adj* **1** IMPORTANT : importante **2** MEANINGFUL : significativo — **significantly** *adv*

signify ['sıgnə,faı] *vt* **-fied; -fying 1** : indicar ⟨he signified his desire for more : haciendo señas indicó que quería más⟩ **2** MEAN : significar

sign language *n* : lenguaje *m* por señas

signpost ['saın,po:st] *n* : poste *m* indicador

silence¹ ['saılənts] *vt* **-lenced; -lencing** : silenciar, acallar

silence² *n* : silencio *m*

silent ['saılənt] *adj* **1** : callado ⟨to remain silent : quedarse callado, guardar silencio⟩ **2** QUIET, STILL : silencioso **3** MUTE : mudo ⟨a silent letter : una letra muda⟩

silently ['saıləntli] *adv* : silenciosamente, calladamente

silhouette¹ [,sılə'wɛt] *vt* **-etted; -etting** : destacar la silueta de ⟨it was silhouetted against the sky : se perfilaba contra el cielo⟩

silhouette² *n* : silueta *f*

silica ['sılıkə] *n* : sílice *f*

silicon ['sılıkən, -,kɑn] *n* : silicio *m*

silk ['sılk] *n* : seda *f*

silken ['sılkən] *adj* **1** : de seda ⟨a silken veil : un velo de seda⟩ **2** SILKY : sedoso ⟨silken hair : cabellos sedosos⟩

silkworm ['sılk,wərm] *n* : gusano *m* de seda

silky ['sılki] *adj* **silkier; -est** : sedoso

sill ['sıl] *n* : alféizar *m* (de una ventana), umbral *m* (de una puerta)

silliness ['sılınəs] *n* : tontería *f*, estupidez *f*

silly ['sıli] *adj* **sillier; -est** : tonto, estúpido, ridículo

silo ['saı,lo:] *n, pl* **silos** : silo *m*

silt ['sılt] *n* : cieno *m*

silver¹ ['sılvər] *adj* **1** : de plata ⟨a silver spoon : una cuchara de plata⟩ **2** → silvery

silver² *n* **1** : plata *f* **2** COINS : monedas *fpl* **3** → silverware **4** : color *m* plata

silverware ['sılvər,wær] *n* **1** : artículos *mpl* de plata, platería *f* **2** FLATWARE : cubertería *f*

silvery ['sılvəri] *adj* : plateado

similar ['sımələr] *adj* : similar, parecido, semejante

similarity [,sımə'lærəti] *n, pl* **-ties** : semejanza *f*, parecido *m*

similarly ['sımələrli] *adv* : de manera similar

simile ['sımə,li:] *n* : símil *m*

simmer ['sımər] *v* : hervir a fuego lento

simper¹ ['sımpər] *vi* : sonreír como un tonto

simper² *n* : sonrisa *f* tonta

simple ['sımpəl] *adj* **simpler; -plest 1** INNOCENT : inocente **2** PLAIN : sencillo, simple **3** EASY : simple, sencillo, fácil **4** STRAIGHTFORWARD : puro, simple ⟨the simple truth : la pura verdad⟩ **5** NAIVE : ingenuo, simple

simpleton ['sımpəltən] *n* : bobo *m*, -ba *f*; tonto *m*, -ta *f*

simplicity [sım'plısəti] *n* : simplicidad *f*, sencillez *f*

simplification [,sımpləfə'keıʃən] *n* : simplificación *f*

simplify ['sımplə,faı] *vt* **-fied; -fying** : simplificar

simply ['sımpli] *adv* **1** PLAINLY : sencillamente **2** SOLELY : simplemente, sólo **3** REALLY : absolutamente

simulate ['sımjə,leıt] *vt* **-lated; -lating** : simular

simulation [,sımjə'leıʃən] *n* : simulación *f*

simultaneous [,saıməl'teınıəs] *adj* : simultáneo — **simultaneously** *adv*

sin¹ ['sın] *vi* **sinned; sinning** : pecar

sin² *n* : pecado *m*

since¹ ['sınts] *adv* **1** : desde entonces ⟨they've been friends ever since : desde entonces han sido amigos⟩ ⟨she's since become mayor : más tarde se hizo alcalde⟩ **2** AGO : hace ⟨he's long since dead : murió hace mucho⟩

since² *conj* **1** : desde que ⟨since he was born : desde que nació⟩ **2** INASMUCH AS : ya que, puesto que, dado que

since³ *prep* : desde

sincere [sın'sır] *adj* **-cerer; -est** : sincero — **sincerely** *adv*

sincerity [sın'serəti] *n* : sinceridad *f*

sinew ['sın,ju:, 'sı,nu:] *n* **1** TENDON : tendón *m*, nervio *m* (en la carne) **2** POWER : fuerza *f*

sinewy ['sınjui, 'sınui] *adj* **1** STRINGY : fibroso **2** STRONG, WIRY : fuerte, nervudo

sinful ['sınfəl] *adj* : pecador (dícese de las personas), pecaminoso

sing ['sıŋ] *v* **sang** ['sæŋ] *or* **sung** ['sʌŋ]; **sung; singing** : cantar

singe ['sındʒ] *vt* **singed; singeing** : chamuscar, quemar

singer ['sıŋər] *n* : cantante *mf*

single¹ ['sıŋgəl] *vt* **-gled; -gling** *or* **to single out 1** SELECT : escoger **2** DISTINGUISH : señalar

single² *adj* **1** UNMARRIED : soltero **2** SOLE : solo ⟨a single survivor : un solo sobreviviente⟩ ⟨every single one : cada uno, todos⟩

single³ *n* **1** : soltero *m*, -ra *f* ⟨for married couples and singles : para los matrimonios y los solteros⟩ **2** *or* **single room** : habitación *f* individual **3** DOLLAR : billete *m* de un dólar

single–handed [ˈsɪŋɡəlˈhændəd] *adj* : sin ayuda, solo

singly [ˈsɪŋɡli] *adv* : individualmente, uno por uno

singular¹ [ˈsɪŋɡjələr] *adj* **1** : singular (en gramática) **2** OUTSTANDING : singular, sobresaliente **3** STRANGE : singular, extraño

singular² *n* : singular *m*

singularity [ˌsɪŋɡjəˈlærəti] *n, pl* **-ties** : singularidad *f*

singularly [ˈsɪŋɡjələrli] *adv* : singularmente

sinister [ˈsɪnəstər] *adj* : siniestro

sink¹ [ˈsɪŋk] *v* **sank** [ˈsæŋk] *or* **sunk** [ˈsʌŋk]; **sunk; sinking** *vi* **1** : hundirse (dícese de un barco) **2** DROP, FALL : descender, caer ⟨to sink into a chair : dejarse caer en una silla⟩ ⟨her heart sank : se le cayó el alma a los pies⟩ **3** DECREASE : bajar — *vt* **1** : hundir (un barco, etc.) **2** EXCAVATE : excavar (un pozo para minar), perforar (un pozo de agua) **3** PLUNGE, STICK : clavar, hincar **4** INVEST : invertir (fondos)

sink² *n* **1** kitchen sink : fregadero *m*, lavaplatos *m* Chile, Col, Mex **2** bathroom sink : lavabo *m*, lavamanos *m*

sinner [ˈsɪnər] *n* : pecador *m*, -dora *f*

sinuous [ˈsɪnjuəs] *adj* : sinuoso — **sinuously** *adv*

sinus [ˈsaɪnəs] *n* : seno *m*

sip¹ [ˈsɪp] *v* **sipped; sipping** *vt* : sorber — *vi* : beber a sorbos

sip² *n* : sorbo *m*

siphon¹ [ˈsaɪfən] *vt* : sacar con sifón

siphon² *n* : sifón *m*

sir [ˈsər] *n* **1** (*in titles*) : sir *m* **2** (*as a form of address*) : señor *m* ⟨Dear Sir : Muy señor mío⟩ ⟨yes sir! : ¡sí, señor!⟩

sire¹ [ˈsaɪr] *vt* **sired; siring** : engendrar, ser el padre de

sire² *n* : padre *m*

siren [ˈsaɪrən] *n* : sirena *f*

sirloin [ˈsərˌlɔɪn] *n* : solomillo *m*

sirup → syrup

sisal [ˈsaɪsəl, -zəl] *n* : sisal *m*

sissy [ˈsɪsi] *n, pl* **-sies** : mariquita *f fam*

sister [ˈsɪstər] *n* **1** : hermana *f* **2** Sister : hermana *f*, Sor *f* ⟨Sister Mary : Sor María⟩

sisterhood [ˈsɪstərˌhʊd] *n* **1** : condición *f* de ser hermana **2** : sociedad *f* de mujeres

sister–in–law [ˈsɪstərɪnˌlɔ] *n, pl* **sisters–in–law** : cuñada *f*

sisterly [ˈsɪstərli] *adj* : de hermana

sit [ˈsɪt] *v* **sat** [ˈsæt]; **sitting** *vi* **1** : sentarse, estar sentado ⟨he sat down : se sentó⟩ **2** ROOST : posarse **3** : sesionar ⟨the legislature is sitting : la legislatu-

ra está en sesión⟩ **4** POSE : posar (para un retrato) **5** LIE, REST : estar (ubicado) ⟨the house sits on a hill : la casa está en una colina⟩ — *vt* SEAT : sentar, colocar ⟨I sat him on the sofa : lo senté en el sofá⟩

sitcom [ˈsɪtˌkʌm] → **situation comedy**

site [ˈsaɪt] *n* **1** PLACE : sitio *m*, lugar *m* **2** LOCATION : emplazamiento *m*, ubicación *f*

sitter [ˈsɪtər] → **baby–sitter**

sitting room → living room

situated [ˈsɪtʃuˌeɪtəd] *adj* LOCATED : ubicado, situado

situation [ˌsɪtʃuˈeɪʃən] *n* **1** LOCATION : situación *f*, ubicación *f*, emplazamiento *m* **2** CIRCUMSTANCES : situación *f* **3** JOB : empleo *m*

situation comedy *n* : comedia *f* de situación

six¹ [ˈsɪks] *adj* : seis

six² *n* : seis *m*

six–gun [ˈsɪksˌɡʌn] *n* : revólver *m* (con seis cámaras)

six hundred¹ *adj* : seiscientos

six hundred² *n* : seiscientos *m*

six–shooter [ˈsɪksˌʃuːtər] → **six–gun**

sixteen¹ [sɪksˈtiːn] *adj* : dieciséis

sixteen² *n* : dieciséis *m*

sixteenth¹ [sɪksˈtiːnθ] *adj* : decimosexto

sixteenth² *n* **1** : decimosexto *m*, -ta *f* (en una serie) **2** : dieciseisavo *m*, dieciseisava parte *f*

sixth¹ [ˈsɪksθ, ˈsɪkst] *adj* : sexto

sixth² *n* **1** : sexto *m*, -ta *f* (en una serie) **2** : sexto *m*, sexta parte *f*

sixtieth¹ [ˈsɪkstiəθ] *adj* : sexagésimo

sixtieth² *n* **1** : sexagésimo *m*, -ma *f* (en una serie) **2** : sesentavo *m*, sesentava parte *f*

sixty¹ [ˈsɪksti] *adj* : sesenta

sixty² *n, pl* **-ties** : sesenta *m*

sizable *or* **sizeable** [ˈsaɪzəbəl] *adj* : considerable

size¹ [ˈsaɪz] *vt* **sized; sizing 1** : clasificar según el tamaño **2 to size up** : evaluar, apreciar

size² *n* **1** DIMENSIONS : tamaño *m*, talla *f* (de ropa), número *m* (de zapatos) **2** MAGNITUDE : magnitud *f*

sizzle [ˈsɪzəl] *vi* **-zled; -zling** : chisporrotear

skate¹ [ˈskeɪt] *vi* **skated; skating** : patinar

skate² *n* **1** : patín *m* ⟨roller skate : patín de ruedas⟩ **2** : raya *f* (pez)

skateboard [ˈskeɪtˌbord] *n* : monopatín *m*

skater [ˈskeɪtər] *n* : patinador *m*, -dora *f*

skein [ˈskeɪn] *n* : madeja *f*

skeletal [ˈskɛlətəl] *adj* **1** : óseo (en anatomía) **2** EMACIATED : esquelético

skeleton [ˈskɛlətən] *n* **1** : esqueleto *m* (anatómico) **2** FRAMEWORK : armazón *mf*

skeptic [ˈskɛptɪk] *n* : escéptico *m*, -ca *f*

skeptical [ˈskɛptɪkəl] *adj* : escéptico

skepticism [ˈskɛptəˌsɪzəm] *n* : escepticismo *m*

sketch¹ ['skɛtʃ] *vt* : bosquejar — *vi* : hacer bosquejos

sketch² *n* **1** DRAWING, OUTLINE : esbozo *m*, bosquejo *m* **2** ESSAY : ensayo *m*

sketchy ['skɛtʃi] *adj*; **-est** : incompleto, poco detallado

skewer¹ ['skju:ər] *vt* : ensartar (carne, etc.)

skewer² *n* : brocheta *f*, broqueta *f*

ski¹ ['ski:] *vi* **skied; skiing** : esquiar

ski² *n, pl* **skis** : esquí *m*

skid¹ ['skɪd] *vi* **skidded; skidding** : derrapar, patinar

skid² *n* : derrape *m*, patinazo *m*

skier ['ski:ər] *n* : esquiador *m*, -dora *f*

skiff ['skɪf] *n* : esquife *m*

skill ['skɪl] *n* **1** DEXTERITY : habilidad *f*, destreza *f* **2** CAPABILITY : capacidad *f*, arte *m*, técnica *f* ⟨organizational skills : la capacidad para organizar⟩

skilled ['skɪld] *adj* : hábil, experto

skillet ['skɪlət] *n* : sartén *mf*

skillful ['skɪlfəl] *adj* : hábil, diestro

skillfully ['skɪlfəli] *adv* : con habilidad, con destreza

skim¹ ['skɪm] *vt* **skimmed; skimming 1** *or* **to skim off** : espumar, descremar (leche) **2** : echarle un vistazo a (un libro, etc.), pasar rozando (una superficie)

skim² *adj* : descremado ⟨skim milk : leche descremada⟩

skimp ['skɪmp] *vi* **to skimp on** : escatimar

skimpy ['skɪmpi] *adj* **skimpier; -est** : exiguo, escaso, raquítico

skin¹ ['skɪn] *vt* **skinned; skinning** : despellejar, desollar

skin² *n* **1** : piel *f*, cutis *m* (de la cara) ⟨dark skin : piel morena⟩ **2** RIND : piel *f*

skin diving *n* : buceo *m*, submarinismo *m*

skinflint ['skɪn,flɪnt] *n* : tacaño *m*, -ña *f*

skinned ['skɪnd] *adj* : de piel ⟨tough-skinned : de piel dura⟩

skinny ['skɪni] *adj* **skinnier; -est** : flaco

skip¹ ['skɪp] *v* **skipped; skipping** *vi* : ir dando brincos — *vt* : saltarse

skip² *n* : brinco *m*, salto *m*

skipper ['skɪpər] *n* : capitán *m*, -tana *f*

skirmish¹ ['skərmɪʃ] *vi* : escaramuzar

skirmish² *n* : escaramuza *f*, refriega *f*

skirt¹ ['skərt] *vt* **1** BORDER : bordear **2** EVADE : evadir, esquivar

skirt² *n* : falda *f*, pollera *f*

skit ['skɪt] *n* : sketch *m* (teatral)

skittish ['skɪtɪʃ] *adj* : asustadizo, nervioso

skulk ['skʌlk] *vi* : merodear

skull ['skʌl] *n* **1** : cráneo *m*, calavera *f* **2 skull and crossbones** : calavera *f* (bandera pirata)

skunk ['skʌŋk] *n* : zorrillo *m*, mofeta *f*

sky ['skaɪ] *n, pl* **skies** : cielo *m*

skylark ['skaɪ,lɑrk] *n* : alondra *f*

skylight ['skaɪ,laɪt] *n* : claraboya *f*, tragaluz *m*

skyline ['skaɪ,laɪn] *n* : horizonte *m*

skyrocket ['skaɪ,rɑkət] *vi* : dispararse

skyscraper ['skaɪ,skreɪpər] *n* : rascacielos *m*

slab ['slæb] *n* : losa *f* (de piedra), tabla *f* (de madera), pedazo *m* grueso (de pan, etc.)

slack¹ ['slæk] *adj* **1** CARELESS : descuidado, negligente **2** LOOSE : flojo **3** SLOW : de poco movimiento

slack² *n* **1** : parte *f* floja ⟨to take up the slack : tensar (una cuerda, etc.)⟩ **2 slacks** *npl* : pantalones *mpl*

slacken ['slækən] *vt* : aflojar — *vi* : aflojarse

slacker ['slækər] *n* : vago *m*, -ga *f*; holgazán *m*, -zana *f*

slag ['slæg] *n* : escoria *f*

slain → **slay**

slake ['sleɪk] *vt* **slaked; slaking** : saciar (la sed), satisfacer (la curiosidad)

slam¹ ['slæm] *v* **slammed; slamming** *vt* **1** : cerrar de golpe ⟨he slammed the door : dio un portazo⟩ **2** : tirar o dejar caer de golpe ⟨he slammed down the book : dejó caer el libro de un golpe⟩ — *vi* : cerrarse de golpe **2 to slam into** : chocar contra

slam² *n* : golpe *m*, portazo *m* (de una puerta)

slander¹ ['slændər] *vt* : calumniar, difamar

slander² *n* : calumnia *f*, difamación *f*

slanderous ['slændərəs] *adj* : difamatorio, calumnioso

slang ['slæŋ] *n* : argot *m*, jerga *f*

slant¹ ['slænt] *vi* : inclinarse, ladearse — *vt* **1** SLOPE : inclinar **2** ANGLE : sesgar, orientar, dirigir ⟨a story slanted towards youth : un artículo dirigido a los jóvenes⟩

slant² *n* **1** INCLINE : inclinación *f* **2** PERSPECTIVE : perspectiva *f*, enfoque *m*

slap¹ ['slæp] *vt* **slapped; slapping** : bofetear, cachetear, dar una palmada (en la espalda, etc.)

slap² *n* : bofetada *f*, cachetada *f*, palmada *f*

slash¹ ['slæʃ] *vt* **1** GASH : cortar, hacer un tajo en **2** REDUCE : reducir, rebajar (precios)

slash² *n* : tajo *m*, corte *m*

slat ['slæt] *n* : tablilla *f*, listón *m*

slate ['sleɪt] *n* **1** : pizarra *f* ⟨a slate roof : un techo de pizarra⟩ **2** : lista *f* de candidatos (políticos)

slaughter¹ ['slɔtər] *vt* **1** BUTCHER : matar (animales) **2** MASSACRE : masacrar (personas)

slaughter² *n* **1** : matanza *f* (de animales) **2** MASSACRE : masacre *f*, carnicería *f*

slaughterhouse ['slɔtər,haʊs] *n* : matadero *m*

Slav ['slɑv, 'slæv] *n* : eslavo *m*, -va *f*

slave¹ ['sleɪv] *vi* **slaved; slaving** : trabajar como un burro

slave² *n* : esclavo *m*, -va *f*

slaver ['slævər, 'sleɪ-] *vi* : babear

slavery ['sleɪvəri] *n* : esclavitud *f*
Slavic ['slɑvɪk, 'slæ-] *adj* : eslavo
slavish ['sleɪvɪʃ] *adj* **1** SERVILE : servil **2** IMITATIVE : poco original
slay ['sleɪ] *vt* **slew** ['slu:]; **slain** ['sleɪn]; **slaying** : asesinar, matar
slayer ['sleɪər] *n* : asesino *m*, -na *f*
sleazy ['sli:zi] *adj* **sleazier; -est 1** SHODDY : chapucero, de mala calidad **2** DILAPIDATED : ruinoso **3** DISREPUTABLE : de mala fama
sled[1] ['slɛd] *v* **sledded; sledding** *vi* : ir en trineo — *vt* : transportar en trineo
sled[2] *n* : trineo *m*
sledge ['slɛʤ] *n* **1** : trineo *m* (grande) **2** → **sledgehammer**
sledgehammer ['slɛʤ,hæmər] *n* : almádena *f*, combo *m Chile, Peru*
sleek[1] ['sli:k] *vt* SLICK : alisar
sleek[2] *adj* : liso y brillante
sleep[1] ['sli:p] *vi* **slept** ['slɛpt]; **sleeping** : dormir
sleep[2] *n* **1** : sueño *m* **2 to go to sleep** : dormirse
sleeper ['sli:pər] *n* **1** : durmiente *mf* ⟨to be a light sleeper : tener el sueño ligero⟩ **2** *or* **sleeping car** : coche *m* cama, coche *m* dormitorio
sleepily ['sli:pəli] *adv* : de manera somnolienta
sleepiness ['sli:pinəs] *n* : somnolencia *f*
sleepless ['sli:pləs] *adj* : sin dormir, desvelado ⟨to have a sleepless night : pasar la noche en blanco⟩
sleepwalker ['sli:p,wɔkər] *n* : sonámbulo *m*, -la *f*
sleepy ['sli:pi] *adj* **sleepier; -est 1** DROWSY : somnoliento, soñoliento ⟨to be sleepy : tener sueño⟩ **2** LETHARGIC : aletargado, letárgico
sleet[1] ['sli:t] *vi* **to be sleeting** : caer aguanieve
sleet[2] *n* : aguanieve *f*
sleeve ['sli:v] *n* : manga *f* (de una camisa, etc.)
sleeveless ['sli:vləs] *adj* : sin mangas
sleigh[1] ['sleɪ] *vi* : ir en trineo
sleigh[2] *n* : trineo *m* (tirado por caballos)
sleight of hand [ˌslaɪtəv'hænd] : prestidigitación *f*, juegos *mpl* de manos
slender ['slɛndər] *adj* **1** SLIM : esbelto, delgado **2** SCANTY : exiguo, escaso ⟨a slender hope : una esperanza lejana⟩
sleuth ['slu:θ] *n* : detective *mf*; sabueso *m*, -sa *f*
slew → **slay**
slice[1] ['slaɪs] *vt* **sliced; slicing** : cortar
slice[2] *n* : rebanada *f*, tajada *f*, lonja *f* (de carne, etc.), rodaja *f* (de una verdura, fruta, etc.), trozo *m* (de pastel, etc.)
slick[1] ['slɪk] *vt* : alisar
slick[2] *adj* **1** SLIPPERY : resbaladizo, resbaloso **2** CRAFTY : astuto, taimado
slicker ['slɪkər] *n* : impermeable *m*
slide[1] ['slaɪd] *v* **slid** ['slɪd]; **sliding** ['slaɪdɪŋ] *vi* **1** SLIP : resbalar **2** GLIDE : deslizarse **3** DECLINE : bajar ⟨to let

things slide : dejar pasar las cosas⟩ — *vt* : correr, deslizar
slide[2] *n* **1** SLIDING : deslizamiento *m* **2** SLIP : resbalón *m* **3** : tobogán *m* (para niños) **4** TRANSPARENCY : diapositiva *f* (fotográfica) **5** DECLINE : descenso *m*
slier, sliest → **sly**
slight[1] ['slaɪt] *vt* : desairar, despreciar
slight[2] *adj* **1** SLENDER : esbelto, delgado **2** FLIMSY : endeble **3** TRIFLING : leve, insignificante ⟨a slight pain : un leve dolor⟩ **4** SMALL : pequeño, ligero ⟨not in the slightest : en absoluto⟩
slight[3] *n* SNUB : desaire *m*
slightly ['slaɪtli] *adv* : ligeramente, un poco
slim[1] ['slɪm] *v* **slimmed; slimming** : adelgazar
slim[2] *adj* **slimmer; slimmest 1** SLENDER : esbelto, delgado **2** SCANTY : exiguo, escaso
slime ['slaɪm] *n* **1** : baba *f* (secretada por un animal) **2** MUD, SILT : fango *m*, cieno *m*
slimy ['slaɪmi] *adj* **slimier; -est** : viscoso
sling[1] ['slɪŋ] *vt* **slung** ['slʌŋ]; **slinging 1** THROW : lanzar, tirar **2** HANG : colgar
sling[2] *n* **1** : honda *f* (arma) **2** : cabestrillo *m* ⟨my arm is in a sling : llevo el brazo en cabestrillo⟩
slingshot ['slɪŋ,ʃɑt] *n* : tiragomas *m*, resortera *f Mex*
slink ['slɪŋk] *vi* **slunk** ['slʌŋk]; **slinking** : caminar furtivamente
slip[1] ['slɪp] *v* **slipped; slipping** *vi* **1** STEAL : ir sigilosamente ⟨to slip away : escabullirse⟩ ⟨to slip out the door : escaparse por la puerta⟩ **2** SLIDE : resbalarse, deslizarse **3** LAPSE : caer ⟨to slip into error : equivocarse⟩ **4 to let slip** : dejar escapar **5 to slip into** PUT ON : ponerse — *vt* **1** PUT : meter, poner **2** PASS : pasar ⟨she slipped me a note : me pasó una nota⟩ **3 to slip one's mind** : olvidársele a uno
slip[2] *n* **1** PIER : atracadero *m* **2** MISHAP : percance *m*, contratiempo *m* **3** MISTAKE : error *m*, desliz *m* ⟨a slip of the tongue : un lapsus⟩ **4** PETTICOAT : enagua *f* **5** : injerto *m*, esqueje *m* (de una planta) **6 slip of paper** : papelito *m*
slipper ['slɪpər] *n* : zapatilla *f*, pantufla *f*
slipperiness ['slɪpərinəs] *n* **1** : lo resbaloso, lo resbaladizo **2** TRICKINESS : astucia *f*
slippery ['slɪpəri] *adj* **slipperier; -est 1** : resbaloso, resbaladizo ⟨a slippery road : un camino resbaloso⟩ **2** TRICKY : artero, astuto, taimado **3** ELUSIVE : huidizo, escurridizo
slipshod ['slɪp,ʃɑd] *adj* : descuidado, chapucero
slip up *vi* : equivocarse
slit[1] ['slɪt] *vt* **slit; slitting** : cortar, abrir por lo largo

slit² *n* **1** OPENING : abertura *f*, rendija *f* **2** CUT : corte *m*, raja *f*, tajo *m*

slither ['slɪðər] *vi* : deslizarse

sliver ['slɪvər] *n* : astilla *f*

slob ['slɑb] *n* : persona *f* desaliñada ⟨what a slob! : ¡qué cerdo!⟩

slobber¹ ['slɑbər] *vi* : babear

slobber² *n* : baba *f*

slogan ['slo:gən] *n* : lema *m*, eslogan *m*

sloop ['slu:p] *n* : balandra *f*

slop¹ ['slɑp] *v* **slopped; slopping** *vt* : derramar — *vi* : derramarse

slop² *n* : bazofia *f*

slope¹ ['slo:p] *vi* **sloped; sloping** : inclinarse ⟨the road slopes upward : el camino sube (en pendiente)⟩

slope² *n* : inclinación *f*, pendiente *f*, declive *m*

sloppy ['slɑpi] *adj* **sloppier; -est** **1** MUDDY, SLUSHY : lodoso, fangoso **2** UNTIDY : descuidado (en el trabajo, etc.), desaliñado (de aspecto)

slot ['slɑt] *n* : ranura *f*

sloth ['slɔθ, 'slo:θ] *n* **1** LAZINESS : pereza *f* **2** : perezoso *m* (animal)

slouch¹ ['slaʊtʃ] *vi* : andar con los hombros caídos, repantigarse (en un sillón)

slouch² *n* **1** SLUMPING : mala postura *f* **2** BUNGLER, IDLER : haragán *m*, -gana *f*; inepto *m*, -ta *f* ⟨to be no slouch : no quedarse atrás⟩

slough¹ ['slʌf] *vt* : mudar de (piel)

slough² ['slu:, 'slaʊ] *n* SWAMP : ciénaga *f*

Slovak ['slo:ˌvɑk, -ˌvæk] *or* **Slovakian** [slo:'vɑkiən, -'væ-] *n* : eslovaco *m*, -ca *f* — **Slovak** *or* **Slovakian** *adj*

Slovene ['slo:ˌvi:n] *or* **Slovenian** [slo:-'vi:niən] *n* : esloveno *m*, -na *f* — **Slovene** *or* **Slovenian** *adj*

slovenly ['slavənli, 'slʌv-] *adj* : descuidado (en el trabajo, etc.), desaliñado (de aspecto)

slow¹ [slo:] *vt* : retrasar, reducir la marcha de — *vi* : ir más despacio

slow² *adv* : despacio, lentamente

slow³ *adj* **1** : lento ⟨a slow process : un proceso lento⟩ **2** : atrasado ⟨my watch is slow : mi reloj está atrasado, mi reloj se atrasa⟩ **3** SLUGGISH : lento, poco activo **4** STUPID : lento, torpe, corto de alcances

slowly [slo:li] *adv* : lentamente, despacio

slowness [slo:nəs] *n* : lentitud *f*, torpeza *f*

sludge ['slʌdʒ] *n* : aguas *fpl* negras, aguas *fpl* residuales

slug¹ ['slʌg] *vt* **slugged; slugging** : pegarle un porrazo (a alguien)

slug² *n* **1** : babosa *f* (molusco) **2** BULLET : bala *f* **3** TOKEN : ficha *f* **4** BLOW : porrazo *m*, puñetazo *m*

sluggish ['slʌgɪʃ] *adj* : aletargado, lento

sluice¹ ['slu:s] *vt* **sluiced; sluicing** : lavar en agua corriente

sluice² *n* : canal *m*

slum ['slʌm] *n* : barriada *f*, barrio *m* bajo

slumber¹ ['slʌmbər] *vi* : dormir

slumber² *n* : sueño *m*

slump¹ ['slʌmp] *vi* **1** DECLINE, DROP : disminuir, bajar **2** SLOUCH : encorvarse, dejarse caer (en una silla, etc.)

slump² *n* : bajón *m*, declive *m* (económico)

slung → **sling**

slunk → **slink**

slur¹ ['slər] *vt* **slurred; slurring** : ligar (notas musicales), tragarse (las palabras)

slur² *n* **1** : ligado *m* (en música), mala pronunciación *f* (de las palabras) **2** ASPERSION : calumnia *f*, difamación *f*

slurp¹ ['slərp] *vi* : beber o comer haciendo ruido — *vt* : sorber ruidosamente

slurp² *n* : sorbo *m* (ruidoso)

slush ['slʌʃ] *n* : nieve *f* medio derretida

slut ['slʌt] *n* PROSTITUTE : ramera *f*, fulana *f*

sly ['slaɪ] *adj* **slier** ['slaɪər]; **sliest** ['slaɪəst] **1** CUNNING : astuto, taimado **2** UNDERHANDED : soplado — **slyly** *adv*

slyness ['slaɪnəs] *n* : astucia *f*

smack¹ ['smæk] *vi* **to smack of** : oler a, saber a — *vt* **1** KISS : besar, plantarle un beso (a alguien) **2** SLAP : pegarle una bofetada (a alguien) **3 to smack one's lips** : relamerse

smack² *adv* : justo, exactamente ⟨smack in the face : en plena cara⟩

smack³ *n* **1** TASTE, TRACE : sabor *m*, indicio *m* **2** : chasquido *m* (de los labios) **3** SLAP : bofetada *f* **4** KISS : beso *m*

small ['smɔl] *adj* **1** : pequeño, chico ⟨a small house : una casa pequeña⟩ ⟨small change : monedas de poco valor⟩ **2** TRIVIAL : pequeño, insignificante

smallness ['smɔlnəs] *n* : pequeñez *f*

smallpox ['smɔlˌpɑks] *n* : viruela *f*

smart¹ ['smɑrt] *vi* **1** STING : escocer, picar, arder **2** HURT : dolerse, resentirse ⟨to smart under a rejection : dolerse ante un rechazo⟩

smart² *adj* **1** BRIGHT : listo, vivo, inteligente **2** STYLISH : elegante — **smartly** *adv*

smart³ *n* **1** PAIN : escozor *m*, dolor *m* **2 smarts** *npl* : inteligencia *f*

smartness ['smɑrtnəs] *n* **1** INTELLIGENCE : inteligencia *f* **2** ELEGANCE : elegancia *f*

smash¹ ['smæʃ] *vt* **1** BREAK : romper, quebrar, hacer pedazos **2** WRECK : destrozar, arruinar **3** CRASH : estrellar, chocar — *vi* **1** SHATTER : hacerse pedazos, hacerse añicos **2** COLLIDE, CRASH : estrellarse, chocar

smash² *n* **1** BLOW : golpe *m* **2** COLLISION : choque *m* **3** BANG, CRASH : estrépito *m*

smattering ['smætərɪŋ] *n* **1** : nociones *fpl* ⟨she has a smattering of programming : tiene nociones de programación⟩ **2** : un poco, unos cuantos ⟨a smattering of spectators : unos cuantos espectadores⟩

smear[1] ['smɪr] *vt* **1** DAUB : embadurnar, untar (mantequilla, etc.) **2** SMUDGE : emborronar **3** SLANDER : calumniar, difamar

smear[2] *n* **1** SMUDGE : mancha *f* **2** SLANDER : calumnia *f*

smell[1] ['smɛl] *v* **smelled** *or* **smelt** ['smɛlt]; **smelling** *vt* : oler, olfatear ⟨to smell danger : olfatear el peligro⟩ — *vi* : oler ⟨to smell good : oler bien⟩

smell[2] *n* **1** : olfato *m*, sentido *m* del olfato **2** ODOR : olor *m*

smelly ['smɛli] *adj* **smellier; -est** : maloliente

smelt[1] ['smɛlt] *vt* : fundir

smelt[2] *n, pl* **smelts** *or* **smelt** : eperlano *m* (pez)

smile[1] ['smaɪl] *vi* **smiled; smiling** : sonreír

smile[2] *n* : sonrisa *f*

smirk[1] ['smərk] *vi* : sonreír con suficiencia

smirk[2] *n* : sonrisa *f* satisfecha

smite ['smaɪt] *vt* **smote** ['smo:t]; **smitten** ['smɪtən] *or* **smote; smiting 1** STRIKE : golpear **2** AFFLICT : afligir

smith ['smɪθ] *n* : herrero *m*, -ra *f*

smithy ['smɪθi] *n, pl* **smithies** : herrería *f*

smock ['smɑk] *n* : bata *f*, blusón *m*

smog ['smɑg, 'smɔg] *n* : smog *m*

smoke[1] ['smo:k] *v* **smoked; smoking** *vi* **1** : echar humo, humear ⟨a smoking chimney : una chimenea que echa humo⟩ **2** : fumar ⟨I don't smoke : no fumo⟩ — *vt* : ahumar (carne, etc.)

smoke[2] *n* : humo *m*

smoke detector [dɪ'tɛktər] *n* : detector *m* de humo

smoker ['smo:kər] *n* : fumador *m*, -dora *f*

smokestack ['smo:k,stæk] *n* : chimenea *f*

smoky ['smo:ki] *adj* **smokier; -est 1** SMOKING : humeante **2** : a humo ⟨a smoky flavor : un sabor a humo⟩ **3** : lleno de humo ⟨a smoky room : un cuarto lleno de humo⟩

smolder ['smo:ldər] *vi* **1** : arder sin llama **2** : arder (en el corazón) ⟨his anger smoldered : su rabia ardía⟩

smooth[1] ['smu:ð] *vt* : alisar

smooth[2] *adj* **1** : liso (dícese de una superficie) ⟨smooth skin : piel lisa⟩ **2** : suave (dícese de un movimiento) ⟨a smooth landing : un aterrizaje suave⟩ **3** : sin grumos ⟨a smooth sauce : una salsa sin grumos⟩ **4** : fluido ⟨smooth writing : escritura fluida⟩

smoothly ['smu:ðli] *adv* **1** GENTLY, SOFTLY : suavemente **2** EASILY : con facilidad, sin problemas

smoothness ['smu:ðnəs] *n* : suavidad *f*

smother ['smʌðər] *vt* **1** SUFFOCATE : ahogar, sofocar **2** COVER : cubrir **3** SUPPRESS : contener — *vi* : asfixiarse

smudge[1] ['smʌdʒ] *v* **smudged; smudging** *vt* : emborronar — *vi* : correrse

smudge[2] *n* : mancha *f*, borrón *m*

smug ['smʌg] *adj* **smugger; smuggest** : suficiente, pagado de sí mismo

smuggle ['smʌgəl] *vt* **-gled; -gling** : contrabandear, pasar de contrabando

smuggler ['smʌgələr] *n* : contrabandista *mf*

smugly ['smʌgli] *adv* : con suficiencia

smut ['smʌt] *n* **1** SOOT : tizne *m*, hollín *m* **2** FUNGUS : tizón *m* **3** OBSCENITY : obscenidad *f*, inmundicia *f*

smutty ['smʌti] *adj* **smuttier; -est 1** SOOTY : tiznado **2** OBSCENE : obsceno, indecente

snack ['snæk] *n* : refrigerio *m*, bocado *m*, tentempié *m fam* ⟨an afternoon snack : una merienda⟩

snag[1] ['snæg] *v* **snagged; snagging** *vt* : enganchar — *vi* : engancharse

snag[2] *n* : problema *m*, inconveniente *m*

snail ['sneɪl] *n* : caracol *m*

snake ['sneɪk] *n* : culebra *f*, serpiente *f*

snakebite ['sneɪk,baɪt] *n* : mordedura *f* de serpiente

snap[1] ['snæp] *v* **snapped; snapping** *vi* **1** : intentar morder (dícese de un perro, etc.), picar (dícese de un pez) **2** : hablar con severidad ⟨he snapped at me! : ¡me gritó!⟩ **3** BREAK : romperse, quebrarse (haciendo un chasquido) — *vt* **1** BREAK : partir (en dos), quebrar **2** : hacer (algo) de un golpe ⟨to snap open : abrir de golpe⟩ **3** RETORT : decir bruscamente **4** CLICK : chasquear ⟨to snap one's fingers : chasquear los dedos⟩

snap[2] *n* **1** CLICK, CRACK : chasquido *m* **2** FASTENER : broche *m* **3** CINCH : cosa *f* fácil ⟨it's a snap : es facilísimo⟩

snapdragon ['snæp,drægən] *n* : dragón *m* (flor)

snapper ['snæpər] → **red snapper**

snappy ['snæpi] *adj* **snappier; -est 1** FAST : rápido ⟨make it snappy! : ¡date prisa!⟩ **2** LIVELY : vivaz **3** CHILLY : frío **4** STYLISH : elegante

snapshot ['snæp,ʃɑt] *n* : instantánea *f*

snare[1] ['snær] *vt* **snared; snaring** : atrapar

snare[2] *n* : trampa *f*, red *f*

snare drum *n* : tambor *m* con bordón

snarl[1] ['snɑrl] *vi* **1** TANGLE : enmarañar, enredar **2** GROWL : gruñir

snarl[2] *n* **1** TANGLE : enredo *m*, maraña *f* **2** GROWL : gruñido *m*

snatch[1] ['snætʃ] *vt* : arrebatar

snatch[2] *n* : fragmento *m*

sneak[1] ['sni:k] *vi* : ir a hurtadillas — *vt* : hacer furtivamente ⟨to sneak a look : mirar con disimulo⟩ ⟨he sneaked a smoke : fumó un cigarrillo a escondidas⟩

sneak[2] *n* : soplón *m*, -plona *f*

sneakers ['sni:kərz] *npl* : tenis *mpl*, zapatillas *fpl*

sneaky ['sni:ki] *adj* **sneakier; -est** : solapado

sneer[1] ['snɪr] *vi* : sonreír con desprecio
sneer[2] *n* : sonrisa *f* de desprecio
sneeze[1] ['sni:z] *vi* **sneezed; sneezing** : estornudar
sneeze[2] *n* : estornudo *m*
snicker[1] ['snɪkər] *vi* : reírse disimuladamente
snicker[2] *n* : risita *f*
snide ['snaɪd] *adj* : sarcástico
sniff[1] ['snɪf] *vi* **1** SMELL : oler, husmear (dícese de los animales) **2 to sniff at** : despreciar, desdeñar — *vt* **1** SMELL : oler **2 to sniff out** : olerse, husmear
sniff[2] *n* **1** SNIFFING : aspiración *f* por la nariz **2** SMELL : olor *m*
sniffle ['snɪfəl] *vi* **-fled; -fling** : respirar con la nariz congestionada
sniffles ['snɪfəlz] *npl* : resfriado *m*
snip[1] ['snɪp] *vt* **snipped; snipping** : cortar (con tijeras)
snip[2] *n* : tijeretada *f*, recorte *m*
snipe[1] ['snaɪp] *vi* **sniped; sniping** : disparar
snipe[2] *n, pl* **snipes** *or* **snipe** : agachadiza *f*
sniper ['snaɪpər] *n* : francotirador *m*, -dora *f*
snippet ['snɪpət] *n* : fragmento *m* (de un texto, etc.)
snivel ['snɪvəl] *vi* **-veled** *or* **-velled; -veling** *or* **-velling** **1** → **snuffle 2** WHINE : lloriquear
snob ['snɑb] *n* : esnob *mf*, snob *mf*
snobbery ['snɑbəri] *n, pl* **-beries** : esnobismo *m*
snobbish ['snɑbɪʃ] *adj* : esnob, snob
snobbishness ['snɑbɪʃnəs] *n* : esnobismo *m*
snoop[1] ['snu:p] *vi* : husmear, curiosear
snoop[2] *n* : fisgón *m*, -gona *f*
snooze[1] ['snu:z] *vi* **snoozed; snoozing** : dormitar
snooze[2] *n* : siestecita *f*, siestita *f*
snore[1] ['snor] *vi* **snored; snoring** : roncar
snore[2] *n* : ronquido *m*
snort[1] ['snɔrt] *vi* : bufar, resoplar
snort[2] *n* : bufido *m*, resoplo *m*
snout ['snaʊt] *n* : hocico *m*, morro *m*
snow[1] ['sno:] *vi* **1** : nevar ⟨I'm snowed in : estoy aislado por la nieve⟩ **2 to be snowed under** : estar inundado
snow[2] *n* : nieve *f*
snowball ['sno:,bɔl] *n* : bola *f* de nieve
snowdrift ['sno:,drɪft] *n* : ventisquero *m*
snowfall ['sno:,fɔl] *n* : nevada *f*
snowplow ['sno:,plaʊ] *n* : quitanieves *m*
snowshoe ['sno:,ʃu:] *n* : raqueta *f* (para nieve)
snowstorm ['sno:,stɔrm] *n* : tormenta *f* de nieve, ventisca *f*
snowy ['sno:i] *adj* **snowier; -est** : nevoso ⟨a snowy road : un camino nevado⟩
snub[1] ['snʌb] *vt* **snubbed; snubbing** : desairar
snub[2] *n* : desaire *m*
snub–nosed ['snʌb,no:zd] *adj* : de nariz respingada

snuff[1] ['snʌf] *vt* **1** : apagar (una vela) **2** : sorber (algo) por la nariz
snuff[2] *n* : rapé *m*
snuffle ['snʌfəl] *vi* **-fled; -fling** : respirar con la nariz congestionada
snug ['snʌg] *adj* **snugger; snuggest 1** COMFORTABLE : cómodo **2** TIGHT : ajustado, ceñido ⟨snug pants : pantalones ajustados⟩
snuggle ['snʌgəl] *vi* **-gled; -gling** : acurrucarse ⟨to snuggle up to someone : arrimársele a alguien⟩
snugly ['snʌgli] *adv* **1** COMFORTABLY : cómodamente **2** : de manera ajustada ⟨the shirt fits snugly : la camisa queda ajustada⟩
so[1] ['so:] *adv* **1** (*referring to something indicated or suggested*) ⟨do you think so? : ¿tú crees?⟩ ⟨so it would seem : eso parece⟩ ⟨I told her so : se lo dije⟩ ⟨he's ready, or so he says : según dice, está listo⟩ ⟨it so happened that . . . : resultó que . . . ⟩ ⟨do it like so : hazlo así⟩ ⟨so be it : así sea⟩ **2** ALSO : también ⟨so do I : yo también⟩ **3** THUS : así, de esta manera **4** : tan ⟨he'd never been so happy : nunca había estado tan contento⟩ **5** CONSEQUENTLY : por lo tanto
so[2] *conj* **1** THEREFORE : así que **2** *or* **so that** : para que, así que, de manera que **3 so what?** : ¿y qué?
soak[1] ['so:k] *vi* : estar en remojo — *vt* **1** : poner en remojo **2 to soak up** ABSORB : absorber
soak[2] *n* : remojo *m*
soap[1] ['so:p] *vt* : enjabonar
soap[2] *n* : jabón *m*
soapsuds ['so:p,sʌdz] → **suds**
soapy ['so:pi] *adj* **soapier; -est** : jabonoso ⟨a soapy taste : un gusto a jabón⟩ ⟨a soapy texture : una textura de jabón⟩
soar ['sor] *vi* **1** FLY : volar **2** RISE : remontar el vuelo (dícese de las aves) ⟨her hopes soared : su esperanza renació⟩ ⟨prices are soaring : los precios están subiendo vertiginosamente⟩
sob[1] ['sɑb] *vi* **sobbed; sobbing** : sollozar
sob[2] *n* : sollozo *m*
sober ['so:bər] *adj* **1** : sobrio ⟨he's not sober enough to drive : está demasiado borracho para manejar⟩ **2** SERIOUS : serio
soberly ['so:bərli] *adv* **1** : sobriamente **2** SERIOUSLY : seriamente
sobriety [sə'braɪəṭi, so-] *n* **1** : sobriedad *f* ⟨sobriety test : prueba de alcoholemia⟩ **2** SERIOUSNESS : seriedad *f*
so–called ['so:'kɔld] *adj* : supuesto, presunto ⟨the so-called experts : los expertos, así llamados⟩
soccer ['sɑkər] *n* : futbol *m*, fútbol *m*
sociable ['so:ʃəbəl] *adj* : sociable
social[1] ['so:ʃəl] *adj* : social — **socially** *adv*
social[2] *n* : reunión *f* social

socialism ['so:ʃə,lɪzəm] *n* : socialismo *m*
socialist[1] ['so:ʃəlɪst] *adj* : socialista
socialist[2] *n* : socialista *mf*
socialize ['so:ʃə,laɪz] *v* **-ized; -izing** *vt* 1 NATIONALIZE : nacionalizar 2 : socializar (en psicología) — *vi* : alternar, circular ⟨to socialize with friends : alternar con amigos⟩
social work *n* : asistencia *f* social
society [sə'saɪəṭi] *n, pl* **-eties** 1 COMPANIONSHIP : compañía *f* 2 : sociedad *f* ⟨a democratic society : una sociedad democrática⟩ ⟨high society : alta sociedad⟩ 3 ASSOCIATION : sociedad *f*, asociación *f*
socioeconomic [,so:sio,i:kə'namɪk, -,ekə-] *adj* : socioeconómico
sociology [,so:si'aləʤi] *n* : sociología *f*
sociological [,so:siə'laʤɪkəl] *adj* : sociológico
sociologist [,so:si'aləʤɪst] *n* : sociólogo *m*, -ga *f*
sock[1] ['sak] *vt* : pegar, golpear, darle un puñetazo a
sock[2] *n* 1 *pl* **socks** *or* **sox** ['saks] : calcetín *m*, media *f* ⟨shoes and socks : zapatos y calcetines⟩ 2 *pl* **socks** ['saks] PUNCH : puñetazo *m*
socket ['sakət] *n* 1 *or* **electric socket** : enchufe *m*, toma *f* de corriente 2 : glena *f* (de una articulación) ⟨shoulder socket : glena del hombro⟩ 3 **eye socket** : órbita *f*, cuenca *f*
sod[1] ['sad] *vt* **sodded; sodding** : cubrir de césped
sod[2] *n* TURF : césped *m*, tepe *m*
soda ['so:də] *n* 1 *or* **soda water** : soda *f* 2 *or* **soda pop** : gaseosa *f*, refresco *m* 3 *or* **ice–cream soda** : refresco *m* con helado
sodden ['sadən] *adj* SOGGY : empapado
sodium ['so:diəm] *n* : sodio *m*
sodium bicarbonate *n* : bicarbonato *m* de soda
sodium chloride → **salt**
sofa ['so:fə] *n* : sofá *m*
soft ['sɔft] *adj* 1 : blando ⟨a soft pillow : una almohada blanda⟩ 2 SMOOTH : suave (dícese de las texturas, de los sonidos, etc.) 3 NONALCOHOLIC : no alcohólico ⟨a soft drink : un refresco⟩
softball ['sɔft,bɔl] *n* : softbol *m*
soften ['sɔfən] *vt* : ablandar (algo sólido), suavizar (la piel, un golpe, etc.), amortiguar (un impacto) — *vi* : ablandarse, suavizarse
softly ['sɔftli] *adv* : suavemente ⟨she spoke softly : habló en voz baja⟩
softness ['sɔftnəs] *n* 1 : blandura *f*, lo blando (de una almohada, de la mantequilla, etc.) 2 SMOOTHNESS : suavidad *f*
software ['sɔft,wær] *n* : software *m*
soggy ['sagi] *adj* **soggier; -est** : empapado
soil[1] ['sɔɪl] *vt* : ensuciar — *vi* : ensuciarse

soil[2] *n* 1 DIRTINESS : suciedad *f* 2 DIRT, EARTH : suelo *m*, tierra *f* 3 COUNTRY : patria *f* ⟨her native soil : su tierra natal⟩
sojourn[1] ['so:,ʤərn, so:'ʤərn] *vi* : pasar una temporada
sojourn[2] *n* : estadía *f*, estancia *f*, permanencia *f*
solace ['saləs] *n* : consuelo *m*
solar ['so:lər] *adj* : solar ⟨the solar system : el sistema solar⟩
sold → **sell**
solder[1] ['sadər, 'sɔ-] *vt* : soldar
solder[2] *n* : soldadura *f*
soldier[1] ['so:lʤər] *vi* : servir como soldado
soldier[2] *n* : soldado *mf*
sole[1] ['so:l] *adj* : único
sole[2] *n* 1 : suela *f* (de un zapato) 2 : lenguado *m* (pez)
solely ['so:li] *adv* : únicamente, sólo
solemn ['saləm] *adj* : solemne, serio — **solemnly** *adv*
solemnity [sə'lɛmnəṭi] *n, pl* **-ties** : solemnidad *f*
solicit [sə'lɪsət] *vt* : solicitar
solicitous [sə'lɪsəṭəs] *adj* : solícito
solicitude [sə'lɪsə,tu:d, -,tju:d] *n* : solicitud *f*
solid[1] ['saləd] *adj* 1 : macizo ⟨a solid rubber ball : una bola maciza de caucho⟩ 2 CUBIC : tridimensional 3 COMPACT : compacto, denso 4 STURDY : sólido 5 CONTINUOUS : seguido, continuo ⟨two solid hours : dos horas seguidas⟩ ⟨a solid line : una línea continua⟩ 6 UNANIMOUS : unánime 7 DEPENDABLE : serio, fiable 8 PURE : macizo, puro ⟨solid gold : oro macizo⟩
solid[2] *n* : sólido *m*
solidarity [,salə'dærəṭi] *n* : solidaridad *f*
solidify [sə'lɪdə,faɪ] *v* **-fied; -fying** *vt* : solidificar — *vi* : solidificarse
solidity [sə'lɪdəṭi] *n, pl* **-ties** : solidez *f*
solidly ['salədli] *adv* 1 : sólidamente 2 UNANIMOUSLY : unánimemente
soliloquy [sə'lɪləkwi] *n, pl* **-quies** : soliloquio *m*
solitaire ['salə,tær] *n* : solitario *m*
solitary ['salə,teri] *adj* 1 ALONE : solitario 2 SECLUDED : apartado, retirado 3 SINGLE : solo
solitude ['salə,tu:d, -,tju:d] *n* : soledad *f*
solo[1] ['so:,lo:] *vi* : volar en solitario (dícese de un piloto)
solo[2] *adv & adj* : en solitario, a solas
solo[3] *n, pl* **solos** : solo *m*
soloist ['so:loɪst] *n* : solista *mf*
solstice ['salstɪs] *n* : solsticio *m*
soluble ['saljəbəl] *adj* : soluble
solution [sə'lu:ʃən] *n* : solución *f*
solve ['salv] *vt* **solved; solving** : resolver, solucionar
solvency ['salvəntsi] *n* : solvencia *f*
solvent ['salvənt] *n* : solvente *m*
Somali [so'mali, sə-] *n* : somalí *mf* — **Somali** *adj*
somber ['sambər] *adj* 1 DARK : sombrío, oscuro ⟨somber colors : colores

oscuros⟩ **2** GRAVE : sombrío, serio **3**
MELANCHOLY : sombrío, lúgubre
sombrero [səm'brer₁o:] *n, pl* **-ros** : sombrero *m* (mexicano)
some¹ ['sʌm] *adj* **1** : un, algún ⟨some lady stopped me : una mujer me detuvo⟩ ⟨some distant galaxy : alguna galaxia lejana⟩ **2** : algo de, un poco de ⟨he drank some water : tomó (un poco de) agua⟩ **3** : unos ⟨do you want some apples? : ¿quieres unas manzanas?⟩ ⟨some years ago : hace varios años⟩
some² *pron* **1** : algunos ⟨some went, others stayed : algunos se fueron, otros se quedaron⟩ **2** : un poco, algo ⟨there's some left : queda un poco⟩ ⟨I have gum; do you want some? : tengo chicle, ¿quieres?⟩
somebody ['sʌmbədi, -₁badi] *pron* : alguien
someday ['sʌm₁deɪ] *adv* : algún día
somehow ['sʌm₁haʊ] *adv* **1** : de alguna manera, de algún modo ⟨I'll do it somehow : lo haré de alguna manera⟩ **2** : por alguna razón ⟨somehow I don't trust her : por alguna razón no me fío de ella⟩
someone ['sʌm₁wʌn] *pron* : alguien
someplace ['sʌm₁pleɪs] → **somewhere**
somersault¹ ['sʌmər₁sɔlt] *vi* : dar volteretas, dar un salto mortal
somersault² *n* : voltereta *f*, salto *m* mortal
something ['sʌmθɪŋ] *pron* : algo ⟨I want something else : quiero otra cosa⟩ ⟨she's writing a novel or something : está escribiendo una novela o no sé qué⟩
sometime ['sʌm₁taɪm] *adv* : algún día, en algún momento ⟨sometime next month : durante el mes que viene⟩
sometimes ['sʌm₁taɪmz] *adv* : a veces, algunas veces, de vez en cuando
somewhat ['sʌm₁hwʌt, -₁hwɑt] *adv* : algo, un tanto
somewhere ['sʌm₁hwer] *adv* **1** (*indicating location*) : en algún lugar ⟨it must be somewhere else : estará en otra parte⟩ **2** (*indicating destination*) : a algún lugar
son ['sʌn] *n* : hijo *m*
sonar ['so:₁nɑr] *n* : sonar *m*
sonata [sə'nɑtə] *n* : sonata *f*
song ['sɔŋ] *n* : canción *f*, canto *m* (de un pájaro)
songbird ['sɔŋ₁bərd] *n* : pájaro *m* cantor
songwriter ['sɔŋ₁raɪtər] *n* : compositor *m*, -tora *f*
sonic ['sɑnɪk] *adj* **1** : sónico **2** **sonic boom** : estampido *m* sónico
son-in-law ['sʌnɪn₁lɔ] *n, pl* **sons-in-law** : yerno *m*, hijo *m* político
sonnet ['sɑnət] *n* : soneto *m*
sonorous ['sɑnərəs, sə'norəs] *adj* : sonoro
soon ['su:n] *adv* **1** : pronto, dentro de poco ⟨he'll arrive soon : llegará pron-

to⟩ **2** QUICKLY : pronto ⟨as soon as possible : lo más pronto posible⟩ ⟨the sooner the better : cuanto antes mejor⟩ **3** : de buena gana ⟨I'd sooner walk : prefiero caminar⟩
soot ['sʊt, 'su:t, 'sʌt] *n* : hollín *m*, tizne *m*
soothe ['su:ð] *vt* **soothed; soothing 1** CALM : calmar, tranquilizar **2** RELIEVE : aliviar
soothsayer ['su:θ₁seɪər] *n* : adivino *m*, -na *f*
sooty ['sʊti, 'su:-, 'sʌ-] *adj* **sootier; -est** : cubierto de hollín, tiznado
sop¹ ['sɑp] *vt* **sopped; sopping 1** DIP : mojar **2** SOAK : empapar **3 to sop up** : rebañar, absorber
sop² *n* **1** CONCESSION : concesión *f* **2** BRIBE : soborno *m*
sophisticated [sə'fɪstə₁keɪtəd] *adj* **1** COMPLEX : complejo **2** WORLDLY-WISE : sofisticado
sophistication [sə₁fɪstə'keɪʃən] *n* **1** COMPLEXITY : complejidad *f* **2** URBANITY : sofisticación *f*
sophomore ['sɑf₁mor, 'sɑfə₁mor] *n* : estudiante *mf* de segundo año
soporific [₁sɑpə'rɪfɪk, ₁so:-] *adj* : soporífero
soprano [sə'præ₁no:] *n, pl* **-nos** : soprano *mf*
sorcerer ['sɔrsərər] *n* : hechicero *m*, brujo *m*, mago *m*
sorceress ['sɔrsərəs] *n* : hechicera *f*, bruja *f*, maga *f*
sorcery ['sɔrsəri] *n* : hechicería *f*, brujería *f*
sordid ['sɔrdɪd] *adj* : sórdido
sore¹ ['sor] *adj* **sorer; sorest 1** PAINFUL : dolorido, doloroso ⟨I have a sore throat : me duele la garganta⟩ **2** ACUTE, SEVERE : extremo, grande ⟨in sore straits : en grandes apuros⟩ **3** ANGRY : enojado, enfadado
sore² *n* : llaga *f*
sorely ['sorli] *adv* : muchísimo ⟨it was sorely needed : se necesitaba urgentemente⟩ ⟨she was sorely missed : la echaban mucho de menos⟩
soreness ['sornəs] *n* : dolor *m*
sorghum ['sɔrgəm] *n* : sorgo *m*
sorority [sə'rɔrəti] *n, pl* **-ties** : hermandad *f* (de estudiantes femeninas)
sorrel ['sɔrəl] *n* **1** : alazán *m* (color o animal) **2** : acedera *f* (hierba)
sorrow ['sar₁o:] *n* : pesar *m*, dolor *m*, pena *f*
sorrowful ['sarofəl] *adj* : triste, afligido, apenado
sorrowfully ['sarofəli] *adv* : con tristeza
sorry ['sari] *adj* **sorrier; -est 1** PITIFUL : lastimero, lastimoso **2 to be sorry** : sentir, lamentar ⟨I'm sorry : lo siento⟩ **3 to feel sorry for** : compadecer ⟨I feel sorry for him : me da pena⟩
sort¹ ['sɔrt] *vt* **1** : dividir en grupos **2** CLASSIFY : clasificar **3 to sort out** ORGANIZE : poner en orden **4 to sort out** RESOLVE : resolver

sort[2] *n* **1** KIND : tipo *m*, clase *f* ⟨a sort of writer : una especie de escritor⟩ **2** NATURE : índole *f* **3 out of sorts** : de mal humor

sortie ['sɔrʈi, sɔr'ti:] *n* : salida *f*

SOS [ˌɛsˌoːˈɛs] *n* : SOS *m*

so–so ['soːˈsoː] *adj & adv* : así así, de modo regular

soufflé [suːˈfleɪ] *n* : suflé *m*

sought → **seek**

soul ['soːl] *n* **1** SPIRIT : alma *f* **2** ESSENCE : esencia *f* **3** PERSON : persona *f*, alma *f*

soulful ['soːlfəl] *adj* : conmovedor, lleno de emoción

sound[1] ['saʊnd] *vt* **1** : sondar (en navegación) **2** *or* **to sound out** PROBE : sondear **3** : hacer sonar, tocar (una trompeta, etc.) — *vi* **1** : sonar ⟨the alarm sounded : la alarma sonó⟩ **2** SEEM : parecer

sound[2] *adj* **1** HEALTHY : sano ⟨safe and sound : sano y salvo⟩ ⟨of sound mind and body : en pleno uso de sus facultades⟩ **2** FIRM, SOLID : sólido **3** SENSIBLE : lógico, sensato **4** DEEP : profundo ⟨a sound sleep : un sueño profundo⟩

sound[3] *n* **1** : sonido *m* ⟨the speed of sound : la velocidad del sonido⟩ **2** NOISE : sonido *m*, ruido *m* ⟨I heard a sound : oí un sonido⟩ **3** CHANNEL : brazo *m* de mar, canal *m* (ancho)

soundless ['saʊndləs] *adj* : sordo

soundlessly ['saʊndləsli] *adv* : silenciosamente

soundly ['saʊndli] *adv* **1** SOLIDLY : sólidamente **2** SENSIBLY : lógicamente, sensatamente **3** DEEPLY : profundamente ⟨sleeping soundly : durmiendo profundamente⟩

soundness ['saʊndnəs] *n* **1** SOLIDITY : solidez *f* **2** SENSIBLENESS : sensatez *f*, solidez *f*

soundproof ['saʊndˌpruːf] *adj* : insonorizado

soundtrack ['saʊndˌtræk] *n* : banda *f* sonora

sound wave *n* : onda *f* sonora

soup ['suːp] *n* : sopa *f*

sour[1] ['saʊər] *vi* : agriarse, cortarse (dícese de la leche) — *vt* : agriar, cortar (leche)

sour[2] *adj* **1** ACID : agrio, ácido (dícese de la fruta, etc.), cortado (dícese de la leche) **2** DISAGREEABLE : desagradable, agrio

source ['sɔrs] *n* : fuente *f*, origen *m*, nacimiento *m* (de un río)

sourness ['saʊərnəs] *n* : acidez *f*

south[1] ['saʊθ] *adv* : al sur, hacia el sur ⟨the window looks south : la ventana mira al sur⟩ ⟨she continued south : continuó hacia el sur⟩

south[2] *adj* : sur, del sur ⟨the south entrance : la entrada sur⟩ ⟨South America : Sudamérica, América del Sur⟩

south[3] *n* : sur *m*

South African *n* : sudafricano *m*, -na *f*

— **South African** *adj*

South American[1] *adj* : sudamericano, suramericano

South American[2] *n* : sudamericano *m*, -na *f*; suramericano *m*, -na *f*

southbound ['saʊθˌbaʊnd] *adj* : con rumbo al sur

southeast[1] [saʊˈθiːst] *adj* : sureste, sudeste, del sureste

southeast[2] *n* : sureste *m*, sudeste *m*

southeasterly [saʊˈθiːstərli] *adv & adj* **1** : del sureste (dícese del viento) **2** : hacia el sureste

southeastern [saʊˈθiːstərn] *adj* → **southeast**[1]

southerly ['sʌðərli] *adv & adj* : del sur

southern ['sʌðərn] *adj* : sur, sureño, meridional, austral ⟨a southern city : una ciudad del sur del país, una ciudad meridional⟩ ⟨the southern side : el lado sur⟩

Southerner ['sʌðərnər] *n* : sureño *m*, -ña *f*

South Pole : Polo *m* Sur

southward ['saʊθwərd] *or* **southwards** [-wərdz] *adv & adj* : hacia el sur

southwest[1] [saʊθˈwest, *as a nautical term often* saʊˈwest] *adj* : suroeste, sudoeste, del suroeste

southwest[2] *n* : suroeste *m*, sudoeste *m*

southwesterly [saʊθˈwestərli] *adv & adj* **1** : del suroeste (dícese del viento) **2** : hacia el suroeste

southwestern [saʊθˈwestərn] *adj* → **southwest**[1]

souvenir [ˌsuːvəˈnɪr, ˈsuːvəˌ-] *n* : recuerdo *m*, souvenir *m*

sovereign[1] ['savərən] *adj* : soberano

sovereign[2] *n* **1** : soberano *m*, -na *f* (monarca) **2** : soberano *m* (moneda)

sovereignty ['savərənti] *n*, *pl* **-ties** : soberanía *f*

Soviet ['soːviˌɛt, 'sa-, -viət] *adj* : soviético

sow[1] ['soː] *vt* **sowed; sown** ['soːn] *or* **sowed; sowing** **1** PLANT : sembrar **2** SCATTER : esparcir

sow[2] ['saʊ] *n* : cerda *f*

sox → **sock**

soy ['sɔɪ] *n* : soya *f*, soja *f*

soybean ['sɔɪˌbiːn] *n* : soya *f*, soja *f*

spa ['spa] *n* : balneario *m*

space[1] ['speɪs] *vt* **spaced; spacing** : espaciar

space[2] *n* **1** PERIOD : espacio *m*, lapso *m*, período *m* **2** ROOM : espacio *m*, sitio *m*, lugar *m* ⟨is there space for me? : ¿hay sitio para mí?⟩ **3** : espacio *m* ⟨blank space : espacio en blanco⟩ **4** : espacio *m* (en física) **5** PLACE : plaza *f*, sitio *m* ⟨to reserve space : reservar plazas⟩ ⟨parking space : sitio para estacionarse⟩

spacecraft ['speɪsˌkræft] *n* : nave *f* espacial

spaceflight ['speɪsˌflaɪt] *n* : vuelo *m* espacial

spaceman ['speɪsmən, -ˌmæn] *n, pl* **-men** [-mən, -ˌmɛn] : astronauta *m*, cosmonauta *m*
spaceship ['speɪsˌʃɪp] *n* : nave *f* espacial
space shuttle *n* : transbordador *m* espacial
space suit *n* : traje *m* espacial
spacious ['speɪʃəs] *adj* : espacioso, amplio
spade[1] ['speɪd] *v* **spaded; spading** *vt* : palear — *vi* : usar una pala
spade[2] *n* **1** SHOVEL : pala *f* **2** : pica *f* (naipe)
spaghetti [spə'gɛti] *n* : espagueti *m*, espaguetis *mpl*, spaghetti *mpl*
spam ['spæm] *n* : spam *m*, correo *m* electrónico no solicitado
span[1] ['spæn] *vt* **spanned; spanning** : abarcar (un período de tiempo), extenderse sobre (un espacio)
span[2] *n* **1** : lapso *m*, espacio *m* (de tiempo) ⟨life span : duración de la vida⟩ **2** : luz *f* (entre dos soportes)
spangle ['spæŋgəl] *n* : lentejuela *f*
Spaniard ['spænjərd] *n* : español *m*, -ñola *f*
spaniel ['spænjəl] *n* : spaniel *m*
Spanish[1] ['spænɪʃ] *adj* : español
Spanish[2] *n* **1** : español *m* (idioma) **2 the Spanish** *npl* : los españoles
spank ['spæŋk] *vt* : darle nalgadas (a alguien)
spar[1] ['spɑr] *vi* **sparred; sparring** : entrenarse (en boxeo)
spar[2] *n* : palo *m*, verga *f* (de un barco)
spare[1] ['spær] *vt* **spared; sparing 1** : perdonar ⟨to spare someone's life : perdonarle la vida a alguien⟩ **2** SAVE : ahorrar, evitar ⟨I'll spare you the trouble : le evitaré la molestia⟩ **3** : prescindir de ⟨I can't spare her : no puedo prescindir de ella⟩ ⟨can you spare a dollar? : ¿me das un dólar?⟩ **4** STINT : escatimar ⟨they spared no expense : no repararon en gastos⟩ **5 to spare** : de sobra
spare[2] *adj* **1** : de repuesto, de recambio ⟨spare tire : llanta de repuesto⟩ **2** EXCESS : de más, de sobra ⟨spare time : tiempo libre⟩ **3** LEAN : delgado
spare[3] *n or* **spare part** : repuesto *m*, recambio *m*
sparing ['spærɪŋ] *adj* : parco, económico — **sparingly** *adv*
spark[1] ['spɑrk] *vi* : chispear, echar chispas — *vt* PROVOKE : despertar, provocar ⟨to spark interest : despertar interés⟩
spark[2] *n* **1** : chispa *f* ⟨to throw off sparks : echar chispas⟩ **2** GLIMMER, TRACE : destello *m*, pizca *f*
sparkle[1] ['spɑrkəl] *vi* **-kled; -kling 1** FLASH, SHINE : destellar, centellear, brillar **2** : estar muy animado (dícese de una conversación, etc.)
sparkle[2] *n* : destello *m*, centelleo *m*
sparkler ['spɑrklər] *n* : luz *f* de bengala
spark plug *n* : bujía *f*

sparrow ['spæro:] *n* : gorrión *m*
sparse ['spɑrs] *adj* **sparser; -est** : escaso — **sparsely** *adv*
spasm ['spæzəm] *n* **1** : espasmo *m* (muscular) **2** BURST, FIT : arrebato *m*
spasmodic [spæz'mɑdɪk] *adj* **1** : espasmódico **2** SPORADIC : irregular, esporádico — **spasmodically** [-dɪkli] *adv*
spastic ['spæstɪk] *adj* : espástico
spat[1] → **spit**[1]
spat[2] ['spæt] *n* : discusión *f*, disputa *f*, pelea *f*
spatial ['speɪʃəl] *adj* : espacial
spatter[1] ['spætər] *v* : salpicar
spatter[2] *n* : salpicadura *f*
spatula ['spætʃələ] *n* : espátula *f*, paleta *f* (para servir)
spawn[1] ['spɔn] *vi* : desovar, frezar — *vt* GENERATE : generar, producir
spawn[2] *n* : hueva *f*, freza *f*
spay ['speɪ] *vt* : esterilizar (una perra, etc.)
speak ['spi:k] *v* **spoke** ['spo:k]; **spoken** ['spo:kən]; **speaking** *vi* **1** TALK : hablar ⟨to speak to someone : hablar con alguien⟩ ⟨who's speaking? : ¿de parte de quien?⟩ ⟨so to speak : por así decirlo⟩ **2 to speak out** : hablar claramente **3 to speak out against** : denunciar **4 to speak up** : hablar en voz alta **5 to speak up for** : defender — *vt* **1** SAY : decir ⟨she spoke her mind : habló con franqueza⟩ **2** : hablar (un idioma)
speaker ['spi:kər] *n* **1** : hablante *mf* ⟨a native speaker : un hablante nativo⟩ **2** : orador *m*, -dora *f* ⟨the keynote speaker : el orador principal⟩ **3** LOUDSPEAKER : altavoz *m*, altoparlante *m*
spear[1] ['spɪr] *vt* : atravesar con una lanza
spear[2] *n* : lanza *f*
spearhead[1] ['spɪrˌhɛd] *vt* : encabezar
spearhead[2] *n* : punta *f* de lanza
spearmint ['spɪrmɪnt] *n* : menta *f* verde
special ['spɛʃəl] *adj* : especial ⟨nothing special : nada en especial, nada en particular⟩ — **specially** *adv*
specialist ['spɛʃəlɪst] *n* : especialista *mf*
specialization [ˌspɛʃələ'zeɪʃən] *n* : especialización *f*
specialize ['spɛʃəˌlaɪz] *vi* **-ized; -izing** : especializarse
specialty ['spɛʃəlti] *n, pl* **-ties** : especialidad *f*
species ['spi:ˌʃi:z, -ˌsi:z] *ns & pl* : especie *f*
specific [spɪ'sɪfɪk] *adj* : específico, determinado — **specifically** [-fɪkli] *adv*
specification [ˌspɛsəfə'keɪʃən] *n* : especificación *f*
specify ['spɛsəˌfaɪ] *vt* **-fied; -fying** : especificar
specimen ['spɛsəmən] *n* **1** SAMPLE : espécimen *m*, muestra *f* **2** EXAMPLE : espécimen *m*, ejemplar *m*
speck ['spɛk] *n* **1** SPOT : manchita *f* **2** BIT, TRACE : mota *f*, pizca *f*, ápice *m*
speckled ['spɛkəld] *adj* : moteado

spectacle ['spɛktɪkəl] n 1 : espectáculo m 2 **spectacles** npl GLASSES : lentes fpl, gafas fpl, anteojos mpl, espejuelos mpl

spectacular [spɛk'tækjələr] adj : espectacular

spectator ['spɛk,teɪtər] n : espectador m, -dora f

specter or **spectre** ['spɛktər] n : espectro m, fantasma m

spectrum ['spɛktrəm] n, pl **spectra** [-trə] or **spectrums** 1 : espectro m (de colores, etc.) 2 RANGE : gama f, abanico m

speculate ['spɛkjə,leɪt] vi -**lated; -lating** 1 : especular (en finanzas) 2 WONDER : preguntarse, hacer conjeturas

speculation [,spɛkjə'leɪʃən] n : especulación f

speculative ['spɛkjə,leɪtɪv] adj : especulativo

speculator ['spɛkjə,leɪtər] n : especulador m, -dora f

speech ['spi:tʃ] n 1 : habla f, modo m de hablar, expresión f 2 ADDRESS : discurso m

speechless ['spi:tʃləs] adj : enmudecido, estupefacto

speed¹ ['spi:d] v **sped** ['spɛd] or **speeded; speeding** vi 1 : ir a toda velocidad, correr a toda prisa ⟨he sped off : se fue a toda velocidad⟩ 2 : conducir a exceso de velocidad ⟨a ticket for speeding : una multa por exceso de velocidad⟩ — vt **to speed up** : acelerar

speed² n 1 SWIFTNESS : rapidez f 2 VELOCITY : velocidad f

speedboat ['spi:d,bo:t] n : lancha f motora

speed bump n : badén m

speed limit n : velocidad f máxima, límite m de velocidad

speedometer [spɪ'dɑmətər] n : velocímetro m

speedup ['spi:d,ʌp] n : aceleración f

speedy ['spi:di] adj **speedier; -est** : rápido — **speedily** [-dəli] adv

spell¹ ['spɛl] vt 1 : escribir, deletrear (verbalmente) ⟨how do you spell it? : ¿cómo se escribe?, ¿cómo se deletrea?⟩ 2 MEAN : significar ⟨that could spell trouble : eso puede significar problemas⟩ 3 RELIEVE : relevar

spell² n 1 TURN : turno m 2 PERIOD, TIME : período m (de tiempo) 3 ENCHANTMENT : encanto m, hechizo m, maleficio m

spellbound ['spɛl,baʊnd] adj : embelesado

speller ['spɛlər] n : persona f que escribe ⟨she's a good speller : tiene buena ortografía⟩

spelling ['spɛlɪŋ] n : ortografía f

spend ['spɛnd] vt **spent** ['spɛnt]; **spending** 1 : gastar (dinero, etc.) 2 PASS : pasar (el tiempo) ⟨to spend time on : dedicar tiempo a⟩

spendthrift ['spɛnd,θrɪft] n : derrochador m, -dora f; despilfarrador m, -dora f

sperm ['spərm] n, pl **sperm** or **sperms** : esperma mf

spew ['spju:] vi : salir a chorros — vt : vomitar, arrojar (lava, etc.)

sphere ['sfɪr] n : esfera f

spherical ['sfɪrɪkəl, 'sfɛr-] adj : esférico

spice¹ ['spaɪs] vt **spiced; spicing** 1 SEASON : condimentar, sazonar 2 or **to spice up** : salpimentar, hacer más interesante

spice² n 1 : especia f 2 FLAVOR, INTEREST : sabor m ⟨the spice of life : la sal de la vida⟩

spick–and–span ['spɪkənd'spæn] adj : limpio y ordenado

spicy ['spaɪsi] adj **spicier; -est** 1 SPICED : condimentado, sazonado 2 HOT : picante 3 RACY : picante

spider ['spaɪdər] n : araña f

spigot ['spɪgət, -kət] n : llave f, grifo m, canilla Arg, Uru

spike¹ ['spaɪk] vt **spiked; spiking** 1 FASTEN : clavar (con clavos grandes) 2 PIERCE : atravesar 3 : añadir alcohol a ⟨he spiked her drink with rum : le puso ron a la bebida⟩

spike² n 1 : clavo m grande 2 CLEAT : clavo m 3 : remache m (en voleibol) 4 PEAK : pico m

spill¹ ['spɪl] vt 1 SHED : derramar, verter ⟨to spill blood : derrame sangre⟩ 2 DIVULGE : revelar, divulgar — vi : derramarse

spill² n 1 SPILLING : derrame m, vertido m ⟨oil spill : derrame de petróleo⟩ 2 FALL : caída f

spin¹ ['spɪn] v **spun** ['spʌn]; **spinning** vi 1 : hilar 2 TURN : girar 3 REEL : dar vueltas ⟨my head is spinning : la cabeza me está dando vueltas⟩ — vt 1 : hilar (hilo, etc.) 2 : tejer ⟨to spin a web : tejer una telaraña⟩ 3 TWIRL : hacer girar

spin² n : vuelta f, giro m ⟨to go for a spin : dar una vuelta (en coche)⟩

spinach ['spɪnɪtʃ] n : espinacas fpl, espinaca f

spinal column ['spaɪnəl] n BACKBONE : columna f vertebral

spinal cord n : médula f espinal

spindle ['spɪndəl] n 1 : huso m (para hilar) 2 : eje m (de un mecanismo)

spindly ['spɪndli] adj : larguirucho fam, largo y débil (dícese de una planta)

spine ['spaɪn] n 1 BACKBONE : columna f vertebral, espina f dorsal 2 QUILL : púa f (de un animal) 3 THORN : espina f 4 : lomo m (de un libro)

spineless ['spaɪnləs] adj 1 : sin púas, sin espinas 2 INVERTEBRATE : invertebrado 3 WEAK : débil (de carácter)

spinet ['spɪnət] n : espineta f

spinster ['spɪntstər] n : soltera f

spiny ['spaɪni] adj **spinier; -est** : con púas (dícese de los animales), espinoso (dícese de las plantas)

spiral[1] ['spaɪrəl] *vi* **-raled** *or* **-ralled; -raling** *or* **-ralling** : ir en espiral

spiral[2] *adj* : espiral, en espiral ⟨a spiral staircase : una escalera de caracol⟩

spiral[3] *n* : espiral *f*

spire ['spaɪr] *n* : aguja *f*

spirit[1] ['spɪrət] *vt* **to spirit away** : hacer desaparecer

spirit[2] *n* **1** : espíritu *m* ⟨body and spirit : cuerpo y espíritu⟩ **2** GHOST : espíritu *m*, fantasma *m* **3** MOOD : espíritu *m*, humor *m* ⟨in the spirit of friendship : en el espíritu de amistad⟩ ⟨to be in good spirits : estar de buen humor⟩ **4** ENTHUSIASM, VIVACITY : espíritu *m*, ánimo *m*, brío *m* **5 spirits** *npl* : licores *mpl*

spirited ['spɪrətəd] *adj* : animado, energético

spiritless ['spɪrətləs] *adj* : desanimado

spiritual[1] ['spɪrɪtʃuəl, -tʃəl] *adj* : espiritual — **spiritually** *adv*

spiritual[2] *n* : espiritual *m* (canción)

spiritualism ['spɪrɪtʃuə,lɪzəm, -tʃə-] *n* : espiritismo *m*

spirituality [,spɪrɪtʃu'ælət̪i] *n, pl* **-ties** : espiritualidad *f*

spit[1] ['spɪt] *v* **spit** *or* **spat** ['spæt]; **spitting** : escupir

spit[2] *n* **1** SALIVA : saliva *f* **2** ROTISSERIE : asador *m* **3** POINT : lengua *f* (de tierra)

spite[1] ['spaɪt] *vt* **spited; spiting** : fastidiar, molestar

spite[2] *n* **1** : despecho *m*, rencor *m* **2 in spite of** : a pesar de (que), pese a (que)

spiteful ['spaɪtfəl] *adj* : malicioso, rencoroso

spitting image *n* **to be the spitting image of** : ser el vivo retrato de

spittle ['spɪtəl] *n* : saliva *f*

splash[1] ['splæʃ] *vt* : salpicar — *vi* **1** : salpicar **2 to splash around** : chapotear

splash[2] *n* **1** SPLASHING : salpicadura *f* **2** SQUIRT : chorrito *m* **3** SPOT : mancha *f*

splatter ['splætər] → **spatter**

splay ['spleɪ] *vt* : extender (hacia afuera) ⟨to splay one's fingers : abrir los dedos⟩ — *vi* : extenderse (hacia afuera)

spleen ['spli:n] *n* **1** : bazo *m* (órgano) **2** ANGER, SPITE : ira *f*, rencor *m*

splendid ['splendəd] *adj* : espléndido — **splendidly** *adv*

splendor ['splendər] *n* : esplendor *m*

splice[1] ['splaɪs] *vt* **spliced; splicing** : empalmar, unir

splice[2] *n* : empalme *m*, unión *f*

splint ['splɪnt] *n* : tablilla *f*

splinter[1] ['splɪntər] *vt* : astillar — *vi* : astillarse

splinter[2] *n* : astilla *f*

split[1] ['splɪt] *v* **split; splitting** *vt* **1** CLEAVE : partir, hender ⟨to split wood : partir madera⟩ **2** BURST : romper, rajar ⟨to split open : abrir⟩ **3** DIVIDE, SHARE : dividir, repartir — *vi* **1** : partirse (dícese de la madera, etc.) **2** BURST, CRACK : romperse, rajarse **3** *or* **to split up** : dividirse

split[2] *n* **1** CRACK : rajadura *f* **2** TEAR : rotura *f* **3** DIVISION : división *f*, escisión *f*

splurge[1] ['splərdʒ] *v* **splurged; splurging** *vt* : derrochar — *vi* : derrochar dinero

splurge[2] *n* : derroche *m*

spoil[1] ['spɔɪl] *vt* **1** PILLAGE : saquear **2** RUIN : estropear, arruinar **3** PAMPER : consentir, mimar — *vi* : estropearse, echarse a perder

spoil[2] *n* PLUNDER : botín *m*

spoke[1] → **speak**

spoke[2] ['spo:k] *n* : rayo *m* (de una rueda)

spoken → **speak**

spokesman ['spo:ksmən] *n, pl* **-men** [-mən, -,mɛn] : portavoz *mf*; vocero *m*, -ra *f*

spokeswoman ['spo:ks,wʊmən] *n, pl* **-women** [-,wɪmən] : portavoz *f*, vocera *f*

sponge[1] ['spʌndʒ] *vt* **sponged; sponging** : limpiar con una esponja

sponge[2] *n* : esponja *f*

spongy ['spʌndʒi] *adj* **spongier; -est** : esponjoso

sponsor[1] ['spantsər] *vt* : patrocinar, auspiciar, apadrinar (a una persona)

sponsor[2] *n* : patrocinador *m*, -dora *f*; padrino *m*, madrina *f*

sponsorship ['spantsər,ʃɪp] *n* : patrocinio *m*, apadrinamiento *m*

spontaneity [,spantə'ni:əti, -'neɪ-] *n* : espontaneidad *f*

spontaneous [span'teɪniəs] *adj* : espontáneo — **spontaneously** *adv*

spoof ['spu:f] *n* : burla *f*, parodia *f*

spook[1] ['spu:k] *vt* : asustar

spook[2] *n* : fantasma *m*, espíritu *m*, espectro *m*

spooky ['spu:ki] *adj* **spookier; -est** : que da miedo, espeluzante

spool ['spu:l] *n* : carrete *m*

spoon[1] ['spu:n] *vt* : comer, servir, o echar con cuchara

spoon[2] *n* : cuchara *f*

spoonful ['spu:n,fʊl] *n* : cucharada *f* ⟨by the spoonful : a cucharadas⟩

spoor ['spʊr, 'spɔr] *n* : rastro *m*, pista *f*

sporadic [spə'rædɪk] *adj* : esporádico — **sporadically** [-dɪkli] *adv*

spore ['spɔr] *n* : espora *f*

sport[1] ['sport] *vi* FROLIC : retozar, juguetear — *vt* SHOW OFF : lucir, ostentar

sport[2] *n* **1** : deporte *m* ⟨outdoor sports : deportes al aire libre⟩ **2** JEST : broma *f* **3 to be a good sport** : tener espíritu deportivo

sporting ['sportɪŋ] *adj* : deportivo ⟨a sporting chance : buenas posibilidades⟩

sportsman ['sportsmən] *n, pl* **-men** [-mən, -,mɛn] : deportista *m*

sportsmanship ['sportsmən‚ʃɪp] *n* : espíritu *m* deportivo, deportividad *f* *Spain*

sportswoman ['sports‚wʊmən] *n, pl* **-women** [-‚wɪmən] : deportista *f*

sporty ['sporṭi] *adj* **sportier; -est** : deportivo

spot¹ ['spɑt] *v* **spotted; spotting** *vt* **1** STAIN : manchar **2** RECOGNIZE, SEE : ver, reconocer ⟨to spot an error : descubrir un error⟩ — *vi* : mancharse

spot² *adj* : hecho al azar ⟨a spot check : un vistazo, un control aleatorio⟩

spot³ *n* **1** STAIN : mancha *f* **2** DOT : punto *m* **3** PIMPLE : grano *m* ⟨to break out in spots : salirle granos a alguien⟩ **4** PREDICAMENT : apuro *m*, aprieto *m*, lío *m* ⟨in a tight spot : en apuros⟩ **5** PLACE : lugar *m*, sitio *m* ⟨to be on the spot : estar en el lugar⟩

spotless ['spɑtləs] *adj* : impecable, inmaculado — **spotlessly** *adv*

spotlight¹ ['spɑt‚laɪt] *vt* **-lighted** *or* **-lit** [-‚lɪt]; **-lighting 1** LIGHT : iluminar (con un reflector) **2** HIGHLIGHT : destacar, poner en relieve

spotlight² *n* **1** : reflector *m*, foco *m* **2** **to be in the spotlight** : ser el centro de atención

spotty ['spɑṭi] *adj* **spottier; -est** : irregular, desigual

spouse ['spaʊs] *n* : cónyuge *mf*

spout¹ ['spaʊt] *vt* **1** : lanzar chorros de **2** DECLAIM : declamar — *vi* : salir a chorros

spout² *n* **1** : pico *m* (de una jarra, etc.) **2** STREAM : chorro *m*

sprain¹ ['spreɪn] *vt* : sufrir un esguince en

sprain² *n* : esguince *m*, torcedura *f*

sprawl¹ ['sprɔl] *vi* **1** LIE : tumbarse, echarse, despatarrarse **2** EXTEND : extenderse

sprawl² *n* **1** : postura *f* despatarrada **2** SPREAD : extensión *f*, expansión *f*

spray¹ ['spreɪ] *vt* : rociar (una superficie), pulverizar (un líquido)

spray² *n* **1** BOUQUET : ramillete *m* **2** MIST : rocío *m* **3** ATOMIZER : atomizador *m*, pulverizador *m*

spray gun *n* : pistola *f*

spread¹ ['sprɛd] *v* **spread; spreading** *vt* **1** *or* **to spread out** : desplegar, extender **2** SCATTER, STREW : esparcir **3** SMEAR : untar (mantequilla, etc.) **4** DISSEMINATE : difundir, sembrar, propagar — *vi* **1** : difundirse, correr, propagarse **2** EXTEND : extenderse

spread² *n* **1** EXTENSION : extensión *f*, difusión *f* (de noticias, etc.), propagación *f* (de enfermedades, etc.) **2** : colcha *f* (para una cama), mantel *m* (para una mesa) **3** PASTE : pasta *f* ⟨cheese spread : pasta de queso⟩

spreadsheet ['sprɛd‚ʃi:t] *n* : hoja *f* de cálculo

spree ['spri] *n* **1** : acción *f* desenfrenada ⟨to go on a shopping spree : comprar como loco⟩ **2** BINGE : parranda *f*, juerga *f* ⟨on a spree : de parranda, de juerga⟩

sprig ['sprɪg] *n* : ramita *f*, ramito *m*

sprightly ['spraɪtli] *adj* **sprightlier; -est** : vivo, animado ⟨with a sprightly step : con paso ligero⟩

spring¹ ['sprɪŋ] *v* **sprang** ['spræŋ] *or* **sprung** ['sprʌŋ]; **sprung; springing** *vi* **1** LEAP : saltar **2** : mover rápidamente ⟨the lid sprang shut : la tapa se cerró de un golpe⟩ ⟨he sprang to his feet : se paró de un salto⟩ **3 to spring up** : brotar (dícese de las plantas), surgir **4 to spring from** : surgir de — *vt* **1** RELEASE : soltar (de repente) ⟨to spring the news on someone : sorprender a alguien con las noticias⟩ ⟨to spring a trap : hacer saltar una trampa⟩ **2** ACTIVATE : accionar (un mecanismo) **3 to spring a leak** : hacer agua

spring² *n* **1** SOURCE : fuente *f*, origen *m* **2** : manantial *m*, fuente *f* ⟨hot spring : fuente termal⟩ **3** : primavera *f* ⟨spring and summer : la primavera y el verano⟩ **4** : resorte *m*, muelle *m* (de metal, etc.) **5** LEAP : salto *m*, brinco *m* **6** RESILIENCE : elasticidad *f*

springboard ['sprɪŋ‚bord] *n* : trampolín *m*

springtime ['sprɪŋ‚taɪm] *n* : primavera *f*

springy ['sprɪŋi] *adj* **springier; -est 1** RESILIENT : elástico **2** LIVELY : enérgico

sprinkle¹ ['sprɪŋkəl] *vt* **-kled; -kling** : rociar (con agua), espolvorear (con azúcar, etc.), salpicar

sprinkle² *n* : llovizna *f*

sprinkler ['sprɪŋkələr] *n* : rociador *m*, aspersor *m*

sprint¹ ['sprɪnt] *vi* : echar la carrera, esprintar (en deportes)

sprint² *n* : esprint *m* (en deportes)

sprinter ['sprɪntər] *n* : esprínter *mf*

sprite ['spraɪt] *n* : hada *f*, elfo *m*

sprocket ['sprɑkət] *n* : diente *m* (de una rueda dentada)

sprout¹ ['spraʊt] *vi* : brotar

sprout² *n* : brote *m*, retoño *m*, vástago *m*

spruce¹ ['spru:s] *v* **spruced; sprucing** *vt* : arreglar — *vi or* **to spruce up** : arreglarse, acicalarse

spruce² *adj* **sprucer; sprucest** : pulcro, arreglado

spruce³ *n* : picea *f* (árbol)

spry ['spraɪ] *adj* **sprier** *or* **spryer** ['spraɪər]; **spriest** *or* **spryest** ['spraɪəst] : ágil, activo

spun → **spin**

spunk ['spʌŋk] *n* : valor *m*, coraje *m*, agallas *fpl fam*

spunky ['spʌŋki] *adj* **spunkier; -est** : animoso, corajudo

spur¹ ['spər] *vt* **spurred; spurring** *or* **to spur on** : espolear (un caballo), motivar (a una persona, etc.)

spur² *n* **1** : espuela *f*, acicate *m* **2** STIM-ULUS : acicate *m* **3** : espolón *m* (de aves gallináceas)

spurious ['spjʊriəs] *adj* : espurio

spurn ['spərn] *vt* : desdeñar, rechazar

spurt¹ ['spərt] *vt* SQUIRT : lanzar un chorro de — *vi* SPOUT : salir a chorros

spurt² *n* **1** : actividad *f* repentina ⟨a spurt of energy : una explosión de energía⟩ ⟨to do in spurts : hacer por rachas⟩ **2** JET : chorro *m* (de agua, etc.)

sputter¹ ['spʌtər] *vi* **1** JABBER : farfullar **2** : chisporrotear (dícese de la grasa, etc.), petardear (dícese de un motor)

sputter² *n* **1** JABBER : farfulla *f* **2** : chisporroteo *m* (de grasa, etc.), petardeo *m* (de un motor)

spy¹ ['spaɪ] *v* **spied; spying** *vt* SEE : ver, divisar — *vi* : espiar ⟨to spy on someone : espiar a alguien⟩

spy² *n* : espía *mf*

squab ['skwɑb] *n, pl* **squabs** *or* **squab** : pichón *m*

squabble¹ ['skwɑbəl] *vi* **-bled; -bling** : reñir, pelearse, discutir

squabble² *n* : riña *f*, pelea *f*, discusión *f*

squad ['skwɑd] *n* : pelotón *m* (militar), brigada *f* (de policías), cuadrilla *f* (de obreros, etc.)

squadron ['skwɑdrən] *n* : escuadrón *m* (de militares), escuadrilla *f* (de aviones), escuadra *f* (de naves)

squalid ['skwɑlɪd] *adj* : miserable

squall ['skwɔl] *n* **1** : aguacero *m* tormentoso, chubasco *m* tormentoso **2** **snow squall** : tormenta *f* de nieve

squalor ['skwɑlər] *n* : miseria *f*

squander ['skwɑndər] *vt* : derrochar (dinero, etc.), desaprovechar (una oportunidad, etc.), desperdiciar (talentos, energías, etc.)

square¹ ['skwær] *vt* **squared; squaring 1** : cuadrar **2** : elevar al cuadrado (en matemáticas) **3** CONFORM : conciliar (con), ajustar (con) **4** SETTLE : saldar (una cuenta) ⟨I squared it with him : lo arreglé con él⟩

square² *adj* **squarer; -est 1** : cuadrado ⟨a square house : una casa cuadrada⟩ **2** RIGHT-ANGLED : a escuadra, en ángulo recto **3** : cuadrado (en matemáticas) ⟨a square mile : una milla cuadrada⟩ **4** HONEST : justo ⟨a square deal : un buen acuerdo⟩ ⟨fair and square : en buena lid⟩

square³ *n* **1** : escuadra *f* (instrumento) **2** : cuadrado *m*, cuadro *m* ⟨to fold into squares : plegar en cuadrados⟩ **3** : plaza *f* (de una ciudad) **4** : cuadrado *m* (en matemáticas)

squarely ['skwærli] *adv* **1** EXACTLY : exactamente, directamente, justo **2** HONESTLY : honradamente, justamente

square root *n* : raíz *f* cuadrada

squash¹ ['skwɑʃ, 'skwɔʃ] *vt* **1** CRUSH : aplastar **2** SUPPRESS : acallar (protestas), sofocar (una rebelión)

squash² *n* **1** *pl* **squashes** *or* **squash** : calabaza *f* (vegetal) **2** *or* **squash racquets** : squash *m* (deporte)

squat¹ ['skwɑt] *vi* **squatted; squatting 1** CROUCH : agacharse, ponerse en cuclillas **2** : ocupar un lugar sin derecho

squat² *adj* **squatter; squattest** : bajo y ancho, rechoncho *fam* (dícese de una persona)

squat³ *n* **1** : posición *f* en cuclillas **2** : ocupación *f* ilegal (de un lugar)

squaw ['skwɔ] *n* : india *f* (norteamericana)

squawk¹ ['skwɔk] *vi* : graznar (dícese de las aves), chillar

squawk² *n* : graznido *m* (de un ave), chillido *m*

squeak¹ ['skwi:k] *vi* : chillar (dícese de un animal), chirriar (dícese de un objeto)

squeak² *n* : chillido *m*, chirrido *m*

squeaky ['skwi:ki] *adj* **squeakier; -est** : chirriante ⟨a squeaky voice : una voz chillona⟩

squeal¹ ['skwi:l] *vi* **1** : chillar (dícese de las personas o los animales), chirriar (dícese de los frenos, etc.) **2** PROTEST : quejarse

squeal² *n* **1** : chillido *m* (de una persona o un animal) **2** SCREECH : chirrido *m* (de frenos, etc.)

squeamish ['skwi:mɪʃ] *adj* : impresionable, sensible ⟨he's squeamish about cockroaches : las cucarachas le dan asco⟩

squeeze¹ ['skwi:z] *vt* **squeezed; squeezing 1** PRESS : apretar, exprimir (naranjas, etc.) **2** EXTRACT : extraer (jugo, etc.)

squeeze² *n* : apretón *m*

squelch ['skwelʧ] *vt* : aplastar (una rebelión, etc.)

squid ['skwɪd] *n, pl* **squid** *or* **squids** : calamar *m*

squint¹ ['skwɪnt] *vi* : mirar con los ojos entornados

squint² *adj or* **squint–eyed** ['skwɪnt‚aɪd] : bizco

squint³ *n* : ojos *mpl* bizcos, bizquera *f*

squire ['skwaɪr] *n* : hacendado *m*, -da *f*; terrateniente *mf*

squirm ['skwərm] *vi* : retorcerse

squirrel ['skwərəl] *n* : ardilla *f*

squirt¹ ['skwərt] *vt* : lanzar un chorro de — *vi* SPURT : salir a chorros

squirt² *n* : chorrito *m*

stab¹ [stæb] *vt* **stabbed; stabbing 1** KNIFE : acuchillar, apuñalar **2** STICK : clavar (con una aguja, etc.), golpear (con el dedo, etc.)

stab² *n* **1** : puñalada *f*, cuchillada *f* **2** JAB : pinchazo *m* (con una aguja, etc.), golpe *m* (con un dedo, etc.) **3 to take a stab at** : intentar

stability [stə'bɪləti] *n, pl* **-ties** : estabilidad *f*

stabilize ['steɪbə‚laɪz] *v* **-lized; -lizing** *vt* : estabilizar — *vi* : estabilizarse

stable[1] ['steɪbəl] *vt* **-bled; -bling** : poner (ganado) en un establo, poner (caballos) en una caballeriza

stable[2] *adj* **-bler; -blest 1** FIXED, STEADY : fijo, sólido, estable 2 LASTING : estable, perdurable ⟨a stable government : un gobierno estable⟩ 3 : estacionario (en medicina), equilibrado (en psicología)

stable[3] *n* : establo *m* (para ganado), caballeriza *f* o cuadra *f* (para caballos)

staccato [stə'kɑto:] *adj* : staccato

stack[1] ['stæk] *vt* **1** PILE : amontonar, apilar **2** COVER : cubrir, llenar ⟨he stacked the table with books : cubrió la mesa de libros⟩

stack[2] *n* **1** PILE : montón *m*, pila *f* **2** SMOKESTACK : chimenea *f*

stadium ['steɪdiəm] *n, pl* **-dia** [-diə] *or* **-diums** : estadio *m*

staff[1] ['stæf] *vt* : proveer de personal

staff[2] *n, pl* **staffs** ['stæfs, stævz] *or* **staves** ['stævz, 'steɪvz] **1** : bastón *m* (de mando), báculo *m* (de obispo) **2** *pl* **staffs** PERSONNEL : personal *m* **3** *or* **stave** : pentagrama *m* (en música)

stag[1] ['stæg] *adv* : solo, sin pareja ⟨to go stag : ir solo⟩

stag[2] *adj* : sólo para hombres

stag[3] *n, pl* **stags** *or* **stag** : ciervo *m*, venado *m*

stage[1] ['steɪdʒ] *vt* **staged; staging** : poner en escena (una obra de teatro)

stage[2] *n* **1** PLATFORM : estrado *m*, tablado *m*, escenario *m* (de un teatro) **2** PHASE, STEP : fase *f*, etapa *f* ⟨stage of development : fase de desarrollo⟩ ⟨in stages : por etapas⟩ **3 the stage** : el teatro *m*

stagecoach ['steɪdʒ,koːtʃ] *n* : diligencia *f*

stagger[1] ['stægər] *vi* TOTTER : tambalearse — *vt* **1** ALTERNATE : alternar, escalonar (turnos de trabajo) **2** : hacer tambalear ⟨to be staggered by : quedarse estupefacto por⟩

stagger[2] *n* : tambaleo *m*

staggering ['stægərɪŋ] *adj* : asombroso

stagnant ['stægnənt] *adj* : estancado

stagnate ['stæg,neɪt] *vi* **-nated; -nating** : estancarse

staid ['steɪd] *adj* : serio, sobrio

stain[1] ['steɪn] *vt* **1** DISCOLOR : manchar **2** DYE : teñir (madera, etc.) **3** SULLY : manchar, empañar

stain[2] *n* **1** SPOT : mancha *f* **2** DYE : tinte *m*, tintura *f* **3** BLEMISH : mancha *f*, mácula *f*

stainless ['steɪnləs] *adj* : sin mancha ⟨stainless steel : acero inoxidable⟩

stair ['stær] *n* **1** STEP : escalón *m*, peldaño *m* **2 stairs** *npl* : escalera *f*, escaleras *fpl*

staircase ['stær,keɪs] *n* : escalera *f*, escaleras *fpl*

stairway ['stær,weɪ] *n* : escalera *f*, escaleras *fpl*

stake[1] ['steɪk] *vt* **staked; staking 1** : estacar, marcar con estacas (una propiedad) **2** BET : jugarse, apostar **3 to stake a claim to** : reclamar, reivindicar

stake[2] *n* **1** POST : estaca *f* **2** BET : apuesta *f* ⟨to be at stake : estar en juego⟩ **3** INTEREST, SHARE : interés *m*, participación *f*

stalactite [stə'læk,taɪt] *n* : estalactita *f*

stalagmite [stə'læg,maɪt] *n* : estalagmita *f*

stale ['steɪl] *adj* **staler; stalest** : viejo ⟨stale bread : pan duro⟩ ⟨stale news : viejas noticias⟩

stalemate ['steɪl,meɪt] *n* : punto *m* muerto, impasse *m*

stalk[1] ['stɔk] *vt* : acechar — *vi* : caminar rígidamente (por orgullo, ira, etc.)

stalk[2] *n* : tallo *m* (de una planta)

stall[1] ['stɔl] *vt* **1** : parar (un motor) **2** DELAY : entretener (a una persona), demorar — *vi* **1** : pararse (dícese de un motor) **2** DELAY : demorar, andar con rodeos

stall[2] *n* **1** : compartimiento *m* (de un establo) **2** : puesto *m* (en un mercado), etc.)

stallion ['stæljən] *n* : caballo *m* semental

stalwart ['stɔlwərt] *adj* **1** STRONG : fuerte ⟨a stalwart supporter : un firme partidario⟩ **2** BRAVE : valiente, valeroso

stamen ['steɪmən] *n* : estambre *m*

stamina ['stæmənə] *n* : resistencia *f*

stammer[1] ['stæmər] *vi* : tartamudear, titubear

stammer[2] *n* : tartamudeo *m*, titubeo *m*

stamp[1] ['stæmp] *vt* **1** : pisotear (con los pies) ⟨to stamp one's feet : patear, dar una patada⟩ **2** IMPRESS, IMPRINT : sellar (una factura, etc.), acuñar (monedas) **3** : franquear, ponerle estampillas a (correo)

stamp[2] *n* **1** : sello *m* (para documentos, etc.) **2** DIE : cuño *m* (para monedas) **3** *or* **postage stamp** : sello *m*, estampilla *f*, timbre *m* *CA, Mex*

stampede[1] [stæm'piːd] *vi* **-peded; -peding** : salir en estampida

stampede[2] *n* : estampida *f*

stance ['stænts] *n* : postura *f*

stanch ['stɔntʃ, 'stantʃ] *vt* : detener, estancar (un líquido)

stand[1] ['stænd] *v* **stood** ['stʊd]; **standing** *vi* **1** : estar de pie, estar parado ⟨I was standing on the corner : estaba parada en la esquina⟩ **2** *or* **to stand up** : levantarse, pararse, ponerse de pie **3** (*indicating a specified position or location*) ⟨they stand third in the country : ocupan el tercer lugar en el país⟩ ⟨the machines are standing idle : las máquinas están paradas⟩ **4** (*referring to an opinion*) ⟨how does he stand on the matter? : ¿cuál es su postura respecto al asunto?⟩ **5** BE : estar ⟨the house stands on a hill : la casa está en una colina⟩ **6** CONTINUE : seguir ⟨the order still stands : el mandato sigue vigente⟩ — *vt* **1** PLACE, SET : poner, colocar ⟨he stood them in a row : los colocó en hilera⟩ **2** TOLERATE : aguantar, soportar ⟨he can't stand her : no la puede tragar⟩ **3 to stand firm** : mantenerse firme **4 to stand guard** : hacer la guardia

stand² *n* **1** RESISTANCE : resistencia *f* ⟨to make a stand against : resistir a⟩ **2** BOOTH, STALL : stand *m*, puesto *m*, kiosko *m* (para vender periódicos, etc) **3** BASE : pie *m*, base *f* **4** : grupo *m* (de árboles, etc.) **5** POSITION : posición *f*, postura *f* **6 stands** *npl* GRANDSTAND : tribuna *f*

standard¹ [ˈstændərd] *adj* **1** ESTABLISHED : estándar, oficial ⟨standard measures : medidas oficiales⟩ ⟨standard English : el inglés estándar⟩ **2** NORMAL : normal, estándar, común **3** CLASSIC : estándar, clásico ⟨a standard work : una obra clásica⟩

standard² *n* **1** BANNER : estandarte *m* **2** CRITERION : criterio *m* **3** RULE : estándar *m*, norma *f*, regla *f* **4** LEVEL : nivel *m* ⟨standard of living : nivel de vida⟩ **5** SUPPORT : poste *m*, soporte *m*

standardization [ˌstændərdəˈzeɪʃən] *n* : estandarización *f*

standardize [ˈstændərˌdaɪz] *vt* **-ized; -izing** : estandarizar

standard time *n* : hora *f* oficial

stand by *vt* : atenerse a, cumplir con (una promesa, etc.) — *vi* **1** : mantenerse aparte ⟨to stand by and do nothing : mirar sin hacer nada⟩ **2** : estar preparado, estar listo (para un anuncio, un ataque, etc.)

stand for *vt* **1** REPRESENT : significar **2** PERMIT, TOLERATE : permitir, tolerar

standing [ˈstændɪŋ] *n* **1** POSITION, RANK : posición *f* **2** DURATION : duración *f*

stand out *vi* **1** : destacar(se) ⟨she stands out from the rest : se destaca entre los otros⟩ **2 to stand out against** RESIST : oponerse a

standpoint [ˈstændˌpɔint] *n* : punto *m* de vista

standstill [ˈstændˌstɪl] *n* **1** STOP : detención *f*, paro *m* ⟨to come to a standstill : pararse⟩ **2** DEADLOCK : punto *m* muerto, impasse *m*

stand up *vt* : dejar plantado ⟨he stood me up again : otra vez me dejó plantado⟩ — *vi* **1** ENDURE : durar, resistir **2 to stand up for** : defender **3 to stand up to** : hacerle frente (a alguien)

stank → **stink**

stanza [ˈstænzə] *n* : estrofa *f*

staple¹ [ˈsteɪpəl] *vt* **-pled; -pling** : engrapar, grapar

staple² *adj* : principal, básico ⟨a staple food : un alimento básico⟩

staple³ *n* **1** : producto *m* principal **2** : grapa *f* (para engrapar papeles)

stapler [ˈsteɪplər] *n* : engrapadora *f*, grapadora *f*

star¹ [ˈstɑr] *v* **starred; starring** *vt* **1** : marcar con una estrella o un aster-isco **2** FEATURE : estar protagonizado por — *vi* : tener el papel principal ⟨to star in : protagonizar⟩

star² *n* : estrella *f*

starboard [ˈstɑrbərd] *n* : estribor *m*

starch¹ [ˈstɑrtʃ] *vt* : almidonar

starch² *n* : almidón *m*, fécula *f* (comida)

starchy [ˈstɑrtʃi] *adj* **starchier; -est** : lleno de almidón ⟨a starchy diet : una dieta feculenta⟩

stardom [ˈstɑrdəm] *n* : estrellato *m*

stare¹ [ˈstær] *vi* **stared; staring** : mirar fijamente

stare² *n* : mirada *f* fija

starfish [ˈstɑrˌfɪʃ] *n* : estrella *f* de mar

stark¹ [ˈstɑrk] *adv* : completamente ⟨stark raving mad : loco de remate⟩ ⟨stark naked : completamente desnudo⟩

stark² *adj* **1** ABSOLUTE : absoluto **2** BARREN, DESOLATE : desolado, desierto **3** BARE : desnudo **4** HARSH : severo, duro

starlight [ˈstɑrˌlaɪt] *n* : luz *f* de las estrellas

starling [ˈstɑrlɪŋ] *n* : estornino *m*

starry [ˈstɑri] *adj* **starrier; -est** : estrellado

start¹ [ˈstɑrt] *vi* **1** JUMP : levantarse de un salto, sobresaltarse, dar un respingo **2** BEGIN : empezar, comenzar **3** SET OUT : salir (de viaje, etc.) **4** : arrancar (dícese de un motor) — *vt* **1** BEGIN : empezar, comenzar, iniciar **2** CAUSE : provocar, causar **3** ESTABLISH : fundar, montar, establecer ⟨to start a business : montar un negocio⟩ **4** : arrancar, poner en marcha, encender ⟨to start the car : arrancar el motor⟩

start² *n* **1** JUMP : sobresalto *m*, respingo *m* **2** BEGINNING : principio *m*, comienzo *m* ⟨to get an early start : salir temprano⟩

starter [ˈstɑrtər] *n* **1** : participante *mf* (en una carrera, etc.); jugador *m* titular, jugadora *f* titular (en beisbol, etc.) **2** APPETIZER : entremés *m*, aperitivo *m* **3** *or* **starter motor** : motor *m* de arranque

startle [ˈstɑrtəl] *vt* **-tled; -tling** : asustar, sobresaltar

start–up [ˈstɑrtˌʌp] *adj* : de puesta en marcha

starvation [stɑrˈveɪʃən] *n* : inanición *f*, hambre *f*

starve [ˈstɑrv] *v* **starved; starving** *vi* : morirse de hambre — *vt* : privar de comida

stash [ˈstæʃ] *vt* : esconder, guardar (en un lugar secreto)

stat [ˈstæt] → **statistic**

state¹ [ˈsteɪt] *vt* **stated; stating 1** REPORT : puntualizar, exponer (los hechos, etc.) ⟨state your name : diga su nombre⟩ **2** ESTABLISH, FIX : establecer, fijar

state² *n* **1** CONDITION : estado *m*, condición *f* ⟨a liquid state : un estado líquido⟩ ⟨state of mind : estado de ánimo⟩

⟨in a bad state : en malas condiciones⟩ **2** NATION : estado *m*, nación *f* **3** : estado *m* (dentro de un país) ⟨the States : los Estados Unidos⟩
stateliness ['steɪtlɪnəs] *n* : majestuosidad *f*
stately ['steɪtli] *adj* **statelier; -est** : majestuoso
statement ['steɪtmənt] *n* **1** DECLARATION : declaración *f*, afirmación *f* **2** *or* **bank statement** : estado *m* de cuenta
stateroom ['steɪt,ruːm, -,rʊm] *n* : camarote *m*
statesman ['steɪtsmən] *n*, *pl* -**men** [-mən, -,mɛn] : estadista *mf*
static[1] ['stætɪk] *adj* : estático
static[2] *n* : estática *f*, interferencia *f*
station[1] ['steɪʃən] *vt* : apostar, estacionar
station[2] *n* **1** : estación *f* (de trenes, etc.) **2** RANK, STANDING : condición *f* (social) **3** : canal *m* (de televisión), estación *f* o emisora *f* (de radio) **4 police station** : comisaría *f* **5 fire station** : estación *f* de bomberos, cuartel *m* de bomberos
stationary ['steɪʃə,nɛri] *adj* **1** IMMOBILE : estacionario, inmovible **2** UNCHANGING : inmutable, inalterable
stationery ['steɪʃə,nɛri] *n* : papel *m* y sobres *mpl* (para correspondencia)
station wagon *n* : camioneta *f* ranchera, camioneta *f* guayín *Mex*
statistic [stə'tɪstɪk] *n* : estadística *f* ⟨according to statistics : según las estadísticas⟩
statistical [stə'tɪstɪkəl] *adj* : estadístico
statistician [,stætə'stɪʃən] *n* : estadístico *m*, -ca *f*
statue ['stæ,tʃuː] *n* : estatua *f*
statuesque [,stætʃu'ɛsk] *adj* : escultural
statuette [,stætʃu'ɛt] *n* : estatuilla *f*
stature ['stætʃər] *n* **1** HEIGHT : estatura *f*, talla *f* **2** PRESTIGE : talla *f*, prestigio *m*
status ['steɪtəs, 'stæ-] *n* : condición *f*, situación *f*, estatus *m* (social) ⟨marital status : estado civil⟩
statute ['stæ,tʃuːt] *n* : ley *f*, estatuto *m*
staunch ['stɔntʃ] *adj* : acérrimo, incondicional, leal ⟨a staunch supporter : un partidario incondicional⟩ — **staunchly** *adv*
stave[1] ['steɪv] *vt* **staved** *or* **stove** ['stoːv]; **staving 1** to stave in : romper **2** to stave off : evitar (un ataque), prevenir (un problema)
stave[2] *n* : duela *f* (de un barril)
staves → **staff**
stay[1] ['steɪ] *vi* **1** REMAIN : quedarse, permanecer ⟨to stay in : quedarse en casa⟩ ⟨he stayed in the city : permaneció en la ciudad⟩ **2** CONTINUE : seguir, quedarse ⟨it stayed cloudy : siguió nublado⟩ ⟨stay awake : mantenerse despierto⟩ **3** LODGE : hospedarse, alojarse (en un hotel, etc.) — *vt* **1** HALT : detener, suspender (una ejecución, etc.) **2 to stay the course** : aguantar hasta el final

stay[2] *n* **1** SOJOURN : estadía *f*, estancia *f*, permanencia *f* **2** SUSPENSION : suspensión *f* (de una sentencia) **3** SUPPORT : soporte *m*
stead ['stɛd] *n* **1** : lugar *m* ⟨she went in his stead : fue en su lugar⟩ **2 to stand (someone) in good stead** : ser muy útil a, servir de mucho a
steadfast ['stɛd,fæst] *adj* : firme, resuelto ⟨a steadfast friend : un fiel amigo⟩ ⟨a steadfast refusal : una negativa categórica⟩
steadily ['stɛdəli] *adv* **1** CONSTANTLY : continuamente, sin parar **2** FIRMLY : con firmeza **3** FIXEDLY : fijamente
steady[1] ['stɛdi] *v* **steadied; steadying** *vt* : sujetar ⟨she steadied herself : recobró el equilibrio⟩ — *vi* : estabilizarse
steady[2] *adj* **steadier; -est 1** FIRM, SURE : seguro, firme ⟨to have a steady hand : tener buen pulso⟩ **2** FIXED, REGULAR : fijo ⟨a steady income : ingresos fijos⟩ **3** CALM : tranquilo, ecuánime ⟨she has steady nerves : es imperturbable⟩ **4** DEPENDABLE : responsable, fiable **5** CONSTANT : constante
steak ['steɪk] *n* : bistec *m*, filete *m*, churrasco *m*, bife *m Arg*, *Chile*, *Uru*
steal ['stiːl] *v* **stole** ['stoːl]; **stolen** ['stoːlən]; **stealing** *vt* : robar, hurtar — *vi* **1** : robar, hurtar **2** : ir sigilosamente ⟨to steal away : escabullirse⟩
stealth ['stɛlθ] *n* : sigilo *m*
stealthily ['stɛlθəli] *adv* : furtivamente
stealthy ['stɛlθi] *adj* **stealthier; -est** : furtivo, sigiloso
steam[1] ['stiːm] *vi* : echar vapor ⟨to steam away : moverse echando vapor⟩ — *vt* **1** : cocer al vapor (en cocina) **2 to steam open** : abrir con vapor
steam[2] *n* **1** : vapor *m* **2 to let off steam** : desahogarse
steamboat ['stiːm,boːt] → **steamship**
steam engine *n* : motor *m* de vapor
steamroller ['stiːm,roːlər] *n* : apisonadora *f*
steamship ['stiːm,ʃɪp] *n* : vapor *m*, barco *m* de vapor
steamy ['stiːmi] *adj* **steamier; -est 1** : lleno de vapor **2** EROTIC : erótico ⟨a steamy romance : un tórrido romance⟩
steed ['stiːd] *n* : corcel *m*
steel[1] ['stiːl] *vt* **to steel oneself** : armarse de valor
steel[2] *adj* : de acero
steel[3] *n* : acero *m*
steely ['stiːli] *adj* **steelier; -est** : como acero ⟨a steely gaze : una mirada fría⟩ ⟨steely determination : determinación férrea⟩
steep[1] ['stiːp] *vt* : remojar, dejar (té, etc.) en infusión
steep[2] *adj* **1** : empinado, escarpado ⟨a steep cliff : un precipicio escarpado⟩ **2** CONSIDERABLE : considerable, marcado **3** EXCESSIVE : excesivo ⟨steep prices : precios muy altos⟩
steeple ['stiːpəl] *n* : aguja *f*, campanario *m*

steeplechase ['sti:pəlˌtʃeɪs] *n* : carrera *f* de obstáculos

steeply ['sti:pli] *adv* : abruptamente

steer[1] ['stɪr] *vt* **1** : conducir (un coche), gobernar (un barco) **2** GUIDE : dirigir, guiar

steer[2] *n* : buey *m*

steering wheel *n* : volante *m*

stein ['staɪn] *n* : jarra *f* (para cerveza)

stellar ['stɛlər] *adj* : estelar

stem[1] ['stɛm] *v* **stemmed; stemming** *vt* : detener, contener, parar ⟨to stem the tide : detener el curso⟩ — *vi* **to stem from** : provenir de, ser el resultado de

stem[2] *n* : tallo *m* (de una planta)

stench ['stɛntʃ] *n* : hedor *m*, mal olor *m*

stencil[1] ['stɛntsəl] *vt* **-ciled** *or* **-cilled; -ciling** *or* **-cilling** : marcar utilizando una plantilla

stencil[2] *n* : plantilla *f* (para marcar)

stenographer [stəˈnɑgrəfər] *n* : taquígrafo *m*, -fa *f*

stenographic [ˌstɛnəˈgræfɪk] *adj* : taquigráfico

stenography [stəˈnɑgrəfi] *n* : taquigrafía *f*

step[1] ['stɛp] *vi* **stepped; stepping 1** : dar un paso ⟨step this way, please : pase por aquí, por favor⟩ ⟨he stepped outside : salió⟩ **2 to step on** : pisar

step[2] *n* **1** : paso *m* ⟨step by step : paso por paso⟩ **2** STAIR : escalón *m*, peldaño *m* **3** RUNG : escalón *m*, travesaño *m* **4** MEASURE, MOVE : medida *f*, paso *m* ⟨to take steps : tomar medidas⟩ **5** STRIDE : paso *m* ⟨with a quick step : con paso rápido⟩

stepbrother ['stɛpˌbrʌðər] *n* : hermanastro *m*

stepdaughter ['stɛpˌdɔtər] *n* : hijastra *f*

stepfather ['stɛpˌfɑðər, -ˌfa-] *n* : padrastro *m*

stepladder ['stɛpˌlædər] *n* : escalera *f* de tijera

stepmother ['stɛpˌmʌðər] *n* : madrastra *f*

steppe ['stɛp] *n* : estepa *f*

stepping–stone ['stɛpɪŋˌstoːn] *n* : pasadera *f* (en un río, etc.), trampolín *m* (al éxito)

stepsister ['stɛpˌsɪstər] *n* : hermanastra *f*

stepson ['stɛpˌsʌn] *n* : hijastro *m*

step up *vt* INCREASE : aumentar

stereo[1] ['stɛriˌoː, 'stɪr-] *adj* : estéreo

stereo[2] *n, pl* **stereos** : estéreo *m*

stereophonic [ˌstɛriˈofɑnɪk, ˌstɪr-] *adj* : estereofónico

stereotype[1] ['stɛrioˌtaɪp, 'stɪr-] *vt* **-typed; -typing** : estereotipar

stereotype[2] *n* : estereotipo *m*

sterile ['stɛrəl] *adj* : estéril

sterility [stəˈrɪləti] *n* : esterilidad *f*

sterilization [ˌstɛrələˈzeɪʃən] *n* : esterilización *f*

sterilize ['stɛrəˌlaɪz] *vt* **-ized; -izing** : esterilizar

sterling ['stərlɪŋ] *adj* **1** : de ley ⟨sterling silver : plata de ley⟩ **2** EXCELLENT : excelente

stern[1] ['stərn] *adj* : severo, adusto — **sternly** *adv*

stern[2] *n* : popa *f*

sternness ['stərnnəs] *n* : severidad *f*

sternum ['stərnəm] *n, pl* **sternums** *or* **sterna** [-nə] : esternón *m*

stethoscope ['stɛθəˌskoːp] *n* : estetoscopio *m*

stevedore ['sti:vəˌdor] *n* : estibador *m*, -dora *f*

stew[1] ['stu:, 'stju:] *vt* : estofar, guisar — *vi* **1** : cocer (dícese de la carne, etc.) **2** FRET : preocuparse

stew[2] *n* **1** : estofado *m*, guiso *m* **2 to be in a stew** : estar agitado

steward ['stu:ərd, 'stju:-] *n* **1** MANAGER : administrador *m* **2** : auxiliar *m* de vuelo (en un avión), camarero *m* (en un barco)

stewardess ['stu:ərdəs, 'stju:-] *n* **1** MANAGER : administradora *f* **2** : camarera *f* (en un barco) **3** : auxiliar *f* de vuelo, azafata *f* (en un avión)

stick[1] ['stɪk] *v* **stuck** ['stʌk]; **sticking** *vt* **1** STAB : clavar **2** ATTACH : pegar **3** PUT : poner **4 to stick out** : sacar (la lengua, etc.), extender (la mano) — *vi* **1** ADHERE : pegarse, adherirse **2** JAM : atascarse **3 to stick around** : quedarse **4 to stick out** PROJECT : sobresalir (de una superficie), asomar (por detrás o debajo de algo) **5 to stick to** : no abandonar ⟨stick to your guns : manténgase firme⟩ **6 to stick up** : estar parado (dícese del pelo, etc.), sobresalir (de una superficie) **7 to stick with** : serle fiel a (una persona), seguir con (una cosa) ⟨I'll stick with what I know : prefiero lo conocido⟩

stick[2] *n* **1** BRANCH, TWIG : ramita *f* **2** : palo *m*, vara *f* ⟨a walking stick : un bastón⟩

sticker ['stɪkər] *n* : etiqueta *f* adhesiva

stickler ['stɪklər] *n* : persona *f* exigente ⟨to be a stickler for : insistir mucho en⟩

sticky ['stɪki] *adj* **stickier; -est 1** ADHESIVE : pegajoso, adhesivo **2** MUGGY : bochornoso **3** DIFFICULT : difícil

stiff ['stɪf] *adj* **1** RIGID : rígido, tieso ⟨a stiff dough : una masa firme⟩ **2** : agarrotado, entumecido ⟨stiff muscles : músculos entumecidos⟩ **3** STILTED : acartonado, poco natural **4** STRONG : fuerte (dícese del viento, etc.) **5** DIFFICULT, SEVERE : severo, difícil, duro

stiffen ['stɪfən] *vt* **1** STRENGTHEN : fortalecer, reforzar (tela, etc.) **2** : hacer más duro (un castigo, etc.) — *vi* **1** HARDEN : endurecerse **2** : entumecerse (dícese de los músculos)

stiffly ['stɪfli] *adv* **1** RIGIDLY : rígidamente **2** COLDLY : con frialdad

stiffness ['stɪfnəs] *n* **1** RIGIDITY : rigidez *f* **2** COLDNESS : frialdad *f* **3** SEVERITY : severidad *f*

stifle ['staɪfəl] vt **-fled; -fling** SMOTHER, SUPPRESS : sofocar, reprimir, contener ⟨to stifle a yawn : reprimir un bostezo⟩

stigma ['stɪgmə] n, pl **stigmata** [stɪg-'mɑtə, 'stɪgmətə] or **stigmas** : estigma m

stigmatize ['stɪgmə,taɪz] vt **-tized; -tizing** : estigmatizar

stile ['staɪl] n : escalones mpl para cruzar un cerco

stiletto [stə'lɛ,to:] n, pl **-tos** or **-toes** : estilete m

still¹ ['stɪl] vt CALM : pacificar, apaciguar — vi : pacificarse, apaciguarse

still² adv **1** QUIETLY : quieto ⟨sit still! : ¡quédate quieto!⟩ **2** : de todos modos, aún, todavía ⟨she still lives there : aún vive allí⟩ ⟨it's still the same : sigue siendo lo mismo⟩ **3** IN ANY CASE : de todos modos, aún así ⟨he still has doubts : aún así le quedan dudas⟩ ⟨I still prefer that you stay : de todos modos prefiero que te quedes⟩

still³ adj **1** MOTIONLESS : quieto, inmóvil **2** SILENT : callado

still⁴ n **1** SILENCE : quietud f, calma f **2** : alambique m (para destilar alcohol)

stillborn ['stɪl,bɔrn] adj : nacido muerto

stillness ['stɪlnəs] n : calma f, silencio m

stilt ['stɪlt] n : zanco m

stilted ['stɪltəd] adj : afectado, poco natural

stimulant ['stɪmjələnt] n : estimulante m — **stimulant** adj

stimulate ['stɪmjə,leɪt] vt **-lated; -lating** : estimular

stimulation [,stɪmjə'leɪʃən] n **1** STIMULATING : estimulación f **2** STIMULUS : estímulo m

stimulus ['stɪmjələs] n, pl **-li** [-,laɪ] **1** : estímulo m **2** INCENTIVE : acicate m

sting¹ ['stɪŋ] v **stung** ['stʌŋ]; **stinging** vt **1** : picar ⟨a bee stung him : le picó una abeja⟩ **2** HURT : hacer escocer (físicamente), herir (emocionalmente) — vi **1** : picar (dícese de las abejas, etc.) **2** SMART : escocer, arder

sting² n : picadura f (herida), escozor m (sensación)

stinger ['stɪŋər] n : aguijón m (de una abeja, etc.)

stinginess ['stɪndʒinəs] n : tacañería f

stingy ['stɪndʒi] adj **stingier; -est 1** MISERLY : tacaño, avaro **2** PALTRY : mezquino, mísero

stink¹ ['stɪŋk] vi **stank** ['stæŋk] or **stunk** ['stʌŋk]; **stunk; stinking** : apestar, oler mal

stink² n : hedor m, mal olor m, peste f

stint¹ ['stɪnt] vt : escatimar ⟨to stint oneself of : privarse de⟩ — vi **to stint on** : escatimar

stint² n : período m

stipend ['staɪ,pɛnd, -pənd] n : estipendio m

stipulate ['stɪpjə,leɪt] vt **-lated; -lating** : estipular

stipulation [,stɪpjə'leɪʃən] n : estipulación f

stir¹ ['stər] v **stirred; stirring** vt **1** AGITATE : mover, agitar **2** MIX : revolver, remover **3** INCITE : incitar, impulsar, motivar **4** or **to stir up** AROUSE : despertar (memorias, etc.), provocar (ira, etc.) — vi : moverse, agitarse

stir² n **1** MOTION : movimiento m **2** COMMOTION : revuelo m

stirrup ['stərəp, 'stɪr-] n : estribo m

stitch¹ ['stɪtʃ] vt : coser, bordar (para decorar) — vi : coser

stitch² n **1** : puntada f **2** TWINGE : punzada f, puntada f

stock¹ ['stɑk] vt : surtir, abastecer, vender — vi **to stock up** : abastecerse

stock² n **1** SUPPLY : reserva f, existencias fpl (en comercio) ⟨to be out of stock : estar agotadas las existencias⟩ **2** SECURITIES : acciones fpl, valores mpl **3** LIVESTOCK : ganado m **4** ANCESTRY : linaje m, estirpe f **5** BROTH : caldo m **6 to take stock** : evaluar

stockade [stɑ'keɪd] n : estacada f

stockbroker ['stɑk,bro:kər] n : corredor m, -dora f de bolsa

stockholder ['stɑk,ho:ldər] n : accionista mf

stocking ['stɑkɪŋ] n : media f ⟨a pair of stockings : unas medias⟩

stock market n : bolsa f

stockpile¹ ['stɑk,paɪl] vt **-piled; -piling** : acumular, almacenar

stockpile² n : reservas fpl

stocky ['stɑki] adj **stockier; -est** : robusto, fornido

stockyard ['stɑk,jɑrd] n : corral m

stodgy ['stɑdʒi] adj **stodgier; -est 1** DULL : aburrido, pesado **2** OLD-FASHIONED : anticuado

stoic¹ ['sto:ɪk] or **stoical** [-ɪkəl] adj : estoico — **stoically** [-ɪkli] adv

stoic² n : estoico m, -ca f

stoicism ['sto:ə,sɪzəm] n : estoicismo m

stoke ['sto:k] vt **stoked; stoking** : atizar (un fuego), echarle carbón a (un horno)

stole¹ → **steal**

stole² ['sto:l] n : estola f

stolen → **steal**

stolid ['stɑlɪd] adj : impasible, imperturbable — **stolidly** adv

stomach¹ ['stʌmɪk] vt : aguantar, soportar

stomach² n **1** : estómago m **2** BELLY : vientre m, barriga f, panza f **3** DESIRE : ganas fpl ⟨he had no stomach for a fight : no quería pelea⟩

stomachache ['stʌmɪk,eɪk] n : dolor m de estómago

stomp ['stɑmp, 'stɔmp] vt : pisotear — vi : pisar fuerte

stone¹ ['sto:n] vt **stoned; stoning** : apedrear, lapidar

stone² n **1** : piedra f **2** PIT : hueso m, pepa f (de una fruta)

Stone Age n : Edad f de Piedra

stony ['sto:ni] *adj* **stonier; -est 1** ROCKY : pedregoso **2** UNFEELING : insensible, frío ⟨a stony stare : una mirada glacial⟩

stood → **stand**

stool ['stu:l] *n* **1** SEAT : taburete *m*, banco *m* **2** FOOTSTOOL : escabel *m* **3** FECES : deposición *f* de heces

stoop¹ ['stu:p] *vi* **1** CROUCH : agacharse **2 to stoop to** : rebajarse a

stoop² *n* **1** : espaldas *fpl* encorvadas ⟨to have a stoop : ser encorvado⟩ **2** : entrada *f* (de una casa)

stop¹ ['stɑp] *v* **stopped; stopping** *vt* **1** PLUG : tapar **2** PREVENT : impedir, evitar ⟨she stopped me from leaving : me impidió que saliera⟩ **3** HALT : parar, detener **4** CEASE : dejar de ⟨he stopped talking : dejó de hablar⟩ — *vi* **1** HALT : detenerse, parar **2** CEASE : cesar, terminar ⟨the rain won't stop : no deja de llover⟩ **3** STAY : quedarse ⟨she stopped with friends : se quedó en casa de unos amigos⟩ **4 to stop by** : visitar

stop² *n* **1** STOPPER : tapón *m* **2** HALT : parada *f*, alto *m* ⟨to come to a stop : pararse, detenerse⟩ ⟨to put a stop to : poner fin a⟩ **3** : parada *f* ⟨bus stop : parada de autobús⟩

stopgap ['stɑp,gæp] *n* : arreglo *m* provisorio

stoplight ['stɑp,laɪt] *n* : semáforo *m*

stoppage ['stɑpɪdʒ] *n* : acto *m* de parar ⟨a work stoppage : un paro⟩

stopper ['stɑpər] *n* : tapón *m*

storage ['storɪdʒ] *n* : almacenamiento *m*, almacenaje *m*

storage battery *n* : acumulador *m*

store¹ ['stor] *vt* **stored; storing** : guardar, almacenar

store² *n* **1** RESERVE, SUPPLY : reserva *f* **2** SHOP : tienda *f* ⟨grocery store : tienda de comestibles⟩

storehouse ['stor,haʊs] *n* : almacén *m*, depósito *m*

storekeeper ['stor,ki:pər] *n* : tendero *m*, -ra *f*

storeroom ['stor,ru:m, -,rʊm] *n* : almacén *m*, depósito *m*

stork ['stork] *n* : cigüeña *f*

storm¹ ['storm] *vi* **1** : llover o nevar tormentosamente **2** RAGE : ponerse furioso, vociferar **3 to storm out** : salir echando pestes — *vt* ATTACK : asaltar

storm² *n* **1** : tormenta *f*, tempestad *f* **2** UPROAR : alboroto *m*, revuelo *m*, escándalo *m* ⟨a storm of abuse : un torrente de abusos⟩

stormy ['stormi] *adj* **stormier; -est** : tormentoso

story ['stori] *n, pl* **stories 1** NARRATIVE : cuento *m*, relato *m* **2** ACCOUNT : historia *f*, relato *m* **3** : piso *m*, planta *f* (de un edificio) ⟨first story : planta baja⟩

stout ['staʊt] *adj* **1** FIRM, RESOLUTE : firme, resuelto **2** STURDY : fuerte, robusto, sólido **3** FAT : corpulento, gordo

stove¹ ['sto:v] *n* : cocina *f* (para cocinar), estufa *f* (para calentar)

stove² → **stave¹**

stow ['sto:] *vt* **1** STORE : poner, meter, guardar **2** LOAD : cargar — *vi* **to stow away** : viajar de polizón

stowaway ['sto:ə,weɪ] *n* : polizón *m*

straddle ['strædəl] *vt* **-dled; -dling** : sentarse a horcajadas sobre

straggle ['strægəl] *vi* **-gled; -gling** : rezagarse, quedarse atrás

straggler ['strægələr] *n* : rezagado *m*, -da *f*

straight¹ ['streɪt] *adv* **1** : derecho, directamente ⟨go straight, then turn right : sigue derecho, luego gira a la derecha⟩ **2** HONESTLY : honestamente ⟨to go straight : enmendarse⟩ **3** CLEARLY : con claridad **4** FRANKLY : francamente, con franqueza

straight² *adj* **1** : recto (dícese de las líneas, etc.), derecho (dícese de algo vertical), lacio (dícese del pelo) **2** HONEST, JUST : honesto, justo **3** NEAT, ORDERLY : arreglado, ordenado

straighten ['streɪtən] *vt* **1** : enderezar, poner derecho **2 to straighten up** : arreglar, ordenar ⟨he straightened up the house : arregló la casa⟩

straightforward [streɪt'forwərd] *adj* **1** FRANK : franco, sincero **2** CLEAR, PRECISE : puro, simple, claro

straightway ['streɪt'weɪ, -,weɪ] *adv* : inmediatamente

strain¹ ['streɪn] *vt* **1** EXERT : forzar (la vista, la voz) ⟨to strain oneself : hacer un gran esfuerzo⟩ **2** FILTER : colar, filtrar **3** INJURE : lastimarse, hacerse daño en ⟨to strain a muscle : sufrir un esguince⟩

strain² *n* **1** LINEAGE : linaje *m*, abolengo *m* **2** STREAK, TRACE : veta *f* **3** VARIETY : tipo *m*, variedad *f* **4** STRESS : tensión *f*, presión *f* **5** SPRAIN : esguince *m*, torcedura *f* (del tobillo, etc.) **6 strains** *npl* TUNE : melodía *f*, acordes *mpl*, compases *fpl*

strainer ['streɪnər] *n* : colador *m*

strait ['streɪt] *n* **1** : estrecho *m* **2 straits** *npl* DISTRESS : aprietos *mpl*, apuros *mpl* ⟨in dire straits : en serios aprietos⟩

straitened ['streɪtənd] *adj* **in straitened circumstances** : en apuros económicos

strand¹ ['strænd] *vt* **1** : varar **2 to be left stranded** : quedar(se) varado, quedar colgado ⟨they left me stranded : me dejaron abandonado⟩

strand² *n* **1** : hebra *f* (de hilo, etc.) ⟨a strand of hair : un pelo⟩ **2** BEACH : playa *f*

strange ['streɪndʒ] *adj* **stranger; -est 1** QUEER, UNUSUAL : extraño, raro **2** UNFAMILIAR : desconocido, nuevo

strangely ['streɪndʒli] *adv* ODDLY : de manera extraña ⟨to behave strangely : portarse de una manera rara⟩ ⟨strangely, he didn't call : curiosamente, no llamó⟩

strangeness ['streɪndʒnəs] *n* 1 ODD-NESS : rareza *f* 2 UNFAMILIARITY : lo desconocido

stranger ['streɪndʒər] *n* : desconocido *m*, -da *f*; extraño *m*, -ña *f*

strangle ['stræŋɡəl] *vt* **-gled; -gling** : estrangular

strangler ['stræŋɡlər] *n* : estrangulador *m*, -dora *f*

strap[1] ['stræp] *vt* **strapped; strapping** 1 FASTEN : sujetar con una correa 2 FLOG : azotar (con una correa)

strap[2] *n* 1 : correa *f* 2 **shoulder strap** : tirante *m*

strapless ['stræpləs] *n* : sin tirantes

strapping ['stræpɪŋ] *adj* : robusto, fornido

stratagem ['stræt̬ədʒəm, -ˌdʒɛm] *n* : estratagema *f*, artimaña *f*

strategic [strə'ti:dʒɪk] *adj* : estratégico

strategist ['stræt̬ədʒɪst] *n* : estratega *mf*

strategy ['stræt̬ədʒi] *n*, *pl* **-gies** : estrategia *f*

stratified ['stræt̬əˌfaɪd] *adj* : estratificado

stratosphere ['stræt̬əˌsfɪr] *n* : estratosfera *f*

stratospheric [ˌstræt̬ə'sfɪrɪk, -'sfɛr-] *adj* : estratosférico

stratum ['streɪt̬əm, 'stræ-] *n*, *pl* **strata** [-t̬ə] : estrato *m*, capa *f*

straw *n* 1 : paja *f* ⟨the last straw : el colmo⟩ 2 *or* **drinking straw** : pajita *f*, popote *m Mex*

strawberry ['strɔˌbɛri] *n*, *pl* **-ries** : fresa *f*

stray[1] ['streɪ] *vi* 1 WANDER : alejarse, extraviarse ⟨the cattle strayed away : el ganado se descarrió⟩ 2 DIGRESS : desviarse, divagar

stray[2] *adj* : perdido, callejero (dícese de un perro o un gato), descarriado (dícese del ganado)

stray[3] *n* : animal *m* perdido, animal *m* callejero

streak[1] ['stri:k] *vt* : hacer rayas en ⟨blue streaked with grey : azul veteado con gris⟩ — *vi* : ir como una flecha

streak[2] *n* 1 : raya *f*, veta *f* (en mármol, queso, etc.), mechón *m* (en el pelo) 2 : rayo *m* (de luz) 3 TRACE : veta *f* 4 : racha *f* ⟨a streak of luck : una racha de suerte⟩

stream[1] ['stri:m] *vi* : correr, salir a chorros ⟨tears streamed from his eyes : las lágrimas brotaban de sus ojos⟩ — *vt* : derramar, dejar correr ⟨to stream blood : derramar sangre⟩

stream[2] *n* 1 BROOK : arroyo *m*, riachuelo *m* 2 RIVER : río *m* 3 FLOW : corriente *f*, chorro *m*

streamer ['stri:mər] *n* 1 PENNANT : banderín *m* 2 RIBBON : serpentina *f* (de papel), cinta *f* (de tela)

streamlined ['stri:mˌlaɪnd] *adj* 1 : aerodinámico (dícese de los automóviles, etc.) 2 EFFICIENT : eficiente, racionalizado

street ['stri:t] *n* : calle *f*

streetcar ['stri:tˌkɑr] *n* : tranvía *m*

strength ['streŋkθ] *n* 1 POWER : fuerza *f* 2 SOLIDITY, TOUGHNESS : solidez *f*, resistencia *f*, dureza *f* 3 INTENSITY : intensidad *f* (de emociones, etc.), lo fuerte (de un sabor, etc.) 4 : punto *m* fuerte ⟨strengths and weaknesses : virtudes y defectos⟩ 5 NUMBER : número *m*, complemento *m* ⟨in full strength : en gran número⟩

strengthen ['streŋkθən] *vt* 1 : fortalecer (los músculos, el espíritu, etc.) 2 REINFORCE : reforzar 3 INTENSIFY : intensificar, redoblar (esfuerzos, etc.) — *vi* 1 : fortalecerse, hacerse más fuerte 2 INTENSIFY : intensificarse

strenuous ['strɛnjuəs] *adj* 1 VIGOROUS : vigoroso, enérgico 2 ARDUOUS : duro, riguroso

strenuously ['strɛnjuəsli] *adv* : vigorosamente, duro

stress[1] ['strɛs] *vt* 1 : someter a tensión (física) 2 EMPHASIZE : enfatizar, recalcar 3 **to stress out** : estresar

stress[2] *n* 1 : tensión *f* (en un material) 2 EMPHASIS : énfasis *m*, acento *m* (en lingüística) 3 TENSION : tensión *f* (nerviosa), estrés *m*

stressful ['strɛsfəl] *adj* : estresante

stretch[1] ['strɛtʃ] *vt* 1 EXTEND : estirar, extender, desplegar (alas) 2 **to stretch the truth** : forzar la verdad, exagerar — *vi* : estirarse

stretch[2] *n* 1 STRETCHING : extensión *f*, estiramiento *m* (de músculos) 2 ELASTICITY : elasticidad *f* 3 EXPANSE : tramo *m*, trecho *m* ⟨the home stretch : la recta final⟩ 4 PERIOD : período *m* (de tiempo)

stretcher ['strɛtʃər] *n* : camilla *f*

strew ['stru:] *vt* **strewed; strewed** *or* **strewn** ['stru:n]; **strewing** 1 SCATTER : esparcir (semillas, etc.), desparramar (papeles, etc.) 2 **to strew with** : cubrir de

stricken ['strɪkən] *adj* **stricken with** : aquejado de (una enfermedad), afligido por (tristeza, etc.)

strict ['strɪkt] *adj* : estricto — **strictly** *adv*

strictness ['strɪktnəs] *n* : severidad *f*, lo estricto

stricture ['strɪktʃər] *n* : crítica *f*, censura *f*

stride[1] ['straɪd] *vi* **strode** ['stro:d]; **stridden** ['strɪdən]; **striding** : ir dando trancos, ir dando zancadas

stride[2] *n* : tranco *m*, zancada *f*

strident ['straɪdənt] *adj* : estridente

strife ['straɪf] *n* : conflictos *mpl*, disensión *f*

strike[1] ['straɪk] *v* **struck** ['strʌk]; **striking** *vt* 1 HIT : golpear (a una persona) ⟨to strike a blow : pegar un golpe⟩ 2 DELETE : suprimir, tachar 3 COIN, MINT : acuñar (monedas) 4 : dar (la hora) 5 AFFLICT : sobrevenir ⟨he was stricken with a fever : le sobrevino una fiebre⟩ **6** IMPRESS : impresionar, parecer ⟨her voice struck me : su voz me impresionó⟩ ⟨it struck him as funny : le pareció chistoso⟩ **7** : encender (un fósforo) **8** FIND : descubrir (oro, petróleo) **9** ADOPT : adoptar (una pose, etc.) — *vi* **1** HIT : golpear ⟨to strike against : chocar contra⟩ **2** ATTACK : atacar **3** : declararse en huelga

strike² *n* **1** BLOW : golpe *m* **2** : huelga *f*, paro *m* ⟨to be on strike : estar en huelga⟩ **3** ATTACK : ataque *m*

strikebreaker ['straık‚breıkər] *n* : rompehuelgas *mf*, esquirol *mf*

strike out *vi* **1** HEAD : salir (para) **2** : ser ponchado (en béisbol) ⟨the batter struck out : poncharon al bateador⟩

striker ['straıkər] *n* : huelguista *mf*

strike up *vt* START : entablar, empezar

striking ['straıkıŋ] *adj* : notable, sorprendente, llamativo ⟨a striking beauty : una belleza imponente⟩ — **strikingly** *adv*

string¹ ['strıŋ] *vt* **strung** ['strʌŋ]; **stringing** **1** THREAD : ensartar ⟨to string beads : ensartar cuentas⟩ **2** HANG : colgar (con un cordel)

string² *n* **1** : cordel *m*, cuerda *f* **2** SERIES : serie *f*, sarta *f* (de insultos, etc.) **3 strings** *npl* : cuerdas *fpl* (en música)

string bean *n* : judía *f*, ejote *m Mex*

stringent ['strınʤənt] *adj* : estricto, severo

stringy ['strıŋi] *adj* **stringier**; **-est** : fibroso

strip¹ ['strıp] *v* **stripped**; **stripping** *vt* : quitar (ropa, pintura, etc.), desnudar, despojar — *vi* UNDRESS : desnudarse

strip² *n* : tira *f* ⟨a strip of land : una faja⟩

stripe¹ ['straıp] *vt* **striped** ['straıpt]; **striping** : marcar con rayas o listas

stripe² *n* **1** : raya *f*, lista *f* **2** BAND : franja *f*

striped ['straıpt, 'straıpəd] *adj* : a rayas, de rayas, rayado, listado

strive ['straıv] *vi* **strove** ['stro:v]; **striven** ['strıvən] *or* **strived**; **striving 1 to strive for** : luchar por lograr **2 to strive to** : esforzarse por

strobe ['stro:b] *or* **strobe light** *n* : luz *f* estroboscópica

strode → **stride**

stroke¹ ['stro:k] *vt* **stroked**; **stroking** : acariciar

stroke² *n* : golpe *m* ⟨a stroke of luck : un golpe de suerte⟩

stroll¹ ['stro:l] *vi* : pasear, pasearse, dar un paseo

stroll² *n* : paseo *m*

stroller ['stro:lər] *n* : cochecito *m* (para niños)

strong ['strɔŋ] *adj* **1** : fuerte **2** HEALTHY : sano **3** ZEALOUS : ferviente

stronghold ['strɔŋ‚ho:ld] *n* : fortaleza *f*, fuerte *m*, bastión *m* ⟨a cultural stronghold : un baluarte de la cultura⟩

strongly ['strɔŋli] *adv* **1** POWERFULLY : fuerte, con fuerza **2** STURDILY

: fuertemente, sólidamente **3** INTENSELY : intensamente, profundamente **4** WHOLEHEARTEDLY : totalmente

struck → **strike¹**

structural ['strʌkʧərəl] *adj* : estructural

structure¹ ['strʌkʧər] *vt* **-tured**; **-turing** : estructurar

structure² *n* **1** BUILDING : construcción *f* **2** ARRANGEMENT, FRAMEWORK : estructura *f*

struggle¹ ['strʌgəl] *vi* **-gled**; **-gling 1** CONTEND : forcejear (físicamente), luchar, contender **2** : hacer con dificultad ⟨she struggled forward : avanzó con dificultad⟩

struggle² *n* : lucha *f*, pelea *f* (física)

strum ['strʌm] *vt* **strummed**; **strumming** : rasguear

strung → **string¹**

strut¹ ['strʌt] *vi* **strutted**; **strutting** : pavonearse

strut² *n* **1** : pavoneo *m* ⟨he walked with a strut : se pavoneaba⟩ **2** : puntal *m* (en construcción, etc.)

strychnine ['strık‚naın, -nən, -‚ni:n] *n* : estricnina *f*

stub¹ ['stʌb] *vt* **stubbed**; **stubbing 1 to stub one's toe** : darse en el dedo (del pie) **2 to stub out** : apagarse

stub² *n* : colilla *f* (de un cigarrillo), cabo *m* (de un lápiz, etc.), talón *m* (de un cheque)

stubble ['stʌbəl] *n* **1** : rastrojo *m* (de plantas) **2** BEARD : barba *f*

stubborn ['stʌbərn] *adj* **1** OBSTINATE : terco, obstinado, empecinado **2** PERSISTENT : pertinaz, persistente — **stubbornly** *adv*

stubbornness ['stʌbərnnəs] *n* **1** OBSTINACY : terquedad *f*, obstinación *f* **2** PERSISTENCE : persistencia *f*

stubby ['stʌbi] *adj* **stubbier**; **-est** : corto y grueso ⟨stubby fingers : dedos regordetes⟩

stucco ['stʌko:] *n, pl* **stuccos** *or* **stuccoes** : estuco *m*

stuck → **stick¹**

stuck–up ['stʌk'ʌp] *adj* : engreído, creído *fam*

stud¹ ['stʌd] *vt* **studded**; **studding** : tachonar, salpicar

stud² *n* **1** *or* **stud horse** : semental *m* **2** : montante *m* (en construcción) **3** HOBNAIL : tachuela *f*, tachón *m*

student ['stu:dənt, 'stju:-] *n* : estudiante *mf*; alumno *m*, -na *f* (de un colegio)

studied ['stʌdid] *adj* : intencionado, premeditado

studio ['stu:di‚o:, 'stju:-] *n, pl* **studios** : estudio *m*

studious ['stu:diəs, 'stju:-] *adj* : estudioso — **studiously** *adv*

study¹ ['stʌdi] *v* **studied**; **studying 1** : estudiar **2** EXAMINE : examinar, estudiar

study² *n, pl* **studies 1** STUDYING : estudio *m* **2** OFFICE : estudio *m*, gabinete *m* (en una casa) 3 RESEARCH : investigación *f*, estudio *m*

stuff¹ ['stʌf] *vt* : rellenar, llenar, atiborrar ⟨a stuffed toy : un juguete de peluche⟩

stuff² *n* 1 POSSESSIONS : cosas *fpl* 2 ESSENCE : esencia *f* 3 SUBSTANCE : cosa *f*, cosas *fpl* ⟨some sticky stuff : una cosa pegajosa⟩ ⟨she knows her stuff : es experta⟩

stuffing ['stʌfɪŋ] *n* : relleno *m*

stuffy ['stʌfi] *adj* **stuffier; -est** 1 CLOSE : viciado, cargado ⟨a stuffy room : una sala mal ventilada⟩ ⟨stuffy weather : tiempo bochornoso⟩ 2 : tapado (dícese de la nariz) 3 STODGY : pesado, aburrido

stumble¹ ['stʌmbəl] *vi* **-bled; -bling** 1 TRIP : tropezar, dar un traspié 2 FLOUNDER : quedarse sin saber qué hacer o decir 3 **to stumble across** *or* **to stumble upon** : dar con, tropezar con

stumble² *n* : tropezón *m*, traspié *m*

stump¹ ['stʌmp] *vt* : dejar perplejo ⟨to be stumped : no tener respuesta⟩

stump² *n* 1 : muñón *m* (de un brazo o una pierna) 2 *or* **tree stump** : cepa *f*, tocón *m* 3 STUB : cabo *m*

stun ['stʌn] *vt* **stunned; stunning** 1 : aturdir (con un golpe) 2 ASTONISH, SHOCK : dejar estupefacto, dejar atónito, aturdir

stung → **sting¹**

stunk → **stink¹**

stunning ['stʌnɪŋ] *adj* 1 ASTONISHING : asombroso, pasmoso, increíble 2 STRIKING : imponente, impresionante (dícese de la belleza)

stunt¹ ['stʌnt] *vt* : atrofiar

stunt² *n* : proeza *f* (acrobática)

stupefy ['stupə,fai, 'stju-] *vt* **-fied; -fying** 1 : aturdir, atontar (con drogas, etc.) 2 AMAZE : dejar estupefacto, dejar atónito

stupendous [stʊ'pɛndəs, stju-] *adj* 1 MARVELOUS : estupendo, maravilloso 2 TREMENDOUS : tremendo — **stupendously** *adv*

stupid ['stupəd, 'stju-] *adj* 1 IDIOTIC, SILLY : tonto, bobo, estúpido 2 DULL, OBTUSE : lento, torpe, lerdo

stupidity [stʊ'pɪdəti, stju-] *n* : tontería *f*, estupidez *f*

stupidly ['stupədli, 'stju-] *adv* 1 IDIOTICALLY : estúpidamente, tontamente 2 DENSELY : torpemente

stupor ['stupər, 'stju-] *n* : estupor *m*

sturdily ['stərdəli] *adv* : sólidamente

sturdiness ['stərdinəs] *n* : solidez *f* (de muebles, etc.), robustez *f* (de una persona)

sturdy ['stərdi] *adj* **sturdier; -est** : fuerte, robusto, sólido

sturgeon ['stərdʒən] *n* : esturión *m*

stutter¹ ['stʌtər] *vi* : tartamudear

stutter² *n* STAMMER : tartamudeo *m*

sty ['stai] *n* 1 *pl* **sties** PIGPEN : chiquero *m*, pocilga *f* 2 *pl* **sties** *or* **styes** : orzuelo *m* (en el ojo)

style¹ ['stail] *vt* **styled; styling** 1 NAME : llamar 2 : peinar (pelo), diseñar (vestidos, etc.) ⟨carefully styled prose : prosa escrita con gran esmero⟩

style² *n* 1 : estilo *m* ⟨that's just his style : él es así⟩ ⟨to live in style : vivir a lo grande⟩ 2 FASHION : moda *f*

stylish ['staɪlɪʃ] *adj* : de moda, elegante, chic

stylishly ['staɪlɪʃli] *adv* : con estilo

stylishness ['staɪlɪʃnəs] *n* : estilo *m*

stylist ['staɪlɪst] *n* : estilista *mf*

stylize ['staɪ,laɪz, 'staɪə-] *vt* : estilizar

stylus ['staɪləs] *n*, *pl* **styli** ['staɪ,laɪ] 1 PEN : estilo *m* 2 NEEDLE : aguja *f* (de un tocadiscos)

stymie ['staɪmi] *vt* **-mied; -mieing** : obstaculizar

suave ['swav] *adj* : fino, urbano

sub¹ ['sʌb] *vi* **subbed; subbing** → **substitute¹**

sub² *n* 1 → **substitute²** 2 → **submarine**

subcommittee ['sʌbkə,mɪti] *n* : subcomité *m*

subconscious¹ [səb'kɑntʃəs] *adj* : subconsciente — **subconsciously** *adv*

subconscious² *n* : subconsciente *m*

subcontract [,sʌb'kɑn,trækt] *vt* : subcontratar

subculture ['sʌb,kʌltʃər] *n* : subcultura *f*

subdivide [,sʌbdə'vaɪd, 'sʌbdə,vaɪd] *vt* **-vided; -viding** : subdividir

subdivision ['sʌbdə,vɪʒən] *n* : subdivisión *f*

subdue [səb'du:, -'dju:] *vt* **-dued; -duing** 1 OVERCOME : sojuzgar (a un enemigo), vencer, superar 2 CONTROL : dominar 3 SOFTEN : suavizar, atenuar (luz, etc.), moderar (lenguaje)

subgroup ['sʌb,gru:p] *n* : subgrupo *m*

subhead ['sʌb,hɛd] *or* **subheading** [-,hɛdɪŋ] *n* : subtítulo *m*

subject¹ [səb'dʒɛkt] *vt* 1 CONTROL, DOMINATE : controlar, dominar 2 : someter ⟨they subjected him to pressure : lo sometieron a presiones⟩

subject² ['sʌbdʒɪkt] *adj* 1 : subyugado, sometido ⟨a subject nation : una nación subyugada⟩ 2 PRONE : sujeto, propenso ⟨subject to colds : sujeto a resfriarse⟩ 3 **subject to** : sujeto a ⟨subject to congressional approval : sujeto a la aprobación del congreso⟩

subject³ ['sʌbdʒɪkt] *n* 1 : súbdito *m*, -ta *f* (de un gobierno) 2 TOPIC : tema *m* 3 : sujeto *m* (en gramática)

subjection [səb'dʒɛkʃən] *n* : sometimiento *m*

subjective [səb'dʒɛktɪv] *adj* : subjetivo — **subjectively** *adv*

subjectivity [,sʌb,dʒɛk'tɪvəti] *n* : subjetividad *f*

subjugate ['sʌbdʒɪ,geɪt] *vt* **-gated; -gating** : subyugar, someter, sojuzgar

subjunctive [səb'dʒʌŋktɪv] *n* : subjuntivo *m* — **subjunctive** *adj*

sublet ['sʌb,lɛt] *vt* **-let; -letting** : subarrendar

sublime [sə'blaɪm] *adj* : sublime

sublimely [sə'blaɪmli] *adv* **1** : de manera sublime **2** UTTERLY : absolutamente, completamente

submarine[1] ['sʌbmə,ri:n, ,sʌbmə'-] *adj* : submarino

submarine[2] *n* : submarino *m*

submerge [səb'mərdʒ] *v* **-merged; -merging** *vt* : sumergir — *vi* : sumergirse

submission [səb'mɪʃən] *n* **1** YIELDING : sumisión *f* **2** PRESENTATION : presentación *f*

submissive [səb'mɪsɪv] *adj* : sumiso, dócil

submit [səb'mɪt] *v* **-mitted; -mitting** *vi* YIELD : rendirse ⟨to submit to : someterse a⟩ — *vt* PRESENT : presentar

subnormal [,sʌb'nɔrməl] *adj* : por debajo de lo normal

subordinate[1] [sə'bɔrdən,eɪt] *vt* **-nated; -nating** : subordinar

subordinate[2] [sə'bɔrdənət] *adj* : subordinado ⟨a subordinate clause : una oración subordinada⟩

subordinate[3] *n* : subordinado *m*, -da *f*; subalterno *m*, -na *f*

subordination [sə,bɔrdən'eɪʃən] *n* : subordinación *f*

subpoena[1] [sə'pi:nə] *vt* **-naed; -naing** : citar

subpoena[2] *n* : citación *f*, citatorio *m*

subscribe [səb'skraɪb] *vi* **-scribed; -scribing 1** : suscribirse (a una revista, etc.) **2 to subscribe to** : suscribir (una opinión, etc.), estar de acuerdo con

subscriber [səb'skraɪbər] *n* : suscriptor *m*, -tora *f* (de una revista, etc.); abonado *m*, -da *f* (de un servicio)

subscription [səb'skrɪpʃən] *n* : suscripción *f*

subsequent ['sʌbsɪkwənt, -sə,kwɛnt] *adj* : subsiguiente ⟨subsequent to : posterior a⟩

subsequently ['sʌb,sɪkwɛntli, -kwənt-] *adv* : posteriormente

subservient [səb'sərviənt] *adj* : servil

subside [səb'saɪd] *vi* **-sided; -siding 1** SINK : hundirse, descender **2** ABATE : calmarse (dícese de las emociones), amainar (dícese del viento, etc.)

subsidiary[1] [səb'sɪdi,ɛri] *adj* : secundario

subsidiary[2] *n, pl* **-ries** : filial *f*, subsidiaria *f*

subsidize ['sʌbsə,daɪz] *vt* **-dized; -dizing** : subvencionar, subsidiar

subsidy ['sʌbsədi] *n, pl* **-dies** : subvención *f*, subsidio *m*

subsist [səb'sɪst] *vi* : subsistir, mantenerse, vivir

subsistence [səb'sɪstənts] *n* : subsistencia *f*

substance ['sʌbstənts] *n* **1** ESSENCE : sustancia *f*, esencia *f* **2** : sustancia *f* ⟨a toxic substance : una sustancia tóxica⟩ **3** WEALTH : riqueza *f* ⟨a woman of substance : una mujer acaudalada⟩

substandard [,sʌb'stændərd] *adj* : inferior, deficiente

substantial [səb'stæntʃəl] *adj* **1** ABUNDANT : sustancioso ⟨a substantial meal : una comida sustanciosa⟩ **2** CONSIDERABLE : considerable, apreciable **3** SOLID, STURDY : sólido

substantially [səb'stæntʃəli] *adv* : considerablemente

substantiate [səb'stæntʃi,eɪt] *vt* **-ated; -ating** : confirmar, probar, justificar

substitute[1] ['sʌbstə,tu:t, -,tju:t] *v* **-tuted; -tuting** *vt* : sustituir — *vi* **to substitute for** : sustituir

substitute[2] *n* **1** : sustituto *m*, -ta *f*; suplente *mf* (persona) **2** : sucedáneo *m* ⟨sugar substitute : sucedáneo de azúcar⟩

substitute teacher *n* : profesor *m*, -sora *f* suplente

substitution [,sʌbstə'tu:ʃən, -'tju:-] *n* : sustitución *f*

subterfuge ['sʌbtər,fju:dʒ] *n* : subterfugio *m*

subterranean [,sʌbtə'reɪniən] *adj* : subterráneo

subtitle ['sʌb,taɪtəl] *n* : subtítulo *m*

subtle ['sʌtəl] *adj* **-tler; -tlest 1** DELICATE, ELUSIVE : sutil, delicado **2** CLEVER : sutil, ingenioso

subtlety ['sʌtəlti] *n, pl* **-ties** : sutileza *f*

subtly ['sʌtəli] *adv* : sutilmente

subtotal ['sʌb,to:təl] *n* : subtotal *m*

subtract [səb'trækt] *vt* : restar, sustraer

subtraction [səb'trækʃən] *n* : resta *f*, sustracción *f*

suburb ['sʌ,bərb] *n* : municipio *m* periférico, suburbio *m*

suburban [sə'bərbən] *adj* : de las afueras (de una ciudad), suburbano

subversion [səb'vərʒən] *n* : subversión *f*

subversive [səb'vərsɪv] *adj* : subversivo

subway ['sʌb,weɪ] *n* : metro *m*, subterráneo *m Arg, Uru*

succeed [sək'si:d] *vt* FOLLOW : suceder a — *vi* : tener éxito (dícese de las personas), dar resultado (dícese de los planes, etc.) ⟨she succeeded in finishing : logró terminar⟩

success [sək'sɛs] *n* : éxito *m*

successful [sək'sɛsfəl] *adj* : exitoso, logrado — **successfully** *adv*

succession [sək'sɛʃən] *n* : sucesión *f* ⟨in succesion : sucesivamente⟩

successive [sək'sɛsɪv] *adj* : sucesivo, consecutivo — **successively** *adv*

successor [sək'sɛsər] *n* : sucesor *m*, -sora *f*

succinct [sək'sɪŋkt, sə'sɪŋkt] *adj* : sucinto — **succinctly** *adv*

succor[1] ['sʌkər] *vt* : socorrer

succor[2] *n* : socorro *m*

succotash ['sʌkə,tæʃ] *n* : guiso *m* de maíz y frijoles

succulent[1] ['sʌkjələnt] *adj* : suculento, jugoso

succulent[2] *n* : suculenta *f* (planta)

succumb [sə'kʌm] *vi* : sucumbir

such[1] ['sʌtʃ] *adv* **1** SO : tan ⟨such tall buildings : edificios tan grandes⟩ **2** VERY : muy ⟨he's not in such good shape : anda un poco mal⟩ **3 such that** : de tal manera que

such[2] *adj* : tal ⟨there's no such thing : no existe tal cosa⟩ ⟨in such cases : en tales casos⟩ ⟨animals such as cows and sheep : animales como vacas y ovejas⟩

such[3] *pron* **1** : tal ⟨such was the result : tal fue el resultado⟩ ⟨he's a child, and acts as such : es un niño, y se porta como tal⟩ **2** : algo o alguien semejante ⟨books, papers and such : libros, papeles y cosas por el estilo⟩

suck ['sʌk] *vi* **1** : chupar (por la boca), aspirar (dícese de las máquinas) **2** SUCKLE : mamar — *vt* : sorber (bebidas), chupar (dulces, etc.)

sucker ['sʌkər] *n* **1** : ventosa *f* (de un insecto, etc.) **2** : chupón *m* (de una planta) **3** → **lollipop 4** FOOL : tonto *m*, -ta *f*; idiota *mf*

suckle ['sʌkəl] *v* **-led; -ling** *vt* : amamantar — *vi* : mamar

suckling ['sʌklɪŋ] *n* : lactante *mf*

sucrose ['su:,kro:s, -,kro:z] *n* : sacarosa *f*

suction ['sʌkʃən] *n* : succión *f*

Sudanese [,su:də'ni:z, -'i:s] *n* : sudanés *m*, -nesa *f* — **Sudanese** *adj*

sudden ['sʌdən] *adj* **1** : repentino, súbito ⟨all of a sudden : de pronto, de repente⟩ **2** UNEXPECTED : inesperado, improviso **3** ABRUPT, HASTY : precipitado, brusco

suddenly ['sʌdənli] *adv* **1** : de repente, de pronto **2** ABRUPTLY : bruscamente

suddenness ['sʌdənnəs] *n* **1** : lo repentino **2** ABRUPTNESS : brusquedad *f* **3** HASTINESS : lo precipitado

suds ['sʌdz] *npl* : espuma *f* (de jabón)

sue ['su:] *v* **sued; suing** *vt* : demandar — *vi* **to sue for** : demandar por (daños, etc.)

suede ['sweɪd] *n* : ante *m*, gamuza *f*

suet ['su:ət] *n* : sebo *m*

suffer ['sʌfər] *vi* : sufrir — *vt* **1** : sufrir, padecer (dolores, etc.) **2** PERMIT : permitir, dejar

sufferer ['sʌfərər] *n* : persona que padece (una enfermedad, etc.)

suffering ['sʌfərɪŋ] *n* : sufrimiento *m*

suffice [sə'faɪs] *vi* **-ficed; -ficing** : ser suficiente, bastar

sufficient [sə'fɪʃənt] *adj* : suficiente

sufficiently [sə'fɪʃəntli] *adv* : (lo) suficientemente, bastante

suffix ['sʌ,fɪks] *n* : sufijo *m*

suffocate ['sʌfə,keɪt] *v* **-cated; -cating** *vt* : asfixiar, ahogar — *vi* : asfixiarse, ahogarse

suffocation [,sʌfə'keɪʃən] *n* : asfixia *f*, ahogo *m*

suffrage ['sʌfrɪdʒ] *n* : sufragio *m*, derecho *m* al voto

suffuse [sə'fju:z] *vt* **-fused; -fusing** : impregnar (de olores, etc.), bañar (de luz), teñir (de colores), llenar (de emociones)

sugar[1] ['ʃʊgər] *vt* : azucarar

sugar[2] *n* : azúcar *mf*

sugarcane ['ʃʊgər,keɪn] *n* : caña *f* de azúcar

sugary ['ʃʊgəri] *adj* **1** : azucarado ⟨sugary desserts : postres azucarados⟩ **2** SACCHARINE : empalagoso

suggest [səg'dʒɛst, sə-] *vt* **1** PROPOSE : sugerir **2** IMPLY : indicar, dar a entender

suggestible [səg'dʒɛstəbəl, sə-] *adj* : influenciable

suggestion [səg'dʒɛstʃən, sə-] *n* **1** PROPOSAL : sugerencia *f* **2** INDICATION : indicio *m* **3** INSINUATION : insinuación *f*

suggestive [səg'dʒɛstɪv, sə-] *adj* : insinuante — **suggestively** *adv*

suicidal [,su:ə'saɪdəl] *adj* : suicida

suicide ['su:ə,saɪd] *n* **1** : suicidio *m* (acto) **2** : suicida *mf* (persona)

suit[1] ['su:t] *vt* **1** ADAPT : adaptar **2** BEFIT : convenir a, ser apropiado a **3** BECOME : favorecer, quedarle bien (a alguien) ⟨the dress suits you : el vestido te queda bien⟩ **4** PLEASE : agradecer, satisfacer, convenirle bien (a alguien) ⟨does Friday suit you? : ¿le conviene el viernes?⟩ ⟨suit yourself! : ¡como quieras!⟩

suit[2] *n* **1** LAWSUIT : pleito *m*, litigio *m* **2** : traje *m* (ropa) **3** : palo *m* (de naipes)

suitability [,su:tə'bɪləti] *n* : idoneidad *f*, lo apropiado

suitable ['su:təbəl] *adj* : apropiado, idóneo — **suitably** [-bli] *adv*

suitcase ['su:t,keɪs] *n* : maleta *f*, valija *f*, petaca *f Mex*

suite ['swi:t, *for 2 also* 'su:t] *n* **1** : suite *f* (de habitaciones) **2** SET : juego *m* (de muebles)

suitor ['su:tər] *n* : pretendiente *m*

sulfur ['sʌlfər] *n* : azufre *m*

sulfuric acid [,sʌl'fjʊrɪk] *adj* : ácido *m* sulfúrico

sulfurous [,sʌl'fjʊrəs, 'sʌlfərəs, 'sʌlfjə-] *adj* : sulfuroso

sulk[1] ['sʌlk] *vi* : estar de mal humor, enfurruñarse *fam*

sulk[2] *n* : mal humor *m*

sulky ['sʌlki] *adj* **sulkier; -est** : malhumorado, taimado *Chile*

sullen ['sʌlən] *adj* **1** MOROSE : hosco, taciturno **2** DREARY : sombrío, deprimente

sullenly ['sʌlənli] *adv* **1** MOROSELY : hoscamente **2** GLOOMILY : sombríamente

sully ['sʌli] *vt* **sullied; sullying** : manchar, empañar

sultan ['sʌltən] *n* : sultán *m*
sultry ['sʌltri] *adj* **sultrier; -est 1** : bochornoso ⟨sultry weather : tiempo sofocante, tiempo bochornoso⟩ **2** SENSUAL : sensual, seductor
sum¹ ['sʌm] *vt* **summed; summing 1** : sumar (números) **2** → **sum up**
sum² *n* **1** AMOUNT : suma *f*, cantidad *f* **2** TOTAL : suma *f*, total *f* **3** : suma *f*, adición *f* (en matemáticas)
sumac ['ʃuːˌmæk, 'suː-] *n* : zumaque *m*
summarize ['sʌməˌraɪz] *v* **-rized; -rizing** : resumir, compendiar
summary¹ ['sʌməri] *adj* **1** CONCISE : breve, conciso **2** IMMEDIATE : inmediato ⟨a summary dismissal : un despido inmediato⟩
summary² *n, pl* **-ries** : resumen *m*, compendio *m*
summer ['sʌmər] *n* : verano *m*
summery ['sʌməri] *adj* : veraniego
summit ['sʌmət] *n* **1** : cumbre *f*, cima *f* (de una montaña) **2** *or* **summit conference** : cumbre *f*
summon ['sʌmən] *vt* **1** CALL : convocar (una reunión, etc.), llamar (a una persona) **2** : citar (en derecho) **3 to summon up** : armarse de (valor, etc.) ⟨to summon up one's strength : reunir fuerzas⟩
summons ['sʌmənz] *n, pl* **summonses 1** SUBPOENA : citación *f*, citatorio *m* *Mex* **2** CALL : llamada *f*, llamamiento *m*
sumptuous ['sʌmptʃʊəs] *adj* : suntuoso
sum up *vt* **1** SUMMARIZE : resumir **2** EVALUATE : evaluar — *vi* : recapitular
sun¹ ['sʌn] *vt* **sunned; sunning 1** : poner al sol **2 to sun oneself** : asolearse, tomar el sol
sun² *n* **1** : sol *m* **2** SUNSHINE : luz *f* del sol
sunbeam ['sʌnˌbiːm] *n* : rayo *m* de sol
sunblock ['sʌnˌblɑk] *n* : filtro *m* solar
sunburn¹ ['sʌnˌbərn] *vi* **-burned** [-ˌbərnd] *or* **-burnt** [-ˌbərnt]; **-burning** : quemarse por el sol
sunburn² ['sʌnˌbərn] *n* : quemadura *f* de sol
sundae ['sʌndi] *n* : sundae *m*
Sunday ['sʌnˌdeɪ, -di] *n* : domingo *m*
sundial ['sʌnˌdaɪl] *n* : reloj *m* de sol
sundown ['sʌnˌdaʊn] → **sunset**
sundries ['sʌndriz] *npl* : artículos *mpl* diversos
sundry ['sʌndri] *adj* : varios, diversos
sunflower ['sʌnˌflaʊər] *n* : girasol *m*, mirasol *m*
sung → **sing**
sunglasses ['sʌnˌglæsəz] *npl* : gafas *fpl* de sol, lentes *mpl* de sol
sunk → **sink¹**
sunken ['sʌŋkən] *adj* : hundido
sunlight ['sʌnˌlaɪt] *n* : sol *m*, luz *f* del sol
sunny ['sʌni] *adj* **sunnier; -est** : soleado
sunrise ['sʌnˌraɪz] *n* : salida *f* del sol
sunscreen ['sʌnˌskriːn] *n* : filtro *m* solar

sunset ['sʌnˌsɛt] *n* : puesta *f* del sol
sunshine ['sʌnˌʃaɪn] *n* : sol *m*, luz *f* del sol
sunspot ['sʌnˌspɑt] *n* : mancha *f* solar
sunstroke ['sʌnˌstroːk] *n* : insolación *f*
suntan ['sʌnˌtæn] *n* : bronceado *m*
sup ['sʌp] *vi* **supped; supping** : cenar
super ['suːpər] *adj* : súper ⟨super! : ¡fantástico!⟩
superabundance [ˌsuːpərə'bʌndənts] *n* : superabundancia *f*
superb [sʊ'pərb] *adj* : magnífico, espléndido — **superbly** *adv*
supercilious [ˌsuːpər'siliəs] *adj* : altivo, altanero, desdeñoso
supercomputer ['suːpərkəmˌpjuːtər] *n* : supercomputadora *f*
superficial [ˌsuːpər'fɪʃəl] *adj* : superficial — **superficially** *adv*
superfluous [sʊ'pərfluəs] *adj* : superfluo
superhighway ['suːpərˌhaɪˌweɪ, ˌsuː-pər'-] *n* : autopista *f*
superhuman [ˌsuːpər'hjuːmən] *adj* **1** SUPERNATURAL : sobrenatural **2** HERCULEAN : sobrehumano
superimpose [ˌsuːpərɪm'poːz] *vt* **-posed; -posing** : superponer, sobreponer
superintend [ˌsuːpərɪn'tɛnd] *vt* : supervisar
superintendent [ˌsuːpərɪn'tɛndənt] *n* : portero *m*, -ra *f* (de un edificio); director *m*, -tora *f* (de una escuela, etc.); superintendente *mf* (de policía)
superior¹ [sʊ'pɪriər] *adj* **1** BETTER : superior **2** HAUGHTY : altivo, altanero
superior² *n* : superior *m*
superiority [sʊˌpɪri'ɔrəti] *n, pl* **-ties** : superioridad *f*
superlative¹ [sʊ'pərlətɪv] *adj* **1** : superlativo (en gramática) **2** SUPREME : supremo **3** EXCELLENT : excelente, excepcional
superlative² *n* : superlativo *m*
supermarket ['suːpərˌmɑrkət] *n* : supermercado *m*
supernatural [ˌsuːpər'nætʃərəl] *adj* : sobrenatural
supernaturally [ˌsuːpər'nætʃərəli] *adv* : de manera sobrenatural
superpower ['suːpərˌpaʊər] *n* : superpotencia *f*
supersede [ˌsuːpər'siːd] *vt* **-seded; -seding** : suplantar, reemplazar, sustituir
supersonic [ˌsuːpər'sɑnɪk] *adj* : supersónico
superstar ['suːpərˌstɑr] *n* : superestrella *f*
superstition [ˌsuːpər'stɪʃən] *n* : superstición *f*
superstitious [ˌsuːpər'stɪʃəs] *adj* : supersticioso
superstructure ['suːpərˌstrʌktʃər] *n* : superestructura *f*
supervise ['suːpərˌvaɪz] *vt* **-vised; -vising** : supervisar, dirigir
supervision [ˌsuːpər'vɪʒən] *n* : supervisión *f*, dirección *f*

supervisor ['su:pər,vaɪzər] *n* : supervisor *m*, -sora *f*

supervisory [,su:pər'vaɪzəri] *adj* : de supervisor

supine [su'paɪn] *adj* **1** : en decúbito supino, en decúbito dorsal **2** ABJECT, INDIFFERENT : indiferente, apático

supper ['sʌpər] *n* : cena *f*, comida *f*

supplant [sə'plænt] *vt* : suplantar

supple ['sʌpəl] *adj* **-pler; -plest** : flexible

supplement[1] ['sʌplə,mɛnt] *vt* : complementar, completar

supplement[2] ['sʌpləmənt] *n* **1** : complemento *m* ⟨dietary supplement : complemento alimenticio⟩ **2** : suplemento *m* (de un libro o periódico)

supplementary [,sʌplə'mɛntəri] *adj* : suplementario

supplicate ['sʌplə,keɪt] *v* **-cated; -cating** *vi* : rezar — *vt* : suplicar

supplier [sə'plaɪər] *n* : proveedor *m*, -dora *f*; abastecedor *m*, -dora *f*

supply[1] [sə'plaɪ] *vt* **-plied; -plying** : suministrar, proveer de, proporcionar

supply[2] *n, pl* **-plies** **1** PROVISION : provisión *f*, suministro *m* ⟨supply and demand : la oferta y la demanda⟩ **2** STOCK : reserva *f*, existencias *fpl* (de un negocio) **3** **supplies** *npl* PROVISIONS : provisiones *fpl*, víveres *mpl*, despensa *f*

support[1] [sə'port] *vt* **1** BACK : apoyar, respaldar **2** MAINTAIN : mantener, sostener, sustentar **3** PROP UP : sostener, apoyar, apuntalar, soportar

support[2] *n* **1** : apoyo *m* (moral), ayuda *f* (económica) **2** PROP : soporte *m*, apoyo *m*

supporter [sə'portər] *n* : partidario *m*, -ria *f*

supportive [sə'portɪv] *adj* : que apoya ⟨his family is very supportive : su familia lo apoya mucho⟩

suppose [sə'po:z] *vt* **-posed; -posing** **1** ASSUME : suponer, imaginarse **2** BELIEVE : suponer, creer **3** **to be supposed to** : tener que, deber

supposed [sə'po:zd, -'po:zəd] *adj* : supuesto — **supposedly** [sə'po:zədli] *adv*

supposition [,sʌpə'zɪʃən] *n* : suposición *f*

suppository [sə'pɑzə,tori] *n, pl* **-ries** : supositorio *m*

suppress [sə'prɛs] *vt* **1** SUBDUE : sofocar, suprimir, reprimir (una rebelión, etc.) **2** : suprimir, ocultar (información) **3** REPRESS : reprimir, contener ⟨to suppress a yawn : reprimir un bostezo⟩

suppression [sə'prɛʃən] *n* **1** SUBDUING : represión *f* **2** : supresión *f* (de información) **3** REPRESSION : represión *f*, inhibición *f*

supremacy [su'prɛməsi] *n, pl* **-cies** : supremacía *f*

supreme [su'pri:m] *adj* : supremo

Supreme Being *n* : Ser *m* Supremo

supremely [su'pri:mli] *adv* : totalmente, sumamente

surcharge ['sər,tʃɑrdʒ] *n* : recargo *m*

sure[1] ['ʃur] *adv* **1** ALL RIGHT : por supuesto, claro **2** (*used as an intensifier*) ⟨it sure is hot! : ¡hace tanto calor!⟩ ⟨she sure is pretty! : ¡qué linda es!⟩

sure[2] *adj* **surer; -est** : seguro ⟨to be sure about something : estar seguro de algo⟩ ⟨a sure sign : una clara señal⟩ ⟨for sure : seguro, con seguridad⟩

surely ['ʃurli] *adv* **1** CERTAINLY : seguramente **2** (*used as an intensifier*) ⟨you surely don't mean that! : ¡no me digas que estás hablando en serio!⟩

sureness ['ʃurnəs] *n* : certeza *f*, seguridad *f*

surety ['ʃurəti] *n, pl* **-ties** : fianza *f*, garantía *f*

surf[1] ['sərf] *n* **1** WAVES : oleaje *m* **2** FOAM : espuma *f*

surface[1] ['sərfəs] *v* **-faced; -facing** *vi* : salir a la superficie — *vt* : revestir (una carretera)

surface[2] *n* **1** : superficie *f* **2** **on the surface** : en apariencia

surfboard ['sərf,bord] *n* : tabla *f* de surf, tabla *f* de surfing

surfeit ['sərfət] *n* : exceso *m*

surfer ['sərfər] *n* : surfista *mf*

surfing ['sərfɪŋ] *n* : surf *m*, surfing *m*

surge[1] ['sərdʒ] *vi* **surged; surging** **1** : hincharse (dícese del mar), levantarse (dícese de las olas) **2** SWARM : salir en tropel (dícese de la gente, etc.)

surge[2] *n* **1** : oleaje *m* (del mar), oleada *f* (de gente) **2** FLUSH : arranque *m*, arrebato *m* (de ira, etc.) **3** INCREASE : aumento *m* (súbito)

surgeon ['sərdʒən] *n* : cirujano *m*, -na *f*

surgery ['sərdʒəri] *n, pl* **-geries** : cirugía *f*

surgical ['sərdʒɪkəl] *adj* : quirúrgico — **surgically** [-kli] *adv*

surly ['sərli] *adj* **surlier; -est** : hosco, arisco

surmise[1] [sər'maɪz] *vt* **-mised; -mising** : conjeturar, suponer, concluir

surmise[2] *n* : conjetura *f*

surmount [sər'maunt] *vt* **1** OVERCOME : superar, vencer, salvar **2** CLIMB : escalar **3** CAP, TOP : coronar

surname ['sər,neɪm] *n* : apellido *m*

surpass [sər'pæs] *vt* : superar, exceder, rebasar, sobrepasar

surplus ['sər,plʌs] *n* : excedente *m*, sobrante *m*, superávit *m* (de dinero)

surprise[1] [sə'praɪz, sər-] *vt* **-prised; -prising** : sorprender

surprise[2] *n* : sorpresa *f* ⟨to take by surprise : sorprender⟩

surprising [sə'praɪzɪŋ, sər-] *adj* : sorprendente — **surprisingly** *adv*

surrender[1] [sə'rɛndər] *vt* **1** : entregar, rendir **2** **to surrender oneself** : entregarse — *vi* : rendirse

surrender[2] *n* : rendición *m* (de una ciudad, etc.), entrega *f* (de posesiones)

surreptitious [ˌsərəpˈtɪʃəs] *adj* : subrepticio — **surreptitiously** *adv*

surrogate [ˈsərəgət, -ˌgeɪt] *n* : sustituto *m*

surround [səˈraʊnd] *vt* : rodear

surroundings [səˈraʊndɪŋz] *npl* : ambiente *m*, entorno *m*

surveillance [sərˈveɪlənts, -ˈveɪljənts, -ˈveɪənts] *n* : vigilancia *f*

survey[1] [sərˈveɪ] *vt* **-veyed; -veying 1** : medir (un terreno) **2** EXAMINE : inspeccionar, examinar, revisar **3** POLL : hacer una encuesta de, sondear

survey[2] [ˈsərˌveɪ] *n, pl* **-veys 1** INSPECTION : inspección *f*, revisión *f* **2** : medición *f* (de un terreno) **3** POLL : encuesta *f*, sondeo *m*

surveyor [sərˈveɪər] *n* : agrimensor *m*, -sora *f*

survival [sərˈvaɪvəl] *n* : supervivencia *f*, sobrevivencia *f*

survive [sərˈvaɪv] *v* **-vived; -viving** *vi* : sobrevivir — *vt* OUTLIVE : sobrevivir a

survivor [sərˈvaɪvər] *n* : superviviente *mf*, sobreviviente *mf*

susceptibility [səˌsɛptəˈbɪləti] *n, pl* **-ties** : vulnerabilidad *f*, propensión *f* (a enfermedades, etc.)

susceptible [səˈsɛptəbəl] *adj* **1** VULNERABLE : vulnerable, sensible ⟨susceptible to flattery : sensible a halagos⟩ **2** PRONE : propenso ⟨susceptible to colds : propenso a resfriarse⟩

suspect[1] [səˈspɛkt] *vt* **1** DISTRUST : dudar de **2** : sospechar (algo), sospechar de (una persona) **3** IMAGINE, THINK : imaginarse, creer

suspect[2] [ˈsʌsˌpɛkt, səˈspɛkt] *adj* : sospechoso, dudoso, cuestionable

suspect[3] [ˈsʌsˌpɛkt] *n* : sospechoso *m*, -sa *f*

suspend [səˈspɛnd] *vt* : suspender

suspenders [səˈspɛndərz] *npl* : tirantes *mpl*

suspense [səˈspɛnts] *n* : incertidumbre *f*, suspenso *m* (en una película, etc.)

suspenseful [səˈspɛntsfəl] *adj* : de suspenso

suspension [səˈspɛnʧən] *n* : suspensión *f*

suspicion [səˈspɪʃən] *n* **1** : sospecha *f* **2** TRACE : pizca *f*, atisbo *m*

suspicious [səˈspɪʃəs] *adj* **1** QUESTIONABLE : sospechoso, dudoso **2** DISTRUSTFUL : suspicaz, desconfiado

suspiciously [səˈspɪʃəsli] *adv* : de modo sospechoso, con recelo

sustain [səˈsteɪn] *vt* **1** NOURISH : sustentar **2** PROLONG : sostener **3** SUFFER : sufrir **4** SUPPORT, UPHOLD : apoyar, respaldar, sostener

sustainable [səˈsteɪnəbəl] *adj* : sostenible

sustenance [ˈsʌstənənts] *n* **1** NOURISHMENT : sustento *m* **2** SUPPORT : sostén *m*

svelte [ˈsfɛlt] *adj* : esbelto

swab[1] [ˈswɑb] *vt* **swabbed; swabbing 1** CLEAN : lavar, limpiar **2** : aplicar a (con hisopo)

swab[2] *n or* **cotton swab** : hisopo *m* (para aplicar medicinas, etc.)

swaddle [ˈswɑdəl] *vt* **-dled; -dling** [ˈswɑdəlɪŋ] : envolver (en pañales)

swagger[1] [ˈswæɡər] *vi* : pavonearse

swagger[2] *n* : pavoneo *m*

swallow[1] [ˈswɑloː] *vt* **1** : tragar (comida, etc.) **2** ENGULF : tragarse, envolver **3** REPRESS : tragarse (insultos, etc.) — *vi* : tragar

swallow[2] *n* **1** : golondrina *f* (pájaro) **2** GULP : trago *m*

swam → **swim**[1]

swamp[1] [ˈswɑmp] *vt* : inundar

swamp[2] *n* : pantano *m*, ciénaga *f*

swampy [ˈswɑmpi] *adj* **swampier; -est** : pantanoso, cenagoso

swan [ˈswɑn] *n* : cisne *f*

swap[1] [ˈswɑp] *vt* **swapped; swapping** : cambiar, intercambiar ⟨to swap places : cambiarse de sitio⟩

swap[2] *n* : cambio *m*, intercambio *m*

swarm[1] [ˈswɔrm] *vi* : enjambrar

swarm[2] *n* : enjambre *m*

swarthy [ˈswɔrði, -θi] *adj* **swarthier; -est** : moreno

swashbuckling [ˈswɑʃˌbʌklɪŋ] *adj* : de aventurero

swat[1] [ˈswɑt] *vt* **swatted; swatting** : aplastar (un insecto), darle una palmada (a alguien)

swat[2] *n* : palmada *f* (con la mano), golpe *m* (con un objeto)

swatch [ˈswɑʧ] *n* : muestra *f*

swath [ˈswɑθ, ˈswɔθ] *or* **swathe** [ˈswɑð, ˈswɔð, ˈsweɪð] *n* : franja *f* (de grano segado)

swathe [ˈswɑð, ˈswɔð, ˈsweɪð] *vt* **swathed; swathing** : envolver

swatter [ˈswɑtər] → **flyswatter**

sway[1] [ˈsweɪ] *vi* : balancearse, mecerse — *vt* INFLUENCE : influir en, convencer

sway[2] *n* **1** SWINGING : balanceo *m* **2** INFLUENCE : influjo *m*

swear [ˈswær] *v* **swore** [ˈswor]; **sworn** [ˈsworn]; **swearing** *vi* **1** VOW : jurar **2** CURSE : decir palabrotas — *vt* : jurar

swearword [ˈswærˌwərd] *n* : mala palabra *f*, palabrota *f*

sweat[1] [ˈswɛt] *vi* **sweat** *or* **sweated; sweating 1** PERSPIRE : sudar, transpirar **2** OOZE : rezumar **3 to sweat over** : sudar la gota gorda por

sweat[2] *n* : sudor *m*, transpiración *f*

sweater [ˈswɛtər] *n* : suéter *m*

sweatshirt [ˈswɛtˌʃərt] *n* : sudadera *f*

sweaty [ˈswɛti] *adj* **sweatier; -est** : sudoroso, sudado, transpirado

Swede [ˈswiːd] *n* : sueco *m*, -ca *f*

Swedish[1] [ˈswiːdɪʃ] *adj* : sueco

Swedish[2] *n* **1** : sueco *m* (idioma) **2 the Swedish** *npl* : los suecos

sweep[1] [ˈswiːp] *v* **swept** [ˈswɛpt]; **sweeping** *vt* **1** : barrer (el suelo, etc.), limpiar (suciedad, etc.) ⟨he swept the books aside : apartó los libros de un manotazo〉 **2** *or* **to sweep through** : extenderse por (dícese del fuego, etc.), azotar (dícese de una tormenta) — *vi* **1** : barrer, limpiar **2** : extenderse (en una curva), describir una curva 〈the sun swept across the sky : el sol describía una curva en el cielo〉

sweep² *n* **1** : barrido *m*, barrida *f* (con una escoba) **2** : movimiento *m* circular **3** SCOPE : alcance *m*

sweeper ['swi:pər] *n* : barrendero *m*, -ra *f*

sweeping ['swi:pɪŋ] *adj* **1** WIDE : amplio (dícese de un movimiento) **2** EXTENSIVE : extenso, radical **3** INDISCRIMINATE : indiscriminado, demasiado general **4** OVERWHELMING : arrollador, aplastante

sweepstakes ['swi:p,steɪks] *ns & pl* **1** : carrera *f* (en que el ganador se lleva el premio entero) **2** LOTTERY : lotería *f*

sweet¹ ['swi:t] *adj* **1** : dulce 〈sweet desserts : postres dulces〉 **2** FRESH : fresco **3** : sin sal (dícese de la mantequilla, etc.) **4** PLEASANT : dulce, agradable **5** DEAR : querido

sweet² *n* : dulce *m*

sweeten ['swi:tən] *vt* : endulzar

sweetener ['swi:tənər] *n* : endulzante *m*

sweetheart ['swi:t,hɑrt] *n* : novio *m*, -via *f* 〈thanks, sweetheart : gracias, cariño〉

sweetly ['swi:tli] *adv* : dulcemente

sweetness ['swi:tnəs] *n* : dulzura *f*

sweet potato *n* : batata *f*, boniato *m*

swell¹ ['swɛl] *vi* **swelled**; **swelled** *or* **swollen** ['swo:lən, 'swʌl-]; **swelling 1** *or* **to swell up** : hincharse 〈her ankle swelled : se le hinchó el tobillo〉 **2** *or* **to swell out** : inflarse, hincharse (dícese de las velas, etc.) **3** INCREASE : aumentar, crecer

swell² *n* **1** : oleaje *m* (del mar) **2** → **swelling**

swelling ['swɛlɪŋ] *n* : hinchazón *f*

swelter ['swɛltər] *vi* : sofocarse de calor

swept → **sweep¹**

swerve¹ ['swərv] *vi* **swerved**; **swerving** : virar bruscamente

swerve² *n* : viraje *m* brusco

swift¹ ['swɪft] *adj* **1** FAST : rápido, veloz **2** SUDDEN : repentino, súbito — **swiftly** *adv*

swift² *n* : vencejo *m* (pájaro)

swiftness ['swɪftnəs] *n* : rapidez *f*, velocidad *f*

swig¹ ['swɪg] *vi* **swigged**; **swigging** : tomar a tragos, beber a tragos

swig² *n* : trago *m*

swill¹ ['swɪl] *vt* : chupar, beber a tragos grandes

swill² *n* **1** SLOP : bazofia *f* **2** GARBAGE : basura *f*

swim¹ ['swɪm] *vi* **swam** ['swæm]; **swum** ['swʌm]; **swimming 1** : nadar **2** FLOAT : flotar **3** REEL : dar vueltas 〈his head was swimming : la cabeza le daba vueltas〉

swim² *n* : baño *m*, chapuzón *m* 〈to go for a swim : ir a nadar〉

swimmer ['swɪmər] *n* : nadador *m*, -dora *f*

swindle¹ ['swɪndəl] *vt* **-dled**; **-dling** : estafar, timar

swindle² *n* : estafa *f*, timo *m fam*

swindler ['swɪndələr] *n* : estafador *m*, -dora *f*; timador *m*, -dora *f*

swine ['swaɪn] *ns & pl* : cerdo *m*, -da *f*

swing¹ ['swɪŋ] *v* **swung** ['swʌŋ]; **swinging** *vt* **1** : describir una curva con 〈he swung the ax at the tree : le dio al arbol con el hacha〉 **2** : balancear (los brazos, etc.), hacer oscilar **3** SUSPEND : colgar — *vi* **1** SWAY : balancearse (dícese de los brazos, etc.), oscilar (dícese de un objeto), columpiarse, mecerse (en un columpio) **2** SWIVEL : girar (en un pivote) 〈the door swung shut : la puerta se cerró〉 **3** CHANGE : virar, cambiar (dícese de las opiniones, etc.)

swing² *n* **1** SWINGING : vaivén *m*, balanceo *m* **2** CHANGE, SHIFT : viraje *m*, movimiento *m* **3** : columpio *m* (para niños) **4 to take a swing at someone** : intentar pegarle a alguien

swipe¹ ['swaɪp] *vt* **swiped**; **swiping 1** STRIKE : dar, pegar (con un movimiento amplio) **2** WIPE : limpiar **3** STEAL : birlar *fam*, robar

swipe² *n* BLOW : golpe *m*

swirl¹ ['swərl] *vi* : arremolinarse

swirl² *n* **1** EDDY : remolino *m* **2** SPIRAL : espiral *f*

swish¹ ['swɪʃ] *vt* : mover (produciendo un sonido) 〈she swished her skirt : movía la falda〉 — *vi* : moverse (produciendo un sonido) 〈the cars swished by : se oían pasar los coches〉

swish² *n* : silbido *m* (de un látigo, etc.), susurro *m* (de agua), crujido *m* (de ropa, etc.)

Swiss ['swɪs] *n* : suizo *m*, -za *f* — **Swiss** *adj*

swiss chard *n* : acelga *f*

switch¹ ['swɪtʃ] *vt* **1** LASH, WHIP : azotar **2** CHANGE : cambiar de **3** EXCHANGE : intercambiar **4 to switch on** : encender, prender **5 to switch off** : apagar — *vi* **1** : moverse de un lado al otro **2** CHANGE : cambiar **3** SWAP : intercambiarse

switch² *n* **1** WHIP : vara *f* **2** CHANGE, SHIFT : cambio *m* **3** : interruptor *m*, llave *f* (de la luz, etc.)

switchboard ['swɪtʃ,bord] *n* : conmutador *m*, centralita *f*

swivel¹ ['swɪvəl] *vi* **-veled** *or* **-velled**; **-veling** *or* **-velling** : girar (sobre un pivote)

swivel² *n* : base *f* giratoria

swollen *pp* → **swell¹**

swoon¹ ['swu:n] *vi* : desvanecerse, desmayarse

swoon² *n* : desvanecimiento *m*, desmayo *m*

swoop[1] ['swu:p] *vi* : abatirse (dícese de las aves), descender en picada (dícese de un avión)

swoop[2] *n* : descenso *m* en picada

sword ['sɔrd] *n* : espada *f*

swordfish ['sɔrd,fɪʃ] *n* : pez *m* espada

swore, sworn → **swear**

swum *pp* → **swim**[1]

swung → **swing**[1]

sycamore ['sɪkə,mor] *n* : sicomoro *m*

sycophant ['sɪkəfənt, -,fænt] *n* : adulador *m*, -dora *f*

syllabic [sə'læbɪk] *adj* : silábico

syllable ['sɪləbəl] *n* : sílaba *f*

syllabus ['sɪləbəs] *n, pl* **-bi** [-,baɪ] *or* **-bus-es** : programa *m* (de estudios)

symbol ['sɪmbəl] *n* : símbolo *m*

symbolic [sɪm'balɪk] *adj* : simbólico — **symbolically** [-kli] *adv*

symbolism ['sɪmbə,lɪzəm] *n* : simbolismo *m*

symbolize ['sɪmbə,laɪz] *vt* **-ized; -izing** : simbolizar

symmetrical [sə'mɛtrɪkəl] *or* **symmetric** [-trɪk] *adj* : simétrico — **symmetrically** [-trɪkli] *adv*

symmetry ['sɪmətri] *n, pl* **-tries** : simetría *f*

sympathetic [,sɪmpə'θɛtɪk] *adj* **1** PLEASING : agradable **2** RECEPTIVE : receptivo, favorable **3** COMPASSIONATE, UNDERSTANDING : comprensivo, compasivo

sympathetically [,sɪmpə'θɛtɪkli] *adv* : con compasión, con comprensión

sympathize ['sɪmpə,θaɪz] *vi* **-thized; -thizing** : compadecer ⟨I sympathize with you : te compadezco⟩

sympathy ['sɪmpəθi] *n, pl* **-thies 1** COMPASSION : compasión *f* **2** UNDERSTANDING : comprensión *f* **3** AGREEMENT : solidaridad *f* ⟨in sympathy with : de acuerdo con⟩ **4** CONDOLENCES : pésame *m*, condolencias *fpl*

symphonic [sɪm'fanɪk] *adj* : sinfónico

symphony ['sɪmpfəni] *n, pl* **-nies** : sinfonía *f*

symposium [sɪm'po:ziəm] *n, pl* **-sia** [-ziə] *or* **-siums** : simposio *m*

symptom ['sɪmptəm] *n* : síntoma *m*

symptomatic [,sɪmptə'mætɪk] *adj* : sintomático

synagogue ['sɪnə,gag, -,gɔg] *n* : sinagoga *f*

sync ['sɪŋk] *n* : sincronización *f* ⟨in sync : sincronizado⟩

synchronize ['sɪŋkrə,naɪz, 'sɪn-] *v* **-nized; -nizing** *vi* : estar sincronizado — *vt* : sincronizar

syncopate ['sɪŋkə,peɪt, 'sɪn-] *vt* **-pated; -pating** : sincopar

syncopation [,sɪŋkə'peɪʃən, ,sɪn-] *n* : síncopa *f*

syndicate[1] ['sɪndə,keɪt] *vi* **-cated; -cating** : formar una asociación

syndicate[2] ['sɪndɪkət] *n* : asociación *f*, agrupación *f*

syndrome ['sɪn,dro:m] *n* : síndrome *m*

synonym ['sɪnə,nɪm] *n* : sinónimo *m*

synonymous [sə'nanəməs] *adj* : sinónimo

synopsis [sə'napsɪs] *n, pl* **-opses** [-,si:z] : sinopsis *f*

syntactic [sɪn'tæktɪk] *adj* : sintáctico

syntax ['sɪn,tæks] *n* : sintaxis *f*

synthesis ['sɪnθəsɪs] *n, pl* **-theses** [-,si:z] : síntesis *f*

synthesize ['sɪnθə,saɪz] *vt* **-sized; -sizing** : sintetizar

synthetic[1] [sɪn'θɪtɪk] *adj* : sintético, artificial — **synthetically** [-ţɪkli] *adv*

synthetic[2] *n* : producto *m* sintético

syphilis ['sɪfələs] *n* : sífilis *f*

Syrian ['sɪriən] *n* : sirio *m*, -ria *f* — **Syrian** *adj*

syringe [sə'rɪndʒ, 'sɪrɪndʒ] *n* : jeringa *f*, jeringuilla *f*

syrup ['sərəp, 'sɪrəp] *n* : jarabe *m*, almíbar *m* (de azúcar y agua)

system ['sɪstəm] *n* **1** METHOD : sistema *m*, método *m* **2** APPARATUS : sistema *m*, instalación *f*, aparato *m* ⟨electrical system : instalación eléctrica⟩ ⟨digestive system : aparato digestivo⟩ **3** BODY : organismo *m*, cuerpo *m* ⟨diseases that affect the whole system : enfermedades que afectan el organismo entero⟩ **4** NETWORK : red *f*

systematic [,sɪstə'mætɪk] *adj* : sistemático — **systematically** [-ţɪkli] *adv*

systematize ['sɪstəmə,taɪz] *vt* **-tized; -tizing** : sistematizar

systemic [sɪs'tɛmɪk] *adj* : sistémico

T

t ['ti:] *n, pl* **t's** *or* **ts** ['ti:z] : vigésima letra del alfabeto inglés

tab ['tæb] *n* **1** FLAP, TAG : lengüeta *f* (de un sobre, una caja, etc.), etiqueta *f* (de ropa) **2** → **tabulator 3** BILL, CHECK : cuenta *f* **4** to keep tabs on : tener bajo vigilancia

tabby ['tæbi] *n, pl* **-bies 1** *or* **tabby cat** : gato *m* atigrado **2** : gata *f*

tabernacle ['tæbər,nækəl] *n* : tabernáculo *m*

table ['teɪbəl] *n* **1** : mesa *f* ⟨a table for two : una mesa para dos⟩ **2** LIST : tabla *f* ⟨multiplication table : tabla de multiplicar⟩ **3** table of contents : índice *m* de materias

tableau [tæ'blo:, 'tæ,-] *n, pl* **-leaux** [-'blo:z, -,blo:z] : retablo *m*, cuadro *m* vivo (en teatro)

tablecloth ['teɪbəl,klɔθ] *n* : mantel *m*

tablespoon ['teɪbəl,spu:n] *n* **1** : cuchara *f* (de mesa) **2** → **tablespoonful**

tablespoonful [ˈteɪbəlˌspuːnˌfʊl] *n* : cucharada *f*

tablet [ˈtæblət] *n* **1** PLAQUE : placa *f* **2** PAD : bloc *m* (de papel) **3** PILL : tableta *f*, pastilla *f*, píldora *f* ⟨an aspirin tablet : una tableta de aspirina⟩

table tennis *n* : tenis *m* de mesa

tableware [ˈteɪbəlˌwær] *n* : vajillas *fpl*, cubiertos *mpl* (de mesa)

tabloid [ˈtæˌblɔɪd] *n* : tabloide *m*

taboo¹ [təˈbuː, tæ-] *adj* : tabú

taboo² *n* : tabú *m*

tabular [ˈtæbjələr] *adj* : tabular

tabulate [ˈtæbjəˌleɪt] *vt* **-lated; -lating** : tabular

tabulator [ˈtæbjəˌleɪtər] *n* : tabulador *m*

tacit [ˈtæsɪt] *adj* : tácito, implícito — **tacitly** *adv*

taciturn [ˈtæsɪˌtərn] *adj* : taciturno

tack¹ [ˈtæk] *vt* **1** : sujetar con tachuelas **2 to tack on** ADD : añadir, agregar

tack² *n* **1** : tachuela *f* **2** COURSE : rumbo *m* ⟨to change tack : cambiar de rumbo⟩

tackle¹ [ˈtækəl] *vt* **-led; -ling 1** : taclear (en futbol americano) **2** CONFRONT : abordar, enfrentar, emprender (un problema, un trabajo, etc.)

tackle² *n* **1** EQUIPMENT, GEAR : equipo *m*, aparejo *m* **2** : aparejo *m* (de un buque) **3** : tacleada *f* (en futbol americano)

tacky [ˈtæki] *adj* **tackier; -est 1** STICKY : pegajoso **2** CHEAP, GAUDY : de mal gusto, naco *Mex*

tact [ˈtækt] *n* : tacto *m*, delicadeza *f*, discreción *f*

tactful [ˈtæktfəl] *adj* : discreto, diplomático, de mucho tacto

tactfully [ˈtæktfəli] *adv* : discretamente, con mucho tacto

tactic [ˈtæktɪk] *n* : táctica *f*

tactical [ˈtæktɪkəl] *adj* : táctico, estratégico

tactics [ˈtæktɪks] *ns & pl* : táctica *f*, estrategia *f*

tactile [ˈtæktəl, -ˌtaɪl] *adj* : táctil

tactless [ˈtæktləs] *adj* : indiscreto, poco delicado

tactlessly [ˈtæktləsli] *adv* : rudamente, sin tacto

tadpole [ˈtædˌpoːl] *n* : renacuajo *m*

taffeta [ˈtæfətə] *n* : tafetán *m*, tafeta *f Arg, Mex, Uru*

taffy [ˈtæfi] *n, pl* **-fies** : caramelo *m* de melaza, chicloso *m Mex*

tag¹ [ˈtæg] *v* **tagged; tagging** *vt* **1** LABEL : etiquetar **2** TAIL : seguir de cerca **3** TOUCH : tocar (en varios juegos) — *vi* **to tag along** : pegarse, acompañar

tag² *n* **1** LABEL : etiqueta *f* **2** SAYING : dicho *m*, refrán *m*

tail¹ [ˈteɪl] *vt* FOLLOW : seguir de cerca, pegarse

tail² *n* **1** : cola *f*, rabo *m* (de un animal) **2** : cola *f*, parte *f* posterior ⟨a comet's tail : la cola de un cometa⟩ **3 tails** *npl* : cruz *f* (de una moneda) ⟨heads or tails : cara o cruz⟩

tailed [ˈteɪld] *adj* : que tiene cola

tailgate¹ [ˈteɪlˌgeɪt] *vi* **-gated; -gating** : seguir a un vehículo demasiado de cerca

tailgate² *n* : puerta *f* trasera (de un vehículo)

taillight [ˈteɪlˌlaɪt] *n* : luz *f* trasera (de un vehículo), calavera *f Mex*

tailor¹ [ˈteɪlər] *vt* **1** : confeccionar o alterar (ropa) **2** ADAPT : adaptar, ajustar

tailor² *n* : sastre *m*, -tra *f*

tailpipe [ˈteɪlˌpaɪp] *n* : tubo *m* de escape

tailspin [ˈteɪlˌspɪn] *n* : barrena *f*

taint¹ [ˈteɪnt] *vt* : contaminar, corromper

taint² *n* : corrupción *f*, impureza *f*

take¹ [ˈteɪk] *v* **took** [ˈtʊk]; **taken** [ˈteɪkən]; **taking** *vt* **1** CAPTURE : capturar, apresar **2** GRASP : tomar, agarrar ⟨to take the bull by the horns : tomar al toro por los cuernos⟩ **3** CATCH : tomar, agarrar ⟨taken by surprise : tomado por sorpresa⟩ **4** CAPTIVATE : encantar, fascinar **5** INGEST : tomar, ingerir ⟨take two pills : tome dos píldoras⟩ **6** REMOVE : sacar, extraer ⟨take an orange : saca una naranja⟩ **7** : tomar, coger (un tren, un autobús, etc.) **8** NEED, REQUIRE : tomar, requerir ⟨these things take time : estas cosas toman tiempo⟩ **9** BRING, CARRY : llevar, sacar, cargar ⟨take them with you : llévalos contigo⟩ ⟨take the trash out : saca la basura⟩ **10** BEAR, ENDURE : soportar, aguantar (dolores, etc.) **11** ACCEPT : aceptar (un cheque, etc.), seguir (consejos), asumir (la responsabilidad) **12** SUPPOSE : suponer ⟨I take it that . . . : supongo que . . . ⟩ **13** (*indicating an action or an undertaking*) ⟨to take a walk : dar un paseo⟩ ⟨to take a class : tomar una clase⟩ **14 to take place** HAPPEN : tener lugar, suceder, ocurrir — *vi* : agarrar (dícese de un tinte), prender (dícese de una vacuna)

take² *n* **1** PROCEEDS : recaudación *f*, ingresos *mpl*, ganancias *fpl* **2** : toma *f* (de un rodaje o una grabación)

take back *vt* : retirar (palabras, etc.)

take in *vt* **1** : tomarle a, achicar (un vestido, etc.) **2** INCLUDE : incluir, abarcar **3** ATTEND : ir a ⟨to take in a movie : ir al cine⟩ **4** GRASP, UNDERSTAND : captar, entender **5** DECEIVE : engañar

takeoff [ˈteɪkˌɔf] *n* **1** PARODY : parodia *f* **2** : despegue *m* (de un avión o cohete)

take off *vt* REMOVE : quitar ⟨take off your hat : quítate el sombrero⟩ — *vi* **1** : despegar (dícese de un avión o un cohete) **2** LEAVE : irse, partir

take on *vt* **1** TACKLE : abordar, emprender (problemas, etc.) **2** ACCEPT : aceptar, encargarse de, asumir (una responsabilidad) **3** CONTRACT : contratar (trabajadores) **4** ASSUME : adoptar, asumir, adquirir ⟨the neighborhood took on a dingy look : el barrio asumió una apariencia deprimente⟩

takeover ['teɪk,o:vər] *n* : toma *f* (de poder o de control), adquisición *f* (de una empresa por otra)

take over *vt* : tomar el poder de, tomar las riendas de — *vi* : asumir el mando

taker ['teɪkər] *n* : persona *f* interesada ⟨available to all takers : disponible a cuantos estén interesados⟩

take up *vt* **1** LIFT : levantar **2** SHORTEN : acortar (una falda, etc.) **3** BEGIN : empezar, dedicarse a (un pasatiempo, etc.) **4** OCCUPY : ocupar, llevar (tiempo, espacio) **5** PURSUE : volver a (una cuestión, un asunto) **6** CONTINUE : seguir con

talc ['tælk] *n* : talco *m*

talcum powder ['tælkəm] *n* : talco *m*, polvos *mpl* de talco

tale ['teɪl] *n* **1** ANECDOTE, STORY : cuento *m*, relato *m*, anécdota *f* **2** FALSEHOOD : cuento *m*, mentira *f*

talent ['tælənt] *n* : talento *m*, don *m*

talented ['tæləntəd] *adj* : talentoso

talisman ['tælɪsmən, -lɪz-] *n*, *pl* **-mans** : talismán *m*

talk¹ ['tɔk] *vi* **1** : hablar ⟨he talks for hours : se pasa horas hablando⟩ **2** CHAT : charlar, platicar — *vt* **1** SPEAK : hablar ⟨to talk French : hablar francés⟩ ⟨to talk business : hablar de negocios⟩ **2** PERSUADE : influenciar, convencer ⟨she talked me out of it : me convenció que no lo hiciera⟩ **3 to talk over** DISCUSS : hablar de, discutir

talk² *n* **1** CONVERSATION : charla *f*, plática *f*, conversación *f* **2** GOSSIP, RUMOR : chisme *m*, rumores *mpl*

talkative ['tɔkətɪv] *adj* : locuaz, parlanchín, charlatán

talker ['tɔkər] *n* : conversador *m*, -dora *f*; hablador *m*, -dora *f*

talk show *n* : programa *m* de entrevistas

tall ['tɔl] *adj* : alto ⟨how tall is he? : ¿cuánto mide?⟩

tallness ['tɔlnəs] *n* HEIGHT : estatura *f* (de una persona), altura *f* (de un objeto)

tallow ['tælo:] *n* : sebo *m*

tally¹ ['tæli] *v* **-lied; -lying** *vt* RECKON : contar, hacer una cuenta de — *vi* MATCH : concordar, corresponder, cuadrar

tally² *n*, *pl* **-lies** : cuenta *f* ⟨to keep a tally : llevar la cuenta⟩

talon ['tælən] *n* : garra *f* (de un ave de rapiña)

tambourine [,tæmbə'ri:n] *n* : pandero *m*, pandereta *f*

tame¹ ['teɪm] *vt* **tamed; taming** : domar, amansar, domesticar

tame² *adj* **tamer; -est 1** DOMESTICATED : domesticado, manso **2** DOCILE : manso, dócil **3** DULL : aburrido, soso

tamely ['teɪmli] *adv* : mansamente, dócilmente

tamer ['teɪmər] *n* : domador *m*, -dora *f*

tamp ['tæmp] *vt* : apisonar

tamper ['tæmpər] *vi* **to tamper with** : adulterar (una sustancia), forzar (un sello, una cerradura), falsear (documentos), manipular (una máquina)

tampon ['tæm,pɑn] *n* : tampón *m*

tan¹ ['tæn] *v* **tanned; tanning** *vt* **1** : curtir (pieles) **2** : broncear — *vi* : broncearse

tan² *n* **1** SUNTAN : bronceado *m* ⟨to get a tan : broncearse⟩ **2** : color *m* canela, color *m* café con leche

tandem¹ ['tændəm] *adv or* **in tandem** : en tándem

tandem² *n* : tándem *m* (bicicleta)

tang ['tæŋ] *n* : sabor *m* fuerte

tangent ['tændʒənt] *n* : tangente *f* ⟨to go off on a tangent : irse por la tangente⟩

tangerine ['tændʒə,ri:n, ,tændʒə'-] *n* : mandarina *f*

tangible ['tændʒəbəl] *adj* : tangible, palpable — **tangibly** [-bli] *adv*

tangle¹ ['tæŋɡəl] *v* **-gled; -gling** *vt* : enredar, enmarañar — *vi* : enredarse

tangle² *n* : enredo *m*, maraña *f*

tango¹ ['tæŋ,ɡo:] *vi* : bailar el tango

tango² *n*, *pl* **-gos** : tango *m*

tangy ['tæŋi] *adj* **tangier; -est** : que tiene un sabor fuerte

tank ['tæŋk] *n* : tanque *m*, depósito *m* ⟨fuel tank : depósito de combustibles⟩

tankard ['tæŋkərd] *n* : jarra *f*

tanker ['tæŋkər] *n* : buque *m* cisterna, camión *m* cisterna, avión *m* cisterna ⟨an oil tanker : un petrolero⟩

tanner ['tænər] *n* : curtidor *m*, -dora *f*

tannery ['tænəri] *n*, *pl* **-neries** : curtiduría *f*, tenería *f*

tannin ['tænən] *n* : tanino *m*

tantalize ['tæntə,laɪz] *vt* **-lized; -lizing** : tentar, atormentar (con algo inasequible)

tantalizing ['tæntə,laɪzɪŋ] *adj* : tentador, seductor

tantamount ['tæntə,maʊnt] *adj* : equivalente

tantrum ['tæntrəm] *n* : rabieta *f*, berrinche *m* ⟨to throw a tantrum : hacer un berrinche⟩

tap¹ ['tæp] *vt* **tapped; tapping 1** : ponerle una espita a, sacar líquido de (un barril, un tanque, etc.) **2** : intervenir (una línea telefónica) **3** PAT, TOUCH : tocar, golpear ligeramente ⟨he tapped me on the shoulder : me tocó en el hombro⟩

tap² *n* **1** FAUCET : llave *f*, grifo *m* ⟨beer on tap : cerveza de barril⟩ **2** : extracción *f* (de líquido) ⟨a spinal tap : una punción lumbar⟩ **3** PAT, TOUCH : golpecito *m*, toque *m*

tape¹ ['teɪp] *vt* **taped; taping 1** : sujetar o arreglar con cinta adhesiva **2** RECORD : grabar

tape² *n* **1** : cinta *f* (adhesiva, magnética, etc.) **2** → **tape measure**

tape measure *n* : cinta *f* métrica

taper¹ ['teɪpər] *vi* **1** : estrecharse gradualmente ⟨its tail tapers towards the tip : su cola va estrechándose hacia la punta⟩ **2** *or* **to taper off** : disminuir gradualmente

taper² *n* **1** CANDLE : vela *f* larga y delgada **2** TAPERING : estrechamiento *m* gradual

tapestry ['tæpəstri] *n, pl* **-tries** : tapiz *m*

tapeworm ['teɪp,wərm] *n* : solitaria *f*, tenia *f*

tapioca [,tæpi'o:kə] *n* : tapioca *f*

tar¹ ['tɑr] *vt* **tarred; tarring** : alquitranar

tar² *n* : alquitrán *m*, brea *f*, chapopote *m* *Mex*

tarantula [tə'ræntʃələ, -'ræntələ] *n* : tarántula *f*

tardiness ['tɑrdinəs] *n* : tardanza *f*, retraso *m*

tardy ['tɑrdi] *adj* **-dier; -est** LATE : tardío, de retraso

target¹ ['tɑrgət] *vt* : fijar como objetivo, dirigir, destinar

target² *n* **1** : blanco *m* ⟨target practice : tiro al blanco⟩ **2** GOAL, OBJECTIVE : meta *f*, objetivo *m*

tariff ['tærɪf] *n* DUTY : tarifa *f*, arancel *m*

tarnish¹ ['tɑrnɪʃ] *vt* **1** DULL : deslustrar **2** SULLY : empañar, manchar (una reputación, etc.) — *vi* : deslustrarse

tarnish² *n* : deslustre *m*

tarpaulin [tɑr'pɔlən, 'tɑrpə-] *n* : lona *f* (impermeable)

tarragon ['tærə,gɑn, -gən] *n* : estragón *m*

tarry¹ ['tæri] *vi* **-ried; -rying** : demorarse, entretenerse

tarry² ['tɑri] *adj* **1** : parecido al alquitrán **2** : cubierto de alquitrán

tart¹ ['tɑrt] *adj* **1** SOUR : ácido, agrio **2** CAUSTIC : mordaz, acrimonioso — **tartly** *adv*

tart² *n* : tartaleta *f*

tartan ['tɑrtən] *n* : tartán *m*

tartar ['tɑrtər] *n* **1** : tártaro *m* ⟨tartar sauce : salsa tártara⟩ **2** : sarro *m* (dental)

tartness ['tɑrtnəs] *n* **1** SOURNESS : acidez *f* **2** ACRIMONY, SHARPNESS : mordacidad *f*, acrimonia *f*, acritud *f*

task ['tæsk] *n* : tarea *f*, trabajo *m*

taskmaster ['tæsk,mæstər] *n* **to be a hard taskmaster** : ser exigente, ser muy estricto

tassel ['tæsəl] *n* : borla *f*

taste¹ ['teɪst] *v* **tasted; tasting** *vt* : probar (alimentos), degustar, catar (vinos) ⟨taste this soup : prueba esta sopa⟩ — *vi* : saber ⟨this tastes good : esto sabe bueno⟩

taste² *n* **1** SAMPLE : prueba *f*, bocado *m* (de comida), trago *m* (de bebidas) **2** FLAVOR : gusto *m*, sabor *m* **3** : gusto *m* ⟨she has good taste : tiene buen gusto⟩ ⟨in bad taste : de mal gusto⟩

taste bud *n* : papila *f* gustativa

tasteful ['teɪstfəl] *adj* : de buen gusto

tastefully ['teɪstfəli] *adv* : con buen gusto

tasteless ['teɪstləs] *adj* **1** FLAVORLESS : sin sabor, soso, insípido **2** : de mal gusto ⟨a tasteless joke : un chiste de mal gusto⟩

taster ['teɪstər] *n* : degustador *m*, -dora *f*; catador *m*, -dora *f* (de vinos)

tastiness ['teɪstinəs] *n* : lo sabroso

tasty ['teɪsti] *adj* **tastier; -est** : sabroso, gustoso

tatter ['tætər] *n* **1** SHRED : tira *f*, jirón *m* (de tela) **2 tatters** *npl* : andrajos *mpl*, harapos *mpl* ⟨to be in tatters : estar por los suelos⟩

tattered ['tætərd] *adj* : andrajoso, en jirones

tattle ['tætəl] *vi* **-tled; -tling 1** CHATTER : parlotear *fam*, cotorrear *fam* **2 to tattle on someone** : acusar a alguien

tattletale ['tætəl,teɪl] *n* : soplón *m*, -plona *f fam*

tattoo¹ [tæ'tu:] *vt* : tatuar

tattoo² *n* : tatuaje *m* ⟨to get a tattoo : tatuarse⟩

taught → **teach**

taunt¹ ['tɔnt] *vt* MOCK : mofarse de, burlarse de

taunt² *n* : mofa *f*, burla *f*

Taurus ['tɔrəs] *n* : Tauro *mf*

taut ['tɔt] *adj* : tirante, tenso — **tautly** *adv*

tautness ['tɔtnəs] *n* : tirantez *f*, tensión *f*

tavern ['tævərn] *n* : taberna *f*

tawdry ['tɔdri] *adj* **-drier; -est** : chabacano, vulgar

tawny ['tɔni] *adj* **-nier; -est** : leonado

tax¹ ['tæks] *vt* **1** : gravar, cobrar un impuesto sobre **2** CHARGE : acusar ⟨they taxed him with neglect : fue acusado de incumplimiento⟩ **3 to tax someone's strength** : ponerle a prueba las fuerzas (a alguien)

tax² *n* **1** : impuesto *m*, tributo *m* **2** BURDEN : carga *f*

taxable ['tæksəbəl] *adj* : sujeto a un impuesto

taxation [tæk'seɪʃən] *n* : impuestos *mpl*

tax–exempt ['tæksɪg'zempt, -ɛg-] *adj* : libre de impuestos

taxi¹ ['tæksi] *vi* **taxied; taxiing** *or* **taxying; taxis** *or* **taxies 1** : ir en taxi **2** : rodar sobre la pista de aterrizaje (dícese de un avión)

taxi² *n, pl* **taxis** : taxi *m*, libre *m Mex*

taxicab ['tæksi,kæb] *n* → **taxi²**

taxidermist ['tæksə,dərmɪst] *n* : taxidermista *mf*

taxidermy ['tæksə,dərmi] *n* : taxidermia *f*

taxpayer ['tæks,peɪər] *n* : contribuyente *mf*, causante *mf Mex*

TB [,ti:'bi:] → **tuberculosis**

tea ['ti:] *n* **1** : té *m* (planta y bebida) **2** : merienda *f*, té *m* (comida)

teach ['ti:tʃ] *v* **taught** ['tɔt]; **teaching** *vt* : enseñar, dar clases de ⟨she teaches math : da clases de matemáticas⟩ ⟨she taught me everything I know : me enseñó todo lo que sé⟩ — *vi* : enseñar, dar clases

teacher ['tiːtʃər] *n* : maestro *m*, -tra *f* (de enseñanza primaria); profesor *m*, -sora *f* (de enseñanza secundaria)

teaching ['tiːtʃɪŋ] *n* : enseñanza *f*

teacup ['tiːˌkʌp] *n* : taza *f* para té

teak ['tiːk] *n* : teca *f*

teakettle ['tiːˌkɛtəl] *n* : tetera *f*

teal ['tiːl] *n*, *pl* **teal** *or* **teals** : cerceta *f* (pato)

team¹ ['tiːm] *vi or* **to team up** **1** : formar un equipo (en deportes) **2** COLLABO-RATE : asociarse, juntarse, unirse

team² *adj* : de equipo

team³ *n* **1** : tiro *m* (de caballos), yunta *f* (de bueyes o mulas) **2** : equipo *m* (en deportes, etc.)

teammate ['tiːmˌmeɪt] *n* : compañero *m*, -ra *f* de equipo

teamster ['tiːmstər] *n* : camionero *m*, -ra *f*

teamwork ['tiːmˌwərk] *n* : trabajo *m* en equipo, cooperación *f*

teapot ['tiːˌpat] *n* : tetera *f*

tear¹ ['tær] *v* **tore** ['tor]; **torn** ['torn]; **tearing** *vt* **1** RIP : desgarrar, romper, rasgar (tela) ⟨to tear to pieces : hacer pedazos⟩ **2** *or* **to tear apart** DIVIDE : dividir **3** REMOVE : arrancar ⟨torn from his family : arrancado de su familia⟩ **4** **to tear down** : derribar — *vi* **1** RIP : desgarrarse, romperse **2** RUSH : ir a gran velocidad ⟨she went tearing down the street : se fue como rayo por la calle⟩

tear² *n* : desgarradura *f*, rotura *f*, desgarro *m* (muscular)

tear³ ['tɪr] *n* : lágrima *f*

teardrop ['tɪrˌdrap] *n* → **tear³**

tearful ['tɪrfəl] *adj* : lloroso, triste — **tearfully** *adv*

tease¹ ['tiːz] *vt* **teased; teasing 1** MOCK : burlarse de, mofarse de **2** ANNOY : irritar, fastidiar

tease² *n* **1** TEASING : burla *f*, mofa *f* **2** : bromista *mf*; guasón *m*, -sona *f*

teaspoon ['tiːˌspuːn] *n* **1** : cucharita *f* **2** → **teaspoonful**

teaspoonful ['tiːˌspuːnˌfʊl] *n*, *pl* **-spoonfuls** [-ˌfʊlz] *or* **-spoonsful** [-ˌspuːnzˌfʊl] : cucharadita *f*

teat ['tiːt] *n* : tetilla *f*

technical ['tɛknɪkəl] *adj* : técnico — **technically** [-kli] *adv*

technicality [ˌtɛknəˈkæləti] *n*, *pl* **-ties** : detalle *m* técnico

technician [tɛkˈnɪʃən] *n* : técnico *m*, -ca *f*

technique [tɛkˈniːk] *n* : técnica *f*

technological [ˌtɛknəˈladʒɪkəl] *adj* : tecnológico

technology [tɛkˈnalədʒi] *n*, *pl* **-gies** : tecnología *f*

teddy bear ['tɛdi] *n* : oso *m* de peluche

tedious ['tiːdiəs] *adj* : aburrido, pesado, monótono — **tediously** *adv*

tediousness ['tiːdiəsnəs] *n* : lo aburrido, lo pesado

tedium ['tiːdiəm] *n* : tedio *m*, pesadez *f*

tee ['tiː] *n* : tee *mf*

teem ['tiːm] *vi* **to teem with** : estar repleto de, estar lleno de

teenage ['tiːnˌeɪdʒ] *or* **teenaged** [-eɪdʒd] *adj* : adolescente, de adolescencia

teenager ['tiːnˌeɪdʒər] *n* : adolescente *mf*

teens ['tiːnz] *npl* : adolescencia *f*

teepee → **tepee**

teeter¹ ['tiːtər] *vi* : balancearse, tambalearse

teeter² *n or* **teeter–totter** ['tiːtərˌtatər] → **seesaw**

teeth → **tooth**

teethe ['tiːð] *vi* **teethed; teething** : formársele a uno los dientes ⟨the baby's teething : le están saliendo los dientes al niño⟩

telecast¹ ['tɛləˌkæst] *vt* **-cast; -casting** : televisar, transmitir por televisión

telecast² *n* : transmisión *f* por televisión

telecommunication [ˌtɛləkəˌmjuːnəˈkeɪʃən] *n* : telecomunicación *f*

telegram ['tɛləˌgræm] *n* : telegrama *m*

telegraph¹ ['tɛləˌgræf] *v* : telegrafiar

telegraph² *n* : telégrafo *m*

telepathic [ˌtɛləˈpæθɪk] *adj* : telepático — **telepathically** [-θɪkli] *adv*

telepathy [təˈlɛpəθi] *n* : telepatía *f*

telephone¹ ['tɛləˌfoːn] *v* **-phoned; -phoning** *vt* : llamar por teléfono a, telefonear — *vi* : telefonear

telephone² *n* : teléfono *m*

telescope¹ ['tɛləˌskoːp] *vi* **-scoped; -scoping** : plegarse (como un telescopio)

telescope² *n* : telescopio *m*

telescopic [ˌtɛləˈskapɪk] *adj* : telescópico

televise ['tɛləˌvaɪz] *vt* **-vised; -vising** : televisar

television ['tɛləˌvɪʒən] *n* : televisión *f*

tell ['tɛl] *v* **told** ['toːld]; **telling** *vt* **1** COUNT : contar, enumerar ⟨all told : en total⟩ **2** INSTRUCT : decir ⟨he told me how to fix it : me dijo cómo arreglarlo⟩ ⟨they told her to wait : le dijeron que esperara⟩ **3** RELATE : contar, relatar, narrar ⟨to tell a story : contar una historia⟩ **4** DIVULGE, REVEAL : revelar, divulgar ⟨he told me everything about her : me contó todo acerca de ella⟩ **5** DISCERN : discernir, notar ⟨I can't tell the difference : no noto la diferencia⟩ — *vi* **1** SAY : decir ⟨I won't tell : no voy a decírselo a nadie⟩ **2** KNOW : saber ⟨you never can tell : nunca se sabe⟩ **3** SHOW : notarse, hacerse sentir ⟨the strain is beginning to tell : la tensión se empieza a notar⟩

teller ['tɛlər] *n* **1** NARRATOR : narrador *m*, -dora *f* **2** *or* **bank teller** : cajero *m*, -ra *f*

temerity [təˈmɛrəti] *n*, *pl* **-ties** : temeridad *f*

temp ['tɛmp] *n* : empleado *m*, -da *f* temporal

temper¹ ['tɛmpər] *vt* **1** MODERATE : moderar, temperar **2** ANNEAL : templar (acero, etc.)

temper² *n* **1** DISPOSITION : carácter *m*, genio *m* **2** HARDNESS : temple *m*, dureza *f* (de un metal) **3** COMPOSURE : calma *f*, serenidad *f* ⟨to lose one's temper : perder los estribos⟩ **4** RAGE : furia *f* ⟨to fly into a temper : ponerse furioso⟩

temperament ['tɛmpərmənt, -prə-, -pərə-] *n* : temperamento *m*

temperamental [ˌtɛmpər'mɛntəl, -prə-, -pərə-] *adj* : temperamental

temperance ['tɛmprənts] *n* : templanza *f*, temperancia *f*

temperate ['tɛmpərət] *adj* : templado (dícese del clima, etc.)

temperature ['tɛmpərˌtʃur, -prə-, -pərə-, -tʃər] *n* **1** : temperatura *f* **2** FEVER : calentura *f*, fiebre *f*

tempest ['tɛmpəst] *n* : tempestad *f*

tempestuous [tɛm'pɛstʃuəs] *adj* : tempestuoso

temple ['tɛmpəl] *n* **1** : templo *m* (en religión) **2** : sien *f* (en anatomía)

tempo ['tɛmˌpoː] *n, pl* **-pi** [-ˌpiː] *or* **-pos** : ritmo *m*, tempo *m* (en música)

temporal ['tɛmpərəl] *adj* : temporal

temporarily [ˌtɛmpə'rɛrəli] *adv* : temporalmente, provisionalmente

temporary ['tɛmpəˌrɛri] *adj* : temporal, provisional, provisorio

tempt ['tɛmpt] *vt* : tentar

temptation [tɛmp'teɪʃən] *n* : tentación *f*

tempter ['tɛmptər] *n* : tentador *m*

temptress ['tɛmptrəs] *n* : tentadora *f*

ten¹ ['tɛn] *adj* : diez

ten² *n* **1** : diez *m* (número) **2** : decena *f* ⟨tens of thousands : decenas de millares⟩

tenable ['tɛnəbəl] *adj* : sostenible, defendible

tenacious [tə'neɪʃəs] *adj* : tenaz

tenacity [tə'næsəti] *n* : tenacidad *f*

tenancy ['tɛnəntsi] *n, pl* **-cies** : tenencia *f*, inquilinato *m* (de un inmueble)

tenant ['tɛnənt] *n* : inquilino *m*, -na *f*; arrendatario *m*, -ria *f*

tend ['tɛnd] *vt* : atender, cuidar (de), ocuparse de — *vi* : tender ⟨it tends to benefit the consumer : tiende a beneficiar al consumidor⟩

tendency ['tɛndəntsi] *n, pl* **-cies** : tendencia *f*, proclividad *f*, inclinación *f*

tender¹ ['tɛndər] *vt* : entregar, presentar ⟨I tendered my resignation : presenté mi renuncia⟩

tender² *adj* **1** : tierno, blando ⟨tender steak : bistec tierno⟩ **2** AFFECTIONATE, LOVING : tierno, cariñoso, afectuoso **3** DELICATE : tierno, sensible, delicado

tender³ *n* **1** OFFER : propuesta *f*, oferta *f* (en negocios) **2** legal tender : moneda *f* de curso legal

tenderize ['tɛndəˌraɪz] *vt* **-ized; -izing** : ablandar (carnes)

tenderloin ['tɛndrˌlɔɪn] *n* : lomo *f* (de res o de puerco)

tenderly ['tɛndərli] *adv* : tiernamente, con ternura

tenderness ['tɛndərnəs] *n* : ternura *f*

tendon ['tɛndən] *n* : tendón *m*

tendril ['tɛndrɪl] *n* : zarcillo *m*

tenement ['tɛnəmənt] *n* : casa *f* de vecindad

tenet ['tɛnət] *n* : principio *m*

tennis ['tɛnəs] *n* : tenis *m*

tenor ['tɛnər] *n* **1** PURPORT : tenor *m*, significado *m* **2** : tenor *m* (en música)

tenpins ['tɛnˌpɪnz] *npl* : bolos *mpl*, boliche *m*

tense¹ ['tɛnts] *v* **tensed; tensing** *vt* : tensar — *vi* : tensarse, ponerse tenso

tense² *adj* **tenser; tensest** **1** TAUT : tenso, tirante **2** NERVOUS : tenso, nervioso

tense³ *n* : tiempo *m* (de un verbo)

tensely ['tɛntsli] *adv* : tensamente

tenseness ['tɛntsnəs] → **tension**

tension ['tɛntʃən] *n* **1** TAUTNESS : tensión *f*, tirantez *f* **2** STRESS : tensión *f*, nerviosismo *m*, estrés *m*

tent ['tɛnt] *n* : tienda *f* de campaña

tentacle ['tɛntɪkəl] *n* : tentáculo *m*

tentative ['tɛntətɪv] *adj* **1** HESITANT : indeciso, vacilante **2** PROVISIONAL : sujeto a cambios, provisional

tentatively ['tɛntətɪvli] *adv* : provisionalmente

tenth¹ ['tɛnθ] *adj* : décimo

tenth² *n* **1** : décimo *m*, -ma *f* (en una serie) **2** : décimo *m*, décima parte *f*

tenuous ['tɛnjuəs] *adj* : tenue, débil ⟨tenuous reasons : razones poco convincentes⟩

tenuously ['tɛnjuəsli] *adv* : tenuemente, ligeramente

tenure ['tɛnjər] *n* : tenencia *f* (de un cargo o una propiedad), titularidad *f* (de un puesto académico)

tepee ['tiːˌpiː] *n* : tipi *m*

tepid ['tɛpɪd] *adj* : tibio

tequila [tə'kiːlə] *n* : tequila *m*

term¹ ['tərm] *vt* : calificar de, llamar, nombrar

term² *n* **1** PERIOD : término *m*, plazo *m*, período *m* **2** : término *m* (en matemáticas) **3** WORD : término *m*, vocablo *m* ⟨legal terms : términos legales⟩ **4 terms** *npl* CONDITIONS : términos *mpl*, condiciones *fpl* **5 terms** *npl* RELATIONS : relaciones *fpl* ⟨to be on good terms with : tener buenas relaciones con⟩ **6 in terms of** : con respecto a, en cuanto a

terminal¹ ['tərmənəl] *adj* : terminal

terminal² *n* **1** : terminal *m*, polo *m* (en electricidad) **2** : terminal *m* (de una computadora) **3** STATION : terminal *f*, estación *f* (de transporte público)

terminate ['tərməˌneɪt] *v* **-nated; -nating** *vi* : terminar(se), concluirse — *vt* : terminar, poner fin a

termination [ˌtərmə'neɪʃən] *n* : cese *m*, terminación *f*

terminology [ˌtərmə'nɑlədʒi] *n, pl* **-gies** : terminología *f*

terminus ['tərmənəs] *n, pl* **-ni** [-ˌnaɪ] *or* **-nuses** **1** END : término *m*, fin *m* **2** : terminal *f* (de transporte público)

termite ['tər,maɪt] *n* : termita *f*
tern ['tərn] *n* : golondrina *f* de mar
terrace¹ ['tɛrəs] *vt* **-raced; -racing** : formar en terrazas, disponer en bancales
terrace² *n* **1** PATIO : terraza *f*, patio *m* **2** : terraplén *m*, terraza *f*, bancal *m* (en agricultura)
terra–cotta [,tɛrə'kɑtə] *n* : terracota *f*
terrain [tə'reɪn] *n* : terreno *m*
terrapin ['tɛrəpɪn] *n* : galápago *m* norteamericano
terrarium [tə'ræriəm] *n, pl* **-ia** [-iə] *or* **-iums** : terrario *m*
terrestrial [tə'rɛstriəl] *adj* : terrestre
terrible ['tɛrəbəl] *adj* : atroz, horrible, terrible
terribly ['tɛrəbli] *adv* **1** BADLY : muy mal **2** EXTREMELY : terriblemente, extremadamente
terrier ['tɛriər] *n* : terrier *mf*
terrific [tə'rɪfɪk] *adj* **1** FRIGHTFUL : aterrador **2** EXTRAORDINARY : extraordinario, excepcional **3** EXCELLENT : excelente, estupendo
terrify ['tɛrə,faɪ] *vt* **-fied; -fying** : aterrorizar, aterrar, espantar
terrifying ['tɛrə,faɪɪŋ] *adj* : espantoso, aterrador
territory ['tɛrə,tori] *n, pl* **-ries** : territorio *m* — **territorial** [,tɛrə'toriəl] *adj*
terror ['tɛrər] *n* : terror *m*
terrorism ['tɛrər,ɪzəm] *n* : terrorismo *m*
terrorist¹ ['tɛrərɪst] *adj* : terrorista
terrorist² *n* : terrorista *mf*
terrorize ['tɛrər,aɪz] *vt* **-ized; -izing** : aterrorizar
terry ['tɛri] *n, pl* **-ries** *or* **terry cloth** : (tela de) toalla *f*
terse ['tərs] *adj* **terser; tersest** : lacónico, conciso, seco — **tersely** *adv*
tertiary ['tərʃi,ɛri] *adj* : terciario
test¹ ['tɛst] *vt* : examinar, evaluar — *vi* : hacer pruebas
test² *n* : prueba *f*, examen *m*, test *m* ⟨to put to the test : poner a prueba⟩
testament ['tɛstəmənt] *n* **1** WILL : testamento *m* **2** : Testamento *m* (en la Biblia) ⟨the Old Testament : el Antiguo Testamento⟩
testicle ['tɛstɪkəl] *n* : testículo *m*
testify ['tɛstə,faɪ] *v* **-fied; -fying** *vi* : testificar, atestar, testimoniar — *vt* : testificar
testimonial [,tɛstə'mo:niəl] *n* **1** REFERENCE : recomendación *f* **2** TRIBUTE : homenaje *m*, tributo *m*
testimony ['tɛstə,mo:ni] *n, pl* **-nies** : testimonio *m*, declaración *f*
test tube *n* : probeta *f*, tubo *m* de ensayo
testy ['tɛsti] *adj* **-tier; -est** : irritable
tetanus ['tɛtənəs] *n* : tétano *m*, tétanos *m*
tête–à–tête [,tɛtə'tɛt, ,teɪtə'teɪt] *n* : conversación *f* en privado
tether¹ ['tɛðər] *vt* : atar (con una cuerda), amarrar
tether² *n* : atadura *f*, cadena *f*, correa *f*

text ['tɛkst] *n* **1** : texto *m* **2** TOPIC : tema *m* **3** → **textbook**
textbook ['tɛkst,bʊk] *n* : libro *m* de texto
textile ['tɛk,staɪl, 'tɛkstəl] *n* : textil *m*, tela *f* ⟨the textile industry : la industria textil⟩
textual ['tɛkstʃʊəl] *adj* : textual
texture ['tɛkstʃər] *n* : textura *f*
Thai ['taɪ] *n* **1** : tailandés *m*, -desa *f* **2** : tailandés *m* (idioma) — **Thai** *adj*
than¹ ['ðæn] *conj* : que, de ⟨it's worth more than that : vale más que esto⟩ ⟨more than you think : más de lo que piensas⟩
than² *prep* : que, de ⟨you're better than he is : eres mejor que él⟩ ⟨more than once : más de una vez⟩
thank ['θæŋk] *vt* : agradecer, darle (las) gracias (a alguien) ⟨thank you! : ¡gracias!⟩ ⟨I thanked her for the present : le di las gracias por el regalo⟩ ⟨I thank you for your help : le agradezco su ayuda⟩
thankful ['θæŋkfəl] *adj* : agradecido
thankfully ['θæŋkfəli] *adv* **1** GRATEFULLY : con agradecimiento **2** FORTUNATELY : afortunadamente, por suerte ⟨thankfully, it's over : se acabó, gracias a Dios⟩
thankfulness ['θæŋkfəlnəs] *n* : agradecimiento *m*, gratitud *f*
thankless ['θæŋkləs] *adj* : ingrato ⟨a thankless task : un trabajo ingrato⟩
thanks ['θæŋks] *npl* **1** : agradecimiento *m* **2 thanks!** : ¡gracias!
Thanksgiving [θæŋks'gɪvɪŋ, 'θæŋks,-] *n* : el día de Acción de Gracias (fiesta estadounidense)
that¹ ['ðæt] *adv* (*in negative constructions*) : tan ⟨it's not that expensive : no es tan caro⟩ ⟨not that much : no tanto⟩
that² *adj, pl* **those** : ese, esa, aquel, aquella ⟨do you see those children? : ¿ves a aquellos niños?⟩
that³ *conj & pron* : que ⟨he said that he was afraid : dijo que tenía miedo⟩ ⟨the book that he wrote : el libro que escribió⟩
that⁴ *pron, pl* **those** ['ðo:z] **1** : ése, ésa, eso ⟨that's my father : ése es mi padre⟩ ⟨those are the ones he likes : ésos son los que le gustan⟩ ⟨what's that? : ¿qué es eso?⟩ **2** (*referring to more distant objects or time*) : aquél, aquélla, aquello ⟨those are maples and these are elms : aquéllos son arces y éstos son olmos⟩ ⟨that came to an end : aquello se acabó⟩
thatch¹ ['θætʃ] *vt* : cubrir o techar con paja
thatch² *n* : paja *f* (usada para techos)
thaw¹ ['θɔ] *vt* : descongelar — *vi* : derretirse (dícese de la nieve), descongelarse (dícese de los alimentos)
thaw² *n* : deshielo *m*

the¹ [ðə, *before vowel sounds usu* ði:] *adv*
1 (*used to indicate comparison*) ⟨the
sooner the better : cuanto más pronto,
mejor⟩ ⟨she likes this one the best : éste
es el que más le gusta⟩ **2** (*used as a conjunction*) : cuanto ⟨the more I learn,
the less I understand : cuanto más
aprendo, menos entiendo⟩

the² *art* : el, la, los, las ⟨the gloves : los
guantes⟩ ⟨the suitcase : la maleta⟩
⟨forty cookies to the box : cuarenta
galletas por caja⟩

theater *or* **theatre** [ˈθiːətər] *n* **1** : teatro
m (edificio) **2** DRAMA : teatro *m*, drama *m*

theatrical [θiˈætrɪkəl] *adj* : teatral,
dramático

thee [ˈðiː] *pron* : te, ti

theft [ˈθɛft] *n* : robo *m*, hurto *m*

their [ˈðɛr] *adj* : su ⟨their friends : sus
amigos⟩

theirs [ˈðɛrz] *pron* : (el) suyo, (la) suya,
(los) suyos, (las) suyas ⟨they came for
theirs : vinieron por el suyo⟩ ⟨theirs is
bigger : la suya es más grande, la de ellos es más grande⟩ ⟨a brother of theirs
: un hermano suyo, un hermano de
ellos⟩

them [ˈðɛm] *pron* **1** (*as a direct object*)
: los (*Spain sometimes* les), las ⟨I know
them : los conozco⟩ **2** (*as an indirect object*) : les, se ⟨I sent them a letter : les
mandé una carta⟩ ⟨give it to them
: dáselo (a ellos)⟩ **3** (*as object of a preposition*) : ellos, ellas ⟨go with them : ve
con ellos⟩ **4** (*for emphasis*) : ellos,
ellas ⟨I wasn't expecting them : no los
esperaba a ellos⟩

thematic [θiˈmætɪk] *adj* : temático

theme [ˈθiːm] *n* **1** SUBJECT, TOPIC : tema
m **2** COMPOSITION : composición *f*, trabajo *m* (escrito) **3** : tema *m* (en música)

themselves [ðəmˈsɛlvz, ðɛm-] *pron* **1**
(*as a reflexive*) : se, sí ⟨they enjoyed
themselves : se divirtieron⟩ ⟨they divided it among themselves : lo
repartieron entre sí, se lo repartieron⟩
2 (*for emphasis*) : ellos mismos, ellas
mismas ⟨they built it themselves : ellas
mismas lo construyeron⟩

then¹ [ˈðɛn] *adv* **1** : entonces, en ese
tiempo ⟨I was sixteen then : tenía entonces dieciséis años⟩ ⟨since then : desde entonces⟩ **2** NEXT : después, luego
⟨we'll go to Toronto, then to Winnipeg
: iremos a Toronto, y luego a Winnipeg⟩
3 BESIDES : además, aparte ⟨then
there's the tax : y aparte está el impuesto⟩ **4** : entonces, en ese caso ⟨if
you like music, then you should attend
: si te gusta la música, entonces deberías asistir⟩

then² *adj* : entonces ⟨the then governor
of Georgia : el entonces gobernador de
Georgia⟩

thence [ˈðɛnts, ˈθɛnts] *adv* : de ahí, de ahí
en adelante

theologian [ˌθiːəˈloːdʒən] *n* : teólogo *m*,
-ga *f*

theological [ˌθiːəˈlɑdʒɪkəl] *adj* : teológico

theology [θiˈɑlədʒi] *n, pl* **-gies** : teología
f

theorem [ˈθiːərəm, ˈθɪrəm] *n* : teorema
m

theoretical [ˌθiːəˈrɛtɪkəl] *adj* : teórico —
theoretically *adv*

theorist [ˈθiːərɪst] *n* : teórico *m*, -ca *f*

theorize [ˈθiːəˌraɪz] *vi* **-rized; -rizing**
: teorizar

theory [ˈθiːəri, ˈθɪri] *n, pl* **-ries** : teoría *f*

therapeutic [ˌθɛrəˈpjuːtɪk] *adj* : terapéutico — **therapeutically** *adv*

therapist [ˈθɛrəpɪst] *n* : terapeuta *mf*

therapy [ˈθɛrəpi] *n, pl* **-pies** : terapia *f*

there¹ [ˈðɛr] *adv* **1** : ahí, allí, allá ⟨stand
over there : párate ahí⟩ ⟨over there
: por allí, por allá⟩ ⟨who's there?
: ¿quién es?⟩ **2** : ahí, en esto, en eso
⟨there is where we disagree : en eso es
donde no estamos de acuerdo⟩

there² *pron* **1** (*introducing a sentence or
clause*) ⟨there comes a time to decide
: llega un momento en que tiene uno
que decidir⟩ **2 there is, there are** : hay
⟨there are many children here : aquí
hay muchos niños⟩ ⟨there's a good hotel downtown : hay un buen hotel en
el centro⟩

thereabouts [ˌðɛrəˈbaʊts, ˈðɛrəˌ-] *or*
thereabout [-ˈbaʊt, -ˌbaʊt] *adv* **or**
thereabouts : por ahí, más o menos ⟨at
five o'clock or thereabouts : por ahí de
las cinco⟩

thereafter [ðɛrˈæftər] *adv* : después
⟨shortly thereafter : poco después⟩

thereby [ðɛrˈbaɪ, ˈðɛrˌbaɪ] *adv* : de tal
modo, de ese manera, así

therefore [ˈðɛrˌfor] *adv* : por lo tanto,
por consiguiente

therein [ðɛrˈɪn] *adv* **1** : allí adentro, ahí
adentro ⟨the contents therein : lo que
allí se contiene⟩ **2** : allí, en ese aspecto ⟨therein lies the problem : allí está
el problema⟩

thereof [ðɛrˈʌv, -ˈav] *adv* : de eso, de
esto

thereupon [ˈðɛrəˌpɑn, -ˌpɔn; ˌðɛrəˈpɑn,
-ˈpɔn] *adv* : acto seguido, inmediatamente (después)

therewith [ðɛrˈwɪð, -ˈwɪθ] *adv* : con eso,
con ello

thermal [ˈθərməl] *adj* **1** : térmico (en física) **2** HOT : termal

thermodynamics [ˌθərmodaɪˈnæmɪks]
ns & pl : termodinámica *f*

thermometer [θərˈmɑmətər] *n* : termómetro *m*

thermos [ˈθərməs] *n* : termo *m*

thermostat [ˈθərməˌstæt] *n* : termostato
m

thesaurus [θɪˈsɔrəs] *n, pl* **-sauri** [-ˈsɔrˌaɪ]
or **-sauruses** [-ˈsɔrəsəz] : diccionario *m*
de sinónimos

these → **this**

thesis ['θi:sɪs] *n, pl* **theses** ['θi:ˌsi:z] : tesis *f*

they ['ðeɪ] *pron* : ellos, ellas ⟨they are here : están aquí⟩ ⟨they don't know : ellos no saben⟩

they'd ['ðeɪd] (*contraction of* **they had** *or* **they would**) → **have, would**

they'll ['ðeɪl, 'ðɛl] (*contraction of* **they shall** *or* **they will**) → **shall, will**

they're ['ðɛr] (*contraction of* **they are**) → **be**

they've ['ðeɪv] (*contraction of* **they have**) → **have**

thiamine ['θaɪəmɪn, -ˌmi:n] *n* : tiamina *f*

thick[1] ['θɪk] *adj* **1** : grueso ⟨a thick plank : una tabla gruesa⟩ **2** : espeso, denso ⟨thick syrup : jarabe espeso⟩ — **thickly** *adv*

thick[2] *n* **1 in the thick of** : en medio de ⟨in the thick of the battle : en lo más reñido de la batalla⟩ **2 through thick and thin** : a las duras y a las maduras

thicken ['θɪkən] *vt* : espesar (un líquido) — *vi* : espesarse

thickener ['θɪkənər] *n* : espesante *m*

thicket ['θɪkət] *n* : matorral *m*, maleza *f*, espesura *f*

thickness ['θɪknəs] *n* : grosor *m*, grueso *m*, espesor *m*

thickset ['θɪk'sɛt] *adj* STOCKY : robusto, fornido

thick–skinned ['θɪk'skɪnd] *adj* : poco sensible, que no se ofende fácilmente

thief ['θi:f] *n, pl* **thieves** ['θi:vz] : ladrón *m*, -drona *f*

thieve ['θi:v] *v* **thieved; thieving** : hurtar, robar

thievery ['θi:vəri] *n* : hurto *m*, robo *m*, latrocinio *m*

thigh ['θaɪ] *n* : muslo *m*

thighbone ['θaɪˌbo:n] *n* : fémur *m*

thimble ['θɪmbəl] *n* : dedal *m*

thin[1] ['θɪn] *v* **thinned; thinning** *vt* : hacer menos denso, diluir, aguar (un líquido), enrarecer (un gas) — *vi* : diluirse, aguarse (dícese de un líquido), enrarecerse (dícese de un gas)

thin[2] *adj* **thinner; -est 1** LEAN, SLIM : delgado, esbelto, flaco **2** SPARSE : ralo, escaso ⟨a thin beard : una barba rala⟩ **3** WATERY : claro, aguado, diluido **4** FINE : delgado, fino ⟨thin slices : rebanadas finas⟩

thing ['θɪŋ] *n* **1** AFFAIR, MATTER : cosa *f*, asunto *m* ⟨don't talk about those things : no hables de esas cosas⟩ ⟨how are things? : ¿cómo van las cosas?⟩ **2** ACT, EVENT : cosa *f*, suceso *m*, evento *m* ⟨the flood was a terrible thing : la inundación fue una cosa terrible⟩ **3** OBJECT : cosa *f*, objeto *m* ⟨don't forget your things : no olvides tus cosas⟩

think ['θɪŋk] *v* **thought** ['θɔt]; **thinking** *vt* **1** : pensar ⟨I thought to return early : pensaba regresar temprano⟩ **2** BELIEVE : pensar, creer, opinar **3** PONDER : pensar, reflexionar **4** CONCEIVE : ocurrirse, concebir ⟨we've thought up a plan : se nos ha ocurrido un plan⟩ —

vi **1** REASON : pensar, razonar **2** CONSIDER : pensar, considerar ⟨think of your family first : primero piensa en tu familia⟩

thinker ['θɪŋkər] *n* : pensador *m*, -dora *f*

thinly ['θɪnli] *adv* **1** LIGHTLY : ligeramente **2** SPARSELY : escasamente ⟨thinly populated : poco populado⟩ **3** BARELY : apenas

thinness ['θɪnnəs] *n* : delgadez *f*

thin–skinned ['θɪn'skɪnd] *adj* : susceptible, muy sensible

third[1] ['θərd] *or* **thirdly** [-li] *adv* : en tercer lugar ⟨she came in third : llegó en tercer lugar⟩

third[2] *adj* : tercero ⟨the third day : el tercer día⟩

third[3] *n* **1** : tercero *m*, -ra *f* (en una serie) **2** : tercero *m*, tercera parte *f*

third world *n* **the Third World** : el Tercer Mundo *m*

thirst[1] ['θərst] *vi* **1** : tener sed **2 to thirst for** DESIRE : tener sed de, estar sediento de

thirst[2] *n* : sed *f*

thirsty ['θərsti] *adj* **thirstier; -est** : sediento, que tiene sed ⟨I'm thirsty : tengo sed⟩

thirteen[1] [ˌθər'ti:n] *adj* : trece

thirteen[2] *n* : trece *m*

thirteenth[1] [ˌθər'ti:nθ] *adj* : décimo tercero

thirteenth[2] *n* **1** : decimotercero *m*, -ra *f* (en una serie) **2** : treceavo *m*, treceava parte *f*

thirtieth[1] ['θərt̬iəθ] *adj* : trigésimo

thirtieth[2] *n* **1** : trigésimo *m*, -ma *f* (en una serie) **2** : treintavo *m*, treintava parte *f*

thirty[1] ['θərt̬i] *adj* : treinta

thirty[2] *n, pl* **thirties** : treinta *m*

this[1] ['ðɪs] *adv* : así, a tal punto ⟨this big : así de grande⟩

this[2] *adj, pl* **these** ['ði:z] : este ⟨these things : estas cosas⟩ ⟨read this book : lee este libro⟩

this[3] *pron, pl* **these** : esto ⟨what's this? : ¿qué es esto?⟩ ⟨this wasn't here yesterday : esto no estaba aquí ayer⟩

thistle ['θɪsəl] *n* : cardo *m*

thong ['θɔŋ] *n* **1** STRAP : correa *f*, tira *f* **2** FLIP-FLOP : chancla *f*, chancleta *f*

thorax ['θor,æks] *n, pl* **-raxes** *or* **-races** ['θorəˌsi:z] : tórax *m*

thorn ['θɔrn] *n* : espina *f*

thorny ['θɔrni] *adj* **thornier; -est** : espinoso

thorough ['θəro:] *adj* **1** CONSCIENTIOUS : concienzudo, meticuloso **2** COMPLETE : absoluto, completo — **thoroughly** *adv*

thoroughbred ['θərəˌbrɛd] *adj* : de pura sangre (dícese de un caballo)

Thoroughbred *n* *or* **Thoroughbred horse** : pura sangre *mf*

thoroughfare ['θərəˌfær] *n* : vía *f* pública, carretera *f*

thoroughness ['θəronəs] *n* : esmero *m*, meticulosidad *f*

those · through

674

those → **that**

thou ['ðaʊ] *pron* : tú

though[1] ['ðo:] *adv* **1** HOWEVER, NEVERTHELESS : sin embargo, no obstante **2 as ∼** : como si ⟨as though nothing had happened : como si nada hubiera pasado⟩

though[2] *conj* : aunque, a pesar de ⟨though it was raining, we went out : salimos a pesar de la lluvia⟩

thought[1] → **think**

thought[2] ['θɔt] *n* **1** THINKING : pensamiento *m*, ideas *fpl* ⟨Western thought : el pensamiento occidental⟩ **2** COGITATION : pensamiento *m*, reflexión *f*, raciocinio *m* **3** IDEA : idea *f*, ocurrencia *f* ⟨it was just a thought : fue sólo una idea⟩

thoughtful ['θɔtfəl] *adj* **1** PENSIVE : pensativo, meditabundo **2** CONSIDERATE : considerado, atento, cortés — **thoughtfully** *adv*

thoughtfulness ['θɔtfəlnəs] *n* : consideración *f*, atención *f*, cortesía *f*

thoughtless ['θɔtləs] *adj* **1** CARELESS : descuidado, negligente **2** INCONSIDERATE : desconsiderado — **thoughtlessly** *adv*

thousand[1] ['θaʊzənd] *adj* : mil

thousand[2] *n, pl* **-sands** *or* **-sand** : mil *m*

thousandth[1] ['θaʊzəntθ] *adj* : milésimo

thousandth[2] *n* **1** : milésimo *m*, -ma *f* (en una serie) **2** : milésimo *m*, milésima parte *f*

thrash ['θræʃ] *vt* **1** → **thresh 2** BEAT : golpear, azotar, darle una paliza (a alguien) **3** FLAIL : sacudir, agitar bruscamente

thread[1] ['θrɛd] *vt* **1** : enhilar, enhebrar (una aguja) **2** STRING : ensartar (cuentas en un hilo) **3 to thread one's way** : abrirse paso

thread[2] *n* **1** : hilo *m*, hebra *f* ⟨needle and thread : aguja e hilo⟩ ⟨the thread of an argument : el hilo de un debate⟩ **2** : rosca *f*, filete *m* (de un tornillo)

threadbare ['θrɛd,bær] *adj* **1** SHABBY, WORN : raído, gastado **2** TRITE : trillado, tópico, manido

threat ['θrɛt] *n* : amenaza *f*

threaten ['θrɛtən] *v* : amenazar

threatening ['θrɛtənɪŋ] *adj* : amenazador — **threateningly** *adv*

three[1] ['θri:] *adj* : tres

three[2] *n* : tres *m*

3–D ['θri:'di:] *adj* → **three–dimensional**

three–dimensional ['θri:də'mɛntʃənəl] *adj* : tridimensional

threefold ['θri:,fo:ld] *adj* TRIPLE : triple

three hundred[1] *adj* : trescientos

three hundred[2] *n* : trescientos *m*

threescore ['θri:'skor] *adj* SIXTY : sesenta

thresh ['θrɛʃ] *vt* : trillar (grano)

thresher ['θrɛʃər] *n* : trilladora *f*

threshold ['θrɛʃ,ho:ld, -,o:ld] *n* : umbral *m*

threw → **throw**[1]

thrice ['θraɪs] *adv* : tres veces

thrift ['θrɪft] *n* : economía *f*, frugalidad *f*

thriftless ['θrɪftləs] *adj* : despilfarrador, manirroto

thrifty ['θrɪfti] *adj* **thriftier; -est** : económico, frugal — **thriftily** ['θrɪftəli] *adv*

thrill[1] ['θrɪl] *vt* : emocionar — *vi* **to thrill to** : dejarse conmover por, estremecerse con

thrill[2] *n* : emoción *f*

thriller ['θrɪlər] *n* **1** : evento *m* emocionante **2** : obra *f* de suspenso

thrilling ['θrɪlɪŋ] *adj* : emocionante, excitante

thrive ['θraɪv] *vi* **throve** ['θro:v] *or* **thrived; thriven** ['θrɪvən] **1** FLOURISH : florecer, crecer abundantemente **2** PROSPER : prosperar

throat ['θro:t] *n* : garganta *f*

throaty ['θro:ti] *adj* **throatier; -est** : ronco (dícese de la voz)

throb[1] ['θrɑb] *vi* **throbbed; throbbing** : palpitar, latir (dícese del corazón), vibrar (dícese de un motor, etc.)

throb[2] *n* : palpitación *f*, latido *m*, vibración *f*

throe ['θro:] *n* **1** PAIN, SPASM : espasmo *m*, dolor *m* ⟨the throes of childbirth : los dolores de parto⟩ **2 throes** *npl* : lucha *f* larga y ardua ⟨in the throes of : en el medio de⟩

throne ['θro:n] *n* : trono *m*

throng[1] ['θrɔŋ] *vt* CROWD : atestar, atiborrar, llenar — *vi* : aglomerarse, amontonarse

throng[2] *n* : muchedumbre *f*, gentío *m*, multitud *f*

throttle[1] ['θrɑtəl] *vt* **-tled; -tling 1** STRANGLE : estrangular, ahogar **2 to throttle down** : desacelerar (un motor)

throttle[2] *n* **1** : válvula *f* reguladora **2 at full throttle** : a toda máquina

through[1] ['θru:] *adv* **1** : a través, de un lado a otro ⟨let them through : déjenlos pasar⟩ **2** : de principio a fin ⟨she read the book through : leyó el libro de principio a fin⟩ **3** COMPLETELY : completamente ⟨soaked through : completamente empapado⟩

through[2] *adj* **1** DIRECT : directo ⟨a through train : un tren directo⟩ **2** FINISHED : terminado, acabado ⟨we're through : hemos terminado⟩

through[3] *prep* **1** : a través de, por ⟨through the door : por la puerta⟩ ⟨a road through the woods : un camino que atraviesa el bosque⟩ **2** BETWEEN : entre ⟨a path through the trees : un sendero entre los árboles⟩ **3** BECAUSE OF : a causa de, como consecuencia de **4** (*in expressions of time*) ⟨through the night : durante la noche⟩ ⟨to go through an experience : pasar por una experiencia⟩ **5** : a, hasta ⟨from Monday through Friday : de lunes a viernes⟩

throughout¹ [θru:'aʊt] *adv* **1** EVERY-WHERE : por todas partes **2** THROUGH : desde el principio hasta el fin de (algo)

throughout² *prep* **1** : en todas partes de, a través de ⟨throughout the United States : en todo Estados Unidos⟩ **2** : de principio a fin de, durante ⟨throughout the winter : durante todo el invierno⟩

throve → **thrive**

throw¹ ['θro:] *vt* **threw** ['θru:]; **thrown** ['θro:n]; **throwing 1** TOSS : tirar, lanzar, echar, arrojar, aventar *Col, Mex* ⟨to throw a ball : tirar una pelota⟩ **2** UNSEAT : desmontar (a un jinete) **3** CAST : proyectar ⟨it threw a long shadow : proyectó una sombra larga⟩ **4 to throw a party** : dar una fiesta **5 to throw into confusion** : desconcertar **6 to throw out** DISCARD : botar, tirar (en la basura)

throw² *n* TOSS : tiro *m*, tirada *f*, lanzamiento *m*, lance *m* (de dados)

thrower ['θro:ər] *n* : lanzador *m*, -dora *f*

throw up *v* VOMIT : vomitar, devolver

thrush ['θrʌʃ] *n* : tordo *m*, zorzal *m*

thrust¹ ['θrʌst] *vt* **thrust**; **thrusting 1** SHOVE : empujar bruscamente **2** PLUNGE, STAB : apuñalar, clavar ⟨he thrust a dagger into her heart : la apuñaló en el corazón⟩ **3 to thrust one's way** : abrirse paso **4 to thrust upon** : imponer a

thrust² *n* **1** PUSH, SHOVE : empujón *m*, empellón *m* **2** LUNGE : estocada *f* (en esgrima) **3** IMPETUS : ímpetu *m*, impulso *m*, propulsión *f* (de un motor)

thud¹ ['θʌd] *vi* **thudded**; **thudding** : producir un ruido sordo

thud² *n* : ruido *m* sordo (que produce un objeto al caer)

thug ['θʌg] *n* : matón *m*

thumb¹ ['θʌm] *vt* : hojear (con el pulgar)

thumb² *n* : pulgar *m*, dedo *m* pulgar

thumbnail ['θʌm,neɪl] *n* : uña *f* del pulgar

thumbtack ['θʌm,tæk] *n* : tachuela *f*, chinche *f*

thump¹ ['θʌmp] *vt* POUND : golpear, aporrear — *vi* : latir con vehemencia (dícese del corazón)

thump² *n* THUD : ruido *m* sordo

thunder¹ ['θʌndər] *vi* **1** : tronar ⟨it rained and thundered all night : llovió y tronó durante la noche⟩ **2** BOOM : retumbar, bramar, resonar — *vt* ROAR, SHOUT : decir a gritos, vociferar

thunder² *n* : truenos *mpl*

thunderbolt ['θʌndər,bo:lt] *n* : rayo *m*

thunderclap ['θʌndər,klæp] *n* : trueno *m*

thunderous ['θʌndərəs] *adj* : atronador, ensordecedor, estruendoso

thundershower ['θʌndər,ʃaʊər] *n* : lluvia *f* con truenos y relámpagos

thunderstorm ['θʌndər,stɔrm] *n* : tormenta *f* con truenos y relámpagos

thunderstruck ['θʌndər,strʌk] *adj* : atónito

Thursday ['θərz,deɪ, -di] *n* : jueves *m*

thus ['ðʌs] *adv* **1** : así, de esta manera **2** SO : hasta (cierto punto) ⟨the weather's been nice thus far : hasta ahora ha hecho buen tiempo⟩ **3** HENCE : por consiguiente, por lo tanto

thwart ['θwɔrt] *vt* : frustrar

thy ['ðaɪ] *adj* : tu

thyme ['taɪm, 'θaɪm] *n* : tomillo *m*

thyroid ['θaɪ,rɔɪd] *n* *or* **thyroid gland** : tiroides *mf*, glándula *f* tiroidea

thyself [ðaɪ'sɛlf] *pron* : ti, ti mismo

tiara [ti'ærə, -'ɑr-] *n* : diadema *f*

Tibetan [tə'bɛtən] *n* **1** : tibetano *m*, -na *f* **2** : tibetano *m* (idioma) — **Tibetan** *adj*

tibia ['tɪbiə] *n*, *pl* **-iae** [-bi,i:] : tibia *f*

tic ['tɪk] *n* : tic *m*

tick¹ ['tɪk] *vi* **1** : hacer tictac **2** OPERATE, RUN : operar, andar (dícese de un mecanismo) ⟨what makes him tick? : ¿qué es lo que lo mueve?⟩ — *vt or* **to tick off** CHECK : marcar

tick² *n* **1** : tictac *m* (de un reloj) **2** CHECK : marca *f* **3** : garrapata *f* (insecto)

ticket¹ ['tɪkət] *vt* LABEL : etiquetar

ticket² *n* **1** : boleto *m*, entrada *f* (de un espectáculo), pasaje *m* (de avión, tren, etc.) **2** SLATE : lista *f* de candidatos

tickle¹ ['tɪkəl] *v* **-led**; **-ling** *vt* **1** AMUSE : divertir, hacerle gracia (a alguien) **2** : hacerle cosquillas (a alguien) ⟨don't tickle me! : ¡no me hagas cosquillas!⟩ — *vi* : picar

tickle² *n* : cosquilleo *m*, cosquillas *fpl*, picor *m* (en la garganta)

ticklish ['tɪklɪʃ] *adj* **1** : cosquilloso (dícese de una persona) **2** DELICATE, TRICKY : delicado, peliagudo

tidal ['taɪdəl] *adj* : de marea, relativo a la marea

tidal wave *n* : maremoto *m*

tidbit ['tɪd,bɪt] *n* **1** BITE, SNACK : bocado *m*, golosina *f* **2** : dato *m* o noticia *f* interesante ⟨useful tidbits of information : informaciones útiles⟩

tide¹ ['taɪd] *vt* **tided**; **tiding** *or* **to tide over** : proveer lo necesario para aguantar una dificultad ⟨this money will tide you over until you find work : este dinero te mantendrá hasta que encuentres empleo⟩

tide² *n* **1** : marea *f* **2** CURRENT : corriente *f* (de eventos, opiniones, etc.)

tidily ['taɪdəli] *adv* : ordenadamente

tidiness ['taɪdinəs] *n* : aseo *m*, limpieza *f*, orden *m*

tidings ['taɪdɪŋz] *npl* : nuevas *fpl*

tidy¹ ['taɪdi] *vt* **-died**; **-dying** : asear, limpiar, poner en orden

tidy² *adj* **-dier**; **-est 1** CLEAN, NEAT : limpio, aseado, en orden **2** SUBSTANTIAL : grande, considerable ⟨a tidy sum : una suma considerable⟩

tie¹ ['taɪ] *v* **tied**; **tying** *or* **tieing** *vt* **1** : atar, amarrar ⟨to tie a knot : atar un nudo⟩ ⟨to tie one's shoelaces : atarse los cordones⟩ **2** BIND, UNITE : ligar, atar **3** : empatar ⟨they tied the score : empataron el marcador⟩ — *vi* : empatar ⟨the two teams were tied : los dos equipos empataron⟩

tie² *n* **1** : ligadura *f*, cuerda *f*, cordón *m* (para atar algo) **2** BOND, LINK : atadura *f*, ligadura *f*, vínculo *m*, lazo *m* ⟨family ties : lazos familiares⟩ **3** *or* **railroad tie** : traviesa *f* **4** DRAW : empate *m* (en deportes) **5** NECKTIE : corbata *f*

tier ['tɪr] *n* : hilera *f*, escalón *m*

tiff ['tɪf] *n* : disgusto *m*, disputa *f*

tiger ['taɪgər] *n* : tigre *m*

tight¹ ['taɪt] *adv* TIGHTLY : bien, fuerte ⟨shut it tight : ciérralo bien⟩

tight² *adj* **1** : bien cerrado, hermético ⟨a tight seal : un cierre hermético⟩ **2** STRICT : estricto, severo **3** TAUT : tirante, tenso **4** SNUG : apretado, ajustado, ceñido ⟨a tight dress : un vestido ceñido⟩ **5** DIFFICULT : difícil ⟨to be in a tight spot : estar en un aprieto⟩ **6** STINGY : apretado, avaro, agarrado *fam* **7** CLOSE : reñido ⟨a tight game : un juego reñido⟩ **8** SCARCE : escaso ⟨money is tight : escasea el dinero⟩

tighten ['taɪtən] *vt* : tensar (una cuerda, etc.), apretar (un nudo, un tornillo, etc.), apretarse (el cinturón), reforzar (las reglas)

tightly ['taɪtli] *adv* : bien, fuerte

tightness ['taɪtnəs] *n* : lo apretado, lo tenso, tensión *f*

tightrope ['taɪt,ro:p] *n* : cuerda *f* floja

tights ['taɪts] *npl* : leotardo *m*, malla *f*

tightwad ['taɪt,wɑd] *n* : avaro *m*, -ra *f*; tacaño *m*, -ña *f*

tigress ['taɪgrəs] *n* : tigresa *f*

tile¹ ['taɪl] *vt* **tiled; tiling** : embaldosar (un piso), revestir de azulejos (una pared), tejar (un techo)

tile² *n* **1** *or* **floor tile** : losa *f*, baldosa *f*, mosaico *m* *Mex* (de un piso) **2** : azulejo *m* (de una pared) **3** : teja *f* (de un techo)

till¹ ['tɪl] *vt* : cultivar, labrar

till² *n* : caja *f*, caja *f* registradora

till³ *prep & conj* → **until**

tiller ['tɪlər] *n* **1** : cultivador *m*, -dora *f* (de la tierra) **2** : caña *f* del timón (de un barco)

tilt¹ ['tɪlt] *vt* : ladear, inclinar — *vi* : ladearse, inclinarse

tilt² *n* **1** SLANT : inclinación *f* **2 at full tilt** : a toda velocidad

timber ['tɪmbər] *n* **1** : madera *f* (para construcción) **2** BEAM : viga *f*

timberland ['tɪmbər,lænd] *n* : bosque *m* maderero

timbre ['tæmbər, 'tɪm-] *n* : timbre *m*

time¹ ['taɪm] *vt* **timed; timing 1** SCHEDULE : fijar la hora de, calcular el momento oportuno para **2** CLOCK : cronometrar, medir el tiempo de (una competencia, etc.)

time² *n* **1** : tiempo *m* ⟨the passing of time : el paso del tiempo⟩ ⟨she doesn't have time : no tiene tiempo⟩ **2** MOMENT : tiempo *m*, momento *m* ⟨this is not the time to bring it up : no es el momento

de sacar el tema⟩ **3** : vez *f* ⟨she called you three times : te llamó tres veces⟩ ⟨three times greater : tres veces mayor⟩ **4** AGE : tiempo *m*, era *f* ⟨in your grandparents' time : en el tiempo de tus abuelos⟩ **5** TEMPO : tiempo *m*, ritmo *m* (en música) **6** : hora *f* ⟨what time is it? : ¿qué hora es?⟩ ⟨it's time for dinner : es hora de comer⟩ ⟨at the usual time : a la hora acostumbrada⟩ ⟨to keep time : ir a la hora⟩ ⟨to lose time : atrasar⟩ **7** EXPERIENCE : rato *m*, experiencia *f* ⟨we had a nice time together : pasamos juntos un rato agradable⟩ ⟨to have a rough time : pasarlo mal⟩ ⟨have a good time! : ¡que se diviertan!⟩ **8 at times** SOMETIMES : a veces **9 for the time being** : por el momento, de momento **10 from time to time** OCCASIONALLY : de vez en cuando **11 in time** PUNCTUALLY : a tiempo **12 in time** EVENTUALLY : con el tiempo **13 time after time** : una y otra vez

timekeeper ['taɪm,ki:pər] *n* : cronometrador *m*, -dora *f*

timeless ['taɪmləs] *adj* : eterno

timely ['taɪmli] *adj* **-lier; -est** : oportuno

timepiece ['taɪm,pi:s] *n* : reloj *m*

timer ['taɪmər] *n* : temporizador *m*, cronómetro *m*

times ['taɪmz] *prep* : por ⟨3 times 4 is 12 : 3 por 4 son 12⟩

timetable ['taɪm,teɪbəl] *n* : horario *m*

timid ['tɪmɪd] *adj* : tímido — **timidly** *adv*

timidity [tə'mɪdəti] *n* : timidez *f*

timorous ['tɪmərəs] *adj* : timorato, miedoso

timpani ['tɪmpəni] *npl* : timbales *mpl*

tin ['tɪn] *n* **1** : estaño *m*, hojalata *f* (metal) **2** CAN : lata *f*, bote *m*, envase *m*

tincture ['tɪŋktʃər] *n* : tintura *f*

tinder ['tɪndər] *n* : yesca *f*

tine ['taɪn] *n* : diente *m* (de un tenedor, etc.)

tinfoil ['tɪn,fɔɪl] *n* : papel *m* (de) aluminio

tinge¹ ['tɪndʒ] *vt* **tinged; tingeing** *or* **tinging** ['tɪndʒɪŋ] TINT : matizar, teñir ligeramente

tinge² *n* **1** TINT : matiz *m*, tinte *m* sutil **2** TOUCH : dejo *m*, sensación *f* ligera

tingle¹ ['tɪŋgəl] *vi* **-gled; -gling** : sentir (un) hormigueo, sentir (un) cosquilleo

tingle² *n* : hormigueo *m*, cosquilleo *m*

tinker ['tɪŋkər] *vi* **to tinker with** : arreglar con pequeños ajustes, toquetear (con intento de arreglar)

tinkle¹ ['tɪŋkəl] *vi* **-kled; -kling** : tintinear

tinkle² *n* : tintineo *m*

tinsel ['tɪntsəl] *n* : oropel *m*

tint¹ ['tɪnt] *vt* : teñir, colorear

tint² *n* : tinte *m*

tiny ['taɪni] *adj* **-nier; -est** : diminuto, minúsculo

tip¹ ['tɪp] *v* **tipped; tipping** *vt* **1** *or* **to tip over** : volcar, voltear, hacer caer **2** TILT : ladear, inclinar ⟨to tip one's hat : saludar con el sombrero⟩ **3** TAP : tocar, golpear ligeramente **4** : darle una propina (a un mesero, etc.) 〈I tipped him $5 : le di $5 de propina〉 **5** : adornar o cubrir la punta de 〈wings tipped in red : alas que tienen las puntas rojas〉 **6 to tip off** : dar información a — *vi* TILT : ladearse, inclinarse

tip² *n* **1** END, POINT : punta *f*, extremo *m* 〈on the tip of one's tongue : en la punta de la lengua〉 **2** GRATUITY : propina *f* **3** ADVICE, INFORMATION : consejo *m*, información *f* (confidencial)

tip-off ['tɪpˌɔf] *n* **1** SIGN : indicación *f*, señal *f* **2** TIP : información *f* (confidencial)

tipple ['tɪpəl] *vi* **-pled; -pling** : tomarse unas copas

tipsy ['tɪpsi] *adj* **-sier; -est** : achispado

tiptoe¹ ['tɪpˌto:] *vi* **-toed; -toeing** : caminar de puntillas

tiptoe² *adv* : de puntillas

tiptoe³ *n* : punta *f* del pie

tip-top¹ ['tɪp'tɑp, -ˌtɑp] *adj* EXCELLENT : excelente

tip-top² *n* SUMMIT : cumbre *f*, cima *f*

tirade ['taɪˌreɪd] *n* : diatriba *f*

tire¹ ['taɪr] *v* **tired; tiring** *vt* : cansar, agotar, fatigar — *vi* : cansarse

tire² *n* : llanta *f*, neumático *m*, goma *f*

tired ['taɪrd] *adj* : cansado, agotado, fatigado 〈to get tired : cansarse〉

tireless ['taɪrləs] *adj* : incansable, infatigable — **tirelessly** *adv*

tiresome ['taɪrsəm] *adj* : fastidioso, pesado, tedioso — **tiresomely** *adv*

tissue ['tɪˌʃu:] *n* **1** : pañuelo *m* de papel **2** : tejido *m* 〈lung tissue : tejido pulmonar〉

titanic [taɪ'tænɪk, tə-] *adj* GIGANTIC : titánico, gigantesco

titanium [taɪ'teɪniəm, tə-] *n* : titanio *m*

titillate ['tɪtəlˌeɪt] *vt* **-lated; -lating** : excitar, estimular placenteramente

title¹ ['taɪtəl] *vt* **-tled; -tling** : titular, intitular

title² *n* : título *m*

titter¹ ['tɪtər] *vi* GIGGLE : reírse tontamente

titter² *n* : risita *f*, risa *f* tonta

tizzy ['tɪzi] *n, pl* **tizzies** : estado *m* agitado o nervioso 〈I'm all in a tizzy : estoy todo alterado〉

TNT [ˌtiːˌɛn'tiː] *n* : TNT *m*

to¹ ['tu:] *adv* **1** : a un estado consciente 〈to come to : volver en sí〉 **2 to and fro** : de aquí para allá, de un lado para otro

to² *prep* **1** (*indicating a place*) : a 〈to go to the doctor : ir al médico〉 〈I'm going to John's : voy a la casa de John〉 **2** TOWARD : a, hacia 〈two miles to the south : dos millas hacia el sur〉 **3** ON : en, sobre 〈apply salve to the wound : póngale ungüento a la herida〉 **4** UP TO : hasta, a 〈to a degree : hasta cierto grado〉 〈from head to toe : de pies a cabeza〉 **5** (*in expressions of time*) 〈it's quarter to seven : son las siete menos

cuarto〉 **6** UNTIL : a, hasta 〈from May to December : de mayo a diciembre〉 **7** (*indicating belonging or possession*) : de, a 〈the key to the lock : la llave del candado〉 **8** (*indicating response*) : a 〈dancing to the rhythm : bailando al compás〉 **9** (*indicating comparison or proportion*) : a 〈it's similar to mine : es parecido al mío〉 〈they won 4 to 2 : ganaron 4 a 2〉 **10** (*indicating agreement or conformity*) : a, de acuerdo con 〈made to order : hecho a la orden〉 〈to my knowledge : a mi saber〉 **11** (*indicating inclusion*) : en cada, por 〈twenty to the box : veinte por caja〉 **12** (*used to form the infinitive*) 〈to understand : entender〉 〈to go away : irse〉

toad ['to:d] *n* : sapo *m*

toadstool ['to:dˌstu:l] *n* : hongo *m* (no comestible)

toady ['to:di] *n, pl* **toadies** : adulador *m*, -dora *f*

toast¹ ['to:st] *vt* **1** : tostar (pan) **2** : brindar por 〈to toast the victors : brindar por los vencedores〉 **3** WARM : calentar 〈to toast oneself : calentarse〉

toast² *n* **1** : pan *m* tostado, tostadas *fpl* **2** : brindis *m* 〈to propose a toast : proponer un brindis〉

toaster ['to:stər] *n* : tostador *m*

tobacco [tə'bæko:] *n, pl* **-cos** : tabaco *m*

toboggan¹ [tə'bagən] *vi* : deslizarse en tobogán

toboggan² *n* : tobogán *m*

today¹ [tə'deɪ] *adv* **1** : hoy 〈she arrives today : hoy llega〉 **2** NOWADAYS : hoy en día

today² *n* : hoy *m* 〈today is a holiday : hoy es día de fiesta〉

toddle ['tadəl] *vi* **-dled; -dling** : hacer pininos, hacer pinitos

toddler ['tadələr] *n* : niño *m* pequeño, niña *f* pequeña (que comienza a caminar)

to-do [tə'du:] *n, pl* **to-dos** [-'du:z] FUSS : lío *m*, alboroto *m*

toe ['to:] *n* : dedo *m* del pie

toenail ['to:ˌneɪl] *n* : uña *f* del pie

toffee *or* **toffy** ['tɔfi, 'tɑ-] *n, pl* **toffees** *or* **toffies** : caramelo *m* elaborado con azúcar y mantequilla

toga ['to:gə] *n* : toga *f*

together [tə'gɛðər] *adv* **1** : juntamente, juntos (el uno con el otro) 〈Susan and Sarah work together : Susan y Sarah trabajan juntas〉 **2 ~ with** : junto con

togetherness [tə'gɛðərnəs] *n* : unión *f*, compañerismo *m*

togs ['tagz, 'tɔgz] *npl* : ropa *f*

toil¹ ['tɔɪl] *vi* : trabajar arduamente

toil² *n* : trabajo *m* arduo

toilet ['tɔɪlət] *n* **1** : arreglo *m* personal **2** BATHROOM : (cuarto de) baño *m*, servicios *mpl* (públicos), sanitario *m* Col, Mex, Ven **3** : inodoro *m* 〈to flush the toilet : jalar la cadena〉

toilet paper *n* : papel *m* higiénico

toiletries ['tɔɪlətriz] *npl* : artículos *mpl* de tocador

token ['to:kən] *n* **1** PROOF, SIGN : prueba *f*, muestra *f*, señal *m* **2** SYMBOL : símbolo *m* **3** SOUVENIR : recuerdo *m* **4** : ficha *f* (para transporte público, etc.)

told → **tell**

tolerable ['talərəbəl] *adj* : tolerable — **tolerably** [-bli] *adv*

tolerance ['talərənts] *n* : tolerancia *f*

tolerant ['talərənt] *adj* : tolerante — **tolerantly** *adv*

tolerate ['talə,reɪt] *vt* **-ated; -ating 1** ACCEPT : tolerar, aceptar **2** BEAR, ENDURE : tolerar, aguantar, soportar

toleration [,talə'reɪʃən] *n* : tolerancia *f*

toll[1] ['to:l] *vt* : tañer, sonar (una campana) — *vi* : sonar, doblar (dícese de las campanas)

toll[2] *n* **1** : peaje *m* (de una carretera, un puente, etc.) **2** CASUALTIES : pérdida *f*, número *m* de víctimas **3** TOLLING : tañido *m* (de campanas)

tollbooth ['to:l,bu:θ] *n* : caseta *f* de peaje

tollgate ['to:l,geɪt] *n* : barrera *f* de peaje

tomahawk ['tamə,hɔk] *n* : hacha *f* de guerra (de los indígenas norteamericanos)

tomato [tə'meɪţo, -'ma-] *n*, *pl* **-toes** : tomate *m*

tomb ['tu:m] *n* : sepulcro *m*, tumba *f*

tomboy ['tam,bɔɪ] *n* : marimacho *mf*; niña *f* que se porta como muchacho

tombstone ['tu:m,sto:n] *n* : lápida *f*

tomcat ['tam,kæt] *n* : gato *m* (macho)

tome ['to:m] *n* : tomo *m*

tomorrow[1] [tə'maro] *adv* : mañana

tomorrow[2] *n* : mañana *m*

tom–tom ['tam,tam] *n* : tam-tam *m*

ton ['tən] *n* : tonelada *f*

tone[1] ['to:n] *vt* **toned; toning 1** *or* **to tone down** : atenuar, suavizar, moderar **2** *or* **to tone up** STRENGTHEN : tonificar, vigorizar

tone[2] *n* : tono *m* ⟨in a friendly tone : en tono amistoso⟩ ⟨a greyish tone : un tono grisáceo⟩

tongs ['taŋz, 'tɔŋz] *npl* : tenazas *fpl*

tongue ['tʌŋ] *n* **1** : lengua *f* **2** LANGUAGE : lengua *f*, idioma *m*

tongue–tied ['tʌŋ,taɪd] *adj* **to get tongue–tied** : trabársele la lengua a uno

tonic[1] ['tanɪk] *adj* : tónico

tonic[2] *n* **1** : tónico *m* **2** *or* **tonic water** : tónica *f*

tonight[1] [tə'naɪt] *adv* : esta noche

tonight[2] *n* : esta noche *f*

tonsil ['tantsəl] *n* : amígdala *f*, angina *f* Mex

tonsillitis [,tantsə'laɪţəs] *n* : amigdalitis *f*, anginas *fpl* Mex

too ['tu:] *adv* **1.** ALSO : también **2** EXCESSIVELY : demasiado ⟨it's too hot in here : aquí hace demasiado calor⟩

took → **take**[1]

tool[1] ['tu:l] *vt* **1** : fabricar, confeccionar (con herramientas) **2** EQUIP : instalar maquinaria en (una fábrica)

tool[2] *n* : herramienta *f*

toolbox ['tu:l,baks] *n* : caja *f* de herramientas

toot[1] ['tu:t] *vt* : sonar (un claxon o un pito)

toot[2] *n* : pitido *m*, bocinazo *m* (de un claxon)

tooth ['tu:θ] *n*, *pl* **teeth** ['ti:θ] : diente *m*

toothache ['tu:θ,eɪk] *n* : dolor *m* de muelas

toothbrush ['tu:θ,brʌʃ] *n* : cepillo *m* de dientes

toothless ['tu:θləs] *adj* : desdentado

toothpaste ['tu:θ,peɪst] *n* : pasta *f* de dientes, crema *f* dental, dentífrico *m*

toothpick ['tu:θ,pɪk] *n* : palillo *m* (de dientes), mondadientes *m*

top[1] ['tap] *vt* **topped; topping 1** COVER : cubrir, coronar **2** SURPASS : sobrepasar, superar **3** CLEAR : pasar por encima de

top[2] *adj* : superior ⟨the top shelf : la repisa superior⟩ ⟨one of the top lawyers : uno de los mejores abogados⟩

top[3] *n* **1** : parte *f* superior, cumbre *f*, cima *f* (de un monte, etc.) ⟨to climb to the top : subir a la cumbre⟩ **2** COVER : tapa *f*, cubierta *f* **3** : trompo *m* (juguete) **4 on top of** : encima de

topaz ['to:,pæz] *n* : topacio *m*

topcoat ['tap,ko:t] *n* : sobretodo *m*, abrigo *m*

topic ['tapɪk] *n* : tema *m*, tópico *m*

topical ['tapɪkəl] *adj* : de interés actual

topmost ['tap,mo:st] *adj* : más alto

top–notch ['tap'natʃ] *adj* : de lo mejor, de primera categoría

topographic [,tapə'græfɪk] *or* **topographical** [-fɪkəl] *adj* : topográfico

topography [tə'pagrəfi] *n*, *pl* **-phies** : topografía *f*

topple ['tapəl] *v* **-pled; -pling** *vi* : caerse, venirse abajo — *vt* : volcar, derrocar (un gobierno, etc.)

topsoil ['tap,sɔɪl] *n* : capa *f* superior del suelo

topsy–turvy [,tapsi'tərvi] *adv & adj* : patas arriba, al revés

torch ['tɔrtʃ] *n* : antorcha *f*

tore → **tear**[1]

torment[1] [tɔr'mɛnt, 'tɔr,-] *vt* : atormentar, torturar, martirizar

torment[2] ['tɔr,mɛnt] *n* : tormento *m*, suplicio *m*, martirio *m*

tormentor [tɔr'mɛntər] *n* : atormentador *m*, -dora *f*

torn *pp* → **tear**[1]

tornado [tɔr'neɪdo] *n*, *pl* **-does** *or* **-dos** : tornado *m*

torpedo[1] [tɔr'pi:do] *vt* : torpedear

torpedo[2] *n*, *pl* **-does** : torpedo *m*

torpid ['tɔrpɪd] *adj* **1** SLUGGISH : aletargado **2** APATHETIC : apático

torpor ['tɔrpər] *n* : letargo *m*, apatía *f*

torrent ['tɔrənt] *n* : torrente *m*

torrential [tɔ'rɛntʃəl, tə-] *adj* : torrencial

torrid ['tɔrɪd] *adj* : tórrido

torso ['tɔr,so:] *n*, *pl* **-sos** *or* **-si** [-,si:] : torso *m*

tortilla [tɔr'tiːjə] *n* : tortilla *f* (de maíz)
tortoise ['tɔrʈəs] *n* : tortuga *f* (terrestre)
tortoiseshell ['tɔrʈəsˌʃɛl] *n* : carey *m*, concha *f*
tortuous ['tɔrʈʊəs] *adj* : tortuoso
torture¹ ['tɔrʈər] *vt* **-tured; -turing** : torturar, atormentar
torture² *n* : tortura *f*, tormento *m* ⟨it was sheer torture! : ¡fue un verdadero suplicio!⟩
torturer ['tɔrʈərər] *n* : torturador *m*, -dora *f*
toss¹ ['tɔs, 'tɑs] *vt* **1** AGITATE, SHAKE : sacudir, agitar, mezclar (una ensalada) **2** THROW : tirar, echar, lanzar — *vi* : sacudirse, moverse agitadamente ⟨to toss and turn : dar vueltas⟩
toss² *n* THROW : lanzamiento *m*, tiro *m*, tirada *f*, lance *m* (de dados, etc.)
toss–up ['tɔsˌʌp] *n* : posibilidad *f* igual ⟨it's a toss-up : quizá sí, quizá no⟩
tot ['tɑt] *n* : pequeño *m*, -ña *f*
total¹ ['toːtəl] *vt* **-taled** *or* **-talled; -taling** *or* **-talling 1** *or* **to total up** ADD : sumar, totalizar **2** AMOUNT TO : ascender a, llegar a
total² *adj* : total, completo, absoluto — **totally** *adv*
total³ *n* : total *m*
totalitarian [toːˌtælə'tɛriən] *adj* : totalitario
totalitarianism [toːˌtælə'tɛriəˌnɪzəm] *n* : totalitarismo *m*
totality [toː'tæləʈi] *n, pl* **-ties** : totalidad *f*
tote ['toːt] *vt* **toted; toting** : cargar, llevar
totem ['toːtəm] *n* : tótem *m*
totter ['tɑtər] *vi* : tambalearse
touch¹ ['tʌtʃ] *vt* **1** FEEL, HANDLE : tocar, tentar **2** AFFECT, MOVE : conmover, afectar, tocar ⟨his gesture touched our hearts : su gesto nos tocó el corazón⟩ — *vi* : tocarse
touch² *n* **1** : tacto *m* (sentido) **2** DETAIL : toque *m*, detalle *m* ⟨a touch of color : un toque de color⟩ **3** BIT : pizca *f*, gota *f*, poco *m* **4** ABILITY : habilidad *f* ⟨to lose one's touch : perder la habilidad⟩ **5** CONTACT : contacto *m*, comunicación *f* ⟨to keep in touch : mantenerse en contacto⟩
touchdown ['tʌtʃˌdaʊn] *n* : touchdown *m* (en futbol americano)
touching ['tʌtʃɪŋ] *adj* MOVING : conmovedor
touchstone ['tʌtʃˌstoːn] *n* : piedra *f* de toque
touch up *vt* : retocar
touchy ['tʌtʃi] *adj* **touchier; -est 1** : sensible, susceptible (dícese de una persona) **2** : delicado ⟨a touchy subject : un tema delicado⟩
tough¹ ['tʌf] *adj* **1** STRONG : fuerte, resistente (dícese de materiales) **2** LEATHERY : correoso ⟨a tough steak : un bistec duro⟩ **3** HARDY : fuerte, robusto (dícese de una persona) **4** STRICT

: severo, exigente **5** DIFFICULT : difícil **6** STUBBORN : terco, obstinado
tough² *n* : matón *m*, persona *f* ruda y brusca
toughen ['tʌfən] *vt* : fortalecer, endurecer — *vi* : endurecerse, hacerse más fuerte
toughness ['tʌfnəs] *n* : dureza *f*
toupee [tu'peɪ] *n* : peluquín *m*, bisoñé *m*
tour¹ ['tʊr] *vi* : tomar una excursión, viajar — *vt* : recorrer, hacer una gira por
tour² *n* **1** : gira *f*, tour *m*, excursión *f* **2 tour of duty** : período *m* de servicio
tourism ['tʊrˌɪzəm] *n* : turismo *m*
tourist ['tʊrɪst, 'tər-] *n* : turista *mf*
tournament ['tərnəmənt, 'tʊr-] *n* : torneo *m*
tourniquet ['tərnɪkət, 'tʊr-] *n* : torniquete *m*
tousle ['taʊzəl] *vt* **-sled; -sling** : desarreglar, despeinar (el cabello)
tout ['taʊt] *vt* : promocionar, elogiar (con exageración)
tow¹ ['toː] *vt* : remolcar
tow² *n* : remolque *m*
toward ['tord, tə'word] *or* **towards** ['tordz, tə'wordz] *prep* **1** (*indicating direction*) : hacia, rumbo a ⟨heading toward town : dirigiéndose rumbo al pueblo⟩ ⟨efforts towards peace : esfuerzos hacia la paz⟩ **2** (*indicating time*) : alrededor de ⟨toward midnight : alrededor de la medianoche⟩ **3** REGARDING : hacia, con respecto a ⟨his attitude toward life : su actitud hacia la vida⟩ **4** FOR : para, como pago parcial de (una compra o deuda)
towel ['taʊəl] *n* : toalla *f*
tower¹ ['taʊər] *vi* **to tower over** : descollar sobre, elevarse sobre, dominar
tower² *n* : torre *f*
towering ['taʊərɪŋ] *adj* : altísimo, imponente
town ['taʊn] *n* : pueblo *m*, ciudad *f* (pequeña)
township ['taʊnˌʃɪp] *n* : municipio *m*
tow truck ['toːˌtrʌk] *n* : grúa *f*
toxic ['tɑksɪk] *adj* : tóxico
toxicity [tɑk'sɪsəʈi] *n, pl* **-ties** : toxicidad *f*
toxin ['tɑksɪn] *n* : toxina *f*
toy¹ ['tɔɪ] *vi* : juguetear, jugar
toy² *adj* : de juguete ⟨a toy rifle : un rifle de juguete⟩
toy³ *n* : juguete *m*
trace¹ ['treɪs] *vt* **traced; tracing 1** : calcar (un dibujo, etc.) **2** OUTLINE : delinear, trazar (planes, etc.) **3** TRACK : describir (un curso, una historia) **4** FIND : localizar, ubicar
trace² *n* **1** SIGN, TRACK : huella *f*, rastro *m*, indicio *m*, vestigio *m* ⟨he disappeared without a trace : desapareció sin dejar rastro⟩ **2** BIT, HINT : pizca *f*, ápice *m*, dejo *m*
trachea ['treɪkiə] *n, pl* **-cheae** [-kiˌiː] : tráquea *f*

tracing paper *n* : papel *m* de calcar

track¹ ['træk] *vt* **1** TRAIL : seguir la pista de, rastrear **2** : dejar huellas de ⟨he tracked mud all over : dejó huellas de lodo por todas partes⟩

track² *n* **1** : rastro *m*, huella *f* (de animales), pista *f* (de personas) **2** PATH : pista *f*, sendero *m*, camino *m* **3** *or* **railroad track** : vía *f* (férrea) **4** → **racetrack 5** : oruga *f* (de un tanque, etc.) **6** : pista *f* (deporte) **7 to keep track of** : llevar la cuenta de

track–and–field ['trækənd'fi:ld] *adj* : de pista y campo

tract ['trækt] *n* **1** AREA : terreno *m*, extensión *f*, área *f* **2** : tracto *m* ⟨digestive tract : tracto digestivo⟩ **3** PAMPHLET : panfleto *m*, folleto *m*

traction ['trækʃən] *n* : tracción *f*

tractor ['træktər] *n* **1** : tractor *m* (vehículo agrícola) **2** TRUCK : camión *m* (con remolque)

trade¹ ['treɪd] *v* **traded; trading** *vi* : comerciar, negociar — *vt* EXCHANGE : intercambiar, canjear

trade² *n* **1** OCCUPATION : oficio *m*, profesión *f*, ocupación *f* ⟨a carpenter by trade : carpintero de oficio⟩ **2** COMMERCE : comercio *m*, industria *f* ⟨free trade : libre comercio⟩ ⟨the book trade : la industria del libro⟩ **3** EXCHANGE : intercambio *m*, canje *m*

trade–in ['treɪd‚ɪn] *n* : artículo *m* que se canjea por otro

trademark ['treɪd‚mɑrk] *n* **1** : marca *f* registrada **2** CHARACTERISTIC : sello *m* característico (de un grupo, una persona, etc.)

trader ['treɪdər] *n* : negociante *mf*, tratante *mf*, comerciante *mf*

tradesman ['treɪdzmən] *n, pl* **-men** [-mən, -‚mɛn] **1** CRAFTSMAN : artesano *m*, -na *f* **2** SHOPKEEPER : tendero *m*, -ra *f*; comerciante *mf*

trade wind *n* : viento *m* alisio

tradition [trə'dɪʃən] *n* : tradición *f*

traditional [trə'dɪʃənəl] *adj* : tradicional — **traditionally** *adv*

traffic¹ ['træfɪk] *vi* **trafficked; trafficking** : traficar (con)

traffic² *n* **1** COMMERCE : tráfico *m*, comercio *m* ⟨the drug traffic : el narcotráfico⟩ **2** : tráfico *m*, tránsito *m*, circulación *f* (de vehículos, etc.)

traffic circle *n* : rotonda *f*, glorieta *f*

trafficker ['træfɪkər] *n* : traficante *mf*

traffic light *n* : semáforo *m*, luz *f* (de tránsito)

tragedy ['trædʒədi] *n, pl* **-dies** : tragedia *f*

tragic ['trædʒɪk] *adj* : trágico — **tragically** *adv*

trail¹ ['treɪl] *vi* **1** DRAG : arrastrarse **2** LAG : quedarse atrás, retrasarse **3 to trail away** *or* **to trail off** : disminuir, menguar, desvanecerse — *vt* **1** DRAG : arrastrar **2** PURSUE : perseguir, seguir la pista de

trail² *n* **1** TRACK : rastro *m*, huella *f*, pista *f* ⟨a trail of blood : un rastro de sangre⟩ **2** : cola *f*, estela *f* (de un meteoro) **3** PATH : sendero *m*, camino *m*, vereda *f*

trailer ['treɪlər] *n* **1** : remolque *m*, tráiler *m* (de un camión) **2** : caravana *f* (vivienda ambulante)

train¹ ['treɪn] *vt* **1** : adiestrar, entrenar (atletas), capacitar (trabajadores), amaestrar (animales) **2** POINT : apuntar (un arma, etc.) — *vi* : entrenar(se) (físicamente), prepararse (profesionalmente) ⟨she's training at the gym : se está entrenando en el gimnasio⟩

train² *n* **1** : cola *f* (de un vestido) **2** RETINUE : cortejo *m*, séquito *m* **3** SERIES : serie *f* (de eventos) **4** : tren *m* ⟨passenger train : tren de pasajeros⟩

trainee [treɪ'ni:] *n* : aprendiz *m*, -diza *f*

trainer ['treɪnər] *n* : entrenador *m*, -dora *f*

training ['treɪnɪŋ] *n* : adiestramiento *m*, entrenamiento *m* (físico), capacitación *f* (de trabajadores)

traipse ['treɪps] *vi* **traipsed; traipsing** : andar de un lado para otro, vagar

trait ['treɪt] *n* : rasgo *m*, característica *f*

traitor ['treɪtər] *n* : traidor *m*, -dora *f*

traitorous ['treɪtərəs] *adj* : traidor

trajectory [trə'dʒɛktəri] *n, pl* **-ries** : trayectoria *f*

tramp¹ ['træmp] *vi* : caminar (a paso pesado) — *vt* : deambular por, vagar por ⟨to tramp the streets : vagar por las calles⟩

tramp² *n* **1** VAGRANT : vagabundo *m*, -da *f* **2** HIKE : caminata *f*

trample ['træmpəl] *vt* **-pled; -pling** : pisotear, hollar

trampoline [‚træmpə'li:n, 'træmpə‚-] *n* : trampolín *m*, cama *f* elástica

trance ['trænts] *n* : trance *m*

tranquil ['træŋkwəl] *adj* : calmo, tranquilo, sereno — **tranquilly** *adv*

tranquilize ['træŋkwə‚laɪz] *vt* **-ized; -izing** : tranquilizar

tranquilizer ['træŋkwə‚laɪzər] *n* : tranquilizante *m*

tranquillity *or* **tranquility** [træŋ'kwɪləti] *n* : sosiego *m*, tranquilidad *f*

transact [træn'zækt] *vt* : negociar, gestionar, hacer (negocios)

transaction [træn'zækʃən] *n* **1** : transacción *f*, negocio *m*, operación *f* **2 transactions** *npl* RECORDS : actas *fpl*

transatlantic [‚træntsət'læntɪk, ‚trænz-] *adj* : transatlántico

transcend [træn'sɛnd] *vt* : trascender, sobrepasar

transcendent [træn'sɛndənt] *adj* : trascendente — **transcendence** [trænt'sɛndənts] *n*

transcendental [‚træn‚sɛn'dɛntəl, -sən-] *adj* : trascendental ⟨transcendental meditation : meditación trascendental⟩

transcribe [træn'skraɪb] vt **-scribed; -scribing** : transcribir

transcript ['træn,skrɪpt] n : copia f oficial

transcription [træn'skrɪpʃən] n : transcripción f

transfer¹ [træn**t**s'fər, 'trænts,fər] v **-ferred; -ferring** vt **1** : trasladar (a una persona), transferir (fondos) **2** : transferir, traspasar, ceder (propiedad) **3** PRINT : imprimir (un diseño) — vi **1** MOVE : trasladarse, cambiarse **2** CHANGE : transbordar, cambiar (de un transporte a otro) ⟨he transfers at E Street : hace un transborde a la calle E⟩

transfer² ['træn**t**s,fər] n **1** TRANSFERRING : transferencia f (de fondos, de propiedad, etc.), traslado m (de una persona) **2** DECAL : calcomanía f **3** : boleto m (para cambiar de un avión, etc., a otro)

transferable [træn**t**s'fərəbəl] adj : transferible

transference [træn**t**s'fərən**t**s] n : transferencia f

transfigure [træn**t**s'fɪgjər] vt **-ured; -uring** : transfigurar, transformar

transfix [træn**t**s'fɪks] vt **1** PIERCE : traspasar, atravesar **2** IMMOBILIZE : paralizar

transform [træn**t**s'fɔrm] vt : transformar

transformation [,træn**t**sfər'meɪʃən] n : transformación f

transformer [træn**t**s'fɔrmər] n : transformador m

transfusion [træn**t**s'fju:ʒən] n : transfusión f

transgress [træn**t**s'grɛs, trænz-] vt : transgredir, infringir

transgression [træn**t**s'grɛʃən, trænz-] n : transgresión f

transient¹ ['trænʃənt, 'trænsiənt] adj : pasajero, transitorio — **transiently** adv

transient² n : transeúnte mf

transistor [træn'zɪstər, -'sɪs-] n : transistor m

transit ['træn**t**sɪt, 'trænzɪt] n **1** PASSAGE : pasaje m, tránsito m ⟨in transit : en tránsito⟩ **2** TRANSPORTATION : transporte m (público) **3** : teodolito m (instrumento topográfico)

transition [træn'sɪʃən, -'zɪʃ-] n : transición f

transitional [træn'sɪʃənəl, -'zɪʃ-] adj : de transición

transitive ['træn**t**sətɪv, 'trænzə-] adj : transitivo

transitory ['træn**t**sə,tori, 'trænzə-] adj : transitorio

translate [træn**t**s'leɪt, trænz-; 'træn**t**s,-, 'træns,-] vt **-lated; -lating** : traducir

translation [træn**t**s'leɪʃən, trænz-] n : traducción f

translator [træn**t**s'leɪtər, trænz-; 'træn**t**s,-, 'træns,-] n : traductor m, -tora f

translucent [træn**t**s'lu:sənt, trænz-] adj : translúcido

transmission [træn**t**s'mɪʃən, trænz-] n : transmisión f

transmit [træn**t**s'mɪt, trænz-] vt **-mitted; -mitting** : transmitir

transmitter [træn**t**s'mɪtər, trænz-; 'træn**t**s,-, 'træns,-] n : transmisor m, emisor m

transom ['træn**t**səm] n : montante m (de una puerta), travesaño m (de una ventana)

transparency [træn**t**s'pærən**t**si] n, pl **-cies** : transparencia f

transparent [træn**t**s'pærənt] adj **1** : transparente, traslúcido ⟨a transparent fabric : una tela transparente⟩ **2** OBVIOUS : transparente, obvio, claro — **transparently** adv

transpiration [,træn**t**spə'reɪʃən] n : transpiración f

transpire [træn**t**s'paɪr] vi **-spired; -spiring 1** : transpirar (en biología y botánica) **2** TURN OUT : resultar **3** HAPPEN : suceder, ocurrir, tener lugar

transplant¹ [træn**t**s'plænt] vt : trasplantar

transplant² ['træn**t**s,plænt] n : trasplante m

transport¹ [træn**t**s'port, 'træn**t**s,-] vt **1** CARRY : transportar, acarrear **2** ENRAPTURE : transportar, extasiar

transport² ['træn**t**s,port] n **1** TRANSPORTATION : transporte m, transportación f **2** RAPTURE : éxtasis m **3** or **transport ship** : buque m de transporte (de personal militar)

transportation [,træn**t**spər'teɪʃən] n : transporte m, transportación f

transpose [træn**t**s'po:z] vt **-posed; -posing** : transponer, trasladar, transportar (una composición musical)

transverse [træn**t**s'vərs, trænz-] adj : transversal, transverso, oblicuo — **transversely** adv

trap¹ ['træp] vt **trapped; trapping** : atrapar, apresar (en una trampa)

trap² n : trampa f ⟨to set a trap : tender una trampa⟩

trapdoor ['træp'dor] n : trampilla f, escotillón m

trapeze [træ'pi:z] n : trapecio m

trapezoid ['træpə,zɔɪd] n : trapezoide m, trapecio m

trapper ['træpər] n : trampero m, -ra f; cazador m, -dora f (que usa trampas)

trappings ['træpɪŋz] npl **1** : arreos mpl, jaeces mpl (de un caballo) **2** ADORNMENTS : adornos mpl, pompa f

trash ['træʃ] n : basura f

trashy ['træʃi] adj : de pacotilla

trauma ['trɔmə, 'trau-] n : trauma m

traumatic [trə'mætɪk, trɔ-, trau-] adj : traumático

travel¹ ['trævəl] vi **-eled** or **-elled; -eling** or **-elling 1** JOURNEY : viajar **2** GO, MOVE : desplazarse, moverse, ir ⟨the waves travel at uniform speed : las ondas se desplazan a una velocidad uniforme⟩

travel[2] *n or* **travels** *npl* : viajes *mpl*

traveler *or* **traveller** ['trævələr] *n* : viajero *m*, -ra *f*

traverse [trə'vərs, træ'vərs, 'trævərs] *vt* **-versed; -versing** CROSS : atravesar, extenderse a través de, cruzar

travesty ['trævəsti] *n, pl* **-ties** : parodia *f*

trawl[1] ['trɔl] *vi* : pescar con red de arrastre, rastrear

trawl[2] *n or* **trawl net** : red *f* de arrastre

trawler ['trɔlər] *n* : barco *m* de pesca (utilizado para rastrear)

tray ['treɪ] *n* : bandeja *f*, charola *f Bol, Mex, Peru*

treacherous ['trɛtʃərəs] *adj* **1** TRAITOROUS : traicionero, traidor **2** DANGEROUS : peligroso

treacherously ['trɛtʃərəsli] *adv* : a traición

treachery ['trɛtʃəri] *n, pl* **-eries** : traición *f*

tread[1] ['trɛd] *v* **trod** ['trɑd]; **trodden** ['trɑdən] *or* **trod; treading** *vt* TRAMPLE : pisotear, hollar — *vi* **1** WALK : caminar, andar **2 to tread on** : pisar

tread[2] *n* **1** STEP : paso *m*, andar *m* **2** : banda *f* de rodadura (de un neumático, etc.) **3** : escalón *m* (de una escalera)

treadle ['trɛdəl] *n* : pedal *m* (de una máquina)

treadmill ['trɛd,mɪl] *n* **1** : rueda *f* de andar **2** ROUTINE : rutina *f*

treason ['tri:zən] *n* : traición *f* (a la patria, etc.)

treasure[1] ['trɛʒər, 'treɪ-] *vt* **-sured; -suring** : apreciar, valorar

treasure[2] *n* : tesoro *m*

treasurer ['trɛʒərər, 'treɪ-] *n* : tesorero *m*, -ra *f*

treasury ['trɛʒəri, 'treɪ-] *n, pl* **-suries** : tesorería *f*, tesoro *m*

treat[1] ['tri:t] *vt* **1** DEAL WITH : tratar (un asunto) ⟨the article treats of poverty : el artículo trata de la pobreza⟩ **2** HANDLE : tratar (a una persona), manejar (un objeto) ⟨to treat something as a joke : tomar(se) algo a broma⟩ **3** INVITE : invitar, convidar ⟨he treated me to a meal : me invitó a comer⟩ **4** : tratar, atender (en medicina) **5** PROCESS : tratar ⟨to treat sewage : tratar las aguas negras⟩

treat[2] *n* : gusto *m*, placer *m* ⟨it was a treat to see you : fue un placer verte⟩ ⟨it's my treat : yo invito⟩

treatise ['tri:tɪs] *n* : tratado *m*, estudio *m*

treatment ['tri:tmənt] *n* : trato *m*, tratamiento *m* (médico)

treaty ['tri:ti] *n, pl* **-ties** : tratado *m*, convenio *m*

treble[1] ['trɛbəl] *vt* **-bled; -bling** : triplicar

treble[2] *adj* **1** → **triple 2** : de tiple, soprano (en música) **3 treble clef** : clave *f* de sol

treble[3] *n* : tiple *m*, parte *f* de soprano

tree ['tri:] *n* : árbol *m*

treeless ['tri:ləs] *adj* : carente de árboles

trek[1] ['trɛk] *vi* **trekked; trekking** : hacer un viaje largo y difícil

trek[2] *n* : viaje *m* largo y difícil

trellis ['trɛlɪs] *n* : enrejado *m*, espaldera *f*, celosía *f*

tremble ['trɛmbəl] *vi* **-bled; -bling** : temblar

tremendous [trɪ'mɛndəs] *adj* : tremendo — **tremendously** *adv*

tremor ['trɛmər] *n* : temblor *m*

tremulous ['trɛmjələs] *adj* : trémulo, tembloroso

trench ['trɛntʃ] *n* **1** DITCH : zanja *f* **2** : trinchera *f* (militar)

trenchant ['trɛntʃənt] *adj* : cortante, mordaz

trend[1] ['trɛnd] *vi* : tender, inclinarse

trend[2] *n* **1** TENDENCY : tendencia *f* **2** FASHION : moda *f*

trendy ['trɛndi] *adj* **trendier; -est** : de moda

trepidation [,trɛpə'deɪʃən] *n* : inquietud *f*, ansiedad *f*

trespass[1] ['trɛspəs, -,pæs] *vi* **1** SIN : pecar, transgredir **2** : entrar ilegalmente (en propiedad ajena)

trespass[2] *n* **1** SIN : pecado *m*, transgresión *f* ⟨forgive us our trespasses : perdónanos nuestras deudas⟩ **2** : entrada *f* ilegal (en propiedad ajena)

tress ['trɛs] *n* : mechón *m*

trestle ['trɛsəl] *n* **1** : caballete *m* (armazón) **2** *or* **trestle bridge** : puente *m* de caballete

triad ['traɪ,æd] *n* : tríada *f*

trial[1] ['traɪəl] *adj* : de prueba ⟨trial period : período de prueba⟩

trial[2] *n* **1** : juicio *m*, proceso *m* ⟨to stand trial : ser sometido a juicio⟩ **2** AFFLICTION : aflicción *f*, tribulación *f* **3** TEST : prueba *f*, ensayo *m*

triangle ['traɪ,æŋgəl] *n* : triángulo *m*

triangular [traɪ'æŋgjələr] *adj* : triangular

tribal ['traɪbəl] *adj* : tribal

tribe ['traɪb] *n* : tribu *f*

tribesman ['traɪbzmən] *n, pl* **-men** [-mən, -,mɛn] : miembro *m* de una tribu

tribulation [,trɪbjə'leɪʃən] *n* : tribulación *f*

tribunal [traɪ'bju:nəl, trɪ-] *n* : tribunal *m*, corte *f*

tributary ['trɪbjə,tɛri] *n, pl* **-taries** : afluente *m*

tribute ['trɪb,ju:t] *n* : tributo *m*

trick[1] ['trɪk] *vt* : engañar, embaucar

trick[2] *n* **1** RUSE : trampa *f*, treta *f*, artimaña *f* **2** PRANK : broma *f* ⟨we played a trick on her : le gastamos una broma⟩ **3** : truco *m* ⟨magic tricks : trucos de magia⟩ ⟨the trick is to wait five minutes : el truco está en esperar cinco minutos⟩ **4** MANNERISM : peculiaridad *f*, manía *f* **5** : baza *f* (en juegos de naipes)

trickery ['trɪkəri] *n* : engaños *mpl*, trampas *fpl*

trickle[1] ['trɪkəl] *vi* **-led; -ling** : gotear, chorrear

trickle² *n* : goteo *m*, hilo *m*

trickster ['trɪkstər] *n* : estafador *m*, -dora *f*; embaucador *m*, -dora *f*

tricky ['trɪki] *adj* **trickier; -est 1** SLY : astuto, taimado **2** DIFFICULT : delicado, peliagudo, difícil

tricycle ['traɪsəkəl, -ˌsɪkəl] *n* : triciclo *m*

trident ['traɪdənt] *n* : tridente *m*

triennial ['traɪ'eniəl] *adj* : trienal

trifle¹ ['traɪfəl] *vi* **-fled; -fling** : jugar, juguetear

trifle² *n* : nimiedad *f*, insignificancia *f*

trifling ['traɪflɪŋ] *adj* : trivial, insignificante

trigger¹ ['trɪgər] *vt* : causar, provocar

trigger² *n* : gatillo *m*

trigonometry [ˌtrɪgə'namətri] *n* : trigonometría *f*

trill¹ ['trɪl] *vi* QUAVER : trinar, gorjear — *vt* : vibrar ⟨to trill the *r* : vibrar la *r*⟩

trill² *n* **1** QUAVER : trino *m*, gorjeo *m* **2** : vibración *f* (en fonética)

trillion ['trɪljən] *n* : billón *m*

trilogy ['trɪlədʒi] *n, pl* **-gies** : trilogía *f*

trim¹ ['trɪm] *vt* **trimmed; trimming 1** DECORATE : adornar, decorar **2** CUT : recortar **3** REDUCE : recortar, reducir ⟨to trim the excess : recortar el exceso⟩

trim² *adj* **trimmer; trimmest 1** SLIM : esbelto **2** NEAT : limpio y arreglado, bien cuidado

trim³ *n* **1** CONDITION : condición *f*, estado *m* ⟨to keep in trim : mantenerse en buena forma⟩ **2** CUT : recorte *m* **3** TRIMMING : adornos *mpl*

trimming ['trɪmɪŋ] *n* : adornos *mpl*, accesorios *mpl*

Trinity ['trɪnəti] *n* : Trinidad *f*

trinket ['trɪŋkət] *n* : chuchería *f*, baratija *f*

trio ['tri:ˌo:] *n, pl* **trios** : trío *m*

trip¹ ['trɪp] *v* **tripped; tripping** *vi* **1** : caminar (a paso ligero) **2** STUMBLE : tropezar **3 to trip up** ERR : equivocarse, cometer un error — *vt* **1** : hacerle una zancadilla (a alguien) ⟨you tripped me on purpose! : ¡me hiciste la zancadilla a propósito!⟩ **2** ACTIVATE : activar (un mecanismo) **3 to trip up** : hacer equivocar (a alguien)

trip² *n* **1** JOURNEY : viaje *m* ⟨to take a trip : hacer un viaje⟩ **2** STUMBLE : tropiezo *m*, traspié *m*

tripartite [traɪ'pɑr,taɪt] *adj* : tripartito

tripe ['traɪp] *n* **1** : mondongo *m*, callos *mpl*, pancita *f* Mex **2** TRASH : porquería *f*

triple¹ ['trɪpəl] *vt* **-pled; -pling** : triplicar

triple² *adj* : triple

triple³ *n* : triple *m*

triplet ['trɪplət] *n* **1** : terceto *m* (en poesía, música, etc.) **2** : trillizo *m*, -za *f* (persona)

triplicate ['trɪplɪkət] *n* : triplicado *m*

tripod ['traɪ,pad] *n* : trípode *m*

trite ['traɪt] *adj* **triter; tritest** : trillado, tópico, manido

triumph¹ ['traɪəmpf] *vi* : triunfar

triumph² *n* : triunfo *m*

triumphal [traɪ'ʌmpfəl] *adj* : triunfal

triumphant [traɪ'ʌmpfənt] *adj* : triunfante, triunfal — **triumphantly** *adv*

trivia ['trɪviə] *ns & pl* : trivialidades *fpl*, nimiedades *fpl*

trivial ['trɪviəl] *adj* : trivial, intrascendente, insignificante

triviality [ˌtrɪvi'æləti] *n, pl* **-ties** : trivialidad *f*

trod, trodden → **tread¹**

troll ['tro:l] *n* : duende *m* o gigante *m* de cuentos folklóricos

trolley ['trali] *n, pl* **-leys** : tranvía *m*

trombone [tram'bo:n] *n* : trombón *m*

trombonist [tram'bo:nɪst] *n* : trombón *m*

troop¹ ['tru:p] *vi* : desfilar, ir en tropel

troop² *n* **1** : escuadrón *m* (de caballería) **2** GROUP : grupo *m*, banda *f* (de personas) **3 troops** *npl* SOLDIERS : tropas *fpl*, soldados *mpl*

trooper ['tru:pər] *n* **1** : soldado *m* (de caballería) **2** : policía *m* montado **3** : policía *m* (estatal)

trophy ['tro:fi] *n, pl* **-phies** : trofeo *m*

tropic¹ ['trapɪk] *or* **tropical** [-pɪkəl] *adj* : tropical

tropic² *n* **1** : trópico *m* ⟨tropic of Cancer : trópico de Cáncer⟩ **2 the tropics** : el trópico

trot¹ ['trat] *vi* **trotted; trotting** : trotar

trot² *n* : trote *m*

trouble¹ ['trʌbəl] *v* **-bled; -bling** *vt* **1** DISTURB, WORRY : molestar, perturbar, inquietar **2** AFFLICT : afligir, afectar — *vi* : molestarse, hacer un esfuerzo ⟨they didn't trouble to come : no se molestaron en venir⟩

trouble² *n* **1** PROBLEMS : problemas *mpl*, dificultades *fpl* ⟨to be in trouble : estar en un aprieto⟩ ⟨heart trouble : problemas de corazón⟩ **2** EFFORT : molestia *f*, esfuerzo *m* ⟨to take the trouble : tomarse la molestia⟩ ⟨it's not worth the trouble : no vale la pena⟩

troublemaker ['trʌbəlˌmeɪkər] *n* : agitador *m*, -dora *f*; alborotador *m*, -dora *f*

troublesome ['trʌbəlsəm] *adj* : problemático, dificultoso — **troublesomely** *adv*

trough ['trɔf] *n, pl* **troughs** ['trɔfs, 'trɔvz] **1** : comedero *m*, bebedero *m* (de animales) **2** CHANNEL, HOLLOW : depresión *f* (en el suelo), seno *m* (de olas)

trounce ['traʊnts] *vt* **trounced; trouncing 1** THRASH : apalear, darle una paliza (a alguien) **2** DEFEAT : derrotar contundentemente

troupe ['tru:p] *n* : troupe *f*

trousers ['traʊzərz] *npl* : pantalón *m*, pantalones *mpl*

trout ['traʊt] *n, pl* **trout** : trucha *f*

trowel ['traʊəl] *n* **1** : llana *f*, paleta *f* (de albañil) **2** : desplantador *m* (de jardinero)

truant ['tru:ənt] *n* : alumno *m*, -na *f* que falta a clase sin permiso

truce ['truːs] *n* : tregua *f*, armisticio *m*

truck[1] ['trʌk] *vt* : transportar en camión

truck[2] *n* **1** : camión *m* (vehículo automóvil), carro *m* (manual) **2** DEALINGS : tratos *mpl* ⟨to have no truck with : no tener nada que ver con⟩

trucker ['trʌkər] *n* : camionero *m*, -ra *f*

truculent ['trʌkjələnt] *adj* : agresivo, beligerante

trudge ['trʌdʒ] *vi* **trudged; trudging** : caminar a paso pesado

true[1] ['truː] *vt* **trued; trueing** : aplomar (algo vertical), nivelar (algo horizontal), centrar (una rueda)

true[2] *adv* **1** TRUTHFULLY : lealmente, sinceramente **2** ACCURATELY : exactamente, certeramente

true[3] *adj* **truer; truest 1** LOYAL : fiel, leal **2** : cierto, verdadero, verídico ⟨it's true : es cierto, es la verdad⟩ ⟨a true story : una historia verídica⟩ **3** GENUINE : auténtico, genuino — **truly** *adv*

true–blue ['truː'bluː] *adj* LOYAL : leal, fiel

truffle ['trʌfəl] *n* : trufa *f*

truism ['truːˌɪzəm] *n* : perogrullada *f*, verdad *f* obvia

trump[1] ['trʌmp] *vt* : matar (en juegos de naipes)

trump[2] *n* : triunfo *m* (en juegos de naipes)

trumped–up ['trʌmpt'ʌp] *adj* : inventado, fabricado ⟨trumped-up charges : falsas acusaciones⟩

trumpet[1] ['trʌmpət] *vi* **1** : sonar una trompeta **2** : berrear, bramar (dícese de un animal) — *vt* : proclamar a los cuatro vientos

trumpet[2] *n* : trompeta *f*

trumpeter ['trʌmpətər] *n* : trompetista *mf*

truncate ['trʌŋˌkeɪt, 'trʌn-] *vt* **-cated; -cating** : truncar

trundle ['trʌndəl] *v* **-dled; -dling** *vi* : rodar lentamente — *vt* : hacer rodar, empujar lentamente

trunk ['trʌŋk] *n* **1** : tronco *m* (de un árbol o del cuerpo) **2** : trompa *f* (de un elefante) **3** CHEST : baúl *m* **4** : maletero *m*, cajuela *f Mex* (de un auto) **5 trunks** *npl* : traje *m* de baño (de caballero)

truss[1] ['trʌs] *vt* : atar (con fuerza)

truss[2] *n* **1** FRAMEWORK : armazón *m* (de una estructura) **2** : braguero *m* (en medicina)

trust[1] ['trʌst] *vi* : confiar, esperar ⟨to trust in God : confiar en Dios⟩ — *vt* **1** ENTRUST : confiar, encomendar **2** : confiar en, tenerle confianza a ⟨I trust you : te tengo confianza⟩

trust[2] *n* **1** CONFIDENCE : confianza *f* **2** HOPE : esperanza *f*, fe *f* **3** CREDIT : crédito *m* ⟨to sell on trust : fiar⟩ **4** : fideicomiso *m* ⟨to hold in trust : guardar en fideicomiso⟩ **5** : trust *m* (consorcio empresarial) **6** CUSTODY : responsabilidad *f*, custodia *f*

trustee [ˌtrʌs'tiː] *n* : fideicomisario *m*, -ria *f*; fiduciario *m*, -ria *f*

trustful ['trʌstfəl] *adj* : confiado — **trustfully** *adv*

trustworthiness ['trʌstˌwərðinəs] *n* : integridad *f*, honradez *f*

trustworthy ['trʌstˌwərði] *adj* : digno de confianza, confiable

trusty ['trʌsti] *adj* **trustier; -est** : fiel, confiable

truth ['truːθ] *n*, *pl* **truths** ['truːðz, 'truːθs] : verdad *f*

truthful ['truːθfəl] *adj* : sincero, veraz — **truthfully** *adv*

truthfulness ['truːθfəlnəs] *n* : sinceridad *f*, veracidad *f*

try[1] ['traɪ] *v* **tried; trying** *vt* **1** : enjuiciar, juzgar, procesar ⟨he was tried for murder : fue procesado por homicidio⟩ **2** : probar ⟨did you try the salad? : ¿probaste la ensalada?⟩ **3** TEST : tentar, poner a prueba ⟨to try one's patience : tentarle la paciencia a uno⟩ **4** ATTEMPT : tratar (de), intentar **5** *or* **to try on** : probarse (ropa) — *vi* : tratar, intentar

try[2] *n*, *pl* **tries** : intento *m*, tentativa *f*

tryout ['traɪˌaʊt] *n* : prueba *f*

tsar ['zɑr, 'tsɑr, 'sɑr] → **czar**

T–shirt ['tiːˌʃərt] *n* : camiseta *f*

tub ['tʌb] *n* **1** CASK : cuba *f*, barril *m*, tonel *m* **2** CONTAINER : envase *m* (de plástico, etc.) ⟨a tub of margarine : un envase de margarina⟩ **3** BATHTUB : tina *f* (de baño), bañera *f*

tuba ['tuːbə, 'tjuː-] *n* : tuba *f*

tube ['tuːb, 'tjuːb] *n* **1** PIPE : tubo *m* **2** : tubo *m* (de dentífrico, etc.) **3** *or* **inner tube** : cámara *f* **4** : tubo *m* (de un aparato electrónico) **5** : trompa *f* (en anatomía)

tubeless ['tuːbləs, 'tjuːb-] *adj* : sin cámara (dícese de una llanta)

tuber ['tuːbər, 'tjuː-] *n* : tubérculo *m*

tubercular [tʊ'bərkjələr, tjʊ-] → **tuberculous**

tuberculosis [tʊˌbərkjə'loːsɪs, tjʊ-] *n*, *pl* **-loses** [-ˌsiːz] : tuberculosis *f*

tuberculous [tʊ'bərkjələs, tjʊ-] *adj* : tuberculoso

tuberous ['tuːbərəs, 'tjuː-] *adj* : tuberoso

tubing ['tuːbɪŋ, 'tjuː-] *n* : tubería *f*

tubular ['tuːbjələr, 'tjuː-] *adj* : tubular

tuck[1] ['tʌk] *vt* **1** PLACE, PUT : meter, colocar ⟨tuck in your shirt : métete la camisa⟩ **2** : guardar, esconder ⟨to tuck away one's money : guardar uno bien su dinero⟩ **3** COVER : arropar (a un niño en la cama)

tuck[2] *n* : pliegue *m*, alforza *f*

Tuesday ['tuːzˌdeɪ, 'tjuːz-, -di] *n* : martes *m*

tuft ['tʌft] *n* : penacho *m* (de plumas), copete *m* (de pelo)

tug[1] ['tʌg] *v* **tugged; tugging** *vi* : tirar, jalar, dar un tirón — *vt* : jalar, arrastrar, remolcar (con un barco)

tug[2] *n* **1** : tirón *m*, jalón *m* **2** → **tugboat**

tugboat ['tʌgˌboːt] *n* : remolcador *m*

tug–of–war [ˌtʌgəˈwɔr] *n, pl* **tugs–of–war** : tira y afloja *m*

tuition [tuˈɪʃən] *n or* **tuition fees** : tasas *fpl* de matrícula, colegiatura *f Mex*

tulip [ˈtuːlɪp, ˈtjuː-] *n* : tulipán *m*

tumble[1] [ˈtʌmbəl] *v* **-bled; -bling** *vi* 1 : dar volteretas (en acrobacia) 2 FALL : caerse, venirse abajo — *vt* 1 TOPPLE : volcar 2 TOSS : hacer girar

tumble[2] *n* : voltereta *f*, caída *f*

tumbler [ˈtʌmblər] *n* 1 ACROBAT : acróbata *mf*, saltimbanqui *mf* 2 GLASS : vaso *m* (de mesa) 3 : clavija *f* (de una cerradura)

tummy [ˈtʌmi] *n, pl* **-mies** BELLY : panza *f*, vientre *m*

tumor [ˈtuːmər, ˈtjuː-] *n* : tumor *m*

tumult [ˈtuːˌmʌlt, ˈtjuː-] *n* : tumulto *m*, alboroto *m*

tumultuous [tʊˈmʌltʃʊəs, tjuː-] *adj* : tumultuoso

tuna [ˈtuːnə, ˈtjuː-] *n, pl* **-na** *or* **-nas** : atún *m*

tundra [ˈtʌndrə] *n* : tundra *f*

tune[1] [ˈtuːn, ˈtjuːn] *v* **tuned; tuning** *vt* 1 ADJUST : ajustar, hacer más preciso, afinar (un motor) 2 : afinar (un instrumento musical) 3 : sintonizar (un radio o televisor) — *vi* **to tune in** : sintonizar (con una emisora)

tune[2] *n* 1 MELODY : tonada *f*, canción *f*, melodía *f* 2 **in tune** : afinado (dícese de un instrumento o de la voz), sintonizado, en sintonía

tuneful [ˈtuːnfəl, ˈtjuːn-] *adj* : armonioso, melódico

tuner [ˈtuːnər, ˈtjuː-] *n* : afinador *m*, -dora *f* (de instrumentos); sintonizador *m* (de un radio o un televisor)

tungsten [ˈtʌŋkstən] *n* : tungsteno *m*

tunic [ˈtuːnɪk, ˈtjuː-] *n* : túnica *f*

tuning fork *n* : diapasón *m*

Tunisian [tuˈniːʒən, tjuːˈnɪziən] *n* : tunecino *m*, -na *f* — **Tunisian** *adj*

tunnel[1] [ˈtʌnəl] *vi* **-neled** *or* **-nelled; -neling** *or* **-nelling** : hacer un túnel

tunnel[2] *n* : túnel *m*

turban [ˈtərbən] *n* : turbante *m*

turbid [ˈtərbɪd] *adj* : turbio

turbine [ˈtərbən, -ˌbaɪn] *n* : turbina *f*

turboprop [ˈtərboˌprɑp] *n* : turbopropulsor *m* (motor), avión *m* turbopropulsado

turbulence [ˈtərbjələnts] *n* : turbulencia *f*

turbulent [ˈtərbjələnt] *adj* : turbulento — **turbulently** *adv*

tureen [təˈriːn, tjuː-] *n* : sopera *f*

turf [ˈtərf] *n* SOD : tepe *m*

turgid [ˈtərdʒɪd] *adj* 1 SWOLLEN : turgente 2 : ampuloso, hinchado ⟨turgid style : estilo ampuloso⟩

Turk [ˈtərk] *n* : turco *m*, -ca *f*

turkey [ˈtərki] *n, pl* **-keys** : pavo *m*

Turkish[1] [ˈtərkɪʃ] *adj* : turco

Turkish[2] *n* : turco *m* (idioma)

turmoil [ˈtərˌmɔɪl] *n* : agitación *f*, desorden *m*, confusión *f*

turn[1] [ˈtərn] *vt* 1 : girar, voltear, volver ⟨to turn one's head : voltear la cabeza⟩ ⟨she turned her chair toward the fire : giró su asiento hacia la hoguera⟩ 2 ROTATE : darle vuelta a, hacer girar ⟨turn the handle : dale vuelta a la manivela⟩ 3 SPRAIN, WRENCH : dislocar, torcer 4 UPSET : revolver (el estómago) 5 TRANSFORM : convertir ⟨to turn water into wine : convertir el agua en vino⟩ 6 SHAPE : tornear (en carpintería) — *vi* 1 ROTATE : girar, dar vueltas 2 : girar, doblar, dar una vuelta ⟨turn left : doble a la izquierda⟩ ⟨to turn around : dar la media vuelta⟩ 3 BECOME : hacerse, volverse, ponerse 4 SOUR : agriarse, cortarse (dícese de la leche) 5 **to turn to** : recurrir a ⟨they have no one to turn to : no tienen quien les ayude⟩

turn[2] *n* 1 : vuelta *f*, giro *m* ⟨a sudden turn : una vuelta repentina⟩ 2 CHANGE : cambio *m* 3 CURVE : curva *f* (en un camino) 4 : turno *m* ⟨they're awaiting their turn : están esperando su turno⟩ ⟨whose turn is it? : ¿a quién le toca?⟩

turnaround [ˈtərnəˌraʊnd] *n* PROCESSING : procesamiento *m*

turncoat [ˈtərnˌkoːt] *n* : traidor *m*, -dora *f*

turn down *vt* 1 REFUSE : rehusar, rechazar ⟨they turned down our invitation : rehusaron nuestra invitación⟩ 2 LOWER : bajar (el volumen)

turn in *vt* : entregar ⟨to turn in one's work : entregar uno su trabajo⟩ ⟨they turned in the suspect : entregaron al sospechoso⟩ — *vi* : acostarse, irse a la cama

turnip [ˈtərnəp] *n* : nabo *m*

turn off *vt* : apagar (la luz, la radio, etc.)

turn on *vt* : prender (la luz, etc.), encender (un motor, etc.)

turnout [ˈtərnˌaʊt] *n* : concurrencia *f*

turn out *vt* 1 EVICT, EXPEL : expulsar, echar, desalojar 2 PRODUCE : producir 3 → **turn off** — *vi* 1 : concurrir, presentarse ⟨many turned out to vote : muchos concurrieron a votar⟩ 2 PROVE, RESULT : resultar

turnover [ˈtərnˌoːvər] *n* 1 : empanada *f* (salada o dulce) 2 : volumen *m* (de ventas) 3 : rotación *f* (de personal) ⟨a high turnover : un alto nivel de rotación⟩

turn over *vt* 1 TRANSFER : entregar, transferir (un cargo o una responsabilidad) 2 : voltear, darle la vuelta a ⟨turn the cassette over : voltea el cassette⟩

turnpike [ˈtərnˌpaɪk] *n* : carretera *f* de peaje

turnstile [ˈtərnˌstaɪl] *n* : torniquete *m* (de acceso)

turntable [ˈtərnˌteɪbəl] *n* : tornamesa *mf*

turn up *vi* 1 APPEAR : aparecer, presentarse 2 HAPPEN : ocurrir, suceder (inesperadamente) — *vt* : subir (el volumen)

turpentine [ˈtərpənˌtaɪn] *n* : aguarrás *m*, trementina *f*

turquoise ['tər,kɔɪz, -,kwɔɪz] *n* : turquesa *f*

turret ['tərət] *n* **1** TOWER : torre *f* pequeña **2** : torreta *f* (de un tanque, un avión, etc.)

turtle ['tərtəl] *n* : tortuga *f* (marina)

turtledove ['tərtəl,dʌv] *n* : tórtola *f*

turtleneck ['tərtəl,nɛk] *n* : cuello *m* de tortuga, cuello *m* alto

tusk ['tʌsk] *n* : colmillo *m*

tussle[1] ['tʌsəl] *vi* **-sled; -sling** SCUFFLE : pelearse, reñir

tussle[2] *n* : riña *f*, pelea *f*

tutor[1] ['tuːtər, 'tjuː-] *vt* : darle clases particulares (a alguien)

tutor[2] *n* : tutor *m*, -tora *f*; maestro *m*, -tra *f* (particular)

tuxedo [,tək'siː,doː] *n, pl* **-dos** *or* **-does** : esmoquin *m*, smoking *m*

TV [,tiː'viː, 'tiː,viː] → **television**

twain ['tweɪn] *n* : dos *m*

twang[1] ['twæŋ] *vt* : pulsar la cuerda de (una guitarra) — *vi* : hablar en tono nasal

twang[2] *n* **1** : tañido *m* (de una cuerda de guitarra) **2** : tono *m* nasal (de voz)

tweak[1] ['twiːk] *vt* : pellizcar

tweak[2] *n* : pellizco *m*

tweed ['twiːd] *n* : tweed *m*

tweet[1] ['twiːt] *vi* : piar

tweet[2] *n* : gorjeo *m*, pío *m*

tweezers ['twiːzərz] *npl* : pinzas *fpl*

twelfth[1] ['twɛlfθ] *adj* : duodécimo

twelfth[2] *n* **1** : duodécimo *m*, -ma *f* (en una serie) **2** : doceavo *m*, doceava parte *f*

twelve[1] ['twɛlv] *adj* : doce

twelve[2] *n* : doce *m*

twentieth[1] ['twʌntiəθ, 'twɛn-] *adj* : vigésimo

twentieth[2] *n* **1** : vigésimo *m*, -ma *f* (en una serie) **2** : veinteavo *m*, veinteava parte *f*

twenty[1] ['twʌnti, 'twɛn-] *adj* : veinte

twenty[2] *n, pl* **-ties** : veinte *m*

twice ['twaɪs] *adv* : dos veces ⟨twice a day : dos veces al día⟩ ⟨it costs twice as much : cuesta el doble⟩

twig ['twɪg] *n* : ramita *f*

twilight ['twaɪ,laɪt] *n* : crepúsculo *m*

twill ['twɪl] *n* : sarga *f*, tela *f* cruzada

twin[1] ['twɪn] *adj* : gemelo, mellizo

twin[2] *n* : gemelo *m*, -la *f*; mellizo *m*, -za *f*

twine[1] ['twaɪn] *v* **twined; twining** *vt* : entrelazar, entrecruzar — *vi* : enroscarse (alrededor de algo)

twine[2] *n* : cordel *m*, cuerda *f*, mecate *m* CA, Mex, Ven

twinge[1] ['twɪndʒ] *vi* **twinged; twinging** *or* **twingeing** : sentir punzadas

twinge[2] *n* : punzada *f*, dolor *m* agudo

twinkle[1] ['twɪŋkəl] *vi* **-kled; -kling 1** : centellear, titilar (dícese de las estrellas o de la luz) **2** : chispear, brillar (dícese de los ojos)

twinkle[2] *n* : centelleo *m* (de las estrellas), brillo *m* (de los ojos)

twirl[1] ['twərl] *vt* : girar, darle vueltas a — *vi* : girar, dar vueltas (rápidamente)

twirl[2] *n* : giro *m*, vuelta *f*

twist[1] ['twɪst] *vt* : torcer, retorcer ⟨he twisted my arm : me torció el brazo⟩ — *vi* : retorcerse, enroscarse, serpentear (dícese de un río, un camino, etc.)

twist[2] *n* **1** BEND : vuelta *f*, recodo *m* (en el camino, el río, etc.) **2** TURN : giro *m* ⟨give it a twist : hazlo girar⟩ **3** SPIRAL : espiral *f* ⟨a twist of lemon : una rodajita de limón⟩ **4** : giro *m* inesperado (de eventos, etc.)

twisted ['twɪstəd] *adj* : retorcido ⟨a twisted mind : una mente retorcida⟩

twister ['twɪstər] **1** → **tornado 2** → **waterspout**

twitch[1] ['twɪtʃ] *vi* : moverse nerviosamente, contraerse espasmódicamente (dícese de un músculo)

twitch[2] *n* : espasmo *m*, sacudida *f* ⟨a nervous twitch : un tic nervioso⟩

twitter[1] ['twɪtər] *vi* CHIRP : gorjear, cantar (dícese de los pájaros)

twitter[2] *n* : gorjeo *m*

two[1] ['tuː] *adj* : dos

two[2] *n, pl* **twos** : dos *m*

twofold[1] ['tuː'foːld] *adv* : al doble

twofold[2] ['tuː,foːld] *adj* : doble

two hundred[1] *adj* : doscientos

two hundred[2] *n* : doscientos *m*

twosome ['tuːsəm] *n* COUPLE : pareja *f*

tycoon [taɪ'kuːn] *n* : magnate *mf*

tying → **tie**[1]

type[1] ['taɪp] *v* **typed; typing** *vt* **1** TYPEWRITE : escribir a máquina, pasar (un texto) a máquina **2** CATEGORIZE : categorizar, identificar — *vi* : escribir a máquina

type[2] *n* **1** KIND : tipo *m*, clase *f*, categoría *f* **2** *or* **printing type** : tipo *m*

typeface ['taɪp,feɪs] *n* : tipo *m* de imprenta

typewrite ['taɪp,raɪt] *v* **-wrote; -written** : escribir a máquina

typewriter ['taɪp,raɪtər] *n* : máquina *f* de escribir

typhoid[1] ['taɪ,fɔɪd, taɪ'-] *adj* : relativo al tifus o a la tifoidea

typhoid[2] *n or* **typhoid fever** : tifoidea *f*

typhoon [taɪ'fuːn] *n* : tifón *m*

typhus ['taɪfəs] *n* : tifus *m*, tifo *m*

typical ['tɪpɪkəl] *adj* : típico, característico — **typically** *adv*

typify ['tɪpə,faɪ] *vt* **-fied; -fying** : ser típico o representativo de (un grupo, una clase, etc.)

typist ['taɪpɪst] *n* : mecanógrafo *m*, -fa *f*

typographic [,taɪpə'græfɪk] *or* **typographical** [-fɪkəl] *adj* : tipográfico — **typographically** [-fɪkli] *adv*

typography [taɪ'pɑgrəfi] *n* : tipografía *f*

tyrannical [tə'rænɪkəl, taɪ-] *adj* : tiránico — **tyrannically** [-nɪkli] *adv*

tyrannize ['tɪrə,naɪz] *vt* **-nized; -nizing** : tiranizar

tyranny ['tɪrəni] *n, pl* **-nies** : tiranía *f*

tyrant ['taɪrənt] *n* : tirano *m*, -na *f*

tzar ['zɑr, 'tsɑr, 'sɑr] → **czar**

U

u ['ju:] *n, pl* **u's** *or* **us** ['ju:z] : vigésima primera letra del alfabeto inglés

ubiquitous [ju:'bɪkwəṭəs] *adj* : ubicuo, omnipresente

udder ['ʌdər] *n* : ubre *f*

UFO [ˌju:ˌɛf'o:, 'ju:ˌfo:] *n, pl* **UFO's** *or* **UFOs** (*unidentified flying object*) : ovni *m*, OVNI *m*

Ugandan [ju:'gændən, -'gɑn-; u:'gɑn-] *n* : ugandés *m*, -desa *f* — **Ugandan** *adj*

ugliness ['ʌglinəs] *n* : fealdad *f*

ugly ['ʌgli] *adj* **uglier; -est 1** UNATTRACTIVE : feo **2** DISAGREEABLE : desagradable, feo ⟨ugly weather : tiempo feo⟩ ⟨to have an ugly temper : tener mal genio⟩

Ukrainian [ju:'kreɪniən, -'kraɪ-] *n* **1** : ucraniano *m*, -na *f* **2** : ucraniano *m* (idioma) — **Ukrainian** *adj*

ukulele [ˌju:kə'leɪli] *n* : ukelele *m*

ulcer ['ʌlsər] *n* : úlcera *f* (interna), llaga *f* (externa)

ulcerate ['ʌlsəˌreɪt] *vi* **-ated; -ating** : ulcerarse

ulceration [ˌʌlsə'reɪʃən] *n* **1** : ulceración *f* **2** ULCER : úlcera *f*, llaga *f*

ulcerous ['ʌlsərəs] *adj* : ulceroso

ulna ['ʌlnə] *n* : cúbito *m*

ulterior [ˌʌl'tɪriər] *adj* : oculto ⟨ulterior motive : motivo oculto, segunda intención⟩

ultimate ['ʌltəmət] *adj* **1** FINAL : último, final **2** SUPREME : supremo, máximo **3** FUNDAMENTAL : fundamental, esencial

ultimately ['ʌltəmətli] *adv* **1** FINALLY : por último, finalmente **2** EVENTUALLY : a la larga, con el tiempo

ultimatum [ˌʌltə'meɪṭəm, -'mɑ-] *n, pl* **-tums** *or* **-ta** [-ṭə] : ultimátum *m*

ultrasound ['ʌltrəˌsaʊnd] *n* **1** : ultrasonido *m* **2** : ecografía *f* (técnica o imagen)

ultraviolet [ˌʌltrə'vaɪələt] *adj* : ultravioleta

umbilical cord [ˌʌm'bɪlɪkəl] *n* : cordón *m* umbilical

umbrage ['ʌmbrɪdʒ] *n* **to take umbrage at** : ofenderse por

umbrella [ˌʌm'brɛlə] *n* **1** : paraguas *m* **2 beach umbrella** : sombrilla *f*

umpire¹ ['ʌmˌpaɪr] *v* **-pired; -piring** : arbitrar

umpire² *n* : árbitro *m*, -tra *f*

umpteenth [ˌʌmp'ti:nθ] *adj* : enésimo

unable [ˌʌn'eɪbəl] *adj* : incapaz ⟨to be unable to : no poder⟩

unabridged [ˌʌnə'brɪdʒd] *adj* : íntegro

unacceptable [ˌʌnɪk'sɛptəbəl] *adj* : inaceptable

unaccompanied [ˌʌnə'kʌmpənid] *adj* : solo, sin acompañamiento (en música)

unaccountable [ˌʌnə'kaʊntəbəl] *adj* : inexplicable, incomprensible — **unaccountably** [-bli] *adv*

unaccustomed [ˌʌnə'kʌstəmd] *adj* **1** UNUSUAL : desacostumbrado, inusual **2** UNUSED : inhabituado ⟨unaccustomed to noise : inhabituado al ruido⟩

unacquainted [ˌʌnə'kweɪntəd] *adj* **to be unacquainted with** : desconocer, ignorar

unadorned [ˌʌnə'dɔrnd] *adj* : sin adornos, puro y simple

unadulterated [ˌʌnə'dʌltəˌreɪṭəd] *adj* **1** PURE : puro ⟨unadulterated food : comida pura⟩ **2** ABSOLUTE : completo, absoluto

unaffected [ˌʌnə'fɛktəd] *adj* **1** : no afectado, indiferente **2** NATURAL : sin afectación, natural

unaffectedly [ˌʌnə'fɛktədli] *adv* : de manera natural

unafraid [ˌʌnə'freɪd] *adj* : sin miedo

unaided [ˌʌn'eɪdəd] *adj* : sin ayuda, solo

unambiguous [ˌʌnæm'bɪgjuəs] *adj* : inequívoco

unanimity [ˌju:nə'nɪməṭi] *n* : unanimidad *f*

unanimous [jʊ'nænəməs] *adj* : unánime — **unanimously** *adv*

unannounced [ˌʌnə'naʊnst] *adj* : sin dar aviso

unanswered [ˌʌn'æntsərd] *adj* : sin contestar

unappealing [ˌʌnə'pi:lɪŋ] *adj* : desagradable

unappetizing [ˌʌn'æpəˌtaɪzɪŋ] *adj* : poco apetitoso, poco apetecible

unarmed [ˌʌn'ɑrmd] *adj* : sin armas, desarmado

unassisted [ˌʌnə'sɪstəd] *adj* : sin ayuda

unassuming [ˌʌnə'su:mɪŋ] *adj* : modesto, sin pretensiones

unattached [ˌʌnə'tætʃt] *adj* **1** LOOSE : suelto **2** INDEPENDENT : independiente **3** : solo (ni casado ni prometido)

unattractive [ˌʌnə'træktɪv] *adj* : poco atractivo

unauthorized [ˌʌn'ɔθəˌraɪzd] *adj* : sin autorización, no autorizado

unavailable [ˌʌnə'veɪləbəl] *adj* : no disponible

unavoidable [ˌʌnə'vɔɪdəbəl] *adj* : inevitable, ineludible

unaware¹ [ˌʌnə'wær] *adv* → **unawares**

unaware² *adj* : inconsciente

unawares [ˌʌnə'wærz] *adv* **1** : por sorpresa ⟨to catch someone unawares : agarrar a alguien desprevenido⟩ **2** UNINTENTIONALLY : inconscientemente, inadvertidamente

unbalanced [ˌʌn'bæləntst] *adj* : desequilibrado

unbearable [ˌʌn'bærəbəl] *adj* : insoportable, inaguantable — **unbearably** [-bli] *adv*

unbecoming [ˌʌnbɪ'kʌmɪŋ] *adj* **1** UNSEEMLY : impropio, indecoroso **2** UNFLATTERING : poco favorecedor

unbelievable [ˌʌnbə'li:vəbəl] *adj* : increíble — **unbelievably** [-bli] *adv*

unbend [ˌʌn'bɛnd] *vi* **-bent** [-'bɛnt]; **-bending** RELAX : relajarse

unbending [ˌʌn'bɛndɪŋ] *adj* : inflexible

unbiased [ˌʌn'baɪəst] *adj* : imparcial, objetivo

unbind [ˌʌn'baɪnd] *vt* **-bound** [-'baʊnd]; **-binding 1** UNFASTEN, UNTIE : desatar, desamarrar **2** RELEASE : liberar

unbolt [ˌʌn'bo:lt] *vt* : abrir el cerrojo de, descorrer el pestillo de

unborn [ˌʌn'bɔrn] *adj* : aún no nacido, que va a nacer

unbosom [ˌʌn'buzəm, -'bu:-] *vt* : revelar, divulgar

unbreakable [ˌʌn'breɪkəbəl] *adj* : irrompible

unbridled [ˌʌn'braɪdəld] *adj* : desenfrenado

unbroken [ˌʌn'bro:kən] *adj* **1** INTACT : intacto, sano **2** CONTINUOUS : continuo, ininterrumpido

unbuckle [ˌʌn'bʌkəl] *vt* **-led; -ling** : desabrochar

unburden [ˌʌn'bərdən] *vt* **1** UNLOAD : descargar **2 to unburden oneself** : desahogarse

unbutton [ˌʌn'bʌtən] *vt* : desabrochar, desabotonar

uncalled–for [ˌʌn'kɔld,fɔr] *adj* : inapropiado, innecesario

uncanny [ən'kæni] *adj* **-nier; -est 1** STRANGE : extraño **2** EXTRAORDINARY : raro, extraordinario — **uncannily** [-'kænəli] *adv*

unceasing [ˌʌn'si:sɪŋ] *adj* : incesante, continuo — **unceasingly** *adv*

unceremonious [ˌʌn,sɛrə'mo:niəs] *adj* **1** INFORMAL : sin ceremonia, sin pompa **2** ABRUPT : abrupto, brusco — **unceremoniously** *adv*

uncertain [ˌʌn'sərtən] *adj* **1** INDEFINITE : indeterminado **2** UNSURE : incierto, dudoso **3** CHANGEABLE : inestable, variable ⟨uncertain weather : tiempo inestable⟩ **4** HESITANT : indeciso **5** VAGUE : poco claro

uncertainly [ˌʌn'sərtənli] *adv* : dudosamente, con desconfianza

uncertainty [ˌʌn'sərtənti] *n, pl* **-ties** : duda *f*, incertidumbre *f*

unchangeable [ˌʌn'tʃeɪndʒəbəl] *adj* : inalterable, inmutable

unchanged [ˌʌn'tʃeɪndʒd] *adj* : sin cambiar

unchanging [ˌʌn'tʃeɪndʒɪŋ] *adj* : inalterable, inmutable, firme

uncharacteristic [ˌʌn,kærɪktə'rɪstɪk] *adj* : inusual, desacostumbrado

uncharged [ˌʌn'tʃɑrdʒd] *adj* : sin carga (eléctrica)

uncivilized [ˌʌn'sɪvə,laɪzd] *adj* **1** BARBAROUS : incivilizado, bárbaro **2** WILD : salvaje

uncle ['ʌŋkəl] *n* : tío *m*

unclean [ˌʌn'kli:n] *adj* **1** IMPURE : impuro **2** DIRTY : sucio

unclear [ˌʌn'klɪr] *adj* : confuso, borroso, poco claro

Uncle Sam ['sæm] *n* : el Tío Sam

unclog [ˌʌn'klɑg] *vt* **-clogged; -clogging** : desatascar, destapar

unclothed [ˌʌn'klo:ðd] *adj* : desnudo

uncomfortable [ˌʌn'kʌmpfərtəbəl] *adj* **1** : incómodo (dícese de una silla, etc.) **2** UNEASY : inquieto, incómodo

uncommitted [ˌʌnkə'mɪtəd] *adj* : sin compromisos

uncommon [ˌʌn'kamən] *adj* **1** UNUSUAL : raro, poco común **2** REMARKABLE : excepcional, extraordinario

uncommonly [ˌʌn'kamənli] *adv* : extraordinariamente

uncompromising [ˌʌn'kamprə,maɪzɪŋ] *adj* : inflexible, intransigente

unconcerned [ˌʌnkən'sərnd] *adj* : indiferente — **unconcernedly** [-'sərnədli] *adv*

unconditional [ˌʌnkən'dɪʃənəl] *adj* : incondicional — **unconditionally** *adv*

unconscious¹ [ˌʌn'kantʃəs] *adj* : inconsciente — **unconsciously** *adv*

unconscious² *n* : inconsciente *m*

unconsciousness [ˌʌn'kantʃəsnəs] *n* : inconsciencia *f*

unconstitutional [ˌʌn,kantʃɪstə'tu:ʃənəl, -'tju:-] *adj* : inconstitucional

uncontrollable [ˌʌnkən'tro:ləbəl] *adj* : incontrolable, incontenible — **uncontrollably** [-bli] *adv*

uncontrolled [ˌʌnkən'tro:ld] *adj* : incontrolado

unconventional [ˌʌnkən'vɛntʃənəl] *adj* : poco convencional

unconvincing [ˌʌnkən'vɪntsɪŋ] *adj* : poco convincente

uncouth [ˌʌn'ku:θ] *adj* CRUDE, ROUGH : grosero, rudo

uncover [ˌʌn'kʌvər] *vt* **1** : destapar (un objeto), dejar al descubierto **2** EXPOSE, REVEAL : descubrir, revelar, exponer

uncultivated [ˌʌn'kʌltə,veɪtəd] *adj* : inculto

uncurl [ˌʌn'kərl] *vt* UNROLL : desenrollar — *vi* : desenrollarse, desrizarse (dícese del pelo)

uncut [ˌʌn'kʌt] *adj* **1** : sin cortar ⟨uncut grass : hierba sin cortar⟩ **2** : sin tallar, en bruto ⟨an uncut diamond : un diamante en bruto⟩ **3** UNABRIDGED : completo, íntegro

undaunted [ˌʌn'dɔntəd] *adj* : impávido

undecided [ˌʌndi'saɪdəd] *adj* **1** IRRESOLUTE : indeciso, irresoluto **2** UNRESOLVED : pendiente, no resuelto

undefeated [ˌʌndi'fi:təd] *adj* : invicto

undeniable [ˌʌndi'naɪəbəl] *adj* : innegable — **undeniably** [-bli] *adv*

under¹ ['ʌndər] *adv* **1** LESS : menos ⟨$10 or under : $10 o menos⟩ **2** UNDERWATER : debajo del agua **3** : bajo los efectos de la anestesia

under² *adj* **1** LOWER : (más) bajo, inferior **2** SUBORDINATE : inferior **3** : insuficiente ⟨an under dose of medicine : una dosis insuficiente de medicina⟩

under³ *prep* **1** BELOW, BENEATH : debajo de, abajo de ⟨under the table : abajo de la mesa⟩ ⟨we walked under the arch : pasamos por debajo del arco⟩ ⟨under the sun : bajo el sol⟩ **2** : menos de ⟨in under 20 minutes : en menos de 20 minutos⟩ **3** (*indicating rank or authority*) : bajo ⟨under the command of : bajo las órdenes de⟩ **4** SUBJECT TO : bajo ⟨under suspicion : bajo sospecha⟩ ⟨under the circumstances : dadas las circunstancias⟩ **5** ACCORDING TO : según, de acuerdo con, conforme a ⟨under the present laws : según las leyes actuales⟩

underage [ˌʌndərˈeɪʤ] *adj* : menor de edad

underbrush [ˈʌndərˌbrəʃ] *n* : maleza *f*

underclothes [ˈʌndərˌkloːz, -ˌkloːðz] → **underwear**

underclothing [ˈʌndərˌkloːðɪŋ] → **underwear**

undercover [ˌʌndərˈkʌvər] *adj* : secreto, clandestino

undercurrent [ˈʌndərˌkərənt] *n* **1** : corriente *f* submarina **2** UNDERTONE : corriente *f* oculta, trasfondo *m*

undercut [ˌʌndərˈkʌt] *vt* -**cut**; -**cutting** : vender más barato que

underdeveloped [ˌʌndərdɪˈvɛləpt] *adj* : subdesarrollado, atrasado

underdog [ˈʌndərˌdɔg] *n* : persona *f* que tiene menos posibilidades

underdone [ˌʌndərˈdʌn] *adj* RARE : poco cocido

underestimate [ˌʌndərˈɛstəˌmeɪt] *vt* -**mated**; -**mating** : subestimar, menospreciar

underexposed [ˌʌndərɪkˈspoːzd] *adj* : subexpuesto (en fotografía)

underfoot [ˌʌndərˈfʊt] *adv* **1** : bajo los pies ⟨to trample underfoot : pisotear⟩ **2 to be underfoot** : estorbar ⟨they're always underfoot : están siempre estorbando⟩

undergarment [ˈʌndərˌgɑrmənt] *n* : prenda *f* íntima

undergo [ˌʌndərˈgoː] *vt* -**went** [-ˈwɛnt]; -**gone** [-ˈgɔn]; -**going** : sufrir, experimentar ⟨to undergo an operation : someterse a una intervención quirúrgica⟩

undergraduate [ˌʌndərˈgræʤuət] *n* : estudiante *m* universitario, estudiante *f* universitaria

underground¹ [ˌʌndərˈgraʊnd] *adv* **1** : bajo tierra **2** SECRETLY : clandestinamente, en secreto ⟨to go underground : pasar a la clandestinidad⟩

underground² [ˈʌndərˌgraʊnd] *adj* **1** SUBTERRANEAN : subterráneo **2** SECRET : secreto, clandestino

underground³ [ˈʌndərˌgraʊnd] *n* : movimiento *m* o grupo *m* clandestino

undergrowth [ˈʌndərˌgroːθ] *n* : maleza *f*, broza *f*

underhand¹ [ˈʌndərˌhænd] *adv* **1** SECRETLY : de manera clandestina **2** or

underhanded : sin levantar el brazo por encima del hombro (en deportes)

underhand² *adj* **1** SLY : solapado **2** : por debajo del hombro (en deportes)

underhanded [ˌʌndərˈhændəd] *adj* **1** SLY : solapado **2** SHADY : turbio, poco limpio

underline [ˈʌndərˌlaɪn] *vt* -**lined**; -**lining** **1** : subrayar **2** EMPHASIZE : subrayar, acentuar, hacer hincapié en

underlying [ˌʌndərˈlaɪɪŋ] *adj* **1** : subyacente ⟨the underlying rock : la roca subyacente⟩ **2** FUNDAMENTAL : fundamental, esencial

undermine [ˌʌndərˈmaɪn] *vt* -**mined**; -**mining** **1** : socavar (una estructura, etc.) **2** SAP, WEAKEN : minar, debilitar

underneath¹ [ˌʌndərˈniːθ] *adv* : debajo, abajo ⟨the part underneath : la parte de abajo⟩

underneath² *prep* : debajo de, abajo de

undernourished [ˌʌndərˈnərɪʃt] *adj* : desnutrido

underpants [ˈʌndərˌpænts] *npl* : calzoncillos *mpl*, calzones *mpl*

underpass [ˈʌndərˌpæs] *n* : paso *m* a desnivel

underprivileged [ˌʌndərˈprɪvlɪʤd] *adj* : desfavorecido

underrate [ˌʌndərˈreɪt] *vt* -**rated**; -**rating** : subestimar, menospreciar

underscore [ˈʌndərˌskor] *vt* -**scored**; -**scoring** → **underline**

undersea¹ [ˌʌndərˈsiː] *or* **underseas** [-ˈsiːz] *adv* : bajo la superficie del mar

undersea² *adj* : submarino

undersecretary [ˌʌndərˈsɛkrəˌtɛri] *n, pl* -**ries** : subsecretario *m*, -ria *f*

undersell [ˌʌndərˈsɛl] *vt* -**sold**; -**selling** : vender más barato que

undershirt [ˈʌndərˌʃərt] *n* : camiseta *f*

undershorts [ˈʌndərˌʃorts] *npl* : calzoncillos *mpl*

underside [ˈʌndərˌsaɪd, ˌʌndərˈsaɪd] *n* : parte *f* de abajo

undersized [ˌʌndərˈsaɪzd] *adj* : más pequeño de lo normal

understand [ˌʌndərˈstænd] *v* -**stood** [-ˈstʊd]; -**standing** *vt* **1** COMPREHEND : comprender, entender ⟨I don't understand it : no lo entiendo⟩ ⟨that's understood : eso se comprende⟩ ⟨to make oneself understood : hacerse entender⟩ **2** BELIEVE : entender ⟨to give someone to understand : dar a alguien a entender⟩ **3** INFER : tener entendido ⟨I understand that she's leaving : tengo entendido que se va⟩ — *vi* : comprender, entender

understandable [ˌʌndərˈstændəbəl] *adj* : comprensible

understanding¹ [ˌʌndərˈstændɪŋ] *adj* : comprensivo, compasivo

understanding² *n* **1** GRASP : comprensión *f*, entendimiento *m* **2** SYMPATHY : comprensión *f* (mutua) **3** INTERPRETATION : interpretación *f* ⟨it's my understanding that ... : tengo la impresión de que ..., tengo entendido que . . . ⟩ **4** AGREEMENT : acuerdo *m*, arreglo *m*

understate [ˌʌndər'steɪt] *vt* **-stated; -stating** : minimizar, subestimar

understatement [ˌʌndər'steɪtmənt] *n* : atenuación *f* ⟨that's an understatement : decir sólo eso es quedarse corto⟩

understudy² ['ʌndərˌstʌdi] *n, pl* **-dies** : sobresaliente *mf*, suplente *mf* (en el teatro)

undertake [ˌʌndər'teɪk] *vt* **-took** [-'tʊk]; **-taken** [-'teɪkən]; **-taking 1** : emprender (una tarea), asumir (una responsabilidad) **2** PROMISE : comprometerse (a hacer algo)

undertaker ['ʌndərˌteɪkər] *n* : director *m*, -tora *f* de funeraria

undertaking ['ʌndərˌteɪkɪŋ, ˌʌndər'-] *n* **1** ENTERPRISE, TASK : empresa *f*, tarea *f* **2** PLEDGE : promesa *f*, garantía *f*

undertone ['ʌndərˌtoːn] *n* **1** : voz *f* baja ⟨to speak in an undertone : hablar en voz baja⟩ **2** HINT, UNDERCURRENT : trasfondo *m*, matiz *m*

undertow ['ʌndərˌtoː] *n* : resaca *f*

undervalue [ˌʌndər'væl.juː] *vt* **-ued; -uing** : menospreciar, subestimar

underwater¹ [ˌʌndər'wɔtər, -'wɑ-] *adv* : debajo (del agua)

underwater² *adj* : submarino

under way [ˌʌndər'weɪ] *adv* : en marcha, en camino ⟨to get under way : ponerse en marcha⟩

underwear ['ʌndərˌwær] *n* : ropa *f* interior, ropa *f* íntima

underworld ['ʌndərˌwərld] *n* **1** HELL : infierno *m* **2 the underworld** CRIMINALS : la hampa, los bajos fondos

underwrite ['ʌndərˌraɪt, ˌʌndər'-] *vt* **-wrote** [-ˌroːt, -'roːt]; **-written** [-ˌrɪtən, -'rɪtən]; **-writing 1** INSURE : asegurar **2** FINANCE : financiar **3** BACK, ENDORSE : suscribir, respaldar

underwriter ['ʌndərˌraɪtər, ˌʌndər'-] *n* INSURER : asegurador *m*, -dora *f*

undeserving [ˌʌndi'zərvɪŋ] *adj* : indigno

undesirable¹ [ˌʌndi'zaɪrəbəl] *adj* : indeseable

undesirable² *n* : indeseable *mf*

undeveloped [ˌʌndi'vɛləpt] *adj* : sin desarrollar, sin revelar (dícese de una película)

undies ['ʌndiːz] → **underwear**

undignified [ʌn'dɪgnəfaɪd] *adj* : indecoroso

undiluted [ˌʌndaɪ'luːtəd, -də-] *adj* : sin diluir, concentrado

undiscovered [ˌʌndɪ'skʌvərd] *adj* : no descubierto

undisputed [ˌʌndɪ'spjuːtəd] *adj* : indiscutible

undisturbed [ˌʌndɪ'stərbd] *adj* : tranquilo (dícese de una persona), sin tocar (dícese de un objeto)

undivided [ˌʌndɪ'vaɪdəd] *adj* : íntegro, completo

undo [ʌn'duː] *vt* **-did** [-'dɪd]; **-done** [-'dʌn]; **-doing 1** UNFASTEN : desabrochar, desatar, abrir **2** ANNUL : anular **3** REVERSE : deshacer, reparar (daños, etc.) **4** RUIN : arruinar, destruir

undoing [ʌn'duːɪŋ] *n* : ruina *f*, perdición *f*

undoubted [ʌn'daʊtəd] *adj* : cierto, indudable — **undoubtedly** *adv*

undress [ʌn'drɛs] *vt* : desvestir, desabrigar, desnudar — *vi* : desvestirse, desnudarse

undrinkable [ʌn'drɪŋkəbəl] *adj* : no potable

undue [ˌʌn'duː, -'djuː] *adj* : excesivo, indebido — **unduly** *adv*

undulate ['ʌndʒəˌleɪt] *vi* **-lated; -lating** : ondular

undulation [ˌʌndʒə'leɪʃən] *n* : ondulación *f*

undying [ʌn'daɪɪŋ] *adj* : perpetuo, imperecedero

unearth [ʌn'ərθ] *vt* **1** EXHUME : desenterrar, exhumar **2** DISCOVER : descubrir

unearthly [ʌn'ərθli] *adj* **-lier; -est** : sobrenatural, de otro mundo

uneasily [ˌʌn'iːzəli] *adv* : inquietamente, con inquietud

uneasiness [ˌʌn'iːzinəs] *n* : inquietud *f*

uneasy [ˌʌn'iːzi] *adj* **-easier; -est 1** AWKWARD : incómodo **2** WORRIED : preocupado, inquieto **3** RESTLESS : inquieto, agitado

uneducated [ˌʌn'ɛdʒəˌkeɪtəd] *adj* : inculto, sin educación

unemployed [ˌʌnɪm'plɔɪd] *adj* : desempleado

unemployment [ˌʌnɪm'plɔɪmənt] *n* : desempleo *m*

unending [ˌʌn'ɛndɪŋ] *adj* : sin fin, interminable

unendurable [ˌʌnɪn'dʊrəbəl, -ɛn-, -'djʊr-] *adj* : insoportable, intolerable

unequal [ˌʌn'iːkwəl] *adj* **1** : desigual **2** INADEQUATE : incapaz, incompetente ⟨to be unequal to a task : no estar a la altura de una tarea⟩

unequaled *or* **unequalled** [ˌʌn'iːkwəld] *adj* : sin igual

unequivocal [ˌʌnɪ'kwɪvəkəl] *adj* : inequívoco, claro — **unequivocally** *adv*

unerring [ˌʌn'ɛrɪŋ, -'ər-] *adj* : infalible

unethical [ˌʌn'ɛθɪkəl] *adj* : poco ético

uneven [ˌʌn'iːvən] *adj* **1** ODD : impar (dícese de un número) **2** : desigual, desnivelado (dícese de una superficie) ⟨uneven terrain : terreno accidentado⟩ **3** IRREGULAR : irregular, poco uniforme **4** UNEQUAL : desigual

unevenly [ˌʌn'iːvənli] *adv* : desigualmente, irregularmente

uneventful [ˌʌnɪ'vɛntfəl] *adj* : sin incidentes, tranquilo

unexpected [ˌʌnɪk'spɛktəd] *adj* : imprevisto, inesperado — **unexpectedly** *adv*

unfailing [ˌʌn'feɪlɪŋ] *adj* **1** CONSTANT : constante **2** INEXHAUSTIBLE : inagotable **3** SURE : a toda prueba, indefectible

unfair [ˌʌnˈfær] *adj* : injusto — **unfairly** *adv*

unfairness [ˌʌnˈfærnəs] *n* : injusticia *f*

unfaithful [ˌʌnˈfeɪθfəl] *adj* : desleal, infiel — **unfaithfully** *adv*

unfaithfulness [ˌʌnˈfeɪθfəlnəs] *n* : infidelidad *f*, deslealtad *f*

unfamiliar [ˌʌnfəˈmɪljər] *adj* **1** STRANGE : desconocido, extraño ⟨an unfamiliar place : un lugar nuevo⟩ **2 to be unfamiliar with** : no estar familiarizado con, desconocer

unfamiliarity [ˌʌnfəˌmɪliˈærəti] *n* : falta *f* de familiaridad

unfashionable [ˌʌnˈfæʃənəbəl] *adj* : fuera de moda

unfasten [ˌʌnˈfæsən] *vt* : desabrochar, desatar (una cuerda, etc.), abrir (una puerta)

unfavorable [ˌʌnˈfeɪvərəbəl] *adj* : desfavorable, mal — **unfavorably** [-bli] *adv*

unfeeling [ˌʌnˈfiːlɪŋ] *adj* : insensible — **unfeelingly** *adv*

unfinished [ˌʌnˈfɪnɪʃd] *adj* : inacabado, incompleto

unfit [ˌʌnˈfɪt] *adj* **1** UNSUITABLE : inadecuado, impropio **2** UNSUITED : no apto, incapaz **3** : incapacitado (físicamente) ⟨to be unfit : no estar en forma⟩

unflappable [ˌʌnˈflæpəbəl] *adj* : imperturbable

unflattering [ˌʌnˈflætərɪŋ] *adj* : poco favorecedor

unfold [ˌʌnˈfoːld] *vt* **1** EXPAND : desplegar, desdoblar, extender ⟨to unfold a map : desplegar un mapa⟩ **2** DISCLOSE, REVEAL : revelar, exponer (un plan, etc.) — *vi* **1** DEVELOP : desarrollarse, desenvolverse ⟨the story unfolded : el cuento se desarrollaba⟩ **2** EXPAND : extenderse, desplegarse

unforeseeable [ˌʌnforˈsiːəbəl] *adj* : imprevisible

unforeseen [ˌʌnforˈsiːn] *adj* : imprevisto

unforgettable [ˌʌnfərˈɡɛtəbəl] *adj* : inolvidable, memorable — **unforgettably** [-bli] *adv*

unforgivable [ˌʌnfərˈɡɪvəbəl] *adj* : imperdonable

unfortunate¹ [ˌʌnˈfɔrtʃənət] *adj* **1** UNLUCKY : desgraciado, infortunado, desafortunado ⟨how unfortunate! : ¡qué mala suerte!⟩ **2** INAPPROPRIATE : inoportuno ⟨an unfortunate comment : un comentario poco feliz⟩

unfortunate² *n* : desgraciado *m*, -da *f*

unfortunately [ˌʌnˈfɔrtʃənətli] *adv* : desafortunadamente

unfounded [ˌʌnˈfaʊndəd] *adj* : infundado

unfreeze [ˌʌnˈfriːz] *v* **-froze** [-ˈfroːz]; **-frozen** [-ˈfroːzən]; **-freezing** *vt* : descongelar — *vi* : descongelarse

unfriendliness [ˌʌnˈfrɛndlinəs] *n* : hostilidad *f*, antipatía *f*

unfriendly [ˌʌnˈfrɛndli] *adj* **-lier; -est** : poco amistoso, hostil

unfurl [ˌʌnˈfərl] *vt* : desplegar, desdoblar — *vi* : desplegarse

unfurnished [ˌʌnˈfərnɪʃt] *adj* : desamueblado

ungainly [ˌʌnˈɡeɪnli] *adj* : desgarbado

ungodly [ˌʌnˈɡɔdli, -ˈɡɑd-] *adj* **1** IMPIOUS : impío **2** OUTRAGEOUS : atroz, terrible ⟨at an ungodly hour : a una hora intempestiva⟩

ungrateful [ˌʌnˈɡreɪtfəl] *adj* : desagradecido, ingrato — **ungratefully** *adv*

ungratefulness [ˌʌnˈɡreɪtfəlnəs] *n* : ingratitud *f*

unhappily [ˌʌnˈhæpəli] *adv* **1** SADLY : tristemente **2** UNFORTUNATELY : desafortunadamente, lamentablemente

unhappiness [ˌʌnˈhæpinəs] *n* : infelicidad *f*, tristeza *f*, desdicha *f*

unhappy [ˌʌnˈhæpi] *adj* **-pier; -est 1** UNFORTUNATE : desafortunado, desventurado **2** MISERABLE, SAD : infeliz, triste, desdichado **3** INOPPORTUNE : inoportuno, poco feliz

unharmed [ˌʌnˈhɑrmd] *adj* : salvo, ileso

unhealthy [ˌʌnˈhɛlθi] *adj* **-thier; -est 1** UNWHOLESOME : insalubre, malsano, nocivo a la salud ⟨an unhealthy climate : un clima insalubre⟩ **2** SICKLY : de mala salud, enfermizo

unheard-of [ˌʌnˈhərdəv] *adj* : sin precedente, inaudito, insólito

unhinge [ˌʌnˈhɪndʒ] *vt* **-hinged; -hinging 1** : desquiciar (una puerta, etc.) **2** DISRUPT, UNSETTLE : trastornar, perturbar

unholy [ˌʌnˈhoːli] *adj* **-lier; -est 1** : profano, impío **2** UNGODLY : atroz, terrible

unhook [ˌʌnˈhʊk] *vt* **1** : desenganchar, descolgar (de algo) **2** UNDO : desabrochar

unhurt [ˌʌnˈhərt] *adj* : ileso

unicorn [ˈjuːnəˌkɔrn] *n* : unicornio *m*

unidentified [ˌʌnaɪˈdɛntəˌfaɪd] *adj* : no identificado ⟨unidentified flying object : objeto volador no identificado⟩

unification [ˌjuːnəfəˈkeɪʃən] *n* : unificación *f*

uniform¹ [ˈjuːnəˌfɔrm] *adj* : uniforme, homogéneo, constante

uniform² *n* : uniforme *m*

uniformed [ˈjuːnəˌfɔrmd] *adj* : uniformado

uniformity [ˌjuːnəˈfɔrməti] *n, pl* **-ties** : uniformidad *f*

unify [ˈjuːnəˌfaɪ] *vt* **-fied; -fying** : unificar, unir

unilateral [ˌjuːnəˈlætərəl] *adj* : unilateral — **unilaterally** *adv*

unimaginable [ˌʌnɪˈmædʒənəbəl] *adj* : inimaginable, inconcebible

unimportant [ˌʌnɪmˈpɔrtənt] *adj* : intrascendente, insignificante, sin importancia

uninhabited [ˌʌnɪnˈhæbətəd] *adj* : deshabitado, desierto, despoblado

uninhibited [ˌʌnɪnˈhɪbətəd] *adj* : desenfadado, desinhibido, sin reservas

uninjured [ˌʌnˈɪndʒərd] *adj* : ileso

unintelligent [ˌʌnɪnˈtɛlədʒənt] *adj* : poco inteligente

unintelligible [ˌʌnɪnˈtɛlədʒəbəl] *adj* : ininteligible, incomprensible

unintentional [ˌʌnɪnˈtɛntʃənəl] *adj* : no deliberado, involuntario

unintentionally [ˌʌnɪnˈtɛntʃənəli] *adv* : involuntariamente, sin querer

uninterested [ˌʌnˈɪntəˌrɛstəd, -trəstəd] *adj* : indiferente

uninteresting [ˌʌnˈɪntəˌrɛstɪŋ, -trəstɪŋ] *adj* : poco interesante, sin interés

uninterrupted [ˌʌnˌɪntəˈrʌptəd] *adj* : ininterrumpido, continuo

union [ˈjuːnjən] *n* 1 : unión *f* 2 *or* **labor union** : sindicato *m*, gremio *m*

unionize [ˈjuːnjəˌnaɪz] *v* **-ized; -izing** *vt* : sindicalizar, sindicar — *vi* : sindicalizarse

unique [juˈniːk] *adj* 1 SOLE : único, solo 2 UNUSUAL : extraordinario

uniquely [juˈniːkli] *adv* 1 EXCLUSIVELY : exclusivamente 2 EXCEPTIONALLY : excepcionalmente

unison [ˈjuːnəsən, -zən] *n* 1 : unísono *m* (en música) 2 CONCORD : acuerdo *m*, armonía *f*, concordia *f* 3 **in ~** SIMULTANEOUSLY : simultáneamente, al unísono

unit [ˈjuːnɪt] *n* 1 : unidad *f* 2 : módulo *m* (de un mobiliario)

unitary [ˈjuːnəˌteri] *adj* : unitario

unite [juˈnaɪt] *v* **united; uniting** *vt* : unir, juntar, combinar — *vi* : unirse, juntarse

unity [ˈjuːnəti] *n, pl* **-ties** 1 UNION : unidad *f*, unión *f* 2 HARMONY : armonía *f*, acuerdo *m*

universal [ˌjuːnəˈvərsəl] *adj* 1 GENERAL : general, universal ⟨a universal rule : una regla universal⟩ 2 WORLDWIDE : universal, mundial — **universally** *adv*

universe [ˈjuːnəˌvərs] *n* : universo *m*

university [ˌjuːnəˈvərsəti] *n, pl* **-ties** : universidad *f*

unjust [ˌʌnˈdʒʌst] *adj* : injusto — **unjustly** *adv*

unjustifiable [ˌʌnˌdʒʌstəˈfaɪəbəl] *adj* : injustificable

unjustified [ˌʌnˈdʒʌstəˌfaɪd] *adj* : injustificado

unkempt [ˌʌnˈkɛmpt] *adj* : descuidado, desaliñado, despeinado (dícese del pelo)

unkind [ˌʌnˈkaɪnd] *adj* : poco amable, cruel — **unkindly** *adv*

unkindness [ˌʌnˈkaɪndnəs] *n* : crueldad *f*, falta *f* de amabilidad

unknowing [ˌʌnˈnoːɪŋ] *adj* : inconsciente, ignorante — **unknowingly** *adv*

unknown [ˌʌnˈnoːn] *adj* : desconocido

unlawful [ˌʌnˈlɔfəl] *adj* : ilícito, ilegal — **unlawfully** *adv*

unleash [ˌʌnˈliːʃ] *vt* : soltar, desatar

unless [ənˈlɛs] *conj* : a menos que, salvo que, a no ser que

unlike¹ [ˌʌnˈlaɪk] *adj* 1 DIFFERENT : diferente, distinto 2 UNEQUAL : desigual

unlike² *prep* 1 : diferente de, distinto de ⟨unlike the others : distinto a los demás⟩ 2 : a diferencia de ⟨unlike her sister, she is shy : a diferencia de su hermana, es tímida⟩

unlikelihood [ˌʌnˈlaɪkliˌhʊd] *n* : improbabilidad *f*

unlikely [ˌʌnˈlaɪkli] *adj* **-lier; -est** 1 IMPROBABLE : improbable, poco probable 2 UNPROMISING : poco prometedor

unlimited [ˌʌnˈlɪmətəd] *adj* : ilimitado

unload [ˌʌnˈloːd] *vt* 1 REMOVE : descargar, desembarcar (mercancías o pasajeros) 2 : descargar (un avión, un camión, etc.) 3 DUMP : deshacerse de — *vi* : descargar (dícese de un avión, un camión, etc.)

unlock [ˌʌnˈlɑk] *vt* 1 : abrir (con llave) 2 DISCLOSE, REVEAL : revelar

unluckily [ˌʌnˈlʌkəli] *adv* : desgraciadamente

unlucky [ˌʌnˈlʌki] *adj* **-luckier; -est** 1 : de mala suerte, desgraciado, desafortunado ⟨an unlucky year : un año de mala suerte⟩ 2 INAUSPICIOUS : desfavorable, poco propicio 3 REGRETTABLE : lamentable

unmanageable [ˌʌnˈmænɪdʒəbəl] *adj* : difícil de controlar, poco manejable, ingobernable

unmarried [ˌʌnˈmærid] *adj* : soltero

unmask [ˌʌnˈmæsk] *vt* EXPOSE : desenmascarar

unmerciful [ˌʌnˈmərsɪfəl] *adj* MERCILESS : despiadado — **unmercifully** *adv*

unmistakable [ˌʌnmɪˈsteɪkəbəl] *adj* : evidente, inconfundible, obvio — **unmistakably** [-bli] *adv*

unmoved [ˌʌnˈmuːvd] *adj* : impasible ⟨to be unmoved by : permanecer impasible ante⟩

unnatural [ˌʌnˈnætʃərəl] *adj* 1 ABNORMAL, UNUSUAL : anormal, poco natural, poco normal 2 AFFECTED : afectado, forzado ⟨an unnatural smile : una sonrisa forzada⟩ 3 PERVERSE : perverso, antinatural

unnecessary [ˌʌnˈnɛsəˌseri] *adj* : innecesario — **unnecessarily** [-ˌnɛsəˈsɛrəli] *adv*

unnerve [ˌʌnˈnərv] *vt* **-nerved; -nerving** : turbar, desconcertar, poner nervioso

unnoticed [ˌʌnˈnoːtəst] *adj* : inadvertido ⟨to go unnoticed : pasar inadvertido⟩

unobstructed [ˌʌnəbˈstrʌktəd] *adj* : libre, despejado

unobtainable [ˌʌnəbˈteɪnəbəl] *adj* : inasequible

unobtrusive [ˌʌnəbˈstruːsɪv] *adj* : discreto

unoccupied [ˌʌnˈɑkjəˌpaɪd] *adj* 1 IDLE : desempleado, desocupado 2 EMPTY : desocupado, libre, deshabitado

unofficial [ˌʌnəˈfɪʃəl] *adj* : extraoficial, oficioso, no oficial

unorganized [ˌʌnˈɔrgəˌnaɪzd] *adj* : desorganizado

unorthodox [ˌʌnˈɔrθəˌdɑks] *adj* : poco ortodoxo, poco convencional

unpack [ˌʌnˈpæk] *vt* : desempacar — *vi* : desempacar, deshacer las maletas

unpaid [ˌʌnˈpeɪd] *adj* : no remunerado, no retribuido ⟨an unpaid bill : una cuenta pendiente⟩

unparalleled [ˌʌnˈpærəˌlɛld] *adj* : sin igual

unpatriotic [ˌʌnˌpeɪtriˈɑtɪk] *adj* : antipatriótico

unpleasant [ˌʌnˈplɛzənt] *adj* : desagradable — **unpleasantly** *adv*

unplug [ˌʌnˈplʌg] *vt* **-plugged; -plugging** **1** UNCLOG : destapar, desatascar **2** DISCONNECT : desconectar, desenchufar

unpopular [ˌʌnˈpɑpjələr] *adj* : impopular, poco popular

unpopularity [ˌʌnˌpɑpjəˈlærəti] *n* : impopularidad *f*

unprecedented [ˌʌnˈprɛsəˌdɛntəd] *adj* : sin precedentes, inaudito, nuevo

unpredictable [ˌʌnpriˈdɪktəbəl] *adj* : impredecible

unprejudiced [ˌʌnˈprɛʤədəst] *adj* : imparcial, objetivo

unprepared [ˌʌnpriˈpærd] *adj* : no preparado ⟨an unprepared speech : un discurso improvisado⟩

unpretentious [ˌʌnpriˈtɛntʃəs] *adj* : modesto, sin pretensiones

unprincipled [ˌʌnˈprɪntsəpəld] *adj* : sin principios, carente de escrúpulos

unproductive [ˌʌnprəˈdʌktɪv] *adj* : improductivo

unprofitable [ˌʌnˈprɑfətəbəl] *adj* : no rentable, poco provechoso

unpromising [ˌʌnˈprɑməsɪŋ] *adj* : poco prometedor

unprotected [ˌʌnprəˈtɛktəd] *adj* : sin protección, desprotegido

unprovoked [ˌʌnprəˈvoːkt] *adj* : no provocado

unpublished [ˌʌnˈpʌblɪʃt] *adj* : inédito

unpunished [ˌʌnˈpʌnɪʃt] *adj* : impune ⟨to go unpunished : escapar sin castigo⟩

unqualified [ˌʌnˈkwɑləˌfaɪd] *adj* **1** : no calificado, sin título **2** COMPLETE : completo, absoluto ⟨an unqualified denial : una negación incondicional⟩

unquestionable [ˌʌnˈkwɛstʃənəbəl] *adj* : incuestionable, indudable, indiscutible — **unquestionably** [-bli] *adv*

unquestioning [ˌʌnˈkwɛstʃənɪŋ] *adj* : incondicional, absoluto, ciego

unravel [ˌʌnˈrævəl] *v* **-eled** *or* **-elled; -eling** *or* **-elling** *vt* **1** DISENTANGLE : desenmarañar, desenredar **2** SOLVE : aclarar, desenmarañar, desentrañar — *vi* : deshacerse

unreal [ˌʌnˈriːl] *adj* : irreal

unrealistic [ˌʌnˌriːəˈlɪstɪk] *adj* : poco realista

unreasonable [ˌʌnˈriːzənəbəl] *adj* **1** IRRATIONAL : poco razonable, irrazonable, irracional **2** EXCESSIVE : excesivo ⟨unreasonable prices : precios excesivos⟩

unreasonably [ˌʌnˈriːzənəbli] *adv* **1** IRRATIONALLY : irracionalmente, de manera irrazonable **2** EXCESSIVELY : excesivamente

unrefined [ˌʌnriˈfaɪnd] *adj* **1** : no refinado, sin refinar (dícese del azúcar, de la harina, etc.) **2** : poco refinado, inculto (dícese de una persona)

unrelated [ˌʌnriˈleɪtəd] *adj* : no relacionado, inconexo

unrelenting [ˌʌnriˈlɛntɪŋ] *adj* **1** STERN : severo, inexorable **2** CONSTANT, RELENTLESS : constante, implacable

unreliable [ˌʌnriˈlaɪəbəl] *adj* : que no es de fiar, de poca confianza, inestable (dícese del tiempo)

unrepentant [ˌʌnriˈpɛntənt] *adj* : impenitente

unresolved [ˌʌnriˈzɑlvd] *adj* : pendiente, no resuelto

unrest [ˌʌnˈrɛst] *n* : inquietud *f*, malestar *m* ⟨political unrest : disturbios políticos⟩

unrestrained [ˌʌnriˈstreɪnd] *adj* : desenfrenado, incontrolado

unrestricted [ˌʌnriˈstrɪktəd] *adj* : sin restricción ⟨unrestricted access : libre acceso⟩

unrewarding [ˌʌnriˈwɔrdɪŋ] *adj* THANKLESS : ingrato

unripe [ˌʌnˈraɪp] *adj* : inmaduro, verde

unrivaled *or* **unrivalled** [ˌʌnˈraɪvəld] *adj* : incomparable

unroll [ˌʌnˈroːl] *vt* : desenrollar — *vi* : desenrollarse

unruffled [ˌʌnˈrʌfəld] *adj* **1** SERENE : sereno, tranquilo **2** SMOOTH : tranquilo, liso ⟨unruffled waters : aguas tranquilas⟩

unruliness [ˌʌnˈruːlinəs] *n* : indisciplina *f*

unruly [ˌʌnˈruːli] *adj* : indisciplinado, díscolo, rebelde

unsafe [ˌʌnˈseɪf] *adj* : inseguro

unsaid [ˌʌnˈsɛd] *adj* : sin decir ⟨to leave unsaid : quedar por decir⟩

unsanitary [ˌʌnˈsænəˌteri] *adj* : antihigiénico

unsatisfactory [ˌʌnˌsætəsˈfæktəri] *adj* : insatisfactorio

unsatisfied [ˌʌnˈsætəsˌfaɪd] *adj* : insatisfecho

unscathed [ˌʌnˈskeɪðd] *adj* UNHARMED : ileso

unscheduled [ˌʌnˈskɛˌʤuːld] *adj* : no programado, imprevisto

unscientific [ˌʌnˌsaɪənˈtɪfɪk] *adj* : poco científico

unscrupulous [ˌʌnˈskruːpjələs] *adj* : inescrupuloso, sin escrúpulos — **unscrupulously** *adv*

unseal [ˌʌnˈsiːl] *vt* : abrir, quitarle el sello a

unseasonable [ˌʌnˈsiːzənəbəl] *adj* **1** : extemporáneo ⟨unseasonable rain

: lluvia extemporánea⟩ 2 UNTIMELY : extemporáneo, inoportuno

unseemly [ˌʌnˈsiːmli] *adj* **-lier; -est 1** INDECOROUS : indecoroso **2** INAPPROPRIATE : impropio, inapropiado

unseen [ˌʌnˈsiːn] *adj* **1** UNNOTICED : inadvertido **2** INVISIBLE : oculto, invisible

unselfish [ˌʌnˈsɛlfɪʃ] *adj* : generoso, desinteresado — **unselfishly** *adv*

unselfishness [ˌʌnˈsɛlfɪʃnəs] *n* : generosidad *f*, desinterés *m*

unsettle [ˌʌnˈsɛtəl] *vt* **-tled; -tling** DISTURB : trastornar, alterar, perturbar

unsettled [ˌʌnˈsɛtəld] *adj* **1** CHANGEABLE : inestable, variable ⟨unsettled weather : tiempo inestable⟩ **2** DISTURBED : agitado, inquieto ⟨unsettled waters : aguas agitadas⟩ **3** UNDECIDED : pendiente (dícese de un asunto), indeciso (dícese de una persona) **4** UNPAID : sin saldar, pendiente **5** UNINHABITED : despoblado, no colonizado

unshaped [ˌʌnˈʃeɪpt] *adj* : sin forma, informe

unsightly [ˌʌnˈsaɪtli] *adj* UGLY : feo, de aspecto malo

unskilled [ˌʌnˈskɪld] *adj* : no calificado

unskillful [ˌʌnˈskɪlfəl] *adj* : inexperto, poco hábil

unsnap [ˌʌnˈsnæp] *vt* **-snapped; -snapping** : desabrochar

unsociable *adj* : poco sociable

unsolved [ˌʌnˈsɑlvd] *adj* : no resuelto, sin resolver

unsophisticated [ˌʌnsəˈfɪstəˌkeɪtəd] *adj* **1** NAIVE, UNWORLDLY : ingenuo, de poco mundo **2** SIMPLE : simple, poco sofisticado, rudimentario

unsound [ˌʌnˈsaʊnd] *adj* **1** UNHEALTHY : enfermizo, de mala salud **2** : poco sólido, defectuoso (dícese de una estructura, etc.) **3** INVALID : inválido, erróneo **4 of unsound mind** : mentalmente incapacitado

unspeakable [ˌʌnˈspiːkəbəl] *adj* **1** INDESCRIBABLE : indecible, inexpresable, incalificable **2** HEINOUS : atroz, nefando, abominable — **unspeakably** [-bli] *adv*

unspecified [ˌʌnˈspɛsəˌfaɪd] *adj* : indeterminado, sin especificar

unspoiled [ˌʌnˈspɔɪld] *adj* **1** : conservado, sin estropear (dícese de un lugar) **2** : que no está mimado (dícese de un niño)

unstable [ˌʌnˈsteɪbəl] *adj* **1** CHANGEABLE : variable, inestable, cambiable ⟨an unstable pulse : un pulso irregular⟩ **2** UNSTEADY : inestable, poco sólido (dícese de una estructura)

unsteadily [ˌʌnˈstɛdəli] *adv* : de modo inestable

unsteadiness [ˌʌnˈstɛdinəs] *n* : inestabilidad *f*, inseguridad *f*

unsteady [ˌʌnˈstɛdi] *adj* **1** UNSTABLE : inestable, variable **2** SHAKY : tembloroso

unstoppable [ˌʌnˈstɑpəbəl] *adj* : irrefrenable, incontenible

unsubstantiated [ˌʌnsəbˈstænʧiˌeɪtəd] *adj* : no corroborado, no demostrado

unsuccessful [ˌʌnsəkˈsɛsfəl] *adj* : fracasado, infructuoso

unsuitable [ˌʌnˈsuːt̬əbəl] *adj* : inadecuado, impropio, inapropiado ⟨an unsuitable time : una hora inconveniente⟩

unsuited [ˌʌnˈsuːtəd] *adj* : inadecuado, inepto

unsung [ˌʌnˈsʌŋ] *adj* : olvidado

unsure [ˌʌnˈʃʊr] *adj* : incierto, dudoso

unsurpassed [ˌʌnsərˈpæst] *adj* : sin par, sin igual

unsuspecting [ˌʌnsəˈspɛktɪŋ] *adj* : desprevenido, desapercibido, confiado

unsympathetic [ˌʌnˌsɪmpəˈθɛtɪk] *adj* : poco comprensivo, indiferente

untangle [ˌʌnˈteɪŋɡəl] *vt* **-gled; -gling** : desenmarañar, desenredar

unthinkable [ˌʌnˈθɪŋkəbəl] *adj* : inconcebible, impensable

unthinking [ˌʌnˈθɪŋkɪŋ] *adj* : irreflexivo, inconsciente — **unthinkingly** *adv*

untidy [ˌʌnˈtaɪdi] *adj* **1** SLOVENLY : desaliñado **2** DISORDERLY : desordenado, desarreglado

untie [ˌʌnˈtaɪ] *vt* **-tied; -tying** *or* **-tieing** : desatar, deshacer

until[1] [ˌʌnˈtɪl] *prep* : hasta ⟨until now : hasta ahora⟩

until[2] *conj* : hasta que ⟨until they left : hasta que salieron⟩ ⟨don't answer until you're sure : no contestes hasta que (no) estés seguro⟩

untimely [ˌʌnˈtaɪmli] *adj* **1** PREMATURE : prematuro ⟨an untimely death : una muerte prematura⟩ **2** INOPPORTUNE : inoportuno, intempestivo

untold [ˌʌnˈtoːld] *adj* **1** : nunca dicho ⟨the untold secret : el secreto sin contar⟩ **2** INCALCULABLE : incalculable, indecible

untouched [ˌʌnˈtʌʧt] *adj* **1** INTACT : intacto, sin tocar, sin probar (dícese de la comida) **2** UNAFFECTED : insensible, indiferente

untoward [ˌʌnˈtɔrd, -ˈtoːərd, -təˈwɔrd] *adj* **1** : indecoroso, impropio (dícese del comportamiento) **2** ADVERSE, UNFORTUNATE : desafortunado, adverso ⟨untoward effects : efectos perjudiciales⟩ **3** UNSEEMLY : indecoroso

untrained [ˌʌnˈtreɪnd] *adj* : inexperto, no capacitado

untreated [ˌʌnˈtriːtəd] *adj* : no tratado (dícese de una enfermedad, etc.), sin tratar (dícese de un material)

untroubled [ˌʌnˈtrʌbəld] *adj* : tranquilo ⟨to be untroubled by : no estar afectado por⟩

untrue [ˌʌnˈtruː] *adj* **1** UNFAITHFUL : infiel **2** FALSE : falso

untrustworthy [ˌʌnˈtrʌstˌwərði] *adj* : de poca confianza (dícese de una persona), no fidedigno (dícese de la información)

untruth [ˌʌnˈtruːθ, ˈʌnˌ-] *n* : mentira *f*, falsedad *f*

untruthful [ˌʌnˈtruːθfəl] *adj* : mentiroso, falso

unusable [ˌʌnˈjuːzəbəl] *adj* : inútil, inservible

unused [ˌʌnˈjuːzd, *in sense 1 usually* -ˈjuːst] *adj* **1** UNACCUSTOMED : inhabituado **2** NEW : nuevo **3** IDLE : no utilizado (dícese de la tierra) **4** REMAINING : restante ⟨the unused portion : la porción restante⟩

unusual [ˌʌnˈjuːʒəl] *adj* : inusual, poco común, raro

unusually [ˌʌnˈjuːʒəli, -ˈjuːʒəli] *adv* : excepcionalmente, extraordinariamente, fuera de lo común

unwanted [ˌʌnˈwɑntəd] *adj* : superfluo, de sobre

unwarranted [ˌʌnˈwɔrəntəd] *adj* : injustificado

unwary [ˌʌnˈwæri] *adj* : incauto

unwavering [ˌʌnˈweɪvərɪŋ] *adj* : firme, inquebrantable ⟨an unwavering gaze : una mirada fija⟩

unwelcome [ˌʌnˈwɛlkəm] *adj* : importuno, molesto

unwell [ˌʌnˈwɛl] *adj* : enfermo, mal

unwholesome [ˌʌnˈhoːlsəm] *adj* **1** UNHEALTHY : malsano, insalubre **2** PERNICIOUS : pernicioso **3** LOATHSOME : repugnante, muy desagradable

unwieldy [ˌʌnˈwiːldi] *adj* CUMBERSOME : difícil de manejar, torpe y pesado

unwilling [ˌʌnˈwɪlɪŋ] *adj* : poco dispuesto ⟨to be unwilling to : no estar dispuesto a⟩

unwillingly [ˌʌnˈwɪlɪŋli] *adv* : a regañadientes, de mala gana

unwind [ˌʌnˈwaɪnd] *v* **-wound** [-ˈwaʊnd]; **-winding** *vt* UNROLL : desenrollar — *vi* **1** : desenrollarse **2** RELAX : relajar

unwise [ˌʌnˈwaɪz] *adj* : imprudente, desacertado, poco aconsejable

unwisely [ˌʌnˈwaɪzli] *adv* : imprudentemente

unwitting [ˌʌnˈwɪtɪŋ] *adj* **1** UNAWARE : inconsciente **2** INADVERTENT : involuntario, inadvertido ⟨an unwitting mistake : un error inadvertido⟩ — **unwittingly** *adv*

unworthiness [ˌʌnˈwərðinəs] *n* : falta *f* de valía

unworthy [ˌʌnˈwərði] *adj* **1** UNDESERVING : indigno ⟨to be unworthy of : no ser digno de⟩ **2** UNMERITED : inmerecido

unwrap [ˌʌnˈræp] *vt* **-wrapped; -wrapping** : desenvolver, deshacer

unwritten [ˌʌnˈrɪtən] *adj* : no escrito

unyielding [ˌʌnˈjiːldɪŋ] *adj* : firme, inflexible, rígido

unzip [ˌʌnˈzɪp] *vt* **-zipped; -zipping** : abrir el cierre de

up¹ [ˈʌp] *v* **upped** [ˈʌpt]; **upping; ups** *vt* INCREASE : aumentar, subir ⟨they upped the prices : aumentaron los precios⟩ — *vi* **to up and** : agarrar y *fam* ⟨she up and left : agarró y se fue⟩

up² *adv* **1** ABOVE : arriba, en lo alto ⟨up in the mountains : arriba en las montañas⟩ **2** UPWARDS : hacia arriba ⟨push it up : empújalo hacia arriba⟩ ⟨the sun came up : el sol salió⟩ ⟨prices went up : los precios subieron⟩ **3** (*indicating an upright position or waking state*) ⟨to sit up : ponerse derecho⟩ ⟨they got up late : se levantaron tarde⟩ ⟨I stayed up all night : pasé toda la noche sin dormir⟩ **4** (*indicating volume or intensity*) ⟨to speak up : hablar más fuerte⟩ **5** (*indicating a northerly direction*) ⟨the climate up north : el clima del norte⟩ ⟨I'm going up to Canada : voy para Canadá⟩ **6** (*indicating the appearance or existence of something*) ⟨the book turned up : el libro apareció⟩ **7** (*indicating consideration*) ⟨she brought the matter up : mencionó el asunto⟩ **8** COMPLETELY : completamente ⟨eat it up : cómetelo todo⟩ **9** : en pedazos ⟨he tore it up : lo rompió en pedazos⟩ **10** (*indicating a stopping*) ⟨the car pulled up to the curb : el carro paró al borde de la acera⟩ **11** (*indicating an even score*) ⟨the game was 10 up : empataron a 10⟩

up³ *adj* **1** (*risen above the horizon*) ⟨the sun is up : ha salido el sol⟩ **2** (*being above a normal or former level*) ⟨prices are up : los precios han aumentado⟩ ⟨the river is up : las aguas están altas⟩ **3** : despierto, levantado ⟨up all night : despierto toda la noche⟩ **4** BUILT : construido ⟨the house is up : la casa está construida⟩ **5** OPEN : abierto ⟨the windows are up : las ventanas están abiertas⟩ **6** (*moving or going upward*) ⟨the up staircase : la escalera para subir⟩ **7** ABREAST : enterado, al día, al corriente ⟨to be up on the news : estar al corriente de las noticias⟩ **8** PREPARED : preparado ⟨we were up for the test : estuvimos preparados para el examen⟩ **9** FINISHED : terminado, acabado ⟨time is up : se ha terminado el tiempo permitido⟩ **10 to be up** : pasar ⟨what's up? : ¿qué pasa?⟩

up⁴ *prep* **1** (*to, toward, or at a higher point of*) ⟨he went up the stairs : subió la escalera⟩ **2** (*to or toward the source of*) ⟨to go up the river : ir río arriba⟩ **3** ALONG : a lo largo, por ⟨up the coast : a lo largo de la costa⟩ ⟨just up the way : un poco más adelante⟩ ⟨up and down the city : por toda la ciudad⟩

upbraid [ˌʌpˈbreɪd] *vt* : reprender, regañar

upbringing [ˈʌpˌbrɪŋɪŋ] *n* : crianza *f*, educación *f*

upcoming [ˌʌpˈkʌmɪŋ] *adj* : próximo

update¹ [ˌʌpˈdeɪt] *vt* **-dated; -dating** : poner al día, poner al corriente, actualizar

update² [ˈʌpˌdeɪt] *n* : actualización *f*, puesta *f* al día

upend [ˌʌpˈɛnd] *vt* **1** : poner vertical **2** OVERTURN : volcar

upgrade¹ ['ʌpˌgreɪd, ˌʌp'-] *vt* **-graded; -grading 1** PROMOTE : ascender **2** IMPROVE : mejorar

upgrade² ['ʌpˌgreɪd] *n* **1** SLOPE : cuesta *f*, pendiente *f* **2** RISE : aumento *m* de categoría (de un puesto), ascenso *m* (de un empleado) **3** IMPROVEMENT : mejoramiento *m*

upheaval [ˌʌp'hiːvəl] *n* **1** : levantamiento *m* (en geología) **2** DISTURBANCE, UPSET : trastorno *m*, agitación *f*, conmoción *f*

uphill¹ [ˌʌp'hɪl] *adv* : cuesta arriba

uphill² ['ʌpˌhɪl] *adj* **1** ASCENDING : en subida **2** DIFFICULT : difícil, arduo

uphold [ˌʌp'hoːld] *vt* **-held; -holding 1** SUPPORT : sostener, apoyar, mantener **2** RAISE : levantar **3** CONFIRM : confirmar (una decisión judicial)

upholster [ˌʌp'hoːlstər] *vt* : tapizar

upholsterer [ˌʌp'hoːlstərər] *n* : tapicero *m*, -ra *f*

upholstery [ˌʌp'hoːlstəri] *n*, *pl* **-steries** : tapicería *f*

upkeep ['ʌpˌkiːp] *n* : mantenimiento *m*

upland ['ʌplənd, -ˌlænd] *n* : altiplanicie *f*, altiplano *m*

uplift¹ [ˌʌp'lɪft] *vt* **1** RAISE : elevar, levantar **2** ELEVATE : elevar, animar (el espíritu, la mente, etc.)

uplift² ['ʌpˌlɪft] *n* : elevación *f*

upon [ə'pɔn, ə'pɑn] *prep* : en, sobre ⟨upon the desk : sobre el escritorio⟩ ⟨upon leaving : al salir⟩ ⟨questions upon questions : pregunta tras pregunta⟩

upper¹ ['ʌpər] *adj* **1** HIGHER : superior ⟨the upper classes : las clases altas⟩ **2** : alto (en geografía) ⟨the upper Mississippi : el alto Mississippi⟩

upper² *n* : parte *f* superior (del calzado, etc.)

uppercase [ˌʌpər'keɪs] *adj* : mayúsculo

upper hand *n* : ventaja *f*, dominio *m*

uppermost ['ʌpərˌmoːst] *adj* : más alto ⟨it was uppermost in his mind : era lo que más le preocupaba⟩

upright¹ ['ʌpˌraɪt] *adj* **1** VERTICAL : vertical **2** ERECT : erguido, derecho **3** JUST : recto, honesto, justo

upright² *n* : montante *m*, poste *m*, soporte *m*

uprising ['ʌpˌraɪzɪŋ] *n* : insurrección *f*, revuelta *f*, alzamiento *m*

uproar ['ʌpˌror] *n* COMMOTION : alboroto *m*, jaleo *m*, escándalo *m*

uproarious [ˌʌp'roriəs] *adj* **1** CLAMOROUS : estrepitoso, clamoroso **2** HILARIOUS : muy divertido, hilarante — **uproariously** *adv*

uproot [ˌʌp'ruːt, -'rʊt] *vt* : desarraigar

upset¹ [ˌʌp'sɛt] *vt* **-set; -setting 1** OVERTURN : volcar **2** SPILL : derramar **3** DISTURB : perturbar, disgustar, inquietar, alterar **4** SICKEN : sentar mal a ⟨it upsets my stomach : me sienta mal al estómago⟩ **5** DISRUPT : trastornar, desbaratar (planes, etc.) **6** DEFEAT : derrotar (en deportes)

upset² *adj* **1** DISPLEASED, DISTRESSED : disgustado, alterado **2 to have an upset stomach** : estar mal del estómago, estar descompuesto (de estómago)

upset³ ['ʌpˌsɛt] *n* **1** OVERTURNING : vuelco *m* **2** DISRUPTION : trastorno *m* (de planes, etc.) **3** DEFEAT : derrota *f* (en deportes)

upshot ['ʌpˌʃɑt] *n* : resultado *m* final

upside–down [ˌʌpˌsaɪd'daʊn] *adj* : al revés

upside down [ˌʌpˌsaɪd'daʊn] *adv* **1** : al revés **2** : en confusión, en desorden

upstairs¹ [ˌʌp'stærz] *adv* : arriba, en el piso superior

upstairs² ['ʌpˌstærz, ˌʌp'-] *adj* : de arriba

upstairs³ ['ʌpˌstærz, ˌʌp'-] *ns & pl* : piso *m* de arriba, planta *f* de arriba

upstanding [ˌʌp'stændɪŋ, 'ʌpˌ-] *adj* HONEST, UPRIGHT : honesto, íntegro, recto

upstart ['ʌpˌstɑrt] *n* : advenedizo *m*, -za *f*

upswing ['ʌpˌswɪŋ] *n* : alza *f*, mejora *f* notable ⟨to be on the upswing : estar mejorándose⟩

uptight [ˌʌp'taɪt] *adj* : tenso, nervioso

up to *prep* **1** : hasta ⟨up to a year : hasta un año⟩ ⟨in mud up to my ankles : en barro hasta los tobillos⟩ **2 to be up to** : estar a la altura de ⟨I'm not up to going : no estoy en condiciones de ir⟩ **3 to be up to** : depender de ⟨it's up to the director : depende del director⟩

up–to–date [ˌʌptə'deɪt] *adj* **1** CURRENT : corriente, al día ⟨to keep up-to-date : mantenerse al corriente⟩ **2** MODERN : moderno

uptown ['ʌp'taʊn] *adv* : hacia la parte alta de la ciudad, hacia el distrito residencial

upturn ['ʌpˌtərn] *n* : mejora *f*, auge *m* (económico)

upward¹ ['ʌpwərd] *or* **upwards** [-wərdz] *adv* **1** : hacia arriba **2 ~ of** : más de

upward² *adj* : ascendente, hacia arriba

upwind [ˌʌp'wɪnd] *adv & adj* : contra el viento

uranium [jʊ'reɪniəm] *n* : uranio *m*

Uranus [jʊ'reɪnəs, 'jʊrənəs] *n* : Urano *m*

urban ['ərbən] *adj* : urbano

urbane [ˌər'beɪn] *adj* : urbano, cortés

urchin ['ərtʃən] *n* **1** SCAMP : granuja *mf*; pillo *m*, -lla *f* **2 sea urchin** : erizo *m* de mar

Urdu ['ʊrduː, 'ər-] *n* : urdu *m*

urethra [jʊ'riːθrə] *n*, *pl* **-thras** *or* **-thrae** [-ˌθriː] : uretra *f*

urge¹ ['ərdʒ] *vt* **urged; urging 1** PRESS : instar, apremiar, insistir ⟨we urged him to come : insistimos en que viniera⟩ **2** ADVOCATE : recomendar, abogar por **3 to urge on** : animar, alentar

urge² *n* : impulso *m*, ganas *fpl*, compulsión *f*

urgency ['ərdʒəntsi] *n*, *pl* **-cies** : urgencia *f*

urgent ['ərdʒənt] *adj* **1** PRESSING : urgente, apremiante **2** INSISTENT : insistente **3 to be urgent** : urgir

urgently ['ərdʒəntli] *adv* : urgentemente

urinal ['jʊrənəl, *esp Brit* jʊ'raɪnəl] *n* : orinal *m* (recipiente), urinario *m* (lugar)

urinary ['jʊrə,neri] *adj* : urinario

urinate ['jʊrə,neɪt] *vi* **-nated; -nating** : orinar

urination [,jʊrə'neɪʃən] *n* : orinación *f*

urine ['jʊrən] *n* : orina *f*

urn ['ərn] *n* **1** VASE : urna *f* **2** : recipiente *m* (para servir café, etc.)

Uruguayan [,ʊrə'gwaɪən, ,jʊr-, -'gweɪ-] *n* : uruguayo *m*, -ya *f* — **Uruguayan** *adj*

us ['ʌs] *pron* **1** (*as direct object*) : nos ⟨they were visiting us : nos visitaban⟩ **2** (*as indirect object*) : nos ⟨he gave us a present : nos dio un regalo⟩ **3** (*as object of preposition*) : nosotros, nosotras ⟨stay with us : quédese con nosotros⟩ ⟨both of us : nosotros dos⟩ **4** (*for emphasis*) : nosotros ⟨it's us! : ¡somos nosotros!⟩

usable ['ju:zəbəl] *adj* : utilizable

usage ['ju:sɪdʒ, -zɪdʒ] *n* **1** HABIT : costumbre *f*, hábito *m* **2** USE : uso *m*

use¹ ['ju:z] *v* **used** ['ju:zd, *in phrase "used to" usually* 'ju:stu:]; **using** *vt* **1** EMPLOY : emplear, usar **2** CONSUME : consumir, tomar (drogas, etc.) **3** UTILIZE : usar, utilizar ⟨to use tact : usar tacto⟩ ⟨he used his friends to get ahead : usó a sus amigos para mejorar su posición⟩ **4** TREAT : tratar ⟨they used the horse cruelly : maltrataron al caballo⟩ **5 to use up** : agotar, consumir, gastar — *vi* (*used in the past with* **to** *to indicate a former fact or state*) : soler, acostumbrar ⟨winters used to be colder : los inviernos solían ser más fríos, los inviernos eran más fríos⟩ ⟨she used to dance : acostumbraba bailar⟩

use² ['ju:s] *n* **1** APPLICATION, EMPLOYMENT : uso *m*, empleo *m*, utilización *f* ⟨out of use : en desuso⟩ ⟨ready for use : listo para usar⟩ ⟨to be in use : usarse, estar funcionando⟩ ⟨to make use of : servirse de, aprovechar⟩ **2** USEFULNESS : utilidad *f* ⟨to be of no use : no servir (para nada)⟩ ⟨it's no use! : ¡es inútil!⟩ **3 to have the use of** : poder usar, tener acceso a **4 to have no use for** : no necesitar ⟨she has no use for po-

etry : a ella no le gusta la poesía⟩

used ['ju:zd] *adj* **1** SECONDHAND : usado, de segunda mano ⟨used cars : coches usados⟩ **2** ACCUSTOMED : acostumbrado ⟨used to the heat : acostumbrado al calor⟩

useful ['ju:sfəl] *adj* : útil, práctico — **usefully** *adv*

usefulness ['ju:sfəlnəs] *n* : utilidad *f*

useless ['ju:sləs] *adj* : inútil — **uselessly** *adv*

uselessness ['ju:sləsnəs] *n* : inutilidad *f*

user ['ju:zər] *n* : usuario *m*, -ria *f*

usher¹ ['ʌʃər] *vt* **1** ESCORT : acompañar, conducir **2 to usher in** : hacer pasar (a alguien) ⟨to usher in a new era : anunciar una nueva época⟩

usher² *n* : acomodador *m*, -dora *f*

usherette [,ʌʃə'rɛt] *n* : acomodadora *f*

usual ['ju:ʒəl] *adj* **1** NORMAL : usual, normal **2** CUSTOMARY : acostumbrado, habitual, de costumbre **3** ORDINARY : ordinario, típico

usually ['ju:ʒəli, 'ju:ʒəli] *adv* : usualmente, normalmente

usurp [jʊ'sərp, -'zərp] *vt* : usurpar

usurper [jʊ'sərpər, -'zər-] *n* : usurpador *m*, -dora *f*

utensil [jʊ'tɛntsəl] *n* **1** : utensilio *m* (de cocina) **2** IMPLEMENT : implemento *m*, útil *m* (de labranza, etc.)

uterine ['ju:tə,raɪn, -rən] *adj* : uterino

uterus ['ju:tərəs] *n, pl* **uteri** [-,raɪ] : útero *m*, matriz *f*

utilitarian [ju:,tɪlə'tɛriən] *adj* : utilitario

utility [ju:'tɪləti] *n, pl* **-ties** **1** USEFULNESS : utilidad *f* **2 public utility** : empresa *f* de servicio público

utilization [,ju:tələ'zeɪʃən] *n* : utilización *f*

utilize ['ju:təl,aɪz] *vt* **-lized; -lizing** : utilizar, hacer uso de

utmost¹ ['ʌt,mo:st] *adj* **1** FARTHEST : extremo, más lejano **2** GREATEST : sumo, mayor ⟨of the utmost importance : de suma importancia⟩

utmost² *n* : lo más posible ⟨to the utmost : al máximo⟩

utopia [jʊ'to:piə] *n* : utopía *f*

utopian [jʊ'to:piən] *adj* : utópico

utter¹ ['ʌtər] *vt* : decir, articular, pronunciar (palabras)

utter² *adj* : absoluto — **utterly** *adv*

utterance ['ʌtərənts] *n* : declaración *f*, articulación *f*

V

v ['vi:] *n, pl* **v's** *or* **vs** ['vi:z] : vigésima segunda letra del alfabeto inglés

vacancy ['veɪkəntsi] *n, pl* **-cies** **1** EMPTINESS : vacío *m*, vacuidad *f* **2** : vacante *f*, puesto *m* vacante ⟨to fill a vacancy

: ocupar un puesto⟩ **3** : habitación *f* libre (en un hotel) ⟨no vacancies : completo⟩

vacant ['veɪkənt] *adj* **1** EMPTY : libre, desocupado (dícese de los edificios,

etc.) **2** : vacante (dícese de los puestos) **3** BLANK : vacío, ausente ⟨a vacant stare : una mirada ausente⟩
vacate ['veɪˌkeɪt] *vt* **-cated; -cating** : desalojar, desocupar
vacation¹ [veɪ'keɪʃən, və-] *vi* : pasar las vacaciones, vacacionar *Mex*
vacation² *n* : vacaciones *fpl* ⟨to be on vacation : estar de vacaciones⟩
vacationer [veɪ'keɪʃənər, və-] *n* : turista *mf*, veraneante *mf*, vacacionista *mf CA, Mex*
vaccinate ['væksəˌneɪt] *vt* **-nated; -nating** : vacunar
vaccination [ˌvæksə'neɪʃən] *n* : vacunación *f*
vaccine [væk'siːn, 'vækˌ-] *n* : vacuna *f*
vacillate ['væsəˌleɪt] *vi* **-lated; -lating 1** HESITATE : vacilar **2** SWAY : oscilar
vacillation [ˌvæsə'leɪʃən] *n* : indecisión *f*, vacilación *f*
vacuous ['vækjuəs] *adj* **1** EMPTY : vacío **2** INANE : vacuo, necio, estúpido
vacuum¹ ['væˌkjuːm, -kjəm] *vt* : limpiar con aspiradora, pasar la aspiradora por
vacuum² *n, pl* **vacuums** *or* **vacua** ['vækjuə] : vacío *m*
vacuum cleaner *n* : aspiradora *f*
vagabond¹ ['vægəˌbɑnd] *adj* : vagabundo
vagabond² *n* : vagabundo *m*, -da *f*
vagary ['veɪgəri, və'geri] *n, pl* **-ries** : capricho *m*
vagina [və'dʒaɪnə] *n, pl* **-nae** [-ˌniː, -ˌnaɪ] *or* **-nas** : vagina *f*
vagrancy ['veɪgrəntsi] *n, pl* **-cies** : vagancia *f*
vagrant¹ ['veɪgrənt] *adj* : vagabundo
vagrant² *n* : vagabundo *m*, -da *f*
vague ['veɪg] *adj* **vaguer; -est 1** IMPRECISE : vago, impreciso ⟨a vague feeling : una sensación indefinida⟩ ⟨I haven't the vaguest idea : no tengo la más remota idea⟩ **2** UNCLEAR : borroso, poco claro ⟨a vague outline : un perfil indistinto⟩ **3** ABSENTMINDED : distraído
vaguely ['veɪgli] *adv* : vagamente, de manera imprecisa
vagueness ['veɪgnəs] *n* : vaguedad *f*, imprecisión *f*
vain ['veɪn] *adj* **1** WORTHLESS : vano **2** FUTILE : vano, inútil ⟨in vain : en vano⟩ **3** CONCEITED : vanidoso, presumido
vainly ['veɪnli] *adv* : en vano, vanamente, inútilmente
valance ['vælənts, 'veɪ-] *n* **1** FLOUNCE : volante *m* (de una cama, etc.) **2** : galería *f* de cortina (sobre una ventana)
vale ['veɪl] *n* : valle *m*
valedictorian [ˌvælədɪk'toriən] *n* : estudiante *mf* que pronuncia el discurso de despedida en ceremonia de graduación
valedictory [ˌvælə'dɪktəri] *adj* : de despedida
valentine ['væləntaɪn] *n* : tarjeta *f* que se manda el Día de los Enamorados (el 14 de febrero)

Valentine's Day *n* : Día *m* de los Enamorados
valet ['væˌleɪ, væ'leɪ, 'vælət] *n* : ayuda *m* de cámara
valiant ['væljənt] *adj* : valiente, valeroso
valiantly ['væljəntli] *adv* : con valor, valientemente
valid ['væləd] *adj* : válido
validate ['væləˌdeɪt] *vt* **-dated; -dating** : validar, dar validez a
validity [və'lɪdəti, væ-] *n* : validez *f*
valise [və'liːs] *n* : maleta *f* (de mano)
valley ['væli] *n, pl* **-leys** : valle *m*
valor ['vælər] *n* : valor *m*, valentía *f*
valorous ['vælərəs] *adj* : valeroso, valiente
valuable¹ ['væljuəbəl, 'væljəbəl] *adj* **1** EXPENSIVE : valioso, de valor **2** WORTHWHILE : valioso, apreciable
valuable² *n* : objeto *m* de valor
valuation [ˌvæljuˈeɪʃən] *n* **1** APPRAISAL : valoración *f*, tasación *f* **2** VALUE : valuación *f*
value¹ ['vælˌjuː] *vt* **-ued; -uing 1** APPRAISE : valorar, avaluar, tasar **2** APPRECIATE : valorar, apreciar
value² *n* **1** : valor *m* ⟨of little value : de poco valor⟩ ⟨to be a good value : estar bien de precio, tener buen precio⟩ ⟨at face value : en su sentido literal⟩ **2 values** *npl* : valores *mpl* (morales), principios *mpl*
valueless ['vælju:ləs] *adj* : sin valor
valve ['vælv] *n* : válvula *f*
vampire ['væmˌpaɪr] *n* **1** : vampiro *m* **2** *or* **vampire bat** : vampiro *m*
van¹ ['væn] → **vanguard**
van² *n* : furgoneta *f*, camioneta *f*
vanadium [və'neɪdiəm] *n* : vanadio *m*
vandal ['vændəl] *n* : vándalo *m*
vandalism ['vændəlˌɪzəm] *n* : vandalismo *m*
vandalize ['vændəlˌaɪz] *vt* : destrozar, destruir, estropear
vane ['veɪn] *n or* **weather vane** : veleta *f*
vanguard ['vænˌgɑrd] *n* : vanguardia *f*
vanilla [və'nɪlə, -'nɛ-] *n* : vainilla *f*
vanish ['vænɪʃ] *vi* : desaparecer, disiparse, desvanecerse
vanity ['vænəti] *n, pl* **-ties 1** : vanidad *f* **2** *or* **vanity table** : tocador *m*
vanquish ['væŋkwɪʃ, 'væn-] *vt* : vencer, conquistar
vantage point ['væntɪdʒ] *n* : posición *f* ventajosa
vapid ['væpəd, 'veɪ-] *adj* : insípido, insulso
vapor ['veɪpər] *n* : vapor *m*
vaporize ['veɪpəˌraɪz] *v* **-rized; -rizing** *vt* : vaporizar — *vi* : vaporizarse, evaporarse
vaporizer ['veɪpəˌraɪzər] *n* : vaporizador *m*
variability [ˌvɛriə'bɪləti] *n, pl* **-ties** : variabilidad *f*
variable¹ ['vɛriəbəl] *adj* : variable ⟨variable cloudiness : nubosidad variable⟩

variable² *n* : variable *f*, factor *m*

variance ['vɛriənts] *n* **1** DISCREPANCY : varianza *f*, discrepancia *f* **2** DISAGREEMENT : desacuerdo *m* ⟨at variance with : en desacuerdo con⟩

variant¹ ['vɛriənt] *adj* : variante, divergente

variant² *n* : variante *f*

variation [,vɛri'eɪʃən] *n* : variación *f*, diferencias *fpl*

varicose ['værə,ko:s] *adj* : varicoso

varicose veins *npl* : varices *fpl*, várices *fpl*

varied ['vɛrid] *adj* : variado, dispar, diferente

variegated ['vɛriə,geɪtd] *adj* : abigarrado, multicolor

variety [və'raɪəti] *n, pl* **-ties 1** DIVERSITY : diversidad *f*, variedad *f* **2** ASSORTMENT : surtido *m* ⟨for a variety of reasons : por diversas razones⟩ **3** SORT : clase *f* **4** BREED : variedad *f* (de plantas)

various ['vɛriəs] *adj* : varios, diversos

varnish¹ ['vɑrnɪʃ] *vt* : barnizar

varnish² *n* : barniz *f*

varsity ['vɑrsəti] *n, pl* **-ties** : equipo *m* universitario

vary ['vɛri] *v* **varied; varying** *vt* : variar, diversificar — *vi* **1** CHANGE : variar, cambiar **2** DEVIATE : desviarse

vascular ['væskjələr] *adj* : vascular

vase ['veɪs, 'veɪz, 'vɑz] *n* : jarrón *m*, florero *m*

vassal ['væsəl] *n* : vasallo *m*, -lla *f*

vast ['væst] *adj* : inmenso, enorme, vasto

vastly ['væstli] *adv* : enormemente

vastness ['væstnəs] *n* : vastedad *f*, inmensidad *f*

vat ['væt] *n* : cuba *f*, tina *f*

vaudeville ['vɔdvəl, -,vɪl; 'vɔdə,vɪl] *n* : vodevil *m*

vault¹ ['vɔlt] *vi* LEAP : saltar

vault² *n* **1** JUMP : salto *m* ⟨pole vault : salto de pértiga, salto con garrocha⟩ **2** DOME : bóveda *f* **3** : bodega *f* (para vino), bóveda *f* de seguridad (de un banco) **4** CRYPT : cripta *f*

vaulted ['vɔltəd] *adj* : abovedado

vaunted ['vɔntəd] *adj* : cacareado, alardeado ⟨a much vaunted wine : un vino muy alardeado⟩

VCR [,vi:,si:'ɑr] *n* : video *m*, videocasetera *f*

veal ['vi:l] *n* : ternera *f*, carne *f* de ternera

veer ['vɪr] *vi* : virar (dícese de un barco), girar (dícese de un coche), torcer (dícese de un camino)

vegetable¹ ['vɛdʒtəbəl, 'vɛdʒətə-] *adj* : vegetal

vegetable² *n* **1** : vegetal *m* ⟨the vegetable kingdom : el reino vegetal⟩ **2** : verdura *f*, hortaliza *f* (para comer)

vegetarian [,vɛdʒə'tɛriən] *n* : vegetariano *mf*

vegetarianism [,vɛdʒə'tɛriə,nɪzəm] *n* : vegetarianismo *m*

vegetate ['vɛdʒə,teɪt] *vi* **-tated; -tating** : vegetar

vegetation [,vɛdʒə'teɪʃən] *n* : vegetación *f*

vegetative ['vɛdʒə,teɪtɪv] *adj* : vegetativo

vehemence ['vi:əmənts] *n* : intensidad *f*, vehemencia *f*

vehement ['vi:əmənt] *adj* : intenso, vehemente

vehemently ['vi:əməntli] *adv* : vehementemente, con vehemencia

vehicle ['vi:əkəl, 'vi:,hɪkəl] *n* **1** *or* motor vehicle : vehículo *m* **2** MEDIUM : vehículo *m*, medio *m*

vehicular [vi'hɪkjələr, və-] *adj* : vehicular ⟨vehicular homicide : muerte por atropello⟩

veil¹ ['veɪl] *vt* **1** CONCEAL : velar, disimular **2** : cubrir con un velo ⟨to veil one's face : cubrirse con un velo⟩

veil² *n* : velo *m* ⟨bridal veil : velo de novia⟩

vein ['veɪn] *n* **1** : vena *f* (en anatomía, botánica, etc.) **2** LODE : veta *f*, vena *f*, filón *m* **3** STYLE : vena *f* ⟨in a humorous vein : en vena humorística⟩

veined ['veɪnd] *adj* : veteado (dícese del queso, de los minerales, etc.)

velocity [və'lɑsəti] *n, pl* **-ties** : velocidad *f*

velour [və'lʊr] *or* **velours** [-'lʊrz] *n* : velour *m*

velvet¹ ['vɛlvət] *adj* **1** : de terciopelo **2** → velvety

velvet² *n* : terciopelo *m*

velvety ['vɛlvəti] *adj* : aterciopelado

venal ['vi:nəl] *adj* : venal, sobornable

vend ['vɛnd] *vt* : vender

vendetta [vɛn'dɛtə] *n* : vendetta *f*

vendor ['vɛndər] *n* : vendedor *m*, -dora *f*; puestero *m*, -ra *f*

veneer¹ [və'nɪr] *vt* : enchapar, chapar

veneer² *n* **1** : enchapado *m*, chapa *f* **2** APPEARANCE : apariencia *f*, barniz *m* ⟨a veneer of culture : un barniz de cultura⟩

venerable ['vɛnərəbəl] *adj* : venerable

venerate ['vɛnə,reɪt] *vt* **-ated; -ating** : venerar

veneration [,vɛnə'reɪʃən] *n* : veneración *f*

venereal disease [və'nɪriəl] *n* : enfermedad *f* venérea

venetian blind [və'ni:ʃən] *n* : persiana *f* veneciana

Venezuelan [,vɛnə'zweɪlən, -zʊ'eɪ-] *n* : venezolano *m*, -na *f* — **Venezuelan** *adj*

vengeance ['vɛndʒənts] *n* : venganza *f* ⟨to take vengeance on : vengarse de⟩

vengeful ['vɛndʒfəl] *adj* : vengativo

venial ['vi:niəl] *adj* : venial ⟨a venial sin : un pecado venial⟩

venison ['vɛnəsən, -zən] *n* : venado *m*, carne *f* de venado

venom ['vɛnəm] *n* **1** : veneno *m* **2** MALICE : veneno *m*, malevolencia *f*

venomous · veto

venomous ['vɛnəməs] *adj* : venenoso
vent¹ ['vɛnt] *vt* : desahogar, dar salida a ⟨to vent one's feelings : desahogarse⟩
vent² *n* **1** OPENING : abertura *f* (de escape), orificio *m* **2** *or* **air vent** : respiradero *m*, rejilla *f* de ventilación **3** OUTLET : desahogo *m* ⟨to give vent to one's anger : desahogar la ira⟩
ventilate ['vɛntəl,eɪt] *vt* **-lated; -lating** : ventilar
ventilation [,vɛntəl'eɪʃən] *n* : ventilación *f*
ventilator ['vɛntəl,eɪtər] *n* : ventilador *m*
ventricle ['vɛntrɪkəl] *n* : ventrículo *m*
ventriloquism [vɛn'trɪlə,kwɪzəm] *n* : ventriloquia *f*
ventriloquist [vɛn'trɪlə,kwɪst] *n* : ventrílocuo *m*, -cua *f*
venture¹ ['vɛntʃər] *v* **-tured; -turing** *vt* **1** RISK : arriesgar **2** OFFER : aventurar ⟨to venture an opinion : aventurar una opinión⟩ — *vi* : arriesgarse, atreverse, aventurarse
venture² *n* **1** UNDERTAKING : empresa *f* **2** GAMBLE, RISK : aventura *f*, riesgo *m*
venturesome ['vɛntʃərsəm] *adj* **1** ADVENTUROUS : audaz, atrevido **2** RISKY : arriesgado
venue ['vɛn,ju:] *n* **1** PLACE : lugar *m* **2** : jurisdicción *f* (en derecho)
Venus ['vi:nəs] *n* : Venus *m*
veracity [və'ræsəti] *n, pl* **-ties** : veracidad *f*
veranda *or* **verandah** [və'rændə] *n* : terraza *f*, veranda *f*
verb ['vərb] *n* : verbo *m*
verbal ['vərbəl] *adj* : verbal
verbalize ['vərbə,laɪz] *vt* **-ized; -izing** : expresar con palabras, verbalizar
verbally ['vərbəli] *adv* : verbalmente, de palabra
verbatim¹ [vər'beɪtəm] *adv* : palabra por palabra, textualmente
verbatim² *adj* : literal, textual
verbose [vər'bo:s] *adj* : verboso, prolijo
verdant ['vərdənt] *adj* : verde, verdeante
verdict ['vərdɪkt] *n* **1** : veredicto *m* (de un jurado) **2** JUDGMENT, OPINION : juicio *m*, opinión *f*
verge¹ ['vərdʒ] *vi* **verged; verging** : estar al borde, rayar ⟨it verges on madness : raya en la locura⟩
verge² *n* **1** EDGE : borde *m* **2** **to be on the verge of** : estar a pique de, estar al borde de, estar a punto de
verification [,vɛrəfə'keɪʃən] *n* : verificación *f*
verify ['vɛrə,faɪ] *vt* **-fied; -fying** : verificar, comprobar, confirmar
veritable ['vɛrətəbəl] *adj* : verdadero — **veritably** *adv*
vermicelli [,vərmə'tʃɛli, -'sɛli] *n* : fideos *mpl* finos
vermin ['vərmən] *ns & pl* : alimañas *fpl*, bichos *mpl*, sabandijas *fpl*
vermouth [vər'mu:th] *n* : vermut *m*
vernacular¹ [vər'nækjələr] *adj* : vernáculo

vernacular² *n* : lengua *f* vernácula
versatile ['vərsətəl] *adj* : versátil
versatility [,vərsə'tɪləti] *n* : versatilidad *f*
verse ['vərs] *n* **1** LINE, STANZA : verso *m*, estrofa *f* **2** POETRY : poesía *f* **3** : versículo *m* (en la Biblia)
versed ['vərst] *adj* : versado ⟨to be well versed in : ser muy versado en⟩
version ['vərʒən] *n* : versión *f*
versus ['vərsəs] *prep* : versus
vertebra ['vərtəbrə] *n, pl* **-brae** [-,breɪ, -,bri:] *or* **-bras** : vértebra *f*
vertebrate¹ ['vərtəbrət, -,breɪt] *adj* : vertebrado
vertebrate² *n* : vertebrado *m*
vertex ['vər,tɛks] *n, pl* **vertices** ['vərtə,si:z] **1** : vértice *m* (en matemáticas y anatomía) **2** SUMMIT, TOP : ápice *m*, cumbre *f*, cima *f*
vertical¹ ['vərtɪkəl] *adj* : vertical — **vertically** *adv*
vertical² *n* : vertical *f*
vertigo ['vərtɪ,go:] *n, pl* **-goes** *or* **-gos** : vértigo *m*
verve ['vərv] *n* : brío *m*
very¹ ['vɛri] *adv* **1** EXTREMELY : muy, sumamente ⟨very few : muy pocos⟩ ⟨I am very sorry : lo siento mucho⟩ **2** (*used for emphasis*) ⟨at the very least : por lo menos, como mínimo⟩ ⟨the very same dress : el mismo vestido⟩
very² *adj* **verier; -est 1** EXACT, PRECISE : mismo, exacto ⟨at that very moment : en ese mismo momento⟩ ⟨it's the very thing : es justo lo que hacía falta⟩ **2** BARE, MERE : solo, mero ⟨the very thought of it : sólo pensarlo⟩ **3** EXTREME : extremo, de todo ⟨at the very top : arriba de todo⟩
vesicle ['vɛsɪkəl] *n* : vesícula *f*
vespers ['vɛspərz] *npl* : vísperas *fpl*
vessel ['vɛsəl] *n* **1** CONTAINER : vasija *f*, recipiente *m* **2** BOAT, CRAFT : nave *f*, barco *m*, buque *m* **3** : vaso *m* ⟨blood vessel : vaso sanguíneo⟩
vest¹ ['vɛst] *vt* **1** CONFER : conferir ⟨to vest authority in : conferirle la autoridad a⟩ **2** CLOTHE : vestir
vest² *n* **1** : chaleco *m* **2** UNDERSHIRT : camiseta *f*
vestibule ['vɛstə,bju:l] *n* : vestíbulo *m*
vestige ['vɛstɪdʒ] *n* : vestigio *m*, rastro *m*
vestment ['vɛstmənt] *n* : vestidura *f*
vestry ['vɛstri] *n, pl* **-tries** : sacristía *f*
vet ['vɛt] *n* **1** → **veterinarian 2** → **veteran²**
veteran¹ ['vɛtərən, 'vɛtrən] *adj* : veterano
veteran² *n* : veterano *m*, -na *f*
Veterans Day *n* : día *m* del Armisticio (celebrado el 11 de noviembre en los Estados Unidos)
veterinarian [,vɛtərə'nɛriən, ,vɛtə'nɛr-] *n* : veterinario *m*, -ria *f*
veterinary ['vɛtərə,nɛri] *adj* : veterinario
veto¹ ['vi:to] *vt* **1** FORBID : prohibir **2** : vetar ⟨to veto a bill : vetar un proyecto de ley⟩

veto[2] *n, pl* **-toes** **1** : veto *m* ⟨the power of veto : el derecho de veto⟩ **2** BAN : veto *m*, prohibición *f*

vex [ˈvɛks] *vt* : contrariar, molestar, irritar

vexation [vɛkˈseɪʃən] *n* : contrariedad *f*, irritación *f*

via [ˈvaɪə, ˈviːə] *prep* : por, vía

viability [ˌvaɪəˈbɪləti] *n* : viabilidad *f*

viable [ˈvaɪəbəl] *adj* : viable

viaduct [ˈvaɪəˌdʌkt] *n* : viaducto *m*

vial [ˈvaɪəl] *n* : frasco *m*

vibrant [ˈvaɪbrənt] *adj* **1** LIVELY : vibrante, animado, dinámico **2** BRIGHT : fuerte, vivo (dícese de los colores)

vibrate [ˈvaɪˌbreɪt] *vi* **-brated; -brating** **1** OSCILLATE : vibrar, oscilar **2** THRILL : bullir ⟨to vibrate with excitement : bullir de emoción⟩

vibration [vaɪˈbreɪʃən] *n* : vibración *f*

vicar [ˈvɪkər] *n* : vicario *m*, -ria *f*

vicarious [vaɪˈkæriːəs, vɪ-] *adj* : indirecto — **vicariously** *adv*

vice [ˈvaɪs] *n* : vicio *m*

vice admiral *n* : vicealmirante *mf*

vice president *n* : vicepresidente *m*, -ta *f*

viceroy [ˈvaɪsˌrɔɪ] *n* : virrey *m*, -rreina *f*

vice versa [ˌvaɪsˈvərsə, ˌvaɪsˈvər-] *adv* : viceversa

vicinity [vəˈsɪnəti] *n, pl* **-ties** **1** NEIGHBORHOOD : vecindad *f*, inmediaciones *fpl* **2** NEARNESS : proximidad *f*

vicious [ˈvɪʃəs] *adj* **1** DEPRAVED : depravado, malo **2** SAVAGE : malo, fiero, salvaje ⟨a vicious dog : un perro feroz⟩ **3** MALICIOUS : malicioso

viciously [ˈvɪʃəsli] *adv* : con saña, brutalmente

viciousness [ˈvɪʃəsnəs] *n* : brutalidad *f*, ferocidad *f* (de un animal), malevolencia *f* (de un comentario, etc.)

vicissitudes [vəˈsɪsəˌtuːdz, vaɪ-, -ˌtjuːdz] *npl* : vicisitudes *fpl*

victim [ˈvɪktəm] *n* : víctima *f*

victimize [ˈvɪktəˌmaɪz] *vt* **-mized; -mizing** : tomar como víctima, perseguir, victimizar *Arg, Mex*

victor [ˈvɪktər] *n* : vencedor *m*, -dora *f*

Victorian [vɪkˈtoːriən] *adj* : victoriano

victorious [vɪkˈtoːriəs] *adj* : victorioso — **victoriously** *adv*

victory [ˈvɪktəri] *n, pl* **-ries** : victoria *f*, triunfo *m*

victuals [ˈvɪtəlz] *npl* : víveres *mpl*, provisiones *fpl*

video[1] [ˈvɪdiˌoː] *adj* : de video ⟨video recording : grabación de video⟩

video[2] *n* **1** : video *m* (medio o grabación) **2** → **videotape**[2]

video camera *n* : videocámara *f*

videocassette [ˌvɪdiokəˈsɛt] *n* : videocasete *m*, videocassette *m*

videocassette recorder → **VCR**

video game *n* : videojuego *m*, juego *m* de video

videotape[1] [ˈvɪdioˌteɪp] *vt* **-taped; -taping** : grabar en video, videograbar

videotape[2] *n* : videocinta *f*

vie [ˈvaɪ] *vi* **vied; vying** [ˈvaɪɪŋ] : competir, rivalizar

Vietnamese [viˌɛtnəˈmiːz, -ˈmiːs] *n* **1** : vietnamita *mf* **2** : vietnamita *m* (idioma) — **Vietnamese** *adj*

view[1] [ˈvjuː] *vt* **1** OBSERVE : mirar, ver, observar **2** CONSIDER : considerar, contemplar

view[2] *n* **1** SIGHT : vista *f* ⟨to come into view : aparecer⟩ **2** ATTITUDE, OPINION : opinión *f*, parecer *m*, actitud *f* ⟨in my view : en mi opinión⟩ **3** SCENE : vista *f*, panorama *f* **4** INTENTION : idea *f*, vista *f* ⟨with a view to : con vistas a, con la idea de⟩ **5 in view of** : dado que, en vista de (que)

viewer [ˈvjuːər] *n or* **television viewer** : telespectador *m*, -dora *f*; televidente *mf*

viewpoint [ˈvjuːˌpɔɪnt] *n* : punto *m* de vista

vigil [ˈvɪdʒəl] *n* **1** : vigilia *f*, vela *f* **2 to keep vigil** : velar

vigilance [ˈvɪdʒələnts] *n* : vigilancia *f*

vigilant [ˈvɪdʒələnt] *adj* : vigilante

vigilante [ˌvɪdʒəˈlænˌtiː] *n* : integrante *mf* de un comité de vigilancia (que actúa como policía)

vigilantly [ˈvɪdʒələntli] *adv* : con vigilancia

vigor [ˈvɪɡər] *n* : vigor *m*, energía *f*, fuerza *f*

vigorous [ˈvɪɡərəs] *adj* : vigoroso, enérgico — **vigorously** *adv*

Viking [ˈvaɪkɪŋ] *n* : vikingo *m*, -ga *f*

vile [ˈvaɪl] *adj* **viler; vilest** **1** WICKED : vil, infame **2** REVOLTING : asqueroso, repugnante **3** TERRIBLE : horrible, atroz ⟨vile weather : tiempo horrible⟩ ⟨to be in a vile mood : estar de un humor de perros⟩

vilify [ˈvɪləˌfaɪ] *vt* **-fied; -fying** : vilipendiar, denigrar, difamar

villa [ˈvɪlə] *n* : casa *f* de campo, quinta *f*

village [ˈvɪlɪdʒ] *n* : pueblo *m* (grande), aldea *f* (pequeña)

villager [ˈvɪlɪdʒər] *n* : vecino *m*, -na *f* (de un pueblo); aldeano *m*, -na *f* (de una aldea)

villain [ˈvɪlən] *n* : villano *m*, -na *f*; malo *m*, -la *f* (en ficción, películas, etc.)

villainess [ˈvɪlənɪs, -nəs] *n* : villana *f*

villainous [ˈvɪlənəs] *adj* : infame, malvado

villainy [ˈvɪləni] *n, pl* **-lainies** : vileza *f*, maldad *f*

vim [ˈvɪm] *n* : brío *m*, vigor *m*, energía *f*

vindicate [ˈvɪndəˌkeɪt] *vt* **-cated; -cating** **1** EXONERATE : vindicar, disculpar **2** JUSTIFY : justificar

vindication [ˌvɪndəˈkeɪʃən] *n* : vindicación *f*, justificación *f*

vindictive [vɪnˈdɪktɪv] *adj* : vengativo

vine [ˈvaɪn] *n* **1** GRAPEVINE : vid *f*, parra *f* **2** : planta *f* trepadora, enredadera *f*

vinegar [ˈvɪnɪɡər] *n* : vinagre *m*

vinegary ['vɪnɪgəri] *adj* : avinagrado

vineyard ['vɪnjərd] *n* : viña *f*, viñedo *m*

vintage¹ ['vɪntɪdʒ] *adj* **1** : añejo (dícese de un vino) **2** CLASSIC : clásico, de época

vintage² *n* **1** : cosecha *f* ⟨the 1947 vintage : la cosecha de 1947⟩ **2** ERA : época *f*, era *f* ⟨slang of recent vintage : argot de la época reciente⟩

vinyl ['vaɪnəl] *n* : vinilo

viola [vi:'o:lə] *n* : viola *f*

violate ['vaɪə,leɪt] *vt* **-lated; -lating 1** BREAK : infringir, violar, quebrantar ⟨to violate the rules : violar las reglas⟩ **2** RAPE : violar **3** DESECRATE : profanar

violation [,vaɪə'leɪʃən] *n* **1** : violación *f*, infracción *f* (de una ley) **2** DESECRATION : profanación *f*

violence ['vaɪlənts, 'vaɪə-] *n* : violencia *f*

violent ['vaɪlənt, 'vaɪə-] *adj* : violento

violently ['vaɪləntli, 'vaɪə-] *adv* : violentamente, con violencia

violet ['vaɪlət, 'vaɪə-] *n* : violeta *f*

violin [,vaɪə'lɪn] *n* : violín *m*

violinist [,vaɪə'lɪnɪst] *n* : violinista *mf*

violoncello [,vaɪələn'tʃelo:, ,vi:-] → **cello**

VIP [,vi:,aɪ'pi:] *n, pl* **VIPs** [-'pi:z] : VIP *mf*, persona *f* de categoría

viper ['vaɪpər] *n* : víbora *f*

viral ['vaɪrəl] *adj* : viral, vírico ⟨viral pneumonia : pulmonía viral⟩

virgin¹ ['vərdʒən] *adj* **1** CHASTE : virginal ⟨the virgin birth : el alumbramiento virginal⟩ **2** : virgen, intacto ⟨a virgin forest : una selva virgen⟩ ⟨virgin wool : lana virgen⟩

virgin² *n* : virgen *mf*

virginity [vər'dʒɪnəti] *n* : virginidad *f*

Virgo ['vər,go:, 'vɪr-] *n* : Virgo *mf*

virile ['vɪrəl, -,aɪl] *adj* : viril, varonil

virility [və'rɪləti] *n* : virilidad *f*

virtual ['vərtʃuəl] *adj* : virtual ⟨a virtual dictator : un virtual dictador⟩ ⟨virtual reality : realidad virtual⟩

virtually ['vərtʃuəli, 'vərtʃəli] *adv* : en realidad, de hecho, casi

virtue ['vər,tʃu:] *n* **1** : virtud *f* **2 by virtue of** : en virtud de, debido a

virtuosity [,vərtʃu'asəti] *n, pl* **-ties** : virtuosismo *m*

virtuoso [,vərtʃu'o:so:, -zo:] *n, pl* **-sos** *or* **-si** [-,si:, -,zi:] : virtuoso *m*, -sa *f*

virtuous ['vərtʃuəs] *adj* : virtuoso, bueno — **virtuously** *adv*

virulence ['vɪrələnts, 'vɪrjə-] *n* : virulencia *f*

virulent ['vɪrələnt, 'vɪrjə-] *adj* : virulento

virus ['vaɪrəs] *n* : virus *m*

visa ['vi:zə, -sə] *n* : visa *f*

vis-à-vis [,vi:zə'vi:, -sə-] *prep* : con relación a, con respecto a

viscera ['vɪsərə] *npl* : vísceras *fpl*

visceral ['vɪsərəl] *adj* : visceral

viscosity [vɪs'kasəti] *n, pl* **-ties** : viscosidad *f*

viscount ['vaɪ,kaʊnt] *n* : vizconde *m*

viscountess ['vaɪ,kæʊntɪs] *n* : vizcondesa *f*

viscous ['vɪskəs] *adj* : viscoso

vise ['vaɪs] *n* : torno *m* de banco, tornillo *m* de banco

visibility [,vɪzə'bɪləti] *n, pl* **-ties** : visibilidad *f*

visible ['vɪzəbəl] *adj* **1** : visible ⟨the visible stars : las estrellas visibles⟩ **2** OBVIOUS : evidente, patente

visibly ['vɪzəbli] *adv* : visiblemente

vision ['vɪʒən] *n* **1** EYESIGHT : vista *f*, visión *f* **2** APPARITION : visión *f*, aparición *f* **3** FORESIGHT : visión *f* (del futuro), previsión *f* **4** IMAGE : imagen *f* ⟨she had visions of a disaster : se imaginaba un desastre⟩

visionary¹ ['vɪʒə,nɛri] *adj* **1** FARSIGHTED : visionario, con visión de futuro **2** UTOPIAN : utópico, poco realista

visionary² *n, pl* **-ries** : visionario *m*, -ria *f*

visit¹ ['vɪzət] *vt* **1** : visitar, ir a ver **2** AFFLICT : azotar, afligir ⟨visited by troubles : afligido con problemas⟩ — *vi* : hacer (una) visita

visit² *n* : visita *f*

visitor ['vɪzətər] *n* : visitante *mf* (a una ciudad, etc.), visita *f* (a una casa)

visor ['vaɪzər] *n* : visera *f*

vista ['vɪstə] *n* : vista *f*

visual ['vɪʒuəl] *adj* : visual ⟨the visual arts : las artes visuales⟩ — **visually** *adv*

visualize ['vɪʒuə,laɪz] *vt* **-ized; -izing** : visualizar, imaginarse, hacerse una idea de — **visualization** [,vɪʒəwələ'zeɪʃən] *n*

vital ['vaɪtəl] *adj* **1** : vital ⟨vital organs : órganos vitales⟩ **2** CRUCIAL : esencial, crucial, decisivo ⟨of vital importance : de suma importancia⟩ **3** LIVELY : enérgico, lleno de vida, vital

vitality [vaɪ'tæləti] *n, pl* **-ties** : vitalidad *f*, energía *f*

vitally ['vaɪtəli] *adv* : sumamente

vital statistics *npl* : estadísticas *fpl* demográficas

vitamin ['vaɪtəmən] *n* : vitamina *f* ⟨vitamin deficiency : carencia vitamínica⟩

vitreous ['vɪtriəs] *adj* : vítreo

vitriolic [,vɪtri'alɪk] *adj* : mordaz, virulento

vituperation [vaɪ,tu:pə'reɪʃən, -,tju:-] *n* : vituperio *m*

vivacious [və'veɪʃəs, vaɪ-] *adj* : vivaz, animado, lleno de vida

vivaciously [və'veɪʃəsli, vaɪ-] *adv* : con vivacidad, animadamente

vivacity [və'væsəti, vaɪ-] *n* : vivacidad *f*

vivid ['vɪvəd] *adj* **1** LIVELY : lleno de vitalidad **2** BRILLIANT : vivo, intenso ⟨vivid colors : colores vivos⟩ **3** INTENSE, SHARP : vívido, gráfico ⟨a vivid dream : un sueño vívido⟩

vividly ['vɪvədli] *adv* **1** BRIGHTLY : con colores vivos **2** SHARPLY : vívidamente

vividness ['vɪvədnəs] *n* **1** BRIGHTNESS : intensidad *f*, viveza *f* **2** SHARPNESS : lo gráfico, nitidez *f*

vivisection [ˌvɪvəˈsɛkʃən, ˈvɪvəˌ-] *n* : vivisección *f*

vixen [ˈvɪksən] *n* : zorra *f*, raposa *f*

vocabulary [voˈkæbjəˌlɛri] *n*, *pl* **-laries** 1 : vocabulario *m* 2 LEXICON : léxico *m*

vocal [ˈvoːkəl] *adj* 1 : vocal 2 LOUD, OUTSPOKEN : ruidoso, muy franco

vocal cords *npl* : cuerdas *fpl* vocales

vocalist [ˈvoːkəlɪst] *n* : cantante *mf*, vocalista *mf*

vocalize [ˈvoːkəlˌaɪz] *vt* **-ized; -izing** : vocalizar

vocation [voˈkeɪʃən] *n* : vocación *f* ⟨to have a vocation for : tener vocación de⟩

vocational [voˈkeɪʃənəl] *adj* : profesional ⟨vocational guidance : orientación profesional⟩

vociferous [voˈsɪfərəs] *adj* : ruidoso, vociferante

vodka [ˈvɑdkə] *n* : vodka *m*

vogue [ˈvoːg] *n* : moda *f*, boga *f* ⟨to be in vogue : estar de moda, estar en boga⟩

voice¹ [ˈvɔɪs] *vt* **voiced; voicing** : expresar

voice² *n* 1 : voz *f* ⟨in a low voice : en voz baja⟩ ⟨to lose one's voice : quedarse sin voz⟩ ⟨the voice of the people : la voz del pueblo⟩ 2 **to make one's voice heard** : hacerse oír

voice box → larynx

voiced [ˈvɔɪst] *adj* : sonoro

voice mail *n* : correo *m* de voz

void¹ [ˈvɔɪd] *vt* : anular, invalidar ⟨to void a contract : anular un contrato⟩

void² *adj* 1 EMPTY : vacío, desprovisto ⟨void of content : desprovisto de contenido⟩ 2 INVALID : inválido, nulo

void³ *n* : vacío *m*

volatile [ˈvɑlətəl] *adj* : volátil, inestable

volatility [ˌvɑləˈtɪləti] *n* : volatilidad *f*, inestabilidad *f*

volcanic [vɑlˈkænɪk] *adj* : volcánico

volcano [vɑlˈkeɪˌnoː] *n*, *pl* **-noes** *or* **-nos** : volcán *m*

vole [ˈvoːl] *n* : campañol *m*

volition [voˈlɪʃən] *n* : volición *f*, voluntad *f* ⟨of one's own volition : por voluntad propia⟩

volley [ˈvɑli] *n*, *pl* **-leys** 1 : descarga *f* (de tiros) 2 : torrente *m*, lluvia *f* (de insultos, etc.) 3 : salva *f* (de aplausos) 4 : volea *f* (en deportes)

volleyball [ˈvɑliˌbɔl] *n* : voleibol *m*

volt [ˈvoːlt] *n* : voltio *m*

voltage [ˈvoːltɪdʒ] *n* : voltaje *m*

volubility [ˌvɑljəˈbɪləti] *n* : locuacidad *f*

voluble [ˈvɑljəbəl] *adj* : locuaz

volume [ˈvɑljəm, -ˌjuːm] *n* 1 BOOK : volumen *m*, tomo *m* 2 SPACE : capacidad *f*, volumen *m* (en física) 3 AMOUNT : cantidad *f*, volumen *m* 4 LOUDNESS : volumen *m*

voluminous [vəˈluːmənəs] *adj* : voluminoso

voluntary [ˈvɑlənˌtɛri] *adj* : voluntario — **voluntarily** [ˌvɑlənˈtɛrəli] *adv*

volunteer¹ [ˌvɑlənˈtɪr] *vt* : ofrecer, dar ⟨to volunteer one's assistance : ofrecer la ayuda⟩ — *vi* : ofrecerse, alistarse como voluntario

volunteer² *n* : voluntario *m*, -ria *f*

voluptuous [vəˈlʌptʃuəs] *adj* : voluptuoso

vomit¹ [ˈvɑmət] *v* : vomitar

vomit² *n* : vómito *m*

voodoo [ˈvuːˌduː] *n*, *pl* **voodoos** : vudú *m*

voracious [vɔˈreɪʃəs, və-] *adj* : voraz

voraciously [vɔˈreɪʃəsli, və-] *adv* : vorazmente, con voracidad

vortex [ˈvɔrˌtɛks] *n*, *pl* **vortices** [ˈvɔrtəˌsiːz] : vórtice *m*

vote¹ [ˈvoːt] *vi* **voted; voting** : votar ⟨to vote Democratic : votar por los demócratas⟩

vote² *n* 1 : voto *m* 2 SUFFRAGE : sufragio *m*, derecho *m* al voto

voter [ˈvoːtər] *n* : votante *mf*

voting [ˈvoːtɪŋ] *n* : votación *f*

vouch [ˈvæʊtʃ] *vi* **to vouch for** : garantizar (algo), responder de (algo), responder por (alguien)

voucher [ˈvæʊtʃər] *n* 1 RECEIPT : comprobante *m* 2 : vale *m* ⟨travel voucher : vale de viajar⟩

vow¹ [væʊ] *vt* : jurar, prometer, hacer voto de

vow² *n* : promesa *f*, voto *m* (en la religión) ⟨a vow of poverty : un voto de pobreza⟩

vowel [ˈvæʊəl] *n* : vocal *m*

voyage¹ [ˈvɔɪɪdʒ] *vi* **-aged; -aging** : viajar

voyage² *n* : viaje *m*

voyager [ˈvɔɪɪdʒər] *n* : viajero *m*, -ra *f*

vulcanize [ˈvʌlkəˌnaɪz] *vt* **-nized; -nizing** : vulcanizar

vulgar [ˈvʌlgər] *adj* 1 COMMON, PLEBIAN : ordinario, populachero, del vulgo 2 COARSE, CRUDE : grosero, de mal gusto, majadero *Mex* 3 INDECENT : indecente, colorado (dícese de un chiste, etc.)

vulgarity [ˌvʌlˈgærəti] *n*, *pl* **-ties** : grosería *f*, vulgaridad *f*

vulgarly [ˈvʌlgərli] *adv* : vulgarmente, groseramente

vulnerability [ˌvʌlnərəˈbɪləti] *n*, *pl* **-ties** : vulnerabilidad *f*

vulnerable [ˈvʌlnərəbəl] *adj* : vulnerable

vulture [ˈvʌltʃər] *n* : buitre *m*, zopilote *m* *CA*, *Mex*

vying → vie

W

w ['dʌbəlˌjuː] *n, pl* **w's** *or* **ws** [-ˌjuːz] : vigésima tercera letra del alfabeto inglés

wad¹ ['wɑd] *vt* **wadded; wadding 1** : hacer un taco con, formar en una masa **2** STUFF : rellenar

wad² *n* : taco *m* (de papel), bola *f* (de algodón, etc.), fajo *m* (de billetes)

waddle¹ ['wɑdəl] *vi* **-dled; -dling** : andar como un pato

waddle² *n* : andar *m* de pato

wade ['weɪd] *v* **waded; wading** *vi* **1** : caminar por el agua **2 to wade through** : leer (algo) con dificultad — *vt or* **to wade across** : vadear

wading bird *n* : zancuda *f*, ave *f* zancuda

wafer ['weɪfər] *n* : barquillo *m*, galleta *f* de barquillo

waffle ['wɑfəl] *n* **1** : wafle *m* **2 waffle iron** : waflera *f*

waft ['wɑft, 'wæft] *vt* : llevar por el aire — *vi* : flotar

wag¹ ['wæg] *v* **wagged; wagging** *vt* : menear — *vi* : menearse, moverse

wag² *n* **1** : meneo *m* (de la cola) **2** JOKER, WIT : bromista *mf*

wage¹ ['weɪdʒ] *vt* **waged; waging** : hacer, librar ⟨to wage war : hacer la guerra⟩

wage² *n or* **wages** *npl* : sueldo *m*, salario *m* ⟨minimum wage : salario mínimo⟩

wager¹ ['weɪdʒər] *v* : apostar

wager² *n* : apuesta *f*

waggish ['wægɪʃ] *adj* : burlón, bromista (dícese de una persona), chistoso (dícese de un comentario)

waggle ['wægəl] *vt* **-gled; -gling** : menear, mover (de un lado a otro)

wagon ['wægən] *n* **1** : carro *m* (tirado por caballos) **2** CART : carrito *m* **3** → **station wagon**

waif ['weɪf] *n* : niño *m* abandonado, animal *m* sin hogar

wail¹ ['weɪl] *vi* : gemir, lamentarse

wail² *n* : gemido *m*, lamento *m*

wainscot ['weɪnskət, -ˌskɑt, -ˌskoːt] *or* **wainscoting** [-skətɪŋ, -ˌskɑ-, -ˌskoː-] *n* : boiserie *f*, revestimiento *m* de paneles de madera

waist ['weɪst] *n* : cintura *f* (del cuerpo humano), talle *m* (de ropa)

waistline ['weɪstˌlaɪn] → **waist**

wait¹ ['weɪt] *vi* : esperar ⟨to wait for something : esperar algo⟩ ⟨wait and see! : ¡espera y verás!⟩ ⟨I can't wait : me muero de ganas⟩ — *vt* **1** AWAIT : esperar **2** DELAY : retrasar ⟨don't wait lunch : no retrase el almuerzo⟩ **3** SERVE : servir, atender ⟨to wait tables : servir (a la mesa)⟩

wait² *n* **1** : espera *f* **2 to lie in wait** : estar al acecho

waiter ['weɪtər] *n* : mesero *m*, camarero *m*, mozo *m* *Arg, Chile, Col, Peru*

waiting room *n* : sala *f* de espera

waitress ['weɪtrəs] *n* : mesera *f*, camarera *f*, moza *f* *Arg, Chile, Col, Peru*

waive ['weɪv] *vt* **waived; waiving** : renunciar a ⟨to waive one's rights : renunciar a sus derechos⟩ ⟨to waive the rules : no aplicar las reglas⟩

waiver ['weɪvər] *n* : renuncia *f*

wake¹ ['weɪk] *v* **woke** ['woːk]; **woken** ['woːkən] *or* **waked; waking** *vi or* **to wake up** : despertar(se) ⟨he woke at noon : se despertó al mediodía⟩ ⟨wake up! : ¡despiértate!⟩ — *vt* : despertar

wake² *n* **1** VIGIL : velatorio *m*, velorio *m* (de un difunto) **2** TRAIL : estela *f* (de un barco, un huracán, etc.) **3** AFTERMATH : consecuencias *fpl* ⟨in the wake of : tras, como consecuencia de⟩

wakeful ['weɪkfəl] *adj* **1** SLEEPLESS : desvelado **2** VIGILANT : alerta, vigilante

waken ['weɪkən] → **awake**

walk¹ ['wɔk] *vi* **1** : caminar, andar, pasear ⟨you're walking too fast : estás caminando demasiado rápido⟩ ⟨to walk around the city : pasearse por la ciudad⟩ **2** : ir andando, ir a pie ⟨we had to walk home : tuvimos que ir a casa a pie⟩ **3** : darle base por bolas (a un bateador) — *vt* **1** : recorrer, caminar ⟨she walked two miles : caminó dos millas⟩ **2** ACCOMPANY : acompañar **3** : sacar a pasear (a un perro)

walk² *n* **1** : paseo *m*, caminata *f* ⟨to go for a walk : ir a caminar, dar un paseo⟩ **2** PATH : camino *m* **3** GAIT : andar *m* **4** : marcha *f* (en beisbol) **5 walk of life** : esfera *f*, condición *f*

walker ['wɔkər] *n* **1** : paseante *mf* **2** HIKER : excursionista *mf* **3** : andador *m* (aparato)

walking stick *n* : bastón *m*

walkout ['wɔkˌaʊt] *n* STRIKE : huelga *f*

walk out *vi* **1** STRIKE : declararse en huelga **2** LEAVE : salir, irse **3 to walk out on** : abandonar, dejar

walkway ['wɔkˌweɪ] *n* **1** SIDEWALK : acera *f* **2** PATH : sendero *m* **3** PASSAGEWAY : pasadizo *m*

wall¹ ['wɔl] *vt* **1 to wall in** : cercar con una pared o un muro, tapiar, amurallar **2 to wall off** : separar con una pared o un muro **3 to wall up** : tapiar, condenar (una ventana, etc.)

wall² *n* **1** : muro *m* (exterior) ⟨the walls of the city : las murallas de la ciudad⟩ **2** : pared *f* (interior) **3** BARRIER : barrera *f* ⟨a wall of mountains : una barrera de montañas⟩ **4** : pared *f* (en anatomía)

wallaby ['wɑləbi] *n, pl* **-bies** : ualabí *m*

walled ['wɔld] *adj* : amurallado

wallet ['wɑlət] *n* : billetera *f*, cartera *f*

wallflower ['wɔlˌflaʊər] *n* **1** : alhelí *m* (flor) **2 to be a wallflower** : comer pavo

wallop¹ ['wɑləp] *vt* **1** TROUNCE : darle una paliza (a alguien) **2** SOCK : pegar fuerte

wallop² *n* : golpe *m* fuerte, golpazo *m*
wallow¹ ['wɑˌloː] *vi* **1** : revolcarse ⟨to wallow in the mud : revolcarse en el lodo⟩ **2** DELIGHT : deleitarse ⟨to wallow in luxury : nadar en lujos⟩
wallow² *n* : revolcadero *m* (para animales)
wallpaper¹ ['wɔlˌpeɪpər] *vt* : empapelar
wallpaper² *n* : papel *m* pintado
walnut ['wɔlˌnʌt] *n* **1** : nuez *f* (fruta) **2** : nogal *m* (árbol y madera)
walrus ['wɔlrəs, 'wɑl-] *n, pl* **-rus** *or* **-ruses** : morsa *f*
waltz¹ ['wɔlts] *vi* **1** : valsar, bailar el vals **2** BREEZE : pasar con ligereza ⟨to waltz in : entrar tan campante⟩
waltz² *n* : vals *m*
wan ['wɑn] *adj* **wanner; -est 1** PALLID : pálido **2** DIM : tenue ⟨wan light : luz tenue⟩ **3** LANGUID : lánguido ⟨a wan smile : una sonrisa lánguida⟩ — **wanly** *adv*
wand ['wɑnd] *n* : varita *f* (mágica)
wander ['wɑndər] *vi* **1** RAMBLE : deambular, vagar, vagabundear **2** STRAY : alejarse, desviarse, divagar ⟨she let her mind wander : dejó vagar la imaginación⟩ — *vt* : recorrer ⟨to wander the streets : vagar por las calles⟩
wanderer ['wɑndərər] *n* : vagabundo *m*, -da *f*; viajero *m*, -ra *f*
wanderlust ['wɑndərˌlʌst] *n* : pasión *f* por viajar
wane¹ ['weɪn] *vi* **waned; waning 1** : menguar (dícese de la luna) **2** DECLINE : disminuir, decaer, menguar
wane² *n* **on the wane** : decayendo, en decadencia
wangle ['wæŋgəl] *vt* **-gled; -gling** FINAGLE : arreglárselas para conseguir
wannabe ['wɑnəˌbiː] *n* : aspirante *mf* (a algo); imitador *m*, -dora *f* (de alguien)
want¹ ['wɑnt, 'wɔnt] *vt* **1** LACK : faltar **2** REQUIRE : requerir, necesitar **3** DESIRE : querer, desear
want² *n* **1** LACK : falta *f* **2** DESTITUTION : indigencia *f*, miseria *f* **3** DESIRE, NEED : deseo *m*, necesidad *f*
wanting ['wɑntɪŋ, 'wɔn-] *adj* **1** ABSENT : ausente **2** DEFICIENT : deficiente ⟨he's wanting in common sense : le falta sentido común⟩
wanton ['wɑntən, 'wɔn-] *adj* **1** LEWD, LUSTFUL : lascivo, lujurioso, licencioso **2** INHUMANE, MERCILESS : despiadado ⟨wanton cruelty : crueldad despiadada⟩
wapiti ['wɑpəˌti] *n, pl* **-ti** *or* **-tis** : uapití *m*
war¹ ['wɔr] *vi* **warred; warring** : combatir, batallar, hacer la guerra
war² *n* : guerra *f* ⟨to go to war : entrar en guerra⟩
warble¹ ['wɔrbəl] *vi* **-bled; -bling** : gorjear, trinar
warble² *n* : trino *m*, gorjeo *m*
warbler ['wɔrblər] *n* : pájaro *m* gorjeador, curruca *f*
ward¹ ['wɔrd] *vt* **to ward off** : desviar, protegerse contra

ward² *n* **1** : sala *f* (de un hospital, etc.) ⟨maternity ward : sala de maternidad⟩ **2** : distrito *m* electoral o administrativo (de una ciudad) **3** : pupilo *m*, -la *f* (de un tutor, etc.)
warden ['wɔrdən] *n* **1** KEEPER : guarda *mf*; guardián *m*, -diana *f* ⟨game warden : guardabosque⟩ **2** *or* **prison warden** : alcaide *m*
wardrobe ['wɔrdˌroːb] *n* **1** CLOSET : armario *m* **2** CLOTHES : vestuario *m*, guardarropa *f*
ware ['wær] *n* **1** POTTERY : cerámica *f* **2 wares** *npl* GOODS : mercancía *f*, mercadería *f*
warehouse ['wærˌhaʊs] *n* : depósito *m*, almacén *m*, bodega *f* *Chile, Col, Mex*
warfare ['wɔrˌfær] *n* **1** WAR : guerra *f* **2** STRUGGLE : lucha *f* ⟨the warfare against drugs : la lucha contra las drogas⟩
warhead ['wɔrˌhɛd] *n* : ojiva *f*, cabeza *f* (de un misil)
warily ['wærəli] *adv* : cautelosamente, con cautela
wariness ['wærinəs] *n* : cautela *f*
warlike ['wærˌlaɪk] *adj* : belicoso, guerrero
warm¹ ['wɔrm] *vt* **1** HEAT : calentar, recalentar **2 to warm one's heart** : reconfortar a uno, alegrar el corazón **3 to warm up** : calentar (los músculos, un automóvil, etc.) — *vi* **1** : calentarse **2 to warm to** : tomarle simpatía (a alguien), entusiasmarse con (algo)
warm² *adj* **1** LUKEWARM : tibio, templado **2** : caliente, cálido, caluroso ⟨a warm wind : un viento cálido⟩ ⟨a warm day : un día caluroso, un día de calor⟩ ⟨warm hands : manos calientes⟩ **3** : caliente, que abriga ⟨warm clothes : ropa de abrigo⟩ ⟨I feel warm : tengo calor⟩ **4** CARING, CORDIAL : cariñoso, cordial **5** : cálido (dícese de colores) **6** FRESH : fresco, reciente ⟨a warm trail : un rastro reciente⟩ **7** (*used for riddles*) : caliente
warm–blooded ['wɔrm'blʌdəd] *adj* : de sangre caliente
warmhearted ['wɔrm'hɑrtəd] *adj* : cariñoso
warmly ['wɔrmli] *adv* **1** AFFECTIONATELY : calurosamente, afectuosamente **2 to dress warmly** : abrigarse
warmonger ['wɔrˌmɑŋgər, -ˌmʌn-] *n* : belicista *mf*
warmth ['wɔrmpθ] *n* **1** : calor *m* **2** AFFECTION : cariño *m*, afecto *m* **3** ENTHUSIASM : ardor *m*, entusiasmo *m*
warm–up ['wɔrmˌʌp] *n* : calentamiento *m*
warn ['wɔrn] *vt* **1** CAUTION : advertir, alertar **2** INFORM : avisar, informar
warning ['wɔrnɪŋ] *n* **1** ADVICE : advertencia *f*, aviso *m* **2** ALERT : alerta *f*, alarma *f*
warp¹ ['wɔrp] *vt* **1** : alabear, combar **2** PERVERT : pervertir, deformar — *vi* : pandearse, alabearse, combarse

warp² *n* **1** : urdimbre *f* ⟨the warp and the weft : la urdimbre y la trama⟩ **2** : alabeo *m* (en la madera, etc.)

warrant¹ ['wɔrənt] *vt* **1** ASSURE : asegurar, garantizar **2** GUARANTEE : garantizar **3** JUSTIFY, MERIT : justificar, merecer

warrant² *n* **1** AUTHORIZATION : autorización *f*, permiso *m* ⟨an arrest warrant : una orden de detención⟩ **2** JUSTIFICATION : justificación *f*

warranty ['wɔrənti, ˌwɔrən'ti:] *n, pl* **-ties** : garantía *f*

warren ['wɔrən] *n* : madriguera *f* (de conejos)

warrior ['wɔriər] *n* : guerrero *m*, -ra *f*

warship ['wɔrˌʃɪp] *n* : buque *m* de guerra

wart ['wɔrt] *n* : verruga *f*

wartime ['wɔrˌtaɪm] *n* : tiempo *m* de guerra

wary ['wæri] *adj* **warier; -est** : cauteloso, receloso ⟨to be wary of : desconfiar de⟩

was → **be**

wash¹ ['wɔʃ, 'wɑʃ] *vt* **1** CLEAN : lavar(se), limpiar, fregar ⟨to wash the dishes : lavar los platos⟩ ⟨to wash one's hands : lavarse las manos⟩ **2** DRENCH : mojar **3** LAP : bañar ⟨waves were washing the shore : las olas bañaban la orilla⟩ **4** CARRY, DRAG : arrastrar **5 to wash away** : llevarse (un puente, etc.) — *vi* **1** : lavarse (dícese de una persona o la ropa) ⟨the dress washes well : el vestido se lava bien⟩ **2 to wash against** *or* **to wash over** : bañar

wash² *n* **1** : lavado *m* ⟨to give something a wash : lavar algo⟩ **2** LAUNDRY : artículos *mpl* para lavar, ropa *f* sucia **3** : estela *f* (de un barco)

washable ['wɔʃəbəl, 'wɑ-] *adj* : lavable

washboard ['wɔʃˌbord, 'wɑʃ-] *n* : tabla *f* de lavar

washbowl ['wɔʃˌboːl, 'wɑʃ-] *n* : lavabo *m*, lavamanos *m*

washcloth ['wɔʃˌklɔθ, 'wɑʃ-] *n* : toallita *f* (para lavarse)

washed–out ['wɔʃtˌaʊt, 'wɑʃt-] *adj* **1** : desvaído (dícese de colores) **2** EXHAUSTED : agotado, desanimado

washed–up ['wɔʃt'ʌp, 'wɑʃt-] *adj* : acabado (dícese de una persona), fracasado (dícese de un negocio, etc.)

washer ['wɔʃər, 'wɑ-] *n* **1** → **washing machine 2** : arandela *f* (de una llave, etc.)

washing ['wɔʃɪŋ, 'wɑ-] *n* WASH : ropa *f* para lavar

washing machine *n* : máquina *f* de lavar, lavadora *f*

washout ['wɔʃˌaʊt, 'wɑʃ-] *n* **1** : erosión *f* (de la tierra) **2** FAILURE : fracaso *m* ⟨she's a washout : es un desastre⟩

washroom ['wɔʃˌruːm, 'wɑʃ-, -ˌrʊm] *n* : servicios *mpl* (públicos), baño *m*, sanitario *m* Col, Mex, Ven

wasn't ['wʌzənt] (*contraction of* **was not**) → **be**

wasp ['wɑsp] *n* : avispa *f*

waspish ['wɑspɪʃ] *adj* **1** IRRITABLE : irritable, irascible **2** CAUSTIC : cáustico, mordaz

waste¹ ['weɪst] *v* **wasted; wasting** *vt* **1** DEVASTATE : arrasar, arruinar, devastar **2** SQUANDER : desperdiciar, despilfarrar, malgastar ⟨to waste time : perder tiempo⟩ — *vi or* **to waste away** : consumirse, chuparse

waste² *adj* **1** BARREN : yermo, baldío **2** DISCARDED : de desecho **3** EXCESS : sobrante

waste³ *n* **1** → **wasteland 2** MISUSE : derroche *m*, desperdicio *m*, despilfarro *m* ⟨a waste of time : una pérdida de tiempo⟩ **3** RUBBISH : basura *f*, desechos *mpl*, desperdicios *mpl* **4** EXCREMENT : excremento *m*

wastebasket ['weɪstˌbæskət] *n* : cesto *m* (de basura), papelera *f*, zafacón *m* Car

wasteful ['weɪstfəl] *adj* : despilfarrador, derrochador, pródigo

wastefulness ['weɪstfəlnəs] *n* : derroche *m*, despilfarro *m*

wasteland ['weɪstˌlænd, -lənd] *n* : baldío *m*, yermo *m*, desierto *m*

watch¹ ['wɑtʃ] *vi* **1** *or* **to keep watch** : velar **2** OBSERVE : mirar, ver, observar **3 to watch for** AWAIT : esperar, quedar a la espera de **4 to watch out** : tener cuidado ⟨watch out! : ¡ten cuidado!, ¡ojo!⟩ — *vt* **1** OBSERVE : mirar, observar **2** *or* **to watch over** : vigilar, cuidar **3** : tener cuidado de ⟨watch what you do : ten cuidado con lo que haces⟩

watch² *n* **1** : guardia *f* ⟨to be on watch : estar de guardia⟩ **2** SURVEILLANCE : vigilancia *f* **3** LOOKOUT : guardia *mf*, centinela *f*, vigía *mf* **4** TIMEPIECE : reloj *m*

watchdog ['wɑtʃˌdɔg] *n* : perro *m* guardián

watcher ['wɑtʃər] *n* : observador *m*, -dora *f*

watchful ['wɑtʃfəl] *adj* : alerta, vigilante, atento

watchfulness ['wɑtʃfəlnəs] *n* : vigilancia *f*

watchman ['wɑtʃmən] *n, pl* **-men** [-mən, -ˌmen] : vigilante *m*, guarda *m*

watchword ['wɑtʃˌwərd] *n* **1** PASSWORD : contraseña *f* **2** SLOGAN : lema *m*, eslogan *m*

water¹ ['wɔtər, 'wɑ-] *vt* **1** : regar (el jardín, etc.) **2 to water down** DILUTE : diluir, aguar — *vi* : lagrimear (dícese de los ojos), hacérsele agua la boca a uno ⟨my mouth is watering : se me hace agua la boca⟩

water² *n* : agua *f*

water buffalo *n* : búfalo *m* de agua

watercolor ['wɔtərˌkʌlər, 'wɑ-] *n* : acuarela *f*

watercourse ['wɔtərˌkors, 'wɑ-] *n* : curso *m* de agua

watercress ['wɔtərˌkrɛs, 'wɑ-] *n* : berro *m*

waterfall ['wɔtər,fɔl, 'wɑ-] *n* : cascada *f*, salto *m* de agua, catarata *f*

waterfowl ['wɔtər,faʊl, 'wɑ-] *n* : ave *f* acuática

waterfront ['wɔtər,frʌnt, 'wɑ-] *n* **1** : tierra *f* que bordea un río, un lago, o un mar **2** WHARF : muelle *m*

water lily *n* : nenúfar *m*

waterlogged ['wɔtər,lɔgd, 'wɑtər-,lɑgd] *adj* : lleno de agua, empapado, inundado (dícese del suelo)

watermark ['wɔtər,mɑrk, 'wɑ-] *n* **1** : marca *f* del nivel de agua **2** : filigrana *f* (en el papel)

watermelon ['wɔtər,mɛlən, 'wɑ-] *n* : sandía *f*

water moccasin → **moccasin**

waterpower ['wɔtər,paʊər, 'wɑ-] *n* : energía *f* hidráulica

waterproof[1] ['wɔtər,pruːf, 'wɑ-] *vt* : hacer impermeable, impermeabilizar

waterproof[2] *adj* : impermeable, a prueba de agua

watershed ['wɔtər,ʃɛd, 'wɑ-] *n* **1** : línea *f* divisoria de aguas **2** BASIN : cuenca *f* (de un río)

waterskiing ['wɔtər,skiːɪŋ, 'wɑ-] *n* : esquí *m* acuático

waterspout ['wɔtər,spaʊt, 'wɑ-] *n* WHIRLWIND : tromba *f* marina

watertight ['wɔtər,taɪt, 'wɑ-] *adj* **1** : hermético **2** IRREFUTABLE : irrebatible, irrefutable ⟨a watertight contract : un contrato sin lagunas⟩

waterway ['wɔtər,weɪ, 'wɑ-] *n* : vía *f* navegable

waterworks ['wɔtər,wərks, 'wɑ-] *npl* : central *f* de abastecimiento de agua

watery ['wɔtəri, 'wɑ-] *adj* **1** : acuoso, como agua **2** : aguado, diluido ⟨watery soup : sopa aguada⟩ **3** : lloroso ⟨watery eyes : ojos llorosos⟩ **4** WASHED-OUT : desvaído (dícese de colores)

watt ['wɑt] *n* : vatio *m*

wattage ['wɑtɪdʒ] *n* : vataje *m*

wattle ['wɑtəl] *n* : carúncula *f* (de un ave, etc.)

wave[1] ['weɪv] *v* **waved; waving** *vi* **1** : saludar con la mano, hacer señas con la mano ⟨she waved at him : lo saludó con la mano⟩ **2** FLUTTER, SHAKE : ondear, agitarse **3** UNDULATE : ondular — *vt* **1** SHAKE : agitar **2** BRANDISH : blandir **3** CURL : ondular, marcar (el pelo) **4** SIGNAL : hacerle señas a (con la mano) ⟨he waved farewell : se despidió con la mano⟩

wave[2] *n* **1** : ola *f* (de agua) **2** CURL : onda *f* (en el pelo) **3** : onda *f* (en física) **4** SURGE : oleada *f* ⟨a wave of enthusiasm : una oleada de entusiasmo⟩ **5** GESTURE : señal *f* con la mano, saludo *m* con la mano

wavelength ['weɪv,lɛŋkθ] *n* : longitud *f* de onda

waver ['weɪvər] *vi* **1** VACILLATE : vacilar, fluctuar **2** FLICKER : parpadear, titilar, oscilar **3** FALTER : flaquear, tambalearse

wavy ['weɪvi] *adj* **wavier; -est** : ondulado

wax[1] ['wæks] *vi* **1** : crecer (dícese de la luna) **2** BECOME : volverse, ponerse ⟨to wax indignant : indignarse⟩ — *vt* : encerar

wax[2] *n* **1** BEESWAX : cera *f* de abejas **2** : cera *f* ⟨floor wax : cera para el piso⟩ **3** *or* **earwax** ['ɪr,wæks] : cerilla *f*, cerumen *m*

waxen ['wæksən] *adj* : de cera

waxy ['wæksi] *adj* **waxier; -est** : ceroso

way ['weɪ] *n* **1** PATH, ROAD : camino *m*, vía *f* **2** ROUTE : camino *m*, ruta *f* ⟨to go the wrong way : equivocarse de camino⟩ ⟨I'm on my way : estoy de camino⟩ **3** : línea *f* de conducta, camino *m* ⟨he chose the easy way : optó por el camino fácil⟩ **4** MANNER, MEANS : manera *f*, modo *m*, forma *f* ⟨in the same way : del mismo modo, igualmente⟩ ⟨there are no two ways about it : no cabe la menor duda⟩ ⟨no way! : ¡de ninguna manera!⟩ **5** (*indicating a wish*) ⟨have it your way : como tú quieras⟩ ⟨to get one's own way : salirse uno con la suya⟩ **6** STATE : estado *m* ⟨things are in a bad way : las cosas marchan mal⟩ **7** RESPECT : aspecto *m*, sentido *m* **8** CUSTOM : costumbre *f* ⟨to mend one's ways : dejar las malas costumbres⟩ **9** PASSAGE : camino *m* ⟨to get in the way : meterse en el camino⟩ **10** DISTANCE : distancia *f* ⟨to come a long way : hacer grandes progresos⟩ **11** DIRECTION : dirección *f* ⟨come this way : venga por aquí⟩ ⟨which way did he go? : ¿por dónde fue?⟩ **12 by the way** : a propósito, por cierto **13 by way of** VIA : vía, pasando por **14 out of the way** REMOTE : remoto, recóndito **15** → **under way**

wayfarer ['weɪ,færər] *n* : caminante *mf*

waylay ['weɪ,leɪ] *vt* **-laid** [-,leɪd]**; -laying** ACCOST : abordar

wayside ['weɪ,saɪd] *n* : borde *m* del camino

wayward ['weɪwərd] *adj* **1** UNRULY : díscolo, rebelde **2** UNTOWARD : adverso

we ['wiː] *pron* : nosotros, nosotras

weak ['wiːk] *adj* **1** FEEBLE : débil, endeble **2** : flojo, pobre ⟨a weak excuse : una excusa poco convincente⟩ **3** DILUTED : aguado, diluido ⟨weak tea : té poco cargado⟩ **4** FAINT : tenue (dícese de los colores, las luces, los sonidos, etc.)

weaken ['wiːkən] *vt* : debilitar — *vi* : debilitarse, flaquear

weakling ['wiːklɪŋ] *n* : alfeñique *m fam*; debilucho *m*, -cha *f*

weakly[1] ['wiːkli] *adv* : débilmente

weakly[2] *adj* **weaklier; -est** : débil, enclenque

weakness ['wiːknəs] *n* **1** FEEBLENESS : debilidad *f* **2** FAULT, FLAW : flaqueza *f*, punto *m* débil

wealth ['wɛlθ] *n* **1** RICHES : riqueza *f* **2** PROFUSION : abundancia *f*, profusión *f*

wealthy ['wɛlθi] *adj* **wealthier; -est** : rico, acaudalado, adinerado

wean ['wi:n] *vt* **1** : destetar (a los niños o las crías) **2 to wean someone away from** : quitarle a alguien la costumbre de

weapon ['wɛpən] *n* : arma *f*

weaponless ['wɛpənləs] *adj* : desarmado

weaponry ['wɛpənri] *n* : armamento *m*

wear¹ ['wær] *v* **wore** ['wor]; **worn** ['worn]; **wearing** *vt* **1** : llevar (ropa, un reloj, etc.), calzar (zapatos) ⟨to wear a happy smile : sonreír alegremente⟩ **2** *or* **to wear away** : desgastar, erosionar (rocas, etc.) **3 to wear out** : gastar ⟨he wore out his shoes : gastó sus zapatos⟩ **4 to wear out** EXHAUST : agotar, fatigar ⟨to wear oneself out : agotarse⟩ — *vi* **1** LAST : durar **2 to wear off** DIMINISH : disminuir **3 to wear out** : gastarse

wear² *n* **1** USE : uso *m* ⟨for everyday wear : para todos los días⟩ **2** CLOTHING : ropa *f* ⟨children's wear : ropa de niños⟩ **3** DETERIORATION : desgaste *m* ⟨to be the worse for wear : estar deteriorado⟩

wearable ['wærəbəl] *adj* : que puede ponerse (dícese de una prenda)

wear and tear *n* : desgaste *m*

weariness ['wɪrinəs] *n* : fatiga *f*, cansancio *m*

wearisome ['wɪrisəm] *adj* : aburrido, pesado, cansado

weary¹ ['wɪri] *v* **-ried; -rying** *vt* **1** TIRE : cansar, fatigar **2** BORE : hastiar, aburrir — *vi* : cansarse

weary² *adj* **-rier; -est 1** TIRED : cansado **2** FED UP : harto **3** BORED : aburrido

weasel ['wi:zəl] *n* : comadreja *f*

weather¹ ['wɛðər] *vt* **1** WEAR : erosionar, desgastar **2** ENDURE : aguantar, sobrellevar, capear ⟨to weather the storm : capear el temporal⟩

weather² *n* : tiempo *m*

weather–beaten ['wɛðər,bi:tən] *adj* : curtido

weatherman ['wɛðər,mæn] *n, pl* **-men** [-mən, -,mɛn] METEOROLOGIST : meteorólogo *m*, -ga *f*

weatherproof ['wɛðər,pru:f] *adj* : que resiste a la intemperie, impermeable

weather vane → **vane**

weave¹ ['wi:v] *v* **wove** ['wo:v] *or* **weaved; woven** ['wo:vən] *or* **weaved; weaving** *vt* **1** : tejer (tela) **2** INTERLACE : entretejer, entrelazar **3 to weave one's way through** : abrirse camino por — *vi* **1** : tejer **2** WIND : serpentear, zigzaguear

weave² *n* : tejido *m*, trama *f*

weaver ['wi:vər] *n* : tejedor *m*, -dora *f*

web¹ ['wɛb] *vt* **webbed; webbing** : cubrir o proveer con una red

web² *n* **1** COBWEB, SPIDERWEB : telaraña *f*, tela *f* de araña **2** ENTANGLEMENT, SNARE : red *f*, enredo *m* ⟨a web of intrigue : una red de intriga⟩ **3** : membrana *f* interdigital (de aves) **4** NETWORK : red *f* ⟨a web of highways : una red de carreteras⟩ **5 the Web** : la web

webbed ['wɛbd] *adj* : palmeado ⟨webbed feet : patas palmeadas⟩

Web site *n* : sitio *m* web

wed ['wɛd] *vt* **wedded; wedding 1** MARRY : casarse con **2** UNITE : ligar, unir

we'd ['wi:d] (*contraction of* **we had, we should,** *or* **we would**) → **have, should, would**

wedding ['wɛdɪŋ] *n* : boda *f*, casamiento *m*

wedge¹ ['wɛdʒ] *vt* **wedged; wedging 1** : apretar (con una cuña) ⟨to wedge open : mantener abierto con una cuña⟩ **2** CRAM : meter, embutir

wedge² *n* **1** : cuña *f* **2** PIECE : porción *f*, trozo *m*

wedlock ['wɛd,lɑk] → **marriage**

Wednesday ['wɛnz,deɪ, -di] *n* : miércoles *m*

wee ['wi:] *adj* : pequeño, minúsculo ⟨in the wee hours : a las altas horas⟩

weed¹ ['wi:d] *vt* **1** : desherbar, desyerbar **2 to weed out** : eliminar, quitar

weed² *n* : mala hierba *f*

weedy ['wi:di] *adj* **weedier; -est 1** : cubierto de malas hierbas **2** LANKY, SKINNY : flaco, larguirucho *fam*

week ['wi:k] *n* : semana *f*

weekday ['wi:k,deɪ] *n* : día *m* laborable

weekend ['wi:k,ɛnd] *n* : fin *m* de semana

weekly¹ ['wi:kli] *adv* : semanalmente

weekly² *adj* : semanal

weekly³ *n, pl* **-lies** : semanario *m*

weep ['wi:p] *v* **wept** ['wɛpt]; **weeping** : llorar

weeping willow *n* : sauce *m* llorón

weepy ['wi:pi] *adj* **weepier; -est** : lloroso, triste

weevil ['wi:vəl] *n* : gorgojo *m*

weft ['wɛft] *n* : trama *f*

weigh ['weɪ] *vt* **1** : pesar **2** CONSIDER : considerar, sopesar **3 to weigh anchor** : levar anclas **4 to weigh down** : sobrecargar (con una carga), abrumar (con preocupaciones, etc.) — *vi* **1** : pesar ⟨it weighs 10 pounds : pesa 10 libras⟩ **2** COUNT : tener importancia, contar **3 to weigh on one's mind** : preocuparle a uno

weight¹ ['weɪt] *vt* **1** : poner peso en, sujetar con un peso **2** BURDEN : cargar, oprimir

weight² *n* **1** HEAVINESS : peso *m* ⟨to lose weight : bajar de peso, adelgazar⟩ **2** : peso *m* ⟨weights and measures : pesos y medidas⟩ **3** : pesa *f* ⟨to lift weights : levantar pesas⟩ **4** BURDEN : peso *m*, carga *f* ⟨to take a weight off one's mind : quitarle un peso de encima a uno⟩ **5**

IMPORTANCE : peso *m* **6** INFLUENCE : influencia *f*, autoridad *f* ⟨to throw one's weight around : hacer sentir su influencia⟩

weighty ['weɪți] *adj* **weightier; -est 1** HEAVY : pesado **2** IMPORTANT : importante, de peso

weird ['wɪrd] *adj* **1** MYSTERIOUS : misterioso **2** STRANGE : extraño, raro — **weirdly** *adv*

welcome¹ ['wɛlkəm] *vt* **-comed; -coming** : darle la bienvenida a, recibir

welcome² *adj* : bienvenido ⟨to make someone welcome : acoger bien a alguien⟩ ⟨you're welcome! : ¡de nada!, ¡no hay de qué!⟩

welcome³ *n* : bienvenida *f*, recibimiento *m*, acogida *f*

weld¹ ['wɛld] *v* : soldar

weld² *n* : soldadura *f*

welder ['wɛldər] *n* : soldador *m*, -dora *f*

welfare ['wɛl,fær] *n* **1** WELL-BEING : bienestar *m* **2** : asistencia *f* social

well¹ ['wɛl] *vi or* **to well up** : brotar, manar

well² *adv* **better** ['bɛțər]; **best** ['bɛst] **1** RIGHTLY : bien, correctamente **2** SATISFACTORILY : bien ⟨to turn out well : resultar bien, salir bien⟩ **3** COMPLETELY : completamente ⟨well-hidden : completamente escondido⟩ **4** INTIMATELY : bien ⟨I knew him well : lo conocía bien⟩ **5** CONSIDERABLY, FAR : muy, bastante ⟨well ahead : muy adelante⟩ ⟨well before the deadline : bastante antes de la fecha⟩ **6 as well** ALSO : también **7** — **as well as**

well³ *adj* **1** SATISFACTORY : bien ⟨all is well : todo está bien⟩ **2** DESIRABLE : conveniente ⟨it would be well if you left : sería conveniente que te fueras⟩ **3** HEALTHY : bien, sano

well⁴ *n* **1** : pozo *m* (de agua, petróleo, gas, etc.), aljibe *m* (de agua) **2** SOURCE : fuente *f* ⟨a well of information : una fuente de información⟩ **3** *or* **stairwell** : caja *f*, hueco *m* (de la escalera)

well⁵ *interj* **1** (*used to introduce a remark*) : bueno **2** (*used to express surprise*) : ¡vaya!

we'll ['wi:l, wɪl] (*contraction of* **we shall** *or* **we will**) → **shall, will**

well-balanced ['wɛl'bælənst] *adj* : equilibrado

well-being ['wɛl'bi:ɪŋ] *n* : bienestar *m*

well-bred ['wɛl'brɛd] *adj* : fino, bien educado

well-defined [,wɛldi'faɪnd] *adj* : bien definido

well-done ['wɛl'dʌn] *adj* **1** : bien hecho ⟨well-done! : ¡bravo!⟩ **2** : bien cocido

well-known ['wɛl'no:n] *adj* : famoso, bien conocido

well-meaning ['wɛl'mi:nɪŋ] *adj* : bienintencionado, que tiene buenas intenciones

well-nigh ['wɛl'naɪ] *adv* : casi ⟨well-nigh impossible : casi imposible⟩

well-off ['wɛl'ɔf] → **well-to-do**

well-rounded ['wɛl'raʊndəd] *adj* : completo, equilibrado

well-to-do [,wɛltə'du:] *adj* : próspero, adinerado, rico

Welsh ['wɛlʃ] *n* **1** : galés *m*, galesa *f* **2** : galés *m* (idioma) — **Welsh** *adj*

welt ['wɛlt] *n* **1** : vira *f* (de un zapato) **2** WHEAL : verdugón *m*

welter ['wɛltər] *n* : fárrago *m*, revoltijo *m* ⟨a welter of data : un fárrago de datos⟩

wend ['wɛnd] *vi* **to wend one's way** : ponerse en camino, encaminar sus pasos

went → **go¹**

wept → **weep**

were → **be**

we're ['wɪr, wər, wi:ər] (*contraction of* **we are**) → **be**

werewolf ['wɪr,wʊlf, 'wɛr-, 'wər-, -,wʌlf] *n, pl* **-wolves** [-,wʊlvz, -,wʌlvz] : hombre *m* lobo

west¹ ['wɛst] *adv* : al oeste

west² *adj* : oeste, del oeste, occidental ⟨west winds : vientos del oeste⟩

west³ *n* **1** : oeste *m* **2 the West** : el Oeste, el Occidente

westerly ['wɛstərli] *adv & adj* : del oeste

western ['wɛstərn] *adj* **1** : Occidental, del Oeste **2** : occidental, oeste

Westerner ['wɛstərnər] *n* : habitante *mf* del oeste

West Indian *n* : antillano *m*, -na *f* — **West Indian** *adj*

westward ['wɛstwərd] *adv & adj* : hacia el oeste

wet¹ ['wɛt] *vt* **wet** *or* **wetted; wetting** : mojar, humedecer

wet² *adj* **wetter; wettest 1** : mojado, húmedo ⟨wet clothes : ropa mojada⟩ **2** RAINY : lluvioso **3 wet paint** : pintura *f* fresca

wet³ *n* **1** MOISTURE : humedad *f* **2** RAIN : lluvia *f*

we've ['wi:v] (*contraction of* **we have**) → **have**

whack¹ ['ʰwæk] *vt* : golpear (fuertemente), aporrear

whack² *n* **1** : golpe *m* fuerte, porrazo *m* **2** ATTEMPT : intento *m*, tentativa *f*

whale¹ ['ʰweɪl] *vi* **whaled; whaling** : cazar ballenas

whale² *n, pl* **whales** *or* **whale** : ballena *f*

whaleboat ['ʰweɪl,bo:t] *n* : ballenero *m*

whalebone ['ʰweɪl,bo:n] *n* : barba *f* de ballena

whaler ['ʰweɪlər] *n* **1** : ballenero *m*, -ra *f* **2** → **whaleboat**

wharf ['ʰwɔrf] *n, pl* **wharves** ['ʰwɔrvz] : muelle *m*, embarcadero *m*

what¹ ['ʰwɑt, 'ʰwʌt] *adv* **1** HOW : cómo, cuánto ⟨what he suffered! : ¡cómo sufría!⟩ **2 what with** : entre ⟨what with one thing and another : entre una cosa y otra⟩

what² *adj* **1** (*used in questions*) : qué ⟨what more do you want? : ¿qué más quieres?⟩ ⟨what color is it? : ¿de qué

color es?⟩ **2** (*used in exclamations*)
: qué ⟨what an idea! : ¡qué idea!⟩ **3**
ANY, WHATEVER : cualquier ⟨give what
help you can : da cualquier contribución que puedas⟩
what³ *pron* **1** (*used in direct questions*)
: qué ⟨what happened? : ¿qué pasó?⟩
⟨what does it cost? : ¿cuánto cuesta?⟩
2 (*used in indirect statements*) : lo que,
que ⟨I don't know what to do : no sé
que hacer⟩ ⟨do what I tell you : haz lo
que te digo⟩ **3 what for** WHY : porqué
4 what if : y si ⟨what if he knows? : ¿y
si lo sabe?⟩
whatever¹ [ˌʍɑt̬ˈɛvər, ˌʍʌt̬-] *adj* **1** ANY
: cualquier, cualquier ... que ⟨what-
ever way you prefer : de cualquier
manera que prefiera, como prefiera⟩ **2**
(*in negative constructions*) ⟨there's no
chance whatever : no hay ninguna posi-
bilidad⟩ ⟨nothing whatever : nada en
absoluto⟩
whatever² *pron* **1** ANYTHING : (todo) lo
que ⟨I'll do whatever I want : haré lo
que quiera⟩ **2** (*no matter what*) ⟨what-
ever it may be : sea lo que sea⟩ **3** WHAT
: qué ⟨whatever do you mean? : ¿qué
quieres decir?⟩
whatsoever¹ [ˌʍɑtsoˈɛvər, ˌʍʌt̬-] *adj*
→ **whatever¹**
whatsoever² *pron* → **whatever²**
wheal [ˈʍiːl] *n* : verdugón *m*
wheat [ˈʍiːt] *n* : trigo *m*
wheaten [ˈʍiːt̬ən] *adj* : de trigo
wheedle [ˈʍiːdəl] *vt* -**dled**; -**dling** CA-
JOLE : engatusar ⟨to wheedle some-
thing out of someone : sonsacarle algo
a alguien⟩
wheel¹ [ˈʍiːl] *vt* : empujar (una bicicleta, etc.), mover (algo sobre ruedas)
— *vi* **1** ROTATE : girar, rotar **2 to wheel
around** TURN : darse la vuelta
wheel² *n* **1** : rueda *f* **2** *or* **steering wheel**
: volante *m* (de automóviles, etc.),
timón *m* (de barcos o aviones) **3**
wheels *npl* : maquinaria *f*, fuerza *f* im-
pulsora ⟨the wheels of government : la
maquinaria del gobierno⟩
wheelbarrow [ˈʍiːlˌbær̩o:] *n* : carretilla *f*
wheelchair [ˈʍiːlˌtʃær] *n* : silla *f* de
ruedas
wheeze¹ [ˈʍiːz] *vi* **wheezed; wheezing**
: resollar, respirar con dificultad
wheeze² *n* : resuello *m*
whelk [ˈʍɛlk] *n* : buccino *m*
whelp¹ [ˈʍɛlp] *vi* : parir
whelp² *n* : cachorro *m*, -rra *f*
when¹ [ˈʍɛn] *adv* : cuándo ⟨when will
you return? : ¿cuándo volverás?⟩ ⟨he
asked me when I would be home : me
preguntó cuándo estaría en casa⟩
when² *conj* **1** (*referring to a particular
time*) : cuando, en que ⟨when you are
ready : cuando estés listo⟩ ⟨the days
when I clean the house : los días en que
limpio la casa⟩ **2** IF : cuando, si ⟨how
can I go when I have no money?

: ¿cómo voy a ir si no tengo dinero?⟩
3 ALTHOUGH : cuando ⟨you said it was
big when actually it's small : dijiste que
era grande cuando en realidad es pe-
queño⟩
when³ *pron* : cuándo ⟨since when are
you the boss? : ¿desde cuándo eres el
jefe?⟩
whence [ˈʍɛnts] *adv* : de donde
whenever¹ [ʍɛnˈvər] *adv* **1** : cuando
sea ⟨tomorrow or whenever : mañana
o cuando sea⟩ **2** (*in questions*) : cuándo
whenever² *conj* **1** : siempre que, cada
vez que ⟨whenever I go, I'm disappointed : siempre que voy, quedo de-
silusionado⟩ **2** WHEN : cuando ⟨when-
ever you like : cuando quieras⟩
where¹ [ˈʍɛr] *adv* : dónde, adónde
⟨where is he? : ¿dónde está?⟩ ⟨where
did they go? : ¿adónde fueron?⟩
where² *conj* : donde, adonde ⟨she knows
where the house is : sabe donde está la
casa⟩ ⟨she goes where she likes : va
adonde quiera⟩
where³ *pron* : donde ⟨Chicago is where
I live : Chicago es donde vivo⟩
whereabouts¹ [ˈʍɛrəˌbauts] *adv*
: dónde, por dónde ⟨whereabouts is the
house? : ¿dónde está la casa?⟩
whereabouts² *ns & pl* : paradero *m*
whereas [ʍɛrˈæz] *conj* **1** : consideran-
do que (usado en documentos legales)
2 : mientras que ⟨I like the white one
whereas she prefers the black : me gusta el blanco mientras que ella prefiere
el negro⟩
whereby [ʍɛrˈbai] *adv* : por lo cual
wherefore [ˈʍɛrˌfor] *adv* : por qué
wherein [ʍɛrˈɪn] *adv* : en el cual, en el
que
whereof [ʍɛrˈʌv, -ɑv] *conj* : de lo cual
whereupon [ˈʍɛrəˌpɑn, -ˌpɔn] *conj*
: con lo cual, después de lo cual
wherever¹ [ʍɛrˈɛvər] *adv* **1** WHERE
: dónde, adónde **2** : en cualquier parte
⟨or wherever : o donde sea⟩
wherever² *conj* : dondequiera que,
donde sea ⟨wherever you go : dondequiera que vayas⟩
wherewithal [ˈʍɛrwɪˌðɔl, -ˌθɔl] *n*
: medios *mpl*, recursos *mpl*
whet [ˈʍɛt] *vt* **whetted; whetting 1**
SHARPEN : afilar **2** STIMULATE : estimular ⟨to whet the appetite : estím-
ular el apetito⟩
whether [ˈʍɛðər] *conj* **1** : si ⟨I don't
know whether it is finished : no sé si
está acabado⟩ ⟨we doubt whether he'll
show up : dudamos que aparezca⟩ **2**
(*used in comparisons*) ⟨whether I like
it or not : tanto si quiero como si no⟩
⟨whether he comes or he doesn't : venga o no⟩
whetstone [ˈʍɛtˌsto:n] *n* : piedra *f* de
afilar
whey [ˈʍei] *n* : suero *m* (de la leche)
which¹ [ˈʍɪtʃ] *adj* : qué, cuál ⟨which tie
do you prefer? : ¿cuál corbata pre-

fieres?⟩ ⟨which ones? : ¿cuáles?⟩ ⟨tell me which house is yours : dime qué casa es la tuya⟩

which² [*h*wɪtʃˈevər] *pron* **1** : cuál ⟨which is the right answer? : ¿cuál es la respuesta correcta?⟩ **2** : que, el (la) cual ⟨the cup which broke : la taza que se quebró⟩ ⟨the house, which is made of brick : la casa, la cual es de ladrillo⟩

whichever¹ [*h*wɪtʃˈevər] *adj* : el (la) que, cualquiera que ⟨whichever book you like : cualquier libro que te guste⟩

whichever² *pron* : el (la) que, cualquiera que ⟨take whichever you want : toma el que quieras⟩ ⟨whichever I choose : cualquiera que elija⟩

whiff¹ [ˈ*h*wɪf] *v* PUFF : soplar

whiff² *n* **1** PUFF : soplo *m*, ráfaga *f* **2** SNIFF : olor *m* **3** HINT : dejo *m*, pizca *f*

while¹ [ˈ*h*waɪl] *vt* whiled; whiling : pasar ⟨to while away the time : matar el tiempo⟩

while² *n* **1** TIME : rato *m*, tiempo *m* ⟨after a while : después de un rato⟩ ⟨in a while : dentro de poco⟩ **2 to be worth one's while** : valer la pena

while³ *conj* **1** : mientras ⟨whistle while you work : silba mientras trabajas⟩ **2** WHEREAS : mientras que **3** ALTHOUGH : aunque ⟨while it's very good, it's not perfect : aunque es muy bueno, no es perfecto⟩

whim [ˈ*h*wɪm] *n* : capricho *m*, antojo *m*

whimper¹ [ˈ*h*wɪmpər] *vi* : lloriquear, gimotear

whimper² *n* : quejido *m*

whimsical [ˈ*h*wɪmzɪkəl] *adj* **1** CAPRICIOUS : caprichoso, fantasioso **2** ERRATIC : errático — **whimsically** *adv*

whine¹ [ˈ*h*waɪn] *vi* whined; whining **1** : lloriquear, gimotear, gemir **2** COMPLAIN : quejarse

whine² *n* : quejido *m*, gemido *m*

whinny¹ [ˈ*h*wɪni] *vi* -nied; -nying : relinchar

whinny² *n, pl* -nies : relincho *m*

whip¹ [ˈ*h*wɪp] *v* whipped; whipping *vt* **1** SNATCH : sacar (rápidamente), arrebatar ⟨she whipped the cloth off the table : arrebató el mantel de la mesa⟩ **2** LASH : azotar **3** DEFEAT : vencer, derrotar **4** INCITE : incitar, despertar ⟨to whip up enthusiasm : despertar el entusiasmo⟩ **5** BEAT : batir (huevos, crema, etc.) — *vi* FLAP : agitarse

whip² *n* **1** : látigo *m*, azote *m*, fusta *f* (de jinete) **2** : miembro *m* de un cuerpo legislativo encargado de disciplina

whiplash [ˈ*h*wɪpˌlæʃ] *n or* **whiplash injury** : traumatismo *m* cervical

whippet [ˈ*h*wɪpət] *n* : galgo *m* pequeño, galgo *m* inglés

whir¹ [ˈ*h*wər] *vi* whirred; whirring : zumbar

whir² *n* : zumbido *m*

whirl¹ [ˈ*h*wərl] *vi* **1** SPIN : dar vueltas, girar ⟨my head is whirling : la cabeza me

está dando vueltas⟩ **2 to whirl about** : arremolinarse, moverse rápidamente

whirl² *n* **1** SPIN : giro *m*, vuelta *f*, remolino *m* (dícese del polvo, etc.) **2** BUSTLE : bullicio *m*, torbellino *m* (de actividad, etc.) **3 to give it a whirl** : intentar hacer, probar

whirlpool [ˈ*h*wərlˌpuːl] *n* : vorágine *f*, remolino *m*

whirlwind [ˈ*h*wərlˌwɪnd] *n* : remolino *m*, torbellino *m*, tromba *f*

whisk¹ [ˈ*h*wɪsk] *vt* **1** : llevar ⟨she whisked the children off to bed : llevó a los niños a la cama⟩ **2** : batir ⟨to whisk eggs : batir huevos⟩ **3 to whisk away** *or* **to whisk off** : sacudir

whisk² *n* **1** WHISKING : sacudida *f* (movimiento) **2** : batidor *m* (para batir huevos, etc.)

whisk broom *n* : escobilla *f*

whisker [ˈ*h*wɪskər] *n* **1** : pelo *m* (de la barba o el bigote) **2 whiskers** *npl* : bigotes *mpl* (de animales)

whiskey *or* **whisky** [ˈ*h*wɪski] *n, pl* -keys *or* -kies : whisky *m*

whisper¹ [ˈ*h*wɪspər] *vi* : cuchichear, susurrar — *vt* : decir en voz baja, susurrar

whisper² *n* **1** WHISPERING : susurro *m*, cuchicheo *m* **2** RUMOR : rumor *m* **3** TRACE : dejo *m*, pizca *f*

whistle¹ [ˈ*h*wɪsəl] *v* -tled; -tling *vi* : silbar, chiflar, pitar (dícese de un tren, etc.) — *vt* : silbar ⟨to whistle a tune : silbar una melodía⟩

whistle² *n* **1** WHISTLING : chiflido *m*, silbido *m* **2** : silbato *m*, pito *m* (instrumento)

whit [ˈ*h*wɪt] *n* BIT : ápice *m*, pizca *f*

white¹ [ˈ*h*waɪt] *adj* whiter; -est : blanco

white² *n* **1** : blanco *m* (color) **2** : clara *f* (de huevos) **3** *or* **white person** : blanco *m*, -ca *f*

white blood cell *n* : glóbulo *m* blanco

whitecaps [ˈ*h*waɪtˌkæps] *npl* : cabrillas *fpl*

white–collar [ˈ*h*waɪtˈkɑlər] *adj* **1** : de oficina **2 white–collar worker** : oficinista *mf*

whitefish [ˈ*h*waɪtˌfɪʃ] *n* : pescado *m* blanco

whiten [ˈ*h*waɪtən] *vt* : blanquear — *vi* : ponerse blanco

whiteness [ˈ*h*waɪtnəs] *n* : blancura *f*

white–tailed deer [ˈ*h*waɪtˈteɪld] *n* : ciervo *f* de Virginia

whitewash¹ [ˈ*h*waɪtˌwɔʃ] *vt* **1** : enjalbegar, blanquear ⟨to whitewash a fence : enjalbegar una valla⟩ **2** CONCEAL : encubrir (un escándalo, etc.)

whitewash² *n* **1** : jalbegue *m*, lechada *f* **2** COVER-UP : encubrimiento *m*

whither [ˈ*h*wɪðər] *adv* : adónde

whiting [ˈ*h*waɪtɪŋ] *n* : merluza *f*, pescadilla *f* (pez)

whitish [ˈ*h*waɪtɪʃ] *adj* : blancuzco

whittle [ˈ*h*wɪtəl] *vt* -tled; -tling **1** : tallar (madera) **2 to whittle down** : reducir, recortar ⟨to whittle down expenses : reducir los gastos⟩

whiz¹ *or* **whizz** [ˈʰwɪz] *vi* **whizzed; whizzing 1** BUZZ : zumbar **2 to whiz by** : pasar muy rápido, pasar volando

whiz² *or* **whizz** *n, pl* **whizzes 1** BUZZ : zumbido *m* **2 to be a whiz** : ser un prodigio, ser muy hábil

who [ˈhu:] *pron* **1** (*used in direct and indirect questions*) : quién ⟨who is that? : ¿quién es ése?⟩ ⟨who did it? : ¿quién lo hizo?⟩ ⟨we know who they are : sabemos quiénes son⟩ **2** (*used in relative clauses*) : que, quien ⟨the lady who lives there : la señora que vive allí⟩ ⟨for those who wait : para los que esperan, para quienes esperan⟩

whodunit [hu:ˈdʌnɪt] *n* : novela *f* policíaca

whoever [hu:ˈɛvər] *pron* **1** : quienquiera que, quien ⟨whoever did it : quienquiera que lo hizo⟩ ⟨give it to whoever you want : dalo a quien quieras⟩ **2** (*used in questions*) : quién ⟨whoever could that be? : ¿quién podría ser?⟩

whole¹ [ˈho:l] *adj* **1** UNHURT : ileso **2** INTACT : intacto, sano **3** ENTIRE : entero, íntegro ⟨the whole island : toda la isla⟩ ⟨whole milk : leche entera⟩ **4 a whole lot** : muchísimo

whole² *n* **1** : todo *m* **2 as a whole** : en conjunto **3 on the whole** : en general

wholehearted [ˈho:lˈhɑrtəd] *adj* : sin reservas, incondicional

whole number *n* : entero *m*

wholesale¹ [ˈho:lˌseɪl] *v* **-saled; -saling** *vt* : vender al por mayor — *vi* : venderse al por mayor

wholesale² *adv* : al por mayor

wholesale³ *adj* **1** : al por mayor ⟨wholesale grocer : tendero al por mayor⟩ **2** TOTAL : total, absoluto ⟨wholesale slaughter : matanza sistemática⟩

wholesale⁴ *n* : mayoreo *m*

wholesaler [ˈho:lˌseɪlər] *n* : mayorista *mf*

wholesome [ˈho:lsəm] *adj* **1** : sano ⟨wholesome advice : consejo sano⟩ **2** HEALTHY : sano, saludable

whole wheat *adj* : de trigo integral

wholly [ˈho:li] *adv* **1** COMPLETELY : completamente **2** SOLELY : exclusivamente, únicamente

whom [ˈhu:m] *pron* **1** (*used in direct questions*) : a quién ⟨whom did you choose? : ¿a quién elegiste?⟩ **2** (*used in indirect questions*) : de quién, con quién, en quién ⟨I don't know whom to consult : no sé con quién consultar⟩ **3** (*used in relative clauses*) : que, a quien ⟨the lawyer whom I recommended to you : el abogado que te recomendé⟩

whomever [hu:mˈɛvər] *pron* WHOEVER : quienquiera, quien ⟨marry whomever you please : cásate con quien quieras⟩

whoop¹ [ˈʰwu:p, ˈʰwʊp] *vi* : gritar, chillar

whoop² *n* : grito *m*

whooping cough *n* : tos *f* ferina

whopper [ˈʰwɑpər] *n* **1** : cosa *f* enorme **2** LIE : mentira *f* colosal

whopping [ˈʰwɑpɪŋ] *adj* : enorme

whore [ˈhor] *n* : puta *f*, ramera *f*

whorl [ˈʰworl, ˈʰwərl] *n* : espiral *f*, espira *f* (de una concha), línea *f* (de una huella digital)

whose¹ [ˈhu:z] *adj* **1** (*used in questions*) : de quién ⟨whose truck is that? : ¿de quién es ese camión?⟩ **2** (*used in relative clauses*) : cuyo ⟨the person whose work is finished : la persona cuyo trabajo está terminado⟩

whose² *pron* : de quién ⟨tell me whose it was : dime de quién era⟩

why¹ [ˈʰwaɪ] *adv* : por qué ⟨why did you do it? : ¿por qué lo hizo?⟩

why² *n, pl* **whys** REASON : porqué *m*, razón *f*

why³ *conj* : por qué ⟨I know why he left : yo sé por qué salió⟩ ⟨there's no reason why it should exist : no hay razón para que exista⟩

why⁴ *interj* (*used to express surprise*) : ¡vaya!, ¡mira!

wick [ˈwɪk] *n* : mecha *f*

wicked [ˈwɪkəd] *adj* **1** EVIL : malo, malvado **2** MISCHIEVOUS : travieso, pícaro ⟨a wicked grin : una sonrisa traviesa⟩ **3** TERRIBLE : terrible, horrible ⟨a wicked storm : una tormenta horrible⟩

wickedly [ˈwɪkədli] *adv* : con maldad

wickedness [ˈwɪkədnəs] *n* : maldad *f*

wicker¹ [ˈwɪkər] *adj* : de mimbre

wicker² *n* **1** : mimbre *m* **2** → **wickerwork**

wickerwork [ˈwɪkərˌwərk] *n* : artículos *mpl* de mimbre

wicket [ˈwɪkət] *n* **1** WINDOW : ventanilla *f* **2** *or* **wicket gate** : postigo *m* **3** : aro *m* (en croquet), palos *mpl* (en críquet)

wide¹ [ˈwaɪd] *adv* **wider; widest 1** WIDELY : por todas partes ⟨to travel far and wide : viajar por todas partes⟩ **2** COMPLETELY : completamente, totalmente ⟨wide open : abierto de par en par⟩ **3 wide apart** : muy separados

wide² *adj* **wider; widest 1** VAST : vasto, extensivo ⟨a wide area : una área extensiva⟩ **2** : ancho ⟨three meters wide : tres metros de ancho⟩ **3** BROAD : ancho, amplio **4** *or* **wide-open** : muy abierto **5 wide of the mark** : desviado, lejos del blanco

wide-awake [ˈwaɪdəˈweɪk] *adj* : (completamente) despierto

wide-eyed [ˈwaɪdˈaɪd] *adj* **1** : con los ojos muy abiertos **2** NAIVE : inocente, ingenuo

widely [ˈwaɪdli] *adv* : extensivamente, por todas partes

widen [ˈwaɪdən] *vt* : ampliar, ensanchar — *vi* : ampliarse, ensancharse

widespread [ˈwaɪdˈspred] *adj* : extendido, extenso, difuso

widow¹ [ˈwɪˌdo:] *vt* : dejar viuda ⟨to be widowed : enviudar⟩

widow² *n* : viuda *f*

widower ['wɪdowər] *n* : viudo *m*
width ['wɪdθ] *n* : ancho *m*, anchura *f*
wield ['wi:ld] *vt* **1** USE : usar, manejar ⟨to wield a broom : usar una escoba⟩ **2** EXERCISE : ejercer ⟨to wield influence : influir⟩
wiener ['wi:nər] → **frankfurter**
wife ['waɪf] *n, pl* **wives** ['waɪvz] : esposa *f*, mujer *f*
wifely ['waɪfli] *adj* : de esposa, conyugal
wig ['wɪg] *n* : peluca *f*
wiggle[1] ['wɪgəl] *v* **-gled; -gling** *vt* : menear, contonear ⟨to wiggle one's hips : contonearse⟩ — *vi* : menearse
wiggle[2] *n* : meneo *m*, contoneo *m*
wiggly ['wɪgəli] *adj* **-glier; -est 1** : que se menea **2** WAVY : ondulado
wigwag ['wɪg,wæg] *vi* **-wagged; -wagging** : comunicar por señales
wigwam ['wɪg,wɑm] *n* : wigwam *m*
wild[1] ['waɪld] *adv* **1** → **wildly 2 to run wild** : descontrolarse
wild[2] *adj* **1** : salvaje, silvestre, cimarrón ⟨wild horses : caballos salvajes⟩ ⟨wild rice : arroz silvestre⟩ **2** DESOLATE : yermo, agreste **3** UNRULY : desenfrenado **4** CRAZY : loco, fantástico ⟨wild ideas : ideas locas⟩ **5** BARBAROUS : salvaje, bárbaro **6** ERRATIC : errático ⟨a wild throw : un tiro errático⟩
wild[3] *n* → **wilderness**
wild card *n* **1** : factor *m* desconocido **2** : comodín *m* (carta o símbolo)
wildcat ['waɪld,kæt] *n* **1** : gato *m* montés **2** BOBCAT : lince *m* rojo
wilderness ['wɪldərnəs] *n* : yermo *m*, desierto *m*
wildfire ['waɪld,faɪr] *n* **1** : fuego *m* descontrolado **2 to spread like wildfire** : propagarse como un reguero de pólvora
wildflower ['waɪld,flauər] *n* : flor *f* silvestre
wildfowl ['waɪld,faul] *n* : ave *f* de caza
wildlife ['waɪld,laɪf] *n* : fauna *f*
wildly ['waɪldli] *adv* **1** FRANTICALLY : frenéticamente, como un loco **2** EXTREMELY : extremadamente ⟨wildly happy : loco de felicidad⟩
wile[1] ['waɪl] *vt* **wiled; wiling** LURE : atraer
wile[2] *n* : ardid *m*, artimaña *f*
will[1] ['wɪl] *v, past* **would** ['wʊd]; *pres sing & pl* **will** *vt* WISH : querer ⟨do what you will : haz lo que quieras⟩ — *v aux* **1** (*expressing willingness*) ⟨no one would take the job : nadie aceptaría el trabajo⟩ ⟨I won't do it : no lo haré⟩ **2** (*expressing habitual action*) ⟨he will get angry over nothing : se pone furioso por cualquier cosa⟩ **3** (*forming the future tense*) ⟨tomorrow we will go shopping : mañana iremos de compras⟩ **4** (*expressing capacity*) ⟨the couch will hold three people : en el sofá cabrán tres personas⟩ **5** (*expressing determination*) ⟨I will go despite them : iré a pesar de

ellos⟩ **6** (*expressing probability*) ⟨that will be the mailman : eso ha de ser el cartero⟩ **7** (*expressing inevitability*) ⟨accidents will happen : los accidentes ocurrirán⟩ **8** (*expressing a command*) ⟨you will do as I say : harás lo que digo⟩
will[2] *vt* **1** ORDAIN : disponer, decretar ⟨if God wills it : si Dios lo dispone, si Dios quiere⟩ **2** : lograr a fuerza de voluntad ⟨they were willing him to succeed : estaban deseando que tuviera éxito⟩ **3** BEQUEATH : legar
will[3] *n* **1** DESIRE : deseo *m*, voluntad *f* **2** VOLITION : voluntad *f* ⟨free will : libre albedrío⟩ **3** WILLPOWER : voluntad *f*, fuerza *f* de voluntad ⟨a will of iron : una voluntad férrea⟩ **4** : testamento *m* ⟨to make a will : hacer testamento⟩
willful *or* **wilful** ['wɪlfəl] *adj* **1** OBSTINATE : obstinado, terco **2** INTENTIONAL : intencionado, deliberado — **willfully** *adv*
willing ['wɪlɪŋ] *adj* **1** INCLINED, READY : listo, dispuesto **2** OBLIGING : servicial, complaciente
willingly ['wɪlɪŋli] *adv* : con gusto
willingness ['wɪlɪŋnəs] *n* : buena voluntad *f*
willow ['wɪ,lo:] *n* : sauce *m*
willowy ['wɪlowi] *adj* : esbelto
willpower ['wɪl,pauər] *n* : voluntad *f*, fuerza *f* de voluntad
wilt ['wɪlt] *vi* **1** : marchitarse (dícese de las flores) **2** LANGUISH : debilitarse, languidecer
wily ['waɪli] *adj* **wilier; -est** : artero, astuto
wimp ['wɪmp] *n* **1** COWARD : gallina *f*, cobarde *mf* **2** WEAKLING : debilucho *m*, -cha *f*; alfeñique *m*
win[1] ['wɪn] *v* **won** ['wʌn]; **winning** *vi* : ganar — *vt* **1** : ganar, conseguir **2 to win over** : ganarse a **3 to win someone's heart** : conquistar a alguien
win[2] *n* : triunfo *m*, victoria *f*
wince[1] ['wɪnts] *vi* **winced; wincing** : estremecerse, hacer una mueca de dolor
wince[2] *n* : mueca *f* de dolor
winch ['wɪntʃ] *n* : torno *m*
wind[1] ['wɪnd] *vt* : dejar sin aliento ⟨to be winded : quedarse sin aliento⟩
wind[2] ['waɪnd] *v* **wound** ['waund]; **winding** *vi* MEANDER : serpentear — *vt* **1** COIL, ROLL : envolver, enrollar **2** TURN : hacer girar ⟨to wind a clock : darle cuerda a un reloj⟩
wind[3] ['wɪnd] *n* **1** : viento *m* ⟨against the wind : contra el viento⟩ **2** BREATH : aliento *m* **3** FLATULENCE : flatulencia *f*, ventosidad *f* **4 to get wind of** : enterarse de
wind[4] ['waɪnd] *n* **1** TURN : vuelta *f* **2** BEND : recodo *m*, curva *f*
windbreak ['wɪnd,breɪk] *n* : barrera *f* contra el viento, abrigadero *m*
windfall ['wɪnd,fɔl] *n* **1** : fruta *f* caída **2** : beneficio *m* imprevisto
wind instrument *n* : instrumento *m* de viento

windlass ['wɪndləs] *n* : cabrestante *m*
windmill ['wɪnd,mɪl] *n* : molino *m* de viento
window ['wɪn,do:] *n* **1** : ventana *f* (de un edificio o una computadora), ventanilla *f* (de un vehículo o avión), vitrina *f* (de una tienda) **2** → **windowpane**
windowpane ['wɪn,do:,peɪn] *n* : vidrio *m*
window–shop ['wɪndo:,ʃɑp] *vi* -**shopped**; -**shopping** : mirar las vitrinas
windpipe ['wɪnd,paɪp] *n* : tráquea *f*
windshield ['wɪnd,ʃi:ld] *n* **1** : parabrisas *m* **2 windshield wiper** : limpiaparabrisas *m*
windup ['waɪnd,ʌp] *n* : conclusión *f*
wind up *vt* END : terminar, concluir — *vi* : terminar, acabar
windward¹ ['wɪndwərd] *adj* : de barlovento
windward² *n* : barlovento *m*
windy ['wɪndi] *adj* **windier**; -**est 1** : ventoso ⟨it's windy : hace viento⟩ **2** VERBOSE : verboso, prolijo
wine¹ ['waɪn] *v* **wined**; **wining** *vi* : beber vino — *vt* **to wine and dine** : agasajar
wine² *n* : vino *m*
wing¹ ['wɪŋ] *vi* FLY : volar
wing² *n* **1** : ala *f* (de un ave, un avión, o un edificio) **2** FACTION : ala *f* ⟨the right wing of the party : el ala derecha del partido⟩ **3 wings** *npl* : bastidores *mpl* (de un teatro) **4 on the wing** : al vuelo, volando **5 under one's wing** : bajo el cargo de uno
winged ['wɪŋd, 'wɪŋəd] *adj* : alado
wink¹ ['wɪŋk] *vi* **1** : guiñar el ojo **2** BLINK : pestañear, parpadear **3** FLICKER : parpadear, titilar
wink² *n* **1** : guiño *m* (del ojo) **2** NAP : siesta *f* ⟨not to sleep a wink : no pegar el ojo⟩
winner ['wɪnər] *n* : ganador *m*, -dora *f*
winning ['wɪnɪŋ] *adj* **1** VICTORIOUS : ganador **2** CHARMING : encantador
winnings ['wɪnɪŋz] *npl* : ganancias *fpl*
winnow ['wɪ,no:] *vt* : aventar (el grano, etc.)
winsome ['wɪnsəm] *adj* CHARMING : encantador
winter¹ ['wɪntər] *adj* : invernal, de invierno
winter² *n* : invierno *m*
wintergreen ['wɪntər,gri:n] *n* : gaultería *f*
wintertime ['wɪntər,taɪm] *n* : invierno *m*
wintry ['wɪntri] *adj* **wintrier**; -**est 1** WINTER : invernal, de invierno **2** COLD : frío ⟨she gave us a wintry greeting : nos saludó fríamente⟩
wipe¹ ['waɪp] *vt* **wiped**; **wiping 1** : limpiar, pasarle un trapo a ⟨to wipe one's feet : limpiarse los pies⟩ **2 to wipe away** : enjugar (lágrimas), borrar (una memoria) **3 to wipe out** ANNIHILATE : aniquilar, destruir
wipe² *n* : pasada *f* (con un trapo, etc.)

wire¹ ['waɪr] *vt* **wired**; **wiring 1** : instalar el cableado en (una casa, etc.) **2** BIND : atar con alambre **3** TELEGRAPH : telegrafiar, mandarle un telegrama (a alguien)
wire² *n* **1** : alambre *m* ⟨barbed wire : alambre de púas⟩ **2** : cable *m* (eléctrico o telefónico) **3** CABLEGRAM, TELEGRAM : telegrama *m*, cable *m*
wireless ['waɪrləs] *adj* : inalámbrico
wiretapping ['waɪr,tæpɪŋ] *n* : intervención *f* electrónica
wiring ['waɪrɪŋ] *n* : cableado *m*
wiry ['waɪri] *adj* **wirier**; -**est 1** : hirsuto, tieso (dícese del pelo) **2** : esbelto y musculoso (dícese del cuerpo)
wisdom ['wɪzdəm] *n* **1** KNOWLEDGE : sabiduría *f* **2** JUDGMENT, SENSE : sensatez *f*
wisdom tooth *n* : muela *f* de juicio
wise¹ ['waɪz] *adj* **wiser**; **wisest 1** LEARNED : sabio **2** SENSIBLE : sabio, sensato, prudente **3** KNOWLEDGEABLE : entendido, enterado ⟨they're wise to his tricks : conocen muy bien sus mañas⟩
wise² *n* : manera *f*, modo *m* ⟨in no wise : de ninguna manera⟩
wisecrack ['waɪz,kræk] *n* : broma *f*, chiste *m*
wisely ['waɪzli] *adv* : sabiamente, sensatamente
wish¹ ['wɪʃ] *vt* **1** WANT : desear, querer **2 to wish (something) for** : desear ⟨they wished me well : me desearon lo mejor⟩ — *vi* **1** : pedir (como deseo) **2** : querer ⟨as you wish : como quieras⟩
wish² *n* **1** : deseo *m* ⟨to grant a wish : conceder un deseo⟩ **2 wishes** *npl* : saludos *mpl*, recuerdos *mpl* ⟨to send best wishes : mandar muchos recuerdos⟩
wishbone ['wɪʃ,bo:n] *n* : espoleta *f*
wishful ['wɪʃfəl] *adj* **1** HOPEFUL : deseoso, lleno de esperanza **2 wishful thinking** : ilusiones *fpl*
wishy–washy ['wɪʃi,wɔʃi, -,wɑʃi] *adj* : insípido, soso
wisp ['wɪsp] *n* **1** BUNCH : manojo *m* (de paja) **2** STRAND : mechón *m* (de pelo) **3** : voluta *f* (de humo)
wispy ['wɪspi] *adj* **wispier**; -**est** : tenue, ralo (dícese del pelo)
wisteria [wɪs'tɪriə] *n* : glicinia *f*
wistful ['wɪstfəl] *adj* : añorante, anhelante, melancólico — **wistfully** *adv*
wistfulness ['wɪstfəlnəs] *n* : añoranza *f*, melancolía *f*
wit ['wɪt] *n* **1** INTELLIGENCE : inteligencia *f* **2** CLEVERNESS : ingenio *m*, gracia *f*, agudeza *f* **3** HUMOR : humorismo *m* **4** JOKER : chistoso *m*, -sa *f* **5 wits** *npl* : razón *f*, buen juicio *m* ⟨scared out of one's wits : muerto de miedo⟩ ⟨to be at one's wits' end : estar desesperado⟩
witch ['wɪtʃ] *n* : bruja *f*
witchcraft ['wɪtʃ,kræft] *n* : brujería *f*, hechicería *f*

witch doctor *n* : hechicero *m*, -ra *f*

witchery [ˈwɪtʃəri] *n*, *pl* **-eries** **1** → **witch-craft** **2** CHARM : encanto *m*

witch–hunt [ˈwɪtʃˌhʌnt] *n* : caza *f* de brujas

with [ˈwɪð, ˈwɪθ] *prep* **1** : con ⟨I'm going with you : voy contigo⟩ ⟨coffee with milk : café con leche⟩ **2** AGAINST : con ⟨to argue with someone : discutir con alguien⟩ **3** (*used in descriptions*) : con, de ⟨the girl with red hair : la muchacha de pelo rojo⟩ **4** (*indicating manner, means, or cause*) : con ⟨to cut with a knife : cortar con un cuchillo⟩ ⟨fix it with tape : arréglalo con cinta⟩ ⟨with luck : consuerte⟩ **5** DESPITE : a pesar de, aún con ⟨with all his work, the business failed : a pesar de su trabajo, el negocio fracasó⟩ **6** REGARDING : con respecto a, con ⟨the trouble with your plan : el problema con su plan⟩ **7** ACCORDING TO : según ⟨it varies with the season : varía según la estación⟩ **8** (*indicating support or understanding*) : con ⟨I'm with you all the way : estoy contigo hasta el fin⟩

withdraw [wɪðˈdrɔ, wɪθ-] *v* **-drew** [-ˈdruː]; **-drawn** [-ˈdrɔn]; **-drawing** *vt* **1** REMOVE : retirar, apartar, sacar (dinero) **2** RETRACT : retractarse de — *vi* : retirarse, recluirse (de la sociedad)

withdrawal [wɪðˈdrɔəl, wɪθ-] *n* **1** : retirada *f*, retiro *m* (de fondos, etc.), retraimiento *m* (social) **2** RETRACTION : retractación *f* **3 withdrawal symptoms** : síndrome *m* de abstinencia

withdrawn [wɪðˈdrɔn, wɪθ-] *adj* : retraído, reservado, introvertido

wither [ˈwɪðər] *vt* : marchitar, agostar — *vi* **1** WILT : marchitarse **2** WEAKEN : decaer, debilitarse

withhold [wɪθˈhoːld, wɪð-] *vt* **-held** [-ˈhld]; **-holding** : retener (fondos), aplazar (una decisión), negar (permiso, etc.)

within[1] [wɪðˈɪn, wɪθ-] *adv* : dentro

within[2] *prep* **1** : dentro de ⟨within the limits : dentro de los límites⟩ **2** (*in expressions of distance*) : a menos de ⟨within 10 miles of the ocean : a menos de 10 millas del mar⟩ **3** (*in expressions of time*) : dentro de ⟨within an hour : dentro de una hora⟩ ⟨within a month of her birthday : a poco menos de un mes de su cumpleaños⟩

without[1] [wɪðˈaut, wɪθ-] *adv* **1** OUTSIDE : fuera **2 to do without** : pasar sin algo

without[2] *prep* **1** OUTSIDE : fuera de **2** : sin ⟨without fear : sin temor⟩ ⟨he left without his briefcase : se fue sin su portafolios⟩

withstand [wɪθˈstænd, wɪð-] *vt* **-stood** [-ˈstʊd]; **-standing** **1** BEAR : aguantar, soportar **2** RESIST : resistir, resistirse a

witless [ˈwɪtləs] *adj* : estúpido, tonto

witness[1] [ˈwɪtnəs] *vt* **1** SEE : presenciar, ver, ser testigo de **2** : atestiguar (una firma, etc.) — *vi* TESTIFY : atestiguar, testimoniar

witness[2] *n* **1** TESTIMONY : testimonio *m* ⟨to bear witness : atestiguar, testimoniar⟩ **2** : testigo *mf* ⟨witness for the prosecution : testigo de cargo⟩

witticism [ˈwɪtəˌsɪzəm] *n* : agudeza *f*, ocurrencia *f*

witty [ˈwɪti] *adj* **-tier; -est** : ingenioso, ocurrente, gracioso

wives → **wife**

wizard [ˈwɪzərd] *n* **1** SORCERER : mago *m*, brujo *m*, hechicero *m* **2** : genio *m* ⟨a math wizard : un genio en matemáticas⟩

wizened [ˈwɪzənd, ˈwiː-] *adj* : arrugado, marchito

wobble[1] [ˈwabəl] *vi* **-bled; -bling** : bambolearse, tambalearse, temblar (dícese de la voz)

wobble[2] *n* : tambaleo *m*, bamboleo *m*

wobbly [ˈwabəli] *adj* : bamboleante, tambaleante, inestable

woe [ˈwoː] *n* **1** GRIEF, MISFORTUNE : desgracia *f*, infortunio *m*, aflicción *f* **2 woes** *npl* TROUBLES : penas *fpl*, males *mpl*

woeful [ˈwoːfəl] *adj* **1** SORROWFUL : afligido, apenado, triste **2** UNFORTUNATE : desgraciado, infortunado **3** DEPLORABLE : lamentable

woke, woken → **wake**[1]

wolf[1] [ˈwʊlf] *vt or* **to wolf down** : engullir

wolf[2] *n, pl* **wolves** [ˈwʊlvz] : lobo *m*, -ba *f*

wolfram [ˈwʊlfrəm] → **tungsten**

wolverine [ˌwʊlvəˈriːn] *n* : glotón *m* (animal)

woman [ˈwʊmən] *n, pl* **women** [ˈwɪmən] : mujer *f*

womanhood [ˈwʊmənˌhʊd] *n* **1** : condición *f* de mujer **2** WOMEN : mujeres *fpl*

womanly [ˈwʊmənli] *adj* : femenino

womb [ˈwuːm] *n* : útero *m*, matriz *f*

won → **win**

wonder[1] [ˈwʌndər] *vi* **1** SPECULATE : preguntarse, pensar ⟨to wonder about : preguntarse por⟩ **2** MARVEL : asombrarse, maravillarse — *vt* : preguntarse ⟨I wonder if they're coming : me pregunto si vendrán⟩

wonder[2] *n* **1** MARVEL : maravilla *f*, milagro *m* ⟨to work wonders : hacer maravillas⟩ **2** AMAZEMENT : asombro *m*

wonderful [ˈwʌndərfəl] *adj* : maravilloso, estupendo

wonderfully [ˈwʌndərfəli] *adv* : maravillosamente, de maravilla

wonderland [ˈwʌndərˌlænd, -lənd] *n* : país *m* de las maravillas

wonderment [ˈwʌndərmənt] *n* : asombro *m*

wondrous [ˈwʌndrəs] → **wonderful**

wont[1] [ˈwɔnt, ˈwoːnt, ˈwant] *adj* : acostumbrado, habituado

wont[2] *n* : hábito *m*, costumbre *f*

won't [ˈwoːnt] (*contraction of* **will not**) → **will**[1]

woo [ˈwuː] *vt* **1** COURT : cortejar **2** : buscar el apoyo de (clientes, votantes, etc.)

wood¹ ['wʊd] *adj* : de madera

wood² *n* **1** *or* **woods** *npl* FOREST : bosque *m* **2** : madera *f* (materia) **3** FIREWOOD : leña *f*

woodchuck ['wʊd,ʧʌk] *n* : marmota *f* de América

woodcut ['wʊd,kʌt] *n* **1** : plancha *f* de madera (para imprimir imágenes) **2** : grabado *m* en madera

woodcutter ['wʊd,kʌt̬ər] *n* : leñador *m*, -dora *f*

wooded ['wʊdəd] *adj* : arbolado, boscoso

wooden ['wʊdən] *adj* **1** : de madera ⟨a wooden cross : una cruz de madera⟩ **2** STIFF : rígido, inexpresivo (dícese del estilo, de la cara, etc.)

woodland ['wʊdlənd, -,lænd] *n* : bosque *m*

woodpecker ['wʊd,pɛkər] *n* : pájaro *m* carpintero

woodshed ['wʊd,ʃɛd] *n* : leñera *f*

woodsman ['wʊdzmən] → **woodcutter**

woodwind ['wʊd,wɪnd] *n* : instrumento *m* de viento de madera

woodworking ['wʊd,wərkɪŋ] *n* : carpintería *f*

woody ['wʊdi] *adj* **woodier; -est 1** → **wooded 2** : leñoso ⟨woody plants : plantas leñosas⟩ **3** : leñoso (dícese de la textura), a madera (dícese del aroma, etc.)

woof ['wʊf] → **weft**

wool ['wʊl] *n* : lana *f*

woolen¹ *or* **woollen** ['wʊlən] *adj* : de lana

woolen² *or* **woollen** *n* **1** : lana *f* (tela) **2 woolens** *npl* : prendas *fpl* de lana

woolly ['wʊli] *adj* **-lier; -est 1** : lanudo **2** CONFUSED : confuso, vago

woozy ['wu:zi] *adj* **-zier; -est** : mareado

word¹ ['wərd] *vt* : expresar, formular, redactar

word² *n* **1** : palabra *f*, vocablo *m*, voz *f* ⟨word for word : palabra por palabra⟩ ⟨in one's own words : en sus propias palabras⟩ ⟨words fail me : me quedo sin habla⟩ **2** REMARK : palabra *f* ⟨by word of mouth : de palabra⟩ ⟨to have a word with : hablar (dos palabras) con⟩ **3** COMMAND : orden *f* ⟨to give the word : dar la orden⟩ ⟨just say the word : no tienes que decirlo⟩ **4** MESSAGE, NEWS : noticias *fpl* ⟨is there any word from her? : ¿hay noticias de ella?⟩ ⟨to send word : mandar un recado⟩ **5** PROMISE : palabra *f* ⟨to keep one's word : cumplir uno su palabra⟩ **6 words** *npl* QUARREL : palabra *f*, riña *f* ⟨to have words with : tener unas palabras con, reñir con⟩ **7 words** *npl* TEXT : letra *f* (de una canción, etc.)

wordiness ['wərdinəs] *n* : verbosidad *f*

wording ['wərdɪŋ] *n* : redacción *f*, lenguaje *m* (de un documento)

word processing *n* : procesamiento *m* de textos

word processor *n* : procesador *m* de textos

wordy ['wərdi] *adj* **wordier; -est** : verboso, prolijo

wore → **wear¹**

work¹ ['wərk] *v* **worked** ['wərkt] *or* **wrought** ['rɔt]; **working** *vt* **1** OPERATE : trabajar, operar ⟨to work a machine : operar una máquina⟩ **2** : lograr, conseguir (algo) con esfuerzo ⟨to work one's way up : lograr subir por sus propios esfuerzos⟩ **3** EFFECT : efectuar, llevar a cabo, obrar (milagros) **4** MAKE, SHAPE : elaborar, fabricar, formar ⟨a beautifully wrought vase : un florero bellamente elaborado⟩ **5 to work up** : estimular, excitar ⟨don't get worked up : no te agites⟩ — *vi* **1** LABOR : trabajar ⟨to work full-time : trabajar a tiempo completo⟩ **2** FUNCTION : funcionar, servir

work² *adj* : laboral

work³ *n* **1** LABOR : trabajo *m*, labor *f* **2** EMPLOYMENT : trabajo *m*, empleo *m* **3** TASK : tarea *f*, faena *f* **4** DEED : obra *f*, labor *f* ⟨works of charity : obras de caridad⟩ **5** : obra *f* (de arte o literatura) **6** → **workmanship 7 works** *npl* FACTORY : fábrica *f* **8 works** *npl* MECHANISM : mecanismo *m*

workable ['wərkəbəl] *adj* **1** : explotable (dícese de una mina, etc.) **2** FEASIBLE : factible, realizable

workaday ['wərkə,deɪ] *adj* : ordinario, banal

workbench ['wərk,bɛnʧ] *n* : mesa *f* de trabajo

workday ['wərk,deɪ] *n* **1** : jornada *f* laboral **2** WEEKDAY : día *m* hábil, día *m* laborable

worker ['wərkər] *n* : trabajador *m*, -dora *f*; obrero *m*, -ra *f*

working ['wərkɪŋ] *adj* **1** : que trabaja ⟨working mothers : madres que trabajan⟩ ⟨the working class : la clase obrera⟩ **2** : de trabajo ⟨working hours : horas de trabajo⟩ **3** FUNCTIONING : que funciona, operativo **4** SUFFICIENT : suficiente ⟨a working majority : una mayoría suficiente⟩ ⟨working knowledge : conocimientos básicos⟩

workingman ['wərkɪŋ,mæn] *n*, *pl* **-men** [-mən, -,mɛn] : obrero *m*

workman ['wərkmən] *n*, *pl* **-men** [-mən, -,mɛn] **1** → **workingman 2** ARTISAN : artesano *m*

workmanlike ['wərkmən,laɪk] *adj* : bien hecho, competente

workmanship ['wərkmən,ʃɪp] *n* **1** WORK : ejecución *f*, trabajo *m* **2** CRAFTSMANSHIP : artesanía *f*, destreza *f*

workout ['wərk,aʊt] *n* : ejercicios *mpl* físicos, entrenamiento *m*

work out *vt* **1** DEVELOP, PLAN : idear, planear, desarrollar **2** RESOLVE : solucionar, resolver ⟨to work out the answer : calcular la solución⟩ — *vi* **1** TURN OUT : resultar **2** SUCCEED : lograr, dar resultado, salir bien **3** EXERCISE : hacer ejercicio

workroom ['wərk,ruːm, -,rʊm] *n* : taller *m*

workshop ['wərk,ʃɑp] *n* : taller *m* ⟨ceramics workshop : taller de cerámica⟩

workstation ['wərk,steɪʃən] *n* : estación *f* de trabajo (en informática)

world[1] ['wərld] *adj* : mundial, del mundo ⟨world championship : campeonato mundial⟩

world[2] *n* : mundo *m* ⟨around the world : alrededor del mundo⟩ ⟨a world of possibilities : un mundo de posibilidades⟩ ⟨to think the world of someone : tener a alguien en alta estima⟩ ⟨to be worlds apart : no tener nada que ver (uno con otro)⟩

worldly ['wərldli] *adj* **1** : mundano ⟨wordly goods : bienes materiales⟩ **2** SOPHISTICATED : sofisticado, de mundo

worldwide[1] ['wərld,waɪd] *adv* : mundialmente, en todo el mundo

worldwide[2] *adj* : global, mundial

World Wide Web *n* : World Wide Web *f*

worm[1] ['wərm] *vi* CRAWL : arrastrarse, deslizarse (como gusano) — *vt* **1** : desparasitar (un animal) **2 to worm one's way into** : introducirse en ⟨he wormed his way into her confidence : se ganó su confianza⟩ **3 to worm something out of someone** : sonsacarle algo a alguien

worm[2] *n* **1** : gusano *m*, lombriz *f* **2 worms** *npl* : lombrices *fpl* (parásitos)

wormy ['wərmi] *adj* **wormier; -est** : infestado de gusanos

worn *pp* → **wear**[1]

worn–out ['worn'aʊt] *adj* **1** USED : gastado, desgastado **2** TIRED : agotado

worried ['wərid] *adj* : inquieto, preocupado

worrier ['wəriər] *n* : persona *f* que se preocupa mucho

worrisome ['wərisəm] *adj* **1** DISTURBING : preocupante, inquietante **2** : que se preocupa mucho (dícese de una persona)

worry[1] ['wəri] *v* **-ried; -rying** *vt* : preocupar, inquietar — *vi* : preocuparse, inquietarse, angustiarse

worry[2] *n*, *pl* **-ries** : preocupación *f*, inquietud *f*, angustia *f*

worse[1] ['wərs] *adv* (*comparative of* **bad** *or of* **ill**) : peor

worse[2] *adj* (*comparative of* **bad** *or of* **ill**) : peor ⟨from bad to worse : de mal en peor⟩ ⟨to get worse : empeorar⟩ ⟨to feel worse : sentirse peor⟩

worse[3] *n* : estado *m* peor ⟨to take a turn for the worse : ponerse peor⟩ ⟨so much the worse : tanto peor⟩

worsen ['wərsən] *vt* : empeorar — *vi* : empeorar(se)

worship[1] ['wərʃəp] *v* **-shiped** *or* **-shipped; -shiping** *or* **-shipping** *vt* : adorar, venerar ⟨to worship God : adorar a Dios⟩ — *vi* : practicar una religión

worship[2] *n* : adoración *f*, culto *m*

worshiper *or* **worshipper** ['wərʃəpər] *n* : devoto *m*, -ta *f*; adorador *m*, -dora *f*

worst[1] ['wərst] *vt* DEFEAT : derrotar

worst[2] *adv* (*superlative of* **ill** *or of* **bad** *or* **badly**) : peor ⟨the worst dressed of all : el peor vestido de todos⟩

worst[3] *adj* (*superlative of* **bad** *or of* **ill**) : peor ⟨the worst movie : la peor película⟩

worst[4] *n* **the worst** : lo peor, el (la) peor ⟨the worst is over : ya ha pasado lo peor⟩

worsted ['wʊstəd, 'wərstəd] *n* : estambre *m*

worth[1] ['wərθ] *n* **1** : valor *m* (monetario) ⟨ten dollars' worth of gas : diez dólares de gasolina⟩ **2** MERIT : valor *m*, mérito *m*, valía *f* ⟨an employee of great worth : un empleado de gran valía⟩

worth[2] *prep* **to be worth** : valer ⟨her holdings are worth a fortune : sus propiedades valen una fortuna⟩ ⟨it's not worth it : no vale la pena⟩

worthiness ['wərðinəs] *n* : mérito *m*

worthless ['wərθləs] *adj* **1** : sin valor ⟨worthless trinkets : chucherías sin valor⟩ **2** USELESS : inútil

worthwhile [wərθ'hwaɪl] *adj* : que vale la pena

worthy ['wərði] *adj* **-thier; -est 1** : digno ⟨worthy of promotion : digno de un ascenso⟩ **2** COMMENDABLE : meritorio, encomiable

would ['wʊd] *past of* **will 1** (*expressing preference*) ⟨I would rather go alone than with her : preferiría ir sola que con ella⟩ **2** (*expressing intent*) ⟨those who would ban certain books : aquellos que prohibirían ciertos libros⟩ **3** (*expressing habitual action*) ⟨he would often take his kids to the park : solía llevar a sus hijos al parque⟩ **4** (*expressing contingency*) ⟨I would go if I had the money : iría yo si tuviera el dinero⟩ **5** (*expressing probability*) ⟨she would have won if she hadn't tripped : habría ganado si no hubiera tropezado⟩ **6** (*expressing a request*) ⟨would you kindly help me with this? : ¿tendría la bondad de ayudarme con esto?⟩

would–be ['wʊd'biː] *adj* : potencial ⟨a would-be celebrity : un aspirante a celebridad⟩

wouldn't ['wʊd'ənt] (*contraction of* **would not**) → **would**

wound[1] ['wuːnd] *vt* : herir

wound[2] *n* : herida *f*

wound[3] ['waʊnd] → **wind**[2]

wove, woven → **weave**[1]

wow ['waʊ] *interj* : ¡guau!, ¡híjole! *Mex*, ¡hala! *Spain*

wrangle[1] ['ræŋgəl] *vi* **-gled; -gling** : discutir, reñir ⟨to wrangle over : discutir por⟩

wrangle[2] *n* : riña *f*, disputa *f*

wrap[1] ['ræp] *v* **wrapped; wrapping** *vt* **1** COVER : envolver, cubrir ⟨to wrap a package : envolver un paquete⟩

⟨wrapped in mystery : envuelto en misterio⟩ **2** ENCIRCLE : rodear, ceñir ⟨to wrap one's arms around someone : estrechar a alguien⟩ **3 to wrap up** FINISH : darle fin a (algo) — *vi* **1** COIL : envolverse, enroscarse **2 to wrap up** DRESS : abrigarse ⟨wrap up warmly : abrígate bien⟩

wrap² *n* **1** WRAPPER : envoltura *f* **2** : prenda *f* que envuelve (como un chal, una bata, etc.)

wrapper ['ræpər] *n* : envoltura *f*, envoltorio *m*

wrapping ['ræpɪŋ] *n* : envoltura *f*, envoltorio *m*

wrath ['ræθ] *n* : ira *f*, cólera *f*

wrathful ['ræθfəl] *adj* : iracundo

wreak ['ri:k] *vt* : infligir, causar ⟨to wreak havoc : crear caos, causar estragos⟩

wreath ['ri:θ] *n, pl* **wreaths** ['ri:ðz, 'ri:θs] : corona *f* (de flores, etc.)

wreathe ['ri:ð] *vt* **wreathed; wreathing** **1** ADORN : coronar (de flores, etc.) **2** ENVELOP : envolver ⟨wreathed in mist : envuelto en niebla⟩

wreck¹ ['rɛk] *vt* : destruir, arruinar, estrellar (un automóvil), naufragar (un barco)

wreck² *n* **1** WRECKAGE : restos *mpl* (de un buque naufragado, un avión siniestrado, etc.) **2** RUIN : ruina *f*, desastre *m* ⟨this place is a wreck! : ¡este lugar está hecho un desastre!⟩ ⟨to be a nervous wreck : tener los nervios destrozados⟩

wreckage ['rɛkɪʤ] *n* : restos *mpl* (de un buque naufragado, un avión siniestrado, etc.), ruinas *fpl* (de un edificio)

wrecker ['rɛkər] *n* **1** TOW TRUCK : grúa *f* **2** : desguazador *m* (de autos, barcos, etc.), demoledor *m* (de edificios)

wren ['rɛn] *n* : chochín *m*

wrench¹ ['rɛntʃ] *vt* **1** PULL : arrancar (de un tirón) **2** SPRAIN, TWIST : torcerse (un tobillo, un músculo, etc.)

wrench² *n* **1** TUG : tirón *m*, jalón *m* **2** SPRAIN : torcedura *f* **3** *or* **monkey wrench** : llave *f* inglesa

wrest ['rɛst] *vt* : arrancar

wrestle¹ ['rɛsəl] *v* **-tled; -tling** *vi* **1** : luchar, practicar la lucha (en deportes) **2** STRUGGLE : luchar ⟨to wrestle with a dilemma : lidiar con un dilema⟩ — *vt* : luchar contra

wrestle² *n* STRUGGLE : lucha *f*

wrestler ['rɛsələr] *n* : luchador *m*, -dora *f*

wrestling ['rɛsəlɪŋ] *n* : lucha *f*

wretch ['rɛtʃ] *n* : infeliz *mf*; desgraciado *m*, -da *f*

wretched ['rɛtʃəd] *adj* **1** MISERABLE, UNHAPPY : desdichado, afligido ⟨I feel wretched : me siento muy mal⟩ **2** UNFORTUNATE : miserable, desgraciado, lastimoso ⟨wretched weather : tiempo espantoso⟩ **3** INFERIOR : inferior, malo

wretchedly ['rɛtʃədli] *adv* : miserablemente, lamentablemente

wriggle ['rɪgəl] *vi* **-gled; -gling** : retorcerse, menearse

wring ['rɪŋ] *vt* **wrung** ['rʌŋ]; **wringing** **1** *or* **to wring out** : escurrir, exprimir (el lavado) **2** EXTRACT : arrancar, sacar (por la fuerza) **3** TWIST : torcer, retorcer **4 to wring someone's heart** : partirle el corazón a alguien

wringer ['rɪŋər] *n* : escurridor *m*

wrinkle¹ ['rɪŋkəl] *v* **-kled; -kling** *vt* : arrugar — *vi* : arrugarse

wrinkle² *n* : arruga *f*

wrinkly ['rɪŋkəli] *adj* **wrinklier; -est** : arrugado

wrist ['rɪst] *n* **1** : muñeca *f* (en anatomía) **2** *or* **wristband** ['rɪst-ˌbænd] CUFF : puño *m*

writ ['rɪt] *n* : orden *f* (judicial)

write ['raɪt] *v* **wrote** ['ro:t]; **written** ['rɪtən]; **writing** : escribir

write down *vt* : apuntar, anotar

write off *vt* CANCEL : cancelar

writer ['raɪtər] *n* : escritor *m*, -tora *f*

writhe ['raɪð] *vi* **writhed; writhing** : retorcerse

writing ['raɪtɪŋ] *n* **1** : escritura *f* **2** HANDWRITING : letra *f* **3 writings** *npl* WORKS : escritos *mpl*, obra *f*

wrong¹ ['rɔŋ] *vt* **wronged; wronging** : ofender, ser injusto con

wrong² *adv* : mal, incorrectamente

wrong³ *adj* **wronger** ['rɔŋər]; **wrongest** ['rɔŋəst] **1** EVIL, SINFUL : malo, injusto, inmoral **2** IMPROPER, UNSUITABLE : inadecuado, inapropiado, malo **3** INCORRECT : incorrecto, erróneo, malo ⟨a wrong answer : una mala respuesta⟩ **4 to be wrong** : equivocarse, estar equivocado

wrong⁴ *n* **1** INJUSTICE : injusticia *f*, mal *m* **2** OFFENSE : ofensa *f*, agravio *m* (en derecho) **3 to be in the wrong** : haber hecho mal, estar equivocado

wrongdoer ['rɔŋˌdu:ər] *n* : malhechor *m*, -chora *f*

wrongdoing ['rɔŋˌdu:ɪŋ] *n* : fechoría *f*, maldad *f*

wrongful ['rɔŋfəl] *adj* **1** UNJUST : injusto **2** UNLAWFUL : ilegal

wrongly ['rɔŋli] *adv* **1** : injustamente **2** INCORRECTLY : erróneamente, incorrectamente

wrote → **write**

wrought ['rɔt] *adj* **1** SHAPED : formado, forjado ⟨wrought iron : hierro forjado⟩ **2** *or* **wrought up** : agitado, excitado

wrung → **wring**

wry ['raɪ] *adj* **wrier** ['raɪər]; **wriest** ['raɪəst] **1** TWISTED : torcido ⟨a wry neck : un cuello torcido⟩ **2** : irónico, sardónico (dícese del humor)

X

x¹ *n, pl* **x's** *or* **xs** ['ɛksəz] **1** : vigésima cuarta letra del alfabeto inglés **2** : incógnita *f* (en matemáticas)

x² ['ks] *vt* **x–ed** ['ɛkst]; **x–ing** *or* **x'ing** ['ɛksɪŋ] DELETE : tachar

xenon ['ziː,nɑn, 'zɛ-] *n* : xenón *m*

xenophobia [,zɛnə'foːbiə, ,ziː-] *n* : xenofobia *f*

Xmas ['krɪsməs] *n* : Navidad *f*

x-ray ['ɛks,reɪ] *vt* : radiografiar

X ray ['ɛks,reɪ] *n* **1** : rayo *m* X **2** *or* **X–ray photograph** : radiografía *f*

xylophone ['zaɪlə,foːn] *n* : xilófono *m*

Y

y ['waɪ] *n, pl* **y's** *or* **ys** ['waɪz] : vigésima quinta letra del alfabeto inglés

yacht¹ ['jɑt] *vi* : navegar (a vela), ir en yate ⟨to go yachting : irse a navegar⟩

yacht² *n* : yate *m*

yak ['jæk] *n* : yac *m*

yam ['jæm] *n* **1** : ñame *m* **2** SWEET POTATO : batata *f*, boniato *m*

yank¹ ['jæŋk] *vt* : tirar de, jalar, darle un tirón a

yank² *n* : tirón *m*

Yankee ['jæŋki] *n* : yanqui *mf*

yap¹ ['jæp] *vi* **yapped; yapping 1** BARK, YELP : ladrar, gañir **2** CHATTER : cotorrear *fam*, parlotear *fam*

yap² *n* : ladrido *m*, gañido *m*

yard ['jɑrd] *n* **1** : yarda *f* (medida) **2** SPAR : verga *f* (de un barco) **3** COURTYARD : patio *m* **4** : jardín *m* (de una casa) **5** : depósito *m* (de mercancías, etc.)

yardage ['jɑrdɪʤ] *n* : medida *f* en yardas

yardarm ['jɑrd,ɑrm] *n* : penol *m*

yardstick ['jɑrd,stɪk] *n* **1** : vara *f* **2** CRITERION : criterio *m*, norma *f*

yarn ['jɑrn] *n* **1** : hilado *m* **2** TALE : historia *f*, cuento *m* ⟨to spin a yarn : inventar una historia⟩

yawl ['jɔl] *n* : yola *f*

yawn¹ ['jɔn] *vi* **1** : bostezar **2** OPEN : abrirse

yawn² *n* : bostezo *m*

ye ['jiː] *pron* : vosotros, vosotras

yea¹ ['jeɪ] *adv* YES : sí

yea² *n* : voto *m* a favor

year ['jɪr] *n* **1** : año *m* ⟨last year : el año pasado⟩ ⟨he's ten years old : tiene diez años⟩ **2** : curso *m*, año *m* (escolar) **3 years** *npl* AGES : siglos *mpl*, años *mpl* ⟨I haven't seen them in years : hace siglos que no los veo⟩

yearbook ['jɪr,bʊk] *n* : anuario *m*

yearling ['jɪrlɪŋ, 'jərlən] *n* : animal *m* menor de dos año

yearly¹ ['jɪrli] *adv* : cada año, anualmente

yearly² *adj* : anual

yearn ['jərn] *vi* : anhelar, ansiar

yearning ['jərnɪŋ] *n* : anhelo *m*

yeast ['jiːst] *n* : levadura *f*

yell¹ ['jɛl] *vi* : gritar, chillar — *vt* : gritar

yell² *n* : grito *m*, alarido *m* ⟨to let out a yell : dar un grito⟩

yellow¹ ['jɛlo] *vi* : ponerse amarillo, volverse amarillo

yellow² *adj* **1** : amarillo **2** COWARDLY : cobarde

yellow³ *n* : amarillo *m*

yellow fever *n* : fiebre *f* amarilla

yellowish ['jɛloɪʃ] *adj* : amarillento

yellow jacket *n* : avispa *f* (con rayas amarillas)

yelp¹ ['jɛlp] *vi* : dar un gañido (dícese de un animal), dar un grito (dícese de una persona)

yelp² *n* : gañido *m* (de un animal), grito *m* (de una persona)

yen ['jɛn] *n* **1** DESIRE : deseo *m*, ganas *fpl* **2** : yen *m* (moneda japonesa)

yeoman ['joːmən] *n, pl* **-men** [-mən, -mɛn] : suboficial *mf* de marina

yes¹ ['jɛs] *adv* : sí ⟨to say yes : decir que sí⟩

yes² *n* : sí *m*

yesterday¹ ['jɛstər,deɪ, -di] *adv* : ayer

yesterday² *n* **1** : ayer *m* **2 the day before yesterday** : anteayer

yet¹ ['jɛt] *adv* **1** BESIDES, EVEN : aún ⟨yet more problems : más problemas aún⟩ ⟨yet again : otra vez⟩ **2** SO FAR : aún, todavía ⟨not yet : todavía no⟩ ⟨as yet : hasta ahora, todavía⟩ **3** : ya ⟨has he come yet? : ¿ya ha venido?⟩ **4** EVENTUALLY : todavía, algún día **5** NEVERTHELESS : sin embargo

yet² *conj* : pero

yew ['juː] *n* : tejo *m*

yield¹ ['jiːld] *vt* **1** SURRENDER : ceder ⟨to yield the right of way : ceder el paso⟩ **2** PRODUCE : producir, dar, rendir (en finanzas) — *vi* **1** GIVE : ceder ⟨to yield under pressure : ceder por la presión⟩ **2** GIVE IN, SURRENDER : ceder, rendirse, entregarse

yield² *n* : rendimiento *m*, rédito *m* (en finanzas)

yin and yang ['jɪnænd'jæŋ, -'jɑŋ] *n* : yin *m* y yang *f*

yodel¹ ['joːdəl] *vi* **-deled** *or* **-delled; -deling** *or* **-delling** : cantar al estilo tirolés

yodel² *n* : canción *f* al estilo tirolés

yoga ['joːgə] *n* : yoga *m*

yogurt ['joːgərt] *n* : yogur *m*, yogurt *m*

yoke¹ ['joːk] *vt* **yoked; yoking** : uncir (animales)

yoke² *n* **1** : yugo *m* (para uncir animales)

⟨the yoke of oppression : el yugo de la opresión⟩ **2** TEAM : yunta *f* (de bueyes) **3** : canesú *m* (de ropa)

yokel [ˈjoːkəl] *n* : palurdo *m*, -da *f*

yolk [ˈjoːk] *n* : yema *f* (de un huevo)

Yom Kippur [ˌjoːmkɪˈpʊr, ˌjɑm-, -ˈkɪpər] *n* : el Día *m* del Perdón, Yom Kippur

yon [ˈjɑn] → **yonder**

yonder[1] [ˈjɑndər] *adv* : allá ⟨over yonder : allá lejos⟩

yonder[2] *adj* : aquel ⟨yonder hill : aquella colina⟩

yore [ˈjoːr] *n* **in days of yore** : antaño

you [ˈjuː] *pron* **1** (*used as subject — familiar*) : tú; vos (*in some Latin American countries*); ustedes *pl*; vosotros, vosotras *pl* Spain **2** (*used as subject — formal*) : usted, ustedes *pl* **3** (*used as indirect object — familiar*) : te, les *pl* (se before lo, la, los, las), os *pl* Spain ⟨he told it to you : te lo contó⟩ ⟨I gave them to (all of, both of) you : se los di⟩ **4** (*used as indirect object — formal*) : lo (*Spain sometimes* le), la; los (*Spain sometimes* les), las *pl* **5** (*used after a preposition — familiar*) : ti; vos (*in some Latin American countries*); ustedes *pl*; vosotros, vosotras *pl* Spain **6** (*used after a preposition — formal*) : usted, ustedes *pl* **7** (*used as an impersonal subject*) ⟨you never know : nunca se sabe⟩ ⟨you have to be aware : hay que ser consciente⟩ ⟨you mustn't do that : eso no se hace⟩ **8 with you** (*familiar*) : contigo; con ustedes *pl*; con vosotros, con vosotras *pl* Spain **9 with you** (*formal*) : con usted, con ustedes *pl*

you'd [ˈjuːd, ˈjʊd] (*contraction of* **you had** *or* **you would**) → **have, would**

you'll [ˈjuːl, ˈjʊl] (*contraction of* **you shall** *or* **you will**) → **shall, will**

young[1] [ˈjʌŋ] *adj* **younger** [ˈjʌŋgər]; **youngest** [-gəst] **1** : joven, pequeño, menor ⟨young people : los jóvenes⟩ ⟨my younger brother : mi hermano menor⟩ ⟨she is the youngest : es la más pequeña⟩ **2** FRESH, NEW : tierno (dícese de las verduras), joven (dícese del vino) **3** YOUTHFUL : joven, juvenil

young[2] *npl* : jóvenes *mfpl* (de los humanos), crías *fpl* (de los animales)

youngster [ˈjʌŋkstər] *n* **1** YOUTH : joven *mf* **2** CHILD : chico *m*, -ca *f*; niño *m*, -ña *f*

your [ˈjʊr, ˈjoːr, jər] *adj* **1** (*familiar singular*) : tu ⟨your cat : tu gato⟩ ⟨your books : tus libros⟩ ⟨wash your hands : lávate las manos⟩ **2** (*familiar plural*) : su, vuestro Spain ⟨your car : su coche, el coche de ustedes⟩ **3** (*formal*) : su ⟨your houses : sus casas⟩ **4** (*impersonal*) : el, la, los, las ⟨on your left : a la izquierda⟩

you're [ˈjʊr, ˈjoːr, ˈjər, ˈjuːər] (*contraction of* **you are**) → **be**

yours [ˈjʊrz, ˈjoːrz] *pron* **1** (*belonging to one person — familiar*) : (el) tuyo, (la) tuya, (los) tuyos, (las) tuyas ⟨those are mine; yours are there : ésas son mías; las tuyas están allí⟩ ⟨is this one yours? : ¿éste es tuyo?⟩ **2** (*belonging to more than one person — familiar*) : (el) suyo, (la) suya, (los) suyos, (las) suyas; (el) vuestro, (la) vuestra, (los) vuestros, (las) vuestras *Spain* ⟨our house and yours : nuestra casa y la suya⟩ **3** (*formal*) : (el) suyo, (la) suya, (los) suyos, (las) suyas

yourself [jərˈsɛlf] *pron, pl* **yourselves** [-ˈslvz] **1** (*used reflexively — familiar*) : te, se *pl*, os *pl* Spain ⟨wash yourself : lávate⟩ ⟨you dressed yourselves : se vistieron, os vestisteis⟩ **2** (*used reflexively — formal*) : se ⟨did you hurt yourself? : ¿se hizo daño?⟩ ⟨you've gotten yourselves dirty : se ensuciaron⟩ **3** (*used for emphasis*) : tú mismo, tú misma; usted mismo, usted misma; ustedes mismos, ustedes mismas *pl*; vosotros mismos, vosotras mismas *pl* Spain ⟨you did it yourselves? : ¿lo hicieron ustedes mismos?, ¿lo hicieron por sí solos?⟩

youth [ˈjuːθ] *n, pl* **youths** [ˈjuːðz, ˈjuːθs] **1** : juventud *f* ⟨in her youth : en su juventud⟩ **2** BOY : joven *m* **3** : jóvenes *mfpl*, juventud *f* ⟨the youth of our city : los jóvenes de nuestra ciudad⟩

youthful [ˈjuːθfəl] *adj* **1** : de juventud **2** YOUNG : joven **3** JUVENILE : juvenil

youthfulness [ˈjuːθfəlnəs] *n* : juventud *f*

you've [ˈjuːv] (*contraction of* **you have**) → **have**

yowl[1] [ˈjæʊl] *vi* : aullar

yowl[2] *n* : aullido *m*

yo-yo [ˈjoːˌjoː] *n, pl* **-yos** : yoyo *m*, yoyó *m*

yucca [ˈjʌkə] *n* : yuca *f*

Yugoslavian [ˌjuːgoˈslɑviən] *n* : yugoslavo *m*, -va *f* — **Yugoslavian** *adj*

yule [ˈjuːl] *n* CHRISTMAS : Navidad *f*

yuletide [ˈjuːlˌtaɪd] *n* : Navidades *fpl*

yuppie [ˈjʌpi] *n* : yuppy *mf*

Z

z ['zi:] *n, pl* **z's** *or* **zs** : vigésima sexta letra del alfabeto inglés

Zambian ['zæmbiən] *n* : zambiano *m*, -na *f* — **Zambian** *adj*

zany¹ ['zeɪni] *adj* **-nier; -est** : alocado, disparatado

zany² *n, pl* **-nies** : bufón *m*, -fona *f*

zap¹ ['zæp] *vt* **zapped; zapping** 1 ELIMINATE : eliminar 2 : enviar o transportar rápidamente — *vi* : ir rápidamente

zap² *n* 1 ZEST : sabor *m*, sazón *f* 2 BLAST : golpe *m* fuerte

zap³ *interj* : ¡zas!

zeal ['zi:l] *n* : fervor *m*, celo *m*, entusiasmo *m*

zealot ['zɛlət] *n* : fanático *m*, -ca *f*

zealous ['zɛləs] *adj* : celoso — **zealously** *adv*

zebra ['zi:brə] *n* : cebra *f*

zenith ['zi:nəθ] *n* 1 : cenit *m* (en astronomía) 2 PEAK : apogeo *m*, cenit *m* ⟨at the zenith of his career : en el apogeo de su carrera⟩

zephyr ['zɛfər] *n* : céfiro *m*

zeppelin ['zɛplən, -pəlɪn] *n* : zepelín *m*

zero¹ ['zi:ro, 'zɪro] *vi* **to zero in on** : apuntar hacia, centrarse en (un problema, etc.)

zero² *adj* : cero, nulo ⟨zero degrees : cero grados⟩ ⟨zero opportunities : oportunidades nulas⟩

zero³ *n, pl* **-ros** : cero *m* ⟨below zero : bajo cero⟩

zest ['zɛst] *n* 1 GUSTO : entusiasmo *m*, brío *m* 2 FLAVOR : sabor *m*, sazón *f*

zestful ['zɛstfəl] *adj* : brioso

zigzag¹ ['zɪg,zæg] *vi* **-zagged; -zagging** : zigzaguear

zigzag² *adv & adj* : en zigzag

zigzag³ *n* : zigzag *m*

Zimbabwean [zɪm'bɑbwiən, -bweɪ] *n* : zimbabuense *mf* — **Zimbabwean** *adj*

zinc ['zɪŋk] *n* : cinc *m*, zinc *m*

zing ['zɪŋ] *n* 1 HISS, HUM : zumbido *m*, silbido *m* 2 ENERGY : brío *m*

zinnia ['zɪniə, 'zi:-, -njə] *n* : zinnia *f*

Zionism ['zaɪə,nɪzəm] *n* : sionismo *m*

Zionist ['zaɪənɪst] *n* : sionista *mf*

zip¹ ['zɪp] *v* **zipped; zipping** *vt* *or* **to zip up** : cerrar el cierre de — *vi* 1 SPEED : pasarse volando ⟨the day zipped by : el día se pasó volando⟩ 2 HISS, HUM : silbar, zumbar

zip² *n* 1 ZING : zumbido *m*, silbido *m* 2 ENERGY : brío *m*

zip code *n* : código *m* postal

zipper ['zɪpər] *n* : cierre *m*, cremallera *f*, zíper *m CA, Mex*

zippy ['zɪpi] *adj* **-pier; -est** : brioso

zircon ['zər,kɑn] *n* : circón *m*, zircón *m*

zirconium [,zər'ko:niəm] *n* : circonio *m*

zither ['zɪðər, -θər] *n* : cítara *f*

zodiac ['zo:di,æk] *n* : zodíaco *m*

zombie ['zɑmbi] *n* : zombi *mf*, zombie *mf*

zone¹ ['zo:n] *vt* **zoned; zoning** 1 : dividir en zonas 2 DESIGNATE : declarar ⟨to zone for business : declarar como zona comercial⟩

zone² *n* : zona *f*

zoo ['zu:] *n, pl* **zoos** : zoológico *m*, zoo *m*

zoological [,zo:ə'lɑʤɪkəl, ,zu:ə-] *adj* : zoológico

zoologist [zo'ɑləʤɪst, zu:-] *n* : zoólogo *m*, -ga *f*

zoology [zo'ɑləʤi, zu:-] *n* : zoología *f*

zoom¹ ['zu:m] *vi* 1 : zumbar, ir volando ⟨to zoom past : pasar volando⟩ 2 CLIMB : elevarse ⟨the plane zoomed up : el avión se elevó⟩

zoom² *n* 1 : zumbido *m* ⟨the zoom of an engine : el zumbido de un motor⟩ 2 : subida *f* vertical (de un avión, etc.) 3 *or* **zoom lens** : zoom *m*

zucchini [zʊ'ki:ni] *n, pl* **-ni** *or* **-nis** : calabacín *m*, calabacita *f Mex*

Zulu ['zu:lu:] *n* 1 : zulú *mf* 2 : zulú *m* (idioma) — **Zulu** *adj*

zygote ['zaɪ,go:t] *n* : zigoto *m*, cigoto *m*

Common Spanish Abbreviations

SPANISH ABBREVIATION AND EXPANSION		ENGLISH EQUIVALENT	
abr.	abril	**Apr.**	April
A.C., a.C.	antes de Cristo	**BC**	before Christ
a. de J.C.	antes de Jesucristo	**BC**	before Christ
admon., admón.	administración	—	administration
a/f	a favor	—	in favor
ago.	agosto	**Aug.**	August
Apdo.	apartado (de correos)	—	P.O. box
aprox.	aproximadamente	**approx.**	approximately
Aptdo.	apartado (de correos)	—	P.O. box
Arq.	arquitecto	**arch.**	architect
A.T.	Antiguo Testamento	**O.T.**	Old Testament
atte.	atentamente	—	sincerely
atto., atta.	atento, atenta	—	kind, courteous
av., avda.	avenida	**ave.**	avenue
a/v.	a vista	—	on receipt
BID	Banco Interamericano de Desarrollo	**IDB**	Interamerican Development Bank
Bo	banco	—	bank
BM	Banco Mundial	—	World Bank
c/, C/	calle	**st.**	street
C	centígrado, Celsius	**C**	centigrade, Celsius
C.	compañía	**Co.**	company
CA	corriente alterna	**AC**	alternating current
cap.	capítulo	**ch., chap.**	chapter
c/c	cuenta corriente	—	current account, checking account
c.c.	centímetros cúbicos	**cu. cm**	cubic centimeters
CC	corriente continua	**DC**	direct current
c/d	con descuento	—	with discount
Cd.	ciudad	—	city
CE	Comunidad Europea	**EC**	European Community
CEE	Comunidad Económica Europea	**EEC**	European Economic Community
cf.	confróntese	**cf.**	compare
cg.	centígramo	**cg**	centigram
CGT	Confederación General de Trabajadores *or* del Trabajo	—	confederation of workers, workers' union
CI	coeficiente intelectual *or* de inteligencia	**IQ**	intelligence quotient
Cía.	compañía	**Co.**	company
cm.	centímetro	**cm**	centimeter
Cnel.	coronel	**Col.**	colonel
col.	columna	**col.**	column
Col. *Mex*	colonia	—	residential area
Com.	comandante	**Cmdr.**	commander
comp.	compárese	**comp.**	compare
Cor.	coronel	**Col.**	colonel

SPANISH ABBREVIATION AND EXPANSION		ENGLISH EQUIVALENT	
C.P.	código postal	—	zip code
CSF, c.s.f.	coste, seguro y flete	**c.i.f.**	cost, insurance, and freight
cta.	cuenta	**ac., acct.**	account
cte.	corriente	**cur.**	current
c/u	cada uno, cada una	**ea.**	each
CV	caballo de vapor	**hp**	horsepower
D.	Don	—	—
Da., D.^a	Doña	—	—
d.C.	después de Cristo	**AD**	anno Domini (in the year of Our Lord)
dcha.	derecha	—	right
d. de J.C.	después de Jesucristo	**AD**	anno Domini (in the year of Our Lord)
dep.	departamento	**dept.**	department
DF, D.F.	Distrito Federal	—	Federal District
dic.	diciembre	**Dec.**	December
dir.	director, directora	**dir.**	director
dir.	dirección	—	address
Dña.	Doña	—	—
do.	domingo	**Sun.**	Sunday
dpto.	departamento	**dept.**	department
Dr.	doctor	**Dr.**	doctor
Dra.	doctora	**Dr.**	doctor
dto.	descuento	—	discount
E, E.	Este, este	**E**	East, east
Ed.	editorial	—	publishing house
Ed., ed.	edición	**ed.**	edition
edif.	edificio	**bldg.**	building
edo.	estado	**st.**	state
EEUU, EE.UU.	Estados Unidos	**US, U.S.**	United States
ej.	por ejemplo	**e.g.**	for example
E.M.	esclerosis multiple	**MS**	multiple sclerosis
ene.	enero	**Jan.**	January
etc.	etcétera	**etc.**	et cetera
ext.	extensión	**ext.**	extension
F	Fahrenheit	**F**	Fahrenheit
f.a.b.	franco a bordo	**f.o.b.**	free on board
FC	ferrocarril	**RR**	railroad
feb.	febrero	**Feb.**	February
FF AA, FF.AA.	Fuerzas Armadas	—	armed forces
FMI	Fondo Monetario Internacional	**IMF**	International Monetary Fund
g.	gramo	**g., gm, gr.**	gram
G.P.	giro postal	**M.O.**	money order
gr.	gramo	**g., gm, gr.**	gram
Gral.	general	**Gen.**	general
h.	hora	**hr.**	hour
Hnos.	hermanos	**Bros.**	brothers
I + D, I & D, I y D	investigación y desarrollo	**R & D**	research and development
i.e.	esto es, es decir	**i.e.**	that is
incl.	inclusive	**incl.**	inclusive, inclusively
Ing.	ingeniero, ingeniera	**eng.**	engineer

SPANISH ABBREVIATION AND EXPANSION		ENGLISH EQUIVALENT	
IPC	índice de precios al consumo	**CPI**	consumer price index
IVA	impuesto al valor agregado	**VAT**	value-added tax
izq.	izquierda	**l.**	left
juev.	jueves	**Thurs.**	Thursday
jul.	julio	**Jul.**	July
jun.	junio	**Jun.**	June
kg.	kilogramo	**kg**	kilogram
km.	kilómetro	**km**	kilometer
km/h	kilómetros por hora	**kph**	kilometers per hour
kv, kV	kilovatio	**kw, kW**	kilowatt
l.	litro	**l, lit.**	liter
Lic.	licenciado, licenciada	—	
Ltda.	limitada	**Ltd.**	limited
lun.	lunes	**Mon.**	Monday
m	masculino	**m**	masculine
m	metro	**m**	meter
m	minuto	**m**	minute
mar.	marzo	**Mar.**	March
mart.	martes	**Tues.**	Tuesday
mg.	miligramo	**mg**	milligram
miérc.	miércoles	**Wednes.**	Wednesday
min	minuto	**min.**	minute
mm.	milímetro	**mm**	millimeter
M-N, m/n	moneda nacional	—	national currency
Mons.	monseñor	**Msgr.**	monsignor
Mtra.	maestra	—	teacher
Mtro.	maestro	—	teacher
N, N.	Norte, norte	**N, no.**	North, north
n/o	nuestro	—	our
n.º	número	**no.**	number
N. de (la) R.	nota de (la) redacción	—	editor's note
NE	nordeste	**NE**	northeast
NN.UU.	Naciones Unidas	**UN**	United Nations
NO	noroeste	**NW**	northwest
nov.	noviembre	**Nov.**	November
N.T.	Nuevo Testamento	**N.T.**	New Testament
ntra., ntro.	nuestra, nuestro	—	our
NU	Naciones Unidas	**UN**	United Nations
núm.	número	**num.**	number
O, O.	Oeste, oeste	**W**	West, west
oct.	octubre	**Oct.**	October
OEA, O.E.A.	Organización de Estados Americanos	**OAS**	Organization of American States
OMS	Organización Mundial de la Salud	**WHO**	World Health Organization
ONG	organización no gubernamental	**NGO**	non-governmental organization
ONU	Organización de las Naciones Unidas	**UN**	United Nations
OTAN	Organización del Tratado del Atlántico Norte	**NATO**	North Atlantic Treaty Organization
p.	página	**p.**	page
P, P.	padre	**Fr.**	father

SPANISH ABBREVIATION AND EXPANSION		ENGLISH EQUIVALENT	
pág.	página	**pg.**	page
pat.	patente	**pat.**	patent
PCL	pantalla de cristal líquido	**LCD**	liquid crystal display
P.D.	post data	**P.S.**	postscript
p. ej.	por ejemplo	**e.g.**	for example
PNB	Producto Nacional Bruto	**GNP**	gross national product
p^o	paseo	**Ave.**	avenue
p.p.	porte pagado	**ppd.**	postpaid
PP, p.p.	por poder, por poderes	**p.p.**	by proxy
prom.	promedio	**av., avg.**	average
ptas., pts.	pesetas	—	—
q.e.p.d.	que en paz descanse	**R.I.P.**	may he/she rest in peace
R, R/	remite	—	sender
RAE	Real Academia Española	—	—
ref., ref.^{a}	referencia	**ref.**	reference
rep.	república	**rep.**	republic
r.p.m.	revoluciones por minuto	**rpm.**	revolutions per minute
rte.	remite, remitente	—	sender
s.	siglo	**c., cent.**	century
s/	su, sus	—	his, her, your, their
S, S.	Sur, sur	**S, so.**	South, south
S.	san, santo	**St.**	saint
S.A.	sociedad anónima	**Inc.**	incorporated (company)
sáb.	sábado	**Sat.**	Saturday
s/c	su cuenta	—	your account
SE	sudeste, sureste	**SE**	southeast
seg.	segundo, segundos	**sec.**	second, seconds
sep., sept.	septiembre	**Sept.**	September
s.e.u.o.	salvo error u omisión	—	errors and omissions excepted
Sgto.	sargento	**Sgt.**	sergeant
S.L.	sociedad limitada	**Ltd.**	limited (corporation)
S.M.	Su Majestad	**HM**	His Majesty, Her Majesty
s/n	sin número	—	no (street) number
s.n.m.	sobre el nivel de mar	**a.s.l.**	above sea level
SO	sudoeste/suroeste	**SW**	southwest
S.R.C.	se ruega contestación	**R.S.V.P.**	please reply
ss.	siguientes	—	the following ones
SS, S.S.	Su Santidad	**H.H.**	His Holiness
Sta.	santa	**St.**	Saint
Sto.	santo	**St.**	saint
t, t.	tonelada	**t., tn.**	ton
TAE	tasa anual efectiva	**APR**	annual percentage rate
tb.	también	—	also
tel., Tel.	teléfono	**tel.**	telephone
Tm.	tonelada métrica	**MT**	metric ton
Tn.	tonelada	**t., tn.**	ton
trad.	traducido	**tr., trans., transl.**	translated

SPANISH ABBREVIATION AND EXPANSION		ENGLISH EQUIVALENT	
UE	Unión Europea	**EU**	European Union
Univ.	universidad	**Univ., U.**	university
UPC	unidad procesadora central	**CPU**	central processing unit
Urb.	urbanización	—	residential area
v	versus	**v., vs.**	versus
v	verso	**v., ver., vs.**	verse
v.	véase	**vid.**	see
Vda.	viuda	—	widow
v.g., v.gr.	verbigracia	**e.g.**	for example
vier., viern.	viernes	**Fri.**	Friday
V.M.	Vuestra Majestad	—	Your Majesty
VºBº, V.ºB.º	visto bueno	—	OK, approved
vol, vol.	volumen	**vol.**	volume
vra., vro.	vuestra, vuestro	—	your

Common English Abbreviations

ENGLISH ABBREVIATION AND EXPANSION		SPANISH EQUIVALENT	
AAA	American Automobile Association	—	—
AD	anno Domini (in the year of Our Lord)	**d.C., d. de J.C.**	después de Cristo, después de Jesucristo
AK	Alaska	—	Alaska
AL, Ala.	Alabama	—	Alabama
Alas.	Alaska	—	Alaska
a.m., AM	ante meridiem	**a.m.**	ante meridiem (de la mañana)
Am., Amer.	America, American	—	América, americano
amt.	amount	—	cantidad
anon.	anonymous	—	anónimo
ans.	answer	—	respuesta
Apr.	April	**abr.**	abril
AR	Arkansas	—	Arkansas
Ariz.	Arizona	—	Arizona
Ark.	Arkansas	—	Arkansas
asst.	assistant	**ayte.**	ayudante
atty.	attorney	—	abogado, -da
Aug.	August	**ago.**	agosto
ave.	avenue	**av., avda.**	avenida
AZ	Arizona	—	Arizona
BA	Bachelor of Arts	**Lic.**	Licenciado, -da en Filosofía y Letras
BA	Bachelor of Arts (degree)	—	Licenciatura en Filosofía y Letras
BC	before Christ	**a.C., A.C., a. de J.C.**	antes de Cristo, antes de Jesucristo
BCE	before the Christian Era, before the Common Era	—	antes de la era cristiana, antes de la era común
bet.	between	—	entre
bldg.	building	**edif.**	edificio
blvd.	boulevard	**blvar., br.**	bulevar
Br., Brit.	Britain, British	—	Gran Bretaña, británico
Bro(s).	brother(s)	**Hno(s).**	hermano(s)
BS	Bachelor of Science	**Lic.**	Licenciado, -da en Ciencias
BS	Bachelor of Science (degree)	—	Licenciatura en Ciencias
c	carat	—	quilate
c	cent	—	centavo
c	centimeter	**cm.**	centímetro
c	century	**s.**	siglo
c	cup	—	taza
C	Celsius, centigrade	**C**	Celsius, centígrado
CA, Cal., Calif.	California	—	California
Can., Canad.	Canada, Canadian	—	Canadá, canadiense
cap.	capital	—	capital
cap.	capital	—	mayúscula
Capt.	captain	—	capitán

ENGLISH ABBREVIATION AND EXPANSION		SPANISH EQUIVALENT	
cent.	century	**s.**	siglo
CEO	chief executive officer	—	presidente, -ta (de una corporación)
ch., chap.	chapter	**cap.**	capítulo
CIA	Central Intelligence Agency	—	—
cm	centimeter	**cm.**	centímetro
Co.	company	**C., Cía.**	compañía
co.	county	—	condado
CO	Colorado	—	Colorado
c/o	care of	**a/c**	a cargo de
COD	cash on delivery, collect on delivery	—	(pago) contra reembolso
col.	column	**col.**	columna
Col., Colo.	Colorado	—	Colorado
Conn.	Connecticut	—	Connecticut
corp.	corporation	—	corporación
CPR	cardiopulmonary resuscitation	**RCP**	reanimación cardiopulmonar, resucitación cardiopulmonar
ct.	cent	—	centavo
CT	Connecticut	—	Connecticut
D.A.	district attorney	—	fiscal (del distrito)
DC	District of Columbia	—	—
DDS	Doctor of Dental Surgery	—	doctor de cirugía dental
DE	Delaware	—	Delaware
Dec.	December	**dic.**	diciembre
Del.	Delaware	—	Delaware
DJ	disc jockey	—	disc-jockey
dept.	department	**dep., dpto.**	departamento
DMD	Doctor of Dental Medicine	—	doctor de medicina dental
doz.	dozen	—	docena
Dr.	doctor	**Dr., Dra.**	doctor, doctora
DST	daylight saving time	—	—
DVM	Doctor of Veterinary Medicine	—	doctor de medicina veterinaria
E	East, east	**E, E.**	Este, este
ea.	each	**c/u**	cada uno, cada una
e.g.	for example (exempli gratia)	**v.g., v.gr.**	verbigracia
EMT	emergency medical technician	—	técnico, -ca en urgencias médicas
Eng.	England, English	—	Inglaterra, inglés
esp.	especially	—	especialmente
EST	eastern standard time	—	—
etc.	et cetera	**etc.**	etcétera
f	false	—	falso
f	female	**f**	femenino
F	Fahrenheit	**F**	Fahrenheit
FBI	Federal Bureau of Investigation	—	—
Feb.	February	**feb.**	febrero
fem.	feminine	—	femenino
FL, Fla.	Florida	—	Florida

ENGLISH ABBREVIATION AND EXPANSION		SPANISH EQUIVALENT	
Fri.	Friday	**vier., viern.**	viernes
ft.	feet, foot	—	pie(s)
g	gram	**g., gr.**	gramo
Ga., GA	Georgia	—	Georgia
gal.	gallon	—	galón
Gen.	general	**Gral.**	general
gm	gram	**g., gr.**	gramo
gov.	governor	—	gobernador, -dora
govt.	government	—	gobierno
gr.	gram	**g., gr.**	gramo
HI	Hawaii	—	Hawai, Hawaii
hr.	hour	**h.**	hora
HS	high school	—	colegio secundario
ht.	height	—	altura
Ia., IA	Iowa	—	Iowa
ID	Idaho	—	Idaho
i.e.	that is (id est)	**i.e.**	id est (esto es, es decir)
IL, Ill.	Illinois	—	Illinois
in.	inch	—	pulgada
IN	Indiana	—	Indiana
Inc.	incorporated	**S.A.**	sociedad anónima
Ind.	Indian, Indiana	—	Indiana
Jan.	January	**ene.**	enero
Jul.	July	**jul.**	julio
Jun.	June	**jun.**	junio
Jr., Jun.	Junior	**Jr.**	Júnior
Kan., Kans.	Kansas	—	Kansas
kg	kilogram	**kg.**	kilogramo
km	kilometer	**km.**	kilómetro
KS	Kansas	—	Kansas
Ky., KY	Kentucky	—	Kentucky
l	liter	**l.**	litro
l.	left	**izq.**	izquierda
L	large	**G**	(talla) grande
La., LA	Louisiana	—	Luisiana, Louisiana
lb.	pound	—	libra
Ltd.	limited	**S.L.**	sociedad limitada
m	male	**m**	masculino
m	meter	**m**	metro
m	mile	—	milla
M	medium	**M**	(talla) mediana
MA	Massachusetts	—	Massachusetts
Maj.	major	—	mayor
Mar.	March	**mar.**	marzo
masc.	masculine	—	masculino
Mass.	Massachusetts	—	Massachusetts
Md., MD	Maryland	—	Maryland
M.D.	Doctor of Medicine	—	doctor de medicina
Me., ME	Maine	—	Maine
Mex.	Mexican, Mexico	**Méx.**	mexicano, México
mg	milligram	**mg.**	miligramo
mi.	mile	—	milla
MI, Mich.	Michigan	—	Michigan
min.	minute	**min**	minuto
Minn.	Minnesota	—	Minnesota
Miss.	Mississippi	—	Mississippi, Misisipí
ml	mililiter	**ml.**	mililitro

ENGLISH ABBREVIATION AND EXPANSION		SPANISH EQUIVALENT	
mm	millimeter	**mm.**	milímetro
MN	Minnesota	—	Minnesota
mo.	month	—	mes
Mo., MO	Missouri	—	Missouri
Mon.	Monday	**lun.**	lunes
Mont.	Montana	—	Montana
mpg	miles per gallon	—	millas por galón
mph	miles per hour	—	millas por hora
MS	Mississippi	—	Mississippi, Misisipí
mt.	mount, mountain	—	monte, montaña
MT	Montana	—	Montana
mtn.	mountain	—	montaña
N	North, north	**N**	Norte, norte
NASA	National Aeronautics and Space Administration	—	—
NC	North Carolina	—	Carolina del Norte, North Carolina
ND, N. Dak.	North Dakota	—	Dakota del Norte, North Dakota
NE	northeast	**NE**	nordeste
NE, Neb., Nebr.	Nebraska	—	Nebraska
Nev.	Nevada	—	Nevada
NH	New Hampshire	—	New Hampshire
NJ	New Jersey	—	Nueva Jersey, New Jersey
NM, N. Mex.	New Mexico	—	Nuevo México, New Mexico
no.	north	**N**	norte
no.	number	**n.⁰**	número
Nov.	November	**nov.**	noviembre
N.T.	New Testament	**N.T.**	Nuevo Testamento
NV	Nevada	—	Nevada
NW	northwest	**NO**	noroeste
NY	New York	**NY**	Nueva York, New York
O	Ohio	—	Ohio
Oct.	October	**oct.**	octubre
OH	Ohio	—	Ohio
OK, Okla.	Oklahoma	—	Oklahoma
OR, Ore., Oreg.	Oregon	—	Oregon
O.T.	Old Testament	**A.T.**	Antiguo Testamento
oz.	ounce, ounces	—	onza, onzas
p.	page	**p.**	página
Pa., PA	Pennsylvania	—	Pennsylvania, Pensilvania
pat.	patent	**pat.**	patente
PD	police department	—	departamento de policía
PE	physical education	—	educación física
Penn., Penna.	Pennsylvania	—	Pennsylvania, Pensilvania
pg.	page	**pág.**	página
PhD	Doctor of Philosophy	—	doctor, -tora (en filosofía)

ENGLISH ABBREVIATION AND EXPANSION		SPANISH EQUIVALENT	
pkg.	package	—	paquete
p.m., PM	post meridiem	**p.m.**	post meridiem (de la tarde)
P.O.	post office	—	oficina de correos, correo
pp.	pages	**págs.**	páginas
PR	Puerto Rico	**PR**	Puerto Rico
pres.	present	—	presente
pres.	president	—	presidente, -ta
prof.	professor	—	profesor, -sora
P.S.	postscript	**P.D.**	postdata
P.S.	public school	—	escuela pública
pt.	pint	—	pinta
pt.	point	**pto.**	punto
PTA	Parent-Teacher Association	—	—
PTO	Parent-Teacher Organization	—	—
q, qt.	quart	—	cuarto de galón
r.	right	**dcha.**	derecha
rd.	road	**c/, C/**	calle
RDA	recommended daily allowance	—	consumo diario recomendado
recd.	received	—	recibido
Rev.	reverend	**Rdo.**	reverendo
RI	Rhode Island	—	Rhode Island
rpm	revolutions per minute	**r.p.m.**	revoluciones por minuto
RR	railroad	**FC**	ferrocarril
R.S.V.P.	please reply (répondez s'il vous plaît)	**S.R.C.**	se ruega contestación
rt.	right	**dcha.**	derecha
rte.	route	—	ruta
S	small	**P**	(talla) pequeña
S	South, south	**S**	Sur, sur
S.A.	South America	—	Sudamérica, América del Sur
Sat.	Saturday	**sáb.**	sábado
SC	South Carolina	—	Carolina del Sur, South Carolina
SD, S. Dak.	South Dakota	—	Dakota del Sur, South Dakota
SE	southeast	**SE**	sudeste, sureste
Sept.	September	**sep., sept.**	septiembre
so.	south	**S**	sur
sq.	square	—	cuadrado
Sr.	Senior	**Sr.**	Sénior
Sr.	sister	—	sor
st.	state	—	estado
st.	street	**c/, C/**	calle
St.	saint	**S., Sto., Sta.**	santo, santa
Sun.	Sunday	**dom.**	domingo
SW	southwest	**SO**	sudoeste, suroeste
t.	teaspoon	—	cucharadita
T, tb., tbsp.	tablespoon	—	cucharada (grande)
Tenn.	Tennessee	—	Tennessee

ENGLISH ABBREVIATION AND EXPANSION		SPANISH EQUIVALENT	
Tex.	Texas	—	Texas
Thu., Thur., Thurs.	Thursday	**juev.**	jueves
TM	trademark	—	marca (de un producto)
TN	Tennessee	—	Tennessee
tsp.	teaspoon	—	cucharadita
Tue., Tues.	Tuesday	**mart.**	martes
TX	Texas	—	Texas
UN	United Nations	**NU, NN.UU.**	Naciones Unidas
US	United States	**EEUU, EE.UU.**	Estados Unidos
USA	United States of America	**EEUU, EE.UU.**	Estados Unidos de América
usu.	usually	—	usualmente
UT	Utah	—	Utah
v.	versus	**v**	versus
Va., VA	Virginia	—	Virginia
vol.	volume	**vol.**	volumen
VP	vice president	—	vicepresidente, -ta
vs.	versus	**v**	versus
Vt., VT	Vermont	—	Vermont
W	West, west	**O**	Oeste, oeste
WA, Wash.	Washington (estado)	—	Washington
Wed.	Wednesday	**miérc.**	miércoles
WI, Wis., Wisc.	Wisconsin	—	Wisconsin
wt.	weight	—	peso
WV, W. Va.	West Virginia	—	Virginia del Oeste, West Virginia
WY, Wyo.	Wyoming	—	Wyoming
yd.	yard	—	yarda
yr.	year	—	año

Spanish Numbers

Cardinal Numbers

1	uno	28	veintiocho
2	dos	29	veintinueve
3	tres	30	treinta
4	cuatro	31	treinta y uno
5	cinco	40	cuarenta
6	seis	50	cincuenta
7	siete	60	sesenta
8	ocho	70	setenta
9	nueve	80	ochenta
10	diez	90	noventa
11	once	100	cien
12	doce	101	ciento uno
13	trece	200	doscientos
14	catorce	300	trescientos
15	quince	400	cuatrocientos
16	dieciséis	500	quinientos
17	diecisiete	600	seiscientos
18	dieciocho	700	setecientos
19	diecinueve	800	ochocientos
20	veinte	900	novecientos
21	veintiuno	1,000	mil
22	veintidós	1,001	mil uno
23	veintitrés	2,000	dos mil
24	veinticuatro	100,000	cien mil
25	veinticinco	1,000,000	un millón
26	veintiséis	1,000,000,000	mil millones
27	veintisiete	1,000,000,000,000	un billón

Ordinal Numbers

1st	primero, -ra	18th	decimoctavo, -va
2nd	segundo, -da	19th	decimonoveno, -na;
3rd	tercero, -ra		*or* decimonono, -na
4th	cuarto, -ta	20th	vigésimo, -ma
5th	quinto, -ta	21st	vigésimoprimero,
6th	sexto, -ta		vigésimaprimera
7th	séptimo, -ta	22nd	vigésimosegundo,
8th	octavo, -ta		vigésimasegunda
9th	noveno, -na	30th	trigésimo, -ma
10th	décimo, -ma	40th	cuadragésimo, -ma
11th	undécimo, -ca	50th	quincuagésimo, -ma
12th	duodécimo, -ma	60th	sexagésimo, -ma
13th	decimotercero, -ra	70th	septuagésimo, -ma
14th	decimocuarto, -ta	80th	octogésimo, -ma
15th	decimoquinto, -ta	90th	nonagésimo, -ma
16th	decimosexto, -ta	100th	centésimo, -ma
17th	decimoséptimo, -ma	1,000th	milésimo, -ma

English Numbers

Cardinal Numbers

1	one	50	fifty
2	two	60	sixty
3	three	70	seventy
4	four	80	eighty
5	five	90	ninety
6	six	100	one hundred
7	seven	101	one hundred and one
8	eight	200	two hundred
9	nine	300	three hundred
10	ten	400	four hundred
11	eleven	500	five hundred
12	twelve	600	six hundred
13	thirteen	700	seven hundred
14	fourteen	800	eight hundred
15	fifteen	900	nine hundred
16	sixteen	1,000	one thousand
17	seventeen	1,001	one thousand and one
18	eighteen	2,000	two thousand
19	nineteen	10,000	ten thousand
20	twenty	100,000	one hundred thousand
21	twenty-one	1,000,000	one million
30	thirty	1,000,000,000	one billion
40	forty	1,000,000,000,000	one trillion

Ordinal Numbers

1st	first	17th	seventeenth
2nd	second	18th	eighteenth
3rd	third	19th	nineteenth
4th	fourth	20th	twentieth
5th	fifth	21st	twenty-first
6th	sixth	30th	thirtieth
7th	seventh	40th	fortieth
8th	eighth	50th	fiftieth
9th	ninth	60th	sixtieth
10th	tenth	70th	seventieth
11th	eleventh	80th	eightieth
12th	twelfth	90th	ninetieth
13th	thirteenth	100th	hundredth
14th	fourteenth	1,000th	thousandth
15th	fifteenth	1,000,000th	millionth
16th	sixteenth	1,000,000,000th	billionth

Nations of the World

Africa/África

ENGLISH	SPANISH
Algeria	Argelia
Angola	Angola
Benin	Benin
Botswana	Botswana, Botsuana
Burkina Faso	Burkina Faso
Burundi	Burundi
Cameroon	Camerún
Cape Verde	Cabo Verde
Central African Republic	República Centroafricana
Chad	Chad
Comoro Islands	Islas Comores, Comoras
Congo	Congo
Democratic Republic of Congo	Congo, República Democrática del
Djibouti	Djibouti, Djibuti
Egypt	Egipto
Equatorial Guinea	Guinea Ecuatorial
Eritrea	Eritrea
Ethiopia	Etiopía
Gabon	Gabón
Gambia	Gambia
Ghana	Ghana
Guinea	Guinea
Guinea-Bissau	Guinea-Bissau
Ivory Coast	Costa de Marfil
Kenya	Kenya, Kenia
Lesotho	Lesotho, Lesoto
Liberia	Liberia
Libya	Libia
Madagascar	Madagascar
Malawi	Malawi, Malaui
Mali	Malí
Mauritania	Mauritania
Mauritius	Mauricio
Morocco	Marruecos
Mozambique	Mozambique
Namibia	Namibia
Niger	Níger
Nigeria	Nigeria
Rwanda	Ruanda, Rwanda
São Tomé and Principe	Santo Tomé y Príncipe
Senegal	Senegal
Seychelles	Seychelles
Sierra Leone	Sierra Leona
Somalia	Somalia
South Africa, Republic of	Sudáfrica, República de
Sudan	Sudán
Swaziland	Suazilandia, Swazilandia
Tanzania	Tanzanía, Tanzania
Togo	Togo

ENGLISH	SPANISH
Tunisia	Túnez
Uganda	Uganda
Zambia	Zambia
Zimbabwe	Zimbabwe, Zimbábue

Antarctica/Antártida
No independent countries

Asia/Asia

Afghanistan	Afganistán
Armenia	Armenia
Azerbaijan	Azerbaiyán, Azerbaiján
Bahrain	Bahrein
Bangladesh	Bangladesh
Bhutan	Bhután, Bután
Brunei	Brunei
Cambodia	Camboya
China	China
Cyprus	Chipre
Georgia, Republic of	Georgia
India	India
Indonesia	Indonesia
Iran	Irán
Iraq	Iraq, Irak
Israel	Israel
Japan	Japón
Jordan	Jordania
Kazakhstan	Kazajstán
Korea, North	Corea del Norte
Korea, South	Corea del Sur
Kuwait	Kuwait
Kyrgyzstan	Kirguistán, Kirguizistán
Laos	Laos
Lebanon	Líbano
Malaysia	Malasia
Maldive Islands	Maldivas
Mongolia	Mongolia
Myanmar	Myanmar
Nepal	Nepal
Oman	Omán
Pakistan	Pakistán
Philippines	Filipinas
Qatar	Qatar
Saudi Arabia	Arabia Saudita, Arabia Saudí
Singapore	Singapur
Sri Lanka	Sri Lanka
Syria	Siria
Taiwan	Taiwán
Tajikistan	Tayikistán
Thailand	Tailandia
Turkey	Turquía
Turkmenistan	Turkmenistán

ENGLISH	SPANISH
United Arab Emirates	Emiratos Árabes Unidos
Uzbekistan	Uzbekistán
Vietnam	Vietnam
Yemen	Yemen

Europe/Europa

Albania	Albania
Andorra	Andorra
Austria	Austria
Belarus	Belarús
Belgium	Bélgica
Bosnia and Herzegovina	Bosnia y Hercegovina, Bosnia y Herzegovina
Bulgaria	Bulgaria
Croatia	Croacia
Czech Republic	República Checa
Denmark	Dinamarca
Estonia	Estonia
Finland	Finlandia
France	Francia
Germany	Alemania
Greece	Grecia
Hungary	Hungría
Iceland	Islandia
Ireland	Irlanda
Italy	Italia
Latvia	Letonia
Liechtenstein	Liechtenstein
Lithuania	Lituania
Luxembourg	Luxemburgo
Macedonia	Macedonia
Malta	Malta
Moldavia	Moldavia
Monaco	Mónaco
Netherlands	Países Bajos
Norway	Noruega
Poland	Polonia
Portugal	Portugal
Romania	Rumania, Rumanía
Russian Federation	Rusia, Federación de
San Marino	San Marino
Serbia and Montenegro	Serbia y Montenegro
Slovakia	Eslovaquia
Slovenia	Eslovenia
Spain	España
Sweden	Suecia
Switzerland	Suiza
Ukraine	Ucrania
United Kingdom	Reino Unido
Vatican City	Ciudad del Vaticano

ENGLISH   SPANISH

North America/Norteamérica

Antigua and Barbuda	Antigua y Barbuda
Bahamas	Bahamas
Barbados	Barbados
Belize	Belice
Bermuda	Bermudas
Canada	Canadá
Costa Rica	Costa Rica
Cuba	Cuba
Dominica	Dominica
Dominican Republic	República Dominicana
El Salvador	El Salvador
Grenada	Granada
Guatemala	Guatemala
Haiti	Haití
Honduras	Honduras
Jamaica	Jamaica
Mexico	México, Méjico
Nicaragua	Nicaragua
Panama	Panamá
Saint Kitts-Nevis	Saint Kitts y Nevis
Saint Lucia	Santa Lucía
Saint Vincent and the Grenadines	San Vicente y las Granadinas
Trinidad and Tobago	Trinidad y Tobago
United States of America	Estados Unidos de América

Oceania/Oceanía

Australia	Australia
Fiji	Fiji
Kiribati	Kiribati
Marshall Islands	Islas Marshall
Nauru	Nauru
New Zealand	Nueva Zelanda, Nueva Zelandia
Papua New Guinea	Papua Nueva Guinea
Solomon Islands	Islas Salomón
Tonga	Tonga
Tuvalu	Tuvalu
Vanuatu	Vanuatu
Western Samoa	Samoa del Oeste

South America/Sudamérica

Argentina	Argentina
Bolivia	Bolivia
Brazil	Brasil
Chile	Chile
Colombia	Colombia
Ecuador	Ecuador
Guyana	Guyana
Paraguay	Paraguay
Peru	Perú
Suriname	Surinam
Uruguay	Uruguay
Venezuela	Venezuela

Metric System: Conversions

Length

unit	number of meters	approximate U.S. equivalents	
millimeter	0.001	0.039	inch
centimeter	0.01	0.39	inch
meter	1	39.37	inches
kilometer	1,000	0.62	mile

Longitud

unidad	número de metros	equivalentes aproximados de los EE.UU.	
milímetro	0.001	0.039	pulgada
centímetro	0.01	0.39	pulgada
metro	1	39.37	pulgadas
kilómetro	1,000	0.62	milla

Area

unit	number of square meters	approximate U.S. equivalents	
square centimeter	0.0001	0.155	square inch
square meter	1	10.764	square feet
hectare	10,000	2.47	acres
square kilometer	1,000,000	0.3861	square mile

Superficie

unidad	número de metros cuadrados	equivalentes aproximados de los EE.UU.	
centímetro cuadrado	0.0001	0.155	pulgada cuadrada
metro cuadrado	1	10.764	pies cuadrados
hectárea	10,000	2.47	acres
kilómetro cuadrado	1,000,000	0.3861	milla cuadrada

Volume

unit	number of cubic meters	approximate U.S. equivalents	
cubic centimeter	0.000001	0.061	cubic inch
cubic meter	1	1.307	cubic yards

Volumen

unidad	número de metros cúbicos	equivalentes aproximados de los EE.UU	
centímetro cúbico	0.000001	0.061	pulgada cúbica
metro cúbico	1	1.307	yardas cúbicas

Capacity

unit	number of liters	approximate U.S. equivalents		
		CUBIC	DRY	LIQUID
liter	1	61.02 cubic inches	0.908 quart	1.057 quarts

Capacidad

unidad	número de litros	equivalentes aproximados de los EE.UU.		
		CÚBICO	SECO	LÍQUIDO
litro	1	61.02 pulgadas cúbicas	0.908 cuarto	1.057 cuartos

Mass and Weight

unit	number of grams	approximate U.S. equivalents	
milligram	0.001	0.015	grain
centigram	0.01	0.154	grain
gram	1	0.035	ounce
kilogram	1,000	2.2046	pounds
metric ton	1,000,000	1.102	short tons

Masa y peso

unidad	número de gramos	equivalentes aproximados de los EE.UU.	
miligramo	0.001	0.015	grano
centigramo	0.01	0.154	grano
gramo	1	0.035	onza
kilogramo	1.000	2.2046	libras
tonelada métrica	1,000,000	1.102	toneladas cortas